DOCUMENTS

of

AMERICAN HISTORY

eighth edition

DOCUMENTS

of

AMERICAN HISTORY

edited by

Henry Steele Commager

APPLETON-CENTURY-CROFTS
EDUCATIONAL DIVISION
New York   **MEREDITH CORPORATION**

To

EVAN

WHO LIKED THEM

FOREWORD BY THE GENERAL EDITOR

Here are the fundamental sources of American history which all students of the subject read about, but for the most part, have not read; in this they share embarrassment with many of their teachers, well-read scholars though they be. It is reassuring, nevertheless, that such confessions are now made with shame, whereas our grandfathers, unless they were lawyers, would have quoted fifth-hand testimony with as clear a conscience as documents themselves. The literary historians in the mid-years of the nineteenth century cared little where they found material, so long as it molded well into a moving narrative. Joel T. Headley, one of the most popular American historical writers of his time, while secretary of state in Albany thought New York was wasting money in the elaborate publication of its colonial documents; and at the end of the century John Fiske could make a great reputation as an historian without much concern for original sources. But appreciation of their high importance and zeal to gather and present them in convenient form had appeared long before, even in young America. Hezekiah Niles had compiled his *Principles and Acts of the Revolution* in 1822 and between 1837 and 1853 Peter Force produced nine massive folios of *American Archives,* which, unfortunately, a stupid federal government refused to continue. The credit for establishing contemporary sources as materials for teaching must go chiefly to Albert Bushnell Hart, who nearly forty years ago began to publish, for classes from elementary school to college, books of source-extracts illustrating the history of the United States,—flavorous samples from diaries and pamphlets, satires and sermons, prose and poetry. Others in their compilations held more strictly to archival records. The present generation knows it does not know a fact until it has checked with the primary source. But inconvenience mocks at duty, and few there are who form the habit of consulting documents before they speak.

Effective educational use of documents is practically impossible without a compilation. It is not likely, for example, that a college library could afford space for more than one set of the *United States Statutes at Large.* Suppose a conscientious class of forty were told to examine the Civil Rights Act of April 9, 1866, before tomorrow morning; it is easy to imagine what would happen to Volume XIV, and, since a book can be read by but one at a time, the disappointment of the thirty, at the least, who had to appear next day unprepared. Probably the library would contain no set of the Laws of Mississippi or of Louisiana and even the five or ten fortunate enough to have read the Act in question could have no first-hand knowledge of the state policies that brought it forth. With the present volume on his own table the student has not only the Act immediately before him in Document 252 but also six statutes of the Black Codes, in Documents 246 and 247, from which he can better understand it; he has in the brief editorial comment a clear idea of the setting of each and, all told, fourteen authors cited, from which, if time and disposition will permit, he may get the general background and detail. By such procedure he will acquire the habit of historical investigation, an objective more important than the amassing of information to be poured back on examination day.

The novelty in the present work is in its successful essay toward practical completeness. Naturally, the compiler would make no claim that he has included here every document of significance in the development of the United States, but he has certainly brought together a larger and perhaps a better balanced collection than any predecessor. Difficult it is to annotate such documents without erring on the side of spare obviousness or on that of wearisome pedantry. In his introductory notes Professor Commager has nicely stopped at the point where essential helpfulness is completed and has referred to special works for

v

extended comment. The volume becomes, therefore, a bibliographical guide in addition to its other usefulness.

These documents distil the spirit of the American people as understood by organized groups, parties, governmental bodies and responsible officials; in general they represent concerted and matured opinion or binding public action. These are not personal vagaries, interesting as those might be, but statements which have mirrored and directed the trend of our national growth. Without disparaging the infinitely various and voluminous testimony on which what is called social history must be predicated, the touchstone here has generally been the bearing of a document upon the transactions of politics. But the compiler knows full well that political forces do not rise alone in halls of legislation or of justice or in party conclaves; hence he properly includes such documents as Garrison's manifesto in the *Liberator* and that of Tillman in the *Charleston Courier,* the Declaration of Purpose of the National Grange and the solemn pledge of the W. C. T. U. No one can foresee the ways in which these documents can be used, nor bracket them in logical relation so as to suit all users; Professor Commager has wisely chosen strict chronology as his principle of arrangement. This in itself is logical and exhibits the manysidedness of public life in any decade.

Commager's *Documents,* we dare to prophesy, will be cited everywhere as a convenient form in which most basic sources of our political history may be consulted. In the college classroom, either as the foundation of a course or as supplementary reading, they will perform but one of many services. Everywhere that swift convenience is essential in historical inquiry this volume, we like to think, will many times repay its cost. Its wide-spread use, in its provision of the basic texts, will go far to dissolve the reputation of glib and careless volubility sometimes fixed upon our countrymen and supplant it with that of accuracy and security in historical statement. Over six hundred fifty messages from the past, serious and well-considered, are here open to instruct us.

DIXON RYAN FOX

PREFACE

These documents are designed to illustrate the course of American history from the Age of Discovery to the present. Exigencies of space and of circumstance have required that the term document be interpreted in a very narrow sense. Properly speaking, almost everything of an original character is a document: letters, memoirs, ballads, folk-lore, poetry, fiction, newspaper reports and editorials, sermons and speeches, to say nothing of inscriptions, stamps, coins, buildings, painting and sculpture, and all the innumerable memorials which man has left in his effort to understand and organize his world. I have tried to limit my selection to documents of an official and quasi-official character, though I have been no more consistent in this than in other things. I have not included selections often, and mistakenly, referred to as "readings"; even partially to illuminate American history from letters, memoirs, travelers' descriptions, etc. would require many volumes; this material, too, should be read in its entirety rather than in excerpt, and is readily available to students.

What is presented here, then, is part of the official record, and students know that the official record is neither the whole record nor in every case the real record. I cannot say that I have been guided in my choice of material by any rigid principles of selection. The choice has been determined by the experience of the class-room, by personal interest, and by availability. I have attempted to include those documents with which students should be familiar, such as the Northwest Ordinance or *Marbury* v. *Madison;* those which are illustrative or typical, such as colonial charters and land laws; those which focussed upon themselves the attention of the country, such as the Missouri Compromise or the Lincoln-Douglas Debates; those which serve as a convenient point of departure for the study of some economic or political development, such as labor cases or party platforms; those which illuminate some phase of our social life, such as the constitution of the Brook Farm Association or the Mooney-Billings Report; those which have certain qualities of interest, eloquence or beauty, such as Lee's Farewell to his Army or Holmes' dissent in the Abrams Case.

No one can be more acutely conscious of the inadequacies of such a collection than is the editor. Students familiar with the sources of American history will find many omissions and will discover many episodes unilluminated. To most of these charges I can plead only the exigencies of space; to some I must confess personal idiosyncrasy and fallibility. Students will look in vain for Webster's Reply to Hayne or Stephen's Cornerstone speech, for Hamilton's Report on Manufactures or the Federal Reserve Act, for the diplomatic correspondence on the X.Y.Z. affair or the Trent episode. These, and scores of similar selections, were omitted because I was not able to achieve a satisfactory condensation and did not feel that they could be included *in extenso.* While I have made efforts to find documents which would illustrate phases of our social and economic history, there are fewer of these than is desirable. Such documents are hard to come by: spiritual forces do not readily translate themselves into documents. I would have liked to have included Emerson's *Divinity School Address,* Fitzhugh's *Pro-Slavery Argument,* the platform of the American Economic Association; to have yielded to this temptation would have opened the flood-gates of miscellaneous source material. It cannot be pretended that presidential messages, supreme court decisions, or statutes, reveal much of the undercurrents of our social life. To discover these it would be necessary to go to church records, school reports, the minutes of fraternal orders, the records of labor organizations and agricultural societies, the records of probate courts, etc. American historians have been distressingly backward in the appreciation and publication of such material. These records therefore are not readily available, nor would a lifetime be sufficient to canvass them and take from them that which is typical.

Neither the notes nor the bibliographies which accompany these documents pretend to be extensive. In the notes I have attempted to state only what is essential for an understanding of the background of the document; the bibliographies are designed to indicate additional reading for the orientation of the document and additional bibliographical references. I have only occasionally included references to the rich deposits of material in periodicals and the publications of learned societies: for these the student will have to go to specialized bibliographical guides and to the invaluable *Writings on American History* which Miss Griffin has compiled. The documents themselves have been taken from and collated with the sources indicated. No effort has been made to standardize spelling, capital·ization or punctuation, or even to correct obvious errors in the originals: to have under-taken this, even granting its propriety, would have produced confusion. I have taken very few liberties with these documents. Omissions have been indicated by the customary ellipsis sign, but I have omitted such phrases as "be it also enacted" and "done at the city of Washington, etc." without any indication. I have in most instances abbreviated Article to Art. and Section to Sec., and I have frequently substituted numbered dates for the lengthier form. I have no doubt that in the many processes of copying, collating, and printing, num-erous errors have crept in; for these I beg the indulgence of the reader.

I am under obligation to many people for coöperation in the compilation of this volume. The officials of the libraries of New York University bore patiently with my demands. To my colleagues in the Department of History, Mr. Cochran, Mr. Craven, Mr. Hoffman, Mr. Musser, and Mr. Wettereau, to Mr. Stein of the Department of Economics, Mr. Thach of the Department of Government, and Dean Sommer of the Law School of New York University, I am grateful for suggestions. Without the faithful and intelligent assistance of Miss Margaret Carroll this volume could never have been prepared.

HENRY STEELE COMMAGER

PREFACE TO THE EIGHTH EDITION

In order to avoid an enlargement which would make *Documents of American History* un-wieldy, I have reluctantly had to drop a number of documents which were included in the seventh edition. In every case the documents illustrated events which, from the perspective of 1968, seem somewhat less important than they did when the last edition was prepared. By eliminating these I have made room for twenty-six new documents from the period since 1962—as eventful a period as any in American history. In the selection and the editing of these documents I have been greatly aided by Professor Christopher Lasch of North-western University.

HENRY STEELE COMMAGER

TABLE OF CONTENTS

Volume I

DOCUMENTS
of
AMERICAN HISTORY
To 1898

DOCUMENTS OF
AMERICAN HISTORY

1. PRIVILEGES AND PREROGATIVES GRANTED TO COLUMBUS
April 30, 1492

(F. N. Thorpe, ed. *Federal and State Constitutions*, Vol. I, p. 39 ff.)

For years Columbus had been presenting his scheme of sailing westward to the Indies to the sovereigns of Spain, Portugal, France and England, but without success. Finally in January 1492, the Spanish forces captured Granada and drove the Moors out of Spain, and Ferdinand and Isabella were free to consider seriously the proposals of Columbus. At first these terms were considered exorbitant and negotiations were broken off. Columbus was actually on his way to France when he was summoned back to Court, and the following terms accepted by Ferdinand and Isabella as King and Queen of Castile. The literature on Columbus is extensive. See, J. Winsor, *Christopher Columbus;* C. R. Markham, *Columbus;* H. Harrisse, *Christophe Colomb*, 2 Vols.; J. B. Thacher, *Christopher Columbus*, 3 Vols. The Hakluyt Society has published the *Journal of Christopher Columbus* and two volumes of *Letters*.

FERDINAND and ELIZABETH, . . .

For as much of you, *Christopher Columbus,* are going by our command, with some, of our vessels and men, to discover and subdue some Islands and Continent in the ocean, and it is hoped that by God's assistance, some of the said Islands and Continent in the ocean will be discovered and conquered by your means and conduct, therefore it is but just and reasonable, that since you expose yourself to such danger to serve us, you should be rewarded for it. And we being willing to honour and favour you for the reasons aforesaid; Our will is, That you, *Christopher Columbus,* after discovering and conquering the said Islands and Continent in the said ocean, or any of them, shall be our Admiral of the said Islands and Conti-

nent you shall so discover and conquer; and that you be our Admiral, Vice-Roy, and Governour in them, and that for the future, you may call and stile yourself, D. *Christopher Columbus,* and that your sons and successors in the said employment, may call themselves Dons, Admirals, Vice-Roys, and Governours of them; and that you may exercise the office of Admiral, with the charge of Vice-Roy and Governour of the said Islands and Continent, which you and your Lieutenants shall conquer, and freely decide all causes, civil and criminal, appertaining to the said employment of Admiral, Vice-Roy, and Governour, as you shall think fit in justice, and as the Admirals of our kingdoms use to do; and that you have power to punish offenders; and you and your Lieutenants exercise the employments of Admiral, Vice-Roy, and Governour, in all things belonging to the said offices, or any of them; and that you enjoy the perquisites and salaries belonging to the said employments, and to each of them, in the same manner as the High Admiral of our kingdoms does. And by this our letter, or a copy of it signed by a *Public Notary:* We command Prince *John,* our most dearly beloved Son, the Infants, Dukes, Prelates, Marquesses, Great Masters and Military Orders, Priors, Commendaries, our Counsellors, Judges, and other Officers of Justice whatsoever, belonging to our Household, Courts, and Chancery, and Constables of Castles, Strong Houses, and others, and all Corporations, Bayliffs, Governours, Judges, Commanders, Sea Officers; and the Aldermen, Common Council, Officers, and

Good People of all Cities, Lands, and Places in our Kingdoms and Dominions, and in those you shall conquer and subdue, and the captains, masters, mates, and other officers and sailors, our natural subjects now being, or that shall be for the time to come, and any of them, that when you shall have discovered the said Islands and Continent in the ocean; and you, or any that shall have your commission, shall have taken the usual oath in such cases, that they for the future, look upon you as long as you live, and after you, your son and heir, and so from one heir to another forever, as our Admiral on our said Ocean, and as Vice-Roy and Governour of the said Islands and Continent, by you, *Christopher Columbus,* discovered and conquered; and that they treat you and your Lieutenants, by you appointed, for executing the employments of Admiral, Vice-Roy, and Governour, as such in all respects, and give you all the perquisites and other things belonging and appertaining to the said offices; and allow, and cause to be allowed you, all the honours, graces, concessions, prehaminences, prerogatives, immunities, and other things, or any of them which are due to you, by virtue of your commands of Admiral, Vice-Roy, and Governour, and to be observed completely, so that nothing be diminished; and that they make no objec-

tion to this, or any part of it, nor suffer it to be made; forasmuch as we from this time forward, by this our letter, bestow on you the employments of Admiral, Vice-Roy, and perpetual Governour forever; and we put you into possession of the said offices, and of every of them, and full power to use and exercise them, and to receive the perquisites and salaries belonging to them, or any of them, as was said above. Concerning all which things, if it be requisite, and you shall desire it, We command our Chancellour, Notaries, and other Officers, to pass, seal, and deliver to you, our Letter of Privilege, in such form and legal manner, as you shall require or stand in need of. And that none of them presume to do any thing to the contrary, upon pain of our displeasure, and fortfeiture of 30 ducats for each offence. And we command him, who shall show them this our Letter, that he summon them to appear before us at our Court, where we shall then be, within fifteen days after such summons, under the said penalty. Under which same, we also command any Public Notary whatsoever, that he give to him that shows it him, a certificate under his seal, that we may know how our command is obeyed.

GIVEN at *Granada,* on the 30th of April, in the year of our Lord, 1492.—

I, THE KING, I, THE QUEEN.

2. THE PAPAL BULL *INTER CAETERA* (ALEXANDER VI)
May 4, 1493

(F. G. Davenport, ed. *European Treaties bearing on the History of the United States and its Dependencies to 1648,* p. 75 ff.)

Columbus returned from his first voyage in March, 1493, and the news of his discoveries was promptly communicated to the rulers of Spain and Portugal and to the Pope. Considerable uncertainty as to the lands discovered by Columbus existed: King John II of Portugal believed that Columbus's discoveries had really been in the region south and west of Guinea. Portuguese control over Guinea and the region to the south of Cape Bojador rested upon discoveries, papal bulls, and a treaty with Spain of 1480. King John was anxious therefore to have some decision as to the effects of Columbus's discoveries on the territorial claims of Portugal and Spain. Under these circumstances the matter was submitted to Pope Alexander VI. By the Bulls of May 3 and May 4 he drew an imaginary line of demarcation one hundred leagues west of the

Cape Verde Islands: east of this line Portugal was to have all the rights and possessions which she already held; west of this line Spain was to have the right to explore, trade, colonize, etc. The Bull of May 4 was amended by another Bull of September, 1493, specifically granting to the Spanish rulers the right to hold lands to the "eastern regions and to India". The line of demarcation of 1493 was changed the following year, Doc. No. 3. See, J. Fiske, *The Discovery of America,* Vol. II, ch. vi; E. G. Bourne, *Spain in America,* ch. iii; J. Winsor, ed. *Narrative and Critical History of America,* Vol. II; J. Winsor, *Christopher Columbus;* O. Peschel, *Die Theilung der Erde unter Papst Alexander VI und Julius II;* H. Harrisse, *Diplomatic History of America: Its First Chapter, 1452–1494.*

Alexander, bishop, servant of the servants of God, to the illustrious sovereigns, our very dear son in Christ, Ferdinand, king, and our very dear daughter in Christ, Isabella, queen of Castile. . . . We have indeed learned that you, who for a long time had intended to seek out and discover certain islands and mainlands remote and unknown and not hitherto discovered by others, to the end that you might bring to the worship of our Redeemer and the profession of the Catholic faith their residents and inhabitants, having been up to the present time greatly engaged in the siege and recovery of the kingdom itself of Granada were unable to accomplish this holy and praiseworthy purpose; but the said kingdom having at length been regained, as was pleasing to the Lord, with a wish to fulfill your desire, chose our beloved son, Christopher Columbus . . . whom you furnished with ships and men equipped for like designs, not without the greatest hardships, dangers, and expenses, to make diligent quest for these remote and unknown mainlands and islands through the sea, where hitherto no one had sailed; and they at length with divine aid and with the utmost diligence sailing in the ocean sea, discovered certain very remote islands and even mainlands that hitherto had not been discovered by others; wherein dwell very many peoples living in peace, and, as reported, going unclothed, and not eating flesh. . . . Wherefore, as becomes Catholic kings and princes . . . you have purposed . . . to bring under your sway the said mainlands and islands. . . . And in order that you may enter upon so great an undertaking with greater readiness and heartiness endowed with the benefit of our apostolic favor, we, of our own accord, not at your instance nor the request of anyone else in your regard, but out of our own sole largess and certain knowledge and out of the fullness of our apostolic power, by the authority of Almighty God conferred upon us in blessed Peter and of the vicarship of Jesus Christ, which we hold on earth, do by tenor of these presents, should any of said islands have been found by your envoys and captains, give, grant, and assign to you and your heirs and successors, kings of Castile and Leon, forever, together with all their dominions, cities, camps, places, and villages, and all rights, jurisdictions, and appurtenances, all islands and mainlands found and to be found, discovered and to be discovered towards the west and the south, by drawing and establishing a line from the Arctic pole, namely the north, to the Antarctic pole, namely the south, no matter whether the said mainlands and islands are found and to be found in the direction of India or towards any other quarter, the said line to be distant one hundred leagues towards the west and south from any of the islands commonly known as the Azores and Cape Verde. With this proviso, however, that none of the islands and mainlands, found and to be found, discovered and to be discovered, beyond that said line towards the west and south, be in the actual possession of any Christian king or prince up to the birthday of our Lord Jesus Christ just past from which the present year 1493 begins. . . . Furthermore, under penalty of excommunication *late sententie* to be incurred *ipso facto,* should anyone thus contravene, we strictly forbid all persons of whatsoever rank, even imperial and royal, or of whatsoever estate, degree, order, or condition, to dare without your special permit or that of your aforesaid heirs and successors, to go for the purpose of trade or any other reason to the islands or mainlands . . . apostolic constitutions and ordinances and other decrees whatsoever to the contrary notwithstanding. . . . Let no one therefore, infringe, or with rash boldness contravene, this our recommendation, exhortation, requisition, gift, grant, assignment, constitution, deputation, decree, mandate, prohibition, and will. Should anyone presume to attempt this, be it known to him that he will incur the wrath of Almighty God and of the blessed apostles Peter and Paul. Given at Rome, at St. Peter's, in the year of the incarnation of our Lord 1493, the fourth of May, and the first year of our pontificate.

3. THE TREATY OF TORDESILLAS
June 7, 1494

(F. G. Davenport, ed. European Treaties bearing on the History of the United States and its Dependencies to 1648, p. 84 ff.)

King John of Portugal was not satisfied with the provisions of the Bull Inter Caetera, and by the Treaty of Tordesillas persuaded the Spanish crown to consent to moving the line of demarcation 370 leagues west from the Cape Verde Islands. This change gave Portugal a claim to Brazil. See, J. Fiske, *The Discovery of America*, Vol. II, ch. vi; E. G. Bourne, *Spain in America*, ch. iii; J. Winsor, ed. *Narrative and Critical History of America*, Vol. II; O. Peschel, *Die Theilung der Erde unter Papst Alexander VI und Julius II*.

. . . Whereas a certain controversy exists between the said lords, their constituents, as to what lands, of all those discovered in the ocean sea up to the present day, the date of this treaty, pertain to each one of the said parts respectively; therefore, for the sake of peace and concord, and for the preservation of the relationship and love of the said King of Portugal for the said King and Queen of Castile, Aragon, etc. it being the pleasure of their Highnesses, they . . . covenanted and agreed that a boundary or straight line be determined and drawn north and south, from pole to pole, on the said ocean sea, from the Arctic to the Antarctic pole. This boundary or line shall be drawn straight, as aforesaid, at a distant of three hundred and seventy leagues west of the Cape Verde Islands, being calculated by degrees. . . . And all lands, both islands and mainlands, found and discovered already, or to be found and discovered hereafter, by the said King of Portugal and by his vessels on this side of the said line and bound determined as above, toward the east, in either north or south latitude, on the eastern side of the said bound, provided the said bound is not crossed, shall belong to and remain in the possession of, and pertain forever to, the said King of Portugal and his successors. And all other lands, both islands and mainlands, found or to be found hereafter, . . . by the said King and Queen of Castile, Aragon, etc. and by their vessels, on the western side of the said bound, determined as above, after having passed the said bound toward the west, in either its north or south latitude, shall belong to . . . the said King and Queen of Castile, Leon, etc. and to their successors.

Item, the said representatives promise and affirm . . . that from this date no ships shall be dispatched—namely as follows: the said King and Queen of Castile, Leon, Aragon etc. for this part of the bound . . . which pertains to the said King of Portugal . . . nor the said King of Portugal to the other side of the said bound which pertains to the said King and Queen of Castile, Aragon, etc.—for the purpose of discovering and seeking any mainlands or islands, or for the purpose of trade, barter, or conquest of any kind. But should it come to pass that the said ships of the said King and Queen of Castile . . . on sailing thus on this side of the said bound, should discover any mainlands or islands in the region pertaining, as abovesaid, to the said King of Portugal, such mainlands or islands shall belong forever to the said King of Portugal and his heirs, and their Highnesses shall order them to be surrendered to him immediately. And if the said ships of the said King of Portugal discover any islands or mainlands in the regions of the said King and Queen of Castile . . . all such lands shall belong to and remain forever in the possession of the said King and Queen of Castile . . . and their heirs, and the said King of Portugal shall cause such lands to be surrendered immediately. . . .

And by this present agreement, they . . . entreat our most Holy Father that his Holiness be pleased to confirm and approve this said agreement, according to what is set forth therein; and that he order his bulls in regard to it to be issued to the parties or to whichever of the parties may solicit them with the tenor of this agreement incorporated therein, and that he lay his censures upon those who shall violate or oppose it at any time whatsoever. . . .

4. LETTERS PATENT TO JOHN CABOT
March 5, 1496

(F. N. Thorpe, ed. *Federal and State Constitutions*, Vol. I, p. 46–7)

Giovanni Caboto was a Genoese; he came to England some time between 1484 and 1490, and settled among the merchant adventurers of Bristol. Eventually he interested Henry VII in the project of a northern route to the East, and secured a patent to find lands unknown to Christians. He set sail from Bristol May 2, 1497 and made a landfall on the Labrador coast; the expenses of the voyage were borne by the Bristol merchants. On Cabot, see C. R. Beazley, *John and Sebastian Cabot;* H. Harrisse, *John Cabot the Discoverer of North America;* C. Deane, *The Voyages of the Cabots,* in J. Winsor, *Narrative and Critical History,* Vol. III; J. A. Williamson, ed. *The Voyages of the Cabots;* J. B. Brebner, *Explorers of North America,* ch. vii.

The Letters patents of King Henry the seuenth granted vnto Iohn Cabot and his three sonnes, Lewis, Sebastian, and Sancius for the discouerie of new and vnknowen lands.

HEnry, by the grace of God, king of England and France, and lord of Ireland, to all to whom these presents shall come, Greeting.

Be it knowen that we haue giuen and granted, and by these presents do giue and grant for vs and our heires, to our welbeloued Iohn Cabot citizen of Venice, to Lewis, Sebastian, and Santius, sonnes of the sayd Iohn, and to the heires of them, and euery of them, and their deputies, full and free authority, leaue, and power to saile to all parts, countreys, and seas of the East, of the West, and of the North, vnder our banners and ensignes, with fiue ships of what burthen or quantity soeuer they be, and as many mariners or men as they will haue with them in the sayd ships, vpon their owne proper costs and charges, to seeke out, discouer, and finde whatsoeuer isles, countreys, regions or prouinces of the heathen and infidels whatsoeuer they be, and in what part of the world soeuer they be, which before this time haue bene vnknowen to all Christians: we haue granted to them, and also to euery of them, the heires of them, and euery of them, and their deputies, and haue giuen them licence to set vp our banners and ensignes in euery village, towne, castle, isle, or maine land of them newly found. And that the aforesayd Iohn and his sonnes, or their heires and assignes may subdue, occupy and possesse all such townes, cities, castles and isles of them found, which they can subdue, occupy and possesse, as our vassals, and lieutenants, getting vnto vs the rule, title, and iurisdiction of the same villages, townes, castles, & firme land so found. Yet so that the aforesayd Iohn, and his sonnes and heires, and their deputies, be holden and bounden of all the fruits, profits, gaines, and commodities growing of such nauigation, for euery their voyage, as often as they shall arriue at our port of Bristoll (at which port they shall be bound and holden onely to arriue) all manner of necessary costs and charges by them made, being deducted, to pay vnto vs in wares or money the fift part of the capitall gaine so gotten. We giuing and granting vnto them and to their heires and deputies, that they shall be free from all paying of customes of all and singular such merchandize as they shall be free from all paying of customes of all and singular they shall bring with them from those places so newlie found.

And moreouer, we haue given and granted to them, their heires and deputies, that all the firme lands, isles, villages, townes, castles and places whatsoeuer they be that they shall chance to finde, may not of any other of our subjects be frequented or visited without the licence of the foresayd Iohn and his sonnes, and their deputies, vnder payne of forfeiture as well of their ships as of all and singular goods of all them that shall presume to saile to those places so found. Willing, and most straightly commanding all and singular our subjects as well on land as on sea, appointed officers, to giue good assistance to the aforesaid Iohn, and his sonnes and deputies, and that as well in arming and furnishing their ships or vessels, as in prouision of quietnesse, and in buying of victuals for their money, and all other things by them to be prouided necessary for the sayd nauigation, they do giue them all their helpe and fauour. In witnesse whereof we have caused to be made these our lettres patents. Witnesse our selfe at Westminister, the fift day of March, in the eleuenth yeere of our reigne.—

5. CHARTER TO SIR WALTER RALEGH
March 25, 1584

(F. N. Thorpe, ed. *Federal and State Constitutions,* Vol. I, p. 53 ff.)

English colonization in America may be dated from the letters patent to Sir Humphrey Gilbert of 1578. Under this grant Gilbert made two efforts to establish a colony in America; both were unsuccessful, and the second ended in the tragic death of the gallant adventurer. Sir Walter Raleigh, Gilbert's half-brother, had participated in both of Gilbert's ventures, and planned to carry on the work of colonization. Six months after Gilbert's death Raleigh received a patent couched in almost identical language as the patent of 1578. Under his charter, Raleigh sent out five expeditions to the new world, and succeeded in planting a colony on Roanoke Island, Virginia. Altogether Raleigh spent a personal fortune of some forty thousand pounds in his efforts to plant a colony in the new world, but he ended his life in the Tower of London. Raleigh, writes Professor Andrews, "was the first Englishman to demonstrate the practicability of transporting English men and women overseas to find new homes on a new soil. His colony of husbands and wives, mothers and nursing children . . . represents a new departure in English history." See, C. M. Andrews, *Our Earliest Colonial Settlements,* ch. i; L. G. Tyler, *England in America,* ch. ii; M. Waldman, *Sir Walter Raleigh;* L. Creighton, *Sir Walter Raleigh;* I. N. Tarbox, *Sir Walter Raleigh;* W. Stebbing, *Sir Walter Raleigh;* E. Edwards, *Life of Ralegh;* E. J. Payne, ed. *Voyages of the Elizabethan Seamen to America,* 1880 ed.

ELIZABETH, by the Grace of God of England, Fraunce and Ireland Queene, defender of the faith, &c. To all people to whome these presents shall come, greeting.

Knowe yee that of our especial grace, certaine science, and meere motion, . . . we give and graunt to our trustie and welbeloved servant *Walter Ralegh,* Esquire, and to his heires assignes for ever, free libertie and licence from time to time, and at all times for ever hereafter, to discover, search, finde out, and view such remote, heathen and barbarous lands, countries, and territories, not actually possessed of any Christian Prince, nor inhabited by Christian People, as to him, . . . shall seeme good, and the same to have, holde occupie and enjoy to him, . . . for ever, with all prerogatives, . . . thereto or thereabouts both by sea and land, whatsoever we by our letters patent may graunt, . . . and the said *Walter Ralegh,* his heires and assignes, . . . shall goe or travaile thither to inhabite or remaine, there to build and fortifie, at the discretion of the said *Walter Ralegh,* . . .

And we do likewise . . . give and graunt full authoritie, libertie and power to the said *Walter Ralegh,* . . . that he . . . shall . . . have, take, and leade in the saide voyage, and travaile thitherward, or to inhabit there with him, or them, and every or any of them, such and so many of our subjects as shall willingly accompanie him or them, . . .

And further that the said *Walter Ralegh,* . . . shall have . . . all the soile of all such lands, territories, and Countreis, so to bee discovered and possessed as aforesaide, and of all such Cities, castles, townes, villages, and places in the same, with the right, royalties, franchises, and jurisdictions, as well marine as other within the saide landes, or Countreis, or the seas thereunto adjoining, to be had, or used, with full power to dispose thereof, and of every part in fee-simple or otherwise, according to the order of the lawes of England, . . . : reserving always to us our heires, and successors, for all services, duties, and demaundes, the fift part of all the oare of golde and silver, that from time to time, and at all times . . . shal be there gotten and obtained: . . .

And moreover, we doe . . . give and graunt licence to the said *Walter Ralegh,* . . . that he, . . . shall and may . . . for his and their defence, encounter and expulse, repell and resist . . . all . . . as without the especiall liking and licence of the said *Walter Ralegh,* . . . shall attempt to inhabite within the said Countreis, . . . or within the space of two hundreth leagues neere to the place or places within such Countreis, . . . where the saide *Walter Ralegh,* . . . shall within sixe yeeres . . . make their dwellings. . . . And for uniting in more perfect league and amitie, of such Countreis, landes, and territories so to bee possessed and inhabited as aforesaide with our Realmes of Englande, and Ireland, and the better incouragement of men to these enterprises: we do . . . declare that all such Countreis, so hereafter to be possessed and inhabited as is aforesaide, from thencefoorth shall bee of the allegiance of us, our heires and successours. And wee doe graunt to the saide *Walter Ralegh,* . . . and to all and every of them, . . . that they . . . being either borne within our saide Realmes of Englande, . . . shall and may have all the priviledges of free Denizens, and persons native of England. . . .

And . . . we . . . do give and graunt to the said *Walter Ralegh,* . . . that hee . . . shall, within the said mentioned remote landes . . . have full and meere power and authoritie to correct, punish, pardon, governe, and rule by their and every or any of their good discretions and pollicies, as well in causes capital, or criminall, as civil, . . . all such our subjects as shall from time to time adventure themselves in the said journies or voyages, or that shall at any time hereafter inhabite any such landes, countreis, or territories as aforesaide, . . . according to such statutes, lawes and ordinances, as shall bee by him the saide *Walter Ralegh* . . . devised, or established, for the better government of the said people as aforesaid. So always as the said statutes, lawes, and ordinances may be as neere as conveniently may be, agreeable to the forme of the lawes, statutes, governement, or pollicie of England, . . .

Provided alwayes, and our will and pleasure is, and wee do hereby declare to all Christian kings, princes and states, that if the saide *Walter Ralegh,* his heires or assignes, or any of them, or any other by their licence or appointment, shall at any time or times hereafter, robbe or spoile by sea or by lande, or do any acte of unjust or unlawful hostilitie, to any of the subjects of us, our heires or successors, or to any of the subjects of any the kings, princes, rulers, governors, or estates, being then in perfect

league and amitie with us, our heires and successors, and that upon such injury, or upon just complaint of any such prince, ruler, governoir, or estate, or their subjects, wee, our heires and successours, shall make open proclamation within any the portes of our Realme of England, that the saide *Walter Ralegh,* his heires and assignes, and adherents, or any to whome these our letters patents may extende, shall within the termes to be limitted, by such proclamation, make full restitution, and satisfaction of all such injuries done, so as both we and the said princes, or other so complayning, may holde us and themselves fully contented. And that if the saide *Walter Ralegh,* his heires and assignes, shall ·not make or cause to be made satisfaction accordingly, within such time so to be limitted, that then it shall be lawfull to us our heires and successors, to put the saide *Walter Ralegh,* his heires and assignes and adherents, and all the inhabitants of the said places to be discovered (as is aforesaide) or any of them out of our allegiance and protection, and that from and after such time of putting out of protection the said *Walter Ralegh,* his heires, assignes and adherents, and others so to be put out, and the said places within their habitation, possession and rule, shal be out of our allegeance and protection, and free for all princes and others, to pursue with hostilitie, as being not our subjects, nor by us any way to be avouched, maintained or defended, nor to be holden as any of ours, nor to our protection or dominion, or allegiance any way belonging, for that expresse mention of the cleer yeerely value of the certaintie of the premisses, or any part thereof, or of any other gift, or grant by us, or any our progenitors, or predecessors to the said *Walter Ralegh,* before this time made in these presents be not expressed, or any other grant, ordinance, provision, proclamation, or restraint to the contrarye thereof, before this time given, ordained, or provided, or any other thing, cause, or matter whatsoever, in any wise notwithstanding. In witness whereof, we have caused these our letters to be made patents. Witnesse our selves, at *Westminster,* the 25. day of March, in the sixe and twentieth yeere of our Raigne.

6. FIRST CHARTER OF VIRGINIA
April 10, 1606

(Poore, ed. *The Federal and State Constitutions,* Part II, p. 1889 ff.)

The charter to the Virginia Company granted by King James provided for the incorporation of two companies: the London Company and the Plymouth Company. It was the London Company that established the first permanent English colony in America; the expedition of one hundred and twenty settlers who left England in December, 1606, made their first landfall at Cape Henry, April 29, 1607, and planted a colony at Jamestown May 14. On the three charters of Virginia and the early history of the Colony see, W. Stith, *History of Virginia,* with numerous documents; A. Brown, *Genesis of the United States,* 2 Vols; A. Brown, *First Republic in America;* J. Fiske, *Old Virginia and her Neighbours,* Vol. I; C. M. Andrews, *The Colonial Period of American History,* Vol. I, ch. v.; L. G. Tyler, *England in America,* chs. iii–v. The records of the Virginia Company are being published by S. M. Kingsbury, ed. *Records of the Virginia Company.* On the Company see also A. Brown, *English Politics in Early Virginia History;* E. D. Neill, *History of the Virginia Company of London;* and W. F. Craven, *The Dissolution of the Virginia Company.*

I. *JAMES,* by the Grace of God, King of *England, Scotland, France,* and *Ireland,* Defender of the Faith, &c. WHEREAS our loving and well-disposed Subjects, Sir *Thomas Gates,* and Sir *George Somers,* Knights, *Richard Hackluit,* Clerk, Prebendary of *Westminster,* and *Edward-Maria Wingfield, Thomas Hanham,* and *Ralegh Gilbert,* Esqrs. *William Parker,* and *George Popham,* Gentlemen, and divers others of our loving Subjects, have been humble Suitors unto us, that We would vouchsafe unto them our Licence, to make Habitation, Plantation, and to deduce a Colony of sundry of our People into that Part of *America,* commonly called VIRGINIA, and other Parts and Territories in *America,* either appertaining unto us, or which are not now actually possessed by any *Christian* Prince or People, situate, lying, and being all along the Sea Coasts, between four and thirty Degrees of *Northerly* Latitude from the Equinoctial Line, and five and forty Degrees of the same Latitude, and in the main Land between the same four and thirty and five and forty Degrees,

and the Islands thereunto adjacent, or within one hundred Miles of the Coast thereof;

And to that End, and for the more speedy Accomplishment of their said intended Plantation and Habitation there, are desirous to divide themselves into two several Colonies and Companies; The one consisting of certain Knights, Gentlemen, Merchants, and other Adventurers, of our City of *London* and elsewhere, which are, and from time to time shall be, joined unto them, which do desire to begin their Plantation and Habitation in some fit and convenient Place, between four and thirty and one and forty Degrees of the said Latitude, alongst the Coasts of *Virginia* and Coasts of *America* aforesaid; And the other consisting of sundry Knights, Gentlemen, Merchants, and other Adventurers, of our Cities of *Bristol* and *Exeter,* and of our Town of *Plimouth,* and of other Places, which do join themselves unto that Colony, which do desire to begin their Plantation and Habitation in some fit and convenient Place, between eight and thirty Degrees and five and forty Degrees of the said Latitude, all alongst the said Coast of *Virginia* and *America,* as that Coast lyeth:

We, greatly commending, and graciously accepting of, their Desires for the Furtherance of so noble a Work, which may, by the Providence of Almighty God, hereafter tend to the Glory of his Divine Majesty, in propagating of *Christian* Religion to such People, as yet live in Darkness and miserable Ignorance of the true Knowledge and Worship of God, and may in time bring the Infidels and Savages, living in those Parts, to human Civility, and to a settled and quiet Government; Do, by these our Letters Patents, graciously accept of, and agree to, their humble and well-intended Desires;

AND do therefore, for Us, our Heirs, and Successors, GRANT and agree, that the said Sir *Thomas Gates,* Sir *George Somers, Richard Hackluit,* and *Edward-Maria Wingfield,* Adventurers of and for our City of *London,* and all such others, as are, or shall be, joined unto them of that Colony, shall be called the *first Colony;* And they shall and may begin their said first Plantation and Habitation, at any Place upon the said Coast of *Virginia* or *America,* where they shall think fit and convenient, between the said four and thirty and one and forty Degrees of the said Latitude; And that they shall have all the Lands, . . . from the said first Seat of their Plantation and Habitation by the Space of fifty Miles of *English* Statute Measure, all along the said Coast of *Virginia* and *America,* towards the *West* and *Southwest,* as the Coast lyeth, . . . And also all the Lands . . . from the said Place of their first Plantation and Habitation for the space of fifty like *English* Miles, all alongst the said Coast of *Virginia* and *America,* towards the *East* and *Northeast,* or towards the *North,* as the Coast lyeth, . . . And also all the Lands . . . from the same fifty Miles every way on the Sea Coast, directly into the main Land by the Space of one hundred like *English* Miles; . . .

AND we do likewise . . . GRANT and agree, that the said *Thomas Hanham,* and *Ralegh Gilbert, William Parker,* and *George Popham,* and all others of the Town of *Plimouth* in the County of *Devon,* or elsewhere, which are, or shall be, joined unto them of that Colony, shall be called the *second Colony;* And that they shall and may begin their said Plantation and Seat of their first Abode and Habitation, at any Place upon the said Coast of *Virginia* and *America,* where they shall think fit and convenient, between eight and thirty Degrees of the said Latitude, and five and forty Degrees of the same Latitude; And that they shall have all the Lands . . . from the first Seat of their Plantation and Habitation by the Space of fifty like *English* Miles, as is aforesaid, all alongst the said Coast of *Virginia* and *America,* towards the *West* and *Southwest,* or towards the *South,* . . . And also all the Lands . . . from the said Place of their first Plantation and Habitation for the Space of fifty like Miles, all alongst the said Coast of *Virginia* and *America,* towards the *East* and *Northeast,* . . . And also all the Lands . . . from the same fifty Miles every way on the Sea Coast, directly into the main Land, by the Space of one hundred like *English* Miles. . . .

Provided always, and our Will and Pleasure herein is, that the Plantation and Habitation of such of the said Colonies, as shall last plant themselves, as aforesaid, shall not be made within one hundred like *English* Miles of the other of them, that first began to make their Plantation, as aforesaid.

AND we do also ordain . . . that each of the said Colonies shall have a Council, which shall govern and order all Matters and Causes, which shall arise, grow, or happen, to or within the same several Colonies, according to such Laws, Ordinances, and Instructions, as shall be, in that behalf, given and signed with Our Hand or Sign Manual, and pass under the Privy Seal of our Realm of *England;* Each of which Councils shall consist of thirteen Persons, to be ordained, made, and removed, from time to time, according as shall be directed and comprised in the same instructions. . . .

AND that also there shall be a Council established here in *England,* which shall, in like Manner, consist of thirteen Persons, to be, for that Purpose, appointed by Us, . . . which shall be called our *Council of Virginia;* And shall, from time to time, have the superior Managing and Direction, only of and for all Matters, that shall or may concern the Government, as well of the said several Colonies, as of and for any other Part or Place, within the aforesaid Precincts of four and thirty and five and forty Degrees, above mentioned. . . .

AND moreover, we do GRANT . . . that the said several Councils, of and for the said several Colonies, shall and lawfully may, by Virtue hereof, from time to time, without any Interruption of Us . . . , give and take Order, to dig, mine, and search for all Manner of Mines of Gold, Silver, and Copper, as well within any part of their said several Colonies, as for the said main Lands on the Backside of the same Colonies. . . . YIELDING therefore, to Us . . . the fifth Part only of all the same Gold and Silver, and the fifteenth Part of all the same Copper, so to be gotten or had. . . .

Giving and granting, by these Presents, unto the said Sir *Thomas Gates* . . . and their Associates of the said first Colony, and unto the said *Thomas Hanham* . . . and their Associates of the said second Colony . . . Power and Authority to take and surprise, by all Ways and Means whatsoever, all and every Person and Persons, with their Ships, Vessels, Goods and other Furniture, which shall be found trafficking, into any Harbour or Harbours, Creek or Creeks, or Place, within the Limits or Precincts of the said several Colonies and Plantations, not being of the same Colony, until such time, as they, being of any Realms or Dominions under our Obedience, shall pay, or agree to pay, to the Hands of the Treasurer of that Colony, within whose Limits and Precincts they shall so traffick, two and a half upon every Hundred, of any thing, so by them trafficked, bought, or sold; And being Strangers, and not Subjects under our Obeysance, until they shall pay five upon every Hundred, of such Wares and Merchandises, as they shall traffick, buy, or sell, within the Precincts of the said several Colonies, wherein they shall so traffick, buy, or sell, as aforesaid; WHICH Sums of Money, or Benefit, as aforesaid, for and during the Space of one and twenty Years, next ensuing the Date hereof, shall be wholly emploied to the Use, Benefit, and Behoof of the said several Plantations, where such Traffick shall be made; And after the said one and twenty Years ended, the same shall be taken to the Use of Us. . . .

Also we do . . . DECLARE . . . that all and every the Persons, being our Subjects, which shall dwell and inhabit within every or any of the said several Colonies and Plantations, and every of their children, which shall happen to be born within any of the Limits and Precincts of the said several Colonies and Plantations, shall HAVE and enjoy all Liberties, Franchises, and Immunities, within any of our other Dominions, to all Intents and Purposes, as if they had been abiding and born, within this our Realm of *England,* or any other of our said Dominions. . . .

And finally, we do . . . GRANT and agree, to and with the said Sir *Thomas Gates* . . . and all others of the said first Colony, that We . . . , upon Petition in that Behalf to be made, shall, . . . GIVE and GRANT unto such Persons, their Heirs, and Assigns, as the Council of that Colony, or the most Part of them, shall, for that Purpose nominate and assign, all the Lands, Tenements, and Hereditaments, which shall be within the Precincts limited for that Colony, as is aforesaid, To BE HOLDEN of Us, our Heirs, and Successors, as of our Manor at *East-Greenwich* in the County of *Kent,* in free and common Soccage only, and not in Capite: . . .

7. SECOND CHARTER OF VIRGINIA
May 23, 1609

(Poore, ed. *The Federal and State Constitutions,* Part II, p. 1893 ff.)

During the first three years of its history the affairs of the Virginia Company, both the Virginia and the Maine plantations, were badly mismanaged. The second charter made some essential changes in the first: the London and the Plymouth companies were separated; the royal council was replaced by a company council; and control of the colony was vested in the treasurer and his council. For references, see Doc. No. 6.

[After reciting the grant of 1606, the charter continues].

Now, forasmuch as divers and sundry of our loving Subjects, as well Adventurers, as Planters, of the said first Colony . . . have of late been humble Suitors unto Us, that . . . We would be pleased to grant them a further Enlargement and Explanation of the said Grant, Privileges, and Liberties, and that

such Counsellors, and other Officers, may be appointed amongst them, to manage and direct their affairs, as are willing and ready to adventure with them, as also whose Dwellings are not so far remote from the City of *London,* but that they may, at convenient Times, be ready at Hand, to give their Advice and Assistance, upon all occasions requisite.

WE . . . do . . . GIVE, GRANT, and CONfirm, to our trusty and well-beloved Subjects, [enumerates grantees] . . . , and to such, and so many, as they do, or shall hereafter, admit to be joined with them, in form hereafter in these presents expressed, whether they go in their Persons, to be Planters there in the said Plantation, or whether they go not, but adventure their monies, goods, or Chattels, that they shall be one Body or Commonalty perpetual, and shall have perpetual Succession, and one common Seal, to serve for the said Body or Commonalty, and that they, and their Successors, shall be known, called, and incorporated by the Name of, *The Treasurer and Company of Adventurers and Planters of the City of London for the first Colony in Virginia.* . . .

And we do also . . . give, grant and confirm, unto the said Treasurer and Company, and their Successors, under the Reservations, Limitations, and Declarations, hereafter expressed, all those Lands, Countries, and Territories, situate, lying, and being, in that Part of *America* called *Virginia,* from the Point of Land, called Cape or *Point Comfort,* all along the Sea Coast, to the Northward two hundred Miles, and from the said Point of *Cape Comfort,* all along the Sea Coast, to the Southward two hundred Miles, and all that Space and Circuit of Land, lying from the Sea Coast of the Precinct aforesaid, up into the Land, throughout from Sea to Sea, West, and Northwest; . . .

AND forasmuch, as the good and prosperous Success of the said Plantation cannot but chiefly depend, next under the Blessing of God, and the Support of our Royal Authority, upon the provident and good Direction of the whole Enterprize, by a careful and understanding Council, and that it is not convenient, that all the Adventurers shall be so often drawn to meet and assemble, as shall be requisite for them to have Meetings and Conference about the Affairs thereof; Therefore we DO ORDAIN, establish, and confirm, that there shall be perpetually one COUNCIL here resident, according to the Tenour of our former Letters-patents. . . .

AND further . . . we do . . . GIVE and GRANT full Power and Authority to our said Council, here resident, . . . to nominate, make, constitute, ordain, and confirm, by such Name or Names, Stile or Stiles, as to them shall seem good, And likewise to revoke, discharge, change, and alter, as well all and singular Governors, Officers, and Ministers, which already have been made, as also which hereafter shall be by them thought fit and needful to be made or used, for the Government of the said Colony and Plantation: AND also to make, ordain, and establish all Manner of Orders, Laws, Directions, In-

structions, Forms, and Ceremonies of Government and Magistracy, fit and necessary, for and concerning the Government of the said Colony and Plantation; And the same, at all times hereafter, to abrogate, revoke, or change, . . . as they, in their good Discretion, shall think to be fittest for the Good of the Adventurers and inhabitants there. . . .

AND we do further . . . ORDAIN and establish, that the said Treasurer and Council here resident, and their Successors, or any four of them, being assembled (the Treasurer being one) shall, from time to time, have full Power and Authority, to admit and receive any other Person into their Company, Corporation, and Freedom; And further, in a General Assembly of the Adventurers, with the Consent of the greater Part, upon good Cause, to disfranchise and put out any Person or Persons, out of the said Freedom or Company. . . .

ALSO we do . . . DECLARE . . . that all and every the Persons being our Subjects, which shall go and inhabit within the said Colony and Plantation, and every their Children and Posterity; which shall happen to be born within any of the Limits thereof, shall HAVE and ENJOY all Liberties, Franchizes, and Immunities of Free Denizens and natural Subjects within any of our other Dominions to all Interests and Purposes, as if they had been abiding and born within this our realm of *England.* . . .

AND forasmuch, as it shall be necessary for all such our loving Subjects, as shall inhabit within the said Precincts of *Virginia,* aforesaid, to determine to live together, in the Fear and true Worship of Almighty God, Christian Peace, and civil Quietness, each with other, whereby every one may, with more Safety, Pleasure, and Profit, enjoy that, whereunto they shall attain with great Pain and Peril; We . . . do GIVE and GRANT unto the said Treasurer and Company, . . . and to such Governors, Officers, and Ministers, as shall be, by our said Council, constituted and appointed, . . . that they shall and may, from time to time for ever hereafter, within the said Precincts of *Virginia,* . . . have full and absolute Power and Authority, to correct, punish, pardon, govern, and rule, all such the Subjects of Us . . . as shall, from time to time, adventure themselves in any Voyage thither, or that shall, at any time hereafter, inhabit in the Precincts and Territories of the said Colony, . . .

AND further . . . in all Questions and Doubts that shall arise upon any Difficulty of Construction or Interpretation of Any thing contained either in this, or in our former Letters-patents, the same shall be . . . interpreted in most ample and beneficial manner for the said Treasurer and Company . . .

AND lastly, because the principal Effect, which we can desire or expect of this Action, is the Conversion and Reduction of the People in those Parts unto the true Worship of God and Christian Religion, in which Respect we should be loath, that any Person should be permitted to pass, that we suspected to affect the Superstitions of the Church of *Rome,* we do hereby DECLARE, that it is our Will and Pleasure, that none be permitted to pass in any Voyage, from time to time to be made into the said Country, but such, as first shall have taken the Oath of Supremacy; . . .

8. THE THIRD CHARTER OF VIRGINIA
March 12, 1612

(F. N. Thorpe, ed. *Federal and State Constitutions,* Vol. VII, p. 3803 ff.)

The third charter of Virginia added the island of Bermuda, which had been discovered by the English in 1609, to the jurisdictions of the Company, provided for more democratic government and a greater degree of independence for the Company, enlarged the powers of the Company, and instituted a lottery. The Company subsequently sold Bermuda. This charter of 1612 was annulled in 1624, when Virginia became a royal colony. See, references under Doc. 6 and W. F. Craven, *The Dissolution of the Virginia Company.*

. . . Now forasmuch as we are given to understand, that in those Seas adjoining to the said Coasts of *Virginia,* and without the Compass of those two hundred Miles by Us so granted unto the said Treasurer and Company as aforesaid, and yet not far distant from the said Colony in *Virginia,* there are or may be divers Islands lying desolate and uninhabited, some of which are already made known and discovered by the Industry, Travel, and Expences of the said Company, and others also are supposed to be and remain as yet unknown and undiscovered, all and every of which it may import the said Colony both in Safety and Policy of Trade to populate and plant; in Regard whereof, as well for the preventing of Peril, as for the better Commodity of the said Colony, they have been humble suitors unto Us, that We would be pleased to grant unto them an Enlargement of our said former Letters-patents, as well for a more ample Extent of their Limits and Territories into the Seas adjoining to and upon the Coast of *Virginia,* as also for some other Matters and Articles concerning the better government of the said Company and Colony, . . .

We therefore . . . do by these Presents give, grant, and confirm to the said Treasurer and Company of Adventurers and Planters of the city of *London* for the first Colony in *Virginia* and to their Heirs and Successors for ever, all and singular those Islands whatsoever situate and being in any Part of the Ocean Seas bordering upon the Coast of our said first Colony in *Virginia,* and being within three Hundred Leagues of any of the Parts heretofore granted to the said Treasurer and Company in our said former Letters-patents as aforesaid, and being within or between the one-and-fortieth and thirtieth Degrees of Northerly Latitude . . . Provided always, that the said Islands or any Premises herein mentioned, or by these Presents intended or meant to be granted, be not actually possessed or inhabited by any other Christian Prince or Estate, nor be within the Bounds, Limits, or Territories of the Northern Colony heretofore by Us granted to be planted by divers of our loving Subjects in the North Parts of *Virginia.* . . .

And we do hereby ordain and grant by these Presents, that the said Treasurer and Company of Adventurers and Planters aforesaid, shall and may, once every week, or oftener, at their Pleasure, hold, and keep a Court and Assembly for the better Order and Government of the said Plantation, and such Things as shall concern the same: And that any five Persons of our Council for the said first Colony in *Virginia*, for the Time being, of which Company the Treasurer, or his Deputy, to be always one, and the Number of fifteen others, at the least, of the Generality of the said Company, assembled together in such Manner, as is and hath been heretofore used and accustomed, shall be said, taken, held, and reputed to be, and shall be a *sufficient Court* of the said Company, for the handling and ordering, and dispatching of all such casual and particular Occurrences, and accidental Matters, of less Consequence and Weight, as shall from Time to Time happen, touching and concerning the said Plantation. . . .

9. ORDINANCE FOR VIRGINIA
July 24, 1621

(F. N. Thorpe, ed. *Federal and State Constitutions,* Vol. VII, p. 3810 ff.)

The first Assembly of Virginia was convened July 30, 1619 by Governor Yeardley, under the authority of the Virginia Company, and marks the beginning of representative government in America. The document authorizing the convening of this first assembly has been lost; the Ordinance of 1621 is believed to be an almost exact reproduction of the earlier one. See references to Doc. No. 6.

An ordinance and Constitution of the Treasurer, Council, and Company in England, for a Council of State and General Assembly. Dated July 24, 1621.

To all People, to whom these Presents shall come, be seen, or heard The Treasurer, Council, and Company of Adventurers and Planters for the City of *London* for the first colony of *Virginia*, send Greeting. Know ye that we, the said Treasurer, Council, and Company, taking into our careful Consideration the present State, of the said Colony of *Virginia*, and intending, by the Divine Assistance, to settle such a Form of Government there as may be to the greatest Benefit and Comfort of the People, and whereby all Injustice, Grievances, and Oppression may be prevented and kept off as much as possible from the said Colony, have thought fit to make our Entrance, by ordering and establishing such Supreme Councils, as may not only be assisting to the Governor for the time being, in the Administration of Justice, and the executing of other Duties for this office belonging, but also, by their vigilant care and Prudence, may provide, as well for a Remedy of all Inconveniences, growing from time to time, as also for advancing of Increase, Strength, Stability, and Prosperity of the said Colony:

II. We therefore, the said Treasurer, Council, and Company, by Authority directed to us from his Majesty under the Great Seal, upon mature Deliberation, do hereby order and declare, that, from hence forward, there shall be Two SUPREME COUNCILS in *Virginia*, for the better Government of the said Colony aforesaid.

III. The one of which Councils, to be called THE COUNCIL OF S TATE (and whose Office shall chiefly be assisting, with their Care, Advise, and Circumspection, to the said Governor) shall be chosen, nominated, placed and displaced, from time to time, by Us, the said Treasurer, Council, and Company, and our Successors: Which Council of State shall consist, for the present, only of these Persons, as are here inserted, *viz.* Sir *Francis Wyat*, Governor of *Virginia*, Captain *Francis West*, Sir *George Yeardley*, Knight, Sir *William Neuce*, Knight Marshal of *Virginia*, Mr. *George Sandys*, Treasurer, Mr. *George Thorpe*, Deputy of the College, Captain *Thomas Neuce*, Deputy for the Company, Mr. *Pawlet*, Mr. *Leech*, Captain *Nathaniel Powel*, Mr. *Harwood*, Mr. *Samuel Macock*, Mr. *Christopher Davison*, Secretary, *Doctor Pots* Physician to the Company, Mr. *Roger Smith*, Mr. *John Berkley*, Mr. *John Rolfe*, Mr. *Ralph Hamer*, Mr. *John Pountis*, Mr. *Michael Lapworth*. Which said Counsellors and Council we earnestly pray and desire, and in his Majesty's Name strictly charge and command, that (all Factions, Partialities, and sinister Respect laid aside) they bend their Care and Endeavors to assist the said Governor; first and principally in the Advancement of the Honour and Service of God, and the Enlargement of his Kingdom amongst the Heathen People; and next, in erecting of the said Colony in due obedience to his Majesty, and all lawful Authority from his Majesty's Directions; and lastly, in maintaining the said People in Justice and *Christian* Conversation amongst themselves, and in Strength and Ability to withstand their Enemies. And this Council, to be always, or for the most Part, residing about or near the Governor.

IV. The other Council, more generally to be called by the Governor, once yearly, and no oftener, but for very extraordinary and important occasions, shall consist, for the present, of the said Council of State, and of two Burgesses out of every Town, Hundred, or other particular Plantation, to be respectively chosen by the Inhabitants; Which Council shall be called THE GENERAL ASSEMBLY, wherein (as also in the said Council of State) all Matter shall be decided, determined, and ordered, by the greater Part of the Voices then present; reserving to the Governor always a Negative Voice. And this General Assembly shall have free Power to treat, consult, and conclude, as well of all emergent Occasions concerning the Publick Weal of the said Colony and every Part thereof, as also to make, ordain, and enact such general Laws and Orders, for the Behoof of the said Colony, and the good Government thereof, as shall, from time to time, appear necessary or requisite;

V. Whereas in all other Things, we require the said General Assembly, as also the said Council of State, to imitate and follow the Policy of the Form of Government—Laws, Customs, and Manner of Trial, and other Administration of Justice, used in the Realm of *England,* as near as may be, even as ourselves, by his Majesty's Letters Patent, are required.

VI. Provided, that no Law or Ordinance, made in the said General Assembly, shall be or continue in Force or Validity, unless the same shall be solemnly ratified and confirmed, in a General Quarter Court of the said Company here in England and so ratified, be returned to them under our Seal; It being our Intent to afford the like Measure also unto the said Colony, that after the Government of the said Colony shall once have been well framed, and settled accordingly, which is to be done by Us, as by Authority derived from his Majesty, and the same shall have been so by Us declared, no Orders of Court afterwards shall bind the said Colony, unless they be ratified in like Manner in the General Assemblies. IN WITNESS whereof we have here unto set our Common Seal, the 24th of *July* 1621, and in the Year of the Reign of our Sovereign Lord, JAMES, King of *England,* &c., the —— and of Scotland the ——

10. THE LEYDEN AGREEMENT
1618

(W. Walker, *The Creeds and Platforms of Congregationalism,* p. 89–90.)

A group of London Separatists had settled in Amsterdam as early as 1593. In 1607–08 Separatists from the Scrooby Congregation joined the congregation in Amsterdam, but shortly moved to Leyden. In 1617 the Scrooby-Leyden group determined to move to America and applied to the Virginia Company for a patent to land in Virginia. To further this application, the congregation drew up these Seven Articles as assurance to the King of loyalty and orthodoxy. The King however promised only that "he would connive at them and not molest them provided they carried themselves peaceably." Eventually they secured a patent from the Virginia Company. See Doc. No. 11. On the Leyden Agreement and the Scrooby-Leyden Congregation see W. Bradford, *History of the Plymouth Plantation;* J. E. Goodwin, *The Pilgrim Republic;* L. Bacon, *The Gene-*

sis of the New England Churches; H. M. Dexter, *Congregationalism of the Last Three Hundred Years as Seen in its Literature,* Lectures v–vii; A. E. Dunning, *Congregationalists in America,* ch. iii; G. Bancroft, in New York Hist. Soc. *Collections,* Second Ser. Vol. III; D. Plooij, *The Pilgrim Fathers from a Dutch Point of View.*

Seven Artikes which ye Church of Leyden sent to ye Counsell of England to bee considered of in respeckt of their judgements occationed about theer going to Virginia Anno 1618

1. To ye confession of fayth published in ye name of ye Church of England & to every artikell theerof wee do wth ye reformed

churches wheer wee live & also els where assent wholy.

2. As wee do acknolidg ye docktryne of fayth theer tawght so do wee ye fruites and effeckts of ye same docktrynε to ye begetting of saving fayth in thousands in ye land (conformistes and reformistes as ye are called) wth whom also ás wth our bretheren wee do desyer to keepe spirituall communion in peace and will pracktis in our parts all lawfull thinges.

3. The Kings Majesty wee acknoledge for Supreame Governer in his Dominion in all causes and over all parsons, and ye none maye decklyne or apeale from his authority or judgement in any cause whatsoever, byt y in all thinges obedience is dewe unto him, ether active, if ye thing commanded be not agaynst God's woord, or passive yf itt bee, except pardon can bee obtayned.

4. Wee judg itt lawfull for his Majesty to apoynt bishops; civill overseers, or officers in awthority onder hime, in ye severall provinces, dioses, congregatíons or parrishes to oversee ye Churches and governe them civilly according to ye Lawes of ye Land, untto whom ye ar in all thinges to give an account & by them to bee ordered according to Godlynes.

5. The authoryty of ye present bishops in ye Land wee do acknowlidg so far forth as ye same is indeed derived from his Majesty untto them and as ye proseed in his name, whom we will also theerein honor in all things and hime in them.

6. Wee beleeve yt no sinod, classes, convocation or assembly of Ecclesiasticall officers hath any power or awthoryty att all but as ye same by ye Majestraet geven unto them.

7. And lastly, wee desyer to geve untto all Superiors dew honnor to preserve ye untiy of ye speritt wth all ye feare God, to have peace wth all men what in us lyeth & wheerin wee err to bee instructed by any.

> Subscribed by
> John Robinson
> and
> Willyam Bruster

11. THE MAYFLOWER COMPACT
November 11, 1620

(Poore, ed. *The Federal and State Constitutions*, Part I, p. 931.)

The Separatists living in Leyden, Holland, desired for various reasons to transplant their colony to America. In 1619 they secured from the Virginia Company a patent for a private plantation. The Pilgrims, reinforced by some seventy persons from London, sailed from Plymouth in September, 1620, and arrived off Cape Cod in November. Some of the London recruits were an "undesirable lot" and, Bradford tells us, boasted that they were not under the jurisdiction of the Virginia Company and "would use their owne libertie". In order to establish some form of government, therefore, the Pilgrim leaders drew up the famous Mayflower Compact. The Compact was not intended as a constitution, but was an extension of the customary church covenant to civil circumstances. Inasmuch as the Plymouth settlers were never able to secure a charter, the Mayflower compact remained the only form of constitution of the colony. See, W. Bradford, *History of the Plymouth Plantation*, various eds.; A. Young, *Chronicles of the Pilgrim Fathers, 1602-25;* E. Arber, ed. *Story of the Pilgrim Fathers, 1606-23;* J. Fiske, *Beginnings of New England;* J. G. Palfrey, *History of New England*, Vol. I; J. A. Doyle, *The English Colonies in America*, Vol. II, pt. I; E. Eggleston, *The Beginners of a Nation;* J. T. Adams, *The Founding of New England;* C. M. Andrews, *The Fathers of New England;* C. M. Andrews, *The Colonial Period of American History*, Vol. I, ch xiii; L. G. Tyler, *England in America*, ch. ix; H. L. Osgood, *American Colonies in the Seventeenth Century*, Vol. I; J. A. Goodwin, *The Pilgrim Republic;* A. Lord, "The Mayflower Compact," *Proceedings* of the Am. Antiquarian Soc., 1921; A. C. McLaughlin, *Foundations of American Constitutionalism*, ch. i; V. L. Parrington, *The Colonial Mind*, p. 16 ff.

IN The Name of God, Amen. We, whose names are underwritten, the Loyal Subjects of our dread Sovereign Lord King *James*, by the Grace of God, of *Great Britain*, *France*, and *Ireland*, King, *Defender of the Faith*, &c. Having undertaken for the Glory of God, and Advancement of the Christian Faith, and the Honour of our King and Country, a Voyage to plant the first colony in the northern Parts of Virginia; Do by these Presents, solemnly and mutually in the

Presence of God and one another, covenant and combine ourselves together into a civil Body Politick, for our better Ordering and Preservation, and Furtherance of the Ends aforesaid; And by Virtue hereof do enact, constitute, and frame, such just and equal Laws, Ordinances, Acts, Constitutions, and Offices, from time to time, as shall be thought most meet and convenient for the general Good of the Colony; unto which we promise all due Submission and Obedience. In WITNESS whereof we have hereunto subscribed our names at *Cape Cod* the eleventh of *November,* in the Reign of our Sovereign Lord King *James* of *England, France,* and *Ireland,* the eighteenth and of *Scotland,* the fifty-fourth. *Anno Domini,* 1620

Mr. John Carver   Mr. Stephen Hopkins
Mr. William Bradford Digery Priest

Mr. Edward Winslow   Thomas Williams
Mr. William Brewster Gilbert Winslow
Isaac Allerton   Edmund Margesson
Miles Standish   Peter Brown
John Alden   Richard Bitteridge
John Turner   George Soule
Francis Eaton   Edward Tilly
James Chilton   John Tilly
John Craxton   Francis Cooke
John Billington   Thomas Rogers
Joses Fletcher   Thomas Tinker
John Goodman   John Ridgate
Mr. Samuel Fuller   Edward Fuller
Mr. Christopher   Richard Clark
  Martin   Richard Gardiner
Mr. William Mullins   Mr. John Allerton
Mr. William White   Thomas English
Mr. Richard Warren   Edward Doten
John Howland   Edward Liester.

12. THE FIRST CHARTER OF MASSACHUSETTS
March 4, 1629

(F. N. Thorpe, ed. *Federal and State Constitutions,* Vol. III, p. 1846 ff.)

In 1620 the survivors of the Plymouth Company applied to the crown for a charter for settlement in New England, and were granted the land from the 40th to the 48th parallel, under the name of the Council for New England. It was from this body that the Pilgrims secured their patent in 1621. In 1623 the "Dorchester Adventurers" had established a fishing settlement at Cape Ann; subsequently the Adventurers, under the leadership of the Rev. John White, secured from the Council for New England a patent to this territory. This company was enlarged, and under the name of the Governor and Company of the Massachusetts Bay in New England secured the royal charter of March 4, 1629. In as much as this charter granted to the Massachusetts Bay Company territory previously granted to the Council for New England, there was some doubt about its legality. The Massachusetts Bay Company had the support of the powerful Earl of Warwick, who was titular President of the Council for New England. "Probably no one," concludes Professor C. M. Andrews, "would deny that the charter of the Massachusetts Bay Company was covertly and even 'surreptitiously' obtained". For the process by which the charter of the Company became the constitution of a colony, see Doc. No. 13. On the Charter, see, J. T. Adams, *The Founding of New England;* C. M. Andrews, *Fathers of New England;* J. Fiske, *The Beginnings of New England;* A. P. Newton, *Colonizing Activities of the English Puritans;* S. E. Morison, *Builders of the Bay Colony;* F. Rose-Troup, *The Massachusetts Bay Company and its Predecessors;* F. Rose-Troup, *John White;* the charter and other related source material is in The Founding of Massachusetts, Mass. Hist. Society, *Proceedings,* Vol. LXII.

CHARLES, BY THE GRACE OF GOD Kinge of England . . . [there follows a recital of the patent of 1620 and the grant to Sir Henry Rosewell of 1628, which grant is by this charter confirmed, and continues:]

AND FURTHER, know yee, . . . Wee . . . doe . . . give and graunte vnto the saide Sir Henry Rosewell, Sir John Younge, Sir Richard Saltonstall, Thomas Southcott, John Humfrey, John Endecott, Symon Whetcombe, Isaak Johnson, Samuell Aldersey, John Ven, Mathewe Cradock, George Harwood, Increase Nowell, Richard Pery, Richard Bellingham, Nathaniel Wright, Samuell Vassall, Theophilus Eaton, Thomas Goffe, Thomas Adams, John Browne, Samuell Browne, Thomas Hutchins, William Vassall, William Pinchion, and George Foxcrofte, their Heires and Assignes, all that Part of Newe England in America, which lyes and extendes betweene a great River there, comonlie called Monomack River, alias Merrimack River, and a certen other River there, called Charles River, being in the Bottome of a certain Bay there, comonlie called Massachusetts, . . . ; and also all and singuler those Landes and Hereditaments whatsoever, lying within the Space of Three Englishe Myles on the South Parte of the said River, called Charles River, . . . also all and singular the Landes . . . , lying and being within the Space of Three Englishe Miles to the southward of the southermost Parte of the said Baye, called Massachusetts, ... And also all those Landes and Hereditaments whatsoever, which lye and be within the Space of Three Englishe Myles to the Northward of the saide River, called Monomack, alias Merrymack, . . . and all Landes and Hereditaments whatsoever, lyeing within the Lymitts aforesaide, North and South, in Latitude and Bredth, and in Length and Longitude, of and within all the Bredth aforesaide, throughout the mayne Landes there, from the Atlantick and Westerne Sea and Ocean on the Easte Parte, to the South Sea on the West Parte; . . . and also all Islandes in America aforesaide, in the saide Seas, . . . and all Mynes and Mynerals as well Royal mynes of Gold and Silver . . . whatsoever, in the said Landes and Premisses, . . . and free Libertie of fishing in or within any the Rivers or Waters within the Boundes and Lymytts aforesaid, and the Seas therevnto adjoining; . . .

WEE HAVE FURTHER . . . Given, graunted and confirmed, . . . vnto Sir Henry Rosewell, [etc.], and all such others as shall hereafter be admitted . . . shall . . . be, . . . one Body corporate and politique in Fact and Name, by the Name of the Governor and Company of the Massachusetts Bay in Newe-England, . . . Wee doe . . . ordeyne, . . . that by that name they shall have perpetuall Succession, and . . . shall and maie be capeable and enabled aswell to implead, and to be impleaded, and to prosecute, demaund, and aunswere, and be aunsweared vnto, in all and singuler Suites, Causes, Querrells, and Accons, of what kinde or nature soever. And also to have, take, possesse, acquire, and purchase any Landes, Tenements, or Hereditaments, or any Goodes or Chattells, . . .

AND FURTHER, . . . That . . . there shalbe one Governor, one Deputy Governor, and eighteene Assitants of the same Company, to be from tyme to tyme constituted, elected and chosen out of the Freemen of the saide Company, . . . which said Officers shall applie themselves to take care for the best disposeing and ordering of the generall buysines and Affaires of, for, and concerning the said Landes and Premisses . . . and the Government of the People there. . . .

AND FURTHER, . . . That the Governor of the saide Company . . . shall have Authoritie from tyme to tyme . . . to give order for the assembling of the saide Company, and . . . saide Company, . . . maie once every Moneth, or oftener at their Pleasures, assemble and houlde and keepe a Courte or Assemblie of themselves, for the better ordering and directing of their Affaires, and that any seaven or more persons of the Assistants, togither with the Governor, or Deputie Governor soe assembled, . . . shalbe a full and sufficient Courte or Assemblie of the said Company, . . . and . . . WEE DOE . . . give and graunte . . . That the Governor, . . . and six of the Assistants at the least to be seaven, shall have full Power and authoritie to choose, nominate, and appointe, such and soe many others as they shall thinke fitt, . . . to be free of the said Company and Body, and them into the same to admitt; and to elect and constitute such Officers as they shall think fitt and requisite, for the ordering, mannaging, and dispatching of the Affaires of the saide Governor and Company, and their Successors; And to make Lawes and Ordinances for the Good and Welfare of the saide Company, and for the Government and ordering of the saide Landes and Plantačon, and the People inhabiting . . . the same, as to them from tyme to tyme shalbe thought meete, . . .

AND, . . . Wee doe graunte to the saide, Governor and Company, . . . That all and every the Subiects of Vs, . . . which shall . . . inhabite within the saide Landes . . . , shall have and enjoy all liberties and Immunities of free and naturall Subjects within any of the Domynions of Vs, . . . And . . . it shall and maie be lawfull, to and for the Governor . . . and such of the Assistants and Freemen of the said Company for the Tyme being as shalbe assembled in any of their generall Courts aforesaide, or in any other Courtes to be specially sumoned and assembled for that Purpose, or the greater

Parte of them . . . from tyme to tyme, to make, ordeine, and establishe all Manner of wholesome and reasonable Orders, Lawes, Statutes, and Ordinnces, Direcčons, and In-strucčons, not contrairie to the Lawes of this our Realme of England, aswell for setling of the Formes and Ceremonies of Governm[t] and Magistracy, . . . and for the directing, . . . of all other Matters and Thinges, whereby our said People, . . . may be soe religiously, peaceablie, and civilly governed, as their good Life and orderlie Conversacon,

maie wynn and incite the Natives of Country, to the Knowledg and Obedience of the onlie true God and Sauior of Mankinde, and the Christian Fayth, which in our Royall In-tencon, and the Adventurers free Profession, is the principall Ende of this Plantacion. . . .

Witnes ourself, at Westminster, the fourth day of March in the fourth Yeare of our Raigne.

Per Breve de Privato Sigillo,

Wolseley.

13. THE CAMBRIDGE AGREEMENT
August 26, 1629

(T. Hutchinson, *Collection of Original Papers relative to the History of the Colony of Massachusetts-Bay*, p. 25 ff.)

By this agreement some of the leading members of the Massachusetts Bay Company bound them-selves to embark for America and take the charter with them. The transfer of the charter meant that a business company would be meta-morphosed into a plantation. The purpose of this drastic and probably illegal action was to secure the enterprise from interference by the Govern-ment of England. For the significance of this transfer of the charter see, C. M. Andrews, *Our Earliest Colonial Settlements*, p. 67 ff.; C. M. Andrews, *The Colonial Period of American History*, Vol. I, ch. xviii.

The True Coppie of the agreement at Cambridge, August 26, 1629.

Upon due consideration of the state of the plantation now in hand for New England, wherein wee (whose names are hereunto sub-scribed) have engaged ourselves: and having weighed the greatnes of the worke in re-gard of the consequence, God's glory and the churches good: As also in regard of the difficultyes and discouragements which in all probabilityes must be forecast upon the ex-ecution of this businesse: Considering withall that this whole adventure growes upon the joint confidence we have in each others fidelity and resolution herein, so as no man of us would have adventured it without as-surance of the rest: Now, for the better en-couragement of ourselves and others that shall joyne with us in this action, and to the end that every man may without scruple dis-pose of his estate and afayres as may best fitt his preparation for this voyage, it is fully and faithfully agreed amongst us, and every of us doth hereby freely and sincerely prom-

ise and bind himself in the word of a chris-tian and in the presence of God who is the searcher of all hearts, that we will so really endeavour the execution of this worke, as by God's assistance we will be ready . . . in our persons, and with such of our severall familyes as are to go with us, and such pro-vision as we are able conveniently to furnish ourselves withall, to embarke for the said plantation by the first of March next, . . . at such port or ports of this land as shall be agreed upon by the Companie, to the end to passe the seas (under God's protection) to inhabite and continue in New England. Pro-vided always, that before the last of Septem-ber next the whole government together with the patent for the said plantation be first by an order of court legally transferred and established to remain with us and others which shall inhabite upon the said plantation . . . And we do further promise every one for himselfe, that shall fayle to be ready through his own default by the day ap-pointed, to pay for every day's default the sum of 3£ to the use of the rest of the Com-panie who shall be ready by the same day and time.

This was done by order of court the 29th of August, 1629.

Richard Saltonstall	Tho: Sharp
Tho: Dudley	Increase Nowell
William Vassall	John Winthrop
Nicko: West	Will: Pinchon
Isaack Johnson	Kellam Browne
John Humfrey	William Colbron

14. CHARTER OF FREEDOMS AND EXEMPTIONS TO PATROONS
June 7, 1629

(E. B. O'Callaghan, ed. *Documents Relative to the Colonial History of the State of New York,* Vol. II, p. 553 ff.)

This charter of privileges to the patroons established the patroon system of land tenure in New Netherland and New York. Under this charter a few patroons secured control of most of the land along the Hudson River; some of the land grants, such as those to Killian Van Rensselaer, were enormous. On the Dutch settlement of New Netherland, see E. B. O'Callaghan, *History of New Netherland,* 2 Vols.; T. A. Janvier, *Dutch Founding of New York;* A. C. Flick, ed. *History of the State of New York,* Vol. I, chs. vii–x; C. W. Rife, "Land Tenure in New Netherland"; *Essays in Colonial History presented to C. M. Andrews,* p. 41 ff.; H. L. Osgood, *American Colonies in the XVII century,* Vol. II, ch. v.

.   .   .   .

III. All such shall be acknowledged Patroons of New Netherland who shall, within the space of four years next after they have given notice to any of the Chambers of the Company here, or to the Commander or Council there, undertake to plant a Colonie there of fifty souls, upwards of fifteen years old; one-fourth part within one year, and within three years after the sending of the first, making together four years, the remainder, to the full number of fifty persons . . . ; but it is to be observed that the Company reserve the Island of the Manhattes to themselves.

IV. They shall, from the time they make known the situation of the places where they propose to settle Colonies, have the preference to all others of the absolute property of such lands as they have there chosen; but in case the situation should not afterwards please them, or they should have been mistaken as to the quality of the land, they may, after remonstrating concerning the same to the Commander and Council there, be at liberty to choose another place.

V. The Patroons, by virtue of their power, shall and may be permitted, at such places as they shall settle their Colonies, to extend their limits four leagues along the shore, that is, on one side of a navigable river, or two leagues on each side of a river, and so far into the country as the situation of the occupiers will permit; provided and conditioned that the Company keep to themselves the lands lying and remaining between the limits of Colonies, to dispose thereof, when and at such time as they shall think proper, in such manner that no person shall be allowed to come within seven or eight leagues of them without their consent, unless the situation of the land thereabout be such that the Commander and Council, for good reasons, should order otherwise. . . .

VI. They shall forever possess and enjoy all the lands lying within the aforesaid limits, together with the fruits, rights, minerals, rivers and fountains thereof; as also the chief command and lower jurisdictions, fishing, fowling and grinding, to the exclusion of all others, to be holden from the Company as a perpetual inheritance, without it ever devolving again to the Company, and in case it should devolve, to be redeemed and repossessed with twenty guilders per Colonie, to be paid to this Company, at the Chamber here or to their Commander there, within a year and six weeks after the same occurs, each at the Chamber where he originally sailed from; and further, no person or persons whatsoever shall be privileged to fish and hunt but the Patroons and such as they shall permit. And in case any one should in time prosper so much as to found one or more cities, he shall have power and authority to establish officers and magistrates there, and to make use of the title of his Colonie, acording to his pleasure and to the quality of the persons. . . .

X. The Patroons and colonists shall be privileged to send their people and effects thither, in ships belonging to the Company, provided they take the oath, and pay to the Company for bringing over the people, as mentioned in the first article. . . .

XII. Inasmuch as it is intended to people the Island of the Manhattes first, all fruits and wares that are produced on the lands situate on the North river, and lying thereabout, shall, for the present, be brought there before being sent elsewhere, . . .

XIII. All the Patroons of Colonies in New Netherland, and of Colonies on the Island of Manhattes, shall be at liberty to sail and traffic all along the coast, from Florida to Terra Neuf, provided that they do again return with all such goods as they shall get in trade to the Island of Manhattes, and pay five per cent duty to the Company, in order, if possible, that, after the necessary inventory of the goods shipped be taken, the same may be sent hither. . . .

XV. It shall be also free for the aforesaid Patroons to traffic and trade all along the coast of New Netherland and places circumjacent, with such goods as are consumed there, and receive in return for them all sorts of merchandise that may be had there, except beavers, otters, minks, and all sorts of peltry, which trade the Company reserve to themselves. But the same shall be permitted at such places where the Company have no factories, conditioned that such traders shall be obliged to bring all the peltry they can procure to the Island of Manhattes, in case it may be, at any rate, practicable, and there deliver to the Director, to be by him shipped hither with the ships and goods; or, if they should come here without going there, then to give notice thereof to the Company, that a proper account thereof may be taken, in order that they may pay to the Company one guilder for each merchantable beaver and otter skin; the property, risk and all other charges remaining on account of the Patroons or owners.

XVI. All coarse wares that the Colonists of the Patroons there shall consume, such as pitch, tar, weed-ashes, wood, grain, fish, salt, hearthstone and such like things shall be conveyed in the Company's ships, at the rate of eighteen guilders per last. . . .

XVIII. The Company promises the colonists of the Patroons that they shall be free from customs, taxes, excise, imposts or any other contributions for the space of ten years; and after the expiration of the said ten years, at the highest, such customs as the goods pay here for the present. . . .

XX. From all judgments given by the Courts of the Patroons for upwards of fifty guilders, there may be an appeal to the Company's Commander and Council in New Netherland.

XXI. In regard to such private persons as on their own account, . . . shall be inclined to go thither and settle, they shall, with the approbation of the Director and Council there, be at liberty to take up and take possession of as much land as they shall be able properly to improve, . . .

XXIII. Whosoever, whether colonists of Patroons for their Patroons, or free persons for themselves, or others for their masters, shall discover any shores, bays or other fit places for erecting fisheries, or the making of salt ponds, they may take possession thereof, and begin to work on them as their own absolute property, to the exclusion of all others. And it is consented to that the Patroons of colonists may send ships along the coast of New Netherland, on the cod fishery, . . .

XXVI. Whoever shall settle any Colonie out of the limits of the Manhattes Island, shall be obliged to satisfy the Indians for the land they shall settle upon, and they may extend or enlarge the limits of their Colonies if they settle a proportionate number of colonists thereon.

XXVII. The Patroons and colonists shall in particular, and in the speediest manner, endeavor to find out ways and means whereby they may support a Minister and Schoolmaster, that thus the service of God and zeal for religion may not grow cool and be neglected among them, and they shall, for the first, procure a Comforter of the sick there. . . .

XXIX. The Colonists shall not be permitted to make any woolen, linen or cotton cloth, nor weave any other stuffs there, on pain of being banished, and as perjurers, to be arbitrarily punished.

XXX. The Company will use their endeavors to supply the colonists with as many Blacks as they conveniently can, on the conditions hereafter to be made, in such manner, however, that they shall not be bound to do it for a longer time than they shall think proper.

XXXI. The Company promise to finish the fort on the Island of the Manhattes, and to put it in a posture of defence without delay.

15. THE CHARTER OF MARYLAND
June 20, 1632

(F. N. Thorpe, ed. *Federal and State Constitutions,* Vol. III, p. 1677 ff.)

George Calvert, first Lord Baltimore, had attempted to found a colony in Newfoundland, but discouraged by the uninviting character of his grant there persuaded Charles I to grant him a patent to land north of the Potomac. George Calvert died in April, 1632, and the charter was issued to his son, Cecil, second Lord Baltimore. The charter of Maryland was modeled after the earlier charter to the Newfoundland plantation, Avalon, which was in turn modeled after the county Palatine of Durham, a crown fief, the powers of whose lord were second only to those of the King. See, C. C. Hall, *The Lords Baltimore and the Maryland Palatinate;* M. P. Andrews, *The Founding of Maryland;* B. C. Steiner, *Beginnings of Maryland;* N. D. Mereness, *Maryland as a Proprietary Province;* W. H. Browne, *Georgius and Cecilius Calvert;* B. C. Steiner, "The First Lord Baltimore and his Colonial Projects," American Hist. Assoc. *Reports,* 1905.

. . . II. Whereas our well beloved and right trusty Subject Caecilius Calvert, Baron of Baltimore, in our Kingdom of Ireland, . . . being animated with a laudable, and pious Zeal for extending the Christian Religion, and also the Territories of our Empire, hath humbly besought Leave of Us, that he may transport, by his own Industry, and Expence, a numerous Colony of the English Nation, to a certain Region, herein after described, in a Country hitherto uncultivated, in the Parts of America, and partly occupied by Savages, having no Knowledge of the Divine Being, and that all that Region, with some certain Privileges, and Jurisdictions, appertaining unto the wholesome Government, and State of his Colony and Region aforesaid, may by our Royal Highness be given, granted, and confirmed unto him, and his Heirs.

III. Know Ye therefore, that We . . . by this our present Charter . . . do Give, Grant, and Confirm, unto the aforesaid Caecilius, now Baron of Baltimore, his Heirs, and Assigns, all that Part of the Peninsula, or Chersonese, lying in the Parts of America, between the Ocean on the East, and the Bay of Chesopeake on the West, [boundaries defined] . . .

IV. Also We do Grant . . . unto the said Baron of Baltimore . . . all Islands and Islets within the Limits aforesaid, all and singular the Islands and Islets, from the Eastern Shore of the aforesaid Region, towards the East, which have been, or shall be formed in the Sea, situate within Ten marine Leagues from the said Shore; . . . And further more the Patronages, and Advowsons of all Churches which (with the increasing Worship and Religion of Christ) within the said Region . . . , hereafter shall happen to be built, together with Licence, and Faculty of erecting and founding Churches, Chapels, and Places of Worship, in convenient and suitable Places within the Premises, and of causing the same to be dedicated and consecrated according to the Ecclesiastical Laws of our Kingdom of England, with all, and singular such, and as ample Rights, Jurisdictions, Privileges, Prerogatives, Royalties, Liberties, Immunities, and royal Rights, and Temporal Franchises whatsoever, as well by Sea as by Land, within the Region . . . aforesaid, to be had, exercised, used, and enjoyed, as any Bishop of Durham, within the Bishoprick or County Palatine of Durham, in our Kingdom of England, ever heretofore, hath had, held, used, or enjoyed or of Right could, or ought to have, hold, use, or enjoy.

V. And We do by these Presents . . . Make, Create, and Constitute Him, the now Baron of Baltimore, and his Heirs, the True and Absolute Lords and Proprietaries of the Region aforesaid, and of all other the Premises (except the before excepted) saving always the Faith and Allegiance and Sovereign Dominion due to Us . . . ; To Hold of Us as of our Castle of Windsor, in our County of Berks, in free and common Soccage, by Fealty only for all Services, and not in capite, nor by Knight's Service, Yielding therefore unto Us . . . two Indian Arrows of these Parts, to be delivered at the said Castle of Windsor, every Year, on Tuesday in Easter-Week: And also the fifth Part of all Gold and Silver Ore, which shall happen from Time to Time, to be found within the aforesaid limits.

VI. Now, That the aforesaid Region, . . . may be eminently distinguished above all other Regions of that Territory, . . . Know Ye, that . . . We do . . . Erect and Incorporate the same into a Province, and nominate the same Maryland, by which name We will that it shall from henceforth be called.

VII. And . . . We . . . do grant unto the said now Baron . . . for the good and happy Government of the said Province, free, full, and absolute Power, by the tenor of these Presents, to Ordain, Make, and Enact Laws, of what kind soever, according to their sound Discretions, whether relating to the Public State of the said Province, or the private Utility of Individuals, of and with the Advice, Assent, and Approbation of the Free-Men of the same Province, or of the greater Part of them, or of their Delegates or Deputies, whom We will shall be called together for the framing of Laws, when, and as often as Need shall require, by the aforesaid now Baron of Baltimore . . . , and in the Form which shall seem best to him . . . and duly to execute the same upon all Persons, for the Time being, within the aforesaid Province, and the Limits thereof, or under his or their Government and Power, . . . by the Imposition of Fines, Imprisonment, and other Punishment whatsoever; even if it be necessary, and the Quality of the Offence require it, by Privation of Member, or Life . . . So Nevertheless. that the Laws aforesaid be consonant to Reason and be not repugnant or contrary, but (so far as conveniently may be) agreeable to the Laws, Statutes, Customs and Rights of this Our Kingdom of England. . . .

XVII. Moreover, We will, appoint, and ordain, and by these Presents, for Us, our Heirs and Successors, do grant unto the aforesaid now Baron of Baltimore, his Heirs and Assigns, that the same Baron of Baltimore, his Heirs and Assigns, from Time to Time, forever, shall have, and enjoy the Taxes and Subsidies payable, or arising within the Ports, Harbors, and other Creeks and Places aforesaid, within the Province aforesaid, for Wares bought and sold, and Things there to be laden, or unladen, to be reasonably assessed by them, and the People there as aforesaid, on emergent Occasion; to whom We grant Power by these Presents, for Us, our Heirs and Successors, to assess and impose the said Taxes and Subsidies there, upon just Cause and in due Proportion.

XVIII. And Furthermore . . . We . . . do give . . . unto the aforesaid now Baron of Baltimore . . . full and absolute Licence, Power, and Authority . . . that he assign, alien, grant, demise, or enfeoff so many, such, and proportionate Parts and Parcels of the Premises, to any Person or Persons willing to purchase the same, as they shall think convenient, to have and to hold . . . in Fee-simple, or Fee-tail, or for Term of Life, Lives, or Years; to hold of the aforesaid now Baron of Baltimore . . . by . . . such . . . Services, Customs and Rents Of This Kind, as to the same now Baron of Baltimore . . . shall seem fit and agreeable, and not immediately of Us . . .

XIX. We also . . . do . . . grant Licence to the same Baron of Baltimore . . . to erect any Parcels of Land within the Province aforesaid, into Manors, and in every of those Manors, to have and to hold a Court-Baron, and all Things which to a Court-Baron do belong; . . .

16. FUNDAMENTAL ORDERS OF CONNECTICUT
January 14, 1639

(Poore, ed. *The Federal and State Constitutions*, Part I, p. 249 ff.)

In 1636 the Rev. Thomas Hooker led his New Town congregation into the inviting Connecticut Valley, and founded the town of Hartford. These pioneers were soon followed by others from Massachusetts Bay, and in January 1639 the freemen of the towns of Hartford, Windsor and Wethersfield assembled at Hartford and drew up the Fundamental Orders—the first written constitution that created a government. See, J. G. Palfrey, *History of New England*, Vol. I; J. Fiske, *Beginnings of New England;* B. Trumbull, *History of Connecticut*, Vol. I; J. A. Doyle, *English Colonies in America: The Puritan Colonies*, Vol. I; B. Long, *Genesis of the Constitution of the United States,* ch. iv. On Hooker, see, G. L. Walker, *Thomas Hooker;* V. L. Parrington, *The Colonial Mind,* p. 53 ff.

Forasmuch as it hath pleased the Allmighty God by the wise disposition of his divyne pruvidence so to Order and dispose of things that we the Inhabitants and Residents of Windsor, Harteford and Wethersfield are now cohabiting and dwelling in and uppon the River of Conectecotte and the Lands thereunto adioyneing; And well knowing where a people are gathered togather the word of God requires that to mayntayne the peace and union of such a people there should be an orderly and decent Government established according to God, to order and dispose of the affayres of the people at all seasons as occasion shall require; doe therefore assotiate and conioyne our selves to be as one Publike State or Commonwelth; and doe, for our selves and our Successors and such as shall be adioyned to us att any tyme hereafter, enter into Combination and Confederation togather, to mayntayne and presearve the liberty and purity of the gospell of our Lord Jesus which we now professe, as also the disciplyne of the Churches, which according to the truth of the said gospell is now practised amongst us; As also in our Civell Affaires to be guided and governed according to such Lawes, Rules, Orders and decrees as shall be made, ordered & decreed, as followeth:—

1. It is Ordered . . . that there shall be yerely two generall Assemblies or Courts, the one the second thursday in Aprill, the other the second thursday in September, following; the first shall be called the Courte of Election, wherein shall be yerely Chosen . . . soe many Magestrats and other publike Officers as shall be found requisitte: Whereof one to be chosen Governour for the yeare ensueing and untill another be chosen, and noe other Magestrate to be chosen for more than one yeare; provided allwayes there be six chosen besids the Governour; which being chosen and sworne according to an Oath recorded for that purpose shall have power to administer iustice according to the Lawes here established, and for want thereof according to the rule of the word of God; which choise shall be made by all that are admitted freemen and

have taken the Oath of Fidellity, and doe cohabitte within this Jurisdiction, (having beene admitted Inhabitants by the major part of the Towne wherein they live,) or the major parte of such as shall be then present.

4. It is Ordered . . . that noe person be chosen Governor above once in two yeares, and that the Governor be alwayes a member of some approved congregation, and formerly of the Magestracy within this Jurisdiction; and all the Magestrats Freemen of this Commonwelth: . . .

5. It is Ordered . . . that to the aforesaid Courte of Election the severall Townes shall send their deputyes, and when the Elections are ended they may proceed in any publike searvice as at other Courts. Also the other Generall Courte in September shall be for makeing of lawes, and any other publike occasion, which conserns the good of the Commonwelth.

7. It is Ordered . . . that after there are warrants given out for any of the said Generall Courts, the Constable . . . of ech Towne shall forthwith give notice distinctly to the inhabitants of the same, . . . that at a place and tyme by him or them lymited and sett, they meet and assemble them selves together to elect and chuse certen deputyes to be att the Generall Courte then following to agitate the afayres of the commonwelth; which said Deputyes shall be chosen by all that are admitted Inhabitants in the severall Townes and have taken the oath of fidellity; provided that non be chosen a Deputy for any Generall Courte which is not a Freeman of this Commonwelth. . . .

8. It is Ordered . . . that Wyndsor, Hartford and Wethersfield shall have power, ech Towne, to send fower of their freemen as their deputyes to every Generall Courte; and whatsoever other Townes shall be hereafter added to this Jurisdiction, they shall send so many deputyes as the Courte shall judge meete, a resonable proportion to the number of Freemen that are in the said Townes being to be attended therein; which deputyes shall have the power of the whole Towne to give their voats and alowance to all such lawes and orders as may be for the publike good, and unto which the said Townes are to be bownd.

9. It is ordered . . . that the deputyes thus chosen shall have power and liberty to appoynt a tyme and a place of meeting togather before any Generall Courte to advise and consult of all such things as may concerne the good of the publike, as also to examine their owne Elections. . . .

10. It is Ordered . . . that every Generall Courte . . . shall consist of the Governor, or some one chosen to moderate the Court, and 4 other Magestrats at lest, with the major parte of the deputyes of the severall Townes legally chosen; and in case the Freemen or major parte of them, through neglect or refusall of the Governor and major parte of the magestrats, shall call a Courte, it shall consist of the major parte of Freemen that are present or their deputyes, with a Moderator chosen by them: In which said Generall Courts shall consist the supreme power of the Commonwelth, and they only shall have power to make lawes or repeale them, to graunt levyes, to admitt of Freemen, dispose of lands undisposed of, to severall Townes or persons, and also shall have power to call ether Courte or Magestrate or any other person whatsoever into question for any misdemeanour, and may for just causes displace or deale otherwise according to the nature of the offence; and also may deale in any other matter that concerns the good of this commonwelth, excepte election of Magestrats, which shall be done by the whole boddy of Freemen.

In which Courte the Governour or Moderator shall have power to order the Courte to give liberty of spech, and silence unceasonable and disorderly speakeings, to put all things to voate, and in case the vote be equall to have the casting voice. But non of these Courts shall be adjorned or dissolved without the consent of the major parte of the Court.

11. It is ordered . . . that when any Generall Courte upon the occasions of the Commonwelth have agreed uppon any summe or sommes of mony to be levyed uppon the severall Townes within this Jurisdiction, that a Committee be chosen to sett out and appoynt what shall be the proportion of every Towne to pay of the said levy, provided the Committees be made up of an equall number out of each Towne.

17. PLANTATION AGREEMENT AT PROVIDENCE
August 27, 1640

(F. N. Thorpe, ed. *Federal and State Constitutions*, Vol. VI, p. 3205 ff.)

In 1636 Roger Williams led a small band of settlers from Massachusetts Bay to Narragansett Bay and founded the town of Providence. In 1638 and 1639 other settlements were established, but all of these towns remained separate and independent until the charter of 1644 went into effect. In 1640 the inhabitants of Providence drew up an agreement in which, among other things, they covenanted "to hould forth liberty of conscience." On Roger Williams and the early history of Rhode Island, see O. S. Strauss, *Roger Williams;* E. Easton, *Roger Williams;* J. Ernst, *Roger Williams;* J. Ernst, *The Political Thought of Roger Williams;* V. L. Parrington, *The Colonial Mind,* p. 62 ff.; S. G. Arnold, *Rhode Island;* I. B. Richman, *Rhode Island;* E. Field, *Rhode Island,* Vol. I; J. Fiske, *Beginnings of New England;* J. T. Adams, *The Founding of New England;* J. Winsor, ed. *Narrative and Critical History,* Vol. III.

Wee, Robert Coles, Chad Browne, William Harris, and John Warner, being freely chosen by the consent of our loving friends and neighbors the Inhabitants of this Towne of Providence, having many differences amongst us, they being freely willing and also bound themselves to stand to our Arbitration in all differences amongst us to rest contented in our determination, being so betrusted we have seriously and carefully indeavoured to weigh and consider all those differences, being desirous to bringe to unity and peace, although our abilities are farr short in the due examination of such weighty things, yet so farre as we conceive in laying all things together we have gone the fairest and equalist way to produce our peace.

II. Agreed. We have with one consent agreed that for the disposeing, of these lands that shall be disposed belonging to this towne of Providence to be in the whole Inhabitants by the choise of five men for generall disposeall of lands and also of the towne Stocke, and all Generall things and not to receive in any six dayes at townesmen, but first to give the Inhabitants notice to consider if any have just cause to shew against the receiving of him as you can apprehend, and to receive none but such as subscribe to this our determination. Also, we agree that if any of our neighbours doe apprehend himselfe wronged by these or any of these 5 disposers, that at the Generall towne meeting he may have a tryall.

Also wee agree for the towne to choose beside the other five men one or more to keepe Record of all things belonging to the towne and lying in Common.

Wee agree, as formerly hath bin the liberties of the town, so still, to hould forth liberty of Conscience.

III. Agreed, that after many Considerations and Consultations of our owne State and alsoe of States abroad in way of government, we apprehend, no way so suitable to our Condition as government by way of Arbitration. But if men agree themselves by arbitration, no State we know of disallows that, neither doe we: But if men refuse that which is but common humanity betweene man and man, then to compel such unreasonable persons to a reasonable way, we agree that the 5 disposers shall have power to compel him to choose two men himselfe, or if he refuse, for them to choose two men to arbitrate his cause, and if these foure men chosen by every partie do end the cause, then to see theire determination performed and the faultive to pay the Arbitrators for theire time spent in it: But if these foure men doe not end it, then for the 5 disposers to choose three men to put an end to it, and for the certainty thereof, wee agree the major part of the 5 disposers to choose the 3 men, and the major part of the 3 men to end the cause haveing power from the 5 disposers by a note under theire hand to performe it, and the faultive not agreeing in the first to pay the charge of the last, and for the Arbitrators to follow no imployment til the cause be ended without consent of the whole that have to doe with the cause.

Instance. In the first Arbitration the offender may offer reasonable terms of peace, and the offended may exact upon him and refuse and trouble men beyond reasonable satisfaction; so for the last arbitrators to judge where the fault was, in not agreeing in the first, to pay the charge of the last.

IV. Agreed, that if any person damnify any man, either in goods or good name, and the person offended follow not the cause upon the offendor, that if any person give notice to the 5 Disposers, they shall call the party delinquent to answer by Arbitration.

Instance. Thus, if any person abuse an other person or goods, may be for peace sake, a man will at present put it up, and it may so be resolve to revenge: therefore, for the peace of the state, the disposers are to look to it in the first place.

V. Agreed, for all the whole Inhabitants to combine ourselves to assist any man in the pursuit of any party delinquent, with all best endeavours to attack him: but if any man raise a hubbub, and there be no just cause, then for the party that raised the hubbub to satisfy men for their time lost in it.

VI. Agreed, that if any man have a difference with any of the 5 Disposers which cannot be deferred till general meeting of the towne, then he may have the Clerk call the towne together at his (discretion) for a tryall.

Instance. It may be, a man may be to depart the land, or to a farr parte of the land; or his estate may lye yppon a speedy tryall or the like case may fall out.

VII. Agreed, that the towne, by the five men shall give every man a deed of all his lands lying within the bounds of the Plantations, to hould it by for after ages.

VIII. Agreed, that the 5 disposers shall from the date hereof, meete every monthday uppon General things and at the quarterday to yeeld a new choise and give up their old Accounts.

IX. Agreed, that the Clerke shall call the 5 Disposers together at the month-day, and the generall towne together every quarter, to meete uppon general occasions from the date hereof. . . .

XI. Agreed, that all acts of disposall on both sides to stand since the difference.

XII. Agreed, that every man that hath not paid in his purchase money for his Plantation shall make up his 10s. to be 30s.

equal with the first purchasers: and for all that are received townsmen hereafter, to pay the like somme of money to the towne stocke.

These being those things wee have gener-ally concluded on, for our peace, we desireing our loving friends to receive as our absolute determination, laying ourselves downe as subjects to it.

18. THE NEW ENGLAND CONFEDERATION
May 19, 1643

(F. N. Thorpe, *Federal and State Constitutions*, Vol. I, p. 77 ff.)

The first suggestion for a union of the New England Colonies came from the magistrates and ministers of Connecticut in 1637. The proposal was renewed in 1638 and 1639; in 1640 the magistrates of Massachusetts Bay indicated acceptance of the proposal, but insisted that Rhode Island should not be admitted to the group. In 1642 the civil wars in England led to a renewal of the proposal from Massachusetts Bay, and in May 1642, delegates from Plymouth, Connecticut and New Haven met with those of the Bay colony in Boston and agreed upon the articles of Confederation. Rhode Island was consistently excluded from the Confederation. The union of the colonies of Connecticut and New Haven and the grant of a charter to Rhode Island practically put an end to the Confederation, but commissioners continued to hold meetings until 1684. See, R. Frothingham, *Rise of the Republic of the United States*, ch. ii; J. A. Doyle, *The English in America; The Puritan Colonies*, Vol. I; J. G. Palfrey, *History of New England*, Vols. I, II; L. G. Tyler, *England in America*, ch. xviii; J. Fiske, *Beginnings of New England*, ch. iv.

The Articles of Confederation between the Plantations under the Government of the Massachusetts, the Plantations under the Government of New Plymouth, the Plantations under the Government of Connecticut, and the Government of New Haven with the Plantations in Combination therewith:

Whereas we all came into these parts of America with one and the same end and aim, namely, to advance the Kingdom of our Lord Jesus Christ and to enjoy the liberties of the Gospel in purity with peace; and whereas in our settling (by a wise providence of God) we are further dispersed upon the sea coasts and rivers than was at first intended, so that we can not according to our desire with convenience communicate in one government and jurisdiction; and whereas we live encompassed with people of several nations and strange languages which hereafter may prove injurious to us or our posterity. And forasmuch as the natives have formerly committed sundry insolence and outrages upon several Plantations of the English and have of late combined themselves against us: and seeing by reason of those sad distractions in England which they have heard of, and by which they know we are hindered from that humble way of seeking advice, or reaping those comfortable fruits of protection, which at other times we might well expect. We therefore do conceive it our bounden duty, without delay to enter into a present Cosociation amongst ourselves, for mutual help and strength in all our future concernments: That, as in nation and religion, so in other respects, we be and continue one according to the tenor and true meaning of the ensuing articles; Wherefore it is fully agreed and concluded by and between the parties or Jurisdictions above named, and they jointly and severally do by these presents agree and conclude that they all be and henceforth be called by the name of the United Colonies of New England.

2. The said United Colonies for themselves and their posterities do jointly and severally hereby enter into a firm and perpetual league of friendship and amity for offence and defence, mutual advice and succor upon all just occasions both for preserving and propagating the truth and liberties of the Gospel and for their own mutual safety and welfare.

3. . . . And in reference to the Plantations which already are settled, or shall hereafter be erected, or shall settle within their limits respectively; provided no other Jurisdiction shall hereafter be taken in as a distinct head or member of this Confederation, nor shall any other Plantation or

Jurisdiction in present being, and not already in combination or under the jurisdiction of any of these Confederates, be received by any of them; nor shall any two of the Confederates join in one Jurisdiction without consent of the rest, which consent to be interpreted as is expressed in the sixth article ensuing.

4. It is by these Confederates agreed that the charge of all just wars, whether offensive or defensive, upon what part or member of this Confederation soever they fall, shall both in men, provisions, and all other disbursements be borne by all the parts of this Confederation in different proportions according to their different ability in manner following, namely, . . . that according to the different numbers which from time to time shall be found in each Jurisdiction upon a true and just account, the service of men and all charges of the war be borne by the poll: each Jurisdiction or Plantation being left to their own just course and custom of rating themselves and people according to their different estates with due respects to their qualities and exemptions amongst themselves though the Confederation take no notice of any such privilege: and that according to their different charge of each Jurisdiction and Plantation the whole advantage of the war (if it please God so to bless their endeavors) whether it be in lands, goods, or persons, shall be proportionately divided among the said Confederates.

5. It is further agreed, that if any of these Jurisdictions or any Plantation under or in combination with them, be invaded by any enemy whomsoever, upon notice and request of any three magistrates of that Jurisdiction so invaded, the rest of the Confederates without any further meeting or expostulation shall forthwith send aid to the Confederate in danger but in different proportions; namely, the Massachusetts an hundred men sufficiently armed and provided for such a service and journey, and each of the rest, forty-five so armed and provided, or any less number, if less be required according to this proportion. . . . But in any such case of sending men for present aid, whether before or after such order or alteration, it is agreed that at the meeting of the Commissioners for this Confederation,

the cause of such war or invasion be duly considered: and if it appear that the fault lay in the parties so invaded then that Jurisdiction or Plantation make just satisfaction, both to the invaders whom they have injured, and bear all the charges of the war themselves, without requiring any allowance from the rest of the Confederates towards the same. And further that if any Jurisdiction see any danger of invasion approaching, and there be time for a meeting, that in such a case three magistrates of the Jurisdiction may summon a meeting at such convenient place as themselves shall think meet, to consider and provide against the threatened danger; . . .

6. It is also agreed, that for the managing and concluding of all affairs proper, and concerning the whole Confederation two Commissioners shall be chosen by and out of each of these four Jurisdictions: namely, two for the Massachusetts, two for Plymouth, two for Connecticut, and two for New Haven, being all in Church-fellowship with us, which shall bring full power from their several General Courts respectively to hear, examine, weigh, and determine all affairs of our war, or peace, leagues, aids, charges, and numbers of men for war, division of spoils and whatsoever is gotten by conquest, receiving of more Confederates for Plantations into combination with any of the Confederates, and all things of like nature, which are the proper concomitants or consequents of such a Confederation for amity, offence, and defence: not intermeddling with the government of any of the Jurisdictions, which by the third article is preserved entirely to themselves. . . . It is further agreed that these eight Commissioners shall meet once every year besides extraordinary meetings (according to the fifth article) to consider, treat, and conclude of all affairs belonging to this Confederation, . . .

8. It is also agreed that the Commissioners for this Confederation hereafter at their meetings, whether ordinary or extraordinary, as they may have commission or opportunity, do endeavor to frame and establish agreements and orders in general cases of a civil nature, wherein all the Plantations are interested, for preserving of peace among themselves, for preventing

as much as may be all occasion of war or differences with others, as about the free and speedy passage of justice in every Jurisdiction, to all the Confederates equally as to their own, receiving those that remove from one Plantation without due certificate, how all the Jurisdictions may carry it towards the Indians, that they neither grow insolent nor be injured without due satisfaction, lest war break in upon the Confederates through such miscarriages. It is also agreed that if any servant run away from his master into any other of these confederated Jurisdictions, that in such case, upon the certificate of one magistrate in the Jurisdiction out of which the said servant fled, or upon other due proof; the said servant shall be delivered, either to his master, or any other that pursues and brings such certificate or proof. And that upon the escape of any prisoner whatsoever, or fugitive for any criminal cause, whether breaking prison, or getting from the officer, or otherwise escaping, upon the certificate of two magistrates of the Jurisdiction out of which the escape is made, that he was a prisoner, or such an offender at the time of the escape, the magistrates, or some of them of that Jurisdiction where for the present the said prisoner or fugitive abideth, shall forthwith grant such a warrant as the case will bear, for the apprehending of any such person, and the delivery of him into the hands of the officer or other person who pursues him. And if there be help required,

for the safe returning of any such offender, then it shall be granted to him that craves the same, he paying the charges thereof.

9. And for that the justest wars may be of dangerous consequence, especially to the smaller Plantations in these United Colonies, it is agreed that neither the Massachusetts, Plymouth, Connecticut, nor New Haven, nor any of the members of them, shall at any time hereafter begin, undertake, or engage themselves, or this Confederation, or any part thereof in any war whatsoever . . . without the consent and agreement of the forementioned eight Commissioners, or at least six of them, as in the sixth article is provided: and that no charge be required of any of the Confederates, in case of a defensive war, till the said Commissioners have met, and approved the justice of the war, and have agreed upon the sum of money to be levied, which sum is then to be paid by the several Confederates in proportion according to the fourth article. . . .

11. It is further agreed that if any of the Confederates shall hereafter break any of these present articles, or be any other ways injurious to any one of the other Jurisdictions; such breach of agreement or injury shall be duly considered and ordered by the Commissioners for the other Jurisdictions, that both peace and this present Confederation may be entirely preserved without violation. . . .

19. MASSACHUSETTS SCHOOL LAW OF 1642
April 14, 1642

(E. P. Cubberley, ed. *Readings in the History of Education,* p. 298–9)

This is the earliest known law on education in the American colonies. Similar laws were adopted, somewhat later, by Connecticut, New Haven, and Plymouth. See also, the law of 1647, Doc. No. 20. See bibliography in M. W. Jernegan, *The American Colonies,* p. 164.

This Co^{rt}, taking into consideration the great neglect of many parents & masters in training up their children in learning & labo^r, & other implyments which may be proffitable to the common wealth, do hereupon order and decree, that in euery towne ye chosen men appointed for managing the prudentiall affajres of the same shall hence-

forth stand charged with the care of the redresse of this evill, so as they shalbee sufficiently punished by fines for the neglect thereof, upon presentment of the grand iury, or other information or complaint in any Court within this iurisdiction; and for this end they, or the greater numbe^r of them, shall have power to take account from time to time of all parents and masters, and of their children, concerning their calling and implyment of their children, especially of their ability to read & understand the principles of religion & the capitall lawes of this country, and to impose fines upon such as shall refuse to render such accounts to them when they shall be required; and they shall have power, with consent of any Court or the magistrate, to put forth apprentices the children of such as they shall (find) not to be able & fitt to employ and bring them up. They shall take . . . that boyes and girles be not suffered to converse together, so as may occasion any wanton, dishonest, or immodest behavio^r; & for their better performance of this trust committed to them, they may divide the towne amongst them, appointing to every of the said townesmen a certaine number of families to have special oversight of. They are also to provide that a sufficient quantity of materialls, as hemp, flaxe, ec^{ra}, may be raised in their severall townes, & tooles & implements provided for working out the same; & for their assistance in this so needfull and beneficiall imploym^t, if they meete wth any difficulty or opposition wch they cannot well master by their own power, they may have reco^{r}se to some of the ma^{trats}, who shall take such course for their help & incuragm^t as the occasion shall require according to iustice; & the said townesmen, at the next Co^{r}t in those limits, after the end of their year, shall give a briefe account in writing of their proceedings herein, provided that they have bene so required by some Co^{r}t or magistrate a month at least before; & this order to continew for two yeares, & till the Co^{r}t shall take further order.

20. MASSACHUSETTS SCHOOL LAW OF 1647

(Records of the Governor and Company of the Massachusetts Bay in New England, Vol. II, p. 203)

This "old deluder Satan" law established the first system of public education in the American colonies. A number of towns had already established schools, and the law of 1642, Doc. No. 19, had provided for the instruction of children in reading. The purpose of the law of 1647 was that "learning might not be buried in the grave of our fathers in Church and commonwealth." Other New England States followed the example of Massachusetts within the next generation. See, G. H. Martin, *Evolution of the Massachusetts School System;* H. Suzzalo, *Rise of Local School Supervision in Massachusetts;* and articles by M. W. Jernegan in *School Review,* Vols. XXIII, XXVI–XXVIII.

It being one chiefe proiect of ye ould deluder, Satan, to keepe men from the knowledge of ye Scriptures, as in form^r times by keeping y^m in an unknowne tongue, so in these latt^r times by perswading from ye use of tongues, y^t so at least ye true sence & meaning of ye originall might be clouded by false glosses of saint seeming deceivers, y^t learning may not be buried in ye grave of o^r fath^{rs} in ye church and commonwealth, the Lord assisting o^r endeavo^{r}s,—

It is therefore ord^{r}ed, y^t ev^{r}y towneship in this iurisdiction, aft^r ye Lord hath increased y^m number to 50 houshold^{r}s, shall then forthwth appoint one wth in their towne to teach all such children as shall resort to him to write & reade, whose wages shall be paid eith^r by ye parents or mast^{r}s of such children, or by ye inhabitants in gen^{r}all, by way of supply, as ye maior part of those y^t ord^r ye prudentials ye twone shall appoint; provided, those y^t send their children be not oppressed by paying much more y^m they can have y^m taught for in oth^r townes; & it is furth^r ordered, y^t where any towne shall increase to ye numb^r of 100 families or household^{r}s, they shall set up a grammer schoole, ye m^r thereof being able to instruct youth so farr as they shall be fitted for ye university, provided, y^t if any towne neglect ye performance hereof above one yeare, y^t every such towne shall pay 5 pounds to ye next schoole till they shall performe this order.

21. THE CAMBRIDGE PLATFORM
1648

(W. Walker, Creeds and Platforms of Congregationalism, p. 194 ff.)

The Cambridge Platform grew out of the challenge of the authority of the Congregational Church by William Vassall and others who petitioned for the removal of civil disabilities of non-members of the Church. A synod met at Cambridge, September 1, 1646, "to discuss, dispute, & cleare up . . . such questions of church government & discipline . . . as they shall thinke needfull & meete." The third session of this synod, in August 1648, adopted the Westminster Confession as its creed, and formulated the relations of church and state and the duties of the clergy in the Cambridge Platform. In 1649 this platform was laid before the Congregations and by 1651 was adopted. "This event", says Fiske, "may be regarded as completing the theocratic organization of the Puritan Commonwealth." See C. Mather, *Magnalia*, Vol. II; W. Hubbard, *General History of New England*, p. 532 ff.; J. G. Palfrey, *History of New England*, Vol. II, p. 165 ff.; H. M. Dexter, *Congregationalism*, p. 435 ff.; B. Adams, *The Emancipation of Massachusetts*, p. 79 ff.; P. Miller, *Orthodoxy in Massachusetts;* J. T. Adams, *The Founding of New England*, ch. xi.

CHAP: XVII

Of The Civil Magistrates powr in Matters Ecclesiastical

It is lawfull, profitable, & necessary for christians to gather themslves into Church estate, and therin to exercise all the ordinances of christ according unto the word, although the consent of Magistrate could not be had therunto, because the Apostles & christians in their time did frequently thus practise, when the Magistrates being all of them Jewish or pagan, & mostly persecuting enemies, would give no countenance or consent to such matters.

2. Church-government stands in no opposition to civil government of commonwelths, nor any intrencheth upon the authority of Civil Magistrates in their jurisdictions; nor any whit weakneth their hands in governing; but rather strengthneth them, & furthereth the people in yielding more hearty & conscionable obedience unto them, whatsoever some ill affected persons to the wayes of Christ have suggested to alienate the affections of Kings & Princes from the ordinances of Christ; as if the kingdome of Christ in his church could not rise & stand, without the falling and weakning of their government, which is also of Christ: whereas the contrary is most true, that they may both stand together & flourish the one being helpfull unto the other, in their distinct and due administrations.

The powr & authority of Magistrates is not for the restraining of churches, or any other good workes, but for helping in and furthering therof; & therfore the consent & countenance of Magistrates when it may be had, is not to be sleighted, or lightly esteemed; but on the contrary; it is part of that honour due to christian Magistrates to desire & crave their consent & approbation therin: which being obtayned, the churches may then proceed in their way with much more encouragement, & comfort.

4. It is not in the powr of Magistrates to compell their subjects to become church-members, & to partake at the Lords table: for the priests are reproved, that brought unworthy ones into the sanctuarie: then, as it was unlawfull for the priests, so it is unlawfull to be done by civil Magistrates. Those whom the church is to cast out if they were in, the Magistrate ought not to thrust into the church, nor to hold them therin.

5. As it is unlawfull for church-officers to meddle with the sword of the Magistrate, so it is unlawfull for the Magistrate to meddle with the work proper to church-officers. the Acts of Moses & David, who were not only Princes, but Prophets, were extraordinary; therfore not imitable. Against such usurpation the Lord witnessed, by smiting Uziah with leprosie, for presuming to offer incense.

6. It is the duty of the Magistrate, to take care of matters of religion, & to improve his civil authority for the observing of the duties commanded in the first, as well as for observing of the duties commanded in the second table. . . .

7. The object of the powr of the Magistrate, are not things meerly inward, & so not subject to his cognisance & view, as in unbeliefe hardness of heart, erronious opinions not vented; but only such things as are acted by the outward man; neither is their powr to be exercised, in commanding such acts of the outward man, & punishing the neglect therof, as are but meer inventions, & devices of men; but about such acts, as are commanded & forbidden in the word; yea such as the word doth clearly determine, though not always clearly the judgment of the Magistrate or others, yet clearly in it selfe. In these he of right ought to putt

forth his authority, though oft-times actually he doth it not.

8. Idolatry, Blasphemy, Heresy, venting corrupt & pernicious opinions, that destroy the foundation, open contempt of the word preached, prophanation of the Lords day, disturbing the peaceable administration & exercise of the worship & holy things of God, & the like, are to be restrayned, & punished by civil authority.

9. If any church one or more shall grow schismaticall, rending it self from the communion of other churches, or shall walke incorrigibly or obstinately in any corrupt way of their own, contrary to the rule of the word; in such case, the Magistrate is to put forth his coercive powr, as the matter shall require. The tribes on this side Jordan intended to make warr against the other tribes, for building the altar of witness, whom they suspected to have turned away therin from following of the Lord.

Finis

22. MARYLAND TOLERATION ACT
April 21, 1649

(The Archives of Maryland, ed. by W. H. Browne, Vol. I, p. 244 ff.)

This so-called Toleration Act, passed in accordance with instructions from Lord Baltimore, was designed to secure Maryland from the charge of intolerance toward Protestantism. In 1654 the Puritans gained control of Maryland and the protection given to Catholics was withdrawn, but upon the restoration of Lord Baltimore to control, the act of 1649 was revived. The harsh provisions of the act against blasphemy were never enforced. See, G. Petrie, *Church and State in Maryland,* J. H. U. *Studies,* Vol. X; M. P. Andrews, *The Founding of Maryland,* ch. x.

Fforasmuch as in a well governed and Christian Common Wealth matters concerning Religion and the honor of God ought in the first place to bee taken, into serious consideration and endeavoured to bee settled. Be it therefore . . . enacted. . . . That whatsoever person or persons within this Province . . . shall from henceforth blaspheme God, . . . or shall deny our Saviour Jesus Christ to bee the sonne of God, or shall deny the holy Trinity the ffather sonne and holy Ghost, or the Godhead of any of the said Three persons of the Trinity or the Unity of the Godhead . . . shall be punished with death and confiscation or forfeiture of all his or her lands. . . .

. . . And whereas the inforceing of the conscience in matters of Religion hath frequently fallen out to be of dangerous Consequence in those commonwealthes where it hath been practised, And for the more quiett and peaceable governement of this Province, and the better to preserve mutuall Love and amity amongst the Inhabitants thereof. Be it

Therefore . . . enacted (except as in this present Act is before Declared and sett forth) that noe person or persons whatsoever within this Province, or the Islands, Ports, Harbors, Creekes, or havens thereunto belonging professing to believe in Jesus Christ, shall from henceforth bee any waies troubled, Molested or discountenanced for or in respect of his or her religion nor in the free exercise thereof within this Province or the Islands thereunto belonging nor any way compelled to the beleife or exercise of any other Religion against his or her consent, soe as they be not unfaithful to the Lord Proprietary, or molest or conspire against the civill Government established or to bee established in this Province under him or his heires. And that all & every person and persons that shall presume Contrary to this Act and the true intent and meaning thereof directly or indirectly either in person or estate willfully to wronge disturbe trouble or molest any person whatsoever within this Province professing to believe in Jesus Christ for or in respect of his or her religion or the free exercise thereof within this Province other than is provided for in this Act that such person or persons soe offending, shalbe compelled to pay trebble damages to the party soe wronged or molested, and for every such offence shall also forfeit 20ˢ sterling in money or the value thereof. . . , Or if the parties soe offending as aforesaid shall refuse or bee unable to recompense the party soe wronged, or to satisfy such ffyne or forfeiture, then such offender shalbe severely punished by publick whipping & imprisonment during the pleasure of the Lord proprietary, or his Leiuetenant or cheife Governor of this Province for the tyme being without baile or maineprise. . . .

23. THE NAVIGATION ACT OF 1660

(D. Pickering, *Statutes at Large,* Vol. VII, p. 452 ff.)

The Navigation laws provided the mechanism for the policy of mercantilism practiced by Great Britain as well as by the other colonizing powers of Europe. The first navigation laws were enacted in 1645; others followed in the decade of the fifties. The Act of 1660, often referred to as the First Navigation Act, systematized the laws and regulations of the preceding fifteen years. See, A. L. Beer, *Commercial Policy of England Towards the American Colonies;* A. L. Beer, *Origin of the British Colonial System, 1578–1660;* A. L. Beer, *The Old Colonial System, 1660–1754,* 2 Vols.; *Cambridge History of the British Empire,* Vol. I, ch. ix; H. E. Egerton, *Short History of British Colonial Policy;* J. T. Adams, *The Founding of New England,* ch. xii; W. J. Ashley, "The Commercial Legislation of England and the American Colonies, 1660–1760," *Quarterly Journal of Economics,* Vol. XIV; E. Channing, "The Navigation Laws," American Antiquarian Society, *Proceedings,* 1889.

An act for the encouraging and increasing of shipping and navigation

For the increase of shipping and encouragement of the navigation of this nation, wherein, under the good providence and protection of God, the wealth, safety and strength of this kingdom is so much concerned; be it enacted by the King's most excellent majesty, and by the lords and commons in this present parliament assembled, and by the authority thereof, That from and after the first day of *December* one thousand six hundred and sixty, and from thenceforward, no goods or commodities whatsoever shall be imported into or exported out of any lands, islands, plantations or territories to his Majesty belonging or in his possession, or which may hereafter belong unto or be in the possession of his Majesty, his heirs and successors, in *Asia, Africa* or *America,* in any other ship or ships, vessel or vessels whatsoever, but in such ships or vessels as do truly and without fraud belong only to the people of *England* or *Ireland,* dominion of *Wales* or town of *Berwick* upon *Tweed,* or are of the built of and belonging to any the said lands, islands, plantations or territories, as the proprietors and right owners thereof, and whereof the master and three fourths of the mariners at least are *English;* under the penalty of the forfeiture and loss of all the goods and commodities which shall be imported into or exported out of any the aforesaid places in any other ship or vessel, as also of the ship or vessel. . . .

II. And be it enacted, That no alien or person not born within the allegiance of our sovereign lord the King, his heirs and successors, or naturalized, or made a free denizen, shall from and after the first day of *February,* 1661, exercise the trade or occupation of a merchant or factor in any the said places; upon pain of the forfeiture and loss of all his goods and chattels, . . . and all governors of the said lands, islands, plantations or territories, and every of them, are hereby strictly required and commanded, and all who hereafter shall be made governors of any such islands, plantations or territories, by his Majesty, his heirs or successors, shall before their entrance into their government take a solemn oath, to do their utmost, that every the aforementioned clauses, and all the matters and things therein contained, shall be punctually and *bona fide* observed according to the true intent and meaning thereof; and upon complaint and proof made before his Majesty, his heirs or successors, or such as shall be by him or them thereunto authorized and appointed, that any the said governors have been willingly and wittingly negligent in doing their duty accordingly, that the said governor so offending shall be removed from his government.

III. And it is further enacted . . . , That no goods or commodities whatsoever, of the growth, production or manufacture of *Africa, Asia* or *America,* or of any part thereof, or which are described or laid down in the usual maps or cards of those places, be imported into *England, Ireland* or *Wales,* islands of *Guernsey* and *Jersey,* or town of *Berwick* upon *Tweed,* in any other ship or ships, vessel or vessels whatsoever, but in such as do truly and without fraud belong only to the people of *England* or *Ireland,* dominion of *Wales,* or town of *Berwick* upon *Tweed* or of the lands, islands, plantations or territories in *Asia, Africa* or *America,* to his Majesty belonging, as the proprietors and right owners thereof, and whereof the master, and three fourths at least of the mariners are *English;* (2) under the penalty of the forfeiture of all such goods and commodities, and of the ship or vessel in which they were imported. . . .

IV. And it is further enacted . . . , That no goods or commodities that are of foreign growth, production or manufacture, and which are to be brought into *England, Ireland, Wales,* the islands of *Guernsey* and *Jersey,* or town of *Berwick* upon *Tweed,* in *English*-built shipping, or other shipping belonging to some of the aforesaid places, and navigated by *English* mariners, as aforesaid, shall be shipped or brought from any other place or places, country or countries, but only from those of the said growth, production or manufacture, or from those ports where the said goods and commodities can only, or are, or usually have been, first shipped for transportation, and from none other places or countries; under the penalty of the forfeiture of all such of the aforesaid goods as shall be imported from any other place or country contrary to the true intent and meaning hereof, as also of the ship in which they were imported, . . .

V. And it is further enacted . . . , That any sort of ling, stock-fish, pilchard, or any other kind of dried or salted fish, usually fished for and caught by the people of *England, Ireland, Wales,* or town of *Berwick* upon *Tweed;* or any sort of cod-fish or herring, or any oil or blubber made or that shall be made of any kind of fish whatsoever, or any whale-fins or whale-bones, which shall be imported into *England, Ireland, Wales,* or town of *Berwick* upon *Tweed,* not having been caught in vessels truly and properly belonging thereunto as proprietors and right owners thereof, and the said fish cured saved and dried, and the oil and blubber aforesaid (which shall be accounted and pay as oil) not

made by the people thereof, and shall be imported into *England, Ireland* or *Wales,* or town of *Berwick* upon *Tweed,* shall pay double aliens custom.

VI. And be it further enacted, . . . That from henceforth it shall not be lawful to any person or persons whatsoever, to load or cause to be loaden and carried in any bottom or bottoms, ship or ships, vessel or vessels whatsoever, whereof any stranger or strangers-born (unless such as shall be denizens or naturalized) be owners, part-owners or master, and whereof three fourths of the mariners at least shall not be *English,* any fish, victual, wares, goods, commodities or things, of what kind or nature soever the fame shall be, from one port or creek of *England, Ireland, Wales,* islands of *Guernsey* or *Jersey,* or town of *Berwick* upon *Tweed,* to another port or creek of the fame, or of any of them; under penalty for every one that shall offend contrary to the true meaning of this branch of this present act, to forfeit all such goods shall be loaden and carried in any such ship or vessel, together with the ship or vessel, . . .

VIII. And it is further enacted . . . That no goods or commodities of the growth, production or manufacture of *Muscovy,* or to any the countries, dominions or territories to the . . . emperor of *Muscovy* or *Russia* belonging, as also that no sort of masts, timber or boards, no foreign salt, pitch, tar, rosin, hemp or flax, raisins, figs, prunes, olive-oils, no sorts of corn or grain, sugar, potashes, wines, vinegar, or spirits called *aqua-vitae,* or brandy-wine, shall from after the first day of April, 1662, be imported into *England, Ireland, Wales,* or town of *Berwick* upon *Tweed,* in any ship or ships . . . but in such as do truly and without fraud belong to the people thereof . . . and whereof the master and three fourths of the mariners at least are *English:* and that no currans nor commodities of the growth, production or manufacture of any of the countries, islands, dominions or territories to the *Othoman* or *Turkish* empire belonging, shall from after the first day of *September,* 1661, be imported into any of the afore-mentioned places in any ship or vessel, but which is of *English*-built, and navigated. . . .

XIII. Provided also, That this act or any thing therein contained, extend not, or be meant, to restrain the importing of any *East-*

India commodities loaden in *English* built shipping, and whereof the master and three-fourths of the mariners at least are English, from the usual place or places for lading of them in any part of those seas, to the southward and eastward of *Cabo bona Esperanza*, although the said ports be not the very places of their growth. . . .

XVIII. And it is further enacted . . . That from and after the first day of *April*, 1661,

no sugars, tobacco, cotton-wool, indicoes, ginger, fustick, or other dying wood, of the growth, production or manufacture of any *English* plantations in *America, Asia* or *Africa*, shall be shipped, carried, conveyed or transported from any of the said *English* plantations to any land . . . other than to such other *English* plantations as do belong to his Majesty. . . .

24. INDEPENDENCY IN COLONIAL MASSACHUSETTS
1661, 1678

The charter of 1629 did not specifically provide that Massachusetts was bound by the laws of Parliament, and on numerous occasions leaders of the Puritan colony insisted that Massachusetts was bound only by laws passed by its legal representatives. Both John Winthrop and John Cotton apparently held this view and it is implicit in the Massachusetts Body of Liberties of 1641. The two documents below indicate the theory that "the lawes of England doe not reach America". The first, submitted to the General Court June 10, 1661, is a Declaration of Rights;

the second the reply of the General Court to certain objections from the Lords of Council for Trade and Plantation to the Massachusetts laws. See, C. F. Mullett, *Fundamental Law and the American Revolution*, ch. ii; B. F. Wright, *American Interpretations of Natural Law;* A. B. Hart, ed. *Commonwealth History of Massachusetts*, Vol. I. chs. v, xvii; J. T. Adams, *Founding of New England*, ch. xii; J. Goebel, "King's Law and local custom in seventeenth century New England", *Columbia Law Rev.*, Vol. XXXI.

1. DECLARATION OF LIBERTIES. At Sessions of General Court, June 10, 1661. The Answer of the Committee unto the Matters proposed to their Consideration by the honored General Court.
(*Records of the Governor and Company of the Massachusetts Bay in New England*, Vol. IV, part 2, p. 25–6.)

Concerning our liberties

1. Wee conceive the pattent (under God) to be the first & maine foundation of our civil politye, by a Gouvernor & Company, according as is therein exprest.

2. The Gouvernor & Company are, by the pattent, a body politicke, in fact & name.

3. This body politicke is vested with power to make freemen. . . .

6. The Gouvernor, Deputy Gouvernor, Asistants, & select representatives or depu-

ties have full power and authoritie, both legislative & executive, for the gouvernment of all the people heere, whither inhabitants or straingers, both concerning eclesiasticks & in civils, without appeale, excepting lawe or lawes repugnant to the lawes of England. . . .

8. Wee conceive any imposition prejudiciall to the country contrary to any just lawe of ours, not repugnant to the lawes of England, to be an infringement of our right.

2. ANSWER TO MR. SOLICITOR'S OBJECTIONS AS TO WHAT IS DEFECTIVE IN THE LAWS OF THE COLONY. October 2, 1678.
(*Records of the Governor and Company of the Massachusetts Bay in New England*, Vol. V, p. 200–201.)

. . . To obj. 7. Your answer also therein being aprooved, the Court adds, viz, That for the acts passed in Parliament for incouraging trade and navigation, wee humbly conceive, according to the usuall sayings of the learned in the lawe, that the lawes of England are bounded within the fower seas,

and doe not reach America. The subjects of his majestie here being not represented in Parliament, so wee have not looked at ourselves to be impeded in our trade by them, nor yet wee abated in our relative allegiance to his majestie. However, so soone as wee understood his majesty's pleasure, that those acts should be observed by his majesties subjects of the Massachusetts, which could not be without invading the liberties and propperties of the subject, untill the Generall Court made provission therein by a law, which they did in October, 1677, and should be strictly attended from time to time, although the same be a discouragement to trade, and a great damage to his majesties plantation, untill wee shall obteyne his majesties gracious favour for that liberty of trade, which wee are not without hopes but that his majestie will see just occasion to grant to us, for the encouraging of his good subjects in a wilderness & hard country, who, by Gods speciall blessing upon their industry, have promoted the worke of navigation, by building ships, raising seamen, and navigating them from country to country; and wee doubt not but it will appeare, upon enquiry, that this restreint upon us will be an abstraction of his majesties customes in England, and not an inlargement thereof, for that the endeavour of the merchant here is to have his bancke in England; nor doe wee beleive that ever it cann be demonstrated, that that liberty hath binn a losse to his majesties customes, especially of late yeares, for that for whatever goods from any of his majesties plantations wee pay his customes before wee have them; and having paid the duties, it seemes hard that wee may not have liberty with our fellow-subjects in England. Wee speake not thus to capitulate with his majesty, but humbly submitt the same to his royall clemency & grace. . . .

25. CONCESSIONS TO THE PROVINCE OF PENNSYLVANIA
July 11, 1681

(F. N. Thorpe, ed. *Federal and State Constitutions,* Vol. V, p. 3044 ff.)

William Penn secured a charter to Pennsylvania March 4, 1681 and immediately began to advertise his land and organize a colony. He drew up an account of the province and its advantages which was widely circulated in England and on the Continent. At the same time he began to sell shares to those who wished to join him in the enterprise and to arrange for land sales and grants. To regulate these matters he drafted a body of Conditions and Concessions, dealing chiefly with land and with Indian relations. These Concessions were not designed as a constitution or body of laws. The Frame of Government, comprising both a constitution and a series of "laws agreed upon in England" bore the dates of April 25 and May 3, 1682. The Frame of Government can be found in Thorpe, *Federal and State Constitutions,* Vol. V. The Charter, the Concessions, and numerous related documents have been conveniently collected in *Charter to William Penn and Laws of the Province of Pennsylvania,* ed. by S. George, B. M. Nead and T. McCamant. On Penn and the founding of Pennsylvania, see S. G. Fisher, *The True Willliam Penn;* B. Dobree, *William Penn;* M. R. Brailsford, *The Making of William Penn;* W. R. Shepherd, *History of Proprietary Government in Pennsylvania;* I. Sharpless, *History of Quaker Government in Pennsylvania,* 2 Vols.

Certain conditions, *or* concessions, *agreed upon by* William Penn, *Proprietary and Governor of the province of Pennsylvania, and those who are the adventurers and purchasers in the same province.* . . .

I. That so soon as it pleaseth God that the abovesaid persons arrive there, a certain quantity of land, or ground plat, shall be laid out, for a large town or city, in the most convenient place, upon the river, for health and navigation; and every purchaser and adventurer shall, by lot, have so much land therein as will answer to the proportion, which he hath bought, or taken up, upon rent: but it is to be noted, that the surveyors shall consider what roads or highways will be necessary to the cities, towns or through the lands. Great roads from city to city not to contain less than *forty* foot, in breadth, shall be first laid out and declared to be for high-ways, before the dividend of acres be laid out for the purchaser, and the like observation to be had for the streets in the towns and cities, that there may be convenient roads and streets preserved, not to be encroached upon by any planter or builder, that none may build irregularly to the damage of another. *In this, custom governs.* . . .

III. That, when the country lots are laid out, every purchaser, from *one thousand,* to *ten thousand* acres, or more, not to have above *one thousand* acres together, unless in *three* years they plant a family upon every *thousand* acres; but that all such as purchase together, lie together; and, if as many as comply with this condition, that the whole be laid out together,

VII. That, for every *fifty* acres, that shall be allotted to a servant, at the end of his service, his quit-rent shall be *two shillings* per annum, and the master, or owner of the servant, when he shall take up the other *fifty acres,* his quit-rent, shall be *four shillings* by the year, or, if the master of the servant (by reason in the indentures he is so obliged to do) allot out to the servant *fifty* acres in his own division, the said master shall have, on demand, allotted him, from the governor, the *one hundred* acres, at the chief rent of six shillings per annum.

VIII. And, for the encouragement of such as are ingenious and willing to search out gold and silver mines in this province, it is hereby agreed, that they have liberty to bore and dig in any man's property, fully paying the damages done; and in case a discovery should be made, that the discoverer have *one-fifth,* the owner of the soil (if not the discoverer) a tenth part, the Governor, *two-fifths,* and the rest to the public treasury, saving to the king the share reserved by patent.

IX. In every *hundred thousand* acres, the Governor and Proprietary, by lot, reserveth ten to himself, what shall lie but in one place.

X. That every man shall be bound to plant, or man, so much of his share of land as shall be set out and surveyed, within *three* years after it is so set out and surveyed, or else it shall be lawful for newcomers to be settled thereupon, paying to them their survey money, and they go up higher for their shares.

XI. There shall be no buying and selling, be it with an *Indian,* or one among another, of any goods to be exported, but what shall be performed in public market, when such places shall be set apart, or erected, where they shall pass the public stamp, or mark. If bad ware, and prized as good, or deceitful in proportion or weight, to forfeit the value, as if good and full weight and proportion, to the public treasury of this province, whether it be the merchandize of the *Indian,* or that of the planters.

XII. And forasmuch, as it is usual with the planters to over-reach the poor natives of the country, in trade, by goods not being good of the kind, or debased with mixtures, with which they are sensibly aggrieved, it is agreed, whatever is sold to the *Indians,* in consideration of their furs, shall be sold in the market place, and there suffer the test, whether good or bad; if good, to pass; if not good, not to be sold for good, that the natives may not be abused, nor provoked.

XIII. That no man shall, by any ways or means, in word, or deed, affront, or wrong any *Indian,* but he shall incur the same penalty of the law, as if he had committed it against his fellow planter, and if any *Indian* shall abuse, in word, or deed, any planter of this province, that he shall not be his own judge upon the *Indian,* but he shall make his complaint to the governor of the province, or his lieutenant, or deputy, or some inferior magistrate near him, who shall, to the utmost of his power, take care with the king of the said *Indian,* that all reasonable satisfaction be made to the said injured planter. . . .

XV. That the *Indians* shall have liberty to do all things relating to improvement of their ground, and providing sustenance for their families, that any of the planters shall enjoy.

XVI. That the laws, as to slanders, drunkenness, swearing, cursing, pride in apparel, trespasses, distriesses, replevins, weights, and measures, shall be the same as in *England,* till altered by law in this province. . . .

XVIII. That, in clearing the ground, care be taken to leave *one* acre of trees for every *five* acres cleared, especially to preserve oak and mulberries, for silk and shipping. . . .

WILLIAM PENN.

26. THE EARLIEST PROTEST AGAINST SLAVERY
Resolutions of Germantown Mennonites.
February 18, 1688

(P. G. Mode, ed. *Source Book and Bibliographical Guide for American Church History*, p. 552–553)

Negro slavery was first introduced to the English colonies in America in 1619; though the number of negro slaves in the seventeenth century was comparatively small, there was some protest against the institution, especially from the Quakers and Mennonites. The protest of 1688 is the earliest known protest against slavery in the American colonies. See, M. S. Locke, *Anti-Slavery in America, 1619–1808* (Radcliffe College Monographs).

This is to the monthly meeting held at Richard Worrell's:

These are the reasons why we are against the traffic of men-body, as followeth: Is there any that would be done or handled at this manner? viz., to be sold or made a slave for all the time of his life? How fearful and faint-hearted are many at sea, when they see a strange vessel, being afraid it should be a Turk, and they should be taken, and sold for slaves into Turkey. Now, what is *this* better done, than Turks do? Yea, rather it is worse for them, which say they are Christians; for we hear that the most part of such negers are brought hither against their will and consent, and that many of them are stolen. Now, though they are black, we cannot conceive there is more liberty to have them slaves, as it is to have other white ones. There is a saying, that we should do to all men like as we will be done ourselves; making no difference of what generation, descent, or colour they are. And those who steal or rob men, and those who buy or purchase them, are they not all alike? Here is liberty of conscience, which is right and reasonable; here ought to be likewise liberty of the body, except of evil-doers, which is another case. But to bring men hither, or to rob and sell them against their will, we stand against. In Europe there are many oppressed for conscience-sake; and here there are those oppressed which are of a black colour. And we who know that men must not commit adultery—some do commit adultery *in* others, separating wives from their husbands, and giving them to others: and some sell the children of these poor creatures to other men. Ah! do consider well this thing, you who do it, if you would be done at this manner—and if it is done according to Christianity! You surpass Holland and Germany in this thing. This makes an ill report in all those countries of Europe, where they hear of [it], that the Quakers do here handel men as they handel there the cattle. And for that reason some have no mind or inclination to come hither. And who shall maintain this your cause, or plead for it? Truly, we cannot do so, except you shall inform us better hereof, viz.: that Christians have liberty to practice these things. Pray, what thing in the world can be done worse towards us, than if men should rob or steal us away, and sell us for slaves to strange countries; separating husbands from their wives and children. Being now this is not done in the manner we would be done at; therefore, we contradict, and are against this traffic of men-body. And we who profess that it is not lawful to steal, must, likewise, avoid to purchase such things as are stolen, but rather help to stop this robbing and stealing, if possible. And such men ought to be delivered out of the hands of the robbers, and set free as in Europe. Then is Pennsylvania to have a good report, instead, it hath now a bad one, for this sake, in other countries; Especially whereas the Europeans are desirous to know in what manner *the Quakers* do rule in *their* province; and most of them do look upon us with an envious eye. But if this is done well, what shall we say is done evil?

If once these slaves (which they say are so wicked and stubborn men,) should join themselves—fight for their freedom, and handel their masters and mistresses, as they did handel them before; will these masters and mistresses take the sword at hand and war against these poor slaves, like, as we are able to believe, some will not refuse to do? Or, have these poor negers not as much right to fight for their freedom, as you have to keep them slaves?

Now consider well this thing, if it is good or bad. And in case you find it to be good to handel these blacks in that manner, we desire and require you hereby lovingly, that you may inform us herein, which at this time never was done, viz., that Christians have such a liberty to do so. To the end we shall be satisfied on this point, and satisfy likewise our good friends and acquaintances in our native country, to whom it is a terror, or fearful thing, that men should be handelled so in Pennsylvania.

This is from our meeting at Germantown, held ye 18th of the 2d month, 1688, to be delivered to the monthly meeting at Richard Worrell's.

> Garret Henderich,
> Derick op de Graeff,
> Francis Daniel Pastorius,
> Abram op de Graeff.

27. THE NAVIGATION ACT OF 1696

(D. Pickering, *Statutes at Large*, Vol. IX, p. 428 ff.)

The Navigation Act of 1696 was designed to put an end to the widespread violations and evasions of the earlier navigation acts. This act, says Professor Channing, "may be said to have added the finishing touch to the colonial system so far as shipping was concerned." For references see Doc. No. 23.

An act for preventing frauds, and regulating abuses in the plantation trade.

II. Be it enacted . . . That after the five and twentieth day of *March,* 1698, no goods or merchandizes whatsoever shall be imported into, or exported out of, any colony or plantation to his Majesty, in *Asia, Africa,* or *America,* belonging, or in his possession, . . . or shall be laden in, or carried from any one port or place in the said colonies or plantations to any other port or place in the same, the kingdom of *England,* dominion of *Wales,* or town of *Berwick* upon *Tweed,* in any ship or bottom, but what is or shall be of the built of *England,* or of the built of *Ireland,* or the said colonies or plantations, and wholly owned by the people thereof, or any of them, and navigated with the masters and three fourths of the mariners of the said places only . . . under pain of forfeiture of ship and goods. . . .

III. [Goods may be imported and exported in prize ships, the master and three fourths the mariners being English.]

VI. And for the more effectual preventing of frauds, and regulating abuses in the plantation trade in *America,* be it further enacted . . . that the officers for the collecting and managing his Majesty's revenue, and inspecting the plantation trade, in any of the said plantations, shall have the same powers and authorities, for visiting and searching of ships, and taking their entries, and for seizing and securing or bringing on shore any of the goods prohibited to be imported or exported . . . or for which any duties are payable or ought to have been paid . . . as are provided for the officers of the customs in England by the said last mentioned act made in the fourteenth year of the reign of King *Charles* the Second, and also to enter houses or warehouses, to search for and seize any such goods. . . .

IX. And it is further enacted . . . That all laws, by-laws, usages or customs, at this time, or which hereafter shall be in practice . . . in any of the said plantations, which are in any wise repugnant to the before mentioned laws, or any of them, so far as they do relate to the said plantations, or any of them, or which are any ways repugnant to this present act, or to any other law hereafter to be made in this kingdom, so far as such law shall relate to and mention the said plantations, are illegal, null and void, to all intents and purposes whatsoever. . . .

XIV. *And whereas several ships and vessels laden with tobacco, sugars, and other goods of the growth and product of his Majesty's plantations in* America, *have been discharged in several ports of the kingdoms of* Scotland *and* Ireland, *contrary to the laws and statutes now in being, under pretence that the said ships and vessels were driven thither by stress of weather, or for want of provisions, and other disabilities could not proceed on their voyage:* for remedy whereof be it enacted . . . That from and after the first day of *December,* 1696, it shall not be lawful, on any pretence whatsoever, to put on shore in the said kingdoms of *Scotland* or *Ireland,* any goods or merchandize of the growth or product of any of his Majesty's plantations aforesaid, unless the same shall have been first landed in the kingdom of *England,* dominion of *Wales,* or town of *Berwick* upon *Tweed,* and paid the rates and duties wherewith they are chargeable by law. . . .

XVI. And be it further enacted . . . That all persons and their assignees, claiming any right or propriety in any islands or tracts of land upon the continent of *America,* by charter or letters patents, shall not at any time hereafter aliene, sell or dispose of any of the said islands, tracts of lands or proprieties, other than to the natural-born subjects of *England, Ireland,* dominion of *Wales,* and town of *Berwick* upon *Tweed,* without the licence and consent of his Majesty . . . ; and all governors nominated and appointed by any such persons or proprietors, who shall be intitled to make such nomination, shall be allowed and approved of by his Majesty . . .

and shall take the oaths injoined by this or any other act to be taken by the governors or commanders in chief in other his Majesty's colonies and plantations, before their entering upon their respective governments, under the like penalty, as his Majesty's governors and commanders in chief are by the said acts liable to.

XVII. And for the more effectual prevention of frauds which may be used to elude the intention of this act, by colouring foreign ships under *English* names, be it further enacted . . . that from and after the five and twentieth day of *March,* 1698, no ship or vessel whatsoever shall be deemed or pass as a ship of the built of *England, Ireland, Wales, Berwick, Guernsey, Jersey,* or any of his Majesty's plantations in *America,* so as to be qualified to trade to, from or in any of the plantations, until the person or persons claiming property in such ship or vessel shall register the same. . . .

28. PENN'S PLAN OF UNION
1697

(E. B. O'Callaghan, ed. *Documents Relative to the Colonial History of the State of New York,* Vol. IV, p. 296–7)

This is probably the earliest of the plans of union for the English colonies in America. For Penn's plan, and other early plans such as that of Daniel Coxe, see, R. Frothingham, *Rise of the Republic of the United States,* p. 110 ff. See also, S. G. Fisher, *The True William Penn.*

A brief and plain scheme how the English colonies in the North parts of America,—viz., Boston, Connecticut, Rhode Island, New York, New Jerseys, Pennsylvania, Maryland, Virginia, and Carolina,—may be made more useful to the crown and one another's peace and safety with an universal concurrence.

1. That the several colonies before mentioned do meet once a year, and oftener if need be during the war, and at least once in two years in times of peace, by their stated and appointed deputies, to debate and resolve of such measures as are most advisable for their better understanding and the public tranquillity and safety.

2. That, in order to it, two persons, well qualified for sense, sobriety, and substance, be appointed by each province as their

representatives or deputies, which in the whole make the congress to consist of twenty persons.

3. That the king's commissioner, for that purpose specially appointed, shall have the chair and preside in the said congress.

4. That they shall meet as near as conveniently may be to the most central colony for ease of the deputies.

5. Since that may in all probability be New York, both because it is near the centre of the colonies and for that it is a frontier and in the king's nomination, the governor of that colony may therefore also be the king's high commissioner during the session, after the manner of Scotland.

6. That their business shall be to hear and adjust all matters of complaint or difference between province and province. As, 1st, where persons quit their own province and go to another, that they may avoid their just debts, though they be able to pay them; 2d, where offenders fly justice, or justice cannot well be had upon such offenders in the

provinces that entertain them; 3d, to prevent or cure injuries in point of commerce; 4th, to consider the ways and means to support the union and safety of these provinces against the public enemies. In which congress the quotas of men and charges will be much easier and more equally set than it is possible for any establishment made here to do; for the provinces, knowing their own condition and one another's, can debate that matter with more freedom and satisfaction, and better adjust and balance their affairs in all respects for their common safety.

7. That, in times of war, the king's high commissioner shall be general or chief commander of the several quotas upon service against the common enemy, as he shall be advised, for the good and benefit of the whole.

29. PENNSYLVANIA CHARTER OF PRIVILEGES
October 28, 1701

(F. N. Thorpe, ed. *Federal and State Constitutions*, Vol. V, p. 3076 ff.)

The Frame of Government of 1682, proving cumbersome and unsatisfactory in detail, was replaced by the Great Charter and Frame of April 2, 1683. The following year Penn returned to England. He soon fell into disfavor with King William and in 1692 his colony was taken away from him and placed under the authority of Governor Fletcher of New York. Two years later it was restored to Penn, but Penn was not able to return to America until 1699, and meanwhile affairs became thoroughly unsatisfactory and disorganized. Under these circumstances, Penn agreed to the appointment of committees from the council and assembly to draft a new frame of government. This charter, finally agreed upon October 28, 1701, remained in force until the Revolution. For references see Doc. No. 25.

William Penn, Proprietary and Governor of the Province of *Pensilvania* and Territories thereunto belonging, To all to whom these Presents shall come, sendeth Greeting. Whereas King Charles *the Second,* by His Letters Patents, under the Great Seal of *England,* bearing Date the *Fourth* Day of *March,* in the Year *One Thousand Six Hundred and Eighty-one,* was graciously pleased to give and grant unto me, and my Heirs and Assigns for ever, this Province of *Pensilvania,* with divers great Powers and Jurisdictions for the well Government thereof. . . .

KNOW YE THEREFORE, That for the further Well-being and good Government of the said Province, and Territories and in Pursuance of the Rights and Powers beforementioned, I the said *William Penn* do declare, grant and confirm, unto all the Freemen, Planters and Adventurers, and other Inhabitants of this Province and Territories, these following Liberties, Franchises and Privileges, so far as in me lieth, to be held, enjoyed and kept, by the Freemen, Planters and Adventurers, and other Inhabitants of and in the said Province and Territories thereunto annexed, for ever.

FIRST

BECAUSE no People can be truly happy, though under the greatest Enjoyment of Civil Liberties, if abridged of the Freedom of their Consciences, as to their Religious Profession and Worship: And Almighty God being the only Lord of Conscience, Father of Lights and Spirits; and the Author as well as Object of all divine Knowledge, Faith and Worship, who only doth enlighten the Minds, and persuade and convince the Understandings of People, I do hereby grant and declare, That no Person or Persons, inhabiting in this province or Territories, who shall confess and acknowledge *One* almighty God, the Creator, Upholder and Ruler of the World; and profess him or themselves obliged to live quietly under the Civil Government, shall be in any Case molested or prejudiced, in his or their Person or Estate, because of his or their conscientious Persuasion or Practice, nor be compelled to frequent or maintain any religious Worship, Place or Ministry, contrary to his or their Mind, or to do or suffer any other Act or Thing, contrary to their religious Persuasion.

AND that all Persons who also profess to believe in *Jesus Christ,* the Saviour of the World, shall be capable (notwithstanding their other Persuasions and Practices in

Point of Conscience and Religion) to serve this Government in any Capacity, both legislatively and executively, he or they solemnly promising, when lawfully required, Allegiance to the King as Sovereign, and Fidelity to the Proprietary and Governor, and taking the Attests as now established by the Law made at *New-Castle,* in the Year *One Thousand and Seven Hundred,* entitled, *An Act directing the Attests of several Officers and Ministers,* as now amended and confirmed this present Assembly.

II For the well governing of this Province and Territories, there shall be an Assembly yearly chosen, by the Freemen thereof, to consist of *Four* Persons out of each County, of most Note for Virtue, Wisdom and Ability. . . . Which Assembly shall have Power to chuse a Speaker and other their Officers; and shall be Judges of the Qualifications and Elections of their own Members; sit upon their own Adjournments; appoint Committees; prepare Bills in order to pass into Laws; impeach Criminals, and redress Grievances; and shall have all other Powers and Privileges of an Assembly, according to the Rights of the free-born Subjects of *England,* and as is usual in any of the King's Plantations in *America.* . . .

III THAT the Freemen in each respective County, at the Time and Place of Meeting for Electing their Representatives to serve in Assembly, may as often as there shall be Occasion, chuse a double Number of Persons to present to the Governor for Sheriffs and Coroners to serve for *Three* Years, if so long they behave themselves well; out of which respective Elections and Presentments, the Governor shall nominate and commissionate one for each of the said Offcers, the *Third* Day after such Presentment, or else the *First* named in such Presentment, for each Office as aforesaid, shall stand and serve in that Office for the Time before respectively limited; and in Case of Death or Default, such Vacancies shall be supplied by the Governor, to serve to the End of the said Term. . . .

AND that the Justices of the respective Counties shall or may nominate and present to the Governor *Three* Persons, to serve for Clerk of the Peace for the said County, when there is a Vacancy, one of which the Governor shall commissionate within *Ten* Days after such Presentment, or else the *First*

nominated shall serve in the said Office during good Behavior.

IV THAT the Laws of this Government shall be in this Stile, viz. *By the Governor, with the Consent and Approbation of the Freemen in General Assembly met;* and shall be, after Confirmation by the Governor, forthwith recorded in the Rolls Office, and kept at *Philadelphia,* unless the Governor and Assembly shall agree to appoint another Place.

V THAT all Criminals shall have the same Privileges of Witnesses and Council as their Prosecutors.

VI THAT no Person or Persons shall or may, at any Time hereafter, be obliged to answer any Complaint, Matter or Thing whatsoever, relating to Property, before the Governor and Council, or in any other Place, but in ordinary Course of Justice, unless Appeals thereunto shall be hereafter by Law appointed.

VII THAT no Person within this Government, shall be licensed by the Governor to keep an Ordinary, Tavern or House of Publick Entertainment, but such who are first recommended to him, under the Hands of the Justices of the respective Counties, signed in open Court; which Justices are and shall be hereby impowered, to suppress and forbid any Person, keeping such Publick-House as aforesaid, upon their Misbehavior, on such Penalties as the Law doth or shall direct; and to recommend others from time to time, as they shall see Occasion. . . .

VIII BUT because the Happiness of Mankind depends so much upon the Enjoying of Liberty of their Consciences as aforesaid, I do hereby solemnly declare, promise and grant, for me, my Heirs and Assigns, That the *First* Article of this Charter relating to Liberty of Conscience, and every Part and Clause therein, according to the true Intent and Meaning thereof, shall be kept and remain, without any Alteration, inviolably for ever.

AND LASTLY, I the said *William Penn,* Proprietary and Governor of the Province of *Pensilvania,* and Territories thereunto belonging, for myself, my Heirs and Assigns, have solemnly declared, granted and confirmed, and do hereby solemnly declare, grant and confirm, That neither I, my Heirs or Assigns, shall procure or do any Thing or Things whereby the Liberties in this Charter contained and expressed, nor any Part thereof, shall be infringed or broken: And if any thing shall be procured or done, by any Person or Persons, contrary to these Presents, it shall be held of no Force or Effect. . . .

30. THE MOLASSES ACT
May 17, 1733

(D. Pickering, *Statutes at Large,* Vol. XVI, p. 374 ff.)

This Act, placing heavy duties upon the importation of rum and molasses from the French West Indies to the American colonies, was passed in response to the demand of the English merchants with interests in the British West Indies. Had it been enforced, it would have played havoc with the triangle trade of the New England merchants; fortunately for them it was not enforced. See, G. L. Beer, *Commercial Policy of England Toward the American Colonies;* E. B. Greene, *Provincial America,* ch. xvii; J. T. Adams, *Revolutionary New England,* ch. viii; W. J. Ashley, *Surveys, Historic and Economic;* C. M. Andrews, "Anglo-French Commercial Rivalry, 1700–1750", *American Hist. Rev.,* Vol. XX.

An act for the better securing and encouraging the trade of his Majesty's sugar colonies in America.

WHEREAS *the welfare and prosperity of your Majesty's sugar colonies in* America *are of the greatest consequence and importance to the trade, navigation and strength of this kingdom: and whereas the planters of the said sugar colonies have of late years fallen under such great discouragements, that they are unable to improve or carry on the sugar trade upon an equal footing with the foreign sugar colonies, without some advantage and relief be given to them from* Great Britain: for remedy whereof . . . be it enacted . . . , That from and after [December 25, 1733,] there shall be raised, levied, collected and paid, unto and for the use of his Majesty . . . , upon all rum or spirits of the produce or manufacture of any of the colonies or plantations in *America,* not in the possession or under the dominion of his Majesty . . . , which at any time or times within or during the continuance of this act, shall be imported or brought into any of the colonies or plantations in *America,* which now are or hereafter may be in the possession or under the dominion of his Majesty . . . , the sum of nine pence, money of *Great Britain,* . . . for every gallon thereof, and after that rate for any greater or lesser quantity: and upon all molasses or syrups of such foreign produce or manufacture as aforesaid, which shall be imported or brought into any of the said colonies or plantations of or belonging to his Majesty, the sum of six pence of like money for every gallon thereof . . . ; and upon all sugars and paneles of such foreign growth, produce or manufacture as aforesaid, which shall be imported into any of the said colonies or plantations . . . , a duty after the rate of five shillings of like money, for every hundred weight *Avoirdupoize.* . . .

IV. And be it further enacted . . . , That from and after December 25, 1733, no sugars, paneles, syrups or molasses, of the growth, product and manufacture of any of the colonies or plantations in *America,* nor any rum or spirits of *America,* except of the growth or manufacture of his Majesty's sugar colonies there, shall be imported by any person or persons whatsoever into the kingdom of *Ireland,* but such only as shall be fairly and *bona fide* loaden and shipped in *Great Britain* in ships navigated according to the several laws now in being in that behalf, under the penalty of forfeiting all such sugar, paneles, syrups or molasses, rum or spirits, or the value thereof, together with the ship or vessel in which the same shall be imported, . . .

IX. And it is hereby further enacted . . . , That in case any sugar or paneles of the growth, produce or manufacture of any of the colonies or plantations belonging to or in the possession of his Majesty . . . , which shall have been imported into *Great Britain* after June 24, 1733, shall at any time within one year after the importation thereof, be again exported out of *Great Britain,* . . . all the residue and remainder of the subsidy or duty, by any former act or acts of parliament granted and charged on such sugar or paneles as aforesaid, shall without any delay or reward be repaid to such merchant or merchants, who do export the same, within one month after demand thereof.

X. And it is hereby further enacted . . . , That from and after June 24, 1733, for every hundred weight of sugar refined in *Great Britain* . . . , which shall be exported out of this kingdom, there shall be, by virtue of this act, repaid at the customhouse to the exporter, within one month after the demand thereof, over and above the several sums of three shillings and one shilling *per* hundred, payable by two former acts of parliament, one of them made in the ninth and tenth years of the reign of his late Majesty King *William* the Third, and the other in the second and third years of the reign of her late Majesty Queen *Anne,* the further sum of two shillings, oath or solemn affirmation as aforesaid, being first made by the refiner, that the

said sugar so exported, was produced from brown and muscovado sugar, and that as he verily believes, the same was imported from some of the colonies or plantations in *America* belonging to and in the possession of the crown of *Great Britain,* and that as he verily believes the duty of the said brown and muscovado sugar was duly paid at the time of the importation thereof, and that the same was duly exported. . . .

XIII. Provided nevertheless, That nothing herein contained shall extend . . . to hinder or restrain the importation of any sugars . . . of any of the dominions belonging to the King of *Spain,* or the King of *Portugal,* from any part or place from whence such sugars might lawfully have been imported before the making of this act. . . .

31. THE ALBANY PLAN OF UNION
1754

(Works of Benjamin Franklin, ed. by J. Sparks, Vol. III, p. 36 ff.)

This plan of union, devised by Franklin, contained the germs of the solution of the problem of imperial order, ultimately solved by the Federal Constitution of the United States. An interesting discussion of the Plan is in R. Frothingham, *Rise of the Republic of the United States,* ch. iv; H. L. Osgood, *American Colonies in the Eighteenth Century,* Vol. IV, ch. xiv; A. C. McLaughlin, "The Background of American Federalism," *America and Britain,* p. 147 ff. In the document Franklin's explanatory notes are omitted.

It is proposed that humble application be made for an act of Parliament of Great Britain, by virtue of which one general government may be formed in America, including all the said colonies, within and under which government each colony may retain its present constitution, except in the particulars wherein a change may be directed by the said act, as hereafter follows.

1. That the said general government be administered by a President-General, to be appointed and supported by the crown; and a Grand Council, to be chosen by the representatives of the people of the several Colonies met in their respective assemblies.

2. That within —— months after the passing such act, the House of Representatives that happen to be sitting within that time, or

that shall be especially for that purpose convened, may and shall choose members for the Grand Council, in the following proportion, that is to say,

Massachusetts Bay	7
New Hampshire	2
Connecticut	5
Rhode Island	2
New York	4
New Jersey	3
Pennsylvania	6
Maryland	4
Virginia	7
North Carolina	4
South Carolina	4
	48

3. ——who shall meet for the first time at the city of Philadelphia, being called by the President-General as soon as conveniently may be after his appointment.

4. That there shall be a new election of the members of the Grand Council every three years; and, on the death or resignation of any member, his place should be supplied by a new choice at the next sitting of the Assembly of the Colony he represented.

5. That after the first three years, when the proportion of money arising out of each Colony to the general treasury can be known,

the number of members to be chosen for each Colony shall, from time to time, in all ensuing elections, be regulated by that proportion, yet so as that the number to be chosen by any one Province be not more than seven, nor less than two.

6. That the Grand Council shall meet once in every year, and oftener if occasion require, at such time and place as they shall adjourn to at the last preceding meeting, or as they shall be called to meet at by the President-General on any emergency; he having first obtained in writing the consent of seven of the members to such call, and sent duly and timely notice to the whole.

7. That the Grand Council have power to choose their speaker; and shall neither be dissolved, prorogued, nor continued sitting longer than six weeks at one time, without their own consent or the special command of the crown.

8. That the members of the Grand Council shall be allowed for their service ten shillings sterling per diem, during their session and journey to and from the place of meeting; twenty miles to be reckoned a day's journey.

9. That the assent of the President-General be requisite to all acts of the Grand Council, and that it be his office and duty to cause them to be carried into execution.

10. That the President-General, with the advice of the Grand Council, hold or direct all Indian treaties, in which the general interest of the Colonies may be concerned; and make peace or declare war with Indian nations.

11. That they make such laws as they judge necessary for regulating all Indian trade.

12. That they make all purchases from Indians, for the crown, of lands not now within the bounds of particular Colonies, or that shall not be within their bounds when some of them are reduced to more convenient dimensions.

13. That they make new settlements on such purchases, by granting lands in the King's name, reserving a quitrent to the crown for the use of the general treasury.

14. That they make laws for regulating and governing such new settlements, till the crown shall think fit to form them into particular governments.

15. That they raise and pay soldiers and build forts for the defence of any of the Colonies, and equip vessels of force to guard the coasts and protect the trade on the ocean, lakes, or great rivers; but they shall not impress men in any Colony, without the consent of the Legislature.

16. That for these purposes they have power to make laws, and lay and levy such general duties, imposts, or taxes, as to them shall appear most equal and just (considering the ability and other circumstances of the inhabitants in the several Colonies), and such as may be collected with the least inconvenience to the people; rather discouraging luxury, than loading industry with unnecessary burdens.

17. That they may appoint a General Treasurer and Particular Treasurer in each government when necessary; and, from time to time, may order the sums in the treasuries of each government into the general treasury; or draw on them for special payments, as they find most convenient.

18. Yet no money to issue but by joint orders of the President-General and Grand Council; except where sums have been appropriated to particular purposes, and the President-General is previously empowered by an act to draw such sums.

19. That the general accounts shall be yearly settled and reported to the several Assemblies.

20. That a quorum of the Grand Council, empowered to act with the President-General, do consist of twenty-five members; among whom there shall be one or more from a majority of the Colonies.

21. That the laws made by them for the purposes aforesaid shall not be repugnant, but, as near as may be, agreeable to the laws of England, and shall be transmitted to the King in Council for approbation, as soon as may be after their passing; and if not disapproved within three years after presentation, to remain in force.

22. That, in case of the death of the President-General, the Speaker of the Grand Council for the time being shall succeed, and be vested with the same powers and authorities, to continue till the King's pleasure be known.

23. That all military commission officers, whether for land or sea service, to act under this general constitution, shall be nominated

by the President-General; but the approbation of the Grand Council is to be obtained, before they receive their commissions. And all civil officers are to be nominated by the Grand Council, and to receive the President-General's approbation before they officiate.

24. But, in case of vacancy by death or removal of any officer, civil or military, under this constitution, the Governor of the Province in which such vacancy happens may appoint, till the pleasure of the President-General and Grand Council can be known.

25. That the particular military as well as civil establishments in each Colony remain in their present state, the general constitution notwithstanding; and that on sudden emergencies any Colony may defend itself, and lay the accounts of expense thence arising before the President-General and General Council, who may allow and order payment of the same, as far as they judge such accounts 'just and reasonable.

32. JAMES OTIS' SPEECH AGAINST THE WRITS OF ASSISTANCE
February 24, 1761

(The Works of John Adams, ed. by C. F. Adams, Vol. II, p. 521 ff.)

This famous case involved the question of the constitutionality of the writs of assistance issued from the court of exchequer in England. On the application of the surveyor-general of the port of Boston for the grant of these writs, some Boston merchants engaged Oxenbridge Thacher and James Otis to argue against their issuance. No formal record of Otis's argument exists. John Adams, however, took notes of the speech, and these are given in the first extract below. G. R. Minot in his *History of Massachusetts, 1748–1765,* Vol. II, p. 87–99, expanded these notes into a version of the argument. Adams's revision of the Minot version, is given in the second extract below. For a learned discussion of the whole question see the Appendix to J. Quincy, *Reports of Cases Argued and Adjudged in the Superior Court of Judicature of the Province of Massachusetts Bay between 1761 and 1772,* p. 479 ff., by Justice Horace Gray. Otis's argument contains one of the earliest statements of the doctrine that a law against natural law is void. For the history of this theory see, C. F. Mullett, *Fundamental Law and the American Revolution.* A copy of a writ of Assistance can be found in W. MacDonald, ed. *Select Charters, etc.,* p. 258 ff.

1. *Otis.* This writ is against the fundamental principles of law. The privilege of the House. A man who is quiet, is as secure in his house, as a prince in his castle—notwithstanding all his debts and civil processes of any kind. But—

For flagrant crimes and in cases of great public necessity, the privilege may be infringed on. For felonies an officer may break upon process and oath, that is, by a special warrant to search such a house, sworn to be suspected, and good grounds of suspicion appearing.

Make oath *coram* Lord Treasurer, or Exchequer in England, or a magistrate here, and get a special warrant for the public good, to infringe the privilege of house.

General warrant to search for felonies. Hawkins, Pleas of the Crown. Every petty officer, from the highest to the lowest; and if some of them are common, others are uncommon.

Government justices used to issue such perpetual edicts. (*Q.* With what particular reference.) But one precedent, and that in the reign of Charles II., when star chamber powers and all powers but lawful and useful powers, were pushed to extremity.

The authority of this modern practice of the Court of Exchequer. It has an Imprimatur. But what may not have? It may be owing to some ignorant Clerk of the Exchequer. But all precedents, and this among the rest, are under the control of the principles of law. Lord Talbot. Better to observe the known principles of law than any one precedent, though in the House of Lords.

As to Acts of Parliament. An act against the Constitution is void; an act against natural equity is void; and if an act of Parliament should be made, in the very words of this petition it would be void. The executive Courts must pass such acts into disuse.

8 Rep. 118 from Viner. Reason of the common law to control an act of Parliament. Iron manufacture. Noble Lord's proposal, that we should send our horses to England to be shod. If an officer will justify under a

writ, he must return it. 12. Mod. 396, perpetual writ. Statute Charles II. We have all as good right to inform as custom-house officers, and every man may have a general irreturnable commission to break houses.

By 12 of Charles, on oath before Lord Treasurer, Barons of Exchequer, or Chief Magistrate, to break, with an officer. 14 C. to issue a warrant requiring sheriffs, &c. to assist the officers to search for goods not entered or prohibited. 7 & 8. W. & M. gives officers in plantations same powers with officers in England.

Continuance of writs and processes proves no more, nor so much, as I grant a special writ of assistance on special oath for special purpose.

Pew indorsed warrant to Ware. Justice Walley searched House. Province Law. p. 114.

Bill in chancery. This Court confined their chancery power to revenue, &c.

2. . . . In the first place, may it please your Honors, I will admit that writs of one kind may be legal; that is, special writs, directed to special officers, and to search certain houses, &c. specially set forth in the writ, may be granted by the Court of Exchequer at home, upon oath made before the Lord Treasurer by the person who asks it, that he suspects such goods to be concealed in those very places he desires to search. The act of 14 Charles II, which Mr. Gridley mentions, proves this. And in this light the writ appears like a warrant from a Justice of the Peace to search for stolen goods. Your Honors will find in the old books concerning the office of a Justice of the Peace, precedents of general warrants to search suspected houses. But in more modern books you will find only special warrants to search such and such houses specially named, in which the complainant has before sworn that he suspects his goods are concealed; and you will find it adjudged that special warrants only are legal. In the same manner I rely on it, that the writ prayed for in this petition, being general, is illegal. It is a power, that places the liberty of every man in the hands of every petty officer. I say I admit that special writs of assistance, to search special places, may be granted to certain persons on oath; but I deny that the writ now prayed for

can be granted, for I beg leave to make some observations on the writ itself, before I proceed to other acts of Parliament. In the first place, the writ is universal, being directed "to all and singular Justices, Sheriffs, Constables, and other officers and subjects;" so, that, in short, it is directed to every subject in the King's dominions. Every one with this writ may be a tyrant; if this commission be legal, a tyrant in a legal manner also may control, imprison, or murder any one within the realm. In the next place, it is perpetual; there is no return. A man is accountable to no person for his doings. Every man may reign secure in his petty tyranny, and spread terror and desolation around him. In the third place, a person with this writ, in the daytime, may enter all houses, shops, &c. at will, and command all to assist him. Fourthly, by this writ not only deputies &c. but even their menial servants, are allowed to lord it over us. Now one of the most essential branches of English liberty is the freedom of one's house. A man's house is his castle; and whilst he is quiet, he is as well guarded as a prince in his castle. This writ, if it should be declared legal, would totally annihilate this privilege. Custom-house officers may enter our houses, when they please; we are commanded to permit their entry. Their menial servants may enter, may break locks, bars, and every thing in their way; and whether they break through malice or revenge, no man, no court, can inquire. Bare suspicion without oath is sufficient. This wanton exercise of his power is not a chimerical suggestion of a heated brain. I will mention some facts. Mr. Pew had one of these writs, and when Mr. Ware succeeded him, he endorsed this writ over to Mr. Ware; so that these writs are negotiable from one officer to another; and so your Honors have no opportunity of judging the persons to whom this vast power is delegated. Another instance is this: Mr. Justice Walley had called this same Mr. Ware before him, by a constable, to answer for a breach of Sabbath-day acts, or that of profane swearing. As soon as he had finished, Mr. Ware asked him if he had done. He replied, Yes/ Well then, said Mr. Ware, I will show you a little of my power. I command you to permit me to search your house for uncustomed goods. And went on to search his house from the garret to the cellar; and then served the constable in the same manner. But to show another absurdity in this writ; if it should be established, I insist upon it, every person by the 14 Charles II. has this power as well as custom-house officers. The words are, "It shall be lawful for any person or persons authorized," &c. What a scene does this open! Every man, prompted by revenge, ill humor, or wantonness, to inspect the inside of his neighbor's house, may get a writ of assistance. Others will ask it from self-defence; one arbitrary exertion will provoke another, until society be involved in tumult and in blood.

Again, these writs are not returned. Writs in their nature are temporary things. When the purposes for which they are issued are answered, they exist no more; but these live forever; no one can be called to account. Thus reason and the constitution are both against this writ. Let us see what authority there is for it. Not more than one instance can be found of it in all our law-books; and that was in the zenith of arbitrary power,

namely, in the reign of Charles II, when star-chamber powers were pushed to extremity by some ignorant clerk of the exchequer. But had this writ been in any book whatever, it would have been illegal. All precedents are under the control of the principles of law. Lord Talbot says it is better to observe these than any precedents, though in the House of Lords, the last resort of the subject. No Acts of Parliament can establish such a writ; though it should be made in the very words of the petition, it would be void. An act against the constitution is void. (vid. Viner.) But these prove no more than what I before observed, that special writs may be granted *on oath and probable suspicion*. The act of 7 & 8 William III. that the officers of the plantation shall have the same powers, &c., is confined to this sense; that an officer should show probable ground; should take his oath of it; should do this before a magistrate; and that such magistrate, if he thinks proper, should issue a special warrant to a constable to search the places. That of 6 Anne can prove no more.

33. THE PROCLAMATION OF 1763
October 7, 1763
(*Annual Register,* 1763, p. 208 ff.)

The immediate background of this famous proclamation was Pontiac's Rebellion, and its provisions were designed to be of a temporary character. The reservation of the lands west of the Appalachians appeared to deprive the Colonies of their western lands and to put an end to the widespread private speculation in these lands. See, C. W. Alvord, *The Mississippi Valley in British Politics,* 2 Vols.; C. E. Carter, *Great Britain and the Illinois Country;* V. Coffin, *Quebec and the American Revolution,* ch. v.

Whereas we have taken into our royal consideration the extensive and valuable acquisitions in America secured to our Crown by the late definitive treaty of peace concluded at Paris the 10th day of February last; and being desirous that all our loving subjects, as well of our kingdom as of our colonies in America, may avail themselves, with all convenient speed, of the great benefits and advantages which must accrue therefrom to their commerce, manufactures, and navigation; we have thought fit, with the

advice of our Privy Council, to issue this our Royal Proclamation, hereby to publish and declare to all our loving subjects that we have, with the advice of our said Privy Council, granted our letters patent under our Great Seal of Great Britain, to erect within the countries and islands ceded and confirmed to us by the said treaty, four distinct and separate governments, styled and called by the names of Quebec, East Florida, West Florida, and Grenada, and limited and bounded as follows, viz:

First, the government of Quebec, bounded on the Labrador coast by the river St. John, and from thence by a line drawn from the head of that river, through the lake St. John, to the South end of the lake Nipissim; from whence the said line, crossing the river St. Lawrence and the Lake Champlain in 45 degrees of North latitude, passes along the High Lands, which divide the rivers that empty themselves into the said river St. Lawrence, from those which fall into the sea; and also along the North coast of the Bayes des Chaleurs, and the coast of the Gulph of St. Lawrence to Cape Rosieres, and from thence crossing the mouth of the river St. Lawrence by the West end of the island of Anticosti, terminates at the aforesaid river St. John.

Secondly, The government of East Florida, bounded to the Westward by the Gulph of Mexico and the Apalachicola river; to the Northward, by a line drawn from that part of the said river where the Catahoochee and Flint rivers meet, to the source of St. Mary's river, and by the course of the said river to the Atlantic Ocean; and to the East and South by the Atlantic Ocean, and the Gulph of Florida, including all islands within six leagues of the sea coast.

Thirdly, The government of West Florida, bounded to the Southward by the Gulph of Mexico, including all islands within six leagues of the coast from the river Apalachicola to lake Pontchartrain; to the Westward by the said lake, the lake Maurepas, and the river Mississippi; to the Northward, by a line drawn due East from that part of the river Mississippi which lies in thirty-one degrees North latitude, to the river Apalachicola, or Catahoochee; and to the Eastward by the said river.

Fourthly, The government of Grenada, comprehending the island of that name, together with the Grenadines, and the islands of Dominico, St. Vincent, and Tobago.

And to the end that the open and free fishery of our subjects may be extended to, and carried on upon the coast of Labrador and the adjacent islands, we have thought fit . . . to put all that coast, from the river St. John's to Hudson's Streights, together with the islands of Anticosti and Madelane, and all other smaller islands lying upon the said coast, under the care and inspection of our governor of Newfoundland.

We have also . . . thought fit to annex the islands of St. John and Cape Breton, or Isle Royale, with the lesser islands adjacent thereto, to our government of Nova Scotia.

We have also . . . annexed to our province of Georgia, all the lands lying between the rivers Atamaha and St. Mary's.

And . . . we have . . . given express power and direction to our governors of our said colonies respectively, that so soon as the state and circumstances of the said colonies will admit thereof, they shall, with the advice and consent of the members of our council, summon and call general assemblies within the said governments respectively, in such manner and form as is used and directed in those colonies and provinces in America, which are under our immediate government; and we have also given power to the said governors, with the consent of our said councils, and the representatives of the people, so to be summoned as aforesaid, to make, constitute, and ordain laws, statutes, and ordinances for the public peace, welfare, and good government of our said colonies, and of the people and inhabitants thereof, as near as may be, agreeable to the laws of England, and under such regulations and restrictions as are used in other colonies; and in the mean time, and until such assemblies can be called as aforesaid, all persons inhabiting in, or resorting to, our said colonies, may confide in our royal protection for the enjoyment of the benefit of the laws of our realm of England: for which purpose we have given power under our great seal to the governors of our said colonies respectively, to erect and constitute, with the advice of our said councils respectively, courts of judicature and public justice within our said colonies, for the hearing and determining all causes as well criminal as civil, according to law and equity, and as near as may be, agreeable to the laws of England, with liberty to all persons who may think themselves aggrieved by the sentence of such courts, in all civil cases, to appeal, under the usual limitations and restrictions, to us, in our privy council.

And whereas it is just and reasonable, and essential to our interest and the security of our colonies, that the several nations or tribes of Indians with whom we are connected, and who live under our protection, should not be molested or disturbed in the possession of such parts of our dominions and territories as, not having been ceded to or purchased by us, are reserved to them, or any of them, as their hunting-grounds; we do therefore, with the advice of our Privy Council, declare it to be our royal will and pleasure, that no Governor or commander in chief, in any of our colonies of Quebec, East Florida, or West Florida, do presume, upon any pretence whatever, to grant warrants of survey, or pass any patents for lands beyond the bounds of their respective governments, as described in their commissions; as also that no Governor or commander in chief of our other colonies or plantations in America do presume for the present, and until our further pleasure be known, to grant warrants of survey or pass patents for any lands beyond the heads or sources of any of the rivers which fall into the Atlantic Ocean from the west or northwest; or upon any lands whatever, which, not having been ceded to or purchased by us, as aforesaid, are reserved to the said Indians, or any of them.

And we do further declare it to be our royal will and pleasure, for the present as aforesaid, to reserve under our sovereignty, protection, and dominion, for the use of the said Indians, all the land and territories not included within the limits of our said three new governments, or within the limits of the territory granted to the Hudson's Bay Company; as also all the land and territories lying to the westward of the sources of the rivers which fall into the sea from the west and northwest as aforesaid; and we do hereby strictly forbid, on pain of our displeasure, all our loving subjects from making any purchases or settlements whatever, or taking possession of any of the lands above reserved, without our special leave and license for that purpose first obtained.

And we do further strictly enjoin and require all persons whatever, who have either wilfully or inadvertently seated themselves upon any lands within the countries above described, or upon any other lands which, not having been ceded to or purchased by us, are still reserved to the said Indians as aforesaid, forthwith to remove themselves from such settlements.

And whereas great frauds and abuses have been committed in the purchasing lands of the Indians, to the great prejudice of our interests, and to the great dissatisfaction of the said Indians; in order, therefore, to prevent such irregularities for the future, and to the end that the Indians may be convinced of our justice and determined resolution to remove all reasonable cause of discontent, we do, with the advice of our Privy Council, strictly enjoin and require, that no

private person do presume to make any purchase from the said Indians of any lands reserved to the said Indians within those parts of our colonies where we have thought proper to allow settlement; but that if at any time any of the said Indians should be inclined to dispose of the said lands, the same shall be purchased only for us, in our name, at some public meeting or assembly of the said Indians, to be held for that purpose by the Governor or commander in chief of our colony respectively within which they shall lie: and in case they shall lie within the limits of any proprietary government, they shall be purchased only for the use and in the name of such proprietaries, conformable to such directions and instructions as we or they shall think proper to give for that purpose. And we do, by the advice of our Privy Council, declare and enjoin, that the trade with the said Indians shall be free and open to all our subjects whatever, provided that every person who may incline to trade with the said Indians do take out a license for carrying on such trade, from the Governor or commander in chief of any of our colonies respectively where such person shall reside, and also give security to observe such regulations as we shall at any time think fit, by ourselves or commissaries to be appointed for this purpose, to direct and appoint for the benefit of the said trade. And we do hereby authorize, enjoin, and require the Governors and commanders in chief of all our colonies respectively, as well those under our immediate government as those under the government and direction of proprietaries, to grant such licenses without fee or reward, taking especial care to insert therein a condition that such license shall be void, and the security forfeited, in case the person to whom the same is granted shall refuse or neglect to observe such regulations as we shall think proper to prescribe as aforesaid.

And we do further expressly enjoin and require all officers whatever, as well military as those employed in the management and direction of Indian affairs within the territories reserved as aforesaid, for the use of the said Indians, to seize and apprehend all persons whatever who, standing charged with treasons, misprisions of treason, murders, or other felonies or misdemeanors, shall fly from justice and take refuge in the said territory, and to send them under a proper guard to the colony where the crime was committed of which they shall stand accused, in order to take their trial for the same.

Given at our Court at St. James's, the 7th day of October 1763, in the third year of our reign.

34. FRONTIER GRIEVANCES

A Remonstrance of the distressed and bleeding Frontier Inhabitants of the Province of Pennsylvania
February 13, 1764

(Minutes of the Provincial Council of Pennsylvania, Vol. IX, p. 138 ff.)

The various manifestations of sectionalism on the eve of the Revolution are nowhere better illustrated than in this remonstrance from the inhabitants of the frontier counties of Pennsylvania. The immediate background of the remonstrance was Pontiac's Rebellion and the raid of the so-called Paxton Boys on the civilized Conestogo Indians. See Franklin's "Narrative of the Massacres", *Works,* ed. by J. Bigelow, Vol. III, p. 260 ff. On sectionalism in Pennsylvania see W. R. Shepherd, *Proprietary Government in Pennsylvania;* C. R. Lincoln, *The Revolutionary Movement in Pennsylvania;* F. J. Turner, *The Frontier in American History,* ch. iii; G. A. Cribbs, *Frontier Policy of Pennsylvania.*

To the Honourable John Penn, Esquire, Governor of the Province of *Pennsylvania,* & of the Counties of *New Castle, Kent,* and *Sussex,* on *Delaware,* and to the Representatives of the Freemen of the said Province, in General Assembly met:

WE Matthew Smith and James Gibson, in behalf of ourselves and His Majesty's faithful and loyal Subjects, the Inhabitants of the Frontier Counties of Lancaster, York, Cumberland, Berks, and Northampton, humbly beg leave to remonstrate and to lay before you the following Grievances, which we submit to your Wisdom for Redress.

First. We apprehend that as Freemen and English Subjects, we have an indisputable Title to the same Privileges & immunities with His Majesty's other Subjects who reside in the interior Counties of Philadelphia, Chester, and Bucks, and therefore ought not to be excluded from an equal share with them in the very important Privilege of Legislation; nevertheless, contrary to the Proprietor's Charter and the acknowledged principles of common Justice & Equity, our five counties are restrained from electing more than ten Representatives, viz: four for Lancaster, two for York, two for Cumberland, one for Berks, and one for Northampton; while the three Counties and City of Philadelphia, Chester, and Bucks, elect Twenty-Six. This we humbly conceive is oppressive, unequal, and unjust, the cause of many of our Grievances, and an infringement of our Natural privileges of Freedom & Equality; wherefore we humbly pray that we may be no longer deprived of an equal number with the three aforesaid Counties, to represent us in Assembly.

Secondly. We understand that a Bill is now before the House of Assembly, wherein it is provided that such Persons as shall be charged with killing any Indians in Lancaster County, shall not be tried in the County where the Fact was committed, but in the Counties of Philadelphia, Chester, or Bucks. This is manifestly to deprive British Subjects of their known Privileges, to cast an eternal Reproach upon whole Counties, as if they were unfit to serve their Country in the quality of Jurymen, and to contradict the well-known Laws of the British Nation in a point whereon Life, Liberty, and security essentially depend, namely, that of being tried by their equals in the neighborhood where their own, their Accusers', and the Witnesses' Character and Credit, with the Circumstances of the Fact, are best known, & instead thereof putting their Lives in the hands of Strangers who may as justly be suspected of partiallity to, as the Frontier Counties can be of prejudices against Indians; and this, too, in favour of Indians only, against His Majesty's faithful & loyal subjects. . . .

Thirdly. During the late and present

Indian War, the Frontiers of this Province have been repeatedly attacked and ravaged by Skulking parties of the Indians, who have with the most Savage Cruelty murdered Men, Women, and Children without distinction, and have reduced near a thousand Families to the most extream distress. It grieves us to the very heart to see such of our Frontier Inhabitants as have escaped Savage Fury with the loss of their parents, their Children, their Wives or Relatives, left destitute by the public, and exposed to the most cruel Poverty and Wretchedness while upwards of an Hundred and twenty of these Savages, who are with great reason suspected of being guilty of these horrid Barbarities under the Mask of Friendship, have procured themselves to be taken under the protection of the Government, with a view to elude the Fury of the brave Relatives of the murdered, and are now maintained at the public Expence. Some of these Indians now in the Barracks of Philadelphia, are confessedly a part of the Wyalusing Indians, which Tribe is now at war with us, and the others are the Moravian Indians, who, living amongst us under the Cloak of Friendship, carried on a Correspondence with our known Enemies on the Great Island. We cannot but observe with sorrow & indignation that some Persons in this Province are at pains to extenuate the barbarous Cruelties practised by these Savages on our murdered Brethren & Relatives, which are shocking to human Nature, and must pierce every Heart but that of the hardened perpetrators or their Abettors; Nor is it less distressing to hear others pleading that although the Wyalusing Tribe is at War with us, yet that part of it which is under the Protection of the Government may be friendly to the English and innocent. In what nation under the Sun was it ever the custom that when a neighboring Nation took up Arms, not an individual should be touched but only the Persons that offered Hostilities? Who ever proclaimed War with a part of a Nation, and not with the Whole? Had these Indians disapproved of the Perfidy of their Tribe, & been willing to cultivate and preserve Friendship with us, why did they not give notice of the War before it happened, as it is known to be the Result of long Deliberations, and a preconcerted Combination amongst them? Why did they not leave their Tribe immediately, and come amongst us before there was Ground to suspect them, or War was actually waged with their Tribe? No, they stayed amongst them, were privy to their murders & Ravages, until we had destroyed their Provisions; and when they could no longer subsist at home, they come not as Deserters, but as Friends to be maintained through the Winter, that they may be able to Scalp and butcher us in the Spring.

And as to the Moravian Indians, there are strong Grounds at least to suspect their Friendship, as it is known they carried on a Correspondence with our Enemies on the Great Island. We killed three Indians going from Bethlehem to the Great Island with Blankets, Ammunition, & Provisions, which is an undeniable Proof that the Moravian Indians were in confederacy with our open Enemies; And we cannot but be filled with Indignation to hear this action of ours painted in the most odious and detestable Colours, as if we had inhumanly murdered our Guides who preserved us from perishing in the Woods, when we only killed three of our known Enemies, who attempted to shoot us when we surprized them. And besides all this, we understand that one of these very Indians is proved by the oath of Stinton's Widow, to be the very Person that murdered her Husband. How then comes it to pass that he alone, of all the Moravian Indians, should join with the enemy to murder that family? Or can it be supposed that any Enemy Indians, contrary to their known custom of making War, should penetrate into the Heart of a settled Country to burn, plunder and murder the Inhabitants, and not molest any Houses in their return, or ever be seen or heard of? Or how can we account for it, that no ravages have been committed in Northampton County, since the removal of the Moravian Indians, when the Great Cove has been struck since? These things put it beyond doubt with us that the Indians now at Philadelphia are His Majesty's Perfidious Enemies, & therefore to protect and maintain them at the Public Expence, while our suffering Brethren on the Frontiers are almost destitute of the necessaries of Life and are neglected by the Public, is sufficient to make us mad with rage, and tempt us to do what nothing but the most violent necessity can vindicate. We humbly and earnestly pray, therefore, that those Enemies of His Majesty may be removed as soon as possible out of the Province.

Fourthly. We humbly conceive that it is contrary to the maxims of good Policy, and extreamely dangerous to our Frontiers, to suffer any Indians of what tribe soever to live within the Inhabited parts of this Province while we are engaged in an Indian War, as Experience has taught us that they are all perfidious, and their claim to Freedom & Independency, puts it in their power to act as Spies, to entertain & give intelligence to our Enemies, and to furnish them with Provisions and Warlike Stores. To this fatal intercourse between our pretended Friends and open Enemies, we must ascribe the greatest of the Ravages and Murders that have been committed in the course of this and the last Indian War. We therefore pray that this grievance be taken under consideration and remedied.

Fifthly. We cannot help lamenting that no Provision has been hitherto made, that such of our Frontier Inhabitants as have been wounded in defence of the Province, their Lives and Liberties, may be taken care of and cured of their Wounds at the publick Expence. We therefore pray that this Grievance may be redressed.

Sixthly. In the late Indian war this Province, with others of His Majesty's Colonies, gave rewards for Indian Scalps, to encourage the seeking them in their own Country, as the most likely means of destroying or reducing them to reason; but no such Encouragement has been given in this War, which has damped the Spirits of many brave Men who are willing to venture their Lives in parties against the Enemy. We therefore pray that public rewards may be proposed for Indian Scalps, which may be adequate to the Dangers attending Enterprizes of this nature.

Seventhly. We daily lament that numbers of our nearest & dearest relatives are still in Captivity among the Savage Heathen, to be trained up in all their Ignorance & Barbarity, or to be tortured to death with all the contrivances of Indian Cruelty, for attempting to make their escape from Bondage; We see they pay no regard to the many solemn Promises which they have made to restore our Friends who are in Bondage amongst them. We therefore earnestly pray that no trade may hereafter be permitted to be carried on with them, until our Brethren and Relatives are brought home to us.

Eightly. We complain that a certain Society of People in this Province, in the late Indian War, & at several Treaties held by the King's representatives, openly loaded the Indians with Presents, and that J. P., a leader of the said Society, in Defiance of all Government, not only abetted our Indian Enemies, but kept up a private intelligence with them, and publickly received from them a Belt of Wampum, as if he had been our Governor or authorized by the King to treat with his Enemies. By this means the Indians have been taught to despise us as a weak and disunited people, and from this fatal Source have arose many of our Calamities under which we groan. We humbly pray therefore that this Grievance may be redressed, and that no private subject be hereafter permitted to treat with, or carry on a Correspondence with our Enemies.

Ninthly. We cannot but observe with sorrow that Fort Augusta, which has been very expensive to this Province, has afforded us but little assistance during this or the last War. The men that were stationed at that place neither helped our distressed Inhabitants to save their Crops, nor did they attack our Enemies in their Towns, or patrole on our Frontiers. We humbly request that proper measures may be taken to make that Garrison more serviceable to us in our Distress, if it can be done.

N.B. We are far from intending any Reflection against the Commanding Officer stationed at Augusta, as we presume his Conduct was always directed by those from whom he received his Orders.

SIGNED on Behalf of ourselves, and by appointment of a great number of the Frontier Inhabitants.

MATTHEW SMITH.
JAMES GIBSON.

February 13th, 1764.

35. THE STAMP ACT
March 22, 1765

(D. Pickering, *Statutes at Large,* Vol. XXVI, p. 179 ff.)

The reorganization of the Empire inaugurated in 1763 required the raising of additional revenue in the American Colonies, and as early as 1764 Grenville announced his intention of introducing a stamp tax. The colonial agents were given the opportunity to suggest alternative means of raising revenue, but though all of them protested against the stamp tax they were unable to suggest any effective alternative. The Stamp Act passed Parliament with little opposition or attention; the debate on the bill was "languid." The measure was designed to raise an additional £60,000, and the ministry optimistically hoped that it would arouse little opposition in the Colonies. For the American reaction to the Stamp Act see Docs. No. 36–39. On the Act, see R. Frothingham, *Rise of the Republic,* ch. v; G. Bancroft, *History of the United States,* author's last revision, Vol. III, chs. v–viii; C. H. Van Tyne, *Causes of the War of Independence,* ch. vi.

An act for granting and applying certain stamp duties, and other duties, in the British *colonies and plantations in* America, *towards further defraying the expences of defending, protecting, and securing the same; and for amending such parts of the several acts of parliament relating to the trade and revenues of the said colonies and plantations, as direct the manner of determining and recovering the penalties and forfeitures therein mentioned.*

WHEREAS by an act made in the last session of parliament, several duties were granted, continued, and appropriated, towards defraying the expences of defending, protecting, and securing, the British *colonies and plantations in* America: *and whereas it is just and necessary, that provision be made for raising a further revenue within your Majesty's dominions in* America, *towards defraying the said expences:* . . . be it enacted . . . , That from and after [November 1, 1765,] there shall be raised, levied, collected, and paid unto his Majesty, his heirs, and successors, throughout the colonies and plantations in *America* which now are, or hereafter may be, under the dominion of his Majesty, his heirs and successors,

For every skin or piece of vellum or parchment, or sheet or piece of paper, on which shall be ingrossed, written or printed, any declaration, plea, replication, rejoinder, demurrer, or other pleading, or any copy thereof, in any court of law within the *British* colonies and plantations in *America,* a stamp duty of three pence.

For every skin . . . on which shall be ingrossed . . . any donation, presentation, collation, or institution of or to any benefice, or any writ or instrument for the like purpose, or any register, entry, testimonial, or certificate of any degree taken in any university, academy, college, or seminary of learning . . . a stamp duty of two pounds. . . .

For every skin . . . on which shall be ingrossed . . . any note or bill of lading, which shall be signed for any kind of goods, wares, or merchandize, to be exported from, or any cocket or clearance granted within the said colonies and plantations, a stamp duty of four pence. . . .

For every skin . . . on which shall be ingrossed . . . any grant, appointment, or admission of or to any publick beneficial office or employment, for the space of one year, or any lesser time, of or above the value of twenty pounds *per annum* sterling money, in salary, fees, and perquisites . . . , (except commissions and appointments of officers of the army, navy, ordnance, or militia, of judges, and of justices of the peace) a stamp duty of ten shillings. . . .

For every skin . . . on which shall be ingrossed . . . any licence for retailing of spirituous liquors, to be granted to any person who shall take out the same . . . , a stamp duty of twenty shillings. . . .

For every skin . . . on which shall be ingrossed . . . any probate of a will, letters of administration, or of guardianship for any estate above the value of twenty pounds sterling money; within the *British* colonies and plantations upon the continent of *America,* the islands belonging thereto, and the *Bermuda* and *Bahama* islands, a stamp duty of five shillings. . . .

For every skin . . . on which shall be ingrossed . . . any bond for securing the payment of any sum of money, not exceeding the sum of ten pounds sterling money, within the *British* colonies and plantations upon the continent of *America,* the islands belonging thereto, and the *Bermuda* and *Bahama* islands, a stamp duty of six pence. . . .

For every skin . . . on which shall be ingrossed . . . any order or warrant for surveying or setting out any quantity of land, not exceeding one hundred acres, issued by any governor, proprietor, or any publick officer alone, or in conjunction with any other person or persons, or with any council, or any council and assembly, within the *British* colonies and plantations in *America,* a stamp duty of six pence. . . .

For every skin . . . on which shall be ingrossed . . . any such original grant . . . by which any quantity of land not exceeding one hundred acres shall be granted . . . within all other parts of the *British* dominions in *America,* a stamp duty of three shillings. [Further provision for larger grants.]

For every skin . . . on which shall be ingrossed . . . any grant, appointment, or admission, of or to any publick beneficial office or employment, not herein before charged, above the value of twenty pounds *per annum* sterling money in salary, fees, and perquisites, or any exemplification of the same, within the *British* colonies and plantations upon the continent of *America,* the islands belonging thereto, and the *Bermuda* and *Bahama* islands (except commissions of officers of the army, navy, ordnance, or militia, and of justices of the peace) a stamp duty of four pounds. . . .

For every skin . . . on which shall be ingrossed . . . any indenture, lease, conveyance, contract, stipulation, bill of sale, charter party, protest, articles of apprenticeship, or covenant (except for the hire of servants not apprentices, and also except such other matters as are herein before charged) within the *British* colonies and plantations in *America,* a stamp duty of two shillings and six pence. . . .

For every skin . . . on which shall be ingrossed . . . any notarial act, bond, deed, letter of attorney, procuration, mortgage, release, or other obligatory instrument, not

herein before charged . . . , a stamp duty of two shillings and three pence. . . .

And for and upon every pack of playing cards, and all dice, which shall be sold or used . . . , the several stamp duties following (that is to say)

For every pack of such cards, the sum of one shilling.

And for every pair of such dice, the sum of ten shillings.

And for and upon every paper, commonly called a *pamphlet,* and upon every news paper . . . and for and upon such advertisements as are herein after mentioned, the respective duties following (that is to say)

For every such pamphlet and paper contained in half a sheet, or any lesser piece of paper . . . , a stamp duty of one halfpenny, for every printed copy thereof.

For every such pamphlet and paper (being larger than half a sheet, and not exceeding one whole sheet) . . . , a stamp duty of one penny, for every printed copy thereof.

For every pamphlet and paper being larger than one whole sheet, and not exceeding six sheets in octavo, or in a lesser page, or not exceeding twelve sheets in quarto, or twenty sheets in folio . . . , a duty after the rate of one shilling for every sheet of any kind of paper which shall be contained in one printed copy thereof.

For every advertisement to be contained in any gazette, news paper, or other paper, or any pamphlet . . . , a duty of two shillings.

For every almanack or calendar, for any one particular year, or for any time less than a year, which shall be written or printed on one side only of any one sheet, skin, or piece of paper parchment, or vellum . . . , a stamp duty of two pence.

For every other almanack or calendar for any one particular year . . . , a stamp duty of four pence.

And for every almanack or calendar written or printed . . . , to serve for several years, duties to the same amount respectively shall be paid for every such year.

For every skin . . . on which any instrument, proceeding, or other matter or thing aforesaid, shall be ingrossed . . . , in any other than the *English* language, a stamp duty of double the amount of the respective duties before charged thereon. . . .

II. And also a duty of one shilling for every twenty shillings, in any sum exceeding fifty pounds, which shall be given, paid, contracted, or agreed, for, with, or in relation to any such clerk or apprentice. . . .

V. And be it further enacted . . . , That all books and pamphlets serving chiefly for the purpose of an almanack, by whatsoever name or names intituled or described, are and shall be charged with the duty imposed by this act on almanacks, but not with any of the duties charged by this act on pamphlets, or other printed papers . . .

VI. Provided always, that this act shall not extend to charge any bills of exchange, accompts, bills of parcels, bills of fees, or any bills or notes not sealed for payment of money at sight, or upon demand, or at the end of certain days of payment. . . .

XII. And be it further enacted . . . , That the said several duties shall be under the management of the commissioners, for the time being, of the duties charged on stamped vellum, parchment, and paper, in *Great Britain:* and the said commissioners are hereby impowered and required to employ such officers under them, for that purpose, as they shall think proper. . . .

XVI. And be it further enacted . . . , That no matter or thing whatsoever, by this act charged with the payment of a duty, shall be pleaded or given in evidence, or admitted in any court within the said colonies and plantations, to be good, useful, or available in law or equity, unless the same shall be marked or stamped, in pursuance of this act, with the respective duty hereby charged thereon, or with a higher duty. . . .

LIV. And be it further enacted . . . , That all the monies which shall arise by the several rates and duties hereby granted (except the necessary charges of raising, collecting, recovering, answering, paying, and accounting for the same and the necessary charges from time to time incurred in relation to this act, and the execution thereof) shall be paid into the receipt of his Majesty's exchequer, and shall be entered separate and apart from all other monies, and shall be there reserved to be from time to time disposed of by parliament, towards further defraying the necessary expences of defending, protecting, and securing, the said colonies and plantations. . . .

LVII. . . . offences committed against any other act or acts of Parliament relating to the trade or revenues of the said colonies or plantations; shall and may be prosecuted, sued for, and recovered, in any court of record, or in any court of admiralty, in the respective colony or plantation where the offence shall be committed, or in any court of vice admiralty appointed or to be appointed, and which shall have jurisdiction within such colony, plantation, or place, (which courts of admiralty or vice admiralty are hereby respectively authorized and required to proceed, hear, and determine the same) at the election of the informer or prosecutor. . . . .

36. VIRGINIA STAMP ACT RESOLUTIONS
May 30, 1765

(Journal of the House of Burgesses of Virginia, 1761–65, p. 360)

On May 29 the Virginia House of Burgesses resolved itself into a committee of the whole to consider the Stamp Act. Patrick Henry, a new member from Louisa County, introduced seven resolutions; these were bitterly opposed by many of the tidewater leaders, but, after "torrents of sublime eloquence" from Henry, were passed. The following day, however, the House adopted the first five only, and rejected the last two. After Henry's departure, the House expunged the fifth resolution from the record. The entire series of resolutions, however, was published in the newspapers. It is in connection with the debate on these resolutions that Henry made his "Caesar had his Brutus" speech, the actual context of which is apparently very different from that generally given. See, S. E. Morison, *Sources and Documents Illustrating the American Revolution,* p. 14 ff.; M. C. Tyler, *Patrick Henry,* p. 61 ff.; G. E. Howard, *Preliminaries of the Revolution,* ch. viii; R. Frothingham, *Rise of the Republic,* ch. v.

THE RESOLVES

Resolved, That the first adventurers and settlers of this His Majesty's Colony and Dominion of Virginia brought with them, and transmitted to their posterity, and all other His Majesty's subjects since inhabiting in this His Majesty's said Colony, all the liberties, privileges, franchises, and immunities, that have at any time been held, enjoyed, and possessed, by the people of Great Britain.

Resolved, That by two royal charters, granted by King James the First, the colonists aforesaid are declared entitled to all liberties, privileges, and immunities of denizens and natural subjects, to all intents and purposes, as if they had been abiding and born within the realm of England.

Resolved, That the taxation of the people by themselves, or by persons chosen by themselves to represent them, who can only know what taxes the people are able to bear, or the easiest method of raising them, and must themselves be affected by every tax laid on the people, is the only security against a burthensome taxation, and the distinguishing characteristick of British freedom, without which the ancient constitution cannot exist.

Resolved, That His Majesty's liege people of this his most ancient and loyal Colony have without interruption enjoyed the inestimable right of being governed by such laws, respecting their internal polity and taxation, as are derived from their own consent, with the approbation of their sovereign, or his substitute; and that the same hath never been forfeited or yielded up, but hath been constantly recognized by the kings and people of Great Britain.

Resolved therefore, That the General Assembly of this Colony have the only and sole exclusive right and power to lay taxes and impositions upon the inhabitants of this Colony, and that every attempt to vest such power in any person or persons whatsoever other than the General Assembly aforesaid has a manifest tendency to destroy British as well as American freedom.

Resolved. That His Majesty's liege people, the inhabitants of this Colony, are not bound to yield obedience to any law or ordinance whatever, designed to impose any taxation whatsoever upon them, other than the laws or ordinances of the General Assembly aforesaid.

Resolved, That any person who shall, by speaking or writing, assert or maintain that any person or persons other than the General Assembly of this Colony, have any right or power to impose or lay any taxation on the people here, shall be deemed an enemy to His Majesty's Colony.

37. INSTRUCTIONS OF THE TOWN OF BRAINTREE MASSACHUSETTS ON THE STAMP ACT
October 14, 1765

(The Works of John Adams, ed. by C. F. Adams, Vol. III, p. 465 ff.)

These instructions have a peculiar interest because they were drafted by John Adams, and announced his entrance into Massachusetts politics and into the struggle between the colonies and the mother country. The instructions were widely copied throughout Massachusetts. See, G. Chinard, *Honest John Adams,* ch. iii.

To EBENEZER THAYER, ESQ.

SIR,— . . . We can no longer forbear complaining, that many of the measures of the late ministry, and some of the late acts of Parliament, have a tendency, in our apprehension, to divest us of our most essential rights and liberties. We shall confine ourselves, however, chiefly to the act of Parliament, commonly called the Stamp Act, by which a very burthensome, and, in our opinion, unconstitutional tax, is to be laid upon us all; and we subjected to numerous and enormous penalties, to be prosecuted, sued for, and recovered, at the option of an informer, in a court of admiralty, without a jury.

We have called this a burthensome tax, because the duties are so numerous and so high, and the embarrassments to business in this infant, sparsely-settled country so great, that it would be totally impossible for the people to subsist under it, if we had no controversy at all about the right and authority of imposing it. Considering the present scarcity of money, we have reason to think, the execution of that act for a short space of time would drain the country of its cash, strip multitudes of all their property, and reduce them to absolute beggary. And what the consequence would be to the peace of the province, from so sudden a shock and such a convulsive change in the whole course of our business and subsistence, we tremble to consider. We further apprehend this tax to be unconstitutional. We have always understood it to be a grand and fundamental principle of the constitution, that no freeman should be subject to any tax to which he has not given his own consent, in person or by proxy. And the maxims of the law, as we have constantly received them, are to the same effect, that no freeman can be separated from his property but by his own act or fault. We take it clearly, therefore, to be inconsistent with the spirit of the common law, and of the essential fundamental principles of the British constitution, that we should be subject to any tax imposed by the British Parliament; because we are not represented in that assembly in any sense, unless it be by a fiction of law, as insensible in theory as it would be injurious in practice, if such a taxation should be grounded on it.

But the most grievous innovation of all, is the alarming extension of the power of courts of admiralty. In these courts, one judge presides alone! No juries have any concern there! The law and the fact are both to be decided by the same single judge, whose commission is only during pleasure, and with whom, as we are told, the most mischievous of all customs has become established, that of taking commissions on all condemnations; so that he is under a pecuniary temptation always against the sub-

ject. . . . We have all along thought the acts of trade in this respect a grievance; but the Stamp Act has opened a vast number of sources of new crimes, which may be committed by any man, and cannot but be committed by multitudes, and prodigious penalties are annexed, and all these are to be tried by such a judge of such a court! . . . We cannot help asserting, therefore, that this part of the act will make an essential change in the constitution of juries, and it is directly repugnant to the Great Charter itself; for, by that charter, "no americament shall be assessed, but by the oath of honest and lawful men of the vicinage;" and, "no freeman shall be taken, or imprisoned, or disseized of his freehold, or liberties of free customs, nor passed upon, nor condemned, but by lawful judgment of his peers, or by the law of the land." So that this act will "make such a distinction, and create such a difference between" the subjects in Great Britain and those in America, as we could not have expected from the guardians of liberty in "both".

As these, sir, are our sentiments of this act, we, the freeholders and other inhabitants, legally assembled for this purpose, must enjoin it upon you, to comply with no measures or proposals for countenancing the same, or assisting in the execution of it, but by all lawful means, consistent with our allegiance to the King, and relation to Great Britain, to oppose the execution of it, till we can hear the success of the cries and petitions of America for relief.

We further recommend the most clear and explicit assertion and vindication of our rights and liberties to be entered on the public records, that the world may know, in the present and all future generations, that we have a clear knowledge and a just sense of them, and, with submission to Divine Providence, that we never can be slaves. . . .

38. RESOLUTIONS OF THE STAMP ACT CONGRESS
October 19, 1765

(Journal of the First Congress of the American Colonies in opposition to the Tyrannical Acts of the British Parliament, p. 27 ff.)

On the motion of James Otis, the Massachusetts House of Representatives adopted, June 8, a circular letter to the other colonies recommending a meeting of committees from the various houses of representatives in New York City in October "to consult together on the present circumstances of the colonies". The Congress met at City Hall, New York, October 7. Twenty-eight delegates from nine colonies were present: Virginia, New Hampshire, North Carolina and Georgia did not send delegates. The Congress drew up Resolutions, an address to the King, a memorial to the Lords and a petition to the House of Commons. The Resolutions were probably drafted by John Dickinson, though there is some support to the claim that they are from the pen of John Cruger of New York. For references see Doc. No. 35.

THE members of this Congress, sincerely devoted with the warmest sentiments of affection and duty to His Majesty's person and Government, inviolably attached to the present happy establishment of the Protestant succession, and with minds deeply impressed by a sense of the present and impending misfortunes of the British colonies on this continent; having considered as maturely as time will permit the circumstances of the said colonies, esteem it our indispensable duty to make the following declarations of our humble opinion respecting the most essential rights and liberties of the colonists, and of the grievances under which they labour, by reason of several late Acts of Parliament.

I. That His Majesty's subjects in these colonies owe the same allegiance to the Crown of Great Britain that is owing from his subjects born within the realm, and all due subordination to that august body the Parliament of Great Britain.

II. That His Majesty's liege subjects in these colonies are intitled to all the inherent rights and liberties of his natural born subjects within the kingdom of Great Britain.

III. That it is inseparably essential to the freedom of a people, and the undoubted right of Englishmen, that no taxes be imposed on them but with their own consent, given personally or by their representatives.

IV. That the people of these colonies are not, and from their local circumstances cannot be, represented in the House of Commons in Great Britain.

V. That the only representatives of the people of these colonies are persons chosen therein by themselves, and that no taxes ever have been, or can be constitutionally imposed on them, but by their respective legislatures.

VI. That all supplies to the Crown being free gifts of the people, it is unreasonable and inconsistent with the principles and spirit of the British Constitution, for the people of Great Britain to grant to His Majesty the property of the colonists.

VII. That trial by jury is the inherent and invaluable right of every British subject in these colonies.

VIII. That the late Act of Parliament, entitled *An Act for granting and applying certain stamp duties, and other duties, in the British colonies and plantations in America, etc.,* by imposing taxes on the inhabitants of these colonies; and the said Act, and several other Acts, by extending the jurisdiction of the courts of Admiralty beyond its ancient limits, have a manifest tendency to subvert the rights and liberties of the colonists.

IX. That the duties imposed by several late Acts of Parliament, from the peculiar circumstances of these colonies, will be extremely burthensome and grievous; and from the scarcity of specie, the payment of them absolutely impracticable.

X. That as the profits of the trade of these colonies ultimately center in Great Britain, to pay for the manufactures which they are obliged to take from thence, they eventually contribute very largely to all supplies granted there to the Crown.

XI. That the restrictions imposed by several late Acts of Parliament on the trade of these colonies will render them unable to purchase the manufactures of Great Britain.

XII. That the increase, prosperity, and happiness of these colonies depend on the full and free enjoyments of their rights and liberties, and an intercourse with Great Britain mutually affectionate and advantageous.

XIII. That it is the right of the British subjects in these colonies to petition the King or either House of Parliament.

Lastly, That it is the indispensable duty of these colonies to the best of sovereigns, to the mother country, and to themselves, to endeavour by a loyal and dutiful address to His Majesty, and humble applications to both Houses of Parliament, to procure the repeal of the Act for granting and applying certain stamp duties, of all clauses of any other Acts of Parliament, whereby the jurisdiction of the Admiralty is extended as aforesaid, and of the other late Acts for the restriction of American commerce.

39. NORTHAMPTON COUNTY RESOLUTIONS ON THE STAMP ACT
February 11, 1766

(A. C. McLaughlin, *Foundations of American Constitutionalism*, p. 126 n.)

This declaration of the county court of Northampton County, Virginia, is given as an example of the local reaction to the Stamp Act; it was one of the earliest declarations to the effect that an unconstitutional act was not binding.

Williamsburg, March 21. The following is a copy of a late order of Northampton Court, on the eastern Shore of this colony, which we are desired to insert. At a court held for Northampton county, Feb. 11, 1766.

"On the motion of the Clerk and other Officers of this Court, praying their opinion whether the act entitled 'An Act for granting and applying certain Stamp Duties, and other Duties, in America, &c,' was binding on the inhabitants of this colony, and whether they the said Officers should incur any penalties by not using stamped paper, agreeable to the directions of the said act, the Court unanimously declared it to be their opinion that the said act did not bind, affect or concern the inhabitants of this colony, in as much as they conceive the same to be unconstitutional, and that the said several officers may proceed to the execution of their respective offices without incurring any penalties by means thereof; which opinion this court doth order to be recorded. Griffin Stith, C.N.C."

Virginia Gazette, March 21, 1766.

40. PETITION OF LONDON MERCHANTS AGAINST THE STAMP ACT
January 17, 1766

(*The Parliamentary History of England*, Vol. XVI, p. 133 ff.)

The American policy of non-importation had severely injured English trade, and Parliament received numerous petitions from merchants throughout the Kingdom urging the repeal of the act. See, W. T. Laprade, "The Stamp Act in British Politics", *American Hist. Review*, Vol. XXXV, p. 735 ff.; C. H. Van Tyne, *Causes of the War of Independence*, ch. vii; D. M. Clark, *British Opinion and the American Revolution*, ch. ii.

A petition of the merchants of London, trading to North America, was presented to the House, and read; setting forth;

"That the petitioners have been long concerned in carrying on the trade between this country and the British colonies on the continent of North America; and that they have annually exported very large quantities of British manufactures, consisting of woollen goods of all kinds, cottons, linens, hardware, shoes, household furniture, and almost without exception of every other species of goods manufactured in these kingdoms, besides other articles imported from abroad, chiefly purchased with our manufactures and with the produce of our colonies; by all which, many thousand manufacturers, seamen and labourers, have been employed, to the very great and increasing benefit of this nation; and that, in return for these exports, the petitioners have received from the colonies, rice, indigo, tobacco, naval stores, oil, whale fins, furs, and lately potash, with other commodities, besides remittances by bills of exchange and bullion, obtained by the colonists in payment for articles of their produce, not required for the British market, and therefore exported to other places; and that, from the nature of this trade, consisting of British manufactures exported, and of the import of raw materials from America, many of them used in our manufactures, and all of them tending to lessen our dependence on neighbouring states, it must be deemed of the highest importance in the commercial system of this nation; and that this commerce, so beneficial to the state, and so necessary for the support of multitudes, now lies under such difficulties and discouragement, that nothing less than its utter ruin is apprehended, without the immediate interposition of parliament; and that, in consequence of the trade between the colonies and the mother country, as established and as permitted for many years, and of the experience which the petitioners have had of the readiness of the Americans to make their just remittances to the utmost of their real ability, they have been induced to make and venture such large exportations of British manufactures, as to leave the colonies indebted to the merchants of Great Britain in the sum of several millions sterling; and that at this time the colonists, when pressed for payment, appeal to past experience, in proof of their willingness; but declare it is not in their power, at present, to make good their engagements, alleging, that the taxes and restrictions laid upon them, and the extension of the jurisdiction of vice admiralty courts established by some late acts of parliament, particularly by an act passed in the fourth year of his present Majesty, for granting certain duties in the British colonies and plantations in America, and by an act passed in the fifth year of his present Majesty, for granting and applying certain stamp duties, and other duties, in the British colonies and plantations in America, with several regulations and restraints, which, if founded in acts of parliament for defined purposes, are represented to have been extended in such a manner as to disturb legal commerce and harass the fair trader, have so far interrupted the usual and former most fruitful branches of their commerce, restrained the sale of their produce, thrown the state of the several provinces into confusion, and brought on so great a number of actual bankruptcies, that the former opportunities and means of remittances and payments are utterly lost and taken from them; and that the petitioners are, by these unhappy events, reduced to the necessity of applying to the House, in order to secure themselves and their families from impending ruin; to prevent a multitude of manufacturers from becoming a burthen to the community, or else seeking their bread in other countries, to the irretrievable loss of this kingdom; and to preserve the strength of this nation entire, its commerce flourishing, the revenues increasing, our navigation, the bulwark of the kingdom, in a state of growth and extension, and the colonies, from inclination, duty, and interest, firmly attached to the mother country; and therefore praying the consideration of the premises, and entreating such relief, as to the House shall seem expedient. . . ."

41. THE DECLARATORY ACT
March 18, 1766

(D. Pickering, *Statutes at Large,* Vol. XXVII, p. 19–20.)

The obvious inability of royal officials in the colonies to enforce the Stamp Act, together with the injury to English trade resulting from the non-importation agreements, persuaded the Rockingham ministry of the expediency of a repeal of the Act. The famous examination of Franklin before the House confirmed members in their opinion that repeal was necessary. Repeal encountered firm opposition in the Lords, however, and was carried only by pressure from the King, and with the salve of the Declaratory Act. The Declaratory Act was couched in the same terms as the odious Irish Declaratory Act of 1719. For references see Docs. No. 35, 36. Franklin's examination is in his *Works,* ed. by J. Sparks, Vol. IV. For an analysis of the political theory behind the Declaratory Act see two opposing interpretations: C. H. Mc Ilwain, *The American Revolution; a Constitutional Interpretation;* R. L. Schuyler, *Parliament and the British Empire.*

An act for the better securing the dependency of his Majesty's dominions in America upon the crown and parliament of Great Britain.

WHEREAS *several of the houses of representatives in his Majesty's colonies and plantations in America, have of late, against law, claimed to themselves, or to the general assemblies of the same, the sole and exclusive right of imposing duties and taxes upon his Majesty's subjects in the said colonies and plantations; and have, in pursuance of such claim, passed certain votes, resolutions, and orders, derogatory to the legislative authority of parliament, and inconsistent with the dependency of the said colonies and plantations upon the crown of* Great Britain: . . . be it declared . . . , That the said colonies and plantations in *America* have been, are, and of right ought to be, subordinate unto, and dependent upon the imperial crown and parliament of *Great Britain;* and that the King's majesty, by and with the advice and consent of the lords spiritual and temporal, and commons of *Great Britain,* in parliament assembled, had, hath, and of right ought to have, full power and authority to make laws and statutes of sufficient force and validity to bind the colonies and people of *America,* subjects of the crown of *Great Britain,* in all cases whatsoever.

II. And be it further declared . . . , That all resolutions, votes, orders, and proceedings, in any of the said colonies or plantations, whereby the power and authority of the parliament of *Great Britain,* to make laws and statutes as aforesaid, is denied, or drawn into question, are, and are hereby declared to be, utterly null and void to all intents and purposes whatsoever.

42. QUARTERING ACT
March 24, 1765

(D. Pickering, *Statutes at Large,* Vol. XXVI, p. 305 ff.)

This Act, passed at the express request of General Gage, was designed to supplement the Stamp Act and the Revenue Act of 1764. The failure of New York to comply in full with the terms of the Quartering Act led to the suspension of the legislative privileges of the assembly. See E. Channing, *History of the United States,* Vol. III, p. 44 ff.; C. Becker, *Political Parties in the Province of New York.* An excellent study of the working of the Quartering Act is in S. M. Pargellis, *Lord Loudoun in North America,* ch. vii.

An act to amend and render more effectual, in his Majesty's dominions in America, *an act passed in this present session of parliament, intituled,* An act for punishing mutiny and desertion, and for the better payment of the army and their quarters. WHEREAS . . . [by the Mutiny Act of 1765] . . . *several regulations are made and enacted for the better government of the army, and their observing strict discipline, and for providing quarters for the army, and carriages on marches and other necessary occasions, and inflicting penalties on offenders against the same act, and for many other good purposes therein mentioned; but the same may not be sufficient for the forces that may be employed in his Majesty's dominions in* America: *and whereas, during the continuance of the said act, there may be occasion for marching and quartering of regiments and companies of his Majesty's forces in several parts of his Majesty's dominions in* America: *and whereas the publick houses and barracks, in his Majesty's dominions in* America, *may not be sufficient to supply quarters for such forces: and whereas it is expedient and necessary that carriages and other conveniences, upon the march of troops in his Majesty's dominions in* America, *should be supplied for that purpose:* be it enacted . . . , That for and during the continuance of this act, and no longer, it shall and may be lawful to and for the constables, tithingmen, magistrates, and other civil officers of villages, towns, townships, cities, districts, and other places, within his Majesty's dominions in *America,* and in their default or absence, for any one justice of the peace inhabiting in or near any such village, township, city, district or place, and for no others; and such constables . . . and other civil officers as aforesaid, are hereby required to billet and quarter the officers and soldiers, in his Majesty's service, in the barracks provided by the colonies; and if there shall not be sufficient room in the said barracks for the officers and soldiers, then and in such case only, to quarter and billet the residue of such officers and soldiers for whom there shall not be room in such barracks, in inns, livery stables, ale-houses, victualling-houses, and the houses of sellers of wine by retail to be drank in their own houses or places thereunto belonging, and all houses of persons selling of rum, brandy, strong water, cyder or metheglin, by retail, to be drank in houses; and in case there shall not be sufficient room for the officers and soldiers in such barracks, inns, victualling and other publick ale-houses, that in such and no other case, and upon no other account, it shall and may be lawful for the governor and council of each respective province in his Majesty's dominions in *America,* to authorize and appoint, and they are hereby directed and impowered to authorize and appoint, such proper person or persons as they shall think fit, to take, hire and make fit, and, in default of the said governor and council appointing and authorizing such person or persons, or in default of such person or persons so appointed neglecting or refusing to do their duty, in that case it shall and may be lawful for any two or more of his Majesty's justices of the peace in or near the said villages, towns, townships, cities, districts, and other places, and they are hereby required to take, hire, and make fit for the reception of his Majesty's forces, such and so many uninhabited houses, outhouses, barns, or other buildings, as shall be necessary, to quarter therein the residue of such officers and soldiers for whom there should not be room in such barracks and publick houses as aforesaid. . . .

II. And it is hereby declared and enacted, That there shall be no more billets at any time ordered, than there are effective soldiers present to be quartered therein: and in order that this service may be effectually provided for, the commander in chief in *America,* or other officer under whose orders any regiment or company shall march, shall, from time to time, give . . . as early notice as conveniently may be, in writing, signed by such commander or officer of their march, specifying their numbers and time of marching as near as may be, to the respective governors of each province through which they are to march. . . .

III. [Military officers taking upon themselves to quarter soldiers contrary to this act, or using any menace to a civil officer to deter them from their duty, to be cashiered. Persons aggrieved by being quartered on may complain to the justices, and be relieved.]

V. Provided nevertheless, and it is hereby enacted, That the officers and soldiers so quartered and billeted as aforesaid (except such as shall be quartered in the barracks, and hired uninhabited houses, or other buildings as aforesaid) shall be received and furnished with diet, and small beer, cyder, or rum mixed with water, by the owners of the inns, livery stables, alehouses, victualling-houses, and other houses in which they are allowed to be quartered and billeted by this act; paying and allowing for the same the several rates herein after mentioned to be payable, out of the subsistence-money, for diet and small beer, cyder, or rum mixed with water.

VI. Provided always, That in case any innholder, or other person, on whom any non-commission officers or private men shall be quartered by virtue of this act, . . . (except on a march, or employed in recruiting, and likewise except the recruits by them raised, for the space of seven days at most, for such non-commission officers and soldiers who are recruiting, and recruits by them raised) shall be desirous to furnish such non-commission officers or soldiers with candles, vinegar, and salt, and with small beer or cyder, not exceeding five pints, or half a pint of rum mixed with a quart of water, for each man *per diem, gratis,* and allow to such non-commission officers or soldiers the use of fire, and the necessary u[n]tensils for dressing and eating their meat, and shall give notice of such his desire to the commanding officer, and shall furnish and allow the same accordingly; then . . . the non-commission officers and soldiers so quartered shall provide their own victuals; and the officer to whom it belongs to receive, or that actually does receive, the pay and subsistence of such non-commission officers and soldiers, shall pay the several sums herein after-mentioned to be payable, out of the subsistence-money, for diet and small beer, to the non-commission officers and soldiers aforesaid. . . .

VII. And whereas there are several barracks in several places in his Majesty's said dominions in *America,* or some of them, provided by the colonies, for the lodging and covering of soldiers in lieu of quarters, for the ease and conveniency as well of the inhabitants of and in such colonies, as of the soldiers; it is hereby further enacted, That all such officers and soldiers, so put and placed in such barracks, or in hired uninhabited houses, outhouses, barns, or other buildings, shall, from time to time, be furnished and supplied there by the persons to be authorized or appointed for that purpose by the governor and council of each respective province, or upon neglect or refusal of such governor and council in any province, then by two or more justices of the peace residing in or near such place, with fire, candles, vinegar, and salt, bedding, utensils for dressing their victuals, and small beer or cyder, not exceeding five pints, or half a pint of rum mixed with a quart of water, to each man, without paying any thing for the same. . . .

XXX. And be it further enacted . . . That this act . . . shall continue and be in force in all his Majesty's dominions in *America* from [March 24, 1765] until [March 24, 1767].

43. THE TOWNSHEND REVENUE ACT
June 29, 1767

(D. Pickering, *Statutes at Large,* Vol. XXVII, p. 505 ff.)

On the reorganization of the Ministry in July 1766, 'Champagne Charlie' Townshend became chancellor of the exchequer; on the retirement of Chatham in October Townshend assumed the leadership in the ministry. "From this time," says Lecky, "the English government of America is little more than a series of deplorable blunders" (*History of England in the Eighteenth Century,* Vol. III, p. 379). In May 1767 Townshend brought forward three acts dealing with American affairs: a bill to suspend the New York assembly until it complied with the mutiny act; the establishment of a board of commissioners of the customs for the colonies; and a revenue act. It was expected that the revenue act would yield some £40,000, part of which was to be used for the salaries of royal governors and judges in America. Townshend died in September 1767, but the acts were enforced by his successors. On the surface the revenue acts and the reorganizations of the customs office were highly successful. Prior to 1767 the American customs had brought in some two thousand pounds annually at a cost of some nine thousand pounds; from 1768 to 1774 the American customs brought in an average of thirty thousand pounds annually, at a cost of thirteen thousand pounds. The new revenue measures excited the liveliest dissatisfaction in the American colonies. See Docs. No. 45, 46 for non-importation agreements and the Massachusetts Circular Letter. On the Townshend Acts, see, G. E. Howard, *Preliminaries of the Revolution,* ch. x; E. Channing, *History of the United States,* Vol. III, ch. iv; R. Frothingham, *Rise of the Republic,* ch. vi; C. H. Van Tyne, *Causes of the War of Independence,* ch. x; D. A. Winstanley, *Lord Chatham and the Whig Opposition.*

An act for granting certain duties in the British *colonies and plantations in* America; *for allowing a drawback of the duties of customs upon the exportation from this kingdom, of coffee and cocoa nuts of the produce of the said colonies or plantations; for discontinuing the drawbacks payable on china earthen ware exported to* America; *and˙for*

more effectually preventing the clandestine running of goods in the said colonies and plantations.

WHEREAS *it is expedient that a revenue should be raised, in your Majesty's dominions in* America, *for making a more certain and adequate provision for defraying the charge of the administration of justice, and the support of civil government, in such provinces as it shall be found necessary; and towards further defraying the expenses of defending, protecting and securing the said dominions;* . . . be it enacted. . . . That from and after the twentieth day of *November,* one thousand seven hundred and sixty seven, there shall be raised, levied, collected, and paid, unto his Majesty, his heirs, and successors, for upon and the respective Goods here in after mentioned, which shall be imported from *Great Britain* into any colony or plantation in *America* which now is or hereafter may be, under the dominion of his Majesty, his heirs, or successors, the several Rates and Duties following; that is to say,

For every hundredweight avoirdupois of crown, plate, flint, and white glass, four shillings and eight pence.

For every hundred weight avoirdupois of red lead, two shillings.

For every hundred weight avoirdupois of green glass, one shilling and two pence.

For every hundred weight avoirdupois of white lead, two shillings.

For every hundred weight avoirdupois of painters colours, two shillings.

For every pound weight avoirdupois of tea, three pence.

For every ream of paper, usually called or known by the name of *Atlas fine,* twelve shillings. . . .

IV. . . . and that all the monies that shall arise by the said duties (except the necessary charges of raising, collecting, levying, recovering, answering, paying, and accounting for the same) shall be applied, in the first place, in such manner as is herein after mentioned, in making a more certain and adequate provision for the charge of the administration of justice, and the support of civil government in such of the said colonies and plantations where it shall be found necessary; and that the residue of such duties shall be payed into the receipt of his Majesty's exchequer, and shall be entered separate and apart from all other monies paid or payable to his Majesty . . . ; and shall be there reserved, to be from time to time disposed of by parliament towards defraying the necessary expense of defending, protecting, and securing, the *British* colonies and plantations in *America.*

V. And be it further enacted . . . , That his Majesty and his successors shall be, and are hereby, impowered, from time to time, by any warrant or warrants under his or their royal sign manual or sign manuals, countersigned by the high treasurer, or any three or more of the commissioners of the treasury for the time being, to cause such monies to be applied, out of the produce of the duties granted by this act, as his Majesty, or his successors, shall think proper or necessary, for defraying the charges of the administration of justice, and the support of the civil government, within all or any of the said colonies or plantations. . . .

X. *And whereas by an act of parliament made in the fourteenth year of the reign of King Charles the Second,* intituled, An act for preventing frauds, and regulating abuses, in his Majesty's customs, *and several other acts now in force, it is lawful for any officer of his Majesty's customs, authorized by writ of assistance under the seal of his Majesty's court of exchequer, to take a constable, headborough, or other public officer inhabiting near unto the place, and in the daytime to enter and go into any house, shop cellar, warehouse, or room or other place and, in case of resistance, to break open doors, chests, trunks, and other pakage there, to seize, and from thence to bring, any kind of goods or merchandise whatsoever prohibited or uncustomed, and to put and secure the same in his Majesty's storehouse next to the place where such seizure shall be made; and whereas by an act made in the seventh and eighth years of the reign of King William the Third, intituled An act for preventing frauds, and regulating abuses, in the plantation trade, it is, amongst otherthings, enacted, that the officers for collecting and managing his Majesty's revenue, and inspecting the plantation trade, in America, shall have the same powers and authorities to enter houses or warehouses, to search or seize goods prohibited to be imported or exported into or out of any of the said plantations, or for which any duties are payable, or ought to have been paid; and that the like assistance shall be given to the said officers in the execution of their office, as, by the said recited act of the fourteenth year of King Charles the Second, is provided for the officers of* England: *but, no authority being expressly given by the said act, made in the seventh and eighth years of the reign of King William the Third, to any particular court to grant such writs of assistance for the officers of the customs in the said plantations, it is doubted whether such officers can legally enter houses and other places on land, to search for and seize goods, in the manner directed by the said recited acts:* To obviate which doubts for the future, and in order to carry the intention of the said recited acts into effectual execution, be it enacted . . . , That from and after the said twentieth day of *November,* one thousand seven hundred and sixty seven, such writs of assistance, to authorize and impower the officers of his Majesty's customs to enter and go into any house, warehouse, shop, cellar, or other place, in the *British* colonies or plantations in *America,* to search for and seize prohibited and uncustomed goods, in the manner directed by the said recited acts, shall and may be granted by the said superior or supreme court of justice having jurisdiction within such colony or plantation respectively. . . .

44. FUNDAMENTAL LAW AND THE BRITISH CONSTITUTION
Letters of the Massachusetts House to Ministry
January, 1768

(Bradford's *Massachusetts State Papers,* p. 137 ff.)

These addresses to the British Ministry were part of the protest of the Massachusetts General Court against the Townshend Acts of 1767. In January 1768 the Massachusetts House drew up a long letter to the Massachusetts agent, Dennis De Bredt, addresses to Shelburne, Chatham, Rockingham, Conway and Camden, the Lords of the Treasury, a petition to the King, and a circular letter to the other American colonies, Doc. No. 45. All of these documents were drafted by Samuel Adams. The extracts given below present one of the earliest formulations of the doctrine of fundamental law in the British constitution. The theory that Parliament could not pass acts contrary to fundamental law became a basic theory in American constitutional law. See also Otis's Speech on the Writs of Assistance, Doc. No. 32, the Resolutions of Virginia on the Stamp Act, Doc. No. 36, and the Massachusetts Circular Letter. The addresses of the House are given in full in Bradford's *Massachusetts State Papers;* an account of their authorship is in W. V. Wells, *Life and Public Services of Samuel Adams,* Vol. I, ch. vii. See also, C. F. Mullett, *Fundamental Law and the American Revolution;* R. G. Adams, *Political Ideas of the American Revolution;* A. C. McLaughlin, *Courts, Constitution and Parties,* ch. i.

1. LETTER OF THE MASSACHUSETTS HOUSE TO THE EARL OF SHELBURNE
January 15, 1768

There are, my Lord, fundamental rules of the constitution, which it is humbly presumed, neither the supreme legislative nor the supreme executive can alter. In all free states, the constitution is fixed; it is from thence, that the legislative derives its authority; therefore it cannot change the constitution without destroying its own foundation. If, then, the constitution of Great Britain is the common right of all British subjects, it is humbly referred to your Lordship's judgment, whether the supreme legislative of the empire may rightly leap the bounds of it, in the exercise of power over the subjects in America, any more than over those in Britain.

2. LETTER OF THE MASSACHUSETTS HOUSE TO THE MARQUIS OF ROCKINGHAM
January 22, 1768

My Lord, the superintending power of that high court over all his Majesty's subjects in the empire, and in all cases which can consist with the fundamental rules of the Constitution, was never questioned in this Province, nor, as the House concieve, in any other. But, in all free states the constitution is fixed; it is from thence that the supreme legislative as well as the supreme executive derives its authority. Neither, then, can break through the fundamental rules of the constitution without destroying their own foundation.

3. LETTER OF THE MASSACHUSETTS HOUSE TO LORD CAMDEN
January 29, 1768

If in all free states, the constitution is fixed, and the supreme legislative power of the nation, from thence derives its authority; can that power overleap the bounds of the constitution, without subverting its own foundation? If the remotest subjects, are bound by the ties of allegiance, which this people and their forefathers have ever acknowledged; are they not by the rules of equity, intitled to all rights of that constitution, which ascertains and limits both sovereignty and allegiance? If it is an essential unalterable right in nature, ingrafted into the British constitution as a fundamental law, and ever held sacred and irrevocable by the subjects within the realm, and that what is a man's own is absolutely his own; and that no man hath a right to take it from him without his consent; may not the subjects of this province, with a decent firmness, which has always distinguished the happy subjects of Britain, plead and maintain this natural constitutional right?

45. MASSACHUSETTS CIRCULAR LETTER
February 11, 1768

(Works of Samuel Adams, ed. by H. A. Cushing, Vol. I, p. 184 ff.)

This circular letter, drawn up by Samuel Adams, informed the assemblies of the other American colonies of the measures which the Massachusetts General Court had taken with regard to the Townshend acts. On the failure of the Massachusetts House to rescind the resolution under which this letter was prepared, Governor Bernard dissolved the General Court. The Circular Letter elicited favorable responses from several of the other colonies, notably from Virginia. See, R. Frothingham, *Rise of the Republic of the United States,* ch. vi; W. V. Wells, *Life and Public Services of Samuel Adams,* Vol. I, p. 152 ff.; T. Hutchinson, *History of the Province of Massachusetts Bay,* 1749–1774.

Pro. of Massachusetts Bay, February 11, 1768.
SIR,

The House of Representatives of this Province, have taken into their serious Consideration, the great difficulties that must accrue to themselves and their Constituents, by the operation of several acts of Parliament, imposing Duties & Taxes on the American colonys. As it is a Subject in which every Colony is deeply interested, they have no reason to doubt but your Assembly is deeply impressed with its importance, & that such constitutional measures will be come into, as are proper. . . .

The House have humbly represented to the ministry, their own Sentiments that his Majesty's high Court of Parliament is the supreme legislative Power over the whole Empire; That in all free States the Constitution is fixed; & as the supreme Legislative derives its Power & Authority from the Constitution, it cannot overleap the Bounds of it, without destroying its own foundation; That the constitution ascertains & limits both Sovereignity and allegiance, &, therefore, his Majesty's American Subjects, who acknowledge themselves bound by the Ties of Allegiance, have an equitable Claim to the full enjoyment of the fundamental Rules of the British Constitution: That it is an essential, unalterable Right, in nature, ungrafted into the British Constitution, as a fundamental Law, & ever held sacred & irrevocable by the Subjects within the Realm, that what a man has honestly acquired is absolutely his own, which he may freely give, but cannot be taken from him without his consent: That the American Subjects may, therefore, exclusive of any Consideration of Charter Rights, with a decent firmness, adapted to the Character of free men & subjects assert this natural and constitutional Right.

It is, moreover, their humble opinion, which they express with the greatest Deference to the Wisdom of the Parliament, that the Acts made there, imposing Duties on the People of this province, with the sole & express purpose of raising a Revenue, are Infringements of their natural & constitutional Rights: because, as they are not represented in the British Parliament, his Majestys Commons in Britain, by those Acts grant their Property without their consent.

This House further are of Opinion, that their Constituents, considering their local Circumstances cannot by any possibility, be represented in the Parliament, & that it will forever be impracticable, that they should be equally represented there, & consequently not at all; being separated by an Ocean of a thousand leagues: and that his Majestys Royal Predecessors, for this reason, were graciously pleased to form a subordinate legislature here, that their subjects might enjoy the unalienable Right of a Representation: Also that considering the utter impracticability of their ever being fully & equally represented in parliament, & the great Expence that must unavoidably attend even a partial representation there, this House think that a taxaticn of their Constituents, even without their Consent, grievous as it is, would be preferable to any Representation that could be admitted for them there.

Upon these principles, & also considering that were the right in Parliament ever so clear, yet, for obvious reasons, it would be beyond the rules of Equity that their Constituents should be taxed, on the manufactures of Great Britain here, in Addition to the dutys they pay for them in England, & other advantages arising to G Britain from the Acts of trade, this House have preferred a humble, dutifull, & loyal Petition, to our most gracious Sovereign, & made such Representations to his Majesty's Ministers, as they apprehended would tend to obtain redress.

They have also submitted to Consideration whether any People can be said to enjoy any degree of Freedom if the Crown in addition to its undoubted Authority of constituting a Governor, should appoint him such a Stipend as it may judge proper, without the Consent of the people & at their expence; & whether, while the Judges of the Land & other Civil officers hold not their Commissions during good Behaviour, their having salarys appointed for them by the Crown independent of the people hath not a tendency to subvert the principles of Equity & endanger the Happiness and Security of the Subject. . . .

These are the Sentiments & proceedings of this House; & as they have too much reason to believe that the enemys of the Colonies have represented them to his Majestys Ministers & the parliament as factious disloyal &

having a disposition to make themselves independent of the Mother Country, they have taken occasion, in the most humble terms, to assure his Majesty & his Ministers that with regard to the People of this province, & as they doubt not, of all the colonies the charge is unjust.

The House is fully satisfied, that your Assembly is too generous & liberal in sentiment, to believe, that this Letter proceeds from an Ambition to take the lead, or dictating to the other Assemblys: They freely submit their opinions to the Judgment of others, & shall take it kind in your house to point out to them any thing further, that may be thought necessary.

This House cannot conclude, without expressing their firm Confidence in the King our common head & Father, that the united & dutifull Supplications of his distressed American Subjects will meet with his Royal & favorable Acceptance.

46. BOSTON NON-IMPORTATION AGREEMENT
August 1, 1768
(*The Annual Register,* 1768, p. 235)

The enactment of the Townshend measures led to a renewal of the non-importation measures which had been employed at the time of the Stamp Act. As early as March 1768 merchants of Boston agreed not to import from England if merchants from New York and Philadelphia would make similar promises. The effort to establish a non-importation league, however, was unsuccessful. In August 1768 the merchants of Boston acted independently: within a few weeks similar action was taken by the merchants of other New England towns and by those of New York. Philadelphia did not fall into line until late in the following year. These and other non-importation agreements reduced importations from England by over one-half in 1768 and 1769. See, A. M. Schlesinger, *The Colonial Merchants and the American Revolution;* C. M. Andrews, *Boston Merchants and the Non-Importation Movement;* C. H. Van Tyne, *Causes of the War of Independence,* ch. x.

Agreement entered into by the Inhabitants of Boston

The merchants and traders in the town of Boston having taken into consideration the deplorable situation of the trade, and the many difficulties it at present labours under on account of the scarcity of money, which is daily increasing for want of the other remittances to discharge our debts in Great Britain, and the large sums collected by the officers of the customs for duties on goods imported; the heavy taxes levied to discharge the debts contracted by the government in the late war; the embarrassments and restrictions laid on trade by several late acts of parliament; together with the bad success of our cod fishery, by which our principal sources of remittance are like to be greatly diminished, and we thereby rendered unable to pay the debts we owe the merchants in Great Britain, and to continue the importation of goods from thence;

We, the subscribers, in order to relieve the trade under those discouragements, to promote industry, frugality, and economy, and to discourage luxury, and every kind of extravagance, do promise and engage to and with each other as follows:

First, That we will not send for or import from Great Britain, either upon our own account, or upon commission, this fall, any other goods than what are already ordered for the fall supply.

Secondly, That we will not send for or import any kind of goods or merchandize from Great Britain, either on our own account, or on commissions, or any otherwise, from the 1st of January 1769, to the 1st of January 1770, except salt, coals, fish-hooks and lines, hemp, and duck bar lead and shot, wool-cards and card-wire.

Thirdly, That we will not purchase of any factor, or others, any kind of goods imported from Great Britain, from January 1769, to January 1770.

Fourthly, That we will not import, on our own account, or on commissions or purchase of any who shall import from any other colony in America, from January 1769, to January 1770, any tea, glass, paper, or other goods commonly imported from Great Britain.

Fifthly, That we will not, from and after the 1st of January 1769, import into this province any tea, paper, glass, or painters colours, until the act imposing duties on those articles shall be repealed.

In witness whereof, we have hereunto set our hands, this first day of August, 1768.

47. THE REGULATORS OF NORTH CAROLINA
Petition of the Inhabitants of Anson County, North Carolina
October 9, 1769

(Colonial Records of North Carolina, ed. by W. L. Saunders, Vol. VIII, p. 75 ff.)

Sectionalism, which played so important a part in colonial history, was particularly significant in the southern colonies. From Virginia to South Carolina, the backcountry of small farmers, non-slaveholding, dissenting in religion, under-represented in politics, was aligned against the tidewater. In North and South Carolina this opposition came to an open rupture. In both colonies the upcountry yeomen organized in "Regulator" bands and interfered with the courts, with the collection of rents, etc. See, J. S. Bassett, "The Regulators of North Carolina", *American Hist. Assoc. Report,* 1894; M. De L. Haywood, *Governor William Tryon;* W. A. Schaper, "Sectionalism in South Carolina," *American Hist. Assoc. Report,* 1900; F. J. Turner, *The Frontier in American History,* ch. iii.

MR. SPEAKER AND GENTLEMEN OF THE AS-
    SEMBLY:
The Petition of the Inhabitants of Anson County, being part of the Remonstrance of the Province of North Carolina,
HUMBLY SHEWETH, That the Province in general labour under general grievances, and the Western part thereof under particular ones; which we not only see but very sensibly feel, being crouch'd beneath our sufferings: and, notwithstanding our sacred privi-ledges, have too long yielded ourselves slaves to remorseless oppression.—Permit us to conceive it to be our inviolable right to make known our grievances, and to petition for redress; as appears in the Bill of Rights

pass'd in the reign of King Charles the first, as well as the act of Settlement of the Crown of the Revolution. We therefore beg leave to lay before you a specimen thereof; that your compassionate endeavours may tend to the relief of your injured Constituents, whose distressed condition calls aloud for aid. The alarming cries of the oppressed possibly may reach your Ears; but without your zeal how shall they ascend the throne. How relentless is the breast without sympathy, the heart that cannot bleed on a View of our calamity; to see tenderness removed, cruelty stepping in; and all our liberties and priviledges invaded and abridg'd by (as it were) domesticks who are conscious of their guilt and void of remorse. O how daring! how relentless! whilst impending Judgments loudly threaten and gaze upon them, with every emblem of merited destruction.

A few of the many grievances are as follows, viz.,

1. That the poor Inhabitants in general are much oppress'd by reason of disproportionate Taxes, and those of the western Counties in particular; as they are generally in mean circumstances.

2. That no method is prescribed by Law for the payment of the Taxes of the Western counties in produce (in lieu of a Currency) as is in other Counties within this Province; to the Peoples great oppression.

3. That Lawyers, Clerks, and other pen-

tioners, in place of being obsequious Servants for the Country's use, are become a nuisance, as the business of the people is often transacted without the least degree of fairness, the intention of the law evaded, exorbitant fees extorted, and the sufferers left to mourn under their oppressions.

4. That an Attorney should have it in his power, either for the sake of ease or interest or to gratify their malevolence and spite, to commence suits to what Courts he pleases, however inconvenient it may be to the Defendant: is a very great oppression.

5. That all unlawful fees taken on Indictment, where the Defendant is acquitted by his Country (however customary it may be) is an oppression.

6. That Lawyers, Clerks, and others extorting more fees than is intended by law; is also an oppression.

7. That the violation of the King's Instructions to his delegates, their artfulness in concealing the same from him; and the great Injury the People thereby sustains: is a manifest oppression.

And for remedy whereof, we take the freedom to recommend the following mode of redress, not doubting audience and acceptance; which will not only tend to our relief, but command prayers as a duty from your humble Petitioners.

1. That at all elections each suffrage be given by Ticket & Ballot.

2. That the mode of Taxation be altered, and each person to pay in proportion to the profits arising from his Estate.

3. That no future tax be laid in Money, untill a currency is made.

4. That there may be established a Western as well as a Northern and Southern District, and a Treasurer for the same.

5. That when a currency is made it may be let out by a Loan office on Land security, and not to be call'd in by a Tax.

6. That all debts above 40s. and under £10 be tried and determined without Lawyers, by a jury of six freeholders impanneled by a Justice, and that their verdict be enter'd by the said Justice, and be a final judgment.

7. That the Chief Justice have no perquisites, but a Sallary only.

8. That Clerks be restricted in respect to fees, costs, and other things within the course of their office.

9. That Lawyers be effectually Barr'd from exacting and extorting fees.

10. That all doubts may be removed in respect to the payment of fees and costs on Indictments where the Defendant is not found guilty by the jury, and therefore acquitted.

11. That the Assembly make known by Remonstrance to the King, the conduct of the cruel and oppressive Receiver of the Quit Rents, for omitting the customary easie and effectual method of collecting by distress, and pursuing the expensive mode of commencing suits in the most distant Courts.

12. That the Assembly in like manner make known that the Governor and Council do frequently grant Lands to as many as they think proper without regard to head rights, notwithstanding the contrariety of His Majesties Instructions; by which means immense sums has been collected and numerous Patents granted, for much of the most fertile lands in this Province, that is yet uninhabited and uncultivated, environed by great numbers of poor people who are necessitated to toil in the cultivation of bad Lands whereon they hardly can subsist, who are thereby deprived of His Majesties liberality and Bounty: nor is there the least regard paid to the cultivation clause in said Patent mentioned, as many of the said Council as well as their friends and favorites enjoy large Quantities of Lands under the above-mentioned circumstances.

13. That the Assembly communicates in like manner the Violation of His Majesties Instructions respecting the Land Office by the Governor and Council, and of their own rules, customs and orders; if it be sufficiently proved that after they had granted Warrants for many Tracts of Land, and that the same was in due time survey'd and return'd, and the Patent fees timely paid into the said office; and that if a private Council was called on purpose to avoid spectators, and peremptory orders made that Patents should not be granted; and Warrants by their orders arbitrarily to have issued in the names of other Persons for the same Lands, and if when intreated by a solicitor they refus'd to render so much as a reason for their so doing, or to refund any part of the money by them extorted.

14. That some method may be pointed out

that every improvement on Lands in any of the Proprietor's part be proved when begun, by whom, and every sale made, that the eldest may have the preference of at least 300 Acres.

15. That all taxes in the following counties be paid as in other Counties in the Province, (i. e.) in the produce of the Country and that ware Houses be erected as follows, (viz.) in Anson County, at Isom Haley's ferry landing on Pe Dee river; Rowan and Orange, . . . Cumberland . . . Mecklenburg . . . and in Tryon County. . . .

16. That every denomination of People may marry according to their respective Mode, Ceremony, and custom, after due publication or Licence.

17. That Doctr Benjamin Franklin or some other known patriot be appointed Agent, to represent the unhappy state of this Province to His Majesty, and to solicit the several Boards in England:—

48. NEW YORK SONS OF LIBERTY RESOLUTIONS ON TEA
November 29, 1773

(H. Niles, *Principles and Acts of the Revolution,* 1822 ed. p. 188–9)

An act of May 1773 permitted the East India Company to export tea directly to the American Colonies free from all duties except the threepenny tax payable in America. The Company disposed of its enormous quantities of tea through its own agents, and thus had a practical monopoly on the tea business in the Colonies. It was the danger of this monopoly rather than the principle of the tea tax that aroused resentment in the Colonies. In Charleston the tea was allowed to enter but was placed in government warehouses. In Philadelphia, New York and elsewhere ships bearing tea were forced to turn back. In Boston the attempt to land tea led to the notorious Boston Tea Party of December 16, 1773. The Resolutions of the New York Sons of Liberty are given as typical of the methods employed by the Colonists. See, A. M. Schlesinger, *Colonial Merchants and the American Revolution;* C. L. Becker, *History of Political Parties in New York, 1760–1776;* H. Dawson, *The Sons of Liberty in New York;* A. C. Flick, *The American Revolution in New York;* I. Q. Leake, *Memoir of the Life and Times of General John Lamb;* M. Farrand, "The Taxation of Tea", *American Hist. Review,* Vol. III.

. . . To prevent a calamity which, of all others, is the most to be dreaded—slavery, and its terrible concomitants—we, subscribers being influenced from a regard to liberty, and disposed to use all lawful endeavors in our power, to defeat the pernicious project, and to transmit to our posterity, those blessings of freedom which our ancestors have handed down to us; and to contribute to the support of the common liberties of America, which are in danger to be subverted, *do,* for those important purposes, agree to associate together, under the name and style of the *sons of liberty of New York,* and engage our honor to, and with each other, faithfully to observe and perform the following *resolutions, viz.*

1st. *Resolved,* That whoever shall aid, or abet, or in any manner assist in the introduction of tea, from any place whatsoever, into this colony, while it is subject, by a British act to parliament, to the payment of a duty, for the purpose of raising a revenue in America, he shall be deemed an enemy to the liberties of America.

2d. *Resolved,* That whoever shall be aiding, or assisting, in the landing, or carting, or such tea, from any ship or vessel, or shall hire any house, store-house, or cellar or any place whatsoever to deposit the tea, subject to a duty as aforesaid, he shall be deemed an enemy to the liberties of America.

3d. *Resolved,* That whoever shall sell, or buy, . . . tea, or shall aid . . . in transporting such tea, . . . from this city, until the . . . revenue act shall be totally and clearly repealed, he shall be deemed an enemy to the liberties of America.

4th. *Resolved,* That whether the duties on tea, imposed by this act, be paid in Great Britain or in America, our liberties are equally affected.

5th. *Resolved,* That whoever shall transgress any of these resolutions, we will not deal with, or employ, or have any connection with him.

49. THE INTOLERABLE ACTS
1774

The Boston Tea Party of December 16, 1773 and the disturbances in Boston and Massachusetts, led Lord North to ask Parliament to vote a series of measures adequate to the emergency. March 14, the first of these notorious "intolerable acts" was laid before Parliament—the Boston Port Act. The introduction of these measures led to one of the most notable debates in Parliamentary history; see Hansard, *Parliamentary History,* Vol. XVII, *passim.* Ultimately five coercive acts received the royal signature: the Boston Port Act; the Massachusetts Government Act; the Administration of Justice Act; the Quartering Act; and the Quebec Act. The provisions of the Quartering Act, approved June 2, 1774, are essentially similar to those of the Quartering Act of 1765, Doc. No. 42. On the Intolerable Acts, see G. Bancroft, *History of the United States,* author's last revision, Vol. III, ch. xxxv, Vol. IV, chs. i, v.; E. Channing, *History,* Vol. III, ch. v.; G. E. Howard, *Preliminaries of the Revolution,* cn. xv; C. H. Van Tyne, *Causes of the War of Independence,* ch. xv; Lord Fitzmaurice, *Life of William, Earl of Shelburne,* Vol. II; F. A. Mumby, *George III and the American Revolution:* G. O. Trevelyan, *The American Revolution,* Vol. I.

1. THE BOSTON PORT ACT
March 31, 1774
(D. Pickering, *Statutes at Large,* Vol. XXX, p. 336 ff.)

The Boston Port Act, the first and most odious of the intolerable acts, was designed specifically as a punishment of Boston for the lawlessness of the Tea Party. The re-opening of the Port was made conditional upon the payment of damages for losses sustained by the East India Company. For the reaction of the colonies to the Boston Port Bill see Docs. No. 50, 51.

An act to discontinue, in such manner, and for such time as are therein mentioned, the landing and discharging, lading or shipping, of goods, wares, and merchandise, at the town, and within the harbour, of Boston, *in the province of* Massachuset's Bay, *in* North America.

WHEREAS *dangerous commotions and insurrections have been fomented and raised in the town of* Boston, *in the province of* Massachuset's Bay, *in* New England, *by divers ill-affected persons, to the subversion of his Majesty's government, and to the utter destruction of the publick peace, and good order of the said town; in which commotions and insurrections certain valuable cargoes of teas, being the property of the* East India Company, *and on board certain vessels lying within the bay or harbour of* Boston, *were seized and destroyed: And whereas, in the present condition of the said town and harbour, the commerce of his Majesty's subjects cannot be safely carried on there, nor the customs payable to his Majesty duly collected; and it is therefore expedient that the officers of his Majesty's customs should be forthwith removed from the said town:* . . . be it enacted . . . , That from and after June 1, 1774, it shall not be lawful for any person or persons whatsoever to lade, put, . . . off or from any quay, wharf, or other place, within the said town of *Boston,* or in or upon any part of the bay, commonly called *The Harbour of Boston,* between a certain headland or point called *Nahant Point,* . . . and a certain other headland or point called *Alderton Point,* . . . or in or upon any island, creek, landing-place, bank, or other place, within the said bay or headlands, into any ship, vessel, lighter, boat, or bottom, any goods, wares, or merchandise whatsoever, to be transported or carried into any other country, province, or place whatsoever, or into any other part of the said province of the *Massachuset's Bay,* in *New England;* or to take up, . . . within the said town, or in or upon any of the places aforesaid, out of any boat, . . . any goods, . . . to be brought from any other country, province, or place, or any other part of the said province, of the *Massachuset's Bay* in *New England,* upon pain of the forfeiture of the said goods, . . . and of the said boat, . . . and of the guns, ammunition, tackle, furniture, and stores, in or belonging to the same: And if any such goods, . . . shall, within the said town, or in any the places aforesaid, be laden or taken in from the shore into any barge, . . . to be carried on board any ship or vessel outward-bound to any other country or provinc**e**, . . . or to be laden into such barge, . . . from or out of any ship or vessel coming in . . . from any other country, such barge, . . . shall be forfeited and lost. . . .

IV. Provided always, That nothing in this act contained shall extend . . . to any military or other stores of his Majesty's use, or to the ships . . . whereon the same shall be laden, which shall be commissioned by, and in the immediate pay of, his Majesty . . . ; nor to any fuel or victual brought coastwise from any part of the continent of America, for the necessary use and sustenance of the inhabitants of the town of Boston, provided the vessels wherein the same are to be carried shall be duly furnished with a cocket and let-pass, after having been duly searched by the proper officers . . . at Marblehead, in the port of Salem, . . . ; and that some officer of his Majesty's customs be also there put on board the same vessel, who is hereby authorized to go on board, and proceed with the said vessel, together with a sufficient number of persons properly armed, for his defence to the said harbour of Boston; nor in any ships . . . which may happen to be within the said harbour of Boston on or before the first day of June (1774) and may have either laden or taken on board, or be there with intent to load or take on board, or to land or discharge any goods, wares . . . provided the said ships . . . do depart . . . within fourteen days after (1 June 1774). . . .

X. Provided also, . . . That nothing herein contained . . . be construed, to enable his Majesty to appoint such port, . . . or officers, in the said town of *Boston,* or in the said bay or islands, until it shall sufficiently appear to his Majesty that full satisfaction hath been made by or on behalf of the inhabitants of the said town of *Boston* to the united company of merchants of *England* trading to the *East Indies,* for the damage sustained by the said company by the destruction of their goods sent to the said town of *Boston,* . . . and until it shall be certified to his Majesty, in council, by the governor, . . . of the said province, that reasonable satisfaction hath been made to the officers of his Majesty's revenue, and others, who suffered by the riots and insurrections above mentioned, in 1773 and 1774.

2. MASSACHUSETTS GOVERNMENT ACT
May 20, 1774
(D. Pickering, *Statutes at Large,* Vol. XXX, p. 381 ff.)

On March 28 Lord North, insisting that he wished "to take the executive power from the hands of the democratic part of the government", introduced an act for "the better regulating the government of the Province of Massachusetts Bay", which would "effectually purge the constitution of all its crudities." The Bill passed by large majorities, but eleven Lords entered a protest against it. Massachusetts largely nullified the administration of the new Act. See, G. Bancroft, *History,* author's last rev. Vol. IV, ch. iii; R. Frothingham, *Rise of the Republic,* ch. ix.

An act for the better regulating the government of the province of the Massachuset's Bay, *in* New England.
And whereas the method of electing such counsellors or assistants, . . . hath, by repeated experience, been found to be extremely ill adapted to the plan of government established in the province of the Massachusets Bay . . . , *and hath . . . for some time past, been such as had the most manifest tendency to obstruct, and, in great measure, defeat, the execution of the laws; . . . : And it hath accordingly happened, that an open resistance to the execution of the laws hath actually taken place in the town of* Boston, *and the neighbourhood thereof, . . . And whereas it is, under these circumstances, become absolutely necessary, . . . that the appointment of the said counsellors or assistants should henceforth be put upon the like footing as is established in such other of his Majesty's colonies . . . in* America, *the governors whereof are appointed by his Majesty's commission, under the great seal of* Great Britain: Be it therefore enacted . . . , that from and after August 1, 1774, so much of the charter . . . [of 1691] which relates to the time and manner of electing the assistants or counsellors for the said province, be revoked, . . . and that the offices of all counsellors and assistants, elected and appointed in pursuance thereof, shall from thenceforth cease and determine: And that, from and after the said August 1, 1774, the council, or court of assistants of the said province for the time being, shall be composed of such of the inhabitants or

proprietors of lands within the same as shall be thereunto nominated and appointed by his Majesty . . . , provided, that the number of the said assistants or counsellors shall not, at any one time, exceed thirty-six, nor be less than twelve.

II. And it is hereby further enacted, That the said assistants or counsellors, so to be appointed as aforesaid, shall hold their offices respectively, for and during the pleasure of his Majesty. . . .

III. And be it further enacted . . . , That from and after July 1, 1774, it shall and may be lawful for his Majesty's governor for the time Leing of the said province, or, in his absence, for the lieutenant-governor, to nominate and appoint, under the seal of the province, from time to time, and also to remove, without the consent of the council, all judges of the inferior courts of common pleas, commissioners of *Oyer* and *Terminer,* the attorney general, provosts, marshals, justices of the peace, and other officers to the council or courts of justice belonging; . . .

VI. And be it further enacted . . . , That, upon every vacancy of the offices of chief justice and judges of the superior court of the said province, from and after July 1, 1774, the governor for the time being, or, in his absence, the lieutenant-governor, without the consent of the council, shall have full power and authority to nominate and appoint the persons to suceed to the said offices, who shall hold their commissions during the pleasure of his Majesty . . . ;

VII. *And whereas, by several acts of the general court, . . . the freeholders and inhabitants of the several townships, districts, and precincts, qualified, as is therein expressed, are authorized to assemble together, annually, or occasionally, upon notice given, in such manner as the said acts direct, for the choice of selectmen, constables, and other officers, and for the making and agreeing upon such necessary rules, orders, and byelaws, for the directing, managing, and ordering, the prudential affairs of such townships, districts, and precincts, and for other purposes: and whereas a great abuse has been made of the power of calling such meetings, and the inhabitants have, contrary to the design of their institution, been misled to treat upon matters of the most general con-*

cern, and to pass many dangerous and unwarrantable resolves: for remedy whereof, be it enacted, that from and after August 1, 1774, no meeting shall be called by the select men, or at the request of any number of freeholders of any township, district, or precinct, without the leave of the governor, or, in his absence, of the lieutenant-governor, in writing, expressing the special business of the said meeting, except the annual meeting in the months of *March* or *May,* for the choice of select men, constables, and other officers, or except for the choice of persons to fill up the offices aforesaid, on the death or removal of any of the persons first elected to such offices, and also, except any meeting for the election of a representative or representatives in the general court; and that no other matter shall be treated of at such meetings. . . .

3. ADMINISTRATION OF JUSTICE ACT
May 20, 1774
(D. Pickering, *Statutes at Large,* Vol. XXX, p. 367 ff.)

This act was designed to provide for a more impartial administration of justice by transferring certain trials to another Province or to Great Britain. It was directed not only toward the maintenance of order but to the more efficient administration of the customs laws.

An act for the impartial administration of justice in the cases of persons questioned for any acts done by them in the execution of the law, or for the suppression of riots and tumults, in the province of the Massachuset's Bay, *in* New England.

WHEREAS *in his Majesty's province of* Massachuset's Bay, *in* New England, *an attempt hath lately been made to throw off the authority of the parliament of* Great Britain *over the said province, and an actual and avowed resistance, by open force, to the execution of certain acts of parliament, hath been suffered to take place, uncontrouled and unpunished, . . . : and whereas, in the present disordered state of the said province, it is of the utmost importance . . . to the re-establishment of lawful authority throughout the same, that neither the magistrates acting in support of the laws, nor any of his Majesty's subjects aiding and assisting them therein, or in the suppression of riots and tumults, . . . should be discouraged from the proper discharge of their duty, by an apprehension, that in case of their being questioned for any acts done therein, they may be liable to be brought to trial for the same before persons who do not acknowledge the validity of the laws, in the execution thereof, or the authority of the magistrate in support of whom, such acts had been done: in order therefore to remove every such discouragement from the minds of his Majesty's subjects, and to induce them, upon all proper occasions, to exert themselves in support of the public peace of the province, and of the authority of the King and Parliament of* Great Britain *over the same;* be it enacted . . . , That if any inquisition or indictment shall be found, or if any appeal shall be sued or preferred against any person, for murther, or other capital offence, in the province of the *Massachuset's Bay,* and it shall appear, by information given upon oath to the governor . . . of the said province, that the fact was committed by the person against whom such inquisition or indictment shall be found, or against whom such appeal shall be sued or preferred, as aforesaid, either in the execution of his duty as a magistrate, for the suppression of riots, or in the support of the laws of revenue, or in acting in his duty as an officer of revenue, or in acting under the direction and order of any magistrate, for the suppression of riots, or for the carrying into effect the laws of revenue, or in aiding and assisting in any of the cases aforesaid; and if it shall also appear, to the satisfaction of the said governor . . . that an indifferent trial cannot be had within the said province, in that case, it shall and may be lawful for the governor . . . , to direct, with the advice and consent of the council, that the inquisition, indictment, or appeal, shall be tried in some other of his Majesty's colonies, or in *Great Britain;* and for that purpose, to order the person against whom such inquisition or indictment shall be found, . . . to be sent, under sufficient custody, to the place appointed for his trial, or to admit such person to bail, taking a recognizance . . . from such person, with sufficient sureties, . . . in such sums of money as the said governor . . . shall deem reasonable, for the personal appearance of such person, if the trial shall be appointed to be had in any other colony, before the governor, . . . of such colony; and if the trial shall be appointed to be had in *Great Britain,* then before his Majesty's court of *King's Bench,* at a time to be mentioned in such recognizances; and the governor, . . . or court of *King's Bench,* where the trial is appointed to be had in *Great Britain,* upon the appearance of such person, according to such recognizance, or in custody, shall either commit such person, or admit him to bail, until such trial. . . .

II. *And, to prevent a failure of justice, from the want of evidence on the trial of any such inquisition, indictment or appeal,* be it further enacted, That the governor . . . is hereby authorised and required, to bind in recognizances to his Majesty all such witnesses as the prosecutor or person against whom such inquisition or indictment shall be found, or appeal sued or preferred, shall desire to attend the trial of the said inquisition, . . . for their personal appearance, at the time and place of such trial, to give evidence: and the said governor . . . shall thereupon appoint a reasonable sum to be allowed for the expences of every such witness . . .

VI. [Persons brought before justices etc. accused of any capital crime in the execution of their duty, to be admitted to bail.]

VIII. And be it further enacted . . . That this act . . . shall . . . be, and continue in force, for and during the term of three years.

4. THE QUEBEC ACT
June 22, 1774
(D. Pickering, *Statutes at Large,* Vol. XXX, p. 549)

The Quebec Act was not, properly speaking, one of the coercive acts. It was not designed with reference to conditions in Massachusetts or the other seaboard colonies. Nevertheless Americans regarded its provisions for religious toleration to Catholics, and for the extension of the territory of Quebec westward, as "intolerable". As a matter of fact the Quebec Act was one of the most enlightened pieces of colonial administration in the history of European colonial expansion. On the Quebec Act see V. Coffin, *The Province of Quebec and the American Revolution,* which is critical, and R. Coupland, *The Quebec Act: a Study in Statesmanship.* For the American background, see C. W. Alvord, *The Mississippi Valley in British Politics,* 2 Vols.; W. Kingsford,

History of Canada, Vol. V; A. L. Burt, *The Old Province of Quebec.*

An Act for making effectual Provision for the Government of the Province of Quebec, *in North America.*

. . . May it therefore please Your most Excellent Majesty,

That it may be enacted: [Boundaries defined, Boundaries of Proclamation of 1763 extended to include territory west to the Mississippi, north to the frontiers of the Hudson's Bay territory, and the islands in the mouth of the St. Lawrence.]

. . . And whereas the Provisions made by the said Proclamation, in respect to the Civil Government of the said Province of *Quebec,* and the Powers and Authorities given to the Governor and other Civil Officers of the said Province, by the Grants and Commissions issued in consequence thereof, have been found, upon Experience, to be inapplicable to the State and Circumstances of the said Province, the Inhabitants whereof amounted at the Conquest, to above Sixty five thousand Persons, professing the Religion of the Church of *Rome.* . . .

It is hereby declared, That His Majesty's Subjects professing the Religion of the Church of *Rome,* of, and in the said Province of *Quebec,* may have, hold, and enjoy, the free Exercise of the Religion of the Church of *Rome,* subject to the King's Supremacy, declared and established by an Act made in the First Year of the Reign of Queen Elizabeth, over all the Dominions and Countries which then did, or thereafter should, belong to the Imperial Crown of this Realm; and that the Clergy of the said Church may hold, receive, and enjoy their accustomed Dues and Rights, with respect to such Persons only as shall profess the said Religion.

Provided nevertheless, That it shall be lawful for His Majesty, His Heirs or Successors, to make such Provisions out of the rest of the said accustomed Dues and Rights, for the Encouragement of the Protestant Religion, and for the Maintenance and Support of a Protestant Clergy within the said Province, as he or they shall, from Time to Time, think necessary or expedient. . . .

And be it further enacted by the Authority aforesaid, That all His Majesty's *Canadian* Subjects within the Province of *Quebec,* the Religious Orders and Communities only excepted, may also hold and enjoy their Property and Possessions, together with all Customs and Usages, relative thereto, and all other their Civil Rights, in as large, ample and beneficial Manner, as if the said Proclamation, Commissions, Ordinances, and other Acts and Instruments, had not been made, and as may consist with their Allegiance to His Majesty, and Subjection to the Crown and Parliament of *Great Britain;* and that in all Matters of Controversy relative to Property and Civil Rights, Resort shall be had to the Laws of *Canada,* as the Rule for the Decision of the same; and all Causes that shall hereafter be instituted in any of the Courts of Justice, to be appointed within and for the said Province by His Majesty, His Heirs and Successors, shall, with respect to such Property and Rights, be determined agreeably to the said Laws and Customs of *Canada,* . . .

And whereas the Certainty and Lenity of the Criminal Law of *England,* and the Benefits and Advantages resulting from the Use of it, have been sensibly felt by the Inhabitants from an Experience of more than Nine Years, during which it has been uniformly administered; be it therefore further enacted by the Authority aforesaid, That the same shall continue to be administered, and shall be observed as Law, in the Province of *Quebec,* as well in the Description and Quality of the Offense, as in the Method of Prosecution and Trial, and the Punishment and Forfeitures thereby inflicted, to the Exclusion of every other Rule of Criminal Law, or Mode of Proceeding thereon, which did or might prevail in the said Province before the Year of our Lord One thousand seven hundred and sixtyfour; any Thing in this Act to the Contrary thereof in any Respect notwithstanding; . . .

And whereas it may be necessary to ordain many Regulations, for the future Welfare and good Government of the Province of *Quebec,* the Occasions of which cannot now be foreseen, nor without much Delay and Inconvenience be provided for, without entrusting that Authority for a certain Time, and upon proper Restrictions to Persons resident there:

And whereas it is at present inexpedient

to call an Assembly; be it therefore enacted by the Authority aforesaid, That it shall and may be lawful for His Majesty, . . . and with the Advice of the Privy Council, to constitute and appoint a Council for the Affairs of the Province of *Quebec,* to consist of such Persons resident there, not exceeding Twenty-three, nor less than Seventeen, as His Majesty, . . . shall be pleased to appoint; . . . which Council, so appointed and nominated, or the major Part thereof, shall have Power and Authority to make Ordinances for the Peace, Welfare, and good Government of the said Province with the Consent of His Majesty's Governor, or, in his Absence, of the Lieutenant Governor, or Commander in Chief for the Time being . . .

50. PENNSYLVANIA RESOLUTIONS ON THE BOSTON PORT ACT
June 20, 1774

(H. Niles, ed. *Principles and Acts of the Revolution,* 1822 ed. p. 180)

This convention, said to have been attended by over eight thousand persons, inaugurated the Revolutionary movement in Pennsylvania. The committee provided for by these resolutions instructed the regular Assembly as to the delegates and instructions for the Continental Congress. For general colonial reaction to the Boston Port Act see Docs. No. 56–57. On Pennsylvania, see C. H. Lincoln, *Revolutionary Movement in Pennsylvania;* C. J. Stillé, *Life and Times of John Dickinson,* ch. vi.

Philadelphia, June 1774

At a very large and respectable meeting of the freeholders and freemen of the city and county of Philadelphia, on June 18, 1774. Thomas Willing, John Dickinson, chairmen.
I. Resolved, That the act of parliament, for shutting up the port of Boston, is unconstitutional, oppressive to the inhabitants of that town, dangerous to the liberties of the British colonies, and that therefore, considering our brethren, at Boston, as suffering in the common cause of America.
II. That a congress of deputies from the several colonies, in North America, is the most probable and proper mode of procuring relief for our suffering brethren, obtaining redress of American grievances, securing our rights and liberties, and re-establishing peace and harmony between Great Britain and these colonies, on a constitutional foundation.
III. That a large and respectable committee be immediately appointed for the city and county of Philadelphia, to correspond with the sister colonies and with the several counties in this province, in order that all may unite in promoting and endeavoring to attain the great and valuable ends, mentioned in the foregoing resolution.
IV. That the committee nominated by this meeting shall consult together, and on mature deliberation determine, what is the most proper mode of collecting the sense of this province, and appointing deputies for the same, to attend a general congress, and having determined thereupon, shall take such measures, as by them shall be judged most expedient, for procuring this province to be represented at the said congress, in the best manner that can be devised for promoting the public welfare.
V. That the committee be instructed immediately to set on foot a subscription for the relief of such poor inhabitants of the town of Boston, as may be deprived of their means of subsistence. . . .
VI. That the committee consist of forty-three persons. . . .

51. NEW YORK CITY RESOLUTIONS ON THE BOSTON PORT ACT
July 6, 1774

(H. Niles, ed. *Principles and Acts of the Revolution,* 1822 ed. p. 174–5)

At a numerous meeting of the inhabitants of the city of New-York, convened in the fields, by a public advertisement, on Wednesday the 6th of July, 1774, Mr. Alexander M'Dougall, Chairman—

The business of the meeting being fully explained by the chairman, and the dangerous tendency of the numerous and vile arts used by the enemies of America, to divide and distract her councils, as well as the misrepresentation of the virtuous intentions of the citizens of this metropolis, in this interesting and alarming state of the liberties of America, the following resolutions were twice read, and the question being separately put on each of them, they were passed without one dissentient.

1st. Resolved, *nem. con.* That the statute commonly called the Boston port act, is oppressive to the inhabitants of that town, unconstitutional in its principles, and dangerous to the liberties of British Americans; and that, therefore, we consider our brethren at Boston, as now suffering in the common cause of these colonies.

2d. Resolved. *nem. con.* That any attack or attempt to abridge the liberties, or invade the constitution, of any of our sister colonies, is immediately an attack upon the liberties and constitution of all the British colonies.

3d. Resolved. *nem. con.* That the shutting up of any of the ports in America, with intent to exact from Americans, a submission to Parliamentary taxation, or extort a reparation of private injuries, is highly unconstitutional, and subversive of the commercial rights of the inhabitants of this continent.

4th. Resolved. *nem. con.* That it is the opinion of this meeting, that if a principal colony on this continent shall come into a joint resolution to stop all importation from, and exportation to Great Britain, till the Act of Parliament for blocking up the harbour of Boston be repealed, the same will prove the salvation of North America and her liberties, and that, on the other hand, if they continue their exports and imports, there is great reason to fear that fraud, power, and the most odious oppression, will triumph over right, justice, social happiness, and freedom:—therefore,

5th. Resolved, *nem. con.* That the deputies who shall represent this colony in the Congress of American deputies, to be held at Philadelphia, about the first of September next, are hereby instructed, empowered, and directed to engage with a majority of the principal colonies, to agree for this city, upon a non-importation from Great Britain, of all goods, wares and merchandizes until the act for blocking up the harbour of Boston be repealed, and American grievances be redressed; and also to agree to all such other measures as the Congress shall, in their wisdom, judge advansive of these great objects, and a general security of the rights and privileges of America.

6th. Resolved, *nem. con.* That this meeting will abide by, obey and observe all such resolutions, determinations and measures, which the Congress aforesaid shall come into, and direct or recommend to be done, for obtaining and securing the important ends mentioned in the foregoing resolution. And that an engagement to this effect be immediately entered into and sent to the Congress, to evince to them, our readiness and determination to co-operate with our sister colonies, for the relief of our distressed brethren of Boston as well as for the security of our common rights and privileges. . . .

8th. Resolved, *nem. con.* That a subscription should immediately be set on foot, for the relief of such poor inhabitants of Boston as are, or may be deprived of the means of subsistence, by the operation of the act of parliament for stopping up the port of Boston. . . .

9th. Resolved, *nem. con.* That the city committee of correspondence be, and they are hereby instructed to use their utmost endeavors to carry these resolutions into execution.

52. RESOLUTIONS OF FREEHOLDERS OF ALBEMARLE COUNTY VIRGINIA
July 26, 1774

(The Writings of Thomas Jefferson, ed. by P. L. Ford, Vol. I, p. 418 ff.)

Pursuant to the instructions of the House of Burgesses of May 27, 1774—Doc. No. 53—the freeholders of Albemarle County held a meeting and subscribed to the following resolutions. The resolutions were drafted by Thomas Jefferson, and contain philosophical principles of the relations of the colonies to Parliament somewhat in advance of those generally subscribed to by the Americans. See, for an elaboration of Jefferson's position, his *Summary View of the Rights of*

British America, in *Writings,* Vol. I., and
C. F. Mullett, *Fundamental Law and the
American Revolution.*

At a meeting of the Freeholders of the
County of Albemarle, assembled in their
collective body, at the Court House of the
said County, on the 26th of *July,* 1774:

Resolved, That the inhabitants of the Several States of *British America* are subject to
the laws which they adopted at their first
settlement, and to such others as have been
since made by their respective Legislatures,
duly constituted and appointed with their
own consent. That no other Legislature whatever can rightly exercise authority over them;
and that these privileges they hold as the
common rights of mankind, confirmed by the
political constitutions they have respectively
assumed, and also by several charters of compact from the Crown.

Resolved, That these their natural and
legal rights have in frequent instances been
invaded by the Parliament of Great Britain
and particularly that they were so by an act
lately passed to take away the trade of the
inhabitants of the town of *Boston,* in the
province of *Massachusetts Bay;* that all such
assumptions of unlawful power are dangerous
to the right of the *British* empire in general,
and should be considered as its common
cause, and that we will ever be ready to join
with our fellow-subjects in every part of
the same, in executing all those rightful powers which God has given us, for the re-establishment and guaranteeing such their constitutional rights, when, where, and by
whomsoever invaded.

It is the opinion of this meeting, that the
most eligible means of effecting these purposes, will be to put an immediate stop to
all imports from *Great Britain,* (cotton,
osnabrigs, striped duffil, medicines, gun-
powder, lead, books and printed papers, the

necessary tools and implements for the handicraft arts and manufactures excepted, for a
limited term) and to all exports thereto,
after the first day of *October,* which shall be
in the year of our Lord, 1775; and immediately to discontinue all commercial intercourse with every part of the *British* Empire
which shall not in like manner break off their
commerce with *Great Britain.*

It is the opinion of this meeting, that we
immediately cease to import all commodities
from every part of the world, which are subjected by the *British* Parliament to the payment of duties in *America.*

It is the opinion of this meeting, that
these measures should be pursued until a repeal be obtained of the Act for blocking up the
harbour of *Boston;* of the Acts prohibiting or
restraining internal manufactures in *America;*
of the Acts imposing on any commodities
duties to be paid in America; and of the Act
laying restrictions on the *American* trade;
and that on such repeal it will be reasonable
to grant to our brethren of *Great Britain*
such privileges in commerce as may amply
compensate their fraternal assistance, past
and future.

Resolved, However, that this meeting do
submit these their opinions to the Convention of Deputies from the several counties
of this Colony, and appointed to be held at
Williamsburg on the first day of *August* next,
and also to the General Congress of Deputies
from the several *American* States, when and
wheresoever held; and that they will concur
in these or any other measures which such
Convention or such Congress shall adopt as
most expedient for the *American* good; and
we do appoint *Thomas Jefferson* and *John
Walker* our Deputies to act for this county
at the said Convention, and instruct them to
conform themselves to these our Resolutions
and Opinions.

53. VIRGINIA INSTRUCTIONS TO THE CONTINENTAL CONGRESS
August 1, 1774

(H. Niles, ed. *Principles and Acts of the Revolution,* 1822 ed. p. 201 ff.)

On May 27, eighty-one members of the House
of Burgesses of Virginia had met at the
Raleigh Tavern in Williamsburg and recommended a meeting of delegates from all the
colonies to a continental congress. These members requested their fellow-members of the

House of Burgesses to sound out their constituents on the question of a congress and to meet at
Williamsburg August 1, 1774. At this meeting the
following resolutions were drawn up and delegates chosen to the Congress. The convention
further declared that it was lawful to meet the

lawless acts of General Gage with force—a statement that was looked upon in England as an act of rebellion. See, R. Frothingham, *Rise of the Republic*, p. 332 ff.; C. H. Van Tyne, *Causes of the War of Independence*, p. 426 ff.; C. R. Lingley, *The Transition in Virginia*; H. J. Eckenrode, *The Revolution in Virginia*; J. M. Leake, *The Virginia Committee System and the American Revolution*.

Instructions for the deputies appointed to meet in general congress on the part of the colony of Virginia.

The unhappy disputes between Great Britain and her American colonies, . . . have compelled them to take the same into their most serious consideration; and being deprived of their usual and accustomed mode of making known their grievances, have appointed us their representatives to consider what is proper to be done in this dangerous crisis of American affairs. It being our opinion that the united wisdom of North America should be collected in a general congress of all the colonies, we have appointed the honorable Peyton Randolph, esquire, Richard Henry Lee, George Washington, Patrick Henry, Richard Bland, Benjamin Harrison, and Edmund Pendleton, esquires, deputies to represent this colony in the said congress, to be held at Philadelphia on the first Monday in September next.

And that they be the better informed of our sentiments, touching the conduct we wish them to observe on this important occasion, we desire they will express, in the first place, our faith and true allegiance to his majesty king George the third, our lawful and rightful sovereign; and that we are determined, with our lives and fortunes, to support him in the *legal* exercise of all his just rights and prerogatives; and however misrepresented, we sincerely approve of a constitutional connexion with Great Britain, and wish most ardently a return of that intercourse of affection and commercial connexion that formerly united both countries, which can only be affected by a removal of those causes of discontent which have of late unhappily divided us.

It cannot admit of a doubt but that British subjects in America, are entitled to the same rights and privileges as their fellow subjects possess in Britain; and therefore, that the power assumed by the British parliament to bind America by their statutes, in all cases whatsoever, is unconstitutional, and the source of these unhappy differences.

The end of government would be defeated by the British parliament exercising a power over the lives, the property, and the liberty of the American subjects; who are not, and from their local circumstances cannot, be there represented. Of this nature we consider the several acts of parliament for raising a revenue in America, for extending the jurisdiction of the courts of admiralty, for seizing American subjects and transporting them to Britain to be tried for crimes committed in America, and the several late oppressive acts respecting the town of Boston, and province of the Massachusetts-Bay.

The original constitution of the American colonies possessing their assemblies with the sole right of directing their internal polity, it is absolutely destructive of the end of their institution that their legislatures should be suspended, or prevented, by hasty dissolutions, from exercising their legislative powers.

Wanting the protection of Britain, we have long *acquiesced* in their acts of navigation restrictive of our commerce, which we consider as an ample recompense for such protection; but as those acts derive their efficacy from that foundation alone, we have reason to expect they will be restrained, so as to produce the reasonable purposes of Britain, without being injurious to us.

To obtain a redress of those grievances, without which the people of America can neither be safe, free, nor happy, they are willing to undergo the great inconvenience that will be derived to them from stopping all imports whatsoever from Great Britain, after the first day of November next, and also to cease exporting any commodity whatsoever, to the same place, after the 10th day of August, 1775. . . .

The proclamation issued by general Gage, in the government of the province of the Massachusetts-Bay, declaring it treason for the inhabitants of that province to assemble themselves to consider of their grievances, and form associations for their common conduct on the occasion, and requiring the civil magistrates and officers to apprehend all such persons to be tried for their supposed offences, is the most alarming process that ever appeared in a British government; . . .

That, if the said general Gage conceives he is empowered to act in this manner, as the commander in chief of his majesty's forces in America, this *odious* and *illegal* proclamation must be considered as a plain and full declaration that this *despotic viceroy* will be bound by *no law,* nor regard the constitutional rights of his majesty's subjects, whenever they interfere with the plan he has formed for oppressing the good people of the Massachusetts-Bay; and therefore, that the *executing,* or *attempting to execute* such proclamation, will justify RESISTANCE and REPRISAL.

54. VIRGINIA NON-IMPORTATION AGREEMENT
August 1, 1774

(H. Niles, ed. *Principles and Acts of the Revolution,* 1822 ed. p. 198 ff.)

The Boston Port Act aroused expressions of sympathy everywhere in the American colonies. The Boston Committee of Correspondence drew up a circular letter to the committees in other colonies recommending a suspension of trade with Great Britain; on the receipt of this letter the Virginia House of Burgesses passed a series of resolutions, drafted by Jefferson, "to oppose by all just and proper means every injury to American rights." This led to the dissolution of the House; subsequent meetings were held in the Raleigh Tavern in Williamsburg. The policy of non-intercourse was recommended by several other semi-official bodies, and was formally adopted by the Continental Congress. See Doc. No. 57; R. Frothingham, *Rise of the Republic of the United States,* ch. viii. On the relief of Boston, see Mass. Hist. Soc. *Collections,* 4th Series, Vol. IV.

At a very full meeting of the delegates from the different counties in the colony and dominion of Virginia, begun in Williamsburg, August 1st, 1774 . . .

1st. We do hereby resolve and declare that we will not either directly or indirectly, after the first day of November next, import from Great Britain, any goods, wares, or merchandize, whatever (medicines excepted) nor will we after that day import any British manufactures, either from the West Indies, or any other place. . . .

2dly. We will neither ourselves import, nor purchase any slave, or slaves, imported by any person, after the first day of November next, either from Africa, the West Indies, or any other place.

3dly. Considering the article of tea as the detestable instrument which laid the foundation of the present sufferings of our distressed friends in the town of Boston, we view it with horror, and therefore resolve that we will not, from this day, either import tea of any kind whatever, nor will we use or suffer, even such of it as is now at hand, to be used in any of our families. . . .

5thly. We do resolve, that unless American grievances be redressed before the 10th day of August, 1775, we will not, after that day, directly or indirectly, export tobacco or any other article whatever, to Great Britain, nor will we sell any such articles as we think can be exported to Great Britain with a prospect of gain. . . . And that this resolution may be the more effectually carried into execution, we do hereby recommend it to the inhabitants of this colony to refrain from the cultivation of tobacco as much as conveniently may be. . . .

8thly. In order the better to distinguish such worthy merchants and traders, who are well wishers to this colony, from those who may attempt, through motives of self-interest, to obstruct our views, we do hereby resolve that we will not, after the first day of November next, deal with any merchant or trader, who will not sign this association. . . .

9thly. Resolved. That if any person or persons shall export tobacco, or any other commodity, to Great Britain, after the 10th day of August, 1775, . . . we shall hold ourselves obliged to consider such persons . . . as inimical to the community, and as an *approver* of American *grievances;* and give it as our opinion that the public should be advertised of his conduct. . . .

55. GALLOWAY'S PLAN OF UNION
September 28, 1774

(Journals of the Continental Congress, ed. by W. C. Ford, Vol. I, p. 49 ff.)

Joseph Galloway, long a distinguished figure in Pennsylvania politics, proposed to solve the problem of colonial home rule by a plan which would give to the American colonies something approaching dominion status. This plan, at first favorably received, was ultimately defeated by a single vote, and subsequently expunged from the minutes of the Congress. John Adams observed in his Diary: "Among all the difficulties in the way of effective and united action in 1774 . . . no more alarming one happened than the plan of a proposed union between Great Britain and the Colonies presented, on the 28th of September, by Mr. Joseph Galloway." (The *Works* of John Adams, Vol. II, p. 387.) On the history of the Plan see Galloway, *Historical and Political Reflections on the Rise and Progress of the American Revolution*. See also, M. C. Tyler, *Literary History of the American Revolution*, Vol. I. p. 369 ff.; W. H. Seibert, *The Loyalists of Pennsylvania;* C. H. Lincoln, *Revolutionary Movement in Pennsylvania*.

Resolved, That this Congress will apply to His Majesty for a redress of grievances, under which his faithful subjects in America labour, and assure him that the colonies hold in abhorrence the idea of being considered independent communities on the British Government, and most ardently desire the establishment of a political union, not only among themselves, but with the mother state, upon those principles of safety and freedom which are essential in the constitution of all free governments, and particularly that of the British Legislature. And as the colonies from their local circumstances cannot be represented in the Parliament of Great Britain, they will humbly propose to His Majesty, and his two Houses of Parliament, the following plan, under which the strength of the whole Empire may be drawn together on any emergency; the interests of both countries advanced; and the rights and liberties of America secured.

A Plan of a proposed Union between Great Britain and the Colonies.

That a British and American legislature, for regulating the administration of the general affairs of America, be proposed and established in America, including all the said colonies; within and under which government, each colony shall retain its present constitution and powers of regulating and governing its own internal police in all cases whatsoever.

That the said government be administered by a President General, to be appointed by the King, and a grand council to be chosen by the Representatives of the people of the several colonies in their respective assemblies, once in every three years.

That the several assemblies shall choose members for the grand council in the following proportions, viz.: . . .

Who shall meet at the city of   for the first time, being called by the President General as soon as conveniently may be after his appointment. That there shall be a new election of members for the grand council every three years; and on the death, removal, or resignation of any member, his place shall be supplied by a new choice at the next sitting of Assembly of the colony he represented.

That the grand council shall meet once in every year if they shall think it necessary, and oftener, if occasions shall require, at such time and place as they shall adjourn to at the last preceding meeting; or as they shall be called to meet at, by the President General on any emergency.

That the grand council shall have power to choose their Speaker, and shall hold and exercise all the like rights, liberties, and privileges as are held and exercised by and in the House of Commons of Great Britain.

That the President General shall hold his office during the pleasure of the King, and his assent shall be requisite to all Acts of the grand council, and it shall be his office and duty to cause them to be carried into execution.

That the President General, by and with the advice and consent of the grand council, hold and exercise all the legislative rights, powers, and authorities, necessary for regulating and administering all the general police and affairs of the colonies, in which

Great Britain and the colonies, or any of them, the colonies in general, or more than one colony, are in any manner concerned, as well civil and criminal as commercial.

That the said President General and grand council, be an inferior and distinct branch of the British legislature, united and incorporated with it for the aforesaid general purposes; and that any of the said general regulations may originate, and be formed and digested, either in the Parliament of Great Britain, or in the said grand council; and being prepared, transmitted to the other for their approbation or dissent; and that the assent of both shall be requisite to the validity of all such general acts and statutes.

That in time of war, all bills for granting aides to the Crown, prepared by the grand council and approved by the President General, shall be valid and passed into a law, without the assent of the British Parliament.

56. DECLARATION AND RESOLVES OF THE FIRST CONTINENTAL CONGRESS
October 14, 1774

(Journals of the Continental Congress, ed. by W. C. Ford, Vol. I, p. 63 ff.)

The passage of the Intolerable Acts brought widespread demands for a congress of all the American colonies. On June 17, 1774 Samuel Adams submitted to the Massachusetts House, then assembled at Salem, a resolution that "a meeting of committees from the several colonies on this continent is highly expedient and necessary to consult upon the present state of the colonies . . . and to deliberate and determine upon wise and proper measures to be by them recommended to all the colonies for the recovery and establishment of just rights and liberties, civil and religious, and the restoration of union and harmony between Great Britain and the colonies," and that such a meeting convene in Philadelphia September 1. The resolution was adopted, and Samuel Adams, John Adams, Robert T. Paine, James Bowdoin and James Cushing were appointed delegates from Massachusetts. Most of the other colonies responded favorably to this proposal, and on September 5, delegates from all the colonies except North Carolina and Georgia assembled at Philadelphia; when the North Carolina delegation arrived, a week later, there were some fifty-five delegates in the convention. The best and liveliest account of the convention is in the Diary of John Adams, *Works*, Vol. II. See also, E. C. Burnett, ed. *Letters of Members of the Continental Congress*, Vol. I; R. Frothingham, *Rise of the Republic of the United States*, chs. viii–ix; G. E. Howard, *Preliminaries of the Revolution*, ch. xvi; C. H. Van Tyne, *Causes of the War of Independence*, chs. xvi–xvii.

Whereas, since the close of the last war, the British parliament, claiming a power of right to bind the people of America by statute in all cases whatsoever, hath, in some acts expressly imposed taxes on them, and in others, under various pretences, but in fact for the purpose of raising a revenue, hath imposed rates and duties payable in these colonies, established a board of commissioners with unconstitutional powers, and extended the jurisdiction of courts of Admiralty not only for collecting the said duties, but for the trial of causes merely arising within the body of a county.

And whereas, in consequence of other statutes, judges who before held only estates at will in their offices, have been made dependent on the Crown alone for their salaries, and standing armies kept in times of peace. And it has lately been resolved in Parliament, that by force of a statute made in the thirty-fifth year of the reign of king Henry the Eighth, colonists may be transported to England, and tried there upon accusations for treasons and misprisions, or concealments of treasons committed in the colonies; and by a late statute, such trials have been directed in cases therein mentioned.

And whereas, in the last session of Parliament, three statutes were made . . . [the Boston Port Act, the Massachusetts Government Act, the Administration of Justice Act], and another statute was then made [the Quebec Act] . . . All which statutes are impolitic, unjust, and cruel, as well as unconstitutional, and most dangerous and destructive of American rights.

And whereas, Assemblies have been frequently dissolved, contrary to the rights of the people, when they attempted to deliberate on grievances; and their dutiful, humble, loyal, & reasonable petitions to the crown for redress, have been repeatedly treated with contempt, by His Majesty's ministers of state:

The good people of the several Colonies of New-hampshire, Massachusetts-bay, Rhode-island and Providence plantations, Connecticut, New-York, New-Jersey, Pennsylvania, Newcastle Kent and Sussex on Delaware, Maryland, Virginia, North-Carolina, and South-Carolina, justly alarmed at these arbitrary proceedings of parliament and administration, have severally elected, constituted, and appointed deputies to meet, and sit in general Congress, in the city of Philadelphia, in order to obtain such establishment, as that their religion, laws, and liberties, may not be subverted:

Whereupon the deputies so appointed being now assembled, in a full and free representation of these Colonies, taking into their most serious consideration the best means of attaining the ends aforesaid, do in the first place, as Englishmen their ancestors in like cases have usually done, for asserting and vindicating their rights and liberties, declare,

That the inhabitants of the English Colonies in North America, by the immutable laws of nature, the principles of the English constitution, and the several charters or compacts, have the following Rights:

Resolved, N. C. D.

1. That they are entitled to life, liberty, and property, & they have never ceded to any sovereign power whatever, a right to dispose of either without their consent.

2. That our ancestors, who first settled these colonies, were at the time of their emigration from the mother country, entitled to all the rights, liberties, and immunities of free and natural-born subjects within the realm of England.

3. That by such emigration they by no means forfeited, surrendered, or lost any of those rights, but that they were, and their descendants now are entitled to the exercise and enjoyment of all such of them, as their local and other circumstances enable them to exercise and enjoy.

4. That the foundation of English liberty, and of all free government, is a right in the people to participate in their legislative council: and as the English colonists are not represented, and from their local and other circumstances, cannot properly be represented in the British parliament, they are entitled to a free and exclusive power of legislation in their several provincial legislatures, where their right of representation can alone be preserved, in all cases of taxation and internal polity, subject only to the negative of their sovereign, in such manner as has been heretofore used and accustomed. But, from the necessity of the case, and a regard to the mutual interest of both countries, we cheerfully consent to the operation of such acts of the British parliament, as are bona fide restrained to the regulation of our external commerce, for the purpose of securing the commercial advantages of the whole empire to the mother country, and the commercial benefits of its respective members excluding every idea of taxation, internal or external, for raising a revenue on the subjects in America without their consent.

5. That the respective colonies are entitled to the common law of England, and more especially to the great and inestimable privilege of being tried by their peers of the vicinage, according to the course of that law.

6. That they are entitled to the benefit of such of the English statutes, as existed at the time of their colonization; and which they have, by experience, respectively found to be applicable to their several local and other circumstances.

7. That these, his majesty's colonies, are likewise entitled to all the immunities and privileges granted and confirmed to them by royal charters, or secured by their several codes of provincial laws.

8. That they have a right peaceably to assemble, consider of their grievances, and petition the King; and that all prosecutions, prohibitory proclamations, and commitments for the same, are illegal.

9. That the keeping a Standing army in these colonies, in times of peace, without the consent of the legislature of that colony in which such army is kept, is against law.

10. It is indispensably necessary to good government, and rendered essential by the English constitution, that the constituent branches of the legislature be independent of each other; that, therefore, the exercise of legislative power in several colonies, by a council appointed during pleasure, by the crown, is unconstitutional, dangerous, and

destructive to the freedom of American legislation.

All and each of which the aforesaid deputies, in behalf of themselves, and their constituents, do claim, demand, and insist on, as their indubitable rights and liberties; which cannot be legally taken from them, altered or abridged by any power whatever, without their own consent, by their representatives in their several provincial legislatures.

In the course of our inquiry, we find many infringments and violations of the foregoing rights, which, from an ardent desire that harmony and mutual intercourse of affection and interest may be restored, we pass over for the present, and proceed to state such acts and measures as have been adopted since the last war, which demonstrate a system formed to enslave America.

Resolved, That the following acts of Parliament are infringements and violations of the rights of the colonists; and that the repeal of them is essentially necessary, in order to restore harmony between Great Britain and the American colonies, . . . viz.:

The several Acts of 4 Geo. 3, ch. 15 & ch. 34; 5 Geo. 3, ch. 25; 6 Geo. 3, ch. 52; 7 Geo. 3, ch. 41 & 46; 8 Geo. 3, ch. 22; which impose duties for the purpose of raising a revenue in America, extend the powers of the admiralty courts beyond their ancient limits, deprive the American subject of trial by jury, authorize the judges' certificate to indemnify the prosecutor from damages that he might otherwise be liable to, requiring oppressive security from a claimant of ships and goods seized before he shall be allowed to defend his property; and are subversive of American rights.

Also the 12 Geo. 3, ch. 24, entitled "An act for the better preserving his Majesty's dockyards, magazines, ships, ammunition, and stores," which declares a new offense in America, and deprives the American subject of a constitutional trial by jury of the vici-

nage, by authorizing the trial of any person charged with the committing any offense described in the said act, out of the realm, to be indicted and tried for the same in any shire or county within the realm.

Also the three acts passed in the last session of parliament, for stopping the port and blocking up the harbour of Boston, for altering the charter & government of the Massachusetts-bay, and that which is entitled "An Act for the better administration of Justice," &c.

Also the act passed the same session for establishing the Roman Catholick Religion in the province of Quebec, abolishing the equitable system of English laws, and erecting a tyranny there, to the great danger, from so great a dissimilarity of Religion, law, and government, of the neighbouring British colonies. . . .

Also the act passed the same session for the better providing suitable quarters for officers and soldiers in his Majesty's service in North America.

Also, that the keeping a standing army in several of these colonies, in time of peace, without the consent of the legislature of that colony in which the army is kept, is against law.

To these grievous acts and measures Americans cannot submit, but in hopes that their fellow subjects in Great-Britain will, on a revision of them, restore us to that state in which both countries found happiness and prosperity, we have for the present only resolved to pursue the following peaceable measures: 1st. To enter into a non-importation, non-consumption, and non-exportation agreement or association. 2. To prepare an address to the people of Great-Britain, and a memorial to the inhabitants of British America, & 3. To prepare a loyal address to his Majesty, agreeable to resolutions already entered into.

57. THE ASSOCIATION
October 20, 1774

(Journals of the Continental Congress, ed. by W. C. Ford, Vol. I, p. 75 ff.)

On September 27 the Continental Congress voted non-intercourse with Great Britain, and three days later a committee was appointed charged with drafting a plan to carry this resolution into effect. The committee reported October 12, and the report was adopted on the 18 and signed on the 20 October. "The signature of the Association," says Hildreth, "may be considered as the commencement of the American Union." Of particular interest are the provisions prohibiting the importation of slaves, and providing for committees of correspondence to enforce the rules of the Association. Several of the Colonies had already adopted non-importation agreements. The effect of the non-intercourse resolutions can be read in the petitions of English merchants to Parliament; see, for example, Doc. No. 58. On the Association, see R. Frothingham. *Rise of the Republic,* p. 372 ff.; A. W. Small, *The Beginnings of American Nationality;* G. E. Howard, *Preliminaries of the Revolution,* ch. xvi.

We, his majesty's most loyal subjects, the delegates of the several colonies of New-Hampshire, Massachusetts-Bay, Rhode-Island, Connecticut, New-York, New-Jersey, Pennsylvania, the three lower counties of Newcastle, Kent and Sussex on Delaware, Maryland, Virginia, North-Carolina, and South-Carolina, deputed to represent them in a continental Congress, held in the city of Philadelphia, on the 5th day of September, 1774, avowing our allegiance to his majesty, our affection and regard for our fellow-subjects in Great-Britain and elsewhere, affected with the deepest anxiety, and most alarming apprehensions, at those grievances and distresses, with which his Majesty's American subjects are oppressed; and having taken under our most serious deliberation, the state of the whole continent, find, that the present unhappy situation of our affairs is occasioned by a ruinous system of colony administration, adopted by the British ministry about the year 1763, evidently calculated for enslaving these colonies, and, with them, the British Empire. In prosecution of which system, various acts of parliament have been passed, for raising a revenue in America, for depriving the American subjects, in many instances, of the constitutional trial by jury, exposing their lives to danger, by directing a new and illegal trial beyond the seas, for crimes alleged to have been committed in America: And in prosecution of the same system, several late, cruel, and oppressive acts have been passed, respecting the town of Boston and the Massachusetts-Bay, and also an act for extending the province of Quebec, so as to border on the western frontiers of these colonies, establishing an arbitrary government therein, and discouraging the settlement of British subjects in that wide extended coun-

try; thus, by the influence of civil principles and ancient prejudices, to dispose the inhabitants to act with hostility against the free Protestant colonies, whenever a wicked ministry shall chuse so to direct them.

To obtain redress of these grievances, which threaten destruction to the lives, liberty, and property of his majesty's subjects, in North-America, we are of opinion, that a non-importation, non-consumption, and non-exportation agreement, faithfully adhered to, will prove the most speedy, effectual, and peaceable measure: And, therefore, we do, for ourselves, and the inhabitants of the several colonies, whom we represent, firmly agree and associate, under the sacred ties of virtue, honour and love of our country, as follows:

1. That from and after the first day of December next, we will not import, into British America, from Great-Britain or Ireland, any goods, wares, or merchandize whatsoever, or from any other place, any such goods, wares, or merchandise, as shall have been exported from Great-Britain or Ireland; nor will we, after that day, import any East-India tea from any part of the world; nor any molasses, syrups, paneles, coffee, or pimento, from the British plantations or from Dominica; nor wines from Madeira, or the Western Islands; nor foreign indigo.

2. We will neither import nor purchase, any slave imported after the first day of December next; after which time, we will wholly discontinue the slave trade, and will neither be concerned in it ourselves, nor will we hire our vessels, nor sell our commodities or manufactures to those who are concerned in it.

3. As a non-consumption agreement, strictly adhered to, will be an effectual security for the observation of the non-importation, we, as above, solemnly agree and associate, that from this day, we will not purchase or use any tea, imported on account of the East-India company, or any on which a duty hath been or shall be paid; and from and after the first day of March next, we will not purchase or use any East-India tea whatever; nor will we, nor shall any person for or under us, purchase or use any of those goods, wares, or merchandize, we have agreed not to import, which we shall know, or have cause to suspect, were imported after the first day of December, except such as come

under the rules and directions of the tenth article hereafter mentioned.

4. The earnest desire we have not to injure our fellow-subjects in Great-Britain, Ireland, or the West-Indies, induces us to suspend a non-exportation, until the tenth day of September, 1775; at which time, if the said acts and parts of acts of the British parliament herein after mentioned, are not repealed, we will not directly or indirectly, export any merchandize or commodity whatsoever to Great-Britain, Ireland, or the West-Indies, except rice to Europe.

5. Such as are merchants, and use the British and Irish trade, will give orders, as soon as possible, to their factors, agents and correspondents, in Great-Britain and Ireland, not to ship any goods to them, on any pretence whatsoever, as they cannot be received in America; and if any merchant, residing in Great-Britain or Ireland, shall directly or indirectly ship any goods, wares or merchandize, for America, in order to break the said non-importation agreement, or in any manner contravene the same, on such unworthy conduct being well attested, it ought to be made public; and, on the same being so done, we will not, from thenceforth, have any commercial connexion with such merchant.

6. That such as are owners of vessels will give positive orders to their captains, or masters, not to receive on board their vessels any goods prohibited by the said non-importation agreement, on pain of immediate dismission from their service.

7. We will use our utmost endeavours to improve the breed of sheep, and increase their number to the greatest extent; and to that end, we will kill them as seldom as may be, especially those of the most profitable kind; nor will we export any to the West-Indies or elsewhere; and those of us, who are or may become overstocked with, or can conveniently spare any sheep, will dispose of them to our neighbours, especially to the poorer sort, on moderate terms.

8. We will, in our several stations, encourage frugality, œconomy, and industry, and promote agriculture, arts and the manufactures of this country, especially that of wool; and will discountenance and discourage every species of extravagance and dissipation, especially all horse-racing, and all kinds of gaming, cock fighting, exhibitions of shews, plays, and other expensive diversions and entertainments; and on the death of any relation or friend, none of us, or any of our families will go into any further mourning-dress, than a black crape or ribbon on the arm or hat, for gentlemen, and a black ribbon and necklace for ladies, and we will discontinue the giving of gloves and scarves at funerals.

9. Such as are venders of goods or merchandize will not take advantage of the scarcity of goods, that may be occasioned by this association, but will sell the same at the rates we have been respectively accustomed to do, for twelve months last past. —And if any vender of goods or merchandize shall sell such goods on higher terms, or shall, in any manner, or by any device whatsoever, violate or depart from this agreement, no person ought, nor will any of us deal with any such person, or his or her factor or agent, at any time thereafter, for any commodity whatever.

10. In case any merchant, trader, or other person, shall import any goods or merchandize, after the first day of December, and before the first day of February next, the same ought forthwith, at the election of the owner, to be either re-shipped or delivered up to the committee of the country or town, wherein they shall be imported, to be stored at the risque of the importer, until the non-importation agreement shall cease, or be sold under the direction of the committee aforesaid; and in the last-mentioned case, the owner or owners of such goods shall be reimbursed out of the sales, the first cost and charges, the profit, if any, to be applied towards relieving and employing such poor inhabitants of the town of Boston, as are immediate sufferers by the Boston port-bill; and a particular account of all goods so returned, stored, or sold, to be inserted in the public papers; and if any goods or merchandizes shall be imported after the said first day of February, the same ought forthwith to be sent back again, without breaking any of the packages thereof.

11. That a committee be chosen in every county, city, and town, by those who are qualified to vote for representatives in the legislature, whose business it shall be attentively to observe the conduct of all persons touching this association; and when it shall

be made to appear, to the satisfaction of a majority of any such committee, that any person within the limits of their appointment has violated this association, that such majority do forthwith cause the truth of the case to be published in the. gazette; to the end, that all such foes to the rights of British-America may be publicly known, and universally contemned as the enemies of American liberty; and thenceforth we respectively will break off all dealings with him or her.

12. That the committee of correspondence, in the respective colonies, do frequently inspect the entries of their customhouses, and inform each other, from time to time, of the true state thereof, and of every other material circumstance that may occur relative to this association.

13. That all manufactures of this country be sold at reasonable prices, so that no undue advantage be taken of a future scarcity of goods.

14. And we do further agree and resolve, that we will have no trade, commerce, dealings or intercourse whatsoever, with any colony or province, in North-America, which shall not accede to, or which shall hereafter violate this association, but will hold them as unworthy of the rights of freemen, and as inimical to the liberties of their country.

And we do solemnly bind ourselves and our constituents, under the ties aforesaid, to adhere to this association, until such parts of the several acts of parliament passed since the close of the last war, as impose or continue duties on tea, wine, molasses, syrups, paneles, coffee, sugar, pimento, indigo, foreign paper, glass, and painters' colours, imported into America, and extend the powers of the admiralty courts beyond their ancient limits, deprive the American subject of trial by jury, authorize the judge's certificate to indemnify the prosecutor from damages, that he might otherwise be liable to from a trial by his peers, require oppressive security from a claimant of ships or goods seized, before he shall be allowed to defend his property, are repealed.—And until that part of the act of the 12 G. 3. ch. 24, entitled "An act for the better securing his majesty's dock-yards, magazines, ships, ammunition, and stores," by which any persons charged with committing any of the offences therein described, in America, may be tried in any shire or county within the realm, is repealed—and until the four acts, passed the last session of parliament, viz. that for stopping the port and blocking up the harbour of Boston—that for altering the charter and government of the Massachusetts-Bay—and that which is entitled "An act for the better administration of justice, &c."—and that "for extending the limits of Quebec, &c." are repealed. And we recommend it to the provincial conventions, and to the committees in the respective colonies, to establish such farther regulations as they may think proper, for carrying into execution this association.

The foregoing association being determined upon by the Congress, was ordered to be subscribed by the several members thereof; and thereupon, we have hereunto set our respective names accordingly.

IN CONGRESS, PHILADELPHIA, *October 20, 1774.*

Signed, PEYTON RANDOLPH, *President.*

58. PETITION OF LONDON MERCHANTS FOR RECONCILIATION WITH AMERICA
January 23, 1775

(The Parliamentary History of England, Vol. XVIII, 1774–1777, p. 168 ff.)

Exports from England to the American colonies dropped from some two and one half million pounds in 1774 to about one-tenth that sum in 1775. Not only did the success of the Association thus threaten English merchants with ruin, but the imminent danger of hostilities with the colonies raised serious doubts as to the ability of English merchants to collect the large debts owed them by American planters. On trade, see, D. M. Clark, *British Opinion and the American Revolution,* ch. iii; on debts, see, I. Harrell, *Loyalism in Virginia.*

Mr. Alderman *Hayley* said he had a petition from the merchants of the city of London concerned in the commerce to North America, to that honourable House, and desired leave to present the same, which being given, it was brought up and read, setting forth;

"That the petitioners are all essentially interested in the trade to North America, either as exporters and importers, or as venders of British and foreign goods for exportation to that country; and that the petitioners have exported, or sold for exportation, to the British colonies in North America, very large quantities of the manufacture of Great Britain and Ireland, and in particular the staple articles of woollen, iron, and linen, also those of cotton, silk, leather, pewter, tin, copper, and brass, with almost every British manufacture; . . . and that the petitioners have likewise exported, or sold for exportation, great quantities of the various species of goods imported into this kingdom from the East-Indies, part of which receive additional manufacture in Great Britain; and that the petitioners receive returns from North America to this kingdom directly, viz. pig and bar iron, timber, staves, naval stores, tobacco, rice, indigo, deer, and other skins, beaver and furs, train oil, whalebone, bees wax, pot and pearl ashes, drugs and dyeing woods, with some bullion, and also wheat flour, Indian corn and salted provisions, when, on account of scarcity in Great Britain, those articles are permitted to be imported; . . . and that the petitioners have great reason to believe, from the best informations they can obtain, that on the balance of this extensive commerce, there is now due from the colonies in North America, to the said city only, 2,000,000 l. sterling, and upwards; and that, by the direct commerce with the colonies, and the circuitous trade thereon depending, some thousands of ships and vessels are employed, and many thousands of seamen are bred and maintained, thereby increasing the naval strength and power of Great Britain; and that, in the year 1765, there was a great stagnation of the commerce between Great Britain and her colonies, in consequence of an Act for granting and applying certain stamp duties, and other duties, in the British colonies and plantations in America, by which the merchants trading to North America, and the artificers employed in the various manufactures consumed in those countries, were subjected to many hardships; and that, in the following year, the said Act was repealed, under an ex-

press declaration of the legislature, that the continuance of the said Act would be attended with many inconveniences, and might be productive of consequences greatly detrimental to the commercial interests of these kingdoms; upon which repeal, the trade to the British colonies immediately resumed its former flourishing state; and that in the year 1767 an Act passed for granting certain duties in the British colonies and plantations in America, which imposed certain duties, to be paid in America, on tea, glass, red and white lead, painters' colours, paper, paste-board, mill-board, and scale-board, when the commerce with the colonies was again interrupted; and that in the year 1770, such parts of the said Act as imposed duties on glass, red and white lead, painters' colours, paper, paste-board, mill-board, and scale-board, were repealed, when the trade to America soon revived, except in the article of tea, on which a duty was continued, to be demanded on its importation into America, whereby that branch of our commerce was nearly lost; and that, in the year 1773, an Act passed, to allow a drawback of the duties of customs on the exportation of tea to his Majesty's colonies or plantations in America, and to empower the commissioners of the Treasury to grant licenses to the East India Company, to export tea, duty free; and by the operation of those and other laws, the minds of his Majesty's subjects in the British colonies have been greatly disquieted, a total stop is now put to the export trade with the greatest and most important part of North America, the public revenue is threatened with a large and fatal diminution, the petitioners with grievous distress, and thousands of industrious artificers and manufacturers with utter ruin; under these alarming circumstances, the petitioners receive no small comfort, from a persuasion that the representatives of the people, newly delegated to the most important of all trusts, will take the whole of these weighty matters into their most serious consideration; and therefore praying the House, that they will enter into a full and immediate examination of that system of commercial policy, which was formerly adopted, and uniformly maintained, to the happiness and advantage of both countries, and will apply such healing remedies as can alone restore and establish the commerce between Great Britain and her colonies on a permanent foundation; and that the petitioners may be heard by themselves, or agents, in support of the said petition."

59. THE BATTLE OF LEXINGTON
1775

The following two extracts present the official American and English versions of.the hostilities at Lexington, April 19, 1775. It is, apparently, impossible to determine at this time who fired the first shot at Lexington, but see A. C. Mc Laughlin, et.al. eds. *Source Problems in United States History,* ch. i; A. French, *The Day of Concord and Lexington;* A. French, *General Gage's Informers,* chs. i–iii; H. Murdock, *Concord Fight.*

1. AMERICAN ACCOUNT OF THE BATTLE OF LEXINGTON: Account by the Provincial Congress at Watertown, Massachusetts
April 26, 1775
(H. Niles, ed. *Principles and Acts of the Revolution,* 1822 ed. p. 434–5.)
Watertown, April 26th, 1775.
In provincial congress of Massachusetts, to the inhabitants of Great Britain.

Friends and fellow subjects—Hostilities are at length commenced in this colony by the troops under the command of general Gage, and it being of the greatest importance, that an early, true, and authentic account of this inhuman proceeding should be known to you, the congress of this colony have transmitted the same, and from want of a session of the hon. continental congress, think it proper to address you on the alarming occasion.

By the clearest depositions relative to this transaction, it will appear that on the night preceding the nineteenth of April instant, a body of the king's troops, under the command of colonel Smith, were secretly landed at Cambridge, with an apparent design to take or destroy the military and other stores, provided for the defence of this colony, and deposited at Concord—that some inhabitants of the colony, on the night aforesaid, whilst travelling peaceably on the road, between Boston and Concord, were seized and greatly abused by armed men, who appeared to be officers of general Gage's army; that the town of Lexington, by these means, was alarmed, and a company of the inhabitants mustered on the occasion—that the regular troops on their way to Concord, marched into the said town of Lexington, and the said company, on their approach, began to disperse—that, notwithstanding this, the regulars rushed on with great violence and first began hostilities, by firing on said Lexington company, whereby they killed eight, and wounded several others —that the regulars continued their fire, until those of said company, who were neither killed nor wounded, had made their escape— that colonel Smith, with the detachment then marched to Concord, where a number of provincials were again fired on by the troops, two of them killed and several wounded, before the provincials fired on them, and provincials were again fired on by the troops, produced an engagement that lasted through the day, in which many of the provincials and more of the regular troops were killed and wounded.

To give a particular account of the ravages of the troops, as they retreated from Concord to Charlestown, would be very difficult, if not impracticable; let it suffice to say, that a great number of the houses on the road were plundered and rendered unfit for use, several were burnt, women in child-bed were driven by the soldiery naked into the streets, old men peaceably in their houses were shot dead, and such scenes exhibited as would disgrace the annals of the most uncivilized nation.

These, brethren, are marks of ministerial vengeance against this colony, for refusing, with her sister colonies, a submission to slavery; but they have not yet detached us from our royal sovereign. We profess to be his loyal and dutiful subjects, and so hardly dealt with as we have been, are still ready, with our lives and fortunes, to defend his person, family, crown and dignity. Nevertheless, to the persecution and tyranny of his cruel ministry we will not tamely submit— appealing to Heaven for the justice of our cause, we determine to die or be free. . . .

By order,
Joseph Warren, President.

2. ENGLISH ACCOUNT OF THE BATTLE OF
LEXINGTON: Report of Lieutenant-Colonel
Smith to Governor Gage
April 22, 1775
(Mass. Historical Society, *Proceedings*, 1876,
p. 350 ff.)

SIR,—In obedience to your Excellency's
commands, I marched on the evening of the
18th inst. with the corps of grenadiers and
light infantry for Concord, to execute your
Excellency's orders with respect to destroying all ammunition, artillery, tents, &c, collected there, which was effected, having
knocked off the trunnions of three pieces of
iron ordnance, some new gun-carriages, a
great number of carriage-wheels burnt, a considerable quantity of flour, some gun-powder
and musquet-balls, with other small articles
thrown into the river. Notwithstanding we
marched with the utmost expedition and
secrecy, we found the country had intelligence
or strong suspicion of our coming, and fired
many signal guns, and rung the alarm bells
repeatedly; and were informed, when at Concord, that some cannon had been taken out
of the town that day, that others, with some
stores, had been carried three days before,
which prevented our having an opportunity
of destroying so much as might have been
expected at our first setting off.

I think it proper to observe, that when I
had got some miles on the march from
Boston, I detached six light infantry companies to march with all expedition to seize
the two bridges on different roads beyond
Concord. On these companies' arrival at Lexington, I understand, from the report of
Major Pitcairn, who was with them, and from
many officers, that they found on a green
close to the road a body of the country people
drawn up in military order, with arms and
accoutrements, and, as appeared after,
loaded; and that they had posted some men
in a dwelling and Meeting-house. Our troops
advanced towards them, without any intention of injuring them, further than to inquire
the reason of their being thus assembled,
and, if not satisfactory, to have secured their
arms; but they in confusion went off, principally to the left, only one of them fired
before he went off, and three or four more
jumped over a wall and fired from behind it
among the soldiers; on which the troops returned it, and killed several of them. They
likewise fired on the soldiers from the Meeting and dwelling-houses. . . . Rather earlier
than this, on the road, a countryman from
behind a wall had snapped his piece at Lieutenants Adair and Sutherland, but it flashed
and did not go off. After this we saw some
in the woods, but marched on to Concord
without anything further happening. While
at Concord we saw vast numbers assembling
in many parts; at one of the bridges they
marched down, with a very considerable
body, on the light infantry posted there. On
their coming pretty near, one of our men
fired on them, which they returned; on which
an action ensued, and some few were killed
and wounded. In this affair, it appears that,
after the bridge was quitted, they scalped
and otherwise ill-treated one or two of the
men who were either killed or severely
wounded. . . . On our leaving Concord to
return to Boston, they began to fire on us
from behind the walls, ditches, trees, &c.,
which, as we marched, increased to a very
great degree, and continued without intermission of five minutes altogether, for, I
believe, upwards of eighteen miles; so that
I can't think but it must have been a preconcerted scheme in them, to attack the
King's troops the first favorable opportunity
that offered, otherwise, I think they could
not, in so short a time from our marching
out, have raised such a numerous body, and
for so great a space of ground. Notwithstanding the enemy's numbers, they did not make
one gallant attempt during so long an action,
though our men were so very much fatigued,
but kept under cover.

I have the honor, &c.,

F. Smith, Lieutenant-Colonel 10th Foot.

60. ADDRESS OF THE CONTINENTAL CONGRESS TO THE INHABITANTS OF CANADA
May 29, 1775

(Journals of the Continental Congress, ed. by W. C. Ford, Vol. II, p. 68 ff.)

One of the first acts of the second Continental Congress which met May 10, 1775, was an Appeal to the inhabitants of Canada. The appeal was drafted by John Jay. Americans continued, through the early years of the war, to hug to themselves the delusion that Canadians wished to bring Canada into the American Union. In the fall of 1775 the appeal of Congress was reenforced by a military expedition under Montgomery and Arnold which was disastrously defeated. Nothing daunted, Congress in March 1776 appointed three commissioners,—Franklin, Samuel Chase, and Charles Carroll—to proceed to Canada and persuade the Canadians to join the Americans. Even after the failure of this move, Congress provided, in the Articles of Confederation, for the admission of Canada. See J. H. Smith, *Our Struggle for the Fourteenth Colony,* Vol. I.

To the oppressed Inhabitants of Canada.
FRIENDS AND COUNTRYMEN,

Alarmed by the designs of an arbitrary Ministry, to extirpate the Rights and liberties of all America, a sense of common danger conspired with the dictates of humanity, in urging us to call your attention, by our late address, to this very important object.

Since the conclusion of the late war, we have been happy in considering you as fellow-subjects, and from the commencement of the present plan for subjugating the continent, we have viewed you as fellow-sufferers with us. As we were both entitled by the bounty of an indulgent creator to freedom, and being both devoted by the cruel edicts of a despotic administration, to common ruin, we perceived the fate of the protestant and catholic colonies to be strongly linked together, and therefore invited you to join with us in resolving to be free, and in rejecting, with disdain, the fetters of slavery, however artfully polished.

We most sincerely condole with you on the arrival of that day, in the course of which, the sun could not shine on a single freeman in all your extensive dominion. Be assured, that your unmerited degradation has engaged the most unfeigned pity of your sister colonies; and we flatter ourselves you will not, by tamely bearing the yoke, suffer that pity to be supplanted by contempt.

When hardy attempts are made to deprive men of rights, bestowed by the almighty, when avenues are cut thro' the most solemn compacts for the admission of despotism, when the plighted faith of government ceases to give security to loyal and dutiful subjects, and when the insidious stratagems and manoeuvres of peace become more terrible than the sanguinary operations of war, it is high time for them to assert those rights, and, with honest indignation, oppose the torrent of oppression rushing in upon them.

By the introduction of your present form of government, or rather present form of tyranny, you and your wives and your children are made slaves. You have nothing that you can call your own, and all the fruits of your labour and industry may be taken from you, whenever an avaritious governor and a rapacious council may incline to demand them. You are liable by their edicts to be transported into foreign countries to fight Battles in which you have no interest, and to spill your blood in conflicts from which neither honor nor emolument can be derived: Nay, the enjoyment of your very religion, in the present system, depends on a legislature in which you have no share, and over which you have no controul, and your priests are exposed to expulsion, banishment, and ruin, whenever their wealth and possessions furnish sufficient temptation. They cannot be sure that a virtuous prince will always fill the throne, and should a wicked or a careless king concur with a wicked ministry in extracting the treasure and strength of your country, it is impossible to conceive to what variety and to what extremes of wretchedness you may, under the present establishment, be reduced.

We are informed you have already been called upon to waste your lives in a contest with us. Should you, by complying in this instance, assent to your new establishment, and a war break out with France, your wealth and your sons may be sent to perish in ex-

peditions against their islands in the West indies.

It cannot be presumed that these considerations will have no weight with you, or that you are so lost to all sense of honor. We can never believe that the present race of Canadians are so degenerated as to possess neither the spirit, the gallantry, nor the courage of their ancestors. You certainly will not permit the infamy and disgrace of such pusillanimity to rest on your own heads, and the consequences of it on your children forever.

We, for our parts, are determined to live free, or not at all; and are resolved, that posterity shall never reproach us with having brought slaves into the world.

Permit us again to repeat that we are your friends, not your enemies, and be not imposed upon by those who may endeavour to create animosities. The taking of the fort and military stores at Ticonderoga and Crown-Point, and the armed vessels on the lake, was dictated by the great law of self-preservation. They are intended to annoy us, and to cut off that friendly intercourse and communication, which has hitherto subsisted between you and us. We hope it has given you no uneasiness, and you may rely on our assurances, that these colonies will pursue no measures whatever, but such as friendship and a regard for our mutual safety and interest may suggest.

As our concern for your welfare entitles us to your friendship, we presume you will not, by doing us injury, reduce us to the disagreeable necessity of treating you as enemies.

We yet entertain hopes of your uniting with us in the defence of our common liberty, and there is yet reason to believe, that should we join in imploring the attention of our sovereign, to the unmerited and unparalleled oppressions of his American subjects, he will at length be undeceived, and forbid a licentious Ministry any longer to riot in the ruins of the rights of Mankind. . . .

61. DECLARATION OF THE CAUSES AND NECESSITY OF TAKING UP ARMS
July 6, 1775

(Journals of the Continental Congress, ed. by W. C. Ford, Vol. II, p. 140 ff.)

Franklin, Jay, Rutledge, Livingston, Johnson, Jefferson and Dickinson were the members of the committee appointed to draw up this declaration. The final draft is the work of Dickinson and Jefferson. On the authorship of the Declaration, see Appendix IV to C. J. Stillé, *Life and Times of John Dickinson*, Vol. I, p. 353 ff.; C. H. Van Tyne, *The War of Independence: American Phase.*

If it was possible for men, who exercise their reason to believe, that the divine Author of our existence intended a part of the human race to hold an absolute property in, and an unbounded power over others, marked out by his infinite goodness and wisdom, as the objects of a legal domination never rightfully resistible, however severe and oppressive, the inhabitants of these colonies might at least require from the parliament of Great-Britain some evidence, that this dreadful authority over them, has been granted to that body. But a reverence for our great Creator, principles of humanity, and the dictates of common sense, must convince all those who reflect upon the subject, that government was instituted to promote the welfare of mankind, and ought to be administered for the attainment of that end. The legislature of Great-Britain, however, stimulated by an inordinate passion for a power not only unjustifiable, but which they know to be peculiarly reprobated by the very constitution of that kingdom, and desperate of success in any mode of contest, where regard should be had to truth, law, or right, have at length, deserting those, attempted to effect their cruel and impolitic purpose of enslaving these colonies by violence, and have thereby rendered it necessary for us to close with their last appeal from reason to arms.—Yet, however blinded that assembly may be, by their intemperate rage for unlimited domination, so to slight justice and the opinion of mankind, we esteem ourselves bound by obligations of respect to the rest of the world, to make known the justice of our cause.

Our forefathers, inhabitants of the island of Great-Britain, left their native land, to seek on these shores a residence for civil and religious freedom. At the expense of their blood, at the hazard of their fortunes, without the least charge to the country from which they removed, by unceasing labour, and an unconquerable spirit, they effected settlements in the distant and inhospitable wilds of America, then filled with numerous and warlike nations of barbarians.—Societies or governments, vested with perfect legislatures, were formed under charters from the crown, and an harmonious intercourse was established between the colonies and the kingdom from which they derived their origin. The mutual benefits of this union became in a short time so extraordinary, as to excite astonishment. It is universally confessed, that the amazing increase of the wealth, strength, and navigation of the realm, arose from this source; and the minister, who so wisely and successfully directed the measures of Great-Britain in the late war, publicly declared, that these colonies enabled her to triumph over her enemies.—Towards the conclusion of that war, it pleased our sovereign to make a change in his counsels.— From that fatal moment, the affairs of the British empire began to fall into confusion, and gradually sliding from the summit of glorious prosperity, to which they had been advanced by the virtues and abilities of one man, are at length distracted by the convulsions, that now shake it to its deepest foundations.—The new ministry finding the brave foes of Britain, though frequently defeated, yet still contending, took up the unfortunate idea of granting them a hasty peace, and of then subduing her faithful friends.

These devoted colonies were judged to be in such a state, as to present victories without bloodshed, and all the easy emoluments of statuteable plunder.—The uninterrupted tenor of their peaceable and respectful behaviour from the beginning of colonization, their dutiful, zealous, and useful services during the war, though so recently and amply acknowledged in the most honourable manner by his majesty, by the late king, and by parliament, could not save them from the meditated innovations.—Parliament was influenced to adopt the pernicious project, and assuming a new power over them, have in the course of eleven years, given such decisive specimens of the spirit and consequences attending this power, as to leave no

doubt concerning the effects of acquiescence under it. They have undertaken to give and grant our money without our consent, though we have ever exercised an exclusive right to dispose of our own property; statutes have been passed for extending the jurisdiction of courts of admiralty, and vice-admiralty beyond their ancient limits; for depriving us of the accustomed and inestimable privilege of trial by jury, in cases affecting both life and property; for suspending the legislature of one of the colonies; for interdicting all commerce to the capital of another; and for altering fundamentally the form of government established by charter, and secured by acts of its own legislature solemnly confirmed by the crown; for exempting the "murderers" of colonists from legal trial, and in effect, from punishment; for erecting in a neighbouring province, acquired by the joint arms of Great-Britain and America, a despotism dangerous to our very existence; and for quartering soldiers upon the colonists in time of profound peace. It has also been resolved in parliament, that colonists charged with committing certain offences, shall be transported to England to be tried.

But why should we enumerate our injuries in detail? By one statute it is declared, that parliament can "of right make laws to bind us in all cases whatsoever." What is to defend us against so enormous, so unlimited a power? Not a single man of those who assume it, is chosen by us; or is subject to our controul or influence; but, on the contrary, they are all of them exempt from the operation of such laws, and an American revenue, if not diverted from the ostensible purposes for which it is raised, would actually lighten their own burdens in proportion, as they increase ours. We saw the misery to which such despotism would reduce us. We for ten years incessantly and ineffectually besieged the throne as supplicants; we reasoned, we remonstrated with parliament, in the most mild and decent language. But administration sensible that we should regard these oppressive measures as freemen ought to do, sent over fleets and armies to enforce them. The indignation of the Americans was roused, it is true; but it was the indignation of a virtuous, loyal, and affectionate people. A Congress of delegates from the United Colonies was assembled at Philadelphia, on the fifth day of last September. We resolved again to offer an humble and dutiful petition to the king, and also addressed our fellow-subjects of Great-Britain. We have pursued every temperate, every respectful measure: we have even proceeded to break off our commercial intercourse with our fellow-subjects, as the last peaceable admonition, that our attachment to no nation upon earth should supplant our attachment to liberty.—This, we flattered ourselves, was the ultimate step of the controversy: but subsequent events have shewn, how vain was this hope of finding moderation in our enemies.

Several threatening expressions against the colonies were inserted in his majesty's speech; our petition, tho' we were told it was a decent one, and that his majesty had been pleased to receive it graciously, and to promise laying it before his parliament, was huddled into both houses among a bundle of American papers, and there neglected. The lords and commons in their address, in the month of February, said, that "a rebellion at that time actually existed within the province of Massachusetts-Bay; and that those concerned in it, had been countenanced and encouraged by unlawful combinations and engagements, entered into by his majesty's subjects in several of the other colonies; and therefore they besought his majesty, that he would take the most effectual measures to inforce due obedience to the laws and authority of the supreme legislature."—Soon after, the commercial intercourse of whole colonies, with foreign countries, and with each other, was cut off by an act of parliament; by another several of them were intirely prohibited from the fisheries in the seas near their coasts, on which they always depended for their sustenance; and large reinforcements of ships and troops were immediately sent over to general Gage.

Fruitless were all the entreaties, arguments, and eloquence of an illustrious band of the most distinguished peers, and commoners, who nobly and stren[u]ously asserted the justice of our cause, to stay, or even to mitigate the heedless fury with which these accumulated and unexampled outrages were hurried on. . . .

. . . General Gage, who in the course of the last year had taken possession of the town of Boston, in the province of Massachusetts-Bay, . . . on the 19th day of April, sent out from that place a large detachment of his army, who made an unprovoked assault on the inhabitants of the said province, at the town of Lexington, as appears by the affidavits of a great number of persons, some of whom were officers and soldiers of that detachment, murdered eight of the inhabitants, and wounded many others. From thence the troops proceeded in warlike array to the town of Concord, where they set upon another party of the inhabitants of the same province, killing several and wounding more, until compelled to retreat by the country people suddenly assembled to repel this cruel aggression. Hostilities, thus commenced by the British troops, have been since prosecuted by them without regard to faith or reputation.—The inhabitants of Boston being confined within that town by the general their governor, and having, in order to procure their dismission, entered into a treaty with him, it was stipulated that the said inhabitants having deposited their arms with their own magistrates, should have liberty to depart, taking with them their other effects. They accordingly delivered up their arms, but in open violation of honour, in defiance of the obligation of treaties, which even savage nations esteemed sacred, the governor ordered the arms deposited as aforesaid, that they might be preserved for their owners, to be seized by a body of soldiers; detained the greatest part of the inhabitants in the town, and compelled the few who were permitted to retire, to leave their most valuable effects behind. . . .

The General, further emulating his ministerial masters, by a proclamation bearing date on the 12th day of June, after venting the grossest falsehoods and calumnies against the good people of these colonies, proceeds to "declare them all, either by name or description, to be rebels and traitors, to supersede the course of the common law, and instead thereof to publish and order the use and exercise of the law martial."—His troops have butchered our countrymen, have wantonly burnt Charlestown, besides a considerable number of houses in other places; our ships and vessels are seized; the necessary supplies of provisions are intercepted, and he is exerting his utmost power to spread destruction and devastation around him.

We have received certain intelligence, that General Carleton, the Governor of Canada, is instigating the people of that province and the Indians to fall upon us; and we have but too much reason to apprehend, that schemes have been formed to excite domestic enemies against us. In brief, a part of these colonies now feel, and all of them are sure of feeling, as far as the vengeance of administration can inflict them, the complicated calamities of fire, sword, and famine. We are reduced to the alternative of chusing an unconditional submission to the tyranny of irritated ministers, or resistance by force.—The latter is our choice.—We have counted the cost of this contest, and find nothing so dreadful as voluntary slavery. —Honour, justice, and humanity, forbid us tamely to surrender that freedom which we received from our gallant ancestors, and which our innocent posterity have a right to receive from us. We cannot endure the infamy and guilt of resigning succeeding generations to that wretchedness which inevitably awaits them, if we basely entail hereditary bondage upon them.

Our cause is just. Our union is perfect. Our internal resources are great, and, if necessary, foreign assistance is undoubtedly attainable.—We gratefully acknowledge, as signal instances of the Divine favour towards us, that his Providence would not permit us to be called into this severe controversy, until we were grown up to our present strength, had been previously exercised in warlike operation, and possessed of the means of defending ourselves. With hearts fortified with these animating reflections, we most solemnly, before God and the world, declare, that, exerting the utmost energy of those powers, which our beneficent Creator hath graciously bestowed upon us, the arms we have been compelled by our enemies to assume, we will, in defiance of every hazard, with unabating firmness and perseverance, employ for the preservation of our liberties; being with one mind resolved to die freemen rather than to live slaves.

Lest this declaration should disquiet the minds of our friends and fellow-subjects in any part of the empire, we assure them that we mean not to dissolve that union which has so long and so happily subsisted between us, and which we sincerely wish to see restored.—Necessity has not yet driven us into that desperate measure, or induced us to excite any other nation to war against them.—We have not raised armies with ambitious designs of separating from Great-Britain, and establishing independent states. We fight not for glory or for conquest. We exhibit to mankind the remarkable spectacle of a people attacked by unprovoked enemies, without any imputation or even suspicion of offence. They boast of their privileges and civilization, and yet proffer no milder conditions than servitude or death.

In our own native land, in defence of the freedom that is our birth-right, and which we ever enjoyed till the late violation of it—for the protection of our property, acquired solely by the honest industry of our fore-fathers and ourselves, against violence actually offered, we have taken up arms. We shall lay them down when hostilities shall cease on the part of the aggressors, and all danger of their being renewed shall be removed, and not before.

With an humble confidence in the mercies of the supreme and impartial Judge and Ruler of the Universe, we most devoutly implore his divine goodness to protect us happily through this great conflict, to dispose our adversaries to reconciliation on reasonable terms, and thereby to relieve the empire from the calamities of civil war.

By order of Congress

JOHN HANCOCK
President.

62. PROCLAMATION OF REBELLION
August 23, 1775

(Force's *American Archives,* Fourth Series, Vol. III, p. 240)

Despite Lexington and Concord and Bunker Hill, the moderates in the Continental Congress still hoped for a reconciliation. Two days after Bunker Hill, Dickinson, the leader of the moderates, reported a draft for a final petition to the King; this was accepted by Congress July 8, 1775, and Richard Penn was authorized to present it to the King. The news of American resistance, however, determined the King to proclaim a state of rebellion. News of the Proclamation arrived in America October 31. See, R. Frothingham, *Rise of the Republic of the United States*, p. 435 ff.; C. J. Stillé, *Life and Times of John Dickinson*, Vol. I; J. Fiske, *The American Revolution*, Vol. I, ch. v.

A PROCLAMATION BY THE KING FOR SUP-
    PRESSING REBELLION AND SEDITION
GEORGE R.

Whereas many of our subjects in divers parts of our Colonies and Plantations in *North America*, misled by dangerous and ill designing men, and forgetting the allegiance which they owe to the power that has protected and supported them; after various disorderly acts committed in disturbance of the publick peace, to the obstruction of lawful commerce, and to the oppression of our loyal subjects carrying on the same; have at length proceeded to open and avowed rebellion, by arraying themselves in a hostile manner, to withstand the execution of the law, and traitorously preparing, ordering and levying war against us: And whereas, there is reason to apprehend that such rebellion hath been much promoted and encouraged by the traitorous correspondence, counsels and comfort of divers wicked and desperate persons within this realm: To the end therefore, that none of our subjects may neglect or violate their duty through ignorance thereof, or through any doubt of the

protection which the law will afford to their loyalty and zeal, we have thought fit, by and with the advice of our Privy Council, to issue our Royal Proclamation, hereby declaring, that not only all our Officers, civil and military, are obliged to exert their utmost endeavours to suppress such rebellion, and to bring the traitors to justice, but that all our subjects of this Realm, and the dominions thereunto belonging, are bound by law to be aiding and assisting in the suppression of such rebellion, and to disclose and make known all traitorous conspiracies and attempts against us, our crown and dignity; and we do accordingly strictly charge and command all our Officers, as well civil as military, and all others our obedient and loyal subjects, to use their utmost endeavours to withstand and suppress such rebellion, and to disclose and make known all treasons and traitorous conspiracies which they shall know to be against us, our crown and dignity; and for that purpose, that they transmit to one of our principal Secretaries of State, or other proper officer, due and full information of all persons who shall be found carrying on correspondence with, or in any manner or degree aiding or abetting the persons now in open arms and rebellion against our Government, within any of our Colonies and Plantations in *North America*, in order to bring to condign punishment the authors, prepetrators, and abetters of such traitorous designs.

Given at our Court at *St. James's* the twenty-third day of *August*, one thousand seven hundred and seventy-five, in the fifteenth year of our reign.

GOD *save the* KING.

63. THE MOVEMENT FOR INDEPENDENCE

Instructions from the Town of Malden, Massachusetts, for a Declaration
of Independence
May 27, 1776

(H. Niles, ed. *Principles and Acts of the Revolution,* 1822 ed. p. 156-7)

On May 9 the Massachusetts House of Representatives, then sitting at Watertown, appointed a committee to bring in a resolve that the Towns of the colony instruct their representatives with respect to independence. The following day the House resolved that "The Inhabitants of each Town, in this Colony, ought in full Meeting warned for that Purpose, to advise the Person or Persons who shall be

chosen to Represent them in the next General Court, whether if the honorable Congress should, for the Safety of the said Colonies, declare them Independent of the Kingdom of Great-Britain, they the said Inhabitants will solemnly engage with their Lives and Fortunes to Support the Congress in the Measure." The instructions from Malden are typical of many voted by the towns of Massachusetts. See A. B.

Hart, ed. *Commonwealth History of Massachusetts*, Vol. III, p. 93 ff.; K. Colegrove, "New England Town Mandates", Colonial Society of Massachusetts, *Publications*, Vol. XXI, p. 411 ff.

At a legal meeting of the inhabitants of the town of Malden, (Mass.), May 27, 1776, it was voted unanimously that the following instructions be given to their represenative, viz. to Mr Ezra Sargeant.

Sir—A resolution of the hon. house of representatives, calling upon the several towns in this colony to express their minds in respect to the important question of American independence, is the occasion of our now instructing you. The time was, sir, when we loved the king and the people of Great Britain with an affection truly filial; we felt ourselves interested in their glory; we shared in their joys and sorrows; we cheerfully poured the fruit of all our labours into the lap of our mother country, and without reluctance expended our blood and our treasure in their cause.

These were our sentiments toward Great Britain while she continued to act the part of a parent state; we felt ourselves happy in our connection with her, nor wished it to be dissolved; but our sentiments are altered, it is now the ardent wish of our soul that America may become a free and independent state.

A sense of unprovoked injuries will arouse the resentment of the most peaceful. Such injuries these colonies have received from Britain. Unjustifiable claims have been made by the king and his minions to tax us without our consent; these claims have been prosecuted in a manner cruel and unjust to the highest degree. The frantic policy of administration hath induced them to send fleets and armies to America; that, by depriving us of our trade, and cutting the throats of our brethren, they might awe us into submission, and erect a system of despotism in America, which should so far enlarge the influence of the crown as to enable it to rivet their shackles upon the people of Great Britain.

This plan was brought to a crisis upon the ever memorable nineteenth of April. We remember the fatal day! the expiring groans of our countrymen yet vibrate on our ears! and we now behold the flames of their peaceful dwellings ascending to Heaven! we hear their blood crying to us from the ground for vengeance! charging us, as we value the peace of their names, to have no further connection with—,who can unfeelingly hear of the slaughter of—, and composedly sleep with their blood upon his soul. The manner in which the war has been prosecuted hath confirmed us in these sentiments; piracy and murder, robbery and breach of faith, have been conspicuous in the conduct of the king's troops: defenceless towns have been attacked and destroyed: the ruins of Charlestown, which are daily in our view, daily reminds of this: the cries of the widow and the orphan demand our attention; they demand that the hand of pity should wipe the tear from their eye, and that the sword of their country should avenge their wrongs. We long entertained hope that the spirit of the British nation would once more induce them to assert their own and our rights, and bring to condign punishment the elevated villains who have trampled upon the sacred rights of men and affronted the majesty of the people. We hoped in vain; they have lost their love to freedom, they have lost their spirit of just resentment; we therefore renounce with disdain our connexion with a kingdom of slaves; we bid a final adieu to Britain.

Could an accommodation now be effected, we have reason to think that it would be fatal to the liberties of America; we should soon catch the contagion of venality and dissipation, which hath Britains to lawless domination. Were we placed in the situation we were in 1763: were the powers of appointing to offices, and commanding the militia, in the hands of governors, our arts, trade and manufactures, would be cramped; nay, more than this, the life of every man who has been active in the cause of his country would be endangered.

For these reasons, as well as many others which might be produced, we are confirmed in the opinion, that the present age would be deficient in their duty to God, their posterity and themselves, if they do not establish an American republic. This is the only form of government which we wish to see established; for we can never be willingly subject to any other King than he who, being possessed of infinite wisdom, goodness and rectitude, is alone fit to possess unlimited power.

We have freely spoken our sentiments upon this important subject, but we mean not to dictate; we have unbounded confidence in the wisdom and uprightness of the continental congress: with pleasure we recollect that this affair is under their direc-

tion; and we now instruct you, sir, to give them the strongest assurance, that, if they should declare America to be a free and independent republic, your constituents will support and defend the measure, to the last drop of their blood, and the last farthing of their treasure.

64. MECKLENBURG COUNTY RESOLUTIONS
May 20, 1775

(Documents Illustrative of the Formation of the Union of the American States, p. 6 ff.)

These resolutions, adopted in Charlotte Town, Mecklenburg County, North Carolina, were entrusted to the North Carolina delegation to the Continental Congress, but never presented. In 1819 an account of these resolutions was published, embellished with phrases taken from the Declaration of Independence; this spurious account gave rise to the persistent myth of the Mecklenburg "Declaration of Independence." Subsequent investigation indicated that no such "declaration" had been adopted at the time, and established the real character of the resolutions. See, W. H. Hoyt, *Mecklenberg Declaration of Independence;* E. W. Sikes, *Transition of North Carolina from Colony to Commonwealth;* J. Fiske, *The American Revolution,* Vol. I, p. 150 ff.

This day the Committee met, and passed the following

RESOLVES

Whereas by an address presented to his Majesty by both Houses of Parliament in February last, the American Colonies are declared to be in a State of actual Rebellion, we conceive that all Laws and Commissions confirmed by, or derived from the Authority of the King or Parliament, are annulled and vacated, and the former civil Constitution of these Colonies for the present wholly suspended. To provide in some degree for the Exigencies of the County in the present alarming Period, we deem it proper and necessary to pass the following Resolves, *viz.*

1. That all Commissions, civil and military, heretofore granted by the Crown, to be exercised in these Colonies, are null and void, and the Constitution of each particular Colony wholly suspended.
2. That the Provincial Congress of each

Province, under the Direction of the Great Continental Congress, is invested with all legislative and executive Powers within their respective Provinces; and that no other Legislative or Executive does or can exist, at this Time, in any of these Colonies.
3. As all former Laws are now suspended in this Province, and the Congress have not yet provided others, we judge it necessary, for the better Preservation of good Order, to form certain Rules and Regulations for the internal Government of this County, until Laws shall be provided for us by the Congress.
4. That the Inhabitants of this County do meet on a certain Day appointed by this Committee, and having formed themselves into nine Companies, to *wit,* eight for the County and one for the Town of *Charlotte,* do choose a Colonel and other military Officers, who shall hold and exercise their several Powers by Virtue of this Choice, and independent of *Great-Britain,* and former Constitution of this Province.
5. That for the better Preservation of the Peace and Administration of Justice, each of these Companies do choose from their own Body two discreet Freeholders, who shall be impowered each by himself, and singly, to decide and determine all Matters of Controversy arising within the said Company under the Sum of Twenty Shillings, and jointly and together all Controversies under the Sum of Forty Shillings, yet so as their Decisions may admit of Appeals to the Convention of the Select Men of the whole County; and also, that any one of these shall have Power to examine, and commit to Confinement, Persons accused of Petit Larceny.

6. That those two Select Men, thus chosen, do, jointly and together, choose from the Body of their particular Company two Persons, properly qualified to serve as Constables, who may assist them in the Execution of their Office.

7. That upon the Complaint of any Person to either of these Select Men, he do issue his Warrant, directed to the Constable, commanding him to bring the Aggressor before him or them to answer the said Complaint.

8. That these eighteen Select Men, thus appointed, to meet every third Tuesday in January, April, July, and October, at the Courthouse in *Charlotte*, to hear and determine all Matters of Controversy for Sums exceeding Forty Shillings; also Appeals: and in Cases of Felony, to commit the Person or Persons convicted thereof to close Confinement, until the Provincial Congress shall provide and establish Laws and Modes of Proceeding in all such Cases.

9. That these Eighteen Select Men, thus convened, do choose a Clerk to record the Transactions of said Convention; and that the said Clerk, upon the Application of any Persons or Persons aggrieved, do issue his Warrant to one of the Constables, to summons and warn said Offender to appear before the Convention at their next sitting, to answer the aforesaid Complaint.

10. That any Person making complaint under Oath to the Clerk, or any Member of the Convention, that he has reason to suspect that any Person or Persons indebted to him in a Sum above Forty Shillings, do intend clandestinely to withdraw from the County without paying such Debt; the Clerk, or such Member, shall issue his Warrant to the Constable, commanding him to take the said Person or Persons into safe Custody, until the next sitting of the Convention. . . .

12. That all Receivers and Collectors of Quitrents, Public and County Taxes, do pay the same into the Hands of the Chairman of this Committee, to be by them disbursed as the public Exigencies may require. And that such Receivers and Collectors proceed no farther in their Office until they be approved of by, and have given to this Committee good and sufficient Security for a faithful Return of such Monies when collected. . . .

14. That all these Officers hold their Commissions during the Pleasure of their respective Constituents.

15. That this Committee will sustain all Damages that may ever hereafter accrue to all or any of these Officers thus appointed, and thus acting, on Account of their Obedience and Conformity to these Resolves.

16. That whatever person shall hereafter receive a Commission from the Crown, or attempt to exercise any such Commission heretofore received, shall be deemed an Enemy to his Country; and upon Information being made to the Captain of the Company where he resides, the said Captain shall cause him to be apprehended, and conveyed before the two Select Men of the said Company, who upon Proof of the Fact shall commit him the said Offender, into safe Custody, until the next sitting of the Convention who shall deal with him as Prudence may direct.

17. That any Person refusing to yield Obedience to the above Resolves shall be deemed equally criminal and liable to the same Punishments as the Offenders above last mentioned.

18. That these Resolves be in full Force and Virtue, until Instructions from the General Congress of this Province, regulating the Jurisprudence of this Province, shall provide otherwise, or the legislative body of *Great-Britain* resign its unjust and arbitrary Pretentions with Respect to America.

19. That the several Militia Companies in this county do provide themselves with proper Arms and Accoutrements, and hold themselves in Readiness to execute the commands and Directions of the Provincial Congress, and of this committee.

20. That this committee do appoint Colonel Thomas Polk, and Doctor Joseph Kennedy, to purchase 300 lb. of Powder, 600 lb. of Lead, and 1000 Flints, and deposit the same in some safe place, hereafter to be appointed by the committee.

Signed by Order of the Committee.

EPH. BREVARD, Clerk of the Committee.

65. RESOLUTION FOR INDEPENDENCE
June 7, 1776

(Journals of the Continental Congress, ed. by W. C. Ford, Vol. V, p. 425)

These resolutions were introduced by Richard Henry Lee of Virginia and seconded by John Adams. The first resolution was not voted until July 2; the others were acted upon later. See, R. Frothingham, *Rise of the Republic of the United States,* p. 513 ff.

RESOLVED, That these United Colonies are, and of right ought to be, free and independent States, that they are absolved from all allegiance to the British Crown, and that all political connection between them and the State of Great Britain is, and ought to be totally dissolved.

That it is expedient forthwith to take the most effectual measures for forming foreign Alliances.

That a plan of confederation be prepared and transmitted to the respective Colonies for their consideration and approbation.

66. THE DECLARATION OF INDEPENDENCE
July 4, 1776

(F. N. Thorpe, ed. *Federal and State Constitutions,* Vol. I, p. 3 ff. The text is taken from the version in the Revised Statutes of the United States, 1878 ed., and has been collated with the facsimile of the original as printed in the original Journal of the old Congress.)

On June 7, 1776, Richard Henry Lee of Virginia introduced three resolutions one of which stated that the "colonies are, and of right ought to be, free and independent States." On the 10th a committee was appointed to prepare a declaration of independence; the committee consisted of Jefferson, John Adams, Franklin, Sherman and R. R. Livingston. This committee brought in its draft on the 28th of June, and on the 2nd of July a resolution declaring independence was adopted. July 4 the Declaration of Independence was agreed to, engrossed, signed by Hancock, and sent to the legislatures of the States. The engrossed copy of the Declaration was signed by all but one signer on August 2. On the Declaration, see C. L. Becker, *The Declaration of Independence,* esp. ch. v with its analysis of Jefferson's draft; H. Friedenwald, *The Declaration of Independence;* J. H. Hazelton, *Declaration of Independence;* J. Sanderson, *Lives of the Signers to the Declaration;* R. Frothingham, *Rise of the Republic,* ch. xi.; C. H. Van Tyne, *The War of Independence, American Phase.*

In Congress, July 4, 1776,

THE UNANIMOUS DECLARATION OF THE THIRTEEN UNITED STATES OF AMERICA,

When in the Course of human events, it becomes necessary for one people to dissolve the political bands which have connected them with another, and to assume among the Powers of the earth, the separate and equal station to which the Laws of Nature and of Nature's God entitle them, a decent respect to the opinions of mankind requires that they should declare the causes which impel them to the separation.

We hold these truths to be self-evident, that all men are created equal, that they are endowed by their Creator with certain unalienable Rights, that among these are Life, Liberty and the pursuit of Happiness. That to secure these rights, Governments are instituted among Men, deriving their just powers from the consent of the governed, That whenever any Form of Government becomes destructive of these ends, it is the Right of the People to alter or to abolish it, and to institute new Government, laying its foundation on such principles and organizing its powers in such form, as to them shall seem most likely to effect their Safety and Happiness. Prudence, indeed, will dictate that Governments long established should not be changed for light and transient causes; and accordingly all experience hath shown, that mankind are more disposed to suffer, while evils are sufferable, than to right themselves by abolishing the forms to which they are accustomed. But when a long train of abuses and usurpations, pursuing invariably the same Object evinces a design to reduce them under absolute Despotism, it is their right, it is their duty, to throw off such Government, and to provide new Guards for their future security.—Such has been the patient sufferance of these Colonies; and such is now the necessity which constrains them to alter their former Systems of Government. The history of the present King of Great Britain is a history of repeated injuries and usurpations, all having in direct object the establishment of an absolute Tyranny over these States. To prove this, let Facts be submitted to a candid world.

He has refused his Assent to Laws, the most wholesome and necessary for the public good.

He has forbidden his Governors to pass Laws of immediate and pressing importance, unless suspended in their operation till his Assent should be obtained; and when so suspended, he has utterly neglected to attend to them.

He has refused to pass other Laws for the accommodation of large districts of people, unless those people would relinquish the right of Representation in the Legislature, a right inestimable to them and formidable to tyrants only.

He has called together legislative bodies at places unusual, uncomfortable, and distant from the depository of their Public Records, for the sole purpose of fatiguing them into compliance with his measures.

He has dissolved Representative Houses repeatedly, for opposing with manly firmness his invasions on the rights of the people.

He has refused for a long time, after such dissolutions, to cause others to be elected; whereby the Legislative Powers, incapable of Annihilation, have returned to the People at large for their exercise; the State remaining in the mean time exposed to all the dangers of invasion from without, and convulsions within.

He has endeavoured to prevent the population of these States; for that purpose obstructing the Laws of Naturalization of Foreigners; refusing to pass others to encourage their migration hither, and raising the conditions of new Appropriations of Lands.

He has obstructed the Administration of Justice, by refusing his Assent to Laws for establishing Judiciary Powers.

He has made Judges dependent on his Will alone, for the tenure of their offices, and the amount and payment of their salaries.

He has erected a multitude of New Offices, and sent hither swarms of Officers to harass our People, and eat out their substance.

He has kept among us, in times of peace, Standing Armies without the Consent of our legislature.

He has affected to render the Military independent of and superior to the Civil Power.

He has combined with others to subject us to a jurisdiction foreign to our constitution, and unacknowledged by our laws; giving his Assent to their acts of pretended legislation:

For quartering large bodies of armed troops among us:

For protecting them, by a mock Trial, from Punishment for any Murders which they should commit on the Inhabitants of these States:

For cutting off our Trade with all parts of the world:

For imposing taxes on us without our Consent:

For depriving us in many cases, of the benefits of Trial by Jury:

For transporting us beyond Seas to be tried for pretended offences:

For abolishing the free System of English Laws in a neighbouring Province, establishing therein an Arbitrary government, and enlarging its Boundaries so as to render it at once an example and fit instrument for introducing the same absolute rule into these Colonies:

For taking away our Charters, abolishing our most valuable Laws, and altering fundamentally the Forms of our Governments:

For suspending our own Legislature, and declaring themselves invested with Power to legislate for us in all cases whatsoever.

He has abdicated Government here, by declaring us out of his Protection and waging War against us.

He has plundered our seas, ravaged our Coasts, burnt our towns, and destroyed the lives of our people.

He is at this time transporting large armies of foreign mercenaries to compleat the works of death, desolation and tyranny, already begun with circumstances of Cruelty & perfidy scarcely paralleled in the most barbarous ages, and totally unworthy the Head of a civilized nation.

He has constrained our fellow Citizens taken Captive on the high Seas to bear Arms against their Country, to become the executioners of their friends and Brethren, or to fall themselves by their Hands.

He has excited domestic insurrections amongst us, and has endeavoured to bring on the inhabitants of our frontiers, the merciless Indian Savages, whose known rule of warfare, is an undistinguished destruction of all ages, sexes and conditions.

In every stage of these Oppressions We have Petitioned for Redress in the most humble terms: Our repeated Petitions have been answered only by repeated injury. A Prince, whose character is thus marked by every act which may define a Tyrant, is unfit to be the ruler of a free People.

Nor have We been wanting in attention to our Brittish brethren. We have warned them from time to time of attempts by their legislature to extend an unwarrantable jurisdiction over us. We have reminded them of the circumstances of our emigration and settlement here. We have appealed to their native justice and magnanimity, and we have conjured them by the ties of our common kindred to disavow these usurpations, which, would inevitably interrupt our connections and correspondence. They too have been deaf to the voice of justice and of consanguinity. We must, therefore, acquiesce in the necessity, which denounces our Separation, and hold them, as we hold the rest of mankind, Enemies in War, in Peace Friends.

We, therefore, the Representatives of the united States of America, in General Congress, Assembled, appealing to the Supreme Judge of the world for the rectitude of our intentions, do, in the Name, and by Authority of the good People of these Colonies, solemnly publish and declare, That these United Colonies are, and of Right ought to be Free and Independent States; that they are Absolved from all Allegiance to the British Crown, and that all political connection between them and the State of Great Britain, is and ought to be totally dissolved; and that as Free and Independent States, they have full Power to levy War, conclude Peace, contract Alliances, establish Commerce, and to do all other Acts and Things which Independent States may of right do. And for the support of this Declaration, with a firm reliance on the Protection of Divine Providence, we mutually pledge to each other our Lives, our Fortunes and our sacred Honor.

JOHN HANCOCK.

New Hampshire
JOSIAH BARTLETT,
WM. WHIPPLE,
MATTHEW THORNTON.

Massachusetts-Bay
SAML. ADAMS,
JOHN ADAMS,
ROBT. TREAT PAINE,
ELBRIDGE GERRY.

Rhode Island
STEP. HOPKINS,
WILLIAM ELLERY.

Connecticut
ROGER SHERMAN,
SAM'EL HUNTINGTON,
WM. WILLIAMS,
OLIVER WOLCOTT.

New York
WM. FLOYD,
PHIL. LIVINGSTON,
FRANS. LEWIS,
LEWIS MORRIS.

Pennsylvania
ROBT. MORRIS,
BENJAMIN RUSH,
BENJA. FRANKLIN,
JOHN MORTON,
GEO. CLYMER,
JAS. SMITH,
GEO. TAYLOR,
JAMES WILSON,
GEO. ROSS.

Delaware
CAESAR RODNEY,
GEO. READ,
THO. M'KEAN.

Georgia
  BUTTON GWINNETT,
  LYMAN HALL,
  GEO. WALTON.

Maryland
  SAMUEL CHASE,
  WM. PACA,
  THOS. STONE,
  CHARLES CARROLL of Carrollton.

Virginia
  GEORGE WYTHE,
  RICHARD HENRY LEE,
  TH. JEFFERSON,
  BENJA. HARRISON,
  THS. NELSON, JR.,
  FRANCIS LIGHTFOOT LEE,
  CARTER BRAXTON.

North Carolina
  WM. HOOPER,
  JOSEPH HEWES,
  JOHN PENN.

South Carolina
  EDWARD RUTLEDGE,
  THOS. HEYWARD, JUNR.,
  THOMAS LYNCH, JUNR.,
  ARTHUR MIDDLETON.

New Jersey
  RICHD. STOCKTON,
  JNO. WITHERSPOON,
  FRAS. HOPKINSON,
  JOHN HART,
  ABRA. CLARK.

67. THE VIRGINIA BILL OF RIGHTS
June 12, 1776

(Poore, ed. *The Federal and State Constitutions,* Part. II, p. 1908–9)

This most famous of the Declarations of Rights of the original state constitutions was drafted by George Mason and adopted with slight changes and two additions, by the Virginia Convention of 1776. It exerted a wide influence not only in this country but in France. The article on religious freedom was drafted by Patrick Henry. See, K. Rowland, *Life of George Mason,* 2 Vols.; H. B. Grigsby, *The Virginia Convention of 1776;* G. Jellinek, *The Declaration of the Rights of Man;* B. Faÿ, *Revolutionary Spirit in France and America,* p. 263 ff.

A declaration of rights made by the representatives of the good people of Virginia, assembled in full and free convention; which rights do pertain to them and their posterity, as the basis and foundation of government.

1. That all men are by nature equally free and independent, and have certain inherent rights, of which, when they enter into a state of society, they cannot by any compact deprive or divest their posterity; namely, the enjoyment of life and liberty, with the means of acquiring and possessing property, and pursuing and obtaining happiness and safety.

2. That all power is vested in, and consequently derived from, the people; that magis-

trates are their trustees and servants, and at all times amenable to them.

3. That government is, or ought to be instituted for the common benefit, protection, and security of the people, nation, or community; of all the various modes and forms of government, that is best which is capable of producing the greatest degree of happiness and safety, and is most effectually secured against the danger of maladministration; and that when any government shall be found inadequate or contrary to these purposes, a majority of the community hath an indubitable, unalienable and indefeasible right to reform, alter or abolish it, in such manner as shall be judged most conducive to the public weal.

4. That no man, or set of men, are entitled to exclusive or separate emoluments or privileges from the community, but in consideration of publick services; which, not being descendible, neither ought the offices of magistrate, legislator or judge to be hereditary.

5. That the legislative and executive powers of the state should be separate and distinct from the judiciary; and that the members of the two first may be restrained from oppression, by feeling and participating the

burthens of the people, they should, at fixed periods, be reduced to a private station, return into that body from which they were originally taken, and the vacancies be supplied by frequent, certain, and regular elections, in which all, or any part of the former members to be again eligible or ineligible, as the laws shall direct.

6. That elections of members to serve as representatives of the people in assembly, ought to be free; and that all men having sufficient evidence of permanent common interest with, and attachment to the community, have the right of suffrage, and cannot be taxed or deprived of their property for publick uses, without their own consent, or that of their representatives so elected, nor bound by any law to which they have not, in like manner, assented for the public good.

7. That all power of suspending laws, or the execution of laws, by any authority without consent of the representatives of the people, is injurious to their rights, and ought not to be exercised.

8. That in all capital or criminal prosecutions a man hath a right to demand the cause and nature of his accusation, to be confronted with the accusers and witnesses, to call for evidence in his favour, and to a speedy trial by an impartial jury of his vicinage, without whose unanimous consent he cannot be found guilty; nor can he be compelled to give evidence against himself; that no man be deprived of his liberty, except by the law of the land or the judgment of his peers.

9. That excessive bail ought not to be required, nor excessive fines imposed, nor cruel and unusual punishments inflicted.

10. That general warrants, whereby an officer or messenger may be commanded to search suspected places without evidence of a fact committed, or to seize any person or persons not named, or whose offence is not particularly described and supported by evidence, are grievous and oppressive, and ought not to be granted.

11. That in controversies respecting property, and in suits between man and man, the ancient trial by jury is preferable to any other, and ought to be held sacred.

12. That the freedom of the press is one of the great bulwarks of liberty, and can never be restrained but by despotick governments.

13. That a well-regulated militia, composed of the body of the people trained to arms, is the proper, natural and safe defence of a free state; that standing armies in time of peace should be avoided as dangerous to liberty; and that in all cases the military should be under strict subordination to, and governed by, the civil power.

14. That the people have a right to uniform government; and, therefore, that no government separate from, or independent of the government of Virginia, ought to be erected or established within the limits thereof.

15. That no free government, or the blessings of liberty, can be preserved to any people, but by a firm adherence to justice, moderation, temperance, frugality and virtue, and by frequent recurrence to fundamental principles.

16. That religion, or the duty which we owe to our Creator, and the manner of discharging it, can be directed only by reason and conviction, not by force or violence; and therefore all men are equally entitled to the free exercise of religion, according to the dictates of conscience; and that it is the mutual duty of all to practise Christian forbearance, love, and charity towards each other.

68. THE CONCORD TOWN MEETING DEMANDS A CONSTITUTIONAL CONVENTION

Resolutions of the Concord Town Meeting
October 21, 1776

(Facsimile in Massachusetts, *Manual of the Constitutional Convention, 1917*)

As early as May 10, 1776 Congress had passed a resolution advising the colonies to form new governments "such as shall best conduce to the happiness and safety of their constituents." The actual transformation of Colony into Commonwealth, however, was a task that challenged the talents of the wisest statesmen. How could governments be established in harmony with the principles of the Revolution; how could the theory that government originates with the people be transformed into reality? The first suggestion of the method eventually perfected by Americans—the constitutional convention— came from the town of Concord. The advice of the Concord Town Meeting, however, was not followed in the construction of the first Massachusetts constitution. Not until 1779 did Massachusetts work out a system in harmony with the Concord Resolutions. See, S. E. Morison, "History of the Constitution of Massachusetts" in *Manual of the Constitutional Convention of 1917.*

At a meeting of the Inhabitants of the Town of Concord being free & twenty one years of age and upward, met by adjournment on the twenty first Day of october 1776 to take into Consideration a Resolve of the Honourable house of Representatives of this State on the 17th of September Last the Town Resolved as followes—

Resolve 1st: That this State being at Present destitute of a Properly established form of Government, it is absolutely necessary that one should be emmediatly formed and established.

Resolved 2. That the Supreme Legislative, either in their Proper Capacity or in Joint Committee, are by no means a body proper to form & Establish a Constitution or form of Government; for Reasons following. first Because we Conceive that a Constitution in its Proper Idea intends a System of Principles Established to Secure the Subject in the Possession & enjoyment of their Rights & Priviliges, against any Encroachments of the Governing Part. 2—Because the Same Body that forms a Constitution have of Consequence a power to alter it. 3—because a Constitution alterable by the Supreme Legislative is no Security at all to the Subject against any Encroachment of the Governing part on any, or on all of their Rights and priviliges.

Resolved 3d. That it appears to this Town highly necessary & Expedient that a Convention, or Congress be immediately Chosen, to form & establish a Constitution, by the inhabitants of the Respective Towns in this State, being free & of twenty-one years of age and upward, in Proportion as the Representatives of this State formerly were Chosen: the Convention or Congress not to Consist of a greater number than the house of assembly of this State heretofore might Consist of, Except that each Town & District shall have the Liberty to Send one Representative, or otherwise as Shall appear meet to the Inhabitants of this State in General.

Resolve 4th. that when the Convention or Congress have formed a Constitution they adjourn for a Short time and Publish their Proposed Constitution for the Inspection and Remarks of the Inhabitants of this State.

Resolved 5ly. that the honourable house of assembly of this State be Desired to Recommend it to the Inhabitents of the State to Proceed to Chuse a Convention or Congress for the Purpas abovesaid as soon as Possable.

CONCORD, October the 22d, 1776.

69. TREATY OF ALLIANCE WITH FRANCE
February 6, 1778

(Malloy, ed. *Treaties, Conventions, etc.*, Vol. I, p. 479 ff.)

This was one of two treaties concluded by the American Commissioners, Franklin, Deane, and Lee; the other was a Treaty of Amity and Commerce. The Treaty of Alliance was not warranted by the instructions from Congress, but Congress ratified it May 4, 1778. This was the first treaty of alliance ever made by the United States. The literature on the American diplomatic negotiations with France and the Treaty of Alliance is voluminous: see, F. Wharton, *Diplomatic Correspondence of the* *American Revolution,* Vol. I; W. H. Trescot, *Diplomacy of the American Revolution;* E. S. Corwin, *French Policy and the American Alliance of 1778;* J. B. Perkins, *France in the American Revolution;* E. E. Hale, *Franklin in France;* and the monumental work of H. Doniol, *Histoire de la Participation de la France à l'Établissement des États-Unis d'Amérique,* 5 Vols.

ART. I.—If war should break out between France and Great Britain during the continuance of the present war between the United States and England, His Majesty and the said United States shall make it a common cause and aid each other mutually with their good offices, their counsels and their forces, according to the exigence of conjunctures, as becomes good and faithful allies.

ART. II.—The essential and direct end of the present defensive alliance is to maintain effectually the liberty, sovereignty and independence absolute and unlimited, of the said United States, as well in matters of government as of commerce.

ART. III.—The two contracting parties shall each on its own part, and in the manner it may judge most proper, make all the efforts in its power against their common enemy, in order to attain the end proposed.

ART. IV.—The contracting parties agree that in case either of them should form any particular enterprise in which the concurrence of the other may be desired, the party whose concurrence is desired, shall readily, and with good faith, join to act in concert for that purpose, as far as circumstances and its own particular situation will permit; and in that case, they shall regulate, by a particular convention, the quantity and kind of succour to be furnished, and the time and manner of its being brought into action, as well as the advantages which are to be its compensation.

ART. V.—If the United States should think fit to attempt the reduction of the British power, remaining in the northern parts of America, or the islands of Bermudas, those countries or islands, in case of success, shall be confederated with or dependent upon the said United States.

ART. VI.—The Most Christian King renounces forever the possession of the islands of Bermudas, as well as of any part of the continent of North America, which before the treaty of Paris in 1763, or in virtue of that treaty, were acknowledged to belong to the Crown of Great Britain, or to the United States, heretofore called British Colonies, or which are at this time, or have lately been under the power of the King and Crown of Great Britain.

ART. VII.—If His Most Christian Majesty shall think proper to attack any of the islands situated in the Gulph of Mexico, or near that Gulph, which are at present under the power of Great Britain, all the said isles, in case of success, shall appertain to the Crown of France.

ART. VIII.—Neither of the two parties shall conclude either truce or peace with Great Britain without the formal consent of the other first obtained; and they mutually engage not to lay down their arms until the independence of the United States shall have been formally or tacitly assured by the treaty or treaties that shall terminate the war.

ART. IX.—The contracting parties declare, that being resolved to fulfil each on its own part the clauses and conditions of the present treaty of alliance, according to its own power and circumstances, there shall be no afterclaim of compensation on one side or the other, whatever may be the event of the war.

ART. X.—The Most Christian King and the United States agree to invite or admit other powers who may have received injuries from England, to make common cause with them, and to accede to the present alliance, under such conditions as shall be freely agreed to and settled between all the parties.

ART. XI.—The two parties guarantee mutually from the present time and forever against all other powers, to wit: The United States to His Most Christian Majesty, the present possessions of the Crown of France in America, as well as those which it may acquire by the future treaty of peace: And His Most Christian Majesty guarantees on his part to the United States their liberty, sovereignty and independence, absolute and unlimited, as well in matters of government as commerce, and also their possessions, and the additions or conquests that their confederation may obtain during the war, from any of the dominions now, or heretofore possessed by Great Britain in North America, conformable to the 5th and 6th articles above written, the whole as their possessions shall be fixed and assured to the said States, at the moment of the cessation of their present war with England.

ART. XII.—In order to fix more precisely the sense and application of the preceding article, the contracting parties declare, that in case of a rupture between France and England the reciprocal guarantee declared in the said article shall have its full force and effect the moment such war shall break out; and if such rupture shall not take place, the mutual obligations of the said guarantee shall not commence until the moment of the cessation of the present war between the United States and England shall have ascertained their possessions. . . .

Done at Paris, this sixth day of February, one thousand seven hundred and seventy-eight.

70. MASSACHUSETTS BILL OF RIGHTS
1780

(Poore, ed. *The Federal and State Constitutions*, Part. I, p. 956 ff.)

The Constitution of Massachusetts of 1778 had contained no Bill of Rights; when submitted to the vote of the freemen it was defeated by an overwhelming majority. John Adams was the chief architect of the constitution of 1780. He was responsible for the whole of the Bill of Rights with the exception of the article on Religious Freedom. See S. E. Morison in *Manual of the Constitutional Convention of 1917;* A. Nevins, *American States During and After the Revolution,* ch. v; C. F. Adams, *Life of John Adams,* ch. vi. On the Revolutionary Bills of Rights, see Doc. No. 67.

The end of the institution, maintenance, and administration of government, is to secure the existence of the body-politic, to protect it, and to furnish the individuals who compose it with the power of enjoying in safety and tranquillity their natural rights, and the blessings of life: and whenever these great objects are not obtained, the people have a right to alter the government, and to take measures necessary for their safety, prosperity, and happiness.

The body-politic is formed by a voluntary association of individuals; it is a social compact by which the whole people covenants with each citizen and each citizen with the whole people that all shall be governed by certain laws for the common good. It is the duty of the people, therefore, in framing a constitution of government, to provide for an equitable mode of making laws, as well as for an impartial interpretation and a faithful execution of them; that every man may, at all times, find his security in them.

We, therefore, the people of Massachusetts, acknowledging, with grateful hearts, the goodness of the great Legislator of the universe, in affording us, in the course of His Providence, an opportunity, deliberately and peaceably, without fraud, violence, or surprise, of entering into an original, explicit, and solemn compact with each other; and of forming a new constitution of civil government, for ourselves and posterity; and devoutly imploring His direction in so interesting a design, do agree upon, ordain, and establish, the following Declaration of Rights, and Frame of Government, as the Constitution of the Commonwealth of Massachusetts.

PART THE FIRST

A DECLARATION OF THE RIGHTS OF THE INHABITANTS OF THE COMMONWEALTH OF MASSACHUSETTS

ARTICLE I. All men are born free and equal, and have certain natural, essential, and unalienable rights; among which may be reckoned the right of enjoying and defending their lives and liberties; that of acquiring, possessing, and protecting property; in fine, that of seeking and obtaining their safety and happiness.

II. It is the right as well as the duty of all men in society, publicly, and at stated seasons, to worship the Supreme Being, the great Creator and Preserver of the universe. And no subject shall be hurt, molested, or restrained, in his person, liberty, or estate, for worshipping God in the manner and season most agreeable to the dictates of his own conscience; or for his religious profession of sentiments; provided he doth not disturb the public peace, or obstruct others in their religious worship. . . .

As the happiness of a people and the good order and preservation of civil government essentially depend upon piety, religion, and morality, and as these cannot be generally diffused through a community but by the institution of the public worship of God and of public instructions, in piety, religion, and morality. Therefore to promote their happiness and secure the good order and preservation of their government, the people of this commonwealth have a right to invest their legislature with power to authorize and require, and the legislature shall from time to time authorize and require, the several towns . . . and other bodies—politic or religious societies, to make suitable provision, at their own expense, for the institution of the public worship of God and the support and maintenance of public Protestant teachers of piety, religion, and morality. . . .

And the people of this commonwealth . . . do invest their legislature with authority to enjoin upon all the subjects an attendance upon the instructions of the public teachers aforesaid. . . .

And every denomination of Christians, demeaning themselves peaceably and as good subjects of the commonwealth, shall be equally under the protection of the law; and no subordination of any one sect or denomination to another shall ever be established by law.

IV. The people of this commonwealth have the sole and exclusive right of governing themselves, as a free, sovereign, and independent State, and do, and forever hereafter shall, exercise and enjoy every power, jurisdiction, and right, which is not, or may not hereafter be, by them expressly delegated to the United States of America, in Congress assembled.

V. All power residing originally in the people, and being derived from them, the several magistrates and officers of government, vested with authority, whether legislative, executive, or judicial, are their substitutes and agents, and are at all times accountable to them.

VI. No man, nor corporation, or association of men, have any other title to obtain advantages, or particular and exclusive privileges, distinct from those of the community, than what arises from the consideration of services rendered to the public; and this title being in nature neither hereditary, nor transmissible to children, or descendants, or relations by blood; the idea of a man born a magistrate, lawgiver, or judge, is absurd and unnatural.

VII. Government is instituted for the common good, for the protection, safety, prosperity, and happiness of the people and not for the profit, honor or private interest of any one man, family, or class of men;

therefore the people alone have an incontestible unalienable, and indefeasible right to institute government; and to reform, alter, or totally change the same, when their protection, safety, prosperity, and happiness require it.

VIII. In order to prevent those who are vested with authority from becoming oppressors, the people have a right, at such periods and in such manner as they shall establish by their frame of government, to cause their public officers to return to private life; and to fill up vacant places by certain and regular elections and appointments.

IX. All elections ought to be free; and all the inhabitants of this commonwealth, having such qualifications as they shall establish by their frame of government, have an equal right to elect officers, and to be elected, for public employments.

X. Each individual of the society has a right to be protected by it in the enjoyment of his life, liberty, and property. . . . No part of the property of any individual can, with justice, be taken from him, or applied to public uses, without his own consent, or that of the representative body of the people. . . . And whenever the public exigencies require that the property of any individual should be appropriated to public uses, he shall receive a reasonable compensation therefor.

XI. Every subject of the commonwealth ought to find a certain remedy, by having recourse to the laws, for all injuries or wrongs which he may receive in his person, property, or character. He ought to obtain right and justice freely, and without being obliged to purchase it; completely, and without any denial; promptly, and without delay, conformably to the laws.

XII. No subject shall be held to answer for any crimes or offence, until the same is fully and plainly . . . described to him; or be compelled to accuse, or furnish evidence against himself. And every subject shall have a right to produce all proofs that may be favorable to him; to meet the witnesses against him face to face, and to be fully heard in his defence by himself, or his counsel, at his election. And no subject shall be arrested, . . . or deprived of his life, liberty, or estate, but by the judgment of his peers, or the law of the land.

And the legislature shall not make any law that shall subject any person to a capital or infamous punishment, excepting for the government of the army and navy, without trial by jury. . . .

XIV. Every subject has a right to be secure from all unreasonable searches, and seizures, of his person, his houses, his papers, and all his possessions. . . . And no warrant ought to be issued but in cases, and with the formalities prescribed by the laws.

XV. In all controversies concerning property, and in all suits between two or more persons, . . . the parties have a right to a trial by jury; and this method of procedure shall be held sacred. . . .

XVI. The liberty of the press is essential to the security of freedom in a state it ought not, therefore, to be restricted in this commonwealth.

XVII. The people have a right to keep and to bear arms for the common defence. And as, in time of peace, armies are dangerous to liberty, they ought not to be maintained without the consent of the legislature; and the military power shall always be held in an exact subordination to the civil authority, and be governed by it.

XVIII. A frequent recurrence to the fundamental principles of the constitution, and a constant adherence to those of piety, justice, moderation, temperance, industry and frugality, are absolutely necessary to preserve the advantages of liberty, and to maintain a free government. The people ought, consequently, to have a particular attention to all those principles, in the choice of their officers and representatives: and they have a right to require of their lawgivers and magistrates an exact and constant observance of them, in the formation and execution of the laws necessary for the good administration of the commonwealth.

XIX. The people have a right, in an orderly and peaceable manner to assemble to consult upon the common good; give instructions to their representatives, and to request of the legislative body, by the way of addresses, petitions, or remonstrances, redress of the wrongs done them, and of the grievances they suffer.

XX. The power of suspending the laws, or the execution of the laws, ought never to be exercised but by the legislature, or by authority derived from it, to be exercised in such particular cases only as the legislature shall expressly provide for.

XXI. The freedom of deliberation, speech, and debate, in either house of the legislature, is so essential to the rights of the people, that it cannot be the foundation of any accusation or prosecution, action or complaint, in any other court or place whatsoever.

XXII. The legislature ought frequently to assemble for the redress of grievances, for correcting, strengthening, and confirming the laws, and for making new laws, as the common good may require.

XXIII. No subsidy, charge, tax, impost, or duties ought to be established, fixed, laid, or levied, under any pretext whatsoever, without the consent of the people or their representatives in the legislature.

XXIV. Laws made to punish for actions done before the existence of such laws, and which have not been declared crimes by preceding laws, are unjust, oppressive, and inconsistent with the fundamental principles of a free government.

XXV. No subject ought, in any case, or in any time, to be declared guilty of treason or felony by the legislature.

XXVI. No magistrate or court of law shall demand excessive bail or sureties, impose excessive fines, or inflict cruel or unusual punishments.

XXVII. In time of peace, no soldier ought to be quartered in any house without the consent of the owner; and in time of war, such quarters ought not to be made but by the civil magistrate, in a manner ordained by the legislature.

XXVIII. No person can in any case be subject to law-martial, or to any penalties or pains, by virtue of that law, except those employed in the army or navy, and except the militia in actual service, but by authority of the legislature.

XXIX. It is essential to the preservation of the rights of every individual, his life, liberty, property, and character, that there be an impartial interpretation of the laws, and administration of justice. It is the right of every citizen to be tried by judges as free, impartial, and independent as the lot of humanity will admit. It is, therefore, not only the best policy, but for the security of the rights of the people, and of every citizen, that the judges of the supreme judicial court should hold their offices as long as they behave themselves well; and that they should have honorable salaries ascertained and established by standing laws.

XXX. In the government of this commonwealth, the legislative department shall never exercise the executive and judicial powers, or either of them: the executive shall never exercise the legislative and judicial powers, or either of them: the judicial shall never exercise the legislative and executive powers, or either of them: to the end it may be a government of laws and not of men.

71. THE QUOCK WALKER CASE
Massachusetts, 1783

(A. B. Hart, ed. *Commonwealth History of Massachusetts,* Vol. IV, p. 37–8)

The status of slavery in Massachusetts was, throughout the Revolutionary period, a matter of uncertainty. As early as 1770—two years before Lord Mansfield's decision in the famous Somerset case, in the case of *James* v. *Lechmere* the Superior Court of Massachusetts ruled that the plaintiff, a negro, was entitled to his freedom under the laws of the province and the terms of the royal charter. In the course of his decision in the case of *Winchendon* v. *Hatfield,* Chief Justice Parsons said, "Several negroes born in this country of imported slaves demanded their freedom of their masters by suit at law, and obtained it by a judgement of court. The defence of the master was faintly made, for such was the temper of the times, that a restless, discontented slave was worth little; and when his freedom was obtained in a course of legal proceedings, the master was not holden for his future support if he became poor. But in the first action, involving the right of the master, which came before the Supreme Judicial Court after the establishment of the Constitution, the judges declared that by virtue of the first article of the Declaration of Rights, slavery in this State was no more". This was the case of *Quock Walker* v. *Nathaniel Jennison,* 1783. Jennison, indicted for assault on Walker, justified his assault on the ground that Walker was his slave. The Court, however, speaking through Chief Justice Cushing, ruled that the first article of the Declaration of Rights had abolished slavery in Massachusetts. The case was not reported, but in 1874 Chief Justice Horace Gray read from the original notebook of Chief Justice Cushing, the following extract from his decision. See, G. H. Moore, *Notes on the History of Slavery in Massachusetts;* M. S. Locke, *Anti-Slavery in America, 1619–1808;* J. C. Hurd, *The Law of Freedom and of Bondage,* Vol. I, p. 263–4, Vol. II, p. 28–30.

CUSHING, C. J. As to the doctrine of slavery and the right of Christians to hold Africans in perpetual servitude, and sell and treat them as we do our horses and cattle, that (it is true) has been heretofore countenanced by the Province Laws formerly, but nowhere is it expressly enacted or established. It has been a usage—a usage which took its origin from the practice of some of the European nations, and the regulations of British government respecting the then Colonies, for the benefit of trade and wealth. But whatever sentiments have formerly prevailed in this particular or slid in upon us by the example of others, a different idea has taken place with the people of America, more favorable to the natural rights of mankind, and to that natural, innate desire of Liberty, which with Heaven (without regard to color, complexion, or shape of noses-features) has inspired all the human race. And upon this ground our Constitution of Government, by which the people of this Commonwealth have solemnly bound themselves, sets out with declaring that all men are born free and equal—and that every subject is entitled to liberty, and to have it guarded by the laws, as well as life and property—and in short is totally repugnant to the idea of being born slaves. This being the case, I think the idea of slavery is inconsistent with our own conduct and Constitution; and there can be no such thing as perpetual servitude of a rational creature, unless his liberty is forfeited by some criminal conduct or given up by personal consent or contract . . . *Verdict Guilty.*

72. THE ARTICLES OF CONFEDERATION

Agreed to by Congress November 15, 1777; ratified and in force, March 1, 1781

(Richardson, ed. *Messages and Papers,* Vol. I, p. 9 ff.)

Congress resolved June 11, 1776, that a committee should be appointed to draw up articles of confederation between the Colonies. A plan proposed by John Dickinson formed the basis of the articles as proposed to Congress and, after some debate and a few changes, adopted, November 15, 1777. Representatives of the States signed the Articles during 1778 and 1779; Maryland alone refused to ratify the Articles until Congress had arrived at some satisfactory solution of the land question. The debates on the Articles, Jefferson's Notes on the Debates, and the Official Letter of Congress accompanying the Articles, can be found in Elliot's *Debates* (1861 ed.) Vol. I, p. 69 ff. The Articles of Confederation constituted the first effort of Americans to solve the problem of imperial order, and should be studied in comparison with the Albany Plan of Union and the Constitution. On the Articles of Confederation see, R. Frothingham, *Rise of the Republic of the United States,* ch. xii; G. Bancroft, *History* Author's last rev. Vol. V, ch. xiv; A. C. McLaughlin, *Confederation and Constitution,* ch. iii; G. T. Curtis, *Constitutional History of the United States,* Vol. I.

To ALL TO WHOM these Presents shall come, we the undersigned Delegates of the States affixed to our Names send greeting. Whereas the Delegates of the United States of America in Congress assembled did on the fifteenth day of November in the Year of our Lord One Thousand Seven Hundred and Seventy seven, and in the Second Year of the Independence of America agree to certain articles of Confederation and perpetual Union between the States of Newhampshire, Massachusetts-bay, Rhodeisland and Providence Plantations, Connecticut, New York, New Jersey, Pennsylvania, Delaware, Maryland, Virginia, North-Carolina, South-Carolina and Georgia in the Words following, viz. "Articles of Confederation and perpetual Union between the states of New-hampshire, Massachusetts-bay, Rhodeisland and Providence Plantations, Connecticut, New-York, New-Jersey, Pennsylvania, Delaware, Maryland, Virginia, North-Carolina, South-Carolina and Georgia.

Art. I. The Stile of this confederacy shall be "The United States of America."

Art. II. Each state retains its sovereignty, freedom and independence, and every Power, Jurisdiction and right, which is not by this confederation expressly delegated to the United States, in Congress assembled.

Art. III. The said states hereby severally enter into a firm league of friendship with each other, for their common defence, the security of their Liberties, and their mutual and general welfare, binding themselves to assist each other, against all force offered to, or attacks made upon them, or any of them, on account of religion, sovereignty, trade, or any other pretence whatever.

Art. IV. The better to secure and perpetuate mutual friendship and intercourse among the people of the different states in this union, the free inhabitants of each of these states, paupers, vagabonds and fugitives from Justice excepted, shall be entitled to all privileges and immunities of free citizens in the several states; and the people of each state shall have free ingress and regress to and from any other state, and shall enjoy therein all the privileges of trade and commerce, subject to the same duties, impositions and restrictions as the inhabitants thereof respectively, provided that such restriction shall not extend so far as to prevent the removal of property imported into any state, to any other state of which the Owner is an inhabitant; provided also that no imposition, duties or restriction shall be laid by any state, on the property of the united states, or either of them.

If any Person guilty of, or charged with treason, felony, or other high misdemeanor in any state, shall flee from Justice, and be found in any of the united states, he shall upon demand of the Governor or executive power, of the state from which he fled, be delivered up and removed to the state having jurisdiction of his offence.

Full faith and credit shall be given in each of these states to the records, acts and judicial proceedings of the courts and magistrates of every other state.

Art. V. For the more convenient management of the general interests of the united states, delegates shall be annually appointed in such manner as the legislature of each state shall direct, to meet in Congress on the first Monday in November, in every year, with a power reserved to each state, to recal its delegates, or any of them, at any time within the year, and to send others in their stead, for the remainder of the Year.

No state shall be represented in Congress by less than two, nor by more than seven Members; and no person shall be capable of being a delegate for more than three years in any term of six years; nor shall any person, being a delegate, be capable of holding any office under the united states, for which he, or another for his benefit receives any salary, fees or emolument of any kind.

Each state shall maintain its own delegates in a meeting of the states, and while they act as members of the committee of the states.

In determining questions in the united states, in Congress assembled, each state shall have one vote.

Freedom of speech and debate in Congress shall not be impeached or questioned in any Court, or place out of Congress, and the members of congress shall be protected in their persons from arrests and imprisonments, during the time of their going to and from, and attendance on congress, except for treason, felony, or breach of the peace.

Art. VI. No state without the Consent of the united states in congress assembled, shall send any embassy to, or receive any embassy from, or enter into any conference, agreement, or alliance or treaty with any King, prince or state; nor shall any person holding any office of profit or trust under the united states, or any of them, accept of any present, emolument, office or title of any kind whatever from any king, prince or foreign state; nor shall the united states in congress assembled, or any of them, grant any title of nobility.

No two or more states shall enter into any treaty, confederation or alliance whatever between them, without the consent of the united states in congress assembled, specifying accurately the purposes for which the same is to be entered into, and how long it shall continue.

No state shall lay any imposts or duties, which may interfere with any stipulations in treaties, entered into by the united states in congress assembled, with any king, prince or state, in pursuance of any treaties already proposed by congress, to the courts of France and Spain.

No vessels of war shall be kept up in time of peace by any state, except such number only, as shall be deemed necessary by the united states in congress assembled, for the defence of such state, or its trade; nor shall any body of forces be kept up by any state, in time of peace, except such number only, as in the judgment of the united states, in congress assembled, shall be deemed requisite to garrison the forts necessary for the defence of such state; but every state shall always keep up a well regulated and disciplined militia, sufficiently armed and accoutred, and shall provide and constantly have ready for use, in public stores, a due number of field pieces and tents, and a proper quantity of arms, ammunition and camp equipage.

No state shall engage in any war without the consent of the united states in congress assembled, unless such state be actually invaded by enemies, or shall have received certain advice of a resolution being formed by some nation of Indians to invade such state, and the danger is so imminent as not to admit of a delay, till the united states in congress assembled can be consulted: nor shall any state grant commissions to any ships or vessels of war, nor letters of marque or reprisal, except it be after a declaration of war by the united states in congress assembled, and then only against the kingdom or state and the subjects thereof, against which war has been so declared, and under such regulations as shall be established by the united states in congress assembled, unless such state be infested by pirates, in which case vessels of war may be fitted out for that occasion, and kept so long as the danger shall continue, or until the united states in congress assembled shall determine otherwise.

Art. VII. When land-forces are raised by any state for the common defence, all officers of or under the rank of colonel, shall be appointed by the legislature of each state respectively by whom such forces shall be raised, or in such manner as such state shall direct, and all vacancies shall be filled up by the state which first made the appointment.

Art. VIII. All charges of war, and all other expences that shall be incurred for the common defence or general welfare, and allowed by the united states in congress assembled, shall be defrayed out of a common treasury, which shall be supplied by the several states, in proportion to the value of all land within each state, granted to or surveyed for any Person, as such land and the buildings and improvements thereon shall be estimated according to such mode as the united states in congress assembled, shall from time to time direct and appoint. The taxes for paying that proportion shall be laid and levied by the authority and direction of the legislatures of the several states within the time agreed upon by the united states in congress assembled.

Art. IX. The united states in congress assembled, shall have the sole and exclusive right and power of determining on peace and war, except in the cases mentioned in the sixth article—of sending and receiving ambassadors—entering into treaties and alliances, provided that no treaty of commerce shall be made whereby the legislative power of the respective states shall be restrained from imposing such imposts and duties on foreigners, as their own people are subjected to, or from prohibiting the exportation or importation of any species of goods or commodities whatsoever—of establishing rules for deciding in all cases, what captures on land or water shall be legal, and in what manner prizes taken by land or naval forces in the service of the united states shall be divided or appropriated.—of granting letters of marque and reprisal in times of peace—appointing courts for the trial of piracies and felonies committed on the high seas and establishing courts for receiving and determining finally appeals in all cases of captures, provided that no member of congress shall be appointed a judge of any of the said courts.

The united states in congress assembled shall also be the last resort on appeal in all disputes and differences now subsisting or that hereafter may arise between two or more states concerning boundary, jurisdiction or any other cause whatever; which authority shall always be exercised in the manner following. Whenever the legislative or executive authority or lawful agent of any state in controversy with another shall present a petition to congress. stating the matter in question and praying for a hearing, notice thereof shall be given by order of congress to the legislative or executive authority of the other state in controversy, and a day assigned for the appearance of the parties by their lawful agents, who shall then be directed to appoint by joint consent, commissioners or judges to constitute a court for hearing and determining the matter in question: but if they cannot agree, congress shall name three persons out of each of the united states, and from the list of such persons each party shall alternately strike out one, the petitioners beginning, until the number shall be reduced to thirteen; and from that number not less than seven, nor more than nine names as congress shall direct, shall in the presence of congress be drawn out by lot, and the persons whose names shall be so drawn or any five of them, shall be commissioners or judges, to hear and finally determine the controversy, so always as a major part of the judges who shall hear the cause shall agree in the determination: and if either party shall neglect to attend at the day appointed, without shewing reasons, which congress shall judge sufficient, or being present shall refuse to strike, the congress shall proceed to nominate three persons out of each state, and the secretary of congress shall strike in behalf of such party absent or refusing; and the judgment and sentence of the court to be appointed, in the manner before prescribed, shall be final and conclusive; and if any of the parties shall refuse to submit to the authority of such court, or to appear to defend their claim or cause, the court shall nevertheless proceed to pronounce sentence, or judgment, which shall in like manner be final and decisive, the judgment or sentence and other proceedings being in either case transmitted to congress, and lodged among the acts of congress for the security of the parties concerned: provided that every commissioner, before he sits in judgment, shall take an oath to be administered by one of the judges of the supreme or superior court of the state, where the cause shall be tried, "well and truly to hear and determine the matter in question, according to the best of his judgment, without favour, affection or hope of reward:" provided also that no state shall be deprived of territory for the benefit of the united states.

All controversies concerning the private right of soil claimed under different grants of two or more states, whose jurisdictions as they may respect such lands, and the states which passed such grants are adjusted, the said grants or either of them being at the same time claimed to have originated antecedent to such settlement of jurisdiction, shall on the petition of either party to the congress of the united states, be finally determined as near as may be in the same manner as is before prescribed for deciding disputes respecting territorial jurisdiction between different states.

The united states in congress assembled shall also have the sole and exclusive right and power of regulating the alloy and value of coin struck by their own authority, or by that of the respective states—fixing the standard of weights and measures throughout the united states.—regulating the trade and managing all affairs with the Indians, not members of any of the states, provided that the legislative right of any state within its own limits be not infringed or violated—establishing and regulating post-offices from one state to another, throughout all the united states, and exacting such postage on the papers passing thro' the same as may be requisite to defray the expences of the said office—appointing all officers of the land forces, in the service of the united states, excepting regimental officers.—appointing all the officers of the naval forces, and commissioning all officers whatever in the service of the united states—making rules for the government and regulation of the said land and naval forces, and directing their operations.

The united states in congress assembled shall have authority to appoint a committee, to sit in the recess of congress, to be denominated "A Committee of the States," and to consist of one delegate from each state; and to appoint such other committees and

civil officers as may be necessary for managing the general affairs of the united states under their direction—to appoint one of their number to preside, provided that no person be allowed to serve in the office of president more than one year in any term of three years; to ascertain the necessary sums of Money to be raised for the service of the united states, and to appropriate and apply the same for defraying the public expences—to borrow money, or emit bills on the credit of the united states, transmitting every half year to the respective states an account of the sums of money so borrowed or emitted,—to build and equip a navy—to agree upon the number of land forces, and to make requisitions from each state for its quota, in proportion to the number of white inhabitants in such state; which requisition shall be binding, and thereupon the legislature of each state shall appoint the regimental officers, raise the men and cloath, arm and equip them in a soldier like manner, at the expence of the united states, and the officers and men so cloathed, armed and equipped shall march to the place appointed, and within the time agreed on by the united states in congress assembled: But if the united states in congress assembled shall, on consideration of circumstances judge proper that any state should not raise men, or should raise a smaller number than its quota, and that any other state should raise a greater number of men than the quota thereof, such extra number shall be raised, officered, cloathed, armed and equipped in the same manner as the quota of such state, unless the legislature of such state shall judge that such extra number cannot be safely spared out of the same, in which case they shall raise officer, cloath, arm and equip as many of such extra number as they judge can be safely spared. And the officers and men so cloathed, armed and equipped, shall march to the place appointed, and within the time agreed on by the united states in congress assembled.

The united states in congress assembled shall never engage in a war, nor grant letters of marque and reprisal in time of peace, nor enter into any treaties or alliances, nor coin money, nor regulate the value thereof, nor ascertain the sums and expences necessary for the defence and welfare of the united states, or any of them, nor emit bills, nor borrow money on the credit of the united states, nor appropriate money, nor agree upon the number of vessels of war, to be built or purchased, or the number of land or sea forces to be raised, nor appoint a commander in chief of the army or navy, unless nine states assent to the same: nor shall a question on any other point, except for adjourning from day to day be determined, unless by the votes of a majority of the united states in congress assembled.

The congress of the united states shall have power to adjourn to any time within the year, and to any place within the united states, so that no period of adjournment be for a longer duration than the space of six Months, and shall publish the Journal of their proceedings monthly, except such parts thereof relating to treaties, alliances or military operations as in their judgment require secresy; and the yeas and nays of the delegates of each state on any question shall be entered on the Journal, when it is desired by any delegate; and the delegates of a state, or any of them, at his or their request shall be furnished with a transcript of the said Journal, except such parts as are above excepted, to lay before the legislatures of the several states.

Art. X. The committee of the states, or any nine of them, shall be authorised to execute, in the recess of congress, such of the powers of congress as the united states in congress assembled, by the consent of nine states, shall from time to time think expedient to vest them with; provided that no power be delegated to the said committee, for the exercise of which, by the articles of confederation, the voice of nine states in the congress of the united states assembled is requisite.

Art. XI. Canada acceding to this confederation, and joining in the measures of the united states, shall be admitted into, and entitled to all the advantages of this union: but no other colony shall be admitted into the same, unless such admission be agreed to by nine states.

Art. XII. All bills of credit emitted, monies borrowed and debts contracted by, or under the authority of congress, before the assembling of the united states, in pursuance of the present confederation, shall be deemed and considered as a charge against the united states, for payment and satisfaction whereof the said united states, and the public faith are hereby solemnly pledged.

Art. XIII. Every state shall abide by the determinations of the united states in congress assembled, on all questions which by this confederation are submitted to them. And the Articles of this confederation shall be inviolably observed by every state, and the union shall be perpetual; nor shall any alteration at any time hereafter be made in any of them; unless such alteration be agreed to in a congress of the united states, and be afterwards confirmed by the legislatures of every state.

AND WHEREAS it hath pleased the Great Governor of the World to incline the hearts of the legislatures we respectively represent in congress, to approve of, and to authorize us to ratify the said articles of confederation and perpetual union. KNOW YE that we the under-signed delegates, by virtue of the power and authority to us given for that purpose, do by these presents, in the name and in behalf of our respective constituents, fully and entirely ratify and confirm each and every of the said articles of confederation and perpetual union, and all and singular the matters and things therein contained: And we do further solemnly plight and engage the faith of our respective constituents, that they shall abide by the determinations of the united states in congress assembled, on all questions, which by the said confederation are submitted to them. And that the articles thereof shall be inviolably observed by the states we respectively represent, and that the union shall be perpetual. In Witness whereof we have hereunto set our hands in Congress. Done at Philadelphia in the state of Pennsylvania the ninth Day of July in the Year of our Lord one Thousand seven Hundred and Seventy-eight, and in the third year of the independence of America.

JOSIAH BARTLETT
JOHN   WENTWORTH
Junr August 8th 1778 } On the part & behalf of the State of New Hampshire

JOHN HANCOCK
SAMUEL ADAMS
ELBRIDGE GERRY
FRANCIS DANA
JAMES LOVELL
SAMUEL HOLTEN } On the part and behalf of The State of Massachusetts Bay

WILLIAM ELLERY
HENRY MARCHANT
JOHN COLLINS } On the part and behalf of the State of Rhode-Island and Providence Plantations

ROGER SHERMAN
SAMUEL HUNTINGTON
OLIVER WOLCOTT
TITUS HOSMER
ANDREW ADAMS } On the part and behalf of the State of Connecticut

JA^S DUANE
FRA^S LEWIS
W^M DUER
GOUV MORRIS } On the Part and Behalf of the State of New York

JNO WITHERSPOON
NATH^L SCUDDER } On the Part and in Behalf of the State of New Jersey. Novr 26, 1778.—

ROB^T MORRIS
DANIEL ROBERDEAU
JON^A BAYARD SMITH.
WILLIAM CLINGAN
JOSEPH   REED   22^d
   July 1778 } On the part and behalf of the State of Pennsylvania

THO M:KEAN Feby
   12 1779
JOHN   DICKINSON
   May 5th 1779
NICHOLAS VAN DYKE, } On the part & behalf of the State of Delaware

JOHN HANSON
   March 1 1781
DANIEL CARROLL d^o } On the part and behalf of the State of Maryland

RICHARD HENRY LEE
JOHN BANISTER
THOMAS ADAMS
JN^O HARVIE
FRANCIS   LIGHTFOOT
   LEE } On the Part and Behalf of the State of Virginia

JOHN   PENN   July
   21st 1778
CORN^S HARNETT
JN^O WILLIAMS } On the part and Behalf of the State of N^o Carolina

HENRY LAURENS
WILLIAM   HENRY
   DRAYTON
JN^O MATHEWS
RICH^D HUTSON
THO^S HEYWARD Junr } On the part & behalf of the State of South-Carolina

JN^O   WALTON   24th
   July 1778
EDW^D TELFAIR
EDW^D LANGWORTHY } On the part & behalf of the State of Georgia

73. COMMONWEALTH v. CATON ET. AL.
Virginia Reports, 4 Call, 5
1782

John Caton was condemned for treason by the General Court of Virginia, under the act of the assembly concerning that offence, passed in 1776, which took from the executive the power of granting pardon in such cases. The House of delegates, by resolution of June, 1782, granted him a pardon and sent it to the senate for concurrence, which was refused. Caton continued in jail under the sentence, and in October, 1782, the attorney-general moved in the general court that execution of the judgement might be awarded. The prisoner pleaded the pardon granted by the house of delegates; the attorney-general denied the validity of the pardon, as the senate had not concurred in it, and the general court adjourned the case for novelty and difficulty, to the court of appeals. This is one of the very earliest cases in the United States where the question of the validity of an unconstitutional act was considered. It is of interest that John Marshall studied law under Judge Wythe.

WYTHE, J.: Among all the advantages which have arisen to mankind, from the study of letters, and the universal diffusion of knowledge, there is none of more importance, than the tendency they have had to produce discussions upon the respective rights of the sovereign and the subject; and upon the powers which the different branches of the government may exercise. For, by this means, tyranny has been sapped, the departments kept within their own spheres, the citizens protected, and general liberty promoted. But this beneficial result attains to higher perfection, when those who hold the purse and the sword, differing as to the powers which each may exercise, the tribunals, who hold neither, are called upon to declare the law impartially between them. For thus the pretensions of each party are fairly examined, their respective powers ascertained, and the boundaries of authority peaceably established. Under these impressions I approach the question which has been submitted to us: and although it was said the other day by one of the judges that, imitating that great and good man Lord Hale, he would sooner quit the bench than determine it, I feel no alarm; but will meet the crisis as I ought; and in the language of my oath of office, will decide it according to the best of my skill and judgement.

I have heard of an English chancellor who said, and it was nobly said, that it was his duty to protect the rights of the subject against the encroachments of the crown; and that he would do it at every hazard. But if it was his duty to protect a solitary individual against the rapacity of the sovereign, surely it is equally mine to protect one branch of the legislature and, consequently, the whole community, against the usurpations of the other: and whenever the proper occasion occurs, I shall feel the duty; and fearlessly perform it. Whenever traitors shall be fairly convicted, by the verdict of their peers, before the competent tribunal, if one branch of the legislature, without the concurrence of the other, shall attempt to rescue the offenders from the sentence of the law, I shall not hesitate, sitting in this place, to say to the general court, *Fiat justitia, ruat coelum;* and, to the usurping branch of the legislature, you attempt worse than a vain thing; for although you cannot succeed, you set an example which may convulse society to its centre. Nay more, if the whole legislature, an event to be deprecated, should attempt to overleap the bounds prescribed to them by the people, I, in administering the public justice of the country, will meet the united powers at my seat in this tribunal; and, pointing to the constitution, will say to them, here is the limit of your authority; and, hither shall you go, but no further. . . .

I am therefore of the opinion that the pardon pleaded by the prisoners, is not valid; and that it ought to be so certified to the general court.

74. TREATY OF PEACE WITH GREAT BRITAIN
September 3, 1783

(Malloy, ed. *Treaties, Conventions, etc.*, Vol. I, p. 586 ff.)

The surrender of Cornwallis at Yorktown, October 19, 1781, brought an end to the British effort to subdue the American colonies. February 27, 1782, a motion urging King George to end the war passed the House of Commons; a month later Lord North resigned, and the Rockingham Ministry entered into negotiations for a definitive peace. Congress appointed John Adams, Benjamin Franklin, John Jay, Henry Laurens, and Thomas Jefferson to conduct the negotiations, but Jefferson did not leave America, and Laurens was released from prison too late to take part in the peace conferences. The chief burden of the negotiations fell upon Franklin, and the treaty is largely a tribute to his shrewdness, persistence, and sagacity. On the Treaty, see the scholarly account by J. B. Scott, in S. F. Bemis, ed. *American Secretaries of State*, Vol. I, chs. iv–v; A. C. McLaughlin, *Confederation and Constitution*, chs. i–ii; E. G. Petty, Lord Fitzmaurice, *Life of William, Earl of Shelburne*, Vol. III.

. . . ART. I.—His Britannic Majesty acknowledges the said United States, viz. New Hampshire, Massachusetts Bay, Rhode Island, and Providence Plantations, Connecticut, New York, New Jersey, Pennsylvania, Delaware, Maryland, Virginia, North Carolina, South Carolina, and Georgia, to be free, sovereign and independent States; that he treats with them as such, and for himself, his heirs and successors, relinquishes all claims to the Government, proprietary and territorial rights of the same, and every part thereof.

ART. II.—And that all disputes which might arise in future, on the subject of the boundaries of the said United States may be prevented, it is hereby agreed and declared, that the following are, and shall be their boundaries, viz.: From the northwest angle of Nova Scotia, viz.: that angle which is formed by a line drawn due north from the source of Saint Croix River to the Highlands; along the said Highlands which divide those rivers that empty themselves into the river St. Lawrence, from those which fall into the Atlantic Ocean, to the northwesternmost head of Connecticut River; thence down along the middle of that river, to the forty-fifth degree of north latitude; from thence, by a line due west on said latitude, until it strikes the river Iroquois or Cataraquy; thence along the middle of said river into Lake Ontario, through the middle of said lake until it strikes the communication by water between that lake and Lake Erie; thence along the middle of said communication into Lake Erie, through the middle of said lake until it arrives at the water communication between that lake and Lake Huron; thence along the middle of said water communication into the Lake Huron; thence through the middle of said lake to the water communication between that lake and Lake Superior; thence through Lake Superior northward of the Isles Royal and Phelipeaux, to the Long Lake; thence through the middle of said Long Lake, and the water communication between it and the Lake of the Woods, to the said Lake of the Woods; thence through the said lake to the most northwestern point thereof, and from thence on a due west course to the river Mississippi; thence by a line to be drawn along the middle of the said river Mississippi until it shall intersect the northernmost part of the thirty-first degree of north latitude. South, by a line to be drawn due east from the determination of the line last mentioned, in the latitude of thirty-one degrees north of the Equator, to the middle of the river Appalachicola or Catahouche; thence along the middle thereof to its junction with the Flint River; thence straight to the head of St. Mary's River; and thence down along the middle of St. Mary's River to the Atlantic Ocean. East, by a line to be drawn along the middle of the river St. Croix, from its mouth in the Bay of Fundy to its source, and from its source directly north to the aforesaid Highlands, which divide the rivers that fall into the Atlantic Ocean from those which fall into the river St. Lawrence; comprehending all islands within twenty leagues of any part of the shores of the United States, and lying between lines to be drawn due east from the points where the aforesaid boundaries between Nova Scotia on the one part, and East Florida on the other, shall respectively touch the Bay of Fundy and the Atlantic Ocean; excepting such islands as now are, or heretofore have been, within the limits of the said province of Nova Scotia.

ART. III.—It is agreed that the people of the United States shall continue to enjoy unmolested the right to take fish of every kind on the Grand Bank, and on all the other banks of Newfoundland; also in the Gulph of Saint Lawrence, and at all other places in the sea where the inhabitants of both countries used at any time heretofore to fish. And also that the inhabitants of the United States shall have liberty to take fish of every kind on such part of the coast of Newfoundland as British fishermen shall use (but not to dry or cure the same on that island) and also on the coasts, bays and creeks of all other of His Britannic Majesty's dominions in America; and that the American fishermen shall have liberty to dry and cure fish in any of the unsettled bays, harbours and creeks of Nova Scotia, Magdalen Islands, and Labrador, so long as the same shall remain unsettled; but so soon as the same or either of them shall be settled, it shall not be lawful for the said fishermen to dry or cure fish at such settlements, without a previous agreement for that purpose with the inhabitants, proprietors or possessors of the ground.

ART. IV.—It is agreed that creditors on either side shall meet with no lawful impediment to the recovery of the full value in sterling money, of all *bona fide* debts heretofore contracted.

ART. V.—It is agreed that the Congress shall earnestly recommend it to the legislatures of the respective States, to provide for the restitution of all estates, rights and properties which have been confiscated, belonging to real British subjects, and also of the estates, rights and properties of persons resident in districts in the possession of His Majesty's arms, and who have not borne arms against the said United States. And that persons of any other description shall have free liberty to go to any part or parts of any of the thirteen United States, and therein to remain twelve months, unmolested in their endeavours to obtain the restitution of such of their estates, rights and properties as may have been confiscated; and that Congress shall also earnestly recommend to the several States a reconsideration and revision of all acts or laws regarding the premises, so as to render the said laws or acts perfectly consistent, not only with justice and equity, but with that spirit of conciliation which, on the return of the blessings of peace, should universally prevail. And that Congress shall also earnestly recommend to the several States, that the estates, rights and properties of such last mentioned persons, shall be restored to them, they refunding to any persons who may be now in possession, the *bona fide* price (where any has been given) which such persons may have paid on purchasing any of the said lands, rights or properties, since the confiscation. And it is agreed, that all persons who have any interest in confiscated lands, either by debts, marriage settlements or otherwise, shall meet with no lawful impediment in the prosecution of their just rights.

ART. VI.—That there shall be no future confiscations made, nor any prosecutions commenced against any person or persons for, or by reason of the part which he or they may have taken in the present war; and that no person shall, on that account, suffer any future loss or damage, either in his person, liberty or property; and that those who may be in confinement on such charges, at the time of the ratification of the treaty in America, shall be immediately set at liberty, and the prosecutions so commenced be discontinued.

ART. VII.—There shall be a firm and perpetual peace between His Britannic Majesty and the said States, and between the subjects of the one and the citizens of the other, wherefore all hostilities, both by sea and land, shall from henceforth cease; All prisoners on both sides shall be set at liberty, and His Britannic Majesty shall, with all convenient speed, and without causing any destruction, or carrying away any negroes or other property of the American inhabitants, withdraw all his armies, garrisons and fleets from the said United States, and from every post, place and harbour within the same; leaving in all fortifications the American artillery that may be therein; And shall also order and cause all archives, records, deeds and papers, belonging to any of the said States, or their citizens, which, in the course of the war, may have fallen into the hands of his officers, to be forthwith restored and deliver'd to the proper States and persons to whom they belong.

ART. VIII.—The navigation of the river Mississippi, from its source to the ocean, shall forever remain free and open to the subjects of Great Britain, and the citizens of the United States.

ART. IX.—In case it should so happen that any place or territory belonging to Great Britain or to the United States, should have been conquer'd by the arms of either from the other, before the arrival of the said provisional articles in America, it is agreed, that the same shall be restored without difficulty, and without requiring any compensation. . . .

75. RESOLUTION OF CONGRESS ON PUBLIC LANDS
October 10, 1780

(Journals of the Continental Congress, ed. by G. Hunt, Vol. XVIII, p. 915)

The ownership, control and administration of the western lands was one of the most acute and perplexing of the problems of the old Empire. By their charters, many of the American colonies were entitled to lands west of the Appalachians, and the Proclamation of 1763, closing these lands to settlement, aroused general resentment. With the outbreak of the Revolution, the States resumed their titles to their western lands. Many of these titles were conflicting and uncertain, and there was a widespread feeling, especially in those States that did not have title to western lands, that these lands should be surrendered to the central government. Congress, by the resolution of October 10, 1780, indicated the policy which it would follow toward any lands ceded to it by the States. See, in this connection, and for references, Docs. No. 76–79.

Resolved, that the unappropriated lands that may be ceded or relinquished to the United States, by any particular States, pursuant to the recommendation of Congress on the 6 day of September last, shall be disposed of for the common benefit of the United States, and be settled and formed into distinct republican States, which shall become members of the Federal Union, and shall have the same rights of sovereignty, freedom and independence, as the other States; that each State which shall be so formed shall contain a suitable extent of territory, not less than one hundred nor more than one hundred and fifty miles square, or as near thereto as circumstances will admit;

That the necessary and reasonable expences which any particular State shall have incurred since the commencement of the present war, in subduing any of the British posts, or in maintaining forts or garrisons within and for the defence, or in acquiring any part of the territory that may be ceded or relinquished to the United States, shall be reimbursed;

That the said lands shall be granted and settled at such times and under such regulations as shall hereafter be agreed on by the United States in Congress assembled, or any nine or more of them.

76. VIRGINIA'S CESSION OF WESTERN LANDS TO THE UNITED STATES
December 20, 1783

(F. N. Thorpe, ed. *Federal and State Constitutions,* Vol. II, p. 955–6)

The Resolution of Congress of October 10, 1780 and the attitude of Maryland toward ratification of the Articles of Confederation gave a powerful impulse to the cession of the land claims of the States to the United States. New York and Connecticut expressed their willingness to cede their claims as early as 1781. The following year Congress accepted the New York cession. The claims of Virginia were the most extensive and the strongest of those of any State: they were based not only on charter rights but on the achievements of Clark in the Northwest. Virginia's first cession, in 1781, was coupled with conditions that were not acceptable to Congress: the cession of 1783 was promptly accepted, and the deed signed March 1, 1784. The clauses in the cession reserving military bounty lands north of the Ohio are of particular importance. See, A. C. McLaughlin, *Confederation and Constitution,* ch. vii; B. A. Hinsdale, *The Old Northwest;* F. L. Paxson, *History of the American Frontier,* chs. v–vi.

Sec. 1. Whereas the Congress of the United States did, by their act of the 6th day of September, in the year 1780, recommend to the several States in the Union, having claims to waste and unappropriated lands in the western country, a liberal cession to the United States of a portion of their respective claims for the common benefit of the Union:

Sec. 2. And whereas this commonwealth did, on the 2d day of January, in the year 1781, yield to the Congress of the United States, for the benefit of the said States, all right, title, and claim which the said commonwealth had to the territory northwest of the river Ohio, subject to the conditions annexed to the said act of cession:

Sec. 3. And whereas the United States in Congress assembled have, by their act of the 13th of September last, stipulated the terms on which they agreed to accept the cession of this State, should the legislature approve thereof, which terms, although they do not come up to the proposition of this commonwealth, are conceived, on the whole, to approach so nearly to them as to induce this State to accept thereof, in full confidence that Congress will, in justice to this State for the liberal cession she hath made, earnestly press upon the other States claiming large tracts of waste and uncultivated territory the propriety of making cessions equally liberal for the common benefit and support of the Union:

Be it enacted by the general assembly,

That it shall and may be lawful for the delegates of this State to the Congress of the United States, . . . to . . . make over unto the United States, in Congress assembled, for the benefit of the said States, all right, title, and claim, as well of soil as jurisdiction, which this commonwealth hath to the territory or tract of country within the limits of the Virginia charter, situate, lying, and being to the northwest of the river Ohio, subject to the terms and conditions contained in the before-recited act of Congress of the 13th day of September last, that is to say: Upon condition that the territory so ceded shall be laid out and formed into States, containing a suitable extent of territory, not less than one hundred nor more than one hundred and fifty miles square, or as near thereto as circumstances will admit; and the States so formed shall be distinct republican States, and admitted members of the Federal Union, having the same rights of sovereignty, freedom, and independence as the other States; that the necessary and reasonable expences incurred by this State in subduing any British posts, or in maintaining forts or garrisons within and for the defence, or in acquiring any part of the territory so ceded or relinquished, shall be fully reimbursed by the United States; and that one commissioner shall be appointed by Congress, one by this commonwealth and another by those two commissioners, who, or a majority of them, shall be authorized and empowered to adjust and liquidate the account of the necessary and reasonable expenses incurred by the State, which they shall judge to be comprised within the intent and meaning of the act of Congress of the 10th of October, 1780, respecting such expenses. That of the French and Canadian inhabitants, and other settlers of the Kaskaskies, Saint Vincents and the neighboring villages, who have professed themselves citizens of Virginia, shall have their possessions and titles confirmed to them, and be protected in the enjoyment of their rights and liberties. That a quantity, not exceeding one hundred and fifty thousand acres, of land, promised by this State, shall be allowed and granted to the then Colonel, now General, George Rogers Clark, and to the officers and soldiers of his regiment who marched with him when the posts of Kaskaskies and Saint Vincents were reduced, and to the officers and soldiers that have been since incorporated into the said regiment, to be laid off in one tract, the length of which not to exceed double the breadth, in such place on the northwest side of the Ohio as a majority of the officers shall choose, and to be afterwards divided among the said officers and soldiers in due proportion according to the law of Virginia. That in case the quantity of good lands on the southeast side of the Ohio, upon the waters of Cumberland River, and between Green River and Tennessee River, which have been reserved by law for the Virginia troops upon continental establishment, should, from the North Carolina line bearing in further upon the Cumberland lands than was expected, prove insufficient for their legal bounties, the deficiency should be made up to the said troops in good lands, to be laid off between the rivers Scioto and Little Miami, on the northwest side of the river Ohio, in such proportions as have been engaged to them by the laws of Virginia. That all the lands within the territory so ceded to the United States, and not reserved for or appropriated to any of the before-mentioned purposes, or disposed of in bounties to the officers and soldiers of the American Army, shall be considered as a common fund for the use and benefit of such of the United States as have become, or shall become members of the confederation or federal alliance of the said States, Virginia inclusive, according to their usual respective proportions in the general charge and expenditure, and shall be faithfully and *bona fide* disposed of for that purpose, and for no other use or purpose whatsoever: *Provided,* That the trust hereby reposed in the delegates of this State shall not be executed unless three of them, at least, are present in Congress.

77. REPORT OF GOVERNMENT FOR THE WESTERN TERRITORY
April 23, 1784

(*Journals of the Continental Congress,* ed. by J. C. Fitzpatrick, Vol. XXVI, p. 275 ff.)

Shortly after Virginia's cession of western lands had been formally completed, Jefferson introduced to Congress a plan for the organization of government in the western territory. The original plan contained two important provisions that were not finally incorporated in the Act of April 23. In the first place Jefferson proposed to create ten States out of the territory between the Ohio and the Mississippi Rivers, and provided for these potential states such names as Dolypotamia, Assenisippia and Metropotamia. In the second place Jefferson's plan contained a clause, "That after the year 1800 there shall be neither slavery nor involuntary servitude in in any of the sd. states." This clause was defeated by a vote of seven to six, even Virginia voting against its retention. Jefferson's plan can be found in various editions of his *Works,* or in Randall's *Jefferson,* Vol. I, p. 397, or in *Old South Leaflets,* Vol. VI. The Report of 1784 never went into effect. See references in Doc. No. 79.

The Committee to whom was recommitted the report of a plan for a temporary government of the western territory have agreed to the following resolutions.

Resolved, that so much of the territory ceded or to be ceded by individual states to the United States as is already purchased or shall be purchased of the Indian inhabitants & offered for sale by Congress, shall be divided into distinct states, in the following manner, as nearly as such cessions will admit; that is to say, by parallels of latitude, so that each state shall comprehend from north to south two degrees of latitude beginning to count from the completion of forty-five degrees north of the equator; and by meridians of longitude, one of which shall pass thro' the lowest point of the rapids of Ohio, and the other through the Western Cape of the mouth of the Great Kanhaway, . . .

That the settlers on any territory so purchased, and offered for sale, shall, either on their own petition, or on the order of Congress, receive authority from them with appointments of time and place for their free males of full age, within the limits of their state to meet together for the purpose of establishing a temporary government, to adopt the constitution and laws of any one of the original states, so that such laws nevertheless shall be subject to alteration by their ordinary legislature; & to erect, subject to a like alteration, counties or townships for the election of members for their legislature.

That when any such State shall have acquired twenty thousand inhabitants, on giving due proof thereof to Congress, they shall receive from them authority with appointment of time and place to call a convention of representatives to establish a permanent Constitution and Government for themselves. Provided that both the temporary and permanent governments be established on these principles as their basis.

First. That they shall forever remain a part of this confederacy of the United States of America. Second. That they shall be subject to the articles of Confederation in all those cases in which the original states shall be so subject and to all the acts and ordinances of the United States in Congress assembled, conformable thereto. Third. That they shall in no case interfere with the primary disposal of the soil by the United States . . . nor with the ordinances and regulations which Congress may find necessary for securing the title to such soil to the bona fide purchasers. Fourth. That they shall be subject to pay a part of the federal debts contracted or to be contracted, to be apportioned on them by Congress, according to the same common rule & measure, by which apportionments thereof shall be made on the other states. Fifth. That no tax shall be imposed on lands, the property of the United States. Sixth. That their respective governments shall be republican. Seventh. That the lands of non-resident proprietors shall in no case, be taxed higher than those of residents . . . before the admission thereof to a vote by its delegates in Congress.

That whensoever any of the sd states shall have, of free inhabitants, as many as shall then be in any one the least numerous of the thirteen Original states, such State shall be admitted by it's delegates into the Congress of the United States on an equal footing with the said original states: provided the consent of so many states in Congress is first obtained as may at the time be competent to such admission. And in order to adopt the said Articles of Confederation to the state of Congress when it's numbers shall be thus increased, it shall be proposed to the legislatures of the states originally parties thereto, to require the assent of two thirds of the United States in Congress assembled in all those cases wherein by the said articles the assent of nine states is now required; which being agreed to by them shall be binding on the new states. Until such admission by their delegates into Congress, any of the said states after the establishment of their temporary government shall have authority to keep a sitting member in Congress, with a right of debating, but not of voting.

That measures not inconsistent with the principles of the Confedn. & necessary for the preservation of peace & good order among the settlers in any of the said new states until they shall assume a temporary Government as aforesaid, may from time to time be taken by the United States in Congress assembled.

That the preceding articles shall be formed into a charter of compact, shall be duly executed by the President of the United States in Congress assembled, under his hand & the seal of the United States, shall be promulgated and shall stand as fundamental constitutions between the thirteen original states and each of the several states now newly described, unalterable . . . but by the joint consent of the United States in Congress assembled, and of the particular state within which such alteration is proposed to be made.

78. LAND ORDINANCE OF 1785
May 20, 1785

(Journals of the Continental Congress, ed. by J. C. Fitzpatrick, Vol. XXVIII, p. 375 ff.)

This land ordinance laid the foundations for the public land system, followed in most essentials until 1862. Of particular importance were the provisions reserving certain lands for educational purposes. See, P. J. Treat, *The National Land System, 1785–1820;* A. C. Ford, *Colonial Precedents of our National Land System;* G. W. Knight, "History of National Land Grants for Education in the Northwest Territory," Am. Hist. Assoc. *Papers,* Vol. I.

An Ordinance for ascertaining the mode of disposing of Lands in the Western Territory.

BE it ordained by the United States in Congress assembled, that the territory ceded by individual States to the United States, which has been purchased of the Indian inhabitants, shall be disposed of in the following manner:

A surveyor from each state shall be appointed by Congress or a Committee of the States, who shall take an oath for the faithful discharge of his duty, before the Geographer of the United States. . . .

The Surveyors, as they are respectively qualified, shall proceed to divide the said territory into townships of six miles square, by lines running due north and south, and others crossing these at right angles, as near as may be, unless where the boundaries of the late Indian purchases may render the same impracticable, . . .

The first line, running due north and south as aforesaid, shall begin on the river Ohio,

at a point that shall be found to be due north from the western termination of a line, which has been run as the southern boundary of the State of Pennsylvania; and the first line, running east and west, shall begin at the same point, and shall extend throughout the whole territory. Provided, that nothing herein shall be construed, as fixing the western boundary of the State of Pennsylvania. The geographer shall designate the townships, or fractional parts of townships, by numbers progressively from south to north; always beginning each range with No. 1; and the ranges shall be distinguished by their progressive numbers to the westward. The first range, extending from the Ohio to the lake Erie, being marked No. 1. The Geographer shall personally attend to the running of the first east and west line; and shall take the latitude of the extremes of the first north and south line, and of the mouths of the principal rivers.

The lines shall be measured with a chain; shall be plainly marked by chaps on the trees, and exactly described on a plat; whereon shall be noted by the surveyor, at their proper distances, all mines, salt-springs, salt-licks and mill-seats, that shall come to his knowledge, and all water-courses, mountains and other remarkable and permanent things, over and near which such lines shall pass, and also the quality of the lands.

The plats of the townships respectively,

shall be marked by subdivisions into lots of one mile square, or 640 acres, in the same direction as the external lines, and numbered from 1 to 36; always beginning the succeeding range of the lots with the number next to that with which the preceding one concluded. . . .

. . . And the geographer shall make . . . returns, from time to time, of every seven ranges as they may be surveyed. The Secretary of War shall have recourse thereto, and shall take by lot therefrom, a number of townships . . . as will be equal to one seventh part of the whole of such seven ranges, . . . for the use of the late Continental army. . . .

The board of treasury shall transmit a copy of the original plats, previously noting thereon the townships and fractional parts of townships, which shall have fallen to the several states, by the distribution aforesaid, to the commissioners of the loan-office of the several states, who, after giving notice . . . shall proceed to sell the townships or fractional parts of townships, at public vendue, in the following manner, viz.: The township or fractional part of a township No. 1, in the first range, shall be sold entire; and No. 2, in the same range, by lots; and thus in alternate order through the whole of the first range . . . provided, that none of the lands, within the said territory, be sold under the price of one dollar the acre,

to be paid in specie, or loan-office certificates, reduced to specie value, by the scale of depreciation, or certificates of liquidated debts of the United States, including interest, besides the expense of the survey and other charges thereon, which are hereby rated at thirty six dollars the township, . . . on failure of which payment, the said lands shall again be offered for sale.

There shall be reserved for the United States out of every township the four lots, being numbered 8,11,26,29, and out of every fractional part of a township, so many lots of the same numbers as shall be found thereon, for future sale. There shall be reserved the lot No. 16, of every township, for the maintenance of public schools within the said township; also one-third part of all gold, silver, lead and copper mines, to be sold, or otherwise disposed of as Congress shall hereafter direct. . . .

And Whereas Congress . . . stipulated grants of land to certain officers and soldiers of the late Continental army . . . for complying with such engagements, Be it ordained, That the secretary of war . . . determine who are the objects of the above resolutions and engagements . . . and cause the townships, or fractional parts of townships, hereinbefore reserved for the use of the late Continental army, to be drawn for in such manner as he shall deem expedient. . . .

79. RELIGIOUS LIBERTY IN VIRGINIA
Memorial of the Presbytery of Hanover
October 24, 1776

(W. H. Foote, *Sketches of Virginia, Historical and Biographical*, p. 323 ff.)

Parallel with the movement for political liberty went a demand for religious liberty. This movement was strongest in the South, where the Anglican Church had long been established by law. Ever since the days of the Great Awakening, the dissenting churches had flourished in the up-country of Virginia. The Presbyterian Church was particularly strong in the Valley, where Scotch-Irish were found in large numbers. Numerous petitions protesting against religious discrimination had been presented to the Virginia House of Burgesses in the fifties and sixties; with the coming of the Revolution these memorials became even more numerous and more emphatic. See. Doc. No. 80 and references.

To the Honorable the General Assembly of Virginia:

The Memorial of the Presbytery of Hanover humbly represents:

. . . It is well known, that in the frontier counties, which are justly supposed to contain a fifth part of the inhabitants of Virginia, the dissenters have borne the heavy burdens of purchasing glebes, building churches, and supporting the established clergy, where there are very few Episcopalians, either to assist in bearing the expense, or to reap the advantage; and that throughout the other parts of the country, there are also many thousands of zealous friends and defenders of our State, who, besides the invidious, and disadvantageous restrictions to which they have been subjected, annually pay large taxes to support an establishment, from which their consciences and principles oblige them to dissent: all which are confessedly so many violations of their natural rights; and in their consequences, a restraint upon freedom of inquiry, and private judgment.

In this enlightened age, and in a land where all, of every denomination are united in the most strenuous efforts to be free, we hope and expect that our representatives will cheerfully concur in removing every species of religious, as well as civil bondage. Certain it is, that every argument for civil liberty, gains additional strength when applied to liberty in the concerns of religion; and there is no argument in favour of establishing the Christian religion, but what may be pleaded, with equal propriety, for establishing the tenets of Mahomed by those who believe the Alcoran: or if this be not true, it is at least impossible for the magistrate to adjudge the right of preference among the various sects that profess the Christian faith, without erecting a chair of infallibility, which would lead us back to the church of Rome.

80. VIRGINIA STATUTE OF RELIGIOUS LIBERTY
January 16, 1786

(W. W. Hening, ed. *Statutes at Large of Virginia*, Vol. XII, p. 84 ff.)

The Declaration of Rights of 1776 had announced the principle of religious liberty, but the Anglican Church was still the established church. In 1777 the liberals succeeded in repealing the statutes requiring church attendance and universal support of the established church, but it was not until 1779 that the church was disestablished. Even this was not satisfactory, and Jefferson prepared a bill for absolute religious freedom and equality. This complete divorcement of church and state was bitterly opposed not only by the Episcopal but by the Presbyterian and other dissenting churches as well. The proposal to make all Christian churches state religions on equal standing and support them by taxation found favor with such men as Patrick Henry, Washington, and other conservatives. Jefferson characterized the long struggle for religious freedom as "the severest contest in which I have ever been engaged," and it was not until 1785 that his bill, sponsored in his absence by Mason, Madison, Taylor, George and W. C. Nicholas, passed the House: in January 1786 it was accepted by the Senate and became law. "Thus," wrote Madison, "in Virginia was extinguished forever the ambitious hope of making laws for the human mind", while Jefferson regarded it as one of his three memorable contributions to history. The Bill was translated into French and Italian, and aroused world-wide remark. See, H. J. Eckenrode, *Separation of Church and State in Virginia*; C. F. James, *Documentary History of the Struggle for Religious Liberty in Virginia*; R. B. Semple, *Rise and Progress of Baptists in Virginia*; F. W. Hirst, *Jefferson*, p. 130 ff.; G. Hunt, *Madison;* A. C. McLaughlin, et.al., *Source Problems in United States History*, No. iv.

An Act for establishing Religious Freedom.

I. WHEREAS Almighty God hath created the mind free; that all attempts to influence it by temporal punishments or burthens, or by civil incapacitations, tend only to beget habits of hypocrisy and meanness, and are a departure from the plan of the Holy author of our religion, who being Lord both of body and mind, yet chose not to propagate it by coercions on either, as was in his Almighty power to do; that the impious presumption of legislators and rulers, civil as well as ecclesiastical, who being themselves but fallible and uninspired men, have assumed dominion over the faith of others, setting up their own opinions and modes of thinking as the only true and infallible, and as such endeavouring to impose them on others, hath established and maintained false religions over the greatest part of the world, and through all time; that to compel a man to furnish contributions of money for the propagation of opinions which he disbelieves, is sinful and tyrannical; that even the forcing him to support this or that teacher of his own religious persuasion, is depriving him of the comfortable liberty of giving his contributions to the particular pastor whose morals he would make his pattern, and whose powers he feels most persuasive to righteousness, and is withdrawing from the ministry those temporary rewards, which proceeding from an approbation of their personal conduct, are an additional incitement to earnest and unremitting labours for the instruction of mankind; that our civil rights have no dependence on our religious opinions, any more than our opinions in physics or geometry; that therefore the proscribing any citizen as unworthy the public confidence by laying upon him an incapacity of being called to offices of trust and emolument, unless he profess or renounce this or that religious opinion, is depriving him injuriously of those privileges and advantages to which in common with his fellow-citizens he has a natural right, that it tends only to corrupt the principles of that religion it is meant to encourage, by bribing with a monopoly of worldly honours and emoluments, those who will externally profess and conform to it; that though indeed these are criminal who do not withstand such temptation, yet neither are those innocent who lay the bait in their way; that to suffer the civil magistrate to intrude his powers into the field of opinion, and to restrain the profession or propagation of principles on supposition of their ill tendency, is a dangerous fallacy, which at once destroys all religious liberty, because he being of course judge of that tendency will make his opinions the rule of judgment, and approve or condemn the sentiments of others only as they shall square with or differ from his own; that it is time enough for the rightful purposes of

civil government, for its officers to interfere when principles break out into overt acts against peace and good order; and finally, that truth is great and will prevail if left to herself, that she is the proper and sufficient antagonist to error, and has nothing to fear from the conflict, unless by human interposition disarmed of her natural weapons, free argument and debate, errors ceasing to be dangerous when it is permitted freely to contradict them.

II. *Be it enacted by the General Assembly,* that no man shall be compelled to frequent or support any religious worship, place or ministry whatsoever, nor shall be enforced, restrained, molested, or burthened in his body or goods, nor shall otherwise suffer on account of his religious opinions or belief; but that all men shall be free to profess, and by argument to maintain, their opinion in matters of religion, and that the same shall in no wise diminish, enlarge or affect their civil capacities.

III. And though we well know that this assembly, elected by the people for the ordinary purposes of legislation only, have no power to restrain the acts of succeeding assemblies, constituted with powers equal to our own, and that therefore to declare this act to be irrevocable would be of no effect in law; yet as we are free to declare, and do declare, that the rights hereby asserted are of the natural rights of mankind, and that if any act shall hereafter be passed to repeal the present, or to narrow its operation, such act will be an infringement of natural right.

81. SHAYS'S REBELLION
1786

(G. R. Minot, *History of the Insurrection in Massachusetts,* p. 82 ff.)

The commercial depression of 1785–86 hit Massachusetts with particular severity. The West India trade was stopped, farm prices fell sharply, and taxation, unfairly apportioned, was intolerably heavy: the poll tax, for example, accounted for forty per cent of the entire taxes. Foreclosures on lands led to a widespread hostility against lawyers and courts, and all through the summer of 1786, town meetings demanded reforms or direct action. The legislature, however, was deaf to the appeals for reform, and in the fall of 1786 a minor rebellion broke out

in central and western Massachusetts. Under the leadership of Captain Daniel Shays, infuriated mobs broke up the meetings of courts, and threatened the armory at Springfield. The outbreak excited fear and despair in the hearts of many observers, and was not without influence in persuading Americans of the desirability of a stronger central government. After the uprising had been suppressed, the legislature enacted many of the reforms advocated by the Shaysites. Minot's *History of the Insurrection* gives many of the petitions and resolutions of the town meetings. On the Rebellion see also, A. C. McLaughlin, *Confederation and Constitution,* ch. x; J. T. Adams, *New England in the Republic,* ch. vi; J. P. Warren, "The Confederation and the Shays Rebellion," *American Hist. Review,* Vol. XI; W. V. Wells, *Life and Public Services of Samuel Adams,* Vol. III, ch. lix.; A. E. Morse, *The Federalist Party in Massachusetts,* ch. iii.

1. An ADDRESS to the People of the several towns in the county of Hampshire, now at arms.

GENTLEMEN,

We have thought proper to inform you of some of the principal causes of the late risings of the people, and also of their present movement, viz.

1st. The present expensive mode of collecting debts, which by reason of the great scarcity of cash, will of necessity fill our gaols with unhappy debtors; and thereby a reputable body of people rendered incapable of being serviceable either to themselves or the community.

2d. The monies raised by impost and excise being appropriated to discharge the interest of governmental securities, and not the foreign debt, when these securities are not subject to taxation.

3d. A suspension of the writ of Habeas Corpus, by which those persons who have stepped forth to assert and maintain the rights of the people, are liable to be taken and conveyed even to the most distant part of the Commonwealth, and thereby subjected to an unjust punishment.

4th. The unlimited power granted to Justices of the Peace and Sheriffs, Deputy Sheriffs, and Constables, by the Riot Act, indemnifying them to the prosecution thereof; when perhaps, wholly actuated from a principle of revenge, hatred, and envy.

Furthermore, Be assured, that this body, now at arms, despise the idea of being instigated by British emissaries, which is so strenuously propagated by the enemies of our liberties: And also wish the most proper and speedy measures may be taken, to discharge both our foreign and domestick debt.

Per Order,

DANIEL GRAY, Chairman
of the Committee.

2. To the Printer of the Hampshire Herald.

SIR,

It has some how or other fallen to my lot to be employed in a more conspicuous manner than some others of my fellow citizens, in stepping forth on defence of the rights and privileges of the people, more especially of the county of Hampshire.

Therefore, upon the desire of the people now at arms, I take this method to publish to the world of mankind in general, particularly the people of this Commonwealth, some of the principal grievances we complain of, . . .

In the first place, I must refer you to a draught of grievances drawn up by a committee of the people, now at arms, under the signature of Daniel Gray, chairman, which is heartily approved of; some others also are here added, viz.

1st. The General Court, for certain obvious reasons, must be removed out of the town of Boston.

2d. A revision of the constitution is absolutely necessary.

3d. All kinds of governmental securities, now on interest, that have been bought of the original owners for two shillings, and the highest for six shillings and eight pence on the pound, and have received more interest than the principal cost the speculator who purchased them—that if justice was done, we verily believe, nay positively know, it would save this Commonwealth thousands of pounds.

4th. Let the lands belonging to this Commonwealth, at the eastward, be sold at the best advantage to pay the remainder of our domestick debt.

5th. Let the monies arising from impost and excise be appropriated to discharge the foreign debt.

6th. Let that act, passed by the General Court last June by a small majority of only seven, called the Supplementary Act, for twenty-five years to come, be repealed.

7th. The total abolition of the Inferiour Court of Common Pleas and General Sessions of the Peace.

8th. Deputy Sheriffs totally set aside, as a useless set of officers in the community; and Constables who are really necessary, be empowered to do the duty, by which means a large swarm of lawyers will be banished from their wonted haunts, who have been more damage to the people at large, especially the common farmers, than the savage beasts of prey.

To this I boldly sign my proper name, as a hearty wellwisher to the real rights of the people.

THOMAS GROVER

Worcester, December 7, 1786.

82. THE NORTHWEST ORDINANCE
July 13, 1787

(F. N. Thorpe, ed. *Federal and State Constitutions*, Vol. II, p. 957 ff.)

The Ordinance of April 23, 1784, Doc. No. 77, laid down the general principles of the American colonial system, but it did not provide in detail for the establishment of an administrative structure, and it was never put into effect. The immediate impulse for the Ordinance of 1787 came from a group of land speculators, members of the Ohio Company of Associates and of the Society of the Cincinnati, who wished to establish colonies in the Ohio country. The spokesmen of these groups were the Rev. Manasseh Cutler, Samuel Parsons, and General Rufus Putnam. These men succeeded in lobbying through a moribund Congress the famous Ordinance establishing a government in the Northwest territory. The authorship of the Ordinance is a matter of controversy, but it seems probable that Nathan Dane and Rufus King were the principal authors; fundamentally, of course, the Ordinance followed Jefferson's Ordinance of 1784. See B. A. Hinsdale, *The Old Northwest;* J. A. Barrett, *Evolution of the Ordinance of 1787;* W. P. and J. P. Cutler, *Life, Journals, and Correspondence of Manasseh Cutler,* 2 Vols.; R. Buell, *Memoirs of Rufus Putnam;* A. B. Hulbert, ed. *Records of the Ohio Company;* C. S. Hall, *Life and Letters of Samuel Holden Parsons;* R. King, *Ohio;* J. P. Dunn, *Indiana;* B. W. Bond, *Civilization of the Old Northwest;* J. M. Merriam, "Legislative History of the Ordinance of 1787", Am. Antiquarian Soc. *Proceedings,* N.S. Vol. V; C. R. King, *Rufus King.* Vol. I.; A. C. McLaughlin, *Confederation and Constitution,* ch. vii; F. L. Paxson, *History of the American Frontier,* chs. vii–viii; J. B. McMaster, *History of the People of the United States,* Vol. I, ch. v.

An Ordinance for the government of the Territory of the United States northwest of the River Ohio.

Be it ordained by the United States in Congress assembled, That the said territory, for the purposes of temporary government, be one district, subject, however, to be di-

vided into two districts, as future circumstances may, in the opinion of Congress, make it expedient.

Be it ordained by the authority aforesaid, That the estates, both of resident and nonresident proprietors in the said territory, dying intestate, shall descend to, and be distributed among their children, and the descendants of a deceased child, in equal parts; the descendants of a deceased child or grandchild to take the share of their deceased parent in equal parts among them: And where there shall be no children or descendants, then in equal parts to the next of kin in equal degree; and among collaterals, the children of a deceased brother or sister of the intestate shall have, in equal parts among them, their deceased parents' share; and there shall in no case be a distinction between kindred of the whole and half-blood; saving, in all cases, to the widow of the intestate her third part of the real estate for life, and one-third part of the personal estate; and this law relative to descents and dower, shall remain in full force until altered by the legislature of the district. And until the governor and judges shall adopt laws as hereinafter mentioned, estates in the said territory may be devised or bequeathed by wills in writing, signed and sealed by him or her in whom the estate may be (being of full age), and attested by three witnesses; and real estates may be conveyed by lease and release, or bargain and sale, signed sealed and delivered by the person, being of full age, in whom the estate may be, and attested by two witnesses, provided such wills be duly proved, and such conveyances be acknowledged, or the execution thereof duly proved, and be recorded within one year after proper magistrates, courts, and registers shall be appointed for that purpose; and personal property may be transferred by delivery; saving, however to the French and Canadian inhabitants, and other settlers of the Kaskaskies, St. Vincents and the neighboring villages who have heretofore professed themselves citizens of Virginia, their laws and customs now in force among them, relative to the descent and conveyance, of property.

Be it ordained by the authority aforesaid, That there shall be appointed from time to time by Congress, a governor, whose commission shall continue in force for the term of three years, unless sooner revoked by Congress; he shall reside in the district, and have a freehold estate therein in 1,000 acres of land, while in the exercise of his office.

There shall be appointed from time to time by Congress, a secretary, whose commission shall continue in force for four years unless sooner revoked; he shall reside in the district, and have a freehold estate therein in 500 acres of land, while in the exercise of his office. It shall be his duty to keep and preserve the acts and laws passed by the legislature, and the public records of the district, and the proceedings of the governor in his executive department, and transmit authentic copies of such acts and proceedings, every six months, to the Secretary of Congress: There shall also be appointed a court to consist of three judges, any two of whom to form a court, who shall have a common law jurisdiction, and reside in the district, and have each therein a freehold estate in 500 acres of land while in the exercise of their offices; and their commissions shall continue in force during good behavior.

The governor and judges, or a majority of them, shall adopt and publish in the district such laws of the original States, criminal and civil, as may be necessary and best suited to the circumstances of the district, and report them to Congress from time to time: which laws shall be in force in the district until the organization of the General Assembly therein, unless disapproved of by Congress; but afterwards the Legislature shall have authority to alter them as they shall think fit.

The governor, for the time being, shall be commander-in-chief of the militia, appoint and commission all officers in the same below the rank of general officers; all general officers shall be appointed and commissioned by Congress.

Previous to the organization of the general assembly, the governor shall appoint such magistrates and other civil officers in each county or township, as he shall find necessary for the preservation of the peace and good order in the same: After the general assembly shall be organized, the powers and duties of the magistrates and other civil officers shall be regulated and defined by the said assembly; but all magistrates and other civil officers not herein otherwise directed, shall, during the continuance of this temporary government, be appointed by the governor.

For the prevention of crimes and injuries, the laws to be adopted or made shall have force in all parts of the district, and for the execution of process, criminal and civil, the governor shall make proper divisions thereof; and he shall proceed from time to time as circumstances may require, to lay out the parts of the district in which the Indian titles shall have been extinguished, into counties and townships, subject however to such alterations as may thereafter be made by the legislature.

So soon as there shall be five thousand free male inhabitants of full age in the district, upon giving proof thereof to the governor, they shall receive authority, with time and place, to elect representatives from their counties or townships to represent them in the general assembly: *Provided,* That, for every five hundred free male inhabitants, there shall be one representative, and so on progressively with the number of free male inhabitants shall the right of representation increase, until the number of representatives shall amount to twenty-five; after which, the number and proportion of representatives shall be regulated by the legislature: *Provided,* That no person be eligible or qualified to act as a representative unless he shall have been a citizen of one of the United States three years, and be a resident in the district, or unless he shall have resided in the district three years; and, in either case, shall likewise hold in his own right, in fee simple, two hundred acres of land within the same: *Provided, also,* That a freehold in fifty acres of land in the district, having been a citizen of one of the states, and being resident in the district, or the like freehold and two years residence in the district, shall be necessary to qualify a man as an elector of a representative.

The representatives thus elected, shall serve for the term of two years; and, in case of the death of a representative, or removal from office, the governor shall issue a writ to the county or township for which he was a member, to elect another in his stead, to serve for the residue of the term.

The general assembly or legislature shall consist of the governor, legislative council, and a house of representatives. The Legislative Council shall consist of five members, to continue in office five years, unless sooner removed by Congress; any three of whom to be a quorum: and the members of the Council shall be nominated and appointed in the following manner, to wit: As soon as representatives shall be elected, the Governor shall appoint a time and place for them to meet together; and, when met, they shall nominate ten persons, residents in the district, and each possessed of a freehold in five hundred acres of land, and return their names to Congress; five of whom Congress shall appoint and commission to serve as aforesaid; and, whenever a vacancy shall happen in the council, by death or removal from office, the house of representatives shall nominate two persons, qualified as aforesaid, for each vacancy, and return their names to Congress; one of whom Congress shall appoint and commission for the residue of the term. And every five years, four months at least before the expiration of the time of service of the members of council, the said house shall nominate ten persons, qualified as aforesaid, and return their names to Congress; five of whom Congress shall appoint and commission to serve as members of the council five years, unless sooner removed. And the governor, legislative council, and house of representatives, shall have authority to make laws in all cases, for the good government of the district, not repugnant to the principles and articles in this ordinance established and declared. And all bills, having passed by a majority in the house, and by a majority in the council, shall be referred to the governor for his assent; but no bill, or legislative act whatever, shall be of any force without his as-

sent. The governor shall have power to convene, prorogue, and dissolve the general assembly, when, in his opinion, it shall be expedient.

The governor, judges, legislative council, secretary, and such other officers as Congress shall appoint in the district, shall take an oath or affirmation of fidelity and of office; the governor before the president of congress, and all other officers before the Governor. As soon as a legislature shall be formed in the district, the council and house assembled in one room, shall have authority, by joint ballot, to elect a delegate to Congress, who shall have a seat in Congress, with a right of debating but not of voting during this temporary government.

And, for extending the fundamental principles of civil and religious liberty, which form the basis whereon these republics, their laws and constitutions are erected; to fix and establish those principles as the basis of all laws, constitutions, and governments, which forever hereafter shall be formed in the said territory: to provide also for the establishment of States, and permanent government therein, and for their admission to a share in the federal councils on an equal footing with the original States, at as early periods as may be consistent with the general interest:

It is hereby ordained and declared by the authority aforesaid, That the following articles shall be considered as articles of compact between the original States and the people and States in the said territory and forever remain unalterable, unless by common consent, to wit:

ART. 1. No person, demeaning himself in a peaceable and orderly manner, shall ever be molested on account of his mode of worship or religious sentiments, in the said territory.

ART. 2. The inhabitants of the said territory shall always be entitled to the benefits of the writ of *habeas corpus,* and of the trial by jury; of a proportionate representation of the people in the legislature; and of judicial proceedings according to the course of the common law. All persons shall be bailable, unless for capital offences, where the proof shall be evident or the presumption great. All fines shall be moderate; and no cruel or unusual punishments shall be inflicted. No man shall be deprived of his liberty or property, but by the judgment of his peers or the law of the land; and, should the public exigencies make it necessary, for the common preservation, to take any person's property, or to demand his particular services, full compensation shall be made for the same. And, in the just preservation of rights and property, it is understood and declared, that no law ought ever to be made, or have force in the said territory, that shall, in any manner whatever, interfere with or affect private contracts or engagements, *bona fide,* and without fraud, previously formed.

ART. 3. Religion, morality, and knowledge, being necessary to good government and the happiness of mankind, schools and the means of education shall forever be encouraged. The utmost good faith shall always be observed towards the Indians; their lands and property shall never be taken from them without their consent; and, in their property, rights, and liberty, they shall never be invaded or disturbed, unless in just and lawful wars authorized by Congress; but laws founded in justice and humanity, shall from time to time be made for preventing wrongs being done to them, and for preserving peace and friendship with them.

ART. 4. The said territory, and the States which may be formed therein, shall forever remain a part of this Confederacy of the United States of America, subject to the Articles of Confederation, and to such alterations therein as shall be constitutionally made; and to all the acts and ordinances of the United States in Congress assembled, conformable thereto. The inhabitants and settlers in the said territory shall be subject to pay a part of the federal debts contracted or to be contracted, and a proportional part of the expenses of government, to be apportioned on them by Congress according to the same common rule and measure by which apportionments thereof shall be made on the other States; and the taxes for paying their proportion shall be laid and levied by the authority and direction of the legislatures of the district or districts, or new States, as in the original States, within the time agreed upon by the United States in Congress assembled. The legislatures of those districts or new States, shall never interfere with the primary disposal of the soil by the United States in Congress assembled, nor with any regulations Congress may find necessary for securing the title in such soil to the *bona fide* purchasers. No tax shall be imposed on lands the property of the United States; and, in no case, shall non-resident proprietors be taxed higher than residents. The navigable waters leading into the Mississippi and St. Lawrence, and the carrying places between the same, shall be common highways and forever free, as well to the inhabitants of the said territory as to the citizens of the United States, and those of any other States that may be admitted into the confederacy, without any tax, impost, or duty therefor.

ART. 5. There shall be formed in the said territory, not less than three nor more than five States; and the boundaries of the States, as soon as Virginia shall alter her act of cession, and consent to the same, shall become fixed and established as follows, to wit: The western State in the said territory, shall be bounded by the Mississippi, the Ohio, and Wabash Rivers; a direct line drawn from the Wabash and Post Vincents, due North, to the territorial line between the United States and Canada; and, by the said territorial line, to the Lake of the Woods and Mississippi. The middle State shall be bounded by the said direct line, the Wabash from Post Vincents to the Ohio, by the Ohio, by a direct line, drawn due north from the mouth of the Great Miami, to the said territorial line, and by the said territorial line. The eastern State shall be bounded by the last mentioned direct line, the Ohio, Pennsylvania, and the said territorial line: *Provided, however,* and it is further understood and declared, that the boundaries of these three States shall be subject so far to be altered, that, if Congress shall hereafter find it expedient, they shall have authority to form one or two States in that part of the said territory which lies north of an east and west line drawn through the southerly bend or extreme of lake Michigan. And, whenever any of the said States shall have sixty thousand free inhabitants therein, such State shall be admitted, by its delegates, into the Congress of the United States, on an equal footing with the original States in all respects whatever, and shall be at liberty to form a permanent constitution and State government: *Provided*, the constitution and government so to be formed, shall be republican, and in conformity to the principles contained in these articles; and, so far as it can be consistent with the general interest of the confederacy, such admission shall be allowed at an earlier period, and when there may be a less number of free inhabitants in the State than sixty thousand.

ART. 6. There shall be neither slavery nor involuntary servitude in the said territory, otherwise than in the punishment of crimes whereof the party shall have been duly convicted: *Provided, always,* That any person escaping into the same, from whom labor or service is lawfully claimed in any one of the original States, such fugitive may be lawfully reclaimed and conveyed to the person claiming his or her labor or service as aforesaid.

Be it ordained by the authority aforesaid, That the resolutions of the 23rd of April 1784, relative to the subject of this ordinance, be, and the same are hereby repealed and declared null and void.

83. THE ANNAPOLIS CONVENTION

Proceedings of the Commissioners To Remedy Defects of the Federal
Government, Annapolis in the State of Maryland.
Sept. 14, 1786

(*Documents Illustrative of the Formation of the Union of the American States,* p. 39 ff.)

Dissatisfaction with the Articles of Confederation had been growing ever since their ratification. The inability of the government of the Confederation to conclude commercial treaties with foreign nations, the mounting financial and currency difficulties, and the apparent impossibility of amending the Articles by ordinary processes, all led to a demand for a drastic revision of the Articles of Confederation. The immediate impulse for the Annapolis Convention came from a group of men who wished to open up navigation on the Potomac. In 1785 Washington invited the commissioners of Virginia and Maryland to meet at Mount Vernon and discuss the problem of communication between the East and the West. These commissioners drew up resolutions asking the co-operation of Pennsylvania in the project. Acting upon this suggestion Madison pushed through the legislature of Virginia a resolution appointing a commission to meet with other commissioners to take into consideration the state of the union. These commissioners met at Annapolis the first Monday in September 1786. See, A. C. McLaughlin, *Confederation and Constitution,* ch. xi; G. Hunt, *James Madison;* W. C. Rives, *Madison.*

To the Honorable, the Legislatures of Virginia, Delaware, Pennsylvania, New Jersey, and New York—

The Commissioners from the said States, respectively assembled at Annapolis, humbly beg leave to report.

That, pursuant to their several appointments, they met, at Annapolis in the State of Maryland, on the eleventh day of September Instant, and having proceeded to a Communication of their Powers; they found that the States of New York, Pennsylvania, and Virginia, had, in substance, and nearly in the same terms, authorized their respective Commissioners "to meet such other Commissioners as were, or might be, appointed by the other States in the Union, at such time and place as should be agreed upon by the said Commissioners to take into consideration the trade and commerce of the United States, to consider how far an uniform system in their commercial intercourse and regulations might be necessary to their common interest and permanent harmony, and to report to the several States such an Act, relative to this great object, as when unanimously ratified by them would enable the United States in Congress assembled effectually to provide for the same." . . .

That the State of New Jersey had enlarged the object of their appointment, empowering their Commissioners, "to consider how far an uniform system in their commercial regulations and *other important matters,* might be necessary to the common interest and permanent harmony of the several States," and to report such an Act on the subject, as when ratified by them, "would enable the United States in Congress assembled, effectually to provide for the exigencies of the Union."

That appointments of Commissioners have also been made by the States of New Hampshire, Massachusetts, Rhode Island, and North Carolina, none of whom however have attended; but that no information has been received by your Commissioners, of any appointment having been made by the States of Connecticut, Maryland, South Carolina or Georgia.

That the express terms of the powers of your Commissioners supposing a deputation from all the States, and having for object the Trade and Commerce of the United States, Your Commissioners did not conceive it advisable to proceed on the business of their mission, under the Circumstance of so partial and defective a representation.

Deeply impressed however with the magnitude and importance of the object confided to them on this occasion, your Commissioners cannot forbear to indulge an expression of their earnest and unanimous wish, that speedy measures be taken, to effect a general meeting, of the States, in a future Convention, for the same, and such other purposes, as the situation of public affairs may be found to require.

If in expressing this wish, or in intimating any other sentiment, your Commissioners should seem to exceed the strict bounds of their appointment, they entertain a full confidence, that a conduct, dictated by an anxiety for the welfare of the United States, will not fail to receive an indulgent construction.

In this persuasion, your Commissioners submit an opinion, that the Idea of extending the powers of their Deputies, to other objects, than those of Commerce, which has been adopted by the State of New Jersey, was an improvement on the original plan, and will deserve to be incorporated into that of a future Convention; they are the more naturally led to this conclusion, as in the course of their reflections on the subject, they have been induced to think, that the power of regulating trade is of such comprehensive extent, and will enter so far into the general System of the foederal government, that to give it efficacy, and to obviate questions and doubts concerning its precise nature and limits, may require a correspondent adjustment of other parts of the Foederal System.

That there are important defects in the system of the Foederal Government is acknowledged by the Acts of all those States, which have concurred in the present Meeting; That the defects, upon a closer examination, may be found greater and more numerous, than even these acts imply, is at least so far probable, from the embarrassments which characterise the present State of our national affairs, foreign and domestic, as may reasonably be supposed to merit a deliberate and candid discussion, in some mode, which will unite the Sentiments and Councils of all the States. In the choice of the mode, your Commissioners are of opinion, that a Convention of Deputies from the different States, for the special and sole purpose of entering into this investigation, and digesting a plan for supplying such defects as may be discovered to exist, will be entitled to a preference from considerations, which will occur without being particularised.

Your Commissioners decline an enumeration of those national circumstances on which their opinion respecting the propriety of a future Convention, with more enlarged powers, is founded; as it would be an useless intrusion of facts and observations, most of which have been frequently the subject of public discussion, and none of which can have escaped the penetration of those to whom they would in this instance be addressed. They are however of a nature so serious, as, in the view of your Commissioners, to render the situation of the United States delicate and critical, calling for an exertion of the united virtue and wisdom of all the members of the Confederacy.

Under this impression, Your Commissioners, with the most respectful deference, beg leave to suggest their unanimous conviction that it may essentially tend to advance the interests of the union if the States, by whom they have been respectively delegated, would themselves concur, and use their endeavours to procure the concurrence of the other States, in the appointment of Commissioners, to meet at Philadelphia on the second Monday in May next, to take into consideration the situation of the United States, to devise such further provisions as shall appear to them necessary to render the constitution of the Foederal Government adequate to the exigencies of the Union; and to report such an Act for that purpose to the United States in Congress assembled, as when agreed to, by them, and afterwards confirmed by the Legislatures of every State, will effectually provide for the same.

Though your Commissioners could not with propriety address these observations and sentiments to any but the States they have the honor to represent, they have nevertheless concluded from motives of respect, to transmit copies of this Report to the United States in Congress assembled, and to the executives of the other States.

84. THE VIRGINIA or RANDOLPH PLAN

Presented to the Federal Convention
May 29, 1787

(Hunt, G., and Scott, J. B., eds. *Debates in the Federal Convention of 1787 Reported by James Madison,* p. 23 ff. For variant texts see, *Documents Illustrative of the Formation of the Union of the American States,* p. 953 ff.)

The Randolph or Large State Plan looked to the creation of a new national government rather than a mere revision of the Articles of Confederation. Of the various plans presented to the Convention, it was not only the first, but the one which most closely approximates the finished Constitution. Note however, that the "Supreme law of the land" clause—the central clause of the Constitution—was taken not from the Randolph but from the New Jersey plan. All of the histories of the Federal Convention deal at length with the Randolph Plan. See, C. Warren, *The Making of the Constitution,* esp. p. 139 ff.; A. C. McLaughlin, *Confederation and Constitution,* ch. xii; J. B. McMaster, *History of the People of the United States,* Vol. I, p. 438 ff.

1. Resolved that the Articles of Confederation ought to be so corrected and enlarged as to accomplish the objects proposed by their institution; namely "common defence, security of liberty and general welfare."

2. Resolved therefore that the rights of suffrage in the National Legislature ought to be proportioned to the Quotas of contribution, or to the number of free inhabitants, as the one or the other rule may seem best in diffent cases.

3. Resolved that the National Legislature ought to consist of two branches.

4. Resolved that the members of the first branch of the National Legislature ought to be elected by the people of the several States every   for the terms of   ; to be of the age of   years at least, to receive liberal stipends by which they may be compensated for the devotion of their time to public service, to be ineligible to any office established by a particular State, or under the authority of the United States, except those peculiarly belonging to the functions of the first branch, during the term of service, and for the space of   after its expiration; to be incapable of reelection for the space of   after the expiration of their term of service, and to be subject to recall.

5. Resolved that the members of the second branch of the National Legislature ought to be elected by those of the first, out of a proper number of persons nominated by the individual Legislatures, to be of the age of   years at least; to hold their offices for a term sufficient to ensure their independency; to receive liberal stipends, by which they may be compensated for the devotion of their time to public service; and to be ineligible to any office established by a particular State, or under the authority of the United States, except those peculiarly belonging to the functions of the second branch, during the term of service, and for the space of   after the expiration thereof.

6. Resolved that each branch ought to possess the right of originating Acts; that the National Legislature ought to be impowered to enjoy the Legislative Rights vested in Congress by the Confederation and moreover to legislate in all cases to which the separate States are incompetent, or in which the harmony of the United States may be interrupted by the exercise of individual Legislation; to negative all laws passed by the several States, contravening in the opin-

ion of the National Legislature the articles of Union; and to call forth the force of the Union against any member of the Union failing in its duty under the articles thereof.

7. Resolved that a National Executive be instituted; to be chosen by the National Legislature for the term of   years; to receive punctually, at stated times, a fixed compensation for the services rendered, in which no increase or diminution shall be made so as to affect the Magistracy, existing at the time of the increase or diminution, and to be ineligible a second time; and that besides a general authority to execute the National laws, it ought to enjoy the Executive rights vested in Congress by the Confederation.

8. Resolved that the Executive and a convenient number of the National Judiciary, ought to compose a Council or revision with authority to examine every act of the National Legislature before it shall operate, and every act of a particular Legislature before a Negative thereon shall be final; and that the dissent of the said Council shall amount to a rejection, unless the Act of the National Legislature be passed again, or that of a particular Legislature be again negatived by   of the members of each branch.

9. Resolved that a National Judiciary be established to consist of one or more supreme tribunals, and of inferior tribunals to be chosen by the National Legislature, to hold their offices during good behaviour; and to receive punctually at stated times fixed compensation for their services, in which no increase or diminution shall be made so as to affect the persons actually in office at the time of such increase or diminution. That the jurisdiction of the inferior tribunals shall be to hear and determine in the first instance, and of the supreme tribunal to hear and determine in the dernier resort, all

piracies and felonies on the high seas, captures from an enemy; cases in which foreigners or citizens of other States applying to such jurisdictions may be interested, or which respect the collection of the National revenue; impeachments of any National officers, and questions which may involve the national peace and harmony.

10. Resolved that provision ought to be made for the admission of States lawfully arising within the limits of the United States, whether from a voluntary junction of Government and Territory or otherwise, with the consent of a number of voices in the National legislature less than the whole.

11. Resolved that a Republican Government and the territory of each State, except in the instance of a voluntary junction of Government and territory, ought to be guaranteed by the United States to each State.

12. Resolved that provision ought to be made for the continuance of Congress and their authorities and privileges, until a given day after the reform of the articles of Union shall be adopted, and for the completion of all their engagements.

13. Resolved that provision ought to be made for the amendment of the Articles of Union whensoever it shall seem necessary, and that the assent of the National Legislature ought not to be required thereto.

14. Resolved that the Legislative Executive and Judiciary powers within the several States ought to be bound by oath to support the articles of Union.

15. Resolved that the amendments which shall be offered to the Confederation, by the Convention ought at a proper time, or times, after the approbation of Congress to be submitted to an assembly or assemblies of Representatives, recommended by the several Legislatures to be expressly chosen by the people, to consider and decide thereon.

85. THE PATERSON OR NEW JERSEY PLAN

Presented to the Federal Convention
June 15, 1787

(Hunt, G., and Scott, J. B., eds. *Debates in the Federal Convention of 1787 Reported by James Madison*, p. 102–4. For variant texts see *Documents Illustrative of the Formation of the Union of the American States*, p. 967–8)

On the Paterson plan, see McLaughlin, *Confederation and Constitution*, p. 212 ff. Note particularly Section 6, which contains the germ of the central clause of the Constitution.

1. Resolved that the Articles of Confederation ought to be so revised, corrected, and enlarged as to render the federal Constitution adequate to the exigencies of Government, and the preservation of the Union.

2. Resolved that in addition to the powers vested in the United States in Congress, by the present existing articles of Confederation, they be authorized to pass acts for raising a revenue, by levying a duty or duties on all goods or merchandizes of foreign growth or manufacture, imported into any part of the United States, by Stamps on paper, vellum or parchment, and by a postage on all letters or packages passing through the general post-office, to be applied to such federal purposes as they shall deem proper and expedient; to make rules and regulations for the collection thereof; and the same from time to time, to alter and amend in such manner as they shall think proper: to pass Acts for the regulation of trade and commerce as well with foreign nations as with each other; provided that all punishments, fines, forfeitures and penalties to be incurred for contravening such acts rules and regulations shall be adjudged by the Common law Judiciaries of the State in which any offence contrary to the true intent and meaning of such Acts rules and regulations shall have been committed or perpetrated, with liberty of commencing in the first instance all suits and prosecutions for that purpose, in the superior common law Judiciary in such state, subject nevertheless, for the correction of errors, both in law and fact in rendering Judgement, to an appeal to the Judiciary of the United States.

3. Resolved that whenever requisitions shall be necessary, instead of the rule for making requisitions mentioned in the articles of Confederation, the United States in Congress be authorized to make such requisitions in proportion to the whole number of white and other free citizens and inhabitants of every age sex and condition including those bound to servitude for a term of years and three fifths of all other persons not comprehended in the foregoing description, except Indians not paying taxes; that if such requisitions be not complied with, in the time specified therein, to direct the collection thereof in the non-complying States and for that purpose to devise and pass acts directing and authorizing the same; provided that none of the powers hereby vested in the United States in Congress shall be exercised without the consent of at least   States, and in that proportion if the number of Confederated States should hereafter be increased or diminished.

4. Resolved that the United States in Congress be authorized to elect a federal Executive to consist of   persons, to continue in office for the term of   years, to receive punctually at stated times a fixed compensation for their services, in which no increase or diminution shall be made so as to affect the persons composing the Executive at the time of such increase or diminution, to be paid out of the federal treasury; to be incapable of holding any other office or appointment during their time of service and for   years thereafter; to be ineligible a second time, and removeable by Congress on application by a majority of the Executives of the several States; that the Executives besides their general authority to execute the federal acts ought to appoint all federal officers not otherwise provided for, and to direct all military operations; provided that none of the persons composing the federal Executive shall on any occasion take command of any troops so as personally to conduct any enterprise as General or in other capacity.

5. Resolved that a federal Judiciary be established to consist of a supreme tribunal the Judges of which to be appointed by the Executive, and to hold their offices during good behaviour, to receive punctually at stated times a fixed compensation for their services in which no increase or diminution shall be made so as to affect persons actually in office at the time of such increase or diminution; that the Judiciary so established shall have authority to hear and determine in the first instance on all impeachments of federal officers, and by way of appeal in the dernier resort in all cases touching the rights of Ambassadors, in all cases of captures from an enemy, in all cases of piracies and felonies on the high Seas, in all cases in which foreigners may be interested, in the construction of any treaty or treaties, or which may arise on any of the Acts for regulation of trade, or the collection of the federal Revenue: that none of the Judiciary shall during the time they remain in office be capable of receiving or holding any other office or appointment during the time of service, or for thereafter.
6. Resolved that all Acts of the United States in Congress made by virtue and in pursuance of the powers hereby and by the articles of Confederation vested in them, and all Treaties made and ratified under the authority of the United States, shall be the supreme law of the respective States so far forth as those Acts or Treaties shall relate to the said States or their Citizens, and that the Judiciary of the several States shall be bound thereby in their decisions, any thing in the respective laws of the Individual States to the contrary notwithstanding; and that if any State, or any body of men in any State shall oppose or prevent carrying into execution such acts or treaties, the federal Executive shall be authorized to call forth the power of the Confederated States, or so much thereof as may be necessary to enforce and compel an obedience to such Acts or an observance of such Treaties.
7. Resolved that provision be made for the admission of new States into the Union.
8. Resolved the rule for naturalization ought to be the same in every State.
9. Resolved that a Citizen of one State committing an offence in another State of the Union, shall be deemed guilty of the same offence as if it had been committed by a Citizen of the State in which the offence was committed.

86. HAMILTON'S PLAN OF UNION
Presented to the Federal Convention
June 18, 1787

(*The Works of Alexander Hamilton,* ed. by H. C. Lodge, Vol. I, p. 331 ff. For variant texts, see *Documents Illustrative of the Formation of the Union of the American States,* p. 979 ff.)

Hamilton, who had long been active in the movement for strengthening the central government, and who had attended the Annapolis Convention, was a delegate to the Federal Convention from New York. He was distinctly out of sympathy with the work of the Federal Convention, as he was with the final Constitution. On June 18 he presented his own plan of Union, and explained it in an elaborate speech. The speech can be found in Madison's Notes, *Documents Illustrative, etc.,* p. 215 ff., and see note, p. 225; a somewhat different version is in the notes of Yates, *Documents Illustrative, etc.,* p. 776 ff. Hamilton's plan had no perceptible influence on the character of the Constitution.

1. The Supreme Legislative power of the United States of America to be vested in two distinct bodies of men; the one to be called the Assembly, the other the Senate who together shall form the Legislature of the United States with power to pass all laws whatsoever subject to the Negative hereafter mentioned.
2. The Assembly to consist of persons elected by the people to serve for three years.
3. The Senate to consist of persons elected to serve during good behaviour; their election to be made by electors chosen for that purpose by the people. In order to this, the States to be divided into election districts. On the death, removal or resignation of any Senator his place to be filled out of the district from which he came.

4. The supreme Executive authority of the United States to be vested in a Governor, to be elected to serve during good behaviour —His election to be made by Electors chosen by electors chosen by the people in the Election Districts aforesaid; or by electors chosen for that purpose by the respective Legislatures—provided that if an election be not made within a limited time, the President of the Senate shall be the Governor. The Governor to have a negative upon all laws about to be passed—and the execution of all laws passed—to be the Commander-in-Chief of the land and naval forces and of the militia of the United States—to have the entire direction of war when authorized or begun—to have, with the advice and approbation of the Senate, the power of making all treaties—to have the appointment of the heads or chief officers of the departments of finance, war, and foreign affairs—to have the nomination of all other officers (ambassadors to foreign nations included) subject to the approbation or rejection of the Senate— to have the power of pardoning all offences but treason, which he shall not pardon without the approbation of the Senate.

5. On the death, resignation, or removal of the Governor, his authorities to be exercised by the President of the Senate (until a successor be appointed).

6. The Senate to have the sole power of declaring war—the power of advising and approving all treaties—the power of approving or rejecting all appointments of officers except the heads or chiefs of the departments of finance, war, and foreign affairs.

7. The supreme judicial authority of the United States to be vested in twelve judges, to hold their offices during good behavior, with adequate and permanent salaries. This court to have original jurisdiction in all causes of capture, and an appellate jurisdiction (from the courts of the several States) in all causes in which the revenues of the General Government or the citizens of foreign nations are concerned.

8. The Legislature of the United States to have power to institute courts in each State for the determination of all causes of capture and of all matters relating to their revenues, or in which the citizens of foreign nations are concerned.

9. The Governor, Senators, and all officers of the United States to be liable to impeachment for mal and corrupt conduct, and upon conviction to be removed from office, and disqualified for holding any place of trust or profit. All impeachments to be tried by a court, to consist of the judges of the Supreme Court, chief or senior judge of the Superior Court of law of each State—provided that such judge hold his place during good behavior and have a permanent salary.

10. All laws of the particular States contrary to the Constitution or laws of the United States to be utterly void. And the better to prevent such laws being passed the Governor or President of each State shall be appointed by the General Government, and shall have a negative upon the laws about to be passed in the State of which he is Governor or President.

11. No State to have any forces, land or naval—and the militia of all the States to be under the sole and exclusive direction of the United States, the officers of which to be appointed and commissioned by them.

87. THE CONSTITUTION OF THE UNITED STATES

(Richardson, ed. *Messages and Papers*, Vol. I, p. 21 ff.)

Following the recommendation of the Annapolis Convention, Congress adopted, February 21, 1787, a resolution that "it is expedient that on the second Monday in May next a Convention of delegates who shall have been appointed by the several states be held at Philadelphia for the sole and express purpose of revising the Articles of Confederation." A quorum, however, did not assemble at Philadelphia until May 25, when the convention proceeded to organize. The convention continued its work throughout the summer of 1787 and on September 15 agreed to the Constitution as reported from the Committee on Style. On the 17th September the Constitution was signed, and submitted to Congress. By resolution of September 28, Congress submitted the Constitution to the States. By June 21, 1788, nine States had ratified the Constitution; Rhode Island, the last of the thirteen States to ratify, acted on May 29, 1790. Congress by resolution of September 13, 1788, fixed the date for the election of a President and the organization of the new government under the Constitution. The resolutions of Congress, the Debates and Proceedings of the Convention, the ratifications of the several States, and related material can be found in *Documents Illustrative of the Formation of the Union of the American States,* ed. by C. C. Tansill. The literature on the Constitution is voluminous. The classic analysis is the *Federalist,* written by Madison, Hamilton and Jay. Almost equally valuable is Judge Story's *Commentaries on the Constitution,* 2 vols. More recent accounts are: C. Warren, *The Making of the Constitution;* A. C. McLaughlin, *Confederation and Constitution;* M. Farrand, *Fathers of the Constitution;* M. Farrand, *Framing of the Constitution;* C. A. Beard, *Economic Interpretation of the Constitution.* The struggle over ratification can be followed in J. Elliot's *Debates in the Several State Conventions,* etc. 5 Vols.; and O. G. Libby, *Geographical Distribution of the Vote on the Federal Convention;* J. B. McMaster and F. D. Stone, *Pennsylvania and the Federal Constitution;* S. B. Harding, *Contest over Ratification in Massachusetts;* C. E. Miner, *Ratification of the Federal Constitution by the State of New York;* L. I. Trenholme, *Ratification of the Federal Constitution in North Carolina;* B. C. Steiner, *Maryland's Adoption of the Federal Constitution;* F. G. Bates, *Rhode Island and the Union;* H. G. Grigsby, *History of the Virginia Federal Convention of 1788,* 2 Vols. On the amendments, see C. Borgeaud, *Adoption and Amendment of Constitutions.*

WE THE PEOPLE of the United States, in Order to form a more perfect Union, establish Justice, insure domestic Tranquility, provide for the common defence, promote the general Welfare, and secure the Blessings of Liberty to ourselves and our Posterity, do ordain and establish this Constitution for the United States of America.

ART. I

Sec. 1. All legislative Powers herein granted shall be vested in a Congress of the United States, which shall consist of a Senate and House of Representatives.

Sec. 2. The House of Representatives shall be composed of Members chosen every second Year by the People of the several States, and the Electors in each State shall have the Qualifications requisite for Electors of the most numerous Branch of the State Legislature.

No Person shall be a Representative who shall not have attained to the Age of twenty five Years, and been seven Years a Citizen of the United States, and who shall not, when elected, be an Inhabitant of that State in which he shall be chosen.

Representatives and direct Taxes shall be apportioned among the several States which may be included within this Union, according to their respective Numbers, which shall be determined by adding to the whole Number of free Persons, including those bound to Service for a Term of Years, and excluding Indians not taxed, three fifths of all other Persons. The actual Enumeration shall be made within three Years after the first Meeting of the Congress of the United States, and within every subsequent Term of ten Years, in such Manner as they shall by Law direct. The Number of Representatives shall not exceed one for every thirty Thousand, but each State shall have at Least one Representative; and until such enumeration shall be made, the State of New Hampshire shall be entitled to chuse three, Massachusetts eight, Rhode-Island and Providence Plantations one, Connecticut five, New-York six, New Jersey four, Pennsylvania eight, Delaware one, Maryland six, Virginia ten, North Carolina five, South Carolina five, and Georgia three.

When vacancies happen in the Representation from any State, the Executive Authority thereof shall issue Writs of Election to fill such Vacancies.

The House of Representatives shall chuse their Speaker and other Officers; and shall have the sole Power of Impeachment.

Sec. 3. The Senate of the United States shall be composed of two Senators from each State, chosen by the Legislature thereof, for six Years; and each Senator shall have one Vote.

Immediately after they shall be assembled in Consequence of the first Election, they shall be divided as equally as may be into three Classes. The Seats of the Senators of the first Class shall be vacated at the Expiration of the second Year, of the second Class at the Expiration of the fourth Year, and of the third Class at the Expiration of the sixth Year, so that one third may be chosen every second Year; and if Vacancies happen by Resignation, or otherwise, during the Recess of the Legislature of any State, the Executive thereof may make temporary Appointments until the next Meeting of the Legislature, which shall then fill such Vacancies.

No Person shall be a Senator who shall not have attained to the Age of thirty Years, and been nine Years a Citizens of the United States, and who shall not, when elected, be an Inhabitant of that State for which he shall be chosen.

The Vice President of the United States shall be President of the Senate, but shall have no Vote, unless they be equally divided.

The Senate shall chuse their other Officers, and also a President pro tempore, in the Absence of the Vice President, or when he shall exercise the Office of President of the United States.

The Senate shall have the sole Power to try all Impeachments. When sitting for that Purpose, they shall be on Oath or Affirmation. When the President of the United States is tried, the Chief Justice shall preside: And no Person shall be convicted without the Concurrence of two thirds of the Members present.

Judgment in Cases of Impeachment shall not extend further than to removal from Office, and disqualification to hold and enjoy any Office of honor, Trust or Profit under the United States: but the Party convicted shall nevertheless be liable and subject to Indictment, Trial, Judgment and Punishment, according to Law.

Sec. 4. The Times, Places and Manner of holding Elections for Senators and Representatives, shall be prescribed in each State by the Legislature thereof; but the Congress may at any time by Law make or alter such Regulations, except as to the Places of chusing Senators.

The Congress shall assemble at least once in every Year, and such Meeting shall be on the first Monday in December, unless they shall by Law appoint a different Day.

Sec. 5. Each House shall be the Judge of the Elections, Returns and Qualifications of its own Members, and a Majority of each shall constitute a Quorum to do Business; but a smaller Number may adjourn from day to day, and may be authorized to compel the Attendance of absent Members, in such Manner, and under such Penalties as each House may provide.

Each House may determine the Rules of its Proceedings, punish its Members for disorderly Behaviour, and, with the Concurrence of two thirds, expel a Member.

Each House shall keep a Journal of its Proceedings, and from time to time publish the same, excepting such Parts as may in their Judgment require Secrecy; and the Yeas and Nays of the Members of either House on any question shall, at the Desire of one fifth of those Present, be entered on the Journal.

Neither House, during the Session of Congress, shall, without the Consent of the other, adjourn for more than three days, nor to any other Place than that in which the two Houses shall be sitting.

Sec. 6. The Senators and Representatives shall receive a Compensation for their Services, to be ascertained by Law, and paid out of the Treasury of the United States. They shall in all Cases, except Treason, Felony and Breach of the Peace, be privileged from Arrest during their Attendance at the Session of their respective Houses, and in going to and returning from the same; and for any Speech or Debate in either House, they shall not be questioned in any other Place.

No Senator or Representative shall, during the Time for which he was elected, be appointed to any civil Office under the Authority of the United States which shall have been created, or the Emoluments whereof shall have been encreased during such time; and no Person holding any Office under the United States, shall be a Member of either House during his Continuance in Office.

Sec. 7. All Bills for raising Revenue shall originate in the House of Representatives; but the Senate may propose or concur with Amendments as on other Bills.

Every Bill which shall have passed the House of Representatives and the Senate, shall, before it become a Law, be presented to the President of the United States; If he approve he shall sign it, but if not he shall return it, with his Objections to that House in which it shall have originated, who shall enter the Objections at large on their Journal, and proceed to reconsider it. If after such Reconsideration two thirds of that House shall agree to pass the Bill, it shall be sent, together with the Objections, to the other House, by which it shall likewise be reconsidered, and if approved by two thirds of that House, it shall become a Law. But in all such Cases the Votes of both Houses shall be determined by yeas and Nays, and the Names of the Persons voting for and against the Bill shall be entered on the Journal of each House respectively. If any Bill shall not be returned by the President within ten Days (Sundays excepted) after it shall have been presented to him, the Same shall be a Law, in like Manner as if he had signed it, unless the Congress by their Adjournment prevent its Return, in which Case it shall not be a Law.

Every Order, Resolution, or Vote to which the Concurrence of the Senate and House of Representatives may be necessary (except on a question of Adjournment) shall be presented to the President of the United States; and before the Same shall take Effect, shall be approved by him, or being disapproved by him, shall be repassed by two thirds of the Senate and House of Representatives, according to the Rules and Limitations prescribed in the Case of a Bill.

Sec. 8. The Congress shall have Power To lay and collect Taxes, Duties, Imposts and Excises, to pay the Debts and provide for the common Defence and general Welfare of the United States; but all Duties, Imposts and Excises shall be uniform throughout the United States;

To borrow Money on the credit of the United States;

To regulate Commerce with foreign Nations, and among the several States, and with the Indian Tribes;

To establish an uniform Rule of Naturalization, and uniform Laws on the subject of Bankruptcies throughout the United States;

To coin Money, regulate the Value thereof, and of foreign Coin, and fix the Standard of Weights and Measures;

To provide for the Punishment of counterfeiting the Securities and current Coin of the United States;

To establish Post Offices and post Roads;

To promote the Progress of Science and useful Arts, by securing for limited Times to Authors and Inventors the exclusive Right to their respective Writings and Discoveries;

To constitute Tribunals inferior to the supreme Court;

To define and punish Piracies and Felonies committed on the high Seas, and Offences against the Law of Nations;

To declare War, grant Letters of Marque and Reprisal, and make Rules concerning Captures on Land and Water;

To raise and support Armies, but no Appropriation of Money to that Use shall be for a longer Term than two Years;

To provide and maintain a Navy;

To make Rules for the Government and Regulation of the land and naval Forces;

To provide for calling forth the Militia to execute the Laws of the Union, suppress Insurrections and repel Invasions;

To provide for organizing, arming, and disciplining, the Militia, and for governing such Part of them as may be employed in the Service of the United States, reserving to the States respectively, the Appointment of the Officers, and the Authority of training .the Militia according to the discipline prescribed by Congress;

To exercise exclusive Legislation in all Cases whatsoever, over such District (not exceeding ten Miles square) as may, by Cession of particular States, and the Acceptance of Congress, become the Seat of the Government of the United States, and to exercise like Authority over all Places purchased by the Consent of the Legislature of the State in which the Same shall be, for the Erection of Forts, Magazines, Arsenals, dock-Yards, and other needful Buildings;—And

To make all Laws which shall be necessary and proper for carrying into Execution the foregoing Powers, and all other Powers vested by this Constitution in the Government of the United States, or in any Department or Officer thereof.

Sec. 9. The Migration or Importation of such Persons as any of the States now existing shall think proper to admit, shall not be prohibited by the Congress prior to the Year one thousand eight hundred and eight, but a Tax or duty may be imposed on such Importation, not exceeding ten dollars for each Person.

The Privilege of the Writ of Habeas Corpus shall not be suspended, unless when in Cases of Rebellion or Invasion the public Safety may require it.

No Bill of Attainder or ex post facto Law shall be passed.

No Capitation, or other direct, Tax shall

be laid, unless in Proportion to the Census or Enumeration herein before directed to be taken.

No Tax or Duty shall be laid on Articles exported from any State.

No Preference shall be given by any Regulation of Commerce or Revenue to the Ports of one State over those of another: nor shall Vessels bound to, or from, one State, be obliged to enter, clear, or pay Duties in another.

No Money shall be drawn from the Treasury, but in Consequence of Appropriations made by Law; and a regular Statement and Account of the Receipts and Expenditures of all public Money shall be published from time to time.

No Title of Nobility shall be granted by the United States: And no Person holding any Office of Profit or Trust under them, shall, without the Consent of the Congress, accept of any present, Emolument, Office, or Title, of any kind whatever, from any King, Prince or foreign State.

Sec. 10. No State shall enter into any Treaty, Alliance, or Confederation; grant Letters of Marque and Reprisal; coin Money; emit Bills of Credit; make any Thing but gold and silver Coin a Tender in Payment of Debts; pass any Bill of Attainder, ex post facto Law, or Law impairing the Obligation of Contracts, or grant any Title of Nobility.

No State shall, without the Consent of the Congress, lay any Imposts or Duties on Imports or Exports, except what may be absolutely necessary for executing it's inspection Laws: and the net Produce of all Duties and Imposts, laid by any State on Imports or Exports, shall be for the Use of the Treasury of the United States; and all such Laws shall be subject to the Revision and Controul of the Congress.

No State shall, without the Consent of Congress, lay any Duty of Tonnage, keep Troops, or Ships of War in time of Peace, enter into any Agreement or Compact with another State, or with a foreign Power, or engage in War, unless actually invaded, or in such imminent Danger as will not admit of delay.

Art. II

Sec. 1. The executive Power shall be vested in a President of the United States of America. He shall hold his Office during the Term of four Years, and, together with the Vice President, chosen for the same Term, be elected, as follows

Each State shall appoint, in such Manner as the Legislature thereof may direct, a Number of Electors, equal to the whole Number of Senators and Representatives to which the State may be entitled in the Congress: but no Senator or Representative, or Person holding an Office of Trust or Profit under the United States, shall be appointed an Elector.

The Electors shall meet in their respective States, and vote by Ballot for two Persons, of whom one at least shall not be an Inhabitant of the same State with themselves. And they shall make a List of all the Persons voted for, and of the Number of Votes for each; which List they shall sign and certify, and transmit sealed to the Seat of the Government of the United States, directed to the President of the Senate. The President of the Senate shall, in the Presence of the Senate and House of Representatives, open all the Certificates, and the Votes shall then be counted. The Person having the greatest Number of Votes shall be the President, if such Number be a Majority of the whole Number of Electors appointed; and if there be more than one who have such Majority, and have an equal Number of Votes, then the House of Representatives shall immediately chuse by Ballot one of them for President; and if no person have a Majority, then from the five highest on the List the said House shall in like Manner chuse the President. But in chusing the President, the Votes shall be taken by States, the Representation from each State having one Vote; A quorum for this Purpose shall consist of a Member or Members from two thirds of the States, and a Majority of all the States shall be necessary to a Choice. In every Case, after the Choice of the President, the Person having the greatest Number of Votes of the Electors shall be the Vice President. But if there should remain two or more who have equal Votes, the Senate shall chuse from them by Ballot the Vice President.

The Congress may determine the Time of chusing the Electors, and the Day on which they shall give their Votes; which Day shall be the same throughout the United States.

No Person except a natural born Citizen, or a Citizen of the United States, at the time of the Adoption of this Constitution, shall be eligible to the Office of President; neither shall any Person be eligible to that Office who shall not have attained to the Age of thirty five Years, and been fourteen Years a Resident within the United States.

In Case of the Removal of the President from Office, or of his Death, Resignation, or Inability to discharge the Powers and Duties of the said Office, the Same shall devolve on the Vice President, and the Congress may by Law provide for the Case of Removal, Death, Resignation or Inability, both of the President and Vice President, declaring what Officer shall then act as President, and such Officer shall act accordingly, until the Disability be removed, or a President shall be elected.

The President shall, at stated Times, receive for his Services, a Compensation, which shall neither be encreased nor diminished during the Period for which he shall have been elected, and he shall not receive within that Period any other Emolument from the United States, or any of them.

Before he enter on the Execution of his Office, he shall take the following Oath or Affirmation:—"I do solemnly swear (or affirm) that I will faithfully execute the Office of President of the United States, and will to the best of my Ability, preserve, protect and defend the Constitution of the United States."

Sec. 2. The President shall be Commander in Chief of the Army and Navy of the United States, and of the Militia of the several States, when called into the actual Service of the United States; he may require the Opinion, in writing, of the principal Officer in each of the executive Departments, upon any Subject relating to the Duties of their respective Offices, and he shall have Power to grant Reprieves and Pardons for Offences against the United States, except in Cases of Impeachment.

He shall have Power, by and with the Advice and Consent of the Senate, to make Treaties, provided two thirds of the Senators present concur; and he shall nominate, and by and with the Advice and Consent of the Senate, shall appoint Ambassadors, other

public Ministers and Consuls, Judges of the supreme Court, and all other Officers of the United States, whose Appointments are not herein otherwise provided for, and which shall be established by Law: but the Congress may by Law vest the Appointment of such inferior Officers, as they think proper, in the President alone, in the Courts of Law, or in the Heads of Departments.

The President shall have Power to fill up all Vacancies that may happen during the Recess of the Senate, by granting Commissions which shall expire at the End of their next Session.

Sec. 3. He shall from time to time give to the Congress Information of the State of the Union, and recommend to their Consideration such Measures as he shall judge necessary and expedient; he may, on extraordinary Occasions, convene both Houses, or either of them, and in Case of Disagreement between them, with Respect to the Time of Adjournment, he may adjourn them to such Time as he shall think proper; he shall receive Ambassadors and other public Ministers; he shall take Care that the Laws be faithfully executed, and shall Commission all the Officers of the United States.

Sec. 4. The President, Vice President and all civil Officers of the United States, shall be removed from Office on Impeachment for, and Conviction of, Treason, Bribery, or other high Crimes and Misdemeanors.

ART. III

Sec. 1. The judicial Power of the United States, shall be vested in one supreme Court, and in such inferior Courts as the Congress may from time to time ordain and establish. The Judges, both of the supreme and inferior Courts, shall hold their Offices during good Behaviour, and shall, at stated Times, receive for their Services, a Compensation, which shall not be diminished during their Continuance in Office.

Sec. 2. The judicial Power shall extend to all Cases, in Law and Equity, arising under this Constitution, the Laws of the United States, and Treaties made, or which shall be made, under their Authority;—to all Cases affecting Ambassadors, other public Ministers and Consuls;—to all Cases of admiralty and maritime Jurisdiction;—to Controversies to which the United States shall be a Party;—

to Controversies between two or more States;
—between a State and Citizens of another
State;—between Citizens of different States,
—between Citizens of the same State claiming Lands under Grants of different States,
and between a State, or the Citizens thereof,
and foreign States, Citizens or Subjects.

In all Cases affecting Ambassadors, other
public Ministers and Consuls, and those in
which a State shall be Party, the supreme
Court shall have original Jurisdiction. In all
the other Cases before mentioned, the supreme Court shall have appellate Jurisdiction, both as to Law and Fact, with such
Exceptions, and under such Regulations as
the Congress shall make.

The Trial of all Crimes, except in Cases
of Impeachment, shall be by Jury; and such
Trial shall be held in the State where the
said Crimes shall have been committed; but
when not committed within any State, the
Trial shall be at such Place or Places as the
Congress may by Law have directed.

Sec. 3. Treason against the United States,
shall consist only in levying War against
them, or in adhering to their Enemies, giving
them Aid and Comfort. No Person shall be
convicted of Treason unless on the Testimony
of two Witnesses to the same overt Act, or
on Confession in open Court.

The Congress shall have Power to declare
the Punishment of Treason, but no Attainder
of Treason shall work Corruption of Blood,
or Forfeiture except during the Life of the
Person attainted.

ART. IV

Sec. 1. Full Faith and Credit shall be given
in each State to the Public Acts, Records,
and judicial Proceedings of every other
State. And the Congress may by general
Laws prescribe the Manner in which such
Acts, Records and Proceedings shall be
proved, and the Effect thereof.

Sec. 2. The Citizens of each State shall be
entitled to all Privileges and Immunities of
Citizens in the several States.

A Person charged in any State with Treason, Felony, or other Crime, who shall flee
from Justice, and be found in another State,
shall on Demand of the executive Authority
of the State from which he fled, be delivered
up, to be removed to the State having Jurisdiction of the Crime.

No Person held to Service or Labour in
one State, under the Laws thereof, escaping
into another, shall, in Consequence of any
Law or Regulation therein, be discharged
from such Service or Labour, but shall be
delivered up on Claim of the Party to whom
such Service or Labour may be due.

Sec. 3. New States may be admitted by the
Congress into this Union; but no new States
shall be formed or erected within the Jurisdiction of any other State; nor any State be
formed by the Junction of two or more
States, or Parts of States, without the Consent of the Legislatures of the States concerned as well as of the Congress.

The Congress shall have Power to dispose
of and make all needful Rules and Regulations respecting the Territory or other Property belonging to the United States; and
nothing in this Constitution shall be so construed as to Prejudice any Claims of the
United States, or of any particular State.

Sec. 4. The United States shall guarantee to
every State in this Union a Republican Form
of Government, and shall protect each of
them against Invasion; and on Application
of the Legislature, or of the Executive (when
the Legislature cannot be convened) against
domestic Violence.

ART. V

The Congress, whenever two thirds of both
Houses shall deem it necessary, shall propose
Amendments to this Constitution, or, on the
Application of the Legislatures of two thirds
of the several States, shall call a Convention
for proposing Amendments, which, in either
Case, shall be valid to all Intents and Purposes, as Part of this Constitution, when
ratified by the Legislatures of three fourths
of the several States, or by Conventions in
three fourths thereof, as the one or the other
Mode of Ratification may be proposed by the
Congress; Provided that no Amendment
which may be made prior to the Year One
thousand eight hundred and eight shall in
any Manner affect the first and fourth
Clauses in the Ninth Section of the first
Article; and that no State, without its Consent, shall be deprived of it's equal Suffrage
in the Senate.

ART. VI

All Debts contracted and Engagements

entered into, before the Adoption of this Constitution, shall be as valid against the United States under this Constitution, as under the Confederation.

This Constitution, and the Laws of the United States which shall be made in Pursuance thereof; and all Treaties made, or which shall be made, under the Authority of the United States, shall be the supreme Law of the Land; and the Judges in every State shall be bound thereby, any Thing in the Constitution or Laws of any State to the Contrary notwithstanding.

The Senators and Representatives before mentioned, and the Members of the several State Legislatures, and all executive and judicial Officers, both of the United States and of the several States, shall be bound by Oath or Affirmation, to support this Constitution; but no religious Test shall ever be required as a Qualification to any Office or public Trust under the United States.

ART. VII

The Ratification of the Conventions of nine States, shall be sufficient for the Establishment of this Constitution between the States so ratifying the Same.

Done in Convention by the Unanimous Consent of the States present the Seventeenth Day of September in the Year of our Lord one thousand seven hundred and Eighty seven and of the Independence of the United States of America the Twelfth. In witness whereof We have hereunto subscribed our Names,

G⁰ WASHINGTON—Presid^t
and deputy from Virginia

New Hampshire	JOHN LANGDON NICHOLAS GILMAN	Delaware	GEO: READ GUNNING BEDFORD jun JOHN DICKINSON RICHARD BASSETT JACO: BROOM
Massachusetts	NATHANIEL GORHAM RUFUS KING		
Connecticut	W^M SAM^L JOHNSON ROGER SHERMAN	Maryland	JAMES M^CHENRY DAN OF S^T THO^S JENIFER DAN^L CARROLL
New York	ALEXANDER HAMILTON	Virginia	JOHN BLAIR— JAMES MADISON JR.
New Jersey	WIL: LIVINGSTON DAVID BREARLEY W^M PATERSON JONA: DAYTON	North Carolina	W^M BLOUNT RICH^D DOBBS SPAIGHT HU WILLIAMSON
Pensylvania	B FRANKLIN THOMAS MIFFLIN ROB^T MORRIS GEO. CLYMER THO^S FITZSIMONS JARED INGERSOLL JAMES WILSON GOUV MORRIS	South Carolina	J. RUTLEDGE CHARLES COTESWORTH PINCKNEY CHARLES PINCKNEY PIERCE BUTLER
		Georgia	WILLIAM FEW ABR BALDWIN

Articles in addition to, and Amendment of the Constitution of the United States of America, proposed by Congress, and ratified by the Legislatures of the several States, pursuant to the fifth Article of the original Constitution.

[The first ten amendments went into effect November 3, 1791.]

ART. I

Congress shall make no law respecting an establishment of religion, or prohibiting the free exercise thereof; or abridging the freedom of speech, or of the press; or the right of the people peaceably to assemble, and to petition the government for a redress of grievances.

ART. II

A well regulated Militia, being necessary to the security of a free State, the right of the people to keep and bear Arms, shall not be infringed.

ART. III

No Soldier shall, in time of peace be quartered in any house, without the consent of the Owner, nor in time of war, but in a manner to be prescribed by law.

ART. IV

The right of the people to be secure in their persons, houses, papers, and effects, against unreasonable searches and seizures, shall not be violated, and no Warrants shall issue, but upon probable cause, supported by Oath or affirmation, and particularly describing the place to be searched, and the persons or things to be seized.

ART. V

No person shall be held to answer for a capital, or otherwise infamous crime, unless on a presentment or indictment of a Grand Jury, except in cases arising in the land or naval forces, or in the Militia, when in actual service in time of War or public danger; nor shall any person be subject for the same offence to be twice put in jeopardy of life or limb; nor shall be compelled in any criminal case to be a witness against himself, nor be deprived of life, liberty, or property, without due process of law; nor shall private property be taken for public use, without just compensation.

ART. VI

In all criminal prosecutions, the accused shall enjoy the right to a speedy and public trial, by an impartial jury of the State and district wherein the crime shall have been committed, which district shall have been previously ascertained by law, and to be informed of the nature and cause of the accusation; to be confronted with the witnesses against him; to have compulsory process for obtaining witnesses in his favor, and to have the Assistance of Counsel for his defence.

ART. VII

In Suits at common law, where the value in controversy shall exceed twenty dollars, the right of trial by jury shall be preserved, and no fact tried by a jury, shall be otherwise re-examined in any Court of the United States, than according to the rules of the common law.

ART. VIII

Excessive bail shall not be required, nor excessive fines imposed, nor cruel and unusual punishments inflicted.

ART. IX

The enumeration in the Constitution, of certain rights, shall not be construed to deny or disparage others retained by the people.

ART. X

The powers not delegated to the United States by the Constitution, nor prohibited by it to the States, are reserved to the States respectively, or to the people.

ART. XI

Jan. 8, 1798

The Judicial power of the United States shall not be construed to extend to any suit in law or equity, commenced or prosecuted against one of the United States by Citizens of another State, or by Citizens or Subjects of any Foreign State.

ART. XII

Sept. 25, 1804

The Electors shall meet in their respective states, and vote by ballot for President and Vice-President, one of whom, at least, shall not be an inhabitant of the same state with themselves; they shall name in their ballots the person voted for as President, and in distinct ballots the person voted for as

Vice-President, and they shall make distinct lists of all persons voted for as President, and of all persons voted for as Vice-President, and of the number of votes for each, which lists they shall sign and certify, and transmit sealed to the seat of the government of the United States, directed to the President of the Senate;—The President of the Senate shall, in the presence of the Senate and House of Representatives, open all the certificates and the votes shall then be counted;—The person having the greatest number of votes for President, shall be the President, if such number be a majority of the whole number of Electors appointed; and if no person have such majority, then from the persons having the highest numbers not exceeding three on the list of those voted for as President, the House of Representatives shall choose immediately, by ballot, the President. But in choosing the President, the votes shall be taken by states, the representation from each state having one vote; a quorum for this purpose shall consist of a member or members from two-thirds of the states, and a majority of all the states shall be necessary to a choice. And if the House of Representatives shall not choose a President whenever the right of choice shall devolve upon them, before the fourth day of March next following, then the Vice-President shall act as President, as in the case of the death or other constitutional disability of the President.—The person having the greatest number of votes as Vice-President, shall be the Vice-President, if such number be a majority of the whole number of Electors appointed, and if no person have a majority, then from the two highest numbers on the list, the Senate shall choose the Vice-President; a quorum for the purpose shall consist of two-thirds of the whole number of Senators, and a majority of the whole number shall be necessary to a choice. But no person constitutionally ineligible to the office of President shall be eligible to that of Vice-President of the United States.

Art. XIII
Dec. 18, 1865

Sec. 1. Neither slavery nor involuntary servitude, except as a punishment for crime whereof the party shall have been duly convicted, shall exist within the United States, or any place subject to their jurisdiction.

Sec. 2. Congress shall have power to enforce this article by appropriate legislation.

Art. XIV
July 28, 1868

Sec. 1. All persons born or naturalized in the United States, and subject to the jurisdiction thereof, are citizens of the United States and of the State wherein they reside. No State shall make or enforce any law which shall abridge the privileges or immunities of citizens of the United States; nor shall any State deprive any person of life, liberty, or property, without due process of law; nor deny to any person within its jurisdiction the equal protection of the laws.

Sec. 2. Representatives shall be apportioned among the several States according to their respective numbers, counting the whole number of persons in each State, excluding Indians not taxed. But when the right to vote at any election for the choice of electors for President and Vice President of the United States, Representatives in Congress, the Executive and Judicial officers of a State, or the members of the Legislature thereof, is denied to any of the male inhabitants of such State. being twenty-one years of age, and citizens of the United States, or in any way abridged, except for participation in rebellion, or other crime, the basis of representation therein shall be reduced in the proportion which the number of such male citizens shall bear to the whole number of male citizens twenty-one years of age in such State.

Sec. 3. No person shall be a Senator or Representative in Congress, or elector of President and Vice President, or hold any office, civil or military, under the United States, or under any State, who, having previously taken an oath, as a member of Congress, or as an officer of the United States, or as a member of any State legislature, or as an executive or judicial officer of any State, to support the Constitution of the United States, shall have engaged in insurrection or rebellion against the same, or given aid or comfort to the enemies thereof. But Congress may by a vote of two-thirds of each House, remove such disability.

Sec. 4. The validity of the public debt of the United States, authorized by law, including debts incurred for payment of pensions and bounties for services in suppressing insurrection or rebellion, shall not be questioned. But neither the United States nor any State shall assume or pay any debt or obligation incurred in aid of insurrection or rebellion against the United States, or any claim for the loss or emancipation of any slave; but all such debts, obligations and claims shall be held illegal and void.

Sec. 5. The Congress shall have power to enforce, by appropriate legislation, the provisions of this article.

ART. XV
March 30, 1870

Sec. 1. The right of citizens of the United States to vote shall not be denied or abridged by the United States or by any State on account of race, color, or previous condition of servitude—

Sec. 2. The Congress shall have power to enforce this article by appropriate legislation—

ART. XVI
February 25, 1913

The Congress shall have power to lay and collect taxes on incomes, from whatever source derived, without apportionment among the several States and without regard to any census or enumeration.

ART. XVII
May 31, 1913

The Senate of the United States shall be composed of two senators from each State, elected by the people thereof, for six years; and each Senator shall have one vote. The electors in each State shall have the qualifications requisite for electors of the most numerous branch of the State legislature.

When vacancies happen in the representation of any State in the Senate, the executive authority of such State shall issue writs of election to fill such vacancies: *Provided,* That the legislature of any State may empower the executive thereof to make temporary appointments until the people fill the vacancies by election as the legislature may direct.

This amendment shall not be so construed as to affect the election or term of any senator chosen before it becomes valid as part of the Constitution.

ART. XVIII
January 29, 1919

After one year from the ratification of this article, the manufacture, sale, or transportation of intoxicating liquors within, the importation thereof into, or the exportation thereof from the United States and all territory subject to the jurisdiction thereof for beverage purposes is hereby prohibited.

The Congress and the several States shall have concurrent power to enforce this article by appropriate legislation.

This article shall be inoperative unless it shall have been ratified as an amendment to the Constitution by the legislatures of the several States, as provided in the Constitution, within seven years from the date of the submission hereof to the States by Congress.

ART. XIX
August 26, 1920

The right of citizens of the United States to vote shall not be denied or abridged by the United States or by any States on account of sex.

The Congress shall have power by appropriate legislation to enforce the provisions of this article.

ART. XX
February 6, 1933

Sec. 1. The terms of the President and Vice-President shall end at noon on the twentieth day of January, and the terms of Senators and Representatives at noon on the third day of January, of the years in which such terms would have ended if this article had not been ratified; and the terms of their successors shall then begin.

Sec. 2. The Congress shall assemble at least once in every year, and such meeting shall begin at noon on the third day of January, unless they shall by law appoint a different day.

Sec. 3. If, at the time fixed for the beginning of the term of the President, the President-elect shall have died, the Vice-President-elect shall become President. If a President shall not have been chosen before the time fixed for the beginning of his term, or if the President-elect shall have failed to qualify, then the Vice-President-elect shall act as President until a President shall have qualified; and the Congress may by law provide for the case wherein neither a President-elect nor a Vice-President-elect shall have qualified, declaring who shall then act as President, or the manner in which one who is to act shall be selected, and such person shall act accordingly until a President or Vice-President shall have qualified.

Sec. 4. The Congress may by law provide for the case of the death of any of the persons from whom the House of Representatives may choose a President whenever the right of choice shall have devolved upon them, and for the case of the death of any of the persons from whom the Senate may choose a Vice-President whenever the right of choice shall have devolved upon them.

Sec. 5. Sections 1 and 2 shall take effect on the 15th day of October following the ratification of this article.

Sec. 6. This article shall be inoperative unless it shall have been ratified as an amendment to the Constitution by the legislatures of three-fourths of the several States within seven years from the date of its submission.

ART. XXI
December 5, 1933

Sec. 1. The eighteenth article of amendment to the Constitution of the United States is hereby repealed. . . .

ART. XXII
February 26, 1951

Sec. 1. No person shall be elected to the office of the President more than twice, and no person who has held the office of President, or acted as President for more than two years of a term to which some other person was elected President shall be elected to the office of the President more than once. But this Article shall not apply to any person holding the office of President when this Article was proposed by the Congress, and shall not prevent any person who may be holding the office of President, or acting as President, during the term within which this Article becomes operative from holding the office of President or acting as President during the remainder of such term.

For articles subsequent to Article XXII see page 633.

88. OBJECTIONS TO THE FEDERAL CONSTITUTION
Letter of Robert Yates and John Lansing to the Governor of New York
1787
(J. Elliot, ed. *Debates in the Several State Conventions on the Adoption of the Federal Constitution,* 1861 ed., Vol. I, p. 480 ff.)

Yates and Lansing, delegates to the Federal Convention from New York, refused to sign the Constitution; Alexander Hamilton alone signed from New York State. Opposition to the new Constitution in New York was intense, and ratification was secured only after nine other States had already ratified. See, E. W. Spaulding, *New York in the Critical Period, 1783–1789;* O. G. Libby, *Geographical Distribution of the Vote of the Thirteen States on the Federal Constitution;* C. E. Miner, *Ratification of the Federal Constitution by the State of New York.*

. . . We beg leave, briefly, to state some cogent reasons, which, among others, influenced us to decide against a consolidation of the states. These are reducible into two heads:—

1st. The limited and well-defined powers under which we acted, and which could not, on any possible construction, embrace an idea of such magnitude as to assent to a general constitution, in subversion of that of the state.

2nd. A conviction of the impracticability of establishing a general government, pervading every part of the United States, and extending essential benefits to all.

Our powers were explicit, and confined to the sole and express purpose of revising the Articles of Confederation, and reporting such alterations and provisions therein, as should render the Federal Constitution adequate to the exigencies of government, and the preservation of the Union.

From these expressions, we were led to believe that a system of consolidated government could not, in the remotest degree, have been in contemplation of the legislature of this state; for that so important a trust, as the adopting measures which tended to deprive the state government of its most essential rights of sovereignty, and to place it in a dependent situation, could not have been confided by implication; and the circumstance, that the acts of the Convention were to receive a state approbation in the last resort.

forcibly corroborated the opinion that our powers could not involve the subversion of a Constitution which, being immediately derived from the people, could only be abolished by their express consent, and not by a legislature, possessing authority vested in them for its preservation. Nor could we suppose that, if it had been the intention of the legislature to abrogate the existing confederation, they would, in such pointed terms, have directed the attention of their delegates to the revision and amendment of it, in total exclusion of every other idea.

Reasoning in this manner, we were of opinion that the leading feature of every amendment ought to be the preservation of the individual states in their uncontrolled constitutional rights, and that, in reserving these, a mode might have l een devised of granting to the Confederacy, the moneys arising from a general system of revenue, the power of regulating commerce and enforcing the observance of foreign treaties, and other necessary matters of less moment.

Exclusive of our objections originating from the want of power, we entertained an opinion that a general government, however guarded by declarations of rights, or cautionary provisions, must unavoidably, in a short time, be productive of the destruction of the civil liberty of such citizens who could be effectually coerced by it, by reason of the extensive territory of the United States, the dispersed situation of its inhabitants, and the insuperable difficulty of controlling or counteracting the views of a set of men (however unconstitutional and oppressive their acts might be) possessed of all the powers of government, and who, from their remoteness from their constituents, and necessary permanency of office, could not be supposed to be uniformly actuated by an attention to their welfare and happiness; that, however wise and energetic the principles of the general government might be, the extremities of the United States could not be kept in due submission and obedience to its laws, at the distance of many hundred miles from the seat of government; that, if the general legislature was composed of so numerous a body of men as to represent the interests of all the inhabitants of the United States, in the usual and true ideas of representation, the expense of supporting it would become intolerably burdensome; and that, if a few only were vested with a power of legislation, the interests of a great majority of the inhabitants of the United States must necessarily be unknown; or, if known, even in the first stages of the operations of the new government, unattended to.

These reasons were, in our opinion, conclusive against any system of consolidated government: to that recommended by the Convention, we suppose most of them very forcibly apply. . . .

89. BAYARD & WIFE v. SINGLETON
North Carolina Reports, 1 Martin, 42
1797

The Assembly of North Carolina, in 1785, passed a law requiring the Court to dismiss on motion any suit brought by a person whose property had been confiscated by the State during the War of Independence, against the purchasers, on affidavit of the defendants that they were purchasers from the commissioners of confiscated property. The decision of the Court is one of the earliest discussions of the right of a court to declare a legislative act void.

The Court made a few observations on our constitution and system of government. . . .

In the course of which the Judges observed that the obligation of their oaths, and the duty of their office required them in that situation, to give their opinion on that important and momentous subject; and that notwithstanding the great reluctance they might feel against involving themselves in a dispute with the Legislature of the State, yet no object of concern or respect could come in competition or authorize them to dispense with the duty they owed the public, in consequence of the trust they were invested with under the solemnity of their oaths.

That they therefore were bound to declare that they considered, that whatever disabilities the persons under whom the plaintiffs were said to derive their titles, might justly have incurred, against their maintaining or prosecuting any suits in the Courts of this State; yet that such disabilities in their nature were merely personal, and not by any means capable of being transferred to the present plaintiffs, either by descent or purchase; and that these plaintiffs being citizens of one of the United States, are citizens of this State, by the confederation of all the States; which is to be taken as a part of the law of the land, unrepealable by any act of the General Assembly.

That by the constitution every citizen had undoubtedly a right to a decision of his property by a trial by jury. For that if the Legislature could take away this right, and require him to stand condemned in his property without a trial, it might with as much authority require his life to be taken away without a trial by jury, and that he should stand condemned to die, without the formality of any trial at all: that if the members of the General Assembly could do this, they

might with equal authority, not only render themselves the Legislators of the State for life, without any further election of the people, but from thence transmit the dignity and authority of legislation down to their heirs male forever.

But that it was clear, that no act they could pass, could by any means repeal or alter the constitution, because if they could do this, they would at the same instant of time, destroy their own existence as a Legislature, and dissolve the government thereby established. Consequently the constitution (which the judicial was bound to take notice of as much as of any other law whatever) standing in full force as the fundamental law of the land, notwithstanding the act on which the present motion was grounded, the same act must of course, in that instance, stand as abrogated and without any effect.

90. WASHINGTON'S FIRST INAUGURAL ADDRESS
April 30, 1789

(Richardson, ed. *Messages and Papers*, Vol. I, p. 51)

The first Congress was supposed to meet March 4, 1789, but not until April 2 did the House have a quorum, and the Senate did not organize until April 5. On the 6th of April the electoral votes were counted, and Washington and Adams were announced as President and Vice-President. Charles Thomson was sent to notify Washington of his election, and on April 16 Washington set out from Mount Vernon for New York. For a description of the inauguration, see, *The Journal of William Maclay*, ch. i; C. Bowers, *Jefferson and Hamilton*, ch. i; R. W. Griswold, *The Republican Court;* J. B. McMaster, *With the Fathers*, p. 150 ff.

Fellow-Citizens of the Senate and of the House of Representatives:

Among the vicissitudes incident to life no event could have filled me with greater anxieties than that of which the notification was transmitted by your order, and received on the 14th day of the present month. On the one hand, I was summoned by my country, whose voice I can never hear but with veneration and love, from a retreat which I had chosen with the fondest predilection, and, in my flattering hopes, with an immutable decision, as the asylum of my declining years— a retreat which was rendered every day more necessary as well as more dear to me by the addition of habit to inclination, and of fre-

quent interruptions in my health to the gradual waste committed on it by time. On the other hand, the magnitude and difficulty of the trust to which the voice of my country called me, being sufficient to awaken in the wisest and most experienced of her citizens a distrustful scrutiny into his qualifications, could not but overwhelm with despondence one who (inheriting inferior endowments from nature and unpracticed in the duties of civil administration) ought to be peculiarly conscious of his own deficiencies. In this conflict of emotions all I dare aver is that it has been my faithful study to collect my duty from a just appreciation of every circumstance by which it might be affected. All I dare hope is that if, in executing this task, I have been too much swayed by a grateful remembrance of former instances, or by an affectionate sensibility to this transcendent proof of the confidence of my fellow-citizens, and have thence too little consulted my incapacity as well as disinclination for the weighty and untried cares before me, my error will be palliated by the motives which mislead me, and its consequences be judged by my country with some share of the partiality in which they originated.

Such being the impressions under which I

have, in obedience to the public summons, repaired to the present station, it would be peculiarly improper to omit in this first official act my fervent supplications to that Almighty Being who rules over the universe, who presides in the councils of nations, and whose providential aids can supply every human defect, that His benediction may consecrate to the liberties and happiness of the people of the United States a Government instituted by themselves for these essential purposes, and may enable every instrument employed in its administration to execute with success the functions allotted to his charge. . . . No people can be bound to acknowledge and adore the Invisible Hand which conducts the affairs of men more than those of the United States. Every step by which they have advanced to the character of an independent nation seems to have been distinguished by some token of providential agency; and in the important revolution just accomplished in the system of their united government the tranquil deliberations and voluntary consent of so many distinct communities from which the event has resulted can not be compared with the means by which most governments have been established without some return of pious gratitude, along with an humble anticipation of the future blessings which the past seem to presage. . . .

By the article establishing the executive department it is made the duty of the President "to recommend to your consideration such measures as he shall judge necessary and expedient." The circumstances under which I now meet you will acquit me from entering into that subject further than to refer to the great constitutional charter under which you are assembled, and which, in defining your powers, designates the objects to which your attention is to be given. It will be more consistent with those circumstances, and far more congenial with the feelings which actuate me, to substitute, in place of a recommendation of particular measures, the tribute that is due to the talents, the rectitude, and the patriotism which adorn the characters selected to devise and adopt them. In these honorable qualifications I behold the surest pledges that as on one side no local prejudices or attachments, no separate views nor party animosities, will misdirect the comprehensive and equal eye which ought to watch over this great assemblage of communities and interests, so, on another, that the foundation of our national policy will be laid in the pure and immutable principles of private morality, and the preëminence of free government be exemplified by all the attributes which can win the affections of its citizens and command the respect of the world. I dwell on this prospect with every satisfaction which an ardent love for my country can inspire, since there is no truth more thoroughly established than that there exists in the economy and course of nature an indissoluble union between virtue and happiness; between duty and advantage; between the genuine maxims of an honest and magnanimous policy and the solid rewards of public prosperity and felicity; since we ought to be no less persuaded that the propitious smiles of Heaven can never be expected on a nation that disregards the eternal rules of order and right which Heaven itself has ordained; and since the preservation of the sacred fire of liberty and the destiny of the republican model of government are justly considered, perhaps, as *deeply,* as *finally,* staked on the experiment intrusted to the hands of the American people.

Besides the ordinary objects submitted to your care, it will remain with your judgment to decide how far an exercise of the occasional power delegated by the fifth article of the Constitution is rendered expedient at the present juncture by the nature of objections which have been urged against the system, or by the degree of inquietude which has given birth to them. . . .

To the foregoing observations I have one to add, which will be most properly addressed to the House of Representatives. It concerns myself, and will therefore be as brief as possible. When I was first honored with a call into the service of my country, then on the eve of an arduous struggle for its liberties, the light in which I contemplated my duty required that I should renounce every pecuniary compensation. From this resolution I have in no instance departed; and being still under the impressions which produced it, I must decline as inapplicable to myself any share in the personal emoluments which may be indispensably included in a permanent provision for the executive department, and must accordingly pray that the pecuniary estimates for the station in which I am placed may during my continuance in it be limited to such actual expenditures as the public good may be thought to require.

Having thus imparted to you my sentiments as they have been awakened by the occasion which brings us together, I shall take my present leave; but not without resorting once more to the benign Parent of the Human Race in humble supplication that, since He has been pleased to favor the American people with opportunities for deliberating in perfect tranquillity, and dispositions for deciding with unparalleled unanimity on a form of government for the security of their union and the advancement of their happiness, so His divine blessing may be equally *conspicuous* in the enlarged views, the temperate consultations, and the wise measures on which the success of this Government must depend.

91. THE JUDICIARY ACT OF 1789
September 24, 1789

(*U. S. Statutes at Large*, Vol. I, p. 73 ff.)

The Constitution provided only for a Supreme Court and "such inferior Courts as the Congress may from time to time establish", thus leaving the whole question of the nature and the organization of the judiciary to the discretion of Congress. The framework of the American judicial system was created in the Act of 1789. The determination of the first Congress to create a federal judiciary was of immense importance in developing American nationalism. See, C. Warren, *Congress, The Constitution, and the Supreme Court;* S. E. Baldwin, *The American Judiciary;* C. Warren, *The Supreme Court in United States History,* 1928 ed. Vol. I, ch. i.

An Act to establish the Judicial Courts of the United States.

SEC. 1. *Be it enacted,* That the supreme court of the United States shall consist of a chief justice and five associate justices, any four of whom shall be a quorum, and shall hold annually at the seat of government two sessions, the one commencing the first Monday of February, and the other the first Monday of August. That the associate justices shall have precedence according to the date of their commissions, or when the commissions of two or more of them bear date on the same day, according to their respective ages.

SEC. 2. That the United States shall be, and they hereby are, divided into thirteen districts, to be limited and called as follows, . . .

SEC. 3. That there be a court called a District Court in each of the aforementioned districts, to consist of one judge, who shall reside in the district for which he is appointed, and shall be called a District Judge, and shall hold annually four sessions, . . .

SEC. 4. That the beforementioned districts, except those of Maine and Kentucky, shall be divided into three circuits, and be called the eastern, the middle, and the southern circuit. That the eastern circuit shall consist of the districts of New Hampshire, Massachusetts, Connecticut, and New York; that the middle circuit shall consist of the districts of New Jersey, Pennsylvania, Delaware, Maryland, and Virginia; and that the southern circuit shall consist of the districts of South Carolina and Georgia; and that there shall be held annually in each district of said circuits two courts which shall be called Circuit Courts, and shall consist of any two justices of the Supreme Court and the district judge of such districts, any two of whom shall constitute a quorum. *Provided,* That no district judge shall give a vote in any case of appeal or error from his own decision; but may assign the reasons of such his decision. . . .

SEC. 9. That the district courts shall have, exclusively of the courts of the several States, cognizance of all crimes and offences that shall be cognizable under the authority of the United States, committed within their respective districts, or upon the high seas; where no other punishment than whipping, not exceeding thirty stripes, a fine not exceeding one hundred dollars, or a term of imprisonment not exceeding six months, is to be inflicted; and shall also have exclusive original cognizance of all civil cases of admiralty and maritime jurisdiction, including all seizures under laws of impost, navigation, or trade of the United States. . . . And shall also have cognizance, concurrent with the courts of the several States, or the circuit courts, as the case may be, of all causes where an alien sues for a tort only in violation of the law of nations or a treaty of the United States. And shall also have cognizance, concurrent as last mentioned, of all suits at common law where the United States sue, and the matter in dispute amounts, exclusive of costs, to the sum or value of one hundred dollars. And shall also have jurisdiction exclusively of the courts of the several States, of all suits against consuls or vice-consuls, except for offences above the description aforesaid. And the trial of issues in fact, in the district courts, in all cases except civil causes of admiralty and maritime jurisdiction, shall be by jury. . . .

SEC. 11. That the circuit courts shall have original cognizance, concurrent with the courts of the several States, of all suits of a civil nature at common law or in equity, where the matter in dispute exceeds, exclusive of costs, the sum or value of five hundred dollars, and the United States are plaintiffs or petitioners; or an alien is a party, or the suit is between a citizen of the State where the suit is brought and a citizen of another State. And shall have exclusive cognizance of all crimes and offences cognizable under the authority of the United States, except where this act otherwise provides, or the laws of the United States shall otherwise direct, and concurrent jurisdiction with the district courts of the crimes and offences cognizable therein. . . . And the circuit courts shall also have appellate jurisdiction from the district courts under the regulations and restrictions hereinafter provided. . . .

SEC. 13. That the Supreme Court shall have exclusive jurisdiction of all controversies of a civil nature, where a state is a party, except between a state and its citizens; and except also between a state and citizens of other states, or aliens, in which latter case it shall have original but not exclusive jurisdiction. And shall have exclusively all such jurisdiction of suits or proceedings against ambassadors or other public ministers, or their domestics, or domestic servants, as a court of law can have or exercise consistently with the law of nations; and original, but not exclusive jurisdiction of all suits brought by ambassadors or other public ministers, or in which a consul or vice-consul shall be a party. And the trial of issues in fact in the Supreme Court in all actions at law against citizens of

the United States shall be by jury. The Supreme Court shall also have appellate jurisdiction from the circuit courts and courts of the several states in the cases hereinafter specially provided for; and shall have power to issue writs of prohibition to the district courts, when proceeding as courts of admiralty and maritime jurisdiction, and writs of *mandamus,* in cases warranted by the principle and usages of law, to any courts appointed, or persons holding office under the authority of the United States. . . .

SEC. 25. That a final judgment or decree in any suit, in the highest court of law or equity of a State in which a decision in the suit could be had, where is drawn in question the validity of a treaty or statute of, or an authority exercised under, the United States, and the decision is against their validity; or where is drawn in question the validity of a statute of, or an authority exercised under, any State, on the ground of their being repugnant to the constitution, treaties, or laws of the United States, and the decision is in favour of such their validity, or where is drawn in question the construction of any clause of the constitution, or of a treaty, or statute of, or commission held under, the United States, and the decision is against the title, right, privilege, or exemption, specially set up or claimed by either party, under such clause of the said Constitution, treaty, statute, or commission, may be re-examined, and reversed or affirmed in the Supreme Court of the United States upon a writ of error, the citation being signed by the chief justice, or judge or chancellor of the court rendering or passing the judgment or decree complained of, or by a justice of the Supreme Court of the United States, in the same manner and under the same regulations, and the writ shall have the same effect as if the judgment or decree complained of had been rendered or passed in a circuit court, and the proceedings upon the reversal shall also be the same, except that the Supreme Court, instead of remanding the cause for a final decision as before provided, may, at their discretion, if the cause shall have been once remanded before, proceed to a final decision of the same, and award execution. But no other error shall be assigned or regarded as a ground of reversal in any such case as aforesaid, than such as appears on the face of the record, and immediately respects the before-mentioned questions of validity or construction of the said constitution, treaties, statutes, commissions, or authorities in dispute. . . .

SEC. 35. . . . And there shall also be appointed a meet person learned in the law to act as attorney-general for the United States, who shall be sworn or affirmed to a faithful execution of his office; whose duty it shall be to prosecute and conduct all suits in the Supreme Court in which the United States shall be concerned, and to give his advice and opinion upon questions of law when required by the President of the United States, or when requested by the heads of any of the departments, touching any matters that may concern their departments, and shall receive such compensation for his services as shall by law be provided.

92. VIRGINIA RESOLUTIONS ON THE ASSUMPTION OF STATE DEBTS
December 16, 1790

(W. W. Hening, ed. *Statutes at Large of Virginia,* Vol. XIII, p. 237 ff.)

The opposition of Virginia to Hamilton's plan for the assumption of the State debts arose from the fact that Virginia had already made provision for a large part of her Revolutionary debt. The Virginia remonstrance was drafted by Patrick Henry, and caused Hamilton to remark, "This is the first symptom of a spirit which must either be killed, or will kill the Constitution of the United States."

In the House of Delegates,
Thursday, the 16th of December, 1790.

The General Assembly of the Commonwealth of Virginia to the United States in Congress assembled.

Represent,

That it is with great concern they find themselves compelled, from a sense of duty, to call the attention of Congress to an act of their last session, intitled "An act making provision for the debt of the United States," which the General Assembly conceive neither policy, justice nor the constitution warrants. Republican policy in the opinion of your memorialists could scarcely have suggested those clauses in the aforesaid act, which limit the right of the United States, in their redemption of the public debt. On the contrary they discern a striking resemblance between this system and that which was introduced into England, at the revolution; a system which has perpetuated upon that nation an enormous debt, and has moreover insinuated into the hands of the executive, an unbounded influence, which pervading every branch of the government, bears down all opposition, and daily threatens the destruction of everything that appertains to English liberty. The same causes produce the same effects! In an agricultural country like this, therefore to erect, and concentrate, and perpetuate a large monied interest, is a measure which your memorialists apprehend must in the course of human events produce one or other of two evils, the prostration of agriculture at the feet of commerce, or a change in the present form of foederal government, fatal to the existence of American liberty.

The General Assembly pass by various other parts of the said act which they apprehend will have a dangerous and impolitic tendency, and proceed to show the injustice of it as it applies to this Commonwealth. . . . Your memorialists turn away from the impolicy and injustice of the said act, and view it in another light, in which to them it appears still more odious and deformed.

During the whole discussion of the foederal constitution by the convention of Virginia, your memorialists were taught to believe "That every power not granted was retained;" under this impression and upon this positive condition, declared in the instrument of ratification, the said government was adopted by the people of this Commonwealth; but your memorialists can find no clause in the constitution authorizing Congress to assume the debts of the states! As the guardians then of the rights and interests of their constituents, as sentinels placed by them over the ministers of the foederal government, to shield it from their encroachments, or at least to sound the alarm when it is threatened with invasion, they can never reconcile it to their consciences, silently to acquiesce in a measure, which violates that hallowed maxim: a maxim on the truth and sacredness of which the foederal government depended for its adoption in this Commonwealth. But this injudicious act not only deserves the censure of the General Assembly, because it is not warranted by the constitution of the United States, but because it is repugnant to an express provision of that constitution; this provision is "That all debts contracted and engagements entered into, before the adoption of this constitution, shall be as valid against the United States under this constitution as under the confederation," which amounts to a constitutional ratification of the contracts respecting the state debts in the situation in which they existed under the confederation, and resorting to that standard there can be no doubt that in the present question the rights of states as contracting with the United States must be considered as sacred.

The General Assembly of the Commonwealth of Virginia confide so fully in the justice and wisdom of Congress upon the present occasion, as to hope that they will revise and amend the aforesaid act generally, and repeal in particular, so much of it as relates to the assumption of the state debts.

December the 23d., 1790. Agreed to by the Senate.

93. HAMILTON'S OPINION ON THE CONSTITUTIONALITY OF THE BANK
February 23, 1791

(The Works of Alexander Hamilton, ed. by J. C. Hamilton, Vol. IV, p. 104 ff.)

December 14, 1790, Hamilton presented to Congress his plan for the establishment of a national bank. A bill embodying most of the features of Hamilton's plan passed Congress February 8, 1791. Washington, doubtful of the constitutionality of the measure, requested Hamilton, Jefferson, and Randolph to submit written opinions on this question. For Jefferson's opinion, see Doc. No. 94. Randolph submitted two opinions, one adverse, one ambiguous. Hamilton's opinion is one of the ablest of his papers: it contained the substance of the argument subsequently adopted by Marshall in his decision in the case of *Mc Culloch* v. *Maryland*. Washington accepted Hamilton's argument, and signed the bill, February 25. On the First Bank, see, M. St. C. Clarke and D. A. Hall, *Legislative and Documentary History of the Bank of the United States;* W. G. Sumner, *History of Banking in the United States,* Vol. I.

. . . In entering upon the argument it ought to be premised that the objections of the Secretary of State and the Attorney-General are founded on a general denial of the authority of the United States to erect corporations. The latter, indeed, expressly admits, that if there be anything in the bill which is not warranted by the Constitution, it is the clause of incorporation.

Now it appears to the Secretary of the Treasury that this *general principle* is *inherent* in the very *definition* of government, and *essential* to every step of the progress to be made by that of the United States, namely:

That every power vested in a government is in its nature *sovereign,* and includes, by *force* of the *term* a right to employ all the *means* requisite and fairly applicable to the attainment of the ends of such power, and which are not precluded by restrictions and exceptions specified in the Constitution, or not immoral, or not contrary to the *essential ends* of political society. . . .

If it would be necessary to bring proof to a proposition so clear, as that which affirms that the powers of the federal government, as to *its objects,* were sovereign, there is a clause of the Constitution which would be decisive. It is that which declares that the Constitution, and the laws of the United States made in pursuance of it, . . . shall be the *supreme law of the land.* The power which can create a *supreme law of the land,* in any case, is doubtless *sovereign* as to such case.

This general and indisputable principle puts at once an end to the *abstract* question, whether the United States have power to erect a corporation; that is to say, to give a *legal* or *artificial capacity* to one or more persons, distinct from the *natural.* For it is unquestionably incident to *sovereign power* to erect corporations, and consequently to *that* of the United States, in *relation* to the *objects* intrusted to the management of the government. The difference is this: where the authority of the government is general, it can create corporations in *all cases;* where it is confined to certain branches of legislation, it can create corporations *only* in those cases. . . .

It is not denied that there are *implied* as well as *express powers,* and that the *former* are as effectually delegated as the *latter.* And for the sake of accuracy it shall be mentioned, that there is another class of powers, which may be properly denominated *resulting powers.* It will not be doubted, that if the United States should make a conquest of any of the territories of its neighbours, they would possess sovereign jurisdiction over the conquered territory. This would be rather a result, from the whole mass of the powers of the government, and from the nature of political society, than a consequence of either of the powers specially enumerated. . . .

It is conceded that *implied powers* are to be considered as delegated equally with *express ones.* Then it follows, that as a power of erecting a corporation may as well be *implied* as any other thing, it may as well be employed as an *instrument* or *mean* of carrying into execution any of the specified powers, as any other *instrument* or *mean* whatever. The only question must be, in this, as in every other case, whether the mean to be employed, or in this instance, the corporation to be erected, has a natural relation to any of the acknowledged objects or lawful ends of the government. Thus a corporation may not be erected by Congress for superintending the police of the city of Philadelphia, because they are not authorized to *regulate* the *police* of that city. But one may be erected in relation to the collection of taxes, or to the trade with foreign countries, or to the trade between the States, or with the Indian tribes; because it is the province of the federal government to *regulate* those objects and because it is incident to a general *sovereign* or *legislative* power to *regulate* a thing, to employ all the means which relate to its regulation to the best and greatest advantage. . . .

Through this mode of reasoning respecting the right of employing all the means requisite to the execution of the specified powers of the government, it is objected, that none but necessary and proper means are to be employed; and the Secretary of State maintains, that no means are to be considered as *necessary* but those without which the grant of the power would be *nugatory.* . . .

It is essential to the being of the national government, that so erroneous a conception of the meaning of the word *necessary* should be exploded.

It is certain, that neither the grammatical nor popular sense of the term requires that construction. According to both, *necessary* often means no more than *needful, requisite, incidental, useful,* or *conducive to.* . . . And it is the true one in which it is to be understood as used in the Constitution. The whole turn of the clause containing it indicates, that it was the intent of the Convention, by that clause, to give a liberal latitude to the exercise of the specified powers. The expressions have peculiar comprehensiveness. They are "to make all *laws* necessary and proper for *carrying into execution* the *foregoing powers,* and *all other powers,* vested by the Constitution in the *government* of the United States, or in any *department* or *officer* thereof.

To understand the word as the Secretary of State does, would be to depart from its obvious and popular sense, and to give it a restrictive operation, an idea never before entertained. It would be to give it the same force as if the word *absolutely* or *indispensably* had been prefixed to it. . . .

The *degree* in which a measure is necessary, can never be a *test* of the legal right to adopt it; that must be a matter of opinion, and can only be a *test* of expediency. The *relation* between the *measure* and the *end;* between the *nature* of the *mean* employed towards the execution of a power, and the object of that power, must be the criterion of constitutionality, not the more or less of *necessity* or *utility.* . . .

This restrictive interpretation of the word *necessary* is also contrary to this sound maxim of construction; namely, that the powers contained in a constitution of government, especially those which concern the general administration of the affairs of a country, its finances, trade, defence &c., ought to be construed liberally in advancement of the public good. . . . The means by which national exigencies are to be provided for, national inconveniences obviated, national prosperity promoted, are of such infinite variety, extent, and complexity, that there must of necessity be great latitude of discretion in the selection and application of those means. Hence, consequently, the necessity and propriety of exercising the authorities intrusted to a government on principles of liberal construction. . . .

But the doctrine which is contended for is not chargeable with the consequences imputed to it. It does not affirm that the national government is sovereign in all respects, but that it is sovereign to a certain extent; that is is, to the extent of the objects of its specified powers.

It leaves, therefore, a criterion of what is constitutional and of what is not so. This criterion is the *end*, to which the measure relates as a *mean*. If the *end* be clearly comprehended within any of the specified powers, and if the measure have an obvious relation to that *end*, and is not forbidden by any particular provision of the Constitution, it may safely be deemed to come within the compass of the national authority. There is also this further criterion, which may materially assist the decision; Does the proposed measure abridge a pre-existing right of any State or of any individual? If it does not, there is a strong presumption in favor of its constitutionality, and slighter relations to any declared object of the Constitution may be permitted to turn the scale. . . .

It is presumed to have been satisfactorily shown in the course of the preceding observations:

1. That the power of the government, *as to* the objects intrusted to its management, is, in its nature, sovereign.
2. That the right of erecting corporations is one inherent in, and inseparable from, the idea of sovereign power.
3. That the position, that the government of the United States can exercise no power but such as is delegated to it by its Constitution, does not militate against this principle.
4. That the word *necessary*, in the general

clause, can have no *restrictive* operation derogating from the force of this principle; indeed, that the degree in which a measure is or is not *necessary*, cannot be a *test* of *constitutional right*, but of *expediency only*.
5. That the power to erect corporations is not to be considered as an *independent* or *substantive* power, but as an *incidental* and *auxiliary* one, and was therefore more properly left to implication than expressly granted.
6. That the principle in question does not extend the power of the government beyond the prescribed limits, because it only affirms a power to *incorporate* for purposes *within the sphere* of the *specified powers*.

And lastly, that the right to exercise such a power in certain cases is unequivocally granted in the most *positive* and *comprehensive* terms. . . .

A hope is entertained that it has, by this time, been made to appear, to the satisfaction of the President, that a bank has a natural relation to the power of collecting taxes—to that of regulating trade—to that of providing for the common defence—and that, as the bill under consideration contemplates the government in the light of a joint proprietor of the stock of the bank, it brings the case within the provision of the clause of the Constitution which immediately respects the property of the United States.

Under a conviction that such a relation subsists, the Secretary of the Treasury, with all deference, conceives, that it will result as a necessary consequence from the position, that all the specified powers of government are sovereign, as to the proper objects; that the incorporation of a bank is a constitutional measure; and that the objections taken to the bill, in this respect, are illfounded. . . .

94. JEFFERSON'S OPINION ON THE CONSTITUTIONALITY OF THE BANK
February 15, 1791

(*The Writings of Thomas Jefferson*, ed. by H. E. Bergh, Vol. III, p. 145 ff.)

The bill for establishing a national bank, in 1791, undertakes, among other things,—
1. To form the subscribers into a corporation.
2. To enable them, in their corporate capaci-

ties, to receive grants of lands; and, so far, is against the laws of *mortmain*.
3. To make *alien* subscribers capable of holding lands; and so far is against the laws of *alienage*.

4. To transmit these lands, on the death of a proprietor, to a certain line of successors; and so far, changes the course of *descents*.

5. To put the lands out of the reach of forfeiture, or escheat; and so far, is against the laws of *forfeiture* and *escheat*.

6. To transmit personal chattels to successors, in a certain line; and so far, is against the laws of *distribution*.

7. To give them the sole and exclusive right of banking, under the national authority; and, so far, is against the laws of *monopoly*.

8. To communicate to them a power to make laws, paramount to the laws of the states; for so they must be construed, to protect the institution from the control of the state legislatures; and so probably they will be construed.

I consider the foundation of the Constitution as laid on this ground—that *all powers not delegated to the United States, by the Constitution, nor prohibited by it to the states, are reserved to the states, or to the people* (10th amend.). To take a single step beyond the boundaries thus specially drawn around the powers of Congress, is to take possession of a boundless field of power, no longer susceptible of any definition.

The incorporation of a bank, and the powers assumed by this bill, have not, in my opinion, been delegated to the United States by the Constitution.

I. *They are not among the powers specially enumerated. For these are,—*

1. A power to *lay taxes* for the purpose of paying the debts of the United States. But no debt is paid by this bill, nor any tax laid. Were it a bill to raise money, its organization in the Senate would condemn it by the Constitution.

2. To "borrow money". But this bill neither borrows money nor insures the borrowing of it. The proprietors of the bank will be just as free as any other money-holders to lend, or not to lend, their money to the public. The operation proposed in the bill, first to lend them two millions, and then borrow them back again, cannot change the nature of the latter act, which will still be a payment, and not a loan, call it by what name you please.

3. "To regulate commerce with foreign nations, and among the states, and with the Indian tribes." To erect a bank, and to regu-

late commerce, are very different acts. He who erects a bank creates a subject of commerce in its bills; so does he who makes a bushel of wheat, or digs a dollar out of the mines; yet neither of these persons regulates commerce thereby. To make a thing which may be bought and sold, is not to prescribe regulations for buying and selling. Besides, if this were an exercise of the power of regulating commerce, it would be void, as extending as much to the internal commerce of every state, as it is external. For the power given to Congress by the Constitution does not extend to the internal regulation of the commerce of a state . . . which remains exclusively with its own legislature; but to its external commerce only, that is to say, its commerce with another state, or with foreign nations, or with the Indian tribes. Accordingly, the bill does not propose the measure as a "regulation of trade", but as "productive of considerable advantage to trade."

Still less are these powers covered by any other of the special enumerations.

II Nor are they within either of the general phrases, which are the two following:—

1. "To lay taxes to provide for the general welfare of the United States;" that is to say, "to lay taxes *for the purpose* of providing for the general welfare;" for the laying of taxes is the *power,* and the general welfare the *purpose* for which the power is to be exercised. Congress are not to lay taxes *ad libitum, for any purpose they please;* but only to *pay the debts, or provide for the welfare, of the Union.* In like manner, they are not *to do anything they please,* to provide for the general welfare, but only *to lay taxes* for that purpose. To consider the latter phrase, not as describing the purpose of the first, but as giving a distinct and independent power to do any act they please which might be for the good of the Union, would render all the preceding and subsequent enumerations of power completely useless. It would reduce the whole instrument to a single phrase—that of instituting a Congress with power to do whatever would be for the good of the United States; and, as they would be the sole judges of the good or evil, it would be also a power to do whatever evil they pleased. It is an established rule of construction, where a phrase

will bear either of two meanings, to give it that which will allow some meaning to the other parts of the instrument, and not that which will render all the others useless. Certainly no such universal power was meant to be given them. It was intended to lace them up straitly within the enumerated powers, and those without which, as means, these powers could not be carried into effect. It is known that the very power now proposed *as a means,* was rejected *as an end by the Convention which formed the Constitution.* A proposition was made to them, to authorize Congress to open canals, and an amendatory one to empower them to incorporate. But the whole was rejected; and one of the reasons of objection urged in debate was, that they then would have a power to erect a bank, which would render great cities, where there were prejudices and jealousies on that subject, adverse to the reception of the Constitution.

2. The second general phrase is, "to make all laws *necessary* and proper for carrying into execution the enumerated powers." But they can all be carried into execution without a bank. A bank, therefore, is not *necessary,* and consequently not authorized by this phrase.

It has been much urged that a bank will give great facility or convenience in the collection of taxes. Suppose this were true; yet the Constitution allows only the means which are "necessary", not those which are merely "convenient", for effecting the enumerated powers. If such a latitude of construction be allowed to this phrase as to give any non-enumerated power, it will go to every one; for there is no one which ingenuity may not torture into a *convenience, in some way or other, to some one* of so long a list of enumerated powers. It would swallow up all the delegated powers, and reduce the whole to one phrase, as before observed. Therefore it was that the Constitution restrained them to the *necessary* means; that is to say, to those means without which

the grant of the power would be nugatory. . . .

Perhaps bank bills may be a more *convenient* vehicle than treasury orders. But a little *difference* in the degree of convenience cannot constitute the necessity which the Constitution makes the ground for assuming any non-enumerated power. . . .

Can it be thought that the Constitution intended that, for a shade or two of *convenience,* more or less, Congress should be authorized to break down the most ancient and fundamental laws of the several states such as those against mortmain, the laws of alienage, the rules of descent, the acts of distribution, the laws of escheat and forfeiture, and the laws of monopoly.

Nothing but a necessity invincible by other means, can justify such a prostration of laws, which constitute the pillars of our whole system of jurisprudence. Will Congress be too strait-laced to carry the Constitution into honest effect, unless they may pass over the foundation laws of the state governments, for the slightest convenience to theirs?

The negative of the President is the shield provided by the Constitution to protect, against the invasions of the legislature, 1. *The rights of the executive;* 2. *Of the judiciary;* 3. *Of the states and state legislatures.* The present is the case of a right remaining exclusively with the states, and is, consequently, one of those intended by the Constitution to be placed under his protection.

It must be added, however, that, unless the President's mind, on a view of everything which is urged for and against this bill, is tolerably clear that it is unauthorized by the Constitution, if the *pro* and the *con* hang so evenly as to balance his judgment, a just respect for the wisdom of the legislature would naturally decide the balance in favor of their opinion. It is chiefly for cases where they are clearly misled by error, ambition, or interest, that the Constitution has placed a check in the negative of the President.

95. CHISHOLM v. GEORGIA
2 Dallas, 419
1793

This is probably the most important of the early cases which came before the Supreme Court, and in the decision of the Court can be found a foreshadowing of the nationalism enunciated by Marshall a decade later. The case of *Chisholm* v. *Georgia* arose out of the effort of Chisholm and others, citizens of South Carolina and executors of the estate of an English creditor, to secure compensation from Georgia for property confiscated during the Revolution. The Constitution of the United States provided, Art. III. Sec. 2, that the judicial power of the United States should extend to controversies between States and between a State and the citizens of another State. Under this provision, could a citizen sue a State in the Federal Courts? That this clause authorized such suits against States was denied by Hamilton in the *Federalist,* and by Madison in the debates in the Virginia ratifying Convention. "It is not," said Madison, "in the power of individuals to call any state into court. The only operation it can have, is that, if a state should wish to bring a suit against a citizen, it must be brought before the federal court." (Elliot's *Debates,* 1861 ed. Vol. III, p. 533.) Yet in this case, the Supreme Court upheld the right of Chisholm to sue Georgia in the Supreme Court. Georgia refused to appear before the Court, denied the validity of the judgement, and threatened to punish by death any official who should attempt to execute the decree of the court. Other states also protested, and shortly after the decision an amendment was introduced which deprived the federal courts of jurisdiction in cases against one of the States by citizens of another State. This, the eleventh amendment, was ratified January 8, 1798. See C. Warren, *The Supreme Court in United States History,* 1928 ed. Vol. I, ch. ii; L. B. Boudin, *Government by Judiciary,* Vol. I, ch. vii; H. L. Carson, *The Supreme Court;* G. J. Mc Ree, *James Iredell,* Vol. II; U. B. Phillips, "Georgia and State Rights," American Hist. Assoc. *Reports,* 1901, Vol. II.

WILSON, J. This is a case of uncommon magnitude. One of the parties to it is a State, certainly respectable, claiming to be sovereign. The question to be determined is, whether this State, so respectable and whose claim soars so high, is amenable to the jurisdiction of the Supreme Court of the United States? This question, important in itself, will depend on others, more important still; and may perhaps, be ultimately resolved into one, no less radical than this— "Do the People of the United States form a nation?". . .

To the Constitution of the United States the term sovereignty is totally unknown. There is but one place where it could have

been used with propriety. But even in that place it would not, perhaps, have comported with the delicacy of those who ordained and established that Constitution. They might have announced themselves sovereign people of the United States; but serenely conscious of the fact, they avoided the ostentatious declaration. . . .

III. I am, thirdly, and chiefly, to examine the important question now before us, by the Constitution of the United States, and the legitimate result of that valuable instrument. Under this view, the question is naturally subdivided into two others. 1. Could the Constitution of the United States vest a jurisdiction over the State of Georgia? 2. Has the Constitution vested such jurisdiction in this Court? I have already remarked, that in the practice, and even in the science of politics, there has been frequently a strong current against the natural order of things; and an inconsiderate or an interested disposition to sacrifice the end to the means. This remark deserves a more particular illustration. Even in almost every nation, which has been denominated free, the state has assumed a supercilious preëminence above the people, who have formed it: Hence the haughty notions of state independence, state sovereignty, and state supremacy. . . .

In the United States and in the several States which compose the Union, we go not so far: but still we go one step farther than we ought to go in this unnatural and inverted order of things. The states rather than the People for whose sakes the states exist, are frequently the objects which attract and arrest our principal attention. This, I believe, has produced much of the confusion and perplexity, which have appeared in several proceedings and several publications on state-politics, and on the politics, too, of the United States. Sentiments and expressions of this inaccurate kind prevail in our common, even in our convivial, language. . . . A State, I cheerfully admit, is the noblest work of Man: But, Man, himself, free and honest, is, I speak as to this world, the noblest work of God. . . .

With the strictest propriety, therefore, classical and political, our national scene opens with the most magnificent object which the nation could present: "The People of the United States" are the first personages introduced. Who were these people? They were the citizens of thirteen States, each of which had a separate constitution and government, and all of which were connected together by articles of confederation. To the purposes of public strength and felicity, that confederacy was totally inadequate. A requisition on the several States terminated its legislative authority; executive or judicial authority it had none. In order, therefore, to form a more perfect union, to establish justice, to insure domestic tranquillity, to provide for the common defense, and to secure the blessings of liberty, those people, among whom were the people of Georgia, ordained and established the present Constitution. By that Constitution legislative power is vested, executive power is vested, judicial power is vested.

The question now opens fairly to our view, could the people of those States, among whom were those of Georgia, bind those States, and Georgia among the others, by the legislative, executive, and judicial power so vested? If the principles on which I have founded myself are just and true, this question must unavoidably receive an affirmative answer. If those States were the work of those people, those people, and, that I may apply the case closely, the people of Georgia in particular, could alter, as they pleased, their former work; to any degree, they could diminish as well as enlarge it. Any or all of the former state powers they could extinguish or transfer. The inference which necessarily results is that the Constitution ordained and established by those people, and, still closely to apply the case, in particular, by the people of Georgia, could vest jurisdiction or judicial power over those States and over the State of Georgia in particular.

The next question under this head is— Has the Constitution done so? . . .

Whoever considers in a combined and comprehensive view the general texture of the Constitution will be satisfied that the people of the United States intended to form themselves into a nation for national purposes. They instituted, for such purposes, a national government, complete in all its parts, with powers legislative, executive and judiciary; and in all those powers extending over the whole nation. Is it congruous that, with regard to such purposes, any person, natural or artificial, should be permitted to claim successfully an entire exemption from the jurisdiction of the national government? Would not such claims, crowned with success, be repugnant to our very existence as a nation? When so many trains of deduction, coming from different quarters, converge and unite at last in the same point, we may safely conclude, as the legitimate result of this Constitution, that the State of Georgia is amenable to the jurisdiction of this court.

But, in my opinion, this doctrine rests not upon the legitimate result of fair and conclusive deduction from the Constitution; it is confirmed beyond all doubt by the direct and explicit declaration of the Constitution itself. "The judicial power of the United States shall extend to controversies between two States.". . . Can the most consummate degree of professional ingenuity devise a mode by which this "controversy between two States" can be brought before a court of law, and yet neither of those States be a defendant? "The judicial power of the United States shall extend to controversies between a State and citizens of another State". Could the strictest legal language . . . describe with more precise accuracy the cause now depending before the tribunal? . . .

From all, the combined inference is, that the action lies. Chief Justice Jay and Justices Blair and Cushing concurred. Justice Iredell dissented.

96. WASHINGTON'S PROCLAMATION OF NEUTRALITY
April 22, 1793

(Richardson, ed. *Messages and Papers,* Vol. I, p. 156)

The proclamation of Neutrality had the support of all the members of Washington's cabinet. Note that the word "neutrality" is nowhere used. The proclamation precipitated a pamphlet controversy between Hamilton, writing as "Pacificus" and Madison, writing as "Helvidius".

See, J. S. Bassett, *The Federalist System*, p. 86 ff.; R. Hildreth, *History of the United States*, Vol. IV, p. 411 ff.; C. M. Thomas, *American Neutrality in 1793*.

BY THE PRESIDENT OF THE UNITED STATES
OF AMERICA
A PROCLAMATION

Whereas it appears that a state of war exists between Austria, Prussia, Sardinia, Great Britain, and the United Netherlands on the one part and France on the other, and the duty and interest of the United States require that they should with sincerity and good faith adopt and pursue a conduct friendly and impartial toward the belligerent powers:

I have therefore thought fit by these presents to declare the disposition of the United States to observe the conduct aforesaid toward those powers respectively, and to exhort and warn the citizens of the United States carefully to avoid all acts and proceeding whatsoever which may in any manner tend to contravene such disposition.

And I do hereby also make known that whosoever of the citizens of the United States shall render himself liable to punishment or forfeiture under the law of nations by committing, aiding, or abetting hostilities against any of the said powers, or by carrying to any of them those articles which are deemed contraband by the modern usage of nations, will not receive the protection of the United States against such punishment or forfeiture; and further, that I have given instructions to those officers to whom it belongs to cause prosecutions to be instituted against all persons who shall, within the cognizance of the courts of the United States, violate the law of nations with respect to the powers at war, or any of them. . . .

Philadelphia, the 22d of April, 1793,

G⁰. WASHINGTON.

97. WASHINGTON'S PROCLAMATION ON THE WHISKEY REBELLION
August 7, 1794

(Richardson, ed. *Messages and Papers*, Vol. I, p. 158)

The excise tax of March 3, 1791 upon distilled spirits and stills was part of Hamilton's financial policy. It bore with peculiar hardship upon the inhabitants of western Pennsylvania and Virginia who were accustomed to turn their corn into whiskey because that was the only way in which it could be transported economically to the coast. The dissatisfaction of the west was so intense that it resulted in a general flouting of the law, accompanied by some violence, and Washington, on Hamilton's recommendation, ordered out the militia in order to suppress the "rebellion." See, H. H. Brackenridge, *Incidents of the Insurrection in the Western Parts of Pennsylvania;* H. Adams, *Gallatin*, p. 86 ff.; W. Findley, *History of the Insurrection in the Four Western Counties of Pennsylvania; Proceedings of the Executive of the United States Respecting the Insurgents*, 1794, with Hamilton's Report. Washington reported to Congress on his handling of the situation in his Sixth Annual Message, Richardson, ed. *Messages and Papers*, Vol. I. p. 162 ff.

BY THE PRESIDENT OF THE UNITED STATES
OF AMERICA
A PROCLAMATION

Whereas combinations to defeat the execution of the laws laying duties upon spirits distilled within the United States and upon stills have from the time of the commencement of those laws existed in some of the western parts of Pennsylvania; and

Whereas the said combinations, proceeding in a manner subversive equally of the just authority of government and of the rights of individuals, have hitherto effected their dangerous and criminal purpose by the influence of certain irregular meetings whose proceedings have tended to encourage and uphold the spirit of opposition by misrepresentations of the laws calculated to render them odious; by endeavors to deter those who might be so disposed from accepting offices under them through fear of public resentment and of injury to person and property, and to compel those who had accepted such offices by actual violence to surrender or forbear the execution of them; by circulating vindictive menaces against all those who should otherwise, directly or indirectly, aid in the execution of the said laws, or who, yielding to the dictates of conscience and to a sense of obligation, should themselves comply therewith; by actually injuring and destroying the property of persons who were understood to have so complied; by inflicting cruel and humiliating punishments upon private citizens for no other cause than that of appearing to be the friends of the laws; by intercepting the public officers on the highways, abusing, assaulting, and otherwise ill treating them; by going to their houses in the night, gaining admittance by force, taking away their papers, and committing other outrages, employing for these unwarrantable purposes the agency of armed banditti disguised in such manner as for the most part to escape discovery; and

Whereas the endeavors of the Legislature to obviate objections to the said laws by lowering the duties and by other alterations conducive to the convenience of those whom they immediately affect . . . and the endeavors of the executive officers to conciliate a compliance with the laws by explanations, by forbearance, and even by particular accommodations founded on the suggestion of local considerations, have been disappointed of their effect by the machinations of persons whose industry to excite resistance has increased with every appearance of a disposition among the people to relax in their opposition and to acquiesce in the laws, insomuch that many persons in the said western parts of Pennsylvania have at length been hardy enough to perpetrate acts which I am advised amount to treason, being overt acts of levying war against the United States, . . . avowing as the motives of these outrageous proceedings an intention to prevent by force of arms the execution of the said laws, . . . to withstand by open violence the lawful authority of the Government of the United States, and to compel thereby an alteration in the measures of the Legislature and a repeal of the laws aforesaid; and

Whereas by a law of the United States entitled "An act to provide for calling forth the militia to execute the laws of the Union, suppress insurrections, and repel invasions," it is enacted "that whenever the laws of the United States shall be opposed or the execution thereof obstructed in any State by combinations too powerful to be suppressed by the ordinary course of judicial proceedings . . . it shall be lawful for the President of the United States to call forth the militia of such State to suppress such combinations and to cause the laws to be duly executed. And if the militia of a State where such combinations may happen shall refuse or be insufficient to suppress the same, it shall be lawful for the President, if the Legislature of the United States shall not be in session, to call forth and employ such numbers of the militia of any other State or States most convenient thereto as may be necessary; . . . *Provided always,* That whenever it may be necessary in the judgment of the President to use the military force hereby directed to be called forth, the President shall forthwith, and previous thereto, by proclamation, command such insurgents to disperse and retire peaceably to their respective abodes within a limited time;" and . . .

Whereas it is in my judgment necessary under the circumstances of the case to take measures for calling forth the militia in order to suppress the combinations aforesaid, and to cause the laws to be duly executed; and I have accordingly determined so to do, feeling the deepest regret for the occasion, but withal the most solemn conviction that the essential interests of the Union demand it, that the very existence of Government and the fundamental principles of social order are materially involved in the issue, and that the patriotism and firmness of all good citizens are seriously called upon, as occasions may require, to aid in the effectual suppression of so fatal a spirit:

Wherefore, and in pursuance of the proviso above recited, I, George Washington, President of the United States, do hereby command all persons being insurgents as aforesaid, and all others whom it may concern, on or before the 1st day of September next to disperse and retire peaceably to their respective abodes. And I do moreover warn all persons whomsoever against aiding, abetting, or comforting the perpetrators of the aforesaid treasonable acts, and do require all officers and other citizens, according to their respective duties and the laws of the land, to exert their utmost endeavors to prevent and suppress such dangerous proceedings. . . .

Philadelphia, the 7th of August, 1794,

Gº. WASHINGTON.

98. THE JAY TREATY
November 19, 1794

(Malloy, ed. *Treaties, Conventions, etc.,* Vol. I, p. 590 ff.)

Contrary to the provisions of the Treaty of 1783, Great Britain had retained control of the Northwest posts and had failed to make any compensation for slaves carried away during the Revolution. In addition to these grievances, of old standing, there were more recent ones arising from interference with neutral trade. War seemed imminent in 1794, when Washington nominated Chief Justice John Jay as envoy extraordinary to conclude a treaty of peace and commerce. The Jay Treaty solved some of the most important matters of dispute between the two nations, and averted war, but it contained certain features profoundly unsatisfactory to the majority of Americans. Washington hesitated some time before sending it to the Senate for ratification. After a bitter contest in the Senate, the Treaty was ratified June 24, 1795, with a reservation which suspended the obnoxious Article XII. For the debate on the Jay Treaty, see H. Adams, *Albert Gallatin;* C. Bowers, *Jefferson and Hamilton,* chs. xi–xii. A thorough history of the Treaty is S. F. Bemis, *Jay's Treaty.* The full text of the adjudications provided for by Articles 5, 6, and 7, have been edited by J. B. Moore, *International Adjudications,* Vols. I–IV. The question of appropriations for carrying out the provisions of the Treaty raised a serious constitutional problem in the House. The appropriations were finally made, but only after one of the greatest political debates in American history. For the speeches of Gallatin and Fisher Ames on appropriations for the Treaty, see A. Johnston, ed. *American Orations,* Vol. I, p. 84 ff.

ART. I. There shall be a firm, inviolable and universal peace, and a true and sincere friendship between his Britannic Majesty, his heirs and successors, and the United States of America; and between their respective countries, territories, cities, towns and people of every degree, without exception of persons or places.

ART. II. His Majesty will withdraw all his troops and garrisons from all posts and places within the boundary lines assigned by the treaty of peace to the United States. This evacuation shall take place on or before [June 1, 1796,] . . . : The United States in the mean time at their discretion, extending their settlements to any part within the said boundary line, except within the precincts or jurisdiction of any of the said posts. All settlers and traders, within the precincts or jurisdiction of the said posts, shall continue to enjoy, unmolested, all their property of every kind, and shall be protected therein. They shall be at full liberty to remain there, or to remove with all or any part of their effects; and it shall also be free to them to sell their lands, houses, or effects, or to retain the property thereof, at their discretion; such of them as shall continue to reside within the said boundary lines, shall not be compelled to become citizens of the United States, or to take any oath of allegiance to the government thereof; but they shall be at full liberty so to do if they think proper, and they shall make and declare their election within one year after the evacuation aforesaid. And all persons who shall continue there after the expiration of the said year, without having declared their intention of remaining subjects of his Britannic Majesty, shall be considered as having elected to become citizens of the United States.

ART. III. It is agreed that it shall at all times be free to his Majesty's subjects, and to the citizens of the United States, and also to the Indians dwelling on either side of the said boundary line, freely to pass and repass by land or inland navigation, into the respective territories and countries of the two parties, on the continent of America (the country within the limits of the Hudson's bay Company only excepted) and to navigate all the lakes, rivers and waters thereof, and freely to carry on trade and commerce with each other. . . . The river Mississippi shall, however, according to the treaty of peace, be entirely open to both parties; and it is further agreed, that all the ports and places on its eastern side, to whichsoever of the parties belonging, may freely be resorted to and used by both parties, in as ample a manner as any of the Atlantic ports or places of the United States, or any of the ports or places of his Majesty in Great-Britain. . . .

Art. IV. Whereas it is uncertain whether the river Mississippi extends so far to the northward, as to be intersected by a line to be drawn due west from the Lake of the Woods, in the manner mentioned in the treaty of peace . . . it is agreed, that measures shall be taken . . . for making a joint survey of the said river from one degree of latitude below the falls of St. Anthony, to the principal source or sources of the said river, and also of the parts adjacent thereto; and that if on the result of such survey, it should appear that the said river, would not be intersected by such a line as is above mentioned, the two parties will thereupon proceed by amicable negociation, to regulate the boundary line in that quarter, . . .

Art. V. Whereas doubts have arisen what river was truly intended under the name of the river St. Croix, mentioned in the said treaty of peace, and forming a part of the boundary therein described; that question shall be referred to the final decision of commissioners to be appointed. . . . The said commissioners shall, by a declaration, under their hands and seals, decide what river is the river St. Croix, intended by the treaty. . . . And both parties agree to consider such decision as final and conclusive, so as that the same shall never thereafter be called into question, or made the subject of dispute or difference between them.

Art. VI. Whereas it is alleged by divers British merchants and others his Majesty's subjects, that debts, to a considerable amount, which were bona fide contracted before the peace, still remain owing to them by citizens or inhabitants of the United States, and that by the operation of various lawful impediments since the peace, not only the full recovery of the said debts has been delayed, but also the value and security thereof have been, in several instances, impaired and lessened, so that by the ordinary course of judicial proceedings, the British creditors cannot now obtain, and actually have and receive full and adequate compensation for the losses and damages which they have thereby sustained. It is agreed, that in all such cases, where full compensation for such losses and damages cannot, for whatever reason, be actually obtained, had and

received by the said creditors in the ordinary course of justice, the United States will make full and complete compensation for the same to the said creditors: But it is distinctly understood, that this provision is to extend to such losses only as have been occasioned by the lawful impediments aforesaid, . . .

Art. VII. Whereas complaints have been made by divers merchants and others, citizens of the United States, that during the course of the war in which his Majesty is now engaged, they have sustained considerable losses and damage, by reason of irregular or illegal captures or condemnations of their vessels and other property, under colour of authority or commissions from his Majesty, and that from various circumstances belonging to the said cases, adequate compensation for the losses and damages so sustained cannot now be actually obtained, had and received by the ordinary course of judicial proceedings; it is agreed, that in all such cases, where adequate compensation cannot, for whatever reason, be now actually obtained, had and received by the said merchants and others, in the ordinary course of justice, full and complete compensation for the same will be made by the British government to the said complainants. But it is distinctly understood, that this provision is not to extend to such losses or damages as have been occasioned by the manifest delay or negligence, or wilful omission of the claimant. . . .

Art. X. Neither the debts due from individuals of the one nation to individuals of the other, nor shares, nor monies which they may have in the public funds, or in the public or private banks, shall ever in any event of war or national differences be sequestered or confiscated. . . .

Art. XI. It is agreed between his Majesty and the United States of America, that there shall be a reciprocal and entirely perfect liberty of navigation and commerce between their respective people, in the manner, under the limitations and on the condtions specified in the following articles:

[Art. XII., relating to trade with the West Indies, was suspended.]

Art. XIII. His Majesty consents that the vessels belonging to the citizens of the United States of America, shall be admitted and hospitably received, in all the sea-ports and harbours of the British territories in the East-Indies. And that the citizens of the said United States, may freely carry on a trade between the said territories and the said United States, in all articles of which the importation or exportation respectively, to or from the said territories, shall not be entirely prohibited. . . . The citizens of the United States shall pay for their vessels when admitted into the said ports no other or higher tonnage-duty than shall be payable on British vessels when admitted into the ports of the United States. And they shall pay no other or higher duties or charges, on the importation or exportation of the cargoes of the said vessels, than shall be payable on the same articles when imported or exported in British vessels. But it is expressly agreed, that the vessels of the United States shall not carry any of the articles exported by them from the said British territories, to any port or place, except to some port or place in America, where the same shall be unladen, and such regulations shall be adopted by both parties, as shall from time to time be found necessary to enforce the due and faithful observance of this stipulation. It is also understood that the permission granted by this article, is not to extend to allow the vessels of the United States to carry on any part of the coasting-trade of the said British territories; but vessels going with their original cargoes, or part thereof, from one port of discharge to another, are not to be considered as carrying on the coasting-trade. Neither is this article to be construed to allow the citizens of the said states to settle or reside within the said territories, or to go into the interior parts thereof, without the permission of the British government established there. . . .

ART. XIV. There shall be between all the dominions of his Majesty in Europe and the territories of the United States, a reciprocal and perfect liberty of commerce and navigation. The people and inhabitants of the two countries respectively, shall have liberty freely and securely, and without hindrance and molestation, to come with their ships and cargoes to the lands, countries, cities, ports, places and rivers, within the dominions and territories aforesaid, to enter into the same, to resort there, and to remain and reside there, without any limitation of time.

Also to hire and possess houses and warehouses for the purposes of their commerce, and generally the merchants and traders on each side, shall enjoy the most complete protection and security for their commerce; but subject always as to what respects this article to the laws and statutes of the two countries respectively.

ART. XV. It is agreed that no other or higher duties shall be paid by the ships or merchandize of the one party in the ports of the other, than such as are paid by the like vessels or merchandize of all other nations. Nor shall any other or higher duty be imposed in one country on the importation of any articles the growth, produce or manufacture of the other, than are or shall be payable on the importation of the like articles being of the growth, produce, or manufacture of any other foreign country. Nor shall any prohibition be imposed on the exportation or importation of any articles to or from the territories of the two parties respectively, which shall not equally extend to all other nations. . . .

The two parties agree to treat for the more exact equalization of the duties on the respective navigation of their subjects and people, in such manner as may be most beneficial to the two countries. . . . In the interval it is agreed, that the United States will not impose any new or additional tonnage duties on British vessels, nor increase the now-subsisting difference between the duties payable on the importation of any articles in British or in American vessels. . . .

ART. XVII. It is agreed, that in all cases where vessels shall be captured or detained on just suspicion of having on board enemy's property, or of carrying to the enemy any of the articles which are contraband of war; the said vessel shall be brought to the nearest or most convenient port; and if any property of an enemy should be found on board such vessel, that part only which belongs to the enemy shall be made prize, and the vessel shall be at liberty to proceed with the remainder without any impediment. . . .

ART. IX. And that more abundant care may be taken for the security of the respective subjects and citizens of the contracting parties, and to prevent their suffering injuries by the men of war, or privateers of either party, all commanders of ships of war and privateers, and all others the said subjects and citizens, shall forbear doing any damage to those of the other party, or committing any outrage against them, and if they act to the contrary, they shall be punished, and shall also be bound in their persons and estates to make satisfaction and reparation for all damages, and the interest thereof, of whatever nature the said damages may be. . . .

ART. XXII. It is expressly stipulated, that neither of the said contracting parties will order or authorize any acts of reprisal against the other, on complaints of injuries or damages, until the said party shall first have presented to the other a statement thereof, verified by competent proof and evidence, and demanded justice and satisfaction, and the same shall either have been refused or unreasonably delayed.

ART. XXVI. If at any time a rupture should take place, (which God forbid) between his Majesty and the United States, the merchants and others of each of the two nations, residing in the dominions of the other, shall have the privilege of remaining and continuing their trade, so long as they behave peaceably, and commit no offence against the laws; and in case their conduct should render them suspected, and the respective governments should think proper to order them to remove, the term of twelve months from the publication of the order shall be allowed them for that purpose, to remove with their families, effects and property; but this favour shall not be extended to those who shall act contrary to the established laws; . . .

ART. XXVIII. It is agreed, that the first ten articles of this treaty shall be permanent, and that the subsequent articles, except the twelfth, shall be limited in their duration to twelve years, . . .

99. THE PINCKNEY TREATY
October 27, 1795

Treaty of Friendship, Boundaries, Commerce and Navigation Between the United States of America, and the King of Spain.

(Malloy, ed. *Treaties, Conventions, etc.* Vol. II, p. 1640 ff.)

On the conclusion of the Revolutionary War Spain, refusing to recognize the right of Great Britain to give to the United States the right to navigate the Mississippi, closed that river to Americans. Other matters of dispute between the United States and Spain concerned the boundaries of West Florida and the activities of the Spanish authorities in fomenting discontent among the Indians. Efforts of the United States to conclude a satisfactory treaty with Spain were unsuccessful in 1781 and again in 1785-6. In the early seventeen-nineties western discontent grew alarmingly and intrigues looking to separation or to an attack upon Spanish possessions attracted wide attention. The conclusion of Jay's Treaty inspired the Spanish Court with the fear that Great Britain and the United States might combine to attack Spanish possessions in the new world, and the Spanish minister, Godoy, promptly concluded with Thomas Pinckney a treaty whose provisions were highly satisfactory to Americans. The terms of the treaty, however, were not carried out for almost three years. For Pinckney's Treaty see S. F. Bemis, *Pinckney's Treaty;* A. P. Whitaker, *The Spanish-American Frontier, 1783-1795;* A. P. Whitaker, *The Mis-*

sissippi Question, 1795-1803; P. C. Phillips, *The West in the Diplomacy of the American Revolution.*

ART. I. THERE shall be a firm and inviolable peace and sincere friendship between His Catholic Majesty, his successors and subjects, and the United States, and their citizens, without exception of persons or places.

ART. II. To prevent all disputes on the subject of the boundaries which separate the territories of the two high contracting parties, it is hereby declared and agreed to as follows, to wit. The southern boundary of the United States, which divides their territory from the Spanish colonies of East and West Florida, shall be designated by a line beginning in the River Mississippi, at the northernmost part of the thirty-first degree of latitude north of the equator, which from thence shall be drawn due east to the middle of the River Apalachicola, or Catahouche, thence along the middle thereof to its junction with the Flint: thence straight to the head of St. Mary's river, and thence down the middle thereof to the Atlantic ocean. . . .

ART. IV. It is likewise agreed that the western boundary of the United States which separates them from the Spanish colony of Louissiana, is in the middle of the channel or bed of the River Missisippi, from the northern boundary of the said states to the completion of the thirty-first degree of latitude north of the equator. And His Catholic Majesty has likewise agreed that the navigation of the said river, in its whole breadth from its source to the ocean, shall be free only to his subjects and the citizens of the United States, unless he should extend this privilege to the subject of other Powers by special convention.

ART. V. The two high contracting parties shall, by all the means in their power, maintain peace and harmony among the several Indian nations who inhabit the country adjacent to the lines and rivers, which, by the preceding articles, form the boundaries of the two Floridas. . . .

And whereas several treaties of friendship exist between the two contracting parties and the said nations of Indians, it is hereby agreed that in future no treaty of alliance, or other whatever (except treaties of peace,) shall be made by either party with the Indians living within the boundary of the other, but both parties will endeavour to make the advantages of the Indian trade common and mutually beneficial to their respective subjects and citizens, observing in all things the most complete reciprocity. . . .

ART. XXII. . . . And in consequence of the stipulations contained in the IV. article, His Catholic Majesty will permit the citizens of the United States, for the space of three years from this time, to deposit their merchandizes and effects in the port of New-Orleans, and to export them from thence without paying any other duty than a fair price for the hire of the stores, and His Majesty promises either to continue this permission, if he finds during that time that it is not prejudicial to the interests of Spain, or if he should not agree to continue it there, he will assign to them, on another part of the banks of the Missisippi, an equivalent establishment. . . .

THOMAS PINCKNEY,
EL PRINCIPE DE LA PAZ,

100. WASHINGTON'S FAREWELL ADDRESS
September 17, 1796

(Richardson, ed. *Messages and Papers,* Vol. I, p. 213 ff.)

This memorable address was Washington's valedictory to the American people; its advice and injunctions have influenced American history far more than Washington himself could have anticipated. The immediate occasion for Washington's Address was the necessity of eliminating himself from the contest for the Presidency. Washington had seriously considered retiring from that office at the end of his first term, and on May 20, 1792, he had written Madison a letter containing many of the points later developed in the Farewell Address. There has been considerable controversy over the question of the authorship of the Address, and Hamilton's admirers claim that he was principally responsible for it. In July 1796 Washington sent his earlier draft of a farewell address, together with Madison's answer, to Hamilton with a request for suggestions and literary alterations. Hamilton proceeded to write an address, based almost entirely upon Washington's draft; Washington returned it to Hamilton with further suggestions, and Hamilton and John Jay polished up this draft. This second draft, however, did not please Washington as much as Hamilton's first draft, and he asked Hamilton to polish up the first draft for him. This draft was returned to Washington, who made some slight alterations and omissions, and sent it to a printer, Claypoole, who published it in the "American Daily Advertiser," September 17. Washington's, Madison's and Hamilton's drafts of the Address are given in W. C. Ford, ed. *The Writings of George Washington,* Vol. XIII. See, H. Binney, *An Inquiry into the Formation of Washington's Farewell Address;* J. C. Fitzpatrick, *George Washington Himself,* ch. lxxii.

UNITED STATES, *September 17, 1796.*
Friends and Fellow-Citizens:

The period for a new election of a citizen to administer the Executive Government of the United States being not far distant, and the time actually arrived when your thoughts must be employed in designating the person who is to be clothed with that important trust, it appears to me proper, especially as it may conduce to a more distinct expression of the public voice, that I should now apprise you of the resolution I have formed to decline being considered among the number of those out of whom a choice is to be made. . . .

The impressions with which I first undertook the arduous trust were explained on the proper occasion. In the discharge of this trust I will only say that I have, with good intentions, contributed toward the organization and administration of the Government the best exertions of which a very fallible judgment was capable. Not unconscious in the outset of the inferiority of my qualifications, experience in my own eyes, perhaps still more in the eyes of others, has strengthened the motives to diffidence of myself; and every day the increasing weight of years admonishes me more and more that the shade of retirement is as necessary to me as it will be welcome. Satisfied that if any circumstances have given peculiar value to my services they were temporary, I have the consolation to believe that, while choice and prudence invite me to quit the political scene, patriotism does not forbid it. . . .

Here, perhaps, I ought to stop. But a solicitude for your welfare which can not end with my life, and the apprehension of danger natural to that solicitude, urge me on an occasion like the present to offer to your solemn contemplation and to recommend to your frequent review some sentiments which are the result of much reflection, of no inconsiderable observation, and which appear to me all important to the permanency of your felicity as a people. . . .

Interwoven as is the love of liberty with every ligament of your hearts, no recommendation of mine is necessary to fortify or confirm the attachment.

The unity of government which constitutes you one people is also now dear to you. It is justly so, for it is a main pillar in the edifice of your real independence, the support of your tranquillity at home, your peace abroad, of your safety, of your prosperity, of that very liberty which you so highly prize. But as it is easy to foresee that from different causes and from different quarters much pains will be taken, many artifices employed, to weaken in your minds the conviction of this truth, as this is the point in your political fortress against which the batteries of internal and external enemies will be most constantly and actively (though often covertly and insidiously) directed, it is of infinite moment that you should properly estimate the immense value of your national union to your collective and individual happiness; that you should cherish a cordial, habitual, and immovable attachment to it; accustoming yourselves to think and speak of it as of the palladium of your political safety and prosperity; watching for its preservation with jealous anxiety; discountenancing whatever may suggest even a suspicion that it can in any event be abandoned, and indignantly frowning upon the first dawning of every attempt to alienate any portion of our country from the rest or to enfeeble the sacred ties which now link together the various parts.

For this you have every inducement of sympathy and interest. Citizens by birth or choice of a common country, that country has a right to concentrate your affections. The name of American, which belongs to you in your national capacity, must always exalt the just pride of patriotism more than any appellation derived from local discriminations. With slight shades of difference, you have the same religion, manners, habits, and political principles. You have in a common cause fought and triumphed together. The independence and liberty you possess are the work of joint councils and joint efforts, of common dangers, sufferings, and successes.

But these considerations, however powerfully they address themselves to your sensibility, are greatly outweighed by those which apply more immediately to your interest. Here every portion of our country finds the most commanding motives for carefully guarding and preserving the union of the whole.

The *North*, in an unrestrained intercourse with the *South*, protected by the equal laws of a common government, finds in the productions of the latter great additional resources of maritime and commercial enterprise and precious materials of manufacturing industry. The *South*, in the same intercourse, benefiting by the same agency of the *North*, sees its agriculture grow and its commerce expand. Turning partly into its own channels the seamen of the *North*, it finds its particular navigation invigorated; and while it contributes in different ways to nourish and increase the general mass of the national navigation, it looks forward to the protection of a maritime strength to which itself is unequally adapted. The *East*, in a like intercourse with the *West*, already finds, and in the progressive improvement of interior communications by land and water will more and more find, a valuable vent for the commodities which it brings from abroad or manufactures at home. The *West* derives from the *East* supplies requisite to its growth and comfort, and what is perhaps of still greater consequence, it must of necessity owe the *secure* enjoyment of indispensable *outlets* for its own productions to the weight, influence, and the future maritime strength of the Atlantic side of the Union, directed by an indissoluble community of interest as *one nation*. Any other tenure by which the *West* can hold this essential advantage, whether derived from its own separate strength or from an apostate and unnatural connection with any foreign power, must be intrinsically precarious.

While, then, every part of our country thus feels an immediate and particular interest in union, all the parts combined can not fail to find in the united mass of means and efforts greater strength, greater resource, proportionably greater security from external danger, a less frequent interruption of their peace by foreign nations, and what is of inestimable value, they must derive from union an exemption from those broils and wars between themselves which so frequently afflict neighboring countries not tied together by the same governments, which their own rivalships alone would be sufficient to produce, but which opposite foreign alliances, attachments, and intrigues would stimulate and imbitter. Hence, likewise, they will avoid the necessity of those overgrown military establishments which, under any form of government, are inauspicious to liberty, and which are to be regarded as particularly hostile to republican liberty. In this sense it is that your union ought to be considered as a main prop of your liberty, and that the love of the one ought to endear to you the preservation of the other. . . .

Is there a doubt whether a common government can embrace so large a sphere? Let experience solve it. To listen to mere speculation in such a case were criminal. It is well worth a fair and full experiment. With such powerful and obvious motives to union affecting all parts of our country, while experience shall not have demonstrated its impracticability, there will always be reason to distrust the patriotism of those who in any quarter may endeavor to weaken its bands.

In contemplating the causes which may disturb our union it occurs as matter of serious concern that any ground should have been furnished for characterizing parties by *geographical* discriminations—*Northern* and *Southern*, *Atlantic* and *Western*—whence designing men may endeavor to excite a belief that there is a real difference of local interests and views. One of the expedients of party to acquire influence within particular districts is to misrepresent the opinions and aims of other districts. You can not shield yourselves too much against the jealousies and heartburnings which spring from these misrepresentations; they tend to render alien to each other those who ought to be bound together by fraternal affection. . . .

To the efficacy and permanency of your union a government for the whole is indispensable. No alliances, however strict, between the parts can be an adequate substitute. They must inevitably experience the infractions and interruptions which all alliances in all times have experienced. Sensible of this momentous truth, you have improved upon your first essay by the adoption of a Constitution of Government better calculated than your former for an intimate union and for the efficacious management of your common concerns. This Government, the offspring of our own choice, uninfluenced and unawed, adopted upon full investigation and mature deliberation, completely free in its principles, in the distribution of its powers, uniting security with energy, and containing within itself a provision for its own amendment, has a just claim to your confidence and your support. Respect for its authority, compliance with its laws, acquiescence in its measures, are duties enjoined by the fundamental maxims of true liberty. The basis of our political systems is the right of the people to make and to alter their constitutions of government. But the constitution which at any time exists till changed by an explicit and authentic act of the whole people is sacredly obligatory upon all. The very idea of the power and the right of the people to establish government presupposes the duty of every individual to obey the established government. . . .

Toward the preservation of your Government and the permanency of your present happy state, it is requisite not only that you steadily discountenance irregular oppositions to its acknowledged authority, but also that you resist with care the spirit of innovation upon its principles, however specious the pretexts. One method of assault may be to effect in the forms of the Constitution alterations which will impair the energy of the system, and thus to undermine what can not be directly overthrown. In all the changes to which you may be invited remember that time and habit are at least as necessary to fix the true character of governments as of other human institutions; that experience is the surest standard by which to test the real tendency of the existing constitution of a country; that facility in changes upon the credit of mere hypothesis and opinion exposes to perpetual change, from the endless variety of hypothesis and opinion; and remember especially that for the efficient management of your common interests in a country so extensive as ours a government of as much vigor as is consistent with the perfect security of liberty is indispensable. Liberty itself will find in such a government, with powers properly distributed and adjusted, its surest guardian. It is, indeed, little else than a name where the government is too feeble to withstand the enterprises of faction, to confine each member of the society within the limits prescribed by the laws, and to maintain all in the secure and tranquil enjoyment of the rights of person and property.

I have already intimated to you the danger of parties in the State, with particular reference to the founding of them on geographical discriminations. Let me now take a more comprehensive view, and warn you in the most solemn manner against the baneful effects of the spirit of party generally.

This spirit, unfortunately, is inseparable from our nature, having its root in the strongest passions of the human mind. It exists under different shapes in all governments, more or less stifled, controlled, or repressed; but in those of the popular form it is seen in its greatest rankness and is truly their worst enemy. . . .

It serves always to distract the public councils and enfeeble the public administration. It agitates the community with ill-founded jealousies and false alarms; kindles the animosity of one part against another; foments occasionally riot and insurrection. It opens the door to foreign influence and corruption, which find a facilitated access to the government itself through the channels of party passion. Thus the policy and the will of one country are subjected to the policy and will of another.

There is an opinion that parties in free countries are useful checks upon the administration of the government, and serve to keep alive the spirit of liberty. This within certain limits is probably true; and in governments of a monarchical cast patriotism may look with indulgence, if not with favor, upon the spirit of party. But in those of the popular character, in governments purely elective, it is a spirit not to be encouraged. From their natural tendency it is certain there will always be enough of that spirit for every salutary purpose; and there being constant danger of excess, the effort ought to be by force of public opinion to mitigate and assuage it. A fire not to be quenched, it demands a uniform vigilance to prevent its bursting into a flame, lest, instead of warming, it should consume.

It is important, likewise, that the habits of thinking in a free country should inspire caution in those intrusted with its administration to confine themselves within their respective constitutional spheres, avoiding in the exercise of the powers of one department to encroach upon another. The spirit of encroachment tends to consolidate the powers of all the departments in one, and thus to create, whatever the form of government, a real despotism. . . . If in the opinion of the people the distribution or modification of the constitutional powers be in any particular wrong, let it be corrected by an amendment in the way which the Constitution designates. But let there be no change by usurpation; for though this in one instance may be the instrument of good, it is the customary weapon by which free governments are destroyed. The precedent must always greatly overbalance in permanent evil any partial or transient benefit which the use can at any time yield.

Of all the dispositions and habits which lead to political prosperity, religion and morality are indispensable supports. In vain would that man claim the tribute of patriotism who should labor to subvert these great pillars of human happiness—these firmest props of the duties of men and citizens. The mere politician, equally with the pious man, ought to respect and to cherish them. A volume could not trace all their connections with private and public felicity. Let it simply be asked, Where is the security for property, for reputation, for life, if the sense of religious obligation *desert* the oaths which are the instruments of investigation in courts of justice? And let us with caution indulge the supposition that morality can be maintained without religion. Whatever may be conceded to the influence of refined education on minds of peculiar structure, reason and experience both forbid us to expect that national morality can prevail in exclusion of religious principle.

It is substantially true that virtue or morality is a necessary spring of popular government. The rule indeed extends with more or less force to every species of free government. Who that is a sincere friend to it can look with indifference upon attempts to shake the foundation of the fabric? Promote, then, as an object of primary importance, institutions for the general diffusion of knowledge. In proportion as the structure of a government gives force to public opinion, it is essential that public opinion should be enlightened.

As a very important source of strength and security, cherish public credit. One method of preserving it is to use it as sparingly as possible, avoiding occasions of expense by cultivating peace, but remembering also that timely disbursements to prepare for danger frequently prevent much greater disbursements to repel it; avoiding

likewise the accumulation of debt, not only by shunning occasions of expense, but by vigorous exertions in time of peace to discharge the debts which unavoidable wars have occasioned, not ungenerously throwing upon posterity the burthen which we ourselves ought to bear. . . .

Observe good faith and justice toward all nations. Cultivate peace and harmony with all. Religion and morality enjoin this conduct. And can it be that good policy does not equally enjoin it? It will be worthy of a free, enlightened, and at no distant period a great nation to give to mankind the magnanimous and too novel example of a people always guided by an exalted justice and benevolence. Who can doubt that in the course of time and things the fruits of such a plan would richly repay any temporary advantages which might be lost by a steady adherence to it? Can it be that Providence has not connected the permanent felicity of a nation with its virtue? The experiment, at least, is recommended by every sentiment which ennobles human nature. Alas! is it rendered impossible by its vices?

In the execution of such a plan nothing is more essential than that permanent, inveterate antipathies against particular nations and passionate attachments for others should be excluded, and that in place of them just and amicable feelings toward all should be cultivated. The nation which indulges toward another an habitual hatred or an habitual fondness is in some degree a slave. It is a slave to its animosity or to its affection, either of which is sufficient to lead it astray from its duty and its interest. Antipathy in one nation against another disposes each more readily to offer insult and injury, to lay hold of slight causes of umbrage, and to be haughty and intractable when accidental or trifling occasions of dispute occur

So, likewise, a passionate attachment of one nation for another produces a variety of evils. Sympathy for the favorite nation, facilitating the illusion of an imaginary common interest in cases where no real common interest exists, and infusing into one the enmities of the other, betrays the former into a participation in the quarrels and wars of the latter without adequate inducement or justification. It leads also to concessions to the favorite nation of privileges denied to others, which is apt doubly to injure the nation making the concessions by unnecessarily parting with what ought to have been retained, and by exciting jealousy, ill will, and a disposition to retaliate in the parties from whom equal privileges are withheld; and it gives to ambitious, corrupted, or deluded citizens (who devote themselves to the favorite nation) facility to betray or sacrifice the interests of their own country without odium, sometimes even with popularity, gilding with the appearances of a virtuous sense of obligation, a commendable deference for public opinion, or a laudable zeal for public good the base or foolish compliances of ambition, corruption, or infatuation. . . .

Against the insidious wiles of foreign influence (I conjure you to believe me, fellow-citizens) the jealousy of a free people ought to be *constantly* awake, since history and experience prove that foreign influence is one of the most baneful foes of republican government. But that jealousy, to be useful, must be impartial, else it becomes the instrument of the very influence to be avoided, instead of a defense against it. Excessive partiality for one foreign nation and excessive dislike of another cause those whom they actuate to see danger only on one side, and serve to veil and even second the arts of influence on the other. Real patriots who may resist the intrigues of the favorite are liable to become suspected and odious, while its tools and dupes usurp the applause and confidence of the people to surrender their interests.

The great rule of conduct for us in regard to foreign nations is, in extending our commercial relations to have with them as little *political* connection as possible. So far as we have already formed engagements let them be fulfilled with perfect good faith. Here let us stop.

Europe has a set of primary interests which to us have none or a very remote relation. Hence she must be engaged in frequent controversies, the causes of which are essentially foreign to our concerns. Hence, therefore, it must be unwise in us to implicate ourselves by artificial ties in the ordinary vicissitudes of her politics or the

ordinary combinations and collisions of her friendships or enmities.

Our detached and distant situation invites and enables us to pursue a different course. If we remain one people, under an efficient government, the period is not far off when we may defy material injury from external annoyance; when we may take such an attitude as will cause the neutrality we may at any time resolve upon to be scrupulously respected; when belligerent nations, under the impossibility of making acquisitions upon us, will not lightly hazard the giving us provocation; when we may choose peace or war, as our interest, guided by justice, shall counsel.

Why forego the advantages of so peculiar a situation? Why quit our own to stand upon foreign ground? Why, by interweaving our destiny with that of any part of Europe, entangle our peace and prosperity in the toils of European ambition, rivalship, interest, humor, or caprice?

It is our true policy to steer clear of permanent alliances with any portion of the foreign world, so far, I mean, as we are now at liberty to do it; for let me not be understood as capable of patronizing infidelity to existing engagements. I hold the maxim no less applicable to public than to private affairs that honesty is always the best policy. I repeat, therefore, let those engagements be observed in their genuine sense. But in my opinion it is unnecessary and would be unwise to extend them.

Taking care always to keep ourselves by suitable establishments on a respectable defensive posture, we may safely trust to temporary alliances for extraordinary emergencies.

Harmony, liberal intercourse with all nations are recommended by policy, humanity, and interest. But even our commercial policy should hold an equal and impartial hand, neither seeking nor granting exclusive favors or preferences; consulting the natural course of things; diffusing and diversifying by gentle means the streams of commerce, but forcing nothing; establishing with powers so disposed, in order to give trade a stable course, to define the rights of our merchants, and to enable the Government to support them, conventional rules of intercourse, the best that present circumstances and mutual opinion will permit, but temporary and liable to be from time to time abandoned or varied as experience and circumstances shall dictate; constantly keeping in view that it is folly in one nation to look for disinterested favors from another; that it must pay with a portion of its independence for whatever it may accept under that character; that by such acceptance it may place itself in the condition of having given equivalents for nominal favors, and yet of being reproached with ingratitude for not giving more. There can be no greater error than to expect or calculate upon real favors from nation to nation. It is an illusion which experience must cure, which a just pride ought to discard. . . .

Though in reviewing the incidents of my Administration I am unconscious of intentional error, I am nevertheless too sensible of my defects not to think it probable that I may have committed many errors. Whatever they may be, I fervently beseech the Almighty to avert or mitigate the evils to which they may tend. I shall also carry with me the hope that my country will never cease to view them with indulgence, and that, after forty-five years of my life dedicated to its service with an upright zeal, the faults of incompetent abilities will be consigned to oblivion, as myself must soon be to the mansions of rest.

Relying on its kindness in this as in other things, and actuated by that fervent love toward it which is so natural to a man who views in it the native soil of himself and his progenitors for several generations, I anticipate with pleasing expectation that retreat in which I promise myself to realize without alloy the sweet enjoyment of partaking in the midst of my fellow-citizens the benign influence of good laws under a free government—the ever-favorite object of my heart, and the happy reward, as I trust, of our mutual cares, labors, and dangers.

G°. WASHINGTON.

101. THE ALIEN AND SEDITION ACTS
1798

The publication, in the spring of 1798, of the X Y Z correspondence raised among the Federalists a spirit of nationalism that found expression in the four acts known collectively as the Alien and Sedition Acts. The animus of these acts was directed particularly against a group of anti-Federalist editors and pamphleteers of French and English extraction, such as Thomas Cooper, Joseph Priestley, James Callender, Benjamin F. Bache, Count de Volney, V. du Pont and others. There was grave doubt as to the constitutionality of the Sedition Act, which extended the jurisdiction of the federal courts, but the question of validity never came before the courts, though in 1812 the supreme court ruled that the federal courts do not have common law jurisdiction in criminal cases. Though the Alien Acts were never enforced, a number of French refugees fled the country or went into hiding. Some twenty-five persons were arrested under the Sedition Act, and ten convicted. See, F. M. Anderson, "The Enforcement of the Alien and Sedition Laws," American Hist. Assoc. *Reports*, 1912; C. G. Bowers, *Jefferson and Hamilton*, ch. xvi-xvii; J. S. Bassett, *The Federalist System*, ch. xvii; J. F. Mc Laughlin, *Matthew Lyon;* D. Malone, *Thomas Cooper;* B. Faÿ, *The Two Franklins*.

1. THE NATURALIZATION ACT
June 18, 1798
(*U. S. Statutes at Large,* Vol. I, p. 566 ff.)

An Act supplementary to and to amend the act, intituled "An act to establish an uniform rule of naturalization;" and to repeal the act heretofore passed on that subject.

SECTION 1. *Be it enacted . . . ,* That no alien shall be admitted to become a citizen of the United States, or of any state, unless . . . he shall have declared his intention to become a citizen of the United States, five years, at least, before his admission, and shall, at the time of his application to be admitted, declare and prove, to the satisfaction of the court having jurisdiction in the case, that he has resided within the United States fourteen years, at least, and within the state or territory where, or for which such court is at the time held, five years, at least, besides conforming to the other declarations, renunciations and proofs, by the said act required, any thing therein to the contrary hereof notwithstanding: *Provided,* that any alien, who was residing within the limits, and under the jurisdiction of the United States, before . . . [January 29, 1795,] . . . may, within one year after the passing of this act—and any alien who shall have made the declaration of his intention to become a citizen of the United States, in conformity to the provisions of the act [of Jan. 29, 1795], may, within four years after having made the declaration aforesaid, be admitted to become a citizen, in the manner prescribed by the said act, . . . *And provided also,* that no alien, who shall be a native, citizen, denizen or subject of any nation or state with whom the United States shall be at war, at the time of his application, shall be then admitted to become a citizen of the United States. . . .

SEC. 4. *And be it further enacted,* That all white persons, aliens, . . . who, after the passing of this act, shall continue to reside, or who shall arrive, or come to reside in any port or place within the territory of the United States, shall be reported, . . . to the clerk of the district court of the district, if living within ten miles of the port or place, in which their residence or arrival shall be, and otherwise, to the collector of such port or place, or some officer or other person there, or nearest thereto, who shall be authorized by the President of the United States, to register aliens: And report, as aforesaid, shall be made in all cases of residence, within six months from and after the passing of this act, and in all after cases, within forty-eight hours after the first arrival or coming into the territory of the United States, and shall ascertain the sex, place of birth, age, nation, place of allegiance or citizenship, condition or occupation, and place of actual or intended residence within the United States, of the alien or aliens reported, and by whom the report is made. . . .

Sec. 5. *And be it further enacted,* That every alien who shall continue to reside, or who shall arrive, as aforesaid, of whom a report is required as aforesaid, who shall refuse or neglect to make such report, and to receive a certificate thereof, shall forfeit and pay the sum of two dollars; and any justice of the peace, or other civil magistrate, who has authority to require surety of the peace, shall and may, on complaint to him made thereof, cause such alien to be brought be-

fore him, there to give surety of the peace and good behaviour during his residence within the United States, or for such term as the justice or other magistrate shall deem reasonable, and until a report and registry of such alien shall be made, and a certificate thereof, received as aforesaid; and in failure of such surety, such alien shall and may be committed to the common gaol, and shall be there held, until the order which the justice or magistrate shall and may reasonably make, in the premises, shall be performed. . . .

2. THE ALIEN ACT
June 25, 1798
(*U. S. Statutes at Large,* Vol. I, p. 570 ff.)

An Act concerning Aliens.

SEC. 1. *Be it enacted* . . . , That it shall be lawful for the President of the United States at any time during the continuance of this act, to *order* all such *aliens* as he shall judge dangerous to the peace and safety of the United States, or shall have reasonable grounds to suspect are concerned in any treasonable or secret machinations against the government thereof, to depart out of the territory of the United States, within such time as shall be expressed in such order, which order shall be served on such alien by delivering him a copy thereof, or leaving the same at his usual abode, and returned to the office of the Secretary of State, by the marshal or other person to whom the same shall be directed. And in case any alien, so ordered to depart, shall be found at large within the United States after the time limited in such order for his departure, and not having obtained a *license* from the President to reside therein, or having obtained such *license* shall not have conformed thereto, every such alien shall, on conviction thereof, be imprisoned for a term not exceeding three years, and shall never after be admitted to become a citizen of the United States. *Provided always, and be it further enacted,* that if any alien so ordered to depart shall prove to the satisfaction of the President, by evidence to be taken before such person or persons as the President shall direct, who are for that purpose hereby authorized to administer oaths, that no injury or danger to the United States will arise from suffering such alien to reside therein, the President may grant a *license* to such alien to remain within the United States for such time as he shall judge proper, and at such place as he may designate. And the President may also require of such alien to enter into a bond to the United States, in such penal sum as he may direct, with one or more sufficient sureties to the satisfaction of the person authorized by the President to take the same, conditioned for the good behavior of such alien during his residence in the United States, and not violating his license, which license the President may revoke, whenever he shall think proper.

Sec. 2. *And be it further enacted,* That it shall be lawful for the President of the United States, whenever he may deem it necessary for the public safety, to order to be removed out of the territory thereof, any alien who may or shall be in prison in pursuance of this act; and to cause to be arrested and sent out of the United States such of those aliens as shall have been ordered to depart therefrom and shall not have obtained a license as aforesaid, in all cases where, in the opinion of the President, the public safety requires a speedy removal. And if any alien so removed or sent out of the United States by the President shall voluntarily return thereto, unless by permission of the President of the United States, such alien on conviction thereof, shall be imprisoned so long as, in the opinion of the President, the public safety may require. . . .

Sec. 6. *And be it further enacted,* That this act shall continue and be in force for and during the term of two years from the passing thereof.

3. THE ALIEN ENEMIES ACT
July 6, 1798
(U. S. Statutes at Large, Vol. I, p. 577 ff.)

An Act respecting Alien Enemies.

SECTION 1. *Be it enacted . . . ,* That whenever there shall be a declared war between the United States and any foreign nation or government, or any invasion or predatory incursion shall be perpetrated, attempted, or threatened against the territory of the United States, by any foreign nation or government, . . . all natives, citizens, denizens, or subjects of the hostile nation or government, being males of the age of fourteen years and upwards, who shall be within the United States, and not actually naturalized, shall be liable to be apprehended, re-

strained, secured and removed, as alien enemies. And the President of the United States shall be, and he is hereby authorized, . . . to direct the conduct to be observed, on the part of the United States, towards the aliens who shall become liable, as aforesaid; the manner and degree of the restraint to which they shall be subject, and in what cases, and upon what security their residence shall be permitted, and to provide for the removal of those, who, not being permitted to reside within the United States, shall refuse or neglect to depart therefrom; and to establish any other regulations which shall be found necessary in the premises and for the public safety: . . .

4. THE SEDITION ACT
July 14, 1798
(U. S. Statutes at Large, Vol. I, p. 596–7)

An Act in addition to the act, entitled "An act for the punishment of certain crimes against the United States."

SEC. 1. *Be it enacted . . . ,* That if any persons shall unlawfully combine or conspire together, with intent to oppose any measure or measures of the government of the United States, which are or shall be directed by proper authority, or to impede the operation of any law of the United States, or to intimidate or prevent any person holding a place or office in or under the government of the United States, from undertaking, performing or executing his trust or duty; and if any person or persons, with intent as aforesaid, shall counsel, advise or attempt to procure any insurrection, riot, unlawful assembly, or combination, whether such conspiracy, threatening, counsel, advice, or attempt shall have the proposed effect or not, he or they shall be deemed guilty of a high misdemeanor, and on conviction, before any court of the United States having jurisdiction thereof, shall be punished by a fine not exceeding five thousand dollars, and by imprisonment during a term not less than six months nor exceeding five years; and further, at the discretion of the court may be holden to find sureties for his good behaviour in such sum, and for such time, as the said court may direct.

SEC. 2. That if any person shall write, print, utter, or publish, or shall cause or procure to be written, printed, uttered or published. or shall knowingly and willingly assist or aid in writing, printing, uttering or publishing any false, scandalous and malicious writing or writings against the government of the United States, or either house of the Congress of the United States, or the President of the United States, with intent to defame the said government, or either house of the said Congress, or the said President. or to bring them, or either of them, into contempt or disrepute; or to excite against them, or either or any of them, the hatred of the good people of the United States, or to stir up sedition within the United States, or to excite any unlawful combinations therein, for opposing or resisting any law of the United States, or any act of the President of the United States, done in pursuance of any such law, or of the powers in him vested by the constitution of the United States, or to resist, oppose, or defeat any such law or act, or to aid, encourage or abet any hostile designs of any foreign nation against the United States, their people or government, then such person, being thereof convicted before any court of the United States having jurisdiction thereof, shall be punished by a fine not exceeding two thousand dollars, and by imprisonment not exceeding two years.

SEC. 3. That if any person shall be prosecuted under this act, for the writing or publishing any libel aforesaid, it shall be lawful for the defendant, upon the trial of the cause, to give in evidence in his defence, the truth of the matter contained in the publication charged as a libel. And the jury who shall try the cause, shall have a right to determine the law and the fact, under the direction of the court, as in other cases.

SEC. 4. That this act shall continue to be in force until March 3, 1801, and no longer. . . .

102. THE KENTUCKY AND VIRGINIA RESOLUTIONS OF 1798

The Kentucky and Virginia Resolutions of 1798 were evoked by the Alien and Sedition Acts. The Kentucky Resolutions were drafted by Jefferson, and sponsored in the Kentucky legislature by John Breckenridge. The Virginia Resolutions were drafted by Madison, and introduced by John Taylor of Caroline. These resolutions represented not so much a constitutional as a social philosophy: they were drawn up with the primary purpose not of presenting a constitutional theory but of presenting a democratic protest against what was considered a dangerous usurpation of power by the central government. The perplexing question of the proper authority to pass on problems of constitutionality had not yet been resolved in favor of the Courts, and it was not unreasonable for those who feared the centralizing tendencies of the federal government to assert that the States were the proper parties to decide this question. The resolutions of 1798 drew forth replies from several states; see Doc. No. 104. On the resolutions, see E. D. Warfield, *The Kentucky Resolutions* of 1798; N. S. Shaler, *Kentucky*, ch. x; C. W. Loring, *Nullification, Secession;* H. Von Holst, *Constitutional and Political History of the United States,* Vol. I; G. Hunt, *James Madison;* E. P. Powell, *Nullification and Secession in the United States;* A. C. McLaughlin, *Courts, Constitution and Parties,* ch. iv.

1. KENTUCKY RESOLUTIONS
November 16, 1798
(N. S. Shaler, *Kentucky,* p. 409 ff.)

I. *Resolved,* that the several States composing the United States of America, are not united on the principle of unlimited submission to their general government; but that by compact under the style and title of a Constitution for the United States and of amendments thereto, they constituted a general government for special purposes, delegated to that government certain definite powers, reserving each State to itself, the residuary mass of right to their own self-government; and that whensoever the general government assumes undelegated powers, its acts are unauthoritative, void, and of no force: That to this compact each State acceded as a State, and is an integral party, its co-States forming, as to itself, the other party: That the government created by this compact was not made the exclusive or final judge of the extent of the powers delegated to itself; since that would have made its discretion, and not the Constitution, the measure of its powers; but that as in all other cases of compact among parties having no common Judge, *each party has an equal right to judge for itself, as well of infractions as of the mode and measure of redress.*

II. *Resolved,* that the Constitution of the United States having delegated to Congress a power to punish treason, counterfeiting the securities and current coin of the United States, piracies and felonies committed on the high seas, and offenses against the laws of nations, and no other crimes whatever, and it being true as a general principle, and one of the amendments to the Constitution having also declared "that the powers not delegated to the United States by the Constitution, nor prohibited by it to the States, are reserved to the States respectively, or to the people," therefore also [the Sedition Act of July 14, 1798]; as also the act passed by them on the 27th day of June, 1798, entitled "An act to punish frauds committed on the Bank of the United States" (and all other their acts which assume to create, define, or punish crimes other than those enumerated in the Constitution), are altogether void and of no force, and that the power to create, define, and punish such other crimes is reserved, and of right appertains solely and exclusively to the respective States, each within its own Territory.

III. *Resolved,* that it is true as a general principle, and is also expressly declared by one of the amendments to the Constitution that "the powers not delegated to the United States by the Constitution, nor prohibited by it to the States, are reserved to the States respectively or to the people;" and that no power over the freedom of religion, freedom of speech, or freedom of the press being delegated to the United States by the Constitution, nor prohibited by it to the States, all lawful powers respecting the same did of right remain, and were reserved to the States, or to the people: That thus was manifested their determination to retain to themselves the right of judging how far the licentiousness of speech and of the press may be abridged without lessening their useful freedom, and how far those abuses which cannot be separated from their use should be tolerated rather than the use be destroyed; and thus also they guarded against all abridgment by the United States of the freedom of religious opinions and exercises, and retained to them-

selves the right of protecting the same, as this State, by a law passed on the general demand of its citizens, had already protected them from all human restraint or interference: And that in addition to this general principle and express declaration, another and more special provision has been made by one of the amendments to the Constitution which expressly declares, that "Congress shall make no law respecting an establishment of religion, or prohibiting the free exercise thereof, or abridging the freedom of speech, or of the press," thereby guarding in the same sentence, and under the same words, the freedom of religion, of speech, and of the press, insomuch, that whatever violates either, throws down the sanctuary which covers the others, and that libels, falsehoods, defamation equally with heresy and false religion, are withheld from the cognizance of Federal tribunals. That therefore [the Sedition Act], which does abridge the freedom of the press, is not law, but is altogether void and of no effect.

IV. *Resolved,* that alien friends are under the jurisdiction and protection of the laws of the State wherein they are; that no power over them has been delegated to the United States, nor prohibited to the individual States distinct from their power over citizens; and it being true as a general principle, and one of the amendments to the Constitution having also declared that "the powers not delegated to the United States by the Constitution, nor prohibited by it to the States, are reserved to the States respectively, or to the people," the [Alien Act of June 22, 1798], which assumes power over alien friends not delegated by the Constitution, is not law, but is altogether void and of no force.

V. *Resolved,* that in addition to the general principle as well as the express declaration, that powers not delegated are reserved, another and more special provision inserted in the Constitution from abundant caution has declared, "that the migration or importation of such persons as any of the States now existing shall think proper to admit, shall not be prohibited by the Congress prior to the year 1808." That this Commonwealth does admit the migration of alien friends described as the subject of the said act concerning aliens; that a provision against prohibiting their migration is a provision against all acts equivalent thereto, or it would be nugatory;

that to remove them when migrated is equivalent to a prohibition of their migration, and is therefore contrary to the said provision of the Constitution, and void.

VI. *Resolved,* that the imprisonment of a person under the protection of the laws of this Commonwealth on his failure to obey the simple order of the President to depart out of the United States, as is undertaken by the said act entitled "An act concerning aliens," is contrary to the Constitution, one amendment to which has provided, that "no person shall be deprived of liberty without due process of law," and that another having provided "that in all criminal prosecutions, the accused shall enjoy the right to a public trial by an impartial jury, to be informed of the nature and cause of the accusation, to be confronted with the witnesses against him, to have compulsory process for obtaining witnesses in his favour, and to have the assistance of counsel for his defense," the same act undertaking to authorize the President to remove a person out of the United States who is under the protection of the law, on his own suspicion, without accusation, without jury, without public trial, without confrontation of the witnesses against him, without having witnesses in his favour, without defense, without counsel, is contrary to these provisions also of the Constitution, is therefore not law, but utterly void and of no force. That transferring the power of judging any person who is under the protection of the laws, from the courts to the President of the United States, as is undertaken by the same act concerning aliens, is against the article of the Constitution which provides, that "the judicial power of the United States shall be vested in courts, the judges of which shall hold their offices during good behavior," and that the said act is void for that reason also; and it is further to be noted, that this transfer of judiciary power is to that magistrate of the general government who already possesses all the executive, and a qualified negative in all the legislative powers.

VII. *Resolved,* that the construction applied by the general government (as is evinced by sundry of their proceedings) to those parts of the Constitution of the United States which delegate to Congress a power to lay and collect taxes, duties, imposts, and excises; to pay the debts, and provide for the common defense, and general welfare of the United States, and to make all laws which shall be necessary and proper for carrying into execution the powers vested by the Constitution in the government of the United States, or any department thereof, goes to the destruction of all the limits prescribed to their power by the Constitution: That words meant by that instrument to be subsidiary only to the execution of the limited powers ought not to be so construed as themselves to give unlimited powers, nor a part so to be taken as to destroy the whole residue of the instrument: That the proceedings of the general government under color of these articles will be a fit and necessary subject for revisal and correction at a time of greater tranquillity, while those specified in the preceding resolutions call for immediate redress.

VIII. *Resolved,* that the preceding Resolutions be transmitted to the Senators and Representatives in Congress from this Commonwealth, who are hereby enjoined to present the same to their respective Houses, and to use their best endeavors to procure, at the next session of Congress, a repeal of the aforesaid unconstitutional and obnoxious acts.

IX. *Resolved,* lastly, that the Governor of this Commonwealth be, and is hereby authorized and requested to communicate the preceding Resolutions to the Legislatures of the several States, to assure them that this Commonwealth considers Union for specified National purposes, and particularly for those specified in their late Federal Compact, to be friendly to the peace, happiness, and prosperity of all the States: that faithful to that compact according to the plain intent and meaning in which it was understood and acceded to by the several parties, it is sincerely anxious for its preservation: that it does also believe, that to take from the States all the powers of self-government, and transfer them to a general and consolidated government, without regard to the special delegations and reservations solemnly agreed to in that compact, is not for the peace, happiness, or prosperity of these States: And that, therefore, this Commonwealth is determined, as it doubts not its co-States are, tamely to submit to undelegated and consequently unlimited powers in no man or body of men on earth: that if the acts before specified should stand, these conclusions would flow from them; that the general government may place any act they think proper on the list of crimes and punish it themselves, whether enumerated or not enumerated by the Constitution as cognizable by them: that they may transfer its cognizance to the President or any other person, who may himself be the accuser, counsel, judge, and jury, whose suspicions may be the evidence, his order the sentence, his officer the executioner, and his breast the sole record of the transaction: that a very numerous and valuable description of the inhabitants of these States being by this precedent reduced as outlaws to the absolute dominion of one man, and the barrier of the Constitution thus swept away from us all, no rampart now remains against the passions and the powers of a majority of Congress, to protect from a like exportation or other more grievous punishment the minority of the same body, the legislatures, judges, governors, and counselors of the States, nor their other peaceable inhabitants who may venture to reclaim the constitutional rights and liberties of the State and people, or who for other causes, good or bad, may be obnoxious to the views or marked by the suspicions of the President, or be thought dangerous to his or their elections or other interests, public or personal: that the friendless alien has indeed been selected as the safest subject of a first experiment, but the citizen will soon follow, or rather has already followed: for, already has a sedition act marked him as its prey: that these and successive acts of the same character, unless arrested on the threshold, may tend to drive these States into revolution and blood, and will furnish new calumnies against Republican governments, and new pretexts for those who wish it to be believed, that man cannot be governed but by a rod of iron: that it would be a dangerous delusion were a confidence in the men of our choice to silence our fears for the safety of our rights: that confidence is everywhere the parent of despotism: free government is founded in jealousy and not in confidence; it is jealousy and not confidence which prescribes limited Constitutions to bind down those whom we are obliged to trust with power: that our Constitution has accordingly fixed the limits to which and no further our confidence may go; and let the honest advocate of confidence read the alien and sedition acts, and say if

the Constitution has not been wise in fixing limits to the government it created, and whether we should be wise in destroying those limits; let him say what the government is if it be not a tyranny, which the men of our choice have conferred on the President, and the President of our choice has assented to and accepted over the friendly strangers, to whom the mild spirit of our country and its laws had pledged hospitality and protection: that the men of our choice have more respected the bare suspicions of the President than the solid rights of innocence, the claims of justification, the sacred force of truth, and the forms and substance of law and justice. In questions of power then let no more be heard of confidence in man, but bind him down from mischief by the claims of the Constitution. That this Commonwealth does therefore call on its co-States for an expression of their sentiments on the acts concerning aliens, and for the punishment of certain crimes herein before specified, plainly declaring whether these acts are or are not authorized by the Federal Compact. And it doubts not that their sense will be so announced as to prove their attachment unaltered to limited government, whether general or particular, and that the rights and liberties of their co-States will be exposed to no dangers by remaining embarked on a common bottom with their own: That they will concur with this Commonwealth in considering the said acts so palpably against the Constitution as to amount to an undisguised declaration, that the compact is not meant to be the measure of the powers of the general government, but that it will proceed in the exercise over these States of all powers whatsoever: That they will view this as seizing the rights of the States and consolidating them in the hands of the general government with a power assumed to bind the States (not merely in cases made Federal) but in all cases whatsoever, by laws made, not with their consent, but by others against their consent: That this would be to surrender the form of government we have chosen, and to live under one deriving its powers from its own will, and not from our authority; and that the co-States, recurring to their natural right in cases not made Federal, will concur in declaring these acts void and of no force, and will each unite with this Commonwealth in requesting their repeal at the next session of Congress.

2. VIRGINIA RESOLUTIONS
December 24, 1798

(Elliot's *Debates,* 1861 ed., Vol. IV, p. 528–529)

Resolved, That the General Assembly of Virginia doth unequivocally express a firm resolution to maintain and defend the Constitution of the United States, and the Constitution of this state, against every aggression either foreign or domestic; and that they will support the Government of the United States in all measures warranted by the former.

That this Assembly most solemnly declares a warm attachment to the union of the states, to maintain which it pledges all its powers; and that, for this end, it is their duty to watch over and oppose every infraction of those principles which constitute the only basis of that Union, because a faithful observance of them can alone secure its existence and the public happiness.

That this Assembly doth explicitly and peremptorily declare that it views the powers of the Federal Government as resulting from the compact to which the states are parties, as limited by the plain sense and intention of the instrument constituting that compact; as no further valid than they are authorized by the grants enumerated in that compact; and that, in case of a deliberate, palpable, and dangerous exercise of other powers not granted by the said compact, the states, who are parties thereto, have the right and are in duty bound to interpose for arresting the progress of the evil, and for maintaining within their respective limits the authorities, rights, and liberties appertaining to them.

That the General Assembly doth also express its deep regret, that a spirit has in sundry instances been manifested by the Federal Government to enlarge its powers by forced constructions of the constitutional charter which defines them; and that indications have appeared of a design to expound certain general phrases (which, having been copied from the very limited grant of powers in the former Articles of Confederation, were the less liable to be misconstrued) so as to destroy the meaning and effect of the particular enumeration which necessarily explains and limits the general phrases; and so as to

consolidate the states, by degrees, into one sovereignty, the obvious tendency and inevitable consequence of which would be to transform the present republican system of the United States into an absolute, or, at best, a mixed monarchy.

That the General Assembly doth particularly PROTEST against the palpable and alarming infractions of the Constitution in the two late cases of the "Alien and Sedition Acts," passed at the last session of Congress; the first of which exercises a power nowhere delegated to the Federal Government, and which, by uniting legislative and judicial powers to those of [the] executive, subverts the general principles of free government, as well as the particular organization and positive provisions of the Federal Constitution: and the other of which acts exercises, in like manner, a power not delegated by the Constitution, but, on the contrary, expressly and positively forbidden by one of the amendments thereto,—a power which, more than any other, ought to produce universal alarm, because it is levelled against the right of freely examining public characters and measures, and of free communication among the people thereon, which has ever been justly deemed the only effectual guardian of every other right.

That this state having, by its Convention which ratified the Federal Constitution, expressly declared that, among other essential rights, "the liberty of conscience and of the press cannot be cancelled, abridged, restrained or modified by any authority of the United States," and from its extreme anxiety to guard these rights from every possible attack of sophistry or ambition, having, with other states, recommended an amendment for that purpose, which amendment was in due time annexed to the Constitution,—it would mark a reproachful inconsistency and criminal degeneracy, if an indifference were now shown to the palpable violation of one of the rights thus declared and secured, and to the establishment of a precedent which may be fatal to the other.

That the good people of this commonwealth, having ever felt and continuing to feel the most sincere affection for their brethren of the other states, the truest anxiety for establishing and perpetuating the union of all and the most scrupulous fidelity to that Constitution, which is the pledge of mutual friendship, and the instrument of mutual happiness, the General Assembly doth solemnly appeal to the like dispositions of the other states, in confidence that they will concur with this Commonwealth in declaring, as it does hereby declare, that the acts aforesaid are unconstitutional; and that the necessary and proper measures will be taken by each for co-operating with this state, in maintaining unimpaired the authorities, rights, and liberties reserved to the states respectively, or to the people. . . .

103. THE KENTUCKY RESOLUTIONS OF 1799
February 22, 1799
(Elliot's *Debates,* 1861 ed. Vol. IV, p. 544 ff.)

The unfavorable character of the replies of various States to the Resolutions of 1798 led to a reassertion of the principles expressed in those resolutions. The Kentucky legislature not only reaffirmed its attachment to the original resolutions, but added a resolution asserting that nullification by the States was the rightful remedy with which to meet infractions of the Constitution. In Virginia, the replies of the States were referred to a special committee of which James Madison was chairman. The report of the committee, drafted by Madison, can be found in Madison's *Writings,* ed. by G. Hunt, Vol. VI. For references, see Doc. No. 102.

The representatives of the good people of this commonwealth, in General Assembly convened, having maturely considered the answers of sundry states in the Union, to their resolutions passed the last session, respecting certain unconstitutional laws of Congress, commonly called the Alien and Sedition Laws, would be faithless, indeed, to themselves and to those they represent, were they silently to acquiesce in the principles and doctrines attempted to be maintained in all those answers, that of Virginia only excepted. To again enter the field of argument, and attempt more fully or forcibly to expose the unconstitutionality of those obnoxious laws, would, it is apprehended, be as unnecessary as unavailing. We cannot, however, but lament, that, in the discussion of those interesting subjects, by sundry of the legislatures of our sister states, unfounded suggestions, and uncandid insinuations, derogatory to the true character and principles of this commonwealth have been substituted in place of fair reasoning and sound argument. Our opinions of these alarming measures of the general government, together with our reasons for those opinions, were detailed with decency, and with temper, and submitted to the discussion and judgment of our fellow-citizens throughout the Union. Whether the like decency and temper have been observed in the answers of most of those States, who have denied or attempted to obviate the great truths contained in those resolutions, we have now only to submit to a candid world. Faithful to the true principles of the federal Union, unconscious of any designs to disturb the harmony of that Union, and anxious only to escape the fangs of despotism, the good people of this commonwealth are regardless of censure or calumniation. Lest, however, the silence of this commonwealth should be construed into an acquiescence in the doctrines and principles advanced and attempted to be maintained by the said answers, or at least those of our fellow-citizens throughout the Union who so widely differ from us on those important subjects, should be deluded by the expectation, that we shall be deterred from what we conceive our duty, or shrink from the principles contained in those resolutions—therefore,

Resolved, That this commonwealth considers the federal Union, upon the terms and for the purposes specified in the late compact, conducive to the liberty and happiness of the several states: That it does now unequivocally declare its attachment to the Union, and to that compact, agreeably to its obvious and real intention, and will be among the last to seek its dissolution: That if those who administer the general government be permitted to transgress the limits fixed by that compact, by a total disregard to the special delegations of power therein contained, an annihilation of the state governments, and the creation upon their ruins of a general consolidated government, will be the inevitable consequence: That the principle and construction contended for by sundry of the state legislatures, that the general government is the exclusive judge of the extent of the powers delegated to it, stop not short of *despotism*—since the discretion of those who administer the government, and not the *Constitution*, would be the measure of their powers: That the several states who formed that instrument being sovereign and independent, have the unquestionable right to judge of the infraction; and, *That a nullification of those sovereignties, of all unauthorized acts done under color of that instrument is the rightful remedy:* That this commonwealth does, under the most deliberate reconsideration, declare, that the said Alien and Sedition Laws are, in their opinion, palpable violations of the said Constitution; and, however cheerfully it may be disposed to surrender its opinion to a majority of its sister states, in matters of ordinary or doubtful policy, yet, in momentous regulations like the present, which so vitally wound the best rights of the citizen, it would consider a silent acquiescence as highly criminal: That although this commonwealth, as a party to the federal compact, will bow to the laws of the Union, yet, it does, at the same time declare, that it will not now, or ever hereafter, cease to oppose in a constitutional manner, every attempt at what quarter soever offered, to violate that compact. And, finally, in order that no pretext or arguments may be drawn from a supposed acquiescence, on the part of this commonwealth in the constitutionality of those laws, and be thereby used as precedents for similar future violations of the federal compact—this commonwealth does now enter against them its solemn PROTEST.

104. STATE REPLIES TO THE VIRGINIA AND KENTUCKY RESOLUTIONS
1799
(Elliot's *Debates*, 1861 ed., Vol. IV, p. 533, 539)

Every State from Maryland north replied to the Virginia and Kentucky Resolutions, disavowing, with varying degrees of indignation, the constitutional principles set forth in these Resolutions. The replies of the States are particularly interesting because of the general assertion that the judiciary rather than the legislative is the proper body to pass on the constitutionality of Congressional acts. Many of the replies are given in Elliot's *Debates*, Vol. IV, p. 532–539. See, F. M. Anderson, "Contemporary Opinion of the Virginia and Kentucky Resolutions", *American Historical Review*, Vol. V.

1. THE STATE OF RHODE ISLAND AND PROVIDENCE PLANTATIONS TO VIRGINIA
February, 1799

Certain resolutions of the Legislature of Virginia, passed on the 21st of December last, being communicated to the Assembly,—

1. *Resolved*, That, in the opinion of this legislature, the second section of the third article of the Constitution of the United States, in these words, to wit,—"The judicial power shall extend to all cases arising under the laws of the United States,"—vests in the Federal Courts, exclusively, and in the Supreme Court of the United States, ultimately, the authority of deciding on the constitutionality of any act or law of the Congress of the United States.

2. *Resolved*, That for any state legislature to assume that authority would be—

1st. Blending together legislative and judicial powers;

2d. Hazarding an interruption of the peace of the states by civil discord, in case of a diversity of opinions among the state legislatures; each state having, in that case, no resort, for vindicating its own opinions, but the strength of its own arm;

3d. Submitting most important questions of law to less competent tribunals; and,

4th. An infraction of the Constitution of the United States, expressed in plain terms.

3. *Resolved*, That, although, for the above reasons, this legislature, in their public capacity, do not feel themselves authorized to consider and decide on the constitutionality of the Sedition and Alien laws, (so called,) yet they are called upon, by the exigency of this occasion, to declare that, in their private opinions, these laws are within the powers delegated to Congress, and promotive of the welfare of the United States.

4. *Resolved,* That the governor communicate these resolutions to the supreme executive of the state of Virginia, and at the same time express to him that this legislature cannot contemplate, without extreme concern and regret, the many evil and fatal consequencies which may flow from the very unwarrantable resolutions aforesaid, of the legislature of Virginia, passed on the twenty-first day of December last.

2. NEW HAMPSHIRE RESOLUTION ON THE VIRGINIA AND KENTUCKY RESOLUTIONS
June 15, 1799

The legislature of New Hampshire, having taken into consideration certain resolutions of the General Assembly of Virginia, dated December 21, 1798; also certain resolutions of the legislature of Kentucky, of the 10th of November 1798:—

Resolved, That the legislature of New Hampshire unequivocally express a firm resolution to maintain and defend the Constitution of the United States, and the Constitution of this State, against every aggression, either foreign or domestic, and that they will support the government of the United States in all measures warranted by the former.

That the state legislatures are not the proper tribunals to determine the constitutionality of the laws of the general government; that the duty of such decision is properly and exclusively confided to the judicial department.

That, if the legislature of New Hampshire, for mere speculative purposes, were to express an opinion on the acts of the general government, commonly called "the Alien and Sedition Bills", that opinion would unreservedly be, that those acts are constitutional, and, in the present critical situation of our country, highly expedient.

That the constitutionality and expediency of the acts aforesaid have been very ably advocated and clearly demonstrated by many citizens of the United States, more especially by the minority of the General Assembly of Virginia. The legislature of New Hampshire, therefore, deem it unnecessary, by any train of arguments, to attempt further illustration of the propositions, the truth of which, it is confidently believed, at this day, is very generally seen and acknowledged.

Which report, . . . was unanimously received and adopted, one hundred and thirty-seven members being present.

105. LAND ACT OF 1800
May 10, 1800
(*U. S. Statutes at Large,* Vol. II, p. 73 ff.)

Sales under the Land Act of 1796 were disappointingly slow; in order to attract settlers and dispose of the public domain the government provided for land purchases on credit. The result was somewhat unfortunate: the credit system encouraged speculation and made collections difficult. It was discontinued by the land act of 1820, Doc. No. 122. See, P. J. Treat, *The National Land System, 1785–1820;* R. T. Hill, *The Public Domain and Democracy;* B. W. Bond, *The Civilization of the Old Northwest,* ch. x.

An Act to amend the act intituled "An act for providing for the sale of the lands of the United States, in the territory northwest of the Ohio, and above the mouth of the Kentucky River."

Sec. 1. *Be it enacted,* That for the disposal of the lands of the United States, directed to be sold by the act, intituled "An act providing for the sale of the lands of the United States, in the territory northwest of the Ohio, and above the mouth of Kentucky river," there shall be four land offices established in the said territory: one at Cincinnati . . . one at Chilicothe . . . one at Marietta . . . and one at Steubenville. . . . Each of the said offices shall be under the direction of an officer, . . . who shall be appointed by the President of the United States, by and with the advice and consent of the Senate, . . .

Sec. 3. That the surveyor-general shall cause the townships west of the Muskingum, which by the above-mentioned act are directed to be sold in quarter townships, to be subdivided into half sections of three hundred and twenty acres each. . . .

Sec. 4. That the lands thus subdivided

. . . shall be offered for sale in sections and half sections, subdivided as before directed at the following places and times, . . . All lands, remaining unsold, at the closing of either of the public sales, may be disposed of at private sale by the registers of these respective land offices, in the manner herein after prescribed; . . .

Sec. 5. That no lands shall be sold by virtue of this act, at either public or private sale, for less than two dollars per acre, and payment may be made for the same by all purchasers, either in specie, or in evidences of the public debt of the United States, . . . and shall be made in the following manner, and under the following conditions, to wit:

1. At the time of purchase, every purchaser shall, exclusively of the fees hereafter mentioned, pay six dollars for every section, and three dollars for every half section, he may have purchased, for surveying expenses, and deposit one twentieth part of the amount of purchase money, to be forfeited, if within forty days one fourth part of the purchase money, including the said twentieth part, is not paid.

2. One fourth part of the purchase money shall be paid within forty days after the day of sale as aforesaid; another fourth part shall be paid within two years; another fourth part within three years; and another fourth part within four years after the day of sale.

3. Interest, at the rate of six per cent. a year from the day of sale shall be charged upon each of the three last payments, . . .

4. A discount at the rate of eight per cent., a year, shall be allowed on any of the three last payments, which shall be paid before the same shall become due, . . .

5. If the first payment of one fourth part of the purchase money shall not be made within forty days after the sale, the deposit, payment and fees, paid and made by the purchaser, shall be forfeited, and the lands shall . . . be disposed of at private sale, on the same terms and conditions, and in the same manner as the other lands directed by this act to be disposed of at private sale: *Provided*, that the lands which shall have been sold at public sale, and which shall, on account of such failure of payment, revert to the United States, shall not be sold at private sale, for a price less than the price that shall have been offered for the same at public sale. . . .

Sec. 16. That each person who, before the passing of this act, shall have erected . . . a grist-mill or saw-mill upon any of the lands herein directed to be sold, shall be entitled to the pre-emption of the section . . . at the rate of two dollars per acre. . . .

106. JEFFERSON'S FIRST INAUGURAL ADDRESS
March 4, 1801

(Richardson, ed. *Messages and Papers*, Vol. I, p. 322)

This address is a classic exposition of democratic philosophy, memorable alike for its confession of faith and for its literary beauty. For a brilliant but critical analysis, see H. Adams, *History of the United States During the Administration of Thomas Jefferson*, Vol. I, ch. vii. For Jefferson, see biographies by H. S. Randall, J. Parton, A. J. Nock, P. L. Ford, D. S. Muzzey, G. Chinard, F. W. Hirst, and J. T. Morse.

Friends and Fellow-Citizens:

Called upon to undertake the duties of the first executive office of our country, I avail myself of the presence of that portion of my fellow-citizens which is here assembled to express my grateful thanks for the favor with which they have been pleased to look toward me, to declare a sincere consciousness that the task is above my talents, and that I approach it with those anxious and awful presentiments which the greatness of the charge and the weakness of my powers so justly inspire. A rising nation, spread over a wide and fruitful land, traversing all the seas with the rich productions of their industry, engaged in commerce with nations who feel power and forget right, advancing rapidly to destinies beyond the reach of mortal eye—when I contemplate these transcendent objects, and see the honor, the happiness, and the hopes of this beloved country committed to the issue and the auspices of this day, I shrink from the contemplation, and humble myself before the magnitude of the undertaking. Utterly, indeed, should I despair did not the presence of many whom I here see remind me that in the other high authorities provided by our Constitution I shall find resources of wisdom, of virtue, and of zeal on which to rely under all difficulties. To you, then, gentlemen, who are charged with the sovereign functions of legislation, and to those associated with you, I look with encouragement for that guidance and support which may enable us to steer with safety the vessel in which we are all embarked amidst the conflicting elements of a troubled world.

During the contest of opinion through which we have passed the animation of discussions and of exertions has sometimes worn an aspect which might impose on strangers unused to think freely and to speak and to write what they think; but this being now decided by the voice of the nation, announced according to the rules of the Constitution, all will, of course, arrange themselves under the will of the law, and unite in common efforts for the common good. All, too, will bear in mind this sacred principle, that though the will of the majority is in all cases to prevail, that will to be rightful must be reasonable; that the minority possess their equal rights, which equal law must protect, and to violate would be oppression. Let us, then, fellow-citizens, unite with one heart and one mind. Let us restore to social intercourse that harmony and affection without which liberty and even life itself are but dreary things. And let us reflect that, having banished from our land that religious intolerance under which mankind so long bled and suffered, we have yet gained little if we countenance a political intolerance as despotic, as wicked, and capable of as bitter and bloody persecutions. During the throes and convulsions of the ancient world, during the agonizing spasms of infuriated man, seeking through blood and slaughter his long-lost liberty, it was not wonderful that the agitation of the billows should reach even this distant and peaceful shore; that this should be more felt and feared by some and less by others, and should divide opinions as to measures of safety. But every difference of opinion is not a difference of principle. We have called by different names

brethren of the same principle. We are all Republicans, we are all Federalists. If there be any among us who would wish to dissolve this Union or to change its republican form, let them stand undisturbed as monuments of the safety with which error of opinion may be tolerated where reason is left free to combat it. I know, indeed, that some honest men fear that a republican government can not be strong, that this Government is not strong enough; but would the honest patriot, in the full tide of successful experiment, abandon a government which has so far kept us free and firm on the theoretic and visionary fear that this Government, the world's best hope, may by possibility want energy to preserve itself? I trust not. I believe this, on the contrary, the strongest Government on earth. I believe it the only one where every man, at the call of the law, would fly to the standard of the law, and would meet invasions of the public order as his own personal concern. Sometimes it is said that man can not be trusted with the government of himself. Can he, then, be trusted with the government of others? Or have we found angels in the forms of kings to govern him? Let history answer this question.

Let us, then, with courage and confidence pursue our own Federal and Republican principles, our attachment to union and representative government. Kindly separated by nature and a wide ocean from the exterminating havoc of one quarter of the globe; too high-minded to endure the degradations of the others; possessing a chosen country, with room enough for our descendants to the thousandth and thousandth generation; entertaining a due sense of our equal right to the use of our own faculties, to the acquisitions of our own industry, to honor and confidence from our fellow-citizens, resulting not from birth, but from our actions and their sense of them; enlightened by a benign religion, professed, indeed, and practiced in various forms, yet all of them inculcating honesty, truth, temperance, gratitude, and the love of man; acknowledging and adoring an overruling Providence, which by all its dispensations proves that it delights in the happiness of man here and his greater happiness hereafter—with all these blessings, what more is necessary to make us a happy and a prosperous people? Still one thing more, fellow-citizens—a wise and frugal Government, which shall restrain men from injuring one another, shall leave them otherwise free to regulate their own pursuits of industry and improvement, and shall not take from the mouth of labor the bread it has earned. This is the sum of good government, and this is necessary to close the circle of our felicities.

About to enter, fellow-citizens, on the exercise of duties which comprehend everything dear and valuable to you, it is proper you should understand what I deem the essential principles of our Government, and consequently those which ought to shape its Administration. I will compress them within the narrowest compass they will bear, stating the general principle, but not all its limitations. Equal and exact justice to all men, of whatever state or persuasion, religious or political; peace, commerce, and honest friendship with all nations, entangling alliances with none; the support of the State governments in all their rights, as the most competent administrations for our domestic concerns and the surest bulwarks against antirepublican tendencies; the preservation of the General Government in its whole constitutional vigor, as the sheet anchor of our peace at home and safety abroad; a jealous care of the right of election by the people—a mild and safe corrective of abuses which are lopped by the sword of revolution where peaceable remedies are unprovided; absolute acquiescence in the decisions of the majority, the vital principle of republics, from which is no appeal but to force, the vital principle and immediate parent of despotism; a well-disciplined militia, our best reliance in peace and for the first moments of war, till regulars may relieve them; the supremacy of the civil over the military authority; economy in the public expense, that labor may be lightly burthened; the honest payment of our debts and sacred preservation of the public faith; encouragement of agriculture, and of commerce as its handmaid; the diffusion of information and arraignment of all abuses at the bar of the public reason; freedom of religion; freedom of the press, and freedom

of person under the protection of the habeas corpus, and trial by juries impartially selected. These principles form the bright constellation which has gone before us and guided our steps through an age of revolution and reformation. The wisdom of our sages and blood of our heroes have been devoted to their attainment. They should be the creed of our political faith, the text of civic instruction, the touchstone by which to try the services of those we trust; and should we wander from them in moments of error or of alarm, let us hasten to retrace our steps and to regain the road which alone leads to peace, liberty, and safety.

I repair, then, fellow-citizens, to the post you have assigned me. With experience enough in subordinate offices to have seen the difficulties of this the greatest of all, I have learnt to expect that it will rarely fall to the lot of imperfect man to retire from this station with the reputation and the favor which bring him into it. Without pretensions to that high confidence you reposed in our first and greatest revolutionary character, whose preëminent services had entitled him to the first place in his country's love and destined for him the fairest page in the volume of faithful history, I ask so much confidence only as may give firmness and effect to the legal administration of your affairs. I shall often go wrong through defect of judgment. When right, I shall often be thought wrong by those whose positions will not command a view of the whole ground. I ask your indulgence for my own errors, which will never be intentional, and your support against the errors of others, who may condemn what they would not if seen in all its parts. The approbation implied by your suffrage is a great consolation to me for the past, and my future solicitude will be to retain the good opinion of those who have bestowed it in advance, to conciliate that of others by doing them all the good in my power, and to be instrumental to the happiness and freedom of all.

Relying, then, on the patronage of your good will, I advance with obedience to the work, ready to retire from it whenever you become sensible how much better choice it is in your power to make. And may that

Infinite Power which rules the destinies of the universe lead our councils to what is best, and give them a favorable issue for your peace and prosperity.

107. JEFFERSON ON THE IMPORTANCE OF NEW ORLEANS

Letter to Robert R. Livingston
April 18, 1802

(The Writings of Thomas Jefferson, ed. by H. E. Bergh, Vol. X, p. 311 ff.)

This famous letter to the American minister to France anticipated the formal instructions of May 1 requesting Livingston to ascertain the terms upon which France would sell New Orleans and the Floridas to the United States. At the same time Jefferson was writing to our minister in England, Rufus King, that we would "marry ourselves to the British fleet and nation" rather than see France control the Mississippi and the Gulf. For reference see Doc. No. 108.

Washington, April 18, 1802.

. . . The cession of Louisiana and the Floridas by Spain to France, works most sorely on the United States. On this subject the Secretary of State has written to you fully, yet I cannot forbear recurring to it personally, so deep is the impression it makes on my mind. It completely reverses all the political relations of the United States, and will form a new epoch in our political course. Of all nations of any consideration, France is the one which, hitherto, has offered the fewest points on which we could have any conflict of right, and the most points of a communion of interests. From these causes, we have ever looked to her as our *natural friend,* as one with which we could never have an occasion of difference. Her growth, therefore, we viewed as our own, her misfortunes ours. There is on the globe one single spot, the possessor of which is our natural and habitual enemy. It is New Orleans, through which the produce of three-eighths of our territory must pass to market, and from its fertility it will ere long yield more than half of our whole produce, and contain more than half of our inhabitants. France, placing herself in that door, assumes to us the attitude of defiance. Spain might have retained it quietly for years. Her pacific dispositions, her feeble state, would induce her to increase our facilities there, so that her possession of the place would hardly be felt by us, and it would

not, perhaps, be very long before some circumstance might arise, which might make the cession of it to us the price of something of more worth to her. Not so can it ever be in the hands of France: the impetuosity of her temper, the energy and restlessness of her character, placed in a point of eternal friction with us, and our character, which, though quiet and loving peace and the pursuit of wealth, is high-minded, despising wealth in competition with insult or injury, enterprising and energetic as any nation on earth; these circumstances render it impossible that France and the United States can continue long friends, when they meet in so irritable a position. They, as well as we, must be blind if they do not see this; and we must be very improvident if we do not begin to make arrangements on that hypothesis. The day that France takes possession of New Orleans, fixes the sentence which is to restrain her forever within her low-water mark. It seals the union of two nations, who, in conjunction, can maintain exclusive possession of the ocean. From that moment, we must marry ourselves to the British fleet and nation. We must turn all our attention to a maritime force, for which our resources place us on very high ground; and having formed and connected together a power which may render reënforcement of her settlements here impossible to France, make the first cannon which shall be fired in Europe the signal for the tearing up of any settlement she may have made, and for holding the two continents of America in sequestration for the common purposes of the United British and American nations. This is not a state of things we seek or desire. . . .

If France considers Louisiana, however, as indispensable for her views, she might perhaps be willing to look about for arrangements which might reconcile it to our interests. If anything could do this, it would be the ceding to us the island of New Orleans and the Floridas. This would certainly, in a great degree, remove the causes of jarring and irritation between us, and perhaps for such a length of time, as might produce other means of making the measure permanently conciliatory to our interests and friendships. It would, at any rate, relieve us from the necessity of taking immediate measures for countervailing such an operatio.1 by arrangements in another quarter. But still we should consider New Orleans and the Floridas as no equivalent for the risk of a quarrel with France, produced by her vicinage.

I have no doubt you have urged these con-

siderations, on every proper occasion, with the government where you are. They are such as must have effect, if you can find means of producing thorough reflection on them by that government. . . . Every eye in the United States is now fixed on the affairs of Louisiana. Perhaps nothing since the revolutionary war, has produced more uneasy sensations through the body of the nation. Notwithstanding temporary bickerings have taken place with France, she has still a strong hold on the affections of our citizens generally. I have thought it not amiss, by way of supplement to the letters of the Secretary of State, to write you this private one, to impress you with the importance we affix to this transaction. . . .

108. THE CESSION OF LOUISIANA
April 30, 1803

(Malloy, ed. *Treaties, Conventions, etc.,* Vol. I, p. 508 ff.)

By the Treaty of Fontainebleau of 1762, France ceded Louisiana west of the Mississippi to Spain. See Shepherd, "Cession of Louisiana to Spain", *Pol. Sci. Qt.,* Vol. XIX, p. 439. By the secret Treaty of St. Ildefonso, Spain ceded this territory back to France. This substitution of a powerful for a weak neighbour along the Mississippi and at New Orleans caused consternation in the West and to Jefferson and his advisers. Congress appropriated $2,000,000 for the purchase of New Orleans, and Jefferson dispatched Monroe to co-operate with Livingston to negotiate the purchase. For reasons primarily concerned with the critical military situation on the Continent, Napoleon decided to sell to the United States the whole of Louisiana, and the cession was accordingly made. By a convention of April 30, 1803, the United States agreed to pay sixty million francs for Louisiana. The most thorough history of the negotiations is, H. Adams, *History of the United States,* Vol. I, chs. xiv–xvii, Vol. II, chs. i–vi. See also, E. W. Lyon, *Louisiana in French Diplomacy, 1759–1804;* A. P. Whitaker, *The Mississippi Question, 1795–1803;* J. K. Hosmer, *The Louisiana Purchase;* S. F. Bemis, ed. *American Secretaries of State,* Vol. III, p. 9 ff. For the Louisiana Boundary, T. M. Marshall, *History of the Western Boundary of the Louisiana Purchase.* For the constitutional questions, see *American Insurance Co.* v. *Canter,* Doc. No. 134; and E. S. Brown, *Constitutional History of the Louisiana Purchase.*

ART. I. Whereas, by the article the third of the treaty concluded at St. Idelfonso, the

1st October, 1800 between the First Consul of the French Republic and his Catholic Majesty, it was agreed as follows: "His Catholic Majesty promises and engages on his part, to cede to the French Republic, six months after the full and entire execution of the conditions and stipulations herein relative to his royal highness the duke of Parma, the colony or province of Louisiana, with the same extent that it now has in the hands of Spain, and that it had when France possessed it; and such as it should be after the treaties subsequently entered into between Spain and other states." And *whereas,* in pursuance of the Treaty, and particularly of the third article, the French Republic has an incontestible title to the domain and to the possession of the said territory:—The First Consul of the French Republic desiring to give to the United States a strong proof of his friendship, doth hereby cede to the said United States, in the name of the French Republic, forever and in full sovereignty, the said territory with all its rights and appurtenances, as fully and in the same manner as they have been acquired by the French Republic, in virtue of the above-mentioned Treaty, concluded with his Catholic Majesty.

ART. II. In the cession made by the preceding article are included the adjacent islands belonging to Louisiana, all public lots and squares, vacant lands, and all public buildings, fortifications, barracks, and other edifices which are not private property.— The Archives, papers, and documents, relative to the domain and sovereignty of Louisiana, and its dependencies, will be left in the possession of the Commissaries of the United States, and copies will be afterwards given in due form to the Magistrates and Municipal officers, of such of the said papers and documents as may be necessary to them.

ART. III. The inhabitants of the ceded territory shall be incorporated in the Union of the United States, and admitted as soon as possible, according to the principles of the Federal Constitution, to the enjoyment of all the rights, advantages and immunities of citizens of the United States; and in the mean time they shall be maintained and protected in the free enjoyment of their liberty, property, and the Religion which they profess. . . .

ART. VII. It has been agreed between the contracting parties, that the French ships coming directly from France or any of her colonies, loaded only with the produce and manufactures of France or her said Colonies; and the ships of Spain coming directly from Spain or any of her colonies, loaded only with the produce or manufactures of Spain or her Colonies, shall be admitted during the space of twelve years in the ports of New Orleans, and in all other legal ports of entry within the ceded territory, in the same manner as the ships of the United States coming directly from France or Spain, or any of their colonies, without being subject to any other or greater duty on merchandize, or other or greater tonnage than that paid by the citizens of the United States. . . .

109. MARBURY v. MADISON
1 Cranch, 137
1803

Original proceeding for mandamus. Under the authority of the Judiciary Act of February 27, 1801, the President appointed one William Marbury justice of the peace; because of the negligence of Secretary of State Marshall the commission was not delivered, and President Jefferson instructed his Secretary of State Madison not to deliver the commission. Marbury sued for a writ of mandamus requiring Madison to deliver his commission. Marshall's opinion embraced two questions: the ethics of withholding the commission, and the right of the Supreme Court to issue a writ of mandamus. On the first question Marshall declared, in what is generally considered *obiter dicta,* that the President had no right to withhold Marbury's commission. On the second, Marshall decided that the provision of the Judiciary Act of 1789 authorizing the Supreme Court to issue a writ of mandamus, was contrary to the Constitution and therefore void. This is the first case in which the Supreme Court held a law of Congress void: not until the Dred Scott decision did the Court hold another act of Congress void. On this famous case see, A. Beveridge, *Life of John Marshall,* Vol. III, ch. iii; E. S. Corwin, *The Doctrine of Judicial Review;* A. C. McLaughlin. *The Courts, The Constitution and Parties,* ch. i; L. B. Boudin, *Government by Judiciary,* Vol. I, ch. x; C. Warren, *The Supreme Court in United States History,* (1928 ed.) Vol. I, ch. v.

MARSHALL, C. J. . . . The peculiar delicacy of this case, the novelty of some of its circumstances, and the real difficulty attending the points which occur in it, require a complete exposition of the principles on which the opinion to be given by the court is founded. . . .

In the order in which the court has viewed this subject, the following questions have been considered and decided:

1st. Has the applicant a right to the commission he demands?

2dly. If he has a right, and that right has been violated, do the laws of his country afford him a remedy?

3dly. If they do afford him a remedy, is it a *mandamus* issuing from this court? . . .

The first object of enquiry is,

Has the applicant a right to the commission he demands? . . .

It is therefore decidedly the opinion of the court, that when a commission has been signed by the President, the appointment is made; and that the commission is complete, when the seal of the United States has been affixed to it by the secretary of state. . . .

Mr. Marbury, then, since his commission was signed by the President, and sealed by the secretary of state, was appointed; and as the law creating the office, gave the officer a right to hold for five years, independent of the executive, the appointment was not revocable; but vested in the officer legal rights, which are protected by the laws of his country.

To withhold his commission, therefore, is an act deemed by the court not warranted by law, but violative of a vested legal right.

2. This brings us to the second enquiry: which is,

If he has a right, and that right has been violated, do the laws of his country afford him a remedy? . . .

The government of the United States has been emphatically termed a government of laws, and not of men. It will certainly cease to deserve this high appellation, if the laws furnish no remedy for the violation of a vested legal right.

If this obloquy is to be cast on the jurisprudence of our country, it must arise from the peculiar character of the case. . . .

By the constitution of the United States, the President is invested with certain important political powers, in the exercise of which he is to use his own discretion, and is accountable only to his country in his political character, and to his own conscience. To aid him in the performance of these duties, he is authorized to appoint certain officers, who act by his authority and in conformity with his orders.

In such cases, their acts are his acts; and whatever opinion may be entertained of the manner in which executive discretion may be used, still there exists, and can exist, no power to control that discretion. The subjects are political. . . .

The conclusion from this reasoning is, that where the heads of departments are the political or confidential agents of the executive, merely to execute the will of the President, or rather to act in cases in which the executive possesses a constitutional or legal discretion, nothing can be more perfectly clear than that their acts are only politically examinable. But where a specific duty is assigned by law, and individual rights depend upon the performance of that duty, it seems equally clear that the individual who considers himself injured, has a right to resort to the laws of his country for a remedy. . . .

It is, then, the opinion of the Court,

1st. That by signing the commission of Mr. Marbury, the president of the United States appointed him a justice of peace for the county of Washington in the district of Columbia; and that the seal of the United States, affixed thereto by the secretary of state, is conclusive testimony of the verity of the signature, and of the completion of the appointment; and that the appointment conferred on him a legal right to the office for the space of five years.

2dly. That, having this legal title to the office, he has a consequent right to the commission; a refusal to deliver which, is a plain violation of that right, for which the laws of his country afford him a remedy.

It remains to be enquired whether,

3dly. He is entitled to the remedy for which he applies. This depends on

1st. The nature of the writ applied for, and

2dly. The power of this court. . . .

This, then, is a plain case for a mandamus, either to deliver the commission, or a copy of it from the record; and it only remains to be enquired,

Whether it can issue from this court.

The act to establish the judicial courts of the United States authorizes the supreme court "to issue writs of mandamus, in cases warranted by the principles and usages of law, to any courts appointed, or persons holding office, under the authority of the United States."

The secretary of state, being a person holding an office under the authority of the United States is precisely within the letter of the description; and if this court is not authorized to issue a writ of mandamus to such an officer, it must be because the law is unconstitutional, and therefore absolutely incapable of conferring the authority and assigning the duties which its words purport to confer and assign.

The constitution vests the whole judicial power of the United States in one supreme court, and such inferior courts as congress shall, from time to time, ordain and establish. This power is expressly extended to all cases arising under the laws of the United States; and consequently, in some form, may be exercised over the present case; because the right claimed is given by a law of the United States.

In the distribution of this power it is declared, that "the supreme court shall have original jurisdiction in all cases affecting ambassadors, other public ministers and consuls, and those in which a state shall be a party. In all other cases, the supreme court shall have appellate jurisdiction." . . .

If it had been intended to leave it in the discretion of the legislature to apportion the judicial power between the supreme and inferior courts according to the will of that body, it would certainly have been useless to have proceeded further than to have defined the judicial power, and the tribunals in which it should be vested. The subsequent part of the section is mere surplusage, is entirely without meaning, if such is to be the construction. If congress remains at liberty to give this court appellate jurisdiction, where the constitution has declared their jurisdiction shall be original; and original jurisdiction where the constitution has declared it shall be appellate; the distribution of jurisdiction, made in the constitution, is form without substance.

Affirmative words are often, in their operation, negative of other objects than those affirmed; and in this case, a negative or exclusive sense must be given to them or they have no operation at all.

It cannot be presumed, that any clause in the constitution is intended to be without effect; and therefore such a construction is inadmissible, unless the words require it. . . .

The authority, therefore, given to the supreme court, by the act establishing the judicial courts of the United States, to issue writs of mandamus to public officers, appears not to be warranted by the constitution; and it becomes necessary to inquire whether a jurisdiction so conferred can be exercised.

The question whether an act repugnant to the constitution can become the law of the land, is a question deeply interesting to the United States; but, happily not of an intricacy proportioned to its interest. It seems only necessary to recognize certain principles supposed to have been long and well established, to decide it.

That the people have an original right to establish for their future government such principles as, in their opinion, shall most conduce to their own happiness, is the basis on which the whole American fabric has been erected. The exercise of this original right is a very great exertion, nor can it nor ought it to be frequently repeated. The principles therefore so established are deemed fundamental. And as the authority from which they proceed is supreme and can seldom act, they are designed to be permanent.

This original and supreme will organizes the government, and assigns to different departments their respective powers. It may either stop here or establish certain limits not to be transcended by those departments.

The government of the United States is of the latter description. The powers of the legislature are defined and limited; and that those limits may not be mistaken or forgotten, the constitution is written. To what purpose are powers limited, and to what purpose is that limitation committed to writing, if these limits may, at any time, be passed by those intended to be restrained? The distinction between a government with limited and unlimited powers is abolished if those limits do not confine the persons on whom they are imposed and if acts prohibited and acts allowed are of equal obligation. It is a proposition too plain to be contested, that the constitution controls any legislative act repugnant to it; or, that the legislature may alter the constitution by an ordinary act.

Between these alternatives there is no middle ground. The constitution is either a superior paramount law, unchangeable by ordinary means, or it is on a level with ordinary legislative acts, and, like other acts, is alterable when the legislature shall please to alter it.

If the former part of the alternative be true, then a legislative act contrary to the constitution is not law; if the latter part be true, then written constitutions are absurd attempts, on the part of the people, to limit a power in its own nature illimitable.

Certainly all those who have framed written constitutions contemplate them as forming the fundamental and paramount law of the nation, and consequently the theory of every such government must be that an act of the legislature repugnant to the Constitution is void.

This theory is essentially attached to a written constitution, and is consequently to be considered, by this court as one of the fundamental principles of our society. It is not, therefore, to be lost sight of in the further consideration of this subject.

If an act of the legislature repugnant to the constitution is void, does it, notwithstanding its invalidity, bind the courts and oblige them to give it effect? Or, in other words, though it be not law, does it constitute a rule as operative as if it was a law? This would be to overthrow in fact what was established in theory, and would seem, at first view, an absurdity too gross to be insisted on. It shall, however, receive a more attentive consideration.

It is emphatically the province and duty of the judicial department to say what the law is. Those who apply the rule to particular cases must of necessity expound and interpret that rule. If two laws conflict with each other, the courts must decide on the operation of each.

So if a law be in opposition to the constitution; if both the law and the constitution apply to a particular case, so that the court must either decide that case conformably to the law, disregarding the constitution, or conformably to the constitution, disregarding the law, the court must determine which of these conflicting rules governs the case. This is of the very essence of judicial duty.

If, then, the courts are to regard the constitution, and the constitution is superior to any ordinary act of the legislature, the constitution, and not such ordinary act, must govern the case to which they both apply.

Those, then, who controvert the principle that the constitution is to be considered in court as a paramount law, are reduced to the necessity of maintaining that courts must close their eyes on the constitution and see only the law.

This doctrine would subvert the very foundation of all written constitutions. It would declare that an act which, according to the principles and theory of our government, is entirely void, is yet, in practice, completely obligatory. It would declare that if the legislature shall do what is expressly forbidden, such act, notwithstanding the express prohibition, is in reality effectual. It would be giving to the legislature a practical and real omnipotence with the same breath which professes to restrict their powers within narrow limits. It is prescribing limits

and declaring that those limits may be passed at pleasure.

That it thus reduces to nothing what we have deemed the greatest improvement on political institutions, a written constitution, would of itself be sufficient, in America, where written constitutions have been viewed with so much reverence, for rejecting the construction. But the peculiar expressions of the constitution of the United States furnish additional arguments in favor of its rejection.

The judicial power of the United States is extended to all cases arising under the constitution.

Could it be the intention of those who gave this power to say that in using it the constitution should not be looked into? That a case arising under the constitution should be decided without examining the instrument under which it arises?

This is too extravagant to be maintained.

In some cases, then, the constitution must be looked into by the judges. And if they can open it at all, what part of it are they forbidden to read or to obey?

There are many other parts of the constitution which serve to illustrate this subject.

It is declared that "no tax or duty shall be laid on articles exported from any state." Suppose a duty on the export of cotton, of tobacco, or of flour, and a suit instituted to recover it, ought judgment to be rendered in such a case? Ought the judges to close their eyes on the constitution, and only see the law?

The constitution declares "that no bill of attainder or *ex post facto* law shall be passed." If, however, such a bill should be passed, and a person should be prosecuted under it, must the court condemn to death those victims whom the constitution endeavors to preserve?

"No person," says the constitution, "shall be convicted of treason unless on the testimony of two witnesses to the same overt act, or on confession in open court."

Here the language of the constitution is addressed especially to the courts. It prescribes, directly for them, a rule of evidence not to be departed from. If the legislature should change that rule, and declare one witness, or a confession out of court, sufficient for conviction, must the constitutional principle yield to the legislative act?

From these, and many other selections which might be made, it is apparent that the framers of the constitution contemplated that instrument as a rule for the government of *courts,* as well as of the legislature. Why otherwise does it direct the judges to take an oath to support it? This oath certainly applies in an especial manner to their conduct in their official character. How immoral to impose it on them if they were to be used as the instruments, and the knowing instruments, for violating what they swear to support!

The oath of office, too, imposed by the legislature, is completely demonstrative of the legislative opinion on this subject. It is in these words: "I do solemnly swear that I will administer justice without respect to persons, and do equal right to the poor and to the rich; and that I will faithfully and impartially discharge all the duties incumbent on me as ———, according to the best of my abilities and understanding, agreeably to *the constitution* and laws of the United States." Why does a judge swear to discharge his duties agreeably to the constitution of the United States, if that constitution forms no rule for his government?—if it is closed upon him, and cannot be inspected by him?

If such be the real state of things, this is worse than solemn mockery. To prescribe, or to take this oath, becomes equally a crime.

It is also not entirely unworthy of observation, that in declaring what shall be the *supreme* law of the land, the constitution itself is first mentioned, and not the laws of the United States generally, but those only which shall be made in *pursuance* of the constitution, have that rank.

Thus, the particular phraseology of the constitution of the United States confirms and strengthens the principle, supposed to be essential to all written constitutions, that a law repugnant to the constitution is void, and that courts, as well as other departments, are bound by that instrument.

[Mandamus denied.]

110. JEFFERSON'S MESSAGE ON THE BURR CONSPIRACY
January 22, 1807

(Richardson, ed. *Messages and Papers,* Vol. I, p. 412 ff.)

On November 27, 1806, Jefferson had issued a proclamation warning citizens of the Burr conspiracy. The message below contains a more detailed account of the information upon which this proclamation was issued. Burr had surrendered to the acting Governor of Louisiana Territory January 17, 1807, but subsequently attempted to escape, only to be apprehended and sent on to Richmond for trial on the charge of treason. Two different interpretations of the Burr conspiracy are in H. Adams, *History of the United States,* Vol. III, chs. x–xiv, xix, and W. F. McCaleb, *Aaron Burr Conspiracy.* An account of the trial is in A. Beveridge, *Life of John Marshall,* Vol. III, chs. vi–ix. For Burr, see J. Parton, *Aaron Burr.*

JANUARY 22, 1807.
To the Senate and House of Representatives of the United States:
Agreeably to the request of the House of Representatives communicated in their resolution of the 16th instant, I proceed to state, under the reserve therein expressed, information received touching an illegal combination of private individuals against the peace and safety of the Union, and a military expedition planned by them against the territories of a power in amity with the United States, with the measures I have pursued for suppressing the same. . . .

Some time in the latter part of September I received intimations that designs were in agitation in the Western country unlawful and unfriendly to the peace of the Union, and that the prime mover in these was Aaron Burr, heretofore distinguished by the favor of his country. The grounds of these intimations being inconclusive, the objects uncertain, and the fidelity of that country known to be firm, the only measure taken was to urge the informants to use their best endeavors to get further insight into the designs and proceedings of the suspected persons and to communicate them to me.

It was not till the latter part of October that the objects of the conspiracy began to be perceived, but still so blended and involved in mystery that nothing distinct could be singled out for pursuit. In this state of uncertainty . . . I thought it best to send to the scene where these things were principally in transaction a person in whose integrity, understanding, and discretion entire confidence could be reposed, with instructions to investigate the plots going on, . . . and . . . to do on the spot whatever should be necessary to discover the designs of the conspirators, arrest their means, bring their persons to punishment, and to call out the force of the country to suppress any unlawful enterprise in which it should be found they were engaged. By this time it was known that many boats were under preparation, stores of provisions collecting, and an unusual number of suspicious characters in motion on the Ohio and its waters. Besides dispatching the confidential agent to that quarter, orders were at the same time sent to the governors of the Orleans and Mississippi Territories and to the commanders of the land and naval forces there to be on their guard against surprise and in constant readiness to resist any enterprise which might be attempted on the vessels, posts, or other objects under their care; and on the 8th of November instructions were forwarded to General Wilkinson to hasten an accommodation with the Spanish commandant on the Sabine, and as soon as that was effected to fall back with his principal force to the hither bank of the Mississippi for the defense of the interesting points on that river. By a letter received from that officer on the 25th of November, we learnt that a confidential agent of Aaron Burr had been deputed to him with communications, partly written in cipher and partly oral, explaining his designs, exaggerating his resources, and making such offers of emolument and command to engage him and the army in his unlawful enterprise as he had flattered himself would be successful. The General, . . . immediately dispatched a trusty officer to me with information of what had passed, . . .

The General's letter, . . . and some other information received a few days earlier, when brought together developed Burr's general designs, . . . It appeared that he contemplated two distinct objects, which might be carried on either jointly or separately, and either the one or the other first, as circumstances should direct. One of these was the severance of the Union of these States by the Alleghany Mountains; the other an attack on Mexico. A third object was provided, merely ostensible, to wit, the settlement of a pretended purchase of a tract of country on the Washita claimed by a Baron Bastrop. This was to serve as the pretext for all his preparations, an allurement for such followers as really wished to acquire settlements in that country and a cover under which to retreat in the event of a final discomfiture of both branches of his real design.

He found at once that the attachment of the Western country to the present Union was not to be shaken; that its dissolution could not be effected with the consent of its inhabitants, and that his resources were inadequate as yet to effect it by force. He took his course then at once, determined to seize on New Orleans, plunder the bank there, possess himself of the military and naval stores, and proceed on his expedition to Mexico, and to this object all his means and preparations were now directed. He collected from all the quarters where himself or his agents possessed influence all the ardent, restless, desperate, and disaffected persons who were ready for any enterprise analogous to their characters. He seduced good and well-meaning citizens, some by assurances that he possessed the confidence of the Government and was acting under its secret patronage, a pretense which procured some credit from the state of our differences with Spain, and others by offers of land in Bastrop's claim on the Washita. . . .

. . . Surmises have been hazarded that this enterprise is to receive aid from certain foreign powers; but these surmises are without proof or probability. . . .

By letters from General Wilkinson of the 14th and 18th of December, which came to hand two days after the date of the resolution of the House of Representatives— . . . I received the important affidavit a copy of which I now communicate, with extracts of so much of the letters as comes within the scope of the resolution. By these it will be seen that of three of the principal emissaries of Mr. Burr whom the General had caused to be apprehended, one had been liberated by habeas corpus, and two others, being those particularly employed in the endeavor to corrupt the general and army of the United States, have been embarked by him for ports in the Atlantic States, probably on the consideration that an impartial trial could not be expected during the present agitations of New Orleans, and that that city was not as yet a safe place for confinement. As soon as these persons shall arrive they will be delivered to the custody of the law and left to such course of trial, both as to place and process, as its functionaries may direct. The presence of the highest judicial authorities, to be assembled at this place within a few days, the means of pursuing a sounder course of proceedings here than elsewhere, and the aid of the Executive means, should the judges have occasion to use them, render it equally desirable for the criminals as for the public that, being already removed from the place where they were first apprehended, the first regular arrest should take place here, and the course of proceedings receive here its proper direction.

TH: JEFFERSON.

111. ACT TO PROHIBIT THE IMPORTATION OF SLAVES
March 2, 1807

(U. S. Statutes at Large, Vol. II, p. 426 ff.)

Article I, section 9 of the Constitution provided that "the importation of such persons as any of the States shall think proper to admit, shall not be prohibited by the Congress prior to the Year 1808. . . ." In his Sixth Annual Message, December 2, 1806 (Richardson, Vol. I, p. 405 ff.) Jefferson wrote, "I congratulate you, fellow-citizens, on the approach of the period at which you may interpose your authority constitutionally to withdraw the citizens of the United States from all further participation in those violations of human rights which have been so long continued on the unoffending inhabitants of Africa." Bills to prohibit the importation of slaves were promptly introduced into the House and the Senate. See W. E. B. Du Bois, *Suppression of the African Slave Trade;* M. S. Locke, *Anti-Slavery in America, 1619–1808;* H. Wilson, *Rise and Fall of the Slave Power in America,* Vol. I.

An Act to prohibit the importation of Slaves into any port or place within the jurisdiction of the United States, from and after the first day of January, in the year of our Lord one thousand eight hundred and eight.

Be it enacted, That from and after the first day of January, one thousand eight hundred and eight, it shall not be lawful to import or bring into the United States or the territories thereof from any foreign kingdom, place, or country, any negro, mulatto, or person of colour, as a slave, or to be held to service or labour.

Sec. 2. That no citizen of the United States, or any other person, shall, from and after the first day of January, in the year of our Lord one thousand eight hundred and eight, for himself, or themselves, or any other person whatsoever, either as master, factor, or owner, build, fit, equip, load or to otherwise prepare any ship or vessel, in any port or place within the jurisdiction of the United States, nor shall cause any ship or vessel to sail from any port or place within the same, for the purpose of procuring any negro, mulatto, or person of colour, from any foreign kingdom, place, or country, to be transported to any port or place whatsoever within the jurisdiction of the United States, to be held, sold, or disposed of as slaves, or to be held to service or labour: and if any ship or vessel shall be so fitted out for the purpose aforesaid, or shall be caused to sail so as aforesaid, every such ship or vessel, her tackle, apparel, and furniture, shall be forfeited to the United States, and shall be liable to be seized, prosecuted, and condemned in any of the circuit courts or district courts, for the district where the said ship or vessel may be found or seized. . . .

Sec. 4. If any citizen or citizens of the United States, or any person resident within the jurisdiction of the same, shall, from and after the first day of January, one thousand eight hundred and eight, take on board, receive or transport from any of the coasts or kingdoms of Africa, or from any other foreign kingdom, place, or country, any negro, mulatto, or person of colour in any ship or vessel, for the purpose of selling them in any port or place within the jurisdiction of the United States as slaves, or to be held to service or labour, or shall be in any ways aiding or abetting therein, such citizen or citizens, or person, shall severally forfeit and pay five thousand dollars, one moiety thereof to the use of any person or persons who shall sue for and prosecute the same to effect. . . .

Sec. 6. That if any person or persons whatsoever, shall, from and after the first day of January, one thousand eight hundred and eight, purchase or sell any negro, mulatto, or person, of colour, for a slave, or to be held to service or labour, who shall have been imported, or brought from any foreign kingdom, place, or country, or from the dominions of any foreign state, immediately adjoining to the United States, after the last day of December, one thousand eight hundred and seven, knowing at the time of such purchase or sale, such negro, mulatto, or person of colour, was so brought within the jurisdiction of the United States, as aforesaid, such purchaser and seller shall severally forfeit and pay for every negro, mulatto, or person of colour, so purchased or sold as aforesaid, eight hundred dollars. . . .

Sec. 7. That if any ship or vessel shall be found, from and after the first day of January, one thousand eight hundred and eight, in any river, port, bay, or harbor, or on the high seas, within the jurisdictional limits of the United States, or hovering on the coast thereof, having on board any negro, mulatto, or person of colour, for the purpose of selling them as slaves, or with intent to land the same, in any port or place within the jurisdiction of the United States, contrary to the prohibition of the act, every such ship or vessel, together with her tackle, apparel, and furniture, and the goods or effects which shall be found on board the same, shall be forfeited to the use of the United States, and may be seized, prosecuted, and condemned, in any court of the United States, having jurisdiction thereof. And it shall be lawful for the President of the United States, and he is hereby authorized, should he deem it expedient, to cause any of the armed vessels of the United States to be manned and employed to cruise on any part of the coast of the United States, or territories thereof, where he may judge attempts will be made to violate the provisions of this act, and to instruct and direct the commanders of armed vessels of the United States, to seize, take, and bring into any port of the United States all such ships or vessels, and moreover to seize, take, or bring into any port of the U. S. all ships or vessel of the U. S. wheresoever found on the high seas, contravening the provisions of this act, to be proceeded against according to law. . . .

112. COMMERCIAL WARFARE
1806–1810

The Peace of Amiens was of short duration, and in 1803 came a renewal of the European wars which soon involved the commerce of the United States. In 1805 Great Britain seized and condemned the vessel *Essex,* engaged in trade with the French West Indies: a year later Monroe reported that over 120 American vessels had been seized by the British. These depredations on neutral commerce were aggravated by the British practice of impressment. Protests proving vain, Congress on April 18, 1806, passed a nonimportation act excluding many articles from importation from Great Britain. April 8, the so-called Fox's Blockade was established around the mouths of the Elbe, Weser, Trave, etc., and May 16 this blockade was extended to include all the coast from the Elbe to Brest. Napoleon retaliated with the Berlin Decree of November 21, 1806. Great Britain replied with the Order in Council of January 7, 1807 prohibiting any vessel from trading with any port of France or her Allies and the additional Order in Council of November 11 blockading all ports in Europe from which the British flag was excluded. Napoleon retaliated with the Milan Decree of December 17 declaring the British Isles in a state of blockade and that every ship searched by the British was to be regarded as enemy property. These decrees and counter-decrees not only bore severely upon American commerce, they also touched American pride and honor. The effort of William Pinkney to conclude a satisfactory treaty with Great Britain having failed, the United States established, December 22, 1807, an embargo. The Embargo Act of December 22 was supplemented by acts of January 9, 1808 and March 12, 1808. The Embargo, which Jefferson fondly believed would bring the warring Powers to terms, proved unenforceable, and it was withdrawn, March 1, 1809, in favor of another non-intercourse law. Section 11 of this act permitted the President, by proclamation, to re-open trade with Great Britain or France if either of these nations ceased to violate American rights. The British Minister Erskine having given assurances that the odious Orders in Council would be withdrawn, President Madison, by Proclamation of April 19, 1809, permitted trade with Great Britain. The action of

Erskine was disavowed by the British Government, however, and President Madison was forced, August 9, to revoke his earlier proclamation and declare the non-intercourse Act in force. This Act, however, expired in 1810, and Nathaniel Macon, Chairman of the Foreign Affairs Committee, introduced the bill known as Macon's Bill Number 2 which provided that in case either France or England should cease their violations of American commerce the non-intercourse act should be revived against the other. Meantime, by the Rambouillet Decree of March 23, 1810 Napoleon had ordered the seizure of all vessels in French ports flying the flag of the United States. Despite this chicanery, Napoleon's assurances of August 5, 1810 that in response to the proffer of the Macon Bill he would revoke all obnoxious Decrees, was accepted in good faith. By Proclamation of November 2, the President therefore withdrew restrictions on commerce with France, and on March 2, 1811 Congress passed a new non-intercourse Act directed against Great Britain. Under the circumstances English opinion demanded a revocation of the Orders in Council: at the critical moment, in May, 1812, Prime Minister Perceval was assassinated, and the revocation did not actually take place until June 23—too late to avoid war. The literature on commercial warfare of these years is extensive. Most of the documents of the controversy can be found in *American State Papers, Foreign Relations,* Vol. III; the Congressional Debates can be found in T. H. Benton, *Abridgement of the Debates of Congress, 1789–1856,* Vols. III, IV. Numerous documents are given in M. Carey, *The Olive Branch,* 10th ed. For political and diplomatic background see H. Adams, *History of the United States,* Vols. IV–VI. See also, L. Sears, *Jefferson and the Embargo;* E. Channing, *The Jeffersonian System;* chs. xvi–xx; E. Channing, *History of the United States,* Vol. IV, chs. xiv–xvi; A. T. Mahan, *Sea Power and the War of 1812;* K. C. Babcock, *Rise of American Nationality,* chs. i–iii; J. Shouler, *History of the United States,* Vol. II; H. Adams, *Albert Gallatin;* W. E. Dodd, *Nathaniel Macon;* biographies of Jefferson and Madison. On the constitutionality of the Embargo see *U. S.* v. *Brigantine William,* Hall's American Law Journal (1808) II, Federal Cases No. 16700, and C. Warren, *The Supreme Court,* (1928 ed.) Vol. II, p. 341 ff.

1. THE BERLIN DECREE
November 21, 1806
(State Papers and Publick Documents of the United States, Vol. V, p. 478)

Art. I. The British islands are declared in a state of blockade.

II. All commerce and correspondence with the British islands are prohibited. In consequence, letters or packets, addressed either to England, to an Englishman, or in the English language, shall not pass through the post-office and shall be seized.

III. Every subject of England, of whatever rank and condition soever, who shall be found in the countries occupied by our troops, or by those of our allies, shall be made a prisoner of war.

IV. All magazines, merchandise, or property whatsoever, belonging to a subject of England, shall be declared lawful prize.

V. The trade in English merchandise is forbidden; all merchandise belonging to England, or coming from its manufactories and colonies, is declared lawful prize.

VI. One half of the proceeds of the confiscation of the merchandise and property, declared good prize by the preceding articles, shall be applied to indemnify the merchants for the losses which they have suffered by the capture of merchant vessels by English cruisers.

VII. No vessel coming directly from England, or from the English colonies, or having been there since the publication of the present decree, shall be received into any port.

VIII. Every vessel contravening the above clause, by means of a false declaration, shall be seized, and the vessel and cargo confiscated, as if they were English property.

IX. Our tribunal of prizes at Paris is charged with the definitive adjudication of all the controversies, which by the French army, relative to the execution of the present decree. Our tribunal of prizes at Milan shall be charged with the definitive adjudication of the said controversies, which may arise within the extent of our kingdom of Italy.

X. The present decree shall be communicated by our minister of exterior relations, to the kings of Spain, of Naples, of Holland, and of Etruria, and to our allies, whose subjects, like ours, are the victims of the injustice and the barbarism of the English maritime laws. Our finances, our police, and our post masters general, are charged each, in what concerns him, with the execution of the present decree.

2. BRITISH ORDER IN COUNCIL
January 7, 1807
(American State Papers, Foreign Relations,
Vol. III, p. 267)

Whereas the French Government has issued certain orders, which, in violation of the usages of war, purport to prohibit the commerce of all neutral nations with His Majesty's dominions, and also to prevent such nations from trading with any other country in any articles, the growth, produce, or manufacture of His Majesty's dominions; and whereas the said Government has also taken upon itself to declare all His Majesty's dominions to be in a state of blockade, at the time when the fleets of France and her allies are themselves confined within their own ports by the superior valor and discipline of the British navy; and whereas such attempts, on the part of the enemy, would give to His Majesty an unquestionable right of retaliation, and would warrant His Majesty in enforcing the same prohibition of all commerce with France, which that power vainly hopes to effect against the commerce of His Majesty's subjects, a prohibition which the superiority of His Majesty's naval forces might enable him to support by actually investing the ports and coasts of the enemy with numerous squadrons and cruisers, so as to make the entrance or approach thereto manifestly dangerous; and whereas His Majesty, though unwilling to follow the example of his enemies by proceeding to an extremity so distressing to all nations not engaged in the war, and carrying on their accustomed trade, yet feels himself bound, by due regard to the just defense of the rights and interests of his people not to suffer such measures to be taken by the enemy, without taking some steps on his part to restrain this violence, and to retort upon them the evils of their own injustice; His Majesty is thereupon pleased, by and with the advice of his privy council, to order, and it is hereby ordered, that no vessel shall be permitted to trade from one port to another, both which ports shall belong to or be in the possession of France or her allies, or shall be so far under their control as that British vessels may not trade freely thereat; and the commanders of His Majesty's ships of war and privateers shall be, and are hereby, instructed to warn every neutral vessel coming from any such port, and destined to another such port, to discontinue her voyage, and not to proceed to any such port; and any vessel, after being so warned, or any vessel coming from any such port, after a reasonable time shall have been afforded for receiving information of this His Majesty's order, which shall be found proceeding to another such port, shall be captured and brought in, and together with her cargo shall be condemned as lawful prize; and His Majesty's principal Secretaries of State, the Lords Commissioners of the Admiralty, and the Judges of the High Court of Admiralty, and the Courts of Vice-admiralty, are to take the necessary measures herein as to them shall respectively appertain.

3. BRITISH ORDER IN COUNCIL
November 11, 1807
(Annals of the Congress of the United States,
10th Congress, 2d. session, 1808–1809, p. 1698 ff.)

Whereas certain orders, establishing an unprecedented system of warfare against this kingdom, and aimed especially at the destruction of its commerce and resources, were, sometime since, issued by the government of France, by which "the British islands were declared to be in a state of blockade," thereby subjecting to capture and condemnation all vessels, with their cargoes, which should continue to trade with his majesty's dominions:

And whereas, by the same order, "all trading in English merchandise is prohibited, and every article of merchandise belonging to England, or coming from her colonies, or of her manufacture, is declared lawful prize:"

And whereas the nations in alliance with France, and under her control, were required to give, and have given, and do give, effect to such orders:

And whereas his majesty's order of the 7th of January last has not answered the desired purpose, either of compelling the enemy to recall those orders, or of inducing neutral nations to interpose, with effect, to obtain their revocation, but, on the contrary, the same have been recently enforced with increased rigor:

And, whereas, his majesty, under these circumstances, finds himself compelled to take further measures for asserting and vindicating his just rights. . . .

His majesty is therefore pleased, by and with the advice of his privy council, to order, and it is hereby ordered, that all the ports and places of France and her allies, or of any country at war with his majesty, and all other ports or places in Europe, from which, although not at war with his majesty, the British flag is excluded, and all ports or places in the colonies belonging to his majesty's enemies, shall, from henceforth, be subject to the same restrictions in point of trade and navigation, with the exceptions hereinafter mentioned, as if the same were actually blockaded by his majesty's naval forces, in the most strict and rigorous manner: And it is hereby further ordered and declared, that all trade in articles which are of the produce or manufacture of the said countries or colonies, shall be deemed and considered to be unlawful; and that every vessel trading from or to the said countries or colonies, together with all goods and merchandise on board, and all articles of the produce or manufacture of the said countries or colonies, shall be captured and condemned as prize to the captors. . . .

And the commanders of his majesty's ships of war and privateers, and other vessels acting under his majesty's commission, shall be, and are hereby, instructed to warn every vessel which shall have commenced her voyage prior to any notice of this order, and shall be destined to any port of France, or of her allies, or of any other country at war with his majesty, or to any port or place from which the British flag, as aforesaid, is excluded, or to any colony belonging to his majesty's enemies, and which shall not have cleared out as is hereinbefore allowed, to discontinue her voyage, and to proceed to some port or place in this kingdom, or to Gibraltar or Malta; and any vessel which, after having been so warned, or after a reasonable time shall have been afforded for the arrival of information of this his majesty's order at any port or place from which she sailed, or which, after having notice of this order, shall be found in the prosecution of any voyage contrary to the restrictions contained in this order, shall be captured, and, together with her cargo, condemned as lawful prize to the captors.

And whereas countries not engaged in the war have acquiesced in these orders of France, prohibiting all trade in any articles the produce or manufacture of his majesty's dominions; and the merchants of those countries have given countenance and effect to those prohibitions by accepting from persons, styling themselves commercial agents of the enemy, resident at neutral ports, certain documents, termed "certificates of origin," being certificates obtained at the ports of shipment, declaring that the articles of the cargo are not of the produce or manufacture of his majesty's dominions, or to that effect:

And whereas this expedient has been directed by France, and submitted to by such merchants, as part of the new system of warfare directed against the trade of this kingdom, and as the most effectual instrument of accomplishing the same, and it is therefore essentially necessary to resist it:

His majesty is therefore pleased, by and with the advice of his privy council, to order, and it is hereby ordered, that if any vessel, after reasonable time shall have been afforded for receiving notice of this his majesty's order, at the port or place from which such vessel shall have cleared out, shall be found carrying any such certificate or document as aforesaid, or any document referring to or authenticating the same, such vessel shall be adjudged lawful prize to the captor, together with the goods laden therein, belonging to the person or persons by whom, or on whose behalf, any such document was put on board.

And the right honorable the lords commissioners of his majesty's treasury, his majesty's principal secretaries of state, the lords commissioners of the admiralty, and the judges of the high court of admiralty and courts of vice admiralty, are to take the necessary measures herein as to them shall respectively appertain.

W. FAWKENER.

4. THE MILAN DECREE
December 17, 1807

(State Papers and Publick Documents of the United States, Vol. VI, p. 74)

NAPOLEON, emperor of the French, king of Italy, and protector of the Rhenish confederation.

Observing the measures adopted by the British government, on the 11th November last, by which vessels belonging to neutral, friendly, or even powers the allies of England, are made liable, not only to be searched by English cruisers, but to be compulsorily detained in England, and to have a tax laid on them of so much per cent on the cargo, to be regulated by the British legislature.

Observing that by these acts the British government *denationalizes* ships of every nation in Europe, that it is not competent for any government to detract from its own independence and rights, all the sovereigns of Europe having in trust the sovereignties and independence of the flag; that if by an unpardonable weakness, and which in the eyes of posterity would be an indelible stain, if such a tyranny was allowed to be established into principles, and consecrated by useage, the English would avail themselves of it to assert it as a right, as they have availed themselves of the tolerance of government to establish the infamous principle, that the flag of a nation does not cover goods, and to have to their right of blockade an arbitrary extension, and which infringes on the sovereignty of every state; we have decreed and do decree as follows:

Art. I. Every ship, to whatever nation it may belong, that shall have submitted to be searched by an English ship, or to a voyage to England, or shall have paid any tax whatsoever to the English government, is thereby and for that alone, declared to be *denationalized,* to have forfeited the protection of its king, and to have become English property.

Art. II. Whether the ships thus *denationalized* by the arbitrary measures of the English government, enter into our ports, or those of our allies, or whether they fall into the hands of our ships of war, or of our privateers, they are declared to be good and lawful prize.

Art. III. The British islands are declared to be in a state of blockade, both by land and sea. Every ship, of whatever nation, or whatsoever the nature of its cargo may be, that sails from the ports of England, or those of the English colonies, and of the countries occupied by English troops, and proceeding to England or to the English colonies, or to countries occupied by English troops, is good and lawful prize, as contrary to the present decree, and may be captured by our ships of war, or our privateers, and adjudged to the captor.

Art. IV. These measures, which are resorted to only in just retaliation of the barbarous system adopted by England, which assimilates its legislation to that of Algiers, shall cease to have any effect with respect to all nations who shall have the firmness to compel the English government to respect their flag. They shall continue to be rigorously in force as long as that government does not return to the principle of the law of nations, which regulates the relations of civilized states in a state of war. The provisions of the present decree shall be abrogated and null, in fact, as soon as the English abide again by the principles of the law of nations, which are also the principles of justice and of honour.

All our ministers are charged with the execution of the present decree, which shall be inserted in the bulletin of the laws.

NAPOLEON.

5. THE EMBARGO ACT
December 22, 1807

(*U. S. Statutes at Large,* Vol. II, p. 451 ff.)

An Act laying an Embargo on all ships and vessels in the ports and harbors of the United States.

Be it enacted, That an embargo be, and hereby is laid on all ships and vessels in the ports and places within the limits or jurisdiction of the United States, cleared or not cleared, bound to any foreign port or place; and that no clearance be furnished to any ship or vessel bound to such foreign port or place, except vessels under the immediate direction of the President of the United States: and that the President be authorized to give such instructions to the officers of the revenue, and of the navy and revenue cutters of the United States, as shall appear best adapted for carrying the same into full effect: *Provided,* that nothing herein contained shall be construed to prevent the departure of any foreign ship or vessel, either in ballast, or with the goods, wares and merchandise on board of such foreign ship or vessel, when notified of this act.

Sec. 2. That during the continuance of this act, no registered, or sea letter vessel, having on board goods, wares and merchandise, shall be allowed to depart from one port of the United States to any other within the same, unless the master, owner, consignee or factor of such vessel shall first give bond, with one or more sureties to the collector of the district from which she is bound to depart, in a sum of double the value of the vessel and cargo, that the said goods, wares, or merchandise shall be relanded in some port of the United States, dangers of the seas excepted, which bond, and also a certificate from the collector where the same may be relanded, shall by the collector respectively be transmitted to the Secretary of the Treasury. All armed vessels possessing public commissions from any foreign power, are not to be considered as liable to the embargo laid by this act.

6. The Non-Intercourse Act
March 1, 1809

(*U. S. Statutes at Large*, Vol. II, p. 528 ff.)

An Act to interdict the commercial intercourse between the United States and Great Britain and France, and their dependencies; and for other purposes.

Be it enacted, That from and after the passing of this act, the entrance of the harbors and waters of the United States and of the territories thereof, be, and the same is hereby interdicted to all public ships and vessels belonging to Great Britain or France. . . . And if any public ship or vessel as aforesaid, not being included in the exception above mentioned, shall enter any harbor or waters within the jurisdiction of the United States, or of the territories thereof, it shall be lawful for the President of the United States, or such other person as he shall have empowered for that purpose, to employ such part of the land and naval forces, or of the militia of the United States, or the territories thereof, as he shall deem necessary, to compel such ship or vessel to depart.

Sec. 2. That it shall not be lawful for any citizen or citizens of the United States or the territories thereof, nor for any person or persons residing or being in the same, to have any intercourse with, or to afford any aid or supplies to any public ship or vessel as aforesaid, which shall, contrary to the provisions of this act, have entered any harbor or waters within the jurisdiction of the United States or the territories thereof; and if any person shall, contrary to the provisions of this act, have any intercourse with such ship or vessel, or shall afford any aid to such ship or vessel,

either in repairing the said vessel or in furnishing her, her officers and crew with supplies of any kind or in any manner whatever, . . . every person so offending, shall forfeit and pay a sum not less than one hundred dollars, nor exceeding ten thousand dollars; and shall also be imprisoned for a term not less than one month, nor more than one year.

Sec. 3. That from and after the twentieth day of May next, the entrance of the harbors and waters of the United States and the territories thereof be, and the same is hereby interdicted to all ships or vessels sailing under the flag of Great Britain or France, or owned in whole or in part by any citizen or subject of either. . . . And if any ship or vessel sailing under the flag of Great Britain or France, . . . shall after the said twentieth day of May next, arrive either with or without a cargo, within the limits of the United States or of the territories thereof, such ship or vessel, together with the cargo, if any, which may be found on board, shall be forfeited, and may be seized and condemned in any court of the United States or the territories thereof, having competent jurisdiction, . . .

Sec. 4. That from and after the twentieth day of May next, it shall not be lawful to import into the United States or the territories thereof, any goods, wares or merchandise whatever, from any port or place situated in Great Britain or Ireland, or in any of the colonies or dependencies of Great Britain, nor from any port or place situated in France, or in any of her colonies or dependencies, nor from any port or place in the actual possession of either Great Britain or France. Nor shall it be lawful to import into the United States, or the territories thereof, from any foreign port or place whatever, any goods, wares or merchandise whatever, being of the growth, produce or manufacture of France, or of any of her colonies or dependencies, or being of the growth, produce or manufacture of Great Britain or Ireland, or of any of the colonies or dependencies of Great Britain, or being of the growth, produce or manufacture of any place or country in the actual possession of either France or Great Britain. . . .

Sec. 11. That the President of the United States be, and he hereby is authorized, in case either France or Great Britain shall so revoke or modify her edicts, as that they shall cease to violate the neutral commerce of the United States, to declare the same by proclamation; after which the trade of the United States, suspended by this act, and by the [Embargo Act] and the several acts supplementary thereto, may be renewed with the nation so doing. . . .

SEC. 12. That so much of the . . . [Embargo Act] and of the several acts supplementary thereto, as forbids the departure of vessels owned by citizens of the United States, and the exportation of domestic and foreign merchandise to any foreign port or place, be and the same is hereby repealed, after March 15, 1809, except so far as they relate to Great Britain or France, or their colonies or dependencies, or places in the actual possession of either. . . .

SEC. 19. That this act shall continue and be in force until the end of the next session of Congress, and no longer; and that the act laying an embargo on all ships and vessels in the ports and harbors of the United States, and the several acts supplementary thereto, shall be, and the same are hereby repealed from and after the end of the next session of Congress.

7. MACON'S BILL, No. 2
May 1, 1810
(U. S. Statutes at Large, Vol. II, p. 605–6)

An Act concerning the commercial intercourse between the United States and Great Britain and France and their dependencies, and for other purposes.

BE it enacted. That from and after the passage of this act, no British or French armed vessel shall be permitted to enter the harbor or waters under the jurisdiction of the United States; . . . except when they shall be forced in by distress . . . or when charged with despatches or business from their government, or coming as a public packet for the conveyance of letters; . . .

Sec. 2. That all pacific intercourse with any interdicted foreign armed vessels, the officers or crew thereof, is hereby forbidden, . . .

Sec. 4. That in case either Great Britain or France shall, before the third day of March next, so revoke or modify her edicts as that they shall cease to violate the neutral commerce of the United States, which fact

the President of the United States shall declare by proclamation, and if the other nation shall not within three months thereafter so revoke or modify her edicts in like manner, then the third, fourth, fifth, sixth, seventh, eighth, ninth, tenth, and eighteenth sections of the act, entituled "An act to interdict the commercial intercourse between the United States and Great Britain and France . . ." shall, from and after the expiration of three months from the date of the proclamation aforesaid, be revived and have full force and effect, so far as relates to the dominions, colonies, and dependencies, and to the articles the growth, produce or manufacture of the dominions, colonies and dependencies of the nation thus refusing or neglecting to revoke or modify her edicts in the manner aforesaid. And the restrictions imposed by this act shall, from the date of such proclamation, cease and be discontinued in relation to the nation revoking or modifying her decrees in the manner aforesaid.

8. THE RAMBOUILLET DECREE
March 23, 1810
(State Papers and Publick Documents of the United States, Vol. VII, p. 467–8)

NAPOLEON, &c.

Considering that the government of the United States, by an act dated 1st March, 1809, which forbids the entrance of the ports, harbours, and rivers of the said States, to all French vessels, orders, 1st. That after the 20th of May following, vessels under the French flag, which shall arrive in the United States, shall be seized and confiscated, as well as their cargoes; 2d. That after the same epoch, no merchandise or produce, the growth or manufacture of France or her colonies, can be imported into the said United States from any port or place whatsoever, under the penalty of seizure, confiscation, and a fine of three times the value of the merchandise; 3d. That American vessels cannot go to any port of France, of her colonies, or dependencies: We have decreed, and do decree, what follows:

ART. 1. All vessels navigating under the flag of the United States, or possessed, in whole or in part, by any citizen or subject of that power, which, counting from the 20th of May, 1809, have entered or shall enter into the ports of our empire, of our colonies, or of the countries occupied by our arms, shall be seized, and the product of the sales shall be deposited in the surplus fund (*caisse d'amortissement.*)

There shall be excepted from this regulation the vessels which shall be charged with despatches, or with commissions of the government of the said States, and who shall not have either cargoes or merchandise on board. . . .

NAPOLEON.

113. FLETCHER v. PECK
6 Cranch, 87
1810

Error to the U. S. circuit court of the district of Massachusetts. In 1795 the legislature of Georgia passed an act for the sale of enormous areas of her western lands. The following year a new legislature annulled the act of 1795 on the ground that it was passed fraudulently. The celebrated case of *Fletcher* v. *Peck* involved two major constitutional questions: the interpretation of the contract clause of the Federal Constitution, and the power of the court to inquire into the motives and circumstances attending the passage of a legislative act. This was the first case in which the Supreme Court held a state law void under the Constitution. See, Beveridge, *Marshall*, Vol. III ch. x; C. H. Haskins, *The Yazoo Land Companies.*

MARSHALL, C. J. . . . That the legislature of Georgia, unless restrained by its own constitution, possesses the power of disposing of the unappropriated lands within its own limits, in such manner as its own judgment shall dictate, is a proposition not to be controverted. The only question, then, presented by this demurrer, for the consideration of the court, is this, did the then constitution of the state of Georgia prohibit the legislature to dispose of the lands, which were the subject of this contract, in the manner stipulated by the contract? . . .

In the constitution of Georgia, adopted in the year 1789, the court can perceive no restriction on the legislative power, which inhibits the passage of the act of 1795. The court cannot say that, in passing that act, the legislature has transcended its powers, and violated the constitution. In overruling the demurrer, therefore, to the first plea, the circuit court committed no error. . . .

That corruption should find its way into the governments of our infant republics, and contaminate the very source of legislation, or that impure motives should contribute to the passage of a law, or the formation of a legislative contract, are circumstances most deeply to be deplored. How far a court of justice would, in any case, be competent, on proceedings instituted by the state itself, to vacate a contract thus formed, and to annul rights acquired, under that contract, by third persons having no notice of the improper means by which it was obtained, is a question which the court would approach with much circumspection. It may well be doubted, how far the validity of a law depends upon the motives of its framers, and how far the particular inducements, operating on members the supreme sovereign power of a state, to the formation of a contract by that power, are examinable in a court of justice. If the principle be conceded, that an act of the supreme sovereign power might be declared null by a court, in consequence of the means which procured it, still would there be much difficulty in saying to what extent those means must be applied to produce this effect. Must it be direct corruption? or would interest or undue influence of any kind be sufficient? Must the vitiating cause operate on a majority? or on what number of the members? Would the act be null, whatever might be the wish of the nation? or would its obligation or nullity depend upon the public sentiment? If the majority of the legislature be corrupted, it may well be doubted, whether it be within the province of the judiciary to control their conduct, and, if less than a majority act from impure motives, the principle by which judicial interference would be regulated, is not clearly discerned. Whatever difficulties this subject might present, when viewed under aspects of which it may be susceptible, this court can perceive none in the particular pleadings now under consideration. . . .

The case, as made out in the pleadings, is simply this: One individual who holds lands in the state of Georgia, under a deed covenanting that the title of Georgia was in the grantor, brings an action of covenant upon this deed and assigns as a breach that some of the members of the legislature were induced to vote in favor of the law which constituted the contract by being promised an interest in it, and that therefore the act is a mere nullity.

This solemn question cannot be brought thus collaterally and incidentally before the court. It would be indecent in the extreme, upon a private contract between two individuals, to enter into an inquiry respecting the corruption of the sovereign power of a state. If the title be plainly deduced from a legislative act which the legislature might constitutionally pass, if the act be clothed with all the requisite forms of a law, a court, sitting as a court of law, cannot sustain a suit brought by one individual against another founded on the allegation that the act is a nullity in consequence of the impure motives which influenced certain members of the legislature which passed the law. . . .

It is not intended to speak with disrespect of the legislature of Georgia, or of its acts. Far from it. The question is a general question, and is treated as one. For although such powerful objections to a legislative grant, as are alleged against this, may not again exist, yet the principle, on which alone this rescinding act is to be supported, may be applied to every case to which it shall be the will of any legislature to apply it. The principle is this: that a legislature may, by its own act, divest the vested estate of any man whatever, for reasons which shall, by itself, be deemed sufficient. . . .

In this case the legislature may have had ample proof that the original grant was obtained by practices which can never be too much reprobated, and which would have justified its abrogation so far as respected those to whom crime was imputable. But the grant, when issued, conveyed an estate in fee-simple to the grantees, clothed with all the solemnities which law can bestow. This estate was transferable; and those who purchased parts of it were not stained by that guilt which infected the original transaction. . . .

Is the power of the legislature competent to the annihilation of such title, and to a resumption of the property thus held? The principle asserted is, that one legislature is competent to repeal any act which a former legislature was competent to pass; and that one legislature cannot abridge the powers of a succeeding legislature. The correctness of this principle, so far as respects general legislation, can never be controverted. But if an act be done under a law, a succeeding legislature cannot undo it. The past cannot be recalled by the most absolute power. Conveyances have been made, those conveyances have vested legal estates, and, if those estates may be seized by the sovereign authority, still, that they originally vested is a fact, and cannot cease to be a fact. When, then, a law is in its nature a contract, when absolute rights have vested under that contract, a repeal of the law cannot divest those rights; and the act of annulling them, if legitimate, is rendered so by a power applicable to the case of every individual in the community.

It may well be doubted whether the nature of society and of the government does not prescribe some limits to the legislative power; and if any be prescribed, where are they to be found, if the property of an individual, fairly and honestly acquired, may be seized without compensation? To the legislature all legislative power is granted; but the question whether the act of transferring the property of an individual to the public be in the nature of legislative power, is well worthy of serious reflection. . . .

The validity of this rescinding act, then, might well be doubted, were Georgia a single sovereign power. But Georgia cannot be viewed as a single, unconnected, sovereign power, on whose legislature no other restrictions are imposed than may be found in its own constitution. She is a part of a large empire; she is a member of the American union; and that union has a constitution, the supremacy of which all acknowledge, and which imposes limits to the legislatures of the several states, which none claim a right to pass. The constitution of the United States declares that no state shall pass any bill of attainder, *ex post facto* law, or law impairing the obligation of contracts.

Does the case now under consideration come within this prohibitory section of the Constitution? In considering this very interesting question, we immediately ask ourselves what is a contract? Is a grant a contract? A contract is a compact between two or more parties, and is either executory or executed. An executory contract is one in which a party binds himself to do, or not to do, a particular thing; such was the law under which the conveyance was made by the governor. A contract executed is one in which the object of contract is performed; and this, says Blackstone, differs in nothing from a grant. The contract between Georgia and the purchasers was executed by the grant. A contract executed, as well as one which is executory, contains obligations binding on the parties. A grant, in its own nature, amounts to an extinguishment of the right of the grantor, and implies a contract not to reassert that right. A party is, therefore, always estopped by his own grant.

Since, then, in fact, a grant is a contract executed, the obligation of which still continues, and since the constitution uses the general term "contracts," without distinguishing between those which are executory and those which are executed, it must be construed to comprehend the latter as well as the former. A law annulling conveyances between individuals, and declaring that the grantors should stand seized of their former estates, notwithstanding those grants, would be as repugnant to the constitution as a law discharging the vendors of property from the obligation of executing their contracts by conveyances. It would be strange if a contract to convey was secured by the constitution, while an absolute conveyance remained unprotected.

If, under a fair construction of the constitution, grants are comprehended under the term "contracts," is a grant from the state excluded from the operation of the provision? Is the clause to be considered as inhibiting the State from impairing the obligation of contracts between two individuals, but as excluding from that inhibition contracts made with itself? The words themselves contain no such distinction. They are general, and are applicable to contracts of every description. If contracts made with the state are to be exempted from their operation, the exception must arise from the character of the contracting party, not from the words which are employed. . . .

It is, then, the unanimous opinion of the court, that, in this case, the estate having passed into the hands of a purchaser for a valuable consideration, without notice, the state of Georgia was restrained, either by general principles which are common to our free institutions, or by the particular provisions of the Constitution of the United States, from passing a law whereby the estate of the plaintiff in the premises so purchased could be constitutionally and legally impaired and rendered null and void. . . .

Judgment affirmed.

114. MADISON'S WAR MESSAGE
June 1, 1812

(Richardson, ed. *Messages and Papers,* Vol. I, p. 499 ff.)

Congress declared war on Great Britain June 18, 1812. On the diplomatic background of the war, see H. Adams, *History of the United States,* Vols. V–VI; on the political background, J. Pratt, *Expansionists of 1812.* It was long charged that the War Hawks forced Madison to recommend a declaration of war as the price for re-election; for a careful analysis of this charge, see T. C. Smith, "War Guilt in 1812", Massachusetts Hist. Soc. *Proceedings,* Vol. LXIV, p. 319 ff.

WASHINGTON, *June 1, 1812.*
To the Senate and House of Representatives of the United States:

I communicate to Congress certain documents, being a continuation of those heretofore laid before them on the subject of our affairs with Great Britain.

Without going back beyond the renewal in 1803 of the war in which Great Britain is engaged, and omitting unrepaired wrongs of inferior magnitude, the conduct of her Government presents a series of acts hostile to the United States as an independent and neutral nation.

British cruisers have been in the continued practice of violating the American flag on the great highway of nations, and of seizing and carrying off persons sailing under it, not in the exercise of a belligerent right founded on the law of nations against an enemy, but of a municipal prerogative over British subjects. British jurisdiction is thus extended to neutral vessels in a situation where no laws can operate but the law of nations and the laws of the country to which the vessels belong, and a self-redress is assumed which, if British subjects were wrongfully detained and alone concerned, is that substitution of force for a resort to the responsible sovereign which falls within the definition of war. . . .

The practice, hence, is so far from affecting British subjects alone that, under the pretext of searching for these, thousands of American citizens, under the safeguard of public law and of their national flag, have been torn from their country and from everything dear to them; have been dragged on board ships of war of a foreign nation and exposed, under the severities of their discipline, to be exiled to the most distant and deadly climes, to risk their lives in the battles of their oppressors, and to be the melancholy instruments of taking away those of their own brethren.

Against this crying enormity, which Great Britain would be so prompt to avenge if committed against herself, the United States have in vain exhausted remonstrances and expostulations, and that no proof might be wanting of their conciliatory dispositions, and no pretext left for a continuance of the practice, the British Government was formally assured of the readiness of the United States to enter into arrangements such as could not be rejected if the recovery of British subjects were the real and the sole object. The communication passed without effect.

British cruisers have been in the practice also of violating the rights and the peace of our coasts. They hover over and harass our entering and departing commerce. To the most insulting pretensions they have added the most lawless proceedings in our very harbors, and have wantonly spilt American blood within the sanctuary of our territorial jurisdiction. . . .

Under pretended blockades, without the presence of an adequate force and sometimes without the practicability of applying one, our commerce has been plundered in every sea, the great staples of our country have been cut off from their legitimate markets, and a destructive blow aimed at our agricultural and maritime interests. In aggravation of these predatory measures they have been considered as in force from the dates of their notification, a retrospective effect being thus added, as has been done in other important cases, to the unlawfulness of the course pursued. And to render the outrage the more signal these mock blockades have been reiterated and enforced in the face of official communications from the British Government declaring as the true definition of a legal blockade "that particular ports must be actually invested and previous warning given to vessels bound to them not to enter."

Not content with these occasional expedients for laying waste our neutral trade, the cabinet of Britain resorted at length to the sweeping system of blockades, under the name of orders in council, which has been molded and managed as might best suit its political views, its commercial jealousies, or the avidity of British cruisers. . . .

Abandoning still more all respect for the neutral rights of the United States and for its own consistency, the British Government now demands as prerequisites to a repeal of its orders as they relate to the United States that a formality should be observed in the repeal of the French decrees nowise necessary to their termination nor exemplified by British usage, and that the French repeal, besides including that portion of the decrees which operates within a territorial jurisdiction, as well as that which operates on the high seas, against the commerce of the United States should not be a single and special repeal in relation to the United States, but should be extended to whatever other neutral nations unconnected with them may be affected by those decrees. . . .

It has become, indeed, sufficiently certain that the commerce of the United States is to be sacrificed, not as interfering with the belligerent rights of Great Britain; not as supplying the wants of her enemies, which she herself supplies; but as interfering with the monopoly which she covets for her own commerce and navigation. She carries on a war against the lawful commerce of a friend that she may the better carry on a commerce with an enemy—a commerce polluted by the forgeries and perjuries which are for the most part the only passports by which it can succeed. . . .

In reviewing the conduct of Great Britain toward the United States our attention is necessarily drawn to the warfare just renewed by the savages on one of our extensive frontiers—a warfare which is known to spare neither age nor sex and to be distinguished by features peculiarly shocking to humanity. It is difficult to account for the activity and combinations which have for some time been developing themselves among tribes in constant intercourse with British traders and garrisons without connecting their hostility with that influence and without recollecting the authenticated examples of such interpositions heretofore furnished by the officers and agents of that Government.

Such is the spectacle of injuries and indignities which have been heaped on our country, and such the crisis which its unexampled forbearance and conciliatory efforts have not been able to avert. . . .

Our moderation and conciliation have had no other effect than to encourage perseverance and to enlarge pretensions. We behold our seafaring citizens still the daily victims of lawless violence, committed on the great common and highway of nations, even within sight of the country which owes them protection. We behold our vessels, freighted with the products of our soil and industry, or returning with the honest proceeds of them, wrested from their lawful destinations, confiscated by prize courts no longer the organs of public law but the instruments of

arbitrary edicts, and their unfortunate crews dispersed and lost, or forced or inveigled in British ports into British fleets, whilst arguments are employed in support of these aggressions which have no foundation but in a principle equally supporting a claim to regulate our external commerce in all cases whatsoever.

We behold, in fine, on the side of Great Britain a state of war against the United States, and on the side of the United States a state of peace toward Great Britain.

Whether the United States shall continue passive under these progressive usurpations and these accumulating wrongs, or, opposing force to force in defense of their national rights, shall commit a just cause into the hands of the Almighty Disposer of Events, avoiding all connections which might entangle it in the contest or views of other powers, and preserving a constant readiness to concur in an honorable reëstablishment of peace and friendship, is a solemn question which the Constitution wisely confides to the legislative department of the Government. In recommending it to their early deliberations I am happy in the assurance that the decision will be worthy the enlightened and patriotic councils of a virtuous, a free, and a powerful nation. . . .

115. REPORT AND RESOLUTIONS OF THE HARTFORD CONVENTION
January 4, 1815
(T. Dwight, *History of the Hartford Convention*, p. 368 ff.)

The dissatisfaction of New England Federalists with the Republican administration, with the accession of western territory, and with the War of 1812, culminated in the Hartford Convention of December 1814. The convention was attended by delegates from Massachusetts, Connecticut, Rhode Island, Vermont and New Hampshire. George Cabot of Massachusetts was President of the Convention; among its members were H. G. Otis, N. Dane, C. Goodrich, and Samuel Ward. Cabot exercised a moderating influence on the Convention, and the report and resolutions adopted were far from radical or treasonable. Commissioners went to Washington with the Resolutions of the Convention, but arriving just after the news of Jackson's victory at New Orleans and the Treaty of Ghent, abandoned their mission. On the Convention see Theodore Dwight, *History of the Hartford Convention;* S. E. Morison, *Harrison Gray Otis,* Vol. II, chs. xxii–xxviii; H. C. Lodge, *George Cabot;* H. Adams, *History of the United States,* Vol VIII, ch. xi.

. . . To investigate and explain the means whereby this fatal reverse has been effected, would require a voluminous discussion. Nothing more can be attempted in this report than a general allusion to the principal outlines of the policy which has produced this vicissitude. Among these may be enumerated—

First.—A deliberate and extensive system for effecting a combination among certain states, by exciting local jealousies and ambition, so as to secure to popular leaders in one section of the Union, the controul of public affairs in perpetual succession. To which primary object most other characteristics of the system may be reconciled.

Secondly.—The political intolerance displayed and avowed in excluding from office men of unexceptionable merit, for want of adherence to the executive creed.

Thirdly.—The infraction of the judiciary authority and rights, by depriving judges of their offices in violation of the constitution.

Fourthly.—The abolition of existing taxes, requisite to prepare the country for those changes to which nations are always exposed, with a view to the acquisition of popular favour.

Fifthly.—The influence of patronage in the distribution of offices, which in these states has been almost invariably made among men the least entitled to such distinction, and who have sold themselves as ready instruments for distracting public opinion, and encouraging administration to hold in contempt the wishes and remonstrances of a people thus apparently divided.

Sixthly.—The admission of new states into the Union formed at pleasure in the western region, has destroyed the balance of power which existed among the original States, and deeply affected their interest.

Seventhly.—The easy admission of naturalized foreigners, to places of trust, honour or profit, operating as an inducement to the malcontent subjects of the old world to come to these States, in quest of executive patronage, and to repay it by an abject devotion to executive measures.

Eighthly.—Hostility to Great Britain, and partiality to the late government of France, adopted as coincident with popular prejudice, and subservient to the main object, party power. Connected with these must be ranked erroneous and distorted estimates of the power and resources of those nations, of the probable results of their controversies, and of our political relations to them respectively.

Lastly and principally.—A visionary and superficial theory in regard to commerce, accompanied by a real hatred but a feigned regard to its interests, and a ruinous perseverance in efforts to render it an instrument of coercion and war.

But it is not conceivable that the obliquity of any administration could, in so short a period, have so nearly consummated the work of national ruin, unless favoured by defects in the constitution.

To enumerate all the improvements of which that instrument is susceptible, and to propose such amendments as might render it in all respects perfect, would be a task which this convention has not thought proper to assume. They have confined their attention to such as experience has demonstrated to be essential, and even among these, some are considered entitled to a more serious attention than others. They are suggested without any intentional disrespect to other states, and are meant to be such as all shall find an interest in promoting. Their object is to strengthen, and if possible to perpetuate, the union of the states, by removing the grounds of existing jealousies, and providing for a fair and equal representation, and a limitation of powers, which have been misused. . . . [There follows an analysis of the proposed amendments.]

THEREFORE RESOLVED,

That it be and hereby is recommended to the legislatures of the several states represented in this Convention, to adopt all such measures as may be necessary effectually to protect the citizens of said states from the operation and effects of all acts which have been or may be passed by the Congress of the United States, which shall contain provisions, subjecting the militia or other citizens to forcible drafts, conscriptions, or impressments, not authorised by the constitution of the United States.

Resolved, That it be and hereby is recommended to the said Legislatures, to authorize an immediate and earnest application to be made to the government of the United States, requesting their consent to some arrangement, whereby the said states may, separately or in concert, be empowered to assume upon themselves the defence of their territory against the enemy; and a reasonable portion of the taxes, collected within said States, may be paid into the respective treasuries thereof, and appropriated to the payment of the balance due said states, and to the future defence of the same. The amount so paid into the said treasuries to be credited, and the disbursements made as aforesaid to be charged to the United States.

Resolved, That it be, and hereby is, recommended to the legislatures of the aforesaid states, to pass laws (where it has not already been done) authorizing the governors or commanders-in-chief of their militia to make detachments from the same, or to form voluntary corps, as shall be most convenient and conformable to their constitutions, and to cause the same to be well armed, equipped, and disciplined, and held in readiness for service; and upon the request of the governor of either of the other states to employ the whole of such detachment or corps, as well as the regular forces of the state, or such part thereof as may be required and can be spared consistently with the safety of the state, in assisting the state, making such request to repel any invasion thereof which shall be made or attempted by the public enemy.

Resolved, That the following amendments of the constitution of the United States be recommended to the states represented as aforesaid, to be proposed by them for adoption by the state legislatures, and in such cases as may be deemed expedient by a convention chosen by the people of each state.

And it is further recommended, that the said states shall persevere in their efforts to obtain such amendments, until the same shall be effected.

First. Representatives and direct taxes shall be apportioned among the several states which may be included within this Union, according to their respective numbers of free persons, including those bound to serve for a term of years, and excluding Indians not taxed, and all other persons.

Second. No new state shall be admitted into the Union by Congress, in virtue of the power granted by the constitution, without the concurrence of two thirds of both houses.

Third. Congress shall not have power to lay any embargo on the ships or vessels of the citizens of the United States, in the ports or harbours thereof, for more than sixty days.

Fourth. Congress shall not have power, without the concurrence of two thirds of both houses, to interdict the commercial intercourse between the United States and any foreign nation, or the dependencies thereof.

Fifth. Congress shall not make or declare war, or authorize acts of hostility against any foreign nation, without the concurrence of two thirds of both houses, except such acts of hostility be in defence of the territories of the United States when actually invaded.

Sixth. No person who shall hereafter be naturalized, shall be eligible as a member of the senate or house of representatives of the United States, nor capable of holding any civil office under the authority of the United States.

Seventh. The same person shall not be elected president of the United States a second time; nor shall the president be elected from the same state two terms in succession.

Resolved, That if the application of these states to the government of the United States, recommended in a foregoing resolution, should be unsuccessful and peace should not be concluded, and the defence of these states should be neglected, as it has since the commencement of the war, it will, in the opinion of this convention, be expedient for the legislatures of the several states to appoint delegates to another convention, to meet at Boston . . . with such powers and instructions as the exigency of a crisis so momentous may require.

116. MADISON'S VETO OF BONUS BILL
March 3, 1817

(Richardson, ed. *Messages and Papers,* Vol. I, p. 584–5)

In December 1816 Calhoun introduced a bill to provide for setting aside the Bank bonus of $1,500,000 as a permanent fund for internal improvements. The bill passed Congress February, 1817; Madison's veto was his last official act. See, H. Adams, *History of the United States,* Vol. IX, p. 148 ff.; P. J. Treat, *The National Land System.*

MARCH 3, 1817.
To the House of Representatives of the United States:

Having considered the bill this day presented to me entitled "An act to set apart and pledge certain funds for internal improvements," and which sets apart and pledges funds "for constructing roads and canals, and improving the navigation of water courses, in order to facilitate, promote, and give security to internal commerce among the several States, and to render more easy and less expensive the means and provisions for the common defense," I am constrained by the insuperable difficulty I feel in reconciling the bill with the Constitution of the United States to return it with that objection to the House of Representatives, in which it originated.

The legislative powers vested in Congress are specified and enumerated in the eighth section of the first article of the Constitution, and it does not appear that the power proposed to be exercised by the bill is among the enumerated powers, or that it falls by any just interpretation within the power to make laws necessary and proper for carrying into execution those or other powers vested by the Constitution in the Government of the United States.

"The power to regulate commerce among the several States" can not include a power to construct roads and canals, and to improve the navigation of water courses in order to facilitate, promote, and secure such a commerce without a latitude of construction departing from the ordinary import of the terms strengthened by the known inconveniences which doubtless led to the grant of this remedial power to Congress.

To refer the power in question to the clause "to provide for the common defense and general welfare" would be contrary to the established and consistent rules cf interpretation, as rendering the special and careful enumeration of powers which follow the clause nugatory and improper. Such a view of the Constitution would have the effect of giving to Congress a general power of legislation instead of the defined and limited one hitherto understood to belong to them, the terms "common defense and general welfare" embracing every object and act within the purview of a legislative trust. It would have the effect of subjecting both the Constitution and laws of the several States in all cases not specifically exempted to be superseded by laws of Congress, it being expressly declared "that the Constitution of the United States and laws made in pursuance thereof shall be the supreme law of the land, and the judges of every State shall be bound thereby, anything in the constitution or laws of any State to the contrary notwithstanding." Such a view of the Constitution, finally, would have the effect of excluding the judicial authority

of the United States from its participation in guarding the boundary between the legislative powers of the General and the State Governments, inasmuch as questions relating to the general welfare, being questions of policy and expediency, are unsusceptible of judicial cognizance and decision.

A restriction of the power "to provide for the common defense and general welfare" to cases which are to be provided for by the expenditure of money would still leave within the legislative power of Congress all the great and most important measures of Government, money being the ordinary and necessary means of carrying them into execution.

If a general power to construct roads and canals, and to improve the navigation of water courses, with the train of powers incident thereto, be not possessed by Congress, the assent of the States in the mode provided in the bill can not confer the power. The only cases in which the consent and cession of particular States can extend the power of Congress are those specified and provided for in the Constitution.

I am not unaware of the great importance of roads and canals and the improved navigation of water courses, and that a power in the National Legislature to provide for them might be exercised with signal advantage to the general prosperity. But seeing that such a power is not expressly given by the Constitution, and believing that it can not be deduced from any part of it without an inadmissible latitude of construction and a reliance on insufficient precedents; believing also that the permanent success of the Constitution depends on a definite partition of powers between the General and the State Governments, and that no adequate landmarks would be left by the constructive extension of the powers of Congress as proposed in the bill, I have no option but to withhold my signature from it, and to cherishing the hope that its beneficial objects may be attained by a resort for the necessary powers to the same wisdom and virtue in the nation which established the Constitution in its actual form and providently marked out in the instrument itself a safe and practicable mode of improving it as experience might suggest.

117. THE RUSH-BAGOT AGREEMENT
April 28, 1818
(Malloy, ed. *Treatises, Conventions, etc.,* Vol. I, p. 628 ff.)

This famous agreement neutralized the waters of the Great Lakes and provided for an unfortified frontier between the United States and Canada. See, J. M. Callahan, "Neutrality of the American lakes and the Anglo-American Relations" Johns Hopkins U. *Studies,* Ser. XVI.

ARRANGEMENT

BETWEEN, *the United States and Great Britain, between Richard Rush, Esq., acting as Secretary of the Department of State, and Charles Bagot, His Britannic Majesty's Envoy Extraordinary, &c.*

The naval force to be maintained upon the American lakes, by his majesty and the government of the United States, shall henceforth be confined to the following vessels on each side; that is—

On lake Ontario, to one vessel not exceeding one hundred tons burden, and armed with one eighteen pound cannon.

On the upper lakes, to two vessels, not exceeding like burden each, and armed with like force.

On the waters of lake Champlain, to one vessel not exceeding like burden, and armed with like force.

All other armed vessels on these lakes shall be forthwith dismantled, and no other vessels of war shall be there built or armed.

If either party should hereafter be desirous of annulling this stipulation, and should give notice to that effect to the other party, it shall cease to be binding after the expiration of six months from the date of such notice.

The naval force so to be limited shall be restricted to such services as will, in no respect, interfere with the proper duties of the armed vessels of the other party.

118. M'CULLOCH v. MARYLAND
4 Wheaton, 316
1819

Error to the Court of Appeals of Maryland. In 1818 Maryland passed an act imposing a tax upon the notes of all banks not chartered by the State. M'Culloch, cashier of the branch Bank of the United States at Baltimore, refused to pay the tax, and action was brought against him by the state of Maryland. Two questions were involved in this case: did Congress have the right to incorporate a bank, and was a state tax upon the bank constitutional. In his consideration of the first of these questions, Marshall relied to a large extent upon Hamilton's argument on the constitutionality of the bank, see Doc. No. 93. This was one of the most notable of Marshall's opinions, and one of the most important in construing the powers of the National Government. See, A. Beveridge, *Marshall,* Vol. IV, p. 282 ff.; C. Warren, *The Supreme Court,* (1928 ed.) Vol. I, ch. xii. This decision evoked a thorough and powerful criticism from Judge Spencer Roane of Virginia: the articles have been reprinted in the *John P. Branch Historical Papers,* 1905.

MARSHALL, C. J. . . . The first question made in this cause is, has Congress power to incorporate a bank?

It has been truly said, that this can scarcely be considered as an open question, entirely unprejudiced by the former proceedings of the nation respecting it. The principle now contested was introduced at a very early period of our history, has been recognized by many successive legislatures, and has been acted upon by the judicial department, in cases of peculiar delicacy, as a law of undoubted obligation. . . .

In discussing this question, the counsel for the State of Maryland have deemed it of some importance, in the construction of the constitution, to consider that instrument not as emanating from the people, but as the act of sovereign and independent States. The powers of the general government, it has been said, are delegated by the States, who alone are truly sovereign; and must be exercised in subordination to the States, who alone possess supreme dominion.

It would be difficult to sustain this proposition. The convention which framed the constitution was, indeed, elected by the State legislatures. But the instrument, when it came from their hands, was a mere proposal, without obligation, or pretensions to it. It was reported to the then existing Congress of the United States, with a request that it might "be submitted to a convention of Delegates, chosen in each State, by the people thereof, under the recommendation of its legislature, for their assent and ratification." This mode of proceeding was adopted; and by the Convention, by Congress, and by the State Legislatures, the instrument was submitted to the people. They acted upon it, in the only manner in which they can act safely, effectively, and wisely, on such a subject, by assembling in Convention. It is true, they assembled in their several States; and where else should they have assembled? No political dreamer was ever wild enough to think of breaking down the lines which separate the States, and of compounding the American people into one common mass. Of consequence, when they act, they act in their States. But the measures they adopt do not, on that account cease to be the measures of the people themselves, or become the measures of the state governments.

From these Conventions the constitution derives its whole authority. The government proceeds directly from the people; is "ordained and established" in the name of the people; and is declared to be ordained, "in order to form a more perfect union, establish justice, insure domestic tranquillity, and secure the blessings of liberty to themselves and to their posterity." The assent of the States, in their sovereign capacity, is implied in calling a Convention, and thus submitting that instrument to the people. But the people were at perfect liberty to accept or reject it; and their act was final. It required not the affirmance, and could not be negatived, by the State governments. The constitution, when thus adopted, was of complete obligation, and bound the State sovereignties. . . .

. . . The government of the Union, then (whatever may be the influence of this fact on the case), is emphatically and truly a government of the people. In form and in substance it emanates from them, its powers are granted by them, and are to be exercised directly on them, and for their benefit.

This government is acknowledged by all to be one of enumerated powers. The principle,

that it can exercise only the powers granted to it, would seem too apparent to have required to be enforced by all those arguments which its enlightened friends, while it was depending before the people, found it necessary to urge. That principle is now universally admitted. But the question respecting the extent of the powers actually granted, is perpetually arising, and will probably continue to arise, as long as our system shall exist. In discussing these questions, the conflicting powers of the State and general governments must be brought into view, and the supremacy of their respective laws, when they are in opposition, must be settled.

If any one proposition could command the universal assent of mankind, we might expect it would be this: that the government of the Union, though limited in its powers, is supreme within its sphere of action. This would seem to result necessarily from its nature. It is the government of all; its powers are delegated by all; it represents all, and acts for all. Though any one State may be willing to control its operations, no State is willing to allow others to control them. The nation, on those subjects on which it can act, must necessarily bind its component parts. But this question is not left to mere reason: the people have, in express terms, decided it, by saying, "this constitution, and the laws of the United States, which shall be made in pursuance thereof," "shall be the supreme law of the land," and by requiring that the members of the State legislatures, and the officers of the executive and judicial departments of the States, shall take the oath of fidelity to it.

The government of the United States, then, though limited in its powers, is supreme; and its laws, when made in pursuance of the constitution, form the supreme law of the land, "anything in the constitution or laws of any State, to the contrary, notwithstanding."

Among the enumerated powers, we do not find that of establishing a bank or creating a corporation. But there is no phrase in the instrument which, like the articles of confederation, excludes incidental or implied powers; and which requires that everything granted shall be expressly and minutely described. Even the 10th amendment, which was framed for the purpose of quieting the excessive jealousies which had been excited, omits the word "expressly," and declares only that the powers "not delegated to the United States, nor prohibited to the States, are reserved to the States or to the people;" thus leaving the question, whether the particular power which may become the subject of contest, has been delegated to the one government, or prohibited to the other, to depend on a fair construction of the whole instrument. The men who drew and adopted this amendment, had experienced the embarrassments resulting from the insertion of this word in the articles of confederation, and probably omitted it to avoid those embarrassments. A constitution, to contain an accurate detail of all the subdivisions of which its great powers will admit, and of all the means by which they may be carried into execution, would partake of the prolixity of a legal code, and could scarcely be embraced by the human mind. It would probably never be understood by the public. Its nature, therefore, requires that only its great outlines should be marked, its important objects designated, and the minor ingredients which compose those objects be deduced from the nature of the objects themselves. That this idea was entertained by the framers of the American constitution, is not only to be inferred from the nature of the instrument, but from the language. Why else were some of the limitations, found in the 9th section of the first article, introduced? It is also, in some degree, warranted by their having omitted to use any restrictive term which might prevent its receiving a fair and just interpretation. In considering this question, then, we must never forget, that it is *a constitution* we are expounding.

Although, among the enumerated powers of government, we do not find the word "bank," or "incorporation," we find the great powers to lay and collect taxes; to borrow money; to regulate commerce; to declare and conduct a war; and to raise and support armies and navies. The sword and the purse, all the external relations, and no inconsiderable portion of the industry of the nation, are intrusted to its government. It can never be pretended that these vast powers draw after them others of inferior importance, merely because they are inferior. Such an idea can never be advanced. But it may, with great

reason, be contended, that a government, intrusted with such ample powers, on the due execution of which the happiness and prosperity of the nation so vitally depends, must also be intrusted with ample means for their execution. The power being given, it is the interest of the nation to facilitate its execution. It can never be their interest, and cannot be presumed to have been their intention, to clog and embarrass its execution by withholding the most appropriate means. Throughout this vast republic, from the St. Croix to the Gulph of Mexico, from the Atlantic to the Pacific, revenue is to be collected and expended, armies are to be marched and supported. The exigencies of the nation may require, that the treasure raised in the north should be transported to the south, *that* raised in the east conveyed to the west, or that this order should be reversed. Is that construction of the constitution to be preferred which would render these operations difficult, hazardous, and expensive? Can we adopt that construction (unless the words imperiously require it) which would impute to the framers of that instrument, when granting these powers for the public good, the intention of impeding their exercise by withholding a choice of means? If, indeed, such be the mandate of the constitution, we have only to obey; but that instrument does not profess to enumerate the means by which the powers it confers may be executed; nor does it prohibit the creation of a corporation, if the existence of such a being be essential to the beneficial exercise of those powers. It is, then, the subject of fair inquiry, how far such means may be employed.

It is not denied that the powers given to the government imply the ordinary means of execution. That, for example, of raising revenue and applying it to national purposes, is admitted to imply the power of conveying money from place to place, as the exigencies of the nation may require, and of employing the usual means of conveyance. But it is denied that the government has its choice of means, or that it may employ the most convenient means, if to employ them it be necessary to erect a corporation. . . .

The government which has a right to do an act, and has imposed on it the duty of performing that act, must, according to the dictates of reason, be allowed to select the means; and those who contend that it may not select any appropriate means, that one particular mode of effecting the object is excepted, take upon themselves the burden of establishing that exception.

The creation of a corporation, it is said, appertains to sovereignty. This is admitted. But to what portion of sovereignty does it appertain? Does it belong to one more than to another? In America, the powers of sovereignty are divided between the government of the Union, and those of the States. They are each sovereign, with respect to the objects committed to it, and neither sovereign with respect to the objects committed to the other. We cannot comprehend that train of reasoning which would maintain, that the extent of power granted by the people is to be ascertained, not by the nature and terms of the grant, but by its date. Some State constitutions were formed *before,* some *since* that of the United States. We cannot believe that their relation to each other is in any degree dependent upon this circumstance. Their respective powers must, we think, be precisely the same, as if they had been formed at the same time. Had they been formed at the same time, and had the people conferred on the general government the power contained in the constitution, and on the States the whole residuum of power, would it have been asserted that the government of the Union was not sovereign, with respect to those objects which were entrusted to it, in relation to which its laws were declared to be supreme? If this could not have been asserted, we cannot well comprehend the process of reasoning which maintains, that a power appertaining to sovereignty cannot be connected with that vast portion of it which is granted to the general government, so far as it is calculated to subserve the legitimate objects of that government. The power of creating a corporation, though appertaining to sovereignty, is not, like the power of making war, or levying taxes, or of regulating commerce, a great substantive and independent power, which cannot be implied as incidental to other powers, or used as a means of executing them. It is never the end for which other powers are exercised, but a means by which other objects are accomplished. No contributions are made to charity for the sake of an incorporation, but a corporation is created to administer the charity; no seminary of learning is instituted in order to be incorporated, but the corporate character is conferred to subserve the purposes of education. No city was ever built with the sole object of being incorporated, but is incorporated as affording the best means of being well governed. The power of creating a corporation is never used for its own sake, but for the purpose of effecting something else. No sufficient reason is, therefore, perceived, why it may not pass as incidental to those powers which are expressly given, if it be a direct mode of executing them.

But the constitution of the United States has not left the right of Congress to employ the necessary means, for the execution of the powers conferred on the government, to general reasoning. To its enumeration of powers is added that of making "all laws which shall be necessary and proper, for carrying into execution the foregoing powers, and all other powers vested by this constitution, in the government of the United States, or in any department thereof."

The counsel for the State of Maryland have urged various arguments, to prove that this clause, though in terms a grant of power, is not so in effect; but is really restrictive of the general right, which might otherwise be implied, of selecting means of executing the enumerated powers. . . .

But the argument on which most reliance is placed, is drawn from the peculiar language of this clause. Congress is not empowered by it to make all laws, which may have relation to the powers conferred on the government, but such only as may be *"necessary and proper"* for carrying them into execution. The word *"necessary"* is considered as controlling the whole sentence, and as limiting the right to pass laws for the execution of the granted powers, to such as are indispensable, and without which the power would be nugatory. That it excludes the choice of means, and leaves to Congress, in each case, that only which is most direct and simple.

Is it true, that this is the sense in which the word "necessary" is always used? Does it always import an absolute physical necessity, so strong, that one thing, to which another may be termed necessary cannot exist without that other? We think it does not.

If reference be had to its use, in the common affairs of the world, or in approved authors, we find that it frequently imports no more than that one thing is convenient, or useful, or essential to another. To employ the means necessary to an end, is generally understood as employing any means calculated to produce the end, and not as being confined to those single means, without which the end would be entirely unattainable. Such is the character of human language, that no word conveys to the mind, in all situations one single definite idea; and nothing is more common than to use words in a figurative sense. Almost all compositions contain words, which, taken in their rigorous sense, would convey a meaning different from that which is obviously intended. It is essential to just construction, that many words which import something excessive, should be understood in a more mitigated sense—in that sense which common usage justifies. The word "necessary" is of this description. It has not a fixed character peculiar to itself. It admits of all degrees of comparison; and is often connected with other words, which increase or diminish the impression the mind receives of the urgency it imports. A thing may be necessary, very necessary, absolutely or indispensably necessary. To no mind would the same idea be conveyed, by these several phrases. . . . This word, then, like others, is used in various senses; and, in its construction, the subject, the context, the intention of the person using them, are all to be taken into view.

Let this be done in the case under consideration. The subject is the execution of those great powers on which the welfare of a nation essentially depends. It must have been the intention of those who gave these powers, to insure, as far as human prudence could insure, their beneficial execution. This could not be done by confining the choice of means to such narrow limits as not to leave it in the power of Congress to adopt any which might be appropriate, and which were conducive to the end. This provision is made in a constitution intended to endure for ages to come, and, consequently, to be adapted to the various crises of human affairs. To have prescribed the means by which government should, in all future time, execute its powers, would have been to change, entirely, the character of the instrument, and give it the properties of a legal code. It would have been an unwise attempt to provide, by immutable rules, for exigencies which, if foreseen at all, must have been seen dimly, and which can be best provided for as they occur. To have declared that the best means shall not be used, but those alone without which the power given would be nugatory, would have been to deprive the legislature of the capacity to avail itself of experience, to exercise its reason, and to accommodate its legislation to circumstances. . . .

This clause, as construed by the State of Maryland, would abridge and almost annihilate this useful and necessary right of the legislature to select its means. That this could not be intended is, we should think, had it not been already controverted, too apparent for controversy. . . .

The result of the most careful and attentive consideration bestowed upon this clause is, that if it does not enlarge, it cannot be construed to restrain the powers of Congress, or to impair the right of the legislature to exercise its best judgment in the selection of measures to carry into execution the constitutional powers of the government. If no other motive for its insertion can be suggested, a sufficient one is found in the desire to remove all doubts respecting the right to legislate on that vast mass of incidental powers which must be involved in the constitution, if that instrument be not a splendid bauble.

We admit, as all must admit, that the powers of the government are limited, and that its limits are not to be transcended. But we think the sound construction of the constitution must allow to the national legislature that discretion, with respect to the means by which the powers it confers are to be carried into execution, which will enable that body to perform the high duties assigned to it, in the manner most beneficial to the people. Let the end be legitimate, let it be within the scope of the constitution, and all means which are appropriate, which are plainly adapted to that end, which are not prohibited, but consist with the letter and spirit of the constitution, are constitutional. . . .

If a corporation may be employed indiscriminately with other means to carry into execution the powers of the government, no particular reason can be assigned for excluding the use of a bank, if required for its fiscal operations. To use one, must be within the discretion of Congress, if it be an appropriate mode of executing the powers of government. That it is a convenient, a useful, and essential instrument in the prosecution of its fiscal operations, is not now a subject of controversy. . . .

But were its necessity less apparent, none can deny its being an appropriate measure; and if it is, the degree of its necessity as has been very justly observed, is to be discussed in another place. Should Congress, in the execution of its powers, adopt measures which are prohibited by the constitution; or should Congress, under the pretext of executing its powers, pass laws for the accomplishment of objects not intrusted to the government, it would become the painful duty of this tribunal, should a case requiring such a decision come before it, to say that such an act was not the law of the land. But where the law is not prohibited, and is really calculated to effect any of the objects intrusted to the government, to undertake here to inquire into the degree of its necessity, would be to pass the line which circumscribes the judicial department, and to tread on legislative ground. This court disclaims all pretensions to such a power. . . .

After the most deliberate consideration, it is the unanimous and decided opinion of this court, that the act to incorporate the Bank of the United States is a law made in pursuance of the constitution, and is a part of the supreme law of the land. . . .

It being the opinion of the Court, that the act incorporating the bank is constitutional; and that the power of establishing a branch in the State of Maryland might be properly exercised by the bank itself, we proceed to inquire—

2. Whether the State of Maryland may, without violating the constitution, tax that branch?

That the power of taxation is one of vital importance; that it is retained by the States; that it is not abridged by the grant of a similar power to the government of the Union; that it is to be concurrently exercised by the two governments: are truths which have never been denied. But, such is the paramount character of the constitution,

that its capacity to withdraw any subject from the action of even this power, is admitted. The States are expressly forbidden to lay any duties on imports or exports, except what may be absolutely necessary for executing their inspection laws. If the obligation of this prohibition must be conceded—if it may restrain a state from the exercise of its taxing power on imports and exports, the same paramount character would seem to restrain, as it certainly may restrain, a state from such other exercise of this power, as is in its nature incompatible with, and repugnant to, the constitutional laws of the Union. A law, absolutely repugnant to another, as entirely repeals that other as if express terms of repeal were used.

On this ground the counsel for the bank place its claim to be exempted from the power of a State to tax its operations. There is no express provision for the case, but the claim has been sustained on a principle which so entirely pervades the constitution, is so intermixed with the materials which compose it, so interwoven with its web, so blended with its texture, as to be incapable of being separated from it, without rending it into shreds.

This great principle is, that the constitution and the laws made in pursuance thereof are supreme; that they control the constitution and laws of the respective States, and cannot be controlled by them. From this, which may be almost termed an axiom, other propositions are deduced as corollaries, on the truth or error of which, and on their application to this case, the cause has been supposed to depend. These are, 1. That a power to create implies a power to preserve. 2. That a power to destroy, if wielded by a different hand, is hostile to, and incompatible with, these powers to create and preserve. 3. That where this repugnancy exists, that authority which is supreme must control, not yield to that over which it is supreme. . . .

The power of Congress to create, and of course to continue, the bank, was the subject of the preceding part of this opinion; and is no longer to be considered as questionable.

That the power of taxing it by the States may be exercised so as to destroy it, is too obvious to be denied. But taxation is said to be an absolute power, which acknowledges no other limits than those expressly prescribed in the constitution, and like sovereign power of every other description, is trusted to the discretion of those who use it. . . .

The argument on the part of the State of Maryland, is, not that the states may directly resist a law of Congress, but that they may exercise their acknowledged powers upon it, and that the Constitution leaves them this right in the confidence that they will not abuse it. . . .

. . . That the power to tax involves the power to destroy; that the power to destroy may defeat and render useless the power to create; that there is a plain repugnance, in conferring on one government a power to control the constitutional measures of another, which other, with respect to those very measures, is declared to be supreme over that which exerts the control, are propositions not to be denied. But all inconsistencies are to be reconciled by the magic of the word CONFIDENCE. Taxation, it is said, does not necessarily and unavoidably destroy. To carry it to the excess of destruction would be an abuse, to presume which, would banish that confidence which is essential to all government.

But is this a case of confidence? Would the people of any one State trust those of another with a power to control the most insignificant operations of their State government? We know they would not. Why, then, should we suppose that the people of any one State should be willing to trust those of another with a power to control the operations of a government to which they have confided their most important and most valuable interests? In the legislature of the Union alone, are all represented. The legislature of the Union alone, therefore, can be trusted by the people with the power of controlling measures which concern all, in the confidence that it will not be abused. This, then, is not a case of confidence, and we must consider it as it really is.

If we apply the principle for which the State of Maryland contends, to the constitution generally, we shall find it capable of changing totally the character of that instrument. We shall find it capable of arresting all the measures of the government, and of prostrating it at the foot of the states. The American people have declared their consti-

tution, and the laws made in pursuance thereof, to be supreme; but this principle would transfer the supremacy, in fact, to the States.

If the States may tax one instrument, employed by the government in the execution of its powers, they may tax any and every other instrument. They may tax the mail; they may tax the mint; they may tax patent rights; they may tax the papers of the custom-house; they may tax judicial process; they may tax all the means employed by the government, to an excess which would defeat all the ends of government. This was not intended by the American people. They did not design to make their government dependent on the States. . . .

The question is, in truth, a question of supremacy; and if the right of the States to tax the means employed by the general government be conceded, the declaration that the constitution, and the laws made in pursuance thereof, shall be the supreme law of the land, is empty and unmeaning declamation. . . .

It has also been insisted, that, as the power of taxation in the general and State governments is acknowledged to be concurrent, every argument which would sustain the right of the general government to tax banks chartered by the States, will equally sustain the right of the States to tax banks chartered by the general government.

But the two cases are not on the same reason. The people of all the States have created the general government, and have conferred upon it the general power of taxation. The people of all the States, and the States themselves, are represented in Congress, and, by their representatives, exercise this power. When they tax the chartered institutions of the States, they tax their constitutents; and these taxes must be uniform. But when a State taxes the operations of the government of the United States, it acts upon institutions created, not by their own constituents, but by people over whom they claim no control. It acts upon the measures of a government created by others as well as themselves, for the benefit of others in common with themselves. The difference is that which always exists, and always must exist, between the action of the whole on a part, and the action of a part on the whole—between the laws of a government declared to be supreme, and those of a government which, when in opposition to those laws, is not supreme. . . .

The Court has bestowed on this subject its most deliberate consideration. The result is a conviction that the States have no power, by taxation or otherwise, to retard, impede, burden, or in any manner control, the operations of the constitutional laws enacted by Congress to carry into execution the powers vested in the general government. This is, we think, the unavoidable consequence of that supremacy which the constitution has declared. We are unanimously of opinion, that the law passed by the legislature of Maryland, imposing a tax on the Bank of the United States, is unconstitutional and void. . . .

Judgment Reversed.

119. TRUSTEES OF DARTMOUTH COLLEGE v. WOODWARD
4 Wheaton, 518
1819

Error to the supreme court of New Hampshire. Dartmouth College had been established in 1769 by a charter granted by King George III. In 1816 the State of New Hampshire altered this charter, and organized, under the new charter, a new board of trustees. The old board of trustees refused to accept this change, and argued that the act of New Hampshire was unconstitutional, because an impairment of contract contrary to the Federal Constitution. The opinion of the Court that a corporation charter was a contract was of considerable importance in the subsequent business history of the country. Its significance, however, was limited by the decision of the court in the *Charles River Bridge* v. *Warren Bridge* case, Doc. No. 155. There is a voluminous literature on the Dartmouth College case. See, J. M. Shirley, *Dartmouth College Causes;* A. Beveridge, *Marshall,* Vol. IV, ch. v.; E. S. Corwin, *John Marshall and the Constitution,* p. 155 ff.; C. Warren, *Supreme Court* (1928 ed.), Vol. I, p. 475 ff.; G. T. Curtis, Daniel Webster, Vol. II; C. Fuess, *Daniel Webster,* Vol. I; and the illuminating note in J. R. Long, *Cases on Constitutional Law,* p. 240.

MARSHALL, C. J.:

. . . This court can be insensible neither to the magnitude nor delicacy of this question. The validity of a legislative act is to be examined; and the opinion of the highest law tribunal of a state is to be revised: an opinion which carries with it intrinsic evidence of the diligence, of the ability, and the integrity with which it was formed. . . .

It can require no argument to prove that the circumstances of this case constitute a contract. An application is made to the crown for a charter to incorporate a religious and literary institution. In the application it is stated that large contributions have been made for the object, which will be conferred on the corporation as soon as it shall be created. The charter is granted, and on its faith the property is conveyed. Surely in this transaction every ingredient of a complete and legitimate contract is to be found. The points for consideration are, 1. Is this contract protected by the constitution of the United States? 2. Is it impaired by the acts under which the defendant holds?

1. On the first point it has been argued that the word "contract," in its broadest sense, would comprehend the political relations between the government and its citizens, would extend to offices held within a state for state purposes, and to many of those laws concerning civil institutions, which must change with circumstances, and be modified by ordinary legislation; which deeply concern the public, and which, to preserve good government, the public judgment must control. That even marriage is a contract, and its obligations are affected by the laws respecting divorces. That the clause in the constitution, if construed in its greatest latitude, would prohibit these laws. Taken in its broad, unlimited sense, the clause would be an unprofitable and vexatious interference with the internal concerns of a state, would unnecessarily and unwisely embarrass its legislation, and render immutable those civil institutions which are established for purposes of internal government, and which, to subserve those purposes, ought to vary with varying circumstances. That as the framers of the constitution could never have intended to insert in that instrument a provision so unnecessary, so mischievous, and so repugnant to its general spirit, the term "contract" must be un-

derstood in a more limited sense. That it must be understood as intended to guard against a power of at least doubtful utility, the abuse of which had been extensively felt, and to restrain the legislature in future from violating the right to property. That anterior to the formation of the constitution, a course of legislation had prevailed in many, if not in all, of the states, which weakened the confidence of man in man, and embarrassed all transactions between individuals, by dispensing with a faithful performance of engagements. To correct this mischief, by restraining the power which produced it, the state legislatures were forbidden "to pass any law impairing the obligation of contracts," that is, of contracts respecting property, under which some . . . individual could claim a right to something beneficial to himself; and that, since the clause in the constitution must in construction receive some limitation, it may be confined, and ought to be confined, to cases of this description, to cases within the mischief it was intended to remedy.

The general correctness of these observations cannot be controverted. That the framers of the constitution did not intend to restrain the states in the regulation of their civil institutions, adopted for internal government, and that the instrument they have given us is not to be so construed, may be admitted. The provision of the constitution never has been understood to embrace other contracts than those which respect property or some object of value, and confer rights which may be asserted in a court of justice. It has never been understood to restrict the general right of the legislature to legislate on the subject of divorces. . . .

The parties in this case differ less on general principles, less on the true construction of the constitution in the abstract, than on the application of those principles to this case, and on the true construction of the charter of 1769. This is the point on which the cause essentially depends. If the act of incorporation be a grant of political power, if it create a civil institution to be employed in the administration of the government, or if the funds of the college be public property, or if the state of New Hampshire, as a government, be alone interested in its transactions, the subject is one in which the legislature of the state may act according to its own judgment, unrestrained by any limitation of its power imposed by the constitution of the United States.

But if this be a *private eleemosynary institution,* endowed with a capacity to take property for objects *unconnected with government,* whose funds are bestowed by individuals on the faith of the charter; if the donors have stipulated for the future disposition and management of those funds in the manner prescribed by themselves; there may be more difficulty in the case, although neither the persons who have made these stipulations, nor those for whose benefit they were made, should be parties to the cause. Those who are no longer interested in the property may yet retain such an interest in the preservation of their own arrangements as to have a right to insist that those arrangements shall be held sacred. Or, if they have themselves disappeared, it becomes a subject of serious and anxious inquiry whether those whom they have legally empowered to represent them forever may not assert all the rights which they possessed while in being; whether, if they be without personal representatives who may feel injured by a violation of the compact, the trustees be not so completely their representatives in the eye of the law as to stand in their place, not only as respects the government of the college, but also as respects the maintenance of the college charter. It becomes then the duty of the court most seriously to examine this charter, and to ascertain its true character. . . .

Whence, then, can be derived the idea that Dartmouth College has become a public institution, and its trustees public officers. . . . Not from the source whence its funds were drawn; for its foundation is purely private and eleemosynary—not from the application of those funds, for money may be given for education and the persons receiving it do not, by being employed in the education of youth, become members of the civil government. Is it from the act of incorporation? Let this subject be considered.

A corporation is an artificial being, invisible, intangible, and existing only in contemplation of law. Being the mere creature of law, it possesses only those properties which the charter of its creation confers upon it, either expressly or as incidental to its very existence. These are such as are supposed best calculated to effect the object for which it was created. Among the most important are immortality, and, if the expression may be allowed, individuality; properties, by which a perpetual succession of many persons are considered as the same, and may act as a single individual. They enable a corporation to manage its own affairs, and to hold property without the perplexing intricacies, the hazardous and endless necessity, of perpetual conveyances for the purpose of transmitting it from hand to hand. It is chiefly for the purpose of clothing bodies of men in succession with these qualities and capacities that corporations were invented and are in use. By these means, a perpetual succession of individuals are capable of acting for the promotion of the particular object, like one immortal being. . . .

From this review of the charter, it appears that Dartmouth College is an eleemosynary institution, incorporated for the purpose of perpetuating the application of the bounty of the donors to the specified objects of that bounty; that its trustees or governors were originally named by the founder, and invested with the power of perpetuating themselves; that they are not public officers, nor is it a civil institution, participating in the administration of government; but a charity school, or a seminary of education, incorporated for the preservation of its property, and the perpetual application of that property to the objects of its creation. . . .

According to the theory of the British constitution, their Parliament is omnipotent. To annul corporate rights might give a shock to public opinion, which that government has chosen to avoid; but its power is not questioned. Had Parliament, immediately after the emanation of this charter and the execution of those conveyances which followed it, annulled the instrument, so that the living donors would have witnessed the disappointment of their hopes, the perfidy of the transaction would have been universally acknowledged. Yet then, as now, the donors would have had no interest in the property; then, as now, those who might be students would have had no rights to be violated; then, as now, it might be said that the trustees, in whom the rights of all were combined, possessed no private, individual, beneficial interest in the property confided to their protection. Yet the contract would at that time have been deemed sacred by all. What has since occurred to strip it of its inviolability? Circumstances have not changed it. In reason, in justice, and in law, it is now what it was in 1769.

This is plainly a contract to which the donors, the trustees, and the crown (to whose rights and obligations New Hampshire succeeds) were the original parties. It is a contract made on a valuable consideration. It is a contract for the security and disposition of property. It is a contract on the faith of which real and personal estate has been conveyed to the corporation. It is then a contract within the letter of the constitution, and within its spirit also, unless the fact that the property is invested by the donors in trustees for the promotion of religion and education, for the benefit of persons who are perpetually changing, though the objects remain the same, shall create a particular exception, taking this case out of the prohibition contained in the constitution.

It is more than possible that the preservation of rights of this description was not particularly in the view of the framers of the constitution when the clause under consideration was introduced into that instrument. It is probable that interferences of more frequent recurrence, to which the temptation was stronger and of which the mischief was more extensive, constituted the great motive for imposing this restriction on the state legislatures. But although a particular and a rare case may not in itself be of sufficient magnitude to induce a rule, yet it must be governed by the rule, when established, unless some plain and strong reason for excluding it can be given. It is not enough to say that this particular case was not in the mind of the convention when the article was framed, nor of the American people when it was adopted. It is necessary to go farther, and to say that, had this particular case been suggested, the language would have been so varied as to exclude it, or it would have been made a special exception. The case, being within the words of the rule, must be within its operation likewise, unless there be something in the literal construction so obviously absurd, or mischievous, or repugnant to the general spirit of the instrument as to justify those who expound the constitution in making it an exception.

On what safe and intelligible ground can this exception stand? There is no expression in the constitution, no sentiment delivered by its contemporaneous expounders, which would justify us in making it. . . .

Almost all eleemosynary corporations, those which are created for the promotion of religion, of charity, or of education, are of the same character. The law of this case is the law of all. . . .

The opinion of the court, after mature deliberation, is, that this is a contract, the obligation of which cannot be impaired without violating the constitution of the United States. This opinion appears to us to be equally supported by reason and by the former decisions of this court.

2. We next proceed to the inquiry whether its obligation has been impaired by those acts of the legislature of New Hampshire to which the special verdict refers. . . .

The obligations, then, which were created by the charter to Dartmouth College were the same in the new that they had been in the old government. The power of the government was also the same. A repeal of this charter at any time prior to the adoption of the present constitution of the United States would have been an extraordinary and unprecedented act of power, but one which could have been contested only by the restrictions upon the legislature to be found in the constitution of the state. But the constitution of the United Sates has imposed this additional limitation, that the legislature of a state shall pass no act "impairing the obligation of contracts."

It has been already stated that the act "to amend the charter and enlarge and improve the corporation of Dartmouth College" increases the number of trustees to twenty-one, gives the appointment of the additional members to the executive of the state, and creates a board of overseers, to consist of twenty-five persons, of whom twenty-one are also appointed by the executive of New Hampshire, who have power to inspect and control the most important acts of the trustees.

On the effect of this law two opinions cannot be entertained. Between acting directly and acting through the agency of trustees and overseers no essential difference is perceived. The whole power of governing the college is transformed from trustees appointed according to the will of the founder, expressed in the charter, to the executive of New Hampshire. The management and application of the funds of this eleemosynary institution, which are placed by the donors in the hands of trustees named in the charter, and empowered to perpetuate themselves, are placed by this act under the control of the government of the state. The will of the state is substituted for the will of the donors in every essential operation of the college. This is not an immaterial change. . . . This system is totally changed. The charter of 1769 exists no longer. It is reorganized; and reorganized in such a manner as to convert a literary institution, molded according to the will of its founders and placed under the control of private literary men, into a machine entirely subservient to the will of government. This may be for the advantage of this college in particular, and may be for the advantage of literature in general; but it is not according to the will of the donors, and is subversive of that contract on the faith of which their property was given. . . .

It results from this opinion, that the acts of the legislature of New Hampshire, which are stated in the special verdict found in this cause, are repugnant to the constitution of the United States; and that the judgment on this special verdict ought to have been for the plaintiffs. The judgment of the state court must, therefore, be reversed.

Mr. Justice Washington and Mr. Justice Story rendered separate concurring cpinions. Mr. Justice Duvall dissented.

120. FLORIDA TREATY
February 22, 1819

(Malloy, ed. *Treaties, Conventions, etc.* Vol. II, p. 1651 ff.)

This treaty concluded long-drawn out negotiations for the cession of Florida, and marked out the western boundaries of the United States. It was later charged that Sec. J. Q. Adams had surrendered our title to Texas by this treaty. Spain held up ratification in an effort to secure from the United States a pledge not to recognize the revolting Spanish Colonies. On the Treaty, see H. B. Fuller, *Purchase of Florida;* T. M. Marshall, *Western Boundary of the Louisiana Purchase;* S. F. Bemis, ed. *American Secretaries of State,* Vol. IV, p. 7 ff.

. . . ART. II. His Catholic Majesty cedes to the United States, in full property and sovereignty, all the territories which belonged to him, situated to the eastward of the Mississippi, known by the name of East and West Florida. The adjacent islands dependent on said provinces, all public lots and squares, vacant lands, public edifices, fortifications, barracks, and other buildings, which are not private property, archives and documents, which relate directly to the property and sovereignty of said provinces, are included in this article. . . .

ART. III. The boundary line between the two countries, west of the Mississippi, shall begin on the Gulph of Mexico, at the mouth of the river Sabine, in the sea, continuing north, along the western bank of that river, to the 32d degree of latitude; thence, by a line due north, to the degree of latitude where it strikes the Rio Roxo of Natchitoches, or Red River; thence following the course of the Rio Roxo westward, to the degree of longitude 100 west from London and 23 from Washington; then, crossing the said Red River, and running thence, by a line due north, to the river Arkansas, thence, following the course of the southern bank of the Arkansas, to its source, in latitude 42 north; and thence, by that parallel of latitude, to the South Sea. The whole being as laid down in Melish's map of the United States, published at Philadelphia, improved to the first of January, 1818. But if the source of the Arkansas River shall be found to fall north or south of latitude 42, then the line shall run from the said source due north or south, as the case may be, till it meets the said parallel of latitude 42, and

thence, along the said parallel, to the South Sea: All the islands in the Sabine, and the said Red and Arkansas Rivers, throughout the course thus described, to belong to the United States; but the use of the waters, and the navigation of the Sabine to the sea, and of the said rivers Roxo and Arkansas, throughout the extent of the said boundary, on their respective banks, shall be common to the respective inhabitants of both nations. . . .

ART. V. The inhabitants of the ceded territories shall be secured in the free exercise of their religion, without any restriction. . . .

ART. VI. The inhabitants of the territories which His Catholic Majesty cedes to the United States, by this treaty, shall be incorporated in the Union of the United States, as soon as may be consistent with the principles of the Federal Constitution, and admitted to the enjoyment of all the privileges, rights, and immunities of the citizens of the United States. . . .

ART. XI. The United States, exonerating Spain from all demands in future, on account of the claims of their citizens to which the renunciations herein contained extend, and considering them entirely cancelled, undertake to make satisfaction for the same, to an amount not exceeding five millions of dollars. To ascertain the full amount and validity of those claims, a commission, to consist of three Commissioners, citizens of the United States, shall be appointed by the President, by and with the advice and consent of the Senate. . . .

ART. XV. Spanish vessels, laden only with productions of Spanish growth or manufacture, coming directly from Spain, or her colonies, "shall be admitted, for the term of twelve years, to the ports of Pensacola and St. Augustine, without paying other or higher duties on their cargoes, or of tonnage, than will be paid by the vessels of the United States. During the said term no other nation shall enjoy the same privileges within the ceded territories. . . .

121. THE MISSOURI COMPROMISE
1819–1821

The Territory of Missouri was part of the Louisiana Purchase; by the terms of this purchase the inhabitants of the Territory were guaranteed in their liberty, property, and religion. When in 1818 Missouri petitioned for admission to the Union as a State, the question arose whether this guaranty covered property in slaves of whom there were some two or three thousand in the Territory. In the course of the discussion of the enabling act, Representative Tallmadge of New York offered an amendment excluding slavery from the State. This amendment passed the House but failed in the Senate. That summer and fall the Missouri question was the chief political issue before the country; Congress was bombarded with petitions from State legislatures and other bodies on the slavery issue. In the new Congress the positions of the House and the Senate are indicated by the passage in the House of the Taylor Amendment, in the Senate of the Thomas Amendment. The application of Maine for admission as a State offered Congress a way out of the difficulty. A conference committee reported bills to admit Maine to Statehood, and to admit Missouri with the Thomas Amendment. An act authorizing Missouri to form a state government was approved March 6, but the constitution which the Missouri Convention drew up contained a clause obnoxious to the anti-slavery element, and probably unconstitutional, and Congress refused to admit the State under this constitution. A conference committee worked out a solution to the problem which was provided in the Resolutions for the admission of Missouri of March 2. The conditions laid down were accepted by the legislature of Missouri in June, and Missouri was admitted to Statehood by proclamation of August 10. On the Missouri Compromise see F. J. Turner, *Rise of the New West*, ch. x; H. Von Holst, *Constitutional and Political History of the United States*, Vol. I, p. 324 ff.; J. B. Mc Master, *History of the People of the United States*, Vol. IV, ch. xxxix; F. C. Shoemaker, *Missouri's Struggle for Statehood, 1804–1821;* J. A. Woodburn, "Historical Significance of the Missouri Compromise," Amer. Hist. Assoc. *Report*, 1893; F. R. Hodder, "Side Lights on the Missouri Compromises" Amer. Hist. Assoc. *Report*, 1909; H. A. Trexler, *Slavery in Missouri, 1804–1865;* H. V. Ames, *State Documents on Federal Relations*, p. 193 ff.; C. R. King, *Life and Correspondence of Rufus King*, Vol. VI.

1. THE TALLMADGE AMENDMENT
February 13, 1819

(*Journal of the House of Representatives,* 15th Congress, 2nd. Sess. p. 272)

And provided also, That the further introduction of slavery or involuntary servitude be prohibited, except for the punishment of crimes, whereof the party shall be duly convicted; and that all children of slaves, born within the said state, after the admission thereof into the Union, shall be free but may be held to service until the age of twenty-five years.

2. THE TAYLOR AMENDMENT
January 26, 1820

(*Annals of the Congress of the United States,* 16th Cong. 1st. Sess. Vol. I, p. 947)

The reading of the bill proceeded as far as the fourth section; when

MR. TAYLOR, of New York, proposed to amend the bill by incorporating in that section the following provision:

Section 4, line 25, insert the following after the word "States"; "And shall ordain and establish, that there shall be neither slavery nor involuntary servitude in the said State, otherwise than in the punishment of crimes, whereof the party shall have been duly convicted: *Provided, always,* That any person escaping into the same, from whom labor or service is lawfully claimed in any other State, such fugitive may be lawfully reclaimed, and conveyed to the person claiming his or her labor or service as aforesaid: *And provided, also,* That the said provision shall not be construed to alter the condition or civil rights of any person now held to service or labor in the said Territory."

3. THE THOMAS AMENDMENT
February 17, 1820

(*Annals of the Congress of the United States,* 16th Cong. 1st Sess. Vol. I, p. 427)

And be it further enacted, That, in all that territory ceded by France to the United States, under the name of Louisiana, which lies north of thirty-six degrees and thirty minutes north latitude, excepting only such part thereof as is included within the limits of the State contemplated by this act, slavery and involuntary servitude, otherwise than in the punishment of crimes whereof the party shall have been duly convicted, shall be and is hereby forever prohibited: *Provided always,* That any person escaping into the same, from whom labor or service is lawfully claimed in any State or Territory of the United States, such fugitive may be lawfully reclaimed, and conveyed to the person claiming his or her labor or service, as aforesaid.

4. MISSOURI ENABLING ACT
March 6, 1820

(U. S. Statutes at Large, Vol. III, p. 545 ff.)

An Act to authorize the people of the Missouri territory to form a constitution and state government, and for the admission of such state into the Union on an equal footing with the original states, and to prohibit slavery in certain territories.

Be it enacted That the inhabitants of that portion of the Missouri territory included within the boundaries hereinafter designated, be, and they are hereby, authorized to form for themselves a constitution and state government, and to assume such name as they shall deem proper; and the said state, when formed, shall be admitted into the Union, upon an equal footing with the original states, in all respects whatsoever.

SEC. 2. That the said state shall consist of all the territory included within the following boundaries, to wit: Beginning in the middle of the Mississippi river, on the parallel of thirty-six degrees of north latitude; thence west, along that parallel of latitude, to the St. Francois river; thence up, and following the course of that river, in the middle of the main channel thereof, to the parallel of latitude of thirty-six degrees and thirty minutes; thence west, along the same, to a point where the said parallel is intersected by a meridian line passing through the middle of the mouth of the Kansas river, where the same empties into the Missouri river, thence, from the point aforesaid north, along the said meridian line, to the intersection of the parallel of latitude which passes through the rapids of the river Des Moines, making the said line to correspond with the Indian boundary line; thence east, from the point of intersection last aforesaid, along the said parallel of latitude, to the middle of the channel of the main fork of the said river Des Moines; thence down and along the middle of the main channel of the said river Des Moines, to the mouth of the same, where it empties into the Mississippi river; thence, due east, to the middle of the main channel of the Mississippi river; thence down, and following the course of the Mississippi river, in the middle of the main channel thereof, to the place of beginning: . . .

SEC. 3. That all free white male citizens of the United States, who shall have arrived at the age of twenty-one years, and have resided in said territory three months previous to the day of election, and all other persons qualified to vote for representatives to the general assembly of the said territory, shall be qualified to be elected, and they are hereby qualified and authorized to vote, and choose representatives to form a convention. . . .

SEC. 8. That in all that territory ceded by France to the United States, under the name of Louisiana, which lies north of thirty-six degrees and thirty minutes north latitude, not included within the limits of the state, contemplated by this act, slavery and involuntary servitude, otherwise than in the punishment of crimes, whereof the parties shall have been duly convicted, shall be, and is hereby, forever prohibited: *Provided always,* That any person escaping into the same, from whom labour or service is lawfully claimed, in any state or territory of the United States, such fugitive may be lawfully reclaimed and conveyed to the person claiming his or her labour or service as aforesaid.

5. THE CONSTITUTION OF MISSOURI
July 19, 1820

(Poore, ed., Federal and State Constitutions, Vol. II, p. 1107–8)

SEC. 26. The general assembly shall not have power to pass laws—

1. For the emancipation of slaves without the consent of their owners; or without paying them, before such emancipation, a full equivalent for such slaves so emancipated; and,

2. To prevent *bona-fide* immigrants to this State, or actual settlers therein, from bringing from any of the United States, or from any of their Territories, such persons as may there be deemed to be slaves, so long as any persons of the same description are allowed to be held as slaves by the laws of this State.

They shall have power to pass laws—

1. To prevent *bona-fide* immigrants to this State of any slaves who may have committed any high crime in any other State or Territory;

2. To prohibit the introduction of any slave for the purpose of speculation, or as an article of trade or merchandise;

3. To prohibit the introduction of any

slave, or the offspring of any slave, who heretofore may have been, or who hereafter may be, imported from any foreign country into the United States, or any Territory thereof, in contravention of any existing statute of the United States; and,

4. To permit the owners of slaves to emancipate them, saving the right of creditors, where the person so emancipating will give security that the slave so emancipated shall not become a public charge.

It shall be their duty, as soon as may be, to pass such laws as may be necessary—

1. To prevent free negroes end [and] mulattoes from coming to and settling in this State, under any pretext whatsoever; and,

2. To oblige the owners of slaves to treat them with humanity, and to abstain from all injuries to them extending to life or limb.

6. RESOLUTION FOR THE ADMISSION OF MISSOURI
March 2, 1821

(U. S. Statutes at Large, Vol. III, p. 645)

Resolution *providing for the admission of the State of Missouri into the Union, on a certain condition.*

Resolved, That Missouri shall be admitted into this union on an equal footing with the original states, in all respects whatever, upon the fundamental condition, that the fourth clause of the twenty-sixth section of the third article of the constitution submitted on the part of said state to Congress, shall never be construed to authorize the passage of any law, and that no law shall be passed in conformity thereto, by which any citizen, of either of the states in this Union, shall be excluded from the enjoyment of any of the privileges and immunities to which such citizen is entitled under the constitution of the United States: *Provided,* That the legislature of the said state, by a solemn public act, shall declare the assent of the said state to the said fundamental condition, and shall transmit to the President of the United States, on or before the fourth Monday in November next, an authentic copy of the said act; upon the receipt whereof, the President, by proclamation, shall announce the fact; whereupon, and without any further proceeding on the part of Congress, the admission of the said state into this Union shall be considered as complete.

122. LAND LAW OF 1820
April 24, 1820

(U. S. Statutes at Large, Vol. III, p. 566–7)

This law reduced the price of public land and put an end to the credit system established by the Act of 1800. See, P. J. Treat, *National Land System, 1785–1820;* T. Donaldson, *The Public Domain: its History with Statistics.*

An act making further provision for the sale of the public lands.

Be it enacted, That from and after the first day of July next, all the public lands of the United States, the sale of which is, or may be authorized by law, shall, when offered at public sale, to the highest bidder, be offered in half quarter sections; and when offered at private sale, may be purchased, at the option of the purchaser, either in entire sections, half sections, quarter sections, or half quarter sections; . . .

SEC. 2. That credit shall not be allowed for the purchase money on the sale of any of the public lands which shall be sold after the first day of July next, but every purchaser of land sold at public sale thereafter, shall, on

the day of purchase, make complete payment therefor; . . .

SEC. 3. That from and after the first day of July next, the price at which the public lands shall be offered for sale, shall be one dollar and twenty-five cents an acre; and at every public sale, the highest bidder, who shall make payment as aforesaid, shall be the purchaser; but no land shall be sold, either at public or private sale, for a less price than one dollar and twenty-five cents an acre; and all the public lands which shall have been offered at public sale before the first day of July next, and which shall then remain unsold, as well as the lands that shall thereafter be offered at public sale, according to law, and remain unsold at the close of such public sales, shall be subject to be sold at private sale, by entry at the land office, at one dollar and twenty-five cents an acre, to be paid at the time of making such entry as aforesaid; . . .

123. COHENS v. VIRGINIA
6 Wheaton, 264
1821

Error to the Quarterly Session Court of Norfolk, Virginia. P. J. and M. J. Cohen were prosecuted for selling lottery tickets in violation of a Virginia statute. The defendants claimed the protection of an act of Congress of 1802 establishing a lottery, but they were convicted and fined in the Virginia Court. The defendants sued out a writ of error to the Supreme Court under Sec. 25 of the Judiciary Act of 1789. This case involved the constitutionality of that Section, and the interpretation of the 11th Amendment to the Constitution. See, Beveridge, *Marshall,* Vol. IV, p. 344 ff.; Warren, *Supreme Court,* ch. xiii.

MARSHALL, C. J. . . . . 1st. The first question to be considered is, whether the jurisdiction of this Court is excluded by the character of the parties, one of them being a State, and the other a citizen of that State.

The second section of the third article of the constitution defines the extent of the judicial power of the United States. Jurisdiction is given to the Courts of the Union, in two classes of cases. In the first, their jurisdiction depends on the character of the cause, whoever may be the parties. This class comprehends "all cases in law and equity arising under this constitution, the laws of the United States, and treaties made, or which shall be made, under their authority." This clause extends the jurisdiction of the Court to all the cases described, without making in its terms any exception whatever, and without any regard to the condition of the party. If there be any exception, it is to be implied against the express words of the article.

In the second class, the jurisdiction depends entirely on the character of the parties. In this are comprehended "controversies between two or more States, between a State and citizens of another State," and "between a State and foreign States, citizens or subjects." If these be the parties, it is entirely unimportant what may be the subject of controversy. Be it what it may, these parties have a constitutional right to come into the courts of the Union. . . .

A case in law or equity . . . may truly be said to arise under the constitution or a law of the United States whenever its correct solution depends on the construction of either. . . .

The jurisdiction of the Court, then, being extended by the letter of the constitution to all cases arising under it or under the laws of the United States, it follows that those who would withdraw any case of this description from that jurisdiction must sustain the exemption they claim on the spirit and true meaning of the constitution, which spirit and true meaning must be so apparent as to overrule the words which its framers have employed.

The counsel for the defendant in error have undertaken to do this; and have laid down the general proposition, that a sovereign independent State is not suable, except by its own consent.

This general proposition will not be controverted. But its consent is not requisite in each particular case. It may be given in a general law. And if a State has surrendered any portion of its sovereignty, the question, whether a liability to suit be a part of this portion, depends on the instrument by which the surrender is made. If, upon a just construction of that instrument it shall appear that the State has submitted to be sued, then it has parted with this sovereign right of judging in every case on the justice of its own pretensions, and has intrusted that power to a tribunal in whose impartiality it confides.

The American States, as well as the American people, have believed a close and firm union to be essential to their liberty and to their happiness. They have been taught by experience that this union cannot exist without a government for the whole; and they have been taught by the same experience that this government would be a mere shadow, that must disappoint all their hopes, unless invested with large portions of that sovereignty which belongs to independent States. Under the influence of this opinion, and thus instructed by experience, the American people, in the conventions of their respective States, adopted the present constitution.

If it could be doubted, whether, from its

nature, it were not supreme in all cases where it is empowered to act, that doubt would be removed by the declaration, that "this constitution, and the laws of the United States which shall be made in pursuance thereof, and all treaties made, or which shall be made, under the authority of the United States, shall be the supreme law of the land; and the judges in every State shall be bound thereby, anything in the constitution or laws of any State to the contrary notwithstanding." This is the authoritative language of the American people; and, if gentlemen please, of the American States. It marks, with lines too strong to be mistaken, the characteristic distinction between the government of the Union, and those of the States. The general government, though limited as to its objects, is supreme with respect to those objects. This principle is a part of the constitution; and if there be any who deny its necessity, none can deny its authority.

To this supreme government ample powers are confided; and if it were possible to doubt the great purposes for which they were so confided, the people of the United States have declared, that they are given "in order to form a more perfect union, establish justice, insure domestic tranquillity, provide for the common defense, promote the general welfare, and secure the blessings of liberty to themselves and their posterity." With the ample powers confided to this supreme government for these interesting purposes are connected many express and important limitations on the sovereignty of the States, which are made for the same purposes. The powers of the Union, on the great subjects of war, peace and commerce, and on many others, are in themselves limitations of the sovereignty of the States; but in addition to these, the sovereignty of the States is surrendered in many instances where the surrender can only operate to the benefit of the people, and where, perhaps, no other power is conferred on Congress than a conservative power to maintain the principles established in the constitution. The maintenance of these principles in their purity is certainly among the great duties of the government. One of the instruments by which this duty may be peaceably performed is the judicial department. It is authorized to decide all cases, of every description, arising under the constitution or laws of the United States. From this general grant of jurisdiction no exception is made of those cases in which a State may be a party. When we consider the situation of the government of the Union and of a State in relation to each other, the nature of our constitution, the subordination of the state governments to that constitution, the great purpose for which jurisdiction over all cases arising under the constitution and laws of the United States is confided to the judicial department, are we at liberty to insert in this general grant, an exception of those cases in which a State may be a party? Will the spirit of the constitution justify this attempt to control its words? We think it will not. We think a case arising under the constitution or laws of the United States is cognizable in the Courts of the Union, whoever may be the parties to that case.

Had any doubt existed with respect to the just construction of this part of the section, that doubt would have been removed by the enumeration of those cases to which the jurisdiction of the federal Courts is extended, in consequence of the character of the parties. In that enumeration, we find "controversies between two or more States, between a State and citizens of another State, and between a State and foreign States, citizens or subjects."

One of the express objects, then, for which the judicial department was established, is the decision of controversies between States, and between a State and individuals. The mere circumstance, that a State is a party, gives jurisdiction to the Court. How, then, can it be contended, that the very same instrument, in the very same section, should be so construed, as that this same circumstance should withdraw a case from the jurisdiction of the court, where the constitution or laws of the United States are supposed to have been violated? . . . The mischievous consequences of the construction contended for on the part of Virginia, are also entitled to great consideration. It would prostrate, it has been said, the government and its laws at the feet of every State in the Union. And would not this be its effect? What power of the government could be executed by its own means, in any State disposed to resist its execution by a course of legislation? The laws must be executed by individuals acting within the several States. If these individuals may be exposed to penalties, and if the Courts of the Union cannot correct the judgments by which these penalties may be enforced, the course of the government may be, at any time, arrested by the will of one of its members. Each member will possess a *veto* on the will of the whole. . . .

Different States may entertain different opinions on the true construction of the constitutional powers of Congress. . . .

But a constitution is framed for ages to come, and is designed to approach immortality as nearly as human institutions can approach it. Its course cannot always be tranquil. It is exposed to storms and tempests, and its framers must be unwise statesmen indeed, if they have not provided it, so far as its nature will permit, with the means of self-preservation from the perils it may be destined to encounter. No government ought to be so defective in its organization as not to contain within itself the means of securing the execution of its own laws against other dangers than those which occur every day. Courts of justice are the means most usually employed; and it is reasonable to expect that a government should repose on its own Courts, rather than on others. There is certainly nothing in the circumstances under which our constitution was formed, nothing in the history of the times, which would justify the opinion that the confidence reposed in the States was so implicit as to leave in them and their tribunals the power of resisting or defeating, in the form of law, the legitimate measures of the Union. . . .

It has been also urged, as an additional objection to the jurisdiction of the Court, that cases between a State and one of its own citizens, do not come within the general scope of the constitution; and were obviously never intended to be made cognizable in the federal Courts. . . .

If jurisdiction depended entirely on the character of the parties, and was not given where the parties have not an original right to come into Court, that part of the 2d section of the 3d article, which extends the judicial power to all cases arising under the constitution and laws of the United States, would be mere surplusage. It is to give jurisdiction where the character of the parties would not give it, that this very important part of the clause was inserted. It may be true, that the partiality of the State tribunals, in ordinary controversies between a State and its citizens, was not apprehended, and therefore the judicial power of the Union was not extended to such cases; but this was not the sole nor the greatest object for which this department was created. A more important, a much more interesting object, was the preservation of the constitution and laws of the United States, so far as they can be preserved by judicial authority; and therefore the jurisdiction of the Courts of the Union was expressly extended to all cases arising under that constitution and those laws. If the constitution or laws may be violated by proceedings instituted by a State against its own citizens, and if that violation may be such as essentially to affect the constitution and the laws, such as to arrest the progress of government in its constitutional course, why should these cases be excepted from that provision which expressly extends the judicial power of the Union to *all* cases arising under the constitution and laws?

After bestowing on this subject the most attentive consideration, the Court can perceive no reason founded on the character of the parties for introducing an exception which the constitution has not made; and we think that the judicial power, as originally given, extends to all cases arising under the constitution or a law of the United States, whoever may be the parties. . . .

This leads to the consideration of the 11th Amendment. . . .

It is, then, the opinion of the Court, that the defendant who removes a judgment rendered against him by a State Court into this Court, for the purpose of re-examining the question, whether that judgment be in violation of the constitution or laws of the United States, does not commence or prosecute a suit against the State, whatever may be its opinion where the effect of the writ may be to restore the party to the possession of a thing which he demands.

But should we in this be mistaken the error does not affect the case now before the Court. If this writ of error be a suit in the sense of the 11th amendment, it is not a suit commenced or prosecuted "by a citizen of another State or by a citizen or subject of any foreign State." It is not then within the amendment, but is governed by the constitution as originally framed, and we have already seen, that in its origin, the judicial power was extended to all cases arising under the constitution or laws of the United States, without respect to parties.

2d. The second objection to the jurisdiction of the Court is that its appellate power cannot be exercised, in any case, over the judgment of a State Court. This objection is sustained chiefly by arguments drawn from the supposed total separation of the judiciary of a State from that of the Union, and their entire independence of each other. The argument considers the federal judiciary as completely foreign to that of a State; and as being no more connected with it, in any respect whatever, than the Court of a foreign State. If this hypothesis be just, the argument founded on it is equally so; but if the hypothesis be not supported by the constitution, the argument fails with it.

This hypothesis is not founded on any words in the constitution which might seem to countenance it, but on the unreasonableness of giving a contrary construction to words which seem to require it, and on the incompatibility of the application of the appellate jurisdiction to the judgments of state courts with that constitutional relation which subsists between the government of the Union and the governments of those States which compose it.

Let this unreasonableness, this total incompatibility, be examined.

That the United States form, for many and for most important purposes, a single nation, has not yet been denied. In war we are one people. In making peace we are one people. In all commercial regulations we are one and the same people. In many other respects the American people are one, and the government which is alone capable of controlling and managing their interests in all these respects, is the government of the Union. It is their government, and in that character they have no other. America has chosen to be, in many respects, and to many purposes, a nation; and for all these purposes her government is complete; to all these objects it is competent. The people have declared that in the exercise of all the powers given for these objects it is supreme. It can, then, in effecting these objects, legitimately control all individuals or governments within the American territory. The constitution and laws of a State, so far as they are repugnant to the constitution and laws of the United States, are absolutely void. These States are constituent parts of the United States. They are members of one great empire—for some purposes sovereign, for some purposes subordinate.

In a government so constituted is it unreasonable that the judicial power should be competent to give efficacy to the constitutional laws of the legislature? That department can decide on the validity of the constitution or law of a State, if it be repugnant to the constitution or to a law of the United States. Is it unreasonable that it should also be empowered to decide on the judgment of a State tribunal enforcing such unconstitutional law? Is it so very unreasonable as to furnish a justification for controlling the words of the constitution? We think it is not. We think that, in a government acknowledgedly supreme with respect to objects of vital interest to the nation, there is nothing inconsistent with sound reason, nothing incompatible with the nature of government, in making all its departments supreme, so far as respects those objects, and so far as is necessary to their attainment. The exercise of the appellate power over those judgments of the state tribunals which may contravene the constitution or laws of the United States, is, we believe, essential to the attainment of those objects.

The propriety of intrusting the construction of the constitution, and laws made in pursuance thereof, to the judiciary of the Union, has not, we believe, as yet been drawn in question. It seems to be a corollary from this political axiom that the federal Courts should either possess exclusive jurisdiction in such cases, or a power to revise the judgment rendered in them by State tribunals. . . .

We are not restrained, then, by the political relations between the general and State governments from construing the words of the constitution defining the judicial power in their true sense. We are not bound to construe them more restrictively than they naturally import.

They give to the Supreme Court appellate jurisdiction in all cases arising under the constitution, laws, and treaties of the United

States. The words are broad enough to comprehend all cases of this description, in whatever court they may be decided. . . .

After having bestowed upon this question the most deliberate consideration of which we are capable, the Court is unanimously of opinion that the objections to its jurisdiction are not sustained, and that the motion ought to be overruled.

Motion denied.

After the jurisdiction of the court was thus established the case was then heard and decided on its merits. The court held that the act of Congress authorizing the lottery was confined in its operation to the city of Washington and gave the defendants no right to sell lottery tickets in Virginia, and that the Norfolk court therefore had the right to convict the defendants for violating a law of Virginia, and its judgment was therefore affirmed.

124. CHANCELLOR KENT ON UNIVERSAL SUFFRAGE

Remarks of Chancellor Kent to the New York Constitutional Convention of 1821

(*Reports of the Proceedings and Debates of the Convention of 1821,* ed. by H. N. Carter, W. L. Stone, and M. T. C. Gould, sec. 219 ff.)

The second decade of the nineteenth century witnessed a liberalizing of the constitutions of the seaboard states, resulting in part from the democratic influence of the new western states. The proposal to abolish the property qualification for suffrage in New York State aroused intense opposition from the conservatives, which was eloquently voiced by Chief Justice Ambrose Spencer and Chancellor James Kent. Despite this opposition the liberals carried the day. See, D. S. Alexander, *Political History of the State of New York,* Vol. II, ch. xxvii; J. B. Mc Master, *Acquisition of Political, Social and Industrial Rights of Man in America;* E. H. Roberts, *New York,* Vol. II; J. D. Hammond, *Political History of the State of New York,* Vol. II. On Kent, see W. J. Curtis, *James Kent;* W. Kent, *Memoirs and Letters of James Kent;* J. Horton, *James Kent.*

Chancellor Kent. . . . These are some of the fruits of our present government; and yet we seem to be dissatisfied with our present condition, and we are engaged in the bold and hazardous experiment of remodelling the constitution. Is it not fit and discreet: I speak as to wise men; is it not fit and proper that we should pause in our career, and reflect well on the immensity of the innovation in contemplation? Discontent in the midst of so much prosperity, and with such abundant means of happiness, looks like ingratitude, and as if we were disposed to arraign the goodness of Providence. Do we not expose ourselves to the danger of being deprived of the blessings we have enjoyed? . . .

The senate has hitherto been elected by the farmers of the state—by the free and independent lords of the soil, worth at least $250 in freehold estate, over and above all debts charged thereon. The governor has been chosen by the same electors, and we have hitherto elected citizens of elevated rank and character. Our assembly has been chosen by freeholders, possessing a freehold of the value of $50, or by persons renting a tenement of the yearly value of $5, and who have been rated and actually paid taxes to the state. By the report before us, we propose to annihilate, at one stroke, all those property distinctions and to bow before the idol of universal suffrage. That extreme democratic principle, when applied to the legislative and executive departments of the government, has been regarded with terror, by the wise men of every age, because in every European republic, ancient and modern, in which it has been tried, it has terminated disastrously, and been productive of corruption, injustice, violence, and tyranny. And dare we flatter ourselves that we are a peculiar people, who can run the career of history, exempted from the passions which have disturbed and corrupted the rest of mankind? If we are like other races of men, with similar follies and vices, then I greatly fear that our posterity will have reason to deplore in sackcloth and ashes, the delusion of the day. . . .

Now, sir, I wish to preserve our senate as the representative of the landed interest. I wish those who have an interest in the soil, to retain the exclusive possession of a branch in the legislature, as a strong hold in which they may find safety through all the vicissitudes which the state may be destined, in the course of Providence, to experience. I wish them to be always enabled to say that their freeholds cannot be taxed without their consent. The men of no property, together with the crowds of dependents connected with great manufacturing and commercial establishments, and the motley and undefinable population of crowded ports, may, perhaps, at some future day, under skilful management predominate in the assembly, and yet we should be perfectly safe if no laws could pass without the free consent of the owners of the soil. That security we at present enjoy; and it is that security which I wish to retain.

The apprehended danger from the experiment of universal suffrage applied to the whole legislative department, is no dream of the imagination. It is too mighty an excitement for the moral constitution of men to endure. The tendency of universal suffrage, is to jeopardize the rights of property, and the principles of liberty. There is a constant tendency in human society, and the history of every age proves it; there is a tendency in the poor to covet a share in the plunder of the rich; in the debtor to relax or avoid the obligation of contracts; in the majority to tyrannize over the minority, and trample down their rights; in the indolent and profligate, to cast the whole burthens of society upon the industrious and the virtuous; and *here is a tendency in ambitious and wicked men, to inflame these combustible materials.* It requires a vigilant government, and a firm administration of justice, to counteract that

tendency. Thou shalt not covet; thou shalt not steal; are divine injunctions induced by this miserable depravity of our nature. Who can undertake to calculate with any precision, how many millions of people, this great state will contain in the course of this and the next century, and who can estimate the future extent and magnitude of our commercial ports? The disproportion between the men of property, and the men of no property, will be in every society in a ratio to its commerce, wealth, and population. We are no longer to remain plain and simple republics of farmers, like the New-England colonists, or the Dutch settlements on the Hudson. We are fast becoming a great nation, with great commerce, manufactures, population, wealth, luxuries, and with the vices and miseries that they engender. One seventh of the population of the city of Paris at this day subsists on charity, and one third of the inhabitants of that city die in the hospitals; what would become of such a city with universal suffrage? France has upwards of four, and England upwards of five millions of manufacturing and commercial labourers without property. Could these Kingdoms sustain the weight of universal suffrage? The radicals in England, with the force of that mighty engine, would at once sweep away the property, the laws, and the liberties of that island like a deluge.

The growth of the city of New-York is enough to startle and awaken those who are pursuing the *IGNIS FATUUS* of universal suffrage. . . .

125. MONROE'S VETO OF CUMBERLAND ROAD BILL
May 4, 1822
(Richardson, ed. *Messages and Papers,* Vol. II, p. 142 ff.)

A detailed and comprehensive exposition of President Monroe's constitutional objections to the Cumberland Road Bill can be found in the paper accompanying this message, Richardson, Vol. II, p. 144–183. See, J. S. Young, *Cumberland Road;* P. J. Treat, *The National Land System;* F. J. Turner, *Rise of the New West,* p. 230 ff.

WASHINGTON, *May 4, 1822.*
To the House of Representatives:
Having duly considered the bill entitled "An act for the preservation and repair of the Cumberland road," it is with deep regret,

approving as I do the policy, that I am compelled to object to its passage and to return the bill to the House of Representatives, in which it originated, under a conviction that Congress do not possess the power under the Constitution to pass such a law.

A power to establish turnpikes with gates and tolls, and to enforce the collection of tolls by penalties, implies a power to adopt and execute a complete system of internal improvement. A right to impose duties to be paid by all persons passing a certain road, and on horses and carriages, as is done by this bill, involves the right to take the land from the proprietor on a valuation and to pass laws for the protection of the road from injuries, and if it exist as to one road it exists as to any other, and to as many roads as Congress may think proper to establish. A right to legislate for one of these purposes is a right to legislate for the others. It is a complete right of jurisdiction and sovereignty for all the purposes of internal improvement, and not merely the right of applying money under the power vested in Congress to make appropriations, under which power, with the consent of the States through which this road passes, the work was originally commenced, and has been so far executed. I am of opinion that Congress do not possess this power; that the States individually can not grant it, for although they may assent to the appropriation of money within their limits for such purposes, they can grant no power of jurisdiction or sovereignty by special compacts with the United States. This power can be granted only by an amendment to the Constitution and in the mode prescribed by it.

If the power exist, it must be either because it has been specifically granted to the United States or that it is incidental to some power which has been specifically granted. If we examine the specific grants of power we do not find it among them, nor is it incidental to any power which has been specifically granted.

It has never been contended that the power was specifically granted. It is claimed only as being incidental to some one or more of the powers which are specifically granted. The following are the powers from which it is said to be derived:

First, from the right to establish post-offices and post-roads; second, from the right to declare war; third, to regulate commerce; fourth, to pay the debts and provide for the common defense and general welfare; fifth, from the power to make all laws necessary and proper for carrying into execution all the powers vested by the Constitution in the Government of the United States or in any department or officer thereof; sixth and lastly, from the power to dispose of and make all needful rules and regulations respecting the territory and other property of the United States.

According to my judgment it can not be derived from either of those powers, nor from all of them united, and in consequence it does not exist. . . .

126. THE ENGLISH BACKGROUND OF THE MONROE DOCTRINE
Letter from George Canning to Richard Rush
August 20, 1823
(R. Rush, *Memoranda of a Residence at the Court of London*, p. 412)

George Canning, who was contemptuous of the Holy Alliance and its activities, became prime minister of Great Britain in September 1822. The following month the powers of Europe met at the Congress of Verona to consider the feasibility of the restoration of the Spanish monarchy in the countries of South America. Great Britain withdrew from this Congress and in March 1823 Canning instructed the English minister to Paris that England could not permit France to acquire any of the former Spanish colonies in America. August 16 Canning made informal overtures to the American minister, Rush, looking to joint action on Latin-American affairs. The letter of August 20 contains a succinct statement of Canning's position, but it did not embrace recognition of the Latin American Republics. For this reason, and because Secretary Adams felt that it would be better not "to come in as a cock-boat in the wake of the British man-of-war"

the United States did not respond to Canning's proposals. Meantime Canning had secured from Prince Polignac assurance that France would not under any circumstances act against the former Spanish colonies by force of arms. Canning was satisfied with this understanding, and did not press his original idea of a joint declaration with the United States. See references to Doc. No. 127 and H. W. V. Temperley, *The Life of Canning;* A. G. Stapleton, *Political Life of George Canning,* 3 Vols; H. W. V. Temperley, *The Foreign Policy of Canning.*

Foreign Office, Aug. 20, 1823
Private and Confidential

My dear Sir:—Before leaving Town I am desirous of bringing before you in a more distinct, but still in an unofficial and confidential shape, the question which we shortly discussed the last time that I had the pleasure of seeing you.

Is not the moment come when our Governments might understand each other as to the Spanish American Colonies? And if we can arrive at such an understanding, would it not be expedient for ourselves, and beneficial for all the world, that the principles of it should be clearly settled and plainly avowed?

For ourselves we have no disguise.

1. We conceive the recovery of the Colonies by Spain to be hopeless.

2. We conceive the question of the recognition of them, as Independent States, to be one of time and circumstances.

3. We are, however, by no means disposed to throw any impediment in the way of an arrangement between them and the mother country by amicable negotiations.

4. We aim not at the possession of any portion of them ourselves.

5. We could not see any portion of them transferred to any other Power, with indifference.

If these opinions and feelings are, as I firmly believe them to be, common to your Government with ours, why should we hesitate mutually to confide them to each other; and to declare them in the face of the world?

If there be any European Power which cherishes other projects, which looks to a forcible enterprise for reducing the colonies to subjugation, on the behalf or in the name of Spain; or which meditates the acquisition of any part of them to itself, by cession or by conquest; such a declaration on the part of your government and ours would be at once the most effectual and the least offensive mode of intimating our joint misapprobation of such projects.

It would at the same time put an end to all the jealousies of Spain with respect to her remaining Colonies, and to agitation which prevails in those Colonies, an agitation which it would be but humane to allay; being determined (as we are) not to profit by encouraging it.

Do you conceive that under the power which you have recently received, you are authorized to enter into negotiation and to sign any Convention upon this subject? Do you conceive, if that be not within your competence, you could exchange with me ministerial notes upon it?

Nothing could be more gratifying to me than to join with you in such a work, and, I am persuaded, there has seldom, in the history of the world, occurred an opportunity when so small an effort of two friendly Governments might produce so unequivocal a good and prevent such extensive calamities.

I shall be absent from London but three weeks at the utmost; but never so far distant but that I can receive and reply to any communication within three or four days.

I have the honor to be

My Dear Sir, with great respect and esteem

Your obedient and faithful servant

George Canning

R. Rush, Esqr.

127. THE MONROE DOCTRINE
Extracts from President Monroe's Seventh Annual Message to Congress
December 2, 1823
(Richardson, ed. *Messages and Papers,* Vol. II, p. 207 ff.)

The literature on the Monroe Doctrine is too voluminous to detail here. See the bibliographies in F. J. Turner, *Rise of the New West*, p. 351; Channing, Hart and Turner, *Guide to the Study and Reading of American History*, Sec. 198; H. B. Meyer, *List of References on the Monroe Doctrine*. For more recent literature, see, D. Perkins, *The Monroe Doctrine, 1823–1826;* S. Bemis, ed. *American Secretaries of State and Their Diplomacy*, Vol. IV, p. 36 ff. and bibliography, p. 347 ff.; H. W. V. Temperley, *The Foreign Policy of Canning;* A. Alvarez, *The Monroe Doctrine*, especially the annexes. On the authorship of the Doctrine, W. C. Ford, "John Quincy Adams: His Connection with the Monroe Doctrine" in Massachusetts Hist. Soc. *Proceedings*, 2d Ser. Vol. XV, p. 373 ff. has not yet been superseded. On recognition of the Latin-American Republics, F. L. Paxson, *The Independence of the South American Republics* is still the standard treatise. The diplomatic correspondence has been collected in three volumes, W. R. Manning, ed. *Diplomatic Correspondence of the United States Concerning the Independence of the Latin Amer-*

ican Nations. A quasi-official statement of the doctrine is J. R. Clark, *Memorandum on the Monroe Doctrine.*

. . . At the proposal of the Russian Imperial Government, made through the minister of the Emperor residing here, a full power and instructions have been transmitted to the minister of the United States at St. Petersburg to arrange by amicable negotiation the respective rights and interests of the two nations on the northwest coast of this continent. A similar proposal had been made by His Imperial Majesty to the Government of Great Britain, which has likewise been acceded to. The Government of the United States has been desirous by this friendly proceeding of manifesting the great value which they have invariably attached to the friendship of the Emperor and their solicitude to cultivate the best understanding with his Government. In the discussions to which this interest has given rise and in the arrangements by which they may terminate the occasion has been judged proper for asserting, as a principle in which the rights and interests of the United States are involved, that the American continents, by the free and independent condition which they have assumed and maintain, are henceforth not to be considered as subjects for future colonization by any European powers. . . .

It was stated at the commencement of the last session that a great effort was then making in Spain and Portugal to improve the condition of the people of those countries, and that it appeared to be conducted with extraordinary moderation. It need scarcely be remarked that the result has been so far very different from what was then anticipated. Of events in that quarter of the globe, with which we have so much intercourse and from which we derive our origin, we have always been anxious and interested spectators. The citizens of the United States cherish sentiments the most friendly in favor of the liberty and happiness of their fellow-men on that side of the Atlantic. In the wars of the European powers in matters relating to themselves we have never taken any part, nor does it comport with our policy so to do. It is only when our rights are invaded or seriously menaced that we resent injuries or make preparation for our defense. With the movements in this hemisphere we are of ne-

cessity more immediately connected, and by causes which must be obvious to all enlightened and impartial observers. The political system of the allied powers is essentially different in this respect from that of America. This difference proceeds from that which exists in their respective Governments; and to the defense of our own, which has been achieved by the loss of so much blood and treasure, and matured by the wisdom of their most enlightened citizens, and under which we have enjoyed unexampled felicity, this whole nation is devoted. We owe it, therefore, to candor and to the amicable relations existing between the United States and those powers to declare that we should consider any attempt on their part to extend their system to any portion of this hemisphere as dangerous to our peace and safety. With the existing colonies or dependencies of any European power we have not interfered and shall not interfere. But with the Governments who have declared their independence and maintained it, and whose independence we have, on great consideration and on just principles, acknowledged, we could not view any interposition for the purpose of oppressing them, or controlling in any other manner their destiny, by any European power in any other light than as the manifestation of an unfriendly disposition toward the United States. In the war between those new Governments and Spain we declared our neutrality at the time of their recognition, and to this we have adhered, and shall continue to adhere, provided no change shall occur which, in the judgment of the competent authorities of this Government, shall make a corresponding change on the part of the United States indispensable to their security.

The late events in Spain and Portugal shew that Europe is still unsettled. Of this important fact no stronger proof can be adduced than that the allied powers should have thought it proper, on any principle satisfactory to themselves, to have interposed by force in the internal concerns of Spain. To what extent such interposition may be carried, on the same principle, is a question in which all independent powers whose governments differ from theirs are interested, even those most remote, and surely none more so than the United States. Our policy in regard to Europe, which was adopted at an early stage of the wars which have so long agitated that quarter of the globe, nevertheless remains the same, which is, not to interfere in the internal concerns of any of its powers; to consider the government *de facto* as the legitimate government for us; to cultivate friendly relations with it, and to preserve those relations by a frank, firm, and manly policy, meeting in all instances the just claims of every power, submitting to injuries from none. But in regard to those continents circumstances are eminently and conspicuously different. It is impossible that the allied powers should extend their political system to any portion of either continent without endangering our peace and happiness; nor can anyone believe that our southern brethren, if left to themselves, would adopt it of their own accord. It is equally impossible, therefore, that we should behold such interposition in any form with indifference. If we look to the comparative strength and resources of Spain and those new Governments, and their distance from each other, it must be obvious that she can never subdue them. It is still the true policy of the United States to leave the parties to themselves, in the hope that other powers will pursue the same course. . . .

128. PROTEST AGAINST THE CAUCUS BY THE GENERAL ASSEMBLY OF THE STATE OF TENNESSEE
1823

(Niles Register, Vol. XXV, p. 137–138)

With the breakdown of the machinery provided by the Constitution for the election of the President, there arose the practice of nominations by party caucus. The growth of the caucus system aroused widespread discontent, and the defeat of Crawford, the choice of the rump caucus of the Republican Party in 1824, marked the death of "King Caucus". The caucus system of nominations was supplanted by nominations by State legislatures and eventually by national conventions. For the origin of the caucus, see A. C. McLaughlin and A. B. Hart, *Cyclopaedia of American Government,* "caucus"; F. W. Dallinger, *Nominations for Elective Office in the United States.*

The general assembly of the State of Tennessee has taken into consideration the practice which, on former occasions, has prevailed at the City of Washington, of members of the Congress of the United States meeting in caucus, and nominating persons to be voted for as president and vice-president of the United States: and, upon the best view of the subject which this general assembly has been able to take, it is believed that the practice of congressional nominations is a violation of the spirit of the Constitution of the United States.

That instrument provides that there shall be three separate and distinct departments of the government, and great care and caution seems to have been exercised by its framers to prevent any one department from exercising the smallest degree of influence over another; and such solicitude was felt on this subject, that, in the second section of the second article, it is expressly declared, "That no *senator or representative,* or person holding an office of trust or profit under the United States, shall be appointed an elector." From this provision, it is apparent that the convention intended that the members of Congress should not be the principal and primary agents or actors in electing the president and vice-president of the United States —so far from it, they are expressly disqualified from being placed in a situation to vote for these high officers. Is there not more danger of undue influence to be apprehended, when the members of Congress meet in caucus and mutually and solemnly pledge themselves to support the individuals who may have the highest number of votes in such meeting, than there would be in permitting them to be eligible to the appointment of electors? In the latter case, a few characters, rendered ineligible by the Constitution, might succeed; but in the former, a powerful combination of influential men is formed, who may fix upon the American people their highest officers against the consent of a clear majority of the people themselves; and this may be done by the very men whom the Constitution intended to prohibit from acting on the subject. Upon an examination of the Constitution of the United States, there is but one case in which the members of Congress are permitted to act, which is in the event of a failure to make an election by the electoral college; and then the members of the House of Representatives vote by States. With what propriety the same men, who, in the year 1825, may be called on to discharge a constitutional duty, can, in the year 1824, go into a caucus and pledge themselves to support the men then nominated, cannot be discerned, especially when it might so happen that the persons thus nominated, could [not] under any circumstances, obtain a single vote from the State whose members stand pledged to support them. . . .

Upon a review of the whole question, the following reasons which admit of much amplification and enlargement, more than has been urged in the foregoing, might be conclusively relied on, to prove the impolicy and unconstitutionality of the Congressional nominations of candidates for the presidency and vice-presidency of the United States: 1st. A caucus nomination is against the spirit of the Constitution. 2nd. It is both inexpedient and impolitic. 3rd. Members of Congress may become the final electors, and therefore ought not to prejudge the case by pledging themselves previously to support particular candidates. 4th. It violates the equality intended to be secured by the Constitution to the weaker States. 5th. Caucus nominations may, in time (by the interference of the States), acquire the force of precedents and become authoritative, and thereby endanger the liberties of the American people.

129. GIBBONS v. OGDEN
9 Wheaton, 1
1824

Error to the New York Court for the Trial of Impeachments and Correction of Errors. The legislature of New York granted to Robert Livingston and Robert Fulton the exclusive right to navigate the waters of New York State by steamboats. This right passed to one Ogden, who sued to restrain Gibbons from operating steamboats on the Hudson River between New Jersey and New York. This is the most notable of all cases involving the interpretation of the commerce clause of the Constitution. See Beveridge, *Marshall,* Vol. IV, ch. viii; Warren, *Supreme Court,* ch. xv.

MARSHALL, C. J. The appellant contends that this decree is erroneous because the laws which purport to give the exclusive privilege it sustains are repugnant to the constitution and laws of the United States. They are said to be repugnant—1st. To that clause in the constitution which authorizes congress to regulate commerce. 2d. To that which authorizes congress to promote the progress of science and useful arts. . . .

As preliminary to the very able discussions of the constitution which we have heard from the bar, and as having some influence on its construction, reference has been made to the political situation of these states, anterior to its formation. It has been said that they were sovereign, were completely independent, and were connected with each other only by a league. This is true. But, when these allied sovereigns converted their league into a government, when they converted their congress of ambassadors, deputed to deliberate on their common concerns, and to recommend measures of general utility, into a legislature, empowered to enact laws on the most interesting subjects, the whole character in which the states appear underwent a change, the extent of which must be determined by a fair consideration of the instrument by which that change was effected.

This instrument contains an enumeration of powers expressly granted by the people to their government. It has been said that these powers ought to be construed strictly. But why ought they to be so construed? Is there one sentence in the constitution which gives countenance to this rule? In the last of the enumerated powers, that which grants, expressly, the means for carrying all others into execution, congress is authorized "to make all laws which shall be necessary and proper" for the purpose. But this limitation on the means which may be used, is not extended to the powers which are conferred; nor is there one sentence in the constitution, which has been pointed out by the gentlemen of the bar, or which we have been able to discern, that prescribes this rule. We do not, therefore, think ourselves justified in adopting it. What do gentlemen mean by a strict construction? If they contend only against that enlarged construction which would extend words beyond their natural and obvious import, we might question the application of the term, but should not controvert the principle. If they contend for that narrow construction which, in support of some theory not to be found in the constitution, would deny to the government those powers which the words of the grant, as usually understood, import, and which are consistent with the general views and objects of the instrument; for that narrow construction, which would cripple the government, and render it unequal to the objects for which it is declared to be instituted, and to which the powers given, as fairly understood, render it competent; then we cannot perceive the propriety of this strict contruction, nor adopt it as the rule by which the constitution is to be expounded. As men whose intentions require no concealment, generally employ the words which most directly and aptly express the ideas they intend to convey, the enlightened patriots who framed our constitution, and the people who adopted it, must be understood to have employed words in their natural sense, and to have intended what they have said.

The words are: "congress shall have power to regulate commerce with foreign nations, and among the several States, and with the Indian tribes." The subject to be regulated is commerce; and our constitution being, as was aptly said at the bar, one of enumeration, and not of definition, to ascertain the extent of the power, it becomes necessary to settle the meaning of the word. The counsel for the appellee would limit it to traffic, to buying and selling, or the interchange of commodities, and do not admit that it comprehends navigation. This would restrict a general term, applicable to many objects, to one of its significations. Commerce, undoubtedly, is traffic, but it is something more,—it is intercourse. It describes the commercial intercourse between nations, and parts of nations, in all its branches, and is regulated by prescribing rules for carrying on that intercourse. The mind can scarcely conceive a system for regulating commerce between nations which shall exclude all laws concerning navigation, which shall be silent on the admission of the vessels of the one nation into the ports of the other, and be confined to prescribing rules for the conduct of individuals, in the actual employment of buying and selling, or of barter. If commerce does not include navigation, the government of the Union has no direct power over that subject, and can make no law prescribing what shall constitute American vessels, or requiring that they shall be navigated by American seamen. Yet this power has been exercised from the commencement of the government, has been exercised with the consent of all, and has been understood by all to be a commercial regulation. All America understands, and has uniformly understood, the word "commerce" to comprehend navigation. It was so understood, and must have been so understood, when the constitution was framed. The power over commerce, including navigation, was one of the primary objects for which the people of America adopted their government, and must have been contemplated in forming it. The convention must have used the word in that sense, because all have understood it in that sense; and the attempt to restrict it comes too late.

If the opinion that "commerce," as the word is used in the constitution, comprehends navigation also, requires any additional confirmation, that additional confirmation is, we think, furnished by the words of the instrument itself. . . .

The word used in the constitution, then, comprehends, and has been always understood to comprehend, navigation within its meaning; and a power to regulate navigation is as expressly granted as if that term had been added to the word "commerce." To what commerce does this power extend? The constitution informs us, to commerce "with foreign nations, and among the several states, and with the Indian tribes." It has, we believe, been universally admitted that these words comprehend every species of commercial intercourse between the United States and foreign nations. No sort of trade can be carried on between this country and any other to which this power does not extend. It has been truly said that commerce, as the word is used in the constitution, is a unit, every part of which is indicated by the term.

If this be the admitted meaning of the word, in its application to foreign nations, it must carry the same meaning throughout the sentence, and remain a unit, unless there be some plain intelligible cause which alters it. The subject to which the power is next applied is to commerce "among the several states." The word "among" means intermingled with. A thing which is among others is intermingled with them. Commerce among the states cannot stop at the external boundary-line of each state, but may be introduced into the interior. It is not intended to say that these words comprehend that commerce which is completely internal, which is carried on between man and man in a state, or between different parts of the same state, and which does not extend to or affect other States. Such a power would be inconvenient and is certainly unnecessary. Comprehensive as the word "among" is, it may very properly be restricted to that commerce which concerns more States than one. The phrase is not one which would probably have been selected to indicate the completely interior traffic of a state, because it is not an apt phrase for that purpose; and the enumeration of the particular classes of commerce to which the power was to be extended would not have been made had the intention been to extend the power to every description. The enumeration presupposes something not enumerated; and that something, if we regard the language or the subject of the sentence, must be the exclusively internal commerce of a state. The genius and character of the whole government seem to be, that its action is to be applied to all the external concerns of the nation, and to those internal concerns which affect the states generally; but not to those which are completely within a particular state, which do not affect other states, and with which it is not necessary to interfere for the purpose of executing some of the general powers of the government. The completely internal commerce of a state then, may be considered as reserved for the state itself.

But, in regulating commerce with foreign nations, the power of congress does not stop at the jurisdictional lines of the several states. It would be a very useless power if it could not pass those lines. The commerce of the United States with foreign nations is that of the whole United States. Every district has a right to participate in it. The deep streams which penetrate our country in every direction pass through the interior of almost every state in the Union, and furnish the means of exercising this right. If congress has the power to regulate it, that power must be exercised whenever the subject exists. If it exists within the states, if a foreign voyage may commence or terminate at a port within a state, then the power of congress may be exercised within a state. . . .

The power of congress, then, whatever it may be, must be exercised within the territorial jurisdiction of the several States. The sense of the nation on this subject is unequivocally manifested by the provisions made in the laws for transporting goods by land between Baltimore and Providence, between New York and Philadelphia, and between Philadelphia and Baltimore.

We are now arrived at the inquiry, What is this power? It is the power to regulate; that is, to prescribe the rule by which commerce is to be governed. This power, like all others vested in congress, is complete in itself, may be exercised to its utmost extent, and acknowledges no limitations other than are prescribed in the constitution. These are expressed in plain terms, and do not affect the questions which arise in this case, or which have been discussed at the bar. If, as has always been understood, the sovereignty of congress, though limited to specified objects, is plenary as to those objects, the power over commerce with foreign nations, and among the several states, is vested in congress as absolutely as it would be in a single government, having in its constitution the same restrictions on the exercise of the power as are found in the constitution of the United States. . . . The power of congress, then, comprehends navigation within the limits of every state in the Union, so far as that navigation may be, in any manner, connected with "commerce with foreign nations, or among the several States, or with the Indian tribes." It may, of consequence, pass the jurisdiction line of New York, and act upon the very waters to which the prohibition now under consideration applies.

But it has been urged with great earnestness that, although the power of congress to regulate commerce with foreign nations, and among the several states, be coextensive with the subject itself, and have no other limits than are prescribed in the constitution, yet the states may severally exercise the same power within their respective jurisdictions. In support of this argument, it is said that they possessed it as an inseparable attribute of sovereignty before the formation of the constitution, and still retain it, except so far as they have surrendered it by that instrument; that this principle results from the nature of the government, and is secured by the tenth amendment; that an affirmative grant of power is not exclusive, unless in its own nature it be such that the continued exercise of it by the former possessor is inconsistent with the grant, and that this is not of that description. . . .

In discussing the question, whether this power is still in the states, in the case under consideration, we may dismiss from it the inquiry, whether it is surrendered by the mere grant to congress, or is retained until congress shall exercise the power. We may dismiss that inquiry, because it has been exercised, and the regulations which congress deemed it proper to make, are now in full operation. The sole question is, Can a State regulate commerce with foreign nations and among the States while Congress is regulating it? . . .

[Here the Chief Justice examined the acts of Congress of 1796 and 1799 directing federal officers to assist in the execution of the quarantine and health laws of a State, the act of 1803 prohibiting the importation of slaves into any State which shall itself prohibit their importation, and the act of 1789 acknowledging a concurrent power in the States to regulate the conduct of pilots.]

These acts were cited at the bar for the purpose of showing an opinion in congress, that the states possess, concurrently with the legislature of the Union, the power to regulate commerce with foreign nations and among the states. Upon reviewing them, we think, they do not establish the proposition they were intended to prove. They show the opinion that the states retain powers enabling them to pass the laws to which allusion has been made, not that those laws proceed from the particular power which has been delegated to congress.

It has been contended by the counsel for the appellant that, as the word "to regulate" implies in its nature full power over the thing to be regulated, it excludes, necessarily, the action of all others that would perform the same operation on the same thing. That regulation is designed for the entire result, applying to those parts which remain as they were, as well as to those which are altered. It produces a uniform whole, which is as much disturbed and deranged by changing what the regulating power designs to leave untouched as that on which it has operated. There is great force in this argument, and the court is not satisfied that it has been refuted.

Since, however, in exercising the power of regulating their own purely internal affairs, whether of trading or police, the states may sometimes enact laws the validity of which depends on their interfering with, and being contrary to, an act of congress passed in pursuance of the constitution, the court will enter upon the inquiry, whether the laws of New York, as expounded by the highest tribunal of that state, have, in their application to this case, come into collision with an act of congress, and deprived a citizen of a right to which that act entitles him. Should this collision exist, it will be immaterial whether those laws were passed in virtue of a concurrent power "to regulate commerce with foreign nations and among the several states," or in virtue of a power to regulate their domestic trade and police. In one case and the other the acts of New York must yield to the law of congress; and the decision sustaining the privilege they confer against a right given by a law of the Union, must be erroneous. This opinion has been frequently expressed in this court, and is founded as well on the nature of the government as on the words of the constitution. In argument, however, it has been contended that, if a law passed by a state in the exercise of its acknowledged sovereignty, comes into conflict with a law passed by congress in pursuance of the constitution, they affect the subject, and each other, like equal opposing powers. But the framers of the constitution foresaw this state of things, and provided for it by declaring the supremacy not only of itself but of the laws made in pursuance of it. The nullity of any act inconsistent with the constitution is produced by the declaration that the constitution is supreme law. . . . In every such case the act of congress, or treaty, is supreme; and the law of the state, though enacted in the exercise of powers not controverted, must yield to it. . . .

The court is aware that in stating the train of reasoning by which we have been conducted to this result, much time has been consumed in the attempt to demonstrate propositions which may have been thought axioms. . . . But it was unavoidable. . . .

Powerful and ingenious minds, taking as postulates that the powers expressly granted to the government of the Union are to be contracted, by construction, into the narrowest possible compass, and that the original powers of the states are to be retained, if any possible construction will retain them, may, by a course of well-digested, but refined and metaphysical reasoning, founded on these premises, explain away the constitution of our country and leave it a magnificent structure indeed, to look at, but totally unfit for use. They may so entangle and perplex the understanding as to obscure principles which were before thought quite plain, and induce doubts where, if the mind were to pursue its own course none would be perceived. In such a case, it is peculiarly necessary to recur to safe and fundamental principles, to sustain those principles, and, when sustained, to make them the tests of the arguments to be examined.

Decree of Court of New York reversed and annulled and bill of Aaron Ogden dismissed.

130. THE NATIONALISM OF PRESIDENT J. Q. ADAMS

Extract from First Annual Message to Congress
December 6, 1825

(Richardson, ed. *Messages and Papers,* Vol. II, p. 311 ff.)

President Adams was firmly committed to a policy of internal improvements, and the development of education and the sciences at government expense. He proposed to finance such projects by carefully conserving the public lands. Adams himself, while Secretary of State, prepared a monumental *Report on Weights and Measures,* and one of his last public acts was the dedication of an astronomical observatory. For the philosophical principles underlying this doctrine, see Brooks Adams, ed. *The Degradation of the Democratic Dogma,* introduction; B. C. Clark, *John Quincy Adams,* p. 235 ff.; F. J. Turner, *Rise of the New West,* ch. xvii; a history of internal improvement legislation is in H. G. Wheeler, *History of Congress,* Vol. II, p. 109 ff.

. . . Upon this first occasion of addressing the Legislature of the Union, with which I have been honored, in presenting to their view the execution so far as it has been effected of the measures sanctioned by them for promoting the internal improvement of our country, I can not close the communication without recommending to their calm and persevering consideration the general principle in a more enlarged extent. The great object of the institution of civil government is the improvement of the condition of those who are parties to the social compact, and no government, in whatever form constituted, can accomplish the lawful ends of its institution but in proportion as it improves the condition of those over whom it is established. Roads and canals, by multiplying and facilitating the communications and intercourse between distant regions and multitudes of men, are among the most important means of improvement. But moral, political, intellectual improvement are duties assigned by the Author of Our Existence to social no less than to individual man. For the fulfillment of those duties governments are invested with power, and to the attainment of the end—the progressive improvement of the condition of the governed —the exercise of delegated powers is a duty as sacred and indispensable as the usurpation of powers not granted is criminal and odious. Among the first, perhaps the very first, instrument for the improvement of the condition of men is knowledge, and to the acquisition of much of the knowledge adapted to the wants, the comforts, and enjoyments of human life public institutions and seminaries of learning are essential. So convinced of this was the first of my predecessors in this office, now first in the memory, as, living, he was first in the hearts, of our countrymen, that once and again in his addresses to the Congresses with whom he coöperated in the public service he earnestly recommended the establishment of seminaries of learning, to prepare for all the emergencies of peace and war—a national university and a military academy. With respect to the latter, had he lived to the present day, in turning his eyes to the institution at West Point he would have enjoyed the gratification of his most earnest wishes; but in surveying the city which has been honored with his name he would have seen the spot of earth which he had destined and bequeathed to the use and benefit of his country as the site for an university still bare and barren.

In assuming her station among the civilized nations of the earth it would seem that our country had contracted the engagement to contribute her share of mind, of labor, and of expense to the improvement of those parts of knowledge which lie beyond the reach of individual acquisition, and particularly to geographical and astronomical science. Looking back to the history only of the half century since the declaration of our independence, and observing the generous emulation with which the Governments of France, Great Britain, and Russia have devoted the genius, the intelligence, the treasures of their respective nations to the common improvement of the species in these branches of science, is it not incumbent upon us to inquire whether we are not bound by obligations of a high and honorable character to contribute our portion of energy and exertion to the common stock? The voyages of discovery prosecuted in the course of that time at the expense of those nations have not only redounded to their glory, but to the improvement of human knowledge. We have been partakers of that improvement and owe for it a sacred debt, not only of gratitude, but of equal or proportional exertion in the same common cause. Of the cost of these undertakings, if the mere expenditures of outfit, equipment, and completion of the expeditions were to be considered the only charges, it would be unworthy of a great and generous nation to take a second thought. One hundred expeditions of circumnavigation like those of Cook and La Pérouse would not burden the exchequer of the nation fitting them out so much as the ways and means of defraying a single campaign in war. But if we take into the account the lives of those benefactors of mankind of which their services in the cause of their species were the purchase, how shall the cost of those heroic

enterprises be estimated, and what compensation can be made to them or to their countries for them? Is it not by bearing them in affectionate remembrance? Is it not still more by imitating their example—by enabling countrymen of our own to pursue the same career and to hazard their lives in the same cause?

In inviting the attention of Congress to the subject of internal improvements upon a view thus enlarged it is not my design to recommend the equipment of an expedition for circumnavigating the globe for purposes of scientific research and inquiry. We have objects of useful investigation nearer home, and to which our cares may be more beneficially applied. The interior of our own territories has yet been very imperfectly explored. Our coasts along many degrees of latitude upon the shores of the Pacific Ocean, though much frequented by our spirited commercial navigators, have been barely visited by our public ships. The River of the West, first fully discovered and navigated by a countryman of our own, still bears the name of the ship in which he ascended its waters, and claims the protection of our armed national flag at its mouth. With the establishment of a military post there or at some other point of that coast, recommended by my predecessor and already matured in the deliberations of the last Congress, I would suggest the expediency of connecting the equipment of a public ship for the exploration of the whole northwest coast of this continent.

The establishment of an uniform standard of weights and measures was one of the specific objects contemplated in the formation of our Constitution, and to fix that standard was one of the powers delegated by express terms in that instrument to Congress. The Governments of Great Britain and France have scarcely ceased to be occupied with inquiries and speculations on the same subject since the existence of our Constitution, and with them it has expanded into profound, laborious, and expensive researches into the figure of the earth and the comparative length of the pendulum vibrating seconds in various latitudes from the equator to the pole. These researches have resulted in the composition and publication of several works highly interesting to the cause of science.

The experiments are yet in the process of performance. Some of them have recently been made on our own shores, within the walls of one of our own colleges, and partly by one of our own fellow-citizens. It would be honorable to our country if the sequel of the same experiments should be countenanced by the patronage of our Government, as they have hitherto been by those of France and Britain.

Connected with the establishment of an university, or separate from it, might be undertaken the erection of an astronomical observatory, with provision for the support of an astronomer, to be in constant attendance of observation upon the phenomena of the heavens, and for the periodical publication of his observations. It is with no feeling of pride as an American that the remark may be made that on the comparatively small terri-torial surface of Europe there are existing upward of 130 of these light-houses of the skies, while throughout the whole American hemisphere there is not one. If we reflect a moment upon the discoveries which in the last four centuries have been made in the physical constitution of the universe by the means of these buildings and of observers stationed in them, shall we doubt of their usefulness to every nation? And while scarcely a year passes over our heads without bringing some new astronomical discovery to light, which we must fain receive at second hand from Europe, are we not cutting ourselves off from the means of returning light for light while we have neither observatory nor observer upon our half of the globe and the earth revolves in perpetual darkness to our unsearching eyes? . . .

131. THE PANAMA CONGRESS

Message of President Adams on the Participation of the United States in the
Panama Congress
December 26, 1825

(Richardson, ed. *Messages and Papers*, Vol. II, p. 318 ff.)

A Congress of the American nations was called by Bolívar to meet in Panama in the summer of 1826. Though Bolívar did not originally invite the United States, invitations were extended by Colombia and Mexico. President Adams adverted to the Congress in his message of December 6, 1825. The message of December 26 presents his definite acceptance of the invitation and the nominations for delegates. A subsequent message of March 15, 1826 contains a lengthy argument for American participation in the Congress. The proposal to send delegates to the Congress aroused bitter opposition in Congress, partly of a factional and partisan character, partly because it was believed that the objects of the Congress were inimical to slavery. Though the Foreign Affairs Committee of the Senate reported adversely on the mission, both Houses finally voted for participation. This action, however, came too late: Mr. Anderson died on the way to Panama, and Mr. Sergeant arrived after the Congress had adjourned. Séc. Clay's instructions to the American delegates can be found in Department of State, *Instructions,* Vol. XI; President Adams's message of March 15 in Richardson, Vol. II, p. 329 ff. Other documents are in International American Conference, Vol. IV: *The Congress of 1826 at Panama.* See also, I. B. Lockey, *Pan-Americanism: Its Beginnings;* S. F. Bemis, ed. *American Secretaries of State,* Vol. IV, p. 137 ff.; C. Schurz, *Henry Clay,* Vol. I. On Bolívar see T. R. Ybarra, *Bolívar;* H. Augell, *Bolívar;* F. L. Petre, *Bolívar. To the Senate of the United States:*

In the message to both Houses of Congress at the commencement of the session it was mentioned that the Governments of the Republics of Colombia, of Mexico, and of Central America had severally invited the Government of the United States to be represented at the Congress of American nations to be assembled at Panama to deliberate upon objects of peculiar concernment to this hemisphere, and that this invitation had been accepted.

Although this measure was deemed to be within the constitutional competency of the Executive, I have not thought proper to take any step in it before ascertaining that my opinion of its expediency will concur with that of both branches of the Legislature, first, by the decision of the Senate upon the nominations to be laid before them, and, secondly, by the sanction of both Houses to the appropriations, without which it can not be carried into effect. . . .

It will be seen that the United States neither intend nor are expected to take part in any deliberations of a belligerent character; that the motive of their attendance is neither to contract alliances nor to engage in any undertaking or project importing hostility to any other nation.

But the Southern American nations, in the infancy of their independence, often find themselves in positions with reference to other countries with the principles applicable to which, derivable from the state of independence itself, they have not been familiarized by experience. The result of this has been that sometimes in their intercourse with the United States they have manifested dispositions to reserve a right of granting special favors and privileges to the Spanish nation as the price of their recognition. At others they have actually established duties and impositions operating unfavorably to the United States to the advantage of other European powers, and sometimes they have appeared to consider that they might interchange among themselves mutual concessions of exclusive favor, to which neither European powers nor the United States should be admitted. In most of these cases their regulations unfavorable to us have yielded to friendly expostulation and remonstrance. But it is believed to be of infinite moment that the principles of a liberal commercial intercourse should be exhibited to them, and urged with disinterested and friendly persuasion upon them when all assembled for the avowed purpose of consulting together upon the establishment of such principles as may have an important bearing upon their future welfare.

The consentaneous adoption of principles of maritime neutrality, and favorable to the navigation of peace, and commerce in time of war, will also form a subject of consideration to this Congress. The doctrine that free ships make free goods and the restrictions of reason upon the extent of blockades may be established by general agreement with far more ease, and perhaps with less danger, by the general engagement to adhere to them concerted at such a meeting, than by partial treaties or conventions with each of the nations separately. An agreement between all the parties represented at the meeting that each will guard by its own means against the establishment of any future European colony within its borders may be found advisable. This was more than two years since announced by my predecessor to the world as a principle resulting from the emancipation of both the American continents. It may be so developed to the new southern nations that they will all feel it as an essential appendage to their independence.

There is yet another subject upon which, without entering into any treaty, the moral influence of the United States may perhaps be exerted with beneficial consequences at such a meeting—the advancement of religious liberty. Some of the southern nations are even yet so far under the dominion of prejudice that they have incorporated with their political constitutions an exclusive church, without toleration of any other than the dominant sect. The abandonment of this last badge of religious bigotry and oppression may be pressed more effectually by the united exertions of those who concur in the principles of freedom of conscience upon those who are yet to be convinced of their justice and wisdom than by the solitary efforts of a minister to any one of the separate Governments. . . .

In fine, a decisive inducement with me for acceding to the measure is to show by this token of respect to the southern Republics the interest that we take in their welfare and our disposition to comply with their wishes. Having been the first to recognize their independence, and sympathized with them so far as was compatible with our neutral duties in all their struggles and sufferings to acquire it, we have laid the foundation of our future intercourse with them in the broadest principles of reciprocity and the most cordial feelings of fraternal friendship. To extend those principles to all our commercial relations with them and to hand down that friendship to future ages is congenial to the highest policy of the Union, as it will be to that of all those nations and their posterity. In the confidence that these sentiments will meet the approbation of the Senate, I nominate Richard C. Anderson, of Kentucky, and John Sergeant, of Pennsylvania, to be envoys extraordinary and ministers plenipotentiary to the assembly of American nations at Panama, and William B. Rochester, of New York, to be secretary to the mission.

132. MARTIN v. MOTT
12 Wheaton, 19
1827

The War of 1812 was violently opposed in New England and parts of New York State. In some instances this opposition took the form of denying the right of the President to call out the militia of a State. In Massachusetts, for example, the Chief Justice of the Supreme Court advised the Governor that he, and not the President, had the right to decide when the Constitutional exigency existed which required the calling of the State militia. It was this question which came before the Supreme Court in the following case. For the background of opposition to the War of 1812 see, S. E. Morison, *Life of Harrison Gray Otis,* ch. xxi; H. Adams, *History of the United States During the Administration of James Madison,* Vol. VI, ch. xvi; T. Roosevelt, *Gouverneur Morris.*

STORY, J. This is a writ of error to the judgment of the court for the trial of impeachments and the correction of errors of the State of New York, being the highest court of that state, and is brought here in virtue of the 25th section of the judiciary act of 1789, ch. 20. . . . The avowry, in substance, asserts a justification of . . . a fine and forfeiture imposed upon the original plaintiff by a court-martial, for a failure to enter the service of the United States as a militia-man, when thereto required by the President of the United States in pursuance of the act of the 28th of February, 1795. . . .

The constitution declares that Congress shall have power "to provide for calling forth the militia, to execute the laws of the Union, suppress insurrections, and repel invasions" and also "to provide for organizing, arming and disciplining the militia, and for governing such part of them as may be employed in the service of the United States". In pursuance of this authority, the act of 1795 has provided "that whenever the United States shall be invaded, or be in imminent danger of invasion from any foreign nation or Indian tribe, it shall be lawful for the President of the United States to call for such number of the militia of the state or states most convenient to the place of danger, or scene of action, as he may judge necessary to repel such invasion, and to issue his order for that purpose, to such officer or officers of the militia as he shall think proper." . . . It has not been denied here that the act of 1795 is within the constitutional authority of Congress, or that Congress may not lawfully provide for cases of imminent danger of invasion, as well as for cases where an invasion has actually taken place. In our opinion there is no ground for a doubt on this point, even if it had been relied on, for the power to provide for repelling invasions includes the power to provide against the attempt and danger of invasion, as the necessary and proper means to effectuate the object.

. . . The power thus confided by Congress to the President is doubtless of a very high and delicate nature. A few people are naturally jealous of the exercise of military power; and the power to call the militia into actual service was certainly felt to be one of no ordinary magnitude. But it is not a power which can be executed without a correspondent responsiblity. It is, in its terms, a limited power, confined to cases of actual invasion, or of imminent danger of invasion. If it be a limited power, the question arises, by whom is the exigency to be judged of and decided? Is the President the sole and exclusive judge whether the exigency has arisen, or is it to be considered as an open question, upon which every officer to whom the orders of the President are addressed may decide for himself, and equally open to be contested by every militia-man who shall refuse to obey the orders of the President? We are all of the opinion that the authority to decide whether the exigency has arisen, belongs exclusively to the President, and that his decision is conclusive upon all other persons. We think that this construction necessarily results from the nature of the power itself, and from the manifest object contemplated by the act of Congress. . . .

If we look at the language of the act of 1795, every conclusion drawn from the nature of the power itself is strongly fortified. . . . The power itself is confined to the executive of the Union, to him who is, by the constitution, "the Commander-in-chief of the militia, when called into the actual service of the United States," whose duty it is to "take care that the laws be faithfully executed," and whose responsibility for an honest discharge of his official obligations is secured by the highest sanctions. He is necessarily constituted the judge of the existence of the exigency in the first instance, and is bound to act according to his belief of the facts. If he does so act, and decides to call forth the militia, his orders for this purpose are in strict conformity with the provisions of the law; and it would seem to follow as a necessary consequence, that every act done by a subordinate officer, in obedience to such orders, is equally justifiable. The law contemplates, under such circumstances, orders shall be given to carry the power into effect; and it cannot therefore be a correct inference that any other person has a just right to disobey them. The law does not provide for any appeal from the judgement of the President, or for any right in subordinate officers to review his decision, and in effect defeat it. Wherever a statute gives a discretionary power to any person, to be exercised by him, upon his own opinion of certain facts, it is a sound rule of construction that the statute constitutes him the sole and exclusive judge of the existence of those facts. And, in the present case, we are all of opinion that such is the true construction of the act of 1795. It is no answer that such a power may be abused, for there is no power which is not susceptible of abuse. The remedy for this, as well as for all other official misconduct, if it should occur, is to be found in the constitution itself. In a free government the danger must be remote, since in addition to the high qualities which the Executive must be presumed to possess, of public virtue and honest devotion to the public interests, the frequency of elections, and the watchfulness of the representatives of the nation, carry with them all the checks which can be useful to guard against usurpation or wanton tyranny.

Judgement reversed.

133. MASSACHUSETTS HIGH SCHOOL LAW
1827

(*Laws of Massachusetts,* January session, 1827, ch. cxliii)

This is the first American law providing for the establishment of high schools. Note that its provisions are mandatory rather than merely permissive. The law was not adequately enforced, however, until Horace Mann assumed control of the Massachusetts Board of Education, in 1837. Even in 1840 there were only 18 high schools in the State: by 1860 the number had increased to over one hundred. See, G. H. Martin, *Evolution of the Massachusetts Public School System.*

Be it enacted, That each town or district within this Commonwealth, containing fifty families, or householders, shall be provided with a teacher or teachers, of good morals, to instruct children in orthography, reading, writing, English grammar, geography, arithmetic, and good behavior, for such term of time as shall be equivalent to six months for one school in each year; and every town or district containing one hundred families or householders, shall be provided with such teacher or teachers, for such term of time as shall be equivalent to eighteen months, for one school in each year. In every city, town, or district, containing five hundred families, or householders shall be provided with such teacher or teachers for such term of time as shall be equivalent to twenty-four months, shall also be provided with a master of good morals, competent to instruct, in addition to the branches of learning aforesaid, in the history of the United States, bookkeeping by single entry, geometry, surveying, algebra; and shall employ such master to instruct a school in such city, town, or district, for the benefit of all the inhabitants thereof, at least ten months in each year, exclusive of vacations, in such convenient places, or alternately at such places in such city, town, or district, as said inhabitants, at their meeting in March, or April, annually, shall determine; and in every city, or town, and district, containing four thousand inhabitants, such master shall be competent in addition to all the foregoing branches, to instruct the Latin and Greek languages, history, rhetoric, and logic.

134. AMERICAN INSURANCE COMPANY v. CANTER
1 Peters, 511
1828

Appeal from the United States circuit court for the district of South Carolina. This was a suit by the American Insurance Co. to recover a cargo of cotton which had been sold by order of the territorial legislature of Florida. The plaintiffs alleged that the territorial court which ordered the sale was not a legally constituted court because the acquisition of Florida by the United States was unconstitutional. This is the leading case on the constitutionality of the acquisition of territory. See A. Beveridge, *John Marshall*, Vol. IV, p. 142 ff.; C. Warren, *Supreme Court*, (1928 ed.) Vol. I, p. 700.

MARSHALL, C. J. The plaintiffs filed their libel in this cause in the District Court of South Carolina to obtain restitution of 356 bales of cotton . . . which had been insured by them on a voyage from New Orleans to Havre de Grace, in France. The *Point à Petre* was wrecked on the coast of Florida, the cargo saved by the inhabitants, and carried into Key West, where it was sold for the purpose of satisfying the salvors; by virtue of a decree of a court, consisting of a notary and five jurors, which was erected by an act of the territorial Legislature of Florida. The owners abandoned to the underwriters, who proceeded against the property; alleging that the sale was not made by order of a court competent to change the property. . . .

David Canter claimed the cotton as a *bona fide* purchaser, under the decree of a competent court. . . .

The district judge pronounced the decree of the Territorial Court a nullity, and awarded restitution to the libelants. . . .

The libelants and claimant both appealed. . . .

The cause depends mainly on the question whether the property in the cargo saved, was changed, by the sale at Key West. . . . Its validity has been denied, on the ground, that it was ordered by an incompetent tribunal. The tribunal was constituted by an act of the territorial legislature of Florida, passed on the 4th July, 1823, which is inserted in the record. That act purports to give the power which has been exercised; consequently, the sale is valid, if the territorial legislature was competent to enact the law.

The course which the argument has taken, will require, that, in deciding this question, the court should take into view the relation in which Florida stands to the United States.

The Constitution confers absolutely on the government of the Union the powers of making war and of making treaties; consequently, that government possesses the power of acquiring territory, either by conquest or by treaty. The usage of the world is, if a nation be not entirely subdued, to consider the holding of conquered territory as a mere military occupation, until its fate shall be determined at the treaty of peace. If it be ceded by the treaty, the acquisition is confirmed, and the ceded territory becomes a part of the nation to which it is annexed; either on the terms stipulated in the treaty of cession, or on such as its new master shall impose. On such transfer of territory, it has never been held that the relations of the inhabitants with each other undergo any change. Their relations with their former sovereign are dissolved, and new relations are created between them and the government which has acquired their territory. The same act which transfers their country transfers the allegiance of those who remain in it; and the law which may be denominated political is necessarily changed, although that which regulates the intercourse and general conduct of individuals remains in force, until altered by the newly created power of the state.

On the 2d of February, 1819, Spain ceded Florida to the United States. The 6th article of the treaty of cession contains the following provision: "The inhabitants of the territories which his Catholic Majesty cedes to the United States by this treaty shall be incorporated in the Union of the United States, as soon as may be consistent with the principles of the federal Constitution; and admitted to the enjoyment of the privileges, rights, and immunities of the citizens of the United States."

This treaty is the law of the land, and admits the inhabitants of Florida to the enjoyment of the privileges, rights and immunities of the citizens of the United States. It is unnecessary to inquire whether this is not their condition, independent of stipulation. They do not, however, participate in political power; they do not share in the government till Florida shall become a State. In the meantime Florida continues to be a territory of the United States, governed by virtue of that clause in the Constitution which empowers Congress "to make all needful rules and regulations respecting the territory or other property belonging to the United States."

Perhaps the power of governing a territory belonging to the United States which has not by becoming a State acquired the means of self-government may result necessarily from the facts that it is not within the jurisdiction of any particular State, and is within the power and jurisdiction of the United States. The right to govern may be the inevitable consequence of the right to acquire territory. Whichever may be the source whence the power is derived, the possession of it is unquestioned. In execution of it Congress, in 1822, passed "An Act for the Establishment of a Territorial Government in Florida;" and on the 3d of March, 1823, passed another act to amend the act of 1822. Under this act the territorial legislature enacted the law now under consideration. . . .

It has been contended that, by the Constitution, the judicial power of the United States extends to all cases of admiralty and maritime jurisdiction; and that the whole of this judicial power must be vested "in one supreme court, and in such inferior courts as Congress shall from time to time ordain and establish." Hence, it has been argued that Congress cannot vest admiralty jurisdiction in courts created by the territorial legislature.

We have only to pursue this subject one step further, to perceive that this provision of the Constitution does not apply to it. The next sentence declares, that "the judges both of the supreme and inferior courts, shall hold their offices during good behavior." The judges of the superior courts of Florida hold their offices for four years. These courts, then, are not constitutional courts, in which the judicial power conferred by the Constitution on the general government can be deposited. They are incapable of receiving it. They are legislative courts, created in virtue of the general right of sovereignty which exists in the government, or in virtue of that clause which enables Congress to make all needful rules and regulations, respecting the territory belonging to the United States. The jurisdiction with which they are invested, is not a part of that judicial power which is defined in the third article of the Constitution, but is conferred by Congress, in the execution of those general powers which that body possesses over the territories of the United States. Although admiralty jurisdiction can be exercised in the States, in those courts only which are established in pursuance of the third article of the Constitution; the same limitation does not extend to the territories. In legislating for them, Congress exercises the combined powers of the general, and of a state government.

We think, then, that the act of the territorial legislature erecting the court by whose decree the cargo of the *Point à Petre* was sold, is not "inconsistent with the laws and Constitution of the United States," and is valid. Consequently, the sale made in pursuance of it changed the property, and the decree of the circuit court, awarding restitution of the property to the claimant, ought to be affirmed, with costs.

Decree affirmed.

135. THE SOUTH CAROLINA PROTEST AGAINST THE TARIFF OF 1828
December 19, 1828

(Elliot's *Debates,* 1861 ed. Vol. IV, p. 580)

This protest against the "tariff of abominations" of May 20, 1828 was the concluding part of the South Carolina Exposition, drafted by Calhoun, then Vice-President of the United States. The Exposition is in Calhoun's *Works,* 1855 ed. Vol. VI. See also, references in Doc. No. 143. On Calhoun see H. Von Holst, *Calhoun;* G. Hunt, *Calhoun;* W. C. Meigs, *Calhoun,* 2 Vols. For earlier

protests against the tariff and for protests from other States, see, H. V. Ames, *State Documents on Federal Relations.*

The Senate and House of Representatives of South Carolina, now met, and sitting in General Assembly, through the Hon. William Smith and the Hon. Robert Y. Hayne, their representatives in the Senate of the United States, do, in the name and on behalf of the good people of the said commonwealth, solemnly PROTEST against the system of protecting duties, lately adopted by the federal government, for the following reasons:—

1st. *Because* the good people of this commonwealth believe that the powers of Congress were delegated to it in trust for the accomplishment of certain specified objects which limit and control them, and that every exercise of them for any other purposes, is a violation of the Constitution as unwarrantable as the undisguised assumption of substantive, independent powers not granted or expressly withheld.

2d. *Because* the power to lay duties on imports is, and in its very nature can be, only a means of effecting objects specified by the Constitution; since no free government, and least of all a government of enumerated powers, can of right impose any tax, any more than a penalty, which is not at once justified by public necessity, and clearly within the scope and purview of the social compact; and since the right of confining appropriations of the public money to such legitimate and constitutional objects is as essential to the liberty of the people as their unquestionable privilege to be taxed only by their consent.

3d. *Because* they believe that the tariff law passed by Congress at its last session, and all other acts of which the principal object is the protection of manufactures, or any other branch of domestic industry, if they be considered as the exercise of a power in Congress to tax the people at its own good will and pleasure, and to apply the money raised to objects not specified in the Constitution, is a violation of these fundamental principles, a breach of a well-defined trust, and a perversion of the high powers vested in the federal government for federal purposes only.

4th. *Because* such acts, considered in the light of a regulation of commerce, are equally liable to objection; since, although the power to regulate commerce may, like all other powers, be exercised so as to protect domestic manufactures, yet it is clearly distinguishable from a power to do so *eo nomine,* both in the nature of the thing and in the common acception of the terms; and because the confounding of them would lead to the most extravagant results, since the encouragement of

domestic industry implies an absolute control over all the interests, resources, and pursuits of a people, and is consistent with the idea of any other than a simple, consolidated government.

5th. *Because,* from the contemporaneous exposition of the Constitution in the numbers of the *Federalist,* (which is cited only because the Supreme Court has recognized its authority), it is clear that the power to regulate commerce was considered by the Convention as only incidentally connected with the encouragement of agriculture and manufactures; and because the power of laying imposts and duties on imports was not understood to justify in any case, a prohibition of foreign commodities, except as a means of extending commerce, by coercing foreign nations to a fair reciprocity in their intercourse with us, or for some *bona fide* commercial purpose.

6th. *Because,* whilst the power to protect manufactures is nowhere expressly granted to Congress, nor can be considered as necessary and proper to carry into effect any specified power, it seems to be expressly reserved to the states, by the 10th section of the 1st article of the Constitution.

7th. *Because* even admitting Congress to have a constitutional right to protect manufactures by the imposition of duties, or by regulations of commerce, designed principally for that purpose, yet a tariff of which the operation is grossly unequal and oppressive, is such an abuse of power as is incompatible with the principles of a free government and the great ends of civil society, justice, and equality of rights and protection.

8th. *Finally,* because South Carolina, from her climate, situation, and peculiar institutions, is, and must ever continue to be, wholly dependent upon agriculture and commerce, not only for her prosperity, but for her very existence as a state; because the valuable products of her soil—the blessings by which Divine Providence seems to have designed to compensate for the great disadvantages under which she suffers in other respects—are among the very few that can be cultivated with any profit by slave labor; and if, by the loss of her foreign commerce, these products should be confined to an inadequate market, the fate of this fertile state would be poverty and utter desolation; her citizens, in despair, would emigrate to more fortunate regions, and the whole frame and constitution of her civil policy be impaired and deranged, if not dissolved entirely.

Deeply impressed with these considerations, the representatives of the good people of this commonwealth, anxiously desiring to live in peace with their fellow-citizens, and to do all that in them lies to preserve and perpetuate the union of the states, and liberties of which it is the surest pledge, but feeling it to be their bounden duty to expose and resist all encroachments upon the true spirit of the Constitution, lest an apparant acquiescence in the system of protecting duties should be drawn into precedent—do, in the name of the commonwealth of South Carolina, claim to enter upon the Journal of the Senate their *protest* against it as unconstitutional, oppressive, and unjust.

136. THE CONSTITUTION OF A LYCEUM
1829

(*Old South Leaflets* No. 139)

The Lyceum movement was part of the general educational reform movement of the eighteen thirties. It was organized in 1826 by Josiah Holbrook of Massachusetts, and the various lyceums of New England were federated in 1831. In many respects similar to the Chautauqua movement of the late nineteenth and early twentieth century, the lyceums attracted to their platforms some of the most eminent intellectual leaders of the day. See, H. B. Adams, "Educational Extension in the United States," U. S. Commissioner of Education, *Report,* 1899–1900; J. S. Noffsinger, *Correspondence Schools, Lyceums, and Chautauquas.*

Constitution

Many Lyceums have adopted the following or similar articles for their Constitution:—
1. The objects of the Lyceum are the improvement of its members in useful knowledge and the advancement of Popular Education.
2. To effect these objects, they will hold meetings for reading, conversation, discussions, dissertations, illustrating the sciences, or other exercises which shall be thought expedient, and, as it is found convenient, will procure a cabinet consisting of books, apparatus for illustrating the sciences, plants, minerals, and other natural or artificial productions.
3. Any person may be Member of the Lyceum by paying into the treasury annually Two Dollars; and Twenty Dollars paid at any one time will entitle a person, his or her heirs or assigns, to one membership forever. Persons under eighteen years of age will be entitled to all the privileges of the Society, except voting, for one-half the annual sum above named. . . .

5. The delegates will meet delegates from other branches of the Lyceum in this county semi-annually, to adopt regulations for their general and mutual benefit, or to take measures to introduce uniformity and improvements into common schools, and to diffuse useful and practical knowledge generally through the community, particularly to form and aid a BOARD OF EDUCATION.
6. To raise the standard of common education, and to benefit the juvenile members of the Lyceum, a portion of the books procured shall be fitted to young minds; and teachers of schools may be permitted to use for the benefit of their pupils who are members of the Lyceum the apparatus and minerals under such restrictions as the association shall prescribe. . . .

RECOMMENDATIONS

The undersigned hereby express their opinion that popular education would be greatly advanced by measures to concentrate the views and efforts of those disposed to act in its behalf to different parts of the country.

That the formation of a Society would be the most direct and efficient measure to concentrate such views and efforts.

That the institution denominated the AMERICAN LYCEUM embraces in its plan the important objects of a National Society, for the advancement of popular education.

That it is highly desirable that an auxiliary to this Society, or a branch Lyceum, should be established in every town.

That some simple articles of apparatus are important to render Lyceums interesting, useful, and permanent, and that the articles proposed by MR. HOLBROOK are fitted to this object, and that a portion of them would be useful in district and other schools.

That a weekly meeting of teachers for us-ing apparatus, and other exercises in relation to their schools, would have a tendency to raise their qualifications and to increase the value of their services.

137. CRAIG ET. AL. V. THE STATE OF MISSOURI
4 Peters, 410
1830

Writ of error to the Supreme Court of the State of Missouri. This case concerned the constitutionality of an act of the legislature of Missouri, 27 June, 1821, to establish loan offices which were empowered to issue certificates to the amount of two hundred thousand dollars, which certificates were to be receivable at the treasury of the State of Missouri in discharge of taxes or debts due to the State and by all officers in the State in discharge of salaries and fees of office.

MARSHALL, C. J. . . . This brings us to the great question in the cause: Is the act of the Legislature of Missouri repugnant to the Constitution of the United States?

The counsel for the plaintiffs in error maintain that it is repugnant to the Constitution, because its object is the emission of bills of credit contrary to the express prohibition contained in the tenth section of the first article. . . . The clause in the Constitution which this act is supposed to violate is in these words: "No state shall emit bills of credit".

What is a bill of credit? What did the Constitution mean to forbid?

In its enlarged, and perhaps its literal sense, the term "bill of credit" may comprehend any instrument by which a State engages to pay money at a future day; thus including a certificate given for money borrowed. But the language of the Constitution itself, and the mischief to be prevented, which we know from the history of our country, equally limit the interpretation of the terms. . . . To "emit bills of credit" conveys to the mind the idea of issuing paper intended to circulate through the community for its ordinary purposes, as money, which paper is redeemable at a future day. This is the sense in which the terms have always been understood. . . .

What is the character of the certificates issued by authority of the act under consideration? What office are they to perform? Certificates signed by the auditor and treasurer of the State are to be issued by those officers to the amount of two hundred thousand dollars, of denominations not exceeding ten dollars nor less than fifty cents. The paper purports on its face to be receivable at the treasury, or at any loan-office of the State of Missouri, in discharge of taxes or debts due to the State. The law . . . also pledges the faith and funds of the State for their redemption.

It seems impossible to doubt the intention of the Legislature in passing this act, or to mistake the character of these certificates, or the office they were to perform. The denominations of the bills—from ten dollars to fifty cents—fitted them for the purpose of ordinary circulation and their reception in payment of taxes and debts to the government and to corporations, and of salaries and fees, would give them currency. They were to be put into circulation; that is, emitted by the government. . . .

But it is contended that though these certificates should be deemed bills of credit, according to the common acceptation of the term, they are not so in the sense of the Constitution because they are not made legal tender.

The Constitution itself furnishes no countenance to this distinction. The prohibition is general. It extends to all bills of credit, not to bills of a particular description. That tribunal must be bold indeed, which, without the aid of other explanatory words, could venture on this construction. It is the less admissible in this case, because the same clause of the Constitution contains a substantive prohibition to the enactment of tender laws. The Constitution, therefore, considers the emission of bills of credit and the enactment of tender laws as distinct operations, independent of each other, which may be separately performed. Both are forbidden. To sustain the one because it is not also the other; to say that bills of credit may be emitted if they be not made a tender in payment of debts, is, in effect, to expunge that distinct independent prohibition, and to read the clause as if it had been entirely omitted. We are not at liberty to do this. . . .

A majority of the court feels constrained to say that the consideration on which the note in this case was given is against the highest law of the land, and that the note itself is utterly void. In rendering judgement for the plaintiff the Court for the State of Missouri decided in favor of the validity of a law which is repugnant to the Constitution of the United States.

In the argument we have been reminded by one side of the dignity of a sovereign State; of the humiliation of her submitting herself to this tribunal; of the dangers which may result from inflicting a wound on that dignity; by the other, of the still superior dignity of the people of the United States, who have spoken their will in terms which we cannot misunderstand.

To these admonitions we can only answer, that if the exercise of that jurisdiction which has been imposed upon us by the Constitution and laws of the United States shall be calculated to bring on those dangers which have been indicated, or if it shall be indispensable to the preservation of the Union, and consequently, of the independence and liberty of these States, these are considerations which address themselves to those departments which may with perfect propriety be influenced by them. This department can listen only to the mandates of law, and can thread only that path which is marked out by duty.

The judgement of the Supreme Court of Missouri is reversed.

138. JACKSON'S VETO OF MAYSVILLE ROAD BILL
May 27, 1830

(Richardson, ed. *Messages and Papers,* Vol. II, p. 483 ff.)

President J. Q. Adams had supported a policy of internal improvements at national expense, but Jackson, nationalistic in many respects, subscribed to doctrines of narrow construction of this question. On the veto, see, W. MacDonald, *Jacksonian Democracy,* ch. viii; E. C. Mason, *The Veto Power,* sec. 83 ff.

MAY 27, 1830.
To the House of Representatives.

Gentlemen: I have maturely considered the bill proposing to authorize "a subscription of stock in the Maysville, Washington, Paris, and Lexington Turnpike Road Company," and now return the same to the House of Representatives, in which it originated, with my objections to its passage. . . .

The constitutional power of the Federal Government to construct or promote works of internal improvement presents itself in two points of view—the first as bearing upon the sovereignty of the States within whose limits their execution is contemplated, if jurisdiction of the territory which they may occupy be claimed as necessary to their preservation and use; the second as asserting the simple right to appropriate money from the National Treasury in aid of such works when undertaken by State authority, sur-

rendering the claim of jurisdiction. In the first view the question of power is an open one, and can be decided without the embarrassments attending the other, arising from the practice of the Government. Although frequently and strenuously attempted, the power to this extent has never been exercised by the Government in a single instance. It does not, in my opinion, possess it; and no bill, therefore, which admits it can receive my official sanction.

But in the other view of the power the question is differently situated. The ground taken at an early period of the Government was "that whenever money has been raised by the general authority and is to be applied to a particular measure, a question arises whether the particular measure be within the enumerated authorities vested in Congress. If it be, the money requisite for it may be applied to it; if not, no such application can be made." The document in which this principle was first advanced is of deservedly high authority, and should be held in grateful remembrance for its immediate agency in rescuing the country from much existing abuse and for its conservative effect upon some of the most valuable principles of the Constitution. The symmetry and purity of the Government would doubtless have been better preserved if this restriction of the power of appropriation could have been maintained without weakening its ability to fulfill the general objects of its institution, an effect so likely to attend its admission, notwithstanding its apparent fitness, that every subsequent Administration of the Government, embracing a period of thirty out of the forty-two years of its existence, has adopted a more enlarged construction of the power. It is not my purpose to detain you by a minute recital of the acts which sustain this assertion, but it is proper that I should notice some of the most prominent in order that the reflections which they suggest to my mind may be better understood. . . .

The bill before me does not call for a more definite opinion upon the particular circumstances which will warrant appropriations of money by Congress to aid works of internal improvement, for although the extension of the power to apply money beyond that of carrying into effect the object for which it is appropriated has, as we have seen, been long claimed and exercised by the Federal Government, yet such grants have always been professedly under the control of the general principle that the works which might be thus aided should be "of a general, not local, national, not State," character. A disregard of this distinction would of necessity lead to the subversion of the federal system. That even this is an unsafe one, arbitrary in its nature, and liable, consequently, to great abuses, is too obvious to require the confirmation of experience. It is, however, sufficiently definite and imperative to my mind to forbid my approbation of any bill having the character of the one under consideration. I have given to its provisions all the reflection demanded by a just regard for the interests of those of our fellow-citizens who have desired its passage, and by the respect which is due to a coördinate branch of the Government, but I am not able to view it in any other light than as a measure of purely local character; or, if it can be considered national, that no further distinction between the appropriate duties of the General and State Governments need be attempted, for there can be no local interest that may not with equal propriety be

denominated national. It has no connection with any established system of improvements; is exclusively within the limits of a State, starting at a point on the Ohio River and running out 60 miles to an interior town, and even as far as the State is interested conferring partial instead of general advantages.

Considering the magnitude and importance of the power, and the embarrassments to which, from the very nature of the thing, its exercise must necessarily be subjected, the real friends of internal improvement ought not to be willing to confide it to accident and chance. . . .

In the other view of the subject, and the only remaining one which it is my intention to present at this time, is involved the expediency of embarking in a system of internal improvement without a previous amendment of the Constitution explaining and defining the precise powers of the Federal Government over it. Assuming the right to appropriate money to aid in the construction of national works to be warranted by the contemporaneous and continued exposition of the Constitution, its insufficiency for the successful prosecution of them must be admitted by all candid minds. If we look to usage to define the extent of the right, that will be found so variant and embracing so much that has been overruled as to involve the whole subject in great uncertainty and to render the execution of our respective duties in relation to it replete with difficulty and embarrassment. It is in regard to such works and the acquisition of additional territory that the practice obtained its first footing. In most, if not all, other disputed questions of appropriation the construction of the Constitution may be regarded as unsettled if the right to apply money in the enumerated cases is placed on the ground of usage. . . .

If it be the wish of the people that the construction of roads and canals should be conducted by the Federal Government, it is not only highly expedient, but indispensably necessary, that a previous amendment of the Constitution, delegating the necessary power and defining and restricting its exercise with reference to the sovereignty of the States, should be made. Without it nothing extensively useful can be effected. The right to exercise as much jurisdiction as is necessary to preserve the works and to raise funds by the collection of tolls to keep them in repair can not be dispensed with. . . .

139. THE SPOILS OF VICTORY
Extract from a Speech by Mr. Marcy
1831

(Niles' Register, Vol. XLIII, p. 8, September 1, 1832)

In the course of the debate on Van Buren's appointment as Minister to England, Clay referred to the spoils system in New York and alleged that Van Buren had introduced this political principle into national politics. Mr. Marcy, in defending Van Buren, announced the notorious doctrine that "to the victor belong the spoils." Though the spoils system has been traced back to the Federalist machine in New York politics, this speech of Marcy's, observes Dr. Alexander, "forever . . . confirmed the belief that Van Buren was an inveterate spoilsman." For the origins of the spoils system, see H. L. McBain, *De Witt Clinton and the Origin of the Spoils System in New York;* D. R. Fox, *The Decline of Aristocracy in the Politics of New York.*

Mr. *Marcy,* one of the senators of the United States from New York, in the course of the debate on the nomination of Mr. Van Buren said—

"It may be, sir, that the politicians of New York are not so fastidious as some gentlemen are, as to disclosing the principles on which they act. They boldly *preach* what they *practice.* When they are contending for *victory,* they avow their intention of enjoying the fruits of it. If they are defeated, they expect to retire from office. If they are successful, they claim, as a matter of right, the advantages of success. They see nothing wrong in the rule that to the VICTOR belongs the spoils of the ENEMY."

140. CHEROKEE NATION v. GEORGIA
5 Peters, 1
1831

Suit for injunction to restrain the State of Georgia. In 1827 the Cherokee Indians, occupying extensive lands in northwestern Georgia, set up a government and declared themselves an independent nation. Thereupon the legislature of Georgia passed resolutions alleging ownership of all Cherokee territory and extending the laws of Georgia over the Cherokee Indians, and annulling all laws, usages and customs of the Indians. The Indians appealed to the Supreme Court for an injunction to prevent the execution of these laws. The opinion of Marshall is notable for its definition of the legal relations of the Indians with the United States government: the Indians constituted not foreign nations but domestic dependent nations in a state of pupilage. See, Beveridge, *Marshall,* Vol. IV, p. 539 ff.; A. Abel, "History of Events Resulting in Indian Consolidation West of the Mississippi River," in Am. Hist. Assoc. *Reports,* 1906, Vol. I; and references in Docs. No. 141–142.

MARSHALL, C. J. This bill is brought by the Cherokee nation, praying an injunction to restrain the state of Georgia from the ex-

ecution of certain laws of that state, which, as is alleged, go directly to annihilate the Cherokee as a political society, and to seize for the use of Georgia, the lands of the nation which have been assured to them by the United States, in solemn treaties repeatedly made and still in force.

If courts were permitted to indulge their sympathies, a case better calculated to excite them can scarcely be imagined. A people, once numerous, powerful, and truly independent, found by our ancestors in the quiet and uncontrolled possession of an ample domain, gradually sinking beneath our superior policy, our arts and our arms, have yielded their lands, by successive treaties, each of which contains a solemn guarantee of the residue, until they retain no more of their formerly extensive territory than is deemed necessary to their comfortable subsistence. To preserve this remnant, the present application is made.

Before we can look into the merits of the case, a preliminary inquiry presents itself.

Has this court jurisdiction of the cause? The third article of the constitution describes the extent of the judicial power. The second section closes an enumeration of the cases to which it is extended, with "controversies between a state or citizens thereof, and foreign states, citizens or subjects." A subsequent clause of the same section gives the supreme court original jurisdiction, in all cases in which a state shall be a party. The party defendant may then unquestionably be sued in this court. May the plaintiff sue in it? Is the Cherokee nation a foreign state, in the sense in which that term is used in the constitution? The counsel for the plaintiffs have maintained the affirmative of this proposition with great earnestness and ability. So much of the argument as was intended to prove the character of the Cherokees as a state, as a distinct political society, separated from others, capable of managing its own affairs and governing itself, has in the opinion of a majority of the judges, been completely successful. They have been uniformly treated as a state, from the settlement of our country. The numerous treaties made with them by the United States, recognise them as a people capable of maintaining the relations of peace and war, of being responsible in their political character for any violation of their engagements, or for any aggression committed on the citizens of the United States, by any individual of their community. Laws have been enacted in the spirit of these treaties. The acts of our government plainly recognise the Cherokee nation as a state, and the courts are bound by those acts.

A question of much more difficulty remains. Do the Cherokees constitute a foreign state in the sense of the constitution? The counsel have shown conclusively, that they are not a state of the Union, and have insisted that, individually, they are aliens, not owing allegiance to the United States. An aggregate of aliens composing a state must, they say, be a foreign state; each individual being foreign, the whole must be foreign.

This argument is imposing, but we must examine it more closely, before we yield to it. The condition of the Indians in relation to the United States is, perhaps, unlike that of any other two people in existence. In general, nations not owing a common allegiance, are foreign to each other. The term foreign nation is, with strict propriety, applicable by either to the other. But the relation of the Indians to the United States is marked by peculiar and cardinal distinctions which exist nowhere else. The Indian territory is admitted to compose a part of the United States. In all our maps, geographical treaties, histories and laws, it is so considered. In all our intercourse with foreign nations, in our commercial regulations, in any attempt at intercourse between Indians and foreign nations, they are considered as within the jurisdictional limits of the United States, subject to many of those restraints which are imposed upon our own citizens. They acknowledge themselves, in their treaties, to be under the protection of the United States; they admit, that the United States shall have the sole and exclusive right of regulating the trade with them, and managing all their affairs as they think proper; and the Cherokees in particular were allowed by the treaty of Hopewell, which preceded the constitution, "to send a deputy of their choice, whenever they think fit, to congress." Treaties were made with some tribes, by the state of New York, under a then unsettled construction of the confederation, by which they ceded all their lands to that state, taking back a limited grant to themselves, in which they admit their dependence. Though the Indians are acknowledged to have an unquestionable, and heretofore unquestioned, right to the lands they occupy, until that right shall be extinguished by a voluntary cession to our government; yet it may well be doubted, whether those tribes which reside within the acknowledged boundaries of the United States can, with accuracy, be denominated foreign nations. They may, more correctly, perhaps, be denominated domestic dependent nations. They occupy a territory to which we assert a title independent of their will, which must take effect in point of possession, when their right of possession ceases. Meanwhile, they are in a state of pupilage; their relation to the United States resembles that of a ward to his guardian. They look to our government for protection; rely upon its kindness and its power; appeal to it for relief to their wants; and address the president as their great father. They and their country are considered by foreign nations, as well as by ourselves, as being so completely under the sovereignty and dominion of the United States, that any attempt to acquire their lands, or to form a political connection with them would be considered by all as an invasion of our territory and an act of hostility. These considerations go far to support the opinion, that the framers of our constitution had not the Indian tribes in view, when they opened the courts of the Union to controversies between a state or the citizens thereof and foreign states.

In considering this subject, the habits and usages of the Indians, in their intercourse with their white neighbors, ought not to be entirely disregarded. At the time the constitution was framed, the idea of appealing to an American court of justice for an assertion of right or a redress of wrong, had perhaps never entered the mind of an Indian or of his tribe. Their appeal was to the tomahawk, or to the government. This was well understood by the statesmen who framed the constitution of the United States, and might furnish some reason for omitting to enumerate them among the parties who might sue in the courts of the Union. Be this as it may, the peculiar relations between the United States and the Indians occupying our territory are such, that we should feel much difficulty in considering them as designated by the term foreign state, were there no other part of the constitution which might shed light on the meaning of these words. But we think that in construing them, considerable aid is furnished by that clause in the eighth section of the third article, which empowers congress to "regulate commerce with foreign nations, and among the several states, and with the Indian tribes." In this clause, they are as clearly contradistinguished, by a name appropriate to themselves, from foreign nations, as from the several states composing the Union. They are designated by a distinct appellation; and as this appellation can be applied to neither of the others, neither can the application distinguishing either of the others be, in fair construction, applied to them. The objects to which the power of regulating commerce might be directed, are divided into three distinct classes—foreign nations, the several states, and Indian tribes. When forming this article, the convention considered them as

entirely distinct. We cannot assume that the distinction was lost, in framing a subsequent article, unless there be something in its language to authorize the assumption.

The counsel for the plaintiffs contend, that the words "Indian tribes" were introduced into the article, empowering congress to regulate commerce, for the purpose of removing those doubts in which the management of Indian affairs was involved by the language of the ninth article of the confederation. Intending to give the whole of managing those affairs to the government about to be instituted, the convention conferred it explicitly; and omitted those qualifications which embarrassed the exercise of it, as granted in the confederation. This may be admitted, without weakening the construction which has been intimated. Had the Indian tribes been foreign nations, in the view of the convention, this exclusive power of regulating intercourse with them might have been, and, most probably, would have been, specifically given, in language indicating that idea, not in language contradistinguishing them from foreign nations. Congress might have been empowered "to regulate commerce with foreign nations, including the Indian tribes, and among the several states." This language would have suggested itself to statesmen who considered the Indian tribes as foreign nations, and were yet desirous of mentioning them particularly.

It has been also said, that the same words have not necessarily the same meaning attached to them, when found in different parts of the same instrument; their meaning is controlled by the context. This is undoubtedly true. In common language, the same word has various meanings, and the peculiar sense in which it is used in any sentence, is to be determined by the context. This may not be equally true with respect to proper names. "Foreign nations" is a general term, the application of which to Indian tribes, when used in the American constitution, is, at best, extremely questionable. In one article, in which a power is given to be exercised in regard to foreign nations generally, and to the Indian tribes particularly, they are mentioned as separate, in terms clearly contradistinguishing them from each other. We perceive plainly, that the constitution, in this article, does not comprehend Indian tribes in the general term "foreign nations;" not, we presume, because a tribe may not be a nation, but because it is not foreign to the United States. When, afterwards, the term "foreign state" is introduced, we cannot impute to the convention, the intention to desert its former meaning, and to comprehend Indian tribes within it, unless the context force that construction on us. We find nothing in the context, and nothing in the subject of the article, which leads to it.

The court has bestowed its best attention on this question, and, after mature deliberation, the majority is of opinion, that an Indian tribe or nation within the United States is not a foreign state, in the sense of the constitution, and cannot maintain an action in the courts of the United States.

A serious additional objection exists to the jurisdiction of the court. Is the matter of the bill the proper subject for judicial inquiry and decision? It seeks to restrain a state from the forcible exercise of legislative power over a neighboring people, asserting their independence; their right to which the state denies. On several of the matters alleged in the bill, for example, on the laws making it criminal to exercise the usual powers of self-government in their own country, by the Cherokee nation, this court cannot interpose; at least, in the form in which those matters are presented.

That part of the bill which respects the land occupied by the Indians, and prays the aid of the court to protect their possession, may be more doubtful. The mere question of right might, perhaps, be decided by this court, in a proper case, with proper parties. But the court is asked to do more than decide on the title. The bill requires us to control the legislature of Georgia, and to restrain the exertion of its physical force. The propriety of such an interposition by the court may be well questioned; it savors too much of the exercise of political power, to be within the proper province of the judicial department. But the opinion on the point respecting parties makes it unnecessary to decide this question.

If it be true, that the Cherokee nation have rights, this is not the tribunal in which those rights are to be asserted. If it be true, that wrongs have been inflicted, and that still greater are to be apprehended, this is not the tribunal which can redress the past or prevent the future. The motion for an injunction is denied.

141. WORCESTER v. GEORGIA
6 Peters, 515
1832

Error to the Superior Court for the County of Gwinnett, Georgia. The facts are stated in the opinion below. It is of this opinion that President Jackson is reputed to have remarked: "John Marshall has made his opinion, now let him enforce it." Georgia was so incensed at judicial interference with what she considered her sovereign affairs that she refused to appear before the Court in this case, and refused likewise to obey the mandate of the Court. For the historical background of the case, see Beveridge, *Marshall*, Vol. IV, p. 547 ff.; E. M. Coulter, *Short History of Georgia*, ch. xvii; W. Lumpkin, *Removal of the Cherokee Indians from Georgia*, 2 vols.; U. B. Phillips, *Georgia and State Rights*, p. 66 ff. See also, *Cherokee Nation* v. *State of Georgia*, Doc. No. 140.

MARSHALL, C. J. This cause, in every point of view in which it can be placed, is of the deepest interest.

The defendant is a State, a member of the Union, which has exercised the powers of government over a people who deny its jurisdiction, and are under the protection of the United States.

The plaintiff is a citizen of the State of Vermont, condemned to hard labor for four years in the penitentiary of Georgia under color of an act which he alleges to be repugnant to the Constitution, laws, and treaties of the United States.

The legislative power of a State, the controlling power of the Constitution and laws of the United States, the rights, if they have any, the political existence of a once numerous and powerful people, the personal liberty of a citizen, all are involved in the subject now to be considered. . . .

We must inquire and decide whether the act of the Legislature of Georgia under which the plaintiff in error has been prosecuted and condemned, be consistent with, or repugnant to the Constitution, laws and treaties of the United States.

It has been said at the bar that the acts of the Legislature of Georgia seize on the whole Cherokee country, parcel it out among the neighboring counties of the State, extend her code over the whole country, abolish its institutions and its laws, and annihilate its political existence.

If this be the general effect of the system, let us inquire into the effect of the particular statute and section on which the indictment is founded.

It enacts that "all white persons, residing within the limits of the Cherokee Nation on the 1st day of March next, or at any time thereafter, without a licence or permit from his excellency the governor . . . and who shall not have taken the oath hereinafter required, shall be guilty of a high misdemeanor, and, upon conviction thereof, shall be punished by confinement to the penitentiary at hard labor for a term not less than four years." . . .

The extraterritorial power of every Legislature being limited in its action to its own citizens or subjects, the very passage of this act is an assertion of jurisdiction over the Cherokee Nation, and of the rights and powers consequent on jurisdiction.

The first step, then, in the inquiry which the Constitution and the laws impose on this court, is an examination of the rightfulness of this claim. . . .

From the commencement of our government Congress has passed acts to regulate trade and intercourse with the Indians; which treat them as nations, respect their rights, and manifest a firm purpose to afford that protection which treaties stipulate. All these acts, and especially that of 1802, which is still in force, manifestly consider the several Indian nations as distinct political communities, having territorial boundaries, within which their authority is exclusive, and having

a right to all the lands within those boundaries, which is not only acknowledged, but guaranteed by the United States. . . .

The Cherokee Nation, then, is a distinct community, occupying its own territory, with boundaries accurately described, in which the laws of Georgia can have no force, and which the citizens of Georgia have no right to enter but with the assent of the Cherokees themselves or in conformity with treaties and with the acts of Congress. The whole intercourse between the United States and this nation is, by our Constitution and laws, vested in the government of the United States.

The act of the State of Georgia under which the plaintiff in error was prosecuted is consequently void, and the judgement a nullity. . . . The Acts of Georgia are repugnant to the Constitution, laws, and treaties of the United States.

They interfere forcibly with the relations established between the United States and the Cherokee Nation, the regulation of which according to the settled principles of our Constitution, are committed exclusively to the government of the Union.

They are in direct hostility with treaties, repeated in a succession of years, which mark out the boundary that separates the Cherokee country from Georgia; guarantee to them all the land within their boundary; solemnly pledge the faith of the United States to restrain their citizens from trespassing on it; and recognize the preexisting power of the nation to govern itself.

They are in equal hostility with the acts of Congress for regulating this intercourse, and giving effect to the treaties.

The forcible seizure and abduction of the plaintiff, who was residing in the nation with its permission, and by authority of the President of the United States, is also a violation of the acts which authorize the chief magistrate to exercise this authority. . . .

Judgement reversed.

142. REMOVAL OF SOUTHERN INDIANS TO INDIAN TERRITORY
Extract from Jackson's Seventh Annual Message to Congress
December 7, 1835
(Richardson, ed. *Messages and Papers*, Vol. III, p. 171 ff.)

Georgia's Indian policy, and the refusal of Jackson to sustain the Supreme Court in its in- terpretation of the rights of the Indians, led to the plan of removing the remaining Creeks,

Cherokees, and other Indian tribes of the South to a reservation west of the Mississippi. This policy had been outlined by Jackson in his first message to Congress, and in 1830 Congress had appropriated half a million dollars for the removal of the Indians to the west. In 1834 Congress created a special Indian Territory, and by a treaty of December 29, 1835, the Indians surrendered their lands east of the Mississippi in return for five million dollars, the expenses of removal, and land. See G. Foreman, *Indian Removal;* G. Foreman, *Indians and Pioneers,* ch. xxi; W. MacDonald, *Jacksonian Democracy,* ch. x.

WASHINGTON, *December 7, 1835.*

. . . The plan of removing the aboriginal people who yet remain within the settled portions of the United States to the country west of the Mississippi River approaches its consummation. It was adopted on the most mature consideration of the condition of this race, and ought to be persisted in till the object is accomplished, and prosecuted with as much vigor as a just regard to their circumstances will permit, and as fast as their consent can be obtained. All preceding experiments for the improvement of the Indians have failed. It seems now to be an established fact that they can not live in contact with a civilized community and prosper. Ages of fruitless endeavors have at length brought us to a knowledge of this principle of intercommunication with them. The past we can not recall, but the future we can provide for. Independently of the treaty stipulations into which we have entered with the various tribes for the usufructuary rights they have ceded to us, no one can doubt the moral duty of the Government of the United States to protect and if possible to preserve and perpetuate the scattered remnants of this race which are left within our borders. In the discharge of this duty an extensive region in the West has been assigned for their permanent residence. It has been divided into districts and allotted among them. Many have already removed and others are preparing to go, and with the exception of two small bands living in Ohio and Indiana, not exceeding 1,500 persons, and of the Cherokees, all the tribes on the east side of the Mississippi, and extending from Lake Michigan to Florida, have entered into engagements which will lead to their transplantation.

The plan for their removal and reëstablishment is founded upon the knowledge we have gained of their character and habits, and has been dictated by a spirit of enlarged liberality. A territory exceeding in extent that relinquished has been granted to each tribe. Of its climate, fertility, and capacity to support an Indian population the representations are highly favorable. To these districts the Indians are removed at the expense of the United States, and with certain supplies of clothing, arms, ammunition, and other indispensable articles; they are also furnished gratuitously with provisions for the period of a year after their arrival at their new homes. In that time, from the nature of the country and of the products raised by them, they can subsist themselves by agricultural labor, if they choose to resort to that mode of life; if they do not they are upon the skirts of the great prairies, where countless herds of buffalo roam, and a short time suffices to adapt their own habits to the changes which a change of the animals destined for their food may require. Ample arrangements have also been made for the support of schools; in some instances council houses and churches are to be erected, dwellings constructed for the chiefs, and mills for common use. Funds have been set apart for the maintenance of the poor; the most necessary mechanical arts have been introduced, and blacksmiths, gunsmiths, wheelwrights, millwrights, etc., are supported among them. Steel and iron, and sometimes salt, are purchased for them, and plows and other farming utensils, domestic animals, looms, spinning wheels, cards, etc., are presented to them. And besides these beneficial arrangements, annuities are in all cases paid, amounting in some instances to more than $30 for each individual of the tribe, and in all cases sufficiently great, if justly divided and prudently expended, to enable them, in addition to their own exertions, to live comfortably. And as a stimulus for exertion, it is now provided by law that "in all cases of the appointment of interpreters or other persons employed for the benefit of the Indians a preference shall be given to persons of Indian descent, if such can be found who are properly qualified for the discharge of the duties."

Such are the arrangements for the physical comfort and for the moral improvement of the Indians. The necessary measures for their political advancement and for their separation from our citizens have not been neglected. The pledge of the United States has been given by Congress that the country destined for the residence of this people shall be forever "secured and guaranteed to them." A country west of Missouri and Arkansas has been assigned to them, into which the white settlements are not to be pushed. No political communities can be formed in that extensive region, except those which are established by the Indians themselves or by the United States for them and with their concurrence. A barrier has thus been raised for their protection against the encroachment of our citizens, and guarding the Indians as far as possible from those evils which have brought them to their present condition. Summary authority has been given by law to destroy all ardent spirits found in their country, without waiting the doubtful result and slow process of a legal seizure. I consider the absolute and unconditional interdiction of this article among these people as the first and great step in their melioration. Halfway measures will answer no purpose. These can not successfully contend against the cupidity of the seller and the overpowering appetite of the buyer. And the destructive effects of the traffic are marked in every page of the history of our Indian intercourse. . . .

143. SOUTH CAROLINA ORDINANCE OF NULLIFICATION
November 24, 1832
(*Statutes at Large of South Carolina,* Vol. I, p. 329 ff.)

The tariff of July 14, 1832 was only less unpopular than the "tariff of abominations" of 1828. The legislature of South Carolina met in special session in October, 1832 and provided for a convention to consider the tariff: the convention met in November and adopted the Ordinance of Nullification. For Jackson's Proclamation, see Doc. No. 144. See, D. F. Houston, *Critical Study of Nullification in South Carolina;* C. S. Boucher, *Nullification Movement in South Carolina;* J. G. Van Deusen, *Economic Basis of Disunion in South Carolina;* H. Von Holst, *Calhoun;* G. Hunt, *Calhoun;* J. S. Bassett, *Andrew Jackson,* Vol. II; J. Parton, *Andrew Jackson,* Vol. III; C. Bowers, *Party Battles of the Jackson Period,* ch. x.

An Ordinance to Nullify certain acts of the Congress of the United States, purporting to be laws laying duties and imposts on the importation of foreign commodities.

Whereas the Congress of the United States, by various acts, purporting to be acts laying duties and imposts on foreign imports, but in reality intended for the protection of domestic manufactures, and the giving of bounties to classes and individuals engaged in particular employments, at the expense and to the injury and oppression of other classes and individuals, and by wholly exempting from taxation certain foreign commodities, such as are not produced or manufactured in the United States, to afford a pretext for imposing higher and excessive duties on articles similar to those intended to be protected, hath exceeded its just powers under the Constitution, which confers on it no authority to afford such protection, and hath violated the true meaning and intent of the Constitution, which provides for equality in imposing the burthens of taxation upon the several States and portions of the Confederacy: *And whereas* the said Congress, exceeding its just power to impose taxes and collect revenue for the purpose of effecting and accomplishing the specific objects and purposes which the Constitution of the United States authorizes it to effect and accomplish, hath raised and collected unnecessary revenue for objects unauthorized by the Constitution:—

We, therefore, the people of the State of South Carolina in Convention assembled, do declare and ordain, . . . That the several acts and parts of acts of the Congress of the United States, purporting to be laws for the imposing of duties and imposts on the importation of foreign commodities, . . . and, more especially, . . . [the tariff acts of 1828 and 1832] . . . , are unauthorized by the Constitution of the United States, and violate the true meaning and intent thereof, and are null, void, and no law, nor binding upon this State, its officers or citizens; and all promises, contracts, and obligations, made or entered into, or to be made or entered into, with purpose to secure the duties imposed by the said acts, and all judicial proceedings which shall be hereafter had in affirmance thereof, are and shall be held utterly null and void.

And it is further Ordained, That it shall not be lawful for any of the constituted authorities, whether of this State or of the United States, to enforce the payment of duties imposed by the said acts within the limits of this State; but it shall be the duty of the Legislature to adopt such measures and pass such acts as may be necessary to give full effect to this Ordinance, and to prevent the enforcement and arrest the operation of the said acts and parts of acts of the Congress of the United States within the limits of this State, from and after the 1st day of February next, . . .

And it is further Ordained, That in no case of law or equity, decided in the courts of this State, wherein shall be drawn in question the authority of this ordinance, or the validity of such act or acts of the Legislature as may be passed for the purpose of giving effect thereto, or the validity of the aforesaid acts of Congress, imposing duties, shall any appeal be taken or allowed to the Supreme Court of the United States, nor shall any copy of the record be printed or allowed for that purpose; and if any such appeal shall be attempted to be taken, the courts of this State shall proceed to execute and enforce their judgments, according to the laws and usages of the State, without reference to such attempted appeal, and the person or persons attempting to take such appeal may be dealt with as for a contempt of the court.

And it is further Ordained, That all persons now holding any office of honor, profit, or trust, civil or military, under this State, (members of the Legislature excepted), shall, within such time, and in such manner as the Legislature shall prescribe, take an oath well and truly to obey, execute, and enforce, this Ordinance, and such act or acts of the Legislature as may be passed in pursuance thereof, according to the true intent and meaning of the same; and on the neglect or omission of any such person or persons so to do, his or their office or offices shall be forthwith vacated, . . . and no person hereafter elected to any office of honor, profit, or trust, civil or military, (members of the Legislature excepted), shall, until the Legislature shall otherwise provide and direct, enter on the execution of his office, . . . until he shall, in like manner, have taken a similar oath; and no juror shall be empannelled in any of the courts of this State, in any cause in which shall be in question this Ordinance, or any act of the Legislature passed in pursuance thereof, unless he shall first, in addition to the usual oath, have taken an oath that he will well and truly obey, execute, and enforce this Ordinance, and such act or acts of the Legislature as may be passed to carry the same into operation and effect, according to the true intent and meaning thereof.

And we, the People of South Carolina, to the end that it may be fully understood by the Government of the United States, and the people of the co-States, that we are determined to maintain this, our Ordinance and Declaration, at every hazard, *Do further Declare* that we will not submit to the application of force, on the part of the Federal Government, to reduce this State to obedience; but that we will consider the passage, by Congress, of any act . . . to coerce the State, shut up her ports, destroy or harass her commerce, or to enforce the acts hereby declared to be null and void, otherwise than through the civil tribunals of the country, as inconsistent with the longer continuance of South Carolina in the Union: and that the people of this State will thenceforth hold themselves absolved from all further obligation to maintain or preserve their political connexion with the people of the other States, and will forthwith proceed to organize a separate Government, and do all other acts and things which sovereign and independent States may of right to do.

144. JACKSON'S PROCLAMATION TO THE PEOPLE OF SOUTH CAROLINA
December 10, 1832

(Richardson, ed. *Messages and Papers*, Vol. II, p. 640 ff.)

Jackson's Proclamation was primarily concerned with the constitutional issues of nullification. January 16, 1833 Jackson reported to Congress on nullification and presented concrete recommendations for action. See, Richardson, *Messages and Papers,* Vol. II, p. 610 ff. For references, see Doc. No. 143.

Whereas a convention assembled in the State of South Carolina have passed an ordinance by which they declare "that the several acts and parts of acts of the Congress of the United States purporting to be laws for the imposing of duties and imposts on the importation of foreign commodities, . . . are unauthorized by the Constitution of the United States, and violate the true meaning and intent thereof, and are null and void and no law," nor binding on the citizens of that State or its officers; and by the said ordinance it is further declared to be unlawful for any of the constituted authorities of the State or of the United States to enforce the payment of the duties imposed by the said acts within the same State, and that it is the duty of the legislature to pass such laws as may be necessary to give full effect to the said ordinance; and

Whereas by the said ordinance it is further ordained that in no case of law or equity decided in the courts of said State wherein shall be drawn in question the validity of the said ordinance, or of the acts of the legislature that may be passed to give it effect, or of the said laws of the United States, no appeal shall be allowed to the Supreme Court of the United States, nor shall any copy of the record be permitted or allowed for that purpose, and that any person attempting to take such appeal shall be punished as for contempt of court; and . . .

Whereas the said ordinance prescribes to the people of South Carolina a course of conduct in direct violation of their duty as citizens of the United States, contrary to the laws of their country, subversive of its Constitution, and having for its object the destruction of the Union—

To preserve this bond of our political existence from destruction, to maintain inviolate this state of national honor and prosperity, and to justify the confidence my fellow-citizens have reposed in me, I, Andrew Jackson, President of the United States, have thought proper to issue this my proclamation, stating my views of the Constitution and laws applicable to the measures adopted by the convention of South Carolina and to the reasons they have put forth to sustain them,

declaring the course which duty will require me to pursue, and, appealing to the understanding and patriotism of the people, warn them of the consequences that must inevitably result from an observance of the dictates of the convention. . . .

The ordinance is founded, not on the indefeasible right of resisting acts which are plainly unconstitutional and too oppressive to be endured, but on the strange position that any one State may not only declare an act of Congress void, but prohibit its execution; that they may do this consistently with the Constitution; that the true construction of that instrument permits a State to retain its place in the Union and yet be bound by no other of its laws than those it may choose to consider as constitutional. It is true, they add, that to justify this abrogation of a law it must be palpably contrary to the Constitution; but it is evident that to give the right of resisting laws of that description, coupled with the uncontrolled right to decide what laws deserve that character, is to give the power of resisting all laws; for as by the theory there is no appeal, the reasons alleged by the State, good or bad, must prevail. If it should be said that public opinion is a sufficient check against the abuse of this power, it may be asked why it is not deemed a sufficient guard against the passage of an unconstitutional act by Congress? There is, however, a restraint in this last case which makes the assumed power of a State more indefensible, and which does not exist in the other. There are two appeals from an unconstitutional act passed by Congress—one to the judiciary, the other to the people and the States. There is no appeal from the State decision in theory, and the practical illustration shows that the courts are closed against an application to review it, both judges and jurors being sworn to decide in its favor. But reasoning on this subject is superfluous when our social compact, in express terms, declares that the laws of the United States, its Constitution, and treaties made under it are the supreme law of the land, and, for greater caution, adds "that the judges in every State shall be bound thereby, anything in the constitution or laws of any State to the contrary notwithstanding." And it may be asserted without fear of refutation that no federative government could exist without a similar provision. Look for a moment to the consequence. If South Carolina considers the revenue laws unconstitutional and has a right to prevent their execution in the port of Charleston, there would be a clear constitutional objection to their collection in every other port; and no revenue could be collected anywhere, for all imposts must be equal. It is no answer to repeat that an unconstitutional law is no law so long as the question of its legality is to be decided by the State itself, for every law operating injuriously upon any local interest will be perhaps thought, and certainly represented, as unconstitutional, and, as has been shown, there is no appeal.

If this doctrine had been established at an earlier day, the Union would have been dissolved in its infancy. The excise law in Pennsylvania, the embargo and nonintercourse law in the Eastern States, the carriage tax in Virginia, were all deemed unconstitutional, and were more unequal in their operation than any of the laws now complained of; but, fortunately, none of those States discovered that they had the right now claimed by South Carolina. The war into which we were forced to support the dignity of the nation and the rights of our citizens might have ended in defeat and disgrace, instead of victory and honor, if the States who supposed it a ruinous and unconstitutional measure had thought they possessed the right of nullifying the act by which it was declared and denying supplies for its prosecution. Hardly and unequally as those measures bore upon several members of the Union, to the legislatures of none did this efficient and peaceable remedy, as it is called, suggest itself. The discovery of this important feature in our Constitution was reserved to the present day. To the statesmen of South Carolina belongs the invention, and upon the citizens of that State will unfortunately fall the evils of reducing it to practice.

If the doctrine of a State veto upon the laws of the Union carries with it internal evidence of its impracticable absurdity, our constitutional history will also afford abundant proof that it would have been repudiated with indignation had it been proposed to form a feature in our Government.

Our present Constitution was formed . . . in vain if this fatal doctrine prevails. It was

formed for important objects that are announced in the preamble, made in the name and by the authority of the people of the United States, whose delegates framed and whose conventions approved it. The most important among these objects—that which is placed first in rank, on which all the others rest—is *"to form a more perfect union."* Now, is it possible that even if there were no express provision giving supremacy to the Constitution and laws of the United States over those of the States, can it be conceived that an instrument made for the purpose of *"forming a more perfect union"* than that of the Confederation could be so constructed by the assembled wisdom of our country as to substitute for that Confederation a form of government dependent for its existence on the local interest, the party spirit, of a State, or of a prevailing faction in a State? Every man of plain, unsophisticated understanding who hears the question will give such an answer as will preserve the Union. Metaphysical subtlety, in pursuit of an impracticable theory, could alone have devised one that is calculated to destroy it.

I consider, then, the power to annul a law of the United States, assumed by one State, *incompatible with the existence of the Union, contradicted expressly by the letter of the Constitution, unauthorized by its spirit, inconsistent with every principle on which it was founded, and destructive of the great object for which it was formed.*

After this general view of the leading principle, we must examine the particular application of it which is made in the ordinance.

The preamble rests its justification on these grounds: It assumes as a fact that the obnoxious laws, although they purport to be laws for raising revenue, were in reality intended for the protection of manufactures, which purpose it asserts to be unconstitutional; that the operation of these laws is unequal; that the amount raised by them is greater than is required by the wants of the Government; and, finally, that the proceeds are to be applied to objects unauthorized by the Constitution. These are the only causes alleged to justify an open opposition to the laws of the country and a threat of seceding from the Union if any attempt should be made to enforce them. The first virtually acknowledges that the law in question was passed under a power expressly given by the Constitution to lay and collect imposts; but its constitutionality is drawn in question from the *motives* of those who passed it. However apparent this purpose may be in the present case, nothing can be more dangerous than to admit the position that an unconstitutional purpose entertained by the members who assent to a law enacted under a constitutional power shall make that law void. For how is that purpose to be ascertained? Who is to make the scrutiny? How often may bad purposes be falsely imputed, in how many cases are they concealed by false professions, in how many is no declaration of motive made? Admit this doctrine, and you give to the States an uncontrolled right to decide, and every law may be annulled under this pretext. If, therefore, the absurd and dangerous doctrine should be admitted that a State may annul an unconstitutional law, or one that it deems such, it will not apply to the present case.

The next objection is that the laws in question operate unequally. This objection may be made with truth to every law that has been or can be passed. The wisdom of man never yet contrived a system of taxation that would operate with perfect equality. If the unequal operation of a law makes it unconstitutional, and if all laws of that description may be abrogated by any State for that cause, then, indeed, is the Federal Constitution unworthy of the slightest effort for its preservation. . . . Nor did the States, when they severally ratified it, do so under the impression that a veto on the laws of the United States was reserved to them or that they could exercise it by implication. Search the debates in all their conventions, examine the speeches of the most zealous opposers of Federal authority, look at the amendments that were proposed; they are all silent—not a syllable uttered, not a vote given, not a motion made to correct the explicit supremacy given to the laws of the Union over those of the States, or to show that implication, as is now contended, could defeat it. No; we have not erred. The Constitution is still the object of our reverence, the bond of our Union, our defense in danger, the source of our prosperity in peace. It shall descend, as we have received it, uncorrupted by sophistical construction, to our posterity; and the sacrifices of local interest, of State prejudices, of personal animosities, that were made to bring it into existence, will again be patriotically offered for its support.

The two remaining objections made by the ordinance to these laws are that the sums intended to be raised by them are greater than are required and that the proceeds will be unconstitutionally employed. . . .

The ordinance, with the same knowledge of the future that characterizes a former objection, tells you that the proceeds of the tax will be unconstitutionally applied. If this could be ascertained with certainty, the objection would with more propriety be reserved for the law so applying the proceeds, but surely can not be urged against the laws levying the duty.

These are the allegations contained in the ordinance. Examine them seriously, my fellow-citizens; judge for yourselves. I appeal to you to determine whether they are so clear, so convincing, as to leave no doubt of their correctness; and even if you should come to this conclusion, how far they justify the reckless, destructive course which you are directed to pursue. Review these objections and the conclusions drawn from them once more. What are they? Every law, then, for raising revenue, according to the South Carolina ordinance, may be rightfully annulled, unless it be so framed as no law ever will or can be framed. Congress have a right to pass laws for raising revenue and each State have a right to oppose their execution— two rights directly opposed to each other; and yet is this absurdity supposed to be contained in an instrument drawn for the express purpose of avoiding collisions between the States and the General Government by an assembly of the most enlightened statesmen and purest patriots ever embodied for a similar purpose.

In vain have these sages declared that Congress shall have power to lay and collect taxes, duties, imposts, and excises; in vain have they provided that they shall have power to pass laws which shall be necessary and proper to carry those powers into execution, that those laws and that Constitution shall be the "supreme law of the land, and that the judges in every State shall be bound thereby, anything in the constitution or laws of any State to the contrary notwithstanding;" . . . if a bare majority of the voters in any one State may, on a real or supposed knowledge of the intent with which a law has been passed, declare themselves free from its operation; . . .

The Constitution declares that the judicial powers of the United States extend to cases arising under the laws of the United States, and that such laws, the Constitution, and treaties shall be paramount to the State constitutions and laws. The judiciary act prescribes the mode by which the case may be brought before a court of the United States by appeal when a State tribunal shall decide against this provision of the Constitution. The ordinance declares there shall be no appeal—makes the State law paramount to the Constitution and laws of the United States, forces judges and jurors to swear that they will disregard their provisions, and even makes it penal in a suitor to attempt relief by appeal. It further declares that it shall not be lawful for the authorities of the United States or of that State to enforce the payment of duties imposed by the revenue laws within its limits.

Here is a law of the United States, not even pretended to be unconstitutional, repealed by the authority of a small majority of the voters of a single State. Here is a provision of the Constitution which is solemnly abrogated by the same authority.

On such expositions and reasonings the ordinance grounds not only an assertion of the right to annul the laws of which it complains, but to enforce it by a threat of seceding from the Union if any attempt is made to execute them.

This right to secede is deduced from the nature of the Constitution, which, they say, is a compact between sovereign States who have preserved their whole sovereignty and therefore are subject to no superior; that because they made the compact they can break it when in their opinion it has been departed from by the other States. Fallacious as this course of reasoning is, it enlists State pride and finds advocates in the honest prejudices of those who have not studied the nature of our Government sufficiently to see the radical error on which it rests. . . .

The Constitution of the United States, then, forms a *government,* not a league; and whether it be formed by compact between the States or in any other manner, its character is the same. It is a Government in which all the people are represented, which operates directly on the people individually, not upon the States; they retained all the power they did not grant. But each State, having expressly parted with so many powers as to constitute, jointly with the other States, a single nation, can not, from that period, possess any right to secede, because such secession does not break a league, but destroys the unity of a nation; and any injury to that unity is not only a breach which would result from the contravention of a compact, but it is an offense against the whole Union. To say that any State may at pleasure secede from the Union is to say that the United States are not a nation, because it would be a solecism to contend that any part of a nation might dissolve its connection with the other parts, to their injury or ruin, without committing any offense. Secession, like any other revolutionary act, may be morally justified by the extremity of oppression; but to call it a constitutional right is confounding the meaning of terms, and can only be done through gross error or to deceive those who are willing to assert a right, but would pause before they made a revolution or incur the penalties consequent on a failure.

Because the Union was formed by a compact, it is said the parties to that compact may, when they feel themselves aggrieved, depart from it; but it is precisely because it is a compact that they can not. A compact is an agreement or binding obligation. It may by its terms have a sanction or penalty for its breach, or it may not. If it contains no sanction, it may be broken with no other consequence than moral guilt; if it have a sanction, then the breach incurs the designated or implied penalty. A league between independent nations generally has no sanction other than a moral one; or if it should contain a penalty, as there is no common superior it can not be enforced. A government, on the contrary, always has a sanction, express or implied; and in our case it is both necessarily implied and expressly given. An attempt, by force of arms, to destroy a government is an offense, by whatever means the constitutional compact may have been formed; and such government has the right by the law of self-defense to pass acts for punishing the offender, unless that right is modified, restrained, or resumed by the constitutional act. In our system, although it is modified in the case of treason, yet authority is expressly given to pass all laws necessary to carry its powers into effect, and under this grant provision has been made for punishing acts which obstruct the due administration of the laws.

It would seem superfluous to add anything to show the nature of that union which connects us, but as erroneous opinions on this subject are the foundation of doctrines the most destructive to our peace, I must give some further development to my views on this subject. . . .

The States severally have not retained their entire sovereignty. It has been shown that in becoming parts of a nation, not members of a league, they surrendered many of their essential parts of sovereignty. The right to make treaties, declare war, levy taxes, exercise exclusive judicial and legislative powers, were all of them functions of sovereign power. The States, then, for all these important purposes were no longer sovereign. . . . How, then, with all these proofs that under all changes of our position we had, for designated purposes and with defined powers, created national governments, how is it that the most perfect of those several modes of union should now be considered as a mere league that may be dissolved at pleasure? It is from an abuse of terms. Compact is used as synonymous with league, although the true term is not employed, because it would at once show the fallacy of the reasoning. It would not do to say that our Constitution was only a league, but it is labored to prove it a compact (which in one sense is is) and then to argue that as a league is a compact every compact between nations must of course be a league, and that from such an engagement every sovereign power has a right to recede. But it has been shown that in this sense the States are not sovereign, and that even if they were, and the national Constitution had been formed by compact, there would be no right in any one State to exonerate itself from its obligations.

This, then, is the position in which we stand: A small majority of the citizens of one State in the Union have elected delegates to a State convention; that convention has ordained that all the revenue laws of the United States must be repealed, or that they are no longer a member of the Union. The governor of that State has recommended to the legislature the raising of an army to carry the secession into effect, and that he may be empowered to give clearances to vessels in the name of the State. No act of violent opposition to the laws has yet been committed, but such a state of things is hourly apprehended. And it is the intent of this instrument to *proclaim,* not only that the duty imposed on me by the Constitution "to take care that the laws be faithfully executed" shall be performed to the extent of the powers already vested in me by law, or of such others as the wisdom of Congress shall devise and intrust to me for that purpose, but to warn the citizens of South Carolina who have been deluded into an opposition to the laws of the danger they will incur by obedience to the illegal and disorganizing ordinance of the convention; to exhort those who have refused to support it to persevere in their determination to uphold the Constitution and laws of their country; and to point out to all the perilous situation into which the good people of that State have been led, and that the course they are urged to pursue is one of ruin and disgrace to the very State whose rights they affect to support. . . .

If your leaders could succeed in establishing a separation, what would be your situation? Are you united at home? Are you free from the apprehension of civil discord, with all its fearful consequences? Do our neighboring republics, every day suffering some new revolution or contending with some new insurrection, do they excite your envy? But the dictates of a high duty oblige me solemnly to announce that you can not succeed. The laws of the United States must be executed. I have no discretionary power on the subject; my duty is emphatically pronounced in the Constitution. Those who told you that you might peaceably prevent their execution deceived you; they could not have been deceived themselves. They know that a forcible opposition could alone prevent the execution of the laws, and they know that such opposition must be repelled. Their object is disunion. But be not deceived by names. Disunion by armed force is *treason*. Are you really ready to incur its guilt? If you are, on the heads of the instigators of the act be the dreadful consequences; on their heads be the dishonor, but on yours may fall the punishment. On your unhappy State will inevitably fall all the evils of the conflict you force upon the Government of your country. It can not accede to the mad project of disunion, of which you would be the first victims. Its First Magistrate can not, if he would, avoid the performance of his duty. The consequence must be fearful for you, distressing to your fellow-citizens here and to the friends of good government throughout the world. Its enemies have beheld our prosperity with a vexation they could not conceal; it was a standing refutation of their slavish doctrines, and they will point to our discord with the triumph of malignant joy. It is yet in your power to disappoint them. . . .

Fellow-citizens of the United States, the threat of unhallowed disunion, the names of those once respected by whom it is uttered, the array of military force to support it, denote the approach of a crisis in our affairs on which the continuance of our unexampled prosperity, our political existence, and perhaps that of all free governments may depend. The conjuncture demanded a free, a full, and explicit enunciation, not only of my intentions, but of my principles of action; and as the claim was asserted of a right by a State to annul the laws of the Union, and even to secede from it at pleasure, a frank exposition of my opinions in relation to the origin and form of our Government and the construction I give to the instrument by which it was created seemed to be proper.

Having the fullest confidence in the justness of the legal and constitutional opinion of my duties which has been expressed, I rely with equal confidence on your undivided support in my determination to execute the laws, to preserve the Union by all constitutional means, to arrest, if possible, by moderate and firm measures the necessity of a recourse to force; and if it be the will of Heaven that the recurrence of its primeval curse on man for the shedding of a brother's blood should fall upon our land, that it be not called down by any offensive act on the part of the United States.

Fellow-citizens, the momentous case is before you. On your undivided support of your Government depends the decision of the great question it involves—whether your sacred Union will be preserved and the blessing it secures to us as one people shall be perpetuated. No one can doubt that the unanimity with which that decision will be expressed will be such as to inspire new confidence in republican institutions, and that the prudence, the wisdom, and the courage which it will bring to their defense will transmit them unimpaired and invigorated to our children.

May the Great Ruler of Nations grant that the signal blessings with which He has favored ours may not, by the madness of party or personal ambition, be disregarded and lost; and may His wise providence bring those who have produced this crisis to see the folly before they feel the misery of civil strife, and inspire a returning veneration for that Union which, if we may dare to penetrate His designs, He has chosen as the only means of attaining the high destinies to which we may reasonably aspire.

ANDREW JACKSON.

145. SOUTH CAROLINA'S REPLY TO JACKSON'S PROCLAMATION
December 20, 1832
(Statutes at Large of South Carolina Vol. I, p. 356–7)

The Committee on federal relations, to which was referred the proclamation of the President of the United States, has had it under consideration, and recommends the adoption of the following resolutions:

Resolved, That the power vested by the Constitution and laws in the President of the United States, to issue his proclamation, does not authorize him in that mode, to interfere whenever he may think fit, in the affairs of the respective states, or that he should use it as a means of promulgating executive expositions of the Constitution, with the sanction of force thus superseding the action of other departments of the general government.

Resolved, That it is not competent to the

President of the United States, to order by proclamation the constituted authorities of a state to repeal their legislation, and that the late attempt of the President to do so is unconstitutional, and manifests a disposition to arrogate and exercise a power utterly destructive of liberty.

Resolved, That the opinions of the President, in regard to the rights of the States, are erroneous and dangerous, leading not only to the establishment of a consolidated government in the stead of our free confederacy, but to the concentration of all powers in the chief executive.

Resolved, That the proclamation of the President is the more extraordinary, that he had silently, and as it is supposed, with entire approbation, witnessed our sister state of Georgia avow, act upon, and carry into effect, even to the taking of life, principles identical with those now denounced by him in South Carolina.

Resolved, That each state of the Union has the right, whenever it may deem such a course necessary for the preservation of its liberties or vital interests, to secede peaceably from the Union, and that there is no constitutional power in the general government, much less in the executive department, of that government, to retain by force such state in the Union.

Resolved, That the primary and paramount allegiance of the citizens of this state, native or adopted, is of right due to this state.

Resolved, That the declaration of the President of the United States in his said proclamation, of his personal feelings and relations towards the State of South Carolina, is rather an appeal to the loyalty of subjects, than to the patriotism of citizens, and is a blending of official and individual character, heretofore unknown in our state papers, and revolting to our conception of political propriety.

Resolved, That the undisguised indulgence of personal hostility in the said proclamation would be unworthy of the animadversion of this legislature, but for the seldom and official form of the instrument which is made its vehicle.

Resolved, That the principles, doctrines and purposes, contained in the said proclamation are inconsistent with any just idea of a limited government, and subversive of the rights of the states and liberties of the people, and if submitted to in silence would lay a broad foundation for the establishment of monarchy.

Resolved, That while this legislature has witnessed with sorrow such a relaxation of the spirit of our institutions, that a President of the United States dare venture upon this high handed measure, it regards with indignation the menaces which are directed against it, and the concentration of a standing army on our borders—that the state will repel force by force, and relying upon the blessings of God, will maintain its liberty at all hazards.

Resolved, That copies of these resolutions be sent to our members in Congress, to be laid before that body.

146. NULLIFICATION OF THE FORCE BILL
March 18, 1833

(Statutes at Large of South Carolina, Vol. I, p. 400–401)

AN ORDINANCE
To Nullify an Act of the Congress of the United States, entitled "An Act further to provide for the Collection of Duties on Imports," commonly called the Force Bill.

We, the People of the State of South Carolina in Convention assembled, do *Declare and Ordain,* that the Act of the Congress of the United States, entitled "An Act further to provide for the collection of duties on imports," approved the second day of March, 1833, is unauthorized by the Constitution of the United States, subversive of that Constitution, and destructive of public liberty; and that the same is, and shall be deemed, null and void, within the limits of this State; and it shall be the duty of the Legislature, at such time as they may deem expedient, to adopt such measures and pass such acts as may be necessary to prevent the enforcement thereof, and to inflict proper penalties on any person who shall do any act in execution or enforcement of the same within the limits of this State.

We do further Declare and Ordain, That the allegiance of the citizens of this State, while they continue such, is due to the said State; and that obedience only, and not allegiance, is due by them to any other power or authority, to whom a control over them has been, or may be delegated by the State; and the General Assembly of the said State is hereby empowered, from time to time, when they may deem it proper, to provide for the administration to the citizens and officers of the State, or such of the said officers as they may think fit, of suitable oaths or affirmations, binding them to the observance of such allegiance; and abjuring all other allegiance; and, also, to define what shall amount to a violation of their allegiance, and to provide the proper punishment for such violation.

147. JACKSON'S VETO OF THE BANK BILL
July 10, 1832
(Richardson, ed. *Messages and Papers,* Vol. II, p. 576 ff.)

The Bill for the recharter of the Second Bank passed the Senate, June 11, and the House, July 3, 1832, with amendments in which the Senate concurred. The attempt to pass the bill over Jackson's veto failed. The veto of the recharter of the bank became the principal issue of the presidential campaign. Particularly interesting is Jackson's rejection of the finality or binding character of the opinion of the Supreme Court on a question of constitutionality. For background see, R. C. H. Catterall, *The Second Bank of the United States;* W. MacDonald, *Jacksonian Democracy,* ch. vii; W. L. Royall, *Andrew Jackson and the Bank;* J. S. Bassett, *Andrew Jackson,* Vol. II, chs. xxvii–xxviii; D. R. Dewey, *Financial History,* ch. ix.

WASHINGTON, *July 10, 1832.*
To the Senate:

The bill "to modify and continue" the act entitled "An act to incorporate the subscribers to the Bank of the United States" was presented to me on the 4th July instant. Having . . . come to the conclusion that it ought not to become a law, I herewith return it to the Senate, in which it originated, with my objections.

A bank of the United States is in many respects convenient for the Government and useful to the people. Entertaining this opinion, and deeply impressed with the belief that some of the powers and privileges possessed by the existing bank are unauthorized by the Constitution, subversive of the rights of the States, and dangerous to the liberties of the people, I felt it my duty at an early period of my Administration to call the attention of Congress to the practicability of organizing an institution combining all its advantages and obviating these objections. I sincerely regret that in the act before me I can perceive none of those modifications of the bank charter which are necessary, in my opinion, to make it compatible with justice, with sound policy, or with the Constitution of our country.

The present corporate body . . . enjoys an exclusive privilege of banking under the authority of the General Government, a monopoly of its favor and support, and, as a necessary consequence, almost a monopoly of the foreign and domestic exchange. The powers, privileges, and favors bestowed upon it in the original charter, by increasing the value of the stock far above its par value, operated as a gratuity of many millions to the stockholders. . . .

The act before me proposes another gratuity to the holders of the same stock, . . . On all hands it is conceded that its passage will increase at least 20 or 30 per cent more the market price of the stock, subject to the payment of the annuity of $200,000 per year secured by the act, thus adding in a moment one-fourth to its par value. It is not our own citizens only who are to receive the bounty of our Government. More than eight millions of the stock of this bank are held by foreigners. By this act the American Republic proposes virtually to make them a present of some millions of dollars. For these gratuities to foreigners and to some of our own opulent citizens the act secures no equivalent whatever. . . .

Every monopoly and all exclusive privileges are granted at the expense of the public, which ought to receive a fair equivalent. The many millions which this act proposes to bestow on the stockholders of the existing bank must come directly or indirectly out of the earnings of the American people. It is due to them, therefore, if their Government sell monopolies and exclusive privileges, that they should at least exact for them as much as they are worth in open market. The value of the monopoly in this case may be correctly ascertained. The twenty-eight millions of stock would probably be at an advance of 50 per cent, and command in market at least $42,000,000, subject to the payment of the present bonus. The present value of the monopoly, therefore, is $17,000,000, and this the act proposes to sell for three millions, payable in fifteen annual installments of $200,000 each.

It is not conceivable how the present stockholders can have any claim to the special favor of the Government. The present corporation has enjoyed its monopoly during the period stipulated in the original contract. If we must have such a corporation, why should not the Government sell out the whole stock and thus secure to the people the full market value of the privileges granted? Why should not Congress create and sell twenty-eight millions of stock, incorporating the purchasers with all the powers and privileges secured in this act and putting the premium upon the sales into the Treasury? . . .

The modifications of the existing charter proposed by this act are not such, in my view, as make it consistent with the rights of the States or the liberties of the people. The qualification of the right of the bank to hold real estate, the limitation of its power to establish branches, and the power reserved to Congress to forbid the circulation of small notes are restrictions comparatively of little value or importance. All the objectionable principles of the existing corporation, and most of its odious features, are retained without alleviation. . . .

Is there no danger to our liberty and independence in a bank that in its nature has so little to bind it to our country? The president of the bank has told us that most of the State banks exist by its forbearance. Should its influence become concentered, as it may under the operation of such an act as this, in the hands of a self-elected directory whose interests are identified with those of the foreign stockholders, will there not be cause to tremble for the purity of our elections in peace and for the independence of our country in war? Their power would be great whenever they might choose to exert it; but if this monopoly were regularly renewed every fifteen or twenty years on terms proposed by themselves, they might seldom in peace put forth their strength to influence elections or control the affairs of the nation. But if any private citizen or public functionary should interpose to curtail its powers or prevent a renewal of its privileges, it can not be doubted that he would be made to feel its influence. . . .

If we must have a bank with private stockholders, every consideration of sound policy and every impulse of American feeling admonishes that it should be *purely American.* Its stockholders should be composed exclusively of our own citizens, who at least ought to be friendly to our Government and willing to support it in times of difficulty and danger. . . . To a bank exclusively of American stockholders, possessing the powers and privileges granted by this act, subscriptions for $200,000,000 could be readily obtained. . . .

It is maintained by the advocates of the bank that its constitutionality in all its features ought to be considered as settled by precedent and by the decision of the Supreme Court. To this conclusion I can not assent. Mere precedent is a dangerous source of authority, and should not be regarded as deciding questions of constitutional power except where the acquiescence of the people and the States can be considered as well settled. So far from this being the case on this subject, an argument against the bank might be based on precedent. One Congress, in 1791, decided in favor of a bank; another, in 1811, decided against it. One Congress, in 1815, decided against a bank; another, in 1816, decided in its favor. Prior to the present Congress, therefore, the precedents drawn from that source were equal. If we resort to the States, the expressions of legislative, judicial, and executive opinions against the bank have been probably to those in its favor as 4 to 1. . . .

If the opinion of the Supreme Court covered the whole ground of this act, it ought not to control the coördinate authorities of this Government. The Congress, the Executive, and the Court must each for itself be guided by its own opinion of the Constitution. Each public officer who takes an oath to support the Constitution swears that he will support it as he understands it, and not as it is understood by others. It is as much the duty of the House of Representatives, of the Senate, and of the President to decide upon the constitutionality of any bill or resolution which may be presented to them for passage or approval as it is of the supreme judges when it may be brought before them for judicial decision. The opinion of the judges has no more authority over Congress than the opinion of Congress has over the judges, and on that point the President is independent of both. The authority of the Supreme Court must not, therefore, be permitted to control the Congress or the Executive when acting in their legislative capacities, but to have only such influence as the force of their reasoning may deserve.

But in the case relied upon the Supreme Court have not decided that all the features of this corporation are compatible with the Constitution. It is true that the court have said that the law incorporating the bank is a constitutional exercise of power by Congress; but taking into view the whole opinion of the court and the reasoning by which they have come to that conclusion, I understand them to have decided that inasmuch as a bank is an appropriate means for carrying into effect the enumerated powers of the General Government, therefore the law incorporating it is in accordance with that provision of the Constitution which declares that Congress shall have power "to make all laws which shall be necessary and proper for carrying those powers into execution." Having satisfied themselves that the word *"necessary"* in the Constitution means *"needful,"* *"requisite,"* *"essential,"* *"conducive to,"* and that "a bank" is a convenient, a useful, and essential instrument in the prosecution of the Government's "fiscal operations," they conclude that to "use one must be within the discretion of Congress" and that "the act to incorporate the Bank of the United States is a law made in pursuance of the Constitution;" "but," say they, *"where the law is not prohibited and is really calculated to effect any of the objects intrusted to the Govern-*

ment, to undertake here to inquire into the degree of its necessity would be to pass the line which circumscribes the judicial department and to tread on legislative ground."

The principle here affirmed is that the "degree of its necessity," involving all the details of a banking institution, is a question exclusively for legislative consideration. A bank is constitutional, but it is the province of the Legislature to determine whether this or that particular power, privilege, or exemption is "necessary and proper" to enable the bank to discharge its duties to the Government, and from their decision there is no appeal to the courts of justice. Under the decision of the Supreme Court, therefore, it is the exclusive province of Congress and the President to decide whether the particular features of this act are *necessary* and *proper* in order to enable the bank to perform conveniently and efficiently the public duties assigned to it as a fiscal agent, and therefore constitutional, or *unnecessary* and *improper,* and therefore unconstitutional.

Without commenting on the general principle affirmed by the Supreme Court, let us examine the details of this act in accordance with the rule of legislative action which they have laid down. It will be found that many of the powers and privileges conferred on it can not be supposed necessary for the purpose for which it is proposed to be created, and are not, therefore, means necessary to attain the end in view, and consequently not justified by the Constitution. . . .

The Constitution declares that "the Congress shall have power to exercise exclusive legislation in all cases whatsoever" over the District of Columbia. Its constitutional power, therefore, to establish banks in the district of Columbia and increase their capital at will is unlimited and uncontrollable by any other power than that which gave authority to the Constitution. Yet this act declares that Congress shall *not* increase the capital of existing banks, nor create other banks with capitals exceeding in the whole $6,000,000. The Constitution declares that Congress *shall* have power to exercise exclusive legislation over this District *"in all cases whatsoever,"* and this act declares they shall not. Which is the supreme law of the land? This provision can not be *"necessary"* or *"proper"* or *constitutional* unless the absurdity be admitted that whenever it be "necessary and proper" in the opinion of Congress they have a right to barter away one portion of the powers vested in them by the Constitution as a means of executing the rest. . . .

The Government is the only *"proper"* judge where its agents should reside and keep their offices, because it best knows where their presence will be *"necessary."* It can not, therefore, be *"necessary"* or *"proper"* to authorize the bank to locate branches where it pleases to perform the public service, without consulting the Government, and contrary to its will. The principle laid down by the Supreme Court concedes that Congress can not establish a bank for purposes of private speculation and gain, but only as a means of executing the delegated powers of the General Government. By the same principle a branch bank can not constitutionally be established for other than public purposes. The power which this act gives to establish two branches in any State, without the injunction or request of the Government and for other than public purposes, is not *"necessary"* to the due *execution* of the powers delegated to Congress. . . .

The principle is conceded that the States can not rightfully tax the operations of the General Government. They can not tax the money of the Government deposited in the State banks, nor the agency of those banks in remitting it; but will any man maintain that their mere selection to perform this public service for the General Government would exempt the State banks and their ordinary business from State taxation? Had the United States, instead of establishing a bank at Philadelphia, employed a private banker to keep and transmit their funds, would it have deprived Pennsylvania of the right to tax his bank and his usual banking operations? . . .

It can not be *necessary* to the character of the bank as a fiscal agent of the Government that its private business should be exempted from that taxation to which all the State banks are liable, nor can I conceive it *"proper"* that the substantive and most essential powers reserved by the States shall be thus attacked and annihilated as a means of executing the powers delegated to the General Government. It may be safely assumed that none of those sages who had an agency in forming or adopting our Constitu-

tion ever imagined that any portion of the taxing power of the States not prohibited to them nor delegated to Congress was to be swept away and annihilated as a means of executing certain powers delegated to Congress.

If our power over means is so absolute that the Supreme Court will not call in question the constitutionality of an act of Congress the subject of which "is not prohibited, and is really calculated to effect any of the objects intrusted to the Government," although, as in the case before me, it takes away powers expressly granted to Congress and rights scrupulously reserved to the States, it becomes us to proceed in our legislation with the utmost caution. Though not directly, our own powers and the rights of the States may be indirectly legislated away in the use of means to execute substantive powers. We may not enact that Congress shall not have the power of exclusive legislation over the District of Columbia, but we may pledge the faith of the United States that as a means of executing other powers it shall not be exercised for twenty years or forever. We may not pass an act prohibiting the States to tax the banking business carried on within their limits, but we may, as a means of executing our powers over other objects, place that business in the hands of our agents and then declare it exempt from State taxation in their hands. Thus may our own powers and the rights of the States, which we can not directly curtail or invade, be frittered away and extinguished in the use of means employed by us to execute other powers. That a bank of the United States, competent to all the duties which may be required by the Government, might be so organized as not to infringe on our own delegated powers or the reserved rights of the States I do not entertain a doubt. . . .

Under such circumstances the bank comes forward and asks a renewal of its charter for a term of fifteen years upon conditions which not only operate as a gratuity to the stockholders of many millions of dollars, but will sanction any abuses and legalize any encroachments. . . .

The bank is professedly established as an agent of the executive branch of the Government, and its constitutionality is maintained on that ground. Neither upon the propriety of present action nor upon the provisions of this act was the Executive consulted. It has had no opportunity to say that it neither needs nor wants an agent clothed with such powers and favored by such exemptions. There is nothing in its legitimate functions which makes it necessary or proper. Whatever interest or influence, whether public or private, has given birth to this act, it can not be found either in the wishes or necessities of the executive department, by which present action is deemed premature, and the powers conferred upon its agent not only unnecessary, but dangerous to the Government and country. . . .

There are no necessary evils in government. Its evils exist only in its abuses. If it would confine itself to equal protection, and, as Heaven does its rains, shower its favors alike on the high and the low, the rich and the poor, it would be an unqualified blessing. In the act before me there seems to be a wide and unnecessary departure from these just principles. . . .

Experience should teach us wisdom. Most of the difficulties our Government now encounters and most of the dangers which impend over our Union have sprung from an abandonment of the legitimate objects of Government by our national legislation, and the adoption of such principles as are embodied in this act. Many of our rich men have not been content with equal protection and equal benefits, but have besought us to make them richer by act of Congress. By attempting to gratify their desires we have in the results of our legislation arrayed section against section, interest against interest, and man against man, in a fearful commotion which threatens to shake the foundations of our Union. It is time to pause in our career to review our principles, and if possible revive that devoted patriotism and spirit of compromise which distinguished the sages of the Revolution and the fathers of our Union.

ANDREW JACKSON.

148. THE REMOVAL OF THE PUBLIC DEPOSITS

Jackson's Paper read to the Cabinet
September 18, 1833

(Richardson, ed. *Messages and Papers,* Vol. III, p. 5 ff.)

The veto of the bill to recharter the Bank was the principal issue of the campaign of 1832. Jackson looked upon his re-election as a public endorsement of his policy, and proceeded to the next step of his "war on the Bank" by withdrawing the public deposits from it. Secretary Duane refused to issue the order removing the deposits, and was forced to give up his office to R. B. Taney, who, on September 26, issued the order for removal and designated the Girard Bank of Philadelphia as a place of deposit. Jackson's paper read to the Cabinet and drafted by Taney, is, according to Professor MacDonald, "the most explicit statement we have of Jackson's theory regarding the status and function of a cabinet officer in our constitutional system." See, W. MacDonald, *Jacksonian Democracy,* ch. xiii; J. S. Bassett, *Andrew Jackson.* Vol. II, ch. xxix; S. Tyler, *R. B. Taney,* p. 191 ff.; D. R. Dewey, *Financial History,* p. 203 ff.

Having carefully and anxiously considered all the facts and arguments which have been submitted to him relative to a removal of the public deposits from the Bank of the United States, the President deems it his duty to communicate in this manner to his Cabinet the final conclusions of his own mind and the reasons on which they are founded, in order to put them in durable form and to prevent misconceptions. . . .

Of all the substitutes for the present bank which have been suggested, none seems to have united any considerable portion of the public in its favor. Most of them are liable to the same constitutional objections for which the present bank has been condemned, and perhaps to all there are strong objections on the score of expediency. . . .

On the whole, the President considers it as conclusively settled that the charter of the Bank of the United States will not be renewed, and he has no reasonable ground to believe that any substitute will be established. Being bound to regulate his course by the laws as they exist, and not to anticipate the interference of the legislative power for the purpose of framing new systems, it is proper for him seasonably to consider the means by which the services rendered by the Bank of the United States are to be performed after its charter shall expire.

The existing laws declare that—

The deposits of the money of the United States in places in which the said bank and branches thereof may be established shall be made in said bank or branches thereof unless the Secretary of the Treasury shall at any time otherwise order and direct, in which case the Secretary of the Treasury shall immediately lay before Congress, if in session, and, if not, immediately after the commencement of the next session, the reasons of such order or direction.

The power of the Secretary of the Treasury over the deposits is *unqualified*. The provision that he shall report his reasons to Congress is no limitation. Had it not been inserted he would have been responsible to Congress had he made a removal for any other than good reasons, and his responsibility now ceases upon the rendition of sufficient ones to Congress. The only object of the provision is to make his reasons accessible to Congress and enable that body the more readily to judge of their soundness and purity, and thereupon to make such further provision by law as the legislative power may think proper in relation to the deposit of the public money. . . .

It is a matter of surprise that a power which in the infancy of the bank was freely asserted as one of the ordinary and familiar duties of the Secretary of the Treasury should now be gravely questioned, and attempts made to excite and alarm the public mind as if some new and unheard-of power was about to be usurped by the executive branch of the Government.

It is but a little more than two and a half years to the termination of the charter of the present bank. It is considered as the decision of the country that it shall then cease to exist, and no man, the President believes, has reasonable ground for expectation that any other Bank of the United States will be created by Congress.

To the Treasury Department is intrusted the safe-keeping and faithful application of the public moneys. A plan of collection different from the present must therefore be introduced and put in complete operation before the dissolution of the present bank.

When shall it be commenced? Shall no step be taken in this essential concern until the charter expires and the Treasury finds itself without an agent, its accounts in confusion, with no depository for its funds, and the whole business of the Government deranged, or shall it be delayed until six months, or a year, or two years before the expiration of the charter? It is obvious that any new system which may be substituted in the place of the Bank of the United States could not be suddenly carried into effect on the termination of its existence without serious inconvenience to the Government and the people. Its vast amount of notes are then to be redeemed and withdrawn from circulation and its immense debt collected. These operations must be gradual, otherwise much suffering and distress will be brought upon the community.

It ought to be not a work of months only, but of years, and the President thinks it can not, with due attention to the interests of the people, be longer postponed. It is safer to begin it too soon than to delay it too long. . . .

As the President presumes that the charter to the bank is to be considered as a contract on the part of the Government, it is not now in the power of Congress to disregard its stipulations; and by the terms of that contract the public money is to be deposited in the bank during the continuance of its charter unless the Secretary of the Treasury shall otherwise direct. Unless, therefore, the Secretary of the Treasury first acts, Congress have no power over the subject, for they can not add a new clause to the charter or strike one out of it without the consent of the bank, and consequently the public money must remain in that institution to the last hour of its existence unless the Secretary of the Treasury shall remove it at an earlier day. The responsibility is thus thrown upon the executive branch of the Government of deciding how long before the expiration of the charter the public interest will require the deposits to be placed elsewhere; . . . it being the duty of one of the Executive Departments to decide in the first instance, . . . whether the public deposits shall remain in the Bank of the United States until the end of its existence or be withdrawn some time before, the President has felt himself bound to examine the question carefully . . . and in his opinion the near approach of the termination of the charter and the public considerations heretofore mentioned are of themselves amply sufficient to justify the removal of the deposits, without reference to the conduct of the bank or their safety in its keeping.

But in the conduct of the bank may be found other reasons, very imperative in their character, and which require prompt action. Developments have been made from time to time of its faithlessness as a public agent, its misapplication of public funds, its interference in elections, its efforts by the machinery of committees to deprive the Government directors of a full knowledge of its concerns, and, above all, its flagrant misconduct as recently and unexpectedly disclosed in placing all the funds of the bank, including the money of the Government, at the disposition of the president of the bank as means of operating upon public opinion and procuring a new charter, without requiring him to render a voucher for their disbursement. A brief recapitulation of the facts which justify these charges, and which have come to the knowledge of the public and the President, will, he thinks, remove every reasonable doubt as to the course which it is now the duty of the President to pursue. . . .

With these facts before him in an official report from the Government directors, the President would feel that he was not only responsible for all the abuses and corruptions the bank has committed or may commit, but almost an accomplice in a conspiracy against that Government which he has sworn honestly to administer, if he did not take every step within his constitutional and legal power likely to be efficient in putting an end to these enormities. If it be possible within the scope of human affairs to find a reason for removing the Government deposits and leaving the bank to its own resource for the means of effecting its criminal designs, we have it here. Was it expected when the moneys of the United States were directed to be placed in that bank that they would be put under the control of one man empowered to spend millions without rendering a voucher or specifying the object? Can they be considered safe with the evidence before us that tens of thousands have been spent for highly improper, if not corrupt, purposes, and that the same

motive may lead to the expenditure of hundreds of thousands, and even millions, more? And can we justify ourselves to the people by longer lending to it the money and power of the Government to be employed for such purposes?

It has been alleged by some as an objection to the removal of the deposits that the bank has the power, and in that event will have the disposition, to destroy the State banks employed by the Government, and bring distress upon the country. It has been the fortune of the President to encounter dangers which were represented as equally alarming, and he has seen them vanish before resolution and energy. . . . But if the President believed the bank possessed all the power which has been attributed to it, his determination would only be rendered the more inflexible. If, indeed, this corporation now holds in its hands the happiness and prosperity of the American people, it is high time to take the alarm. If the despotism be already upon us and our only safety is in the mercy of the despot, recent developments in relation to his designs and the means he employs show how necessary it is to shake it off. The struggle can never come with less distress to the people or under more favorable auspices than at the present moment.

All doubt as to the willingness of the State banks to undertake the service of the Government to the same extent and on the same terms as it is now performed by the Bank of the United States is put to rest by the report of the agent recently employed to collect information, and from that willingness their own safety in the operation may be confidently inferred. Knowing their own resources better than they can be known by others, it is not to be supposed that they would be willing to place themselves in a situation which they can not occupy without danger of annihilation or embarrassment. . . .

From all these considerations the President thinks that the State banks ought immediately to be employed in the collection and disbursement of the public revenue, and the funds now in the Bank of the United States drawn out with all convenient dispatch. . . .

As one of the most serious objections to the Bank of the United States is the power which it concentrates, care must be taken in finding other agents for the service of the Treasury not to raise up another power equally formidable. . . .

It is the desire of the President that the control of the banks and the currency shall, as far as possible, be entirely separated from the political power of the country as well as wrested from an institution which has already attempted to subject the Government to its will. In his opinion the action of the General Government on this subject ought not to extend beyond the grant in the Constitution, which only authorizes Congress "to coin money and regulate the value thereof;" all else belongs to the States and the people, and must be regulated by public opinion and the interests of trade.

In conclusion, the President must be permitted to remark that he looks upon the pending question as of higher consideration than the mere transfer of a sum of money from one bank to another. Its decision may affect the character of our Government for ages to come. Should the bank be suffered longer to use the public moneys in the accomplishment of its purposes, with the proofs of its faithlessness and corruption before our eyes, the patriotic among our citizens will despair of success in struggling against its power, and we shall be responsible for entailing it upon our country forever. Viewing it as a question of transcendent importance, both in the principles and consequences it involves, the President could not, in justice to the responsibility which he owes to the country, refrain from pressing upon the Secretary of the Treasury his view of the considera-

tions which impel to immediate action. . . .

In the remarks he has made on this all-important question he trusts the Secretary of the Treasury will see only the frank and respectful declarations of the opinions which the President has formed on a measure of great national interest deeply affecting the character and usefulness of his Administration, and not a spirit of dictation, which the President would be as careful to avoid as ready to resist. Happy will he be if the facts now disclosed produce uniformity of opinion and unity of action among the members of the Administration.

The President again repeats that he begs his Cabinet to consider the proposed measure as his own, in the support of which he shall require no one of them to make a sacrifice of opinion or principle. Its responsibility has been assumed after the most mature deliberation and reflection as necessary to preserve the morals of the people, the freedom of the press, and the purity of the elective franchise, without which all will unite in saying that the blood and treasure expended by our forefathers in the establishment of our happy system of government will have been vain and fruitless. Under these convictions he feels that a measure so important to the American people can not be commenced too soon, and he therefore names the 1st day of October next as a period proper for the change of the deposits, or sooner, provided the necessary arrangements with the State banks can be made.

ANDREW JACKSON.

149. THE LIBERATOR, Vol. I., No. 1.
January 1, 1831

(William Lloyd Garrison, 1805–1879: the Story of his Life Told by his Children, Vol. I, p. 224 ff.)

About 1828 Garrison met Benjamin Lundy, and the following year joined with him in editing the *Genius for Universal Emancipation*. Jailed for libel, he was bailed out by the philanthropist Arthur Tappan, and shortly betook himself to Boston where, with Isaac Knapp, he issued the *Liberator*. The entrance of Garrison into the anti-slavery agitation gave that movement a particularly violent and fanatical character, and he came eventually to be regarded as the leading abolitionist in the country. On Garrison see the

biography by his children, above, and L. Swift, *William Lloyd Garrison.* A severely critical estimate is in G. H. Barnes, *The Antislavery Impulse, 1830–1844.* See also bibliography in A. B. Hart, *Slavery and Abolition.*

To the Public.

In the month of August, I issued proposals for publishing *"The Liberator"* in Washington City; but the enterprise, though hailed in different sections of the country, was palsied by public indifference. Since that time, the removal of the *Genius of Universal Emancipation* to the Seat of Government has rendered less imperious the establishment of a similar periodical in that quarter.

During my recent tour for the purpose of exciting the minds of the people by a series of discourses on the subject of slavery, every place that I visited gave fresh evidence of the fact, that a greater revolution in public sentiment was to be effected in the free states —*and particularly in New England*—than at the south. I found contempt more bitter, opposition more active, detraction more relentless, prejudice more stubborn, and apathy more frozen, than among slave owners themselves. Of course, there were individual exceptions to the contrary. This state of things afflicted, but did not dishearten me. I determined, at every hazard, to lift up the standard of emancipation in the eyes of the nation, *within sight of Bunker Hill and in the birth place of liberty.* That standard is now unfurled; and long may it float, unhurt by the spoliations of time or the missiles of a desperate foe—yea, till every chain be broken, and every bondman set free! Let Southern oppressors tremble—let their secret abettors tremble—let their Northern apologists tremble—let all the enemies of the persecuted blacks tremble.

I deem the publication of my original Prospectus unnecessary, as it has obtained a wide circulation. The principles therein inculcated will be steadily pursued in this paper, excepting that I shall not array myself as the political partisan of any man. In defending the great cause of human rights, I wish to derive the assistance of all religions and of all parties.

Assenting to the "self evident truth" maintained in the American Declaration of Independence, "that all men are created equal, and endowed by their Creator with certain inalienable rights—among which are life, liberty and the pursuit of happiness," I shall strenuously contend for the immediate enfranchisement of our slave population. In Park-Street Church, on the Fourth of July, 1829, in an address on slavery, I unreflectingly assented to the popular but pernicious doctrine of *gradual* abolition. I seize this opportunity to make a full and unequivocal recantation, and thus publicly to ask pardon of my God, of my country, and of my brethren the poor slaves, for having uttered a sentiment so full of timidity, injustice and absurdity. A similar recantation, from my pen, was published in the *Genius of Universal Emancipation* at Baltimore, in September, 1829. My conscience is now satisfied.

I am aware, that many object to the severity of my language; but is there not cause for severity? I *will be* as harsh as truth, and as uncompromising as justice. On this subject, I do not wish to think, or speak, or write, with moderation. No! No! Tell a man whose house is on fire, to give a moderate alarm; tell him to moderately rescue his wife from the hands of the ravisher; tell the mother to gradually extricate her babe from the fire into which it has fallen;—but urge me not to use moderation in a cause like the present. I am in earnest —I will not equivocate—I will not excuse— I will not retreat a single inch—*AND I WILL BE HEARD.* The apathy of the people is enough to make every statue leap from its pedestal, and to hasten the resurrection of the dead.

It is pretended, that I am retarding the cause of emancipation by the coarseness of my invective, and the precipitancy of my measures. *The charge is not true.* On this question my influence,—humble as it is,—is felt at this moment to a considerable extent, and shall be felt in coming years—not perniciously, but beneficially—not as a curse, but as a blessing; and posterity will bear testimony that I was right. I desire to thank God, that he enables me to disregard "the fear of man which bringeth a snare," and to speak his truth in its simplicity and power. . . .

William Lloyd Garrison.

150. THE AMERICAN ANTI-SLAVERY SOCIETY: CONSTITUTION
December 4, 1833

The enactment of the West Indian Emancipation bill by Parliament in 1833 precipitated the organization of abolitionist sentiment in the United States in an Anti-Slavery Society. Though there was considerable opposition to such organization at the time, the insistence of Garrison carried the day, and a convention was called to meet in Philadelphia, December 4, 1833. Only a handful of delegates met, and these were dominated by Garrison, who drew up the Declaration of Sentiments. See, *William Lloyd Garrison: The Story of His Life Told by His Children,* Vol. I; A. B. Hart, *Slavery and Abolition,* ch. xii; L. Tappan, *Arthur Tappan;* S. T. Pickard, *Life and Works of J. G. Whittier;* G. H. Barnes, *The Antislavery Impulse, 1830–1844.*

1. CONSTITUTION OF THE AMERICAN ANTI-SLAVERY SOCIETY

(*Platform of the American Anti-Slavery Society and its Auxiliaries,* New York, 1860, p. 3–4)

Whereas the Most High God "hath made of one blood all nations of men to dwell on all the face of the earth," and hath commanded them to love their neighbors as themselves; and whereas, our National Existence is based upon this principle, as recognized in the Declaration of Independence, "that all mankind are created equal, and that they are endowed by their Creator with certain inalienable rights, among which are life, liberty, and the pursuit of happiness"; and whereas, after the lapse of nearly sixty years, since the faith and honor of the American people were pledged to this avowal, before Almighty God and the World, nearly one-sixth part of the nation are held in bondage by their fellow-citizens; and whereas, Slavery is contrary to the principles of natural justice, of our republican form of government, and of the Christian religion, and is destructive of the prosperity of the country, while it is endangering the peace, union, and liberties of the States; and whereas, we believe it the duty and interest of the masters immediately to emancipate their slaves, and that no scheme of expatriation, either voluntary or by compulsion, can remove this great and increasing evil; and whereas, we believe that it is practicable, by appeals to the consciences, hearts, and interests of the people, to awaken a public sentiment throughout the nation that will be opposed to the continuance of Slavery in any part of the Republic, and by effecting the speedy abolition of Slavery, prevent a general convulsion; and whereas, we believe we owe it to the oppressed, to our fellow-citizens who hold slaves, to our whole country, to posterity, and to God, to do all that is lawfully in our power to bring about the extinction of Slavery, we do hereby agree, with a prayerful reliance on the Divine aid, to form ourselves into a society, to be governed by the following Constitution:—

ART. I.—This Society shall be called the AMERICAN ANTI-SLAVERY SOCIETY.

ART. II.—The object of this Society is the entire abolition of Slavery in the United States. While it admits that each State, in which Slavery exists, has, by the Constitution of the United States, the exclusive right to *legislate* in regard to its abolition in said State, it shall aim to convince all our fellow-citizens, by arguments addressed to their understandings and consciences, that Slaveholding is a heinous crime in the sight of God, and that the duty, safety, and best interests of all concerned, require its *immediate abandonment,* without expatriation. The Society will also endeavor, in a constitutional way to influence Congress to put an end to the domestic Slave trade, and to abolish Slavery in all those portions of our common country which come under its control, especially in the District of Columbia,—and likewise to prevent the extension of it to any State that may be hereafter admitted to the Union.

ART. III.—This Society shall aim to elevate the character and condition of the people of color, by encouraging their intellectual, moral. and religious improvement, and by removing public prejudice, that thus they may, according to their intellectual and moral worth, share an equality with the whites, of civil and religious privileges; but this Society will never, in any way, countenance the oppressed in vindicating their rights by resorting to physical force.

ART. IV.—Any person who consents to the principles of this Constitution, who contributes to the funds of this Society, and is not a Slaveholder, may be a member of this Society, and shall be entitled to vote at the meetings. . . .

151. SOUTH CAROLINA RESOLUTIONS ON ABOLITIONIST PROPAGANDA
December 16, 1835
(*Acts and Resolutions of South Carolina*, 1835, p. 26 ff.)

The Southern States met abolitionist propaganda with regulatory or prohibitory legislation; most of the states south of Virginia provided severe penalties for printing or speaking anything that might incite insurrection among the slaves, or even for arguing against the institution of slavery. Several states demanded that the Federal government close the mails to abolitionist literature: the resolutions of South Carolina are given as an example of these demands. See, A. B. Hart, *Slavery and Abolition*, ch. xvi.

1. *Resolved,* That the formation of the abolition societies, and the acts and doings of certain fanatics. calling themselves abolitionists, in the non-slaveholding states of this confederacy, are in direct violation of the obligations of the compact of the union, dissocial, and incendiary in the extreme.

2. *Resolved,* That no state having a just regard for her own peace and security can acquiesce in a state of things by which such conspiracies are engendered within the limits of a friendly state, united to her by the bonds of a common league of political association, without either surrendering or compromising her most essential rights.

3. *Resolved,* That the Legislature of South Carolina, having every confidence in the justice and friendship of the non-slaveholding states, announces to her co-states her confident expectation, and she earnestly requests that the governments of these states will promptly and effectually suppress all those associations within their respective limits, purporting to be abolition societies, and that they will make it highly penal to print, publish, and distribute newspapers, pamphlets, tracts and pictorial representations calculated and having an obvious tendency to excite the slaves of the southern states to insurrection and revolt.

4. *Resolved,* That, regarding the domestic slavery of the southern states as a subject exclusively within the control of each of the said states, we shall consider every interference, by any other state of the general government, as a direct and unlawful interference, to be resisted at once, and under every possible circumstance.

5. *Resolved,* In order that a salutary negative may be put on the mischievous and unfounded assumption of some of the abolitionists—the non-slaveholding states are requested to disclaim by legislative declaration, all right, either on the part of themselves or the government of the United States, to interfere in any manner with domestic slavery, either in the states, or in the territories where it exists.

6. *Resolved,* That we should consider the abolition of slavery in the District of Columbia, as a violation of the rights of the citizens of that District, derived from the implied conditions on which that territory was ceded to the general government, and as an usurpation to be at once resisted as nothing more than the commencement of a scheme of much more extensive and flagrant injustice.

7. *Resolved,* That the legislature of South Carolina, regards with decided approbation, the measures of security adopted by the Post Office Department of the United States, in relation to the transmission of incendiary tracts. But if this highly essential and protective policy, be counteracted by congress, and the United States mail becomes a vehicle for the transmission of the mischievous documents, with which it was recently freighted we, in this contingency, expect that the Chief Magistrate of our state, will forthwith call the legislature together, that timely measures may be taken to prevent its traversing our territory. (Resolutions of transmission.)

152. TEXAS DECLARATION OF INDEPENDENCE
March 2, 1836
(Thorpe, ed., *Federal and State Constitutions*, VI, 3528)

The Texas revolution against Mexico, simmering all through the early thirties, broke out in the fall of 1835. Early in November a "consultation" at San Filipe de Austin issued a preliminary but somewhat ambiguous declaration of independence. Early in 1836, a Mexican army under Santa Anna crossed the border and the war for independence began. The first week of March witnessed the attack on the Alamo. While Travis and his 188 men were preparing to defend the Alamo, a convention met at Washington, Texas, and drew up this Declaration of Independence. On March 16, the same convention completed a constitution modeled closely upon that of the United States. On April 21, 1836, Santa Anna was defeated at San Jacinto, and Texas had won its independence. See John H. Brown, *History of Texas*, Vol. I; G. P. Garrison, *Texas;* W. C. Binkley, *The Texas Revolution;* E. C. Barker, *Life of Stephen F. Austin;* Marquis James, *The Raven: A Biography of Sam Houston;* William R. Hogan, *The Texas Republic.*

When a government has ceased to protect the lives liberty and property of its people, from whom its legitimate powers are derived, and for the advancement of whose happiness it was instituted, and so far from being a guarantee for the enjoyment of those inestimable and inalienable rights, becomes an instrument in the hands of evil rulers for their oppression: When the Federal Republican Constitution of their country, which they have sworn to support, no longer has a substantial existence, and the whole nature of their government has been forcibly changed without their consent, from a restricted federative republic, composed of sovereign states to a consolidated central military despotism in which every interest is disregarded but that of the army and the priesthood—both the eternal enemies of civil liberty, the ever-ready minions of power, and the usual instruments of tyrants:

When, long after the spirit of the constitution has departed, moderation is at length so far lost by those in power that even the semblance of freedom is removed, and the forms, themselves, of the constitution discontinued; and so far from their petitions and remonstrances being regarded, the agents who bear them are thrown into dungeons; and mercenary armies sent forth to force a new government upon them at the point of the bayonet: When, in consequence of such acts of malfeasance and abdication, on the part of the government, anarchy prevails, and Civil Society is dissolved into its original elements. In such a crisis, the first law of nature, the right of self-preservation —the inherent and unalienable right of the people to appeal to first principles and take their political affairs into their own hands in extreme cases enjoins it as a right towards themselves and a sacred obligation to their posterity to abolish such government and create another in its stead, calculated to rescue them from impending dangers, and to secure their future welfare and happiness.

Nations, as well as individuals, are amenable for their acts to the public opinion of mankind. Statement of a part of our grievance is, therefore, submitted to an impartial world, in justification of the hazardous but unavoidable step now taken of severing our political connection with the Mexican people, and assuming an independent attitude among the nations of the earth.

The Mexican government, by its colonization laws, invited and induced the Anglo-American population of Texas to colonize its wilderness under the pledged faith of a written constitution that they should continue to enjoy that constitutional liberty and republican government to which they had been habituated in the land of their birth, the United States of America. In this expectation they have been cruelly disappointed, in as much as the Mexican nation has acquiesced in the late changes made in the government by General Antonio Lopez de Santa Anna, who, having overturned the constitution of his country, now offers as the cruel alternative either to abandon our homes, acquired by so many privations, or submit to the most intolerable of all tyranny, the combined despotism of the sword and the priesthood.

It has sacrificed our welfare to the State of Coahuila, by which our interests have been continually depressed through a jealous and partial course of legislation carried on at a far distant seat of government by a hostile majority, in an unknown tongue; and this to, notwithstanding we have petitioned in the humblest terms, for the establishment of a separate state government, and have, in accordance with the provisions of the national constitution presented to the General Congress a republican constitution which was, without just cause, contemptuously rejected.

It incarcerated in a dungeon, for a long time, one of our citizens, for no other cause but a zealous endeavor to procure the acceptance of our constitution and the establishment of a state government.

It has failed and refused to secure on a firm basis, the right of trial by jury, that palladium of civil liberty, and only safe guarantee for the life, liberty, and property of the citizen.

It has failed to establish any public system of education, although possessed of almost boundless resources (the public domain) and although it is an axiom in political science, that unless a people are educated and enlightened it is idle to expect the continuance of civil liberty, or the capacity for self-government.

It has suffered the military commandants stationed among us to exercise arbitrary acts of oppression and tyranny; thus trampling upon the most sacred rights of the citizen and rendering the military superior to the civil power.

It has dissolved by force of arms, the State Congress of Coahuila and Texas, and obliged our representatives to fly for their lives from the seat of government; thus depriving us of the fundamental political right of representation.

It has demanded the surrender of a number of our citizens and ordered military detachments to seize and carry them into the interior for trial; in contempt of the civil authorities, and in defiance of the laws and the constitution.

It has made piratical attacks upon our commerce, by commissioning foreign desperadoes, and authorizing them to seize our vessels, and convey the property of our citizens to far distant ports for confiscation.

It denies us the right of worshipping the Almighty according to the dictates of our own conscience, by the support of a national religion calculated to promote the temporal interest of its human functionaries rather than the glory of the true and living God.

It has demanded us to deliver up our arms, which are essential to our defence, the rightful property of freemen, and formidable only to tyrannical governments.

It has invaded our country by sea and by land, with intent to lay waste our territory and drive us from our homes, and has now a large mercenary army advancing to carry on against us a war of extermination.

It has, through its emissaries, incited the merciless savage, with the tomahawk and scalping knife, to massacre the inhabitants of our defenceless frontiers.

It hath been, during the whole time of our connection with it, the contemptible sport and victim of successive military revolutions, and hath continually exhibited every characteristic of a weak, corrupt, and tyrannical government.

These, and other grievances, were patiently borne by the people of Texas until they reached that point at which forbearance ceases to be a virtue. We then took up arms in defence of the national constitution. We appealed to our Mexican brethren for assistance. Our appeal has been made in vain. Though months have elapsed, no sympathetic response has yet been heard from the interior. We are, therefore, forced to the melancholy conclusion that the Mexican people have acquiesced in the destruction of their liberty and the substitution therefore of a Military Government—that they are unfit to be free and incapable of self-government.

The necessity of self-preservation, therefore, now decrees our eternal political separation.

We therefore, the delegates with plenary powers, of the people of Texas, in solemn convention assembled, appealing to a candid world for the necessities of our condition, do hereby resolve and declare that our political connection with the Mexican Nation has forever ended; and that the people of Texas do now constitute a free sovereign and independent republic, and are fully invested with all the rights and attributes which properly belong to independent nations; and conscious of the rectitude of our intentions, we fearlessly and confidently commit the issue to the decision of the Supreme Arbiter of the destinies of Nations.

RICHARD ELLIS, *President*

Test:

H. S. KIMBLE, *Secretary*

153. THE SPECIE CIRCULAR
July 11, 1836

(American State Papers, Public Lands, Vol. VIII, p. 910)

The distribution of government funds in "pet" banks, the distribution of the surplus, and apparent prosperity led to violent speculation in public lands in the west during the second Jackson administration. Land sales rose from $2,623,-000, in 1832 to $14,757,000 in 1835, and $24,877,000 in 1836. Payment, however, was frequently in notes of local banks based on other notes of speculators. Under these circumstances Benton drafted the specie circular which was promulgated by the Secretary of the Treasury, July 11, 1836. The result of the specie circular was to check sharply the sales of public lands and to reveal the unsoundness of many of the smaller western banks. For Jackson's explanation and defence of the specie circular see Doc. No. 154. On the specie circular, see W. MacDonald, *Jacksonian Democracy,* ch. xvi; D. R. Dewey, *Financial History of the United States,* ch. x; R. G. Wellington, *Political and Sectional Influence of the Public Lands, 1828–1842;* E. G. Bourne, *History of the Surplus Revenue of 1837.*

Circular to Receivers of Public Money, and to the Deposite Banks

TREASURY DEPARTMENT, *July* 11, 1836

In consequence of complaints which have been made of frauds, speculations, and monopolies, in the purchase of the public lands, and the aid which is said to be given to effect these objects by excessive bank credits, and dangerous if not partial facilities through bank drafts and bank deposites, and the general evil influence likely to result to the public interests, and especially the safety of the great amount of money in the Treasury, and the sound condition of the currency of the country, from the further exchange of the national domain in this manner, the President of the United States has given directions, and you are hereby instructed, after the 15th day of August next, to receive in payment of the public lands nothing except what is directed by the existing laws, viz: gold and silver, and in the proper cases, Virginia land scrip; provided that till the 15th of December next, the same indulgences heretofore extended as to the kind of money received, may be continued for any quantity of land not exceeding 320 acres to each purchaser who is an actual settler or bona fide resident in the State where the sales are made.

In order to ensure the faithful execution of these instructions, all receivers are strictly prohibited from accepting for land sold, any draft, certificate, or other evidence of money, or deposite, though for specie, unless signed by the Treasurer of the United States, in conformity to the act of April 24, 1820. . . .

The principal objects of the President in adopting this measure being to repress alleged frauds, and to withhold any countenance or facilities in the power of the Government from the monopoly of the public lands in the hands of speculators and capitalists, to the injury of the actual settlers in the new States, and of emigrants in search of new homes, as well as to discourage the ruinous extension of bank issues, and bank credits, by which those results are generally supposed to be promoted, your utmost vigilance is required, and relied on, to carry this order into complete execution.

LEVI WOODBURY.

154. JACKSON'S MESSAGE ON THE SPECIE CIRCULAR

Extract from Eighth Annual Message to Congress
December 5, 1836

(Richardson, ed. *Messages and Papers*, Vol. III, p. 249)

. . . The effects of an extension of bank credits and overissues of bank paper have been strikingly illustrated in the sales of the public lands. From the returns made by the various registers and receivers in the early part of last summer it was perceived that the receipts arising from the sales of the public lands were increasing to an unprecedented amount. In effect, however, these receipts amounted to nothing more than credits in bank. The banks lent out their notes to speculators. They were paid to the receivers and immediately returned to the banks, to be lent out again and again, being mere instruments to transfer to speculators the most valuable public land and pay the Government by a credit on the books of the banks. Those credits on the books of some of the Western banks, usually called deposits, were already greatly beyond their immediate means of payment, and were rapidly increasing. Indeed, each speculation furnished means for another; for no sooner had one individual or company paid in the notes than they were immediately lent to another for a like purpose, and the banks were extending their business and their issues so largely as to alarm considerate men and render it doubtful whether these bank credits if permitted to accumulate would ultimately be of the least value to the Government. The spirit of expansion and speculation was not confined to the deposit banks, but pervaded the whole multitude of banks throughout the Union and was giving rise to new institutions to aggravate the evil.

The safety of the public funds and the interest of the people generally required that these operations should be checked; and it became the duty of every branch of the General and State Governments to adopt all legitimate and proper means to produce that salutary effect. Under this view of my duty I directed the issuing of the order which will be laid before you by the Secretary of the Treasury, requiring payment for the public lands sold to be made in specie, with an exception until the 15th of the present month in favor of actual settlers. This measure has produced many salutary consequences. It checked the career of the Western banks and gave them additional strength in anticipation of the pressure which has since pervaded our Eastern as well as the European commercial cities. By preventing the extension of the credit system it measurably cut off the means of speculation and retarded its progress in monopolizing the most valuable of the public lands. It has tended to save the new States from a nonresident proprietorship, one of the greatest obstacles to the advancement of a new country and the prosperity of an old one. It has tended to keep open the public lands for entry by emigrants at Government prices instead of their being compelled to purchase of speculators at double or triple prices. And it is conveying into the interior large sums in silver and gold, there to enter permanently into the currency of the country and place it on a firmer foundation. It is confidently believed that the country will find in the motives which induced that order and the happy consequences which will have ensued much to commend and nothing to condemn.

It remains for Congress if they approve the policy which dictated this order to follow it up in its various bearings. Much good, in my judgment, would be produced by prohibiting sales of the public lands except to actual settlers at a reasonable reduction of price, and to limit the quantity which shall be sold to them. Although it is believed the General Government never ought to receive anything but the constitutional currency in exchange for the public lands, that point would be of less importance if the lands were sold for immediate settlement and cultivation. Indeed, there is scarcely a mischief arising out of our present land system, including the accumulating surplus of revenues, which would not be remedied at once by a restriction on land sales to actual settlers; and it promises other advantages to the country in general and to the new States in particular which can not fail to receive the most profound consideration of Congress. . . .

155. CHARLES RIVER BRIDGE v. WARREN BRIDGE
11 Peters, 420
1837

Error to the supreme court of Massachusetts. By act of 1785 the legislature of Massachusetts granted to the Charles River Bridge Company the right to build and maintain a toll bridge over the Charles River. The bridge was opened in 1786, and in 1792 the charter was extended to a period of seventy years. The charter was not, however, exclusive. In 1828 the legislature incorporated the Warren Bridge Company for the purpose of erecting a competing bridge only a few rods from the Charles River Bridge. The Warren Bridge was to be surrendered to the State as soon as the cost of construction should be recovered. The Charles River Bridge Company sued for an injunction on the ground that the construction of a competing bridge constituted an impairment of contract. The question before the court was whether the original grant should be so construed as to constitute an exclusive grant. The decision, Chief Justice Taney's first constitutional opinion, was of utmost importance in establishing the principle that legislative grants are to be construed narrowly in favor of the State, and that any ambiguity in a grant must operate against the corporation and in favor of the public. This decision modified the significance of the decision of the court in the Dartmouth College Case, and marked what some students have regarded as a retreat from the advanced position taken by the Court under Marshall. See, Warren, *Supreme Court*, (1928 ed.) Vol. II, p. 21 ff.; Boudin, *Government by Judiciary*, Vol. I, p. 385 ff.; S. Tyler, *Memoir of Roger B. Taney;* B. C. Steiner, *Life of R. B. Taney;* G. W. Biddle, "Constitutional History of the United States as Influenced by Chief-Justice Taney" in *Constitutional History of the United States as seen in the Development of American Law.*

TANEY, C. J. . . . Borrowing, as we have done, our system of jurisprudence from the English law . . . it would present a singular spectacle, if, while the courts in England are restraining, within the strictest limits, the spirit of monopoly, and exclusive privileges in nature of monopolies, and confining corporations to the privileges plainly given to them in their charter, the courts of this country should be found enlarging these privileges by implication; and construing a statute more unfavorably to the public, and to the rights of the community, than would be done in a like case in an English court of justice.

But we are not now left to determine for the first time the rules by which public grants are to be construed in this country. The subject has already been considered in this court, and the rules of construction above stated fully established. In the case of the *United States* v. *Arredondo,* 8 Pet. 738, the leading cases upon this subject are collected together by the learned judge who delivered the opinion of the court, and the principle recognized that, in grants by the public nothing passes by implication. . . .

But the case most analogous to this, and in which the question came more directly before the court, is the case of *Providence Bank* v. *Billings,* 4 Pet. 514, which was decided in 1830. In that case it appeared that the legislature of Rhode Island had chartered the bank, in the usual form of such acts of incorporation. The charter contained no stipulation on the part of the State that it would not impose a tax on the bank, nor any reservation of the right to do so. It was silent on this point. Afterwards a law was passed imposing a tax on all banks in the State, and the right to impose this tax was resisted by the Providence Bank upon the ground that if the State could impose a tax, it might tax so heavily as to render the franchise of no value, and destroy the institution; that its charter was a contract, and that a power which may in effect destroy the charter is inconsistent with it, and is impliedly renounced in granting it. But the court said that the taxing power is of vital importance and essential to the existence of government, and that the relinquishment of such a power is never to be assumed. . . . The case now before the court is, in principle, precisely the same. It is a charter from a state; the act of incorporation is silent in relation to the contested power. The argument in favor of the proprietors of the Charles River bridge, is the same, almost in words, with that used by the Providence Bank; that is, that the power claimed by the state, if it exists, may be so used as to destroy the value of the franchise they have granted to the corporation. The argument must receive the same answer; and the fact that the power has been already exercised, so as to destroy the value of the franchise, cannot in any degree affect the principle. The existence of the power does not, and cannot, depend upon the circumstance of its having been exercised or not.

It may, perhaps, be said, that in the case of the Providence Bank, this court were speaking of the taxing power; which is of vital importance to the very existence of every government. But the object and end of all government is to promote the happiness and prosperity of the community by which it is established; and it can never be assumed, that the government intended to diminish its power of accomplishing the end for which it was created. And in a country like ours, free, active and enterprising, continually advancing in numbers and wealth, new channels of communication are daily found necessary, both for travel and trade, and are essential to the comfort, convenience and prosperity of the people. A state ought never to be presumed to surrender this power, because, like the taxing power, the whole community have an interest in preserving it undiminished. And when a corporation alleges, that a state has surrendered, for seventy years, its power of improvement and public accommodation, in a great and important line of travel, along which a vast number of its citizens must daily pass, the community have a right to insist, in the language of this court, above quoted, "that its abandonment ought not to be presumed, in a case, in which the deliberate purpose of the state to abandon it does not appear." The continued existence of a government would be of no great value, if, by implications and presumptions, it was disarmed of the powers necessary to accomplish the ends of its creation, and the functions it was designed to perform, transferred to the hands of privileged corporations. The rule of construction announced by the court, was not confined to the taxing power, nor is it so limited, in the opinion delivered. On the contrary, it was distinctly placed on the ground, that the interests of the community were concerned in preserving, undiminished, the power then in question; and whenever any power of the state is said to be surrendered or diminished, whether it be the taxing power, or any other affecting the public interest, the same principle applies, and the rule of construction must be the same. No one will question, that the interests of the great body of the people of the state, would, in this instance, be affected by the surrender of this great line of travel to a single corporation, with the right to exact toll, and exclude competition, for seventy years. While the rights of private property are sacredly guarded, we must not forget, that the community also have rights, and that the happiness and well-being of every citizen depends on their faithful preservation.

Adopting the rule of construction above stated as the settled one, we proceed to apply it to the charter of 1785 to the proprietors of the Charles River bridge. This act of incorporation is in the usual form, and the privileges such as are commonly given to corporations of that kind. It confers on them the ordinary faculties of a corporation, for the purpose of building the bridge; and establishes certain rates of toll, which the company are authorized to take. This is the whole grant. There is no exclusive privilege given to them over the waters of Charles river, above or below their bridge; no right to erect another bridge themselves, nor to prevent other persons from erecting one, no engagement from the State, that another shall not be erected; and no undertaking not to sanction competition, nor to make improvements that may diminish the amount of its income. Upon all these subjects the charter is silent; and nothing is said in it about a line of travel, so much insisted on in the argument, in which they are to have exclusive privileges. No words are used from which an intention to grant any of these rights can be inferred. If the plaintiff is entitled to them, it must be implied, simply from the nature of the grant, and cannot be inferred from the words by which the grant is made. . . .

The inquiry then is, does the charter contain such a contract on the part of the State? Is there any such stipulation to be found in that instrument? It must be admitted on all hands, that there is none—no words that even relate to another bridge, or to the diminution of their tolls, or to the line of travel. If a contract on that subject can be gathered from the charter, it must be by implication, and cannot be found in the words used. Can such an agreement be implied? The rule of construction before stated is an answer to the question. In charters of this description, no rights are taken from the public, or given to the corporation, beyond those which the words of the charter, by their natural and proper construction, purport to convey. There are no words which import such a contract as the plaintiffs in error contend for, and none can be implied; and the same answer must be given to them that was given by this court to the Providence Bank. The whole community are interested in this inquiry, and they have a right to require that the power of promoting their comfort and convenience, and of advancing the public prosperity, by providing safe, convenient, and cheap ways for the transportation of produce and the purposes of travel, shall not be construed to have been surrendered or diminished by the State, unless it shall appear by plain words that it was intended to be done. . . .

Indeed, the practice and usage of almost every State in the Union old enough to have commenced the work of internal improvement, is opposed to the doctrine contended for on the part of the plaintiffs in error. Turnpike roads have been made in succession, on the same line of travel; the later ones interfering materially with the profits of the first. These corporations have, in some instances, been utterly ruined by the introduction of newer and better modes of transportation and travelling. In some cases, railroads have rendered the turnpike roads on the same line of travel so entirely useless, that the franchise of the turnpike corporation is not worth preserving. Yet in none of these cases have the corporations supposed that their privileges were invaded, or any contract violated on the part of the State. . . .

And what would be the fruits of this doctrine of implied contracts on the part of the States, and of property in a line of travel by a corporation, if it should now be sanctioned by this court? To what results would it lead us? If it is to be found in the charter to this bridge, the same process of reasoning must discover it, in the various acts which have been passed, within the last forty years, for turnpike companies. . . . If this court should establish the principles now contended for, what is to become of the numerous railroads established on the same line of travel with turnpike companies, and which have rendered the franchises of the turnpike corporations of no value? Let it once be understood that such charters carry with them these implied contracts, and give this unknown and undefined property in a line of travelling, and you will soon find the old turnpike corporations awakening from their sleep and calling upon this court to put down the improvements which have taken their place. The millions of property which have been invested in railroads and canals upon lines of travel which had been before occupied by turnpike corporations will be put in jeopardy. We shall be thrown back to the improvements of the last century, and obliged to stand still until the claims of the old turnpike corporations shall be satisfied, and they shall consent to permit these States to avail themselves of the lights of modern science, and to partake of the benefit of those improvements which are now adding to the wealth and prosperity, and the convenience and comfort, of every other part of the civilized world. . . .

Judgment affirmed.

STORY, J., delivered a dissenting opinion in which THOMPSON, J., concurred.

156. THE *CAROLINE* AFFAIR
Message of President Van Buren
January 8, 1838

(Richardson, ed. *Messages and Papers*, Vol. III, p. 401 ff.)

Upon the failure of the Canadian Rebellion of 1837, a number of refugees seized Navy Island in the Niagara River, and from there made attacks upon the Canadian border. On December

29, Canadian militia seized the steamer, *Caroline*, then in the service of the insurgents, but on the New York shore. This invasion of American territory led to a diplomatic controversy with Great Britain that was subsequently aggravated by the arrest in New York City of a British subject, Alexander Mc Leod, on the charge of murder in connection with the attack on the *Caroline*. The documents appended to Van Buren's message give the history of the affair. See, O. E. Tiffany "Relations of the United States to the Rebellion of 1837," *Publications* of the Buffalo Historical Society, Vol. VIII; J. B. McMaster, *History of the People of the United States*, Vol. VI, p. 434 ff.; and *British and Foreign State Papers*, Vols. XXVI, XXIX, *passim*.

WASHINGTON, *January 8, 1838.*
To the Senate and House of Representatives of the United States:

In the highly excited state of feeling on the northern frontier, occasioned by the disturbances in Canada, it was to be apprehended that causes of complaint might arise on the line dividing the United States from Her Britannic Majesty's dominions. Every precaution was therefore taken on our part authorized by the existing laws, and as the troops of the Provinces were embodied on the Canadian side it was hoped that no serious violation of the rights of the United States would be permitted to occur. I regret, however, to inform you that an outrage of a most aggravated character has been committed, accompanied by a hostile though temporary invasion of our territory, producing the strongest feelings of resentment on the part of our citizens in the neighborhood and on the whole border line, and that the excitement previously existing has been alarmingly increased. To guard against the possible recurrence of any similar act I have thought it indispensable to call out a portion of the militia, to be posted on that frontier. The documents herewith presented to Congress show the character of the outrage committed, the measures taken in consequence of its occurrence, and the necessity for resorting to them. . . .

M. VAN BUREN.

STATE OF NEW YORK, *Niagara County, ss:*
Gilman Appleby, of the city of Buffalo, being sworn, says that he left the port of Buffalo on the morning of the 29th instant in the steamboat *Caroline*, owned by William Wells, of Buffalo, and bound for Schlosser, upon the east side of the Niagara River and within the United States; that this deponent commanded the said *Caroline,* and that she was cleared from Buffalo with a view to run between said Buffalo and Schlosser, carrying passengers, freight, etc.; that this deponent caused the said *Caroline* to be landed at Black Rock on her way down, and that while at Black Rock this deponent caused the American flag to be run up, and that soon after leaving Black Rock Harbor a volley of musketry was discharged at the *Caroline* from the Canada shore, but without injury; that the said *Caroline* continued her course down the Niagara River unmolested and landed outside of certain scows or boats attached to Navy Island, where a number of passengers disembarked and, as this deponent supposes, certain articles of freight were landed; . . . that at about 6 o'clock in the evening this deponent caused the said *Caroline* to be landed at Schlosser; that the crew and officers of the *Caroline* numbered ten, and that in the course of the evening twenty-three individuals, all of whom were citizens of the United States, came on board of the *Caroline* and requested this deponent and other officers of the boat to permit them to remain on board during the night, as they were unable to get lodgings at the tavern near by; these requests were acceded to, and the persons thus coming on board retired to rest, as did also the crew and officers of the *Caroline,* except such as were stationed to watch during the night; that about midnight this deponent was informed by one of the watch that several boats filled with men were making toward the *Caroline* from the river, and this deponent immediately gave the alarm, and before he was able to reach the dock the *Caroline* was boarded by some seventy or eighty men, all of whom were armed; that they immediately commenced a warfare with muskets, swords, and cutlasses upon the defenseless crew and passengers of the *Caroline* under a fierce cry of "G—d d—n them, give them no quarters; kill every man. Fire! fire!"; that the *Caroline* was abandoned without resistance, and the only effort made by either the crew or passengers seemed to be to escape slaughter; that this deponent narrowly escaped, having received several wounds, none of which, however, are of a

serious character; that immediately after the *Caroline* fell into the hands of the armed force who boarded her she was set on fire, cut loose from the dock, was towed into the current of the river, there abandoned, and soon after descended the Niagara Falls; that this deponent has made vigilant search after the individuals, thirty-three in number, who are known to have been on the *Caroline* at the time she was boarded, and twenty-one only are to be found, . . . the twelve individuals who are missing, this deponent has no doubt, were either murdered upon the steamboat or found a watery grave in the cataract of the Falls; and this deponent further says that immediately after the *Caroline* was got into the current of the stream and abandoned, as before stated, beacon lights were discovered upon the Canada shore near Chippewa, and after sufficient time had elapsed to enable the boats to reach that shore this deponent distinctly heard loud and vociferous cheering at that point; that this deponent has no doubt that the individuals who boarded the *Caroline* were a part of the British forces now stationed at Chippewa.

[Subscribed and sworn to before a commissioner, etc.]

TORONTO, UPPER CANADA, *January 8, 1838.*
His Excellency HENRY S. FOX,

Her Majesty's Minister, Washington. . . .

The governor of the State of New York complains of the cutting out and burning of the steamboat *Caroline* by order of Colonel McNab, commanding Her Majesty's forces at Chippewa, in the Province of Upper Canada, and of the destruction of the lives of some American citizens who were on board of the boat at the time she was attacked.

The act complained of was done under the following circumstances:

In Upper Canada, which contains a population of about 450,000 souls, the most perfect tranquillity prevailed up to the 4th day of December last, although in the adjoining Province of Lower Canada many of the French Canadian inhabitants had been in open rebellion against the Government for about a month preceding.

At no time since the treaty of peace with the United States in 1815 had Upper Canada been more undisturbed. The real causes of the insurrection in Lower Canada, namely, the national antipathy of the French inhabitants, did not in any degree apply in the upper Province, whose population, like the British and American inhabitants of Lower Canada, were wholly opposed to the revolt and anxious to render every service in their power in support of the Queen's authority. . . .

On the night of the 4th December the inhabitants of the city of Toronto were alarmed by the intelligence that about 500 persons armed with rifles were approaching the city; that they had murdered a gentleman of great respectability in the highway, and had made several persons prisoners. . . .

On the 7th of December an overwhelming force of militia went against them and dispersed them without losing a man, taking many prisoners, who were instantly by my order released and suffered to depart to their homes. The rest, with their leaders, fled; some have since surrendered themselves to justice; many have been taken, and some have escaped from the Province. . . .

After the dispersion of the armed insurgents near Toronto Mr. McKenzie, their leader, escaped in disguise to the Niagara River and crossed over to Buffalo. Reports had been spread there and elsewhere along the American frontier that Toronto had been burnt and that the rebels were completely successful, but the falsehood of these absurd rumors was well known before McKenzie arrived on the American side. . . .

Nevertheless, a number of American citizens in Buffalo and other towns on the frontier of the State of New York enlisted as soldiers, with the avowed object of invading Canada and establishing a provisional government. Public meetings were held to forward this design of invading a country with which the United States were at peace. Volunteers were called for, and arms, ammunition, and provisions were supplied by contributions openly made. All this was in direct and flagrant violation of the express laws of the United States, as well as of the law of nations.

The civil authority of Buffalo offered some slight shew of resistance to the movement, being urged to interpose by many of the most respectable citizens. But no real impediment was offered, and on the 13th of

December some hundreds of the citizens of the State of New York, as an armed body under the command of a Mr. Van Rensselaer, an American citizen, openly invaded and took possession of Navy Island, a part of Upper Canada, situate in the Niagara River.

Not believing that such an outrage would really be committed, no force whatever was assembled at the time to counteract this hostile movement.

In a very short time this lawless band obtained from some of the arsenals of the State of New York (clandestinely, as it is said) several pieces of artillery and other arms, which in broad daylight were openly transported to Navy Island without resistance from the American authorities. The people of Buffalo and the adjacent country continued to supply them with stores of various kinds, and additional men enlisted in their ranks.

In a few days their force was variously stated from 500 to 1,500, of whom a small proportion were rebels who had fled from Upper Canada. They began to intrench themselves, and threatened that they would in a short time make a landing on the Canadian side of the Niagara River. . . .

An official statement of the unfriendly proceedings at Buffalo was without delay (on the 13th December) made by me to his excellency the governor of the State of New York, to which no answer has been received. And after this open invasion of our territory, and when it became evident that nothing was effected at Buffalo for preventing the violation of neutrality, a special messenger was sent to your excellency at Washington to urge your interposition in the matter. . . . Soon after his departure this band of outlaws on Navy Island, . . . opened a fire from several pieces of ordnance upon the Canadian shore, which in this part is thickly settled, . . . They put several balls through a house in which a party of militiamen were quartered. . . . They killed a horse on which a man at the time was riding, but happily did no further mischief, though they fired also repeatedly with cannon and musketry upon our boats.

They continued daily to render their position more formidable, receiving constant supplies of men and warlike stores from the State of New York, . . . On the 28th De-

cember positive information was given to Colonel McNab by persons from Buffalo that a small steamboat called the *Caroline,* of about 50 tons burthen, had been hired by the pirates, who called themselves "patriots," and was to be employed in carrying down cannon and other stores and in transporting men and anything else that might be required between Fort Schlosser and Navy Island.

He resolved if she came down and engaged in this service to take or destroy her. She did come down agreeably to the information he received. She transported a piece of artillery and other stores to the island, and made repeated passages during the day between the island and the main shore.

In the night he sent a party of militia in boats, with orders to take or destroy her. They proceeded to execute the order. They found the *Caroline* moored to the wharf opposite to the inn at Fort Schlosser. In the inn there was a guard of armed men to protect her—part of the pirate force, or acting in their support. On her deck there was an armed party and a sentinel, who demanded the countersign.

Thus identified as she was with the force which in defiance of the law of nations and every principle of natural justice had invaded Upper Canada and made war upon its unoffending inhabitants, she was boarded, and after a resistance in which some desperate wounds were inflicted upon the assailants she was carried. If any peaceable citizens of the United States perished in the conflict, it was and is unknown to the captors, and it was and is equally unknown to them whether any such were there. . . .

No wanton injury was committed by the party who gallantly effected this service. They loosed the vessel from the wharf, and finding they could not tow her against the rapid current of the Niagara, they abandoned the effort to secure her, set her on fire, and let her drift down the stream.

The prisoners taken were a man who, it will be seen by the documents accompanying this dispatch, avowed himself to be a subject of Her Majesty, inhabiting Upper Canada, who had lately been traitorously in arms in that Province, and, having fled to' the United States, was then on board for the purpose of going to the camp at Navy Island; and a boy, who, being born in Lower

Canada, was probably residing in the United States, and who, being afraid to land from the boat in consequence of the firing kept up by the guard on the shore, was placed in one of the boats under Captain Drew and taken over to our side, from whence he was sent home the next day by the Falls ferry with money given him to bear his expenses. . . .

The exact position, then, of affairs on our frontier may be thus described:

An army of American citizens, joined to a very few traitors from Upper Canada, and under the command of a subject of the United States, has been raised and equipped in the State of New York against the laws of the United States and the treaties now subsisting, and are using artillery plundered from the arsenals of the State of New York in carrying on this piratical warfare against a friendly country.

The officers and Government of the United States and of the State of New York have attempted to arrest these proceedings and to control their citizens, but they have failed. Although this piratical assemblage are thus defying the civil authorities of both coun-

tries, Upper Canada alone is the object of their hostilities. The Government of the United States has failed to enforce its authority by any means, civil or military, and the single question (if it be a question) is whether Upper Canada was bound to refrain from necessary acts of self-defense against a people whom their own Government either could not or would not control.

In perusing the message of His Excellency Governor Marcy to the legislature of the State of New York your excellency will probably feel some degree of surprise that after three weeks' continued hostility carried on by the citizens of New York against the people of Upper Canada his excellency seems to have considered himself not called upon to make this aggression the subject of remark for any other purpose than to complain of a solitary act of self-defense on the part of Her Majesty's Province of Upper Canada, to which such unprovoked hostilities have unavoidably led.

I have the honor to be, sir, your excellency's most obedient, humble servant,

F. B. HEAD.

157. PRE-EMPTION ACT OF 1841
September 4, 1841

(*U. S. Statutes at Large,* Vol. V, p. 453 ff.)

The occupation of the west, pushing ahead faster than the government land surveys, created a problem of a grave character. Individual settlers squatted on the public domain, and considered it a gross injustice when lands which they had cleared, cultivated, and improved were put up for public sale. To circumvent the government, settlers organized "Claims Associations", whose members were bound not to bid higher than a pre-arranged price. Congress, in 1841, recognized the rights of squatters and the force of public opinion by enacting a pre-emption law by which settlers were allowed to settle on a quarter section of unsurveyed public land with the right of purchase at the minimum price when such land was placed on sale. See, B. H. Hibbard, *History of Public Land Policies,* ch. ix; S. Sato, *History of the Land Question in the United States,* p. 148 ff.; R. G. Wellington, *Political and Sectional Influence of the Public Lands, 1828–1842.*

An Act to appropriate the proceeds of the

sales of public lands and to grant pre-emption rights.

Sec. 8. That there shall be granted to each State . . . five hundred thousand acres of land for . . . internal improvements. *Provided,* that to each of the States which has already received grants for said purposes, there is hereby granted no more than a quantity of land which shall, together with the amount said State has already received . . . make five hundred thousand acres. . . .

Sec. 9. . . . That the net proceeds of the sale of said lands shall be faithfully applied to objects of internal improvement . . . namely, roads, railways, bridges, canals and improvement of water-courses, and draining of swamps. . . .

Sec. 10. That from and after the passage of this act, every . . . man, over the age of twenty-one years, and being a citizen of the United States, or having filed his declaration of intention to become a citizen . . . who since the first day of June, A. D. eighteen hundred and forty, has made . . . a settlement in person on the public lands to which the Indian title had been . . . extinguished, and which . . . shall have been surveyed prior thereto, and who shall inhabit and improve the same, and who . . . shall erect a dwelling thereon, . . . is hereby, authorized to enter with . . . the land office . . . by legal subdivisions, any number of acres not exceeding one hundred and sixty, or a quarter section of land, to include the residence of such claimant, upon paying to the United States the minimum price of such land, subject, however, to the following limitations and exceptions: No person shall be entitled to more than one pre-emptive right by virtue of this act; no person who is the proprietor of three hundred and twenty acres of land in any State or Territory of the United States, and no person who shall quit or abandon his residence on his own land to reside on the public land in the same State or Territory, shall acquire any right of preemption under this act; no lands included in any reservation . . . no lands reserved for the support of schools, nor the lands . . . to which the title has been or may be extinguished by the United States at any time during the operation of this act; no sections of land reserved to the United States alternate to other sections granted to any of the States for the construction of any canal, railroad, or other . . . public improvement; no sections . . . included within the limits of any incorporated town; no portions of the public lands which have been selected as the site for a city or town; no parcel or lot of land actually settled and occupied for the purposes of trade and not agriculture; and no lands on which are situated any known salines or mines, shall be liable to entry under and by virtue of the provisions of this act. . . .

Sec. 11. That when two or more persons shall have settled on the same quarter section of land, the right of pre-emption shall be in him or her who made the first settlement, provided such persons shall conform to the other provisions of this act; and all questions as to the right of pre-emption arising between different settlers shall be settled by the register and receiver of the district within which the land is situated, subject to an appeal to and a revision by the Secretary of the Treasury of the United States. . . .

158. PRIGG v. THE COMMONWEALTH OF PENNSYLVANIA
16 Peters, 539
1842

Error to the Supreme Court of Pennsylvania. The facts of the case are stated in the opinion below. The decision of the Court, that Congress had exclusive power over the rendition of fugitive slaves, and that the states could not be obliged to enforce fugitive slave laws through state officers, led to a series of Personal Liberty Laws in northern states which largely nullified the Fugitive Slave Laws. See, for example, Doc. No. 182. See, Warren, *Supreme Court,* (1928 ed.) Vol. II, p. 83 ff.; A. B. Hart, *Slavery and Abolition,* ch. xix; M. G. Mc Dougall, *Fugitive Slaves, 1619–1865;* J. C. Hurd, *The Law of Freedom and Bondage,* Vol. II.

STORY, J. This is a writ of error to the Supreme Court of Pennsylvania, brought under the 25th section of the Judiciary Act of 1789, for the purpose of revising the judgement of that court, in a case involving the construction of the Constitution and laws of the United States.

The facts are briefly these: the plaintiff in error was indicted in the Court of Oyer and Terminer for York County for having, . . . taken and carried away from that county to the State of Maryland, a certain negro woman, named Margaret Morgan, with a design and intention of selling and disposing of, and keeping her as a slave or servant for life, contrary to a statute of Pennsylvania, passed on the 26th of March 1826. That statute in the first section, . . . provides, that if any person or persons shall from and after the passing of the act, by force and violence take and carry away . . . and shall by fraud and false pretense seduce . . . any negro or mulatto from any part of that Commonwealth, . . . shall on conviction thereof, be deemed guilty of a felony, and shall forfeit and pay a sum not less than five hundred, nor more than one thousand dollars; . . . and shall be confined and kept to hard labor, etc. . . .

The plaintiff in error pleaded not guilty to the indictment; and at the trial the jury found a special verdict, which, in substance, states, that the negro woman, Margaret Morgan was a slave for life, and held to labor and service . . . to a certain Margaret Ashmore, a citizen of Maryland; that the slave escaped and fled from Maryland into Pennsylvania in 1832; that the plaintiff in error . . . caused the said negro woman to be taken . . . as a fugitive from labor by a State constable under a warrant from a Pennsylvania magistrate; that the said negro woman was thereupon brought before the said magistrate who refused to take further cognizance of the case; and thereupon the plaintiff . . . did . . . carry away the said negro woman and her children out of Pennsylvania into Maryland. . . . The special verdict further finds, that one of the children was born in Pennsylvania, more than a year after the said negro woman had fled and escaped from Maryland. . . .

The question arising in the case as to the constitutionality of the statute of Pennsylvania, has been most elaborately argued at the bar. The counsel for the plaintiff have contended that the statute of Pennsylvania is unconstitutional; First, because Congress has the exclusive power of legislation upon the subject matter under the constitution of the United States, and under the act of the 12th of February 1793, which was passed in pursuance thereof; second, that if this power is not exclusive in Congress, still the concurrent power of the State Legislatures is suspended by the actual exercise of the power by Congress; and third, that if not suspended, still the statute of Pennsylvania, in all its provisions applicable to this case, is in direct collision with the act of Congress, and therefore is unconstitutional and void. The counsel for Pennsylvania maintain the negative of all these points.

Few questions which have ever come before this court involve more delicate and important considerations; and few upon which the public at large may be presumed to feel a more profound and pervading interest. . . .

(Upholds constitutionality of fugitive slave act of 1793.)

The remaining question is, whether the power of legislation upon this subject is exclusive in the national government, or concurrent in the States, until it is exercised by Congress. In our opinion it is exclusive; and we shall now proceed briefly to state our reasons for that opinion. . . .

In the first place it is material to state . . . that the right to seize and retake fugitive slaves and the duty to deliver them up, in whatever State of the Union they may be found, and of course the corresponding power of Congress to use the appropriate means to enforce the right and duty, derive their whole validity and obligation exclusively from the Constitution of the United States. . . . Under the Constitution it is recognized as an absolute and positive right and duty, pervading the whole Union with an equal and supreme force, uncontrolled and uncontrollable by State sovereignty or State legislation. It is therefore in a just sense a new and positive right, independent of comity, confined to no territorial limits, and bounded by no State institutions or policy. The natural inference deducible from this consideration certainly is, in the absence of any positive delegation of power to the State Legislatures, that it belongs to the legislative department of the national government, to which it owes its origin and establishment. It would be a strange anomaly, and forced construction, to suppose that the national government meant to rely for the due fulfillment of its own proper duties and the rights which it intended to secure upon State legislation, and not upon that of the Union. *A fortiori,* it would be more objectionable to suppose that a power, which was to be the same throughout the Union, should be confided to State sovereignty, which could not rightfully act beyond its own territorial limits.

In the next place, the nature of the provision and the objects to be attained by it, require that it should be controlled by one and the same will, and act uniformly by the same system of regulations throughout the Union. . . .

It is scarcely conceivable that the slaveholding States would have been satisfied with leaving to the legislation of the non-slaveholding States a power of regulation, in the absence of that of Congress, which would or might practically amount to a power to destroy the rights of the owner. . . . On the other hand, construe the right of legislation as exclusive in Congress, and every evil and every danger vanishes. The right and the duty are then co-extensive and uniform in remedy and operation throughout the whole Union. The owner has the same security, and the same remedial justice, and the same exemption from State regulation and control, through however many States he may pass with his fugitive slave in his possession. . . .

These are some of the reasons but by no means all upon which we hold the power of legislation on this subject to be exclusive in Congress. To guard, however, against any possible misconstruction of our views, it is proper to state that we are by no means to be understood, in any manner whatsoever to doubt or to interfere with the police power belonging to the States in virtue of their general sovereignty. That police power extends over all subjects within the territorial limits of the States, and has never been conceded to the United States. . . . But such regulations can never be permitted to interfere with or to obstruct the just rights of the owner to reclaim his slave, derived from the Constitution of the United States, or with the remedies prescribed by Congress to aid and enforce the same.

Upon these grounds we are of opinion that the act of Pennsylvania upon which this indictment is founded, is unconstitutional and void. . . .

Judgement reversed . . .

M'LEAN, J., dissenting. . . . The slave is found in a State where every man, black or white, is presumed to be free; and this State, to preserve the peace of its citizens, and its soil and jurisdiction from acts of violence, has prohibited the forcible abduction of persons of color. Does this law conflict with the Constitution? It clearly does not in its terms. . . .

No conflict can arise between the act of Congress and this State law. The conflict can only arise between the forcible acts of the master and the law of the State. The master exhibits no proof of right to the services of the slave, but seizes him and is about to remove him by force. I speak only of the force exerted on the slave. The law of the State presumes him to be free and prohibits his removal. Now, which shall give

way, the master or the State? The law of the State does in no case discharge, in the language of the Constitution, the slave from the service of his master.

It is a most important police regulation. And if the master violate it, is he not amenable? The offence consists in abduction of a person of color. And this is attempted to be justified upon the simple ground that the slave is property. That a slave is property must be admitted. The State law is not violated by the seizure of the slave by the master, for this is authorized by the act of Congress; but by removing him out of the State by force, and without proof of right, which the act does not authorize. Now, is not this an act which a State may prohibit? . . .

The important point is, shall the presumption of right set up by the master, unsustained by any proof, or the presumption which arises from the laws and institutions of the State, prevail. This is the true issue. The sovereignty of the State is on one side, and the asserted interest of the master on the other. That interest is protected by the paramount law, and a special, a summary, and an effectual mode of redress is given. But this mode is not pursued, and the remedy is taken into his own hands by the master.

The presumption of the State that the colored person is free may be erroneous in fact; and if so, there can be no difficulty in proving it. But may not the assertion of the master be erroneous also; and if so, how is his act of force to be remedied? The colored person is taken, and forcibly conveyed beyond the jurisdiction of the State. This force, not being authorized by the act of Congress nor by the Constitution, may be prohibited by the State. As the act covers the whole power in the Constitution, and carries out, by special enactments, its provisions, we are, in my judgement, bound by the act. We can no more, under such circumstances, administer a remedy under the Constitution in disregard of the act than we can exercise a commercial or other power in disregard of an act of Congress on the same subject.

This view respects the rights of the master and the rights of the State. It neither jeopards nor retards the reclamation of the slave. It removes all State action prejudicial to the rights of the master; and recognizes in the State a power to guard and protect its own jurisdiction, and the peace of its citizens. . . .

159. THE PEOPLE v. FISHER
N. Y. Reports, 14 Wend. 9
1835

This case illustrates the attitude of the Courts toward combinations of laborers organized for the purpose of securing higher wages, in the early decades of the nineteenth century. See Doc. No. 160.

SAVAGE, C. J. The legislature have given us their definition of conspiracies, and abrogated the common law on the subject. We must therefore see whether this case comes within the statute. The legislature have said, ". . . (6) *To commit any act injurious to the public health, to public morals, or to trade or commerce;* or for the perversion or obstruction of justice of the due administration of the laws—they shall be deemed guilty of a misdemeanor." And in section 9, it is declared that "no conspiracies, other than such as are enumerated in the last section, are punishable criminally." If the conspiracy charged in the indictment is an offence under this statute, it must be embraced under the sixth subdivision, and *is an act injurious to trade or commerce.* . . .

The question therefore is, is a conspiracy to raise the wages of journeymen shoemakers an act injurious to trade or commerce? The words *trade* and *commerce* are said by *Jacobs,* in his Law Dictionary, not to be synonymous; that commerce relates to dealings with foreign nations; trade, on the contrary, means mutual traffic among ourselves, or the buying, selling, or exchange of articles between members of the same community. That the raising of wages and a conspiracy, confederacy, or mutual agreement among journeymen for that purpose is a matter of public concern, and in which the public have a deep interest, there can be no doubt. That it was an indictable offence at common law is established by legal adjudications. . . . Such was the construction of the common law; but in *England* the subject has been thought sufficiently important to require the special attention of the legislature, and statutes were enacted in the reign of Edward 6th and George 3d, which subject workmen,

conspiring either to reduce the time of labor or to raise their wages, to the punishment of fine and imprisonment. I have found but few adjudications upon this subject; but *precedents,* in the absence of *adjudications* are some evidence of what the law is. Among these we find precedents at common law against journeymen for conspiring to raise their wages and lessen the time of labor, and to compel masters to pay for a whole day's work; against journeymen lamp-lighters, for conspiring to raise wages, and against journeymen curriers for the like offence; against salt makers, for conspiring to enhance the price of salt; . . . The immediate object in those cases, as in this, probably was to benefit the conspirators themselves; but if their individual benefit is to work a public injury, a conspiracy for such an object is against the spirit of the common law. . . .

Whatever disputes may exist among political economists upon the point, I think there can be no doubt, in a legal sense, but what the wages of labor compose a material portion of the value of manufactured articles. The products of mechanical labor compose a large proportion of the materials with which trade is carried on. By trade, I now understand traffic or mutual dealings between members of the same community, or internal trade. Coarse boots and shoes are made in many parts of our country; not for particular persons who are to wear them, but as an article of trade and commerce. Probably such is the case in Geneva, where this offence was committed. If journeymen bootmakers, by extravagant demands for wages, so enhance the price of boots made in *Geneva,* for instance, that boots made elsewhere, in *Auburn,* for example, can be sold cheaper, is not such an act injurious to trade? It is surely so to the trade of Geneva in that particular article, and that I apprehend is all that is necessary to bring the offence within the statute. It is important to the best interests of society that the price of labor be left to regulate itself, or rather be limited by the demand for it. Combinations and confederacies to *enhance* or *reduce* the prices of labor, or of any articles of trade or commerce, are injurious. They may be oppressive, by compelling the public to give more for an article of necessity or of convenience than it is worth; or on the other hand, of compelling the labor of the mechanic for less than its value. Without any officious and improper interference of the subject, the price of labor or the wages of mechanics will be regulated by the demand for the manufactured article, and the value of that which is paid for it; but the right does not exist either to enhance the price of the article, or the wages of the mechanic, by any forced and artificial means. The man who owns an article of trade or commerce is not obliged to sell it for any particular price, nor is the mechanic obliged by law to labor for any particular price. He may say that he will not make coarse boots for less than one dollar per pair, but *he has no right to say that no other mechanic shall make them for less.* The cloth merchant may say that he will not sell his goods for less than so much per yard, but has no right to say that any other merchant shall not sell for a less price. If one individual does not possess such a right over the conduct of another, no number of individuals can possess such a right. All combinations therefore to effect such an object are injurious, not only to the individual particularly oppressed, but to the public at large. . . . It is true that no great danger is to be apprehended on account of the impracticability of . . . universal combinations. But if universally or even generally entered into, they would be prejudicial to trade and to the public; they are wrong in each particular case. Truth is, that industry requires no such means to support it. Competition is the life of trade. If the defendants cannot make coarse boots for less than one dollar per pair, let them refuse to do so; but let them not directly or indirectly undertake to say that others shall not do the work for a less price. It may be that *Pennock,* from greater industry or greater skill, made more profit by making boots at seventy-five cents per pair than the defendants at a dollar. He had a right to work for what he pleased. His employer had a right to employ him for such price as they could agree upon. The interference of the defendants was unlawful; its tendency is not only to individual oppression, but to public inconvenience and embarrassment.

I am of the opinion that the offence is indictable, and that the judgment of the general sessions of Ontario county should be reversed, and that a *venire de novo* should issue.

Judgment accordingly.

160. COMMONWEALTH v. HUNT
Mass. Reports, 4 Metcalf 45
1842

By the common law, which obtained in most American States, any combination of working men for the purpose of regulating the terms of employment or raising wages was a conspiracy. See, for example, the *Trial of James Melvin and Others for Conspiracy to Raise Wages, New York City, 1810,* American State Trials, Vol. XIII, p. 576 ff.; and *People* v. *Fisher,* Doc. No. 159. In the famous case of *Commonwealth* v. *Hunt,* Chief Justice Shaw held that a combination of working men for this purpose was not illegal.

This was an indictment against the defendants, (seven in number,) for a conspiracy. The first count alleged that the defendants, together with divers other persons unknown to the grand jurors, "on the first Monday of September 1840, at Boston, being workmen and journeymen in the art and manual occupation of boot-makers, unlawfully, perniciously and deceitfully designing and intending to continue, keep up, form, and unite themselves into an unlawful club, society and combination, . . . did unlawfully assemble and meet together, and, . . . did then and there unjustly and corruptly . . . agree together, that none of them would work for any master or person whatsoever, in the said art, mystery or occupation, who should employ any workman or journeyman, or other person, in the said art, who was not a member of said club, society or combination, after notice given him to discharge such workman from the employ of such master; to the great damage and oppression, not only of their said masters employing them in said art and occupation, but also of divers other workmen and journeymen in the said art, mystery and occupation; to the evil example of all others in like case offending, and against the peace and dignity of the Commonwealth."

The second count charged that the defendants, and others unknown, at the time and place mentioned in the first count, "did unlawfully assemble, meet, conspire, confederate and agree together, not to work for any master or person who should employ any workman not being a member of a club, society or combination, called the Boston Journeymen Bootmakers' Society in Boston, in Massachusetts, or should break any of their by-laws, unless such workman should pay to said club and society such sum as should be agreed upon as a penalty for the breach of such unlawful rules, orders and by-laws; and by means of said conspiracy, they did compel one Isaac B. Wait, a master cordwainer in said Boston, to turn out of his employ one Jeremiah Horne, a journeyman bootmaker, because said Horne would not pay a sum of money to said society for an alleged penalty of some of said unjust rules, orders and by-laws.". . .

The defendants were found guilty, at the October term, 1840, of the municipal court, and thereupon several exceptions were alleged by them to the ruling of the judge at the trial. The only exception, which was considered in this court, was this: "The defendants' counsel contended that the indictment did not set forth any agreement to do a criminal act, or to do any lawful act by criminal means; and that the agreements, therein set forth, did not constitute a conspiracy indictable by any law of this Commonwealth; and they moved the court so to instruct the jury: But the judge refused so to do, and instructed the jury that the indictment against the defendants did, in his opinion, describe a confederacy among the defendants to do an unlawful act, and to effect the same by unlawful means: That the society, organized and associated for the purpose described in the indictment, was an un-

lawful conspiracy, against the laws of this Commonwealth. . . .

SHAW, C. J. . . . We have no doubt, that by the operation of the constitution of this Commonwealth, the general rules of the common law, making conspiracy an indictable offence, are in force here, and that this is included in the description of laws which had, before the adoption of the constitution, been used and approved in the Province, Colony, or State of Massachusetts Bay, and usually practised in the courts of law. . . . Still it is proper in this connexion to remark, that although the common law in regard to conspiracy in this Commonwealth is in force, yet it will not necessarily follow that every indictment at common law for this offence is a precedent for a similar indictment in this State. The general rule of the common law is, that it is a criminal and indictable offence, for two or more to confederate and combine together, by concerted means, to do that which is unlawful or criminal, to the injury of the public, or portions or classes of the community, or even to the rights of an individual. This rule of law may be equally in force as a rule of the common law, in England and in this Commonwealth; and yet it must depend upon the local laws of each country to determine, whether the purpose to be accomplished by the combination, or the concerted means of accomplishing it, be unlawful or criminal in the respective countries. All those laws of the parent country, whether rules of the common law, or early English statutes, which were made· for the purpose of regulating the wages of laborers, the settlement of paupers, and making it penal for anyone to use a trade or handicraft to which he had not served a full apprenticeship—not being adapted to the circumstances of our colonial condition—were not adopted, used or approved, and therefore do not come within the description of the laws adopted and confirmed by the provision of the constitution already cited. . . .

Stripped then of these introductory recitals and alleged injurious consequences, and of the qualifying epithets attached to the facts, the averment is this; that the defendants and others formed themselves into a society, and agreed not to work for any person who should employ any journeyman or other person, not a member of such society, after notice given him to discharge such workman. The manifest intent of the association is, to induce all those engaged in the same occupation to become members of it. Such a purpose is not unlawful. It would give them a power which might be exerted for useful and honorable purposes, or for dangerous and pernicious ones. If the latter were the real and actual object, and susceptible of proof, it should have been specially charged. Such an association might be used to afford each other assistance in times of poverty, sickness and distress; or to raise their intellectual, moral and social condition; or to make improvement in their art; or for other proper purposes. Or the association might be designed for purposes of oppression and injustice. . . .

Nor can we perceive that the objects of this association, whatever they may have been, were to be attained by criminal means. The means which they proposed to employ, as averred in this count, and which, as we are now to presume, were established by the proof, were, that they would not work for a person, who, after due notice, should employ a journeyman not a member of the society. Supposing the object of the association to be laudable and lawful, or at least not unlawful, are these means criminal? The case supposes that these persons are not bound by contract, but free to work for whom they please, or not to work, if they so prefer. In this state of things, we cannot

perceive, that it is criminal for men to agree together to exercise their own acknowledged rights, in such a manner as best to subserve their own interests. One way to test this is, to consider the effect of such an agreement, where the object of the association is acknowledged on all hands to be a laudable one. Suppose a class of workmen, impressed with the manifold evils on intemperance, should agree with each other not to work in a shop in which ardent spirit was furnished, or not to work in a shop with any one who used it, or not to work for an employer, who should, after notice, employ a journeyman who habitually used it. The consequences might be the same. A workman, who should still persist in the use of ardent spirit, would find it more difficult to get employment; a master employing such an one might, at times, experience inconvenience in his work, in losing the services of a skilful but intemperate workman. Still it seems to us, that as the object would be lawful, and the means not unlawful, such an agreement could not be pronounced a criminal conspiracy. . . .

We think, therefore, that associations may be entered into, the object of which is to adopt measures that may have a tendency to impoverish another, that is, to diminish his gains and profits, and yet so far from being criminal or unlawful, the object may be highly meritorious and public spirited. The legality of such an association will therefore depend upon the means to be used for its accomplishment. . . .

161. THE WEBSTER-ASHBURTON TREATY
August 9, 1842

(Malloy, ed. *Treaties, Conventions, etc.* Vol. I, p. 650 ff.)

This treaty finally settled the long-standing northeastern boundary dispute between the United States and Canada. In 1827 a convention had referred the dispute to the arbitration of the King of the Netherlands, but his award had been rejected by both Great Britain and the United States. In 1838 the dispute precipitated the "Aroostook War" between the inhabitants of Maine and New Brunswick. The Webster-Ashburton Treaty embraced other outstanding disputes, particularly those which had grown out of the *Caroline* and McLeod affairs, see Doc. No. 156. The negotiations were conducted with amiability on both sides: Ashburton, the American representative of the Barings, was a per-

sonal friend of Webster's. On the northeastern boundary dispute and the Treaty, see Webster's speech, in Works, Vol. V, p. 78 ff.; J. B. Moore, *History of International Arbitrations,* Vol. I, chs. i ff.; W. F. Ganong, *The Boundaries of New Brunswick;* H. S. Burrage, *Maine in the Northeastern Boundary Controversy;* E. D. Adams, "Lord Ashburton and the Treaty of Washington," *American Hist. Rev.,* July, 1912; S. F. Bemis, ed. *American Secretaries of State,* Vol. V, p. 20 ff.

Treaty to Settle and Define Boundaries; for the Final Suppression of the African Slave-Trade; and for the Giving up of Criminals Fugitive from Justice.

ART. I. It is hereby agreed and declared that the line of boundary shall be as follows: Beginning at the monument at the source of the river St. Croix as designated and agreed to by the Commissioners under the fifth article of the treaty of 1794, between the Governments of the United States and Great Britain; thence, north, following the exploring line run and marked by the surveyors of the two Governments in the years 1817 and 1818, under the fifth article of the treaty of Ghent, to its intersection with the river St. John, and to the middle of the channel thereof; thence, up the middle of the main channel of the said river St. John, to the mouth of the river St. Francis; thence, up the middle of the channel of the said river St. Francis, and of the lakes through which it flows, to the outlet of the Lake Pohenagamook: thence, southwesterly, in a straight line, to a point on the northwest branch of the river St. John, which point shall be ten miles distant from the main branch of· the St. John, in a straight line, and in the nearest direction; but if the said point shall be found to be less than seven miles from the nearest point of the summit or crest of the highlands that divide those rivers which empty themselves into the river St. Lawrence from those which fall into the river St. John, then, the said point shall be made to recede down the said northwest branch of the river St. John, to a point seven miles in a straight line from the said summit or crest; thence, in a straight line, in a course about south, eight degrees west, to the point where the parallel of latitude of 46° 25′ north intersects the southwest branch of the St. John's; thence, southerly, by the said branch, to the source thereof in the highlands at the Metjarmette portage; thence, down along the said highlands which divide the waters which empty themselves into the river St. Lawrence from those which fall into the Atlantic Ocean, to the head of Hall's Stream; thence, down the middle of said stream, till the line thus run intersects the old line of boundary surveyed and marked by Valentine and Collins, previously to the year 1774, as the 45th degree of north latitude, and which has been known and understood to be the line of actual division between the States of New York and Vermont on one side, and the British province of

Canada on the other; and from said point of intersection, west, along the said dividing line, as heretofore known and understood, to the Iroquois or St. Lawrence River. . . .

ART. II. It is moreover agreed, that, from the place where the joint commissioners terminated their labors under the sixth article of the treaty of Ghent, to wit: at a point in the Neebish channel, near Muddy Lake, the line shall run into and along the ship channel between St. Joseph and St. Tammany islands, to the division of the channel at or near the head of St. Joseph's island; thence, turning eastwardly and northwardly around the lower end of St. George's or Sugar island, and following the middle of the channel which divides St. George's from St. Joseph's island; thence up the east Neebish channel, nearest to St. George's island, through the middle of Lake George; thence, west of Jonas' island, into St. Mary's river, to a point in the middle of that river, about one mile above St. George's or Sugar island, so as to appropriate and assign the said island to the United States; thence, adopting the line traced on the maps by the commissioners, through the river St. Mary and Lake Superior, to a point north of Ile Royale, in said lake, one hundred yards to the north and east of Ile Chapeau, which last-mentioned island lies near the northeastern point of Ile Royale, where the line marked by the commissioners terminates; and from the last-mentioned point, southwesterly, through the middle of the sound between Ile Royale and the northwestern main land, to the mouth of Pigeon river, and up the said river, to and through the north and south Fowl Lakes, to the lakes of the height of land between Lake Superior and the Lake of the Woods; thence, along the water communication to Lake Saisaginaga, and through that lake; thence, to and through Cypress Lake, Lac du Bois Blanc, Lac la Croix, Little Vermilion Lake, and Lake Namecan, and through the several smaller lakes, straits, or streams, connecting the lakes here mentioned, to that point in Lac la Pluie, or Rainy Lake, at the Chaudière Falls, from which the commissioners traced the line to the most northwestern point of the Lake of the Woods; thence, along the said line, to the said most northwestern point, being in latitude 49° 23′ 55″ north, and in longitude 95° 14′ 38″

west from the observatory at Greenwich; thence, according to existing treaties, due south to its intersection with the 49th parallel of north latitude, and along that parallel to the Rocky mountains. It being understood that all the water communications and all the usual portages along the line from Lake Superior to the Lake of the Woods, and also Grand portage, from the shore of Lake Superior to the Pigeon river, as now actually used, shall be free and open to the use of the citizens and subjects of both countries. . . .

ART. VIII. The parties mutually stipulate that each shall prepare, equip, and maintain in service, on the coast of Africa, a sufficient and adequate squadron, or naval force of vessels, of suitable numbers and descriptions, to carry in all not less than eighty guns, to enforce, separately and respectively, the laws, rights, and obligations, of each of the two countries, for the suppression of the slave trade; the said squadrons to be independent of each other; but the two Governments stipulating, nevertheless, to give such orders to the officers commanding their respective forces as shall enable them most effectually to act in concert and co-operation, upon mutual consultation, as exigencies may arise, for the attainment of the true object of this article; copies of all such orders to be communicated by each Government to the other, respectively.

162. THE CONSTITUTION OF THE BROOK FARM ASSOCIATION
1841

(O. B. Frothingham, *Transcendentalism in New England,* p. 159 ff.)

Brook Farm, by virtue of the distinguished character of its membership and of its literary associations, is the most famous of those Utopian experiments which flourished in the generation preceding the Civil War. It was established at West Roxbury, Massachusetts, some nine miles south of Boston, and among its members were George Ripley, J. S. Dwight, Charles A. Dana, and Nathaniel Hawthorne, while almost the whole of literary Boston and Concord frequented its halls. A disastrous fire brought the experiment to an untimely end in 1846. See, L. Swift, *Brook Farm;* O. B. Frothingham, *George Ripley,* chs. iii–iv; O. B. Frothingham, *Transcendentalism in New England,* ch. vii; J. T. Codman, *Brook Farm;* J. H. Noyes, *History of American Socialisms;* M. Hillquit, *History of Socialism in the United States;* H. Semler, *Geschichte der Socialismus und Communismus in Nord America.* For other communistic experiments, see C. Nordhoff, *The Communistic Societies of the United States;* W. A. Hinds, *American Communities and Co-operative Colonies;* G. B. Lockwood, *The New Harmony Movement;* B. M. H. Shambaugh, *Amana;* A. Shaw, *Icaria;* M. A. Mikkelsen, *Bishop Hill Colony;* R. J. Hendricks, *Bethel and Aurora.* Hawthorne's *Blithedale Romance* gives a somewhat unfair picture of Brook Farm.

CONSTITUTION

In order more effectually to promote the great purposes of human culture; to establish the external relations of life on a basis of wisdom and purity; to apply the principles of justice and love to our social organization in accordance with the laws of Divine Providence; to substitute a system of brotherly coöperation for one of selfish competition; to secure to our children and those who may be entrusted to our care, the benefits of the highest physical, intellectual and moral education, which in the progress of knowledge the resources at our command will permit; to institute an attractive, efficient, and productive system of industry; to prevent the exercise of worldly anxiety, by the competent supply of our necessary wants; to diminish the desire of excessive accumulation, by making the acquisition of individual property subservient to upright and disinterested uses; to guarantee to each other forever the means of physical support, and of spiritual progress; and thus to impart a greater freedom, simplicity, truthfulness, refinement, and moral dignity, to our mode of life;—we the undersigned do unite in a voluntary Association, and adopt and ordain the following articles of agreement, to wit:

ARTICLE I

Sec. 1. The name of this Association shall be "THE BROOK-FARM ASSOCIATION FOR INDUSTRY AND EDUCATION." All persons who shall hold one or more shares in its stock, or whose labor and skill shall be considered an equivalent for capital, may be admitted by the vote of two-thirds of the Association, as members thereof.

Sec. 2. No member of the Association shall ever be subjected to any religious test; nor shall any authority be assumed over individual freedom of opinion by the Association, nor by any one member over another; nor shall any one be held accountable to the Association, except for such overt acts, omissions of duty, as violate the principles of justice, purity, and love, on which it is founded; and in such cases the relation of any member may be suspended, or discontinued, at the pleasure of the Association.

ARTICLE II

Sec. 1. The members of this Association shall own and manage such real and personal estate in joint stock proprietorship, divided into shares of one hundred dollars, each, as may from time to time be agreed on. . . .

Sec. 4. The shareholders on their part, for themselves, their heirs and assigns, do renounce all claim on any profits accruing to the Association for the use of their capital invested in the stock of the Association, except five per cent, interest on the amount of stock held by them, payable in the manner described in the preceding section.

ARTICLE III

Sec. 1. The Association shall provide such employment for all its members as shall be adapted to their capacities, habits, and tastes; and each member shall select and perform such operations of labor, whether corporal or mental, as shall be deemed best suited to his own endowments, and the benefit of the Association.

Sec. 2. The Association guarantees to all its members, their children, and family dependents, house-rent, fuel, food, and clothing, and the other necessaries of life, without charge, not exceeding a certain fixed amount to be decided annually by the Association; no charge shall ever be made for support during inability to labor from sickness or old age, or for medical or nursing attendance, except in case of shareholders, who shall be charged therefor . . . but no charge shall be made to any members for education or the use of library and public rooms. . . .

ARTICLE V

Sec. 1. The government of the Association shall be vested in a board of Directors, divided into four departments as follows; 1st., General Direction; 2d, Direction of Education; 3d., Direction of Industry; 4th, Direction of Finance; consisting of three persons each. . . .

Sec. 5. The departments of Education and Finance shall be under the control each of its own Direction, which shall select, and in concurrence with the General Direction, shall appoint such teachers, officers, and agents, as shall be necessary to the complete and systematic organization of the department. No Directors or other officers shall be deemed to possess any rank superior to the other members of the Association, nor shall they receive any extra remuneration for their official services.

Sec. 6. The department of Industry shall be arranged in groups and series, as far as practicable, and shall consist of three primary series; to wit, Agricultural, Mechanical, and Domestic Industry. The chief of each series shall be elected every two months by the members thereof. . . .

163. DOROTHEA DIX'S MEMORIAL TO THE LEGISLATURE OF MASSACHUSETTS
January, 1843
(Old South Leaflets, No. 148)

In March 1841, Dorothea Dix, visiting a jail in East Cambridge, Massachusetts, found insane persons kept in an unheated room. The following two years she spent investigating the jails and almshouses of Massachusetts, and in January 1843 her report, dated from Dr. Channing's house, was presented to the Legislature by some of her influential friends. The Memorial produced a profound sensation: it was referred to a committee of which Dr. Samuel G. Howe was chairman and reported with recommendations for relief. Within a short time Massachusetts made more adequate provision for her insane, and Miss Dix entered upon a larger field of philanthropic work which embraced most of the States of the American Union and several European countries. See, F. Tiffany, *Life of Dorothea Lynde Dix;* A. S. Roe, *Dorothea Dix.*

Gentlemen,—I respectfully ask to present this Memorial, believing that the cause, which actuates to and sanctions so unusual a movement, presents no equivocal claim to public consideration and sympathy. . . .

About two years since leisure afforded opportunity and duty prompted me to visit several prisons and almshouses in the vicinity of this metropolis. I found, near Boston, in the jails and asylums for the poor, a numerous class brought into unsuitable connection with criminals and the general mass of paupers. I refer to idiots and insane persons, dwelling in circumstances not only adverse to their own physical and moral improvement, but productive of extreme disadvantages to all other persons brought into association with them. I applied myself diligently to trace the causes of these evils, and sought to supply remedies. As one obstacle was surmounted, fresh difficulties appeared. Every new investigation has given depth to the conviction that it is only by decided, prompt, and vigorous legislation the evils to which I refer, and which I shall proceed more fully to illustrate, can be remedied. I shall be obliged to speak with great plainness, and to reveal many things revolting to the taste, and from which my woman's nature shrinks with peculiar sensitiveness. But truth is the highest consideration. *I tell what I have seen*—painful and shocking as the details often are—that from them you may feel more deeply the imperative obligation which lies upon you to prevent the possibility of a repetition or continuance of such outrages upon humanity. . . .

I come to present the strong claims of suffering humanity. I come to place before the Legislature of Massachusetts the condition of the miserable, the desolate, the outcast. I come as the advocate of helpless, forgotten, insane, and idiotic men and women; of beings sunk to a condition from which the most unconcerned would start with real horror; of beings wretched in our prisons, and more wretched in our almshouses. . . .

I must confine myself to few examples,

but am ready to furnish other and more complete details, if required.

If my pictures are displeasing, coarse, and severe, my subjects, it must be recollected, offer no tranquil, refined, or composing features. The condition of human beings, reduced to the extremest states of degradation and misery cannot be exhibited in softened language, or adorn a polished page.

I proceed, gentlemen, briefly to call your attention to the *present* state of insane persons confined within this Commonwealth, in *cages, closets, cellars, stalls, pens! Chained, naked, beaten with rods,* and *lashed* into obedience. . . .

It is the Commonwealth, not its integral parts, that is accountable for most of the abuses which have lately and do still exist. I repeat it, it is defective legislation which perpetuates and multiplies these abuses. In illustration of my subject, I offer the following extracts from my Note-book and Journal:—

Springfield. In the jail, one lunatic woman, furiously mad, a State pauper, improperly situated, both in regard to the prisoners, the keepers, and herself. It is a case of extreme self-forgetfulness and oblivion to all the decencies of life, to describe which would be to repeat only the grossest scenes. She is much worse since leaving Worcester. In the almshouse of the same town is a woman apparently only needing judicious care, and some well-chosen employment, to make it unnecessary to confine her in solitude, in a dreary unfurnished room. Her appeals for employment and companionship are most touching, but the mistress replied "she had no time to attend to her.". . .

Lincoln. A woman in a cage. *Medford.* One idiotic subject chained, and one in a close stall for seventeen years. *Pepperell.* One often doubly chained, hand and foot; another violent; several peaceable now. *Brookfield.* One man caged, comfortable. *Granville.* One often closely confined; now losing the use of his limbs from want of exercise. *Charlemont.* One man caged. *Savoy.* One man caged. *Lenox.* Two in the jail, against whose unfit condition there the jailer protests.

Dedham. The insane disadvantageously placed in the jail. In the almshouse, two females in stalls, situated in the main building; lie in wooden bunks filled with straw; always shut up. One of these subjects is supposed curable. The overseers of the poor have declined giving her a trial at the hospital, as I was informed, on account of expense. . . .

Besides the above, I have seen many who, part of the year, are chained or caged. The use of cages all but universal. Hardly a town but can refer to some not distant period of using them; chains are less common; negligences frequent; wilful abuse less frequent than sufferings proceeding from ignorance, or want of consideration. I encountered during the last three months many poor creatures wandering reckless and unprotected through the country. . . . But I cannot particularize. In traversing the State, I have found hundreds of insane persons in every variety of circumstance and condition, many whose situation could not and need not be improved; a less number, but that very large, whose lives are the saddest pictures of human suffering and degradation.

I give a few illustrations; but description fades before reality.

Danvers. November. Visited the almshouse. A large building, much out of repair. Understand a new one is in contemplation. Here are from fifty-six to sixty inmates, one idiotic, three insane; one of the latter in close confinement at all times.

Long before reaching the house, wild shouts, snatches of rude songs, imprecations and obscene language, fell upon the ear, proceeding from the occupant of a low building, rather remote from the principal building to which my course was directed. Found the mistress, and was conducted to the place which was called "the home" of the *forlorn* maniac, a young woman, exhibiting a condition of neglect and misery blotting out the faintest idea of comfort, and outraging every sentiment of decency. She had been, I learnt, "a respectable person, industrious and worthy. Disappointments and trials shook her mind, and, finally, laid prostrate reason and self-control. She became a maniac for life. She had been at Worcester Hospital for a considerable time, and had been returned as incurable." The mistress told me she understood that, "while there, she was comfortable and decent." Alas, what a change was here exhibited! She had passed from one degree of violence to another, in swift progress. There she stood, clinging to or beating upon the bars of her caged apartment, the contracted size of which afforded space only for increasing accumulations of filth, a *foul* spectacle. There she stood with naked arms and dishevelled hair, the unwashed frame invested with fragments of unclean garments, the air so extremely offensive, though ventilation was afforded on all sides save one, that it was not possible to remain beyond a few moments without retreating for recovery to the outward air. Irritation of body, produced by utter filth and exposure, incited her to the horrid process of tearing off her skin by inches. Her face, neck, and person were thus disfigured to hideousness. She held up a fragment just rent off. To my exclamation of horror, the mistress replied: "Oh, we can't help it. Half the skin is off sometimes. We can do nothing with her; and it makes no difference what she eats, for she consumes her own filth as readily as the food which is brought her."

Men of Massachusetts, I beg, I implore, I demand pity and protection for these of my suffering, outraged sex. Fathers, husbands, brothers, I would supplicate you for this boon; but what do I say? I dishonor you, divest you at once of Christianity and humanity, does this appeal imply distrust. If it comes burdened with a doubt of your righteousness in this legislation, then blot it out; while I declare confidence in your honor, not less than your humanity. Here you will put away the cold, calculating spirit of selfishness and self-seeking; lay off the armor of local strife and political opposition; here and now, for once, forgetful of the earthly and perishable, come up to these halls and consecrate them with one heart and one mind to works of righteousness and just judgment.

Become the benefactors of your race, the just guardians of the solemn rights you hold in trust. Raise up the fallen, succor the desolate, restore the outcast, defend the helpless, and for your eternal and great reward receive the benediction, "Well done, good and faithful servants, become rulers over many things!"

Injustice is also done to the *convicts:* it is certainly very wrong that they should be doomed day after day and night after night to listen to the ravings of madmen and madwomen. This is a kind of punishment that is not recognized by our statutes, and is what the criminal ought not to be called upon to undergo. The confinement of the criminal and of the insane in the same building is subversive of that good order and discipline which should be observed in every well-regulated prison. I do most sincerely hope that more permanent provision will be made for the pauper insane by the State, either to restore Worcester Insane Asylum to what it was originally designed to be or else make some just appropriation for the benefit of this very unfortunate class of our "fellow-beings."

Gentlemen, I commit to you this sacred cause. Your action upon this subject will affect the present and future condition of hundreds and of thousands. In this legislation, as in all things, may you exercise that "wisdom which is the breath of the power of God."

Respectfully submitted,

D. L. DIX.

164. CLAY'S RALEIGH LETTER
April 17, 1844

(*Niles' National Register,* Vol. LXVI, p. 152–3)

It was apparent, early in 1844, that Clay would be the Whig nominee for the Presidency, and it was commonly believed that Van Buren would be nominated by the Democrats. Early in 1844 Van Buren visited Clay at Ashland and came to an agreement with him to eliminate the Texas question from the campaign. Accordingly on April 17 both candidates published letters opposing immediate annexation. Van Buren's letter in all probability cost him the nomination. Clay's letter so embarrassed him in the campaign that he sought to explain it away in a series of letters known as the "Alabama letters"—but without success. Clay was defeated by Polk who was pledged to immediate annexation. The letters of Clay and Van Buren and the subsequent Alabama letters can be found in *Niles Register,* Vol. LXVI. See, C. Schurz, *Henry Clay,* Vol. II; T. C. Smith, *The Liberty and Free Soil Parties;* E. M. Shepard, *Martin Van Buren.*

TO THE EDITORS OF THE NATIONAL INTELLIGENCER

Raleigh, April 17, 1844.

Gentlemen: Subsequent to my departure from Ashland, in December last, I received various communications from popular assemblages and private individuals, requesting an expression of my opinion upon the question of the annexation of Texas to the United States. . . . The rejection of the overture of Texas, some years ago, to become annexed to the United States, had met with general acquiescence. Nothing had since occurred materially to vary the question. I had seen no evidence of a desire being entertained, on the part of any considerable portion of the American people, that Texas should become an integral part of the United States. . . . To the astonishment of the whole nation, we are now informed that a treaty of annexation has been actually concluded, and is to be submitted to the senate for its consideration. The motives for my silence, therefore, no longer remain, and I feel it to be my duty to present an exposition of my views and opinions upon the question, for what they may be worth, to the public consideration. I adopt this method as being more convenient than several replies to the respective communications which I have received.

I regret that I have not the advantage of a view of the treaty itself, so as to enable me to adapt an expression of my opinion to the actual conditions and stipulations which it contains. Not possessing that opportunity, I am constrained to treat the question according to what I presume to be the terms of the treaty. If, without the loss of national character, without the hazard of foreign war, with the general concurrence of the nation, without any danger to the integrity of the Union, and without giving an unreasonable price for Texas, the question of annexation were presented, it would appear in quite a different light from that in which, I apprehend, it is now to be regarded. . . .

Annexation and war with Mexico are identical. Now, for one, I certainly am not willing to involve this country in a foreign war for the object of acquiring Texas. I know there are those who regard such a war with indifference and as a trifling affair, on account of the weakness of Mexico, and her inability to inflict serious injury upon this country. But I do not look upon it thus lightly. I regard all wars as great calamities, to be avoided, if possible, and honorable peace as the wisest and truest policy of this country. What the United States most need are union, peace, and patience. Nor do I think that the weakness of a power should form a motive, in any case, for inducing us to engage in or to depreciate the evils of war.—Honor and good faith and justice are equally due from this country towards the weak as towards the strong. And, if an act of injustice were to be perpetrated towards any power, it would be more compatible with the dignity of the nation, and, in my judgment, less dishonorable, to inflict it upon a powerful instead of a weak foreign nation. But are we perfectly sure that we should be free from injury in a state of war with Mexico? Have we any security that countless numbers of foreign vessels, under the authority and flag of Mexico, would not prey upon our defenceless commerce in the Mexican gulf, on the Pacific ocean, and on every other sea and ocean? What commerce, on the other hand, does Mexico offer, as an indemnity for our losses, to the gallantry and enterprise of our countrymen? This view of the subject supposes that the war would be confined to the United States and Mexico as the only belligerents. But have we any certain guaranty that Mexico would obtain no allies among the great European powers? . . .

Assuming that the annexation of Texas is war with Mexico, is it competent to the treaty-making power to plunge this country into war, not only without the concurrence of, but without deigning to consult congress, to which, by the constitution, belongs exclusively the power of declaring war?

I have hitherto considered the question upon the supposition that the annexation is attempted without the assent of Mexico. If she yields her consent, that would materially affect the foreign aspect of the question, if it did not remove all foreign difficulties. On the assumption of that assent, the question would be confined to the domestic considerations which belong to it, embracing the terms and conditions upon which annexation is proposed. I do not think that Texas ought to be received into the Union, as an integral part

of it, in decided opposition to the wishes of a considerable and respectable portion of the confederacy. I think it far more wise and important to compose and harmonize the present confederacy, as it now exists, than to introduce a new element of discord and distraction into it. . . . Mr. Jefferson expressed the opinion, and others believed, that it never was in the contemplation of the framers of the constitution to add foreign territory to the confederacy, out of which new states were to be formed. The acquisitions of Louisiana and Florida may be defended upon the peculiar ground of the relation in which they stood to the states of the Union. After they were admitted, we might well pause a while, people our vast wastes, develop our resources, prepare the means of defending what we possess, and augment our strength, power, and greatness. If hereafter further territory should be wanted for an increased population, we need entertain no apprehensions but that it will be acquired by means, it is to be hoped, fair, honorable, and constitutional.

It is useless to disguise that there are those who espouse and those who oppose the annexation of Texas upon the ground of the influence which it would exert, in the balance of political power, between two great sections of the Union. I conceive that no motive for the acquisition of foreign territory would be more unfortunate, or pregnant with more fatal consequences, than that of obtaining it for the purpose of strengthening one part against another part of the common confederacy. Such a principle, put into practical operation, would menace the existence, if it did not certainly sow the seeds of a dissolution of the Union. It would be to proclaim to the world an insatiable and unquenchable thirst for foreign conquest or acquisition of territory. For if today Texas be acquired to strengthen one part of the confederacy, tomorrow Canada may be required to add strength to another. And, after that might have been obtained, still other and further acquisitions would become necessary to equalize and adjust the balance of political power. Finally, in the progress of this spirit of universal dominion, the part of the confederacy which is now weakest, would find itself still weaker from the impossibility of securing new theatres for those peculiar institutions which it is charged with being desirous to extend.

But would Texas, ultimately, really add strength to that which is now considered the weakest part of the confederacy? If my information be correct, it would not. According to that, the territory of Texas is susceptible of a division into five states of convenient size and form. Of these, two only would be adapted to those peculiar institutions to which I have referred, and the other three, lying west and north of San Antonio, being only adapted to farming and grazing purposes, from the nature of their soil, climate, and productions, would not admit of those institutions. In the end, therefore, there would be two slave and three free states probably added to the Union. If this view of the soil and geography of Texas be correct, it might serve to diminish the zeal both of those who oppose and those who are urging annexation. . . .

In the future progress of events, it is probable that there will be a voluntary or forcible separation of the British North American possessions from the parent country. I am strongly inclined to think that it will be best for the happiness of all parties that, in that event, they should be erected into a separate and independent republic. With the Canadian republic on one side, that of Texas on the other, and the United States,

the friend of both, between them, each could advance its own happiness by such constitutions, laws, and measures, as were best adapted to its peculiar condition. They would be natural allies, ready, by co-operation, to repel any European or foreign attack upon either. Each would afford a secure refuge to the persecuted and oppressed driven into exile by either of the others. They would emulate each other in improvements, in free institutions, and in the science of self-government. Whilst Texas has adopted our constitution as the model of hers, she has, in several important particulars, greatly improved upon it.

Although I have felt compelled, from the nature of the inquiries addressed to me, to extend this communication to a much greater length than I could have wished, I could not do justice to the subject, and fairly and fully expose my own opinions in a shorter space. In conclusion, they may be stated in a few words to be, that I consider the annexation of Texas, at this time, without the assent of Mexico, as a measure compromising the national character, involving us certainly in war with Mexico, probably with other foreign powers, dangerous to the integrity of the Union, inexpedient in the present financial condition of the country, and not called for by any general expression of public opinion.

I am, respectfully, your obedient servant,

HENRY CLAY.

165. THE ANNEXATION OF TEXAS

Joint Resolution of Congress annexing Texas to the United States
March 1, 1845

(*U. S. Statutes at Large,* Vol. V, p. 797–8)

Texas, inhabited largely by Americans, achieved independence from Mexico in 1836; independence was recognized by the United States and most of the powers of Europe, but not by Mexico. The project of annexation to the United States was continually agitated, and a treaty of annexation negotiated in 1844 which had been rejected by the Senate became the major issue of the campaign of 1844. The triumph of Polk on a platform calling for the "re-annexation" of Texas, appeared to give a mandate from the American people for annexation, and accordingly a joint resolution for annexation was pushed through Congress and approved March 1. This was the first occasion of the use of the joint resolution to achieve a desired result in foreign relations instead of a treaty, which demanded a

two-thirds vote in the Senate. Fear of English designs in Texas played a considerable rôle in hastening annexation. See, J. H. Smith, *The Annexation of Texas;* E. D. Adams, *British Interests and Activities in Texas;* S. F. Bemis, ed. *American Secretaries of State,* Vol. V, *passim;* J. S. Reeves, *American Diplomacy under Tyler and Polk.*

Resolved . . . , That Congress doth consent that the territory properly included within, and rightfully belonging to the Republic of Texas, may be erected into a new State, to be called the State of Texas, with a republican form of government, to be adopted by the people of said republic, by deputies in convention assembled, with the consent of the existing government, in order that the same may be admitted as one of the States of this Union.

2. That the foregoing consent of Congress is given upon the following conditions, and with the following guarantees, to wit: *First,* Said State to be formed, subject to the adjustment by this government of all questions of boundary that may arise with other governments; and the constitution thereof, with the proper evidence of its adoption by the people of said Republic of Texas, shall be transmitted to the President of the United States, to be laid before Congress for its final action, on or before the first day of January, one thousand eight hundred and forty-six. *Second,* Said State, when admitted into the Union, after ceding to the United States, all public edifices, fortifications, barracks, ports and harbors, navy and navy-yards, docks, magazines, arms, armaments, and all other property and means pertaining to the public defence belonging to said Republic of Texas, shall retain all the public funds, debts, taxes, and dues of every kind, which may belong to or be due and owing said republic; and shall also retain all the vacant and unappropriated lands lying within its limits, to be applied to the payment of the debts and liabilities of said Republic of Texas, and the residue of said lands, after discharging said debts and liabilities, to be disposed of as said State may direct; but in no event are said debts and liabilities to become a charge upon the Government of the United States. *Third.* New States, of convenient size, not exceeding four in number, in addition to said State of Texas, and having sufficient population, may hereafter, by the consent of said State, be formed out of the territory thereof, which shall be entitled to admission under the provisions of the federal constitution. And such States as may be formed out of that portion of said territory lying south of thirty-six degrees thirty minutes north latitude, commonly known as the Missouri compromise line, shall be admitted into the Union with or without slavery, as the people of each State asking admission may desire. And in such State or States as shall be formed out of said territory north of said Missouri compromise line, slavery, or involuntary servitude, (except for crime,) shall be prohibited.

3. That if the President of the United States shall in his judgment and discretion deem it most advisable, instead of proceeding to submit the foregoing resolution to the Republic of Texas, as an overture on the part of the United States for admission, to negotiate with that Republic; then,

Be it resolved, That a State, to be formed out of the present Republic of Texas, with suitable extent and boundaries, and with two representatives in Congress, until the next apportionment of representation, shall be admitted into the Union, by virtue of this act, on an equal footing with the existing States, as soon as the terms and conditions of such admission, and the cession of the remaining Texian territory to the United States shall be agreed upon by the Governments of Texas and the United States: And that the sum of one hundred thousand dollars be, and the same is hereby, appropriated to defray the expenses of missions and negotiations, to agree upon the terms of said admission and cession, either by treaty to be submitted to the Senate, or by articles to be submitted to the two houses of Congress, as the President may direct.

166. TEXAS AND OREGON

Extract from Polk's Inaugural Address
March 4, 1845

(Richardson, ed. *Messages and Papers,* Vol. IV, p. 379 ff.)

The Democratic campaign of 1844 had been fought on the platform of the "re-annexation of Texas and the re-occupation of Oregon". Polk, a confirmed expansionist, announced his adherence to these policies in his inaugural address. Of particular interest is Polk's statement that "our title to the country of Oregon is clear and unquestionable." See, E. I. McCormac, *James K. Polk;* J. S. Reeves, *American Diplomacy under Tyler and Polk.*

. . . The Republic of Texas has made known her desire to come into our Union, to form a part of our Confederacy and enjoy with us the blessings of liberty secured and guaranteed by our Constitution. Texas was once a part of our country—was unwisely ceded away to a foreign power—is now independent, and possesses an undoubted right to dispose of a part or the whole of her territory and to merge her sovereignty as a separate and independent state in ours. I congratulate my country that by an act of the late Congress of the United States the assent of this Government has been given to the reunion, and it only remains for the two countries to agree upon the terms to consummate an object so important to both.

I regard the question of annexation as belonging exclusively to the United States and Texas. They are independent powers competent to contract, and foreign nations have no right to interfere with them or to take exceptions to their reunion. Foreign powers do not seem to appreciate the true character of our Government. Our Union is a confederation of independent States, whose policy is peace with each other and all the world. To enlarge its limits is to extend the dominions of peace over additional territories and increasing millions. The world has nothing to fear from military ambition in our Government. While the Chief Magistrate and the popular branch of Congress are elected for short terms by the suffrages of those millions who must in their own persons bear all the burdens and miseries of war, our Government can not be otherwise than pacific. Foreign powers should therefore look on the annexation of Texas to the United States not as the conquest of a nation seeking to extend her dominions by arms and violence, but as the peaceful acquisition of a territory once her own, by adding another member to our confederation, with the consent of that member, thereby diminishing the chances of war and opening to them new and ever-increasing markets for their products.

To Texas the reunion is important, because the strong protecting arm of our Government would be extended over her, and the vast resources of her fertile soil and genial climate would be speedily developed, while the safety of New Orleans and of our whole southwestern frontier against hostile aggression, as well as the interests of the whole Union, would be promoted by it. . . .

None can fail to see the danger to our safety and future peace if Texas remains an independent state or becomes an ally or dependency of some foreign nation more powerful than herself. Is there one among our citizens who would not prefer perpetual peace with Texas to occasional wars, which so often occur between bordering independent nations? Is there one who would not prefer free intercourse with her to high duties on all our products and manufactures which enter her ports or cross her frontiers? Is there one who would not prefer an unrestricted communication with her citizens to the frontier obstructions which must occur if she remains out of the Union? Whatever is good or evil in the local institutions of Texas will remain her own whether annexed to the United States or not. None of the present States will be responsible for them any more than they are for the local institutions of each other. They have confederated together for certain specified objects. Upon the same principle that they would refuse to form a perpetual union with Texas because of her local institutions our forefathers would have been prevented from forming our present Union. Perceiving no valid objection to the measure and many reasons for its adoption vitally affecting the peace, the safety, and the prosperity of both countries, I shall on the broad principle which formed the basis and produced the adoption of our Constitution, and not in any narrow spirit of sectional policy, endeavor by all constitutional, honorable, and appropriate means to consummate the expressed will of the people and Government of the United States by the reannexation of Texas to our Union at the earliest practicable period.

Nor will it become in a less degree my duty to assert and maintain by all constitutional means the right of the United States to that portion of our territory which lies beyond the Rocky Mountains. Our title to the country of the Oregon is "clear and unquestionable," and already are our people preparing to perfect that title by occupying it with their wives and children. But eighty years ago our population was confined on the west by the ridge of the Alleghanies. Within that period—within the lifetime, I might say, of some of my hearers—our people, increasing to many millions, have filled the eastern valley of the Mississippi, adventurously ascended the Missouri to its headsprings, and are already engaged in establishing the blessings of self-government in valleys of which the rivers flow to the Pacific. The world beholds the peaceful triumphs of the industry of our emigrants. To us belongs the duty of protecting them adequately wherever they may be upon our soil. The jurisdiction of our laws and the benefits of our republican institutions should be extended over them in the distant regions which they have selected for their homes. The increasing facilities of intercourse will easily bring the States, of which the formation in that part of our territory can not be long delayed, within the sphere of our federative Union. In the meantime every obligation imposed by treaty or conventional stipulations should be sacredly respected. . . .

167. THE REASSERTION OF THE MONROE DOCTRINE

Extract from President Polk's First Annual Message to Congress December 2, 1845

(Richardson, ed. *Messages and Papers*, Vol. IV, p. 398 ff.)

This message of Polk's was, according to Professor Perkins, "second only in importance" to the original Monroe Doctrine. It inaugurated a new era in the history of the doctrine, and was closely connected with Polk's policy toward Oregon and Texas. Note that Polk speaks of "this continent" rather than, as in the case of Monroe, of "these continents". On the revival of the Doctrine, see, D. Perkins. *The Monroe Doctrine, 1826–1867*, ch. ii, and notes.

. . . The rapid extension of our settlements over our territories heretofore unoccupied, the addition of new States to our Confederacy, the expansion of free principles, and our rising greatness as a nation are attracting the attention of the powers of Europe, and lately the doctrine has been broached in some of them of a "balance of power" on this continent to check our advancement. The United States, sincerely desirous of preserving relations of good understanding with all nations, can not in silence permit any European interference on the North American continent, and should any such interference be attempted will be ready to resist it at any and all hazards.

It is well known to the American people and to all nations that this Government has never interfered with the relations subsisting between other governments. We have never made ourselves parties to their wars or their alliances; we have not sought their territories by conquest; we have not mingled with parties in their domestic struggles; and believing our own form of government to be the best, we have never attempted to propagate it by intrigues, by diplomacy, or by force. We may claim on this continent a like exemption from European interference. The nations of America are equally sovereign and independent with those of Europe. They possess the same rights, independent of all foreign interposition, to make war, to conclude peace, and to regulate their internal affairs. The people of the United States can not, therefore, view with indifference attempts of European powers to interfere with the independent action of the nations on this continent. The American system of government is entirely different from that of Europe. Jealousy among the different sovereigns of Europe, lest any one of them might become too powerful for the rest, has caused them anxiously to desire the establishment of what they term the "balance of power." It can not be permitted to have any application on the North American continent, and especially to the United States. We must ever maintain the principle that the people of this continent alone have the right to decide their own destiny. Should any portion of them, constituting an independent state, propose to unite themselves with our Confederacy, this will be a question for them and us to determine without any foreign interposition. We can never consent that European powers shall interfere to prevent such a union because it might disturb the "balance of power" which they may desire to maintain upon this continent. Near a quarter of a century ago the principle was distinctly announced to the world, in the annual message of one of my predecessors, that—

The American continents, by the free and independent condition which they have assumed and maintain, are henceforth not to be considered as subjects for future colonization by any European powers.

This principle will apply with greatly increased force should any European power attempt to establish any new colony in North America. In the existing circumstances of the world the present is deemed a proper occasion to reiterate and reaffirm the principle avowed by Mr. Monroe and to state my cordial concurrence in its wisdom and sound policy. The reassertion of this principle, especially in reference to North America, is at this day but the promulgation of a policy which no European power should cherish the disposition to resist. Existing rights of every European nation should be respected, but it is due alike to our safety and our interests that the efficient protection of our laws should be extended over our whole territorial limits, and that it should be distinctly announced to the world as our settled policy that no future European colony or dominion shall with our consent be planted or established on any part of the North American continent. . . .

168. POLK'S MESSAGE ON WAR WITH MEXICO
May 11, 1846

(Richardson, ed. *Messages and Papers*, Vol. IV, p. 437 ff.)

This notorious message, declaring that "Mexico . . . has shed American blood upon the American soil," led to a declaration of war, May 13. Whether the territory between the Nueces and the Rio Grande, where this act of war took place, was actually American Territory, is highly controversial. In any event Polk and his Cabinet had determined upon war as early as May 9, so that the alleged provocation for the war was not the real one. Whether Polk deserved the appellation of "the mendacious Polk" or not is a matter of opinion among historians. On the origins of the Mexican War, see, J. H. Smith, *The War with Mexico*, Vol. I; J. S. Reeves, *The Diplomacy of Tyler and Polk;* E. C. McCormac, *James K. Polk;* L. M. Sears, *John Slidell;* G. L. Rives, *The United States and Mexico*, Vol. I; N. W. Stephenson, *Texas and the Mexican War;* G. P. Garrison, *Westward Extension*, chs. xiii–xv.

To the Senate and House of Representatives:

The existing state of the relations between the United States and Mexico renders it proper that I should bring the subject to the consideration of Congress. . . .

In my message at the commencement of the present session I informed you that upon the earnest appeal both of the Congress and convention of Texas I had ordered an efficient military force to take a position "between the Nueces and the Del Norte." This had become necessary to meet a threatened invasion of Texas by the Mexican forces, for which extensive military preparations had been made. The invasion was threatened solely because Texas had determined, in accordance with a solemn resolution of the Congress of the United States, to annex herself to our Union, and under these circumstances it was plainly our duty to extend our protection over her citizens and soil.

This force was concentrated at Corpus Christi, and remained there until after I had received such information from Mexico as rendered it probable, if not certain, that the Mexican Government would refuse to receive our envoy.

Meantime Texas, by the final action of our Congress, had become an integral part of our Union. The Congress of Texas, by its act of December 19, 1836, had declared the Rio del Norte to be the boundary of that Republic. Its jurisdiction had been extended and exercised beyond the Nueces. The country between that river and the Del Norte had been represented in the Congress and in the convention of Texas, had thus taken part in the act of annexation itself, and is now included within one of our Congressional districts. Our own Congress had, moreover, with great unanimity, by the act approved December 31, 1845, recognized the country beyond the Nueces as a part of our territory by including it within our own revenue system, and a revenue officer to reside within that district has been appointed by and with the advice and consent of the Senate. It became, therefore, of urgent necessity to provide for the defense of that portion of our country. Accordingly, on the 13th of January last instructions were issued to the general in command of these troops to occupy the left bank of the Del

Norte. This river, which is the southwestern boundary of the State of Texas, is an exposed frontier.

The movement of the troops to the Del Norte was made by the commanding general under positive instructions to abstain from all aggressive acts toward Mexico or Mexican citizens and to regard the relations between that Republic and the United States as peaceful unless she should declare war or commit acts of hostility indicative of a state of war. . . .

The Mexican forces at Matamoras assumed a belligerent attitude, and on the 12th of April General Ampudia, then in command, notified General Taylor to break up his camp within twenty-four hours and to retire beyond the Nueces River, and in the event of his failure to comply with these demands announced that arms, and arms alone, must decide the question. But no open act of hostility was committed until the 24th of April. On that day General Arista, who had succeeded to the command of the Mexican forces, communicated to General Taylor that "he considered hostilities commenced and should prosecute them." A party of dragoons of 63 men and officers were on the same day dispatched from the American camp up the Rio del Norte, on its left bank, to ascertain whether the Mexican troops had crossed or were preparing to cross the river, "became engaged with a large body of these troops, and after a short affair, in which some 16 were killed and wounded, appear to have been surrounded and compelled to surrender." . . .

The cup of forbearance had been exhausted even before the recent information from the frontier of the Del Norte. But now, after reiterated menaces, Mexico has passed the boundary of the United States, has invaded our territory and shed American blood upon the American soil. She has proclaimed that hostilities have commenced, and that the two nations are now at war.

As war exists, and, notwithstanding all our efforts to avoid it, exists by the act of Mexico herself, we are called upon by every consideration of duty and patriotism to vindicate with decision the honor, the rights, and the interests of our country. . . .

In further vindication of our rights and defense of our territory, I invoke the prompt action of Congress to recognize the existence of the war, and to place at the disposition of the Executive the means of prosecuting the war with vigor, and thus hastening the restoration of peace. . . .

169. THE OREGON TREATY
June 15, 1846

(Malloy, ed. *Treaties, Conventions, etc.*, Vol. I, p. 656)

The Oregon Treaty, establishing the boundary between the United States and British America along the 49th parallel, concluded half a century of boundary controversy in a manner highly favorable to the United States. By the convention of 1818 the United States and Great Britain had joint occupancy of the territory between the 42nd and the 54th parallels; this arrangement had been extended indefinitely in 1827, with provision for termination on one year's notice. A resolution of April 27, 1846 authorized the President to give notice of the termination of the joint occupancy agreement at his discretion. On the Oregon Treaty, see J. S. Reeves, *American Diplomacy under Tyler and Polk;* J. C. Bell, *Opening a Highway to the Pacific, 1838–1846;* F. Merk, "Oregon Pioneers and the Boundary," *American Hist. Rev.,* Vol. XXIX, p. 681 ff.; H. S. Commager, "England and the Oregon Treaty of 1846," *Oregon Historical Qt.* Vol. XXVIII.

ART. I. From the point on the forty-ninth parallel of north latitude. where the boundary laid down in existing treaties and conventions between the United States and Great Britain terminates, the line of boundary between the territories of the United States and those of her Britannic Majesty shall be continued westward along the said forty-ninth parallel of north latitude to the middle of the channel which separates the continent from Vancouver's Island, and thence southerly through the middle of the said channel, and of Fuca's Straits, to the Pacific Ocean: *Provided, however,* That the navigation of the whole of the said channel and straits, south of the forty-ninth parallel of north latitude, remain free and open to both parties.

ART. II. From the point at which the forty-ninth parallel of north latitude shall be found to intersect the great northern branch of the Columbia River, the navigation of the said branch shall be free and open to the Hudson's Bay Company, and to all British subjects trading with the same, to the point where the said branch meets the main stream of the Columbia, and thence down the said main stream to the ocean, with free access into and through the said river or rivers, it being understood that all the usual portages along the line thus described shall, in like manner, be free and open. In navigating the said river or rivers, British subjects, with their goods and produce, shall be treated on the same footing as citizens of the United States; it being, however, always understood that nothing in this article shall be construed as preventing, or intended to prevent, the government of the United States from making any regulations respecting the navigation of the said river or rivers not inconsistent with the present treaty.

ART. III. In the future appropriation of the territory south of the forty-ninth parallel of north latitude, as provided in the first article of this treaty, the possessory rights of the Hudson's Bay Company, and of all British subjects who may be already in the occupation of land or other property lawfully acquired within the said territory, shall be respected.

ART. IV. The farms, lands, and other property of every description, belonging to the Puget's Sound Agricultural Company, on the north side of the Columbia River, shall be confirmed to the said company. In case, however, the situation of those farms and lands should be considered by the United States to be of public and political importance, and the United States government should signify a desire to obtain possession of the whole, or of any part thereof, the property so required shall be transferred to the said government, at a proper valuation, to be agreed upon between the parties. . . .

170. INDEPENDENT TREASURY ACT
August 8, 1846
(*U. S. Statutes at Large,* Vol. IX, p. 69 ff.)

Van Buren, upon his accession to the Presidency, recommended the establishment of a sub-treasury system as a substitute for the National Bank. A bill incorporating this suggestion was three times defeated, but finally passed July 4, 1840, only to be repealed by the incoming Harrison administration, August 13, 1841. The victory of the Democrats in the election of 1844 insured the repassage af the act. See, D. Kinley, *The Independent Treasury System;* E. M. Shepard, *Martin Van Buren;* J. P. Phillips, *Methods of Keeping the Public Money;* A. S. Bolles, *Financial History of the United States,* Vol. II.

An Act to provide for the better Organization of the Treasury, and for the Collection, Safe-Keeping, Transfer, and Disbursement of the public Revenue.

Be it enacted . . . , That the rooms prepared and provided in the new treasury building at the seat of government for the use of the treasurer of the United States, his assistants, and clerks, and occupied by them, and also the fireproof vaults and safes erected in said rooms for the keeping of the public moneys in the possession and under the immediate control of said treasurer, and such other apartments as are provided for in this act as places of deposit of the public money, are hereby constituted and declared to be the treasury of the United States. And all moneys paid into the same shall be subject to the draft of the treasurer, drawn agreeably to appropriations made by law. . . .

SEC. 6. That the treasurer of the United States, the treasurer of the mint of the United States, the treasurers, and those acting as such, of the various branch mints, all collectors of the customs, all surveyors of the customs acting also as collectors, all assistant treasurers, all receivers of public moneys at the several land offices, all postmasters, and all public officers of whatsoever character, be, and they are hereby, required to keep safely, without loaning, using, depositing in banks, or exchanging for other funds than as allowed by this act, all the public money collected by them, or otherwise at any time placed in their possession and custody, till the same is ordered, by the proper department or officer of the government, to be transferred or paid out; and when such orders for transfer or payment are received, faithfully and promptly to make the same as directed, and to do and perform all other duties as fiscal agents of the government which may be imposed by this or any other acts of Congress, or by any regulation of the treasury department made in conformity to law; and also to do and perform all acts and duties required by law, or by direction of any of the Executive departments of the government, as agents for paying pensions, or for making any other disbursements which either of the heads of these departments may be required by law to make, and which are of a character to be made by the depositaries hereby constituted, consistently with the other official duties imposed upon them. . . .

SEC. 9. That all collectors and receivers of public money, of every character and description, within the District of Columbia, shall, as frequently as they may be directed by the Secretary of the Treasury, or the Postmaster-General so to do, pay over to the treasurer of the United States, at the treasury, all public moneys collected by them, or in their hands; . . .

SEC. 18. That on January 1, 1847, and thereafter, all duties, taxes, sales of public lands, debts, and sums of money accruing or becoming due to the United States, and also all sums due for postages or otherwise, to the general post-office department, shall be paid in gold and silver coin only, or in treasury notes issued under the authority of the United States. . . .

SEC. 19. That on April 1, 1847, and thereafter, every officer or agent engaged in making disbursements on account of the United States, or of the general post-office, shall make all payments in gold and silver coin, or in treasury notes, if the creditor agree to receive said notes in payment. . . .

171. TREATY OF GUADALUPE HIDALGO
Signed, February 2, 1848; Ratified May 30, 1848

(Malloy, ed. *Treaties, Conventions, etc.*, Vol. I, p. 1107 ff.)

This Treaty, ending the War with Mexico, was negotiated by N. P. Trist. He had been instructed to demand the cession of New Mexico and California, Lower California, and a right of way across the Isthmus of Tehuantepec. Trist's blundering, and a growing sentiment for the annexation of even more Mexican territory, led to Trist's recall; he disregarded his recall, however, and concluded the Treaty of Guadalupe Hidalgo. Polk, after some hesitation, sent the treaty to the Senate for ratification, at the same time confiding to his Diary, "if the treaty was now to be made, I should demand more territory". On the Treaty, see, J. S. Reeves, "Treaty of Guadalupe Hidalgo", *American Hist. Rev.* Vol. X, pp. 309–324; R. S. Ripley, *The War with Mexico,* Vol. II; J. H. Smith, *The War with Mexico,* Vol. II: and see, L. M. Sears, "Nicholas P. Trist, A Diplomat with Ideals," *Miss. Valley Hist. Rev.* Vol. XI, p. 85 ff.

ART. I. THERE shall be firm and universal peace between the United States of America and the Mexican Republic, and between their respective countries, territories, cities, towns, and people, without exception of place or persons. . . .

ART. V. The boundary line between the two Republics shall commence in the Gulf of Mexico, three leagues from land, opposite the mouth of the Rio Grande, otherwise called Rio Bravo del Norte, or opposite the mouth of its deepest branch, if it should have more than one branch emptying directly into the sea; from thence up the middle of that river, following the deepest channel, where it has more than one, to the point where it strikes the southern boundary of New Mexico; thence, westwardly, along the whole southern boundary of New Mexico (which runs north of the town called *Paso*) to its western termination; thence, northward, along the western line of New Mexico, until it intersects the first branch of the River Gila; (or if it should not intersect any branch of that river, then to the point on the said line nearest to such branch, and thence in a direct line to the same;) thence down the middle of the said branch and of the said river, until it empties into the Rio Colorado; thence across the Rio Colorado, following the division line between Upper and Lower California, to the Pacific Ocean. . . .

ART. VII. The River Gila, and the part of

the Rio Bravo del Norte lying below the southern boundary of New Mexico, being, agreeably to the fifth article, divided in the middle between the two republics, the navigation of the Gila and of the Bravo below said boundary shall be free and common to the vessels and citizens of both countries; and neither shall, without the consent of the other, construct any work that may impede or interrupt, in whole or in part, the exercise of this right; not even for the purpose of favoring new methods of navigation. . . .

ART. VIII. Mexicans now established in territories previously belonging to Mexico, and which remain for the future within the limits of the United States, as defined by the present treaty, shall be free to continue where they now reside, or to remove at any time to the Mexican republic, retaining the property which they possess in the said territories, or disposing thereof, and removing the proceeds wherever they please, without their being subjected, on this account, to any contribution, tax, or charge whatever. . . .

ART. XII. In consideration of the extension acquired by the boundaries of the United States, as defined in the fifth article of the present treaty, the Government of the United States engages to pay to that of the Mexican Republic the sum of fifteen millions of dollars. . . .

ART. XIII. The United States engage, moreover, to assume and pay to the claimants all the amounts now due them, and those hereafter to become due, by reason of the claims already liquidated and decided against the Mexican Republic, under the conventions between the two republics severally concluded on the eleventh day of April, eighteen hundred and thirty-nine, and on the thirtieth day of January, eighteen hundred and forty-three; so that the Mexican Republic shall be absolutely exempt, for the future, from all expense whatever on account of the said claims.

ART. XIV. The United States do furthermore discharge the Mexican Republic from all claims of citizens of the United States, not heretofore decided against the Mexican Government, which may have arisen previously to the date of the signature of this treaty; which discharge shall be final and perpetual, whether the said claims be rejected or be allowed by the board of commissioners provided for in the following article, and whatever shall be the total amount of those allowed. . . .

ART. XV. The United States, exonerating Mexico from all demands on account of the claims of their citizens mentioned in the preceding article, and considering them entirely and forever cancelled, whatever their amount may be, undertake to make satisfaction for the same, to an amount not exceeding three and one quarter millions of dollars. . . .

ART. XXI. If unhappily any disagreement should hereafter arise between the governments of the two republics, whether with respect to the interpretation of any stipulation in this treaty, or with respect to any other particular concerning the political or commercial relations of the two nations, the said governments, in the name of those nations, do promise to each other that they will endeavor, in the most sincere and earnest manner, to settle the differences so arising, and to preserve the state of peace and friendship in which the two countries are now placing themselves; using, for this end, mutual representations and pacific negotiations. And if, by these means, they should not be enabled to come to an agreement, a resort shall not, on this account, be had to reprisals, aggression, or hostility of any kind, by the one republic against the other, until the Government of that which deems itself aggrieved shall have maturely considered, in the spirit of peace and good neighborship, whether it would not be better that such difference should be settled by the arbitration of commissioners appointed on each side, or by that of a friendly nation. And should such course be proposed by either party, it shall be acceded to by the other, unless deemed by it altogether incompatible with the nature of the difference, or circumstances of the case.

172. WOMAN'S RIGHTS

The Seneca Falls Declaration of Sentiments and Resolutions
July 19, 1848

(The History of Woman Suffrage, ed. by E. C. Stanton, S. B. Anthony and M. J. Gage, Vol. I, p. 70 ff.)

Though Frances Wright, Ernestine Rose, and others had championed the cause of woman's rights early in the century, the immediate origin of the woman's rights movement of the mid-century was in the anti-slavery crusade. When at the World Anti-Slavery Convention in London, in 1840, a group of American women delegates found themselves excluded, they determined that the cause of emancipation affected them as well as slaves. The Seneca Falls Convention was the first of its kind ever held. On the early woman's rights movement, see *The History of Woman Suffrage,* Vol. I; E. A. Hecker, *Short History of Women's Rights;* B. A. Rembaugh, *The Political Status of Women in the United States;* T. Stanton and H. S. Baltch, *Elizabeth Cady Stanton;* A. D. Hallowell, *Life and Letters of James and Lucretia Mott;* K. Anthony, *Margaret Fuller.* Some interesting comments on the philosophical implications of the movement are in T. V. Smith, *The American Philosophy of Equality.*

1. DECLARATION OF SENTIMENTS

When, in the course of human events, it becomes necessary for one portion of the family of man to assume among the people of the earth a position different from that which they have hitherto occupied, but one to which the laws of nature and of nature's God entitle them, a decent respect to the opinions of mankind requires that they should declare the causes that impel them to such a course.

We hold these truths to be self-evident: that all men and women are created equal; that they are endowed by their Creator with certain inalienable rights; that among these are life, liberty, and the pursuit of happiness; that to secure these rights governments are instituted, deriving their just powers from the consent of the governed. Whenever any form of government becomes destructive of these ends, it is the right of those who suffer from it to refuse allegiance to it, and to insist upon the institution of a new government, laying its foundation on such principles, and organizing its powers in such form, as to them shall seem most likely to effect their safety and happiness. Prudence, indeed, will dictate that governments long established should not be changed for light and transient causes; and accordingly all experience hath shown that mankind are more disposed to suffer while evils are sufferable, than to right themselves by abolishing the forms to which they are accustomed. But when a long train of abuses and usurpations, pursuing invariably the same object, evinces a design to reduce them under absolute despotism, it is their duty to throw off such government, and to provide new guards for their future security. Such has been the patient sufferance of the women under this government, and such is now the necessity which constrains them to demand the equal station to which they are entitled.

The history of mankind is a history of repeated injuries and usurpations on the part of man toward woman, having in direct object the establishment of an absolute tyranny over her. To prove this, let facts be submitted to a candid world.

He has never permitted her to exercise her inalienable right to the elective franchise.

He has compelled her to submit to laws, in the formation of which she had no voice.

He has withheld from her rights which are given to the most ignorant and degraded men—both natives and foreigners.

Having deprived her of this first right of a citizen, the elective franchise, thereby leaving her without representation in the halls of legislation, he has oppressed her on all sides.

He has made her, if married, in the eye of the law, civilly dead.

He has taken from her all right in property, even to the wages she earns.

He has made her, morally, an irresponsible being, as she can commit many crimes with impunity, provided they be done in the presence of her husband. In the covenant of marriage, she is compelled to promise obedience to her husband, he becoming, to all intents and purposes, her master—the law giving him power to deprive her of her liberty, and to administer chastisement.

He has so framed the laws of divorce, as to what shall be the proper causes, and in case of separation, to whom the guardianship of the children shall be given, as to be wholly regardless of the happiness of women—the law, in all cases, going upon a false supposition of the supremacy of man, and giving all power into his hands.

After depriving her of all rights as a married woman, if single, and the owner of property, he has taxed her to support a government which recognizes her only when her property can be made profitable to it.

He has monopolized nearly all the profitable employments, and from those she is permitted to follow, she receives but a scanty remuneration. He closes against her all the avenues to wealth and distinction which he considers most honorable to himself. As a teacher of theology, medicine, or law, she is not known.

He has denied her the facilities for obtaining a thorough education, all colleges being closed against her.

He allows her in Church, as well as State, but a subordinate position, claiming Apostolic authority for her exclusion from the ministry, and, with some exceptions, from any public participation in the affairs of the Church.

He has created a false public sentiment by giving to the world a different code of morals for men and women, by which moral delinquencies which exclude women from society, are not only tolerated, but deemed of little account in man.

He has usurped the prerogative of Jehovah himself, claiming it as his right to assign for her a sphere of action, when that belongs to her conscience and to her God.

He has endeavored, in every way that he could, to destroy her confidence in her own powers, to lessen her self-respect and to make her willing to lead a dependent and abject life.

Now, in view of this entire disfranchisement of one-half the people of this country, their social and religious degradation—in view of the unjust laws above mentioned, and because women do feel themselves aggrieved, oppressed, and fraudulently deprived of their most sacred rights, we insist that they have immediate admission to all the rights and privileges which belong to them as citizens of the United States.

In entering upon the great work before us, we anticipate no small amount of misconception, misrepresentation, and ridicule; but we shall use every instrumentality within our power to effect our object. We shall employ agents, circulate tracts, petition the State and National legislatures, and endeavor to enlist the pulpit and the press in our behalf. We hope this Convention will be followed by a series of Conventions embracing every part of the country.

2. RESOLUTIONS

WHEREAS, The great precept of nature is conceded to be, that "man shall pursue his own true and substantial happiness." Blackstone in his Commentaries remarks, that this law of Nature being coeval with mankind, and dictated by God himself, is of course superior in obligation to any other. It is binding over all the globe, in all countries and at all times; no human laws are of any validity if contrary to this, and such of them as are valid, derive all their force, and all their validity, and all their authority, mediately and immediately, from this original; therefore,

Resolved, That all laws which prevent woman from occupying such a station in society as her conscience shall dictate, or which place her in a position inferior to that of man, are contrary to the great precept of nature, and therefore of no force or authority.

Resolved, That woman is man's equal—was intended to be so by the Creator, and the highest good of the race demands that she should be recognized as such.

Resolved, That the women of this country ought to be enlightened in regard to the laws under which they live, that they may no longer publish their degradation by declaring themselves satisfied with their present position, nor their ignorance, by asserting that they have all the rights they want.

Resolved, That inasmuch as man, while claiming for himself intellectual superiority, does accord to woman moral superiority, it is pre-eminently his duty to encourage her to speak and teach, as she has an opportunity, in all religious assemblies.

Resolved, That the same amount of virtue, delicacy, and refinement of behavior that is required of woman in the social state, should also be required of man, and the same transgressions should be visited with equal severity on both man and woman.

Resolved, That the objection of indelicacy and impropriety, which is so often brought against woman when she addresses a public audience, comes with a very ill-grace from those who encourage, by their attendance, her appearance on the stage, in the concert, or in feats of the circus.

Resolved, That woman has too long rested satisfied in the circumscribed limits which corrupt customs and a perverted application of the Scriptures have marked out for her, and that it is time she should move in the enlarged sphere which her great Creator has assigned her.

Resolved, That it is the duty of the women of this country to secure to themselves their sacred right to the elective franchise.

Resolved, That the equality of human rights results necessarily from the fact of the identity of the race in capabilities and responsibilities.

Resolved, That the speedy success of our cause depends upon the zealous and untiring efforts of both men and women, for the overthrow of the monopoly of the pulpit, and for the securing to women an equal participation with men in the various trades, professions, and commerce.

Resolved, therefore, That, being invested by the creator with the same capabilities, and the same consciousness of responsibility for their exercise, it is demonstrably the right and duty of woman, equally with man, to promote every righteous cause by every righteous means; and especially in regard to the great subjects of morals and religion, it is self-evidently her right to participate with her brother in teaching them, both in private and in public, by writing and by speaking, by any instrumentalities proper to be used, and in any assemblies proper to be held; and this being a self-evident truth growing out of the divinely implanted principles of human nature, any custom or authority adverse to it, whether modern or wearing the hoary sanction of antiquity, is to be regarded as a self-evident falsehood, and at war with mankind.

173. HORACE MANN ON EDUCATION AND NATIONAL WELFARE
1848

(Twelfth Annual Report of Horace Mann as Secretary of Massachusetts State Board of Education)

Horace Mann's appointment as Secretary of the newly organized Board of Education, in 1837, inaugurated a new era in the history of American education. In his annual reports Mann discussed the larger implications of education in a democracy. These reports can be found in *The Life and Work of Horace Mann,* Vols. II–V. On Mann, see biography by Mrs. Mary Mann, in Vol. I of the *Life and Work;* B. A. Hinsdale, *Horace Mann and the Common School Revival in the United States;* A. E. Winship, *Horace Mann, the Educator.*

. . . . A cardinal object which the government of Massachusetts, and all the influential men in the State, should propose to themselves, is the physical well-being of all the people,—the sufficiency, comfort, competence, of every individual in regard to food, raiment, and shelter. And these necessaries and conveniences of life should be obtained by each individual for himself, or by each family for themselves, rather than accepted from the hand of charity or extorted by poor-laws. It is not averred that this most desirable result can, in all instances, be obtained; but it is, nevertheless, the end to be aimed at. True statesmanship and true political economy, not less than true philanthropy, present this perfect theory as the goal, to be more and more closely approximated by our imperfect practice. The desire to achieve such a result cannot be regarded as an unreasonable ambition; for, though all mankind were well fed, well clothed, and well housed, they might still be half civilized.

According to the European theory, men are divided into classes,—some to toil and earn, others to seize and enjoy. According to the Massachusetts theory, all are to have an equal chance for earning, and equal security in the enjoyment of what they earn. The latter tends to equality of condition; the former, to the grossest inequalities. Tried by any Christian standard of morals, or even by any of the better sort of heathen standards, can any one hesitate, for a moment, in declaring which of the two will produce the greater amount of human welfare, and which, therefore, is the more conformable to the divine will? The European theory is blind to what constitutes the highest glory as well as the highest duty of a State. . . .

Our ambition as a State should trace itself to a different origin, and propose to itself a different object. Its flame should be lighted at the skies. Its radiance and its warmth should reach the darkest and the coldest of abodes of men. It should seek the solution of such problems as these: To what extent can competence displace pauperism? How nearly can we free ourselves from the low-minded and the vicious, not by their expatriation, but by their elevation? To what extent can the resources and powers of Nature be converted into human welfare, the peaceful arts of life be advanced, and the vast treasures of human talent and genius be developed? How much of suffering, in all its forms, can be relieved? or, what is better than relief, how much can be prevented? Cannot the classes of crimes be lessened, and the number of criminals in each class be diminished? . . .

Now two or three things will doubtless be admitted to be true, beyond all controversy, in regard to Massachusetts. By its industrial condition, and its business operations, it is exposed, far beyond any other State in the Union, to the fatal extremes of overgrown wealth and desperate poverty. Its population is far more dense than that of any other State. It is four or five times more dense than the average of all the other States taken together; and density of population has always been one of the proximate causes of social inequality. According to population and territorial extent there is far more capital in Massachusetts—capital which is movable, and instantaneously available—than in any other State in the Union; and probably both these qualifications respecting population and territory could be omitted without endangering the truth of the assertion. . . .

Now surely nothing but universal education can counterwork this tendency to the domination of capital and the servility of labor. If one class possesses all the wealth and the education, while the residue of society is ignorant and poor, it matters not by what

name the relation between them may be called: the latter, in fact and in truth, will be the servile dependents and subjects of the former. But, if education be equally diffused, it will draw property after it by the strongest of all attractions; for such a thing never did happen, and never can happen, as that an intelligent and practical body of men should be permanently poor. Property and labor in different classes are essentially antagonistic; but property and labor in the same class are essentially fraternal. The people of Massachusetts have, in some degree, appreciated the truth that the unexampled prosperity of the State—its comfort, its competence, its general intelligence and virtue—is attributable to the education, more or less perfect, which all its people have received; but are they sensible of a fact equally important,— namely, that it is to this same education that two-thirds of the people are indebted for not being to-day the vassals of as severe a tyranny, in the form of capital, as the lower classes of Europe are bound to in any form of brute force?

Education then, beyond all other devices of human origin, is a great equalizer of the conditions of men,—the balance wheel of the social machinery. I do not here mean that it so elevates the moral nature as to make men disdain and abhor the oppression of their fellow men. This idea pertains to another of its attributes. But I mean that it gives each man the independence and the means by which he can resist the selfishness of other men. It does better than to disarm the poor of their hostility toward the rich: it prevents being poor. Agrarianism is the revenge of poverty against wealth. The wanton destruction of the property of others—the burning of hay-ricks, and corn-ricks, the demolition of machinery because it supersedes hand-labor, the sprinkling of vitriol on rich dresses—is only agrarianism run mad. Education prevents both the revenge and the madness. On the other hand, a fellow-feeling for one's class or caste is the common instinct of hearts not wholly sunk in selfish regard for a person or for a family. The spread of education, by enlarging the cultivated class or caste, will open a wider area over which the social feelings will expand; and, if this education should be universal and complete, it would do more than all things else to obliterate factitious distinctions in society. . . .

For the creation of wealth, then,—for the existence of a wealthy people and a wealthy nation,—intelligence is the grand condition. The number of improvers will increase as the intellectual constituency, if I may so call it, increases. In former times, and in most parts of the world even at the present day, not one man in a million has ever had such a development of mind as made it possible for him to become a contributor to art or science. . . . Let this development proceed, and contributions . . . of inestimable value, will be sure to follow. That political economy, therefore, which busies itself about capital and labor, supply and demand, interests and rents, favorable and unfavorable balances of trade, but leaves out of account the elements of a wide-spread mental development, is naught but stupendous folly. The greatest of all the arts in political economy is to change a consumer into a producer; and the next greatest is to increase the producing power,—and this to be directly obtained by increasing his intelligence. For mere delving, an ignorant man is but little better than a swine, whom he so much resembles in his appetites, and surpasses in his power of mischief. . . .

174. THE COMPROMISE OF 1850

The new territorial accessions that resulted from the War with Mexico precipitated the slavery question into politics in an inescapable manner. As early as August, 1846, David Wilmot of Pennsylvania had introduced into the House a resolution "That as an express and fundamental condition to the acquisition of any territory from the republic of Mexico by the United States, by virtue of any treaty which may be negotiated between them . . . neither slavery nor involuntary servitude shall ever exist in any part of said territory." This resolution was never passed by Congress, but the principle it expressed was aggressively maintained by the anti-slavery element. In 1848 Oregon was organized as a Territory and the principle of the Northwest Ordinance applied, but efforts to organize California and New Mexico failed. In 1849 the people of California took matters into their own hands by adopting a constitution which prohibited slavery. With the entire country seething with excitement and threats of secession coming from everywhere in the South, the stage was set for the greatest debate in Congressional history. Clay, Webster, Calhoun, Davis, Seward, Chase and others participated in the discussion. January 29 Clay introduced his compromise resolutions. The resolutions were submitted to a committee of which Clay was chairman and reported as two bills: an Omnibus Bill covering the organization of the Territories, and a bill to prohibit the slave trade in the District of Columbia. In the course of the debates on these bills Calhoun, too feeble to speak, presented his last denunciation of Northern aggressions, Webster made his famous Seventh of March speech, and Clay his last effort to save the Union. The Omnibus Bill was finally passed in separate acts. The Bill to admit California as a State was passed and approved September 9. On the Compromise of 1850 see J. F. Rhodes, *History of the United States Since the Compromise of 1850,* Vol. I; H. Von Holst, *Constitutional History of the United States,* Vol. III; J. Shouler, *History of the United States,* Vol. V; E. Channing, *History of the United States,* Vol. VI, chs. iii–iv; C. Schurz, *Henry Clay,* Vol. II; C. Fuess, *Daniel Webster,* Vol. II; H. Von Holst, *Calhoun;* W. E. Dodd, *Jefferson Davis;* A. Johnson, *Stephen A. Douglas;* A. B. Hart, *Samuel P. Chase.* The important debates can be found in T. H. Benton's *Abridgement of the Debates in Congress,* Vol. XVI. The speeches of Calhoun, Webster and Clay are reprinted in A. Johnston and J. A. Woodburn, *American Orations,* Vol. II. Many interesting letters are preserved in J. S. Pike, *First Blows of the Civil War.*

1. CLAY'S RESOLUTIONS
January 29, 1850

(U. S. *Senate Journal,* 31st Congress, 1st Session, p. 118 ff.)

It being desirable, for the peace, concord, and harmony of the Union of these States, to settle and adjust amicably all existing questions of controversy between them arising out of the institution of slavery upon a fair, equitable and just basis: therefore,

1. *Resolved,* That California, with suitable boundaries, ought, upon her application to be admitted as one of the States of this Union, without the imposition by Congress of any restriction in respect to the exclusion or introduction of slavery within those boundaries.

2. *Resolved,* That as slavery does not exist by law, and is not likely to be introduced into any of the territory acquired by the United

States from the republic of Mexico, it is inexpedient for Congress to provide by law either for its introduction into, or exclusion from, any part of the said territory; and that appropriate territorial governments ought to be established by Congress in all of the said territory, not assigned as the boundaries of the proposed State of California, without the adoption of any restriction or condition on the subject of slavery.

3. *Resolved,* That the western boundary of the State of Texas ought to be fixed on the Rio del Norte, commencing one marine league from its mouth, and running up that river to the southern line of New Mexico; thence with that line eastwardly, and so continuing in the same direction to the line as established between the United States and Spain, excluding any portion of New Mexico, whether lying on the east or west of that river.

4. *Resolved,* That it be proposed to the State of Texas, that the United States will provide for the payment of all that portion of the legitimate and bona fide public debt of that State contracted prior to its annexation to the United States, and for which the duties on foreign imports were pledged by the said State to its creditors, not exceeding the sum of —— dollars, in consideration of the said duties so pledged having been no longer applicable to that object after the said annexation, but having thenceforward become payable to the United States; and upon the condition, also, that the said State of Texas shall, by some solemn and authentic act of her legislature or of a convention, relinquish to the United States any claim which it has to any part of New Mexico.

5. *Resolved,* That it is inexpedient to abolish slavery in the District of Columbia whilst that institution continues to exist in the State of Maryland, without the consent of that State, without the consent of the people of the District, and without just compensation to the owners of slaves within the District.

6. *But, resolved,* That it is expedient to prohibit, within the District, the slave trade in slaves brought into it from States or places beyond the limits of the District, either to be sold therein as merchandise, or to be transported to other markets without the District of Columbia.

7. *Resolved,* That more effectual provision ought to be made by law, according to the requirement of the constitution, for the restitution and delivery of persons bound to service or labor in any State, who may escape into any other State or Territory in the Union. And,

8. *Resolved,* That Congress has no power to promote or obstruct the trade in slaves between the slaveholding States; but that the admission or exclusion of slaves brought from one into another of them, depends exclusively upon their own particular laws.

2. THE TEXAS AND NEW MEXICO ACT
September 9, 1850
(U. S. Statutes at Large, Vol. IX, p. 446 ff.)

An Act proposing to the State of Texas the Establishment of her Northern and Western Boundaries, the Relinquishment by the said State of all Territory claimed by her exterior to said Boundaries, and of all her claims upon the United States, and to establish a territorial Government for New Mexico.

Be it enacted, That the following propositions shall be, and the same hereby are, offered to the State of Texas, which, when agreed to by the said State, and in an act passed by the general assembly, shall be binding and obligatory, upon the United States, and upon the said State of Texas: *Provided,* The said agreement by the said general assembly shall be given on or before the first day of December, eighteen hundred and fifty:

FIRST. The State of Texas will agree that her boundary on the north shall commence at the point at which the meridian of one hundred degrees west from Greenwich is intersected by the parallel of thirty-six degrees thirty minutes north latitude, and shall run from said point due west to the meridian of one hundred and three degrees west from Greenwich; thence her boundary shall run due south to the thirty-second degree of north latitude; thence on the said parallel of thirty-two degrees of north latitude to the Rio Bravo del Norte, and thence with the channel of said river to the Gulf of Mexico.

SECOND. The State of Texas cedes to the United States all her claim to territory exterior to the limits and boundaries which she agrees to establish by the first article of this agreement.

THIRD. The State of Texas relinquishes all claim upon the United States for liability of the debts of Texas, and for compensation or indemnity for the surrender to the United States of her ships, forts, arsenals, custom-houses, custom-house revenue, arms and munitions of war, and public buildings with their sites, which became the property of the United States at the time of the annexation.

FOURTH. The United States, in consideration of said establishment of boundaries, cession of claim to territory, and relinquishment of claims, will pay to the State of Texas the sum of ten millions of dollars in a stock bearing five per cent. interest, and redeemable at the end of fourteen years, the interest payable half-yearly at the treasury of the United States. . . .

Sec. 2. And that all that portion of the Territory of the United States bounded as follows (boundaries) . . . is hereby erected into a temporary government, by the name of the Territory of New Mexico: *Provided,* That nothing in this act contained shall be construed to inhibit the government of the United States from dividing said Territory into two or more Territories, in such manner and at such times as Congress shall deem convenient and proper, or from attaching any portion thereof to any other Territory or State: *And provided, further,* That, when admitted as a State, the said Territory, or any portion of the same, shall be received into the Union, with or without slavery, as their constitution may prescribe at the time of their admission.

3. THE UTAH ACT
(September 9, 1850)
(*U. S. Statutes at Large,* Vol. IX, p. 453 ff.)
An Act to establish a Territorial Government for Utah

Be it enacted, That all that part of the territory of the United States included within the following limits, to wit: bounded on the west by the State of California, on the north by the Territory of Oregon, and on the east by the summit of the Rocky Mountains, and on the south by the thirty-seventh parallel of north latitude, be, and the same is hereby, created into a temporary government, by the name of the Territory of Utah; and, when admitted as a State, the said Territory, or any portion of the same, shall be received into the Union, with or without slavery, as their constitution may prescribe at the time

of their admission: *Provided,* That nothing in this act contained shall be construed to inhibit the government of the United States from dividing said Territory into two or more Territories, in such manner and at such times as Congress shall deem convenient and proper, or from attaching any portion of said Territory to any other State or Territory of the United States. . . .

4. FUGITIVE SLAVE ACT
(September 18, 1850)
(*U. S. Statutes at Large,* Vol. IX, p. 462 ff.)
An Act to amend, and supplementary to, the Act entitled "An Act respecting Fugitives from Justice, and Persons escaping from the Service of their Masters," approved—[February 12, 1793].

. . . SEC. 5. That it shall be the duty of all marshals and deputy marshals to obey and execute all warrants and precepts issued under the provisions of this act, when to them directed; and should any marshal or deputy marshal refuse to receive such warrant, or other process, when tendered, or to use all proper means diligently to execute the same, he shall, on conviction thereof, be fined in the sum of one thousand dollars, to the use of such claimant, . . . and after arrest of such fugitive, by such marshal or his deputy, or whilst at any time in his custody under the provisions of this act, should such fugitive escape, whether with or without the assent of such marshal or his deputy, such marshal shall be liable, on his official bond, to be prosecuted for the benefit of such claimant, for the full value of the service or labor of said fugitive in the State, Territory, or District whence he escaped: and the better to enable the said commissioners, when thus appointed, to execute their duties faithfully and efficiently, in conformity with the requirements of the Constitution of the United States and of this act, they are hereby authorized and empowered, within their counties respectively, to appoint, . . . any one or more suitable persons, from time to time, to execute all such warrants and other process as may be issued by them in the lawful performance of their respective duties; with authority to such commissioners, or the persons to be appointed by them, to execute process as aforesaid, to summon and call to their aid the bystanders, or *posse comitatus* of the proper county, when necessary to ensure a faithful observance of the clause of the Constitution referred to, in conformity with the provisions of this act; and all good citizens are hereby commanded to aid and assist in the prompt and efficient execution of this law, whenever their services may be required, as aforesaid, for that purpose; and said warrants shall run, and be executed by said officers, any where in the State within which they are issued.

SEC. 6. That when a person held to service or labor in any State or Territory of the United States, has heretofore or shall hereafter escape into another State or Territory of the United States, the person or persons to whom such service or labor may be due, . . . may pursue and reclaim such fugitive person, either by procuring a warrant from some one of the courts, judges, or commissioners aforesaid, of the proper circuit, district, or county, for the apprehension of such fugitive from service or labor, or by seizing and arresting such fugitive, where the same can be done without process, and by taking, or causing such person to be taken, forthwith before such court, judge, or commissioner, whose duty it shall be to hear and determine the case of such claimant in a summary manner; and upon satisfactory proof being made, by deposition or affidavit, in writing, to be taken and certified by such court, judge, or commissioner, or by other satisfactory testimony, duly taken and certified by some court, . . . and with proof, also by affidavit, of the identity of the person whose service or labor is claimed to be due as aforesaid, that the person so arrested does in fact owe service or labor to the person or persons claiming him or her, in the State or Territory from which such fugitive may have escaped as aforesaid, and that said person escaped, to make out and deliver to such claimant, his or her agent or attorney, a certificate setting forth the substantial facts as to the service or labor due from such fugitive to the claimant, and of his or her escape from the State or Territory in which he or she was arrested, with authority to such claimant, . . . to use such reasonable force and restraint as may be necessary, under the circumstances of the case, to take and remove such fugitive person back to the State or Territory whence he or she may

have escaped as aforesaid. In no trial or hearing under this act shall the testimony of such alleged fugitive be admitted in evidence; and the certificates in this and the first [fourth] section mentioned, shall be conclusive of the right of the person or persons in whose favor granted, to remove such fugitive to the State or Territory from which he escaped, and shall prevent all molestation of such person or persons by any process issued by any court, judge, magistrate, or other person whomsoever.

SEC. 7. That any persons who shall knowingly and willingly obstruct, hinder, or prevent such claimant, his agent or attorney, or any person or persons lawfully assisting him, her, or them, from arresting such a fugitive from service or labor, either with or without process as aforesaid, or shall rescue, or attempt to rescue, such fugitive from service or labor, from the custody of such claimant, . . . or other person or persons lawfully assisting as aforesaid, when so arrested, . . . or shall aid, abet, or assist such person so owing service or labor as aforesaid, directly or indirectly, to escape from such claimant, . . . or shall harbor or conceal such fugitive, so as to prevent the discovery and arrest of such person, after notice or knowledge of the fact that such person was a fugitive from service or labor . . . shall, for either of said offences, be subject to a fine not exceeding one thousand dollars, and imprisonment not exceeding six months . . . ; and shall moreover forfeit and pay, by way of civil damages to the party injured by such illegal conduct, the sum of one thousand dollars, for each fugitive so lost as aforesaid. . . .

SEC. 9. That, upon affidavit made by the claimant of such fugitive, . . . that he has reason to apprehend that such fugitive will be rescued by force from his or their possession before he can be taken beyond the limits of the State in which the arrest is made, it shall be the duty of the officer making the arrest to retain such fugitive in his custody, and to remove him to the State whence he fled, and there to deliver him to said claimant, his agent, or attorney. And to this end, the officer aforesaid is hereby authorized and required to employ so many persons as he may deem necessary to overcome such force, and to retain them in his service so long as circumstances may require. . . .

SEC. 10. That when any person held to service or labor in any State or Territory, or in the District of Columbia, shall escape therefrom, the party to whom such service or labor shall be due, . . . may apply to any court of record therein, . . . and make satisfactory proof to such court, . . . of the escape aforesaid, and that the person escaping owed service or labor to such party. Whereupon the court shall cause a record to be made of the matters so proved, and also a general description of the person so escaping, with such convenient certainty as may be; and a transcript of such record, . . . being produced in any other State, Territory, or district in which the person so escaping may be found, . . . shall be held and taken to be full and conclusive evidence of the fact of escape, and that the service or labor of the person escaping is due to the party in such record mentioned. And upon the production by the said party of other and further evidence if necessary, either oral or by affidavit, in addition to what is contained in the said record of the identity of the person escaping, he or she shall be delivered up to the claimant. And the said court, commissioner, judge, or other person authorized by this act to grant certificates to claimants of fugitives, shall, upon the production of the record and other evidences aforesaid, grant to such claimant a certificate of his right to take any such person identified and proved to be owing service or labor as aforesaid, which certificate shall authorize such claimant to seize or arrest and transport such person to the State or Territory from which he escaped . . .

5. ACT ABOLISHING THE SLAVE TRADE IN THE DISTRICT OF COLUMBIA
September 20, 1850

(*U. S. Statutes at Large,* Vol. IX, p. 467 ff.)

An Act to suppress the Slave Trade in the District of Columbia.

Be it enacted . . . , That from and after January 1, 1851, it shall not be lawful to bring into the District of Columbia any slave whatever, for the purpose of being sold, or for the purpose of being placed in depot, to be subsequently transferred to any other State or place to be sold as merchandize. And if any slave shall be brought into the said District by its owner, or by the authority or consent of its owner, contrary to the provisions of this act, such slave shall thereupon become liberated and free.

Sec. 2. That it shall and may be lawful for each of the corporations of the cities of Washington and Georgetown, from time to time, and as often as may be necessary, to abate, break up, and abolish any depot or place of confinement of slaves brought into the said District as merchandize, contrary to the provisions of this act, by such appropriate means as may appear to either of the said corporations expedient and proper. And the same power is hereby vested in the Levy Court of Washington county, if any attempt shall be made, within its jurisdictional limits, to establish a depot or place of confinement for slaves brought into the said District as merchandize for sale contrary to this act.

175. THE GEORGIA PLATFORM
1850

(A. H. Stephens, *The War Between the States,* Vol. II, app. B.)

Resolutions of a Convention held at Milledgeville, Georgia, to consider the Compromise of 1850. This platform was written by Charles J. Jenkins, and represented the point of view of the Union element in Georgia. See, R. H. Shryock, *Georgia and the Union in 1850;* U. B. Phillips, "Georgia and State Rights," Am. Hist. Assoc. *Reports,* 1901, Vol. II; and references to Doc. No. 176.

To the end that the position of this State may be clearly apprehended by her Confederates of the South and of the North, and that she may be blameless of all future consequences—

Be it resolved by the people of Georgia in Convention assembled, First. That we hold the American Union secondary in importance only to the rights and principles it was designed to perpetuate. That past associations, present fruition, and future prospects, will bind us to it so long as it continues to be the safe-guard of those rights and principles.

Second. That if the thirteen original Parties to the Compact, bordering the Atlantic in a narrow belt, while their separate interests were in embryo, their peculiar tendencies scarcely developed, their revolutionary trials and triumphs still green in memory, found Union impossible without compromise, the thirty-one of this day may well yield somewhat in the conflict of opinion and policy, to preserve that Union which has extended the sway of Republican Government over a vast wilderness to another ocean, and proportionately advanced their civilization and national greatness.

Third. That in this spirit the State of Georgia has maturely considered the action of Congress, embracing a series of measures for the admission of California into the Union, the organization of Territorial Governments for Utah and New Mexico, the establishment of a boundary between the latter and the State of Texas, the suppression of the slave-trade in the District of Columbia, and the extradition of fugitive slaves, and (connected with them) the rejection of propositions to exclude slavery from the Mexican Territories, and to abolish it in the District

of Columbia; and, whilst she does not wholly approve, will abide by it as a permanent adjustment of this sectional controversy.

Fourth. That the State of Georgia, in the judgment of this Convention, will and ought to resist, even (as a last resort) to a disruption of every tie which binds her to the Union, any future Act of Congress abolishing Slavery in the District of Columbia, without the consent and petition of the slaveholders thereof, or any Act abolishing Slavery in places within the slave-holding States, purchased by the United States for the erection of forts, magazines, arsenals, dockyards, navy-yards, and other like purposes; or in any Act suppressing the slave-trade between slave-holding States; or in any refusal to admit as a State any Territory applying because of the existence of Slavery therein; or in any Act prohibiting the introduction of slaves into the Territories of Utah and New Mexico; or in any Act repealing or materially modifying the laws now in force for the recovery of fugitive slaves.

Fifth. That it is the deliberate opinion of this Convention, that upon the faithful execution of the Fugitive Slave Bill by the proper authorities, depends the preservation of our much loved Union.

176. RESOLUTIONS OF THE NASHVILLE CONVENTION
June 10, 1850

(Resolutions, Addresses, and Journal of Proceedings of the Southern Convention, p. 57 ff.)

The Nashville Convention was called by the more radical of the Southern leaders to consider what action should be taken on the Compromise of 1850. Nine slave States were represented, but the moderates were from the beginning in control of the Convention, and from the point of view of its original sponsors it was a fiasco. A second convention, attended by only a handful of delegates, met in November and drew up resolutions denouncing the Compromise and reasserting the right of secession. See, J. W. Du-Bose, *Life and Times of William Lowndes Yancey;* L. A. White, *Robert Barnwell Rhett;* J. Hodgson, *The Cradle of the Confederacy, or the Times of Troup, Quitman, and Yancey;* P. M. Hamer, *The Secession Movement in South Carolina, 1847–1852;* M. J. White, *Secession Movement in the United States, 1847–1852;* D. T. Herndon, "The Nashville Convention of 1850",

Alabama Hist. Soc. *Transactions,* Vol. V; A. C. Cole, "The South and the Right of Secession in the Early Fifties," *Miss. Valley Hist. Rev.,* Vol. I; R. P. Brooks, "Howell Cobb and the Crisis of 1850", *Miss. Valley Hist. Review,* Vol. IV.

1. *Resolved,* That the territories of the United States belong to the people of the several States of this Union as their common property. That the citizens of the several States have equal rights to migrate with their property to these territories, and are equally entitled to the protection of the federal government in the enjoyment of that property so long as the territories remain under the charge of that government.

2. *Resolved,* That Congress has no power to exclude from the territory of the United

States any property lawfully held in the States of the Union, and any act which may be passed by Congress to effect this result is a plain violation of the Constitution of the United States. . . .

4. *Resolved,* That to protect property existing in the several States of the Union the people of these States invested the federal government with the powers of war and negotiation and of sustaining armies and navies, and prohibited to State authorities the exercise of the same powers. They made no discrimination in the protection to be afforded or the description of the property to be defended, nor was it allowed to the federal government to determine what should be held as property. Whatever the States deal with as property the federal government is bound to recognize and defend as such. Therefore it is the sense of this Convention that all acts of the federal government which tend to denationalize property of any description recognized in the Constitution and laws of the States, or that discriminate in the degree and efficiency of the protection to be afforded to it, or which weaken or destroy the title of any citizen upon American territories, are plain and palpable violations of the fundamental law under which it exists.

5. *Resolved,* That the slaveholding States cannot and will not submit to the enactment by Congress of any law imposing onerous conditions or restraints upon the rights of masters to remove with their property into the territories of the United States, or to any law making discrimination in favor of the proprietors of other property against them. . . .

8. *Resolved,* That the performance of its duties, upon the principle we declare, would enable Congress to remove the embarrassments in which the country is now involved. The vacant territories of the United States, no longer regarded as prizes for sectional rapacity and ambition, would be gradually occupied by inhabitants drawn to them by their interests and feelings. The institutions fitted to them would be naturally applied by governments formed on American ideas, and approved by the deliberate choice of their constituents. The community would be edu-

cated and disciplined under a republican administration in habits of self government. and fitted for an association as a State, and to the enjoyment of a place in the confederacy. A community so formed and organized might well claim admission to the Union and none would dispute the validity of the claim. . . .

9. *Resolved,* That a recognition of this principle would deprive the questions between Texas and the United States of their sectional character, and would leave them for adjustment, without disturbance from sectional prejudices and passions, upon considerations of magnanimity and justice. . . .

11. *Resolved,* That in the event a dominant majority shall refuse to recognize the great constitutional rights we assert, and shall continue to deny the obligations of the Federal Government to maintain them, it is the sense of this convention that the territories should be treated as property, and divided between the sections of the Union, so that the rights of both sections be adequately secured in their respective shares. That we are aware this course is open to grave objections, but we are ready to acquiesce in the adoption of the line of 36 deg. 30 min. north latitude, extending to the Pacific ocean, as an extreme concession, upon consideration of what is due to the stability of our institution.

12. *Resolved,* That it is the opinion of this Convention that this controversy should be ended, either by a recognition of the constitutional rights of the Southern people, or by an equitable partition of the territories. That the spectacle of a confederacy of States, involved in quarrels over the fruits of a war in which the American arms were crowned with glory, is humiliating. That the incorporation of the Wilmot Proviso in the offer of settlement, a proposition which fourteen States regard as disparaging and dishonorable, is degrading to the country. A termination to this controversy by the disruption of the confederacy or by the abandonment of the territories to prevent such a result, would be a climax to the shame which attaches to the controversy which it is the paramount duty of Congress to avoid. . . .

177. CLAYTON-BULWER TREATY
April 19, 1850
(Malloy, ed. *Treaties, Conventions, etc.* Vol. I, p. 659 ff.)

The project of a canal across the Isthmus had long been agitated, and was part of Polk's foreign policy. In as much as Great Britain controlled the eastern terminus of the Nicaragua route and was expanding in Central America, the Clayton-Bulwer Treaty represented a diplomatic victory for the United States. For the abrogation of this treaty, see Doc. No. 354. On the Isthmian project see I. D. Travis, *History of the Clayton-Bulwer Treaty;* L. M. Keasby, *The Nicaragua Canal and the Monroe Doctrine;* C. H. Huberich, *The Trans-Isthmian Canal: a Study in American Diplomatic History, 1825–1904;* D. Perkins, *The Monroe Doctrine, 1826–1867,* ch. iv.

ART. I. The Governments of the United States and Great Britain hereby declare that neither the one nor the other will ever obtain or maintain for itself any exclusive control over the said ship canal; agreeing that neither will ever erect or maintain any fortifications commanding the same, or in the vicinity thereof, or occupy, or fortify, or colonize or assume, or exercise any dominion over Nicaragua, Costa Rica, the Mosquito coast, or any part of Central America; nor will either make use of any protection which either affords or may afford, or any alliance which either has or may have to or with any state or people, for the purpose of erecting or maintaining any such fortifications, or of occupying, fortifying, or colonizing Nicaragua, Costa Rica, the Mosquito coast, or any part of Central America, or of assuming or exercising dominion over the same; nor will the United States or Great Britain take advantage of any intimacy, or use any alliance, connection or influence that either may possess with any State or Government through whose territory the said canal may pass, for the purpose of acquiring or holding, directly or indirectly, for the citizens or subjects of the one, any rights or advantages in regard to commerce or navigation through the said canal which shall not be offered on the same terms to the citizens or subjects of the other.

ART. II. Vessels of the United States or Great Britain traversing the said canal shall, in case of war between the contracting parties, be exempted from blockade, detention or capture by either of the belligerents; and this provision shall extend to such a distance from the two ends of the said canal as may hereafter be found expedient to establish.

ART. III. In order to secure the construction of the said canal, the contracting parties engage that if any such canal shall be undertaken upon fair and equitable terms by any parties having the authority of the local Government or Governments through whose territory the same may pass, then the persons employed in making the said canal, and their property used, or to be used, for that object, shall be protected, from the commencement of the said canal to its completion, by the Governments of the United States and Great Britain, from unjust detention, confiscation, seizure or any violence whatsoever. . . .

ART. V. The contracting parties further engage, that when the said canal shall have been completed, they will protect it from interruption, seizure or unjust confiscation, and that they will guarantee the neutrality thereof, so that the said canal may forever be open and free, and the capital invested therein secure. Nevertheless, the Governments of the United States and Great Britain, in according their protection to the construction of the said canal, and guaranteeing its neutrality and security when completed, always understand that this protection and guarantee are granted conditionally, and may be withdrawn by both Governments, or either Government, if both Governments, or either Government, should deem that the persons or company undertaking or managing the same adopt or establish such regulations concerning the traffic thereupon as are contrary to the spirit and intention of this convention, either by making unfair discriminations in favor of the commerce of one of the contracting parties over the commerce of the other, or by imposing oppressive exactions or unreasonable tolls upon the passengers, vessels, goods, wares, merchandise or other articles. Neither party, however, shall withdraw the aforesaid protection and guarantee without first giving six months' notice to the other.

ART. VI. The contracting parties in this convention engage to invite every State with which both or either have friendly intercourse to enter into stipulations with them similar to those which they have entered into with each other, to the end that all other States may share in the honor and advantage of having contributed to a work of such general interest and importance as the canal herein contemplated. And the contracting parties likewise agree that each shall enter into treaty stipulations with such of the Central American States as they may deem advisable, for the purpose of more effectually carrying out the great design of this convention, namely, that of constructing and maintaining the said canal as a ship communication between the two oceans for the benefit of mankind, on equal terms to all, and of protecting the same; and they also agree that the good offices of either shall be employed, when requested by the other, in aiding and assisting the negotiation of such treaty stipulations; and should any differences arise as to right or property over the territory through which the said canal shall pass between the States or Governments of Central America, and such differences should in any way impede or obstruct the execution of the said canal, the Governments of the United States and Great Britain will use their good offices to settle such differences in the manner best suited to promote the interests of the said canal, and to strengthen the bonds of friendship and alliance which exist between the contracting parties.

ART. VII. It being desirable that no time should be unnecessarily lost in commencing and constructing the said canal, the Governments of the United States and Great Britain determine to give their support and encouragement to such persons or company as may first offer to commence the same, with the necessary capital, the consent of the local authorities, and on such principles as accord with the spirit and intention of this convention. . . .

ART. VIII. The Governments of the United States and Great Britain having not only desired, in entering into this convention, to accomplish a particular object, but also to establish a general principle, they hereby agree to extend their protection, by treaty stipulations, to any other practicable communications, whether by canal or railway, across the isthmus which connects North and South America, and especially to the interoceanic communications, should the same prove to be practicable, whether by canal or railway, which are now proposed to be established by the way of Tehuantepec or Panama. In granting, however, their joint protection to any such canals or railways as are by this article specified, it is always understood by the United States and Great Britain that the parties constructing or owning the same shall impose no other charges or conditions of traffic thereupon than the aforesaid Governments shall approve of as just and equitable; and that the same canals or railways, being open to the citizens and subjects of the United States and Great Britain on equal terms, shall also be open on like terms to the citizens and subjects of every other State which is willing to grant thereto such protection as the United States and Great Britain engage to afford.

178. TRIAL OF MRS. DOUGLAS FOR TEACHING COLORED CHILDREN TO READ
Norfolk, Virginia, 1853
(*American State Trials,* ed. J. D. Lawson, Vol. VII, p. 56 ff.)

The slave codes of most Southern states forbade teaching slaves to read or write; some, as those of Virginia, extended the prohibition to all negroes. Though these laws were generally disregarded, the decision of the Court below indicates that they were at times enforced. Mrs. Douglas was convicted and spent one month in jail. See U. B. Phillips, *American Negro Slavery;* C S. Sydnor, *Slavery in Mississippi.*

BAKER, J. Upon an indictment found against you for assembling with negroes to instruct them to read and write, and for associating with them in an unlawful as-

sembly, you were found guilty, and a mere
nominal fine imposed, on the last day of this
court held in the month of November. . . .
The Court is not called on to vindicate the
policy of the law in question, for so long as
it remains upon the statute book, and unrepealed, public and private justice and
morality require that it should be respected
and sustained. There are persons, I believe,
in our community, opposed to the policy
of the law in question. They profess to believe that universal intellectual culture is
necessary to religious instruction and education, and that such culture is suitable to a
state of slavery; and there can be no misapprehension as to your opinions on this subject, judging from the indiscreet freedom
with which you spoke of your regard for the
colored race in general. Such opinions in
the present state of our society I regard
as manifestly mischievous. It is not true
that our slaves cannot be taught religious
and moral duty, without being able to read
the Bible and use the pen. . . .
A valuable report or document recently
published in the city of New York by the
Southern Aid Society sets forth many valuable and important truths upon the condition
of the Southern slaves, and the utility of
moral and religious instruction, apart from
a knowledge of books. I recommend the careful perusal of it to all whose opinions concur
with your own. It shows that a system of
catechetical instruction, with a clear and
simple exposition of Scripture, has been employed with gratifying success; that the slave
population of the South are peculiarly susceptible of good religious influences. Their
mere residence among a Christian people has
wrought a great and happy change in their
condition: they have been raised from the
night of heathenism to the light of Christianity, and thousands of them have been
brought to a saving knowledge of the Gospel.
Of the one hundred millions of the negro
race, there cannot be found another so large
a body as the three millions of slaves in the
United States, at once so intelligent, so inclined to the Gospel, and so blessed by the
elevating influence of civilization and Christianity. Occasional instances of cruelty and
oppression, it is true, may sometimes occur,
and probably will ever continue to take place
under any system of laws; but this is not
confined to wrongs committed upon the
negro; wrongs are committed and cruelly
practiced in a like degree by the lawless
white man upon his own color; and while the
negroes of our town and State are known
to be surrounded by most of the substantial
comforts of life, and invited both by precept
and example to participate in proper, moral
and religious duties, it argues, it seems to
me, a sickly sensibility towards them to say
their persons, and feelings, and interests are
not sufficiently respected by our laws, which
in effect, tend to nullify the act of our
Legislature passed for the security and protection of their masters.
. . . The first legislative provision upon
this subject was introduced in the year 1831
immediately succeeding the bloody scenes of
the memorable Southampton insurrection
and that law being found not sufficiently
penal to check the wrongs complained of
was re-enacted with additional penalties in
the year 1848, which last mentioned act
after several years' trial and experience, has
been re-affirmed by adoption, and incorporated into our present code. After these several and repeated recognitions of the wisdom
and propriety of the said act, it may well
be said that bold and open opposition to it
is a matter not to be slightly regarded
especially as we have reason to believe that
every Southern slave state in our country
as a measure of self-preservation and protection, has deemed it wise and just to adopt
laws with similar provisions.
There might have been no occasion for
such enactments in Virginia, or elsewhere, on
the subject of negro education, but as a
matter of self-defense against the schemes
of Northern incendiaries, and the outcry
against holding our slaves in bondage. Many
now living well remember how, and when
and why the anti-slavery fury began, and
by what means its manifestations were made
public. Our mails were clogged with abolition
pamphlets and inflammatory documents, to be
distributed among our Southern negroes to in
duce them to cut our throats. Sometimes, it
may be, these libelous documents were dis
tributed by Northern citizens professing
Southern feelings, and at other times by
Southern people professing Northern feel
ings. These, however, were not the only
means resorted to by the Northern fanatics

o stir up insubordination among our slaves. They scattered far and near pocket handkerchiefs, and other similar articles, with frightful engravings, and printed over with anti-slavery nonsense, with the view to work upon the feeling and ignorance of our negroes, who otherwise would have remained comfortable and happy. Under such circumstances there was but one measure of protection for the South, and that was adopted. . . . In vindication of the policy and justness of our laws, which every individual should be taught to respect, the judgment of the Court is, in addition to the proper fine and costs, that you be imprisoned for the period of one month in the jail of this city. . . .

179. APPEAL OF THE INDEPENDENT DEMOCRATS
January 19, 1854

(J. W. Schuckers, *Life and Public Services of S. P. Chase*, p. 140 ff.)

The effort of Douglas to push through the Kansas-Nebraska Bill was the immediate occasion for this "appeal", signed by six of the most prominent abolitionists in the country. More moderate Democrats like Seward refused to sign the document. The Appeal had a profound effect: it was reprinted in all of the important papers of the country, and was partly responsible for the organization of the Republican Party. For Douglas's reply to the Appeal, see *Congressional Globe*, 33 Cong. 1st Sess. XXVIII, pt. I, p. 275 ff. See A. Beveridge, *Abraham Lincoln*, Vol. II, p. 184 ff.; J. F. Rhodes, *History of the United States from the Compromise of 1850*, Vol. I, ch. v; A. Johnson, *S. A. Douglas;* A. B. Hart, *S. P. Chase.*

As Senators and Representatives in the Congress of the United States it is our duty to warn our constituents, whenever imminent danger menaces the freedom of our institutions or the permanency of the Union.

Such danger, as we firmly believe, now impends, and we earnestly solicit your prompt attention to it.

At the last session of Congress a bill for the organization of the Territory of Nebraska passed the House of Representatives by an overwhelming majority. That bill was based on the principle of excluding slavery from the new Territory. It was not taken up for consideration in the Senate and consequently failed to become a law.

At the present session a new Nebraska bill has been reported by the Senate Committee on Territories, which, should it unhappily receive the sanction of Congress, will open all the unorganized Territories of the Union to the ingress of slavery.

We arraign this bill as a gross violation of a sacred pledge; as a criminal betrayal of precious rights; as part and parcel of an atrocious plot to exclude from a vast unoccupied region immigrants from the Old World and free laborers from our own States, and convert it into a dreary region of despotism, inhabited by masters and slaves.

Take your maps, fellow citizens, we entreat you, and see what country it is which this bill gratuitously and recklessly proposes to open to slavery. . . .

This immense region, occupying the very heart of the North American Continent, and larger, by thirty-three thousand square miles, than all the existing free States—including California . . . this immense region the bill now before the Senate, without reason and without excuse, but in flagrant disregard of sound policy and sacred faith, purposes to open to slavery.

We beg your attention, fellow-citizens, to a few historical facts:

The original settled policy of the United States, clearly indicated by the Jefferson proviso of 1784 and the Ordinance of 1787, was non-extension of slavery.

In 1803 Louisiana was acquired by purchase from France. . . .

In 1818, six years later, the inhabitants of the Territory of Missouri applied to Congress for authority to form a State constitution, and for admission into the Union. There were, at that time, in the whole territory acquired from France, outside of the State of Louisiana, not three thousand slaves.

There was no apology, in the circumstances of the country, for the continuance of slavery. The original national policy was against it, and not less the plain language of the treaty under which the territory had been acquired from France.

It was proposed, therefore, to incorporate in the bill authorizing the formation of a State government, a provision requiring that the constitution of the new State should contain an article providing for the abolition of existing slavery, and prohibiting the further introduction of slaves.

This provision was vehemently and pertinaciously opposed, but finally prevailed in the House of Representatives by a decided vote. In the Senate it was rejected, and—in consequence of the disagreement between the two Houses—the bill was lost.

At the next session of Congress, the controversy was renewed with increased violence. It was terminated at length by a compromise. Missouri was allowed to come into the Union with slavery; but a section was inserted in the act authorizing her admission, excluding slavery forever from all the territory acquired from France, not included in the new State, lying north of 36° 30′. . . .

The question of the constitutionality of this prohibition was submitted by President Monroe to his cabinet. John Quincy Adams was then Secretary of State; John C. Calhoun was Secretary of War; William H. Crawford was Secretary of the Treasury; and William Wirt was Attorney-General. Each of these eminent gentlemen—three of them being from the slave states—gave a written opinion, affirming its constitutionality, and thereupon the act received the sanction of the President himself, also from a slave State.

Nothing is more certain in history than the fact that Missouri could not have been admitted as a slave State had not certain members from the free States been reconciled to the measure by the incorporation of this prohibition into the act of admission. Nothing is more certain than that this prohibition has been regarded and accepted by the whole country as a solemn compact against the extension of slavery into any part of the territory acquired from France lying north of 36° 30′, and not included in the new State of Missouri. The same act— let it be ever remembered—which authorized the formation of a constitution by the State, without a clause forbidding slavery, consecrated, beyond question and beyond honest recall, the whole remainder of the Territory

to freedom and free institutions forever. For more than thirty years—during more than half our national existence under our present Constitution—this compact has been universally regarded and acted upon as inviolable American law. In conformity with it, Iowa was admitted as a free State and Minnesota has been organized as a free Territory.

It is a strange and ominous fact, well calculated to awaken the worst apprehensions and the most fearful forebodings of future calamities, that it is now deliberately proposed to repeal this prohibition, by implication or directly—the latter certainly the manlier way—and thus to subvert the compact, and allow slavery in all the yet unorganized territory.

We cannot, in this address, review the various pretenses under which it is attempted to cloak this monstrous wrong, but we must not altogether omit to notice one.

It is said that Nebraska sustains the same relations to slavery as did the territory acquired from Mexico prior to 1850, and that the pro-slavery clauses of the bill are necessary to carry into effect the compromise of that year.

No assertion could be more groundless. . . .

The statesmen whose powerful support carried the Utah and New Mexico acts never dreamed that their provisions would be ever applied to Nebraska. . . .

Here is proof beyond controversy that the principle of the Missouri act prohibiting slavery north of 36° 30′, far from being abrogated by the Compromise Acts, is expressly affirmed; and that the proposed repeal of this prohibition, instead of being an affirmation of the Compromise Acts, is a repeal of a very prominent provision of the most important act of the series. It is solemnly declared in the very Compromise Acts "that nothing herein contained shall be construed to impair or qualify" the prohibition of slavery north of 36° 30′; and yet in the face of this declaration, that sacred prohibition is said to be overthrown. Can presumption further go? To all who, in any way, lean upon these compromises, we commend this exposition.

These pretenses, therefore, that the territory covered by the positive prohibition of

1820, sustains a similar relation to slavery with that acquired from Mexico, covered by no prohibition except that of disputed constitutional or Mexican law, and that the Compromises of 1850 require the incorporation of the pro-slavery clauses of the Utah and New Mexico Bill in the Nebraska act, are mere inventions, designed to cover from public reprehension meditated bad faith. Were he living now, no one would be more forward, more eloquent, or more indignant in his denunciation of that bad faith, than Henry Clay, the foremost champion of both compromises. . . .

We confess our total inability properly to delineate the character or describe the consequences of this measure. Language fails to express the sentiments of indignation and abhorrence which it inspires; and no vision less penetrating and comprehensive than that of the All-Seeing can reach its evil issues. . . .

We appeal to the people. We warn you that the dearest interests of freedom and the Union are in imminent peril. Demagogues may tell you that the Union can be maintained only by submitting to the demands of slavery. We tell you that the Union can only be maintained by the full recognition of the just claims of freedom and man. The Union was formed to establish justice and secure the blessings of liberty. When it fails to accomplish these ends it will be worthless, and when it becomes worthless it cannot long endure.

We entreat you to be mindful of that fundamental maxim of Democracy—EQUAL RIGHTS AND EXACT JUSTICE FOR ALL MEN. Do not submit to become agents in extending legalized oppression and systematized injustice over a vast territory yet exempt from these terrible evils.

We implore Christians and Christian ministers to interpose. Their divine religion requires them to behold in every man a brother, and to labor for the advancement and regeneration of the human race.

Whatever apologies may be offered for the toleration of slavery in the States, none can be offered for its extension into Territories where it does not exist, and where that extension involves the repeal of ancient law and the violation of solemn compact. Let all protest, earnestly and emphatically, by correspondence, through the press, by memorials, by resolutions of public meetings and legislative bodies, and in whatever other mode may seem expedient, against this enormous crime.

For ourselves, we shall resist it by speech and vote, and with all the abilities which God has given us. Even if overcome in the impending struggle, we shall not submit. We shall go home to our constituents, erect anew the standard of freedom, and call on the people to come to the rescue of the country from the domination of slavery. We will not despair; for the cause of human freedom is the cause of God.

> S. P. Chase
> Charles Sumner
> J. R. Giddings
> Edward Wade
> Gerritt Smith
> Alexander De Witt.

180. THE KANSAS–NEBRASKA ACT
May 30, 1854

(*U. S. Statutes at Large*, Vol. X, p. 277 ff.)

This momentous measure organized two Territories, Kansas and Nebraska, divided by the fortieth parallel; it specifically repealed the Missouri Compromise, which had come to be regarded as sacrosanct by many people in the North, and recognized the principle of "squatter sovereignty." Probably no bill ever introduced to Congress was fraught with graver consequences. Senator Douglas, who sponsored the Bill, became anathema to a large part of the North; a group of Northern Democrats, headed by Chase, issued an "Appeal of the Independent Democrats", Doc. No. 179, calling for the organization of an anti-slavery party, and in February and July of 1854 the new Republican Party came into existence. The passage of the Kansas-Nebraska Bill with its provision for "popular sovereignty" led to a struggle for the control of Kansas that soon earned for that Territory the name of "Bleeding" Kansas. Lincoln, in his debates with Douglas, attacked the theory of popular sovereignty with such skill as seriously to damage Douglas's popularity in the South and to earn for himself a national reputation. It was charged and long believed that Douglas, in his championship of this bill, was actuated solely by ambition for the Presidency. It is probable, however, that Douglas sincerely believed that the territory opened up by the Kansas-Nebraska bill would become, because of its geography and climate, free territory. He was also profoundly interested in the construction of a trans-continental railway along a Northern route, and anxious therefore to throw open the region west of Iowa to settlement. The literature on the Kansas-Nebraska Act is extensive. See, P. O. Ray, *The Repeal of the Missouri Compromise;* S. B. Dixon, *A True History of the Missouri Compromise and Its Repeal;* F. H. Hodder, "Genesis of the Kansas-Nebraska Act," Wisconsin Hist. Soc. *Proceedings,* 1912; J. F. Rhodes, *History of the United States,* Vol. I, ch. v; A. Johnson, *S. A. Douglas,* chs. viii-ix; A. J. Beveridge, *Abraham Lincoln,* Vol. II, chs. iii-iv; G. F. Milton, *The Eve of the Conflict,* ch. vii. ff.

An Act to Organize the Territories of Nebraska and Kansas.

Be it enacted . . . , That all that part of the territory of the United States included within the following limits, except such portions thereof as are hereinafter expressly exempted from the operations of this act, to wit: beginning at a point in the Missouri River where the fortieth parallel of north latitude crosses the same; thence west on said parallel to the east boundary of the Territory of Utah, on the summit of the Rocky Mountains; thence on said summit northward to the forty-ninth parallel of north latitude; thence east on said parallel to the western boundary of the territory of Minnesota; thence southward on said boundary to the Missouri River; thence down the main channel of said river to the place of beginning, be, and the same is hereby, created into a temporary government by the name of the Territory of Nebraska; and when admitted as a State or States, the said Territory, or any portion of the same, shall be received into the Union with or without slavery, as their constitution may prescribe at the time of their admission: . . .

SEC. 14. *And be it further enacted, . . .* That the Constitution, and all laws of the United States which are not locally inap-

plicable, shall have the same force and effect within the said Territory of Nebraska as elsewhere within the United States, except the eighth section of the act preparatory to the admission of Missouri into the Union, approved March 6, 1820, which, being inconsistent with the principle of non-intervention by Congress with slavery in the States and Territories, as recognized by the legislation of eighteen hundred and fifty, commonly called the Compromise Measures, is hereby declared inoperative and void; it being the true intent and meaning of this act not to legislate slavery into any Territory or State, nor to exclude it therefrom, but to leave the people thereof perfectly free to form and regulate their domestic institutions in their own way, subject only to the Constitution of the United States: *Provided,* That nothing herein contained shall be construed to revive or put in force any law or regulation which may have existed prior to the act of March 6, 1820, either protecting, establishing, prohibiting, or abolishing slavery. . . .

SEC. 19. *And be it further enacted,* That all that part of the Territory of the United States included within the following limits, except such portions thereof as are hereinafter expressly exempted from the operations of this act, to wit, beginning at a point on the western boundary of the State of Missouri, where the thirty-seventh parallel of north latitude crosses the same; thence west on said parallel to the eastern boundary of New Mexico; thence north on said boundary to latitude thirty-eight; thence following said boundary westward to the east boundary of the Territory of Utah, on the summit of the Rocky Mountains; thence northward on said summit to the fortieth parallel of latitude; thence east on said parallel to the western boundary of the State of Missouri; thence south with the western boundary of said State to the place of beginning, be, and the same is hereby, created into a temporary government by the name of the Territory of Kansas; and when admitted as a State or States, the said Territory, or any portion of the same, shall be received into the Union with or without slavery, as their constitution may prescribe at the time of their admission: . . .

181. THE OSTEND MANIFESTO
October 18, 1854

(U. S. 33d Congress, 2d Session, House Executive Doc. No. 93)

In August, 1854, Secretary of State Marcy instructed our minister to Spain, Pierre Soulé, to negotiate for the purchase of Cuba, and suggested a consultation with our ministers to France and England, Mr. Mason and Mr. Buchanan, for the purpose of considering European opposition to such a purchase. The three ministers accordingly met at Ostend, Belgium, and drew up the notorious Ostend Manifesto. The report was repudiated by Marcy, and Soulé resigned his mission. Buchanan's participation in the Manifesto recommended him to the Southern Democrats as a suitable candidate for the Presidency. See, S. F. Bemis, ed. *American Secretaries of State,* Vol. VI, p. 183 ff.; R. F. Nichols, *Franklin Pierce,* chs, xlvi-xlviii, and appendix; S. Webster, "Mr. Marcy, the Cuban Question and the Ostend Manifesto," *Pol. Sci. Quart.,* Vol. VIII; A. A. Ettinger, *Mission to Spain of Pierre Soulé, 1853–1855.*

Aix la Chapelle, October 18, 1854.

Sir:—The undersigned, in compliance with the wish expressed by the President in the several confidential despatches you have addressed to us, respectively, to that effect, have met in conference, first at Ostend, in Belgium, on the 9th, 10th, and 11th instant, and then at Aix la Chapelle, in Prussia, on the days next following, up to the date hereof. . . .

We have arrived at the conclusion, and are thoroughly convinced, that an immediate and earnest effort ought to be made by the government of the United States to purchase Cuba from Spain at any price for which it can be obtained, not exceeding the sum of $—.

The proposal should, in our opinion, be made in such a manner as to be presented through the necessary diplomatic forms to the Supreme Constituent Cortes about to assemble. On this momentous question, in which the people both of Spain and the United States are so deeply interested, all our proceedings ought to be open, frank, and public. They should be of such a character as to challenge the approbation of the world.

We firmly believe that, in the progress of human events, the time has arrived when the vital interests of Spain are as seriously involved in the sale, as those of the United States in the purchase, of the island and that the transaction will prove equally honorable to both nations.

Under these circumstances we cannot anticipate a failure, unless possibly through the malign influence of foreign powers who possess no right whatever to interfere in the matter.

We proceed to state some of the reasons which have brought us to this conclusion, and, for the sake of clearness, we shall specify them under two distinct heads:

1. The United States ought, if practicable, to purchase Cuba with as little delay as possible.

2. The probability is great that the government and cortes of Spain will prove willing to sell it, because this would essentially promote the highest and best interests of the Spanish people.

Then, 1. It must be clear to every reflecting mind that, from the peculiarity of its geographical position, and the considerations attendant on it, Cuba is as necessary to the North American republic as any of its present members, and that it belongs naturally to that great family of States of which the Union is the providential nursery. . . .

The natural and main outlet to the products of this entire population, the highway of their direct intercourse with the Atlantic and the Pacific States, can never be secure, but must ever be endangered whilst Cuba is a dependency of a distant power in whose possession it has proved to be a source of constant annoyance and embarrassment to their interests.

Indeed, the Union can never enjoy repose, nor possess reliable security, as long as Cuba is not embraced within its boundaries.

Its immediate acquisition by our government is of paramount importance, and we cannot doubt but that it is a consummation devoutly wished for by its inhabitants.

The intercourse which its proximity to our

coasts begets and encourages between them and the citizens of the United States, has, in the progress of time, so united their interests and blended their fortunes that they now look upon each other as if they were one people and had but one destiny.

Considerations exist which render delay in the acquisition of this island exceedingly dangerous to the United States. . . .

Cuba has thus become to us an unceasing danger, and a permanent cause of anxiety and alarm.

But we need not enlarge on these topics. It can scarcely be apprehended that foreign powers, in violation of international law, would interpose their influence with Spain to prevent our acquisition of the island. . . .

Besides, the commercial nations of the world cannot fail to perceive and appreciate the great advantages which would result to their people from a dissolution of the forced and unnatural connexion between Spain and Cuba, and the annexation of the latter to the United States. The trade of England and France with Cuba would, in that event, assume at once an important and profitable character, and rapidly extend with the increasing population and prosperity of the island.

2. But if the United States and every commercial nation would be benefited by this transfer, the interests of Spain would also be greatly and essentially promoted.

She cannot but see what such a sum of money as we are willing to pay for the island would effect in the development of her vast natural resources. . . .

Should Spain reject the present golden opportunity for developing her resources, and removing her financial embarrassments, it may never again return. . . .

Under no probable circumstances can Cuba ever yield to Spain one per cent. on the large amount which the United States are willing to pay for its acquisition. But Spain is in imminent danger of losing Cuba, without remuneration. . . .

It is not improbable, therefore, that Cuba may be wrested from Spain by a successful revolution; and in that event she will lose both the island and the price which we are now willing to pay for it—a price far beyond what was ever paid by one people to another for any province.

It may also be remarked that the settle-ment of this vexed question, by the cession of Cuba to the United States, would forever prevent the dangerous complications between nations to which it may otherwise give birth.

It is certain that, should the Cubans themselves organize an insurrection against the Spanish government, and should other independent nations come to the aid of Spain in the contest, no human power could, in our opinion, prevent the people and government of the United States from taking part in such a civil war in support of their neighbors and friends.

But if Spain, dead to the voice of her own interest, and actuated by stubborn pride and a false sense of honor, should refuse to sell Cuba to the United States, then the question will arise, What ought to be the course of the American government under such circumstances? Self-preservation is the first law of nature, with States as well as with individuals. All nations have, at different periods, acted upon this maxim. Although it has been made the pretext for committing flagrant injustice, as in the partition of Poland and other similar cases which history records, yet the principle itself, though often abused, has always been recognized. . . .

Our past history forbids that we should acquire the island of Cuba without the consent of Spain, unless justified by the great law of self-preservation. We must, in any event, preserve our own conscious rectitude and our own self-respect.

Whilst pursuing this course we can afford to disregard the censures of the world, to which we have been so often and so unjustly exposed.

After we shall have offered Spain a price for Cuba far beyond its present value, and this shall have been refused, it will then be time to consider the question, does Cuba, in the possession of Spain, seriously endanger our internal peace and existence of our cherished Union?

Should this question be answered in the affirmative, then, by every law, human and divine, we shall be justified in wresting it from Spain if we possess the power; and this upon the very same principle that would justify an individual in tearing down the burning house of his neighbor if there were no other means of preventing the flames from destroying his own home.

Under such circumstances we ought neither to count the cost nor regard the odds which Spain might enlist against us. We forbear to enter into the question, whether the present condition of the island would justify such a measure? We should, however, be recreant to our duty, be unworthy of our gallant forefathers, and commit base treason against our posterity, should we permit Cuba to be Africanized and become a second St. Domingo, with all its attendant horrors to the white race, and suffer the flames to extend to our own neighboring shores seriously to endanger or actually to consume the fair fabric of our Union.

We fear that the course and current of events are rapidly tending towards such a catastrophe. We, however, hope for the best, though we ought certainly to be prepared for the worst. . . .

Yours, very respectfully,
James Buchanan.
J. Y. Mason.
Pierre Soulé.

Hon. Wm. L. Marcy, Secretary of State.

182. MASSACHUSETTS PERSONAL LIBERTY ACT
May 21, 1855

(Acts and Resolves Passed by the General Court of Massachusetts in the year 1855, p. 924 ff.)

This remarkably stringent personal liberty act which practically nullified the Fugitive Slave Act of 1850, resulted from the revulsion of feeling at the time of the capture of Anthony Burns in 1854. The bill was passed over the veto of Governor Gardner. Section fourteen was directed against Judge E. G. Loring, who had returned Burns to slavery. Governor Gardner refused to remove Loring, but he was subsequently removed in 1858. See J. Parker, *Personal Liberty Laws;* J. Hurd, *The Law of Freedom and Bondage;* R. C. Hurd, *Personal Liberty and Habeas Corpus;* H. Wilson, *History of the Rise and Fall of the Slave Power,* Vol. I; C. E. Stevens, *Anthony Burns, a History;* A. B. Hart, ed. *Commonwealth History of Massachusetts,* Vol. IV, ch. xvi; C. M. Fuess, *Life of Caleb Cushing;* T. Parker, *Discourses of Slavery,* Vol. II.

An Act to protect the Rights and Liberties of the People of the Commonwealth of Massachusetts.

Sec. 1. [Act of 1842 extended.]

Sec. 2. The meaning of the one hundred and eleventh chapter of the Revised Statutes is hereby declared to be, that every person imprisoned or restrained of his liberty is entitled, as of right and of course, to the writ of *habeas corpus,* except in the cases mentioned in the second section of that chapter.

Sec. 3. The writ of *habeas corpus* may be issued by the supreme judicial court, the court of common pleas, by any justice's court or police court of any town or city, by any court of record, or by any justice of either of said courts, or by any judge of probate; and it may be issued by any justice of the peace, if no magistrate above named is known to said justice of the peace to be within five miles of the place where the party is imprisoned or restrained, and it shall be returnable before the supreme judicial court, or any one of the justices thereof, whether the court may be in session or not, and in term time or vacation. . . .

Sec. 6. If any claimant shall appear to demand the custody or possession of the person for whose benefit such writ is sued out, such claimant shall state in writing the facts on which he relies, with precision and certainty; and neither the claimant of the alleged fugitive, nor any person interested in his alleged obligation to service or labor, nor the alleged fugitive, shall be permitted to testify at the trial of the issue; and no confessions, admissions or declarations of the alleged fugitive against himself shall be given in evidence. Upon every question of fact involved in the issue, the burden of proof shall be on the claimant, and the facts alleged and necessary to be established, must be proved by the testimony of at least two credible witnesses, or other legal evidence equivalent thereto, and by the rules of evidence known and secured by the common law; and no *ex parte* deposition or affidavit shall be received in proof in behalf of the claimant, and no presumption shall arise in favor of the claimant from any proof that the alleged fugitive or any of his ancestors had actually been held as a slave, without proof that such holding was legal.

Sec. 7. If any person shall remove from the limits of this Commonwealth, or shall assist in removing therefrom, or shall come into the Commonwealth with the intention of removing or of assisting in the removing therefrom, or shall procure or assist in procuring to be so removed, any person being in the peace thereof who is not "held to service or labor" by the "party" making "claim," or who has not "escaped" from the "party" making "claim," within the meaning of those words in the constitution of the United States, on the pretence that such person is so held or has so escaped, or that his "service or labor" is so "due," or with the intent to subject him to such "service or labor," he shall be punished by a fine of not less than one thousand, nor more than five thousand dollars, and by imprisonment in the State Prison not less than one, nor more than five years. . . .

Sec. 9. No person, while holding any office of honor, trust, or emolument, under the laws of this Commonwealth, shall, in any capacity, issue any warrant or other process, or grant any certificate, under or by virtue of an act of congress [February 12, 1793] . . . or under or by virtue of an act of congress [September 18, 1853] . . . or shall in any capacity, serve any such warrant or other process.

Sec. 10. Any person who shall grant any certificate under or by virtue of the acts of congress, mentioned in the preceding section, shall be deemed to have resigned any commission from the Commonwealth which he may possess, his office shall be deemed vacant, and he shall be forever thereafter ineligible to any office of trust, honor or emolument under the laws of this Commonwealth.

Sec. 11. Any person who shall act as counsel or attorney for any claimant of any alleged fugitive from service or labor, under or by virtue of the acts of congress mentioned in the ninth section of this act, shall be deemed to have resigned any commission from the Commonwealth that he may possess, and he shall be thereafter incapacitated from appearing as counsel or attorney in the courts of this Commonwealth. . . .

Sec. 14. Any person holding any judicial office under the constitution or laws of this Commonwealth, who shall continue, for ten days after the passage of this act, to hold the office of United States commissioner, or any office . . . which qualifies him to issue any warrant or other process . . . under the [Fugitive Slave Acts] shall be deemed to have violated good behavior, to have given reason for the loss of public confidence, and furnished sufficient ground either for impeachment or for removal by address.

Sec. 15. Any sheriff, deputy sheriff, jailer, coroner, constable, or other officer of this Commonwealth, or the police of any city or town, or any district, county, city or town officer, or any officer or other member of the volunteer militia of this Commonwealth, who shall hereafter arrest . . . any person for the reason that he is claimed or adjudged to be a fugitive from service or labor, shall be punished by fine . . . and by imprisonment. . . .

Sec. 16. The volunteer militia of the Commonwealth shall not act in any manner in the seizure . . . of any person for the reason that he is claimed or adjudged to be a fugitive from service or labor. . . .

Sec. 19. No jail, prison, or other place of confinement belonging to, or used by, either the Commonwealth of Massachusetts or any county therein, shall be used for the detention or imprisonment of any person accused or convicted of any offence created by [the Federal Fugitive Slave Acts] . . . or accused or convicted of obstructing or resisting any process, warrant, or order issued under either of said acts, or of rescuing, or attempting to rescue, any person arrested or detained under any of the provisions of either of the said acts. . . .

183. AMERICAN PARTY PLATFORM
1856

(A Political Text-book for 1860, p. 23 ff.)

The American or Know-Nothing Party represented the nativist sentiment, but it attracted large numbers, North and South, who hoped that its program might distract attention from the slavery struggle and that it might effect some reconciliation between the sections. The Party nominated ex-president Millard Fillmore, and secured almost nine hundred thousand votes. It was particularly strong in Massachusetts, New York, and Maryland. On the Know-Nothings see, L. D. Scisco, *Political Nativism in New York;* L. F. Schmeckebier, *Know-Nothing Party in Maryland;* C. Stickney, *Know-Nothingism in Rhode Island;* H. J. Desmond, *The Know-Nothing Party;* T. C. Smith, *Parties and Slavery,* chs, viii, x, xii.

. . . .

2. The perpetuation of the Federal Union and Constitution, as the palladium of our civil and religious liberties, and the only sure bulwarks of American Independence.

3. *Americans must rule America;* and to this end *native*-born citizens should be selected for all State, Federal and municipal offices of government employment, in preference to all others. *Nevertheless,*

4. Persons born of American parents residing temporarily abroad, should be entitled to all the rights of native-born citizens.

5. No person should be selected for political station (whether of native or foreign birth), who recognizes any allegiance or obligation of any description to any foreign prince, potentate or power, or who refuses to recognize the Federal and State Constitutions (each within its sphere) as paramount to all other laws, as rules of political action.

6. The unqualified recognition and maintenance of the reserved rights of the several States, and the cultivation of harmony and fraternal good will between the citizens of the several States, and to this end, non-interference by Congress with questions appertaining solely to the individual States, and non-intervention by each State with the affairs of any other State.

7. The recognition of the right of native-born and naturalized citizens of the United States, permanently residing in any territory thereof, to frame their constitution and laws, and to regulate their domestic and social affairs in their own mode, subject only to the provisions of the Federal Constitution, with the privilege of admission into the Union whenever they have the requisite population for one Representative in Congress: *Provided, always,* that none but those who are citizens of the United States, under the Constitution and laws thereof, and who have a fixed residence in any such Territory, ought to participate in the formation of the Constitution, or in the enactment of laws for said Territory or State.

8. An enforcement of the principles that no State or Territory ought to admit others than citizens to the right of suffrage, or of holding political offices of the United States.

9. A change in the laws of naturalization, making a continued residence of twenty-one years, of all not heretofore provided for, an indispensable requisite for citizenship hereafter, and excluding all paupers, and persons convicted of crime, from landing upon our shores; but no interference with the vested rights of foreigners.

10. Opposition to any union between Church and State; no interference with religious faith or worship, and no test oaths for office. . . .

13. Opposition to the reckless and unwise policy of the present Administration in the general management of our national affairs, and more especially as shown in removing "Americans" (by designation) and Conservatives in principle, from office, and placing foreigners and Ultraists in their places; as shown in a truckling subserviency to the stronger, and an insolent and cowardly bravado toward the weaker powers; as shown in reopening sectional agitation, by the repeal of the Missouri Compromise; as shown in granting to unnaturalized foreigners the right of suffrage in Kansas and Nebraska; as shown in its vacillating course on the Kansas and Nebraska question; as shown in the corruptions which pervade some of the Departments of the Government; as shown in disgracing meritorious naval officers through prejudice or caprice: and as shown in the

blundering mismanagement of our foreign relations.

14. Therefore, to remedy existing evils, and prevent the disastrous consequences otherwise resulting therefrom, we would build up the "American Party" upon the principles herein before stated. . . .

184. CONSTITUTION OF THE COMMITTEE OF VIGILANTES OF SAN FRANCISCO
May 15, 1856
(*American State Trials*, ed. J. D. Lawson, Vol. XV, p. 65 ff.)

The influx of lawless elements to California at the time of the Gold Rush had led, in 1851, to the organization of Vigilance Committees who took the law into their own hands. A new outbreak of lawlessness, together with the apparent breakdown of the machinery of law-enforcement, led in 1856 to the organization of the famous San Francisco Committee of Vigilantes which H. H. Bancroft designated as "the greatest demonstration in the cause of civil righteousness, without subversion of the law or of the government that the world has ever seen." On the work of the Committee, see, H. H. Bancroft, *Popular Tribunals*, Vol. II; F. Tuthill, *History of California*. For the earlier Vigilante organization, see M. F. Williams, *History of the San Francisco Vigilance Committee of 1851*, University of California Publications in History, Vol. XII. For the workings of vigilante committees elsewhere, see N. P. Langford, *Vigilante Days and Ways;* T. J. Dimsdale, *Vigilantes of Montana*. The records of the Trial of criminals by the Vigilante Committee of 1856 can be found in *American State Trials*, Vol. XV.

Whereas, it has become apparent to the citizens of San Francisco that there is no security for life and property, either under the regulations of society, as it at present exists, or under the laws as now administered; and that by the association together of bad characters, our ballot boxes have been stolen and others substituted, or stuffed with votes that were not polled, and thereby our elections nullified, our dearest rights violated, and no other method left by which the will of the people can be manifested; therefore, the citizens whose names are hereunto attached, do unite themselves into an association for maintenance of peace and good order of society—the preservation of our lives and property, and to insure that our ballot boxes shall hereafter express the actual and unforged will of the majority of our citizens; and we do bind ourselves, each unto the other, by a solemn oath, to do and perform every just and lawful act for the maintenance of law and order, and to sustain the laws when faithfully and properly administered; but we are determined that no thief, burglar, incendiary, assassin, ballot-box stuffer, or other disturbers of the peace, shall escape punishment, either by the quibbles of the law, the insecurity of prisons, the carelessness or corruption of police, or a laxity of those who pretend to administer justice; and to secure the objects of this association, we do hereby agree:

1st. That the name and style of this association shall be the Committee of Vigilance, for the protection of the ballot-box, the lives, liberty and property of the citizens and residents of the City of San Francisco.

2d. That there shall be rooms for the deliberations of the Committee, at which there shall be some one or more members of the Committee appointed for that purpose, in constant attendance at all hours of the day and night, to receive the report of any member of the association, or of any other person or persons of any act of violence done to the person or property of any citizen of San Francisco; and if, in the judgment of the member or members of the Committee present, it be such an act as justifies or demands the interference of this Committee, either in aiding in the execution of the laws, or the prompt and summary punishment of the offender, the Committee shall be at once assembled for the purpose of taking such action as the majority of them, when assembled, shall determine upon.

3d. That it shall be the duty of any member or members of the Committee on duty at the committee rooms, whenever a general assemblage of the Committee be deemed necessary, to cause a call to be made, in such a manner as shall be found advisable.

4th. That whereas, an Executive Committee, has been chosen by the General Committee, it shall be the duty of said Executive Committee to deliberate and act upon all important questions, and decide upon all measures necessary to carry out the objects for which this association was formed.

5th. That whereas, this Committee has been organized into subdivisions, the Executive Committee shall have the power to call, when they shall so determine, upon a board of delegates, to consist of three representatives from each division, to confer with them upon matters of vital importance.

6th. That all matters of detail and government shall be embraced in a code of By-Laws.

7th. That the action of this body shall be entirely and vigorously free from all consideration of, or participation in the merits or demerits, or opinion or acts, of any and all sects, political parties, or sectional divisions in the community; and every class of orderly citizens, of whatever sect, party, or nativity, may become members of this body. No discussion of political, sectional, or sectarian subjects shall be allowed in the rooms of the association.

8th. That no persons, accused before this body, shall be punished until after fair and impartial trial and conviction.

9th. That whenever the General Committee have assembled for deliberation, the decision of the majority, upon any question that may be submitted to them by the Executive Committee, shall be binding upon the whole; provided nevertheless, that when the delegates are deliberating upon the punishment to be awarded to any criminals, no vote inflicting the death penalty shall be binding, unless passed by two-thirds of those present and entitled to vote.

10th. That all good citizens shall be eligible for admission to this body, under such regulations as may be prescribed by a committee on qualifications; and if any unworthy persons gain admission, they shall on due proof be expelled; and believing ourselves to be executors of the will of the majority of our citizens, we do pledge our sacred honor, to defend and sustain each other in carrying out the determined action of this committee, at the hazard of our lives and our fortunes.

185. DRED SCOTT v. SANDFORD
19 Howard, 393
1857

Error to the U.S. circuit court for the district of Missouri. In 1834 Dred Scott, a negro slave, was taken by his master from Missouri, a slave state, to Illinois, a free state, and hence to Wisconsin Territory where slavery was forbidden by the Missouri Compromise of 1820. Subsequently Scott was brought back to Missouri, and in 1846 he began suit to obtain his freedom, on the ground that he had become free when taken into free territory. The case was eventually brought on appeal to the Supreme Court. Three major questions were involved: whether Scott was a citizen of the State of Missouri, so as to give the Federal courts jurisdiction; whether he had been set free by his sojourn in the free state of Illinois; whether he had been set free by his sojourn in the free Territory of Wisconsin, e.g., whether the Missouri Compromise was constitutional. The Court ruled that Scott was not a citizen of the United States or of the State of Missouri and therefore not competent to sue in the Federal courts. Having thus refused jurisdiction, the court went on to pass on the other questions presented,

all of the judges giving separate opinions. Of the dissenting opinions, that by Justice Curtis dealt most elaborately with the question of citizenship.

This case, probably the most famous in the history of the Court, has been the subject of an extensive literature. See the discussion of the case and bibliographical notes in Warren, *Supreme Court,* Vol. II, ch. xxvi; C. B. Swisher, *R. B. Taney;* Hodder, "Some Phases of the Dred Scott Case," *Miss. Valley Hist. Rev.* Vol. XVI; Corwin, "Dred Scott Decision in the Light of Contemporary Legal Doctrines," A. H. R., Vol. XVII; Cattarall, "Some Antecedents of the Dred Scott Case," A. H. R., Vol. XXX; Cohn, "Dred Scott Decision in the Light of Later Events," 46 Am. Law Rev. 548.

TANEY, C. J. . . . There are two leading questions presented by the record:

1. Had the Circuit Court of the United States jurisdiction to hear and determine the case between these parties? And,

2. If it had jurisdiction, is the judgment it has given erroneous or not?

The plaintiff in error, who was also the plaintiff in the court below, was, with his wife and children, held as slaves by the defendant, in the State of Missouri, and he brought this action in the Circuit Court of the United States for that district, to assert the title of himself and his family to freedom.

The declaration is . . . that he and the defendant are citizens of different States; that is, that he is a citizen of Missouri, and the defendant a citizen of New York.

The defendant pleaded in abatement to the jurisdiction of the court, that the plaintiff was not a citizen of the State of Missouri, as alleged in his declaration, being a negro of African descent whose ancestors were of pure African blood, and who were brought into this country and sold as slaves.

To this plea the plaintiff demurred, and the defendant joined in demurrer. . . .

Before we speak of the pleas in bar, it will be proper to dispose of the questions which have arisen on the plea in abatement.

That plea denies the right of the plaintiff to sue in a court of the United States, for the reasons therein stated.

If the question raised by it is legally before us, and the court should be of opinion that the facts stated in it disqualify the plaintiff from becoming a citizen, in the sense in which that word is used in the Constitution of the United States, then the judgment of the Circuit Court is erroneous, and must be reversed. . . .

The question to be decided is, whether the facts stated in the plea are sufficient to show that the plaintiff is not entitled to sue as a citizen in a court of the United States.

This is certainly a very serious question, and one that now for the first time has been brought for decision before this court. But it is brought here by those who have a right to bring it, and it is our duty to meet it and decide it.

The question is simply this: Can a negro, whose ancestors were imported into this country, and sold as slaves, become a member of the political community formed and brought into existence by the Constitution of the United States, and as such become entitled to all the rights, and privileges, and immunities, guaranteed by that instrument to the citizen? One of which rights is the privilege of suing in a court of the United States in the cases specified in the Constitution.

It will be observed, that the plea applies to that class of persons only whose ancestors were negroes of the African race, and imported into this country, and sold and held as slaves. The only matter in issue before the court, therefore, is, whether the descendants of such slaves, when they shall be emancipated, or who are born of parents who had become free before their birth, are citizens of a State, in the sense in which the word citizen is used in the Constitution of the United States. And this being the only matter in dispute on the pleadings, the court must be understood as speaking in this opinion of that class only, that is of persons who are the descendants of Africans who were imported into this country and sold as slaves. . . .

We proceed to examine the case as presented by the pleadings.

The words "people of the United States" and "citizens" are synonymous terms, and mean the same thing. They both describe the political body who, according to our republican institutions, form the sovereignty, and who hold the power and conduct the government through their representatives. They are what we familiarly call the "sovereign people," and every citizen is one of this people, and a constituent member of this sovereignty. The question before us is, whether the class of persons described in the plea in abatement compose a portion of this people, and are constituent members of this sovereignty? We think they are not, and that they are not included, and were not intended to be included, under the word "citizens" in the Constitution, and can, therefore, claim none of the rights and privileges which that instrument provides for and secures to citizens of the United States. On the contrary, they were at that time considered as a subordinate and inferior class of beings, who had been subjugated by the dominant race, and whether emancipated or not, yet remained subject to their authority, and had no rights or privileges but such as those who held the power and the government might choose to grant them. . . .

In discussing this question, we must not confound the rights of citizenship which a state may confer within its own limits, and he rights of citizenship as a member of the Union. It does not by any means follow, because he has all the rights and privileges of a citizen of a State, that he must be a citizen of the United States. He may have all of the rights and privileges of the citizen of a State, and yet not be entitled to the rights and privileges of a citizen in any other State. For, previous to the adoption of the Constitution of the United States, every State had the undoubted right to confer on whomsoever it pleased the character of a citizen, and to endow him with all its rights. But this character, of course, was confined to the boundaries of the State, and gave him no rights or privileges in other States beyond those secured to him by the laws of nations and the comity of States. Nor have the several States surrendered the power of conferring these rights and privileges by adopting the Constitution of the United States. Each State may still confer them upon an alien, or any one it thinks proper, or upon any class or description of persons; yet he would not be a citizen in the sense in which that word is used in the Constitution of the United States, nor entitled to sue as such in one of its courts, nor to the privileges and immunities of a citizen in other States. The rights which he would acquire would be restricted to the State which gave them. . . .

It is very clear, therefore, that no State can, by any Act or law of its own, passed since the adoption of the Constitution, introduce a new member into the political community created by the Constitution of the United States. It cannot make him a member of this community by making him a member of its own. And for the same reason it cannot introduce any person, or description of persons, who were not intended to be embraced in this new political family, which the Constitution brought into existence, but were intended to be excluded from it.

The question then arises, whether the provisions of the Constitution, in relation to the personal rights and privileges to which the citizen of a State should be entitled, embraced the negro African race, at that time in this country, or who might afterwards be imported, who had then or should afterwards be made free in any State; and to put it in the power of a single State to make him a citizen of the United States, and endue him with the full rights of citizenship in every other State without their consent. Does the Constitution of the United States act upon him whenever he shall be made free under the laws of a State, and raised there to the rank of a citizen, and immediately clothe him with all the privileges of a citizen in every other State, and in its own courts?

The court think the affirmative of these propositions cannot be maintained. And if it cannot, the plaintiff in error could not be a citizen of the State of Missouri, within the meaning of the Constitution of the United States, and, consequently, was not entitled to sue in its courts.

It is true, every person, and every class and description of persons, who were at the time of the adoption of the Constitution recognized as citizens in the several States, became also citizens of this new political body; but none other; it was formed by them, and for them and their posterity, but for no one else. And the personal rights and privileges guarantied to citizens of this new sovereignty were intended to embrace those only who were then members of the several state communities, or who should afterwards, by birthright or otherwise, become members, according to the provisions of the Constitution and the principles on which it was founded. . . .

It becomes necessary, therefore, to determine who were citizens of the several States when the Constitution was adopted. And in order to do this, we must recur to the governments and institutions of the thirteen Colonies, when they separated from Great Britain and formed new sovereignties. . . . We must inquire who, at that time, were recognized as the people or citizens of a State. . . .

In the opinion of the court, the legislation and histories of the times, and the language used in the Declaration of Independence, show, that neither the class of persons who had been imported as slaves, nor their descendants, whether they had become free or not, were then acknowledged as a part of the people, nor intended to be included in the general words used in that memorable instrument.

It is difficult at this day to realize the state of public opinion in relation to that unfortunate race, which prevailed in the civilized and enlightened portions of the world at the time of the Declaration of Independence, and when the Constitution of the United States was framed and adopted. . . .

They had for more than a century before been regarded as beings of an inferior order; and altogether unfit to associate with the white race, either in social or political relations; and so far inferior that they had no rights which the white man was bound to respect; and that the negro might justly and lawfully be reduced to slavery for his benefit. . . . This opinion was at that time fixed and universal in the civilized portion of the white race. It was regarded as an axiom in morals as well as in politics, which no one thought of disputing, or supposed to be open to dispute; and men in every grade and position in society daily and habitually acted upon it in their private pursuits, as well as in matters of public concern, without doubting for a moment the correctness of this opinion. . . .

The legislation of the different Colonies furnishes positive and undisputable proof of this fact. . . .

The language of the Declaration of Independence is equally conclusive. . . .

This state of public opinion had undergone no change when the Constitution was adopted, as is equally evident from its provisions and language. . . .

But there are two clauses in the Constitution which point directly and specifically to the negro race as a separate class of persons, and show clearly that they were not regarded as a portion of the people or citizens of the Government then formed.

One of these clauses reserves to each of the thirteen States the right to import slaves until the year 1808, if he thinks it proper. And the importation which it thus sanctions was unquestionably of persons of the race of which we are speaking, as the traffic in slaves in the United States had always been confined to them. And by the other provision the States pledge themselves to each other to maintain the right of property of the master, by delivering up to him any slave who may have escaped from his service, and be found within their respective territories. . . . And these two provisions show, conclusively, that neither the description of persons therein referred to, nor their descendants, were embraced in any of the other provisions of the Constitution; for certainly these two clauses were not intended to confer on them or their

posterity the blessings of liberty, or any of the personal rights so carefully provided for the citizen. . . .

Indeed, when we look to the condition of this race in the several States at the time, it is impossible to believe that these rights and privileges were intended to be extended to them. . . .

The legislation of the States therefore shows, in a manner not to be mistaken, the inferior and subject condition of that race at the time the Constitution was adopted, and long afterwards, throughout the thirteen States by which that instrument was framed; and it is hardly consistent with the respect due to these States, to suppose that they regarded at that time, as fellow-citizens and members of the sovereignty, a class of beings whom they had thus stigmatized; . . . More especially, it cannot be believed that the large slave-holding States regarded them as included in the word "citizens," or would have consented to a constitution which might compel them to receive them in that character from another State. For if they were so received, and entitled to the privileges and immunities of citizens, it would exempt them from the operation of the special laws and from the police regulations which they considered to be necessary for their own safety. . . . And all of this would be done in the face of the subject race of the same color, both free and slaves, inevitably producing discontent and insubordination among them, and endangering the peace and safety of the State. . . .

But it is said that a person may be a citizen, and entitled to that character, although he does not possess all the rights which may belong to other citizens; as, for example, the right to vote, or to hold particular offices; and that yet, when he goes into another State, he is entitled to be recognized there as a citizen, although the State may measure his rights by the rights which it allows to persons of a like character or class, resident in the State, and refuse to him the full rights of citizenship.

This argument overlooks the language of the provision in the Constitution of which we are speaking.

Undoubtedly, a person may be a citizen, that is, a member of the community who form the sovereignty, although he exercises no share of the political power, and is incapacitated from holding particular offices. . . .

So, too, a person may be entitled to vote by the law of the State, who is not a citizen even of the State itself. And in some of the States of the Union foreigners not naturalized are allowed to vote. And the State may give the right to free negroes and mulattoes, but that does not make them citizens of the State, and still less of the United States. And the provision in the Constitution giving privileges and immunities in other States, does not apply to them.

Neither does it apply to a person who, being the citizen of a State, migrates to another State. For then he becomes subject to the laws of the State in which he lives, and he is no longer a citizen of the State from which he removed. And the State in which he resides may then, unquestionably, determine his *status* or condition, and place him among the class of persons who are not recognized as citizens, but belong to an inferior and subject race; and may deny him the privileges and immunities enjoyed by its citizens. . . .

. . . But if he ranks as a citizen of the State to which he belongs, within the meaning of the Constitution of the United States, then, whenever he goes into another State, the Constitution clothes him, as to the rights of person, with all the privileges and immunities which belong to citizens of the State. And if persons of the African race are citizens of a state, and of the United States, they would be entitled to all of these privileges and immunities in every State, and the State could not restrict them; for they would hold these privileges and immunities, under the paramount authority of the Federal Government, and its courts would be bound to maintain and enforce them, the Constitution and laws of the State to the contrary notwithstanding. . . .

And upon a full and careful consideration of the subject, the court is of opinion that, upon the facts stated in the plea in abatement, Dred Scott was not a citizen of Missouri within the meaning of the Constitution of the United States, and not entitled as such to sue in its courts; and, consequently, that the Circuit Court had no jurisdiction of the case, and that the judgment on the plea in abatement is erroneous. . . .

We proceed, therefore, to inquire whether the facts relied on by the plaintiff entitled him to his freedom. . . .

In considering this part of the controversy, two questions arise: 1st. Was he, together with his family, free in Missouri by reason of the stay in the territory of the United States hereinbefore mentioned? And 2d, If they were not, is Scott himself free by reason of his removal to Rock Island, in the State of Illinois, as stated in the above admissions?

We proceed to examine the first question.

The Act of Congress, upon which the plaintiff relies, declares that slavery and involuntary servitude, except as a punishment for crime, shall be forever prohibited in all that part of the territory ceded by France, under the name of Louisiana, which lies north of thirty-six degrees thirty minutes north latitude, and not included within the limits of Missouri. And the difficulty which meets us at the threshold of this part of the inquiry is, whether Congress was authorized to pass this law under any of the powers granted to it by the Constitution; for if the authority is not given by that instrument, it is the duty of this court to declare it void and inoperative, and incapable of conferring freedom upon any one who is held as a slave under the laws of any one of the States.

The counsel for the plaintiff has laid much stress upon that article in the Constitution which confers on Congress the power "to dispose of and make all needful rules and regulations respecting the territory or other property belonging to the United States;" but, in the judgment of the court, that provision has no bearing on the present controversy, and the power there given, whatever it may be, is confined, and was intended to be confined, to the territory which at that time belonged to, or was claimed by, the United States, and was within their boundaries as settled by the treaty with Great Britain, and can have no influence upon a territory afterwards acquired from a foreign Government. It was a special provision for a known and particular territory, and to meet a present emergency, and nothing more. . . .

If this clause is construed to extend to territory acquired by the present Government from a foreign nation, outside of the limits of any charter from the British Government to a colony, it would be difficult to say, why it was deemed necessary to give the Government the power to sell any vacant lands belonging to the sovereignty which might be found within it; and if this was necessary, why the grant of this power should precede the power to legislate over it and establish a Government there; and still more difficult to say, why it was deemed necessary so specially and particularly to grant the power to make needful rules and regulations in relation to any personal or movable property it might acquire there. For the words, *other property* necessarily, by every known rule of interpretation, must mean property of a different description from territory or land. And the difficulty would perhaps be insurmountable in endeavoring to account for the last member of the sentence, which provides that "nothing in this Constitution shall be so construed as to prejudice any claims of the United States or any particular State," or to say how any particular State could have claims in or to a territory ceded by a foreign Government, or to account for associating this provision with the preceding provisions of the clause, with which it would appear to have no connection. . . .

But the power of Congress over the person or property of a citizen can never be a mere discretionary power under our Constitution and form of Government. The powers of the Government and the rights and privileges of the citizen are regulated and plainly defined by the Constitution itself. And when the Territory becomes a part of the United States, the Federal Government enters into possession in the character impressed upon it by those who created it. It enters upon it with its powers over the citizen strictly defined, and limited by the Constitution, from which it derives its own existence, and by virtue of which alone it continues to exist and act as a Government and sovereignty. It has no power of any kind beyond it; and it cannot, when it enters a Territory of the United States, put off its character, and assume discretionary or despotic powers which the Constitution has denied to it. It cannot create for itself a new character separated from the citizens of the United States, and the duties it owes them under the provisions of the Constitution. The Territory being a part of the United States, the Government and the citizen both enter it under the authority of the Constitution, with their respective rights defined and marked

out; and the Federal Government can exercise no power over his person or property, beyond what that instrument confers, nor lawfully deny any right which it has reserved. . . .

The rights of private property have been guarded with equal care. Thus the rights of property are united with the rights of person, and placed on the same ground by the fifth amendment to the Constitution. . . . An Act of Congress which deprives a person of the United States of his liberty or property merely because he came himself or brought his property into a particular Territory of the United States, and who had committed no offense against the laws, could hardly be dignified with the name of due process of law. . . .

And this prohibition is not confined to the States, but the words are general, and extend to the whole territory over which the Constitution gives it power to legislate, including those portions of it remaining under territorial government, as well as that covered by States. It is a total absence of power everywhere within the dominion of the United States, and places the citizens of a territory, so far as these rights are concerned, on the same footing with citizens of the States, and guards them as firmly and plainly against any inroads which the general government might attempt, under the plea of implied or incidental powers. And if Congress itself cannot do this—if it is beyond the powers conferred on the Federal Government—it will be admitted, we presume, that it could not authorize a territorial government to exercise them. It could confer no power on any local government, established by its authority, to violate the provisions of the Constitution.

It seems, however, to be supposed, that there is a difference between property in a slave and other property, and that different rules may be applied to it in expounding the Constitution of the United States. And the laws and usages of nations, and the writings of eminent jurists upon the relation of master and slave and their mutual rights and duties, and the powers which governments may exercise over it, have been dwelt upon in the argument.

But . . . if the Constitution recognizes the right of property of the master in a slave, and makes no distinction between that description of property and other property owned by a citizen, no tribunal, acting under the authority of the United States, whether it be legislative, executive, or judicial, has a right to draw such a distinction, or deny to it the benefit of the provisions and guarantees which have been provided for the protection of private property against the encroachments of the Government.

Now . . . the right of property in a slave is distinctly and expressly affirmed in the Constitution. The right to traffic in it, like an ordinary article of merchandise and property, was guaranteed to the citizens of the United States, in every State that might desire it, for twenty years. And the Government in express terms is pledged to protect it in all future time, if the slave escapes from his owner. . . . And no word can be found in the Constitution which gives Congress a greater power over slave property, or which entitles property of that kind to less protection than property of any other description. The only power conferred is the power coupled with the duty of guarding and protecting the owner in his rights.

Upon these considerations, it is the opinion of the court that the Act of Congress which prohibited a citizen from holding and owning property of this kind in the territory of the United States north of the line therein mentioned, is not warranted by the Constitution, and is therefore void; and that neither Dred Scott himself, nor any of his family, were made free by being carried into this territory; even if they had been carried there by the owner, with the intention of becoming a permanent resident. . . .

Upon the whole, therefore, it is the judgment of this court, that it appears by the record before us that the plaintiff in error is not a citizen of Missouri, in the sense in which that word is used in the Constitution; and that the Circuit Court of the United States, for that reason, had no jurisdiction in the case, and could give no judgment in it.

Its judgment for the defendant must, consequently, be reversed, and a mandate issued directing the suit to be dismissed for want of jurisdiction.

WAYNE, J., NELSON, J., GRIER, J., DANIEL, J., CAMPBELL, J., AND CATRON, J., filed separate concurring opinions. McLEAN, J. and CURTIS, J. dissented.

186. LINCOLN'S HOUSE DIVIDED SPEECH
Springfield, Illinois, June 17, 1858

(*Writings of Abraham Lincoln*, Constitutional ed., Vol. III, p. 1 ff.)

This speech was delivered at the close of the Republican State Convention, in the Hall of the House of Representatives. Though the "house divided" phrase had been used frequently before, it was this speech of Lincoln's that gave currency and familiarity to the phrase and the idea. For an analysis of the speech and a description of the setting, see A. Beveridge, *Abraham Lincoln*, Vol. II, p. 575 ff.

MR. PRESIDENT AND GENTLEMEN OF THE CONVENTION: If we could first know where we are, and whither we are tending, we could better judge what to do, and how to do it. We are now far into the fifth year since a policy was initiated with the avowed object and confident promise of putting an end to slavery agitation. Under the operation of that policy, that agitation has not only not ceased, but has constantly augmented. In my opinion, it will not cease until a crisis shall have been reached and passed. "A house divided against itself cannot stand." I believe this government cannot endure permanently half slave and half free. I do not expect the Union to be dissolved; I do not expect the house to fall; but I do expect it will cease to be divided. It will become all one thing, or all the other. Either the opponents of slavery will arrest the further spread of it, and place it where the public mind shall rest in the belief that it is in the course of ultimate extinction, or its advocates will push it forward till it shall become alike lawful in all the States, old as well as new, North as well as South.

Have we no tendency to the latter condition?

Let any one who doubts, carefully contemplate that now almost complete legal combination—piece of machinery, so to speak—compounded of the Nebraska doctrine and the Dred Scott decision. Let him consider, not only what work the machinery is adapted to do, and how well adapted, but also let him study the history of its construction, and trace, if he can, or rather fail, if he can, to trace the evidences of design, and concert of action, among its chief architects, from the beginning.

The new year of 1854 found slavery excluded from more than half the States by State Constitutions, and from most of the National territory by Congressional prohibition. Four days later, commenced the struggle which ended in repealing that Congressional prohibition. This opened all the National territory to slavery, and was the first point gained. . . .

While the Nebraska Bill was passing through Congress, a *law case,* involving the question of a negro's freedom, by reason of his owner having voluntarily taken him first into a free State, and then into a territory covered by the Congressional prohibition, and held him as a slave for a long time in each, was passing through the United States Circuit Court for the District of Missouri; and both Nebraska Bill and lawsuit were brought to a decision in the same month of May, 1854. The negro's name was "Dred Scott," which name now designates the decision finally made in the case. Before the then next Presidential election, the law case came to, and was argued in, the Supreme Court of the United States; but the decision of it was deferred until after the election. Still, before the election, Senator Trumbull, on the floor of the Senate, requested the leading advocate of the Nebraska Bill to state *his opinion* whether the people of a Territory can constitutionally exclude slavery from their limits; and the latter answers: "That is a question for the Supreme Court."

The election came. Mr. Buchanan was elected, and the indorsement, such as it was, secured. That was the second point gained. . . . The Presidential inauguration came, and still no decision of the court; but the incoming President, in his inaugural address, fervently exhorted his people to abide by the forthcoming decision, whatever it might be. Then, in a few days, came the decision.

The reputed author of the Nebraska Bill finds an early occasion to make a speech at this capital indorsing the Dred Scott decision, and vehemently denouncing all opposition to it. The new President, too, seizes the early occasion of the Silliman letter to indorse and strongly construe that decision, and to express his astonishment that any different view had ever been entertained!

At length a squabble springs up between the President and the author of the Nebraska Bill, on the mere question of *fact,* whether the Lecompton Constitution was or was not in any just sense made by the people of Kansas; and in that quarrel the latter declares that all he wants is a fair vote for the people, and that he cares not whether slavery be voted *down* or voted *up.* I do not understand his declaration, that he cares not whether slavery be voted down or voted up, to be intended by him other than as an apt definition of the policy he would impress upon the public mind. . . . That principle is the only shred left of his original Nebraska doctrine. Under the Dred Scott decision "squatter sovereignty" squatted out of existence, tumbled down like temporary scaffolding; like the mould at the foundry, served through one blast, and fell back into loose sand; helped to carry an election, and then was kicked to the winds. His late joint struggle with the Republicans, against the Lecompton Constitution, involves nothing of the original Nebraska doctrine. That struggle was made on a point—the right of a people to make their own constitution—upon which he and the Republicans have never differed.

The several points of the Dred Scott decision, in connection with Senator Douglas's "care not" policy, constitute the piece of machinery, in its present state of advancement. This was the third point gained. The working points of that machinery are:

Firstly, That no negro slave, imported as such from Africa, and no descendant of such slave, can ever be a citizen of any State, in the sense of that term as used in the Constitution of the United States. This point is made in order to deprive the negro, in every possible event, of the benefit of that provision of the United States Constitution which declares that "The citizens of each State shall be entitled to all privileges and immunities of citizens in the several States."

Secondly, That, "subject to the Constitution of the United States," neither Congress nor a Territorial Legislature can exclude slavery from any United States Territory. This point is made in order that individual men may fill up the Territories with slaves, without danger of losing them as property, and thus to enhance the chances of permanency to the institution through all the future.

Thirdly, That whether the holding a negro in actual slavery in a free State makes him free, as against the holder, the United States courts will not decide, but will leave to be decided by the courts of any slave State the negro may be forced into by the master. This point is made, not to be pressed immediately; but, if acquiesced in for a while, and apparently indorsed by the people at an election, then to sustain the logical conclusion that what Dred Scott's master might lawfully do with Dred Scott, in the free State of Illinois, every other master may lawfully do with any other one, or one thousand slaves, in Illinois, or in any other free State.

Auxiliary to all this, and working hand in hand with it, the Nebraska doctrine, or what is left of it, is to educate and mould public opinion, at least Northern public opinion, not to care whether slavery is voted down or voted up. This shows exactly where we now are; and partially, also, whither we are tending. . . .

Why was the amendment, expressly declaring the right of the people, voted down? Plainly enough now,—the adoption of it would have spoiled the niche for the Dred Scott decision. Why was the court decision held up? Why even a Senator's individual opinion withheld, till after the Presidential election? Plainly enough now,—the speaking

out then would have damaged the "perfectly free" argument upon which the election was to be carried. Why the outgoing President's felicitation on the indorsement? Why the delay of a reargument? Why the incoming President's advance exhortation in favor of the decision? These things look like the cautious patting and petting of a spirited horse preparatory to mounting him, when it is dreaded that he may give the rider a fall. And why the hasty after-indorsement of the decision by the President and others?

We cannot absolutely know that all these exact adaptations are the result of preconcert. But when we see a lot of framed timbers, different portions of which we know have been gotten out at different times and places and by different workmen,—Stephen, Franklin, Roger, and James, for instance,—and when we see these timbers joined together, and see they exactly make the frame of a house or a mill, all the tenons and mortises exactly fitting, and all the lengths and proportions of the different pieces exactly adapted to their respective places, and not a piece too many or too few,—not omitting even scaffolding,—or, if a single piece be lacking, we see the place in the frame exactly fitted and prepared yet to bring such piece in,—in such a case, we find it impossible not to believe that Stephen and Franklin and Roger and James all understood one another from the beginning, and all worked upon a common plan or draft drawn up before the first blow was struck. . . .

187. THE LINCOLN–DOUGLAS DEBATES
1858
(The Writings of Abraham Lincoln, Constitutional ed., Vols. III–IV)

Lincoln had been a candidate for the United States Senate in 1854–55; on that memorable occasion he had thrown his vote to Lyman Trumbull and thus secured the election of Trumbull over Douglas. In June, 1858 Lincoln was chosen as the Republican candidate for the Senatorship (Doc. No. 186), and on July 24 he challenged his opponent, Douglas, to a series of joint debates. The challenge was accepted, and seven joint debates arranged for. The debates were held at Ottawa, Freeport, Jonesboro, Charleston, Galesburg, Quincy, and Alton, Illinois, from August 21 to October 15. Perhaps the most important of the debates was the second, held at

Freeport, where Lincoln forced Douglas to announce the so-called Freeport Doctrine. In the election Lincoln carried districts containing a larger population than those which Douglas carried, but Douglas received the majority of the votes of the legislature. The Debates dramatized Lincoln before the country and paved the way for his candidacy in 1860, while they distinctly embarrassed Douglas in the south. Extracts from the second, third and seventh debates are given below. The Debates have been reprinted in numerous editions. See, A. Beveridge, *Abraham Lincoln,* Vol. II, chs. ix, x; C. Sandburg, *Abraham Lincoln, The Prairie Years;* A. Johnson, *Stephen*

A. *Douglas;* G. F. Milton, *The Eve of Conflict,* ch. xx; A. C. Cole, *The Era of the Civil War,* Centennial History of Illinois, Vol. IV.

1. THE SECOND JOINT DEBATE
Freeport, August 27, 1858
LINCOLN'S OPENING SPEECH AND DOUGLAS'S REPLY

Mr. Lincoln's Speech

. . . I now proceed to propound to the Judge the interrogatories, so far as I have framed them. I will bring forward a new installment when I get them ready. I will bring them forward now only reaching to number four.

The first one is:

Question 1.—If the people of Kansas shall, by means entirely unobjectionable in all other respects, adopt a State constitution, and ask admission into the Union under it, *before* they have the requisite number of inhabitants according to the English bill,—some ninety-three thousand,—will you vote to admit them?

Q. 2. Can the people of a United States Territory, in any lawful way, against the wish of any citizen of the United States, exclude slavery from its limits prior to the formation of a State constitution?

Q. 3. If the Supreme Court of the United States shall decide that States cannot exclude slavery from their limits, are you in favor of acquiescing in, adopting, and following such decision as a rule of political action?

Q. 4. Are you in favor of acquiring additional territory, in disregard of how such acquisition may affect the nation on the slavery question? . . .

Senator Douglas's Reply

First, he desires to know if the people of Kansas shall form a constitution by means entirely proper and unobjectionable, and ask admission into the Union as a State, before they have the requisite population for a member of Congress, whether I will vote for that admission. . . . I will answer his question. In reference to Kansas, it is my opinion that as she has population enough to constitute a slave State, she has people enough for a free State. I will not make Kansas an exceptional case to the other States of the Union. I hold it to be a sound rule, of uni-

versal application, to require a Territory to contain the requisite population for a member of Congress before it is admitted as a State into the Union. I made that proposition in the Senate in 1856, and I renewed it during the last session, in a bill providing that no Territory of the United States should form a constitution and apply for admission until it had the requisite population. On another occasion I proposed that neither Kansas nor any other Territory should be admitted until it had the requisite population. Congress did not adopt any of my propositions containing this general rule, but did make an exception of Kansas. I will stand by that exception. Either Kansas must come in as a free State, with whatever population she may have, or the rule must be applied to all the other Territories alike. I therefore answer at once, that, it having been decided that Kansas has people enough for a slave State, I hold that she has enough for a free State. I hope Mr. Lincoln is satisfied with my answer; . . .

The next question propounded to me by Mr. Lincoln is, Can the people of a Territory in any lawful way, against the wishes of any citizen of the United States, exclude slavery from their limits prior to the formation of a State constitution? I answer emphatically, as Mr. Lincoln has heard me answer a hundred times from every stump in Illinois, that in my opinion the people of a Territory can, by lawful means, exclude slavery from their limits prior to the formation of a State constitution. Mr. Lincoln knew that I had answered that question over and over again. He heard me argue the Nebraska Bill on that principle all over the State in 1854, in 1855, and in 1856, and he has no excuse for pretending to be in doubt as to my position on that question. It matters not what way the Supreme Court may hereafter decide as to the abstract question whether slavery may or may not go into a Territory under the Constitution, the people have the lawful means to introduce it or exclude it as they please, for the reason that slavery cannot exist a day or an hour anywhere, unless it is supported by local police regulations. Those police regulations can only be established by the local legislature; and if the people are opposed to slavery, they will elect representatives to that body who will by unfriendly legislation effectually prevent the introduction of it into their midst. If, on the contrary, they are for it, their legislation will favor its extension. Hence, no matter what the decision of the Supreme Court may be on that abstract question, still the right of the people to make a slave Territory or a free Territory is perfect and complete under the Nebraska Bill. I hope Mr. Lincoln deems my answer satisfactory on that point. . . .

. . . The third question which Mr. Lincoln presented is, if the Supreme Court of the United States shall decide that a State of this Union cannot exclude slavery from its own limits, will I submit to it? . . . He casts an imputation upon the Supreme Court of the United States, by supposing that they would violate the Constitution of the United States. I tell him that such a thing is not possible. It would be an act of moral treason that no man on the bench could ever descend to. Mr. Lincoln himself would never in his partisan feelings so far forget what was right as to be guilty of such an act.

The fourth question of Mr. Lincoln is, Are you in favor of acquiring additional territory, in disregard as to how such acquisition may affect the Union on the slavery question? This question is very ingeniously and cunningly put.

The Black Republican creed lays it down expressly that under no circumstances shall we acquire any more territory, unless slavery is first prohibited in the country. . . . I answer that whenever it becomes necessary, in our growth and progress, to acquire more territory, that I am in favor of it, without reference to the question of slavery; and when we have acquired it, I will leave the people free to do as they please, either to make it slave or free territory, as they prefer. It is idle to tell me or you that we have territory enough. . . . I tell you, increase, and multiply, and expand, is the law of this nation's existence. You cannot limit this great Republic by mere boundary lines, saying, "Thus far shalt thou go, and no farther." Any one of you gentlemen might as well say to a son twelve years old that he is big enough, and must not grow any larger; and in order to prevent his growth, put a hoop around him to keep him to his present size. What would be the result? Either the hoop must burst and be rent asunder, or the child must die. So it would be with this great

nation. With our natural increase, growing with a rapidity unknown in any part of the globe, with the tide of emigration that is fleeing from despotism in the Old World to seek refuge in our own, there is a constant torrent pouring into this country that requires more land, more territory upon which to settle; and just as fast as our interests and our destiny require additional territory in the North, in the South, or on the islands of the ocean, I am for it; and when we acquire it, will leave the people, according to the Nebraska Bill, free to do as they please on the subject of slavery and every other question. . . .

2. THE THIRD JOINT DEBATE
Jonesboro, September 15, 1858
Lincoln's Reply to Douglas

. . . At Freeport I propounded four interrogatories to him, claiming it as a right that he should answer as many interrogatories for me as I did for him, and I would reserve myself for a future installment when I got them ready. The Judge, in answering me upon that occasion, put in what I suppose he intends as answers to all four of my interrogatories. The first one of these interrogatories I have before me, and it is in these words:

"*Question* 1. If the people of Kansas shall, by means entirely unobjectionable in all other respects, adopt a State constitution, and ask admission into the Union under it, *before* they have the requisite number of inhabitants according to the English bill,"—some ninety-three thousand,—"will you vote to admit them?"

As I read the Judge's answer in the newspaper, and as I remember it as pronounced at the time, he does not give any answer which is equivalent to yes or no,—I will or I won't. He answers at very considerable length, rather quarrelling with me for asking the question, and insisting that Judge Trumbull had done something that I ought to say something about, and finally getting out such statements as induce me to infer that he means to be understood he will, in that supposed case, vote for the admission of Kansas. I only bring this forward now for the purpose of saying that if he chooses to put a different construction upon his answer, he may do it. But if he does not, I shall from this time forward assume that he will vote for the admission of Kansas in disregard of the English bill. He has the right to remove any misunderstanding I may have. I only mention it now, that I may hereafter assume this to be the true construction of his answer, if he does not now choose to correct me.

The second interrogatory that I propounded to him was this:

"Question 2. Can the people of a United States Territory, in any lawful way, against the wish of any citizen of the United States, exclude slavery from its limits prior to the formation of a State Constitution?"

To this Judge Douglas answered that they can lawfully exclude slavery from the Territory prior to the formation of a constitution. He goes on to tell us how it can be done. As I understand him, he holds that it can be done by the Territorial Legislature refusing to make any enactments for the protection of slavery in the Territory, and especially by adopting unfriendly legislation to it. For the sake of clearness, I state it again: that they can exclude slavery from the Territory, 1st, by withholding what he assumes to be an indispensable assistance to it in the way of legislation; and, 2d, by unfriendly legislation. If I rightly understand him, I wish to ask your attention for a while to his position.

In the first place, the Supreme Court of the United States has decided that any Congressional prohibition of slavery in the Territories is unconstitutional; that they have reached this proposition as a conclusion from their former proposition, that the Constitution of the United States expressly recognizes property in slaves, and from that other Constitutional provision, that no person shall be deprived of property without due process of law. Hence they reach the conclusion that as the Constitution of the United States expressly recognizes property in slaves, and prohibits any person from being deprived of property without due process of law, to pass an Act of Congress by which a man who owned a slave on one side of a line would be deprived of him if he took him on the other side, is depriving him of that property without due process of law. That I understand to be the decision of the Supreme Court. I understand also that Judge Douglas adheres most firmly to that decision; and the difficulty is, how is it possible for any power to

exclude slavery from the Territory, unless in violation of that decision? That is the difficulty. . . .

I hold that the proposition that slavery cannot enter a new country without police regulations is historically false. It is not true at all. I hold that the history of this country shows that the institution of slavery was originally planted upon this continent *without* these "police regulations" which the Judge now thinks necessary for the actual establishment of it. Not only so, but is there not another fact: how came this Dred Scott decision to be made? It was made upon the case of a negro being taken and actually held in slavery in Minnesota Territory, claiming his freedom because the Act of Congress prohibited his being so held there. *Will the Judge pretend that Dred Scott was not held there without police regulations?* There is at least one matter of record as to his having been held in slavery in the Territory, not only without police regulations, but in the teeth of Congressional legislation supposed to be valid at the time. This shows that there is vigor enough in slavery to plant itself in a new country even against unfriendly legislation. It takes not only law, but the *enforcement* of law to keep it out. That is the history of this country upon the subject.

I wish to ask one other question. It being understood that the Constitution of the United States guarantees property in slaves in the Territories, if there is any infringement of the right of that property, would not the United States courts, organized for the government of the Territory, apply such remedy as might be necessary in that case? It is a maxim held by the courts that there is no wrong without its remedy; and the courts have a remedy for whatever is acknowledged and treated as a wrong.

Again: I will ask you, my friends, if you were elected members of the Legislature, what would be the first thing you would have to do before entering upon your duties? *Swear to support the Constitution of the United States.* Suppose you believe, as Judge Douglas does, that the Constitution of the United States guarantees to your neighbor the right to hold slaves in that Territory; that they are his property: how can you clear your oaths unless you give him such legislation as is necessary to enable him to enjoy that property? What do you understand by supporting the Constitution of a State, or of the United States? Is it not to give such constitutional helps to the rights established by that Constitution as may be practically needed? Can you, if you swear to support the Constitution, and believe that the Constitution establishes a right, clear your oath, without giving it support? Do you support the Constitution if, knowing or believing there is a right established under it which needs specific legislation, you withhold that legislation? Do you not violate and disregard your oath? I can conceive of nothing plainer in the world. There can be nothing in the words "support the Constitution," if you may run counter to it by refusing support to any right established under the Constitution. And what I say here will hold with still more force against the Judge's doctrine of "unfriendly legislation." How could you, having sworn to support the Constitution, and believing it guaranteed the right to hold slaves in the Territories, assist in legislation *intended to defeat that right?* That would be violating your own view of the Constitution. Not only so, but if you were to do so, how long would it take the courts to hold your votes unconstitutional and void? Not a moment.

Lastly, I would ask: Is not Congress itself under obligation to give legislative support to any right that is established under the United States Constitution? I repeat the question: Is not Congress itself bound to give legislative support to any right that is established in the United States Constitution? A member of Congress swears to support the Constitution of the United States: and if he sees a right established by that Constitution which needs specific legislative protection, can he clear his oath without giving that protection? Let me ask you why many of us who are opposed to slavery upon principle give our acquiescence to a Fugitive Slave law? Why do we hold ourselves under obligations to pass such a law, and abide by it when it is passed? Because the Constitution makes provision that the owners of slaves shall have the right to reclaim them. It gives the right to reclaim slaves; and that right is, as Judge Douglas says, a barren right, unless there is legislation that will enforce it.

The mere declaration, "No person held to service or labor in one State under the laws thereof, escaping into another, shall in consequence of any law or regulation therein be discharged from such service or labor, but shall be delivered up on claim of the party to whom such service or labor may be due," is powerless without specific legislation to enforce it. Now, on what ground would a member of Congress, who is opposed to slavery in the abstract, vote for a Fugitive law, as I would deem it my duty to do? Because there is a constitutional right which needs legislation to enforce it. And although it is distasteful to me, I have sworn to support the Constitution; and having so sworn, I cannot conceive that I do support it if I withhold from that right any necessary legislation to make it practical. And if that is true in regard to a Fugitive Slave law, is the right to have fugitive slaves reclaimed any better fixed in the Constitution than the right to hold slaves in the Territories? For this decision is a just exposition of the Constitution, as Judge Douglas thinks. Is the one right any better than the other? Is there any man who, while a member of Congress, would give support to the one any more than the other? If I wished to refuse to give legislative support to slave property in the Territories, if a member of Congress, I could not do it, holding the view that the Constitution establishes that right. If I did it at all, it would be because I deny that this decision properly construes the Constitution. But if I acknowledge, with Judge Douglas, that this decision properly construes the Constitution, I cannot conceive that I would be less than a perjured man if I should refuse in Congress to give such protection to that property as in its nature it needed.

3. THE SEVENTH JOINT DEBATE
Alton, October 15, 1858

DOUGLAS'S SPEECH, LINCOLN'S REPLY, AND DOUGLAS'S REJOINDER

Senator Douglas's Speech

LADIES AND GENTLEMEN: It is now nearly four months since the canvass between Mr. Lincoln and myself commenced. On the 16th of June the Republican Convention assembled at Springfield and nominated Mr. Lincoln as their candidate for the United States Senate, and he, on that occasion, delivered a speech in which he laid down what he understood to be the Republican creed, and the platform on which he proposed to stand during the contest. The principal points in that speech of Mr. Lincoln's were: First, that this government could not endure permanently divided into free and slave States, as our fathers made it; that they must all become free or all become slave; all become one thing, or all become the other,—otherwise this Union could not continue to exist. I give you his opinions almost in the identical language he used. His second proposition was a crusade against the Supreme Court of the United States because of the Dred Scott decision, urging as an especial reason for his opposition to that decision that it deprived the negroes of the rights and benefits of that clause in the Constitution of the United States which guarantees to the citizens of each State all the rights, privileges, and immunities of the citizens of the several States. On the 10th of July I returned home, and delivered a speech to the people of Chicago, in which I announced it to be my purpose to appeal to the people of Illinois to sustain the course I had pursued in Congress. In that speech I joined issue with Mr. Lincoln on the points which he had presented. Thus there was an issue clear and distinct made up between us on these two propositions laid down in the speech of Mr. Lincoln at Springfield, and controverted by me in my reply to him at Chicago. On the next day, the 11th of July, Mr. Lincoln replied to me at Chicago, explaining at some length and reaffirming the positions which he had taken in his Springfield speech. In that Chicago speech he even went further than he had before, and uttered sentiments in regard to the negro being on an equality with the white man. He adopted in support of this position the argument which Lovejoy and Codding and other Abolition lecturers had made familiar in the northern and central portions of the State: to wit, that the Declaration of Independence having declared all men free and equal, by divine law, also that negro equality was an inalienable right, of which they could not be deprived. He insisted, in that speech, that the Declaration of Independence included the negro in the clause asserting that all men were created equal, and went so far as to say that if one man was allowed to take the position that it did

not include the negro, others might take the position that it did not include other men. He said that all these distinctions between this man and that man, this race and the other race, must be discarded, and we must all stand by the Declaration of Independence, declaring that all men were created equal.

The issue thus being made up between Mr. Lincoln and myself on three points, we went before the people of the State. During the following seven weeks, between the Chicago speeches and our first meeting at Ottawa, he and I addressed large assemblages of the people in many of the central counties. In my speeches I confined myself closely to those three positions which he had taken, controverting his proposition that this Union could not exist as our fathers made it, divided into free and slave States, controverting his proposition of a crusade against the Supreme Court because of the Dred Scott decision, and controverting his proposition that the Declaration of Independence included and meant the negroes as well as the white men, when it declared all men to be created equal. . . . I took up Mr. Lincoln's three propositions in my several speeches, analyzed them, and pointed out what I believed to be the radical errors contained in them. First, in regard to his doctrine that this government was in violation of the law of God, which says that a house divided against itself cannot stand, I repudiated it as a slander upon the immortal framers of our Constitution. I then said, I have often repeated, and now again assert, that in my opinion our government can endure forever, divided into free and slave States as our fathers made it,—each State having the right to prohibit, abolish, or sustain slavery, just as it pleases. This government was made upon the great basis of the sovereignty of the States, the right of each State to regulate its own domestic institutions to suit itself; and that right was conferred with the understanding and expectation that, inasmuch as each locality had separate interests, each locality must have different and distinct local and domestic institutions, corresponding to its wants and interests. Our fathers knew when they made the government that the laws and institutions which were well adapted to the Green Mountains of Vermont were unsuited to the rice plantations of South

Carolina. They knew then, as well as we know now, that the laws and institutions which would be well adapted to the beautiful prairies of Illinois would not be suited to the mining regions of California. They knew that in a republic as broad as this, having such a variety of soil, climate, and interest, there must necessarily be a corresponding variety of local laws,—the policy and institutions of each State adapted to its condition and wants. For this reason this Union was established on the right of each State to do as it pleased on the question of slavery, and every other question; and the various States were not allowed to complain of, much less interfere with, the policy of their neighbors. . . .

. . . These measures [Compromise of 1850] passed on the joint action of the two parties. They rested on the great principle that the people of each State and each Territory should be left perfectly free to form and regulate their domestic institutions to suit themselves. You Whigs and we Democrats justified them in that principle. In 1854, when it became necessary to organize the Territories of Kansas and Nebraska, I brought forward the bill on the same principle. In the Kansas-Nebraska Bill you find it declared to be the true intent and meaning of the act not to legislate slavery into any State or Territory, nor to exclude it therefrom, but to leave the people thereof perfectly free to form and regulate their domestic institutions in their own way. I stand on that same platform in 1858 that I did in 1850, 1854, and 1856. . . . It has occurred to me that in 1854 the author of the Kansas and Nebraska Bill was considered a pretty good Democrat. It has occurred to me that in 1856, when I was exerting every nerve and every energy for James Buchanan, standing on the same platform then that I do now, that I was a pretty good Democrat. They now tell me that I am not a Democrat, because I assert that the people of a Territory, as well as those of a State, have the right to decide for themselves whether slavery can or cannot exist in such Territory. . . .

I . . . further . . . say that while, under the decision of the Supreme Court, as recorded in the opinion of Chief Justice Taney, slaves are property like all other property, and can be carried into any Territory of the United States the same as any other description of property, yet when you get them there they are subject to the local law of the Territory just like all other property. You will find in a recent speech delivered by that able and eloquent statesman Hon. Jefferson Davis, at Bangor, Maine, that he took the same view of this subject that I did in my Freeport speech. He there said:

"If the inhabitants of any Territory should refuse to enact such laws and police regulations as would give security to their property or to his, it would be rendered more or less valueless in proportion to the difficulties of holding it without such protection. In the case of property in the labor of man, or what is usually called slave property, the insecurity would be so great that the owner could not ordinarily retain it. Therefore, though the right would remain, the remedy being withheld, it would follow that the owner would be practically debarred, by the circumstances of the case, from taking slave property into a Territory where the sense of the inhabitants was opposed to its introduction. So much for the oft-repeated fallacy of forcing slavery upon any community."

You will also find that the distinguished Speaker of the present House of Representatives, Hon. Jas. L. Orr, construed the Kansas and Nebraska Bill in this same way in 1856, and also that great intellect of the South, Alex. H. Stephens, put the same construction upon it in Congress that I did in my Freeport speech. The whole South are rallying to the support of the doctrine that if the people of a Territory want slavery, they have a right to have it, and if they do not want it, that no power on earth can force it upon them. I hold that there is no principle on earth more sacred to all the friends of freedom than that which says that no institution, no law, no constitution, should be forced on an unwilling people contrary to their wishes; and I assert that the Kansas and Nebraska Bill contains that principle. It is the great principle contained in that bill. It is the principle on which James Buchanan was made President. Without that principle, he never would have been made President of the United States. I will never violate or abandon that doctrine, if I have to stand alone. I have resisted the blandishments and threats of power on the one side, and seduction on the other, and have stood immovably for that principle, fighting for it when assailed by Northern mobs, or threatened by Southern hostility. I have defended it against the North and the South, and I will defend it against whoever assails it, and I will follow it wherever its logical conclusions lead me. I say to you that there is but one hope, one safety for this country, and that is to stand immovably by that principle which declares the right of each State and each Territory to decide these questions for themselves. This government was founded on that principle, and must be administered in the same sense in which it was founded. . . .

Mr. Lincoln's Reply

. . . Now, irrespective of the moral aspect of this question as to whether there. is a right or wrong in enslaving a negro, I am still in favor of our new Territories being in such a condition that white men may find a home,—may find some spot where they can better their condition; where they can settle upon new soil and better their condition in life. I am in favor of this, not merely (I must say it here as I have elsewhere) for our own people who are born amongst us, but as an outlet for *free white people everywhere*—the world over—in which Hans, and Baptiste, and Patrick, and all other men from all the world, may find new homes and better their conditions in life.

I have stated upon former occasions, and I may as well state again, what I understand to be the real issue in this controversy between Judge Douglas and myself. . . . The real issue in this controversy—the one pressing upon every mind—is the sentiment on the part of one class that looks upon the institution of slavery *as a wrong*, and of another class that *does not* look upon it as a wrong. The sentiment that contemplates the institution of slavery in this country as a wrong is the sentiment of the Republican party. It is the sentiment around which all their actions, all their arguments, circle, from which all their propositions radiate. They look upon it as being a moral, social, and political wrong; and while they contemplate it as such, they nevertheless have due regard for its actual existence among us, and

the difficulties of getting rid of it in any satisfactory way, and to all the constitutional obligations thrown about it. Yet, having a due regard for these, they desire a policy in regard to it that looks to its not creating any more danger. They insist that it should, as far as may be, *be treated* as a wrong; and one of the methods of treating it as a wrong is to *make provision that it shall grow no larger*. They also desire a policy that looks to a peaceful end of slavery at some time, as being wrong. These are the views they entertain in regard to it as I understand them; and all their sentiments, all their arguments and propositions, are brought within this range. I have said, and I repeat it here, that if there be a man amongst us who does not think that the institution of slavery is wrong in any one of the aspects of which I have spoken, he is misplaced, and ought not to be with us. And if there be a man amongst us who is so impatient of it as a wrong as to disregard its actual presence among us and the difficulty of getting rid of it suddenly in a satisfactory way, and to disregard the constitutional obligations thrown about it, that man is misplaced if he is on our platform. We disclaim sympathy with him in practical action. He is not placed properly with us.

On this subject of treating it as a wrong, and limiting its spread, let me say a word. Has anything ever threatened the existence of this Union save and except this very institution of slavery? What is it that we hold most dear amongst us? Our own liberty and prosperity. What has ever threatened our liberty and prosperity, save and except this institution of slavery? If this is true, how do you propose to improve the condition of things by enlarging slavery,—by spreading it out and making it bigger? You may have a wen or cancer upon your person, and not be able to cut it out, lest you bleed to death; but surely it is no way to cure it, to engraft it and spread it over your whole body. That is no proper way of treating what you regard a wrong. You see this peaceful way of dealing with it as a wrong,—restricting the spread of it, and not allowing it to go into new countries where it has not already existed. That is the peaceful way, the old-fashioned way, the way in which the fathers themselves set us the example.

On the other hand, I have said there is a sentiment which treats it as *not* being wrong. That is the Democratic sentiment of this day. . . .

. . . The Democratic policy in regard to that institution will not tolerate the merest breath, the slightest hint, of the least degree of wrong about it. Try it by some of Judge Douglas's arguments. He says he "don't care whether it is voted up or voted down" in the Territories. I do not care myself, in dealing with that expression, whether it is intended to be expressive of his individual sentiments on the subject, or only of the national policy he desires to have established. It is alike valuable for my purpose. Any man can say that who does not see anything wrong in slavery; but no man can logically say it who does see a wrong in it, because no man can logically say he don't care whether a wrong is voted up or voted down. He may say he don't care whether an indifferent thing is voted up or down, but he must logically have a choice between a right thing and a wrong thing. He contends that whatever community wants slaves has a right to have them. So they have, if it is not a wrong. But if it is a wrong, he cannot say people have a right to do wrong. He says that upon the score of equality slaves should be allowed to go in a new Territory, like other property. This is strictly logical if there is no difference between it and other property. If it and other property are equal, this argument is entirely logical. But if you insist that one is wrong and the other right, there is no use to institute a comparison between right and wrong. You may turn over everything in the Democratic policy from beginning to end, whether in the shape it takes on the statute book, in the shape it takes in the Dred Scott decision, in the shape it takes in conversation, or the shape it takes in short maxim-like arguments,—it everywhere carefully excludes the idea that there is anything wrong in it.

That is the real issue. That is the issue that will continue in this country when these poor tongues of Judge Douglas and myself shall be silent. It is the eternal struggle between these two principles—right and wrong—throughout the world. They are the two principles that have stood face to face from the beginning of time, and will ever continue to struggle. The one is the common right of humanity, and the other the divine right of kings. . . . And whenever we can get rid of the fog which obscures the real question, when we can get Judge Douglas and his friends to avow a policy looking to its perpetuation,—we can get out from among that class of men and bring them to the side of those who treat it as a wrong. Then there will soon be an end of it, and that end will be its "ultimate extinction." Whenever the issue can be distinctly made, and all extraneous matter thrown out so that men can fairly see the real difference between the parties, this controversy will soon be settled, and it will be done peaceably too. There will be no war, no violence. It will be placed again where the wisest and best men of the world placed it. . . .

I understand I have ten minutes yet. I will employ it in saying something about this argument Judge Douglas uses, while he sustains the Dred Scott decision, that the people of the Territories can still somehow exclude slavery. The first thing I ask attention to is the fact that Judge Douglas constantly said, before the decision, that whether they could or not, *was a question for the Supreme Court.* But after the court had made the decision he virtually says it is *not* a question for the Supreme Court, but for the people. And how is it he tells us they can exclude it? He says it needs "police regulations," and that admits of "unfriendly legislation." Although it is a right established by the Constitution of the United States to take a slave into a Territory of the United States and hold him as property, yet unless the Territorial Legislature will give friendly legislation, and more especially if they adopt unfriendly legislation, they can practically exclude him. Now, without meeting this proposition as a matter of fact, I pass to consider the real constitutional obligation. Let me take the gentleman who looks me in the face before me, and let us suppose that he is a member of the Territorial Legislature. The first thing he will do will be to swear that he will support the Constitution of the United States. His neighbor by his side in the Territory has slaves and needs Territorial legislation to enable him to enjoy that constitutional right. Can he withhold the legislation which his neighbor needs for the enjoyment of a right which is fixed in his favor in the Constitution of the United States which he has sworn to support? Can he withhold it without violating his oath? And, more especially, can he pass unfriendly legislation to violate his oath? Why, this is a *monstrous* sort of talk about the Constitution of the United States! *There has never been as outlandish or lawless a doctrine from the mouth of any respectable man on earth.* I do not believe it is a constitutional right to hold slaves in a Territory of the United States. I believe the decision was improperly made and I go for reversing it. Judge Douglas is furious against those who go for reversing a decision. But he is for legislating it out of all force while the law itself stands. I repeat that there has never been so monstrous a doctrine uttered from the mouth of a respectable man. . . .

I say that no man can deny his obligation to give the necessary legislation to support slavery in a Territory, who believes it is a constitutional right to have it there. No man can, who does not give the Abolitionists an argument to deny the obligation enjoined by the Constitution to enact a Fugitive State law. Try it now. It is the strongest Abolition argument ever made. I say if that Dred Scott decision is correct, then the right to hold slaves in a Territory is equally a constitutional right with the right of a slaveholder to have his runaway returned. No one can show the distinction between them. The one is express, so that we cannot deny it. The other is construed to be in the Constitution, so that he who believes the decision to be correct believes in the right. And the man who argues that by unfriendly legislation, in spite of that constitutional right, slavery may be driven from the Territories, cannot avoid furnishing an argument by which Abolitionists may deny the obligation to return fugitives, and claim the power to pass laws unfriendly to the right of the slaveholder to reclaim his fugitive. I do not know how such an argument may strike a popular assembly like this, but I defy anybody to go before a body of men whose minds are educated to estimating evidence and reasoning, and show that there is an iota of difference between the constitutional right to reclaim a fugitive and the constitutional right to hold a slave, in a Territory, provided this Dred Scott decision is correct. I defy any man to make an argument that will justify unfriendly legislation to deprive a slaveholder of his right to hold his slave in a Territory, that will not equally, in all its length, breadth, and thickness, furnish an argument for nullifying the Fugitive Slave law. Why, there is not such an Abolitionist in the nation as Douglas, after all!

Mr. Douglas's Rejoinder

Mr. Lincoln tries to avoid the main issue by attacking the truth of my proposition that our fathers made this government divided into free and slave States, recognizing the right of each to decide all its local questions for itself. Did they not thus make it? It is true that they did not establish slavery in any of the States, or abolish it in any of them; but finding thirteen States, twelve of which were slave and one free, they agreed to form a government uniting them together as they stood, divided into free and slave States, and to guarantee forever to each State the right to do as it pleased on the slavery question. Having thus made the government, and conferred this right upon each State forever, I assert that this government can exist as they made it, divided into free and slave States, if any one State chooses to retain slavery. He says that he looks forward to a time when slavery shall be abolished everywhere. I look forward to a time when each State shall be allowed to do as it pleases. If it chooses to keep slavery forever, it is not my business, but its own; if it chooses to abolish slavery, it is its own business,—not mine. I care more for the great principle of self-government, the right of the people to rule, than I do for all the negroes in Christendom. I would not endanger the perpetuity of this Union, I would not blot out the great inalienable rights of the white man, for all the negroes that ever existed. Hence, I say, let us maintain this government on the principles that our fathers made it, recognizing the right of each State to keep slavery as long as its people determine, or to abolish it when they please. But Mr. Lincoln says that when our fathers made this government they did not look forward to the state of things now existing, and therefore he thinks the doctrine was wrong; . . .

Our fathers, I say, made this government on the principle of the right of each State to do as it pleases in its own domestic affairs, subject to the Constitution, and allowed the people of each to apply to every new change of circumstances such remedy as they may see fit to improve their condition. This right they have for all time to come.

Mr. Lincoln went on to tell you that he does not at all desire to interfere with slavery in the States where it exists, nor does his party. I expected him to say that down here. Let me ask him, then, how he expects to put slavery in the course of ultimate extinction everywhere, if he does not intend to interfere with it in the States where it exists? He says that he will prohibit it in all Territories, and the inference is, then, that unless they make free States out of them he will keep them out of the Union; for, mark you, he did not say whether or not he would vote to admit Kansas with slavery or not, as her people might apply (he forgot that, as usual, etc.): he did not say whether or not he was in favor of bringing the Territories now in existence into the Union on the principle of Clay's Compromise measures on the slavery question. I told you that he would not. His idea is that he will prohibit slavery in all the Territories and thus force them all to become free States, surrounding the slave States with a cordon of free States, and hemming them in, keeping the slaves confined to their present limits whilst they go on multiplying, until the soil on which they live will no longer feed them, and he will thus be able to put slavery in a course of ultimate extinction by starvation. He will extinguish slavery in the Southern States as the French general exterminated the Algerines when he smoked them out. He is going to extinguish slavery by surrounding the Slave States, hemming in the slaves, and starving them out of existence, as you smoke a fox out of his hole. He intends to do that in the name of humanity and Christianity, in order that we may get rid of the terrible crime and sin entailed upon our fathers of holding slaves. . . .

I ask you to look into these things, and then tell me whether the Democracy or the Abolitionists are right. I hold that the people of a Territory, like those of a State . . . have the right to decide for themselves whether slavery shall or shall not exist within their limits. The point upon which Chief Justice Taney expresses his opinion is simply this, that slaves, being property, stand on an equal footing with other property, and consequently that the owner has the same right to carry that property into a Territory that he has any other, subject to the same conditions. Suppose that one of your merchants was to take fifty or one hundred thousand dollars' worth of liquors to Kansas. He has a right to go there, under that decision; but when he gets there he finds the Maine liquor law in force, and what can he do with his property after he gets it there? He cannot sell it, he cannot use it; it is subject to the local law, and that law is against him, and the best thing he can do with it is to bring it back into Missouri or Illinois and sell it. If you take negroes to Kansas, as Colonel Jefferson Davis said in his Bangor speech, from which I have quoted to-day, you must take them there subject to the local law. If the people want the institution of slavery, they will protect and encourage it; but if they do not want it, they will withhold that protection, and the absence of local legislation protecting slavery excludes it as completely as a positive prohibition. You slaveholders of Missouri might as well understand, what you know practically, that you cannot carry slavery where the people do not want it. All you have a right to ask is that the people shall do as they please: if they want slavery, let them have it; if they do not want it, allow them to refuse to encourage it.

My friends, if, as I have said before, we will only live up to this great fundamental principle, there will be peace between the North and the South. Mr. Lincoln admits that, under the Constitution, on all domestic questions, except slavery, we ought not to interfere with the people of each State. What right have we to interfere with slavery any more than we have to interfere with any other question? He says that this slavery question is now the bone of contention. Why? Simply because agitators have combined in all the free States to make war upon it. Suppose the agitators in the States should combine in one half of the Union to make war upon the railroad system of the other half? They would thus be driven to the same sectional strife. Suppose one section makes war upon any other peculiar institution of the opposite section, and the same strife is produced. The only remedy and safety is that we shall stand by the Constitution as our fathers made it, obey the laws as they are passed, while they stand the proper test, and sustain the decisions of the Supreme Court and the constituted authorities.

188. ABLEMAN v. BOOTH
21 Howard, 506
1859

Two writs of custody to the supreme court of Wisconsin. Booth was held by Ableman, United States marshal, for violation of the fugitive slave law of September 18, 1850. The supreme court of Wisconsin discharged him from custody on a writ of *habeas corpus*. He was subsequently tried again before the United States district court, sentenced to imprisonment and fine. The supreme court of Wisconsin again ordered his release on the ground that the fugitive slave law was unconstitutional. See Warren, *Supreme Court,* (1928 ed.) Vol. II. ch. xxvii; J. Hurd, *The Law of Freedom and Bondage,* Vol. II.

TANEY, C. J. . . . It will be seen, from the foregoing statement of facts, that a judge of the supreme court of the State of Wisconsin, in the first of these cases, claimed and exercised the right to supervise and annul the proceedings of a commissioner of the United States, and to discharge a prisoner who had been committed by the commissioner for an offense against the laws of this government, and that this exercise of power by the judge was afterwards sanctioned and affirmed by the supreme court of the State.

In the second case, the state court has gone a step further, and . . . claimed and exercised this jurisdiction, but have also determined that their decision is final and conclusive upon all the courts of the United States, and ordered their clerk to disregard and refuse obedience to the writ of error issued by this court, pursuant to the act of Congress of 1789, to bring here for examination and revision the judgment of the state court.

These propositions are new in the jurisprudence of the United States, as well as of the States; and the supremacy of the state courts over the courts of the United States, in cases arising under the Constitution and laws of the United States, is now for the first time asserted and acted upon in the supreme court of a State. . . .

If the judicial power exercised in this instance has been reserved to the States, no offence against the laws of the United States can be punished by their own courts, without the permission and according to the judgement of the courts of the State in which the party happens to be imprisoned; for if the Supreme Court of Wisconsin possessed the power it has exercised in relation to offences against the act of Congress in question, it necessarily follows that they must have the same judicial authority in relation to any other law of the United States; and, consequently, their supervising and controlling power would embrace the whole criminal code of the United States, and extend to offences against our revenue laws, or any other law, intended to guard the different departments of the General Government from fraud or violence. And it would embrace all crimes, from the highest to the lowest; including felonies which are punished with death, as well as misdemeanours, which are punished by imprisonment. . . .

It would seem to be hardly necessary to do more than state the result to which these decisions of the State courts must inevitably lead. It is, of itself, a sufficient and conclusive answer; for no one will suppose that a Government which has now lasted nearly seventy years, enforcing its laws by its own tribunals, and preserving the union of the States could have lasted a single year, or fulfilled the high trusts committed to it, if offences against its laws could not have been punished without the consent of the State in which the culprit was found.

The judges of the supreme court of Wisconsin do not distinctly state from what source they suppose they have derived this judicial power. There can be no such thing as judicial authority, unless it is conferred by a government or sovereignty; and if the judges and courts of Wisconsin possess the jurisdiction they claim, they must derive it either from the United States or the State. It certainly has not been conferred on them by the United States; and it is equally clear that it was not in the power of the State to confer it, even if it had attempted to do so; for no State can authorize one of its judges or courts to exercise judicial power, by habeas corpus or otherwise, within the jurisdiction of another and independent government. And although the State of Wisconsin is sovereign within its territorial limits to a certain extent, yet that sovereignty is limited and restricted by the Constitution of the United States. . . . And the State of Wisconsin had no more power to authorize these proceedings of its judges and courts, than it would have had if the prisoner had been confined in Michigan, or in any other State of the Union, for an offense against the laws of the State in which he was imprisoned. . . .

But, as we have already said, questions of this kind must always depend upon the Constitution and laws of the United States, and not of a State. The Constitution was not formed merely to guard the States against danger from foreign nations, but mainly to secure union and harmony at home; for if this object could be attained, there would be but little danger from abroad; and to accomplish this purpose, it was felt by the statesmen who framed the Constitution, and by the people who adopted it, that it was necessary that many of the rights of sovereignty which the States then possessed should be ceded to the general government; and that, in the sphere of action assigned to it, it should be supreme, and strong enough to execute its own laws by its own tribunals, without interruption from a State or from state authorities. And it was evident that anything short of this would be inadequate to the main object for which the government was established; and that local interests, local passions or prejudices, incited and fostered by individuals for sinister purposes, would lead to acts of aggression and injustice by one State upon the rights of another, which would ultimately terminate in violence and force, unless there was a common arbiter between them, armed with power enough to protect and guard the rights of all, by appropriate laws, to be carried into execution peaceably by its judicial tribunals.

The language of the Constitution, by which this power is granted is too plain to admit of doubt or to need comment. It declares that "this Constitution, and the laws of the United States which shall be passed in pursuance thereof, and all treaties made, or which shall be made, under the authority of the United States, shall be the supreme law of the land, and the judges in every State shall be bound thereby, anything in the constitution or laws of any State to the contrary notwithstanding."

But the supremacy thus conferred on this government could not peaceably be maintained, unless it was clothed with judicial power, equally paramount in authority to carry it into execution; for if left to the courts of justice of the several States, conflicting decisions would unavoidably take place, and the local tribunals could hardly be expected to be always free from the local influences of which we have spoken. And the Constitution and laws and treaties of the United States, and the powers granted to the federal government, would soon receive different interpretations in different States, and the government of the United States would soon become one thing in one State and another thing in another. It was essential, therefore, to its very existence as a government, that it should have the power of establishing courts of justice, altogether independent of state power, to carry into effect its own laws; and that a tribunal should be established in which all cases which might arise under the Constitution and laws and treaties of the United States, whether in a state court or in a court of the United States, should be finally and conclusively decided. Without such a tribunal, it is obvious that there would be no uniformity of judicial decision; and that the supremacy (which is but another name for independence), so carefully provided in the clause of the Constitution above referred to, could not possibly be maintained peaceably, unless it was associated with this paramount judicial authority.

Accordingly, it was conferred on the general government, in clear, precise, and comprehensive terms. . . .

The importance which the framers of the Constitution attached to such a tribunal for the purpose of preserving internal tranquillity, is strikingly manifested by the clause which gives this court jurisdiction over the sovereign States which compose this Union, when a controversy arises between them. . . . Experience has demonstrated that this power was not unwisely surrendered by the States; for in the time that has already elapsed since this government came into existence, several irritating and angry controversies have taken place between adjoining States, in relation to their respective boundaries, and which have sometimes threatened to end in force and violence, but for the power vested in this court to hear them and decide between them.

The same purposes are clearly indicated by the different language employed when conferring supremacy upon the laws of the United States, and jurisdiction upon its courts. In the first case, it provides that "this Constitution, and the laws of the United States *which shall be made in pursuance thereof,* shall be the supreme law of the land, and obligatory upon the judges in every State." The words in italics show the precision and forethought which marks every clause in the instrument. The sovereignty to be created was to be limited in its powers of legislation, and if it passed a law not authorized by its enumerated powers, it was not to be regarded as the supreme law of the land, nor were the state judges bound to carry it into execution. And as the courts of a State, and the courts of the United States, might, and indeed certainly would, often differ as to the extent of the powers conferred by the general government, it was manifested that serious controversies would arise between the authorities of the United States and of the States, which must be settled by force of arms, unless some tribunal was created to decide between them finally and without appeal.

The Constitution has accordingly provided, as far as human foresight could provide, against this danger. And in conferring judicial power upon the federal government, it declares that the jurisdiction of its courts shall extend to all cases arising under "this constitution" and the laws of the United States—leaving out the words of restriction contained in the grant of legislative power which we have above noticed. The judicial power covers every legislative act of Congress, whether it be made within the limits of its delegated powers, or be an assumption of power beyond the grants in the Constitution.

This judicial power was justly regarded as indispensable, not merely to maintain the supremacy of the laws of the United States, but also to guard the States from any encroachment upon their reserved rights by the general government. And as the Constitution is the fundamental and supreme law, if it appears that an act of Congress is not pursuant to and within the limits of the power assigned to the federal government, it is the duty of the courts of the United States to declare it unconstitutional and void. . . .

We do not question the authority of a state court, or judge, who is authorized by the laws of the State to issue the writ of habeas corpus, to issue it in any case where the party is imprisoned within its territorial limits, provided it does not appear, when the application is made, that the person imprisoned is in custody under the authority of the United States. . . . But, after the return is made, and the state judge or court judicially apprized that the party is in custody under the authority of the United States, they can proceed no further. No State judge or Court after they are judicially informed that the party is imprisoned under the authority of the United States, has any right to interfere with him, or to require him to be brought before them. And if the authority of a State, in the form of judicial process or otherwise, should attempt to control the marshal or other authorized officer or agent of the United States, in any respect, in the custody of his prisoner, it would be his duty to resist it, and to call to his aid any force that might be necessary to maintain the authority of law against illegal interference. No judicial process, whatever form it may assume, can have any lawful authority outside of the limits of the jurisdiction of the court or judge by whom it is issued; and an attempt to enforce it beyond these boundaries is nothing less than lawless violence.

And no power is more clearly conferred by the Constitution and the laws of the United States, than the power of this court to decide ultimately and finally, all cases arising under such Constitution and laws; and for that purpose to bring here for revision, by writ of error, the judgement of a state court, where such questions have arisen, and the right claimed under them is denied by the highest judicial tribunal in the State. . . .

If there was any defect of power in the commissioner, or in his mode of proceeding, it was for the tribunals of the United States to revise and correct it, and not for a state court. . . .

But although we think it unnecessary to discuss these questions, yet, as they have been decided by the state court, and are before us on the record, and we are not willing to be misunderstood, it is proper to say that, in the judgement of this court, the act of Congress commonly called the fugitive slave law is, in all of its provisions, fully authorized by the Constitution of the United States; that the commissioner had lawful authority to issue the warrant and commit the party, and that his proceedings were regular and conformable to law. . . .

Judgement of the state court reversed.

189. JOHN BROWN'S LAST SPEECH
November 2, 1859

(*American State Trials,* ed. by J. D. Lawson, Vol. VI, p. 800 ff.)

John Brown, most fanatical of abolitionists, planned to incite a general insurrection of slaves in Virginia and form a free state somewhere in the mountains of western Maryland and Virginia. With the aid of funds gathered in New England and New York he collected supplies and arms at a farmhouse near Harper's Ferry, Virginia, and on the night of October 16 moved on the town of Harper's Ferry and captured the government armory. United States marines under the command of Col. R. E. Lee carried the armory by assault, and captured Brown and some of his followers. He was indicted for treason and for conspiring with slaves to commit murder, convicted, and sentenced to be hanged. On Brown, see O. G. Villard, *John Brown;* F. B. Sanborn, *Life and Letters of John Brown;* R. P. Warren, *John Brown.* The trial is given in full in *American State Trials,* Vol. VI.

I have, may it please the Court, a few words to say.

In the first place, I deny everything but what I have all along admitted,—the design on my part to free the slaves. I intended certainly to have made a clean thing of that matter, as I did last winter, when I went into Missouri and there took slaves without the snapping of a gun on either side, moved them through the country, and finally left them in Canada. I designed to have done the same thing again, on a larger scale. That was all I intended. I never did intend murder, or treason, or the destruction of property, or to excite or incite slaves to rebellion, or to make insurrection.

I have another objection; and that is, it is unjust that I should suffer such a penalty. Had I interfered in the manner which I admit, and which I admit has been fairly proved (for I admire the truthfulness and candor of the greater portion of the witnesses who have testified in this case),—had I so interfered in behalf of the rich, the powerful, the intelligent, the so-called great, or in behalf of any of their friends,—either father, mother, brother, sister, wife, or children, or any of that class,—and suffered and sacrificed what I have in this interference, it would have been all right; and every man in this court would have deemed it an act worthy of reward rather than punishment.

This court acknowledges, as I suppose, the validity of the law of God. I see a book kissed here which I suppose to be the Bible, or at least the New Testament. That teaches me that all things whatsoever I would that men should do to me, I should do even so to them. It teaches me, further, to "remember them that are in bonds, as bound with them." I endeavored to act up to that instruction. I say, I am yet too young to understand that God is any respecter of persons. I believe that to have interfered as I have done—as I have always freely admitted I have done—in behalf of His despised poor, was not wrong, but right. Now, if it is deemed necessary that I should forfeit my life for the furtherance of the ends of justice, and mingle my blood further with the blood of my children and with the blood of millions in this slave country whose rights are disregarded by wicked, cruel, and unjust enactments,—I submit; so let it be done!

Let me say one word further.

I feel entirely satisfied with the treatment I have received on my trial. Considering all the circumstances, it has been more generous than I expected. But I feel no consciousness of guilt. I have stated from the first what was my intention, and what was not. I never had any design against the life of any person, nor any disposition to commit treason, or excite slaves to rebel, or make any general insurrection. I never encouraged any man to do so, but always discouraged any idea of that kind.

Let me say, also, a word in regard to the statements made by some of those connected with me. I hear it has been stated by some of them that I have induced them to join me. But the contrary is true. I do not say this to injure them, but as regretting their weakness. There is not one of them but joined me of his own accord, and the greater part of them at their own expense. A number of them I never saw, and never had a word of conversation with, till the day they came to me; and that was for the purpose I have stated.

Now I have done.

190. RESOLUTIONS ON SECESSION FROM FLOYD COUNTY, GEORGIA
1860

(The Confederate Records of the State of Georgia, ed. by A. D. Candler, Vol. I, p. 115 ff.)

These resolutions are typical of the resolutions which were passed by many counties in Georgia on the eve of secession. The struggle between the Unionists and the dis-unionists in Georgia was more severe than elsewhere in the South with the exception of Virginia. See, I. W. Avery, *History of the State of Georgia from 1850 to 1881;* G. M. Battey, *History of Rome and Floyd County;* U. B. Phillips, *Georgia and State Rights;* H. Fielder, *Sketch of the Life and Times of Joseph E. Brown;* H. J. Pearce, *Benjamin H. Hill;* U. B. Phillips, *Life of Robert Toombs;* P. S. Flippin, *Herschel V. Johnson;* L. Pendleton, *Alexander H. Stephens.*

Whereas, the abolition sentiment of the *Northern States* first openly manifested in 1820, has for the last forty years, steadily and rapidly increased in volume, and in the intensity of hostility to the form of society, existing in the *Southern States,* and to the rights of these States as equal, independent and sovereign members of the Union; has led to long continued and ever increasing abuse and hatred of the Southern people; to ceaseless war upon their plainest Constitutional rights; to an open and shameless nullification of that provision of the constitution intended to secure the rendition of fugitive slaves, and of the laws of Congress to give it ef-

fect; . . . has prompted the armed invasion of Southern soil, by stealth . . . for the diabolical purpose of inaugurating a ruthless war of the blacks against the whites throughout the Southern States; has prompted large masses of Northern people openly to sympathize with the treacherous and traitorous invaders of our country, and elevate the leader of a band of midnight assassins, and robbers . . . to the rank of a hero and a martyr . . . ; has disrupted the churches, and destroyed all national parties, and has now finally organized a party confined to a *hostile section,* and composed even there of those only who have encouraged, sympathized with, instigated, or perpetuated their long series of insults, outrages and wrongs, for the avowed purpose of making a common government, armed by us with power only for our protection, an instrument, in the hands of enemies of our destruction.

Therefore we, a portion of the people of Floyd County . . . do hereby declare:

1st. That Georgia is and of right ought to be a free, sovereign and independent State.

2d. That she came into the Union with the other States, as a sovereignty, and by virtue of that sovereignty, has the right to secede whenever, in her sovereign capacity, she shall judge such a step necessary.

3d. That in our opinion, she ought not to submit to the inauguration of Abraham Lincoln and Hannibal Hamlin, as her President and Vice-President; but should leave them to rule over those by whom alone they were elected.

4th. That we request the Legislature to announce this opinion . . . and to co-operate with the Governor in calling a Convention of the people to determine on the mode and measure of redress. . . .

6th. That we respectfully suggest to the Legislature to take immediate steps to organize and arm the forces of the State. . . .

191. CONSTITUTIONAL UNION PLATFORM
May, 1860

(K. Porter, ed. *National Party Platforms*, p. 52)

The Constitutional Union Party met at Baltimore in May, 1860, and nominated John Bell of Tennessee for President and Edward Everett of Massachusetts for the Vice-President. Bell secured the electoral votes of Tennessee, Kentucky, and Virginia, and a popular vote of some 590,000.

Whereas, Experience has demonstrated that Platforms adopted by the partisan Conventions of the country have had the effect to mislead and deceive the people, and at the same time to widen the political divisions of the country, by the creation and encouragement of geographical and sectional parties; therefore

Resolved, that it is both the part of patriotism and of duty to *recognize* no political principle other than THE CONSTITUTION OF THE COUNTRY, THE UNION OF THE STATES, AND THE ENFORCEMENT OF THE LAWS, and that, as representatives of the Constitutional Union men of the country, in National Convention assembled, we hereby pledge ourselves to maintain, protect, and defend, separately and unitedly, these great principles of public liberty and national safety, against all enemies, at home and abroad; believing that thereby peace may once more be restored to the country; the rights of the People and of the States reëstablished, and the Government again placed in that position of justice, fraternity and equality, which, under the example and Constitution of our fathers, has solemnly bound every citizen of the United States to maintain a more perfect union, establish justice, insure domestic tranquillity, provide for the common defense, promote the general welfare, and secure the blessings of liberty to ourselves and our posterity.

192. REPUBLICAN PARTY PLATFORM
Chicago, Illinois, May 16, 1860

(*A Political Text-book for 1860,* p. 26 ff.)

The reaffirmation of the Declaration of Independence was included only after Joshua Giddings of Ohio had threatened to bolt the convention if it was omitted. This platform revealed the influence of the eastern element of the party more largely than did that of 1856. On the conventions and the election, see, E. D. Fite, *The Presidential Campaign of 1860,* ch. vi.

Resolved, That we, the delegated representatives of the Republican electors of the United States, in Convention assembled, in discharge of the duty we owe to our constituents and our country, unite in the following declarations:

1. That the history of the nation, during the last four years, has fully established the propriety and necessity of the organization and perpetuation of the Republican party, and that the causes which called it into existence are permanent in their nature, and now, more than ever before, demand its peaceful and constitutional triumph.

2. That the maintenance of the principles promulgated in the Declaration of Independence and embodied in the Federal Constitution, "That all men are created equal; that they are endowed by their Creator with certain inalienable rights; that among these

are life, liberty and the pursuit of happiness; that, to secure these rights, governments are instituted among men, deriving their just powers from the consent of the governed," is essential to the preservation of our Republican institutions; and that the Federal Constitution, the Rights of the States, and the Union of the States, must and shall be preserved.

3. That to the Union of the States this nation owes its unprecedented increase in population, its surprising development of material resources, its rapid augmentation of wealth, its happiness at home and its honor abroad; and we hold in abhorrence all schemes for Disunion, come from whatever source they may; And we congratulate the country that no Republican member of Congress has uttered or countenanced the threats of Disunion so often made by Democratic members, without rebuke and with applause from their political associates; and we denounce those threats of Disunion, in case of a popular overthrow of their ascendency, as denying the vital principles of a free government, and as an avowal of contemplated treason, which it is the imperative duty of an indignant People sternly to rebuke and forever silence.

4. That the maintenance inviolate of the rights of the States, and especially the right of each State to order and control its own domestic institutions according to its own judgment exclusively, is essential to that balance of powers on which the perfection and endurance of our political fabric depends; and we denounce the lawless invasion by armed force of the soil of any State or Territory, no matter under what pretext, as among the gravest of crimes.

5. That the present Democratic Administration has far exceeded our worst apprehensions, in its measureless subserviency to the exactions of a sectional interest, as especially evinced in its desperate exertions to force the infamous Lecompton constitution upon the protesting people of Kansas; in construing the personal relation between master and servant to involve an unqualified property in persons; in its attempted enforcement, everywhere, on land and sea, through the intervention of Congress and of the Federal Courts of the extreme pretensions of a purely local interest; and in its

general and unvarying abuse of the power intrusted to it by a confiding people. . . .

7. That the new dogma that the Constitution, of its own force, carries Slavery into any or all of the Territories of the United States, is a dangerous political heresy, at variance with the explicit provisions of that instrument itself, with contemporaneous exposition, and with legislative and judicial precedent; is revolutionary in its tendency, and subversive of the peace and harmony of the country.

8. That the normal condition of all the territory of the United States is that of freedom; That as our Republican fathers, when they had abolished slavery in all our national territory, ordained that "no person should be deprived of life, liberty, or property, without due process of law," it becomes our duty, by legislation, whenever such legislation is necessary, to maintain this provision of the Constitution against all attempts to violate it; and we deny the authority of Congress, of a territorial legislature, or of any individuals, to give legal existence to Slavery in any Territory of the United States.

9. That we brand the recent re-opening of the African slave-trade, under the cover of our national flag, aided by perversions of judicial power, as a crime against humanity and a burning shame to our country and age; and we call upon Congress to take prompt and efficient measures for the total and final suppression of that execrable traffic.

10. That in the recent vetoes, by their Federal Governors, of the acts of the Legislatures of Kansas and Nebraska, prohibiting Slavery in those Territories, we find a practical illustration of the boasted Democratic principle of Non-Intervention and Popular Sovereignty embodied in the Kansas-Nebraska bill, and a demonstration of the deception and fraud involved therein.

11. That Kansas should, of right, be immediately admitted as a State under the Constitution recently formed and adopted by her people, and accepted by the House of Representatives.

12. That, while providing revenue for the support of the General Government by duties upon imports, sound policy requires such an adjustment of these imposts as to encourage the development of the industrial interests

of the whole country; and we commend that policy of national exchanges which secures to the working men liberal wages, to agriculture remunerating prices, to mechanics and manufacturers an adequate reward for their skill, labor and enterprise, and to the nation commercial prosperity and independence.

13. That we protest against any sale or alienation to others of the Public Lands held by actual settlers, and against any view of the Homestead policy which regards the settlers as paupers or supplicants for public bounty; and we demand the passage by Congress of the complete and satisfactory Homestead measure which has already passed the house.

14. That the Republican Party is opposed to any change in our Naturalization Laws or any State legislation by which the rights of our citizenship hitherto accorded to immigrants from foreign lands shall be abridged or impaired; and in favor of giving a full and efficient protection to the rights of all classes of citizens, whether native or naturalized, both at home and abroad.

15. That appropriations by Congress for River and Harbor improvements of a National character, required for the accommodation and security of an existing commerce, are authorized by the Constitution, and justified by the obligations of Government to protect the lives and property of its citizens.

16. That a Railroad to the Pacific Ocean is imperatively demanded by the interests of the whole country; that the Federal Government ought to render immediate and efficient aid in its construction; and that, as preliminary thereto, a daily Overland Mail should be promptly established. . . .

193. THE DEMOCRATIC PARTY PLATFORM OF 1860
June 18, 1860
(K. Porter, ed. *National Party Platforms*, p. 53)

The Democratic convention met at Charleston, S. C. in April 1860, but a victory of the Douglas forces on the floor of the convention resulted in the secession of the delegations from Alabama, Louisiana, Mississippi, Texas, Florida and a majority of those from South Carolina, Georgia and Arkansas. The remaining delegates were unable to agree upon a candidate, and the convention adjourned to Baltimore. The seceders, after a hasty meeting in Charleston, adjourned to Richmond. When the convention met in Baltimore, June 18, it was faced with contesting delegations from the Southern States, and a second secession followed. The remaining delegates nominated Douglas for the Presidency and Fitzpatrick for the Vice-Presidency. See E. D. Fite, *The Presidential Campaign of 1860,* ch. v; G. F. Milton, *The Eve of Conflict,* chs. xxv–xxix.

1. *Resolved,* That we, the Democracy of the Union in Convention assembled, hereby declare our affirmation of the resolutions unanimously adopted and declared as a platform of principles by the Democratic Convention at Cincinnati, in the year 1856, believing that Democratic principles are unchangeable in their nature, when applied to the same subject matters; and we recommend, as the only further resolutions, the following:

2. Inasmuch as difference of opinion exists in the Democratic party as to the nature and extent of the powers of a Territorial Legislature, and as to the powers and duties of Congress, under the Constitution of the United States, over the institution of slavery within the Territories,

Resolved, That the Democratic party will abide by the decision of the Supreme Court of the United States upon these questions of Constitutional law.

3. *Resolved,* That it is the duty of the United States to afford ample and complete protection to all its citizens, whether at home or abroad, and whether native or foreign born.

4. *Resolved,* That one of the necessities of the age, in a military, commercial, and postal point of view, is speedy communication between the Atlantic and Pacific States; and the Democratic party pledge such Constitutional Government aid as will insure the construction of a Railroad to the Pacific coast, at the earliest practicable period.

5. *Resolved,* That the Democratic party are in favor of the acquisition of the Island of Cuba on such terms as shall be honorable to ourselves and just to Spain.

6. *Resolved,* That the enactments of the State Legislatures to defeat the faithful execution of the Fugitive Slave Law, are hostile in character, subversive of the Constitution, and revolutionary in their effect.

7. *Resolved,* That it is in accordance with the interpretation of the Cincinnati platform, that during the existence of the Territorial Governments the measure of restriction, whatever it may be, imposed by the Federal Constitution on the power of the Territorial Legislature over the subject of the domestic relations, as the same has been, or shall hereafter be finally determined by the Supreme Court of the United States, should be respected by all good citizens, and enforced with promptness and fidelity by every branch of the general government.

194. THE DEMOCRATIC (BRECKENRIDGE FACTION) PLATFORM OF 1860
June, 1860
(K. Porter, ed. *National Party Platforms,* p. 54)

The seceders from the Baltimore Convention of the regular Democratic Party nominated Vice-President Breckenridge for the Presidency and Senator Lane for the Vice-Presidency. The platform and the nominations were ratified by the delegations convened at Richmond.

Resolved, That the platform adopted by the Democratic party at Cincinnati be affirmed, with the following explanatory resolutions:

1. That the Government of a Territory organized by an act of Congress is provisional and temporary, and during its existence all citizens of the United States have an equal right to settle with their property in the Territory, without their rights, either of person or property being destroyed or impaired by Congressional or Territorial legislation.

2. That it is the duty of the Federal Government, in all its departments, to protect, when necessary, the rights of persons and property in the Territories, and wherever else its constitutional authority extends.

3. That when the settlers in a Territory, having an adequate population, form a State Constitution, the right of sovereignty commences, and being consummated by admission into the Union, they stand on an equal footing with the people of other States, and the State thus organized ought to be admitted into the Federal Union, whether its Constitution prohibits or recognizes the institution of slavery.

Resolved, That the Democratic party are in favor of the acquisition of the Island of Cuba, on such terms as shall be honorable to ourselves and just to Spain, at the earliest practicable moment.

Resolved, That the enactments of State Legislatures to defeat the faithful execution of the Fugitive Slave Law are hostile in character, subversive of the Constitution, and revolutionary in their effect.

Resolved, That the Democracy of the United States recognize it as the imperative duty of this Government to protect the naturalized citizen in all his rights, whether at home or in foreign lands, to the same extent as its native-born citizens.

WHEREAS, One of the greatest necessities of the age, in a political, commercial, postal and military point of view, is a speedy communication between the Pacific and Atlantic coasts, Therefore be it

Resolved, That the National Democratic party do hereby pledge themselves to use every means in their power to secure the passage of some bills, to the extent of the constitutional authority of Congress for the construction of a Pacific Railroad from the Mississippi River to the Pacific Ocean, at the earliest practicable moment.

195. PRESIDENT BUCHANAN ON SECESSION
Extract from the Fourth Annual Message to Congress
December 3, 1860
(Richardson, ed. *Messages and Papers,* Vol. V, p. 626 ff.)

The process of secession was already under way in the South when Buchanan sent his last annual message to Congress. This message, deprecating the disruption of the Union, nevertheless announced the impotence of the Federal Government to prevent secession by force. In this opinion, Buchanan relied upon the opinion of his Attorney-general, Jeremiah S. Black, who declared that while the President should use all the force at his command to enforce the laws, he did not have the right to coerce a state. "If this view of the subject be as correct as I think it is," wrote Black, "then the Union must utterly perish at the moment when Congress shall arm one part of the people against another for any purpose beyond that of merely protecting the General Government in the exercise of its proper constitutional functions." Black's opinion is given in E. McPherson, *Political History of the Great Rebellion*, p. 51–2. On Buchanan, see G. T. Curtis, *Life of James Buchanan;* and Buchanan's own defence, *Mr. Buchanan's Administration on the Eve of the Rebellion;* P. G. Auchampaugh, *Buchanan and his Cabinet on the Eve of Secession;* and the forthcoming volume of R. F. Nichols, *The Administrative Policies of James Buchanan and his cabinet as contributing causes to the outbreak of the Civil War.*

WASHINGTON CITY, *December 3, 1860.*
Fellow-Citizens of the Senate and House of Representatives:
. . . The long-continued and intemperate interference of the Northern people with the question of slavery in the Southern States has at length produced its natural effects. The different sections of the Union are now arrayed against each other, and the time has arrived, so much dreaded by the Father of his Country, when hostile geographical parties have been formed. . . .

It can not be denied that for five and twenty years the agitation at the North against slavery has been incessant. In 1835 pictorial handbills and inflammatory appeals were circulated extensively throughout the South of a character to excite the passions of the slaves, and, in the language of General Jackson, "to stimulate them to insurrection and produce all the horrors of a servile war." This agitation has ever since been continued by the public press, by the proceedings of State and county conventions and by abolition sermons and lectures. The time of Congress has been occupied in violent speeches on this never-ending subject, and appeals, in pamphlet and other forms, indorsed by distinguished names, have been sent forth from this central point and spread broadcast over the Union.

How easy would it be for the American people to settle the slavery question forever and to restore peace and harmony to this distracted country! They, and they alone, can do it. All that is necessary to accomplish the object, and all for which the slave States have ever contended, is to be let alone and permitted to manage their domestic institutions in their own way. As sovereign States, they, and they alone, are responsible before God and the world for the slavery existing among them. For this the people of the North are not more responsible and have no more right to interfere than with similar institutions in Russia or in Brazil.

Upon their good sense and patriotic forbearance I confess I still greatly rely. Without their aid it is beyond the power of any President, no matter what may be his own political proclivities, to restore peace and harmony among the States. Wisely limited and restrained as is his power under our Constitution and laws, he alone can accomplish but little for good or for evil on such a momentous question.

And this brings me to observe that the election of any one of our fellow-citizens to the office of President does not of itself afford just cause for dissolving the Union. This is more especially true if his election has been effected by a mere plurality, and not a majority of the people, and has resulted from transient and temporary causes, which may probably never again occur. . .

After all, he is no more than the chief executive officer of the Government. His province is not to make but to execute the laws. And it is a remarkable fact in our history that, notwithstanding the repeated efforts of the antislavery party, no single act has ever passed Congress, unless we may possibly except the Missouri compromise, impairing in the slightest degree the rights of the South to their property in slaves; and it may also be observed, judging from present indications, that no probability exists of the passage of such an act by a majority of both Houses, either in the present or the next Congress. . . .

I have purposely confined my remarks to revolutionary resistance, because it has been claimed within the last few years that any State, whenever this shall be its sovereign will and pleasure, may secede from the Union in accordance with the Constitution and without any violation of the constitutional rights of the other members of the Confederacy; that as each became parties to the Union by the vote of its own people assembled in convention, so any one of them may retire from the Union in a similar manner by the vote of such a convention.

In order to justify secession as a constitutional remedy, it must be on the principle that the Federal Government is a mere voluntary association of States, to be dissolved at pleasure by any one of the contracting parties. If this be so, the Confederacy is a rope of sand, to be penetrated and dissolved by the first adverse wave of public opinion in any of the States.

Such a principle is wholly inconsistent with the history as well as the character of the Federal Constitution. . . .

It was intended to be perpetual, and not to be annulled at the pleasure of any one of the contracting parties. . . .

It may be asked, then, Are the people of the States without redress against the tyranny and oppression of the Federal Government? By no means. The right of resistance on the part of the governed against the oppression of their governments can not be denied. It exists independently of all constitutions, and has been exercised at all periods of the world's history. Under it old governments have been destroyed and new ones have taken their place. It is embodied in strong and express language in our own Declaration of Independence. But the distinction must ever be observed that this is revolution against an established government, and not a voluntary secession from it by virtue of an inherent constitutional right. In short, let us look the danger fairly in the face. Secession is neither more nor less than revolution. It may or it may not be a justifiable revolution, but still it is revolution.

What, in the meantime, is the responsibility and true position of the Executive? He is bound by solemn oath, before God and the country, "to take care that the laws be faithfully executed," and from this obligation he can not be absolved by any human power. But what if the performance of this duty, in whole or in part, has been rendered impracticable by events over which he could have exercised no control? Such at the present moment is the case throughout the State of South Carolina so far as the laws of the United States to secure the administration of justice by means of the Federal judiciary are concerned. All the Federal officers within its limits through whose agency alone these laws can be carried into execution have already resigned. We no longer have a district judge, a district attorney, or a marshal in South Carolina. In fact, the whole machinery of the Federal Government necessary for the distribution of remedial justice among the people has been demolished, and it would be difficult, if not impossible, to replace it.

The only acts of Congress on the statute book bearing upon this subject are those of February 28, 1795, and March 3, 1807. These authorize the President, after he shall have ascertained that the marshal, with his *posse comitatus,* is unable to execute civil or criminal process in any particular case, to call forth the militia and employ the Army and Navy to aid him in performing this service, having first by proclamation commanded the insurgents "to disperse and retire peaceably to their respective abodes within a limited time." This duty can not by possibility be performed in a State where no judicial authority exists to issue process, and where there is no marshal to execute it, and where, even if there were such an officer, the entire population would constitute one solid combination to resist him.

The bare enumeration of these provisions proves how inadequate they are without further legislation to overcome a united opposition in a single State, not to speak of other States who may place themselves in a similar attitude. Congress alone has power to decide whether the present laws can or can not be amended so as to carry out more effectually the objects of the Constitution. . . .

Apart from the execution of the laws, so far as this may be practical, the Executive has no authority to decide what shall be the relations between the Federal Government and South Carolina. He has been invested with no such discretion. He possesses no power to change the relations heretofore existing between them, much less to acknowledge the independence of that State. This would be to invest a mere executive officer with the power of recognizing the dissolution of the confederacy among our thirty-three sovereign States.

It bears no resemblance to the recognition of a foreign *de facto* government, involving no such responsibility. Any attempt to do this would, on his part, be a naked act of usurpation. It is therefore my duty to submit to Congress the whole question in all its bearings. The course of events is so rapidly hastening forward that the emergency may soon arise when you may be called upon to decide the momentous question whether you possess the power by force of arms to compel a State to remain in the Union. I should feel myself recreant to my duty were I not to express an opinion on this important subject.

The question fairly stated is, Has the Constitution delegated to Congress the power to coerce a State into submission which is attempting to withdraw or has actually withdrawn from the Confederacy? If answered in the affirmative, it must be on the principle that the power has been conferred upon Congress to declare and to make war against a State. After much serious reflection I have arrived at the conclusion that no such power has been delegated to Congress or to any other department of the Federal Government. It is manifest upon an inspection of the Constitution that this is not among the specific and enumerated powers granted to Congress, and it is equally apparent that its exercise is not "necessary and proper for carrying into execution" any one of these powers. So far from this power having been delegated to Congress, it was expressly refused by the Convention which framed the Constitution. . . .

But if we possessed this power, would it be wise to exercise it under existing circumstances? The object would doubtless be to preserve the Union. War would not only present the most effectual means of destroying it, but would vanish all hope of its peaceable reconstruction. Besides, in the fraternal conflict a vast amount of blood and treasure would be expended, rendering future reconciliation between the States impossible. In the meantime, who can foretell what would be the sufferings and privations of the people during its existence?

The fact is that our Union rests upon public opinion, and can never be cemented by the blood of its citizens shed in civil war. If it can not live in the affections of the people, it must one day perish. Congress possesses many means of preserving it by conciliation, but the sword was not placed in their hand to preserve it by force. . . .

196. CRITTENDEN PEACE RESOLUTIONS
December 18, 1860

(E. McPherson, *Political History of the Great Rebellion,* p. 64–5)

The secession of the Southern States and the imminent danger of war led to numerous efforts to patch up some sort of a compromise. A Committee of Thirty Three, appointed to work out some compromise measures, achieved nothing. Senator Crittenden of Kentucky, bitterly opposed to secession, introduced the following resolutions to Congress, but they were rejected. While not entirely unsatisfactory to the South, they were unacceptable to Lincoln who, through Thurlow Weed, advised their rejection. Another effort to patch up peace, the Peace Conference held at the request of the legislature of Virginia, recommended a number of amendments to the Constitution, but these recommendations, too, were rejected by Congress. For various resolutions and reports, see McPherson, *Political History of the Great Rebellion,* p. 49–77. See, D. L. Dumond, *The Secession Movement, 1860–1861,* chs. viii–xii; C. Coleman, *The Life of John J.* Crittenden; M. Scrugham, *The Peaceable Americans, 1860–1861.*

Whereas, serious and alarming dissensions have arisen between the Northern and Southern States, concerning the rights and security of the rights of the slave-holding States, and especially their rights in the common territory of the United States; and whereas it is eminently desirable and proper that these dissensions which now threaten the very existence of this Union, should be permanently quieted and settled, by constitutional provision, which shall do equal justice to all sections, and thereby restore to the people that peace and good will which ought to prevail between all the citizens of the United States: Therefore,

Resolved by the Senate and House of Representatives of the United States of America in Congress Assembled, That the following articles be, and are hereby, proposed and submitted as amendments to the Constitution of the United States, . . .

Article 1. In all the territory of the United States now held, or hereafter acquired, situate North of Latitude 36° 30′, slavery or involuntary servitude, except as a punishment for crime, is prohibited while such territory shall remain under territorial government. In all the territory south of said line of latitude, slavery of the African race is hereby recognized as existing, and shall not be interfered with by Congress, but shall be protected as property by all the departments of the territorial government during its continuance. And when any Territory, north or south of said line, within such boundaries as Congress may prescribe, shall contain the population requisite for a member of Congress according to the then Federal ratio, of representation of the people of the United States, it shall, if its form of government be republican, be admitted into the Union, on an equal footing with the original States, with or without slavery, as the constitution of such new State may provide.

Art. 2. Congress shall have no power to abolish slavery in places under its exclusive jurisdiction, and situate within the limits of States that permit the holding of slaves.

Art. 3. Congress shall have no power to abolish slavery within the district of Columbia so long as it exists in the adjoining States of Virginia and Maryland, or either, not without the consent of the inhabitants, nor without just compensation first made to such owners of slaves as do not consent to such abolishment. Nor shall Congress at any time prohibit officers of the Federal Government, or members of Congress, whose duties require them to be in said District, from bringing with them their slaves, and holding them as such during the time their duties may require them to remain there, and afterwards taking them from the District.

Art. 4. Congress shall have no power to prohibit or hinder the transportation of slaves from one State to another, or to a Territory in which slaves are by law permitted to be held, whether that transportation be by land, navigable rivers, or by the sea. . . .

Art. 6. No future amendment of the Constitution shall affect the five preceding articles . . . and no amendment shall be made to the Constitution which shall authorize or give to Congress any power to abolish or interfere with slavery in any of the States by whose laws it is, or may be, allowed or permitted.

And whereas, also, besides these causes of dissension embraced in the foregoing amendments proposed to the Constitution of the United States, there are others which come within the jurisdiction of Congress, and may be remedied by its legislative power; Therefore

1. Resolved. . . . That the laws now in force for the recovery of fugitive slaves are in strict pursuance of the plain and mandatory provisions of the Constitution, and have been sanctioned as valid and constitutional by the judgment of the Supreme Court of the United States; that the slave-holding States are entitled to the faithful observance and execution of those laws, and that they ought not to be repealed, or so modified or changed as to impair their efficiency; and that laws ought to be made for the punishment of those who attempt by rescue of the slave, or other illegal means, to hinder or defeat the due execution of said laws.

2. That all State laws which conflict with the fugitive slave acts of Congress, or any other Constitutional acts of Congress, or which, in their operation, impede, hinder, or delay, the free course and due execution of any of said acts, are null and void by the present provisions of the Constitution of the United States; yet those State laws, void as they are, have given color to practices, and led to consequences which have obstructed the due administration and execution of acts of Congress, and especially the acts for the delivery of fugitive slaves, and have thereby contributed much to the discord and commotion now prevailing. Congress, therefore, in the present perilous juncture, does not deem it improper, respectfully and earnestly to recommend the repeal of those laws to the several States which have enacted them, or such legislative corrections or explanations of them as may prevent their being used or perverted to such mischievous purposes.

3. That the Act of the 18th of September, 1850, commonly called the fugitive slave law, . . . the last clause of the fifth section of said act, which authorizes a person holding a

warrant for the arrest or detention of a fugitive slave, to summon to his aid the *posse comitatus,* and which declares it to be the duty of all good citizens to assist him in its execution, ought to be so amended as to expressly limit the authority and duty to cases in which there shall be resistance or danger of resistance or rescue.

4. That the laws for the suppression of the African slave trade, and especially those prohibiting the importation of slaves in the United States, ought to be made effectual, and ought to be thoroughly executed: and all further enactments necessary to those ends ought to be promptly made.

197. MISSISSIPPI RESOLUTIONS ON SECESSION
November 30, 1860

(*Laws of Mississippi,* 1860, p. 43 ff.)

On secession in Mississippi, see D. L. Dumond, *The Secession Movement,* ch. x; J. F. H. Claiborne, *Life and Correspondence of John A. Quitman;* J. F. Garner, "The First Struggle over Secession in Mississippi," Mississippi Hist. Soc., *Publications,* Vol. IV.

Whereas, The Constitutional Union was formed by the several States in their separate sovereign capacity for the purpose of mutual advantage and protection;

That the several States are distinct sovereignties, whose supremacy is limited so far only as the same has been delegated by voluntary compact to a Federal Government, and when it fails to accomplish the ends for which it was established, the parties to the compact have the right to resume, each State for itself, such delegated powers;

That the institution of slavery existed prior to the formation of the Federal Constitution, and is recognized by its letter, and all efforts to impair its value or lessen its duration by Congress, or any of the free States, is a violation of the compact of Union and is destructive of the ends for which it was ordained, but in defiance of the principles of the Union thus established, the people of the Northern States have assumed a revolutionary position towards the Southern States;

That they have set at defiance that provision of the Constitution which was intended to secure domestic tranquillity among the States and promote their general welfare, namely: "No person held to service or labor in one State, under the laws thereof, escaping into another, shall, in consequence of any law or regulation therein, be discharged from such service or labor, but shall be delivered up on claim of the party to whom such service or labor may be due;"

That they have by voluntary associations, individual agencies and State legislation interfered with slavery as it prevails in the slaveholding States;

That they have enticed our slaves from us, and by State intervention obstructed and prevented their rendition under the fugitive slave law;

That they continue their system of agitation obviously for the purpose of encouraging other slaves to escape from service, to weaken the institution in the slave-holding States by rendering the holding of such property insecure, and as a consequence its ultimate abolition certain;

That they claim the right and demand its execution by Congress to exclude slavery from the Territories, but claim the right of protection for every species of property owned by themselves;

That they declare in every manner in which public opinion is expressed their unalterable determination to exclude from admittance into the Union any new State that tolerates slavery in its Constitution, and thereby force Congress to a condemnation of that species of property;

That they thus seek by an increase of abolition States "to acquire two-thirds of both houses" for the purpose of preparing an amendment to the Constitution of the United States, abolishing slavery in the States, and so continue the agitation that the proposed amendment shall be ratified by the Legislatures of three-fourths of the States;

That they have in violation of the comity of all civilized nations, and in violation of the comity established by the Constitution of the United States, insulted and outraged our citizens when travelling among them for pleasure, health or business, by taking their servants and liberating the same, under the forms of State laws, and subjecting their owners to degrading and ignominious punishment;

That to encourage the stealing of our property they have put at defiance that provision of the Constitution which declares that fugitives from justice (escaping) into another State, on demand of the Executive authority of that State from which he fled, shall be delivered up;

That they have sought to create domestic discord in the Southern States by incendiary publications;

That they encouraged a hostile invasion of a Southern State to excite insurrection, murder and rapine;

That they have deprived Southern citizens of their property and continue an unfriendly agitation of their domestic institutions, claiming for themselves perfect immunity from external interference with their domestic policy; . . .

That they have elected a majority of Electors for President and Vice-President on the ground that there exists an irreconcilable conflict between the two sections of the Confederacy in reference to their respective systems of labor and in pursuance of their hostility to us and our institutions, thus declaring to the civilized world that the powers of this Government are to be used for the dishonor and overthrow of the Southern Section of this great Confederacy. Therefore,

Be it resolved by the Legislature of the State of Mississippi, That in the opinion of those who now constitute the said Legislature, the secession of each aggrieved State is the proper remedy for these injuries.

198. SOUTH CAROLINA ORDINANCE OF SECESSION
December 20, 1860

(F. Moore, ed. *The Rebellion Record,* Vol. I, p. 2)

Immediately on the election of Lincoln to the Presidency, the legislature of South Carolina called a convention to meet December 17 to consider the question of secession. The convention, chosen by popular vote, was overwhelmingly in favor of immediate secession. It met at Charleston and on December 20 voted unanimously for secession. See, L. A. White, *Robert Barnwell Rhett,* ch. ix; J. J. Van Deusen, *Economic Basis of Disunion in South Carolina;* E. Merritt, *James Henry Hammond,* ch. vii; H. D. Capers, *Life and Times of C. G. Memminger.* See also, C. P. Denman; *The Secession Movement in Alabama;* B. B. Munford, *Virginia's Attitude Toward Slavery and Secession;* H. T. Shanks, *The Secession Movement in Virginia;* D. Dumond, *The Secession Movement, 1860–1861.*

An Ordinance to Dissolve the Union between the State of South Carolina and other

States united with her under the compact entitled the Constitution of the United States of America:

We, the people of the State of South Carolina, in Convention assembled, do declare and ordain, and it is hereby declared and ordained, that the ordinance adopted by us in Convention, on the 23d day of May, in the year of our Lord 1788, whereby the Constitution of the United States of America was ratified, and also all Acts and parts of Acts of the General Assembly of this State ratifying the amendments of the said Constitution, are hereby repealed, and that the union now subsisting between South Carolina and other States under the name of the United States of America is hereby dissolved.

199. SOUTH CAROLINA DECLARATION OF CAUSES OF SECESSION
December 24, 1860

(F. Moore, ed. *The Rebellion Record,* Vol. I, p. 3 ff.)

In justification of secession, the South Carolina Convention adopted two papers: one an Address to the People of the Slaveholding States, reported by R. B. Rhett; the other a Declaration of the Causes of Secession, reported by C. G. Memminger. An extract from the second is given below. The Address to the People can be found conveniently in E. McPherson, *Political History* of the Great Rebellion, p. 12 ff.; L. A. White, Robert Barnwell Rhett, p. 187 ff.; H. D. Capers, Life and Times of C. G. Memminger.

The people of the State of South Carolina in Convention assembled, on the 2d day of April, A. D. 1852, declared that the frequent violations of the Constitution of the United States by the Federal Government, and its encroachments upon the reserved rights of the States, fully justified this State in their withdrawal from the Federal Union; but in deference to the opinions and wishes of the other Slaveholding States, she forbore at that time to exercise this right. Since that time these encroachments have continued to increase, and further forbearance ceases to be a virtue.

And now the State of South Carolina having resumed her separate and equal place among nations, deems it due to herself, to the remaining United States of America, and to the nations of the world, that she should declare the immediate causes which have led to this act.

In 1787, Deputies were appointed by the States to revise the articles of Confederation; and on 17th September, 1787, these Deputies recommended, for the adoption of the States, the Articles of Union, known as the Constitution of the United States.

. . . Thus was established by compact between the States, a Government with defined objects and powers, limited to the express words of the grant. . . . We hold that the Government thus established is subject to the two great principles asserted in the Declaration of Independence; and we hold further, that the mode of its formation subjects it to a third fundamental principle, namely, the law of compact. We maintain that in every compact between two or more parties, the obligation is mutual; that the failure of one of the contracting parties to perform a material part of the agreement, entirely releases the obligation of the other; and that, where no arbiter is provided, each party is remitted to his own judgment to determine the fact of failure, with all its consequences.

In the present case, that fact is established with certainty. We assert that fourteen of the States have deliberately refused for years past to fulfil their constitutional obligations, and we refer to their own statutes for the proof.

The Constitution of the United States, in its fourth Article, provides as follows:

"No person held to service or labor in one State under the laws thereof, escaping into another, shall, in consequence of any law or regulation therein, be discharged from such service or labor, but shall be delivered up, on claim of the party to whom such service or labor may be due."

This stipulation was so material to the compact that without it that compact would not have been made. The greater number of the contracting parties held slaves, and they had previously evinced their estimate of the value of such a stipulation by making it a condition in the Ordinance for the government of the territory ceded by Virginia, which obligations, and the laws of the General Government, have ceased to effect the objects of the Constitution. The States of Maine, New Hampshire, Vermont, Massachusetts, Connecticut, Rhode Island, New York, Pennsylvania, Illinois, Indiana, Michigan, Wisconsin and Iowa, have enacted laws which either nullify the acts of Congress, or render useless any attempt to execute them. In many of these States the fugitive is discharged from the service of labor claimed, and in none of them has the State Government complied with the stipulation made in the Constitution. The State of New Jersey, at an early day, passed a law in conformity with her constitutional obligation; but the current of Anti-Slavery feeling has led her more recently to enact laws which render inoperative the remedies provided by her own laws and by the laws of Congress. In the State of New York even the right of transit for a slave has been denied by her tribunals; and the States of Ohio and Iowa have refused to surrender to justice fugitives charged with murder, and with inciting servile insurrection in the State of Virginia. Thus the constitutional compact has been deliberately broken and disregarded by the non-slaveholding States; and the consequence follows that South Carolina is released from her obligation. . . .

We affirm that these ends for which this Government was instituted have been defeated, and the Government itself has been destructive of them by the action of the non-slaveholding States. Those States have assumed the right of deciding upon the propriety of our domestic institutions; and have denied the rights of property established in fifteen of the States and recognized by the Constitution; they have denounced as sinful the institution of Slavery; they have permitted the open establishment among them of societies, whose avowed object is to disturb the peace of and eloin the property of the citizens of other States. They have encouraged and assisted thousands of our slaves to leave their homes; and those who remain, have been incited by emissaries, books, and pictures, to servile insurrection.

For twenty-five years this agitation has been steadily increasing, until it has now secured to its aid the power of the common Government. Observing the *forms* of the Constitution, a sectional party has found within that article establishing the Executive Department, the means of subverting the Constitution itself. A geographical line has been drawn across the Union, and all the States north of that line have united in the election of a man to the high office of President of the United States whose opinions and purposes are hostile to Slavery. He is to be intrusted with the administration of the common Government, because he has declared that "Government cannot endure permanently half slave, half free," and that the public mind must rest in the belief that Slavery is in the course of ultimate extinction.

This sectional combination for the subversion of the Constitution has been aided, in some of the States, by elevating to citizenship persons who, by the supreme law of the land, are incapable of becoming citizens; and their votes have been used to inaugurate a new policy, hostile to the South, and destructive of its peace and safety.

On the 4th of March next this party will take possession of the Government. It has announced that the South shall be excluded from the common territory, that the Judicial tribunal shall be made sectional, and that a war must be waged against Slavery until it shall cease throughout the United States.

The guarantees of the Constitution will then no longer exist; the equal rights of the States will be lost. The Slaveholding States will no longer have the power of self-government, or self-protection, and the Federal Government will have become their enemy.

Sectional interest and animosity will deepen the irritation; and all hope of remedy is rendered vain, by the fact that the public opinion at the North has invested a great political error with the sanctions of a more erroneous religious belief.

We, therefore, the people of South Carolina, by our delegates in Convention assembled, appealing to the Supreme Judge of the world for the rectitude of our intentions, have solemnly declared that the Union heretofore existing between this State and the other States of North America is dissolved, and that the State of South Carolina has resumed her position among the nations of the world, as a separate and independent state, with full power to levy war, conclude peace, contract alliances, establish commerce, and to do all other acts and things which independent States may of right do.

200. MAYOR FERNANDO WOOD'S RECOMMENDATION FOR THE SECESSION OF NEW YORK CITY
January 6, 1861

(E. McPherson, ed. *The Political History of the Great Rebellion*, p. 42 ff.)

The financial and commercial interests of New York City, with their heavy investments in the South and in the textile industries, were particularly hostile to a war policy on the part of the Federal government. Thurlow Weed made strenuous efforts to commit Lincoln to a compromise policy; Governor Morgan of New York urged moderation; and even Horace Greeley wished to let the "erring sisters go in peace." For historical background, see, D. A. Alexander, *Political History of the State of New York*, Vol. II, ch. xxvi; S. D. Brummer, *Political His-* tory of New York State during the period of the Civil War.

To the Honorable the Common Council:
Gentlemen: We are entering upon the public duties of the year under circumstances as unprecedented as they are gloomy and painful to contemplate. . . .

It would seem that a dissolution of the Federal Union is inevitable. . . .

If these forebodings shall be realized, and

a separation of the States shall occur, momentous considerations will be presented to the corporate authorities of this city. We must provide for the new relations which will necessarily grow out of the new condition of public affairs.

It will not only be necessary for us to settle the relations which we shall hold to other cities and States, but to establish if we can, new ones with a portion of our own State. Being the child of the Union, having drawn our sustenance from its bosom, and arisen to our present power and strength through the vigor of our mother—when deprived of her maternal advantages, we must rely upon our own resources and assume a position predicated upon the new phase which public affairs will present, and upon the inherent strength which our geographical, commercial, political, and financial preëminence imparts to us.

With our aggrieved brethren of the Slave States, we have friendly relations and a common sympathy. We have not participated in the warfare upon their constitutional rights or their domestic institutions. . . . Our ships have penetrated to every clime, and so have New York capital, energy, and enterprise found their way to every State, and, indeed, to almost every county and town of the American Union. If we have derived sustenance from the Union, so have we in return disseminated blessings for the common benefit of all. Therefore, New York has a right to expect, and should endeavor to preserve a continuance of uninterrupted intercourse with every section.

It is, however, folly to disguise the fact that, judging from the past, New York may have more cause of apprehension from the aggressive legislation of our own State than from external dangers. We have already suffered largely from this cause. For the past five years, our interests and corporate rights have been repeatedly trampled upon. Being an integral portion of the State, it has been assumed, and in effect tacitly admitted on our part by nonresistance, that all political and governmental power over us rested in the State Legislature. Even the common right of taxing ourselves for our own government, has been yielded, and we are not permitted to do so without this authority. . . .

Thus it will be seen that the political connection between the people of the city and the State has been used by the latter to our injury. The Legislature, in which the present partizan majority has the power, has become an instrument by which we are plundered to enrich their speculators, lobby agents, and Abolition politicians. . . .

How we shall rid ourselves of this odious and oppressive connection, it is not for me to determine. It is certain that a dissolution cannot be peacefully accomplished, except by the consent of the Legislature itself. Whether this can be obtained or not, is, in my judgement, doubtful. Deriving so much advantage from its power over the city, it is not probable that a partizan majority will consent to a separation—and the resort to force by violence and revolution must not be thought of for an instant. We have been distinguished as an orderly and law-abiding people. Let us do nothing to forfeit this character, or to add to the present distracted condition of public affairs.

Much, no doubt, can be said in favor of the justice and policy of a separation. . . . Why should not New York city, instead of supporting by her contributions in revenue two-thirds of the expenses of the United States, become also equally independent? As a free city, with but nominal duty on imports, her local Government could be supported without taxation upon her people. Thus we could live free from taxes, and have cheap goods nearly duty free. In this she would have the whole and united support of the Southern States, as well as all the other States to whose interests and rights under the Constitution she has always been true.

It is well for individuals or communities to look every danger squarely in the face and to meet it calmly and bravely. As dreadful as the severing of the bonds that have hitherto united the States has been in contemplation, it is now apparently a stern and inevitable fact. We have now to meet it with all the consequences, whatever they may be. If the Confederacy is broken up, the Government is dissolved, and it behooves every distinct community, as well as every individual, to take care of themselves.

When Disunion has become a fixed and certain fact, why may not New York disrupt the bands which bind her to a venal and corrupt master—to a people and a party that have plundered her revenues, attempted to ruin her commerce, taken away the power of self-government, and destroyed the Confederacy of which she was the proud Empire City? Amid the gloom which the present and prospective condition of things must cast over the country, New York, as a *Free City*, may shed the only light and hope of a future reconstruction of our once blessed Confederacy.

But I am not prepared to recommend the violence implied in these views. In stating this argument in favor of freedom "peace-

ably if we can, forcibly if we must," let me not be misunderstood. The redress can be found only in appeals to the magnanimity of the people of the whole State. The events of the past two months have no doubt effected a change in the popular sentiment of the State and National politics. This change may bring us the desired relief, and we may be able to obtain a repeal of the law to which I have referred, and a consequent restoration of our corporate rights.

FERNANDO WOOD, Mayor.

201. THE CONSTITUTION OF THE CONFEDERATE STATES OF AMERICA
March 11, 1861

(Richardson, ed. *Messages and Papers of the Confederacy*, Vol. I, p. 37 ff.)

A Provisional Constitution had been adopted February 8, 1861: it is reproduced in Jefferson Davis, *Rise and Fall of the Confederate Government*, Vol. II, appendix K. The permanent Constitution closely resembled the Constitution of the United States. Even the African slave trade was prohibited. Professor Stephenson observes that "the framers of 1861 left unstated most of their distinctive views". See, N. W. Stephenson, *The Day of the Confederacy*, ch. i.

WE, the people of the Confederate States, each State acting in its sovereign and independent character, in order to form a permanent federal government, establish justice, insure domestic tranquillity, and secure the blessings of liberty to ourselves and our posterity—invoking the favor and guidance of Almighty God—do ordain and establish this Constitution for the Confederate States of America.

ART. I

SEC. 1.—All legislative powers herein delegated shall be vested in a Congress of the Confederate States, which shall consist of a Senate and House of Representatives.

SEC. 2. (1) The House of Representatives shall be chosen every second year by the people of the several States; and the electors in each State shall be citizens of the Confederate States, and have the qualifications requisite for electors of the most numerous branch of the State Legislature; but no person of foreign birth, not a citizen of the Confederate

States, shall be allowed to vote for any officer, civil or political, State or Federal.

(2) No person shall be a Representative who shall not have attained the age of twenty-five years, and be a citizen of the Confederate States, and who shall not, when elected, be an inhabitant of that State in which he shall be chosen.

(3) Representatives and direct taxes shall be apportioned among the several States which may be included within this Confederacy, according to their respective numbers, which shall be determined by adding to the whole number of free persons, including those bound to service for a term of years, and excluding Indians not taxed, three-fifths of all slaves. The actual enumeration shall be made within three years after the first meeting of the Congress of the Confederate States, and within every subsequent term of ten years, in such manner as they shall by law direct. The number of Representatives shall not exceed one for every fifty thousand, but each State shall have at least one Representative; and until such enumeration shall be made, the State of South Carolina shall be entitled to choose six; the State of Georgia ten; the State of Alabama nine; the State of Florida two; the State of Mississippi seven; the State of Louisiana six; and the State of Texas six.

(4) When vacancies happen in the representation of any State, the Executive authority thereof shall issue writs of election to fill such vacancies.

(5) The House of Representatives shall choose their Speaker and other officers; and shall have the sole power of impeachment; except that any judicial or other federal officer resident and acting solely within the limits of any State, may be impeached by a vote of two-thirds of both branches of the Legislature thereof.

SEC. 3. (1) The Senate of the Confederate States shall be composed of two Senators from each State, chosen for six years by the Legislature thereof, at the regular session next immediately preceding the commencement of the term of service; and each Senator shall have one vote.

(2) Immediately after they shall be assembled, in consequence of the first election, they shall be divided as equally as may be into three classes. The seats of the Senators of the first class shall be vacated at the expiration of the second year; of the second class at the expiration of the fourth year; and of the third class at the expiration of the sixth year; so that one-third may be chosen every second year; and if vacancies happen by resignation or otherwise during the recess of the Legislature of any State, the Executive thereof may make temporary appointments until the next meeting of the Legislature, which shall then fill such vacancies.

(3) No person shall be a Senator, who shall not have attained the age of thirty years, and be a citizen of the Confederate States; and who shall not, when elected, be an inhabitant of the State for which he shall be chosen.

(4) The Vice-President of the Confederate States shall be President of the Senate, but shall have no vote, unless they be equally divided.

(5) The Senate shall choose their other officers, and also a President *pro tempore*, in the absence of the Vice-President, or when he shall exercise the office of President of the Confederate States.

(6) The Senate shall have sole power to try all impeachments. When sitting for that purpose they shall be on oath or affirmation. When the President of the Confederate States is tried, the Chief-Justice shall preside; and no person shall be convicted without the concurrence of two-thirds of the members present.

(7) Judgment in cases of impeachment shall not extend further than removal from office, and disqualification to hold and enjoy any office of honor, trust, or profit, under the Confederate States; but the party convicted shall, nevertheless, be liable to and subject to indictment, trial, judgment, and punishment according to law.

SEC. 4. (1) The times, places, and manner of holding elections for Senators and Representatives, shall be prescribed in each State by the Legislature thereof, subject to the provisions of this Constitution; but the Congress may, at any time, by law, make or alter such regulations, except as to the times and places of choosing Senators.

(2) The Congress shall assemble at least once in every year; and such meeting shall be on the first Monday in December, unless they shall, by law, appoint a different day.

SEC. 5. (1) Each House shall be the judge of the elections, returns, and qualifications of its own members, and a majority of each shall constitute a quorum to do business; but a smaller number may adjourn from day to day, and may be authorized to compel the attendance of absent members, in such manner and under such penalties as each House may provide.

(2) Each House may determine the rules of its proceedings, punish its members for disorderly behavior, and, with the concurrence of two-thirds of the whole number, expel a member.

(3) Each House shall keep a journal of its proceedings, and from time to time publish the same, excepting such part as may in its judgment require secrecy, and the ayes and nays of the members of either House, on any question, shall, at the desire of one-fifth of those present, be entered on the journal.

(4) Neither House, during the session of Congress, shall, without the consent of the other, adjourn for more than three days, nor to any other place than that in which the two Houses shall be sitting.

SEC. 6. (1) The Senators and Representatives shall receive a compensation for their services, to be ascertained by law, and paid out of the Treasury of the Confederate States. They shall, in all cases except treason and breach of the peace, be privileged from arrest during their attendance at the session of their respective Houses, and in going to and returning from the same; and for any speech or debate in either House, they shall not be questioned in any other place.

(2) No Senator or Representative shall, during the time for which he was elected, be appointed to any civil office under the authority of the Confederate States, which shall have been created, or the emoluments whereof shall have been increased during such time; and no person holding any office under the Confederate States shall be a member of either House during his continuance in office. But Congress may, by law, grant to the principal officer in each of the Executive Departments a seat upon the floor of either House, with the privilege of discussing any measure appertaining to his department.

SEC. 7. (1) All bills for raising revenue shall originate in the House of Representatives; but the Senate may propose or concur with amendments as on other bills.

(2) Every bill which shall have passed both Houses shall, before it becomes a law, be presented to the President of the Confederate States; if he approve he shall sign it; but if not, he shall return it with his objections to that House in which it shall have originated, who shall enter the objections at large on their journal, and proceed to reconsider it. If, after such reconsideration, two-thirds of that House shall agree to pass the bill, it shall be sent, together with the objections, to the other House, by which it shall likewise be reconsidered, and if approved by two-thirds of that House, it shall become a law. But in all such cases, the votes of both Houses shall be determined by yeas and nays, and the names of the persons voting for and against the bill shall be entered on the journal of each House respectively. If any bill shall not be returned by the President within ten days (Sundays excepted) after it shall have been presented to him, the same shall be a law, in like manner as if he had signed it, unless the Congress, by their adjournment, prevent its return; in which case it shall not be a law. The President may approve any appropriation and disapprove any other appropriation in the same bill. In such case he shall, in signing the bill, designate the appropriations disapproved; and shall return a copy of such appropriations, with his objections, to the House in which the bill shall have originated; and the same proceedings shall then be had as in case of other bills disapproved by the President.

(3) Every order, resolution, or vote, to which the concurrence of both Houses may be necessary (except on questions of adjournment) shall be presented to the President of the Confederate States; and before the same shall take effect shall be approved by him; or being disapproved by him, may be repassed by two-thirds of both Houses, according to the rules and limitations prescribed in case of a bill.

SEC. 8.—The Congress shall have power—

(1) To lay and collect taxes, duties, imposts, and excises, for revenue necessary to pay the debts, provide for the common defence, and carry on the Government of the Confederate States; but no bounties shall be granted from the treasury; nor shall any duties or taxes on importations from foreign nations be laid to promote or foster any branch of industry; and all duties, imposts, and excises shall be uniform throughout the Confederate States.

(2) To borrow money on the credit of the Confederate States.

(3) To regulate commerce with foreign nations, and among the several States, and with the Indian tribes; but neither this, nor any other clause contained in the Constitution shall be construed to delegate the power to Congress to appropriate money for any internal improvement intended to facilitate commerce; except for the purpose of furnishing lights, beacons, and buoys, and other aids to navigation upon the coasts, and the improvement of harbors, and the removing of obstructions in river navigation, in all which cases, such duties shall be laid on the navigation facilitated thereby, as may be necessary to pay the costs and expenses thereof.

(4) To establish uniform laws of naturalization, and uniform laws on the subject of bankruptcies throughout the Confederate States, but no law of Congress shall discharge any debt contracted before the passage of the same.

(5) To coin money, regulate the value thereof, and of foreign coin, and fix the standard of weights and measures.

(6) To provide for the punishment of counterfeiting the securities and current coin of the Confederate States.

(7) To establish post-offices and post-routes; but the expenses of the Post-office Department, after the first day of March, in the year of our Lord eighteen hundred and sixty-three, shall be paid out of its own revenues.

(8) To promote the progress of science and useful arts, by securing for limited times to authors and inventors the exclusive right to their respective writings and discoveries.

(9) To constitute tribunals inferior to the Supreme Court.

(10) To define and punish piracies and felonies committed on the high seas, and offences against the law of nations.

(11) To declare war, grant letters of marque and reprisal, and make rules concerning captures on land and water.

(12) To raise and support armies; but no appropriation of money to that use shall be for a longer term than two years.

(13) To provide and maintain a navy.

(14) To make rules for government and regulation of the land and naval forces.

(15) To provide for calling forth the militia to execute the laws of the Confederate States; suppress insurrections, and repel invasions.

(16) To provide for organizing, arming, and disciplining the militia, and for governing such part of them as may be employed in the service of the Confederate States; reserving to the States, respectively, the appointment of the officers, and the authority of training the militia according to the discipline prescribed by Congress.

(17) To exercise exclusive legislation, in all cases whatsoever, over such district (not exceeding ten miles square) as may, by cession of one or more States, and the acceptance of Congress, become the seat of the Government of the Confederate States; and to exercise a like authority over all places purchased by the consent of the Legislature of the State in which the same shall be, for the erection of forts, magazines, arsenals, dock-yards, and other needful buildings, and

(18) To make all laws which shall be necessary and proper for carrying into execution the foregoing powers, and all other powers vested by this Constitution in the Government of the Confederate States, or in any department or officer thereof.

SEC. 9. (1) The importation of negroes of the African race, from any foreign country, other than the slaveholding States or Territories of the United States of America, is hereby forbidden; and Congress is required to pass such laws as shall effectually prevent the same.

(2) Congress shall also have power to prohibit the introduction of slaves from any State not a member of, or Territory not belonging to, this Confederacy.

(3) The privilege of the writ of *habeas corpus* shall not be suspended, unless when in cases of rebellion or invasion the public safety may require it.

(4) No bill of attainder, or *ex post facto* law, or law denying or impairing the right of property in negro slaves shall be passed.

(5) No capitation or other direct tax shall be laid unless in proportion to the census or enumeration hereinbefore directed to be taken.

(6) No tax or duty shall be laid on articles exported from any State, except by a vote of two-thirds of both Houses.

(7) No preference shall be given by any regulation of commerce or revenue to the ports of one State over those of another.

(8) No money shall be drawn from the treasury but in consequence of appropriations made by law; and a regular statement and account of the receipts and expenditures of all public money shall be published from time to time.

(9) Congress shall appropriate no money from the treasury except by a vote of two-thirds of both Houses, taken by yeas and nays, unless it be asked and estimated for by some one of the heads of departments, and submitted to Congress by the President; or for the purpose of paying its own expenses and contingencies; or for the payment of claims against the Confederate States, the justice of which shall have been judicially declared by a tribunal for the investigation of claims against the Government, which it is hereby made the duty of Congress to establish.

(10) All bills appropriating money shall specify in federal currency the exact amount of each appropriation and the purposes for which it is made; and Congress shall grant no extra compensation to any public con-

tractor, officer, agent, or servant, after such contract shall have been made or such service rendered.

(11) No title of nobility shall be granted by the Confederate States; and no person holding any office of profit or trust under them shall, without the consent of the Congress, accept of any present, emoluments, office, or title of any kind whatever, from any king, prince, or foreign state.

(12) Congress shall make no law respecting an establishment of religion, or prohibiting the free exercise thereof; or abridging the freedom of speech or of the press; or the right of the people peaceably to assemble and petition the Government for a redress of grievances.

(13) A well-regulated militia being necessary to the security of a free State, the right of the people to keep and bear arms shall not be infringed.

(14) No soldier shall, in time of peace, be quartered in any house without the consent of the owner; nor in time of war, but in a manner prescribed by law.

(15) The right of the people to be secure in their persons, houses, papers, and against unreasonable searches and seizures, shall not be violated; and no warrant shall issue but upon probable cause, supported by oath or affirmation, and particularly describing the place to be searched, and the person or things to be seized.

(16) No person shall be held to answer for a capital or otherwise infamous crime, unless on a presentment or indictment of a grand jury, except in cases arising in the land or naval forces, or in the militia, when in actual service, in time of war, or public danger; nor shall any person be subject for the same offence to be twice put in jeopardy of life or limb; nor be compelled in any criminal case to be a witness against himself; nor be deprived of life, liberty, or property, without due process of law; nor shall any private property be taken for public use without just compensation.

(17) In all criminal prosecutions the accused shall enjoy the right to a speedy and public trial, by an impartial jury of the State and district wherein the crime shall have been committed, which district shall have been previously ascertained by law, and to be informed of the nature and cause of the accusation; to be confronted with the witnesses against him; to have compulsory process for obtaining witnesses in his favor; and to have the assistance of counsel for his defence.

(18) In suits at common law, where the value in controversy shall exceed twenty dollars, the right of trial by jury shall be preserved; and no fact so tried by a jury shall be otherwise reëxamined in any court of the Confederacy, than according to the rules of the common law.

(19) Excessive bail shall not be required, nor excessive fines imposed, nor cruel or unusual punishment inflicted.

(20) Every law, or resolution having the force of law, shall relate to but one subject, and that shall be expressed in the title.

SEC. 10. (1) No State shall enter into any treaty, alliance, or confederation; grant letters of marque and reprisals; coin money; make any thing but gold and silver coin a tender in payment of debts; pass any bill of attainder, or *ex post facto* law, or law impairing the obligation of contracts; or grant any title of nobility.

(2) No State shall, without the consent of Congress, lay any imposts or duties on imports or exports, except what may be absolutely necessary for executing its inspection laws; and the net produce of all duties and imposts, laid by any State on imports or exports, shall be for the use of the Treasury of the Confederate States; and all such laws shall be subject to the revision and control of Congress.

(3) No State shall, without the consent of Congress, lay any duty of tonnage, except on sea-going vessels, for the improvement of its rivers and harbors navigated by the said vessels; but such duties shall not conflict with any treaties of the Confederate States with foreign nations; and any surplus of revenue, thus derived, shall, after making such improvement, be paid into the common treasury; nor shall any State keep troops or ships of war in time of peace, enter into any agreement or compact with another State, or with a foreign power, or engage in war, unless actually invaded, or in such imminent danger as will not admit of delay. But when any river divides or flows through two or more

States, they may enter into compacts with each other to improve the navigation thereof.

ART. II.

SEC. 1. (1) The Executive power shall be vested in a President of the Confederate States of America. He and the Vice-President shall hold their offices for the term of six years; but the President shall not be reëligible. The President and Vice-President shall be elected as follows:

(2) Each State shall appoint, in such manner as the Legislature thereof may direct, a number of electors equal to the whole number of Senators and Representatives to which the State may be entitled in Congress; but no Senator or Representative, or person holding an office of trust or profit under the Confederate States, shall be appointed an elector.

(3) The electors shall meet in their respective States and vote by ballot for President and Vice-President, one of whom, at least, shall not be an inhabitant of the same State with themselves; they shall name in their ballots the person voted for as President, and in distinct ballots the person voted for as Vice-President, and they shall make distinct lists of all persons voted for as President, and of all persons voted for as Vice-President, and of the number of votes for each; which list they shall sign, and certify, and transmit, sealed, to the Government of the Confederate States, directed to the President of the Senate. The President of the Senate shall, in the presence of the Senate and House of Representatives, open all the certificates, and the votes shall then be counted; the person having the greatest number of votes for President shall be the President, if such number be a majority of the whole number of electors appointed; and if no person shall have such a majority, then, from the persons having the highest numbers, not exceeding three, on the list of those voted for as President, the House of Representatives shall choose immediately, by ballot, the President. But, in choosing the President, the votes shall be taken by States, the Representative from each State having one vote; a quorum for this purpose shall consist of a member or members from two-thirds of the States, and a majority of all the States shall be necessary

to a choice. And if the House of Representatives shall not choose a President, whenever the right of choice shall devolve upon them, before the fourth day of March next following, then the Vice-President shall act as President, as in case of the death, or other constitutional disability of the President.

(4) The person having the greatest number of votes as Vice-President shall be the Vice-President, if such number be a majority of the whole number of electors appointed; and if no person have a majority, then from the two highest numbers on the list, the Senate shall choose the Vice-President; a quorum for the purpose shall consist of two-thirds of the whole number of Senators, and a majority of the whole number shall be necessary for a choice.

(5) But no person constitutionally ineligible to the office of President shall be eligible to that of Vice-President of the Confederate States.

(6) The Congress may determine the time of choosing the electors, and the day on which they shall give their votes; which day shall be the same throughout the Confederate States.

(7) No person except a natural born citizen of the Confederate States, or a citizen thereof, at the time of the adoption of this Constitution, or a citizen thereof born in the United States prior to the 20th December, 1860, shall be eligible to the office of President; neither shall any person be eligible to that office who shall not have attained the age of thirty-five years, and been fourteen years a resident within the limits of the Confederate States, as they may exist at the time of his election.

(8) In case of the removal of the President from office, or of his death, resignation, or inability to discharge the powers and duties of the said office, the same shall devolve on the Vice-President; and the Congress may, by law, provide for the case of the removal, death, resignation, or inability both of the President and the Vice-President, declaring what officer shall then act as President, and such officer shall then act accordingly until the disability be removed or a President shall be elected.

(9) The President shall, at stated times, receive for his services a compensation, which

shall neither be increased nor diminished during the period for which he shall have been elected; and he shall not receive within that period any other emolument from the Confederate States, or any of them.

(10) Before he enters on the execution of the duties of his office, he shall take the following oath or affirmation:

"I do solemnly swear (or affirm) that I will faithfully execute the office of President of the Confederate States, and will, to the best of my ability, preserve, protect, and defend the Constitution thereof."

SEC. 2. (1) The President shall be commander-in-chief of the army and navy of the Confederate States, and of the militia of the several States, when called into the actual service of the Confederate States; he may require the opinion, in writing, of the principal officer in each of the Executive Departments, upon any subject relating to the duties of their respective offices; and he shall have power to grant reprieves and pardons for offences against the Confederate States, except in cases of impeachment.

(2) He shall have power, by and with the advice and consent of the Senate, to make treaties, provided two-thirds of the Senators present concur; and he shall nominate, and, by and with the advice and consent of the Senate, shall appoint ambassadors, other public ministers, and consuls, Judges of the Supreme Court, and all other officers of the Confederate States, whose appointments are not herein otherwise provided for, and which shall be established by law; but the Congress may by law vest the appointment of such inferior officers, as they think proper, in the President alone, in the courts of law, or in the heads of departments.

(3) The principal officer in each of the Executive Departments, and all persons connected with the diplomatic service, may be removed from office at the pleasure of the President. All other civil officers of the Executive Department may be removed at any time by the President, or other appointing power, when their services are unnecessary, or for dishonesty, incapacity, inefficiency, misconduct, or neglect of duty; and when so removed, the removal shall be reported to the Senate, together with the reasons therefor.

(4) The President shall have power to fill all vacancies that may happen during the recess of the Senate, by granting commissions which shall expire at the end of the next session; but no person rejected by the Senate shall be reappointed to the same office during their ensuing recess.

SEC. 3. (1) The President shall, from time to time, give to the Congress information of the state of the Confederacy, and recommend to their consideration such measures as he shall judge necessary and expedient; he may, on extraordinary occasions, convene both Houses, or either of them; and, in case of disagreement between them, with respect to the time of adjournment he may adjourn them to such time as he shall think proper; he shall receive ambassadors and other public ministers; he shall take care that the laws be faithfully executed, and shall commission all the officers of the Confederate States.

SEC. 4. (1) The President and Vice-President, and all civil officers of the Confederate States, shall be removed from office on impeachment for, or conviction of, treason, bribery, or other high crimes and misdemeanors.

ART. III.

SEC. 1. (1) The judicial power of the Confederate States shall be vested in one Superior Court, and in such inferior courts as the Congress may from time to time ordain and establish. The judges, both of the Supreme and inferior courts, shall hold their offices during good behavior, and shall, at stated times, receive for their services a compensation, which shall not be diminished during their continuance in office.

SEC. 2. (1) The judicial power shall extend to all cases arising under the Constitution, the laws of the Confederate States, or treaties made or which shall be made under their authority; to all cases affecting ambassadors, other public ministers, and consuls; to all cases of admiralty or maritime jurisdiction; to controversies to which the Confederate States shall be a party; to controversies between two or more States; between a State and citizens of another State, where the State is plaintiff; between citizens claiming lands under grants of different States, and between a State or the citizens thereof, and foreign States, citizens, or subjects; but no State shall be sued by a citizen or subject of any foreign State.

(2) In all cases affecting ambassadors, other public ministers, and consuls, and those in which a State shall be a party, the Supreme Court shall have original jurisdiction. In all the other cases before mentioned, the Supreme Court shall have appellate jurisdiction, both as to law and fact, with such exceptions, and under such regulations as the Congress shall make.

(3) The trial of all crimes, except in cases of impeachment, shall be by jury, and such trial shall be held in the State where the said crimes shall have been committed; but when not committed within any State, the trial shall be at such place or places as the Congress may by law have directed.

SEC. 3. (1) Treason against the Confederate States shall consist only in levying war against them, or in adhering to their enemies, giving them aid and comfort. No person shall be convicted of treason unless on the testimony of two witnesses to the same overt act, or on confession in open court.

(2) The Congress shall have power to declare the punishment of treason, but no attainder of treason shall work corruption of blood, or forfeiture, except during the life of the person attainted.

ART. IV.

SEC. 1. (1) Full faith and credit shall be given in each State to the public acts, records, and judicial proceedings of every other State. And the Congress may, by general laws, prescribe the manner in which such acts, records, and proceedings shall be proved, and the effect thereof.

SEC. 2. (1) The citizens of each State shall be entitled to all the privileges and immunities of citizens of the several States, and shall have the right of transit and sojourn in any State of this Confederacy, with their slaves and other property; and the right of property in said slaves shall not be thereby impaired.

(2) A person charged in any State with treason, felony, or other crime against the laws of such State, who shall flee from justice, and be found in another State, shall, on demand of the executive authority of the State from which he fled, be delivered up to be removed to the State having jurisdiction of the crime.

(3) No slave or other person held to service or labor in any State or Territory of the Confederate States, under the laws thereof, escaping or unlawfully carried into another, shall, in consequence of any law or regulation therein, be discharged from such service or labor; but shall be delivered up on claim of the party to whom such slave belongs, or to whom such service or labor may be due.

SEC. 3. (1) Other States may be admitted into this Confederacy by a vote of two-thirds of the whole House of Representatives, and two-thirds of the Senate, the Senate voting by States; but no new State shall be formed or erected within the jurisdiction of any other State; nor any State be formed by the junction of two or more States, or parts of States, without the consent of the Legislatures of the States concerned as well as of the Congress.

(2) The Congress shall have power to dispose of and make all needful rules and regulations concerning the property of the Confederate States, including the lands thereof.

(3) The Confederate States may acquire new territory; and Congress shall have power to legislate and provide governments for the inhabitants of all territory belonging to the Confederate States, lying without the limits of the several States, and may permit them, at such times, and in such manner as it may by law provide, to form States to be admitted into the Confederacy. In all such territory, the institution of negro slavery, as it now exists in the Confederate States, shall be recognized and protected by Congress and by the territorial government; and the inhabitants of the several Confederate States and Territories shall have the right to take to such territory any slaves lawfully held by them in any of the States or Territories of the Confederate States.

(4) The Confederate States shall guarantee to every State that now is or hereafter may become a member of this Confederacy, a Republican form of Government, and shall protect each of them against invasion; and on application of the Legislature, (or of the Executive when the Legislature is not in session,) against domestic violence.

ART. V.

SEC. 1. (1) Upon the demand of any three States, legally assembled in their several Conventions, the Congress shall summon a Convention of all the States, to take into consideration such amendments to the Constitution as the said States shall concur in suggesting at the time when the said demand is made; and should any of the proposed amendments to the Constitution be agreed on by the said Convention—voting by States—and the same be ratified by the Legislatures of two-thirds of the several States, or by conventions in two-thirds thereof—as the one or the other mode of ratification may be proposed by the general convention—they shall thenceforward form a part of this Constitution. But no State shall, without its consent, be deprived of its equal representation in the Senate.

ART. VI.

1.—The Government established by this Constitution is the successor of the Provisional Government of the Confederate States of America, and all the laws passed by the latter shall continue in force until the same shall be repealed or modified; and all the officers appointed by the same shall remain in office until their successors are appointed and qualified, or the offices abolished.

2. All debts contracted and engagements entered into before the adoption of this Constitution, shall be as valid against the Confederate States under this Constitution as under the Provisional Government.

3. This Constitution, and the laws of the Confederate States, made in pursuance thereof, and all treaties made, or which shall be made, under the authority of the Confederate States, shall be the supreme law of the land; and the judges in every State shall be bound thereby, any thing in the Constitution or laws of any State to the contrary notwithstanding.

4. The Senators and Representatives before mentioned, and the members of the several State Legislatures, and all executive and judicial offices, both of the Confederate States and of the several States, shall be bound, by oath or affirmation, to support this Constitution; but no religious test shall ever be required as a qualification to any office or public trust under the Confederate States.

5. The enumeration, in the Constitution, of certain rights, shall not be construed to deny or disparage others retained by the people of the several States.

6. The powers not delegated to the Confederate States by the Constitution, nor prohibited by it to the States, are reserved to the States, respectively, or to the people thereof.

ART. VII.

1.—The ratification of the conventions of five States shall be sufficient for the establishment of this Constitution between the States so ratifying the same.

2. When five States shall have ratified this Constitution in the manner before specified, the Congress, under the provisional Constitution, shall prescribe the time for holding the election of President and Vice-President, and for the meeting of the electoral college, and for counting the votes and inaugurating the President. They shall also prescribe the time for holding the first election of members of Congress under this Constitution, and the time for assembling the same. Until the assembling of such Congress, the Congress under the provisional Constitution shall continue to exercise the legislative powers granted them; not extending beyond the time limited by the Constitution of the Provisional Government.

Adopted unanimously by the Congress of the Confederate States of South Carolina, Georgia, Florida, Alabama, Mississippi, Louisiana, and Texas, sitting in convention at the capitol, in the city of Montgomery, Ala., on the eleventh day of March, in the year eighteen hundred and sixty-one.

Howell Cobb
President of the Congress.

[Signatures]

202. LINCOLN'S FIRST INAUGURAL ADDRESS
March 4, 1861

(Richardson, ed. *Messages and Papers*, Vol. VI, p. 5 ff.)

In his first inaugural address Lincoln reiterated his constitutional doctrine that the Union was older than the States and that the contract between the States was binding and irrevocable. The last paragraph of the Inaugural was phrased by Seward. See, J. G. Nicolay and J. Hay, *Abraham Lincoln*, Vol. III; W. E. Barton, *President Lincoln*, Vol. I, ch. xiii.

FELLOW-CITIZENS OF THE UNITED STATES: —In compliance with a custom as old as the Government itself, I appear before you to address you briefly, and to take in your presence the oath prescribed by the Constitution of the United States to be taken by the President "before he enters on the execution of his office.". . .

Apprehension seems to exist among the people of the Southern States that by the accession of a Republican administration their property and their peace and personal security are to be endangered. There has never been any reasonable cause for such apprehension. Indeed, the most ample evidence to the contrary has all the while existed and been open to their inspection. It is found in nearly all the published speeches of him who now addresses you. I do but quote from one of those speeches when I declare that "I have no purpose, directly or indirectly, to interfere with the institution of slavery in the States where it exists. I believe I have no lawful right to do so, and I have no inclination to do so." . . .

I now reiterate these sentiments; and, in doing so, I only press upon the public attention the most conclusive evidence of which the case is susceptible, that the property, peace and security of no section are to be in any wise endangered by the now incoming administration. I add, too, that all the protection which, consistently with the Constitution and the laws, can be given, will be cheerfully given to all the States when lawfully demanded, for whatever cause —as cheerfully to one section as to another. . . .

I take the official oath to-day with no mental reservations, and with no purpose to construe the Constitution or laws by any hypercritical rules. And, while I do not choose now to specify particular acts of Congress as proper to be enforced, I do suggest that it will be much safer for all, both in official and private stations, to conform to and abide by all those acts which stand unrepealed, than to violate any of them, trusting to find impunity in having them held to be unconstitutional. . . .

A disruption of the Federal Union, heretofore only menaced, is now formidably attempted.

I hold that, in contemplation of universal law and of the Constitution, the Union of these States is perpetual. Perpetuity is implied, if not expressed, in the fundamental law of all national governments. It is safe to assert that no government proper ever had a provision in its organic law for its own termination. Continue to execute all the express provisions of our national Constitution, and the Union will endure forever—it being impossible to destroy it except by some action not provided for in the instrument itself.

Again, if the United States be not a government proper, but an association of States in the nature of contract merely, can it as a contract be peaceably unmade by less than all the parties who made it? One party to a contract may violate it—break it, so to speak; but does it not require all to lawfully rescind it?

Descending from these general principles, we find the proposition that in legal contemplation the Union is perpetual confirmed by the history of the Union itself. The Union is much older than the Constitution. It was formed, in fact, by the Articles of Association in 1774. It was matured and continued by the Declaration of Independence in 1776. It was further matured, and the faith of all the then thirteen States expressly plighted and engaged that it should be perpetual, by the Articles of Confederation in 1778. And, finally, in 1787 one of the declared objects for ordaining and establishing the Constitution was "to form a more perfect Union."

But if the destruction of the Union by one or by a part only of the States be lawfully possible, the Union is less perfect than before the Constitution, having lost the vital element of perpetuity.

It follows from these views that no State upon its own mere motion can lawfully get out of the Union; that resolves and ordinances to that effect are legally void; and that acts of violence, within any State or States, against the authority of the United States, are insurrectionary or revolutionary, according to circumstances.

I therefore consider that, in view of the Constitution and the laws, the Union is unbroken; and to the extent of my ability I shall take care, as the Constitution itself expressly enjoins upon me, that the laws of the Union be faithfully executed in all the States. Doing this I deem to be only a simple duty on my part; and I shall perform it so far as practicable, unless my rightful masters, the American people, shall withhold the requisite means, or in some authoritative manner direct the contrary. I trust this will not be regarded as a menace, but only as the declared purpose of the Union that it will constitutionally defend and maintain itself.

In doing this there needs to be no bloodshed or violence; and there shall be none, unless it be forced upon the national authority. The power confided to me will be used to hold, occupy, and possess the property and places belonging to the Government, and to collect the duties and imposts; but beyond what may be necessary for these objects, there will be no invasion, no using of force against or among the people anywhere. Where hostility to the United States, in any interior locality, shall be so great and universal as to prevent competent resident citizens from holding the Federal offices, there will be no attempt to force obnoxious strangers among the people for that object. While the strict legal right may exist in the government to enforce the exercise of these offices, the attempt to do so would be so irritating, and so nearly impracticable withal, that I deem it better to forego for the time the uses of such offices.

The mails, unless repelled, will continue to be furnished in all parts of the Union. So far as possible, the people everywhere shall have that sense of perfect security which is most favorable to calm thought and reflection. The course here indicated will be followed unless current events and experience shall show a modification or change to be proper, and in every case and exigency my best discretion will be exercised according to circumstances actually existing, and with a view and a hope of a peaceful solution of the national troubles and the restoration of fraternal sympathies and affections.

That there are persons in one section or another who seek to destroy the Union at all events, and are glad of any pretext to do it, I will neither affirm nor deny; but if there be such, I need address no word to them. To those, however, who really love the Union may I not speak?

Before entering upon so grave a matter as the destruction of our national fabric, with all its benefits, its memories, and its hopes, would it not be wise to ascertain precisely why we do it? Will you hazard so desperate a step while there is any possibility that any portion of the ills you fly from have no real existence? Will you, while the certain ills you fly to are greater than all the real ones you fly from—will you risk the commission of so fearful a mistake?

All profess to be content in the Union if all constitutional rights can be maintained. Is it true, then, that any right, plainly written in the Constitution, has been denied? I think not. Happily the human mind is so constituted that no party can reach to the audacity of doing this. Think, if you can, of a single instance in which a plainly written provision of the Constitution has ever been denied. If by the mere force of numbers a majority should deprive a minority of any clearly written constitutional right, it might, in a moral point of view, justify revolution—certainly would if such a right were a vital one. But such is not our case. All the vital rights of minorities and of individuals are so plainly assured to them by affirmations and negations, guaranties and prohibitions, in the Constitution, that controversies never arise concerning them. But no organic law can ever be framed with a provision specifically applicable to every question which may occur in practical administration. No foresight can anticipate, nor any document of reasonable length contain, express provisions for all possible questions. Shall fugitives from labor be surrendered by national or by State authority? The Constitution does not expressly say. *May* Congress prohibit slavery in the Territories? The Constitution does not expressly say. *Must* Congress protect slavery in the Territories? The Constitution does not expressly say.

From questions of this class spring all our constitutional controversies, and we divide upon them into majorities and minorities. If the minority will not acquiesce, the majority must, or the Government must cease. There is no other alternative; for continuing the Government is acquiescence on one side or the other.

If a minority in such case will secede rather than acquiesce, they make a precedent which in turn will divide and ruin them; for a minority of their own will secede from them whenever a majority refuses to be controlled by such minority. For instance, why may not any portion of a new confederacy a year or two hence arbitrarily secede again, precisely as portions of the present Union now claim to secede from it? All who cherish disunion sentiments are now being educated to the exact temper of doing this.

Is there such perfect identity of interests among the States to compose a new Union as to produce harmony only, and prevent renewed secession?

Plainly, the central idea of secession is the essence of anarchy. A majority held in restraint by constitutional checks and limitations, and always changing easily with deliberate changes of popular opinions and sentiments, is the only true sovereign of a free people. Whoever rejects it does, of necessity, fly to anarchy or to despotism. Unanimity is impossible; the rule of a minority, as a permanent arrangement, is wholly inadmissible; so that, rejecting the majority principle, anarchy or despotism in some form is all that is left.

I do not forget the position assumed by some, that constitutional questions are to be decided by the Supreme Court; nor do I deny that such decisions must be binding, in any case, upon the parties to a suit, as to the object of that suit, while they are also entitled to a very high respect and consideration in all parallel cases by all other departments of the government. And, while it is

obviously possible that such decision may be erroneous in any given case, still the evil effect following it, being limited to that particular case, with the chance that it may be overruled and never become a precedent for other cases, can better be borne than could the evils of a different practice. At the same time, the candid citizen must confess that if the policy of the government, upon vital questions affecting the whole people, is to be irrevocably fixed by decisions of the Supreme Court, the instant they are made, in ordinary litigation between parties in personal actions, the people will have ceased to be their own rulers, having to that extent practically resigned the government into the hands of that eminent tribunal. Nor is there in this view any assault upon the court or the judges. It is a duty from which they may not shrink to decide cases properly brought before them, and it is no fault of theirs if others seek to turn their decisions to political purposes.

One section of our country believes slavery is right, and ought to be extended, while the other believes it is wrong, and ought not to be extended. This is the only substantial dispute. The fugitive slave clause of the Constitution and the law for the suppression of the foreign slave trade are each as well enforced, perhaps, as any law can ever be in a community where the moral sense of the people imperfectly supports the law itself. The great body of the people abide by the dry legal obligation in both cases, and a few break over in each. This, I think, cannot be perfectly cured; and it would be worse in both cases after the separation of the sections than before. The foreign slave trade, now imperfectly suppressed, would be ultimately revived, without restriction, in one section, while fugitive slaves, now only partially surrendered, would not be surrendered at all by the other.

Physically speaking, we cannot separate. We cannot remove our respective sections from each other, nor build an impassable wall between them. A husband and wife may be divorced and go out of the presence and beyond the reach of each other; but the different parts of our country cannot do this. They cannot but remain face to face, and intercourse, either amicable or hostile, must continue between them. Is it possible, then, to make that intercourse more advantageous or more satisfactory after separation than before? Can aliens make treaties easier than friends can make laws? Can treaties be more faithfully enforced between aliens than laws can among friends? Suppose you go to war, you cannot fight always; and when, after much loss on both sides, and no gain on either, you cease fighting, the identical old questions as to terms of intercourse are again upon you.

This country, with its institutions, belongs to the people who inhabit it. Whenever they shall grow weary of the existing government, they can exercise their constitutional right of amending it, or their revolutionary right to dismember or overthrow it. I cannot be ignorant of the fact that many worthy and patriotic citizens are desirous of having the national Constitution amended. While I make no recommendation of amendments, I fully recognize the rightful authority of the people over the whole subject, to be exercised in either of the modes prescribed in the instrument itself, and I should, under existing circumstances, favor rather than oppose a fair opportunity being afforded the people to act upon it. I will venture to add that to me the convention mode seems preferable, in that it allows amendments to originate with the people themselves, instead of only permitting them to take or reject propositions originated by others not especially chosen for the purpose, and which might not be precisely such as they would wish to either accept or refuse. I understand a proposed amendment to the Constitution—which amendment, however, I have not seen—has passed Congress, to the effect that the Federal Government shall never interfere with the domestic institutions of the States, including that of persons held to service. To avoid misconstruction of what I have said, I depart from my purpose not to speak of particular amendments so far as to say that, holding such a provision to now be implied constitutional law, I have no objection to its being made express and irrevocable. . . .

Why should there not be a patient confidence in the ultimate justice of the people? Is there any better or equal hope in the world? In our present differences is either party without faith of being in the right? If the Almighty Ruler of nations, with his eternal truth and justice, be on your side of the North, or on yours of the South, that truth and that justice will surely prevail by the judgment of this great tribunal of the American people.

By the frame of the government under which we live, this same people have wisely given their public servants but little power for mischief; and have, with equal wisdom, provided for the return of that little to their own hands at very short intervals. While the people retain their virtue and vigilance, no administration, by any extreme of wickedness or folly, can very seriously injure the government in the short space of four years.

My countrymen, one and all, think calmly and well upon this whole subject. Nothing valuable can be lost by taking time. If there be an object to hurry any of you in hot haste to a step which you would never take deliberately, that object will be frustrated by taking time; but no good object can be frustrated by it. Such of you as are now dissatisfied still have the old Constitution unimpaired, and, on the sensitive point, the laws of your own framing under it; while the new administration will have no immediate power, if it would, to change either. If it were admitted that you who are dissatisfied hold the right side in the dispute, there still is no single good reason for precipitate action. Intelligence, patriotism, Christianity, and a firm reliance on Him who has never yet forsaken this favored land, are still competent to adjust in the best way all our present difficulty.

In your hands, my dissatisfied fellow-countrymen, and not in mine, is the momentous issue of civil war. The government will not assail you. You can have no conflict without being yourselves the aggressors. You have no oath registered in heaven to destroy the government, while I shall have the most solemn one to "preserve, protect, and defend" it.

I am loath to close. We are not enemies, but friends. We must not be enemies. Though passion may have strained, it must not break, our bonds of affection. The mystic chords of memory, stretching from every battle-field and patriot grave to every living heart and hearthstone all over this broad land, will yet swell the chorus of the Union when again touched, as surely they will be, by the better angels of our nature.

203. DAVIS'S MESSAGE TO CONGRESS
April 29, 1861

(Richardson, ed. *Messages and Papers of the Confederacy,* Vol. I, p. 63 ff.)

Davis called the Confederate Congress together in special session April 29, 1861. In his message he analyzed again the theory of the Union and the logic of secession. In this message he also asked for authority to prosecute the war: in response to his requests Congress at this session authorized him to use all the land and naval force of the Confederacy, to issue letters of marque, raise volunteers, make loans, etc. See, J. Davis, *Rise and Fall of the Confederate Government,* Vol. I, Part IV, ch. iv.

Gentlemen of the Congress. . . .

The declaration of war made against this Confederacy by Abraham Lincoln, the President of the United States, in his proclamation issued on the 15th day of the present month, rendered it necessary, in my judgment, that you should convene at the earliest practicable moment to devise the measures necessary for the defense of the country. The occasion is indeed an extraordinary one. It justifies me in a brief review of the relations heretofore existing between us and the States which now unite in warfare against us and in a succinct statement of the events which have resulted in this warfare, to the end that mankind may pass intelligent and impartial judgment on its motives and objects. During the war waged against Great Britain by her colonies on this continent a common danger impelled them to a close alliance and to the formation of a Confederation, by the terms of which the colonies, styling themselves States, entered *"severally* into a firm league of friendship with each other for their common defense, the security of their liberties, and their mutual and general welfare. binding themselves to assist each other against all force offered to or attacks made upon them, or any of them, on account of religion, sovereignty, trade, or any other pretense whatever." In order to guard against any misconstruction of their compact, the several States made explicit declaration in a distinct article—that *"each* State *retains its* sovereignty, freedom, and independence, and every power, jurisdiction, and right which is not by this Confederation *expressly delegated* to the United States in Congress assembled."

Under this contract of alliance, the war of the Revolution was successfully waged, and resulted in the treaty of peace with Great Britain in 1783, by the terms of which the several States were *each by name* recognized to be independent. The Articles of Confederation contained a clause whereby all alterations were prohibited unless confirmed by the Legislatures of *every State* after being agreed to by the Congress; and in obedience to this provision, under the resolution of Congress of the 21st of February, 1787, the several States appointed delegates who attended a convention "for the *sole and express purpose* of revising the Articles of Confederation and reporting to Congress and the several Legislatures such alterations and provisions therein as shall, when agreed to in Congress *and confirmed by the States,* render the Federal Constitution adequate to the exigencies of Government and the preservation of the Union." It was by the delegates chosen by the *several States* under the resolution just quoted that the Constitution of the United States was framed in 1787 and submitted to the *several States* for ratification, as shown by the seventh article, which is in these words: "The ratification of the *conventions of nine States* shall be sufficient for the establishment of this Constitution *between the States* so ratifying the same." . . . The Constitution of 1787, having, however, omitted the clause already recited from the Articles of Confederation, which provided in explicit terms that each State *retained* its sovereignty and independence, some alarm was felt in the States, when invited to ratify the Constitution, lest this omission should be construed into an abandonment of their cherished principle, and they refused to be satisfied until amendments were added to the Constitution placing beyond any pretense of doubt the reservation by the States of all their sovereign rights and powers not expressly delegated to the United States by the Constitution.

Strange, indeed, must it appear to the impartial observer, but it is none the less true that all these carefully worded clauses proved unavailing to prevent the rise and growth in the Northern States of a political school which has persistently claimed that the government thus formed was not a compact *between* States, but was in effect a national government, set up *above* and *over* the States. An organization created by the States to secure the blessings of liberty and independence against *foreign* aggression, has been gradually perverted into a machine for their control in their *domestic* affairs. The *creature* has been exalted above its *creators;* the *principals* have been made subordinate to the *agent* appointed by themselves. The people of the Southern States, whose almost exclusive occupation was agriculture, early perceived a tendency in the Northern States to render the common government subservient to their own purposes by imposing burdens on commerce as a protection to their manufacturing and shipping interests. . . . By degrees, as the Northern States gained preponderance in the National Congress, self-interest taught their people to yield ready assent to any plausible advocacy of their right as a majority to govern the minority without control. They learned to listen with impatience to the suggestion of any constitutional impediment to the exercise of their will, and so utterly have the principles of the Constitution been corrupted in the Northern mind that, in the inaugural address delivered by President Lincoln in March last, he asserts as an axiom, which he plainly deems to be undeniable, that the theory of the Constitution requires that in all cases the majority shall govern; . . . This is the lamentable and fundamental error on which rests the policy that has culminated in his declaration of war against these Confederate States. In addition to the long-continued and deep-seated resentment felt by the Southern States at the persistent abuse of the powers they had delegated to the Congress, for the purpose of enriching the manufacturing and shipping classes of the North at the expense of the South, there has existed for nearly half a century another subject of discord, involving interests of such transcendent magnitude as at all times to create the apprehension in the minds of many devoted lovers of the Union that its permanence was impossible. When the several States delegated certain powers to the United States Congress, a

large portion of the laboring population consisted of African slaves imported into the colonies by the mother country. In twelve out of the thirteen States negro slavery existed, and the right of property in slaves was protected by law. This property was recognized in the Constitution, and provision was made against its loss by the escape of the slave. The increase in the number of slaves by further importation from Africa was also secured by a clause forbidding Congress to prohibit the slave trade anterior to a certain date, and in no clause can there be found any delegation of power to the Congress authorizing it in any manner to legislate to the prejudice, detriment, or discouragement of the owners of that species of property, or excluding it from the protection of the Government.

The climate and soil of the Northern States soon proved unpropitious to the continuance of slave labor, whilst the converse was the case at the South. Under the unrestricted free intercourse between the two sections, the Northern States consulted their own interests by selling their slaves to the South and prohibiting slavery within their limits. The South were willing purchasers of property suitable to their wants, and paid the price of the acquisition without harboring a suspicion that their quiet possession was to be disturbed by those who were inhibited not only by want of constitutional authority, but by good faith as vendors, from disquieting a title emanating from themselves. As soon, however, as the Northern States that prohibited African slavery within their limits had reached a number sufficient to give their representation a controlling voice in the Congress, a persistent and organized system of hostile measures against the rights of the owners of slaves in the Southern States was inaugurated and gradually extended. A continuous series of measures was devised and prosecuted for the purpose of rendering insecure the tenure of property in slaves. . . . Emboldened by success, the theatre of agitation and aggression against the clearly expressed constitutional rights of the Southern States was transferred to the Congress; Senators and Representatives were sent to the common councils of the nation, whose chief title to this distinction consisted in the display of a spirit of ultra-fanaticism, and whose business was not "to promote the general welfare or insure domestic tranquillity," but to awaken the bitterest hatred against the citizens of sister States, by violent denunciation of their institutions; the transaction of public affairs was impeded by repeated efforts to usurp powers not delegated by the Constitution, for the purpose of impairing the security of property in slaves, and reducing those States which held slaves to a condition of inferiority. Finally a great party was organized for the purpose of obtaining the administration of the Government, with the avowed object of using its power for the total exclusion of the slave States from all participation in the benefits of the public domain acquired by all the States in common, whether by conquest or purchase; of surrounding them entirely by States in which slavery should be prohibited; of those rendering the property in slaves so insecure as to be comparatively worthless, and thereby annihilating in effect property worth thousands of millions of dollars. This party, thus organized, succeeded in the month of November last in the election of its candidate for the Presidency of the United States.

In the meantime, the African slaves had augmented in number from about 600,000, at the date of the adoption of the constitutional compact, to upward of 4,000,000. In moral and social condition they had been elevated from brutal savages into docile, intelligent, and civilized agricultural laborers, and supplied not only with bodily comforts but with careful religious instruction. Under the supervision of a superior race their labor had been so directed as not only to allow a gradual and marked amelioration of their own condition, but to convert hundreds of thousands of square miles of the wilderness into cultivated lands covered with a prosperous people; towns and cities had sprung into existence, and had rapidly increased in wealth and population under the social system of the South; the white population of the Southern slave-holding States had augmented from about 1,250,000 at the date of the adoption of the Constitution to more than 8,500,000, in 1860; and the productions in the South of cotton, rice, sugar, and tobacco, for the full development and continuance of which the labor of African slaves was and is indispensable, had swollen to an amount which formed nearly three-fourths of the exports of the whole United States and had become absolutely necessary to the wants of civilized man. With interests of such overwhelming magnitude imperiled, the people of the Southern States were driven by the conduct of the North to the adoption of some course of action to avert the danger with which they were openly menaced. With this view the Legislatures of the several States invited the people to select delegates to conventions to be held for the purpose of determining for themselves what measures were best adapted to meet so alarming a crisis in their history. Here it may be proper to observe that from a period as early as 1798 there had existed in *all* of the States of the Union a party almost uninterruptedly in the majority based upon the creed that each State was, in the last resort, the sole judge as well of its wrongs as of the mode and measure of redress. . . .

. . . In the exercise of a right so ancient, so well-established, and so necessary for self-preservation, the people of the Confederate States, in their conventions, determined that the wrongs which they had suffered and the evils with which they were menaced required that they should revoke the delegation of powers to the Federal Government which they had ratified in their several conventions. They consequently passed ordinances resuming all their rights as sovereign and independent States and dissolved their connection with the other States of the Union.

Having done this, they proceeded to form a new compact amongst themselves by new articles of confederation, which have been also ratified by the conventions of the several States with an approach to unanimity far exceeding that of the conventions which adopted the Constitution of 1787. They have organized their new Government in all its departments; the functions of the executive, legislative, and judicial magistrates are performed in accordance with the will of the people, as displayed not merely in a cheerful acquiescence, but in the enthusiastic support of the Government thus established by themselves; and but for the interference of the Government of the United States in this legitimate exercise of the right of a people to self-government, peace, happiness, and prosperity would now smile on our land. . . .

Jefferson Davis.

204. SEWARD'S PLAN TO AVERT CIVIL WAR
April 1, 1861

(Writings of Abraham Lincoln, Constitutional ed., Vol. V, p. 278 ff.)

Seward was one of the founders of the Republican Party and the most prominent of the candidates for the Republican nomination in 1860. He looked upon his appointment to the first place in the Cabinet as nothing more than his due, and entertained the idea of dominating the Presidential policy. "Seward," said Gideon Welles, "liked to be called premier". His "Thoughts for the President's Consideration" were intended to establish his dominance over the President: Lincoln's reply was a masterly rebuke, which did not alienate the Secretary of State. The best biography of Seward is F. Bancroft, *Life of William H. Seward,* 2 vols.; see especially Vol. II, chs. xxviii, xxix. See also, C. E. Macartney, *Lincoln and His Cabinet,* ch. v.; G. Bradford, *Union Portraits,* ch. vii.

Some Thoughts for the President's Consideration, April 1, 1861.

First. We are at the end of a month's administration, and yet without a policy either domestic or foreign.

Second. This, however, is not culpable, and it has even been unavoidable. The presence of the Senate, with the need to meet applications for patronage, have prevented attention to other and more grave matters.

Third. But further delay to adopt and prosecute our policies for both domestic and foreign affairs would not only bring scandal on the administration, but danger upon the country.

Fourth. To do this we must dismiss the applicants for office. But how? I suggest that we make the local appointments forthwith, leaving foreign or general ones for ulterior and occasional action.

Fifth. The policy at home. I am aware that my views are singular, and perhaps not sufficiently explained. My system is built upon this idea as a ruling one, namely, that we must

CHANGE THE QUESTION BEFORE THE PUBLIC FROM ONE UPON SLAVERY, OR ABOUT SLAVERY, for a question upon UNION OR DISUNION:

In other words, from what would be regarded as a party question, to one of patriotism or union.

The occupation or evacuation of Fort Sumter, although not in fact a slavery or a party question, is so regarded. Witness the temper manifested by the Republicans in the free States, and even by the Union men in the South.

I would therefore terminate it as a safe means for changing the issue. I deem it fortunate that the last administration created the necessity.

For the rest, I would simultaneously defend and reinforce all the ports in the gulf, and have the navy recalled from foreign stations to be prepared for a blockade. Put the island of Key West under martial law.

This will raise distinctly the question of union or disunion. I would maintain every fort and possession in the South.

FOR FOREIGN NATIONS

I would demand explanations from Spain and France, categorically, at once.

I would seek explanations from Great Britain and Russia, and send agents into Canada, Mexico, and Central America to rouse a vigorous continental spirit of independence on this continent against European intervention.

And, if satisfactory explanations are not received from Spain and France,

Would convene Congress and declare war against them.

But whatever policy we adopt, there must be an energetic prosecution of it.

For this purpose it must be somebody's business to pursue and direct it incessantly.

Either the President must do it himself, and be all the while active in it, or

Devolve it on some member of his Cabinet. Once adopted, debates on it must end, and all agree and abide.

It is not in my especial province;

But I neither seek to evade nor assume responsibility.

REPLY TO SECRETARY SEWARD'S MEMORANDUM

Executive Mansion, April 1, 1861.
HON. W. H. SEWARD.

MY DEAR SIR:—Since parting with you I

have been considering your paper dated this day, and entitled "Some Thoughts for the President's Consideration." The first proposition in it is, *"First,* We are at the end of a month's administration, and yet without a policy either domestic or foreign."

At the beginning of that month, in the inaugural, I said: "The power confided to me will be used to hold, occupy, and possess the property and places belonging to the Government, and to collect the duties and imposts." This had your distinct approval at the time; and, taken in connection with the order I immediately gave General Scott, directing him to employ every means in his power to strengthen and hold the forts, comprises the exact domestic policy you now urge, with the single exception that it does not propose to abandon Fort Sumter.

Again, I do not perceive how the reinforcement of Fort Sumter would be done on a slavery or a party issue, while that of Fort Pickens would be on a more national and patriotic one.

The news received yesterday in regard to St. Domingo certainly brings a new item within the range of our foreign policy; but up to that time we have been preparing circulars and instructions to ministers and the like, all in perfect harmony, without even a suggestion that we had no foreign policy.

Upon your closing propositions—that "whatever policy we adopt, there must be an energetic prosecution of it.

"For this purpose it must be somebody's business to pursue and direct it incessantly.

"Either the President must do it himself, and be all the while active in it, or

"Devolve it on some member of his Cabinet. Once adopted, debates on it must end, and all agree and abide"—I remark that if this must be done, I must do it. When a general line of policy is adopted, I apprehend there is no danger of its being changed without good reason, or continuing to be a subject of unnecessary debate; still, upon points arising in its progress I wish, and suppose I am entitled to have, the advice of all the Cabinet.

Your obedient servant,
A. LINCOLN.

205. LINCOLN'S MESSAGE TO CONGRESS IN SPECIAL SESSION
July 4, 1861

(Richardson, ed. *Messages and Papers,* Vol. VI, p. 20 ff.)

By proclamation of April 15, 1861, Lincoln called Congress to meet in special session July 4, 1861. In the intervening period Lincoln had strained the executive authority in his effort to suppress the rebellion. The special session message informed Congress of the steps that the executive had taken and made specific recommendations for the grant of additional powers. It presented too, in a more elaborate form than the Inaugural Address, Lincoln's conception of the significance of the struggle for the preservation of the Union.

FELLOW-CITIZENS OF THE SENATE AND HOUSE OF REPRESENTATIVES:—Having been convened on an extraordinary occasion, as authorized by the Constitution, your attention is not called to any ordinary subject of legislation.

At the beginning of the present Presidential term, four months ago, the functions of the Federal Government were found to be generally suspended within the several States of South Carolina, Georgia, Alabama, Mississippi, Louisiana, and Florida, excepting only those of the Post-office Department. . . .

. . . The purpose to sever the Federal Union was openly avowed. In accordance with this purpose, an ordinance had been adopted in each of these States, declaring the States respectively to be separated from the national Union. A formula for instituting a combined government of these States had been promulgated; and this illegal organization, in the character of confederate States, was already invoking recognition, aid, and intervention from foreign powers. . . .

And this issue embraces more than the fate of these United States. It presents to the whole family of man the question whether a constitutional republic or democracy—a government of the people by the same people —can or cannot maintain its territorial integrity against its own domestic foes. It presents the question whether discontented individuals, too few in number to control administration according to organic laws in any case, can always, upon the pretenses made in this case, or on any other pretenses, or arbitrarily without any pretense, break up their government, and thus practically put an end to free government upon the earth. It forces us to ask: Is there in all republics this inherent and fatal weakness? Must a government, of necessity, be too strong for the liberties of its own people, or too weak to maintain its own existence?

So viewing the issue, no choice was left but to call out the war power of the government, and so to resist force employed for its destruction by force for its preservation. . . .

The forbearance of this government had been so extraordinary and so long continued as to lead some foreign nations to shape their action as if they supposed the early destruction of our national Union was probable. While this, on discovery, gave the executive some concern, he is now happy to say that the sovereignty and rights of the United States are now everywhere practically respected by foreign powers; and a general sympathy with the country is manifested throughout the world. . . .

It might seem, at first thought, to be of little difference whether the present movement at the South be called "secession" or "rebellion." The movers, however, well understand the difference. At the beginning they knew they could never raise their treason to any respectable magnitude by any name which implies violation of law. They knew their people possessed as much of moral sense, as much of devotion to law and order, and as much pride in and reverence for the history and government of their common country as any other civilized and patriotic people. They knew they could make no advancement directly in the teeth of these strong and noble sentiments. Accordingly, they commenced by an insidious debauching of the public mind. They invented an ingenious sophism which, if conceded, was followed by perfectly logical steps, through all the incidents, to the complete destruction of the Union. The sophism itself is that any State of the Union may consistently with the national Constitution, and therefore lawfully and peacefully, withdraw from the Union without the consent of the Union or of any other State. . . .

This sophism derives much, perhaps the whole, of its currency from the assumption that there is some omnipotent and sacred supremacy pertaining to a State—to each State of our Federal Union. Our States have neither more nor less power than that reserved to them in the Union by the Constitution—no one of them ever having been a State out of the Union. The original ones passed into the Union even before they cast off their British colonial dependence; and the new ones each came into the Union directly from a condition of dependence, excepting Texas. And even Texas in its temporary independence was never designated a State. The new ones only took the designation of States on coming into the Union, while that name was first adopted for the old ones in and by the Declaration of Independence. . . . Having never been States either in substance or in name outside of the Union, whence this magical omnipotence of "State rights," asserting a claim of power to lawfully destroy the Union itself? Much is said about the "sovereignty" of the States; but the word even is not in the national Constitution, nor, as is believed, in any of the State constitutions. What is "sovereignty" in the political sense of the term? Would it be far wrong to define it as "a political community without a political superior"? Tested by this, no one of our States except Texas ever was a sovereignty. . . . The States have their status in the Union, and they have no other legal status. If they break from this, they can only do so against law and by revolution. The Union, and not themselves separately, procured their independence and their liberty. By conquest or purchase the Union gave each of them whatever of independence or liberty it has. The Union is older than any of the States, and, in fact, it created them as States. Originally some dependent colonies made the Union, and, in turn, the Union threw off their old dependence for them, and made them States, such as they are. Not one of them ever had a State constitution independent of the Union. Of course, it is not forgotten that all the new States framed their constitutions before they entered the Union—nevertheless, dependent upon and preparatory to coming into the Union. . . .

What is now combated is the position that secession is consistent with the Constitution —is lawful and peaceful. It is not contended that there is any express law for it; and nothing should ever be implied as law which leads to unjust or absurd consequences. . . .

The seceders insist that our Constitution admits of secession. They have assumed to make a national constitution of their own, in which of necessity they have either discarded or retained the right of secession as they insist it exists in ours. If they have discarded it, they thereby admit that on principle it ought not to be in ours. If they have retained it, by their own construction of ours, they show that to be consistent they must secede from one another whenever they shall find it the easiest way of settling their debts, or effecting any other selfish or unjust object. The principle itself is one of disintegration and upon which no government can possibly endure. . . .

It may well be questioned whether there is to-day a majority of the legally qualified voters of any State except perhaps South Carolina in favor of disunion. There is much reason to believe that the Union men are the majority in many, if not in every other one, of the so-called seceded States. . . .

This is essentially a people's contest. On the side of the Union it is a struggle for maintaining in the world that form and substance of government whose leading object is to elevate the condition of men—to lift artificial weights from all shoulders; to clear the paths of laudable pursuit for all; to afford all an unfettered start, and a fair chance in the race of life. Yielding to partial and temporary departures, from necessity, this is the leading object of the government for whose existence we contend. . . .

Our popular government has often been called an experiment. Two points in it our people have already settled—the successful establishing and the successful administering of it. One still remains—its successful maintenance against a formidable internal attempt to overthrow it. It is now for them to demonstrate to the world that those who can fairly carry an election can also suppress a rebellion; that ballots are the rightful and peaceful successors of bullets; and that when ballots have fairly and constitutionally decided, there can be no successful appeal back to bullets; that there can be no successful appeal, except to ballots themselves, at succeeding elections. Such will be a great lesson of peace: teaching men that what they cannot take by an election, neither can they take it by war; teaching all the folly of being the beginners of a war. . . .

206. THE CRITTENDEN–JOHNSON RESOLUTIONS ON THE OBJECTS OF THE WAR
July, 1861
(Richardson, ed. *Messages and Addresses,* Vol. VI, p. 430)

These resolutions represented a conservative attitude toward the South and the objects of the war that shortly disappeared. The Crittenden Resolutions passed the House, July 22, 1861, with only two dissenting votes; the Johnson Resolutions passed the Senate July 25 with five dissenting votes.

THE CRITTENDEN RESOLUTIONS

Resolved by the House of Representatives of the Congress of the United States, That the present deplorable civil war has been forced upon the country by the disunionists of the Southern States now in revolt against the constitutional Government and in arms around the capital; that in this national emergency Congress, banishing all feelings of mere passion or resentment, will recollect only its duty to the whole country; that this war is not waged upon our part in any spirit of oppression, nor for any purpose of conquest or subjugation, nor purpose of overthrowing or interfering with the rights or established institutions of those States, but to defend and maintain the supremacy of the Constitution and to preserve the Union, with all the dignity, equality, and rights of the several States unimpaired; and that as soon as these objects are accomplished the war ought to cease.

THE JOHNSON RESOLUTIONS

Resolved, That the present deplorable civil war has been forced upon the country by the disunionists of the Southern States now in revolt against the constitutional Government and in arms around the capital; that in this national emergency Congress, banishing all feeling of mere passion or resentment, will recollect only its duty to the whole country; that this war is not prosecuted upon our part in any spirit of oppression, nor for any purpose of conquest or subjugation, nor purpose of overthrowing or interfering with the rights or established institutions of those States, but to defend and maintain the supremacy of the Constitution and all laws made in pursuance thereof and to preserve the Union, with all the dignity, equality, and rights of the several States unimpaired; that as soon as these objects are accomplished the war ought to cease.

207. GENERAL BUTLER'S "CONTRABANDS"

Report of General Butler to the Secretary of War July 30, 1861

(F. Moore, ed. *The Rebellion Record,* Vol. II, p. 437)

The problem of the refugee slaves was one of the most perplexing which the Government had to face. General Butler, commanding at Fortress Monroe, took matters into his own hands, and treated fugitive or captured slaves as "contraband of war". For a somewhat different solution, see Frémont's Proclamation, Doc. No. 208. The fairest discussion of Butler is in C. R. Fish's article in the *Dictionary of American Biography,* Vol. III.

Head-quarters Department of Virginia,
Fortress Monroe, July 30, 1861.
Hon. Simon Cameron, Secretary of War:—
SIR: . . . In the village of Hampton there were a large number of negroes, composed in a great measure of women and children of the men who had fled thither within my lines for protection, who had escaped from maurauding parties of rebels who had been gathering up able-bodied blacks to aid them in constructing their batteries on the James and York Rivers. I have employed the men in Hampton in throwing up intrenchments, and they were working zealously and efficiently at that duty, saving our soldiers from that labor under the gleam of the mid-day sun. The women were earning substantially their own subsistence in washing, marketing, and taking care of the clothes of the soldiers, and rations were being served out to the men who worked for the support of the children. But by the evacuation of Hampton, rendered necessary by the withdrawal of troops, leaving me scarcely 5,000 men outside the Fort, including the force at Newport News, all these black people were obliged to break up their homes at Hampton, fleeing across the creek within my lines for protection and support. Indeed, it was a most distressing sight to see these poor creatures, who had trusted to the protection of the arms of the United States, and who aided the troops of the United States in their enterprise, to be thus obliged to flee from their homes, and the homes of their masters who had deserted them, and become fugitives from fear of the return of the rebel soldiery, who had threatened to shoot the men who had wrought for us, and to carry off the women who had served us, to a worse than Egyptian bondage. I have, therefore, now within the Peninsula, this side of Hampton Creek, 900 negroes, 300 of whom are able-bodied men, 30 of whom are men substantially past hard labor, 175 women, 225 children under the age of 10 years, and 170 between 10 and 18 years, and many more coming in. The questions which this state of facts presents are very embarrassing.

First, What shall be done with them? and, *Second,* What is their state and condition?

Upon these questions I desire the instructions of the Department.

The first question, however, may perhaps be answered by considering the last. Are these men, women, and children, slaves? Are they free? Is their condition that of men, women, and children, or of property, or is it a mixed relation? What their *status* was under the Constitution and laws, we all know. What has been the effect of rebellion and a state of war upon that *status?* When I adopted the theory of treating the able-bodied negro fit to work in the trenches as property liable to be used in aid of rebellion, and so contraband of war, that condition of things was in so far met, as I then and still believe, on a legal and constitutional basis. But now a new series of questions arises. Passing by women, the children, certainly, cannot be treated on that basis; if property, they must be considered the incumbrance rather than the auxiliary of an army, and, of course, in no possible legal relation could be treated as contraband. Are they property? If they were so, they have been left by their masters and owners, deserted, thrown away, abandoned, like the wrecked vessel upon the ocean. Their former possessors and owners have causelessly, traitorously, rebelliously, and, to carry out the figure, practically abandoned them to be swallowed up by the winter storm of starvation. If property, do they not become the property of the salvors? but we, their salvors, do not need and will not hold such property, and will assume no such ownership: has not, therefore, all proprietary relation ceased? Have they not become, thereupon, men, women, and children? No longer under ownership of any kind, the fearful relicts of fugitive masters, have they not by their mas-

ters' acts, and the state of war, assumed the condition, which we hold to be the normal one, of those made in God's image? Is not every constitutional, legal, and moral requirement, as well to the runaway master as their relinquished slaves, thus answered? I confess that my own mind is compelled by this reasoning to look upon them as men and women. If not free born, yet free, manumitted, sent forth from the hand that held them never to be reclaimed. . . .

In a loyal State I would put down a servile insurrection. In a state of rebellion I would confiscate that which was used to oppose my arms, and take all that property, which constituted the wealth of that State, and furnished the means by which the war is prosecuted, beside being the cause of the war; and if, in so doing, it should be objected that human beings were brought to the free enjoyment of life, liberty, and the pursuit of happiness, such objection might not require much consideration.

Pardon me for addressing the Secretary of War directly upon this question, as it involves some political considerations as well as propriety of military action. I am, sir, your obedient servant,

BENJAMIN F. BUTLER.

208. FRÉMONT'S PROCLAMATION ON SLAVES
St. Louis, August 30, 1861

(F. Moore, ed. *The Rebellion Record*, Vol. III, p. 33)

John Charles Frémont, too popular a figure to ignore, was placed in charge of the Department of the West. An ardent abolitionist, he declared martial law and issued the proclamation of August 30 confiscating the property and emancipating the slaves of rebels. While this action inspired applause from the abolitionists, it seriously embarrassed the administration, and Lincoln was forced largely to countermand it. On Frémont, see, A. Nevins, *Frémont*, ch. xxx–xxxi; C. Goodwin, *J. C. Frémont*, ch. xii.

Head-quarters Western Department.
St. Louis, Aug, 30, 1861.

CIRCUMSTANCES in my judgment are of sufficient urgency to render it necessary that the commanding General of this department should assume the administrative powers of the State. Its disorganized condition, helplessness of civil authority and the total in-

security of life, and devastation of property by bands of murderers and marauders, who infest nearly every county in the State, and avail themselves of public misfortunes, in the vicinity of a hostile force, to gratify private and neighborhood vengeance, and who find an enemy wherever they find plunder, finally demand the severest measures to repress the daily increasing crimes and outrages, which are driving off the inhabitants and ruining the State.

In this condition, the public safety and success of our arms require unity of purpose, without let or hindrance to the prompt administration of affairs. In order, therefore, to suppress disorders, maintain the public peace, and give security to the persons and property of loyal citizens, I do hereby extend and declare established martial law throughout the State of Missouri. The lines of the army occupation in this State are for the present declared to extend from Leavenworth, by way of posts of Jefferson City, Rolla, and Ironton, to Cape Girardeau on the Mississippi River. All persons who shall be taken with arms in their hands within these lines shall be tried by court-martial, and if found guilty, will be shot. Real and personal property of those who shall take up arms against the United States, or who shall be directly proven to have taken an active part with their enemies in the field, is declared confiscated to public use, and their slaves, if any they have, are hereby declared free men.

All persons who shall be proven to have destroyed, after the publication of this order, railroad tracks, bridges, or telegraph lines, shall suffer the extreme penalty of the law. All persons engaged in treasonable correspondence, in giving or procuring aid to the enemy, in fermenting turmoil, and disturbing public tranquillity, by creating or circulating false reports, or incendiary documents, are warned that they are exposing themselves.

All persons who have been led away from allegiance, are required to return to their homes forthwith. Any such absence without sufficient cause, will be held to be presumptive evidence against them. The object of this declaration is to place in the hands of military authorities power to give instantaneous effect to the existing laws, and supply such deficiencies as the conditions of the war demand; but it is not intended to suspend the ordinary tribunals of the country, where law will be administered by civil officers in the usual manner, and with their customary authority, while the same can be peaceably administered.

The commanding General will labor vigilantly for the public welfare, and, by his efforts for their safety, hopes to obtain not only acquiescence, but the active support of the people of the country.

J. C. FREMONT,
Major-General Commanding.

209. EX PARTE MERRYMAN
17 Federal Cases, 144.
1861

Circuit Court, District of Maryland. Petition for a writ of *habeas corpus.* John Merryman a citizen of Baltimore, Maryland, was arrested by order of General Keim, and imprisoned at Fort McHenry. No ground having been shown for his arrest, Chief Justice Taney authorized a writ of *habeas corpus,* commanding General Cadwalader in command of Fort McHenry to deliver up the prisoner. General Cadwalader, stating that he was acting under the authority of the President, refused to respect the writ. The Chief Justice then cited him for contempt of court, but the General refused to receive the writ of contempt. It was under these circumstances that the Chief Justice filed the following opinion. For a reply to the argument of the court, see the opinion of the Hon. Reverdy Johnson, in F. Moore, ed. *The Rebellion Record,* Vol. II, p. 185 ff. For a discussion of the case see Warren, *Supreme Court,* ch. xxviii; S. Klaus, ed. *The Milligan Case,* Introduction; J. G. Randall, *Constitutional Problems Under Lincoln;* B. C. Steiner, *Life of Roger Brooke Taney;* G. C. Sellery, *Lincoln's Suspension of Habeas Corpus,* University of Wisconsin, Bull. No. 149.

TANEY, C. J. The application in this case for a writ of *habeas corpus* is made to me under the 14th section of the Judiciary Act of 1789, which renders effectual for the citizen the constitutional privilege of the writ of *habeas corpus.* That act gives to the Courts of the United States, as well as to each justice of the Supreme Court, and to every District Judge, power to grant writs of *habeas corpus* for the purpose of an inquiry into the cause of commitment. The petition was presented to me at Washington, under the impression that I would order the prisoner to be brought before me there, but as he was confined in Fort McHenry, at the City of Baltimore, which is in my circuit, I resolved to hear it in the latter city, as obedience to the writ, under such circumstances, would not withdraw Gen. Cadwalader who had him in charge from the limits of his military command. . . .

A copy of the warrant or order, under which the prisoner was arrested, was demanded by his counsel, and refused. And it is not alleged in the return that any specific act, constituting an offence against the laws of the United States, has been charged against him upon oath; but he appears to have been arrested upon general charges of treason and rebellion, without proof, and without giving the names of the witnesses, or specifying the acts, which in the judgement of the military officer, constituted the crime. And having the prisoner thus in custody on these vague and unsupported accusations, he refuses to obey the writ of *habeas corpus*, upon the ground that he is duly authorized by the President to suspend it.

The case, then, is simply this: A military officer residing in Pennsylvania issues an order to arrest a citizen of Maryland, upon vague and indefinite charges, without any proof, so far as appears. Under this order his house is entered in the night; he is seized as a prisoner, and conveyed to Fort McHenry, and there kept in close confinement. And when a *habeas corpus* is served on the commanding officer, requiring him to produce the prisoner before a justice of the Supreme Court, in order that he may examine into the legality of the imprisonment, the answer of the officer is that he is authorized by the President to suspend the writ of *habeas corpus* at his discretion, and, in the exercise of that discretion, suspends it in this case, and on that ground refuses obedience to the writ.

As the case comes before me, therefore, I understand that the President not only claims the right to suspend the writ of *habeas corpus* himself, at his discretion, but to delegate that discretionary power to a military officer, and to leave it to him to determine whether he will or will not obey judicial process that may be served upon him.

No official notice has been given to the Courts of Justice, or to the public, by proclamation or otherwise, that the President claimed this power and had exercised it in the matter stated in the return. And I certainly listened to it with some surprise, for I had supposed it to be one of those points of constitutional law upon which there was no difference of opinion, and that it was admitted on all hands that the privilege of the writ could not be suspended except by act of Congress. . . .

The clause in the Constitution which authorizes the suspension of the privilege of the writ of *habeas corpus* is in the ninth section of the first article.

This article is devoted to the Legislative Department of the United States, and has not the slightest reference to the Executive Department. It begins by providing "that all legislative powers therein granted shall be vested in a Congress of the United States. . . ." After prescribing the manner in which these two branches of the Legislative department shall be chosen, it proceeds to enumerate specifically the legislative powers which it thereby grants and legislative powers which it expressly prohibits, and at the conclusion of this specification, a clause is inserted giving Congress "the power to make all laws which may be necessary and proper for carrying into execution the foregoing powers, and all other powers vested by this Constitution in the Government of the United States or in any department or office thereof."

The power of legislation granted by this latter clause is by its word carefully confined to the specific objects before enumerated. But as this limitation was unavoidably somewhat indefinite, it was deemed necessary to guard more effectively certain great cardinal principles essential to the liberty of the citizen and to the rights and equality of the States by denying to Congress, in express terms, any power of legislation over them. It was apprehended, it seems, that such legislation might be attempted under the pretext that it was necessary and proper to carry into execution the powers granted; and it was determined that there should be no room to doubt, where rights of such vital importance were concerned, and accordingly this clause is immediately followed by an enumeration of certain subjects to which the powers of legislation shall not extend; and the great importance which the framers of the Constitution attached to the privilege of the writ of *habeas corpus* to protect the liberty of the citizen, is proved by the fact that its suspension, except in cases of invasion and rebellion, is first in the list of prohibited power; and even in these cases the power is denied and its exercise prohibited unless the public safety shall require it. It is true that in the cases mentioned Congress is of necessity to judge whether the public safety does or does not require it; and its judgement is conclusive.

But the introduction of these words is a standing admonition to the legislative body of the danger of suspending it and of the extreme caution they should exercise before they give the Government of the United States such power over the liberty of a citizen.

It is the second Article of the Constitution that provides for the organization of the Executive Department, and enumerates the powers conferred on it, and prescribes its duties. And if the high power over the liberty of the citizens now claimed was intended to be conferred on the President, it would undoubtedly be found in plain words in this article. But there is not a word in it that can furnish the slightest ground to justify the exercise of the power. . . .

And the only power, therefore, which the President possesses, where the "life, liberty and property" of a private citizen is concerned, is the power and duties prescribed in the third section of the Second Article which requires, "that he shall take care that the laws be faithfully executed." He is not authorized to execute them himself, or through agents or officers, civil or military, appointed by himself, but he is to take care that they be faithfully carried into execution as they are expounded and adjudged by the co-ordinate branch of the government, to which that duty is assigned by the Constitution. It is thus made his duty to come in aid of the judicial authority, if it shall be resisted by force too strong to be overcome without the assistance of the Executive arm. But in exercising this power, he acts in subordination to judicial authority, assisting it to execute its process and enforce its judgements.

With such provisions in the Constitution, expressed in language too clear to be misunderstood by anyone, I can see no ground whatever for supposing that the President in any emergency or in any state of things can authorize the suspension of the privilege of the writ of *habeas corpus,* or arrest a citizen except in aid of the judicial power. He certainly does not faithfully execute the laws if he takes upon himself legislative power by suspending the writ of *habeas corpus*—and the judicial power, also, by arresting and imprisoning a person without due process of law. Nor can any argument be drawn from the

nature of sovereignty, or the necessities of government for self-defence, in times of tumult and danger. The Government of the United States is one of delegated and limited powers. It derives its existence and authority altogether from the Constitution, and neither of its branches—executive, legislative, or judicial—can exercise any of the powers of government beyond those specified and granted. . . .

To guide me to a right conclusion, I have the Commentaries on the Constitution of the United States of the late Mr. Justice Story . . . and also the clear and authoritative decision of (the Supreme) Court, given more than a half century since, and conclusively establishing the principles I have above stated. Mr. Story, speaking in his Commentaries of the *habeas corpus* clause in the Constitution, says:

"It is obvious that cases of a peculiar emergency may arise, which may justify, nay, even require, the temporary suspension of any right to the writ. . . . Hitherto no suspension of the writ has ever been authorized by Congress since the establishment of the Constitution. It would seem, as the power is given to Congress to suspend the writ of *habeas corpus* in cases of rebellion or invasion, that the right to judge whether the exigency had arisen must exclusively belong to that body". *Commentaries,* section 1,336.

And Chief Justice Marshall, in delivering the opinion of the Supreme Court in the case *ex parte* Bollman and Swartwout, uses this decisive language, in 4 Cranch, 101:

"If at any time the public safety should require the suspension of the powers vested by this act in the courts of the United States, it is for the Legislature to say so. That question depends on political considerations, on which the Legislature is to decide. Until the legislative will be expressed, this court can only see its duty, and must obey the laws."

I can add nothing to these clear and emphatic words of my great predecessor.

But the documents before me show that the military authority in this case has gone far beyond the mere suspension of the privilege of the writ of *habeas corpus.* It has, by force of arms, thrust aside the judicial authorities and officers to whom the Constitution has confided the power and duty of interpreting and administering the laws, and substituted a military government in its place, to be administered and executed by military officers. . . .

The Constitution provides, as I have before said, that "no person shall be deprived of life, liberty, or property without due process of law". It declares that "the right of the people to be secure in their persons, houses, papers, and effects against unreasonable searches and seizures shall not be violated, and no warrant shall issue but upon probable cause, supported by oath or affirmation, and particularly describing the place to be searched and the persons or things to be seized." It provides that the party accused shall be entitled to a speedy trial in a court of justice.

And these great and fundamental laws, which Congress itself could not suspend, have been disregarded and suspended, like the writ of *habeas corpus*, by a military order, supported by force of arms. Such is the case now before me; and I can only say that if the authority which the Constitution has confided to the judiciary department and judicial officers may thus upon any pretext or under any circumstances be usurped by the military power at its discretion, the people of the United States are no longer living under a Government of laws, but every citizen holds life, liberty, and property at the will and pleasure of the army officer in whose military district he may happen to be found.

In such a case my duty was too plain to be mistaken. I have exercised all the power which the Constitution and laws confer on me, but that power has been resisted by a force too strong for me to overcome. It is possible that the officer who had incurred this grave responsibility may have misunderstood his instructions, and exceeded the authority intended to be given him. I shall therefore order all the proceedings in this case, with my opinion, to be filed and recorded in the Circuit Court of the United States for the District of Maryland, and direct the clerk to transmit a copy . . . to the President of the United States. It will then remain for that high officer, in fulfillment of his constitutional obligation to "take care that the laws be faithfully executed" to determine what measure he will take to cause the civil process of the United States to be respected and enforced.

R. B. Taney

210. SECESSION OF KENTUCKY
November 20, 1861

(F. Moore, ed. *The Rebellion Record,* Vol. XII, p. 164–5)

The regularly elected legislature of Kentucky, after first attempting to maintain neutrality, eventually pledged the loyalty of the State to the Union, and provided for the expulsion of Confederate troops from the State. The Kentucky soldiers in the Confederate Army, however, called a convention to meet at Russellville, November 18, 1861. This convention drew up the following declaration of independence, and took steps to bring Kentucky into the Confederacy. See, W. C. Goodloe, *Kentucky Unionists of 1861;* E. C. Smith, *The Borderland in the Civil War,* chs. ix, xi; N. S. Shaler, *Kentucky;* T. Speed, *The Union Cause in Kentucky.*

DECLARATION OF INDEPENDENCE AND ORDINANCE OF SEPARATION

Whereas, The Federal Constitution, which created the Government of the United States, was declared by the framers thereof to be the supreme law of the land, and was intended to limit, and did expressly limit, the powers of said Government to certain general specified purposes, and did expressly reserve to the States and people all other powers whatever, and the President and Congress have treated this supreme law of the Union with contempt, and usurped to themselves the power to interfere with the rights and liberties of the States and the people, against the express provisions of the Constitution, and have thus substituted for the highest forms of rational liberty and constitutional government a central despotism, founded upon the ignorant prejudices of the masses of Northern society, and instead of giving protection, with the Constitution, to the people of fifteen States of the Union, have turned loose upon them the unrestrained and raging passions of mobs and fanatics; and because we now seek to hold our liberties, our property, our homes.

and our families, under the protection of the reserved powers of the States, have blockaded our ports, invaded our soil, and waged war upon our people, for the purpose of subjugating us to their will;

And whereas, Our own honor and our duty to posterity demand that we shall not relinquish our own liberty, and shall not abandon the rights of our descendants and the world to the inestimable blessings of constitutional government, therefore,

Be it ordained, That we do hereby forever sever our connection with the Government of the United States, and in the name of the people we do hereby declare Kentucky to be a free and independent State, clothed with all the power to fix her own destiny, and to secure her own rights and liberties.

And whereas, The majority of the Legislature of Kentucky have violated their most solemn pledges made before the election, and deceived and betrayed the people; have abandoned the position of neutrality assumed by themselves and the people, and invited into the State the organized armies of Lincoln; have abdicated the Government in favor of the military despotism which they have placed around themselves, but cannot control, and have abandoned the duty of shielding the citizen with their protection; have thrown upon our people and the State the horrors and ravages of war, instead of attempting to preserve the peace; and have voted men and money for the war waged by the North for the destruction of our constitutional rights;

have violated the express words of the Constitution, by borrowing five millions of money for the support of the war, without a vote of the people; have permitted the arrest and imprisonment of our citizens, and transferred the constitutional prerogatives of the executive to a military commission of partisans; have seen the writ of *habeas corpus* suspended, without an effort for its preservation, and permitted our people to be driven in exile from their homes; have subjected our proprty to confiscation, and our persons to confinement in the penitentiary as felons, because we may choose to take part in a contest for civil liberty and constitutional government against a sectional majority, waging war against the people and institutions of thirteen States of the old Federal Union, and have done all these things deliberately, against the warnings and voice of the Governor, and the solemn remonstrances of the minority in the Senate and House of Representatives; therefore,

Be it further ordained, That the unconstitutional edicts of a factious majority of a Legislature, thus false to their pledges, their honor, and their interests, are not law, and that such a Government is unworthy of the support of a brave and free people; and we do hereby declare, that the people are absolved from all allegiance to said Government, and have the right to establish any government which to them may seem best adapted to the preservation of their rights and liberties. . . .

211. COMPENSATED EMANCIPATION

Extracts from Lincoln's Messages to Congress Recommending Compensated Emancipation
1862

(Richardson, ed. *Messages and Papers,* Vol. VI, p. 68 ff., 126 ff.)

Until the very end of the War Lincoln urged on Congress, and on the South, his plan for compensated emancipation. In his message of December 1861 he had recommended this plan to the Border States, but without effect. Shortly after the special message of March 6, Lincoln summoned members of Congress from these States, and appealed for support, but without success. On July 12, 1862, he held a conference with the senators and representatives of these States, and read to them an appeal for this policy, but again without result. The Annual

Message of December 1, 1862 contained a specific plan for compensated emancipation to which Lincoln invited the attention of Congress. See, E. C. Smith, *The Borderland in the Civil War,* p. 375 ff.; I. N. Arnold, *Lincoln and the Overthrow of Slavery.*

1. MESSAGE TO CONGRESS
March 6, 1862

FELLOW-CITIZENS OF THE SENATE AND HOUSE OF REPRESENTATIVES:—I recommend the adoption of a joint resolution by your honorable bodies which shall be substantially as follows:

"*Resolved,* That the United States ought to co-operate with any State which may adopt gradual abolishment of slavery, giving to such State pecuniary aid, to be used by such State, in its discretion, to compensate for the inconveniences, public and private, produced by such change of system."

If the proposition contained in the resolution does not meet the approval of Congress and the country, there is the end; but if it does command such approval, I deem it of importance that the States and people immediately interested should be at once distinctly notified of the fact, so that they may begin to consider whether to accept or reject it. The Federal Government would find its highest interest in such a measure, as one of the most efficient means of self-preservation. The leaders of the existing insurrection entertain the hope that this government will ultimately be forced to acknowledge the independence of some part of the disaffected region, and that all the slave States north of such part will then say, "The Union for which we have struggled being already gone, we now choose to go with the Southern section." To deprive them of this hope substantially ends the rebellion, and the initiation of emancipation completely deprives them of it as to all the States initiating it. The point is not that *all* the States tolerating slavery would very soon, if at all, initiate emancipation; but that, while the offer is equally made to all, the more northern shall by such initiation make it certain to the more southern that in no event will the former ever join the latter in their proposed confederacy. I say "initiation" because, in my judgment, gradual and not sudden emancipation is better for all. In the mere financial or pecuniary view, any member of Congress with the census tables and treasury reports before him can readily see for himself how very soon the current expenditures of this war would purchase, at fair valuation, all the slaves in any named State. Such a proposition on the part of the General Government sets up no claim of a right by Federal authority to interfere with slavery within State limits, referring, as it does, the absolute control of the subject in each case to the State and its people immediately in-

terested. It is proposed as a matter of perfectly free choice with them. . . .

The proposition now made (though an offer only), I hope it may be esteemed no offense to ask whether the pecuniary consideration tendered would not be of more value to the States and private persons concerned than are the institution and property in it in the present aspect of affairs.

While it is true that the adoption of the proposed resolution would be merely initiatory, and not within itself a practical measure, it is recommended in the hope that it would soon lead to important practical results. In full view of my great responsibility to my God and to my country, I earnestly beg the attention of Congress and the people to the subject.

ABRAHAM LINCOLN.

2. MESSAGE TO CONGRESS
December 1, 1862

. . . Our strife pertains to ourselves—to the passing generations of men—and it can without convulsion be hushed forever with the passing of one generation.

In this view I recommend the adoption of the following resolution and articles amendatory to the Constitution of the United States:

Resolved by the Senate and House of Representatives of the United States of America, in Congress assembled, (two thirds of both Houses concurring), That the following articles be proposed to the Legislatures (or conventions) of the several States as amendments to the Constitution of the United States, all or any of which articles, when ratified by three fourths of the said Legislatures (or conventions), to be valid as part or parts of the said Constitution, viz:

ART.—. Every State wherein slavery now exists which shall abolish the same therein at any time or times before the 1st day of January, A.D. 1900, shall receive compensation from the United States as follows, to wit:

The President of the United States shall deliver to every such State bonds of the United States bearing interest at the rate of —per cent. per annum to an amount equal to the aggregate sum of ——— for each slave shown to have been therein by the Eighth Census of the United States, said bonds to be delivered to such State by instalments or in one parcel at the completion of the abolishment, accordingly as the same shall have been gradual or at one time within such State; and interest shall begin to run upon any such bond only from the proper time of its delivery as aforesaid. Any State having received bonds as aforesaid and afterwards reintroducing or tolerating slavery therein shall refund to the United States the bonds so received, or the value thereof, and all interest paid thereon.

ART.—. All slaves who shall have enjoyed actual freedom by the chances of the war at any time before the end of the rebellion shall be forever free; but all owners of such who shall not have been disloyal shall be compensated for them at the same rates as is provided for States adopting abolishment of slavery, but in such way that no slave shall be twice accounted for.

ART.—. Congress may appropriate money and otherwise provide for colonizing free colored persons with their own consent at any place or places without the United States.

I beg indulgence to discuss these proposed articles at some length. Without slavery the rebellion could never have existed; without slavery it could not continue.

Among the friends of the Union there is great diversity of sentiment and of policy in regard to slavery and the African race amongst us. Some would perpetuate slavery; some would abolish it suddenly and without compensation; some would abolish it gradually and with compensation; some would remove the freed people from us, and some would retain them with us; and there are yet other minor diversities. Because of these diversities we waste much strength in struggles among ourselves. By mutual concession we should harmonize and act together. This would be compromise, but it would be compromise among the friends and not with the enemies of the Union. These articles are intended to embody a plan of such mutual concessions. If the plan shall be adopted, it is assumed that emancipation will follow, at least in several of the States.

As to the first article, the main points are, first, the emancipation; secondly, the length of time for consummating it (thirty-seven years); and, thirdly, the compensation.

The emancipation will be unsatisfactory to the advocates of perpetual slavery, but the length of time should greatly mitigate their dissatisfaction. The time spares both races from the evils of sudden derangement—in fact, from the necessity of any derangement—while most of those whose habitual course of thought will be disturbed by the measure will have passed away before its consummation. They will never see it. Another class will hail the prospect of emancipation, but will deprecate the length of time. They will feel that it gives too little to the now living slaves. But it really gives them much. It saves them from the vagrant destitution which must largely attend immediate emancipation in localities where their numbers are very great, and it gives the inspiring assurance that their posterity shall be free forever. The plan leaves to each State choosing to act under it to abolish slavery now or at the end of the century, or at any intermediate time, or by degrees extending over the whole or any part of the period, and it obliges no two States to proceed alike. It also provides for compensation, and generally the mode of making it. This, it would seem, must further mitigate the dissatisfaction of those who favor perpetual slavery, and especially of those who are to receive the compensation. Doubtless some of those who are to pay and not to receive will object. Yet the measure is both just and economical. In a certain sense the liberation of slaves is the destruction of property—property acquired by descent or by purchase, the same as any other property. It is no less true for having been often said that the people of the South are not more responsible for the original introduction of this property than are the people of the North, and when it is remembered how unhesitatingly we all use cotton and sugar and share the profits of dealing in them, it may not be quite safe to say that the South has been more responsible than the North for its continuance. If, then, for a common object this property is to be sacrificed, is it not just that it be done at a common charge?

And if with less money, or money more easily paid, we can preserve the benefits of the Union by this means than we can by the war alone, is it not also economical to do it? Let us consider it, then. Let us ascertain the sum we have expended in the war since compensated emancipation was proposed last March, and consider whether if that measure had been promptly accepted by even some of the slave States the same sum would not have done more to close the war than has been otherwise done. If so, the measure would save money, and in that view would be a prudent and economical measure. . . . The aggregate sum necessary for compensated emancipation of course would be large. But it would require no ready cash, nor the bonds even any faster than the emancipation progresses. This might not, and probably would not, close before the end of the thirty-seven years. At that time we shall probably have a hundred millions of people to share the burden, instead of thirty-one millions as now. . . .

The proposed emancipation would shorten the war, perpetuate peace, insure this increase of population, and proportionately the wealth of the country. With these we should pay all the emancipation would cost, together with our other debt, easier than we should pay our other debt without it. . . .

This fact would be no excuse for delaying payment of what is justly due, but it shows the great importance of time in this connection—the great advantage of a policy by which we shall not have to pay until we number 100,000,000 what by a different policy we would have to pay now, when we number but 31,000,000. In a word, it shows that a dollar will be much harder to pay for the war than will be a dollar for emancipation on the proposed plan. And then the latter will cost no blood, no precious life. It will be a saving of both. . . .

The third article relates to the future of the freed people. It does not oblige, but merely authorizes Congress to aid in colonizing such as may consent. This ought not to be regarded as objectionable on the one hand or on the other, insomuch as it comes to nothing unless by the mutual consent of the people to be deported and the American voters through their representatives in Congress. . . .

The plan consisting of these articles is recommended, not but that a restoration of the national authority would be accepted without its adoption.

Nor will the war nor proceedings under the proclamation of September 22, 1862, be stayed because of the *recommendation* of this plan. Its timely *adoption,* I doubt not, would bring restoration, and thereby stay both.

And notwithstanding this plan, the recommendation that Congress provide by law for compensating any State which may adopt emancipation before this plan shall have been acted upon is hereby earnestly renewed. Such would be only an advance part of the plan, and the same arguments apply to both.

This plan is recommended as a means, not in exclusion of, but additional to, all others for restoring and preserving the national authority throughout the Union. The subject is presented exclusively in its economical aspect. The plan would, I am confident, secure peace more speedily and maintain it more permanently than can be done by force alone, while all it would cost, considering amounts and manner of payment and times of payment, would be easier paid than will be the additional cost of the war if we rely solely upon force. It is much, very much, that it would cost no blood at all.

The plan is proposed as permanent constitutional law. It cannot become such without the concurrence of, first, two thirds of Congress, and afterwards three fourths of the States. The requisite three fourths of the States will necessarily include seven of the slave States. Their concurrence, if obtained, will give assurance of their severally adopting emancipation at no very distant day upon the new constitutional terms. This assurance would end the struggle now and save the Union forever. . . .

Fellow-citizens, *we* can not escape history. We of this Congress and this administration will be remembered in spite of ourselves. No personal significance or insignificance can spare one or another of us. The fiery trial through which we pass will light us down in honor or dishonor to the latest generation. We *say* we are for the Union. The world will not forget that we say this. We know how to save the Union. The world knows we do know how to save it. We, even *we here,* hold the power and bear the responsibility. In *giving* freedom to the *slave* we *assure* freedom to the *free*—honorable alike in what we give and what we preserve. We shall nobly save or meanly lose the last, best hope of earth. Other means may succeed; this could not fail. The way is plain, peaceful, generous, just—a way which if followed the world will forever applaud and God must forever bless.

ABRAHAM LINCOLN.

212. SUMNER'S RESOLUTIONS ON THE THEORY OF SECESSION AND RECONSTRUCTION
February 11, 1862

(E. McPherson, ed. *Political History of the Great Rebellion*, p. 322)

These resolutions contain the famous state-suicide theory. See, W. A. Dunning, *Essays on the Civil War and Reconstruction*, p. 105 ff. See also, Sumner's article on "How to Treat the Rebel States", *Atlantic Monthly*, October 1863.

Resolutions declaratory of the relations between the United States and the territory once occupied by certain States, and now usurped by pretended governments, without constitutional or legal right.

Whereas certain States, rightfully belonging to the Union of the United States, have through their respective governments wickedly undertaken to abjure all those duties by which their connection with the Union was maintained; to renounce all allegiance to the Constitution; to levy war upon the national Government; and, for the consummation of this treason, have unconstitutionally and unlawfully confederated together, with the declared purpose of putting an end by force to the supremacy of the Constitution within their respective limits; and whereas this condition of insurrection, organized by pretended governments, openly exists in South Carolina, Georgia, Florida, Alabama, Mississippi, Louisiana, Texas, Arkansas, Tennessee, and Virginia, except in Eastern Tennessee and Western Virginia, and has been declared by the President of the United States, in a proclamation duly made in conformity with an act of Congress, to exist throughout this territory, with the exceptions already named; and whereas the extensive territory thus usurped by these pretended governments and organized into a hostile confederation, belongs to the United States, as an inseparable part thereof, under the sanctions of the Constitution, to be held in trust for the inhabitants in the present and future generations, and is so completely interlinked with the Union that it is forever dependent thereon; and whereas the Constitution, which is the supreme law of the land, cannot be displaced in its rightful operation within this territory, but must ever continue the supreme law thereof, notwithstanding of the doings of any pretended governments acting singly or in confederation, in order to put an end to its supremacy: Therefore—

1. *Resolved,* That any vote of secession or other act by which any State may undertake to put an end to the supremacy of the Constitution within its territory is inoperative and void against the Constitution, and when sustained by force it becomes a practical *abdication* by the State of all rights under the Constitution, while the treason which it involves still further works an instant *forfeiture* of all those functions and powers essential to the continued existence of the State as a body politic, so that from that time forward the territory falls under the exclusive jurisdiction of Congress as other territory, and the State being, according to the language of the law, *felo-de-se,* ceases to exist.

2. That any combination of men assuming to act in the place of such State, attempting to ensnare or coerce the inhabitants thereof into a confederation hostile to the Union is rebellious, treasonable, and destitute of all moral authority; and that such combination is a usurpation incapable of any constitutional existence and utterly lawless, so that every thing dependent upon it is without constitutional or legal support.

3. That the termination of a State under the Constitution necessarily causes the termination of those peculiar local institutions which, having no origin in the Constitution or in those natural rights which exist independent of the Constitution, are upheld by the sole and exclusive authority of the State.

4. That slavery, being a peculiar local institution, derived from local laws, without any origin in the Constitution or in natural rights, is upheld by the sole and exclusive authority of the State, and must therefore cease to exist legally or constitutionally when the State on which it depends no longer exists; for the incident cannot survive the principal.

5. That in the exercise of its exclusive jurisdiction over the territory once occupied by the States, it is the duty of Congress to see that the supremacy of the Constitution is

maintained in its essential principles, so that everywhere in this extensive territory slavery shall cease to exist practically, as it has already ceased to exist constitutionally or legally.

6. That any recognition of slavery in such territory, or any surrender of slaves under the pretended laws of the extinct States by any officer of the United States, civil or military, is a recognition of the pretended governments, to the exclusion of the jurisdiction of Congress under the Constitution, and is in the nature of aid and comfort to the rebellion that has been organized.

7. That any such recognition of slavery or surrender of pretended slaves, besides being a recognition of the pretended governments, giving them aid and comfort, is a denial of the rights of persons who, by the extinction of the States, have become free, so that under the Constitution, they cannot again be enslaved.

8. That allegiance from the inhabitant and protection from the Government are corresponding obligations, dependent upon each other, so that while the allegiance of every inhabitant of this territory, without distinction of color or class, is due to the United States, and cannot in any way be defeated by the action of any pretended Government, or by any pretence of property or claim to service, the corresponding obligation of protection is at the same time due by the United States to every such inhabitant, without distinction of color or class; and it follows that inhabitants held as slaves, whose paramount allegiance is due to the United States, may justly look to the national Government for protection.

9. That the duty directly cast upon Congress by the extinction of the States is reinforced by the positive prohibition of the Constitution that "no State shall enter into any confederation," or "without the consent of Congress keep troops or ships-of-war in time of peace, or enter into any agreement or compact with another State," or "grant letters of marque and reprisal," or "coin money," or "emit bills of credit," or "without the consent of Congress lay any duties on imports or exports," all of which have been done by these pretended governments, and also by the positive injunction of the Constitution, addressed to the nation, that "the United States shall guaranty to every State in this Union a republican form of government;" and that in pursuance of this duty cast upon Congress, and further enjoined by the Constitution, Congress will assume complete jurisdiction of such vacated territory where such unconstitutional and illegal things have been attempted, and will proceed to establish therein republican forms of government under the Constitution; and in the execution of this trust will provide carefully for the protection of all the inhabitants thereof, for the security of families, the organization of labor, the encouragement of industry, and the welfare of society, and will in every way discharge the duties of a just, merciful, and paternal Government.

213. INAUGURAL ADDRESS OF JEFFERSON DAVIS
February 22, 1862

(Richardson, ed. *Messages and Papers of the Confederacy,* Vol. I, p. 183 ff.)

Davis had been chosen provisional President of the Confederacy by the Montgomery Congress, and was formally inaugurated February 18. A regular election held in accordance with the Confederate Constitution, in October 1861, resulted in his election as President for a term of six years: his inaugural followed on the 22nd of February. On Davis, see his own *Rise and Fall of the Confederate Government,* 2 Vols.; W. E. Dodd, *Jefferson Davis;* A. Tate, *Jefferson Davis;* E. Cutting, *Jefferson Davis.* His writings can be found in D. Rowland, ed. *Jefferson Davis,* *Constitutionalist, His Letters, Papers and Speeches,* 10 vols.

FELLOW-CITIZENS: On this the birthday of the man most identified with the establishment of American Independence, and beneath the monument erected to commemorate his heroic virtues and those of his compatriots, we have assembled to usher into existence the permanent government of the confederate States. Through this instrumentality, under the favor of Divine Providence, we hope to perpetuate the principles of our Revolutionary fathers. The day, the memory and the purpose seem fitly associated. . . .

When a long course of class legislation, directed not to the general welfare, but to the aggrandizement of the Northern section of the Union, culminated in a warfare on the domestic institutions of the Southern States —when the dogmas of a sectional party, substituted for the provisions of the constitutional compact, threatened to destroy the sovereign rights of the States, six of those States, withdrawing from the Union, confederated together to exercise the right and perform the duty of instituting a government which would better secure the liberties for the preservation of which that Union was established.

Whatever of hope some may have entertained that a returning sense of justice would remove the danger with which our rights were threatened, and render it possible to preserve the Union of the Constitution, must have been dispelled by the malignity and barbarity of the Northern States in the prosecution of the existing war. The confidence of the most hopeful among us must have been destroyed by the disregard they have recently exhibited for all the time-honored bulwarks of civil and religious liberty. Bastiles filled with prisoners, arrested without civil process or indictment duly found; the writ of *habeas corpus* suspended by Executive mandate; a State Legislature controlled by the imprisonment of members whose avowed principles suggested to the Federal Executive that there might be another added to the list of seceded States; elections held under threats of a military power; civil officers, peaceful citizens and gentle women incarcerated for opinion's sake, proclaimed the incapacity of our late associates to administer a government as free, liberal and humane as that established for our common use.

For proof of the sincerity of our purpose to maintain our ancient institutions, we may point to the constitution of the Confederacy and the laws enacted under it, as well as to the fact that through all the necessities of an unequal struggle there has been no act on our part to impair personal liberty or the freedom of speech, of thought or of the press. The courts have been open, the judicial functions fully executed, and every right of the peaceful citizen maintained as securely as if a war of invasion had not disturbed the land.

The people of the States now confederated became convinced that the Government of the United States had fallen into the hands of a sectional majority, who would pervert that most sacred of all trusts to the destruction of the rights which it was pledged to protect. They believed that to remain longer in the Union would subject them to a continuance of a disparaging discrimination, submission to which would be inconsistent with their welfare, and intolerable to a proud people. They therefore determined to sever its bonds and establish a new confederacy for themselves.

The experiment instituted by our Revolutionary fathers, of a voluntary union of sovereign States for purposes specified in a solemn compact, had been perverted by those who, feeling power and forgetting right, were determined to respect no law but their own will. The Government had ceased to answer the ends for which it was ordained and established. To save ourselves from a revolution which, in its silent but rapid progress, was about to place us under the despotism of numbers, and to preserve in spirit, as well as in form, a system of government we believed to be peculiarly fitted to our condition, and full of promise for mankind, we determined to make a new association, composed of States homogeneous in interest, in policy and in feeling.

True to our traditions of peace and our love of justice, we sent commissioners to the United States to propose a fair and amicable settlement of all questions of public debt or property which might be in dispute. But the Government at Washington, denying our right to self-government, refused even to listen to any proposals for a peaceful separation. Nothing was then left to us but to prepare for war.

The first year in our history has been the most eventful in the annals of this continent. A new government has been established, and its machinery put in operation over an area exceeding seven hundred thousand square miles. The great principles upon which we have been willing to hazard everything that is dear to man have made conquests for us which could never have been achieved by the sword. Our Confederacy has grown from six to thirteen States; and Maryland, already united to us by hallowed memories and material interests, will, I believe, when able to speak with unstifled voice, connect her destiny with the South. . . .

The period is near at hand when our foes must sink under the immense load of debt which they have incurred, a debt which in their effort to subjugate us has already attained such fearful dimensions as will subject them to burthens which must continue to oppress them for generations to come.

We, too, have had our trials and difficulties. That we are to escape them in future is not to be hoped. It was to be expected when we entered upon this war that it would expose our people to sacrifices and cost them much, both of money and blood. But we knew the value of the object for which we struggle, and understood the nature of the war in which we were engaged. Nothing could be so bad as failure, and any sacrifice would be cheap as the price of success in such a contest. . . .

It was, perhaps, in the ordination of Providence, that we were to be taught the value of our liberties by the price which we pay for them.

The recollections of this great contest, with all its common traditions of glory, of sacrifice and of blood, will be the bond of harmony and enduring affection amongst the people; producing unity in policy, fraternity in sentiment, and joint effort in war.

Nor have the material sacrifices of the past year been made without some corresponding benefits. If the acquiescence of foreign nations in a pretended blockade has deprived us of our commerce with them, it is fast making us a self-supporting and an independent people. The blockade, if effectual and permanent, could only serve to divert our industry from the production of articles for export, and employ it in supplying commodities for domestic use.

It is a satisfaction that we have maintained the war by our unaided exertions. We have neither asked nor received assistance from any quarter. Yet the interest involved is not wholly our own. The world at large is concerned in opening our markets to its commerce. When the independence of the confederate States is recognized by the nations of the earth, and we are free to follow our interests and inclinations by cultivating foreign trade, the Southern States will offer to manufacturing nations the most favorable markets which ever invited their commerce. Cotton, sugar, rice, tobacco, provisions, timber and naval stores, will furnish attractive exchanges. Nor would the constancy of these supplies be likely to be disturbed by war. Our confederate strength will be too great to tempt aggression; and never was there a people whose interests and principles committed them so fully to a peaceful policy as those of the confederate States. By the character of their productions they are too deeply interested in foreign commerce wantonly to disturb it. War of conquest they cannot wage, because the constitution of their confederacy admits of no coërced association. Civil war there can not be between States held together by their volition only. The rule of voluntary association, which cannot fail to be conservative, by securing just and impartial government at home, does not diminish the security of the obligations by which the confederate States may be bound to foreign nations. In proof of this it is to be remembered that, at the first moment of asserting their right of secession, these States proposed a settlement on the basis of a common liability for the obligations of the General Government.

Fellow-citizens, after the struggles of ages had consecrated the right of the Englishman to constitutional representative government, our colonial ancestors were forced to vindicate that birthright by an appeal to arms. Success crowned their efforts, and they provided for their posterity a peaceful remedy against future aggression.

The tyranny of an unbridled majority, the most odious and least responsible form of despotism, has denied us both the right and remedy. Therefore we are in arms to renew such sacrifices as our fathers made to the holy cause of constitutional liberty. At the darkest hour of our struggle the provisional gives place to the permanent government. After a series of successes and victories, which covered our arms with glory, we have recently met with serious disasters. But in the heart of a people resolved to be free, these disasters tend but to stimulate to increased resistance.

To show ourselves worthy of the inheritance bequeathed to us by the patriots of the Revolution, we must emulate that heroic devotion which made reverse to them but the crucible in which their patriotism was refined.

With confidence in the wisdom and virtue of those who will share with me the responsibility, and aid me in the conduct of public affairs; securely relying on the patriotism and courage of the people, of which the present war has furnished so many examples, I deeply feel the weight of the responsibilities I now, with unaffected diffidence, am about to assume; and, fully realizing the inequality of human power to guide and to sustain, my hope is reverently fixed on Him whose favor is ever vouchsafed to the cause which is just. With humble gratitude and adoration, acknowledging the Providence which has so visibly protected the Confederacy during its brief but eventful career, to Thee, O God! I trustingly commit myself, and prayerfully invoke thy blessing on my country and its cause.

214. HOMESTEAD ACT
May 20, 1862
(*U. S. Statutes at Large,* Vol. XII, p. 392 ff.)

A Homestead Act had passed both houses of Congress in 1859 only to be vetoed by President Buchanan. With the success of the Republican. party in 1860, Homestead legislation was assured. The Homestead Act brought to an end one period of American land policy and inaugurated a new policy which, with modifications, has been followed since 1862. See, B. H. Hibbard, *History of Public Land Policies,* chs. xvii-xviii; G. M. Stephenson, *A Political History of the Public Lands from 1840 to 1862;* R. T. Hill, *The Public Domain and Democracy;* J. T. DuBois and G. S. Mathews, *Galusha Grow.*

AN ACT to secure homesteads to actual settlers on the public domain.

Be it enacted, That any person who is the head of a family, or who has arrived at the age of twenty-one years, and is a citizen of the United States, or who shall have filed his declaration of intention to become such, as required by the naturalization laws of the United States, and who has never borne arms against the United States Government or given aid and comfort to its enemies, shall, from and after the first of January, eighteen hundred and sixty-three, be entitled to enter one quarter-section or a less quantity of unappropriated public lands, upon which said person may have filed a pre-emption claim, or which may, at the time the application is made, be subject to pre-emption at one dollar and twenty-five cents, or less, per acre; or eighty acres or less of such unappropriated lands, at two dollars and fifty cents per acre, to be located in a body, in conformity to the legal subdivisions of the public lands, and after the same shall have been surveyed: *Provided,* That any person owning or residing on land may, under the provisions of this act, enter other land lying contiguous to his or her said land, which shall not, with the land so already owned and occupied, exceed in the aggregate one hundred and sixty acres.

Sec. 2. That the person applying for the benefit of this act shall, upon application to the register of the land office in which he or she is about to make such entry, make affidavit before the said register or receiver that he or she is the head of a family, or is twenty-one or more years of age, or shall have performed service in the Army or Navy of the United States, and that he has never borne arms against the Government of the United States or given aid and comfort to its enemies, and that such application is made for his or her exclusive use and benefit, and that said entry is made for the purpose of actual settlement and cultivation, and not, either directly or indirectly, for the use or benefit of any other person or persons whomsoever; and upon filing the said affidavit with the register or receiver, and on payment of ten dollars, he or she shall thereupon be permitted to enter the quantity of land specified: *Provided, however,* That no certificate shall be given or patent issued therefor until the expiration of five years from the date of such entry; and if, at the expiration of such time, or at any time within two years thereafter, the person making such entry—or if he be dead, his widow; or in case of her death, his heirs or devisee; or in case of a widow making such entry, her heirs or devisee, in case of her death—shall prove by two credible witnesses that he, she, or they have resided upon or cultivated the same for the term of five years immediately succeeding the time of filing the affidavit aforesaid, and shall make affidavit that no part of said land has been alienated, and that he has borne true allegiance to the Government of the United States; then, in such case, he, she, or they, if at that time a citizen of the United States, shall be entitled to a patent, as in other cases provided for by law: *And provided, further,* That in case of the death of both father and mother, leaving an infant child or children under twenty-one years of age, the right and fee shall inure to the benefit of said infant child or children; and the executor, administrator, or guardian may, at any time within two years after the death of the surviving parent, and in accordance with the laws of the State in which such children for the time being have their domicile, sell said land for the benefit of said infants, but for no other purpose; and the purchaser shall acquire the absolute title by the purchase, and be entitled to a patent from the United States, on payment of the office fees and sum of money herein specified. . . .

215. THE PACIFIC RAILWAY ACT
July 1, 1862
(*U. S. Statutes at Large,* Vol. XII, p. 489 ff.)

The idea of a transcontinental railroad had been broached in the eighteen-forties, and the rapid growth of California after 1849 brought it sharply to the attention of the country. Throughout the fifties there was general acquiescence in the idea that the road was necessary and should be financed in part by the government, but sectional rivalries prevented any agreement on the route which the road should take. In 1853 Congress authorized a survey of various routes, and the surveys were undertaken under the direction of Secretary of War Davis, but Congress took no action on the reports of the surveys. The secession of the Southern States cleared the way for a northern route, and in 1862 the first Pacific Railway Bill, authorizing the transcontinental railroad and granting generous government aid, was passed. Two years later a second Pacific Railway Act doubled the land grants and provided that the government have a second instead of a first mortgage on the railroad property. (*Stat. at Large,* Vol. XIII, p. 356.) Altogether some 45,000,000 acres of land were granted, and some $60,000,000 lent to the Union and Central Pacific Railroads. See L. H. Haney, *A Congressional History of Railways in the United States, 1850–1887;* J. B. Sanborn, *Congressional Grants of Land in Aid of Railways;* R. E. Riegel, *The Story of the Western Railroads;* N. Trottman, *History of the Union Pacific;* K. White, *History of the Union Pacific Railway;* E. L. Sabin, *Building the Pacific Railway;* G. M. Dodge, *How We Built the Union Pacific;* J. R. Perkins, *Trails, Rails and War: The Life of General Grenville Dodge;* F. A. Cleveland and F. W. Powell, *Railroad Promotion and Capitalization.*

An Act to aid in the Construction of a Railroad and Telegraph Line from the Missouri River to the Pacific Ocean. . . .

Be it enacted, That Walter S. Burgess [names of corporators]; together with five commissioners to be appointed by the Secretary of the Interior . . . are hereby created and erected into a body corporate . . . by the name . . . of "The Union Pacific Railroad Company" . . . ; and the said corporation is hereby authorized and empowered to lay out, locate, construct, furnish, maintain and enjoy a continuous railroad and telegraph . . . from a point on the one hundredth meridian of longitude west from Greenwich, between the south margin of the valley of the Republican River and the north margin of the valley of the Platte River, to the western boundary of Nevada Territory, upon the route and terms hereinafter provided. . . .

Sec. 2. That the right of way through the public lands be . . . granted to said company for the construction of said railroad and telegraph line; and the right . . . is hereby given to said company to take from the public lands adjacent to the line of said road, earth, stone, timber, and other materials for the construction thereof; said right of way is granted to said railroad to the extent of two hundred feet in width on each side of said railroad when it may pass over the public lands, including all necessary grounds for stations, buildings, workshops, and depots, machine shops, switches, side tracks, turn tables, and water stations. The United States shall extinguish as rapidly as may be the Indian titles to all lands falling under the operation of this act. . . .

Sec. 3. That there be . . . granted to the said company, for the purpose of aiding in the construction of said railroad and telegraph line, and to secure the safe and speedy transportation of mails, troops, munitions of war, and public stores thereon, every alternate section of public land, designated by odd numbers, to the amount of five alternate sections per mile on each side of said railroad, on the line thereof, and within the limits of ten miles on each side of said road. . . . *Provided* That all mineral lands shall be excepted from the operation of this act; but where the same shall contain timber, the timber thereon is hereby granted to said company. . . .

Sec. 5. That for the purposes herein mentioned the Secretary of the Treasury shall . . . in accordance with the provisions of this act, issue to said company bonds of the United States of one thousand dollars each, payable in thirty years after date, paying six per centum per annum interest . . . to the amount of sixteen of said bonds per mile for each section of forty miles; and to secure the repayment to the United States . . . of the amount of said bonds . . . the issue of said bonds . . . shall ipso facto constitute a first mortgage on the whole line of the railroad and telegraph. . . .

Sec. 9. That the Leavenworth, Pawnee and Western Railroad Company of Kansas are hereby authorized to construct a railroad and telegraph line . . . upon the same terms and conditions in all respects as are provided [for construction of the Union Pacific Railroad]. . . . The Central Pacific Railroad Company of California are hereby authorized to construct a railroad and telegraph line from the Pacific coast . . . to the eastern boundaries of California, upon the same terms and conditions in all respects [as are provided for the Union Pacific Railroad].

Sec. 10. . . . And the Central Pacific Rail-Road Company of California after completing its road across said State, is authorized to continue the construction of said railroad and telegraph through the Territories of the United States to the Missouri River . . . upon the terms and conditions provided in this act in relation to the Union Pacific Railroad Company, until said roads shall meet and connect. . . .

Sec. 11. That for three hundred miles of said road most mountainous and difficult of construction, to wit: one hundred and fifty miles westerly from the eastern base of the Rocky Mountains, and one hundred and fifty miles eastwardly from the western base of the Sierra Nevada mountains . . . the bonds to be issued to aid in the construction thereof shall be treble the number per mile hereinbefore provided . . . ; and between the sections last named of one hundred and fifty miles each, the bonds to be issued to aid in the construction thereof shall be double the number per mile first mentioned. . . .

216. THE MORRILL ACT
July 2, 1862
(*U. S. Statutes at Large,* Vol. XII, p. 503)

This act, granting public land for the support of industrial and agricultural education, is, with the exception of the Act of 1785, the most important piece of legislation on behalf of education ever passed. Under the terms of this act some 13,000,000 acres of the public domain have been given to the States for the establishment of mechanical and agricultural colleges: the act gave a tremendous impetus to the movement for establishing State Universities. The real "father" of the act was J. B. Turner of the University of Illinois. See, E. J. James, *Origin of the Land Grant Act of 1862;* M. T. Carriel, *Life of* J. B. Turner; W. B. Parker, *Life and Public Services of Justin Smith Morrill;* G. W. Atherton, *Legislative Career of J. S. Morrill.* I. L. Kandel, "Federal Land Grants for Vocational Education" in Carnegie Foundation for the Advancement of Teaching, *Bulletin* No. 10, is unsympathetic to the Turner claim.

An Act donating Public Lands to the several States and Territories which may provide Colleges for the Benefit of Agriculture and the Mechanic Arts.

Be it enacted by the Senate and House of Representatives of the United States of America in Congress assembled, That there be granted to the several States, for the purposes hereinafter mentioned, an amount of public land, to be apportioned to each State a quantity equal to thirty thousand acres for each senator and representative in Congress to which the States are respectively entitled by the apportionment under the census of eighteen hundred and sixty: Provided, That no mineral lands shall be selected or purchased under the provisions of this act.

SEC. 2. And be it further enacted, That the land aforesaid, after being surveyed, shall be apportioned to the several States in sections or subdivisions of sections, not less than one quarter of a section; and whenever there are public lands in a State subject to sale at private entry at one dollar and twenty-five cents per acre, the quantity to which said State shall be entitled shall be selected from such lands within the limits of such State, and the Secretary of the Interior is hereby directed to issue to each of the States in which there is not the quantity of public lands subject to sale at private entry at one dollar and twenty-five cents per acre, to which said State may be entitled under the provisions of this act, land scrip to the amount in acres for the deficiency of its distributive share: said scrip to be sold by said States and the proceeds thereof applied to the uses and purposes prescribed in this act, and for no other use or purpose whatsoever. . . .

SEC. 4. And be it further enacted, That all moneys derived from the sale of the lands aforesaid by the States to which the lands are apportioned, and from the sale of land scrip hereinbefore provided for, shall be invested in stocks of the United States, or of the States, or some other safe stocks, yielding not less than five per centum upon the par value of said stocks; and that the moneys so invested shall constitute a perpetual fund, the capital of which shall remain forever undiminished, (except so far as may be provided in section fifth of this act,) and the interest of which shall be inviolably appropriated, by each State which may take and claim the benefit of this act, to the endowment, support, and maintenance of at least one college where the leading object shall be, without excluding other scientific and classical studies, and including military tactics, to teach such branches of learning as are related to agriculture and mechanic arts, in such manner as the legislatures of the State may respectively prescribe, in order to promote the liberal and practical education of the industrial classes in the several pursuits and professions in life.

SEC. 5. . . .

Sixth. No State while in a condition of rebellion or insurrection against the government of the United States shall be entitled to the benefit of this Act. . . .

217. McCLELLAN OUTLINES A POLICY FOR PRESIDENT LINCOLN

Letter of General McClellan to President Lincoln
July 7, 1862

(E. McPherson, ed. *Political History of the Great Rebellion*, p. 385 ff.)

Seward was not the only prominent man who presumed to advise President Lincoln on matters of policy. McClellan's contempt for Lincoln, and his political ambitions, are well known. McClellan has revealed himself in his autobiography, *McClellan's Own Story.* The best brief interpretation is in G. Bradford, *Union Portraits,* ch. i; a severe but just analysis of his generalship is J. C. Ropes, "General McClellan" in *Critical Sketches of Some of the Federal and Confederate Commanders, Papers* of the Military Historical Society of Massachusetts, Vol. X.

General McClellan's Letter to President Lincoln.

Headquarters Army of the Potomac
July 7, 1862

Mr. President: You have been fully informed that the rebel army is in the front, with the purpose of overwhelming us by attacking our positions or reducing us by blocking our river communications. I cannot but regard our condition as critical, and I earnestly desire, in view of possible contingencies, to lay before your excellency, for your private consideration, my general views concerning the existing state of rebellion, although they do not strictly relate to the situation of this army, or strictly come within the scope of my official duties. . . .

The time has come when the government must determine upon a civil and military policy, covering the whole ground of our national trouble.

The responsibility of determining, declaring, and supporting such civil and military policy, and of directing the whole course of national affairs in regard to the rebellion, must now be assumed and exercised by you, or our cause will be lost. The Constitution gives you power, even for the present terrible exigency.

This rebellion has assumed the character of a war; as such it should be regarded, and it should be conducted upon the highest principles known to Christian civilization. It should not be a war looking to the subjugation of the people of any State, in any event. It should not be at all a war upon a population, but against armed forces and political organizations. Neither confiscation of property, political execution of persons, territorial organization of States, or forcible abolition of slavery, should be contemplated for a moment.

In prosecuting the war, all private property and unarmed persons should be strictly protected, subject only to the necessity of military operation; all private property taken for military use should be paid or receipted for; pillage and waste should be treated as high crimes; all unnecessary trespass sternly prohibited, and offensive demeanor by the military towards citizens promptly rebuked. Military arrests should not be tolerated, except in places where active hostilities exist; and oaths, not required by enactments, constitutionally made, should be neither demanded nor received.

Military government should be confined to the preservation of public order and the protection of political right. Military power should not be allowed to interfere with the relations of servitude either by supporting or impairing the authority of the master, except for repressing disorder, as in other cases. Slaves, contraband under the act of Congress, seeking military protection, should receive it. The right of the government to appropriate permanently to its own service claims to slave labor should be asserted and the right of the owner to compensation therefor should be recognized. This principle might be extended, upon grounds of military necessity and security, to all the slaves of a particular State, thus working manumission in such State; and in Missouri, perhaps in Western Virginia also, and possibly even in Maryland, the expediency of such a measure is only a question of time. A system of policy thus constitutional, and pervaded by the influences of Christianity and freedom, would receive the support of almost all truly loyal men, would deeply impress the rebel masses and all foreign nations, and it might humbly be hoped that it would commend itself to the favor of the Almighty.

Unless the principles governing the future conduct of our struggle shall be made known and approved, the effort to obtain requisite forces will be almost hopeless. A declaration of radical views, especially upon slavery, will rapidly disintegrate our present armies. . . .

In carrying out any system of policy which you may form, you will require a commander-in-chief of the army, one who possesses your confidence, understands your views, and who is competent to execute your orders, by directing the military forces of the nation to the accomplishment of the objects by you proposed. I do not seek that place for myself. I am willing to serve you in such position as you may assign to me, and I will do so as faithfully as ever subordinate served superior.

I may be on the brink of eternity; and as I hope forgiveness from my Maker, I have written this letter with sincerity towards you and from love for my country.

George B. McClellan
Major General Commanding

218. GENERAL POPE'S ADDRESS TO THE ARMY OF VIRGINIA
July 14, 1862

(F. Moore, ed. *The Rebellion Record,* Vol. V, p. 551)

In July 1862 Lincoln appointed General Halleck to the post of General-in-Chief of all the Union armies, and at the same time brought General John Pope from the west and placed him at the head of the Army of Virginia, consisting of the corps of McDowell, Banks and Frémont. Pope signallized his accession to this position by issuing the gasconade of July 14; six weeks later he suffered a disastrous defeat at the Second Battle of Bull Run. See, J. C. Ropes, *The Army Under Pope;* G. H. Gordon, *History of the campaign of the Army of Virginia under John Pope; Papers* of the Military Historical Society of Massachusetts, Vol. II: *The Virginia Campaign of General Pope.*

WASHINGTON, Monday, July 14.
To the Officers and Soldiers of the Army of Virginia:

By special assignment of the President of the United States, I have assumed command of this army. I have spent two weeks in learning your whereabouts, your condition, and your wants; in preparing you for active operations, and in placing you in positions from which you can act promptly and to the purpose.

I have come to you from the West, where we have always seen the backs of our enemies —from an army whose business it has been to seek the adversary, and to beat him when found, whose policy has been attack and not defence.

In but one instance has the enemy been able to place our Western armies in a defensive attitude. I presume that I have been called here to pursue the same system, and to lead you against the enemy. It is my purpose to do so, and that speedily.

I am sure you long for an opportunity to win the distinction you are capable of achieving—that opportunity I shall endeavor to give you.

Meantime I desire you to dismiss from your minds certain phrases which I am sorry to find much in vogue amongst you.

I hear constantly of taking strong positions and holding them—of lines of retreat, and of bases of supplies. Let us discard such ideas.

The strongest position a soldier should desire to occupy is one from which he can most easily advance against the enemy.

Let us study the probable lines of retreat of our opponents, and leave our own to take care of themselves. Let us look before us and not behind. Success and glory are in the advance. Disaster and shame lurk in the rear.

Let us act on this understanding, and it is safe to predict that your banners shall be inscribed with many a glorious deed, and that your names will be dear to your countrymen forever.

JOHN POPE,
Major-General Commanding.

219. LINCOLN AND GREELEY
August 19, 22, 1862

(F. Moore, ed. *The Rebellion Record,* Vol. XII, p. 480 ff.)

Greeley had, at the beginning of the secession movement, advocated letting the "erring sisters go in peace." Though not formally allied with the Garrison abolitionists, he had, through the columns of the *Tribune,* persistently denounced slavery. In his Prayer of Twenty Millions he demanded that Lincoln should definitely commit himself to emancipation: in this attitude Greeley spoke for a large and powerful anti-slavery element in the North, but he certainly did not speak for "twenty millions." Lincoln's reply, justifying the war as one for the preservation of the Union, is one of the most notable of his pronouncements. Greeley subsequently embarrassed the administration and himself by dallying with peace overtures from the South. See, D. Seitz, *Horace Greeley;* D. S. Alexander, *Political History of New York,* Vol. III, p. 35 ff.

1. THE PRAYER OF TWENTY MILLIONS

To Abraham Lincoln, President of the United States:

DEAR SIR: I do not intrude to tell you— for you must know already—that a great proportion of those who triumphed in your election, and of all who desire the unqualified suppression of the rebellion now desolating our country, are sorely disappointed and deeply pained by the policy you seem to be pursuing with regard to the slaves of rebels. I write only to set succinctly and unmistakably before you what we require, what we think we have a right to expect, and of what we complain.

I. We require of you, as the first servant of the Republic, charged especially and pre-eminently with this duty, that you EXECUTE THE LAWS. . . .

II. We think you are strangely and disas-trously remiss in the discharge of your official and imperative duty with regard to the eman-cipating provisions of the new Confiscation Act. Those provisions were designed to fight Slavery with Liberty. They prescribe that men loyal to the Union, and willing to shed their blood in her behalf, shall no longer be held, with the nation's consent, in bondage to persistent, malignant traitors, who for twenty years have been plotting and for sixteen months have been fighting to divide and de-stroy our country. Why these traitors should be treated with tenderness by you, to the prejudice of the dearest rights of loyal men, we cannot conceive.

III. We think you are unduly influenced by the councils, the representations, the men-aces, of certain fossil politicians hailing from the Border Slave States. Knowing well that the heartily, unconditionally loyal portion of the white citizens of those States do not expect nor desire that Slavery shall be upheld to the prejudice of the Union—(for the truth of which we appeal not only to every Republican residing in those States, but to such eminent loyalists as H. Winter Davis, Parson Brown-low, the Union Central Committee of Balti-more, and to *The Nashville Union*)—we ask you to consider that Slavery is everywhere the inciting cause and sustaining base of trea-son: the most slaveholding sections of Mary-land and Delaware being this day, though un-der the Union flag, in full sympathy with the rebellion, while the free labor portions of Tennessee and of Texas, though writhing un-der the bloody heel of treason, are unconquer-ably loyal to the Union. . . . It seems to us the most obvious truth, that whatever strengthens or fortifies Slavery in the Border States strengthens also treason, and drives home the wedge intended to divide the Union. Had you, from the first, refused to recognize in those States, as here, any other than un-conditional loyalty—that which stands for the Union, whatever may become of Slavery —those States would have been, and would be, far more helpful and less troublesome to the defenders of the Union than they have been, or now are.

IV. We think timid counsels in such a crisis calculated to prove perilous, and proba-bly disastrous. It is the duty of a Govern-ment so wantonly, wickedly assailed by re-bellion as ours has been, to oppose force to force in a defiant, dauntless spirit. It can-not afford to temporize with traitors, nor with semi-traitors. It must not bribe them to be-have themselves, nor make them fair prom-ises in the hope of disarming their causeless hostility. Representing a brave and high-spirited people, it can afford to forfeit any thing else better than its own self-respect, or their admiring confidence, For our Govern-ment even to seek, after war has been made on it, to dispel the affected apprehensions of armed traitors that their cherished privi-leges may be assailed by it, is to invite insult and encourage hopes of its own downfall. The rush to arms of Ohio, Indiana, Illinois, is the true answer at once to the rebel raids of John Morgan and the traitorous sophis-tries of Beriah Magoffin.

V. We complain that the Union cause has suffered, and is now suffering immensely, from mistaken deference to rebel Slavery. Had you, sir, in your Inaugural Address, un-mistakably given notice that, in case the rebellion already commenced, were persisted in, and your efforts to preserve the Union and enforce the laws should be resisted by armed force, *you would recognize no loyal person as rightfully held in Slavery by a traitor,* we believe the rebellion would therein have received a staggering if not fatal blow. At that moment, according to the returns of the most recent elections, the Unionists were a large majority of the voters of the slave States. But they were composed in good part of the aged, the feeble, the wealthy, the timid—the young, the reckless, the aspiring, the adventurous, had already been largely lured by the gamblers and negro-traders, the politicians by trade and the conspirators by instinct, into the toils of treason. Had you then proclaimed that rebellion would strike the shackles from the slaves of every traitor, the wealthy and the cautious would have been supplied with a powerful inducement to remain loyal. . . .

VI. We complain that the Confiscation Act which you approved is habitually disre-garded by your Generals, and that no word of rebuke for them from you has yet reached the public ear. Frémont's Proclamation and Hunter's Order favoring Emancipation were promptly annulled by you; while Halleck's Number Three, forbidding fugitives from slavery to rebels to come within his lines— an order as unmilitary as inhuman, and which received the hearty approbation of every traitor in America—with scores of like tendency, have never provoked even your remonstrance. . . . And finally, we complain that you, Mr. President, elected as a Republican, knowing well what an abomination Slavery is, and how emphatically it is the core and essence of this atrocious rebellion, seem never to interfere with these atrocities, and never give a direction to your military subordinates, which does not appear to have been conceived in the interest of Slavery rather than of Freedom.

VIII. On the face of this wide earth, Mr. President, there is not one disinterested, determined, intelligent champion of the Union cause who does not feel that all attempts to put down the rebellion and at the same time uphold its inciting cause are preposterous and futile—that the rebellion, if crushed out to-morrow, would be renewed within a year if Slavery were left in full vigor—that army officers who remain to this day devoted to Slavery can at best be but half-way loyal to the Union—and that every hour of deference to Slavery is an hour of added and deepened peril to the Union. I appeal to the testimony of your ambassadors in Europe. It is freely at your service, not at mine. Ask them to tell you candidly whether the seeming subserviency of your policy to the slaveholding, slavery-upholding interest, is not the perplexity, the despair of statesmen of all parties, and be admonished by the general answer!

IX. I close as I began with the statement that what an immense majority of the loyal millions of your countrymen require of you is a frank, declared, unqualified, ungrudging execution of the laws of the land, more especially of the Confiscation Act. That act gives freedom to the slaves of rebels coming within our lines, or whom those lines may at any time inclose—we ask you to render it due obedience by publicly requiring all your subordinates to recognize and obey it. The rebels are everywhere using the late anti-negro riots in the North, as they have long used your

officers' treatment of negroes in the South, to convince the slaves that they have nothing to hope from a Union success—that we mean in that case to sell them into a bitter bondage to defray the cost of the war. Let them impress this as a truth on the great mass of their ignorant and credulous bondmen, and the Union will never be restored—never. We cannot conquer ten millions of people united in solid phalanx against us, powerfully aided by Northern sympathizers and European allies. We must have scouts, guides, spies, cooks, teamsters, diggers, and choppers from the blacks of the South, whether we allow them to fight for us or not, or we shall be baffled and repelled. As one of the millions who would gladly have avoided this struggle at any sacrifice but that of principle and honor, but who now feel that the triumph of the Union is indispensable not only to the existence of our country but to the wellbeing of mankind, I entreat you to render a hearty and unequivocal obedience to the law of the land.

Yours,   HORACE GREELEY.

2. PRESIDENT LINCOLN'S LETTER

Executive Mansion,
Washington, August 22, 1862.
Hon. Horace Greeley:

DEAR SIR: I have just read yours of the nineteenth, addressed to myself through the New-York *Tribune*. If there be in it any statements or assumptions of fact which I may know to be erroneous, I do not now and here controvert them. If there be in it any inferences which I may believe to be falsely drawn, I do not now and here argue against them. If there be perceptible in it an impatient and dictatorial tone, I waive it in deference to an old friend, whose heart I have always supposed to be right.

As to the policy I "seem to be pursuing," as you say, I have not meant to leave any one in doubt.

I would save the Union. I would save it the shortest way under the Constitution. The sooner the National authority can be restored, the nearer the Union will be "the Union as it was." If there be those who would not save the Union unless they could at the same time *save* Slavery, I do not agree with them. If there be those who would not save the Union unless they could at the same time *destroy*

DOCUMENTS OF AMERICAN HISTORY

Slavery, I do not agree with them. My paramount object in this struggle *is* to save the Union, and is *not* either to save or destroy Slavery. If I could save the Union without freeing *any* slave, I would do it; and if I could save it by freeing *all* the slaves, I would do it; and if I could do it by freeing some and leaving others alone, I would also do that. What I do about Slavery and the colored race, I do because I believe it helps to save this Union; and what I forbear, I forbear because I do *not* believe it would help

to save the Union. I shall do *less* whenever I shall believe what I am doing hurts the cause, and I shall do *more* whenever I shall believe doing more will help the cause. I shall try to correct errors when shown to be errors; and I shall adopt new views so fast as they shall appear to be true views. I have here stated my purpose according to my view of *official* duty, and I intend no modification of my oft-expressed *personal* wish that all men, everywhere, could be free.   Yours,

A. LINCOLN.

220. ADDRESS TO PRESIDENT LINCOLN BY THE WORKING-MEN OF MANCHESTER, ENGLAND
December 31, 1862

(F. Moore, ed. *The Rebellion Record*, Vol. VI, p. 344)

During the Civil War the English government preserved a cautious neutrality: the opinion of the governing classes was on the whole sympathetic toward the South, that of the working-men sympathetic toward the North. Lincoln's preliminary proclamation of emancipation was a determining influence in holding England to neutrality and cementing the friendship of the liberals and the working classes. The address of the working-men of Manchester was subscribed on the eve of the formal proclamation of emancipation. For Lincoln's reply see Doc. No. 221. On the English attitude toward the War, see D. Jordan, and E. J. Pratt, *Europe and the American Civil War*, Part I; E. D. Adams, *Great Britain and the American Civil War*, 2 Vols.; H. Adams, *The Education of Henry Adams;* C. F. Adams, *Trans-Atlantic Historical Solidarity;* B. Villiers and W. H. Chesson, *Anglo-American Relations, 1861–1865;* F. L. Owsley, *King Cotton Diplomacy.*

To Abraham Lincoln, President of the United States:

As citizens of Manchester, assembled at the Free-Trade Hall, we beg to express our fraternal sentiments toward you and your country. We rejoice in your greatness as an outgrowth of England, whose blood and language you share, whose orderly and legal freedom you have applied to new circumstances, over a region immeasurably greater than our own. We honor your Free States, as a singularly happy abode for the working millions where industry is honored. One thing alone has, in the past, lessened our sympathy with your country and our confidence in it—

we mean the ascendency of politicians who not merely maintained negro slavery, but desired to extend and root it more firmly. Since we have discerned, however, that the victory of the free North, in the war which has so sorely distressed us as well as afflicted you, will strike off the fetters of the slave, you have attracted our warm and earnest sympathy. We joyfully honor you, as the President, and the Congress with you, for many decisive steps toward practically exemplifying your belief in the words of your great founders: "All men are created free and equal." You have procured the liberation of the slaves in the district around Washington, and thereby made the centre of your Federation visibly free. You have enforced the laws against the slave-trade, and kept up your fleet against it, even while every ship was wanted for service in your terrible war. You have nobly decided to receive ambassadors from the negro republics of Hayti and Liberia, thus forever renouncing that unworthy prejudice which refuses the rights of humanity to men and women on account of their color. In order more effectually to stop the slave-trade, you have made with our Queen a treaty, which your Senate has ratified, for the right of mutual search. Your Congress has decreed freedom as the law forever in the vast unoccupied or half unsettled Territories which are directly subject to its legislative power. It has offered pecuniary aid to all States which will enact emancipation locally, and has forbidden your

Generals to restore fugitive slaves who seek their protection. You have entreated the slave-masters to accept these moderate offers; and after long and patient waiting, you, as Commander-in-Chief of the Army, have appointed to-morrow, the first of January, 1863, as the day of unconditional freedom for the slaves of the rebel States. Heartily do we congratulate you and your country on this humane and righteous course. We assume that you cannot now stop short of a complete uprooting of slavery. It would not become us to dictate any details, but there are broad principles of humanity which must guide you. If complete emancipation in some States be deferred, though only to a predetermined day, still in the interval, human beings should not be counted chattels. Women must have the rights of chastity and maternity, men the rights of husbands, masters the liberty of manumission. Justice demands for the black, no less than for the white, the protection of law—that his voice be heard in your courts. Nor must any such abomination be tolerated as slave-breeding States, and a slave market—if you are to earn the high reward of all your sacrifices, in the approval of the universal brotherhood and of the Divine Father. It is for your free country to decide whether any thing but immediate and total emancipation can secure the most indispensable rights of humanity against the inveterate wickedness of local laws and local executives. We implore you, for your own honor and welfare, not to faint in your providential mission. While your enthusiasm is aflame, and the tide of events runs high, let the work be finished effectually. Leave no root of bitterness to spring up and work fresh misery to your children. It is a mighty task, indeed, to reörganize the industry not only of four millions of the colored race, but of five millions of whites. Nevertheless, the vast progress you have made in the short space of twenty months fills us with hope that every stain on your freedom will shortly be removed, and that the erasure of that foul blot upon civilization and Christianity —chattel slavery—during your Presidency will cause the name of Abraham Lincoln to be honored and revered by posterity. We are certain that such a glorious consummation will cement Great Britain to the United States in close and enduring regards. Our interests, moreover, are identified with yours. We are truly one people, though locally separate. And if you have any ill-wishers here, be assured they are chiefly those who oppose liberty at home, and that they will be powerless to stir up quarrels between us, from the very day in which your country becomes, undeniably and without exception, the home of the free. Accept our high admiration of your firmness in upholding the proclamation of freedom.

221. LINCOLN'S REPLY TO THE WORKING-MEN OF MANCHESTER, ENGLAND
January 19, 1863

(The Writings of Abraham Lincoln, Constitutional ed., Vol. VI, p. 248)

To the Working-Men of Manchester:

I have the honor to acknowledge the receipt of the address and resolutions which you sent me on the eve of the new year. When I came, on the 4th of March, 1861, through a free and constitutional election to preside in the Government of the United States, the country was found at the verge of civil war. Whatever might have been the cause, or whosoever the fault, one duty, paramount to all others, was before me, namely, to maintain and preserve at once the Constitution and the integrity of the Federal Republic. A conscientious purpose to perform this duty is the key to all the measures of administration which have been and to all which will hereafter be pursued. Under our frame of government and my official oath, I could not depart from this purpose if I would. It is not always in the power of governments to enlarge or restrict the scope of moral results which follow the policies that they may deem it necessary for the public safety from time to time to adopt.

I have understood well that the duty of self-preservation rests solely with the American people; but I have at the same time been aware that favor or disfavor of foreign nations might have a material influence in enlarging or prolonging the struggle with disloyal men in which the country is engaged. A fair examination of history has served to authorize a belief that the past actions and influences of the United States were generally regarded as having been beneficial toward mankind. I have, therefore, reckoned upon the forbearance of nations. Circumstances—to some of which you kindly allude—induce me especially to expect that if justice and good faith should be practised by the United States, they would encounter no hostile influence on the part of Great Britain. It is now a pleasant duty to acknowledge the demonstration you have given of your desire that a spirit of amity and peace toward this country may prevail in the councils of your Queen, who is respected and esteemed in your own country only more than she is by the kindred nation which has its home on this side of the Atlantic.

I know and deeply deplore the sufferings which the working-men at Manchester, and in all Europe, are called to endure in this crisis. It has been often and studiously represented that the attempt to overthrow this government, which was built upon the foundation of human rights, and to substitute for it one which should rest exclusively on the basis of human slavery, was likely to obtain the favor of Europe. Through the action of our disloyal citizens, the working-men of Europe have been subjected to severe trials, for the purpose of forcing their sanction to that attempt. Under the circumstances, I cannot but regard your decisive utterances upon the question as an instance of sublime Christian heroism which has not been surpassed in any age or in any country. It is indeed an energetic and reinspiring assurance of the inherent power of truth and of the ultimate and universal triumph of justice, humanity, and freedom. I do not doubt that the sentiments you have expressed will be sustained by your great nation; and, on the other hand, I have no hesitation in assuring you that they will excite admiration, esteem, and the most reciprocal feelings of friendship among the American people. I hail this interchange of sentiment, therefore, as an augury that whatever else may happen, whatever misfortune may befall your country or my own, the peace and friendship which now exist between the two nations will be, as it shall be my desire to make them, perpetual.

ABRAHAM LINCOLN.

222. THE EMANCIPATION PROCLAMATION
January 1, 1863

(*U. S. Statutes at Large,* Vol. XII, p. 1268-9)

As early as July 22, 1862, Lincoln had read to his Cabinet a preliminary draft of an emancipation proclamation. At this time Secretary Seward suggested that the proclamation should not be issued until a military victory had been won. The battle of Antietam gave Lincoln his desired opportunity; on the 22 of September he read to his Cabinet a second draft of the proclamation. After some modifications this was issued as a preliminary proclamation; the formal and definite proclamation came January 1, 1863. The *Diaries* of Welles, Chase, and Bates give interesting records of the Cabinet meetings. This proclamation was particularly important in its effect upon European, especially English, public opinion. See E. D. Adams, *Great Britain and the American Civil War,* 2 Vols.; D. Jordan and E. J. Pratt, *Europe and the American Civil War;* W. R. West, *Contemporary French Opinion on the American Civil War.* On the constitutionality of emancipation, see J. G. Randall, *Constitutional Problems Under Lincoln,* chs. xv–xvi.

BY THE PRESIDENT OF THE UNITED
STATES OF AMERICA:

A Proclamation.

Whereas on the 22d day of September, A.D. 1862, a proclamation was issued by the President of the United States, containing, among other things, the following, to wit:

"That on the 1st day of January, A.D. 1863, all persons held as slaves within any State or designated part of a State the people whereof shall then be in rebellion against the United States shall be then, thenceforward, and forever free; and the executive government of the United States, including the military and naval authority thereof, will recognize and maintain the freedom of such persons and will do no act or acts to repress such persons, or any of them, in any efforts they may make for their actual freedom.

"That the executive will on the 1st day of January aforesaid, by proclamation, designate the States and parts of States, if any, in which the people thereof, respectively, shall then be in rebellion against the United States; and the fact that any State or the people thereof shall on that day be in good faith represented in the Congress of the United States by members chosen thereto at elections wherein a majority of the qualified voters of such States shall have participated shall, in the absence of strong countervailing testimony, be deemed conclusive evidence that such State and the people thereof are not then in rebellion against the United States."

Now, therefore, I, Abraham Lincoln, President of the United States, by virtue of the power in me vested as Commander-in-Chief of the Army and Navy of the United States in time of actual armed rebellion against the authority and government of the United States, and as a fit and necessary war measure for suppressing said rebellion, do, on this 1st day of January, A.D. 1863, and in accordance with my purpose so to do, publicly proclaimed for the full period of one hundred days from the first day above mentioned, order and designate as the States and parts of States wherein the people thereof, respectively, are this day in rebellion against the United States the following, to wit:

Arkansas, Texas, Louisiana (except the parishes of St. Bernard, Plaquemines, Jefferson, St. John, St. Charles, St. James, Ascension, Assumption, Terrebonne, Lafourche, St. Mary, St. Martin, and Orleans, including the city of New Orleans), Mississippi, Alabama, Florida, Georgia, South Carolina, North Carolina, and Virginia (except the forty-eight counties designated as West Virginia, and also the counties of Berkeley, Accomac, Northhampton, Elizabeth City, York, Princess Anne, and Norfolk, including the cities of Norfolk and Portsmouth), and which excepted parts are for the present left precisely as if this proclamation were not issued.

And by virtue of the power and for the purpose aforesaid, I do order and declare that all persons held as slaves within said designated States and parts of States are, and henceforward shall be, free; and that the Executive Government of the United States, including the military and naval authorities thereof, will recognize and maintain the freedom of said persons.

And I hereby enjoin upon the people so declared to be free to abstain from all violence, unless in necessary self-defense; and I recommend to them that, in all cases when allowed, they labor faithfully for reasonable wages.

And I further declare and make known that such persons of suitable condition will be received into the armed service of the United States to garrison forts, positions, stations, and other places, and to man vessels of all sorts in said service.

And upon this act, sincerely believed to be an act of justice, warranted by the Constitution upon military necessity, I invoke the considerate judgment of mankind and the gracious favor of Almighty God.

223. OPPOSITION TO THE EMANCIPATION PROCLAMATION

Resolutions of Illinois State Legislature
January 7, 1863

(Illinois State Register, January 7, 1863)

Lincoln's emancipation proclamation aroused widespread criticism from Northern democrats who were opposed to a war fought for the purpose of freeing the slaves. The legislature of Illinois was Democratic, and Illinois was one of the strongholds of Copperheadism and of the Knights of the Golden Circle. See, A. C. Cole, *The Era of the Civil War* (Centennial History of Illinois); E. J. Benton, *The Movement for Peace without a Victory During the Civil War.*

The constitutionality of Emancipation is discussed in J. G. Randall, *Constitutional Problems Under Lincoln*, chs. xvi–xvii.

Resolved: That the emancipation proclamation of the President of the United States is as unwarrantable in military as in civil law; a gigantic usurpation, at once converting the war, professedly commenced by the administration for the vindication of the authority of the constitution, into the crusade for the sudden, unconditional and violent liberation of 3,000,000 negro slaves; a result which would not only be a total subversion of the Federal Union but a revolution in the social organization of the Southern States, the immediate and remote, the present and far-reaching consequences of which to both races cannot be contemplated without the most dismal foreboding of horror and dismay. The proclamation invites servile insurrection as an element in this emancipation crusade—a means of warfare, the inhumanity and diabolism of which are without example in civilized warfare, and which we denounce, and which the civilized world will denounce, as an uneffaceable disgrace to the American people.

224. APPOINTMENT OF GENERAL HOOKER TO THE COMMAND OF THE ARMY OF THE POTOMAC

Letter from President Lincoln to Hooker
January 26, 1863

(The Writings of Abraham Lincoln, Constitutional ed., Vol. VI, p. 254)

After the shocking defeat of Burnside at Fredericksburg, Lincoln decided to appoint "Fighting Joe" Hooker to the command of the Army of the Potomac. At the same time the President distrusted Hooker, and many of his closest advisers felt that he was not competent to fill the position. Lincoln's letter is curious in its revelation of Lincoln's character as well as in its criticism of Hooker himself. Hooker was badly defeated at the Battle of Chancellorsville, under circumstances of an unfortunate character; just before the Battle of Gettysburg he was supplanted by General Meade. See, T. A. Dodge, *The Campaign of Chancellorsville;* J. Bigelow, *The Campaign of Chancellorsville;* A. Doubleday, *Chancellorsville and Gettysburg;* J. F. Rhodes, *History,* Vol. IV, p. 202 ff, 256 ff.

Executive Mansion, Washington, D. C.,
January 26, 1863.

MAJOR-GENERAL HOOKER.

GENERAL:—I have placed you at the head of the Army of the Potomac. Of course I have done this upon what appear to me to be sufficient reasons, and yet I think it best for you to know that there are some things in regard to which I am not quite satisfied with you. I believe you to be a brave and skilful soldier, which of course I like. I also believe you do not mix politics with your profession, in which you are right. You have confidence in yourself, which is a valuable if not an indispensable quality. You are ambitious, which within reasonable bounds does good rather than harm; but I think that during General Burnside's command of the army you have taken counsel of your ambition and thwarted him as much as you could, in which you did a great wrong to the country and to a most meritorious and honorable brother officer. I have heard, in such a way as to believe it, of your recently saying that both the army and the government needed a dictator. Of course it was not for this, but in spite of it, that I have given you the command. Only those generals who gain successes can set up dictators. What I now ask of you is military success, and I will risk the dictatorship. The government will support you to the utmost of its ability, which is neither more nor less than it has done and will do for all commanders. I much fear that the spirit that you have aided to infuse into the army, of criticising their commander and withholding confidence from him, will now turn upon you. I shall assist you as far as I can to put it down. Neither you nor Napoleon, if he were alive again, could get any good out of an army while such a spirit prevails in it. And now beware of rashness. Beware of rashness, but with energy and sleepless vigilance go forward and give us victories.

Yours very truly,
A. LINCOLN.

225. RESOLUTIONS AGAINST FOREIGN MEDIATION
March 3, 1863

(E. McPherson, *Political History of the Great Rebellion,* p. 346–7)

These resolutions were reported from the Committee on Foreign Affairs by Charles Sumner, and passed both Houses by large majorities.

WHEREAS it appears from the diplomatic correspondence submitted to Congress that a proposition, friendly in form, looking to pacification through foreign mediation, has been made to the United States by the Emperor of the French and promptly declined by the President; and whereas the idea of mediation or intervention in some shape may be regarded by foreign governments as practicable, and such governments, through this misunderstanding, may be led to proceedings tending to embarrass the friendly relations which now exist between them and the United States; and whereas, in order to remove for the future all chance of misunderstanding on this subject, and to secure for the United States the full enjoyment of that freedom from foreign interference which is one of the highest rights of independent states, it seems fit that Congress should declare its convictions thereon: Therefore—

Resolved, (the House of Representatives concurring,) That while in times past the United States have sought and accepted the friendly mediation or arbitration of foreign powers for the pacific adjustment of *international* questions, where the United States were the party of the one part and some other sovereign power the party of the other part; and while they are not disposed to misconstrue the natural and humane desire of foreign powers to aid in arresting *domestic* troubles, which, widening in their influence, have afflicted other countries, especially in view of the circumstance, deeply regretted by the American people, that the blow aimed by the rebellion at the national life has fallen heavily upon the laboring population of Europe: yet, notwithstanding these things, Congress cannot hesitate to regard every proposition of foreign interference in the present contest as so far unreasonable and inadmissible that its only explanation will be found in a misunderstanding of the true state of the question,

and of the real character of the war in which the republic is engaged.

2. That the United States are now grappling with an unprovoked and wicked rebellion, which is seeking the destruction of the republic that it may build a new power, whose cornerstone, according to the confession of its chief, shall be slavery; that for the suppression of this rebellion, and thus to save the republic and to prevent the establishment of such a power, the national government is now employing armies and fleets, in full faith that through these efforts all the purposes of conspirators and rebels will be crushed; that while engaged in this struggle, on which so much depends, any proposition from a foreign power, whatever form it may take, having for its object the arrest of these efforts, is, just in proportion to its influence, an encouragement to the rebellion, and to its declared pretensions, and, on this account, is calculated to prolong and embitter the conflict, to cause increased expenditure of blood and treasure, and to postpone the much-desired day of peace; that, with these convictions, and not doubting that every such proposition, although made with good intent, is injurious to the national interests, Congress will be obliged to look upon any further attempt in the same direction as an unfriendly act which it earnestly deprecates, to the end that nothing may occur abroad to strengthen the rebellion or to weaken those relations of good will with foreign powers which the United States are happy to cultivate.

3. That the rebellion from its beginning, and far back even in the conspiracy which preceded its outbreak, was encouraged by the hope of support from foreign powers; that its chiefs frequently boasted that the people of Europe were so far dependent upon regular supplies of the great southern staples that, sooner or later, their governments would be constrained to take side with the rebellion in some effective form, even to the extent of forcible intervention, if the milder form did not prevail; that the rebellion is now sustained by this hope,

which every proposition of foreign interference quickens anew, and that, without this life-giving support, it must soon yield to the just and paternal authority of the national government; that, considering these things, which are aggravated by the motive of the resistance thus encouraged, the United States regret that foreign powers have not frankly told the chiefs of the rebellion that the work in which they are engaged is hateful, and that a new government, such as they seek to found, with slavery as its acknowledged cornerstone, and with no other declared object of separate existence, is so far shocking to civilization and the moral sense of mankind that it must not expect welcome or recognition in the commonwealth of nations.

4. That the United States, confident in the justice of their cause, which is the cause, also, of good government and of human rights everywhere among men; anxious for the speedy restoration of peace, which shall secure tranquillity at home and remove all occasion of complaint abroad; and awaiting with well-assured trust the final suppression of the rebellion, through which all these things, rescued from present danger, will be secured forever, and the republic, one and indivisible, triumphant over its enemies, will continue to stand an example to mankind, *hereby announce,* as their unalterable purpose, that the war will be vigorously prosecuted, according to the humane principles of Christian states, until the rebellion shall be overcome; and they reverently invoke upon their cause the blessings of Almighty God. . . .

226. THE FRENCH IN MEXICO
1862–1866

The decision of the Mexican Congress, in July 1861 to suspend for two years all payments on foreign debts, brought to a head a situation which had long been threatening. France, Spain and Great Britain signed an agreement for joint intervention, and in 1862 took possession of Mexican custom houses. Spain and Great Britain reaching a satisfactory agreement with Mexico thereupon withdrew from the coalition, leaving France in control of the situation. A French army defeated Juarez, captured the Mexican capital, and organized a provisional government which promptly voted to establish an Empire and invited the Austrian Archduke Maximilian to the throne. Secretary Seward watched this violation of the Monroe Doctrine with profound dissatisfaction, but hesitated to antagonize Emperor Napoleon III. The despatch of March 3, 1862 sets forth the American position on intervention and assumes the honorable intentions of the signatories of the convention of 1861. The success of the Union arms by 1864 made Congress ready to assume a bolder position, but the resolution of April 4, 1864 was not passed by the Senate. After the War Seward assumed a position of inflexible hostility to the maintenance of the French regime in Mexico, and the despatch of April 16, 1866 sets forth the American attitude toward the project of Austrian military support to Emperor Maximilian. French troops were finally withdrawn from Mexico in 1867 and in June of that year the hapless Maximilian was shot. See J. B. Moore, *A Digest of International Law,* Vol. vi;

D. Perkins, *The Monroe Doctrine,* 1826–1867, ch. vii, and bibliography; E. C. Corti, *Maximilian and Charlotte of Mexico,* Vol. II; J. M. Callahan, *Evolution of Seward's Mexican Policy;* J. F. Rippy, *The United States and Mexico,* ch. xiv; C. A. Duniway, "Reasons for the Withdrawal of the French from Mexico", *American Hist. Assoc. Annual Report,* 1902, Vol. I, p. 313. On Confederate diplomacy in Mexico, see F. L. Owsley, *King Cotton Diplomacy,* ch. xvii.

1. MR. SEWARD TO MR. ADAMS
March 3, 1862

(U. S. 37th Congress, 2d Session, *House Doc.* No. 100, p. 207–8)

Department of State,
Washington, March 3, 1862.

Sir: We observe indications of a growing opinion in Europe that the demonstrations which are being made by Spanish, French, and British forces against Mexico are likely to be attended with a revolution in that country which will bring in a monarchical government there, in which the crown will be assumed by some foreign prince.

This country is deeply concerned in the peace of nations, and aims to be loyal at the same time in all its relations, as well to the allies as to Mexico. The President has therefore instructed me to submit his views on the new aspect of affairs to the parties concerned. He has relied upon the assurances given to this government by the allies that they were seeking no political objects and only a redress of grievances. He does not doubt the sincerity of the allies, and his confidence in their good faith, if it could be shaken, would be reinspired by explanations apparently made in their behalf that the governments of Spain, France, and Great Britain are not intending to intervene and will not intervene to effect a change of the constitutional form of government now existing in Mexico, or to produce any political change there in opposition to the will of the Mexican people. Indeed, he understands the allies to be unanimous in declaring that the proposed revolution in Mexico is moved only by Mexican citizens now in Europe.

The President, however, deems it his duty to express to the allies, in all candor and frankness, the opinion that no monarchical government which could be founded in Mexico, in the presence of foreign navies and armies in the waters and upon the soil of Mexico, would have any prospect of security or permanency. Secondly, that the instability of such a monarchy there would be enhanced if the throne should be assigned to any person not of Mexican nativity. That under such circumstances the new government must speedily fall unless it could draw into its support European alliances, which, relating back to the present invasion, would, in fact, make it the beginning of a permanent policy of armed European monarchical intervention injurious and practically hostile to the most general system of government on the continent of America, and this would be the beginning rather than the ending of revolution in Mexico.

These views are grounded upon some knowledge of the political sentiments and habits of society in America.

In such a case it is not to be doubted that the permanent interests and sympathies of this country would be with the other American republics. It is not intended on this occasion to predict the course of events which might happen as a consequence of the proceeding contemplated, either on this continent or in Europe. It is sufficient to say that, in the President's opinion, the emancipation of this continent from European control has been the principal fea-

ture in its history during the last century. It is not probable that a revolution in the contrary direction would be successful in an immediately succeeding century, while population in America is so rapidly increasing, resources so rapidly developing, and society so steadily forming itself upon principles of democratic American government. Nor is it necessary to suggest to the allies the improbability that European nations could steadily agree upon a policy favorable to such a counter-revolution as one conducive to their own interests, or to suggest that, however studiously the allies may act to avoid lending the aid of their land and naval forces to domestic revolutions in Mexico, the result would nevertheless be traceable to the presence of those forces there, although for a different purpose, since it may be deemed certain that but for their presence there no such revolution could probably have been attempted or even conceived.

The Senate of the United States has not, indeed, given its official sanction to the precise measures which the President has proposed for lending our aid to the existing government in Mexico, with the approval of the allies, to relieve it from its present embarrassments. This, however, is only a question of domestic administration. It would be very erroneous to regard such a disagreement as indicating any serious difference of opinion in this government or among the American people in their cordial good wishes for the safety, welfare, and stability of the republican system of government in that country.

I am, sir, your obedient servant,
William H. Seward.

2. HOUSE RESOLUTION ON FRENCH INTERVENTION IN MEXICO
April 4, 1864

(E. McPherson, *Political History of the Rebellion*, p. 349)

Resolved. That the Congress of the United States are unwilling, by silence, to leave the nations of the world under the impression that they are indifferent spectators of the deplorable events now transpiring in the Republic of Mexico; and they therefore think fit to declare that it does not accord with the policy of the United States to acknowledge a monarchical government, erected on the ruins of any republican government in America, under the auspices of any European power.

3. MR. SEWARD TO MR. MOTLEY
April 16, 1866
(U. S. 39th Congress, 1st Session, *House Doc.* No. 93, p. 46–7)

Department of State,
Washington, April 16, 1866.

SIR: I have had the honor to receive your despatch of the 27th of March, No. 155, which brings the important announcement that a treaty, called a "military supplementary convention," was ratified on the 15th of that month between the Emperor of Austria and the Prince Maximilian, who claims to be an emperor in Mexico.

You inform me that it is expected that about one thousand volunteers will be shipped (under this treaty) from Trieste to Vera Cruz very soon, and that at least as many more will be shipped in autumn.

I have heretofore given you the President's instructions to ask for explanations, and, conditionally, to inform the government of Austria that the despatch of military expeditions by Austria under such an arrangement as the one which seems now to have been consummated would be regarded with serious concern by the United States.

The subject has now been further considered in connexion with the official information thus recently received. The time seems to have arrived when the attitude of this government in relation to Mexican affairs should be once again frankly and distinctly made known to the Emperor of Austria, and all other powers whom it may directly concern. The United States, for reasons which seem to them to be just, and to have their foundation in the laws of nations, maintain that the domestic republican government with which they are in relations of friendly communication is the only legitimate government existing in Mexico; that a war has for a period of several years been waged against that republic by the government of France; which war began with a disclaim of all political or dynastic designs that that war has subsequently taken upon

itself, and now distinctly wears the character of an European intervention to overthrow that domestic republican government, and to erect in its stead a European, imperial, military despotism by military force. The United States, in view of the character of their own political institutions, their proximity and intimate relations towards Mexico, and their just influence in the political affairs of the American continent, cannot consent to the accomplishment of that purpose by the means described. The United States have therefore addressed themselves, as they think, seasonably to the government of France, and have asked that its military forces, engaged in that objectionable political invasion, may desist from further intervention and be withdrawn from Mexico.

A copy of the last communication upon this subject, which was addressed by us to the government of France, is herewith transmitted for your special information. This paper will give you the true situation of the question. It will also enable you to satisfy the government of Vienna that the United States must be no less opposed to military intervention for political objects hereafter in Mexico by the government of Austria, than they are opposed to any further intervention of the same character in that country by France.

You will, therefore, at as early a day as may be convenient, bring the whole case, in a becoming manner, to the attention of the imperial royal government. You are authorized to state that the United States sincerely desire that Austria may find it just and expedient to come upon the same ground of non-intervention in Mexico which is maintained by the United States, and to which they have invited France.

You will communicate to us the answer of the Austrian government to this proposition.

This government could not but regard as a matter of serious concern the despatch of any troops from Austria for Mexico while the subject which you are thus directed to present to the Austrian government remains under consideration.

I am, sir, your obedient servant,
WILLIAM H. SEWARD.

227. NEW JERSEY PEACE RESOLUTIONS
March 18, 1863

(F. Moore, ed. *The Rebellion Record,* Vol. XII, p. 679 ff.)

These resolutions of the legislature of New Jersey did not meet with the approval of the New Jersey soldiers. Their protest is given in the accompanying document below. See, C. M. Knapp, *New Jersey Politics During the Civil War;* J. F. Rhodes, *History,* Vol. V, p. 317 ff.

1. NEW-JERSEY PEACE RESOLUTIONS

1. *Be it Resolved by the Senate and General Assembly of the State of New-Jersey,* That this State, in promptly answering the calls made by the President of the United States, at and since the inauguration of the war, for troops and means to assist in maintaining the power and dignity of the Federal Government, believed and confided in the professions and declarations of the President of the United States, in his inaugural address, and in the resolutions passed by Congress on the twenty-fifth day of July, 1861, in which, among other things, it was declared "that the war is not waged for conquest or subjugation, or interfering with the rights or established institutions of the States, but to maintain and defend the supremacy of the Constitution, with the rights and equality under it unimpaired, and that as soon as these objects shall be accomplished the war ought to cease;". . .

2. *And be it Resolved,* That this State having waited for the redemption of the sacred pledges of the President and Congress with a patience and forbearance only equalled in degree by the unfaltering and unswerving bravery and fidelity of her sons, conceives it to be her solemn duty, as it is her unquestioned right, to urge upon the President and Congress, in the most respectful but decided manner, the redemption of the pledges under which the troops of this State entered upon, and to this moment have continued in, the contest; . . .

3. *And be it Resolved,* That it is the deliberate sense of the people of this State that the war power within the limits of the Constitution is ample for any and all emergencies, and that all assumption of power, under whatever plea, beyond that conferred by the Constitution, is without warrant or

authority, and if permitted to continue without remonstrance, will finally encompass the destruction of the liberties of the people and the death of the Republic; and therefore, to the end that in any event the matured and deliberate sense of the people of New-Jersey may be known and declared, we, their representatives in Senate and General Assembly convened, do, in their name and in their behalf, make unto the Federal Government this our solemn

PROTEST

Against a war waged with the insurgent States for the accomplishment of unconstitutional or partisan purposes;

Against a war which has for its object the subjugation of any of the States, with a view to their reduction to territorial condition; . . .

Against the domination of the military over the civil laws in States, Territories, or districts not in a state of insurrection;

Against all arrests without warrant; against the suspension of the writ of *habeas corpus* in States and Territories sustaining the Federal Government, "where the public safety does not require it," and against the assumption of power by any person to suspend such writ, except under the express authority of Congress;

Against the creation of new States by the division of existing ones, or in any other manner not clearly authorized by the Constitution, and against the right of secession as practically admitted by the action of Congress in admitting as a new State a portion of the State of Virginia;

Against the power assumed in the proclamation of the President made January first, 1863, by which all the slaves in certain States and parts of States are for ever set free; and against the expenditures of the public moneys for the emancipation of slaves or their support at any time, under any pretence whatever;

Against any and every exercise of power upon the part of the Federal Government that is not clearly given and expressed in the Federal Constitution—reasserting that "the powers not delegated to the United States by the Constitution, nor prohibited by it to the States, are reserved to the States respectively, or to the people.". . .

4. *And be it Resolved*, That . . . while abating naught in her devotion to the Union of the States and the dignity and power of the Federal Government, at no time since the commencement of the present war has this State been other than willing to terminate peacefully and honorably to all a war unnecessary in its origin, fraught with horror and suffering in its prosecution, and necessarily dangerous to the liberties of all in its continuance. . . .

2. PROTEST OF THE NEW-JERSEY SOLDIERS

Camp of the Eleventh New-Jersey Volunteers,
Below Falmouth, Va., March 10, 1863.

Whereas, The Legislature of our native States, . . . has sought to tarnish its high honor, and bring upon it disgrace, by the passage of resolutions tending to a dishonorable peace with armed rebels seeking to destroy our great and beneficent Government, the best ever designed for the happiness of the many; and

Whereas, We, her sons, members of the Eleventh regiment New-Jersey volunteers, citizens representing every section of the State, have left our homes to endure the fatigues, privations, and dangers incident to a soldier's life, in order to maintain our Republic in its integrity, willing to sacrifice our lives to that object; fully recognizing the impropriety of a soldier's discussion of the legislative functions of the State, yet deeming it due to ourselves, that the voice of those who offer their all in their country's

cause, be heard when weak and wicked men seek its dishonor; therefore

Resolved, That the Union of the States is the only guarantee for the preservation of our liberty and independence, and that the war for the maintenance of that Union commands *now,* as it ever has done, our best efforts and our heartfelt sympathy.

Resolved, That we consider the passage, or even the introduction of the so-called Peace Resolutions, as wicked, weak, and cowardly, tending to aid by their sympathy, the rebels seeking to destroy the Republic.

Resolved, That we regard as traitors alike the foe in arms and the secret enemies of our Government, who, at home, foment disaffection and strive to destroy confidence in our legally chosen rulers.

Resolved, That the reports spread broadcast throughout the North, by secession sympathizers, prints, and voices, that the army of which we esteem it a high honor to form a part, is demoralized and clamorous for peace on any terms, are the lying utterances of traitorous tongues, and do base injustice to our noble comrades who have never faltered in the great work, and are now not only willing but anxious to follow their gallant and chivalric leader against the strongholds of the enemy.

Resolved, That we put forth every effort, endure every fatigue, and shrink from no danger, until, under the gracious guidance of a kind Providence, every armed rebel shall be conquered, and traitors at home shall quake with fear, as the proud emblem of our national independence shall assert its power from North to South, and crush beneath its powerful folds all who dared to assail its honor, doubly hallowed by the memory of the patriot dead. . . .

228. THE GETTYSBURG ADDRESS
November 19, 1863

(The Writings of Abraham Lincoln, Constitutional ed., Vol. VII, p. 20)

There is considerable variation in phraseology among the various versions of this famous address. For a learned discussion of the address and comparison of facsimile manuscripts, see W. E. Barton, *Lincoln at Gettysburg.* A more popular account is C. E. Carr, *Lincoln at Gettysburg.*

Four score and seven years ago our fathers brought forth on this continent, a new nation, conceived in Liberty, and dedicated to the proposition that all men are created equal.

Now we are engaged in a great civil war,

testing whether that nation or any nation so conceived and so dedicated, can long endure. We are met on a great battle-field of that war. We have come to dedicate a portion of that field, as a final resting place for those who here gave their lives that that nation might live. It is altogether fitting and proper that we should do this.

But, in a larger sense, we can not dedicate —we can not consecrate—we can not hallow —this ground. The brave men, living and dead, who struggled here, have consecrated it, far above our poor power to add or detract. The world will little note, nor long remember what we say here, but it can never forget what they did here. It is for us the living, rather, to be dedicated here to the unfinished work which they who fought here have thus far so nobly advanced. It is rather for us to be here dedicated to the great task remaining before us—that from these honored dead we take increased devotion to that cause for which they gave the last full measure of devotion—that we here highly resolve that these dead shall not have died in vain—that this nation, under God, shall have a new birth of freedom— and that government of the people, by the people, for the people, shall not perish from the earth.

229. RECONSTRUCTION OF TENNESSEE

Lincoln's Letter to Governor Johnson
September 11, 1863

(Writings of Abraham Lincoln, Constitutional ed., Vol. VI, p. 407–8)

This letter is significant for the development of Lincoln's policy of Reconstruction. See references in Doc. No. 230 and C. R. Hall, *Andrew Johnson, Military Governor of Tennessee;* J. W. Fertig, *Secession and Reconstruction of Tennessee;* J. W. Patton, *Unionism and Reconstruction in Tennessee.*

Executive Mansion, Washington, September 11, 1863.
HON. ANDREW JOHNSON.

MY DEAR SIR:—All Tennessee is now clear of armed insurrectionists. You need not to be reminded that it is the nick of time for reinaugurating a loyal State government. Not a moment should be lost. You and the co-operating friends there can better judge of the ways and means than can be judged by any here. I only offer a few suggestions. The reinauguration must not be such as to give control of the State and its representation in Congress to the enemies of the Union, driving its friends there into political exile. The whole struggle for Tennessee will have been profitless to both State and nation if it so ends that Governor Johnson is put down and Governor Harris put up. It must not be so. You must have it otherwise. Let the reconstruction be the work of such men only as can be trusted for the Union. Exclude all others, and trust that your government so organized will be recognized here as being the one of republican form to be guaranteed to the State, and to be protected against invasion and domestic violence. It is something on the question of time to remember that it cannot be known who is next to occupy the position I now hold, nor what he will do. I see that you have declared in favor of emancipation in Tennessee, for which may God bless you. Get emancipation into your new State government—constitution—and there will be no such word as fail for your case. The raising of colored troops, I think, will greatly help every way.

Yours very truly,
A. LINCOLN.

230. LINCOLN'S PLAN OF RECONSTRUCTION

Proclamation of Amnesty and Reconstruction
December 8, 1863

(Richardson, ed. *Messages and Papers,* Vol. VI, p. 213 ff.)

Lincoln had already indicated his reconstruction policy by his action during 1862 in the reconstruction of Tennessee and Louisiana. The Presidential plan, as presented in the message of

December 8, 1863, provided for the restoration of loyal governments in the seceded states when a number, equal to one tenth of the voting population of the State in 1860, should take an oath prescribed and organize a government. This Presidential plan assumed that the States were not out of the Union, and that reconstruction was a Presidential function, to be carried out through the instrumentality of the pardoning power. The opposition to this theory was announced first by the refusal of Congress to admit representatives from the reconstructed States, and, decisively, by the passage of the Wade-Davis Bill, Doc. No. 234. On Lincoln's policy, see, C. H. McCarthy, *Lincoln's Plan of Reconstruction;* C. E. Chadsey, *Reconstruction Prior to the Close of the Civil War;* J. W. Burgess, *Civil War on the Constitution,* 2 Vols.

A Proclamation

Whereas in and by the Constitution of the United States it is provided that the President "shall have power to grant reprieves and pardons for offenses against the United States, except in cases of impeachment;" and

Whereas a rebellion now exists whereby the loyal State governments of several States have for a long time been subverted, and many persons have committed and are now guilty of treason against the United States; and

Whereas, with reference to said rebellion and treason, laws have been enacted by Congress declaring forfeitures and confiscation of property and liberation of slaves, all upon terms and conditions therein stated, and also declaring that the President was thereby authorized at any time thereafter, by proclamation, to extend to persons who may have participated in the existing rebellion in any State or part thereof pardon and amnesty, with such exceptions and at such times and on such conditions as he may deem expedient for the public welfare; and

Whereas the Congressional declaration for limited and conditional pardon accords with well-established judicial exposition of the pardoning power; and

Whereas, with reference to said rebellion, the President of the United States has issued several proclamations with provisions in regard to the liberation of slaves; and

Whereas it is now desired by some persons heretofore engaged in said rebellion to resume their allegiance to the United States and to reinaugurate loyal State governments within and for their respective States:

Therefore, I, Abraham Lincoln, President of the United States, do proclaim, . . . to all persons who have, directly or by implication, participated in the existing rebellion, except as hereinafter excepted, that a full pardon is hereby granted to them and each of them, with restoration of all rights of property, except as to slaves and in property cases where rights of third parties shall have intervened, and upon the condition that every such person shall take and subscribe an oath and thenceforward keep and maintain said oath inviolate, and which oath shall be registered for permanent preservation and shall be of the tenor and effect following, to wit:

I, —— ——, do solemnly swear, in presence of Almighty God, that I will henceforth faithfully support, protect, and defend the Constitution of the United States and the Union of the States thereunder; and that I will in like manner abide by and faithfully support all acts of Congress passed during the existing rebellion with reference to slaves, so long and so far as not repealed, modified, or held void by Congress or by decision of the Supreme Court; and that I will in like manner abide by and faithfully support all proclamations of the President made during the existing rebellion having reference to slaves, so long and so far as not modified or declared void by decision of the Supreme Court. So help me God.

The persons excepted from the benefits of the foregoing provisions are all who are or shall have been civil or diplomatic officers or agents of the so-called Confederate Government; all who have left judicial stations under the United States to aid the rebellion; all who are or shall have been military or naval officers of said so-called Confederate Government above the rank of colonel in the army or of lieutenant in the navy; all who left seats in the United States Congress to aid the rebellion; all who resigned commissions in the Army or Navy of the United States and afterwards aided the rebellion; and all who have engaged in any way in treating colored persons, or white persons in charge of such, otherwise than lawfully as prisoners of war, and which persons may have been found in the United States service as soldiers, seamen, or in any other capacity.

And I do further proclaim, declare, and make known that whenever, in any of the States of Arkansas, Texas, Louisiana, Mississippi, Tennessee, Alabama, Georgia, Florida, South Carolina, and North Carolina, a number of persons, not less than one-tenth in number of the votes cast in such State at the Presidential election of the year A. D. 1860, each having taken oath aforesaid, and not having since violated it, and being a qualified voter by the election law of the State existing immediately before the so-called act of secession, and excluding all others, shall re-establish a State government which shall be republican and in nowise contravening said oath, such shall be recognized as the true government of the State, and the State shall receive thereunder the benefits of the constitutional provision which declares that "the United States shall guarantee to every State in this Union a republican form of government and shall protect each of them against invasion, and, on application of the legislature, or the executive (when the legislature can not be convened), against domestic violence."

And I do further proclaim, declare, and make known that any provision which may be adopted by such State government in relation to the freed people of such State which shall recognize and declare their permanent freedom, provide for their education, and which may yet be consistent as a temporary arrangement with their present condition as a laboring, landless, and homeless class, will not be objected to by the National Executive.

And it is suggested as not improper that in constructing a loyal State government in any State the name of the State, the boundary, the subdivisions, the constitution, and the general code of laws as before the rebellion be maintained, subject only to the modifications made necessary by the conditions hereinbefore stated, and such others, if any, not contravening said conditions and which may be deemed expedient by those framing the new State government.

To avoid misunderstanding, it may be proper to say that this proclamation, so far as it relates to State governments, has no reference to States wherein loyal State governments have all the while been maintained. And for the same reason it may be proper to further say that whether members sent to Congress from any State shall be admitted to seats constitutionally rests exclusively with the respective Houses, and not to any extent with the Executive. And, still further, that this proclamation is intended to present the people of the States wherein the national authority has been suspended and loyal State governments have been subverted a mode in and by which the national authority and loyal State governments may be re-established within said States or in any of them; and while the mode presented is the best the Executive can suggest, with his present impressions, it must not be understood that no other possible mode would be acceptable.

ABRAHAM LINCOLN.

231. THE NATIONAL BANK ACT
June 3, 1864

(U. S. Statutes at Large, Vol. XIII, p. 99 ff.)

This act amended the banking act of February 25, 1863, and created the national banking system that obtained until the passage of the Federal Reserve Act of 1913. For a history of the National Bank Act see, D. R. Dewey, *Financial History of the United States*, p. 299 ff.; J. J. Knox, *History of Banking*, p. 220 ff.; A. B. Hepburn, *History of Currency in the United States*, ch. xvii; A. M. Davis, *The Origin of the National Banking System*.

An Act to provide a National Currency, se-

cured by a Pledge of United States Bonds, and to provide for the Circulation and Redemption thereof.

. . . Sec. 5. That associations for carrying on the business of banking may be formed by any number of persons, not less in any case than five, who shall enter into articles of association, which shall specify in general terms the object for which the association is formed, and may contain any other provisions, not inconsistent with the provisions of this act, which the association may see fit to adopt for the regulation of the business of the association and the conduct of its affairs, which said articles shall be signed by the persons uniting to form the association, and a copy of them forwarded to the comptroller of the currency, to be filed and preserved in his office. . . .

SEC. 7. That no association shall be organized under this act, with a less capital than one hundred thousand dollars, nor in a city whose population exceeds fifty thousand persons, with a less capital than two hundred thousand dollars: *Provided,* That banks with a capital of not less than fifty thousand dollars may, with the approval of the Secretary of the Treasury, be organized in any place the population of which does not exceed six thousand inhabitants.

SEC. 8. That every association formed pursuant to the provisions of this act shall . . . transact no business except such as may be incidental to its organization and necessarily preliminary, until authorized by the comptroller of the currency to commence the business of banking. Such association shall have power to adopt a corporate seal, and shall have succession by the name designated in its organization certificate, for the period of twenty years from its organization, unless sooner dissolved according to the provisions of its articles of association, or by the act of its shareholders owning two thirds of its stock, or unless the franchise shall be forfeited by a violation of this act; by such name it may make contracts . . . , and exercise under this act all such incidental powers as shall be necessary to carry on the business of banking by discounting and negotiating promissory notes, drafts, bills of exchange, and other evidences of debt; by receiving deposits; by buying and selling exchange, coin, and bullion; by loaning money on personal security; by obtaining, issuing, and circulating notes according to the provisions of this act. . . .

The shareholders of each association formed under the provisions of this act, and of each existing bank or banking association that may accept the provisions of this act, shall be held individually responsible, equally and ratably, and not one for another, for all contracts, debts, and engagements of such

association to the extent of the amount of their stock therein at the par value thereof, in addition to the amount invested in such shares; except that shareholders of any banking association now existing under state laws, having not less than five millions of dollars of capital actually paid in, and a surplus of twenty per centum on hand, both to be determined by the comptroller of the currency, shall be liable only to the amount invested in their shares. . . .

SEC. 16. That every association, after having complied with the provisions of this act, preliminary to the commencement of banking business under its provisions, and before it shall be authorized to commence business, shall transfer and deliver to the treasurer of the United States any United States registered bonds bearing interest to an amount not less than thirty thousand dollars nor less than one third of the capital stock paid in, which bonds shall be deposited with the treasurer of the United States and by him safely kept in his office until the same shall be otherwise disposed of, in pursuance of the provisions of this act; and the Secretary of the Treasury is hereby authorized to receive and cancel any United States coupon bonds, and to issue in lieu thereof registered bonds of like amount, bearing a like rate of interest, and having the same time to run; and the deposit of bonds shall be, by every association, increased as its capital may be paid up or increased, so that every association shall at all times have on deposit with the treasurer registered United States bonds to the amount of at least one third of its capital stock actually paid in. . . .

SEC. 21. That upon the transfer and delivery of bonds to the treasurer, as provided in the foregoing section, the association making the same shall be entitled to receive from the comptroller of the currency circulating notes of different denominations, in blank, registered and countersigned as hereinafter provided, equal in amount to ninety per centum of the current market value of the United States bonds so transferred and delivered, but not exceeding ninety per centum of the amount of said bonds at the par value thereof, if bearing interest at a rate not less than five per centum per annum; and at no time shall the total amount of such notes, issued to any such association, exceed the amount at such time actually paid in of its capital stock.

SEC. 22. That the entire amount of notes for circulation to be issued under this act shall not exceed three hundred millions of dollars. . . .

SEC. 23. That after any such association shall have caused its promise to pay such notes on demand to be signed by the president or vice-president and cashier thereof, in such manner as to make them obligatory promissory notes, payable on demand, at its place of business, such association is hereby authorized to issue and circulate the same as money; and the same shall be received at par in all parts of the United States in payment of taxes, excises, public lands, and all other dues to the United States, except for duties on imports; and also for all salaries and other debts and demands owing by the United States to individuals, corporations, and associations within the United States, except interest on the public debt, and in redemption of the national currency. And no such association shall issue post notes or any other notes to circulate as money than such as are authorized by the foregoing provisions of this act. . . .

SEC. 26. That the bonds transferred to and deposited with the treasurer of the United States, as hereinbefore provided, by any banking association for the security of its circulating notes, shall be held exclusively for that purpose, until such notes shall be redeemed, except as provided in this act; but the comptroller of the currency shall give to any such banking association powers of attorney to receive and appropriate to its own use the interest on the bonds which it shall have so transferred to the treasurer; but such powers shall become inoperative whenever such banking association shall fail to redeem its circulating notes as aforesaid. Whenever the market or cash value of any bonds deposited with the treasurer of the United States, as aforesaid, shall be reduced below the amount of the circulation issued for the same, the comptroller of the currency is hereby authorized to demand and receive the amount of such depreciation in other United States bonds at cash value, or in money, from the association receiving said

bills, to be deposited with the treasurer of the United States as long as such depreciation continues. . . .

SEC. 30. That every association may take, receive, reserve, and charge on any loan or discount made, or upon any note, bill of exchange, or other evidences of debt, interest at the rate allowed by the laws of the state or territory where the bank is located, and no more. . . . And when no rate is fixed by the laws of the state or territory, the bank may take, receive, reserve, or charge a rate not exceeding seven per centum. . . .

SEC. 31. That every association in the cities hereinafter named shall, at all times, have on hand, in lawful money of the United States, an amount equal to at least twenty-five per centum of the aggregate amount of its notes in circulation and its deposits; and every other association shall, at all times, have on hand, in lawful money of the United States, an amount equal to at least fifteen per centum of the aggregate amount of its notes in circulation, and of its deposits. . . . *Provided,* That three fifths of said fifteen per centum may consist of balances due to an association available for the redemption of its circulating notes from associations approved by the comptroller of the currency, organized under this act, in the cities of Saint Louis, Louisville, Chicago, Detroit, Milwaukee, New Orleans, Cincinnati, Cleveland, Pittsburg, Baltimore, Philadelphia, Boston, New York, Albany, Leavenworth, San Francisco, and Washington City: *Provided, also,* That clearing-house certificates, representing specie or lawful money specially deposited for the purpose of any clearing-house association, shall be deemed to be lawful money in the possession of any association belonging to such clearing-house holding and owning such certificate, and shall be considered to be a part of the lawful money which such association is required to have under the foregoing provisions of this section: *Provided,* That the cities of Charleston and Richmond may be added to the list of cities in the national associations of which other associations may keep three fifths of their lawful money, whenever, in the opinion of the comptroller of the currency, the condition of the southern states will warrant it. And it shall be competent for the comptroller of the currency to notify any association, whose lawful money reserve as aforesaid shall be below the amount to be kept on hand as aforesaid, to make good such reserve; and if such association shall fail for thirty days thereafter so to make good its reserve of lawful money of the United States, the comptroller may, with the concurrence of the Secretary of the Treasury, appoint a receiver to wind up the business of such association, as provided in this act.

SEC. 32. That each association organized in any of the cities named in the foregoing section shall select, subject to the approval of the comptroller of the currency, an association in the city of New York, at which it will redeem its circulating notes at par. And each of such associations may keep one half of its lawful money reserve in cash deposits in the city of New York. . . .

SEC. 36. That no association shall at any time be indebted, or in any way liable, to an amount exceeding the amount of its capital stock at such time actually paid in and remaining undiminished by losses or otherwise, except on the following accounts, that is to say:—

First. On account of its notes or circulation.

Second. On account of moneys deposited with, or collected by, such association.

Third. On account of bills of exchange or drafts drawn against money actually on deposit to the credit of such association, or due thereto.

Fourth. On account of liabilities to its stockholders for dividends and reserved profits. . . .

SEC. 38. That no association, or any member thereof, shall, during the time it shall continue its banking operations, withdraw, or permit to be withdrawn, either in form of dividends or otherwise, any portion of its capital. And if losses shall at any time have been sustained by any such association equal to or exceeding its undivided profits then on hand, no dividend shall be made; and no dividend shall ever be made by any association, while it shall continue its banking op-

erations, to an amount greater than its net profits then on hand, deducting therefrom its losses and bad debts. . . .

SEC. 41. And in lieu of all existing taxes, every association shall pay to the treasurer of the United States, in the months of January and July, a duty of one half of one per centum each half year from and after [January 1, 1864] upon the average amount of its notes in circulation, and a duty of one quarter of one per centum each half year upon the average amount of its deposits, and a duty of one quarter of one per centum each half year, as aforesaid, on the average amount of its capital stock beyond the amount invested in United States bonds; . . .

SEC. 44. That any bank incorporated by special law, or any banking institution organized under a general law of any state, may, by authority of this act, become a national association under its provisions, by the name prescribed in its organization certificate. . . .

SEC. 45. That all associations under this act, when designated for that purpose by the Secretary of the Treasury, shall be depositaries of public money, except receipts from customs, under such regulations as may be prescribed by the Secretary; and they may also be employed as financial agents of the government; and they shall perform all such reasonable duties, as depositaries of public moneys and financial agents of the government, as may be required of them. And the Secretary of the Treasury shall require of the association thus designated satisfactory security, by the deposit of United States bonds and otherwise, for the safe-keeping and prompt payment of the public money deposited with them, and for the faithful performance of their duties as financial agents of the government: *Provided,* That every association which shall be selected and designated as receiver or depositary of the public money shall take and receive at par all of the national currency bills, by whatever association issued, which have been paid in to the government for internal revenue, or for loans or stocks. . . .

232. PLATFORM OF NATIONAL UNION CONVENTION
Baltimore, Maryland
June 7, 1864

(The Writings of Abraham Lincoln, Constitutional ed., Vol. VII, p. 148 ff.)

The Republican Party took the name of National Union Party during the war period.

1. *Resolved,* That it is the highest duty of every American citizen to maintain against all their enemies the integrity of the Union and the paramount authority of the Constitution and laws of the United States; and that, laying aside all differences of political opinion, we pledge ourselves, as Union men, animated by a common sentiment and aiming at a common object, to do everything in our power to aid the Government in quelling by force of arms the rebellion now raging against its authority, and in bringing to the punishment due to their crimes the rebels and traitors arrayed against it.

2. *Resolved,* That we approve the determination of the Government of the United States not to compromise with rebels, or to offer them any terms of peace, except such as may be based upon an unconditional surrender of their hostility and a return to their just allegiance to the Constitution and laws of the United States, and that we call upon the Government to maintain this position, and to prosecute the war with the utmost possible vigor to the complete suppression of the rebellion, in full reliance upon the self-sacrificing patriotism, the heroic valor, and the undying devotion of the American people to their country and its free institutions.

3. *Resolved,* That as slavery was the cause, and now constitutes the strength, of this rebellion, and as it must be, always and everywhere, hostile to the principles of republican government, justice and the national safety demand its utter and complete extirpation from the soil of the republic; and that while we uphold and maintain the acts and proclamations by which the Government, in its own defense, has aimed a death-blow at this gigantic evil, we are in favor, furthermore, of such an amendment to the Constitution, to be made by the people in conformity with its provisions, as shall terminate and forever prohibit the existence of slavery within the limits or the jurisdiction of the United States.

4. *Resolved,* That the thanks of the American people are due to the soldiers and sailors of the Army and Navy, who have periled their lives in defense of their country and in vindication of the honor of its flag; that the nation owes to them some permanent recognition of their patriotism and their valor, and ample and permanent provision for those of their survivors who have received disabling and honorable wounds in the service of the country; and that the memories of those who have fallen in its defense shall be held in grateful and everlasting remembrance.

5. *Resolved,* That we approve and applaud the practical wisdom, the unselfish patriotism, and the unswerving fidelity to the Constitution and the principles of American liberty, with which Abraham Lincoln has discharged under circumstances of unparalleled difficulty the great duties and responsibilities of the Presidential office; that we approve and indorse as demanded by the emergency and essential to the preservation of the nation, and as within the provisions of the Constitution, the measures and acts which he has adopted to defend the nation against its open and secret foes; that we approve, especially, the Proclamation of Emancipation, and the employment as Union soldiers of men heretofore held in slavery; and that we have full confidence in his determination to carry these and all other constitutional measures essential to the salvation of the country into full and complete effect.

6. *Resolved,* That we deem it essential to the general welfare that harmony should prevail in the national councils, and we regard as worthy of public confidence and official trust those only who cordially indorse the principles proclaimed in these resolutions, and which should characterize the administration of the Government.

7. *Resolved,* That the Government owes to all men employed in its armies, without

regard to distinction of color, the full protection of the laws of war, and that any
violation of these laws, or of the usages of
civilized nations in time of war, by the rebels
now in arms, should be made the subject
of prompt and full redress.

8. *Resolved,* That foreign immigration,
which in the past has added so much to the
wealth, development of resources, and increase of power to this nation, the asylum
of the oppressed of all nations, should be
fostered and encouraged by a liberal and
just policy.

9. *Resolved,* That we are in favor of the
speedy construction of the railroad to the
Pacific coast.

10. *Resolved,* That the national faith,
pledged for the redemption of the public
debt, must be kept inviolate, and that for
this purpose we recommend economy and
rigid responsibility in the public expenditures, and a vigorous and just system of
taxation: and that it is the duty of every
loyal State to sustain the credit and promote
the use of the national currency.

11. *Resolved,* That we approve the position taken by the Government that the people of the United States can never regard
with indifference the attempt of any European power to overthrow by force or to supplant by fraud the institutions of any republican government on the Western Continent,
and that they will view with extreme jealousy, as menacing to the peace and independence of their own country, the efforts of any
such power to obtain new footholds for
monarchical governments, sustained by foreign military force, in near proximity to the
United States.

233. THE CONTRACT LABOR LAW
July 4, 1864
(*U. S. Statutes at Large,* Vol. XIII, p. 386)

This law, giving validity to liens upon the wages
or property of laborers imported on contract,
was repealed in 1868, but the practice itself was
not specifically outlawed until 1885.

Be it enacted . . .

SEC. 2. That all contracts that shall be
made by emigrants to the United States in
foreign countries, in conformity to regulations that may be established . . . whereby
emigrants shall pledge the wages of their
labor for a term not exceeding twelve
months, to repay the expenses of their emigration, shall be held to be valid in law, and
may be enforced in the Courts of the United
States, or of the several states and territories; and such advances, if so stipulated
in the contract . . . shall operate as a lien
upon any land thereafter acquired by the
emigrant. . . .

SEC. 5. That no person shall be qualified
to fill any office under this act who shall be
directly or indirectly interested in any corporation having lands for sale to immigrants,
or in the carrying or transportation of immigrants . . . or who shall receive any fee
or reward, or the promise thereof, for any
service performed. . . .

234. THE WADE–DAVIS BILL
July 8, 1864
(Richardson, ed. *Messages and Papers,* Vol. VI, p. 223 ff.)

Congressional hostility to the Presidential plan
of reconstruction, outlined in the message of
December 8, 1863, grew increasingly emphatic
during the following year and culminated in the
passage by a close vote of the Wade-Davis bill.
This bill embodied the Congressional plan of
reconstruction. Lincoln did not sign the bill, and
after the adjournment of Congress, issued a
proclamation giving his reasons for refusing to
accept the Congressional plan. See, J. G. Nicolay
and J. Hay, *Abraham Lincoln,* Vol. IX, ch. v;
C. H. McCarthy, *Lincoln's Plan of Reconstruction;* B. C. Steiner, *Life of Henry Winter Davis;*
A. G. Riddle, *Life of Benjamin F. Wade.*

*An Act to guarantee to certain States whose
Governments have been usurped or over-*

thrown a Republican Form of Government.

Be it enacted, That in the states declared in rebellion against the United States, the President shall, by and with the advice and consent of the Senate, appoint for each a provisional governor, . . . who shall be charged with the civil administration of such state until a state government therein shall be recognized as hereinafter provided.

SEC. 2. That so soon as the military resistance to the United States shall have been suppressed in any such state, and the people thereof shall have sufficiently returned to their obedience to the constitution and the laws of the United States, the provisional governor shall direct the marshal of the United States, as speedily as may be, to name a sufficient number of deputies, and to enroll all white male citizens of the United States, resident in the state in their respective counties, and to request each one to take the oath to support the constitution of the United States, and in his enrolment to designate those who take and those who refuse to take that oath, which rolls shall be forthwith returned to the provisional governor; and if the persons taking that oath shall amount to a majority of the persons enrolled in the state, he shall, by proclamation, invite the loyal people of the state to elect delegates to a convention charged to declare the will of the people of the state relative to the reëstablishment of a state government subject to, and in conformity with, the constitution of the United States.

SEC. 3. That the convention shall consist of as many members as both houses of the last constitutional state legislature, apportioned by the provisional governor among the counties, parishes, or districts of the state, in proportion to the white population, returned as electors, by the marshal, in compliance with the provisions of this act. The provisional governor shall, . . . provide an adequate force to keep the peace during the election.

SEC. 4. That the delegates shall be elected by the loyal white male citizens of the United States of the age of twenty-one years, and resident at the time in the county, parish, or district in which they shall offer to vote, and enrolled as aforesaid, or absent in the military service of the United States, and who shall take and subscribe the oath of allegiance to the United States in the form contained in the act of July 2, 1862; and all such citizens of the United States who are in the military service of the United States shall vote at the headquarters of their respective commands, under such regulations as may be prescribed by the provisional governor for the taking and return of their votes; but no person who has held or exercised any office, civil or military, state or confederate, under the rebel usurpation, or who has voluntarily borne arms against the United States, shall vote, or be eligible to be elected as delegate, at such election.

SEC. 5. That the said commissioners, . . . shall hold the election in conformity with this act and, . . . shall proceed in the manner used in the state prior to the rebellion. The oath of allegiance shall be taken and subscribed on the poll-book by every voter in the form above prescribed, but every person known by, or proved to, the commissioners to have held or exercised any office, civil or military, state or confederate, under the rebel usurpation, or to have voluntarily borne arms against the United States, shall be excluded, though he offer to take the oath; and in case any person who shall have borne arms against the United States shall offer to vote he shall be deemed to have borne arms voluntarily unless he shall prove the contrary by the testimony of a qualified voter. . . .

SEC. 6. That the provisional governor shall, by proclamation, convene the delegates elected as aforesaid, at the capital of the state, on a day not more than three months after the election, giving at least thirty days' notice of such day. In case the said capital shall in his judgment be unfit, he shall in his proclamation appoint another place. He shall preside over the deliberations of the convention, and administer to each delegate, before taking his seat in the convention, the oath of allegiance to the United States in the form above prescribed.

SEC. 7. That the convention shall declare, on behalf of the people of the state, their submission to the constitution and laws of the United States, and shall adopt the following provisions, hereby prescribed by the

United States in the execution of the constitutional duty to guarantee a republican form of government to every state, and incorporate them in the constitution of the state, that is to say:

First. No person who has held or exercised any office, civil or military, except offices merely ministerial, and military offices below the grade of colonel, state or confederate, under the usurping power, shall vote for or be a member of the legislature, or governor.

Second. Involuntary servitude is forever prohibited, and the freedom of all persons is guaranteed in said state.

Third. No debt, state or confederate, created by or under the sanction of the usurping power, shall be recognized or paid by the state.

SEC. 8. That when the convention shall have adopted those provisions, it shall proceed to reëstablish a republican form of government, and ordain a constitution containing those provisions, which, when adopted, the convention shall by ordinance provide for submitting to the people of the state, entitled to vote under this law, at an election to be held in the manner prescribed by the act for the election of delegates; but at a time and place named by the convention, at which election the said electors, and none others, shall vote directly for or against such constitution and form of state government, and the returns of said election shall be made to the provisional governor, who shall canvass the same in the presence of the electors, and if a majority of the votes cast shall be for the constitution and form of government, he shall certify the same, with a copy thereof, to the President of the United States, who, after obtaining the assent of congress, shall, by proclamation, recognize the government so established, and none other, as the constitutional government of the state, and from the date of such recognition, and not before, Senators and Representatives, and electors for President and Vice-President may be elected in such state, according to the laws of the state and of the United States.

SEC. 9. That if the convention shall refuse to reëstablish the state government on the conditions aforesaid, the provisional governor shall declare it dissolved; but it shall be the duty of the President, whenever he shall have reason to believe that a sufficient number of the people of the state entitled to vote under this act, in number not less than a majority of those enrolled, as aforesaid, are willing to reëstablish a state government on the conditions aforesaid, to direct the provisional governor to order another election of delegates to a convention for the purpose. . . .

SEC. 10. That, until the United States shall have recognized a republican form of state government, the provisional governor in each of said states shall see that this act, and the laws of the United States, and the laws of the state in force when the state government was overthrown by the rebellion, are faithfully executed within the state; but no law or usage whereby any person was heretofore held in involuntary servitude shall be recognized or enforced by any court or officer in such state, and the laws for the trial and punishment of white persons shall extend to all persons, and jurors shall have the qualifications of voters under this law for delegates to the convention. . . .

SEC. 11. That until the recognition of a state government as aforesaid, the provisional governor shall, under such regulations as he may prescribe, cause to be assessed, levied, and collected, for the year eighteen hundred and sixty-four, and every year thereafter, the taxes provided by the laws of such state to be levied during the fiscal year preceding the overthrow of the state government thereof, in the manner prescribed by the laws of the state, as nearly as may be; . . . The proceeds of such taxes shall be accounted for to the provisional governor, and be by him applied to the expenses of the administration of the laws in such state, subject to the direction of the President, and the surplus shall be deposited in the treasury of the United States to the credit of such state, to be paid to the state upon an appropriation therefor, to be made when a republican form of government shall be recognized therein by the United States.

SEC. 12. That all persons held to involuntary servitude or labor in the states aforesaid are hereby emancipated and discharged therefrom, and they and their posterity shall be forever free. And if any such persons or their posterity shall be restrained of liberty, under pretence of any claim to such service or labor, the courts of the United States shall, on habeas corpus, discharge them.

SEC. 13. That if any person declared free by this act, or any law of the United States, or any proclamation of the President, be restrained of liberty, with intent to be held in or reduced to involuntary servitude or labor, the person convicted before a court of competent jurisdiction of such act shall be punished by fine of not less than fifteen hundred dollars, and be imprisoned not less than five nor more than twenty years.

SEC. 14. That every person who shall hereafter hold or exercise any office, civil or military, except offices merely ministerial, and military offices below the grade of colonel, in the rebel service, state or confederate, is hereby declared not to be a citizen of the United States.

235. LINCOLN'S PROCLAMATION ON THE WADE–DAVIS BILL
July 8, 1864

(Richardson, ed. *Messages and Papers,* Vol. VI, p. 222)

BY THE PRESIDENT OF THE UNITED STATES:

A Proclamation.

Whereas at the late session Congress passed a bill "to guarantee to certain States whose governments have been usurped or overthrown a republican form of government," a copy of which is hereunto annexed; and

Whereas, the said bill was presented to the President of the United States for his approval less than one hour before the *sine die* adjournment of said session, and was not signed by him; and

Whereas ·the said bill contains, among other things, a plan for restoring the States in rebellion to their proper practical relation in the Union, which plan expresses the sense of Congress upon that subject, and which plan it is now thought fit to lay before the people for their consideration:

Now, therefore, I, Abraham Lincoln, President of the United States, do proclaim, declare, and make known that while I am (as I was in December last, when, by proclamation, I propounded a plan for restoration) unprepared by a formal approval of this bill to be inflexibly committed to any single plan of restoration, and while I am also unprepared to declare that the free State constitutions and governments already adopted and installed in Arkansas and Louisiana shall be set aside and held for naught, thereby repelling and discouraging the loyal citizens who have set up the same as to further effort, or to declare a constitutional competency in Congress to abolish slavery in States, but am at the same time sincerely hoping and expecting that a constitutional amendment abolishing slavery throughout the nation may be adopted, nevertheless I am fully satisfied with the system for restoration contained in the bill as one very proper plan for the loyal people of any State choosing to adopt it, and that I am and at all times shall be prepared to give the Executive aid and assistance to any such people so soon as the military resistance to the United States shall have been suppressed in any such State and the people thereof shall have sufficiently returned to their obedience to the Constitution and the laws of the United States, in which cases military governors will be appointed with directions to proceed according to the bill. . . .

ABRAHAM LINCOLN.

236. THE WADE–DAVIS MANIFESTO
August 5, 1864

(E. McPherson, ed. *Political History of the Rebellion,* p. 332 ff.)

Lincoln's pocket veto of the Wade-Davis Bill and his statement of opposition to the Congressional plan of reconstruction, provoked a vindictive attack on Lincoln and the Presidential policy by the sponsors of the bill, Benjamin Wade and Henry Winter Davis. The Manifesto was published in the New York *Tribune,* August 5, and shortly thereafter in the other leading papers of the country.

We have read without surprise, but not without indignation, the Proclamation of the President of the 8th of July. . . .

The President, by preventing this bill from becoming a law, holds the electoral votes of the rebel States at the dictation of his personal ambition.

If those votes turn the balance in his favor, is it to be supposed that his competitor, defeated by such means, will acquiesce?

If the rebel majority assert their supremacy in those States, and send votes which elect an enemy of the Government, will we not repel his claims?

And is not that civil war for the Presidency inaugurated by the votes of rebel States?

Seriously impressed with these dangers, Congress, *"the proper constituted authority,"* formally declared that there are no State governments in the rebel States, and provided for their erection at a proper time; and both the Senate and the House of Representatives rejected the Senators and Representatives chosen under the authority of what the President calls the free constitution and government of Arkansas.

The President's proclamation *"holds for naught"* this judgment, and discards the authority of the Supreme Court, and strides headlong toward the anarchy his proclamation of the 8th of December inaugurated.

If electors for President be allowed to be chosen in either of those States, a sinister light will be cast on the motives which induced the President to "hold for naught" the will of Congress rather than his government in Louisiana and Arkansas.

That judgment of Congress which the President defies was the exercise of an authority exclusively vested in Congress by the Constitution to determine what is the established government in a State, and in its own nature and by the highest judicial authority binding on all other departments of the Government. . . .

A more studied outrage on the legislative authority of the people has never been perpetrated.

Congress passed a bill; the President refused to approve it, and then by proclamation puts as much of it in force as he sees fit, and proposes to execute those parts by officers unknown to the laws of the United States and not subject to the confirmation of the Senate!

The bill directed the appointment of Provisional Governors by and with the advice and consent of the Senate.

The President, after defeating the law, proposes to appoint without law, and without the advice and consent of the Senate, *Military* Governors for the rebel States!

He has already exercised this dictatorial usurpation in Louisiana, and he defeated the bill to prevent its limitation. . . .

The President has greatly presumed on the forbearance which the supporters of his Administration have so long practiced, in view of the arduous conflict in which we are engaged, and the reckless ferocity of our political opponents.

But he must understand that our support is of a cause and not of a man; that the authority of Congress is paramount and must be respected; that the whole body of the Union men of Congress will not submit to be impeached by him of rash and unconstitutional legislation; and if he wishes our support, he must confine himself to his executive duties—to obey and execute, not make the laws—to suppress by arms armed rebellion, and leave political reorganization to Congress.

If the supporters of the Government fail to insist on this, they become responsible for the usurpations which they fail to rebuke, and are justly liable to the indignation of the people whose rights and security, committed to their keeping, they sacrifice.

Let them consider the remedy for these usurpations, and, having found it, fearlessly execute it.

237. THE HAMPTON ROADS CONFERENCE
February 3, 1865

(The Works of Abraham Lincoln, Constitutional ed., Vol. VII, p. 290, 319 ff.)

In January 1865 Francis P. Blair, Sr. was permitted to go to Richmond to discuss terms of peace with some of the leaders of the Confederacy: out of this mission came the Hampton Roads conference. Lincoln, as the instructions of January 31 indicate, first appointed Seward to conduct the unofficial negotiations with the representatives of the Confederacy; later he thought it necessary to attend the conference in person. No record was kept of this conference, but the report of Sec. Seward is apparently reliable. See also the discussion and report of the Conference in, A. H. Stephens, *War Between the States,* Vol. II, ch. xxiii, and app. R. For Blair's part in the negotiations, see W. E. Smith, *The Francis Preston Blair Family in Politics,* Vol. II, ch. xxxvii.

1. INSTRUCTIONS TO SECRETARY SEWARD

Executive Mansion,
Washington, January 31, 1865.

HON. WILLIAM H. SEWARD, Secretary of State:

You will proceed to Fortress Monroe, Virginia, there to meet and informally confer with Messrs. Stephens, Hunter, and Campbell, on the basis of my letter to F. P. Blair, Esq., of January 18, 1865, a copy of which you have. You will make known to them that three things are indispensable—to wit:

1. The restoration of the national authority throughout all the States.

2. No receding by the Executive of the United States on the slavery question from the position assumed thereon in the late annual message to Congress, and in preceding documents.

3. No cessation of hostilities short of an end of the war and the disbanding of all forces hostile to the Government.

You will inform them that all propositions of theirs, not inconsistent with the above, will be considered and passed upon in a spirit of sincere liberality. You will hear all they may choose to say and report it to me. You will not assume to definitely consummate anything.

Yours, etc.,
ABRAHAM LINCOLN.

2. MR. SEWARD TO MR. ADAMS

Department of State,
Washington, February 7, 1865.

. . . . . .

On the morning of the 3d, the President, attended by the Secretary, received Messrs. Stephens, Hunter, and Campbell on board the United States steam transport *River Queen* in Hampton Roads. The conference was altogether informal. There was no attendance of secretaries, clerks, or other witnesses. Nothing was written or read. The conversation, although earnest and free, was calm, and courteous, and kind on both sides. The Richmond party approached the discussion rather indirectly, and at no time did they either make categorical demands, or tender formal stipulations or absolute refusals. Nevertheless, during the conference, which lasted four hours, the several points at issue between the Government and the insurgents were distinctly raised, and discussed fully, intelligently, and in an amicable spirit. What the insurgent party seemed chiefly to favor was a postponement of the question of separation, upon which the war is waged, and a mutual direction of efforts of the Government, as well as those of the insurgents, to some extrinsic policy or scheme for a season during which passions might be expected to subside, and the armies be reduced, and trade and intercourse between the people of both sections resumed. It was suggested by them that through such postponement we might now have immediate peace, with some not very certain prospect of an ultimate satisfactory adjustment of political relations between this Government and the States, section, or people now engaged in conflict with it.

This suggestion, though deliberately considered, was nevertheless regarded by the President as one of armistice or truce, and he announced that we can agree to no cessation or suspension of hostilities, except on the basis of the disbandment of the insurgent forces, and the restoration of the national authority throughout all the States in the Union. Collaterally, and in subordination to the proposition which was thus announced, the antislavery policy of the United States was reviewed in all its bearings, and the President announced that he must not be expected to depart from the positions he had heretofore assumed in his proclamation of emancipation and other documents, as these positions were reiterated in his last annual message. It was further declared by the President that the complete restoration of the national authority was an indispensable condition of any assent on our part to whatever form of peace might be proposed. The President assured the other party that, while he must adhere to these positions, he would be prepared, so far as power is lodged with the

Executive, to exercise liberality. His power, however, is limited by the Constitution; and when peace should be made, Congress must necessarily act in regard to appropriations of money and to the admission of representatives from the insurrectionary States. The Richmond party were then informed that Congress had, on the 31st ultimo, adopted by a constitutional majority a joint resolution submitting to the several States the proposition to abolish slavery throughout the Union, and that there is every reason to expect that it will be soon accepted by three fourths of the States, so as to become a part of the national organic law.

The conference came to an end by mutual acquiescence, without producing an agreement of views upon the several matters discussed, or any of them. Nevertheless, it is perhaps of some importance that we have been able to submit our opinions and views directly to prominent insurgents, and to hear them in answer in a courteous and not unfriendly manner.

I am, sir, your obedient servant,

WILLIAM H. SEWARD.

238. LINCOLN'S SECOND INAUGURAL ADDRESS
March 4, 1865

(Richardson, ed. *Messages and Papers*, Vol. VI, p. 276 ff.)

FELLOW-COUNTRYMEN:—At this second appearing to take the oath of the presidential office there is less occasion for an extended address than there was at the first. Then a statement somewhat in detail of a course to be pursued seemed fitting and proper. Now, at the expiration of four years, during which public declarations have been constantly called forth on every point and phase of the great contest which still absorbs the attention and engrosses the energies of the nation, little that is new could be presented. The progress of our arms, upon which all else chiefly depends, is as well known to the public as to myself, and it is, I trust, reasonably satisfactory and encouraging to all. With high hope for the future, no prediction in regard to it is ventured.

On the occasion corresponding to this four years ago all thoughts were anxiously directed to an impending civil war. All dreaded it, all sought to avert it. While the inaugural address was being delivered from this place, devoted altogether to *saving* the Union without war, insurgent agents were in the city seeking to *destroy* it without war—seeking to dissolve the Union and divide effects by negotiation. Both parties deprecated war, but one of them would *make* war rather than let the nation survive, and the other would *accept* war rather than let it perish, and the war came.

One eighth of the whole population was colored slaves, not distributed generally over the Union, but localized in the southern part of it. These slaves constituted a peculiar and powerful interest. All knew that this interest was somehow the cause of the war. To strengthen, perpetuate, and extend this interest was the object for which the insurgents would rend the Union even by war, while the Government claimed no right to do more than to restrict the territorial enlargement of it. Neither party expected for the war the magnitude or the duration which it has already attained. Neither anticipated that the *cause* of the conflict might cease with or even before the conflict itself should cease. Each looked for an easier triumph, and a result less fundamental and astounding. Both read the same Bible and pray to the same God, and each invokes His aid against the other. It may seem strange that any men should dare to ask a just God's assistance in wringing their bread from the sweat of other men's faces, but let us judge not, that we be not judged. The prayers of both could not be answered. That of neither has been answered fully. The Almighty has His own purposes. "Woe unto the world because of offenses; for it must needs be that offenses come, but woe to that man by whom the offense cometh." If we shall suppose that American slavery is one of those offenses which, in the providence of God, must needs come, but which, having continued through His appointed time, He now wills to remove, and that He gives to both North and South this terrible war as the woe due to those by whom the offense came, shall we discern therein any departure from those divine attributes which the believers in a living God always ascribe to Him? Fondly do we hope, fervently do we pray, that this mighty scourge of war may speedily pass away. Yet, if God wills that it continue until all the wealth piled by the bondsman's two hundred and fifty years of unrequited toil shall be sunk, and until every drop of blood drawn with the lash shall be paid by another drawn with the sword, as was said three thousand years ago, so still it must be said, "The judgments of the Lord are true and righteous altogether."

With malice toward none, with charity for all, with firmness in the right as God gives us to see the right, let us strive on to finish the work we are in, to bind up the nation's wounds, to care for him who shall have borne the battle and for his widow and his orphan, to do all which may achieve and cherish a just and lasting peace among ourselves and with all nations.

239. LINCOLN'S TERMS OF PEACE?

Admiral Porter's Report of the City Point Conference March 27, 1865

(W. T. Sherman, *Memoirs*, Vol. II, p. 328 ff.)

On March 27th Lincoln held a conference with Grant and Sherman at City Point, Va., in which he discussed the terms for a cessation of hostilities. Serious doubts have been cast on the accuracy of Admiral Porter's recollections of this important conference.

The day of General Sherman's arrival at City Point (I think the 27th of March, 1865), I accompanied him and General Grant on board the President's flag-ship, the *Queen,* where the President received us in the upper saloon, no one but ourselves being present.

The President was in an exceedingly pleasant mood, and delighted to meet General Sherman, whom he cordially greeted.

It seems that this was the first time he had met Sherman, to remember him, since the beginning of the war, and did not remember when he had seen him before, until the general reminded him of the circumstances of their first meeting. . . .

The conversation soon turned on the events of Sherman's campaign through the South, with every movement of which the President seemed familiar. . . .

The interview between the two generals and the President lasted about an hour and a half, and, as it was a remarkable one, I jotted down what I remembered of the conversation, as I have made a practice of doing during the rebellion, when any thing interesting occurred.

I don't regret having done so, as circumstances afterward occurred (Stanton's ill conduct toward Sherman) which tended to cast odium on General Sherman for allowing such liberal terms to Jos. Johnston.

Could the conversation that occurred on board the *Queen,* between the President and General Sherman, have been known, Sherman would not, and could not, have been censured. Mr. Lincoln, had he lived, would have acquitted the general of any blame, for he was only carrying out the President's wishes.

My opinion is, that Mr. Lincoln came down to City Point with the most liberal views toward the rebels. He felt confident that we would be successful, and was willing that the enemy should capitulate on the most favorable terms.

I don't know what the President would have done had he been left to himself, and had our army been unsuccessful, but he was then wrought up to a high state of excitement. He wanted peace on almost any terms, and there is no knowing what proposals he might have been willing to listen to. His heart was tenderness throughout, and, as long as the rebels laid down their arms, he did not care how it was done. I do not know how far he was influenced by General Grant, but I presume, from their long conferences, that they must have understood each other perfectly, and that the terms given to Lee after his surrender were authorized by Mr. Lincoln. I know that the latter was delighted when he heard that they had been given, and exclaimed, a dozen times, "Good!"

"All right!" "Exactly the thing!" and other similar expressions. Indeed, the President more than once told me what he supposed the terms would be: if Lee and Johnston surrendered, he considered the war ended, and that all the other rebel forces would lay down their arms at once.

In this he proved to be right. Grant and Sherman were both of the same opinion, and so was every one else who knew any thing about the matter. . . .

After hearing General Sherman's account of his own position, and that of Johnston, at that time, the President expressed fears that the rebel general would escape south again by the railroads, and that General Sherman would have to chase him anew, over the same ground; but the general pronounced this to be impracticable. He remarked: "I have him where he cannot move without breaking up his army, which, once disbanded, can never again be got together; and I have destroyed the Southern railroads, so that they cannot be used again for a long time." General Grant remarked, "What is to prevent their laying the rails again?" "Why," said General Sherman, "my 'bummers' don't do things by halves. Every rail, after having been placed over a hot fire, has been twisted as crooked as a ram's horn, and they never can be used again."

This was the only remark made by General Grant during the interview, as he sat smoking a short distance from the President, intent, no doubt, on his own plans, which were being brought to a successful termination.

The conversation between the President and General Sherman, about the terms of surrender to be allowed Jos. Johnston, continued. Sherman energetically insisted that he could command his own terms, and that Johnston would have to yield to his demands;

but the President was very decided about the matter, and insisted that the surrender of Johnston's army must be obtained on any terms.

General Grant was evidently of the same way of thinking, for, although he did not join in the conversation to any extent, yet he made no objections, and I presume had made up his mind to allow the best terms himself.

He was also anxious that Johnston should not be driven into Richmond, to reenforce the rebels there, who, from behind their strong intrenchments, would have given us incalculable trouble.

Sherman, as a subordinate officer, yielded his views to those of the President, and the terms of capitulation between himself and Johnston were exactly in accordance with Mr. Lincoln's wishes. He could not have done any thing which would have pleased the President better.

Mr. Lincoln did, in fact, arrange the (so considered) liberal terms offered General Jos. Johnston, and, whatever may have been General Sherman's private views, I feel sure that he yielded to the wishes of the President in every respect. It was Mr. Lincoln's policy that was carried out, and, had he lived long enough, he would have been but too glad to have acknowledged it. Had Mr. Lincoln lived, Secretary Stanton would have issued no false telegraphic dispatches, in the hope of killing off another general in the regular army, one who by his success had placed himself in the way of his own succession. . . .

D. D. Porter, Vice-Admiral.

(Written by the admiral in 1866, at the United States Naval Academy at Annapolis, Md., and mailed to General Sherman at St. Louis, Mo.)

240. JEFFERSON DAVIS'S LAST MESSAGE TO THE PEOPLE OF THE CONFEDERACY
April 4, 1865

(Richardson, ed. *Messages and Papers of the Confederacy*, Vol. I, p. 568 ff.)

On April 2, the Confederate Government abandoned Richmond and fled to Danville; the following day Richmond fell. President Davis's last appeal to the Confederate people reveals a stubborn determination to continue the war, but in this decision in which he was not supported by Lee, he was overruled by the course of events.

Danville, Va. April 4, 1865.

To the People of the Confederate States of America.

The General in Chief of our Army has found it necessary to make such movements of the troops as to uncover the capital and thus involve the withdrawal of the Government from the city of Richmond.

It would be unwise, even were it possible, to conceal the great moral as well as material injury to our cause that must result from the occupation of Richmond by the enemy. It is equally unwise and unworthy of us, as patriots engaged in a most sacred cause, to allow our energies to falter, our spirits to grow faint, or our efforts to become relaxed under reverses, however calamitous. While it has been to us a source of national pride that for four years of unequaled warfare we have been able, in close proximity to the center of the enemy's power, to maintain the seat of our chosen Government free from the pollution of his presence; while the memories of the heroic dead who have freely given their lives to its defense must ever remain enshrined in our hearts; while the preservation of the capital, which is usually regarded as the evidence to mankind of separate national existence, was an object very dear to us, it is also true, and should not be forgotten, that the loss which we have suffered is not without compensation. For many months the largest and finest army of the Confederacy, under the command of a leader whose presence inspires equal confidence in the troops and the people, has been greatly trammeled by the necessity of keeping constant watch over the approaches to the capital, and has thus been forced to forego more than one opportunity for promising enterprise. The hopes and confidence of the enemy have been constantly excited by the belief that their possession of Richmond would be the signal for our submission to their rule, and relieve them from the burden of war, as their failing resources admonish them it must be abandoned if not speedily brought to a successful close. It is for us, my countrymen, to show by our bearing under reverses how wretched has been the self-deception of those who have believed us less able to endure misfortune with fortitude than to encounter danger with courage. We have now entered upon a new phase of a struggle the memory of which is to endure for all ages and to shed an increasing luster upon our country.

Relieved from the necessity of guarding cities and particular points, important but not vital to our defense, with an army free to move from point to point and strike in detail the detachments and garrisons of the enemy, operating on the interior of our own country, where supplies are more accessible, and where the foe will be far removed from his own base and cut off from all succor in case of reverse, nothing is now needed to render our triumph certain but the exhibition of our own unquenchable resolve. Let us but will it, and we are free; and who, in the light of the past, dare doubt your purpose in the future?

Animated by the confidence in your spirit and fortitude, which never yet has failed me, I announce to you, fellow-countrymen, that it is my purpose to maintain your cause with my whole heart and soul; that I will never consent to abandon to the enemy one foot of the soil of any one of the States of the Confederacy. . . . If by stress of numbers we should ever be compelled to a temporary withdrawal from her limits, or those of any other border State, again and again will we return, until the baffled and exhausted enemy shall abandon in despair his endless and impossible task of making slaves of a people resolved to be free.

Let us not, then, despond, my countrymen; but, relying on the never-failing mercies and protecting care of our God, let us meet the foe with fresh defiance, with unconquered and unconquerable hearts.

Jeff'n Davis.

241. THE BURNING OF COLUMBIA, S. C.

Report of General Sherman on the Campaign of the Carolinas
April 4, 1865

(F. Moore, ed. *The Rebellion Record,* Vol. XI, p. 377)

On the night of February 17, 1865, Columbia, South Carolina, was largely destroyed by fire. It was charged at the time and is still firmly believed in some sections of the country that Sherman deliberately destroyed the city. Sherman himself placed the responsibility for the burning of the city upon Wade Hampton and the weather; subsequently he admitted that a good deal of the account given below was imaginative. General Logan in his report blames the burning upon unnamed parties who spread fire. The problem of responsibility is apparently an insoluble one, but see J. D. Hill, "The Burning of Columbia Reconsidered," *South Atlantic Quarterly,* Vol. XXV, p. 269 ff., and J. F. Rhodes, *History,* Vol. V, p. 90 ff. There is an interesting contemporary account, with some documents, in G. W. Nichols, *The Story of the Great March.*

. . . In anticipation of the occupation of the city, I had made written orders to General Howard touching the conduct of the troops. These were to destroy, absolutely, all arsenals and public property not needed for our own use, as well as all railroads, depots, and machinery useful in war to an enemy, but to spare all dwellings, colleges, schools, asylums, and harmless private property. I was the first to cross the pontoon bridge, and in company with General Howard rode into the city. The day was clear, but a perfect tempest of wind was raging. The brigade of Colonel Stone was already in the city, and was properly posted. Citizens and soldiers were on the streets, and general good order prevailed. General Wade Hampton, who commanded the Confederate rear-guard of cavalry, had, in anticipation of our capture of Columbia, ordered that all cotton, public and private, should be moved into the streets and fired, to prevent our making use of it. Bales were piled everywhere, the rope and bagging cut, and tufts of cotton were blown about in the wind, lodged in the trees and against houses, so as to resemble a snow storm. Some of these piles of cotton were burning, especially one in the very heart of the city, near the Court-house, but the fire was partially subdued by the labor of our soldiers.

During the day the Fifteenth corps passed through Columbia and out on the Camden road. The Seventeenth did not enter the town at all; and, as I have before stated, the left wing and cavalry did not come within two miles of the town.

Before one single public building had been fired by order, the smoldering fires, set by Hampton's order, were rekindled by the wind, and communicated to the buildings around. About dark they began to spread, and got beyond the control of the brigade on duty within the city. The whole of Wood's division was brought in, but it was found impossible to check the flames, which, by midnight, had become unmanageable, and raged until about four A. M., when the wind subsiding, they were got under control. I was up nearly all night, and saw Generals Howard, Logan, Woods, and others, laboring to save houses and protect families thus suddenly deprived of shelter, and of bedding and wearing apparel. I disclaim on the part of my army any agency in this fire, but on the contrary, claim that we saved what of Columbia remains unconsumed. And without hesitation, I charge General Wade Hampton with having burned his own city of Columbia, not with a malicious intent, or as the manifestations of a silly "Roman stoicism," but from folly and want of sense, in filling it with lint, cotton, and tinder. Our officers and men on duty worked well to extinguish the flames; but others not on duty, including the officers who had long been imprisoned there, rescued by us, may have assisted in spreading the fire after it had once begun, and may have indulged in unconcealed joy to see the ruin of the capital of South Carolina. During the eighteenth and nineteenth, the arsenal, railroad depots, machine shops, foundries, and other buildings were properly destroyed by detailed working parties, and the railroad track torn up and destroyed down to Kingsville and the Wateree bridge, and up in the direction of Winnsboro. . . .

242. LEE'S FAREWELL TO HIS ARMY
April 10, 1865

(Recollections and Letters of General Lee, by R. E. Lee, p. 153–4)

After the fall of Richmond, Lee pushed west towards Danville, where large supplies had been concentrated. He hoped that he might be able to effect a juncture with Johnston's army, then in North Carolina. Sheridan cut off Lee's retreat to the west, however, and on April 9 Lee surrendered his army to Grant, at Appomattox Court House. On Lee after the War, see, *Recollections and Letters of General Lee,* by his Son, R. E. Lee, p. 162 ff.; R. Winston, *Robert E. Lee;* F. L. Riley, *General Robert E. Lee After Appomattox.*

Headquarters, Army of Northern Virginia,
April 10, 1865.

After four years of arduous service, marked by unsurpassed courage and fortitude, the Army of Northern Virginia has been compelled to yield to overwhelming numbers and resources. I need not tell the survivors of so many hard-fought battles, who have remained steadfast to the last, that I have consented to this result from no distrust of them; but, feeling that valour and devotion could accomplish nothing that could compensate for the loss that would have attended the continuation of the contest, I have determined to avoid the useless sacrifice of those whose past services have endeared them to their countrymen. By the terms of the agreement, officers and men can return to their homes and remain there until exchanged. You will take with you the satisfaction that proceeds from the consciousness of duty faithfully performed; and I earnestly pray that a merciful God will extend to you His blessing and protection. With an increasing admiration of your constancy and devotion to your country, and a grateful remembrance of your kind and generous consideration of myself, I bid you an affectionate farewell.

R. E. Lee, General.

243. SURRENDER OF GENERAL JOHNSTON

Memorandum made between General Joseph E. Johnston and Major-General William T. Sherman
April 18, 1865

(Memoirs of General W. T. Sherman, Vol. II, p. 356–7)

The failure of Lee to escape from Grant and Sheridan, and the surrender of the Army of Northern Virginia, April 9, left Johnston's army the only large Confederate force still in the field. The terms of Johnston's surrender to Sherman were on the same general lines as those given by Grant to Lee and were apparently outlined by Lincoln, Doc. No. 239. These terms, however, were disapproved by Secretary Stanton, and Sherman was ordered to advance upon Johnston. Johnston agreed to new terms April 26. Stanton's disapproval of Sherman's course led to a violent altercation between the two men, in which the Secretary of War appeared in a very unhappy light. Stanton wrote of Sherman's terms, "I am distressed beyond measure at the terms. . . . They are inadmissible. There should now be literally no terms granted. We should not only brand the leading rebels with infamy, but the whole rebellion should bear the badge of the penitentiary".

(Gorham, G. C., *Life and Public Services of E. M. Stanton,* Vol. II, p. 195). Sherman's account of the incident can be found in his *Memoirs,* Vol. II, ch. xxiii. His testimony before the Committee on the War is given at length in the appendix to Nichols, *The Story of the Great March.*

Memorandum, or Basis of Agreement, made this 18th day of April, A.D. 1865, near Durham's Station, in the State of North Carolina, by and between General Joseph E. Johnston, commanding the Confederate Army, and Major-General William T. Sherman, commanding the Army of the United States in North Carolina, both present:

1. The contending armies now in the field to maintain the *status quo* until notice is

given by the commanding general of any one to its opponent, and reasonable time—say, forty-eight hours—allowed.

2. The Confederate armies now in existence to be disbanded and conducted to their several State capitals, there to deposit their arms and public property in the State Arsenal; and each officer and man to execute and file an agreement to cease from acts of war, and to abide the action of the State and Federal authority. The number of arms and munitions of war to be reported to the Chief of Ordnance at Washington City, subject to the future action of the Congress of the United States, and, in the meantime, to be used solely to maintain peace and order within the borders of the States respectively.

3. The recognition, by the Executive of the United States, of the several State governments, on their officers and Legislatures taking the oaths prescribed by the Constitution of the United States, and, where conflicting State governments have resulted from the war, the legitimacy of all shall be submitted to the Supreme Court of the United States.

4. The reestablishment of all the Federal Courts in the several States, with powers as defined by the Constitution of the United States and of the States respectively.

5. The people and inhabitants of all the States to be guaranteed, so far as the Executive can, their political rights and franchises, as well as their rights of person and property, as defined by the Constitution of the United States and of the States respectively.

6. The Executive authority of the Government of the United States not to disturb any of the people by reason of the late war, so long as they live in peace and quiet, abstain from acts of armed hostility, and obey the laws in existence at the place of their residence.

7. In general terms—the war to cease; a general amnesty, so far as the Executive of the United States can command, on condition of the disbandment of the Confederate armies, the distribution of the arms, and the resumption of peaceful pursuits by the officers and men hitherto composing said armies.

244. LINCOLN'S LAST PUBLIC ADDRESS
April 11, 1865

(Writings of Abraham Lincoln, Constitutional ed., Vol. VII, p. 362 ff.)

On the evening of April 11, a crowd celebrating the end of the war called at the Executive mansion. Lincoln addressed them from the balcony on the question of reconciliation and reconstruction. At the Cabinet meeting of Friday, April 14, Lincoln again spoke of the problem of reconstruction in terms similar to those of the speech of April 11. "If we were wise and discreet," he said, according to Sec. Welles, "we should re-animate the states and get their governments in successful operation, with order prevailing and the Union reëstablished, before Congress came together in December. . . . There were men in Congress who, if their motives were good were nevertheless impracticable, and who possessed feelings of hate and vindictiveness in which he did not sympathize and could not participate. He hoped there would be no persecution, no bloody work, after the war was over. None need expect he would take any part in hanging or killing those men, even the worst of them."

FELLOW-CITIZENS:—We meet this evening not in sorrow, but in gladness of heart. The evacuation of Petersburg and Richmond, and the surrender of the principal insurgent army, give hope of a righteous and speedy peace, whose joyous expression cannot be restrained. In the midst of this, however, He from whom all blessings flow must not be forgotten.

A call for a national thanksgiving is being prepared, and will be duly promulgated. . . . By these recent successes, the reinauguration of the national authority—reconstruction—which has had a large share of thought from the first, is pressed much more closely upon our attention. It is fraught with great difficulty. Unlike a case of war between independent nations, *there is no authorized organ for us to treat with*—no one man has authority to give up the rebellion for any other man. We simply must begin with and mould from disorganized and discordant elements. Nor is it a small additional embarrassment that we, the loyal people, differ among ourselves as to the mode, manner, and measure of reconstruction. As a general rule, I abstain from reading the reports of attacks upon myself, wishing not to be provoked by that to which I cannot properly offer an answer. In spite of this precaution, however, it comes to my knowledge that I am much censured for some supposed agency in setting up and seeking to sustain the new State government of Louisiana. In this I have done just so much and no more than the public knows. In the Annual Message of December, 1863, and the accompanying proclamation, I presented a plan of reconstruction, as the phrase goes, which I promised, if adopted by any State, would be acceptable to and sustained by the Executive Government of the nation. I distinctly stated that this was not the only plan which might possibly be acceptable, and I also distinctly protested that the Executive claimed no right to say when or whether members should be admitted to seats in Congress from such States. This plan was in advance submitted to the then Cabinet, and approved by every member of it. One of them suggested that I should then and in that connection apply the Emancipation Proclamation to the theretofore excepted parts of Virginia and Louisiana; that I should drop the suggestion about apprenticeship for freed people, and that I should omit the protest against my own power in regard to the admission of members of Congress. But even he approved every part and parcel of the plan which has since been employed or touched by the action of Louisiana. The new constitution of Louisiana, declaring emancipation for the whole State, practically applies the proclamation to the part previously excepted. It does not adopt apprenticeship for freed people, and is silent, as it could not well be otherwise, about the admission of members to Congress. So that, as it applied to Louisiana, every member of the Cabinet fully approved the plan. The message went to Congress, and I received many commendations of the plan, written and verbal, and not a single objection to it from any professed emancipationist came to my knowledge until after the news reached Washington that the people of Louisiana had begun to move in accordance with it. From about July, 1862, I had corresponded with different persons supposed to be interested

in seeking a reconstruction of a State government for Louisiana. When the message of 1863, with the plan before mentioned, reached New Orleans, General Banks wrote me that he was confident that the people, with his military co-operation, would reconstruct substantially on that plan. I wrote to him and some of them to try it. They tried it, and the result is known. Such has been my only agency in setting up the Louisiana government. As to sustaining it my promise is out, as before stated. But, as bad promises are better broken than kept, I shall treat this as a bad promise and break it, whenever I shall be convinced that keeping it is adverse to the public interest; but I have not yet been so convinced. I have been shown a letter on this subject, supposed to be an able one, in which the writer expresses regret that my mind has not seemed to be definitely fixed upon the question whether the seceded States, so called, are in the Union or out of it. It would perhaps add astonishment to his regret were he to learn that since I have found professed Union men endeavoring to answer that question, I have purposely forborne any public expression upon it. As appears to me, that question has not been nor yet is a practically material one, and that any discussion of it, while it thus remains practically immaterial, could have no effect other than the mischievous one of dividing our friends. As yet, whatever it may become, that question is bad as the basis of a controversy, and good for nothing at all—a merely pernicious abstraction. We all agree that the seceded States, so called, are out of their proper practical relation with the Union, and that the sole object of the Government, civil and military, in regard to those States, is to again get them into their proper practical relation. I believe that it is not only possible, but in fact easier, to do this without deciding or even considering whether those States have ever been out of the Union, than with it. Finding themselves safely at home, it would be utterly immaterial whether they had been abroad. Let us all join in doing the acts necessary to restore the proper practical relations between these States and the Union, and each forever after innocently indulge his own opinion whether, in doing the acts he brought the States from without into the Union, or only gave them proper assistance, they never having been out of it. The amount of constituency, so to speak, on which the Louisiana government rests, would be more satisfactory to all if it contained fifty thousand, or thirty thousand, or even twenty thousand, instead of twelve thousand, as it does. It is also unsatisfactory to some that the elective franchise is not given to the colored man. I would myself prefer that it were now conferred on the very intelligent, and on those who serve our cause as soldiers. Still, the question is not whether the Louisiana government, as it stands, is quite all that is desirable. The question is, Will it be wiser to take it as it is and help to improve it, or to reject and disperse? Can Louisiana be brought into proper practical relation with the Union sooner by sustaining or by discarding her new State government? Some twelve thousand voters in the heretofore Slave State of Louisiana have sworn allegiance to the Union, assumed to be the rightful political power of the State, held elections, organized a State government, adopted a Free State constitution, giving the benefit of public schools equally to black and white, and empowering the Legislature to confer the elective franchise upon the colored man. This Legislature has already voted to ratify the Constitutional Amendment recently passed by Congress, abolishing slavery throughout the nation. These twelve thousand persons are thus fully committed to the Union and to perpetuate freedom in the State—committed to the very things, and nearly all things, the nation wants—and they ask the nation's recognition and its assistance to make good this committal. Now, if we reject and spurn them, we do our utmost to disorganize and disperse them. We, in fact, say to the white man: You are worthless or worse; we will neither help you nor be helped by you. To the blacks we say: This cup of liberty which these, your old masters, held to your lips, we will dash from you, and leave you to the chances of gathering the spilled and scattered contents in some vague and undefined when, where, and how. If this course, discouraging and paralyzing both white and black, has any tendency to bring Louisiana into proper practical relations with the Union, I have so far been unable to perceive it. If, on the con-

trary, we recognize and sustain the new government of Louisiana, the converse of all this is made true. We encourage the hearts and nerve the arms of twelve thousand to adhere to their work, and argue for it, and proselyte for it, and fight for it, and feed it, and grow it, and ripen it to a complete success. The colored man, too, in seeing all united for him, is inspired with vigilance, and energy, and daring to the same end. Grant that he desires the elective franchise, will he not attain it sooner by saving the already advanced steps towards it, than by running backward over them? Concede that the new government of Louisiana is only to what it should be as the egg is to the fowl, we shall sooner have the fowl by hatching the egg than by smashing it. Again, if we reject Louisiana, we also reject one vote in favor of the proposed amendment to the National Constitution. To meet this proposition, it has been argued that no more than three fourths of those States which have not attempted secession are necessary to validly ratify the amendment. I do not commit myself against this, further than to say that such a ratification would be questionable, and sure to be persistently questioned, while a ratification by three fourths of all the States would be unquestioned and unquestionable. I repeat the question, Can Louisiana be brought into proper practical relation with the Union sooner by sustaining or by discarding her new State government? What has been said of Louisiana will apply to other States. And yet so great peculiarities pertain to each State, and such important and sudden changes occur in the same State, and withal so new and unprecedented is the whole case, that no exclusive and inflexible plan can safely be prescribed as to details and collaterals. Such exclusive and inflexible plan would surely become a new entanglement. Important principles may and must be inflexible. In the present situation as the phrase goes, it may be my duty to make some new announcement to the people of the South. I am considering, and shall not fail to act, when satisfied that action will be proper.

245. THE FREEDMEN'S BUREAU
March 3, 1865

(U. S. Statutes at Large, Vol. XIII, p. 507 ff.)

The Freedmen's Bureau was established to care for the freedmen and for the abandoned lands in the South. It was to continue for one year after the close of the war. An act of February 19, 1866, extending the life of the Freedmen's Bureau was vetoed by President Johnson. (Doc. No. 251.) July 16, 1866, a supplementary Freedmen's Bureau Act, enlarging the scope of the Bureau, was passed over the President's veto. General O. O. Howard was placed in charge of the Bureau. See, P. S. Peirce, *The Freedmen's Bureau;* L. Webster, *The Freedmen's Bureau in South Carolina;* and the documents in W. L. Fleming, *Documentary History of Reconstruction,* Vol. I.

An Act to establish a Bureau for the Relief of Freedmen and Refugees.

Be it enacted, That there is hereby established in the War Department, to continue during the present war of rebellion, and for one year thereafter, a bureau of refugees, freedmen, and abandoned lands, to which shall be committed, as hereinafter provided, the supervision and management of all abandoned lands, and the control of all subjects relating to refugees and freedmen from rebel states, or from any district of country within the territory embraced in the operations of the army, under such rules and regulations as may be prescribed by the head of the bureau and approved by the President. The said bureau shall be under the management and control of a commissioner to be appointed by the President, by and with the advice and consent of the Senate. . . .

SEC. 2. That the Secretary of War may direct such issues of provisions, clothing, and fuel, as he may deem needful for the immediate and temporary shelter and supply of destitute and suffering refugees and freedmen and their wives and children, under such rules and regulations as he may direct.

SEC. 3. That the President may, by and with the advice and consent of the Senate, appoint an assistant commissioner for each of the states declared to be in insurrection, not exceeding ten in number, who shall, under the direction of the commissioner, aid in the execution of the provisions of this act; . . . And any military officer may be detailed and assigned to duty under this act without increase of pay or allowances. . . .

SEC. 4. That the commissioner, under the direction of the President, shall have authority to set apart, for the use of loyal refugees and freedmen, such tracts of land within the insurrectionary states as shall have been abandoned, or to which the United States shall have acquired title by confiscation or sale, or otherwise, and to every male citizen, whether refugee or freedman, as aforesaid, there shall be assigned not more than forty acres of such land, and the person to whom it was so assigned shall be protected in the use and enjoyment of the land for the term of three years at an annual rent not exceeding six per centum upon the value of such land, as it was appraised by the state authorities in the year eighteen hundred and sixty, for the purpose of taxation, and in case no such appraisal can be found, then the rental shall be based upon the estimated value of the land in said year, to be ascertained in such manner as the commissioner may by regulation prescribe. At the end of said term, or at any time during said term, the occupants of any parcels so assigned may purchase the land and receive such title thereto as the United States can convey, upon paying therefor the value of the land, as ascertained and fixed for the purpose of determining the annual rent aforesaid. . . .

246. BLACK CODE OF MISSISSIPPI
1865
(Laws of Mississippi, 1865, p. 82 ff.)

The so-called Black Codes represented the Southern effort to solve the problem of the freedmen. The codes varied in harshness: those of Georgia, for example, were notably lenient; those of Louisiana and Mississippi severe. "The legislation," says Professor Fleming, "showed the combined influence of the old laws for free negroes, the vagrancy laws of the North and South for whites, the customs of slavery times, the British West Indies legislation for ex-slaves, and the regulations of the U. S. War and Treasury Departments and of the Freedmen's Bureau" *(Sequel of Appomattox,* p. 94). The laws below regulate civil rights, apprenticeship, vagrancy, and penal crimes. Most of these black laws were suspended by the military governors of the reconstructed states, and the Civil Rights Act and the Fourteenth Amendment were designed to protect the negro in his civil and legal rights. On the Black Codes, see, W. L. Fleming, *Sequel to Appomattox,* ch. iv; E. P. Oberholtzer, *History of the United States Since the Civil War,* Vol. I; and the numerous monographs on reconstruction in the States, such as those of Fleming, Garner, Reynolds, Hamilton, Ramsdell, Fertig, etc. There is a summary of the Black Codes in E. McPherson, *Political History of Reconstruction,* p. 29 ff.

1. CIVIL RIGHTS OF FREEDMEN IN MISSISSIPPI

Sec.1. *Be it enacted,* . . . That all freedmen, free negroes, and mulattoes may sue and be sued, implead and be impleaded, in all the courts of law and equity of this State, and may acquire personal property, and choses in action, by descent or purchase, and may dispose of the same in the same manner and to the same extent that white persons may: *Provided,* That the provisions of this section shall not be so construed as to allow any freedman, free negro, or mulatto to rent or lease any lands or tenements except in incorporated cities or towns, in which places the corporate authorities shall control the same. . . .

Sec. 3. . . . All freedmen, free negroes, or mulattoes who do now and have herebefore lived and cohabited together as husband and wife shall be taken and held in law as legally married, and the issue shall be taken and held as legitimate for all purposes; that it shall not be lawful for any freedman, free negro, or mulatto to intermarry with any white person; nor for any white person to intermarry with any freedman, free negro, or mulatto; and any person who shall so intermarry, shall be deemed guilty of felony, and on conviction thereof shall be confined in the State penitentiary for life; and those shall be deemed freedmen, free negroes, and mulattoes who are of pure negro blood, and those descended from a negro to the third generation, inclusive, though one ancestor in each generation may have been a white person.

Sec. 4. . . . In addition to cases in which freedmen, free negroes, and mulattoes are now by law competent witnesses, freedmen, free negroes, or mulattoes shall be competent in civil cases, when a party or parties to the suit, either plaintiff or plaintiffs, defendant or defendants, and a white person or white persons, is or are the opposing party or parties, plaintiff or plaintiffs, defendant or defendants. They shall also be competent witnesses in all criminal prosecutions where the crime charged is alleged to have been committed by a white person upon or against the person or property of a freedman, free negro, or mulatto: *Provided,* that in all cases said witnesses shall be examined in open court, on the stand; except, however, they may be examined before the grand jury, and shall in all cases be subject to the rules and tests of the common law as to competency and credibility. . . .

Sec. 6. . . . All contracts for labor made with freedmen, free negroes, and mulattoes for a longer period than one month shall be in writing, and in duplicate, attested and read to said freedman, free negro, or mulatto by a beat, city or county officer, or two disinterested white persons of the county in which the labor is to be performed, of which each party shall have one; and said contracts shall be taken and held as entire contracts, and if the laborer shall quit the service of the employer before the expiration of his term of service, without good cause, he shall forfeit his wages for that year up to the time of quitting.

Sec. 7. . . . Every civil officer shall, and every person may, arrest and carry back to his or her legal employer any freedman, free negro, or mulatto who shall have quit the service of his or her employer before the expiration of his or her term of service without good cause; and said officer and person shall be entitled to receive for arresting and carrying back every deserting employe aforesaid the sum of five dollars, and ten cents per mile from the place of arrest to the place of delivery; and the same shall be paid by the employer, and held as a set-off for so much against the wages of said deserting employe: *Provided,* that said arrested party, after being so returned, may appeal to the justice of the peace or member of the board of police of the county, who, on notice to the alleged employer, shall try summarily whether said appellant is legally employed by the alleged employer, and has good cause to quit said employer; either party shall have the right of appeal to the county court, pending which the alleged deserter shall be remanded to the alleged employer or otherwise disposed of, as shall be right and just; and the decision of the county court shall be final. . . .

Sec. 9. . . . If any person shall persuade or attempt to persuade, entice, or cause any freedman, free negro, or mulatto to desert from the legal employment of any person before the expiration of his or her term of service, or shall knowingly employ any such deserting freedman, free negro, or mulatto, or shall knowingly give or sell to any such deserting freedman, free negro, or mulatto, any food, raiment, or other thing, he or she shall be guilty of a misdemeanor, and, upon conviction, shall be fined not less than twenty-five dollars and not more than two

hundred dollars and the costs; and if said fine and costs shall not be immediately paid, the court shall sentence said convict to not exceeding two months' imprisonment in the county jail, and he or she shall moreover be liable to the party injured in damages: *Provided,* if any person shall, or shall attempt to, persuade, entice, or cause any freedman, free negro, or mulatto to desert from any legal employment of any person, with the view to employ said freedman, free negro, or mulatto without the limits of this State, such person, on conviction, shall be fined not less than fifty dollars, and not more than five hundred dollars and costs; and if said fine and costs shall not be immediately paid, the court shall sentence said convict to not exceeding six months imprisonment in the county jail. . . .

2. MISSISSIPPI APPRENTICE LAW
(*Laws of Mississippi,* 1865, p. 86)

Sec. 1. . . . It shall be the duty of all sheriffs, justices of the peace, and other civil officers of the several counties in this State, to report to the probate courts of their respective counties semi-annually, at the January and July terms of said courts, all freedmen, free negroes, and mulattoes, under the age of eighteen, in their respective counties, beats or districts, who are orphans, or whose parent or parents have not the means or who refuse to provide for and support said minors; and thereupon it shall be the duty of said probate court to order the clerk of said court to apprentice said minors to some competent and suitable person, on such terms as the court may direct, having a particular care to the interest of said minor: *Provided,* that the former owner of said minors shall have the preference when, in the opinion of the court, he or she shall be a suitable person for that purpose.

Sec. 2. . . . The said court shall be fully satisfied that the person or persons to whom said minor shall be apprenticed shall be a suitable person to have the charge and care of said minor, and fully to protect the interest of said minor. The said court shall require the said master or mistress to execute bond and security, payable to the State of Mississippi, conditioned that he or she shall furnish said minor with sufficient food and clothing; to treat said minor humanely;

furnish medical attention in case of sickness; teach, or cause to be taught, him or her to read and write, if under fifteen years old, and will conform to any law that may be hereafter passed for the regulation of the duties and relation of master and apprentice. . . .

Sec. 3. . . . In the management and control of said apprentice, said master or mistress shall have the power to inflict such moderate corporal chastisement as a father or guardian is allowed to inflict on his or her child or ward at common law: *Provided,* that in no case shall cruel or inhuman punishment be inflicted.

Sec. 4. . . . If any apprentice shall leave the employment of his or her master or mistress, without his or her consent, said master or mistress may pursue and recapture said apprentice, and bring him or her before any justice of the peace of the county, whose duty it shall be to remand said apprentice to the service of his or her master or mistress; and in the event of a refusal on the part of said apprentice so to return, then said justice shall commit said apprentice to the jail of said county, on failure to give bond, to the next term of the county court; and it shall be the duty of said court at the first term thereafter to investigate said case, and if the court shall be of opinion that said apprentice left the employment of his or her master or mistress without good cause, to order him or her to be punished, as provided for the punishment of hired freedmen, as may be from time to time provided for by law for desertion, until he or she shall agree to return to the service of his or her master or mistress: . . . if the court shall believe that said apprentice had good cause to quit his said master or mistress, the court shall discharge said apprentice from said indenture, and also enter a judgment against the master or mistress for not more than one hundred dollars, for the use and benefit of said apprentice.... .

3. MISSISSIPPI VAGRANT LAW
(*Laws of Mississippi,* 1865, p. 90)

Sec. 1. *Be it enacted,* etc., . . . That all rogues and vagabonds, idle and dissipated persons, beggars, jugglers, or persons practicing unlawful games or plays, runaways, common drunkards, common night-walkers, pilferers, lewd, wanton, or lascivious persons, in speech or behavior, common railers and brawlers, persons who neglect their calling or employment, misspend what they earn, or do not provide for the support of themselves or their families, or dependents, and all other idle and disorderly persons, including all who neglect all lawful business, habitually misspend their time by frequenting houses of ill-fame, gaming-houses, or tippling shops, shall be deemed and considered vagrants, under the provisions of this act, and upon conviction thereof shall be fined not exceeding one hundred dollars, with all accruing costs, and be imprisoned at the discretion of the court, not exceeding ten days.

Sec. 2. . . . All freedmen, free negroes and mulattoes in this State, over the age of eighteen years, found on the second Monday in January, 1866, or thereafter, with no lawful employment or business, or found unlawfully assembling themselves together, either in the day or night time, and all white persons so assembling themselves with freedmen, free negroes or mulattoes, or usually associating with freedmen, free negroes or mulattoes, on terms of equality, or living in adultery or fornication with a freed woman, free negro or mulatto, shall be deemed vagrants, and on conviction thereof shall be fined in a sum not exceeding, in the case of a freedman, free negro or mulatto, fifty dollars, and a white man two hundred dollars, and imprisoned at the discretion of the court, the free negro not exceeding ten days, and the white man not exceeding six months. . . .

Sec. 7. . . . If any freedman, free negro, or mulatto shall fail or refuse to pay any tax levied according to the provisions of the sixth section of this act, it shall be *prima facie* evidence of vagrancy, and it shall be the duty of the sheriff to arrest such freedman, free negro, or mulatto or such person refusing or neglecting to pay such tax, and proceed at once to hire for the shortest time such delinquent tax-payer to any one who will pay the said tax, with accruing costs, giving preference to the employer, if there be one. . . .

4. PENAL LAWS OF MISSISSIPPI
(*Laws of Mississippi, 1865,* p. 165.)

Sec.1. *Be it enacted,* . . . That no freedman, free negro or mulatto, not in the military service of the United States government, and not licensed so to do by the board of police of his or her county, shall keep or carry fire-arms of any kind, or any ammunition, dirk or bowie knife, and on conviction thereof in the county court shall be punished by fine, not exceeding ten dollars, and pay the costs of such proceedings, and all such arms or ammunition shall be forfeited to the informer; and it shall be the duty of every civil and military officer to arrest any freedman, free negro, or mulatto found with any such arms or ammunition, and cause him or her to be committed to trial in default of bail.

2. . . . Any freedman, free negro, or mulatto committing riots, routs, affrays, trespasses, malicious mischief, cruel treatment to animals, seditious speeches, insulting gestures, language, or acts, or assaults on any person, disturbance of the peace, exercising the function of a minister of the Gospel without a license from some regularly organized church, vending spirituous or intoxicating liquors, or committing any other misdemeanor, the punishment of which is not specifically provided for by law, shall, upon conviction thereof in the county court, be fined not less than ten dollars, and not more than one hundred dollars, and may be imprisoned at the discretion of the court, not exceeding thirty days.

Sec. 3. . . . If any white person shall sell, lend, or give to any freedman, free negro, or mulatto any fire-arms, dirk or bowie knife, or ammunition, or any spirituous or intoxicating liquors, such person or persons so offending, upon conviction thereof in the county court of his or her county, shall be fined not exceeding fifty dollars, and may be imprisoned, at the discretion of the court, not exceeding thirty days. . . .

Sec. 5. . . . If any freedman, free negro, or mulatto, convicted of any of the misdemeanors provided against in this act, shall fail or refuse for the space of five days, after conviction, to pay the fine and costs imposed, such person shall be hired out by the sheriff or other officer, at public outcry, to any white person who will pay said fine and all costs, and take said convict for the shortest time.

247. BLACK CODE OF LOUISIANA
1865

(Acts of the General Assembly of Louisiana Regulating Labor. Extra Session, 1865, p. 3 ff.)

On the Black Codes see Doc. No. 246 and references. See also, E. Lonn, *Reconstruction in Louisiana;* J. R. Flicken, *History of Reconstruction in Louisiana;* H. C. Warmoth, *War, Politics and Reconstruction: Stormy Days in Louisiana.*

1. An Act to Provide for and Regulate Labor Contracts for Agricultural Pursuits.

Sec. 1. Be it enacted by the Senate and House of Representatives of the State of Louisiana in general assembly convened, That all persons employed as laborers in agricultural pursuits shall be required, during the first ten days of the month of January of each year, to make contracts for labor for the then ensuing year, or for the year next ensuing the termination of their present contracts. All contracts for labor for agricultural purposes shall be made in writing, signed by the employer, and shall be made in the presence of a Justice of the Peace and two disinterested witnesses, in whose presence the contract shall be read to the laborer, and when assented to and signed by the latter, shall be considered as binding for the time prescribed. . . .

Sec. 2. Every laborer shall have full and perfect liberty to choose his employer, but, when once chosen, he shall not be allowed to leave his place of employment until the fulfillment of his contract . . . and if they do so leave, without cause or permission, they shall forfeit all wages earned to the time of abandonment. . . .

Sec. 7. All employers failing to comply with their contracts, shall, upon conviction, be fined an amount double that due the laborer . . . to be paid to the laborer; and any inhumanity, cruelty, or neglect of duty on the part of the employer shall be summarily punished by fines . . . to be paid to the injured party. . . .

Sec. 8. Be it further enacted, &c., That in case of sickness of the laborer, wages for the time lost shall be deducted, and where the sickness is feigned for purposes of idleness, and also on refusal to work according to contract, double the amount of wages shall be deducted for the time lost; and also where rations have been furnished; and should the refusal to work continue beyond three days, the offender shall be reported to a Justice of the Peace, and shall be forced to labor on roads, levees, and other public works, without pay, until the offender consents to return to his labor.

Sec. 9. Be it further enacted, &c., That, when in health, the laborer shall work ten hours during the day in summer, and nine hours during the day in winter, unless otherwise stipulated in the labor contract; he shall obey all proper orders of his employer or his agent; take proper care of his work-mules, horses, oxen, stock; also of all agricultural implements; and employers shall have the right to make a reasonable deduction from the laborer's wages for injuries done to animals or agricultural implements committed to his care, or for bad or negligent work. Bad work shall not be allowed. Failing to obey reasonable orders, neglect of duty, and leaving home without permission will be deemed disobedience; impudence, swearing, or indecent language to or in the presence of the employer, his family, or agent, or quarreling and fighting with one another, shall be deemed disobedience. For any disobedience a fine of one dollar shall be imposed on and paid by the offender. For all lost time from work-hours, unless in case of sickness, the laborer shall be fined twenty-five cents per hour. For all absence from home without leave he will be fined at the rate of two dollars per day. Laborers will not be required to labor on the Sabbath unless by special contract. For all thefts of the laborer from the employer of agricultural products, hogs, sheep, poultry, or any other property of the employer, or willful destruction of property or injury, the laborer shall pay the employer double the amount of the value of the property stolen, destroyed, or injured, one-half to be paid to the employer and the other half to be placed in the general fund

provided for in this section. No live stock shall be allowed to laborers without the permission of the employer. Laborers shall not receive visitors during work-hours. All difficulties arising between the employers and laborers, under this section, shall be settled by the former; if not satisfactory to the laborers, an appeal may be had to the nearest Justice of the Peace and two freeholders, citizens, one of said citizens to be selected by the employer and the other by the laborer; and all fines imposed and collected under this section shall be deducted from wages due, and shall be placed in a common fund, to be divided among the other laborers on the plantation, except as provided for above. . . .

Sec. 10. Be it further enacted, &c., That for gross misconduct on the part of the laborer, such as insubordination, habitual laziness, frequent acts of violation of his contract or the laws of the State, he may be dismissed by his employer; nevertheless, the laborer shall have the right to resist his dismissal and to a redress of his wrongs by an appeal to a Justice of the Peace and two freeholders, citizens of the parish, one of the freeholders to be selected by himself and the other by his employer.

2. AN ACT RELATIVE TO APPRENTICES AND INDENTURED SERVANTS

Sec. 1. Be it enacted . . . That it shall be the duty of Sheriffs, Justices of the Peace, and other Civil officers of this State, to report . . . for each and every year, all persons under the age of eighteen years, if females, and twenty-one, if males, who are orphans, or whose parents, . . . have not the means, or who refuse to provide for and maintain said minors; and thereupon it shall be the duty of the Clerk of the District Courts . . . to examine whether the party or parties so reported from time to time, come within the purview and meaning of this Act, and, if so, to apprentice said minor or minors, in manner and form as prescribed by the Civil Code. . . .

Sec. 2. That persons, who have attained the age of majority, . . . may bind themselves to services to be performed in this State, for the term of five years, on such terms as they may stipulate, as domestic servants, and to work on farms, plantations, or in manufacturing establishments, which contracts shall be valid and binding on the parties to the same.

Sec. 3. That in all cases where the age of the minor can not be ascertained by record testimony, the Clerk of the District Courts, Mayor and President of the Police Jury, or Justices of the Peace aforesaid, shall fix the age, according to the best evidence before them. . . .

248. JOHNSON'S AMNESTY PROCLAMATION
May 29, 1865

(Richardson, ed. *Messages and Papers,* Vol. VI, p. 310 ff.)

Johnson's proclamation was similar in most respects to Lincoln's proclamation of December 8, 1863; the most important difference is to be found in section thirteen.

BY THE PRESIDENT OF THE UNITED STATES OF AMERICA.

A PROCLAMATION.

Whereas the President of the United States, on the 8th day of December, A. D. 1863, and on the 26th day of March, A. D. 1864, did, with the object to suppress the existing rebellion, to induce all persons to return to their loyalty, and to restore the authority of the United States, issue proclamations offering amnesty and pardon to certain persons who had, directly or by implication, participated in the said rebellion; and

Whereas many persons who had so engaged in said rebellion have, since the issuance of said proclamations, failed or neglected to take the benefits offered thereby; and

Whereas many persons who have been justly deprived of all claim to amnesty and pardon thereunder by reason of their participation, directly or by implication, in said rebellion and continued hostility to the Government of the United States since the date of said proclamations now desire to apply for and obtain amnesty and pardon.

To the end, therefore, that the authority of the Government of the United States may be restored and that peace, order, and freedom may be established, I, Andrew Johnson, President of the United States, do proclaim and declare that I hereby grant to all persons who have, directly or indirectly, participated in the existing rebellion, except as hereinafter excepted, amnesty and pardon, with restoration of all rights of property, except as to slaves . . . but upon the condition, nevertheless, that every such person shall take and subscribe the following oath (or affirmation) and thenceforward keep and maintain said oath inviolate, and which oath shall be registered for permanent preservation and shall be of the tenor and effect following, to wit:

I, —— ——, do solemnly swear (or affirm), in presence of Almighty God, that I will henceforth faithfully support, protect, and defend the Constitution of the United States and the Union of the States thereunder, and that I will in like manner abide by and faithfully support all laws and proclamations which have been made during the existing rebellion with reference to the emancipation of slaves. So help me God.

The following classes of persons are excepted from the benefits of this proclamation:

First. All who are or shall have been pretended civil or diplomatic officers or otherwise domestic or foreign agents of the pretended Confederate government.

Second. All who left judicial stations under the United States to aid the rebellion.

Third. All who shall have been military or naval officers of said pretended Confederate government above the rank of colonel in the army or lieutenant in the navy.

Fourth. All who left seats in the Congress of the United States to aid the rebellion.

Fifth. All who resigned or tendered resignations of their commissions in the Army or Navy of the United States to evade duty in resisting the rebellion.

Sixth. All who have engaged in any way in treating otherwise than lawfully as prisoners of war persons found in the United States service as officers, soldiers, seamen, or in other capacities.

Seventh. All persons who have been or are absentees from the United States for the purpose of aiding the rebellion.

Eighth. All military and naval officers in the rebel service who were educated by the Government in the Military Academy at West Point or the United States Naval Academy.

Ninth. All persons who held the pretended offices of governors of States in insurrection against the United States.

Tenth. All persons who left their homes within the jurisdiction and protection of the United States and passed beyond the Federal military lines into the pretended Confederate States for the purpose of aiding the rebellion.

Eleventh. All persons who have been engaged in the destruction of the commerce of the United States upon the high seas and all persons who have made raids into the United States from Canada or been engaged in destroying the commerce of the United States upon the lakes and rivers that separate the British Provinces from the United States.

Twelfth. All persons who, at the time when they seek to obtain the benefits hereof by taking the oath herein prescribed, are in military, naval, or civil confinement or custody, or under bonds of the civil, military, or naval authorities or agents of the United States as prisoners of war, or persons detained for offenses of any kind, either before or after conviction.

Thirteenth. All persons who have voluntarily participated in said rebellion and the estimated value of whose taxable property is over $20,000.

Fourteenth. All persons who have taken the oath of amnesty as prescribed in the President's proclamation of December 8, A. D. 1863, or an oath of allegiance to the Government of the United States since the date of said proclamation and who have not thenceforward kept and maintained the same inviolate.

Provided, That special application may be made to the President for pardon by any person belonging to the excepted classes, and such clemency will be liberally extended as may be consistent with the facts of the case and the peace and dignity of the United States.

The Secretary of State will establish rules and regulations for administering and recording the said amnesty oath, so as to insure its benefit to the people and guard the Government against fraud. . . .

249. PRESIDENTIAL RECONSTRUCTION

Proclamation of President Johnson for the Provisional Government of South Carolina

June 30, 1865

(Richardson, ed. *Messages and Papers,* Vol. VI, p. 326 ff.)

Johnson followed, almost *in toto* the reconstruction policy of Lincoln. Under Lincoln provisional governments had been established in four States: Louisiana, Tennessee, Arkansas and Virginia. May 29, 1865, Johnson issued his Amnesty Proclamation, and the same day a proclamation organizing a provisional government for North Carolina. Within the next two months similar proclamations for the other six states were issued. On reconstruction in South Carolina see J. P. Hollis, *Early Reconstruction Period in South Carolina;* J. S. Reynolds, *Reconstruction in South Carolina;* F. P. Simkins and R. H. Woody, *South Carolina during Reconstruction.* For special studies of reconstruction in other States see bibliography in H. K. Beale, *The Critical Year.*

BY THE PRESIDENT OF THE UNITED STATES OF AMERICA.

A PROCLAMATION.

Whereas the fourth section of the fourth article of the Constitution of the United States declares that the United States shall guarantee to every State in the Union a republican form of government and shall protect each of them against invasion and domestic violence; and

Whereas the President of the United States is by the Constitution made Commander in Chief of the Army and Navy, as well as chief civil executive officer of the

United States, and is bound by solemn oath faithfully to execute the office of President of the United States and to take care that the laws be faithfully executed; and

Whereas the rebellion which has been waged by a portion of the people of the United States against the properly constituted authorities of the Government thereof in the most violent and revolting form, but whose organized and armed forces have now been almost entirely overcome, has in its revolutionary progress deprived the people of the State of South Carolina of all civil government; and

Whereas it becomes necessary and proper to carry out and enforce the obligations of the United States to the people of South Carolina in securing them in the enjoyment of a republican form of government:

Now, therefore, in obedience to the high and solemn duties imposed upon me by the Constitution of the United States and for the purpose of enabling the loyal people of said State to organize a State government whereby justice may be established, domestic tranquillity insured, and loyal citizens protected in all their rights of life, liberty, and property, I, Andrew Johnson, President of the United States and Commander in Chief of the Army and Navy of the United States, do hereby appoint Benjamin F. Perry, of South Carolina, provisional governor of the State of South Carolina, whose duty it shall be, at the earliest practicable period, to prescribe such rules and regulations as may be necessary and proper for convening a convention composed of delegates to be chosen by that portion of the people of said State who are loyal to the United States, and no others, for the purpose of altering or amending the constitution thereof, and with authority to exercise within the limits of said State all the powers necessary and proper to enable such loyal people of the State of South Carolina to restore said State to its constitutional relations to the Federal Government and to present such a republican form of State government as will entitle the State to the guaranty of the United States therefor and its people to protection by the United States against invasion, insurrection, and domestic violence: *Provided,* That in any election that may be hereafter held for choosing delegates to any State convention

as aforesaid no person shall be qualified as an elector or shall be eligible as a member of such convention unless he shall have previously taken and subscribed the oath of amnesty as set forth in the President's proclamation of May 29, A. D. 1865, and is a voter qualified as prescribed by the constitution and laws of the State of South Carolina in force immediately before the 17th day of November, A. D. 1860, the date of the so-called ordinance of secession; and the said convention, when convened, or the legislature that may be thereafter assembled, will prescribe the qualification of electors and the eligibility of persons to hold office under the constitution and laws of the State —a power the people of the several States composing the Federal Union have rightfully exercised from the origin of the Government to the present time.

And I do hereby direct—

First. That the military commander of the department and all officers and persons in the military and naval service aid and assist the said provisional governor in carrying into effect this proclamation; and they are enjoined to abstain from in any way hindering, impeding, or discouraging the loyal people from the organization of a State government as herein authorized.

Second. That the Secretary of State proceed to put in force all laws of the United States the administration whereof belongs to the State Department applicable to the geographical limits aforesaid.

Third. That the Secretary of the Treasury proceed to nominate for appointment assessors of taxes and collectors of customs and internal revenue and such other officers of the Treasury Department as are authorized by law and put in execution the revenue laws of the United States within the geographical limits aforesaid. In making appointments the preference shall be given to qualified loyal persons residing within the districts where their respective duties are to be performed; but if suitable residents of the districts shall not be found, then persons residing in other States or districts shall be appointed.

Fourth. That the Postmaster-General proceed to establish post-offices and post routes and put into execution the postal laws of the United States within the said State, giving to loyal residents the preference of appointment; but if suitable residents are not found, then to appoint agents, etc., from other States.

Fifth. That the district judge for the judicial district in which South Carolina is included proceed to hold courts within said State in accordance with the provisions of the act of Congress. The Attorney-General will instruct the proper officers to libel and bring to judgment, confiscation, and sale property subject to confiscation and enforce the administration of justice within said State in all matters within the cognizance and jurisdiction of the Federal courts.

Sixth. That the Secretary of the Navy take possession of all public property belonging to the Navy Department within said geographical limits and put in operation all acts of Congress in relation to naval affairs having application to the said State.

Seventh. That the Secretary of the Interior put in force the laws relating to the Interior Department applicable to the geographical limits aforesaid.

250. GENERAL GRANT'S OBSERVATIONS ON CONDITIONS IN THE SOUTH
December 18, 1865

(U. S. 39th Congress, 1st Session, *Sen. Executive Doc.* No. 2, p. 107 ff.)

In the fall of 1865 President Johnson, anxious to have reliable information on conditions in the South, sent several personal representatives through that section for purposes of observation. Among these emissaries were Carl Schurz, Harvey M. Watterson, Benjamin C. Truman, Chief Justice Chase, and General Grant. Schurz's report was a severe arraignment of the southern people and a plea for the radical policy of reconstruction: it was subsequently revealed that he was under financial obligations to the Radicals. The reports of Truman and Watterson described the South as pacified and conciliatory, and sustained the Presidential policy of reconstruction. General Grant left Washington on his trip of observation November 29, 1865, and visited Raleigh, Charleston, Savannah, Augusta, and Atlanta. His report, presented to the President December 18, was convincing testimony to the wisdom of the Presidential policy. See, L. A. Coolidge, *Life of U. S. Grant*, ch. xxiv. The Report of Schurz is bound together with Grant's; Truman's Report is in 39th Congress, 1 Sess. *Sen. Executive Doc.* No. 43. On Chase's trip, see C. G. Bowers, *The Tragic Era*, ch. iii.

. . . I am satisfied that the mass of thinking men of the south accept the present situation of affairs in good faith. The questions which have heretofore divided the sentiment of the people of the two sections —slavery and State rights, or the right of a State to secede from the Union—they regard as having been settled forever by the highest tribunal—arms—that man can resort to. I was pleased to learn from the leading men whom I met that they not only accepted the decision arrived at as final, but, now that the smoke of battle has cleared away and time has been given for reflection, that this decision has been a fortunate one for the whole country, they receiving like benefits from it with those who opposed them in the field and in council.

Four years of war, during which law was executed only at the point of the bayonet throughout the States in rebellion, have left the people possibly in a condition not to yield that ready obedience to civil authority the American people have generally been in the habit of yielding. This would render the presence of small garrisons throughout those States necessary until such time as labor returns to its proper channel, and civil authority is fully established. I did not meet anyone, either those holding places under the government or citizens of the southern States, who think it practicable to withdraw the military from the south at present. The white and the black mutually require the protection of the general government.

There is such universal acquiescence in the authority of the general government throughout the portions of country visited by me, that the mere presence of a military force, without regard to numbers, is sufficient to maintain order. The good of the country, and economy, require that the force kept in the interior, where there are many freedmen, (elsewhere in the southern States than at forts upon the seacoast no force is necessary,) should all be white troops. The reasons for this are obvious without mentioning many of them. The presence of black troops, lately slaves, demoralizes labor, both by their advice and by furnishing in their camps a resort for the freedmen for long distances around. White troops generally excite no opposition, and therefore a small number of them can maintain order in a given district. Colored troops must be kept in bodies sufficient to defend themselves. It is not the thinking men who would use violence towards any class of troops sent among them by the general government, but the ignorant in some places might; and the late slave seems to be imbued with the idea that the property of his late master should, by right, belong to him, or at least should have no protection from the colored soldier. There is danger of collisions being brought on by such causes.

My observations lead me to the conclusion that the citizens of the southern States are anxious to return to self-government, within the Union, as soon as possible; that whilst reconstructing they want and require protection from the government; that they are in earnest in wishing to do what they think is required by the government, not humiliating to them as citizens, and that if such a course were pointed out they would pursue it in good faith. It is to be regretted that there cannot be a greater commingling, at this time, between the citizens of the two sections, and particularly of those intrusted with the law-making power.

I did not give the operations of the Freedmen's Bureau that attention I would have done if more time had been at my disposal. Conversations on the subject, however, with officers connected with the bureau, lead me to think that, in some of the States, its affairs have not been conducted with good judgment or economy, and that the belief widely spread among the freedmen of the southern States, that the lands of their former owners will, at least in part, be divided among them, has come from the agents of this bureau. This belief is seriously interfering with the willingness of the freedmen to make contracts for the coming year. In some form the Freedmen's Bureau is an absolute necessity until civil law is established and enforced, securing to the freedmen their rights and full protection. At present, however, it is independent of the military establishment of the country, and seems to be operated by the different agents of the bureau according to their individual notions. Everywhere General Howard, the able head of the bureau, made friends by the just and fair instructions and advice he gave; but the complaint in South Carolina was that when he left, things went on as before. Many, perhaps the majority, of the agents of the Freedmen's Bureau advise the freedmen that by their own industry they must expect to live. To this end they endeavor to secure employment for them, and to see that both contracting parties comply with their engagements. In some instances, I am sorry to say, the freedman's mind does not seem to be disabused of the idea that a freedman has the right to live without care or provision for the future. The effect of the belief in division of lands is idleness and accumulation in camps, towns, and cities. In such cases I think it will be found that vice and disease will tend to the extermination or great reduction of the colored race. It cannot be expected that the opinions held by men at the south for years can be changed in a day, and therefore the freedmen require, for a few years, not only laws to protect them, but the fostering care of those who will give them good counsel, and on whom they rely.

The Freedmen's Bureau being separated from the military establishment of the country, requires all the expense of a separate organization. One does not necessarily know what the other is doing, or what orders they are acting under. It seems to me this could be corrected by regarding every officer on duty with troops in the southern States as an agent of the Freedmen's Bureau, and then have all orders from the head of the bureau sent through department commanders. This would create a responsibility that would secure uniformity of action throughout all the south; would insure the orders and instructions from the head of the bureau being carried out, and would relieve from duty and pay a large number of employes of the government.

I have the honor to be, very respectfully, your obedient servant,

U. S. Grant, Lieutenant General.

251. VETO OF FREEDMEN'S BUREAU BILL
February 19, 1866

(Richardson, ed. *Messages and Papers*, Vol. VI, p. 398 ff.)

The Freedmen's Bureau had been established by act of Congress, March 3, 1865. February 19, 1866, a new Freedmen's Bureau bill, extending the life of the bureau and enlarging its powers, was presented to President Johnson. The veto of this bill inaugurated the open warfare between the Radicals and President Johnson. July 16, a supplementary Freedmen's Bureau Act was passed over the President's veto. For the Freedmen's Bureau, see, P. S. Peirce, *The Freedmen's Bureau;* L. Webster, *The Freedmen's Bureau in South Carolina.* For the veto message, see H. Beale, *The Critical Year,* p. 80 ff.; G. F. Milton, *Age of Hate,* p. 284 ff.

WASHINGTON, *February 19, 1866.*
To the Senate of the United States:

I have examined with care the bill, which originated in the Senate and has been passed by the two Houses of Congress, to amend an act entitled "An act to establish a bureau for the relief of freedmen and refugees," and for other purposes. Having with much regret come to the conclusion that it would not be consistent with the public welfare to give my approval to the measure, I return the bill to the Senate with my objections to its becoming a law. . . .

I share with Congress the strongest desire to secure to the freedmen the full enjoyment of their freedom and property and their entire independence and equality in making contracts for their labor, but the bill before me contains provisions which in my opinion are not warranted by the Constitution and are not well suited to accomplish the end in view.

The bill proposes to establish by authority of Congress military jurisdiction over all parts of the United States containing refugees and freedmen. It would by its very nature apply with most force to those parts of the United States in which the freedmen most abound, and it expressly extends the existing temporary jurisdiction of the Freedmen's Bureau, with greatly enlarged powers, over those States "in which the ordinary course of judicial proceedings has been interrupted by the rebellion." The source from which this military jurisdiction is to emanate is none other than the President of the United States, acting through the War Department and the Commissioner of the Freedmen's Bureau. The agents to carry out this military jurisdiction are to be selected either from the Army or from civil life; the country is to be divided into districts and subdistricts, and the number of salaried agents to be employed may be equal to the number of counties or parishes in all the United States where freedmen and refugees are to be found.

The subjects over which this military jurisdiction is to extend in every part of the United States include protection to "all employees, agents, and officers of this bureau in the exercise of the duties imposed" upon them by the bill. In eleven States it is further to extend over all cases affecting freedmen and refugees discriminated against "by local law, custom, or prejudice." In those eleven States the bill subjects any white person who may be charged with depriving a freedman of "any civil rights or immunities belonging to white persons" to imprisonment or fine, or both, without, however, defining the "civil rights and immunities" which are thus to be secured to the freedmen by military law. This military jurisdiction also extends to all questions that may arise respecting contracts. The agent who is thus to exercise the office of a military judge may be a stranger, entirely ignorant of the laws of the place, and exposed to the errors of judgment to which all men are liable. The exercise of power over which there is no legal supervision by so vast a number of agents as is contemplated by the bill must, by the very nature of man, be attended by acts of caprice, injustice, and passion.

The trials having their origin under this bill are to take place without the intervention of a jury and without any fixed rules of law or evidence. The rules on which offenses are to be "heard and determined" by the numerous agents are such rules and regulations as the President, through the War Department, shall prescribe. No previous presentment is required nor any indictment charging the commission of a crime against the laws; but the trial must proceed on charges and specifications. The punishment will be, not what the law declares, but such as a court-martial may think proper; and from these arbitrary tribunals there lies no appeal, no writ of error to any of the courts in which the Constitution of the United States vests exclusively the judicial power of the country.

While the territory and the classes of actions and offenses that are made subject to this measure are so extensive, the bill itself, should it become a law, will have no limitation in point of time, but will form a part of the permanent legislation of the country. I can not reconcile a system of military jurisdiction of this kind with the words of the Constitution which declare that "no person shall be held to answer for a capital or otherwise infamous crime unless on a presentment or indictment of a grand jury, except in cases arising in the land or naval forces, or in the militia when in actual service in time of war or public danger," and that "in all criminal prosecutions the accused shall enjoy the right to a speedy and public trial by an impartial jury of the State and district wherein the crime shall have been committed." The safeguards which the experience and wisdom of ages taught our fathers to establish as securities for the protection of the innocent, the punishment of the guilty, and the equal administration of justice are to be set aside, and for the sake of a more vigorous interposition in behalf of justice we are to take the risks of the many acts of injustice that would necessarily follow from an almost countless number of agents established in every parish or county in nearly a third of the States of the Union, over whose decisions there is to be no supervision or control by the Federal courts. The power that would be thus placed in the hands of the President is such as in time of peace certainly ought never to be intrusted to any one man.

If it be asked whether the creation of such a tribunal within a State is warranted as a measure of war, the question immediately presents itself whether we are still engaged in war. Let us not unnecessarily disturb the commerce and credit and industry of the country by declaring to the American people and to the world that the United States are still in a condition of civil war. At present there is no part of our country in which the

authority of the United States is disputed. Offenses that may be committed by individuals should not work a forfeiture of the rights of whole communities. The country has returned, or is returning, to a state of peace and industry, and the rebellion is in fact at an end. The measure, therefore, seems to be as inconsistent with the actual condition of the country as it is at variance with the Constitution of the United States.

If, passing from general considerations, we examine the bill in detail, it is open to weighty objections. . . .

I can not but add another very grave objection to this bill. The Constitution imperatively declares, in connection with taxation, that each State *shall* have at least one Representative, and fixes the rule for the number to which, in future times, each State shall be entitled. It also provides that the Senate of the United States *shall* be composed of two Senators from each State, and adds with peculiar force "that no State, without its consent, shall be deprived of its equal suffrage in the Senate." The original act was necessarily passed in the absence of the States chiefly to be affected, because their people were then contumaciously engaged in the rebellion. Now the case is changed, and some, at least, of those States are attending Congress by loyal representatives, soliciting the allowance of the constitutional right for representation. At the time, however, of the consideration and the passing of this bill there was no Senator or Representative in Congress from the eleven States which are to be mainly affected by its provisions. The very fact that reports were and are made against the good disposition of the people of that portion of the country is an additional reason why they need and should have representatives of their own in Congress to explain their condition, reply to accusations, and assist by their local knowledge in the perfecting of measures immediately affecting themselves. While the liberty of deliberation would then be free and Congress would have full power to decide according to its judgment, there could be no objection urged that the States most interested had not been permitted to be heard. The principle is firmly fixed in the minds of the American people that there should be no taxation without representation. Great burdens have now to be borne by all the country, and we may best demand that they shall be borne without murmur when they are voted by a majority of the representatives of all the people. I would not interfere with the unquestionable right of Congress to judge, each House for itself, "of the elections, returns, and qualifications of its own members;" but that authority can not be construed as including the right to shut out in time of peace any State from the representation to which it is entitled by the Constitution. . . .

The bill under consideration refers to certain of the States as though they had not "been fully restored in all their constitutional relations to the United States." If they have not, let us at once act together to secure that desirable end at the earliest possible moment. It is hardly necessary for me to inform Congress that in my own judgment most of those States, so far, at least, as depends upon their own action, have already been fully restored, and are to be deemed as entitled to enjoy their constitutional rights as members of the Union. Reasoning from the Constitution itself and from the actual situation of the country, I feel not only entitled but bound to assume that with the Federal courts restored and those of the several States in the full exercise of their functions the rights and interests of all classes of people will, with the aid of the military in cases of resistance to the laws, be essentially protected against unconstitutional infringement or violation. Should this expectation unhappily fail, which I do not anticipate, then the Executive is already fully armed with the powers conferred by the act of March, 1865, establishing the Freedmen's Bureau, and hereafter, as heretofore, he can employ the land and naval forces of the country to suppress insurrection or to overcome obstructions to the laws.

In accordance with the Constitution, I return the bill to the Senate, in the earnest hope that a measure involving questions and interests so important to the country will not become a law, unless upon deliberate consideration by the people it shall receive the sanction of an enlightened public judgment.

ANDREW JOHNSON.

252. THE CIVIL RIGHTS ACT
April 9, 1866
(U. S. Statutes at Large, Vol. XIV, p. 27 ff.)

This measure, designed to protect the freedmen from such discriminating legislation as the Black codes, was first passed March 13. It was vetoed by President Johnson (Doc. No. 253), and passed over his veto April 9. The act conferred citizenship upon the negroes, legislation necessitated by the Dred Scott decision. Doubt as to the constitutionality of the measure induced Congress to enact most of its provisions into the Fourteenth Amendment. See, H. E. Flack, *Adoption of the Fourteenth Amendment;* H. White, *Life of Lyman Trumbull;* J. F. Rhodes, *History of the United States,* Vol. V, 583 ff.

An Act to protect all Persons in the United States in their Civil Rights, and furnish the Means of their Vindication.

Be it enacted, That all persons born in the United States and not subject to any foreign power, excluding Indians not taxed, are hereby declared to be citizens of the United States; and such citizens, of every race and color, without regard to any previous condition of slavery or involuntary servitude, except as a punishment for crime whereof the party shall have been duly convicted, shall have the same right, in every State and Territory in the United States, to make and enforce contracts, to sue, be parties, and give evidence, to inherit, purchase, lease, sell, hold, and convey real and personal property, and to full and equal benefit of all laws and proceedings for the security of person and property, as is enjoyed by white citizens, and shall be subject to like punishment, pains, and penalties, and to none other, any law, statute, ordinance, regulation, or custom, to the contrary notwithstanding.

SEC. 2. *And be it further enacted,* That any person who, under color of any law, statute, ordinance, regulation, or custom, shall subject, or cause to be subjected, any inhabitant of any State or Territory to the deprivation of any right secured or protected by this act, or to different punishment, pains, or penalties on account of such person having at any time been held in a condition of slavery or involuntary servitude, except as a punishment for crime whereof the party shall have been duly convicted, or by reason of his color or race, than is prescribed for the punishment of white persons, shall be deemed guilty of a misdemeanor, and, on conviction, shall be punished by fine not exceeding one thousand dollars, or imprisonment not exceeding one year, or both, in the discretion of the court.

SEC. 3. *And be it further enacted,* That the district courts of the United States, . . . shall have, exclusively of the courts of the several States, cognizance of all crimes and offences committed against the provisions of this act, and also, concurrently with the circuit courts of the United States, of all causes, civil and criminal, affecting persons who are denied or cannot enforce in the courts or judicial tribunals of the State or locality where they may be any of the rights secured to them by the first section of this act. . . .

SEC. 4. *And be it further enacted,* That the district attorneys, marshals, and deputy marshals of the United States, the commissioners appointed by the circuit and territorial courts of the United States, with powers of arresting, imprisoning, or bailing offenders against the laws of the United States, the officers and agents of the Freedmen's Bureau, and every other officer who may be specially empowered by the President of the United States, shall be, and they are hereby, specially authorized and required, at the expense of the United States, to institute proceedings against all and every person who shall violate the provisions of this act, and cause him or them to be arrested and imprisoned, or bailed, as the case may be, for trial before such court of the United States or territorial court as by this act has cognizance of the offence. . . .

SEC. 8. *And be it further enacted,* That whenever the President of the United States shall have reason to believe that offences have been or are likely to be committed against the provisions of this act within any judicial district, it shall be lawful for him, in his discretion, to direct the judge, marshal, and district attorney of such district to attend at such place within the district, and for such time as he may designate, for the purpose of the more speedy arrest and trial of persons charged with a violation of this act; and it shall be the duty of every judge or other officer, when any such requisition shall be received by him, to attend at the place and for the time therein designated.

SEC. 9. *And be it further enacted,* That it shall be lawful for the President of the United States, or such person as he may empower for that purpose, to employ such part of the land or naval forces of the United States, or of the militia, as shall be necessary to prevent the violation and enforce the due execution of this act.

SEC. 10. *And be it further enacted,* That upon all questions of law arising in any cause under the provisions of this act a final appeal may be taken to the Supreme Court of the United States.

253. VETO OF THE CIVIL RIGHTS ACT
March 27, 1866

(Richardson, ed. *Messages and Papers,* Vol. VI, p. 405 ff.)

WASHINGTON, D. C., *March 27, 1866.*
To the Senate of the United States:

I regret that the bill, which has passed both Houses of Congress, entitled "An act to protect all persons in the United States in their civil rights and furnish the means of their vindication," contains provisions which I can not approve consistently with my sense of duty to the whole people and my obligations to the Constitution of the United States. I am therefore constrained to return it to the Senate, the House in which it originated, with my objections to its becoming a law.

By the first section of the bill all persons born in the United States and not subject to any foreign power, excluding Indians not taxed, are declared to be citizens of the United States. . . . It does not purport to give these classes of persons any status as citizens of States, except that which may result from their status as citizens of the United States. The power to confer the right of State citizenship is just as exclusively with the several States as the power to confer the right of Federal citizenship is with Congress.

The right of Federal citizenship thus to be conferred on the several excepted races before mentioned is now for the first time proposed to be given by law. If, as is claimed by many, all persons who are native born already are, by virtue of the Constitution, citizens of the United States, the passage of the pending bill can not be necessary to make them such. If, on the other hand, such persons are not citizens, as may be assumed from the proposed legislation to make them such, the grave question presents itself whether, when eleven of the thirty-six States are unrepresented in Congress at the present time, it is sound policy to make our entire colored population and all other excepted classes citizens of the United States. Four millions of them have just emerged from slavery into freedom. . . . It may also be asked whether it is necessary that they should be declared citizens in order that they may be secured in the enjoyment of the civil rights proposed to be conferred by the bill. Those rights are, by Federal as well as State laws, secured to all domiciled aliens and foreigners, even before the completion of the process of naturalization; and it may safely be assumed that the same enactments are sufficient to give like protection and benefits to those for whom this bill provides special legislation. Besides, the policy of the Government from its origin to the present time seems to have been that persons who are strangers to and unfamiliar with our institutions and our laws should pass through a certain probation, at the end of which, before attaining the coveted prize, they must give evidence of their fitness to receive and to exercise the rights of citizens as contemplated by the Constitution of the United States. The bill in effect proposes a discrimination against large numbers of intelligent, worthy, and patriotic foreigners, and in favor of the negro, to whom, after long years of bondage, the avenues to freedom and intelligence have just now been suddenly opened. . . .

The first section of the bill also contains an enumeration of the rights to be enjoyed by these classes so made citizens "in every State and Territory in the United States." These rights are "to make and enforce contracts; to sue, be parties, and give evidence; to inherit, purchase, lease, sell, hold, and convey real and personal property," and to have "full and equal benefit of all laws and proceedings for the security of person and property as is enjoyed by white citizens." So, too, they are made subject to the same punishment, pains, and penalties in common with white citizens, and to none other. Thus a perfect equality of the white and colored races is attempted to be fixed by Federal law in every State of the Union over the vast field of State jurisdiction covered by these enumerated rights. In no one of these can any State ever exercise any power of discrimination between the different races. . . .

Hitherto every subject embraced in the enumeration of rights contained in this bill has been considered as exclusively belonging to the States. They all relate to the internal police and economy of the respective States. They are matters which in each State concern the domestic condition of its people, varying in each according to its own peculiar circumstances and the safety and well-being of its own citizens. I do not mean to say that upon all these subjects there are not Federal restraints—as, for instance, in the State power of legislation over contracts there is a Federal limitation that no State shall pass a law impairing the obligations of contracts; and, as to crimes, that no State shall pass an *ex post facto* law; and, as to money, that no State shall make anything but gold and silver a legal tender; but where can we find a Federal prohibition against the power of any State to discriminate, as do most of them, between aliens and citizens, between artificial persons, called corporations, and natural persons, in the right to hold real estate? If it be granted that Congress can repeal all State laws discriminating between whites and blacks in the subjects covered by this bill, why, it may be asked, may not Congress repeal in the same way all State laws discriminating between the two races on the subjects of suffrage and office? If Congress can declare by law who shall hold lands, who shall testify, who shall have capacity to make a contract in a State, then Congress can by law also declare who, without regard to color or race, shall have the right to sit as a juror or as a judge, to hold any office, and, finally, to vote "in every State and Territory of the United States." As respects the Territories, they come within the power of Congress, for as to them the lawmaking power is the Federal power; but as to the States no similar provision exists vesting in Congress the power "to make rules and regulations" for them.

The object of the second section of the bill is to afford discriminating protection to colored persons in the full enjoyment of all the rights secured to them by the preceding section. . . .

This provision of the bill seems to be unnecessary, as adequate judicial remedies could be adopted to secure the desired end without invading the immunities of legislators, always important to be preserved in the interest of public liberty; without assailing the independence of the judiciary, always essential to the preservation of individual rights; and without impairing the efficiency of ministerial officers, always necessary for the maintenance of public peace and order. The remedy proposed by this section seems to be in this respect not only anomalous, but unconstitutional; for the Constitution guarantees nothing with certainty if it does not insure to the several States the right of making and executing laws in regard to all matters arising within their jurisdiction, subject only to the restriction that in cases of conflict with the Constitution and constitutional laws of the United States the latter should be held to be the supreme law of the land. . . .

It is clear that in States which deny to persons whose rights are secured by the first section of the bill any one of those rights all criminal and civil cases affecting them will, by the provisions of the third section, come under the exclusive cognizance of the Federal tribunals. It follows that if, in any State which denies to a colored person any one of all those rights, that person should commit a crime against the laws of a State—murder, arson, rape, or any other crime—all protection and punishment through the courts of the State are taken away, and he can only be tried and punished in the Federal courts. How is the criminal to be tried? If the offense is provided for and punished by Federal law, that law, and not the State law, is to govern. It is only when the offense does not happen to be within the purview of Federal law that the Federal courts are to try

and punish him under any other law. Then resort is to be had to "the common law, as modified and changed" by State legislation, "so far as the same is not inconsistent with the Constitution and laws of the United States." So that over this vast domain of criminal jurisprudence provided by each State for the protection of its own citizens and for the punishment of all persons who violate its criminal laws, Federal law, whenever it can be made to apply, displaces State law. The question here naturally arises, from what source Congress derives the power to transfer to Federal tribunals certain classes of cases embraced in this section. . . . This section of the bill undoubtedly comprehends cases and authorizes the exercise of powers that are not, by the Constitution, within the jurisdiction of the courts of the United States. To transfer them to those courts would be an exercise of authority well calculated to excite distrust and alarm on the part of all the States, for the bill applies alike to all of them—as well to those that have as to those that have not been engaged in rebellion. . . .

The fourth section of the bill provides that officers and agents of the Freedmen's Bureau shall be empowered to make arrests, and also that other officers may be specially commissioned for that purpose by the President of the United States. It also authorizes circuit courts of the United States and the superior courts of the Territories to appoint, without limitation, commissioners, who are to be charged with the performance of *quasi* judicial duties. The fifth section empowers the commissioners so to be selected by the courts to appoint in writing, under their hands, one or more suitable persons from time to time to execute warrants and other processes described by the bill. These numerous official agents are made to constitute a sort of police, in addition to the military, and are authorized to summon a *posse comitatus*, and even to call to their aid such portion of the land and naval forces of the United States, or of the militia, "as may be necessary to the performance of the duty with which they are charged." This extraordinary power is to be conferred upon agents irresponsible to the Government and to the people, to whose number the discretion of the commissioners is the only limit, and in whose hands such authority might be made a terrible engine of wrong, oppression, and fraud. . . .

The ninth section authorizes the President, or such person as he may empower for that purpose, "to employ such part of the land or naval forces of the United States, or of the militia, as shall be necessary to prevent the violation and enforce the due execution of this act." This language seems to imply a permanent military force, that is to be always at hand, and whose only business is to be the enforcement of this measure over the vast region where it is intended to operate. . . .

In all our history, in all our experience as a people living under Federal and State law, no such system as that contemplated by the details of this bill has ever before been proposed or adopted. They establish for the security of the colored race safeguards which go infinitely beyond any that the General Government has ever provided for the white race. In fact, the distinction of race and color is by the bill made to operate in favor of the colored and against the white race. They interfere with the municipal legislation of the States, with the relations existing exclusively between a State and its citizens, or between inhabitants of the same State—an absorption and assumption of power by the General Government which, if acquiesced in, must sap and destroy our federative system of limited powers and break down the barriers which preserve the rights of the States. It is another step, or rather stride, toward centralization and the concentration of all legislative powers in the National Government. The tendency of the bill must be to resuscitate the spirit of rebellion and to arrest the progress of those influences which are more closely drawing around the States the bonds of union and peace. . . .

ANDREW JOHNSON.

254. REPORT OF THE JOINT COMMITTEE ON RECONSTRUCTION
June 20, 1866
(*Report of the Joint Committee on Reconstruction,* p. 4 ff.)

A Committee of six Senators and nine Representatives, of which Senator Fessenden was chairman, was appointed in December 1865 "to inquire into the condition of the states which formed the so-called Confederate States of America, and report whether they, or any of them, are entitled to be represented in either house of Congress." The *Report* recommended that the Confederate states were not entitled to representation; it also maintained the authority of Congress, rather than of the Executive, over the process of reconstruction. The *Report* was published separately, and also with a voluminous body of testimony collected by various sub-committees. Of great importance is B. B. Kendrick, *Journal of the Joint Committee of Fifteen on Reconstruction.*

A claim for the immediate admission of senators and representatives from the so-called Confederate States has been urged, which seems to your committee not to be founded either in reason or in law, and which cannot be passed without comment. Stated in a few words, it amounts to this: That inasmuch as the lately insurgent States had no legal right to separate themselves from the Union, they still retain their position as States, and consequently the people thereof have a right to immediate representation in Congress without the interposition of any conditions whatever. . . . It has even been contended that until such admission all legislation affecting their interests is, if not unconstitutional, at least unjustifiable and oppressive.

It is believed by your Committee that these propositions are not only wholly untenable, but, if admitted, would tend to the destruction of the government. . . . It cannot, we think, be denied that the war thus waged was a civil war of the greatest magnitude. The people waging it were necessarily subject to all the rules which, by the law of nations, control a contest of that character, and to all the legitimate consequences following it. One of these consequences was that, within the limits prescribed by humanity, the conquered rebels were at the mercy of the conquerors. . . .

It is moreover contended . . . that from the peculiar nature and character of our government . . . from the moment rebellion lays down its arms and actual hostilities cease all political rights of rebellious communities are at once restored; that because the people of a state of the Union were once an organized community within the Union, they necessarily so remain, and their right to be represented in Congress at any and all times, and to participate in the government of the country under all circumstances, admits of neither question nor dispute. If this is indeed true, then is the government of the United States powerless for its own protection, and flagrant rebellion, carried to the extreme of civil war, is a pastime which any state may play at, not only certain that it can lose nothing in any event, but may even be the gainer by defeat. If rebellion succeeds it accomplishes its purpose and destroys the government. If it fails, the war has been barren of results, and the battle may still be fought out in the legislative halls of the country. Treason, defeated in the field, has only to take possession of Congress, and the cabinet.

Your committee do not deem it either necessary or proper to discuss the question whether the late Confederate States are still States of this Union, or can ever be otherwise. Granting this profitless abstraction about which so many words have been wasted, it by no means follows that the people of those States may not place themselves in a position to abrogate the powers and privileges incident to a State of the Union, and deprive themselves of all pretence of right to exercise those powers and enjoy those privileges. . . .

Equally absurd is the pretence that the legislative authority of the nation must be inoperative so far as they are concerned, while they, by their own act, have lost the right to take part in it. Such a proposition carries its own refutation on its face. . . .

It is the opinion of your committee—

I. That the States lately in rebellion were, at the close of the war, disorganized communities, without civil government, and without constitutions or other forms, by virtue of which political relation could legally exist between them and the federal government.

II. That Congress cannot be expected to recognize as valid the election of representatives from disorganized communities, which, from the very nature of the case, were unable to present their claim to representation under those established and recognized rules, the observance of which has been hitherto required.

III. That Congress would not be justified in admitting such communities to a participation in the government of the country without first providing such constitutional or other guarantees as will tend to secure the civil rights of all citizens of the republic; a just equality of representation; protection against claims founded in rebellion and crime; a temporary restoration of the right of suffrage to those who have not actively participated in the efforts to destroy the Union and overthrow the government, and the exclusion from position of public trust of, at least, a portion of those whose crimes have proved them to be enemies of the Union, and unworthy of public confidence. . . .

We now propose to re-state, as briefly as possible, the general facts and principles applicable to all the States recently in rebellion:

. . . Third. Having voluntarily deprived themselves of representation in Congress for the criminal purpose of destroying the Union, and having reduced themselves, by the act of levying war, to the condition of public enemies, they have no right to complain of temporary exclusion from Congress; but on the contrary . . . the burden now rests upon them, before claiming to be reinstated in their former condition, to show that they are qualified to resume federal relations. . . .

Fourth. Having . . . forfeited all civil and political rights and privileges under the federal Constitution, they can only be restored thereto by the permission and authority of that constitutional power against which they rebelled and by which they were subdued.

Fifth. These rebellious enemies were conquered by the people of the United States acting through all the co-ordinate branches of the government, and not by the executive department alone. The powers of conqueror are not so vested in the President that he can fix and regulate the terms of settlement and confer congressional representation on conquered rebels and traitors. . . . The authority to restore rebels to political power in the federal Government can be exercised only with the concurrence of all the departments in which political power is vested. . . .

. . . Eighth. . . . No proof has been afforded to Congress of a constituency in any one of the so-called Confederate States, unless we except the State of Tennessee, qualified to elect senators and representatives in Congress. No State Constitution, or amendment to a State Constitution, has had the sanction of the people. All the so-called legislation of State conventions and legislatures has been had under military dictation. If the President may, at his will and under his own authority, whether as military commander or chief executive, qualify persons to appoint senators and elect representatives, and empower others to appoint and elect them, he thereby practically controls the organization of the legislative department. The constitutional form of government is thereby practically destroyed, and its power absorbed in the Executive. . . .

Ninth. The necessity of providing adequate safeguards for the future, before restoring the insurrectionary States to a participation in the direction of public affairs, is apparent from the bitter hostility to the government and people of the United States yet existing throughout the conquered territory. . . .

Tenth. The conclusion of your committee therefore is, that the so-called Confederate States are not, at present, entitled to representation in the Congress of the United States. . . .

255. PRESIDENT JOHNSON ON THE RESTORATION OF THE SOUTHERN STATES TO THE UNION

Second Annual Message to Congress
December 3, 1866

(Richardson, ed. *Messages and Papers,* Vol. VI, p. 445 ff.)

WASHINGTON, *December 3, 1866.*
Fellow-Citizens of the Senate and House of Representatives:

. . . In my message of the 4th of December, 1865, Congress was informed of the measures which had been instituted by the Executive with a view to the gradual restoration of the States in which the insurrection occurred to their relations with the General Government. Provisional governors had been appointed, conventions called, governors elected, legislatures assembled, and Senators and Representatives chosen to the Congress of the United States. Courts had been opened for the enforcement of laws long in abeyance. The blockade had been removed, custom-houses reestablished, and the internal-revenue laws put in force, in order that the people might contribute to the national income. Postal operations had been renewed, and efforts were being made to restore them to their former condition of efficiency. The States themselves had been asked to take part in the high function of amending the Constitution, and of thus sanctioning the extinction of African slavery as one of the legitimate results of our internecine struggle.

Having progressed thus far, the executive department found that it had accomplished nearly all that was within the scope of its constitutional authority. One thing, however,

yet remained to be done before the work of restoration could be completed, and that was the admission to Congress of loyal Senators and Representatives from the States whose people had rebelled against the lawful authority of the General Government. This question devolved upon the respective Houses, which by the Constitution are made the judges of the elections, returns, and qualifications of their own members, and its consideration at once engaged the attention of Congress. . . .

All of the States in which the insurrection had existed promptly amended their constitutions so as to make them conform to the great change thus effected in the organic law of the land; declared null and void all ordinances and laws of secession; repudiated all pretended debts and obligations created for the revolutionary purposes of the insurrection, and proceeded in good faith to the enactment of measures for the protection and amelioration of the condition of the' colored race. Congress, however, yet hesitated to admit any of these States to representation, and it was not until toward the close of the eighth month of the session that an exception was made in favor of Tennessee by the admission of her Senators and Representatives.

I deem it a subject of profound regret that

Congress has thus far failed to admit to seats loyal Senators and Representatives from the other States whose inhabitants, with those of Tennessee, had engaged in the rebellion. Ten States—more than one-fourth of the whole number—remain without representation; the seats of fifty members in the House of Representatives and of twenty members in the Senate are yet vacant, not by their own consent, not by a failure of election, but by the refusal of Congress to accept their credentials. Their admission, it is believed, would have accomplished much toward the renewal and strengthening of our relations as one people and removed serious cause for discontent on the part of the inhabitants of those States. It would have accorded with the great principle enunciated in the Declaration of American Independence that no people ought to bear the burden of taxation and yet be denied the right of representation. It would have been in consonance with the express provisions of the Constitution that "each State shall have at least one Representative" and "that no State, without its consent, shall be deprived of its equal suffrage in the Senate." These provisions were intended to secure to every State and to the people of every State the right of representation in each House of Congress; and so important was it deemed by the framers of the Constitution that the equality of the States in the Senate should be preserved that not even by an amendment of the Constitution can any State, without its consent, be denied a voice in that branch of the National Legislature.

It is true it has been assumed that the existence of the States was terminated by the rebellious acts of their inhabitants, and that, the insurrection having been suppressed, they were thenceforward to be considered merely as conquered territories. The legislative, executive, and judicial departments of the Government have, however, with great distinctness and uniform consistency, refused to sanction an assumption so incompatible with the nature of our republican system and with the professed objects of the war. Throughout the recent legislation of Congress the undeniable fact makes itself apparent that these ten political communities are nothing less than States of this Union. At the very commencement of the rebellion each House declared, with a unanimity as remarkable as it was significant, that the war was not "waged upon our part in any spirit of oppression, nor for any purpose of conquest or subjugation, nor purpose of overthrowing or interfering with the rights or established institutions of those States, but to defend and maintain the supremacy of the Constitution and all laws made in pursuance thereof, and to preserve the Union, with all the dignity, equality, and rights of the several States unimpaired; and that as soon as these objects" were "accomplished the war ought to cease." . . .

The action of the executive department of the Government upon this subject has been equally definite and uniform, and the purpose of the war was specifically stated in the proclamation issued by my predecessor on the 2nd day of September, 1862. It was then solemnly proclaimed and declared "that hereafter, as heretofore, the war will be prosecuted for the object of practically restoring the constitutional relation between the United States and each of the States and the people thereof in which States that relation is or may be suspended or disturbed."

The recognition of the States by the judicial department of the Government has also been clear and conclusive in all proceedings affecting them as States had in the Supreme, circuit, and district courts.

In the admission of Senators and Representatives from any and all of the States there can be no just ground of apprehension that persons who are disloyal will be clothed with the powers of legislation, for this could not happen when the Constitution and the laws are enforced by a vigilant and faithful Congress. Each House is made the "judge of the elections, returns, and qualifications of its own members," and may, "with the concurrence of two-thirds, expel a member." . . .

The Constitution of the United States makes it the duty of the President to recommend to the consideration of Congress "such measures as he shall judge necessary and expedient." I know of no measure more imperatively demanded by every consideration of national interest, sound policy, and equal justice than the admission of loyal members from the now unrepresented States. This would consummate the work of restoration and exert a most salutary influence in the reestablishment of peace, harmony, and fraternal feeling. It would tend greatly to renew the confidence of the American people in the vigor and stability of their institutions. It would bind us more closely together as a nation and enable us to show to the world the inherent and recuperative power of a government founded upon the will of the people and established upon the principles of liberty, justice, and intelligence. . . .

In our efforts to preserve "the unity of government which constitutes us one people" by restoring the States to the condition which they held prior to the rebellion, we should be cautious, lest, having rescued our nation from perils of threatened disintegration, we resort to consolidation, and in the end absolute despotism, as a remedy for the recurrence of similar troubles. The war having terminated, and with it all occasion for the exercise of powers of doubtful constitutionality, we should hasten to bring legislation within the boundaries prescribed by the Constitution and to return to the ancient landmarks established by our fathers for the guidance of succeeding generations. . . .

256. EX PARTE MILLIGAN
4 Wallace, 2
1866

Certificate from the United States circuit court for the District of Indiana. By an act of March 3, 1863, Congress authorized the President to suspend the writ of *habeas corpus,* and under this authority President Lincoln, September 15, 1863, suspended the writ in cases where officers held persons for offenses against the military or naval service. Milligan, a civilian, was arrested, tried by a military commission, found guilty of fomenting insurrection, and sentenced to be hanged. He petitioned the United States circuit court for a writ of *habeas corpus.*

The decision of the Court in this case, one of the most notable in our history, condemned military tribunals in sections where the civil courts were open, and, by implication, raised serious doubts as to the legality of Congressional reconstruction. A thorough discussion of the case can be found in *The Milligan Case,* ed. by S. Klaus. See also in this connection the opinion of Taney in *ex parte Merryman,* Doc. No. 209. A standard work on the constitutional problems of the war is W. Whiting, *War Powers under the Constitution of the United States.* An excellent briefer discussion can be found in W. A. Dunning, *Essays on the Civil War and Reconstruction,* chs. i, ii. On Copperhead activities see I. W. Ayer, *The Great Northwest Conspiracy;* F. A. Stiger, *History of the Order of Sons of Liberty;* J. L. Vallandigham, *Life of Clement L. Vallandigham.*

DAVIS, J. . . . The importance of the main question presented by this record cannot be overstated; for it involves the very framework of the government and the fundamental principles of American liberty.

During the late wicked rebellion, the temper of the times did not allow that calmness in deliberation and discussion so necessary to a correct conclusion of a purely judicial question. *Then,* considerations of safety were mingled with the exercise of power; and feelings and interests prevailed which are happily terminated. *Now,* that the public safety is assured, this question, as well as all others, can be discussed and decided without passion or the admixture of any element not required to form a legal judgment. We approach the investigation of this case, fully sensible of the magnitude of the inquiry and the necessity of full and cautious deliberation. . . .

The controlling question in the case is this: Upon the *facts* stated in Milligan's petition, and the exhibits filed, had the military commission mentioned in it *jurisdiction,* legally, to try and sentence him? Milligan, not a resident of one of the rebellious states, or a prisoner of war, but a citizen of Indiana for twenty years past, and never in the military or naval service, is, while at his home, arrested by the military power of the United States, imprisoned, and, on certain criminal charges preferred against him, tried, convicted, and sentenced to be hanged by a military commission, organized under the direction of the military commander of the military district of Indiana. Had this tribunal the legal power and authority to try and punish this man?

No graver question was ever considered by this court, nor one which more nearly concerns the rights of the whole people; for it is the birthright of every American citizen when charged with crime, to be tried and punished according to law. The power of punishment is alone through the means which the laws have provided for that purpose, and if they are ineffectual, there is an immunity from punishment no matter how great an offender the individual may be, or how much his crimes may have shocked the sense of justice of the country, or endangered its safety. By the protection of the law human rights are secured; withdraw that protection, and they are at the mercy of wicked rulers, or the clamor of an excited people. If there was law to justify this military trial, it is not our province to interfere; if there was not, it is our duty to declare the nullity of the whole proceedings. The decision of this question does not depend on argument or judicial precedents, numerous and highly illustrative as they are. These precedents inform us of the extent of the struggle to preserve liberty, and to relieve those in civil life from military trials. The founders of our government were familiar with the history of that struggle, and secured in a written Constitution every right which the people had wrested from power during a contest of ages. By that Constitution and the laws authorized by it this question must be determined. The provisions of that instrument on the administration of criminal justice are too plain and direct to leave room for misconstruction or doubt of their true meaning. Those applicable to this case are found in that clause of the original Constitution which says, "That the trial of all crimes, except in case of impeachment, shall be by jury"; and in the fourth, fifth, and sixth articles of the amendments. . . .

Time has proven the discernment of our ancestors; for even these provisions, expressed in such plain English words, that it would seem the ingenuity of man could not evade them, are *now,* after the lapse of more than seventy years, sought to be avoided. . . . The Constitution of the United States is a law for rulers and people, equally in war and in peace, and covers with the shield of its protection all classes of men, at all times, and under all circumstances. No doctrine involving more pernicious consequences was ever invented by the wit of man than that any of its provisions can be suspended during any of the great exigencies of government. Such a doctrine leads directly to anarchy or despotism, but the theory of necessity on which it is based is false; for the government, within the Constitution, has all the powers granted to it which are necessary to preserve its existence; as has been happily proved by the result of the great effort to throw off its just authority.

Have any of the rights guaranteed by the Constitution been violated in the case of Milligan? and if so, what are they?

Every trial involves the exercise of judicial power; and from what source did the military commission that tried him derive their authority? Certainly no part of the judicial power of the country was conferred on them; because the Constitution expressly vests it "in one Supreme Court and such inferior courts as the Congress may from time to time ordain and establish," and it is not pretended that the commission was a court ordained and established by Congress. They cannot justify on the mandate of the President, because he is controlled by law, and has his appropriate sphere of duty, which is to execute, not to make, the laws; and there is "no unwritten criminal code to which resort can be had as a source of jurisdiction."

But it is said that the jurisdiction is complete under the "laws and usages of war."

It can serve no useful purpose to inquire what those laws and usages are, whence they originated, where found, and on whom they operate; they can never be applied to citizens in states which have upheld the authority of the government, and where the courts are open and their process unobstructed. This court has judicial knowledge that in Indiana the federal authority was always unopposed, and its courts always open to hear criminal accusations and redress grievances; and no usage of war could sanction a military trial there for any offense whatever of a citizen in civil life, in nowise connected with the military service. Congress could grant no such power; and to the honor of our national legislature be it said, it has never been provoked by the state of the country even to attempt its exercise. One of the plainest constitutional provisions was, therefore, infringed when Milligan was tried by a court not ordained and established by Congress, and not composed of judges appointed during good behavior.

Why was he not delivered to the circuit court of Indiana to be proceeded against according to law? No reason of necessity could be urged against it; because Congress had declared penalties against the offenses charged, provided for their punishment, and directed that court to hear and determine them. And soon after this military tribunal was ended, the circuit court met, peacefully transacted its business, and adjourned. It needed no bayonets to protect it, and required no military aid to execute its judgments. It was held in a state, eminently distinguished for patriotism, by judges commissioned during the rebellion who were provided with juries, upright, intelligent, and selected by a marshal appointed by the President. The government had no right to conclude that Milligan, if guilty, would not receive in that court merited punishment; for its records disclose that it was constantly engaged in the trial of similar offenses, and was never interrupted in its administration of criminal justice. If it was dangerous, in the distracted condition of affairs, to leave Milligan unrestrained of his liberty, because he "conspired against the government, afforded aid and comfort to rebels, and incited the people to insurrection," the *law* said, arrest him, confine him closely, render him powerless to do further mischief; and then present his case to the grand jury of the district, with proofs of his guilt, and, if indicted, try him according to the course of the common law. If this had been done, the Constitution would have been vindicated, the law of 1863 enforced, and the securities for personal liberty preserved and defended.

Another guarantee of freedom was broken when Milligan was denied a trial by jury. The great minds of the country have differed on the correct interpretation to be given to the various provisions of the federal Constitution; and judicial decision has been often invoked to settle their true meaning; but until recently no one ever doubted that the right of trial by jury was forfeited in the organic law against the power of attack. It is *now* assailed; but if ideas can be expressed in words, and language has any meaning, *this right*— one of the most valuable in a free country— is preserved to every one accused of crime who is not attached to the army, or navy, or militia in actual service. . . .

It is claimed that martial law covers with its broad mantle the proceedings of this military commission. The proposition is this: that in a time of war the commander of an armed force (if, in his opinion, the exigencies of the country demand it, and of which he is to judge) has the power, within the lines of his military district, to suspend all civil rights and their remedies, and subject citizens as well as soldiers to the rule of *his will;* and in the exercise of his lawful authority cannot be restrained, except by his superior officer or the President of the United States.

If this position is sound to the extent claimed, then when war exists, foreign or domestic, and the country is subdivided into military departments for mere convenience, the commander of one of them can, if he chooses, within his limits, on the plea of necessity, with the approval of the Executive, substitute military force for, and to the exclusion of, the laws, and punish all persons, as he thinks right and proper, without fixed or certain rules.

The statement of this proposition shows its importance; for, if true, republican government is a failure, and there is an end of liberty regulated by law. Martial law, established on such a basis, destroys every guarantee of the Constitution, and effectually renders the "military independent of, and superior to, the civil power,"—the attempt to do which by the king of Great Britain was deemed by our fathers such an offense, that they assigned it to the world as one of the causes which impelled them to declare their independence. Civil liberty and this kind of martial law cannot endure together; the antagonism is irreconcilable; and, in the conflict, one or the other must perish.

This nation, as experience has proved, cannot always remain at peace, and has no right to expect that it will always have wise and humane rulers, sincerely attached to the principles of the Constitution. Wicked men, ambitious of power, with hatred of liberty and contempt of law, may fill the place once occupied by Washington and Lincoln; and if this right is conceded, and the calamities of war again befall us, the dangers to human liberty are frightful to contemplate. If our fathers had failed to provide for just such a contingency, they would have been false to the trust reposed in them. They knew—the history of the world told them—the nation they were founding, be its existence short' or long, would be involved in war; how often or how long continued, human foresight could not tell; and that unlimited power, wherever lodged at such a time, was especially hazardous to freemen. For this, and other equally weighty reasons, they secured the inheritance they had fought to maintain, by incorporating in a written Constitution the safeguards which time had proved were essential to its preservation. Not one of these safeguards can the President, or Congress, or the judiciary disturb, except the one concerning the writ of habeas corpus.

It is essential to the safety of every government that, in a great crisis like the one we have just passed through, there should be a power somewhere of suspending the writ of habeas corpus. In every war, there are men of previously good character, wicked enough to counsel their fellow-citizens to resist the measures deemed necessary by a good government to sustain its just authority and overthrow its enemies; and their influence may lead to dangerous combinations. In the emergency of the times, an immediate public investigation according to law may not be possible; and yet the peril to the country may be too imminent to suffer such persons to go at large. Unquestionably, there is then an exigency which demands that the government, if it should see fit, in the exercise of a proper discretion, to make arrests, should not be required to produce the persons arrested in answer to a writ of habeas corpus. The Constitution goes no further. It does not say after a writ of habeas corpus is denied a citizen, that he shall be tried otherwise than by the course of the common law; if it had intended this result, it was easy by the use of direct words to have accomplished it. The illustrious men who framed that instrument were guarding the foundations of civil liberty against the abuses of unlimited power; they were full of wisdom, and the lessons of history informed them that a trial by an established court, assisted by an impartial jury, was the only sure way of protecting the citizen against oppression and wrong. Knowing this, they limited the suspension to one great right, and left the rest to remain forever inviolable. But, it is insisted that the safety of the country in time of war demands that this broad claim for martial law shall be sustained. If this were true, it could be well said

that a country, preserved at the sacrifice of all the cardinal principles of liberty, is not worth the cost of preservation. Happily, it is not so.

It will be borne in mind that this is not a question of the power to proclaim martial law, when war exists in a community and the courts and civil authorities are overthrown. Nor is it a question what rule a military commander, at the head of his army, can impose on states in rebellion to cripple their resources and quell the insurrection. The jurisdiction claimed is much more extensive. The necessities of the service, during the late rebellion, required that the loyal states should be placed within the limits of certain military districts and commanders appointed in them; and, it is urged, that this, in a military sense, constituted them the theatre of military operations; and, as in this case, Indiana had been and was again threatened with invasion by the enemy, the occasion was furnished to establish martial law. The conclusion does not follow from the premises. If armies were collected in Indiana, they were to be employed in another locality, where the laws were obstructed and the national authority disputed. On *her* soil there was no hostile foot; if once invaded, that invasion was at an end, and with it all pretext for martial law. Martial law cannot arise from a *threatened* invasion. The necessity must be actual and present; the invasion real, such as effectually closes the courts and deposes the civil administration.

It is difficult to see how the *safety* of the country required martial law in Indiana. If any of her citizens were plotting treason, the power of arrest could secure them, until the government was prepared for their trial, when the courts were open and ready to try them. It was as easy to protect witnesses before a civil as a military tribunal; and as there could be no wish to convict, except on sufficient legal evidence, surely an ordained and established court was better able to judge of this than a military tribunal composed of gentlemen not trained to the profession of the law.

It follows, from what has been said on this subject, that there are occasions when martial rule can be properly applied. If, in foreign invasion or civil war, the courts are actually closed, and it is impossible to administer criminal justice according to law, *then*, on the theatre of active military operations, where war really prevails, there is a necessity to furnish a substitute for the civil authority, thus overthrown, to preserve the safety of the army and society; and as no power is left but the military, it is allowed to govern by martial rule until the laws can have their free course. As necessity creates the rule, so it limits its duration; for, if this government is continued *after* the courts are reinstated, it is a gross usurpation of power. Martial rule can never exist where the courts are open, and in the proper and unobstructed ex-ercise of their jurisdiction. It is also confined to the locality of actual war. Because, during the late rebellion it could have been enforced in Virginia, where the national authority was overturned and the courts driven out, it does not follow that it should obtain in Indiana, where that authority was never disputed, and justice was always administered. . . .

Mr. Chief Justice Chase, for himself and Mr. Justice Wayne, Mr. Justice Swayne, and Mr. Justice Miller, delivered an opinion in which he differed from the court in several important points, but concurred in the judge-ment in the case.

257. EFFORTS TO ENCOURAGE IMMIGRATION

South Carolina Immigration Bill
1866

(South Carolina Statutes at Large, Vol. XIII, p. 380)

The demand for industrial labor, the opening up of the west, and the disorganization of the labor system of the South, all led to official as well as unofficial efforts to encourage immigration. Most Southern States attempted to attract immigrants to take the place of the negro worker, but uni-formly without success. In South Carolina a state commissioner of agriculture was created and a pamphlet advertising the attractions of the state published in several languages and dis-tributed widely throughout northern Europe. See, F. B. Simkins and R. H. Woody, *South Caro-lina During Reconstruction*, p. 243 ff.

To Encourage Immigration to South Carolina
1. *Be it enacted* by the Senate and House of Representatives, now met and sitting in General Assembly, and by the authority of the same, That for the.purpose of encourag-ing, promoting and protecting European im-migration to and in this State, the sum of ten thousand dollars be appropriated from the contingent fund, to be expended under the direction of the Government, for the pur-poses and in the manner hereinafter pro-vided.
2. That the Governor, by and with the ad-vice and consent of the Senate, shall appoint a Commissioner of Immigration, who shall open an office in the fire-proof building in Charleston, to perform such duties as may appertain to his office, and shall be paid for his services the salary of fifteen hundred dol-lars per annum out of the fund aforesaid, in quarterly payments.
3. That it shall be the duty of said Com-missioner of Immigration to advertise in all the gazettes of the State for lands for sale; to cause such lands, after having been duly laid off, platted and described, at the expense of the owner or owners of said lands, to be appraised by three disinterested persons, and their titles to be examined by the Attorney General or Solicitors of the State, and en-dorsed by them, as the case may be; to open a book or books for the registry of the same, together with the price demanded and the conditions of payment. And in case such lands be selected by any immigrant, to super-intend the transfer of title and other neces-sary instruments and proceedings of con-veyance.
4. That the said Commissioner shall pe-riodically publish, advertise and cause to be distributed in the Northern and European ports and states, descriptive lists of such lands as have been registered and offered for sale, together with this Act, and a statement of such advantages as this State offers in soil, climate, productions, social improve-ments, etc., to the industrious, orderly and frugal European immigrant.

258. EX PARTE GARLAND
4 Wallace, 333
1867

Petition to the Supreme Court. Garland, a citizen of Arkansas, had been admitted to practice before the Supreme Court in 1860. He subsequently served in the Confederate Army, but received from the President a full pardon for all offences. An Act of Congress of January 24, 1865, excluded from practice before the Supreme Court any one who could not take an oath that he had never fought against the United States. Garland challenged the constitutionality of this law. This is the first case in which an act of Congress was held unconstitutional by a vote of five to four.

FIELD, J. . . . The petitioner . . . now produces his pardon, and asks permission to continue to practise as an attorney and counsellor of the court without taking the oath required by the act of January 24, 1865, and the rule of the court, which he is unable to take, by reason of the offices he held under the Confederate government. He rests his application principally upon two grounds:

1st. That the act of January 24, 1865, so far as it affects his status in the court, is unconstitutional and void; and,

2. That, if the act be constitutional, he is released from compliance with its provisions by the pardon of the President. . . .

The statute is directed against parties who have offended in any of the particulars embraced by these clauses. And its object is to exclude them from the profession of the law, or at least from its practice in the courts of the United States. As the oath prescribed cannot be taken by these parties, the act, as against them, operates as a legislative decree of perpetual exclusion. And exclusion from any of the professions or any of the ordinary avocations of life for past conduct can be regarded in no other light than as punishment for such conduct. The exaction of the oath is the mode provided for ascertaining the parties upon whom the act is intended to operate, and instead of lessening, increases its objectionable character. All enactments of this kind partake of the nature of bills of pains and penalties, and are subject to the constitutional inhibition against the passage of bills of attainder, under which general designation they are included.

In the exclusion which the statute adjudges it imposes a punishment for some of the acts specified which were not punishable at the time they were committed; and for other of the acts it adds a new punishment to that before prescribed, and it is thus brought within the further inhibition of the Constitution against the passage of an ex post facto law. . . .

The profession of an attorney and counsellor is not like an office created by an act of Congress, which depends for its continuance, its powers, and its emoluments upon the will of its creator, and the possession of which may be burdened with any conditions not prohibited by the Constitution. Attorneys and counsellors are not officers of the United States; they are not elected or appointed in the manner prescribed by the Constitution for the election and appointment of such officers. They are officers of the court, admitted as such by its order, upon evidence of their possessing sufficient legal learning and fair private character. . . . They hold their office during good behavior, and can only be deprived of it for misconduct ascertained and declared by the judgment of the court after opportunity to be heard has been afforded. Their admission or their exclusion is not the exercise of a mere ministerial power. It is the exercise of judicial power, and has been so held in numerous cases. . . .

The legislature may undoubtedly prescribe qualifications for the office, to which he must conform, as it may where it has exclusive jurisdiction, prescribe qualifications for the pursuit of any of the ordinary avocations of life. The question, in this case, is not as to the power of Congress to prescribe qualifications, but whether that power has been exercised as a means for the infliction of punishment, against the prohibition of the Constitution. . . .

This view is strengthened by a consideration of the effect of the pardon produced by the petitioner, and the nature of the pardoning power of the President.

The Constitution provides that the President "shall have power to grant reprieves and pardons for offenses against the United

States, except in cases of impeachment."

The power thus conferred is unlimited, with the exception stated. It extends to every offense known to the law, and may be exercised at any time after its commission, either before legal proceedings are taken, or during their pendency, or after conviction and judgment. This power of the President is not subject to legislative control. Congress can neither limit the effect of his pardon, nor exclude from its exercise any class of offenders. The benign prerogative of mercy reposed in him cannot be fettered by any legislative restrictions.

Such being the case, the inquiry arises as to the effect and operation of a pardon, and on this point all the authorities concur. A pardon reaches both the punishment prescribed for the offense and the guilt of the offender; and when the pardon is full, it releases the punishment and blots out of existence the guilt, so that in the eye of the law the offender is as innocent as if he had never committed the offense. If granted before conviction, it prevents any of the penalties and disabilities consequent upon conviction from attaching; if granted after conviction, it removes the penalties and disabilities, and restores him to all his civil rights; it makes him, as it were, a new man, and gives him a new credit and capacity. . . . The pardon produced by the petitioner is a full pardon "for all offenses by him committed, arising from participation, direct or implied, in the Rebellion," and is subject to certain conditions which have been complied with. The effect of this pardon is to relieve the petitioner from all penalties and disabilities attached to the offense of treason, committed by his participation in the Rebellion. So far as that offense is concerned, he is thus placed beyond the reach of punishment of any kind. But to exclude him, by reason of that offense, from continuing in the enjoyment of a previously acquired right, is to enforce a punishment for that offense notwithstanding the pardon. If such exclusion can be effected by the exaction of an expurgatory oath covering the offense, the pardon may be avoided, and that accomplished indirectly which cannot be reached by direct legislation. It is not within the constitutional power of Congress to inflict punishment beyond the reach of executive clemency. From the petitioner, therefore, the oath required by the act of January 24th, 1865, could not be exacted, even if that act were not subject to any other objection than the one thus stated.

It follows, from the views expressed, that the prayer of the petitioner must be granted. . . . And it is so ordered.

MILLER, J., with whom concurred WAITE, C. J., and Justices SWAYNE and DAVIS, delivered a dissenting opinion.

259. MISSISSIPPI v. JOHNSON
4 Wallace, 475
1867

Suit in the Supreme Court by the State of Mississippi to enjoin President Johnson from enforcing the Reconstruction Acts of 1867 on the ground that they were unconstitutional. With the failure of Mississippi to secure a decision from the Court on this question, Georgia filed a suit to restrain Secretary Stanton from enforcing the acts. *Georgia* v. *Stanton*, 6 Wallace, 50. See, W. A. Dunning, *Reconstruction, Political and Economic*, ch. xvi; J. W. Burgess, *Reconstruction and the Constitution*, p. 144 ff.; Warren, *The Supreme Court*, Vol. II, ch. xxx.

CHASE, C. J. A motion was made, some days since, in behalf of the State of Mississippi, for leave to file a bill in the name of the State, praying this court perpetually to enjoin and restrain Andrew Johnson, President of the United States, and E. O. C. Ord, general commanding in the District of Mississippi and Arkansas, from executing, or in any manner carrying out, certain acts of Congress therein named.

The acts referred to are those of March 2d and March 23d, 1867, commonly known as the Reconstruction Acts. . . . The single point which requires consideration is this: Can the President be restrained by injunction from carrying into effect an act of Congress alleged to be unconstitutional?

It is assumed by the counsel for the State of Mississippi, that the President, in the execution of the Reconstruction Acts, is required to perform a mere ministerial duty. In this assumption there is, we think, a confounding of the terms ministerial and executive, which are by no means equivalent in import.

A ministerial duty, the performance of which may, in proper cases, be required of the head of a department, by judicial process, is one in respect to which nothing is left to discretion. It is a simple, definite duty, arising under conditions admitted or proved to exist, and imposed by law. . . .

Very different is the duty of the President in the exercise of the power to see that the laws are faithfully executed, and among these laws the acts named in the bill. By the first of these acts he is required to assign generals to command in the several military districts, and to detail sufficient military force to enable such officers to discharge their duties under the law. By the supplementary act, other duties are imposed on the several commanding generals, and these duties must necessarily be performed under the supervision of the President as commander in chief. The duty thus imposed on the President is in no just sense ministerial. It is purely executive and political.

An attempt on the part of the judicial department of the government to enforce the performance of such duties by the President might be justly characterized, in the language of Chief Justice Marshall, as "an absurd and excessive extravagance."

It is true that in the instance before us the interposition of the court is not sought to enforce action by the executive under constitutional legislation, but to restrain such action under legislation alleged to be unconstitutional. But we are unable to perceive that this circumstance takes the case out of the general principles which forbid judicial interference with the exercise of executive discretion.

It was admitted in the argument that the application now made to us is without a precedent; and this is of much weight against it. . . .

The fact that no such application was ever before made in any case indicates the general judgment of the profession that no such application should be entertained.

It will hardly be contended that Congress [the court?] can interpose, in any case, to restrain the enactment of an unconstitutional law; and yet how can the right to judicial interposition to prevent such an enactment, when the purpose is evident and the execution of that purpose certain, be distinguished, in principle, from the right to such interposition against the execution of such a law by the President?

The Congress is the legislative department of the government; the President is the executive department. Neither can be restrained in its action by the judicial department; though the acts of both, when performed, are, in proper cases, subject to its cognizance.

The impropriety of such interference will be clearly seen upon consideration of its possible consequences.

Suppose the bill filed and the injunction prayed for allowed. If the President refuse obedience, it is needless to observe that the court is without power to enforce its process. If, on the other hand, the President complies with the order of the court and refuses to execute the acts of Congress, is it not clear that a collision may occur between the executive and legislative departments of the government? May not the House of Representatives impeach the President for such refusal? And in that case could this court interfere, in behalf of the President, thus endangered by compliance with its mandate, and restrain by injunction the Senate of the United States from sitting as a court of impeachment? Would the strange spectacle be offered to the public world of an attempt by this court to arrest proceedings in that court?

These questions answer themselves. . . .

It has been suggested that the bill contains a prayer that, if the relief sought cannot be had against Andrew Johnson, as President, it may be granted against Andrew Johnson as a citizen of Tennessee. But it is plain that relief as against the execution of an act of Congress by Andrew Johnson, is relief against its execution by the President. A bill praying an injunction against the execution of an act of Congress by the incumbent of the presidential office cannot be received, whether it describes him as President or as a citizen of a State.

The motion for leave to file the bill is therefore denied.

260. THE FIRST RECONSTRUCTION ACT
March 2, 1867

(*U. S. Statutes at Large*, Vol. XIV, p. 428 ff.)

The triumph of the Radicals in the elections of 1866 gave them a free hand in the development of a reconstruction policy. The famous Act of March 2, 1867, contained the general principles of congressional reconstruction. There was grave doubt about the constitutionality of some of the provisions of this act, but the efforts of Southern States to bring the question before the Supreme Court were unavailing. For the argument against the constitutionality of the measure, see Johnson's veto message, Document No. 261. On the history of the Act, see J. F. Rhodes, *History of the United States*, Vol. VI; J. W. Burgess, *Reconstruction and the Constitution;* W. L. Fleming, *The Sequel of Appomattox,* chs. v–vi; C. E. Chadsey, *The Struggle Between President Johnson and Congress over Reconstruction;* J. A. Woodburn, *Thaddeus Stevens,* chs. xiii–xviii; G. F. Milton, *The Age of Hate,* ch. xvii; B. B. Kendrick, *The Journal of the Joint Committee of Fifteen.* For the political background, H. K. Beale, *The Critical Year,* is invaluable. For military government, see W. A. Dunning, *Essays on the Civil War and Reconstruction,* chs. iii–iv; and the numerous monographs on reconstruction in the States; see bibliographies in W. A. Dunning, *Reconstruction,* and in H. K. Beale, *Critical. Year.*

An Act to provide for the more efficient Government of the Rebel States

WHEREAS no legal State governments or adequate protection for life or property now exists in the rebel States of Virginia, North Carolina, South Carolina, Georgia, Mississippi, Alabama, Louisiana, Florida, Texas, and Arkansas; and whereas it is necessary that peace and good order should be enforced in said States until loyal and republican State governments can be legally established: Therefore,

Be it enacted, That said rebel States shall be divided into military districts and made subject to the military authority of the United States as hereinafter prescribed, and for that purpose Virginia shall constitute the first district; North Carolina and South Carolina the second district; Georgia, Alabama, and Florida the third district; Mississippi and Arkansas the fourth district; and Louisiana and Texas the fifth district.

SEC. 2. That it shall be the duty of the President to assign to the command of each of said districts an officer of the army, not below the rank of brigadier-general, and to detail a sufficient military force to enable such officer to perform his duties and enforce his authority within the district to which he is assigned.

SEC. 3. That it shall be the duty of each officer assigned as aforesaid, to protect all persons in their rights of persons and property, to suppress insurrection, disorder, and violence, and to punish, or cause to be punished, all disturbers of the public peace and criminals; and to this end he may allow local civil tribunals to take jurisdiction of and to try offenders, or, when in his judgment it may be necessary for the trial of offenders, he shall have power to organize military commissions or tribunals for that purpose, and all interference under color of State authority with the exercise of military authority under this act, shall be null and void.

SEC. 4. That all persons put under military arrest by virtue of this act shall be tried without unnecessary delay, and no cruel or unusual punishment shall be inflicted, and no sentence of any military commission or tribunal hereby authorized, affecting the life or liberty of any person, shall be executed until it is approved by the officer in command of the district, and the laws and regulations for the government of the army shall not be affected by this act, except in so far as they conflict with its provisions: *Provided,* That no sentence of death under the provisions of this act shall be carried into effect without the approval of the President.

SEC. 5. That when the people of any one of said rebel States shall have formed a constitution of government in conformity with the Constitution of the United States in all respects, framed by a convention of delegates elected by the male citizens of said State, twenty-one years old and upward, of whatever race, color, or previous condition, who have been resident in said State for one year previous to the day of such election, except such as may be disfranchised for participation in the rebellion or for felony at common law, and when such constitution shall provide that the elective franchise shall be enjoyed by all such persons as have the qualifications herein stated for electors of delegates, and when such constitution shall be ratified by a majority of the persons voting on the question of ratification who are qualified as electors for delegates, and when such constitution shall have been submitted to Congress for examination and approval, and Congress shall have approved the same, and when said State, by a vote of its legislature elected under said constitution, shall have adopted the amendment to the Constitution of the United States, proposed by the Thirty-ninth Congress, and known as article fourteen, and when said article shall have become a part of the Constitution of the United States said State shall be declared entitled to representation in Congress, and senators and representatives shall be admitted therefrom on their taking the oath prescribed by law, and then and thereafter the preceding sections of this act shall be inoperative in said State: *Provided,* That no person excluded from the privilege of holding office by said proposed amendment to the Constitution of the United States, shall be eligible to election as a member of the convention to frame a constitution for any of said rebel States, nor shall any such person vote for members of such convention.

SEC. 6. That, until the people of said rebel States shall be by law admitted to representation in the Congress of the United States, any civil governments which may exist therein shall be deemed provisional only, and in all respects subject to the paramount authority of the United States at any time to abolish, modify, control, or supersede the same; and in all elections to any office under such provisional governments all persons shall be entitled to vote, and none others, who are entitled to vote, under the provisions of the fifth section of this act; and no persons shall be eligible to any office under any such provisional governments who would be disqualified from holding office under the provisions of the third *article* of said constitutional amendment.

261. VETO OF THE FIRST RECONSTRUCTION ACT
March 2, 1867

(Richardson, ed. *Messages and Papers,* Vol. VI, p. 498 ff.)

Dunning states that this veto message was drafted by J. S. Black.

WASHINGTON, *March 2, 1867*
To the House of Representatives:

I have examined the bill "to provide for the more efficient government of the rebel States" with the care and anxiety which its transcendent importance is calculated to awaken. I am unable to give it my assent, for reasons so grave that I hope a statement of them may have some influence on the minds of the patriotic and enlightened men with whom the decision must ultimately rest.

The bill places all the people of the ten States therein named under the absolute domination of military rulers; and the preamble undertakes to give the reason upon which the measure is based and the ground upon which it is justified. It declares that there exists in those States no legal governments and no adequate protection for life or property, and asserts the necessity of enforcing peace and good order within their limits. Is this true as matter of fact?

It is not denied that the States in question have each of them an actual government, with all the powers—executive, judicial, and legislative—which properly belong to a free state. They are organized like the other States of the Union, and, like them, they make, administer, and execute the laws which concern their domestic affairs. An existing *de facto* government, exercising such functions as these, is itself the law of the state upon all matters within its jurisdiction. To pronounce the supreme law-making power of an established state illegal is to say that law itself is unlawful.

The provisions which these governments have made for the preservation of order, the suppression of crime, and the redress of private injuries are in substance and principle the same as those which prevail in the Northern States and in other civilized countries. . . .

The bill, however, would seem to show upon its face that the establishment of peace and good order is not its real object. The fifth section declares that the preceding sections shall cease to operate in any State where certain events shall have happened. . . .

All these conditions must be fulfilled before the people of any of these States can be relieved from the bondage of military domination; but when they are fulfilled, then immediately the pains and penalties of the bill are to cease, no matter whether there be peace and order or not, and without any reference to the security of life or property. The excuse given for the bill in the preamble is admitted by the bill itself not to be real. The military rule which it establishes is plainly to be used, not for any purpose of order or for the prevention of crime, but solely as a means of coercing the people into the adoption of principles and measures to which it is known that they are opposed, and upon which they have an undeniable right to exercise their own judgment.

I submit to Congress whether this measure is not in its whole character, scope, and object without precedent and without authority, in palpable conflict with the plainest provisions of the Constitution, and utterly destructive to those great principles of liberty and humanity for which our ancestors on both sides of the Atlantic have shed so much blood and expended so much treasure.

The ten States named in the bill are divided into five districts. For each district an officer of the Army, not below the rank of a brigadier-general, is to be appointed to rule over the people; and he is to be supported with an efficient military force to enable him to perform his duties and enforce his authority. Those duties and that authority, as defined by the third section of the bill, are "to protect all persons in their rights of person and property, to suppress insurrection, disorder, and violence, and to punish or cause to be punished all disturbers of the public peace or criminals." The power thus given to the commanding officer over all the people of each district is that of an absolute monarch. His mere will is to take the place of all law. The law of the States is now the only rule applicable to the subjects placed under his control, and that is completely displaced by the clause which declares all interference of State authority to be null and void. He alone is permitted to determine what are rights of person or property, and he may protect them in such way as in his discretion may seem proper. It places at his free disposal all the lands and goods in his district, and he may distribute them without let or hindrance to whom he pleases. Being bound by no State law, and there being no other law to regulate the subject, he may make a criminal code of his own; and he can make it as bloody as any recorded in history, or he can reserve the privilege of acting upon the impulse of his private passions in each case that arises. He is bound by no rules of evidence; there is, indeed, no provision by which he is authorized or required to take any evidence at all. Everything is a crime which he chooses to call so, and all persons are condemned whom he pronounces to be guilty. He is not bound to keep and record or make any report of his proceedings. He may arrest his victims wherever he finds them, without warrant, accusation, or proof of probable cause. If he gives them a trial before he inflicts the punishment, he gives it of his grace and mercy, not because he is commanded so to do. . . .

It is also provided that "he shall have power to organize military commissions or tribunals;" but this power he is not commanded to exercise. . . . Instead of mitigating the harshness of his single rule, such a tribunal would be used much more probably to divide the responsibility of making it more cruel and unjust.

Several provisions dictated by the humanity of Congress have been inserted in the bill, apparently to restrain the power of the commanding officer; but it seems to me that they are of no avail for that purpose. . . .

It is plain that the authority here given to the military officer amounts to absolute despotism. But to make it still more unendurable, the bill provides that it may be delegated to as many subordinates as he chooses to appoint, for it declares that he shall "punish or cause to be punished." Such a power has not been wielded by any monarch in England for more than five hundred years. In all that time no people who speak the English language have borne such servitude. It reduces the whole population of the ten States—all persons, of every color, sex, and condition, and every stranger within their limits—to the most abject and degrading slavery. No master ever had a control so absolute over the slaves as this bill gives to the military officers over both white and colored persons. . . .

I come now to a question which is, if possible, still more important. Have we the power to establish and carry into execution a measure like this? I answer, Certainly not, if we derive our authority from the Constitution and if we are bound by the limitations which it imposes.

This proposition is perfectly clear, that no branch of the Federal Government—executive, legislative, or judicial—can have any just powers except those which it derives through and exercises under the organic law of the Union. Outside of the Constitution we have no legal authority more than private citizens, and within it we have only so much as that instrument gives us. This broad principle limits all our functions and applies to all subjects. It protects not only the citizens of States which are within the Union, but it shields every human being who comes or is brought under our jurisdiction. We have no right to do in one place more than in another that which the Constitution says we shall not do at all. If, therefore, the Southern States were in truth out of the Union, we could not treat their people in a way which the fundamental law forbids.

Some persons assume that the success of our arms in crushing the opposition which was made in some of the States to the execution of the Federal laws reduced those States and all their people—the innocent as well as the guilty—to the condition of vassalage and gave us a power over them which the Constitution does not bestow or define or limit. No fallacy can be more transparent than this. Our victories subjected the insurgents to legal obedience, not to the yoke of an arbitrary despotism. . . .

Invasion, insurrection, rebellion, and domestic violence were anticipated when the Government was framed, and the means of repelling and suppressing them were wisely provided for in the Constitution; but it was not thought necessary to declare that the States in which they might occur should be expelled from the Union. Rebellions, which were invariably suppressed, occurred prior to that out of which these questions grow; but the States continued to exist and the Union remained unbroken. In Massachusetts, in Pennsylvania, in Rhode Island, and in New York, at different periods in our history, violent and armed opposition to the United States was carried on; but the relations of those States with the Federal Government were not supposed to be interrupted or changed thereby after the rebellious portions of their population were defeated and put down. It is true that in these earlier cases there was no formal expression of a determination to withdraw from the Union, but it is also true that in the Southern States the ordinances of secession were treated by all the friends of the Union as mere nullities and are now acknowledged to be so by the States themselves. If we admit that they had any force or validity or that they did in fact take the States in which they were passed out of the Union, we sweep from under our feet all the grounds upon which we stand in justifying the use of Federal force to maintain the integrity of the Government.

This is a bill passed by Congress in time of peace. There is not in any one of the States brought under its operation either war or insurrection. The laws of the States and of the Federal Government are all in undisturbed and harmonious operation. The courts, State and Federal, are open and in the full exercise of their proper authority. Over every State comprised in these five military districts, life, liberty, and property are secured by State laws and Federal laws, and the National Constitution is everywhere in force and everywhere obeyed. What, then, is the ground on which this bill proceeds? The title of the bill announces that it is intended "for the more efficient government" of these ten States. It is recited by way of preamble that no legal State governments "nor adequate protection for life or property" exist in those States, and that peace and good order should be thus enforced. The first thing which arrests attention upon these recitals, which prepare the way for martial law, is this, that the only foundation upon which martial law can exist under our form of government is not stated or so much as pretended. Actual war, foreign invasion, domestic insurrection—none of these appear; and none of these, in fact, exist. It is not even recited that any sort of war or insurrection is threatened. Let us pause here to consider, upon this question of constitutional law and the power of Congress, a recent decision of the Supreme Court of the United States in *ex parte* Milligan. . . .

I need not say to the representatives of the American people that their Constitution forbids the exercise of judicial power in any way but one—that is, by the ordained and established courts. It is equally well known that in all criminal cases a trial by jury is made indispensable by the express words of that instrument. I will not enlarge on the inestimable value of the right thus secured to every freeman or speak of the danger to public liberty in all parts of the country which must ensue from a denial of it anywhere or upon any pretense. A very recent decision of the Supreme Court has traced the history, vindicated the dignity, and made known the value of this great privilege so clearly that nothing more is needed. To what extent a violation of it might be excused in time of war or public danger may admit of discussion, but we are providing now for a time of profound peace, when there is not an armed soldier within our borders except those who are in the service of the Government. It is in such a condition of things that an act of Congress is proposed which, if carried out, would deny a trial by the lawful courts and juries to 9,000,000 American citizens and to their posterity for an indefinite period. It seems to be scarcely possible that anyone should seriously believe this consistent with a Constitution which declares in simple, plain, and unambiguous language that all persons shall have that right and that no person shall ever in any case be deprived of it. The Constitution also forbids the arrest of the citizen without judicial warrant, founded on probable cause. This bill authorizes an arrest without warrant, at the pleasure of a military commander. The Constitution declares that "no person shall be held to answer for a capital or otherwise infamous crime unless on presentment by a grand jury." This bill holds every person not a soldier answerable for all crimes and all charges without any presentment. The Constitution declares that "no person shall be deprived of life, liberty, or property without due process of law." This bill sets aside all process of law, and makes the citizen answerable in his person and property to the will of one man, and as to his life to the

will of two. Finally, the Constitution declares that "the privilege of the writ of *habeas corpus* shall not be suspended unless when, in case of rebellion or invasion, the public safety may require it;" whereas this bill declares martial law (which of itself suspends this great writ) in time of peace, and authorizes the military to make the arrest, and gives to the prisoner only one privilege, and that is a trial "without unnecessary delay." He has no hope of release from custody, except the hope, such as it is, of release by acquittal before a military commission.

The United States are bound to guarantee to each State a republican form of government. Can it be pretended that this obligation is not probably broken if we carry out a measure like this, which wipes away every vestige of republican government in ten States and puts the life, property, liberty, and honor of all the people in each of them under the domination of a single person clothed with unlimited authority?

The purpose and object of the bill—the general intent which pervades it from beginning to end—is to change the entire structure and character of the State governments and to compel them by force to the adoption of organic laws and regulations which they are unwilling to accept if left to themselves. The negroes have not asked for the privilege of voting; the vast majority of them have no idea what it means. This bill not only thrusts it into their hands, but compels them, as well as the whites, to use it in a particular way. If they do not form a constitution with prescribed articles in it and afterwards elect a legislature which will act upon certain measures in a prescribed way, neither blacks nor whites can be relieved from the slavery which the bill imposes upon them. Without pausing here to consider the policy or impolicy of Africanizing the southern part of our territory, I would simply ask the attention of Congress to that manifest, well-known, and universally acknowledged rule of constitutional law which declares that the Federal Government has no jurisdiction, authority, or power to regulate such subjects for any State. To force the right of suffrage out of the hands of the white people and into the hands of the negroes is an arbitrary violation of this principle. . . .

The bill also denies the legality of the gov-

ernments of ten of the States which participated in the ratification of the amendment to
the Federal Constitution abolishing slavery
forever within the jurisdiction of the United
States and practically excludes them from the
Union. If this assumption of the bill be correct, their concurrence can not be considered
as having been legally given, and the important fact is made to appear that the consent
of three-fourths of the States—the requisite
number—has not been constitutionally obtained to the ratification of that amendment,
thus leaving the question of slavery where it
stood before the amendment was officially declared to have become a part of the Constitution.

That the measure proposed by this bill does
violate the Constitution in the particulars
mentioned and in many other ways which I
forbear to enumerate is too clear to admit of
the least doubt. . . .

It is a part of our public history which can
never be forgotten that both Houses of Congress, in July, 1861, declared in the form of a
solemn resolution that the war was and should
be carried on for no purpose of subjugation,
but solely to enforce the Constitution and
laws, and that when this was yielded by the
parties in rebellion the contest should cease,
with the constitutional rights of the States
and of individuals unimpaired. This resolution was adopted and sent forth to the world
unanimously by the Senate and with only two
dissenting voices in the House. It was accepted by the friends of the Union in the
South as well as in the North as expressing
honestly and truly the object of the war. On
the faith of it many thousands of persons in
both sections gave their lives and their fortunes to the cause. To repudiate it now by
refusing to the States and to the individuals
within them the rights which the Constitution and laws of the Union would secure
to them is a breach of our plighted honor for
which I can imagine no excuse and to which
I can not voluntarily become a party. . . .

ANDREW JOHNSON.

262. THE TENURE OF OFFICE ACT
March 2, 1867
(*U. S. Statutes at Large*, Vol. XIV, p. 430 ff.)

The struggle between Johnson and the Radicals
over Reconstruction had been referred to the
voters, and the elections of the fall of 1866 were
overwhelmingly favorable to the Radicals. The
thirty-ninth Congress which met in December
1866 was dominated by such Radical leaders as
Stevens, Sumner, Wilson, Boutwell, Wade,
Chandler, and others. The Tenure of Office Act
was one of three momentous bills passed March
2, 1867. The question of the power of the
President to remove officials appointed by and
with the advice of the Senate had long been
a controversial one; it was not, indeed, settled
until 1926 (see Doc. No. 459). It was highly uncertain whether the Act was originally designed
to afford permanence of tenure to the members
of Johnson's cabinet who had been appointed by
President Lincoln. See Johnson's veto message,
Doc. No. 263. Johnson's removal of Secretary
Stanton, in alleged violation of the Tenure of
Office Act, was the principal charge in the
impeachment proceedings. See, C. E. Chadsey,
*The Struggle Between President Johnson and
Congress over Reconstruction;* W. A. Dunning,
Reconstruction, ch. vi; J. F. Rhodes, *History of
the United States,* Vol. VI; J. W. Burgess, *Re-*
construction and the Constitution; biographies
of Johnson by Milton, Stryker, Winston.

An Act regulating the Tenure of certain Civil Offices.

Be it enacted, That every person holding
any civil office to which he has been appointed
by and with the advice and consent of the
Senate, and every person who shall hereafter
be appointed to any such office, and shall become duly qualified to act therein, is, and
shall be entitled to hold such office until a successor shall have been in like manner appointed and duly qualified, except as herein
otherwise provided: *Provided,* That the Secretaries of State, of the Treasury, of War, of
the Navy, and of the Interior, the Postmaster-General, and the Attorney-General, shall
hold their offices respectively for and during
the term of the President by whom they may
have been appointed and for one month thereafter, subject to removal by and with the advice and consent of the Senate.

SEC. 2. That when any officer appointed as aforesaid, excepting judges of the United States courts, shall, during a recess of the Senate, be shown, by evidence satisfactory to the President, to be guilty of misconduct in office, or crime, or for any reason shall become incapable or legally disqualified to perform its duties, in such case, and in no other, the President may suspend such officer and designate some suitable person to perform temporarily the duties of such office until the next meeting of the Senate, and until the case shall be acted upon by the Senate . . . ; and in such case it shall be the duty of the President, within twenty days after the first day of such next meeting of the Senate, to report to the Senate such suspension, with the evidence and reasons for his action in the case, and the name of the person so designated to perform the duties of such office. And if the Senate shall concur in such suspension and advise and consent to the removal of such officer, they shall so certify to the President, who may thereupon remove such officer, and, by and with the advice and consent of the Senate, appoint another person to such office. But if the Senate shall refuse to concur in such suspension, such officer so suspended shall forthwith resume the functions of his office, and the powers of the person so performing its duties in his stead shall cease, and the official salary and emoluments of such officer shall, during such suspension, belong to the person so performing the duties thereof, and not to the officer so suspended. . . .

SEC. 3. That the President shall have power to fill all vacancies which may happen during the recess of the Senate, by reason of death or resignation, by granting commissions which shall expire at the end of their next session thereafter. . . .

SEC. 4. That nothing in this act contained shall be construed to extend the term of any office the duration of which is limited by law.

SEC. 5. That if any person shall, contrary to the provisions of this act, accept any appointment to or employment in any office, or shall hold or exercise or attempt to hold or exercise, any such office or employment, he shall be deemed, and is hereby declared to be, guilty of a high misdemeanor, and, upon trial and conviction thereof, he shall be punished therefor by a fine not exceeding ten thousand dollars, or by imprisonment not exceeding five years, or both said punishments, in the discretion of the court.

SEC. 6. That every removal, appointment, or employment, made, had, or exercised, contrary to the provisions of this act, . . . shall be deemed, and are hereby declared to be, high misdemeanors, and, upon trial and conviction thereof, every person guilty thereof shall be punished by a fine not exceeding ten thousand dollars, or by imprisonment not exceeding five years, or both said punishments, in the discretion of the court. . . .

263. VETO OF TENURE OF OFFICE ACT
March 2, 1867

(Richardson, ed. *Messages and Papers,* Vol. VI, p. 492 ff.)

According to Welles, the veto message was drafted by Secretaries Seward and Stanton.

WASHINGTON, *March 2, 1867.*
To the Senate of the United States:

I have carefully examined the bill "to regulate the tenure of certain civil offices." . . . In effect the bill provides that the President shall not remove from their places any of the civil officers whose terms of service are not limited by law without the advice and consent of the Senate of the United States. The bill in this respect conflicts, in my judgment, with the Constitution of the United States. The question, as Congress is well aware, is by no means a new one. That the power of removal is constitutionally vested in the President of the United States is a principle which has been not more distinctly declared by judicial authority and judicial commentators than it has been uniformly practiced upon by the legislative and executive departments of the Government. . . .

The question has often been raised in subsequent times of high excitement, and the practice of the Government has, nevertheless, conformed in all cases to the decision thus early made.

The question was revived during the Administration of President Jackson, who made, as is well recollected, a very large number of removals, which were made an occasion of close and rigorous scrutiny and remonstrance. The subject was long and earnestly debated in the Senate, and the early construction of the Constitution was, nevertheless, freely accepted as binding and conclusive upon Congress.

The question came before the Supreme Court of the United States in January, 1839, *ex parte* Hennen. It was declared by the court on that occasion that the power of removal from office was a subject much disputed, and upon which a great diversity of opinion was entertained in the early history of the Government. This related, however, to the power of the President to remove officers appointed with the concurrence of the Senate, and the great question was whether the removal was to be by the President alone or with the concurrence of the Senate, both constituting the appointing power. No one denied the power of the President and Senate jointly to remove where the tenure of the office was not fixed by the Constitution, which was a full recognition of the principle that the power of removal was incident to the power of appointment; but it was very early adopted as a practical construction of the Constitution that this power was vested in the President alone, . . .

Thus has the important question presented by this bill been settled, in the language of the late Daniel Webster . . . by construction, settled by precedent, settled by the practice of the Government, and settled by statute. The events of the last war furnished a prac-

tical confirmation of the wisdom of the Constitution as it has hitherto been maintained in many of its parts, including that which is now the subject of consideration. When the war broke out, rebel enemies, traitors, abettors, and sympathizers were found in every Department of the Government, as well in the civil service as in the land and naval military service. They were found in Congress and among the keepers of the Capitol; in foreign missions; in each and all the Executive Departments; in the judicial service; in the post-office, and among the agents for conducting Indian affairs. Upon probable suspicion they were promptly displaced by my predecessor, so far as they held their offices under executive authority, and their duties were confided to new and loyal successors. No complaints against that power or doubts of its wisdom were entertained in any quarter. I sincerely trust and believe that no such civil war is likely to occur again. I can not doubt, however, that in whatever form and on whatever occasion sedition can raise an effort to hinder or embarrass or defeat the legitimate action of this Government, whether by preventing the collection of revenue, or disturbing the public peace, or separating the States, or betraying the country to a foreign enemy, the power of removal from office by the Executive, as it has heretofore existed and been practiced, will be found indispensable.

Under these circumstances, as a depository of the executive authority of the nation, I do not feel at liberty to unite with Congress in reversing it by giving my approval to the bill. . . .

264. COMMAND OF THE ARMY ACT
March 2, 1867

(*U. S. Statutes at Large,* Vol. XIV, p. 485 ff.)

Congress inserted in the Army Appropriation act of March 2, 1867, provisions which virtually deprived the President of the command of the army by requiring that he issue all military orders through the General of the army. Johnson approved of the bill, in order not to defeat the appropriations, but he entered a protest against those sections depriving him of command of the army. See, Richardson, Vol. VI, p. 472. For references, see Doc. No. 262.

An Act making appropriations for the sup-

port of the army for the year ending June, 30, 1868 *and for other purposes.*

SEC. 2. *And be it further enacted,* That the headquarters of the General of the army of the United States shall be at the city of Washington, and all orders and instructions relating to military operations issued by the President or Secretary of War shall be issued through the General of the army, and, in case of his inability, through the next in rank. The General of the army shall not be removed, suspended, or relieved from command, or assigned to duty elsewhere than at said headquarters, except at his own request, without the previous approval of the Senate; and any orders or instructions relating to military operations issued contrary to the requirements of this section shall be null and void; and any officer who shall issue orders or instructions contrary to the provisions of this section shall be deemed guilty of a misdemeanor in office; and any officer of the army who shall transmit, convey, or obey any orders or instructions so issued contrary to the provisions of this section, knowing that such orders were so issued, shall be liable to imprisonment for not less than two nor more than twenty years, upon conviction thereof in any court of competent jurisdiction. . . .

265. THE SECOND RECONSTRUCTION ACT
March 23, 1867

(*U. S. Statutes at Large*, Vol. XV, p. 2 ff.)

This act provided in detail for the processes by which the military commanders were to reconstruct the Southern States. For references see Doc. No. 260.

An Act supplementary to an Act entitled "An Act to provide for the more efficient Government of the Rebel States," passed March 2, 1867, and to facilitate Restoration.

Be it enacted . . . , That before . . . September 1, 1867 . . . , the commanding general in each district defined by . . . [the act of March 2, 1867] . . . , shall cause a registration to be made of the male citizens of the United States, twenty-one years of age and upwards, resident in each county or parish in the State or States included in his district, which registration shall include only those persons who are qualified to vote for delegates by the act aforesaid, and who shall have taken and subscribed the following oath or affirmation: "I, ———— ————, do solemnly swear (or affirm), in the presence of Almighty God, that I am a citizen of the State of ————; that I have resided in said State for ———— months next preceding this day, and now reside in the county of ————, or the parish of ————, in said State (as the case may be); that I am twenty-one years old; that I have not been disfranchised for participation in any rebellion or civil war against the United States, or for felony committed against the laws of any State or of the United States; that I have never been a member of any State legislature, nor held any executive or judicial office in any State, and afterwards engaged in insurrection or rebellion against the United States, or given aid or comfort to the enemies thereof; that I have never taken an oath as a member of Congress of the United States, or as an officer of the United States, or as a member of any State legislature, or as an executive or judicial officer of any State, to support the Constitution of the United States, and afterwards engaged in insurrection or rebellion against the United States, or given aid or comfort to the enemies thereof; that I will faithfully support the Constitution and obey the laws of the United States, and will, to the best of my ability, encourage others so to do, so help me God." . . .

SEC. 2. That after the completion of the registration hereby provided for in any State, at such time and places therein as the commanding general shall appoint and direct, of which at least thirty days' public notice shall be given, an election shall be held of delegates to a convention for the purpose of establishing a constitution and civil government for such State loyal to the Union, said convention in each State, except Virginia, to consist of the same number of members as the most numerous branch of the State legislature of such State . . . [in 1860] . . . , to be apportioned among the several districts, counties, or parishes of such State by the commanding general, giving to each representation in the ration of voters registered as aforesaid as nearly as may be. The convention in Virginia shall consist of the same number of members as represented the territory now constituting Virginia in the most numerous branch of the legislature of said State . . . [in 1860] . . . , to be apportioned as aforesaid.

SEC. 3. That at said election the registered voters of each State shall vote for or against a convention to form a constitution therefor under this act. And the commanding general . . . shall ascertain and declare the total vote in each State . . . If a majority of the votes given on that question shall be for a convention, then such convention shall be held as hereinafter provided; but if a majority of said votes shall be against a convention, then no such convention shall be held under this act: *Provided,* That such convention shall not be held unless a majority of all such registered voters shall have voted on the question of holding such convention.

SEC. 4. That the commanding general of each district shall appoint as many boards of registration as may be necessary, consisting of three loyal officers or persons, to make and complete the registration, superintend the election, and make return to him of the votes, lists of voters, and of the persons elected as delegates by a plurality of the votes cast at said election; and upon receiving said returns he shall open the same, ascertain the persons elected as delegates, according to the returns of the officers who conducted said election, and make proclamation thereof; and if a majority of the votes given on that question shall be for a convention, the commanding general, within sixty days from the date of election, shall notify the delegates to assemble in convention, at a time and place to be mentioned in the notification, and said convention, when organized, shall proceed to frame a constitution and civil government according to the provisions of this act, and the act to which it is supplementary; and when the same shall have been so framed, said constitution shall be submitted by the convention for ratifica-

tion to the persons registered under the provisions of this act at an election to be conducted by the officers or persons appointed or to be appointed by the commanding general, as hereinbefore provided, and to be held after the expiration of thirty days from the date of notice thereof, to be given by said convention; and the returns thereof shall be made to the commanding general of the district.

SEC. 5. That if, according to said returns, the constitution shall be ratified by a majority of the votes of the registered electors . . . at least one half of all the registered voters voting upon the question of such ratification, the president of the convention shall transmit a copy of the same, duly certified, to the President of the United States, who shall forthwith transmit the same to Congress . . . ; and if it shall moreover appear to Congress that the election was one at which all the registered and qualified electors in the State had an opportunity to vote freely and without restraint, fear, or the influence of fraud, and if the Congress shall be satisfied that such constitution meets the approval of a majority of all the qualified electors in the State, and if the said constitution shall be declared by Congress to be in conformity with the provisions of the act to which this is supplementary, and the other provisions of said act shall have been complied with, and the said constitution shall be approved by Congress, the State shall be declared entitled to representation, and senators and representatives shall be admitted therefrom as therein provided.

266. VETO OF THE SECOND RECONSTRUCTION ACT
March 23, 1867

(Richardson, ed. *Messages and Papers,* Vol. VI, p. 531 ff.)

WASHINGTON, *March 23, 1867.*
To the House of Representatives:

I have considered the bill entitled "An act supplementary to an act entitled 'An act to provide for the more efficient government of the rebel States,' passed March 2, 1867, and to facilitate restoration," and now return it to the House of Representatives with my objections.

This bill provides for elections in the ten States brought under the operation of the original act to which it is supplementary. Its

details are principally directed to the elections for the formation of the State constitutions, but by the sixth section of the bill "all elections" in these States occurring while the original act remains in force are brought within its purview. Referring to these details, it will be found that, first of all, there is to be a registration of the voters. No one whose name has not been admitted on the list is to be allowed to vote at any of these elections. To ascertain who is entitled to registration, reference is made necessary, by the express language of the supplement, to the original act and to the pending bill. The fifth section of the original act provides, as to voters, that they shall be "male citizens of the State, 21 years old and upward, of whatever race, color, or previous condition, who have been residents of said State for one year." This is the general qualification, followed, however, by many exceptions. No one can be registered, according to the original act, "who may be disfranchised for participation in the rebellion"—a provision which left undetermined the question as to what amounted to disfranchisement, and whether without a judicial sentence the act itself produced that effect. This supplemental bill superadds an oath, to be taken by every person before his name can be admitted upon the registration, that he has "not been disfranchised for participation in any rebellion or civil war against the United States." It thus imposes upon every person the necessity and responsibility of deciding for himself, under the peril of punishment by a military commission if he makes a mistake, what works disfranchisement by participation in rebellion and what amounts to such participation. . . .

The fourth section of the bill provides "that the commanding general of each district shall appoint as many boards of registration as may be necessary, consisting of three loyal officers or persons." The only qualification stated for these officers is that they must be "loyal." They may be persons in the military service or civilians, residents of the State or strangers. Yet these persons are to exercise most important duties and are vested with unlimited discretion. They are to decide what names shall be placed upon the register and from their decision there is to be no appeal. They are to superintend the elections and to decide all questions which may arise. They are to have the custody of the ballots and to make return of the persons elected. Whatever frauds or errors they may commit must pass without redress. All that is left for the commanding general is to receive the returns of the elections, open the same, and ascertain who are chosen "according to the returns of the officers who conducted said elections." By such means and with this sort of agency are the conventions of delegates to be constituted.

As the delegates are to speak for the people, common justice would seem to require that they should have authority from the people themselves. No convention so constituted will in any sense represent the wishes of the inhabitants of these States, for under the all-embracing exceptions of these laws, by a construction which the uncertainty of the clause as to disfranchisement leaves open to the board of officers, the great body of the people may be excluded from the polls and from all opportunity of expressing their own wishes or voting for delegates who will faithfully reflect their sentiments.

I do not deem it necessary further to investigate the details of this bill. No consideration could induce me to give my approval to such an election law for any purpose, and especially for the great purpose of framing the constitution of a State. If ever the American citizen should be left to the free exercise of his own judgment it is when he is engaged in the work of forming the fundamental law under which he is to live. That work is his work, and it can not properly be taken out of his hands. All this legislation proceeds upon the contrary assumption that the people of each of these States shall have no constitution except such as may be arbitrarily dictated by Congress and formed under the restraint of military rule. A plain statement of facts makes this evident.

In all these States there are existing constitutions, framed in the accustomed way by the people. Congress, however, declares that these constitutions are not "loyal and republican," and requires the people to form them anew. What, then, in the opinion of Congress, is necessary to make the constitution of a State "loyal and republican"? The original act answers the question: It is universal negro suffrage—a question which the Federal Constitution leaves exclusively to the States themselves. All this legislative machinery of martial law, military coercion, and political disfranchisement is avowedly for that purpose and none other. The existing constitutions of the ten States conform to the acknowledged standards of loyalty and republicanism. Indeed, if there are degrees in republican forms of government, their constitutions are more republican now than when these States, four of which were members of the original thirteen, first became members of the Union.

Congress does not now demand that a single provision of their constitutions be changed except such as confine suffrage to the white population. It is apparent, therefore, that these provisions do not conform to the standard of republicanism which Congress seeks to establish. That there may be no mistake, it is only necessary that reference should be made to the original act, which declares "such constitution shall provide that the elective franchise shall be enjoyed by all such persons as have the qualifications herein stated for electors of delegates." What class of persons is here meant clearly appears in the same section; that is to say, "the male citizens of said State 21 years old and upward, of whatever race, color, or previous condition, who have been resident in said State for one year previous to the day of such election."

Without these provisions no constitution which can be framed in any one of the ten States will be of any avail with Congress. This, then, is the test of what the constitution of a State of this Union must contain to make it republican. Measured by such a standard, how few of the States now composing the Union have republican constitutions! If in the exercise of the constitutional guaranty that Congress shall secure to every State a republican form of government universal suffrage for blacks as well as whites is a *sine qua non,* the work of reconstruction may as well begin in Ohio as in Virginia, in Pennsylvania as in North Carolina. . . .

ANDREW JOHNSON

267. THE THIRD RECONSTRUCTION ACT
July 19, 1867
(*U. S. Statutes at Large,* Vol. XV, p. 14 ff.)

This act was designed to clear up the ambiguities of the Acts of March 2 and March 23, 1867, particularly with reference to the oath required by the second of those acts. This act was drafted by Sec. Stanton. See, G. C. Gorham, *Life and Public Services of Stanton,* Vol. II, and references to Doc. No. 260.

An Act supplementary to an Act entitled "An Act to provide for the more efficient Government of the Rebel States," passed [March 2, 1867], *and the Act supplementary thereto, passed* [March 23, 1867].

Be it enacted, That it is hereby declared to have been the true intent and meaning . . . [of the acts of March 2 and March 23, 1867] . . . , that the governments then existing in the rebel States of Virginia, North Carolina, South Carolina, Georgia, Mississippi, Alabama, Louisiana, Florida, Texas, and Arkansas were not legal State governments; and that thereafter said governments, if continued, were to be continued subject in all respects to the military commanders of the respective districts, and to the paramount authority of Congress.

SEC. 2. That the commander of any district named in said act shall have power, subject to the disapproval of the General of the army of the United States, and to have effect till disapproved, whenever in the opinion of such commander the proper administration of said act shall require it, to suspend or remove from office, or from the performance of official duties and the exercise of official powers, any officer or person holding or exercising, or professing to hold or exercise, any civil or military office or duty in such district under any power, election, appointment or authority derived from, or granted by, or claimed under, any so-called State or the government thereof, or any municipal or other division thereof, and upon such suspension or removal such commander, subject to the disapproval of the General as aforesaid, shall have power to provide from time to time for the performance of the said duties of such officer or person so suspended or removed, by the detail of some competent officer or soldier of the army, or by the appointment of some other person, to perform the same, and to fill vacancies occasioned by death, resignation, or otherwise.

SEC. 3. That the General of the army of the United States shall be invested with all the powers of suspension, removal, appointment, and detail granted in the preceding section to district commanders.

SEC. 4. That the acts of the officers of the army already done in removing in said districts persons exercising the functions of civil officers, and appointing others in their stead, are hereby confirmed: *Provided,* That any person heretofore or hereafter appointed by any district commander to exercise the functions of any civil office, may be removed either by the military officer in command of the district, or by the General of the army. And it shall be the duty of such commander to remove from office as aforesaid all persons who are disloyal to the government of the United States, or who use their official influence in any manner to hinder, delay, prevent, or obstruct the due and proper administration of this act and the acts to which it is supplementary.

SEC. 5. That the boards of registration provided for in the act [of March 23, 1867] shall have power, and it shall be their duty before allowing the registration of any person, to ascertain, upon such facts or information as they can obtain, whether such person is entitled to be registered under said act, and the oath required by said act shall not be conclusive on such question, and no person shall be registered unless such board shall decide that he is entitled thereto; and such board shall also have power to examine, under oath, . . . any one touching the qualification of any person claiming registration; . . . *Provided,* That no person shall be disqualified as member of any board of registration by reason of race or color.

SEC. 6. That the true intent and meaning of the oath prescribed in said supplementary act is, (among other things,) that no person who has been a member of the legislature of any State, or who has held any executive or judicial office in any State, whether he has taken an oath to support the Constitution of the United States or not, and whether he was holding such office at the commencement of the rebellion, or had held it before, and who has afterwards engaged in insurrection or rebellion against the United States, or given aid or comfort to the enemies thereof, is entitled to be registered or to vote; and the words "executive or judicial office in any State" in said oath mentioned shall be construed to include all civil offices created by law for the administration of any general law of a State, or for the administration of justice. . . .

SEC. 10. That no district commander or member of the board of registration, or any of the officers or appointees acting under them, shall be bound in his action by any opinion of any civil officer of the United States.

SEC. 11. That all provisions of this act and of the acts to which this is supplementary shall be construed liberally, to the end that all the intents thereof may be fully and perfectly carried out.

268. THE PURCHASE OF ALASKA
March 30, 1867

(Malloy, ed. *Treaties, Conventions, etc.* Vol. II, p. 1521 ff.)

The purchase of Alaska was regarded, at the time, as "Seward's folly"; it was lobbied through Congress by Robert Walker of Mississippi, to the accompaniment of rumors of bribery. See, F. Bancroft, *Seward,* Vol. II, ch. xlii; J. M. Callahan, *The Alaska Purchase and Americo-Canadian Relations,* W. Va. Studies in History, Series I. On Walker, see W. E. Dodd, *Robert J. Walker, Imperialist.*

CONVENTION FOR THE CESSION OF THE RUSSIAN POSSESSIONS IN NORTH AMERICA TO THE UNITED STATES
Concluded March 30, 1867. Ratifications exchanged at Washington, June 20, 1867.
Proclaimed June 20, 1867.
. . . ART. I. . . . His Majesty the Emperor of all the Russias agrees to cede to the United States, by this Convention, immediately upon the exchange of the ratifications

thereof, all the territory and dominion now possessed by his said Majesty on the continent of America and in the adjacent islands, the same being contained within the geographical limits herein set forth, to wit: The eastern limit is the line of demarcation between the Russian and the British possessions in North America, as established by the convention between Russia and Great Britain, of February 28—16, 1825, and described in Articles III. and IV. of said convention, in the following terms: . . .

" 'IV. With reference to the line of demarcation laid down in the preceding article, it is understood—

" '1st. That the island called Prince of Wales Island shall belong wholly to Russia,' . . .

" '2d. That whenever the summit of the

mountains which extend in a direction parallel to the coast from the 56th degree of north latitude to the point of intersection of the 141st degree of west longitude shall prove to be at the distance of more than ten marine leagues from the ocean, the limit between the British possessions and the line of coast which is to belong to Russia as above mentioned, (that is to say, the limit to the possessions ceded by this convention,) shall be formed by a line parallel to the winding of the coast, and which shall never exceed the distance of ten marine leagues therefrom.' " . . .

ART. II. . . . In the cession of territory and dominion made by the preceding article are included the right of property in all public lots and squares, vacant lands, and all public buildings, fortifications, barracks, and other edifices which are not private individual property. It is, however, understood and agreed, that the churches which have been built in the ceded territory by the Russian Government, shall remain the property of such members of the Greek Oriental Church resident in the territory as may choose to worship therein. . . .

ART. III. . . . The inhabitants of the ceded territory, according to their choice, reserving their natural allegiance, may return to Russia within three years; but, if they should prefer to remain in the ceded territory, they, with the exception of uncivilized native tribes, shall be admitted to the enjoyment of all the rights, advantages, and immunities of citizens of the United States, and shall be maintained and protected in the free enjoyment of their liberty, property, and religion. The uncivilized tribes will be subject to such laws and regulations as the United States may from time to time adopt in regard to aboriginal tribes of that country. . . .

ART. VI. In consideration of the cession aforesaid, the United States agree to pay at the Treasury in Washington . . . seven million two hundred thousand dollars in gold. . . .

269. THE IMPEACHMENT OF PRESIDENT JOHNSON
1868

(Richardson, ed. *Messages and Papers*, Vol. VI, p. 709 ff., 755 ff.)

The House of Representatives resolved, February 24, 1868, to impeach President Johnson. On March 2 and 3 articles of impeachment were agreed upon by the House and on March 4 presented to the Senate. J. A. Bingham, G. S. Boutwell, J. F. Wilson, B. F. Butler, T. Williams, J. A. Logan, and T. Stevens were the House managers of the impeachment. The Senate voted on the articles, May 16 and 26, 1868. See, D. M. De Witt, *Impeachment and Trial of Andrew Johnson;* W. A. Dunning, *Essays on Civil War and Reconstruction,* p. 253 ff.; G. F. Milton, *The Age of Hate,* chs. xxi–xxvi; L. P. Stryker, *Andrew Johnson,* chs. lxiii–lxxx; C. G. Bowers, *The Tragic Era,* ch. ix.

IN THE HOUSE OF REPRESENTATIVES,
UNITED STATES,
March 2, 1868.

ARTICLES EXHIBITED BY THE HOUSE OF REPRESENTATIVES OF THE UNITED STATES, IN THE NAME OF THEMSELVES AND ALL THE PEOPLE OF THE UNITED STATES, AGAINST ANDREW JOHNSON, PRESIDENT OF THE UNITED STATES, IN MAINTENANCE AND SUPPORT OF THEIR IMPEACHMENT AGAINST HIM FOR HIGH CRIMES AND MISDEMEANORS IN OFFICE.

ARTICLE I. That said Andrew Johnson, President of the United States, on the 21st day of February, A. D. 1868, at Washington, in the district of Columbia, unmindful of the high duties of his office, of his oath of office, and of the requirement of the Constitution that he should take care that the laws be faithfully executed, did unlawfully and in violation of the Constitution and laws of the United States issue an order in writing for the removal of Edwin M. Stanton from the office of Secretary for the Department of War, said Edwin M. Stanton having been theretofore duly appointed and commissioned, by and with the advice and consent of the Senate of the United States, as such Secretary; and said Andrew Johnson, President of the United States, on the 12th day of August, A. D. 1867, and during the recess of said Senate, having suspended by his order Edwin M. Stanton from said office, and within twenty days after the first day of the next meeting of said Senate—that is to say, on the 12th day of December, in the year last aforesaid— having reported to said Senate such suspension, with the evidence and reasons for his action in the case and the name of the person designated to perform the duties of such office temporarily until the next meeting of the Senate; and said Senate thereafterwards, on the 13th day of January, A. D. 1868, having duly considered the evidence and reasons reported by said Andrew Johnson for said suspension, and having refused to concur in said suspension, whereby and by force of the provisions of an act entitled "An act regulating the tenure of certain civil offices," passed March 2, 1867, said Edwin M. Stanton did forthwith resume the functions of his office, whereof the said Andrew Johnson had then and there due notice; and said Edwin M. Stanton, by reason of the premises, on said 21st day of February, being lawfully entitled to hold said office of Secretary for the Department of War; which said order for the removal of said Edwin M. Stanton is in substance as follows; that is to say:

EXECUTIVE MANSION,
Washington, D. C., February 21, 1868.
HON. EDWIN M. STANTON,
Washington, D. C.

SIR: By virtue of the power and authority vested in me as President by the Constitution and laws of the United States, you are hereby removed from office as Secretary for the Department of War, and your functions as such will terminate upon the receipt of this communication.

You will transfer to Brevet Major-General Lorenzo Thomas, Adjutant-General of the Army, who has this day been authorized and empowered to act as Secretary of War *ad interim,* all records, books, papers, and other public property now in your custody and charge.

Respectfully, yours,
ANDREW JOHNSON.

which order was unlawfully issued with intent then and there to violate the act entitled "An act regulating the tenure of certain civil offices," passed March 2, 1867 . . . whereby said Andrew Johnson, President of the United States, did then and there commit and was guilty of a high misdemeanor in office.

ART. II. That on said 21st day of February, A. D. 1868, at Washington, in the District of Columbia, said Andrew Johnson, President of the United States, . . . did, with intent to violate the Constitution of the United States and the act aforesaid, issue and deliver to one Lorenzo Thomas a letter of authority in substance as follows; that is to say:

EXECUTIVE MANSION,
Washington, D. C., February 21, 1868.
Brevet Major-General LORENZO THOMAS,
Adjutant-General United States Army, Washington, D. C.

SIR: The Hon. Edwin M. Stanton having been this day removed from office as Secretary for the Department of War, you are hereby authorized and empowered to act as Secretary of War *ad interim,* and will immediately enter upon the discharge of the duties pertaining to that office.

Mr. Stanton has been instructed to transfer to you all the records, books, papers, and other public property now in his custody and charge.

Respectfully, yours,
ANDREW JOHNSON.

then and there being no vacancy in said office of Secretary for the Department of War; whereby said Andrew Johnson, President of the United States, did then and there commit and was guilty of a high misdemeanor in office.

ART. III. That said Andrew Johnson, President of the United States, on the 21st day of February, A. D. 1868, at Washington, in the District of Columbia, did commit and was guilty of a high misdemeanor in office in this, that without authority of law, while the Senate of the United States was then and there in session, he did appoint one Lorenzo Thomas to be Secretary for the Department of War *ad interim,* without the advice and consent of the Senate, and with intent to violate the Constitution of the United States, . . .

ART. IV. That said Andrew Johnson, President of the United States, . . . did unlawfully conspire with one Lorenzo Thomas, and with other persons to the House of Representatives unknown, with intent, by intimidation and threats, unlawfully to hinder and prevent Edwin M. Stanton, then and there the Secretary for the Department of War, . . . from holding said office of Secretary for the Department of War, contrary to and in violation of the Constitution of the United States and of the provisions of an act entitled "An act to define and punish certain conspiracies," approved July 31, 1861; . . .

ART. V. That said Andrew Johnson, President of the United States, . . . did unlawfully conspire with one Lorenzo Thomas, and with other persons to the House of Representatives unknown, to prevent and hinder the execution of an act entitled "An act regulating the tenure of certain civil offices," passed March 2, 1867. . . .

ART. VI. That said Andrew Johnson, President of the United States, . . . did unlawfully conspire with one Lorenzo Thomas by force to seize, take, and possess the property of the United States in the Department of War, and then and there in the custody and charge of Edwin M. Stanton, Secretary for said Department, contrary to the provisions of an act entitled "An act to define and punish certain conspiracies," approved July 31, 1861, and with intent to violate and disregard an act entitled "An act regulating the tenure of certain civil offices," passed March 2, 1867; . . .

ART. VII. That said Andrew Johnson, President of the United States, . . . did unlawfully conspire with one Lorenzo Thomas with intent unlawfully to seize, take, and possess the property of the United States in the Department of War, in the custody and charge of Edwin M. Stanton, Secretary for said Department, with intent to violate and disregard the act entitled "An act regulating the tenure of certain civil offices, passed March 2, 1867; . . .

ART. VIII. That said Andrew Johnson, President of the United States, . . . with intent unlawfully to control the disbursement of the moneys appropriated for the military service and for the Department of War, . . . did unlawfully, and in violation of the Constitution of the United States, and without the advice and consent of the Senate of the United States, . . . there being no vacancy in the office of Secretary for the Department of War, and with intent to violate and disregard the act aforesaid, then and there issue and deliver to one Lorenzo Thomas a letter of authority, . . .

ART. IX. That said Andrew Johnson, President of the United States, on the 22d day of February, A. D. 1868, . . . in disregard of

the Constitution and the laws of the United States duly enacted, as Commander in Chief of the Army of the United States, did bring before himself then and there William H. Emory, a major-general by brevet in the Army of the United States, actually in command of the Department of Washington and the military forces thereof, and did then and there, as such Commander in Chief, declare to and instruct said Emory that part of a law of the United States, passed March 2, 1867, entitled "An Act making appropriations for the support of the Army for the year ending June 30, 1868, and for other purposes," especially the second section thereof, which provides, among other things, that "all orders and instructions relating to military operations issued by the President or Secretary of War shall be issued through the General of the Army, and in case of his inability through the next in rank," was unconstitutional . . . with intent thereby to induce said Emory, in his official capacity as commander of the Department of Washington, to violate the provisions of said act and to take and receive, act upon, and obey such orders as he, the said Andrew Johnson, might make and give, and which should not be issued through the General of the Army of the United States, according to the provisions of said act, . . .

March 3, 1868.

The following additional articles of impeachment were agreed to, viz:

ART. X. That said Andrew Johnson, President of the United States, unmindful of the high duties of his office and the dignity and proprieties thereof, and of the harmony and courtesies which ought to exist and be maintained between the executive and legislative branches of the Government of the United States, . . . did attempt to bring into disgrace, ridicule, hatred, contempt, and reproach the Congress of the United States and the several branches thereof, to impair and destroy the regard and respect of all the good people of the United States for the Congress and legislative power thereof (which all officers of the Government ought inviolably to preserve and maintain), and to excite the odium and resentment of all the good people of the United States against Congress and the laws by it duly and constitutionally enacted; and, in pursuance of his said design and intent, openly and publicly, and before divers assemblages of the citizens of the United States, . . . did, on the 18th day of August, A. D. 1866, and on divers other days and times, . . . make and deliver with a loud voice certain intemperate, inflammatory, and scandalous harangues, and did therein utter loud threats and bitter menaces, as well against Congress as the laws of the United States, duly enacted thereby, amid the cries, jeers, and laughter of the multitudes then assembled and in hearing, which are set forth in the several specifications hereinafter written in substance and effect; that is to say:

Specification first.—In this, that at Washington, . . . in the Executive Mansion, to a committee of citizens who called upon the President of the United States, speaking of and concerning the Congress of the United States, said Andrew Johnson, President of the United States, . . . on the 18th day of August, A. D. 1866, did in a loud voice declare in substance and effect, among other things; that is to say: . . .

We have witnessed in one department of the Government every endeavor to prevent the restoration of peace, harmony, and union. We have seen hanging upon the verge of the Government, as it were, a body called, or which assumes to be, the Congress of the United States, while in fact it is a Congress of only a part of the States. We have seen this Congress pretend to be for the Union, when its every step and act tended to perpetuate disunion and make a disruption of the States inevitable. . . . We have seen Congress gradually encroach, step by step, upon constitutional rights, and violate, day after day and month after month, fundamental principles of the Government. We have seen a Congress that seemed to forget that there was a limit to the sphere and scope of legislation. We have seen a Congress in a minority assume to exercise power which, allowed to be consummated, would result in despotism or monarchy itself.

Specification second.—In this, that at Cleveland, in the State of Ohio, . . . on the 3d day of September, A. D. 1866, before a public assemblage of citizens and others, said Andrew Johnson, President of the United States, speaking of and concerning the Congress of the United States, did in a loud voice declare in substance and effect, among other things; that is to say:

I will tell you what I did do. I called upon your Congress that is trying to break up the Government. . . .

In conclusion, besides that, Congress had taken much pains to poison their constituents against him. But what had Congress done? Have they done anything to restore the Union of these States? No. On the contrary, they have done everything to prevent it. And because he stood now where he did when the rebellion commenced, he had been denounced as a traitor. Who had run greater risks or made greater sacrifices than himself? But Congress, factious and domineering, had undertaken to poison the minds of the American people.

Specification third.—In this, that at St. Louis, in the State of Missouri, . . . on the 8th day of September, A. D. 1866, . . . said Andrew Johnson, President of the United States, speaking of and concerning the Congress of the United States, did in a loud voice declare in substance and effect, among other things; that is to say:

Go on . . . if you will go back and ascertain the cause of the riot at New Orleans, perhaps you will not be so prompt in calling out "New Orleans." If you will take up the riot at New Orleans and trace it back to its source or its immediate cause, you will find out who was responsible for the blood that was shed there. If you will take up the riot at New Orleans and trace it back to the Radical Congress, you will find that the riot at New Orleans was substantially planned. . . . You will also find that that convention did assemble, in violation of law, and the intention of that convention was to supersede the reorganized authorities in the State government of Louisiana, which had been recognized by the Government of the United States; and every man engaged in that rebellion in that convention, with the intention of superseding and upturning the civil government which had been recognized by the Government of the United States, I say that he was a traitor to the Constitution of the United States; and hence you find that another rebellion was commenced, *having its origin in the Radical Congress.* . . .

And I have been traduced, I have been slandered, I have been maligned, I have been called Judas Iscariot and all that. Now, my countrymen, here to-night, it is very easy to indulge in epithets; it is easy to call a man a Judas and cry out "traitor;" but when he is called upon to give arguments and facts he is very often found wanting. Judas Iscariot—Judas. There was a Judas, and he was one of the twelve apostles. Oh, yes; the twelve apostles had a Christ. The twelve apostles had a Christ, and he never could have had a Judas unless he had had twelve apostles. If I have played the Judas, who has been my Christ that I have played the Judas with? Was it Thad. Stevens? Was it Wendell Phillips? Was it Charles Sumner? These are the men that stop and compare themselves with the Savior, and everybody that differs with them in opinion, and to try to stay and arrest their diabolical and nefarious policy, is to be denounced as a Judas. . . .

which said utterances, declarations, threats, and harangues, highly censurable in any, are peculiarly indecent and unbecoming in the Chief Magistrate of the United States, by means whereof said Andrew Johnson has brought the high office of the President of the United States into contempt, ridicule, and disgrace, to the great scandal of all good citizens; whereby said Andrew Johnson, President of the United States, did commit and was then and there guilty of a high misdemeanor in office.

ART. XI. That said Andrew Johnson, President of the United States, . . . did on the 18th day of August, A. D. 1866, at the city of Washington, in the District of Columbia, by public speech, declare and affirm in substance that the Thirty-ninth Congress of the United States was not a Congress of the United States authorized by the Constitution to exercise legislative power under the same, but, on the contrary, was a Congress of only part of the States; thereby denying and intending to deny that the legislation of said Congress was valid or obligatory upon him, the said Andrew Johnson, except in so far as he saw fit to approve the same, . . . in pursuance of said declaration the said Andrew Johnson, President of the United States, . . . on the 21st day of February, A. D. 1868, at the city of Washington, in the District of Columbia, did unlawfully, and in disregard of the requirement of the Constitution that he should take care that the laws be faithfully executed, attempt to prevent the execution of an act entitled "An act regulating the tenure of certain civil offices," passed March 2, 1867, by unlawfully devising and contriving, and attempting to devise and contrive, means by which he should prevent Edwin M. Stanton from forthwith resuming the functions of the office of Secretary for the Department of

War, notwithstanding the refusal of the Senate to concur in the suspension theretofore by said Andrew Johnson of said Edwin M. Stanton from said office of Secretary for the Department of War, and also by further unlawfully devising and contriving, and attempting to devise and contrive, means then and there to prevent the execution of an act entitled "An act making appropriations for the support of the Army for the fiscal year ending June 30, 1868, and for other purposes," approved March 2, 1867, and also to prevent the execution of an act entitled "An act to provide for the more efficient government of the rebel States," passed March 2, 1867, whereby the said Andrew Johnson, President of the United States, did then, to wit, on the 21st day of February, A. D. 1868, at the city of Washington, commit and was guilty of a high misdemeanor in office.

SATURDAY, MAY 16, 1868.
THE UNITED STATES vs. ANDREW JOHNSON, PRESIDENT.

The Chief Justice stated that, in pursuance of the order of the Senate, he would first proceed to take the judgment of the Senate on the eleventh article. The roll of the Senate was called, with the following result:

The Senators who voted "guilty" are Messrs. Anthony, Cameron, Cattell, Chandler, Cole, Conkling, Conness, Corbett, Cragin, Drake, Edmunds, Ferry, Frelinghuysen, Harlan, Howard, Howe, Morgan, Morrill of Maine, Morrill of Vermont, Morton, Nye, Patterson of New Hampshire, Pomeroy, Ramsey, Sherman, Sprague, Stewart, Sumner, Thayer, Tipton, Wade, Williams, Willey, Wilson, and Yates—35.

The Senators who voted "not guilty" are Messrs. Bayard, Buckalew, Davis, Dixon, Doolittle, Fessenden, Fowler, Grimes, Henderson, Hendricks, Johnson, McCreery, Norton, Patterson of Tennessee, Ross, Saulsbury, Trumbull, Van Winkle, and Vickers—19.

The Chief Justice announced that upon this article thirty-five Senators had voted "guilty" and nineteen Senators "not guilty," and declared that two-thirds of the Senators present not having pronounced him guilty, Andrew Johnson, President of the United States, stood acquitted of the charges contained in the eleventh article of impeachment.

TUESDAY, MAY 26, 1868.
THE UNITED STATES vs. ANDREW
JOHNSON, PRESIDENT.

The Senate ordered that the vote be taken upon the second article of impeachment. The roll of the Senate was called, with the following result:

The Senators who voted "guilty" are Messrs. Anthony, Cameron, Cattell, Chandler, Cole, Conkling, Conness, Corbett, Cragin, Drake, Edmunds, Ferry, Frelinghuysen, Harlan, Howard, Howe, Morgan, Morrill of Maine, Morrill of Vermont, Morton, Nye, Patterson of New Hampshire, Pomeroy, Ramsey, Sherman, Sprague, Stewart, Sumner, Thayer, Tipton, Wade, Willey, Williams, Wilson, and Yates—35.

The Senators who voted "not guilty" are Messrs. Bayard, Buckalew, Davis, Dixon, Doolittle, Fessenden, Fowler, Grimes, Henderson, Hendricks, Johnson, McCreery, Norton, Patterson of Tennessee, Ross, Saulsbury, Trumbull, Van Winkle, and Vickers—19.

The Chief Justice announced that upon this article thirty-five Senators had voted "guilty" and nineteen Senators had voted "not guilty," and declared that two-thirds of the Senators present not having pronounced him guilty, Andrew Johnson, President of the United States, stood acquitted of the charges contained in the second article of impeachment.

The Senate ordered that the vote be taken upon the third article of impeachment. The roll of the Senate was called, with the following result:

The Senators who voted "guilty" are Messrs. Anthony, Cameron, Cattell, Chandler, Cole, Conkling, Conness, Corbett, Cragin, Drake, Edmunds, Ferry, Frelinghuysen, Harlan, Howard, Howe, Morgan, Morrill of Maine, Morrill of Vermont, Morton, Nye, Patterson of New Hampshire, Pomeroy, Ramsey, Sherman, Sprague, Stewart, Sumner, Thayer, Tipton, Wade, Willey, Williams, Wilson, and Yates—35.

The Senators who voted "not guilty" are Messrs. Bayard, Buckalew, Davis, Dixon, Doolittle, Fessenden, Fowler, Grimes, Henderson, Hendricks, Johnson, McCreery, Norton, Patterson of Tennessee, Ross, Saulsbury,

Trumbull, Van Winkle, and Vickers—19.

The Chief Justice announced that upon this article thirty-five Senators had voted "guilty" and nineteen Senators had voted "not guilty," and declared that two-thirds of the Senators present not having pronounced him guilty, Andrew Johnson, President of the United States, stood acquitted of the charges contained in the third article.

No objection being made, the secretary, by direction of the Chief Justice, entered the judgment of the Senate upon the second, third, and eleventh articles, as follows:

The Senate having tried Andrew Johnson, President of the United States, upon articles of impeachment exhibited against him by the House of Representatives, and two-thirds of the Senators present not having found him guilty of the charges contained in the second, third, and eleventh articles of impeachment, it is therefore

Ordered and adjudged, That the said Andrew Johnson, President of the United States, be, and he is, acquitted of the charges in said articles made and set forth.

A motion "that the Senate sitting for the trial of the President upon articles of impeachment do now adjourn without day" was adopted by a vote of 34 yeas to 16 nays.

Those who voted in the affirmative are Messrs. Anthony, Cameron, Cattell, Chandler, Cole, Conkling, Corbett, Cragin, Drake, Edmunds, Ferry, Frelinghuysen, Harlan, Howard, Morgan, Morrill of Maine, Morrill of Vermont, Morton, Nye, Patterson of New Hampshire, Pomeroy, Ramsey, Sherman, Sprague, Stewart, Sumner, Thayer, Tipton, Van Winkle, Wade, Willey, Williams, Wilson, and Yates.

Those who voted in the negative are Messrs. Bayard, Buckalew, Davis, Dixon, Doolittle, Fowler, Henderson, Hendricks, Johnson, McCreery, Norton, Patterson of Tennessee, Ross, Saulsbury, Trumbull, and Vickers.

The Chief Justice declared the Senate sitting as a court of impeachment for the trial of Andrew Johnson, President of the United States, upon articles of impeachment exhibited against him by the House of Representatives, adjourned without day.

270. FOURTH RECONSTRUCTION ACT
March 11, 1868

(U. S. Statutes at Large, Vol. XV, p. 41)

The Second Reconstruction Act, Doc. No. 265, provided for the ratification of the new state constitutions only where they were accepted by a majority of the registered voters. The defeat of the Alabama Constitution in February 1868 by the absence from the polls of a majority of the registered voters led Congress to pass the Act of March 11, 1868. Under the provisions of this Act a number of constitutions were ratified and in the summer of 1868 Congress admitted seven of the southern States to the Union. For references, see Doc. No. 260.

An Act to amend the Act [of March 23, 1867]

Be it enacted, That hereafter any election authorized by the act [of March 23, 1867], shall be decided by a majority of the votes actually cast; and at the election in which the question of the adoption or rejection of any constitution is submitted, any person duly registered in the State may vote in the election district where he offers to vote when he has resided therein for ten days next preceding such election, upon presentation of his certificate of registration, his affidavit, or other satisfactory evidence, under such regulations as the district commanders may prescribe.

SEC. 2. *And be it further enacted,* That the constitutional convention of any of the States mentioned in the acts to which this is amendatory may provide that at the time of voting upon the ratification of the constitution the registered voters may vote also for members of the House of Representatives of the United States, and for all elective officers provided for by the said constitution; and the same election officers who shall make the return of the votes cast on the ratification or rejection of the constitution, shall enumerate and certify the votes cast for members of Congress.

271. THE KU KLUX KLAN
Organization and Principles
1868

(J. C. Lester and D. L. Wilson, *The Ku Klux Klan* . . . ed. by W. L. Fleming, p. 154 ff.)

The Ku Klux Klan, one of the two largest of the secret organizations that flourished in the South during Reconstruction, was founded in 1865 at Pulaski, Tennessee. The order grew rapidly in 1867 and 1868; a general organization was perfected in May 1867 at which a constitution was adopted. General Bedford Forrest was the first Grand Wizard of the Order. The Order was effective in frightening the negro out of his unnatural alliance with the Union Leagues, but it was used as a cloak for lawlessness and violence and formally disbanded in 1869. Its activities continued, however, for some time after this date. Congress took cognizance of the Order and similar secret societies such as the Knights of the White Camelia, by passing the Ku Klux Klan Acts of May 31, 1870 and April 20, 1871, Doc. No. 273. A Congressional Ku Klux Klan Committee sat during the summer of 1871 and took thirteen volumes of testimony on conditions in the South. See, *Report of the Joint Select Committee* . . . U.S. 42d Cong. 2d Sess. Sen. Report, No. 41. On the Ku Klux Klan see also, W. L. Fleming, *Sequel to Appomattox,* ch. xi; W. G. Brown, *The Lower South in American History,* ch. iv; W. A. Sinclair, *The Aftermath of Slavery.*

Organization and Principles of the Ku Klux Klan

Appellation

This Organization shall be styled and denominated, the Order of the * * *

Creed

We, the Order of the * * * , reverentially acknowledge the majesty and supremacy of the Divine Being, and recognize the goodness and providence of the same. And we recognize our relation to the United States Government, the supremacy of the Constitution, the Constitutional Laws thereof, and the Union of States thereunder.

Character and objects of the Order

This is an institution of Chivalry, Humanity, Mercy, and Patriotism; embodying in its genius and its principles all that is chivalric in conduct, noble in sentiment, generous in manhood, and patriotic in purpose; its peculiar objects being

First: To protect the weak, the innocent, and the defenseless, from the indignities, wrongs, and outrages of the lawless, the violent, and the brutal; to relieve the injured and oppressed; to succor the suffering and unfortunate, and especially the widows and orphans of Confederate soldiers.

Second: To protect and defend the Constitution of the United States, and all laws passed in conformity thereto, and to protect the States and the people thereof from all invasion from any source whatever.

Third: To aid and assist in the execution of all constitutional laws, and to protect the people from unlawful seizure, and from trial except by their peers in conformity to the laws of the land.

Titles

Sec. 1. The officers of this Order shall consist of a Grand Wizard of the Empire, and his ten Genii; a Grand Dragon of the Realm, and his eight Hydras; a Grand Titan of the Dominion, and his six Furies; a Grand Giant of the Province, and his four Goblins; a Grand Cyclops of the Den, and his two Night Hawks; a Grand Magi, a Grand Monk, a Grand Scribe, a Grand Exchequer, a Grand Turk, and a Grand Sentinel.

Sec. 2. The body politic of this Order shall be known and designated as "Ghouls."

Territory and its Divisions

Sec. 1. The territory embraced within the jurisdiction of this Order shall be coterminous with the States of Maryland, Virginia, North Carolina, South Carolina, Georgia, Florida, Alabama, Mississippi, Louisiana, Texas, Arkansas, Missouri, Kentucky, and Tennessee; all combined constituting the Empire.

Sec. 2. The Empire shall be divided into four departments, the first to be styled the Realm, and coterminous with the boundaries of the several States; the second to be styled the Dominion and to be coterminous with such counties as the Grand Dragons of the several Realms may assign to the charge of

the Grand Titan. The third to be styled the Province, and to be coterminous with the several counties; *provided* the Grand Titan may, when he deems it necessary, assign two Grand Giants to one Province, prescribing, at the same time, the jurisdiction of each. The fourth department to be styled the Den, and shall embrace such part of a Province as the Grand Giant shall assign to the charge of a Grand Cyclops. . . .

Interrogations to be asked

1st. Have you ever been rejected, upon application for membership in the * * * , or have you ever been expelled from the same?

2d. Are you now, or have you ever been, a member of the Radical Republican party, or either of the organizations known as the "Loyal League" and the "Grand Army of the Republic?"

3d. Are you opposed to the principles and policy of the Radical party, and to the Loyal League, and the Grand Army of the Republic, so far as you are informed of the character and purposes of those organizations?

4th. Did you belong to the Federal army during the late war, and fight against the South during the existence of the same?

5th. Are you opposed to negro equality, both social and political?

6th. Are you in favor of a white man's government in this country?

7th. Are you in favor of Constitutional liberty, and a Government of equitable laws instead of a Government of violence and oppression?

8th. Are you in favor of maintaining the Constitutional rights of the South?

9th. Are you in favor of the re-enfranchisement and emancipation of the white men of the South, and the restitution of the Southern people to all their rights, alike proprietary, civil, and political?

10th. Do you believe in the inalienable right of self-preservation of the people against the exercise of arbitrary and unlicensed power? . . .

. . . 9. The most profound and rigid secrecy concerning any and everything that relates to the Order, shall at all times be maintained.

10. Any member who shall reveal or betray the secrets of this Order, shall suffer the extreme penalty of the law.

272. THE FOURTEENTH AMENDMENT
July 28, 1868

(F. N. Thorpe, ed. *Federal and State Constitutions*, Vol. I, p. 31)

Widespread doubt as to the constitutionality of the Civil Rights Act, Doc. No. 252, led to the formulation, by the Joint Committee of Fifteen, of this amendment to the Constitution. It was first submitted to the legislatures of the States in June, 1866. Rejected by most of the southern States, its ratification was made a condition of restoration to the Union. Ratification, thus being obtained, was announced July 28, 1868. New Jersey, Ohio, and Oregon subsequently rescinded their ratification. The revolutionary character of the Fourteenth Amendment justifies its insertion at this point. The Amendment for the first time defined citizenship, and for the first time threw the protection of the Federal Government around rights that might be invaded by the State governments—thus reversing the traditional relationship. The first section of the Amendment has given rise to more adjudication than any other part of the Constitution. There appears to be little support to the so-called conspiracy theory that the framers of the amendment deliberately phrased the amendment so that it would protect the property and rights of corporations against State legislation. See, B. B. Kendrick, *The Journal of the Joint Committee of Fifteen on Reconstruction;* H. E. Flack, *The Adoption of the Fourteenth Amendment;* C. Warren, *Supreme Court,* Vol. II, chs. xxx–xxxii; L. Boudin, *Government by Judiciary,* Vol. II, chs. xxiii, xxxvi; Graham, "The Conspiracy Theory of the Fourteenth Amendment," 47 Yale L. J. 371; Boudin, "Truth and Fiction about the Fourteenth Amendment," 16 N. Y. U. L. Qt. Rev. 19. F. J. Swayze, "Judicial Construction of the Fourteenth Amendment," 26 Harv. Law R. 1.

ART. XIV.

SEC. 1. All persons born or naturalized in the United States, and subject to the jurisdiction thereof, are citizens of the United States and of the State wherein they reside. No State shall make or enforce any law which shall abridge the privileges or immunities of citizens of the United States; nor shall any State deprive any person of life, liberty, or property, without due process of law; nor deny to any person within its jurisdiction the equal protection of the laws.

SEC. 2. Representatives shall be apportioned among the several States according to their respective numbers, counting the whole number of persons in each State, excluding Indians not taxed. But when the right to vote at any election for the choice of electors for President and Vice-President of the United States, Representatives in Congress, the Executive and Judicial officers of a State, or the members of the Legislature thereof, is denied to any of the male inhabitants of such State, being twenty-one years of age, and citizens of the United States, or in any way abridged, except for participation in rebellion, or other crime, the basis of representation therein shall be reduced in the proportion which the number of such male citizens shall bear to the whole number of male citizens twenty-one years of age in such State.

SEC. 3. No person shall be a Senator or Representative in Congress, or elector of President and Vice-President, or hold any office, civil or military, under the United States, or under any State, who, having previously taken an oath, as a member of Congress, or as an officer of the United States, or as a member of any State legislature, or as an executive or judicial officer of any State, to support the Constitution of the United States, shall have engaged in insurrection or rebellion against the same, or given aid or comfort to the enemies thereof. But Congress may by a vote of two-thirds of each House, remove such disability.

SEC. 4. The validity of the public debt of the United States, authorized by law, including debts incurred for payment of pensions and bounties for services in suppressing insurrection or rebellion, shall not be questioned. But neither the United States nor any State shall assume or pay any debt or obligation incurred in aid of insurrection or rebellion against the United States, or any claim for the loss or emancipation of any slave; but all such debts, obligations and claims shall be held illegal and void.

SEC. 5. The Congress shall have power to enforce, by appropriate legislation, the provisions of this article.

273. ACT TO ENFORCE THE FOURTEENTH AMENDMENT
April 20, 1871

(*U. S. Statutes at Large,* Vol. XVII, p. 13 ff.)

This so-called Ku Klux Act was the most important of several Civil Rights Acts designed to insure for the negro the full benefits of the thirteenth, fourteenth and fifteenth amendments. Similar acts had been passed May 31, 1870 and February 28, 1871. An act designed to secure social equality for the negro was passed March 1, 1875 (see Doc. No. 291). In 1876 the Supreme Court, in *U. S.* v. *Reese,* 92 U. S. 214 and *U. S.* v. *Cruikshank,* 92 U. S. 542, declared certain sections of the Civil Rights Act of May 31, 1870 unconstitutional, and thus anticipated its attitude toward the Ku Klux and Civil Rights Acts. In 1883, in *U. S.* v. *Harris,* 106 U. S. 629, the Court held parts of the Act of April 20, 1871 unconstitutional; in *The Civil Rights Cases,* 109 U. S. 3, it held the Civil Rights Act unconstitutional. Efforts to repeal these force acts were not successful until the second Cleveland administration. See, W. W. Davis, "The Federal Enforcement Acts," in *Studies in Southern History and Politics;* W. A. Dunning, *Essays on the Civil War and Reconstruction,* p. 353 ff.; C. Warren, *The Supreme Court* (1928 ed.), Vol. II, ch. xxxiv,

An Act to enforce the Provisions of the Fourteenth Amendment to the Constitution of the United States, and for other Purposes.

*Be it enacted . . . ,*That any person who, under color of any law, statute, ordinance, regulation, custom, or usage of any State, shall subject, or cause to be subjected, any person within the jurisdiction of the United States to the deprivation of any rights, privileges, or immunities secured by the Constitution of the United States, shall, any such law, statute, ordinance, regulation, custom, or usage of the State to the contrary notwithstanding, be liable to the party injured in any action at law, suit in equity, or other proper proceeding for redress; such proceeding to be prosecuted in the several district or circuit courts of the United States, with and subject to the same rights of appeal, review upon error, and other remedies provided in like cases in such courts, under the provisions of the [Civil Rights Act of 1866], and the other remedial laws of the United States which are in their nature applicable in such cases.

SEC. 2. That if two or more persons within any State or Territory of the United States shall conspire together to overthrow, or to put down, or to destroy by force the government of the United States, or to levy war against the United States, or to oppose by force the authority of the government of the United States, or by force, intimidation, or threat to prevent, hinder, or delay the execution of any law of the United States, or by force to seize, take, or possess any property of the United States contrary to the authority thereof, or by force, intimidation, or threat to prevent any person from accepting or holding any office or trust or place of confidence under the United States, or from discharging the duties thereof, or by force, intimidation, or threat to induce any officer of the United States to leave any State, district, or place where his duties as such officer might lawfully be performed, or to injure him in his person or property on account of his lawful discharge of the duties of his office, or to injure his person while engaged in the lawful discharge of the duties of his office, or to injure his property so as to molest, interrupt, hinder, or impede him in the discharge of his official duty, or by force, intimidation, or threat to deter any party or witness in any court of the United States from attending such court, or from testifying in any matter pending in such court fully, freely, and truthfully, or to injure any such party or witness in his person or property on account of his having so attended or testified, or by force, intimidation, or threat to influence the verdict, presentment, or indictment, of any juror or grand juror in any court of the United States, or to injure such juror in his person or property on account of any verdict, presentment, or indictment lawfully assented to by him, or on account of his being or having been such juror, or shall conspire together, or go in disguise upon the public highway or upon the premises of another for the purpose, either directly or indirectly, of depriving any person or any class of persons of the equal protection of the laws, or of equal privileges or immunities under the laws, or for the purpose of preventing or hindering the constituted authorities of any State from giving or securing to all persons within such

State the equal protection of the laws, or shall conspire together for the purpose of in any manner impeding, hindering, obstructing, or defeating the due course of justice in any State or Territory, with intent to deny to any citizen of the United States the due and equal protection of the laws, or to injure any person in his person or his property for lawfully enforcing the right of any person or class of persons to the equal protection of the laws, or by force, intimidation, or threat to prevent any citizen of the United States lawfully entitled to vote from giving his support or advocacy in a lawful manner towards or in favor of the election of any lawfully qualified person as an elector of President or Vice-President of the United States, or as a member of the Congress of the United States, or to injure any such citizen in his person or property on account of such support or advocacy, each and every person so offending shall be deemed guilty of a high crime, and, upon conviction thereof in any district or circuit court of the United States or district or supreme court of any Territory of the United States having jurisdiction of similar offences, shall be punished by a fine not less than five hundred nor more than five thousand dollars, or by imprisonment, with or without hard labor, as the court may determine, for a period of not less than six months nor more than six years, as the court may determine, or by both such fine and imprisonment as the court shall determine. . . .

SEC. 3. That in all cases where insurrection, domestic violence, unlawful combinations, or conspiracies in any State shall so obstruct or hinder the execution of the laws thereof, and of the United States, as to deprive any portion or class of the people of such State of any of the rights, privileges, or immunities, or protection, named in the Constitution and secured by this act, and the constituted authorities of such State shall either be unable to protect, or shall, from any cause, fail in or refuse protection of the people in such rights, such facts shall be deemed a denial by such State of the equal protection of the laws to which they are entitled under the Constitution of the United States; and in all such cases . . . it shall be lawful for the President, and it shall be his duty to take such measures, by the employment of the militia or the land and naval forces of the United States, or of either, or by other means, as he may deem necessary for the suppression of such insurrection, domestic violence, or combinations. . . .

SEC. 4. That whenever in any State or part of a State the unlawful combinations named in the preceding section of this act shall be organized and armed, and so numerous and powerful as to be able, by violence, to either overthrow or set at defiance the constituted authorities of such State, and of the United States within such State, or when the constituted authorities are in complicity with, or shall connive at the unlawful purposes of, such powerful and armed combinations; and whenever, by reason of either or all of the causes aforesaid, the conviction of such offenders and the preservation of the public safety shall become in such district impracticable, in every such case such combinations shall be deemed a rebellion against the government of the United States, and during the continuance of such rebellion, and within the limits of the district which shall be so under the sway thereof, such limits to be prescribed by proclamation, it shall be lawful for the President of the United States, when in his judgment the public safety shall require it, to suspend the privileges of the writ of habeas corpus, to the end that such rebellion may be overthrown: *Provided,* That all the provisions of the second section of [the Habeas Corpus Act of March 3, 1863], which relate to the discharge of prisoners other than prisoners of war, and to the penalty for refusing to obey the order of the court, shall be in full force so far as the same are applicable to the provisions of this section: *Provided further,* That the President shall first have made proclamation, as now provided by law, commanding such insurgents to disperse: *And provided also,* That the provisions of this section shall not be in force after the end of the next regular session of Congress.

SEC. 5. That no person shall be a grand or petit juror in any court of the United States upon any inquiry, hearing, or trial of any suit, proceeding, or prosecution based upon or arising under the provisions of this act who shall, in the judgment of the court, be in complicity with any such combination or conspiracy; and every such juror shall, before entering upon any such inquiry, hearing, or trial, take and subscribe an oath in open court that he has never, directly or indirectly, counselled, advised, or voluntarily aided any such combination or conspiracy. . . .

SEC. 6. That any person or persons, having knowledge that any of the wrongs conspired to be done and mentioned in the second section of this act are about to be committed, and having power to prevent or aid in preventing the same, shall neglect or refuse to do so, and such wrongful act shall be committed, such person or persons shall be liable to the person injured . . . for all damages caused by any such wrongful act which such first-named person or persons by reasonable diligence could have prevented. . . .

274. THE DEMOCRATIC PLATFORM OF 1868
July 4, 1868

(K. Porter, ed. *National Party Platforms*, p. 64 ff.)

Reconstruction and the money question were the principal issues of the campaign of 1868. The Democratic Convention met in New York City in July 1868 and adopted a platform incorporating Pendleton's "Ohio idea" on money, but nominated for the Presidency Horatio Seymour of New York, a hard money man. The second place on the ticket went to Frank Blair of Missouri. Seymour polled 2,709,000 votes, but secured only 80 votes in the electoral college. Only the money and reconstruction planks of the platform are given. See, C. H. Coleman, *The Election of 1868;* W. H. Smith, *The Francis Preston Blair Family in Politics,* Vol. II, ch. xlii.

. . . 3. Payment of the public debt of the United States as rapidly as practicable. All moneys drawn from the people by taxation, except so much as is requisite for the necessities of the government, economically administered, being honestly applied to such payment, and where the obligations of the government do not expressly state upon their face, or the law under which they were issued does not provide, that they shall be paid in coin, they ought, in right and in justice, to be paid in the lawful money of the United States. . . .

5. One currency for the government and the people, the laborer and the office-holder, the pensioner and the soldier, the producer and the bond-holder. . . .

8. . . . In demanding these measures and reforms we arraign the Radical party for its disregard of right, and the unparalleled oppression and tyranny which have marked its career.

After the most solemn and unanimous pledge of both Houses of Congress to prosecute the war exclusively for the maintenance of the government and the preservation of the Union under the Constitution, it has repeatedly violated that most sacred pledge, under which alone was rallied that noble volunteer army which carried our flag to victory.

Instead of restoring the Union, it has, so far as in its power, dissolved it, and subjected ten States, in time of profound peace, to military despotism and negro supremacy.

It has nullified there the right of trial by jury; it has abolished the *habeas corpus,* that most sacred writ of liberty; it has overthrown the freedom of speech and of the press; it has substituted arbitrary seizures and arrests, and military trials and secret star-chamber inquisitions, for the constitutional tribunals; it has disregarded in time of peace the right of the people to be free from searches and seizures; it has entered the post and telegraph offices, and even the private rooms of individuals, and seized their private papers and letters without any specific charge or notice of affidavit, as required by the organic law; it has converted the American capitol into a Bastile; it has established a system of spies and official espionage to which no constitutional monarchy of Europe would now dare to resort; it has abolished the right of appeal, on important constitutional questions, to the Supreme Judicial tribunal, and threatens to curtail, or destroy, its original jurisdiction, which is irrevocably vested by the Constitution; while the learned Chief Justice has been subjected to the most atrocious calumnies, merely because he would not prostitute his high office to the support of the false and partisan charges preferred against the President. Its corruption and extravagance have exceeded anything known in history, and by its frauds and monopolies it has nearly doubled the burden of the debt created by the war; it has stripped the President of his constitutional power of appointment, even of his own Cabinet. Under its repeated assaults the pillars of the government are rocking on their base, and should it succeed in November next and inaugurate its President, we will meet, as a subjected and conquered people, amid the ruins of liberty and the scattered fragments of the Constitution.

And we do declare and resolve, That ever since the people of the United States threw off all subjection to the British crown, the privilege and trust of suffrage have belonged to the several States, and have been granted, regulated, and controlled exclusively by the political power of each State respectively, and that any attempt by congress, on any pretext whatever, to deprive any State of this right, or interfere with its exercise, is a flagrant usurpation of power, which can find no warrant in the Constitution; and if sanctioned by the people will subvert our form of government, and can only end in a single centralized and consolidated government, in which the separate existence of the States will be entirely absorbed, and an unqualified despotism be established in place of a federal union of co-equal States; and that we regard the reconstruction acts so-called, of Congress, as such an usurpation, and unconstitutional, revolutionary, and void. . . .

275. PRESIDENT JOHNSON'S RECOMMENDATION FOR THE REVALUATION OF THE PUBLIC DEBT

Extract from Fourth Annual Message to Congress
December 9, 1868

(Richardson, ed. *Messages and Papers,* Vol. VI, p. 677)

President Johnson's biographers have largely ignored his financial ideas and policies. There is a brief discussion in H. Beale, *The Critical Year,* ch. x.

. . . In my message to Congress December 4, 1865, it was suggested that a policy should be devised which, without being oppressive to the people, would at once begin to effect a reduction of the debt, and, if persisted in, discharge it fully within a definite number of years. The Secretary of the Treasury forcibly recommends legislation of this character, and justly urges that the longer it is deferred the more difficult must become its accomplishment. We should follow the wise precedents established in 1789 and 1816, and without further delay make provision for the payment of our obligations at as early a period as may be practicable. The fruits of their labors should be enjoyed by our citizens rather than used to build up and sustain moneyed monopolies in our own and other lands. Our foreign debt is already computed by the Secretary of the Treasury at $850,-000,000; citizens of foreign countries receive interest upon a large portion of our securities, and American taxpayers are made to contribute large sums for their support. The idea that such a debt is to become permanent should be at all times discarded as involving taxation too heavy to be borne, and payment once in every sixteen years, at the present rate of interest, of an amount equal to the original sum. This vast debt, if permitted to become permanent and increasing, must eventually be gathered into the hands of a few, and enable them to exert a dangerous and controlling power in the affairs of the Government. The borrowers would become servants to the lenders, the lenders the masters of the people. We now pride ourselves upon having given freedom to 4,000,000 of the colored race; it will then be our shame that 40,000,000 of people, by their own toleration of usurpation and profligacy, have suffered themselves to become enslaved, and merely exchanged slave owners for new taskmasters in the shape of bondholders and taxgatherers. Besides, permanent debts pertain to monarchical governments, and, tending to monopolies, perpetuities, and class legislation, are totally irreconcilable with free institutions. Introduced into our republican system, they would gradually but surely sap its foundations, eventually subvert our governmental fabric, and erect upon its ruins a moneyed aristocracy. It is our sacred duty to transmit unimpaired to our posterity the blessings of liberty which were bequeathed to us by the founders of the Republic, and by our example teach those who are to follow us carefully to avoid the dangers which threaten a free and independent people.

Various plans have been proposed for the payment of the public debt. However they may have varied as to the time and mode in which it should be redeemed, there seems to be a general concurrence as to the propriety and justness of a reduction in the present rate of interest. The Secretary of the Treasury in his report recommends 5 per cent; Congress, in a bill passed prior to adjournment on the 27th of July last, agreed upon 4 and 4½ per cent; while by many 3 per cent has been held to be an amply sufficient return for the investment. The general impression as to the exorbitancy of the existing rate of interest has led to an inquiry in the public mind respecting the consideration which the Government has actually received for its bonds, and the conclusion is becoming prevalent that the amount which it obtained was in real money three or four hundred per cent less than the obligations which it issued in return. It can not be denied that we are paying an extravagant percentage for the use of the money borrowed, which was paper currency, greatly depreciated below the value of coin. This fact is made apparent when we consider that bondholders receive from the Treasury upon each dollar they own in Government securities 6 per cent in gold, which is nearly or quite equal to 9 per cent in currency; that the bonds are then converted into capital for the national banks, upon which those institutions issue their circulation, bearing 6 per cent interest; and that

they are exempt from taxation by the Government and the States, and thereby enhanced 2 per cent in the hands of the holders. We thus have an aggregate of 17 per cent which may be received upon each dollar by the owners of Government securities. A system that produces such results is justly regarded as favoring a few at the expense of the many, and has led to the further inquiry whether our bondholders, in view of the large profits which they have enjoyed, would themselves be averse to a settlement of our indebtedness upon a plan which would yield them a fair remuneration and at the same time be just to the taxpayers of the nation. Our national credit should be sacredly observed, but in making provision for our creditors we should not forget what is due to the masses of the people. It may be assumed that the holders of our securities have already received upon their bonds a larger amount than their original investment, measured by a gold standard. Upon this statement of facts it would seem but just and equitable that the 6 per cent interest now paid by the Government should be applied to the reduction of the principal in semi-annual installments, which in sixteen years and eight months would liquidate the entire national debt. Six per cent in gold would at present rates be equal to 9 per cent in currency, and equivalent to the payment of the debt one and a half times in a fraction less than seventeen years. This, in connection with all the other advantages derived from their investment, would afford to the public creditors a fair and liberal compensation for the use of their capital, and with this they should be satisfied. The lessons of the past admonish the lender that it is not well to be over-anxious in exacting from the borrower rigid compliance with the letter of the bond. . . .

276. GRANT'S FIRST INAUGURAL ADDRESS
March 4, 1869

(Richardson, ed. Messages and Addresses, Vol. VII, p. 6 ff.)

On the election of 1868, see C. H. Coleman, *The Election of 1868;* for the Grant administration see J. F. Rhodes, *History,* Vol. VII and forthcoming studies by W. B. Hesseltine and by A. Nevins; on Grant after Appomattox, see A.

Badeau, *Grant in Peace;* L. A. Coolidge, *U. S. Grant,* ch. xxx ff.

Citizens of the United States:

Your suffrages having elected me to the

office of President of the United States, I have, in conformity to the Constitution of our country, taken the oath of office prescribed therein. I have taken this oath without mental reservation and with the determination to do to the best of my ability all that is required of me. The responsibilities of the position I feel, but accept them without fear. The office has come to me unsought; I commence its duties untrammeled. I bring to it a conscious desire and determination to fill it to the best of my ability to the satisfaction of the people.

On all leading questions agitating the public mind I will always express my views to Congress and urge them according to my judgment, and when I think it advisable will exercise the constitutional privilege of interposing a veto to defeat measures which I oppose; but all laws will be faithfully executed, whether they meet my approval or not.

I shall on all subjects have a policy to recommend, but none to enforce against the will of the people. Laws are to govern all alike—those opposed as well as those who favor them. I know no method to secure the repeal of bad or obnoxious laws so effective as their stringent execution.

The country having just emerged from a great rebellion, many questions will come before it for settlement in the next four years which preceding Administrations have never had to deal with. In meeting these it is desirable that they should be approached calmly, without prejudice, hate, or sectional pride, remembering that the greatest good to the greatest number is the object to be attained.

This requires security of person, property, and free religious and political opinion in every part of our common country, without regard to local prejudice. All laws to secure these ends will receive my best efforts for their enforcement.

A great debt has been contracted in securing to us and our posterity the Union. The payment of this, principal and interest, as well as the return to a specie basis as soon as it can be accomplished without material detriment to the debtor class or to the country at large, must be provided for. To protect the national honor, every dollar of Government indebtedness should be paid in gold, unless otherwise expressly stipulated in the contract. Let it be understood that no repudiator of one farthing of our public debt will be trusted in public place, and it will go far toward strengthening a credit which ought to be the best in the world, and will ultimately enable us to replace the debt with bonds bearing less interest than we now pay. To this should be added a faithful collection of the revenue, a strict accountability to the Treasury for every dollar collected, and the greatest practicable retrenchment in expenditure in every department of Government.

When we compare the paying capacity of the country now, with the ten States in poverty from the effects of war, but soon to emerge, I trust, into greater prosperity than ever before, with its paying capacity twenty-five years ago, and calculate what it probably will be twenty-five years hence, who can doubt the feasibility of paying every dollar then with more ease than we now pay for useless luxuries? Why, it looks as though Providence had bestowed upon us a strong box in the precious metals locked up in the sterile mountains of the far West, and which we are now forging the key to unlock, to meet the very contingency that is now upon us.

Ultimately it may be necessary to insure the facilities to reach these riches, and it may be necessary also that the General Government should give its aid to secure this access; but that should only be when a dollar of obligation to pay secures precisely the same sort of dollar to use now, and not before. Whilst the question of specie payments is in abeyance the prudent business man is careful about contracting debts payable in the distant future. The nation should follow the same rule. A prostrate commerce is to be rebuilt and all industries encouraged.

The young men of the country—those who from their age must be its rulers twenty-five years hence—have a peculiar interest in maintaining the national honor. A moment's reflection as to what will be our commanding influence among the nations of the earth in their day, if they are only true to themselves, should inspire them with national pride. All divisions—geographical, political, and religious—can join in this common sentiment. How the public debt is to be paid or specie payments resumed is not so important as that a plan should be adopted and acquiesced in. A united determination to do is worth more than divided counsels upon the method of doing. Legislation upon this subject may not be necessary now, nor even advisable, but it will be when the civil law is more fully restored in all parts of the country and trade resumes its wonted channels. . . .

The question of suffrage is one which is likely to agitate the public so long as a portion of the citizens of the nation are excluded from its privileges in any State. It seems to me very desirable that this question should be settled now, and I entertain the hope and express the desire that it may be by the ratification of the fifteenth article of amendment to the Constitution.

In conclusion I ask patient forbearance one toward another throughout the land, and a determined effort on the part of every citizen to do his share toward cementing a happy union; and I ask the prayers of the nation to Almighty God in behalf of this consummation.

277. VEAZIE BANK v. FENNO
8 Wallace, 533
1869

Certificate from the U.S. circuit court for the district of Maine. This case involved the constitutionality of the act of Congress of July 13, 1866 imposing a tax of ten per cent on state bank notes.

CHASE, C. J. . . . It will be seen that when the policy of taxing bank circulation was first adopted in 1863, Congress was inclined to discriminate for, rather than against, the circulation of the State banks; but that when the country had been sufficiently furnished with a national currency by the issues of United States notes and of National bank notes, the discrimination was turned, and very decidedly turned, in the opposite direction.

The general question now before us is, whether or not the tax of ten per cent., imposed on State banks . . . is repugnant to the Constitution of the United States.

In support of the position that the act of Congress, so far as it provides for the levy and collection of this tax, is repugnant to the Constitution, two propositions have been argued with much force and earnestness.

The first is that the tax in question is a direct tax, and has not been apportioned among the States agreeably to the Constitution.

The second is that the act imposing the tax impairs a franchise granted by the State, and that Congress has no power to pass any law with that intent or effect. . . .

The difficulty of defining with accuracy the terms used in the clause of the Constitution which confers the powers of taxation upon Congress, was felt in the Convention which framed that instrument, and has always been experienced by courts when called upon to determine their meaning. . . .

Much diversity of opinion has always prevailed upon the question, what are direct taxes? Attempts to answer it by reference to the definitions of political economists have been frequently made, but without satisfactory results. The enumeration of the different kinds of taxes which Congress was authorized to impose was probably made with very little reference to this question. The great work of Adam Smith, the first comprehensive treatise on political economy in the English language, had then been recently published; but in this work, though there are passages which refer to the characteristic difference between direct and indirect taxation, there is nothing which affords any valuable light on the use of the words "direct taxes" in the Constitution.

We are obliged, therefore, to resort to historical evidence, and to seek the meaning of words in the use and in the opinion of those whose relations to the government, and means of knowledge, warranted them in speaking with authority.

And, considered in this light, the meaning and application of the rule, as to direct taxes, appears to us quite clear.

It is, as we think, distinctly shown in every act of Congress on the subject. . . .

This review shows that personal property, contracts, occupations, and the like, have never been regarded by Congress as proper subjects of direct tax. . . .

It may rightly be affirmed, therefore, that in the practical construction of the Constitution by Congress, direct taxes have been limited to taxes on land and appurtenances, and taxes on polls or capitation taxes.

And this construction is entitled to great consideration especially in the absence of anything adverse to it in the discussions of the Convention which framed, and of the conventions which ratified, the Constitution. . . .

It follows necessarily that the power to tax without apportionment extends to all other objects. Taxes on other objects are included under the heads of taxes not direct, duties, imposts, and excises, and must be laid and collected by the rule of uniformity. The tax under consideration is a tax on bank circulation, and may very well be classed under the head of duties. Certainly it is not, in the sense of the Constitution, a direct tax. It may be said to come within the same category of taxation as the tax on incomes of insurance companies, . . .

It is insisted, however, that the tax in the case before us is excessive, and so excessive as to indicate a purpose on the part of Congress to destroy the franchise of the bank, and is, therefore, beyond the constitutional power of Congress.

The first answer to this is that the judicial cannot prescribe to the legislative departments of the government limitations upon the exercise of its acknowledged powers. The power to tax may be exercised oppressively upon persons, but the responsibility of the legislature is not to the courts, but to the people by whom its members are elected. So if a particular tax bears heavily upon a corporation, or a class of corporations, it cannot, for that reason only, be pronounced contrary to the Constitution.

But there is another answer which vindicates equally the wisdom and power of Congress.

It cannot be doubted that under the Con-stitution the power to provide a circulation of coin is given to Congress. And it is settled by the uniform practice of the government and by repeated decisions, that Congress may constitutionally authorize the emission of bills of credit. It is not important here, to decide whether the quality of legal tender, in payment of debts, can be constitutionally imparted to these bills; it is enough to say, that there can be no question of the power of the government to emit them; to make them receivable in payment of debts to itself; to fit them for use by those who see fit to use them in all the transactions of commerce; to provide for their redemption; to make them a currency, uniform in value and description, and convenient and useful for circulation. These powers, until recently, were only partially and occasionally exercised. Lately, however, Congress has undertaken to supply a currency for the entire country. . . .

Having thus, in the exercise of undisputed constitutional powers, undertaken to provide a currency for the whole country, it cannot be questioned that Congress may, constitutionally, secure the benefit of it to the people by appropriate legislation. To this end, Congress has denied the quality of legal tender to foreign coins, and has provided by law against the imposition of counterfeit and base coin on the community. To the same end, Congress may restrain, by suitable enactments, the circulation as money of any notes not issued under its own authority. Without this power, indeed, its attempts to secure a sound and uniform currency for the country must be futile.

Viewed in this light, as well as in the other light of a duty on contracts or property, we cannot doubt the constitutionality of the tax under consideration. . . .

NELSON, J., delivered a dissenting opinion in which DAVIS, J., concurred.

278. TEXAS v. WHITE
7 Wallace, 700
1869

Suit by Texas in the Supreme Court of the United States. During the Civil War the government of Texas disposed of some United States bonds, in payment of supplies for the Confederate government. The Reconstruction gov-ernment of Texas brought suit to enjoin the defendants from receiving payment on these bonds, on the ground that the State government of the Confederacy was not a legal government and therefore the disposition of the bonds was illegal. This celebrated case is the leading case on the question of the theory of secession and of reconstruction. See, Warren, *The Supreme Court* (1928 ed.), Vol. II, p. 488 ff.; Dunning, *Essays on the Civil War and Reconstruction*, ch. ii.

CHASE, C. J. . . . The first inquiries to which our attention was directed by counsel arose upon the allegations . . . that the State, having severed her relations with a majority of the States of the Union, and having by her ordinance of secession attempted to throw off her allegiance to the Constitution, and the government of the United States, has so far changed her status as to be disabled from prosecuting suits in the National courts. . . .

. . . It is not to be questioned that this court has original jurisdiction of suits by States against citizens of other States, or that the States entitled to invoke this jurisdiction must be States of the Union. But it is equally clear that no such jurisdiction has been conferred upon this court of suits by any other political communities than such States.

If, therefore, it is true that the State of Texas was not at the time of filing this bill, or is not now, one of the United States, we have no jurisdiction of this suit, and it is our duty to dismiss it. . . .

In the Constitution the term "State" most frequently expresses the combined idea just noticed, of people, territory, and government. A State, in the ordinary sense of the Constitution, is a political community of free citizens, occupying a territory of defined boundaries and organized under a government sanctioned and limited by a written constitution, and established by the consent of the governed. It is the union of such States, under a common constitution, which forms the distinct and greater political unit, which the Constitution designates as the United States, and makes of the people and States which compose it one people and one country. . . .

The Republic of Texas was admitted into the Union, as a State, on the 27th of December, 1845. By this act the new State, and the people of the new State, were invested with all the rights, and became subject to all the responsibilities and duties of the original States under the Constitution.

From the date of admission until 1861 the State was represented in the Congress of the United States by her senators and representatives, and her relations as a member of the Union remained unimpaired. In that year, acting upon the theory that the rights of a State under the Constitution might be renounced, and her obligations thrown off at pleasure, Texas undertook to sever the bond thus formed, and to break up her constitutional relations with the United States. . . .

The position thus assumed could only be maintained by arms, and Texas accordingly took part, with the other Confederate States, in the war of rebellion, which these events made inevitable. During the whole of that war there was no governor, or judge, or any other state officer in Texas, who recognized the National authority. Nor was any officer of the United States permitted to exercise any authority whatever under the National government within the limits of the State, except under the immediate protection of the National military forces.

Did Texas, in consequence of these acts, cease to be a State? Or, if not, did the State cease to be a member of the Union?

It is needless to discuss at length the question whether the right of a State to withdraw from the Union for any cause, regarded by itself as sufficient, is consistent with the Constitution of the United States.

The Union of the States was never a purely artificial and arbitrary relation. It began among the Colonies, and grew out of common origin, mutual sympathies, kindred principles, similar interests, and geographical relations. It was confirmed and strengthened by the necessities of war, and received definite form, and character, and sanction from the Articles of Confederation. By these the Union was solemnly declared to be "perpetual." And when these Articles were found to be inadequate to the exigencies of the country, the Constitution was ordained "to form a more perfect Union." It is difficult to convey the idea of indissoluble unity more clearly than by these words. What can be indissoluble if a perpetual Union made more perfect, is not?

But the perpetuity and indissolubility of the Union by no means implies the loss of distinct and individual existence, or of the right of self-government by the States. Under the Articles of Confederation each State retained its sovereignty, freedom, and independence, and every power, jurisdiction, and right not expressly delegated to the United States. Under the Constitution, though the powers of the States were much restricted, still, all powers not delegated to the United States, nor prohibited to the States, are reserved to the States, respectively, or to the people. And we have already had occasion to remark at this term, that "the people of each State compose a State, having, its own government, and endowed with all the functions essential to separate and independent existence," and that "without the States in union, there could be no such political body as the United States." Not only, therefore, can there be no loss of separate and independent autonomy to the States, through their union under the Constitution, but it may be not unreasonably said that the preservation of the States, and the maintenance of their governments, are as much within the design and care of the Constitution as the preservation of the Union and the maintenance of the National government. The Constitution, in all its provisions, looks to an indestructible Union, composed of indestructible States.

When, therefore, Texas became one of the United States, she entered into an indissoluble relation. All the obligations of perpetual union, and all the guaranties of republican government in the Union, attached at once to the State. The act which consummated her admission into the Union was something more than a compact; it was the incorporation of a new member into the political body. And it was final. The union between Texas and the other States was as complete, as perpetual, and as indissoluble as the union between the original States. There was no place for reconsideration or revocation except through revolution, or through consent of the States.

Considered therefore as transactions under the Constitution, the ordinance of secession, adopted by the convention and ratified by a majority of the citizens of Texas, and all the acts of her legislature intended to give effect to that ordinance, were absolutely void. They were utterly without operation in law. The obligations of the State, as a member of the Union, and of every citizen of the State,

remained perfect and unimpaired. It certainly follows that the State did not cease to be a State, nor her citizens to be citizens of the Union. If this were otherwise, the State must have become foreign, and her citizens foreigners. The war must have become a war for conquest and subjugation.

Our conclusion therefore is, that Texas continued to be a State, and a State of the Union, notwithstanding the transactions to which we have referred.

But in order to the exercise by a State, of the right to sue in this court, there needs to be a state government, competent to represent the State in its relations with the National government, so far at least as the institution and prosecution of a suit is concerned.

And it is by no means a logical conclusion, from the premises which we have endeavored to establish, that the governmental relations of Texas to the Union remained unaltered. . . . No one has been bold enough to contend that, while Texas was controlled by a government hostile to the United States, and in affiliation with a hostile confederation, waging war upon the United States, senators chosen by her legislature, or representatives elected by her citizens, were entitled to seats in Congress, or that any suit, instituted in her name, could be entertained in this court. All admit that, during this condition of civil war, the rights of the State as a member, and of her people as citizens of the Union, were suspended. The government and the citizens of the State, refusing to recognize their constitutional obligations, assumed the character of enemies, and incurred the consequences of rebellion.

These new relations imposed new duties upon the United States. The first was that of suppressing the rebellion. The next was that of re-establishing the broken relations of the State with the Union. The first of these duties having been performed, the next necessarily engaged the attention of the National government.

The authority for the performance of the first had been found in the power to suppress insurrection and carry on war; for the performance of the second, authority was derived from the obligation of the United States to guarantee to every State in the Union a republican form of government. The latter, indeed, in the case of a rebellion which involves the government of a State, and for the time excludes the National authority from its limits, seems to be a necessary complement to the former.

Of this the case of Texas furnishes a striking illustration. When the war closed there was no government in the State except that which had been organized for the purpose of waging war against the United States. That government immediately disappeared. . . .

There being no government in Texas in constitutional relations with the Union, it became the duty of the United States to provide for the restoration of such a government. . . .

It is not important to review, at length, the measures which have been taken under this power, by the executive and legislative departments of the National government. It is proper, however, to observe the almost immediately after the cessation of organized hostilities, and while the war yet smouldered in Texas, the President of the United States issued his proclamation appointing a provisional governor for the State, and providing for the assembling of a convention, with a view to the re-establishment of a republican government, under an amended constitution, and to the restoration of the State to her proper constitutional relations. A convention was accordingly assembled, the constitution amended, elections held, and a state government, acknowledging its obligations to the Union, established.

Whether the action thus taken was, in all respects, warranted by the Constitution, it is not now necessary to determine. The power exercised by the President was supposed, doubtless, to be derived from his constitutional functions as commander-in-chief; and, so long as the war continued, it cannot be denied that he might institute temporary government within insurgent districts, occupied by the National forces, or take measures, in any State, for the restoration of state government faithful to the Union, employing, however, in such efforts, only such means and agents as were authorized by constitutional laws.

But the power to carry into effect the clause of the guaranty is primarily a legislative power, and resides in Congress. . . .

The action of the President must, therefore, be considered as provisional, and in that light it seems to have been regarded by Congress. It was taken after the term of the 38th Congress had expired. The 39th Congress, which assembled in December, 1865, followed by the 40th Congress, which met in March, 1867, proceeded, after long deliberation, to adopt various measures for reorganization and restoration. These measures were embodied in proposed amendments to the Constitution, and in the acts known as the Reconstruction Acts, which have been so far carried into effect, that a majority of the States which were engaged in the rebellion have been restored to their constitutional relations, under forms of government, adjudged to be republican by Congress, through the admission of their "Senators and Representatives into the councils of the Union."

Nothing in the case before us requires the court to pronounce judgment upon the constitutionality of any particular provision of these acts. . . .

What has thus been said generally describes, with sufficient accuracy, the situation of Texas. A provisional governor of the State was appointed by the President in 1865; in 1866 a governor was elected by the people under the constitution of that year; at a subsequent date a governor was appointed by the commander of the district. Each of the three exercised executive functions and actually represented the State in the executive department.

In the case before us each has given his sanction to the prosecution of the suit, and we find no difficulty, without investigating the legal title of either to the executive office, in holding that the sanction thus given sufficiently warranted the action of the solicitor and counsel in behalf of the State. The necessary conclusion is that the suit was instituted and is prosecuted by competent authority. . . .

[The court then considered the validity of the acts of the state government during the period of secession and held the transfer of the bonds by that government void.]

It follows that the title of the State was not divested by the act of the insurgent government in entering into this contract. . . .

On the whole case, therefore, our conclusion is that the State of Texas is entitled to the relief sought by her bill, and a decree must be made accordingly.

GRIER, J., delivered a dissenting opinion in which Justices SWAYNE and MILLER concurred.

279. GRANT'S APPEAL FOR THE ANNEXATION OF SANTO DOMINGO
May 31, 1870

(Richardson, ed. *Messages and Papers*, Vol. VII, p. 61 ff.)

Grant, who was anxious to secure the annexation of the Dominican Republic, sent his secretary Babcock to Santo Domingo to survey the situation; Babcock returned with a treaty of annexation. Grant submitted this irregular document to his Cabinet only to meet unanimous opposition. A more formal treaty was then drawn up and submitted to the Senate January 10, 1870; on the 15th of March the Committee on Foreign Relations reported adversely on ratification and Sumner delivered his famous "Naboth's Vineyard" speech, which cost him the Chairmanship of the Foreign Relations Committee. For his opposition to the Treaty, Attorney General E. R. Hoar was forced to resign. See, S. F. Bemis, ed. *American Secretaries of State,* Vol. VII, p. 147 ff.; E. L. Pierce, *Memoir and Letters of Charles Sumner,* Vol. IV, 425 ff.; A. Nevins, *Hamilton Fish and the Grant Administration.*

EXECUTIVE MANSION, *May 31, 1870.*
To the Senate of the United States:

I transmit to the Senate, for consideration with a view to its ratification, an additional article to the treaty of the 29th of November last, for the annexation of the Dominican Republic to the United States, stipulating for an extension of the time for exchanging the ratifications thereof, signed in this city on the 14th instant by the plenipotentiaries of the parties.

It was my intention to have also negotiated with the plenipotentiary of San Domingo amendments to the treaty of annexation to obviate objections which may be urged against the treaty as it is now worded; but on reflection I deem it better to submit to the Senate the propriety of their amending the treaty as follows: First, to specify that the obligations of this Government shall not exceed the $1,500,000 stipulated in the treaty; secondly, to determine the manner of appointing the agents to receive and disburse the same; thirdly, to determine the class of creditors who shall take precedence in the settlement of their claims; and, finally, to insert such amendments as may suggest themselves to the minds of Senators to carry out in good faith the conditions of the treaty submitted to the Senate of the United States in January last, according to the spirit and intent of that treaty. From the most reliable information I can obtain, the sum specified in the treaty will pay every just claim against the Republic of San Domingo and leave a balance sufficient to carry on a Territorial government until such time as new laws for providing a Territorial revenue can be enacted and put in force.

I feel an unusual anxiety for the ratification of this treaty, because I believe it will redound greatly to the glory of the two countries interested, to civilization, and to the extirpation of the institution of slavery.

The doctrine promulgated by President Monroe has been adhered to by all political parties, and I now deem it proper to assert the equally important principle that hereafter no territory on this continent shall be regarded as subject of transfer to a European power.

The Government of San Domingo has voluntarily sought this annexation. It is a weak power, numbering probably less than 120,000 souls, and yet possessing one of the richest territories under the sun, capable of supporting a population of 10,000,000 people in luxury. The people of San Domingo are not capable of maintaining themselves in their present condition, and must look for outside support.

They yearn for the protection of our free institutions and laws, our progress and civilization. Shall we refuse them?

I have information which I believe reliable that a European power stands ready now to offer $2,000,000 for the possession of Samana Bay alone. If refused by us, with what grace can we prevent a foreign power from attempting to secure the prize?

The acquisition of San Domingo is desirable because of its geographical position. It commands the entrance to the Caribbean Sea and the Isthmus transit of commerce. It possesses the richest soil, best and most capacious harbors, most salubrious climate, and the most valuable products of the forest, mine, and soil of any of the West India Islands. Its possession by us will in a few years build up a coastwise commerce of immense magnitude, which will go far toward restoring to us our lost merchant marine. It will give to us those articles which we consume so largely and do not produce, thus equalizing our exports and imports.

In case of foreign war it will give us command of all the islands referred to, and thus prevent an enemy from ever again possessing himself of rendezvous upon our very coast.

At present our coast trade between the States bordering on the Atlantic and those bordering on the Gulf of Mexico is cut into by the Bahamas and the Antilles. Twice we must, as it were, pass through foreign countries to get by sea from Georgia to the west coast of Florida.

San Domingo, with a stable government, under which her immense resources can be developed, will give remunerative wages to tens of thousands of laborers not now on the island.

This labor will take advantage of every available means of transportation to abandon the adjacent islands and seek the blessings of freedom and its sequence—each inhabitant receiving the reward of his own labor. Porto Rico and Cuba will have to abolish slavery, as a measure of self-preservation to retain their laborers.

San Domingo will become a large consumer of the products of Northern farms and manufactories. The cheap rate at which her citizens can be furnished with food, tools, and machinery will make it necessary that the contiguous islands should have the same advantages in order to compete in the production of sugar, coffee, tobacco, tropical fruits, etc. This will open to us a still wider market for our products.

The production of our own supply of these articles will cut off more than one hundred millions of our annual imports, besides largely increasing our exports. With such a picture it is easy to see how our large debt abroad is ultimately to be extinguished. With a balance of trade against us (including interest on bonds held by foreigners and money spent by our citizens traveling in foreign lands) equal to the entire yield of the precious metals in this country, it is not so easy to see how this result is to be otherwise accomplished.

The acquisition of San Domingo is an adherence to the "Monroe doctrine;" it is a measure of national protection; it is asserting our just claim to a controlling influence over the great commercial traffic soon to flow from east to west by the way of the Isthmus of Darien; it is to build up our merchant marine; it is to furnish new markets for the products of our farms, shops, and manufactories; it is to make slavery insupportable in Cuba and Porto Rico at once and ultimately so in Brazil; it is to settle the unhappy condition of Cuba, and end an exterminating conflict; it is to provide honest means of paying our honest debts, without overtaxing the people; it is to furnish our citizens with the necessaries of everyday life at cheaper rates than ever before; and it is, in fine, a rapid stride toward that greatness which the intelligence, industry, and enterprise of the citizens of the United States entitle this country to assume among nations.

U. S. GRANT.

280. THE LEGAL TENDER CASES
12 Wallace, 457
1871

These were two cases involving the constitutionality of the legal tender acts of 1862 and 1863. The first case, *Knox* v. *Lee,* came on a writ of error from the Western District of Texas; the second, *Parker* v. *Davis,* came on a writ of error to the Supreme Judicial Court of Massachusetts. In the case of *Hepburn* v. *Griswold,* 8 Wallace 603, the Court, which then consisted of only eight judges, held the legal tender acts of 1862 and 1863 unconstitutional by a vote of five to three. Shortly before this decision was announced Justice Grier resigned.

There were therefore two vacancies on the Court, and President Grant promptly filled them by the appointment of J. P. Bradley and W. Strong. Both of these justices maintained the constitutionality of the legal tender acts, Justice Strong delivering the opinion of the Court in the Legal Tender Cases. It was at the time freely charged that President Grant had packed the Court. On the Legal Tender Cases see C. Warren, *Supreme Court,* 1928 ed., Vol. II, ch. xxxi; H. L. Carson, *The Supreme Court,* p. 442 ff.; L. Boudin, *Government by Judiciary,* Vol. II, ch. xxv; G. Bancroft, *A Plea for the Constitution of the United States Wounded in the House of its Guardians;* G. F. Hoar, *The Charge of Packing the Court Against President Grant and Attorney-General Hoar;* E. J. James, *The Legal Tender Decisions.*

STRONG, J., The controlling questions in these cases are the following: Are the acts of Congress, known as the legal tender acts, constitutional when applied to contracts made before their passage; and, secondly, Are they valid as applicable to debts contracted since their enactment? . . . It would be difficult to overestimate the consequences which must follow our decision. They will affect the entire business of the country, and take hold of the possible continued existence of the government. If it be held by this court that Congress has no constitutional power, under any circumstances, or in any emergency, to make treasury notes a legal tender for the payment of all debts (a power confessedly possessed by every independent sovereignty other than the United States), the government is without those means of self-preservation which, all must admit, may, in certain contingencies, become indispensable, even if they were not when the acts of Congress now called in question were enacted. . . .

The consequences of which we have spoken, serious as they are, must be accepted, if there is a clear incompatibility between the Constitution and the legal tender acts. But we are unwilling to precipitate them upon the country unless such incompatibility plainly appears. A decent respect for a co-ordinate branch of the government demands that the judiciary should presume, until the contrary is clearly shown, that there has been no transgression of power by Congress—all the members of which act under the obligation of an oath of fidelity to the Constitution. . . .

Nor can it be questioned that, when investigating the nature and extent of the powers conferred by the Constitution upon Congress, it is indispensable to keep in view the objects for which those powers were granted. This is the universal rule of construction applied alike to statutes, wills, contracts, and constitutions. If the general purpose of the instrument is ascertained, the language of its provisions must be construed with reference to that purpose and so as to subserve it. In no other way can the intent of the framers of the instrument be discovered. And there are more urgent reasons for looking to the ultimate purpose in examining the powers conferred by a constitution than there are in construing a statute, a will, or a contract. We do not expect to find in a constitution minute details. It is necessarily brief and comprehensive. It prescribes outlines, leaving the filling up to be deduced from the outlines. . . .

If these are correct principles, if they are proper views of the manner in which the Constitution is to be understood, the powers conferred upon Congress must be regarded as related to each other, and all means for a common end. Each is but part of a system, a constituent of one whole. No single power is the ultimate end for which the Constitution was adopted. It may, in a very proper sense, be treated as a means for the accomplishment of a subordinate object, but that object is itself a means designed for an ulterior purpose. Thus the power to levy and collect taxes, to coin money and regulate its value, to raise and support armies, or to provide for and maintain a navy, are instruments for the paramount object, which was to establish a government, sovereign within its sphere, with capability of self-preservation, thereby forming a union more perfect than that which existed under the old Confederacy.

The same may be asserted also of all the non-enumerated powers included in the authority expressly given "to make all laws which shall be necessary and proper for carrying into execution the specified powers vested in Congress, and all other powers vested by the Constitution in the government of the United States, or in any department or officer thereof." It is impossible to know what those non-enumerated powers are, and what is their nature and extent, without considering the purposes they were intended to subserve. Those purposes, it must be noted, reach beyond the mere execution of all powers definitely intrusted to Congress and mentioned in detail. They embrace the execution of all other powers vested by the Constitution in the government of the United States, or in any department or officer thereof. It certainly was intended to confer upon the government the power of self-preservation. . . .

That would appear, then, to be a most unreasonable construction of the Constitution which denies to the government created by it, the right to employ freely every means, not prohibited, necessary for its preservation, and for the fulfillment of its acknowledged duties. Such a right, we hold, was given by the last clause of the eighth section of its first article. The means or instrumentalities referred to in that clause, and authorized, are not enumerated or defined. In the nature of things enumeration and specification were impossible. But they were left to the discretion of Congress, subject only to the restrictions that they be not prohibited, and be necessary and proper for carrying into execution the enumerated powers given to Congress, and all other powers vested in the government of the United States, or in any department or officer thereof.

And here it is to be observed it is not indispensable to the existence, of any power claimed for the federal government that it can be found specified in the words of the Constitution, or clearly and directly traceable to some one of the specified powers. Its existence may be deduced fairly from more than one of the substantive powers expressly defined, or from them all combined. It is allowable to group together any number of them and infer from them all that the power claimed has been conferred. . . . And it is of importance to observe that Congress has often exercised, without question, powers that are not expressly given nor ancillary to any single enumerated power. Powers thus exercised are what are called by Judge Story, in his Commentaries on the Constitution, resulting powers, arising from the aggregate powers of the government. He instances the right to sue and make contracts. Many others might be given. The oath required by law from officers of the government is one. So is

building a capitol or a presidential mansion, and so also is the penal code. . . .

Indeed, the whole history of the government and of congressional legislation has exhibited the use of a very wide discretion, even in times of peace and in the absence of any trying emergency, in the selection of the necessary and proper means to carry into effect the great objects for which the government was framed, and this discretion has generally been unquestioned, or, if questioned, sanctioned by this court. . . .

Before we can hold the Legal Tender Acts unconstitutional, we must be convinced they were not appropriate means, or means conducive to the execution of any or all of the powers of Congress, or of the government, not appropriate in any plain degree (for we are not judges of the degree of appropriateness), or we must hold that they were prohibited. This brings us to the inquiry whether they were, when enacted, appropriate instrumentalities for carrying into effect, or executing any of the known powers of Congress, or of any department of the government. Plainly, to this inquiry, a consideration of the time when they were enacted, and of the circumstances in which the government then stood, is important. It is not to be denied that acts may be adapted to the exercise of lawful power, and appropriate to it, in seasons of exigency, which would be inappropriate at other times.

We do not propose to dilate at length upon the circumstances in which the country was placed, when Congress attempted to make treasury notes a legal tender. They are of too recent occurrence to justify enlarged description. Suffice it to say that a civil war was then raging which seriously threatened the overthrow of the government and the destruction of the Constitution itself. It demanded the equipment and support of large armies and navies, and the employment of money to an extent beyond the capacity of all ordinary sources of supply. Meanwhile the public treasury was nearly empty, and the credit of the government, if not stretched to its utmost tension, had become nearly exhausted. . . .

It was at such a time and in such circumstances that Congress was called upon to devise means for maintaining the army and navy, for securing the large supplies of money needed, and, indeed, for the preservation of the government created by the Constitution. It was at such a time and in such an emergency that the Legal Tender Acts were passed. Now, if it were certain that nothing else would have supplied the absolute necessities of the treasury, that nothing else would have enabled the government to maintain its armies and navy, that nothing else would have saved the government and the Constitution from destruction, while the Legal Tender Acts would, could any one be bold enough to assert that Congress transgressed its powers? . . .

But if it be conceded that some other means might have been chosen for the accomplishment of these legitimate and necessary ends, the concession does not weaken the

argument. . . . At best this is mere conjecture. But admitting it to be true, what does it prove? Nothing more than that Congress had the choice of means for a legitimate end, each appropriate and adapted to that end, though, perhaps, in different degrees. What then? Can this court say that it ought to have adopted one rather than the other? . . .

We hold the acts of Congress constitutional as applied to contracts made either before or after their passage. In so holding we overrule so much of what was decided in *Hepburn* v. *Griswold,* 8 Wallace, 603, as ruled the acts unwarranted by the Constitution so far as applied to contracts made before their enactment. . . .

Judgment in each case affirmed.

CHASE, C. J. and CLIFFORD, J., NELSON, J. and FIELD, J. dissenting.

281. THE TREATY OF WASHINGTON
May 8, 1871

(Malloy, ed. *Treaties, Conventions, etc.* Vol. I, p. 700 ff.)

The failure of the Johnson-Clarendon Convention of 1869 left Anglo-American relations in an unsatisfactory state. The Treaty of Washington provided for the arbitration of the most pressing problem of our relations with Great Britain —the Alabama Claims. The Treaty represented a triumph of the ideas of Secretary of State Fish over those of Charles Sumner. On the Treaty of Washington, see C. Cushing, *The Treaty of Washington;* J. C. Bancroft Davis, *Mr. Fish and the Treaty of Washington;* D. H. Chamberlain, *Charles Sumner and the Treaty of Washington;* S. F. Bemis, ed. *American Secretaries of State,* Vol. VII, p. 165 ff.; *Papers Relating to the Treaty of Washington,* in *Foreign Relations of the United States,* 1872, Part II.

TREATY RELATIVE TO CLAIMS, FISHERIES, NAVIGATION OF THE ST. LAWRENCE, ETC., AMERICAN LUMBER ON THE RIVER ST. JOHN; BOUNDARY.

ART. I. Whereas differences have arisen between the Government of the United States and the Government of Her Britannic Majesty, and still exist, growing out of the acts committed by the several vessels which have given rise to the claims generically known as the "Alabama Claims:"

And whereas Her Britannic Majesty has authorized her High Commissioners and Plenipotentiaries to express, in a friendly

spirit, the regret felt by Her Majesty's Government for the escape, under whatever circumstances, of the Alabama and other vessels from British ports, and for the depredations committed by those vessels:

Now, in order to remove and adjust all complaints and claims on the part of the United States, and to provide for the speedy settlement of such claims which are not admitted by Her Britannic Majesty's Government, the high contracting parties agree that all the said claims, growing out of acts committed by the aforesaid vessels and generically known as the "Alabama Claims," shall be referred to a tribunal of arbitration to be composed of five Arbitrators, to be appointed in the following manner, that is to say: One shall be named by the President of the United States; one shall be named by Her Britannic Majesty; His Majesty the King of Italy shall be requested to name one; the President of the Swiss Confederation shall be requested to name one; and His Majesty the Emperor of Brazil shall be requested to name one. . . .

ART. II. The Arbitrators shall meet at Geneva, in Switzerland, at the earliest convenient day . . . and shall proceed impartially and carefully to examine and decide all questions that shall be laid before them on the part of the Governments of the United States and Her Britannic Majesty respectively. All questions considered by the tribunal, including the final award, shall be decided by a majority of all the Arbitrators. . . .

ART. VI. In deciding the matters submitted to the Arbitrators, they shall be governed by the following three rules, . . . and by such principles of international law not inconsistent therewith as the Arbitrators shall determine to have been applicable to the case.

RULES.

A neutral Government is bound—

First, to use due diligence to prevent the fitting out, arming, or equipping, within its jurisdiction, of any vessel which it has reasonable ground to believe is intended to cruise or to carry on war against any Power with which it is at peace; and also to use like diligence to prevent the departure from its jurisdiction of any vessel intended to cruise or carry on war as above, such vessel having been specially adapted, in whole or in part, within such jurisdiction, to warlike use.

Secondly, not to permit or suffer either belligerent to make use of its ports or waters as the base of naval operations against the other, or for the purpose of renewal or augmentation of military supplies or arms, or the recruitment of men.

Thirdly, to exercise due diligence in its own ports and waters, and, as to all persons within its jurisdiction, to prevent any violation of the foregoing obligations and duties.

Her Britannic Majesty has commanded her High Commissioners and Plenipotentiaries to declare that Her Majesty's Government cannot assent to the foregoing rules as a statement of principles of international law which were in force at the time when the claims mentioned in Article I. arose, but that Her Majesty's Government, in order to evince its desire of strengthening the friendly relations between the two countries, and of making satisfactory provision for the future, agrees that in deciding the questions between the two countries arising out of those claims, the Arbitrators should assume that Her Majesty's Government had undertaken to act upon the principles set forth in these rules.

And the high contracting parties agree to observe these rules as between themselves in future, and to bring them to the knowledge of other maritime Powers, and to invite them to accede to them.

ART. VII. . . . The said tribunal shall first determine as to each vessel separately whether Great Britain has, by any act or omission, failed to fulfil any of the duties set forth in the foregoing three rules, or recognized by the principles of international law not inconsistent with such rules. . . . In case the tribunal find that Great Britain has failed to fulfil any duty or duties as aforesaid, it may, if it think proper, proceed to award a sum in gross to be paid by Great Britain to the United States for all the claims referred to it. . . .

282. THE COLLECTOR v. DAY
11 Wallace, 113
1871

Error to the U.S. circuit court for the district of Massachusetts. This case involved the constitutionality of a federal income tax on the salary of a State official. The dissenting opinion expresses a view more widely held today than at the time of its announcement.

NELSON, J. The case presents the question whether or not it is competent for Congress, under the Constitution of the United States, to impose a tax upon a salary of a judicial officer of a State?

In *Dobbins* v. *The Commissioners of Erie County,* 16 Peters, 435, it was decided that it was not competent for the legislature of a State to levy a tax upon the salary or emoluments of an officer of the United States. The decision was placed mainly upon the ground that the officer was a means or instrumentality employed for carrying into effect some of the legitimate powers of the government, which could not be interfered with by taxation or otherwise by the States, and that the salary or compensation for the service of the officer was inseparably connected with the office; that if the officer, as such, was exempt, the salary assigned for his support or maintenance while holding the office was also, for like reasons, equally exempt. . . .

We shall now proceed to show that, upon the same construction of that instrument, and for like reasons, that government is prohibited from taxing the salary of the judicial officer of a State. . . .

The general government, and the States, although both exist within the same territorial limits, are separate and distinct sovereignties, acting separately and independently of each other, within their respective spheres. The former in its appropriate sphere is supreme but the States within the limits of their powers not granted, or, in the language of the Tenth Amendment, "reserved," are as independent of the general government as that government within its sphere is independent of the States.

The relations existing between the two governments are well stated by the present Chief Justice [CHASE] in the case of *Lane County v. Oregon,* 7 Wallace, 76. "Both the States and the United States," he observed, "existed before the Constitution. The people, through that instrument, established a more perfect union, by substituting a National government, acting with ample powers directly upon the citizens, instead of the Confederate government, which acted with powers greatly restricted, only upon the States. But, in many of the articles of the Constitution, the necessary existence of the States, and within their proper spheres, the independent authority of the States, are distinctly recognized. To them nearly the whole charge of interior regulation is committed or left; to them, and to the people, all powers, not expressly delegated to the National government, are reserved." Upon looking into the Constitution, it will be found that but few of the articles in that instrument could be carried into practical effect without the existence of the States.

Two of the great departments of the government, the executive and legislative, depend upon the exercise of the powers, or upon the people of the States. The Constitution guarantees to the States a republican form of government, and protects each against invasion or domestic violence. Such being the separate and independent condition of the States in our complex system, as recognized by the Constitution, and the existence of which is so indispensable, that, without them, the general government itself would disappear from the family of nations, it would seem to follow, as a reasonable, if not a necessary consequence, that the means and instrumentalities employed for carrying on the operations of their governments, for preserving their existence, and fulfilling the high and responsible duties assigned to them in the Constitution, should be left free and unimpaired, should not be liable to be crippled, much less defeated, by the taxing power of another government, which power acknowledges no limits but the will of the legislative body imposing the tax. And, more especially, those means and instrumentalities which are the creation of their sovereign and reserved rights, one of which is the establishment of the judicial department, and the appointment of officers to administer their laws. Without this power, and the exercise of it, we risk nothing in saying that no one of the States under the form of government guaranteed by the Constitution could long preserve its existence. . . .

The supremacy of the general government, therefore, so much relied on in the argument of the counsel for the plaintiff in error, in respect to the question before us, cannot be maintained. The two governments are upon an equality, and the question is whether the power "to lay and collect taxes" enables the general government to tax the salary of a judicial officer of the State, which officer is a means or instrumentality employed to carry into execution one of its most important functions, the administration of the laws, and which concerns the exercise of a right reserved to the States?

. . . In respect to the reserved powers, the State is as sovereign and independent as the general government. And if the means and instrumentalities employed by that government to carry into operation the powers granted to it are, necessarily, and, for the sake of self-preservation, exempt from taxation by the States, why are not those of the States depending upon their reserved powers, for like reasons, equally exempt from federal taxation? Their unimpaired existence in the one case is as essential as in the other. It is admitted that there is no express provision in the Constitution that prohibits the general government from taxing the means and instrumentalities of the States, nor is there any prohibiting the States from taxing the means and instrumentalities of that government. In both cases the exemption rests upon necessary implication, and is upheld by the great law of self-preservation; as any government, whose means employed in conducting its operations, if subject to the control of another and distinct government, can exist only at the mercy of that government. Of what avail are these means if another power may tax them at discretion? . . .

Judgment affirmed.

Mr. Justice BRADLEY dissenting,

I dissent from the opinion of the court in this case, because it seems to me that the general government has the same power of taxing the income of officers of the state governments as it has of taxing that of its own officers. It is the common government of all alike; and every citizen is presumed to trust his own government in the matter of taxation. No man ceases to be a citizen of the United States by being an officer under the state government. I cannot accede to the doctrine that the general government is to be regarded as in any sense foreign or antagonistic to the state governments, their officers, or people; nor can I agree that a presumption can be admitted that the general government will act in a manner hostile to the existence or functions of the state governments, which are constituent parts of the system or body politic forming the basis on which the general government is founded. The taxation by the state governments of the instruments em-

ployed by the general government in the exercise of its powers, is a very different thing. Such taxation involves an interference with the powers of a government in which other states and their citizens are equally interested with the state which imposes the taxation. In my judgment, the limitation of the power of taxation in the general government, which the present decision establishes, will be found very difficult of control. Where are we to stop in enumerating the functions of the state governments which will be interfered with by federal taxation? If a state incorporates a railroad to carry out its purposes of internal improvement, or a bank to aid its financial arrangements, reserving, perhaps, a percentage on the stock or profits, for the supply of its own treasury, will the bonds or stock of such an institution be free from federal taxation? How can we now tell what the effect of this decision will be? I cannot but regard it as founded on a fallacy, and that it will lead to mischievous consequences. I am as much opposed as any one can be to any interference by the general government with the just powers of the state governments. But no concession of any of the just powers of the general government can easily be recalled. I, therefore, consider it my duty to at least record my dissent when such concession appears to be made. An extended discussion of the subject would answer no useful purpose.

283. LIBERAL REPUBLICAN PARTY PLATFORM
Cincinnati, Ohio
May 1; 1872

(K. Porter, ed. *National Party Platforms*, p. 77 ff.)

The Liberal Republican movement represented a reaction from the Radical Republican policy toward the South and from the corruption of the Grant administration. The movement had its genesis in Sumner's break with Grant over the Santo Domingo affair and in a party division in Missouri. The Cincinnati convention nominated Horace Greeley for the Presidency, and the Democrats in their Baltimore Convention accepted this candidate. See, E. D. Ross, *The Liberal Republican Movement;* T. S. Barclay, *The Liberal Republican Movement in Missouri;* E. P. Oberholtzer, *History of the United States Since the Civil War,* Vol. III, ch. i.

Cincinnati, Ohio, May 1, 1872

We, the Liberal Republicans of the United States, in National Convention assembled at Cincinnati, proclaim the following principles as essential to just government:

1. We recognize the equality of all men before the law, and hold that it is the duty of Government, in its dealings with the people to mete out equal and exact justice to all, of whatever nativity, race, color, or persuasion, religious or political.

2. We pledge ourselves to maintain the

union of these States, emancipation and enfranchisement, and to oppose any reopening of the questions settled by the Thirteenth, Fourteenth, and Fifteenth Amendments to the Constitution.

3. We demand the immediate and absolute removal of all disabilities imposed on account of the Rebellion, which was finally subdued seven years ago, believing that universal amnesty will result in complete pacification in all sections of the country.

4. Local self-government, with impartial suffrage, will guard the rights of all citizens more securely than any centralized power. The public welfare requires the supremacy of the civil over the military authority, and freedom of person under the protection of the *habeas corpus*. We demand for the individual the largest liberty consistent with public order; for the State self-government, and for the nation a return to the methods of peace and the constitutional limitations of power.

5. The Civil Service of the Government has become a mere instrument of partisan tyranny and personal ambition, and an object of selfish greed. It is a scandal and reproach upon free institutions, and breeds a demoralization dangerous to the perpetuity of republican government. We therefore regard such thorough reforms of the Civil Service as one of the most pressing necessities of the hour; that honesty, capacity, and fidelity, constitute the only valid claims to public employment; that the offices of the Government cease to be a matter of arbitrary favoritism and patronage, and that public station become again a post of honor. To this end it is imperatively required that no President shall be a candidate for re-election.

6. We demand a system of Federal taxation which shall not unnecessarily interfere with the industry of the people, and which

shall provide the means necessary to pay the expenses of the Government economically administered, the pensions, the interest on the public debt, and a moderate reduction annually of the principal thereof; and, recognizing that there are in our midst honest but irreconcilable differences of opinion with regard to the respective systems of Protection and Free Trade, we remit the discussion of the subject to the people in their Congressional Districts, and to the decision of Congress thereon, wholly free of Executive interference or dictation.

7. The public credit must be sacredly maintained, and we denounce repudiation in every form and guise.

8. A speedy return to specie payment is demanded alike by the highest considerations of commercial morality and honest government.

9. We remember with gratitude the heroism and sacrifices of the soldiers and sailors of the republic, and no act of ours shall ever detract from their justly-earned fame, or the full reward of their patriotism.

10. We are opposed to all further grants of land to railroads or other corporations. The public domain should be held sacred to actual settlers.

11. We hold that it is the duty of the Government, in its intercourse with foreign nations, to cultivate the friendship of peace, by treating with all on fair and equal terms, regarding it alike dishonorable either to demand what is not right, or to submit to what is wrong.

12. For the promotion and success of these vital principles, and the support of the candidates nominated by this convention we invite and cordially welcome the cooperation of all patriotic citizens, without regard to previous affiliations.

284. THE SLAUGHTER-HOUSE CASES
16 Wallace, 36
1873

Error to the supreme court of Louisiana. In 1869 the legislature of Louisiana, in order to protect the health of the people of New Orleans, granted to a slaughter-house company for twenty-five years the exclusive privilege of conducting a slaughter-house within the city limits

of New Orleans. The validity of the act was challenged on the ground that it violated the Fourteenth Amendment. The opinion of the court is memorable as one of the earliest interpretations of the Fourteenth Amendment. Note especially the scant consideration given by the Court to the due process clause of the Amendment. See Warren, *Supreme Court,* Vol. II, ch. xxxii.

MILLER, J. . . . The plaintiffs in error . . . allege that the statute is a violation of the Constitution of the United States in these several particulars:

That it creates an involuntary servitude forbidden by the Thirteenth Article of Amendment;

That it abridges the privileges and immunities of citizens of the United States;

That it denies to the plaintiffs the equal protection of the laws; and,

That it deprives them of their property without due process of law; contrary to the provisions of the first section of the Fourteenth Article of Amendment.

This court is thus called upon for the first time to give construction of these articles. . . .

Twelve articles of amendment were added to the federal Constitution soon after the original organization of the government under it in 1789. . . . Within the last eight years three other articles of amendment of vast importance have been added by the voice of the people to that now venerable instrument.

The most cursory glance at these articles discloses a unity of purpose, when taken in connection with the history of the times, which cannot fail to have an important bearing on any question of doubt concerning their true meaning. Nor can such doubts, when any reasonably exist, be safely and rationally solved without a reference to that history; for in it is found the occasion and the necessity for recurring again to the great source of power in this country, the people of the States, for additional guarantees of human rights; additional powers to the federal government; additional restraints upon those of the States. . . .

We repeat, then, in the light of this recapitulation of events, almost too recent to be called history, but which are familiar to us all; and on the most casual examination of the language of these amendments, no one can fail to be impressed with the one pervading purpose found in them all, lying at the foundation of each, and without which none of them would have been even suggested; we mean the freedom of the slave race, the se-

curity and firm establishment of that freedom, and the protection of the newly-made freeman and citizen from the oppressions of those who had formerly exercised unlimited dominion over him. It is true that only the Fifteenth Amendment, in terms, mentions the negro by speaking of his color and his slavery. But it is just as true that each of the other articles was addressed to the grievances of that race, and designed to remedy them as the Fifteenth.

We do not say that no one else but the negro can share in this protection. Both the language and spirit of these articles are to have their fair and just weight in any question of construction. Undoubtedly while negro slavery alone was in the mind of the Congress which proposed the thirteenth article, it forbids any other kind of slavery, now or hereafter. If Mexican peonage or the Chinese coolie labor system shall develop slavery of the Mexican or Chinese race within our territory, this amendment may safely be trusted to make it void. And so if other rights are assailed by the States which properly and necessarily fall within the protection of these articles, that protection will apply, though the party interested may not be of African descent. But what we do say, and what we wish to be understood is, that in any fair and just construction of any section or phrase of these amendments, it is necessary to look to the purpose which we have said was the pervading spirit of them all, the evil which they were designed to remedy, and the process of continued addition to the Constitution, until that purpose was supposed to be accomplished, as far as constitutional law can accomplish it.

The first section of the fourteenth article, to which our attention is more specially invited, opens with a definition of citizenship— not only citizenship of the United States, but citizenship of the States. No such definition was previously found in the Constitution, nor had any attempt been made to define it by act of Congress. . . . It had been said by eminent judges that no man was a citizen of the United States, except as he was a citizen of one of the States composing the Union. Those, therefore, who had been born and resided always in the District of Columbia or in the Territories, though within the United States, were not citizens. Whether this proposition was sound or not had never been judicially decided. But it had been held by this court, in the celebrated Dred Scott Case, only a few years before the outbreak of the civil war, that a man of African descent, whether a slave or not, could not be a citizen of a State or of the United States. This decision, while it met the condemnation of some of the ablest statesmen and constitutional lawyers of the country, had never been overruled; and if it was to be accepted as a constitutional limitation of the right of citizenship, then all the negro race who had recently been made freemen, were still, not only not citizens, but were incapable of becoming so by anything short of an amendment to the Constitution.

To remove this difficulty primarily, and to establish a clear and comprehensive definition of citizenship which should declare what should constitute citizenship of the United States, and also citizenship of a State, the first clause of the first section was framed.

"All persons born or naturalized in the United States, and subject to the jurisdiction thereof, are citizens of the United States and of the State wherein they reside." . . .

It is quite clear, then, that there is a citizenship of the United States, and a citizenship of a State, which are distinct from each other, and which depend upon different characteristics or circumstances in the individual.

We think this distinction and its explicit recognition in this amendment of great weight in this argument, because the next paragraph of this same section, which is the one mainly relied on by the plaintiffs in error, speaks only of privileges and immunities of citizens of the United States, and does not speak of those of citizens of the several States. The argument, however, in favor of the plaintiffs rests wholly on the assumption that the citizenship is the same, and the privileges and immunities guaranteed by the clause are the same.

The language is, "No State shall make or enforce any law which shall abridge the privileges or immunities of citizens of *the United States*." It is a little remarkable, if this clause was intended as a protection to the citizen of a State against the legislative power of his own State, that the word citizen of the State should be left out when it is so carefully used, and used in contradistinction to citizens of the

United States, in the very sentence which precedes it. It is too clear for argument that the change in phraseology was adopted understandingly and with a purpose.

Of the privileges and immunities of the citizen of the United States, and of the privileges and immunities of the citizen of the State, and what they respectively are, we will presently consider; but we wish to state here that it is only the former which are placed by this clause under the protection of the federal Constitution, and that the latter, whatever they may be, are not intended to have any additional protection by this paragraph of the amendment.

If, then, there is a difference between the privileges and immunities belonging to a citizen of the United States as such, and those belonging to the citizen of the State as such, the latter must rest for their security and protection where they have heretofore rested; for they are not embraced by this paragraph of the amendment.

The first occurrence of the words "privileges and immunities" in our constitutional history, is to be found in the fourth of the Articles of the old Confederation. . . .

In the Constitution of the United States, which superseded the Articles of Confederation, the corresponding provision is found in section two of the fourth article, in the following words: "The citizens of each State shall be entitled to all the privileges and immunities of citizens of the several States."

There can be but little question that the purpose of both these provisions is the same, and that the privileges and immunities intended are the same in each. In the Articles of the Confederation we have some of these specifically mentioned, and enough perhaps to give some general idea of the class of civil rights meant by the phrase.

Fortunately we are not without judicial construction of this clause of the Constitution. . . .

The constitutional provision there alluded to did not create those rights, which it called privileges and immunities of citizens of the States. It threw around them in that clause no security for the citizens of the State in which they were claimed or exercised. Nor did it profess to control the power of the state governments over the rights of its own citizens.

Its sole purpose was to declare to the several States, that whatever those rights, as you grant or establish them to your own citizens, or as you limit or qualify, or impose restrictions on their exercise, the same, neither more nor less, shall be the measure of the rights of citizens of other States within your jurisdiction. . . . But with the exception of . . . a few . . . restrictions, the entire domain of the privileges and immunities of citizens of the States, as above defined, lay within the constitutional and legislative power of the States, and without that of the federal government. Was it the purpose of the Fourteenth Amendment, by the simple declaration that no State should make or enforce any law which shall abridge the privileges and immunities of citizens of the United States, to transfer the security and protection of all the civil rights which we have mentioned, from the States to the federal government? And where it is declared that Congress shall have the power to enforce that article, was it intended to bring within the power of Congress the entire domain of civil rights heretofore belonging exclusively to the States?

All this and more must follow, if the proposition of the plaintiffs in error be sound. For not only are these rights subject to the control of Congress whenever in its discretion any of them are supposed to be abridged by state legislation, but that body may also pass laws in advance, limiting and restricting the exercise of legislative power by the States, in their most ordinary and usual functions, as in its judgment it may think proper on all such subjects. And still further, such a construction followed by the reversal of the judgments of the Supreme Court of Louisiana in these cases, would constitute this court a perpetual censor upon all legislation of the States, on the civil rights of their own citizens, with authority to nullify such as it did not approve as consistent with those rights, as they existed at the time of the adoption of this amendment. The argument, we admit, is not always the most conclusive which is drawn from the consequences urged against the adoption of a particular construction of an instrument. But when, as in the case before us, these consequences are so serious, so far-reaching and pervading, so great a departure from the structure and spirit of our institutions; when the effect is to fetter and degrade the state governments by subjecting them to the control of Congress, in the exercise of powers heretofore universally conceded to them of the most ordinary and fundamental character; when in fact it radically changes the whole theory of the relations of the state and federal governments to each other and of both these governments to the people; the argument has a force that is irresistible, in the absence of language which expresses such a purpose too clearly to admit of doubt.

We are convinced that no such results were intended by the Congress which proposed these amendments, nor by the legislatures of the States which ratified them.

Having shown that the privileges and immunities relied on in the argument are those which belong to citizens of the States as such, and that they are left to the state governments for security and protection, and not by this article placed under the special care of the federal government, we may hold ourselves excused from defining the privileges and immunities of citizens of the United States which no State can abridge, until some case involving those privileges may make it necessary to do so. . . .

But it is useless to pursue this branch of the inquiry, since we are of opinion that the rights claimed by these plaintiffs in error, if they have any existence, are not privileges and immunities of citizens of the United States within the meaning of the clause of the Fourteenth Amendment under consideration. . . .

The argument has not been much pressed in these cases that the defendant's charter deprives the plaintiffs of their property without due process of law, or that it denies to them the equal protection of the law. The first of these paragraphs has been in the Constitution since the adoption of the Fifth Amendment, as a restraint upon the federal power. It is also to be found in some form of expression in the constitutions of nearly all the States, as a restraint upon the power of the States. This law, then, has practically been the same as it now is during the existence of the government, except so far as the present amendment may place the restraining power over the States in this matter in the hands of the federal government.

We are not without judicial interpretation, therefore, both state and national, of the meaning of this clause. And it is sufficient to say that under no construction of that provision that we have ever seen, or any that we deem admissible, can the restraint imposed by the State of Louisiana upon the exercise of their trade by the butchers of New Orleans be held to be a deprivation of property within the meaning of that provision.

"Nor shall any State deny to any person within its jurisdiction the equal protection of the laws."

In the light of the history of these amendments, and the pervading purpose of them, which we have already discussed, it is not difficult to give a meaning to this clause. The existence of laws in the States where the newly emancipated negroes resided, which discriminated with gross injustice and hardship against them as a class, was the evil to be remedied by this clause, and by it such laws are forbidden.

If, however, the States did not conform their laws to its requirements, then by the fifth section of the article of amendment Congress was authorized to enforce it by suitable legislation. We doubt very much whether any action of a State not directed by way of discrimination against the negroes as a class, or on account of their race, will ever be held to come within the purview of this provision. It is so clearly a provision for that race and that emergency, that a strong case would be necessary for its application to any other. But as it is a State that is to be dealt with, and not alone the validity of its laws, we may safely leave that matter until Congress shall have exercised its power, or some case of state oppression, by denial of equal justice in its courts, shall have claimed a decision at our hands. We find no such case in the one before us, and do not deem it necessary to go over the argument again, as it may have relation to this particular clause of the amendment. . . .

Judgment affirmed.

Justice FIELD delivered a dissenting opinion in which Chief Justice CHASE and Justices BRADLEY and SWAYNE concurred.

285. "THE CRIME OF '73"
Coinage Act of February 12, 1873

(U. S. Statutes at Large, Vol. XVII, p. 424 ff.)

This act revising the coinage system of the country omitted from the coinage the standard silver dollar of 412½ grains. This demonetization of silver came later to be known as the "crime of '73". What gave significance to the demonetization of silver was the enormous increase in the American production of silver due to new discoveries of silver ore in the west. The charge that the omission of silver dollars from the coinage was part of a gold conspiracy is rejected by most students of our financial history, but it was an article of faith with a large part of the American people for twenty years. See, J. L. Laughlin, *History of Bimetallism;* A. D. Noyes, *Forty Years of American Finance; Report of the Monetary Commission of 1876;* A. B. Hepburn, *History of Currency in the United States,* ch. xv; W. H. Harvey, *Coin's Financial School.*

An Act revising and amending the Laws relative to the Mints, Assay-offices, and Coinage of the United States.

SEC. 14. That the gold coins of the United States shall be a one-dollar piece, which, at the standard weight of twenty-five and eight-tenths grains, shall be the unit of value; a quarter-eagle, or two-and-a-half dollar piece; a three-dollar piece; a half-eagle, or five-dollar piece; an eagle, or ten-dollar piece; and a double eagle, or twenty-dollar piece . . . ; which coins shall be a legal tender in all payments at their nominal value when not below the standard weight and limit of tolerance provided in this act for the single piece, and, when reduced in weight, below said standard and tolerance, shall be a legal tender at valuation in proportion to their actual weight. . . .

SEC. 15. That the silver coins of the United States shall be a trade-dollar, a half-dollar, or fifty-cent piece, a quarter-dollar, or twenty-five-cent piece, a dime, or ten-cent piece; . . . and said coins shall be a legal tender at their nominal value for any amount not exceeding five dollars in any one payment.

SEC. 16. That the minor coins of the

United States shall be a five-cent piece, a three-cent piece, and a one-cent piece . . . ; which coins shall be a legal tender, at their nominal value, for any amount not exceeding twenty-five cents in any one payment.

SEC. 17. That no coins, either of gold, silver, or minor coinage, shall hereafter be issued from the mint other than those of the denominations, standards, and weights herein set forth.

286. CITIZENS' SAVINGS & LOAN ASSOCIATION v. TOPEKA
20 Wallace, 655
1874

Error to the United States circuit court for the district of Kansas. This case involved the validity of an act of the legislature of Kansas authorizing the sale of bonds for the benefit of a bridge manufacturing company. The city of Topeka, which had issued the bonds in the first instance, claimed that the law was void and the issue unconstitutional. This is the leading case for the doctrine that taxes may not be imposed for other than public purposes. For a discussion of the question of what constitutes public purposes, see *Green* v. *Frazier,* Doc. No. 441.

MILLER, J. . . . We find ample reason to sustain the demurrer on the second ground on which it is argued by counsel and sustained by the circuit court.

That proposition is that the act authorizes the towns and other municipalities to which it applies, by issuing bonds or loaning their credit, to take the property of the citizen under the guise of taxation to pay these bonds, and use it in aid of the enterprises of others which are not of a public character, thus perverting the right of taxation, which can only be exercised for a public use, to the aid of individual interests and personal purposes of profit and gain.

The proposition as thus broadly stated is not new, nor is the question which it raises difficult of solution.

If these municipal corporations, which are in fact subdivisions of the State, and which for many reasons are vested with quasi legislative powers, have a fund or other property out of which they can pay the debts which they contract, without resort to taxation, it may be within the power of the legislature of the State to authorize them to use it in aid of projects strictly private or personal, but which would in a secondary manner contribute to the public good; or where there is property or money vested in a corporation of the kind for a particular use, as public worship or charity, the legislature may pass laws

authorizing them to make contracts in reference to this property, and incur debts payable from that source.

But such instances are few and exceptional, and the proposition is a very broad one, that debts contracted by municipal corporations must be paid, if paid at all, out of taxes which they may lawfully levy, and that all contracts creating debts to be paid in future, not limited to payment from some other source, imply an obligation to pay by taxation.

It follows that in this class of cases the right to contract must be limited by the right to tax, and if in the given case no tax can lawfully be levied to pay the debt, the contract itself is void for want of authority to make it. . . . The validity of a contract which can only be fulfilled by a resort to taxation depends on the power to lay the tax for that purpose. . . .

. . . We assume that unless the legislature of Kansas had the right to authorize the counties and towns in that State to lay taxes to be used as an aid of manufacturing enterprises, conducted by individuals, or private corporations, for purposes of gain, the law is void, and the bonds issued under it are also void.

We proceed to the inquiry whether such a power exists in the legislature of the State of Kansas.

We have already said the question is not new. The subject of the aid voted to the railways by counties and towns has been brought to the attention of the courts of almost every State in the Union. It has been thoroughly discussed and is still the subject of discussion in those courts. It is quite true that a decided preponderance of authority is to be found in favor of the proposition that the legislatures of the States, unless restricted by some special provisions of their constitutions, may confer upon those municipal bodies the right to take stock in corporations created to build railroads, and to lend their credit to such corporations. Also to levy the necessary taxes on the inhabitants, and on property within their limits to general taxation, to enable them to pay the debts thus incurred. . . .

In all these cases, however, the decision has turned upon the question whether the taxation by which this aid was afforded to the building of railroads was for a public purpose. Those who came to the conclusion that it was, held the laws for that purpose valid. Those who could not reach that conclusion held them void. In all the controversy this has been the turning point of the judgements of the courts. And it is safe to say that no court has held debts created in aid of railroad companies by counties or towns, valid on any other ground than that the purpose for which the taxes were levied was a public use. . . .

We have referred to this history of the contest over aid to railroads by taxation, to show that the strongest advocates for the validity of these laws never placed it on the ground of the unlimited power in the state legislature to tax the people, but conceded that where the purpose for which the tax was to be issued, could no longer be justly claimed to have this public character, but was purely in aid of private or personal objects, the law authorizing it was beyond the legislative power, and was an unauthorized invasion of private right. . . .

Of all the powers conferred upon government that of taxation is most liable to abuse. Given a purpose or object for which taxation may be lawfully used, and the extent of its exercise is in its very nature unlimited. It is true that express limitation on the amount of tax to be levied or the things to be taxed may be imposed by constitution or statute, but in most instances for which taxes are levied, as the support of government, the prosecution of war, the national defence, any limitation is unsafe. The entire resources of the people should in some instances be at the disposal of the government.

The power to tax is, therefore, the strongest, the most pervading of all the powers of government, reaching directly or indirectly to all classes of the people. It was said by Chief Justice Marshall, in the case of Mc-Culloch v. State of Maryland, that the power to tax is the power to destroy. A striking instance of the truth of the proposition is seen in the fact that the existing tax of ten per cent, imposed by the United States on the circulation of all other banks than the national banks, drove out of existence every state bank of circulation within a year or two after its passage. This power can as readily be employed against one class of individuals and in favor of another, so as to ruin the one class and give unlimited wealth and prosperity to the other, if there is no implied limitation of the uses for which the power may be exercised.

To lay with one hand the power of the government on the property of the citizen, and with the other to bestow it upon favored individuals to aid private enterprises and build up private fortunes, is none the less a robbery because it is done under the forms of law and is called taxation. This is not legislation. It is a decree under legislative forms.

Nor is it taxation. A "tax," says Webster's Dictionary, "is a rate or sum of money assessed on the person or property of a citizen by government for the use of the nation or state." "Taxes are burdens or charges imposed by the legislature upon persons or property to raise money for public purposes." Cooley on Constitutional Limitations, 479. . . .

We have established, we think, beyond cavil that there can be no lawful tax which is not laid for a public purpose. It may not be easy to draw the line in all cases so as to decide what is a public purpose in this sense and what is not.

It is undoubtedly the duty of the legislature which imposes or authorizes municipalities to impose a tax to see that it is not to be used for purposes of private interest instead of a public use, and the courts can only be justified in interposing when a violation of this principle is clear and the reason for interference cogent. And in deciding whether, in the given case, the object for which the taxes are assessed falls upon the one side or the other of this line, they must be governed mainly by the course and usage of the government, the objects for which taxes have been customarily and by long course of legislation levied, what objects or purposes have been considered necessary to the support and for the proper use of the government, whether state or municipal. Whatever lawfully pertains to this and is sanctioned by time and the acquiescence of the people may well be held to belong to the public use, and proper for the maintenance of good government, though this may not be the only criterion of rightful taxation.

But in the case before us, in which the towns are authorized to contribute aid by way of taxation to any class of manufacturers, there is no difficulty in holding that this is not such a public purpose as we have been considering. If it be said that a benefit results to the local public of a town by es-tablishing manufactures, the same may be said of any other business or pursuit which employs capital or labor. The merchant, the mechanic, the inn-keeper, the banker, the builder, the steamboat owner are equally promoters of the public good, and equally deserving the aid of the citizens by forced contributions. No line can be drawn in favor of the manufacturer which would not open the coffers of the public treasury to the importunities of two-thirds of the business men of the city or town. . . .

Judgment affirmed.

CLIFFORD, J. dissenting.

287. THE GRANGER MOVEMENT

The two documents below illustrate the local and the general character of the Granger movement. The first indicates the anti-railroad character of the movement in the middle western States; the second emphasizes the social rather than the economic character of the movement. The first is taken from J. Periam, *The Groundswell*, p. 286 ff.; the second from *Proceedings of the Seventh Session of the National Grange of the Patrons of Husbandry*, Feb. 4, 1874. Both are reprinted in J. R. Commons, ed. *Documentary History of American Industrial Society*, Vol. X. For background, see S. J. Buck, *The Granger Movement; The Agrarian Crusade; A. E. Paine, Granger Movement in Illinois*.

1. RESOLUTIONS OF SPRINGFIELD, ILLINOIS, FARMERS' CONVENTION
April 2, 1873

1. Resolved, by the farmers of Illinois, in mass meeting assembled, that all chartered monopolies, not regulated and controlled by law, have proved detrimental to the public prosperity, corrupting in their management, and dangerous to republican institutions.

2. Resolved, that the railways of the world, except in those countries where they have been held under the strict regulation and supervision of the government, have proved themselves arbitrary, extortionate and as opposed to free institutions and free commerce between states as were the feudal barons of the middle ages.

3. Resolved, that we hold, declare and resolve, that this despotism, which defies our laws, plunders our shippers, impoverishes our people, and corrupts our government, shall be subdued and made to subserve the public interest at whatever cost. . . .

5. Resolved, that in view of the present extortions, we look with alarm upon the future of an interest which can combine in the hands of a few men a capital of nearly $250,-000,000, and we believe it essential to the prosperity of all classes that this contest continue until these corporations acknowledge the supremacy of law.

6. Resolved, that we regard it as the undoubted power, and the imperative duty of the legislature, to pass laws fixing reasonable maximum rates for freight and passengers, without classification of roads, and that we urge upon our General Assembly the passage of such laws. . . .

9. Resolved, that we urge the passage of a bill enforcing the principle that railroads are public highways, and requiring railroads to make connections with all roads whose tracks meet or cross their own, and to receive and transmit cars and trains offered over their roads at reasonable maximum rates, whether offered at such crossings, or at stations along their roads, and empowering the making of connections by municipal corporations for that purpose, and for public use. . . .

12. Resolved, that we indorse most fully the action of those who tender legal rates of fare upon the railroads, and refuse to pay more; and that it is the duty of the legislature to provide by law for the defense by the State of Illinois of suits commenced, or that hereafter may be commenced by rail-

road companies against individuals who have in good faith insisted, or hereafter may insist, upon the right to ride in railroads at legal rates.

13. Resolved, that the presentation of railroad passes to our legislators, whatever may be the spirit and intent with which they are accepted, are demoralizing in their influence; and we look to our legislature, now in session, to rise above personal considerations of pecuniary interest or convenience, and to pass a law making it a misdemeanor for any Senator, or other state or county officers, to accept any railroad pass. . . .

14. Whereas, the constitution of 1848, Article X, prohibits the legislature from granting special railroad charters . . . therefore, Resolved, that it is extremely doubtful whether any railroad charter granted since April 1, 1848, by the legislature of Illinois, is of any validity, and that the vested rights of railroad monopolies in this state exist only by assumption of the monopolies and the sufferance of the people. . . .

15. Whereas, the constitution of 1870, Article XI, Section 13, prohibits any railroad company from issuing watered stock . . . and whereas, this article of the constitution has probably been violated by nearly all the railroad companies in the state; therefore, Resolved, that it is the duty of the railroad commissioners to look carefully into this matter, and to commence proceedings in all clear cases by *quo warranto,* or otherwise, against all railroad companies which have disregarded this important provision of the organic law of the state. . . .

18. Resolved, that we are in favor of the immediate repeal of the protective duties on iron, steel, lumber, and all materials which enter into the construction of railroad cars, steamships, sailing vessels, agricultural implements, etc. and that we urge upon Congress immediate action for this purpose, that cheap railroads and cheap ships are necessary to cheap freights, and that we invite the railroad companies to co-operate with us to that end. . . .

2. DECLARATION OF PURPOSE OF NATIONAL GRANGE
1874

1. PREAMBLE. Profoundly impressed with the truth that the National Grange of the United States should definitely proclaim to the world its general objects, we hereby unanimously make this Declaration of Purposes of the Patrons of Husbandry:

GENERAL OBJECTS. 1. United by the strong and faithful tie of agriculture, we mutually resolve to labor for the good of our Order, our country, and mankind.

2. We heartily indorse the motto: "In essentials, unity; in non-essentials, liberty; in all things, charity."

SPECIFIC OBJECTS. 3. We shall endeavor to advance our cause by laboring to accomplish the following objects:

To develop a better and higher manhood and womanhood among ourselves. To enhance the comforts and attractions of our homes, and strengthen our attachments to our pursuits. To foster mutual understanding and coöperation. To maintain inviolate our laws, and to emulate each other in labor to hasten the good time coming. To reduce our expenses, both individual and corporate. To buy less and produce more, in order to make our farms self-sustaining. To diversify our crops, and crop no more than we can cultivate. To condense the weight of our exports, selling less in the bushel and more on hoof and in fleece; less in lint, and more in warp and woof. To systematize our work, and calculate intelligently on probabilities. To discountenance the credit system, the mortgage system, the fashion system, and every other system tending to prodigality and bankruptcy.

We propose meeting together, talking together, working together, buying together, selling together, and in general acting together for our mutual protection and advancement, as occasion may require. We shall avoid litigation as much as possible by arbitration in the Grange. We shall constantly strive to secure entire harmony, goodwill, vital brotherhood among ourselves, and to make our order perpetual. We shall earnestly endeavor to suppress personal, local, sectional, and national prejudices, all unhealthy rivalry, all selfish ambition. Faithful adherence to these principles will insure our mental, moral, social, and material advancement.

BUSINESS RELATIONS. 4. For our business interests, we desire to bring producers and consumers, farmers and manufacturers into the most direct and friendly relations possible. Hence we must dispense with a surplus of middlemen, not that we are unfriendly to them, but we do not need them. Their surplus and their exactions diminish our profits.

We wage no aggressive warfare against any other interest whatever. On the contrary, all our acts and all our efforts, so far as business is concerned, are not only for the benefit of the producer and consumer, but also for all other interests that tend to bring these two parties into speedy and economical contact. Hence we hold that transportation companies of every kind are necessary to our success, that their interests are intimately connected with our interests, and harmonious action is mutually advantageous, keeping in view the first sentence in our declaration of principles of action that "Individual happiness depends upon general prosperity."

We shall, therefore, advocate for every state the increase in every practicable way, of all facilities for transporting cheaply to the seaboard, or between home producers and consumers, all the productions of our country. We adopt it as our fixed purpose to "open out the channels in nature's great arteries that the life-blood of commerce may flow freely."

We are not enemies of railroads, navigable and irrigating canals, nor of any corporation that will advance our industrial interests, nor of any laboring classes.

In our noble Order there is no communism, no agrarianism.

We are opposed to such spirit and management of any corporation or enterprise as tends to oppress the people and rob them of their just profits. We are not enemies to capital, but we oppose the tyranny of monopolies. We long to see the antagonism between capital and labor removed by common consent, and by an enlightened statesmanship worthy of the nineteenth century. We are opposed to excessive salaries, high rates of interest, and exorbitant per cent profits in trade. They greatly increase our burdens, and do not bear a proper proportion to the profits of producers. We desire only self-protection and the protection of every true interest of our land by legitimate transactions, legitimate trade, and legitimate profits.

EDUCATION. We shall advance the cause of education among ourselves and for our children, by all just means within our power. We especially advocate for our agricultural and industrial colleges that practical agriculture, domestic science, and all the arts which adorn the home, be taught in their courses of study.

THE GRANGE NOT PARTISAN. 5. We emphatically and sincerely assert the oft-repeated truth taught in our organic law, that the Grange, National, State, or Subordinate, is not a political or party organization. No Grange, if true to its obligations, can discuss political or religious questions, nor call political conventions, nor nominate candidates, nor even discuss their merits in its meetings.

Yet the principles we teach underlie all true politics, all true statesmanship, and, if properly carried out, will tend to purify the whole political atmosphere of our country. For we seek the greatest good to the greatest number.

We must always bear in mind that no one, by becoming a Patron of Husbandry, gives up that inalienable right and duty which belongs to every American citizen, to take a proper interest in the politics of his country.

On the contrary, it is right for every member to do all in his power legitimately to influence for good the action of any political party to which he belongs. It is his duty to do all he can in his own party to put down bribery, corruption, and trickery; to see that none but competent, faithful, and honest men, who will unflinchingly stand by our industrial interests, are nominated for all positions of trust; and to have carried out the principle which should always characterize every Patron, that the office should seek the man, and not the man the office.

We acknowledge the broad principle that difference of opinion is no crime, and hold that "progress toward truth is made by differences of opinion," while "the fault lies in bitterness of controversy."

We desire a proper equality, equity, and fairness; protection for the weak, restraint upon the strong; in short, justly distributed burdens and justly distributed power. These are American ideas, the very essence of American independence, and to advocate the contrary is unworthy of the sons and daughters of an American republic.

We cherish the belief that sectionalism is, and of right should be, dead and buried with the past. Our work is for the present and the future. In our agricultural brotherhood and its purposes we shall recognize no north, no south, no east, no west.

It is reserved by every Patron, as the right of a freeman, to affiliate with any party that will best carry out his principles.

OUTSIDE COÖPERATION. 6. Ours being peculiarly a farmers' institution, we cannot admit all to our ranks. Many are excluded by the nature of our organization, not because they are professional men, or artisans, or laborers, but because they have not a sufficient direct interest in tilling the soil, or may have some interest in conflict with our purposes. But we appeal to all good citizens for their cordial coöperation to assist in our efforts toward reform, that we may eventually remove from our midst the last vestige of tyranny and corruption. We hail the general desire for fraternal harmony, equitable compromises, and earnest coöperation, as an omen of our future success.

7. It shall be an abiding principle with us to relieve any of our oppressed and suffering brotherhood by any means at our command.

Last, but not least, we proclaim it among our purposes to inculcate a proper appreciation of the abilities and sphere of woman, as is indicated by admitting her to membership and position in our order.

Imploring the continued assistance of our Divine Master to guide us in our work, we here pledge ourselves to faithful and harmonious labor for all future time, to return by our united efforts to the wisdom, justice, fraternity, and political purity of our forefathers.

288. GRANT'S RECOMMENDATION OF RESUMPTION OF SPECIE PAYMENTS

Extracts from President Grant's First Annual Message and Sixth Annual Message to Congress
December 6, 1869 and December 7, 1874

(Richardson, ed. *Messages and Papers,* Vol. VII, p. 29–30, p. 285 ff.)

For references see Doc. No. 289.

1. . . . Among the evils growing out of the rebellion, and not yet referred to, is that of an irredeemable currency. It is an evil which I hope will receive your most earnest attention. It is a duty, and one of the highest duties, of Government to secure to the citizen a medium of exchange of fixed, unvarying value. This implies a return to a specie basis, and no substitute for it can be devised. It should be commenced now and reached at the earliest practicable moment consistent with a fair regard to the interests of the debtor class. Immediate resumption, if practicable, would not be desirable. It would compel the debtor class to pay, beyond their contracts, the premium on gold at the date of their purchase, and would bring bankruptcy and ruin to thousands. Fluctuation, however, in the paper value of the measure of all values (gold) is detrimental to the interests of trade. It makes the man of business an involuntary gambler, for in all sales where future payment is to be made both parties speculate as to what will be the value of the currency to be paid and received. I earnestly recommend to you, then, such legislation as will insure a gradual return to specie payments and put an immediate stop to fluctuations in the value of currency.

The methods to secure the former of these results are as numerous as are the speculators on political economy. To secure the latter I see but one way, and that is to authorize the Treasury to redeem its own paper, at a fixed price, whenever presented, and to withhold from circulation all currency so redeemed until sold again for gold.

The vast resources of the nation, both developed and undeveloped, ought to make our credit the best on earth. With a less burden of taxation than the citizen has endured for six years past, the entire public debt could be paid in ten years. But it is not desirable that the people should be taxed to pay it in that time. Year by year the ability to pay increases in a rapid ratio. But the burden of interest ought to be reduced as rapidly as can be done without the violation of contract. The public debt is represented in great part by bonds having from five to twenty and from ten to forty years to run, bearing interest at the rate of 6 per cent and 5 per cent, respectively. It is optional with the Government to pay these bonds at any period after the expiration of the least time mentioned upon their face. The time has already expired when a great part of them may be taken up, and is rapidly approaching when all may be. It is believed that all which are now due may be replaced by bonds bearing a rate of interest not exceeding 4½ per cent, and as rapidly as the remainder become due that they may be replaced in the same way. To accomplish this it may be necessary to authorize the interest to be paid at either of three or four of the money centers of Europe, or by any assistant treasurer of the United States, at the option of the holder of the bond. I suggest this subject for the consideration of Congress, and also, simultaneously with this, the propriety of redeeming our currency, as before suggested, at its market value at the time the law goes into effect, increasing the rate at which currency shall be bought and sold from day to day or week to week, at the same rate of interest as Government pays upon its bonds. . . .

2. . . . In view of the pledges of the American Congress when our present legal-tender system was adopted, and debt contracted, there should be no delay—certainly no unnecessary delay—in fixing by legislation a method by which we will return to specie. To the accomplishment of this end I invite your special attention. I believe firmly that there can be no prosperous and permanent revival of business and industries until a policy is adopted—with legislation to carry it out—looking to a return to a specie basis. It is easy to conceive that the debtor and speculative classes may think it of value to them to make so-called money abundant until they can throw a portion of their burdens upon others. But even these, I believe, would be disappointed in the result if a course should be pursued which will keep in doubt the value of the legal-tender medium of exchange. A revival of productive industry is needed by all classes; by none more than the holders of property, of whatever sort, with debts to liquidate from realization upon its

sale. But admitting that these two classes of citizens are to be benefited by expansion, would it be honest to give it? Would not the general loss be too great to justify such relief? Would it not be just as honest and prudent to authorize each debtor to issue his own legal-tenders to the extent of his liabilities? Than to do this, would it not be safer, for fear of overissues by unscrupulous creditors, to say that all debt obligations are obliterated in the United States, and now we commence anew, each possessing all he has at the time free from incumbrance? These propositions are too absurd to be entertained for a moment by thinking or honest people. Yet every delay in preparation for final resumption partakes of this dishonesty, and is only less in degree as the hope is held out that a convenient season will at last arrive for the good work of redeeming our pledges to commerce. It will never come, in my opinion, except by positive action by Congress, or by national disasters which will destroy, for a time at least, the credit of the individual and the State at large. A sound currency might be reached by total bankruptcy and discredit of the integrity of the nation and of individuals. I believe it is in the power of Congress at this session to devise such legislation as will renew confidence, revive all the industries, start us on a career of prosperity to last for many years and to save the credit of the nation and of the people. Steps toward the return to a specie basis are the great requisites to this devoutly to be sought for end. There are others which I may touch upon hereafter.

A nation dealing in a currency below that of specie in value labors under two great disadvantages: First, having no use for the world's acknowledged medium of exchange, gold and silver, these are driven out of the country because there is no need for their use; second, the medium of exchange in use being of a fluctuating value—for, after all, it is only worth just what it will purchase of gold and silver, metals having an intrinsic value just in proportion to the honest labor it takes to produce them—a larger margin must be allowed for profit by the manufacturer and producer. It is months from the date of production to the date of realization. Interest upon capital must be charged, and risk of fluctuation in the value of that which is to be received in payment added. Hence high prices, acting as a protection to the foreign producer, who receives nothing in exchange for the products of his skill and labor except a currency good, at a stable value, the world over. It seems to me that nothing is clearer than that the greater part of the burden of existing prostration, for the want of a sound financial system, falls upon the working man, who must after all produce the wealth, and the salaried man, who superintends and conducts business. The burden falls upon them in two ways—by the deprivation of employment and by the decreased purchasing power of their salaries. It is the duty of Congress to devise the method of correcting the evils which are acknowledged to exist, and not mine. But I will venture to suggest two or three things which seem to me as absolutely necessary to a return to specie payments, the first great requisite in a return to prosperity. The legal-tender clause to the law authorizing the issue of currency by the National Government should be repealed, to take effect as to all contracts entered into after a day fixed in the repealing act—not to apply, however, to payments of salaries by Government, or for other expenditures now provided by law to be paid in currency, in the interval pending between repeal and final resumption. Provision should be made by which the Secretary of the Treasury can obtain gold as it may become necessary from time to time from the date when specie redemption commences. To this might and should be added a revenue sufficiently in excess of expenses to insure an accumulation of gold in the Treasury to sustain permanent redemption.

I commend this subject to your careful consideration, believing that a favorable solution is attainable, and if reached by this Congress that the present and future generations will ever gratefully remember it as their deliverer from a thraldom of evil and disgrace. . . .

289. THE RESUMPTION OF SPECIE PAYMENTS
January 14, 1875

(U. S. Statutes at Large, Vol. XVIII, p. 296)

The financial stringency brought about by the panic of 1873 resulted in an effort to increase the issuance of legal tender notes to $400,000,000 which was defeated only by Grant's veto. This veto was the turning point in the greenback agitation; early in 1875 Congress provided for the resumption of specie payments, and the reduction of greenback circulation to $300,000,000. Hayes, elected in 1876, appointed John Sherman Secretary of the Treasury, and Sherman accumulated a gold reserve sufficient to insure successful resumption January 1, 1879. The result was that greenbacks reached par shortly before resumption. The reduction in the circulation of greenbacks provided for by the act of 1875 was stopped when $346,681,000 was outstanding. See, D. R. Dewey, *Financial History,* ch. xv; J. Sherman, *Recollections,* Vol. I, p. 507 ff., Vol. II, p. 636 ff.; A. D. Noyes, *Forty Years of American Finance;* A. S. Bolles, *Financial History of the United States,* Vol. III; *Specie Resumption and the Refunding of the National Debt,* Executive Doc. XVII, 46th Congress, 2nd Session; D. C. Barrett, *Greenbacks and the Resumption of Specie Payments, 1862–1879;* A. B. Hepburn, *A History of Currency in the United States,* chs. xii, xiii.

An act to provide for the resumption of specie payments.

Be it enacted . . . ,That the Secretary of the Treasury is hereby authorized and required, as rapidly as practicable, to cause to be coined at the mints of the United States, silver coins of the denominations of ten, twenty-five, and fifty cents, of standard value, and to issue them in redemption of an equal number and amount of fractional currency of similar denominations, or, at his discretion, he may issue such silver coins through the mints, the subtreasuries, public depositaries, and post-offices of the United States; and, upon such issue, he is hereby authorized and required to redeem an equal amount of such fractional currency, until the whole amount of such fractional currency outstanding shall be redeemed.

SEC. 2. That so much of section 3524 of the Revised Statutes of the United States as provides for a charge of one-fifth of one per centum for converting standard gold bullion into coin is hereby repealed, and hereafter no charge shall be made for that service.

SEC. 3. That section 5177 of the Revised Statutes of the United States, limiting the aggregate amount of circulating-notes of national banking-associations, be, and is hereby, repealed; and each existing banking-association may increase its circulating-notes in accordance with existing law without respect to said aggregate limit; and new banking-associations may be organized in accordance with existing law without respect to said aggregate limit; and the provisions of law for the withdrawal and redistribution of national-bank currency among the several States and Territories are hereby repealed. And whenever, and so often, as circulating-notes shall be issued to any such banking-association, so increasing its capital or circulating-notes, or so newly organized as aforesaid, it shall be the duty of the Secretary of the Treasury to redeem the legal-tender United States notes in excess only of three hundred million of dollars, to the amount of eighty per centum of the sum of national-bank notes so issued to any such banking-association as aforesaid,

and to continue such redemption as such circulating-notes are issued until there shall be outstanding the sum of three hundred million dollars of such legal-tender United States notes, and no more. And on and after January 1, 1879, the Secretary of the Treasury shall redeem, in coin, the United States legal-tender notes then outstanding on their presentation for redemption, at the office of the assistant treasurer of the United States in the city of New York, in sums of not less than fifty dollars. And to enable the Secretary of the Treasury to prepare and provide for the redemption in this act authorized or required, he is authorized to use any surplus revenues, from time to time, in the Treasury not otherwise appropriated, and to issue, sell, and dispose of, at not less than par, in coin, either of the descriptions of bonds of the United States described in the . . . Act of July 14, 1870 . . . , with like qualities, privileges, and exemptions, to the extent necessary to carry this act into full effect, and to use the proceeds thereof for the purposes aforesaid. . . .

290. MINOR v. HAPPERSETT
21 Wallace, 162
1875

Error to the supreme court of Missouri. This case involved the interpretation of the relation of the Fourteenth Amendment to the right to vote, with particular reference to the privileges and immunities clause of that Amendment.

WAITE, C. J. The question is presented in this case, whether, since the adoption of the Fourteenth Amendment, a woman, who is a citizen of the United States and of the State of Missouri, is a voter in that State, notwithstanding the provision of the constitution and laws of the State, which confine the right of suffrage to men alone. . . .

It is contended that the provisions of the Constitution and laws of the State of Missouri, which confine the right of suffrage and registration therefor to men, are in violation of the Constitution of the United States, and therefore void. The argument is, that as a woman, born or naturalized in the United States and subject to the jurisdiction thereof, is a citizen of the United States and of the State in which she resides, she has the right

of suffrage as one of the privileges and immunities of her citizenship, which the State cannot by its laws or constitution abridge.

There is no doubt that women may be citizens. They are persons, and by the Fourteenth Amendment "all persons born or naturalized in the United States and subject to the jurisdiction thereof" are expressly declared to be "citizens of the United States and of the State wherein they reside." But, in our opinion, it did not need this amendment to give them that position. Before its adoption the Constitution of the United States did not in terms prescribe who should be citizens of the United States or of the several States, yet there were necessarily such citizens without such provision. . . .

For convenience it has been found necessary to give a name to this membership. The object is to designate by a title the person and the relation he bears to the nation. For this purpose the words "subject," "inhabitant," and "citizen" have been used, and the choice between them is sometimes made to depend upon the form of the government. Citizen is now more commonly employed, however, and as it has been considered better suited to the description of one living under a republican government, it was adopted by nearly all of the States upon their separation from Great Britain, and was afterwards adopted in the Articles of Confederation and in the Constitution of the United States. When used in this sense it is understood as conveying the idea of membership of a nation, and nothing more. . . .

. . . Sex has never been made one of the elements of citizenship in the United States. In this respect men have never had an advantage over women. The same laws precisely apply to both. The Fourteenth Amendment did not affect the citizenship of women any more than it did of men. In this particular, therefore, the rights of Mrs. Minor do not depend upon the amendment. She has always been a citizen from her birth, and entitled to all the privileges and immunities of citizenship. . . .

If the right of suffrage is one of the necessary privileges of a citizen of the United States, then the constitution and laws of Missouri confining it to men are in violation of the Constitution of the United States, as amended, and consequently void. The direct question is, therefore, presented whether all citizens are necessarily voters.

The Constitution does not define the privileges and immunities of citizens. For that definition we must look elsewhere. In this case we need not determine what they are, but only whether suffrage is necessarily one of them.

It certainly is nowhere made so in express terms. The United States has no voters in the States of its own creation. The elective officers of the United States are all elected directly or indirectly by state voters. . . .

The Amendment did not add to the privileges and immunities of a citizen. It simply furnished an additional guaranty for the protection of such as he already had. No new voters were necessarily made by it. Indirectly it may have had that effect, because it may have increased the number of citizens entitled to suffrage under the constitution and laws of the States, but it operates for this purpose, if at all, through the States and the state laws, and not directly upon the citizen.

It is clear therefore, we think, that the Constitution has not added the right of suffrage to the privileges and immunities of citizenship as they existed at the time it was adopted. This makes it proper to inquire whether suffrage was co-extensive with the citizenship of the States at the time of its adoption. If it was, then it may with force be argued that suffrage was one of the rights which belonged to citizenship, and in the enjoyment of which every citizen must be protected. But if it was not, the contrary may with propriety be assumed.

When the Federal Constitution was adopted, all the States, with the exception of Rhode Island and Connecticut, had constitutions of their own. . . . Upon an examination of these constitutions we find that in no State were all citizens permitted to vote. . . .

In this condition of the law in respect to suffrage in the several States it cannot for a moment be doubted that if it had been intended to make all citizens of the United States voters, the framers of the Constitution would not have left it to implication. . . .

It is true that the United States guarantees to every State a republican form of government. . . . The guaranty is of a republican form of government. No particular government is designated as republican, neither is the exact form to be guaranteed, in any manner especially designated. Here, as in other parts of the instrument, we are compelled to resort elsewhere to ascertain what was intended.

The guaranty necessarily implies a duty on the part of the States themselves to provide such a government. All the States had governments when the Constitution was adopted. In all the people participated to some extent, through their representatives elected in the manner specially provided. These governments the Constitution did not change. They were accepted precisely as they were, and it is, therefore, to be presumed that they were such as it was the duty of the States to provide. Thus we have unmistakable evidence of what was republican in form, within the meaning of that term as employed in the Constitution.

As we have seen, all the citizens of the States were not invested with the right of suffrage. In all, save perhaps New Jersey, this right was only bestowed upon men and not upon all of them. Under these circumstances it is certainly now too late to contend that a government is not republican, within the meaning of this guaranty in the Constitution, because women are not made voters. . . .

Certainly if the courts can consider any question settled, this is one. For nearly ninety years the people have acted upon the idea that the Constitution, when it conferred citizenship, did not necessarily confer the right of suffrage. . . .

Being unanimously of the opinion that the Constitution of the United States does not confer the right of suffrage upon any one, and that the constitutions and laws of the several States which commit that important trust to men alone are not necessarily void, we affirm the judgement.

291. THE CIVIL RIGHTS ACT
March 1, 1875
(*U. S. Statutes at Large*, Vol. XVIII, p. 335 ff.)

For history and references, see Doc. No. 273.

An act to protect all citizens in their civil and legal rights

Whereas it is essential to just government we recognize the equality of all men before the law, and hold that it is the duty of government in its dealings with the people to mete out equal and exact justice to all, of whatever nativity, race, color, or persuasion, religious or political; and it being the appropriate object of legislation to enact great fundamental principles into law: Therefore,

Be it enacted, That all persons within the jurisdiction of the United States shall be entitled to the full and equal enjoyment of the accommodations, advantages, facilities, and privileges of inns, public conveyances on land or water, theaters, and other places of public amusement; subject only to the conditions and limitations established by law, and applicable alike to citizens of every race and color, regardless of any previous condition of servitude.

SEC. 2. That any person who shall violate the foregoing section by denying to any citizen, except for reasons by law applicable to citizens of every race and color, and regardless of any previous condition of servitude, the full enjoyment of any of the accommodations, advantages, facilities, or privileges in said section enumerated, or by aiding or inciting such denial, shall, for every such offense, forfeit and pay the sum of five hundred dollars to the person aggrieved thereby, . . . and shall also, for every such offense, be deemed guilty of a misdemeanor, and, upon conviction thereof, shall be fined not less than five hundred nor more than one thousand dollars, or shall be imprisoned not less than thirty days nor more than one year . . .

SEC. 3. That the district and circuit courts of the United States shall have, exclusively of the courts of the several States, cognizance of all crimes and offenses against, and violations of, the provisions of this act . . .

SEC. 4. That no citizen possessing all other qualifications which are or may be prescribed by law shall be disqualified for service as grand or petit juror in any court of the United States, or of any State, on account of race, color, or previous condition of servitude; and any officer or other person charged with any duty in the selection or summoning of jurors who shall exclude or fail to summon any citizen for the cause aforesaid shall, on conviction thereof, be deemed guilty of a misdemeanor, and be fined not more than five thousand dollars.

SEC. 5. That all cases arising under the provisions of this act . . . shall be renewable by the Supreme Court of the United States, without regard to the sum in controversy. . . .

292. CIVIL RIGHTS CASES
109 U. S. 3
1883

These were five cases, appealed from different circuit courts, involving the validity and interpretation of the Civil Rights Act of March 1, 1875. (Doc. No. 291.) In each case a colored person had been denied some accommodation or privilege on account of color. The opinion of the Court that the rights which this law attempted to protect were social rather than civil rights, and that the Federal Government had no jurisdiction over these matters, practically put an end to the effort of the Federal Government to enforce the guaranties of the Fourteenth Amendment. See, Warren, *Supreme Court* (1928 ed.), Vol. II, ch. xxxiv; W. A. Dunning, *Essays on Civil War and Reconstruction*, p. 363 ff.; W. W. Davis, "The Federal Enforcement Acts," *Studies in Southern History and Politics.*

BRADLEY, J. [After holding that the statute derived no support from the Fourteenth Amendment].

. . . But the power of Congress to adopt direct and primary, as distinguished from corrective legislation, on the subject in hand, is sought in the second place, from the Thirteenth Amendment, which abolishes slavery. . . .

It is true that slavery cannot exist without law any more than property in lands and goods can exist without law, and therefore the Thirteenth Amendment may be regarded as nullifying all state laws which establish or uphold slavery. But it has a reflex character also, establishing and decreeing universal civil and political freedom throughout the United States; and it is assumed that the power in Congress to enforce the articles by appropriate legislation, clothes Congress with power to pass all laws necessary and proper for abolishing all badges and incidents of slavery in the United States; and upon this assumption it is claimed that this is sufficient authority for declaring by law that all persons shall have equal accommodations and privileges in all inns, public conveyances, and places of public amusement; the argument being that the denial of such equal accommodations and privileges is in itself a subjection to a species of servitude within the meaning of the amendment. Conceding the major proposition to be true, that Congress has a right to enact all necessary and proper laws for the obliteration and prevention of slavery with all its badges and incidents, is the minor proposition also true, that the denial to any person of admission to the accommodations and privileges of an inn, a public conveyance, or a theatre, does subject that person to any form of servitude, or tend to fasten upon him any badge of slavery? If it does not, then

power to pass the law is not found in the Thirteenth Amendment. . . .

But is there any similarity between such servitudes and a denial by the owner of an inn, a public conveyance, or a theatre, of its accommodations and privileges to an individual, even though the denial be founded on the race or color of that individual? Where does any slavery or servitude, or badge of either, arise from such an act of denial? Whether it might not be a denial of a right which, if sanctioned by the state law, would be obnoxious to the prohibitions of the Fourteenth Amendment, is another question. But what has it to do with the question of slavery? . . .

The long existence of African slavery in this country gave us very distinct notions of what it was, and what were its necessary incidents. Compulsory service of the slave for the benefit of the master, restraint of his movements except by the master's will, disability to hold property, to make contracts, to have a standing in court, to be a witness against a white person, and such like burdens and incapacities were the inseparable incidents of the institution. . . . Can the act of a mere individual, the owner of the inn, the public conveyance, or place of amusement, refusing the accommodation, be justly regarded as imposing any badge of slavery or servitude upon the applicant, or only as inflicting an ordinary civil injury, properly cognizable by the laws of the State, and presumably subject to redress by those laws until the contrary appears?

After giving to these questions all the consideration which their importance demands, we are forced to the conclusion that such an act of refusal has nothing to do with slavery or involuntary servitude, and that if it is violative of any right of the party, his redress is to be sought under the laws of the State; or, if those laws are adverse to his rights and do not protect him, his remedy will be found in the corrective legislation which Congress has adopted, or may adopt, for counteracting the effect of state laws, or state action, prohibited by the Fourteenth Amendment. It would be running the slavery argument into the ground to make it apply to every act of discrimination which a person may see fit to make as to the guests he will entertain, or as to the people he will take into his coach or

cab or car, or admit to his concert or theatre, or deal with in other matters of intercourse or business. . . .

When a man has emerged from slavery,
and by the aid of beneficent legislation has
shaken off the inseparable concomitants of
that state, there must be some stage in the
progress of his elevation when he takes the
rank of a mere citizen, and ceases to be the
special favorite of the laws, and when his
rights as a citizen, or a man, are to be protected in the ordinary modes by which other
men's rights are protected. There were thousands of free colored people in this country
before the abolition of slavery, enjoying all
the essential rights of life, liberty and property the same as white citizens; yet no one, at
that time, thought that it was any invasion
of his personal status as a freeman because
he was not admitted to all the privileges enjoyed by white citizens, or because he was

subjected to discriminations in the enjoyment
of accommodations in inns, public conveyances and places of amusement. Mere discriminations on account of race or color were
not regarded as badges of slavery. If, since
that time, the enjoyment of equal rights in
all these respects has become established by
constitutional enactment, it is not by force of
the Thirteenth Amendment (which merely
abolishes slavery), but by force of the Fourteenth and Fifteenth Amendments.

On the whole we are of the opinion that
no countenance of authority for the passage
of the law in question can be found in either
the Thirteenth or Fourteenth Amendment of
the Constitution; and no other ground of
authority for its passage being suggested, it
must necessarily be declared void, at least so
far as its operation in the several States is
concerned. . . .

HARLAN, J., delivered a dissenting opinion.

293. EX PARTE YARBROUGH
110 U. S. 651
1884

Petition for a writ of *habeas corpus* for release of persons convicted and imprisoned for
conspiracy to prevent a negro from voting at
an election for a member of Congress, contrary to Federal laws safeguarding the right to
vote at Congressional elections. It was alleged
by Yarbrough that these laws were unconstitutional.

MILLER, J. . . . Stripped of its technical
verbiage, the offence charged in this indictment is that the defendants conspired to intimidate Berry Saunders, a citizen of African
descent, in the exercise of his right to vote
for a member of the Congress of the United
States, and in the execution of that conspiracy they beat, bruised, wounded and
otherwise maltreated him; and in the second
count, that they did this on account of his
race, color, and previous condition of servitude, by going in disguise and assaulting him
on the public highway and on his own premises. . . .

. . . That a government whose essential
character is republican, whose executive head
and legislative body are both elective, whose
most numerous and powerful branch of the
legislature is elected by the people directly,
has no power by appropriate laws to secure

this election from the influence of violence,
of corruption, and of fraud, is a proposition
so startling as to arrest attention and demand
the gravest consideration.

If this government is anything more than
a mere aggregation of delegated agents of
other states and governments, each of which
is superior to the general government, it must
have the power to protect the elections on
which its existence depends from violence and
corruption.

If it has not this power, it is left helpless
before the two great natural and historical
enemies of all republics, open violence and
insidious corruption.

The proposition that it has no such power
is supported by the old argument often heard,
often repeated, and in this court never assented to, that when a question of the power
of Congress arises the advocate of the power
must be able to place his finger on words
which expressly grant it. . . . Because there
is no *express* power to provide for preventing
violence exercised on the voter as a means of
controlling his vote, no such law can be enacted. It destroys at one blow, in construing
the Constitution of the United States, the
doctrine universally applied to all instruments

of writing, that what is implied is as much a part of the instrument as what is expressed. This principle, in its application to the Constitution of the United States, more than to almost any other writing, is a necessity, by reason of the inherent inability to put into words all derivative powers,—a difficulty which the instrument itself recognizes by conferring on Congress the authority to pass all laws necessary and proper to carry into execution the powers expressly granted, and all other powers vested in the government or any branch of it by the Constitution. Article 1, section 8, clause 18.

We know of no express authority to pass laws to punish theft or burglary of the treasury of the United States. Is there therefore no power in the Congress to protect the treasury by punishing such theft and burglary?

Are the mails of the United States, and the money carried in them, to be left at the mercy of robbers and of thieves who may handle the mail, because the Constitution contains no express words of power in Congress to enact laws for the punishment of those offences? The principle, if sound, would abolish the entire criminal jurisdiction of the courts of the United States, and the laws which confer that jurisdiction.

It is said that the states can pass the necessary law on this subject, and no necessity exists for such action by Congress. But the existence of state laws punishing the counterfeiting of the coin of the United States has never been held to supersede the acts of Congress passed for that purpose, or to justify the United States in failing to enforce its own laws to protect the circulation of the coin which it issues. . . .

So, also, has the Congress been slow to exercise the powers expressly conferred upon it in relation to elections by the fourth section of the first article of the Constitution. This section declares that: "The times, places, and manner of holding elections for Senators and Representatives shall be prescribed in each State by the legislature thereof; but the Congress may at any time make or alter such regulations, except as to the place of choosing Senators." . . .

Will it be denied that it is in the power of that body to provide laws for the proper conduct of those elections? To provide, if necessary, the officers who shall conduct them and make return of the result? And especially to provide, in an election held under its own authority, for security of life and limb to the voter while in the exercise of this function? Can it be doubted that Congress can, by law, protect the act of voting, the place where it is done, and the man who votes from personal violence or intimidation, and the election itself from corruption or fraud?

If this be so, and it is not doubted, are such powers annulled because an election for state officers is held at the same time and place? Is it any less important that the election of members of Congress should be the free choice of all the electors, because state officers are to be elected at the same time?

These questions answer themselves; and it is only because the Congress of the United States, through long habit and long years of forbearance, has, in deference and respect to the states, refrained from the exercise of these powers, that they are now doubted.

But when, in the pursuance of a new demand for action, that body, as it did in the cases just enumerated, finds it necessary to make additional laws for the free, the pure, and the safe exercise of this right of voting, they stand upon the same ground, and are to be upheld for the same reasons.

It is said that the parties assaulted in these cases are not officers of the United States, and their protection in exercising the right to vote by Congress does not stand on the same ground.

But the distinction is not well taken. The power in either case arises out of the circumstance that the function in which the party is engaged or the right which he is about to exercise is dependent on the laws of the United States.

In both cases it is the duty of that government to see that he may exercise this right freely, and to protect him from violence while so doing, or on account of so doing. This duty does not arise solely from the interest of the party concerned, but from the necessity of the government itself that its service shall be free from the adverse influence of force and fraud practiced on its agents, and that the votes by which its members of Congress and its President are elected shall be the *free* votes of the electors, and the officers thus chosen the free and uncorrupted choice of those who have the right to take part in that choice.

This proposition answers, also, another objection to the constitutionality of the laws under consideration, namely, that the right to vote for a member of Congress is not dependent upon the Constitution or laws of the United States, but is governed by the law of each state respectively.

If this were conceded, the importance to the general government of having the actual election—the voting for those members—free from force and fraud is not diminished by the circumstance that the qualification of the voter is determined by the law of the state where he votes. It equally affects the government; it is as indispensable to the proper discharge of the great function of legislating for that government, that those who are to control this legislation shall not owe their election to bribery or violence, whether the class of persons who shall vote is determined by the law of the state, or by the laws of the United States, or by their united result.

But it is not correct to say that the right to vote for a member of Congress does not depend on the Constitution of the United States.

The office, if it be properly called an office, is created by that Constitution, and by that alone. It also declares how it shall be filled, namely, by election. Its language is: "The House of Representatives shall be composed of members chosen every second year by the people of the several States; and the electors in each State shall have the same qualifications requisite for electors of the most numerous branch of the State legislature." Article 1, section 2.

The states, in prescribing the qualifications of voters for the most numerous branch of their own legislatures, do not do this with reference to the election for members of Congress. Nor can they prescribe the qualification for voters for those *eo nomine*. They define who are to vote for the popular branch of their own legislature, and the Constitution of the United States says the same persons shall vote for members of Congress in that state. It adopts the qualification thus furnished as the qualification of its own electors for members of Congress.

It is not true, therefore, that electors for members of Congress owe their right to vote to the state law, in any sense which makes the exercise of the right to depend exclusively on the law of the state.

Counsel for petitioners, seizing upon the expression found in the opinion of the court of the case of *Minor* v. *Happersett*, 21 Wallace 162, that "the Constitution of the United States does not confer the right of suffrage upon any one," without reference to the connection in which it is used, insists that the voters in this case do not owe their right to vote in any sense to that instrument.

But the court was combating the argument that this right was conferred on all citizens, and therefore upon women as well as men.

In opposition to that idea, it was said the Constitution adopts as the qualification for voters of members of Congress that which prevails in the state where the voting is to be done; therefore, said the opinion, the right is not definitely conferred on any person or class of persons by the Constitution alone, because you have to look to the law of the state for the description of the class. But the court did not intend to say that when the class or the person is thus ascertained, his right to vote for a member of Congress was not fundamentally based upon the Constitution, which created the office of member of Congress, and declared it should be elective, and pointed to the means of ascertaining who should be electors. . . .

It is as essential to the successful working of this government that the great organisms of its executive and legislative branches should be the free choice of the people, as that the original form of it should be so. In absolute governments, where the monarch is the source of all power, it is still held to be important that the exercise of that power shall be free from the influence of extraneous violence and internal corruption.

In a republican government, like ours, where political power is reposed in representatives of the entire body of the people, chosen at short intervals by popular elections, the temptations to control these elections by violence and by corruption is a constant source of danger.

Such has been the history of all republics, and, though ours has been comparatively free from both these evils in the past, no lover of his country can shut his eyes to the fear of future danger from both sources.

If the recurrence of such acts as these prisoners stand convicted of are too common in one quarter of the country, and give omen of danger from lawless violence, the free use of money in elections, arising from the vast growth of recent wealth in other quarters, presents equal cause for anxiety.

If the government of the United States has within its constitutional domain no authority to provide against these evils,—if the very sources of power may be poisoned by corruption or controlled by violence and outrage, without legal restraint,—then, indeed, is the country in danger, and its best powers, its highest purposes, the hopes which it inspires, and the love which enshrines it, are at the mercy of the combinations of those who respect no right but brute force on the one hand, and unprincipled corruptionists on the other.

The rule is discharged, and the writ of habeas corpus is denied.

294. MUNN v. ILLINOIS
94 U. S. 113
1877

Error to the supreme court of Illinois. This was the most important of the so-called "Granger cases," and involved the validity of an act of the legislature of Illinois providing for the fixing of maximum charges for the storage of grain in warehouses in Chicago. The law was attacked as in violation of the Fourteenth Amendment. The doctrine which the court laid down in this case is one of the most important principles in American constitutional interpretation, and has never been successfully challenged since that day. Yet note in this connection the remarks of Mr. Justice Brandeis in his dissenting opinion in the Oklahoma Ice Case, Doc. No. 472. For the historical background of the case see, S. J. Buck, *The Granger Movement;* A. E. Paine, *The Granger Movement in Illinois;* Warren, *Supreme Court,* Vol. II, ch. xxxiii.

WAITE, C. J. The question to be determined in this case is whether the general assembly of Illinois can, under the limitations upon the legislative powers of the States imposed by the Constitution of the United States, fix by law the maximum of charges for the storage of grain in warehouses at Chicago and other places in the State having not less than one hundred thousand inhabitants, "in which grain is stored in bulk, and in which the grain of different owners is mixed together, or in which grain is stored in such a manner that the identity of different lots or parcels cannot be accurately preserved."

It is claimed that such a law is repugnant—

1. To that part of sect. 8, art. I, of the Constitution of the United States which confers upon Congress the power "to regulate commerce with foreign nations and among the several States;"

2. To that part of sect. 9 of the same article, which provides that "no preference shall be given by any regulation of commerce or revenue to the ports of one State over those of another;" and

3. To that part of amendment 14 which ordains that no State shall "deprive any person of life, liberty, or property, without due process of law, nor deny to any person within its jurisdiction the equal protection of the laws."

We will consider the last of these objections first. . . .

The Constitution contains no definition of the word "deprive," as used in the Fourteenth Amendment. To determine its signification, therefore, it is necessary to ascertain the effect which usage has given it, when employed in the same or a like connection.

While this provision of the amendment is new in the Constitution of the United States, as a limitation upon the powers of the States, it is old as a principle of civilized government. It is found in Magna Charta, and, in substance if not in form, in nearly or quite all the constitutions that have been from time to time adopted by the several States of the Union. By the Fifth Amendment, it was introduced into the Constitution of the United States as a limitation upon the powers of the national government, and by the Fourteenth, as a guarantee against any encroachment upon an acknowledged right of citizenship by the legislatures of the States. . . .

When one becomes a member of society, he necessarily parts with some rights or privileges which, as an individual not affected by his relations to others, he might retain. "A body politic," as aptly defined in the preamble of the constitution of Massachusetts, "is a social compact by which the whole people covenants with each citizen, and each citizen with the whole people, that all shall be governed by certain laws for the common good." This does not confer power upon the whole people to control rights which are purely and exclusively private; but it does authorize the establishment of laws requiring each citizen to so conduct himself, and so use his own property, as not unnecessarily to injure another. This is the very essence of government, and has found expression in the maxim *sic utere tuo ut alienum non lædas.* From this source come the police powers, which, as was said by Mr. Chief Justice Taney in the License Cases, 5 How. 583, "are nothing more or less than the powers of government inherent in every sovereignty, . . . that is to say, . . . the power to govern men and things." Under these powers the government regulates the conduct of its citizens one towards another, and the manner in which each shall use his own property, when such regulation becomes necessary for the public good. In their exercise it has been customary in England from time immemorial, and in this country from its first colonization, to regulate ferries, common carriers, hackmen, bakers, millers, wharfingers, innkeepers, &c., and in so doing to fix a maximum of charge to be made for services rendered, accommodations furnished, and articles sold. To this day, statutes are to be found in many of the States upon some or all these subjects; and we think it has never yet been successfully contended that such legislation came within any of the constitutional prohibitions against interference with private property. With the Fifth Amendment in force Congress, in 1820, conferred power upon the city of Washington "to regulate . . . the rates of wharfage at private wharves, . . . the sweeping of chimneys, and to fix the rates of fees therefor, . . . and the weight and quality of bread," 3 Stat. 587, § 7; and, in 1848, "to make all necessary regulations respecting hackney carriages and the rates of fare of the same, and the rates of hauling by cartmen, wagoners, carmen, and draymen, and the rates of commission of auctioneers," 9 Id. 224, sect. 2.

From this it is apparent that, down to the

time of the adoption of the Fourteenth Amendment, it was not supposed that statutes regulating the use, or even the price of the use, of private property necessarily deprived an owner of his property without due process of law. Under some circumstances they may, but not under all. The amendment does not change the law in this particular: it simply prevents the States from doing that which will operate as such a deprivation.

This brings us to inquire as to the principles upon which this power of regulation rests, in order that we may determine what is within and what without its operative effect. Looking, then, to the common law, from whence came the right which the Constitution protects, we find that when private property is "affected with a public interest, it ceases to be *juris privati* only." This was said by Lord Chief Justice Hale more than two hundred years ago, in his treatise *De Portibus Maris,* 1 Harg. Law Tracts, 78, and has been accepted without objection as an essential element in the law of property ever since. Property does become clothed with a public interest when used in a manner to make it of public consequence, and affect the community at large. When, therefore, one devotes his property to a use in which the public has an interest, he, in effect, grants to the public an interest in that use, and must submit to be controlled by the public for the common good, to the extent of the interest he has thus created. He may withdraw his grant by discontinuing the use; but, so long as he maintains the use, he must submit to the control. . . .

From the same source comes the power to regulate the charges of common carriers, which was done in England as long ago as the third year of the reign of William and Mary, and continued until within a comparatively recent period. And in the first statute we find the following suggestive preamble, to wit: "And whereas divers waggoners and other carriers, by combination amongst themselves, have raised the prices of carriage of goods in many places to excessive rates, to the great injury of the trade: Be it, therefore, enacted," etc. 3 W. & M. chap. 12, § 24; 3 Stat. at Large (Great Britain) 481.

Common carriers exercise a sort of public office, and have duties to perform in which the public is interested. . . . Their business is, therefore, "affected with a public interest," within the meaning of the doctrine which Lord Hale has so forcibly stated.

But we need not go further. Enough has already been said to show that, when private property is devoted to a public use, it is subject to public regulation. It remains only to ascertain whether the warehouses of these plaintiffs in error, and the business which is carried on there, come within the operation of this principle.

For this purpose we accept as true the statements of fact contained in the elaborate brief of one of the plaintiffs in error. . . .

In this connection it must also be borne in mind that, although in 1874 there were in Chicago fourteen warehouses adapted to this particular business, and owned by about thirty persons, nine business firms controlled them, and that the prices charged and received for storage were such "as have been from year to year agreed upon and established by the different elevators or warehouses in the city of Chicago, and which rates have been annually published in one or more newspapers printed in said city, in the month of January in each year, as the established rates for the year then next ensuing such publication." Thus it is apparent that all the elevating facilities through which these vast productions "of seven or eight great States of the West" must pass on the way "to four or five of the States on the sea-shore" may be a "virtual" monopoly.

Under such circumstances it is difficult to see why, if the common carrier, or the miller, or the ferryman, or the innkeeper, or the wharfinger, or the baker, or the cartman, or the hackney-coachman, pursues a public employment and exercises "a sort of public office," these plaintiffs in error do not. They stand, to use again the language of their counsel, in the very "gateway of commerce," and take toll from all who pass. Their business most certainly "tends to a common charge, and is become a thing of public interest and use." . . . Certainly, if any business can be clothed "with a public interest and cease to be *juris privati* only," this has been. It may not be made so by the operation of the constitution of Illinois or this statute, but it is by the facts. . . .

. . . For our purposes we must assume that

if a state of facts could exist that would justify such legislation, it actually did exist when the statute now under consideration was passed. For us the question is one of power, not of expediency. If no state of circumstances could justify such a statute, then we may declare this one void, because in excess of the legislative power of the State. But if it could we must presume it did. Of the propriety of legislative interference within the scope of legislative power, the legislature is the exclusive judge.

Neither is it a matter of any moment that no precedent can be found for a statute precisely like this. It is conceded that the business is one of recent origin, that its growth has been rapid, and that it is already of great importance. And it must also be conceded that it is a business in which the whole public has a direct and positive interest. It presents, therefore, a case for the application of a long-known and well-established principle in social science, and this statute simply extends the law so as to meet this new development of commercial progress. There is no attempt to compel these owners to grant the public an interest in their property, but to decline their obligations, if they use it in this particular manner.

It matters not in this case that these plaintiffs in error had built their warehouses and established their business before the regulations complained of were adopted. What they did was from the beginning subject to the power of the body politic to require them to conform to such regulations as might be established by the proper authorities for the common good. They entered upon their business and provided themselves with the means to carry it on subject to this condition. If they did not wish to submit themselves to such interference, they should not have clothed the public with an interest in their concerns. The same principle applies to them that does to the proprietor of a hackney-carriage, and as to him it has never been supposed that he was exempt from regulating statutes or ordinances because he had purchased his horses and carriage and established his business before the statute or the ordinance was adopted.

It is insisted, however, that the owner of

property is entitled to a reasonable compensation for its use, even though it be clothed with a public interest, and that what is reasonable is a judicial and not a legislative question.

As has already been shown, the practice has been otherwise. In countries where the common law prevails, it has been customary from time immemorial for the legislature to declare what shall be a reasonable compensation under such circumstances, or perhaps more properly speaking, to fix a maximum beyond which any charge made would be unreasonable. Undoubtedly in mere private contracts, relating to matters in which the public has no interest, what is reasonable must be ascertained judicially. But this is because the legislature has no control over such a contract, So, too, in matters which do not affect the public interest, and as to which legislative control may be exercised . . . the courts must determine what is reasonable. The controlling fact is the power to regulate at all. If that exists, the right to establish the maximum charge, as one of the means of regulation, is implied. . . .

We know that this is a power which may be abused; but that is no argument against its existence. For protection against abuses by legislatures the people must resort to the polls, not to the courts. . . .

We come now to consider the effect upon this statute of the power of Congress to regulate commerce.

. . . The warehouses of these plaintiffs in error are situated and their business carried on exclusively within the limits of the State of Illinois. They are used as instruments by those engaged in State as well as those engaged in inter-state commerce. . . . Incidentally they may become connected with inter-State commerce, but not necessarily so. Their regulation is a thing of domestic concern and, certainly, until Congress acts in reference to their inter-State relations, the State may exercise all the powers of government over them, even though in so doing it may indirectly operate upon commerce outside its immediate jurisdiction. . . .

Judgement affirmed.

FIELD, J. delivered a dissenting opinion.

295. COMMONWEALTH v. HAMILTON MANUFACTURING COMPANY
120 Mass. Reports, 383
1876

Massachusetts was the pioneer state in labor legislation designed to protect women and children from undue exploitation. This case involved the constitutionality of a statute limiting the hours of labor of minors and women in manufacturing establishments to sixty a week. Compare this decision to that of *People* v. *Williams,* Doc. No. 365. See, R. Fuller, *Child Labor and the Constitution;* G. G. Groat, *Attitude of American Courts in Labor Cases;* M. C. Cahill, *Shorter Hours: A History of the Movement Since the Civil War.*

LORD, J. The defendant contends that the St. of 1874, c. 221, under which the complaint in this case is made, is unconstitutional and void. The provision, which it is alleged is without authority under the Constitution, is, that "no minor under the age of eighteen years, and no woman over that age, shall be employed in laboring by any person, firm or corporation in any manufacturing establishment in this Commonwealth more than ten hours in any one day," except in certain cases, and that "in no case shall the hours of labor exceed sixty per week."

The learned counsel for the defendant in his argument did not refer to any particular clause of the Constitution to which this provision is repugnant. His general proposition was, that the defendant's act of incorporation, St. 1824, c. 44, is a contract with the Commonwealth, and that this act impairs that contract. The contract, it is claimed, is an implied one; that is, an act of incorporation to manufacture cotton and woolen goods by necessary implication confers upon the corporation the legal capacity to contract for all the labor needful for this work. If this is conceded to the fullest extent, it is only a contract with the corporation that it may contract for all lawful labor. There is no contract implied that such labor as was then forbidden by law might be employed by the defendant; or that the General Court would not perform its constitutional duty of making such wholesome laws thereafter as the public welfare should demand. The law, therefore, violates no contract with the defendant; and the only other question is, whether it is in violation of any right reserved under the Constitution to the individual citizen. Upon this question, there seems to be no room for debate. It does not forbid any person, firm or corporation from employing as many persons or as much labor as such person, firm or corporation may desire; nor does it forbid any person to work as many hours a day or a week as he chooses. It merely provides that in an employment, which the Legislature has evidently deemed to some extent dangerous to health, no person shall be engaged in labor more than ten hours a day or sixty hours a week. There can be no doubt that such legislation may be maintained either as a health or police regulation, if it were necessary to resort to either of those sources for power. This principle has been so frequently recognized in this Common-

wealth that reference to the decisions is unnecessary.

It is also said that the law violates the right of Mary Shirley to labor in accordance with her own judgment as to the number of hours she shall work. The obvious and conclusive reply to this is, that the law does not limit her right to labor as many hours per day or per week as she may desire; it does not in terms forbid her laboring in any particular business or occupation as many hours per day or per week, as she may desire; it merely prohibits her being employed continuously in the same service more than a certain number of hours per day or week, which is so clearly within the power of the Legislature, that it becomes unnecessary to inquire whether it is a matter of grievance of which this defendant has the right to complain.

Judgment affirmed.

296. PRESIDENT GRANT'S APOLOGY

Extract from Eighth Annual Message to Congress
December 5, 1876

(Richardson, ed. *Messages and Papers,* Vol. VII, p. 399–400)

EXECUTIVE MANSION, *December 5, 1876.*
To the Senate and House of Representatives:

In submitting my eighth and last annual message to Congress it seems proper that I should refer to and in some degree recapitulate the events and official acts of the past eight years.

It was my fortune, or misfortune, to be called to the office of Chief Executive without any previous political training. From the age of 17 I had never even witnessed the excitement attending a Presidential campaign but twice antecedent to my own candidacy, and at but one of them was I eligible as a voter.

Under such circumstances it is but reasonable to suppose that errors of judgment must have occurred. Even had they not, differences of opinion between the Executive, bound by an oath to the strict performance of his duties, and writers and debaters must have arisen. It is not necessarily evidence of

blunder on the part of the Executive because there are these differences of views. Mistakes have been made, as all can see and I admit, but it seems to me oftener in the selections made of the assistants appointed to aid in carrying out the various duties of administering the Government—in nearly every case selected without a personal acquaintance with the appointee, but upon recommendations of the representatives chosen directly by the people. It is impossible, where so many trusts are to be allotted, that the right parties should be chosen in every instance. History shows that no Administration from the time of Washington to the present has been free from these mistakes. But I leave comparisons to history, claiming only that I have acted in every instance from a conscientious desire to do what was right, constitutional, within the law, and for the very best interests of the whole people. Failures have been errors of judgment, not of intent. . . .

297. THE RESTORATION OF WHITE RULE IN SOUTH CAROLINA
Letter of Governor Chamberlain to William Lloyd Garrison
June 11, 1877

(W. Allen, *Governor Chamberlain's Administration in
South Carolina,* appendix III, p. 504)

In the famous 'Red Shirt' campaign of 1876, Wade Hampton was apparently successful over the carpet-bag Governor, Chamberlain. With the withdrawal of Federal support, the Chamberlain government came to a prompt end. On Chamberlain's administration see the volume by Walter Allen, above, and Chamberlain's article "Reconstruction in South Carolina," *Atlantic Monthly,* April, 1901. See also, H. T. Thompson, *Ousting the Carpetbagger from South Carolina;* E. Wells, *Hampton and Reconstruction;* C. G. Bowers, *The Tragic Era,* chs. xxiv–xxv; F. B. Simkins and R. H. Woody, *South Carolina During Reconstruction,* chs. xviii–xix.

New York, June 11, 1877

Dear Mr. Garrison. . . . Your prophecy is fulfilled, and I am not only overthrown, but as a consequence I am now a citizen of New York. It seems to me a remarkable experience indeed, though I hope I do not egotistically exaggerate it, for I am sure it will soon be forgotten by most men in the press and hurry of new events. Why I write this line now and send it to Boston when I know you are in Europe, is because I feel like putting on record my main reflections on my experiences of the last three years. . . .

First, then, my defeat was inevitable under the circumstances of time and place which surrounded me. I mean here exactly that the uneducated negro was too weak, no matter what his numbers, to cope with the whites.

We had lost too, the sympathy of the North, in some large measure, though we never deserved it so certainly as in 1876 in South Carolina.

The Presidential contest also endangered us and doubtless defeated us. The hope of electing Tilden incited our opponents, and the greed of office led the defeated Republicans under Hayes to sell us out. There was just as distinct a bargain to do this at Washington as ever existed which was not signed and sealed on paper. And the South is not to be blamed for it, if anybody is; but rather those leaders, like Evarts, who could never see their Constitutional obligations towards the South until the offices were slipping away from their party.

So the end came, but not as you expected. . . .

Daniel H. Chamberlain.

298. PREAMBLE OF CONSTITUTION OF THE KNIGHTS OF LABOR
January 1, 1878

(T. V. Powderly, *Thirty Years of Labor,* p. 243 ff.)

The Noble Order of the Knights of Labor developed out of a society of garment cutters organized in Philadelphia in 1869. The first General Assembly met in 1878 and drew up a constitution. Under Uriah Stephens and, later, Terence Powderly, the organization grew in power and strength until by 1886 it numbered some three-quarters of a million members. The Knights of Labor advocated the principle of industrial democracy, and its membership included men and women, white and negro, skilled and unskilled laborers. Membership declined rapidly after 1886. The best general discussion of the Knights is in N. J. Ware, *The Labor Movement in the United States, 1860–1895.*

The recent alarming development and aggression of aggregated wealth, which, unless checked, will invariably lead to the pauperization and hopeless degradation of the toiling masses, render it imperative, if we desire to enjoy the blessings of life, that a check should be placed upon its power and upon unjust accumulation, and a system adopted which will secure to the laborer the fruits of his toil; and as this much-desired object can only be accomplished by the thorough unification of labor, and the united efforts of those who obey the divine injunction that "In the sweat of thy brow shalt thou eat bread," we have formed the * * * * * with a view of securing the organization and direction, by co-operative effort, of the power of the industrial classes; and we submit to the world the object sought to be accomplished by our organization, calling upon all who believe in securing "the greatest good to the greatest number" to aid and assist us:—

I. To bring within the folds of organization every department of productive industry, making knowledge a standpoint for action, and industrial and moral worth, not wealth, the true standard of individual and national greatness.

II. To secure to the toilers a proper share of the wealth that they create; more of the leisure that rightfully belongs to them; more societary advantages; more of the benefits, privileges, and emoluments of the world; in a word, all those rights and privileges necessary to make them capable of enjoying, appreciating, defending, and perpetuating the blessings of good government.

III. To arrive at the true condition of the producing masses in their educational, moral, and financial condition, by demanding from the various governments the establishment of bureaus of Labor Statistics.

IV. The establishment of co-operative institutions, productive and distributive.

V. The reserving of the public lands—the heritage of the people—for the actual settler; —not another acre for railroads or speculators.

VI. The abrogation of all laws that do not bear equally upon capital and labor, the removal of unjust technicalities, delays, and discriminations in the administration of justice, and the adopting of measures providing for the health and safety of those en-

gaged in mining, manufacturing, or building pursuits.

VII. The enactment of laws to compel chartered corporations to pay their employes weekly, in full, for labor performed during the preceding week, in the lawful money of the country.

VIII. The enactment of laws giving mechanics and laborers a first lien on their work for their full wages.

IX. The abolishment of the contract system on national, State, and municipal work.

X. The substitution of arbitration for strikes, whenever and wherever employers and employes are willing to meet on equitable grounds.

XI. The prohibition of the employment of children in workshops, mines, and factories before attaining their fourteenth year.

XII. To abolish the system of letting out by contract the labor of convicts in our prisons and reformatory institutions.

XIII. To secure for both sexes equal pay for equal work.

XIV. The reduction of the hours of labor to eight per day, so that the laborers may have more time for social enjoyment and intellectual improvement, and be enabled to reap the advantages conferred by the labor-saving machinery which their brains have created.

XV. To prevail upon governments to establish a purely national circulating medium, based upon the faith and resources of the nation, and issued directly to the people, without the intervention of any system of banking corporations, which money shall be a legal tender in payment of all debts, public or private.

299. THE BLAND–ALLISON ACT
February 28, 1878
(*U. S. Statutes at Large*, Vol. XX, p. 25 ff.)

The demonetization of silver in 1873 inaugurated a quarter century of agitation for the free and unlimited coinage of silver. The Bland-Allison act represented a compromise between the silver west and the gold-standard East, unsatisfactory alike to both groups. The act was vetoed by President Hayes, but passed over his veto. For Hayes's veto message see Doc. No. 300. On the Bland-Allison Act see, D. R. Dewey, *Financial History of the United States*, ch. xvii; J. L. Laughlin, *History of Bimetallism*, p. 209 ff.;

W. V. Byars, *An American Commoner, R. P. Bland*, ch. xii; A. B. Hepburn, *History of Currency*, ch. xv.

An act to authorize the coinage of the standard silver dollar, and to restore its legal-tender character.

Be it enacted . . . , That there shall be coined, at the several mints of the United States, silver dollars of the weight of four hundred and twelve and a half grains Troy of standard silver, as provided in the act of January 18, 1837, . . . which coins together with all silver dollars heretofore coined by the United States, of like weight and fineness, shall be a legal tender, at their nominal value, for all debts and dues public and private, except where otherwise expressly stipulated in the contract. And the Secretary of the Treasury is authorized and directed to purchase, from time to time, silver bullion, at the market price thereof, not less than two million dollars worth per month, and cause the same to be coined monthly, as fast as so purchased, into such dollars. . . . And any gain or seigniorage arising from this coinage shall be accounted for and paid into the Treasury, as provided under existing laws relative to the subsidiary coinage: *Provided,* That the amount of money at any one time invested in such silver bullion, exclusive of such resulting coin shall not exceed five million dollars. *And provided further,* That nothing in this act shall be construed to authorize the payment in silver of certificates of deposit issued under the provisions of section 254 of the Revised Statutes.

Sec. 2. That immediately after the passage of this act, the President shall invite the governments of the countries composing the Latin Union, so-called, and of such other European nations as he may deem advisable, to join the United States in a conference to adopt a common ratio between gold and silver, for the purpose of establishing, internationally, the use of bi-metallic money, and securing fixity of relative value between those metals; such conference to be held at such place, in Europe or in the United States, at such time within six months, as may be mutually agreed upon by the executives of the governments joining in the same, whenever the governments so invited, or any three of them, shall have signified their willingness to unite in the same.

The President shall, by and with the advice and consent of the Senate, appoint three commissioners, who shall attend such conference on behalf of the United States, and shall report the doings thereof to the President, who shall transmit the same to Congress. . . .

Sec. 3. That any holder of the coin authorized by this act may deposit the same with the Treasurer or any assistant treasurer of the United States, in sums not less than ten dollars, and receive therefor certificates of not less than ten dollars each, corresponding with the denominations of the United States notes. The coin deposited for or representing the certificates shall be retained in the Treasury for the payment of the same on demand. Said certificates shall be receivable for customs, taxes, and all public dues, and, when so received, may be reissued.

300. PRESIDENT HAYES'S VETO OF BLAND–ALLISON ACT
Feb. 28, 1878.

(Richardson, ed. *Messages and Papers,* Vol. VII, p. 486 ff.)

EXECUTIVE MANSION, *February 28, 1878.*
To the House of Representatives:

After a very careful consideration of the House bill No. 1093, entitled "An act to authorize the coinage of the standard silver dollar and to restore its legal-tender character," I feel compelled to return it to the House of Representatives, in which it originated, with my objections to its passage.

Holding the opinion, which I expressed in my annual message, that "neither the interests of the Government nor of the people of the United States would be promoted by disparaging silver as one of the two precious metals which furnish the coinage of the world, and that legislation which looks to maintaining the volume of intrinsic money to as full a measure of both metals as their relative commercial values will permit would be neither unjust nor inexpedient," it has been my earnest desire to concur with Congress in the adoption of such measures to increase the silver coinage of the country as would not impair the obligation of contracts, either public or private, nor injuriously affect the public credit. It is only upon the conviction that this bill does not meet these essential requirements that I feel it my duty to withhold from it my approval. . . .

The bill provides for the coinage of silver dollars of the weight of 412½ grains each, of standard silver, to be a legal tender at their nominal value for all debts and dues, public and private, except where otherwise expressly stipulated in the contract. It is well known that the market value of that number of grains of standard silver during the past year has been from 90 to 92 cents as compared with the standard gold dollar. Thus the silver dollar authorized by this bill is worth 8 to 10 per cent less than it purports to be worth, and is made a legal tender for debts contracted when the law did not recognize such coins as lawful money.

The right to pay duties in silver or in certificates for silver deposits will, when they are issued in sufficient amount to circulate, put an end to the receipt of revenue in gold, and thus compel the payment of silver for both the principal and interest of the public debt. $1,143,493,400 of the bonded debt now outstanding was issued prior to February, 1873, when the silver dollar was unknown in circulation in this country, and was only a convenient form of silver bullion for exportation; $583,440,350 of the funded debt has been issued since February, 1873, when gold alone was the coin for which the bonds were sold, and gold alone was the coin in which both parties to the contract understood that the bonds would be paid. These bonds entered into the markets of the world. They were paid for in gold when silver had greatly depreciated, and when no one would have bought them if it had been understood that they would be paid in silver. The sum of $225,000,000 of these bonds has been sold during my Administration for gold coin, and the United States received the benefit of these sales by a reduction of the rate of interest to 4 per cent. During the progress of these sales a doubt was suggested as to the coin in which payment of these bonds would be made. The public announcement was thereupon authorized that it was "not to be anticipated that any future legislation of Congress or any action of any department of the Government would sanction or tolerate the redemption of the principal of these bonds or the payment of the interest thereon in coin of less value than the coin authorized by law at the time of the issue of the bonds, being the coin exacted by the Government in exchange for the same." In view of these facts it will be justly regarded as a grave breach of the public faith to undertake to pay these bonds, principal or interest, in silver coin worth in the market less than the coin received for them.

It is said that the silver dollar made a legal tender by this bill will under its operation be equivalent in value to the gold dollar. Many supporters of the bill believe this, and would not justify an attempt to pay debts, either public or private, in coin of inferior value to the money of the world. The capital defect of the bill is that it contains no provision protecting from its operation preëxisting debts in case the coinage which it creates shall continue to be of less value than that which was the sole legal tender when they were contracted. If it is now proposed, for the purpose of taking advantage of the depreciation of silver in the payment of debts, to coin and make a legal tender a silver dollar of less commercial value than any dollar, whether of gold or paper, which is now lawful money in this country, such measure, it will hardly be questioned, will, in the judgment of mankind, be an act of bad faith. As to all debts heretofore contracted, the silver dollar should be made a legal tender only at its market value. The standard of value should not be changed without the consent of both parties to the contract. National promises should be kept with unflinching fidelity. There is no power to compel a nation to pay its just debts. Its credit depends on its honor. The nation owes what it has led or allowed its creditors to expect. I can not approve a bill which in my judgment authorizes the violation of sacred obligations. The obligation of the public faith transcends all questions of profit or public advantage. Its unquestionable maintenance is the dictate as well of the highest expediency as of the most necessary duty, and should ever be carefully guarded by the Executive, by Congress, and by the people.

It is my firm conviction that if the country is to be benefited by a silver coinage it can be done only by the issue of silver dollars of full value, which will defraud no man. A currency worth less than it purports to be worth will in the end defraud not only creditors, but all who are engaged in legitimate business, and none more surely than those who are dependent on their daily labor for their daily bread.

R. B. HAYES.

301. ENCYCLICAL LETTER, QUOD APOSTOLICI MUNERIS
December 28, 1878

(The Great Encyclical Letters of Pope Leo XIII (Benziger Brothers), p. 22 ff.)

This Encyclical Letter is recited as an illustration of the attitude of the Catholic Church towards socialism. See, W. E. Garrison, *The March of Faith;* W. E. Garrison, *Catholicism and the American Mind.*

. . . You understand as a matter of course, Venerable Brothers, that We are alluding to that sect of men who, under the motley and all but barbarous terms and titles of Socialists, Communists, and Nihilists, are spread abroad throughout the world and, bound intimately together in baneful alliance, no longer look for strong support in secret meetings held in darksome places, but standing forth openly and boldly in the light of day, strive to carry out the purpose long resolved upon, of uprooting the foundations of civilized society at large.

These are they in very truth who, as the sacred text bears witness, *defile the flesh, and despise dominion, and blaspheme majesty.* (Jude 8) They leave nothing scathless or uninjured of that which human and divine laws alike have wisely ordained to ensure the preservation and honor of life. From the heads of States to whom, as the Apostle admonishes, all owe submission, and on whom the rights of authority are bestowed by God Himself, these sectaries withhold obedience and preach up the perfect equality of all men in regard to rights alike and duties. . . . In short, spurred on by greedy hankering after things present, which is the *root of all evils, which some coveting have erred from the faith* (1 Tim. vi. 10) they attack the right of property, sanctioned by the law of nature, and with signal depravity, while pretending to feel solicitous about the needs, and anxious to satisfy the requirements of all, they strain every effort to seize upon and hold in common all that has been individually acquired by title of lawful inheritance, through intellectual or manual labor, or economy in living. These monstrous views they proclaim in public meetings, uphold in booklets, and spread broadcast everywhere through the daily press. Hence the hallowed dignity and authority of rulers has incurred such odium on the part of rebellious subjects

that evil-minded traitors, spurning all control, have many a time within a recent period boldly raised impious hands against even the very heads of States. . . .

For although the Socialists, turning to evil use the Gospel itself so as to deceive more readily the unwary, have been wont to twist it to their meaning, still so striking is the disagreement between their criminal teachings and the pure doctrine of Christ, that no greater can exist: *For what participation hath justice with injustice, or what fellowship hath light with darkness.* (2. Cor. vi. 14) They in good sooth cease not from asserting—as we have already mentioned—that all men are by nature equal, and hence they contend that neither honor nor respect is owed to public authority, nor any obedience to the laws, saving perhaps to those which have been sanctioned according to their good pleasure. Contrariwise, from the Gospel records, equality among men consists in this, that one and all, possessing the same nature, are called to the sublime dignity of being sons of God; and, moreover, that one and the same end being set before all, each and every one has to be judged according to the same laws and to have punishments or rewards meted out according to individual deserts. There is, however, an inequality of right and authority, which emanates from the Author of nature Himself, *of whom all paternity in heaven and earth is named.* (Eph. iii. 15) As regards rulers and subjects, all without exception, according to Catholic teaching and precept, are mutually bound by duties and rights, in such manner that, on the one hand, moderation is enjoined on the appetite for power, and, on the other, obedience is shown to be easy, stable, and wholly honorable. . . .

But to the end that the rulers of the people shall employ the power bestowed for the advancement, and not detriment, of those under rule, the Church of Christ very fittingly warns the rulers themselves that the Sovereign Judge will call them to a strict and speedy account, and evoking the words of divine wisdom, she addresses them one and all in God's name. *Give ear, you that rule the people, and that please yourselves in multitudes of nations; for power is given you by the Lord, and strength by the Most High, who will examine your works, and search out your thoughts; . . . for a most severe judgement shall be for them that bear rule. . . . For God will not accept any man's person, neither will He stand in awe of any one's greatness; for He hath made the little and the great, and He hath equally care of all. But a greater punishment is ready for the more mighty.* (Wisd. vi. 3 seqq.) Should it, however, happen, at any time, that in the public exercise of authority rulers act rashly and arbitrarily, the teaching of the Catholic Church does not allow subjects to rise against them, without further warranty, lest peace and order become more and more disturbed, and society run the risk of greater detriment. And when things have come to such a pass as to hold out no further hope, she teaches that a remedy is to be sought in the virtue of Christian patience and in urgent prayer to God. But should it please legislators and rulers to enjoin or sanction anything repugnant to the divine and natural law, the dignity and duty of the name of Christian and the Apostolic injunction proclaim that *one ought to obey God rather than man.* (Acts. v. 29). . . .

As regards the maintenance of public and private tranquillity Catholic wisdom, sustained by both divine and natural law, prudently provides through what it holds and teaches touching the right of ownership and the apportioning of personal property which has been accumulated for the wants and requirements of life. For the Socialists wrongly assume the right of property to be of mere human invention, repugnant to the natural equality between men, and, preaching up the community of goods, declare that no one should endure poverty meekly, and that all may with impunity seize upon the possessions and usurp the rights of the wealthy. More wisely and profitably the Church recognizes the existence of inequality amongst men, who are by nature unlike in mental endowment and strength of body, and even in amount of fortune; and she enjoins that the right of property and of its disposal, derived from nature, should in the case of every individual remain intact and inviolate. She knows full well indeed that robbery and rapine have been so forbidden by God, the Author and Protector of every right, that it is unlawful even to covet the goods of others, and that thieves and robbers no less than adulterers and idolaters are excluded from the kingdom of heaven. Nor does she, on this account, loving mother as she is, omit solicitude for the poor or fail to provide for their needs; nay, taking them to her arms with maternal affection, and knowing that they in a manner represent the person of Christ Himself, who accounts as done unto Him any benefit conferred upon the lowliest among the poor, she holds them in great account, brings them aid to the utmost of her power, takes thought to have erected in every land in their behoof homes and refuges where they can be received, nurtured, and tended; and takes these charitable foundations under her protecting care. Moreover, she lays the rich under strict command to give of their superfluity to the poor, impressing them with fear of the divine judgement which will exact the penalty of eternal punishment unless they succor the wants of the needy. In fine, she cheers and comforts exceedingly the hearts of the poor, either by setting before them the example of Christ, who, *being rich became poor for our sakes,* (2 Cor. viii. 9) or by reminding them of the words by which Jesus pronounced the poor to be *blessed,* and enjoined them to hope for the reward of eternal bliss. Who then does not perceive that herein lies the best means of appeasing the undying conflict between the rich and the poor? For, as the evidence of things and facts clearly demonstrates, if such conclusion be disallowed or made light of, it must come about either that the vast majority of mankind will fall back into that most abject condition of bondage which through a long lapse of time obtained among pagan nations, or else that human society will be agitated by constant outbreaks and ravaged by plunder and rapine. . . .

302. POWELL'S REPORT ON THE ARID REGION OF THE WEST
1878

Major Powell was director of the U.S. Geological Survey. His report on the arid regions of the west, with recommendations for changes in the land system, though it had no immediate legislative results, was of epoch-making significance. He pointed out that the land system which had obtained from the beginning of our history and for the region east of the 100th meridian, was unsuitable to the arid lands of the west, where access to water was the basic consideration. See also, J. W. Powell, "Institutions for the Arid Lands," *Century Magazine*, May, 1890. For an appreciation of the work of Major Powell, and an elaboration of the thesis which he presented, see W. P. Webb, *The Great Plains*, esp. p. 353 ff.

. . . If the whole of the Arid Region was yet unsettled, it might be wise for the Government to undertake the parceling of the lands and employ skilled engineers to do the work, whose duties could be performed in advance of settlement. . . . Many of the lands surveyed along the minor streams have been entered, and the titles to these lands are in the hands of actual settlers. Many pasturage farms, or ranches, as they are called locally, have been established throughout the country. These remarks are true of every state and territory in the Arid Region. In the main these ranches or pasturage farms are on Government land, and the settlers are squatters, and some are not expecting to make permanent homes. . . . It is now too late for the Government to parcel the pasturage lands in advance of the wants of settlers in the most available way, so as to closely group residences and give water privileges to the several farms. Many of the farmers are actually on the ground, and are clamoring for some means by which they can obtain titles to pasturage farms of an extent adequate to their wants, and the tens of thousands of individual interests would make the problem a difficult one for the officers of the Government to solve. A system less arbitrary than that of the rectangular surveys now in vogue, and requiring unbiased judgement, overlooking the interests of single individuals and considering only the interests of the greatest number, would meet with local opposition. . . .

Under these circumstances it is believed that it is best to permit the people to divide their lands for themselves—not in a way by which each man may take what he pleases for himself, but by providing methods by which these settlers may organize and mutually protect each other from the rapacity of individuals. The lands, as lands, are of but slight value, as they cannot be used for ordinary agricultural purposes, i. e., the cultivation of crops; but their value consists in the scant grasses which they spontaneously produce, and these values can be made available only by the use of the waters necessary for the subsistence of stock, and that necessary for the small amount of irrigable land which should be attached to the several pasturage farms. Thus, practically, all values inhere in the water, and an equitable division of the waters can be made only by a wise system of parcelling the lands; and the people in organized bodies can well be trusted with this right, while individuals could not thus be trusted. These considerations have led to the plan suggested in the bill submitted for the organization of pasturage districts.

In like manner, in the bill designed for the purpose of suggesting a plan for the organization of irrigation districts, the same principle is involved, *viz*, that of permitting the settlers themselves to subdivide the lands into such tracts as they may desire.

The lands along the streams are not valuable for agricultural purposes in continuous bodies or squares, but only in irrigable tracts governed by the levels of the meandering canals which carry the water for irrigation, and it would be greatly to the advantage of every such district if the lands could be divided into parcels, governed solely by the conditions under which the water could be distributed over them; and such parcelling cannot be done prior to the occupancy of the lands, but can only be made *pari passu* with the adoption of a system of canals; and the people settling on these lands should be allowed the privilege of dividing the lands into such tracts as may be most available for such purposes, and they should not be hampered with the present arbitrary system of dividing tracts into rectangular tracts. . . .

The title to no tract of land should be conveyed from the Government to the individual until the proper survey of the same is made and the plat prepared for record. With this precaution, which the Government already invariably takes in disposing of its lands, no fear of uncertainty of identification need be entertained. . . .

. . . The general subject of water rights is one of great importance. In many places in the Arid Region irrigation companies are organized who obtain vested rights in the waters they control, and consequently the rights to such waters do not inhere in any particular tracts of land.

When the area to which it is possible to take the water of any given stream is much greater than the stream is competent to serve, if the land titles and water rights are severed, the owner of any tract of land is at the mercy of the owner of the water right. In general the lands greatly exceed the capacities of the streams. Thus the lands have no value without water. If the water rights fall into the hands of irrigating companies and the lands into the hands of individual farmers, the farmers then will be dependent upon the stock companies, and eventually the monopoly of water rights will be an intolerable burden to the people.

The magnitude of the interests involved must not be overlooked. All the present and future agriculture of more than four-tenths of the area of the United States is dependent upon irrigation, and practically all values for agricultural industries inhere, not in the lands, but in the water. Monopoly of land need not be feared. The question for legislators to solve is to devise some practical means by which water rights may be distributed among individual farmers and water monopolies prevented. . . .

The pioneer is fully engaged in the present with its hopes of immediate remuneration for labor. The present development of the country fully occupies him. For this reason every effort put forth to increase the area of the agricultural land by irrigation is welcomed.

Every man who turns his attention to this department of industry is considered a public benefactor. But if in the eagerness for present development a land and water system shall grow up in which the practical control of agriculture shall fall into the hands of water companies, evils will result therefrom that generations may not be able to correct, and the very men who are now lauded as benefactors to the country will, in the ungovernable reaction which is sure to come, be denounced as oppressors of the people.

The right to use water should inhere in the land to be irrigated, and water rights should go with land titles.

Those unacquainted with the industrial institutions of the far west, involving the use of lands and waters, may without careful thought suppose that the long recognized principles of the common law are sufficient to prevent the severance of land and water rights; but other practices are obtaining which have, or eventually will have, all the force of common law because the necessities of the country require the change, and these practices are obtaining the color of right from state and territorial legislation, and to some extent by national legislation. In all that country the natural channels of the streams cannot be made to govern water rights without great injury to its agricultural and mining industries. For the great purposes of irrigation and hydraulic mining the water has no value in its natural channel. In general the water cannot be used for irrigation on the lands immediately contiguous to the streams—i. e., the flood plains or bottom valleys. . . . The waters must be taken to a greater or less extent on the bench lands to be used in irrigation. All the waters of all the arid lands will eventually be taken from their natural channels, and they can be utilized only to the extent to which they are thus removed, and water rights must of necessity be severed from the natural channels. There is another important factor to be considered. The water when used in irrigation is absorbed by the soil and reëvaporated to the heavens. It cannot be taken from its natural channel, used, and returned. Again, the water cannot in general be properly utilized in irrigation by requiring it to be taken from its natural channel within the limits ordinarily included in a single ownership. In order to conduct the water on the higher bench lands where it is to be used in irrigation, it is necessary to go up the stream until a level is reached from which the waters will flow to the lands to be redeemed. The exceptions to this are so small that the statement scarcely needs qualification. Thus, to use the water it must be diverted from its natural course often miles or scores of miles from where it is to be used.

The ancient principles of common law applying to the use of natural streams, so wise and equitable in a humid region, would, if applied to the Arid Region, practically prohibit the growth of its most important industries. Thus it is that a custom is springing up in the Arid Region which may or may not have color of authority in statutory or common law; on this I do not wish to express an opinion; but certain it is that water rights are practically being severed from the natural channels of the streams; and this must be done. In the change, it is to be feared that water rights will in many cases be separated from all land rights as the system is now forming. If this fear is not groundless, to the extent that such a separation is secured, water will become a property independent of the land, and this property will be gradually absorbed by a few. Monopolies of water will be secured, and the whole agriculture of the country will be tributary thereto—a condition of affairs which an American citizen having in view the interests of the largest number of the people cannot contemplate with favor.

Practically, in that country the right to water is acquired by priority of utilization, and this is as it should be from the necessities of the country. But two important qualifications are needed. The *user right* should attach to the *land* where used, not to the individual or company constructing the canals by which it is used; the priority of usage should secure the right. But this needs some slight modification. A farmer settling on a small tract, to be redeemed by irrigation, should be given a reasonable length of time in which to secure his water right by utilization, that he may secure it by his own labor, either directly by constructing the waterways himself, or indirectly by coöperating with his neighbours in constructing systems of waterways. Without this provision there is little inducement for poor men to commence farming operations, and men of ready capital only will engage in such enterprises. . . .

If there be any doubt of the ultimate legality of the practices of the people in the arid country relating to water and land rights, all such doubts should be speedily quieted through the enactment of appropriate laws by the national legislature. Perhaps an amplification by the courts of what has been designated as the *natural right* to the use of water may be made to cover the practices now obtaining; but it hardly seems wise to imperil interests so great by intrusting them to the possibility of some future court made law.

303. THE PROBLEM OF "RIDERS"

President Hayes's veto of the Army Appropriation Act for 1880
April 29, 1879

(Richardson, ed. *Messages and Papers*, Vol. VII, p. 523 ff.)

The Democratic House of Representatives attached to the Army Appropriation Act for the year ending June 30, 1880 a "rider" practically repealing the acts of 1865 and 1874 which authorized the use of Federal troops in elections. The problem of the "rider" was squarely met in Hayes's veto message.

To the House of Representatives:

I have maturely considered the important questions presented by the bill entitled "An act making appropriations for the support of

the Army for the fiscal year ending June 30, 1880, and for other purposes," and I now return it to the House of Representatives, in which it originated, with my objections to its approval.

The bill provides in the usual form for the appropriations required for the support of the Army during the next fiscal year. If it contained no other provisions, it would receive my prompt approval. It includes, however, further legislation, which, attached, as it is, to appropriations which are requisite for the efficient performance of some of the most necessary duties of the Government, involves questions of the gravest character. The sixth section of the bill is amendatory of the statute now in force in regard to the authority of persons in the civil, military, and naval service of the United States "at the place where any general or special election is held in any State." . . .

The effect of the adoption of this amendment may be considered—

First. Upon the right of the United States Government to use military force to keep the peace at the elections for Members of Congress; and

Second. Upon the right of the Government, by civil authority, to protect these elections from violence and fraud. . . .

This section is, however, not presented to me as a separate and independent measure, but is, as has been stated, attached to the bill making the usual annual appropriations for the support of the Army. It makes a vital change in the election laws of the country, which is in no way connected with the use of the Army. It prohibits, under heavy penalties, any person engaged in the civil service of the United States from having any force at the place of any election, prepared to preserve order, to make arrests, to keep the peace, or in any manner to enforce the laws. This is altogether foreign to the purpose of an Army appropriation bill. The practice of tacking to appropriation bills measures not pertinent to such bills did not prevail until more than forty years after the adoption of the Constitution. It has become a common practice. All parties when in power have adopted it. Many abuses and great waste of public money have in this way crept into appropriation bills. The public opinion of the country is against it. The States which have recently adopted constitutions have generally provided a remedy for the evil by enacting that no law shall contain more than one subject, which shall be plainly expressed in its title. The constitutions of more than half of the States contain substantially this provision. The public welfare will be promoted in many ways by a return to the early practice of the Government and to the true principle of legislation, which requires that every measure shall

stand or fall according to its own merits. If it were understood that to attach to an appropriation bill a measure irrelevant to the general object of the bill would imperil and probably prevent its final passage and approval, a valuable reform in the parliamentary practice of Congress would be accomplished. The best justification that has been offered for attaching irrelevant riders to appropriation bills is that it is done for convenience' sake, to facilitate the passage of measures which are deemed expedient by all the branches of Government which participate in legislation. It can not be claimed that there is any such reason for attaching this amendment of the election laws to the Army appropriation bill. The history of the measure contradicts this assumption. . . .

. . . Upon the assembling of this Congress, in pursuance of a call for an extra session, which was made necessary by the failure of the Forty-fifth Congress to make the needful appropriations for the support of the Government, the question was presented whether the attempt made in the last Congress to ingraft by construction a new principle upon the Constitution should be persisted in or not. This Congress has ample opportunity and time to pass the appropriation bills, and also to enact any political measures which may be determined upon in separate bills by the usual and orderly methods of proceeding. But the majority of both Houses have deemed it wise to adhere to the principles asserted and maintained in the last Congress by the majority of the House of Representatives. That principle is that the House of Representatives has the sole right to originate bills for raising revenue, and therefore has the right to withhold appropriations upon which the existence of the Government may depend unless the Senate and the President shall give their assent to any legislation which the House may see fit to attach to appropriation bills. To establish this principle is to make a radical, dangerous, and unconstitutional change in the character of our institutions. The various departments of the Government and the Army and the Navy are established by the Constitution or by laws passed in pursuance thereof. Their duties are clearly defined and their support is carefully provided for by law. The money required for this purpose has been collected from the people and is now in the Treasury, ready to be paid out as soon as the appropriation bills are passed. Whether appropriations are made or not, the collection of the taxes will go on. The public money will accumulate in the Treasury. It was not the intention of the framers of the Constitution that any single branch of the Government should have the power to dictate conditions upon which this treasure should be applied to the purpose for which it was collected. Any such intention, if it had been entertained, would have been plainly expressed in the Constitution. . . .

The new doctrine, if maintained, will result in a consolidation of unchecked and despotic power in the House of Representatives. A bare majority of the House will become the Government. The Executive will no longer be what the framers of the Constitution intended—an equal and independent branch of the Government. It is clearly the constitutional duty of the President to exercise his discretion and judgment upon all bills presented to him without constraint or duress from any other branch of the Government. To say that a majority of either or both of the Houses of Congress may insist upon the approval of a bill under the penalty of stopping all of the operations of the Government for want of the necessary supplies is to deny to the Executive that share of the legislative power which is plainly conferred by the second section of the seventh article of the Constitution. It strikes from the Constitution the qualified negative of the President. It is said that this should be done because it is the peculiar function of the House of Representatives to represent the will of the people. But no single branch or department of the Government has exclusive authority to speak for the American people. The most authentic and solemn expression of their will is contained in the Constitution of the United States. By that Constitution they have ordained and established a Government whose powers are distributed among coördinate branches, which, as far as possible consistently with a harmonious coöperation, are absolutely independent of each other. The people of this country are unwilling to see the supremacy of the Constitution replaced by the omnipotence of any one department of the Government.

The enactment of this bill into a law will establish a precedent which will tend to destroy the equal independence of the several branches of the Government. Its principle places not merely the Senate and the Executive, but the judiciary also, under the coercive dictation of the House. The House alone will be the judge of what constitutes a grievance, and also of the means and measures of redress. . . .

Believing that this bill is a dangerous violation of the spirit and meaning of the Constitution, I am compelled to return it to the House in which it originated without my approval. . . .

RUTHERFORD B. HAYES.

304. THE INDIAN PROBLEM

Extract from President Arthur's First Annual Message
December 6, 1881

(Richardson, ed. *Messages and Papers*, Vol. VIII, p. 54 ff.)

The recommendations of President Arthur foreshadowed the provisions of the Dawes Act of 1887, Doc. No. 315. In support of Arthur's characterization of our Indian policy, see H. H. Jackson, *A Century of Dishonor*, and the references listed in Doc. No. 315.

. . . Prominent among the matters which challenge the attention of Congress at its present session is the management of our Indian affairs. While this question has been a cause of trouble and embarrassment from the infancy of the Government, it is but recently that any effort has been made for its solution at once serious, determined, consistent, and promising success.

It has been easier to resort to convenient makeshifts for tiding over temporary difficulties than to grapple with the great permanent problem, and accordingly the easier course has almost invariably been pursued.

It was natural, at a time when the national territory seemed almost illimitable and contained many millions of acres far outside the bounds of civilized settlements, that a policy should have been initiated which more than aught else has been the fruitful source of our Indian complications.

I refer, of course, to the policy of dealing with the various Indian tribes as separate nationalities, of relegating them by treaty stipulations to the occupancy of immense reservations in the West, and of encouraging them to live a savage life, undisturbed by any earnest and well-directed efforts to bring them under the influences of civilization.

The unsatisfactory results which have sprung from this policy are becoming apparent to all.

As the white settlements have crowded the borders of the reservations, the Indians, sometimes contentedly and sometimes against their will, have been transferred to other hunting grounds, from which they have again been dislodged whenever their new-found homes have been desired by the adventurous settlers.

These removals and the frontier collisions by which they have often been preceded have led to frequent and disastrous conflicts between the races.

It is profitless to discuss here which of them has been chiefly responsible for the disturbances whose recital occupies so large a space upon the pages of our history.

We have to deal with the appalling fact that though thousands of lives have been sacrificed and hundreds of millions of dollars expended in the attempt to solve the Indian problem, it has until within the past few years seemed scarcely nearer a solution than it was half a century ago. But the Government has of late been cautiously but steadily feeling its way to the adoption of a policy which has already produced gratifying results, and which, in my judgment, is likely, if Congress and the Executive accord in its support, to relieve us ere long from the difficulties which have hitherto beset us.

For the success of the efforts now making to introduce among the Indians the customs and pursuits of civilized life and gradually to absorb them into the mass of our citizens, sharing their rights and holden to their responsibilities, there is imperative need for legislative action.

My suggestions in that regard will be chiefly such as have been already called to the attention of Congress and have received to some extent its consideration.

First. I recommend the passage of an act making the laws of the various States and Territories applicable to the Indian reservations within their borders and extending the laws of the State of Arkansas to the portion of the Indian Territory not occupied by the Five Civilized Tribes.

The Indian should receive the protection of the law. He should be allowed to maintain in court his rights of person and property. He has repeatedly begged for this privilege. Its exercise would be very valuable to him in his progress toward civilization.

Second. Of even greater importance is a measure which has been frequently recommended by my predecessors in office, and in furtherance of which several bills have been from time to time introduced in both Houses of Congress. The enactment of a general law permitting the allotment in severalty, to such Indians, at least, as desire it, of a reasonable quantity of land secured to them by patent, and for their own protection made inalienable for twenty or twenty-five years, is demanded for their present welfare and their permanent advancement.

In return for such considerate action on the part of the Government, there is reason to believe that the Indians in large numbers would be persuaded to sever their tribal relations and to engage at once in agricultural pursuits. Many of them realize the fact that their hunting days are over and that it is now for their best interests to conform their manner of life to the new order of things. By no greater inducement than the assurance of permanent title to the soil can they be led to engage in the occupation of tilling it.

The well-attested reports of their increasing interest in husbandry justify the hope and belief that the enactment of such a statute as I recommend would be at once attended with gratifying results. A resort to the allotment system would have a direct and powerful influence in dissolving the tribal bond, which is so prominent a feature of savage life, and which tends so strongly to perpetuate it.

Third. I advise a liberal appropriation for the support of Indian schools, because of my confident belief that such a course is consistent with the wisest economy. . . .

305. PAN-AMERICANISM

Secretary Blaine's Invitation to Pan-American Congress
November 29, 1881

(Papers Relating to the Foreign Relations of the United States, 1881, p. 13 ff.)

James G. Blaine became Secretary of State for the first time, May 7, 1881; he at once addressed himself to the problem of our relations with the countries of Latin-America. The assassination of Garfield brought Arthur to the Presidency, and Blaine was succeeded in the State Department by Frelinghuysen. Frelinghuysen reversed Blaine's Latin-American policy, and withdrew the invitations to a Pan-American Conference. In 1888 Congress authorized a Pan-American Conference which met in Washington October 1889, and established the Pan-American Union. See, A. F. Tyler, *Foreign Policy of James G. Blaine;* D. S. Muzzey, *James G. Blaine;* S. F. Bemis, ed. *American Secretaries of State,* Vol. VII, p. 275 ff.; J. F. Rippy, *Historical Evolution of Hispanic America,* ch. xxiii.

MR. BLAINE TO MR. OSBORN.

Department of State

Washington, November 29, 1881.

Sir: The attitude of the United States with respect to the question of general peace on the American continent is well known through its persistent efforts for years to avert the evils of warfare, or, these efforts failing, to bring positive conflicts to an end through pacific counsels or the advocacy of impartial arbitration. This attitude has been consistently maintained, and always with such fairness as to leave no room for imputing to our government any motive except the humane and disinterested one of saving the kindred states of the American continent from the burdens of war. The position of the United States as the leading power of the New World might well give its government a claim to authoritative utterance for the purpose of quieting discord among its neighbors, with all of whom the most friendly relations exist. Nevertheless, the good offices of this government are not and have not at any time been tendered with a show of dictation or compulsion, but only as exhibiting the solicitous good-will of a common friend.

For some years past a growing disposition has been manifested by certain states of Central and South America to refer disputes affecting grave questions of international relationship and boundaries to arbitration rather than to the sword. It has been on several such occasions a source of profound satisfaction to the Government of the United States to see that this country is in a large measure looked to by all the American powers as their friend and mediator. The just and impartial counsel of the President in such cases has never been withheld, and his efforts have been rewarded by the prevention of sanguinary strife or angry contentions between peoples whom we regard as brethren.

The existence of this growing tendency convinces the President that the time is ripe for a proposal that shall enlist the good-will and active coöperation of all the states of the western hemisphere, both north and south, in the interest of humanity and for the common weal of nations. He conceives that none of the governments of America can be less alive than our own to the dangers and horrors of a state of war, and especially of war between kinsmen. He is sure that none of the chiefs of governments on the continent can be less sensitive than he is to the sacred duty of making every endeavor to do away with the chances of fratricidal strife. And he looks with hopeful confidence to such active assistance from them as will serve to show the broadness of our common humanity and the strength of the ties which bind us all together as a great and harmonious system of American commonwealths.

Impressed by these views, the President extends to all the independent countries of North and South America an earnest invitation to participate in a general congress to be held in the city of Washington on the 24th day of November, 1882, for the purpose of considering and discussing the methods of preventing war between the nations of America. He desires that the attention of the congress shall be strictly confined to this one great object; that its sole aim shall be to seek a way of permanently averting the horrors of cruel and bloody combat between countries, oftenest of one blood and speech, or the even worse calamity of internal commotion and civil strife; that it shall regard the burdensome and far-reaching consequences of such struggles, the legacies of exhausted finances, of oppressive debt, of onerous taxation, of ruined cities, of paralyzed industries, of devastated fields, of ruthless conscription, of the slaughter of men, of the grief of the widow and the orphan, of embittered resentment that long survive those who provoked them and heavily afflict the innocent generations that come after.

The President is especially desirous to have it understood that, in putting forth this invitation, the United States does not assume the position of counseling or attempting through the voice of the congress, to counsel any determinate solution of existing questions which may now divide any of the countries of America. Such questions can not properly come before the congress. Its mission is higher. It is to provide for the interest of all in the future, not to settle the individual differences of the present. For this reason especially the President has indicated a day for the assembling of the congress so far in the future as to leave good ground for hope that by the time named the present situation on the South Pacific coast will be happily terminated, and that those engaged in the contest may take peaceable part in the discussion and solution of the general question affecting in an equal degree the well-being of all.

It seems also desirable to disclaim in advance any purpose on the part of the United States to prejudge the issues to be presented to the congress. It is far from the intent of this government to appear before the congress as in any sense the protector of its neighbors or the predestined and necessary arbitrator of their disputes. The United States will enter into the deliberations of the congress on the same footing as the other powers represented, and with the loyal determination to approach any proposed solution, not merely in its own interest, or with a view to asserting its power, but as a single member among many coördinate and coequal states. So far as the influence of this government may be potential, it will be exerted in the direction of conciliating whatever conflicting interests of blood, or government, or historical tradition may necessarily come together in response to a call embracing such vast and diverse elements.

I am, &c.,

James G. Blaine.

306. TREATY REGULATING IMMIGRATION FROM CHINA
November 17, 1880

(Malloy, ed. *Treaties, Conventions, etc.* Vol. I, p. 237 ff.)

By the Burlingame Treaty of 1868 Chinese were given the right to immigrate to the United States; shortly after the ratification of this Treaty anti-Chinese sentiment on the Pacific coast became so strong that there was a demand for its abrogation. A bill abrogating the provision insuring reciprocal immigration privileges passed Congress in 1879 but was vetoed by President Hayes. In order to deal with the situation the President appointed a committee to negotiate a new Treaty: the Treaty of November 17, 1880 was the result. In 1882 a bill to prohibit the immigration of Chinese laborers for a period of ten years received the signature of President Arthur; the restriction was subsequently extended until it became permanent. On Oriental Immigration, see M. R. Coolidge, *Chinese Immigration;* R. L. Garis, *Immigration Restriction.*

. . . Whereas the Government of the United States, because of the constantly increasing immigration of Chinese laborers to the territory of the United States, and the embarrassments consequent upon such immigration, now desires to negotiate a modification of the existing Treaties which shall not be in direct contravention of their spirit: . . .

Art. I. Whenever in the opinion of the Government of the United States, the coming of Chinese laborers to the United States, or their residence therein, affects or threatens to affect the interests of that country, or to endanger the good order of the said country or of any locality within the territory thereof, the Government of China agrees that the Government of the United States may regulate, limit, or suspend such coming or residence, but may not absolutely prohibit it. The limitation or suspension shall be reasonable and shall apply only to Chinese who may go to the United States as laborers, other classes not being included in the limitations. Legislation taken in regard to Chinese laborers will be of such a character only as is necessary to enforce the regulation, limitation or suspension of immigration, and immigrants shall not be subject to personal maltreatment or abuse.

ART. II. Chinese subjects, whether proceeding to the United States as teachers, students, merchants, or from curiosity, together with their body and household servants, and Chinese laborers who are now in the United States, shall be allowed to go and come of their own free will and accord, and shall be accorded all the rights, privileges, immunities and exemptions which are accorded to the citizens and subjects of the most favored nation.

ART. III. If Chinese laborers, or Chinese of any other class, now either permanently or temporarily residing in the territory of the United States, meet with ill treatment at the hands of any other persons, the Government of the United States will exert all its power to devise measures for their protection and to secure to them the same rights, privileges, immunities and exemptions as may be enjoyed by the citizens or subjects of the most favored nation, and to which they are entitled by treaty. . . .

307. CHINESE EXCLUSION ACT
May 6, 1882
(*U. S. Statutes at Large,* Vol. XXII, p. 58 ff.)

For references, see Doc. No. 306.

An act to execute certain treaty stipulations relating to Chinese.

WHEREAS, in the opinion of the Government of the United States the coming of Chinese laborers to this country endangers the good order of certain localities within the territory thereof: Therefore,

Be it enacted, That from and after the expiration of ninety days next after the passage of this act, and until the expiration of ten years next after the passage of this act, the coming of Chinese laborers to the United States be, . . . suspended; and during such suspension it shall not be lawful for any Chinese laborer to come, or, having so come after the expiration of said ninety days, to remain within the United States.

SEC. 2. That the master of any vessel who shall knowingly bring within the United States on such vessel, and land or permit to be landed, any Chinese laborer, from any foreign port or place, shall be deemed guilty of a misdemeanor, and on conviction thereof shall be punished by a fine of not more than five hundred dollars for each and every such Chinese laborer so brought, and may be also imprisoned for a term not exceeding one year.

SEC. 3. That the two foregoing sections shall not apply to Chinese laborers who were in the United States on the seventeenth day of November, eighteen hundred and eighty or who shall have come into the same before the expiration of ninety days next after the passage of this act, . . .

SEC. 6. That in order to the faithful execution of articles one and two of the treaty in this act before mentioned, every Chinese person other than a laborer who may be entitled by said treaty and this act to come within the United States, and who shall be about to come to the United States, shall be identified as so entitled by the Chinese Government in each case, such identity to be evidenced by a certificate issued under the authority of said government, which certificate shall be in the English language or (if not in the English language) accompanied by a translation into English, stating such right to come, and which certificate shall state the name, title, or official rank, if any, the age, height, and all physical peculiarities, former and present occupation or profession and place of residence in China of the person to whom the certificate is issued and that such person is entitled conformably to the treaty in this act mentioned to come within the United States. . . .

SEC. 12. That no Chinese person shall be permitted to enter the United States by land without producing to the proper officer of customs the certificate in this act required of Chinese persons seeking to land from a vessel. And any Chinese person found unlawfully within the United States shall be caused to be removed therefrom to the country from whence he came, by direction of the President of the United States, and at the cost of the United States, after being brought before some justice, judge, or commissioner of a court of the United States and found to be one not lawfully entitled to be or remain in the United States.

SEC. 13. That this act shall not apply to diplomatic and other officers of the Chinese Government traveling upon the business of that government, whose credentials shall be taken as equivalent to the certificate in this act mentioned, and shall exempt them and their body and household servants from the provisions of this act as to other Chinese persons.

SEC. 14. That hereafter no State court or court of the United States shall admit Chinese to citizenship; and all laws in conflict with this act are hereby repealed.

SEC. 15. That the words "Chinese laborers," whenever used in this act, shall be construed to mean both skilled and unskilled laborers and Chinese employed in mining.

308. PENDLETON ACT
January 16, 1883

(U. S. Statutes at Large, Vol. XXII, p. 403 ff.)

Agitation for civil service reform dates back to the Grant administration. From 1871 to 1872 Congress appropriated money for a civil service commission, but thereafter no action was taken until 1881. A New York Civil Service Reform Association was founded in 1877, and a National Civil Service Reform League in 1881, under the leadership of G. W. Curtis of New York. The assassination of Garfield by a disappointed office-seeker dramatized the desirability of reform, and President Arthur in his message of December 6 asked for legislation on the subject. The Pendleton Act established the merit system in our national administration. Dorman B. Eaton, long active in the reform movement, drafted the Pendleton Act, and was appointed by Arthur to head the new Civil Service Commission. See, C. R. Fish, *The Civil Service and the Patronage;* L. Mayer, *Federal Service;* D. H. Smith, *The United States Civil Service Commission;* F. M. Stewart, *The National Civil Service Reform League;* J. Bryce, *The American Commonwealth,* 1893 ed. Vol. II, ch. lxv.; and bibliographies accompanying sketches of Carl Schurz, G. W. Curtis, D. B. Eaton, T. A. Jenckes, in the *Dictionary of American Biography.*

An act to regulate and improve the civil service of the United States.

Be it enacted . . . , That the President is authorized to appoint, by and with the advice and consent of the Senate, three persons, not more than two of whom shall be adherents of the same party, as Civil Service Commissioners, and said three commissioners shall constitute the United States Civil Service Commission. Said commissioners shall hold no other official place under the United States.

Sec. 2. That it shall be the duty of said commissioners:

FIRST. To aid the President, as he may request, in preparing suitable rules for carrying this act into effect, and when said rules shall have been promulgated it shall be the duty of all officers of the United States in the departments and offices to which any such rules may relate to aid, in all proper ways, in carrying said rules, and any modifications thereof, into effect.

SECOND. And, among other things, said rules shall provide and declare, as nearly as the conditions of good administration will warrant, as follows:

First, for open, competitive examinations for testing the fitness of applicants for the public service now classified or to be classified hereunder. Such examinations shall be practical in their character, and so far as may be shall relate to those matters which will fairly test the relative capacity and fitness of the persons examined to discharge the duties of the service into which they seek to be appointed.

Second, that all the offices, places, and employments so arranged or to be arranged in classes shall be filled by selections according to grade from among those graded highest as the results of such competitive examinations.

Third, appointments to the public service aforesaid in the departments at Washington shall be apportioned among the several States and Territories and the District of Columbia upon the basis of population as ascertained at the last preceding census. . . .

Fourth, that there shall be a period of probation before any absolute appointment or employment aforesaid.

Fifth, that no person in the public service is for that reason under any obligations to contribute to any political fund, or to render any political service, and that he will not be removed or otherwise prejudiced for refusing to do so.

Sixth, that no person in said service has any right to use his official authority or influence to coerce the political action of any person or body.

Seventh, there shall be non-competitive examinations in all proper cases before the commission, when competent persons do not compete, after notice has been given of the existence of the vacancy, under such rules as may be prescribed by the commissioners as to the manner of giving notice. . . .

THIRD. Said commission shall, subject to the rules that may be made by the President, make regulations for, and have control of, such examinations, . . .

SEC. 3. . . . The commission shall, at Washington, and in one or more places in each State and Territory where examinations are to take place, designate and select a suitable number of persons, not less than three, in the official service of the United States, residing in said State or Territory, after consulting the head of the department or office in which such persons serve, to be members of boards of examiners. . . . Such boards of examiners shall be so located as to make it reasonably convenient and inexpensive for applicants to attend before them; and where there are persons to be examined in any State or Territory, examinations shall be held therein at least twice in each year. . . .

SEC. 6. That within sixty days after the passage of this act it shall be the duty of the Secretary of the Treasury, in as near conformity as may be to the classification of certain clerks now existing under . . . [Section 163] . . . of the Revised Statutes, to arrange in classes the several clerks and persons employed by the collector, naval officer, surveyor, and appraisers, or either of

them, or being in the public service, at their respective offices in each customs district where the whole number of said clerks and persons shall be all together as many as fifty. And thereafter, from time to time, on the direction of the President, said Secretary shall make the like classification or arrangement of clerks and persons so employed, in connection with any said office or offices, in any other customs district. And, upon like request, and for the purposes of this act, said Secretary shall arrange in one or more of said classes, or of existing classes, any other clerks, agents, or persons employed under his department in any said district not now classified; and every such arrangement and classification upon being made shall be reported to the President.

Second. Within said sixty days it shall be the duty of the Postmaster-General, in general conformity to said . . . [Section 163] . . . , to separately arrange in classes the several clerks and persons employed, or in the public service, at each post-office, or under any postmaster of the United States, where the whole number of said clerks and persons shall together amount to as many as fifty. And thereafter, from time to time, on the direction of the President, it shall be the duty of the Postmaster-General to arrange in like classes the clerks and persons so employed in the postal service in connection with any other post-office; and every such arrangement and classification upon being made shall be reported to the President.

Third. That from time to time said Secretary, the Postmaster-General, and each of the heads of departments mentioned in . . . [Section 158] . . . of the Revised Statutes, and each head of an office, shall, on the direction of the President, and for facilitating the execution of this act, respectively revise any then existing classification or arrangement of those in their respective departments and offices, and shall, for the purposes of the examination herein provided for, include in one or more of such classes, so far as practicable, subordinate places, clerks, and officers in the public service pertaining to their respective departments not before classified for examination.

SEC. 7. That after the expiration of six months from the passage of this act no officer or clerk shall be appointed, and no person shall be employed to enter or be promoted in either of the said classes now existing, or that may be arranged hereunder pursuant to said rules, until he has passed an examination, or is shown to be specially exempted from such examination in conformity herewith. But nothing herein contained shall be construed to take from those honorably discharged from the military or naval service any preference conferred by . . . [Section 1754] . . . of the Revised Statutes, nor to take from the President any authority not inconsistent with this act conferred by . . . [Section 1753] . . . of said statutes; nor shall any officer not in the executive branch of the government, or any person merely employed as a laborer or workman, be required to be classified hereunder; nor, unless by direction of the Senate, shall any person who has been nominated for confirmation by the Senate be required to be classified or to pass an examination.

SEC. 8. That no person habitually using intoxicating beverages to excess shall be appointed to, or retained in, any office, appointment, or employment to which the provisions of this act are applicable.

SEC. 9. That whenever there are already two or more members of a family in the public service in the grades covered by this act, no other member of such family shall be eligible to appointment to any of said grades.

SEC. 10. That no recommendation of any person who shall apply for office or place under the provisions of this act which may be given by any Senator or member of the House of Representatives, except as to the character or residence of the applicant, shall be received or considered by any person concerned in making any examination or appointment under this act.

SEC. 11. That no Senator, or Representative, or Territorial Delegate of the Congress, or Senator, Representative, or Delegate elect, or any officer or employee of either of said houses, and no executive, judicial, military, or naval officer of the United States, and no clerk or employee of any department, branch or bureau of the executive, judicial, or military or naval service of the United States, shall, directly or indirectly, solicit or receive, or be in any manner concerned in soliciting or receiving, any assessment, subscription, or contribution for any political purpose whatever, from any officer, clerk, or employee of the United States, or any department, branch, or bureau thereof, or from any person receiving any salary or compensation from moneys derived from the Treasury of the United States. . . .

309. JULLIARD v. GREENMAN
110 U. S. 421
1884

Error to the U.S. Circuit Court for the Southern District of New York. This notable case involved the constitutionality of the Act of May 31, 1878, providing that legal tender notes issued during the Civil War should not be cancelled, but reissued and kept in circulation. The question was whether Congress could, except as an emergency war measure, make anything but gold and silver legal tender in the payment of private debts. Mr. Warren calls the decision of the court in this case "the most sweeping opinion as to the extent of Congressional power which had ever heretofore been rendered". Immediately after the Court had rendered its decision numerous measures were introduced into Congress limiting the power of Congress as to the issue of legal tender notes. See, Warren, *Supreme Court,* 1928 ed. Vol. II, p. 652 ff. and references, p. 657 n. On the dissenting opinion

see C. B. Swisher, *Stephen J. Field, Craftsman of the Law.*

GRAY, J. . . . The act of May 31st, 1878, ch. 146, under which the notes in question were reissued, is entitled "An act to forbid the further retirement of United States legal tender notes," and enacts as follows:

"From and after the passage of this act it shall not be lawful for the Secretary of the Treasury or other officer under him to cancel or retire any more of the United States legal tender notes. And when any of said notes may be redeemed or be received into the Treasury under any law from any source whatever and shall belong to the

United States, they shall not be retired, cancelled or destroyed, but they shall be reissued and paid out again and kept in circulation: Provided, That nothing herein shall prohibit the cancellation and destruction of mutilated notes and the issue of other notes of like denomination in their stead, as now provided by law. All acts and parts of acts in conflict herewith are hereby repealed." 20 Stat. 87.

The manifest intention of this act is that the notes which it directs, after having been redeemed, to be reissued and kept in circulation, shall retain their original quality of being a legal tender. The single question, therefore, to be considered, . . . is whether notes of the United States, issued in time of war, under acts of Congress declaring them to be a legal tender in payment of private debts, and afterwards in time of peace redeemed and paid in gold coin at the treasury, and then reissued under the act of 1878, can, under the Constitution of the United States, be a legal tender in payment of such debts. . . .

The breadth and comprehensiveness of the words of the Constitution are nowhere more strikingly exhibited than in regard to the powers, over the subjects of revenue, finance, and currency, of which there is no other express grant than may be found in these few brief clauses:

"The Congress shall have power—

"To lay and collect taxes, duties, imposts, and excises, to pay the debts and provide for the common defense and general welfare of the United States; but all duties, imposts, and excises shall be uniform throughout the United States."

"To borrow money on the credit of the United States."

"To regulate commerce with foreign nations, and among the several States, and with the Indian tribes."

"To coin money, regulate the value thereof, and of foreign coin, and fix the standard of weights and measures."

The section which contains the grant of these and other principal legislative powers concludes by declaring that the Congress shall have power—

"To make all laws which shall be necessary and proper for carrying into execution the foregoing powers, and all other powers vested by this Constitution in the government of the United States, or any department or officer thereof.". . .

The power "to borrow money on the credit of the United States" is the power to raise money for the public use on a pledge of the public credit, and may be exercised to meet either present or anticipated expenses and liabilities of the government. It includes the power to issue, in return for the money borrowed, the obligations of the United States in any appropriate form, of stock, bonds, bills or notes; and in whatever form they are issued, being instruments of the national government, they are exempt from taxation by the governments of the several States. Congress has authority to issue these obligations in a form adapted to circulation from hand to hand in the ordinary transactions of commerce and business. In order to promote and facilitate such circulation, to adapt them to use as currency, and to make them more current in the market, it may provide for their redemption in coin or bonds, and may make them receivable in payment of debts to the government. So much is settled beyond doubt, and was asserted or distinctly admitted by the judges who dissented from the decision in the *Legal Tender Cases*, as well as by those who concurred in that decision. . . .

The constitutional authority of Congress to provide a currency for the whole country is now firmly established. . . .

By the Constitution of the United States, the several States are prohibited from coining money, emitting bills of credit, or making anything but gold and silver coin a tender in payment of debts. But no intention can be inferred from this to deny to Congress either of these powers. . . . The States are forbidden, but Congress is expressly authorized, to coin money. The States are prohibited from emitting bills of credit; but Congress, which is neither expressly authorized nor expressly forbidden to do so, has, as we have already seen, been held to have the power of emitting bills of credit, and of making every provision for their circulation as currency, short of giving them the quality of legal tender for private debts, even by those who have denied its authority to give them this quality.

It appears to us to follow, as a logical and necessary consequence, that Congress has the power to issue the obligations of the United States in such form, and to impress upon them such qualities as currency for the purchase of merchandise and the payment of debts, as accord with the usage of sovereign governments. The power, as incident to the power of borrowing money and issuing bills or notes of the government for money borrowed, of impressing upon those bills or notes the quality of being a legal tender for the payment of private debts, was a power universally understood to belong to sovereignty, in Europe and America, at the time of the framing and adoption of the Constitution of the United States. . . .

. . . The power of issuing bills of credit, and making them, at the discretion of the legislature, a tender in payment of private debts, had long been exercised in this country by the several colonies and States; and during the Revolutionary War the States, upon the recommendation of the Congress of the Confederation, had made the bills issued by Congress a legal tender. The exercise of this power not being prohibited to Congress by the Constitution, it is included in the power expressly granted to borrow money on the credit of the United States.

This position is fortified by the fact that Congress is vested with the exclusive exercise of the analogous power of coining money and regulating the value of domestic and foreign coin, and also with the paramount power of regulating foreign and interstate commerce. Under the power to borrow money on the credit of the United States, and to issue circulating notes for the money borrowed, its power to define the quality and force of those notes as currency is as broad as the like power over a metallic currency under the power to coin money and to regulate the value thereof. Under the two powers, taken together, Congress is authorized to establish a national currency, either in coin or in paper, and to make that currency lawful money for all purposes, as regards the national government or private individuals.

The power of making the notes of the United States a legal tender in payment of private debts, being included in the power to borrow money and to provide a national currency, is not defeated or restricted by the fact that its exercise may affect the value of private contracts. If, upon a just and fair interpretation of the whole Constitution, a particular power or authority appears to be vested in Congress, it is no constitutional objection to its existence, or to its exercise, that the property or the contracts of individuals may be incidentally affected. . . .

So, under the power to coin money and to regulate its value, Congress may (as it did with regard to gold by the Act of June 28th, 1834, c. 95, and with regard to silver by the Act of February 28th, 1878, c. 20), issue coins of the same denominations as those already current by law, but of less intrinsic value than those, by reason of containing a less weight of the precious metals, and thereby enable debtors to discharge their debts by the payment of coins of the less real value. A contract to pay a certain sum in money, without any stipulation as to the kind of money in which it shall be paid, may always be satisfied by payment of that sum in any currency which is lawful money at the place and time at which payment is to be made. . . .

Congress, as the legislature of a sovereign nation, being expressly empowered by the Constitution, "to lay and collect taxes, to pay the debts and provide for the common defense and general welfare of the United States," and "to borrow money on the credit of the United States," and "to coin money and regulate the value thereof and of foreign coin;" and being clearly authorized, as incidental to the exercise of those great powers, to emit bills of credit, to charter national banks, and to provide a national currency for the whole people, in the form of coin, treasury notes, and national bank bills; and the power to make the notes of the government a legal tender in payment of private debts being one of the powers belonging to sovereignty in other civilized nations, and not expressly withheld from Congress by the Constitution; we are irresistibly impelled to the conclusion that the impressing upon the treasury notes of the United States the quality of being a legal tender in payment of private debts is an appropriate means, conducive and plainly adapted to the execution of the undoubted powers of Congress, consistent with the letter and spirit of the Constitution, and therefore, within the meaning of that instrument, "necessary and proper for carrying into execution the powers vested by this Constitution in the government of the United States."

Such being our conclusion in matter of law, the question whether at any particular time, in war or in peace, the exigency is such by reason of unusual and pressing demands on the resources of the government, or of the inadequacy of the supply of gold and silver coin to furnish the currency needed for the uses of the government and of the people, that it is, as matter of fact, wise and expedient to resort to this means, is a political question, to be determined by Congress when the question of exigency arises, and not a judicial question, to be afterwards passed upon by the courts. . . .

It follows that the act of May 31, 1878, ch. 146, is constitutional and valid, and that the circuit court rightly held that the tender in treasury notes, reissued and kept in circulation under that act, was a tender of lawful money in payment of the defendant's debt to the plaintiff.

Judgment affirmed.

FIELD, J., delivered a dissenting opinion.

310. IN RE JACOBS
98 New York, 98
1885

Appeal from an order of the General Term of the Supreme Court. The case involved an interpretation of the New York Tenement House Law of 1882. "This decision," wrote Theodore Roosevelt, (*Autobiography*, p. 81), "completely blocked tenement-house reform legislation in New York for a score of years, and hampers it to this day. It was one of the most serious setbacks which the cause of industrial and social progress and reform ever received." For background, see R. W. De Forest and L. Veiller, *The Tenement House Problem*, 2 vols.; Jacob Riis, *The Battle With the Slum*.

EARL, J. . . . These facts showed a violation of the provision of the act which took effect immediately upon its passage and the material portions of which are as follows: "Section 1. The manufacture of cigars or preparation of tobacco in any form on any floor, or in any part of any floor, in any tenement-house is hereby prohibited, if such floor or any part of such floor is by any person occupied as a home or residence for the purpose of living, sleeping, cooking or doing any household work therein. . . . Section 6. This act shall apply only to cities having over five hundred thousand inhabitants.". . .

Generally it is for the legislature to determine what laws and regulations are needed to protect the public health and secure the public comfort and safety, and while its measures are calculated, intended, convenient and appropriate to accomplish these ends, the exercise of its discretion is not subject to review by the courts. But they must have some relation to these ends. Under the mere guise of police regulations, personal rights and private property cannot arbitrarily be invaded, and the determination of the legislature is not final or conclusive. If it passes an act ostensibly for the public health, and thereby destroys or takes away the property of a citizen, or interferes with his personal liberty, then it is for the courts to scrutinize the act and see whether it really relates to and is convenient and appropriate to promote the public health. It matters not that the legislature may in the title to the act, or in its body, declare that it is intended for the improvement of the public health. Such a declaration does not conclude the courts, and they must yet determine the fact declared and enforce the supreme law. . . . The legislature may condemn or authorize the condemnation of private property for public use, and it may, in the exercise of its discretion, determine when and upon what property the power of eminent domain may be exercised; but its exercise is not beyond the reach of judicial inquiry. Whether or not a use is a public one, which will justify the exercise of the power, is a judicial question. . . .

We will now once more recur to the law

under consideration. It does not deal with tenement-houses as such; it does not regulate the number of persons who may live in any one of them, or be crowded into one room, nor does it deal with the mode of their construction for the purpose of securing the health and safety of their occupants or of the public generally. It deals mainly with the preparation of tobacco and the manufacture of cigars, and its purpose obviously was to regulate them. We must take judicial notice of the nature and qualities of tobacco. It has been in general use among civilized men for more than two centuries. It is used in some form by a majority of the men in this State; by the good and bad, learned and unlearned, the rich and the poor. Its manufacture into cigars is permitted without any hindrance, except for revenue purposes, in all civilized lands. It has never been said, so far as we can learn, and it was not affirmed even on the argument before us, that its preparation and manufacture into cigars were dangerous to the public health. We are not aware, and are not able to learn, that tobacco is even injurious to the health of those who deal in it, or are engaged in its production or manufacture. We certainly know enough about it to be sure that its manipulation in one room can produce no harm to the health of the occupants of other rooms in the same house. It was proved in this case that the odor of the tobacco did not extend to any of the other rooms of the tenement-house. . . . To justify this law it would not be sufficient that the use of tobacco may be injurious to some persons, or that its manipulation may be injurious to those who are engaged in its preparation and manufacture; but it would have to be injurious to the public health. This law was not intended to protect the health of those engaged in cigar-making, as they are allowed to manufacture cigars everywhere except in the forbidden tenement-houses. It cannot be perceived how the cigar maker is to be improved in his health or his morals by forcing him from his home and its hallowed associations and beneficent influences, to ply his trade elsewhere. It was not intended to protect the health of that portion of the public not residing in the forbidden tenement-houses, as cigars are allowed to be manufactured in private houses, in large factories and shops

in the too crowded cities, and in all other parts of the State. What possible relation can cigarmaking in any building have on the health of the general public? Nor was it intended to improve or protect the health of the occupants of tenement-houses. If there are but three families in the tenement-house, however numerous and gregarious their members may be, manufacture is not forbidden; and it matters not how large the number of the occupants may be if they are not divided into more than three families living and cooking independently. If a store is kept for the sale of cigars on the first floor of one of these houses, and thus more tobacco is kept there than otherwise would be, and the baneful influence of tobacco, if any, is thus increased, that floor, however numerous its occupants, or the occupants of the house, is exempt from the operation of the act. What possible relation to the health of the occupants of a large tenement-house could cigarmaking in one of its remote rooms have? If the legislature had in mind the protection of the occupants of the tenement-houses, why was the act confined in its operation to the two cities only? It is plain that this is not a health law, and that it has no relation whatever to the public health. . . . Such legislation may invade one class of rights to-day and another to-morrow, and if it can be sanctioned under the Constitution, while far removed in time we will not be far away in practical statesmanship from those ages when governmental prefects supervised the building of houses, the rearing of cattle, the sowing of seed and the reaping of grain, and governmental ordinances regulated the movements and labor of artisans, the rate of wages, the price of food, the diet and clothing of the people, and a large range of other affairs long since in all civilized lands regarded as outside of governmental functions. Such governmental interferences disturb the normal adjustments of the social fabric, and usually derange the delicate and complicated machinery of industry and cause a score of ills while attempting the removal of one.

When a health law is challenged in the courts as unconstitutional on the ground that it arbitrarily interferes with personal liberty and private property without due process of law, the courts must be able to see that it has at least in fact some relation to the public health, that the public health is the end actually aimed at, and that it is appropriate and adapted to that end. This we have not been able to see in this law, and we must, therefore, pronounce it unconstitutional and void. . . .

311. CLEVELAND'S RECOMMENDATION OF THE REPEAL OF THE BLAND–ALLISON ACT

Extract from the First Annual Message to Congress
December 8, 1885

(Richardson, ed. *Messages and Papers*, Vol. VIII, p. 342 ff.)

Cleveland's plea for the repeal of the Silver Coinage Act of 1878 was not at this time successful, but he did succeed in defeating projects for free coinage of silver. On his re-election in 1893, Cleveland moved immediately for the repeal of the Sherman Silver Coinage Act, and carried his policy through to success. See Docs. No. 327, 328. On the first phase of Cleveland's silver policy, see A. Nevins, *Grover Cleveland*, ch. xvi.

. . . Nothing more important than the present condition of our currency and coinage can claim your attention.

Since February, 1878, the Government has, under the compulsory provisions of law, purchased silver bullion and coined the same at the rate of more than $2,000,000 every month. By this process up to the present date 215,759,431 silver dollars have been coined. . . .

The necessity for such an addition to the silver currency of the nation as is compelled by the silver-coinage act is negatived by the fact that up to the present time only about 50,000,000 of the silver dollars so coined have actually found their way into circulation, leaving more than 165,000,000 in the possession of the Government, the custody of which has entailed a considerable expense for the construction of vaults for its deposit. Against this latter amount there are outstanding silver certificates amounting to about $93,000,000.

Every month two millions of gold in the public Treasury are paid out for two millions or more of silver dollars, to be added to the idle mass already accumulated.

If continued long enough, this operation will result in the substitution of silver for all the gold the Government owns applicable to its general purposes. . . . The proportion of silver and its certificates received by the Government will probably increase as time goes on, for the reason that the nearer the period approaches when it will be obliged to offer silver in payment of its obligations the greater inducement there will be to hoard gold against depreciation in the value of silver or for the purpose of speculating.

This hoarding of gold has already begun.

When the time comes that gold has been withdrawn from circulation, then will be apparent the difference between the real value of the silver dollar and a dollar in gold, and the two coins will part company. Gold, still the standard of value and necessary in our dealings with other countries, will be at a premium over silver; banks which have substituted gold for the deposits of their customers may pay them with silver bought with such gold, thus making a handsome profit; rich speculators will sell their hoarded gold to their neighbors who need it to liquidate their foreign debts, at a ruinous premium over silver, and the laboring men and women of the land, most defenseless of all, will find that the dollar received for the wage of their toil has sadly shrunk in its purchasing power. It may be said that the latter result will be but temporary, and that ultimately the price of labor will be adjusted to the change; but even if this takes place the wage-worker can not possibly gain, but must inevitably lose, since the price he is compelled to pay for his living will not only be measured in a coin heavily depreciated and fluctuating and uncertain in its value, but this uncertainty in the value of the purchasing medium will be made the pretext for an advance in prices beyond that justified by actual depreciation. . . .

Those who do not fear any disastrous consequences arising from the continued compulsory coinage of silver as now directed by law, and who suppose that the addition to the currency of the country intended as its result will be a public benefit, are reminded that history demonstrates that the point is easily reached in the attempt to float at the same time two sorts of money of different excellence when the better will cease to be in general circulation. The hoarding of gold which has already taken place indicates that we shall not escape the usual experience in such cases. So if this silver coinage be continued we may reasonably expect that gold and its equivalent will abandon the field of circulation to silver alone. This of course must produce a severe contraction of our circulating medium, instead of adding to it.

It will not be disputed that any attempt on the part of the Government to cause the circulation of silver dollars worth 80 cents side by side with gold dollars worth 100 cents, even within the limit that legislation does not run counter to the laws of trade, to be successful must be seconded by the confidence of the people that both coins will retain the same purchasing power and be interchangeable at will. A special effort has been made by the Secretary of the Treasury to increase the amount of our silver coin in circulation; but the fact that a large share of the limited amount thus put out has soon returned to the public Treasury in payment of duties leads to the belief that the people do not now desire to keep it in hand, and this, with the evident disposition to hoard gold, gives rise to the suspicion that there already exists a lack of confidence among the people touching our financial processes. There is certainly not enough silver now in circulation to cause uneasiness, and the whole amount coined and now on hand might after a time be absorbed by the people without apprehension; but it is the ceaseless stream that threatens to overflow the land which causes fear and uncertainty. . . .

The so-called debtor class, for whose benefit the continued compulsory coinage of silver is insisted upon, are not dishonest because they are in debt, and they should not be suspected of a desire to jeopardize the financial safety of the country in order that they may cancel their present debts by paying the same in depreciated dollars. Nor should it be forgotten that it is not the rich nor the money lender alone that must submit to such a readjustment, enforced by the Government and their debtors. The pittance of the widow and the orphan and the incomes of helpless beneficiaries of all kinds would be disastrously reduced. The depositors in savings banks and in other institutions which hold in trust the savings of the poor, when their little accumulations are scaled down to meet the new order of things, would in their distress painfully realize the delusion of the promise made to them that plentiful money would improve their condition.

We have now on hand all the silver dollars necessary to supply the present needs of the people and to satisfy those who from sentiment wish to see them in circulation, and if their coinage is suspended they can be readily obtained by all who desire them. If the need of more is at any time apparent, their coinage may be renewed.

That disaster has not already overtaken us furnishes no proof that danger does not wait upon a continuation of the present silver coinage. We have been saved by the most careful management and unusual expedients, by a combination of fortunate conditions, and by a confident expectation that the course of the Government in regard to silver coinage would be speedily changed by the action of Congress.

Prosperity hesitates upon our threshold because of the dangers and uncertainties surrounding this question. Capital timidly shrinks from trade, and investors are unwilling to take the chance of the questionable shape in which their money will be returned to them, while enterprise halts at a risk against which care and sagacious management do not protect.

As a necessary consequence, labor lacks employment and suffering and distress are visited upon a portion of our fellow-citizens especially entitled to the careful consideration of those charged with the duties of legislation. No interest appeals to us so strongly for a safe and stable currency as the vast army of the unemployed.

I recommend the suspension of the compulsory coinage of silver dollars, directed by the law passed in February, 1878. . . .

312. PRESIDENT CLEVELAND ON PENSION LEGISLATION

Extract from Veto Message
June 21, 1886

(Richardson, ed. *Messages and Papers*, Vol. VIII, p. 437-8)

The practice of granting pensions by special legislation grew during the decade of the eighties to a positive menace. Cleveland did his best to stanch this flow of special legislation, but succeeded only in inspiring charges that he was unfriendly to the veterans of the Civil War. The Harrison administration reversed the Cleveland policy; Corporal Tanner, who was placed in charge of the pension bureau, is said to have remarked, "God help the surplus". The pension act of 1890 increased the annual pension appropriations, within two years, by $68,000,000. See, W. H. Glasson, *Federal Military Pensions;* A. Nevins, *Grover Cleveland,* ch. xix; J. W. Oliver, *History of Civil War Pensions.*

Executive Mansion,
June 21, 1886.

To the Senate:

. . . I am so thoroughly tired of disapproving gifts of public money to individuals who in my view have no right or claim to the same, notwithstanding apparent Congressional sanction, that I interpose with a feeling of relief a veto in a case where I find it unnecessary to determine the merits of the application. In speaking of the promiscuous and ill-advised grants of pensions which have lately been presented to me for approval, I have spoken of their "apparent Congressional sanction" in recognition of the fact that a large proportion of these bills have never been submitted to a majority of either branch of Congress, but are the result of nominal sessions held for the express purpose of their consideration and attended by a small minority of the members of the respective Houses of the legislative branch of Government. . . .

I have not been insensible to the suggestions which should influence every citizen, either in private station or official place, to exhibit not only a just but a generous appreciation of the services of our country's defenders. In reviewing the pension legislation presented to me many bills have been approved upon the theory that every doubt should be resolved in favor of the proposed beneficiary. I have not, however, been able to entirely divest myself of the idea that the public money appropriated for pensions is the soldiers' fund, which should be devoted to the indemnification of those who in the defense of the Union and in the nation's service have worthily suffered, and who in the day of their dependence resulting from such suffering are entitled to the benefactions of their Government. This reflection lends to the bestowal of pensions a kind of sacredness which invites the adoption of such principles and regulations as will exclude perversion as well as insure a liberal and generous application of grateful and benevolent designs. Heedlessness and a disregard of the principle which underlies the granting of pensions is unfair to the wounded, crippled soldier who is honored in the just recognition of his Government. Such a man should never find himself side by side on the pension roll with those who have been tempted to attribute the natural ills to which humanity is heir to service in the Army. Every relaxation of principle in the granting of pensions invites applications without merit and encourages those who for gain urge honest men to become dishonest. This is the demoralizing lesson taught the people that as against the public Treasury the most questionable expedients are allowable.

During the present session of Congress 493 special pension bills have been submitted to me, and I am advised that 111 more have received the favorable action of both Houses of Congress and will be presented within a day or two, making over 600 of these bills which have been passed up to this time during the present session, nearly three times the number passed at any entire session since the year 1861. With the Pension Bureau, fully equipped and regulated by the most liberal rules, in active operation, supplemented in its work by constant special legislation, it certainly is not unreasonable to suppose that in all the years that have elapsed since the close of the war a majority of the meritorious claims for pensions have been presented and determined.

I have now more than 130 of these bills before me awaiting Executive action. It will be impossible to bestow upon them the examination they deserve, and many will probably become operative which should be rejected.

In the meantime I venture to suggest the significance of the startling increase in this kind of legislation and the consequences involved in its continuance.

GROVER CLEVELAND.

313. THE SINGLE-TAX

Platform of Henry George in the Mayoralty Contest, New York
1886

(L. F. Post and F. C. Leubuscher, *An Account of the George-Hewitt Campaign of 1886*)

Henry George published his *Progress and Poverty* in 1879. Within the next six years the single-tax movement gained headway both in the United States and in the British Isles. In 1886 George was tendered the nomination for mayor by various labor and liberal groups in New York City. A fierce campaign, punctuated by unmeasured denunciation from George's opponents, resulted in the election of Abram S. Hewitt, the Tammany candidate. Hewitt was credited with 90,552 votes, George with 68,110, and Theodore Roosevelt, the Republican candidate, with 60,435: it was charged at the time that Tammany Hall counted out George, but these charges have not been substantiated. On the campaign, and Henry George, see Post and Leubuscher, above; the forthcoming biography of Abram Hewitt by A. Nevins; H. George, Jr., *The Life of Henry George*, Vol. II, ch. vii; G. R. Geiger, *The Philosophy of Henry George;* L. F. Post, *The Prophet of San Francisco;* A. N. Young, *The Single Tax Movement in the United States;* R. A. Sawyer, *Henry George and the Single Tax;* J. Chamberlain, *Farewell to Reform.*

The delegates of the trade and labor organizations of New York in conference assembled, make this declaration.

1. Holding that the corruptions of government and the impoverishment of labor result from neglect of the self-evident truths proclaimed by the founders of this Republic that all men are created equal and endowed with inalienable rights, we aim at the abolition of the system which compels men to pay their fellow-creatures for the use of God's gifts to all, and permits monopolies to deprive labor of natural opportunities for employment, . . .

2. Holding, moreover, that the advantages arising from social growth and improvement belong to society at large, we aim at the abolition of the system which makes such beneficent inventions as the railroad and telegraph a means for the oppression of the people, and the aggrandizement of an aristocracy of wealth and power. We declare the true purpose of government to be the maintenance of that sacred right of property which gives to everyone opportunity to employ his labor and security that he shall enjoy its fruits; to prevent the strong from oppressing the weak, and the unscrupulous from robbing the honest; and to do for the equal benefit of all such things as can be better done by organized society than by individuals; and we aim at the abolition of all laws which give to any class of citizens advantages, either judicial, financial, industrial, or political, that are not equally shared by all others. . . .

4. We declare the crowding of so many of our people into narrow tenements at enormous rents, while half the area of the city is yet unbuilt upon to be a scandalous evil, and that to remedy this state of things all taxes on buildings and improvements should be abolished, so that no fine shall be put upon the employment of labor in increasing living accommodations, and that taxes should be levied on land irrespective of improvements, so that those who are now holding land vacant shall be compelled either to build on it themselves, or give up the land to those who will.

5. We declare, furthermore, that the enormous value which the presence of a million and a half people gives to the land of this

city belongs properly to the whole community; that it should not go to the enrichment of individuals and corporations, but should be taken in taxation and applied to the improvement and beautifying of the city, to the promotion of the health, comfort, education, and recreation of its people, and to the providing of means of transit commensurate with the needs of a great metropolis. We also declare that existing means of traffic should not be left in the hands of corporations which, while gaining enormous profits from the growth of population, oppress their employés and provoke strikes that interrupt travel and imperil the public peace, but should by lawful process be assumed by the city and operated for public benefit.

314. WABASH, ST. LOUIS AND PACIFIC RAILROAD COMPANY v. ILLINOIS
118 U. S. 557
1886

Error to the Supreme Court of Illinois. This case involved the legality of an Illinois law prohibiting the "long-and-short-haul" evil. The Wabash Railroad had charged certain shippers fifteen cents a hundred pounds for carrying goods from Peoria, Illinois, to New York City, and twenty-five cents a hundred pounds for carrying goods of the same class for other shippers from Gilman, Illinois, to New York City, although Peoria was 86 miles farther from New York City than was Gilman. The Supreme Court of the State of Illinois upheld the constitutionality of the State law. This case seriously modified the earlier decision of the Court in *Munn* v. *Illinois,* and helped to bring about the passage of the Interstate Commerce Act.

MILLER, J. . . . The matter thus presented, as to the controlling influence of the Constitution of the United States over this legislation of the state of Illinois, raises the question which confers jurisdiction on this court. Although the precise point presented by this case may not have been heretofore decided by this court, the general subject of the power of the State legislatures to regulate taxes, fares, and tolls for passengers and transportation of freight over railroads within their limits has been very much considered recently . . . and the question how far such regulations, made by the States . . . are valid or void, as they may affect the transportation of goods through more than one State, in one voyage, is not entirely new here.

The supreme court of Illinois, in the case now before us, conceding that each of these contracts was in itself a unit, and that the pay received by the Illinois railroad company was the compensation for the entire transportation from the point of departure in the State of Illinois to the city of New York, holds that, while the statute of Illinois is inoperative upon that part of the contract which has reference to the transportation outside of the State, it is binding and effectual as to so much of the transportation as was within the limits of the State of Illinois; and undertaking for itself to apportion the rates charged over the whole route, decides that the contract and the receipt of the money for so much of it as was performed within the State of Illinois violate the statute of the State on that subject.

If the Illinois statute could be construed to apply exclusively to contracts for a carriage which begins and ends within the State, disconnected from a continuous transportation through or into other States, there does not seem to be any difficulty in holding it to be valid. . . .

The supreme court of Illinois does not place its judgment in the present case on the ground that the transportation and the charge are exclusively state commerce, but, conceding that it may be a case of commerce among the States, or interstate commerce, which Congress would have the right to regulate if it had attempted to do so, argues that this statute of Illinois belongs to that class of commercial regulations which may be established by the laws of a State until Congress shall have exercised its power on that subject. In support of its view of the subject the supreme court of Illinois cites the cases of Munn v. Illinois; Chicago, Burlington & Quincy Railroad v. Iowa; and Peik v. Chicago & Northwestern Railway,

. . . It cannot be denied that the general language of the court in these cases, upon the power of Congress to regulate commerce, may be susceptible of the meaning which the Illinois court places upon it. . . . Whatever may be the instrumentalities by which the transportation from one point to the other is effected, it is but one voyage, as much so as that of the steamboat on the Mississippi River.

It is not the railroads themselves that are regulated by this act of the Illinois legislature so much as the charge for transportation, and . . . if each one of the States through whose territories these goods are transported can fix its own rules for prices, for modes of transit, for times and modes of delivery, and all the other incidents of transportation to which the word "regulation" can be applied, it is readily seen that the embarrassments upon interstate transportation, as an element of interstate commerce, might be too oppressive to be submitted to. "It was," in the language of the court cited above, "to meet just such a case that the commerce [commercial] clause of the Constitution was adopted."

It cannot be too strongly insisted upon that the right of continuous transportation, from one end of the country to the other, is essential, in modern times, to that freedom of commerce from the restraints which the States might choose to impose upon it, that the commerce clause was intended to secure. This clause, giving to Congress the power to regulate commerce among the States, and with foreign nations, as this court has said before, was among the most important of the subjects which prompted the formation of the Constitution. And it would be a very feeble and almost useless provision, but poorly adapted to secure the entire freedom of commerce among the States which was deemed essential to a more perfect union by the framers of the Constitution, if, at every stage of the transportation of goods and chattels through the country, the State within whose limits a part of this transportation must be done could impose regulations concerning the price, compensation, or taxation, or any other restrictive regulation interfering with and seriously embarrassing this commerce. . . .

We must therefore hold that it is not, and

never has been, the deliberate opinion of a majority of this court that a statute of a State which attempts to regulate the fares and charges by railroad companies within its limits, for a transportation which constitutes a part of commerce among the States, is a valid law.

Let us see precisely what is the degree of interference with transportation of property or persons from one State to another which this statute proposes. A citizen of New York has goods which he desires to have transported by the railroad companies from that city to the interior of the State of Illinois. A continuous line of rail over which a car loaded with these goods can be carried, and is carried habitually, connects the place of shipment with the place of delivery. He undertakes to make a contract with a person engaged in the carrying business at the end of this route from whence the goods are to start, and he is told by the carrier: "I am free to make a fair and reasonable contract for this carriage to the line of the State of Illinois, but when the car which carries these goods is to cross the line of that State, pursuing at the same time this continuous track, I am met by a law of Illinois which forbids me to make a free contract concerning this transportation within that State, and subjects me to certain rules by which I am to be governed as to the charges which the same railroad company in Illinois may make, or has made, with reference to other persons and other places of delivery." So that while that carrier might be willing to carry these goods from the city of New York to the city of Peoria at the rate of fifteen cents per hundred pounds, he is not permitted to do so, because the Illinois railroad company has already charged at the rate of twenty-five cents per hundred pounds for carriage to Gilman, in Illinois, which is eighty-six miles shorter than the distance to Peoria.

So, also, in the present case, the owner of corn, the principal product of the country, desiring to transport it from Peoria, in Illinois, to New York, finds a railroad company willing to do this at the rate of fifteen cents per hundred pounds for a car-load, but is compelled to pay at the rate of twenty-five cents per hundred pounds, because the railroad company has received from a person residing at Gilman twenty-five cents per hundred pounds for the transportation of a car-load of the same class of freight over the same line of road from Gilman to New York. This is the result of the statute of Illinois, in its endeavor to prevent unjust discrimination, as construed by the supreme court of that State. The effect of it is that whatever may be the rate of transportation per mile charged by the railroad company from Gilman to Sheldon, a distance of twenty-three miles, in which the loading and the unloading of the freight is the largest expense incurred by the railroad company, the same rate per mile must be charged from Peoria to the city of New York.

The obvious injustice of such a rule as this, which railroad companies are by heavy penalties compelled to conform to, in regard to commerce among the States, when applied to transportation which includes Illinois in a long line of carriage through several States, shows the value of the constitutional provision which confides the power of regulating interstate commerce to the Congress of the United States, whose enlarged view of the interests of all the States, and of the railroads concerned, better fits it to establish just and equitable rules.

Of the justice or propriety of the principle which lies at the foundation of the Illinois statute it is not the province of this court to speak. As restricted to a transportation which begins and ends within the limits of the State, it may be very just and equitable, and it certainly is the province of the state legislature to determine that question. But when it is attempted to apply to transportation through an entire series of States a principle of this kind, and each one of the States shall attempt to establish its own rates of transportation, its own methods to prevent discrimination in rates, or to permit it, the deleterious influence upon the freedom of commerce among the States, and upon the transit of goods through those States, cannot be overestimated. That this species of regulation is one which must be, if established at all, of a general and national character, and cannot be safely and wisely remitted to local rules and local regulations, we think is clear from what has already been said. And if it be a regulation of commerce, as we think we have demonstrated it is, and as the Illinois court concedes it to be, it must be of that national character; and the regulation can only appropriately exist by general rules and principles, which demand that it should be done by the Congress of the United States under the commerce clause of the Constitution.

Judgment reversed.

BRADLEY, J., delivered a dissenting opinion, in which WAITE, C. J., and GRAY, J., concurred.

315. THE DAWES ACT
February 8, 1887
(*U. S. Statutes at Large*, Vol. XXIV, p. 388 ff.)

This act marked the end of a quarter of a century of agitation for reform in our treatment of the Indian problem. It was, said one philanthropist, "the end of a century of dishonor." See, for background, F. E. Leupp, *The Indian and His Problem;* G. W. Manypenny, *Our Indian Wards;* and for the subsequent history of the act, L. F. Schmeckebier, *The Office of Indian Affairs;* L. Meriam, et al., *The Problem of Indian Administration.*

An act to provide for the allotment of lands in severalty to Indians on the various reservations, and to extend the protection of the laws of the United States and the

Territories over the Indians, and for other purposes.

Be it enacted, That in all cases where any tribe or band of Indians has been, or shall hereafter be, located upon any reservation created for their use, either by treaty stipulation or by virtue of an act of Congress or executive order setting apart the same for their use, the President of the United States be, and he hereby is, authorized, whenever in his opinion any reservation or any part thereof of such Indians is advantageous for agriculture and grazing purposes to cause said reservation, or any part thereof, to be surveyed, or resurveyed if necessary, and to allot the lands in said reservation in severalty to any Indian located thereon in quantities as follows:

To each head of a family, one-quarter of a section;

To each single person over eighteen years of age, one-eighth of a section;

To each orphan child under eighteen years of age, one-eighth of a section; and,

To each other single person under eighteen years now living, or who may be born prior to the date of the order of the President directing an allotment of the lands embraced in any reservation, one-sixteenth of a section: . . .

SEC. 5. That upon the approval of the allotments provided for in this act by the Secretary of the Interior, he shall . . . declare that the United States does and will hold the land thus allotted, for the period of twenty-five years, in trust for the sole use and benefit of the Indian to whom such allotment shall have been made, . . . and that at the expiration of said period the United States will convey the same by patent to said Indian, or his heirs as aforesaid, in fee, discharged of such trust and free of all charge or incumbrance whatsoever: . . .

SEC. 6. That upon the completion of said allotments and the patenting of the lands to said allottees, each and every member of the respective bands or tribes of Indians to whom allotments have been made shall have the benefit of and be subject to the laws, both civil and criminal, of the State or Territory in which they may reside; . . . And every Indian born within the territorial limits of the United States to whom allotments shall have been made under the provisions of this act, or under any law or treaty, and every Indian born within the territorial limits of the United States who has voluntarily taken up, within said limits, his residence separate and apart from any tribe of Indians therein, and has adopted the habits of civilized life, is hereby declared to be a citizen of the United States, and is entitled to all the rights, privileges, and immunities of such citizens, whether said Indian has been or not, by birth or otherwise, a member of any tribe of Indians within the territorial limits of the United States without in any manner impairing or otherwise affecting the right of any such Indian to tribal or other property. . . .

316. THE HATCH ACT
March 2, 1887
(U. S. Statutes at Large, Vol. XXIV, p. 400 ff.)

This important act established Agricultural Experiment Stations. See, M. Conover, *The Office of Experiment Stations;* B. H. Hibbard, *History of Public Land Policies,* ch. xvi.

An act to establish agricultural experiment stations in connection with the colleges established in the several States under the provisions of an act approved July second, eighteen hundred and sixty-two, and of the acts supplementary thereto.

Be it enacted, That in order to aid in acquiring and diffusing among the people of the United States useful and practical information on subjects connected with agriculture, and to promote scientific investigation and experiment respecting the principles and applications of agricultural science, there shall be established, under direction of the college or colleges or agricultural department of colleges in each State or Territory es-

tablished, or which may hereafter be established, in accordance with the provisions of an act approved July second, eighteen hundred and sixty-two, entitled "An act donating public lands to the several States and Territories which may provide colleges for the benefit of agriculture and the mechanic arts," or any of the supplements of said act, a department to be known and designated as an "agricultural experiment station:" Provided, That in any State or Territory in which two such colleges have been or may be so established the appropriation hereinafter made to such State or Territory shall be equally divided between such colleges, unless the legislature of such State or Territory shall otherwise direct.

SEC. 2. That it shall be the object and duty of said experiment stations to conduct original researches or verify experiments on the physiology of plants and animals; the diseases to which they are severally subject, with the remedies for the same; the chemical composition of useful plants at their different stages of growth; the comparative advantages of rotative cropping as pursued under a varying series of crops; the capacity of new plants or trees for acclimation; the analysis of soils and water; the chemical composition of manures, natural or artificial, with experiments designed to test their comparative effects on crops of different kinds; the adaptation and value of grasses and forage plants; the composition and digestibility of the different kinds of food for domestic animals; the scientific and economic questions involved in the production of butter and cheese; and such other researches or experiments bearing directly on the agricultural industry of the United States as may in each case be deemed advisable, having due regard to the varying conditions and needs of the respective States or Territories. . . .

SEC. 5. That for the purpose of paying the necessary expenses of conducting investigations and experiments and printing and distributing the results as hereinbefore prescribed, the sum of fifteen thousand dollars per annum is hereby appropriated to each State, to be specially provided for by Congress in the appropriations from year to year, and to each Territory entitled under the provisions of section eight of this act, out of any money in the Treasury proceeding from the sales of public lands, to be paid in equal quarterly payments, on the first day of January, April, July, and October in each year, to the treasurer or other officer duly appointed by the governing boards of said colleges to receive the same, the first payment to be made on the first day of October, eighteen hundred and eighty-seven. . . .

317. CLEVELAND'S TARIFF MESSAGE OF 1887
December 6, 1887
(Richardson, ed. *Messages and Papers,* Vol. VIII, p. 579 ff.)

President Cleveland focussed the attention of the nation upon the problem of tariff reform by devoting his third annual message to Congress exclusively to this subject. For background, see A. Nevins, *Grover Cleveland,* chs. xvii, xxi; R. McElroy, *Grover Cleveland,* Vol. I, ch. xi; and histories of the tariff by Stanwood, Tarbell, and Taussig.

WASHINGTON, *December 6, 1887.*
To the Congress of the United States:

You are confronted at the threshold of your legislative duties with a condition of the national finances which imperatively demands immediate and careful consideration.

The amount of money annually exacted, through the operation of present laws, from the industries and necessities of the people largely exceeds the sum necessary to meet the expenses of the Government.

When we consider that the theory of our institutions guarantees to every citizen the full enjoyment of all the fruits of his industry and enterprise, with only such deduction as may be his share toward the careful and economical maintenance of the Government which protects him, it is plain that the exaction of more than this is indefensible extortion and a culpable betrayal of American fairness and justice. This wrong inflicted upon those who bear the burden of national taxation, like other wrongs, multiplies a brood of evil consequences. The public Treasury, which should only exist as a conduit conveying the people's tribute to its legitimate objects of expenditure, becomes a hoarding place for money needlessly withdrawn from trade and the people's use, thus crippling our national energies, suspending our country's development, preventing investment in productive enterprise, threatening financial disturbance, and inviting schemes of public plunder. . . .

In the present state of legislation the only pretense of any existing executive power to restore at this time any part of our surplus revenues to the people by its expenditure consists in the supposition that the Secretary of the Treasury may enter the market and purchase the bonds of the Government not yet due, at a rate of premium to be agreed upon. . . .

In considering the question of purchasing

bonds as a means of restoring to circulation the surplus money accumulating in the Treasury, it should be borne in mind that premiums must of course be paid upon such purchase, that there may be a large part of these bonds held as investments which can not be purchased at any price, and that combinations among holders who are willing to sell may unreasonably enhance the cost of such bonds to the Government. . . .

I have deemed it my duty to thus bring to the knowledge of my countrymen, as well as to the attention of their representatives charged with the responsibility of legislative relief, the gravity of our financial situation. . . .

Our scheme of taxation, by means of which this needless surplus is taken from the people and put into the public Treasury, consists of a tariff or duty levied upon importations from abroad and internal-revenue taxes levied upon the consumption of tobacco and spirituous and malt liquors. . . .

. . . Our present tariff laws, the vicious, inequitable, and illogical source of unnecessary taxation, ought to be at once revised and amended. These laws, as their primary and plain effect, raise the price to consumers of all articles imported and subject to duty by precisely the sum paid for such duties. Thus the amount of the duty measures the tax paid by those who purchase for use these imported articles. Many of these things, however, are raised or manufactured in our own country, and the duties now levied upon foreign goods and products are called protection to these home manufactures, because they render it possible for those of our people who are manufacturers to make these taxed articles and sell them for a price equal to that demanded for the imported goods that have paid customs duty. So it happens that while comparatively a few use the imported articles, millions of our people, who never used and never saw any of the foreign products, purchase and use things of the same kind made in this country, and pay therefor nearly or quite the same enhanced price which the duty adds to the imported articles. Those who buy imports pay the duty charged thereon into the public Treasury, but the great majority of our citizens, who buy domestic articles of the same class, pay a sum at least approximately equal to this duty to the home manufacturer. This reference to the operation of our tariff laws is not made by way of instruction, but in order that we may be constantly reminded of the manner in which they impose a burden upon those who consume domestic products as well as those who consume imported articles, and thus create a tax upon all our people.

It is not proposed to entirely relieve the country of this taxation. It must be extensively continued as the source of the Government's income; and in a readjustment of our tariff the interests of American labor engaged in manufacture should be carefully considered, as well as the preservation of our manufacturers. It may be called protection or by any other name, but relief from the hardships and dangers of our present tariff laws should be devised with especial precaution against imperiling the existence of our manufacturing interests. But this existence should not mean a condition which, without regard to the public welfare or a national exigency, must always insure the realization of immense profits instead of moderately profitable returns. As the volume and diversity of our national activities increase, new recruits are added to those who desire a continuation of the advantages which they conceive the present system of tariff taxation directly affords them. So stubbornly have all efforts to reform the present condition been resisted by those of our fellow-citizens thus engaged that they can hardly complain of the suspicion, entertained to a certain extent, that there exists an organized combination all along the line to maintain their advantage. . . .

It is also said that the increase in the price of domestic manufactures resulting from the present tariff is necessary in order that higher wages may be paid to our workingmen employed in manufactories than are paid for what is called the pauper labor of Europe. . . .

By the last census it is made to appear that of the 17,392,099 of our population engaged in all kinds of industries 7,670,493 are employed in agriculture, 4,074,238 in professional and personal service (2,934,876 of whom are domestic servants and laborers), while 1,810,256 are employed in trade and transportation and 2,623,089 employed in such manufacturing industries as are claimed to be benefited by a high tariff.

Their compensation, as it may be affected by the operation of tariff laws, should at all times be scrupuously kept in view; and yet with slight reflection they will not overlook the fact that they are consumers with the rest; that they too have their own wants and those of their families to supply from their earnings, and that the price of the necessaries of life, as well as the amount of their wages, will regulate the measure of their welfare and comfort. . . .

Nor can the worker in manufactures fail to understand that while a high tariff is claimed to be necessary to allow the payment of remunerative wages, it certainly results in a very large increase in the price of nearly all sorts of manufactures, which, in almost countless forms, he needs for the use of himself and his family. . . .

In speaking of the increased cost to the consumer of our home manufactures resulting from a duty laid upon imported articles of the same description, the fact is not overlooked that competition among our domestic producers sometimes has the effect of keeping the price of their products below the highest limit allowed by such duty. But it is notorious that this competition is too often strangled by combinations quite prevalent at this time, and frequently called trusts, which have for their object the regulation of the supply and price of commodities made and sold by members of the combination. The people can hardly hope for any consideration in the operation of these selfish schemes.

If, however, in the absence of such combination, a healthy and free competition reduces the price of any particular dutiable article of home production below the limit which it might otherwise reach under our tariff laws, and if with such reduced price its manufacture continues to thrive, it is entirely evident that one thing has been discovered which should be carefully scrutinized in an effort to reduce taxation.

The necessity of combination to maintain the price of any commodity to the tariff point furnishes proof that someone is willing to accept lower prices for such commodity and that such prices are remunerative; and lower prices produced by competition prove the same thing. Thus where either of these conditions exists a case would seem to be presented for an easy reduction of taxation.

The considerations which have been presented touching our tariff laws are intended only to enforce an earnest recommendation that the surplus revenues of the Government be prevented by the reduction of our customs duties, and at the same time to emphasize a suggestion that in accomplishing this purpose we may discharge a double duty to our people by granting to them a measure of relief from tariff taxation in quarters where it is most needed and from sources where it can be most fairly and justly accorded. . . .

The difficulty attending a wise and fair revision of our tariff laws is not underestimated. It will require on the part of the Congress great labor and care, and especially a broad and national contemplation of the subject and a patriotic disregard of such local and selfish claims as are unreasonable and reckless of the welfare of the entire country.

Under our present laws more than 4,000 articles are subject to duty. Many of these do not in any way compete with our own manufactures, and many are hardly worth attention as subjects of revenue. A considerable reduction can be made in the aggregate by adding them to the free list. The taxation of luxuries presents no features of hardship; but the necessaries of life used and consumed by all the people, the duty upon which adds to the cost of living in every home, should be greatly cheapened.

The radical reduction of the duties imposed upon raw material used in manufacturies, or its free importation, is of course an important factor in any effort to reduce the price of these necessaries. It would not only relieve them from the increased cost caused by the tariff on such material, but the manufactured product being thus cheapened that part of the tariff now laid upon such product, as a compensation to our manufacturers for the present price of raw material, could be accordingly modified. Such reduction or free importation would serve besides to largely reduce the revenue. It is not apparent how such a change can have any injurious effect upon our manufacturers. On the contrary, it would appear to give them a better chance in foreign markets with the manufacturers of other countries, who cheapen their wares by free material.

Thus our people might have the opportunity of extending their sales beyond the limits of home consumption, saving them from the depression, interruption in business, and loss caused by a glutted domestic market and affording their employees more certain and steady labor, with its resulting quiet and contentment. . . .

Our progress toward a wise conclusion will not be improved by dwelling upon the theories of protection and free trade. This savors too much of bandying epithets. It is a *condition* which confronts us, not a theory.

Relief from this condition may involve a slight reduction of the advantages which we award our home productions, but the entire withdrawal of such advantages should not be contemplated. The question of free trade is absolutely irrelevant, and the persistent claim made in certain quarters that all the efforts to relieve the people from unjust and unnecessary taxation are schemes of so-called free traders is mischievous and far removed from any consideration for the public good. . . .

318. THE INTERSTATE COMMERCE ACT
February 4, 1887
(*U. S. Statutes at Large,* Vol. XXIV, p. 379 ff.)

The exclusive character of Federal regulation of interstate commerce had been established as early as 1824 in *Gibbons* v. *Ogden,* Doc. No. 129, yet it was not until over half a century later that Congress passed any law looking to national regulation of commerce. State regulation of railroads, such as the Granger laws, had proved unsatisfactory, and the Wabash Case, Doc. No. 314, indicated the urgent necessity of national regulation. On the Act, see, D. R. Dewey, *National Problems,* ch. vi; B. H. Meyer, *Railway Legislation in the United States;* W. Z. Ripley, *Railroads: Rates and Regulation;* the Cullom Report, which largely influenced the character of the Act, is in the *Report of the Senate Select Committee on Interstate Commerce,* 49 Cong. 1 Sess. Sen. Report No. 46. See also, C. A. Miller, *Legislative History of the Interstate Commerce Act;* I. L. Sharfman, *The Interstate Commerce Commission,* 4 vols.

An act to regulate commerce.

Be it enacted . . . , That the provisions of this act shall apply to any common carrier or carriers engaged in the transportation of passengers or property wholly by railroad, or partly by railroad and partly by water when both are used, under a common control, management, or arrangement, for a continuous carriage or shipment, from one State or Territory of the United States, or the District of Columbia, to any other State or Territory of the United States, or the District of Columbia, or from any place in the United States to an adjacent foreign country, or from any place in the United States through a foreign country to any other place

in the United States, and also to the transportation in like manner of property shipped from any place in the United States to a foreign country and carried from such place to a port of transshipment, or shipped from a foreign country to any place in the United States and carried to such place from a port of entry either in the United States or an adjacent foreign country: *Provided, however,* That the provisions of this act shall not apply to the transportation of passengers or property, or to the receiving, delivering, storage, or handling of property, wholly within one State, and not shipped to or from a foreign country from or to any State or Territory as aforesaid.

The term "railroad" as used in this act shall include all bridges and ferries used or operated in connection with any railroad, and also all the road in use by any corporation operating a railroad, whether owned or operated under a contract, agreement, or lease; and the term "transportation" shall include all instrumentalities of shipment or carriage.

All charges made for any service rendered or to be rendered in the transportation of passengers or property as aforesaid, or in connection therewith, or for the receiving, delivering, storage, or handling of such property, shall be reasonable and just; and every unjust and unreasonable charge for such service is prohibited and declared to be unlawful.

SEC. 2. That if any common carrier subject to the provisions of this act shall, directly or indirectly, by any special rate, rebate, drawback, or other device, charge, demand, collect, or receive from any person or persons a greater or less compensation for any service rendered, or to be rendered, in the transportation of passengers or property, subject to the provisions of this act, than it charges, demands, collects, or receives from any other person or persons for doing for him or them a like and contemporaneous service in the transportation of a like kind of traffic under substantially similar circumstances and conditions, such common carrier shall be deemed guilty of unjust discrimination, which is hereby prohibited and declared to be unlawful.

SEC. 3. That it shall be unlawful for any common carrier subject to the provisions of this act to make or give any undue or unreasonable preference or advantage to any particular person, company, firm, corporation, or locality, or any particular description of traffic, in any respect whatsoever, or to subject any particular person, company, firm, corporation, or locality, or any particular description of traffic, to any undue or unreasonable prejudice or disadvantage in any respect whatsoever.

Every common carrier subject to the provisions of this act shall, according to their respective powers, afford all reasonable, proper, and equal facilities for the interchange of traffic between their respective lines, and for the receiving, forwarding, and delivering of passengers and property to and from their several lines and those connecting therewith, and shall not discriminate in their rates and charges between such connecting lines; but this shall not be construed as requiring any such common carrier to give the use of its tracks or terminal facilities to another carrier engaged in like business.

SEC. 4. That it shall be unlawful for any common carrier subject to the provisions of this act to charge or receive any greater compensation in the aggregate for the transportation of passengers or of like kind of property, under substantially similar circumstances and conditions, for a shorter than for a longer distance over the same line, in the same direction, the shorter being included within the longer distance; but this shall not be construed as authorizing any common carrier within the terms of this act to charge

and receive as great compensation for a shorter as for a longer distance: *Provided, however,* That upon application to the Commission appointed under the provisions of this act, such common carrier may, in special cases, after investigation by the Commission, be authorized to charge less for longer than for shorter distances for the transportation of passengers or property; and the Commission may from time to time prescribe the extent to which such designated common carrier may be relieved from the operation of this section of this act.

SEC. 5. That it shall be unlawful for any common carrier subject to the provisions of this act to enter into any contract, agreement, or combination with any other common carrier or carriers for the pooling of freights of different and competing railroads, or to divide between them the aggregate or net proceeds of the earnings of such railroads, or any portion thereof; and in any case of an agreement for the pooling of freights as aforesaid, each day of its continuance shall be deemed a separate offense.

SEC. 6. That every common carrier subject to the provisions of this act shall print and keep for public inspection schedules showing the rates and fares and charges for the transportation of passengers and property which any such common carrier has established and which are in force at the time upon its railroad, as defined by the first section of this act. . . . Copies for the use of the public shall be kept in every depot or station upon any such railroad, in such places and in such form that they can be conveniently inspected. . . .

No advance shall be made in the rates, fares, and charges which have been established and published as aforesaid by any common carrier in compliance with the requirements of this section, except after ten days' public notice, which shall plainly state the changes proposed to be made in the schedule then in force, and the time when the increased rates, fares, or charges will go into effect. . . .

And when any such common carrier shall have established and published its rates, fares, and charges in compliance with the provisions of this section, it shall be unlawful for such common carrier to charge, demand, collect, or receive from any person or persons a greater or less compensation for the transportation of passengers or property, or for any services in connection therewith, than is specified in such published schedule of rates, fares, and charges as may at the time be in force.

Every common carrier subject to the provisions of this act shall file with the Commission hereinafter provided for copies of its schedules of rates, fares, and charges which have been established and published in compliance with the requirements of this section, and shall promptly notify said Commission of all changes made in the same. Every such common carrier shall also file with said Commission copies of all contracts, agreements, or arrangements with other common carriers in relation to any traffic affected by the provisions of this act to which it may be a party. . . .

SEC. 9. That any person or persons claiming to be damaged by any common carrier subject to the provisions of this act may either make complaint to the Commission as hereinafter provided for, or may bring suit in his or their own behalf for the recovery of the damages for which such common carrier may be liable under the provisions of this act, in any district or circuit court of the United States of competent jurisdiction . . .

SEC. 10. That any common carrier subject to the provisions of this act, or, whenever such common carrier is a corporation, any director or officer thereof, or any receiver, trustee, lessee, agent, or person acting for or employed by such corporation, who, alone or with any other corporation, company, person, or party, . . . shall be guilty of any infraction of this act, or shall aid or abet therein, shall be deemed guilty of a misdemeanor, and shall, upon conviction thereof in any district court of the United States within the jurisdiction of which such offense was committed, be subject to a fine of not to exceed five thousand dollars for each offense.

SEC. 11. That a Commission is hereby created and established to be known as the Inter-State Commerce Commission, which shall be composed of five Commissioners, who shall be appointed by the President, by and with the advice and consent of the Senate. The Commissioners first appointed under this act shall continue in office for the term of two, three, four, five, and six years, respectively, from January 1, 1887, the term of each to be designated by the President; but their successors shall be appointed for terms of six years. . . . Any Commissioner may be removed by the President for inefficiency, neglect of duty, or malfeasance in office. Not more than three of the Commissioners shall be appointed from the same political party. No person in the employ of or holding any official relation to any common carrier subject to the provisions of this act, or owning stock or bonds thereof, or who is in any manner pecuniarily interested therein, shall enter upon the duties of or hold such office. Said Commissioners shall not engage in any other business, vocation, or employment. No vacancy in the Commission shall impair the right of the remaining Commissioners to exercise all the powers of the Commission.

SEC. 12. That the Commission hereby created shall have authority to inquire into the management of the business of all common carriers subject to the provisions of this act, and shall keep itself informed as to the manner and method in which the same is conducted, and shall have the right to obtain from such common carriers full and complete information necessary to enable the Commission to perform the duties and carry out the objects for which it was created; and for the purposes of this act the Commission shall have power to require the attendance and testimony of witnesses and the production of all books, papers, tariffs, contracts, agreements, and documents relating to any matter under investigation, and to that end may invoke the aid of any court of the United States in requiring the attendance and testimony of witnesses and the production of books, papers, and documents under the provisions of this section. . . .

SEC. 13. That any person, firm, corporation, or association, or any mercantile, agricultural, or manufacturing society, or any body politic or municipal organization complaining of anything done or omitted to be done by any common carrier subject to the provisions of this act in contravention of the provisions thereof, may apply to said Commission by petition, which shall briefly state the facts; whereupon a statement of the charges thus made shall be forwarded by the Commission to such common carrier, who shall be called upon to satisfy the complaint or to answer the same in writing within a reasonable time, to be specified by the Commission. . . . If there shall appear to be any reasonable ground for investigating said complaint, it shall be the duty of the Commission to investigate the matters complained of in such manner and by such means as it shall deem proper.

Said Commission shall in like manner investigate any complaint forwarded by the railroad commissioner or railroad commission of any State or Territory, at the request of such commissioner or commission, and may institute any inquiry on its own motion in the same manner and to the same effect as though complaint had been made. . . .

SEC. 16. That whenever any common carrier, . . . shall violate or refuse or neglect to obey any lawful order or requirement of the Commission in this act named, it shall be the duty of the Commission, and lawful for any company or person interested in such order or requirement, to apply, in a summary way, by petition, to the circuit court of the United States sitting in equity in the judicial district in which the common carrier complained of has its principal office, or in which the violation or disobedience of such order

or requirement shall happen, alleging such violation or disobedience, as the case may be; and the said court shall have power to hear and determine the matter, on such short notice to the common carrier complained of as the court shall deem reasonable. . . .

SEC. 20. That the Commission is hereby authorized to require annual reports from all common carriers subject to the provisions of this act, fix the time and prescribe the manner in which such reports shall be made, and to require from such carriers specific answers to all questions upon which the Commission may need information. Such reports shall also contain such information in relation to rates or regulations concerning fares or freights, or agreements, arrangements, or contracts with other common carriers, as the Commission may require; and the said Commission may, within its discretion, for the purpose of enabling it the better to carry out the purposes of this act, prescribe (if in the opinion of the Commission it is practicable to prescribe such uniformity and methods of keeping accounts) a period of time within which all common carriers subject to the provisions of this act shall have, as near as may be, a uniform system of accounts, and the manner in which such accounts shall be kept. . . .

319. THE JUDICIAL REVIEW OF RAILROAD RATES

Beginning with the Granger laws of the late sixties and early seventies, many mid-western and southern States established railway commissions with the power of fixing railway charges; that the State had the power thus to regulate charges was established in the Granger Cases of 1876. See Doc. No. 294. Obviously the charges fixed by the state, or its instruments, had to be reasonable, and not confiscatory. But who was to decide whether a rate was reasonable, and what was to be the basis upon which these charges were to be predicated? These and related questions have plagued the Courts for the last half-century, and no satisfactory solution has yet been discovered. The opinions below illustrate the process whereby the Court came to insist (1) that due process requires provision for judicial review, and (2) that the rates must be high enough to yield a fair return on a fair valuation of the property. The ingenuity of the Courts, however, has not yet been sufficient to devise a means whereby a fair

valuation of railroad property might be determined and a rate fixed that is fair both to the roads and to the public. For a general treatment of the problem of rate regulation, see, W. Z. Ripley, *Railroads: Rates and Regulation;* A. T. Hadley, *Railroad Transportation, its History and its Law;* F. A. Cleveland and F. W. Powell, *Railway Promotion and Capitalization in the United States.*

1. CHICAGO, MILWAUKEE AND ST. PAUL
   RAILROAD CO. v. MINNESOTA
   134 U.S., 418
   1889

Error to the Supreme Court of Minnesota. BLATCHFORD, J. . . . This being the construction of the statute by which we are bound in considering the present case, we are of the opinion, that, so construed, it conflicts with the Constitution of the United

States in the particulars complained of by the railroad company. It deprives the company of its right to a judicial investigation, by due process of law, under the forms and with the machinery provided by the wisdom of successive ages for the investigation judicially of the truth of a matter in controversy, and substitutes therefor, as an absolute finality, the action of a railroad commission which, in view of the powers conceded to it by the State court, cannot be regarded as clothed with judicial functions or possessing the machinery of a court of justice. . . .

Under the second section of the statute in question, it is provided that all charges made by a common carrier for the transportation of passengers or property shall be equal and reasonable. Under this provision, the carrier has a right to make equal and reasonable charges for such transportation. In the present case, the return alleged that the rate of charge fixed by the commission was not equal or reasonable, and the Supreme Court held that the statute deprived the company of the right to show that judicially. The question of the reasonableness of a rate of charge for transportation by a railroad company, involving as it does the element of reasonableness both as regards the company and as regards the public, is eminently a question for judicial investigation, requiring due process of law for its determination. If the company is deprived of the power of charging reasonable rates for the use of its property, and such deprivation takes place in the absence of an investigation by judicial machinery, it is deprived of the lawful use of its property, and thus, in substance and effect, of the property itself, without due process of law and in violation of the Constitution of the United States; and in so far as it is thus deprived, while other persons are permitted to receive reasonable profits upon their invested capital, the company is deprived of the equal protection of the laws. . . .

BRADLEY, J., dissenting: I cannot agree to the decision of the court in this case. It practically overrules *Munn* v. *Illinois,* and the several railroad cases that were decided at the same time. The governing principle of those cases was that the regulation and settlement of the fares of railroads and other accommodations is a legislative prerogative

and not a judicial one. This is a principle which I regard as of great importance. . . .

It is always a delicate thing for the courts to make an issue with the legislative department of the government, and they should never do so if it is possible to avoid it. By the decision now made we declare, in effect, that the judiciary, and not the legislature, is the final arbiter in the regulation of fares and freights of railroads and the charges of other public accommodations. It is an assumption of authority on the part of the judiciary which, it seems to me, . . . it has no right to make. . . . It is complained that the decisions of the board are final and without appeal. So are the decisions of the courts in matters within their jurisdiction. There must be a final tribunal somewhere for deciding every question in the world. Injustice may take place in all tribunals. All human institutions are imperfect—courts as well as commissions and legislatures. Whatever tribunal has jurisdiction, its decisions are final and conclusive unless an appeal is given therefrom. The important question always is, what is the lawful tribunal for the particular case? In my judgement, in the present case, the proper tribunal was the legislature, or board of commissioners which it created for that purpose. . . .

2. SMYTH V. AMES
169 U.S. 466
1897

Appeal from the Circuit Court of the United States for the district of Nebraska. The legislature of Nebraska by act of April 12, 1893 established a schedule of rates for railroad transportation radically reducing the rates then in effect. Bondholders of the Union Pacific and other railroads affected sought an injunction restraining the railroads from putting the new schedules into effect. The Circuit Court granted the injunction.

HARLAN, J. . . . The power to enact the statute whose validity is now assailed, . . . regulating railroads, classifying freights, fixing reasonable maximum rates, etc., in Nebraska, was referred by counsel to the general legislative power of the state as well as to the 4th section of article 11 of the State Constitution, which provides: "Railways heretofore constructed, or that may hereafter be constructed in this state, are hereby declared public highways. . . . And the legislature may from time to time pass laws establishing reasonable maximum rates of charges for the transportation of passengers and freight on the different railroads in this state." . . .

We are now to inquire whether the Nebraska statute is repugnant to the Constitution of the United States.

By the 14th Amendment it is provided that no state shall deprive any person of property without due process of law nor deny to any person within its jurisdiction the equal protection of the laws. That corporations are persons within the meaning of this Amendment is now settled. What amounts to deprivation of property without due process of law or what is a denial of the equal protection of the laws is often difficult to determine, especially where the question relates to the property of a quasi-public corporation and the extent to which it may be subjected to public control. But this court, speaking by Chief Justice Waite, has said that, while a state has power to fix the charges for railroad companies for the transportation of persons and property within its own jurisdiction, unless restrained by valid contract, or unless what is done amounts to a regulation of foreign or interstate commerce, such power is not without limit; and that "under pretense of regulating fares, and freights, the state cannot require a railroad corporation to carry persons or property without reward; neither can it do that which in law amounts to a taking of private property for public use without just compensation, or without due process of law." . . .

The plaintiffs contended that a railroad company is entitled to exact such charges for transportation as will enable it, at all times, not only to pay operating expenses, but also to meet the interest regularly accruing upon all its outstanding obligations, and justify a dividend upon all its stock; and that to prohibit it from maintaining rates or charges for transportation adequate to *all* those ends will deprive it of its property without due process of law, and deny to it the equal protection of the laws. This contention should not be passed without examination.

In our opinion the broad proposition advanced by counsel involves some misconception of the relations between the public and a railroad corporation. It is unsound in that it practically excludes from consideration the fair value of the property used, omits altogether any consideration of the right of the public to be exempt from unreasonable exactions, and makes the interests of the corporation maintaining a public highway the sole test in determining whether the rates established by or for it are such as may be rightfully prescribed as between it and the public. . . .

What was said in *Covington & L. Turnpike* v. *Sandford* is pertinent to the question under consideration. It was there observed: ". . . It is alleged here that the rates prescribed are unreasonable and unjust to the company and its stockholders. But that involves an inquiry as to what is reasonable and just for the public. . . . The public cannot properly be subjected to unreasonable rates in order simply that stockholders may earn dividends. The legislature has the authority, in every case where its power has not been restrained by contract, to proceed upon the ground that the public may not rightfully be required to submit to unreasonable exactions for the use of a public highway established and maintained under legislative authority. If a corporation cannot maintain such a highway and earn dividends for stockholders it is a misfortune for it and them which the Constitution does not require to be remedied by imposing unjust burdens upon the public."

We hold, however, that the basis of all calculations as to the reasonableness of rates to be charged by a corporation maintaining a highway under legislative sanction must be the fair value of the property being used by it for the convenience of the public. And, in order to ascertain that value, the original cost of construction, the amount expended in permanent improvements, the amount and market value of its bonds and stocks, the present as compared with the original cost of construction, the probable earning capacity of the property, under particular rates prescribed by statute, and the sum required to meet operating expenses, are all matters for consideration, and are to be given such weight as may be just and right in each case.

We do not say that there may not be other matters to be regarded in estimating the value of the property. What the company is entitled to ask is a fair return upon the value of that which it employs for the public convenience. On the other hand, what the public is entitled to demand is that no more be exacted from it for the use of a public highway than the services rendered by it are reasonably worth.

Decree of the Circuit Court affirmed.

3. REGAN V. FARMERS' LOAN AND TRUST COMPANY
154 U.S. 362
1894

Appeal from the United States circuit court for the Western District of Texas.

BREWER, J. . . . Passing from the question of jurisdiction to the act itself, there can be no doubt of the general power of a State to regulate the fares and freights which may be charged and received by railroads or other carriers, and that this regulation may be carried on by means of a commission. Such a commission is merely an administrative board created by the State for carrying into effect the will of the State, as expressed by its legislation. No valid objection, therefore, can be made on account of the general features of this act; those by which the State has created the railroad commission and entrusted it with the duty of prescribing rates of fares and freights as well as other regulations for the management of the railroads of the State. . . .

It appears from the bill that, in pursuance of the powers given to it by this act, the state commission has made a body of rates for fares and freights. This body of rates, as a whole, is challenged by the plaintiff as unreasonable, unjust, and working a destruction of its rights of property. The defendant denies the power of the court to entertain an inquiry into that matter, insisting that the fixing of rates for carriage by a public carrier is a matter wholly within the power of the legislative department of the government and beyond examination by the courts.

It is doubtless true, as a general proposition, that the formation of a tariff of charges for the transportation by a common carrier of persons or property is a legislative or ad-

ministrative rather than a judicial function. Yet it has always been recognized that, if a carrier attempted to charge a shipper an unreasonable sum, the courts had jurisdiction to inquire into that matter and to award to the shipper any amount exacted from him in excess of a reasonable rate; and also in a reverse case to render judgment in favor of the carrier for the amount found to be a reasonable charge. The province of the courts is not changed, nor the limit of judicial inquiry altered, because the legislature instead of the carrier prescribes the rates. The courts are not authorized to revise or change the body of rates imposed by a legislature or a commission; they do not determine whether one rate is preferable to another, or what under all circumstances would be fair and reasonable as between the carriers and the shippers; they do not engage in any mere administrative work; but still there can be no doubt of their power and duty to inquire whether a body of rates prescribed by a legislature or a commission is unjust and unreasonable, and such as to work a practical destruction to rights of property, and, if found to be so, to restrain its operation. In *Chicago, Burlington & Quincy Railroad* v. *Iowa,* and in *Peik* v. *Chicago & Northwestern Railway,* the question of legislative control over railroads was presented, and it was held that the fixing of rates was not a matter within the absolute discretion of the carriers, but was subject to legislative control. . . .

These cases all support the proposition that while it is not the province of the courts to enter upon the merely administrative duty of framing a tariff of rates for carriage, it is within the scope of judicial power and a part of judicial duty to restrain anything which, in the form of a regulation of rates, operates to deny to the owners of property invested in the business of transportation that equal protection which is the constitutional right of all owners of other property. There is nothing new or strange in this. It has always been a part of the judicial function to determine whether the act of one party (whether that party be a single individual, an organized body, or the public as a whole) operates to divest the other party of any rights of person or property. . . . It was, therefore, within the competency of the circuit court of the United States for the Western District of Texas, at the instance of the plaintiff, a citizen of another State, to enter upon an inquiry as to the reasonableness and justice of the rates prescribed by the railroad commission. . . .

320. THE SHERMAN ANTI-TRUST ACT
July 2, 1890
(*U. S. Statutes at Large,* Vol. XXVI, p. 209)

The growth of trusts and corporations, and some of the more notorious malpractices of big business, led to a growing demand for the regulation of trusts by the Federal Government. Both parties demanded such regulation in their platforms of 1888. December 4, 1889, Senator Sherman introduced a bill providing for the regulation of trusts. The final bill, which bears Sherman's name, was written chiefly by Senators Hoar and Edmunds. The first federal act ever passed which attempted to regulate trusts, it was couched in general and often ambiguous language. The bill contains no definition of a trust, or of a monopoly, and no indication of the meaning of the term "restraint". Nor was it clear at the time of the passage of the act whether its terms were meant to embrace combinations of labor as well as of capital. These, and similar questions, were deliberately left to the Courts. The literature on the Sherman Act is extensive. For the legislative background, see *Bills and Debates in Congress relating to Trusts,* 57th Congress, 2nd Sess., Sen. Doc. No. 147; A. H. Walker, *History of the Sherman Law;* J. D. Clark, *The Federal Trust Policy.* The most complete single volume on the trust problem is H. R. Seager and C. A. Gulick, *Trust and Corporation Problems.* The *Anti-Trust Decisions* have been collected in some twelve volumes. On the application of the Sherman Act to labor, see Docs. No. 326, 335. On the "rule of reason" see Doc. No. 375.

An ACT To protect trade and commerce against unlawful restraints and monopolies. . . .

  Be it enacted

  SEC. 1. Every contract, combination in the form of trust or otherwise, or conspiracy, in restraint of trade or commerce among the several States, or with foreign nations, is hereby declared to be illegal. Every person who shall make any such contract or engage in any such combination or conspiracy, shall be deemed guilty of a misdemeanor, and, on conviction thereof, shall be punished by fine not exceeding five thousand dollars, or by imprisonment not exceeding one year, or by both said punishments, in the discretion of the court.

  SEC. 2. Every person who shall monopolize, or attempt to monopolize, or combine or conspire with any other person or persons, to monopolize any part of the trade or commerce among the several States, or with foreign nations, shall be deemed guilty of a misdemeanor, and, on conviction thereof, shall be punished by fine not exceeding five thousand dollars, or by imprisonment not exceeding one year, or by both said punishments, in the discretion of the court.

  SEC. 3. Every contract, combination in form of trust or otherwise, or conspiracy, in restraint of trade or commerce in any Territory of the United States or of the District of Columbia, or in restraint of trade or commerce between any such Territory and another, or between any such Territory or Territories and any State or States or the District of Columbia, or with foreign nations, or between the District of Columbia and any State or States or foreign nations, is hereby declared illegal. Every person who shall make any such contract or engage in any such combination or conspiracy, shall be deemed guilty of a misdemeanor, and, on conviction thereof, shall be punished by fine not exceeding five thousand dollars, or by imprisonment not exceeding one year, or by both said punishments, in the discretion of the court.

  SEC. 4. The several circuit courts of the United States are hereby invested with jurisdiction to prevent and restrain violations of this act; and it shall be the duty of the several district attorneys of the United States, in their respective districts, under the direction of the Attorney-General, to institute proceedings in equity to prevent and restrain such violations. Such proceedings may be by way of petition setting forth the case and praying that such violation shall be enjoined or otherwise prohibited. When the parties complained of shall have been duly notified of such petition the courts shall proceed, as soon as may be, to the hearing and determination of the case; and pending such petition and before final decrees, the court may at any time make such temporary restraining order or prohibition as shall be deemed just in the premises.

SEC. 5. Whenever it shall appear to the court before which any proceeding under Section four of this act may be pending, that the ends of justice require that other parties should be brought before the court, the court may cause them to be summoned, whether they reside in the district in which the court is held or not; and subpœnas to that end may be served in any district by the marshal thereof.

SEC. 6. Any property owned under any contract or by any combination, or pursuant to any conspiracy (and being the subject thereof) mentioned in section one of this act, and being in the course of transportation from one State to another, or to a foreign country, shall be forfeited to the United States, and may be seized and condemned by like proceedings as those provided by law for the forfeiture, seizure, and condemnation of property imported into the United States contrary to law.

SEC. 7. Any person who shall be injured in his business or property by any other person or corporation by reason of anything forbidden or declared to be unlawful by this act, may sue therefor in any circuit court of the United States in the district in which the defendant resides or is found, without respect to the amount in controversy, and shall recover threefold the damages by him sustained, and the costs of suit, including a reasonable attorney's fee.

SEC. 8. That the word "person," or "persons," wherever used in this act shall be deemed to include corporations and associations existing under or authorized by the laws of either the United States, the laws of any of the Territories, the laws of any State, or the laws of any foreign country.

321. THE SHERMAN SILVER PURCHASE ACT
July 14, 1890
(U. S. Statutes at Large, Vol. XXVI, p. 289 ff.)

Both the free silver and the gold elements were dissatisfied with the Bland-Allison Act of 1878. The Sherman Act of 1890 represented another compromise, but one on the whole more favorable to the silver elements, because it provided for the purchase of practically the entire domestic output of silver. The concessions made to silver were in return for western support to the Mc Kinley tariff of 1890. See, D. R. Dewey, *Financial History of the United States*, ch. xix; A. B. Hepburn, *History of Currency*, ch. xvi; A. D. Noyes, *Forty Years of American Finance;* J. Sherman, *Recollections*, Vol. II; F. Wellborn, "Influence of the Silver Republicans, 1889–1891," *Miss. Valley Hist. Rev.*, Vol. XIV.

An act directing the purchase of silver bullion and the issue of Treasury notes thereon, and for other purposes.

Be it enacted . . . , That the Secretary of the Treasury is hereby directed to purchase, from time to time, silver bullion to the aggregate amount of four million five hundred thousand ounces, or so much thereof as may be offered in each month, at the market price thereof, not exceeding one dollar for three hundred and seventy-one and twenty-five hundredths grains of pure silver, and to issue in payment for such purchases of silver bullion Treasury notes of the United States to be prepared by the Secretary of the Treasury, in such form and of such denominations, not less than one dollar nor more than one thousand dollars, as he may prescribe. . . .

SEC. 2. That the Treasury notes issued in accordance with the provisions of this act shall be redeemable on demand, in coin, at the Treasury of the United States, or at the office of any assistant treasurer of the United States, and when so redeemed may be reissued; but no greater or less amount of such notes shall be outstanding at any time than the cost of the silver bullion and the standard silver dollars coined therefrom, then held in the Treasury purchased by such notes; and such Treasury notes shall be a legal tender in payment of all debts, public and private, except where otherwise expressly stipulated in the contract, and shall be receivable for customs, taxes, and all public dues, and when so received may be reissued; and such notes, when held by any national banking association, may be counted as a part of its lawful reserve. That upon demand of the holder of any of the Treasury notes herein provided for the Secretary of the Treasury shall, under such regulations as he may prescribe, redeem such notes in gold or silver coin, at his discretion, it being the established policy of the United States to maintain the two metals on a parity with each other upon the present legal ratio, or such ratio as may be provided by law.

SEC. 3. That the Secretary of the Treasury shall each month coin two million ounces of the silver bullion purchased under the provisions of this act into standard dollars until July 1, 1891, and after that time he shall coin of the silver bullion purchased under the provisions of this act as much as may be necessary to provide for the redemption of the Treasury notes herein provided for, and any gain or seigniorage arising from such coinage shall be accounted for and paid into the Treasury. . . .

322. CLEVELAND'S SILVER LETTER
February 10, 1891
Letter to E. Ellery Anderson of the Reform Club
(*Letters of Grover Cleveland*, ed. by Allan Nevins, p. 245–6)

This letter was one of the dramatic incidents of the silver struggle. In January, 1891, a free silver bill had passed the Senate, largely through Democratic support, and it was widely believed that Cleveland was drifting toward support of the silver cause. This letter to the Reform Club dramatically announced his unalterable opposition to free silver and aligned him with the conservative eastern wing of the Democratic Party. For background, see A. Nevins, *Grover Cleveland*, p. 465 ff.

New York, February 10, 1891

I have this afternoon received your note inviting me to attend tomorrow evening the meeting called for the purpose of voicing the opposition of the business men of our city to the 'free coinage of silver in the United States.'

I shall not be able to attend and address the meeting as you request, but I am glad that the business interests of New York are at last to be heard from on this subject.

It surely cannot be necessary for me to make a formal expression of my agreement with those who believe that the greatest peril would be initiated by the adoption of the scheme embraced in the measure now pending in Congress for the unlimited coinage of silver at our mints. If we have developed an unexpected capacity for the assimilation of a largely increased volume of this currency, and even if we have demonstrated the usefulness of such an increase, these conditions fall far short of insuring us against disaster, if in the present situation we enter upon the dangerous and reckless experiment of free, unlimited and independent silver coinage.

323. TILLMANISM IN SOUTH CAROLINA
The Shell Manifesto
January 23, 1890
(*The Charleston News and Courier*, January 23, 1890)

The century-old sectionalism in South Carolina was partially allayed by the unifying experiences of the Civil War and Reconstruction, but it came to the front again in the late eighties with the agrarian distress of that period. The Populist movement as such made little headway in South Carolina, but the revolt against the Bourbon control of the Democratic party was the political equivalent of the populist revolt elsewhere. The leader of the agrarian and up-country revolt against the Charleston "aristocracy" was Benjamin F. Tillman of Edgefield County. In 1886 and again in 1888 Tillman lost the nomination for governorship, but by 1890 the revolt was too strong to be controlled. The campaign of 1890 was inaugurated by the famous Shell Manifesto, written by Tillman, but published over the name of G. W. Shell, the

President of the Farmers' Association. Tillman and his entire ticket were swept into office in the elections of that year. See, F. P. Simkins, *The Tillman Movement in South Carolina;* J. D. Hicks, *The Populist Revolt;* W. W. Ball, *The State that Forgot.*

THE COMING CAMPAIGN
A CONTEST PROPOSED WITHIN THE DEMOCRATIC PARTY

An Address to the Democrats of South Carolina, Issued by Order of "the Executive Committee of the Farmers' Association of South Carolina."

Mr. W. G. Shell of Laurens, president of the Farmers' Association of South Carolina, requests the News and Courier to publish the following address:

To the Democracy of South Carolina: For four years the Democratic party in the State has been deeply agitated, and efforts have been made at the primaries and conventions to secure retrenchments and reform, and a recognition of the needs and rights of the masses. The first Farmers' Convention met in April 1886. Another in November of the same year perfected a permanent organization under the name of the "Farmers Association of South Carolina." This Association, representing the reform element in the party, has held two annual sessions since, and at each of these four conventions, largely attended by representative farmers from nearly all of the counties, the demands of the people for greater economy in the Government, greater efficiency in its officials, and a fuller recognition of the necessity for cheaper and more practical education have been pressed upon the attention of our Legislature.

In each of the two last Democratic State Conventions the "Farmers' Movement" has had a large following and we only failed of controlling the Convention of 1888 by a small vote—less than twenty-five—and that, too, in the face of the active opposition of nearly every trained politician in the State. We claim that we have always had a majority of the people on our side, and have only failed by reason of the superior political tactics of our opponents and our lack of organization. . . .

The executive committee of the Farmers' Association did not deem it worth while to hold any convention last November, but we

have watched closely every move of the enemies of economy—the enemies of true Jeffersonian Democracy—and we think the time has come to show the people what it is they need and how to accomplish their desires. We will draw up the indictment against these who have been and are still governing our State, because it is at once the cause and justification of the course we intend to pursue.

South Carolina has never had a real Republican Government. Since the days of the "Lords Proprietors" it has been an aristocracy under the forms of Democracy, and whenever a champion of the people has attempted to show them their rights and advocated those rights an aristocratic oligarchy has bought him with an office, or failing in that turned loose the floodgates of misrepresentation and slander in order to destroy his influence.

The peculiar situation now existing in the State, requiring the united efforts of every true white man to preserve white supremacy and our very civilization even has intensified and tended to make permanent the conditions which existed before the war. Fear of a division among us and consequent return of a negro rule has kept the people quiet, and they have submitted to many grievances imposed by the ruling faction because they dreaded to risk such a division.

The "Farmers' Movement" has been hampered and retarded in its work by this condition of the public mind, but we have shown our fealty to race by submitting to the edicts of the party and we intend, as heretofore, to make our fight inside the party lines, feeling assured that truth and justice must finally prevail. The results of the agitation thus far are altogether encouraging. Inch by inch and step by step true Democracy—the rule of the people—has won its way. We have carried all the outposts. Only two strongholds remain to be taken, and with the issues fairly made up and plainly put to the people we have no fear of the result. The House of Representatives has been carried twice, and at last held after a desperate struggle.

The advocates of reform and economy are no longer sneered at as "Three for a quarter statesmen." They pass measures of economy which four years ago would have excited only derision, and with the Farmers' Movement to strengthen their backbone have withstood the cajolery, threats and impotent rage of the old "ring bosses." The Senate is now the main reliance of the enemies of retrenchment and reform, who oppose giving the people their rights. The Senate is the stronghold of "existing institutions" and the main dependence of those who are antagonistic to all progress. As we captured the House we can capture the Senate; but we must control the Democratic State Convention before we can hope to make economy popular in Columbia, or be assured of no more pocket votes.

The General Assembly is largely influenced by the idea and policy of the State officers, and we must elect those before we can say the Farmers' Movement has accomplished its mission. It is true that we have wrenched from the aristocratic coterie who were educated at and sought to monopolize everything for the South Carolina College, the right to control the land script and Hatch fund and a part of the privilege tax on fertilizers for one year, and we have $40,000 with which to commence building a separate agricultural college, where the sons of poor farmers can get a practical education at small expense.

But we dare not relax our efforts or rely upon the loud professions of our opponents as to their willingness now to build and equip this agricultural school. . . .

All the cry about "existing institutions" which must remain inviolate shows that the ring—the South Carolina University, Citadel, Agricultural Bureau, Columbia Club, Greenville building ring—intend in the future, as in the past, to get all they can, and keep all they get. These pets of the aristocracy and its nurseries are only hoping that the people will again sink into their accustomed apathy. . . .

Is it not plain that these people intend to yield obedience to the law only when they are made to do it? The Farmers' Association demands that the land script and Hatch funds and the fertilizer tax shall be consolidated and used for the building and maintenance of a first class industrial school, with experiment stations attached, for farmers and mechanics. We hold that the experimental work, the educational work and the inspection and analysis of fertilizers can all be more efficiently and economically carried on under one board, mostly at one place, and much of it by the same corps of men who teach.

We have never and do not now want any increase of taxes to accomplish these ends. . . .

The bill prepared by the committee of the Farmers' Association for the reorganization of the board of agriculture would have secured our farmers against swindling fertilizer dealers, but it was amended to death by the lawyers in the Senate, who are attorneys for the phosphate miners and fertilizer companies, and the men who were elected on the board over the nominees of the Farmers' Convention were chosen not because they are more loyal to the agricultural interests, or better fitted for the position, but because they are friends of the University and belong or are subservient to our aristocracy —"so called"—and the phosphate miners are too well satisfied with the system of collecting the State royalty to permit a change if they can help it.

How wonderfully perfect or defective this system is, is shown by the fact that during ten years under the same officials not a single indictment has been brought against any one for attempting to swindle the State out of its dues. No wonder Charleston is in love with the agricultural bureau and cannot bear to see the "existing institutions" disturbed.

The recent proposal to sell the State's interest in the phosphate beds is fortunate, because thereby the attention of taxpayers is attracted to this most important matter. The Farmers' Association proposed in 1886 to increase the royalty as a means of lowering taxes, and we believe this can be safely done to the extent of $100,000.

A legislative committee was appointed to "investigate" and report on the subject. This was only done to give time—waiting ten months until the market had been manipulated, etc. This committee proceeded to show how well it had been chosen "not to do it." There was no honest effort made to get at the real facts as to the profits of the business and its ability to stand an increase of royalty, and after it had been "wined and dined" and brought into a suitable frame of mind that committee came to Columbia and actually proposed to give the six largest companies a monopoly for a less annual rental than the State was then receiving. Only one Senator, to whom all honor is due, dissented from this outrageous proposal. What was the result?

Of course the General Assembly did not act favorably upon it, but all thought of an increase of royalty was also abandoned, and this was what the corporation attorneys who were there in the interest of their clients and not of their constitutents had been working for. "The goose that lays the golden egg" was not killed—"existing institutions" were not disturbed. Phosphate rock, which had been manipulated down to $3.40 per ton, advanced in two months after the Legislature adjourned to $6.00 and has since ruled between $5.50 and $7.50 per ton. The golden eggs are still being laid, but not in the State's nest—whether some of them have not gone into pockets which they ought not is an open question.

Now we want to warn the people that the charter of the Coosaw Company—obtained by bribery, it is said, of a Radical Legislature—expires in 1891. This Company which has grown fabulously rich, claims to have a perpetual contract, with exclusive right to mine in Coosaw River and pay only one dollar a ton for the privilege. The next Legislature must act on this question and the next Attorney General may have to test these claims in court. The whole question of phosphate management, or mismanagement, must be settled. Can the taxpayers afford to allow any but true men to go to the Senate or elect a corporation lawyer as Attorney General? Shall the politicians choose him, or shall we, casting about among the many honorable, patriotic lawyers of the State, make the selection ourselves?

The Legislature which has just adjourned has other sins to answer for, or rather the Senate must be held responsible. The people demanded that the railroad commissioners should have something to do besides draw their salaries and spend them. We want protection against the greed of the gigantic corporations owned by the North, which regard South Carolina as a lemon to be squeezed and care nothing for the welfare of our towns, our State or our people. . . .

The railroad commissioners now in office have been "tamed," so to speak, by the railroads, and men who have not been so long

under wing might have done something in the interest of the people; but that same Senate which has again and again thwarted the people, which refused to reduce salaries, which fought the Clemson College and yielded at last to necessity only, which is the stronghold of aristocracy with its non-progressive, impracticable ideas, which, in a word, is dominated by Charleston's rich politicians—that Senate resolved to maintain this "existing institution" too, status quo.

Of all the taxes we pay, the pensions to Confederate Veterans are submitted to most willingly, and we regret that we cannot increase the pittance they receive. But the continuance of men in office as political pensioners, after their ability or willingness to serve the people is gone—when the interests and even rights of the people are thereby sacrificed, this pandering to sentiment, this favoritism—is a crime, nothing more and nothing less. Rotation in office is a cardinal Democratic principle, and the neglect to practice it is the cause of many of the ills we suffer.

We cannot elaborate the other counts in this indictment. We can only point briefly to the mismanagement of the Penitentiary, which is a burden on the taxpayers, even while engaged in no public works which might benefit the State. To the wrong committed against the people of many counties (strongholds of Democracy) by the failure to reapportion representation according to the population, whereby Charleston has five votes in the House and ten votes in the State Convention, which choose our State officers, to which it is not entitled.

To the zeal and extravagance of this aristocratic oligarchy, whose sins we are pointing out, in promising higher education for every class except farmers, while it neglects the free schools which are the only chance for an education to thousands of poor children, whose fathers bore the brunt in the struggle for our redemption in 1876. To the continued recurrence of horrible lynchings—which we can but attribute to bad laws and their inefficient administration. To the impotence of justice to punish criminals who have money. To the failure to call a constitutional convention that we may have an organic law framed by South Carolinians for South Carolinians and suited to our wants, thereby lessening the burdens of taxation and giving us better government.

Fellow Democrats, do not all these things cry out for a change? Is it not opportune, when there is no national election, for the common people who redeemed the State from Radical rule to take charge of it? Can we afford to leave it longer in the hands of those who, wedded to ante-bellum ideas, but possessing little of ante-bellum patriotism and honor, are running it in the interest of a few families and for the benefit of a selfish ring of politicians? As real Democrats and white men, those who here renew our pledge to make the fight inside the Democratic party and abide the result, we call upon every true Carolinian, of all classes and callings, to help us purify and reform the Democratic party and give us a government of the people, by the people and for the people.

If we control the State Democratic Convention, a Legislature in sympathy will naturally follow; failing to do this, we risk losing all we have gained, and have no hope of any change for the better. . . .

We therefore issue this call for a Convention of those Democrats who sympathize with our views and purposes, as herein set forth, . . .

By order of the executive committee of the Farmers' Association of South Carolina.

G. W. Shell,
President and Ex Officio Chairman.

324. THE OCALA DEMANDS
December, 1890

(Proceedings of the Supreme Council of the National Farmers' Alliance and Industrial Union, 1890, p. 32–3)

The Southern Alliance, the Farmers' Mutual Benefit Association, and the Colored Farmers' Alliance, all met at Ocala, Florida, in 1890. The demands drawn up presaged the entry of the Alliance into the political field, and revealed the beginnings of the disintegration of the Alliance. See, J. D. Hicks, *The Populist Revolt*, ch. viii.

1. a. We demand the abolition of national banks.

b. We demand that the government shall establish sub-treasuries or depositories in the several states, which shall loan money direct to the people at a low rate of interest, not to exceed two per cent per annum, on non-perishable farm products, and also upon real estate, with proper limitations upon the quantity of land and amount of money.

c. We demand that the amount of the circulating medium be speedily increased to not less than $50 per capita.

2. We demand that Congress shall pass such laws as will effectually prevent the dealing in futures of all agricultural and mechanical productions; providing a stringent system of procedure in trials that will secure the prompt conviction, and imposing such penalties as shall secure the most perfect compliance with the law.

3. We condemn the silver bill recently passed by Congress, and demand in lieu thereof the free and unlimited coinage of silver.

4. We demand the passage of laws prohibiting alien ownership of land, and that Congress take prompt action to devise some plan to obtain all lands now owned by aliens and foreign syndicates; and that all lands now held by railroads and other corporations in excess of such as is actually used and needed by them be reclaimed by the government and held for actual settlers only.

5. Believing in the doctrine of equal rights to all and special privileges to none, we demand—

a. That our national legislation shall be so framed in the future as not to build up one industry at the expense of another.

b. We further demand a removal of the existing heavy tariff tax from the necessities of life, that the poor of our land must have.

c. We further demand a just and equitable system of graduated tax on incomes.

d. We believe that the money of the country should be kept as much as possible in the hands of the people, and hence we demand that all national and state revenues shall be limited to the necessary expenses of the government economically and honestly administered.

6. We demand the most rigid, honest, and just state and national government control and supervision of the means of public communication and transportation, and if this control and supervision does not remove the abuse now existing, we demand the government ownership of such means of communication and transportation.

7. We demand that the Congress of the United States submit an amendment to the Constitution providing for the election of United States Senators by direct vote of the people of each state.

325. POPULIST PARTY PLATFORM
July 4, 1892
(E. McPherson, *A Handbook of Politics for 1892*, p. 269 ff.)

The Preamble, which appeared first in the St. Louis platform of March 1892, was written by Ignatius Donnelly of Minnesota. The most thorough history of the Populist movement is J. D. Hicks, *The Populist Revolt*, which contains an elaborate bibliography.

Assembled upon the 116th anniversary of the Declaration of Independence, the People's Party of America, in their first national convention, invoking upon their action the blessing of Almighty God, put forth in the name and on behalf of the people of this country, the following preamble and declaration of principles:

PREAMBLE

The conditions which surround us best justify our co-operation; we meet in the midst of a nation brought to the verge of moral, political, and material ruin. Corruption dominates the ballot-box, the Legislatures, the Congress, and touches even the ermine of the bench. The people are demoralized; most of the States have been compelled to isolate the voters at the polling places to prevent universal intimidation and bribery. The newspapers are largely subsidized or muzzled, public opinion silenced, business prostrated, homes covered with mortgages, labor impoverished, and the land concentrating in the hands of capitalists. The urban workmen are denied the right to organize for self-protection, imported pauperized labor beats down their wages, a hireling standing army, unrecognized by our laws, is established to shoot them down, and they are rapidly degenerating into European conditions. The fruits of the toil of millions are boldly stolen to build up colossal fortunes for a few, unprecedented in the history of mankind; and the possessors of these, in turn, despise the Republic and endanger liberty. From the same prolific womb of governmental injustice we breed the two great classes—tramps and millionaires.

The national power to create money is appropriated to enrich bond-holders; a vast public debt payable in legal-tender currency has been funded into gold-bearing bonds, thereby adding millions to the burdens of the people.

Silver, which has been accepted as coin since the dawn of history, has been demonetized to add to the purchasing power of gold by decreasing the value of all forms of property as well as human labor, and the supply of currency is purposely abridged to fatten usurers, bankrupt enterprise, and enslave industry. A vast conspiracy against mankind has been organized on two continents, and it is rapidly taking possession of the world. If not met and overthrown at once it forebodes terrible social convulsions, the destruction of civilization, or the establishment of an absolute despotism.

We have witnessed for more than a quarter of a century the struggles of the two great political parties for power and plunder, while grievous wrongs have been inflicted upon the suffering people. We charge that the controlling influences dominating both these parties have permitted the existing dreadful conditions to develop without serious effort to prevent or restrain them. Neither do they now promise us any substantial reform. They have agreed together to ignore, in the coming campaign, every issue but one. They propose to drown the outcries of a plundered people with the uproar of a sham battle over the tariff, so that capitalists, corporations, national banks, rings, trusts, watered stock, the demonetization of silver and the oppressions of the usurers may all be lost sight of. They propose to sacrifice our homes, lives, and children on the altar of mammon; to destroy the multitude in order to secure corruption funds from the millionaires.

Assembled on the anniversary of the birthday of the nation, and filled with the spirit of the grand general and chief who established our independence, we seek to restore the government of the Republic to the hands of the "plain people," with which class it originated. We assert our purposes to be identical with the purposes of the National Constitution; to form a more perfect union and establish justice, insure domestic tranquillity, provide for the common defence, promote the general welfare, and secure the blessings of liberty for ourselves and our posterity.

We declare that this Republic can only endure as a free government while built upon the love of the people for each other and for the nation; that it cannot be pinned together by bayonets; that the Civil War is over, and that every passion and resentment which grew out of it must die with it, and that we must be in fact, as we are in name, one united brotherhood of free men.

Our country finds itself confronted by conditions for which there is no precedent in the history of the world; our annual agricultural productions amount to billions of dollars in value, which must, within a few weeks or months, be exchanged for billions of dollars' worth of commodities consumed in their production; the existing currency supply is wholly inadequate to make this exchange; the results are falling prices, the formation of combines and rings, the impoverishment of the producing class. We pledge ourselves that if given power we will labor to correct these evils by wise and reasonable legislation, in accordance with the terms of our platform.

We believe that the power of government —in other words, of the people—should be expanded (as in the case of the postal service) as rapidly and as far as the good sense of an intelligent people and the teachings of experience shall justify, to the end that op-pression, injustice, and poverty shall eventually cease in the land.

While our sympathies as a party of reform are naturally upon the side of every proposition which will tend to make men intelligent, virtuous, and temperate, we nevertheless regard these questions, important as they are, as secondary to the great issues now pressing for solution, and upon which not only our individual prosperity but the very existence of free institutions depend; and we ask all men to first help us to determine whether we are to have a republic to administer before we differ as to the conditions upon which it is to be administered, believing that the forces of reform this day organized will never cease to move forward until every wrong is righted and equal rights and equal privileges securely established for all the men and women of this country.

PLATFORM

We declare, therefore—

First.—That the union of the labor forces of the United States this day consummated shall be permanent and perpetual; may its spirit enter into all hearts for the salvation of the Republic and the uplifting of mankind.

Second.—Wealth belongs to him who creates it, and every dollar taken from industry without an equivalent is robbery. "If any will not work, neither shall he eat." The interests of rural and civil labor are the same; their enemies are identical.

Third.—We believe that the time has come when the railroad corporations will either own the people or the people must own the railroads; and should the government enter upon the work of owning and managing all railroads, we should favor an amendment to the constitution by which all persons engaged in the government service shall be placed under a civil-service regulation of the most rigid character, so as to prevent the increase of the power of the national administration by the use of such additional government employes.

FINANCE.—We demand a national currency, safe, sound, and flexible issued by the general government only, a full legal tender for all debts, public and private, and that without the use of banking corporations; a just, equitable, and efficient means of distribution direct to the people, at a tax not to exceed 2 per cent, per annum, to be provided as set forth in the sub-treasury plan of the Farmers' Alliance, or a better system; also by payments in discharge of its obligations for public improvements.

1. We demand free and unlimited coinage of silver and gold at the present legal ratio of 16 to 1.
2. We demand that the amount of circulating medium be speedily increased to not less than $50 per capita.
3. We demand a graduated income tax.
4. We believe that the money of the country should be kept as much as possible in the hands of the people, and hence we demand that all State and national revenues shall be limited to the necessary expenses of the government, economically and honestly administered.
5. We demand that postal savings banks be established by the government for the safe deposit of the earnings of the people and to facilitate exchange.

TRANSPORTATION.—Transportation being a means of exchange and a public necessity, the government should own and operate the railroads in the interest of the people. The telegraph and telephone, like the post-office system, being a necessity for the transmission of news, should be owned and operated by the government in the interest of the people.

LAND.—The land, including all the natural sources of wealth, is the heritage of the people, and should not be monopolized for speculative purposes, and alien ownership of land should be prohibited. All land now held by railroads and other corporations in excess of their actual needs, and all lands now owned by aliens should be reclaimed by the government and held for actual settlers only.

EXPRESSION OF SENTIMENTS

Your Committee on Platform and Resolutions beg leave unanimously to report the following:

Whereas, Other questions have been presented for our consideration, we hereby submit the following, not as a part of the Platform of the People's Party, but as resolutions expressive of the sentiment of this Convention.

1. RESOLVED, That we demand a free ballot and a fair count in all elections. and pledge ourselves to secure it to every legal voter without Federal intervention, through the adoption by the States of the unperverted Australian or secret ballot system.
2. RESOLVED, That the revenue derived from a graduated income tax should be applied to the reduction of the burden of taxation now levied upon the domestic industries of this country.
3. RESOLVED, That we pledge our support to fair and liberal pensions to ex-Union soldiers and sailors.
4. RESOLVED, That we condemn the fallacy of protecting American labor under the present system, which opens our ports to the pauper and criminal classes of the world and crowds out our wage-earners; and we denounce the present ineffective laws against contract labor, and demand the further restriction of undesirable emigration.
5. RESOLVED, That we cordially sympathize with the efforts of organized workingmen to shorten the hours of labor, and demand a rigid enforcement of the existing eight-hour law on Government work, and ask that a penalty clause be added to the said law.
6. RESOLVED, That we regard the maintenance of a large standing army of mercenaries, known as the Pinkerton system, as a menace to our liberties, and we demand its abolition; and we condemn the recent invasion of the Territory of Wyoming by the hired assassins of plutocracy, assisted by Federal officers.
7. RESOLVED, That we commend to the favorable consideration of the people and the reform press the legislative system known as the initiative and referendum.
8. RESOLVED, That we favor a constitutional provision limiting the office of President and Vice-President to one term, and providing for the election of Senators of the United States by a direct vote of the people.
9. RESOLVED, That we oppose any subsidy or national aid to any private corporation for any purpose.

10. RESOLVED, That this convention sympathizes with the Knights of Labor and their righteous contest with the tyrannical combine of clothing manufacturers of Rochester, and declare it to be a duty of all who hate tyranny and oppression to refuse to purchase the goods made by the said manufacturers, or to patronize any merchants who sell such goods.

326. UNITED STATES v. WORKINGMEN'S AMALGAMATED COUNCIL OF NEW ORLEANS ET AL.
54 Fed. 994
1893

Did the prohibitions of the Sherman Anti-Trust Act apply to combinations of labor? The wording of the act was ambiguous—perhaps purposely so—and the question was left for the courts to decide. Compare the opinion below with *Waterhouse* v. *Comer*, 55 Fed. 150, and *United States* v. *Patterson*, 55 Fed. 605. For a careful discussion of the relation of the Sherman Law to labor, see A. T. Mason, *Organized Labor and the Law;* E. Berman, *Labor and the Sherman Act.*

BILLINGS, District Judge.

This cause is submitted upon an application for an injunction on the bill of complaint, answer, and numerous affidavits and exhibits. The bill of complaint in this case is filed by the United States under the act of Congress entitled "An act to protect trade and commerce against unlawful restraint and monopolies," (26 St. at Large, p. 209.) The substance of the bill avers that a disagreement between the warehousemen and their employes and the principal draymen and their subordinates had been adopted by all the organizations named in the bill, until, by this vast combination of men and of organizations, it was threatened that, unless there was an acquiescence in the demands of the subordinate workmen and draymen, all the men in all the defendant organizations would leave work, and would allow no work in any department of business; that violence was threatened and used in support of this demand; and that this demand included the interstate and foreign commerce which flows through the city of New Orleans. The bill further states that the proceedings on the part of the defendants had taken such a vast and ramified proportion that, in consequence of the threats of the defendants, the whole business of the city of New Orleans was paralyzed, and the transit of goods and merchandise which was being conveyed through it from state to state, and to and from foreign countries, was totally interrupted. . . .

. . . The theory of the defense is that this case does not fall within the purview of the statute; that the statute prohibited monopolies and combinations which, using words in a general sense, were of capitalists, and not of laborers. I think the congressional debates show that the statute had its origins in the evils of massed capital; but, when the congress came to formulating the prohibition which is the yardstick for measuring to complainant's right to injunction, . . . the subject had so broadened in the minds of the legislators that the source of the evil was not regarded as material, and the evil in its entirety is dealt with. They made the interdiction include combinations of labor, as well as of capital; in fact, all combinations in restraint of commerce, without reference to the character of the persons who entered into them. It is true this statute has not been much expounded by judges, but, as it seems to me, its meaning, as far as relates to the sort of combinations to which it is to apply, is manifest, and that it includes combinations which are composed of laborers acting in the interest of laborers. . . .

The defendants urge (6) that the combination to secure or compel the employment of none but union men is not in the restraint of commerce. To determine whether the proposition urged as a defense can apply to this case, the case must first be stated as it is made out by the established facts. The case is this: The combination setting out to secure and compel the employment of none but union men in a given business, as a means to effect this compulsion, finally enforced a discontinuance of labor in all kinds of business, including the business of transportation of goods and merchandise which were in transit through the city of New Orleans, from state to state, and to and from foreign countries. When the case is thus stated,— and it must be so stated to embody the facts here proven,—I do not think there can be any question but that the combination of the defendants was in restraint of commerce.

I have thus endeavored to state and deal with the various grounds of defense urged before me. I shall now, as briefly as possible, state the case as it is established in the voluminous record.

. . . The question simply is, do these facts establish a case within the statute? It seems to me this question is tantamount to the question, could there be a case under the statute? It is conceded that the labor organizations were at the outset lawful. But when lawful forces are put into unlawful channels,—i.e. when lawful associations adopt and further unlawful purposes and do unlawful acts,—the associations themselves become unlawful. The evil, as well as the unlawfulness, of the act of the defendants, consists in this: that, until certain demands of theirs were complied with, they endeavored to prevent, and did prevent, everybody from moving the commerce of the country. . . .

It is the successful effort of the combination of the defendants to intimidate and overawe others who were at work in conducting or carrying on the commerce of the country, in which the court finds their error and their violation of the statute. One of the intended results of their combined action was the forced stagnation of all the commerce which flowed through New Orleans. This intent and combined action are none the less unlawful because they included in their scope the paralysis of all other business within the city as well. . . .

327. CLEVELAND'S MESSAGE ON THE REPEAL OF THE SHERMAN SILVER PURCHASE ACT
August 8, 1893

(Richardson, ed. *Messages and Papers,* Vol. IX, p. 401 ff.)

On June 30, 1893, Cleveland issued a call for a special session of Congress to meet August 7. The struggle for the repeal of the Silver Purchase Act of 1890 was the most violent political battle of Cleveland's career. See, A. Nevins, *Grover Cleveland,* ch. xxix; R. McElroy, *Grover Cleveland,* Vol. II, ch. i; W. J. Bryan, *The First Battle,* ch. ii, iii; A. B. Hepburn, *History of Currency in the United States,* ch. xx.

Executive Mansion, *August 8, 1893.*
To the Congress of the United States:

The existence of an alarming and extraordinary business situation, involving the welfare and prosperity of all our people, has constrained me to call together in extra session the people's representatives in Congress, to the end that through a wise and patriotic exercise of the legislative duty, with which they solely are charged, present evils may be mitigated and dangers threatening the future may be averted.

Our unfortunate financial plight is not the result of untoward events nor of conditions related to our natural resources, nor is it traceable to any of the afflictions which frequently check national growth and prosperity. With plenteous crops, with abundant promise of remunerative production and manufacture, with unusual invitation to safe investment, and with satisfactory assurance to business enterprise, suddenly financial distrust and fear have sprung up on every side. . . . Values supposed to be fixed are fast becoming conjectural, and loss and failure have invaded every branch of business.

I believe these things are principally chargeable to Congressional legislation touching the purchase and coinage of silver by the General Government.

This legislation is embodied in a statute passed on the 14th day of July, 1890, which was the culmination of much agitation on the subject involved, and which may be considered a truce, after a long struggle, between the advocates of free silver coinage and those intending to be more conservative. . . .

This law provides that in payment for the 4,500,000 ounces of silver bullion which the Secretary of the Treasury is commanded to purchase monthly there shall be issued Treasury notes redeemable on demand in gold or silver coin, at the discretion of the Secretary of the Treasury, and that said notes may be reissued. It is, however, declared in the act to be "the established policy of the United States to maintain the two metals on a parity with each other upon the present legal ratio or such ratio as may be provided by law." This declaration so controls the action of the Secretary of the Treasury as to prevent his exercising the discretion nominally vested in him if by such action the parity between gold and silver may be disturbed. Manifestly a refusal by the Secretary to pay these Treasury notes in gold if demanded would necessarily result in their discredit and depreciation as obligations payable only in silver, and would destroy the parity between the two metals by establishing a discrimination in favor of gold. . . .

The policy necessarily adopted of paying these notes in gold has not spared the gold reserve of $100,000,000 long ago set aside by the Government for the redemption of other notes, for this fund has already been subjected to the payment of new obligations amounting to about $150,000,000 on account of silver purchases, and has as a consequence for the first time since its creation been encroached upon.

We have thus made the depletion of our gold easy and have tempted other and more appreciative nations to add it to their stock. . . .

Unless Government bonds are to be constantly issued and sold to replenish our exhausted gold, only to be again exhausted, it is apparent that the operation of the silver-purchase law now in force leads in the direction of the entire substitution of silver for the gold in the Government Treasury, and that this must be followed by the payment of all Government obligations in depreciated silver.

At this stage gold and silver must part company and the Government must fail in its established policy to maintain the two metals on a parity with each other. Given over to the exclusive use of a currency greatly depreciated according to the standard of the commercial world, we could no longer claim a place among nations of the first class, nor could our Government claim a performance of its obligation, so far as such an obligation has been imposed upon it, to provide

for the use of the people the best and safest money.

If, as many of its friends claim, silver ought to occupy a larger place in our currency and the currency of the world through general international coöperation and agreement, it is obvious that the United States will not be in a position to gain a hearing in favor of such an arrangement so long as we are willing to continue our attempt to accomplish the result single-handed. . . .

The people of the United States are entitled to a sound and stable currency and to money recognized as such on every exchange and in every market of the world. Their Government has no right to injure them by financial experiments opposed to the policy and practice of other civilized states, nor is it justified in permitting an exaggerated and unreasonable reliance on our national strength and ability to jeopardize the soundness of the people's money.

This matter rises above the plane of party politics. It vitally concerns every business and calling and enters every household in the land. There is one important aspect of the subject which especially should never be overlooked. At times like the present, when the evils of unsound finance threaten us, the speculator may anticipate a harvest gathered from the misfortune of others, the capitalist may protect himself by hoarding or may even find profit in the fluctuations of values; but the wage earner—the first to be injured by a depreciated currency and the last to receive the benefit of its correction—is practically defenseless. He relies for work upon the ventures of confident and contented capital. This failing him, his condition is without alleviation, for he can neither prey on the misfortunes of others nor hoard his labor. . . .

It is of the utmost importance that such relief as Congress can afford in the existing situation be afforded at once. The maxim "He gives twice who gives quickly" is directly applicable. It may be true that the embarrassments from which the business of the country is suffering arise as much from evils apprehended as from those actually existing. We may hope, too, that calm counsels will prevail, and that neither the capitalists nor the wage earners will give way to unreasoning panic and sacrifice their property or their interests under the influence of exaggerated fears. Nevertheless, every day's delay in removing one of the plain and principal causes of the present state of things enlarges the mischief already done and increases the responsibility of the Government for its existence. Whatever else the people have a right to expect from Congress, they may certainly demand that legislation condemned by the ordeal of three years' disastrous experience shall be removed from the statute books as soon as their representatives can legitimately deal with it.

It was my purpose to summon Congress in special session early in the coming September, that we might enter promptly upon the work of tariff reform, which the true interests of the country clearly demand, which so large a majority of the people, as shown by their suffrages, desire and expect, and to the accomplishment of which every effort of the present Administration is pledged. But while tariff reform has lost nothing of its immediate and permanent importance and must in the near future engage the attention of Congress, it has seemed to me that the financial condition of the country should at once and before all other subjects be considered by your honorable body.

I earnestly recommend the prompt repeal of the provisions of the act passed July 14, 1890, authorizing the purchase of silver bullion, and that other legislative action may put beyond all doubt or mistake the intention and the ability of the Government to fulfill its pecuniary obligations in money universally recognized by all civilized countries.

GROVER CLEVELAND.

328. REPEAL OF THE SHERMAN SILVER PURCHASE ACT
November 1, 1893

(*U. S. Statutes at Large,* Vol. XXVIII, p. 4)

The panic of 1893 emphasized to Cleveland the imperative necessity of the repeal of the Sherman Silver Act of 1890. On June 30, Cleveland called a special session of Congress to meet August 7 to repeal the Sherman Act. After one of the most violent debates in our legislative history, the administration was finally successful in securing repeal, but only at the cost of a split in the Democratic party which led finally to the triumph of the silver element of that party in 1896. On repeal, see Cleveland's message, Doc. No. 327, and A. Nevins, *Grover Cleveland*, ch. xxix; J. A. Barnes, *John G. Carlisle*, ch. xii; R. McElroy, *Grover Cleveland*, Vol. II, ch. i; W. J. Bryan, *The First Battle*, chs. i–iii.

An Act to repeal a part of [*the Silver Purchase Act of July 14, 1890*].

Be it enacted . . . , That so much of the [Silver Purchase Act of July 14, 1890], as directs the Secretary of the Treasury to purchase from time to time silver bullion to the aggregate amount of four million five hundred thousand ounces, or so much thereof as may be offered in each month at the market price thereof, not exceeding one dollar for three hundred and seventy-one and twenty-five one-hundredths grains of pure silver, and to issue in payment for such purchases Treasury notes of the United States, be, and the same is hereby, repealed. And it is hereby declared to be the policy of the United States to continue the use of both gold and silver as standard money, and to coin both gold and silver into money of equal intrinsic and exchangeable value, such equality to be secured through international agreement, or by such safeguards of legislation as will insure the maintenance of the parity in value of the coins of the two metals, and the equal power of every dollar at all times in the markets and in the payment of debts. And it is hereby further declared that the efforts of the Government should be steadily directed to the establishment of such a safe system of bimetallism as will maintain at all times the equal power of every dollar coined or issued by the United States, in the markets and in the payment of debts.

329. THE FUR-SEALING CONTROVERSY

Convention Between the United States and Great Britain for the Settlement of the
Controversy and the Award of the Tribunal
1892, 1893

(Malloy, ed. *Treaties, Conventions, etc.* Vol. I, p. 746 ff.)

The most valuable herds of seals in the world were found off the shores of Alaska and in the waters of Bering Sea, particularly on the Pribilof Islands. Russia had claimed jurisdiction over the whole of the Bering Sea, and the United States, after the purchase of Alaska, claimed that this sea was a *mare clausum*. By acts of 1869 and 1870 Congress forbade the killing of seals upon the shores of Alaska or the waters thereof except during the months from June to October. Subsequently the exclusive right of killing seals was leased to the Alaska Commercial Company under careful restrictions. The invasion of the Bering Sea by Canadian sealers led to the seizure and condemnation of three Canadian vessels. Despite the protests of Great Britain the seizures continued during the late eighties. A *modus vivendi* was arrived at by the United States and Great Britain in 1891, and the following year a convention was concluded submitting the questions of sealing and of jurisdiction to a tribunal. This Convention of February 29, 1892, presented a series of five major questions which the Tribunal was called upon to adjudicate. The Tribunal met in Paris in 1893 and decided all points of law adversely to the United States. At the same time it drew up a series of regulations designed to protect the fur seals. These regulations were only moderately effective, and on their expiration in 1898 they were not renewed. In 1906 President Roosevelt suggested the extermination of the seal herd by the United States on humanitarian grounds. Finally in 1911 Great Britain, Russia, Japan and the United States concluded a convention which afforded adequate protection to the seals. On the controversy see J. B. Moore, *International Arbitrations*, Vol. I; J. W. Foster, *Diplomatic Memoirs*, Vol. II; A. F. Tyler, *The Foreign Policy of James G. Blaine;* J. M. Callahan, *American Relations in the Pacific;* S. B. Stanton, *The Behring Sea Controversy;* S. F. Bemis, ed. *American Secretaries of State,* Vol. VIII, p. 128 ff.; J. Stanley-Brown, "The Bering Sea Controversy from an Economic Standpoint," *Yale Review,* Vol. II; T. A. Walker, *International Law,* p. 175 ff.

A CONVENTION FOR THE SETTLEMENT OF
THE DISPUTED RIGHT OF THE UNITED

STATES TO PROTECT THE SEALS IN BEHRING SEA.

Concluded, February 29, 1892.

The United States of America and Her Majesty the Queen of the United Kingdom of Great Britain and Ireland, being desirous to provide for an amicable settlement of the questions which have arisen between their respective governments concerning the jurisdictional rights of the United States in the waters of Behring's Sea, and concerning also the preservation of the fur-seal in, or habitually resorting to, the said Sea, and the rights of the citizens and subjects of either country as regards the taking of fur-seal in, or habitually resorting to, the said waters, have resolved to submit to arbitration the questions involved. . . .

ART. I—The questions which have arisen between the Government of the United States and the Government of Her Britannic Majesty concerning the jurisdictional rights of the United States in the waters of Behring's Sea, and concerning also the preservation of the fur-seal in, or habitually resorting to, the said Sea, and the rights of the citizens and subjects of either country as regards the taking of fur-seal in, or habitually resorting to, the said waters, shall be submitted to a tribunal of Arbitration, to be composed of seven Arbitrators, who shall be appointed in the following manner, that is to say: Two shall be named by the President of the United States; two shall be named by Her Britannic Majesty; His Excellency the President of the French Republic shall be jointly requested by the High Contracting Parties to name one; His Majesty the King of Italy shall be so requested to name one; and His Majesty the King of Sweden and Norway shall be so requested to name one. The seven arbitrators to be so named shall be jurists of distinguished reputation in their respective countries. . . .

ART. II.—The arbitrators shall meet

at Paris within twenty days after the delivery of the counter-case mentioned in Article IV and shall proceed impartially and carefully to examine and decide the questions that have been or shall be laid before them as herein provided on the part of the Governments of the United States and Her Britannic Majesty respectively. All questions considered by the tribunal including the final decision, shall be determined by a majority of all the Arbitrators.

Each of the High Contracting Parties shall also name one person to attend the tribunal as its Agent to represent it generally in all matters connected with the arbitration. . . .

ART. VI.—In deciding the matters submitted to the Arbitrators, it is agreed that the following five points shall be submitted to them, in order that their award shall embrace a distinct decision upon each of said five points, to wit:

1. What exclusive jurisdiction in the sea now known as the Behring's Sea, and what exclusive rights in the seal fisheries therein, did Russia assert and exercise prior and up to the time of the cession of Alaska to the United States?

2. How far were these claims of jurisdiction as to the seal fisheries recognized and conceded by Great Britain?

3. Was the body of water now known as the Behring's Sea included in the phrase "Pacific Ocean," as used in the Treaty of 1825 between Great Britain and Russia; and what rights, if any, in the Behring's Sea were held and exclusively exercised by Russia after said Treaty?

4. Did not all the rights of Russia as to jurisdiction, and as to the seal fisheries in Behring's Sea east of the water boundary, in the Treaty between the United States and Russia of the 30th March, 1867, pass unimpaired to the United States under that treaty?

5. Has the United States any right, and if so, what right of protection or property in the fur-seals frequenting the islands of the United States in Behring Sea when such seals are found outside the ordinary three-mile limit?

ART. VII.—If the determination of the foregoing questions as to the exclusive jurisdiction of the United States shall leave the subject in such position that the concurrence of Great Britain is necessary to the establishment of Regulations for the proper protection and preservation of the fur-seal in, or habitually resorting to, the Behring Sea, the Arbitrators shall then determine what concurrent Regulations outside the jurisdictional limits of the respective Governments are necessary, and over what waters such Regulations should extend, and to aid them in that determination the report of a Joint Commission to be appointed by the respective Governments shall be laid before them, with such other evidence as either Government may submit.

The High Contracting Parties furthermore agree to cooperate in securing the adhesion of other Powers to such Regulations.

ART. VIII.—The High Contracting Parties having found themselves unable to agree upon a reference which shall include the question of the liability of each for the injuries alleged to have been sustained by the other, or by its citizens, in connection with the claims presented and urged by it; and, being solicitous that this subordinate question should not interrupt or longer delay the submission and determination of the main questions, do agree that either may submit to the Arbitrators any question of fact involved in said claims and ask for a finding thereon, the question of the liability of either Government upon the facts found to be the subject of further negotiation. . . .

James G. Blaine.
Julian Pauncefote.

2. ARTICLES OF THE AWARD OF THE TRIBUNAL OF ARBITRATION, AUGUST 15, 1893

"ART. I. The Governments of the United States and Great Britain shall forbid their citizens and subjects, respectively, to kill, capture, or pursue at any time and in any manner whatever the animals commonly called fur seals within a zone of 60 miles around the Pribilof Islands, inclusive of the territorial waters.

"The miles mentioned in the preceding paragraph are geographical miles, of 60 to a degree of latitude.

"ART. 2. The two Governments shall forbid their citizens and subjects, respectively, to kill, capture, or pursue in any manner whatever during the season extending each year from the 1st of May to the 31st of July, both inclusive, the fur seals on the high sea in the part of the Pacific Ocean, inclusive of the Bering Sea, which is situated to the north of the thirty-fifth degree of north latitude and eastward of the one hundred and eightieth degree of longitude from Greenwich till it strikes the water boundary described in Article I of the treaty of 1867 between the United States and Russia, and following that line up to Bering Strait. . . .

"ART. 4. Each sailing vessel authorized to fish for fur seals must be provided with a special license issued for that purpose by its Government, and shall be required to carry a distinguishing flag to be prescribed by its Government.

"ART. 6. The use of nets, firearms, and explosives shall be forbidden in the fur-seal fishing. This restriction shall not apply to shotguns when such fishing takes place outside of Bering Sea during the season when it may be lawfully carried on.

"ART. 9. The concurrent regulations hereby determined with a view to the protection and preservation of the fur seals shall remain in force until they have been in whole or in part abolished or modified by common agreement between the Governments of the United States and of Great Britain. . . .

330. THE ANNEXATION OF HAWAII

Message of President Harrison Transmitting Treaty of Annexation
February 13, 1893

(Richardson, ed. *Messages and Papers,* Vol. IX, p. 348 ff.)

See Docs. No. 331, 348. For the complicated story of the Hawaiian Revolution and the attempted annexation of the Island, see E. J. Carpenter, *America in Hawaii;* H. E. Chambers, *Constitutional History of Hawaii;* J. W. Foster, *American Diplomacy in the Orient,* p. 365 ff.; D. R. Dewey, *National Problems,* ch. xix; A. Nevins, *Grover Cleveland,* ch. xxx. The official documents are in *Foreign Relations of the United States,* 1894, Appendix II.

EXECUTIVE MANSION,
Washington, February 15, 1893.
To the Senate:

I transmit herewith, with a view to its ratification, a treaty of annexation concluded on the 14th day of February, 1893, between John W. Foster, Secretary of State, . . . and Lorin A. Thurston, W. R. Castle, W. C. Wilder, C. L. Carter, and Joseph Marsden, the commissioners on the part of the Government of the Hawaiian Islands. . . .

I do not deem it necessary to discuss at any length the conditions which have resulted in this decisive action. It has been the policy of the Administration not only to respect but to encourage the continuance of an independent government in the Hawaiian Islands so long as it afforded suitable guaranties for the protection of life and property and maintained a stability and strength that gave adequate security against the domination of any other power. The moral support of this Government has continually manifested itself in the most friendly diplomatic relations and in many acts of courtesy to the Hawaiian rulers.

The overthrow of the monarchy was not in any way promoted by this Government, but had its origin in what seems to have been a reactionary and revolutionary policy on the part of Queen Liliuokalani, which put in serious peril not only the large and preponderating interests of the United States in the islands, but all foreign interests, and, indeed, the decent administration of civil affairs and the peace of the islands. It is quite evident that the monarchy had become effete and the Queen's Government so weak and inadequate as to be the prey of designing and unscrupulous persons. The restoration of Queen Liliuokalani to her throne is undesirable, if not impossible, and unless actively supported by the United States would be accompanied by serious disaster and the disorganization of all business interests. The influence and interest of the United States in the islands must be increased and not diminished.

Only two courses are now open—one the establishment of a protectorate by the United States, and the other annexation full and complete. I think the latter course, which has been adopted in the treaty, will be highly promotive of the best interests of the Hawaiian people, and is the only one that will adequately secure the interests of the United States. These interests are not wholly selfish. It is essential that none of the other great powers shall secure these islands. Such a possession would not consist with our safety and with the peace of the world. This view of the situation is so apparent and conclusive that no protest has been heard from any government against proceedings looking to annexation. Every foreign representative at Honolulu promptly acknowledged the Provisional Government, and I think there is a general concurrence in the opinion that the deposed Queen ought not to be restored.

Prompt action upon this treaty is very desirable. . . .

331. CLEVELAND'S WITHDRAWAL OF TREATY FOR ANNEXATION OF HAWAII
December 18, 1893

(Richardson, ed. *Messages and Papers*, Vol. IX, p. 461 ff.)

Cleveland came to office while the treaty for annexation of Hawaii was still pending in the Senate. He at once appointed a special agent, James H. Blount, to investigate into the circumstances of the Hawaiian revolution. Acting on Blount's report he reversed the policy of the Harrison Administration. For the ultimate annexation of Hawaii see Doc. No. 348.

Executive Mansion
Washington, December 18, 1893.
To the Senate and House of Representatives:
. . . I suppose that right and justice should determine the path to be followed in treating this subject. If national honesty is to be disregarded and a desire for territorial extension or dissatisfaction with a form of government not our own ought to regulate our conduct, I have entirely misapprehended the mission and character of our Government and the behavior which the conscience of our people demands of their public servants.

When the present Administration entered upon its duties, the Senate had under consideration a treaty providing for the annexation of the Hawaiian Islands to the territory of the United States. Surely under our Constitution and laws the enlargement of our limits is a manifestation of the highest attribute of sovereignty, and if entered upon as an Executive act all things relating to the transaction should be clear and free from suspicion. Additional importance attached to this particular treaty of annexation because it contemplated a departure from unbroken American tradition in providing for the addition to our territory of islands of the sea more than 2,000 miles removed from our nearest coast.

These considerations might not of themselves call for interference with the completion of a treaty entered upon by a previous Administration, but it appeared from the documents accompanying the treaty when submitted to the Senate that the ownership of Hawaii was tendered to us by a Provisional Government set up to succeed the constitutional ruler of the islands, who had been dethroned, and it did not appear that such Provisional Government had the sanction of either popular revolution or suffrage. Two other remarkable features of the transaction naturally attracted attention. One was the extraordinary haste, not to say precipitancy, characterizing all the transactions connected with the treaty. . . . Thus between the initiation of the scheme for a Provisional Government in Hawaii, on the 14th day of January, and the submission to the Senate of the treaty of annexation concluded with such Government the entire interval was thirty-two days, fifteen of which were spent by the Hawaiian commissioners in their journey to Washington. . . .

But a protest also accompanied said treaty, signed by the Queen and her ministers at the time she made way for the Provisional Government, which explicitly stated that she yielded to the superior force of the United States, whose minister had caused United States troops to be landed at Honolulu and declared that he would support such Provisional Government.

The truth or falsity of this protest was surely of the first importance. If true, nothing but the concealment of its truth could induce our Government to negotiate with the semblance of a government thus created, nor could a treaty resulting from the acts stated in the protest have been knowingly deemed worthy of consideration by the Senate. Yet the truth or falsity of the protest had not been investigated.

I conceived it to be my duty, therefore, to withdraw the treaty from the Senate for examination, and meanwhile to cause an accurate, full, and impartial investigation to be made of the facts attending the subversion of the constitutional Government of Hawaii and the installment in its place of the Provisional Government. . . .

The report, with its accompanying proofs and such other evidence as is now before the Congress or is herewith submitted, justifies, in my opinion, the statement that when the President was led to submit the treaty to the Senate with the declaration that "the overthrow of the monarchy was not in any way promoted by this Government," and when the Senate was induced to receive and discuss it on that basis, both President and Senate were misled. . . .

I believe that a candid and thorough examination of the facts will force the conviction that the Provisional Government owes its existence to an armed invasion by the United States. Fair-minded people, with the evidence before them, will hardly claim that the Hawaiian Government was overthrown by the people of the islands or that the Provisional Government had ever existed with their consent. I do not understand that any member of this Government claims that the people would uphold it by their suffrages if they were allowed to vote on the question.

While naturally sympathizing with every effort to establish a republican form of government, it has been the settled policy of the United States to concede to people of foreign countries the same freedom and independence in the management of their domestic affairs that we have always claimed for ourselves, and it has been our practice to recognize revolutionary governments as soon as it became apparent that they were supported by the people. . . .

As I apprehend the situation, we are brought face to face with the following conditions:

The lawful Government of Hawaii was overthrown without the drawing of a sword or the firing of a shot by a process every step of which, it may safely be asserted, is directly traceable to and dependent for its success upon the agency of the United States acting through its diplomatic and naval representatives.

But for the notorious predilections of the United States minister for annexation the committee of safety, which should be called the committee of annexation, would never have existed.

But for the landing of the United States forces upon false pretexts respecting the danger to life and property the committee would never have exposed themselves to the pains and penalties of treason by undertaking the subversion of the Queen's Government.

But for the presence of the United States forces in the immediate vicinity and in position to afford all needed protection and support the committee would not have proclaimed the Provisional Government from the steps of the Government building.

And finally, but for the lawless occupation of Honolulu under false pretexts by the United States forces, and but for Minister Stevens's recognition of the Provisional Government when the United States forces were its sole support and constituted its only military strength, the Queen and her Government would never have yielded to the Provisional Government, even for a time and for the sole purpose of submitting her case to the enlightened justice of the United States.

Believing, therefore, that the United States could not, under the circumstances disclosed, annex the islands without justly incurring the imputation of acquiring them by unjustifiable methods, I shall not again submit the treaty of annexation to the Senate for its consideration, and in the instructions of Minister Willis, a copy of which accompanies this message, I have directed him to so inform the Provisional Government. . . .

332. COXEY'S PROGRAM
1894

"General" Jacob S. Coxey of Massillon, Ohio, proposed to end the depression of 1893 by a public works program to be undertaken by federal and local authorities. This program would have the added advantage of increasing the amount of money in circulation through issues of legal tender. In order to bring these proposals before Congress, Coxey led an industrial army from Ohio to Washington. See, H. Vincent, *The Story of the Commonwealth;* D. L. McMurray, *Coxey's Army.*

1. NON-INTEREST BEARING BOND BILL
(D. L. McMurray, *Coxey's Army,* p. 302–303)

A Bill to provide for public improvements and employment of the citizens of the United States.

Be it enacted . . . That whenever any State, Territory, County, township, municipality, or incorporated town or village deem it necessary to make any public improvements, they shall deposit with the Secretary of the Treasury of the United States a non-interest bearing twenty-five year bond, not to exceed one-half of the assessed valuation of the property in said State, Territory, County, township, municipality or incorporated town or village, and said bond to be retired at the rate of four per centum per annum.

SEC. 2. That whenever the foregoing section of this Act has been complied with it shall be mandatory upon the Secretary of the Treasury of the United States to have . . . printed Treasury notes in the denomination of one, two, five, and ten dollars each, which shall be full legal tender for all debts, public and private to the face value of said bond, and deliver to said State . . . ninety-nine per centum of said notes, and retain one per centum for expense of engraving and printing same.

SEC. 3. That after the passage of this Act it shall be compulsory upon every incorpo-

rated town or village, municipality, township, County, State or Territory, to give employment to any idle man applying for work, and that the rate be not less than one dollar and fifty cents per day for common labor and three dollars and fifty cents per day for teams and labor, and that eight hours per day shall constitute a day's labor under this act.

2. COXEY'S GOOD ROADS BILL
(H. Vincent, *The Story of the Commonwealth,* p. 51–52)

SEC. 1. Be it enacted . . . That the Secretary of the Treasury of the United States is hereby authorized and instructed to have engraved and printed . . . five hundred millions of dollars of treasury notes, as legal tender for all debts, public and private, said notes to be in denominations of one, two, five and ten dollars, and to be placed in a fund to be known as the "general county road fund system of the United States," and to be expended solely for the said purpose.

SEC. 2. . . . That it shall be the duty of the Secretary of War to take charge of the construction of the General County Road System in the United States, and said construction to commence as soon as . . . said fund is available . . . when it shall be the duty of the Secretary of War to inaugurate the work and expend the sum of twenty millions of dollars per month, pro rata with the number of miles of roads in each state and territory in the United States.

SEC. 3. . . . That all labor other than that of the Secretary of War . . . shall be paid by the day, and that the rate be not less than one dollar and fifty cents per day for common labor, and three dollars and fifty cents per day for teams and labor, and that eight hours shall constitute a day's labor under the provisions of this bill.

333. POLLOCK v. FARMERS' LOAN AND TRUST COMPANY
158 U. S. 601
1894

Appeal from U. S. circuit court for the Southern District of New York. Rehearing. The Wilson tariff bill of 1894 had included provision for

an income tax. The constitutionality of such a tax was challenged on the ground that it was a direct tax and therefore contrary to the Constitutional requirement that all direct taxes be apportioned among the States according to population. The issues before the Court were involved, but on the general question of the legality of a tax on the income from personal property, the court was divided four to four. The opinion below is the opinion of the court on a rehearing of the case. On the constitutionality of the tax on incomes, the Court stood five to four. Justice Jackson, who had not taken part in the first hearing, dissented from the majority opinion in the final case, while one of the other judges changed his position and voted with the majority. It was long believed that it was Justice Shiras who reversed his opinion, but lately Mr. Sidney Ratner has adduced evidence to the effect that it was Mr. Justice Brewer who reversed himself. The decision of the Court in this case aroused widespread and bitter dissatisfaction; it led, eventually, to the Sixteenth Amendment. For background, see, Warren, *The Supreme Court* (1928 ed.) Vol. II, p. 699 ff.; L. B. Boudin, *Government by Judiciary,* Vol. II, ch. xxvii; A. Nevins, *Grover Cleveland,* appendix.

FULLER, C. J. Whenever this court is required to pass upon the validity of an act of Congress, as tested by the fundamental law enacted by the people, the duty imposed demands in its discharge the utmost deliberation and care, and invokes the deepest sense of responsibility. . . .

We have, therefore, with an anxious desire to omit nothing which might in any degree tend to elucidate the questions submitted, and aided by further able arguments embodying the fruits of elaborate research, carefully re-examined these cases, with the result that, while our former conclusions remain unchanged, their scope must be enlarged by the acceptance of their logical consequences. . . .

Our previous decision was confined to the consideration of the validity of the tax on the income from real estate, and on the income from municipal bonds. . . .

We are now permitted to broaden the field of inquiry, and to determine to which of the two great classes a tax upon a person's entire income, whether derived from rents or products, or otherwise, of real estate, or from bonds, stocks, or other forms of personal property, belongs; and we are unable to conclude that the enforced subtraction from the yield of all the owner's real or personal property, in the manner prescribed, is

so different from a tax on the property itself, that it is not a direct, but an indirect, tax in the meaning of the Constitution. . . .

We do not care to retravel ground already traversed, but some observations may be added. . . .

The reasons for the clauses of the Constitution in respect of direct taxation are not far to seek. . . .

The founders anticipated that the expenditures of the States, their counties, cities, and towns, would chiefly be met by direct taxation on accumulated property, while they expected that those of the Federal government would be for the most part met by indirect taxes. And in order that the power of direct taxation by the general government should not be exercised except on necessity, and, when the necessity arose, should be so exercised as to leave the States at liberty to discharge their respective obligations, and should not be so exercised unfairly and discriminatingly, as to particular States or otherwise, by a mere majority vote, possibly of those whose constituents were intentionally not subjected to any part of the burden, the qualified grant was made. . . .

Those who made it knew that the power to tax involved the power to destroy, and that, in the language of Chief Justice Marshall, in *McCulloch* v. *Maryland,* "the only security against the abuse of this power is found in the structure of the government itself." . . . And they retained this security by providing that direct taxation and representation in the lower house of Congress should be adjusted on the same measure.

Moreover, whatever the reasons for the constitutional provisions, there they are, and they appear to us to speak in plain language.

It is said that a tax on the whole income of property is not a direct tax in the meaning of the Constitution, but a duty, and, as a duty, leviable without apportionment, whether direct or indirect. We do not think so. Direct taxation was not restricted in one breath, and the restriction blown to the winds in another. . . .

The Constitution prohibits any direct tax, unless in proportion to numbers as ascertained by the census, and, in the light of the circumstances to which we have referred, is it not an evasion of that prohibition to hold that a general unapportioned tax, imposed upon all property owners as a body for or in respect of their property, is not direct, in the meaning of the Constitution, because confined to the income therefrom?

Whatever the speculative views of political economists or revenue reformers may be, can it be properly held that the Constitution, taken in its plain and obvious sense, and with due regard to the circumstances attending the formation of the government, authorizes a general unapportioned tax on the products of the farm and the rents of real estate, although imposed merely because of ownership, and with no possible means of escape from payment, as belonging to a totally different class from that which includes the property from whence the income proceeds?

There can be but one answer, unless the constitutional restriction is to be treated as utterly illusory and futile, and the object of its framers defeated. We find it impossible to hold that a fundamental requisition deemed so important as to be enforced by two provisions, one affirmative and one negative, can be refined away by forced distinctions between that which gives value to property and the property itself.

Nor can we perceive any ground why the same reasoning does not apply to capital in personalty held for the purpose of income, or ordinarily yielding income, and to the income therefrom. . . .

Personal property of some kind is of general distribution, and so are incomes, though the taxable range thereof might be narrowed through large exemptions. . . .

Nor are we impressed with the contention that, because in the four instances in which the power of direct taxation has been exercised, Congress did not see fit, for reasons of expediency, to levy a tax on personalty, this amounts to such a practical construction of the Constitution that the power did not exist, that we must regard ourselves bound by it. We should regret to be compelled to hold the powers of the general government thus restricted, and certainly we cannot accede to the idea that the Constitution has become weakened by a particular course of inaction under it.

The stress of the argument is thrown, however, on the assertion that an income tax is not a property tax at all; . . . that rents received, crops harvested, interest collected, have lost all connection with their origin, and, though once not taxable, have become transmuted, in their new form, into taxable subject-matter; in other words, that income is taxable, irrespective of the source whence it is derived. . . .

We have unanimously held in this case that, so far as this law operates on the receipts from municipal bonds, it cannot be sustained, because it is a tax on the power of the States and on their instrumentalities to borrow money, and consequently repugnant to the Constitution. But, if, as contended, the interest, when received, has become merely money in the recipient's pocket, and taxable, as such, without reference to the source from which it came, the question is immaterial whether it could have been originally taxed at all or not. This was admitted by the Attorney General, with characteristic candor; and it follows that if the revenue derived from municipal bonds cannot be taxed, because the source cannot be, the same rule applies to revenue from any other source not subject to the tax, and the lack of power to levy any but an apportioned tax on real and personal property equally exists as to the revenue therefrom.

Admitting that this act taxes the income of property, irrespective of its source, still we cannot doubt that such a tax is necessarily a direct tax in the meaning of the Constitution. . . .

The power to tax real and personal property and the income from both, there being an apportionment, is conceded; that such a tax is a direct tax in the meaning of the Constitution has not been, and, in our judgment, cannot be successfully denied; and yet we are thus invited to hesitate in the enforcement of the mandate of the Constitution, which prohibits Congress from laying a direct tax on the revenue from property of the citizen without regard to state lines, and in such manner that the States cannot intervene by payment in regulation of their own resources, lest a government of delegated powers should be found to be, not less powerful, but less absolute, than the imagination of the advocate had supposed.

We are not here concerned with the question whether an income tax be or be not desirable, nor whether such a tax would enable the government to diminish taxes on consumption and duties on imports, and to enter upon what may be believed to be a reform of its fiscal and commercial system. Questions of that character belong to the controversies of political parties, and cannot be settled by judicial decision. In these cases our province is to determine whether this income tax on the revenue from property does or does not belong to the class of direct taxes. If it does, it is, being unapportioned, in violation of the Constitution, and we must so declare. . . .

We have considered the act only in respect of the tax on income derived from real estate, and from invested personal property, and have not commented on so much of it as bears on gains or profits from business, privileges, or employments, in view of the instances in which taxation on business, privileges, or employments has assumed the guise of an excise tax and been sustained as such.

. . . Being of opinion that so much of the section of this law as lays a tax on income from real and personal property is invalid, we are brought to the question of the effect of that conclusion upon these sections as a whole.

It is elementary that the same statute may be in part constitutional and in part unconstitutional, and, if the parts are wholly independent of each other, that which is constitutional may stand while that which is unconstitutional will be rejected. And in the case before us there is no question as to the validity of this act, except sections twenty-seven to thirty-seven, inclusive, which relate to the subject which has been under discussion; and, as to them, we think the rule laid down by Chief Justice Shaw in *Warren* v. *Charlestown*, 2 Gray, 84, is applicable, that if the different parts "are so mutually connected with and dependent on each other, as conditions, considerations, or compensations for each other, as to warrant a belief that the legislature intended them as a whole, and that if all could not be carried into effect the legislature would not pass the residue independently, and some parts are unconstitutional, all the provisions which are thus dependent, conditional, or connected must fall with them." . . .

According to the census, the true valuation of real and personal property in the United States in 1890 was $65,037,091,197, of which real estate with improvements thereon made up $39,544,544,333. Of course, from the latter must be deducted, in applying these sections, all unproductive property and all property whose net yield does not exceed four thousand dollars; but, even with such deductions, it is evident that the income from realty formed a vital part of the scheme for taxation embodied therein. If that be stricken out, and also the income from all invested personal property, bonds, stocks, investments of all kinds, it is obvious that by far the largest part of the anticipated revenue would be eliminated, and this would leave the burden of the tax to be borne by professions, trades, employments, or vocations; and in that way what was intended as a tax on capital would remain in substance a tax on occupations and labor. We cannot believe that such was the intention of Congress. We do not mean to say that an act laying by apportionment a direct tax on all real estate and personal property, or the income thereof, might not also lay excise taxes on business, privileges, employments, and vocations. But this is not such an act; and the scheme must be considered as a whole. Being invalid as to the greater part, and falling, as the tax would, if any part were held valid, in a direction which could not have been contemplated except in connection with the taxation considered as an entirety, we are constrained to conclude that sections twenty-seven to thirty-seven, inclusive, of the act, which became a law, without the signature of the President, on August 28, 1894, are wholly inoperative and void.

Our conclusions may, therefore, be summed up as follows:

First. We adhere to the opinion already announced, that, taxes on real estate being indisputably direct taxes, taxes on the rents or income of real estate are equally direct taxes.

Second. We are of opinion that taxes on personal property, or on the income of personal property, are likewise direct taxes.

Third. The tax imposed by sections twenty-seven to thirty-seven, inclusive, of the act of 1894, so far as it falls on the income of real estate and of personal property, being a direct tax within the meaning of the Constitution, and, therefore, unconstitutional and void because not apportioned according to representation, all those sections, constituting one entire scheme of taxation, are necessarily invalid.

Decrees reversed and relief prayed for granted.

Justices HARLAN, BROWN, JACKSON, and WHITE delivered dissenting opinions.

334. THE ALTGELD-CLEVELAND CONTROVERSY
1894

(W. R. Browne, *Altgeld of Illinois*, p. 154 ff.)

This notable controversy arose out of Cleveland's action in sending federal troops to Chicago during the Pullman Strike. Governor Altgeld had not requested these troops, and there is no convincing evidence that the local and state authorities were not fully competent to handle the situation without outside aid. Cleveland's action broke the strike and earned him contemporary applause, but in perspective it appears unwarranted either by circumstances or by law. See *In re Debs,* Doc. No. 336. On Altgeld, see the biography by Browne; for the controversy, see A. Nevins, *Grover Cleveland,* ch. xxxiii; G. Cleveland, "The Government and the Chicago Strike," in *Presidential Problems.*

1.   Executive Office, State of Illinois
                            July 5, 1894.
Hon. Grover Cleveland, President of the
    United States,
    Washington, D. C.
Sir:—I am advised that you have ordered Federal troops to go into service in the State of Illinois. Surely the facts have not been correctly presented to you in this case, or you would not have taken this step, for it is entirely unnecessary, and, as it seems to me, unjustifiable. Waiving all questions of courtesy, I will say that the State of Illinois is not only able to take care of itself, but it stands ready to furnish the Federal government any assistance it may need elsewhere. Our military force is ample, and consists of as good soldiers as can be found in the country. They have been ordered promptly whenever and wherever they were needed. We have stationed in Chicago alone three Regiments of Infantry, one Battery and one troop of Cavalry, and no better soldiers can be found. They have been ready every moment to go on duty, and have been and are now eager to go into service, but they have not been ordered out because nobody in Cook county, whether official or private citizen, asked to have their assistance, or even intimated in any way that their assistance was desired or necessary.

So far as I have been advised, the local officials have been able to handle the situation. But if any assistance were needed, the State stood ready to furnish a hundred men for every one man required, and stood ready to do so at a moment's notice. Notwithstanding these facts the Federal Government has been applied to by men who had political and selfish motives for wanting to ignore the State Government. We have just gone through a coal strike, more extensive here than in any other State. We have now had ten days of the railroad strike, and we have promptly furnished military aid wherever the local officials needed it.

In two instances the United States marshal for the Southern District of Illinois applied for assistance to enable him to enforce the processes of the United States court, and troops were promptly furnished him, and he was assisted in every way he desired. The law has been thoroughly executed, and every man guilty of violating it during the strike has been brought to justice. If the marshal of the Northern District of Illinois or the authorities of Cook county needed military assistance they had but to ask for it in order to get it from the State.

At present some of our railroads are paralyzed, not by reason of obstruction, but because they cannot get men to operate their trains. For some reason they are anxious to keep this fact from the public, and for this purpose they are making an outcry about obstructions in order to divert attention. Now, I will cite to you two examples which illustrate the situation: . . .

It is true that in several instances a road made efforts to work a few green men and a crowd standing around insulted them and tried to drive them away, and in a few other cases they cut off Pullman sleepers from trains. But all these troubles were local in character and could easily be handled by the State authorities. Illinois has more railroad men than any other State in the Union, but as a rule they are orderly and well-behaved. This is shown by the fact that so very little actual violence has been committed. Only a very small percentage of these men have been guilty of infractions of the law. The newspaper accounts have in many cases been pure fabrications, and in others wild exaggerations.

I have gone thus into details to show that it is not soldiers that the railroads need so much as it is men to operate trains, and that the conditions do not exist here which bring the cause within the Federal statute, a statute that was passed in 1881 (1861) and was in reality a war measure. The statute authorized the use of Federal troops in a State whenever it shall be impracticable to enforce the laws of the United States within such States by the ordinary Judicial proceedings. Such a condition does not exist in Illinois. There have been a few local disturbances, but nothing that seriously interfered with the administration of justice, or that could not be easily controlled by the local or State authorities, for the Federal troops can do nothing that the State troops cannot do.

I repeat that you have been imposed upon in this matter; but even if by a forced construction it were held that the conditions here came within the letter of the statute, then I submit that local self-government is a fundamental principle of our Constitution. Each community shall govern itself so long as it can and is ready and able to enforce the law, and it is in harmony with this fundamental principle that the statute authorizing the President to send troops into States must be construed; especially is this so in matters relating to the exercise of the police power and the preservation of law and order.

To absolutely ignore a local government in matters of this kind, when the local government is ready to furnish assistance needed, and is amply able to enforce the law, not only insults the people of this State by imputing to them an inability to govern themselves, or an unwillingness to enforce the law, but is in violation of a basic principle of our institutions. The question of Federal supremacy is in no way involved. No one disputes it for a moment; but, under our Constitution, Federal supremacy and local self-government must go hand in hand, and to ignore the latter is to do violence to the Constitution.

As Governor of the State of Illinois, I protest against this, and ask the immediate withdrawal of the Federal troops from active duty in this State. Should the situation at any time get so serious that we cannot control it with the State forces, we will promptly ask for Federal assistance; but until such time, I protest, with all due deference, against this uncalled for reflection upon our people, and again ask the immediate withdrawal of these troops. I have the honor to be, yours respectfully,

JOHN P. ALTGELD, Governor of Illinois.

2.   Executive Mansion, Washington, D. C., July 5, 1894.
Hon. John P. Altgeld, Governor of Illinois, Springfield, Ill.
Sir:—Federal troops were sent to Chicago in strict accordance with the Constitution and laws of the United States, upon the demand of the postoffice department that obstruction of the mails should be removed, and upon the representations of the judicial officers of the United States that the process of the Federal courts could not be executed through the ordinary means, and upon competent proof that conspiracies existed against commerce between the States. To meet these conditions, which are clearly within the province of Federal authority, the presence of Federal troops in the city of Chicago was deemed not only proper, but necessary, and there has been no intention of thereby interfering with the plain duty of the local authorities to preserve the peace of the city.

GROVER CLEVELAND.

3.   Executive Office, State of Illinois, July 6, 1894.
Hon. Grover Cleveland, President of the United States,
Sir:—Your answer to my protest involves some startling conclusions and ignores and evades the question at issue—that is, that the principle of local self-government is just as fundamental in our institutions as is that of Federal supremacy.

First—You calmly assume that the executive has the legal right to order Federal troops into any community of the United States, in the first instance, whenever there is the slightest disturbance, and that he can do this without any regard to the question as to whether that community is able and ready to enforce the law itself. Inasmuch as the executive is the sole judge of the question as to whether any disturbance exists in any part of the country, this assumption means that the executive can send Federal troops into any community in the United States at his pleasure, and keep them there as long as he chooses. If this is the law, then the principle of self-government either never did exist in this country or else has been destroyed, for no community can be said to possess local self-government if the executive can, at his pleasure, send military forces to patrol its streets under pretense of enforcing some law. The kind of local self-government that could exist under these circumstances can be found in any of the monarchies of Europe, and it is not in harmony with the spirit of our institutions.

Second—It is also a fundamental principle in our government that except in times of war the military shall be subordinate to the civil authority. In harmony with this provision, the State troops are ordered out to act under and with the civil authorities. The troops you have ordered to Chicago are not under the civil authorities, and are in no way responsible to them for their conduct. They are not even acting under the United States Marshal or any Federal officer of the State, but are acting directly under military orders issued from military headquarters at Washington; and in so far as these troops act at all, it is military government.

Third—The statute authorizing Federal troops to be sent into States in certain cases contemplates that the State troops shall be taken first. This provision has been ignored and it is assumed that the executive is not bound by it. Federal interference with industrial disturbances in the various States is certainly a new departure, and it opens up so large a field that it will require a very little stretch of authority to absorb to itself all the details of local government.

Fourth—You say that troops were ordered into Illinois upon the demand of the post-office department, and upon representations of the judicial officers of the United States that process of the courts could not be served, and upon proof that conspiracies existed. We will not discuss the facts, but look for a moment at the principle involved in your statement. All of these officers are appointed by the executive. Most of them can be removed by him at will. They are not only obliged to do his bidding, but they are in fact a part of the executive. If several of them can apply for troops, one alone can; so that under the law, as you assume it to be, an executive, through any one of his appointees, can apply to himself to have the military sent into any city or number of cities, and base his application on such representations as he sees fit to make. In fact, it will be immaterial whether he makes any showing or not, for the executive is the sole judge, and nobody else has any right to interfere or even inquire about it. Then the executive can pass on his own application, his will being the sole guide—he can hold the application to be sufficient, and order troops to as many places as he wishes and put them in command of anyone he chooses, and have them act, not under the civil officers, either Federal or State, but directly under military orders from Washington, and there is not in the Constitution or laws, whether written or unwritten, any limitation or restraint upon his power. His judgment—that is, his will— is the sole guide; and it being purely a matter of discretion, his decision can never be examined or questioned.

This assumption as to the power of the executive is certainly new, and I respectfully submit that it is not the law of the land. The jurists have told us that this is a government of law, and not a government by the caprice of an individual, and, further, instead of being autocratic, it is a government of limited power. Yet the autocrat of Russia could certainly not possess, or claim to possess, greater power than is possessed by the executive of the United States, if your assumption is correct.

Fifth—The executive has the command not only of the regular forces of all the United States, but of the military forces of all the States, and can order them to any place he sees fit; and as there are always more or less local disturbances over the country, it will be an easy matter under your construction of the law for an ambitious executive to order out the military forces of all of the States, and establish at once a military government. The only chance of failure in such a movement could come from rebellion, and with such a vast military power at command this could readily be crushed, for, as a rule, soldiers will obey orders.

As for the situation in Illinois, that is of no consequence now compared with the far-reaching principle involved. True, according to my advices, Federal troops have now been on duty for over two days, and although the men were brave and the officers valiant and able, yet their very presence proved to be an irritant because it aroused the indignation of a large class of people who, while upholding law and order, had been taught to believe in local self-government, and therefore resented what they regarded as unwarranted interference.

Inasmuch as the Federal troops can do nothing but what the State troops can do there, and believing that the State is amply able to take care of the situation and enforce the law, and believing that the ordering out of the Federal troops was unwarranted, I again ask their withdrawal.

JOHN P. ALTGELD.

4. Executive Mansion, Washington, D. C.
    July 6, 1894.

While I am still persuaded that I have neither transcended my authority nor duty in the emergency that confronts us, it seems to me that in this hour of danger and public distress, discussion may well give way to active efforts on the part of all in authority to restore obedience to law and to protect life and property.

GROVER CLEVELAND.

Hon. John P. Altgeld,
Governor of Illinois.

335. U.S. v. DEBS ET AL.
64 Fed. 724
1894

Proceedings for contempt against Eugene V. Debs and others for violation of injunctions issued in the Pullman strike of 1894. The extract from the decision of the Circuit Court for the Northern District of Illinois bears on the application of the Sherman Anti-Trust Act to the case. The Congressional investigation of the strike can be found in *United States Strike Commission Report*, Sen. Exec. Doc. 7, 53d. Cong. 3d. Sess. See also A. Nevins, *Grover Cleveland*, ch. xxxiii; W. R. Browne, *Altgeld of Illinois*, chs. xii–xvi; and Doc. No. 334. On the use of the injunction in labor disputes see, F. Frankfurter and L. Greene, *The Labor Injunction;* E. E. Witte, *The Government in Labor Disputes;* P. F. Brissenden, "The Labor Injunction," *Pol. Sci. Qt.* Vol. XLVIII.

WOODS, Circuit Judge. . . . The question now to be considered [is] whether or not the injunction was authorized by the act of July 2, 1890. It was under that act that the order was asked and was granted; but it has been seriously questioned in this proceeding, as well as by an eminent judge and by lawyers elsewhere, whether the statute is by its terms applicable, or consistently with constitutional guaranties can be applied, to cases like this.

. . . The position of the defendants in respect to this statute, as stated in one of the briefs, is that it "is directed at capital", "at dangers very generally supposed to result from vast aggregations of capital", that "the evil aimed at is one of a contractual character, and not of force and violence.". . . It is said we may gather from the debates in congress, as from any other source, "the history of the evil which the legislation was intended to remedy." Doubtless this is often true; and in this instance it is perhaps apparent that the original measure, as proposed in the senate, "was directed wholly against trusts, and not at organizations of labor in any form". But it also appears that before the bill left the senate its title had been changed, and material additions made to the text; and it is worthy of note that a proviso to the effect that the act should not be construed to apply "to any arrangements, agreements or combinations made between laborers with a view of lessening hours of labor or of increasing their wages, nor to any arrangements, agreements or combinations among persons engaged in agriculture made with the view of enhancing the price of agricultural . . . products" was not adopted. Such an amendment, doubtless, was not necessary in order to exclude agreements and arrangements of the kind mentioned; but the offering of the proposition shows that the possible application of the statute to cases not in the nature of trusts or monopolies, and in which workmen or farmers should be concerned, was not overlooked. But it is more significant that, upon the introduction of the bill into the house, the chairman of the judiciary committee, . . . made the following statement: "Now just what contracts, what combinations in the form of trusts, or what conspiracies will be in restraint of trade or commerce, mentioned in the bill, will not be known until the courts have construed and interpreted this provision."

It is therefore the privilege and duty of the court, uncontrolled by considerations drawn from other sources, to find the meaning of the statute in the terms of its provisions, interpreted by the settled rules of construction. That the original design to suppress trusts and monopolies created by contract or combination in the form of trust, which of course would be of a "contractual character" was adhered to, is clear; but it is equally clear that a further and more comprehensive purpose came to be entertained, and was embodied in the final form of the enactment. Combinations are condemned, not only when they take the form of trusts, but in whatever form found, if they be in restraint of trade. That is the effect of the words "or otherwise". . . . Any proposed restraint of trade, though it be in itself innocent, if it is to be accomplished by conspiracy, is unlawful. . . .

I have not failed, I think, to appreciate the just force of the argument to the contrary, of my opinion,—it has sometimes entangled me in doubt,—but my conclusion is clear, that under the act of 1890, the court had jurisdiction of the case presented in the application, and that the injunction granted was not without authority of law, nor for any reason invalid. . . .

336. IN RE DEBS
158 U.S. 564
1895

Petition for a writ of *habeas corpus*. The facts of the case are stated in *U.S.* v. *Debs*, Doc. No. 335. It is important to notice that the decision of the Supreme Court was based not upon the Sherman Anti-Trust Act, but upon much broader grounds.

BREWER, J. The case presented by the bill is this: The United States, finding that the interstate transportation of persons and property, as well as the carriage of the mails, is forcibly obstructed, and that a combination and conspiracy exists to subject the control of such transportation to the will of the conspirators, applied to one of their courts, sitting as a court of equity, for an injunction to restrain such obstruction and prevent carrying into effect such conspiracy. Two questions of importance are presented: First. Are the relations of the general government to interstate commerce and the transportation of the mails such as to authorize a direct interference to prevent a forcible obstruction thereof? Second. If authority exists, as authority in governmental affairs implies both power and duty, has a court of equity jurisdiction to issue an injunction in aid of the performance of such duty?

First. What are the relations of the general government to interstate commerce and the transportation of the mails? They are those of direct supervision, control, and management. While under the dual system which prevails with us the powers of government are distributed between the state and the nation, and while the latter is properly styled a government of enumerated powers, yet within the limits of such enumeration it has all the attributes of sovereignty, and, in the exercise of those enumerated powers, acts directly upon the citizen, and not through the intermediate agency of the state. . . .

"We hold it to be an incontrovertible principle, that the government of the United States may, by means of physical force, exercised through its official agents, execute on every foot of American soil the powers and functions that belong to it. This necessarily involves the power to command obedience to its laws, and hence the power to keep the peace to that extent. . . ." Mr. Justice Bradley in *Ex parte Siebold,* 100 U. S. 371, 395. . . .

Among the powers expressly given to the national government are the control of interstate commerce and the creation and management of the postoffice system for the nation. . . .

Obviously these powers given to the national government over interstate commerce and in respect to the transportation of the mails were not dormant and unused. Congress had taken hold of these two matters, and by various and specific acts had assumed and exercised the powers given to it, and was in the full discharge of its duty to regulate interstate commerce and carry the mails. The validity of such exercise and the exclusiveness of its control had been again and again presented to this court for consideration. It is curious to note the fact that in a large proportion of the cases in respect to interstate commerce brought to this court the question presented was of the validity of state legislation in its bearings upon interstate commerce, and the uniform course of decision has been to declare that it is not within the competency of a state to legislate in such a manner as to obstruct interstate commerce. If a state with its recognized powers of sovereignty is impotent to obstruct interstate commerce, can it be that any mere voluntary association of individuals within the limits of that state has a power which the state itself does not possess?

As, under the Constitution, power over interstate commerce and the transportation of the mails is vested in the national government, and Congress by virtue of such grant has assumed actual and direct control, it follows that the national government may prevent any unlawful and forcible interference therewith. But how shall this be accomplished? Doubtless, it is within the competency of Congress to prescribe by legislation that any interference with these matters shall be offenses against the United States, and prosecuted and punished by indictment in the proper courts. But is that the only remedy? Have the vast interests of the nation in interstate commerce, and in the transporta-

tion of the mails, no other protection than lies in the possible punishment of those who interfere with it? To ask the question is to answer it. By article 3, section 2, clause 3, of the federal Constitution it is provided: "The trial of all crimes except in cases of impeachment shall be by jury; and such trial shall be held in the State where the said crime shall have been committed." If all the inhabitants of a state, or even a great body of them, should combine to obstruct interstate commerce or the transportation of the mails, prosecutions for such offenses had in such a community would be doomed in advance to failure. And if the certainty of such failure was known, and the national government had no other way to enforce the freedom of interstate commerce and the transportation of the mails than by prosecution and punishment for interference therewith, the whole interests of the nation in these respects would be at the absolute mercy of a portion of the inhabitants of that single state.

But there is no such impotency in the national government. The entire strength of the nation may be used to enforce in any part of the land the full and free exercise of all national powers and the security of all rights entrusted by the Constitution to its care. The strong arm of the national government may be put forth to brush away all obstructions to the freedom of interstate commerce or the transportation of the mails. If the emergency arises, the army of the nation, and all its militia, are at the service of the nation to compel obedience to its laws.

But passing to the second question, is there no other alternative than the use of force on the part of the executive authorities whenever obstructions arise to the freedom of interstate commerce or the transportation of the mails? Is the army the only instrument by which rights of the public can be enforced and the peace of the nation preserved? Grant that any public nuisance may be forcibly abated either at the instance of the authorities, or by any individual suffering private damage therefrom, the existence of this right of forcible abatement is not inconsistent with nor does it destroy the right of appeal in an orderly way to the court for a judicial determination, and an exercise of their powers by writ of injunction and otherwise to accomplish the same result. . . .

It is obvious from these decisions that while it is not the province of the government to interfere in any mere matter of private controversy between individuals, or to use its great powers to enforce the rights of one against another, yet, whenever the wrongs complained of are such as affect the public at large, and are in respect of matters which by the Constitution are entrusted to the care of the nation, and concerning which the nation owes the duty to all the citizens of securing to them their common rights, then the mere fact that the government has no pecuniary interest in the controversy is not sufficient to exclude it from the courts, or prevent it from taking measures therein to fully discharge those constitutional duties.

The national government, given by the Constitution power to regulate interstate commerce, has by express statute assumed jurisdiction over such commerce when carried upon railroads. It is charged, therefore, with the duty of keeping those highways of interstate commerce free from obstruction, for it has always been recognized as one of the powers and duties of a government to remove obstructions from the highway under its control. . . .

We have given to this case the most careful and anxious attention, for we realize that it touches closely questions of supreme importance to the people of this country. Summing up our conclusions, we hold that the government of the United States is one having jurisdiction over every foot of soil within its territory, and acting directly upon each citizen; that while it is a government of enumerated powers, it has within the limits of those powers all the attributes of sovereignty; that to it is committed power over interstate commerce and the transmission of the mail; that the powers thus conferred upon the national government are not dormant, but have been assumed and put into practical exercise by the legislation of Congress; that in the exercise of those powers it is competent for the nation to remove all obstructions upon highways, natural or artificial, to the passage of interstate commerce or the carrying of the mail; that while it may be competent for the government (through the executive branch and in the use of the entire executive power of the nation)

to forcibly remove all such obstructions, it is equally within its competency to appeal to the civil courts for an inquiry and determination as to the existence and character of any alleged obstructions, and if such are found to exist, or threaten to occur, to invoke the powers of these courts to remove or restrain such obstruction; that the jurisdiction of courts to interfere in such matters by injunction is one recognized from ancient times and by indubitable authority; that such jurisdiction is not ousted by the fact that the obstructions are accompanied by or consist of acts in themselves violations of the criminal law; that the proceeding by injunction is of a civil character, and may be enforced by proceedings in contempt; that such proceedings are not in execution of the criminal laws of the land; that the penalty for a violation of injunction is no substitute for and no defense to a prosecution for any criminal offenses committed in the course of such violation; that the complaint filed in this case clearly showed an existing obstruction of artificial highways for the passage of interstate commerce and the transmission of the mail—an obstruction not only temporarily existing, but threatening to continue; that under such complaint the circuit court had power to issue its process of injunction; that it having been issued and served on these defendants, the circuit court had authority to inquire whether its orders had been disobeyed, and when it found that they had been, then to proceed under section 725, Revised Statutes, which grants power "to punish by fine or imprisonment, . . . disobedience, . . . by any party . . . or other person, to any lawful writ, process, order, rule, decree or command," and enter the order of punishment complained of; and, finally, that, the circuit court, having full jurisdiction in the premises, its finding of the fact of disobedience is not open to review on habeas corpus in this or any other court. . . .

We enter into no examination of the act of July 2, 1890, upon which the Circuit Court relied mainly to sustain its jurisdiction. It must not be understood from this that we dissent from the conclusions of that court in reference to the scope of the act, but simply that we prefer to rest our judgement on the broader ground which has been discussed in this opinion, believing it of importance that the principles underlying it should be fully stated and affirmed.

The petition for a writ of *habeas corpus* is denied.

337. CLEVELAND'S APPEAL FOR A GOLD GUARANTEE ON BONDS
Message to Congress February 8, 1895

(Richardson, ed. *Messages and Papers*, Vol. VIII, p. 567 ff.)

As early as January 1895 it became apparent that the government would have to replenish its gold reserve through a third bond sale. The President and Secretary Carlisle accordingly made an arrangement with a syndicate headed by J. P. Morgan for the sale of $65,000,000 of bonds. These bonds were to yield four per cent. but if Congress would substitute the words "gold bonds" for "coin bonds" the interest rate would be reduced to three per. cent., thus saving the government some $16,000,000 in interest. Cleveland's appeal to Congress to authorize the necessary change was defeated by the silver forces, led by Bland and Bryan. The terms of the third bond deal were considered excessively hard, and both the Government and the syndicate were bitterly criticised for the transaction. See, A. Nevins, *Grover Cleveland*, p. 661 ff.; W. J. Bryan, *The First Battle*, p. 135 ff.; J. A. Barnes, *John G. Carlisle*, ch. xv; L. Corey, *The House of Morgan*, ch. xviii; the bond sale investigation is in 54th Cong. 2d Sess. *Senate Exec. Doc. No. 187*.

EXECUTIVE MANSION, *February 8, 1895.*
To the Congress of the United States:

Since my recent communication to the Congress calling attention to our financial condition and suggesting legislation which I deemed essential to our national welfare and credit the anxiety and apprehension then existing in business circles has continued.

As a precaution, therefore, against the failure of timely legislative aid through Congressional action, cautious preparations have been pending to employ to the best possible advantage, in default of better means, such Executive authority as may without additional legislation be exercised for the purpose of reënforcing and maintaining in our Treasury an adequate and safe gold reserve.

In the judgment of those especially charged with this responsibility the business situation is so critical and the legislative situation is so unpromising, with the omission thus far on the part of Congress to beneficially enlarge the powers of the Secretary of the Treasury in the premises, as to enjoin im-

mediate Executive action with the facilities now at hand.

Therefore, in pursuance of section 3700 of the Revised Statutes, the details of an arrangement have this day been concluded with parties abundantly able to fulfill their undertaking whereby bonds of the United States authorized under the act of July 14, 1875, payable in coin thirty years after their date, with interest at the rate of 4 per cent per annum, to the amount of a little less than $62,400,000, are to be issued for the purchase of gold coin, amounting to a sum slightly in excess of $65,000,000, to be delivered to the Treasury of the United States, which sum added to the gold now held in our reserve will so restore such reserve as to make it amount to something more than $100,000,000. Such a premium is to be allowed to the Government upon the bonds as to fix the rate of interest upon the amount of gold realized at 3¾ per cent per annum. At least one-half of the gold to be obtained is to be supplied from abroad, which is a very important and favorable feature of the transaction.

The privilege is especially reserved to the Government to substitute at par within ten days from this date, in lieu of the 4 per cent coin bonds, other bonds in terms payable in gold and bearing only 3 per cent interest if the issue of the same should in the meantime be authorized by the Congress.

The arrangement thus completed, which after careful inquiry appears in present circumstances and considering all the objects desired to be the best attainable, develops such a difference in the estimation of investors between bonds made payable in coin and those specifically made payable in gold in favor of the latter as is represented by three-fourths of a cent in annual interest. In the agreement just concluded the annual saving in interest to the Government if 3 per cent gold bonds should be substituted for 4 per cent coin bonds under the privilege reserved would be $539,159, amounting in thirty years, or at the maturity of the coin bonds, to $16,174,770.

Of course there never should be a doubt in any quarter as to the redemption in gold of the bonds of the Government which are made payable in coin. Therefore the discrimination, in the judgment of investors, between our bond obligations payable in coin and those specifically made payable in gold is very significant. It is hardly necessary to suggest that, whatever may be our views on the subject, the sentiments or preferences of those with whom we must negotiate in disposing of our bonds for gold are not subject to our dictation.

I have only to add that in my opinion the transaction herein detailed for the information of the Congress promises better results than the efforts previously made in the direction of effectively adding to our gold reserve through the sale of bonds, and I believe it will tend, as far as such action can in present circumstances, to meet the determination expressed in the law repealing the silver-purchasing clause of the act of July 14, 1890, and that, in the language of such repealing act, the arrangement made will aid our efforts to "insure the maintenance of the parity in value of the coins of the two metals and the equal power of every dollar at all times in the markets and in the payment of debts."

GROVER CLEVELAND.

338. APPEAL OF THE SILVER DEMOCRATS
March 5, 1895
(W. J. Bryan, *The First Battle*, p. 156-7)

Ever since the beginning of the second Cleveland administration, the split in the Democratic party between the silver and the gold Democrats had been steadily widening. In the closing days of the Fifty-third Congress, Bryan and Bland, the two outstanding leaders of the silver forces in the House, drew up an appeal to the Democratic party, which was signed by about one fifth of the Democratic members of the lower House and by Evan Howell, editor of the Atlanta Constitution. "This address," wrote Bryan, "was the beginning of the successful effort on the part of the silver Democrats to take control of the Democratic organization". This effort culminated in the control of the 1896 convention by the silver forces. See, W. J. Bryan, *The First Battle*, ch. vi.

An Important Document

To the Democrats of the United States:

We, the undersigned Democrats, present for your consideration the following statement:

We believe that the establishment of gold as the only monetary standard and the elimination of silver as a full legal tender money, will increase the purchasing power of each dollar, add to the burden of all debts, decrease the market value of all other forms of property, continue and intensify business depression, and, finally, reduce the majority of the people to financial bondage.

We believe that no party can hope for enduring success in the United States so long as it advocates a single gold standard, and that the advocacy of such a financial policy would be especially fatal to a party which, like the Democratic party, derives its voting strength from those who may without reproach be called the common people; and we point to the overwhelming defeat of the party in 1894, to the opposition aroused by the veto of the seigniorage bill and to the still more unanimous protest against the issue of gold bonds, as proof that the Democratic party cannot be brought to the support of the gold standard policy.

We believe that the money question will be the paramount issue in 1896, and will so remain until it is settled by the intelligence and patriotism of the American voters.

We believe that a large majority of the Democrats of the United States favor bimetallism, and realize that it can only be secured by the restoration of the free and unlimited coinage of gold and silver at the present ratio, and we assert that the majority have, and should exercise, the right to control the policy of the party and retain the party name.

We believe that it is the duty of the majority, and within their power, to take charge of the party organization and make the Democratic party an effective instrument in the accomplishment of needed reforms. It is necessary that Democrats should surrender their convictions on other questions in order to take an active part in the settlement of the question which at this time surpasses all others in importance.

We believe that the rank and file of the Democratic party should at once assert themselves in the Democratic party and place the party on record in favor of the immediate restoration of the free and unlimited coinage of gold and silver at the present legal ratio of 16 to 1, as such coinage existed prior to 1873, without waiting for the aid or consent of any other nation, such gold and silver coin to be a full legal tender for all debts public and private.

We urge all Democrats who favor the financial policy above set forth to associate themselves together and impress their views upon the party organization; we urge all newspapers in harmony with the above financial policy to place it at the head of the editorial column and assist in the immediate restoration of bimetallism.

339. UNITED STATES v. E. C. KNIGHT COMPANY
156 U. S. 1
1895

Appeal from the United States Circuit Court of Appeals. Bill by the United States against the E. C. Knight Company, and other corporations, charging violation of the Sherman Anti-Trust Act. The E. C. Knight Company, the American Sugar Refining Company, had purchased the stock of four competing sugar refining companies located in Philadelphia, Pennsylvania, and thus secured a practical monopoly on the manufacture of refined sugar in the United States. It was charged that these purchases constituted a combination in restraint of trade. The Circuit Court of Appeals dismissed the bill.

The decision in this case constituted a serious set-back to the enforcement of the Sherman Anti-Trust Act. For a discussion of the case see A. H. Walker, *History of the Sherman Law*, p. 90 ff.

FULLER, C. J. . . . In the view which we take of the case, we need not discuss whether because the tentacles which drew the outlying refineries into the dominant corporation were separately put out, therefore there was no combination to monopolize; or, because according to political economists, aggregations of capital may reduce prices, therefore the objection to concentration of power is relieved; or, because others were theoretically left free to go into the business of refining sugar, and the original stockholders of the Philadelphia refineries after becoming stockholders of the American Company might go into competition with themselves, or, parting with that stock, might set up again for themselves, therefore no objectionable restraint was imposed.

The fundamental question is, whether conceding that the existence of a monopoly in manufacture is established by the evidence, that monopoly can be directly suppressed under the act of Congress in the mode attempted by this bill.

It cannot be denied that the power of a State to protect the lives, health, and property of its citizens, and to preserve good order and the public morals, "the power to govern men and things within the limits of its dominion," is a power originally and always belonging to the States, not surrendered by them to the general government, nor directly restrained by the Constitution of the United States, and essentially exclusive. The relief of the citizens of each State from the burden of monopoly and the evils resulting from the restraint of trade among such citizens was left with the States to deal with. . . . On the other hand, the power of Congress to regulate commerce among the several States is also exclusive. . .

The argument is that the power to control the manufacture of refined sugar is a monopoly over a necessary of life, to the enjoyment of which by a large part of the population of the United States interstate commerce is indispensable, and that, therefore, the general government in the exercise of the power to regulate commerce may suppress such monopoly directly and set aside the instruments which have created it. But this argument cannot be confined to necessaries of life merely, and must include all articles of general consumption. Doubtless the power to control the manufacture of a given thing involves in a certain sense the control of its disposition, but this is a secondary and not the primary sense; and although the exercise of that power may result in bringing the operation of commerce into play, it does not control it, and affects it only incidentally and indirectly. Commerce succeeds to manufacture, and is not a part of it. The power to regulate commerce is the power to prescribe the rule by which commerce shall be governed, and is a power independent of the power to suppress monopoly. But it may operate in repression of monopoly whenever it comes within the rules by which commerce is governed or whenever the transaction is itself a monopoly of commerce.

It is vital that the independence of the commercial power and of the police power, and the delimitation between them, however sometimes perplexing, should always be recognized and observed, for while the one furnishes the strongest bond of union, the other is essential to the autonomy of the States as required by our dual form of government; and acknowledged evils, however grave and urgent they may appear to be, had better be borne, than the risk be run, in the effort to suppress them, of more serious consequences by resort to expedients of even doubtful constitutionality.

It will be perceived how far-reaching the proposition is that the power of dealing with a monopoly directly may be exercised by the general government whenever interstate or international commerce may be ultimately affected. The regulation of commerce applies to the subjects of commerce, and not to matters of internal police. Contracts to buy, sell, or exchange goods to be transported among the several States, the transportation and its instrumentalities, and articles bought, sold, or exchanged for the purposes of such transit among the States, or put in the way of transit, may be regulated, but this is because they form part of interstate trade or commerce. The fact that an article is manufactured for export to another State does not of itself make it an article of interstate commerce, and the intent of the manufacturer does not determine the time when the article or product passes from the control of the State and belongs to commerce. . . .

And Mr. Justice Lamar remarked: "A situation more paralyzing to the state governments, and more provocative of conflicts between the general government and the States, and less likely to have been what the framers of the Constitution intended, it would be difficult to imagine."

Contracts, combinations, or conspiracies to control domestic enterprise in manufacture, agriculture, mining production in all its forms, or to raise or lower prices or wages, might unquestionably tend to restrain external as well as domestic trade, but the restraint would be an indirect result, however inevitable and whatever its extent, and such result would not necessarily determine the object of the contract, combination, or conspiracy.

Again, all the authorities agree that in order to vitiate a contract or combination it is not essential that its result should be a complete monopoly; it is sufficient if it really tends to that end and to deprive the public of the advantages which flow from free competition. Slight reflection will show that if the national power extends to all contracts and combinations in manufacture, agriculture, mining, and other productive industries, whose ultimate result may affect external commerce, comparatively little of business operations and affairs would be left for state control.

It was in the light of well-settled principles that the act of July 2, 1890 was framed. Congress did not attempt thereby to assert the power to deal with monopoly directly as such; or to limit and restrict the rights of corporations created by the States or the citizens of the States in the acquisition, control, or disposition of property; or to regulate or prescribe the price or prices at which such property or the products thereof should be sold; or to make criminal the acts of persons in the acquisition and control of property which the States of their residence or creation sanctioned or permitted. Aside from the provisions applicable where Congress might exercise municipal power, what the law struck at was combinations, contracts, and conspiracies to monopolize trade and commerce among the several States or with foreign nations; but the contracts and acts of the defendants related exclusively to the acquisition of the Philadelphia refineries and the business of sugar refining in Pennsylvania, and bore no direct relation to commerce between the States or with foreign nations. The object was manifestly private gain in the manufacture of the commodity, but not through the control of interstate or foreign commerce. It is true that the bill alleged that the products of these refineries were sold and distributed among the several States, and that all the companies were engaged in trade or commerce with the several States and with foreign nations; but this was no more than to say that trade and commerce served manufacture to fulfil its function. . . . There was nothing in the proofs to indicate any intention to put a restraint upon trade or commerce, and the fact, as we have seen, that trade or commerce might be indirectly affected was not enough to entitle complainants to a decree. . . .

Decree of the Circuit Court of Appeals dismissing the bill affirmed. HARLAN, J. delivered a dissenting opinion.

340. CLEVELAND'S MESSAGE ON THE VENEZUELA BOUNDARY CONTROVERSY
December 17, 1895

(Richardson, ed. *Messages and Papers,* Vol. IX, p. 655 ff.)

The dispute between Great Britain and Venezuela over the boundary of British Guiana was of long standing. The efforts of Venezuela to submit it to arbitration proving vain, Venezuela broke off diplomatic relations with Great Britain in 1887. Cleveland considered that the Monroe Doctrine was involved in the dispute, and in 1895 he determined to force the issue to a conclusion. July 20, Secretary Olney sent a despatch for transmission to Lord Salisbury calling attention to the interest of the United States in the boundary dispute and insisting that the Monroe Doctrine required American intervention on behalf of arbitration. In the course of his letter, Mr. Olney said, "To-day the United States is practically sovereign on this continent, and its fiat is law upon the subjects to which it confines its interposition. Why? . . . It is because in addition to all other grounds, its infinite resources combined with its isolated position render it master of the situation and practically invulnerable against any or all other powers." And Mr. Olney concluded with a definite request for arbitration. Lord Salisbury replied, November 26, in two notes: one denying the applicability of the Monroe Doctrine to the dispute, the other maintaining the correctness of the British position in the boundary controversy. December 17, President Cleveland laid this correspondence before Congress and asked for authority to appoint an independent commission to pass on the merits of the dispute. To many it seemed that war was inevitable, but public opinion in both countries forced an accommodation. Furthermore Great Britain was faced, in 1896, with a serious outbreak of the Boers in South Africa, and on January 3 Kaiser William of Germany sent his famous telegram of sympathy to the Boer leader, Paul Kruger. Under the circumstances Lord Salisbury acquiesced in the American demand. A treaty was negotiated with Venezuela which provided for the appointment of an impartial tribunal to pass on the boundary controversy. The tribunal met in Paris in 1899 and handed down a decision which favored the British contentions. See, G. Cleveland, *The Venezuela Boundary Controversy;* A. Nevins, *Grover Cleveland,* ch. xxxiv; R. McElroy, *Grover Cleveland,* Vol. II, ch. vi; H. James, *Richard Olney;* S. F. Bemis ed., *American Secretaries of State,* Vol. VIII, p. 291 ff.; A. B. Hart, *The Monroe Doctrine;* T. B. Edgington, *The Monroe Doctrine,* ch. xvi; D. Y. Thomas, *One Hundred Years of the Monroe Doctrine.*

Executive Mansion, December 17, 1895.
To the Congress:

In my annual message addressed to the Congress on the 3d instant I called attention to the pending boundary controversy between Great Britain and the Republic of Venezuela and recited the substance of a representation made by this Government to Her Britannic Majesty's Government suggesting reasons why such dispute should be submitted to arbitration for settlement and inquiring whether it would be so submitted.

The answer of the British Government, which was then awaited, has since been received, and, together with the despatch to which it is a reply, is hereto appended.

Such reply is embodied in two communications addressed by the British prime minister to Sir Julian Pauncefote, the British ambassador at this capital. It will be seen that one of these communications is devoted exclusively to observations upon the Monroe doctrine, and claims that in the present instance a new and strange extension and development of this doctrine is insisted on by the United States; that the reasons justifying an appeal to the doctrine enunciated by President Monroe are generally inapplicable "to the state of things in which we live at the present day," and especially inapplicable to a controversy involving the boundary line between Great Britain and Venezuela.

Without attempting extended argument in reply to these positions, it may not be amiss to suggest that the doctrine upon which we stand is strong and sound, because its enforcement is important to our peace and safety as a nation and is essential to the integrity of our free institutions and the tranquil maintenance of our distinctive form of government. It was intended to apply to every stage of our national life and can not become obsolete while our Republic endures. If the balance of power is justly a cause for jealous anxiety among the Governments of the Old World and a subject for our absolute noninterference, none the less is an observance of the Monroe doctrine of vital concern to our people and their Government.

Assuming, therefore, that we may properly insist upon this doctrine without regard to "the state of things in which we live" or any changed conditions here or elsewhere, it is not apparent why its application may not be invoked in the present controversy.

If a European power by an extension of its boundaries takes possession of the territory of one of our neighboring Republics against its will and in derogation of its rights, it is difficult to see why to that extent such European power does not thereby attempt to extend its system of government to that portion of this continent which is thus taken. This is the precise action which President Monroe declared to be "dangerous to our peace and safety," and it can make no difference whether the European system is extended by an advance of frontier or otherwise.

It is also suggested in the British reply that we should not seek to apply the Monroe doctrine to the pending dispute because it does not embody any principle of international law which "is founded on the general consent of nations," and that "no statesman, however eminent, and no nation, however powerful, are competent to insert into the code of international law a novel principle which was never recognized before and which has not since been accepted by the government of any other country."

Practically the principle for which we contend has peculiar, if not exclusive, relation to the United States. It may not have been admitted in so many words to the code of international law, but since in international councils every nation is entitled to the rights belonging to it, if the enforcement of the Monroe doctrine is something we may justly claim it has its place in the code of international law as certainly and as securely as if it were specifically mentioned; and when the United States is a suitor before the high tribunal that administers international law the question to be determined is whether or not we present claims which the justice of that code of law can find to be right and valid.

The Monroe doctrine finds its recognition in those principles of international law which are based upon the theory that every nation shall have its rights protected and its just claims enforced.

Of course this Government is entirely confident that under the sanction of this doctrine we have clear rights and undoubted claims. Nor is this ignored in the British reply. The prime minister, while not admitting that the Monroe doctrine is applicable to present conditions, states:

In declaring that the United States would resist any such enterprise if it was contemplated, President Monroe adopted a policy which received the entire sympathy of the English Government of that date.

He further declares:

Though the language of President Monroe is directed to the attainment of objects which most Englishmen would agree to be salutary, it is impossible to admit that they have been inscribed by any adequate authority in the code of international law.

Again he says:

They [Her Majesty's Government] fully concur with the view which President Monroe apparently entertained, that any disturbance of the existing territorial distribution in that hemisphere by any fresh acquisitions on the part of any European State would be a highly inexpedient change.

In the belief that the doctrine for which

we contend was clear and definite, that it was founded upon substantial considerations and involved our safety and welfare, that it was fully applicable to our present conditions and to the state of the world's progress, and that it was directly related to the pending controversy, and without any conviction as to the final merits of the dispute, but anxious to learn in a satisfactory and conclusive manner whether Great Britain sought under a claim of boundary to extend her possessions on this continent without right, or whether she merely sought possession of territory fairly included within her lines of ownership, this Government proposed to the Government of Great Britain a resort to arbitration as the proper means of settling the question, to the end that a vexatious boundary dispute between the two contestants might be determined and our exact standing and relation in respect to the controversy might be made clear.

It will be seen from the correspondence herewith submitted that this proposition has been declined by the British Government upon grounds which in the circumstances seem to me to be far from satisfactory. It is deeply disappointing that such an appeal, actuated by the most friendly feelings toward both nations directly concerned, addressed to the sense of justice and to the magnanimity of one of the great powers of the world, and touching its relations to one comparatively weak and small, should have produced no better results.

The course to be pursued by this Government in view of the present condition does not appear to admit of serious doubt. Having labored faithfully for many years to induce Great Britain to submit this dispute to impartial arbitration, and having been now finally apprised of her refusal to do so, nothing remains but to accept the situation, to recognize its plain requirements, and deal with it accordingly. Great Britain's present proposition has never thus far been regarded as admissible by Venezuela, though any adjustment of the boundary which that country may deem for her advantage and may enter into of her own free will can not of course be objected to by the United States.

Assuming, however, that the attitude of Venezuela will remain unchanged, the dispute has reached such a stage as to make it now incumbent upon the United States to take measures to determine with sufficient certainty for its justification what is the true divisional line between the Republic of Venezuela and British Guiana. The inquiry to that end should of course be conducted carefully and judicially, and due weight should be given to all available evidence, records, and facts in support of the claims of both parties.

In order that such an examination should be prosecuted in a thorough and satisfactory manner, I suggest that the Congress make an adequate appropriation for the expenses of a commission, to be appointed by the Executive, who shall make the necessary investigation and report upon the matter with the least possible delay. When such report is made and accepted it will, in my opinion, be the duty of the United States to resist by every means in its power, as a wilful aggression upon its rights and interests, the appropriation by Great Britain of any lands or the exercise of governmental jurisdiction over any territory which after investigation we have determined of right belongs to Venezuela.

In making these recommendations I am fully alive to the responsibility incurred and keenly realize all the consequences that may follow.

I am, nevertheless, firm in my conviction that while it is a grievous thing to contemplate the two great English-speaking peoples of the world as being otherwise than friendly competitors in the onward march of civilization and strenuous and worthy rivals in all the arts of peace, there is no calamity which a great nation can invite which equals that which follows a supine submission to wrong and injustice and the consequent loss of national self-respect and honor, beneath which are shielded and defended a people's safety and greatness.

GROVER CLEVELAND.

341. THE REPUBLICAN PLATFORM OF 1896
St. Louis, Missouri
June 16, 1896

(K. Porter, ed. *National Party Platforms,* p. 201 ff.)

The Republican National Convention met in St. Louis, Missouri, June 16, 1896, adopted a platform calling for the gold standard and high tariffs, and nominated William McKinley of Ohio and G. A. Hobart of New Jersey for President and Vice-President. McKinley was elected with an electoral college vote of 271 and a popular vote of over seven million. See Mark Sullivan, *Our Times,* Vol. I; H. T. Peck, *Twenty Years of the Republic;* O. S. Olcott, *William McKinley,* 2 Vols.; H. Croly, *Mark Hanna;* T. Beer, *Mark Hanna;* for the campaign, see W. J. Bryan, *The First Battle.*

. . . For the first time since the civil war the American people have witnessed the calamitous consequence of full and unrestricted Democratic control of the government. It has been a record of unparalleled incapacity, dishonor, and disaster. In administrative management it has ruthlessly sacrificed indispensable revenue, entailed an unceasing deficit, eked out ordinary current expenses with borrowed money, piled up the public debt by $262,000,000, in time of peace, forced an adverse balance of trade, kept a perpetual menace hanging over the redemption fund, pawned American credit to alien syndicates and reversed all the measures and results of successful Republican rule. In the broad effect of its policy it has precipitated panic, blighted industry and trade with prolonged depression, closed factories, reduced work and wages, halted enterprise and crippled American production, while stimulating foreign production for the American market. Every consideration of public safety and individual interest demands that the government shall be wrested from the hands of those who have shown themselves incapable of conducting it without disaster at home and dishonor abroad and shall be restored to the party which for thirty years administered it with unequaled success and prosperity. And in this connection, we heartily endorse the wisdom, patriotism and success of the administration of Benjamin Harrison.

We renew and emphasize our allegiance to the policy of protection as the bulwark of American industrial independence and the foundation of American development and prosperity. This true American policy taxes foreign products and encourages home industry. It puts the burden of revenue on foreign goods; it secures the American market for the American producer. It upholds the American standard of wages for the American workingman; it puts the factory by the side of the farm, and makes the American farmer less dependent on foreign demand and price; it diffuses general thrift, and founds the strength of each. In its reasonable application it is just, fair and impartial, equally opposed to foreign control and domestic monopoly, to sectional discrimination and individual favoritism.

We denounce the present tariff as sectional, injurious to the public credit and destructive to business enterprise. We demand such an equitable tariff on foreign imports which come into competition with the American products as will not only furnish adequate revenue for the necessary expense of the Government, but will protect American labor from degradation and the wage level of other lands. We are not pledged to any particular schedules. The question of rates is a practical question, to be governed by the condition of time and of production. The ruling and uncompromising principle is the protection and development of American labor and industries. The country demands a right settlement, and then it wants a rest.

We believe the repeal of the reciprocity arrangements negotiated by the last Republican Administration was a national calamity, and demand their renewal and extension on such terms as will equalize our trade with other nations, remove the restrictions which now obstruct the sale of American products in the ports of other countries, and secure enlarged markets for the products of our farms, forests, and factories.

Protection and Reciprocity are twin measures of American policy and go hand in hand. Democratic rule has recklessly struck down both, and both must be re-established. Protection for what we produce; reciprocal agreement of mutual interests, which gain open markets for us in return for our open markets for others. Protection builds up domestic industry and trade and secures our own market for ourselves; reciprocity builds up foreign trade and finds an outlet for our surplus. . . .

The Republican party is unreservedly for sound money. It caused the enactment of a law providing for the resumption of specie payments in 1879. Since then every dollar has been as good as gold. We are unalterably opposed to every measure calculated to debase our currency or impair the credit of our country. We are therefore opposed to the free coinage of silver, except by international agreement with the leading commercial nations of the earth, which agreement we pledge ourselves to promote, and until such agreement can be obtained the existing gold standard must be maintained. All of our silver and paper currency must be maintained at parity with gold, and we favor all measures designated to maintain inviolable the obligations of the United States, of all our money, whether coin or paper, at the present standard, the standard of most enlightened nations of the world. . . .

We denounce the practice in the pension bureau so recklessly and unjustly carried on by the present Administration of reducing pensions and arbitrarily dropping names from the rolls, as deserving the severest condemnation of the American people.

Our foreign policy should be at all times firm, vigorous and dignified, and all our interests in the western hemisphere should be carefully watched and guarded.

The Hawaiian Islands should be controlled by the United States, and no foreign power should be permitted to interfere with them. The Nicaragua Canal should be built, owned and operated by the United States. And, by the purchase of the Danish Islands we should secure a much needed Naval station in the West Indies. . . .

342. BRYAN'S CROSS OF GOLD SPEECH
July 8, 1896

(W. J. Bryan, *The First Battle*, p. 199 ff.)

Bryan, a delegate from Nebraska to the Democratic National Convention at Chicago, made the concluding speech in the debate on the adoption of the platform. This speech, the most notable of his career and one of the most notable in the history of American oratory, dramatized Bryan before the Convention and did much to bring about a nomination already highly probable. See, Bryan, *The First Battle, passim; The Memoirs of William Jennings Bryan*, ch. vi; P. Hibben, *The Peerless Leader, William Jennings Bryan*, chs. xv, xvi; M. Sullivan, *Our Times: the Turn of the Century*.

I would be presumptuous, indeed, to present myself against the distinguished gentlemen to whom you have listened if this were a mere measuring of abilities; but this is not a contest between persons. The humblest citizen in all the land, when clad in the armor of a righteous cause, is stronger than all the hosts of error. I come to speak to you in defense of a cause as holy as the cause of liberty—the cause of humanity.

When this debate is concluded, a motion will be made to lay upon the table the resolution offered in commendation of the Administration, and also, the resolution offered in condemnation of the Administration. We object to bringing this question down to the level of persons. The individual is but an atom; he is born, he acts, he dies; but principles are eternal; and this has been a contest over a principle.

Never before in the history of this country has there been witnessed such a contest as that through which we have just passed. Never before in the history of American politics has a great issue been fought out as this issue has been, by the voters of a great party. On the fourth of March 1893, a few Democrats, most of them members of Congress, issued an address to the Democrats of the nation, asserting that the money question was the paramount issue of the hour; declaring that a majority of the Democratic party had the right to control the action of the party on this paramount issue; and concluding with the request that the believers in the free coinage of silver in the Democratic party should organize, take charge of, and control the policy of the Democratic party. Three months later, at Memphis, an organization was perfected, and the silver Democrats went forth openly and courageously proclaiming their belief, and declaring that, if successful, they would crystallize into a platform the declaration which they had made. Then began the struggle. With a zeal approaching the zeal which inspired the Crusaders who followed Peter the Hermit, our silver Democrats went forth from victory unto victory until they are now assembled, not to discuss, not to debate, but to enter up the judgement already rendered by the plain people of this country. In this contest brother has been arrayed against brother, father against son. The warmest ties of love, acquaintance, and association have been disregarded; old leaders have been cast aside when they have refused to give expression to the sentiments of those whom they would lead, and new leaders have sprung up to give direction to this cause of truth. Thus has the contest been waged, and we have assembled here under as binding and solemn instructions as were ever imposed upon representatives of the people.

We do not come as individuals. As individuals we might have been glad to compliment the gentleman from New York [Senator Hill], but we know that the people for whom we speak would never be willing to put him in a position where he could thwart the will of the Democratic party. I saw it was not a question of persons; it was a question of principle, and it is not with gladness, my friends, that we find ourselves brought into conflict with those who are now arrayed on the other side. . . .

When you [turning to the gold delegates] come before us and tell us that we are about to disturb your business interests, we reply that you have disturbed our business interests by your course.

We say to you that you have made the definition of a business man too limited in its application. The man who is employed for wages is as much a business man as his employer; the attorney in a country town is as much a business man as the corporation counsel in a great metropolis; the merchant at the cross-roads store is as much a business man as the merchant of New York; the farmer who goes forth in the morning and toils all day, who begins in the spring and toils all summer, and who by the application of brain and muscle to the natural resources of the country creates wealth, is as much a business man as the man who goes upon the Board of Trade and bets upon the price of grain; the miners who go down a thousand feet into the earth, or climb two thousand feet upon the cliffs, and bring forth from their hiding places the precious metals to be poured into the channels of trade are as much business men as the few financial magnates who, in a back room, corner the money of the world. We come to speak of this broader class of business men.

Ah, my friends, we say not one word against those who live upon the Atlantic Coast, but the hardy pioneers who have braved all the dangers of the wilderness, who have made the desert to bloom as the rose —the pioneers away out there [pointing to the West] who rear their children near to Nature's heart, where they can mingle their voices with the voices of the birds—out there where they have erected schoolhouses for the education of their young, churches where they praise their Creator, and cemeteries where rest the ashes of their dead—these people, we say, are as deserving of the consideration of our party as any people in this country. It is for these that we speak. We do not come as aggressors. Our war is not a war of conquest; we are fighting in the defense of our homes, our families, and posterity. We have petitioned, and our petitions have been scorned; we have entreated, and our entreaties have been disregarded; we have begged, and they have mocked when our calamity came. We beg no longer; we entreat no more; we petition no more. We defy them!

The gentleman from Wisconsin [Vilas] has said that he fears a Robespierre. My friends, in this land of the free you need not fear that a tyrant will spring up from among the people. What we need is an Andrew Jackson to stand, as Jackson stood, against the encroachments of organized wealth.

They tell us that this platform was made to catch votes. We reply to them that changing conditions make new issues; that the principles upon which Democracy rests are as everlasting as the hills, but they must be applied to new conditions as they arise. Conditions have arisen, and we are here to meet those conditions. They tell us that the income tax ought not to be brought in here; that it is a new idea. They criticize us for our criticism of the Supreme Court of the United States. My friends, we have not criticized; we have simply called attention to what you already know. If you want criticisms read the dissenting opinions of the court. There you will find criticisms. They say that we passed an unconstitutional law; we deny it. The income tax was not unconstitutional when it was passed; it was not unconstitutional when it went before the Supreme Court for the first time; it did not become unconstitutional until one of the judges changed his mind, and we cannot be expected to know when a judge will change his mind. The income tax is just. It simply intends to put the burden of government justly upon the backs of the people. I am in favor of an income tax. When I find a man who is not willing to bear his share of the burdens of the government which protects him, I find a man who is unworthy to enjoy the blessings of a government like ours.

They say that we are opposing national bank currency; it is true. If you will read what Thomas Benton said, you will find he said that, in searching history, he could find but one parallel to Andrew Jackson; that was Cicero, he destroyed the conspiracy of Cataline and saved Rome. Benton said that Cicero only did for Rome what Jackson did for us when he destroyed the bank conspiracy and saved America. We say in our platform we believe that the right to coin and issue money is a function of government. We believe it. We believe that it is a part of sovereignty, and can no more with safety be delegated to private individuals than we could afford to delegate to private individuals the power to make penal statutes or levy taxes. Mr. Jefferson, who was once regarded as good Democratic authority, seems to have differed in opinion from the gentleman who has addressed us on the part of the minority. Those who are opposed to this proposition tell us that the issue of paper money is a function of the banks, and that the government ought to go out of the banking business. I stand with Jefferson rather than with them, and tell them, as he did, that the issue

of money is a function of government, and that the banks ought to go out of the governing business.

They complain about the plank which declares against life tenure in office. They have tried to strain it to mean that which it does not mean. What we oppose by that plank is the life tenure which is being built up in Washington, and which excludes from participation in official benefits the humbler members of society. . . .

And now, my friends, let me come to the paramount issue. If they ask us why it is that we say more on the money question than we say upon the tariff question, I reply that, if protection has slain its thousands, the gold standard has slain its tens of thousands. If they ask us why we do not embody in our platforms all the things that we believe in, we reply that when we have restored the money of the Constitution, all other necessary reform will be possible; but that until this is done, there is no other reform that can be accomplished.

Why is it that within three months such a change has come over the country? Three months ago when it was confidently asserted that those who believed in the gold standard would frame our platform and nominate our candidates, even the advocates of the gold standard did not think that we could elect a President. And they had good reason for their doubt, because there is scarcely a State here today asking for the gold standard which is not in the absolute control of the Republican Party. But note the change. Mr. McKinley was nominated at St. Louis upon a platform which declared for the maintenance of the gold standard until it can be changed into bimetallism by international agreement. Mr. McKinley was the most popular man among the Republicans, and three months ago everybody in the Republican Party prophesied his election. How is it today? Why, the man who was once pleased to think that he looked like Napoleon—that man shudders today when he remembers that he was nominated on the anniversary of the battle of Waterloo.

Not only that, but as he listens, he can hear with ever-increasing distinctness the sound of the waves as they beat upon the lonely shores of St. Helena.

Why this change? Ah, my friends, is not

the reason for the change evident to any one who will look at the matter? No private character, however pure, no personal popularity, however great, can protect from the avenging wrath of an indignant people a man who will declare that he is in favor of fastening the gold standard upon this country, or who is willing to surrender the right of self-government and place the legislative control of our affairs in the hands of foreign potentates and powers.

We go forth confident that we shall win. Why? Because upon the paramount issue of this campaign there is not a spot of ground upon which the enemy will dare to challenge battle. If they tell us that the gold standard is a good thing, we shall point to their platform and tell them that their platform pledges the party to get rid of the gold standard and substitute bimetallism. If the gold standard is a good thing why try to get rid of it? I call your attention to the fact that some of the very people who are in this Convention today and who tell us that we ought to declare in favor of international bimetallism—thereby declaring that the gold standard is wrong and that the principle of bimetallism is better—these very people four months ago were open and avowed advocates of the gold standard, and were then telling us that we could not legislate two metals together, even with the aid of all the world. If the gold standard is a good thing, we ought to declare in favor of its retention and not in favor of abandoning it; and if the gold standard is a bad thing why should we wait until other nations are willing to help us to let go? Here is the line of battle, and we care not upon which issue they force the fight; we are prepared to meet them on either issue or on both. If they tell us that the gold standard is the standard of civilization, we reply to them that this, the most enlightened of all the nations of the earth, has never declared for a gold standard and that both the great parties this year are declaring against it. If the gold standard is the standard of civilization, why, my friends, should we not have it? If they come to meet us on that issue we can present the history of our nation. More than that; we can tell them that they will search the pages of history in vain to find a single instance where the common people of any land have ever declared themselves in favor of the gold standard. They can find where the holders of fixed investments have declared for a gold standard, but not where the masses have. Mr. Carlisle said in 1878 that this was a struggle between the "idle holders of idle capital" and "the struggling masses, who produce the wealth and pay the taxes of the country," and, my friends, the question we are to decide is: Upon which side will the Democratic party fight; upon the side of "the idle holders of idle capital" or upon the side of "the struggling masses"? That is the question which the party must answer first, and then it must be answered by each individual hereafter. The sympathies of the Democratic party, as shown by the platform, are on the side of the struggling masses who have ever been the foundation of the Democratic party. There are two ideas of government. There are those who believe that if you will only legislate to make the well-to-do prosperous, their prosperity will leak through on those below. The Democratic idea, however, has been that if you make the masses prosperous, their prosperity will find its way up through every class which rests upon them.

You come to us and tell us that the great cities are in favor of the gold standard; we reply that the great cities rest upon our broad and fertile prairies. Burn down your cities and leave our farms, and your cities will spring up again as if by magic; but destroy our farms and the grass will grow in the streets of every city in the country.

My friends, we declare that this nation is able to legislate for its own people on every question, without waiting for the aid or consent of any other nation on earth; and upon that issue we expect to carry every state in the Union. I shall not slander the inhabitants of the fair state of Massachusetts nor the inhabitants of the state of New York by saying that, when they are confronted with the proposition, they will declare that this nation is not able to attend to its own business. It is the issue of 1776 over again. Our ancestors, when but three million in number, had the courage to declare their political independence of every other nation; shall we, their descendants, when we have grown to seventy millions, declare that we are less independent than our forefathers?

No, my friends, that will never be the verdict of our people. Therefore, we care not upon what lines the battle is fought. If they say bimetallism is good, but that we cannot have it until other nations help us, we reply, that instead of having a gold standard because England has, we will restore bimetallism, and then let England have bimetallism because the United States has it. If they dare to come out in the open field and defend the gold standard as a good thing, we will fight them to the uttermost. Having behind us the producing masses of this nation and the world, supported by the commercial interests, the laboring interests and the toilers everywhere, we will answer their demand for a gold standard by saying to them: You shall not press down upon the brow of labor this crown of thorns, you shall not crucify mankind upon a cross of gold.

343. PLESSY v. FERGUSON

163 U. S. 537
1896

This case wrote the "separate but equal" doctrine into American constitutional law. It was, in effect, reversed in Brown v. Topeka, Doc. no. 617. See Vann Woodward, *The Strange Career of Jim Crow;* Gilbert Stephenson, *Race Distinctions in American Law;* Rayford Logan, *Negro in American Life and Thought 1877–1901;* and refs. to Doc. 617.

BROWN, J. This case turns upon the constitutionality of an act of the general assembly of the state of Louisiana, passed in 1890, providing for separate railway carriages for the white and colored races. . . .

The constitutionality of this act is attacked upon the ground that it conflicts both with the 13th Amendment of the Constitution, abolishing slavery, and the 14th Amendment, which prohibits certain restrictive legislation on the part of the states.

1. That it does not conflict with the 13th Amendment, which abolished slavery and involuntary servitude, except as a punishment for crime, is too clear for argument. . . .

A statute which implies merely a legal distinction between the white and colored races—a distinction which is founded in the color of the two races, and which must always exist so long as white men are distinguished from the other race by color—has no tendency to destroy the legal equality of the two races, or re-establish a state of involuntary servitude. Indeed, we do not understand that the 13th Amendment is strenuously relied upon by the plaintiff in error in this connection. . . .

The object of the amendment was undoubtedly to enforce the absolute equality of the two races before the law, but in the nature of things it could not have been intended to abolish distinctions based upon color, or to enforce social, as distinguished from political, equality, or a commingling of the two races upon terms unsatisfactory to either. Laws permitting, and even requiring their separation in places where they are liable to be brought into contact do not necessarily imply the inferiority of either race to the other, and have been generally, if not universally, recognized as within the competency of the state legislatures in the exercise of their police power. The most common instance of this is connected with the establishment of separate schools for white and colored children, which have been held to be a valid exercise of the legislative power even by courts of states where the political rights of the colored race have been longest and most earnestly enforced. . . .

It is claimed by the plaintiff in error that, in any mixed community, the reputation of belonging to the dominant race, in this instance the white race is *property,* in the same sense that a right of action, or of inheritance, is property. Conceding this to be so, for the purposes of this case, we are unable to see how this statute deprives him of, or in any way affects his right to, such property. If he be a white man and assigned to a colored coach, he may have his action for damages against the company for being deprived of his so-called property. Upon the other hand, if he be a colored man and be so assigned, he has been deprived of no property, since he is not lawfully entitled to the reputation of being a white man. . . .

So far, then, as a conflict with the 14th

Amendment is concerned, the case reduces itself to the question whether the statute of Louisiana is a reasonable regulation, and with respect to this there must necessarily be a large discretion on the part of the legislature. In determining the question of reasonableness it is at liberty to act with reference to the established usages, customs, and traditions of the people, and with a view to the promotion of their comfort, and the preservation of the public peace and good order. Gauged by this standard, we cannot say that a law which authorizes or even requires the separation of the two races in public conveyances is unreasonable or more obnoxious to the 14th Amendment than the acts of Congress requiring separate schools for colored children in the District of Columbia, the constitutionality of which does not seem to have been questioned, or the corresponding acts of state legislatures.

We consider the underlying fallacy of the plaintiff's argument to consist in the assumption that the enforced separation of the two races stamps the colored race with a badge of inferiority. If this be so, it is not by reason of anything found in the act, but solely because the colored race chooses to put that construction upon it. The argument necessarily assumes that if, as has been more than once the case, and is not unlikely to be so again, the colored race should become the dominant power in the state legislature, and should enact a law in precisely similar terms, it would thereby relegate the white race to an inferior position. We imagine that the white race, at least, would not acquiesce in this assumption. The argument also assumes that social prejudice may be overcome by legislation, and that equal rights cannot be secured to the Negro except by an enforced commingling of the two races. We cannot accept this proposition. If the two races are to meet on terms of social equality, it must be the result of natural affinities, a mutual appreciation of each other's merits and a voluntary consent of individuals. . . . Legislation is powerless to eradicate racial instincts or to abolish distinctions based upon physical differences, and the attempt to do so can only result in accentuating the difficulties of the present situation. If the civil and political right of both races be equal,

one cannot be inferior (552) to the other civilly or politically. If one race be inferior to the other socially, the Constitution of the United States cannot put them upon the same plane.

Justice HARLAN, dissenting. . . . In respect of civil rights, common to all citizens, the Constitution of the United States does not, I think, permit any public authority to know the race of those entitled to be protected in the enjoyment of such rights. Every true man has pride of race, and under appropriate circumstances, when the rights of others, his equals before the law, are not to be affected, it is his privilege to express such pride and to take such action based upon it as to him seems proper. But I deny that any legislative body or judicial tribunal may have regard to the race of citizens when the civil rights of those citizens are involved. Indeed such legislation as that here in question is inconsistent, not only with that equality of rights which pertains to citizenship, national and state, but with the personal liberty enjoyed by every one within the United States. . . .

In my opinion, the judgment this day rendered will, in time, prove to be quite as pernicious as the decision made by this tribunal in the Dred Scott Case. It was adjudged in that case that the descendants of Africans who were imported into this country and sold as slaves were not included nor intended to be included under the word "citizens" in the Constitution, and could not claim any of the rights and privileges which that instrument provided for and secured to citizens of the United States; that at the time of the adoption of the Constitution they were "considered as a subordinate and inferior class of beings, who had been subjugated by the dominant race, and, whether emancipated or not, yet remained subject to their authority, and had no rights or privileges but such as those who held the power and the government might choose to grant them." The recent amendments of the Constitution, it was supposed, had eradicated these principles from our institutions. But it seems that we have yet, in some of the states, a dominant race, a superior class of citizens, which assumes to regulate the enjoyment of civil rights, common to all citizens, upon the basis of race. The present decision, it may well be apprehended, will not only stimulate aggressions, more or less brutal and irritating, upon the admitted rights of colored citizens, but will encourage the belief that it is possible, by means of state enactments, to defeat the beneficent purposes which the people of the United States had in view when they adopted the recent amendments of the Constitution, by one of which the blacks of this country were made citizens of the United States and of the states in which they respectively reside and whose privileges and immunities, as citizens, the states are forbidden to abridge. Sixty millions of whites are in no danger from the presence here of eight millions of blacks. The destinies of the two races in this country are indissolubly linked together, and the interests of both require that the common government of all shall not permit the seeds of race hate to be planted under the sanction of law. What can more certainly arouse race hate, what more certainly create and perpetuate a feeling of distrust between these races, than state enactments which in fact proceed on the ground that colored citizens are so inferior and degraded that they cannot be allowed to sit in public coaches occupied by white citizens? That, as all will admit, is the real meaning of such legislation as was enacted in Louisiana. . . .

If evils will result from the commingling of the two races upon public highways established for the benefit of all, they will be infinitely less than those that will surely come from state legislation regulating the enjoyment of civil rights upon the basis of race. We boast of the freedom enjoyed by our people above all other peoples. But it is difficult to reconcile that boast with a state of the law which, practically, puts the brand of servitude and degradation upon a large class of our fellow citizens, our equals before the law. The thin disguise of "equal" accommodations for passengers in railroad coaches will not mislead anyone, or atone for the wrong this day done. . . .

I am of opinion that the statute of Louisiana is inconsistent with the personal liberty of citizens, white and black, in that state, and hostile to both the spirit and letter of the Constitution of the United States. If laws of like character should be enacted in the several states of the Union, the effect would be in the highest degree mischievous. Slavery as an institution tolerated by law would, it is true, have disappeared from our country, but there would remain a power in the states, by sinister legislation, to interfere with the full enjoyment of the blessings of freedom; to regulate civil rights, common to all citizens, upon the basis of race; and to place in a condition of legal inferiority a large body of American citizens, now constituting a part of the political community, called the people of the United States, for whom and by whom, through representatives, our government is administered. Such a system is inconsistent with the guarantee given by the Constitution to each state of a republican form of government, and may be stricken down by Congressional action, or by the courts in the discharge of their solemn duty to maintain the supreme law of the land, anything in the Constitution or laws of any state to the contrary notwithstanding.

For the reasons stated, I am constrained to withhold my assent from the opinion and judgment of the majority.

344. HOLDEN v. HARDY
169 U. S. 366
1898

Error to the Supreme Court of the State of Utah. Compare this decision to *Lochner* v. *New York*, Doc. No. 364.

BROWN, J. This case involves the constitutionality of an act of the legislature of Utah of March 30, 1896, chap. 72, entitled "An Act Regulating the Hours of Employ-ment in Underground Mines and in Smelters and Ore Reduction Works." . . .

The validity of the statute in question is, . . . challenged upon the ground of an alleged violation of the 14th amendment to the Constitution of the United States, in that it abridges the privileges or immunities of citizens of the United States; deprives both the employer and the laborer of his property without due process of law, and denies to them the equal protection of the laws. . . .

In passing upon the validity of state legislation under that Amendment, this court has not failed to recognize the fact that the law is to a certain extent a progressive science; that in some of the states methods of procedure which, at the time the Constitution was adopted, were deemed essential to the protection and safety of the people, or to the liberty of the citizen, have been found to be no longer necessary; that restrictions which had formerly been laid upon the conduct of individuals, or of classes of individuals, had proved detrimental to their interests; while, upon the other hand, certain other classes of persons, particularly those engaged in dangerous or unhealthful employments, have been found to be in need of additional protection. . . .

This right of contract, however, is itself subject to certain limitations which the state may lawfully impose in the exercise of its police powers. While this power is inherent in all governments, it has doubtless been greatly expanded in its application during the past century, owing to an enormous increase in the number of occupations which are dangerous, or so far detrimental to the health of employees as to demand special precaution for their well-being and protection, or the safety of adjacent property. While this court has held that the police power cannot be put forward as an excuse for oppressive and unjust legislation, it may be lawfully resorted to for the purpose of preserving the public health, safety, or morals, or the abatement of public nuisances, and a large discretion "is necessarily vested in the legislature to determine, not only what the interests of the public require, but what measures are necessary for the protection of such interests." . . .

But if it be within the power of a legislature to adopt such means for the protection of the lives of its citizens, it is difficult to see why precautions may not also be adopted for the protection of their health and morals. It is as much for the interest of the state that the public health should be preserved as that life should be made secure.

Upon the principles above stated, we think the act in question may be sustained as a valid exercise of the police power of the state. The enactment does not profess to limit the hours of all workmen, but merely those who are employed in underground mines, or in the smelting, reduction, or refining of ores or metals. These employments when too long pursued the legislature has judged to be detrimental to the health of the employees, and, so long as there are reasonable grounds for believing that this is so, its decision upon this subject cannot be reviewed by the Federal courts.

While the general experience of mankind may justify us in believing that men may engage in ordinary employments more than eight hours per day without injury to their health, it does not follow that labor for the same length of time is innocuous when carried on beneath the surface of the earth, when the operative is deprived of fresh air and sunlight, and is frequently subjected to foul atmosphere and a very high temperature, or to influence of noxious gases, generated by the processes of refining or smelting. . . . That both parties are of full age and competent to contract does not necessarily deprive the state of the power to interfere where the parties do not stand upon an equality, or where the public health demands that one party to the contract shall be protected against himself. "The state still retains an interest in his welfare, however reckless he may be. The whole is no greater than the sum of all the parts, and when the individual health, safety, and welfare are sacrificed or neglected, the state must suffer."

We have no disposition to criticise the many authorities which hold that state statutes restricting the hours of labor are unconstitutional. Indeed, we are not called upon to express an opinion upon this subject. It is sufficient to say of them that they have no application to cases where the legislature had adjudged that a limitation is necessary for the preservation of the health of employees, and there are reasonable grounds for believing that such determination is supported by the facts. The question in each case is whether the legislature has adopted the statute in exercise of a reasonable discretion, or whether its action be a mere excuse for an unjust discrimination, or the oppression, or spoliation of a particular class. . . .

345. THE DE LÔME LETTER
December 1897
(Foreign Relations of the United States, 1898, p. 1007)

This private letter from the Spanish Minister in the United States to a friend was stolen from the Havana post-office by an insurgent spy and held by the Cuban junta in the United States until it could be most effectively used. It was given to the press February 9, 1898. De Lôme at once cabled his resignation. De Lôme had been an exceptionally able diplomat, and his humiliation constitutes one of the unpleasant episodes in the annals of American diplomacy. See, W. Millis, *The Martial Spirit*, p. 96 ff.; M. A. Wilkerson, *Public Opinion and the Spanish American War*, p. 91 ff.

LEGATION OF SPAIN, Washington.
His Excellency Don JOSÉ CANALEJAS.

MY DEAR FRIEND:

You have no reason to ask my excuses for not having written to me. I ought also to have written to you, but I have put off doing so because overwhelmed with work and nous sommes quittes.

The situation here remains the same. Everything depends on the political and military outcome in Cuba. . . .

The message has been a disillusionment to the insurgents, who expected something different; but I regard it as bad (for us).

Besides the ingrained and inevitable bluntness (groseria) with which is repeated all that the press and public opinion in Spain have said about Weyler, it once more shows what McKinley is, weak and a bidder for the admiration of the crowd, besides being a would-be politician (politicastro) who tries to leave a door open behind himself while keeping on good terms with the jingoes of his party.

Nevertheless, whether the practical results of it [the message] are to be injurious and adverse depends only upon ourselves.

I am entirely of your opinions; without a military end of the matter nothing will be accomplished in Cuba, and without a military and political settlement there will always be the danger of encouragement being given to the insurgents by a part of the public opinion if not by the Government. . . .

I do not think sufficient attention has been paid to the part England is playing.

Nearly all the newspaper rabble that swarms in your hotels are Englishmen, and while writing for the Journal they are also correspondents of the most influential journals and reviews of London. It has been so ever since this thing began. As I look at it England's only object is that the Americans should amuse themselves with us and leave her alone; and if there should be a war, that would the better stave off the conflict which she dreads but which will never come about.

It would be very advantageous to take up, even if only for effect, the question of commercial relations, and to have a man of some prominence sent hither in order that I may make use of him here to carry on a propaganda among the Senators and others in opposition to the junta and to try to win over the refugees. . . .

Ever your attached friend and servant,

ENRIQUE DEPUY DE LÔME.

ARTICLES SUBSEQUENT TO ARTICLE XXII

ART. XXIII

March 29, 1961

SEC. 1. The District constituting the seat of Government of the United States shall appoint in such manner as the Congress may direct:

A number of electors of President and Vice-President equal to the whole number of Senators and Representatives in Congress to which the District would be entitled if it were a State, but in no event more than the least populous state; they shall be in addition to those appointed by the states, but they shall be considered, for the purposes of the election of President and Vice-President, to be electors appointed by a state; and they shall meet in the District and perform such duties as provided by the twelfth article of amendment.

SEC. 2. The Congress shall have power to enforce this article by appropriate legislation.

ART. XXIV

January 24, 1964

SEC. 1. The right of citizens of the United States to vote in any primary or other election for President or Vice-President, for electors for President or Vice-President, or for Senator or Representative in Congress, shall not be denied or abridged by the United States or any state by reason of failure to pay any poll tax or other tax.

SEC. 2. The Congress shall have power to enforce this article by appropriate legislation.

ART. XXV

SEC. 1. In case of the removal of the President from office or his death or resignation, the Vice-President shall become President.

SEC. 2. Whenever there is a vacancy in the office of the Vice-President, the President shall nominate a Vice-President who shall take the office upon confirmation by a majority vote of both houses of Congress.

SEC. 3. Whenever the President transmits to the President pro tempore of the Senate and the Speaker of the House of Representatives his written declaration that he is unable to discharge the powers and duties of his office, and until he transmits to them a written declaration to the contrary, such powers and duties shall be discharged by the Vice-President as Acting President.

SEC. 4. Whenever the Vice-President and a majority of either the principal officers of the executive departments, or of such other body as Congress may by law provide, transmit to the President pro tempore of the Senate and the Speaker of the House of Representatives their written declaration that the President is unable to discharge the powers and duties of his office, the Vice-President shall immediately assume the powers and duties of the office as Acting President.

Thereafter, when the President transmits to the President pro tempore of the Senate and the Speaker of the House of Representatives his written declaration that no inability exists, he shall resume the powers and duties of his office unless the Vice-President and a majority of either the principal officers of the executive de-

633

partment, or of such other body as Congress may by law provide, transmit within four days to the President pro tempore of the Senate and the Speaker of the House of Representatives their written declaration that the President is unable to discharge the powers and duties of his office. Thereupon Congress shall decide the issue, assembling within 48 hours for that purpose if not in session. If the Congress, within 21 days after receipt of the latter written declaration, or, if Congress is not in session, within 21 days after Congress is required to assemble, determines by two-thirds vote of both houses that the President is unable to discharge the powers and duties of his office, the Vice-President shall continue to discharge the same as Acting President; otherwise, the President shall resume the powers and duties of his office.

Volume II

DOCUMENTS
of
AMERICAN HISTORY
Since 1898

DOCUMENTS OF
AMERICAN HISTORY
Since 1898

346. McKINLEY'S WAR MESSAGE
April 11, 1898
(Richardson, ed. *Messages and Papers*, Vol. X, p. 139 ff.)

In this message to Congress President McKinley recounted the events which in his opinion justified intervention in Cuba. Filled with suggestion and innuendo, the account is thoroughly misleading, but it struck a responsive note in Congress and in the public mind. In as much as Spain, in the note received by McKinley April 10, promised to order an immediate cessation of hostilities in Cuba, the principal basis for intervention had disappeared. For recognition of Cuban independence, see Doc. No. 347. See W. Millis, *The Martial Spirit;* F. E. Chadwick, *Relations of the United States and Spain,* Vol. I; C. S. Olcott, *Life of William McKinley,* 2 Vols.; J. H. Latané, *America as a World Power,* ch. i. For diplomatic correspondence, see *Foreign Relations of the United States,* 1898; and *Spanish Diplomatic Correspondence and Documents, 1896–1900.* An analysis of this is in H. E. Flack, *Spanish-American Diplomatic Relations Preceding the War of 1898.*

EXECUTIVE MANSION, *April 11, 1898.*
To the Congress of the United States:

Obedient to that precept of the Constitution which commands the President to give from time to time to the Congress information of the state of the Union and to recommend to their consideration such measures as he shall judge necessary and expedient, it becomes my duty to now address your body with regard to the grave crisis that has arisen in the relations of the United States to Spain by reason of the warfare that for more than three years has raged in the neighboring island of Cuba. . . .

The present revolution is but the successor of other similar insurrections which have occurred in Cuba against the dominion of Spain, extending over a period of nearly half a century, each of which during its progress has subjected the United States to great effort and expense in enforcing its neutrality laws, caused enormous losses to American trade and commerce, caused irritation, annoyance, and disturbance among our citizens, and, by the exercise of cruel, barbarous, and uncivilized practices of warfare, shocked the sensibilities and offended the human sympathies of our people. . . .

Our trade has suffered, the capital invested by our citizens in Cuba has been largely lost, and the temper and forbearance of our people have been so sorely tried as to beget a perilous unrest among our own citizens, which has inevitably found its expression from time to time in the National Legislature, so that issues wholly external to our own body politic engross attention and stand in the way of that close devotion to domestic advancement that becomes a self-contained commonwealth whose primal maxim has been the avoidance of all foreign entanglements. All this must needs awaken, and has, indeed, aroused, the utmost concern on the part of this Government, as well during my predecessor's term as in my own.

In April, 1896, the evils from which our country suffered through the Cuban war became so onerous that my predecessor made an effort to bring about a peace through the mediation of this Government in any way that might tend to an honorable adjustment of the contest between Spain and her revolted colony, on the basis of some effective scheme of self-government for Cuba under the flag and sovereignty of Spain. It failed through the refusal of the Spanish government then in power to consider any form of mediation or, indeed, any plan of settlement which did not begin with the actual submission of the insurgents to the mother country, and then only on such terms as Spain herself might see fit to grant. The war continued unabated. The resistance of the insurgents was in no wise diminished. . . .

The overtures of this Government made through its new envoy, General Woodford, and looking to an immediate and effective amelioration of the condition of the island, although not accepted to the extent of admitted mediation in any shape, were met by assurances that home rule in an advanced phase would be forthwith offered to Cuba, without waiting for the war to end, and that more humane methods should thenceforth prevail in the conduct of hostilities. Coincidentally with these declarations the new government of Spain continued and completed the policy, already begun by its predecessor, of testifying friendly regard for this nation by releasing American citizens held under one charge or another connected with the insurrection, so that by the end of November not a single person entitled in any way to our national protection remained in a Spanish prison. . . .

The necessity for a change in the condition of the reconcentrados is recognized by the Spanish Government. Within a few days past the orders of General Weyler have been revoked. The reconcentrados, it is said, are to be permitted to return to their homes and aided to resume the self-supporting pursuits of peace. Public works have been ordered to give them employment and a sum of $600,000 has been appropriated for their relief.

The war in Cuba is of such a nature that, short of subjugation or extermination, a final military victory for either side seems impracticable. The alternative lies in the physical exhaustion of the one or the other party, or perhaps of both—a condition which in effect ended the ten years' war by the truce of Zanjon. The prospect of such a protraction and conclusion of the present strife is a contingency hardly to be contemplated with equanimity by the civilized world, and least of all by the United States, affected and injured as we are, deeply and intimately, by its very existence.

Realizing this, it appeared to be my duty, in a spirit of true friendliness, no less to Spain than to the Cubans, who have so much to lose by the prolongation of the struggle, to seek to bring about an immediate termination of the war. To this end I submitted on the 27th ultimo, as a result of much representation and correspondence, through the United States minister at Madrid, propositions to the Spanish Government looking to an armistice until October 1 for the negotiation of peace with the good offices of the President.

In addition I asked the immediate revocation of the order of reconcentration, so as to permit the people to return to their farms and the needy to be relieved with provisions and supplies from the United States, cooperating with the Spanish authorities, so as to afford full relief.

The reply of the Spanish cabinet was received on the night of the 31st ultimo. It offered, as the means to bring about peace in Cuba, to confide the preparation thereof to the insular parliament, inasmuch as the concurrence of that body would be necessary to reach a final result, it being, however, understood that the powers reserved by the constitution to the central Government are not lessened or diminished. As the Cuban parliament does not meet until the 4th of May next, the Spanish Government would not object for its part to accept at once a suspension of hostilities if asked for by the insurgents from the general in chief, to whom it would pertain in such case to determine the duration and conditions of the armistice. . . .

With this last overture in the direction of immediate peace, and its disappointing reception by Spain, the Executive is brought to the end of his effort.

In my annual message of December last I said.

Of the untried measures there remain only: recognition of the insurgents as belligerents; recognition of the independence of Cuba; neutral intervention to end the war by imposing a rational compromise between the contestants, and intervention in favor of one or the other party. I speak not of forcible annexation, for that can not be thought of. That, by our code of morality, would be criminal aggression.

Thereupon I reviewed these alternatives in the light of President Grant's measured words, uttered in 1875, when, after seven years of sanguinary, destructive, and cruel hostilities in Cuba, he reached the conclusion that the recognition of the independence of Cuba was impracticable and indefensible and that the recognition of belligerence was not warranted by the facts according to the tests of public law. I commented especially upon the latter aspect of the question, pointing out the inconveniences and positive dangers of a recognition of belligerence, which, while adding to the already onerous burdens of neutrality within our own jurisdiction, could not in any way extend our influence or effective offices in the territory of hostilities.

Nothing has since occurred to change my view in this regard, and I recognize as fully now as then that the issuance of a proclamation of neutrality, by which process the so-called recognition of belligerents is published, could of itself and unattended by other action accomplish nothing toward the one end for which we labor—the instant pacification of Cuba and the cessation of the misery that afflicts the island. . . .

There remain the alternative forms of intervention to end the war, either as an impartial neutral, by imposing a rational compromise between the contestants, or as the active ally of the one party or the other.

As to the first, it is not to be forgotten that during the last few months the relation of the United States has virtually been one of friendly intervention in many ways, each not of itself conclusive, but all tending to the exertion of a potential influence toward an ultimate pacific result, just and honorable to all interests concerned. The spirit of all our acts hitherto has been an earnest, unselfish desire for peace and prosperity in Cuba, untarnished by differences between us and Spain and unstained by the blood of American citizens.

The forcible intervention of the United States as a neutral to stop the war, according to the large dictates of humanity and following many historical precedents where neighboring states have interfered to check the hopeless sacrifices of life by internecine conflicts beyond their borders, is justifiable on rational grounds. It involves, however, hostile constraint upon both the parties to the contest, as well to enforce a truce as to guide the eventual settlement.

The grounds for such intervention may be briefly summarized as follows:

First. In the cause of humanity and to put an end to the barbarities, bloodshed, starvation, and horrible miseries now existing there, and which the parties to the conflict are either unable or unwilling to stop or mitigate. It is no answer to say this is all in another country, belonging to another nation, and is therefore none of our business. It is specially our duty, for it is right at our door.

Second. We owe it to our citizens in Cuba to afford them that protection and indemnity for life and property which no government there can or will afford, and to that end to terminate the conditions that deprive them of legal protection.

Third. The right to intervene may be justified by the very serious injury to the commerce, trade, and business of our people and by the wanton destruction of property and devastation of the island.

Fourth, and which is of the utmost importance. The present condition of affairs in Cuba is a constant menace to our peace and entails upon this Government an enormous expense. With such a conflict waged for years in an island so near us and with which our people have such trade and business relations; when the lives and liberty of our citizens are in constant danger and their property destroyed and themselves ruined; where our trading vessels are liable to seizure and are seized at our very door by war ships of a foreign nation; the expeditions of filibustering that we are powerless to prevent altogether, and the irritating questions and entanglements thus arising—all these and others that I need not mention, with the resulting strained relations, are a constant menace to our peace and compel us to keep on a semi-war footing with a nation with which we are at peace.

These elements of danger and disorder already pointed out have been strikingly illustrated by a tragic event which has deeply and justly moved the American people. I have already transmitted to Congress the report of the naval court of inquiry on the destruction of the battle ship *Maine* in the harbor of Havana during the night of the 15th of February. The destruction of that noble vessel has filled the national heart with inexpressible horror. Two hundred and fifty-eight brave sailors and marines and two officers of our Navy, reposing in the fancied security of a friendly harbor, have been hurled to death, grief and want brought to their homes and sorrow to the nation.

The naval court of inquiry, which, it is needless to say, commands the unqualified confidence of the Government, was unanimous in its conclusion that the destruction of the *Maine* was caused by an exterior explosion—that of a submarine mine. It did not assume to place the responsibility. That remains to be fixed.

In any event, the destruction of the *Maine*, by whatever exterior cause, is a patent and impressive proof of a state of things in Cuba that is intolerable. That condition is thus shown to be such that the Spanish Government can not assure safety and security to a vessel of the American Navy in the harbor of Havana on a mission of peace, and rightfully there. . . .

The long trial has proved that the object for which Spain has waged the war can not be attained. The fire of insurrection may flame or may smolder with varying seasons, but it has not been and it is plain that it can not be extinguished by present methods. The only hope of relief and repose from a condition which can no longer be endured is the enforced pacification of Cuba. In the name of humanity, in the name of civilization, in behalf of endangered American interests which give us the right and the duty to speak and to act, the war in Cuba must stop.

In view of these facts and of these considerations I ask the Congress to authorize and empower the President to take measures to secure a full and final termination of hostilities between the Government of Spain and the people of Cuba, and to secure in the island the establishment of a stable government, capable of maintaining order and observing its international obligations, insuring peace and tranquillity and the security of its citizens as well as our own, and to use the military and naval forces of the United States as may be necessary for these purposes.

And in the interest of humanity and to aid in preserving the lives of the starving people of the island I recommend that the distribution of food and supplies be continued and that an appropriation be made out of the public Treasury to supplement the charity of our citizens.

The issue is now with the Congress. It is a solemn responsibility. I have exhausted every effort to relieve the intolerable condition of affairs which is at our doors. Prepared to execute every obligation imposed upon me by the Constitution and the law, I await your action.

Yesterday, and since the preparation of the foregoing message, official information was received by me that the latest decree of the Queen Regent of Spain directs General Blanco, in order to prepare and facilitate peace, to proclaim a suspension of hostilities, the duration and details of which have not yet been communicated to me.

This fact, with every other pertinent consideration, will, I am sure, have your just and careful attention in the solemn deliberations upon which you are about to enter. If this measure attains a successful result, then our aspirations as a Christian, peace-loving people will be realized. If it fails, it will be only another justification for our contemplated action.

WILLIAM McKINLEY.

347. THE INDEPENDENCE OF CUBA
April 20, 1898
(*U. S. Statutes at Large,* Vol. XXX, p. 738)

April 11, McKinley sent his message to Congress recommending intervention in Cuba. See Doc. No. 346. The Joint Resolution of April 20 authorized the use of the army and the navy to effect Cuban independence; the formal declaration of war followed April 25. The most important of the resolutions of April 20 was the fourth, known as the Teller Amendment. See references, Doc. No. 346.

Joint resolution for the recognition of the independence of the people of Cuba, demanding that the Government of Spain relinquish its authority and government in the Island of Cuba, and to withdraw its land and naval forces from Cuba and Cuban waters, and directing the President of the United States to use the land and naval forces of the United States to carry these resolutions into effect.

Whereas the abhorrent conditions which have existed for more than three years in the Island of Cuba, so near our own borders, have shocked the moral sense of the people of the United States, have been a disgrace to Christian civilization, culminating, as they have, in the destruction of a United States battle ship, with two hundred and sixty-six of its officers and crew, while on a friendly visit in the harbor of Havana, and can not longer be endured, as has been set forth by the President of the United States in his message to Congress of April eleventh, eighteen hundred and ninety-eight, upon which the action of Congress was invited: Therefore,

Resolved, First. That the people of the Island of Cuba are, and of right ought to be, free and independent.

Second. That it is the duty of the United States to demand, and the Government of the United States does hereby demand, that the Government of Spain at once relinquish its authority and government in the Island of Cuba and withdraw its land and naval forces from Cuba and Cuban waters.

Third. That the President of the United States be, and he hereby is, directed and empowered to use the entire land and naval forces of the United States, and to call into the actual service of the United States the militia of the several States, to such extent as may be necessary to carry these resolutions into effect.

Fourth. That the United States hereby disclaims any disposition or intention to exercise sovereignty, jurisdiction, or control over said Island except for the pacification thereof, and asserts its determination, when that is accomplished, to leave the government and control of the Island to its people.

348. THE ANNEXATION OF HAWAII
July 7, 1898
(*U. S. Statutes at Large,* Vol. XXX, p. 750–51)

Though President Cleveland withdrew from the Senate the Treaty of 1893 providing for the annexation of the Hawaiian Islands and denounced the methods by which the Hawaiian revolution had been brought about, Queen Liliuokalani was not restored to the throne. In July 1894 the Republic of Hawaii was established, and was recognized by the United States. Agitation for annexation continued, and a second treaty of annexation was concluded in 1897. While this treaty was still pending in the Senate the war with Spain broke out and the United States used the islands as a naval base. The islands were then annexed by joint resolution in order to avoid the danger of rejection by one-third of the Senate.

Joint Resolution To provide for annexing, the Hawaiian Islands to the United States.

WHEREAS the Government of the Republic of Hawaii having, in due form, signified its consent, in the manner provided by its constitution, to cede absolutely and without reserve to the United States of America all rights of sovereignty of whatsoever kind in and over the Hawaiian Islands and their dependencies, and also to cede and transfer to the United States the absolute fee and ownership of all public, Government, or Crown lands, public buildings or edifices, ports, harbors, military equipment, and all other public property of every kind and description belonging to the Government of the Hawaiian Islands, together with every right and appurtenance thereunto appertaining: Therefore,

Resolved, That said cession is accepted, ratified, and confirmed, and that the said Hawaiian Islands and their dependencies be, and they are hereby, annexed as a part of the territory of the United States and are subject to the sovereign dominion thereof, and that all and singular the property and rights hereinbefore mentioned are vested in the United States of America.

The existing laws of the United States relative to public lands shall not apply to such lands in the Hawaiian Islands; but the Congress of the United States shall enact special laws for their management and disposition: *Provided,* That all revenue from or proceeds of the same, except as regards such part thereof as may be used or occupied for the civil, military, or naval purposes of the United States, or may be assigned for the use of the local government, shall be used solely for the benefit of the inhabitants of the Hawaiian Islands for educational and other public purposes.

Until Congress shall provide for the government of such islands all the civil, judicial, and military powers exercised by the officers of the existing government in said islands shall be vested in such person or persons and shall be exercised in such manner as the President of the United States shall direct; and the President shall have power to remove said officers and fill the vacancies so occasioned.

The existing treaties of the Hawaiian Is-

lands with foreign nations shall forthwith cease and determine, being replaced by such treaties as may exist, or as may be hereafter concluded, between the United States and such foreign nations. The municipal legislation of the Hawaiian Islands, not enacted for the fulfillment of the treaties so extinguished, and not inconsistent with this joint resolution nor contrary to the Constitution of the United States nor to any existing treaty of the United States, shall remain in force until the Congress of the United States shall otherwise determine.

Until legislation shall be enacted extending the United States customs laws and regulations to the Hawaiian Islands the existing customs relations of the Hawaiian Islands with the United States and other countries shall remain unchanged.

The public debt of the Republic of Hawaii, lawfully existing at the date of the passage of this joint resolution, including the amounts due to depositors in the Hawaiian Postal Savings Bank, is hereby assumed by the Government of the United States; but the liability of the United States in this regard shall in no case exceed four million dollars. So long, however, as the existing Government and the present commercial relations of the Hawaiian Islands are continued as hereinbefore provided said Government shall continue to pay the interest on said debt.

There shall be no further immigration of Chinese into the Hawaiian Islands, except upon such conditions as are now or may hereafter be allowed by the laws of the United States; and no Chinese, by reason of anything herein contained, shall be allowed to enter the United States from the Hawaiian Islands.

The President shall appoint five commissioners, at least two of whom shall be residents of the Hawaiian Islands, who shall, as soon as reasonably practicable, recommend to Congress such legislation concerning the Hawaiian Islands as they shall deem necessary or proper. . . .

349. TREATY OF PEACE WITH SPAIN
Concluded at Paris
December 10, 1898

(U. S. Statutes at Large, Vol. XXX, p. 1754 ff.)

The American commissioners were William R. Day, Cushman K. Davis, William P. Frye, George Gray, and Whitelaw Reid. For the history of the negotiations see, *Papers relating to the Treaty with Spain,* 56 Cong. 1 Sess. Senate Doc. No. 148; R. Cortissoz, *Whitelaw Reid,* Vol. II, chs. xii, xiii; J. H. Latané, *America as a World Power,* ch. iv; W. S. Holt, *Treaties Defeated by the Senate,* ch. viii. The cession of the Philippines to the United States precipitated a contest over ratification that seriously threatened the fate of the treaty.

ART. I. Spain relinquishes all claim of sovereignty over and title to Cuba.

And as the island is, upon its evacuation by Spain, to be occupied by the United States, the United States will, so long as such occupation shall last, assume and discharge the obligations that may under international law result from the fact of its occupation, for the protection of life and property.

ART. II. Spain cedes to the United States the island of Porto Rico and other islands now under Spanish sovereignty in the West Indies, and the island of Guam in the Marianas or Ladrones.

ART. III. Spain cedes to the United States the archipelago known as the Philippine Islands, and comprehending the islands lying within the following line:

A line running from west to east along or near the twentieth parallel of north latitude, and through the middle of the navigable channel of Bachi, from the one hundred and eighteenth (118th) to the one hundred and twenty seventh (127th) degree meridian of longitude east of Greenwich, thence along the one hundred and twenty seventh (127th) degree meridian of longitude east of Greenwich to the parallel of four degrees and forty five minutes (4° 45′) north latitude, thence along the parellel of four degrees and forty five minutes (4° 45′) north latitude to its intersection with the meridian of longitude one hundred and nineteen degrees and thirty five minutes (119° 35′) east of Greenwich,

thence along the meridian of longitude one hundred and nineteen degrees and thirty five minutes (119° 35′) east of Greenwich to the parallel of latitude seven degrees and forty minutes (7° 40′) north, thence along the parallel of latitude seven degrees and forty minutes (7° 40′) north to its intersection with the one hundred and sixteenth (116th) degree meridian of longitude east of Greenwich, thence by a direct line to the intersection of the tenth (10th) degree parallel of north latitude with the one hundred and eighteenth (118th) degree meridian of longitude east of Greenwich, and thence along the one hundred and eighteenth (118th) degree meridian of longitude east of Greenwich to the point of beginning.

The United States will pay to Spain the sum of twenty million dollars ($20,000,000) within three months after the exchange of the ratifications of the present treaty.

ART. IV. The United States will, for the term of ten years from the date of the exchange of the ratifications of the present treaty, admit Spanish ships and merchandise to the ports of the Philippine Islands on the same terms as ships and merchandise of the United States. . . .

ART. VII. The United States and Spain mutually relinquish all claims for indemnity, national and individual, of every kind, of either Government, or of its citizens or subjects, against the other Government, that may have arisen since the beginning of the late insurrection in Cuba and prior to the exchange of ratifications of the present treaty, including all claims for indemnity for the cost of the war.

The United States will adjudicate and settle the claims of its citizens against Spain relinquished in this article.

ART. VIII. In conformity with the provisions of Articles I, II, and III of this treaty, Spain relinquishes in Cuba, and cedes in Porto Rico and other islands in the West Indies, in the island of Guam, and in the Philippine Archipelago, all the buildings, wharves, barracks, forts, structures, public highways and other immovable property which, in conformity with law, belong to the public domain, and as such belong to the Crown of Spain.

And it is hereby declared that the relinquishment or cession, as the case may be, to which the preceding paragraph refers, cannot in any respect impair the property or rights which by law belong to the peaceful possession of property of all kinds, of provinces, municipalities, public or private establishments, ecclesiastical or civic bodies, or any other associations having legal capacity to acquire and possess property in the aforesaid territories renounced or ceded, or of private individuals, of whatsoever nationality such individuals may be.

The aforesaid relinquishment or cession, as the case may be, includes all documents exclusively referring to the sovereignty relinquished or ceded that may exist in the archives of the Peninsula. Where any document in such archives only in part relates to said sovereignty, a copy of such part will be furnished whenever it shall be requested. Like rules shall be reciprocally observed in favor of Spain in respect of documents in the archives of the islands above referred to.

In the aforesaid relinquishment or cession, as the case may be, are also included such rights as the Crown of Spain and its authorities possess in respect of the official archives and records, executive as well as judicial, in the islands above referred to, which relate to said islands or the rights and property of their inhabitants. Such archives and records shall be carefully preserved, and private persons shall without distinction have the right to require, in accordance with law, authenticated copies of the contracts, wills and other instruments forming part of notarial protocols or files, or which may be contained in the executive or judicial archives, be the latter in Spain or in the islands aforesaid. . . .

ART. X. The inhabitants of the territories over which Spain relinquishes or cedes her sovereignty shall be secured in the free exercise of their religion.

ART. XI. The Spaniards residing in the territories over which Spain by this treaty cedes or relinquishes her sovereignty shall be subject in matters civil as well as criminal to the jurisdiction of the courts of the country wherein they reside, pursuant to the ordinary laws governing the same; and they shall have the right to appear before such courts, and to pursue the same course as citizens of the country to which the courts belong. . . .

ART. XIII. The rights of property secured by copyrights and patents acquired by Spaniards in the Island of Cuba, and in Porto Rico, the Philippines and other ceded territories, at the time of the exchange of the ratifications of this treaty, shall continue to be respected. Spanish scientific, literary and artistic works, not subversive of public order in the territories in question, shall continue to be admitted free of duty into such territories, for the period of ten years, to be reckoned from the date of the exchange of the ratifications of this treaty. . . .

ART. XV. The Government of each country will, for the term of ten years, accord to the merchant vessels of the other country the same treatment in respect of all port charges, including entrance and clearance dues, light dues, and tonnage duties, as it accords to its own merchant vessels, not engaged in the coastwise trade.

This article may at any time be terminated on six months' notice given by either Government to the other.

ART. XVI. It is understood that any obligations assumed in this treaty by the United States with respect to Cuba are limited to the time of its occupancy thereof; but it will upon the termination of such occupancy, advise any Government established in the island to assume the same obligations.

350. THE OPEN DOOR IN CHINA
1899–1900

In both England and the United States there was at the close of the century a growing apprehension that the encroachments of the European powers and of Japan on China would destroy the territorial integrity and sovereignty of China and would lead to discriminations at the expense of English and American rights. In March 1898 the English Ambassador approached the United States with a suggestion for joint action to protect the integrity of China; eventually the agitation of Lord Charles Beresford, the influence of W. W. Rockhill of the American State Department, and of Alfred Hippisley, an Englishman, led to the concrete formulation of the famous Open Door policy. This policy was first announced in the circular note of September 6, 1899. For the various replies of the Powers, many of them far from "final and definitive," see *Foreign Relations of the United States,* 1899, p. 128 ff. Evasive as these replies were, Hay interpreted them to indicate acceptance of the Open Door policy and promptly announced such acquiescence in the circular note of March 20, 1900. Shortly thereafter the outbreak of the Boxer uprising seriously endangered the Open Door policy, and Hay moved once again to formulate and apply that policy. To the note of July 3 there were, however, no satisfactory replies. Of these Open Door notes, Dr. Tyler Dennett says, "It would have taken more than a lawyer to define what new rights had been recognized, or required, or even what had actually been said, but such comment is beside the point. These notes had not been put forward by a lawyer as a contribution to the law of nations, but by a publicist to crystallize public opinion." (*Hay,* p. 293). See, T. Dennett, *John Hay,* chs. xxiv–xxvi; W. W. Willoughby, *Foreign Rights and Interests in China,* 2 Vols.; T. F. Millard, *Democracy and the Eastern Question;* H. Chung, *The Oriental Policy of the United States;* M. J. Bau, *The Open Door Doctrine.* For a critical evaluation of the Open Door policy see J. Barnes, ed. *Empire in the East.* An appreciation of Hay's gesture is "The Quarry" by William Vaughn Moody.

1. HAY'S CIRCULAR LETTER,
September 6, 1899

(Malloy, ed. *Treaties, Conventions, etc.,* Vol. I, p. 246)

MR. HAY TO MR. WHITE

DEPARTMENT OF STATE

WASHINGTON, September 6, 1899.

SIR: At the time when the Government of the United States was informed by that of Germany that it had leased from His Majesty the Emperor of China the port of Kiao-chao and the adjacent territory in the province of Shantung, assurances were given to the ambassador of the United States at Berlin by the Imperial German minister for foreign affairs that the rights and privileges insured by treaties with China to citizens of the United States would not thereby suffer or be in anywise impaired within the area over which Germany had thus obtained control.

More recently, however, the British Government recognized by a formal agreement with Germany the exclusive right of the latter country to enjoy in said leased area and the contiguous "sphere of influence or interest" certain privileges, more especially those relating to railroads and mining enterprises; but, as the exact nature and extent of the rights thus recognized have not been clearly defined, it is possible that serious conflicts of interest may at any time arise, not only between British and German subjects within said area, but that the interests of our citizens may also be jeopardized thereby.

Earnestly desirous to remove any cause of irritation and to insure at the same time to the commerce of all nations in China the undoubted benefits which should accrue from a formal recognition by the various powers claiming "spheres of interest" that they shall enjoy perfect equality of treatment for their commerce and navigation within such "spheres," the Government of the United States would be pleased to see His German Majesty's Government give formal assurances and lend its coöperation in securing like assurances from the other interested powers that each within its respective sphere of whatever influence—

First. Will in no way interfere with any treaty port or any vested interest within any so-called "sphere of interest" or leased territory it may have in China.

Second. That the Chinese treaty tariff of the time being shall apply to all merchandise landed or shipped to all such ports as are within said "sphere of interest" (unless they be "free ports"), no matter to what nationality it may belong, and that duties so leviable shall be collected by the Chinese Government.

Third. That it will levy no higher harbor dues on vessels of another nationality frequenting any port in such "sphere" than shall be levied on vessels of its own nationality, and no higher railroad charges over lines built, controlled, or operated within its "sphere" on merchandise belonging to citizens or subjects of other nationalities transported through such "sphere" than shall be levied on similar merchandise belonging to its own nationals transported over equal distances.

The liberal policy pursued by His Imperial German Majesty in declaring Kiao-chao a free port and in aiding the Chinese Government in the establishment there of a customhouse are so clearly in line with the proposition which this Government is anxious to see recognized that it entertains the strongest hope that Germany will give its acceptance and hearty support.

The recent ukase of His Majesty the Emperor of Russia declaring the port of Ta-lien-wan open during the whole of the lease under which it is held from China, to the merchant ships of all nations, coupled with the categorical assurances made to this Government by His Imperial Majesty's representative at this capital at the time, and since repeated to me by the present Russian ambassador, seem to insure the support of the Emperor to the proposed measure. Our ambassador at the Court of St. Petersburg has, in consequence, been instructed to submit it to the Russian Government and to request their early consideration of it. A copy of my instruction on the subject to Mr. Tower is herewith inclosed for your confidential information.

The commercial interests of Great Britain and Japan will be so clearly served by the desired declaration of intentions, and the views of the Governments of these countries as to the desirability of the adoption of measures insuring the benefits of equality of treatment of all foreign trade throughout China are so similar to those entertained by the United States, that their acceptance of the propositions herein outlined and their co-operation in advocating their adoption by the other powers can be confidently expected. I inclose herewith copy of the instruction which I have sent to Mr. Choate on the subject.

In view of the present favorable conditions, you are instructed to submit the above considerations to His Imperial German Majesty's minister for foreign affairs, and to request his early consideration of the subject. Copy of this instruction is sent to our ambassadors at London and at St. Petersburg for their information.

I have, etc.,   JOHN HAY.

2. HAY'S LETTER OF INSTRUCTION
March 20, 1900

(Malloy, ed. *Treaties, Conventions, etc.,* Vol. I, p. 260)

Instructions sent mutatus mutandis to the United States ambassadors at London, Paris, Berlin, St. Petersburg, and Rome, and to the United States Minister at Tokyo.

Department of State,
Washington, March 20, 1900.

SIR: The —— Government having accepted the declaration suggested by the United States concerning foreign trade in China, the terms of which I transmitted to you in my instruction No. — of ——, and like action having been taken by all the various powers having leased territory or so-called "spheres of interest" in the Chinese Empire, as shown by the notes which I herewith transmit to you, you will please inform the government to which you are accredited, that the condition originally attached to its acceptance— that all other powers concerned should likewise accept the proposals of the United States —having been complied with, this Government will therefore consider the assent given to it by —— as final and definitive.

You will also transmit to the minister of foreign affairs copies of the present inclosures, and by the same occasion convey to him the expression of the sincere gratification which the President feels at the successful termination of these negotiations, in which he sees proof of the friendly spirit which animates the various powers interested in the untrammeled development of commerce and industry in the Chinese Empire and a source of vast benefit to the whole commercial world.

I am, etc.,   JOHN HAY.

3. HAY'S CIRCULAR LETTER OF
July 3, 1900

(Foreign Relations of the United States, 1900, p. 345)

Circular telegram sent to the United States embassies in Berlin, Paris, London, Rome, and St. Petersburg, and to the United States missions in Vienna, Brussels, Madrid, Tokyo, The Hague, and Lisbon.

Department of State,
Washington, July 3, 1900.

In this critical posture of affairs in China it is deemed appropriate to define the attitude of the United States as far as present circumstances permit this to be done. We adhere to the policy initiated by us in 1857, of peace with the Chinese nation, of furtherance of lawful commerce, and of protection of lives and property of our citizens by all means guaranteed under extraterritorial treaty rights and by the law of nations. If wrong be done to our citizens we propose to hold the responsible authors to the uttermost accountability. We regard the condition at Pekin as one of virtual anarchy, whereby power and responsibility are practically devolved upon the local provincial authorities. So long as they are not in overt collusion with rebellion and use their power to protect foreign life and property we regard them as representing the Chinese people, with whom we seek to remain in peace and friendship. The purpose of the President is, as it has been heretofore, to act concurrently with the other powers, first, in opening up communication with Pekin and rescuing the American officials, missionaries, and other Americans who are in danger; secondly, in affording all possible protection everywhere in China to American life and property; thirdly, in guarding and protecting all legitimate American interests; and fourthly, in aiding to prevent a spread of the disorders to the other provinces of the Empire and a recurrence of such disasters. It is, of course, too early to forecast the means of attaining this last result; but the policy of the government of the United States is to seek a solution which may bring about permanent safety and peace to China, preserve Chinese territorial and administrative entity, protect all rights guaranteed to friendly powers by treaty and international law, and safeguard for the world the principle of equal and impartial trade with all parts of the Chinese Empire.

You will communicate the purport of this instruction to the minister for foreign affairs.

Hay.

---

351. PLATFORM OF THE AMERICAN ANTI-IMPERIALIST LEAGUE
October 18, 1899

(C. Schurz, Speeches, Correspondence and Political Speeches, Vol. V, p. 77 ff.)

This platform was adopted at the Anti-imperialist Congress which met in Chicago, October 17, 1899. The league was composed of various local and sectional anti-imperialist leagues; George S. Boutwell of Massachusetts was elected president of the new organization. For anti-imperialism, see M. Lanzar-Carpia, "The Anti-Imperialist League," *Philippine Social Science Review*, Vol. IV; M. A. DeWolfe Howe, *Portrait of an Independent: Moorfield Storey;* M. Storey and M. P. Lichauco, *Conquest of the Philippines by the United States;* R. F. Pettigrew, *The Course of Empire.*

We hold that the policy known as imperialism is hostile to liberty and tends toward militarism, an evil from which it has been our glory to be free. We regret that it has become necessary in the land of Washington and Lincoln to reaffirm that all men, of whatever race or color, are entitled to life, liberty, and the pursuit of happiness. We maintain that governments derive their just powers from the consent of the governed. We insist that the subjugation of any people is "criminal aggression" and open disloyalty to the distinctive principles of our Government.

We earnestly condemn the policy of the present National Administration in the Philippines. It seeks to extinguish the spirit of

1776 in those islands. We deplore the sacrifice of our soldiers and sailors, whose bravery deserves admiration even in an unjust war. We denounce the slaughter of the Filipinos as a needless horror. We protest against the extension of American sovereignty by Spanish methods.

We demand the immediate cessation of the war against liberty, begun by Spain and continued by us. We urge that Congress be promptly convened to announce to the Filipinos our purpose to concede to them the independence for which they have so long fought and which of right is theirs.

The United States have always protested against the doctrine of international law which permits the subjugation of the weak by the strong. A self-governing state cannot accept sovereignty over an unwilling people. The United States cannot act upon the ancient heresy that might makes right.

Imperialists assume that with the destruction of self-government in the Philippines by American hands, all opposition here will cease. This is a grievous error. Much as we abhor the war of "criminal aggression" in the Philippines, greatly as we regret that the blood of the Filipinos is on American hands, we more deeply resent the betrayal of American institutions at home. The real firing line is not in the suburbs of Manila. The foe is of our own household. The attempt of 1861 was to divide the country. That of 1899 is to destroy its fundamental principles and noblest ideals.

Whether the ruthless slaughter of the Filipinos shall end next month or next year is but an incident in a contest that must go on until the Declaration of Independence and the Constitution of the United States are rescued from the hands of their betrayers. Those who dispute about standards of value while the Republic is undermined will be listened to as little as those who would wrangle about the small economies of the household while the house is on fire. The training of a great people for a century, the aspiration for liberty of a vast immigration are forces that will hurl aside those who in the delirium of conquest seek to destroy the character of our institutions.

We deny that the obligation of all citizens to support their Government in times of grave National peril applies to the present situation. If an Administration may with impunity ignore the issues upon which it was chosen, deliberately create a condition of war anywhere on the face of the globe, debauch the civil service for spoils to promote the adventure, organize a truth-suppressing censorship and demand of all citizens a suspension of judgement and their unanimous support while it chooses to continue the fighting, representative government itself is imperiled.

We propose to contribute to the defeat of any person or party that stands for the forcible subjugation of any people. We shall oppose for reëlection all who in the White House or in Congress betray American liberty in pursuit of un-American gains. We still hope that both of our great political parties will support and defend the Declaration of Independence in the closing campaign of the century.

We hold, with Abraham Lincoln, that "no man is good enough to govern another man without that man's consent. When the white man governs himself, that is self-government, but when he governs himself and also governs another man, that is more than self-government—that is despotism". "Our reliance is in the love of liberty which God has planted in us. Our defense is in the spirit which prizes liberty as the heritage of all men in all lands. Those who deny freedom to others deserve it not for themselves, and under a just God cannot long retain it."

We cordially invite the coöperation of all men and women who remain loyal to the Declaration of Independence and the Constitution of the United States.

352. DOWNES v. BIDWELL
182 U. S. 244
1901

Error to the United States circuit court for the Southern district of New York. This was an action brought by Downes against Bidwell, collector of the port of New York, to recover back duties paid under protest upon a consignment shipped to the plaintiff from Porto Rico in November, 1900. The duties were collected under the Foraker Act of April 2, 1900, providing a temporary government for the island. This is one of the earliest of the so-called Insular Cases, dealing with the vexed question of the constitutional relations of the United States with the territories acquired through the War with Spain. Mr. John W. Davis said of these Insular Cases that "there may be found in these opinions the most hotly contested and long continued duel in the life of the Supreme Court." The literature, technical and controversial, on the insular cases and the general question of imperialism is enormous. The briefs and arguments in the insular cases were published in *House Documents,* 56 Cong. 2 Sess. No. 509. For general treatments of the constitutional questions involved, see, W. F. Willoughby, *Territories and Dependencies of the United States;* C. F. Randolph, *Law and Policy of Annexation;* and C. E. Magoon, *Legal Status of the Territory and Inhabitants of the Islands Acquired by the United States during the War with Spain.*

BROWN, J. This case involves the question whether merchandise brought into the port of New York from Porto Rico, since the passage of the Foraker act, is exempt from duty, notwithstanding the third section of that act, which requires the payment of "fifteen per centum of the duties which are required to be levied, collected and paid upon like articles of merchandise imported from foreign countries.". . .

In the case of *De Lima* v. *Bidwell* just decided, we held that upon the ratification of the treaty of peace with Spain, Porto Rico ceased to be a foreign country, and became a territory of the United States, and that duties were no longer collectible upon merchandise brought from that island. We are now asked to hold that it became a part of the *United States* within that provision of the Constitution which declares that "all duties, imposts and excises shall be uniform throughout the United States." Art. I, Sec. 8. If Porto Rico be a part of the United States, the Foraker act imposing duties upon its products is unconstitutional, not only by reason of a violation of the uniformity clause, but because by section 9 "vessels bound to or from one State" cannot "be obliged to enter, clear or pay duties in another."

The case also involves the broader question whether the revenue clauses of the Constitution extend of their own force to our newly acquired territories. The Constitution itself does not answer the question. Its solution must be found in the nature of the government created by that instrument, in the opinion of its contemporaries, in the practical construction put upon it by Congress and in the decisions of this court. . . .

[Here follows some consideration of the Articles of Confederation, the Ordinance of 1787, and the Constitution.]

It is sufficient to observe in relation to these three fundamental instruments that it can nowhere be inferred that the territories were considered a part of the United States. The Constitution was created by the people of the *United States,* as a union of *States,* to be governed solely by representatives of the *States;* and even the provision relied upon here, that all duties, imposts and excises shall be uniform "throughout the United States," is explained by subsequent provisions of the Constitution, that "no tax or duty shall be laid on articles exported from any *State,*" and "no preference shall be given by any regulation of commerce or revenue to the ports of one *State* over those of another; nor shall vessels bound to or from one State be obliged to enter, clear or pay duties in another." In short, the Constitution deals with *States,* their people and their representatives. . . .

The question of the legal relations between the States and the newly acquired territories first became the subject of public discussion in connection with the purchase of Louisiana in 1803. . . .

Notwithstanding these provisions for the incorporation of territories into the Union, Congress, not only in organizing the territory of Louisiana by Act of March 26, 1804, but all other territories carved out of this vast inheritance, has assumed that the Constitution did not extend to them of its own force, and has in each case made special provision, either that their legislatures shall pass no law inconsistent with the Constitution of the United States, or that the Constitution or laws of the United States shall be the supreme law of such territories. Finally, in Rev. Stat., Sec. 1891, a general provision was enacted that "the Constitution and all laws of the United States which are not locally inapplicable shall have the same force and effect within all the organized territories, and in every territory hereafter organized, as elsewhere within the United States". . . .

Indeed, whatever may have been the fluctuations of opinion in other bodies, (and even this court has not been exempt from them), Congress has been consistent in recognizing the difference between the States and territories under the Constitution.

The decisions of this court upon this subject have not been altogether harmonious. Some of them are based upon the theory that the Constitution does not apply to the territories without legislation. Other cases, arising from territories where such legislation has been had, contain language which would justify the inference that such legislation was unnecessary, and that the Constitution took effect immediately upon the cession of the territory to the United States. It may be remarked, upon the threshold of an analysis of these cases, that too much weight must not be given to general expressions found in several opinions that the power of Congress over territories is complete and supreme, because these words may be interpreted as meaning only supreme under the Constitution; nor upon the other hand, to general statements that the Constitution covers the territories as well as the States, since in such cases it will be found that acts of Congress had already extended the Constitution to such territories, and that thereby it subordinated not only its own acts, but those of the territorial legislatures, to what had become the supreme law of the land. . . . [Here follows a review of the decisions.]

Eliminating, then, from the opinions of this court all expressions unnecessary to the disposition of the particular case, and gleaning therefrom the exact point decided in each, the following propositions may be considered as established:

1. That the District of Columbia and the territories are not States, within the judicial clause of the Constitution giving jurisdiction in cases between citizens of different States;

2. That territories are not States, within the meaning of Revised Statutes, sec. 709, permitting writs of error from this court in cases where the validity of a *state* statute is drawn in question;

3. That the District of Columbia and the territories are States, as that word is used in treaties with foreign powers, with respect to the ownership, disposition and inheritance of property;

4. That the territories are not within the clause of the Constitution providing for the creation of a Supreme Court and such inferior courts as Congress may see fit to establish;

5. That the Constitution does not apply to foreign countries or to trials therein conducted, and that Congress may lawfully provide for such trials before consular tribunals, without the intervention of a grand or petit jury;

6. That where the Constitution has been once formally extended by Congress to territories, neither Congress nor the territorial legislature can enact laws inconsistent therewith. . . .

To sustain the judgment in the case under consideration it by no means becomes necessary to show that none of the articles of the Constitution apply to the Island of Porto Rico. There is a clear distinction between such prohibitions as go to the very root of the power of Congress to act at all, irrespective of time or place, and such as are operative only "throughout the United States" or among the several States.

Thus, when the Constitution declares that "no bill of attainder or ex post facto law shall be passed," and that "no title of nobility shall be granted by the United States," it goes to the competency of Congress to pass a bill *of that description*. Perhaps the same remark may apply to the First Amendment, that "Congress shall make no law respecting an establishment of religion, or prohibiting the free exercise thereof, or abridging the freedom of speech, or of the press, or the right of the people to peacefully assemble and to petition the government for a redress of grievances." We do not wish, however, to be understood as expressing an opinion how far the bill of rights contained in the first eight amendments is of general and how far of local application.

Upon the other hand, when the Constitution declares that all duties shall be uniform "throughout the United States," it becomes necessary to inquire whether there be any territory over which Congress has jurisdiction which is not a part of the "United States," by which term we understand the *States* whose people *united* to form the Constitution, and such as have since been admitted to the Union upon an equality with them. Not only did the people in adopting the Thirteenth Amendment thus recognize a distinction between the United States and "any place subject to their jurisdiction," but Congress itself, in the Act of March 27, 1804, c. 56, 2 Stat. 298, providing for the proof of public records, applied the provisions of the act, not only to "every court and office within the United States," but to the "courts and offices of the respective territories of the United States and countries subject to the jurisdiction of the United States.". . . Unless these words are to be rejected as meaningless, we must treat them as a recognition by Congress of the fact that there may be territories subject to the jurisdiction of the United States, which are not *of* the United States. . . .

Indeed, the practical interpretation put by Congress upon the Constitution has been long continued and uniform to the effect that the Constitution is applicable to territories acquired by purchase or conquest only when and so far as Congress shall so direct. . . .

We are also of opinion that the power to acquire territory by treaty implies, not only the power to govern such territory, but to prescribe upon what terms the United States will receive its inhabitants, and what their status shall be in what Chief Justice Marshall termed the "American empire." There seems to be no middle ground between this position and the doctrine that if their inhabitants do not become, immediately upon annexation, citizens of the United States, their children thereafter born, whether savages or civilized, are such, and entitled to all the rights, privileges and immunities of citizens. If such be their status, the consequences will be extremely serious. Indeed, it is doubtful if Congress would ever assent to the annexation of territory upon the condition that its inhabitants, however foreign they may be to our habits, traditions, and modes of life, shall become at once citizens of the United States. In all its treaties hitherto the treaty-making power has made special provisions for this subject. . . . In all these cases there is an implied denial of the right

of the inhabitants to American citizenship until Congress by further action shall signify its assent thereto. . . .

It is obvious that in the annexation of outlying and distant possessions grave questions will arise from differences of race, habits, laws and customs of the people, and from differences of soil, climate and production, which may require action on the part of Congress that would be quite unnecessary in the annexation of contiguous territory inhabited only by people of the same race, or by scattered bodies of native Indians.

We suggest, without intending to decide, that there may be a distinction between certain natural rights enforced in the Constitution by prohibitions against interference with them, and what may be termed artificial or remedial rights which are peculiar to our own system of jurisprudence. Of the former class are the rights to one's own religious opinions and to a public expression of them, or, as sometimes said, to worship God according to the dictates of one's own conscience; the right to personal liberty and individual property; to freedom of speech and of the press; to free access to courts of justice, to due process of law, and to an equal protection of the laws; to immunities from unreasonable searches and seizures, as well as cruel and unusual punishments; and to such other immunities as are indispensable to a free government. Of the latter case are the rights to citizenship, to suffrage (*Minor* v. *Happersett*, 21 Wall. 162), and to the particular methods of procedure pointed out in the Constitution, which are peculiar to Anglo-Saxon jurisprudence, and some of which have already been held by the States to be unnecessary to the proper protection of individuals. . . .

We do not desire, however, to anticipate the difficulties which would naturally arise in this connection, but merely to disclaim any intention to hold that the inhabitants of these territories are subject to an unrestrained power on the part of Congress to deal with them upon the theory that they have no rights which it is bound to respect. . . .

In passing upon the questions involved in this and kindred cases, we ought not to overlook the fact that, while the Constitution was intended to establish a permanent form of government for the States which should elect to take advantage of its conditions, and continue for an indefinite future, the vast possibilities of that future could never have entered the minds of its framers. . . . The difficulties of bringing about a union of the States were so great, the objections to it seemed so formidable, that the whole thought of the convention centered upon surmounting these obstacles. The question of territories was dismissed with a single clause, apparently applicable only to the territories then existing, giving Congress the power to govern and dispose of them. . . .

. . . If it be once conceded that we are at liberty to acquire foreign territory, a presumption arises that our power with respect to such territories is the same power which other nations have been accustomed to exercise with respect to territories acquired by them. If, in limiting the power which Congress was to exercise within the United States, it was also intended to limit it with regard to such territories as the people of the United States should thereafter acquire, such limitations should have been expressed. Instead of that, we find the Constitution speaking only to States, except in the territorial clause, which is absolute in its terms, and suggestive of no limitations upon the power of Congress in dealing with them. . . .

. . . The liberality of Congress in legislating the Constitution into all our contiguous territories has undoubtedly fostered the impression that it went there by its own force, but there is nothing in the Constitution itself, and little in the interpretation put upon it, to confirm that impression. There is not even an analogy to the provisions of an ordinary mortgage for its attachment to after-acquired property, without which it covers only property existing at the date of the mortgage. In short, there is absolute silence upon the subject. The executive and legislative departments of the government have for more than a century interpreted this silence as precluding the idea that the Constitution attached to these territories as soon as acquired, and unless such interpretation be manifestly contrary to the letter or spirit of the Constitution, it should be followed by the judicial department. . . .

Patriotic and intelligent men may differ widely as to the desirableness of this or that acquisition, but this is solely a political question. We can only consider this aspect of the case so far as to say that no construction of the Constitution should be adopted which would prevent Congress from considering each case upon its merits, unless the language of the instrument imperatively demand it. A false step at this time might be fatal to the development of what Chief Justice Marshall called the American empire. Choice in some cases, the natural gravitation of small bodies towards large ones in others, the result of a successful war in still others, may bring about conditions which would render the annexation of distant possessions desirable. If those possessions are inhabited by alien races, differing from us in religion, customs, laws, methods of taxation and modes of thought, the administration of government and justice, according to Anglo-Saxon principles, may for a time be impossible; and the question at once arises whether large concessions ought not to be made for a time, that, ultimately, our own theories may be carried out, and the blessings of a free government under the Constitution extended to them. We decline to hold that there is anything in the Constitution to forbid such action.

We are therefore of opinion that the Island of Porto Rico is a territory appurtenant and belonging to the United States, but not a part of the United States within the revenue clauses of the Constitution; that the Foraker act is constitutional, so far as it imposes duties upon imports from such island, and that the plaintiff cannot recover back the duties exacted in this case.

The judgment of the Circuit Court is therefore affirmed.

[WHITE, J. delivered a separate opinion concurring in the judgment, but for different reasons. Justices SHIRAS and McKENNA concurred in this opinion. Chief Justice FULLER delivered a dissenting opinion, in which Justices HARLAN, BREWER, and PECKHAM concurred. HARLAN, J., also delivered a separate dissenting opinion.]

FULLER, C. J. dissenting. . . . The inquiry is stated to be: "Had Porto Rico, at the time of the passage of the act in question, been incorporated into and become an integral part of the United States?" And the answer being given that it had not, it is held that the rule of uniformity was not applicable. I submit that that is not the question in this case. The question is whether, when Congress has created a civil government for Porto Rico, has constituted its inhabitants a body politic, has given it a governor and other officers, a legislative assembly, and courts, with right of appeal to this court, Congress can, in the same act and in the exercise of the power conferred by the first clause of section eight, impose duties on the commerce between Porto Rico and the States and other territories in contravention of the rule of uniformity qualifying the power. If this can be done, it is because the power of Congress over commerce between the States and any of the territories is not restricted by the Constitution. This was the position taken by the Attorney General, with a candor and ability that did him great credit.

But that position is rejected, and the contention seems to be that, if an organized and settled province of another sovereignty is acquired by the United States, Congress has the power to keep it, like a disembodied shade, in an intermediate state of ambiguous existence for an indefinite period; and, more than that, that after it has been called from that limbo, commerce with it is absolutely subject to the will of Congress, irrespective of constitutional provisions. . . .

Great stress is thrown upon the word "incorporation" as if possessed of some occult meaning, but I take it that the act under consideration made Porto Rico, whatever its situation before, an organized territory of the United States. Being such, and the act undertaking to impose duties by virtue of clause 1 sec. 8, how is it that the rule which qualifies the power does not apply to its

exercise in respect of commerce with that territory? The power can only be exercised as prescribed, and even if the rule of uniformity could be treated as a mere regulation of the granted power—a suggestion as to which I do not assent—the validity of these duties comes up directly, and it is idle to discuss the distinction between a total want of power and a defective exercise of it.

The concurring opinion recognizes the fact that Congress, in dealing with the people of new territories or possessions, is bound to respect the fundamental guarantees of life, liberty, and property, but assumes that Congress is not bound, in those territories or possessions, to follow the rule of taxation prescribed by the Constitution. And yet the power to tax involves the power to destroy, and the levy of duties touches all our people in all places under the jurisdiction of the government.

The logical result is that Congress may prohibit commerce altogether between the States and territories, and may prescribe one rule of taxation in one territory, and a different rule in another.

That theory assumes that the Constitution created a government empowered to acquire countries throughout the world, to be governed by different rules than those obtaining in the original States and territories, and substitutes for the present system of republican government a system of domination over distant provinces in the exercise of unrestricted power.

In our judgment, so much of the Porto Rican act as authorized the imposition of duties is invalid, and plaintiffs were entitled to recover. . . .

353. THE GOLD STANDARD ACT OF 1900
March 14, 1900
(U. S. Statutes at Large, Vol. XXXI, p. 45 ff.)

The election of McKinley in 1896 had temporarily ended the agitation for free silver. The return of prosperity during the McKinley administration, the great increase in world production of gold, and the failure of the half-hearted efforts of the administration to arrive at some international agreement for bimetallism, all

made the enactment of the gold standard inevitable. See, A. B. Hepburn, *History of Currency*, p. 371 ff.; D. R. Dewey, *Financial History*, p. 468 ff.

An act to define and fix the standard of value, to maintain the parity of all forms of money issued or coined by the United States. . . .

Be it enacted, That the dollar consisting of twenty-five and eight-tenths grains of gold nine-tenths fine, as established by section thirty-five hundred and eleven of the Revised Statutes of the United States, shall be the standard unit of value, and all forms of money issued or coined by the United States shall be maintained at a parity of value with this standard, and it shall be the duty of the Secretary of the Treasury to maintain such parity.

Sec. 2. That United States notes, and Treasury notes issued under the Act of July 14, 1890, when presented to the Treasury for redemption, shall be redeemed in gold coin of the standard fixed in the first section of this Act, and in order to secure the prompt and certain redemption of such notes as herein provided it shall be the duty of the Secretary of the Treasury to set apart in the Treasury a reserve fund of one hundred and fifty million dollars in gold coin and bullion, which fund shall be used for such redemption purposes only, and whenever and as often as any of said notes shall be redeemed from said fund it shall be the duty of the Secretary of the Treasury to use said notes so redeemed to restore and maintain such reserve fund. . . .

Sec. 3. That nothing contained in this Act shall be construed to affect the legal-tender quality as now provided by law of the silver dollar, or of any other money coined or issued by the United States. . . .

Sec. 14. That the provisions of this Act are not intended to preclude the accomplishment of international bimetallism whenever conditions shall make it expedient and practicable to secure the same by concurrent action of the leading commercial nations of the world and at a ratio which shall insure permanence of relative value between gold and silver.

354. McKINLEY'S RECIPROCITY SPEECH
Buffalo, New York, September 5, 1901

(Richardson, ed. *Messages and Papers,* Vol. X, p. 393 ff.)

In this, McKinley's last public address, the high-priest of protective tariffs announced that "the period of exclusiveness is past" and suggested a modification of the traditional tariff policy of the Republican party. The following day he was shot by the anarchist Czolgosz, and he died September 14. Roosevelt, who succeeded him, cautiously avoided the tariff issue. See, C. S. Olcott, *Life of William McKinley,* 2 Vols.

. . . My fellow citizens: Trade statistics indicate that this country is in a state of unexampled prosperity. The figures are almost appalling. They show that we are utilizing our fields and forests and mines, and that we are furnishing profitable employment to the millions of working-men throughout the United States, bringing comfort and happiness to their homes, and making it possible to lay by savings for old age and disability. That all the people are participating in this great prosperity is seen in every American community, and shown by the enormous and unprecedented deposits in our savings banks. Our duty is the care and security of these deposits, and their safe investment demands the highest integrity and the best business capacity of those in charge of these depositories of the people's earnings.

We have a vast and intricate business, built up through years of toil and struggle, in which every part of the country has its stake, which will not permit either of neglect or of undue selfishness. No narrow, sordid, policy will subserve it. The greatest skill and wisdom on the part of manufacturers and producers will be required to hold and increase it. Our industrial enterprises, which have grown to such proportions, affect the homes and occupations of the people and the welfare of the country. Our capacity to produce has developed so enormously, and our products have so multiplied, that the problem of more markets requires our urgent and immediate attention. Only a broad and enlightened policy will keep what we have. No other policy will get more. In these times of marvellous business energy and gain we ought to be looking to the future, strengthening the weak places in our industrial and commercial systems, that we may be ready for any storm or strain.

By sensible trade arrangements which will not interrupt our home production, we shall extend the outlets for our increasing surplus. A system which provides a mutual exchange of commodities is manifestly essential to the continued and healthful growth of our export trade. We must not repose in fancied security that we can forever sell everything and buy little or nothing. If such a thing were possible, it would not be best for us or for those with whom we deal. We should take from our customers such of their products as we can use without harm to our industries and labor. Reciprocity is the natural outgrowth of our wonderful industrial development under the domestic policy now firmly established. What we produce beyond our domestic consumption must have a vent abroad. The excess must be relieved through a foreign outlet, and we should sell everywhere we can and buy wherever the buying will enlarge our sales and production, and thereby make a greater demand for home labor.

The period of exclusiveness is past. The expansion of our trade and commerce is the pressing problem. Commercial wars are unprofitable. A policy of good will and friendly trade relations will prevent reprisals. Reciprocity treaties are in harmony with the spirit of the times; measures of retaliation are not.

If perchance some of our tariffs are no longer needed for revenue or to encourage and protect our industries at home, why should they not be employed to extend and promote our markets abroad? . . .

355. HAY-PAUNCEFOTE TREATY
November 18, 1901

(Malloy, ed. *Treaties, Conventions, etc.* Vol. I, p. 782 ff.)

The first Hay-Pauncefote Treaty was ratified by the Senate, December 20, 1900, but with amendments unacceptable to Great Britain. See, T. Dennett, *John Hay*, ch. xxi; L. M. Keasby, *Nicaragua Canal*, chs. xxi, xxii; H. G. Miller, *The Isthmian Highway*, ch. xi; W. S. Holt, *Treaties Defeated by the Senate*, ch. ix.

TREATY TO FACILITATE THE CONSTRUCTION OF A SHIP CANAL

The United States of America and His Majesty Edward the Seventh, of the United Kingdom of Great Britain and Ireland, . . . being desirous to facilitate the construction of a ship canal to connect the Atlantic and Pacific Oceans, by whatever route may be considered expedient, and to that end to remove any objection which may arise out of the convention of the nineteenth of April, 1850, commonly called the Clayton-Bulwer treaty, to the construction of such canal under the auspices of the Government of the United States, without impairing the "general principle" of neutralization established in Article VIII of that convention, have . . . agreed upon the following articles:

ART. I. The High Contracting Parties agree that the present treaty shall supersede the afore-mentioned Convention of the 19th April, 1850.

ART. II. It is agreed that the canal may be constructed under the auspices of the Government of the United States either directly at its own cost, or by gift or loan of money to individuals or Corporations, or through subscription to or purchase of stock or shares, and that, subject to the provisions of the present Treaty, the said Government shall have and enjoy all the rights incident to such construction, as well as the exclusive right of providing for the regulation and management of the canal.

ART. III. The United States adopts, as the basis of the neutralization of such ship canal, the following Rules, substantially as embodied in the Convention of Constantinople signed the twenty-eighth of October,

1888, for the free navigation of the Suez Canal, that is to say:

1. The canal shall be free and open to the vessels of commerce and of war of all nations observing these Rules, on terms of entire equality, so that there shall be no discrimination against any such nation, or its citizens or subjects, in respect of the conditions or charges of traffic or otherwise. Such conditions and charges of traffic shall be just and equitable.

2. The canal shall never be blockaded, nor shall any right of war be exercised nor any act of hostility be committed within it. The United States, however, shall be at liberty to maintain such military police along the canal as may be necessary to protect it against lawlessness and disorder.

3. Vessels of war of a belligerent shall not revictual nor take any stores in the canal except so far as may be strictly necessary; and the transit of such vessels through the canal shall be effected with the least possible delay in accordance with the Regulations in force, and with only such intermission as may result from the necessities of the service.

Prizes shall be in all respects subject to the same rules as vessels of war of the belligerents.

4. No belligerent shall embark or disembark troops, munitions of war, or warlike materials in the canal, except in case of accidental hindrance of the transit, and in such case the transit shall be resumed with all possible dispatch.

5. The provisions of this Article shall apply to waters adjacent to the canal, within 3 marine miles of either end. Vessels of war of a belligerent shall not remain in such waters longer than twenty-four hours at any one time, except in case of distress, and in such case shall depart as soon as possible; but a vessel of war of one belligerent shall not depart within twenty-four hours from the departure of a vessel of war of the other belligerent.

6. The plant, establishments, buildings and all works necessary to the construction, maintenance and operation of the canal shall be deemed to be part thereof, for the purposes of this treaty, and in time of war, as in time of peace, shall enjoy complete immunity from attack or injury by belligerents, and from acts calculated to impair their usefulness as part of the canal.

ART. IV. It is agreed that no change of territorial sovereignty or of international relations of the country or countries traversed by the beforementioned canal shall affect the general principle of neutralization or the obligation of the High Contracting Parties under the present Treaty. . . .

356. PRESIDENT ROOSEVELT AND THE TRUSTS
Extract from First Annual Message to Congress
December 3, 1901

(Richardson, ed. *Messages and Papers*, Vol. X, p. 417 ff.)

With this message President Roosevelt, who succeeded to the Presidency on the death of McKinley, gave warning that he would wield the "big stick" on lawless business. The message was succinctly summarized by Mr. Dooley, "Th' trusts, says he, are heejoous monsthers built up be th' enlightened intherprise iv th' men that have done so much to advance progress in our beloved country, he says. On wan hand I wud stamp thim undher fut; on th' other hand not so fast."

To the Senate and House of Representatives:
. . . The tremendous and highly complex industrial development which went on with ever-accelerated rapidity during the latter half of the nineteenth century brings us face to face, at the beginning of the twentieth, with very serious social problems. The old laws, and the old customs which had almost the binding force of law, were once quite sufficient to regulate the accumulation and

distribution of wealth. Since the industrial changes which have so enormously increased the productive power of mankind, they are no longer sufficient.

The growth of cities has gone on beyond comparison faster than the growth of the country, and the upbuilding of the great industrial centres has meant a startling increase, not merely in the aggregate of wealth, but in the number of very large individual, and especially of very large corporate, fortunes. The creation of these great corporate fortunes has not been due to the tariff nor to any other governmental action, but to natural causes in the business world, operating in other countries as they operate in our own.

The process has aroused much antagonism, a great part of which is wholly without warrant. . . . The captains of industry who have driven the railway systems across this continent, who have built up our commerce, who have developed our manufactures, have on the whole done great good to our people. Without them the material development of which we are so justly proud could never have taken place. Moreover, we should recognize the immense importance of this material development by leaving as unhampered as is compatible with the public good the strong and forceful men upon whom the success of business operations inevitably rests. The slightest study of business conditions will satisfy any one capable of forming a judgment that the personal equation is the most important factor in a business operation; that the business ability of the man at the head of any business concern, big or little, is usually the factor which fixes the gulf between striking success and hopeless failure.

An additional reason for caution in dealing with corporations is to be found in the international commercial conditions of today. The same business conditions which have produced the great aggregations of corporate and individual wealth have made them very potent factors in international commercial competition. Business concerns which have the largest means at their disposal and are managed by the ablest men are naturally those which take the lead in the strife for commercial supremacy among the nations of the world. America has only just begun to assume that commanding position in the international business world which we believe will more and more be hers. It is of the utmost importance that this position be not jeopardized, especially at a time when the overflowing abundance of our own natural resources and the skill, business energy, and mechanical aptitude of our people make foreign markets essential. Under such conditions it would be most unwise to cramp or to fetter the youthful strength of our nation.

Moreover, it cannot too often be pointed out that to strike with ignorant violence at the interests of one set of men almost inevitably endangers the interests of all. The fundamental rule in our national life—the rule which underlies all others—is that, on the whole, and in the long run, we shall go up or down together. . . .

The mechanism of modern business is so delicate that extreme care must be taken not to interfere with it in a spirit of rashness or ignorance. Many of those who have made it their vocation to denounce the great industrial combinations which are popularly, although with technical inaccuracy, known as "trusts", appeal especially to hatred and fear. These are precisely the two emotions, particularly when combined with ignorance, which unfit men for the exercise of cool and steady judgment. In facing new industrial conditions, the whole history of the world shows that legislation will generally be both unwise and ineffective unless undertaken after calm inquiry and with sober self-restraint. . . .

All this is true; and yet it is also true that there are real and grave evils, one of the chief being overcapitalization because of its many baleful consequences; and a resolute and practical effort must be made to correct these evils.

There is a widespread conviction in the minds of the American people that the great corporations known as trusts are in certain of their features and tendencies hurtful to the general welfare. This . . . is based upon sincere conviction that combination and concentration should be, not prohibited, but supervised and within reasonable limits controlled; and in my judgment this conviction is right.

It is no limitation upon property rights or freedom of contract to require that when men receive from government the privilege of doing business under corporate form, which frees them from individual responsibility, and enables them to call into their enterprises the capital of the public, they shall do so upon absolutely truthful representations as to the value of the property in which the capital is to be invested. Corporations engaged in interstate commerce should be regulated if they are found to exercise a license working to the public injury. It should be as much the aim of those who seek for social betterment to rid the business world of crimes of cunning as to rid the entire body politic of crimes of violence. Great corporations exist only because they are created and safeguarded by our institutions; and it is therefore our right and our duty to see that they work in harmony with these institutions.

The first essential in determining how to deal with the great industrial combinations is knowledge of the facts—publicity. In the interest of the public, the government should have the right to inspect and examine the workings of the great corporations engaged in interstate business. Publicity is the only sure remedy which we can now invoke. What further remedies are needed in the way of governmental regulation, or taxation, can only be determined after publicity has been obtained, by process of law, and in the course of administration. The first requisite is knowledge, full and complete—knowledge which may be made public to the world. . . .

The large corporations, commonly called trusts, though organized in one State, always do business in many States, often doing very little business in the State where they are incorporated. There is utter lack of uniformity in the State laws about them; and as no State has any exclusive interest in or power over their acts, it has in practice proved impossible to get adequate regulation through State action. Therefore, in the interest of the whole people, the nation should, without interfering with the power of the States in the matter itself, also assume power of supervision and regulation over all corporations doing an interstate business. This is especially true where the corporation derives a portion of its wealth from the existence of some monopolistic element or tendency in its business. There would be no hardship in such supervision; banks are subject to it, and in their case it is now accepted as a simple matter of course. Indeed, it is now probable that supervision of corporations by the National Government need not go so far as is now the case with the supervision exercised over them by so conservative a State as Massachusetts, in order to produce excellent results.

When the Constitution was adopted, at the end of the eighteenth century, no human wisdom could foretell the sweeping changes, alike in industrial and political conditions, which were to take place by the beginning of the twentieth century. At that time it was accepted as a matter of course that the several States were the proper authorities to regulate, so far as was then necessary, the comparatively insignificant and strictly localized corporate bodies of the day. The conditions are now wholly different and wholly different action is called for. I believe that a law can be framed which will enable the National Government to exercise control along the lines above indicated; profiting by the experience gained through the passage and administration of the Interstate Commerce Act. If, however, the judgment of the Congress is that it lacks the constitutional power to pass such an act, then a constitutional amendment should be submitted to confer the power.

357. W.C.T.U. DECLARATION OF PRINCIPLES
1902

(National Woman's Christian Temperance Union, *Annual Leaflet*, 1902)

The W. C. T. U. was, with the Anti-Saloon League and the Methodist Church, the most effective of the numerous agencies working for prohibition. For background of the prohibition movement see J. A. Krout, *The Origins of Prohibition*. See also, P. Odegard, *Pressure Politics: The Story of the Anti-Saloon League;* E. H. Cherrington, *Evolution of Prohibition in the United States;* D. L. Colvin, *Prohibition in the United States.*

We believe in the coming of His Kingdom whose service is perfect freedom, because His laws, written in our members as well as in nature and in grace, are perfect, converting the soul.

We believe in the gospel of the Golden Rule, and that each man's habits of life should be an example safe and beneficent for every other man to follow.

We believe that God created both man and woman in His own image, and therefore, we believe in one standard of purity for both men and women, and in the equal right of all to hold opinions and to express the same with equal freedom.

We believe in a living wage; in an eight hour day; in courts of conciliation and arbitration; in justice as opposed to greed of gain; in "peace on earth and good-will to men."

We therefore formulate, and for ourselves adopt the following pledge, asking our sisters and brothers of a common danger and a common hope, to make common cause with us, in working its reasonable and helpful precepts into the practice of everyday life:

I hereby solemnly promise GOD HELPING ME, to abstain from all distilled, fermented and malt liquors, including wine, Beer and Cider, and to employ all proper means to discourage the use of and traffic in the same.

To conform and enforce the rationale of this pledge, we declare our purpose to educate the young; to form a better public sentiment; to reform so far as possible, by religious, ethical and scientific means, the drinking classes; to seek the transforming power of divine grace for ourselves and all for whom we work, that they and we may willfully transcend no law of pure and wholesome living; and finally we pledge ourselves to labor and to pray that all of these principles, founded upon the Gospel of Christ, may be worked out into the customs of Society and the Laws of the Land.

358. THE DRAGO DOCTRINE
December 29, 1902
(*Foreign Relations of the United States,* 1903, p. 1 ff.)

This announcement of the doctrine that the use of coercion for the collection of claims would constitute a violation of the principles of the Monroe Doctrine arose out of the Venezuelan situation of 1902. On the failure of Venezuela to make any arrangements for the payment of claims of German, English and other foreign claimants, Great Britain and Germany established a blockade of the Venezuela coast; Italy shortly joined the blockading powers. The claims were eventually arbitrated, and the powers induced to withdraw their blockade. The Drago doctrine was embodied in Convention II of the Second Hague Convention, 1907. See, Malloy, ed. *Treaties, Conventions, etc.,* Vol. II, p. 2254. The Venezuela situation can be followed in Moore's *Digest,* Vol. VI; *Foreign Relations of the United States,* 1903 and 1904; H. C. Hill, *Roosevelt and the Caribbean.*

THE DRAGO DOCTRINE: LETTER OF DR. LUIS

M. DRAGO, MINISTER OF FOREIGN RELATIONS OF THE ARGENTINE REPUBLIC, TO MR. MÉROU, ARGENTINE MINISTER TO THE UNITED STATES, DECEMBER 29, 1902
BUENOS AIRES, *December 29, 1902.*

MR. MINISTER: I have received your excellency's telegram of the 20th instant concerning the events that have lately taken place between the Government of the Republic of Venezuela and the Governments of Great Britain and Germany. According to your excellency's information the origin of the disagreement is, in part, the damages suffered by subjects of the claimant nations during the revolutions and wars that have recently occurred within the borders of the Republic mentioned, and in part also the fact that certain payments on the external debt of the nation have not been met at the proper time.

Leaving out of consideration the first class of claims the adequate adjustments of which it would be necessary to consult the laws of the several countries, this Government has deemed it expedient to transmit to your excellency some considerations with reference to the forcible collection of the public debt suggested by the events that have taken place.

At the outset it is to be noted in this connection that the capitalist who lends his money to a foreign state always takes into account the resources of the country and the probability, greater or less, that the obligations contracted will be fulfilled without delay.

All governments thus enjoy different credit according to their degree of civilization and culture and their conduct in business transactions; and these conditions are measured and weighed before making any loan, the terms being made more or less onerous in accordance with the precise data concerning them which bankers always have on record.

In the first place the lender knows that he is entering into a contract with a sovereign entity, and it is an inherent qualification of all sovereignty that no proceedings for the execution of a judgment may be instituted or carried out against it, since this manner of collection would compromise its very existence and cause the independence and freedom of action of the respective government to disappear.

Among the fundamental principles of public international law which humanity has consecrated, one of the most precious is that which decrees that all states, whatever be the force at their disposal, are entities in law, perfectly equal one to another, and mutually entitled by virtue thereof to the same consideration and respect.

The acknowledgment of the debt, the payment of it in its entirety, can and must be made by the nation without diminution of its inherent rights as a sovereign entity, but the summary and immediate collection at a given moment, by means of force, would occasion nothing less than the ruin of the weakest nations, and the absorption of their governments, together with all the functions inherent in them, by the mighty of the earth. The principles proclaimed on this continent of

America are otherwise. "Contracts between a nation and private individuals are obligatory according to the conscience of the sovereign, and may not be the object of compelling force," said the illustrious Hamilton. "They confer no right of action contrary to the sovereign will."

The United States has gone very far in this direction. The eleventh amendment to its Constitution provided in effect, with the unanimous assent of the people, that the judicial power of the nation should not be extended to any suit in law or equity prosecuted against one of the United States by citizens of another State, or by citizens or subjects of any foreign State. The Argentine Government has made its provinces indictable, and has even adopted the principle that the nation itself may be brought to trial before the supreme court on contracts which it enters into with individuals.

What has not been established, what could in no wise be admitted, is that, once the amount for which it may be indebted has been determined by legal judgment, it should be deprived of the right to choose the manner and the time of payment, in which it has as much interest as the creditor himself, or more, since its credit and its national honor are involved therein.

This is in no wise a defense for bad faith, disorder, and deliberate and voluntary insolvency. It is intended merely to preserve the dignity of the public international entity which may not thus be dragged into war with detriment to those high ends which determine the existence and liberty of nations.

The fact that collection can not be accomplished by means of violence does not, on the other hand, render valueless the acknowledgment of the public debt, the definite obligation of paying it.

The State continues to exist in its capacity as such, and sooner or later the gloomy situations are cleared up, resources increase, common aspirations of equity and justice prevail, and the most neglected promises are kept.

The decision, then, which declares the obligation to pay a debt, whether it be given by the tribunals of the country or by those of international arbitration, which manifest the abiding zeal for justice as the basis of the political relations of nations, constitutes an indisputable title which can not be compared to the uncertain right of one whose claims are not recognized and who sees himself driven to appeal to force in order that they may be satisfied.

As these are the sentiments of justice, loyalty, and honor which animate the Argentine people and have always inspired its policy, your excellency will understand that it has felt alarmed at the knowledge that the failure of Venezuela to meet the payments of its public debt is given as one of the determining causes of the capture of its fleet, the bombardment of one of its ports, and the establishment of a rigorous blockade along its shores. If such proceedings were to be definitely adopted they would establish a precedent dangerous to the security and the peace of the nations of this part of America.

The collection of loans by military means implies territorial occupation to make them effective, and territorial occupation signifies the suppression or subordination of the governments of the countries on which it is imposed.

Such a situation seems obviously at variance with the principles many times proclaimed by the nations of America, and particularly with the Monroe doctrine, sustained and defended with so much zeal on all occasions by the United States, a doctrine to which the Argentine Republic has heretofore solemnly adhered. . . .

But in very recent times there has been observed a marked tendency among the publicists and in the various expressions of European opinion to call attention to these countries as a suitable field for future territorial expansion. . . .

And it will not be denied that the simplest way to the setting aside and easy ejectment of the rightful authorities by European governments is just this way of financial interventions—as might be shown by many examples. We in no wise pretend that the South American nations are, from any point of view, exempt from the responsibilities of all sorts which violations of international law impose on civilized peoples. We do not nor can we pretend that these countries occupy an exceptional position in their relations with European powers, which have the indubitable right to protect their subjects as completely as in any other part of the world against the persecutions and injustices of which they may be the victims. The only principle which the Argentine Republic maintains and which it would, with great satisfaction, see adopted, in view of the events in Venezuela, by a nation that enjoys such great authority and prestige as does the United States, is the principle, already accepted, that there can be no territorial expansion in America on the part of Europe, nor any oppression of the peoples of this continent, because an unfortunate financial situation may compel some one of them to postpone the fulfillment of its promises. In a word, the principle which she would like to see recognized is: that the public debt can not occasion armed intervention nor even the actual occupation of the territory of American nations by a European power.

The loss of prestige and credit experienced by States which fail to satisfy the rightful claims of their lawful creditors brings with it difficulties of such magnitude as to render it unnecessary for foreign intervention to aggravate with its oppression the temporary misfortunes of insolvency.

The Argentine Government could cite its own example to demonstrate the needlessness of armed intervention in these cases. . . .

At this time, then, no selfish feeling animates us, nor do we seek our own advantage in manifesting our desire that the public debt of States should not serve as a reason for an armed attack on such States. Quite as little do we harbor any sentiment of hostility with regard to the nations of Europe. On the contrary, we have maintained with all of them since our emancipation the most friendly relations, especially with England, to whom we have recently given the best proof of the confidence which her justice and equanimity inspire in us by intrusting to her decision the most important of our international questions, which she has just decided, fixing our limits with Chile after a controversy of more than seventy years.

We know that where England goes civilization accompanies her, and the benefits of political and civil liberty are extended. Therefore we esteem her, but this does not mean that we should adhere with equal sympathy to her policy in the improbable case of her attempting to oppress the nationalities of this continent which are struggling for their own progress, which have already overcome the greatest difficulties and will surely triumph—to the honor of democratic institutions. Long, perhaps, is the road that the South American nations still have to travel. But they have faith enough and energy and worth sufficient to bring them to their final development with mutual support.

And it is because of this sentiment of continental brotherhood and because of the force which is always derived from the moral support of a whole people that I address you, in pursuance of instructions from His Excellency the President of the Republic, that you may communicate to the Government of the United States our point of view regarding the events in the further development of which that Government is to take so important a part, in order that it may have it in mind as the sincere expression of the sentiments of a nation that has faith in its destiny and in that of this whole continent, at whose head march the United States, realizing our ideals and affording us examples.

Luis M. Drago.

359. THE LOTTERY CASE (CHAMPION v. AMES)
188 U. S. 321
1903

Appeal from the U. S. circuit court for the Northern district of Illinois. Congress, by act of March 2, 1895, had made it a criminal offense to send lottery tickets through the mails. This case involved the question whether such a prohibition was a valid exercise of the power of Congress over commerce. How far Congress can go in regulating morals, health, etc. under the authority of the commerce clause, is subject to dispute. Compare this case to *Hammer* v. *Dagenhart*, Doc. No. 413.

HARLAN, J. . . . We come then to inquire whether there is any solid foundation upon which to rest the contention that Congress may not regulate the carrying of lottery tickets from one State to another, at least by corporations or companies whose business it is, for hire, to carry tangible property from one State to another.

It was said in argument that lottery tickets are not of any real or substantial value in themselves, and therefore are not subjects of commerce. If that were conceded to be the only legal test as to what are to be deemed subjects of commerce that may be regulated by Congress, we cannot accept as accurate the broad statement that such tickets are of no value. . . .

We are of opinion that lottery tickets are subjects of traffic and therefore are subjects of commerce, and the regulation of the carriage of such tickets from State to State, at least by independent carriers, is a regulation of commerce among the several States.

But it is said that the statute in question does not regulate the carrying of lottery tickets from State to State, but by punishing those who cause them to be so carried Congress in effect prohibits such carrying; that in respect of the carrying from one State to another of articles or things that are, in fact, or according to usage in business, the subjects of commerce, the authority given Congress was not to *prohibit*, but only to *regulate*. This view was earnestly pressed at the bar by learned counsel, and must be examined.

It is to be remarked that the Constitution does not define what is to be deemed a legitimate regulation of interstate commerce. In Gibbons v. Ogden it was said that the power to regulate such commerce is the power to prescribe the rule by which it is to be governed. But this general observation leaves it to be determined, when the question comes before the court, whether Congress in prescribing a particular rule, has exceeded its power under the Constitution. . . .

We have said that the carrying from State to State of lottery tickets constitutes interstate commerce, and that the regulation of such commerce is within the power of Congress under the Constitution. Are we prepared to say that a provision which is, in effect a *prohibition* of the carriage of such articles from State to State is not a fit or appropriate mode for the *regulation* of that particular kind of commerce? If lottery traffic, *carried on through interstate commerce,* is a matter of which Congress may take cognizance and over which its power may be exerted, can it be possible that it must tolerate the traffic, and simply regulate the manner in which it may be carried on? Or may not Congress, for the protection of the people of all the States, and under the power to regulate interstate commerce, devise such means, within the scope of the Constitution, and not prohibited by it, as will drive that traffic out of commerce among the States?

In determining whether regulation may not under some circumstances properly take the form or have the effect of prohibition, the nature of the interstate traffic which it was sought by the act of May 2d, 1895, to suppress cannot be overlooked. . . .

If a State, when considering legislation for the suppression of lotteries within its own limits, may properly take into view the evils that inhere in the raising of money in that mode, why may not Congress, invested with the power to regulate commerce among the several States, provide that such commerce shall not be polluted by the carrying of lottery tickets from one State to another? In this connection it must not be forgotten that the power of Congress to regulate commerce among the States is plenary, is complete in itself, and is subject to no limitations except such as may be found in the Constitution. What provision in that instrument can be regarded as limiting the exercise of the power granted? What clause can be cited which, in any degree, countenances the suggestion that one may, of right, carry or cause to be carried from one State to another that which will harm the public morals? We cannot think of any clause of that instrument that could possibly be invoked by those who assert their right to send lottery tickets from State to State except the one providing that no person shall be deprived of his liberty without due process of law. . . . But surely it will not be said to be a part of anyone's liberty, as recognized by the supreme law of the land, that he shall be allowed to introduce into commerce among the States an element that will be confessedly injurious to the public morals.

If it be said that the act of 1895 is incon-sistent with the Tenth Amendment, reserving to the States respectively, or to the people, the powers not delegated to the United States, the answer is that the power to regulate commerce among the States has been expressly delegated to Congress.

Besides, Congress, by that act, does not assume to interfere with traffic or commerce in lottery tickets carried on exclusively within the limits of any State, but has in view only commerce of that kind among the several States. It has not assumed to interfere with the completely internal affairs of any State, and has only legislated in respect of a matter which concerns the people of the United States. As a State may, for the purpose of guarding the morals of its own people, forbid all sales of lottery tickets within its limits, so Congress, for the purpose of guarding the people of the United States against the "wide-spread pestilence of lotteries" and to protect the commerce which concerns all the States, may prohibit the carrying of lottery tickets from one State to another. In legislating upon the subject of the traffic in lottery tickets, as carried on through interstate commerce, Congress only supplemented the action of those States—perhaps all of them—which, for the protection of the public morals, prohibit the drawing of lotteries, as well as the sale or circulation of lottery tickets, within their respective limits. It said, in effect, that it would not permit the declared policy of the States, which sought to protect their people against the mischiefs of the lottery business, to be overthrown or disregarded by the agency of interstate commerce. We should hesitate long before adjudging that an evil of such appalling character, carried on through interstate commerce, cannot be met and crushed by the only power competent to that end. We say competent to that end, because Congress alone has the power to occupy, by legislation, the whole field of interstate commerce. . . . If the carrying of lottery tickets from one State to another be interstate commerce, and if Congress is of opinion that an effective regulation for the suppression of lotteries, carried on through such commerce, is to make it a criminal offense to cause lottery tickets to be carried from one State to another, we know of no authority in the Courts to hold that the means thus devised are not appropriate and necessary to protect the country at large against a species of interstate commerce which, although in general use and somewhat favored in both national and state legislation in the early history of the country, has grown into disrepute, and has become offensive to the entire people of the nation. It is a kind of traffic which no one can be entitled to pursue as of right. . . .

That regulation may sometimes appropriately assume the form of prohibition is also illustrated by the case of diseased cattle, transported from one State to another. . . .

The Act of July 2, 1890, known as the Sherman Anti-Trust Act . . . is an illustration of the proposition that regulation may take the form of prohibition . . . [Cites other examples].

It is said, however, that if, in order to suppress lotteries carried on through interstate commerce, Congress may exclude lottery tickets from such commerce, that principle leads necessarily to the conclusion that Congress may arbitrarily exclude from commerce among the States any article, commodity, or thing, of whatever kind or nature, or however useful or valuable, which it may choose, no matter with what motive, to declare shall not be carried from one State to another. It will be time enough to consider the constitutionality of such legislation when we must do so. The present case does not require the court to declare the full extent of the power that Congress may exercise in the regulation of commerce among the States. We may, however, repeat, in this connection, what the court has heretofore said, that the power of Congress to regulate commerce among the States, although plenary, cannot be deemed arbitrary, since it is subject to such limitations or restrictions as are prescribed by the

Constitution. This power, therefore, may not be exercised so as to infringe rights secured or protected by that instrument. It would not be difficult to imagine legislation that would be justly liable to such an objection as that stated, and be hostile to the objects for the accomplishment of which Congress was invested with the general power to regulate commerce among the several States. But, as often said, the possible abuse of a power is not an argument against its existence. There is probably no governmental power that may not be exerted to the injury of the public. . . .

The whole subject is too important, and the questions suggested by its consideration are too difficult of solution, to justify any attempt to lay down a rule for determining in advance the validity of every statute that may be enacted under the commerce clause.

We decide nothing more in the present case than that lottery tickets are subjects of traffic among those who choose to sell or buy them; that the carriage of such tickets by independent carriers from one State to another is therefore interstate commerce; that under its power to regulate commerce among the several States Congress—subject to the limitations imposed by the Constitution upon the exercise of the powers granted —has plenary authority over such commerce, and may prohibit the carriage of such tickets from State to State; and that legislation to that end, and of that character, is not inconsistent with any limitation or restriction imposed upon the exercise of the powers granted to Congress.

The judgment is affirmed.

FULLER, C. J., delivered a dissenting opinion in which Justices BREWER, SHIRAS, and PECKHAM concurred.

360. THE PLATT AMENDMENT
Treaty with Cuba Embodying the Platt Amendment
May 22, 1903
(Malloy, ed. *Treaties, Conventions, etc.* Vol. I, p. 362 ff.)

By the so-called Teller Amendment of the Resolutions of April 19, 1898, the United States disclaimed any intention of exercising sovereignty over the Island of Cuba and promised to leave the government in the hands of the Cuban people. On the conclusion of the war, General Leonard Wood, military governor of the island, provided for the meeting of a constitutional convention to draw up a form of government. The convention met in November 1900, and drew up a constitution modeled upon that of the United States, but without any provision for future relations with the United States. The American government was unwilling to acquiesce in this situation, and a series of provisions known as the Platt Amendments were added to the Army Appropriation Bill of March 2, 1901. These Amendments were drafted by Elihu Root, with the exception of the fifth, drafted by General Wood. The Cuban convention duly added them as an appendix to the Cuban Constitution, and in 1903 they were incorporated into a Treaty with the United States. See, *Documentary History of the Inauguration of the Cuban Government*, Annual Report of the Secretary of War, 1902, Appendix A.; Foreign Policy Association *Information Service Reports*, "Cuba and the Platt Amendment," April, 1929; H. Hagedorn, *Leonard Wood*, 2 Vols.; G. H. Stuart, *Cuba and its International Relations;* L. H. Jenks, *Our Cuban Colony;* H. C. Hill, *Roosevelt and the Caribbean;* E. Root, *Military and Colonial Policy of the United States;* A. G. Robinson, *Cuba and the Intervention;* C. J. Chapman, *History of the Cuban Republic.* The Platt Amendment was abrogated by Treaty of May 31, 1934, Doc. No. 485.

ART. I. The Government of Cuba shall never enter into any treaty or other compact with any foreign power or powers which will impair or tend to impair the independence of Cuba, nor in any manner authorize or permit any foreign power or powers to obtain by colonization or for military or naval purposes, or otherwise, lodgement in or control over any portion of said island.

ART. II. The Government of Cuba shall not assume or contract any public debt to pay the interest upon which, and to make reasonable sinking-fund provision for the ultimate discharge of which, the ordinary revenues of the Island of Cuba, after defraying the current expenses of the Government, shall be inadequate.

ART. III. The Government of Cuba consents that the United States may exercise the right to intervene for the preservation of Cuban independence, the maintenance of a government adequate for the protection of life, property, and individual liberty, and for discharging the obligations with respect to Cuba imposed by the treaty of Paris on the United States, now to be assumed and undertaken by the government of Cuba.

ART. IV. All Acts of the United States in Cuba during its military occupancy thereof are ratified and validated, and all lawful rights acquired thereunder shall be maintained and protected.

ART. V. The Government of Cuba will execute, and as far as necessary extend, the plans already devised or other plans to be mutually agreed upon, for the sanitation of the cities of the island, to the end that a recurrence of epidemics and infectious diseases may be prevented thereby assuring protection to the people and commerce of Cuba, as well as to the commerce of the southern ports of the United States and the people residing therein.

ART. VI. The Isle of Pines shall be omitted from the boundaries of Cuba, specified in the Constitution, the title thereto being left to future adjustment by treaty.

ART. VII. To enable the United States to maintain the independence of Cuba, and to protect the people thereof, as well as for its own defense, the government of Cuba will sell or lease to the United States lands necessary for coaling or naval stations at certain specified points to be agreed upon with the President of the United States. . . .

361. CONVENTION WITH PANAMA FOR THE CONSTRUCTION OF A CANAL
Concluded November 18, 1903

(Malloy, ed. *Treaties, Conventions, etc.,* Vol. II, p. 1349 ff.)

Upon the failure of the United States to come   to any satisfactory agreement with Colombia on

the question of an Isthmian Canal, Panama revolted from Colombia and, with the benevolent
protection of the United States, declared her independence. The revolt took place November 3,
1903; our government recognized the Republic of
Panama on the 6th, and concluded a canal
treaty on the 18th of November. The terms are
practically the same as those offered to
Colombia. In order "to remove all misunderstandings growing out of the political events in
Panama in November 1903", the United States
paid to Colombia, in 1922, the sum of $25,-
000,000. The literature on the diplomacy of
the Canal is extensive, but see H. Pringle,
Theodore Roosevelt, Book II, chs. v–vi; W. F.
McCaleb, *Theodore Roosevelt*, p. 145 ff.; H. C.
Hill, *Roosevelt and the Caribbean*; P. Bunau-
Varilla, *Panama*. There is a wealth of material
in Congressional Investigations. See "The Story
of Panama," *Hearings on the Rainey Resolution*,
House Committee on Foreign Affairs, 1912;
Diplomatic History of the Panama Canal, 63d
Congress, 2nd Session, Sen. Doc. No. 474;
Senate.Committee on Inter-Oceanic Canals, 59th
Congress, 2nd Session, Sen. Doc. No. 401.

ART. I. The United States guarantees and
will maintain the independence of the Republic of Panama.

ART. II. The Republic of Panama grants
to the United States in perpetuity the use,
occupation and control of a zone of land and
land under water for the construction, maintenance, operation, sanitation and protection
of said Canal of the width of ten miles extending to the distance of five miles on each
side of the center line of the route of the
canal to be constructed; the said zone beginning in the Caribbean Sea, three marine
miles from mean low water mark, and extending to and across the Isthmus of Panama
into the Pacific Ocean to a distance of three
marine miles from mean low water mark,
with the proviso that the cities of Panama
and Colon and the harbors adjacent to said
cities, which are included within the boundaries of the zone above described, shall not
be included within this grant. The Republic
of Panama further grants to the United
States in perpetuity the use, occupation and
control of any other lands and waters outside of the zone above described which may
be necessary and convenient for the construction, maintenance, operation, sanitation
and protection of the said Canal or of any
auxiliary canals or other works necessary and
convenient for the construction, maintenance,

operation, sanitation and protection of the
said enterprise.

The Republic of Panama further grants
in like manner to the United States in perpetuity all islands within the limits of the
zone above described and in addition thereto
the group of small islands in the Bay of
Panama, named Perico, Naos, Culebra and
Flamenco.

ART. III. The Republic of Panama grants
to the United States all the rights, power
and authority within the zone mentioned and
described in Article II of this agreement and
within the limits of all auxiliary lands and
waters mentioned and described in said Article II which the United States would
possess and exercise if it were the sovereign
of the territory within which said lands and
waters are located to the entire exclusion of
the exercise by the Republic of Panama of
any such sovereign rights, power or authority. . . .

ART. V. The Republic of Panama grants
to the United States in perpetuity a monopoly for the construction, maintenance
and operation of any system of communication by means of canal or railroad across its
territory between the Caribbean Sea and the
Pacific Ocean. . . .

ART. VII. The Republic of Panama grants
to the United States within the limits of the
cities of Panama and Colon and their adjacent harbors and within the territory adjacent thereto the right to acquire by purchase or by the exercise of the right of
eminent domain, any lands, buildings, water
rights or other properties necessary and convenient for the construction, maintenance,
operation and protection of the Canal and of
any works of sanitation, such as the collection and disposition of sewage and the distribution of water in the said cities of Panama and Colon, which, in the discretion of
the United States may be necessary and
convenient for the construction, maintenance,
operation, sanitation and protection of the
said Canal and railroad.

The Republic of Panama agrees that the
cities of Panama and Colon shall comply
in perpetuity with the sanitary ordinances
whether of a preventive or curative character
prescribed by the United States and in case
the Government of Panama is unable or
fails in its duty to enforce this compliance

by the cities of Panama and Colon with the sanitary ordinances of the United States the Republic of Panama grants to the United States the right and authority to enforce the same.

The same right and authority are granted to the United States for the maintenance of public order in the cities of Panama and Colon and the territories and harbors adjacent thereto in case the Republic of Panama should not be, in the judgment of the United States, able to maintain such order.

ART. VIII. The Republic of Panama grants to the United States all rights which it now has or hereafter may acquire to the property of the New Panama Canal Company and the Panama Railroad Company as a result of the transfer of sovereignty from the Republic of Colombia to the Republic of Panama over the Isthmus of Panama and authorizes the New Panama Canal Company to sell and transfer to the United States its rights, privileges, properties and concessions as well as the Panama Railroad and all the shares or part of the shares of that company.

ART. IX. The United States agrees that the ports at either entrance of the Canal and the waters thereof and the Republic of Panama agrees that the towns of Panama and Colon shall be free for all time so that there shall not be imposed or collected custom house tolls, tonnage, anchorage, lighthouse, wharf, pilot or quarantine dues or any other charges or taxes of any kind upon any vessel using or passing through the Canal or belonging to or employed by the United States, directly or indirectly, in connection with the construction, maintenance, operation, sanitation and protection of the main Canal, or auxiliary works, or upon the cargo, officers, crew or passengers of any such vessels, except such tolls and charges as may be imposed by the United States for the use of the Canal and other works, and except tolls and charges imposed by the Republic of Panama upon merchandise destined to be introduced for the consumption of the rest of the Republic of Panama, and upon vessels touching at the ports of Colon and Panama and which do not cross the Canal.

The Government of the Republic of Panama shall have the right to establish in such ports and in the towns of Panama and Colon such houses and guards as it may deem necessary to collect duties on importations destined to other portions of Panama and to prevent contraband trade. The United States shall have the right to make use of the towns and harbors of Panama and Colon as places of anchorage, and for making repairs, for loading, unloading, depositing or trans-shipping cargoes either in transit or destined for the service of the canal and for other works pertaining to the canal.

ART. X. The Republic of Panama agrees that there shall not be imposed any taxes, national, municipal, departmental or of any other class upon the Canal, the railways and auxiliary works, tugs and other vessels employed in the service of the canal, storehouse, workshops, offices, quarters for laborers, factories of all kinds, warehouses, wharves, machinery and other works, property, and effects appertaining to the Canal or railroad and auxiliary works, or their officers or employees, situated within the cities of Panama and Colon, and that there shall not be imposed contributions or charges of a personal character of any kind upon officers, employees, laborers and other individuals in the service of the Canal and railroad and auxiliary works. . . .

ART. XIV. As the price or compensation for the rights, powers and privileges granted in this convention by the Republic of Panama to the United States, the Government of the United States agrees to pay to the Republic of Panama the sum of ten million dollars ($10,000,000) in gold coin of the United States on the exchange of the ratification of this convention and also an annual payment during the life of this convention of two hundred and fifty thousand dollars ($250,-000) in like gold coin, beginning nine years after the date aforesaid.

The provisions of this article shall be in addition to all other benefits assured to the Republic of Panama under this convention.

But no delay or difference of opinion under this article or any other provisions of this treaty shall affect or interrupt the full operation and effect of this convention in all other respects. . . .

ART. XVIII. The Canal, when constructed, and the entrances thereto shall be neutral in perpetuity, and shall be opened upon the terms provided for by Section 1 of Article III of, and in conformity with all the stipulations of, the treaty entered into by the Governments of the United States and Great Britain on November 18, 1901.

ART. XIX. The Government of the Republic of Panama shall have the right to transport over the Canal its vessels and its troops and munitions of war in such vessels at all times without paying charges of any kind. The exemption is to be extended to the auxiliary railway for the transportation of persons in the service of the Republic of Panama, or of the police force charged with the preservation of public order outside of said zone, as well as to their baggage, munitions of war and supplies.

ART. XX. If by virtue of any existing treaty in relation to the territory of the Isthmus of Panama, whereof the obligations shall descend or be assumed by the Republic of Panama, there may be any privilege or concession in favor of the Government or the citizens and subjects of a third power relative to an interoceanic means of communication which in any of its terms may be incompatible with the terms of the present convention, the Republic of Panama agrees to cancel or modify such treaty in due form, for which purpose it shall give to the said third power the requisite notification within the term of four months from the date of the present convention, and in case the existing treaty contains no clause permitting its modifications or annulment, the Republic of Panama agrees to procure its modifications or annulment in such form that there shall not exist any conflict with the stipulations of the present convention. . . .

ART. XXII. The Republic of Panama renounces and grants to the United States the participation to which it might be entitled in the future earnings of the Canal under Article XV of the concessionary contract with Lucien N. B. Wyse, now owned by the New Panama Canal Company, and any and all other rights or claims of a pecuniary nature arising under or relating to said concession, or arising under or relating to the concessions to the Panama Railroad Company or any extension or modification thereof; and it likewise renounces, confirms and grants to the United States, now and hereafter, all the rights and property reserved in the said concessions which otherwise would belong to Panama at or before the expiration of the terms of ninety-nine years of the concessions granted to or held by the above-mentioned party and companies, and all right, title and interest which it now has or may hereafter have, in and to the lands, canal, works, property and rights held by the said companies under said concessions or otherwise, and acquired or to be acquired by the United States from or through the New Panama Canal Company, including any property and rights which might or may in the future either by lapse of time, forfeiture or otherwise, revert to the Republic of Panama under any contracts or concessions, with said Wyse, the Universal Panama Canal Company, the Panama Railroad Company and the New Panama Canal Company.

The aforesaid rights and property shall be and are free and released from any present or reversionary interest in or claims of Panama and the title of the United States thereto upon consummation of the contemplated purchase by the United States from the New Panama Canal Company, shall be absolute, so far as concerns the Republic of Panama, excepting always the rights of the Republic specifically secured under this treaty.

ART. XXIII. If it should become necessary at any time to employ armed forces for the safety or protection of the Canal, or of the ships that make use of the same, or the railways and auxiliary works, the United States shall have the right, at all times and in its discretion, to use its police and its land and naval forces or to establish fortifications for these purposes.

ART. XXIV. No change either in the Government or in the laws and treaties of the Republic of Panama shall, without the consent of the United States, affect any right of the United States under the present convention, or under any treaty stipulation between the two countries that now exists or may hereafter exist touching the subject matter of this convention.

If the Republic of Panama shall hereafter enter as a constituent into any other Government or into any union or confederation of States, so as to merge her sovereignty or independence in such Government, union or confederation, the rights of the United States under this convention shall not be in any respect lessened or impaired.

ART. XXV. For the better performance of the engagements of this convention and to the end of the efficient protection of the Canal and the preservation of its neutrality, the Government of the Republic of Panama will sell or lease to the United States lands adequate and necessary for naval or coaling stations on the Pacific coast and on the western Caribbean coast of the Republic at certain points to be agreed upon with the President of the United States. . . .

JOHN HAY—BUNAU-VARILLA

362. THE ROOSEVELT COROLLARY TO THE MONROE DOCTRINE
1904, 1905

Roosevelt's experience in the Venezuela episode and the outbreak of disorder in Santo Domingo led him to develop the so-called Roosevelt corollary to the Monroe Doctrine—the principle that inasmuch as we permit no European nation to intervene in the affairs of Latin-American countries we must ourselves assume the responsibility of preserving order and protecting life and property in those countries. This principle led to protracted intervention in Santo Domingo and, subsequently, to intervention in Haiti, Nicaragua and Cuba. There is no necessary connection between this principle of moral and police responsibility and the original Monroe Doctrine. Roosevelt formulated his "corollary" in his annual messages of 1904 and 1905. See references, Docs. No. 398, 460, 469.

1. ROOSEVELT'S ANNUAL MESSAGE
December 6, 1904

(Messages and Papers of the Presidents,
Vol. XIV, p. 6923 ff.)

. . . It is not true that the United States feels any land hunger or entertains any projects as regards the other nations of the Western Hemisphere save such as are for their welfare. All that this country desires is to see the neighboring countries stable, orderly, and prosperous. Any country whose people conduct themselves well can count upon our hearty friendship. If a nation shows that it knows how to act with reasonable efficiency and decency in social and political matters, if it keeps order and pays its obligations, it need fear no interference from the United States. Chronic wrongdoing, or an impotence which results in a general loosening of the ties of civilized society, may in America, as elsewhere, ultimately require intervention by some civilized nation, and in the Western Hemisphere the adherence of the United States to the Monroe Doctrine may force the United States, however reluctantly, in flagrant cases of such wrongdoing or impotence, to the exercise of an international police power. If every country washed by the Caribbean Sea would show the progress in stable and just civilization which with the aid of the Platt amendment Cuba has shown since our troops left the island, and which so many of the republics in both Americas are constantly and brilliantly showing, all question of interference by this Nation with their affairs would be at an end. Our interests and those of our southern neighbors are in reality identical. They have great natural riches, and if within their borders the reign of law and justice obtains, prosperity is sure to come to them. While they thus obey the primary laws of civilized society they may rest assured that they will be treated by us in a spirit of cordial and helpful sympathy. We would interfere with them only in the last resort, and then only if it became evident that their inability or unwillingness to do justice at home and abroad had violated the rights of the United States or had invited foreign aggression to the detriment of the entire body of American nations. It is a mere truism to say that every nation, whether in America or anywhere else, which desires to maintain its freedom, its independence, must ultimately realize that the right of such independence can not be separated from the responsibility of making good use of it.

In asserting the Monroe Doctrine, in taking such steps as we have taken in regard to Cuba, Venezuela, and Panama, and in endeavoring to circumscribe the theater of war in the Far East, and to secure the open door in China, we have acted in our own interest as well as in the interest of humanity at large. There are, however, cases in which, while our own interests are not greatly involved, strong appeal is made to our sympathies. . . . But in extreme cases action may be justifiable and proper. What form the action shall take must depend upon the circumstances of the case; that is, upon the degree of the atrocity and upon our power to remedy it. The cases in which we could interfere by force of arms as we interfered to put a stop to intolerable conditions in Cuba are necessarily very few.

2. ROOSEVELT'S ANNUAL MESSAGE
December 5, 1905
(Messages and Papers of the Presidents, Vol. XIV, p. 6994 ff.)

. . . It must be understood that under no circumstances will the United States use the Monroe Doctrine as a cloak for territorial aggression. We desire peace with all the world, but perhaps most of all with the other peoples of the American Continent. There are, of course, limits to the wrongs which any self-respecting nation can endure. It is always possible that wrong actions toward this Nation, or toward citizens of this Nation, in some State unable to keep order among its own people, unable to secure justice from outsiders, and unwilling to do justice to those outsiders who treat it well, may result in our having to take action to protect our rights; but such action will not be taken with a view to territorial aggression, and it will be taken at all only with extreme reluctance and when it has become evident that every other resource has been exhausted.

Moreover, we must make it evident that we do not intend to permit the Monroe Doctrine to be used by any nation on this Continent as a shield to protect it from the consequences of its own misdeeds against foreign nations. If a republic to the south of us commits a tort against a foreign nation. such as an outrage against a citizen of that nation, then the Monroe Doctrine does not force us to interfere to prevent punishment of the tort, save to see that the punishment does not assume the form of territorial occupation in any shape. The case is more difficult when it refers to a contractual obligation. Our own Government has always refused to enforce such contractual obligations on behalf of its citizens by an appeal to arms. It is much to be wished that all foreign governments would take the same view. But they do not; and in consequence we are liable at any time to be brought face to face with disagreeable alternatives. On the one hand, this country would certainly decline to go to war to prevent a foreign government from collecting a just debt; on the other hand, it is very inadvisable to permit any foreign power to take possession, even temporarily, of the custom houses of an American Republic in order to enforce the payment of its obligations; for such temporary occupation might turn into a permanent occupation. The only escape from these alternatives may at any time be that we must ourselves undertake to bring about some arrangement by which so much as possible of a just obligation shall be paid. It is far better that this country should put through such an arrangement, rather than allow any foreign country to undertake it. To do so insures the defaulting republic from having to pay debt of an improper character under duress, while it also insures honest creditors of the republic from being passed by in the interest of dishonest or grasping creditors. Moreover, for the United States to take such a position offers the only possible way of insuring us against a clash with some foreign power. The position is, therefore, in the interest of peace as well as in the interest of justice. It is of benefit to our people; it is of benefit to foreign peoples; and most of all it is really of benefit to the people of the country concerned. . . .

363. NORTHERN SECURITIES COMPANY v. UNITED STATES
193 U. S. 197
1904

Appeal from the circuit court of United States for the district of Minnesota. It was with this celebrated suit that President Roosevelt made his first bid for popularity as a "trust-buster". A struggle between the Harriman and the Hill interests for the control of the stock of the Northern Pacific Railway had ended, in 1901, with the formation of the Northern Securities Company as a holding company to hold the stock of the competing interests. This was the first great holding company, and the question whether such a device constituted a violation of the Sherman Anti-Trust Act was one of great importance. The opinion of Mr. Justice Holmes, who had just been appointed to the Supreme Court, was awaited with particular interest. See, B. H. Meyer, *A History of the Northern Securities Case;* F. B. Clark, *Constitutional Doctrines of Justice Harlan;* D. Richardson, *Constitutional Doctrines of Justice O. W. Holmes.*

HARLAN, J. . . . The Government charges that if the combination was held not to be in violation of the act of Congress, then all efforts of the National Government to preserve to the people the benefits of free competition among carriers engaged in interstate commerce will be wholly unavailing, and all transcontinental lines, indeed the entire railway systems of the country, may be absorbed, merged and consolidated, thus placing the public at the absolute mercy of the holding corporation.

. . . In our judgment, the evidence fully sustains the material allegations of the bill, and shows a violation of the act of Congress, in so far as it declares illegal every combination or conspiracy in restraint of commerce among the several States and with foreign nations, and forbids attempts to monopolize such commerce or any part of it.

. . . Is the act to be construed as forbidding every combination or conspiracy in restraint of trade or commerce among the States or with foreign nations? Or, does it embrace only such restraints as are unreasonable in their nature? Is the motive with which a forbidden combination or conspiracy was formed at all material when it appears that the necessary tendency of the particular combination or conspiracy in question is to restrict or suppress free competition between competing railroads engaged in commerce among the States? Does the act of Congress prescribe, as a *rule* for *interstate* or *international* commerce, that the operation of the natural laws of competition between those engaged in *such* commerce shall not be restricted or interfered with by any contract, combination or conspiracy? . . .

. . . The first case in this court arising under the Anti-Trust Act was *United States* v. *E. C. Knight Co.*, 156 U. S. 1. The next case was that of *United States* v. *Trans-Missouri Freight Association*, 166 U. S. 290. That was followed by *United States* v. *Joint Traffic Association*, 171 U. S. 505, *Hopkins* v. *United States*, 171 U. S. 578, *Anderson* v. *United States*, 171 U. S. 604, *Addyston Pipe & Steel Co.* v. *United States* 175 U. S. 211, and *Montague & Co.* v. *Lowry*, 193 U. S. 38. To these may be added *Pearsall* v. *Great Northern Railway*, 161 U. S. 646, which, although not arising under the Anti-Trust Act, involved an agreement under which the Great Northern and Northern Pacific Railway companies should be consolidated and by which competition between those companies was to cease.

. . . We will not incumber this opinion by extended extracts from the former opinions of this court. It is sufficient to say that from the decisions in the above cases certain propositions are plainly deducible and embrace the present case. Those propositions are:

That although the act of Congress known as the Anti-Trust Act has no reference to the mere manufacture or production of articles or commodities within the limits of the several States, it does embrace and declare to be illegal every contract, combination or conspiracy, in whatever form, of whatever nature, and whoever may be parties to it, which directly or necessarily operates *in restraint* of trade or commerce *among the several States or with foreign nations;*

That the act is not limited to restraints of interstate and international trade or commerce that are unreasonable in their nature, but embraces *all* direct *restraints* imposed by any combination, conspiracy or monopoly upon such trade or commerce;

That railroad carriers engaged in interstate or international commerce are embraced by the act;

That combinations even among *private* manufacturers or dealers whereby interstate or international commerce is restrained are equally embraced by the act;

That Congress has the power to establish *rules* by which *interstate and international* commerce shall be governed, and, by the Anti-Trust Act, has prescribed the rule of free competition among those engaged in such commerce;

That *every* combination or conspiracy which would extinguish competition between otherwise competing railroads engaged in *interstate trade or commerce,* and which would *in that way* restrain such trade or commerce, is made illegal by the act;

That the natural effect of competition is to increase commerce, and an agreement whose direct effect is to prevent this play of competition restrains instead of promotes trade and commerce;

That to vitiate a combination, such as the act of Congress condemns, it need not be shown that the combination, in fact, results or will result in a total suppression of trade or in a complete monopoly, but it is only essential to show that by its necessary operation it tends to restrain interstate or international trade or commerce and to deprive the public of the advantages that flow from free competition;

That the constitutional guarantee of liberty of contract does not prevent Congress from prescribing the rule of free competition for those engaged in *interstate and international* commerce; and,

That under its power to regulate commerce among the several States and with foreign nations, Congress had authority to enact the statute in question. . . .

It is said that whatever may be the power of a State over such subjects Congress cannot forbid single individuals from disposing of their stock in a state corporation, even if such corporation be engaged in interstate and international commerce; that the holding or purchase by a state corporation or the purchase by individuals, of the stock of another

corporation, for whatever purposes, are matters in respect of which Congress has no authority under the Constitution. . . . It is unnecessary in this case to consider such abstract, general questions. The court need not now concern itself with them. . . .

In this connection, it is suggested that the contention of the Government is that the acquisition is itself interstate commerce, if that corporation be engaged in interstate commerce. . . . For instance, it is said that the question here is whether the power of Congress over interstate commerce extends to the regulation of the ownership of the stock in state railroad companies, by reason of their being engaged in such commerce. Again it is said that the only issue in this case is whether the Northern Securities Company can acquire and hold stock in other state corporations. . . . Such statements as to the issues in this case are, we think, wholly unwarranted and are very wide of the mark; it is the setting up of mere men of straw to be easily stricken down. . . . What the Government particularly complains of, indeed, all that it complains of here, is the existence of a combination among the stockholders of competing railroad companies which in violation of the act of Congress restrains interstate and international commerce through the agency of a common corporate trustee designated to act for both companies in repressing free competition between them. . . .

Whether the free operation of the normal laws of competition is a wise and wholesome rule for trade and commerce is an economic question which this court need not consider or determine. Undoubtedly, there are those who think that the general business interests and prosperity of the country will be best promoted if the rule of competition is not applied. But there are others who believe that such a rule is more necessary in these days of enormous wealth than it ever was in any former period of our history. Be all this as it may, Congress has, in effect, recognized the rule of free competition by declaring illegal every combination or conspiracy in restraint of . . . commerce.

Indeed, if the contentions of the defendants are sound, why may not *all* the railway companies in the United States, that are engaged, under state charters, in interstate and international commerce, enter into a combination such as the one here in question, and by the device of a holding corporation obtain the absolute control throughout the entire country of rates for passengers and freight, beyond the power of Congress to protect the public against their exactions? The argument in behalf of the defendants necessarily leads to such results and places Congress, although invested by the people of the United States with full authority to regulate . . . commerce, in a condition of utter helplessness, so far as the protection of the public against such combinations is concerned. . . .

It was said in argument that the circumstances under which the Northern Securities Company obtained the stock of the constituent companies imported simply an investment in the stock of other corporations, a purchase of that stock; which investment or purchase, it was contended was not forbidden by the charter of the company and could not be made illegal by any act of Congress. This view is wholly fallacious. . . . There was no actual investment, in any substantial sense, by the Northern Securities Company in the stock of the two constituent companies. . . . However that company may have acquired for itself the stock in the Great Northern and Northern Pacific Railway companies . . . all the stock it held or acquired in the constituent companies was acquired and held to be used in suppressing competition between those companies. It came into existence only for that purpose. . . .

Guided by these long established rules of construction, it is manifest that if the Anti-Trust Act is held not to embrace a case such as is now before us, the plain intention of the legislative branch of the Government will be defeated. If Congress has not, by the words used in the act, described this and like cases, it would, we apprehend, be impossible to find words that would describe them. . . .

The judgement of the court is that the decree below be and hereby is affirmed. . . .

HOLMES, J., with whom concurred Chief Justice FULLER, Justice WHITE and Justice PECKHAM, dissenting.
. . . Great cases like hard cases make bad law. For great cases are called great, not by reason of their real importance in shaping the law of the future, but because of some accident of immediate overwhelming interest which appeals to the feelings and distorts the judgement. These immediate interests exercise a kind of hydraulic pressure which makes what previously was clear seem doubtful, and before which even well settled principles of law will bend. What we have to do in this case is to find the meaning of some not very difficult words. . . .

. . . We must try, I have tried, to do it with the same freedom of natural and spontaneous interpretation that one would be sure of if the same question arose upon an indictment for a similar act which excited no public attention, and was of importance only to a prisoner before the court. Furthermore, while at times judges need for their work the training of economists or statesmen, and must act in view of their foresight and of consequences, yet when their task is to interpret and apply the words of a statute, their function is merely academic to begin with—to read English intelligently—and a consideration of consequences comes into play, if at all, only when the meaning of the words used is open to reasonable doubt.

The question to be decided is whether, under the act of July 2, 1890, it is unlawful, at any stage of the process, if several men unite to form a corporation for the purpose of buying more than half the stock of each of two competing interstate railroad companies, if they form the corporation, and the corporation buys the stock. I will suppose further that every step is taken, from the beginning, with the single intent of ending competition between the companies. . . .

This act is construed by the Government to affect the purchasers of shares in two railroad companies because of the effect it may have, or, if you like, is certain to have, upon the competition of these roads. If such a remote result of the exercise of an ordinary incident of property and personal freedom is enough to make that exercise unlawful, there is hardly any transaction concerning commerce between the States that may not be made a crime by the finding of a jury or a court. The personal ascendency of one man may be such that it would give to his advice the effect of a command, if he owned but a single share in each road. The tendency of his presence in the stockholders' meetings might be certain to prevent competition, and thus his advice, if not his mere existence, become a crime.

. . . Contracts in restraint of trade are dealt with and defined by the common law. They are contracts with a stranger to the contractor's business, (although in some cases carrying on a similar one,) which wholly or partially restrict the freedom of the contractor in carrying on that business as otherwise he would. The objection of the common law to them was primarily on the contractor's own account. The notion of monopoly did not come in unless the contract covered the whole of England. . . .

. . . The provision of the statute against contracts in restraint of trade has been held to apply to contracts between railroads, otherwise remaining independent, by which they restricted their respective freedom as to rates. This restriction by contract with a stranger to the contractor's business is the ground of the decision in *United States* v. *Joint Traffic Association,* following and affirming *United States* v. *Trans-Missouri Freight Association.* I accept those decisions absolutely, not only as binding upon me, but as decisions which I have no desire to criticize or abridge. But the provision has not been decided, and, it seems to me, could not be decided without perversion of plain language, to apply to an arrangement by which competition is ended through community of interest—an arrangement which leaves the parties without external restriction. That provision, taken alone, does not require that all existing competitions shall be maintained. It does not look primarily, if at all, to competition. It simply requires that a party's freedom in trade between the States shall not be cut down by contract with a stranger. . . .

. . . According to popular speech, every concern monopolizes whatever business it does, and if that business is trade between two States it monopolizes a part of the trade among the States. Of course the statute does not forbid that. It does not mean that all business must cease. A single railroad down a narrow valley or through a mountain gorge monopolizes all the railroad transportation through that valley or gorge. Indeed every railroad monopolizes, in a popular sense, the trade of some area. Yet I suppose that no

one would say that the statute forbids a combination of men into a corporation to build and run such a railroad between the States.

. . . I will suppose that three parties apply to a State for charters; one for each of two new and possibly competing lines respectively, and one for both of these lines, and that the charter is granted to the last. I think that charter would be good, and I think the whole argument to the contrary rests on a popular instead of an accurate and legal conception of what the word "monopolize" in the statute means. I repeat, that in my opinion there is no attempt to monopolize, and what, as I have said, in my judgment amounts to the same thing, that there is no combination in restraint of trade, until something is done with the intent to exclude strangers to the combination from competing with it in some part of the business which it carries on.

Unless I am entirely wrong in my understanding of what a "combination in restraint of trade" means, then the same monopoly may be attempted and effected by an individual, and is made equally illegal in that case by Sec. 2. But I do not expect to hear it maintained that Mr. Morgan could be sent to prison for buying as many shares as he liked of the Great Northern and the Northern Pacific, even if he bought them both at the same time and got more than half the stock of each road. . . .

A partnership is not a contract or combination in restraint of trade between the partners unless the well known words are to be given a new meaning invented for the purpose of this act. . . . The law, I repeat, says nothing about competition, and only prevents its suppression by contracts or combinations in restraint of trade, and such contracts or combinations derive their character as restraining trade from other features than the suppression of competition alone. To see whether I am wrong, the illustrations put in the argument are of use. If I am, then a partnership between two stage drivers who had been competitors in driving across a state line, or two merchants once engaged in rival commerce among the States whether made after or before the act, if now continued, is a crime. For, again I repeat, if the restraint on the freedom of the members of a combination caused by their entering into partnership is a restraint of trade, every such combination, as well the small as the great, is within the act. . . .

I am happy to know that only a minority of my brethren adopt an interpretation of the law which in my opinion would make eternal the *bellum omnium contra omnes* and disintegrate society so far as it could into individual atoms. If that were its intent I should regard calling such a law a regulation of commerce as a mere pretense. It would be an attempt to reconstruct society. I am not concerned with the wisdom of such an attempt, but I believe that Congress was not entrusted by the Constitution with the power to make it and I am deeply persuaded that it has not tried.

364. LOCHNER v. NEW YORK
198 U. S. 45
1905

Error to the County Court of Oneida County, New York. A New York law limited the hours of labor in bakeries to not more than sixty hours a week or ten hours a day. The validity of this law was challenged on the ground that it was not a proper exercise of the police power, but a violation of the rights of contract and of property guaranteed in the Fourteenth Amendment. Compare the decision of the Court here with the decision in *Holden* v. *Hardy*, Doc. No. 344, and *Bunting* v. *Oregon*, Doc. No. 421.

PECKHAM, J. . . . The statute necessarily interferes with the right of contract between the employer and employees, concerning the number of hours in which the latter may labor in the bakery of the employer. The general right to make a contract in relation to his business is part of the liberty of the individual protected by the Fourteenth Amendment of the Federal Constitution. . . . There are, however, certain powers, existing in the sovereignty of each State in the Union, somewhat vaguely termed police powers, the exact description and limitation of which have not been attempted by the courts. These powers, broadly stated and without, at present, any attempt at a more specific definition, relate to the safety, health, morals and general welfare of the public. . . .

The State, therefore, has power to prevent the individual from making certain kinds of contracts, and in regard to them the Federal Constitution offers no protection. If the contract be one which the State, in the legitimate exercise of its police power, has the right to prohibit, it is not prevented from prohibiting it by the Fourteenth Amendment. . . .

. . . This court has recognized the existence and upheld the exercise of the police powers of the States in many cases which might fairly be considered as border ones, and it has, in the course of its determination of questions regarding the asserted invalidity of such statutes, on the ground of their violation of the rights secured by the federal Constitution, been guided by rules of a very liberal nature, the application of which has resulted, in numerous instances, in upholding the validity of state statutes thus assailed. Among the later cases where the state law has been upheld by this court is that of *Holden* v. *Hardy*, 169 U. S. 366. . . .

It will be observed that, even with regard to that class of labor, the Utah statute provided for cases of emergency wherein the provisions of the statute would not apply. The statute now before this court has no emergency clause in it, and, if the statute is valid, there are no circumstances and no emergencies under which the slightest violation of the provisions of the act would be innocent. There is nothing in *Holden* v. *Hardy* which covers the case now before us. . . .

It must, of course, be conceded that there is a limit to the valid exercise of the police power by the State. There is no dispute concerning this general proposition. Otherwise the Fourteenth Amendment would have no efficacy and the legislatures of the States would have unbounded power, and it would be enough to say that any piece of legislation was enacted to conserve the morals, the health, or the safety of the people; such legislation would be valid, no matter how absolutely without foundation the claim might be. The claim of the police power would be a mere pretext—become another and delusive name for the supreme sovereignty of the State to be exercised free from constitutional restraint. This is not contended for. In every case that comes before this court, therefore, where legislation of this character is concerned, and where the protection of the federal Constitution is sought, the question necessarily arises: Is this a fair, reasonable, and appropriate exercise of the police power of the State, or is it an unreasonable, unnecessary, and arbitrary interference with the right of the individual to his personal liberty or to enter into those contracts in relation to labor which may seem to him appropriate or necessary for the support of himself and his family? Of course the liberty of contract relating to labor includes both parties to it. The one has as much right to purchase as the other to sell labor.

This is not a question of substituting the judgment of the court for that of the legislature. If the act be within the power of the State it is valid, although the judgment of the court might be totally opposed to the enactment of such a law. But the question would still remain: Is it within the police power of the State? and that question must be answered by the court.

The question whether this act is valid as a labor law, pure and simple, may be dismissed in a few words. There is no reasonable ground for interfering with the liberty of person or the right of free contract, by determining the hours of labor, in the occupation of a baker. There is no contention that bakers as a class are not equal in intelligence and capacity to men in other trades or manual occupations, or that they are not able to assert their rights and care for themselves without the protecting arm of the State, interfering with their independence of judgment and of action. They are in no sense wards of the State. Viewed in the light of a purely labor law, with no reference whatever to the question of health, we think that a law like the one before us involves neither the safety, the morals, nor the welfare, of the public, and that the interest of the public is not in the slightest degree affected by such an act. The law must be upheld, if at all, as a law pertaining to the health of the individual engaged in the occupation of a baker. It does not affect any other portion of the public than those who are engaged in that occupation. Clean and wholesome bread does not depend upon whether the baker works but ten hours per day or only sixty hours a week. The limitation of the hours of labor does not come within the police power on that ground.

It is a question of which of two powers or rights shall prevail—the power of the State to legislate or the right of the individual to liberty of person and freedom of contract. The mere assertion that the subject relates, though but in a remote degree, to the public health, does not necessarily render the enactment valid. The act must have a more direct relation, as a means to an end, and the end itself must be appropriate and legitimate, before an act can be held to be valid which interferes with the general right of an individual to be free in his person and in his power to contract in relation to his own labor. . . .

We think the limit of the police power has been reached and passed in this case. There is, in our judgment, no reasonable foundation for holding this to be necessary or appropriate as a health law to safeguard the public health, or the health of the individuals who are following the trade of a baker. If this statute be valid, and if, therefore, a proper case is made out in which to deny the right of an individual, *sui juris*, as employer or employee, to make contracts for the labor of the latter under the protection of the provisions of the federal Constitution, there would seem to be no length to which legislation of this nature might not go. . . .

It is impossible for us to shut our eyes to the fact that many of the laws of this character, while passed under what is claimed to be the police power for the purpose of protecting the public health or welfare, are, in reality, passed from other motives. We are justified in saying so when, from the character of the law and the subject upon which it legislates, it is apparent that the public health or welfare bears but the most remote relation to the law. The purpose of a statute must be determined from the natural and legal effect of the language employed; and whether it is or is not repugnant to the Constitution of the United States must be determined from the natural effect of such statutes when put into operation, and not from their proclaimed purpose. . . . The court looks beyond the mere letter of the law in such cases.

. . . The act is not, within any fair meaning of the term, a health law, but is an illegal interference with the rights of individuals, both employers and employees, to make contracts regarding labor upon such terms as they may think best, or which they may agree upon with the other parties to such contracts. Statutes of the nature of that under review, limiting the hours in which grown and intelligent men may labor to earn their living, are mere meddlesome interferences with the rights of the individual, and they are not saved from condemnation by the claim that they are passed in the exercise of the police power and upon the subject of the health of the individual whose rights are interfered with, unless there be some fair ground, reasonable in and of itself, to say that there is material danger to the public health, or to the health of the employees, if the hours of labor are not curtailed. . . .

It is manifest to us that the limitation of the hours of labor as provided for in this section of the statute . . . has no such direct relation to and no such substantial effect upon the health of the employee, as to justify us in regarding the section as really a health law. It seems to us that the real object and purpose were simply to regulate the hours of labor between the master and his employees . . . in a private business, not dangerous in any degree to morals or in any real and substantial degree, to the health of the employees. Under such circumstances the freedom of master and employee to contract with each other in relation to their employment, and in defining the same, cannot be prohibited or interfered with, without violating the Federal Constitution.

Judgement reversed.

HOLMES, J., dissenting. . . . The case is decided upon an economic theory which a large part of the country does not entertain. If it were a question whether I agreed with that theory, I should desire to study it further and long before making up my mind. But I do not conceive that to be my duty, because I strongly believe that my agreement or disagreement has nothing to do with the right of a majority to embody their opinions in law. It is settled by various decisions of this court that state constitutions and state laws may regulate life in many ways which we as legislators might think as injudicious, or if you like as tyrannical, as this, and which, equally with this, interfere with the liberty to contract. Sunday laws and usury laws are ancient examples. A more modern one is the prohibition of lotteries. The liberty of the citizen to do as he likes so long as he does not interfere with the liberty of others to do the same, which has been a shibboleth for some well-known writers, is interfered with by school laws, by the post-office, by every state or municipal institution which takes his money for purposes thought desirable, whether he likes it or not. The Fourteenth Amendment does not enact Mr. Herbert Spencer's Social Statics. . . . United States and state statutes and decisions cutting down the liberty to contract by way of combination are familiar to this court. . . . Some of these laws embody convictions or prejudices which judges are likely to share. Some may not. But a constitution is not intended to embody a particular economic theory, whether of paternalism and the organic relation of the citizen to the state or of *laissez faire*. It is made for people of fundamentally differing views, and the accident of our finding certain opinions natural and familiar, or novel, and even shocking, ought not to conclude our judgement upon the question whether statutes embodying them conflict with the Constitution of the United States.

General propositions do not decide concrete cases. The decision will depend on a judgement or intuition more subtle than any articulate major premise. But I think that the proposition just stated, if it is accepted, will carry us far toward the end. Every opinion tends to become a law. I think that the word "liberty," in the Fourteenth Amendment, is perverted when it is held to prevent the natural outcome of a dominant opinion, unless it can be said that a rational and fair man necessarily would admit that the statute proposed would infringe fundamental principles as they have been understood by the traditions of our people and our law. It does not need research to show that no such sweeping condemnation can be passed upon the statute before us. A reasonable man might think it a proper measure on the score of health. Men whom I certainly could not pronounce unreasonable would uphold it as a first instalment of a general regulation of the hours of work. Whether in the latter aspect it would be open to the charge of inequality I think it unnecessary to discuss.

365. PEOPLE v. WILLIAMS
189 New York, 131
1907

Appeal from order of the Appellate Division of the Supreme Court. Compare the decision in this case to the decision in *Commonwealth* v. *Hamilton Manufacturing Company*, Doc. No. 295.

GRAY, J. The defendant was arrested and convicted upon the charge of having violated the provisions of section 3841 of the Penal Code. . . . The provision of the Labor Law now in question is contained in section 77; which is entitled: "Hours of labor of minors and women" and reads that "No minor under the age of eighteen years, and no female shall be employed, permitted or suffered to work in any factory in this state before six o'clock in the morning, or after nine o'clock in the evening of any day; or for more than ten hours in any one day except to make a shorter work day on the last day of the week; or for more than sixty hours in any one week, or more hours in any one week than will make an average of ten hours per day for the whole number of days so worked." (L. 1903, ch. 184, sec. 2.) The information and the proof were that a female, named Katie Mead, over twenty one years of age, was found by the factory inspector at work in a book binding establishment, in the city of New York, at twenty minutes after ten o'clock in the evening. . . . If the inhibition against employing a female in any factory after that hour was a valid act of legislation, then the defendant came within its operation and he was amenable to punishment. After the defendant had been found guilty, the trial court granted his motion in arrest of judgment and discharged him; holding that the legislative enactment was unconstitutional. The justices of the Appellate Division, in the first department, by a divided vote, have affirmed the order of the trial court.

In my judgment, the determination below was correct. I think that the legislature, in preventing the employment of an adult woman in a factory, and in prohibiting her to work therein, before six o'clock in the morning, or after nine o'clock in the evening has overstepped the limits set by the Constitution of the state to the exercise of power to interfere with the rights of citizens. The fundamental law of the state, as embodied in its Constitution, provides that "no person shall . . . be deprived of life, liberty or property without due process of law." (Art. 1, sec. 6.) The provisions of the State and the Federal Constitutions protect every citizen in the right to pursue any lawful employment in a lawful manner. He enjoys the utmost freedom to follow his chosen pursuit and any arbitrary distinction against, or deprivation of, that freedom by the legislature is an invasion of the constitutional guaranty. Under our laws men and women now stand alike in their constitutional rights and there is no warrant for making any discrimination between them with respect to the liberty of person, or of contract. It is claimed, however, in this case, that the enactment in question can be justified as an exercise of the police power of the state; having for its purpose the general welfare of the state in a measure for the preservation of the health of the female citizens. It is to be observed that it is not a regulation of the number of hours of labor for working women; the enactment goes far beyond this. It attempts to take away the right of a woman to labor before six in the morning, or after nine o'clock in the evening without any reference to other considerations. . . . Except as to women under twenty one years of age, this was the first attempt on the part of the state to restrict their liberty of person, or their freedom of contract, in the pursuit of a vocation. I find nothing in the language of the section which suggests the purpose of promoting health, except as it might be inferred that for a woman to work during the forbidden hours of night would be unhealthful. If the inhibition of the section in question had been framed to prevent the ten hours of work from being performed at night, or to prolong them beyond nine o'clock in the evening, it might, more readily, be appreciated that the health of women was the matter of legislative concern. That is not the effect, nor the sense, of the provision of the section with which, alone, we are dealing. It was not the case upon which this defendant was convicted. If this enactment is to be sustained, then an adult woman, although a citizen and entitled as such to all the rights of citizenship under our laws, may not be employed, nor contract to work, in any factory for any period of time, no matter how short, if it is within the prohibited hours; and this, too, without any regard to the healthfulness of the employment. It is clear, as it seems to me, that this legislation cannot, and should not, be upheld as a proper exercise of the police power. It is, certainly, discriminative against female citizens, in denying to them equal rights with men in the same pursuit. The courts have gone very far in upholding legislative enactments, framed clearly for the welfare, comfort and health of the community, and that a wide range in the exercise of the police power of the state should be conceded, I do not deny; but, when it is sought under the guise of a labor law, arbitrarily, as here, to prevent an adult female citizen from working at any

time of the day that suits her, I think it is time to call a halt. It arbitrarily deprives citizens of their right to contract with each other. The tendency of legislatures, in the form of regulatory measures, to interfere with the lawful pursuits of citizens is becoming a marked one in this country, and it behooves the courts, firmly and fearlessly, to interpose the barriers of their judgments, when invoked to protect against legislative acts, plainly transcending the powers conferred by the Constitution upon the legislative body. . . .

Without extended reference to the cases bearing upon the much discussed subject of the exercise of the police power, I need only refer to the recent case of *Lochner* v. *State of New York*, (198 U. S. 45); where the Supreme Court of the United States had before it a case arising in this state under a provision of the Labor Law, which restricted the hours of labor for the employés of bakers. . . . It was held that bakers "are in no sense wards of the State.". . .

So I think, in this case, that we should say, as an adult female is in no sense a ward of the state, that she is not to be made the special object of the exercise of the paternal power of the state and that the restriction, here imposed upon her privilege to labor, violates the constitutional guarantees. In the gradual course of legislation upon the rights of a woman in this state, she has come to possess all of the responsibilities of the man and she is entitled to be placed upon an equality of rights with the man.

It might be observed that working in a factory in the night hours is not the only situation of menace to the working woman; but such occupation is, arbitrarily, debarred her.

For these reasons, I advise that the order appealed from should be affirmed.

366. MULLER v. OREGON
208 U. S. 412
1908

Error to the supreme court of Oregon. An Oregon law of 1903 prohibited the employment of any female in any factory or laundry for more than ten hours a day. Mr. Louis Brandeis, subsequently Justice of the Supreme Court, was one of the counsel for the state of Oregon, and produced a mass of evidence of a statistical, sociological, and historical character bearing on the reasonableness of the law in question, which was admitted by the court. Mr. Brandeis's brief was printed by the National Consumers' League as *Women in Industry*.

BREWER, J. . . . The single question is the constitutionality of the statute under which the defendant was convicted, so far as affects the work of a female in a laundry. . . .

It is the law of Oregon that women, whether married or single, have equal contractual and personal rights with men. . . .

It thus appears that, putting to one side the elective franchise, in the matter of personal and contractual rights they stand on the same plane as the other sex. Their rights in these respects can no more be infringed than the equal rights of their brothers. We held in Lochner v. New York, 198 U. S. 45, that a law providing that no laborer shall be required or permitted to work in a bakery more than sixty hours in a week or ten hours in a day was not as to men a legitimate exercise of the police power of the State, but an unreasonable, unnecessary, and arbitrary interference with the right and liberty of the individual to contract in relation to his labor, and as such was in conflict with, and void under, the federal Constitution. That decision is invoked by plaintiff in error as decisive of the question before us. But this assumes that the difference between the sexes does not justify a different rule respecting a restriction of the hours of labor.

. . . It may not be amiss, in the present case, before examining the constitutional question, to notice the course of legislation, as well as expressions of opinion from other than judicial sources. In the brief filed by Mr. Louis D. Brandeis for the defendant in error is a very copious collection of all these matters. . . .

The legislation and opinions referred to . . . may not be, technically speaking, authorities, and in them is little or no discussion of the constitutional question presented to us for determination, yet they are significant of a widespread belief that woman's physical structure, and the functions she performs in consequence thereof, justify special legislation restricting or qualifying the conditions under which she should be permitted to toil. Constitutional questions, it is true, are not settled by even a consensus of present public opinion, for it is the peculiar value of a written constitution that it places in unchanging form limitations upon legislative action, and thus gives a permanence and stability to popular government which other-

wise would be lacking. At the same time, when a question of fact is debated and debatable, and the extent to which a special constitutional limitation goes is affected by the truth in respect to that fact, a widespread and long-continued belief concerning it is worthy of consideration. We take judicial cognizance of all matters of general knowledge. . . .

That woman's physical structure and the performance of maternal functions place her at a disadvantage in the struggle for subsistence is obvious. This is especially true when the burdens of motherhood are upon her. Even when they are not, by abundant testimony of the medical fraternity continuance for a long time on her feet at work, repeating this from day to day, tends to injurious effects upon the body, and, as healthy mothers are essential to vigorous offspring, the physical well-being of woman becomes an object of public interest and care in order to preserve the strength and vigor of the race. . . .

Differentiated by these matters from the other sex, she is properly placed in a class by herself, and legislation designed for her protection may be sustained, even when like legislation is not necessary for men, and could not be sustained. It is impossible to close one's eyes to the fact that she still looks to her brother and depends upon him. Even though all restrictions on political, personal, and contractual rights were taken away, and she stood, so far as statutes are concerned, upon an absolutely equal plane with him, it would still be true that she is so constituted that she will rest upon and look to him for protection; that her physical structure and a proper discharge of her maternal functions—having in view not merely her own health, but the well-being of the race—justify legislation to protect her from the greed as well as the passion of man. The limitations which this statute places upon her contractual powers, upon her right to agree with her employer as to the time she shall labor, are not imposed solely for her benefit, but also largely for the benefit of all. Many words cannot make this plainer. The two sexes differ in structure of body, in the functions to be performed by each, in the amount of physical strength, in the capacity for long continued labor, particularly when done standing, the influence of vigorous health upon the future well-being of the race, the self-reliance which enables one to assert full rights, and in the capacity to maintain the struggle for subsistence. This difference justifies a difference in legislation, and upholds that which is designed to compensate for some of the burdens which rest upon her. . . .

For these reasons, and without questioning in any respect the decision in *Lochner* v. *New York*, we are of the opinion that it cannot be adjudged that the act in question is in conflict with the federal Constitution, so far as it respects the work of a female in a laundry, and the judgment of the supreme court of Oregon is
Affirmed.

367. JAPANESE IMMIGRATION—THE GENTLEMEN'S AGREEMENT
1908

(Report of the Commissioner General of Immigration, 1908, p. 125)

The growing number of Japanese in California, and the hostility of labor to Oriental competition, led to an agitation against Japanese immigration that culminated in the San Francisco school laws of 1906. These laws required, in insulting terms, that Chinese, Japanese, and Korean children attend a separate Oriental Public School. The danger of further hostile legislation led President Roosevelt to conclude with Japan the famous Gentlemen's Agreement,—an executive agreement, the exact terms of which have never been revealed. The agreement salved the pride of Japan, and temporarily placated the Californians. By permitting the immigration of wives, it increased the Japanese population in California materially, and was eventually superseded by the Immigration Act of 1924. See, E. G. Mears, *Resident Orientals on the American Pacific Coast;* S. L. Gulick, *The American Japanese Problem;* E. Root, "The Real Questions under the Japanese Treaty and the San Francisco School Board Resolution," *Proc. Am. Soc. of International Law,* 1907; K. K. Amakami, *The Real Japanese Question;* T. Iyenaga and K. Sato, *Japan and the California Problem;* R. D. McKenzie, *Oriental Exclusion;* J. E. Johnsen, ed. *Japanese Exclusion.*

In order that the best results might follow from an enforcement of the regulations, an understanding was reached with Japan that the existing policy of discouraging emigration of its subjects of the laboring classes to continental United States should be continued, and should, by co-operation with the governments, be made as effective as possible. This understanding contemplates that the Japanese government shall issue passports to continental United States only to such of its subjects as are non-laborers or are laborers who, in coming to the continent, seek to resume a formerly acquired domicile, to join a parent, wife, or children residing there, or to assume active control of an already possessed interest in a farming enterprise in this country, so that the three classes of laborers entitled to receive passports have come to be designated "former residents," "parents, wives, or children of residents," and "settled agriculturists."

With respect to Hawaii, the Japanese government of its own volition stated that, experimentally at least, the issuance of passports to members of the laboring classes proceeding thence would be limited to "former residents" and "parents, wives, or children of residents." The said government has also been exercising a careful supervision over the subject of emigration of its laboring class to foreign contiguous territory.

368. ADAIR v. UNITED STATES
208 U. S. 161
1908

Error to the District Court of United States for Eastern District of Kentucky to review conviction of an agent of an interstate carrier for discharging an employee from service because of his membership in a labor organization.

HARLAN, J. This case involves the constitutionality of certain provisions of the act of Congress of June 1, 1898, . . . concerning carriers engaged in interstate commerce and their employees. . . .

The 10th section upon which the present prosecution is based is in these words:

"That any employer subject to the provisions of this act, . . . who shall require any employee, or any person seeking employment, as a condition of such employment, to enter into an agreement, either written or verbal, not to become or remain a member of any labor corporation, association, or organization; . . . is hereby declared to be guilty of a disdemeanor. . . ."

The specific charge . . . was "that said William Adair, agent and employee of said common carrier and employer, . . . did unlawfully and unjustly discriminate against O. B. Coppage, employee, . . . by then and there discharging said O. B. Coppage from such employment . . . *because of his membership in said labor organization and thereby did unjustly discriminate against an employee of a common carrier and employer engaged in interstate commerce because of his membership in a labor organization,* contrary to the forms of the Statute.". . .

May Congress make it a criminal offense against the United States—as, by the 10th section of the Act of 1898 it does,—for an agent or officer of an interstate carrier, . . . to discharge an employee from service simply because of his membership in a labor organization? . . .

The first inquiry is whether the part of the 10th section of the Act of 1898 upon which the first count of the indictment is based is repugnant to the 5th Amendment to the Constitution, declaring that no person shall be deprived of liberty or property without due process of law. In our opinion that section in the particular mentioned is an invasion of the personal liberty, as well as of the right of property, guaranteed by that Amendment. Such liberty and right embrace the right to make contracts for the purchase of the labor of others, and equally the right to make contracts for the sale of one's own labor; each right, however, being subject to the fundamental condition that no contract, whatever its subject-matter, can be sustained which the law, upon reasonable grounds, forbids as inconsistent with the public interest, or as hurtful to the public order, or as detrimental to the common good. . . . It is sufficient in this case to say that, as agent of the railroad company, and, as such, responsible for the conduct of the business of one of its departments, it was the defendant Adair's right—and that right inhered in his personal liberty, and was also a right of property— to serve his employer as best he could, so long as he did nothing that was reasonably forbidden by law as injurious to the public interest. It was the right of the defendant to prescribe the terms upon which the services of Coppage would be accepted, and it was the right of Coppage to become or not, as he chose, an employee of the railroad company upon the terms offered to him. . . .

In every case that comes before this court, therefore, where legislation of this character is concerned, . . . the question necessarily arises: Is this a fair, reasonable, and appropriate exercise of the police power of the state, or is it an unreasonable, unnecessary, and arbitrary interference with the right of the individual to his personal liberty or to enter into those contracts in relation to labor which may seem to him appropriate or necessary for the support of himself and his family? . . .

While, . . . the right of liberty and property guaranteed by the Constitution against deprivation without due process of law is subject to such reasonable restraints as the common good or the general welfare may require, it is not within the functions of government . . . to compel any person in the course of his business and against his will, to accept or retain the personal services of another, or to compel any person, against his will, to perform personal services for another. . . .

As the relations and the conduct of the parties towards each other was not controlled by any contract other than a general employment on one side to accept the services of the employee and a general agreement on the other side to render services to the employer,—no term being fixed for the continuance of the employment,—Congress could not, consistently with the 5th Amendment, make it a crime against the United States to discharge the employee because of his being a member of a labor organization.

But it is suggested that the authority to make it a crime . . . can be referred to the power of Congress to regulate interstate commerce, without regard to any question of personal liberty or right of property arising under the 5th Amendment. This suggestion can have no bearing, in the present discussion unless the statute, in the particular just stated, is, within the meaning of the Constitution, a regulation of commerce among the States. If it be not, then clearly the government cannot invoke the commerce clause of the Constitution as sustaining the indictment against Adair. . . .

Looking alone at the words of the statute for the purpose of ascertaining its scope and effect, and of determining its validity, we hold that there is no such connection between interstate commerce and membership in a labor organization as to authorize Congress to make it a crime against the United States for an agent of an interstate carrier to discharge an employee because of such membership on his part. . . .

It results, on the whole case, that the provision of the statute under which the defendant was convicted must be held to be repugnant to the 5th Amendment and as not embraced by nor within the power of Congress to regulate interstate commerce, but, under the guise of regulating commerce, and as applied to this case, it arbitrarily sanctions an illegal invasion of the personal liberty as well as the right of property of the defendant Adair.

Judgement reversed.

HOLMES, J., dissenting: I . . . think that the statute is Constitutional, and, but for the decision of my brethren, I should have felt pretty clear about it.

As we all know, there are special labor unions of men engaged in the service of carriers. These unions exercise a direct influence upon the employment of labor in that business, upon the terms of such employment, and upon the business itself. Their very existence is directed specifically to the business, and their connection with it is, at least, as intimate and important, as that of safety couplers, and, I should think, as the liability of master to servant,—matters which, it is admitted, Congress might regulate so far as they concerned commerce among the states. I suppose that it hardly would be denied that some of the relations of railroads with unions of railroad employees are closely enough connected with commerce to justify legislation by Congress. If so, legislation to prevent the exclusion of such unions from employment is sufficiently near.

The ground on which this particular law is held bad, is not so much that it deals with matters remote from commerce among the states, as that it interferes with the paramount individual rights secured by the 5th Amendment. The section is, in substance, a very limited interference with freedom of contract, no more. It does not require the carriers to employ anyone. It does not forbid them to refuse to employ anyone, for any reason they deem good, even where the notion of a choice of persons is a fiction and wholesale employment is necessary upon general principles that it might be proper to control. The section simply prohibits the more powerful party to exact certain undertakings, or to threaten dismissal or unjustly discriminate on certain grounds against those already employed. I hardly can suppose that the grounds on which a contract lawfully may be made to end are less open to regulation than other terms. So I turn to the general question whether the employment can be regulated at all. I confess that I think that the right to make contracts at will that has been derived from the word "liberty" in the Amendments, has been stretched to its extreme by the decisions; but they agree that sometimes the right may be restrained. Where there is, or generally is believed to be, an important ground of public policy for restraint, the Constitution does not forbid it, whether this court agrees or disagrees with the policy pursued. It cannot be doubted that to prevent strikes and, so far as possible, to foster its scheme of arbitration, might be deemed by Congress an important point of policy, and I think it impossible to say that Congress might not reasonably think that the provision in question would help a good deal to carry its policy along. But suppose the only effect really were to tend to bring about the complete unionizing of such railroad laborers as Congress can deal with, I think that object alone would justify the act. I quite agree that the question what and how much good labor unions do, is one on which intelligent people may differ; I think that laboring men sometimes attribute to them advantages, as many attribute to combinations of capital, disadvantages, that really are due to economic conditions of a far wider and deeper kind; but I could not pronounce it unwarranted if Congress should decide that to foster a strong union was for the best interests, not only of the men, but of the railroads and the country at large.

369. THE CONSERVATION OF NATURAL RESOURCES
Roosevelt's Seventh Annual Message to Congress
Dec. 3, 1907
(*The Works of Theodore Roosevelt*, Vol. XV, p. 443 ff.)

Of all Roosevelt's policies, that of conservation of the natural resources of the nation was of the most permanent significance. In his first message to Congress he had announced that the forest and water problems were the most vital domestic problems facing the American people, and during his administration he succeeded in setting aside almost 150,000,000 acres of timber land and some 85,000,000 acres of mineral lands in Alaska. More than this, he dramatized the problem of conservation before the country by his speeches, his actions, and by the convening of the Conservation Conference, Doc. No. 370. On Roosevelt and conservation, see, *Theodore Roosevelt, an Autobiography*, ch. xi; the various *Reports* of the Public Lands Commission, the Inland Waterways Commission, and the National Conservation Commission; C. R. Van Hise, *Conservation of Natural Resources in the United States;* F. H. Newell, *Irrigation in the United States;* W. E. Smyth, *The Conquest of Arid America;* G. Pinchot, *The Fight for Conservation;* B. H. Hibbard, *History of Public Land Policies*, ch. xxii; on the enduring nature of the problem, see S. Chase, *The Tragedy of Waste.*

To the Senate and House of Representatives:
    . . . The conservation of our natural resources and their proper use constitute the fundamental problem which underlies almost every other problem of our national life. . . . As a nation we not only enjoy a wonderful measure of present prosperity but if this prosperity is used aright it is an earnest of future success such as no other nation will have. The reward of foresight for this nation is great and easily foretold. But there must be the look ahead, there must be a realization of the fact that to waste, to destroy, our natural resources, to skin and exhaust the land instead of using it so as to increase its usefulness, will result in undermining in the days of our children the very prosperity which we ought by right to hand down to them amplified and developed. For the last few years, through several agencies, the government has been endeavoring to get our people to look ahead and to substitute a planned and orderly development of our resources in place of a haphazard striving for immediate profit. Our great river systems should be developed as national water highways, the Mississippi, with its tributaries, standing first in importance, and the Columbia second, although there are many others of importance on the Pacific, the Atlantic, and the Gulf slopes. The National Government should undertake this work, and I hope a beginning will be made in the present Congress; and the greatest of all our rivers, the Mississippi, should receive special attention. From the Great Lakes to the mouth of the Mississippi there should be a deep waterway, with deep waterways leading from it to the East and the West. Such a waterway would practically mean the extension of our coastline into the very heart of our country. It would be of incalculable benefit to our people. If begun at once it can be carried through in time appreciably to relieve the congestion of our great freight-carrying lines of railroads. The work should be systematically and continuously carried forward in accordance with some well-conceived plan. The main streams should be improved to the highest point of efficiency before the improvement of the branches is attempted; and the work should be kept free from every taint of recklessness or jobbery. The inland waterways which lie just back of the whole Eastern and Southern coasts should likewise be developed. Moreover, the development of our waterways involves many other important water problems, all of which should be considered as part of the same general scheme. The government dams should be used to produce hundreds of thousands of horse-power as an incident to improving nav-

igation; for the annual value of the unused water-power of the United States perhaps exceeds the annual value of the products of all our mines. As an incident to creating the deep waterways down the Mississippi, the government should build along its whole lower length levees which, taken together with the control of the headwaters, will at once and forever put a complete stop to all threat of floods in the immensely fertile delta region. The territory lying adjacent to the Mississippi along its lower course will thereby become one of the most prosperous and populous, as it already is one of the most fertile, farming regions in all the world. I have appointed an inland waterways commission to study and outline a comprehensive scheme of development along all the lines indicated. Later I shall lay its report before the Congress.

Irrigation should be far more extensively developed than at present, not only in the States of the great plains and the Rocky Mountains, but in many others, as, for instance, in large portions of the South Atlantic and Gulf States, where it should go hand in hand with the reclamation of swamp-land. The Federal Government should seriously devote itself to this task, realizing that utilization of waterways and water-power, forestry, irrigation, and the reclamation of lands threatened with overflow, are all interdependent parts of the same problem. The work of the Reclamation Service in developing the larger opportunities of the Western half of our country for irrigation is more important than almost any other movement. The constant purpose of the government in connection with the Reclamation Service has been to use the water resources of the public lands for the ultimate greatest good of the greatest number; in other words, to put upon the land permanent home-makers, to use and develop it for themselves and for their children and children's children. . . .

The effort of the government to deal with the public land has been based upon the same principle as that of the Reclamation Service. The land law system which was designed to meet the needs of the fertile and well-watered regions of the Middle West has largely broken down when applied to the drier regions of the great plains, the mountains, and much of the Pacific slope, where

a farm of 160 acres is inadequate for self-support. . . . Three years ago a public-lands commission was appointed to scrutinize the law, and defects, and recommend a remedy. Their examination specifically showed the existence of great fraud upon the public domain, and their recommendations for changes in the law were made with the design of conserving the natural resources of every part of the public lands by putting it to its best use. Especial attention was called to the prevention of settlement by the passage of great areas of public land into the hands of a few men, and to the enormous waste caused by unrestricted grazing upon the open range. The recommendations of the Public-Lands Commission are sound, for they are especially in the interest of the actual home-maker; and where the small home-maker cannot at present utilize the land they provide that the government shall keep control of it so that it may not be monopolized by a few men. The Congress has not yet acted upon these recommendations, but they are so just and proper, so essential to our national welfare, that I feel confident, if the Congress will take time to consider them, that they will ultimately be adopted.

Some such legislation as that proposed is essential in order to preserve the great stretches of public grazing-land which are unfit for cultivation under present methods and are valuable only for the forage which they supply. These stretches amount in all to some 300,000,000 acres, and are open to the free grazing of cattle, sheep, horses, and goats, without restriction. Such a system, or lack of system, means that the range is not so much used as wasted by abuse. As the West settles, the range becomes more and more overgrazed. Much of it cannot be used to advantage unless it is fenced, for fencing is the only way by which to keep in check the owners of nomad flocks which roam hither and thither, utterly destroying the pastures and leaving a waste behind so that their presence is incompatible with the presence of home-makers. The existing fences are all illegal. . . . All these fences, those that are hurtful and those that are beneficial, are alike illegal and must come down. But it is an outrage that the law should necessitate such action on the part of the Administration. The unlawful fencing of public lands for private grazing must be stopped, but the necessity which occasioned it must be provided for. The Federal Government should have control of the range, whether by permit or lease, as local necessities may determine. Such control could secure the great benefit of legitimate fencing, while at the same time securing and promoting the settlement of the country. . . . The government should part with its title only to the actual home-maker, not to the profit-maker who does not care to make a home. Our prime object is to secure the rights and guard the interests of the small ranchman, the man who ploughs and pitches hay for himself. It is this small ranchman, this actual settler and home-maker, who in the long run is most hurt by permitting thefts of the public land in whatever form.

Optimism is a good characteristic, but if carried to an excess it becomes foolishness. We are prone to speak of the resources of this country as inexhaustible; this is not so. The mineral wealth of the country, the coal, iron, oil, gas, and the like, does not reproduce itself, and therefore is certain to be exhausted ultimately; and wastefulness in dealing with it today means that our descendants will feel the exhaustion a generation or two before they otherwise would. But there are certain other forms of waste which could be entirely stopped—the waste of soil by washing, for instance, which is among the most dangerous of all wastes now in progress in the United States, is easily preventable, so

that this present enormous loss of fertility is entirely unnecessary. The preservation or replacement of the forests is one of the most important means of preventing this loss. We have made a beginning in forest preservation. but . . . so rapid has been the rate of exhaustion of timber in the United States in the past, and so rapidly is the remainder being exhausted, that the country is unquestionably on the verge of a timber famine which will be felt in every household in the land. . . . The present annual consumption of lumber is certainly three times as great as the annual growth; and if the consumption and growth continue unchanged, practically all our lumber will be exhausted in another generation, while long before the limit to complete exhaustion is reached the growing scarcity will make itself felt in many blighting ways upon our national welfare. About twenty per cent of our forested territory is now reserved in national forests; but these do not include the most valuable timberlands, and in any event the proportion is too small to expect that the reserves can accomplish more than a mitigation of the trouble which is ahead for the nation. . . . We should acquire in the Appalachian and White Mountain regions all the forest-lands that it is possible to acquire for the use of the nation. These lands, because they form a national asset, are as emphatically national as the rivers which they feed, and which flow through so many States before they reach the ocean. . . .

370. DECLARATION OF THE CONSERVATION CONFERENCE
May 15, 1908

(Proceedings of a Conference of Governors, May 13–15, 1908, p. 192 ff.)

To cap his work for the conservation of natural resources, President Roosevelt called a conference of governors, congressmen, supreme court justices, members of the cabinet, and other distinguished public men, to consider the broad problem of conservation. The conference adopted the resolution given below, and provided for the appointment of thirty-six state conservation commissions and a national conservation commission. The national commission, of which Gifford Pinchot was chairman, prepared an inventory of the natural resources of the country. On conservation see references in Doc. No. 369.

DECLARATION

We the Governors of the States and Territories of the United States of America, in Conference assembled, do hereby declare the conviction that the great prosperity of our country rests upon the abundant resources of the land chosen by our forefathers for their homes and where they laid the foundation of this great Nation.

We look upon these resources as a heritage to be made use of in establishing and promoting the comfort, prosperity, and happiness of the American People, but not to be wasted, deteriorated, or needlessly destroyed.

We agree that our country's future is involved in this; that the great natural resources supply the material basis on which our civilization must continue to depend, and on which the perpetuity of the Nation itself rests.

We agree, in the light of facts brought to our knowledge and from information received from sources which we can not doubt, that this material basis is threatened with exhaustion. Even as each succeeding generation from the birth of the Nation has performed its part in promoting the progress and development of the Republic, so do we in this generation recognize it as a high duty to perform our part; and this duty in large degree lies in the adoption of measures for the conservation of the natural wealth of the country.

We declare our firm conviction that this conservation of our natural resources is a subject of transcendent importance, which should engage unremittingly the attention of the Nation, the States, and the People in earnest cooperation. These natural resources include the land on which we live and which yields our food; the living waters which fertilize the soil, supply power, and form great avenues of commerce; the forests which yield the materials for our homes, prevent erosion of the soil, and conserve the navigation and other uses of our streams; and the minerals which form the basis of our industrial life, and supply us with heat, light, and power.

We agree that the land should be so used that erosion and soil-wash shall cease; that there should be reclamation of arid and semi-arid regions by means of irrigation, and of swamp and overflowed regions by means of drainage; that the waters should be so conserved and used as to promote navigation, to enable the arid regions to be reclaimed by irrigation, and to develop power in the interests of the People; that the forests which regulate our rivers, support our industries, and promote the fertility and productiveness of the soil should be preserved and perpetuated; that the minerals found so abundantly beneath the surface should be so used as to prolong their utility; that the beauty, healthfulness, and habitability of our country should be preserved and increased; that the

sources of national wealth exist for the benefit of the People, and that monopoly thereof should not be tolerated.

We commend the wise forethought of the President in sounding the note of warning as to the waste and exhaustion of the natural resources of the country, and signify our high appreciation of his action in calling this Conference to consider the same and to seek remedies therefor through cooperation of the Nation and the States.

We agree that this cooperation should find expression in suitable action by the Congress within the limits of and coextensive with the national jurisdiction of the subject, and, complementary thereto, by the legislatures of the several States within the limits of and coextensive with their jurisdiction.

We declare the conviction that in the use of the natural resources our independent States are interdependent and bound together by ties of mutual benefits, responsibilities and duties.

We agree in the wisdom of future conferences between the President, Members of Congress, and the Governors of States on the conservation of our natural resources with a view of continued cooperation and action on the lines suggested; and to this end we advise that from time to time, as in his judgment may seem wise, the President call the Governors of the States and Members of Congress and others into conference.

We agree that further action is advisable to ascertain the present condition of our natural resources and to promote the conservation of the same; and to that end we recommend the appointment by each State of a Commission on the Conservation of Natural Resources, to cooperate with each other and with any similar commission of the Federal Government.

We urge the continuation and extension of forest policies adapted to secure the husbanding and renewal of our diminishing timber supply, the prevention of soil erosion, the protection of headwaters, and the maintenance of the purity and navigability of our streams. We recognize that the private ownership of forest lands entails responsibilities in the interests of all the People, and we favor the enactment of laws looking to the protection and replacement of privately owned forests.

We recognize in our waters a most valuable asset of the People of the United States, and we recommend the enactment of laws looking to the conservation of water resources for irrigation, water supply, power, and navigation, to the end that navigable and source streams may be brought under complete control and fully utilized for every purpose. We especially urge on the Federal Congress the immediate adoption of a wise, active, and thorough waterway policy, providing for the prompt improvement of our streams and the conservation of their water-

sheds required for the uses of commerce and the protection of the interests of our People.

We recommend the enactment of laws looking to the prevention of waste in the mining and extraction of coal, oil, gas, and other minerals with a view to their wise conservation for the use of the People, and to the protection of human life in the mines.

Let us conserve the foundations of our prosperity.

Respectfully submitted,

[SIGNATURES]

371. THE SOCIAL CREED OF THE CHURCHES

Statement Adopted by the General Conference of the Methodist Episcopal Church
May 1908

(*A Year Book of the Church and Social Service in the United States,* ed. by
H. F. Ward, 1916, p. 197–8)

One of the most significant developments in the history of the church in America is the movement for the socialization of Christianity. While the roots of this movement go back to the period of the rise of Unitarianism, it reached its climax in the first two decades of the twentieth century. See, A. M. Schlesinger, *The Rise of the City,* ch. x; W. E. Garrison, *The March of Faith;* W. Gladden, *Recollections;* S. Matthews, "The Development of Social Christianity in America," in G. B. Smith, ed. *Religious Thought in the Last Quarter Century;* J. R. Commons, *Social Reform and the Church;* W. Rauschenbusch, *Christianity and the Social Crisis;* H. F. Ward, *The Social Creed of the Churches;* R. T. Ely, *Social Aspects of Christianity;* F. G. Peabody, *Jesus Christ and the Social Question;* G. Taylor, *Social Idealism and the Changing Theology.*

The Methodist Episcopal Church stands:

For equal rights and complete justice for all men in all stations of life.

For the principle of conciliation and arbitration in industrial dissensions.

For the protection of the worker from dan-

gerous machinery, occupational disease, injuries and mortality.

For the abolition of child labor.

For such regulation of the conditions of labor for women as shall safeguard the physical and moral health of the community.

For the suppression of the "sweating system."

For the gradual and reasonable reduction of the hours of labor to the lowest practical point, with work for all; and for that degree of leisure for all which is the condition of the highest human life.

For a release from employment one day in seven.

For a living wage in every industry.

For the highest wage that each industry can afford, and for the most equitable division of the products in industry that can ultimately be devised.

For the recognition of the Golden Rule, and the mind of Christ as the supreme law of society and the sure remedy for all social ills.

372. THE ROOT-TAKAHIRA AGREEMENT
November 30, 1908

(*Foreign Relations of the United States,* 1908, p. 510–511)

This agreement was brought about by an exchange of notes between the Japanese Ambassador and Secretary of State Root. By it Japan apparently confirmed the Open Door policy in

China, and both nations bound themselves to maintain the existing *status quo* in China. In as much as Japan had, in the preceding years, concluded a number of secret agreements with

China and with Russia, giving to her exceptional privileges in China and Manchuria, the significance of the agreement is somewhat ambiguous. See, W. W. Willoughby, *Foreign Rights and Interests in China,* 2 Vols.; G. H. Blakeslee, ed., *Japan and Japanese-American Relations;* H. K. Norton, *China and the Powers;* P. J. Treat, *Japan and the United States, 1853–1921.*

The Japanese Ambassador to the Secretary of State

Imperial Japanese Embassy
Washington, November 30, 1908

Sir: The exchange of views between us, which has taken place at the several interviews which I have recently had the honor of holding with you, has shown that Japan and the United States holding important outlying insular possessions in the region of the Pacific Ocean, the Governments of the two countries are animated by a common aim, policy, and intention in that region.

Believing that a frank avowal of that aim, policy, and intention would not only tend to strengthen the relations of friendship and good neighborhood, which have immemorially existed between Japan and the United States, but would materially contribute to the preservation of the general peace, the Imperial Government have authorized me to present to you an outline of their understanding of that common aim, policy and intention.

1. It is the wish of the two Governments to encourage the free and peaceful development of their commerce on the Pacific Ocean.

2. The policy of both Governments, uninfluenced by any aggressive tendencies, is directed to the maintenance of the existing status quo in the region above mentioned and to the defense of the principle of equal opportunity for commerce and industry in China.

3. They are accordingly firmly resolved reciprocally to respect the territorial possessions belonging to each other in said region.

4. They are also determined to preserve the common interest of all powers in China by supporting by all pacific means at their disposal the independence and integrity of China and the principle of equal opportunity for commerce and industry of all nations in that Empire.

5. Should any event occur threatening the status quo as above described or the principle of equal opportunity as above defined, it remains for the two Governments to communicate with each other in order to arrive at an understanding as to what measures they may consider it useful to take.

If the foregoing outline accords with the view of the Government of the United States, I shall be gratified to receive your confirmation.

I take this opportunity to renew to your excellency the assurance of my highest consideration.

K. Takahira.

373. THE INJUNCTION IN LABOR DISPUTES

Extract from Inaugural Address of President Taft
March 4, 1909

(Supplement to the Messages and Papers of the Presidents Covering the Administration of W. H. Taft, p. 7758)

Before his entry into politics, Taft had been a Judge of the Circuit Court, and his decisions had aroused the hostility of labor. His position on questions involving the power, prestige, and independence of the judiciary was consistently conservative; see Doc. No. 378. See in connection with the opinion here expressed, the Norris-LaGuardia Anti-Injunction Law, Doc. No. 474. On Taft, see H. S. Duffy, *William Howard Taft,* and the forthcoming biography by Henry Pringle.

. . . Another labor question has arisen which has awakened the most excited discussion. That is in respect to the power of the federal courts to issue injunctions in industrial disputes. As to that, my convictions are fixed. Take away from the courts, if it could be taken away, the power to issue injunctions in labor disputes, and it would create a privileged class among the laborers and save the lawless among their number from a most needful remedy available to all men for the protection of their business against lawless invasion. The proposition that business is not a property or pecuniary right which can be protected by equitable injunction is utterly without foundation in precedent or reason. The proposition is usually linked with one to make the secondary boycott lawful. Such a proposition is at variance with the American instinct, and will find no support, in my judgment, when submitted to the American people. The secondary boycott is an instrument of tyranny, and ought not to be made legitimate.

The issue of a temporary restraining order without notice has in several instances been abused by its inconsiderate exercise, and to remedy this the platform upon which I was elected recommends the formulation in a statute of the conditions under which such a temporary restraining order ought to issue. A statute can and ought to be framed to embody the best modern practice, and can bring the subject so closely to the attention of the court as to make abuses of the process unlikely in the future. The American people, if I understand them, insist that the authority of the courts shall be sustained, and are opposed to any change in the procedure by which the powers of a court may be weakened and the fearless and effective administration of justice be interfered with.

374. TAFT'S DEFENCE OF THE PAYNE-ALDRICH TARIFF

Speech at Winona, Minnesota
September 1909

(Supplement to the Messages and Papers of the Presidents Covering the Administration of W. H. Taft, p. 7773 ff.)

The Republican platform of 1908 called for a revision of the tariff, and shortly after his accession to the Presidency, Taft called a special session of Congress to carry out this pledge. The result was the Payne-Aldrich Tariff which Taft signed August 5, 1909. The high-protectionist character of the tariff aroused widespread dissatisfaction, and partly to allay this dissatisfaction Taft undertook a speaking tour through the mid-western states. In his Winona speech he declared that this bill was the best tariff bill that the Republican Party had ever passed, a statement which brought him a storm of derisive criticism. See, N. W. Stephenson, *Nelson W. Aldrich*, p. 346 ff.; C. G. Bowers, *Beveridge and the Progressive Era*, Book IV; R. M. La Follette, *La Follette's Autobiography*, chs. x–xi; F. A. Ogg, *National Progress*, ch. xxii; F. W. Taussig, *Tariff History of the United States* (5th ed.), ch. viii; I. M. Tarbell, *Tariff in Our Times*, ch. xiii.

. . . The Ways and Means Committee of the House, with Mr. Payne at its head, spent a full year in an investigation, assembling evidence in reference to the rates under the tariff, and devoted an immense amount of work in the study of the question where the tariff rates could be reduced and where they ought to be raised with a view to maintaining a reasonably protective rate, under the principles of the platform, for every indus-

try that deserved protection. They found that the determination of the question, what was the actual cost of production and whether an industry in this country could live under a certain rate and withstand threatened competition from abroad, was most difficult. The manufacturers were prone to exaggerate the injury which a reduction in the duty would give and to magnify the amount of duty that was needed; while the importers, on the other hand, who were interested in developing the importation from foreign shores, were quite likely to be equally biased on the other side.

Mr. Payne reported a bill—the Payne Tariff bill—which went to the Senate and was amended in the Senate by increasing the duty on some things and decreasing it on others. The difference between the House bill and the Senate bill was very much less than the newspapers represented. . . .

One way of stating what was done is to say what the facts show—that under the Dingley law there were 2,024 items. This included dutiable items only. The Payne law leaves 1,150 of these items unchanged. . . .

Now, the promise of the Republican platform was not to revise everything downward, and in the speeches which have been taken as interpreting that platform, which I made in the campaign, I did not promise that everything should go downward. What I promised was, that there should be many decreases, and that in some few things increases would be found to be necessary; but that on the whole I conceived that the change of conditions would make the revision necessarily downward—and that, I contend, under the showing which I have made, has been the result of the Payne bill. I did not agree, nor did the Republican party agree, that we would reduce rates to such a point as to reduce prices by the introduction of foreign competition. That is what the free traders desire. That is what the revenue tariff reformers desire; but that is not what the Republican platform promised, and it is not what the Republican party wished to bring about. To repeat the statement with which I opened this speech, the proposition of the Republican party was to reduce rates so as to maintain a difference between the cost of production abroad and the cost of production here, insuring a reasonable profit to the manufacturer on all articles produced in this country; and the proposition to reduce rates and prevent their being excessive was to avoid the opportunity for monopoly and the suppression of competition, so that the excessive rates could be taken advantage of to force prices up.

With respect to the wool schedule, I agree that it probably represents considerably more than the difference between the cost of production abroad and the cost of production here. The difficulty about the woolen sched-ule is that there were two contending factions early in the history of Republican tariffs, to wit, woolgrowers and the woolen manufacturers, and that finally, many years ago, they settled on a basis by which wool in the grease should have 11 cents a pound, and by which allowance should be made for the shrinkage of the washed wool in the differential upon woolen manufactures. The percentage of duty was very heavy—quite beyond the difference in the cost of production, which was not then regarded as a necessary or proper limitation upon protective duties. . . .

On the whole, however, I am bound to say that I think the Payne tariff bill is the best tariff bill that the Republican party ever passed. . . .

If the country desires free trade, and the country desires a revenue tariff and wishes the manufacturers all over the country to go out of business, and to have cheaper prices at the expense of the sacrifice of many of our manufacturing interests, then it ought to say so and ought to put the Democratic party in power if it thinks that party can be trusted to carry out any affirmative policy in favor of a revenue tariff. Certainly in the discussions in the Senate there was no great manifestation on the part of our Democratic friends in favor of reducing rates on necessities. They voted to maintain the tariff rates on everything that came from their particular sections. If we are to have free trade, certainly it can not be had through the maintenance of Republican majorities in the Senate and House and a Republican administration. . . .

375. THE RULE OF REASON
1897–1911

Did the Sherman Anti-Trust Act prohibit *all* contracts in restraint of trade between the States, or only unreasonable restraints? Unreasonable or undue restraint of trade had long been illegal at common law. Inasmuch as the Federal Courts had no common law jurisdiction, was the Sherman Act intended merely to grant the Federal Courts such jurisdiction, or was the act intended to go further than the common law in outlawing contracts in restraint of trade? The evolution of the so-called "rule of reason" is indicated in the following extracts. The literature on the Sherman Act is voluminous. See, on the question of the rule of reason, P. L. Anderson, *The Rule of Reason;* A. H. Walker, *History of the Sherman*

Law, passim; W. H. Taft, *The Anti-Trust Act and the Supreme Court;* and the illuminating bibliography in Warren, *The Supreme Court* (1928 ed.) Vol. II, p. 733, 734, n.

1 *United States* v. *Trans-Missouri Freight Association,* 166 U. S. 290. (1897)

PECKHAM, J. . . . The next question to be discussed is as to what is the true construction of the statute. . . . What is the meaning of the language as used in the statute "that every contract, combination in the form of trust or otherwise, or conspiracy in restraint of trade or commerce among the several States . . . is hereby declared to be illegal"? Is it confined to a contract or combination which is only in unreasonable restraint of trade or commerce, or does it include what the language of the act plainly and in terms covers, all contracts of that nature? It is now . . . urged that the statute, in declaring illegal every combination in the form of trust or otherwise, or conspiracy in restraint of trade or commerce, does not mean what the language therein plainly imports, but that it only means to declare illegal any such contract which is in *unreasonable* restraint of trade, while leaving all others unaffected by the provisions of that act; that the common law meaning of the term "contract in restraint of trade" includes only such contracts as are in *unreasonable* restraint of trade, and when that term is used in the Federal statute it is not intended to include all contracts in restraint of trade, but only those which are in unreasonable restraint thereof. . . . By the simple use of the term "contract in restraint of trade", all contracts of that nature, whether valid or otherwise, would be included and not alone that kind of contract which was invalid and unenforceable as being in unreasonable restraint of trade. When, therefore, the body of an act pronounces illegal every contract or combination in restraint of trade . . . among the several States etc. the plain and ordinary meaning of such language is not limited to that kind of contract alone which is in unreasonable restraint of trade, but all contracts are included in such language, and no exception or limitation can be added without placing in the act that which has been omitted by Congress. . . . The arguments which have been addressed to us against the inclusion of all contracts in restraint of trade, as provided for by the language of the act, have been based on the alleged presumption that Congress, notwithstanding the language of the act, could not have intended to embrace all contracts, but only such contracts as were in unreasonable restraint of trade. . . . In other words, we are asked to read into the act by way of judicial legislation an exception that is not placed there by the lawmaking branch of the Government, and this is to be done upon the theory that the impolicy of such legislation is so clear that it cannot be supposed Congress intended the natural import of the language to be used. This we cannot and ought not to do. . . . If the act ought to read as contended for by the defendants, Congress is the body to amend it and not this court, by a process of judicial legislation wholly unjustifiable. . . .

2 Report of Senator Nelson, on behalf of Senate Judiciary Committee, in reference to bill to amend the Anti-Trust Act in certain particulars. *Federal Anti-Trust Decisions.* Vol. IV, p. 160 ff. (1909).

. . . The Anti-Trust Act makes it a criminal offense to violate the law, and provides a punishment both by fine and imprisonment. To inject into the act the question of whether an agreement or combination is *reasonable or unreasonable* would render the act as a criminal or penal statute indefinite and uncertain, and hence, to that extent, utterly nugatory and void, and would practically amount to a repeal of that part of the act. . . . And while the same technical objection does not apply to civil prosecutions, the injection of the rule of reasonableness or unreasonableness would lead to the greatest variableness and uncertainty in the enforcement of the law. The defense of reasonable restraint would be made in every case and there would be as many different rules of reasonableness as cases, courts and juries. What one court or jury might deem unreasonable another court or jury might deem reasonable. A court or jury in Ohio might find a given agreement or combination reasonable, while a court and jury in Wisconsin might find the same agreement and combination unreasonable. In the case of *People* v. *Sheldon* 139 N. Y. 264, Chief Justice Andrews remarks, "If agreements and combinations to prevent competition in prices are or may be hurtful to trade, the only sure remedy is to prohibit all agreements of that character. . . ." To amend the Anti-Trust Act, as suggested by this bill, would be to entirely emasculate it, and for all practical purposes render it nugatory as a remedial statute. Criminal prosecutions would not lie and civil remedies would labor under the greatest doubt and uncertainty. The act as it exists is clear, comprehensive, certain, and highly remedial. It practically covers the field of Federal jurisdiction and is in every respect a model law. To destroy or undermine it at the present juncture, when combinations are on the increase . . . would be a calamity.

3 Standard Oil Company of New Jersey et al v. The United States. 221 U. S. 1. (1911) WHITE, C. J. . . . It is certain that only one point of concord between the parties is discernible, which is, that the controversy in every aspect is controlled by a correct conception of the meaning of the first and second sections of the Anti-Trust Act. . . . We shall make our investigation under four separate headings: First, the text of the first and second sections of the act originally considered and its meaning in the light of the common law and the law of this country at the time of its adoption; second, the contentions of the parties concerning the act, and the scope and effect of the decisions of this court upon which they rely. . . .

In view of the common law and the law in this country as to restraint of trade, which we have reviewed, and the illuminating effect which that history must have under the rule to which we have referred, we think it results:

(a) That the context manifests that the statute was drawn in the light of the existing practical conception of the law of restraint of trade, because it groups as within that class, not only contracts which were in restraint of trade in the subjective sense, but all contracts or acts which theoretically were attempts to monopolize, yet which in practice had come to be considered as in restraint of trade in a broad sense.

(b) That in view of the many new forms of contracts and combinations which were being evolved from existing economic conditions, it was deemed essential by an all-embracing enumeration to make sure that no form of contract or combination by which an undue restraint of interstate or foreign commerce was brought about could save such restraint from condemnation. The statute under this view evidenced the intent not to restrain the right to make and enforce contracts, whether resulting from combination or otherwise, which did not unduly restrain interstate or foreign commerce, but to pro-

tect that commerce from being restrained by methods, whether old or new, which would constitute an interference that is an undue restraint.

(c) And as the contracts or acts embraced in the provision were not expressly defined, since the enumeration addressed itself simply to classes of acts, those classes being broad enough to embrace every conceivable contract or combination which could be made concerning trade or commerce or the subjects of such commerce, and thus caused any act done by any of the enumerated methods anywhere in the whole field of human activity to be illegal if in restraint, it inevitably follows that the provision necessarily called for the exercise of judgement which required that some standard should be resorted to for the purpose of determining whether the prohibitions contained in the statute had or had not in any given case been violated. Thus not specifying, but indubitably contemplating and requiring a standard, it follows that it was intended that the standard of reason which had been applied at the common law and in this country in dealing with subjects of the character embraced by the statute, was intended to be the measure used for the purpose of determining whether in a given case a particular act had or had not brought about the wrong against which the statute provided. . . .

4 Dissenting opinion of Justice Harlan in Standard Oil case.

. . . After what has been adjudged, upon full consideration, as to the meaning and the scope of the Anti-Trust Act, and in view of the usages of this court when attorneys for litigants have attempted to reopen questions that have been deliberately decided, I confess to no little surprise as to what has occurred in the present case. The court says that the previous cases, above cited, "cannot by any possible conception be treated as authoritative without the certitude that *reason* was resorted to for the purpose of deciding them." . . . It is more than once intimated, if not suggested, that if the Anti-Trust Act is to be construed as prohibiting *every* contract or combination, of whatever nature, which is in fact in restraint of commerce, regardless of the reasonableness or unreasonableness of such restraint, that fact would show that the court had not proceeded, in its decision, according to "the light of reason", but had disregarded the "rule of reason" . . . Now this court is asked to do that which it has distinctly declared it could not and would not do, and has now done what it then said it could .not constitutionally do. It has, by mere interpretation, modified the act of Congress, and deprived it of practical value as a defensive measure against the evils to be remedied. . . . In effect, the court says, that it will now, for the first time, bring the discussion under the "light of reason" and apply the "rule of reason" to the questions to be decided. I have the authority of this court for saying that such a course of proceeding on its part would be "judicial legislation".

Still more, what is now done involves a serious departure from the settled usages of this court. Counsel have not ordinarily been allowed to discuss questions already settled by previous decisions. . . .

But my brethren, in their wisdom, have deemed it best to pursue a different course. They have now said to those who condemn our former decisions and who object to all legislative prohibitions of contracts, combinations, and trusts in restraint of interstate commerce, "You may now restrain such commerce, provided you are reasonable about it; only take care that the restraint is not undue." . . .

It remains for me to refer, more fully than I have heretofore done, to another, and, in my judgment—if we look to the future—the most important aspect of this case. That aspect concerns the usurpation by the judicial branch of the Government of the functions of the legislative department. . . . I said at the outset that the action of the court in this case might well alarm thoughtful men who revered the Constitution. I meant by this that many things are intimated and said in the court's opinion which will not be regarded otherwise than as sanctioning an invasion by the judiciary of the constitutional domain of Congress—an attempt by interpretation to soften or modify what some regard as a harsh public policy. This court, let me repeat, solemnly adjudged many years ago that it could not, except by *"judicial legislation"* read words into the Anti-Trust Act not put there by Congress, and which,

being inserted, give it a meaning which the words of the act, as passed, if properly interpreted, would not justify. The Court has decided that it could not thus change a public policy formulated and declared by Congress; that Congress has paramount authority to regulate interstate commerce, and that it alone can change a policy once inaugurated by legislation. The courts have nothing to do with the wisdom or policy of an act of Congress. Their duty is to ascertain the will of Congress, and if the statute embodying the expression of that will is constitutional, the courts must respect it. They have no function to declare a public policy, nor to *amend* legislative enactments. . . . Nevertheless, if I do not misapprehend its opinion, the court has now read into the act of Congress words which are not to be found there, and has thereby done that which it adjudged in 1896 and in 1898 could not be done without violating the Constitution, namely, by interpretation of a statute, changed a public policy declared by the legislative department. . . .

5 Extract from Special Message of President Taft, December 5, 1911, *Supplement to the Messages and Papers of the Presidents Covering the Administration of William Howard Taft,* p. 8025–6.

. . . In two early cases, where the statute was invoked to enjoin a transportation rate agreement between interstate railroad companies, it was held that it was no defense to show that the agreement as to rates complained of was reasonable at common law, because it was said that the statute was directed against all contracts and combinations in restraint of trade whether reasonable at common law or not. It was plain from the record, however, that the contracts complained of in those cases would not have been deemed reasonable at common law. In subsequent cases the court said that the statute should be given a reasonable construction and refused to include within its inhibition, certain contractual restraints of trade which it denominated as incidental or as indirect.

These cases of restraint of trade that the court excepted from the operation of the statute were instances which, at common law, would have been called reasonable. In the Standard Oil and Tobacco cases, therefore, the court merely adopted the tests of the common law, and in defining exceptions to the literal application of the statute, only substituted for the test of being incidental or indirect, that of being reasonable, and this, without varying in the slightest the actual scope and effect of the statute. In other words, all the cases under the statute which have now been decided would have been decided the same way if the court had originally accepted in its construction the rule at common law.

It has been said that the court, by introducing into the construction of the statute common-law distinctions, has emasculated it. This is obviously untrue. By its judgment every contract and combination in restraint of interstate trade made with the purpose or necessary effect of controlling prices by stifling competition, or of establishing in whole or in part a monopoly of such trade, is condemned by the statute. The most extreme critics can not instance a case that ought to be condemned under the statute which is not brought within its terms as thus construed.

The suggestion is also made that the Supreme Court by its decision in the last two cases has committed to the court the undefined and unlimited discretion to determine whether a case of restraint of trade is within the terms of the statute. This is wholly untrue. A reasonable restraint of trade at common law is well understood and is clearly defined. It does not rest in the discretion of the court. It must be limited to accomplish the purpose of a lawful main contract to which, in order that it shall be enforceable at all, it must be incidental. If it exceed the needs of that contract, it is void.

The test of reasonableness was never applied by the court at common law to contracts or combinations or conspiracies in restraint of trade whose purpose was or whose necessary effect would be to stifle competition, to control prices, or establish monopolies. The courts never assumed power to say that such contracts or combinations or conspiracies might be lawful if the parties to them were only moderate in the use of the power thus secured and did not exact from the public too great and exorbitant prices. It is true that many theorists, and others engaged in business violating the statute, have hoped that some such line could be drawn by courts; but no court of authority has ever attempted it. Certainly there is nothing in the decisions of the latest two cases from which such a dangerous theory of judicial discretion in enforcing this statute can derive the slightest sanction.

376. DECLARATION OF PRINCIPLES OF THE NATIONAL PROGRESSIVE REPUBLICAN LEAGUE
January 21, 1911
(*The Autobiography of Robert La Follette*, p. 495–6)

Insurgency, which had been stirring in the Republican Party ever since the fight on the Hepburn Act of 1906, was crystallized by the administration support to the Payne-Aldrich Tariff. See Doc. No. 374. Robert La Follette of Wisconsin was by common consent the natural leader of the progressive element in the Republican party. "During the holiday recess in the last days of December, 1910," he says in his *Autobiography*, "I drafted a Declaration of Principles and form of constitution for the organization of a league, and submitted the same to Senators Bourne and Bristow. . . . The organization was effected at a meeting held at my residence on the 21st day of January, 1911. Jonathan Bourne was elected President; Frederic C. Howe, Secretary; Charles R. Crane, Treasurer". For the campaign of 1912 see references, Doc. No. 379. A provoca-tive appreciation of La Follette is in J. Chamberlain, *Farewell to Reform*, ch. viii.

We, the undersigned, associate ourselves together as The National Progressive Republican League.

The object of the League is the promotion of popular government and progressive legislation.

Popular government in America has been thwarted and progressive legislation strangled by the special interests, which control caucuses, delegates, conventions, and party organizations; and, through this control of the machinery of government, dictate nominations and platforms, elect administrations, legislatures, representatives in Congress, United States Senators, and control cabinet officers.

Under existing conditions legislation in the public interest has been baffled and defeated. This is evidenced by the long struggle to secure laws but partially effective for the control of railway rates and services, the revision of the tariff in the interest of the producer and consumer, statutes dealing with trusts and combinations, based on sound economic principles, as applied to modern industrial and commercial conditions; wise, comprehensive and impartial reconstruction of banking and monetary laws, the conservation of coal, oil, gas, timber, waterpowers, and other natural resources belonging to the people, and for the enactment of all legislation solely for the common good.

Just in proportion as popular government has in certain states superseded the delegate convention system, and the people have assumed control of the machinery of government, has government become responsive to the popular will, and progressive legislation been secured.

The Progressive Republican League believes that popular government is fundamental to all other questions. To this end it advocates:

(1) The election of United States Senators by direct vote of the people.

(2) Direct primaries for the nomination of elective officials.

(3) The direct election of delegates to national conventions with opportunity for the voter to express his choice for President and Vice-President.

(4) Amendment to state constitutions providing for the Initiative, Referendum and Recall.

(5) A thoroughgoing corrupt practices act.

377. CANADIAN RECIPROCITY

Special Message of President Taft
January 26, 1911

(Supplement to the Messages and Papers of the Presidents Covering the Administration of W. H. Taft, p. 7961 ff.)

A reciprocity treaty with Canada had been concluded in 1854, only to be denounced by the United States in 1866. The Payne-Aldrich Tariff of 1909 precipitated what appeared to be a dangerous tariff war between the United States and Canada, and Taft attempted to avoid this by concluding another reciprocity agreement. An agreement negotiated by Secretary Knox received the assent of Congress, and was signed by the President July 26, 1911. In the course of the debates on the measure, however, the argument had been advanced that reciprocity was a step toward ultimate annexation; this argument aroused nationalistic sentiment in Canada, and led to the rejection of the agreement by the Dominion Parliament. See, United States Tariff Commission, *Reciprocity with Canada;* S. F. Bemis, ed. *American Secretaries of States,* Vol. IX, p. 344 ff.; H. Keenleyside, *Canada and the United States.*

THE WHITE HOUSE, January 26, 1911.

To the Senate and House of Representatives:

. . . One by one the controversies resulting from the uncertainties which attended the partition of British territory on the American Continent at the close of the Revolution, and which were inevitable under the then conditions, have been eliminated— some by arbitration and some by direct negotiation. The merits of these disputes, many of them extending through a century, need not now be reviewed. They related to the settlement of boundaries, the definition of rights of navigation, the interpretation of treaties, and many other subjects.

The path having been thus opened for the improvement of commercial relations, a reciprocal trade agreement is the logical sequence of all that has been accomplished in disposing of matters of a diplomatic and controversial character. The identity of interest of two peoples linked together by race, language, political institutions, and geographical proximity offers the foundation. . . .

The guiding motive in seeking adjustment of trade relations between two countries so situated geographically should be to give play to productive forces as far as practicable, regardless of political boundaries. While equivalency should be sought in an arrangement of this character, an exact balance of financial gain is neither imperative nor attainable. No yardstick can measure the benefits to the two peoples of this freer commercial intercourse and no trade agreement should be judged wholly by custom house statistics.

We have reached a stage in our own development that calls for a statesmanlike and broad view of our future economic status and its requirements. We have drawn upon our natural resources in such a way as to invite attention to their necessary limit. This has properly aroused effort to conserve them, to avoid their waste, and to restrict their use to our necessities. We have so increased in population and in our consumption of food products and the other necessities of life, hitherto supplied largely from our own country, that unless we materially increase our production we can see before us a change in our economic position, from that of a country selling to the world food and natural products of the farm and forest, to one consuming and importing them. Excluding cotton, which is exceptional, a radical change is already shown in our exports in the falling off in the amount of our agricultural products sold abroad and a correspondingly marked increase in our manufactures exported. A far-sighted policy requires that if we can enlarge our supply of natural resources, and especially of food products and the necessities of life, without substantial injury to any of our producing and manufacturing classes, we should take steps to do so now. We have on the north of us a country contiguous to ours for three thousand miles, with natural resources of the same character as ours which have not been drawn upon as ours have been, and in the development of which the conditions as to wages and character of the wage earner and transportation to market differ but little from those prevailing with us. The difference is not greater than it is between different States of our own country or between different Provinces of the Dominion of Canada. Ought we not, then, to arrange a commercial agreement with Canada, if we can, by which we shall have direct access to her great supply of natural products without an obstructing or prohibitory tariff? This is not a violation of the protective principle, as that has been authoritatively announced by those who uphold it, because that principle does not call for a tariff between this country and one whose conditions as to production, population, and wages are so like ours, and when our common boundary line of three thousand miles in itself must make a radical distinction between our commercial treatment of Canada and of any other country. . . .

In the reciprocal trade agreement numerous additions are made to the free list. These include not only food commodities, such as cattle, fish, wheat and other grains, fresh vegetables, fruits, and dairy products, but also rough lumber and raw materials useful to our own industries. Free lumber we ought to have. By giving our people access to Canadian forests we shall reduce the consumption of our own, which, in the hands of comparatively few owners, now have a value that requires the enlargement of our available timber resources.

Natural, and especially food, products being placed on the free list, the logical development of a policy of reciprocity in rates on secondary food products, or foodstuffs partly manufactured, is, where they cannot also be entirely exempted from duty, to lower the duties in accord with the exemption of the raw material from duty. This has been followed in the trade agreement which has been negotiated. As an example, wheat is made free and the rate on flour is equalized on a lower basis. In the same way, live animals being made free, the duties on fresh meats and on secondary meat products and on canned meats are substantially lowered. Fresh fruits and vegetables being placed on the free list, the duties on canned goods of these classes are reduced. . . .

This trade agreement, if entered into, will cement the friendly relations with the Dominion which have resulted from the satisfactory settlement of the controversies that have lasted for a century, and further promote good feeling between kindred peoples. It will extend the market for numerous products of the United States among the inhabitants of a prosperous neighboring country with an increasing population and an increasing purchasing power. It will deepen and widen the sources of food supply in contiguous territory, and will facilitate the movement and distribution of these foodstuffs.

The geographical proximity, the closer relation of blood, common sympathies, and identical moral and social ideas furnish very real and striking reasons why this agreement ought to be viewed from a high plane.

Since becoming a nation, Canada has been our good neighbor, immediately contiguous across a wide continent without artificial or natural barrier except navigable waters used in common.

She has cost us nothing in the way of preparations for defense against her possible assault, and she never will. She has sought to agree with us quickly when differences have disturbed our relations. She shares with us common traditions and aspirations. I feel I have correctly interpreted the wish of the American people by expressing, in the arrangement now submitted to Congress for its approval, their desire for a more intimate and cordial relationship with Canada. I therefore earnestly hope that the measure will be promptly enacted into law.

WILLIAM H. TAFT.

378. TAFT'S VETO OF ARIZONA ENABLING ACT
August 22, 1911

(Supplement to the Messages and Papers of the Presidents Covering the Administration of W. H. Taft, p. 8016 ff.)

Taft based his veto of the joint resolution admitting New Mexico and Arizona to the Union on the clause in the Arizona constitution providing for the recall of judges. Arizona changed the Constitution to conform to Taft's objections, and, after admission, restored the objectionable provision. Roosevelt, in 1911 and 1912, had given his support to the principle of the recall of judges, and Colorado had an arrangement for the recall of judicial decisions. See, C. A. Beard and B. E. Schultz, *Documents on the Initiative, Referendum, and Recall;* W. B. Munro, *The Initiative, Referendum and Recall.* On the struggle of Arizona and New Mexico for statehood, the most elaborate account is in C. A. Bowers, *Beveridge and the Progressive Era, passim.*

THE WHITE HOUSE, *August 22, 1911.*

To the House of Representatives:

I return herewith, without my approval, House joint resolution No. 14, "To admit the Territories of New Mexico and Arizona as States into the Union on an equal footing with the original States." . . .

I have not approved the Arizona constitution, nor have the two Houses of Congress, except as they have done so by the joint resolution under consideration. The resolution admits [Arizona] to statehood . . . on condition . . . that Arizona shall submit to its electors, at the time of the election of its State officers, a proposed amendment to its constitution by which judicial officers shall be excepted from the section permitting a recall of all elective officers.

If I sign this joint resolution, I do not see how I can escape responsibility for the judicial recall of the Arizona constitution. The joint resolution admits Arizona with the judicial recall, but requires the submission of the question of its wisdom to the voters. In other words, the resolution approves the admission of Arizona with the judicial recall, unless the voters themselves repudiate it. Under the Arizona constitution all elective officers, and this includes county and State judges, six months after their election are subject to the recall. . . .

This provision of the Arizona constitution, in its application to county and State judges, seems to me so pernicious in its effect, so destructive of independence in the judiciary, so likely to subject the rights of the individual to the possible tyranny of a popular majority, and, therefore, to be so injurious to the cause of free government, that I must disapprove a constitution containing it. . . . I am discharging my constitutional function in respect to the enactment of laws, and my discretion is equal to that of the Houses of Congress. I must therefore withhold my approval from this resolution if in fact I do not approve it as a matter of governmental policy. Of course, a mere difference of opinion as to the wisdom of details in a State constitution ought not to lead me to set up my opinion against that of the people of the Territory. It is to be their government, and while the power of Congress to withhold or grant statehood is absolute, the people about to constitute a State should generally know better the kind of government and constitution suited to their needs than Congress or the Executive. But when such a constitution contains something so destructive of free government as the judicial recall, it should be disapproved.

A government is for the benefit of all the people. . . . Now, as the government is for all the people, and is not solely for a majority of them, the majority in exercising control either directly or through its agents is bound to exercise the power for the benefit of the minority as well as the majority. But all have recognized that the majority of a people, unrestrained by law, when aroused and without the sobering effect of deliberation and discussion, may do injustice to the minority or to the individual when the selfish interest of the majority prompts. Hence arises the necessity for a constitution by which the will of the majority shall be permitted to guide the course of the government only under controlling checks that experience has shown to be necessary to secure for the minority its share of the benefit to the whole people that a popular government is established to bestow. A popular government is not a government of a majority, by a majority, for a majority of the people. It is a government of the whole people, by a majority of the whole people under such rules and checks as will secure a wise, just, and beneficent government for all the people. It is said you can always trust the people to do justice. If that means all the people and they all agree, you can. But ordinarily they do not all agree, and the maxim is interpreted to mean that you can always trust a majority of the people. This is not invariably true; and every limitation imposed by the people upon the power of the majority in their constitutions is an admission that it is not always true. No honest, clear-headed man, however great a lover of popular government, can deny that the unbridled expression of the majority of a community converted hastily into law or action would sometimes make a government tyrannical and cruel. Constitutions are checks upon the hasty action of the majority. They are the self-imposed restraints of a whole people upon a majority of them to secure sober action and a respect for the rights of the minority, and

of the individual in his relation to other individuals, and in his relation to the whole people in their character as a state or government. . . .

By the recall in the Arizona constitution it is proposed to give to the majority power to remove arbitrarily, and without delay, any judge who may have the courage to render an unpopular decision. By the recall it is proposed to enable a minority of 25 per cent of the voters of the district or State, for no prescribed cause, after the judge has been in office six months, to submit the question of his retention in office to the electorate. The petitioning minority must say on the ballot what they can against him in 200 words, and he must defend as best he can in the same space. Other candidates are permitted to present themselves and have their names printed on the ballot, so that the recall is not based solely on the record or the acts of the judge, but also on the question whether some other and more popular candidate has been found to unseat him. Could there be a system more ingeniously devised to subject judges to momentary gusts of popular passion than this? We can not be blind to the fact that often an intelligent and respectable electorate may be so roused upon an issue that it will visit with condemnation the decision of a just judge, though exactly in accord with the law governing the case, merely because it affects unfavorably their contest. Controversies over elections, labor troubles, racial or religious issues as to the construction or constitutionality of liquor laws, criminal trials of popular or unpopular defendants, the removal of county seats, suits by individuals to maintain their constitutional rights in obstruction of some popular improvement—these and many other cases could be cited in which a majority of a district electorate would be tempted by hasty anger to recall a conscientious judge if the opportunity were open all the time. No period of delay is interposed for the abatement of popular feeling. The recall is devised to encourage quick action, and to lead the people to strike while the iron is hot. The judge is treated as the instrument and servant of a majority of the people and subject to their momentary will, not after a long term in which his qualities as a judge and his character as a man have been subjected to a test of all the varieties of judicial work and duty so as to furnish a proper means of measuring his fitness for continuance in another term. On the instant of an unpopular ruling, while the spirit of protest has not had time to cool and even while an appeal may be pending from his ruling in which he may be sustained, he is to be haled before the electorate as a tribunal, with no judicial hearing, evidence, or defense, and thrown out of office, and disgraced for life because he has failed, in a single decision, it may be, to satisfy the popular demand. Think of the opportunity such a system would give to unscrupulous political bosses in control, as they have been in control not only of conventions but elections! Think of the enormous power for evil given to the sensational, muckraking portion of the press in rousing prejudice against a just judge by false charges and insinuations, the effect of which in the short period of an election by recall it would be impossible for him to meet and offset! Supporters of such a system seem to think that it will work only in the interest of the poor, the humble, the weak and the oppressed; that it will strike down only the judge who is supposed to favor corporations and be affected by the corrupting influence of the rich. Nothing could be further from the ultimate result. The motive it would offer to unscrupulous combinations to seek to control politics in order to control judges is clear. Those would profit by the recall who have the best opportunity of rousing the majority of the people to action on a sudden impulse. Are they likely to be the wisest or the best people in a community? Do they not include those who have money enough to employ the firebrands and slanderers in a community and the stirrers-up of social hate? Would not self-respecting men well hesitate to accept judicial office with such a sword of Damocles hanging over them? What kind of judgments might those on the unpopular side expect from courts whose judges must make their decisions under such legalized terrorism? The character of the judges would deteriorate to that of trimmers and time-servers, and independent judicial action would be a thing of the past. As the possibilities of such a system pass in review, is it too much to characterize it as one which will destroy the judiciary, its standing, and its usefulness? . . .

Attempt is made to defend the principle of judicial recall by reference to States in which judges are said to have shown themselves to be under corrupt corporate influence and in which it is claimed that nothing but a desperate remedy will suffice. If the political control in such States is sufficiently wrested from corrupting corporations to permit the enactment of a radical constitutional amendment like that of judicial recall, it would seem possible to make provision in its stead for an effective remedy by impeachment in which the cumbrous features of the present remedy might be avoided, but the opportunity for judicial hearing and defense before an impartial tribunal might be retained. Real reforms are not to be effected by patent short cuts or by abolishing those requirements which the experience of ages has shown to be essential in dealing justly with everyone. Such innovations are certain in the long run to plague the inventor or first user and will come readily to the hand of the enemies and corrupters of society after the passing of the just popular indignation that prompted their adoption.

Again judicial recall is advocated on the ground that it will bring the judges more into sympathy with the popular will and the progress of ideas among the people. It is said that now judges are out of touch with the movement toward a wider democracy and a greater control of governmental agencies in the interest and for the benefit of the people. The righteous and just course for a judge to pursue is ordinarily fixed by statute or clear principles of law, and the cases in which his judgment may be affected by his political, economic, or social views are infrequent. But even in such cases, judges are not removed from the people's influence. Surround the judiciary with all the safeguards possible, create judges by appointment, make their tenure for life, forbid diminution of salary during their term, and still it is impossible to prevent the influence of popular opinion from coloring judgments in the long run. Judges are men, intelligent, sympathetic men, patriotic men, and in those fields of the law in which the personal equation unavoidably plays a part, there will be found a response to sober popular opinion as it changes to meet the exigency of social, political, and economic changes. Indeed this should be so. Individual instances of a hidebound and retrograde conservatism on the part of courts in decisions which turn on the individual economic or sociological views of the judges may be pointed out; but they are not many, and do not call for radical action. In treating of courts we are dealing with a human machine, liable like all the inventions of man to err, but we are dealing with a human institution that likens itself to a divine institution because it seeks and preserves justice. It has been the corner stone of our gloriously free government in which the rights of the individual and of the minority have been preserved, while governmental action of the majority has lost nothing of beneficent progress, efficacy, and directness. This balance was planned in the Constitution by its framers and has been maintained by our independent judiciary. . . .

But it is said that the people of Arizona are to become an independent State when created, and even if we strike out judicial recall now, they can reincorporate it in their constitution after statehood.

To this I would answer that in dealing with the courts, which are the corner stone of good government, and in which not only the voters, but the nonvoters and nonresidents, have a deep interest as a security for their rights of life, liberty, and property, no matter what the future action of the State may be, it is necessary for the authority which is primarily responsible for its creation to assert in no doubtful tones the necessity for an independent and untrammeled judiciary. . . .

WILLIAM H. TAFT.

379. ROOSEVELT'S CANDIDACY IN 1912

(*The Works of Theodore Roosevelt,* National ed. Vol. XVII, p. 149–150)

When Roosevelt returned from his European trip in June, 1910, he was drawn, though with apparent reluctance, into State and national politics. As early as August 31, 1910, in his speech at Ossawatomie, Kansas he sounded a note of protest against the conservatism of the Taft administration. With the apparent waning of the La Follette movement, progressives turned to Roosevelt to assume the leadership of the insurgents in the Republican Party. Roosevelt himself had definitely decided to enter the race for the nomination early in 1912, and he was instrumental in having the Progressive Governors draw up the letter of February 10. Roosevelt replied from New York February 24. See H. Pringle, *Theodore Roosevelt,* Book III; J. B. Bishop, *Theodore Roosevelt and His Time,* Vol. II, ch. xx–xxiv; L. Einstein, *Roosevelt: His Mind in Action;* R. La Follette, *Autobiography,* chs. x–xiii; H. S. Duffy, *W. H. Taft,* chs. xxviii–xxix. The speeches of the campaign can be found in Roosevelt's *Works,* Vol. XVII, and in W. Wilson, *The New Freedom.*

Chicago, Illinois, February 10, 1912

We, the undersigned Republican Governors, assembled for the purpose of considering what will best insure the continuation of the Republican Party as a useful agency of good government, declare it our belief, after a careful investigation of the facts, that a large majority of the Republican voters of the country favor your nomination, and a large majority of the people favor your election as the next President of the United States.

We believe that your candidacy will insure success in the next campaign. We believe that you represent as no other man represents those principles and policies upon which we must appeal for a majority of the votes of the American people, and which, in our opinion, are necessary for the happiness and prosperity of the country.

We believe that, in view of this public demand, you should soon declare whether, if the nomination for the presidency comes to you unsolicited and unsought, you will accept it.

In submitting this request we are not considering your personal interests. We do not regard it as proper to consider either the interests or the preference of any man as regards the nomination for the presidency. We are expressing our sincere belief and best judgment as to what is demanded of you in the interests of the people as a whole, and we feel that you would be unresponsive to a plain public duty if you should decline to accept the nomination coming as the voluntary expression of the wishes of a majority of the Republican voters of the United States through the action of their delegates in the next National Convention.

Yours truly,

William E. Glasscock, West Virginia.
Chester H. Aldrich, Nebraska.
Robert P. Bass, New Hampshire.
Joseph M. Cary, Wyoming.
Chase S. Osborn, Michigan.
W. R. Stubbs, Kansas.
Herbert S. Hadley, Missouri.

New York, February 24, 1912

GENTLEMEN:

I deeply appreciate your letter, and I realize to the full the heavy responsibility it puts upon me, expressing as it does the carefully considered convictions of the men elected by popular vote to stand as the heads of government in their several States.

I absolutely agree with you that this matter is not one to be decided with any reference to the personal preferences or interests of any man, but purely from the standpoint of the interests of the people as a whole.

I will accept the nomination for President if it is tendered to me, and I will adhere to this decision until the convention has expressed its preference.

One of the chief principles for which I have stood, and for which I now stand, and which I have always endeavored and always shall endeavor to reduce to action, is the genuine rule of the people, and therefore I hope that so far as possible the people may be given the chance, through direct primaries, to express their preference as to who shall be the nominee of the Republican Presidential Convention.

Very truly yours,

THEODORE ROOSEVELT.

380. ROOSEVELT AND THE NEW NATIONALISM

Speech of Theodore Roosevelt before the Ohio Constitutional Convention, Columbus Ohio

February 21, 1912

(*The Works of Theodore Roosevelt*, National ed. Vol. XVII, p. 119 ff.)

Roosevelt had already decided, when he delivered this speech, to enter the race in 1912. The speech can therefore be regarded as the opening note in the pre-convention campaign. Three days later, February 24, Roosevelt formally accepted the invitation of the Seven Governors to be a candidate on the Republican ticket. The principal interest of this address lies in Roosevelt's energetic advocacy of the recall of judicial decisions. Roosevelt's attitude toward the Courts alienated many of his more conservative followers such as Root, Stimson, Knox, Lodge, etc., and was partly responsible for his subsequent defeat. For the origins of this attitude, see Doc. No. 310.

. . . The only safe course to follow in this great American democracy, is to provide for making the popular judgement really effective.

When this is done, then it is our duty to see that the people, having the full power, realize their heavy responsiblity for exercising that power aright.

But it is a false constitutionalism, a false statesmanship, to endeavor by the exercise of a perverted ingenuity to seem to give the people full power and at the same time to trick them out of it. Yet this is precisely what is done in every case where the State permits its representatives, whether on the bench or in the legislature or in executive office, to declare that it has not the power to right grave social wrongs, or that any of the officers created by the people, and rightfully the servants of the people, can set themselves up to be the masters of the people. Constitution-makers should make it clear beyond shadow of doubt that the people in their legislative capacity have the power to enact into law any measure they deem necessary for the betterment of social and industrial conditions. The wisdom of framing any particular law of this kind is a proper subject of debate; but the power of the people to enact the law should not be subject to debate. To hold the contrary view is to be false to the cause of the people, to the cause of American democracy. . . .

We stand for the rights of property, but we stand even more for the rights of man.

We will protect the rights of the wealthy

man, but we maintain that he holds his wealth subject to the general right of the community to regulate its business use as the public welfare requires. . . .

Moreover, shape your constitutional action so that the people will be able through their legislative bodies, or, failing that, by direct popular vote, to provide workmen's compensation acts to regulate the hours of labor for children and for women, to provide for their safety while at work, and to prevent overwork or work under unhygienic or unsafe conditions. See to it that no restrictions are placed upon legislative powers that will prevent the enactment of laws under which your people can promote the general welfare, the common good. Thus only will the "general welfare" clause of our Constitution become a vital force for progress, instead of remaining a mere phrase. This also applies to the police powers of the government. Make it perfectly clear that on every point of this kind it is your intention that the people shall decide for themselves how far the laws to achieve their purposes shall go, and that their decision shall be binding upon every citizen in the State, official or non-official, unless, of course, the Supreme Court of the nation in any given case decides otherwise. . . .

There remains the question of the recall of judges. . . .

I do not believe in adopting the recall save as a last resort, when it has become clearly evident that no other course will achieve the desired result.

But either the recall will have to be adopted or else it will have to be made much easier than it now is to get rid, not merely of a bad judge, but of a judge who, however virtuous, has grown so out of touch with social needs and facts that he is unfit longer to render good service on the bench.

It is nonsense to say that impeachment meets the difficulty. In actual practice we have found that impeachment does not work, that unfit judges stay on the bench in spite of it, and indeed because of the fact that impeachment is the only remedy that can be used against them. Where such is the actual fact it is idle to discuss the theory of the case. Impeachment as a remedy for the ills of which the people justly complain is a complete failure. A quicker, a more sum-mary, remedy is needed; some remedy at least as summary and as drastic as that embodied in the Massachusetts constitution. And whenever it be found in actual practice that such remedy does not give the needed results, I would unhesitatingly adopt the recall.

But there is one kind of recall in which I very earnestly believe, and the immediate adoption of which I urge.

There are sound reasons for being cautious about the recall of a good judge who has rendered an unwise and improper decision. Every public servant, no matter how valuable—and not omitting Washington or Lincoln or Marshall—at times makes mistakes. Therefore we should be cautious about recalling the judge, and we shall be cautious about interfering in any way with the judge in decisions which he makes in the ordinary course as between individuals. But when a judge decides a constitutional question, when he decides what the people as a whole can or cannot do, the people should have the right to recall that decision if they think it wrong. We should hold the judiciary in all respect; but it is both absurd and degrading to make a fetich of a judge or of any one else. . . .

Again and again in the past justice has been scandalously obstructed by State courts declaring State laws in conflict with the Federal Constitution, although the Supreme Court of the nation had never so decided or had even decided in a contrary sense.

When the supreme court of the State declares a given statute unconstitutional, because in conflict with the State of the National Constitution, its opinion should be subject to revision by the people themselves. Such an opinion ought always to be treated with great respect by the people, and unquestionably in the majority of cases would be accepted and followed by them. But actual experience has shown the vital need of the people reserving to themselves the right to pass upon such opinion. If any considerable number of the people feel that the decision is in defiance of justice, they should be given the right by petition to bring before the voters at some subsequent election, special or otherwise, as might be decided, and after the fullest opportunity for deliberation and debate, the question whether or not the judges' interpretation of the Constitution is to be sustained. If it is sustained, well and good. If not, then the popular verdict is to be accepted as final, the decision is to be treated as reversed, and the construction of the Constitution definitely decided—subject only to action by the Supreme Court of the United States. . . .

381. RECOMMENDATIONS OF THE ALDRICH COMMISSION
1912
(Publications of the National Monetary Commission, Vol. XXVI, p. 6 ff.)

The Monetary Commission was authorized by Act of Congress in 1908, under the chairmanship of Nelson W. Aldrich. It submitted numerous volumes dealing with the financial history of the United States and European nations, and some recommendations for the reconstruction of the American banking system. Some of these were adopted by Congress in 1913–14 in the Federal Reserve Act. On Aldrich and the Monetary Commission, see N. W. Stephenson, *Nelson W. Aldrich,* ch. xxi.

We have made a thorough study of the defects of our banking system, which were largely responsible for these disasters and have sought to provide effective remedies for these and other defects, in the legislation we propose.

The principal defects in our banking system we believe may be summarized as follows:

1. We have no provision for the concentration of the cash reserves of the banks and for their mobilization and use wherever needed in times of trouble. Experience has shown that the scattered cash reserves of our banks are inadequate for purposes of assistance or defense at such times.

2. Antiquated Federal and State laws restrict the use of bank reserves and prohibit the lending power of banks at times when, in the presence of unusual demands, reserves should be freely used and credit liberally extended to all deserving customers.

3. Our banks also lack adequate means available for use at any time to replenish their reserves or increase their loaning powers when necessary to meet normal or unusual demands.

4. Of our various forms of currency the bank-note issue is the only one which we might expect to respond to the changing needs of business by automatic expansion and contraction, but this issue is deprived of all such qualities by the fact that its volume is largely dependent upon the amount and price of United States bonds.

5. We lack means to insure such effective coöperation on the part of banks as is necessary to protect their own and the public interests in times of stress or crisis. There is no coöperation of any kind among banks outside the clearing-house cities. While clearing-house organizations of banks have been able to render valuable services within a limited sphere for local communities, the lack of means to secure their coöperation or affiliation in broader fields makes it impossible to use these or similar local agencies to prevent panics or avert calamitous disturbances affecting the country at large. These organizations have, in fact, never been able to prevent the suspension of cash payments by financial institutions in their own localities in cases of emergency.

6. We have no effective agency covering the entire country which affords necessary facilities for making domestic exchanges between different localities and sections, or which can prevent disastrous disruption of all such exchanges in times of serious trouble.

7. We have no instrumentality that can deal effectively with the broad questions which, from an international standpoint, affect the credit and status of the United States as one of the great financial powers of the world. In times of threatened trouble or of actual panic these questions, which involve the course of foreign exchange and the international movements of gold, are even more important to us from a national than from an international standpoint.

8. The lack of commercial paper of an established standard, issued for agricultural, industrial, and commercial purposes, available for investments by banks, leads to an unhealthy congestion of loanable funds in

great centers and hinders the development of the productive forces of the country.

9. The narrow character of our discount market, with its limited range of safe and profitable investments for banks, results in sending the surplus money of all sections, in excess of reserves and local demands, to New York, where it is usually loaned out on call on Stock Exchange securities, tending to promote dangerous speculation and inevitably leading to injurious disturbances in reserves. This concentration of surplus money and available funds in New York imposes upon the managers of the banks of that city the vast responsibilities which are inherent in the control of a large proportion of the banking resources of the country.

10. The absence of a broad discount market in our system, taken together with the restrictive treatment of reserves, creates at times when serious financial disturbances are anticipated a condition of dependence on the part of individual banks throughout the country, and at the same time places the farmers and others engaged in productive industries at a great disadvantage in securing the credit they require for the growth, retention, and distribution of their products.

11. There is a marked lack of equality in credit facilities between different sections of the country, reflected in less favored communities, in retarded development, and great disparity in rates of discount.

12. Our system lacks an agency whose influence can be made effective in securing greater uniformity, steadiness, and reasonableness of rates of discount in all parts of the country.

13. We have no effective agency that can surely provide adequate banking facilities for different regions promptly and on reasonable terms to meet the ordinary or unusual demands for credit or currency necessary for moving crops or for other legitimate purposes.

14. We have no power to enforce the adoption of uniform standards with regard to capital, reserves, examinations, and the character and publicity of reports of all banks in the different sections of the country.

15. We have no American banking institutions in foreign countries. The organization of such banks is necessary for the development of our foreign trade.

16. The provision that national banks shall not make loans upon real estate restricts their power to serve farmers and other borrowers in rural communities.

17. The provision of law under which the Government acts as custodian of its own funds results in irregular withdrawals of money from circulation and bank reserves in periods of excessive Government revenues, and in the return of these funds into circulation only in periods of deficient revenues. Recent efforts to modify the Independent Treasury system by a partial distribution of the public moneys among national banks have resulted, it is charged, in discrimination and favoritism in the treatment of different banks.

382. SOCIALIST PARTY PLATFORM OF 1912
Indianapolis, Indiana, May 12, 1912

(K. Porter, ed. *National Party Platforms*, p. 361 ff.)

The Socialist Party offered its first candidate in a national election in 1892. The history of the party is closely identified with the career of Eugene V. Debs, who became converted to socialism during his imprisonment at the time of the Pullman Strike. In 1912 the party nominated Debs for the presidency for the fourth time: Emil Seidel of Milwaukee was the nominee for the vice-presidency. Debs polled a popular vote of almost nine hundred thousand. On the Socialist Party, see N. Fine, *Labor and Farmer Parties in the United States, 1828–1928;* J. Macy, *Socialism in the United States;* M. Hillquit, *His-* tory of Socialism in the United States; F. E. Haynes, *Social Politics in the United States,* chs. ix, xii. On Debs see D. Karsner, *Debs, His Authorized Life and Letters;* M. Coleman, *Eugene V. Debs.*

The Socialist party declares that the capitalist system has outgrown its historical function, and has become utterly incapable of meeting the problems now confronting society. We denounce this outgrown system as incompetent and corrupt and the source of unspeakable misery and suffering to the whole working class.

Under this system the industrial equipment of the nation has passed into the absolute control of a plutocracy which exacts an annual tribute of hundreds of millions of dollars from the producers. Unafraid of any organized resistance, it stretches out its greedy hands over the still undeveloped resources of the nation—the land, the mines, the forests and the water powers of every State of the Union.

In spite of the multiplication of labor-saving machines and improved methods in industry which cheapen the cost of production, the share of the producers grows ever less, and the prices of all the necessities of life steadily increase. The boasted prosperity of this nation is for the owning class alone. To the rest it means only greater hardship and misery. The high cost of living is felt in every home. Millions of wage-workers have seen the purchasing power of their wages decrease until life has become a desperate battle for mere existance.

Multitudes of unemployed walk the streets of our cities or trudge from State to State awaiting the will of the masters to move the wheels of industry.

The farmers in every state are plundered by the increasing prices exacted for tools and machinery and by extortionate rents, freight rates and storage charges.

Capitalist concentration is mercilessly crushing the class of small business men and driving its members into the ranks of propertyless wage-workers. The overwhelming majority of the people of America are being forced under a yoke of bondage by this soulless industrial despotism.

It is this capitalist system that is responsible for the increasing burden of armaments, the poverty, slums, child labor, most of the insanity, crime and prostitution, and much of the disease that afflicts mankind.

Under this system the working class is exposed to poisonous conditions, to frightful and needless perils to life and limb, is walled around with court decisions, injunctions and unjust laws, and is preyed upon incessantly for the benefit of the controlling oligarchy of wealth. Under it also, the children of the working class are doomed to ignorance, drudging toil and darkened lives.

In the face of these evils, so manifest that all thoughtful observers are appalled at them, the legislative representatives of the Republican and Democratic parties remain the faithful servants of the oppressors. Measures designed to secure to the wage-earners of this Nation as humane and just treatment as is already enjoyed by the wage-earners of all other civilized nations have been smothered in committee without debate, the laws ostensibly designed to bring relief to the farmers and general consumers are juggled and transformed into instruments for the exaction of further tribute. The growing unrest under oppression has driven these two old parties to the enactment of a variety of regulative measures, none of which has limited in any appreciable degree the power of the plutocracy, and some of which have been perverted into means of increasing that power. Anti-trust laws, railroad restrictions and regulations, with the prosecutions, indictments and investigations based upon such legislation, have proved to be utterly futile and ridiculous.

Nor has this plutocracy been seriously restrained or even threatened by any Republican or Democratic executive. It has continued to grow in power and insolence alike under the administration of Cleveland, McKinley, Roosevelt and Taft.

We declare, therefore, that the longer sufferance of these conditions is impossible, and we purpose to end them all. We declare them to be the product of the present system in which industry is carried on for private greed, instead of for the welfare of society. We declare, furthermore, that for these evils there will be and can be no remedy and no substantial relief except through Socialism under which industry will be carried on for the common good and every worker receive the full social value of the wealth he creates.

Society is divided into warring groups and classes, based upon material interests. Fundamentally, this struggle is a conflict between the two main classes, one of which, the capitalist class, owns the means of production, and the other, the working class, must use these means of production, on terms dictated by the owners.

The capitalist class, though few in numbers, absolutely controls the government, legislative, executive and judicial. This class owns the machinery of gathering and disseminating news through its organized press. It subsidizes seats of learning—the colleges and schools—and even religious and moral agencies. It has also the added prestige which established customs give to any order of society, right or wrong.

The working class, which includes all those who are forced to work for a living whether by hand or brain, in shop, mine or on the soil, vastly outnumbers the capitalist class. Lacking effective organization and class solidarity, this class is unable to enforce its will. Given such a class solidarity and effective organization, the workers will have the power to make all laws and control all industry in their own interest. All political parties are the expression of economic class interests. All other parties than the Socialist party represent one or another group of the ruling capitalist class. Their political conflicts reflect merely superficial rivalries between competing capitalist groups. However they result, these conflicts have no issue of real value to the workers. Whether the Democrats or Republicans win politically, it is the capitalist class that is victorious economically.

The Socialist party is the political expression of the economic interests of the workers. Its defeats have been their defeats and its victories their victories. It is a party founded on the science and laws of social development. It proposes that, since all social necessities to-day are socially produced, the means of their production and distribution shall be socially owned and democratically controlled.

In the face of the economic and political aggressions of the capitalist class the only reliance left the workers is that of their economic organizations and their political power. By the intelligent and class conscious use of these, they may resist successfully the capitalist class, break the fetters of wage slavery, and fit themselves for the future society, which is to displace the capitalist system. The Socialist party appreciates the full significance of class organization and urges the wage-earners, the working farmers and all other useful workers to organize for economic and political action, and we pledge ourselves to support the toilers of the fields as well as those in the shops, factories and mines of the nation in their struggles for economic justice.

In the defeat or victory of the working class party in this new struggle for freedom lies the defeat or triumph of the common people of all economic groups, as well as the failure or triumph of popular government. Thus the Socialist party is the party of the present day revolution which makes the transition from economic individualism to socialism, from wage slavery to free co-operation, from capitalist oligarchy to industrial democracy.

Working Program

As measures calculated to strengthen the working class in its fight for the realization of its ultimate aim, the co-operative commonwealth, and to increase its power against capitalist oppression, we advocate and pledge ourselves and our elected officers to the following program:

Collective Ownership

1. The collective ownership and democratic management of railroads, wire and wireless telegraphs and telephones, express service, steamboat lines, and all other social means of transportation and communication and of all large scale industries.

2. The immediate acquirement by the municipalities, the states or the federal government of all grain elevators, stock yards, storage warehouses, and other distributing agencies, in order to reduce the present extortionate cost of living.

3. The extension of the public domain to include mines, quarries, oil wells, forests and water power.

4. The further conservation and development of natural resources for the use and benefit of all the people: . . .

5. The collective ownership of land whereever practicable, and in cases where such ownership is impracticable, the appropriation by taxation of the annual rental value of all the land held for speculation and exploitation.

6. The collective ownership and democratic management of the banking and currency system.

Unemployment

The immediate government relief of the unemployed by the extension of all useful public works. All persons employed on such works to be engaged directly by the government under a work day of not more than eight hours and at not less than the prevailing union wages. The government also to establish employment bureaus; to lend money to states and municipalities without interest for the purpose of carrying on public works, and to take such other measures within its power as will lessen the widespread misery of the workers caused by the misrule of the capitalist class.

Industrial Demands

The conservation of human resources, particularly of the lives and well-being of the workers and their families:

1. By shortening the work day in keeping with the increased productiveness of machinery.
2. By securing for every worker a rest period of not less than a day and a half in each week.
3. By securing a more effective inspection of workshops, factories and mines.
4. By the forbidding the employment of children under sixteen years of age.
5. By the co-operative organization of the industries in the federal penitentiaries for the benefit of the convicts and their dependents.
6. By forbidding the interstate transportation of the products of child labor, of convict labor and of all uninspected factories and mines.
7. By abolishing the profit system in government work and substituting either the direct hire of labor or the awarding of contracts to co-operative groups of workers.
8. By establishing minimum wage scales.
9. By abolishing official charity and substituting a non-contributary system of old age pensions, a general system of insurance by the State of all its members against unemployment and invalidism and a system of compulsory insurance by employers of their workers, without cost to the latter, against industrial diseases, accidents and death.

Political Demands

1. The absolute freedom of press, speech and assemblage.
2. The adoption of a graduated income tax and the extension of inheritance taxes, graduated in proportion to the value of the estate and to nearness of kin—the proceeds of these taxes to be employed in the socialization of industry.

3. The abolition of the monopoly ownership of patents and the substitution of collective ownership, with direct rewards to inventors by premiums or royalties.
4. Unrestricted and equal suffrage for men and women.
5. The adoption of the initiative, referendum and recall and of proportional representation, nationally as well as locally.
6. The abolition of the Senate and of the veto power of the President.
7. The election of the President and Vice-President by direct vote of the people.
8. The abolition of the power usurped by the Supreme Court of the United States to pass upon the constitutionality of the legislation enacted by Congress. National laws to be repealed only by act of Congress or by a referendum vote of the whole people.
9. Abolition of the present restrictions upon the amendment of the constitution, so that instrument may be made amendable by a majority of the voters in a majority of the States.
10. The granting of the right of suffrage in the District of Columbia with representation in Congress and a democratic form of municipal government for purely local affairs.
11. The extension of democratic government to all United States territory.
12. The enactment of further measures for the conservation of health. The creation of an independent bureau of health, with such restrictions as will secure full liberty to all schools of practice.
13. The enactment of further measures for general education and particularly for vocational education in useful pursuits. The Bureau of Education to be made a department.
14. The separation of the present Bureau of Labor from the Department of Commerce and Labor and its elevation to the rank of a department.
15. Abolition of all federal districts courts and the United States circuit court of appeals. State courts to have jurisdiction in all cases arising between citizens of several states and foreign corporations. The election of all judges for short terms.
16. The immediate curbing of the power of the courts to issue injunctions.
17. The free administration of the law.
18. The calling of a convention for the revision of the constitution of the U. S.

Such measures of relief as we may be able to force from capitalism are but a preparation of the workers to seize the whole powers of government, in order that they may thereby lay hold of the whole system of socialized industry and thus come to their rightful inheritance.

383. BRYAN'S RESOLUTIONS, DEMOCRATIC NATIONAL CONVENTION
June 27, 1912

(*Official Proceedings of the Democratic National Convention, 1912*, p. 149)

With the rupture of the Republican Party, and the probability that the Democratic nominee would be elected to the Presidency, Bryan began an intensive campaign to nominate a liberal candidate. The first step was the contest over the temporary chairmanship of the Convention. The second, designed as a dramatic gesture to influence public opinion, was the Resolution below. "If (the convention) passed the resolution," wrote Bryan, "it excluded anyone who was the representative of Morgan, Belmont, or Ryan or under their influence; if they voted it down, the rebuke from the country would make it impossible for New York to select a candidate." The resolution passed, 883 to 201, even New York voting for it. The second paragraph in these resolutions was withdrawn by Bryan, but this was not generally understood by the delegates. See, Bryan, *A Tale of Two Conventions;* R. S. Baker, *Woodrow Wilson, Life and Letters,* Vol. III, p. 340 ff.

Resolved, That in this crisis in our party's career and in our country's history this convention sends greetings to the people of the United States, and assures them that the party of Jefferson and Jackson is still the champion of popular government and equality before the law. As proof of our fidelity to the people, we hereby declare ourselves opposed to the nomination of any candidate for President who is the representative of or under obligation to J. Pierpont Morgan, Thomas F. Ryan, August Belmont, or any other member of the privilege-hunting and favor-seeking class.

Be It Further Resolved, That we demand the withdrawal from this convention of any delegate or delegates constituting or representing the above-named interests.

384. THE PROGRESSIVE PARTY PLATFORM
August 5, 1912

(K. Porter, ed. *National Party Platforms,* p. 334 ff.)

The steam-roller tactics of the Republican National Convention of 1912 in ruling against the Roosevelt delegates to that convention led to the formation of the Progressive Party. June 22, Roosevelt's followers met at Orchestra Hall, Chicago, and pledged support to him and to his principles. July 7, the call for a nominating convention was issued, and the convention duly met at Chicago August 5 and nominated Roosevelt by acclamation. Hiram Johnson of California was nominated to the Vice-Presidency. The third party succeeded in winning 88 electoral votes and a popular vote of over four millions. See, G. H. Payne, *The Birth of a New Party;* V. Rosewater, *Backstage in 1912;* O. K. Davis, *Released for Publication;* M. Sullivan, *Our Times,* Vol. III; R. M. La Follette, *Autobiography,* chs. xi–xii; H. Pringle, *Theodore Roosevelt.*

The conscience of the people, in a time of grave national problems, has called into being a new party, born of the nation's sense of justice. We of the Progressive party here dedicate ourselves to the fulfillment of the duty laid upon us by our fathers to maintain the government of the people, by the people and for the people whose foundations they laid. . . .

THE OLD PARTIES

Political parties exist to secure responsible government and to execute the will of the people.

From these great tasks both of the old parties have turned aside. Instead of instruments to promote the general welfare, they have become the tools of corrupt interests which use them impartially to serve their selfish purposes. Behind the ostensible government sits enthroned an invisible government owing no allegiance and acknowledging no responsibility to the people.

To destroy this invisible government, to

dissolve the unholy alliance between corrupt business and corrupt politics is the first task of the statesmanship of the day.

The deliberate betrayal of its trust by the Republican party, the fatal incapacity of the Democratic party to deal with the new issues of the new time, have compelled the people to forge a new instrument of government through which to give effect to their will in laws and institutions.

Unhampered by tradition, uncorrupted by power, undismayed by the magnitude of the task, the new party offers itself as the instrument of the people to sweep away old abuses, to build a new and nobler commonwealth. . . .

THE RULE OF THE PEOPLE

. . . In particular, the party declares for direct primaries for the nomination of State and National officers, for nation-wide preferential primaries for candidates for the presidency; for the direct election of United States Senators by the people; and we urge on the States the policy of the short ballot, with responsibility to the people secured by the initiative, referendum and recall. . . .

EQUAL SUFFRAGE

The Progressive party, believing that no people can justly claim to be a true democracy which denies political rights on account of sex, pledges itself to the task of securing equal suffrage to men and women alike.

CORRUPT PRACTICES

We pledge our party to legislation that will compel strict limitation of all campaign contributions and expenditures, and detailed publicity of both before as well as after primaries and elections.

PUBLICITY AND PUBLIC SERVICE

We pledge our party to legislation compelling the registration of lobbyists; publicity of committee hearings except on foreign affairs, and recording of all votes in committee; and forbidding federal appointees from holding office in State or National political organizations, or taking part as officers or delegates in political conventions for the nomination of elective State or National officials.

THE COURTS

The Progressive party demands such restriction of the power of the courts as shall leave to the people the ultimate authority to determine fundamental questions of social welfare and public policy. To secure this end, it pledges itself to provide:

1. That when an Act, passed under the police power of the State, is held unconstitutional under the State Constitution, by the courts, the people, after an ample interval for deliberation, shall have an opportunity to vote on the question whether they desire the Act to become law, notwithstanding such decision.

2. That every decision of the highest appellate court of a State declaring an Act of the Legislature unconstitutional on the ground of its violation of the Federal Constitution shall be subject to the same review by the Supreme Court of the United States as is now accorded to decisions sustaining such legislation.

ADMINISTRATION OF JUSTICE

. . . We believe that the issuance of injunctions in cases arising out of labor disputes should be prohibited when such injunctions would not apply when no labor disputes existed.

We believe also that a person cited for contempt in labor disputes, except when such contempt was committed in the actual presence of the court or so near thereto as to interfere with the proper administration of justice, should have a right to trial by jury.

SOCIAL AND INDUSTRIAL JUSTICE

The supreme duty of the Nation is the conservation of human resources through an enlightened measure of social and industrial justice. We pledge ourselves to work unceasingly in State and Nation for:

Effective legislation looking to the prevention of industrial accidents, occupational diseases, overwork, involuntary unemployment, and other injurious effects incident to modern industry;

The fixing of minimum safety and health standards for the various occupations, and the exercise of the public authority of State and Nation, including the Federal Control over interstate commerce, and the taxing power, to maintain such standards;

The prohibition of child labor;

Minimum wage standards for working women, to provide a "living wage" in all industrial occupations;

The general prohibition of night work for women and the establishment of an eight hour day for women and young persons;

One day's rest in seven for all wage workers;

The eight hour day in continuous twenty-four-hour industries;

The abolition of the convict contract labor system; substituting a system of prison production for governmental consumption only; and the application of prisoners' earnings to the support of their dependent families;

Publicity as to wages, hours and conditions of labor; full reports upon industrial accidents and diseases, and the opening to public inspection of all tallies, weights, measures and check systems on labor products;

Standards of compensation for death by industrial accident and injury and trade disease which will transfer the burden of lost earnings from the families of working people to the industry, and thus to the community;

The protection of home life against the hazards of sickness, irregular employment and old age through the adoption of a system of social insurance adapted to American use;

The development of the creative labor power of America by lifting the last load of illiteracy from American youth and establishing continuation schools for industrial education under public control and encouraging agricultural education and demonstration in rural schools;

The establishment of industrial research laboratories to put the methods and discoveries of science at the service of American producers;

We favor the organization of the workers, men and women, as a means of protecting their interests and of promoting their progress. . . .

CURRENCY

. . . The issue of currency is fundamentally a Government function and the system should have as basic principles soundness and elasticity. The control should be lodged with the Government and should be protected from domination or manipulation by Wall Street or any special interests.

We are opposed to the so-called Aldrich currency bill, because its provisions would place our currency and credit system in private hands, not subject to effective public control. . . .

CONSERVATION

. . . We believe that the remaining forests, coal and oil lands, water powers and other natural resources still in State or National control (except agricultural lands) are more likely to be wisely conserved and utilized for the general welfare if held in the public hands.

In order that consumers and producers, managers and workmen, now and hereafter, need not pay toll to private monopolies of power and raw material, we demand that such resources shall be retained by the State or Nation, and opened to immediate use under laws which will encourage development and make to the people a moderate return for benefits conferred. . . .

385. THE LODGE COROLLARY TO THE MONROE DOCTRINE
August 2, 1912

(*Congressional Record,* 62d Congress, 2d Session, Vol. XXXXVIII, pt. 10, p. 10045)

In 1911 an American syndicate proposed to sell a four hundred thousand acre tract of land in Lower California, including Magdalena Bay, to a Japanese syndicate. On hearing of the proposal, Senator Lodge introduced a resolution which, with slight alterations, was passed by the Senate by a vote of 51 to 4. This resolution was the first extension of the Monroe Doctrine to an Asiatic power, and the first extension of the Doctrine to cover control of American soil which had a potential military value by a foreign corporation. See, T. A. Bailey, "The Lodge Corollary," *Pol. Sci. Qt.,* Vol. XLVIII, p. 220 ff.; S. F. Bemis, ed., *American Secretaries of State,* Vol.

IX, p. 340 ff.; J. M. Callahan, *American Foreign Policy in Mexican Relations.*

Resolved, That when any harbor or other place in the American continents is so situated that the occupation thereof for naval or military purposes might threaten the communications or the safety of the United States, the Government of the United States could not see without grave concern the actual or potential possession of such harbor or other place by any Government, not American, as to give that Government practical power of control for naval or military purposes.

386. DOLLAR DIPLOMACY

Extract from Fourth Annual Message of President Taft
December 3, 1912

(Supplement to the Messages and Papers of the Presidents Covering the Administration of Taft, p. 8152–3)

American surplus capital had flowed largely into South American investments, but prior to the accession of Taft to the Presidency there had been little investment in China. The financing of Chinese development was almost entirely in the hands of English, Japanese and European bankers. In 1909, however, Taft made official representations to the Chinese Government on behalf of some American banking houses for participation in the Hukuang railroad in the Yangtse Valley. As a result American bankers were admitted to a four power consortium. In 1912 American bankers were about to co-operate in floating a Chinese loan for £25,000,000, but the advent of Wilson to the Presidency brought a sharp repudiation of "dollar diplomacy" in the Far East, and the Americans withdrew. For the Hukuang Railroad loan, see *Foreign Relations of the United States,* 1910, 1912, and for the consortium, *Foreign Relations,* 1912. On dollar diplomacy, see, S. Nearing and J. Freeman, *Dollar Diplomacy;* J. W. Overlach, *Foreign Financial Control in China;* B. H. Williams, *Economic Foreign Policy of the United States;* M. C. Hsu, *Railway Problems in China;* H. Croly, *Willard Straight;* F. V. Field, *American Participation in the Chinese Consortiums.*

CHINA

In China the policy of encouraging financial investment to enable that country to help itself has had the result of giving new life and practical application to the open-door policy. The consistent purpose of the present administration has been to encourage the use of American capital in the development of China by the promotion of those essential reforms to which China is pledged by treaties with the United States and other powers. The hypothecation to foreign bankers in connection with certain industrial enterprises, such as the Hukuang railways, of the national revenues upon which these reforms depended, led the Department of State early in the administration to demand for American citizens participation in such enterprises, in order that the United States might have equal rights and an equal voice in all questions pertaining to the disposition of the public reve-

nues concerned. The same policy of promoting international accord among the powers having similar treaty rights as ourselves in the matters of reform, which could not be put into practical effect without the common consent of all, was likewise adopted in the case of the loan desired by China for the reform of its currency. The principle of international cooperation in matters of common interest upon which our policy had already been based in all of the above instances has admittedly been a great factor in that concert of the powers which has been so happily conspicuous during the perilous period of transition through which the great Chinese nation has been passing.

CENTRAL AMERICA NEEDS OUR HELP IN DEBT ADJUSTMENT

In Central America the aim has been to help such countries as Nicaragua and Honduras to help themselves. They are the immediate beneficiaries. The national benefit to the United States is twofold. First, it is obvious that the Monroe doctrine is more vital in the neighborhood of the Panama Canal and the zone of the Caribbean than anywhere else. There, too, the maintenance of that doctrine falls most heavily upon the United States. It is therefore essential that the countries within that sphere shall be removed from the jeopardy involved by heavy foreign debt and chaotic national finances and from the ever-present danger of international complications due to disorder at home. Hence the United States has been glad to encourage and support American bankers who were willing to lend a helping hand to the financial rehabilitation of such countries because this financial rehabilitation and the protection of their customhouses from being the prey of would-be dictators would remove at one stroke the menace of foreign creditors and the menace of revolutionary disorder.

The second advantage of the United States is one affecting chiefly all the southern and

Gulf ports and the business and industry of the South. The Republics of Central America and the Caribbean possess great natural wealth. They need only a measure of stability and the means of financial regeneration to enter upon an era of peace and prosperity, bringing profit and happiness to themselves and at the same time creating conditions sure to lead to a flourishing interchange of trade with this country.

I wish to call your especial attention to the recent occurrences in Nicaragua, for I believe the terrible events recorded there during the revolution of the past summer— the useless loss of life, the devastation of property, the bombardment of defenseless cities, the killing and wounding of women and children, the torturing of noncombatants to exact contributions, and the suffering of thousands of human beings—might have been averted had the Department of State, through approval of the loan convention by the Senate, been permitted to carry out its now well-developed policy of encouraging the extending of financial aid to weak Central American States with the primary objects of avoiding just such revolutions by assisting those Republics to rehabilitate their finances, to establish their currency on a stable basis, to remove the customhouses from the danger of revolutions by arranging for their secure administration, and to establish reliable banks.

387. TAFT'S VETO OF LITERACY TEST FOR IMMIGRANTS
February 14, 1913

(Supplement to the Messages and Papers of the Presidents Covering the Administration of William Howard Taft, p. 8228 ff.)

The veto message is accompanied by the opinion of Secretary of Commerce, Charles Nagel. For Wilson's veto of the literacy test, see Doc. No. 404.

To the Senate:

I return herewith, without my approval, Senate Bill No. 3175.

I do this with great reluctance. The bill contains many valuable amendments to the present immigration law which will insure greater certainty in excluding undesirable immigrants.

The bill received strong support in both Houses and was recommended by an able commission after an extended investigation and carefully drawn conclusions.

But I can not make up my mind to sign a bill which in its chief provision violates a principle that ought, in my opinion, to be upheld in dealing with our immigration. I refer to the literacy test. For the reasons stated in Secretary Nagel's letter to me, I can not approve that test. The Secretary's letter accompanies this.

WM. H. TAFT.

MY DEAR MR. PRESIDENT:

. . . I am of the opinion that this provision can not be defended upon its merits. It was originally urged as a selective test. For some time recommendations in its support upon that ground have been brought to our attention. The matter has been considered from that point of view, and I became completely satisfied that upon that ground the test could not be sustained. The older argument is now abandoned, and in the later conferences, at least, the ground is taken that the provision is to be defended as a practical measure to exclude a large proportion of undesirable immigrants from certain countries. The measure proposes to reach its result by indirection, and is defended purely upon the ground of practical policy, the final purpose being to reduce the quantity of cheap labor in this country. I can not accept this argument. No doubt the law would exclude a considerable percentage of immigration from southern Italy, among the Poles, the Mexicans, and the Greeks. This exclusion would embrace probably in large part undesirable but also a great many desirable people, and the embarrassment, expense, and distress to those who seek to enter would be out of all proportion to any good that can possibly be promised for this measure.

My observation leads me to the conclusion that, so far as the merits of the individual immigrant are concerned, the test is altogether overestimated. The people who come from the countries named are frequently illiterate because opportunities have been denied them. The oppression with which these people have to contend in modern times is not religious, but it consists of a denial of the opportunity to acquire reading and writing. Frequently the attempt to learn to read and write the language of the particular people is discouraged by the Government, and these immigrants in coming to our shores are really striving to free themselves from the conditions under which they have been compelled to live.

So far as the industrial conditions are concerned, I think the question has been superficially considered. We need labor in this country, and the natives are unwilling to do the work which the aliens come over to do. It is perfectly true that in a few cities and localities there are congested conditions. It is equally true that in very much larger areas we are practically without help. In my judgment, no sufficiently earnest and intelligent effort has been made to bring our wants and our supply together, and so far the same forces that give the chief support to this provision of the new bill have stubbornly resisted any effort looking to an intelligent distribution of new immigration to meet the needs of our vast country. In my judgment, no such drastic measure based upon a ground which is untrue and urged for a reason which

we are unwilling to assert should be adopted until we have at least exhausted the possibilities of a rational distribution of these new forces. . . .

The census returns show conclusively that the importance of illiteracy among aliens is overestimated, and that these people are prompt after their arrival to avail [themselves] of the opportunities which this country affords. While, according to the reports of the Bureau of Immigration, about 25 per cent of the incoming aliens are illiterate, the census shows that among the foreign-born people of such States as New York and Massachusetts where most of the congestion complained of has taken place, the proportion of illiteracy represents only about 13 per cent.

I am persuaded that this provision of the bill is in principle of very great consequence, and that it is based upon a fallacy in undertaking to apply a test which is not calculated to reach the truth and to find relief from a danger which really does not exist. This provision of the bill is new, and it is radical. It goes to the heart of the measure. It does not permit of compromise, and, much as I regret it, because the other provisions of the measure are in most respects excellent and in no respect really objectionable, I am forced to advise that you do not approve this bill. Very sincerely, yours,

CHARLES NAGEL, *Secretary.*

388. THE CONCENTRATION OF CONTROL OF MONEY AND CREDIT
Report of the Pujo Committee
1913

(U. S. 62d Congress, 3rd. Session, *House Report,* No. 1593, ch. iii)

Ever since the publication of Henry D. Lloyd's *Wealth Against Commonwealth* in 1894 the charge that a small group of money masters controlled American industry, transportation and credit, had gained acceptance. With the muckraking campaign of the first decade of the new century this charge was substantiated in many details and given wide popularity. In February 1912 the House of Representatives directed the Committee on Banking and Currency to investigate banking and currency with a view to necessary legislation. A subcommittee, headed by Arsene P. Pujo, investigated banking abuses. The chief examiner of the Pujo committee was Samuel Untermeyer of New York. The material unearthed by the

Pujo committee was valuable for the campaign of 1912 and served to strengthen the hands of the reformers in the first Wilson administration. See for relevant material, *The Autobiography of Robert La Follette,* p. 762 ff.; L. Brandeis, *Other Peoples' Money;* J. Moody, *The Truth About the Trusts;* H. W. Laidler, *Concentration of Control in American Industry;* J. Moody, *Masters of Capital;* W. I. King, *Wealth and Income of the People of the United States;* G. Myers, *History of Great American Fortunes,* 3 Vols.; L. Corey, *The House of Morgan;* C. C. Regier, *The Era of the Muckrakers;* A. A. Berle and G. C. Means, *Modern Corporation and Private Property.*

Section 2—Fact of Increasing Concentration Admitted

The resources of the banks and trust companies of the city of New York on 1911 were $5,121,245,175, which is 21.73 per cent of the total banking resources of the country as reported by the Comptroller of the Currency. This takes no account of the unknown resources of the great private banking houses whose affiliations to the New York financial institutions we are about to discuss.

That in recent years concentration of control of the banking resources and consequently of credit by the groups to which we will refer has grown apace in the city of New York is defended by some witnesses and regretted by others, but acknowledged by all to be a fact.

As appears from statistics compiled by accountants for the committee, in 1911, of the total resources of the banks and trust companies in New York City, the 20 largest held 42.97 per cent; in 1906, the 20 largest held 38.24 per cent of the total; in 1901, 34.97 per cent.

Section 3—Processes of Concentration

This increased concentration of control of money and credit has been effected principally as follows:

First, through consolidations of competitive or potentially competitive banks and trust companies, which consolidations in turn have recently been brought under sympathetic management.

Second, through the same powerful interests becoming large stockholders in potentially competitive banks and trust companies. This is the simplest way of acquiring control, but since it requires the largest investment of capital, it is the least used, although the recent investments in that direction for that apparent purpose amount to tens of millions of dollars in present market values.

Third, through the confederation of potentially competitive banks and trust companies by means of the system of interlocking directorates.

Fourth, through the influence which the more powerful banking houses, banks, and trust companies have secured in the management of insurance companies, railroads, producing and trading corporations, and public utility corporations, by means of stockholdings, voting trusts, fiscal agency contracts, or representation upon their boards of directors, or through supplying the money requirements of railway, industrial, and public utilities corporations and thereby being enabled to participate in the determination of their financial and business policies.

Fifth, through partnership or joint account arrangements between a few of the leading banking houses, banks, and trust companies in the purchase of security issues of the great interstate corporations, accompanied by understandings of recent growth—sometimes called "banking ethics"—which have had the effect of effectually destroying competition between such banking houses, banks, and trust companies in the struggle for business or in the purchase and sale of large issues of such securities.

Section 4—Agents of Concentration

It is a fair deduction from the testimony that the most active agents in forwarding and bringing about the concentration of control of money and credit through one or another of the processes above described have been and are—

J. P. Morgan & Co.
First National Bank of New York
National City Bank of New York
Lee, Higginson & Co., of Boston and New York
Kidder, Peabody & Co., of Boston and New York
Kuhn, Loeb & Co.

. . . . . .

Combined Power of Morgan & Co., the First National, and National City Banks.— In earlier pages of the report the power of these three great banks was separately set forth. It is now appropriate to consider their combined power as one group.

First, as regards banking resources:

The resources of Morgan & Co. are unknown; its deposits are $163,000,000. The resources of the First National Bank are $150,-000,000 and those of its appendage, the First Security Co., at a very low estimate, $35,-000,000. The resources of the National City Bank are $274,000,000; those of its appendage, the National City Co., are unknown, though the capital of the latter is alone

$10,000,000. Thus, leaving out of account the very considerable part which is unknown, the institutions composing this group have resources of upward of $632,000,000, aside from the vast individual resources of Messrs. Morgan, Baker, and Stillman.

Further, as heretofore shown, the members of this group, through stockholdings, voting trusts, interlocking directorates, and other relations, have become in some cases the absolutely dominant factor, in others the most important single factor, in the control of the following banks and trust companies in the city of New York:

(a) Bankers Trust Co., resources	$250,000,000
(b) Guaranty Trust Co., resources	232,000,000
(c) Astor Trust Co., resources	27,000,000
(d) National Bank of Commerce, resources	190,000,000
(e) Liberty National Bank, resources	29,000,000
(f) Chase National Bank, resources	150,000,000
(g) Farmers Loan & Trust Co., resources	135,000,000

in all, 7, with total resources of 968,000,000 which, added to the known resources of members of the group themselves, makes $1,600,000,000 as the aggregate of known banking resources in the city of New York under their control or influence.

If there be added also the resources of the Equitable Life Assurance Society controlled through stock ownership of J. P. Morgan 504,000,000

the amount becomes $2,104,000,000

Second, as regards the greater transportation systems.

(a) Adams Express Co.: Members of the group have two representatives in the directorate of this company.

(b) Anthracite coal carriers: With the exception of the Pennsylvania, the Reading, the Central of New Jersey (a majority of whose stock is owned by the Reading), the Lehigh Valley, the Delaware, Lackawanna & Western, the Erie (controlling the New York, Susquehanna & Western), and the New York, Ontario & Western, afford the only transportation outlets from the anthracite coal fields. As before stated, they transport 80 per cent of the output moving from the mines and own and control 88 per cent of the entire deposits. The Reading, as now organized, is the creation of a member of this banking group—Morgan & Co. One or more members of the group are stockholders in that system and have two representatives in its directorate; are stockholders of the Central of New Jersey and have four representatives in its directorate; are stockholders of the Lehigh Valley and have four representatives in its directorate; are stockholders of the Delaware, Lackawanna & Western and have nine representatives in its directorate; are stockholders of the Erie, and have four representatives in its directorate; have two representatives in the directorate of the New York, Ontario & Western; and have purchased or marketed practically all security issues made by these railroads in recent years.

(c) Atchison, Topeka & Sante Fe Railway: One or more members of the group are stockholders and have two representatives in the directorate of the company; and since 1907 have purchased or procured the marketing of its security issues to the amount of $107,244,000.

(d) Chesapeake & Ohio Railway: Members of the group have two directors in common with this company; and since 1907, in association with others, have purchased or procured the marketing of its security issues to the amount of $85,000,000.

(e) Chicago Great Western Railway: Members of the group absolutely control this system through a voting trust.

(f) Chicago, Milwaukee & St. Paul Railway: Members of the group have three directors or officers in common with this company, and since 1909, in association with others, have purchased or procured the marketing of its security issues to the amount of $112,000,000.

(g) Chicago & Northwestern Railway: Members of the group have three directors in common with this company, and since 1909, in association with others, have purchased or procured the marketing of its security issues to the amount of $31,250,000.

(h) Chicago, Rock Island & Pacific Railway: Members of the group have four directors in common with this company.

(i) Great Northern Railway: One or more members of the group are stockholders of and have marketed the only issue of bonds made by this company.

(j) International Mercantile Marine Co.; A member of the group organized this company, is a stockholder, dominates it through a voting trust, and markets its securities.

(k) New York Central Lines: One or more members of the group are stockholders and have four representatives in the directorate of the company, and since 1907 have purchased from or marketed for it and its principal subsidiaries security issues to the extent of $343,000,000, one member of the group being the company's sole fiscal agent.

(l) New York, New Haven & Hartford Railroad: One or more members of the group are stockholders and have three representatives in the directorate of the company, and since 1907 have purchased from or marketed for it and its principal subsidiaries security issues in excess of $150,000,000, one member of the group being the company's sole fiscal agent.

(m) Northern Pacific Railway: One member of the group organized this company and is its fiscal agent, and one or more members are stockholders and have six representatives in its directorate and three in its executive committee.

(n) Southern Railway: Through a voting trust, members of the group have absolutely controlled this company since its reorganization in 1894.

(o) Southern Pacific Co.: Until its separation from the Union Pacific, lately ordered by the Supreme Court of the United States, members of the group had three directors in common with this company.

(p) Union Pacific Railroad: Members of the group have three directors in common with this company.

Third, as regards the greater producing and trading corporations.

(a) Amalgamated Copper Co.: One member of the group took part in the organization of the company, still has one leading director in common with it, and markets its securities.

(b) American Can Co.: Members of the group have two directors in common with this company.

(c) J. L. Case Threshing Machine Co.: The president of one member of the group is a voting trustee of this company and the group also has one representative in its directorate and markets its securities.

(d) William Cramp Ship & Engine Building Co.: Members of the group absolutely control this company through a voting trust.

(e) General Electric Co.: A member of the group was one of the organizers of the company, is a stockholder, and has always had two representatives in its directorate and markets its securities.

(f) International Harvester Co.: A member of the group organized the company, named its directorate and the chairman of its finance committee, directed its management, through a voting trust, and markets its securities.

(g) Lackawanna Steel Co.: Members of the group have four directors in common with the company and, with associates, marketed its last issue of securities.

(h) Pullman Co.: The group has two representatives, Mr. Morgan and Mr. Baker, in the directorate of this company.

(i) United States Steel Corporation: A member of the group organized this company, named its directorate, and the chairman of its finance committee (which also has the powers of an executive committee) is its sole fiscal agent and a stockholder, and has always controlled its management.

Fourth, as regards the great public utility corporations.

(a) American Telephone and Telegraph Co.: One or more members of the group are stockholders, have three representatives in its directorate, and since 1906, with other associates, have marketed for it and its subsidiaries security issues in excess of $300,-000,000.

(b) Chicago Elevated Railways: A member of the group has two officers or directors in common with the company, and in conjunction with others marketed for it in 1911 security issues amounting to $66,000,000.

(c) Consolidated Gas Co. of New York: Members of the group control this company through majority representation on its directorate.

(d) Hudson & Manhattan Railroad: One or more members of the group marketed and have large interests in the securities of this company, though its debt is now being adjusted by Kuhn, Loeb & Co.

(e) Interborough Rapid Transit Co. of New York: A member of the group is the banker of this company, and the group has agreed to market its impending bond issue of $170,000,000.

(f) Philadelphia Rapid Transit Co.: Members of the group have two representatives in the directorate of this company.

(g) Western Union Telegraph Co.: Members of the group have seven representatives in the directorate of this company.

Summary of Directorships Held by These Members of the Group.—Exhibit 134-B . . . shows the combined directorships in the more important enterprises held by Morgan & Co., the First National Bank, the National City Bank, and the Bankers and Guaranty Trust Cos., which latter two, as previously shown, are absolutely controlled by Morgan & Co. through voting trusts. It appears there that firm members or directors of these institutions together hold:

One hundred and eighteen directorships in 34 banks and trust companies having total resources of $2,679,000,000 and total deposits of $1,983,000,000.

Thirty directorships in 10 insurance companies having total assets of $2,293,000,000.

One hundred and five directorships in 32 transportation systems having a total capitalization of $11,784,000,000 and a total mileage (excluding express companies and steamship lines) of 150,200.

Sixty-three directorships in 24 producing and trading corporations having a total capitalization of $3,339,000,000.

Twenty-five directorships in 12 public utility corporations having a total capitalization of $22,245,000,000.

In all, 341 directorships in 112 corporations having aggregate resources or capitalization of $42,340,000,000.

The members of the firm of J. P. Morgan & Co. held 72 directorships in 47 of the greater corporations: George F. Baker, chairman of the board, F. L. Hine, president, and George F. Baker, Jr., and C. D. Norton, vice-presidents, of the First National Bank of New York, hold 46 directorships in 37 of the greater corporations; and James Stillman, chairman of the board, Frank A. Vanderlip, president, and Samuel McRoberts, J. T. Talbert, W. A. Simonson, vice-presidents, of the National City Bank of New York, hold 32 directorships in 26 of the greater corporations; making in all for these members of the group 150 directorships in 110 of the greater corporations. . . .

389. WILSON'S FIRST INAUGURAL ADDRESS
March 4, 1913

(U. S. 63d Congress, Special Session, *Senate Doc.* 3)

In his first Inaugural Address Woodrow Wilson reaffirmed the philosophy of the New Freedom which he had enunciated during his campaign for election. The address is one of the most notable statements of democratic faith in our political literature, and for eloquence compares favorably with Jefferson's First Inaugural and Lincoln's Second Inaugural. On Wilson, see R. S. Baker, *Woodrow Wilson, Life and Letters,* Vol. IV; W. E. Dodd, *Woodrow Wilson;* J. Kerney, *The Political Education of Woodrow Wilson.*

MY FELLOW CITIZENS:

There has been a change of government. It began two years ago, when the House of Representatives became Democratic by a decisive majority. It has now been completed.

The Senate about to assemble will also be Democratic. The offices of President and Vice-President have been put into the hands of Democrats. What does the change mean? That is the question that is uppermost in our minds to-day. That is the question I am going to try to answer, in order, if I may, to interpret the occasion.

It means much more than the mere success of a party. The success of a party means little except when the Nation is using that party for a large and definite purpose. No one can mistake the purpose for which the Nation now seeks to use the Democratic Party. It seeks to use it to interpret a change in its own plans and point of view. Some old things with which we had grown familiar, and which had begun to creep into the very habit of our thought and of our lives, have altered their aspect as we have latterly looked critically upon them, with fresh, awakened eyes; have dropped their disguises and shown themselves alien and sinister. Some new things, as we look frankly upon them, willing to comprehend their real character, have come to assume the aspect of things long believed in and familiar, stuff of our own convictions. We have been refreshed by a new insight into our own life.

We see that in many things that life is very great. It is incomparably great in its material aspects, in its body of wealth, in the diversity and sweep of its energy, in the industries which have been conceived and built up by the genius of individual men and the limitless enterprise of groups of men. It is great, also, very great, in its moral force.

Nowhere else in the world have noble men and women exhibited in more striking forms the beauty and the energy of sympathy and helpfulness and counsel in their efforts to rectify wrong, alleviate suffering, and set the weak in the way of strength and hope. We have built up, moreover, a great system of government, which has stood through a long age as in many respects a model for those who seek to set liberty upon foundations that will endure against fortuitous change, against storm and accident. Our life contains every great thing, and contains it in rich abundance.

But the evil has come with the good, and much fine gold has been corroded. With riches has come inexcusable waste. We have squandered a great part of what we might have used, and have not stopped to conserve the exceeding bounty of nature, without which our genius for enterprise would have been worthless and impotent, scorning to be careful, shamefully prodigal as well as admirably efficient. We have been proud of our industrial achievements, but we have not hitherto stopped thoughtfully enough to count the human cost, the cost of lives snuffed out, of energies overtaxed and broken, the fearful physical and spiritual cost to the men and women and children upon whom the dead weight and burden of it all has fallen pitilessly the years through. The groans and agony of it all had not yet reached our ears, the solemn, moving undertone of our life, coming up out of the mines and factories and out of every home where the struggle had its intimate and familiar seat. With the great Government went many deep secret things which we too long delayed to look into and scrutinize with candid, fearless eyes. The great Government we loved has too often been made use of for private and selfish purposes, and those who used it had forgotten the people.

At last a vision has been vouchsafed us of our life as a whole. We see the bad with the good, the debased and decadent with the sound and vital. With this vision we approach new affairs. Our duty is to cleanse, to reconsider, to restore, to correct the evil without impairing the good, to purify and humanize every process of our common life without weakening or sentimentalizing it. There has been something crude and heartless and unfeeling in our haste to succeed and be great. Our thought has been "Let every man look out for himself, let every generation look out for itself," while we reared giant machinery which made it impossible that any but those who stood at the levers of control should have a chance to look out for themselves. We had not forgotten our morals. We remembered well enough that we had set up a policy which was meant to serve the humblest as well as the most powerful, with an eye single to the standards of justice and fair play, and remembered it with pride. But we were very heedless and in a hurry to be great.

We have come now to the sober second thought. The scales of heedlessness have fallen from our eyes. We have made up our minds to square every process of our national life again with the standards we so proudly set up at the beginning and have always carried at our hearts. Our work is a work of restoration.

We have itemized with some degree of particularity the things that ought to be altered and here are some of the chief items: A tariff which cuts us off from our proper part in the commerce of the world, violates the just principles of taxation, and makes the Government a facile instrument in the hands of private interests; a banking and currency system based upon the necessity of the Government to sell its bonds fifty years ago and perfectly adapted to concentrating cash and restricting credits; an industrial system which, take it on all its sides, financial as well as administrative, holds capital in leading strings, restricts the liberties and limits the opportunities of labor, and exploits without renewing or conserving the natural resources of the country; a body of agricultural activities never yet given the efficiency of great business undertakings or served as it should be through the instrumentality of science taken directly to the farm, or afforded the facilities of credit best suited to its practical needs; water-courses undeveloped, waste places unreclaimed, forests untended, fast disappearing without plan or prospect of renewal, unregarded waste heaps at every mine. We have studied as perhaps no other nation has the most effective means of production, but we have not studied cost or economy as we should either as organizers of industry, as statesmen, or as individuals.

Nor have we studied and perfected the means by which government may be put at the service of humanity, in safeguarding the health of the Nation, the health of its men and its women and its children, as well as their rights in the struggle for existence. This is no sentimental duty. The firm basis of government is justice, not pity. These are matters of justice. There can be no equality or opportunity, the first essential of justice in the body politic, if men and women and children be not shielded in their lives, their very vitality, from the consequences of great industrial and social processes which they can not alter, control, or singly cope with. Society must see to it that it does not itself crush or weaken or damage its own constituent parts. The first duty of law is to keep sound the society it serves. Sanitary laws, pure food laws, and laws determining conditions of labor which individuals are powerless to determine for themselves are intimate parts of the very business of justice and legal efficiency.

These are some of the things we ought to do, and not leave the others undone, the old-fashioned, never-to-be-neglected, fundamental safeguarding of property and of individ-

ual right. This is the high enterprise of the new day: To lift everything that concerns our life as a Nation to the light that shines from the hearthfire of every man's conscience and vision of the right. It is inconceivable that we should do this as partisans; it is inconceivable we should do it in ignorance of the facts as they are or in blind haste. We shall restore, not destroy. We shall deal with our economic system as it is and as it may be modified, not as it might be if we had a clean sheet of paper to write upon; and step by step we shall make it what it should be, in the spirit of those who question their own wisdom and seek counsel and knowledge, not shallow self-satisfaction or the excitement of excursions whither they can not tell. Justice, and only justice, shall alway be our motto.

And yet it will be no cool process of mere science. The Nation has been deeply stirred, stirred by a solemn passion, stirred by the knowledge of wrong, of ideals lost, of government too often debauched and made an instrument of evil. The feelings with which we face this new age of right and opportunity sweep across our heartstrings like some air out of God's own presence, where justice and mercy are reconciled and the judge and the brother are one. We know our task to be no mere task of politics but a task which shall search us through and through, whether we be able to understand our time and the need of our people, whether we be indeed their spokesmen and interpreters, whether we have the pure heart to comprehend and the rectified will to choose our high course of action.

This is not a day of triumph; it is a day of dedication. Here muster, not the forces of party, but the forces of humanity. Men's hearts wait upon us; men's lives hang in the balance; men's hopes call upon us to say what we will do. Who shall live up to the great trust? Who dares fail to try? I summon all honest men, all patriotic, all forward-looking men, to my side. God helping me, I will not fail them, if they will but counsel and sustain me!

390. THE REPUDIATION OF "DOLLAR DIPLOMACY"

Statement from President Wilson
March 19, 1913

(American Journal of International Law, Vol. VII, p. 338–9)

For the history of the Chinese loan see Doc. No. 386. The American bankers acquiesced in the position of the Government and withdrew from the consortium.

We are informed that at the request of the last administration a certain group of American bankers undertook to participate in the loan now desired by the Government of China (approximately $125,000,000.) Our government wished American bankers to participate along with the bankers of other nations, because it desired that the good will of the United States towards China should be exhibited in this practical way, that American capital should have access to that great country, and that the United States should be in a position to share with the other Powers any political responsibilities that might be associated with the development of the foreign relations of China in connection with her industrial and commercial enterprises. The present administration has been asked by this group of bankers whether it would also request them to participate in the loan. The representatives of the bankers through whom the administration was approached declared that they would continue to seek their share of the loan under the proposed agreements only if expressly requested to do so by the government. The administration has declined to make such request because it did not approve the conditions of the loan or the implications of responsibility on its own part which it was plainly told would be involved in the request.

The conditions of the loan seem to us to touch very nearly the administrative independence of China itself; and this administration does not feel that it ought, even by implication, to be a party to those conditions. The responsibility on its part which would be implied in requesting the bankers to undertake the loan might conceivably go to the length in some unhappy contingency of forcible interference in the financial, and even the political, affairs of that great oriental state, just now awakening to a consciousness of its power and its obligations to its people. The conditions include not only the pledging of particular taxes, some of them antiquated and burdensome, to secure the loan, but also the administration of those taxes by foreign agents. The responsibility on the part of our government implied in the encouragement of a loan thus secured and administered is plain enough and is obnoxious to the principles upon which the government of our people rests.

The Government of the United States is not only willing, but earnestly desirous, of aiding the great Chinese people in every way that is consistent with their untrammeled development and its own immemorial principles. The awakening of the people of China to a consciousness of their possibilities under free government is the most significant, if not the most momentous event of our generation. With this movement and aspiration the American people are in profound sympathy. They certainly wish to participate, and participate very generously, in opening to the Chinese and to the use of the world the almost untouched and perhaps unrivalled resources of China.

The Government of the United States is earnestly desirous of promoting the most extended and intimate trade relationships between this country and the Chinese Republic. . . . This is the main material interest of its citizens in the development of China. Our interests are those of the open door—a door of friendship and mutual advantage. This is the only door we care to enter.

391. TARIFF REVISION UNDER WILSON

Address of President Wilson to Congress asking revision of the Payne-Aldrich Tariff
April 8, 1913

(*Congressional Record,* 63d Congress, 1st Session, Vol. L, p. 130 ff.)

Wilson had pledged tariff reform in his campaign for the presidency; immediately upon his accession to office he called Congress into a special session, and on April 8, reviving a custom that had not been observed since Jefferson, addressed Congress in person. In response to Wilson's demand for downward revision Congress promptly passed the Underwood tariff which became law October 3, 1913. See, R. S. Baker, *Woodrow Wilson, Life and Letters,* Vol. IV, ch. iii.; F. W. Taussig, *Tariff History of the United States,* 1931 ed.; H. P. Willis, "The Tariff of 1913," *Journal Pol. Econ.* Vol. XXII.

GENTLEMEN OF THE CONGRESS:

. . . I have called the Congress together in extraordinary session because a duty was laid upon the party now in power at the recent elections which it ought to perform promptly, in order that the burden carried by the people under existing law may be lightened as soon as possible, and in order, also, that the business interests of the country may not be kept too long in suspense as to what the fiscal changes are to be to which they will be required to adjust themselves. It is clear to the whole country that the tariff duties must be altered. They must be changed to meet the radical alteration in the conditions of our economic life which the country has witnessed within the last generation. While the whole face and method of our industrial and commercial life were being changed beyond recognition the tariff schedules have remained what they were before the change began, or have moved in the direction they were given when no large circumstance of our industrial development was what it is to-day. Our task is to square them with the actual facts. The sooner that is done the sooner we shall escape from suffering from the facts and the sooner our men of business will be free to thrive by the law of nature—the nature of free business—instead of by the law of legislation and artificial arrangement.

We have seen tariff legislation wander very far afield in our day—very far indeed from the field in which our prosperity might have had a normal growth and stimulation. No one who looks the facts squarely in the face or knows anything that lies beneath the surface of action can fail to perceive the principles upon which recent tariff legislation has been based. We long ago passed beyond the modest notion of "protecting" the industries of the country and moved boldly forward to the idea that they were entitled to the direct patronage of the Government. For a long time—a time so long that the men now active in public policy hardly remember the conditions that preceded it—we have sought in our tariff schedules to give each group of manufacturers or producers what they themselves thought that they needed in order to maintain a practically exclusive market as against the rest of the world. Consciously or unconsciously, we have built up a set of privileges and exemptions from competition behind which it was easy by any, even the crudest, forms of combination to organize monopoly; until at last nothing is normal, nothing is obliged to stand the tests of efficiency and economy, in our world of big business, but everything thrives by concerted arrangement. Only new principles of action will save us from a final hard crystallization of monopoly and a complete loss of the influences that quicken enterprise and keep independent energy alive.

It is plain what those principles must be. We must abolish everything that bears even the semblance of privilege or of any kind of artificial advantage, and put our business men and producers under the stimulation of a constant necessity to be efficient, economical, and enterprising, masters of competitive supremacy, better workers and merchants than any in the world. Aside from the duties laid upon articles which we do not, and probably can not, produce, therefore, and the duties laid upon luxuries and merely for the sake of the revenues they yield, the object of the tariff duties henceforth laid must be effective competition, the whetting of American wits by contest with the wits of the rest of the world.

It would be unwise to move toward this end headlong, with reckless haste, or with strokes that cut at the very roots of what has grown up amongst us by long process and at our own invitation. It does not alter a thing to upset it and break it and deprive it of a chance to change. It destroys it. We must make changes in our fiscal laws, in our fiscal system, whose object is development, a more free and wholesome development, not revolution or upset or confusion. We must build up trade, especially foreign trade. We need the outlet and the enlarged field of energy more than we ever did before. We must build up industry as well, and must adopt freedom in the place of artificial stimulation only so far as it will build, not pull down. In dealing with the tariff the method by which this may be done will be a matter of judgment exercised item by item. To some not accustomed to the excitements and responsibilities of greater freedom our methods may in some respects and at some points seem heroic but remedies may be heroic and yet be remedies. It is our business to make sure that they are genuine remedies. Our object is clear. If our motive is above just challenge and only an occasional error of judgment is chargeable against us, we shall be fortunate.

We are called upon to render the country a great service in more matters than one. Our responsibility should be met and our methods should be thorough, as thorough as moderate and well considered, based upon the facts as they are, and not worked out as if we were beginners. We are to deal with the facts of our own day, with the facts of no other and to make laws which square with those facts. It is best, indeed it is necessary, to begin with the tariff. . . .

392. WILSON'S DENUNCIATION OF THE TARIFF LOBBY
Statement to the Press
May 26, 1913

(Associated Press Dispatch, Washington, May 26, 1913)

I think that the public ought to know the extraordinary exertions being made by the lobby in Washington to gain recognition for certain alterations of the Tariff bill. Washington has seldom seen so numerous, so industrious or so insidious a lobby. The newspapers are being filled with paid advertisements calculated to mislead the judgement of public men not only, but also the public opinion of the country itself. There is every evidence that money without limit is being spent to sustain this lobby and to create an appearance of a pressure of opinion antagonistic to some of the chief items of the Tariff bill.

It is of serious interest to the country that the people at large should have no lobby and be voiceless in these matters, while great bodies of astute men seek to create an artificial opinion and to overcome the interests of the public for their private profit. It is thoroughly worth the while of the people of this country to take knowledge of this matter. Only public opinion can check and destroy it.

The Government in all its branches ought to be relieved from this intolerable burden and this constant interruption to the calm progress of debate. I know that in this I am speaking for the members of the two Houses who would rejoice as much as I would to be released from this unbearable situation.

393. WILSON'S SPECIAL MESSAGE ON MEXICAN RELATIONS
August 27, 1913

(Congressional Record, 63d Congress, 1st. Sess., Vol. 50, p. 3803–04)

The Mexican situation reached a crisis in the summer of 1913. For the diplomatic and political background of our relations with Mexico at this time, see J. F. Rippy, *The United States and Mexico,* ch. xx; E. E. Robinson and V. J. West, *The Foreign Policy of Woodrow Wilson, passim;* R. S. Baker, *Woodrow Wilson, Life and Letters,* Vol. IV, ch. vi; J. M. Callahan, *American Foreign Policy in Mexican Relations,* ch. xiv.

Gentlemen of the Congress: It is clearly my duty to lay before you, very fully and without reservation, the facts concerning our present relations with the Republic of Mexico. The deplorable posture of affairs in Mexico I need not describe, but I deem it my duty to speak very frankly of what this Government has done and should seek to do in fulfillment of its obligation to Mexico herself, as a friend and neighbor, and to American citizens whose lives and vital interests are daily affected by the distressing conditions which now obtain beyond our southern border. . . .

The peace, prosperity and contentment of Mexico mean more, much more, to us than merely an enlarged field for our commerce and enterprise. They mean an enlargement of the field of self-government and the realization of the hopes and rights of a nation with whose best aspirations, so long suppressed and disappointed, we deeply sympathize. We shall yet prove to the Mexican people that we know how to serve them without first thinking how we shall serve ourselves. . . .

Mexico has a great and enviable future before her, if only she choose and attain the paths of honest constitutional government.

The present circumstances of the Republic, I deeply regret to say, do not seem to promise even the foundations of such a peace. We have waited many months, months full of peril and anxiety for the conditions there to improve, and they have not improved. They have grown worse, rather. . . . War and disorder, devastation and confusion, seem to threaten to become the settled fortune of the distracted country. As friends we could wait no longer for a solution which every week seemed further away. It was our duty at least to volunteer our good offices—to offer to assist, if we might, in effecting some arrangement which would bring relief and peace and set up a universally acknowledged political authority there.

Accordingly, I took the liberty of sending the Hon. John Lind, formerly governor of Minnesota, as my personal spokesman and representative, to the City of Mexico, with the following instructions:
[Instructions follow]. . . .

Mr. Lind executed his delicate and difficult mission with singular tact, firmness, and good judgement, and made clear to the authorities at the City of Mexico not only the purpose of his visit but also the spirit in which it had been undertaken. But the proposals he submitted were rejected. . . .

I am led to believe that they were rejected partly because the authorities at Mexico City had been grossly misinformed and misled upon two points. They did not realize the spirit of the American people in this matter, their earnest friendliness and yet sober determination that some just solution be found for the Mexican difficulties; and they did not believe that the present administration spoke through Mr. Lind for the people of the United States. The effect of this unfortunate misunderstanding on their part is to leave them singularly isolated and without friends who can effectually aid them. So long as the misunderstanding continues we can only await the time of their awakening to a realization of the actual facts. We can not thrust our good offices upon them. The situation must be given a little more time to work itself out in the new circumstances; and I believe that only a little more will be necessary. For the circumstances are new. The rejection of our friendship makes them new and will inevitably bring its own alterations in the whole aspect of affairs. The actual situation of the authorities at Mexico City will presently be revealed.

Meanwhile what is it our duty to do? Clearly everything that we do must be rooted in patience and done with calm and disinterested deliberation. Impatience on our part would be childish, and would be fraught with every risk of wrong and folly. We can afford to exercise the self-restraint of a really great nation which realizes its own strength and scorns to misuse it. It was our duty to offer our active assistance. It is now our duty to show what true neutrality will do to enable the people of Mexico to set their affairs in order again, and wait for a further opportunity to offer our friendly counsels. The door is not closed against the resumption, either upon the initiative of Mexico or upon our own, of the effort to bring order out of the confusion by friendly cooperative action, should fortunate occasion offer.

While we wait, the contest of the rival forces will undoubtedly for a little while be sharper than ever, just because it will be plain that an end must be made of the existing situation, and that very promptly; and with the increased activity of the contending factions will come, it is to be feared, increased danger to the non-combatants in Mexico, as well as to those actually in the field of battle. The position of outsiders is always particularly trying and full of hazard where there is civil strife and a whole country is upset. We should earnestly urge all Americans to leave Mexico at once, and should assist them to get away in every way possible—not because we would mean to slacken in the least our efforts to safeguard their lives and their interests, but because it is imperative that they should take no unnecessary risks when it is physically possible for them to leave the country. We should let every one who assumes to exercise authority in any part of Mexico know in the most unequivocal way that we shall vigilantly watch the fortunes of those Americans who can not get away, and shall hold those responsible for their sufferings and losses to a definite reckoning. That can be and will be made plain beyond the possibility of a misunderstanding.

For the rest, I deem it my duty to exercise the authority conferred upon me by the law of March 14, 1912, to see to it that neither side of the struggle now going on in Mexico receive any assistance from this side the border. I shall follow the best practice of nations in the matter of neutrality by forbidding the exportation of arms or munitions of war of any kind from the United States to any part of the Republic of Mexico—a policy suggested by several interesting precedents and certainly dictated by many manifest considerations of practical expediency. We can not in the circumstances be partisans of either party to the contest that now distracts Mexico, or constitute ourselves the virtual umpire between them.

I am happy to say that several of the great Governments of the world have given this Government their generous moral support in urging upon the provisional authorities at the City of Mexico the acceptance of our proffered offices in the spirit in which they were made. . . .

394. WILSON'S MOBILE ADDRESS
October 27, 1913

(U. S. 63d Congress, 1st Session, *Senate Doc.* 226)

This address delivered before the Southern Commercial Congress at Mobile, Alabama, announced the Wilson policy toward Latin-America. Though the promises of this address were not consistently observed, relations with the Latin-American states were materially improved during the Wilson administrations. See, E. E. Robinson and V. J. West, *The Foreign Policy of Woodrow Wilson;* J. F. Rippy, *The United States and Mexico,* ch. xx; R. S. Baker, *Woodrow Wilson, Life and Letters,* Vol. IV, chs. ii, vi.

. . . The future, ladies and gentlemen, is going to be very different for this hemisphere from the past. These States lying to the south of us, which have always been our neighbors, will now be drawn closer to us by innumerable ties, and, I hope, chief of all, by the tie of a common understanding of each other. Interest does not tie nations together; it sometimes separates them. But sympathy and understanding does unite them, and I believe that by the new route that is just

about to be opened, while we physically cut two continents asunder, we spiritually unite them. It is a spiritual union which we seek. . . .

There is one peculiarity about the history of the Latin American States which I am sure they are keenly aware of. You hear of "concessions" to foreign capitalists in Latin America. You do not hear of concessions to foreign capitalists in the United States. They are not granted concessions. They are invited to make investments. The work is ours, though they are welcome to invest in it. We do not ask them to supply the capital and do the work. It is an invitation, not a privilege; and States that are obliged, because their territory does not lie within the main field of modern enterprise and action, to grant concessions are in this condition, that foreign interests are apt to dominate their domestic affairs, a condition of affairs always dangerous and apt to become intolerable.

What these States are going to see, therefore, is an emancipation from the subordination, which has been inevitable, to foreign enterprise and an assertion of the splendid character which, in spite of these difficulties, they have again and again been able to demonstrate. The dignity, the courage, the self-possession, the self-respect of the Latin American States, their achievements in the face of all these adverse circumstances, deserve nothing but the admiration and applause of the world. They have had harder bargains driven with them in the matter of loans than any other peoples in the world. Interest has been exacted of them that was not exacted of anybody else, because the risk was said to be greater; and then securities were taken that destroyed the risk—an admirable arrangement for those who were forcing the terms! I rejoice in nothing so much as in the prospect that they will now be emancipated from these conditions, and we ought to be the first to take part in assisting in that emancipation. I think some of these gentlemen have already had occasion to bear witness that the Department of State in recent months has tried to serve them in that wise. In the future they will draw closer and closer to us because of circumstances of which I wish to speak with moderation and, I hope, without indiscretion.

We must prove ourselves their friends, and champions upon terms of equality and honor. You cannot be friends upon any other terms than upon the terms of equality. You cannot be friends at all except upon the terms of honor. We must show ourselves friends by comprehending their interest whether it squares with our own interest or not. It is a very perilous thing to determine the foreign policy of a nation in the terms of material interest. It not only is unfair to those with whom you are dealing, but it is degrading as regards your own actions.

Comprehension must be the soil in which shall grow all the fruits of friendship, and there is a reason and a compulsion lying behind all this which is dearer than anything else to the thoughtful men of America. I mean the development of constitutional liberty in the world. Human rights, national integrity, and opportunity as against material interests—that, ladies and gentlemen, is the issue which we now have to face. I want to take this occasion to say that the United States will never again seek one additional foot of territory by conquest. She will devote herself to showing that she knows how to make honorable and fruitful use of the territory she has, and she must regard it as one of the duties of friendship to see that from no quarter are material interests made superior to human liberty and national opportunity. I say this, not with a single thought that anyone will gainsay it, but merely to fix in our consciousness what our real relationship with the rest of America is. It is the relationship of a family of mankind devoted to the development of true constitutional liberty. We know that that is the soil out of which the best enterprise springs. We know that this is a cause which we are making in common with our neighbors, because we have had to make it for ourselves.

Reference has been made here to-day to some of the national problems which confront us as a Nation. What is at the heart of all our national problems? It is that we have seen the hand of material interest sometimes about to close upon our dearest rights and possessions. We have seen material interests threaten constitutional freedom in the United States. Therefore we will now know how to sympathize with those in the rest of America who have to contend with such powers, not only within their borders but from outside their borders also. . . .

In emphasizing the points which must unite us in sympathy and in spiritual interest with the Latin American peoples, we are only emphasizing the points of our own life, and we should prove ourselves untrue to our own traditions if we proved ourselves untrue friends to them. . . .

395. THE TAMPICO INCIDENT

Address of President Wilson to Congress on the Mexican Crisis
April 20, 1914

(Foreign Relations of the United States, 1914, p. 474 ff.)

On April 9 several sailors from the U. S. S. *Dolphin* were arrested at Tampico by officers of President Huerta. Admiral Mayo at once demanded an apology and a salute of twenty-one guns. This demand was sustained by the American government, though in as much as the United States did not recognize Huerta, it presented obvious legal difficulties. Huerta refused to comply with the American demands, and April 20 Wilson appeared before Congress and asked for authority to take such action as the situation required. The House, by a vote of 323–29, and the Senate by a vote of 72–13, gave Wilson the necessary authority. On the 22d, Admiral Fletcher landed marines at Vera Cruz, seized the customs house and prevented the landing of munitions from a German ship. This action brought the United States and Mexico to the verge of war, and threatened, moreover, to unite all of Mexico behind Huerta. From this unhappy situation both nations were rescued by the timely intervention of the A.B.C. powers with the offer of mediation. See Doc. No. 396. For the Tampico incident, see R. S. Baker, *Woodrow Wilson*, Vol. IV, p. 313 ff.; M. E. Curti, *Bryan and World Peace*, p. 181 ff.; C. P. Lamar, *Life of Joseph Rucker Lamar;* J. M. Callahan, *American Foreign Relations in Mexican Policy*. The official correspondence can be found in *Foreign Relations of the United States,* 1914.

Gentlemen of the Congress:

It is my duty to call your attention to a situation which has arisen in our dealings with General Victoriano Huerta at Mexico City which calls for action, and to ask your advice and cooperation in acting upon it. On the 9th of April a paymaster of the U.S.S. *Dolphin* landed at the Iturbide Bridge landing at Tampico with a whaleboat and boat's crew to take off certain supplies needed by his ship, and while engaged in loading the boat was arrested by an officer and squad of men of the army of General Huerta. . . . Admiral Mayo regarded the arrest as so serious an affront that he was not satisfied with the apologies offered, but demanded that the flag of the United States be saluted with special ceremony by the military commander of the port.

The incident can not be regarded as a trivial one, especially as two of the men arrested were taken from the boat itself—that is to say, from the territory of the United States—but had it stood by itself it might have been attributed to the ignorance or arrogance of a single officer. Unfortunately, it was not an isolated case. A series of incidents have recently occurred which can not but create the impression that the representatives of General Huerta were willing to go out of their way to show disregard for the dignity and rights of this Government and felt perfectly safe in doing what they pleased, making free to show in many ways their irritation and contempt. . . .

The manifest danger of such a situation was that such offenses might grow from bad to worse until something happened of so gross and intolerable a sort as to lead directly and inevitably to armed conflict. It was necessary that the apologies of General Huerta and his representatives should go much further, that they should be such as to attract the attention of the whole population to their significance, and such as to impress upon General Huerta himself the necessity of seeing to it that no further occasion for explanations and professed regrets should arise. I, therefore, felt it my duty to sustain Admiral Mayo in the whole of his demand and to insist that the flag of the United States should be saluted in such a way as to indicate a new spirit and attitude on the part of the Huertistas.

Such a salute, General Huerta has refused, and I have come to ask your approval and support in the course I now propose to pursue.

This Government can, I earnestly hope, in no circumstances be forced into war with the people of Mexico. Mexico is torn by civil strife. If we are to accept the tests of its own constitution, it has no government. General Huerta has set his power up in the City of Mexico, such as it is, without right and by methods for which there can be no justification. Only part of the country is under his control. If armed conflict should unhappily come as a result of his attitude of personal resentment toward this Government, we should be fighting only General Huerta and those who adhere to him and give him their support, and our object would be only to restore to the people of the distracted Republic the opportunity to set up again their own laws and their own government.

But I earnestly hope that war is not now in question. I believe I speak for the American people when I say that we do not desire to control in any degree the affairs of our sister Republic. Our feeling for the people of Mexico is one of deep and genuine friendship, and every thing that we have so far done or refrained from doing has proceeded from our desire to help them, not to hinder or embarrass them. We would not wish even to exercise the good offices of friendship without their welcome and consent. The people of Mexico are entitled to settle their own domestic affairs in their own way, and we sincerely desire to respect their right. The present situation need have none of the grave implications of interference if we deal with it promptly, firmly, and wisely.

No doubt I could do what is necessary in the circumstances to enforce respect for our Government without recourse to the Congress, and yet not exceed my constitutional powers as President; but I do not wish to act in a manner possibly of so grave consequence except in close conference and cooperation with both the Senate and House. I, therefore, come to ask your approval that I should use the armed forces of the United States in such ways and to such an extent as may be necessary to obtain from General Huerta and his adherents the fullest recognition of the rights and dignity of the United States, even amidst the distressing conditions now unhappily obtaining in Mexico.

There can in what we do be no thought of aggression or of selfish aggrandizement. We seek to maintain the dignity and authority of the United States only because we wish always to keep our great influence unimpaired for the uses of liberty, both in the United States and wherever else it may be employed for the benefit of mankind.

396. MEDIATION PROTOCOL OF THE A.B.C. CONFERENCE
Niagara Falls, New York, June 12, 1914
(*Foreign Relations of the United States,* 1914, p. 548–9)

President Wilson's opposition to Huerta led to retaliations by Huerta against American citizens; when the Mexican President refused to apologize for arresting American marines at Tampico, Wilson ordered the occupation of Vera Cruz. The situation was rapidly shaping up for war when Wilson was saved by an offer of mediation by Argentina, Brazil and Chile. Huerta was soon driven out of Mexico, and another conference of the A.B.C. powers, several lesser Latin American states and the United States, decided to recognize Carranza. The A.B.C. Conference is important not so much for its accomplishments as for the indication of the willingness of the United States to admit Latin American nations to joint responsibility for the maintenance of American policies. Other documents on the Conference can be found in *Foreign Relations of the United States,* 1914, p. 487 ff. A convenient summary is in *Publications of the World Peace Foundation,* Vol. VI, No. 3. See also, J. F. Rippy, *The United States and Mexico,* ch. xx; E. E. Robinson and V. J. West, *Foreign Policy of Woodrow Wilson;* J. M. Callahan, *American Foreign Policy in Mexican Relations.*

Protocol No. 3, June 12, 1914.

A Provisional Government for the United Mexican States, constituted as hereinafter provided, shall be recognized at Mexico City at noon on the ——— day of ——— 1914, from which time it shall exercise governmental power until the inauguration of a Constitutional President.

Protocol No. 4, June 24, 1914.

I.

The Provisional Government referred to in protocol No. 3 shall be constituted by agreement of the delegates representing the parties between which the internal struggle in Mexico is taking place.

II.

A. Upon the constitution of the Provisional Government in the City of Mexico, the Government of the United States of

America will recognize it immediately and thereupon diplomatic relations between the two countries will be restored.

B. The Government of the United States of America will not in any form whatsoever claim a war indemnity or other international satisfaction.

C. The Provisional Government will proclaim an absolute amnesty to all foreigners for any and all political offenses committed during the period of civil war in Mexico.

D. The Provisional Government will negotiate for the constitution of international commission for the settlement of the claims of foreigners on account of damages sustained during the period of civil war as a consequence of military acts or the acts of national authorities.

III.

The three mediating Governments agree on their part to recognize the Provisional Government organized as provided by Section I of this protocol.

397. WILSON'S PANAMA CANAL TOLLS MESSAGE
Address to Congress March 5, 1914

(Congressional Record, 63d Congress, 2d Session, Vol. LI, p. 4313)

The Panama Canal Act of August 24, 1912 exempted vessels engaged in the coastwise trade of the United States from payment of the customary canal tolls. Great Britain protested that this exemption constituted a breach of the Canal Treaty of 1901, Article III, sec. 1; see Doc. No. 355. Congress yielded to the President's demand and required equality of charges on all vessels. Wilson's position on this question aroused general approval in the United States and Great Britain, and was instrumental in persuading Great Britain to follow Wilson's leadership in Mexican relations. See, R. S. Baker, *Woodrow Wilson,* Vol. IV, ch. viii.

Gentlemen of the Congress:

I have come to you upon an errand which can be very briefly performed, but I beg that you will not measure its importance by the number of sentences in which I state it. No communication I have addressed to the Congress carried with it graver or more far-reaching implications as to the interest of the country, and I come now to speak upon a matter with regard to which I am charged in a peculiar degree, by the Constitution itself, with personal responsibility.

I have come to ask you for the repeal of that provision of the Panama Canal Act of August 24, 1912, which exempts vessels engaged in the coastwise trade of the United States from payment of tolls, and to urge upon you the justice, the wisdom, and the large policy of such a repeal with the utmost earnestness of which I am capable.

In my own judgment, very fully considered and maturely formed, that exemption constitutes a mistaken economic policy from every point of view, and is, moreover, in plain contravention of the treaty with Great Britain concerning the canal concluded on November 18, 1901. But I have not come to urge upon you my personal views. I have come to state to you a fact and a situation. Whatever may be our own differences of opinion concerning this much debated measure, its meaning is not debated outside the United States. Everywhere else the language of the treaty is given but one interpretation, and that interpretation precludes the exemption I am asking you to repeal. We consented to the treaty; its language we accepted, if we did not originate it; and we are too big, too powerful, too self-respecting a nation to interpret with a too strained or refined reading the words of our own promises just because we have power enough to give us leave to read them as we please. The large thing to do is the only thing we can afford to do, a voluntary withdrawal from a position everywhere questioned and misunderstood. We ought to reverse our action without raising the question whether we were right or wrong, and so once more deserve our reputation for generosity and for the redemption of every obligation without quibble or hesitation.

I ask this of you in support of the foreign policy of the administration. I shall not know how to deal with other matters of even greater delicacy and nearer consequence if you do not grant it to me in ungrudging measure.

398. THE BRYAN-CHAMORRO CONVENTION
August 5, 1914

(*U. S. Statutes at Large*, Vol. XXXIX, p. 1661 ff.)

The United States had been interested in an Isthmian canal across Nicaragua for three-quarters of a century. For the first convention granting the United States right of transit, that of 1867, see Malloy, ed., *Treaties, Conventions,* etc., Vol. II, p. 1279 ff. The Bryan-Chamorro Convention by which the United States secured lease to the Great Corn and Little Corn islands and the Gulf of Fonseca was regarded by other Central American States as an infringement on Nicaraguan sovereignty. Costa Rica and Salvador denounced the convention before the Central American Court of Justice. The Court upheld this protest and ruled against the United States. Both Nicaragua and the United States disregarded the ruling of the Court, and it came to an inglorious end. See S. Nearing and J. Freeman, *Dollar Diplomacy;* D. G. Munro, *The Five Republics of Central America;* I. J. Cox, *Nicaragua and the United States;* M. W. Williams, *Anglo-American Isthmian Diplomacy;* H. G. Miller, *The Isthmian Highway,* ch. xvi.

ART. I. The Government of Nicaragua grants in perpetuity to the Government of the United States, forever free from all taxation or other public charge, the exclusive proprietary rights necessary and convenient for the construction, operation and maintenance of an inter-oceanic canal by way of the San Juan River and the great Lake of Nicaragua or by way of any route over Nicaraguan territory, the details of the terms upon which such canal shall be constructed, operated and maintained to be agreed to by the two governments whenever the Government of the United States shall notify the Government of Nicaragua of its desire or intention to construct such canal.

ART. II. To enable the Government of the United States to protect the Panama Canal and the proprietary rights granted to the Government of the United States by the foregoing article, and also to enable the Government of the United States to take any measure necessary to the ends contemplated herein, the Government of Nicaragua hereby leases for a term of ninety-nine years to the Government of the United States the islands in the Caribbean Sea known as Great Corn Island and Little Corn Island; and the Government of Nicaragua further grants to the Government of the United States for a like period of ninety-nine years the right to establish, operate and maintain a naval base at such place on the territory of Nicaragua bordering upon the Gulf of Fonseca as the Government of the United States may select. The Government of the United States shall have the option of renewing for a further term of ninety-nine years the above leases and grants upon the expiration of their respective terms, it being expressly agreed that the territory hereby leased and the naval base which may be maintained under the grant aforesaid shall be subject exclusively to the laws and sovereign authority of the United States during the terms of such lease and grant and of any renewal or renewals thereof.

ART. III. In consideration of the foregoing stipulations and for the purposes contemplated by this Convention and for the purpose of reducing the present indebtedness of Nicaragua, the Government of the United States shall, upon the date of the exchange of ratification of this Convention, pay for the benefit of the Republic of Nicaragua the sum of three million dollars United States gold coin, of the present weight and fineness, to be deposited to the order of the Government of Nicaragua in such bank or banks or with such banking corporation as the Government of the United States may determine, to be applied by Nicaragua upon its indebtedness or other public purposes for the advancement of the welfare of Nicaragua in a manner to be determined by the two High Contracting Parties, all such disbursements to be made by orders drawn by the Minister of Finance of the Republic of Nicaragua and approved by the Secretary of State of the United States or by such person as he may designate.

This Convention shall be ratified by the High Contracting Parties in accordance with their respective laws, and the ratifications thereof shall be exchanged at Washington as soon as possible. . . .

WILLIAM JENNINGS BRYAN.
EMILIANO CHAMORRO.

399. HOUSTON, EAST & WEST TEXAS RAILWAY COMPANY v. UNITED STATES
234 U. S. 342
1914

Appeal from the United States Commerce Court. Suit to set aside order of the Interstate Commerce Commission regulating railway rates. This case is generally known as the Shreveport Case.

HUGHES, C. J. These suits were brought in the commerce court . . . to set aside an order of the Interstate Commerce Commission, dated March 11, 1912, upon the ground that it exceeded the Commission's authority. . . .

The gravamen of the complaint, said the Interstate Commerce Commission, was that the carriers made rates out of Dallas and other Texas points into eastern Texas which were much lower than those which they extended into Texas from Shreveport. The situation may be briefly described: Shreveport, Louisiana, is about 40 miles from the Texas state line, and 231 miles from Houston, Texas, on the line of the Houston, East & West Texas and Houston and Shreveport Companies; it is 189 miles from Dallas, Texas, on the line of the Texas & Pacific. Shreveport competes with both cities for the trade of the intervening territory. The rates on these lines from Dallas and Houston, respectively, eastward to intermediate points, in Texas, were much less, according to distance, than from Shreveport westward to the same points. It is undisputed that the difference was substantial, and injuriously affected the commerce of Shreveport. . . .

The Interstate Commerce Commission found that the interstate class rates out of Shreveport to named Texas points were unreasonable, and it established maximum class rates for this traffic. . . .

The point of the objection to the order is that, as the discrimination found by the Commission to be unjust arises out of the relation of intrastate rates, maintained under state authority, to interstate rates that have been upheld as reasonable, its correction was beyond the Commission's power. . . . The invalidity of the order is challenged upon two grounds:

1. That Congress is impotent to control the intrastate charges of an interstate carrier even to the extent necessary to prevent injurious discrimination against interstate traffic. . . .

Congress is empowered to regulate,—that is, to provide the law for the government of interstate commerce; to enact "all appropriate legislation" for its protection and advancement . . . As it is competent for Congress to legislate to these ends, unquestionably it may seek their attainment by requiring that the agencies of interstate commerce shall not be used in such manner as to cripple, retard, or destroy it. The fact that carriers are instruments of intrastate commerce, as well as of interstate commerce, does not derogate from the complete and paramount authority of Congress over the latter, or preclude the Federal power from being exerted to prevent the intrastate operations of such carriers from being made a means of injury to that which has been confided to Federal care. Wherever the interstate and intrastate transactions of carries are so related that the government of the one involves the control of the other, it is Congress, and not the state, that is entitled to prescribe the final and dominant rule, for otherwise Congress would be denied the exercise of its constitutional authority, and the state, and not the nation, would be supreme within the national field. . . .

It is for Congress to supply the needed correction where the relation between intrastate and interstate rates presents the evil to be corrected, and this it may do completely, by reason of its control over the interstate carrier in all matters having such a close and substantial relation to interstate commerce that it is necessary or appropriate to exercise the control for the effective government of that commerce.

It is also clear that, in removing the injurious discriminations against interstate traffic arising from the relation of intrastate to interstate rates, Congress is not bound to reduce the latter below what it may deem to be a proper standard fair to the carrier and to the public. Otherwise, it could prevent the injury to interstate commerce only by the sacrifice of its judgement as to interstate rates. Congress is entitled to maintain its own standard as to these rates, and to forbid any discriminatory action by interstate carriers which will obstruct the freedom of movement of interstate traffic over their lines in accordance with the terms it establishes.

Having this power, Congress could provide for its execution through the aid of a subordinate body; and we conclude that the order of the Commission now in question cannot be held invalid upon the ground that it exceeded the authority which Congress could lawfully confer. . . .

Decree of the Commerce Court affirmed.

Justices LURTON and PITNEY dissenting.

400. WILSON'S APPEAL FOR NEUTRALITY
Message to Senate, August 19, 1914

(U. S. 63 Congress, 2nd Sess. *Senate Doc.* 566)

The outbreak of the World War in August, 1914 brought an immediate Proclamation of Neutrality, August 4, together with a proposal to "act in the interest of peace". Two weeks later President Wilson reinforced this official proclamation with an appeal for neutrality "in thought as well as in action."

My fellow countrymen: I suppose that every thoughtful man in America has asked himself, during these last troubled weeks, what influence the European war may exert upon the United States, and I take the liberty of addressing a few words to you in order to point out that it is entirely within our own choice what its effects upon us will be and to urge very earnestly upon you the sort of speech and conduct which will best safeguard the Nation against distress and disaster.

The effect of the war upon the United States will depend upon what American citizens say and do. Every man who really loves America will act and speak in the true spirit of neutrality, which is the spirit of impartiality and fairness and friendliness to all concerned. The spirit of the Nation in this critical matter will be determined largely by what individuals and society and those gathered in public meetings do and say, upon what newspapers and magazines contain, upon what ministers utter in their pulpits, and men proclaim as their opinions on the street.

The people of the United States are drawn from many nations, and chiefly from the nations now at war. It is natural and inevitable that there should be the utmost variety of sympathy and desire among them with regard to the issues and circumstances of the conflict. Some will wish one nation, others another, to succeed in the momentous struggle. It will be easy to excite passion and difficult to allay it. Those responsible for exciting it will assume a heavy responsibility, responsibility for no less a thing than that the people of the United States, whose love of their country and whose loyalty to its Government should unite them as Americans all, bound in honor and affection to think first of her and her interests, may be divided in camps of hostile opinion, hot against each other, involved in the war itself in impulse and opinion if not in action.

Such divisions amongst us would be fatal to our peace of mind and might seriously stand in the way of the proper performance of our duty as the one great nation at peace, the one people holding itself ready to play a part of impartial mediation and speak the counsels of peace and accommodation, not as a partisan, but as a friend.

I venture, therefore, my fellow countrymen, to speak a solemn word of warning to you against that deepest, most subtle, most essential breach of neutrality which may spring out of partisanship, out of passionately taking sides. The United States must be neutral in fact as well as in name during these days that are to try men's souls. We must be impartial in thought as well as in action, must put a curb upon our sentiments as well as upon every transaction that might be construed as a preference of one party to the struggle before another.

My thought is of America. I am speaking, I feel sure, the earnest wish and purpose of every thoughtful American that this great country of ours, which is, of course, the first in our thoughts and in our hearts, should show herself in this time of peculiar trial a Nation fit beyond others to exhibit the fine poise of undisturbed judgment, the dignity of self-control, the efficiency of dispassionate action; a Nation that neither sits in judgment upon others nor is disturbed in her own counsels and which keeps herself fit and free to do what is honest and disinterested and truly serviceable for the peace of the world.

Shall we not resolve to put upon ourselves the restraints which will bring to our people the happiness and the great and lasting influence for peace we covet for them?

401. TREATY OF ARBITRATION WITH CHINA
September 15, 1914

(American Journal of International Law, Supplement, Vol. X, p. 268)

When Bryan became Secretary of State he proceeded to put into effect a policy of the arbitration of international disputes that he had advocated since the beginning of his public career. These treaties called for the erection of arbitration commissions to adjudicate issues in dispute between the United States and other nations, and the suspension of all preparation for war for the period of one year. Bryan succeeded in concluding thirty of these treaties, and he regarded them as his most permanent claim to fame. See, M. E. Curti, *Bryan and World Peace;* C. L. Lange, *The American Peace Treaties;* P. Hibben, *The Peerless Leader,* ch. xxvii; the treaties are collected in *Treaties for the Advancement of Peace Negotiated by William Jennings Bryan.*

TREATY BETWEEN CHINA AND THE UNITED STATES FOR THE ADVANCEMENT OF PEACE

Signed at Washington, September 15, 1914; ratifications exchanged, October 22, 1915.

Art. I. Any disputes arising between the Government of the United States of America and the Government of the Republic of China, of whatever nature they may be, shall, when ordinary diplomatic proceedings have failed and the high contracting parties do not have recourse to arbitration, be submitted for investigation and report to a permanent international commission constituted in the manner prescribed in the following article.

The high contracting parties agree not to resort, with respect to each other, to any act of force during the investigation to be made by the commission and before its report is handed in.

Art. II. The international commission shall be composed of five members appointed as follows: each government shall designate two members, only one of whom shall be of its own nationality; the fifth member shall be designated by common consent and shall not belong to any of the nationalities already represented on the commission; he shall perform the duties of president.

In case the two governments should not be able to agree on the choice of the fifth commissioner, the other four shall be called upon to designate him, and failing an understanding between them, the provisions of Article 45 of the Hague Convention of 1907 shall be applied.

The commission shall be organized within six months from the exchange of ratification of the present convention.

The members shall be appointed for one year and their appointment may not be renewed. They shall remain in office until superseded or reappointed, or until the work on which they are engaged at the time their office expires is completed. . . .

Art. III. In case a dispute should arise between the high contracting parties which is not settled by the ordinary methods, each party shall have a right to ask that the investigation thereof be intrusted to the international commission charged with making a report. Notice shall be given to the President of the international commission, who shall at once communicate with his colleagues.

In the same case the president may, after consulting his colleagues and upon receiving the consent of a majority of the commission, offer the services of the latter to each of the contracting parties. Acceptance of that offer declared by one of the two governments shall be sufficient to give jurisdiction of the case to the commission in accordance with the foregoing paragraph.

The place of meeting shall be determined by the commission itself.

Art. IV. The two high contracting parties shall have a right, each on its own part, to state to the president of the commission what is the subject matter of the controversy. No difference in these statements, which shall be furnished by way of suggestion, shall arrest the action of the commission.

In case the cause of the dispute should consist of certain acts already committed or about to be committed, the commission shall as soon as possible indicate what measures to preserve the rights of each party ought in its opinion to be taken provisionally and pending the delivery of its report.

Art. V. . . . The work of the commission shall be completed within one year from the date on which it has taken jurisdiction of the case, unless the high contracting parties should agree to set a different period.

The conclusion of the commission and the terms of its report shall be adopted by a majority. The report, signed by virtue of his office, shall be transmitted by him to each of the contracting parties.

The high contracting parties reserve full liberty as to the action to be taken on the report of the commission.

Art. VI. The present treaty shall be ratified by the President of the United States of America, with the advice and consent of the Senate of the United States, and by the President of the Republic of China.

It shall go into force immediately after the exchange of ratifications and shall last five years.

Unless denounced six months at least before the expiration of the said period of five years, it shall remain in force until the expiration of a period of twelve months after either party shall have notified the other of its intention to terminate it. . . .

WILLIAM JENNINGS BRYAN.

KAI FU SHAH.

402. THE FEDERAL TRADE COMMISSION ACT
September 26, 1914
(*U. S. Statutes at Large,* Vol. XXXVIII, p. 717 ff.)

January 20, President Wilson delivered to Congress a message on trusts in which he recommended, among other things, a law creating a federal trade commission to advise, inform and guide business. A bill in harmony with these suggestions was promptly introduced into Congress and with the energetic support of Senator Newlands and Representatives Adamson, Clayton and others, passed and approved September 26. The purpose of this and the Clayton Bill, according to Wilson, was "to make men in a small way of business as free to succeed as men in a big way, and to kill monopoly in the seed." See, G. C. Henderson, *The Federal Trade Commission;* R. S. Baker, *Woodrow Wilson,* Vol. IV, ch. vii; H. R. Seager and C. A. Gulick, *Trust and Corporation Problems.*

An act to create a Federal Trade Commission, to define its powers and duties, and for other purposes.

Be it enacted, That a commission is hereby created and established, to be known as the Federal Trade Commission (hereinafter referred to as the commission), which shall be composed of five commissioners, who shall be appointed by the President, by and with the advice and consent of the Senate. Not more than three of the commissioners shall be members of the same political party. The first commissioners appointed shall continue in office for terms of three, four, five, six, and seven years, respectively, from the date of the taking effect of this Act, the term of each to be designated by the President, but their successors shall be appointed for terms of seven years, except that any person chosen to fill a vacancy shall be appointed only for the unexpired term of the commissioner whom he shall succeed. . . .

SEC. 3. That upon the organization of the commission and election of its chairman, the Bureau of Corporations and the offices of Commissioner and Deputy Commissioner of Corporations shall cease to exist; and all pending investigations and proceedings of the Bureau of Corporations shall be continued by the commission. . . .

SEC. 5. That unfair methods of competition in commerce are hereby declared unlawful.

The commission is hereby empowered and directed to prevent persons, partnerships, or corporations, except banks, and common carriers subject to the Acts to regulate commerce, from using unfair methods of competition in commerce.

Whenever the commission shall have reason to believe that any such person, partnership, or corporation has been or is using any unfair method of competition in commerce, . . . it shall issue and serve upon such person, partnership, or corporation a complaint stating its charges in that respect, and containing a notice of a hearing upon a day and at a place therein fixed at least thirty days after the service of said complaint. The person, partnership, or corporation so complained of shall have the right to appear at the place and time so fixed and show cause why an order should not be entered by the commission requiring such person, partnership, or corporation to cease and desist from the violation of the law so charged in said complaint. . . . If upon such hearing the commission shall be of the opinion that the method of competition in question is prohibited by this Act, it shall make a report in writing in which it shall state its findings as to the facts, and shall issue and cause to be served on such person, partnership, or corporation an order requiring such person, partnership, or corporation to cease and desist from using such method of competition. . . .

SEC. 6. That the commission shall also have power—

(a) To gather and compile information concerning and to investigate from time to time the organization, business, conduct, practices, and management of any corporation engaged in commerce, excepting banks and common carriers subject to the Act to regulate commerce, and its relation to other corporations and to individuals, associations, and partnerships.

(b) To require, . . . corporations engaged in commerce, excepting banks, and common carriers subject to the Act to regulate commerce, . . . to file with the commission in such form as the commission may prescribe annual or special, or both annual and special, reports or answers in writing to specific questions, furnishing to the commission such information as it may require as to the organization, business, conduct, practices, management, and relation to other corporations, partnerships, and individuals of the respective corporations filing such reports. . . .

(c) Whenever a final decree has been entered against any defendant corporation in any suit brought by the United States to prevent and restrain any violation of the antitrust Acts, to make investigation, . . . of the manner in which the decree has been or is being carried out, . . . it shall be its duty to make such investigation. It shall transmit to the Attorney General a report embodying its findings and recommendations as a result of any such investigation, and the report shall be made public in the discretion of the commission.

403. THE CLAYTON ANTI-TRUST ACT
October 15, 1914
(U. S. Statutes at Large XXXVIII, p. 730 ff.)

This act and the Federal Trade Commission Act embodied a large part of Wilson's ideas of the regulation of business. For a general expression of the Wilsonian policy, see *The New Freedom.* The most important sections of the Clayton law were those dealing with labor. For the judicial construction of these labor provisions, see Doc. No. 445. The legislative history of the Clayton Act is told in R. S. Baker, *Woodrow Wilson, Life and Letters,* Vol. IV.

. . . SEC. 2. That it shall be unlawful for any person engaged in commerce, in the course of such commerce, either directly or indirectly to discriminate in price between different purchasers of commodities which commodities are sold for use, consumption, or resale within the United States or any . . . other place under the jurisdiction of the United States, where the effect of such discrimination may be to substantially lessen competition or tend to create a monopoly in any line of commerce: . . .

SEC. 3. That it shall be unlawful for any person engaged in commerce, to lease or make a sale of goods, . . . or other commodities, . . . for use, consumption or resale within the United States or . . . other place under the jurisdiction of the United States, or fix a price charged therefor, or discount from, or rebate upon, such price, on the condition, . . . that the lessee or purchaser thereof shall not use or deal in the goods, . . . or other commodities of a competitor or competitors of the lessor or seller, where the effect of such lease, sale, or contract for sale or such condition, agreement, or understanding may be to substantially lessen competition or tend to create a monopoly in any line of commerce. . . .

SEC. 6. That the labor of a human being is not a commodity or article of commerce. Nothing contained in the anti-trust laws shall be construed to forbid the existence and operation of labor, agricultural, or horticultural organizations, instituted for the purposes of mutual help, and not having capital stock or conduced for profit, or to forbid or restrain individual members of such organizations from lawfully carrying out the legitimate objects thereof; nor shall such organizations, or the members thereof, be held or construed to be illegal combinations or conspiracies in restraint of trade, under the anti-trust laws.

SEC. 7. That no corporation engaged in commerce shall acquire, directly or indirectly, the whole or any part of the stock or other share capital of another corporation engaged also in commerce, where the effect of such acquisition may be to substantially lessen competition between the corporation whose stock is so acquired and the corporation making the acquisition, or to restrain such commerce in any section or community, or tend to create a monopoly of any line of commerce. . . .

This section shall not apply to corporations purchasing such stock solely for investment and not using the same by voting or otherwise to bring about, or in attempting to bring about, the substantial lessening of competition. . . .

SEC. 8. That from and after two years from the date of the approval of this act no person shall at the same time be a director or other officer or employee of more than one bank, banking association or trust company, organized or operating under the laws of the United States, either of which has deposits, capital, surplus, and undivided profits aggregating more than $5,000,000; and no private banker or person who is a director in any bank or trust company, organized and operating under the laws of a State, having deposits, capital, surplus, and undivided profits aggregating more than $5,000,000, shall be eligible to be a director in any bank or banking association organized or operating under the laws of the United States. . . .

That from and after two years from the date of the approval of this Act no person at the same time shall be a director in any two or more corporations, any one of which has capital, surplus, and undivided profits aggregating more than $1,000,000, engaged in whole or in part in commerce, other than banks, banking associations, trust companies and common carriers subject to the Act to regulate commerce, approved February 4th, 1887, if such corporations are or shall have been theretofore, by virtue of their business and location of operation, competitors, so that the elimination of competition by agreement between them would constitute a violation of any of the provisions of any of the anti-trust laws. . . .

SEC. 10. That after two years from the approval of this Act no common carrier engaged in commerce shall have any dealings in securities, supplies, or other articles of commerce, . . . to the amount of more than $50,000, in the aggregate, in any one year, with another corporation, firm, partnership or association when the said common carrier shall have upon its board of directors or as its president, manager, or as its purchasing or selling officer, or agent in the particular transaction, any person who is at the same time a director, manager, or purchasing or selling officer of, or who has any substantial interest in, such other corporation, firm, partnership, or association, unless and except such purchases shall be made from, or such dealings shall be with, the bidder whose bid is the most favorable to such common carrier, to be ascertained by competitive bidding under regulations to be prescribed by rule or otherwise by the Interstate Commerce Commission. . . .

SEC. 20. That no restraining order or injunction shall be granted by any court of the United States, or a judge or the judges thereof, in any case between an employer and employees or between employers and employees, or between employees, or between persons employed and persons seeking employment, involving, or growing out of, a dispute concerning terms or conditions of employment, unless necessary to prevent irreparable injury to property, or to a property right, of the party making the application, for which injury there is no adequate remedy at law, and such property or property right must be described with a particularity in the application, which must be in writing and sworn to by the applicant or by his agent or attorney.

And no such restraining order or injunction shall prohibit any person or persons, whether singly or in concert, from terminating any relation of employment, or from ceasing to perform any work or labor, or from recommending, advising, or persuading others by peaceful means so to do; or from attending at any place where any such person or persons may lawfully be, for the purpose of peacefully obtaining or communicating information, or from peacefully persuading any person to work or to abstain from working; or from ceasing to patronize or to employ any party to such dispute, or from recommending, advising, or persuading others by peaceful and lawful means so to do; or from paying or giving to, or withholding from, any person engaged in such dispute, any strike benefits or other moneys or things of value; or from peaceably assembling in a lawful manner, and for lawful purposes; or from doing any act or thing which might lawfully be done in the absence of such dispute by any party thereto; nor shall any of the acts specified in this paragraph be considered or held to be violations of any law of the United States.

404. WILSON'S VETO OF LITERACY TEST FOR IMMIGRANTS
January 28, 1915

(*Congressional Record,* 63d Congress, 3d. session, Vol. LII, p. 2481-2)

A similar act had been vetoed by Presidents Cleveland and Taft; a bill incorporating the main features of the Act of 1915 was passed over President Wilson's veto, in 1917.

To the House of Representatives: It is with unaffected regret that I find myself constrained by clear conviction to return this bill without my signature. Not only do I feel it to be a very serious matter to exercise the power of veto in any case, because it involves opposing the single judgement of the President to the judgement of a majority of both Houses of the Congress . . . but also because this particular bill is in so many important respects admirable, well conceived, and desirable. Its enactment into law would undoubtedly enhance the efficiency and improve the methods of handling the important branch of the public service to which it relates. But candor and a sense of duty with regard to the responsibility so clearly imposed upon me by the Constitution in matters of legislation leave me no choice but to dissent.

In two particulars of vital consequence this bill embodies a radical departure from the traditional and long established policy of this country, a policy in which our people have conceived the very character of their Government to be expressed, the very mission and spirit of the Nation in respect of its relations to the peoples of the world outside their borders. It seeks to all but close entirely the gates of asylum which have always been open to those who could find nowhere else the right and opportunity of constitutional agitation for what they conceived to be the natural and inalienable rights of men; and it excludes those to whom the opportunities of elementary education have been denied, without regard to their character, their purposes, or their natural capacity.

Restrictions like these, adopted earlier in our history as a Nation, would very materially have altered the course and cooled the humane ardors of our politics. The right of political asylum has brought to this country many a man of noble character and elevated purpose who was marked as an outlaw in his own less fortunate land, and who has yet become an ornament to our citizenship and to our public councils. The children and compatriots of these illustrious Americans must stand amazed to see the representatives of their Nation now resolved, in the fullness of our national strength and at the maturity of our great institutions, to risk turning such men back from our shores without test of quality or purpose. It is difficult for me to believe that the full effect of this feature of the bill was realized when it was framed and adopted, and it is impossible for me to assent to it in the form in which it is here cast.

The literacy test and the tests and restrictions which accompany it constitute an even more radical change in the policy of the Nation. Hitherto we have generously kept our doors open to all who were not unfitted by reason of disease or incapacity for self-support or such personal records and antecedents as were likely to make them a menace to our peace and order or to the wholesome and essential relationships of life. In this bill it is proposed to turn away from tests of character and of quality and impose tests which exclude and restrict; for the laws here embodied are not tests of quality or of character or of personal fitness, but tests of opportunity. Those who come seeking opportunity are not to be admitted unless they have already had one of the chief of the opportunities they seek, the opportunity of education. The object of such provisions is restriction, not selection.

If the people of this country have made up their minds to limit the number of immigrants by arbitrary tests and so reverse the policy of all the generations of Americans that have gone before them, it is their right to do so. I am their servant and have no license to stand in their way. But I do not believe that they have. I respectfully submit that no one can quote their mandate to that effect. Has any political party ever avowed a policy of restriction in this fundamental matter, gone to the country on it, and been commissioned to control its legislation? Does this bill rest upon the conscious and universal assent and desire of the American people? I doubt it. It is because I doubt it that I make bold to dissent from it. I am willing to bide by the verdict, but not until it has been rendered. Let the platforms of parties speak out upon this policy and the people pronounce their wish. The matter is too fundamental to be settled otherwise.

I have no pride of opinion in this question. I am not foolish enough to profess to know the wishes and ideals of America better than the body of her chosen representatives know them. I only want instruction direct from those whose fortunes with ours, and all men's are involved.

405. THE FIRST *LUSITANIA* NOTE
May 13, 1915

(Foreign Relations of the United States, 1915, Supplement, p. 393 ff.)

On May 7, 1915, the British passenger ship *Lusitania* was torpedoed and sunk by a German submarine with a loss of life of over eleven hundred passengers and crew, including one hundred and twenty-four Americans. This act brought the United States and Germany to the verge of war. The first *Lusitania* note was written by President Wilson, and without the qualifying clauses which Secretary Bryan was anxious to insert. Because of a misunderstanding of a conversation which the Austrian Ambassador Dumba held with Bryan, Germany was at first inclined to take the note less seriously than was required by the circumstances. The German government attempted to justify the act of the submarine commander on the ground that the *Lusitania* was, in fact, armed and carried contraband of war. In his second *Lusitania* note of June 9, Wilson brushed aside these allegations as irrelevant, and again insisted upon a disavowal from the German government and assurances that the German government would recognize "the obligation to take sufficient precaution to ascertain whether a suspected merchantman is in fact of belligerent nationality or is in fact carrying contraband of war under a neutral flag. The Government of the United States therefore deems it reasonable to expect that the Imperial German Government will adopt the measures necessary to put these principles into practice in respect to the safeguarding of American lives and American ships." (*For. Rel. of the U. S., 1915,* Suppl.,

p. 436 ff.) Bryan felt unable to sign this note, and resigned from the Cabinet: the note went out over the signature of Secretary Lansing. The negotiations dragged out for some time, but after a further exchange of notes, and the sinking of the *Arabic*, August 19, 1915, Germany promised to accept the President's terms. See, C. Seymour, *American Diplomacy during the World War*, p. 89 ff.; C. Seymour, *Intimate Papers of Colonel House*, Vol. I, ch. xiv, Vol. II, chs. i–ii; W. J. Bryan, *Memoirs*, Part II, chs. xiv–xv; S. F. Bemis, ed., *American Secretaries of States*, Vol. X, p. 23 ff.; J. B. Scott, *Survey of International Relations Between the United States and Germany, 1914–1917;* C. H. Grattan, *Why We Fought.*

The Secretary of State to Ambassador Gerard.
DEPARTMENT OF STATE,
Washington, May 13, 1915.

Please call on the Minister of Foreign Affairs and after reading to him this communication leave with him a copy.

In view of recent acts of the German authorities in violation of American rights on the high seas which culminated in the torpedoing and sinking of the British steamship *Lusitania* on May 7, 1915, by which over 100 American citizens lost their lives, it is clearly wise and desirable that the Government of the United States and the Imperial German Government should come to a clear and full understanding as to the grave situation which has resulted.

The sinking of the British passenger steamer *Falaba* by a German submarine on March 28, through which Leon C. Thrasher, an American citizen, was drowned; the attack on April 28 on the American vessel *Cushing* by a German aeroplane; the torpedoing on May 1 of the American vessel *Gulflight* by a German submarine, as a result of which two or more American citizens met their death; and, finally, the torpedoing and sinking of the steamship *Lusitania,* constitute a series of events which the Government of the United States has observed with growing concern, distress, and amazement.

Recalling the humane and enlightened attitude hitherto assumed by the Imperial German Government in matters of international right, and particularly with regard to the freedom of the seas; having learned to recognize the German views and the German influence in the field of international obligation as always engaged upon the side of justice and humanity; and having understood the instructions of the Imperial German Government to its naval commanders to be upon the same plane of humane action prescribed by the naval codes of other nations, the Government of the United States was loath to believe—it can not now bring itself to believe—that these acts, so absolutely contrary to the rules, the practices, and the spirit of modern warfare, could have the countenance or sanction of that great Government. It feels it to be its duty, therefore, to address the Imperial German Government concerning them with the utmost frankness and in the earnest hope that it is not mistaken in expecting action on the part of the Imperial German Government which will correct the unfortunate impressions which have been created and vindicate once more the position of that Government with regard to the sacred freedom of the seas.

The Government of the United States has been apprised that the Imperial German Government considered themselves obliged by the extraordinary circumstances of the present war and the measures adopted by their adversaries in seeking to cut Germany off from all commerce, to adopt methods of retaliation which go much beyond the ordinary methods of warfare at sea, in the proclamation of a war zone from which they have warned neutral ships to keep away. This Government has already taken occasion to inform the Imperial German Government that it can not admit the adoption of such measures or such a warning of danger to operate as in any degree an abbreviation of the rights of American shipmasters or of American citizens bound on lawful errands as passengers on merchant ships of belligerent nationality; and that it must hold the Imperial German Government to a strict accountability for any infringement of those rights, intentional or incidental. It does not understand the Imperial German Government to question those rights. It assumes, on the contrary, that the Imperial Government accept, as of course, the rule that the lives of noncombatants, whether they be of neutral citizenship or citizens of one of the nations at war, can not lawfully or rightfully be put in jeopardy by the capture or destruction of an unarmed merchantman, and recognize also, as all other nations do, the obligation to take the usual precaution of visit and search to ascertain whether a suspected merchantman is in fact of belligerent nationality or is in fact carrying contraband of war under a neutral flag.

The Government of the United States, therefore, desires to call the attention of the Imperial German Government with the utmost earnestness to the fact that the objection to their present method of attack against the trade of their enemies lies in the practical impossibility of employing submarines in the destruction of commerce without disregarding those rules of fairness, reason, justice, and humanity which all modern opinion regards as imperative. It is practically impossible for the officers of a submarine to visit a merchantman at sea and examine her papers and cargo. It is practically impossible for them to make a prize of her; and, if they can not put a prize crew on board of her, they can not sink her without leaving her crew and all on board of her to the mercy of the sea in her small boats. These facts it is understood the Imperial German Government frankly admit. We are informed that in the instances of which we have spoken time enough for even that poor measure of safety was not given, and in at least two of the cases cited not so much as a warning was received. Manifestly submarines can not be used against merchantmen, as the last few weeks have shown, without an inevitable violation of many sacred principles of justice and humanity.

American citizens act within their indisputable rights in taking their ships and in traveling wherever their legitimate business calls them upon the high seas, and exercise those rights in what should be the well-justified confidence that their lives will not be endangered by acts done in clear violation of universally acknowledged international obligations, and certainly in the confidence that their own Government will sustain them in the exercise of their rights.

There was recently published in the newspapers of the United States, I regret to inform the Imperial German Government, a formal warning, purporting to come from the Imperial German Embassy at Washington, addressed to the people of the United States, and stating, in effect, that any citizen of the United States who exercised his right of free travel upon the seas would do so at his peril if his journey should take him within the zone of waters within which the Imperial German Navy was using submarines against the commerce of Great Britain and France, notwithstanding the respectful but very earnest protest of his Government, the Government of the United States. I do not refer to this for the purpose of calling the attention of the Imperial German Government at this time to the surprising irregularity of a communication from the Imperial German Embassy at Washington addressed to the people of the United States through the newspapers, but only for the purpose of pointing out that no warning that an unlawful and inhumane act will be committed can possibly be accepted as an excuse or palliation for that act or as an abatement of the responsibility for its commission.

Long acquainted as this Government has been with the character of the Imperial German Government and with the high principles of equity by which they have in the past been actuated and guided, the Government of the United States can not believe that the commanders of the vessels which committed these acts of lawlessness did so except under a misapprehension of the orders issued by the Imperial German naval authorities. It takes it for granted that, at least within the practical possibilities of every such case, the commanders even of submarines were expected to do nothing that would involve the lives of noncombatants or the safety of neutral ships, even at the cost of failing of their object of capture or destruction. It confidently expects, therefore, that the Imperial German Government will disavow the acts of which the Government of the United States complains, that they will make reparation so far as reparation is possible for injuries which are without measure, and that they will take immediate steps to prevent the recurrence of anything so obviously subversive of the principles of warfare for which the Imperial German Government have in the past so wisely and so firmly contended.

The Government and people of the United

States look to the Imperial German Government for just, prompt, and enlightened action in this vital matter with the greater confidence because the United States and Germany are bound together not only by special ties of friendship but also by the explicit stipulations of the treaty of 1828 between the United States and the Kingdom of Prussia.

Expressions of regret and offers of reparation in the case of the destruction of neutral ships sunk by mistake, while they may satisfy international obligations, if no loss of life results, can not justify or excuse a practice, the natural and necessary effect of which is to subject neutral nations and neutral persons to new and immeasurable risks.

The Imperial German Government will not expect the Government of the United States to omit any word or any act necessary to the performance of its sacred duty of maintaining the rights of the United States and its citizens and of safeguarding their free exercise and enjoyment.

BRYAN.

406. ELIHU ROOT ON INVISIBLE GOVERNMENT
Speech to the New York Constitutional Convention
August 30, 1915

(Record of the Constitutional Convention of the State of New York, 1915, Vol. III, p. 3381 ff.)

These remarks by Mr. Root apropos of the reorganization of the executive power in the State, constitute an excellent analysis of "invisible government" and boss rule. On Boss Platt, see *The Autobiography of Thomas Collier Platt;* H. S. Gosnell, *Boss Platt and his New York Machine;* D. S. Alexander, *Four Famous New Yorkers.*

Mr. Chairman, I have had great doubt whether or not I should impose any remarks on this bill upon the Convention, especially after my friend Mr. Quigg has so ingeniously made it difficult for me to speak; but I have been so long deeply interested in the subject of the bill, and I shall have so few opportunities hereafter, perhaps never another, that I cannot refrain from testifying to my faith in the principles of government which underlie the measure, and putting upon this record for whatever it may be worth the conclusions which I have reached upon the teachings of long experience in many positions, through many years of participation in the public affairs of this State and in observation of them. . . .

The governments of our cities: Why, twenty years ago, when James Bryce wrote his "American Commonwealth," the government of American cities was a byword and a shame for Americans all over the world. Heaven be thanked, the government of our cities has now gone far toward redeeming itself and us from that disgrace, and the government of American cities today is in the main far superior to the government of American States. I challenge contradiction to that statement. How has it been reached? How have our cities been lifted up from the low grade of incompetency and corruption on which they stood when the "American Commonwealth" was written? It has been done by applying the principles of this bill to city government, by giving power to the men elected by the people to do the things for which they were elected. But I say it is quite plain that that is not all. It is not all.

I am going to discuss a subject now that goes back to the beginning of the political life of the oldest man in this Convention, and one to which we cannot close our eyes, if we keep the obligations of our oath. We talk about the government of the Constitution. We have spent many days in discussing the powers of this and that and the other officer. What is the government of this State? What has it been during the forty years of my acquaintance with it? The government of the Constitution? Oh, no; not half the time, or half way. When I ask what do the people find wrong in our State government, my mind goes back to those periodic fits of public rage in which the people rouse up and tear down the political leader, first of one party and then of the other party. It goes on to the public feeling of resentment against the control of party organizations, of both parties and of all parties.

Now, I treat this subject in my own mind not as a personal question to any man. I am talking about the system. From the days of Fenton, and Conkling, and Arthur and Cornell, and Platt, from the days of David B. Hill, down to the present time the government of the State has presented two different lines of activity, one of the constitutional and statutory officers of the State, and the other of the party leaders,—they call them party bosses. They call the system —I don't coin the phrase, I adopt it because it carries its own meaning—the system they call "invisible government." For I don't remember how many years, Mr. Conkling was the supreme ruler in this State; the Governor did not count, the legislatures did not count; comptrollers and secretaries of state and what not, did not count. It was what Mr. Conkling said, and in a great outburst of public rage he was pulled down.

Then Mr. Platt ruled the State; for nigh upon twenty years he ruled it. It was not the Governor; it was not the Legislature; it was not any elected officers; it was Mr. Platt. And the capitol was not here; it was at 49 Broadway; Mr. Platt and his lieutenants. It makes no difference what name you give, whether you call it Fenton or Conkling or Cornell or Arthur or Platt, or by the names of men now living. The ruler of the State during the greater part of the forty years of my acquaintance with the State government has not been any man authorized by the Constitution or by the law; and, sir, there is throughout the length and breadth of this State a deep and sullen and long-continued resentment at being governed thus by men not of the people's choosing. The party leader is elected by no one, accountable to no one, bound by no oath of office, removable by no one. Ah! My friends here have talked about this bill's creating an autocracy. The word points with admirable facility the very opposite reason for the bill. It is to destroy autocracy and restore power so far as may be to the men elected by the people, accountable to the people, removable by the people. I don't criticise the men of the invisible government. How can I? I have known them all, and among them have been some of my dearest friends.

I can never forget the deep sense of indignation that I felt in the abuse that was heaped upon Chester A. Arthur, whom I honored and loved, when he was attacked because he held the position of political leader. But it is all wrong. It is all wrong that a government not authorized by the people should be continued superior to the government that is authorized by the people.

How is it accomplished? How is it done? Mr. Chairman, it is done by the use of patronage, and the patronage that my friends on the other side of this question have been arguing and pleading for in this Convention is the power to continue that invisible government against that authorized by the people. Everywhere, sir, that these two systems of government co-exist, there is a conflict day by day, and year by year, between two principles of appointment to office, two radically opposed principles. The elected officer or the appointed officer, the lawful officer who is to be held responsible for the administration of his office, desires to get men into the different positions of his office who will do their work in a way that is creditable to him and his administration. Whether it be a president appointing a judge, or a governor appointing a superintendent of public works, whatever it may be, the officer wants to make a success, and he wants to get the man selected upon the ground of his ability to do the work.

How is it about the boss? What does the boss have to do? He has to urge the appointment of a man whose appointment will consolidate his power and preserve the organization. The invisible government proceeds to build up and maintain its power by a reversal of the fundamental principle of good government, which is that men should be selected to perform the duties of the office; and to substitute the idea that men should be appointed to office for the preservation and enhancement of power of the political leader. The one, the true one, looks upon appointment to office with a view to the service that can be given to the public. The other, the false one, looks upon appointment to office with a view to what can be gotten out of it. Gentlemen of the Convention, I appeal to your knowledge of facts. Every one of you knows that what I say about the use of patronage under the system of invisible government is true. Louis Marshall told us the other day about the appointment of wardens in the Adirondacks, hotel keepers and people living there, to render no service whatever. They were appointed not for the service that they were to render to the State; they were appointed for the service they were to render to promote the power of a political organization. Mr. Chairman, we all know that the halls of this capitol swarm with men during the session of the Legislature on pay day. A great number, seldom here, rendering no service, are put on the payrolls as a matter of patronage, not of service, but of party patronage. Both parties are alike; all parties are alike. The system extends through all. Ah, Mr. Chairman, that system finds its opportunity in the division of powers, in a six headed executive, in which, by the natural workings of human nature there shall be opposition and discord and the playing of one force against the other, and so, when we refuse to make one Governor elected by the people the real chief executive, we make inevitable the setting up of a chief executive not selected by the people, not acting for the people's interest, but for the selfish interest of the few who control the party, whichever party it may be. Think for a moment of what this patronage system means. How many of you are there who would be willing to do to your private client, or customer, or any private trust, or to a friend or neighbor, what you see being done to the State of New York every year of your lives in the taking of money out of her treasury without service? We can, when we are in a private station, pass on without much attention to inveterate abuses. We can say to ourselves, I know it is wrong, I wish it could be set right; it cannot be set right, I will do nothing. But here, here, we face the duty, we cannot escape it, we are bound to do our work, face to face, in clear recognition of the truth, unpalatable, deplorable as it may be and the truth is that what the unerring instinct of the democracy of our State has seen in this government is that a different standard of morality is applied to the conduct of affairs of States than that which is applied in private affairs. I have been told forty times since this Convention met that you cannot change it. We can try, can't we? I deny that we cannot change it. I repel that cynical assumption which is born of the lethargy that comes from poisoned air during all these years. I assert that this perversion of democracy, this robbing democracy of its virility, can be changed as truly as the system under which Walpole governed the commons of England, by bribery, as truly as the atmosphere which made the *credit mobilier* scandal possible in the Congress of the United States has been blown away by the force of public opinion. We cannot change it in a moment, but we can do our share. We can take this one step toward, not robbing the people of their part in government, but toward robbing an irresponsible autocracy of its indefensible and unjust and undemocratic control of government, and restoring it to the people to be exercised by the men of their choice and their control. . . .

407. THE CONCENTRATION OF WEALTH
Final Report of the Commission on Industrial Relations
1915

(U. S. Commission on Industrial Relations: Final Report and Testimony, Vol. I, p. 80 ff. U. S. 64th Congress, 1st Session, *Sen. Doc.* No. 415)

By Act of August 23, 1912, Congress provided for a Commission on Industrial Relations to survey the condition of industry in the United States with special reference to labor. The Commission's Report is in eleven volumes; the first contains the final report and conclusions. For references, see Doc. No. 388, and E. Clark, *American Foundations and Their Fields.*

The Concentration of Wealth and Influence

The evidence developed by the hearings and investigations of the commission is the basis for the following statements:

1. The control of manufacturing, mining, and transportation industries is to an in-

creasing degree passing into the hands of great corporations through stock ownership, and control of credit is centralized in a comparatively small number of enormously powerful financial institutions. These financial institutions are in turn dominated by a very small number of powerful financiers.

2. The final control of American industry rests, therefore, in the hands of a small number of wealthy and powerful financiers.

3. The concentration of ownership and control is greatest in the basic industries upon which the welfare of the country must finally rest.

4. With few exceptions each of the great basic industries is dominated by a single large corporation, and where this is not true the control of the industry through stock ownership in supposedly independent corporations and through credit is almost, if not quite, as potent.

5. In such corporations, in spite of the large number of stockholders, the control through actual stock ownership rests with a very small number of persons. For example, in the United States Steel Corporation, which had in 1911 approximately one hundred thousand share holders, 1.5 percent of the stockholders held 57 percent of the stock, while the final control rested with a single private banking house.

Similarly, in the American Tobacco Company before the dissolution, 10 stockholders owned sixty percent of the stock.

6. Almost without exception the employees of the large corporations are unorganized as a result of the active and aggressive "nonunion" policy of the corporation management.

Furthermore, the labor policy of the large corporations almost inevitably determines the labor policy of the entire industry.

7. A careful and conservative study shows that the corporations controlled by six financial groups and affiliated interests employ 2,651,684 wage earners and have a grand total capitalization of $19,875,200,000. These six financial groups control 28 percent of the total number of wage earners engaged in the industries covered by the report of our investigation. The Morgan-First National Bank group alone controls corporations employing 785,499 wage earners. . . .

8. The lives of millions of wage earners are therefore subject to the dictation of a relatively small number of men.

9. These industrial dictators for the most part are totally ignorant of every aspect of the industries which they control except the finances, and are totally unconcerned with regard to the working and living conditions of the employees in those industries. Even if they were deeply concerned, the position of the employees would be merely that of the subjects of benevolent industrial despots.

10. Except, perhaps, for improvements in safety and sanitation, the labor conditions of these corporation-control industries are subject to great criticism and are a menace to the welfare of the Nation.

11. In order to prevent the organization of employees for the improvement of working conditions, elaborate systems of espionage are maintained by the large corporations which refuse to deal with labor unions, and the employees suspected of union affiliations are discharged.

12. The domination by the men in whose hands the final control of a large part of American industry rests is not limited to their employees, but is being rapidly extended to control the education and "social service" of the Nation.

13. This control is being extended largely through the creation of enormous privately managed funds for indefinite purposes, hereinafter designated "foundations," by the endowment of colleges and universities, by the creation of funds for the pensioning of teachers, by contributions to private charities, as well as through controlling or influencing the public press. . . .

22. The entrance of the foundations into the field of industrial relations, through the creation of a special division by the Rockefeller Foundation, constitutes a menace to the national welfare to which the attention not only of Congress but of the entire country should be directed. Backed by the $100-000,000 of the Rockefeller Foundation, this movement has the power to influence the entire country in the determination of its most vital policy. . . .

26. Apart from these foundations there is developing a degree of control over the teachings of professors in our colleges and

universities which constitutes a most serious menace. In June of this year two professors, known throughout their professions as men of great talent and high character, were dropped from the positions they had occupied and no valid reason for such action was made public. Both were witnesses before the commission, and made statements based upon their own expert knowledge and experience which were given wide publicity. One was a professor of law in a State university, who had acted as counsel for the strikers in Colorado; the other a professor of economics, who had not only been active in fights in behalf of child-labor legislation and other progressive measures, but had recently published a work comparing the incomes paid for all classes of service.

In the face of such an enormous problem one can only frankly confess inability to suggest measures which will protect the Nation from the grave dangers described. It is believed, however, that if Congress will enact the measures already recommended, providing for a heavy tax on large inheritances with a rigid limitation on the total amount of the bequest, for the reclamation by the Federal Government of all parts of the public domain (including mineral rights) which have been secured by fraud, and for a tax on nonproductive land and natural resources, a great step in the right direction will have been taken.

As regards the "foundations" created for unlimited general purposes and endowed with enormous resources, their ultimate possibilities are so grave a menace, not only as regards their own activities and influence but also the benumbing effect which they have on private citizens and public bodies, that if they could be clearly differentiated from other forms of voluntary altruistic effort it would be desirable to recommend their abolition. It is not possible, however, at this time to devise any clear-cut definition upon which they can be differentiated.

As the basis for effective action, it is suggested that the commission recommend:

1. The enactment by Congress of a statute providing that all incorporated nonprofit-making bodies whose present charters empower them to perform more than a single specific function and whose funds exceed $1,000,000 shall be required to secure a Federal charter.

The Federal charter should contain the following provisions:

(a) Definite limitation of the funds to be held by any organization, at least not to exceed the largest amount held by any at the time of the passage of the act.

(b) Definite and exact specifications of the powers and functions which the organization is empowered to exercise, with provision for heavy penalties if its corporate powers are exceeded.

(c) Specific provision against the accumulation of funds by the compounding of unexpended income and against the expenditure in any one year of more than 10 per cent of the principal.

(d) Rigid inspection of the finances as regards both investment and expenditure of funds.

(e) Complete publicity through open reports to the proper Government officials.

(f) Provision that no line of work which is not specifically and directly mentioned in the articles of incorporation shall be entered upon without the unanimous consent and approval of the board of trustees, nor unless Congress is directly informed of such intention through communication to the Clerk of the House and the Clerk of the Senate, which shall be duly published in the Congressional Record, nor until six months after such intention has been declared.

2. Provision by Congress for the thorough investigation, by a special committee or commission, of all endowed institutions, both secular and religious, whose property holdings or income exceeds a moderate amount. The committee or commission should be given full power to compel the production of books and papers and the attendance and testimony of witnesses. It should be authorized and directed to investigate not only the finances of such institutions but all their activities and affiliations.

3. As the only effective means of counteracting the influence of the foundations, as long as they are permitted to exist, consists in the activities of governmental agencies along similar lines, the appropriations of the Federal Government for education and social service should be correspondingly increased.

408. THE GORE-McLEMORE RESOLUTION AND WILSON'S REPLY
February, March, 1916

(Current History, April, 1916, p. 15 ff.)

As Secretary of State Mr. Bryan had urged that many of the most dangerous problems of our relations with belligerents might be avoided if Americans were forbidden to travel on the armed ships of belligerent powers. Mr. Wilson refused to accept this point of view as either reasonable or necessary. The German threat of a renewal of unrestricted submarine warfare March 1, 1916, aroused widespread hostility in Congress to the Wilson program. The Democratic Congressional leaders served notice on the President that unless he placed an embargo upon American travel on armed merchantmen, Congress would recommend such action. The Gore-McLemore Resolution embodied the Bryan attitude toward this perplexing question. President Wilson's letter to Senator Stone indicated his refusal to accept any limitation on American rights or any modification of international law. As a result of Presidential pressure the resolution was defeated in the Senate, 68–14 and in the House 276–142. A considerable part of the administration support came from Republicans. See C. Seymour, *American Diplomacy During the World War* p. 116 ff.; "Armed Liner Issue," *Current History,* April, 1916.

1. THE GORE-McLEMORE RESOLUTION

Resolved . . . That it is the sense of the Congress, vested as it is with the sole power to declare war, that all persons owing allegiance to the United States should in behalf of their own safety and the vital interest of the United States, forbear to exercise the right to travel as passengers on any armed vessel of any belligerent power, whether such vessel be armed for offensive or defensive purposes, and it is the further sense of Congress that no passport should be issued or renewed by the Secretary of State, or anyone acting under him, to be used by any person owing allegiance to the United States for the purpose of travel upon any such armed vessel of a belligerent power.

2. PRESIDENT WILSON'S LETTER TO SENATOR STONE

The White House,
Washington, February 24, 1916.

My Dear Senator: I very warmly appreciate your kind and frank letter of to-day, and feel that it calls for an equally frank reply.

You are right in assuming that I shall do everything in my power to keep the United States out of war. I think the country will feel no uneasiness about my course in that respect. Through many anxious months I have striven for that object, amidst difficulties more manifold than can have been apparent upon the surface, and so far I have succeeded. I do not doubt that I shall continue to succeed. The course which the Central European powers have announced their intention of following in the future with regard to undersea warfare seems for the moment to threaten insuperable obstacles, but its apparent meaning is so manifestly inconsistent with explicit assurances recently given us by those powers with regard to their treatment of merchant vessels on the high seas, that I must believe that explanations will presently ensue which will put a different aspect upon it. We have had no reason to question their good faith or their fidelity to their promises in the past, and I for one feel confident that we shall have none in the future.

But in any event our duty is clear. No nation, no group of nations, has the right while war is in progress to alter or disregard the principles which all nations have agreed upon in mitigation of the horrors and sufferings of war; and if the clear rights of American citizens should ever unhappily be abridged or denied by any such action, we should, it seems to me, have in honor no choice as to what our own course should be.

For my own part, I cannot consent to any abridgment of the rights of American citizens in any respect. The honor and self-respect of the nation is involved. We covet peace, and shall preserve it at any cost but the loss of honor. To forbid our people to exercise their rights for fear we might be called upon to vindicate them would be a deep humiliation indeed. It would be an implicit, all but an explicit, acquiescence in the violation of the rights of mankind everywhere, and of whatever nation or allegiance. It would be a deliberate abdication of our hitherto proud position as spokesmen, even amidst the turmoils of war, for the law and the right. It would make everything this Government has attempted, and everything that it has achieved during this terrible struggle of nations meaningless and futile.

It is important to reflect that if in this instance we allowed expediency to take the place of principle, the door would inevitably be opened to still further concessions. Once accept a single abatement of right, and many other humiliations would certainly follow, and the whole fine fabric of international law might crumble under our hands piece by piece. What we are contending for in this matter is of the very essence of the things that have made America a sovereign nation. She cannot yield them without conceding her own impotency as a nation, and making virtual surrender of her independent position among the nations of the world.

I am speaking, my dear Senator, in deep solemnity, without heat, with a clear consciousness of the high responsibilities of my office, and as your sincere and devoted friend. If we should unhappily differ, we shall differ as friends; but where issues so momentous as these are involved we must, just because we are friends, speak our minds without reservation.

Faithfully yours,
Woodrow Wilson

409. THE *SUSSEX* AFFAIR

Wilson's Address to Congress
April 19, 1916

(U. S. 64th Congress, 1st Session, *House Doc.* 1034)

After the sinking of the *Arabic,* August 18, 1915, Germany gave a pledge that in the future liners would not be sunk by submarines without warning and without safety for the lives of noncombatants. This period of quiet in submarine warfare came to an end with the sinking of the French cross-channel steamer *Sussex,* March 24, 1916. Wilson warned Germany that unless she ceased her unrestricted submarine warfare, the United States would be forced to break off diplomatic relations. On May 4, Germany promised that merchant vessels would not be sunk without warning, unless they should attempt to escape or to offer resistance. The crisis was temporarily passed, but in January, 1917, Germany renewed her policy of unrestricted submarine warfare. See, J. S. Bassett, *Our War with Germany,* chs. i–v; J. B. McMaster, *The United States and the World War,* Vol. I; J. B. Scott, *Survey of International Relations Between the United States and Germany, 1914–1917,* ch. ix.

A situation has arisen in the foreign relations of the country of which it is my plain duty to inform you very frankly. . . .

In February of the present year the Imperial German Government informed this Government . . . that the Imperial German Government felt justified in the circumstances in treating all armed merchantmen of belligerent ownership as auxiliary vessels of war, which it would have the right to destroy without warning. . . .

One of the latest and most shocking instances of this method of warfare was that of the destruction of the French cross-channel steamer *Sussex.* It must stand forth, as the sinking of the *Lusitania* did, as so singularly tragical and unjustifiable as to constitute a truly terrible example of the inhumanity of submarine warfare as the commanders of German vessels have for the past twelvemonth been conducting it. If this instance stood alone, some explanation, some disavowal by the German Government, some evidence of criminal mistake or wilful disobedience on the part of the commander of the vessel that fired the torpedo might be sought or entertained; but unhappily it does not stand alone. . . .

The Government of the United States has been very patient. At every stage of this distressing experience of tragedy after tragedy in which its own citizens were involved, it has sought to be restrained from any extreme course of action or of protest by a thoughtful consideration of the extraordinary circumstances of this unprecedented war, and actuated in all that it said or did by the sentiments of genuine friendship which the people of the United States have always entertained and continue to entertain towards the German nation. It has of course accepted the successive explanations and assurances of the Imperial German Government as given in entire sincerity and good faith, and has hoped, even against hope, that it would prove to be possible for the German Government so to order and control the acts of its naval commanders as to square its policy with the principles of humanity as embodied in the law of nations. It has been willing to wait until the significance of the facts became absolutely unmistakable and susceptible of but one interpretation.

That point has now unhappily been reached. The facts are susceptible of but one interpretation. The Imperial German Government has been unable to put any limits or restraints upon its warfare against either freight or passenger ships. It has therefore become painfully evident that the position which this Government took at the very outset is inevitable, namely, that the use of submarines for the destruction of an enemy's commerce is, of necessity, because of the very character of the vessels employed and the very methods of attack which their employment of course involves, incompatible with the principles of humanity, the long established and incontrovertible rights of neutrals, and the sacred immunities of non-combatants.

I have deemed it my duty, therefore, to say to the Imperial German Government, that if it is still its purpose to prosecute relentless and indiscriminate warfare against vessels of commerce by the use of submarines, notwithstanding the now demon-strated impossibility of conducting that warfare in accordance with what the Government of the United States must consider the sacred and indisputable rules of international law and the universally recognized dictates of humanity, the Government of the United States is at last forced to the conclusion that there is but one course it can pursue; and that unless the Imperial German Government should now immediately declare and effect an abandonment of its present methods of warfare against passenger and freight carrying vessels this Government can have no choice but to sever diplomatic relations with the Government of the German Empire altogether.

This decision I have arrived at with the keenest regret; the possibility of the action contemplated I am sure all thoughtful Americans will look forward to with unaffected reluctance. But we cannot forget that we are in some sort and by the force of circumstances the responsible spokesmen of the rights of humanity, and that we cannot remain silent while those rights seem in process of being swept utterly away in the maelstrom of this terrible war. We owe it to a due regard for our own rights as a nation, to our sense of duty as a representative of the rights of neutrals the world over, and to a just conception of the rights of mankind to take this stand now with the utmost solemnity and firmness. . . .

410. AMERICAN CONTROL OF HAITI

Treaty Between the United States and Haiti
May 3, 1916

(*U. S. Statutes at Large*, Vol. XXXIX, p. 1654)

Long continued anarchy in Haiti led to American intervention in January and February, 1914; in December of that year American naval officers, acting under instructions from the Navy Department, removed half a million dollars of reserve funds from the Banque Nationale and secured them in the National City Bank of New York until monetary reforms had been carried into effect. Continued revolutions led to a demand for American control of the finances, customs and police force of the island, but not until the terrible massacre of July 27, 1915, did the United States invest the capital with marines. Such investment was held imperative in order to establish order and to forestall the intervention of European powers. A Convention satisfactory to the United States was signed September 16, ratified by the Haitian government November 11, and by the United States Senate in February, 1916. American forces continued to occupy Haiti until 1930. The occupations of Haiti and of Santo Domingo are illuminating examples of the effects of the Monroe Doctrine and of economic imperialism. An excellent treatise on American occupation is H. P. Davis, *Black Democracy*, Part II; R. L. Buell, "American Occupation of Haiti," Foreign Policy Association, *Information Service*, Vol. V, C. Kelsey, "American Intervention in Haiti", Am. Academy of Pol. and Social Science, *Annals*, 1922, E. G. Balch, et al., *Occupied Haiti*,

F. Bausman, et al., *The Seizure of Haiti by the United States*, are for the most part critical. See also *Inquiry into the Occupation and Administration of Haiti and Santo Domingo*, United States, 67th Congress, 2nd Sess. Sen. *Report 794*, and A. C. Millspaugh, *Haiti Under American Control, 1915–1930*.

Art. I. The Government of the United States will, by its good offices, aid the Haitian Government in the proper and efficient development of its agricultural, mineral and commercial resources and in the establishment of the finances of Haiti on a firm and solid basis.

Art. II. The President of Haiti shall appoint, upon nomination by the President of the United States, a General Receiver and such aids and employees as may be necessary, who shall collect, receive and apply all customs duties on imports and exports accruing at the several custom houses and ports of entry of the Republic of Haiti.

The President of Haiti shall appoint, upon nomination by the President of the United States, a Financial Adviser, who shall be an officer attached to the Ministry of Finance, to give effect to whose proposals and labours the Minister will lend efficient aid. The Financial Adviser shall devise an adequate system of public accounting, aid in increasing the revenues and adjusting them to the expenses, inquire into the validity of the debts of the Republic, enlighten both Governments with reference to all eventual debts, recommend improved methods of collecting and applying the revenues, and make such other recommendations to the Minister of Finance as may be deemed necessary for the welfare and prosperity of Haiti.

Art. III. The Government of the Republic of Haiti will provide by law or appropriate decrees for the payment of all customs duties to the General Receiver, and will extend to the Receivership, and to the Financial Adviser, all needful aid and full protection in the execution of the powers conferred and duties imposed herein; and the United States on its part will extend like aid and protection.

Art. IV. Upon the appointment of the Financial Adviser, the Government of the Republic of Haiti, in co-operation with the Financial Adviser, shall collate, classify, arrange and make full statement of all the debts of the Republic, the amounts, character, maturity and condition thereof, and the interest accruing and the sinking fund requisite to their final discharge.

Art. V. All sums collected and received by the General Receiver shall be applied, first, to the payment of the salaries and allowances of the General Receiver, his assistants and employees and expenses of the Receivership, including the salary and expenses of the Financial Adviser, which salaries will be determined by previous agreement; second, to the interest and sinking fund of the public debt of the Republic of Haiti; and, third, to the maintenance of the constabulary referred to in Article X, and then the remainder to the Haitian Government for purposes of current expenses. . . .

Art. VI. The expenses of the Receivership, including salaries and allowances of the General Receiver, his assistants and employees, and the salary and expenses of the Financial Adviser, shall not exceed five per centum of the collections and receipts from customs duties, unless by agreement by the two Governments.

Art. VII. The General Receiver shall make monthly reports of all collections, receipts and disbursements to the appropriate officer of the Republic of Haiti and to the Department of State of the United States, which reports shall be open to inspection and verification at all times by the appropriate authorities of each of the said Governments.

The Republic of Haiti shall not increase its public debt except by previous agreement with the President of the United States, and shall not contract any debt or assume any financial obligation unless the ordinary revenues of the Republic available for that purpose, after defraying the expenses of the Government, shall be adequate to pay the interest and provide a sinking fund for the final discharge of such debt.

Art. IX. The Republic of Haiti will not without a previous agreement with the President of the United States, modify the customs duties in a manner to reduce the revenues therefrom; and in order that the revenues of the Republic may be adequate to meet the public debt and the expenses of the Government, to preserve tranquillity and to promote material prosperity, the Republic of Haiti will co-operate with the Financial

Adviser in his recommendations for improvement in the methods of collecting and disbursing the revenues and for new sources of needed income.

Art. X. The Haitian Government obligates itself, for the preservation of domestic peace, the security of individual rights and full observance of the provisions of this treaty, to create without delay an efficient constabulary, urban and rural, composed of native Haitians. This constabulary shall be organized and officered by Americans, appointed by the President of Haiti, upon nomination by the President of the United States. . . . These officers will be replaced by Haitians as they, by examination, conducted under direction of a board to be selected by the senior American officer of this constabulary and in the presence of a representative of the Haitian Government, ; re found to be qualified to assume such duties. The constabulary herein provided for, shall, under the direction of the Haitian Government, have supervision and control of arms and ammunition, military supplies, and traffic therein, throughout the country. The high contracting parties agree that the stipulations in this Article are necessary to prevent factional strife and disturbances.

Art. XI. The Government of Haiti agrees not to surrender any of the territory of the Republic of Haiti by sale, lease or otherwise, or jurisdiction over such territory, to any foreign government or power, not to enter into any treaty or contract with any foreign power or powers that will impair or tend to impair the independence of Haiti.

Art. XII. The Haitian Government agrees to execute with the United States a protocol for the settlement, by arbitration or otherwise, of all pending pecuniary claims of foreign corporations, companies, citizens or subjects against Haiti.

Art. XIII. The Republic of Haiti, being desirous to further the development of its natural resources, agrees to undertake and execute such measures as in the opinion of the high contracting parties may be necessary for the sanitation and public improvement of the Republic, under the supervision and direction of an engineer or engineers, to be appointed by the President of Haiti upon nomination by the President of the United States, and authorized for that purpose by the Government of Haiti.

Art. XIV. The high contracting parties shall have authority to take such steps as may be necessary to insure the complete attainment of any of the objects comprehended in this treaty; and, should the necessity occur, the United States will lend an efficient aid for the preservation of Haitian Independence and the maintenance of a Government adequate for the protection of life, property and individual liberty. . . .

Art. XVI. The present treaty shall remain in full force and virtue for the term of ten years, to be counted from the day of exchange of ratifications, and further for another term of ten years if, for specific reasons presented by either of the high contracting parties, the purpose of this treaty has not been fully accomplished. . . .

411. AGRICULTURAL LEGISLATION IN THE FIRST WILSON ADMINISTRATION

Letter of President Wilson to A. F. Lever
August 11, 1916

(*Congressional Record*, 64th Congress, 1st Session, App., p. 1762–3)

This letter from Wilson to the chairman of the Committee on Agriculture furnishes a succinct summary of the agricultural legislation of the first Wilson administration. See, E. R. A. Seligman, *Economics of Farm Relief;* W. S. Holt, *Federal Farm Loan Bureau;* J. B. Morman, *Farm Credits in the United States and Canada;* E. S. Spahr, *History and Theory of Agricultural Credit in the United States.*

My Dear Mr. Lever: It has given me much satisfaction to approve to-day the bill making appropriations for the Department of Agriculture for the fiscal year ending June 30, 1917, and for other purposes, because the bill not only makes very generous provision for the improvement of farm production in the Nation and for investigations and demonstrations in the field of marketing of farm crops and of the organization of rural life, but also contains three well-conceived measures designed to improve market practices and the storage and financing of staple crops. As the passage of this bill marks the practical completion of an important part of the program for the betterment of rural life which was mapped out at the beginning of the administration, I feel that I cannot let the occasion pass without conveying to you and your associates in both Houses my appreciation of the great service rendered to the nation in strengthening its great agricultural foundations.

The record, legislative as well as administrative, is a remarkable one. It speaks for itself and needs only to be set forth.
1. Appreciation of the importance of agriculture has been shown through greatly and intelligently increased appropriations for its support.
2. Particular pains have been taken to foster production by every promising means, and careful thought has been given especially to the matter of increasing the meat supply of the Nation.
3. Greatly increased provision has been made, through the enactment of the cooperative agricultural extension act, for conveying agricultural information to farmers, and for inducing them to apply it. This piece of legislation is one of the most significant and far-reaching measures for the education of adults ever adopted by any Government. It provides for co-operation between the States and the Federal Government. This is a highly important and significant principle. When the act is in full operation there will be expended annually under its terms, from Federal and State sources alone, a total of over $8,600,000 in the direct education of the farmer; this amount is being and will be increasingly supplemented by contributions from local sources. It will permit the placing in each of the 2,850 rural counties of the Nation two farm demonstrators and specialists, who will assist the demonstrators in the more difficult problems confronting them.
4. Systematic provision for the first time has been made for the solution of problems in that important half of agriculture which concerns distribution marketing, rural finance, and rural organization.
5. Provision was made promptly for the creation of an Office of Markets and Rural Organization, and the appropriations for this office, including those for enforcing new laws designed to promote better marketing, have been increased to $1,200,000. The more difficult problems of marketing are being investigated and plans are in operation for furnishing assistance to producers of perishables through a market news service. A similar service for the live-stock interest will be inaugurated during the year.
6. The problem of securing the uniform grading of staple crops, of regulating dealings and traffic in them, of developing a better system of warehouses, and of providing more available collateral for farm loans has been successfully dealt with.
7. Under the cotton-futures act standards for cotton have been established, the operations of the future exchanges have been put under supervision, and the sale of cotton has been placed on a firmer basis.
8. The United States grain-standards act will secure uniformity in the grading of grain, enable the farmer to obtain fairer prices for his product, and afford him an incentive to raise better grades of grain.
9. The United States warehouse act will enable the Department of Agriculture to license bonded warehouses in the various States. It will lead to the development of better storage facilities for staple crops and will make possible the issuance of reliable warehouse receipts which will be widely and easily negotiable.
10. Of no less importance for agriculture and for national development is the Federal Aid road act. This measure will conduce to the establishment of more effective highway machinery in each State, strongly influence the development of good road building along right lines, stimulate larger production and better marketing, promote a fuller and more attractive rural life, add greatly to the convenience and economic welfare of all the people, and strengthen the national foundations. The act embodies sound principles of road legislation and will safeguard the expenditure of funds arising under the act not only, but will also result in the more efficient

use of the large additional sums made available by States and localities.

11. The Federal Reserve Act benefits the farmer, as it does all the other people of the Nation, by guaranteeing better banking, safeguarding the credit structure of the country, and preventing panics. It takes particular note of the special needs of the farmer by making larger provision for loans through national banks on farm mortgages and by giving farm paper a maturity period of six months.

12. It was essential, however, that banking machinery be devised which would reach intimately into the rural districts, that it should operate on terms suited to the farmer's needs, and should be under sympathetic management. The need was for machinery which would introduce business methods into farm finance, bring order out of chaos, reduce the cost of handling farm loans, place upon the market mortgages which would be a safe investment for private funds, attract into agricultural operations a fair share of the capital of the Nation, and lead to a reduction of interest. These needs and these ideals have been met by the enactment of the Federal farm-loan act. . . .

Faithfully yours,
Woodrow Wilson

412. ORGANIC ACT OF THE PHILIPPINE ISLANDS
August 29, 1916

(*U. S. Statutes at Large*, Vol. XXXIX, p. 545 ff.)

The act of July 1, 1902 had provided a territorial government for the Philippines. Inhabitants of the islands were made citizens of the Philippines, not of the United States; partial self-government was extended to the islands, and these rights were enlarged in 1907. Many Filipinos continued to hope for independence, and their demands met with some support among various idealistic and economic groups in the United States. The Democratic Party in 1912 pledged its support to ultimate independence; in accordance with this traditional Democratic position, President Wilson appointed native Filipinos to a majority of the seats in the Philippine upper house. The Jones Act of August 29, 1916, not only greatly enlarged Philippine self-government, but promised independence as soon as a stable government was established. This promise was finally fulfilled by the Philippine Independence Act of 1934, Doc. No. 484. The literature on the Philippines is extensive and controversial; see D. C. Worcester, *Philippines: Past and Present;* W. C. Forbes, *The Philippine Islands,* 2 Vols.; J. S. Reyes, *Legislative History of America's Economic Policy Toward the Philippines;* C. B. Elliott, *The Philippines to the End of the Commission Government;* F. B. Harrison, *The Cornerstone of Philippine Independence.* On military conquest and occupation, see M. Storey and M. P. Lichauco, *Conquest of the Philippines by the United States, 1898-1925.*

An Act to declare the purpose of the people of the United States as to the future political status of the people of the Philippine Islands, and to provide a more autonomous government for those islands.

Whereas it was never the intention of the people of the United States in the incipiency of the War with Spain to make it a war of conquest or for territorial aggrandizement; and

Whereas it is, as it has always been, the purpose of the people of the United States to withdraw their sovereignty over the Philippine Islands and to recognize their independence as soon as a stable government can be established therein; and

Whereas for the speedy accomplishment of such purpose it is desirable to place in the hands of the people of the Philippines as large a control of their domestic affairs as can be given them without, in the meantime, impairing the exercise of the rights of sovereignty by the people of the United States, in order that, by the use and exercise of popular franchise and governmental powers, they may be the better prepared to fully assume the responsibilities and enjoy all the privileges of complete independence: Therefore

Be it enacted, . . .

SEC. 2. That all inhabitants of the Philippine Islands who were Spanish subjects on [April 11, 1899] and then resided in said islands, and their children born subsequent thereto, shall be deemed and held to be citizens of the Philippine Islands, except such as shall have elected to preserve their allegiance to the Crown of Spain in accordance with the provisions of the treaty of peace between the United States and Spain, . . . and except such others as have since become citizens of some other country: . . .

SEC. 3. [Bill of rights for the Philippines.] . . .

SEC. 5. That the statutory laws of the United States hereafter enacted shall not apply to the Philippines Islands, except when they specifically so provide, or it is so provided in this Act.

SEC. 6. That the laws now in force in the Philippines shall continue in force and effect, except as altered, amended, or modified herein, until altered, amended or repealed by the legislative authority herein provided or by Act of Congress of the United States.

SEC. 7. That the legislative authority herein provided shall have power, when not inconsistent with this Act, by due enactment to amend, alter, modify, or repeal any law, civil or criminal, continued in force by this Act as it may from time to time see fit.

This power shall specifically extend with the limitation herein provided as to the tariff to all laws relating to revenue and taxation in effect in the Philippines.

SEC. 8. That general legislative power, except as otherwise herein provided, is hereby granted to the Philippine Legislature, authorized by this Act. . . .

SEC. 10. That while this Act provides that the Philippine government shall have the authority to enact a tariff law the trade relations between the islands and the United States shall continue to be governed exclusively by laws of the Congress of the United States: *Provided,* That tariff acts or acts amendatory to the tariff of the Philippine Islands shall not become law until they shall receive the approval of the President of the United States, nor shall any act of the Philippine Legislature affecting immigration or the currency or coinage laws of the Philippines become a law until it has been approved by the President of the United States: *Provided further,* That the President shall approve or disapprove any act mentioned in the foregoing proviso within six months from and after its enactment and submission for his approval, and if not disapproved within such

time it shall become a law the same as if it had been specifically approved.

SEC. 11. . . . That the entire indebtedness of the Philippine government . . . shall not exceed at any one time the sum of $15,-000,000. . . .

SEC. 12. That general legislative powers in the Philippines, except as herein otherwise provided, shall be vested in a legislature which shall consist of two houses, one the senate and the other the house of representatives, and the two houses shall be designated "The Philippine Legislature": . . .

SEC. 13. [The Senate]

SEC. 14. [The House of Representatives]

SEC. 15. . . . Until otherwise provided by the Philippine Legislature herein provided for the qualifications of voters for senators and representatives in the Philippines and all officers elected by the people shall be as follows:

Every male person who is not a citizen or subject of a foreign power twenty-one years of age or over . . . who shall have been a resident of the Philippines for one year and of the municipality in which he shall offer to vote for six months next preceding the day of voting, and who is comprised within one of the following classes:

(a) Those who under existing law are legal voters and have exercised the right of suffrage.

(b) Those who own real property to the value of 500 pesos, or who annually pay 30 pesos or more of the established taxes.

(c) Those who are able to read and write either Spanish, English or a native tongue.

. . . The first election under the provisions of this Act shall be held on the first Tuesday of October, nineteen hundred and sixteen, . . . *Provided,* That the Governor General of the Philippine Islands shall appoint, without the consent of the senate and without restriction as to residence, senators and representatives who will, in his opinion, best represent the senate district and those representative districts which may be included in the territory not now represented in the Philippine Assembly: . . .

SEC. 19. . . . Every bill and joint resolution which shall have passed both houses shall, before it becomes a law, be presented to the Governor General. If he approve the same, he shall sign it; but if not, he shall return it with his objections to that house in which it shall have originated, which shall enter the objections at large on its journal and proceed to reconsider it. If, after such reconsideration, two-thirds of the members elected to that house shall agree to pass the same, it shall be sent, together with the objections, to the other house, by which it shall likewise be reconsidered, and if approved by two-thirds of all the members elected to that house it shall be sent to the Governor General, who, in case he shall then not approve, shall transmit the same to the President of the United States. . . . If the President of the United States approve the same, he shall sign it and it shall become a law. If he shall not approve same, he shall return it to the Governor General, so stating, and it shall not become a law: . . .

All laws enacted by the Philippine Legislature shall be reported to the Congress of the United States, which hereby reserves the power and authority to annul the same. If at the termination of any fiscal year the appropriations necessary for the support of government for the ensuing fiscal year shall not have been made, the several sums appropriated in the last appropriation bills for the objects and purposes therein specified, so far as the same may be done, shall be deemed to be reappropriated for the several objects and purposes specified in said last appropriation bill; . . .

SEC. 20. That at the first meeting of the Philippine Legislature created by this Act and triennially thereafter there shall be chosen by the legislature two Resident Commissioners to the United States, who shall hold their office for a term of three years beginning with the fourth day of March following their election, and which shall be entitled to an official recognition as such by all departments upon presentation to the President of a certificate of election by the Governor General of said islands. . . .

SEC. 21. That the supreme executive power shall be vested in an executive officer, whose official title shall be "The Governor General of the Philippine Islands." He shall be appointed by the President, by and with the advice and consent of the Senate of the United States, and hold his office at the pleasure of the President and until his successor is chosen and qualified. The Governor General shall reside in the Philippine Islands during his official incumbency, and maintain his office at the seat of government. He shall, unless otherwise herein provided, appoint, by and with the consent of the Philippine Senate, such officers as may now be appointed by the Governor General, or such as he is authorized by this Act to appoint, or whom he may hereafter be authorized by law to appoint; . . . He . . . shall be commander in chief of all locally created armed forces and militia. . . . He shall be responsible for the faithful execution of the laws of the Philippine Islands and of the United States operative within the Philippine Islands, and whenever it becomes necessary he may call upon the commanders of the military and naval forces of the United States in the islands, or summon the *posse comitatus,* or call out the militia or other locally created armed forces, to prevent or suppress lawless violence, invasion, insurrection, or rebellion; and he may, in case of rebellion or invasion, or imminent danger thereof, when the public safety requires it, suspend the privileges of the writ of habeas corpus, or place the islands, or any part thereof, under martial law. . . .

SEC. 26. . . . The chief justice and associate justices of the Supreme Court shall hereafter be appointed by the President, by and with the advice and consent of the Senate of the United States. The judges of the court of first instance shall be appointed by the Governor General by and with the advice and consent of the Philippine Senate. . . .

SEC. 27. That the Supreme Court of the United States shall have jurisdiction to review, revise, reverse, modify, or affirm the final judgements and decrees of the Supreme Court of the Philippine Islands in all actions, cases, causes, and proceedings now pending therein or hereafter determined thereby in which the Constitution or any statute, treaty, title, right, or privilege of the United States is involved, or in causes in which the value in controversy exceeds $25,000. . . .

SEC. 28. . . . It shall be unlawful for any corporation organized under this Act, or for any person, company, or corporation receiving any grant, franchise, or concession from the government of said islands, to use, employ, or contract for the labor of persons held in involuntary serviture; . . .

SEC. 29. That, except as in this Act otherwise provided, the salaries of all the officials of the Philippines not appointed by the President, including deputies, assistants, and other employees, shall be such and be so paid out of the revenues of the Philippines as shall from time to time be determined by the Philippine Legislature; and

if the legislature shall fail to make an appropriation for such salaries, the salaries so fixed shall be paid without the necessity of further appropriations therefor. The salaries of all officers and all expenses of the offices of the various officials of the Philippines appointed as herein provided by the President shall also be paid out of the revenues of the Philippines. . . .

413. HAMMER v. DAGENHART ET AL.
247 U. S. 251
1918

Appeal from the U. S. district court for the Western District of North Carolina. This case involved the interpretation of the Keating-Owen Act of 1916. *Stat. at Large,* Vol. XXXIX, p. 675.

DAY, J. . . . The attack upon the act rests upon three propositions:

First. It is not a regulation of interstate and foreign commerce.

Second. It contravenes the Tenth Amendment to the Constitution.

Third. It conflicts with the Fifth Amendment to the Constitution.

The controlling question for decision is: Is it within the authority of Congress in regulating commerce among the States to prohibit the transportation in interstate commerce of manufactured goods, the product of a factory in which, within thirty days prior to their removal therefrom, children under the age of fourteen have been employed or permitted to work, or children between the ages of fourteen and sixteen years have been employed or permitted to work more than eight hours in any day, or more than six days in any week, or after the hour of 7 o'clock P. M. or before the hour of 6 o'clock A. M.?

The power essential to the passage of this act, the government contends, is found in the commerce clause of the Constitution which authorizes Congress to regulate commerce with foreign nations and among the States. . . .

But it is insisted that adjudged cases in this court establish the doctrine that the power to regulate given to Congress incidentally includes the authority to prohibit the movement of ordinary commodities, and

therefore that the subject is not open for discussion. The cases demonstrate the contrary. They rest upon the character of the particular subjects dealt with and the fact that the scope of governmental authority, state or national, possessed over them, is such that the authority to prohibit is, as to them, but the exertion of the power to regulate.

The first of these cases is *Champion* v. *Ames,* 188 U. S. 321, the so-called *Lottery Case,* in which it was held that Congress might pass a law having the effect to keep the channels of commerce free from use in the transportation of tickets used in the promotion of lottery schemes. In *Hipolite Egg Co.* v. *United States,* 220 U. S. 45, this court sustained the power of Congress to pass the Pure Food and Drugs Act which prohibited the introduction into the States by means of interstate commerce of impure foods and drugs. In *Hoke* v. *United States,* 227 U. S. 308, this court sustained the constitutionality of the so-called "White Slave Traffic Act" whereby the transportation of a woman in interstate commerce for the purpose of prostitution was forbidden. . . . [Cites other cases.]

In each of these instances the use of interstate transportation was necessary to the accomplishment of harmful results. In other words, although the power over interstate transportation was to regulate, that could only be accomplished by prohibiting the use of the facilities of interstate commerce to effect the evil intended.

This element is wanting in the present case. The thing intended to be accomplished by this statute is the denial of the facilities of interstate commerce to those manufacturers in the States who employ children within the prohibited ages. The act in its effect does not regulate transportation among the States, but aims to standardize the ages at which children may be employed in mining and manufacturing within the States. The goods shipped are of themselves harmless. The act permits them to be freely shipped after thirty days from the time of their removal from the factory. When offered for shipment, and before transportation begins, the labor of their production is over, and the mere fact that they were intended for interstate commerce transportation does not make their production subject to federal control under the commerce power.

Commerce "consists of intercourse and traffic . . . and includes the transportation of persons and property, as well as the purchase, sale and exchange of commodities." The making of goods and the mining of coal are not commerce, nor does the fact that these things are to be afterwards shipped, or used in interstate commerce, make their production a part thereof.

Over interstate transportation, or its incidents, the regulatory power of Congress is ample, but the production of articles intended for interstate commerce is a matter of local regulation. . . . If it were otherwise, all manufacture intended for interstate shipment would be brought under federal control to the practical exclusion of the authority of the states, a result certainly not contemplated by the framers of the Constitution when they vested in Congress the authority to regulate commerce among the states.

It is further contended that the authority of Congress may be exerted to control interstate commerce in the shipment of child-made goods because of the effect of the circulation of such goods in other States where the evil of this class of labor has been recognized by local legislation, and the right to thus employ child labor has been more rigorously restrained than in the state of production. In other words, that the unfair competition thus engendered may be controlled by closing the channels of interstate commerce to manufacturers in those States where the local laws do not meet what

Congress deems to be the more just standard of other States.

There is no power vested in Congress to require the States to exercise their police power so as to prevent possible unfair competition. Many causes may coöperate to give one State, by reason of local laws or conditions, an economic advantage over others. The commerce clause was not intended to give to Congress a general authority to equalize such conditions. In some of the States laws have been passed fixing minimum wages for women, in others the local law regulates the hours of labor of women in various employments. Business done in such States may be at an economic disadvantage when compared with States which have no such regulation; surely, this fact does not give Congress the power to deny transportation in interstate commerce to those who carry on business where the hours of labor and the rate of compensation for women have not been fixed by a standard in use in other States and approved by Congress.

The grant of power to Congress over the subject of interstate commerce was to enable it to regulate such commerce, and not to give it authority to control the States in their exercise of the police power over local trade and manufacture.

The grant of authority over a purely federal matter was not intended to destroy the local power always existing and carefully reserved to the States in the Tenth Amendment to the Constitution. . . .

That there should be limitations upon the right to employ children in mines and factories in the interest of their own and the public welfare, all will admit. That such employment is generally deemed to require regulation is shown by the fact that the brief of counsel states that every state in the Union has a law upon the subject, limiting the right to thus employ children. In North Carolina, the State wherein is located the factory in which the employment was had in the present case, no child under twelve years of age is permitted to work.

It may be desirable that such laws be uniform, but our federal government is one of enumerated powers. . . .

To sustain this statute would not be, in our judgment, a recognition of the lawful exertion of congressional authority over interstate commerce, but would sanction an invasion by the federal power of the control of a matter purely local in its character, and over which no authority has been delegated to Congress in conferring the power to regulate commerce among the states. . . .

In our view the necessary effect of this act is, by means of a prohibition against the movement in interstate commerce of ordinary commercial commodities, to regulate the hours of labor of children in factories and mines within the States, a purely state authority. Thus the act in a twofold sense is repugnant to the Constitution. It not only transcends the authority delegated to Congress over commerce, but also exerts a power as to a purely local matter to which the federal authority does not extend. The far-reaching result of upholding the act cannot be more plainly indicated than by pointing out that if Congress can thus regulate matters intrusted to local authority by prohibition of the movement of commodities in interstate commerce, all freedom of commerce will be at an end, and the power of the states over local matters may be eliminated, and thus our system of government be practically destroyed.

For these reasons we hold that this law exceeds the constitutional authority of Congress. It follows that the decree of the district court must be affirmed.

HOLMES, J., dissenting:

The single question in this case is whether Congress has power to prohibit the shipment in interstate or foreign commerce of any product of cotton mill [etc.]. . . . The objection urged against the power is that the States have exclusive control over their methods of production and that Congress cannot meddle with them, and taking the proposition in the sense of direct intermeddling I agree to it and suppose that no one denies it. But if an act is within the powers specifically conferred upon Congress, it seems to me that it is not made any less constitutional because of the indirect effects that it may have, however obvious it may be that it will have those effects, and that we are not at liberty upon such grounds to hold it void.

The first step in any argument is to make plain what no one is likely to dispute—that the statute in question is within the power expressly given to Congress if considered only as to its immediate effects, and that if invalid it is so only upon some collateral ground. The statute confines itself to prohibiting the carriage of certain goods in interstate or foreign commerce. Congress is given power to regulate such commerce in unqualified terms. It would not be argued to-day that the power to regulate does not include the power to prohibit. Regulation means the prohibition of something, and when interstate commerce is the matter to be regulated I cannot doubt that the regulations may prohibit any part of such commerce that Congress sees fit to forbid. At all events it is established by the Lottery Case and others that have followed it that a law is not beyond the regulative power of Congress merely because it prohibits certain transportation out and out. So I repeat that this statute in its immediate operation is clearly within the Congress's constitutional power.

The question, then, is narrowed to whether the exercise of its otherwise constitutional power by Congress can be pronounced unconstitutional because of its possible reaction upon the conduct of the States in a matter upon which I have admitted that they are free from direct control. I should have thought that that matter had been disposed of so fully as to leave no room for doubt. I should have thought that the most conspicuous decisions of this court had made it clear that the power to regulate commerce and other constitutional powers could not be cut down or qualified by the fact that it might interfere with the carrying out of the domestic policy of any state.

The manufacture of oleomargarine is as much a matter of state regulation as the manufacture of cotton cloth. Congress levied a tax upon the compound when colored so as to resemble butter that was so great as obviously to prohibit the manufacture and sale. In a very elaborate discussion the present chief justice excluded any inquiry into the purpose of an act which, apart from that purpose, was within the power of Congress. *McCray* v. *United States*, 195 U. S. 27. . . . Fifty years ago a tax on state banks, the obvious purpose and actual effect of which was to drive them, or at least their circulation, out of existence, was sustained, although the result was one that Congress had no constitutional power to require. The court made short work of the argument as to the purpose of the act. "The judicial cannot prescribe to the legislative departments of the government limitations upon the exercise of its acknowledged powers." *Veazie Bank* v. *Fenno,* 8 Wallace 533. . . . And to come to cases upon interstate commerce, . . . the Sherman Act has been made an instrument for the breaking up of combinations in restraint of trade and monopolies, using the power to regulate commerce as a foothold, but not proceeding because that commerce was the end actually in mind. The objection that the control of the states over production was interfered with was urged again and again, but always in vain. . . .

The Pure Food and Drug Act which was sustained in *Hipolite Egg Co.* v. *United States,* 220 U. S. 45, with the intimation that "no trade can be carried on between the states to which it [the power of Congress to regulate commerce] does .not extend," applies not merely to articles that the changing opinions of the time condemn as intrinsically harmful, but to others innocent in themselves, simply on the ground that the order for them was induced by a preliminary fraud. It does not matter whether the supposed evil precedes or follows the transportation. It is enough that, in the opinion of Congress, the transportation encourages the evil. . . .

The notion that prohibition is any less prohibition when applied to things now thought evil I do not understand. But if there is any matter upon which civilized countries have agreed,—far more unanimously than they have with regard to intoxicants and some other matters over which this country is now emotionally aroused,—it is the evil of premature and excessive child labor. I should have thought that if we were to introduce our own moral conceptions where, in my opinion, they do not belong, this was preëminently a case for upholding the exercise of all its powers by the United States.

But I had thought that the propriety of the exercise of a power admitted to exist in some cases was for the consideration of Congress alone, and that this court always had disavowed the right to intrude its judgment upon questions of policy or morals. It is not for this court to pronounce when prohibition is necessary to regulation if it ever may be necessary—to say that it is permissible as against strong drink, but not as against the product of ruined lives.

The act does not meddle with anything belonging to the States. They may regulate their internal affairs and their domestic commerce as they like. But when they seek to send their products across the state line they are no longer within their rights. If there were no Constitution and no Congress their power to cross the line would depend upon their neighbors. Under the Constitution such commerce belongs not to the States, but to Congress to regulate. It may carry out its views of public policy whatever indirect effect they may have upon the activities of the States. Instead of being encountered by a prohibitive tariff at her boundaries, the State encounters the public policy of the United States which it is for Congress to express. The public policy of the United States is shaped with a view to the benefit of the nation as a whole. If, as has been the case within the memory of men still living, a State should take a different view of the propriety of sustaining a lottery from that which generally prevails, I cannot believe that the fact would require a different decision from that reached in *Champion* v. *Ames.* Yet in that case it would be said with quite as much force as in this that Congress was attempting to intermeddle with the State's domestic affairs. The national welfare as understood by Congress may require a different attitude within its sphere from that of some self-seeking State. It seems to me entirely constitutional for Congress to enforce its understanding by all the means at its command.

Mr. Justice McKenna, Mr. Justice Brandeis, and Mr. Justice Clarke concur in this opinion.

414. THE ADAMSON ACT
September 3, 5, 1916

(U. S. Statutes at Large, Vol. XXXIX, p. 721 ff.)

In March, 1916, the Four Brotherhoods of Railway workers demanded an eight-hour day without reduction of wages, and threatened a nationwide strike unless their demands were complied with. As a tie-up in our transportation system at that time would have been disastrous, Wilson appeared before Congress and asked for the enactment of a law providing for an eight-hour day without reduction in wages: Congress responded with the Adamson Act. On the constitutionality of the measure, see *Wilson* v. *New,* Doc. No. 415.

An act to establish an eight-hour day for employees of carriers engaged in interstate and foreign commerce, and for other purposes

BE it enacted, That beginning January first, nineteen hundred and seventeen, eight hours shall, in contracts for labor and service, be deemed a day's work and the measure or standard of a day's work for the purpose of reckoning the compensation for services of all employees who are now or may hereafter be employed by any common carrier by railroad, except railroads independently owned and operated not exceeding one hundred miles in length, electric street railroads, and electric interurban railroads, which is subject to the provisions of the Act of February 4, 1887, entitled "An Act to regulate commerce," as amended, and who are now or may hereafter be actually engaged in any capacity in the operation of trains used for the transportation of persons or property on railroads, . . . from any State or Territory of the United States or the District of Columbia to any other State or Territory of the United States or the District of Columbia or from one place in a Territory to another place in the same Territory, or from any place in the United States to an adjacent foreign country, or from any place in the United States through a foreign country to any other place in the United States: *Provided,* That the above exceptions shall not apply to railroads though less than one hundred miles in length whose principal business is leasing or furnishing terminal or transfer facilities to other railroads, or are themselves engaged in transfers of freight between railroads or between railroads and industrial plants. . . .

Sec. 2. That the President shall appoint a commission of three, which shall observe the operation and effects of the institution of the eight-hour standard workday. . . .

Sec. 3. That pending the report of the commission . . . and for a period of thirty days thereafter, the compensation of railway employees subject to this Act for a standard eight-hour workday shall not be reduced below the present standard day's wage. . . .

415. WILSON v. NEW
243 U. S. 332
1917

Appeal from the District Court for Western District of Missouri. Suit to enjoin enforcement of the Adamson Act fixing an eight-hour work day for and regulating wages of railway employees on interstate carriers. On the constitutionality of emergency legislation see the Minnesota Mortgage Moratorium Case, Doc. No. 483.

WHITE, C. J. Was there power in Congress, under the circumstances existing, to deal with the hours of work and wages of railroad employees engaged in interstate commerce, is the principal question here to be considered. . . .

[Review of history of passage of Adamson Act by Congress]

All the propositions relied upon and arguments advanced ultimately come to two questions: first, the entire want of constitutional power to deal with the subjects embraced by the statute, and second, such abuse of the power, if possessed as rendered its exercise unconstitutional. We will consider these subjects under distinct propositions separately.

I. The entire want of constitutional power to deal with the subjects embraced by the statute. . . .

. . . Concretely stated, therefore, the question is this: Did Congress have power, . . . to provide a permanent eight-hour standard and to create by legislative action a standard of wages to be operative upon the employers and employees for such reasonable time as it deemed necessary to afford an opportunity for the meeting of the minds of employers and employees on the subject of wages? Or, in other words, did it have the power, in order to prevent the interruption of interstate commerce, to exert its will to supply the absence of a wage scale resulting from the disagreement as to wages between the employers and employees, and to make its will on that subject controlling for the limited period provided for?

Coming to the general considerations by which both subjects must be controlled, to simplify the analysis for the purpose of considering the question of inherent power, we put the question as to the eight-hour standard entirely out of view, on the ground that the authority to permanently establish it is so clearly sustained as to render the subject not disputable. . . .

That the business of common carriers by rail is in a sense a public business because of the interest of society in the continued operation and rightful conduct of such business, and that the public interest begets a public right of regulation to the full extent necessary to secure and protect it, is settled by so many decisions, state and Federal, and is illustrated by such a continuous exertion of state and Federal legislative power, as to leave no room for question on the subject. It is also equally true that as the right to fix by agreement between the carrier and its employees a standard of wages to control their relations is primarily private, the establishment and giving effect to such agreed-on standard is not subject to be controlled or prevented by public authority. But, taking all these propositions as undoubted, if the situation which we have described and with which the act of Congress dealt be taken into view,—that is, the dispute between the employers and employees

as to a standard of wages, their failure to agree, the resulting absence of such standard, the entire interruption of interstate commerce which was threatened, and the infinite injury to the public interest which was imminent,—it would seem inevitably to result that the power to regulate necessarily obtained and was subject to be applied to the extent necessary to provide a remedy for the situation, which included the power to deal with the dispute, to provide by appropriate action for a standard of wages to fill the want of one caused by the failure to exert the private right on the subject, and to give effect by appropriate legislation to the regulations thus adopted. This must be unless it can be said that the right to so regulate as to save and protect the public interest did not apply to a case where the destruction of the public right was imminent as the result of a dispute between the parties and their consequent failure to establish by private agreement the standard of wages which was essential; in other words, that the existence of the public right and the public power to preserve it was wholly under the control of the private right to establish a standard by agreement. Nor is it an answer to this view to suggest that the situation was one of emergency, and that emergency cannot be made the source of power. The proposition begs the question, since although an emergency may not call into life a power which has never lived, nevertheless emergency may afford a reason for the exertion of a living power already enjoyed. . . .

Let us . . . briefly recapitulate some of the more important of the regulations which have been enacted in the past in order to show how necessarily the exertion of the power to enact them manifests the existence of the legislative authority to ordain the regulation now before us, and how completely the whole system of regulations adopted in the past would be frustrated or rendered unavailing if the power to regulate under the conditions stated, which was exerted by the act before us, was not possessed. . . .

In the presence of this vast body of acknowledged powers there would seem to be no ground for disputing the power which was exercised in the act which is before us . . . to exert the legislative will for the purpose of settling the dispute, and bind both parties to the duty of acceptance and compliance, to the end that no individual dispute or difference might bring ruin to the vast interests concerned in the movement of interstate commerce, for the express purpose of protecting and preserving which the plenary legislative authority granted to Congress was reposed. . . .

We are of the opinion that the reasons stated conclusively establish that, from the point of view of inherent power, the act which is before us was clearly within the legislative power of Congress to adopt, and that, in substance and effect, it amounted to an exertion of its authority under the circumstances disclosed to compulsorily arbitrate the dispute between the parties by establishing as to the subject-matter of that dispute a legislative standard of wages operative and binding as a matter of law upon the parties,—a power none the less efficaciously exerted because exercised by direct legislative act instead of by the enactment of other and appropriate means providing for the bringing about of such result. If it be conceded that the power to enact the statute was in effect the exercise of the right to fix wages where, by reason of the dispute, there had been a failure to fix by agreement, it would simply serve to show the nature and character of the regulation essential to protect the public right and safeguard the movement of interstate commerce, not involving any denial of the authority to adopt it. . . .

We conclude that the court below erred in holding the statute was not within the power of Congress to enact and its decree must therefore be . . . reversed.

Justices Day, Pitney, Van Devanter and McReynolds dissenting.

416. PEACE WITHOUT VICTORY

Address of President Wilson to the United States Senate
January 22, 1917

(U. S. 64th Congress, 2nd Sess., *Sen. Document* 685)

This memorable speech, calling for a peace without victory, anticipated in many respects the Fourteen Points speech, and indicated Wilson's determination to provide machinery for the maintenance of international peace. The term "peace without victory" inspired a great deal of contemporary derision. See C. Seymour, *American Diplomacy During the World War.*

Gentlemen of the Senate: . . .

. . . I have sought this opportunity to address you because I thought that I owed it to you, as the counsel associated with me in the final determination of our international obligations, to disclose to you without reserve the thought and purpose that have been taking form in my mind in regard to the duty of our Government in the days to come when it will be necessary to lay afresh and upon a new plan the foundations of peace among the nations.

It is inconceivable that the people of the United States should play no part in that great enterprise. . . . They cannot in honor withhold the service to which they are now about to be challenged. They do not wish to withhold it. But they owe it to themselves and to the other nations of the world to state the conditions under which they will feel free to render it.

That service is nothing less than this, to add their authority and their power to the authority and force of other nations to guarantee peace and justice throughout the world. Such a settlement cannot now be long postponed. It is right that before it comes this Government should frankly formulate the conditions upon which it would feel justified in asking our people to approve its formal and solemn adherence to a League for Peace. I am here to attempt to state those conditions.

The present war must first be ended; but we owe it to candor and to a just regard for the opinion of mankind to say that, so far as our participation in guarantees of future peace is concerned, it makes a great deal of difference in what way and upon what terms it is ended. The treaties and agreements which bring it to an end must embody terms which will create a peace that is worth guaranteeing and preserving, a peace that will win the approval of mankind, not merely a peace that will serve the several interests and immediate aims of the nations engaged. . . .

No covenant of co-operative peace that does not include the peoples of the New World can suffice to keep the future safe against war; and yet there is only one sort of peace that the peoples of America could join in guaranteeing. The elements of that peace must be elements that engage the confidence and satisfy the principles of the American governments, elements consistent with their political faith and with the practical convictions which the peoples of America have once for all embraced and undertaken to defend. . . .

It will be absolutely necessary that a force be created as a guarantor of the permanency of the settlement so much greater than the force of any nation now engaged or any alliance hitherto formed or projected that no nation, no probable combination of nations could face or withstand it. If the peace presently to be made is to endure, it must be a peace made secure by the organized major force of mankind.

The terms of the immediate peace agreed upon will determine whether it is a peace for which such a guarantee can be secured. The question upon which the whole future peace and policy of the world depends is this: Is the present war a struggle for a just and secure peace, or only for a new balance of power? If it be only a struggle for a new balance of power, who will guarantee, who can guarantee the stable equilibrium of the new arrangement? Only a tranquil Europe can be a stable Europe. There must be, not a balance of power, but a community of power; not organized rivalries, but an organized common peace.

Fortunately we have received very explicit assurances on this point. . . . I think it will be serviceable if I attempt to set forth what we understand them to be.

They imply, first of all, that it must be a peace without victory. It is not pleasant to say this. I beg that I may be permitted to put my own interpretation upon it and that it may be understood that no other interpre-tation was in my thought. I am seeking only to face realities and to face them without soft concealments. Victory would mean peace forced upon the loser, a victor's terms imposed upon the vanquished. It would be accepted in humiliation, under duress, at an intolerable sacrifice, and would leave a sting, a resentment, a bitter memory upon which terms of peace would rest, not permanently, but only as upon quicksand. Only a peace between equals can last. Only a peace the very principle of which is equality and a common participation in a common benefit. The right state of mind, the right feeling between nations, is as necessary for a lasting peace as is the just settlement of vexed questions of territory or of racial and national allegiance.

The equality of nations upon which peace must be founded if it is to last must be an equality of rights; the guarantees exchanged must neither recognize nor imply a difference between big nations and small, between those that are powerful and those that are weak. Right must be based upon the common strength, not upon the individual strength, of the nations upon whose concert peace will depend. Equality of territory or of resources there of course cannot be; nor any sort of equality not gained in the ordinary peaceful and legitimate development of the peoples themselves. But no one asks or expects anything more than an equality of rights. Mankind is looking now for freedom of life, not for equipoises of power.

And there is a deeper thing involved than even equality of right among organized nations. No peace can last, or ought to last, which does not recognize and accept the principle that governments derive all their just powers from the consent of the governed, and that no right anywhere exists to hand peoples about from sovereignty to sovereignty as if they were property. I take it for granted, for instance, if I may venture upon a single example, that statesmen everywhere are agreed that there should be a united, independent, and autonomous Poland, and that henceforth inviolable security of life, of worship, and of industrial and social development should be guaranteed to all peoples who have lived hitherto under the power of governments devoted to a faith and purpose hostile to their own. . . .

So far as practicable, moreover, every great people now struggling towards a full development of its resources and of its powers should be assured a direct outlet to the great highways of the sea. Where this cannot be done by the cession of territory, it can no doubt be done by the neutralization of direct rights of way under the general guarantee which will assure the peace itself. With a right comity of arrangement no nation need be shut away from free access to the open paths of the world's commerce.

And the paths of the sea must alike in law and in fact be free. The freedom of the seas is the *sine qua non* of peace, equality, and co-operation. No doubt a somewhat radical reconsideration of many of the rules of international practice hitherto thought to be established may be necessary in order to make the seas indeed free and common in practically all circumstances for the use of mankind, but the motive for such changes is convincing and compelling. There can be no trust or intimacy between the peoples of the world without them. The free, constant, unthreatened intercourse of nations is an essential part of the process of peace and of development. It need not be difficult either to define or to secure the freedom of the seas if the governments of the world sincerely desire to come to an agreement concerning it.

It is a problem closely connected with the limitation of naval armaments and the co-operation of the navies of the world in keeping the seas at once free and safe. And the question of limiting naval armaments opens the wider and perhaps more difficult question of the limitation of armies and of all programs of military preparation. Difficult and delicate as these questions are, they must be faced with the utmost candor and decided in a spirit of real accommodation if peace is to come with healing in its wings, and come to stay. Peace cannot be had without concession and sacrifice. There can be no sense of safety and equality among the nations if great preponderating armaments are henceforth to continue here and there to be built up and maintained. The statesmen of the world must plan for peace and nations must adjust and accommodate their policy to it as they have planned for war and made ready for pitiless contest and rivalry. The question of armaments, whether on land or sea, is the most immediately and intensely practical question connected with the future fortunes of nations and of mankind.

I have spoken upon these great matters without reserve and with the utmost explicitness because it has seemed to me to be necessary if the world's yearning desire for peace was anywhere to find free voice and utterance. Perhaps I am the only person in high authority amongst all the peoples of the world who is at liberty to speak and hold nothing back. I am speaking as an individual, and yet I am speaking also, of course, as the responsible head of a great government, and I feel confident that I have said what the people of the United States would wish me to say. . . .

I am proposing, as it were, that the nations should with one accord adopt the doctrine of President Monroe as the doctrine of the world: that no nation should seek to extend its polity over any other nation or people, but that every people should be left free to determine its own polity, its own way of development, unhindered, unthreatened, unafraid, the little along with the great and powerful.

I am proposing that all nations henceforth avoid entangling alliances which would draw them into competitions of power; catch them in a net of intrigue and selfish rivalry, and disturb their own affairs with influences intruded from without. There is no entangling alliance in a concert of power. When all unite to act in the same sense and with the same purpose all act in the common interest and are free to live their own lives under a common protection.

I am proposing government by the consent of the governed; that freedom of the seas which in international conference after conference representatives of the United States have urged with the eloquence of those who are the convinced disciples of liberty; and that moderation of armaments which makes of armies and navies a power for order merely, not an instrument of aggression or of selfish violence.

These are American principles, American policies. We could stand for no others. And they are also the principles and policies of forward looking men and women everywhere, of every modern nation, of every enlightened community. They are the principles of mankind and must prevail.

417. THE ZIMMERMANN NOTE
Released March 1, 1917

(J. B. Scott, ed. *Diplomatic Correspondence between the United States and Germany,* p. 338)

This note from the German Foreign Secretary to the German Minister in Mexico, was received by the United States Department of State from the British Naval Intelligence Service, February 26. It was promptly given to the press, and was very effective in consolidating public opinion in favor of war against Germany. See, C. H. Grattan, *Why We Fought;* J. B. Scott, *Survey of International Relations Between the United States and Germany, 1914–1917.*

Berlin, January 19, 1917

On the first of February we intend to begin submarine warfare unrestricted. In spite of this it is our intention to keep neutral the United States of America.

If this attempt is not successful we propose an alliance on the following basis with Mexico: That we shall make war together and together make peace. We shall give general financial support, and it is understood that Mexico is to reconquer the lost territory in New Mexico, Texas, and Arizona. The details are left for your settlement.

You are instructed to inform the President of Mexico of the above in the greatest confidence as soon as it is certain there will be an outbreak of war with the United States, and we suggest that the President of Mexico on his own initiative should communicate with Japan suggesting adherence at once to this plan; at the same time offer to mediate between Germany and Japan.

Please call to the attention of the President of Mexico that the employment of ruthless submarine warfare now promises to compel England to make peace in a few months.

Zimmermann.

418. WILSON'S SPEECH FOR DECLARATION OF WAR AGAINST GERMANY
Address delivered at Joint Session of the Two Houses of Congress, April 2, 1917

(U. S. 65th Congress, 1st Session, *Senate Doc. 5*)

Wilson had been successful during his first administration in avoiding entry into the World War, and the slogan "he kept us out of war" had considerable influence in his re-election in November, 1916. In January, 1917, however, Germany informed the United States that she intended to resume unrestricted submarine warfare; on February 3, Ambassador Bernstorff received his passports, and diplomatic relations with Germany were severed. During March three American merchant ships were sunk by submarines, and Wilson called Congress into extraordinary session, for April 2. Four days later Congress declared war with Germany; war was not declared upon Austria until December 7, 1917. Wilson's speech to Congress was one of the most notable of all his addresses: only the First Inaugural can be compared to it for eloquence. On the causes of the War, see, C. H. Grattan, *Why We Fought;* C. Seymour, ed., *The Intimate Papers of Colonel House,* Vol. II; C. Seymour, *American Diplomacy During the World War.*

I have called the Congress into extraordinary session because there are serious, very serious, choices of policy to be made, and made immediately, which it was neither right nor constitutionally permissible that I should assume the responsibility of making.

On the third of February last I officially laid before you the extraordinary announcement of the Imperial German Government that on and after the first day of February it was its purpose to put aside all restraints of law or of humanity and use its submarines to sink every vessel that sought to approach either the ports of Great Britain and Ireland or the western coasts of Europe or any of the ports controlled by the enemies of Germany within the Mediterranean. That had seemed to be the object of the German submarine warfare earlier in the war, but since April of last year the Imperial Government had somewhat restrained the commanders of its undersea craft in conformity with its promise then given to us that passenger boats should not be sunk and that due warning would be given to all other vessels which its submarines might seek to destroy, when no resistance was offered or escape attempted, and care taken that their crews were given at least a fair chance to save their lives in their open boats. The precautions taken were meager and haphazard enough, as was proved in distressing instance after instance in the progress of the cruel and unmanly business, but a certain degree of restraint was observed. The new policy has swept every restriction aside. Vessels of every kind, whatever their flag, their character, their cargo, their destination, their errand, have been ruthlessly sent to the bottom without warning and without thought of help or mercy for those on board, the vessels of friendly neutrals along with those of belligerents. Even hospital ships and ships carrying relief to the sorely bereaved and stricken people of Belgium, though the latter were provided with safe conduct through the proscribed areas by the German Government itself and were distinguished by unmistakable marks of identity, have been sunk with the same reckless lack of compassion or of principle.

I was for a little while unable to believe that such things would in fact be done by any government that had hitherto subscribed to the humane practices of civilized nations. International law had its origin in the attempt to set up some law which would be respected and observed upon the seas, where no nation had right of dominion and where lay the free highways of the world. . . . This minimum of right the German Government has swept aside under the plea of retaliation and necessity and because it had no weapons which it could use at sea except these which it is impossible to employ as it is employing them without throwing to the winds all scruples of humanity or of respect for the understandings that were supposed to underlie the intercourse of the world. I am not now thinking of the loss of property involved, immense and serious as that is, but only of the wanton and wholesale destruction of the lives of non-combatants, men, women, and children, engaged in pursuits which have always, even in the darkest periods of modern history, been deemed innocent and legitimate. Property can be paid for; the lives of peaceful and innocent people cannot be. The present German submarine warfare against commerce is a warfare against mankind.

It is a war against all nations. American ships have been sunk, American lives taken, in ways which it has stirred us very deeply to learn of, but the ships and people of other neutral and friendly nations have been sunk and overwhelmed in the waters in the same way. There has been no discrimination. The challenge is to all mankind. Each nation must decide for itself how it will meet it. The choice we make for ourselves must be made with a moderation of counsel and a temperateness of judgment befitting our character and our motives as a nation. We must put excited feeling away. Our motive will not be revenge or the victorious assertion of the physical might of the nation, but only the vindication of right, of human right, of which we are only a single champion.

When I addressed the Congress on the twenty-sixth of February last I thought that it would suffice to assert our neutral rights with arms, our right to use the seas against unlawful interference, our right to keep our people safe against unlawful violence. But armed neutrality, it now appears, is impracticable. Because submarines are in effect outlaws when used as the German submarines have been used against merchant shipping, it is impossible to defend ships against their attacks as the law of nations has assumed that merchantmen would defend themselves against privateers or cruisers, visible craft giving chase upon the open sea. It is common prudence in such circumstances, grim necessity indeed, to endeavor to destroy them before they have shown their own intention. They must be dealt with upon sight, if dealt with at all. The German Government denies the right of neutrals to use arms at all within the areas of the sea which it has proscribed, even in the defense of rights which no modern publicist has ever before questioned their right to defend. The intimation is conveyed that the armed guards which we have placed on our merchant ships will be treated as beyond the pale of law and subject to be dealt with as pirates would be. Armed neutrality is ineffectual enough at best; in such circumstances and in the face of such pretensions it is worse than ineffectual: it is likely only to produce what it was meant to prevent; it is practically certain to draw us into the war without either the rights or the effectiveness of belligerents. There is one choice we cannot make, we are incapable of making: we will not choose the path of submission and suffer the most sacred rights of our Nation and our people to be ignored or violated. The wrongs against which we now array ourselves are no common wrongs; they cut to the very roots of human life.

With a profound sense of the solemn and even tragical character of the step I am taking and of the grave responsibilities which it involves, but in unhesitating obedience to what I deem my constitutional duty, I advise that the Congress declare the recent course of the Imperial German Government to be in fact nothing less than war against the government and people of the United States; that it formally accept the status of belligerent which has thus been thrust upon it; and that it take immediate steps not only to put the country in a more thorough state of defense but also to exert all its power and employ all its resources to bring the Government of the German Empire to terms and end the war.

What this will involve is clear. It will involve the utmost practicable coöperation in counsel and action with the governments now at war with Germany, and, as incident to that, the extension to those governments of the most liberal financial credits, in order that our resources may so far as possible be added to theirs. It will involve the organization and mobilization of all the material resources of the country to supply the materials of war and serve the incidental needs of the Nation in the most abundant and yet the most economical and efficient way possible. It will involve the immediate full equipment of the navy in all respects but particularly in supplying it with the best means of dealing with the enemy's submarines. It will involve the immediate addition to the armed forces of the United States already provided for by law in case of war at least five hundred thousand men, who should, in my opinion, be chosen upon the principle of universal liability to service, and also the authorization of subsequent additional increments of equal force so soon as they may be needed and can be handled in training. It will involve also, of course, the granting of adequate credits to the Government, sustained, I hope, so far as they can equitably be sustained by the present generation, by well conceived taxation. . . .

While we do these things, these deeply momentous things, let us be very clear, and make very clear to all the world what our motives and our objects are. My own thought has not been driven from its habitual and normal course by the unhappy events of the last two months, and I do not believe that the thought of the Nation has been altered or clouded by them. I have exactly the same things in mind now that I had in mind when I addressed the Senate on the twenty-second of January last; the same that I had in mind when I addressed the Congress on the third of February and on the twenty-sixth of February. Our object now, as then, is to vindicate the principles of peace and justice in the life of the world as against selfish and autocratic power and to set up amongst the really free and self-governed peoples of the world such a concert of purpose and of action as will henceforth insure the observance of those principles. Neutrality is no longer feasible or desirable where the peace of the world is involved and the freedom of its peoples, and the menace to that peace and freedom lies in the existence of autocratic governments backed by organized force which is controlled wholly by their will, not by the will of their people. We have seen the last of neutrality in such circumstances. We are at the beginning of an age in which it will be insisted that the same standards of conduct and of responsibility for wrong done shall be observed among nations and their governments that are observed among the individual citizens of civilized states.

We have no quarrel with the German people. We have no feeling towards them but one of sympathy and friendship. It was not upon their impulse that their government acted in entering this war. It was not with their previous knowledge or approval. It was a war determined upon as wars used to be determined upon in the old, unhappy days when peoples were nowhere consulted by their rulers and wars were provoked and waged in the interest of dynasties or of little groups of ambitious men who were accustomed to use their fellow men as pawns and tools. . . .

We are accepting this challenge of hostile purpose because we know that in such a Government, following such methods, we can never have a friend; and that in the presence of its organized power, always lying in wait to accomplish we know not what purpose, there can be no assured security for the democratic Governments of the world. We are now about to accept gauge of battle with this natural foe to liberty and shall, if necessary, spend the whole force of the nation to check and nullify its pretensions and its power. We are glad, now that we see the facts with no veil of false pretense about them, to fight thus for the ultimate peace of the world and for the liberation of its peoples, the German peoples included: for the rights of nations great and small and the privilege of men everywhere to choose their way of life and of obedience. The world must be made safe for democracy. Its peace must be planted upon the tested foundations of political liberty. We have no selfish ends to serve. We desire no conquest, no dominion. We seek no indemnities for ourselves, no material compensation for the sacrifices we shall freely make. We are but one of the champions of the rights of mankind. We shall be satisfied when those rights have been made as secure as the faith and the freedom of nations can make them.

Just because we fight without rancor and without selfish object, seeking nothing for ourselves but what we shall wish to share with all free peoples, we shall, I feel confident, conduct our operations as belligerents without passion and ourselves observe with proud punctilio the principles of right and of fair play we profess to be fighting for.

I have said nothing of the Governments allied with the Imperial Government of Germany because they have not made war upon us or challenged us to defend our right and our honor. The Austro-Hungarian Government has, indeed, avowed its unqualified indorsement and acceptance of the reckless and lawless submarine warfare adopted now without disguise by the Imperial German Government, and it has therefore not been possible for this Government to receive Count Tarnowski, the Ambassador recently accredited to this Government by the Imperial and Royal Government of Austria-Hungary; but that Government has not actually engaged in warfare against citizens of the United States on the seas, and I take the liberty, for the present at least, of postponing a discussion of our relations with the authorities at Vienna. We enter this war only where we are clearly forced into it because there are no other means of defending our rights.

It will be all the easier for us to conduct ourselves as belligerents in a high spirit of right and fairness because we act without animus, not in enmity towards a people or with the desire to bring any injury or disadvantage upon them, but only in armed opposition to an irresponsible government which has thrown aside all considerations of humanity and of right and is running amuck. We are, let me say again, the sincere friends of the German people, and shall desire nothing so much as the early reëstablishment of intimate relations of mutual advantage between us,—however hard it may be for them, for the time being, to believe that this is spoken from our hearts. We have borne with their present Government through all these bitter months because of that friendship,—exercising a patience and forbearance which would otherwise have been impossible. We shall, happily, still have an opportunity to prove that friendship in our daily attitude and actions towards the millions of men and women of German birth and native sympathy who live amongst us and share our life, and we shall be proud to prove it towards all who are in fact loyal to their neighbors and to the Government in the hour of test. They are, most of them, as true and loyal Americans as if they had never known any other fealty or allegiance. They will be prompt to stand with us in rebuking and restraining the few who may be of a different mind and purpose. If there should be disloyalty, it will be dealt with with a firm hand of stern repression; but, if it lifts its head at all, it will lift it only here and there and without countenance except from a lawless and malignant few.

It is a distressing and oppressive duty, Gentlemen of the Congress, which I have performed in thus addressing you. There are, it may be, many months of fiery trial and sacrifice ahead of us. It is a fearful thing to lead this great peaceful people into war, into the most terrible and disastrous of all wars, civilization itself seeming to be in the balance. But the right is more precious than peace, and we shall fight for the things which we have always carried nearest our hearts,— for democracy, for the right of those who submit to authority to have a voice in their own Governments, for the rights and liberties of small nations, for a universal dominion of right by such a concert of free peoples as shall bring peace and safety to all nations and make the world itself at last free. To such a task we can dedicate our lives and our fortunes, everything that we are and everything that we have, with the pride of those who know that the day has come when America is privileged to spend her blood and her might for the principles that gave her birth and happiness and the peace which she has treasured. God helping her, she can do no other.

419. THE LEVER ACT
August 10, 1917

(*U. S. Statutes at Large,* Vol. XL, p. 276 ff.)

This act authorized the President to conserve food and fuel during the prosecution of the War. The guarantee of two dollars a bushel for wheat was to last until May 1, 1919; actually the price was fixed at $2.20 a bushel. Herbert Hoover was made Food Commissioner, and H. A. Garfield Fuel Commissioner. See, C. R. Van Hise, *Conservation and Regulation in the United States during the World War;* F. M. Surface, *The Stabilization of the Price of Wheat during the War;* W. F. Willoughby, *Government Organization in War Time and After.*

An Article to provide for the national security and defense by encouraging the production, conserving the supply, and controlling the distribution of food products and fuel.

Be it enacted, That by reason of the existence of a state of war, it is essential to the national security and defense, for the successful prosecution of the war, and for the support and maintenance of the Army and Navy, to assure an adequate supply and equitable distribution, and to facilitate the movement, of foods, feeds, fuel . . . and equipment required for the actual production of foods, feeds, and fuel, hereafter in this Act called necessaries; to prevent, . . . scarcity, monopolization, hoarding, injurious speculation, manipulations . . . and private controls, affecting such supply, . . . and to establish and maintain governmental control of such necessaries during the war. For such purposes the instrumentalities . . . and prohibitions hereinafter set forth are created. The President is authorized to make such regulations and to issue such orders as are essential effectively to carry out the provisions of this Act. . . .

SEC. 14. That whenever the President shall find that an emergency exists requiring stimulation of the production of wheat and that it is essential that the producers of wheat, produced within the United States, shall have the benefits of the guaranty provided for in this section, he is authorized, . . . to determine and fix and to give public notice of what, under specified conditions, is a reasonable guaranteed price for wheat, in order to assure such producers a reasonable profit. The President shall thereupon fix such guaranteed price. . . . Thereupon, the Government of the United States hereby guarantees every producer of wheat produced within the United States, that, upon compliance by him with the regulations prescribed, he shall receive for any wheat produced in reliance upon this guarantee within the period, not exceeding eighteen months, prescribed in the notice, a price not less than the guaranteed price therefor as fixed pursuant to this section. . . . The guaranteed prices for the several standard grades of wheat for the crop of nineteen hundred and eighteen, shall be based upon number one northern spring or its equivalent at not less than $2 per bushel at the principal interior primary markets. This guaranty shall not be dependent upon the action of the President under the first part of this section, but is hereby made absolute and shall be binding until May first, nineteen hundred and nineteen. . . .

For the purpose of making any guaranteed price effective under this section, or whenever he deems it essential . . . the President is authorized also, in his discretion, to purchase any wheat for which a guaranteed price shall be fixed . . . and to hold, transport, or store it, or to sell, dispose of, and deliver the same. . . .

SEC. 15. That from and after thirty days from the date of the approval of this Act no foods, fruits, food materials, or feeds shall be used in the production of distilled spirits for beverage purposes: . . . Nor shall there be imported into the United States any distilled spirits. Whenever the President shall find that limitation, regulation, or prohibition of the use of foods, fruits, food materials, or feeds in the production of malt or vinous liquors for beverage purposes, or that reduction of the alcoholic content of any such malt or vinous liquor, is essential, in order to assure an adequate and continuous supply of food, or that the national security and defense will be subserved thereby, he is authorized, from time to time, to prescribe and give public notice of the extent of the limitation, regulation, prohibition, or reduction so necessitated. . . .

SEC. 16. That the President is authorized and directed to commandeer any or all distilled spirits in bond or in stock at the date of the approval of this Act for redistillation, in so far as such redistillation may be necessary to meet the requirements of the Government in the manufacture of munitions and other military and hospital supplies. . . .

SEC. 24. That the provisions of this Act shall cease to be in effect when the existing state of war between the United States and Germany shall have terminated. . . .

SEC. 25. That the President of the United States shall be, . . . empowered, whenever and wherever in his judgment necessary for the efficient prosecution of the war, to fix the price of coal and coke, wherever and whenever sold . . . to regulate the method of production, sale, shipment, distribution, apportionment, or storage thereof among dealers and consumers. . . .

420. THE LANSING–ISHII AGREEMENT
November 2, 1917

(Foreign Relations of the United States, 1917, p. 264)

In 1915 Japan had given notice to the world that she would not, in fact, be bound by the Open Door policy. At this time she had presented to China the notorious Twenty-One Demands, fifteen of which China was compelled to accept. By a series of secret agreements with the Allied Powers, during 1916 and 1917, she had secured special concessions and promises of territorial acquisitions in the Far East. In the summer of 1917 Viscount Ishii came to the United States on a special mission for the purpose of quieting American apprehensions of Japanese policies and securing from the United States a modification of the Open Door policy. Ishii insisted that the United States recognize Japan's "paramount" interest in China. The Lansing-Ishii agreement, while apparently confirming the Open Door policy, did actually recognize that Japan had "special interests" in China; to that extent it represented a diplomatic victory for Japan. See, S. F. Bemis, ed. *American Secretaries of State,* Vol. X, p. 126 ff.; J. V. A. MacMurray, *Treaties*

and Agreements with and Concerning China, Vol. II; W. W. Willoughby, *Foreign Rights and Interests in China,* 2 Vols.; T. F. Millard, *Democracy and the Eastern Question;* H. Chung, *The Oriental Policy of the United States.*

Department of State
Washington, November 2, 1917

Excellency: I have the honor to communicate herein my understanding of the agreement reached by us in our recent conversations touching the questions of mutual interest to our Governments relating to the Republic of China.

In order to silence mischievous reports that have from time to time been circulated, it is believed by us that a public announcement once more of the desires and intentions shared by our two Governments with regard to China is advisable.

The Governments of the United States and Japan recognize that territorial propinquity creates special relations between countries, and consequently the Government of the United States recognizes that Japan has special interests in China, particularly in that part to which her possessions are contiguous.

The territorial sovereignty of China, nevertheless, remains unimpaired, and the Government of the United States has every confidence in the repeated assurances of the Imperial Japanese Government that while geographical position gives Japan such special interests, they have no desire to discriminate against the trade of other nations or to disregard the commercial rights heretofore granted by China in treaties with other powers.

The Governments of the United States and Japan deny that they have any purpose to infringe in any way the independence or territorial integrity of China, and they declare, furthermore, that they always adhere to the principle of the so-called "open-door" or equal opportunity for commerce and industry in China.

Moreover, they mutually declare that they are opposed to the acquisition by any government of any special rights or privileges that would affect the independence or territorial integrity of China, or that would deny to the subjects or citizens of any country the full enjoyment of equal opportunity in the commerce and industry of China.

I shall be glad to have Your Excellency confirm this understanding of the agreement reached by us.

Robert Lansing.

His Excellency Viscount Kikujiro Ishii

421. BUNTING v. OREGON
243 U. S. 426
1917

Error to the supreme court of Oregon. This case involved the interpretation of an Oregon statute of 1913 establishing a ten hour day for all employees in manufacturing establishments and providing that overtime work not to exceed three hours in one day must be paid at the rate of time and one-half of the regular wage.

McKenna, J. . . . The consonance of the Oregon law with the Fourteenth Amendment is the question in the case, and this depends upon whether it is a proper exercise of the police power of the State, as the supreme court of this State decided that it is.

That the police power extends to health regulations is not denied, but it is denied that the law has such purpose or justification. It is contended that it is a wage law, not a health regulation, and takes the property of plaintiff in error without due process. . . .

There is a certain verbal plausibility in the contention that it was intended to permit thirteen hours' work if there be fifteen and one-half-hours' pay, but the plausibility disappears upon reflection. The provision for overtime is permissive, in the same sense that any penalty may be said to be permissive. Its purpose is to deter by its burden, and its adequacy for this was a matter of legislative judgment under the particular circumstances. . . . We cannot know all of the conditions that impelled the law or its particular form. The supreme court, nearer to them, describes the law as follows: "It is clear that the intent of the law is to make ten hours a regular day's labor in the occupations to which reference is made. Apparently the provisions permitting labor for the overtime on express conditions were made in order to facilitate the enforcement of the law, and in the nature of a mild penalty for employing one not more than three hours overtime. It might be regarded as more difficult to detect violations of the law by an employment for a shorter time than for a longer time. This penalty also goes to the employee in case the employer avails himself of the overtime clause." . . .

But passing general considerations and coming back to our immediate concern, which is the validity of the particular exertion of power in the Oregon law, our judgment of it is that it does not transcend constitutional limits. . . .

There is a contention made that the law, even regarded as regulating hours of service, is not either necessary or useful "for preservation of the health of employees in mills, factories and manufacturing establishments."

The record contains no facts to support the contention, and against it is the judgment of the legislature and the supreme court, which said: "In view of the well-known fact that the custom in our industries does not sanction a longer service than 10 hours per day, it cannot be held, as a matter of law, that the legislative requirement is unreasonable or arbitrary as to hours of labor. Statistics show that the average daily working time among workingmen in different countries is, in Australia, 8 hours; in Great Britain, 9; in the United States, 9¾; in Denmark, 9¾; in Norway, 10; Sweden, France, and Switzerland, 10½; Germany, 10¼; Belgium, Italy, and Austria, 11; and in Russia, 12 hours." . . .

Judgment affirmed.

WHITE, C. J., and VAN DEVANTER, J., and McREYNOLDS, J., dissented. BRANDEIS, J., took no part in the decision.

422. IMMIGRATION RESTRICTION
The Laws of 1917 and 1921

(U. S. Bureau of Immigration, *Annual Report of the Commissioner-General of Immigration*, 1923, p. 2 ff.)

The law of 1917, passed over the veto of President Wilson, marked a definite end to our traditional immigration policy: the act of 1921 with its quota system inaugurated the present policy of severe restriction. This summary of the two important laws is given in lieu of the acts themselves. For a collection of Documents on Immigration, see E. Abbott, *Selected Documents on Immigration; Historical Aspects of the Immigration Problem*. A brief history of the legislation of the nineteen-twenties can be found in C. P. Howland, ed. *Survey of American Foreign Relations: 1929.*

Perhaps it is not very generally realized that the per centum limit law marked the beginning of actual restriction or limitation of immigration to the United States from Europe, Africa, Australia, and a considerable part of Asia. The Chinese exclusion act of 1882, the passport agreement with Japan which became effective in 1908, and the "barred zone" provision in the general immigration law of 1917 had already stopped or greatly reduced the influx of oriental peoples, but so far as others, and particularly Europeans, were concerned, all applicants who met the various tests prescribed in the general law were admitted. This general law, first enacted in 1882 and several times revised and strengthened, was and still is based on the principle of selection rather than of numerical restriction. It is probably true that the provision barring illiterate aliens from admission, which was added to the general law in 1917, was intended as a restrictive measure rather than a quality test, but in its practical effect it was only another addition to the already numerous class of alleged undesirables who were denied admission, and obviously could not be relied upon actually to limit the volume of immigration.

The immigration act of 1882, which, as already indicated, was the first general law upon the subject, provided for the exclusion from the United States of the following classes only: Convicts, lunatics, idiots, and persons likely to become a public charge. This law underwent more or less important revisions in 1891, 1893, 1903, 1907, and 1917, until the last-mentioned act, which is the present general immigration law, denies admission to many classes of aliens, including the following: Idiots, imbeciles, feeble-minded persons, epileptics, insane persons; persons who have had one or more attacks of insanity at any time previously; persons of constitutional psychopathic inferiority; persons with chronic alcoholism; paupers; professional beggars; vagrants; persons afflicted with tuberculosis in any form or with a loathsome or dangerous contagious disease; persons certified by the examining physician as being mentally or physically defective, such physical defect being of a nature which may affect the ability of the alien to earn a living; persons who have been convicted of or admit having committed a felony or other crime or misdemeanor involving moral turpitude; polygamists, or persons who practice polygamy or believe in or advocate the practice of polygamy; anarchists and similar classes; immoral persons and persons coming for an immoral purpose; contract laborers;

persons likely to become a public charge; persons seeking admission within one year of date of previous debarment or deportation; persons whose ticket or passage is paid for with the money of another or who are assisted by others to come, unless it is affirmatively shown that such persons do not belong to one of the foregoing excluded classes; persons whose ticket or passage is paid for by any corporation, association, society, municipality, or foreign government, either directly or indirectly; stowaways; children under 16 years of age unless accompanied by one or both of their parents; persons who are natives of certain geographically defined territory; aliens over 16 years of age who are unable to read some language or dialect; certain accompanying aliens, as described in the last proviso of section 18 of the act; and persons who have arrived in Canada or Mexico by certain steamship lines. Persons who fail to meet certain passport requirements were added to the excluded classes in subsequent legislation.

Obviously it would be difficult to find, or even to invent, many other terms denoting individual undesirability which might be added to the foregoing list, but, as already pointed out, the general law is essentially selective in theory, for even its most rigid application with respect to the excludable classes above enumerated could not be depended upon to prevent the coming of unlimited numbers of aliens who were able to meet the tests imposed.

Even a casual survey of congressional discussions of the immigration problem during the past quarter of a century demonstrates very clearly that while the law makers were deeply concerned with the mental, moral, and physical quality of immigrants, there developed as time went on an even greater concern as to the fundamental racial character of the constantly increasing numbers who came. The record of alien arrivals year by year had shown a gradual falling off in the immigration of northwest European peoples, representing racial stocks which were common to America even in colonial days, and a rapid and remarkably large increase in the movement from southern and eastern European countries and Asiatic Turkey. Immigration from the last-named sources reached an annual average of about 750,000 and in some

years nearly a million came, and there seems to have been a general belief in Congress that it would increase rather than diminish. At the same time no one seems to have anticipated a revival of the formerly large influx from the "old sources," as the countries of northwest Europe came to be known.

This remarkable change in the sources and racial character of our immigrants led to an almost continuous agitation of the immigration problem both in and out of Congress, and there was a steadily growing demand for restriction, particularly of the newer movement from the south and east of Europe. During the greater part of this period of agitation the so-called literacy test for aliens was the favorite weapon of the restrictionists, and its widespread popularity appears to have been based quite largely on a belief, or at least a hope, that it would reduce to some extent the stream of "new" immigration, about one-third of which was illiterate, without seriously interfering with the coming of the older type, among whom illiteracy was at a minimum.

Presidents Cleveland and Taft vetoed immigration bills because they contained a literacy test provision, and President Wilson vetoed two bills largely for the same reason. In 1917, however, Congress passed a general immigration bill which included the literacy provision over the President's veto, and, with certain exceptions, aliens who are unable to read are no longer admitted to the United States. At that time, however, the World War had already had the effect of reducing immigration from Europe to a low level, and our own entry into the conflict a few days before the law in question went into effect practically stopped it altogether. Consequently, the value of the literacy provision as a means of restricting European immigration was never fairly tested under normal conditions.

The Congress, however, seemingly realized that even the comprehensive immigration law of 1917, including the literacy test, would afford only a frail barrier against the promised rush from the war-stricken countries of Europe, and in December, 1920, the House of Representatives, with little opposition, passed a bill to suspend practically all immigration for the time being. The per centum limit plan was substituted by the Senate, however, and the substitute prevailed in Congress, but it failed to become a law at the time because President Wilson withheld executive approval. Nevertheless, favorable action was not long delayed, for at the special session called at the beginning of the present administration the measure was quickly enacted, and, with President Harding's approval, became a law on May 19, 1921. This law expired by limitation June 30, 1922, but by the act of May 11, 1922, its life was extended to June 30, 1924, and some strengthening amendments were added.

The principal provisions of the per centum limit act, or the "quota law," as it is popularly known, are as follows:

The number of aliens of any nationality who may be admitted to the United States in any fiscal year shall not exceed 3 per cent of the number of persons of such nationality who were resident in the United States according to the census of 1910.

Monthly quotas are limited to 20 per cent of the annual quota.

For the purposes of the act, "nationality" is determined by country of birth.

The law does not apply to the following classes of aliens: Government officials; aliens in transit; aliens visiting the United States as tourists or temporarily for business or pleasure; aliens from countries immigration from which is regulated in accordance with treaties or agreement relating solely to immigration, otherwise China and Japan; aliens from the so-called Asiatic barred zone; aliens who have resided continuously for at least five years in Canada, Newfoundland, Cuba, Mexico, Central or South America, or adjacent islands; aliens under the age of 18 who are children of citizens of the United States.

Certain other classes of aliens who are counted against quotas are admissible after a quota is exhausted. The following are included in this category: Aliens returning from a temporary visit abroad; aliens who are professional actors, artists, lecturers, singers, ministers of any religious denomination, professors for colleges or seminaries, members of any recognized learned profession, or aliens employed as domestic servants.

So far as possible preference is given to the wives and certain near relatives of citizens of the United States, applicants for citizenship and honorably discharged soldiers, eligible to citizenship, who served in the United States military or naval forces at any time between April 6, 1917, and November 11, 1918.

Transportation companies are liable to a fine of $200 for each alien brought to a United States port in excess of the quota and where such fine is imposed the amount paid for passage must be returned to the rejected alien.

The quota limit law is in addition to and not in substitution for the provisions of the immigration laws.

423. THE FOURTEEN POINTS
1. Wilson's Address to Congress January 8, 1918

(Supplement to the Messages and Papers of the Presidents Covering the Second Administration of Woodrow Wilson, p. 8421 ff.)

In this famous speech on War Aims and Peace Terms, President Wilson laid down fourteen points as the "only possible" program for world peace. These points were subsequently taken as the basis for peace negotiations. The immediate background of this speech was the failure of the Interallied Conference to agree upon a formulation of war aims, and the overtures of Russia toward Germany. The fourteen points were based on a report prepared for Mr. Wilson by The Inquiry—a commission organized by Mr. House for the purpose of studying Allied and American policy. See, C. Seymour, *American Diplomacy During the World War*, p. 277 ff.; R. S. Baker, *Woodrow Wilson and the World Settlement*, Vol. I, ch. vi. See also, J. B. Scott, ed. *Official Statements of War Aims and Peace Proposals, December 1916 to November 1919.*

Gentlemen of the Congress:
. . . It will be our wish and purpose that the processes of peace, when they are begun, shall be absolutely open and that they shall involve and permit henceforth no secret understandings of any kind. The day of conquest and aggrandizement is gone by; so is also the day of secret covenants entered into

in the interest of particular governments and likely at some unlooked-for moment to upset the peace of the world. It is this happy fact, now clear to the view of every public man whose thoughts do not still linger in an age that is dead and gone, which makes it possible for every nation whose purposes are consistent with justice and the peace of the world to avow now or at any other time the objects it has in view.

We entered this war because violations of right had occurred which touched us to the quick and made the life of our own people impossible unless they were corrected and the world secured once for all against their recurrence. What we demand in this war, therefore, is nothing peculiar to ourselves. It is that the world be made fit and safe to live in; and particularly that it be made safe for every peace-loving nation which, like our own, wishes to live its own life, determine its own institutions, be assured of justice and fair dealing by the other peoples of the world as against force and selfish aggression. All the peoples of the world are in effect partners in this interest, and for our own part we see very clearly that unless justice be done to others it will not be done to us. The program of the world's peace, therefore, is our program; and that program, the only possible program, as we see it, is this:

I. Open covenants of peace, openly arrived at, after which there shall be no private international understandings of any kind but diplomacy shall proceed always frankly and in the public view.

II. Absolute freedom of navigation upon the seas, outside territorial waters, alike in peace and in war, except as the seas may be closed in whole or in part by international action for the enforcement of international covenants.

III. The removal, so far as possible, of all economic barriers and the establishment of an equality of trade conditions among all the nations consenting to the peace and associating themselves for its maintenance.

IV. Adequate guarantees given and taken that national armaments will be reduced to the lowest point consistent with domestic safety.

V. A free, open-minded, and absolutely impartial adjustment of all colonial claims, based upon a strict observance of the principle that in determining all such questions of sovereignty the interests of the populations concerned must have equal weight with the equitable claims of the government whose title is to be determined.

VI. The evacuation of all Russian territory and such a settlement of all questions affecting Russia as will secure the best and freest coöperation of the other nations of the world in obtaining for her an unhampered and unembarrassed opportunity for the independent determination of her own political development and national policy and assure her of a sincere welcome into the society of free nations under institutions of her own choosing; and, more than a welcome, assistance also of every kind that she may need and may herself desire. The treatment accorded Russia by her sister nations in the months to come will be the acid test of their good will, of their comprehension of her needs as distinguished from their own interests, and of their intelligent and unselfish sympathy.

VII. Belgium, the whole world will agree, must be evacuated and restored, without any attempt to limit the sovereignty which she enjoys in common with all other free nations. No other single act will serve as this will serve to restore confidence among the nations in the laws which they have themselves set and determined for the government of their relations with one another. Without this healing act the whole structure and validity of international law is forever impaired.

VIII. All French territory should be freed and the invaded portions restored, and the wrong done to France by Prussia in 1871 in the matter of Alsace-Lorraine, which has unsettled the peace of the world for nearly fifty years, should be righted, in order that peace may once more be made secure in the interest of all.

IX. A readjustment of the frontiers of Italy should be effected along clearly recognizable lines of nationality.

X. The peoples of Austria-Hungary, whose place among the nations we wish to see safeguarded and assured, should be accorded the freest opportunity of autonomous development.

XI. Rumania, Serbia, and Montenegro should be evacuated; occupied territories restored; Serbia accorded free and secure access to the sea; and the relations of the several Balkan states to one another determined by friendly counsel along historically established lines of allegiance and nationality; and international guarantees of the political and economic independence and territorial integrity of the several Balkan states should be entered into.

XII. The Turkish portions of the present Ottoman Empire should be assured a secure sovereignty, but the other nationalities which are now under Turkish rule should be assured an undoubted security of life and an absolutely unmolested opportunity of autonomous development, and the Dardanelles should be permanently opened as a free passage to the ships and commerce of all nations under international guarantees.

XIII. An independent Polish state should be erected which should include the territories inhabited by indisputably Polish populations, which should be assured a free and secure access to the sea, and whose political and economic independence and territorial integrity should be guaranteed by international covenant.

XIV. A general association of nations must be formed under specific covenants for the purpose of affording mutual guarantees of political independence and territorial integrity to great and small states alike.

In regard to these essential rectifications of wrong and assertions of right we feel ourselves to be intimate partners of all the governments and peoples associated together against the Imperialists. We cannot be separated in interest or divided in purpose. We stand together until the end.

For such arrangements and covenants we are willing to fight and to continue to fight until they are achieved; but only because we wish the right to prevail and desire a just and stable peace such as can be secured only by removing the chief provocations to war, which this program does not remove. We have no jealousy of German greatness, and there is nothing in this program that impairs it. We grudge her no achievement or distinction of learning or of pacific enterprise such as have made her record very bright and very enviable. We do not wish to injure her or to block in any way her legitimate influence or power. We do not wish to fight her either with arms or with hostile arrangements of trade if she is willing to associate herself with us and the other peace-loving nations of the world in covenants of justice and law and fair dealing. We wish her only to accept a place of equality among the peoples of the world,—the new world in which we now live, —instead of a place of mastery.

Neither do we presume to suggest to her any alteration or modification of her institutions. But it is necessary, we must frankly say, and necessary as a preliminary to any intelligent dealings with her on our part, that we should know whom her spokesmen speak for when they speak to us, whether for the Reichstag majority or for the military party and the men whose creed is imperial domination.

We have spoken now, surely, in terms too concrete to admit of any further doubt or question. An evident principle runs through the whole program I have outlined. It is the principle of justice to all peoples and nationalities, and their right to live on equal terms of liberty and safety with one another, whether they be strong or weak. Unless this principle be made its foundation no part of the structure of international justice can stand. The people of the United States could act upon no other principle; and to the vindication of this principle they are ready to devote their lives, their honor, and everything that they possess. The moral climax of this the culminating and final war for human liberty has come, and they are ready to put their own strength, their own highest purpose, their own integrity and devotion to the test.

2. The American Interpretation of the Fourteen Points

(*Foreign Relations of the United States*, 1918, Supplement, Vol. I, p. 405 ff.)

This semi-official interpretation of the Fourteen Points was prepared under the supervision of Colonel House by Frank Cobb and Walter Lippman. "These interpretations," wrote Colonel House, "were on the table day after day when we sat in conference. . . . Many times they asked the meaning of this or that point and I would read from the accepted interpretation." (*Intimate Papers of Colonel House,* Vol. IV, p. 154.) See C. Seymour, *American Diplomacy During the World War,* p. 372 ff.

1. The purpose is clearly to prohibit treaties, sections of treaties of understandings that are secret, such as the [Triple Alliance], etc.

The phrase "openly arrived at" need not cause difficulty. In fact, the President explained to the Senate last winter that the phrase was not meant to exclude confidential diplomatic negotiations involving delicate matters. The intention is that nothing which occurs in the course of such confidential negotiations shall be binding unless it appears in the final covenant made public to the world.

The matter may perhaps be put this way: it is proposed that in future every treaty be part of the public law of the world, and that every nation assume a certain obligation in regard to its enforcement. Obviously, nations cannot assume obligations in matters of which they are ignorant; and therefore any secret treaty tends to undermine the solidity of the whole structure of international covenants which it is proposed to erect.

2. This proposition must be read in connection with number 14 which proposes a league of nations. It refers to navigation under the three following conditions: (1) general peace; (2) a general war, entered into by the League of Nations for the purpose of enforcing international covenants; (3) limited war, involving no breach of international covenants.

Under "(1) General peace" no serious dispute exists. There is implied freedom to come and go [on the high seas].

No serious dispute exists as to the intention under "(2) A general war entered into by the League of Nations to enforce international covenants." Obviously such a war is conducted against an outlaw nation and complete nonintercourse with that nation is intended.

"(3) A limited war, involving no breach of international covenants" is the crux of the whole difficulty. The question is, what are to be the rights of neutral shipping and private property on the high seas during a war between a limited number of nations when that war involves no issue upon which the League of Nations cares to take sides. In other words, a war in which the League of Nations remains neutral. Clearly, it is the intention of the proposal that in such a war the rights of neutrals shall be maintained against the belligerents, the rights of both to be clearly and precisely defined in the law of nations.

3. The proposal applies only to those nations which accept the responsibilities of membership in the League of Nations. It means the destruction of all special commercial agreements, each putting the trade of every other nation in the League on the same basis, the most-favored-nation clause applying automatically to all members of the League of Nations. Thus a nation could legally maintain a tariff or a special railroad rate or a port restriction against the whole world, or against all the signatory powers. It could maintain any kind of restriction which it chose against a nation not in the League. But it could not discriminate as between its partners in the League.

This clause naturally contemplates fair and equitable understanding as to the distribution of raw materials.

4. "Domestic safety" clearly implies not only internal policing, but the protection of territory against invasion. The accumulation of armaments above this level would be a violation of the intention of the proposal.

What guarantees should be given and taken, or what are to be the standards of judgment have never been determined. It will be necessary to adopt the general principle and then institute some kind [of international commission of investigation] to prepare detailed projects for its execution.

5. Some fear is expressed in France [and England] that this involves reopening of all colonial questions. Obviously it is not so intended. It applies clearly [to those] colonial claims which have been created by the war. That means the German colonies and any other colonies which may come under international consideration as a result of the war. . . .

What are the "interests of the populations"? That they should not be militarized, that exploitation should be conducted on the principle of the "open door", and under the strictest regulation as to labor conditions, profits and taxes, that a sanitary regime be maintained, that permanent improvements in the way of roads, etc., be made, that native organization and custom be respected, that the protecting authority be stable and experienced enough to thwart intrigue and corruption, that the [protecting] power have adequate resources in money and competent administrators to act successfully.

It would seem as if the principle involved in this proposition is that a colonial power acts not as owner of its colonies, but as trustee for the natives and for the interests of the society of nations, that the terms on which the colonial administration is conducted are a matter of international concern and may legitimately be the subject of international inquiry, and that the peace conference may, therefore, write a code of colonial conduct binding upon [all] colonial powers.

6. The first question is whether Russian territory is synonymous with territory belonging to the former Russian Empire. This is clearly not so, because proposition 13 stipulates an independent Poland, a proposal which excludes the territorial reëstablishment of the Empire. What is recognized as valid for the Poles will certainly have to be recognized for the Finns, the Lithuanians, the Letts, and perhaps also for the Ukrainians. Since the formulating of this condition these subject nationalities have emerged, and there can be no doubt that they will have to be granted an opportunity of free development.

The problem of these nationalities is complicated by two facts: (1) that they have conflicting claims; (2) that the evacuation called for in the proposal may be followed by Bolshevist revolutions in all of them. . . .

This can mean nothing less than the [recognition] by the peace conference of a series of [de facto] governments representing Finns, Esths, Lithuanians, Ukrainians. This primary [act] of recognition should be conditional upon the calling of national assemblies for the creation of de facto governments, as soon as the peace conference has drawn frontiers for these new states. The frontiers should be drawn so far as possible on ethnic lines, but in [every] case the right of unhampered economic [transit] should be reserved. No dynastic ties with German [or] Austrian or Romanoff princes should be permitted, and every inducement should be [given] to encourage federal [relations] between these new states. Under proposition 3 the economic sections of the treaty of Brest-Litovsk are obliterated, but this proposition should not be construed as forbidding a customs union, a monetary union, a railroad union, etc., of these states. Provision should also be made by which Great Russia can federate with these states on the same terms. . . .

The essence of the Russian problem then in the immediate future would seem to be: (1) the recognition of provisional governments; (2) assistance extended to and through these governments. . . .

In any case the treaties of Brest-Litovsk and Bucharest must be cancelled as palpably fraudulent. Provision must be made for the withdrawal of all German troops in Russia and the peace conference [will] have a clean slate on which to write a policy for all the Russian peoples.

7. The only problem raised here is in the word "restored". Whether restoration is to be in kind or how the amount of the indemnity is to be determined is a matter of detail, not of principle. The principle that should be established is that in the case of Belgium there exists no distinction between "legitimate" and "illegitimate" destruction. The initial act of invasion was illegitimate and therefore all the consequences of that act are of the same character. Among the consequences may be put the war debt of Belgium. The recognition of this principle would constitute "the healing act" of which the President speaks.

8. In regard to the restoration of French territory it might well be argued that the invasion of northern France, being the result of the illegal act as regards Belgium, was in itself illegal. But the case is not perfect. As the world stood in 1914, war between France and Germany was not in itself a violation of international law, and great insistence should be put upon keeping the Belgian case distinct and symbolic. Thus Belgium might well, as indicated above, claim reimbursement not only for destruction but for the cost of carrying on the war. France could not claim payment, it would seem, for more than the damage done to her northeastern departments.

The status of Alsace-Lorraine was settled by the official statement issued a few days ago. It is to be restored completely to French sovereignty.

Attention is called to the strong current of French opinion which claims "the boundaries of 1914 [1814]" rather than of 1871. The territory claimed is the valley of the Saar with its coalfields. No claim on grounds of nationality can be established, but the argument leans on the possibility of taking this territory in lieu of indemnity; it would seem to be a clear violation of the President's proposal.

Attention is called also to the fact that no reference is made to status of Luxemburg. The best solution would seem to be a free choice by the [people of] Luxemburg themselves.

9. This proposal is less than the Italian claim; less, of course, than the territory allotted by the treaty of London; less than the arrangement made between the Italian Government and the Jugo-Slav state.

In the region of Trent the Italians claim a strategic rather than ethnic frontier. It should be noted in this connection that [Italy] and Germany will become neighbors if German Austria joins the German Empire. And if Italy obtains the best geographical frontier she will assume sovereignty over a large number of Germans. This is a violation of principle. But it may be argued that by drawing a sharp line along the crest of the Alps, Italy's security will be enormously enhanced and the necessity of heavy armaments reduced. It might, therefore, be provided that Italy should have her claim in the Trentino, but that the northern part, inhabited by Germans, should be completely autonomous and that the population should not be liable to military service in the Italian Army. Italy could thus occupy the uninhabited Alpine peaks for military purposes, but would not govern the cultural life of the alien population to the south of her frontier.

The other problems of the frontier are questions between Italy and Jugo-Slavia, Italy and the Balkans, Italy and Greece.

The agreement reached with Jugo-Slavs may well be allowed to stand, although it should be insisted for [the protection of] the hinterland that both Trieste and Fiume be free ports. This is [essential] to Bohemia, German Austria, Hungary, as well as to prosperity of the cities themselves. . . .

Italy's claims in Turkey belong to the problem of the Turkish Empire.

10. This proposition no longer holds. Instead we have [today] the following elements:

(1) Czecho-Slovakia. Its territories include at least a million Germans for whom some provision must be made.

The independence of Slovakia means the dismemberment of the northwestern countries of Hungary.

(2) Galicia. Western Galicia is clearly Polish. Eastern Galicia is in large measure Ukrainian (or Ruthenian) and does not of right belong to Poland.

There also are several hundred thousand Ukrainians among the north and northeastern borders of Hungary and in parts of Bukowina (which belonged to Austria).

(3) German Austria. This territory should of right be permitted to join Germany, but there is strong objection in [France] because of the increase of [population] involved.

(4) Jugo-Slavia. It faces the following problems: (a) Frontier questions with Italy in Istria and the Dalmatian coast; with Roumania in the Banat. (b) An international problem arises out of the refusal of the Croats to accept the domination of the Serbs of Servian Kingdom. (c) A problem of the Mohammedan Serbs of Bosnia who are said to be loyal to the Hapsburgs. They constitute a little less than one-third of the population.

(5) Transylvania. Will undoubtedly join Roumania, but provision must be made for the protection of the Magyars, Szeklers and Germans who constitute a large minority.

(6) Hungary. Now independent and very democratic in form, but governed by Magyars whose aim is to prevent the detachment of territory of nationalities on the fringe.

The United States is clearly committed to the program of national unity and independence. It must stipulate, however, for the protection of national minorities, for freedom of access to the Adriatic and the Black Sea, and it supports a program aiming at a confederation of southeastern Europe.

11. This proposal is also altered by events. Servia will appear as Jugo-Slavia with access to the Adriatic. Roumania will have acquired the Dobrudja, Bessarabia and probably Transylvania. These two states will have eleven or twelve million inhabitants and will be far greater and stronger than Bulgaria.

Bulgaria should clearly have her frontier in the southern Dobrudja as it stood before the second Balkan War. She should also have Thrace up to the Enos-Midia line and perhaps even to the Midia-Rodosto line.

Macedonia should be allotted after an impartial investigation. The line which might be taken as a basis of investigation is the southern line of the "contested zone" agreed upon by Serbia and Bulgaria before the first Balkan War.

Albania could be under a protectorate, no doubt of Italy, and its frontiers in the north might be essentially those of the London conference.

12. The same difficulty arises here as in the case of Austria-Hungary concerning the word "autonomous".

It is clear that the Straits and Constantinople, while they may remain nominally Turkish, should be under international control. This control may be collective or be in the hands of one power as mandatory of the League.

Anatolia should be reserved for the Turks. The coast lands, where Greeks predominate, should be under special international control, perhaps with Greece as mandatory.

Armenia must be [given] a port on the Mediterranean, and a protecting power established. France may claim it, but the Armenians would prefer Great Britain.

Syria has already been allotted to France by agreement with Great Britain.

Great Britain is clearly the best mandatory for Palestine, Mesopotamia and Arabia.

A general code of guarantees binding upon all mandatories in Asia Minor should be written into the treaty of peace.

This should contain provisions for minorities and the "open door". The trunk railroad lines should be internationalized.

13. The chief problem is whether Poland is to obtain territory west of the Vistula, which would cut off the Germans of East Prussia from the Empire, or whether Danzig can be made a free port and the Vistula internationalized.

On the east, Poland should receive no territory in which Lithuanians or Ukrainians predominate.

If Posen and Silesia go to Poland, rigid protection must be afforded the minorities of Germans and Jews living there, as well as in other parts of the Polish state.

The principle on which frontiers will be [delimited] is contained in the President's word "indisputably". This may imply the taking of an impartial census before frontiers are marked.

14. The principle of a league of nations as the primary essential of a permanent peace has been so clearly presented by President Wilson in his speech of September 27, 1918, that no further elucidation is required. It is the foundation of the whole diplomatic structure of a permanent peace.

3. The Allies Accept the Fourteen Points
November 5, 1918

(*Foreign Relations of the United States,* 1918, Supplement, Vol. I, p. 468–9)

In October, 1918, the German Government opened negotiations with President Wilson looking to an armistice on the basis of the Fourteen Points. While Wilson was willing to conclude an armistice on this basis as far as the United States was concerned, he could not bind the Allies to any such agreement. The diplomacy of Colonel House and the threat from Wilson of independent action by the United States finally forced the Allies to agree to accept the Fourteen Points as a basis for the Armistice, but with an important reservation on the interpretation of the second point—the freedom of the seas. See C. Seymour, *American Diplomacy During the World War,* chs. viii–x; R. S. Baker, *Woodrow Wilson and the World Settlement,* Vol. I, ch. x.

The Allied Governments have given careful consideration to the correspondence which has passed between the President of the United States and the German Government. Subject to the qualifications which follow they declare their willingness to make peace with the Government of Germany on the terms of peace laid down in the President's address to Congress of January, 1918, and the principles of settlement enunciated in his subsequent addresses. They must point out, however, that clause 2, relating to what is usually described as the freedom of the seas, is open to various interpretations, some of which they could not accept. They must, therefore, reserve to themselves complete freedom on this subject when they enter the peace conference.

Further, in the conditions of peace laid down in his address to Congress of January 8, 1918, the President declared that invaded territories must be restored as well as evacuated and freed, the Allies feel that no doubt ought to be allowed to exist as to what this provision implies. By it they understand that compensation will be made by Germany for all damage done to the civilian population of the Allies and their property by the aggression of Germany by land, by sea and from the air.

424. RAILWAY ADMINISTRATION ACT
March   21, 1918
(*U. S. Statutes at Large,* Vol. XL, p. 451 ff.)

Shortly after the outbreak of the war the Railroads created a Railroads' War Board to secure more unified administration of the roads; the results were disappointing and in December 1917 the Government took over control of the railroads. The Act of March 21, 1917 provided for the operation of the 1oads and for compensation to the owners. Gover imental operation aroused considerable criticism on grounds of extravagance, but on the whole the roads were operated efficiently and soundly. For the return of the roads to private ownership and control, see the Transportation Act of 1920, Doc. No. 438. On government operation, see F. H. Dixon, *Railroads and Government, 1910–1921;* W. D. Hines, *War History of American Railroads;* R. MacVeagh, *Transportation Act of 1920.*

An Act To provide for the operation of transportation systems while under Federal control, for the just compensation of their owners, and for other purposes.
BE it enacted . . . That the President, having in time of war taken over the possession, use, control, and operation (called herein Federal control) of certain railroads and systems of transportation (called herein carrier;), is hereby authorized to agree with and to guarantee to any such carrier making operating returns to the Interstate Commerce Commission, that during the period of such Federal control it shall receive as just compensation an annual sum, payable from time to time in reasonable installments, for each year and pro rata for any fractional year of such Federal control, not exceeding a sum equivalent as nearly as may be to its average annual railway operating income for the three years ended June thirtieth, nineteen hundred and seventeen.

That any railway operating income accruing during the period of Federal control in excess of such just compensation shall remain the property of the United States. . . .

Every such agreement shall also contain adequate and appropriate provisions for the maintenance, repair, renewals, and depreciation of the property, for the creation of any reserves or reserve funds found necessary in connection therewith, and for such accounting and adjustments of charges and payments, both during and at the end of Federal control as may be requisite in order that the property of each carrier may be returned to it in substantially as good repair and in substantially as complete equipment as it was in at the beginning of Federal control, and also that the United States may, by deductions from the just compensations or by other proper means and charges, be reimbursed for the cost of any additions, repairs, renewals, and betterments to such property not justly chargeable to the United States; in making such accounting and adjustments, due consideration shall be given to the amounts expended or reserved by each carrier for maintenance, repairs, renewals, and depreciation during the three years ended June thirtieth, nineteen hundred and seventeen, to the condition of the property at the beginning and at the end of Federal control and to any other pertinent facts and circumstances. . . .

SEC. 5. That no carrier while under Federal control shall, without the prior approval of the President, declare or pay any dividend in excess of its regular rate of dividends during the three years ended June thirtieth, nineteen hundred and seventeen: *Provided, however,* That such carriers as have paid no regular dividends or no dividends during said period may, with the prior approval of the President, pay dividends at such rate as the President may determine.

SEC. 6. That the sum of $500,000,000 is hereby appropriated, out of any moneys in the Treasury not otherwise appropriated, which, together with any funds available from any operating income of said carriers, may be used by the President as a revolving fund for the purpose of paying the expenses of the Federal control, and so far as necessary the amount of just compensation, and to provide terminals, motive power, cars, and other necessary equipment, such terminals, motive power, cars, and equipment to be used and accounted for as the President may direct and to be disposed of as Congress may hereafter by law provide.

The President may also make or order any carrier to make any additions, betterments, or road extensions, and to provide terminals, motive power, cars and other equipment necessary or desirable for war purposes or in the public interest on or in connection with the property of any carrier. He may from said revolving fund advance to such carrier all or any part of the expense of such additions, betterments, or road extensions, and to provide terminals, motive power, cars, and other necessary equipment so ordered and constructed by such carrier or by the President, such advances to be charged against such carrier and to bear interest at such rate and be payable on such terms as may be determined by the President, to the end that the United States may be fully reimbursed for any sums so advanced. . . .

From said revolving fund the President may expend such an amount as he may deem necessary or desirable for the utilization and operation of canals, or for the purchase . . . and operation of boats . . . and other transportation facilities on the inland, canal, or coastwise waterways. . . .

SEC. 10. . . . That during the period of Federal control, whenever in his opinion the public interest requires, the President may initiate rates, fares, charges, classifications, regulations, and practices by filing the same with the Interstate Commerce Commission, which said rates, fares, charges, classifications, regulations, and practices shall not be suspended by the commission pending final determination. . . .

SEC. 14. That the Federal control of railroads and transportation systems herein and heretofore provided for shall continue for and during the period of the war and for a reasonable time thereafter, which shall not exceed one year and nine months next following the date of the proclamation by the President of the exchange of ratifications of the treaty of peace: *Provided, however,* That the President may, prior to July first, nineteen hundred and eighteen, relinquish control of all or any part of any railroad or system of transportation, further Federal control of which the President shall deem not needful or desirable; and the President may at any time during the period of Federal control agree with the owners thereof to relinquish all or any part of any railroad or system of transportation. The President may relinquish all railroads and systems of transportation under the Federal control at any time he shall deem such action needful or desirable. No right to compensation shall accrue to such owners from and after the date of relinquishment for the property so relinquished. . . .

SEC. 16. That this Act is expressly declared to be emergency legislation enacted to meet conditions growing out of war; and nothing herein is to be construed as expressing or prejudicing the future policy of the Federal Government concerning the ownership, control, or regulation of carriers or the method or basis of the capitalization thereof.

425. THE ESPIONAGE ACT
May 16, 1918

(*U. S. Statutes at Large,* Vol. XL, p. 553 ff.)

This Act was far more drastic than the act of June 15, 1917, and made the Sedition Act of 1798 look very mild indeed. Under Attorney-General Palmer the Espionage Act was drastically enforced, and freedom of speech and of the press temporarily disappeared. See, Z. Chafee, *Freedom of Speech.* For the judicial interpretation of the act, see *Schenck,* v. *U. S.,* Doc. No. 426 and *Abrams* v. *U. S.,* Doc. No. 427.

Be it enacted, That section three of the Act . . . approved June 15, 1917, be . . . amended so as to read as follows:
"Sec. 3. Whoever, when the United States is

at war, shall wilfully make or convey false reports or false statements with intent to interfere with the operation or success of the military or naval forces of the United States, or to promote the success of its enemies, or shall wilfully make or convey false reports, or false statements, or say or do anything except by way of bona fide and not disloyal advice to an investor . . . with intent to obstruct the sale by the United States of bonds . . . or the making of loans by or to the United States, or whoever, when the United States is at war, shall wilfully cause . . . or incite . . . insubordination, disloyalty, mutiny, or refusal of duty, in the military or naval forces of the United States, or shall wilfully obstruct . . . the recruiting or enlistment service of the United States, and whoever, when the United States is at war, shall wilfully utter, print, write, or publish any disloyal, profane, scurrilous, or abusive language about the form of government of the United States, or the Constitution of the United States, or the military or

naval forces of the United States, or the flag . . . or the uniform of the Army or Navy of the United States, or any language intended to bring the form of government . . . or the Constitution . . . or the military or naval forces . . . or the flag . . . of the United States into contempt, scorn, contumely, or disrepute . . . or shall wilfully display the flag of any foreign enemy, or shall wilfully . . . urge, incite, or advocate any curtailment of production in this country of any thing or things . . . necessary or essential to the prosecution of the war . . . and whoever shall wilfully advocate, teach, defend, or suggest the doing of any of the acts or things in this section enumerated and whoever shall by word or act support or favor the cause of any country with which the United States is at war or by word or act oppose the cause of the United States therein, shall be punished by a fine of not more than $10,000 or imprisonment for not more than twenty years, or both. . . .

426. SCHENCK v. UNITED STATES
249 U. S. 47
1919

Error to the United States district court for the Eastern district of Pennsylvania. This case involved the constitutionality of the Espionage Act of June 15, 1917, Doc. No. 425. The defendants alleged that the act violated the First Amendment to the Constitution. Compare this opinion to the dissenting opinion of Mr. Justice Holmes in the *Abrams* v. *United States,* Doc. No. 427.

HOLMES, J. This is an indictment in three counts. The first charges a conspiracy to violate the Espionage Act of June 15, 1917 . . . by causing and attempting to cause insubordination, &c., in the military and naval forces of the United States, and to obstruct the recruiting and enlistment service of the United States, when the United States was at war with the German Empire, to wit, that the defendants wilfully conspired to have printed and circulated to men who had been called and accepted for military service under the Act of May 18, 1917, a document set forth and alleged to be calculated to cause such insubordination and obstruction. The count alleges overt acts in pursuance of the conspiracy, ending in

the distribution of the document set forth. . . . They set up the First Amendment to the Constitution forbidding Congress to make any law abridging the freedom of speech, or of the press, and bringing the case here on that ground have argued some other points also of which we must dispose.

It is argued that the evidence, if admissible, was not sufficient to prove that the defendant Schenck was concerned in sending the documents. According to the testimony Schenck said he was general secretary of the Socialist party and had charge of the Socialist headquarters from which the documents were sent. He identified a book found there as the minutes of the Executive Committee of the party. The book showed a resolution of August 13, 1917, that 15,000 leaflets should be printed on the other side of one of them in use, to be mailed to men who had passed exemption boards, and for distribution. Schenck personally attended to the printing. On August 20 the general secretary's report said, "Obtained new leaflets from printer and started work addressing envelopes" &c.; and there was a resolve that Comrade Schenck be allowed $125 for sending leaflets through the mail. He said that he had about fifteen or sixteen thousand printed. There were files of the circular in question in the inner office which he said were printed on the other side of the one sided circular and were there for distribution. Other copies were proved to have been sent through the mails to drafted men. Without going into confirmatory details that were proved, no reasonable man could doubt that the defendant Schenck was largely instrumental in sending the circulars about. . . .

The document in question upon its first printed side recited the first section of the Thirteenth Amendment, said that the idea embodied in it was violated by the Conscription Act and that a conscript is little better than a convict. In impassioned language it intimated that conscription was despotism in its worse form and a monstrous wrong against humanity in the interest of Wall Street's chosen few. It said, "Do not submit to intimidation," but in form at least confined itself to peaceful measures such as a petition for the repeal of the act. The other and later printed side of the sheet was headed "Assert Your Rights." It stated reasons for alleging that any one violated the Constitution when he refused to recognize "your right to assert your opposition to the draft," and went on "If you do not assert and support your rights, you are helping to deny or disparage rights which it is the solemn duty of all citizens and residents of the United States to retain." It described the arguments on the other side as coming from cunning politicians and a mercenary capitalist press, and even silent consent to the conscription law as helping to support an infamous conspiracy. It denied the power to send our citizens away to foreign shores to shoot up the people of other lands, and added that words could not express the condemnation such cold-blooded ruthlessness deserves, &c., &c., winding up "You must do your share to maintain, sup-

port and uphold the rights of the people of this country." Of course the document would not have been sent unless it had been intended to have some effect, and we do not see what effect it could be expected to have upon persons subject to the draft except to influence them to obstruct the carrying of it out. The defendants do not deny that the jury might find against them on this point.

But it is said, suppose that that was the tendency of this circular, it is protected by the First Amendment to the Constitution. . . . We admit that in many places and in ordinary times the defendants in saying all that was said in the circular would have been within their constitutional rights. But the character of every act depends upon the circumstances in which it is done. The most stringent protection of free speech would not protect a man in falsely shouting fire in a theatre and causing a panic. It does not even protect a man from an injunction against uttering words that may have all the effect of force. The question in every case is whether the words used are used in such circumstances and are of such a nature as to create a clear and present danger that they will bring about the substantive evils that Congress has a right to prevent. It is a question of proximity and degree. When a nation is at war many things that might be said in time of peace are such a hindrance to its effort that their utterance will not be endured so long as men fight and that no Court could regard them as protected by any constitutional right. It seems to be admitted that if an actual obstruction of the recruiting service were proved, liability for words that produced that effect might be enforced. The statute of 1917 in sec. 4 punishes conspiracies to obstruct as well as actual obstruction. If the act, (speaking, or circulating a paper,) its tendency and the intent with which it is done are the same, we perceive no ground for saying that success alone warrants making the act a crime. . . .

Judgements affirmed.

427. ABRAMS v. UNITED STATES
250 U. S. 616
1919

We have included only the dissenting opinion in this case. The position of the Court on the interpretation of laws limiting freedom of speech can be read in *Schenck* v. *United States,* Doc. No. 426, and *Gitlow* v. *New York,* Doc. No. 456. Mr. Justice Holmes's dissent is significant because it expresses much of his legal philosophy and because of its literary quality. For Mr. Justice Holmes, see, S. Bent, *Mr. Justice Holmes;* F. Frankfurter, ed. *Mr. Justice Holmes;* A. Lief, ed. *The Dissenting Opinions of Mr. Justice Holmes;* D. Richardson, *The Constitutional Doctrines of Justice Holmes.*

HOLMES, J., dissenting. This indictment is found wholly upon the publication of two leaflets which I shall describe in a moment. The first count charges a conspiracy pending the war with Germany to publish abusive language about the form of government of the United States, laying the preparation and publishing of the first leaflet as overt acts. The second count charges a conspiracy pending the war to publish language intended to bring the form of government into contempt, laying the preparation and publishing of the two leaflets as overt acts. The third count alleges a conspiracy to encourage resistance to the United States in the same war and to attempt to effectuate the purpose by publishing the same leaflets. The fourth count lays a conspiracy to incite curtailment of production of things necessary to the prosecution of the war and to attempt to accomplish it by publishing the second leaflet to which I have referred. . . .

No argument seems to me necessary to show that these pronunciamentos in no way attack the form of government of the United States, or that they do not support either of the first two counts. What little I have to say about the third count may be postponed until I have considered the fourth. With regard to that it seems too plain to be denied that the suggestion to workers in the ammunition factories that they are producing bullets to murder their dearest, and the further advocacy of a general strike, both in the second leaflet, do urge curtailment of production of things necessary to the prosecution of the war within the meaning of the Act of May 16, 1918, c. 75, 40 Stat. 553, amending part 3 of the earlier Act of 1917. But to make the conduct criminal that statute requires that it should be "with intent by such curtailment to cripple or hinder the United States in the prosecution of the war." It seems to me that no such intent is proved.

I am aware of course that the word intent as vaguely used in ordinary legal discussion means no more than knowledge at the time of the act that the consequences said to be intended will ensue. Even less than that will satisfy the general principle of civil and criminal liability. A man may have to pay damages, may be sent to prison, at common law might be hanged, if at the time of his act he knew facts from which common experience showed that the consequences would follow, whether he individually could foresee them or not. But, when words are used exactly, a deed is not done with intent to produce a consequence unless that consequence is the aim of the deed. It may be obvious, and obvious to the actor, that the consequence will follow, and he may be liable for it even if he regrets it, but he does not do the act with intent to produce it unless the aim to produce it is the proximate motive of the specific act, although there may be some deeper motive behind. . . .

I do not see how anyone can find the intent required by the statute in any of the defendants' words. The second leaflet is the only one that affords even a foundation for the charge, and there, without invoking the hatred of German militarism expressed in the former one, it is evident from the beginning to the end that the only object of the paper is to help Russia and stop American intervention there against the popular government—not to impede the United States in the war that it was carrying on. To say that two phrases taken literally might import a suggestion of conduct that would have interference with the war as an indirect and probably undesired effect seems to me by no means enough to show an attempt to produce that effect. . . .

In this case sentences of twenty years imprisonment have been imposed for the publishing of two leaflets that I believe the defendants had as much right to publish as the Government has to publish the Constitution of the United States now vainly invoked by them. Even if I am technically wrong and enough can be squeezed from these poor and puny anonymities to turn the color of legal litmus paper; I will add, even if what I think the necessary intent were shown; the most nominal punishment seems to me all that possibly could be inflicted, unless the defendants are to be made to suffer not for what the indictment alleges but for the creed that they avow—a creed that I believe to be the creed of ignorance and immaturity when honestly held, as I see no reason to doubt that it was held here, but which, although made the subject of examination at the trial, no one has a right even to consider in dealing with the charges before the Court.

Persecution for the expression of opinions seems to me perfectly logical. If you have no doubt of your premises or your power and want a certain result with all your heart you naturally express your wishes in law and sweep away all opposition. To allow opposition by speech seems to indicate that you think the speech impotent, as when a man says that he has squared the circle, or that you do not care whole-heartedly for the result, or that you doubt either your power or your premises. But when men have realized that time has upset many fighting faiths, they may come to believe even more than they believe the very foundations of their own conduct that the ultimate good desired is better reached by free trade in ideas—that the best test of truth is the power of the thought to get itself accepted in the competition of the market, and that truth is the only ground upon which their wishes safely can be carried out. That at any rate is the theory of our Constitution. It is an experiment, as all life is an experiment. Every year if not every day we have to wager our salvation upon some prophecy based upon imperfect knowledge. While that experiment is part of our system I think that we should be eternally vigilant against attempts to check the expression of opinions that we loathe and believe to be fraught with death, unless they so imminently threaten immediate interference with the lawful and pressing purposes of the law that an immediate check is required to save the country. I wholly disagree with the argument of the Government that the First Amendment left the common law as to seditious libel in force. History seems to me against the notion. I had conceived that the United States through many years had shown its repentence for the Sedition Act of 1798, by repaying fines that it imposed. Only the emergency that makes it immediately dangerous to leave the correction of evil counsels to time warrants making any exception to the sweeping command, "Congress shall make no law . . . abridging the freedom of speech." Of course I am speaking only of expressions of opinion and exhortations, which were all that were uttered here, but I regret that I cannot put into more impressive words my belief that in their conviction upon this indictment the defendants were deprived of their rights under the Constitution of the United States.

Mr. Justice Brandeis concurs with the foregoing opinion.

428. THE ARCHANGEL EXPEDITION
The Aide-Mémoire of July 17, 1918

(Foreign Relations of the United States, 1918, Russia, Vol. II, p. 287 ff.)

This aide-mémoire states the terms upon which the United States would participate with the Allied Powers in intervention in Russia. Though the mémoire states that "military intervention . . . would be of no advantage" and that the United States "cannot take part in such intervention", it pledges the Government to do just that. In accordance with this agreement, three battalions of infantry and three companies of engineers were sent to Archangel to protect supplies, and a small American force co-operated with the Japanese at Vladivostock. These forces were withdrawn in 1919 and 1920. See, J. R. Moore, ed. *American Expedition in North Russia;* F. L. Schuman, *American Policy Toward Russia since 1917,* chs. v, vii; R. Albertson,

Fighting Without a War; W. S. Graves, *America's Siberian Adventure, 1918–1920;* C. K. Cummins and W. W. Pettit, *Russian-American Relations, 1913–1920: Documents and Papers.*

The Secretary of State to the Allied Ambassadors Aide-Mémoire

. . . It is the clear and fixed judgment of the Government of the United States, arrived at after repeated and very searching reconsiderations of the whole situation in Russia, that military intervention there would add to the present sad confusion in Russia rather than cure it, injure her rather than help her, and that it would be of no advantage in the prosecution of our main design, to win the war against Germany. It can not, therefore, take part in such intervention or sanction it in principle. Military intervention would, in its judgment, even supposing it to be efficacious in its immediate avowed object of delivering an attack upon Germany from the east, be merely a method of making use of Russia, not a method of serving her. Her people could not profit by it, if they profited by it at all, in time to save them from their present distresses, and their substance would be used to maintain foreign armies, not to reconstitute their own. Military action is admissible in Russia, as the Government of the United States sees the circumstances, only to help the Czecho-Slovaks consolidate their forces and get into successful cooperation with their Slavic kinsmen and to steady any efforts at self-government or self-defense in which the Russians themselves may be willing to accept assistance. Whether from Vladivostok or from Murmansk and Archangel, the only legitimate object for which American or Allied troops can be employed, it submits, is to guard military stores which may subsequently be needed by Russian forces and to render such aid as may be acceptable to the Russians in the organization of their own self-defense. For helping the Czecho-Slovaks there is immediate necessity and sufficient justification. Recent developments have made it evident that that is in the interest of what the Russian people themselves desire, and the Government of the United States is glad to contribute the small force at its disposal for that purpose. It yields, also, to the judgment of the Supreme Command in the matter of establishing a small force at Murmansk, to guard the military stores at Kola, and to make it safe for Russian forces to come together in organized bodies in the north. But it owes it to frank counsel to say that it can go no further than these modest and experimental plans. It is not in a position, and has no expectation of being in a position, to take part in organized intervention in adequate force from either Vladivostok or Murmansk and Archangel. It feels that it ought to add, also, that it will feel at liberty to use the few troops it can spare only for the purposes here stated and shall feel obliged to withdraw those forces, in order to add them to the forces at the western front, if the plans in whose execution it is now intended that they should cooperate should develop into others, inconsistent with the policy to which the Government of the United States feels constrained to restrict itself.

At the same time the Government of the United States wishes to say with the utmost cordiality and good will that none of the conclusions here stated is meant to wear the least color of criticism of what the other governments associated against Germany may think it wise to undertake. It wishes in no way to embarrass their choices of policy. All that is intended here is a perfectly frank and definite statement of the policy which the United States feels obliged to adopt for herself and in the use of her own military forces. The Government of the United States does not wish it to be understood that in so restricting its own activities it is seeking, even by implication, to set limits to the action or to define the policies of its associates.

It hopes to carry out the plans for safeguarding the rear of the Czecho-Slovaks operating from Vladivostok in a way that will place it and keep it in close cooperation with a small military force like its own from Japan, and if necessary from the other Allies, and that will assure it of the cordial accord of all the Allied powers; and it proposes to ask all associated in this course of action to unite in assuring the people of Russia in the most public and solemn manner that none of the governments uniting in action either in Siberia or in northern Russia contemplates any interference of any kind with the political sovereignty of Russia, any intervention in her internal affairs, or any impairment of her territorial integrity either now or hereafter, but that each of the associated powers has the single object of affording such aid as shall be acceptable, and only such aid as shall be acceptable, to the Russian people in their endeavor to regain control of their own affairs, their own territory, and their own destiny.

It is the hope and purpose of the Government of the United States to take advantage of the earliest opportunity to send to Siberia a commission of merchants, agricultural experts, labor advisers, Red Cross representatives, and agents of the Young Men's Christian Association accustomed to organizing the best methods of spreading useful information and rendering educational help of a modest sort, in order in some systematic manner to relieve the immediate economic necessities of the people there in every way for which opportunity may open. The execution of this plan will follow and will not be permitted to embarrass the military assistance rendered in the rear of the westward-moving forces of the Czecho-Slovaks.

429. PRESIDENT WILSON'S APPEAL TO THE VOTERS TO RETURN A DEMOCRATIC CONGRESS
October 24, 1918

(Associated Press Dispatch)

With the end of the World War rapidly approaching, President Wilson was preparing to go to Europe to secure a just peace. His appeal for political support met with popular disapproval. The elections of November 5 resulted in Republican majorities in both Houses of Congress. Wilson's partial failure at Paris may be attributed to the fact that European diplomats knew that he had been repudiated by his own people. Just before Wilson sailed for Europe, ex-President Roosevelt issued a statement that "Our allies and our enemies and Mr. Wilson himself should all understand that Mr. Wilson has no authority whatever to speak for the American people at this time. His leadership has just been emphatically repudiated by them. Mr. Wilson and his Fourteen Points and his four supplementary points and his five complementary points and all his utterances every which way have ceased to have any shadow of right to be accepted as expressive of the will of the American people."

My Fellow Countrymen:

The Congressional elections are at hand. They occur in the most critical period our country has ever faced or is likely to face in our time. If you have approved of my leadership and wish me to continue to be your unembarrassed spokesman in affairs at home and abroad, I earnestly beg that you will express yourselves unmistakably to that effect by returning a Democratic majority to both the Senate and the House of Representatives.

I am your servant and will accept your judgment without cavil. But my power to administer the great trust assigned to me by the Constitution would be seriously impaired should your judgment be adverse, and I must frankly tell you so because so many critical issues depend upon your verdict. No scruple or taste must in grim times like these be allowed to stand in the way of speaking the plain truth.

I have no thought of suggesting that any political party is paramount in matters of patriotism. I feel too deeply the sacrifices which have been made in this war by all our citizens, irrespective of party affiliations, to harbor such an idea. I mean only that the difficulties and delicacies of our present task are of a sort that makes it imperatively necessary that the nation should give its undivided support to the Government under a unified leadership, and that a Republican Congress would divide the leadership.

The leaders of the minority in the present Congress have unquestionably been pro-war, but they have been anti-administration. At almost every turn since we entered the war they have sought to take the choice of policy and the conduct of the war out of my hands and put it under the control of instrumentalities of their own choosing.

This is no time either for divided counsels or for divided leadership. Unity of command is as necessary now in civil action as it is upon the field of battle. If the control of the House and the Senate should be taken away from the party now in power an opposing majority could assume control of legislation and oblige all action to be taken amid contest and obstruction.

The return of a Republican majority to either house of the Congress would, moreover, be interpreted on the other side of the water as a repudiation of my leadership. Spokesmen of the Republican party are urging you to elect a Republican Congress in order to back up and support the President, but, even if they should in this impose upon some credulous voters on this side of the water, they would impose on no one on the other side. It is well understood there as well as here that Republican leaders desire not so much to support the President as to control him.

The peoples of the allied countries with whom we are associated against Germany are quite familiar with the significance of elections. They would find it very difficult to believe that the voters of the United States had chosen to support their President by electing to the Congress a majority controlled by those who are not in fact in sympathy with the attitude and action of the Administration.

I need not tell you, my fellow countrymen, that I am asking your support not for my own sake or for the sake of a political party, but for the sake of the nation itself in order that its inward duty of purpose may be evident to all the world. In ordinary times I would not feel at liberty to make such an appeal to you. In ordinary times divided counsels can be endured without permanent hurt to the country. But these are not ordinary times.

If in these critical days it is your wish to sustain me with undivided minds, I beg that you will say so in a way which it will not be possible to misunderstand, either here at home or among our associates on the other side of the sea. I submit my difficulties and my hopes to you.

WOODROW WILSON.

430. THE CHILD LABOR ACT
February 24, 1919

(*U. S. Statutes at Large*, Vol. XL, p. 1138)

The decision of the Supreme Court in *Hammer v. Dagenhart* defeated the effort of Congress to prohibit child labor through the exercise of its control over interstate commerce. In 1919 a section of the general taxation bill assessed a tax upon the products of child labor. For the fate of this section, see Doc. No. 431. In 1924 Congress passed an amendment to the Constitution giving Congress the right to regulate child labor: fifteen years later 28 states had ratified this amendment, but the prospects for obtaining a sufficient number of ratifications were dim. See, R. Fuller, *Child Labor and the Constitution*.

. . . Sec. 1200. Every person (other than a bona fide boys' or girls' canning club recognized by the Agricultural Department of a State and of the United States) operating (a) any mine or quarry situated in the United States in which children under the age of sixteen years have been employed or permitted to work during any portion of the taxable year; or (b) any mill, cannery, workshop, factory, or manufacturing establishment situated in the United States in which children under the age of fourteen years have been employed or permitted to work, or children between the ages of fourteen and sixteen have been employed or permitted to work more than eight hours in any day or more than six days in any week, or after the hour of seven o'clock post meridian, or before the hour of six o'clock ante meridian, during any portion of the taxable year, shall pay for each taxable year, in addition to all other taxes imposed by law, an excise tax equivalent to 10 per centum of the entire net profits received or accrued for such year from the sale or disposition of the product of such mine, quarry, mill, cannery, workshop, factory, or manufacturing establishment. . . .

431. BAILEY v. DREXEL FURNITURE COMPANY
259 U. S. 20
1922

Error to the U. S. district court for the western district of North Carolina. This case involved the constitutionality of the Child Labor tax law of February 24, 1919, Doc. No. 430.

TAFT, C. J. . . . The law is attacked on the ground that it is a regulation of the employment of child labor in the States— an exclusively state function under the Federal Constitution and within the reservations of the Tenth Amendment. It is defended on the ground that it is a mere excise tax levied by the Congress of the United States under its broad power of taxation conferred by § 8, Article I, of the federal Constitution. We must construe the law and interpret the intent and meaning of Congress from the language of the act. The words are to be given their ordinary meaning unless the context shows that they are differently used. Does this law impose a tax with only that incidental restraint and regulation which a tax must inevitably involve? Or does it regulate by the use of the so-called tax as a penalty? If a tax, it is clearly an excise. If it were an excise on a commodity or other thing of value we might not be permitted under previous decisions of this court to infer solely from its heavy burden that the act intends a prohibition instead of a tax. But this act is more. It provides a heavy exaction for a departure from a detailed and specified course of conduct in business. That course of business is that employers shall employ in mines and quarries, children of an age greater than sixteen years; in mills and factories, children of an age greater than fourteen years, and shall prevent children of less than sixteen years in mills and factories from working more than eight hours a day or six days in the week. If an employer departs from this prescribed course of business, he is to pay to the Government one-tenth of his entire net income in the business for a full year. The amount is not to be proportioned in any degree to the frequency of the departures, but is to be paid by the employer in full measure whether he employs five hundred

children for a year, or employs only one for a day. Moreover, if he does not know the child is within the named age limit, he is not to pay; that is to say, it is only where he knowingly departs from the prescribed course that payment is to be exacted. . . .

In the light of these features of the act, a court must be blind not to see that the so-called tax is imposed to stop the employment of children within the age limits prescribed. Its prohibitory and regulatory effect and purpose are palpable. All others can see and understand this. How can we properly shut our minds to it?

It is the high duty and function of this court in cases regularly brought to its bar to decline to recognize or enforce seeming laws of Congress, dealing with subjects not entrusted to Congress but left or committed by the supreme law of the land to the control of the States. We can not avoid the duty even though it requires us to refuse to give effect to legislation designed to promote the highest good. The good sought in unconstitutional legislation is an insidious feature because it leads citizens and legislators of good purpose to promote it without thought of the serious breach it will make in the ark of our covenant or the harm which will come from breaking down recognized standards. In the maintenance of local self government, on the one hand, and the national power on the other, our country has been able to endure and prosper for near a century and a half.

Out of a proper respect for the acts of a co-ordinate branch of the Government, this court has gone far to sustain taxing acts as such, even though there has been ground for suspecting from the weight of the tax it was intended to destroy its subject. But in the act before us the presumption of validity cannot prevail, because the proof of the contrary is found on the very face of its provisions. Grant the validity of this law, and all that Congress would need to do, hereafter, in seeking to take over to its control any one of the great number of subjects of public interests, jurisdiction of which the

States have never parted with, and which are reserved to them by the Tenth Amendment, would be to enact a detailed measure of complete regulation of the subject and enforce it by a so-called tax upon departures from it. To give such magic to the word "tax" would be to break down all constitutional limitation of the powers of Congress and completely wipe out the sovereignty of the State. . . .

For the reasons given, we must hold the Child Labor Tax Law invalid and the judgment of the district court is

Affirmed.

CLARKE, J., dissents.

432. THE VOLSTEAD ACT
October 28, 1919

(*U. S. Statutes at Large,* Vol. XXXXI, p. 305 ff.)

Ratification of the Eighteenth Amendment was proclaimed January 29, 1919: the amendment went into effect January 16, 1920. The National Prohibition Act, known popularly as the Volstead Act after its sponsor, Volstead of Minnesota, was passed over the veto of President Wilson. On the constitutionality of the Act, see Doc. No. 433. The literature on Prohibition is enormous, but most of it is of a controversial character. See E. H. Cherrington, *Evolution of Prohibition in the United States;* P. Odegard, *Pressure Politics;* C. Merz, *The Dry Decade;* H. Feldman, *Prohibition, Its Economic and Industrial Aspects;* I. Fisher, *Prohibition at Its Worst;* F. Franklin, *The A.B.C. of Prohibition;* The Federal Council of Churches of Christ in America, *The Prohibition Situation; Annals* of the American Academy of Pol. and Social Science, Vol. CIX. The famous Wickersham Report is in the U. S. 71st Congress, 3d Sess., *House Doc. No. 722.*

Be it Enacted. . . . That the short title of this Act shall be the "National Prohibition Act."

TITLE I.
TO PROVIDE FOR THE ENFORCEMENT OF WAR PROHIBITION.

The term "War Prohibition Act" used in this Act shall mean the provisions of any Act or Acts prohibiting the sale and manufacture of intoxicating liquors until the conclusion of the present war and thereafter until the termination of demobilization, the date of which shall be determined and proclaimed by the President of the United States. The words "beer, wine, or other intoxicating malt or vinous liquors" in the War Prohibition Act shall be hereafter construed to mean any such beverages which contain one-half of 1 per centum or more of alcohol by volume: . . .

SEC. 2. The Commissioner of Internal Revenue, his assistants, agents, and inspectors, shall investigate and report violations of the War Prohibition Act to the United States attorney for the district in which committed, who shall be charged with the duty of prosecuting, subject to the direction of the Attorney General, the offenders as in the case of other offenses against laws of the United States; and such Commissioner of Internal Revenue, his assistants, agents, and inspectors may swear out warrants before United States commissioners or other officers or courts authorized to issue the same for the apprehension of such offenders, and may, subject to the control of the said United States attorney, conduct the prosecution at the committing trial for the purpose of having the offenders held for action of a grand jury. . . .

TITLE II.
PROHIBITION OF INTOXICATING BEVERAGES.

SEC. 3. No person shall on or after the date when the eighteenth amendment to the Constitution of the United States goes into effect, manufacture, sell, barter, transport, import, export, deliver, furnish or possess any intoxicating liquor except as authorized in this Act, and all the provisions of this Act shall be liberally construed to the end that the use of intoxicating liquor as a beverage may be prevented.

Liquor for nonbeverage purposes and wine for sacramental purposes may be manufactured, purchased, sold, bartered, transported, imported, exported, delivered, furnished and possessed, but only as herein provided, and the commissioner may, upon application, issue permits therefor: *Provided,* That nothing in this Act shall prohibit the purchase and sale of warehouse receipts covering distilled spirits on deposit in Government bonded warehouses, and no special tax liability shall attach to the business of purchasing and selling such warehouse receipts. . . .

SEC. 6. No one shall manufacture, sell, purchase, transport, or prescribe any liquor without first obtaining a permit from the commissioner so to do, except that a person may, without a permit, purchase and use liquor for medicinal purposes when prescribed by a physician as herein provided, and except that any person who in the opinion of the commissioner is conducting a bona fide hospital or sanatorium engaged in the treatment of persons suffering from alcoholism, may, under such rules, regulations, and conditions as the commissioner shall prescribe, purchase and use, in accordance with the methods in use in such institution, liquor, to be administered to the patients of such institution under the direction of a duly qualified physician employed by such institution.

All permits to manufacture, prescribe, sell, or transport liquor, may be issued for one year, and shall expire on the 31st day of December next succeeding the issuance thereof: . . . Permits to purchase liquor shall specify the quantity and kind to be purchased and the purpose for which it is to be used. No permit shall be issued to any person who within one year prior to the application therefor or issuance thereof shall have violated the terms of any permit issued under this Title or any law of the United States or of any State regulating traffic in liquor. No permit shall be issued to anyone to sell liquor at retail, unless the sale is to be made through a pharmacist designated in the permit and duly licensed under the laws of his State to compound and dispense medicine prescribed by a duly licensed physician. No one shall be given a permit to prescribe liquor unless he is a physician duly licensed to practice medicine and actively engaged in the practice of such profession. . . .

Nothing in this title shall be held to apply to the manufacture, sale, transportation, importation, possession, or distribution of wine for sacramental purposes, or like religious rites, except section 6 (save as the same requires a permit to purchase) and section 10 hereof, and the provisions of this Act prescribing penalties for the violation of either of said sections. No person to whom a permit may be issued to manufacture, transport, import, or sell wines for sacramental purposes or like religious rites shall sell, barter, exchange, or furnish any such to any person not a rabbi, minister of the gospel, priest, or an officer duly authorized for the purpose by any church or congregation, nor to any such except upon an application duly subscribed by him, which application, authenticated as regulations may prescribe, shall be filed and preserved by the seller. The head of any conference or diocese or other ecclesiastical jurisdiction may designate any rabbi, minister, or priest to supervise the manufacture of wine to be used for the purposes and rites in this section mentioned, and the person so designated may, in the discretion of the commissioner, be granted a permit to supervise such manufacture.

SEC. 7. No one but a physician holding a permit to prescribe liquor shall issue any prescription for liquor. And no physician shall prescribe liquor unless after careful physical examination of the person for whose use such prescription is sought, or if such examination is found impracticable, then upon the best information obtainable, he in good faith believes that the use of such liquor as a medicine by such person is necessary and will afford relief to him from some known ailment. Not more than a pint of spiritous liquor to be taken internally shall be prescribed for use by the same person within any period of ten days and no prescription shall be filled more than once. Any pharmacist filling a prescription shall at the time indorse upon it over his own signature the word "canceled," together with the date when the liquor was delivered, and then make the same a part of the record that he is required to keep as herein provided. . . .

SEC. 18. It shall be unlawful to advertise, manufacture, sell, or possess for sale any utensil, contrivance, machine, preparation, compound, tablet, substance, formula direction, recipe advertised, designed, or intended for use in the unlawful manufacture of intoxicating liquor. . . .

SEC. 21. Any room, house, building, boat,

vehicle, structure, or place where intoxicating liquor is manufactured, sold, kept, or
bartered in violation of this title, and all
intoxicating liquor and property kept and
used in maintaining the same, is hereby declared to be a common nuisance, and any
person who maintains such a common
nuisance shall be guilty of a misdemeanor
and upon conviction thereof shall be fined
not more than $1,000 or be imprisoned for
not more than one year, or both. . . .

SEC. 25. It shall be unlawful to have or
possess any liquor or property designed for
the manufacture of liquor intended for use
in violating this title or which has been so
used, and no property rights shall exist in
any such liquor or property. . . . No search
warrant shall issue to search any private
dwelling occupied as such unless it is being
used for the unlawful sale of intoxicating
liquor, or unless it is in part used for some
business purposes such as a store, shop,
saloon, restaurant, hotel, or boarding
house. . . .

SEC. 29. Any person who manufactures
or sells liquor in violation of this title shall
for a first offense be fined not more than
$1,000, or imprisoned not exceeding six
months, and for a second or subsequent offense shall be fined not less than $200 nor
more than $2,000 and be imprisoned not less
than one month nor more than five years.

Any person violating the provisions of any
permit, or who makes any false record, report,
or affidavit required by this title, or violates
any of the provisions of this title, for which
offense a special penalty is not prescribed,
shall be fined for a first offense not more
than $500; for a second offense not less than
$100 nor more than $1,000, or be imprisoned
not more than ninety days; for any subsequent offense he shall be fined not less than
$500 and be imprisoned not less than three
months nor more than two years. . . .

SEC. 33. After February 1, 1920, the possession of liquors by any person not legally
permitted under this title to possess liquor
shall be prima facie evidence that such
liquor is kept for the purpose of being sold,
bartered, exchanged, given away, furnished,
or otherwise disposed of in violation of the
Provisions of this title. . . . But it shall not
be unlawful to possess liquors in one's private dwelling while the same is occupied and
used by him as his dwelling only and such
liquor need not be reported, provided such
liquors are for use only for the personal
consumption of the owner thereof and his
family residing in such dwelling and of his
bona fide guests when entertained by him
therein; and the burden of proof shall be
upon the possessor in any action concerning
the same to prove that such liquor was lawfully acquired, possessed, and used. . . .

433. NATIONAL PROHIBITION CASES
253 U. S. 350
1920

These were seven cases involving the constitutionality of the Volstead Act of 1919 and the
validity of the Eighteenth Amendment. This is
the only case in the history of the court where
the court stated its opinion of a question of
constitutional law without giving its reasoning.

VAN DEVANTER, J., announced the conclusions of the court.

Power to amend the Constitution is reserved by Article V, which reads: . . . The
text of the Eighteenth Amendment, proposed
by Congress in 1917 and proclaimed as ratified in 1919, 40 Stat. at L. 1050, 1941, is as
follows: . . .

The cases have been elaborately argued
at the bar and in printed briefs; and the

arguments have been attentively considered,
with the result that we reach and announce
the following conclusions on the questions
involved.

1. The adoption by both houses of Congress, each by a two-thirds vote, of a joint
resolution proposing an amendment to the
Constitution sufficiently shows that the proposal was deemed necessary by all who
voted for it. An express declaration that they
regarded it as necessary is not essential.
None of the resolutions whereby prior
amendments were proposed contained such
a declaration.

2. The two-thirds vote in each house
which is required in proposing an amendment is a vote of two-thirds of the members

present—assuming the presence of a quorum —and not a vote of two thirds of the entire membership, present and absent. *Missouri Pacific Ry. Co. v. Kansas,* 248 U. S. 276.

3. The referendum provisions of state constitutions and statutes cannot be applied, consistently with the Constitution of the United States, in the ratification or rejection of amendments to it. *Hawke v. Smith,* 253 U. S. 221.

4. The prohibition of the manufacture, sale, transportation, importation and exportation of intoxicating liquors for beverage purposes, as embodied in the Eighteenth Amendment, is within the power to amend reserved by Article V of the Constitution.

5. That amendment, by lawful proposal and ratification, has become a part of the Constitution, and must be respected and given effect the same as other provisions of that instrument.

6. The first section of the amendment— the one embodying the prohibition—is operative throughout the entire territorial limits of the United States, binds all legislative bodies, courts, public officers and individuals within those limits, and of its own force invalidates every legislative act— whether by Congress, by a state legislature, or by a territorial assembly—which authorizes or sanctions what the section prohibits.

7. The second section of the amendment— the one declaring "The Congress and the several States shall have concurrent power to enforce this article by appropriate legislation"—does not enable Congress or the several States to defeat or to thwart the prohibition, but only to enforce it by appropriate means.

8. The words "concurrent power" in that section do not mean joint power, or require that legislation thereunder by Congress, to be effective, shall be approved or sanctioned by the several States or any of them; nor

do they mean that the power to enforce is divided between Congress and the several States along the lines which separate or distinguish foreign and interstate commerce from intrastate affairs.

9. The power confided to Congress by that section, while not exclusive, is territorially co-extensive with the prohibition of the first section, embraces manufacture and other intrastate transactions as well as importation, exportation and interstate traffic, and is in no wise dependent on or affected by action or inaction on the part of the several States or any of them.

10. That power may be exerted against the disposal for beverage purposes of liquors manufactured before the amendment became effective just as it may be against subsequent manufacture for those purposes. In either case it is a constitutional mandate or prohibition that is being enforced.

11. While recognizing that there are limits beyond which Congress cannot go in treating beverages as within its power of enforcement, we think these limits are not transcended by the provision of the Volstead Act (Title II, § 1), wherein liquors containing as much as one-half of one per cent. of alcohol by volume and fit for use for beverage purposes are treated as within that power. *Jacob Ruppert v. Caffey,* 251 U. S. 264.

WHITE, C. J., concurring. I profoundly regret that in a case of this magnitude, affecting as it does an amendment to the Constitution dealing with the powers and duties of the national and state governments, and intimately concerning the welfare of the whole people, the court has deemed it proper to state only ultimate conclusions without an exposition of the reasoning by which they have been reached. . . .

McKENNA, J., and CLARKE, J., delivered dissenting opinions.

434. PREAMBLE OF THE INDUSTRIAL WORKERS OF THE WORLD
Chicago, 1919

(P. F. Brissenden, *The I. W. W., A Study of American Syndicalism,* p. 351)

The Industrial Workers of the World was organized in 1905 and lasted about twenty years. It represented the extreme left wing of the American labor movement, advocated the general strike, and practised sabotage and violence.

Its membership, extremely fluctuating and recruited chiefly among the casual laborers of the western lumber camps, mines and harvest fields, never exceeded sixty thousand. See, P. F. Brissenden, *The I. W. W.;* J. S. Gambs, *The Decline of the I. W. W.;* W. D. Haywood, *Bill Haywood's Book;* D. L. Saposs, *Left Wing Unionism;* J. Oneal, *American Communism.*

The working class and the employing class have nothing in common. There can be no peace so long as hunger and want are found among millions of working people and the few, who make up the employing class, have all the good things of life.

Between these two classes a struggle must go on until the workers of the world organize as a class, take possession of the earth and the machinery of production and abolish the wage system.

We find that the centering of the management of industries into fewer and fewer hands makes the trade unions unable to cope with the ever growing power of the employing class. The trade unions foster a state of affairs which allows one set of workers to be pitted against another set of workers in the same industry, thereby helping defeat one another in wage wars. Moreover the trade unions aid the employing class to mislead the workers into the belief that the working class have interests in common with their employers.

These conditions can be changed and the interest of the working class upheld only by an organization formed in such a way that all its members in any one industry, or in all industries if necessary, cease work whenever a strike or lockout is on in any department thereof, thus making an injury to one an injury to all.

Instead of the conservative motto, "A fair day's wage for a fair day's work," we must inscribe on our banner the revolutionary watchword, "Abolition of the wage system." It is the historic mission of the working class to do away with capitalism. The army of production must be organized not only for the everyday struggle with capitalists, but also to carry on production when capitalism shall have been overthrown. By organizing industrially we are forming the structure of the new society within the shell of the old.

435. PRESIDENT WILSON'S EXPOSITION OF THE LEAGUE OF NATIONS TO THE SENATE COMMITTEE ON FOREIGN RELATIONS
August 19, 1919

(U. S. 66th Congress, 1st. Session, *Sen. Doc.* No. 76)

In July, 1919, the Treaty of Versailles and the Covenant of the League of Nations were formally transmitted to the Senate. In order to allay strong Senatorial opposition to ratification, Wilson invited the members of the Senate Committee on Foreign Relations to discuss with him their objections to the Covenant of the League. The most irreconcilable of Wilson's opponents, Senator Lodge of Massachusetts, was chairman of the Foreign Affairs Committee, and Wilson's appeal was without apparent effect. See, H. C. Lodge, *The Senate and the League of Nations;* W. E. Dodd, *Woodrow Wilson;* J. C. Malin, *The United States After the World War,* chs. ii–iv.

MR. CHAIRMAN:

I have taken the liberty of writing out a little statement in the hope that it might faciliate discussion by speaking directly on some points that I know have been points of controversy and upon which I thought an expression of opinion would not be unwelcome. . . .

Nothing, I am led to believe, stands in the way of ratification of the treaty except certain doubts with regard to the meaning and implication of certain articles of the Covenant of the League of Nations; and I must frankly say that I am unable to understand why such doubts should be entertained. You will recall that when I had the pleasure of a conference with your committee and with the committee of the House of Representatives on Foreign Affairs at the White House in March last the questions now most frequently asked about the League of Nations were all canvassed with a view to their immediate clarification. The Covenant of the League was then in its first draft and subject to revision. It was pointed out that no express recognition was given to the Monroe Doctrine; that it was not expressly provided that the League should have no authority to act or to express a judgment on matters of domestic policy; that the right to withdraw from the League was not expressly recognized; and that the constitutional right of the Congress to determine all questions of peace and war was not sufficiently safeguarded. On my return to Paris all these matters were taken up again by the Commission on the League of Nations and every suggestion of the United States was accepted.

The views of the United States with regard to the questions I have mentioned had, in fact, already been accepted by the commission and there was supposed to be nothing inconsistent with them in the draft of the Covenant first adopted—the draft which was the subject of our discussion in March —but no objection was made to saying explicitly in the text what all had supposed to be implicit in it. There was absolutely no doubt as to the meaning of any one of the resulting provisions of the Covenant in the minds of those who participated in drafting them, and I respectfully submit that there is nothing vague or doubtful in their wording.

The Monroe Doctrine is expressly mentioned as an understanding which is in no way to be impaired or interfered with by anything contained in the covenant and the expression "regional understandings like the Monroe Doctrine" was used, not because any one of the conferees thought there was any comparable agreement anywhere else in existence or in contemplation, but only because it was thought best to avoid the appearance of dealing in such a document with the policy of a single nation. Absolutely nothing is concealed in the phrase.

With regard to domestic questions Article 16 of the Covenant expressly provides that, if in case of any dispute arising between members of the League the matter involved is claimed by one of the parties "and is found by the council to arise out of a matter which by international law is solely within the domestic jurisdiction of that party, the council shall so report, and shall make no recommendation as to its settlement." The United States was by no means the only Government interested in the explicit adoption of this provision, and there is no doubt in the mind of any authoritative student of international law that such matters as immigration, tariffs, and naturalization are incontestably domestic questions with which no international body could deal without express authority to do so. No enumeration of domestic questions was undertaken because to undertake it, even by sample, would have involved the danger of seeming to exclude those not mentioned.

The right of any sovereign State to withdraw had been taken for granted, but no objection was made to making it explicit. Indeed, so soon as the views expressed at the White House conference were laid before the commission it was at once conceded that it was best not to leave the answer to so important a question to inference. No proposal was made to set up any tribunal to pass judgment upon the question whether a withdrawing nation had in fact fulfilled "all its international obligations and all its obligations under the covenant." It was recognized that that question must be left to be resolved by the conscience of the Nation proposing to withdraw; and I must say that it did not seem to me worth while to propose that the article be made more explicit, because I knew that the United States would never itself propose to withdraw from the League if its conscience was not entirely clear as to the fulfillment of all its international obligations. It has never failed to fulfill them and never will.

Article 10 is in no respect of doubtful meaning when read in the light of the covenant as a whole. The council of the League can only "advise upon" the means by which the obligations of that great article are to be given effect to. Unless the United States is a party to the policy or action in question, her own affirmative vote in the council is necessary before any advice can be given, for a unanimous vote of the council is required. If she is a party, the trouble is hers anyhow. And the unanimous vote of the council is only advice in any case. Each Government is free to reject it if it pleases. Nothing could have been made more clear to the conference than the right of our Congress under our Constitution to exercise its independent judgment in all matters of peace and war. No attempt was made to question or limit that right.

The United States will, indeed, undertake under Article 10 to "respect and preserve as against external aggression the territorial integrity and existing political independence of all members of the League," and that engagement constitutes a very grave and solemn moral obligation. But it is a moral, not a legal, obligation, and leaves our Congress absolutely free to put its own interpretation upon it in all cases that call for action. It is binding in conscience only, not in law.

Article 10 seems to me to constitute the very backbone of the whole covenant. Without it the League would be hardly more than an influential debating society.

It has several times been suggested, in public debate and in private conference, that interpretations of the sense in which the United States accepts the engagements of the covenant should be embodied in the instrument of ratification. There can be no reasonable objection to such interpretations accompanying the act of ratification provided they do not form a part of the formal ratification itself. Most of the interpretations which have been suggested to me embody what seems to me the plain meaning of the instrument itself. But if such interpretations should constitute a part of the formal resolution of ratification, long delays would be the inevitable consequence, inasmuch as all the many Governments concerned would have to accept, in effect, the language of the Senate as the language of the treaty before ratification would be complete. The assent of the German Assembly at Weimar would have to be obtained, among the rest, and I must frankly say that I could only with the greatest reluctance approach that Assembly for permission to read the treaty as we understand it and as those who framed it quite certainly understood it. If the United States were to qualify the document in any way, moreover, I am confident from what I know of the many conferences and debates which accompanied the formulation of the treaty that our example would immediately be followed in many quarters, in some instances with very serious reservations, and that the meaning and operative force of the treaty would presently be clouded from one end of its clauses to the other.

Pardon me, Mr. Chairman, if I have been entirely unreserved and plain-spoken in speaking of the great matters we all have so much at heart. If excuse is needed, I trust that the critical situation of affairs may serve as my justification. The issues that manifestly hang upon the conclusions of the Senate with regard to peace and upon the time of its action are so grave and so clearly insusceptible of being thrust on one side or postponed that I have felt it necessary in the public interest to make this urgent plea, and to make it as simply and as unreservedly as possible.

I thought that the simplest way, Mr. Chairman, to cover the points that I knew to be points of interest.

436. THE DEFEAT OF THE LEAGUE OF NATIONS

Resolution of Ratification of Treaty of Peace with Germany and the League of Nations
March 19, 1920

(*Congressional Record,* Vol. LIX, p. 4599)

Wilson called Congress into special session for consideration of the Treaty with Germany, May 19, 1919. An unofficial copy of the treaty was read to the Senate June 9, but the treaty was not officially before the Senate until July 10; then debate on the Treaty and the League was under way. After a vigorous and at times embittered debate, the treaty, both with and without reservations, was rejected November 19, 1919. Efforts to arrive at a compromise between the moderate reservationist Republicans and the moderate Democrats were unavailing. The Treaty was brought up for reconsideration again on February 11, but again with reservations dictated largely by Senator Lodge and unacceptable to the President. The final vote on the Treaty, with reservations, came March 19. It resulted in 49 for ratification and 35 against ratification, and the treaty thus lacking the necessary two-thirds vote was defeated. Subsequent efforts to make peace by resolution were defeated in 1920 and successful the following year. See Doc. No. 442. Separate treaties concluding peace with Germany, Austria and Hungary were ratified October 18, 1921. See, H. C. Lodge, *The Senate and the League of Nations;* D. F. Fleming, *The United States and the League of Nations, 1918–1920;* C. P. Howland, ed. *Survey of American Foreign Relations, 1928,* Sec. III; W. S. Holt, *Treaties Defeated by the Senate,* ch. x; J. C. Malin, *The United States After the World War,* chs. i–iv; A. Nevins, *Henry White,* ch. xxiii;

S. F. Bemis, ed. *American Secretaries of State*, Vol. X, p. 47 ff.

The PRESIDENT pro tempore. Upon agreeing to the resolution of ratification the yeas are 49 and the nays are 35. Not having received the affirmative votes of two-thirds of the Senators present and voting, the resolution is not agreed to, and the Senate does not advise and consent to the ratification of the treaty of peace with Germany.

The resolution of ratification voted upon and rejected is as follows:

Resolution of ratification.

Resolved (two-thirds of the Senators present concurring therein), That the Senate advise and consent to the ratification of the treaty of peace with Germany concluded at Versailles on the 28th day of June, 1919, subject to the following reservations and understandings, which are hereby made a part and condition of this resolution of ratification, which ratification is not to take effect or bind the United States until the said reservations and understandings adopted by the Senate have been accepted as a part and a condition of this resolution of ratification by the allied and associated powers and a failure on the part of the allied and associated powers to make objection to said reservations and understandings prior to the deposit of ratification by the United States shall be taken as a full and final acceptance of such reservations and understandings by said powers:

1. The United States so understands and construes article 1 that in case of notice of withdrawal from the League of Nations, as provided in said article, the United States shall be the sole judge as to whether all its international obligations and all its obligations under the said covenant have been fulfilled, and notice of withdrawal by the United States may be given by a concurrent resolution of the Congress of the United States.

2. The United States assumes no obligation to preserve the territorial integrity or political independence of any other country by the employment of its military or naval forces, its resources, or any form of economic discrimination, or to interfere in any way in controversies between nations, including all controversies relating to territorial integrity or political independence, whether members of the league or not, under the provisions of article 10, or to employ the military or naval forces of the United States, under any article of the treaty for any purpose, unless in any particular case the Congress, which, under the Constitution, has the sole power to declare war or authorize the employment of the military or naval forces of the United States, shall, in the exercise of full liberty of action, by act or joint resolution so provide.

3. No mandate shall be accepted by the United States under article 22, part 1, or any other provision of the treaty of peace with Germany, except by action of the Congress of the United States.

4. The United States reserves to itself exclusively the right to decide what questions are within its domestic jurisdiction and declares that all domestic and political questions relating wholly or in part to its internal affairs, including immigration, labor, coastwise traffic, the tariff, commerce, the suppression of traffic in women and children and in opium and other dangerous drugs, and all other domestic questions, are solely within the jurisdiction of the United States and are not under this treaty to be submitted in any way either to arbitration or to the consideration of the council or of the assembly of the League of Nations, or any agency thereof, or to the decision or recommendation of any other power.

5. The United States will not submit to arbitration or to inquiry by the assembly or by the council of the League of Nations, provided for in said treaty of peace, any questions which in the judgment of the United States depend upon or relate to its long-established policy, commonly known as the Monroe doctrine; said doctrine is to be interpreted by the United States alone and is hereby declared to be wholly outside the jurisdiction of said League of Nations and entirely unaffected by any provision contained in the said treaty of peace with Germany.

6. The United States withholds its assent to articles 156, 157, and 158, and reserves full liberty of action with respect to any controversy which may arise under said articles.

7. No person is or shall be authorized to represent the United States, nor shall any citizen of the United States be eligible, as a member of any body or agency established

or authorized by said treaty of peace with Germany, except pursuant to an act of the Congress of the United States providing for his appointment and defining his powers and duties.

8. The United States understands that the reparation commission will regulate or interfere with exports from the United States to Germany, or from Germany to the United States, only when the United States by act or joint resolution of Congress approves such regulation or interference.

9. The United States shall not be obligated to contribute to any expenses of the League of Nations, or of the secretariat, or of any commission, or committee, or conference, or other agency, organized under the League of Nations or under the treaty or for the purpose of carrying out the treaty provisions, unless and until an appropriation of funds available for such expenses shall have been made by the Congress of the United States: *Provided,* That the foregoing limitation shall not apply to the United States' proportionate share of the expense of the office force and salary of the secretary general.

10. No plan for the limitation of armaments proposed by the council of the League of Nations under the provisions of article 8 shall be held as binding the United States until the same shall have been accepted by Congress, and the United States reserves the right to increase its armament without the consent of the council whenever the United States is threatened with invasion or engaged in war.

11. The United States reserves the right to permit, in its discretion, the nationals of a covenant-breaking State, as defined in article 16 of the covenant of the League of Nations, residing within the United States or in countries other than such covenant-breaking State, to continue their commercial, financial, and personal relations with the nationals of the United States.

12. Nothing in articles 296, 297, or in any of the annexes thereto or in any other article, section, or annex of the treaty of peace with Germany shall, as against citizens of the United States, be taken to mean any confirmation, ratification, or approval of any act otherwise illegal or in contravention of the rights of citizens of the United States.

13. The United States withholds its assent to Part XIII (articles 387 to 427, inclusive) unless Congress by act or joint resolution shall hereafter make provision for representation in the organization established by said Part XIII, and in such event the participation of the United States will be governed and conditioned by the provisions of such act or joint resolution.

14. Until Part I, being the covenant of the League of Nations, shall be so amended as to provide that the United States shall be entitled to cast a number of votes equal to that which any member of the league and its self-governing dominions, colonies, or parts of empire, in the aggregate shall be entitled to cast, the United States assumes no obligation to be bound, except in cases where Congress has previously given its consent, by any election, decision, report, or finding of the council or assembly in which any member of the league and its self-governing dominions, colonies, or parts of empire, in the aggregate have cast more than one vote.

The United States assumes no obligation to be bound by any decision, report, or finding of the council or assembly arising out of any dispute between the United States and any member of the league if such member, or any self-governing dominion, colony, empire, or part of empire united with it politically has voted.

15. In consenting to the ratification of the treaty with Germany the United States adheres to the principle of self-determination and to the resolution of sympathy with the aspirations of the Irish people for a government of their own choice adopted by the Senate June 6, 1919, and declares that when such government is attained by Ireland, a consummation it is hoped is at hand, it should promptly be admitted as a member of the League of Nations.

437. MISSOURI v. HOLLAND
252 U. S. 416
1920

Appeal from the United States district court for the Western District of Missouri. This case involved the constitutionality of the Migratory Bird Treaty Act of July 3, 1918, which sought to enforce certain provisions of a convention between the United States and Canada. The important question raised was whether Congress could, in pursuance of the provisions of a treaty, enact legislation otherwise beyond its powers. The opinion of the Court in this case is one of the most far-reaching assertions of national power in our constitutional history.

HOLMES, J. This is a bill in equity brought by the State of Missouri to prevent a game warden of the United States from attempting to enforce the Migratory Bird Treaty Act of July 3, 1918, and the regulations made by the Secretary of Agriculture in pursuance of the same. The ground of the bill is that the statute is an unconstitutional interference with the rights reserved to the States by the Tenth Amendment, and that the acts of the defendant done and threatened under that authority invade the sovereign right of the State and contravene its will manifested in statutes. The State also alleges a pecuniary interest, as owner of the wild birds within its borders and otherwise, admitted by the government to be sufficient, but it is enough that the bill is a reasonable and proper means to assert the alleged quasi sovereign rights of a State. A motion to dismiss was sustained by the district court on the ground that the act of Congress is constitutional. 258 Fed. Rep. 479. The State appeals.

On December 8, 1916, a treaty between the United States and Great Britain was proclaimed by the President. It recited that many species of birds in their annual migrations traversed certain parts of the United States and of Canada, that they were of great value as a source of food and in destroying insects injurious to vegetation, but were in danger of extermination through lack of adequate protection. It therefore provided for specified closed seasons and protection in other forms, and agreed that the two powers would take or propose to their law-making bodies the necessary measures for carrying the treaty out. 39 Stat. 1702. The above mentioned Act of July 3, 1918, entitled an act to give effect to the convention, prohibited the killing, capturing or selling any of the migratory birds included in the terms of the treaty except as permitted by regulations compatible with those terms, to be made by the Secretary of Agriculture. Regulations were proclaimed on July 31, and October 25, 1918. It is unnecessary to go into any details, because, as we have said, the question raised is the general one whether the treaty and statute are void as an interference with the rights reserved to the States.

To answer this question it is not enough to refer to the Tenth Amendment, reserving the powers not delegated to the United States, because by Article II, §2, the power to make treaties is delegated expressly, and by Article VI treaties made under the authority of the United States, along with the Constitution and laws of the United States made in pursuance thereof, are declared the supreme law of the land. If the treaty is valid there can be no dispute about the validity of the statute under Article I, §8, as a necessary and proper means to execute the powers of the Government. The language of the Constitution as to the supremacy of treaties being general, the question before us is narrowed to an inquiry into the ground upon which the present supposed exception is placed.

It is said that a treaty cannot be valid if it infringes the Constitution, that there are limits, therefore, to the treaty-making power, and that one such limit is that what an act of Congress could not do unaided, in derogation of the powers reserved to the States, a treaty cannot do. An earlier act of Congress that attempted by itself and not in pursuance of a treaty to regulate the killing of migratory birds within the States had been held bad in the District Court. *United States* v. *Shauver,* 214 Fed. Rep. 154; *United States* v. *McCullagh,* 221 Fed. Rep. 288. Those decisions were supported by arguments that migratory birds were owned by the States in their sovereign capacity for the benefit of their people, and that under cases like *Geer*

v. *Connecticut,* 161 U. S. 519, this control was one that Congress had no power to displace. The same argument is supposed to apply now with equal force.

Whether the two cases cited were decided rightly or not they cannot be accepted as a test of the treaty power. Acts of Congress are the supreme law of the land only when made in pursuance of the Constitution, while treaties are declared to be so when made under the authority of the United States. It is open to question whether the authority of the United States means more than the formal acts prescribed to make the convention. We do not mean to imply that there are no qualifications to the treaty-making power; but they must be ascertained in a different way. It is obvious that there may be matters of the sharpest exigency for the national well being that an act of Congress could not deal with but that a treaty followed by such an act could, and it is not lightly to be assumed that, in matters requiring national action, "a power which must belong to and somewhere reside in every civilized government" is not to be found. *Andrews* v. *Andrews,* 188 U. S. 14. What was said in that case with regard to the powers of the States applies with equal force to the powers of the nation in cases where the States individually are incompetent to act. We are not yet discussing the particular case before us but only are considering the validity of the test proposed. . . . The treaty in question does not contravene any prohibitory words to be found in the Constitution. The only question is whether it is forbidden by some invisible radiation from the general terms of the Tenth Amendment. We must consider what this country has become in deciding what that amendment has reserved.

The State as we have intimated founds its claim of exclusive authority upon an assertion of title to migratory birds, an assertion that is embodied in statute. No doubt it is true that as between a State and its inhabitants the State may regulate the killing and sale of such birds, but it does not follow that its authority is exclusive of paramount powers. To put the claim of the State upon title is to lean upon a slender reed. Wild birds are not in the possession of anyone; and possession is the beginning of ownership. The whole foundation of the State's rights is the presence within their jurisdiction of birds that yesterday had not arrived, tomorrow may be in another State and in a week a thousand miles away. If we are to be accurate we cannot put the case of the State upon higher ground than that the treaty deals with creatures that for the moment are within the state borders, that it must be carried out by officers of the United States within the same territory, and that but for the treaty the State would be free to regulate this subject itself.

As most of the laws of the United States are carried out within the States and as many of them deal with matters which in the silence of such laws the State might regulate, such general grounds are not enough to support Missouri's claim. Valid treaties of course "are as binding within the territorial limits of the States as they are elsewhere throughout the dominion of the United States." *Baldwin* v. *Franks,* 120 U. S. 678. No doubt the great body of private relations usually fall within the control of the State, but a treaty may override its power. We do not have to invoke the later developments of constitutional law for this proposition; it was recognized as early as *Hopkirk* v. *Bell,* 3 Cranch, 454, with regard to statutes of limitation, and even earlier, as to confiscation, in *Ware* v. *Hylton,* 3 Dall. 199. . . . Further illustration seems unnecessary, and it only remains to consider the application of established rules to the present case.

Here a national interest of very nearly the first magnitude is involved. It can be protected only by national action in concert with that of another power. The subject-matter is only transitorily within the State and has no permanent habitat therein. But for the treaty and the statute there soon might be no birds for any powers to deal with. We see nothing in the Constitution that compels the government to sit by while a food supply is cut off and the protectors of our forests and our crops are destroyed. It is not sufficient to rely upon the States. The reliance is vain, and were it otherwise, the question is whether the United States is forbidden to act. We are of opinion that the treaty and statute must be upheld.

Decree affirmed.

Justices VAN DEVANTER and PITNEY dissented.

438. THE TRANSPORTATION ACT OF 1920
February 28, 1920
(*U. S. Statutes at Large,* Vol. XLI, p. 456 ff.)

This act, sometimes known as the Esch-Cummins Act, terminated the war-time period of government operation of the railroads and provided for the return of the roads to private ownership and operation under careful regulations. The most interesting feature of the Transportation Act of 1920 was the so-called "recapture" clause which provided for the setting aside of a reserve fund from railroad earnings over a "fair return." See A. R. Ellingwood and W. Coombs, *The Government and Railroad Transportation;* W. M. Splawn, *Government Ownership and Operation of Railroads;* R. MacVeagh, *The Transportation Act of 1920;* F. H. Dixon, *Railroads and Government;* W. D. Hines, *War History of American Railroads.*

TITLE II.
TERMINATION OF FEDERAL CONTROL

SEC. 200. (a) Federal control shall terminate at 12.01 A.M., March 1, 1920; and the President shall then relinquish possession and control of all railroads and systems of transportation then under Federal control and cease the use and operation thereof. . . .

SEC. 202. The President shall, as soon as practicable after the termination of Federal control, adjust, settle, liquidate, and wind up all matters, including compensation, and all questions and disputes of whatsoever nature, arising out of or incident to Federal control. . . .

SEC. 208. (a) All rates, fares, and charges, . . . which on February 29, 1920, are in effect on the lines of carriers subject to the Interstate Commerce Act, shall continue in force and effect until thereafter changed by State or Federal authority, respectively, or pursuant to authority of law; but prior to September 1, 1920, no such rate, fare, or charge shall be reduced, . . . unless such reduction or change is approved by the Commission. . . .

SEC. 209. . . .

(c) The United States hereby guarantees—

(1) With respect to any carrier with which a contract . . . has been made . . . that the railway operating income of such carrier for the guaranty period as a whole shall not be less than one-half the amount named in such contract as annual compensation, . . .

TITLE III.
DISPUTES BETWEEN CARRIERS AND THEIR EMPLOYEES AND SUBORDINATE OFFICIALS

SEC. 301. It shall be the duty of all carriers and their officers, employees, and agents, to exert every reasonable effort . . . to avoid any interruption to the operation of any carrier growing out of any dispute between the carrier and the employees or subordinate officials thereof. All such disputes shall be considered and, if possible, decided in conference between representatives designated and authorized so to confer by the carriers, or the employees or subordinate officials thereof, directly interested in the dispute. If any dispute is not decided in such conference, it shall be referred by the parties thereto to the board which under the provisions of this title is authorized to hear and decide such dispute.

SEC. 302. Railroad Boards of Labor Adjustment may be established by agreement between any carrier, . . . or the carriers as a whole, and any employees or subordinate officials of carriers, or organization or group of organizations thereof.

SEC. 303. Each such Adjustment Board shall, (1) upon the application of the chief executive of any carrier or organization of employees or subordinate officials whose members are directly interested in the dispute, (2) upon the written petition signed by not less than 100 unorganized employees or subordinate officials directly interested in the dispute, (3) upon the Adjustment Board's own motion, or (4) upon the request of the Labor Board whenever such board is of the opinion that the dispute is likely substantially to interrupt commerce, receive for hearing, and as soon as practicable and with due diligence decide, any dispute involving only grievances, rules, or working conditions, not decided as provided in section 301, between the carrier and its employees or subordinate officials. . . .

SEC. 304. There is hereby established a board to be known as the "Railroad Labor Board" and to be composed of nine members as follows:

(1) Three members constituting the labor group, representing the employees and subordinate officials of the carriers, to be appointed by the President, by and with the advice and consent of the Senate, from not less than six nominees whose nominations shall be made and offered by such employees in such manner as the Commission shall by regulation prescribe;

(2) Three members, constituting the management group, representing the carriers, to be appointed by the President, by and with the advice and consent of the Senate, from not less than six nominees whose nominations shall be made and offered by the carriers in such manner as the Commission shall by regulation prescribe; and

(3) Three members, constituting the public group, representing the public, to be appointed directly by the President, by and with the advice and consent of the Senate. . . .

SEC. 306. (a) Any member of the Labor Board who during his term of office is an active member or in the employ of or holds any office in any organization of employees or subordinate officials, or any carrier, or owns any stock or bond thereof, or is pecuniarily interested therein, shall at once become ineligible for further membership upon the Labor Board; but no such member is required to relinquish honorary membership in, or his rights in any insurance or pension or other benefit fund maintained by, any organization of employees or subordinate officials or by a carrier.

SEC. 307. (a) The Labor Board shall hear, and . . . decide, any dispute involving grievances, rules, or working conditions, in respect to which any Adjustment Board certifies to the Labor Board that in its opinion the Adjustment Board has failed or will fail to reach a decision within a reasonable time, or in respect to which the Labor Board determines that any Adjustment Board has so failed or is not using due diligence in its consideration thereof. . . .

(b) The Labor Board shall receive for hearing, and as soon as practicable and with due diligence decide, all disputes with respect to the wages or salaries of employees or subordinate officials of carriers, not decided as provided in section 301. . . .

(c) A decision by the Labor Board under the provisions of paragraphs (a) or (b) of this section shall require the concurrence therein of at least 5 of the 9 members of the Labor Board: *Provided,* That in case of any decision under paragraph (b), at least one of the representatives of the public shall concur in such decision. . . .

(d) . . . In determining the justness and reasonableness of . . . wages and salaries or working conditions the board shall, so far as applicable, take into consideration among other relevant circumstances:

(1) The scale of wages paid for similar kinds of work in other industries;

(2) The relation between wages and the cost of living;

(3) The hazards of the employment;

(4) The training and skill required;

(5) The degree of responsibility;

(6) The character and regularity of employment; and

(7) Inequalities of increases in wages or of treatment, the result of previous wage orders or adjustments.

SEC. 407 . . .

(4) The Commission shall as soon as practicable prepare and adopt a plan for the consolidation of the railway properties of the continental United States into a limited number of systems. In the division of such railways into such systems under such plan, competition shall be preserved as fully as possible and wherever practicable the existing routes and channels of trade and commerce shall be maintained. . . .

(6) It shall be lawful for two or more carriers by railroad, subject to this Act, to consolidate their properties or any part thereof, into one corporation for the ownership, management, and operation of the properties theretofore in separate ownership, management, and operation, under the following conditions:

(a) The proposed consolidation must be in harmony with and in furtherance of the complete plan of consolidation mentioned in paragraph (5) and must be approved by the Commission; . . .

(8) The carriers affected by any order made under the foregoing provisions of this section and any corporation organized to effect a consolidation approved and authorized in such order shall be, and they are hereby, relieved from the operation of the "antitrust laws," as designated in section 1 of the Act entitled "An Act to supplement existing laws against unlawful restraints and monopolies, and for other purposes," approved October 15, 1914, and of all other restraints or prohibitions by law, State or Federal, in so far as may be necessary to enable them to do anything authorized or required by any order made under and pursuant to the foregoing provisions of this section. . . .

SEC. 422. . . .

(2) In the exercise of its power to prescribe just and reasonable rates the Commission shall initiate, modify, establish or adjust such rates so that carriers as a whole . . . will, under honest, efficient and economical management and reasonable expenditures for maintenance of way, structures and equipment, earn an aggregate annual net railway operating income equal, as nearly as may be, to a fair return upon the aggregate value of the railway property of such carriers held for and used in the service of transportation. . . .

(3) The Commission shall from time to time determine and make public what percentage of such aggregate property value constitutes a fair return thereon, and such percentage shall be uniform for all rate groups or territories which may be designated by the Commission. In making such determination it shall give due consideration, among other things, to the transportation needs of the country and the necessity . . . of enlarging such facilities in order to provide the people of the United States with adequate transportation: *Provided,* That during the two years beginning March 1, 1920, the Commission shall take as such fair return a sum equal to 5½ per centum of such aggregate value to make provision in whole or in part for improvements, betterments, or equipment, which, according to the accounting system prescribed by the Commission, are chargeable to capital account. . . .

(5) Inasmuch as it is impossible . . . to establish uniform rates upon competitive traffic which will adequately sustain all the carriers which are engaged in such traffic and which are indispensable to the communities to which they render the service of transportation, without enabling some of such carriers to receive a net railway operating income substantially and unreasonably in excess of a fair return upon the value of their railway property held for and used in the service of transportation, it is hereby declared that any carrier which receives such an income so in excess of a fair return, shall hold such part of the excess, as hereinafter prescribed, as trustee for, and shall pay it to, the United States.

(6) If, under the provisions of this section, any carrier receives for any year a net railway operating income in excess of 6 per centum of the value of the railway property held for and used by it in the service of transportation, one-half of such excess shall be placed in a reserve fund established and maintained by such carrier, and the remaining one-half thereof shall, within the first four months following the close of the period for which such computation is made, be recoverable by and paid to the Commission for the purpose of establishing and maintaining a general railroad contingent fund as hereinafter described. . . .

439. RAILROAD COMMISSION OF WISCONSIN v. CHICAGO, BURLINGTON, & QUINCY RAILROAD COMPANY
257 U. S. 563
1922

Appeal from the District Court for Eastern District of Wisconsin. Decree to enjoin state railroad commission from interfering with maintenance of rates fixed by the Interstate Commerce Commission. The Interstate Commerce Commission, acting under authority of the Transportation Act of 1920, ordered an increase of twenty per cent in passenger rates on railroads in the group which embraced the Wisconsin carriers. This order conflicted with a state statute of February 28, 1920, fixing a maximum rate of 2 cents a mile for intrastate passenger transportation. The Interstate Commerce Commission consequently ordered an increase in intrastate rates to bring them into conformity with those charged over interstate transportation.

TAFT, C. J. The Commission's order, interference with which was enjoined by the district court, effects the removal of the unjust discrimination found to exist against persons in interstate commerce, and against interstate commerce, by fixing a minimum for intrastate passenger fares in Wisconsin at 3.6 cents per mile. . . .

We have two questions to decide.

First, Do the intrastate passenger fares work undue prejudice against persons in interstate commerce, such as to justify a horizontal increase of them all?

Second, Are these intrastate fares an undue discrimination against interstate commerce as a whole which it is the duty of the Commission to remove? . . .

The order in this case . . . is much wider than the orders made in the proceedings following the Shreveport and Illinois C. R. Co. Cases. There, as here, the report of the Commission showed discrimination against persons and localities at border points and the orders were extended to include all rates or fares from all points in the state to border points. But this order is not so restricted. It includes fares between all interior points, although neither may be near the border, and the fares between them may not work a discrimination against interstate travelers at all. Nothing in the precedents cited justifies an order affecting all rates of a general description when it is clear that this would include many rates not within the proper class or reason of the order. . . .

Intrastate rates and the income from them must play a most important part in maintaining an adequate national railway system. Twenty per cent of the gross freight receipts of the railroads of the country are from intrastate traffic, and 50 per cent of the passenger receipts. The ratio of the gross intrastate revenue to the interstate revenue is a little less than one to three. If the rates, on which such receipts are based, are to be fixed at a substantially lower level than in interstate traffic, the share which the intrastate

traffic will contribute will be proportionately less. . . .

It is objected here, as it was in the Shreveport Case, that orders of the Commission which raise the intrastate rates to a level of the interstate structure violate the specific proviso of the original Interstate Commerce Act . . . that the Commission is not to regulate traffic wholly within a state. To this the same answer must be made as was made in the Shreveport Case, that such orders as to intrastate traffic are merely incidental to the regulation of interstate commerce, and necessary to its efficiency. Effective control of the one must embrace some control over the other, in view of the blending of both in actual operation. The same rails and the same cars carry both. The same men conduct them. Commerce is a unit and does not regard state lines, and while, under the Constitution, interstate and intrastate commerce are ordinarily subject to regulation by different sovereignties, yet when they are so mingled together that the supreme authority, the nation, cannot exercise complete effective control over interstate commerce without incidental regulation of intrastate commerce, such incidental regulation is not an invasion of state authority or a violation of the proviso. . . .

Congress in its control of its interstate commerce system, is seeking in the Transportation Act to make the system adequate to the needs of the country by securing for it a reasonably compensatory return for all the work it does. The states are seeking to use that same system for intrastate traffic. That entails large duties and expenditures on the interstate commerce which may burden it unless compensation is received for the intrastate business reasonably proportionate to that for the interstate business. Congress, as the dominant controller of interstate commerce, may, therefore, restrain undue limitations of the earning power of the interstate commerce system in doing state work. The affirmative power of Congress in developing interstate commerce agencies is clear. In such development, it can impose any reasonable condition on a state's use of interstate carriers for intrastate commerce it deems necessary or desirable. This is because of the supremacy of the national power in this field. Order of the District Court affirmed.

440. DAYTON-GOOSE CREEK RAILWAY COMPANY v. UNITED STATES
263 U. S. 456
1924

Appeal from decree of District Court for Eastern District of Texas dismissing a bill to restrain enforcement of order from Interstate Commerce Commission. The Transportation Act of 1920 (see Doc. No. 438) provided that any railroad receiving an income in excess of such fair return as shall be established by the Interstate Commerce Commission shall hold the excess earnings as a trustee for the United States. One half of the excess is to constitute a reserve fund to be maintained by the carrier, and the other half a general railroad revolving fund to be maintained and administered by the Interstate Commerce Commission.

TAFT, C. J. The main question in this case is whether the so-called "recapture" paragraphs of the Transportation Act of February 28, 1920 are constitutional. . . .

This court has recently had occasion to construe the Transportation Act. . . . It was pointed out that the Transportation Act adds a new and important object to previous interstate commerce legislation, which was designed primarily to prevent unreasonable or discriminatory rates against persons and localities. The new act seeks affirmatively to build up a system of railways prepared to handle promptly all the interstate traffic of the country. It aims to give the owners of the railways an opportunity to earn enough to maintain their properties and equipment in such a state of efficiency that they can carry well this burden. To achieve this great purpose, it puts the railroad systems of the country more completely than ever under the fostering guardianship and control of the Commission, which is to supervise their issue of securities, their car supply and distribution, their joint use of terminals, their construction of new lines, their abandonment of old lines, and by a proper division of joint rates, and by fixing adequate rates, for interstate commerce, and, in case of discrimination, for intrastate commerce, to secure a fair return upon the properties of the carriers engaged. . . .

We have been greatly pressed with the argument that the cutting down of income actually received by the carrier for its service

to a so-called fair return is a plain appropriation of its property without any compensation; that the income it receives for the use of its property is as much protected by the 5th Amendment as the property itself. The statute declares the carrier to be only a trustee for the excess over a fair return received by it. Though in its possession, the excess never becomes its property, and it accepts custody of the product of all the rates with this understanding. It is clear, therefore, that the carrier never has such a title to the excess as to render the recapture of it by the government a taking without due process.

It is then objected that the government has no right to retain one half of the excess, since, if it does not belong to the carrier, it belongs to the shippers, and should be returned to them. If it were valid, it is an objection which the carrier cannot be heard to make. It would be soon enough to consider such a claim when made by the shipper. But it is not valid. The rates are reasonable from the standpoint of the shipper, as we have shown, though their net product furnishes more than a fair return for the carrier. The excess caused by the discrepancy between the standard of reasonableness for the shipper and that for the carrier, due to the necessity of maintaining uniform rates to be charged the shippers, may properly be appropriated by the government for public uses because the appropriation takes away nothing which equitably belongs either to the shipper or to the carrier. . . .

The third question for our consideration is whether the recapture clause, by reducing the net income from intrastate rates, invades the reserved power of the States and is in conflict with the 10th Amendment. In solving the problem of maintaining the efficiency of an interstate commerce railway system which serves both the states and the nation, Congress is dealing with a unit, in which state and interstate operations are often inextricably commingled. When the adequate maintenance of interstate commerce involves and makes necessary on this account the incidental and partial control of intrastate commerce, the power of Congress to exercise such control has been clearly established. (Minnesota Rate Cases, 230 U. S. 352; Shreveport Case, 234 U. S. 342; Railway Commission v. Chicago B & Q R. R. 257 U. S. 563.) The combination of uniform rates with the recapture clauses is necessary to the better development of the country's in-terstate transportation system as Congress has planned it. The control of the excess profit due to the level of the whole body of rates is the heart of the plan. To divide that excess and attempt to distribute one part to interstate traffic and the other to intrastate traffic would be impracticable and defeat the plan. . . .

Decree of District Court affirmed.

441. GREEN v. FRAZIER
253 U. S. 233
1920

Error to the Supreme Court of the State of North Dakota. This case involved the legality of taxation for the maintenance of State-managed manufacturing and banking institutions. The decision in *Loan Association* v. *Topeka,* Doc. No. 286, had established the rule that public moneys could not be used for the support of private business, but it remained to determine what businesses were private and what public in character. For the background, see P. R. Fossum, *The Agrarian Movement in North Dakota.*

DAY, J. . . . The only ground of attack involving the validity of the legislation which requires our consideration concerns the alleged deprivation of rights secured to the plaintiffs by the Fourteenth Amendment to the federal Constitution. It is contended that taxation under the laws in question has the effect of depriving plaintiffs of property without due process of law.

The legislation involved consists of a series of acts passed under the authority of the state constitution, which are (1) An Act creating an Industrial Commission of North Dakota which is authorized to conduct and manage on behalf of that State certain utilities, enterprises, and business projects, to be established by law . . . (2) The Bank of North Dakota Act, which establishes a Bank operated by the State . . . (4) An Act providing for the issuing of bonds in the sum of not exceeding $10,000,000 . . . These bonds are to be issued for the purpose of raising money to produce funds for the Bank of North Dakota . . . (5) An Act declaring the purpose of the State of North Dakota to engage in the business of manufacturing and marketing farm products and to establish a warehouse, elevator, and flour mill system . . . (6) An Act providing for the issuing of bonds of the State of North Dakota in a sum not exceeding $5,000,000 . . . These bonds are to be issued and sold for the purpose of carrying on the business of the Mill & Elevator Association. The faith and credit of the state are pledged for the payment of the bonds, both principle and interest . . . (7) The Home Building Act. . . .

There are certain principles which must be borne in mind in this connection, and which must control the decision of this court upon the federal question herein involved. This legislation was adopted under the broad power of the state to enact laws raising by taxation such sums as are deemed necessary to promote purposes essential to the general welfare of its people. Before the adoption of the Fourteenth Amendment this power of the state was unrestrained by any federal authority. That amendment introduced a new limitation upon state power into the federal Constitution. The states were forbidden to deprive persons of life, liberty and property without due process of law. What is meant by due process of law this court has had frequent occasion to consider, and has always declined to give a precise meaning, preferring to leave its scope to judicial decisions when cases from time to time arise.

The due process of law clause contains no specific limitation upon the right of taxation in the states, but it has come to be settled that the authority of the states to tax does not include the right to impose taxes for merely private purposes. . . .

Accepting this as settled by the former adjudications of this court, the enforcement of the principle is attended with the application of certain rules equally well settled.

The taxing power of the states is primarily

vested in their legislatures, deriving their authority from the people. When a state legislature acts within the scope of its authority it is responsible to the people, and their right to change the agents to whom they have intrusted the power is ordinarily deemed a sufficient check upon its abuse. When the constituted authority of the state undertakes to exert the taxing power, and the question of the validity of its action is brought before this court, every presumption in its favor is indulged, and only clear and demonstrative usurpation of power will authorize judicial interference with legislative action.

In the present instance under the authority of the constitution and laws prevailing in North Dakota the people, the legislature, and the highest court of the state have declared the purpose for which these several acts were passed to be of a public nature, and within the taxing authority of the state. With this united action of people, legislature and court, we are not at liberty to interfere unless it is clear beyond reasonable controversy that rights secured by the federal Constitution have been violated. What is a public purpose has given rise to no little judicial consideration. Courts, as a rule, have attempted no judicial definition of a "public" as distinguished from a "private" purpose, but have left each case to be determined by its own peculiar circumstances. . . . Questions of policy are not submitted to judicial determination, and the courts have no general authority of supervision over the exercise of discretion which under our system is reposed in the people or other departments of government.

With the wisdom of such legislation, and the soundness of the economic policy involved we are not concerned. Whether it will result in ultimate good or harm it is not within our province to inquire.

We come now to examine the grounds upon which the supreme court of North Dakota held this legislation not to amount to a taking of property without due process of law. The questions involved were given elaborate consideration in that court, and it held, concerning what may in general terms be denominated the "banking legislation," that it was justified for the purpose of providing banking facilities, and to enable the state to carry out the purposes of the other acts, of which the Mill and Elevator Association Act is the principal one. It justified the Mill and Elevator Association Act by the peculiar situation in the State of North Dakota, and particularly by the great agricultural industry of the state. It estimated from facts of which it was authorized to take judicial notice, that 90 per cent. of the wealth produced by the state was from agriculture; and stated that upon the prosperity and welfare of that industry other business and pursuits carried on in the state were largely dependent; that the state produced 125,000,000 bushels of wheat each year. The manner in which the present system of transporting and marketing this great crop prevents the realization of what are deemed just prices was elaborately stated. It was affirmed that the annual loss from these sources (including the loss of fertility to the soil and the failure to feed the byproducts of grain to stock within the state), amounted to fifty-five millions of dollars to the wheat raisers of North Dakota. It answered the contention that the industries involved were private in their nature, by stating that all of them belonged to the State of North Dakota, and therefore the activities authorized by the legislation were to be distinguished from business of a private nature having private gain for its objective.

As to the Home Building Act, that was sustained because of the promotion of the general welfare in providing homes for the people, a large proportion of whom were tenants moving from place to place. It was believed and affirmed by the supreme court of North Dakota that the opportunity to secure and maintain homes would promote the general welfare, and that the provisions of the statutes to enable this feature of the system to become effective would redound to the general benefit.

As we have said, the question for us to consider and determine is whether this system of legislation is violative of the federal Constitution because it amounts to a taking of property without due process of law. The precise question herein involved so far as we have been able to discover has never been presented to this court. The nearest approach to it is found in Jones v. City of Portland, 245 U. S. 217, in which we held that an act of the State of Maine authorizing cities or towns to establish and maintain wood, coal and fuel yards for the purpose of selling these necessaries to the inhabitants of cities and towns, did not deprive taxpayers of due process of law within the meaning of the Fourteenth Amendment. In that case we reiterated the attitude of this court towards state legislation, and repeated what had been said before, that what was or was not a public use was a question concerning which local authority, legislative and judicial, had especial means of securing information to enable them to form a judgment; and particularly that the judgment of the highest court of the state declaring a given use to be public in its nature, would be accepted by this court unless clearly unfounded. In that case the previous decisions of this court, sustaining this proposition, were cited with approval, and a quotation was made from the opinion of the supreme court of Maine justifying the legislation under the conditions prevailing in that state. We think the principle of that decision is applicable here.

This is not a case of undertaking to aid private institutions by public taxation as was the fact in Citizens' Savings and Loan Association v. Topeka, 20 Wallace 655. In many instances states and municipalities have in late years seen fit to enter upon projects to promote the public welfare which in the past have been considered entirely within the domain of private enterprise.

Under the peculiar conditions existing in North Dakota, which are emphasized in the opinion of its highest court, if the state sees fit to enter upon such enterprises as are here involved, with the sanction of its constitution, its legislature and its people, we are not prepared to say that it is within the authority of this court, in enforcing the observance of the Fourteenth Amendment, to set aside such action by judicial decision.

Affirmed.

442. TREATY OF PEACE WITH GERMANY
August 25, 1921

(*U. S. Statutes at Large*, Vol. XXXXII, p. 1939)

The United States of America and Germany:

Considering that the United States, acting in conjunction with its co-belligerents, entered into an Armistice with Germany on November 11, 1918, in order that a Treaty of Peace might be concluded;

Considering that the Treaty of Versailles was signed on June 28, 1919, and came into force according to the terms of its Article 440, but has not been ratified by the United States;

Considering that the Congress of the United States passed a Joint Resolution, approved by the President July 2, 1921, which reads in part as follows:

"Resolved by the Senate and House of Representatives of the United States of America in Congress Assembled:

"That the state of war declared to exist between the Imperial German Government and the United States of America by the joint resolution of Congress approved April 6, 1917, is hereby declared at an end.

"Section 2. That in making this declaration, and as a part of it, there are expressly reserved to the United States of America and its nationals any and all rights, privileges, indemnities, reparations or advantages, together with the right to enforce the same, to which it or they have become entitled under the terms of the Armistice signed November 11, 1918, or any extensions or modifications thereof; or which were acquired by or are in the possession of the United States of America by reason of its participation in the war or to which its nationals have thereby become rightfully entitled; or which, under the Treaty of Versailles, have been stipulated for its or their benefit; or to which it is entitled as one of the Principal Allied and Associated powers; or to which it is entitled by virtue of any Act or Acts of Congress; or otherwise."

. . . Being desirous of restoring the friendly relations existing between the two Nations prior to the outbreak of war:

Have for that purpose appointed their plenipotentiaries:

The President of the United States of America

Ellis Loring Dresel, Commissioner of the United States of America to Germany, and

The President of the German Empire

Dr. Friedrich Rosen, Minister for Foreign Affairs,

Who, having communicated their full powers, found to be in good and due form have agreed as follows:

Art. 1. Germany undertakes to accord to the United States, and the United States shall have and enjoy, all the rights, privileges, indemnities, reparations or advantages specified in the aforesaid Joint Resolution of the Congress of the United States of July 2, 1921, including all the rights and advantages stipulated for the benefit of the United States in the Treaty of Versailles which the United States shall fully enjoy notwithstanding the fact that such Treaty has not been ratified by the United States.

Art. 2. With a view to defining more particularly the obligations of Germany under the foregoing Article with respect to certain provisions in the Treaty of Versailles, it is understood and agreed between the High Contracting Parties:

(1) That the rights and advantages stipulated in that Treaty for the benefit of the United States, which it is intended the United States shall have and enjoy, are those defined in Section 1 of Part IV, and Parts V, VI, VIII, IX, X, XI, XII, XIV, and XV.

The United States, in availing itself of the rights and advantages stipulated in the provisions of that Treaty mentioned in this paragraph, will do so in a manner consistent with the rights accorded to Germany under such provisions.

(2) That the United States shall not be bound by the provisions of Part 1 of that Treaty, nor by any provisions of that Treaty, including those mentioned in Paragraph (1) of this Article, which relate to the Covenant of the League of Nations, or by the Council or by the Assembly thereof, unless the United States shall expressly give the assent to such action.

(3) That the United States assumes no obligations under or with respect to the provisions of Part II, Part III, Sections 2 to 8 inclusive of Part IV, and Part XIII of that Treaty.

(4) That, while the United States is privileged to participate in the Reparation Commission, according to the terms of Part VIII of that Treaty, and in any other Commission established under the Treaty or under any agreement supplemental thereto, the United States is not bound to participate in any such commission unless it shall elect to do so.

(5) That the periods of time to which reference is made in Article 440 of the Treaty of Versailles shall run, with respect to any act or election on the part of the United States, from the date of the coming into force of the present Treaty.

Art. 3. The present Treaty shall be ratified in accordance with the constitutional forms of the High Contracting Parties and shall take effect immediately on the exchange of ratifications, which shall take place as soon as possible at Berlin.

In witness whereof, the respective plenipotentiaries have signed this Treaty and have hereunto affixed their seals.

Done in duplicate in Berlin this twenty-fifth day of August, 1921.

Ellis Loring Dresel.
Rosen.

443. THE SHEPPARD–TOWNER ACT
November 23, 1921

(*U. S. Statutes at Large,* Vol. XXXXII, p. 224 ff.)

This act, extending federal aid to states for welfare work, was regarded by many critics as an unwarranted intrusion on the jurisdiction of the states, and many states refused to avail themselves of the provisions of the act. See A. F. Macdonald, *Federal Aid: a Study of the American Subsidy System;* W. Thompson, *Federal Centralization.*

An Act For the promotion of the welfare and hygiene of maternity and infancy, and for other purposes.

Be it enacted That there is hereby authorized to be appropriated annually, out of any money in the Treasury not otherwise appropriated, the sums specified in section 2 of this Act, to be paid to the several States for the purpose of cooperating with them in promoting the welfare and hygiene of maternity and infancy as hereinafter provided.

Sec. 2. For the purpose of carrying out the provisions of this Act, there is authorized to be appropriated, out of any money in the Treasury not otherwise appropriated, for the current fiscal year $480,000, to be equally apportioned among the several States, and for each subsequent year, for the period of five years, $240,000, to be equally apportioned among the several States in the manner hereinafter provided: Provided, That there is hereby authorized to be appropriated for the use of the States, subject to the provisions of this Act, for the fiscal year ending to June 30, 1922, an additional sum of $1,000,000 and annually thereafter, for the period of five years, an additional sum not to exceed $1,000,000: Provided further, That the additional appropriations herein authorized shall be apportioned $5,000 to each State and the balance among the States in the proportion which their population bears to the total population of the States of the United States, according to the last preceding United States census: And provided further, That no payment out of the additional appropriation herein authorized shall be made in any year to any State until an equal sum has been appropriated for that year by the legislature of such State for the maintenance of the services and facilities provided for in this Act. . . .

Sec. 4. In order to secure the benefits of the appropriations authorized in section 2 of this Act, any State shall, through the legislative authority thereof, accept the provisions of this Act and designate or authorize the creation of a State agency with which the Children's Bureau shall have all necessary powers to co-operate as herein provided in the administration of the provisions of this Act: Provided, That in any State having a child-welfare or child-hygiene division in its State agency of health, the said State agency of health shall administer the provisions of this Act through such divisions. If the legislature of any State has not made provision for accepting the provisions of this Act the governor of such State may in so far as he is authorized to do so by the laws of such State accept the provisions of this Act and designate or create a State agency to co-operate with the Children's Bureau until six months after the adjournment of the first regular session of the legislature in such State following the passage of this Act. . . .

Sec. 8. Any State desiring to receive the benefits of this Act shall, by its agency described in section 4, submit to the Children's Bureau detailed plans for carrying out the provisions of this Act within such State, which plans shall be subject to the approval of the board: . . .

Sec. 14. This Act shall be construed as intending to secure to the various States control of the administration of this Act within their respective States, subject only to the provisions and purposes of this Act.

444. TRUAX v. CORRIGAN
257 U. S. 312
1921

Error to the supreme court of Arizona. This is one of the leading cases on the right of labor to picket or to employ a boycott in labor disputes. The facts of the controversy are stated in the case below. For a general discussion, see F. Frankfurter and N. Greene, *The Labor Injunction;* P. F. Brissenden, "The Labor Injunction," *Pol. Sci. Qt.,* Vol. XLVIII.

TAFT, C. J. . . . The complaint further averred that the defendants were relying for immunity on Paragraph 1464 of the Revised Statutes of Arizona, 1913, which is in part as follows:

"No restraining order or injunction shall be granted by any court of this state, or a judge or the judges thereof, in any case between an employer and employees, or between employers and employees, or between employees, or between persons employed and persons seeking employment, involving or growing out of a dispute concerning terms or conditions of employment, unless necessary to prevent irreparable injury to property or to a property right of the party making the application, for which injury there is no adequate remedy at law, and such property or property right must be described with particularity in the application, which must be in writing and sworn to by the applicant or by his agent or attorney.

"And no such restraining order or injunction shall prohibit any person or persons from terminating any relation of employment, or from ceasing to perform any work or labor, or from recommending, advising, or persuading others by peaceful means so to do; or from attending at or near a house or place where any person resides or works, or carries on business, or happens to be for the purpose of peacefully obtaining or communicating information, or of peacefully persuading any person to work or to abstain from working; or from ceasing to patronize or to employ any party to such dispute; or from recommending, advising, or persuading others by peaceful means so to do; . . ."

The plaintiffs alleged that this paragraph if it made lawful defendants' acts contravened the Fourteenth Amendment to the Constitution of the United States by depriving plaintiffs of their property without due process of law, and by denying to plaintiffs the equal protection of the laws, and was, therefore, void and of no effect. Upon the case thus stated the plaintiffs asked a temporary, and a permanent, injunction. . . . The Superior Court for Chocise County . . . dismissed the complaint, and this judgment was affirmed by the supreme court of Arizona. . . .

The effect of this ruling is that, under the statute, loss may be inflicted upon the plaintiffs' property and business by "picketing" in any form if violence be not used, and that, because no violence was shown or claimed, the campaign carried on, as described in the complaint and exhibits, did not unlawfully invade plaintiffs' rights. . . .

The complaint and its exhibits make this case:

The defendants conspired to injure and destroy plaintiffs' business by inducing their theretofore willing patrons and would be patrons not to patronize them. . . .

The result of this campaign was to reduce the business of the plaintiffs from more than $55,000 a year to one of $12,000.

Plaintiffs' business is a property right (Duplex Printing Press Co. v. Deering, 254 U. S. 443) and free access for employees,

owner, and customers to his place of business is incident to such right. Intentional injury caused to either right or both by a conspiracy is a tort. . . .

A law which operates to make lawful such a wrong as is described in plaintiffs' complaint deprives the owner of the business and the premises of his property without due process, and cannot be held valid under the Fourteenth Amendment. . . .

If, however, contrary to the construction which we put on the opinion of the Supreme Court of Arizona, it does not withhold from the plaintiffs all remedy for the wrongs they suffered, but only the equitable relief of injunction, there still remains the question whether they are thus denied the equal protection of the laws. . . .

The necessary effect of . . . paragraph 1464 is that the plaintiffs in error would have had the right to an injunction against such a campaign as that conducted by the defendants in error, if it had been directed against the plaintiffs' business and property in any kind of a controversy which was not a dispute between employer and former employees. . . .

This brings us to consider the effect in this case of that provision of the Fourteenth Amendment which forbids any State to deny to any person the equal protection of the laws. The clause is associated in the amendment with the due process clause and it is customary to consider them together. . . .

The guaranty was aimed at undue favor and individual or class privilege, on the one hand, and at hostile discrimination or the oppression of inequality, on the other. It sought an equality of treatment of all persons, even though all enjoyed the protection of due process. Mr. Justice Field, delivering the opinion of this court in Barbier v. Connolly, 113 U. S. 27, of the equality clause, said— "Class legislation, discriminating against some and favoring others, is prohibited, but legislation which, in carrying out a public purpose, is limited in its application, if within the sphere of its operation it affects alike all persons similarly situated, is not within the amendment." . . .

Mr. Justice Matthews, in Yick Wo v. Hopkins, 118 U. S. 356, speaking for the court of both the due process and the equality clause of the Fourteenth Amendment, said:

"These provisions are universal in their application, to all persons within the territorial jurisdiction, without regard to any differences of race, of color, or nationality; *and the equal protection of the laws is a pledge of the protection of equal laws.*" . . .

With these views of the meaning of the equality clause, it does not seem possible to escape the conclusion that by the clauses of Paragraph 1464 of the Revised Statutes of Arizona, here relied on by the defendants, as construed by its supreme court, the plaintiffs have been deprived of the equal protection of the law. . . . Here is a direct invasion of the ordinary business and property rights of a person, unlawful when committed by any one, and remediable because of its otherwise irreparable character by equitable process, except when committed by ex-employees of the injured person. If this is not a denial of the equal protection of the laws, then it is hard to conceive what would be. . . .

Classification is the most inveterate of our reasoning processes. We can scarcely think or speak without consciously or unconsciously exercising it. It must therefore obtain in and determine legislation; but it must regard real resemblances and real differences between things and persons, and class them in accordance with their pertinence to the purpose in hand. Classification like the one with which we are here dealing is said to be the development of the philosophic thought of the world and is opening the door to legalized experiment. When fundamental rights are thus attempted to be taken away, however, we may well subject such experiment to attentive judgment. The Constitution was intended, its very purpose was, to prevent experimentation with the fundamental rights of the individual. We said through Mr. Justice Brewer, in Muller v. Oregon, 208 U. S. 412, 52 L. ed. 551, 28 S. Ct. R. 324, that "it is the peculiar value of a written constitution that it places in unchanging form limitations upon legislative action, and thus gives a permanence and stability to popular government which otherwise would be lacking." . . .

We conclude that the demurrer in this case should have been overruled, the defendants required to answer, and that if the evidence sustained the averments of the complaint, an injunction should issue as prayed. . . .

Judgment reversed.

HOLMES, J., dissenting. The dangers of a delusive exactness in the application of the Fourteenth Amendment have been adverted to before now. Delusive exactness is a source of fallacy throughout law. By calling a business "property" you make it seem like land, and lead up to the conclusion that a statute cannot substantially cut down the advantages of ownership existing before the statute was passed. An established business no doubt may have pecuniary value and commonly is protected by law against various unjustified injuries. But you cannot give it definiteness of contour by calling it a thing. It is a course of conduct and like other conduct is subject to substantial modification according to time and circumstances both in itself and in regard to what shall justify doing it harm. I cannot understand the notion that it would be unconstitutional to authorize boycotts and the like in aid of the employees' or the employers' interest by statute when the same result has been reached constitutionally without statute by Courts with whom I agree. In this case it does not even appear that the business was not created under the laws as they now are.

I think further that the selection of the class of employers and employees for special treatment, dealing with both sides alike, is beyond criticism on principles often asserted by this Court. And especially I think that without legalizing the conduct complained of the extraordinary relief by injunction may be denied to the class. Legislation may begin where an evil begins. If, as many intelligent people believe, there is more danger that the injunction will be abused in labor cases than elsewhere I can feel no doubt of the power of the legislature to deny it in such cases. . . .

I must add one general consideration. There is nothing that I more deprecate than the use of the Fourteenth Amendment beyond the absolute compulsion of its words to prevent the making of social experiments that an important part of the community desires, in the insulated chambers afforded by the several States, even though the experiments may seem futile or even noxious to me and to those whose judgment I most respect. I agree with the more elaborate expositions of my brothers PITNEY and BRANDEIS and in their conclusion that the judgment should be affirmed.

(PITNEY, J., delivered a dissenting opinion.

in which CLARKE, J., concurred. BRANDEIS, J., also delivered a dissenting opinion.)

445. DUPLEX PRINTING PRESS COMPANY v. DEERING
254 U. S. 443
1921

Appeal from the U.S. circuit court of appeals for the second district. Suit to enjoin an alleged unlawful conspiracy in restraint of trade. The facts are stated in the opinion. This is the leading case on the interpretation of the labor clauses of the Clayton Anti-Trust Act of 1914. See Doc. No. 403.

PITNEY, J. This was a suit in equity brought by appellant in the District Court for the Southern District of New York for an injunction to restrain a course of conduct carried on by defendants in that district . . . in maintaining a boycott against the products of complainant's factory, in furtherance of a conspiracy to injure and destroy its good will, trade, and business,—especially to obstruct and destroy its interstate trade. . . .

The suit was begun before but brought to hearing after, the passage of the Clayton Act of October 15, 1914. Both parties invoked the provisions of the later act, and both Courts created them as applicable. Complainant relied also upon the common law; but we shall deal first with the effect of the acts of Congress.

The facts . . . may be summarized as follows: Complainant conducts its business on the "open-shop" policy, without discrimination against either union or nonunion men. The individual defendants and the local organization of which they are the representatives are affiliated with the International Association of Machinists . . . and are united in a combination, . . . having the object of compelling complainant to unionize its factory. . . .

In August, 1913 . . . the International Association called a strike at complainant's factory in Battle Creek, as a result of which union machinists to the number of about eleven in the factory, and three who supervised the erection of presses in the field, left complainant's employ. . . . The acts complained of made up the details of an elaborate program adopted and carried out by defendants in their organizations in and

about the city of New York as part of a country-wide program adopted by the International Association, for the purpose of enforcing a boycott of complainant's product. . . .

All the judges of the Circuit Court of Appeals concurred in the view that defendants' conduct consisted essentially of efforts to render it impossible for complainant to carry on any commerce in printing presses between Michigan and New York; and that defendants had agreed to do and were endeavoring to accomplish the very thing pronounced unlawful by this court in *Lowe* v. *Lawler*. The judges also agreed that the interference with interstate commerce was such as ought to be enjoined, unless the Clayton Act of October 15, 1914, forbade such injunction. . . .

That . . . complainant has sustained substantial damage to its interstate trade,—and is threatened with further and irreparable loss and damage in the future,—is proved by clear and undisputed evidence. Hence, the right to an injunction is clear if the threatened loss is due to a violation of the Sherman Act, as amended by the Clayton Act. . . .

The substance of the matters here complained of is an interference with complainant's interstate trade intended to have coercive effect upon complainant, and produced by what is commonly known as a "secondary boycott"; that is, a combination not merely to refrain from dealing with complainant, or to advise or by peaceful means persuade complainant's customers to refrain ("primary boycott") but to exercise coercive pressure. . . .

As we shall see, the recognized distinction between a primary and a secondary boycott is material to be considered upon the question of a proper construction of the Clayton Act. . . .

The principal reliance is upon sec. 20 (of Clayton Act). . . . The second paragraph declares that "no such restraining order or injunction" shall prohibit certain conduct specified,—manifestly still referring to a "case between an employer and an employee, . . . involving, or growing out of, a dispute concerning terms or conditions of employment", as designated in the first paragraph. It is very clear that the restriction upon the use of the injunction is in favor only of those concerned as parties to such a dispute as is described. . . .

The majority of the Circuit Court of Appeals appear to have entertained the view that the words "employers and employees" as used in sec. 20 should be treated as referring to "the business class or clan to which the parties ligitant respectively belong;" and that, . . . sec. 20 operated to permit members of the Machinists' Union elsewhere—some 60,000 in number,—although standing in no relation of employment under complainant, past, present, or prospective, to make that dispute their own, and proceed to instigate sympathetic strikes, picketing, and boycotting against employers wholly unconnected with complainant's factory, and having relations with complainant only in the way of purchasing its product in the ordinary course of interstate commerce, —and this where there was no dispute between such employers and their employees respecting terms or conditions of employment.

We deem this construction altogether inadmissible. . . .

The emphasis placed on the words "lawful" and "lawfully," "peaceful" and "peacefully", and the references to the dispute and the parties to it, strongly rebut a legislative intent to confer a general immunity for conduct violative of the Anti-Trust laws, or otherwise unlawful. The subject of the boycott is dealt with specifically in the "ceasing to patronize" provision, and by the clear force of the language employed the exemption is limited to pressure exerted upon a "party to such dispute" by means of "peaceful and *lawful*" influence upon neutrals. There is nothing here to justify defendants or the organizations they represent in using either threats or persuasion to bring about strikes or a cessation of work on the part of employees of complainant's customers or prospective customers, or of the trucking company employed by the customers, with the object of compelling such customers to withdraw or refrain from commercial relations with complainant, and of thereby constraining complainant to yield the matter in dispute. To instigate a sympathetic strike in aid of a secondary boycott cannot be deemed "peaceful and lawful" persuasion. . . .

The question whether the bill legalized a secondary boycott having been raised (in the House), it was emphatically and unequivocally answered . . . in the negative. The subject . . . was under consideration when the bill was framed, and the section as reported was carefully prepared with the settled purpose of excluding the secondary boycott, and confining boycotting to the parties to the dispute, allowing parties to cease to patronize and to ask others to cease to patronize a party to the dispute; it was the opinion of the committee that it did not legalize the secondary boycott; it was not their purpose to authorize such a boycott; not a member of the committee would vote to do so; clarifying amendment was unnecessary; the section as reported expressed the real purpose so well that it could not be tortured into a meaning authorizing the secondary boycott. . . .

There should be an injunction against defendants and the associations represented by them.

Justices BRANDEIS, HOLMES and CLARKE dissenting.

446. BALZAC v. PORTO RICO
258 U. S. 298
1922

Error to the supreme court of Porto Rico. Balzac, an editor, was convicted for criminal libel without a jury trial. He appealed on the ground that the Sixth Amendment to the Federal Constitution guaranteed him the right of trial by jury. This case involved the question of the application of such procedural rights to the inhabitants of our insular possessions. For the constitutional problems involved, see references under *Downes* v. *Bidwell,* Doc. No. 352.

TAFT, C. J. . . . We have now to inquire whether that part of the Sixth Amendment to the Constitution, which requires that, in all criminal prosecutions, the accused shall enjoy the right to a speedy and public trial, by an impartial jury of the State and district wherein the crime shall have been committed, which district shall have been previously ascertained by law, applies to Porto Rico. Another provision on the subject is in Article III of the Constitution providing that the trial of all crimes, except in cases of impeachment, shall be by jury; and such trial shall be held in the State where the said crimes shall have been committed; but, when not committed within any State, the trial shall be at such place or places as the Congress may by law have directed. The Seventh Amendment of the Constitution provides that in suits at common law, where the value in controversy shall exceed twenty dollars, the right of trial by jury shall be preserved. It is well settled that these provisions for jury trial in criminal and civil cases apply to the territories of the United States. . . . But it is just as clearly settled that they do not apply to territory belonging to the United States, which has not been incorporated into the Union. *Hawaii* v. *Mankichi*, 190 U. S. 197, *Dorr* v. *United States*, 195 U. S. 138. It was further settled in *Downes* v. *Bidwell*, 182 U. S. 244, and confirmed by *Dorr* v. *United States*, 195 U. S. 138, R. 808, that neither the Philippines nor Porto Rico was territory which had been incorporated in the Union or become a part of the United States, as distinguished from merely belonging to it; and that the acts giving temporary governments to the Philippines, 32 Stat. 691, and to Porto Rico, 31 Stat. 77, had no such effect. The *Insular Cases* revealed much diversity of opinion in this court as to the constitutional status of the territory acquired by the Treaty of Paris ending the Spanish War, but the *Dorr Case* shows that the opinion of Mr. Justice White of the majority, in *Downes* v. *Bidwell*, has become the settled law of the court. The conclusion of this court in the *Dorr Case*, 195 U. S. 149, was as follows:

"We conclude that the power to govern territory, implied in the right to acquire it, and given to Congress in the Constitution in Article IV, § 3, to whatever other limitations it may be subject, the extent of which must be decided as questions arise, does not require that body to enact for ceded territory, not made a part of the United States by Congressional action, a system of laws which shall include the right of trial by jury, and that the Constitution does not, without legislation and of its own force, carry such right to territory so situated."

The question before us, therefore, is: Has Congress, since the Foraker Act of April 12, 1900, enacted legislation incorporating Porto Rico into the Union? Counsel for the plaintiff in error give, in their brief, an extended list of acts, to which we shall refer later, which they urge as indicating a purpose to make the island a part of the United States, but they chiefly rely on the Organic Act of Porto Rico of March 2, 1917, known as the Jones Act.

The act is entitled "An Act to provide a civil government for Porto Rico, and for other purposes." It does not indicate by its title that it has a purpose to incorporate the island into the Union. It does not contain any clause which declares such purpose or effect. While this is not conclusive, it strongly tends to show that Congress did not have such an intention. Few questions have been the subject of such discussion and dispute in our country as the status of our territory acquired from Spain in 1899. The division between the political parties in respect to it, the diversity of the views of the members of this court in regard to its constitutional aspects, and the constant recurrence of the subject in the Houses of Congress, fixed the attention of all on the future relation of this acquired territory to the United States. Had Congress intended to take the important step of changing the treaty status of Porto Rico by incorporating it into the Union, it is reasonable to suppose that it would have done so by the plain declaration, and would not have left it to mere inference. Before the question became acute at the close of the Spanish War, the distinction between acquisition and incorporation was not regarded as important, or at least it was not fully understood and had not aroused great controversy. Before that, the purpose of Congress might well be a matter of mere inference from various legislative acts; but in these latter days, incorporation is not to be assumed without express declaration, or an implication so strong as to exclude any other view. . . .

The section of the Jones Act which counsel press on us is § 5. This in effect declares that all persons who under the Foraker Act were made citizens of Porto Rico and certain other residents shall become citizens of the United States, unless they prefer not to become such, in which case they are to declare such preference within six months, and thereafter they lose certain rights under the new government. . . . When Porto Ricans passed from under the government of Spain, they lost the protection of that government as subjects of the King of Spain, a title by which they had been known for centuries. They had a right to expect, in passing under the dominion of the United States, a status entitling them to the protection of their new sovereign. . . . It became a yearning of the Porto Ricans to be American citizens, therefore, and this act gave them the boon. What additional rights did it give them? It enabled them to move into the continental United States and becoming residents of any State there to enjoy every right of any other citizen of the United States, civil, social and political. A citizen of the Philippines must be naturalized before he can settle and vote in this country. Not so the Porto Rican under the Organic Act of 1917.

In Porto Rico, however, the Porto Rican can not insist upon the right of trial by jury, except as his own representatives in his legislature shall confer it on him. The citizen of the United States living in Porto Rico can not there enjoy a right of trial by jury under the Federal Constitution, any more than the Porto Rican. It is locality that is determinative of the application of the Constitution, in such matters as judicial procedure, and not the status of the people who live in it.

It is true that, in the absence of other and countervailing evidence, a law of Congress or a provision in a treaty acquiring territory, declaring an intention to confer political and civil rights on the inhabitants of the new lands as American citizens, may be properly interpreted to mean an incorporation of it into the Union, as in the case of Louisiana and Alaska. This was one of the chief grounds upon which this court placed its conclusion that Alaska had been incorporated in the Union, in *Rassmussen* v. *United States*, 197 U. S. 516. But Alaska was a very different case from that of Porto Rico. It was an enormous territory, very sparsely settled and offering opportunity for immigration and settlement by American citizens. It was on the American Continent and within easy reach of the then United States. It involved none of the difficulties which incorporation of the Philippines and Porto Rico presents, and one of them is in the very matter of trial by jury. This court refers to the difficulties in *Dorr* v. *United States*, 195 U. S. 138, 148:

"If the right to trial by jury were a fundamental right which goes wherever the jurisdiction of the United States extends, or if Congress, in framing laws for outlying territory belonging to the United States was obliged to establish that system by affirmative legislation, it would follow that, no matter what the needs or capacities of the people, trial by jury, and in no other way, must be forthwith established, although the result may be to work injustice and provoke disturbance rather than to aid the orderly administration of justice. . . . Again, if the United States shall acquire by treaty the cession of territory having an established system of jurisprudence, where jury trials are unknown, but a method of fair and orderly trial prevails under an acceptable and long-established code, the preference of the people must be disregarded, their established customs ignored and they themselves coerced to accept, in advance of incorporation into the United States, a system of trial unknown to them and unsuited to their needs. We do not think it was intended, in giving power to Congress to make regulations for the territories, to hamper its exercise with this condition."

The jury system needs citizens trained to the exercise of the responsibilities of jurors. In common-law countries centuries of tradition have prepared a conception of the impartial attitude jurors must assume. The jury system postulates a conscious duty of participation in the machinery of justice which it is hard for people not brought up in fundamentally popular government at once to acquire. One of its greatest benefits is in the security it gives the people that they, as jurors actual or possible, being a part of the judicial system of the country can prevent its arbitrary use or abuse. Congress has thought that a people like the Filipinos or the Porto Ricans, trained to a complete judicial system which knows no juries, living in compact and ancient communities, with definitely formed customs and political conceptions, should be permitted themselves to determine how far they wish to adopt this institution of Anglo-Saxon origin, and when. . . . We cannot find any intention to depart from this policy in making Porto Ricans American citizens. . . .

We need not dwell on another consideration which requires us not lightly to infer, from acts thus easily explained on other grounds, an intention to incorporate in the Union these distant ocean communities of a different origin and language from those of our continental people. Incorporation has always been a step, and an important one, leading to statehood. Without, in the slightest degree, intimating an opinion as to the wisdom

of such a policy, for that is not our province, it is reasonable to assume that when such a step is taken it will be begun and taken by Congress deliberately and with a clear declaration of purpose, and not left a matter of mere inference or construction. . . .

On the whole, therefore, we find no features in the Organic Act of Porto Rico of 1917 from which we can infer the purpose of Congress to incorporate Porto Rico into the United States with the consequences which would follow. . . .

The judgments of the Supreme Court of Porto Rico are affirmed.

Mr. Justice HOLMES concurs in the result.

447. NAVAL LIMITATION TREATY
Signed February 6, 1922
Proclaimed August 21, 1923

(U. S. Statutes at Large, Vol. XXXXIII, p. 1655 ff.)

December 14, 1920, Senator Borah introduced a resolution requesting the President to call an international conference for the reduction of naval armaments. The resolution was appended to the Naval Appropriations Bill for 1921. In accordance with this resolution President Harding invited the principal powers to a conference to consider not only naval disarmaments, but questions relating to the Pacific as well. The conference convened in Washington November 12, 1921, and Secretary Hughes presented the American program for disarmament. That program was embodied in the Naval Limitation Treaty, given below. On the Washington Conference see R. L. Buell, *The Washington Conference;* Y. Ichihashi, *The Washington Conference and After;* G. H. Blakeslee, *The Pacific Area,* World Peace Foundation Pamphlets, Vol. XII, no. 3; S. F. Bemis, ed. *American Secretaries of State,* Vol. X, p. 242 ff. The *Report of the Conference* is in *Senate Document 126,* 67th Congress, 2nd Session. See also, Docs. No. 448, 449.

The United States of America, the British Empire, France, Italy and Japan;

Desiring to contribute to the maintenance of the general peace, and to reduce the burdens of competition in armament;

Have resolved, with a view to accomplishing these purposes, to conclude a treaty to limit their respective naval armament, and to that end have appointed as their Plenipotentiaries; . . .

Who, having communicated to each other

their respective full powers, found to be in good and due form, have agreed as follows:

CHAPTER I

ART. I. The Contracting Powers agree to limit their respective naval armament as provided in the present Treaty.

ART. II. The Contracting Powers may retain respectively the capital ships which are specified in Chapter II, Part 1. On the coming into force of the present Treaty, but subject to the following provisions of this Article, all other capital ships, built or building, of the United States, the British Empire and Japan shall be disposed of as prescribed in Chapter II, Part 2.

In addition to the capital ships specified in Chapter II, Part 1, the United States may complete and retain two ships of the *West Virginia* class now under construction. On the completion of these two ships the *North Dakota* and *Delaware* shall be disposed of as prescribed in Chapter II, Part 2.

The British Empire may, in accordance with the replacement table in Chapter II, Part 3, construct two new capital ships not exceeding 35,000 tons (35,560 metric tons) standard displacement each. On the completion of the said two ships the *Thunderer, King George V, Ajax* and *Centurion* shall be disposed of as prescribed in Chapter II, Part 2.

ART. III. Subject to the provisions of

Article II, the Contracting Powers shall abandon their respective capital ship building programs, and no new capital ships shall be constructed or acquired by any of the Contracting Powers except replacement tonnage which may be constructed or acquired as specified in Chapter II, Part 3.

Ships which are replaced in accordance with Chapter II, Part 3, shall be disposed of as prescribed in Part 2 of that Chapter.

ART. IV. The total capital ship replacement tonnage of the Contracting Powers shall not exceed in standard displacement, for the United States 525,000 tons (533,400 metric tons); for the British Empire 525,000 tons (533,400 metric tons); for France 175,000 tons (177,800 metric tons); for Italy 175,000 tons (177,800 metric tons); for Japan 315,000 tons (320,040 metric tons).

ART. V. No capital ship exceeding 35,000 tons (35,560 metric tons) standard displacement shall be acquired by, or constructed by, for, or within the jurisdiction of, any of the Contracting Powers.

ART. VI. No capital ship of any of the Contracting Powers shall carry a gun with a calibre in excess of 16 inches (405 millimetres).

ART. VII. The total tonnage for aircraft carriers of each of the Contracting Powers shall not exceed in standard displacement, for the United States 135,000 tons (137,160 metric tons); for the British Empire 135,000 tons (137,160 metric tons); for France 60,000 tons (60,960 metric tons); for Italy 60,000 tons (60,960 metric tons); for Japan 81,000 tons (82,296 metric tons). . . .

ART. IX. No aircraft carrier exceeding 27,-000 tons (27,432 metric tons) standard displacement shall be acquired by, or constructed by, for or within the jurisdiction of, any of the Contracting Powers. . . .

ART. XI. No vessel of war exceeding 10,000 tons (10,160 metric tons) standard displacement, other than a capital ship or aircraft carrier, shall be acquired by, or constructed by, for, or within the jurisdiction of, any of the Contracting Powers. Vessels not specifically built as fighting ships nor taken in time of peace under government control for fighting purposes, which are employed on fleet duties or as troop transports or in some other way for the purpose of assisting in the prosecution of hostilities otherwise than as fighting ships, shall not be within the limitations of this Article.

ART. XII. No vessel of war of any of the Contracting Powers, hereafter laid down, other than a capital ship, shall carry a gun with a calibre in excess of 8 inches (203 millimetres).

ART. XIII. Except as provided in Article IX, no ship designated in the present Treaty to be scrapped may be reconverted into a vessel of war.

ART. XIV. No preparations shall be made in merchant ships in time of peace for the installation of warlike armaments for the purpose of converting such ships into vessels of war, . . .

ART. XIX. The United States, the British Empire and Japan agree that the status quo at the time of the signing of the present Treaty, with regard to fortifications and naval bases, shall be maintained in their respective territories and possessions specified hereunder:

(1) The insular possessions which the United States now holds or may hereafter acquire in the Pacific Ocean, except (a) those adjacent to the coast of the United States, Alaska and Panama Canal Zone, not including the Aleutian Islands, and (b) the Hawaiian Islands;

(2) Hongkong and the insular possessions which the British Empire now holds or may hereafter acquire in the Pacific Ocean, east of the meridian of 110° east longitude, except (a) those adjacent to the coast of Canada, (b) the Commonwealth of Australia and its Territories, and (c) New Zealand;

(3) The following insular territories and possessions of Japan in the Pacific Ocean, to wit: the Kurile Islands, the Bonin Islands, Amami-Oshima, the Loochoo Islands, Formosa and the Pescadores, and any insular territories or possessions in the Pacific Ocean which Japan may hereafter acquire.

The maintenance of the status quo under the foregoing provisions implies that no new fortifications or naval bases shall be established in the territories and possessions specified; that no measures shall be taken to increase the existing naval facilities for the repair and maintenance of naval forces, and that no increase shall be made in the coast defences of the territories and possessions above specified. This restriction, however, does not preclude such repair and replacement of worn-out weapons and equipment as is customary in naval and military establishments in time of peace. . . .

CHAPTER II
PART 1.
CAPITAL SHIPS WHICH MAY BE RETAINED BY THE CONTRACTING POWERS
[Lists]

PART 2.
RULES FOR SCRAPPING VESSELS OF WAR.

The following rules shall be observed for the scrapping of vessels of war which are to be disposed of in accordance with Articles II and III.

I. A vessel to be scrapped must be placed in such condition that it cannot be put to combatant use.

II. This result must be finally effected in any one of the following ways:
  (a) Permanent sinking of the vessel;
  (b) Breaking the vessel up.
This shall always involve the destruction or removal of all machinery, boilers and armour, and all deck, side and bottom plating;
  (c) Converting the vessel to target use exclusively. . . . Not more than one capital ship may be retained for this purpose at one time by any of the Contracting Powers. . . .

PART 3.
SEC. I.
RULES FOR REPLACEMENT.

(a) Capital ships and aircraft carriers twenty years after the date of their completion may, except as otherwise provided in Article VIII and in the tables in Section II of this Part, be replaced by new construction, but within the limits prescribed in Article IV and Article VII. The keels of such new construction may, except as otherwise provided in Article VIII and in the tables in Section II of this Part, be laid down not earlier than seventeen years from the date of completion of the tonnage to be replaced, provided, however, that no capital ship tonnage, with the exception of the ships referred to in the third paragraph of Article II, and replacement tonnage specifically mentioned in Section II of this Part, shall be laid down until ten years from November 12, 1921. . . .

CHAPTER III

ART. XXIII. The present Treaty shall remain in force until December 31st, 1936, and in case none of the Contracting Powers shall have given notice two years before that date of its intention to terminate the Treaty, it shall continue in force until the expiration of two years from the date on which notice of termination shall be given by one of the Contracting Powers. . . .

448. THE FOUR-POWER TREATY
December 13, 1921. In Force, August 17, 1923
(*U. S. Statutes at Large,* Vol. XXXXIII, p. 1646 ff.)

This was one of the treaties that emerged from the Washington Arms Conference. For references, see under Doc. No. 447.

Treaty between the United States, the British Empire, France and Japan relating to their Insular Possessions and Insular Dominions in the Region of the Pacific Ocean

The United States of America, the British Empire, France and Japan,

With a view to the preservation of the general peace and the maintenance of their rights in relation to their insular possessions and insular dominions in the region of the Pacific Ocean,

Have determined to conclude a treaty to this effect and have appointed as their plenipotentiaries: . . .

Who, having communicated their full powers, found in good and due form, have agreed as follows:

I. The high contracting parties agree as between themselves to respect their rights in relation to their insular possessions and insular dominions in the region of the Pacific Ocean.

If there should develop between any of the

high contracting parties a controversy arising out of any Pacific question and involving their said rights which is not satisfactorily settled by diplomacy and is likely to affect the harmonious accord now happily subsisting between them, they shall invite the other high contracting parties to a joint conference to which the whole subject will be referred for consideration and adjustment.

II. If the said rights are threatened by the aggressive action of any other power, the high contracting parties shall communicate with one another fully and frankly in order to arrive at an understanding as to the most efficient measures to be taken, jointly or separately, to meet the exigencies of the particular situation.

III. This treaty shall remain in force for 10 years from the time it shall take effect, and after the expiration of said period it shall continue to be in force subject to the right of any of the high contracting parties to terminate it upon 12 months' notice.

IV. This treaty shall be ratified as soon as possible in accordance with the constitutional methods of the high contracting parties and shall take effect on the deposit of ratifications, which shall take place at Washington, and thereupon the agreement between Great Britain and Japan, which was concluded at London on July 13, 1911, shall terminate. . . .

449. THE NINE-POWER TREATY
February 6, 1922. Proclaimed August 5, 1925
(*U.S. Statutes at Large*, Vol. XXXXIV, p. 2113 ff.)

This treaty, one of several to emerge from the Washington Conference, apparently gave international sanction to the traditional Open Door policy toward China. The principles which this treaty attempted to establish were, however, shortly violated by Japan. A number of other treaties and resolutions concerning China were adopted by the Conference. Of these the most important were: a treaty relating to the Chinese tariff; an adjustment of the Shantung controversy; and a resolution providing for a commission to study the problem of extraterritoriality in China. For references, see Doc. No. 447.

A Treaty . . . relating to principles and policies to be followed in matters concerning China.

The United States of America, Belgium, the British Empire, China, France, Italy, Japan, the Netherlands and Portugal:

Desiring to adopt a policy designed to stabilize conditions in the Far East, to safeguard the rights and interests of China, and to promote intercourse between China and the other Powers upon the basis of equality of opportunity;

Have resolved to conclude a treaty for that purpose and to that end have appointed as their respective Plenipotentiaries: . . .

Who, having communicated to each other their full powers, found to be in good and due form, have agreed as follows:

I. The Contracting Powers, other than China, agree:

(1) To respect the sovereignty, the independence, and the territorial and administrative integrity of China;

(2) To provide the fullest and most unembarrassed opportunity to China to develop and maintain for herself an effective and stable government;

(3) To use their influence for the purpose of effectually establishing and maintaining the principle of equal opportunity for the commerce and industry of all nations throughout the territory of China;

(4) To refrain from taking advantage of conditions in China in order to seek special rights or privileges which would abridge the rights of subjects or citizens of friendly States, and from countenancing action inimical to the security of such States.

II. The Contracting Powers agree not to enter into any treaty, agreement, arrangement, or understanding, either with one another, or, individually or collectively, with any Power or Powers, which would infringe or impair the principles stated in Article I.

III. With a view to applying more effectually the principles of the Open Door or equality of opportunity in China for the trade and industry of all nations, the Contracting Powers, other than China, agree that they will not seek nor support their respective nationals, in seeking

(a) any arrangement which might purport to establish in favor of their interests any general superiority of rights with respect to commercial or economic development in any designated region of China.

(b) any such monopoly or preference as would deprive the nationals of any other Power of the right of undertaking any legitimate trade or industry in China, or of participating with the Chinese Government, or with any local authority, in any category of public enterprise, or which by reason of its scope, duration or geographical extent is calculated to frustrate the practical application of the principle of equal opportunity.

It is understood that the foregoing stipulations of this Article are not to be so construed as to prohibit the acquisition of such properties or rights as may be necessary to the conduct of a particular commercial, industrial, or financial undertaking or to the encouragement of invention and research.

China undertakes to be guided by the principles stated in the foregoing stipulations of this Article in dealing with applications for economic rights and privileges from Governments and nationals of all foreign countries, whether parties to the present Treaty or not.

IV. The Contracting Powers agree not to support any agreements by their respective nationals with each other designed to create Spheres of Influence or to provide for the enjoyment of mutually exclusive opportunities in designated parts of Chinese territory.

V. China agrees that, throughout the whole of the railways in China, she will not exercise or permit unfair discrimination of any kind. In particular there shall be no discrimination whatever, direct or indirect, in respect of charges or of facilities on the ground of the nationality of passengers or the countries from which or to which they are proceeding, or the origin or ownership of goods or the country from which or to which they are consigned, or the nationality or ownership of the ship or other means of conveying such passengers or goods before or after their transport on the Chinese railways.

The Contracting Powers, other than China, assume a corresponding obligation in respect of any of the aforesaid railways over which they or their nationals are in a position to exercise any control in virtue of any concession, special agreement or otherwise.

VI. The Contracting Powers, other than China, agree fully to respect China's rights as a neutral in time of war to which China is not a party; and China declares that when she is a neutral she will observe the obligations of neutrality.

VII. The Contracting Powers agree that, whenever a situation arises which in the opinion of any one of them involves the application of the stipulations of the present Treaty, and renders desirable discussion of such application, there shall be full and frank communication between the Contracting Powers concerned.

VIII. Powers not signatory to the present Treaty, which have Governments recognized by the Signatory Powers and which have treaty relations with China, shall be invited to adhere to the present Treaty. To this end the Government of the United States will make the necessary communications to non-signatory Powers and will inform the Contracting Powers of the replies received. Adherence by any Power shall become effective on receipt of notice thereof by the Government of the United States.

IX. The present Treaty shall be ratified by the Contracting Powers in accordance with their respective constitutional methods and shall take effect on the date of the deposit of all the ratifications, which shall take place at Washington as soon as possible. The Government of the United States will transmit to the other Contracting Powers a certified copy of the procès-verbal of the deposit of ratifications.

The present Treaty, of which the French and English texts are both authentic, shall remain deposited in the archives of the Government of the United States, and duly certified copies thereof shall be transmitted by that Government to the other Contracting Powers.

In faith whereof the above-named Plenipotentiaries have signed the Present Treaty.

Done at the City of Washington the sixth day of February One Thousand Nine Hundred and Twenty-Two.

450. WOLFF PACKING CO. v. COURT OF INDUSTRIAL RELATIONS
OF KANSAS
262 U. S. 522
1923

Writ of Error to Supreme Court of Kansas.

TAFT, C. J. This case involves the validity of the Court of Industrial Relations Act of Kansas (1920). The act declares the following to be affected with a public interest: First, manufacture and preparation of food for human consumption; . . . fifth, public utilities and common carriers. The act vests an industrial court of three judges with power, upon its own initiative or on complaint, to summon the parties and hear any dispute over wages or other terms of employment in any such industry, and if it shall find the peace and health of the public imperiled by such controversy, it is required to make findings and fix the wages and other terms for the future conduct of the industry. . . .

The Charles Wolff Packing Co., the plaintiff in error, is a corporation of Kansas engaged in slaughtering hogs and cattle and preparing the meat for sale and shipment. . . .

In January, 1921, the president and secretary of the Meat Cutters Union filed a complaint with the Industrial Court against the Packing Company, respecting the wages its employees were receiving. The Company appeared and answered and a hearing was had. The Court made findings, including one of an emergency, and an order as to wages, increasing them over the figures to which the company had recently reduced them. The Company refused to comply with the order, and the Industrial Court then instituted mandamus proceedings in the Supreme Court to compel compliance. . . . The Industrial Court conceded that the Wolff Company could not operate on the schedule fixed without a loss, but relied on the statement by its president that he hoped for more prosperous times.

The Packing Company brings this case here on the ground that the validity of the Industrial Court Act was upheld, although as in conflict with the provision of the 14th Amendment that no State shall deprive any person of liberty or property without due process of law. . . .

The necessary postulate of the Industrial Court Act is that the state, representing the people, is so much interested in their peace, health, and comfort, that it may compel those engaged in the manufacture of food and clothing, and the production of fuel, whether owners or workers, to continue in their business and employment on terms fixed by an agency of the state, if they cannot agree. Under the construction adopted by the state supreme court, the act gives the Industrial Court authority to permit the owner or employer to go out of the business if he shows that he can only continue on the terms fixed at such heavy loss that collapse will follow; but this privilege, under the circumstances, is generally illusory. A laborer dissatisfied with his wages is permitted to quit, but he may not agree with his fellows to quit, or combine with others to induce them to quit.

These qualifications do not change the essence of the act. It curtails the right of the employer, on the one hand, and that of the employee, on the other, to contract about his affairs. This is part of the liberty of the individual protected by the guaranty of the due process clause of the 14th Amendment. . . .

It is manifest from an examination of the cases cited . . . that the mere declaration by a legislature that a business is affected with a public interest is not conclusive of the question whether its attempted regulation on that ground is justified. The circumstances of its alleged change from the status of a private business and its freedom from regulation into one in which the public have come to have an interest, are always a subject of judicial inquiry. . . .

It has never been supposed, since the adoption of the Constitution, that the business of the butcher, or the baker, the tailor, the woodchopper, the mining operator, or the miner, was clothed with such a public interest that the price of his product or his wages could be fixed by state regulation. . . .

To say that a business is clothed with a public interest is not to determine what regulation is permissible in view of the private rights of the owner. The extent to which an inn or cab system may be regulated may differ widely from that allowable as to a railroad or other common carrier. It is not a matter of legislative discretion solely. It depends upon the nature of the business, on the feature which touches the public, and on the abuses reasonably to be feared. To say that business is clothed with a public interest is not to import that the public may take over its entire management and run it at the expense of the owner. The extent to which regulation may reasonably go varies with different kinds of business. The regulation of rates to avoid monopoly, is one thing. The regulation of wages is another. A business may be of such character that only the first is permissible, while another may involve such a possible danger of monopoly on the one hand, and such disaster from stoppage on the other, that both come within the public concern and power of regulation.

If, as, in effect, contended by counsel for the state, the common callings are clothed with a public interest by a mere legislative declaration, which necessarily authorizes full and comprehensive regulation within legislative discretion, there must be a revolution in the relation of government to general business. This will be running the public-interest argument into the ground. . . . It will be impossible to reconcile such result with the freedom of contract and of labor secured by the 14th Amendment.

This brings to the nature and purpose of the regulation under the Industrial Court Act. The avowed object is continuity of food, clothing, and fuel supply. By sec. 6 reasonable continuity and efficiency of the industries specified are declared to be necessary for the public peace, health, and general welfare, and all are forbidden to hinder, limit, or suspend them. Sec. 7 gives the Industrial Court power, in case of controversy between employers and workers which may endanger the continuity or efficiency of service, to bring the employer and employee before it, and after hearing and investigation, to fix the terms and conditions between them. The employer is bound by this act to pay the wages fixed; and while the worker is not required to work at the wages fixed, he is forbidden on penalty of fine or imprisonment, to strike against them, and thus is compelled to give up that means of putting himself on an equality with his employer which action in concert with his fellows gives him. . . .

The minutely detailed government supervision, including that of their relations to their employees, to which the railroads of the country have been gradually subjected by Congress through its power over interstate commerce, furnishes no precedent for regulation of the business of the plaintiff, whose classification as public is, at the best, doubtful. It is not too much to say that the ruling in *Wilson* v. *New* went to the borderline, although it concerned an interstate common carrier in the presence of a nation-wide emergency and the possibility of great disaster. Certainly there is nothing to justify extending the drastic regulation sustained in that exceptional case to the one before us.

We think that Industrial Court Act . . . in conflict with the 14th Amendment. Judgement reversed.

451. ADKINS v. CHILDREN'S HOSPITAL
261 U. S. 525
1923

Appeal from the Court of Appeals for the District of Columbia. Suit to enjoin the Wage Board for the District of Columbia from enforcing its orders fixing minimum wages for women under authority of an act of Congress of September 19, 1918. The statute authorized the Board to ascertain and declare standards of minimum wages for women and minors adequate to the cost of living and to maintain them in health and protect their morals. The Court of Appeals affirmed decrees granting the injunction. See *The Su-* *preme Court and Minimum Wage Legislation*, pub. by the National Consumers' League.

SUTHERLAND, J. The question presented for determination by these appeals is the constitutionality of the Act of September 19, 1918, providing for the fixing of minimum wages for women and children in the District of Columbia. . . .

It is declared that the purposes of the act

are "to protect the women and minors of the District from conditions detrimental to their health and morals, resulting from wages which are inadequate to maintain decent standards of living; and the act in each of its provisions and in its entirety, shall be interpreted to effectuate these purposes." . . .

The statute now under consideration is attacked upon the ground that it authorizes an unconstitutional interference with the freedom of contract included within the guaranties of the due process clause of the 5th Amendment. That the right to contract about one's affairs is a part of the liberty of the individual protected by this clause is settled by the decisions of this Court and is no longer open to question. Within this liberty are contracts of employment of labor. In making such contracts, generally speaking, the parties have an equal right to obtain from each other the best terms they can as the result of private bargaining. . . .

There is, of course, no such thing as absolute freedom of contract. It is subject to a great variety of restraints. But freedom of contract is, nevertheless, the general rule and restraint the exception; and the exercise of legislative authority to abridge it can be justified only by the existence of exceptional circumstances. Whether these circumstances exist in the present case constitutes the question to be answered. It will be helpful to this end to review some of the decisions where the interference has been upheld and consider the grounds upon which they rest. [Here an elaborate review of the decisions.] . . .

If now, in the light furnished by the foregoing exceptions to the general rule forbidding legislative interference with freedom of contract, we examine and analyze the statute in question, we shall see that it differs from them in every material respect. It is not a law dealing with any business charged with a public interest, or with public work, or to meet and tide over a temporary emergency. It has nothing to do with the character, methods or periods of wage payments. It does not prescribe hours of labor or conditions under which labor is to be done. It is not for the protection of persons under legal disability or for the prevention of fraud. It is simply and exclusively a price-fixing law, confined to adult women (for we are not now considering the provisions relating to minors), who are legally as capable of contracting for themselves as men. It forbids two parties having lawful capacity—under penalties as to the employer—to freely contract with one another in respect of the price for which one shall render service to the other in a purely private employment where both are willing, perhaps anxious, to agree, even though the consequence may be to oblige one to surrender a desirable engagement and the other to dispense with the services of a desirable employee. The price fixed by the board need have no relation to the capacity or earning power of the employee, the number of hours which may happen to constitute the day's work, the character of the place where the work is to be done, or the circumstances or surroundings of the employment; and, while it has no other basis to support its validity than the assumed necessities of the employee, it takes no account of any independent resources she may have. It is based wholly on the opinions of the members of the board and their advisers —perhaps an average of their opinions, if they do not precisely agree—as to what will be necessary to provide a living for a woman, keep her in health and preserve her morals. It applies to any and every occupation in the District, without regard to its nature or the character of the work.

The standard furnished by the statute for the guidance of the board is so vague as to be impossible of practical application with any reasonable degree of accuracy. What is sufficient to supply the necessary cost of living for a woman worker and maintain her in good health and protect her morals is obviously not a precise or unvarying sum—not even approximately so. The amount will depend upon a variety of circumstances: the individual temperament, habits of thrift, care, ability to buy necessaries intelligently, and whether the woman live alone or with her family. To those who practice economy, a given sum will afford comfort, while to those of a contrary habit the same sum will be wholly inadequate. The coöperative economies of the family group are not taken into account though they constitute an important consideration in estimating the cost of living, for it is obvious that the individual expense will be less in the case of a member of a family than in the case of one living alone. The relation between earnings and morals is not capable of standardization. It cannot be shown that well paid women safeguard their morals more carefully than those who are poorly paid. Morality rests upon other considerations than wages; and there is, certainly, no such prevalent connection between the two as to justify a broad attempt to adjust the latter with reference to the former. As a means of safeguarding morals the attempted classification in our opinion, is without reasonable basis. No distinction can be made between women who work for others and those who do not; nor is there ground for distinction between women and men, for, certainly, if women require a minimum wage to preserve their morals men require it to preserve their honesty. For these reasons, and others which might be stated, the inquiry in respect of the necessary cost of living and of the income necessary to preserve health and morals, presents an individual and not a composite question, and must be answered for each individual considered by herself and not by a general formula prescribed by a statutory bureau. . . .

The law takes account of the necessities of only one party to the contract. It ignores the necessities of the employer by compelling him to pay not less than a certain sum, not only whether the employee is capable of earning it, but irrespective of the ability of his business to sustain the burden, generously leaving him, of course, the privilege of abandoning his business as an alternative for going on at a loss. Within the limits of the minimum sum, he is precluded, under penalty of fine and imprisonment, from adjusting compensation to the differing merits of his employees. It compels him to pay at least the sum fixed in any event, because the employee needs it, but requires no service of equivalent value from the employee. It therefore undertakes to solve but one-half of the problem. The other half is the establishment of a corresponding standard of efficiency, and this forms no part of the policy of the legislation, although in practice the former half without the latter must lead to ultimate failure, in accordance with the inexorable law that no one can continue indefinitely to take out more than he puts in without ultimately exhausting the supply. The law . . . takes no account of periods of stress and business depression, of crippling losses, which may leave the employer himself

without adequate means of livelihood. To the extent that the sum fixed exceeds the fair value of the services rendered, it amounts to a compulsory exaction from the employer for the support of a partially indigent person, for whose condition there rests upon him no peculiar responsibility, and therefore, in effect, arbitrarily shifts to his shoulders a burden which, if it belongs to anybody, belongs to society as a whole.

The feature of this statute which perhaps more than any other, puts upon it the stamp of invalidity is that it exacts from the employer an arbitrary payment for a purpose and upon a basis having no causal connection with his business, or the contract or the work the employee engages to do. The declared basis as already pointed out, is not the value of the service rendered but the extraneous circumstances that the employee needs to get a prescribed sum of money to insure her subsistence, health and morals. The ethical right of every worker, man or woman, to a living wage, may be conceded. One of the declared and important purposes of trade organizations is to secure it. And with that principle and with every legitimate effort to realize it in fact, no one can quarrel; but the fallacy of the proposed method of attaining it is that it assumes that every employer is bound at all events to furnish it. . . .

It is said that great benefits have resulted from the operation of such statutes, not alone in the District of Columbia but in the several States, where they have been in force. A mass of reports, opinions of special observers and students of the subject, and the like, has been brought before us in support of this statement, all of which we have found interesting, but only mildly persuasive. . . .

Finally, it may be said that if, in the interest of the public welfare, the police power may be invoked to justify the fixing of a minimum wage, it may, when the public welfare is thought to require it, be invoked to justify a maximum wage. The power to fix high wages connotes, by like reasoning, the power to fix low wages. If, in the face of the guaranties of the 5th Amendment, this form of legislation shall be legally justified, the field for the operation of the police power will have been widened to a great and dangerous degree. If, for example, in the opinion of future lawmakers, wages in the building trades shall become so high as to preclude people of ordinary means from building and owning homes, an authority which sustains the minimum wage will be invoked to support a maximum wage for building laborers and artisans, and the same argument which has been here urged to strip the employer of his constitutional liberty of contract in one direction will be utilized to strip the employee of his constitutional liberty of contract in the opposite direction. A wrong decision does not end with itself; it is a precedent, and, with the swing of sentiment, its bad influence may run from one extremity of the arc to the other.

It has been said that legislation of the kind now under review is required in the interest of social justice, for whose ends freedom of contract may lawfully be subjected to restraint. The liberty of the individual to do as he pleases, even in innocent matters, is not absolute. It must frequently yield to the common good, and the line beyond which the power of interference may not be pressed is neither definite nor unalterable but may be made to move, within limits not well defined, with changing need and circumstance. Any attempt to fix a rigid boundary would be unwise and futile. But, nevertheless, there are limits to the power, and when these have been passed, it becomes the plain duty of the courts in the proper exercise of their authority to so declare. To sustain the individual freedom of action contemplated by the Constitution, is not to strike down the common good but to exalt it; for surely the good of society as a whole cannot be better served than by the preservation against arbitrary restraint of the liberties of its constituent members.

It follows from what has been said that the act in question passes the limit prescribed by the Constitution, and, accordingly, the decrees of the court below are

Affirmed.

TAFT, C. J. dissenting. . . . Legislatures, in limiting freedom of contract between employee and employer by a minimum wage, proceed on the assumption that employees in the class receiving least pay are not upon a full level of equality of choice with their employer, and in their necessitous circumstances are prone to accept pretty much anything that is offered. They are peculiarly subject to the overreaching of the harsh and greedy employer. The evils of the sweating system and of the long hours and low wages which are characteristic of it are well known. Now, I agree that it is a disputable question in the field of political economy, how far a statutory requirement of maximum hours or minimum wages may be a useful remedy for these evils, and whether it may not make the case of the oppressed employee worse than it was before. But it is not the function of this court to hold Congressional acts invalid simply because they are passed to carry out economic views which the court believes to be unwise or unsound. . . .

The right of the legislature under the 5th and 14th Amendments to limit the hours of employment on the score of the health of the employee, it seems to me, has been firmly established. As to that, one would think, the line had been pricked out so that it has become a well-formulated rule. . . .

However, the opinion herein does not overrule the Bunting case in express terms, and therefore I assume that the conclusion in this case rests on the distinction between a minimum of wages and a maximum of hours in the limiting of liberty to contract. I regret to be at variance with the court as to the substance of this distinction. . . .

If it be said that long hours of labor have a more direct effect upon the health of the employee than the low wage, there is every respectable authority from close observers, disclosed in the record and in the literature on the subject, quoted at length in the briefs, that they are equally harmful in this regard; Congress took this view, and we cannot say it was not warranted in so doing. . . .

HOLMES, J., dissenting: The question in this case is the broad one, whether Congress can establish minimum rates of wages for women in the District of Columbia, with due provision for special circumstances, or whether we must say that Congress has no power to meddle with the matter at all. To me, notwithstanding the deference due to the prevailing judgement of the court, the power of Congress seems absolutely free from doubt. The end—to remove conditions leading to ill health, immorality, and the deterioration of the race—no one would deny to be within the scope of constitutional legislation. The means are means that have the approval of Congress, of many states, and of those governments

from which we have learned our greatest lessons. When so many intelligent persons who
have studied the matter more than any of us
can, have thought that the means are effective
and are worth the price, it seems to me impossible to deny that the belief reasonably
may be held by reasonable men. . . . But,
in the present instance, the only objection
that can be urged is founded in the vague
contours of the 5th Amendment, prohibiting
the depriving any person of liberty or of
property without due process of law. To that
I turn.

The earlier decisions upon the same words
in the 14th Amendment began within our
memory, and went no farther than an unpre-
tentious assertion of the liberty to follow the
ordinary callings. Later that innocuous generality was expanded into the dogma Liberty
of Contract. Contract is not specially mentioned in the text that we have to construe.
It is merely an example of doing what you
want to do, embodied in the word "liberty".
But pretty much all law, consists in forbidding men to do some things that they want to
do, and contract is no more exempt from law
than other acts. . . .
[Cites numerous examples.]

The criterion of constitutionality is not
whether we believe the law to be for the public good. We certainly cannot be prepared to
deny that a reasonable man reasonably might
have that belief, in view of the legislation of
Great Britain, Victoria, and a number of the
states of this Union. The belief is fortified
by a very remarkable collection of documents
submitted on behalf of the appellants, material here, I conceive, only as showing that
the belief reasonably may be held. . . .

452. TEAPOT DOME

Joint Resolution of Congress Respecting Prosecution for Cancellation of Oil Leases
February 8, 1924

(*U. S. Statutes at Large,* Vol. XXXXIII, p. 5)

The scandals of the Harding were no less shocking than those of the Grant administration. Of
all the revelations, none more profoundly stirred
the indignation of the nation than those concerning the leasing of rich oil reserves to private
interests by the Secretaries of the Navy and
of the Interior. These reserves, originally under
the control of the Department of the Navy,
were transferred to the Department of the Interior. In 1922, Secretary Albert B. Fall of this
Department secretly leased the Teapot Dome
reserve to Harry F. Sinclair, and the Elk Hill
reserve to E. L. Doheny. The civil suits instituted
for the cancellation of these leases were finally
successful; on the criminal charges arising from
corruption, Secretary Fall was convicted and
imprisoned. See, U.S. 68 Cong. 1st. Sess. *Sen.
Rep.* 794; M. E. Ravage, *Teapot Dome.*

*A joint resolution directing the President
to institute and prosecute suits to cancel certain leases of oil lands and incidental contracts, and for other purposes.*

Whereas it appears from evidence taken by
the Committee on Public Lands and Surveys
of the United States Senate that certain lease
of naval reserve No. 3, in the State of Wyoming, bearing date April 7, 1922, made in form
by the Government of the United States,
through Albert B. Fall, Secretary of the Interior, and Edwin Denby, Secretary of the
Navy, as lessor, to the Mammoth Oil Co., as
lessee, and that certain contract between the
Government of the United States and the Pan
American Petroleum & Transport Co., dated
April 25, 1922, signed by Edward C. Finney,
Acting Secretary of the Interior, and Edwin
Denby, Secretary of the Navy, relating
among other things to the construction of oil
tanks at Pearl Harbor, Territory of Hawaii,
and that certain lease of naval reserve No. 1,
in the State of California, bearing date December 11, 1922, made in form by the Government of the United States through Albert
B. Fall, Secretary of the Interior, and Edwin
Denby, Secretary of the Navy, as lessor, to
the Pan American Petroleum Co., as lessee,
were executed under circumstances indicating
fraud and corruption; and

Whereas the said leases and contract were
entered into without authority on the part of
the officers purporting to act in the execution
of the same for the United States and in violation of the laws of Congress; and

Whereas such leases and contract were made in defiance of the settled policy of the Government adhered to through three successive administrations, to maintain in the ground a great reserve supply of oil adequate to the needs of the Navy in any emergency threatening the national security: Therefore be it

Resolved, etc., That the said leases and contract are against the public interest and that the lands embraced therein should be recovered and held for the purpose to which they were dedicated; and

Resolved further, That the President of the United States be, and he hereby is, authorized and directed immediately to cause suit to be instituted and prosecuted for the annulment and cancellation of the said leases and contract and all contracts incidental or supplemental thereto, to enjoin further extraction of oil from the said reserves under said leases or from the territory covered by the same, to secure any further appropriate incidental relief, and to prosecute such other actions or proceedings, civil and criminal, as may be warranted by the facts in relation to the making of the said leases and contract.

And the President is further authorized and directed to appoint, by and with the advice and consent of the Senate, special counsel who shall have charge and control of the prosecution of such litigation, anything in the statutes touching the powers of the attorney General of the Department of Justice to the contrary notwithstanding.

453. THE IMMIGRATION ACT OF 1924
May 26, 1924

(U. S. Bureau of Immigration, *Annual Report of the Commissioner-General of Immigration,* 1924, p. 24 ff.)

The quotas established by the immigration act of 1921, Doc. No. 422, were unsatisfactory for two reasons: they admitted too large a number of immigrants; they did not discriminate sufficiently in favor of immigration from Northern and Western Europe. The act of 1924 sought to remedy the first defect by reducing the percentage of immigrants admitted in relation to nationals already in the country from three to two, and remedied the second by establishing 1890 rather than 1910 as the basic date. The report and summary of the law of 1924 is given in lieu of the law itself for purposes of conciseness.

. . . The "Immigration act of 1924" . . . which supplants the so-called quota limit act of May 19, 1921, the latter having expired by limitation at the close of the fiscal year just ended, makes several very important changes not only in our immigration policy but also in the administrative machinery of the Immigration Service. Some of the more important changes in these respects will be briefly referred to.

It will be remembered that the quota limit act of May, 1921, provided that the number of aliens of any nationality admissible to the United States in any fiscal year should be limited to 3 per cent of the number of persons of such nationality who were resident in the United States according to the census of 1910, it being also provided that not more than 20 per cent of any annual quota could be admitted in any one month. Under the act of 1924 the number of each nationality who may be admitted annually is limited to 2 per cent of the population of such nationality resident in the United States according to the census of 1890, and not more than 10 per cent of any annual quota may be admitted in any month except in cases where such quota is less than 300 for the entire year.

Under the act of May, 1921, the quota area was limited to Europe, the Near East, Africa, and Australasia. The countries of North and South America, with adjacent islands, and countries immigration from which was otherwise regulated, such as China, Japan, and countries within the Asiatic barred zone, were not within the scope of the quota law. Under the new act, however, immigration from the entire world, with the exception of the Dominion of Canada, Newfoundland, the Republic of Mexico, the Republic of Cuba, the Republic of Haiti, the Dominican Republic, the Canal Zone, and independent countries of Central and South America, is subject to quota limitations. The various quotas established under the new law are shown in the following proclamation of the President, issued on the last day of the present fiscal year:

BY THE PRESIDENT OF THE UNITED STATES OF AMERICA

A PROCLAMATION

Whereas it is provided in the act of Congress approved May 26, 1924, entitled "An act to limit the immigration of aliens into the United States, and for other purposes" that—

"The annual quota of any nationality shall be two per centum of the number of foreign-born individuals of such nationality resident in continental United States as determined by the United States census of 1890, but the minimum quota of any nationality shall be 100 (Sec. 11(a)). . . .

"The Secretary of State, the Secretary of Commerce, and the Secretary of Labor, jointly, shall, as soon as feasible after the enactment of this act, prepare a statement showing the number of individuals of the various nationalities resident in continental United States as determined by the United States census of 1890, which statement shall be the population basis for the purposes of subdivision (a) of section 11 (sec. 12(b)).

"Such officials shall, jointly, report annually to the President the quota of each nationality under subdivision (a) of section 11, together with the statements, estimates, and revisions provided for in this section. The President shall proclaim and make known the quotas so reported." (Sec. 12 (e)).

Now, therefore, I, Calvin Coolidge, President of the United States of America acting under and by virtue of the power in me vested by the aforesaid act of Congress, do hereby proclaim and make known that on and after July 1, 1924, and throughout the fiscal year 1924–1925, the quota of each nationality provided in said Act shall be as follows:

Country or area of birth

	Quota 1924–1925
Afghanistan	100
Albania	100
Andorra	100
Arabian peninsula (1, 2)	100
Armenia	124
Australia, including Papua, Tasmania, and all islands appertaining to Australia	
(3, 4)	121
Austria	785
Belgium (5)	512
Bhutan	100
Bulgaria	100
Cameroon (proposed British mandate)	100
Cameroon (French mandate)	100
China	100
Czechoslovakia	3,073
Danzig, Free City of	228
Denmark (5, 6)	2,789
Egypt	100
Esthonia	124
Ethiopia (Abyssinia)	100
Finland	170
France (1, 5, 6)	3,954
Germany	51,227
Great Britain and Northern Ireland (1, 3, 5, 6)	34,007
Greece	100
Hungary	473
Iceland	100
India (3)	100
Iraq (Mesopotamia)	100
Irish Free State (3)	28,567
Italy, including Rhodes, Dodekanesia, and Castellorizzo (5)	3,845
Japan	100
Latvia	142
Liberia	100
Liechtenstein	100
Lithuania	344
Luxemburg	100
Monaco	100
Morocco (French and Spanish Zones and Tangier)	100
Muscat (Oman)	100
Nauru (proposed British mandate) (4)	100
Nepal	100
Netherlands (1, 5, 6)	1,648
New Zealand (including appertaining islands (3, 4)	100
Norway (5)	6,453
New Guinea, and other Pacific Islands under proposed Australian mandate (4)	100
Palestine (with Trans-Jordan, proposed British mandate)	100

Quota
1924–1925

Persia (1)	100
Poland	5,982
Portugal (1, 5)	503
Ruanda and Urundi (Belgium mandate)	100
Rumania	603
Russia, European and Asiatic (1)	2,248
Samoa, Western (4) (proposed mandate of New Zealand)	100
San Marino	100
Siam	100
South Africa, Union of (3) .	100
South West Africa (proposed mandate of Union of South Africa)	100
Spain (5)	131
Sweden	9,561
Switzerland	2,081
Syria and The Lebanon (French mandate)	100
Tanganyika (proposed British mandate)	100
Togoland (proposed British mandate)	100
Togoland (French mandate)	100
Turkey	100
Yap and other Pacific islands (under Japanese mandate) (4)	100
Yugoslavia	671

1. (a) Persons born in the portions of Persia, Russia, or the Arabian peninsula situated within the barred zone, and who are admissible under the immigration laws of the United States as quota immigrants, will be charged to the quotas of these countries; and (b) persons born in the colonies, dependencies, or protectorates, or portions thereof, within the barred zone, of France, Great Britain, the Netherlands, or Portugal, who are admissible

under the immigration laws of the United States as quota immigrants, will be charged to the quota of the country to which such colony or dependency belongs or by which it is administered as a protectorate.

2. The quota-area denominated "Arabian peninsula" consists of all territory except Muscat and Aden, situated in the portion of that peninsula and adjacent islands, to the southeast of Iraq, of Palestine with Trans-Jordan, and of Egypt.

3. Quota immigrants born in the British self-governing dominions or in the Empire of India, will be charged to the appropriate quota rather than to that of Great Britain and Northern Ireland. There are no quota restrictions for Canada and Newfoundland. . . .

4. Quota immigrants eligible to citizenship in the United States, born in a colony, dependency, or protectorate of any country to which a quota applies will be charged to the quota of that country.

5. In contrast with the law of 1921, the immigration act of 1924 provides that persons born in the colonies or dependencies of European countries situated in Central America, South America, or the islands adjacent to the American continents (except Newfoundland and islands pertaining to Newfoundland, Labrador and Canada), will be charged to the quota of the country to which such colony or dependency belongs.

GENERAL NOTE.—The immigration quotas assigned to the various countries and quota-areas should not be regarded as having any political significance whatever, or as involving recognition of new governments, or of new boundaries, or of transfers of territory except as the United States Government has already made such recognition in a formal and official manner. . . .

CALVIN COOLIDGE.

454. THE LA FOLLETTE PLATFORM OF 1924

(K. Porter, ed. *National Party Platforms,* p. 516 ff.)

The apparent failure of the Farmer-Labor movement in 1920 led to the disintegration of that organization. Its place was taken by the Conference for Progressive Political Action, which had the support of the Four Railroad Brotherhoods. The Conference, dissatisfied with

the nominations and platforms of the two major parties in 1924, offered the nomination on a third party ticket to Robert La Follette of Wisconsin, long leader of the progressive element in the Republican party. The American Federation of Labor, the Socialist Party, and other minor organizations rallied to the La Follette standard, and in the subsequent election he polled 4,822,900 votes—the largest number ever polled by a third party candidate. La Follette's *Autobiography* was written prior to this election: there is no adequate biography of La Follette but several are promised. See N. Fine, *Labor and Farmer Parties in the United States, 1828–1928.*

The great issue before the American people today is the control of government and industry by private monopoly.

For a generation the people have struggled patiently, in the face of repeated betrayals by successive administrations, to free themselves from this intolerable power which has been undermining representative government.

Through control of government, monopoly has steadily extended its absolute dominion to every basic industry.

In violation of law, monopoly has crushed competition, stifled private initiative and independent enterprise, and without fear of punishment now exacts extortionate profits upon every necessity of life consumed by the public.

The equality of opportunity proclaimed by the Declaration of Independence and asserted and defended by Jefferson and Lincoln as the heritage of every American citizen has been displaced by special privilege for the few, wrested from the government of the many.

FUNDAMENTAL RIGHTS IN DANGER

That tyrannical power which the American people denied to a king, they will no longer endure from the monopoly system. The people know they cannot yield to any group the control of the economic life of the nation and preserve their political liberties. They know monopoly has its representatives in the halls of Congress, on the Federal bench, and in the executive departments; that these servile agents barter away the nation's natural resources, nullify acts of Congress by judicial veto and administrative favor, invade the people's rights by unlawful arrests and unconstitutional searches and seizures, direct our foreign policy in the interests of predatory wealth, and make wars and conscript the sons of the common people to fight them.

The usurpation in recent years by the federal courts of the power to nullify laws duly enacted by the legislative branch of the government is a plain violation of the Constitution. . . .

DISTRESS OF AMERICAN FARMERS

The present condition of American agriculture constitutes an emergency of the gravest character. The Department of Commerce report shows that during 1923 there was a steady and marked increase in dividends paid by the great industrial corporations. The same is true of the steam and electric railways and practically all other large corporations. On the other hand, the Secretary of Agriculture reports that in the fifteen principal wheat growing states more than 108,000 farmers since 1920 have lost their farms through foreclosure or bankruptcy; that more than 122,000 have surrendered their property without legal proceedings, and that nearly 375,000 have retained possession of their property only through the leniency of their creditors, making a total of more than 600,000 or 26 percent of all farmers who have virtually been bankrupted since 1920 in these fifteen states alone.

Almost unlimited prosperity for the great corporations and ruin and bankruptcy for agriculture is the direct and logical result of the policies and legislation which deflated the farmer while extending almost unlimited credit to the great corporations; which protected with exorbitant tariffs the industrial magnates, but depressed the prices of the farmers' products by financial juggling while greatly increasing the cost of what he must buy; which guaranteed excessive freight rates to the railroads and put a premium on wasteful management while saddling an unwarranted burden on to the backs of the American farmer; which permitted gambling in the products of the farm by grain speculators to the great detriment of the farmer and to the great profit of the grain gambler.

A COVENANT WITH THE PEOPLE

Awakened by the dangers which menace their freedom and prosperity the American people still retain the right and courage to exercise their sovereign control over their government. In order to destroy the economic and political power of monopoly, which has come between the people and their government, we pledge ourselves to the following principles and policies:

THE HOUSE CLEANING

1. We pledge a complete housecleaning in the Department of Justice, the Department of the Interior, and the other executive departments. We demand that the power of the Federal Government be used to crush private monopoly, not to foster it.

NATURAL RESOURCES

2. We pledge recovery of the navy's oil reserves and all other parts of the public domain which have been fraudulently or illegally leased, or otherwise wrongfully transferred, to the control of private interests; vigorous prosecution of all public officials, private citizens and corporations that participated in these transactions; complete revision of the water-power act, the general leasing act, and all other legislation relating to the public domain. We favor public ownership of the nation's water power and the creation and development of a national super-water-power' system, including Muscle Shoals, to supply at actual cost light and power for the people and nitrate for the farmers, and strict public control and permanent conservation of all the nation's resources, including coal, iron and other ores, oil and timber lands, in the interest of the people.

RAILROADS

3. We favor repeal of the Esch-Cummins railroad law and the fixing of railroad rates upon the basis of actual, prudent investment and cost of service. . . .

TAX REDUCTION

4. We favor reduction of Federal taxes upon individual incomes and legitimate business, limiting tax exactions strictly to the requirements of the government administered with rigid economy, particularly by the curtailment of the eight hundred million dollars now annually expended for the army and navy in preparation for future wars; by the recovery of the hundreds of millions of dollars stolen from the Treasury through fraudulent war contracts and the corrupt leasing of the public resources; and by diligent action to collect the accumulated interest upon the eleven billion dollars owing us by foreign governments.

We denounce the Mellon tax plan as a device to relieve multi-millionaires at the expense of other tax payers, and favor a taxation policy providing for immediate reductions upon moderate incomes, large increases in the inheritance tax rates upon large estates to prevent the indefinite accumulation by inheritance of great fortunes in a few hands; taxes upon excess profits to penalize profiteering, and complete publicity, under proper safeguards, of all Federal tax returns.

THE COURTS

5. We favor submitting to the people, for their considerate judgment, a constitutional amendment providing that Congress may by enacting a statute make it effective over a judicial veto.

We favor such amendment to the constitution as may be necessary to provide for the election of all Federal Judges, without party designation, for fixed terms not exceeding ten years, by direct vote of the people.

THE FARMERS

6. We favor drastic reduction of the exorbitant duties on manufactures provided in the Fordney-McCumber tariff legislation, the prohibiting of gambling by speculators and profiteers in agricultural products; the reconstruction of the Federal Reserve and Federal Farm Loan Systems, so as to eliminate control by usurers, speculators and international financiers, and to make the credit of the nation available upon fair terms to all and without discrimination to business men, farmers, and home-builders. We advocate the calling of a special session of Congress to pass legislation for the relief of American agriculture. We favor such further legislation as may be needful or helpful in promoting and protecting co-operative enterprises. We demand that the Interstate Commerce Commission proceed forthwith to reduce by an approximation to pre-war levels the present freight rates on agricultural products, including live stock, and upon the materials required upon American farms for agricultural purposes.

LABOR

7. We favor abolition of the use of injunctions in labor disputes and declare for complete protection of the right of farmers and industrial workers to organize, bargain collectively through representatives of their own

choosing, and conduct without hindrance co-operative enterprises.

We favor prompt ratification of the Child Labor amendment, and subsequent enactment of a Federal law to protect children in industry. . . .

PEACE ON EARTH

12. We denounce the mercenary system of foreign policy under recent administrations in the interests of financial imperialists, oil monopolies and international bankers, which has at times degraded our State Department from its high service as a strong and kindly intermediary of defenseless governments to a trading outpost for those interests and concession-seekers engaged in the exploitations of weaker nations, as contrary to the will of the American people, destructive of domestic development and provocative of war. We favor an active foreign policy to bring about a revision of the Versailles treaty in accordance with the terms of the armistice, and to promote firm treaty agreements with all nations to outlaw wars, abolish conscription, drastically reduce land, air and naval armaments, and guarantee public referendum on peace and war.

455. PIERCE v. SOCIETY OF THE SISTERS
268 U. S. 510
1925

Appeal from the District Court of United States for Oregon. Suit to enjoin enforcement of Oregon Compulsory Education Act of 1922 requiring children to attend public schools.

McREYNOLDS, J. These appeals are from decrees . . . which granted preliminary orders restraining appellants from threatening or attempting to enforce the Compulsory Education Act adopted November 7, 1922, under the initiative provision of her Constitution by the voters of Oregon. . . .

The challenged act, effective September 1, 1926, requires every parent . . . of a child between eight and sixteen years to send him "to a public school for the period of time a public school shall be held during the current year" in the district where the child resides; and failure to do so is declared a misdemeanor. . . . The manifest purpose is to compel general attendance at public schools by normal children between eight and sixteen, who have not completed the eighth grade. And without doubt enforcement of the statute would seriously impair, perhaps destroy, the profitable features of appellees' business, and greatly diminish the value of their property.

Appellee the Society of Sisters is an Oregon corporation, organized in 1880, with power to care for orphans, educate and instruct the youth, establish and maintain academies or schools, and acquire necessary real and personal property. . . . It conducts interdependent primary and high schools and junior colleges, and maintains orphanages for the custody and control of children between eight and sixteen. In its primary schools many children between those ages are taught the subjects usually pursued in Oregon public schools during the first eight years. Systematic religious instruction and moral training according to the tenets of the Roman Catholic Church are also regularly provided. . . . The business is remunerative . . . and the successful conduct of this business requires long-time contracts with teachers and parents. The Compulsory Education Act of 1922 has already caused the withdrawal from its schools of children who would otherwise continue, and their income has steadily declined. . . .

The bill alleges that the enactment conflicts with the right of parents to choose schools where their children will receive appropriate mental and religious training . . . and the right of schools and teachers therein to engage in a useful business or profession, and is accordingly repugnant to the Constitution and void. . . .

No question is raised concerning the power of the State reasonably to regulate all schools, to inspect, supervise and examine them, their teachers and pupils; to require that all children of proper age attend some school, that teachers shall be of good moral character and patriotic disposition, that certain studies plainly essential to good citizenship must be taught, and that nothing be taught which is manifestly inimical to the public welfare.

The inevitable practical result of enforcing the act under consideration would be destruction of appellees' primary schools, and perhaps all other private primary schools for normal children within the State of Oregon. Appellees are engaged in a kind of undertaking not inherently harmful, but long regarded as useful and meritorious. Certainly there is nothing in the present records to indicate that they have failed to discharge their obligations to patrons, students, or the State. And there are no peculiar circumstances or present emergencies which demand extraordinary measures relative to primary education.

Under the doctrine of *Meyer* v. *Nebraska*, 262 U. S. 390, we think it entirely plain that the Act of 1922 unreasonably interferes with the liberty of parents and guardians to direct the upbringing and education of children under their control. As often heretofore pointed out rights guaranteed by the Constitution may not be abridged by legislation which has no reasonable relation to some purpose within the competency of the State. The fundamental theory of liberty upon which all governments in this Union repose excludes any general power of the State to standardize its children by forcing them to accept instruction from public teachers only. The child is not the mere creature of the State; those who nurture him and direct his destiny have the right, coupled with the high duty, to recognize and prepare him for additional obligations. . . .

Decree affirmed.

456. GITLOW v. PEOPLE OF NEW YORK
268 U. S. 652
1925

Error to the Supreme Court of the State of New York. Both the Federal and the State Constitutions guarantee the right of freedom of speech, but the question of how far that right may be used is one of the most perplexing that the Courts have to face. As Mr. Justice Holmes said in the case of *U.S.* v. *Schenck,* Doc. No. 426, "The most stringent protection of free speech would not protect a man in falsely shouting fire in a theatre and causing a panic." The present case involved the validity of the New York Criminal Anarchy Act of 1902. Compare the opinion of the Court in this case with the opinions in *U.S.* v. *Schenck* and *Abrams* v. *United States,* 250 U.S. 616, and *Patterson* v. *Colorado,* 205 U. S. 454. For a general discussion, see Z. Chafee, *Freedom of Speech.*

SANFORD, J. Benjamin Gitlow was indicted in the supreme court of New York, with three others, for the statutory crime of criminal anarchy. . . .

The contention here is that the statute, by its terms and as applied in this case, is repugnant to the due process clause of the Fourteenth Amendment. Its material provisions are:

"Section 160. *Criminal anarchy defined.*— Criminal anarchy is the doctrine that organized government should be overthrown by force or violence, or by assassination of the executive head or of any of the executive officials of government, or by any unlawful means. The advocacy of such doctrine either by word of mouth or writing is a felony.

"Section 161. *Advocacy of criminal anarchy.*—Any person who:

"1. By word of mouth or writing advocates, advises or teaches the duty, necessity or propriety of overthrowing or overturning organized government by force or violence, or by assassination of the executive head or of any of the executive officials of government, or by any unlawful means; or,

"2. Prints, publishes, edits, issues or knowingly circulates, sells, distributes or publicly displays any book, paper, document, or written or printed matter in any form, containing or advocating, advising or teaching the doctrine that organized government should be overthrown by force, violence or any unlawful means . . . ,

"Is guilty of a felony and punishable" by imprisonment or fine, or both.

The indictment was in two counts. The first charged that the defendants had advocated, advised, and taught the duty, necessity, and propriety of overthrowing and overturning organized government by force, violence, and unlawful means, by certain writings therein set forth, entitled, "The Left Wing Manifesto"; the second, that the defendants had printed, published, and knowingly circulated and distributed a certain paper called "The Revolutionary Age," containing the writings set forth in the first count, advocating, advising, and teaching the doctrine that organized government should be overthrown by force, violence, and unlawful means. . . .

There was no evidence of any effect resulting from the publication and circulation of the Manifesto.

No witnesses were offered in behalf of the defendant.

Extracts from the Manifesto are set forth in the margin. Coupled with a review of the rise of Socialism, it condemned the dominant "moderate Socialism" for its recognition of the necessity of the democratic parliamentary state; repudiated its policy of introducing Socialism by legislative measures; and advocated, in plain and unequivocal language, the necessity of accomplishing the "Communist Revolution" by a militant and "revolutionary Socialism," based on "the class struggle" and mobilizing the "power of the proletariat in action," through mass industrial revolts developing into mass political strikes and "revolutionary mass action," for the purpose of conquering and destroying the parliamentary state and establishing in its place, through a "revolutionary dictatorship of the proletariat," the system of Communist Socialism. The then recent strikes in Seattle and Winnipeg were cited as instances of a development already verging on revolutionary action and suggestive of proletarian dictatorship, in which the strike workers were "trying to usurp the functions of municipal government"; and Revolutionary Socialism, it was urged, must use these mass industrial revolts to broaden the strike, make it general and militant, and develop it into mass political strikes and revolutionary mass action for the annihilation of the parliamentary state. . . .

. . . The sole contention here is, essentially, that, as there was no evidence of any concrete result flowing from the publication of the Manifesto, or of circumstances showing the likelihood of such result, the statute as construed and applied by the trial court penalizes the mere utterance, as such, of "doctrine" having no quality of incitement, without regard either to the circumstances of its utterance or to the likelihood of unlawful sequences; and that, as the exercise of the right of free expression with relation to government is only punishable "in circumstances involving likelihood of substantive evil," the statute contravenes the due process clause of the Fourteenth Amendment. The argument in support of this contention rests primarily upon the following propositions: first, that the "liberty" protected by the Fourteenth Amendment includes the liberty of speech and of the press; and second, that while liberty of expression "is not absolute," it may be restrained "only in circumstances where its exercise bears a causal relation with some substantive evil, consummated, attempted, or likely"; and as the statute "takes no account of circumstances," it unduly restrains this liberty, and is therefore unconstitutional.

The precise question presented, and the only question which we can consider under this writ of error, then, is whether the statute, as construed and applied in this case by the state courts, deprived the defendant of his liberty of expression, in violation of the due process clause of the Fourteenth Amendment.

The statute does not penalize the utterance or publication of abstract "doctrine" or academic discussion having no quality of incitement to any concrete action. It is not aimed against mere historical or philosophical essays. It does not restrain the advocacy of changes in the form of government by constitutional and lawful means. What it prohibits is language advocating, advising, or teaching the overthrow of organized government by unlawful means. . . .

The Manifesto, plainly, is neither the statement of abstract doctrine nor, as suggested by counsel, mere prediction that industrial disturbances and revolutionary mass strikes will result spontaneously in an inevitable process of evolution in the economic system. It advocates and urges in fervent language mass action which shall progressively foment industrial disturbances, and, through political mass strikes and revolutionary mass action, overthrow and destroy organized parliamentary government. . . .

The means advocated for bringing about the destruction of organized parliamentary government, namely, mass industrial revolts usurping the functions of municipal government, political mass strikes directed against the parliamentary state, and revolutionary mass action for its final destruction, necessarily imply the use of force and violence, and in their essential nature are inherently unlawful in a constitutional government of law and order. That the jury was warranted in finding that the Manifesto advocated not merely the abstract doctrine of overwhelming organized government by force, violence, and unlawful means, but action to that end, is clear.

For the present purposes we may and do assume that freedom of speech and of the press—which are protected by the First Amendment from abridgment by Congress—are among the fundamental personal rights and "liberties" protected by the due process clause of the Fourteenth Amendment from impairment by the states. . . .

It is a fundamental principle, long established, that the freedom of speech and of the press which is secured by the Constitution does not confer an absolute right to speak or publish, without responsibility, whatever one may choose, or an unrestricted and unbridled license that gives immunity for every possible use of language, and prevents the punishment of those who abuse this freedom. . . .

That a state, in the exercise of its police power, may punish those who abuse this freedom by utterances inimical to the public welfare, tending to corrupt public morals, incite to crime, or disturb the public peace, is not open to question. . . .

And, for yet more imperative reasons, a State may punish utterances endangering the foundations of organized government and threatening its overthrow by unlawful means. These imperil its own existence as a constitutional state. Freedom of speech and press, said Story (supra), does not protect disturbances of the public peace or the attempt to subvert the government. It does not protect publications or teachings which tend to subvert or imperil the government, or to impede or hinder it in the performance of its governmental duties. It does not protect publications prompting the overthrow of government by force; the punishment of those who publish articles which tend to destroy organized society being essential to the security of

freedom and the stability of the state. And a State may penalize utterances which openly advocate the overthrow of the representative and constitutional form of government of the United States and the several states, by violence or other unlawful means. In short, this freedom does not deprive a State of the primary and essential right of self-preservation, which, so long as human governments endure, they cannot be denied. . . .

By enacting the present statute the State has determined, through its legislative body, that utterances advocating the overthrow of organized government by force, violence, and unlawful means, are so inimical to the general welfare, and involve such danger of substantive evil, that they may be penalized in the exercise of its police power. That determination must be given great weight. Every presumption is to be indulged in favor of the validity of the statute. . . . That utterances inciting to the overthrow of organized government by unlawful means present a sufficient danger of substantive evil to bring their punishment within the range of legislative discretion is clear. Such utterances, by their very nature, involve danger to the public peace and to the security of the state. They threaten breaches of the peace and ultimate revolution. And the immediate danger is none the less real and substantial because the effect of a given utterance cannot be accurately foreseen. The state cannot reasonably be required to measure the danger from every such utterance in the nice balance of a jeweler's scale. A single revolutionary spark may kindle a fire that, smoldering for a time, may burst into a sweeping and destructive conflagration. It cannot be said that the state is acting arbitrarily or unreasonably when, in the exercise of its judgment as to the measures necessary to protect the public peace and safety, it seeks to extinguish the spark without waiting until it has enkindled the flame or blazed into the conflagration. It cannot reasonably be required to defer the adoption of measures for its own peace and safety until the revolutionary utterances lead to actual disturbances of the public peace or imminent and immediate danger of its own destruction; but it may, in the exercise of its judgment, suppress the threatened danger in its incipiency. . . .

We cannot hold that the present statute

is an arbitrary or unreasonable exercise of the police power of the state, unwarrantably infringing the freedom of speech or press; and we must and do sustain its constitutionality.

This being so it may be applied to every utterance—not too trivial to be beneath the notice of the law—which is of such a character and used with such intent and purpose as to bring it within the prohibition of the statute. . . . In other words, when the legislative body has determined generally, in the constitutional exercise of its discretion, that utterances of a certain kind involve such danger of substantive evil that they may be punished, the question whether any specific utterance coming within the prohibited class is likely, in and of itself, to bring about the substantive evil, is not open to consideration. It is sufficient that the statute itself be constitutional, and that the use of the language comes within its prohibition. . . .

And finding, for the reasons stated, that the statute is not in itself unconstitutional, and that it has not been applied in the present case in derogation of any constitutional right, the judgment of the court of appeals is affirmed.

HOLMES, J., dissenting:

Mr Justice Brandeis and I are of opinion that this judgment should be reversed. The general principle of free speech, it seems to me, must be taken to be included in the Fourteenth Amendment, in view of the scope that has been given to the word "liberty" as there used, although perhaps it may be accepted with a somewhat larger latitude of interpretation than is allowed to Congress by the sweeping language that governs, or ought to govern, the laws of the United States. If I am right, then I think that the criterion sanctioned by the full court in *Schenck* v. *United States*, 249 U. S. 47, 52, applies: "The question in every case is whether the words used are used in such circumstances and are of such a nature as to create a clear and present danger that they will bring about the substantive evils that [the state] has a right to prevent." . . . If what I think the correct test is applied, it is manifest that there was no present danger of an attempt to overthrow the government by force on the part of the admittedly small minority who shared the defendant's views. It is said that this Manifesto was more than a theory, that it was an incitement. Every idea is an incitement. It offers itself for belief, and, if believed, it is acted on unless some other belief outweighs it, or some failure of energy stifles the movement at its birth. The only difference between the expression of an opinion and an incitement in the narrower sense is the speaker's enthusiasm for the result. Eloquence may set fire to reason. But whatever may be thought of the redundant discourse before us, it had no chance of starting a present conflagration. If, in the long run, the beliefs expressed in proletarian dictatorship are destined to be accepted by the dominant forces of the community, the only meaning of free speech is that they should be given their chance and have their way.

If the publication of this document had been laid as an attempt to induce an uprising against government at once, and not at some indefinite time in the future, it would have presented a different question. The object would have been one with which the law might deal, subject to the doubt whether there was any danger that the publication could produce any result; or, in other words, whether it was not futile and too remote from possible consequences. But the indictment alleges the publication and nothing more.

457. THE UNITED STATES AND THE WORLD COURT

Senate Reservations to Accession of the United States, and World Court Modifications
January 27, 1926

The World Court of International Justice was provided for by the Covenant of the League of Nations. A committee of ten distinguished jurists, including Mr. Elihu Root, drew up the Rules for the Court; these were adopted by the Assembly of the League of Nations, December 13, 1920, and the Court was organized the following year. Every administration has apparently favored our accession to the Court, but not until 1926 was President Coolidge able to secure the consent of the Senate, and then with the reservations below. These reservations were incorporated with slight modifications into the Protocol of March 19, 1929, and the signature of the United States affixed November 25, 1929. The Senate has not yet (1934) acted upon the ratification of the protocol. The Senate reservations are in *Congressional Record,* Vol. LXVII, p. 2306; the World Court Protocol in Foreign Policy Association, *Information Service,* Vol. V, No. 21. See, P. C. Jessup, *The United States and the World Court,* World Peace Foundation Pamphlets, Vol XII, No. 4.

1. CONDITIONS UPON WHICH THE UNITED STATES WILL ENTER THE WORLD COURT

THE SWANSON RESOLUTION

Whereas the President, under date of February 24, 1923, transmitted a message to the Senate accompanied by a letter from the Secretary of State, dated February 17, 1923, asking the favorable advice and consent of the Senate to the adherence on the part of the United States to the protocol of December 16, 1920, of signature of the statute for the Permanent Court of International Justice, set out in said message of the President (without accepting or agreeing to the optional clause for compulsory jurisdiction contained therein), upon the conditions and understandings hereafter stated, to be made a part of the instrument of adherence: Therefore be it

Resolved (*two-thirds of the Senators present concurring*), That the Senate advise and consent to the adherence on the part of the United States to the said protocol of December 16, 1920, and the adjoined statute for the Permanent Court of International Justice (without accepting or agreeing to the optional clause for compulsory jurisdiction contained in said statute), and that the signature of the United States be affixed to the said protocol, subject to the following reservations and understandings, which are hereby made a part and condition of this resolution, namely:

1. That such adherence shall not be taken to involve any legal relation on the part of the United States to the League of Nations or the assumption of any obligations by the United States under the treaty of Versailles.

2. That the United States shall be permitted to participate, through representatives designated for the purpose and upon an equality with the other states, members, respectively, of the Council and Assembly of the League of Nations, in any and all proceedings of either the council or the assembly for the election of judges or deputy judges of the Permanent Court of International Justice or for the filling of vacancies.

3. That the United States will pay a fair share of the expenses of the court, as determined and appropriated from time to time by the Congress of the United States.

4. That the United States may at any time withdraw its adherence to the said protocol and that the statute for the Permanent Court of International Justice adjoined to the protocol shall not be amended without the consent of the United States.

5. That the court shall not render any advisory opinion except publicly after due notice to all states adhering to the court and to all interested states and after public hearing or opportunity for hearing given to any state concerned; nor shall it, without the consent of the United States, entertain any request for an advisory opinion touching any dispute or question in which the United States has or claims an interest.

The signature of the United States to the said protocol shall not be affixed until the powers signatory to such protocol shall have indicated, through an exchange of notes, their acceptance of the foregoing reservations and understandings as a part and a condition of adherence by the United States to the said protocol.

Resolved further, As a part of this act of ratification that the United States approve the protocol and statute hereinabove mentioned, with the understanding that recourse to the Permanent Court of International Justice for the settlement of differences between the United States and any other state or states can be had only by agreement thereto through general or special treaties concluded between the parties in dispute; and

Resolved further, That adherence to the said protocol and statute hereby approved shall not be so construed as to require the United States to depart from its traditional policy of not intruding upon, interfering with, or entangling itself in the political questions of policy or internal administration of any foreign state; nor shall adherence to the said protocol and statute be construed to imply a relinquishment by the United States of its traditional attitude toward purely American questions.

2. DRAFT PROTOCOL FOR THE ACCESSION OF THE UNITED STATES

The States signatories of the Protocol of Signature of the Permanent Court of International Justice, dated December 16th, 1920, and the United States of America, through the undersigned duly authorized representatives, have mutually agreed upon the following provisions regarding the adherence of the United States of America to the said Protocol, subject to the five reservations formulated by the United States in the resolution adopted by the Senate on January 27th, 1926.

ART. 1. The States signatories of the said Protocol accept the special conditions attached by the United States in the five reservations mentioned above to its adherence to the said Protocol upon the terms and conditions set out in the following Articles.

ART. 2. The United States shall be admitted to participate, through representatives designated for the purpose and upon an equality with the signatory States Members of the League of Nations represented in the Council or in the Assembly, in any and all proceedings of either the Council or the Assembly for the election of judges or deputy-judges of the Permanent Court of International Justice, provided for in the Statute of the Court. The vote of the United States shall be counted in determining the absolute majority of votes required by the Statute.

ART. 3. No amendment of the Statute of the Court may be made without the consent of all the Contracting States.

ART. 4. The Court shall render advisory opinions in public session after notice and opportunity for hearing substantially as provided in the now existing Articles 73 and 74 of the Rules of Court.

ART. 5. With a view to ensuring that the Court shall not, without the consent of the United States, entertain any request for an advisory opinion touching any dispute or question in which the United States has or claims an interest, the Secretary-General of the League of Nations shall, through any channel designated for that purpose by the United States, inform the United States of any proposal before the Council or the Assembly of the League for obtaining an advisory opinion from the Court, and thereupon, if desired, an exchange of views as to whether an interest of the United States is affected shall proceed with all convenient speed between the Council or Assembly of the League and the United States.

Whenever a request for an advisory opinion comes to the Court, the Registrar shall notify the United States thereof, among other States mentioned in the now existing Article 73 of the Rules of Court, stating a reasonable time-limit fixed by the President within which a written statement by the United States concerning the request will be received. If for any reason no sufficient opportunity for an exchange of views upon such request should have been afforded and the United States advises the Court that the question upon which the opinion of the Court is asked is one that affects the interests of the United States, proceedings shall be stayed for a period sufficient to enable such an exchange of views between the Council or the Assembly and the United States to take place.

With regard to requesting an advisory opinion of the Court in any case covered by the preceding paragraphs, there shall be attributed to an objection of the United States the same force and effect as attaches to a vote against asking for the opinion given by a Member of the League of Nations in the Council or in the Assembly.

If, after the exchange of views provided for in paragraphs 1 and 2 of this Article, it shall appear that no agreement can be reached and the United States is not prepared to forego its objection, the exercise of the powers of withdrawal provided for in Article 8 hereof will follow naturally without any imputation of unfriendliness or unwillingness to co-operate generally for peace and goodwill.

ART. 6. Subject to the provisions of Article 8 below, the provisions of the present Protocol shall have the same force and effect as the provisions of the Statute of the Court and any future signature of the Protocol of December 16th, 1920, shall be deemed to be an acceptance of the provisions of the present Protocol.

ART. 7. The present Protocol shall be ratified. Each State shall forward the instrument of ratification to the Secretary-General of the League of Nations, who shall inform all the other signatory States. The instruments of ratification shall be deposited in the archives of the Secretariat of the League of Nations.

The present Protocol shall come into force as soon as all States which have ratified the Protocol of December 16th, 1920, and also the United States, have deposited their ratifications.

ART. 8. The United States may at any time notify the Secretary-General of the League of Nations that it withdraws its adherence to the Protocol of December 16th, 1920. The Secretary-General shall immediately communicate this notification to all the other States signatories of the Protocol.

In such case, the present Protocol shall cease to be in force as from the receipt by the Secretary-General of the notification by the United States.

On their part, each of the other Contracting States may at any time notify the Secretary-General of the League of Nations that it desires to withdraw its acceptance of the special conditions attached by the United States to its adherence to the Protocol of December 16th, 1920. The Secretary-General shall immediately give communication of this notification to each of the States signatories of the present Protocol. The present Protocol shall be considered as ceasing to be in force if and when, within one year from the date of receipt of the said notification, not less than two-thirds of the Contracting States other than the United States shall have notified the Secretary-General of the League of Nations that they desire to withdraw the above-mentioned acceptance.

458. TYSON v. BANTON
273 U. S. 418
1926

Appeal from United States district court for Southern district of New York. The facts of the case are stated in the opinion below. The dissenting opinion of Mr. Justice Holmes is particularly important as foreshadowing the attitude of the Court at the present time.

SUTHERLAND, J. Appellant is engaged in the business of reselling tickets of admission to theatres and other places of entertainment in the city of New York. . . . Section 167 of ch. 590 (New York laws) declares that the price of or charge for admission to theatres, etc., is a matter affected with a public interest and subject to state supervision in order to safeguard the public against fraud, extortion, exorbitant rates, and similar abuses. Section 172 forbids the resale of any ticket . . . to any theatre, etc., "at a price in excess of fifty cents in advance of the price printed on the face of such ticket." . . .

Strictly, the question for determination relates only to the maximum price for which an entrance ticket to a theatre, etc., may be resold. But the answer necessarily must be to a question of greater breadth. The statutory declaration is that the price of or charge for admission to a theatre . . . is a matter af-

fected with a public interest. To affirm the validity of section 172 is to affirm this declaration completely since appellant's business embraces the resale of entrance tickets to all forms of entertainment therein enumerated. And since the ticket broker is a mere appendage of the theatre, etc., and the price of or charge for admission is the essential element in the statutory declaration, it results that the real inquiry is whether every public exhibition, game, contest or performance, to which an admission charge is made, is clothed with a public interest, so as to authorize a law-making body to fix the maximum amount of the charge, which its patrons may be required to pay. . . .

A business is not affected with a public interest merely because it is large or because the public are warranted in having a feeling of concern in respect of its maintenance. Nor is the interest meant such as arises from the mere fact that the public derives benefit, accommodation, ease or enjoyment from the existence or operation of the business; and while the word has not always been limited narrowly as strictly denoting "a right", that synonym, more nearly than any other, expresses the sense in which it is to be understood. . . .

. . . The mere declaration by the legislature that a particular kind of property or business is affected with a public interest is not conclusive upon the question of the validity of the regulation. The matter is one which is always open to judicial inquiry.

From the foregoing review it will be seen that each of the decisions of this court upholding governmental price regulation aside from cases involving legislation to tide over temporary emergencies, has turned upon the existence of conditions, peculiar to the business under consideration, which bore such a substantial and definite relation to the public interest as to justify an indulgence of the legal fiction of a grant by the owner to the public of an interest in the use.

Lord Hale's statement that when private property is "affected with a public interest, it ceases to be *juris privati* only" is accepted by this court as the guiding principle in cases of this character. . . .

A theatre or other place of entertainment does not meet this conception of Lord Hale's aphorism or fall within the reasons of the decisions of this court based upon it. A theatre is a private enterprise, which, in its relation to the public, differs obviously and widely, both in character and degree, from a grain elevator, standing at the gateway of commerce and exacting toll . . .; or stock yards, standing in like relation to the commerce in live stock; or insurance company engaged as a sort of common agency, in collecting and holding a guarantee fund in which definite and substantial rights are enjoyed by a considerable portion of the public. . . . Sales of theatre tickets bear no relation to the commerce of the country; and they are not interdependent transactions, but stand, both in form and effect, separate and apart from each other, "terminating in their effect with the instances." And, certainly a place of entertainment is in no legal sense a public utility; and, quite as certainly, its activities are not such that their enjoyment can be regarded under any conditions from the point of view of an emergency. . . .

The statute assailed contravenes the 14th Amendment, and the decree must be reversed.

HOLMES, J., dissenting. We fear to grant power and are unwilling to recognize it when it exists. The States very generally have stripped jury trials of one of their most important characteristics by forbidding the judges to advise the jury upon the facts, and when legislatures are held to be authorized to do anything considerably affecting public welfare, it is covered by apologetic phrases like the police power, or the statement that the business concerned has been dedicated to a public use. The former expression is convenient, to be sure, to conciliate the mind to something that needs explanation; the fact that the constitutional requirement of compensation when property is taken cannot be pressed to its grammatical extreme; that property rights may be taken for public purposes without pay if you do not take too much; that some play must be allowed to the joints if the machine is to work. But police power often is used in a wide sense to cover and, as I said, to apologize for the general power of the legislature to make a part of the community uncomfortable by a change.

I do not believe in such apologies. I think the proper course is to recognize that a state legislature can do whatever it sees fit to do unless it is restrained by some express prohibition in the Constitution of the United States or of the state, and that courts should be careful not to extend such prohibitions beyond their obvious meaning by reading into them conceptions of public policy that the particular court may happen to entertain.

Coming down to the case before us, I think, as I intimated in *Adkins* v. *Children's Hospital,* that the notion that a business is clothed with a public interest and has been devoted to the public use is little more than a fiction intended to beautify what is disagreeable to the sufferers. The truth seems to me to be that, subject to compensation when compensation is due, the legislature may forbid or restrict any business when it has a sufficient force of public opinion behind it. Lotteries were thought useful adjuncts of the state a century or so ago; now they are believed to be immoral and they have been stopped. Wine has been thought good for man from the time of the Apostles until recent years. But when public opinion changed it did not need the 18th Amendment, notwithstanding the 14th, to enable a state to say that the business should end. What has happened to lotteries and wine might happen to theatres in some moral storm of the future, not because theatres were devoted to a public use, but because people had come to think that way.

But if we are to yield to fashionable conventions, it seems to me that theatres are as much devoted to public use as anything well can be. We have not that respect for art that is one of the glories of France. But to many people the superfluous is the necessary, and it seems to me that government does not go beyond its sphere in attempting to make life livable for them. I am far from saying that I think this particular law a wise and rational provision. That is not my affair. But if the people of the state of New York speaking by their authorized voice say that they want it, I see nothing in the Constitution of the United States to prevent their having their will.

459. MYERS v. UNITED STATES
272 U. S. 52
1926

Appeal from the Court of Claims. It will be remembered that President Johnson challenged the validity of the Tenure of Office Act of March 2, 1867 (see Doc. No. 263) and that his impeachment rested largely on his defiance of this Act. He was unable, at the time, to bring the question of the constitutionality of the Act before the Courts, and not until 1926 did the Court hand down an opinion on the vexed question of the power of removal. The opinion of the Court in this case may be taken as a complete vindication of the position of President Johnson.

TAFT, C. J. This case presents the question whether under the Constitution the President has the exclusive power of removing executive officers of the United States whom he has appointed by and with the advice and consent of the Senate.

Meyers was on July 21, 1917 appointed by the President, by and with the advice and consent of the Senate, to be a postmaster of the first class at Portland, Oregon, for a term of four years. On January 20, 1920, Myers's resignation was demanded. He refused the demand. On February 2, 1920, he was removed from office by order of the Postmaster General, acting by direction of the President. . . .

By the 6th section of the Act of Congress of July 12, 1876, under which Myers was appointed with the advice and consent of the Senate as a first class postmaster, it is provided that "Postmasters of the first, second and third classes shall be appointed and may be removed by the President by and with the advice and consent of the Senate and shall hold their offices for four years unless

sooner removed or suspended according to law".

The Senate did not consent to the President's removal of Myers during his term. If this statute in its requirement that his term should be four years unless sooner removed by the President by and with the consent of the Senate is valid, the appellant . . . is entitled to recover his unpaid salary for his full term and the judgement of the court of claims must be reversed. The government maintains that the requirement is invalid, for the reason that under article 2 of the Constitution, the President's power of removal of executive officers appointed by him with the advice and consent of the Senate is full and complete without consent of the Senate. If this view is sound, the removal of Myers by the President without the Senate's consent was legal. . . .

[There follows a learned discussion of the history of the President's power of removal.]

Our conclusion on the merits sustained by the arguments before stated is that article 2 grants to the President the executive power of the Government, i. e. the general administrative control of those executing the laws, including the power of appointment and removal of executive officers, a conclusion confirmed by his obligation to take care that the laws be faithfully executed; that article 2 excludes the legislative of executive power by Congress to provide for appointments and removals except only as granted therein to Congress in the matter of inferior offices; that Congress is only given power to provide for appointments and removals of inferior officers after it has vested, and on condition that it does vest, their appointment in other authority than the President with the Senate's consent; that the provisions of the second section of article 2, which blend action by the legislative branch, or by part of it, in the work of the executive, are limitations to be strictly construed and not to be extended by implication; that the President's power of removal is further established as an incident to his specifically enumerated function of appointment by and with the advice of the Senate, but that such incident does not by implication extend to removals of the Senate's power of checking appointment; and finally that to hold otherwise would make it impossible for the President in case of political or other difference with the Senate or Congress to take care that the laws be faithfully executed.

We come now to a period in the history of the Government when both houses of Congress attempted to reverse this constitutional construction and to subject the power of removing executive officers appointed by the President and conformed by the Senate to the control of the Senate, indeed finally to the assumed power in Congress to place the removal of such officers anywhere in the Government.

This reversal grew out of the serious political difference between the two Houses of Congress and President Johnson. . . . The chief legislation in support of the reconstruction policy of Congress was the Tenure of Office Act of March 2, 1867, providing that all officers appointed by and with the consent of the Senate should hold their offices until their successors should have in like manner been appointed and qualified, that certain heads of departments, including the Secretary of War, should hold their offices during the terms of the President by whom appointed and one month thereafter subject to removal by consent of the Senate. The Tenure of Office Act was vetoed, but it was passed over the veto. . . .

In spite of the foregoing Presidential declarations, it is contended that since the passage of the Tenure of Office Act, there has been a general acquiescence by the Executive in the power of Congress to forbid the President alone to remove executive officers, an acquiescence which has changed any formerly accepted constitutional construction to the contrary. Instances are cited of the signed approval by President Grant and other Presidents of legislation in derogation of such construction. We think these are all to be explained not by acquiescence therein, but by reason of the otherwise valuable effect of the legislation approved. Such is doubtless the explanation of the executive approval of the Act of 1867, which we are considering, for it was an appropriation act on which the section here in question was imposed as rider. . . .

When, then, are the elements that enter into our decision of this case? We have first a construction of the Constitution made by a Congress which was to provide by legislation for the organization of the Government in accord with the Constitution which had just then been adopted, and in which there were, as representatives and senators, a considerable number of those who had been members of the Convention that framed the Constitution and presented it for ratification. It was the Congress that launched the Government. It was the Congress that rounded out the Constitution itself by the proposing of the first ten amendments which had in effect been promised to the people as a consideration for the ratification. . . . It was a Congress whose constitutional decisions have always been regarded as they should be regarded as of the greatest weight in the interpretation of that fundamental instrument. . . . We are now asked to set aside this construction thus buttressed and adopt an adverse view because the Congress of the United States did so during a heated political difference of opinion between the then President and the majority leaders of Congress over the reconstruction measures adopted as a means of restoring to their proper status the States which attempted to withdraw from the Union at the time of the Civil War. . . . When on the merits we find our conclusions strongly favoring the view which prevailed in the First Congress, we have no hesitation in holding that conclusion to be correct; and it therefore follows that the Tenure of Office Act of 1867, in so far as it attempted to prevent the President from removing executive officers who had been appointed by him by and with the advice and consent of the Senate, was invalid and that subsequent legislation to the same effect was equally so.

For the reasons given we must therefore hold that the provision of the law of 1876 by which the unrestricted power of removal of first class postmasters is denied to the President is in violation of the Constitution and invalid. This leads to an affirmation of the judgement of the Court of Claims. . . .

HOLMES, J., dissenting. . . . The arguments (for the President's power of removal) drawn from the executive power of the President, and from his duty to appoint officers of the United States (when Congress does not vest the appointment elsewhere), to take care that the laws be faithfully executed, and to commission all officers of the United States, seem to me spider's webs inadequate to control the dominant facts.

We have to deal with an office that owes its existence to Congress and that Congress may abolish tomorrow. Its duration and the pay attached to it while it lasts depend on Congress alone. Congress alone confers on the President the power to appoint to it and at any time may transfer the power to other hands. With such power over its own creation, I have no more trouble in believing that Congress has power to prescribe a term of life for it free from any interference than I have in accepting the undoubted power of Congress to decree its end. I have equally little trouble in accepting its power to prolong the tenure of an incumbent until Congress or the Senate shall have assented to his removal. The duty of the President to see that the laws be executed is a duty that does not go beyond the laws or require him to achieve more than Congress sees fit to leave within his power.

MCREYNOLDS, J., and BRANDEIS, J., joined in this dissent.

460. AMERICAN INTERVENTION IN NICARAGUA
Message of President Coolidge to Congress
January 10, 1927
(U. S. 69th Congress, 2d Session, *House Doc.* No. 633)

Dissatisfaction of the liberals in Nicaragua with the Diaz government resulted in disturbances which led in 1927 to a renewal of American intervention. In his special message to Congress of January 10, President Coolidge sketched the background of American intervention and pointed out the circumstances which, in his opinion, made intervention imperative. Within a few months over 5000 American marines were sent to Nicaragua to preserve order. In April Mr. Henry Stimson went to Nicaragua as special commissioner to work out some agreement among the warring factions. He succeeded in providing for a new election to take place in 1928 under American supervision. At this election General Moncada, the liberal candidate, was elected over General Diaz who had been maintained by American arms and diplomacy. Moncada promptly appointed Dr. Sacasa, who had been deposed by Diaz and whose appeal to the United States had been spurned, minister to the United States! Sandino, a Sacasa supporter, refused to be bound by the election of 1928, and for the next four years he carried on a desultory warfare against the government. In 1932 Dr. Sacasa was elected to the Presidency, and Sandino voluntarily laid down his arms. American marines were withdrawn from Nicaragua in 1933. See, I. J. Cox, *Nicaragua and the United States, 1909–1927;* H. A. Stimson, *American Policy in Nicaragua;* C. P. Howland, ed. *Survey of American Foreign Relations, 1929;* M. Winkler, *Investments of United States Capital in Latin America.*

The White House
To the Congress of the United States:

. . . It is well known that in 1912 the United States intervened in Nicaragua with a large force and put down a revolution, and that from that time to 1925 a legation guard of American marines was, with the consent of the Nicaraguan Government, kept in Managua to protect American lives and property. In 1923 representatives of the five Central American countries, namely, Costa Rica, Guatemala, Honduras, Nicaragua, and Salvador, at the invitation of the United States, met in Washington and entered into a series of treaties. These treaties dealt with limitation of armament, a Central American tribunal for arbitration, and the general subject of peace and amity. The treaty last referred to specifically provides in Article II that the Governments of the contracting parties will not recognize any other government which may come into power in any of the five Republics through a coup d'état, or revolution, and disqualifies the leaders of such coup d'état, or revolution, from assuming the presidency or vice presidency. . . .

The United States was not a party to this treaty, but it was made in Washington under the auspices of the Secretary of State, and this Government has felt a moral obligation to apply its principles in order to encourage the Central American States in their efforts to prevent revolution and disorder. . . .

The Nicaraguan constitution provides in article 106 that in the absence of the President and Vice President the Congress shall designate one of its members to complete the unexpired term of President . . . the action of Congress in designating Senor Diaz was perfectly legal and in accordance with the constitution. Therefore the United States Government on November 17 extended recognition to Senor Diaz. . . .

Immediately following the inauguration of President Diaz and frequently since that date he has appealed to the United States for support, has informed this Government of the aid which Mexico is giving to the revolutionists, and has stated that he is unable solely because of the aid given by Mexico to the revolutionists to protect the lives and property of American citizens and other foreigners. When negotiations leading up to the Corinto conferences began, I immediately placed an embargo on the shipment of arms and ammunition to Nicaragua. . . .

. . . At the end of November, after spending some time in Mexico City, Doctor Sacasa went back to Nicaragua, landing at Puerto Cabezas, near Bragmans Bluff. He immediately placed himself at the head of the insurrection and declared himself President of Nicaragua. He has never been recognized by any of the Central American Republics nor by any other government, with the exception of Mexico, which recognized him immediately. As arms and munitions in large quantities were reaching the revolutionists, I deemed it unfair to prevent the recognized government from purchasing arms abroad, and, accordingly, the Secretary of State has notified the Diaz Government that licenses would be issued for the export of arms and munitions purchased in this country. It would be thoroughly inconsistent for this country not to support the government recognized by it while the revolutionists were receiving arms and munitions from abroad. . . .

For many years numerous Americans have been living in Nicaragua, developing its industries and carrying on business. At the present time there are large investments in lumbering, mining, coffee growing, banana culture, shipping, and also in general mercantile and other collateral business.

In addition to these industries now in existence, the Government of Nicaragua, by a treaty entered into on the 5th day of August, 1914, granted in perpetuity to the United States the exclusive proprietary rights necessary and convenient for the construction, operation, and maintenance of an oceanic canal. . . .

There is no question that if the revolution continues American investments and business interests in Nicaragua will be very seriously affected, if not destroyed.

Manifestly the relation of this Government to the Nicaraguan situation and its policy in the existing emergency, are determined by the facts which I have described. The proprietary rights of the United States in the Nicaraguan canal route, with the necessary implications growing out of it affecting the Panama Canal, together with the obligations flowing from the investments of all classes of our citizens in Nicaragua, place us in a position of peculiar responsibility. I am sure it is not the desire of the United States to intervene in the internal affairs of Nicaragua or of any other Central American Republic. Nevertheless it must be said that we have a very definite and special interest in the maintenance of order and good government in Nicaragua at the present time, and that the stability, prosperity, and independence of all Central American countries can never be a matter of indifference to us. The United States can not, therefore, fail to view with deep concern any serious threat to stability and constitutional government in Nicaragua tending toward anarchy and jeopardizing American interests, especially if such state of affairs is contributed to or brought about by outside influences or by any foreign power. It has always been and remains the policy of the United States in such circumstances to take the steps that may be necessary for the preservation and protection of the lives, the property, and the interests of its citizens and of this Government itself. In this respect I propose to follow the path of my predecessors.

Consequently, I have deemed it my duty to use the powers committed to me to insure the adequate protection of all American interests in Nicaragua, whether they be endangered by internal strife or by outside interference in the affairs of that Republic.

Calvin Coolidge.

461. THE McNARY–HAUGEN BILL
February 25, 1927

(*The Congressional Record,* 69th Congress, 2d Session, Vol. LXVIII, part 4, p. 3869 ff.)

The prolonged agricultural depression that set in about 1921 resulted in a persistent demand that the Government extend relief of a more positive character than any heretofore attempted. In the face of an agricultural surplus which tended to level down all prices to the world price, the Farm Bloc in Congress attempted to solve the problem by extending the protective system to the farmers. The McNary-Haugen Act sought to maintain a high domestic price by permitting the government to buy up the surplus agricultural commodities, dispose of them at a loss in the foreign market, and make good the loss through an "equalization fee" to be paid by the farmers. The bill was roundly denounced by President Coolidge as dangerously socialistic in character. It was repassed in May, 1928, and again vetoed by President Coolidge. The second veto can be found in *Supplement to the Messages and Papers of the Presidents Covering the Administration of President Coolidge,* p. 9777 ff. George N. Peek, who drafted the bill, explained it in *Current History,* November 1928. See also E. R. A. Seligman, *The Economics of Farm Relief; J. D. Black, Agricultural Reform in the United States.*

SEC. 1. It is hereby declared to be the policy of Congress to promote the orderly marketing of basic agricultural commodities in interstate and foreign commerce and to that end to provide for the control and disposition of surpluses of such commodities, to enable producers of such commodities to stabilize their markets against undue and excessive fluctuations, to preserve advantageous domestic markets for such commodities, to minimize speculation and waste in marketing such commodities, and to encourage the organization of producers of such commodities into cooperative marketing associations.

SEC. 2. (a) A Federal Farm Board is hereby created which shall consist of the Secretary of Agriculture, who shall be a member ex officio, and 12 members, one from each of the 12 Federal land-bank districts, appointed by the President of the United States, by and with the advice and consent of the Senate, from lists of eligibles submitted by the nominating committee for the district, as hereinafter in this section provided.

(b) There is hereby established a nominating committee in each of the 12 Federal land-bank districts, to consist of seven members. Four of the members of the nominating committee in each district shall be elected by the bona fide farm organizations and cooperative associations in such district at a convention of such organizations and associations, to be held at the office of the Federal land bank in such district, or at such other place, in the city where such Federal land bank is located, to which the convention may adjourn. Two of the members of the nominating committee in each district shall be elected by a majority vote of the heads of the agricultural departments of the several States of each Federal land-bank district, at a meeting to be held in the same city and at the same time of the meeting of the convention of the bona fide farm organizations and cooperative associations in each district. One of the members of the nominating committee in each district shall be appointed by the Secretary of Agriculture. . . .

SEC. 6. (a) For the purposes of this act, cotton, wheat, corn, rice, tobacco, and swine shall be known and are referred to as "basic agricultural commodities," except that the board may, in its discretion, treat as a separate basic agricultural commodity one or more of such classes or types of tobacco as are designated in the classification of the Department of Agriculture.

(b) Whenever the board finds that the conditions of production and marketing of any other agricultural commodity are such that the provisions of this act applicable to a basic agricultural commodity should be made applicable to such other agricultural commodity, the board shall submit its report thereon to Congress.

(c) Whenever the board finds, first, that there is or may be during the ensuing year either (1) a surplus above the domestic requirements for wheat, corn, rice, tobacco, or swine, or (2) a surplus above the requirements for the orderly marketing of cotton, or of wheat, corn, rice, tobacco, or swine; and, second, that both the advisory council hereinafter created for the commodity and a substantial number of cooperative associations or other organizations representing the producers of the commodity favor the full cooperation of the board in the stabilization of the commodity, then the board shall publicly declare its findings and commence, upon a date to be fixed by the board and published in such declaration, the operations in such commodity authorized by this act: . . .

(d) During the continuance of such operations in any basic agricultural commodity, the board is authorized to enter into agreements, for the purpose of carrying out the policy declared in section 1, with any cooperative association engaged in handling the basic agricultural commodity, or with a corporation created by one or more of such cooperative associations, or with processors of the basic agricultural commodity.

(e) Such agreements may provide for (1) removing or disposing of any surplus of the basic agricultural commodity, (2) withholding such surplus, (3) insuring such commodity against undue and excessive fluctuations in market conditions, and (4) financing the purchase, storage, or sale or other disposition of the commodity. The moneys in the stabilization fund of the basic agricultural commodity shall be available for carrying out such agreements. In the case of any agreement in respect of the removal or disposal of the surplus of a basic agricultural commodity, the agreement shall provide both for the payment from the stabilization fund for the commodity of the amount of losses, costs, and charges, arising out of the purchase, storage, or sale or other disposition of the commodity or out of contracts therefor, and for the payment into the stabilization fund for the commodity of profits (after deducting all costs and charges provided for in the agreement) arising out of such purchase, storage, or sale or other disposition, or contracts therefor. In the case of agreements insuring such commodity against undue and excessive fluctuations in market conditions, the board may insure any cooperative marketing association against decline in the market price for the commodity at the time of sale by the association, from the market price for such commodity at the time of delivery to the association.

SEC. 7. (a) The board is hereby authorized and directed to create for each basic agricultural commodity an advisory council of seven members fairly representative of the producers of such commodity. . . .

SEC. 8. In order that each marketed unit of a basic agricultural commodity may contribute ratably its equitable share to the stabilization fund hereinafter established for such commodity; in order to prevent any unjust discrimination against, any direct burden or undue restraint upon, and any suppression of commerce with foreign nations in basic agricultural commodities in favor of interstate or intrastate commerce in such commodities; and in order to stabilize and regulate the current of foreign and interstate commerce in such commodities—there shall be apportioned and paid as a regulation of such commerce an equalization fee as hereinafter provided.

SEC. 9. Prior to the commencement of operations in respect of any basic agricultural commodity, and thereafter from time to time, the board shall estimate the probable advances, losses, costs, and charges to be paid in respect of the operations in such commodity. Having due regard to such estimates, the board shall from time to time determine and publish the amount for each unit of weight, measure, or value designated by it, to be collected upon such unit of such basic agricultural commodity during the operations in such commodity. Such amount is hereinafter referred to as the "equalization fee." At the time of determining and publishing an equalization fee the board shall specify the period during which it shall remain in effect, and the place and manner of its payment and collection.

SEC. 10. (a) Under such regulations as the board may prescribe there shall be paid, during operations in a basic agricultural commodity and in respect of each unit of such commodity, an equalization fee upon one of the following: the transportation, processing, or sale of such unit. . . .

(b) The board may by regulation require any person engaged in the transportation, processing, or acquisition by sale of a basic agricultural commodity—

(1) To file returns under oath and to report, in respect of his transportation, processing, or acquisition of such commodity, the amount of equalization fees payable thereon and such other facts as may be necessary for their payment or collection.

(2) To collect the equalization fee as directed by the board, and to account therefor.

(3) In the case of cotton, to issue to the producer a serial receipt for the commodity which shall be evidence of the participating interest of the producer in the equalization fund for the commodity. The board may in such case prepare and issue such receipts and prescribe the terms and conditions thereof. The Secretary of the Treasury, upon the request of the board, shall have such receipts prepared at the Bureau of Engraving and Printing.

(c) Every person who, in violation of the regulations prescribed by the board, fails to collect or account for any equalization fee shall be liable for its amount and to a penalty equal to one-half its amount. Such amount and penalty may be recovered together in a civil suit brought by the board in the name of the United States.

SEC. 11. (a) In accordance with regulations prescribed by the board, there shall be established a stabilization fund for each basic agricultural commodity. Such funds shall be administered by and exclusively under the control of the board, and the board shall have the exclusive power of expending the moneys in any such fund. There shall be deposited to the credit of the stabilization fund for a basic agricultural commodity, advances from the revolving fund hereinafter established, premiums paid for insurance under section 12, and the equalization fees and profits in connection with operations by the board in

the basic agricultural commodity or its food products. . . .

SEC. 12. (a) The board is authorized, upon such terms and conditions and in accordance with such regulations as it may prescribe, to make loans out of the revolving fund to any cooperative association engaged in the purchase, storage, or sale or other disposition of any agricultural commodity (whether or not a basic agricultural commodity) for the purpose of assisting such cooperative association in controlling the surplus of such commodity in excess of the requirements for orderly marketing.

(b) For the purpose of developing continuity of cooperative services, including unified terminal marketing facilities and equipment, the board is authorized, upon such terms and conditions and in accordance with such regulations as it may prescribe, to make loans out of the revolving fund to any cooperative association engaged in the purchase, storage, sale, or other disposition, or processing of any agricultural commodity, (1) for the purpose of assisting any such association in the acquisition, by purchase, construction, or otherwise, of facilities to be used in the storage, processing, or sale of such agricultural commodity, or (2) for the purpose of furnishing funds to such associations for necessary expenditures in federating, consolidating, or merging cooperative associations, or (3) for the purpose of furnishing to any such association funds to be used by it as capital for any agricultural credit corporation eligible for receiving rediscounts from an intermediate-credit bank. In making any such loan the board may provide for the payment of such charge, to be determined by the board from time to time, upon each unit of the commodity handled by the association, as will within a period of not more than 20 years repay the amount of such loan, together with interest thereon. The aggregate amounts loaned under this subdivision and remaining unpaid shall not exceed at any one time the sum of $25,000,000.

(c) Any loan under subdivision (a) or (b) shall bear interest at the rate of 4 per cent per annum.

(d) The board may at any time enter into a contract with any cooperative marketing association engaged in marketing any basic agricultural commodity, insuring such association for periods of 12 months against decline in the market price for such commodity at the time of sale by the association from the market price for such commodity at the time of delivery to the association. For such insurance the association shall pay such premium, to be determined by the board, upon each unit of the basic agricultural commodity reported by the association for coverage under the insurance contract, as will cover the risks of the insurance. . . .

SEC. 16. (a) There is hereby authorized to be appropriated, out of any money in the Treasury not otherwise appropriated, the sum of $250,000,000, which shall be administered by the board and used as a revolving fund, in accordance with the provisions of this act. . . .

462. COOLIDGE'S VETO OF THE McNARY–HAUGEN BILL
February 25, 1927

(*Congressional Record,* 69th Congress, 2d Session, Vol. LXVIII, p. 4771 ff.)

To the Senate:

THE conditions which Senate bill 4808 is designed to remedy have been, and still are, unsatisfactory in many cases. No one can deny that the prices of many farm products have been out of line with the general price level for several years. No one could fail to want every proper step taken to assure to agriculture a just and secure place in our economic scheme. Reasonable and constructive legislation to that end would be thoroughly justified and would have the hearty support of all who have the interests of the Nation at heart. The difficulty with this particular measure is that it is not framed to aid farmers as a whole, and it is, furthermore, calculated to injure rather than promote the general public welfare.

It is axiomatic that progress is made through building on the good foundations that already exist. For many years—indeed, from before the day of modern agricultural science—balanced and diversified farming has been regarded by thoughtful farmers and scientists as the safeguard of our agriculture. The bill under consideration throws this aside as of no consequence. It says in effect that·all the agricultural scientists and all the thinking farmers of the last 50 years are wrong, that what we ought to do is not to encourage diversified agriculture but instead put a premium on one-crop farming.

The measure discriminates definitely against products which make up what has been universally considered a program of safe farming. The bill upholds as ideals of American farming the men who grow cotton, corn, rice, swine, tobacco, or wheat, and nothing else. These are to be given special favors at the expense of the farmer who has toiled for years to build up a constructive farming enterprise to include a variety of crops and livestock that shall, so far as possible, be safe, and keep the soil, the farmer's chief asset, fertile and productive.

The bill singles out a few products, chiefly sectional, and proposes to raise the prices of those regardless of the fact that thousands of other farmers would be directly penalized. If this is a true farm-relief measure, why does it leave out the producers of beef cattle, sheep, dairy products, poultry products, potatoes, hay, fruit, vegetables, oats, barley, rye, flax, and the other important agricultural lines? So far as the farmers as a whole are concerned this measure is not for them. It is for certain groups of farmers in certain sections of the country. Can it be thought that such legislation could have the sanction of the rank and file of the Nation's farmers?

This measure provides specifically for the payment by the Federal board of all losses, costs, and charges of packers, millers, cotton spinners, or other processors who are operating under contract with the board. It contemplates that the packers may be commissioned by the Government to buy hogs enough to create a near scarcity in this country, slaughter the hogs, sell the pork products abroad at a loss, and have their losses, costs, and charges made good out of the pockets of farm taxpayers. The millers would be similarly commissioned to operate in wheat or corn and have their losses, costs, and charges paid by farm taxpayers. . . .

It seems almost incredible that the producers of hogs, corn, wheat, rice, tobacco, and cotton should be offered a scheme of legislative relief in which the only persons who are guaranteed a profit are the exporters, packers, millers, cotton spinners, and other processors.

Clearly this legislation involves government fixing of prices. It gives the proposed Federal board almost unlimited authority to fix prices on the designated commodities. This is price fixing, furthermore, on some of the Nation's basic foods and materials. Nothing is more certain than that such price fixing would upset the normal exchange relationships existing in the open market and that it would finally have to be extended to cover a multitude of other goods and services. Government price fixing, once started, has alike no justice and no end. It is an economic folly from which this country has every right to be spared.

This legislation proposes, in effect, that Congress shall delegate to a Federal Farm Board, nominated by farmers, the power to fix and collect a tax, called an equalization fee, on certain products produced by those farmers. That certainly contemplates a remarkable delegation of the taxing power. The purpose of that tax, it may be repeated, is to pay the losses incurred in the disposition of the surplus products in order to raise the price on that portion of the products consumed by our own people.

This so-called equalization fee is not a tax for purposes of revenue in the accepted sense. It is a tax for the special benefit of particular groups. As a direct tax on certain of the vital necessaries of life it represents the most vicious form of taxation. Its real effect is an employment of the coercive powers of Government to the end that certain special groups of farmers and processors may profit temporarily at the expense of other farmers and of the community at large.

The chief objection to the bill is that it would not benefit the farmer. Whatever may be the temporary influence of arbitrary interference, no one can deny that in the long run prices will be governed by the law of supply and demand. To expect to increase prices and then to maintain them on a higher level by means of a plan which must of necessity increase production while decreasing consumption, is to fly in the face of an economic law as well established as any law of nature. Experience shows that high prices in any given year mean greater acreage the next year. This does not necessarily mean a larger crop the following year, because adverse weather conditions may produce a smaller crop on a larger acreage, but in the long run a constantly increasing acreage must of necessity mean a larger average crop. . . .

A board of 12 men are granted almost unlimited control of the agricultural industry and can not only fix the price which the producers of five commodities shall receive for their goods, but can also fix the price which the consumers of the country shall pay for these commodities. The board is expected to obtain higher prices for the American farmer by removing the surplus from the home market and dumping it abroad at a below-cost price. To do this, the board is given the authority by implication to fix the domestic price level, either by means of contracts which it may make with processors or cooperatives, or by providing for the purchase of the commodities in such quantities as will bring the prices up to the point which the board may fix.

Except as it may be restrained by fear of foreign importations, the farm board, composed of representatives of producers, is given the power to fix the prices of these necessities of life at any point it sees fit. The law fixes no standards, imposes no restrictions, and requires no regulation of any kind. There could be no appeal from the arbitrary decision of these men, who would be under constant pressure from their constituents to push prices as high as possible. To expect moderation under these circumstances is to disregard experience and credit human nature with qualities it does not possess. It is not so long since the Government was spending vast sums and through the Department of Justice exerting every effort to break up combinations that were raising the cost of living to a point conceived to be excessive. This bill, if it accomplishes its purpose, will raise the price of the specified agricultural commodities to the highest possible point and in doing so the board will operate without any restraints imposed by the antitrust laws. The granting of any such arbitrary power to a Government board is to run counter to our traditions, the philosophy of our Government, the spirit of our institutions, and all principles of equity.

The administrative difficulties involved are sufficient to wreck the plan. No matter how simple an economic conception may be, its application on a large scale in the modern world is attended by infinite complexities and difficulties. The principle underlying this bill, whether fallacious or not, is simple and easy to state; but no one has outlined in definite and detailed terms how the principle is to be carried out in practice. How can the board be expected to carry out after the enactment of the law what can not even be described prior to its passage? In the meanwhile, existing channels and methods of distribution and marketing must be seriously dislocated.

This is even more apparent when we take into consideration the problem of administering the collection of the equalization fee. The bureau states that the fee will have to be collected either from the processors or the transportation companies, and dismisses as impracticable collections at the point of sale. In the case of transportation companies it points out the enormous difficulties of collecting the fee in view of the possibility of shipping commodities by unregistered vehicles. In so far as processors are concerned, it estimates the number at 6,632, without considering the number of factories engaged in the business of canning corn or manufacturing food products other than millers. Some conception of the magnitude of the task may be had when we consider that if the wheat, the corn, and the cotton crops had been under operation in the year 1925, collection would have been required from an aggregate of 16,034,466,679 units. The bureau states that it will be impossible to collect the equalization fee in full.

The bill will not succeed in providing a practical method of controlling the agricultural surplus, which lies at the heart of the whole problem. In the matter of controlling output, the farmer is at a disadvantage as compared with the manufacturer. The latter is better able to gauge his market, and in the face of falling prices can reduce production. The farmer, on the other hand, must operate over a longer period of time in producing his crops and is subject to weather conditions and disturbances in world markets which can never be known in advance. In trying to find a solution for this fundamental problem of the surplus, the present bill offers no constructive suggestion. It seeks merely to increase the prices paid by the consumer, with the inevitable result of stimulating production on the part of the farmer and decreasing consumption on the part of the public. It ignores the fact that production is curbed only by decreased, not increased, prices. In the end the equalization fee and the entire machinery provided by the bill under construction will merely aggravate conditions which are the cause of the farmer's present distress.

We must be careful in trying to help the farmer not to jeopardize the whole agricultural industry by subjecting it to the tyranny of bureaucratic regulation and control. That is what the present bill will do. But aside from all this, no man can foresee what the effect on our economic life will be of disrupting the long-established and delicately adjusted channels of commerce. That it will be far-reaching is undeniable, nor is it beyond the range of possibility that the present bill, if enacted into law, will threaten the very bases of our national prosperity, through dislocation, the slowing up of industry, and the disruption of the farmer's home market, which absorbs 90 per cent of his products. . . .

The effect of this plan will be continuously to stimulate American production and to pile up increasing surpluses beyond the world demand. We are already overproducing. It has been claimed that the plan would only be used in the emergency of occasional surplus which unduly depresses the price. No such limitations are placed in the bill. But on the other hand the definition of surplus is the "surplus over domestic requirements" and as we have had such a surplus in most of the commodities covered in the bill for 50 years and will have for years to come it means continuous action. It is said that by the automatic increase of the equalization fee to meet the increasing losses on enlarged dumping of increasing surplus that there would be restraint on production. This can prove effective only after so great an increase in production as will greatly enlarge our exports on all the commodities except cotton. With such increased surpluses dumped from the United States on to foreign markets the world prices will be broken down and with them American prices upon which the premium is based will likewise be lowered to the point of complete disaster to American farmers. It is impossible to see how this bill can work.

Several of our foreign markets have agriculture of their own to protect and they have laws in force which may be applied to dumping and we may expect reprisals from them against dumping agricultural products which will even more diminish our foreign markets.

The bill is essentially a price-fixing bill, because in practical working the board must arrive in some way at the premium price which will be demanded from the American consumer, and it must fix these prices in the contracts at which it will authorize purchases by flour millers, packers, other manufacturers, and such cooperatives as may be used, for the board must formulate a basis upon which the board will pay losses on the export of their surplus. . . .

The main policy of this bill is an entire reversal of what has been heretofore thought to be sound. Instead of undertaking to secure a method of orderly marketing which will dispose of products at a profit, it proposes to dispose of them at a loss. It runs counter to the principle of conservation, which would require us to produce only what can be done at a profit, not to waste our soil and resources producing what is to be sold at a loss to us for the benefit of the foreign consumer. It runs counter to the well-considered principle that a healthy economic condition is best maintained through a free play of competition by undertaking to permit a legalized restraint of trade in these commodities and establish a species of monopoly under Government protection. . . . For many generations such practices have been denounced by law as repugnant to the public welfare. It can not be that they would now be found to be beneficial to agriculture.

This measure is so long and involved that it is impossible to discuss it without going into many tiresome details. Many other reasons exist why it ought not to be approved, but it is impossible to state them all without writing a book. The most decisive one is that it is not constitutional. This feature is discussed in an opinion of the Attorney General, herewith attached and made a part hereof, so that I shall not consider the details of that phase of my objections. Of course it includes some good features. Some of its provisions, intended to aid and strengthen cooperative marketing, have been borrowed from proposals that do represent the general trend of constructive thought on the agricultural problem. In this measure, however, these provisions are all completely subordinated to the main objective, which is to have the Government dispose of exportable surpluses at a loss and make some farmer taxpayers foot the bill. This is not a measure to help cooperative marketing. Its effect, on the contrary, is to eliminate the very conditions of advantage that now induce farmers to join together to regulate and improve their own business. . . .

CALVIN COOLIDGE.

463. BUCK v. BELL
274 U. S. 200
1927

Error to the Supreme Court of Appeals of State of Virginia. A statute of Virginia, March 20, 1924, provided for the sterilization of inmates of State-supported institutions who should be found to be affected with hereditary insanity.

HOLMES, J. . . . An Act of Virginia . . . recites that the health of the patient and the welfare of society may be promoted in certain cases by the sterilization of mental defectives, under careful safeguard, etc. . . . ; that the Commonwealth is supporting in various institutions many defective persons who if now discharged would become a menace but if incapable of procreating might be discharged with safety and become self-supporting with benefit to themselves and to society. . . .

We have seen more than once that the public welfare may call upon the best citizens for their lives. It would be strange if it could not call upon those who already sap the strength of the State for these lesser sacrifices, often not felt to be such by those concerned, in order to prevent our being swamped with incompetence. It is better for all the world, if instead of waiting to execute degenerate offspring for crime, or to let them starve for their imbecility, society can prevent those who are manifestly unfit from continuing their kind. The principle that sustains compulsory vaccination is broad enough to cover cutting the Fallopian. . . . Three generations of imbeciles are enough.

But, it is said, however it might be if this reasoning were applied generally, it fails when it is confined to the small number who are in the institutions named and is not applied to the multitudes outside. It is the usual last resort of constitutional arguments to point out shortcomings of this sort. But the answer is that the law does all that is needed when it does all that it can, indicates a policy, applies it to all within the lines, and seeks to bring within the lines all similarly situated so far and so fast as its means allow. . . .

Judgment affirmed. BUTLER, J., dissenting.

464. NIXON v. HERNDON (TEXAS WHITE PRIMARY CASE)
273 U. S. 536
1927

Writ of error to the district court of the United States for Western District of Texas. After Reconstruction, the Southern States resorted to a great variety of contrivances to evade the requirements of the Fifteenth Amendment. The most popular of these devices of recent years has been the expedient of excluding negroes from participation in party primaries. This exclusion is generally attained by indirection: the effort of Texas to exclude negroes from participation in the primaries of the Democratic party took the form of an express prohibition. For an excellent discussion of negro participation in politics in the South, see P. Lewinsohn, *Race, Class and Party.*

HOLMES, J. This is an action against the judges of elections for refusing to permit the plaintiff to vote at a primary election in Texas. It lays the damages at $5,000. The petition alleges that the plaintiff is a negro, a citizen of the United States and of Texas and a resident of El Paso, and in every way qualified to vote, as set forth in detail, except that the statute to be mentioned interferes with his right; that on July 26, 1924, a primary election was held at El Paso for the nomination of candidates for a senator and representatives in Congress and state and other offices, upon the Democratic ticket; that the plaintiff, being a member of the Democratic party, sought to vote, but was denied the right by defendants; that the denial was based upon a statute of Texas enacted in May, 1923, and designated article 3093a, by the words of which "in no event shall a negro be eligible to participate in a Democratic party primary election held in the state of Texas," etc., and that this statute is contrary to the 14th and 15th Amendments to the Constitution of the United States. The defendants moved to dismiss upon the ground that the subject matter of the suit was political and not within the jurisdiction of the court and that no violation of the Amendments was shown. The suit was dismissed and a writ of error was taken directly to this court. Here no argument was made on behalf of the defendants but a brief was allowed to be filed by the attorney general of the state. . . .

The important question is whether the statute can be sustained. But although we state it as a question the answer does not seem to us open to a doubt. We find it unnecessary to consider the 15th Amendment, because it seems to us hard to imagine a more direct and obvious infringement of the 14th. That Amendment, while it applies to all, was passed, as we know, with a special intent to protect the blacks from discrimination against them. . . . That Amendment "not only gave citizenship and the privileges of citizenship to persons of color, but it denied to any state the power to withhold from them the equal protection of the laws. . . . What is this but declaring that the law in the states shall be the same for the black as for the white; that all persons, whether colored or white, shall stand equal before the laws of the states, and, in regard to the colored race, for whose protection the Amendment was primarily designed, that no discrimination shall be made against them by law because of their color?" [*Buchanan* v. *Wailey,* 245 U.S. 60] . . . The statute of Texas, in the teeth of the prohibitions referred to, assumes to forbid negroes to take part in a primary election the importance of which we have indicated, discriminating against them by the distinction of color alone. States may do a good deal of classifying that it is difficult to believe rational, but there are limits, and it is too clear for extended argument that color cannot be made the basis of a statutory classification affecting the right set up in this case.

Judgment reversed.

465. BARTOLOMEO VANZETTI'S LAST STATEMENT IN COURT
April 9, 1927

(O. K. Fraenkel, *The Sacco-Vanzetti Case*, p. 138 ff.)

Probably no criminal case in American history attracted as much attention as did the trial of Nicola Sacco and Bartolomeo Vanzetti for the murder of Alexander Beradelli at South Braintree, Massachusetts, April 15, 1920. In the course of the trial much was made of the radical beliefs and activities of the defendants, and it was alleged that Judge Thayer had been guilty of prejudice against the defendants and of conduct unbecoming in a judge. The widespread belief that the defendants had not received a fair trial and that the conviction had been found on grounds having to do with their political doctrines and their foreign character, led to extraordinary efforts on their behalf by liberals throughout the world. After the sentence of death was imposed on the defendants, Governor Fuller was persuaded to appoint a distinguished committee, consisting of President Lowell of Harvard University, President Stratton of the M.I.T. and Judge Robert Grant, to review the case. The committee's report sustained the findings of the Court, but concluded that Judge Thayer had been guilty of a "grave breach of official decorum". The execution of Sacco and Vanzetti on August 23, 1927 was regarded by many as on a par with the execution of witches in seventeenth century Salem. The *Records* of the Trial were published in six volumes by Holt and Co.

Yes. What I say is that I am innocent, not only of the Braintree crime but also of the Bridgewater crime. That I am not only innocent of these two crimes, but in all my life I have never stole and I have never killed and I have never spilled blood. That is what I want to say. And it is not all. Not only am I innocent of these two crimes, not only in all my life I have never stole, never killed, never spilled blood, but I have struggled all my life, since I began to reason, to eliminate crime from the earth.

Everybody that knows these two arms knows very well that I did not need to go in between the street and kill a man to take the money. I can live with my two arms and live well. But besides that, I can live even without work with my arm for other people. I have had plenty of chance to live independently and to live what the world conceives to be a higher life than not to gain our bread with the sweat of our brow. . . .

Well, I want to reach a little point farther, and it is this—that not only have I not been trying to steal in Bridgewater, not only have I not been in Braintree to steal and kill and have never steal or kill or spilt blood in all my life, not only have I struggled hard against crimes, but I have refused myself the commodity or glory of life, the pride of life of a good position because in my consideration it is not right to exploit man. . . .

Now, I should say that I am not only innocent of all these things, not only have I never committed a real crime in my life—though some sins, but not crimes—not only have I struggled all my life to eliminate crimes that the official law and the official moral condemns, but also the crime that the official moral and the official law sanctions and sanctifies,—the exploitation and the oppression of the man by the man, and if there is a reason why I am here as a guilty man, if there is a reason why you in a few minutes can doom me, it is this reason and none else.

I beg your pardon. There is the more good man I ever cast my eyes upon since I lived, a man that will last and will grow always more near and more dear to the people, so far as into the heart of the people, so long as admiration for goodness and for sacrifice will last. I mean Eugene Debs. . . . He know, and not only he but every man of understanding in the world, not only in this country but also in the other countries, men that we have provided a certain amount of a record of the times, they all stick with us, the flower of mankind of Europe, the better writers, the greatest thinkers, of Europe, have pleaded in our favor. The scientists, the greatest scientists, the greatest statesmen of Europe, have pleaded in our favor. The people of foreign nations have pleaded in our favor.

Is it possible that only a few on the jury, only two or three men, who would condemn their mother for worldly honor and for earthly fortune; is it possible that they are right against what the world, the whole world has say it is wrong and that I know that it is wrong? If there is one that I should know it, if it is right or if it is wrong, it is I and this man. You see it is seven years that we are in jail. What we have suffered during those years no human tongue can say, and yet you see me before you, not trembling, you see me looking you in your eyes straight, not blushing, not changing color, not ashamed or in fear. . . .

We have proved that there could not have been another Judge on the face of the earth more prejudiced and more cruel than you have been against us. We have proved that. Still they refuse the new trial. We know, and you know in your heart, that you have been against us from the very beginning, before you see us. Before you see us you already know that we were radicals, that we were underdogs, that we were the enemy of the institution that you can believe in good faith in their goodness—I don't want to condemn that—and that it was easy on the time of the first trial to get a verdict of guiltiness.

We know that you have spoke yourself and have spoke your hostility against us, and your despisement against us with friends of yours on the train, at the University Club, of Boston, on the Golf Club of Worcester, Massachusetts. I am sure that if the people who know all what you say against us would have the civil courage to take the stand, maybe your Honor—I am sorry to say this because you are an old man, and I have an old father—but maybe you would be beside us in good justice at this time.

When you sentenced me at the Plymouth trial you say, to the best part of my memory, of my good faith, that crimes were in accordance with my principle,—something of that sort—and you take off one charge, if I remember it exactly, from the jury. The jury was so violent against me that they found me guilty of both charges, because there were only two. . . .

We were tried during a time that has now passed into history. I mean by that, a time when there was hysteria of resentment and hate against the people of our principles, against the foreigner, against slackers, and it seems to me—rather, I am positive, that both you and Mr. Katzmann has done all what it were in your power in order to work out, in order to agitate still more the passion of the juror, the prejudice of the juror, against us. . . .

Well, I have already say that I not only am not guilty of these crimes, but I never commit a crime in my life,—I have never steal and I have never kill and I have never spilt blood, and I have fought against the crime, and I have fought and I have sacrificed myself even to eliminate the crimes that the law and the church legitimate and sanctify.

This is what I say: I would not wish to a dog or to a snake, to the most low and misfortunate creature on the earth—I would not wish to any of them what I have had to suffer for things that I am not guilty of. But my conviction is that I have suffered for things that I am guilty of. I am suffering because I am a radical and indeed I am a radical; I have suffered because I was an Italian, and indeed I am an Italian; I have suffered more for my family and for my beloved than for myself; but I am so convinced to be right that if you could execute me two times, and if I could be reborn two other times, I would live again to do what I have done already. I have finished. Thank you.

466. TREATIES OF ARBITRATION AND CONCILIATION WITH GERMANY
May 5, 1928

(United States Treaty Series, No. 774, 775)

Article II of the Kellogg Pact provided that "the settlement of all disputes or conflicts . . . shall never be sought except by pacific means." It remained to provide the machinery by which this sentiment might be converted into reality. In December 1927 the United States submitted to France the text of a treaty for arbitration; this was ratified the following February, and the Department of State at once entered into negotiations with other powers for the conclusion of treaties of arbitration and conciliation. Unlike the traditional treaties of arbitration, these treaties made no exception for disputes involving "national honor and vital interest", though the treaty of arbitration did except disputes involving the maintenance of the Monroe Doctrine. The Treaties with Germany are given as examples of those entered into with most of the powers of the world. See references, Doc. No. 467.

1. TREATY OF ARBITRATION

The President of the United States of America and the President of the German Reich

Determined to prevent so far as in their power lies any interruption in the peaceful relations now happily existing between the two nations;

Desirous of reaffirming their adherence to the policy of submitting to impartial decision all justiciable controversies that may arise between them; and

Eager by their example not only to demonstrate their condemnation of war as an instrument of national policy in their mutual relations, but also to hasten the time when the perfection of international arrangements for the pacific settlement of international disputes shall have eliminated forever the possibility of war among any of the powers of the world;

Have decided to conclude a treaty of arbitration and for that purpose they have appointed as their respective plenipotentiaries

The President of the United States of America, Frank B. Kellogg, Secretary of State of the United States, and

The President of the German Reich, Herr Friedrich von Prittwitz und Gaffron, German Ambassador to the United States of America:

Who, having communicated to one another their full powers found in good and due form, have agreed upon the following articles:

ART. I. All differences relating to international matters in which the high contracting parties are concerned by virtue of a claim of right made by one against the other under treaty or otherwise, which it has not been possible to adjust by diplomacy, which have not been adjusted as a result of reference to an appropriate commission of conciliation, and which are justiciable in their nature by reason of being susceptible of decision by the application of the principles of law or equity, shall be submitted to the Permanent Court of Arbitration established at The Hague by the convention of October 18, 1907, or to some other competent tribunal, as shall be decided in each case by special agreement, which special agreement shall provide for the organization of such tribunal if necessary, define its powers, state the question or questions at issue, and settle the terms of reference.

The special agreement in each case shall be made on the part of the United States of America by the President of the United States of America by and with the advice and consent of the Senate thereof, and on the part of Germany in accordance with its constitutional laws.

ART. II. The provisions of this treaty shall not be invoked in respect of any dispute the subject matter of which

(a) is within the domestic jurisdiction of either of the high contracting parties,

(b) involves the interests of third parties.

(c) depends upon or involves the maintenance of the traditional attitude of the United States concerning American questions, commonly described as the Monroe doctrine,

(d) depends upon or involves the observance of the obligations of Germany in accordance with the Covenant of the League of Nations.

ART. III. The present treaty shall be ratified by the President of the United States of America by and with the advice and consent of the Senate thereof and by the President of the German Reich in accordance with German constitutional laws.

The ratifications shall be exchanged at Washington as soon as possible, and the treaty shall take effect on the date of the exchange of the ratifications. It shall thereafter remain in force continuously unless and until terminated by one year's written notice given by either high contracting party to the other.

In faith whereof the respective plenipotentiaries have signed this treaty in duplicate in the English and German languages, both texts having equal force, and hereunto affix their seals.

Done at Washington the fifth day of May in the year of our Lord one thousand nine hundred and twenty-eight.

FRANK B. KELLOGG,
F. VON PRITTWITZ.

2. TREATY OF CONCILIATION

The President of the United States of America and the President of the German Reich, being desirous to strengthen the bonds of amity that bind them together and also to advance the cause of general peace, have resolved to enter into a treaty for that purpose, and have agreed upon and concluded the following articles:

ART. I. Any disputes arising between the Government of the United States of America and the Government of Germany, of whatever nature they may be, shall, when ordinary diplomatic proceedings have failed and the high contracting parties do not have recourse to adjudication by a competent tribunal, be submitted for investigation and report to a permanent International Commission constituted in the manner prescribed in the next succeeding article; the high contracting parties agree not to declare war or begin hostilities during such investigation and before the report is submitted.

ART. II. The International Commission shall be composed of five members, to be appointed as follows: One member shall be chosen from each country, by the Government thereof; one member shall be chosen by each Government from some third country; the fifth member shall be chosen by common agreement between the two Governments, it being understood that he shall not be a citizen of either country. The expenses of the Commission shall be paid by the two Governments in equal proportions.

The International Commission shall be appointed within six months after the exchange of ratifications of this treaty; and vacancies shall be filled according to the manner of the original appointment.

ART. III. In case the high contracting parties shall have failed to adjust a dispute by diplomatic methods, and they do not have recourse to adjudication by a competent tribunal, they shall at once refer it to the International Commission for investigation and report. The International Commission may, however, spontaneously by unanimous agreement offer its services to that effect, and in such case it shall notify both Governments and request their cooperation in the investigation.

The high contracting parties agree to furnish the Permanent International Commission with all the means and facilities required for its investigation and report.

The report of the commission shall be completed within one year after the date on which it shall declare its investigation to have begun, unless the high contracting parties shall shorten or extend the time by mutual agreement. The report shall be prepared in triplicate; one copy shall be presented to each Government, and the third retained by the commission for its files.

The high contracting parties reserve the right to act independently on the subject matter of the dispute after the report of the commission shall have been submitted. . . .

Washington the fifth of May one thousand nine hundred and twenty-eight.

FRANK B. KELLOGG.
F. VON PRITTWITZ.

467. THE KELLOGG PEACE PACT
August 27, 1928
(*U. S. Statutes at Large,* Vol. XXXXVI, p. 2343)

In June, 1927, Aristide Briand proposed to the United States government a treaty outlawing war between France and the United States. Secretary of State Kellogg proposed to broaden the pact to embrace all nations. In April, 1928, notes were forwarded to the major European powers requesting their adherence to the pact, and August 27 the pact was signed by fifteen powers: subsequently sixty-two nations adhered to the agreement. The Treaty was introduced to the Senate December 4, 1928, and passed with only one dissenting vote—that of Senator Blaine of Wisconsin. See, D. P. Myers, *Origin and Conclusion of the Paris Pact;* D. H. Miller, *The*

Peace Pact of Paris; A. J. Toynbee, *Survey of International Relations, 1928,* Part I.

The President of the German Reich, the President of the United States of America, His Majesty the King of the Belgians, the President of the French Republic, His Majesty the King of Great Britain, Ireland and the British Dominions beyond the Seas, Emperor of India, His Majesty the King of Italy, His Majesty the Emperor of Japan, the President of the Republic of Poland, the President of the Czechoslovak Republic,

Deeply sensible of their solemn duty to promote the welfare of mankind;

Persuaded that the time has come when a frank renunciation of war as an instrument of national policy should be made to the end that the peaceful and friendly relations now existing between their peoples may be perpetuated;

Convinced that all changes in their relations with one another should be sought only by pacific means and be the result of a peaceful and orderly process, and that any signatory power which shall hereafter seek to promote its national interests by resort to war should be denied the benefits furnished by this treaty;

Hopeful that, encouraged by their example, all the other nations of the world will join in this humane endeavor and by adhering to the present treaty as soon as it comes into force bring their peoples within the scope of its beneficent provisions, thus uniting the civilized nations of the world in a common renunciation of war as an instrument of their national policy;

Have decided to conclude a treaty and for that purpose have appointed as their respective plenipotentiaries: . . .

Who, having communicated to one another their full powers found in good and due form have agreed upon the following articles:

ART. 1. The high contracting parties solemnly declare in the names of their respective peoples that they condemn recourse to war for the solution of international controversies, and renounce it as an instrument of national policy in their relations with one another.

ART. 2. The high contracting parties agree that the settlement or solution of all disputes or conflicts of whatever nature or of whatever origin they may be, which may arise among them, shall never be sought except by pacific means.

ART. 3. The present treaty shall be ratified by the high contracting parties named in the preamble in accordance with their respective constitutional requirements, and shall take effect as between them as soon as all their several instruments of ratification shall have been deposited at Washington.

This treaty shall, when it has come into effect as prescribed in the preceding paragraph, remain open as long as may be necessary for adherence by all the other powers of the world. Every instrument evidencing the adherence of a power shall be deposited at Washington and the treaty shall immediately upon such deposit become effective as between the power thus adhering and the other powers parties hereto. . . .

468. THE PHILOSOPHY OF RUGGED INDIVIDUALISM

Speech by Herbert Hoover, New York City
October 22, 1928

(The New Day. Campaign Speeches of Herbert Hoover, p. 149 ff.)

With this speech Hoover closed his campaign for the Presidency in 1928. It expresses the philosophy not only of Hoover, but of the Republican party in the years after the World War. For the campaign, see, R. V. Peel and T. C. Donnelly, *The 1928 Campaign: An Analysis.* For an earlier exposition of the doctrines herein announced, see H. Hoover, *American Individualism; The Challenge to Liberty.*

This campaign now draws near a close. The platforms of the two parties defining principles and offering solutions of various national problems have been presented and are being earnestly considered by our people. . . .

In my acceptance speech I endeavored to outline the spirit and ideals by which I would be guided in carrying that platform into administration. Tonight I will not deal with the multitude of issues which have been already well canvassed. I intend rather to discuss some of those more fundamental principles and ideals upon which I believe the government of the United States should be conducted. . . .

After the war, when the Republican party assumed administration of the country, we were faced with the problem of determination of the very nature of our national life. During one hundred and fifty years we have builded up a form of self-government and a social system which is peculiarly our own. It differs essentially from all others in the world. It is the American system. It is just as definite and positive a political and social system as has ever been developed on earth. It is founded upon a particular conception of self-government in which decentralized local responsibility is the very base. Further than this, it is founded upon the conception that only through ordered liberty, freedom, and equal opportunity to the individual will his initiative and enterprise spur on the march of progress. And in our insistence upon equality of opportunity has our system advanced beyond all the world.

During the war we necessarily turned to the government to solve every difficult economic problem. The government having absorbed every energy of our people for war, there was no other solution. For the preservation of the state the Federal Government became a centralized despotism which undertook unprecedented responsibilities, assumed autocratic powers, and took over the business of citizens. To a large degree we regimented our whole people temporarily into a socialistic state. However justified in time of war if continued in peace-time it would destroy not only our American system but with it our progress and freedom as well.

When the war closed, the most vital of all issues both in our own country and throughout the world was whether governments should continue their wartime ownership and operation of many instrumentalities of production and distribution. We were challenged with a peace-time choice between the American system of rugged individualism and a European philosophy of diametrically opposed doctrines—doctrines of paternalism and state socialism. The acceptance of these ideas would have meant the destruction of self-government through centralization of government. It would have meant the undermining of the individual initiative and enterprise through which our people have grown to unparalleled greatness.

The Republican Party from the beginning resolutely turned its face away from these ideas and these war practices. . . . When the Republican Party came into full power it went at once resolutely back to our fundamental conception of the state and the rights and responsibilities of the individual. Thereby it restored confidence and hope in the American people, it freed and stimulated enterprise, it restored the government to its position as an umpire instead of a player in the economic game. For these reasons the American people have gone forward in progress while the rest of the world has halted, and some countries have even gone backwards. If anyone will study the causes of retarded recuperation in Europe, he will find much of it due to stifling of private initiative on one hand, and overloading of the government with business on the other.

There has been revived in this campaign, however, a series of proposals which, if adopted, would be a long step toward the abandonment of our American system and a surrender to the destructive operation of governmental conduct of commercial business. Because the country is faced with difficulty and doubt over certain national problems—that is prohibition, farm relief, and electrical power—our opponents propose that we must thrust government a long way into the businesses which give rise to these problems. In effect, they abandon the tenets of their own party and turn to state socialism as a solution for the difficulties presented by all three. It is proposed that we shall change from prohibition to the state purchase and sale of liquor. If their agricultural relief program means anything, it means that the government shall directly or indirectly buy and sell and fix prices of agricultural products. And we are to go into the hydroelectric power business. In other words, we are confronted with a huge program of government in business.

There is, therefore, submitted to the American people a question of fundamental principle. That is: shall we depart from the principles of our American political and economic system, upon which we have advanced beyond all the rest of the world, in order to adopt methods based on principles destructive of its very foundations? And I wish to emphasize the seriousness of these proposals. I wish to make my position clear; for this goes to the very roots of American life and progress.

I should like to state to you the effect that this projection of government in business would have upon our system of self-government and our economic system. That effect would reach to the daily life of every man and woman. It would impair the very basis of liberty and freedom not only for those left outside the fold of expanded bureaucracy but for those embraced within it.

Let us first see the effect upon self-government. When the Federal Government undertakes to go into commercial business it must at once set up the organization and administration of that business, and it immediately finds itself in a labyrinth, every alley of which leads to the destruction of self-government.

Commercial business requires a concentration of responsibility. Self-government requires decentralization and many checks and balances to safeguard liberty. Our Government to succeed in business would need to become in effect a despotism. There at once begins the destruction of self-government. . . .

It is a false liberalism that interprets itself into the government operation of commercial business. Every step of bureaucratizing of the business of our country poisons the very roots of liberalism—that is, political equality, free speech, free assembly, free press, and equality of opportunity. It is the road not to more liberty, but to less liberty. Liberalism should be found not striving to spread bureaucracy but striving to set bounds to it. True liberalism seeks all legitimate freedom first in the confident belief that without such freedom the pursuit of all other blessings and benefits is vain. That belief is the foundation of all American progress, political as well as economic.

Liberalism is a force truly of the spirit, a force proceeding from the deep realization that economic freedom cannot be sacrificed if political freedom is to be preserved. Even if Governmental conduct of business could give us more efficiency instead of less efficiency, the fundamental objection to it would remain unaltered and unabated. It would destroy political equality. It would increase rather than decrease abuse and corruption. It would stifle initiative and invention. It would undermine the development of leadership. It would cramp and cripple the mental and spiritual energies of our people. It would extinguish equality and opportunity. It would dry up the spirit of liberty and progress. For these reasons primarily it must be resisted. For a hundred and fifty years liberalism has found its true spirit in the American system, not in the European systems.

I do not wish to be misunderstood in this statement. I am defining a general policy. It does not mean that our government is to part with one iota of its national resources without complete protection to the public interest. I have already stated that where the government is engaged in public works for purposes of flood control, of navigation, of irrigation, of scientific research or national defense, or in pioneering a new art, it will at times necessarily produce power or commodities as a by-product. But they must be a by-product of the major purpose, not the major purpose itself.

Nor do I wish to be misinterpreted as believing that the United States is free-for-all and devil-take-the-hindmost. The very essence of equality of opportunity and of American individualism is that there shall be no domination by any group or combination in this republic, whether it be business or political. On the contrary, it demands economic justice as well as political and social justice. It is no system of laissez faire.

I feel deeply on this subject because during the war I had some practical experience with governmental operation and control. I have witnessed not only at home but abroad the many failures of government in business. I have seen its tyrannies, its injustices, its destructions of self-government, its undermining of the very instincts which carry our people forward to progress. I have witnessed the lack of advance, the lowered standards of living, the depressed spirits of people working under such a system. My objection is based not upon theory or upon a failure to recognize wrong or abuse, but I know the adoption of such methods would strike at the very roots of American life and would destroy the very basis of American progress.

Our people have the right to know whether we can continue to solve our great problems without abandonment of our American system. I know we can. . . .

And what have been the results of the American system? Our country has become the land of opportunity to those born without inheritance, not merely because of the wealth of its resources and industry but because of this freedom of initiative and enterprise. Russia has natural resources equal to ours. Her people are equally industrious, but she has not had the blessings of one hundred and fifty years of our form of government and our social system.

By adherence to the principles of decentralized self-government, ordered liberty, equal opportunity, and freedom to the individual, our American experiment in human welfare has yielded a degree of well-being unparalleled in all the world. It has

come nearer to the abolition of poverty, to the abolition of fear of want, than humanity has ever reached before. Progress of the past seven years is the proof of it. This alone furnishes the answer to our opponents, who ask us to introduce destructive elements into the system by which this has been accomplished. . . .

I have endeavored to present to you that the greatness of America has grown out of a political and social system and a method of control of economic forces distinctly its own —our American system—which has carried this great experiment in human welfare farther than ever before in all history. We are nearer today to the ideal of the abolition of poverty and fear from the lives of men and women than ever before in any land. And I again repeat that the departure from our American system by injecting principles destructive to it which our opponents propose, will jeopardize the very liberty and freedom of our people, and will destroy equality of opportunity not alone to ourselves but to our children. . . .

469. THE STIMSON DOCTRINE

Address by Secretary of State Stimson before the Council on Foreign Relations February 6, 1931

(W. Lippmann and W. O. Scroggs, eds. *The United States in World Affairs*, 1931, p. 332 ff.)

President Wilson had attempted to establish moral standards as a test for recognition of new governments in foreign states. This policy had involved the United States in no little embarrassment and difficulty in dealing with Latin American countries. It was abandoned by the Hoover administration, and the abandonment formalized in this statement by Secretary Stimson. President Roosevelt has followed the Stimson rather than the Wilson policy in his dealings with foreign nations.

. . . The practice of this country as to the recognition of new governments has been substantially uniform from the days of the administration of Secretary of State Jefferson in 1792 to the days of Secretary of State Bryan in 1913. There were certain slight departures from this policy during the Civil War, but they were manifestly due to the exigencies of warfare and were abandoned immediately afterwards. This general

policy, as thus observed, was to base the act of recognition not upon the question of the constitutional legitimacy of the new government but upon its *de facto* capacity to fulfill its obligations as a member of the family of nations. This country recognized the right of other nations to regulate their own internal affairs of government and disclaimed any attempt to base its recognition upon the correctness of their constitutional action.

Said Mr. Jefferson in 1792:

We certainly cannot deny to other nations that principle whereon our own Government is founded, that every nation has a right to govern itself internally under what forms it pleases, and to change these forms at its own will; and externally to transact business with other nations through whatever organ it chooses, whether that be a king, convention, assembly, committee, president or whatever it be.

In these essentials our practice corresponded with the practice of the other nations of the world.

The particular considerations upon which our action was regularly based were well stated by Mr. Adee, long the trusted Assistant Secretary of State of this Government, as follows:

Ever since the American Revolution entrance upon diplomatic intercourse with foreign states has been *de facto,* dependent upon the existence of three conditions of fact: the control of the administrative machinery of the state; the general acquiescence of its people; and the ability and willingness of their government to discharge international and conventional obligations. The form of government has not been a conditional factor in such recognition; in other words, the *de jure* element of legitimacy of title has been left aside.

With the advent of President Wilson's administration this policy of over a century was radically departed from in respect to the Republic of Mexico, and, by a public declaration on March 11, 1913, it was announced that

Cooperation (with our sister republics of Central and South America) is possible only when supported at every turn by the orderly processes of just government based upon law, not upon arbitrary or irregular force. We hold, as I am sure that all thoughtful leaders of republican government everywhere hold, that just government rests always upon the consent of the governed, and that there can be no freedom without order based upon law and upon the public conscience and approval. We shall look to make these principles the basis of mutual intercourse, respect, and helpfulness between our sister republics and ourselves.

Mr. Wilson's government sought to put

this new policy into effect in respect to the recognition of the then Government of Mexico held by President Victoriano Huerta. Although Huerta's government was in *de facto* possession, Mr. Wilson refused to recognize it, and he sought through the influence and pressure of his great office to force it from power. Armed conflict followed with the forces of Mexico, and disturbed relations between us and that republic lasted until a comparatively few years ago.

In his sympathy for the development of free constitutional institutions among the people of our Latin American neighbors, Mr. Wilson did not differ from the feelings of the great mass of his countrymen in the United States . . . but he differed from the practice of his predecessors in seeking actively to propagate these institutions in a foreign country by the direct influence of this Government and to do this against the desires of the authorities and people of Mexico.

The present administration has declined to follow the policy of Mr. Wilson and has followed consistently the former practice of this Government since the days of Jefferson. As soon as it was reported to us, through our diplomatic representatives, that the new governments in Bolivia, Peru, Argentina, Brazil, and Panama were in control of the administrative machinery of the state, with the apparent general acquiescence of their people, and that they were willing and apparently able to discharge their international and conventional obligations, they were recognized by our Government. And, in view of the economic depression, with the consequent need for prompt measures of financial stabilization, we did this with as little delay as possible in order to give those sorely pressed countries the quickest possible opportunities for recovering their economic poise.

470. HOOVER'S VETO OF THE MUSCLE SHOALS BILL
Message to the Senate, March 3, 1931

(Message from the President of the United States, Government Printing Office)

In 1918 President Wilson had authorized, as a wartime measure, the construction of government plants at Muscle Shoals on the Tennessee River for the manufacture of nitrates, and of dams to generate electric power. After the war the disposition of these plants and dams became

a matter of prolonged and bitter controversy. Conservatives insisted that they be turned over to private companies; progressives under the leadership of Senator Norris of Nebraska advocated government ownership and operation. Henry Ford at one time offered to take over the plants, but no satisfactory arrangement could be made. In 1928 a bill providing for government operation passed Congress only to be vetoed by President Coolidge. A similar bill of 1931 was vetoed by President Hoover: the veto message reiterated the Republican doctrine of individualism in business and the belief that government ownership and operation was an approach to socialism. For the ultimate settlement of the question, see Doc. No. 478.

To the Senate:

I return herewith, without my approval, Senate Joint Resolution 49, "To provide for the national defense by the creation of a corporation for the operation of the Government properties at and near Muscle Shoals in the State of Alabama; to authorize the letting of the Muscle Shoals properties under certain conditions; and for other purposes."

This bill proposes the transformation of the war plant at Muscle Shoals, together with important expansions, into a permanently operated Government institution for the production and distribution of power and the manufacture of fertilizers. . . .

The plants at Muscle Shoals were originally built for a production of nitrates for use in war explosives. I am advised by the War Department that the very large development in the United States by private enterprise in the manufacture of synthetic nitrogen now affords an ample supply covering any possible requirements of war. It is therefore unnecessary to maintain this plant for any such purposes.

This bill provides that the President for a period of 12 months may negotiate a lease of the nitrate plants for fertilizer manufacture under detailed limitations, but in failure to make such a lease the bill makes it mandatory upon the Government to manufacture nitrogen fertilizers at Muscle Shoals by the employment of existing facilities or by modernizing existing plants or by any other process. . . .

I am firmly opposed to the Government entering into any business the major purpose of which is competition with our citizens. There are national emergencies which require that the Government should temporarily enter the field of business, but they must be emergency actions and in matters where the cost of the project is secondary to much higher considerations. There are many localities where the Federal Government is justified in the construction of great dams and reservoirs, where navigation, flood control, reclamation or stream regulation are of dominant importance, and where they are beyond the capacity or purpose of private or local government capital to construct. In these cases power is often a by-product and should be disposed of by contract or lease. But for the Federal Government deliberately to go out to build up and expand an occasion to the major purpose of a power and manufacturing business is to break down the initiative and enterprise of the American people; it is destruction of equality of opportunity of our people; it is the negation of the ideals upon which our civilization has been based.

This bill raises one of the important issues confronting our people. That is squarely the issue of Federal Government ownership and operation of power and manufacturing business not as a minor by-product but as a major purpose. Involved in this question is the agitation against the conduct of the power industry. The power problem is not to be solved by the project in this bill. The remedy for abuses in the conduct of that industry lies in regulation and not by the Federal Government entering upon the business itself. I have recommended to the Congress on various occasions that action should be taken to establish Federal regulation of interstate power in cooperation with State authorities. This bill would launch the Federal Government upon a policy of ownership and operation of power utilities upon a basis of competition instead of by the proper Government function of regulation for the protection of all the people. I hesitate to contemplate the future of our institutions, of our country if the preoccupation of its officials is to be no longer the promotion of justice and equal opportunity but is to be devoted to barter in the markets. That is not liberalism, it is degeneration.

This proposal can be effectively opposed upon other and perhaps narrower grounds. The establishment of a Federal-operated power business and fertilizer factory in the Tennessee Valley means Federal control from Washington with all the vicissitudes of national politics and the tyrannies of remote bureaucracy imposed upon the people of that valley without voice by them in their own resources, the overriding of State and local government, the undermining of State and local responsibility. The very history of this project over the past 10 years should be a complete demonstration of the ineptness of the Federal Government to administer such enterprise and of the penalties which the local community suffers under it.

This bill distinctly proposes to enter the field of powers reserved to the States. It would deprive the adjacent States of the right to control rates for this power and would deprive them of taxes on property within their borders and would invade and weaken the authority of local government. . . .

The real development of the resources and the industries of the Tennessee Valley can only be accomplished by the people in that valley themselves. Muscle Shoals can only be administered by the people upon the ground, responsible to their own communities, directing them solely for the benefit of their communities and not for purposes of pursuit of social theories or national politics. Any other course deprives them of liberty. . . .

HERBERT HOOVER.

471. THE MOONEY–BILLINGS CASE

Conclusions of the sub-committee of the Section on Lawless Enforcement of Law of the Wickersham Committee
June, 1931

(The Mooney-Billings Report, Suppressed by the Wickersham Committee, p. 242–3)

On July 22, 1916, a bomb was thrown into a Preparedness parade in San Francisco, killing nine and wounding some forty people. Two days later a Bomb Squad was organized and promptly arrested Thomas Mooney, a labor agitator, his wife, Rena Mooney, Warren K. Billings, a machinist, E. D. Nolan, a labor leader, and Israel Weinberg, a jitney driver, and charged them with the crime. The Grand Jury returned indictments against each of the prisoners for murder. Subsequently the charges against all but Mooney and Billings were dismissed. These two were convicted of murder in the first degree; Billings was sentenced to life imprisonment and Mooney to death. In view of the character of the trial and certain doubts as to the justice of the conviction, President Wilson in September 1917 requested the Mediation Commission to investigate the case. The Commission reported the following January that there was a basis for the feeling that an injustice was done the prisoners and recommended that the President intercede on behalf of the prisoners with the Governor of California. Wilson wrote three letters to the Governor, and eventually the sentence of Mooney was commuted to life imprisonment. The case became a *cause célèbre* and attracted world wide attention. Ceaseless efforts of various groups in the United States to re-open the case or to secure a pardon from the executive of California were without avail. In 1931 a sub-committee of the Wickersham Committee on Law Observance and Enforcement, consisting of Professor Z. Chafee, W. H. Pollack and C. S. Stern, made an extensive report on the Mooney-Billings Case. This Report was not published along with the other reports of the Wickersham Committee, because the Committee felt that it was not proper to inquire into particular cases but only into general principles. Allusions to the Mooney-Billings Report, however, brought a demand for a publication of the document, and when Congress failed to provide for publication it was privately printed. The Wickersham Committee *Report* is in 71 Congress, 2d Session, *House Doc.* No. 252, 14 parts. On the Mooney-Billings Case see also H. T. Hart, *The Case of Thomas J. Mooney and Warren K. Billings: Abstract and Analysis of record before Governor Young of California;* E. J. Hopkins, *What Happened in the Mooney Case.* See also, A. G. Hays, *Trial by Prejudice;* E. M. Borchard, *Convicting the Innocent.*

CONCLUSIONS

Considering the records as a whole, we conclude:

(1) There was never any scientific attempt made, by either the police or the prosecution to discover the perpetrators of the crime. The investigation was in reality turned over to a private detective who used his position to cause the arrest of the defendants. The police investigation was reduced to a hunt for evidence to convict the arrested defendants.

(2) There were flagrant violations of the statutory laws of California by both the police and the prosecution in the manner in which the defendants were arrested and held incommunicado and in the subsequent search of their homes to procure evidence against them.

(3) After the arrest of the defendants, witnesses were brought to the jails to "identify" them, and their "identifications" were accepted by the police and the prosecution, despite the fact that these witnesses were never required to pick the defendants out of a line-up, or to demonstrate their accuracy by any other test.

(4) Immediately after the arrests of the defendants there commenced a deliberate attempt to arouse public prejudice against them, by a series of almost daily interviews given to the press by prosecuting officials.

(5) Witnesses were procured at the trials with information in the hands of the prosecution that seriously challenged the credibility of the witnesses, but this information was deliberately concealed.

(6) Witnesses were permitted to testify at the trials, despite such knowledge in the possession of the prosecution of prior contradictory stories told by these witnesses as to make their mere reproduction a vouching for perjured testimony.

(7) Witnesses were coached in their testimony to a degree that approximated subornation of perjury. There is a strong inference that some of this coaching was done by prosecuting officials, and other evidence points to knowledge by the prosecuting officials that such coaching was being practiced on other witnesses.

(8) The prejudice against the defendants, stimulated by newspaper publicity, was further appealed to at the trials by unfair and intemperate arguments to the jury in the opening and closing statements of the prosecuting attorneys.

(9) After the trials, the disclosures casting doubt on the justice of the convictions were minimized, and every attempt made to defeat the liberation of the defendants, by a campaign of misrepresentation and propaganda carried on by the officials who had prosecuted them.

472. NEW STATE ICE COMPANY v. LIEBMANN
285 U. S. 262
1932

Appeal from the United States Circuit Court of Appeals for the Tenth District. An act of the Oklahoma Legislature, 1925, declared that the manufacture, sale, and distribution of ice is a public business, that no one shall be permitted to manufacture, sell or distribute ice within the State without a license, and that the Corporation Commission in granting a license shall take into consideration the necessity for the manufacture, etc. of ice at the place desired, the extent to which the community was already equipped with such facilities, the responsibility, reliability, and capacity of the persons or corporation applying for the license to furnish facilities, conveniences, and services to the public. One Liebmann set up an ice plant in Oklahoma City, without having first obtained a license, and the New State Ice Company, operating under a license, sought to enjoin him from doing business in Oklahoma City. The Circuit Court dismissed the bill.

SUTHERLAND, J. . . . It must be conceded that all businesses are subject to some measure of public regulation. And that the business of manufacturing, selling, or distributing ice, like that of the grocer, the dairyman, the butcher, or the baker, may be subjected to appropriate regulations in the interest of public health cannot be doubted; but the question here is whether the business is so charged with a public use as to justify the particular restriction above stated. If this legislative restriction be within the constitutional power of the state Legislature, it follows that the license or permit, issued to appellant, constitutes a franchise, to which a court of equity will afford protection against one who seeks to carry on the same business without obtaining from the commission a license or permit to do so. . . . In that view, engagement in the business is a privilege to be exercised only in virtue of a public grant, and not a common right to be exercised independently by any competent person conformably to reasonable regulations equally applicable to all who choose to engage therein. . . .

Here we are dealing with an ordinary business, not with a paramount industry, upon which the prosperity of the state in large measure depends. It is a business as essentially private in its nature as the business of the grocer, the dairyman, the butcher, the baker, the shoemaker, or the tailor, each of whom performs a service which, to a greater or less extent, the community is dependent upon and is interested in having maintained; but which bears no such relation to the public as to warrant its inclusion in the category of businesses charged with a public use. It may be quite true that in Oklahoma ice is, not only an article of prime necessity, but indispensable; but certainly not more so than food or clothing or the shelter of a home. . . .

Plainly, a regulation which has the effect of denying or unreasonably curtailing the common right to engage in a lawful private business, such as that under review, cannot be upheld consistent with the Fourteenth Amendment. Under that amendment nothing is more clearly settled than that it is beyond the power of a state "under the guise of protecting the public, arbitrarily to interfere with private business or prohibit lawful occupations or impose unreasonable and unnecessary restrictions upon them." . . .

The particular requirement before us was evidently not imposed to prevent a practical monopoly of the business, since its tendency is quite to the contrary. Nor is it a case of the protection of natural resources. There is nothing in the product that we can perceive on which to rest a distinction, in respect of this attempted control, from other products in common use which enter into free competition, subject, of course, to reasonable regulations prescribed for the protection of the public and applied with appropriate impartiality.

And it is plain that unreasonable or arbitrary interference or restrictions cannot be saved from the condemnation of that amendment merely by calling them experimental. It is not necessary to challenge the authority of the states to indulge in experimental legislation; but it would be strange and unwarranted doctrine to hold that they may do so by enactments which transcend the limitations imposed on them by the Federal Constitution. The principle is imbedded in our constitutional system that there are certain essentials of liberty with which the state is not entitled to dispense in the interests of experiments. . . .

Judgment affirmed

BRANDEIS, J., dissenting. . . . In my opinion the judgment should be reversed.

First. The Oklahoma statute makes entry into the business of manufacturing ice for sale and distribution dependent, in effect, upon a certificate of public convenience and necessity. Such a certificate was unknown to the common law. It is a creature of the machine age, in which plants have displaced tools and businesses are substituted for trades. The purpose of requiring it is to promote the public interest by preventing waste. Particularly in those businesses in which interest and depreciation charges on plant constitute a large element in the cost of production, experience has taught that the financial burdens incident to unnecessary duplication of facilities are likely to bring high rates and poor service. . . . The introduction in the United States of the certificate of public convenience and necessity marked the growing conviction that under certain circumstances free competition might be harmful to the community, and that, when it was so, absolute freedom to enter the business of one's choice should be denied.

Long before the enactment of the Oklahoma statute here challenged, a like requirement had become common in the United States in some lines of business. . . . As applied to public utilities, the validity under the Fourteenth Amendment of the requirement of the certificate has never been successfully questioned.

Second. Oklahoma declared the business of manufacturing ice for sale and distribution a "public-business"; that is, a public utility. . . . But the conception of a public utility is not static. The welfare of the community may require that the business of supplying ice be made a public utility, as well as the business of supplying water or any other necessary commodity or service. If the business is, or can be made, a public utility, it must be possible to make the issue of a certificate a prerequisite to engaging in it.

Whether the local conditions are such as to justify converting a private business into a public one is a matter primarily for the determination of the state Legislature. . . .

. . . Liebmann rests his defense upon the broad claim that the Federal Constitution gives him the right to enter the business of manufacturing ice for sale even if his doing so be found by the properly constituted authority to be inconsistent with the public welfare. He claims that, whatever the local conditions may demand, to confer upon the commission power to deny that right is an unreasonable, arbitrary, and capricious restraint upon his liberty.

The function of the court is primarily to determine whether the conditions in Oklahoma are such that the Legislature could not reasonably conclude (1) that the public welfare required treating the manufacture of ice for sale and distribution as a "public business"; and (2) that, in order to insure to the inhabitants of some communities an adequate supply of ice at reasonable rates, it was necessary to give the commission power to exclude the establishment of an additional ice plant in places where the community was already well served. Unless the Court can say that the Federal Constitution confers an absolute right to engage anywhere in the business of manufacturing ice for sale, it cannot properly decide that the legislators acted unreasonably without first ascertaining what was the experience of Oklahoma in respect to the ice business. . . .

Can it be said in the light of these facts that it was not an appropriate exercise of legislative discretion to authorize the commission to deny a license to enter the business in localities where necessity for another plant did not exist? The need of some remedy for the evil of destructive competition, where competition existed, had been and was widely felt. Where competition did not exist, the propriety of public regulation had been proven. Many communities were not supplied with ice at all. The particular remedy adopted was not enacted hastily. The statute was based upon a long-established state policy recognizing the public importance of the ice business, and upon 17 years' legislative and administrative experience in the regulation of it. The advisability of treating the ice business as a public utility and of applying to it the certificate of convenience and necessity had been under consideration for many years. Similar legislation had been enacted in Oklahoma under similar circumstances with respect to other public services. The measure bore a substantial relation to the evils found to exist. Under these circumstances, to hold the act void as being unreasonable would, in my opinion, involve the exercise, not of the function of judicial review, but the function of a super-Legislature. . . .

A regulation valid for one kind of business may, of course, be invalid for another, since the reasonableness of every regulation is dependent upon the relevant facts. But so far as concerns the power to regulate, there is no difference, in essence, between a business called private and one called a public utility or said to be "affected with a public interest." . . . The notion of a distinct category of business "affected with a public interest," employing property "devoted to a public use," rests upon historical error. The consequences which it is sought to draw from those phrases are belied by the meaning in which they were first used centuries ago, and by the decision of this Court, in *Munn* v. *Illinois,* 94 U.S. 113, which first introduced them into the law of the Constitution. In my opinion, the true principle is that the state's power extends to every regulation of any business reasonably required and appropriate for the public protection. I find in the due process clause no other limitation upon the character or the scope of regulation permissible. . . .

The people of the United States are now confronted with an emergency more serious than war. Misery is widespread, in a time, not of scarcity, but of overabundance. The long-continued depression has brought unprecedented unemployment, a catastrophic fall in commodity prices, and a volume of economic losses which threatens our financial institutions. . . . But rightly or wrongly, many persons think that one of the major contributing causes has been unbridled competition. Increasingly, doubt is expressed whether it is economically wise, or morally right, that men should be permitted to add to the producing facilities of an industry which is already suffering from overcapacity. . . . Many insist there must be some form of economic control. There are plans for pro-ration. There are many proposals for stabilization. And some thoughtful men of wide business experience insist that all projects for stabilization and pro-ration must prove futile unless, in some way, the equivalent of the certificate of public convenience and necessity is made a prerequisite to embarking new capital in an industry in which the capacity already exceeds the production of schedules.

Whether that view is sound nobody knows. The objections to the proposal are obvious and grave. The remedy might bring evils worse than the present disease. The obstacles to success seem insuperable. The economic and social sciences are largely uncharted seas. We have been none too successful in the modest essays in economic control already entered upon. The new proposal involves a vast extension of the area of control. . . .

Some people assert that our present plight is due, in part, to the limitations set by courts upon experimentation in the fields of social and economic science; and to the discouragement to which proposals for betterment there have been subjected otherwise. There must be power in the states and the nation to remould, through experimentation, our economic practices and institutions to meet changing social and economic needs.

I cannot believe that the framers of the Fourteenth Amendment, or the states which ratified it, intended to deprive us of the power to correct the evils of technological unemployment and excess productive capacity which have attended progress in the useful arts.

To stay experimentation in things social and economic is a grave responsibility. Denial of the right to experiment may be fraught with serious consequences to the nation. It is one of the happy incidents of the federal system that a single courageous state may, if its citizens choose, serve as a laboratory, and try novel social economic experiments without risk to the rest of the country. This Court has the power to prevent an experiment. We may strike down the statute which embodies it on the ground that, in our opinion, the measure is arbitrary, capricious, or unreasonable. We have power to do this, because the due process clause has been held by the Court applicable to matters of substantive law as well as to matters of procedure. But, in the exercise of this high power, we must be ever on our guard, lest we erect our prejudices into legal principles. If we would guide by the light of reason, we must let our minds be bold.

473. CONSTITUTION OF THE AMERICAN FEDERATION OF LABOR
1932

(Report of Proceedings of the 52d Annual Convention of the American Federation of Labor, Cincinnati, Ohio, 1932, p. xviii ff.)

The American Federation of Labor was organized first in 1881, and reorganized as a national Federation in 1886. With the decline of the Knights of Labor, it came to be the dominant labor organization in the country, and by 1934 had attained a membership of over five million. The literature on the A. F. of L. is extensive. See, S. Gompers, *Seventy Years of Life and Labor,* 2 Vols.; S. Perlman, *History of Trade Unionism in the United States;* L. Wolman, *Growth of American Trade Unions;* F. T. Carlton, *History and Problems of Organized Labor;* R. F. Hoxie, *Trade Unionism in the United States;* L. L. Lorwin, *The American Federation of Labor.*

PREAMBLE—Whereas, A struggle is going on in all the nations of the civilized world

between the oppressors and the oppressed of all countries, a struggle between the capitalist and the laborer, which grows in intensity from year to year, and will work disastrous results to the toiling millions if they are not combined for mutual protection and benefit. It, therefore, behooves the representatives of the Trade and Labor Unions of America, in convention assembled, to adopt such measures and disseminate such principles among the mechanics and laborers of our country as will permanently unite them to secure the recognition of rights to which they are justly entitled. We, therefore, declare ourselves in favor of the formation of thorough Federation, embracing every Trade and Labor Organization in America, organized under the Trade Union system.

CONSTITUTION

ART. I—Name: This Association shall be known as the American Federation of Labor, and shall consist of such Trade and Labor Unions as shall conform to its rules and regulations.

ART. II—Objects: Sec. 1. The object of this Federation shall be the encouragement and formation of local Trade and Labor Unions, and the closer federation of such societies through the organization of Central Trade and Labor Unions in every city, and the further combination of such bodies into State, Territorial, or Provincial organizations to secure legislation in the interest of the working masses.

Sec. 2. The establishment of National and International Trade Unions, based upon a strict recognition of the autonomy of each trade, and the promotion and advancement of such bodies.

Sec. 3. The establishment of Departments composed of National or International Unions affiliated with the American Federation of Labor, of the same industry, and which Departments shall be governed in conformity with the laws of the American Federation of Labor.

Sec. 4. An American Federation of all National and International Trade Unions, to aid and assist each other; to aid and encourage the sale of union label goods, and to secure legislation in the interest of the working people, and influence public opinion, by peaceful and legal methods, in favor of organized labor.

Sec. 5. To aid and encourage the labor press of America. . . .

Sec. 8. Party politics, whether they be Democratic, Republican, Socialist, Populistic, Prohibition, or any other, shall have no place in the Conventions of the American Federation of Labor. . . .

ART. IX—Executive Council: Sec. 1. It shall be the duty of the Executive Council to watch legislative measures directly affecting the interests of working people, and to initiate, whenever necessary, such legislative action as the Convention may direct.

Sec. 2. The Executive Council shall use every possible means to organize new Na-

tional or International Trade or Labor Unions, and to organize Local Trade and Labor Unions, and connect them with the Federation until such time as there is a sufficient number to form a National or International Union, when it shall be the duty of the President of the Federation to see that such organization is formed. . . .

Sec. 5. While we recognize the right of each trade to manage its own affairs, it shall be the duty of the Executive Council to secure the unification of all labor organizations, so far as to assist each other in any trade dispute. . . .

Sec. 10. All Local Trade Unions and Federal Labor Unions holding charters direct from the American Federation of Labor, desiring the assistance of the American Federation of Labor in trade disputes, shall submit to the President of the American Federation of Labor for approval by the Executive Council the full statement of the grievance, and shall receive within twenty (20) days from the President an answer as to whether they will be sustained or not, and no benefits shall be paid where a strike takes place before the Local Union has received the approval of the Executive Council. . . .

ART. X—Revenue: Sec. 1. The revenue of the Federation shall be derived from a per capita tax to be paid upon the full paid-up membership of all affiliated bodies, as follows: From International or National Trade Unions, a per capita tax of one cent per member per month; from Local Trade Unions and Federal Labor Unions, thirty-five cents per member per month, twelve and one-half cents of which must be set aside to be used only in case of strike or lockout. . . .

ART. XI—Local Central Bodies: . . .

Sec. 2. It shall be the duty of all National and International Unions affiliated with the American Federation of Labor to instruct their Local Unions to join chartered Central Labor Bodies, Departments, and State Federations in their vicinity where such exist. Similar instructions shall be given by the American Federation of Labor to all Trade and Federal Labor Unions under its jurisdiction.

Sec. 3. Where there are one or more Local Unions in any city belonging to any National or International Union affiliated with this Federation they may organize a

Central Labor Union, or shall join such body if already in existence.

Sec. 4. The Executive Council and Local Central Labor Unions shall use all possible means to organize and connect as Local Unions to National or International Unions the organizations in their vicinity to aid the formation of National or International Unions where none exist, and to organize Federal Labor Unions where the number of craftsmen precludes any other form of organization.

Sec. 5. No Central Labor Union, or other central body of delegates, shall have the authority or power to order any organization, affiliated with such Central Labor Union, or other central labor body, on strike, or to take a strike vote, where such organization has a national organization, until the proper authorities of such National or International organization have been consulted and agreed to such action.

Sec. 6. Separate charters may be issued to Central Labor Unions, Local Unions, or Federal Labor Unions, composed exclusively of colored members, where, in the judgment of the Executive Council, it appears advisable and to the best interest of the Trade Union movement to do so.

Sec. 7. No Central Labor Union, or other central body of delegates, shall have authority or power to originate a boycott, nor shall such bodies indorse and order the placing of the name of any person, firm, or corporation on an unfair list until the Local Union desiring the same has, before declaring the boycott, submitted the matter in dispute to the Central Body for investigation, and the best endeavors on its part to effect an amicable settlement. Violation of this section shall forfeit charter. . . .

ART. XII—Assessment in Defense of National and International Unions: Sec. 1. The Executive Council shall have power to declare a levy of one cent per member per week on all affiliated unions for a period not exceeding ten weeks in any one year, to assist in the support of an affiliated National or International Union engaged in a protracted strike or lockout. . . .

ART. XIII—Defense Fund For Local Trade and Federal Labor Unions: Sec. 1. Unless otherwise ordered by the Executive Council the moneys of the defense fund shall be drawn only to sustain strikes or lockouts of Local Trade and Federal Labor Unions when such strikes or lockouts are authorized, indorsed, and conducted in conformity with the following provisions of this Article:

Sec. 2. In the event of a disagreement between a Local Union and an employer which, in the opinion of the Local Union, may result in a strike, such Union shall notify the President of the American Federation of Labor, who shall investigate or cause an investigation to be made of the disagreement, and endeavor to adjust the difficulty. If his efforts should prove futile, he shall take such steps as he shall deem necessary in notifying the Executive Council, and if the majority of said Council shall decide that a strike is necessary such Union shall be authorized to order a strike, but that under no circumstances shall a strike or lockout be deemed legal, or moneys expended from the defense fund on that account, unless the strike or lockout shall have been first authorized and approved by the President and Executive Council. . . .

Sec. 5. When a strike has been inaugurated under the provisions of Sections 2 and 3, the American Federation of Labor shall pay to the bonded officer of the Union involved, or his order, for a period of six weeks, an amount equal to seven ($7) dollars per week for each member. Each Local Union shall require its treasurer to give proper bond for the safekeeping and disbursement of all funds of the Local. No benefit shall be paid for the first two weeks of the strike. The Executive Council shall have the power to authorize the payment of strike benefits for an additional period. . . .

Sec. 7. Any Union inaugurating a strike without the approval of the Executive Council shall not receive benefit on account of said strike. . . .

Sec. 10. Before a strike shall be declared off a special meeting of the Union shall be called for that purpose, and it shall require a majority vote of all members present to decide the question either way.

Sec. 11. In the event of the defense fund becoming dangerously low through protracted strike or lockout, the Executive Council of the American Federation of Labor shall have the power to levy an assessment of ten cents on each member of Local

Trade and Federal Labor Unions, assessments to be restricted to not more than five per year; and further, that there shall always be a surplus of five thousand ($5,000) dollars in the defense fund. . . .

474. NORRIS–LAGUARDIA ANTI-INJUNCTION BILL
March 20, 1932
(*U. S. Statutes at Large,* Vol. XLVII, p. 70 ff.)

This measure was the climax of a quarter century of agitation for the strict limitation of the use of the injunction in labor disputes. The earlier attempt in the Clayton Act, Doc. No. 403, had proved ineffective. See, F. Frankfurter and N. Greene, *The Labor Injunction;* E. E. Witte, *The Government in Labor Disputes;* Brissenden, "The Labor Injunction" 48 Pol. Sci. Qt. 413; Monkemeyer, "Five Years of the Norris-LaGuardia Act," 2 Mo. L. Rev. 1; Hellerstein, "Picketing Legislation and the Courts," 10 N. C. L. Rev. 158; Riddlesbarger, "Federal Anti-Injunction Act," 14 Ore. L. Rev. 242; and note in 48 Yale L. J. 308.

AN ACT to amend the Judicial Code and to define and limit the jurisdiction of courts sitting in equity, and for other purposes.

Be it enacted, That no court of the United States, as herein defined, shall have jurisdiction to issue any restraining order or temporary or permanent injunction in a case involving or growing out of a labor dispute, except in a strict conformity with the provisions of this Act; nor shall any such restraining order or temporary or permanent injunction be issued contrary to the public policy declared in this Act.

Sec. 2. In the interpretation of this Act and in determining the jurisdiction and authority of the courts of the United States, as such jurisdiction and authority are herein defined and limited, the public policy of the United States is hereby declared as follows:

Whereas, under prevailing economic conditions, . . . the individual unorganized worker is commonly helpless to exercise actual liberty of contract and to protect his freedom of labor, and thereby to obtain acceptable terms and conditions of employment, wherefore, though he should be free to decline to associate with his fellows, it is necessary that he should have full freedom of association, self-organization, and designation of representatives of his own choosing, to negotiate the terms and conditions of his employment, and that he shall be free from the interference, restraint, or coercion of employers of labor, or their agents, in the activities for the purpose of collective bargaining or other mutual aid or protection; therefore, the following definitions of, and limitations upon, the jurisdiction and authority of the courts of the United States are hereby enacted.

Sec. 3. Any undertaking or promise, such as is described in this section, or any other undertaking or promise in conflict with the public policy declared in section 2 of this Act, is hereby declared to be contrary to the public policy of the United States, shall not be enforceable in any court of the United States and shall not afford any basis for the granting of legal or equitable relief by any such court, including specifically the following:

Every undertaking or promise hereafter made, whether written or oral, express or implied, constituting or contained in any contract or agreement of hiring or employment between any individual firm, company, association, or corporation, and any employee or prospective employee of the same, whereby,

a—Either party to such contract or agreement undertakes or promises not to join, become, or remain a member of any labor organization or of any employer organization; or

b—Either party to such contract or agreement undertakes or promises that he will withdraw from any employment relation in the event that he joins, becomes, or remains a member of any labor organization or of any employer organization.

Sec. 4. No court of the United States shall have the jurisdiction to issue any restraining order or temporary or permanent injunction in any case involving or growing out of any labor dispute to prohibit any person or persons participating or interested in such dispute (as these terms are herein defined) from doing, whether singly or in concert, any of the following acts:

(a) Ceasing or refusing to perform any

work or to remain in any relation of employment;

(b) Becoming or remaining a member of any labor organization or of any employer organization, regardless of any such undertaking or promise as is described in section 3 of this Act:

(c) Paying or giving to, or withholding from any person participating or interested in such labor dispute, any strike or employment benefits or insurance, or other moneys or things of value;

(d) By all lawful means aiding any person participating or interested in any labor dispute who is being proceeded against in, or is prosecuting, any action or suit in any court in the United States or of any state;

(e) Giving publicity to the extent of, or the facts involved in any labor dispute whether by advertising, speaking, patrolling, or by any other method not involving fraud or violence;

(f) Assembling peaceably to act or to organize to act in promotion of their interests in a labor dispute;

(g) Advising or notifying any persons of any intentions to do any of the acts heretofore specified;

(h) Agreeing with other persons to do or not to do any of the acts heretofore specified; and

(i) Advising, urging, or otherwise causing or inducing without fraud or violence the acts heretofore specified, regardless of any such undertaking or promise as is described in section 3 of this Act.

Sec. 5. No court of the United States shall have jurisdiction to issue a restraining order or temporary or permanent injunction upon the ground that any of the persons participating or interested in a labor dispute constitute or are engaged in an unlawful combination or conspiracy because of the doing in concert of the acts enumerated in section 4 of this Act.

Sec. 6. No officer or member of any organization or association, and no association or organization participating or interested in a labor dispute, shall be held responsible or liable in any court of the United States for the unlawful acts of individual officers, members, or agents, except upon clear proof of actual participation in, or actual authorization of, such acts, or of ratification of such acts after actual knowledge thereof.

Sec. 7. No court of the United States shall have jurisdiction to issue a temporary or permanent injunction in any case involving or growing out of a labor dispute as herein defined except after hearing the testimony of witnesses in open court (with opportunity for cross-examination) in support of the allegations of a complaint made under oath, and testimony in opposition thereto, if offered, and except after findings of fact by the court, to the effect—

(a) That unlawful acts have been threatened and will be committed unless restrained or have been committed and will be continued unless restrained, but no injunction or temporary restraining order shall be issued on account of any threat or unlawful act excepting against the person or persons, association, or organization making the threat or committing the unlawful act or actually authorizing or ratifying the same after actual knowledge thereof;

(b) That substantial and irreparable injury to complainant's property will follow;

(c) That as to each item of relief granted greater injury will be inflicted upon complainant by the denial of relief than will be inflicted upon defendants by the granting of relief;

(d) That complainant has no adequate remedy at law; and

(e) That the public officers charged with the duty to protect complainant's property are unable or unwilling to furnish adequate protection. . . .

Sec. 9. No restraining order or temporary or permanent injunctions shall be granted in a case involving or growing out of a labor dispute, except on the basis of findings of fact made and filed by the court in the record of the case prior to the issuance of such restraining order or injunction; and every restraining order or injunction granted in a case involving or growing out of a labor dispute shall include only a prohibition of such specific act or acts as may be expressly complained of in the bill of complaint or petition filed in such case and as shall be expressly included in said findings of fact made and filed by the court as provided herein. . . .

Sec. 11. In all cases arising under this Act in which a person shall be charged with contempt in a court of the United States (as herein defined), the accused shall enjoy the right to speedy and public trial by an impartial jury of the state and district wherein the contempt shall have been committed: *Provided,* That this right shall not apply to contempt committed in the presence of the court or so near thereto as to interfere directly with the administration of justice or to apply to the misbehavior, misconduct, or disobedience of any officer of the court in respect to the writs, orders, or process of the court. . . .

Sec. 13. . . .

(c) The term "labor dispute" includes any controversy concerning terms or conditions of employment, or concerning the association or representation of persons negotiating, fixing, maintaining, changing, or seeking to arrange terms or conditions of employment, regardless of whether or not the disputants stand in approximate relation of employer and employee. . . .

475. THE DEMOCRATIC PLATFORM OF 1932
June 30, 1932
(*Proceedings* of the Democratic National Convention of 1932, p. 146)

The failure of the Republican administration to solve the problems presented by the great depression made Democratic chances of success in 1932 very bright. In an atmosphere of optimism the Democrats met at Chicago, June 27, and nominated to the Presidency Governor Franklin D. Roosevelt of New York. The vice-Presidential nomination went to John E. Garner of Texas. The Republicans, meeting likewise at Chicago, renominated President Hoover and vice-President Curtis. In the November election the Democratic ticket polled 22,821,857 popular and 472 electoral votes, the Republican 15,761,841 popular and 59 electoral votes. See E. E. Robinson, *The Presidential Vote, 1896–1932;* R. V. Peel and T. C. Donnelly, *The 1932 Campaign;* D. Dumond, *Roosevelt to Roosevelt;* C. A. and M. R. Beard, *America in Midpassage;* E. K. Lindley, *The Roosevelt Revolution.* Roosevelt's campaign speeches can be found in his *Public Papers and Addresses,* Vol. II.

In this time of unprecedented economic and social distress the Democratic Party declares its conviction that the chief causes of this condition were the disastrous policies pursued by our government since the World War, of economic isolation, fostering the merger of competitive businesses into monopolies and encouraging the indefensible expansion and contraction of credit for private profit at the expense of the public.

Those who were responsible for these policies have abandoned the ideals on which the war was won and thrown away the fruits of victory, thus rejecting the greatest opportunity in history to bring peace, prosperity, and happiness to our people and to the world.

They have ruined our foreign trade; destroyed the values of our commodities and products, crippled our banking system, robbed millions of our people of their life savings, and thrown millions more out of work, produced wide-spread poverty and brought the government to a state of financial distress unprecedented in time of peace.

The only hope for improving present conditions, restoring employment, affording permanent relief to the people, and bringing the nation back to the proud position of domestic happiness and of financial, industrial, agricultural and commercial leadership in the world lies in a drastic change in economic governmental policies.

We believe that a party platform is a covenant with the people to be faithfully kept by the party when entrusted with power, and that the people are entitled to know in plain words the terms of the contract to which they are asked to subscribe. We hereby declare this to be the platform of the Democratic Party:

The Democratic Party solemnly promises by appropriate action to put into effect the principles, policies, and reforms herein advocated, and to eradicate the policies, methods, and practices herein condemned. We advocate an immediate and drastic reduction of governmental expenditures by abolishing useless commissions and offices, consolidating departments and bureaus, and eliminating extravagance, to accomplish a saving of not less than twenty-five per cent in the cost of federal government, and we call upon the Democratic Party in the States to make a zealous effort to achieve a proportionate result.

We favor maintenance of the national credit by a federal budget annually balanced on the basis of accurate executive estimates within revenues, raised by a system of taxation levied on the principle of ability to pay.

We advocate a sound currency to be preserved at all hazards and an international monetary conference called on the invitation of our government to consider the rehabilitation of silver and related questions.

We advocate a competitive tariff for revenue, with a fact-finding tariff commission free from executive interference, reciprocal tariff agreements with other nations, and an international economic conference designed to restore international trade and facilitate exchange.

We advocate the extension of federal credit to the states to provide unemployment relief wherever the diminishing resources of the states make it impossible for them to provide for the needy; expansion of the federal program of necessary and useful construction affected with a public interest, such as adequate flood control and waterways.

We advocate the spread of employment by a substantial reduction in the hours of labor, the encouragement of the shorter week by applying that principle in government service. We advocate advance planning of public works.

We advocate unemployment and old age insurance under state laws.

We favor the restoration of agriculture, the nation's basic industry; better financing of farm mortgages through recognized farm bank agencies at low rates of interest on an amortization plan, giving preference to credits for the redemption of farms and homes sold under foreclosure.

Extension and development of Farm Cooperative movement and effective control of crop surpluses so that our farmers may have the full benefit of the domestic market.

The enactment of every constitutional measure that will aid the farmers to receive for their basic farm commodities prices in excess of cost.

We advocate a Navy and an Army adequate for national defense, based on a survey of all facts affecting the existing establishments, that the people in time of peace may not be burdened by an expenditure fast approaching a billion dollars annually.

We advocate strengthening and impartial enforcement of the anti-trust laws, to prevent monopoly and unfair trade practices, and revision thereof for the better protection of labor and the small producer and distributor.

The conservation, development, and use of the nation's water power in the public interest.

The removal of government from all fields of private enterprise except where necessary to develop public works and natural resources in the common interest.

We advocate protection of the investing public by requiring to be filed with the government and carried in advertisements of all offerings of foreign and domestic stocks and bonds true information as to bonuses, commissions, principal invested, and interests of the sellers.

Regulation to the full extent of federal power of

    (a) Holding companies which sell securities in interstate commerce;

    (b) Rates of utility companies operating across state lines;

    (c) Exchanges in securities and commodities.

We advocate quicker methods of realizing on assets for the relief of depositors of suspended banks, and a more rigid supervision of national banks for the protection of depositors and the prevention of the use of their moneys in speculation to the detriment of local credits.

The severance of affiliated security companies from, and the divorce of the investment banking business from, commercial banks, and further restriction of federal reserve banks in permitting the use of federal reserve facilities for speculative purposes.

We advocate the full measure of justice and generosity for all war veterans who have suffered disability or disease caused by or resulting from actual service in time of war and for their dependents.

We advocate a firm foreign policy, including peace with all the world and the settlement of international dispute by arbitration; no interference in the internal affairs of other nations; the sanctity of treaties and the maintenance of good faith and of good will in financial obligations; adherence to the World Court with appending reservations; the Pact of Paris abolishing war as an instrument of national policy, to be made effective by provisions for consultation and conference in case of threatened violations of treaties.

International agreements for reduction of armaments and cooperation with nations of

.he Western Hemisphere to maintain the spirit of the Monroe Doctrine.

We oppose cancellation of the debts owing to the United States by foreign nations.

Independence for the Philippines; ultimate statehood for Porto Rico.

The employment of American citizens in the operation of the Panama Canal.

Simplification of legal procedure and reorganization of the judicial system to make the attainment of justice speedy, certain, and at less cost.

Continuous publicity of political contributions and expenditures; strengthening of the Corrupt Practices Act and severe penalties for misappropriation of campaign funds.

We advocate the repeal of the Eighteenth Amendment. To effect such repeal we demand that the Congress immediately propose a Constitutional Amendment to truly representative conventions in the states called to act solely on that proposal. We urge the enactment of such measures by the several states as will actually promote temperance, effectively prevent the return of the saloon and bring the liquor traffic into the open under complete supervision and control by the states.

We demand that the Federal Government effectively exercise its power to enable the states to protect themselves against importation of intoxicating liquors in violation of their laws.

Pending repeal, we favor immediate modification of the Volstead Act to legalize the manufacture and sale of beer and other beverages of such alcoholic content as is permissible under the Constitution and to provide therefrom a proper and needed revenue.

We advocate continuous responsibility of government for human welfare, especially for the protection of children.

We condemn the improper and excessive use of money in political activities.

We condemn paid lobbies of special interests to influence members of Congress and other public servants by personal contact.

We condemn action and utterances of high public officials designed to influence stock exchange prices.

We condemn the open and covert resistance of administration officials to every effort made by Congressional committees to curtail the extravagant expenditures of the government and to revoke improvident subsidies granted to favorite interests.

We condemn the extravagance of the Farm Board, its disastrous action which made the Government a speculator of farm products and the unsound policy of restricting agricultural products to the demands of domestic markets.

We condemn the usurpation of power by the State Department in assuming to pass upon foreign securities offered by international bankers as a result of which billions of dollars in questionable bonds have been sold to the public upon the implied approval of the Federal Government.

We condemn the Hawley-Smoot Tariff Law, the prohibitive rates of which have resulted in retaliatory action by more than forty countries, created international economic hostilities, destroyed international trade, driven our factories into foreign countries, robbed the American farmer of his foreign markets, and increased the cost of production.

In conclusion, to accomplish these purposes and to recover economic liberty we pledge the nominees of this convention the best efforts of a great party whose founder announced the doctrine which guides us now in the hour of our country's need:

Equal rights to all; special privileges to none.

476. F. D. ROOSEVELT'S FIRST INAUGURAL ADDRESS
March 4, 1933

(Pamphlet, Government Printing Office)

This speech is reproduced, with minor variations, in Vol. II of the *Public Papers and Addresses of F. D. Roosevelt*. On Roosevelt, see this five volume collection of public papers, and E. Looker, *This Man Roosevelt;* E. K. Lindley, *The Roosevelt Revolution, First Phase.* For the New Deal program in general see C. A. and M. R. Beard, *America in Midpassage;* L. Hacker, *Short History of the New Deal;* D. Dumond, *Roosevelt to Roosevelt;* C. A. Beard, *The Future Comes;* S. Chase, *A New Deal;* W. F. Ogburn, ed. *Social Change and the New Deal;* S. Wallace, *The New*

Deal in Action; G. Soule, *The Coming American Revolution;* R. Moley, *After Seven Years;* J. Alsop and R. Kitner, *The Men Around the President.*

President Hoover, Mr. Chief Justice, my friends:

This is a day of national consecration, and I am certain that my fellow-Americans expect that on my induction into the Presidency I will address them with a candor and a decision which the present situation of our nation impels.

This is pre-eminently the time to speak the truth, the whole truth, frankly and boldly. Nor need we shrink from honestly facing conditions in our country today. This great nation will endure as it has endured, will revive and will prosper.

So first of all let me assert my firm belief that the only thing we have to fear is fear itself—nameless, unreasoning, unjustified terror which paralyzes needed efforts to convert retreat into advance.

In every dark hour of our national life a leadership of frankness and vigor has met with that understanding and support of the people themselves which is essential to victory. I am convinced that you will again give that support to leadership in these critical days.

In such a spirit on my part and on yours we face our common difficulties. They concern, thank God, only material things. Values have shrunken to fantastic levels; taxes have risen; our ability to pay has fallen, government of all kinds is faced by serious curtailment of income; the means of exchange are frozen in the currents of trade; the withered leaves of industrial enterprise lie on every side; farmers find no markets for their produce; the savings of many years in thousands of families are gone.

More important, a host of unemployed citizens face the grim problem of existence, and an equally great number toil with little return. Only a foolish optimist can deny the dark realities of the moment.

Yet our distress comes from no failure of substance. We are stricken by no plague of locusts. Compared with the perils which our forefathers conquered because they believed and were not afraid, we have still much to be thankful for. Nature still offers her bounty and human efforts have multiplied it. Plenty is at our doorstep, but a generous use of it languishes in the very sight of the supply.

Primarily, this is because the rulers of the exchange of mankind's goods have failed through their own stubbornness and their own incompetence, have admitted their failure and abdicated. Practices of the unscrupulous money changers stand indicted in the court of public opinion, rejected by the hearts and minds of men.

True, they have tried, but their efforts have been cast in the pattern of an outworn tradition. Faced by failure of credit, they have proposed only the lending of more money.

Stripped of the lure of profit by which to induce our people to follow their false leadership, they have resorted to exhortations, pleading tearfully for restored confidence. They know only the rules of a generation of self-seekers.

They have no vision, and when there is no vision the people perish.

The money changers have fled from their high seats in the temple of our civilization. We may now restore that temple to the ancient truths.

The measure of the restoration lies in the extent to which we apply social values more noble than mere monetary profit.

Happiness lies not in the mere possession of money; it lies in the joy of achievement, in the thrill of creative effort.

The joy and moral stimulation of work no longer must be forgotten in the mad chase of evanescent profits. These dark days will be worth all they cost us if they teach us that our true destiny is not to be ministered unto but to minister to ourselves and to our fellow-men.

Recognition of the falsity of material wealth as the standard of success goes hand in hand with the abandonment of the false belief that public office and high political position are to be valued only by the standards of pride of place and personal profit; and there must be an end to a conduct in banking and in business which too often has given to a sacred trust the likeness of callous and selfish wrongdoing.

Small wonder that confidence languishes, for it thrives only on honesty, on honor, on the sacredness of obligations, on faithful protection, on unselfish performance. Without them it cannot live.

Restoration calls, however, not for changes in ethics alone. This nation asks for action, and action now.

Our greatest primary task is to put people to work. This is no unsolvable problem if we face it wisely and courageously.

It can be accomplished in part by direct recruiting by the government itself, treating the task as we would treat the emergency of a war, but at the same time, through this employment, accomplishing greatly needed projects to stimulate and reorganize the use of our natural resources.

Hand in hand with this, we must frankly recognize the overbalance of population in our industrial centers and, by engaging on a national scale in the redistribution, endeavor to provide a better use of the land for those best fitted for the land.

The task can be helped by definite efforts to raise the values of agricultural products and with this the power to purchase the output of our cities.

It can be helped by preventing realistically the tragedy of the growing loss, through foreclosure, of our small homes and our farms.

It can be helped by insistence that the Federal, State and local governments act forthwith on the demand that their cost be drastically reduced.

It can be helped by the unifying of relief activities which today are often scattered, uneconomical and unequal. It can be helped by national planning for and supervision of all forms of transportation and of communications and other utilities which have a definitely public character.

There are many ways in which it can be helped, but it can never be helped merely by talking about it. We must act, and act quickly.

Finally, in our progress toward a resumption of work we require two safeguards against a return of the evils of the old order; there must be a strict supervision of all banking and credits and investments; there must be an end to speculation with other people's money, and there must be provision for an adequate but sound currency.

These are the lines of attack. I shall presently urge upon a new Congress in special session detailed measures for their fulfillment, and I shall seek the immediate assistance of the several States.

Through this program of action we address ourselves to putting our own national house in order and making income balance outgo.

Our international trade relations, though vastly important, are, in point of time and necessity, secondary to the establishment of a sound national economy.

I favor as a practical policy the putting of first things first. I shall spare no effort to restore world trade by international economic readjustment, but the emergency at home cannot wait on that accomplishment.

The basic thought that guides these specific means of national recovery is not narrowly nationalistic.

It is the insistence, as a first consideration, upon the interdependence of the various elements in, and parts of, the United States—a recognition of the old and permanently important manifestation of the American spirit of the pioneer.

It is the way to recovery. It is the immediate way. It is the strongest assurance that the recovery will endure.

In the field of world policy I would dedicate this nation to the policy of the good neighbor—the neighbor who resolutely respects himself and, because he does so, respects the rights of others—the neighbor who respects his obligations and respects the sanctity of his agreements in and with a world of neighbors.

If I read the temper of our people correctly, we now realize as we have never before, our interdependence on each other; that we cannot merely take, but we must give as well; that if we are to go forward we must move as a trained and loyal army willing to sacrifice for the good of a common discipline, because, without such discipline, no progress is made, no leadership becomes effective.

We are, I know, ready and willing to submit our lives and property to such discipline because it makes possible a leadership which aims at a larger good.

This I propose to offer, pledging that the larger purposes will bind upon us all as a sacred obligation with a unity of duty hitherto evoked only in time of armed strife.

With this pledge taken, I assume unhesitatingly the leadership of this great army of our people, dedicated to a disciplined attack upon our common problems.

Action in this image and to this end is feasible under the form of government which we have inherited from our ancestors.

Our Constitution is so simple and practical that it is possible always to meet extraordinary needs by changes in emphasis and arrangement without loss of essential form.

That is why our constitutional system has proved itself the most superbly enduring political mechanism the modern world has produced. It has met every stress of vast expansion of territory, of foreign wars, of bitter internal strife, of world relations.

It is to be hoped that the normal balance of executive and legislative authority may be wholly adequate to meet the unprecedented task before us. But it may be that an unprecedented demand and need for undelayed .ction may call for temporary departure from that normal balance of public procedure.

I am prepared under my constitutional duty to recommend the measures that a stricken nation in the midst of a stricken world may require.

These measures, or such other measures as the Congress may build out of its experience and wisdom, I shall seek, within my constitutional authority, to bring to speedy adoption.

But in the event that the Congress shall fail to take one of these two courses, and in the event that the national emergency is still critical, I shall not evade the clear course of duty that will then confront me.

I shall ask the Congress for the one remaining instrument to meet the crisis—broad executive power to wage a war against the emergency as great as the power that would be given me if we were in fact invaded by a foreign foe.

For the trust reposed in me I will return the courage and the devotion that befit the time. I can do no less.

We face the arduous days that lie before us in the warm courage of national unity; with the clear consciousness of seeking old and precious moral values; with the clean satisfaction that comes from the stern performance of duty by old and young alike.

We aim at the assurance of a rounded and permanent national life.

We do not distrust the future of essential democracy. The people of the United States have not failed. In their need they have registered a mandate that they want direct, vigorous action.

They have asked for discipline and direction under leadership. They have made me the present instrument of their wishes. In the spirit of the gift I take it.

In this dedication of a nation we humbly ask the blessing of God. May He protect each and every one of us! May He guide me in the days to come!

477. THE AGRICULTURAL ADJUSTMENT ACT
May 12, 1933

(U. S. Statutes at Large, Vol. XLVIII, p. 31)

The failure of the Hoover farm relief program made it imperative that the new Democratic administration give emergency relief to the farmers. This Agricultural Adjustment Act was the most important of several acts which attempted to afford temporary relief from the most pressing ills of the farmer and at the same time to rehabilitate agriculture. One of the major purposes of the Act was to raise the general level of agricultural commodity prices to that of the pre-War period, chiefly through voluntary crop reduction. This Act also authorized the President to devalue the gold dollar by not more than fifty per cent. Parts of the AAA were subsequently nullified by the Court (Doc. No. 478) but those parts were later substantially reënacted. See, H. Wallace, *America Must Choose,* and *New Frontiers;* M. Ezekiel and L. H. Bean, *Economic Bases of the AAA;* E. G. Nourse, et. al. *Three Years of the AAA;* E. G. Nourse, *Marketing Agreements under the AAA;* J. Davis, *Wheat and the AAA;* H. T. Richards, *Cotton and the AAA;* J. D. Black, *Dairy Industry and the AAA.*

AN ACT To relieve the existing national economic emergency by increasing agricultural purchasing power, . . . to provide for the orderly liquidation of joint-stock land banks, and for other purposes.

TITLE I—AGRICULTURAL ADJUST-MENT

DECLARATION OF EMERGENCY

That the present acute economic emergency being in part the consequence of a severe and increasing disparity between the prices of agricultural and other commodities, which disparity has largely destroyed the purchasing power of farmers for industrial products, has broken down the orderly exchange of commodities, and has seriously impaired the agricultural assets supporting the national credit structure, it is hereby declared that these conditions in the basic industry of agriculture have affected transactions in agricultural commodities with a national public interest, have burdened and obstructed the normal currents of commerce in such commodities, and render imperative the immediate enactment of title I of this Act.

DECLARATION OF POLICY

SEC. 2. It is hereby declared to be the policy of Congress—

(1) To establish and maintain such balance between the production and consumption of agricultural commodities, and such marketing conditions therefor, as will reestablish prices to farmers at a level that will give agricultural commodities a purchasing power with respect to articles that farmers buy, equivalent to the purchasing power of agricultural commodities in the base period. The base period in the case of all agricultural commodities except tobacco shall be the prewar period, August 1909–July 1914. In the case of tobacco, the base period shall be the postwar period, August 1919–July 1929.

(2) To approach such equality of purchasing power by gradual correction of the present inequalities therein at as rapid a rate as is deemed feasible in view of the current consumptive demand in domestic and foreign markets.

(3) To protect the consumers' interest by readjusting farm production at such level as will not increase the percentage of the consumers' retail expenditures for agricultural commodities, or products derived therefrom, which is returned to the farmer, above the percentage which was returned to the farmer in the prewar period, August 1909–July 1914. . . .

SEC. 6. (a) The Secretary of Agriculture is hereby authorized to enter into option contracts with the producers of cotton to sell to any such producer an amount of cotton to be agreed upon not in excess of the amount of reduction in production of cotton by such producer below the amount produced by him in the preceding crop year, in all cases where such producer agrees in writing to reduce the amount of cotton produced by him in 1933, below his production in the previous year, by not less than 30 per centum, without increase in commercial fertilization per acre.

(b) To any such producer so agreeing to reduce production the Secretary of Agriculture shall deliver a nontransferable-option contract agreeing to sell to said producer an amount, equivalent to the amount of his agreed reduction, of the cotton in the possession and control of the Secretary.

(c) The producer is to have the option to buy said cotton at the average price paid by the Secretary for the cotton procured under section 3, and is to have the right at any time up to January 1, 1934, to exercise his option, upon proof that he has complied with his contract and with all the rules and regulations of the Secretary of Agriculture with respect thereto, by taking said cotton upon payment by him of his option price and all actual carrying charges on such cotton; or the Secretary may sell such cotton for the account of such producer, paying him the excess of the market price at the date of sale over the average price above referred to after deducting all actual and necessary carrying charges: *Provided,* That in no event shall the producer be held responsible or liable for financial loss incurred in the holding of such cotton or on account of the carrying charges therein: *Provided further,* That such agreement to curtail cotton production shall contain a further provision that such cotton producer shall not use the land taken out of cotton production for the production for sale, directly or indirectly, of any other nationally produced agricultural commodity or product. . . .

PART 2—COMMODITY BENEFITS

GENERAL POWERS

SEC. 8. In order to effectuate the declared policy, the Secretary of Agriculture shall have power—

(1) To provide for reduction in the acreage or reduction in the production for market, or both, of any basic agricultural commodity, through agreements with producers or by other voluntary methods, and to provide for rental or benefit payments in connection therewith or upon that part of the production of any basic agricultural commodity required for domestic consumption, in such amounts as the Secretary deems fair and reasonable, to be paid out of any moneys available for such payments. . . .

(2) To enter into marketing agreements with processors, associations of producers, and others engaged in the handling, in the current of interstate or foreign commerce of any agricultural commodity or project thereof, after due notice and opportunity for hearing to interested parties. The making of any such agreement shall not be held to be in violation of any of the antitrust laws of the United States, and any such agreement shall be deemed to be lawful. . . .

PROCESSING TAX

SEC. 9. (a) To obtain revenue for extraordinary expenses incurred by reason of the national economic emergency, there shall be levied processing taxes as hereinafter provided. When the Secretary of Agriculture determines that rental or benefit payments are to be made with respect to any basic agricultural commodity, he shall proclaim such determination, and a processing tax shall be in effect with respect to such commodity from the beginning of the marketing year therefor next following the date of such proclamation. The processing tax shall be levied, assessed, and collected upon the first domestic processing of the commodity, whether of domestic production or imported, and shall be paid by the processor. . . .

(b) The processing tax shall be at such rate as equals the difference between the current average farm price for the commodity and the fair exchange value of the commodity; except that if the Secretary has reason to believe that the tax at such rate will cause such reduction in the quantity of the commodity or products thereof domestically consumed as to result in the accumulation of surplus stocks of the commodity or products thereof or in the depression of the farm price of the commodity, then he shall cause

an appropriate investigation to be made and afford due notice and opportunity for hearing to interested parties. If thereupon the Secretary finds that such result will occur, then the processing tax shall be at such rate as will prevent such accumulation of surplus stocks and depression of the farm price of the commodity. . . .

(c) For the purposes of part 2 of this title, the fair exchange value of a commodity shall be the price therefor that will give the commodity the same purchasing power, with respect to articles farmers buy, as such commodity had during the base period specified in section 2. . . .

(d) As used in part 2 of this title—

(1) In case of wheat, rice, and corn, the term "processing" means the milling or other processing (except cleaning and drying) of wheat, rice, or corn for market, including custom milling for toll as well as commercial milling, but shall not include the grinding or cracking thereof not in the form of flour for feed purposes only.

(2) In case of cotton, the term "processing" means the spinning, manufacturing, or other processing (except ginning) of cotton; and the term "cotton" shall not include cotton linters.

(3) In case of tobacco, the term "processing" means the manufacturing or other processing (except drying or converting into insecticides and fertilizers) of tobacco.

(4) In case of hogs, the term "processing" means the slaughter of hogs for market.

(5) In the case of any other commodity, the term "processing" means any manufacturing or other processing involving a change in the form of the commodity or its preparation for market, as defined by regulations of the Secretary of Agriculture; and in prescribing such regulations the Secretary shall give due weight to the customs of the industry.

(e) When any processing tax, or increase or decrease therein, takes effect in respect of a commodity the Secretary of Agriculture, in order to prevent pyramiding of the processing tax and profiteering in the sale of the products derived from the commodity, shall make public such information as he deems necessary regarding (1) the relationship between the processing tax and the price paid to producers of the commodity, (2) the effect of the processing tax upon prices to consumers of products of the commodity, (3) the relationship, in previous periods, between prices paid to the producers of the commodity and prices to consumers of the products thereof, and (4) the situation in foreign countries relating to prices paid to producers of the commodity and prices to consumers of the products thereof. . . .

PART 8

"Emergency Farm Mortgage Act of 1933."

TITLE III—FINANCING—AND EXERCISING POWER CONFERRED BY SECTION 8 OF ARTICLE I OF THE CONSTITUTION: TO COIN MONEY AND TO REGULATE THE VALUE THEREOF

SEC. 43. Whenever the President finds, upon investigation, that (1) the foreign commerce of the United States is adversely affected by reason of the depreciation in the value of the currency of any other government or governments in relation to the present standard value of gold, or (2) action under this section is necessary in order to regulate and maintain the parity of currency issues of the United States, or (3) an economic emergency requires an expansion of credit, or (4) an expansion of credit is necessary to secure by international agreement a stabilization at proper levels of the currencies of various governments, the President is authorized, in his discretion— . . .

(1) To direct the Secretary of the Treasury to cause to be issued in such amount or amounts as he may from time to time order, United States notes, . . . in the same size and of similar color to the Federal Reserve notes heretofore issued and in denominations of $1, $5, $10, $20, $50, $100, $500, $1,000, and $10,000; but notes issued under this subsection shall be issued only for the purpose of meeting maturing Federal obligations to repay sums borrowed by the United States and for purchasing United States bonds and other interest-bearing obligations of the United States: *Provided,* That when any such notes are used for such purpose the bond or other obligation so acquired or taken up shall be retired and canceled. Such notes shall be issued at such times and in such amounts as the President may approve but the aggregate amount of such notes outstanding at any time shall not exceed $3,000,000,-000. There is hereby appropriated, out of any money in the Treasury not otherwise appropriated, an amount sufficient to enable the Secretary of the Treasury to retire and cancel 4 per centum annually of such outstanding notes, and the Secretary of the Treasury is hereby directed to retire and cancel annually 4 per centum of such outstanding notes. Such notes and all other coins and currencies heretofore or hereafter coined or issued by or under the authority of the United States shall be legal tender for all debts public and private.

(2) By proclamation to fix the weight of the gold dollar in grains nine tenths fine and also to fix the weight of the silver dollar in grains nine tenths fine at a definite fixed ratio in relation to the gold dollar at such amounts as he finds necessary from his investigation to stabilize domestic prices or to protect the foreign commerce against the adverse effect of depreciated foreign currencies, and to provide for the unlimited coinage of such gold and silver at the ratio so fixed, or in case the Government of the United States enters into an agreement with any government or governments under the terms of which the ratio between the value of gold and other currency issued by the United States and by any such government or governments is established, the President may fix the weight of the gold dollar in accordance with the ratio so agreed upon, and such gold dollar, the weight of which is so fixed, shall be the standard unit of value, and all forms of money issued or coined by the United States shall be maintained at a parity with this standard and it shall be the duty of the Secretary of the Treasury to maintain such parity, but in no event shall the weight of the gold dollar be fixed so as to reduce its present weight by more than 50 per centum. . . .

SEC. 45. (a) The President is authorized for a period of six months from the date of the passage of this Act, to accept silver in payment of the whole or any part of the principal or interest now due, or to become due within six months after such date, from any foreign government or governments on account of any indebtedness to the United States, such silver to be accepted at not to exceed the price of 50 cents an ounce in United States currency. The aggregate value of the silver accepted under this section shall not exceed $200,000,000. . . .

(d) The Secretary of the Treasury shall cause silver certificates to be issued in such denominations as he deems advisable to the total number of dollars for which such silver was accepted in payment of debts. Such silver certificates shall be used by the Treasurer of the United States in payment of any obligations of the United States.

(e) The silver so accepted and received under this section shall be coined into standard silver dollars and subsidiary coins sufficient, in the opinion of the Secretary of the Treasury, to meet any demands for redemption of such silver certificates issued under the provisions of this section, and such coins shall be retained in the Treasury for the payment of such certificates on demand. The silver so accepted and received under this section, except so much thereof as is coined under the provisions of this section, shall be held in the Treasury for the sole purpose of aiding in maintaining the parity of such certificates as provided in existing law. Any such certificates or reissued certificates, when presented at the Treasury, shall be redeemed in standard silver dollars, or in subsidiary silver coin, at the option of the holder of the certificates: . . .

(f) When any silver certificates issued under the provisions of this section are redeemed or received into the Treasury from any source whatsoever, and belong to the United States, they shall not be retired, canceled, or destroyed, but shall be reissued and paid out again and kept in circulation; . . .

SEC. 46. Section 19 of the Federal Reserve Act, as amended, is amended by inserting immediately after paragraph (c) thereof the following new paragraph:

"Notwithstanding the foregoing provisions of this section, the Federal Reserve Board, upon the affirmative vote of not less than five of its members and with the approval of the President, may declare that an emergency exists by reason of credit expansion, and may by regulation during such emergency increase or decrease from time to time, in its discretion, the reserve balances required to be maintained against either demand or time deposits."

478. THE UNITED STATES v. BUTLER et. al.
297 U. S. 1
1936

On Writ of Certiorari to the U. S. Circuit Court of Appeals for the First Circuit. The invalidation of the AAA was perhaps the severest blow which the Supreme Court struck at the New Deal and was in large part responsible for the demand for judicial reform (see Doc. No. 515). While apparently accepting the doctrine of the McCulloch case, the Court here took the position that the end here aimed at—e.g., the rehabilitation of agriculture—was not a legitimate one, but was solely under the jurisdiction of the states. The major provisions of the AAA were reënacted by Congress in the Soil Conservation and Domestic Allotment Act of 1936 and the AAA Act of 1938. The literature on this case is large, but see especially: Holmes, "Federal Spending Power and State Rights," 34 Mich. Law. Rev. 637; Hart, "Processing Taxes and Protective Tariffs," 49 Harv. L. Rev. 610; Brebner-Smith, "The Hoosac Mills Case," 25 Georgetown L. J. 2; Post, "Constitutionality of Government Spending for General Welfare," 22 Va. L. Rev. 1; Collier, "Judicial Bootstraps and the General Welfare Clause," 4 Geo. Wash. L. Rev. 211; D. Alfange, *The Supreme Court and the National Will*; W. Hamilton and O. Adair, *The Power to Govern.*

ROBERTS, J. In this case we must determine whether certain provisions of the Agricultural Adjustment Act, 1933, conflict with the federal Constitution.

Title I of the statute is captioned "Agricultural Adjustment." Section 1 recites that an economic emergency has arisen, due to disparity between the prices of agricultural and other commodities, with consequent destruction of farmers' purchasing power and breakdown in orderly exchange, which, in turn, have affected transactions in agricultural commodities with a national public interest and burdened and obstructed the normal currents of commerce, calling for the enactment of legislation.

Section 2 declares it to be the policy of Congress:

"To establish and maintain such balance between the production and consumption of agricultural commodities, and such marketing, conditions therefor, as will reëstablish prices to farmers at a level that will give agricultural commodities a purchasing power with respect to articles that farmers buy, equivalent to the purchasing power of agricultural commodities in the base period."

The base period, in the case of cotton, and all other commodities except tobacco, is designated as that between August, 1909, and July, 1914.

The further policies announced are an approach to the desired equality by gradual correction of present inequalities "at as rapid a rate as is deemed feasible in view of the current consumptive demand in domestic and foreign markets," and the protection of consumers' interest by readjusting farm production at such level as will not increase the percentage of the consumers' retail expenditures for agricultural commodities or products derived therefrom, which is returned to the farmer, above the percentage returned to him in the base period.

Section 8 provides, amongst other things, that "In order to effectuate the declared policy," the Secretary of Agriculture shall have power

"(1) To provide for reduction in the acreage or reduction in the production for market, or both, of any basic agricultural commodity, through agreements with producers or by other voluntary methods, and to provide for rental or benefit payments in connection therewith or upon that part of the production of any basic agricultural commodity required for domestic consumption, in such amounts as the Secretary deems fair and reasonable, to be paid out of any moneys available for such payments." . . .

"(2) To enter into marketing agreements with processors, associations of producers, and others engaged in the handling, in the current of interstate or foreign commerce of any agricultural commodity or product thereof, after due notice and opportunity for hearing to interested parties." . . .

"(3) To issue licenses permitting processors, associations of producers, and others to engage in the handling, in the current of interstate or foreign commerce, of any agricultural commodity or product thereof, or any competing commodity or product thereof."

It will be observed that the Secretary is not required, but is permitted, if, in his un-controlled judgment, the policy of the act will so be promoted, to make agreements with individual farmers for a reduction of acreage or production upon such terms as he may think fair and reasonable.

Section 9 (a) enacts:

"To obtain revenue for extraordinary expenses incurred by reason of the national economic emergency, there shall be levied processing taxes as hereinafter provided. When the Secretary of Agriculture determines that rental or benefit payments are to be made with respect to any basic agricultural commodity, he shall proclaim such determination, and a processing tax shall be in effect with respect to such commodity from the beginning of the marketing year therefor next following the date of such proclamation. The processing tax shall be levied, assessed, and collected upon the first domestic processing of the commodity, whether of domestic production or imported, and shall be paid by the processor." . . .

Section 9 (b) fixes the tax "at such rate as equals the difference between the current average farm price for the commodity and the fair exchange value," with power in the Secretary, after investigation, notice, and hearing, to readjust the tax so as to prevent the accumulation of surplus stocks and depression of farm prices.

Section 9 (c) directs that the fair exchange value of a commodity shall be such a price as will give that commodity the same purchasing power with respect to articles farmers buy as it had during the base period and that the fair exchange value and the current average farm price of a commodity shall be ascertained by the Secretary from available statistics in his department.

Section 12 (a) appropriates $100,000,000 "to be available to the Secretary of Agriculture for administrative expenses under this title and for rental and benefit payments . . .";　and Section 12 (b) appropriates the proceeds derived from all taxes imposed under the act "to be available to the Secretary of Agriculture for expansion of markets and removal of surplus agricultural products . . . Administrative expenses, rental and benefit payments, and refunds on taxes."

Section 15 (d) permits the Secretary, upon certain conditions to impose compensating taxes on commodities in competition with those subject to the processing tax. . . .

On July 14, 1933, the Secretary of Agriculture, with the approval of the President, proclaimed that he had determined rental and benefit payments should be made with respect to cotton; that the marketing year for that commodity was to begin August 1, 1933; and calculated and fixed the rates of processing and floor taxes on cotton in accordance with the terms of the act.

The United States presented a claim to the respondents as receivers of the Hoosac Mills Corporation for processing and floor taxes on cotton levied under sections 9 and 16 of the act. The receivers recommended that the claim be disallowed. The District Court found the taxes valid and ordered them paid. Upon appeal to Circuit Court of Appeals reversed the order. The judgment under review was entered prior to the adoption of the amending act of August 24, 1935, and we are therefore concerned only with the original act.

First. At the outset the United States contends that the respondents have no standing to question the validity of the tax. The position is that the act is merely a revenue measure levying an excise upon the activity of processing cotton,—a proper subject for the imposition of such a tax,—the proceeds of which go into the federal treasury and thus become available for appropriation for any purpose. It is said that what the respondents are endeavoring to do is to challenge the intended use of the money pursuant to Congressional appropriation when, by confession, that money will have become the property of the Government and the taxpayer will no longer have any interest in it. . . .

The tax can only be sustained by ignoring the avowed purpose and operation of the act, and holding it a measure merely laying on excise upon processors to raise revenue for the support of government. Beyond cavil the sole object of the legislation is to restore the purchasing power of agricultural products to a parity with that prevailing in an earlier day; to take money from the processor and bestow it upon farmers who will reduce their acreage for the accomplishment of the proposed end, and, meanwhile, to aid these farmers during the period required to bring the prices of their crops to the desired level.

The tax plays an indispensable part in the plan of regulation. As stated by the Agricultural Adjustment Administrator, it is "the heart of the law"; a means of "accomplishing one or both of two things intended to help farmers attain parity prices and purchasing power." . . .

The statute not only avows an aim foreign to the procurement of revenue for the support of government, but by its operation shows the exaction laid upon processors to be the necessary means for the intended control of agricultural production. . . .

It is inaccurate and misleading to speak of the exaction from processors prescribed by the challenged act as a tax, or to say that as a tax it is subject to no infirmity. A tax, in the general understanding of the term, and as used in the Constitution, signifies an exaction for the support of the Government. The word has never been thought to connote the expropriation of money from one group for the benefit of another. We may concede that the latter sort of imposition is constitutional when imposed to effectuate regulation of a matter in which both groups are interested and in respect of which there is a power of legislative regulation. But manifestly no justification for it can be found unless as an integral part of such regulation. The exaction cannot be rested out of its setting, denominated an excise for raising revenue and legalized by ignoring its purpose as a mere instrumentality for bringing about a desired end. To do this would be to shut our eyes to what all others than we can see and understand. *Child Labor Tax Case,* 259 U. S. 20, 37.

We conclude that the act is one regulating agricultural production; that the tax is a mere incident of such regulation and that the respondents have standing to challenge the legality of the exaction.

It does not follow that as the act is not an exertion of the taxing power and the exaction not a true tax, the statute is void or the exaction uncollectible. For, to paraphrase what was said in *The Head Money Cases (supra),* p. 596, if this is an expedient regulation by Congress, of a subject within one of its granted powers, "and the end to be attained is one falling within that power, the act is not void, because, within a loose and more extended sense than was used in the Constitution," the exaction is called a tax.

Second. The Government asserts that even if the respondents may question the propriety of the appropriation embodied in the statute their attack must fail because Article I, Section 8 of the Constitution authorizes the contemplated expenditure of the funds raised by the tax. This contention presents the great and the controlling question in the case. We approach its decision with a sense of our grave responsibility to render judgment in accordance with the principles established for the governance of all three branches of the Government.

There should be no misunderstanding as to the function of this court in such a case. It is sometimes said that the court assumes a power to overrule or control the action of the people's representatives. This is a misconception. The Constitution is the supreme law of the land ordained and established by the people. All legislation must conform to the principles it lays down. When an act of Congress is appropriately challenged in the courts as not conforming to the constitutional mandate the judicial branch of the Government has only one duty,—to lay the article of the Constitution which is invoked beside the statute which is challenged and to decide whether the latter squares with the former. All the court does, or can do, is to announce its considered judgment upon the question. The only power it has, if such it may be called, is the power of judgment. This court neither approves nor condemns any legislative policy. Its delicate and difficult office is to ascertain and declare whether the legislation is in accordance with, or in contravention of, the provisions of the Constitution; and, having done that, its duty ends.

The question is not what power the federal Government ought to have but what powers in fact have been given by the people. It hardly seems necessary to reiterate that ours is a dual form of government; that in every state there are two governments,—the state and the United States. Each State has all governmental powers save such as the people, by their Constitution, have conferred upon the United States, denied to the States, or reserved to themselves. The federal union is a government of delegated powers. It has only such as are expressly conferred upon it and such as are reasonably to be implied from those granted. In this respect we differ radically from nations where all legislative power, without restriction or limitation, is vested in a parliament or other legislative body subject to no restrictions except the discretion of its members.

Article I, Section 8, of the Constitution vests sundry powers in the Congress. But two of its clauses have any bearing upon the validity of the statute under review.

The third clause endows the Congress with power "to regulate Commerce . . . among the several States." Despite a reference in its first section to a burden upon, and an obstruction of the normal currents of commerce, the act under review does not purport to regulate transactions in interstate or foreign commerce. Its stated purpose is the control of agricultural production, a purely local activity in an effort to raise the prices paid the farmer. Indeed, the Government does not attempt to uphold the validity of the act on the basis of the commerce clause, which, for the purpose of the present case, may be put aside as irrelevant.

The clause thought to authorize the legislation,—the first,—confers upon the Congress power "to lay and collect Taxes, Duties, Imposts and Excises, to pay the Debts and provide for the common Defence and general Welfare of the United States. . . ." It is not contended that this provision grants power to regulate agricultural production upon the theory that such legislation would promote the general welfare. The Government concedes that the phrase "to provide for the general welfare" qualifies the power "to lay and collect taxes." The view that the clause grants power to provide for the general welfare, independently of the taxing power, has never been authoritatively accepted. . . . The true construction undoubtedly is that the only thing granted is the power to tax for the purpose of providing funds for payment of the nation's debts and making provision for the general welfare.

Nevertheless the Government asserts that warrant is found in this clause for the adoption of the Agricultural Adjustment Act. The argument is that Congress may appropriate and authorize the spending of moneys for the "general welfare"; that the phrase should be liberally construed to cover anything conducive to national welfare; that decision as to what will promote such welfare rests with Congress alone, and the courts may not review its determination; and finally that the appropriation under attack was in fact for the general welfare of the United States. . . .

Since the foundation of the nation sharp differences of opinion have persisted as to the true interpretation of the phrase. Madison asserted it amounted to no more than a reference to the other powers enumerated in the subsequent clauses of the same section; that, as the United States is a government of limited and enumerated powers, the grant of power to tax and spend for the general national welfare must be confined to the enumerated legislative fields committed to the Congress. In this view the phrase is mere tautology, for taxation and appropriation are or may be necessary incidents of the exercise of any of the enumerated legislative powers. Hamilton, on the other hand, maintained the clause confers a power separate and distinct from those later enumerated, is not restricted in meaning by the grant of them, and Congress consequently has a substantive power to tax and to appropriate, limited only by the requirement that it shall be exercised to provide for the general welfare of the United States. Each contention has had the support of those whose views are entitled to weight. This court has noticed the question, but has never found it necessary to decide which is the true construction. Mr. Justice Story, in his Commentaries, espouses the Hamiltonian position. We shall not review the writings of public men and commentators or discuss the legislative practice. Study of all these leads us to conclude that the reading advocated by Mr. Justice Story is the correct one. While, therefore, the power to tax is not unlimited, its confines are set in the clause which confers it, and not in those of section 8 which bestow and define the legislative powers of the Congress. It results that the power of Congress to authorize expenditure of public moneys for public purposes is not limited by the direct grants of legislative power found in the Constitution.

But the adoption of the broader construction leaves the power to spend subject to limitations. . . .

That the qualifying phrase must be given effect all advocates of broad construction admit. Hamilton, in his well known Report on Manufactures, states that the purpose must be "general, and not local.". . .

We are not now required to ascertain the scope of the phrase "general welfare of the United States" or to determine whether an appropriation in aid of agriculture falls within it. Wholly apart from that question, another principle embedded in our Constitution prohibits the enforcement of the Agricultural Adjustment Act. The act invades the reserved rights of the states. It is a statutory plan to regulate and control agricultural production, a matter beyond the powers delegated to the federal government. The tax, the appropriation of the funds raised, and the direction for their disbursement, are but parts of the plan. They are but means to an unconstitutional end.

From the accepted doctrine that the United States is a government of delegated powers, it follows that those not expressly granted, or reasonably to be implied from such as are conferred, are reserved to the states or to the people. To forestall any suggestion to the contrary, the Tenth Amendment was adopted. The same proposition, otherwise stated, is that powers not granted are prohibited. None to regulate agricultural production is given, and therefore legislation by Congress for that purpose is forbidden.

It is an established principle that the attainment of a prohibited end may not be accomplished under the pretext of the exertion of powers which are granted. . . .

These principles are as applicable to the power to lay taxes as to any other federal power. . . .

The power of taxation, which is expressly granted, may, of course, be adopted as a means to carry into operation another power also expressly granted. But resort to the taxing power to effectuate an end which is not legitimate, not within the scope of the Constitution, is obviously inadmissible. . . .

Third. If the taxing power may not be used as the instrument to enforce a regulation of matters of state concern with respect to which the Congress has no authority to interfere, may it, as in the present case, be employed to raise the money necessary to purchase a compliance which the Congress is powerless to command? The Government asserts that whatever might be said against the validity of the plan, if compulsory, it is constitutionally sound because the end is accomplished by voluntary cooperation. There are two sufficient answers to the contention. The regulation is not in fact voluntary. The farmer, of course, may refuse to comply, but the price of such refusal is the loss of benefits. The amount offered is intended to be sufficient to exert pressure on him to agree to the proposed regulation. The power to confer or withhold unlimited benefits is the power to coerce or destroy. If the cotton grower elects not to accept the benefits, he will receive less for his crops; those who receive payments will be able to undersell him. The result may well be financial ruin. The coercive purpose and intent of the statute is not obscured by the fact that it has not been perfectly successful. It is pointed out that, because there still remained a minority whom the rental and benefit payments were insufficient to induce to surrender their independence of action, the Congress has gone further and, in the Bankhead Cotton Act, used the taxing power in a more directly minatory fashion to compel submission. This progression only serves more fully to expose the coercive purpose of the so-called tax imposed by the present act. It is clear that the Department of Agriculture has properly described the plan as one to keep a non-cooperating minority in line. This is coercion by economic pressure. The asserted power of choice is illusory. . . .

But if the plan were one for purely voluntary cooperation it would stand no better so far as federal power is concerned. At best it is a scheme for purchasing with federal funds submission to federal regulation of a subject reserved to the states.

It is said that Congress has the undoubted right to appropriate money to executive officers for expenditure under contracts between the government and individuals; that much of the total expenditures is so made. But appropriations and expenditures under contracts for proper governmental purposes cannot justify contracts which are not within federal power. And contracts for the reduction of acreage and the control of production are outside the range of that power. An appropriation to be expended by the United States under contracts calling for violation of a state law clearly would offend the Constitution. Is a statute less objectionable which authorizes expenditure of federal moneys to induce action in a field in which the United States has no power to intermeddle? The Congress cannot invade state jurisdiction to compel individual action; no more can it purchase such action.

We are referred to numerous types of federal appropriation which have been made in the past, and it is asserted no question has been raised as to their validity. We need not stop to examine or consider them. . . .

Congress has no power to enforce its commands on the farmer to the ends sought by the Agricultural Adjustment Act. It must follow that it may not indirectly accomplish those ends by taxing and spending to purchase compliance. The Constitution and the entire plan of our government negative any such use of the power to tax and to spend as the act undertakes to authorize. It does not help to declare that local conditions throughout the nation have created a situation of national concern; for this is but to say that whenever there is a widespread similarity of local conditions, Congress may ignore constitutional limitations upon its own powers and usurp those reserved to the states. If, in lieu of compulsory regulation of subjects within the states' reserved jurisdiction, which is prohibited, the Congress could invoke the taxing and spending power as a means to accomplish the same end, clause 1 of Section 8 of Article I would become the instrument for total subversion of the governmental powers reserved to the individual states.

If the act before us is a proper exercise of the federal taxing power, evidently the regulation of all industry throughout the United States may be accomplished by similar exercises of the same power. It would be possible to exact money from one branch of an industry and pay it to another branch in every field of activity which lies within the province of the states. The mere threat of such a procedure might well induce the surrender of rights and the compliance with federal regulation as the price of continuance in business. A few instances will illustrate the thought. . . .

A possible result of sustaining the claimed federal power would be that every business group which thought itself under-privileged might demand that a tax be laid on its vendors or vendees the proceeds to be appropriated to the redress of its deficiency of income. . . .

Until recently no suggestion of the existence of any such power in the federal government has been advanced. The expressions of the framers of the Constitution, the decisions of this court interpreting that instrument and the writings of great commentators will be searched in vain for any suggestion that there exists in the clause under discussion or elsewhere in the Constitution, the authority whereby every provision and every fair implication from that instrument may be subverted, the independence of the individual states obliterated, and the United States converted into a central government exercising uncontrolled police power in every state of the Union, superseding all local control or regulation of the affairs or concerns of the states.

Hamilton himself, the leading advocate of broad interpretation of the power to tax and to appropriate for the general welfare, never suggested that any power granted by the Constitution could be used for the destruction of local self-government in the states. Story countenances no such doctrine. It seems never to have occurred to them, or to those who have agreed with them, that the general welfare of the United States, (which has aptly been termed "an indestructible Union, composed of indestructible States,") might be served by obliterating the constituent members of the Union. But to this fatal conclusion the doctrine contended for would inevitably lead. And its sole premise is that, though the makers of the Constitution, in erecting the federal government, intended sedulously to limit and define its powers, so as to reserve to the states and the people sovereign power, to be wielded by the states and their citizens and not to be invaded by the United States, they nevertheless by a single clause gave power to the Congress to tear down the barriers, to invade the states' jurisdiction, and to become a parliament of the whole people, subject to no restrictions save such as are self-imposed. The argument when seen in its true character and in the light of its inevitable results must be rejected.

The judgment is affirmed.

Mr. Justice STONE, dissenting. I think the judgment should be reversed.

The present stress of widely held and strongly expressed differences of opinion of the wisdom of the Agricultural Adjustment Act makes it important, in the interest of clear thinking and sound result, to emphasize at the outset certain propositions which should have controlling influence in determining the validity of the Act. They are:

1. The power of courts to declare a statute unconstitutional is subject to two guiding principles of decision which ought never to be absent from judicial consciousness. One is that courts are concerned only with the power to enact statutes, not with their wisdom. The other is that while unconstitutional exercise of power by the executive and legislative branches of the government is subject to judicial restraint, the only check upon our own exercise of power is our own sense of self-restraint. For the removal of unwise laws from the statute books appeal lies not to the courts but to the ballot and to the processes of democratic government.

2. The constitutional power of Congress to levy an excise tax upon the processing of agricultural products is not questioned. The present levy is held invalid, not for any want of power in Congress to lay such a tax to defray public expenditures, including those for the general welfare, but because the use to which its proceeds are put is disapproved.

3. As the present depressed state of agriculture is nation wide in its extent and effects, there is no basis for saying that the expenditure of public money in aid of farmers is not within the specifically granted power of Congress to levy taxes to "provide for the . . . general welfare." The opinion of the Court does not declare otherwise. . . .

It is with these preliminary and hardly controverted matters in mind that we should direct our attention to the pivot on which the decision of the Court is made to turn. It is that a levy unquestionably within the taxing power of Congress may be traced as invalid because it is a step in a plan to regulate agricultural production and is thus a forbidden infringement of state power. The levy is not any the less an exercise of taxing power because it is intended to defray an expenditure for the general welfare rather than for some other support of government. Nor is the levy and collection of the tax pointed to as effecting the regulation. While all federal taxes inevitably have some influence on the internal economy of the states, it is not contended that the levy of a processing tax upon manufacturers using agricultural products as raw material has any perceptible regulatory effect upon either their production or manufacture. . . .

Of the assertion that the payments to farmers are coercive, it is enough to say that no such contention is pressed by the taxpayer, and no such consequences were to be anticipated or appear to have resulted from the administration of the Act. The suggestion of coercion finds no support in the record or in any data showing the actual operation of the Act. Threat of loss, not hope of gain, is the essence of economic coercion. . . . The presumption of constitutionality of a statute is not to be overturned by an assertion of its coercive effect which rests on nothing more substantial than groundless speculation.

It is upon the contention that state power is infringed by purchased regulation of agricultural production that chief reliance is placed. It is insisted that, while the Constitution gives to Congress, in specific and unambiguous terms, the power to tax and spend, the power is subject to limitations which do not find their origin in any express provision of the Constitution and to which other expressly delegated powers are not subject.

The Constitution requires that public funds shall be spent for a defined purpose, the promotion of the general welfare. Their expenditure usually involves payment on terms which will insure use by the selected recipients within the limits of the constitutional purpose. Expenditures would fail of their purpose and thus lose their constitutional sanction if the terms of payment were not such that by their influence on the action of the recipients the permitted end would be attained. The power of Congress to spend is inseparable from persuasion to action over which Congress has no legislative control. Congress may not command that the science of agriculture be taught in state universities. But if it would aid the teaching of that science by grants to state institutions, it is appropriate, if not necessary, that the grant be on the condition, incorporated in the Morrill Act, that it be used for the intended purpose. Similarly it would seem to be compliance with the Constitution, not violation of it, for the government to take and the university to give a contract that the grant would be so used.

It makes no difference that there is a promise to do an act which the condition is calculated to induce. Condition and promise are alike valid since both are in furtherance of the national purpose for which the money is appropriated.

These effects upon individual action, which are but incidents of the authorized expenditure of government money, are pronounced to be themselves a limitation upon the granted power, and so the time-honored principle of constitutional interpretation that the granted power includes all those which are incident to it is reversed. "Let the end be legitimate," said the great Chief Justice, "let it be within the scope of the Constitution, and all means which are appropriate, which are plainly adapted to that end, which are not prohibited, but consist with the letter and spirit of the Constitution, are constitutional." *McCulloch* v. *Maryland*. This cardinal guide to constitutional exposition must now be rephrased so far as the spending power of the federal government is concerned. Let the expenditure be to promote the general welfare, still, if it is needful in order to insure its use for the intended purpose to influence any action which Congress cannot command because within the sphere of state government, the expenditure is unconstitutional. And taxes otherwise lawfully levied are likewise unconstitutional if they are appropriated to the expenditure whose incident is condemned. . . .

Such a limitation is contradictory and destructive of the power to appropriate for the public welfare, and is incapable of practical application. The spending power of Congress is in addition to the legislative power and not subordinate to it. This independent grant of the power of the purse, and its very nature, involving in its exercise the duty to insure expenditure within the granted power, presuppose freedom of selection among divers ends and aims, and the capacity to impose such conditions as will render the choice effective. It is a contradiction in terms to say that there is power to spend for the national welfare, while rejecting any power to impose conditions reasonably adapted to the attainment of the end which alone would justify the expenditure.

The limitation now sanctioned must lead to absurd consequences. The government may give seeds to farmers, but may not condition the gift upon their being planted in places where they are most needed or even planted at all. The government may give money to the unemployed, but may not ask that those who get it shall give labor in return, or even use it to support their families. It may give money to sufferers from earthquake, fire, tornado, pestilence or flood, but may not impose conditions—health precautions designed to prevent the spread of disease, or induce the movement of population to safer or more sanitary areas. All that, because it is purchased regulation infringing state powers, must be left for the states, who are unable or unwilling to supply the necessary relief. The government may spend its money for vocational rehabilitation, but it may not, with the consent of all concerned, supervise the process which it undertakes to aid. It may spend its money for the suppression of the boll weevil, but may not compensate the farmers for suspending the growth of cotton in the infected areas. It may aid state reforestation and forest fire prevention agencies, but may not be permitted to supervise their conduct. It may support rural schools, but may not condition its grant by the requirement that certain standards be maintained. It may appropriate moneys to be expended by the Reconstruction Finance Corporation "to aid in financing agriculture, commerce and industry," and to facilitate "the exportation of agricultural and other products." Do all its activities collapse because, in order to effect the permissible purpose, in myriad ways the money is paid out upon terms and conditions which influence action of the recipients within the states, which Congress cannot command? The answer would seem plain. If the expenditure is for a national public purpose, that purpose will not be thwarted because payment is on condition which will advance that purpose. The action which Congress induces by payments of money to promote the general welfare, but which it does not command or coerce, is but an incident to a specifically granted power, but a permissible means to a legitimate end. If appropriation in aid of a program of curtailment of agricultural production is constitutional, and it is not denied that it is, payment to farmers on condition that they reduce their crop acreage is constitutional. It is not any the less so be-

cause the farmer at his own option promises to fulfill the condition.

That the governmental power of the purse is a great one is not now for the first time announced. Every student of the history of government and economics is aware of its magnitude and of its existence in every civilized government. Both were well understood by the framers of the Constitution when they sanctioned the grant of the spending power to the federal government, and both were recognized by Hamilton and Story, whose views of the spending power as standing on a parity with the other powers specifically granted, have hitherto been generally accepted.

The suggestion that it must now be curtailed by judicial fiat because it may be abused by unwise use hardly rises to the dignity of argument. So may judicial power be abused. . . . "It must be remembered that legislators are the ultimate guardians of the liberties and welfare of the people in quite as great a degree as the courts." Justice Holmes, in *Missouri, Kansas & Texas R. R. Co.* v. *May.*

A tortured construction of the Constitution is not to be justified by recourse to extreme examples of reckless congressional spending which might occur if courts could not prevent expenditures which, even if they could be thought to effect any national purpose, would be possible only by action of a legislature lost to all sense of public responsibility. Such suppositions are addressed to the mind accustomed to believe that it is the business of courts to sit in judgment on the wisdom of legislative action. Courts are not the only agency of government that must be assumed to have capacity to govern. Congress and the courts both unhappily may falter or be mistaken in the performance of their constitutional duty. But interpretation of our great charter of government which proceeds on any assumption that the responsibility for the preservation of our institutions is the exclusive concern of any one of the three branches of government, or that it alone can save them from destruction is far more likely, in the long run, "to obliterate the constituent members" of "an indestructible union of indestructible states" than the frank recognition that language, even of a constitution, may mean what it says: that the power to tax and spend includes the power to relieve a nation-wide economic maladjustment by conditional gifts of money.

Mr. Justice BRANDEIS and Mr. Justice CARDOZO join in this opinion.

479. THE TENNESSEE VALLEY ACT
May 18, 1933

(U. S. Statutes at Large, Vol. XLVIII, p. 58)

The Tennessee Valley Authority, established by this Act, undertook a broad program of economic and social reconstruction of the Tennessee Valley region. The TVA not only constructed dams and transmission lines, but undertook rural electrification, withdrawal of marginal lands, promotion of public health, and many similar activities. The success of the experiment led to the demand for the construction of other power sites and for regional planning by the federal government. See, S. Chase, *Rich Land, Poor Land;* R. Lord, *Behold Our Land;* H. S. Raushenbush, *The Power Fight;* H. S. Raushenbush and H. W. Laidler, *Power Control;* Martell, "Legal Aspects of the TVA," 7 Geo. Wash. L. Rev. 983. On Sen. Norris, chiefly responsible for the passage of the act, see R. L. Neuberger and S. B. Kahn, *George W. Norris.*

AN ACT to improve the navigability and to provide for the flood control of the Tennessee River; to provide for reforestation and the proper use of marginal lands in the Tennessee Valley; to provide for the agricultural and industrial development of said valley; to provide for the national defense by the creation of a corporation for the operation of Government properties at and near Muscle Shoals in the State of Alabama, and for other purposes. . . .

Be it enacted, That for the purpose of maintaining and operating the properties now owned by the United States in the vicinity of Muscle Shoals, Alabama, . . . there is hereby created a body corporate by the name of the "Tennessee Valley Authority." . . .

SEC. 2. . . .

(f) No director shall have financial interest in any public-utility corporation engaged in the business of distributing and selling power to the public nor in any corporation engaged in the manufacture, selling, or distribution of fixed nitrogen or fertilizer, or any ingredients thereof, nor shall any member have any interest in any business that may be adversely affected by the success of the Corporation as a producer of concen-

trated fertilizers or as a producer of electric power. . . .

(h) All members of the board shall be persons who profess a belief in the feasibility and wisdom of this Act. . . .

SEC. 3. . . .

All contracts to which the Corporation is a party and which require the employment of laborers and mechanics in the construction, alteration, maintenance, or repair of buildings, dams, locks, or other projects shall contain a provision that not less than the prevailing rate of wages for work of a similar nature prevailing in the vicinity shall be paid to such laborers or mechanics. . . .

SEC. 4. Except as otherwise specifically provided in this Act, the Corporation—

(f) May purchase or lease and hold such real and personal property as it deems necessary or convenient in the transaction of its business, and may dispose of any such personal property held by it. . . .

(h) Shall have power in the name of the United States of America to exercise the right of eminent domain, and in the purchase of any real estate or the acquisition of real estate by condemnation proceedings, the title to such real estate shall be taken in the name of the United States of America, . . .

(i) Shall have power to acquire real estate for the construction of dams, reservoirs, transmission lines, power houses, and other structures, and navigation projects at any point along the Tennessee River, or any of its tributaries, . . .

(j) Shall have power to construct dams, reservoirs, power houses, power structures, transmission lines, navigation projects, and incidental works in the Tennessee River and its tributaries, and to unite the various power installations into one or more systems by transmission lines.

SEC. 5. The board is hereby authorized— . . .

(b) To arrange with farmers and farm organizations for large-scale practical use of the new forms of fertilizers under conditions permitting an accurate measure of the economic return they produce.

(c) To cooperate with National, State, district, or county experimental stations or demonstration farms, for the use of new forms of fertilizer or fertilizer practices during the initial or experimental period of their introduction.

(d) The board in order to improve and cheapen the production of fertilizer is authorized to manufacture and sell fixed nitrogen, fertilizer, and fertilizer ingredients at Muscle Shoals by the employment of existing facilities, by modernizing existing plants, or by any other process or processes that in its judgment shall appear wise and profitable for the fixation of atmospheric nitrogen or the cheapening of the production of fertilizer.

(e) Under the authority of this Act the board may make donations or sales of the product of the plant or plants operated by it to be fairly and equitably distributed through the agency of county demonstration agents, agricultural colleges, or otherwise as the board may direct, for experimentation, education, and introduction of the use of such products in cooperation with practical farmers so as to obtain information as to the value, effect, and best methods of their use.

(f) The board is authorized to make alterations, modifications, or improvements in existing plants and facilities, and to construct new plants.

(g) In the event it is not used for the fixation of nitrogen for agricultural purposes or leased, then the board shall maintain in standby condition nitrate plant numbered 2, or its equivalent, for the fixation of atmospheric nitrogen, for the production of explosives in the event of war or a national emergency, until the Congress shall by joint resolution release the board from this obligation, and if any part thereof be used by the board for the manufacture of phosphoric acid or potash, the balance of nitrate plant numbered 2 shall be kept in stand-by condition.

(h) To establish, maintain, and operate laboratories and experimental plants, and to undertake experiments for the purpose of enabling the Corporation to furnish nitrogen products for military purposes, and nitrogen and other fertilizer products for agricultural purposes in the most economical manner and at the highest standard of efficiency. . . .

(l) To produce, distribute, and sell electric power, as herein particularly specified.

(m) No products of the Corporation shall be sold for use outside of the United States, its Territories and possessions, except to the United States Government for the use of its Army and Navy, or to its allies in case of war.

SEC. 10. The board is hereby empowered and authorized to sell the surplus power not used in its operations, and for operation of locks and other works generated by it, to States, counties, municipalities, corporations, partnerships, or individuals, according to the policies hereinafter set forth; and to carry out said authority, the board is authorized to enter into contracts for such sale for a term not exceeding twenty years, and in the sale of such current by the board it shall give preference to States, counties, municipalities, and cooperative organizations of citizens or farmers, not organized or doing business for profit, but primarily for the purpose of supplying electricity to its own citizens or members: . . . In order to promote and encourage the fullest possible use of electric light and power on farms within reasonable distance of any of its transmission lines the board in its discretion shall have power to construct transmission lines to farms and small villages that are not otherwise supplied with electricity at reasonable rates, and to make such rules and regulations governing such sale and distribution of such electric power as in its judgment may be just and equitable: *Provided further,* That the board is hereby authorized and directed to make studies, experiments, and determinations to promote the wider and better use of electric power for agricultural and domestic use, or for small or local industries, and it may cooperate with State governments, or their subdivisions or agencies, with educational or research institutions, and with cooperatives or other organizations, in the application of electric power to the fuller and better balanced development of the resources of the region.

SEC. 11. It is hereby declared to be the policy of the Government so far as practical to distribute and sell the surplus power generated at Muscle Shoals equitably among the States, counties, and municipalities within transmission distance. This policy is further declared to be that the projects herein provided for shall be considered primarily as for the benefit of the people of the section as a whole and particularly the domestic and rural consumers to whom the power can economically be made available, and accordingly that sale to and use by industry shall be a secondary purpose, to be utilized principally to secure a sufficiently high load factor and revenue returns which will permit domestic and rural use at the lowest possible rates and in such manner as to encourage increased domestic and rural use of electricity. It is further hereby declared to be the policy of the Government to utilize the Muscle Shoals properties so far as may be necessary to improve, increase, and cheapen the production of fertilizer and fertilizer ingredients by carrying out the provision of this Act. . . .

SEC. 22. To aid further the proper use, conservation, and development of the natural resources of the Tennessee River drainage basin and of such adjoining territory as may be related to or materially affected by the development consequent to this Act, and to provide for the general welfare of the citizens of said areas, the President is hereby authorized, by such means or methods as he may deem proper within the limits of appropriations made therefor by Congress, to make such surveys of and general plans for said Tennessee basin and adjoining territory as may be useful to the Congress and to the several States in guiding and controlling the extent, sequence, and nature of development that may be equitably and economically advanced through the expenditure of public funds, or through the guidance or control of public authority, all for the general purpose of fostering an orderly and proper physical, economic, and social development of said areas; and the President is further authorized in making said surveys and plans to cooperate with the States affected thereby, or subdivisions or agencies of such States, or with cooperative or other organizations, and to make such studies, experiments, or demonstrations as may be necessary and suitable to that end.

SEC. 23. The President shall, from time to time, as the work provided for in the preceding section progresses, recommend to Congress such legislation as he deems proper to carry out the general purposes stated in said section, and for the especial purpose of bringing about in said Tennessee drainage basin and adjoining territory in conformity with said general purposes (1) the maximum amount of flood control; (2) the maximum development of said Tennessee River for navigation purposes; (3) the maximum generation of electric power consistent with flood control and navigation; (4) the proper use of marginal lands; (5) the proper method of reforestation of all lands in said drainage basin suitable for reforestation; and (6) the economic and social well-being of the people living in said river basin. . . .

480. ASHWANDER et. al. v. TENNESSEE VALLEY AUTHORITY
297 U. S. 288
1936

On Writs of Certiorari to the U. S. Circuit Court of Appeals for the Fifth District. This decision was one of the few notable victories of the government in the Courts during the first Roosevelt administration. Justices Brandeis, Stone, Roberts and Cardozo concurred in the result but insisted that the plaintiffs should have had no standing in the Court. See, Albertsworth, "Constitutional Issues of the Federal Power Program," 29 Ills. L. Rev. 883; Grant, "Commerce, Production and the Fiscal Powers of Congress," 45 Yale L. J. 751, 991; Boyd, "The Tennessee Valley Litigation," 11 Indiana L. J. 368; and notes in 84 U. of Pa. L. Rev. 787; 34 Mich. L. Rev. 680; 5 U. of Chicago L. Rev. 639.

HUGHES, C. J. On January 4, 1934, the Tennessee Valley Authority, an agency of the Federal Government, entered into a contract with the Alabama Power Company, providing (1) for the purchase by the Authority from the Power Company of certain transmission lines, sub-stations, and auxiliary properties for $1,000,000, (2) for the purchase by the Authority from the Power Company of certain real property for $150,000, (3) for an interchange of hydroelectric energy, and in addition for the sale by the Authority to the Power Company of its "surplus power," on stated terms, and (4) for mutual restrictions as to the areas to be served in the sale of power. The contract was amended and supplemented in minor particulars on February 13 and May 24, 1934.

The Alabama Power Company is a corporation organized under the laws of Alabama and is engaged in the generation of electric energy and its distribution generally throughout that State, its lines reaching 66 counties. The transmission lines to be purchased by the Authority extend from Wilson Dam, at the Muscle Shoals plant owned by the United States on the Tennessee River in northern Alabama, into seven counties in that State, within a radius of about 50 miles. These lines serve a population of approximately 190,000, including about 10,000 individual customers, or about one-tenth of the total number served directly by the Power Company. The real property to be acquired by the Authority (apart from the transmission lines above mentioned and related properties) is adjacent to the area known as the "Joe Wheeler dam site," upon which the Authority is constructing the Wheeler Dam. . . .

Plaintiffs are holders of preferred stock of the Alabama Power Company. Conceiving the contract with the Tennessee Valley Authority to be injurious to the corporate interests and also invalid, because beyond the constitutional power of the Federal Government, they submitted their protest to the board of directors of the Power Company and demanded that steps should be taken to have the contract annulled. . . . Going beyond that particular challenge, and setting for the pronouncements, policies and programs of the Authority, plaintiffs sought a decree restraining these activities as repugnant to the Constitution, and also asked a general declaratory decree with respect to the rights of the Authority in various relations.

The defendants, including the Authority and its directors, the Power Company and its mortgage trustee, and the municipalities within the described area, filed answers and the case was heard upon evidence. The District Court made elaborate findings and entered a final decree annulling the contract of January 4, 1934, and enjoining the transfer of the transmission lines and auxiliary properties. The court also enjoined the defendant municipalities from making or performing any contracts with the Authority for the purchase of power, and from accepting or expending any funds received from the Authority or the Public Works Administration for the purpose of constructing a public distribution system to distribute power which the Authority supplied. The court gave no consideration to plaintiff's request for a general declaratory decree.

The Authority, its directors, and the city of Florence appealed from the decree and the case was severed as to the other defendants. Plaintiffs took a cross appeal.

The Circuit Court of Appeals limited its discussion to the precise issue with respect to the effect and validity of the contract of January 4, 1934. The District Court had found that the electric energy required for the territory served by the transmission lines to be purchased under that contract is available at Wilson Dam without the necessity for any interconnection with any other dam or power plant. The Circuit Court of Appeals accordingly considered the constitutional authority for the construction of Wilson Dam and for the disposition of the electric energy there created. In the view that the Wilson Dam had been constructed in the exercise of the war and commerce powers of the Congress and that the electric energy there available was the property of the United States and subject to its disposition, the Circuit Court of Appeals decided that the decree of the District Court was erroneous and should be reversed. The court also held that plaintiffs should take nothing by their cross appeal. 78 F. (2d) 578. On plaintiffs' application we granted writs of certiorari, 296 U. S.—.

First. The right of plaintiffs to bring this suit. . . .

We think that plaintiffs have made a sufficient showing to entitle them to bring suit and that a constitutional question is properly presented and should be decided.

Second. The scope of the issue. We agree with the Circuit Court of Appeals that the question to be determined is limited to the validity of the contract of January 4, 1934. The pronouncements, policies and program of the Tennessee Valley Authority and its directors, their motives and desires, did not give rise to a justiciable controversy save as they had fruition in action of a definite and concrete character constituting an actual or threatened interference with the rights of the persons complaining. The judicial power does not extend to the determination of abstract questions. . . .

As it appears that the transmission lines in question run from the Wilson Dam and that the electric energy generated at that dam is more than sufficient to supply all the requirements of the contract, the questions that are properly before us relate to the constitutional authority for the construction of the Wilson Dam and for the disposition, as provided in the contract, of the electric energy there generated.

Third. The constitutional authority for the construction of the Wilson Dam. The Congress may not, "under the pretext of executing its powers, pass laws for the accomplishment of objects not entrusted to the government." Chief Justice Marshall, in *McCulloch* v. *Maryland; Linder* v. *United States,* 268 U. S. 15, 17. The Government's argument recognizes this essential limitation. The Government's contention is that the Wilson Dam was constructed, and the power plant connected with it was installed, in the exercise by the Congress of its war and commerce powers, that is, for the purposes of national defense and the improvement of navigation. . . .

We may take judicial notice of the international situation at the time the Act of 1916 was passed, and it cannot be successfully disputed that the Wilson Dam and its auxiliary plants, including the hydro-electric power plant, are, and were intended to be, adapted to the purposes of national defense. While the District Court found that there is no intention to use the nitrate plants or the hydro-electric units installed at Wilson Dam for the production of war materials in time of peace, "the maintenance of said properties in operating condition and the assurance of an abundant supply of electric energy is the event of war, constitute national defense assets." This finding has ample support.

The Act of 1916 also had in view "improvements to navigation." Commerce includes navigation. "All America understands.

and has uniformly understood," said Chief Justice Marshall in *Gibbons* v. *Ogden,* "the word 'commerce,' to comprehend navigation." The power to regulate interstate commerce embraces the power to keep the navigable rivers of the United States free from obstructions to navigation and to remove such obstructions when they exist. "For these purposes," said the Court in *Gilman* v. *Philadelphia,* 3 Wall. 713, 725, "Congress possesses all the powers which existed in the States before the adoption of the national Constitution, and which have always existed in the Parliament in England." . . .

The Tennessee River is a navigable stream, although there are obstructions at various points because of shoals, reefs and rapids. The improvement of navigation on this river has been a matter of national concern for over a century. . . .

While, in its present condition, the Tennessee River is not adequately improved for commercial navigation, and traffic is small, we are not at liberty to conclude either that the river is not susceptible of development as an important waterway, or that Congress has not undertaken that development, or that the construction of the Wilson Dam was not an appropriate means to accomplish a legitimate end.

The Wilson Dam and its power plant must be taken to have been constructed in the exercise of the constitutional functions of the Federal Government.

Fourth. The constitutional authority to dispose of electric energy generated at the Wilson Dam. The Government acquired full title to the dam site, with all riparian rights. The power of falling water was an inevitable incident of the construction of the dam. That water power came into the exclusive control of the Federal Government. The mechanical energy was convertible into electric energy, and the water power, the right to convert it into electric energy, and the electric energy thus produced, constitute property belonging to the United States.

Authority to dispose of property constitutionally acquired by the United States is expressly granted to the Congress by section 3 of Article IV of the Constitution. This section provides:

"The Congress shall have Power to dispose of and make all needful Rules and Regulations respecting the Territory or other Property belonging to the United States; and nothing in this Constitution shall be so construed as to Prejudice any Claims of the United States, or of any particular State."

To the extent that the power of disposition is thus expressly conferred, it is manifest that the Tenth Amendment is not applicable. And the Ninth Amendment (which petitioners also invoke) in insuring the maintenance of the rights retained by the people does not withdraw the rights which are expressly granted to the Federal Government. The question is as to the scope of the grant and whether there are inherent limitations which render invalid the disposition of property with which we are now concerned.

The occasion for the grant was the obvious necessity of making provision for the government of the vast territory acquired by the United States. The power to govern and to dispose of that territory was deemed to be indispensable to the purposes of the cessions made by the States. . . . The grant was made in broad terms, and the power of regulation and disposition was not confined to territory, but extended to "other property belonging to the United States," so that the power may be applied, as Story says, "to the due regulation of all other personal and real property rightfully belonging to the United States." And so, he adds, "it has been constantly understood and acted upon."

This power of disposal was early construed to embrace leases, thus enabling the Government to derive profit through royalties. . . . The policy, early adopted and steadily pursued, of segregating mineral lands from other public lands and providing for leases, pointed to the recognition both of the full power of disposal and of the necessity of suitably adapting the methods of disposal to different sorts of property. . . .

But when Congress thus reserved mineral lands for special disposal, can it be doubted that Congress could have provided for mining directly by its own agents, instead of giving that right to lessees on the payment of royalties? Upon what ground could it be said that the Government could not mine its own gold, silver, coal, lead, or phosphates in the public domain, and dispose of them as property belonging to the United States? That it could dispose of its land but not of what the land contained? It would seem to be clear that under the same power of disposition which enabled the Government to lease and obtain profit from sales by its lessees, it could mine and obtain profit from its own sales.

The question is whether a more limited power of disposal should be applied to the water power, convertible into electric energy, and to the electric energy thus produced at the Wilson Dam constructed by the Government in the exercise of its constitutional functions. If so, it must be by reason either of (1) the nature of the particular property, or (2) the character of the "surplus" disposed of, or (3) the manner of disposition.

(1) That the water power and the electric energy generated at the dam are susceptible of disposition as property belonging to the United States is well established. . . .

(2) The argument is stressed that, assuming that electric energy generated at the dam belongs to the United States, the Congress has authority to dispose of this energy only to the extent that it is a surplus necessarily created in the course of making munitions of war or operating the works for navigation purposes; that is, that the remainder of the available energy must be lost or go to waste. We find nothing in the Constitution which imposes such a limitation. It is not to be deduced from the mere fact that the electric energy is only potentially available until the generators are operated. The Government has no less right to the energy thus available by letting the water course over its turbines than it has to use the appropriate processes to reduce to possession other property within its control, as, for example, oil which it may recover from a pool beneath its lands, and which is reduced to possession by boring oil wells and otherwise might escape its grasp. And it would hardly be contended that, when the Government reserves coal on its lands, it can mine the coal and dispose of it only for the purpose of heating public buildings or for other governmental operations. Or, if the Government owns a silver mine, that it can obtain the silver only for the purpose of storage or coinage. Or that when the Government extracts the oil it has reserved, it has no constitutional power to sell it. Our decisions recognize no such restriction. The United States owns the coal, or the silver, or the lead, or the oil, it obtains

from its lands, and it lies in the discretion of the Congress, acting in the public interest, to determine of how much of the property it shall dispose.

We think that the same principle is applicable to electric energy. The argument pressed upon us leads to absurd consequences in the denial, despite the broad terms of the constitutional provision, of a power of disposal which the public interest may imperatively require. Suppose, for example, that in the erection of a dam for the improvement of navigation, it became necessary to destroy a dam and power plant which had previously been erected by a private corporation engaged in the generation and distribution of energy which supplied the needs of neighboring communities and business enterprises. Would anyone say that, because the United States had built its own dam and plant in the exercise of its constitutional functions, and had complete ownership and dominion over both, no power could be supplied to the communities and enterprises dependent on it, not because of any unwillingness of the Congress to supply it, or of any overriding governmental need, but because there was no constitutional authority to furnish the supply? Or that, with abundant power available, which must otherwise be wasted, the supply to the communities and enterprises whose very life may be at stake must be limited to the slender amount of surplus unavoidably involved in the operation of the navigation works, because the Constitution does not permit any more energy to be generated and distributed? In the case of the *Green Bay Canal Company,* where the government works supplanted those of the Canal Company, the Court found no difficulty in sustaining the Government's authority to grant to the Canal Company the water powers which it had previously enjoyed, subject, of course, to the dominant control of the Government. And in the case of *United States* v. *Chandler-Dunbar Company, supra,* the statutory provision, to which the Court referred, was "that any excess of water in the St. Marys River at Sault Sainte Marie over and above the amount now or hereafter required for the uses of navigation shall be leased for power purposes by the Secretary of War upon such terms and conditions as shall be best calculated in his judgment to insure the develop-

ment thereof." It was to the leasing, under this provision, "of any excess of power over the needs of the Government" that the Court saw no valid objection. . . .

(3) We come then to the question as to the validity of the method which had been adopted in disposing of the surplus energy generated at the Wilson Dam. The constitutional provision is silent as to the method of disposing of property belonging to the United States. That method, of course, must be an appropriate means of disposition according to the nature of the property, it must be one adopted in the public interest as distinguished from private or personal ends, and we may assume that it must be consistent with the foundation principles of our dual system of government and must not be contrived to govern the concerns reserved to the States. In this instance, the method of disposal embraces the sale of surplus energy by the Tennessee Valley Authority to the Alabama Power Company, the interchange of energy between the Authority and the Power Company, and the purchase by the Authority from the Power Company of certain transmission lines.

As to the mere sale of surplus energy, nothing need be added to what we have said as to the constitutional authority to dispose. The Government could lease or sell and fix the terms. Sales of surplus energy to the Power Company by the Authority continued a practice begun by the Government several years before. The contemplated interchange of energy is a form of disposition and presents no questions which are essentially different from those that are pertinent to sales.

The transmission lines which the Authority undertakes to purchase from the Power Company lead from the Wilson Dam to a large area within about fifty miles of the dam. These lines provide the means of distributing the electric energy, generated at the dam, to a large population. They furnish a method of reaching a market. The alternative method is to sell the surplus energy at the dam, and the market there appears to be limited to one purchaser, the Alabama Power Company, and its affiliated interests. We know of no constitutional ground upon which the Federal Government can be denied the right to seek a wider market. We suppose that in the early days of mining in the West, if the

Government had undertaken to operate a silver mine on its domain, it could have acquired the mules or horses and equipment to carry its silver to market. And the transmission lines for electric energy are but a facility for conveying to market that particular sort of property, and the acquisition of these lines raises no different constitutional question, unless in some way there is an invasion of the rights reserved to the State or to the people. We find no basis for concluding that the limited undertaking with the Alabama Power Company amounts to such an invasion. Certainly, the Alabama Power Company has no constitutional right to insist that it shall be the sole purchaser of the energy generated at the Wilson Dam; that the energy shall be sold to it or go to waste.

We limit our decision to the case before us, as we have defined it. The argument is earnestly presented that the Government by virtue of its ownership of the dam and power plant could not establish a steel mill and make and sell steel products, or a factory to manufacture clothing or shoes for the public, and thus attempt to make its ownership of energy, generated at its dam, a means of carrying on competitive commercial enterprises and thus drawing to the Federal Government the conduct and management of business having no relation to the purposes for which the Federal Government was established. The picture is eloquently drawn but we deem it to be irrelevant to the issue here. The Government is not using the water power at the Wilson Dam to establish any industry or business. It is not using the energy generated at the dam to manufacture commodities of any sort for the public. The Government is disposing of the energy itself which simply is the mechanical energy, incidental to falling water at the dam, converted into the electric energy which is susceptible of transmission. The question here is simply as to the acquisition of the transmission lines as a facility for the disposal of that energy. And the Government rightly conceded at the bar, in substance, that it was without constitutional authority to acquire or dispose of such energy except as it comes into being in the operation of works constructed in the exercise of some power delegated to the United States. As we have said, these transmission lines lead directly from the dam, which has been lawfully constructed, and the question of the constitutional right of the Government to acquire or operate local or urban distribution systems is not involved. We express no opinion as to the validity of such an effort, as to the status of any other dam or power development in the Tennessee Valley, whether connected with or apart from the Wilson Dam, or as to the validity of the Tennessee Valley Authority Act or of the claims made in the pronouncements and program of the Authority apart from the questions we have discussed in relation to the particular provisions of the contract of January 4, 1934, affecting the Alabama Power Company.

The decree of the Circuit Court of Appeals is affirmed.

Affirmed.

Brandeis, J. delivered a separate opinion in which Justices Stone, Roberts and Cardozo concurred. McReynolds, J. dissented.

481. THE ABANDONMENT OF THE GOLD STANDARD

Joint Resolution of Congress Voiding the Gold Clause in Government Obligations
June 5, 1933

(*U. S. Statutes at Large,* Vol. XLVIII, p. 113)

By executive order of April, 1933, all holders of gold were required to turn their gold into the Federal Reserve Banks by May 1. An executive order of April 20 put an end to the export of gold and formally took the nation off the gold standard. The Joint Resolution of June 5, 1933, repudiated the gold clause not only in all private but in government obligations. See J. Donaldson, *The Dollar;* A. Nussbaum, *Money in the Law;*

J. D. Paris, *Monetary Policies of the United States, 1932–1938;* G. Cassel, *The Downfall of the Gold Standard.* For the constitutional aspects of the Resolution see references to Doc. No. 482.

JOINT RESOLUTION to assure uniform value to the coins and currencies of the United States.

Whereas the holding of or dealing in gold

affect the public interest, and are therefore subject to proper regulation and restriction; and

Whereas the existing emergency has disclosed that provisions of obligations which purport to give the obligee a right to require payment in gold or a particular kind of coin or currency of the United States, or in an amount of money of the United States measured thereby, obstruct the power of the Congress to regulate the value of the money of the United States, and are inconsistent with the declared policy of the Congress to maintain at all times the equal power of every dollar, coined or issued by the United States, in the markets and in the payment of debts. Now, therefore, be it

Resolved by the Senate and House of Representatives of the United States of America in Congress assembled, That (a) every provision contained in or made with respect to any obligation which purports to give the obligee a right to require payment in gold or a particular kind of coin or currency, or in an amount in money of the United States measured thereby, is declared to be against public policy; and no such provision shall be contained in or made with respect to any obligation hereafter incurred. Every obligation, heretofore or hereafter incurred, whether or not any such provision is contained therein or made with respect thereto, shall be discharged upon payment, dollar for dollar, in any coin or currency which at the time of payment is legal tender for public and private debts. Any such provision contained in any law authorizing obligations to be issued by or under authority of the United States, is hereby repealed, but the repeal of any such provision shall not invalidate any other provision or authority contained in such law.

(b) As used in this resolution, the term "obligation" means an obligation (including every obligation of and to the United States, excepting currency) payable in money of the United States; and the term "coin or currency" means coin or currency of the United States, including Federal Reserve notes and circulating notes of Federal Reserve banks and national banking associations.

Sec. 2. The last sentence of paragraph (1) of subsection (b) of section 43 of the act entitled "An act to relieve the existing national economic emergency by increasing agricultural purchasing power, to raise revenue for extraordinary expenses incurred by reason of such emergency, to provide emergency relief with respect to agricultural indebtedness, to provide for the orderly liquidation of joint-stock land banks, and for other purposes," approved May 12, 1933, is amended to read as follows:

"All coins and currencies of the United States (including Federal Reserve notes and circulating notes of Federal Reserve banks and national banking associations) heretofore or hereafter coined or issued shall be legal tender for all debts, public and private, public charges, taxes, duties, and dues, except that gold coins, when below the standard weight and limit of tolerance provided by law for the single piece, shall be legal tender only at valuation in proportion to their actual weight."

482. THE GOLD CLAUSE CASES
1935

These were five cases, appealed from various courts, involving the validity of the Joint Resolution of June 5, 1933 repudiating the gold clause in private and public contracts. (Doc. No. 481). Two decisions are given here, the first involving the validity of the resolution with respect to private, the second with respect to government contracts. In the first case the Court sustained unequivocally the right of Congress to alter private contracts. In the second the Court held that the gold clause violated the legal and binding character of the government contract but that plaintiff had failed to show damages. In this case Justice Stone delivered a separate opinion holding that the Court should have confined itself to answering the first question raised. Justice McReynolds, dissenting sharply from both opinions, warned that "the impending legal and moral chaos is appalling." On these cases see, A. Nussbaum, *Money in the Law;* J. D. Paris, *Monetary Policies of the United States, 1932–1938;* Dawson, "The Gold Clause Decisions," 33 Mich. L. Rev. 647; Dickinson, "The Gold Decisions," 85 U. of Pa. L. Rev. 715; Hart, "The Gold Clause in U. S. Bonds," 48 Harv. L. Rev. 1057; Eder, "The Gold Clauses in the Light of History," 23 Georgetown L. J. 359; Carpenter, "The Gold Clause Cases," 8 So. Calif. L. Rev. 181.

1. *Norman v. The Baltimore and Ohio Railroad Company.*

HUGHES, C. J. These cases present the question of the validity of the Joint Resolution
of the Congress, of June 5, 1933, with respect
to the "gold clauses" of private contracts for
the payment of money. . . .

In No. 270, the suit was brought upon a
coupon of a bond made by the Baltimore
and Ohio Railroad Company under date of
February 1, 1930, for the payment of $1,000
on February 1, 1960, and interest from date
at the rate of 4½ per cent. per annum, payable semi-annually. The bond provided that
the payment of principal and interest "will
be made . . . in gold coin of the United
States of America of or equal to the standard
of weight and fineness existing on February 1,
1930." . . . The coupon in suit, for $22.50
was payable on February 1, 1934. On presentation of the coupon, defendant refused to pay
the amount in gold, or the equivalent of gold
in legal tender of the United States which was
alleged to be, on February 1, 1934, according
to the standard of weight and fineness existing on February 1, 1930, the sum of $38.10,
and plaintiff demanded judgment for that
amount. . . .

The Joint Resolution of June 5, 1933, was
one of a series of measures relating to the currency. These measures disclose not only the
purposes of the Congress but also the situations which existed at the time the Joint Resolution was adopted and when the payments
under the "gold clauses" were sought. . . .

On January 30, 1934, the Congress passed
the "Gold Reserve Act of 1934" (48 Stat.
337) which, by section 13, ratified and confirmed all the actions, regulations and orders taken or made by the President and
the Secretary of the Treasury under the Act
of March 9, 1933, or under Section 43 of the
Act of May 12, 1933, and, by section 12, with
respect to the authority of the President to
fix the weight of the gold dollar, provided
that it should not be fixed "in any event at
more than 60 per centum of its present
weight." On January 31, 1934, the President
issued his proclamation declaring that he
fixed "the weight of the gold dollar to be
15⁵⁄₂₁ grains nine tenths fine," from and
after that date.

We have not attempted to summarize all
the provisions of these measures. We are not
concerned with their wisdom. The question
before the Court is one of power, not of
policy. And that question touches the validity
of these measures at but a single point, that
is, in relation to the Joint Resolution denying
effect to "gold clauses" in existing contracts.
The Resolution must, however, be considered in its legislative setting and in the light
of other measures *in pari materia.*

*First. The Interpretation of the gold
clauses in suit.* In the case of the *Baltimore
and Ohio Railroad Company,* the obligor considers the obligation to be one "for the payment of money and not for the delivery of
a specified number of grains or ounces of
gold"; that it is an obligation payable in
money of the United States and not less so
because payment is to be made "in a particular kind of money"; that it is not a "commodity contract" which could be discharged
by "tender of bullion." . . .

We are of the opinion that the gold clauses
now before us were not contracts for payment in gold coin as a commodity, or in
bullion, but were contracts for the payment
of money. The bonds were severally for the
payment of one thousand dollars. We also
think that, fairly construed, these clauses
were intended to afford a definite standard or
measure of value, and thus to protect against
a depreciation of the currency and against
the discharge of the obligation by a payment
of lesser value than that prescribed. When
these contracts were made they were not repugnant to any action of the Congress. In
order to determine whether effect may now
be given to the intention of the parties in
the face of the action taken by the Congress,
or the contracts may be satisfied by the payment dollar for dollar, in legal tender, as
the Congress has now prescribed, it is necessary to consider (1) the power of the Congress to establish a monetary system and
the necessary implications of that power;
(2) the power of the Congress to invalidate
the provisions of existing contracts which
interfere with the exercise of its constitutional authority; and (3) whether the clauses
in question do constitute such an interference as to bring them within the range of
that power.

*Second. The power of the Congress to es-
tablish a monetary system.* It is unnecessary
to review the historic controversy as to the

extent of this power, or again to go over the ground traversed by the Court in reaching the conclusion that the Congress may make treasury notes legal tender in payment of debts previously contracted, as well as of those subsequently contracted, whether that authority be exercised in course of war or in time of peace. *Knox* v. *Lee, 12* Wall. 457; *Juilliard* v. *Greenman,* 110 U. S. 421. . . .

The question of the validity of the Joint Resolution of June 5, 1933, must be determined in the light of these settled principles.

Third. The power of the Congress to invalidate the provisions of existing contracts which interfere with the exercise of its constitutional authority. The instant cases involve contracts between private parties, but the question necessarily relates as well to the contracts or obligations of States and municipalities, or of their political subdivisions, that is, to such engagements as are within the reach of the applicable national power. . . .

The contention is that the power of the Congress, broadly sustained by the decisions we have cited in relation to private contracts for the payment of money generally, does not extend to the striking down of express contracts for gold payments. . . .

Here, the Congress has enacted an express interdiction. The argument against it does not rest upon the mere fact that the legislation may cause hardship or loss. Creditors who have not stipulated for gold payments may suffer equal hardship or loss with creditors who have so stipulated. The former, admittedly, have no constitutional grievance. And, while the latter may not suffer more, the point is pressed that their express stipulations for gold payments constitute property, and that creditors who have not such stipulations are without that property right. And the contestants urge that the Congress is seeking not to regulate the currency, but to regulate contracts, and thus has stepped beyond the power conferred.

This argument is in the teeth of another established principle. Contracts, however express, cannot fetter the constitutional authority of the Congress. Contracts may create rights of property, but when contracts deal with a subject matter which lies within the control of the Congress, they have a congenital infirmity. Parties cannot remove their transactions from the reach of dominant constitutional power by making contracts about them. . . .

The principle is not limited to the incidental effect of the exercise by the Congress of its constitutional authority. There is no constitutional ground for denying to the Congress the power expressly to prohibit and invalidate contracts although previously made, and valid when made, when they interfere with the carrying out of the policy it is free to adopt. . . . To subordinate the exercise of the Federal authority to the continuing operation of previous contracts would be to place to this extent the regulation of interstate commerce in the hands of private individuals and to withdraw from the control of the Congress so much of the field as they might choose by "prophetic discernment" to bring within the range of their agreements. The Constitution recognizes no such limitation.

The same reasoning applies to the constitutional authority of the Congress to regulate the currency and to establish the monetary system of the country. If the gold clauses now before us interfere with the policy of the Congress in the exercise of that authority, they cannot stand.

Fourth. The effect of the gold clauses in suit in relation to the monetary policy adopted by the Congress. Despite the wide range of the discussion at the bar and the earnestness with which the arguments against the validity of the Joint Resolution have been pressed, these contentions necessarily are brought, under the dominant principles to which we have referred, to a single and narrow point. That point is whether the gold clauses do constitute an actual interference with the monetary policy of the Congress in the light of its broad power to determine that policy. Whether they may be deemed to be such an interference depends upon an appraisement of economic conditions and upon determinations of questions of fact. With respect to those conditions and determinations, the Congress is entitled to its own judgment. We may inquire whether its action is arbitrary or capricious, that is, whether it has reasonable relation to a legitimate end. If it is an appropriate means to such an end, the decisions of the Congress as to the degree of the necessity for the adoption of that means, is final. . . .

Can we say that this determination is so destitute of basis that the interdiction of the gold clauses must be deemed to be without any reasonable relation to the monetary policy adopted by the Congress? . . .

The devaluation of the dollar placed the domestic economy upon a new basis. In the currency as thus provided, States and municipalities must receive their taxes; railroads, their rates and fares; public utilities, their charges for services. The income out of which they must meet their obligations is determined by the new standard. Yet, according to the contentions before us, while that income is thus controlled by law, their indebtedness on their "gold bonds" must be met by an amount of currency determined by the former gold standard. Their receipts, in this view, would be fixed on one basis; their interest charges, and the principal of their obligations, on another. It is common knowledge that the bonds issued by these obligors have generally contained gold clauses, and presumably they account for a large part of the outstanding obligations of that sort. It is also common knowledge that a similar situation exists with respect to numerous industrial corporations that have issued their "gold bonds" and must now receive payments for their products in the existing currency. It requires no acute analysis or profound economic inquiry to disclose the dislocation of the domestic economy which would be caused by such a disparity of conditions in which, it is insisted, those debtors under gold clauses should be required to pay one dollar and sixty-nine cents in currency while respectively receiving their taxes, rates, charges and prices on the basis of one dollar of that currency.

We are not concerned with consequences, in the sense that consequences, however serious, may excuse an invasion of constitutional right. We are concerned with the constitutional power of the Congress over the monetary system of the country and its attempted frustration. Exercising that power, the Congress has undertaken to establish a uniform currency, and parity between kinds of currency, and to make that currency, dollar for dollar, legal tender for the payment of debts. In the light of abundant experience, the Congress was entitled to choose such a uniform monetary system, and to reject a dual system, with respect to all obligations within the range of the exercise of its constitutional authority. The contention that these gold clauses are valid contracts and cannot be struck down proceeds upon the assumption that private parties, and States and municipalities, may make and enforce contracts which may limit that authority. Dismissing that untenable assumption, the facts must be faced. We think that it is clearly shown that these clauses interfere with the exertion of the power granted to the Congress and certainly it is not established that the Congress arbitrarily or capriciously decided that such an interference existed.

The judgment and decree, severally under review, are affirmed.

2. *John N. Perry* v. *The United States.* 294 U. S. 330.

HUGHES, C. J. The certificate from the Court of Claims shows the following facts:

Plaintiff brought suit as the owner of an obligation of the United States for $10,000 known as "Fourth Liberty Loan 4¼% Gold Bond of 1933–1938." This bond was issued pursuant to the Act of September 24, 1917, as amended, and Treasury Department circular No. 121 dated September 28, 1918. The bond provided: "The principal and interest hereof are payable in United States gold coin of the present standard of value." . . .

The Court of Claims has certified the following questions:

1. Is the claimant, being the holder and owner of a Fourth Liberty Loan 4¼% bond of the United States, of the principal amount of $10,000, issued in 1918, which was payable on and after April 15, 1934, and which bond contained a clause that the principal is "payable in United States gold coin of the present standard of value," entitled to receive from the United States an amount in legal tender currency in excess of the face amount of the bond?

2. Is the United States, as obligor in a Fourth Liberty Loan 4¼% gold bond, Series of 1933–1938, as stated in Question One liable to respond in damages in a suit in the Court of Claims on such bond as an express contract by reason of the change in or impossibility of performance in accordance with the tenor thereof, due to the provisions of Public Resolution No. 10, 73rd Congress, abrogating the gold clause in all obligations?

First. The import of the obligation. The bond in suit differs from an obligation of private parties, or of States or municipalities, whose contracts are necessarily made in subjection to the dominant power of the Congress. *Norman* v. *Baltimore & Ohio R. R. Co.*, decided this day. The bond now before us is an obligation of the United States. The terms of the bond are explicit. They were not only expressed in the bond itself, but they were definitely prescribed by the Congress. The Act of September 24, 1917, both in its original and amended form, authorized the moneys to be borrowed, and the bonds to be issued, "on the credit of the United States" in order to meet expenditures needed "for the national security and defense and other public purposes authorized by law." 40 Stat. 288, 503. The circular of the Treasury Department of September 28, 1918, to which the bond refers "for a statement of the further rights of the holders of bonds of said series" also provided that the principal and interest "are payable in United States gold coin of the present standard of value."

This obligation must be fairly construed. The *"present* standard of value" stood in contradistinction to a *lower* standard of value. The promise obviously was intended to afford protection against loss. That protection was sought to be secured by setting up a standard or measure of the Government's obligation. We think that the reasonable import of the promise is that it was intended to assure one who lent his money to the Government and took its bond that he would not suffer loss through depreciation in the medium of payment. . . .

Second. The binding quality of the obligation. The question is necessarily presented whether the Joint Resolution of June 5, 1933 (48 Stat. 113) is a valid enactment so far as it applies to the obligations of the United States. The Resolution declared that provisions requiring "payment in gold or a particular kind of coin or currency" were "against public policy," and provided that "every obligation, heretofore or hereafter incurred, whether or not any such provision is contained therein," shall be discharged "upon payment, dollar for dollar, in any coin or currency which at the time of payment is legal tender for public and private debts." This enactment was expressly extended to obligations of the United States and provisions for payment in gold, "contained in any law authorizing obligations to be issued by or under

authority of the United States," were repealed.

There is no question as to the power of the Congress to regulate the value of money, that is, to establish a monetary system and thus to determine the currency of the country. The question is whether the Congress can use that power so as to invalidate the terms of the obligations which the Government has theretofore issued in the exercise of the power to borrow money on the credit of the United States. In attempted justification of the Joint Resolution in relation to the outstanding bonds of the United States, the Government argues that "earlier Congresses could not validly restrict the 73rd Congress from exercising its constitutional powers to regulate the value of money, borrow money, or regulate foreign and interstate commerce"; and, from this premise, the Government seems to deduce the proposition that when, with adequate authority, the Government borrows money and pledges the credit of the United States, it is free to ignore that pledge and alter the terms of its obligations in case a later Congress finds their fulfillment inconvenient. The Government's contention thus raises a question of far greater importance than the particular claim of the plaintiff. On that reasoning, if the terms of the Government's bond as to the standard of payment can be repudiated, it inevitably follows that the obligation as to the amount to be paid may also be repudiated. The contention necessarily imports that the Congress can disregard the obligations of the Government at its discretion and that, when the Government borrows money, the credit of the United States is an illusory pledge.

We do not so read the Constitution. There is a clear distinction between the power of the Congress to control or interdict the contracts of private parties when they interfere with the exercise of its constitutional authority, and the power of the Congress to alter or repudiate the substance of its own engagements when it has borrowed money under the authority which the Constitution confers. In authorizing the Congress to borrow money, the Constitution empowers the Congress to fix the amount to be borrowed and the terms of payment. By virtue of the power to borrow money *"on the credit of the United States,"* the Congress is authorized to pledge that

credit as an assurance of payment as stipulated,—as the highest assurance the Government can give, its plighted faith. To say that
the Congress may withdraw or ignore that
pledge is to assume that the Constitution contemplates a vain promise, a pledge having no
other sanction than the pleasure and convenience of the pledgor. This Court has given
no sanction to such a conception of the obligations of our Government. . . .

When the United States, with constitutional authority, makes contracts, it has rights
and incurs responsibilities similar to those of
individuals who are parties to such instruments. . . .

The argument in favor of the Joint Resolution, as applied to government bonds, is in
substance that the Government cannot by
contract restrict the exercise of a sovereign
power. But the right to make binding obligations is a competence attaching to sovereignty.
In the United States, sovereignty resides in
the people who act through the organs established by the Constitution. The Congress as
the instrumentality of sovereignty is endowed
with certain powers to be exerted on behalf
of the people in the manner and with the effect the Constitution ordains. The Congress
cannot invoke the sovereign power of the people to override their will as thus declared. The
powers conferred upon the Congress are harmonious. The Constitution gives to the Congress the power to borrow money on the credit
of the United States, an unqualified power, a
power vital to the Government,—upon which
in an extremity its very life may depend. The
binding quality of the promise of the United
States is of the essence of the credit which is
so pledged. Having this power to authorize
the issue of definite obligations for the payment of money borrowed, the Congress has
not been vested with authority to alter or destroy those obligations. The fact that the
United States may not be sued without its
consent is a matter of procedure which does
not affect the legal and binding character of
its contracts. While the Congress is under no
duty to provide remedies through the courts,
the contractual obligation still exists and, despite infirmities of procedure, remains binding
upon the conscience of the sovereign.

The Fourteenth Amendment, in its fourth
section, explicitly declares: "The validity of
the public debt of the United States, authorized by law, . . . shall not be questioned."
While this provision was undoubtedly inspired
by the desire to put beyond question the obligations of the Government issued during the
Civil War, its language indicates a broader
connotation. We regard it as confirmatory of
a fundamental principle which applies as well
to the government bonds in question, and to
others duly authorized by the Congress, as to
those issued before the Amendment was
adopted. Nor can we perceive any reason for
not considering the expression "the *validity*
of the public debt" as embracing whatever
concerns the integrity of the public obligations.

We conclude that the Joint Resolution of
June 5, 1933, in so far as it attempted to
override the obligation created by the bond
in suit, went beyond the congressional power.

Third. The question of damages. In this
view of the binding quality of the Government's obligations, we come to the question
as to the plaintiff's right to recover damages.
That is a distinct question. Because the Government is not at liberty to alter or repudiate
its obligations, it does not follow that the
claim advanced by the plaintiff should be sustained. The action is for breach of contract.
As a remedy for breach, plaintiff can recover
no more than the loss he has suffered and of
which he may rightfully complain. He is not
entitled to be enriched. Plaintiff seeks judgment for $16,931.25, in present legal tender
currency, on his bond for $10,000. The ques-
tion is whether he has shown damage to that
extent, or any actual damage, as the Court of
Claims has no authority to entertain an action
for nominal damages. . . .

The change in the weight of the gold dollar
did not necessarily cause loss to the plaintiff
of the amount claimed. The question of actual loss cannot fairly be determined without
considering the economic situation at the time
the Government offered to pay him the
$10,000, the face of his bond, in legal tender
currency. The case is not the same as if gold
coin had remained in circulation. That was
the situation at the time of the decisions under the legal tender acts of 1862 and 1863.

Before the change in the weight of the
gold dollar in 1934, gold coin had been withdrawn from circulation. The Congress had authorized the prohibition of the exportation of
gold coin and the placing of restrictions upon

transactions in foreign exchange. . . . And the holder of an obligation, or bond, of the United States, payable in gold coin of the former standard, so far as the restraint upon the right to export gold coin or to engage in transactions in foreign exchange is concerned, was in no better case than the holder of gold coin itself.

In considering what damages, if any, the plaintiff has sustained by the alleged breach of his bond, it is hence inadmissible to assume that he was entitled to obtain gold coin for recourse to foreign markets or for dealings in foreign exchange or for other purposes contrary to the control over gold coin which the Congress had the power to exert, and had exerted, in its monetary regulation. Plaintiff's damages could not be assessed without regard to the internal economy of the country at the time the alleged breach occurred. The discontinuance of gold payments and the establishment of legal tender currency on a standard unit of value with which "all forms of money" of the United States were to be "maintained at a parity," had a controlling influence upon the domestic economy. It was adjusted to the new basis. A free domestic market for gold was non-existent.

Plaintiff demands the "equivalent" in currency of the gold coin promised. But "equivalent" cannot mean more than the amount of money which the promised gold coin would be worth to the bondholder for the purposes for which it could legally be used. That equivalence or worth could not properly be ascertained save in the light of the domestic and restricted market which the Congress had lawfully established. In the domestic transactions to which the plaintiff was limited, in the absence of special license, determination of the value of the gold coin would necessarily have regard to its use as legal tender and as a medium of exchange under a single monetary system with an established parity of all currency and coins. And in view of the control of export and foreign exchange, and the restricted domestic use, the question of value, in relation to transactions legally available to the plaintiff, would require a consideration of the purchasing power of the dollars which the plaintiff has received. Plaintiff has not shown, or attempted to show, that in relation to buying power he has sustained any loss whatever. On the contrary, in view of the adjustment of the internal economy to the single measure of value as established by the legislation of the Congress, and the universal availability and use throughout the country of the legal tender currency in meeting all engagements, the payment to the plaintiff of the amount which he demands would appear to constitute not a recoupment of loss in any proper sense but an unjustified enrichment.

Plaintiff seeks to make his case solely upon the theory that by reason of the change in the weight of the dollar he is entitled to one dollar and sixty-nine cents in the present currency for every dollar promised by the bond, regardless of any actual loss he has suffered with respect to any transaction in which his dollars may be used. We think that position is untenable.

In the view that the facts alleged by the petition fail to show a cause of action for actual damages, the first question submitted by the Court of Claims is answered in the negative. It is not necessary to answer the second question.

Question No. 1 is answered "No."

483. EMERGENCY RAILROAD TRANSPORTATION ACT
June 16, 1933
(*U. S. Statutes at Large*, Vol. XLVIII, p. 211)

The railroads had suffered more seriously than had any other public utility from the depression of 1929—, and throughout the Hoover administration plans for a consolidation of resources and service had been broached. One of the first acts of the Roosevelt administration was to provide for the reorganization of the railroads. The Emergency Act of 1933 provided for mergers and consolidation of terminals, etc. under the direction of a federal coördinator. Mr. Joseph Eastman was appointed first federal coördinator, and in his first report of January 20, 1934, recommended eventual government ownership of railroads. See, E. R. Johnson, *Government Regulation of Transportation.*

AN ACT to relieve the existing national emergency in relation to interstate railroad transportation.

TITLE I—EMERGENCY POWERS

. . . SEC. 2. In order to foster and protect interstate commerce in relation to railroad transportation by preventing and relieving obstructions and burdens thereon resulting from the present acute economic emergency, and in order to safeguard and maintain an adequate national system of transportation, there is hereby created the office of Federal Coordinator of Transportation, who shall be appointed by the President, by and with the advice and consent of the Senate, or be designated by the President from the membership of the Commission. If so designated, the Coordinator shall be relieved from other duties as Commissioner during his term of service to such extent as the President may direct; except that the Coordinator shall not sit as a member of the Commission in any proceedings for the review or suspension of any order issued by him as Coordinator. . . .

SEC. 3. The Coordinator shall divide the lines of the carriers into three groups, to wit, an eastern group, a southern group, and a western group, and may from time to time make such changes or subdivisions in such groups as he may deem to be necessary or desirable. At the earliest practicable date . . . three regional coordinating committees shall be created, one for each group, and each committee shall consist of five regular members and two special members. The carriers in each group, acting each through its board of directors . . . shall select the regular members of the committee representing that group, and shall prescribe the rules under which such committee shall operate; but no railroad system shall have more than one representative on any such committee. In such selection each carrier shall have a vote in proportion to its mileage lying within the group. The two special members of each committee shall be selected in such manner as the Coordinator may approve, one to represent the steam railroads within the group which had in 1932 railway operating revenues of less than $1,000,000 and the other to represent electric railways within the group not owned by a steam railroad or operated as a part of a general steam railroad system of transportation. . . .

SEC. 4. The purposes of this title are (1) to encourage and promote or require action on the part of the carriers and of subsidiaries subject to the Interstate Commerce Act, as amended, which will (a) avoid unnecessary duplication of services and facilities of whatsoever nature and permit the joint use of terminals and trackage incident thereto or requisite to such joint use: *Provided,* That no routes now existing shall be eliminated except with the consent of all participating lines or upon order of the Coordinator, (b) control allowances, accessorial services and the charges therefor, and other practices affecting service or operation, to the end that undue impairment of net earnings may be prevented, and (c) avoid other wastes and preventable expense; (2) to promote financial reorganization of the carriers, with due regard to legal rights, so as to reduce fixed charges to the extent required by the public interest and improve carrier credit; and (3) to provide for the immediate study of other means of improving conditions surrounding transportation in all its forms and the preparation of plans therefor. . . .

SEC. 6. (a) The Coordinator shall confer freely with the committees and give them the benefit of his advice and assistance. At his request, the committees, the carriers, the subsidiaries, and the Commission shall furnish him, or his assistants and agents, such information and reports as he may desire in investigating any matter within the scope of his duties under this title; and the Coordinator, his assistants, and agents, and the Commission, shall at all times have access to all accounts, records, and memoranda of the carriers and subsidiaries. . . .

SEC. 7. (a) A labor committee for each regional group of carriers may be selected by those railroad labor organizations which, as representatives duly designated and authorized to act in accordance with the requirements of the Railway Labor Act, entered into the agreements of January 31, 1932, and December 21, 1932, with duly authorized representatives of the carriers, determining the wage payments of the employees of the carriers. A similar labor committee for each regional group of carriers may be selected by such other railroad labor organizations as may be duly designated and authorized to represent employees in accordance with the requirements of the Railway Labor Act. It shall be the duty of the regional coordinating committees and the Coordinator to give reasonable notice to, and to confer with, the appropriate regional labor committee or committees upon the subject matter prior to taking any action or issuing any order which will affect the interest of the employees, and to afford the said labor committee or committees reasonable opportunity to present views upon said contemplated action or order.

(b) The number of employees in the service of a carrier shall not be reduced by reason of any action taken pursuant to the authority of this title below the number as shown by the pay rolls of employees in service during the month of May, 1933, . . . but not more in any one year than 5 per centum of said number in service during May, 1933; nor shall any employee in such service be deprived of employment such as he had during said month of May or be in a worse position with respect to his compensation for such employment, by reason of any action taken pursuant to the authority conferred by this title.

(c) The Coordinator is authorized and directed to establish regional boards of adjustment whenever and wherever action taken pursuant to the authority conferred by this title creates conditions that make necessary such boards of adjustment to settle controversies between carriers and employees. Carriers and their employees shall have equal representation on such boards of adjustment for settlement of such controversies, and said boards shall exercise the functions of boards of adjustment provided for by the Railway Labor Act.

(d) The Coordinator is authorized and directed to provide means for determining the amount of, and to require the carriers to make just compensation for, property losses and expenses imposed upon employees by reason of transfers of work from one locality to another in carrying out the purposes of this title. . . .

SEC. 10. (a) The carriers or subsidiaries subject to the Interstate Commerce Act, as amended, affected by any order of the Coordinator or Commission made pursuant to this title shall, so long as such order is in effect, be, and they are hereby, relieved from the operation of the antitrust laws. . . . *Provided, however,* That nothing herein shall be construed to repeal, amend, suspend, or modify any of the requirements of the Railway Labor Act or the duties and obligations imposed thereunder or through contracts entered into in accordance with the provisions of said Act. . . .

SEC. 13. It shall further be the duty of the Coordinator, and he is hereby authorized and directed, forthwith to investigate and consider means, not provided for in this title, of improving transportation conditions throughout the country, including cost finding in rail transportation and the ability, financial or otherwise, of the carriers to improve their properties and furnish service and charge rates which will promote the commerce and industry of the country and including, also, the stability of railroad labor employment and other improvement of railroad labor conditions and relations; and from time to time he shall submit to the Commission such recommendations calling for further legislation to these ends as he may deem necessary or desirable in the public interest. The Commission shall promptly transmit such recommendations, together with its comments thereon, to the President and to the Congress. . . .

484. THE NATIONAL RECOVERY ACT
June 16, 1933

(U. S. Statutes at Large, Vol. XLVIII, p. 195)

The National Industrial Recovery Act, approved the last day of the notable first session of the 73rd Congress, was in some respects the most extraordinary law ever passed by an American Congress. It provided for the federal control of the entire industrial structure of the country through the mechanism of codes drawn up by government administrators and special industries. For a typical code see Doc. No. 485. Gen. Hugh S. Johnson was appointed chief administrator. Widespread dissatisfaction with the actual workings of the NRA led to a sweeping reorganization in September, 1934. Six months later the Supreme Court invalidated the code system (see

Doc. No. 486), whereupon the President terminated the life of the National Recovery Administration as of Jan. 1, 1936. Some important features of the NRA were later reënacted. See, H. Johnson, *The Blue Eagle, from Egg to Earth;* L. Mayers, ed. *A Handbook of the N.R.A.;* L. S. Lyon, et. al. *The National Recovery Administration;* C. L. Dearing, et. al., *The ABC of the NRA;* D. V. Brown, et. al., *The Economics of the Recovery Program;* C. Dougherty, *Labor under the NRA;* A. A. Berle, et. al., *America's Recovery Program;* F. Perkins, *People at Work;* H. Ickes, *Back to Work;* M. F. Gallagher, *Government Rules Industry,* and references for Doc. No. 486.

AN ACT to encourage national industrial recovery, to foster fair competition, and to provide for the construction of certain useful public works, and for other purposes.

TITLE I—INDUSTRIAL RECOVERY

DECLARATION OF POLICE

SEC. 1. A national emergency productive of widespread unemployment and disorganization of industry, which burdens interstate and foreign commerce, affects the public welfare, and undermines the standards of living of the American people, is hereby declared to exist. It is hereby declared to be the policy of Congress to remove obstructions to the free flow of interstate and foreign commerce which tend to diminish the amount thereof; and to provide for the general welfare by promoting the organization of industry for the purpose of cooperative action among trade groups, to induce and maintain united action of labor and management under adequate governmental sanctions and supervision, to eliminate unfair competitive practices, to promote the fullest possible utilization of the present productive capacity of industries, to avoid undue restriction of production (except as may be temporarily required), to increase the consumption of industrial and agricultural products by increasing purchasing power, to reduce and relieve unemployment, to improve standards of labor, and otherwise to rehabilitate industry and to conserve natural resources.

ADMINISTRATIVE AGENCIES

SEC. 2. . . . . (c) This title shall cease to be in effect and any agencies established hereunder shall cease to exist at the expiration of two years after the date of enactment of this Act, or sooner if the President shall by proclamation or the Congress shall by joint resolution declare that the emergency recognized by section 1 has ended.

CODES OF FAIR COMPETITION

SEC. 3. (a) Upon the application to the President by one or more trade or industrial associations or groups, the President may approve a code or codes of fair competition for the trade or industry or subdivision thereof, represented by the applicant or applicants, if the President finds (1) that such associations or groups impose no inequitable restrictions on admission to membership therein and are truly representative of such trades or industries or subdivisions thereof, and (2) that such code or codes are not designed to promote monopolies or to eliminate or oppress small enterprises and will not operate to discriminate against them, and will tend to effectuate the policy of this title: *Provided,* That such code or codes shall not permit monopolies or monopolistic practices: *Provided further,* That where such code or codes affect the services and welfare of persons engaged in other steps of the economic process, nothing in this section shall deprive such persons of the right to be heard prior to approval by the President of such code or codes. The President may, as a condition of his approval of any such code, impose such conditions (including requirements for the making of reports and the keeping of accounts) for the protection of consumers, competitors, employees, and others, and in furtherance of the public interest, and may provide such exceptions to and exemptions from the provisions of such code, as the President in his discretion deems necessary to effectuate the policy herein declared.

(b) After the President shall have approved any such code, the provisions of such code shall be the standards of fair competition for such trade or industry or subdivision thereof. Any violation of such standards in any transaction in or affecting interstate or foreign commerce shall be deemed an unfair method of competition in commerce within the meaning of the Federal Trade Commission Act, as amended; but nothing in this title shall be construed to impair the powers of the Federal Trade Commission under such Act, as amended. . . .

(d) Upon his own motion, or if complaint is made to the President that abuses inimical to the public interest and contrary to the policy herein declared are prevalent in any trade or industry or subdivision thereof, and if no code of fair competition therefor has theretofore been approved by the President, the President, after such public notice and hearing as he shall specify, may prescribe and approve a code of fair competition for such trade or industry or subdivision thereof, which shall have the same effect as a code of fair competition approved by the President under subsection (a) of this section. . . .

AGREEMENTS AND LICENSES

SEC. 4. (a) The President is authorized to enter into agreements with, and to approve voluntary agreements between and among, persons engaged in a trade or industry, labor organizations, and trade or industrial organizations, associations, or groups, relating to any trade or industry, if in his judgment such agreements will aid in effectuating the policy of this title with respect to transactions in or affecting interstate or foreign commerce, and will be consistent with the requirements of clause (2) of subsection (a) of section 3 for a code of fair competition.

(b) Whenever the President shall find that destructive wage or price cutting or other activities contrary to the policy of this title are being practiced in any trade or industry or any subdivision thereof, and, after such public notice and hearing as he shall specify, shall find it essential to license business enterprises in order to make effective a code of fair competition or an agreement under this title or otherwise to effectuate the policy of this title, and shall publicly so announce, no person shall, after a date fixed in such announcement, engage in or carry on any business, in or affecting interstate or foreign commerce, specified in such announcement, unless he shall have first obtained a license issued pursuant to such regulations as the President shall prescribe. The President may suspend or revoke any such license, after due notice and opportunity for hearing, for violations of the terms or conditions thereof. Any order of the President suspending or revok-

ing any such license shall be final if in accordance with law. . . .

SEC. 5. While this title is in effect . . . and for sixty days thereafter, any code, agreement, or license approved, prescribed, or issued and in effect under this title, and any action complying with the provisions thereof taken during such period, shall be exempt from the provisions of the antitrust laws of the United States.

Nothing in this Act, and no regulation thereunder, shall prevent an individual from pursuing the vocation of manual labor and selling or trading the products thereof; nor shall anything in this Act, or regulation thereunder, prevent anyone from marketing or trading the produce of his farm.

LIMITATIONS UPON APPLICATION OF TITLE

SEC. 6. (a) No trade or industrial association or group shall be eligible to receive the benefit of the provisions of this title until it files with the President a statement containing such information relating to the activities of the association or group as the President shall by regulation prescribe. . . .

SEC. 7. (a) Every code of fair competition, agreement, and license approved, prescribed, or issued under this title shall contain the following conditions: (1) That employees shall have the right to organize and bargain collectively through representatives of their own choosing, and shall be free from the interference, restraint, or coercion of employers of labor, or their agents, in the designation of such representatives or in self-organization or in other concerted activities for the purpose of collective bargaining or other mutual aid or protection; (2) that no employee and no one seeking employment shall be required as a condition of employment to join any company union or to refrain from joining, organizing, or assisting a labor organization of his own choosing; and (3) that employers shall comply with the maximum hours of labor, minimum rates of pay, and other conditions of employment, approved or prescribed by the President.

(b) The President shall, so far as practicable, afford every opportunity to employers and employees in any trade or industry or subdivision thereof with respect to which the conditions referred to in clauses (1) and (2) of subsection (a) prevail, to establish by mutual agreement, the standards as to the maximum hours of labor, minimum rates of pay, and such other conditions of employment as may be necessary in such trade or industry or subdivision thereof to effectuate the policy of this title; and the standards established in such agreements, when approved by the President, shall have the same effect as a code of fair competition. . . .

(c) Where no such mutual agreement has been approved by the President he may investigate the labor practices, policies, wages, hours of labor, and conditions of employment in such trade or industry or subdivision thereof; and upon the basis of such investigations, and after such hearings as the President finds advisable, he is authorized to prescribe a limited code of fair competition fixing such maximum hours of labor, minimum rates of pay, and other conditions of employment in the trade or industry or subdivision thereof investigated as he finds to be necessary to effectuate the policy of this title, which shall have the same effect as a code of fair competition approved by the President under subsection (a) of section 3. The President may differentiate according to experience and skill of the employees affected and according to the locality of employment; but no attempt shall be made to introduce any classification according to the nature of the work involved which might tend to set a maximum as well as a minimum wage.

(d) As used in this title, the term "person" includes any individual, partnership, association, trust, or corporation; . . .

OIL REGULATION

SEC. 9. (a) The President is further authorized to initiate before the Interstate Commerce Commission proceedings necessary to prescribe regulations to control the operations of oil pipe lines and to fix reasonable, compensatory rates for the transportation of petroleum and its products by pipe lines, and the Interstate Commerce Commission shall grant preference to the hearings and determination of such cases.

(b) The President is authorized to institute proceedings to divorce from any holding company any pipe-line company controlled by such holding company which pipe-line company by unfair practices or by exorbitant rates in the transportation of petroleum or its products tends to create a monopoly.

(c) The President is authorized to prohibit the transportation in interstate and foreign commerce of petroleum and the products thereof produced or withdrawn from storage in excess of the amount permitted to be produced or withdrawn from storage by any State law or valid regulation or order prescribed thereunder, by any board, commission, officer, or other duly authorized agency of a State. . . .

TITLE II—PUBLIC WORKS AND CONSTRUCTION PROJECTS
FEDERAL EMERGENCY ADMINISTRATION OF PUBLIC WORKS

SECTION 201. (a) To effectuate the purposes of this title, the President is hereby authorized to create a Federal Emergency Administration of Public Works, all the powers of which shall be exercised by a Federal Emergency Administrator of Public Works, . . . and to establish such agencies, to accept and utilize such voluntary and uncompensated services, to appoint, without regard to the civil service laws, such officers and employees, and to utilize such Federal officers and employees, and, with the consent of the State, such State and local officers and employees as he may find necessary, to prescribe their authorities, duties, responsibilities, and tenure, and, without regard to the Classification Act of 1923, as amended, to fix the compensation of any officers and employees so appointed. The President may delegate any of his functions and powers under this title to such officers, agents, and employees as he may designate or appoint.

(b) The Administrator may, without regard to the civil service laws or the Classification Act of 1923, as amended, appoint and fix the compensation of such experts and such other officers and employees as are necessary to carry out the provisions of this title; and may make such expenditures (including expenditures for personal services and rent at the seat of government and elsewhere, for law books and books of reference, and for paper, printing and binding) as are necessary to carry out the provisions of this title. . . .

(d) After the expiration of two years after the date of the enactment of this Act, or sooner if the President shall by proclamation or the Congress shall by joint resolution declare that the emergency recognized by section 1 has ended, the President shall not make any further loans or grants or enter upon any new construction under this title, and any agencies established hereunder shall cease to exist and any of their remaining functions shall be transferred to such departments of the Government as the President shall designate: . . .

SEC. 202. The Administrator, under the direction of the President, shall prepare a comprehensive program of public works, which shall include among other things the following: (a) Construction, repair, and improvement of public highways and park ways, public buildings, and any publicly owned instrumentalities and facilities; (b) conservation and development of natural resources, including control, utilization, and purification of waters, prevention of soil or coastal erosion, development of water power, transmission of electrical energy, and construction of river and harbor improvements and flood control and also the construction of any river or drainage improvement required to perform or satisfy any obligation incurred by the United States through a treaty with a foreign Government heretofore ratified and to restore or develop for the use of any State or its citizens water taken from or denied to them by performance on the part of the United States of treaty obligations heretofore assumed: *Provided,* That no river or harbor improvements shall be carried out unless they shall have heretofore or hereafter been adopted by the Congress or are recommended by the Chief of Engineers of the United States Army; (c) any projects of the character heretofore constructed or carried on either directly by public authority or with public aid to serve the interests of the general public; (d) construction, reconstruction, alteration, or repair under public regulation or control of low-cost housing and slum-clearance projects; (e) any project (other than those included in the foregoing classes) of any character heretofore eligible for loans under subsection (a) of section 201 of the Emergency Relief and Construction Act of 1932, as amended, and paragraph (3) of such subsection (a) shall for such purposes be held to include loans for the construction or

completion of hospitals the operation of which is partly financed from public funds, and of reservoirs and pumping plants and for the construction of dry docks; and if in the opinion of the President it seems desirable, the construction of naval vessels within the terms and/or limits established by the London Naval Treaty of 1930 and of aircraft required therefor and construction of heavier-than-air aircraft and technical construction for the Army Air Corps and such Army housing projects as the President may approve, and provision of original equipment for the mechanization or motorization of such Army tactical units as he may designate: *Provided, however,* That in the event of an international agreement for the further limitation of armament, to which the United States is signatory, the President is hereby authorized and empowered to suspend, in whole or in part, any such naval or military construction or mechanization and motorization of Army units. . . .

SEC. 203. (a) With a view to increasing employment quickly (while reasonably securing any loans made by the United States) the President is authorized and empowered, through the Administrator or through such other agencies as he may designate or create, (1) to construct, finance, or aid in the construction or financing of any public-works project included in the program prepared pursuant to section 202; (2) upon such terms as the President shall prescribe, to make grants to States, municipalities, or other public bodies for the construction, repair, or improvement of any such project, but no such grant shall be in excess of 30 per centum of the cost of the labor and materials employed upon such project; (3) to acquire by purchase, or by exercise of the power of eminent domain, any real or personal property in connection with the construction of any such project, and to sell any security acquired or any property so constructed or acquired or to lease any such property with or without the privilege of purchase: *Provided,* That all moneys received from any such sale or lease or the repayment of any loan shall be used to retire obligations issued pursuant to section 209 of this Act, in addition to any other moneys required to be used for such purpose; (4) to aid in the financing of such railroad maintenance and equipment as may be approved by the Interstate Commerce Commission as desirable for the improvement of transportation facilities; . . . *Provided,* That in deciding to extend any aid or grant hereunder to any State, county, or municipality the President may consider whether action is in process or in good faith assured therein reasonably designed to bring the ordinary current expenditures thereof within the prudently estimated revenues thereof. . . .

(d) The President, in his discretion, and under such terms as he may prescribe, may extend any of the benefits of this title to any State, county, or municipality notwithstanding any constitutional or legal restriction or limitation on the right or power of such State, county, or municipality to borrow money or incur indebtedness.

SEC. 204. (a) For the purpose of providing for emergency construction of public highways and related projects, the President is authorized to make grants to the highway departments of the several States in an amount not less than $400,000,000, to be expended by such departments in accordance with the provisions of the Federal Highway Act, approved November 9, 1921, as amended and supplemented. . . .

SEC. 205. (a) Not less than $50,000,000 of the amount made available by this Act shall be allotted for (A) national forest highways, (B) national forest roads, trails, bridges, and related projects, (C) national park roads and trails in national parks owned or authorized, (D) roads on Indian reservations, and (E) roads through public lands, to be expended in the same manner as provided in paragraph (2) of section 301 of the Emergency Relief and Construction Act of 1932, in the case of appropriations allocated for such purposes, respectively, in such section 301, to remain available until expended. . . .

SEC. 206. All contracts let for construction projects and all loans and grants pursuant to this title shall contain such provisions as are necessary to insure (1) that no convict labor shall be employed on any such project; (2) that (except in executive, administrative, and supervisory positions), so far as practicable and feasible, no individual directly employed on any such project shall be permitted to work more than thirty hours in any one week; (3) that all employees shall be paid just and reasonable wages which shall be compensation sufficient to provide, for the hours of labor as limited, a standard of living in decency and comfort; (4) that in the employment of labor in connection with any such project, preference shall be given, where they are qualified, to ex-service men with dependents, and then in the following order: (A) To citizens of the United States and aliens who have declared their intention of becoming citizens, who are bona fide residents of the political subdivision and/or county in which the work is to be performed, and (B) to citizens of the United States and aliens who have declared their intention of becoming citizens, who are bona fide residents of the State, Territory, or district in which the work is to be performed: *Provided,* That these preferences shall apply only where such labor is available and qualified to perform the work to which the employment relates; and (5) that the maximum of human labor shall be used in lieu of machinery wherever practicable and consistent with sound economy and public advantage. . . .

SUBSISTENCE HOMESTEADS

SEC. 208. To provide for aiding the redistribution of the overbalance of population in industrial centers $25,000,000 is hereby made available to the President, to be used by him through such agencies as he may establish and under such regulations as he may make, for making loans for and otherwise aiding in the purchase of subsistence homesteads. The moneys collected as repayment of said loans shall constitute a revolving fund to be administered as directed by the President for the purposes of this section.

485. COTTON TEXTILE CODE
July 17, 1933

(J. D. Magee, W. E. Atkins, E. Stein, *The National Recovery Program,* p. 11 ff.)

This Code of Fair Competition for the cotton textile industry was drawn up in accordance with the provisions of Sec. 3 of the National Recovery Act of 1933. The most significant section of the code provided for the abolition of child labor in the textile industries.

To effectuate the policy of Title I of the National Industrial Recovery Act, during the period of the emergency, by reducing and relieving unemployment, improving the standards of labor, eliminating competitive practices destructive of the interests of the public, employee and employers, relieving the disastrous effects of over-capacity, and otherwise rehabilitating the cotton textile industry and by increasing the consumption of industrial and agricultural products by increasing purchasing power, and in other respects, the following provisions are established as a Code of fair competition for the cotton textile industry: . . .

Definitions

II. On and after the effective date, the minimum wage that shall be paid by employers in the cotton textile industry to any of their employees—except learners during a six weeks' apprenticeship, cleaners and outside employees—shall be at the rate of $12 per week when employed in the Southern section of the industry and at the rate of $13 per week when employed in the Northern section for 40 hours of labor.

III. On and after the effective date, employers in the cotton textile industry shall not operate on a schedule of hours of labor for their employees—except repair shop crews, engineers, electricians, firemen, office and supervisory staff, shipping, watching and outside crews, and cleaners—in excess of 40 hours per week and they shall not operate productive machinery in the cotton textile industry for more than two shifts of 40 hours each per week.

IV. On and after the effective date, employers in the cotton textile industry shall not employ any minor under the age of 16 years. . . . Each person engaged in the cotton textile industry will furnish duly certified reports in substance as follows and in such form as may hereafter be provided: . . .

V. The Cotton-Textile Institute, Inc., 320 Broadway, New York City, is constituted the agency to collect and receive such reports.

VI. To further effectuate the policies of the Act, the Cotton Textile Industry Committee, . . . is set up to co-operate with the Administrator as a planning and fair practice agency for the cotton textile industry. Such agency may from time to time present to the Administrator recommendations based on conditions in the industry as they may develop from time to time which will tend to effectuate the operation of the provisions of this Code and the policy of the National Industrial Recovery Act. . . .

Such agency is also set up to co-operate with the Administrator in making investigations as to the functioning and observance of any of the provisions of this Code, at its own instance or on complaint by any person affected, and to report the same to the Administrator.

Such agency is also set up for the purpose of investigating and informing the Administrator on behalf of the cotton textile industry as to the importation of competitive articles into the United States in substantial quantities or increasing ratio to domestic production on such terms or under such conditions as to render ineffective or seriously to endanger the maintenance of this Code and as an agency for making complaint to the President on behalf of the cotton textile industry under the provisions of the National Industrial Recovery Act, with respect thereto.

VII. Where the costs of executing contracts entered into in the cotton textile industry prior to the presentation of Congress of the National Industrial Recovery Act are increased by the application of the provisions of that Act to the industry, it is equitable and promotive of the purposes of the Act that appropriate adjustments of such contracts to reflect such increased costs be arrived at by arbitral proceedings or otherwise, and the Cotton Textile Industry Committee, the applicant for this Code, is constituted an agency to assist in effecting such adjustments.

VIII. Employers in the cotton textile industry shall comply with the requirements of the National Industrial Recovery Act as follows: "(1) That employees shall have the right to organize and bargain collectively through representatives of their own choosing, and shall be free from the interference, restraint, or coercion of employers of labor, or their agents, in the designation of such representatives or in self-organization or in other concerted activities for the purpose of collective bargaining or other mutual aid or

protection; (2) that no employee and no one seeking employment shall be required as a condition of employment to join any company union or to refrain from joining, organizing or assisting a labor organization of his own choosing, and (3) that employers shall comply with the maximum hours of labor, minimum rates of pay, and other conditions of employment, approved or prescribed by the President." . . .

486. SCHECHTER POULTRY CORP. v. UNITED STATES
295 U. S. 495
1935

On Writs of Certiorari to the U. S. Circuit Court of Appeals for the Second Circuit. This unanimous opinion invalidating the NRA was the first of a series of judicial onslaughts upon New Deal legislation. The invalidation rested upon two grounds: that the NRA act improperly delegated legislative powers to the executive, and that the provisions of the Poultry Code constituted a regulation of intrastate, not interstate, commerce. It was upon this second count, representing an extreme retreat from the historic position of the Court, that criticism was chiefly focussed. See, Black, "Commerce Clause and the New Deal," 20 Corn. L. Qt. 169; Black, "NRA delegation to the President," 19 Corn L. Qt. 389; Boudin, "Is Economic Planning Constitutional?" 21 Georgetown L. J. 253; Carpenter, "Constitutionality of the NIRA and the AAA," 7 So. Calif. L. Rev. 125; Corwin, "The Schechter Case—Landmark or what?" 13 N. Y. U. L. Qt. Rev. 151; Dickinson, "The Major Issues Presented by the Industrial Recovery Act," 33 Col. L. Rev. 1095; Field, "Constitutional Theory of the NIRA," 18 Minn. L. Rev. 269; Grant, "Commerce, Production, and Fiscal Powers of Congress," 44 Yale L. J. 751; McGowen, "An Economic Interpretation of the Doctrine of Delegation of Governmental Powers," 12 Tulane L. Rev. 179; Powell, "Commerce, Pensions, and Codes, II" 49 Harv. L. Rev. 193.

HUGHES, C. J. Petitioners were convicted in the District Court of the United States for the Eastern District of New York on eighteen counts of an indictment charging violations of what is known as the "Live Poultry Code," and on an additional count for conspiracy to commit such violations. By demurrer to the indictment and appropriate motions on the trial, the defendants contended (1) that the Code had been adopted pursuant to an unconstitutional delegation by Congress of legislative power; (2) that it attempted to regulate intrastate transactions which lay outside the authority of Congress; and (3) that in certain provisions it was repugnant to the due process clause of the Fifth Amendment.

The defendants are slaughterhouse operators. . . . A. L. A. Schechter Poultry Corporation and Schechter Live Poultry Market are corporations conducting wholesale poultry slaughterhouse markets in Brooklyn, New York City. Defendants ordinarily purchase their live poultry from commission men at the West Washington Market in New York City or at the railroad terminals serving the City, but occasionally they purchase from commission men in Philadelphia. They buy the poultry for slaughter and resale. After the poultry is trucked to their slaughterhouse markets in Brooklyn, it is there sold, usually within twenty-four hours, to retail poultry dealers and butchers who sell directly to consumers. The poultry purchased from defendants is immediately slaughtered, prior to delivery, by shochtim in defendants' employ. Defendants do not sell poultry in interstate commerce.

The "Live Poultry Code" was promulgated under section 3 of the National Industrial Recovery Act. That section authorizes the President to approve "codes of fair competition." Such a code may be approved for a trade or industry, upon application by one or more trade or industrial associations or groups, if the President finds (1) that such associations or groups "impose no inequitable restrictions on admission to membership therein and are truly representative," and (2) that such codes are not designed "to promote monopolies or to eliminate or oppress small enterprises and will not operate to discriminate against them, and will tend to effectuate the policy" of Title I of the act. Such codes "shall not permit monopolies or monopolistic practices." As a condition of his approval, the President may "impose such conditions (including requirements for the making of reports and the keeping of accounts) for the protection of consumers, competitors, employees, and others, and in furtherance of the public interest, and may provide such exceptions to and exemptions from the provisions of such code as the President in his discretion deems necessary to effectuate the policy herein declared." Where such a code has not been approved, the President may prescribe one, either on his own motion or on complaint. Violation of any provision of a code (so approved or prescribed) "in any transaction in or affecting interstate or foreign commerce" is made a misdemeanor punishable by a fine of not more than $500 for each offense, and each day the violation continues is to be deemed a separate offense.

The "Live Poultry Code" was approved by the President on April 13, 1934. Its divisions indicate its nature and scope. The Code has eight articles entitled (1) purposes, (2) definitions, (3) hours, (4) wages (5) general labor provisions, (6) administration, (7) trade practice provisions, and (8) general.

The declared purpose is "To effect the policies of title I of the National Industrial Recovery Act." The Code is established as "a code for fair competition for the live poultry industry of the metropolitan area in and about the City of New York." That area is described as embracing the five boroughs of New York City, the counties of Rockland, Westchester, Nassau and Suffolk in the State of New York, the counties of Hudson and Bergen in the State of New Jersey, and the county of Fairfield in the State of Connecticut.

The "industry" is defined as including "every person engaged in the business of selling, purchasing for resale, transporting, or handling and/or slaughtering live poultry, from the time such poultry comes into the New York metropolitan area to the time it is first sold in slaughtered form," and such "related branches" as may from time to time be included by amendment. Employers are styled "members of the industry," and the term employee is defined to embrace "any and all persons engaged in the industry, however compensated," except "members."

The Code fixes the number of hours for work-days. It provides that no employee, with certain exceptions, shall be permitted to work in excess of forty (40) hours in any one week, and that no employee, save as stated, "shall be paid in any pay period less than at the rate of fifty (50) cents per hour." The article containing "general labor provisions" prohibits the employment of any person under sixteen years of age, and declares that employees shall have the right of "collective bargaining," and freedom of choice with respect to labor organizations, in the terms of section 7 (a) of the Act. The minimum number of employees, who shall be employed by slaughterhouse operators, is fixed, the number being graduated according to the average volume of weekly sales.

The seventh article, containing "trade practice provisions," prohibits various practices which are said to constitute "unfair methods of competition."

Of the eighteen counts of the indictment upon which the defendants were convicted, aside from the count for conspiracy, two counts charged violation of the minimum wage and maximum hour provisions of the Code, and ten counts were for violation of the requirement (found in the "trade practice provisions") of "straight killing." The charges in the ten counts, respectively, were that the defendants in selling to retail dealers and butchers had permitted "selections of individual chickens taken from particular coops and half coops."

Of the other six counts, one charged the sale to a butcher of an unfit chicken; two counts charged the making of sales without having the poultry inspected or approved in accordance with regulations or ordinances of the City of New York; two counts charged the making of false reports or the failure to make reports relating to the range of daily prices and volume of sales for certain periods; and the remaining count was for sales to slaughterers or dealers who were without licenses required by the ordinances and regulations of the City of New York.

First. Two preliminary points are stressed by the Government with respect to the appropriate approach to the important questions presented. We are told that the provision of the statute authorizing the adoption of codes must be viewed in the light of the grave national crisis with which Congress was confronted. Undoubtedly, the conditions to which power is addressed are always to be considered when the exercise of power is challenged. Extraordinary conditions may call for extraordinary remedies. But the argument necessarily stops short of an attempt to justify action which lies outside the sphere of constitutional authority. Extraordinary conditions do not create or enlarge constitutional power. The Constitution established a national government with powers deemed to be adequate, as they have proved to be both in war and peace, but these powers of the national government are limited by the constitutional grants. Those who act under these grants are not at liberty to transcend the imposed limits because they believe that more or different power is necessary. Such assertions of extraconstitutional authority were anticipated and precluded by the explicit terms of the Tenth Amendment,—"The powers not delegated to the United States by the Constitution, nor prohibited by it to the States, are reserved to the States respectively, or to the people."

The further point is urged that the national crisis demanded a broad and intensive cooperative effort by those engaged in trade and industry, and that this necessary cooperation was sought to be fostered by permitting them to initiate the adoption of codes. But the statutory plan is not simply one for voluntary effort. It does not seek merely to endow voluntary trade or industrial associations or groups with privileges or immunities. It involves the coercive exercise of the lawmaking power. The codes of fair competition, which the statute attempts to authorize, are codes of laws. If valid, they place all persons within their reach under the obligation of positive law, binding equally those who assent and those who do not assent. Violations of the provisions of the codes are punishable as crimes.

Second. The question of the delegation of legislative power. For a statement of the authorized objectives and content of the "codes of fair competition" we are referred repeatedly to the "Declaration of Policy" in section one of Title I of the Recovery Act. Thus, the approval of a code by the President is conditioned on his finding that it "will tend to effectuate the policy of this title." Sec. 3 (a). The President is authorized to impose such conditions "for the protection of consumers, competitors, employees, and others, and in furtherance of the public interest, and may provide such exceptions to and exemptions from the provisions of such code as the President in his discretion deems necessary to ef-

fectuate the policy herein declared." *Id.* The "policy herein declared" is manifestly that set forth in section one. That declaration embraces a broad range of objectives. Among them we find the elimination of "unfair competitive practices." . . .

We think the conclusion is inescapable that the authority sought to be conferred by section 3 was not merely to deal with "unfair competitive practices" which offend against existing law, and could be the subject of judicial condemnation without further legislation, or to create administrative machinery for the application of established principles of law to particular instances of violation. Rather, the purpose is clearly disclosed to authorize new and controlling prohibitions through codes of laws which would embrace what the formulators would propose, and what the President would approve, or prescribe, as wise and beneficent measures for the government of trades and industries in order to bring about their rehabilitation, correction and development, according to the general declaration of policy in section one. Codes of laws of this sort are styled "codes of fair competition."

We find no real controversy upon this point and we must determine the validity of the Code in question in this aspect.

The question, then, turns upon the authority which section 3 of the Recovery Act vests in the President to approve or prescribe. If the codes have standing as penal statutes, this must be due to the effect of the executive action. But Congress cannot delegate legislative power to the President to exercise an unfettered discretion to make whatever laws he thinks may be needed or advisable for the rehabilitation and expansion of trade or industry.

Accordingly we turn to the Recovery Act to ascertain what limits have been set to the exercise of the President's discretion. *First,* the President, as a condition of approval, is required to find that the trade or industrial associations or groups which propose a code, "impose no inequitable restrictions on admission to membership" and are "truly representative." That condition, however, relates only to the status of the initiators of the new laws and not to the permissible scope of such laws. *Second,* the President is required to find that the code is not "designed to promote monopolies or to eliminate or oppress small enterprises and will not operate to discriminate against them." And, to this is added a proviso that the code "shall not permit monopolies or monopolistic practices." But these restrictions leave virtually untouched the field of policy envisaged by section one, and, in that wide field of legislative possibilities, the proponents of a code, refraining from monopolistic designs, may roam at will and the President may approve or disapprove their proposals as he may see fit.

Nor is the breadth of the President's discretion left to the necessary implications of this limited requirement as to his findings. As already noted, the President in approving a code may impose his own conditions, adding to or taking from what is proposed, as "in his discretion" he thinks necessary "to effectuate the policy" declared by the Act. Of course, he has no less liberty when he prescribes a code of his own motion or on complaint, and he is free to prescribe one if a code has not been approved. The Act provides for the creation by the President of administrative agencies to assist him, but the action or reports of such agencies, or of his other assistants,—their recommendations and findings in relation to the making of codes— have no sanction beyond the will of the President, who may accept, modify or reject them as he pleases. Such recommendations or findings in no way limit the authority which section 3 undertakes to vest in the President with no other conditions than those there specified. And this authority relates to a host of different trades and industries, thus extending the President's discretion to all the varieties of laws which he may deem to be beneficial in dealing with the vast array of commercial and industrial activities throughout the country.

Such a sweeping delegation of legislative power finds no support in the decisions upon which the Government especially relies.

To summarize and conclude upon this point: Section 3 of the Recovery Act is without precedent. It supplies no standards for any trade, industry or activity. It does not undertake to prescribe rules of conduct to be applied to particular states of fact determined by appropriate administrative procedure. Instead of prescribing rules of conduct, it authorizes the making of codes to prescribe them. For that legislative undertaking, section 3 sets up no standards, aside from the statement of the general aims of rehabilitation, correction and expansion described in section one. In view of the scope of that broad declaration, and of the nature of the few restrictions that are imposed, the discretion of the President in approving or prescribing codes, and thus enacting laws for the government of trade and industry throughout the country, is virtually unfettered. We think that the code-making authority thus conferred is an unconstitutional delegation of legislative power.

Second. The question of the application of the provisions of the Live Poultry Code to intrastate transactions. This aspect of the case presents the question whether the particular provisions of the Live Poultry Code, which the defendants were convicted for violating and for having conspired to violate, were within the regulating power of Congress.

These provisions relate to the hours and wages of those employed by defendants in their slaughterhouses in Brooklyn and to the sales there made to retail dealers and butchers.

(1) Were these transactions *"in"* interstate commerce? Much is made of the fact that almost all the poultry coming to New York is sent there from other States. But the code provisions, as here applied, do not concern the transportation of the poultry from other States to New York, or the transactions of the commission men or others to whom it is consigned, or the sales made by such consignees to defendants. When defendants had made their purchases, whether at the West Washington Market in New York City or at the railroad terminals serving the City, or elsewhere, the poultry was trucked to their slaughterhouses in Brooklyn for local disposition. The interstate transactions in relation to that poultry then ended. Defendants held the poultry at their slaughterhouse markets for slaughter and local sale to retail dealers and butchers who in turn sold directly to consumers. Neither the slaughtering nor the sales by defendants were transactions in interstate commerce.

The undisputed facts thus afford no warrant for the argument that the poultry handled by defendants at their slaughterhouse markets was in a *"current"* or *"flow"* of interstate commerce and was thus subject to congressional regulation. The mere fact that there may be a constant flow of commodities into a State does not mean that the flow continues after the property has arrived and has become commingled with the mass of property within the State and is there held solely for local disposition and use. So far as the poultry here in question is concerned, the flow in interstate commerce had ceased. The poultry had come to a permanent rest within the State. It was not held, used, or sold by defendants in relation to any further transactions in interstate commerce and was not destined for transportation to other states. Hence, decisions which deal with a stream of interstate commerce—where goods come to rest within a State temporarily and are later to go forward in interstate commerce—and with the regulations of transactions involved in that practical continuity of movement, are not applicable here.

(2) Did the defendants' transactions directly *"affect"* interstate commerce so as to be subject to federal regulation? The power of Congress extends not only to the regulation of transactions which are part of interstate commerce, but to the protection of that commerce from injury.

In determining how far the federal government may go in controlling intrastate transactions upon the ground that they "affect" interstate commerce, there is a necessary and well-established distinction between direct and indirect effects. The precise line can be drawn only as individual cases arise, but the distinction is clear in principle. Direct effects are illustrated by the railroad cases we have cited, as *e. g.*, the effect of failure to use prescribed safety appliances on railroads which are the highways of both interstate and intrastate commerce, injury to an employee engaged in interstate transportation by the negligence of an employee engaged in an intrastate movement, the fixing of rates for intrastate transportation which unjustly discriminate against interstate commerce. But where the effect of intrastate transactions upon interstate commerce is merely indirect, such transactions remain within the domain of state power. If the commerce clause were construed to reach all enterprises and transactions which could be said to have an indirect effect upon interstate commerce, the

federal authority would embrace practically all the activities of the people and the authority of the State over its domestic concerns would exist only by sufferance of the federal government. Indeed, on such a theory, even the development of the State's commercial facilities would be subject to federal control.

The distinction between direct and indirect effects has been clearly recognized in the application of the Anti-Trust Act. Where a combination or conspiracy is formed, with the intent to restrain interstate commerce or to monopolize any part of it, the violation of the statute is clear. But where that intent is absent, and the objectives are limited to intrastate activities, the fact that there may be an indirect effect upon interstate commerce does not subject the parties to the federal statute, notwithstanding its broad provisions.

While these decisions related to the application of the federal statute, and not to its constitutional validity, the distinction between direct and indirect effects of intrastate transactions upon interstate commerce must be recognized as a fundamental one, essential to the maintenance of our constitutional system. Otherwise as we have said, there would be virtually no limit to the federal power and for all practical purposes we should have a completely centralized government. We must consider the provisions here in question in the light of this distinction.

The question of chief importance relates to the provisions of the Code as to the hours and wages of those employed in defendants' slaughterhouse markets. It is plain that these requirements are imposed in order to govern the details of defendants' management of their local business. The persons employed in slaughtering and selling in local trade are not employed in interstate commerce. Their hours and wages have no direct relation to interstate commerce. The question of how many hours these employees should work and what they should be paid differs in no essential respect from similar questions in other local businesses which handle commodities brought into a State and there dealt in as a part of its internal commerce. This appears from an examination of the considerations urged by the Government with respect to conditions in the poultry trade. Thus, the Government argues that hours and wages affect prices; that slaughterhouse men sell at a small margin above operating costs; that labor represents 50 to 60 per cent of these costs; that a slaughterhouse operator paying lower wages or reducing his cost by exacting long hours of work, translates his saving into lower prices; that this results in demands for a cheaper grade of goods; and that the cutting of prices brings about demoralization of the price structure. Similar conditions may be adduced in relation to other businesses. The argument of the Government proves too much. If the federal government may determine the wages and hours of employees in the internal commerce of a State, because of their relation to cost and prices and their indirect effect upon interstate commerce, it would seem that a similar control might be exerted over other elements of cost, also affecting prices, such as the number of employees, rents, advertising, methods of doing business, etc. All the processes of production and distribution that enter into cost could likewise be controlled. If the cost of doing an intrastate business is in itself the permitted object of federal control, the extent of the regulation of cost would be a question of discretion and not of power.

The Government also makes the point that efforts to enact state legislation establishing high labor standards have been impeded by the belief that unless similar action is taken generally, commerce will be diverted from the States adopting such standards, and that this fear of diversion has led to demands for federal legislation on the subject of wages and hours. The apparent implication is that the federal authority under the commerce clause should be deemed to extend to the establishment of rules to govern wages and hours in intrastate trade and industry generally throughout the country, thus overriding the authority of the States to deal with domestic problems arising from labor conditions in their internal commerce.

It is not the province of the Court to consider the economic advantages or disadvantages of such a centralized system. It is sufficient to say that the Federal Constitution does not provide for it. Our growth and development have called for wide use of the commerce power of the federal government in its control over the expanded activities of interstate commerce, and in protecting that commerce from burdens, interferences, and conspiracies to restrain and monopolize it. But the authority of the federal government may not be pushed to such an extreme as to destroy the distinction, which the commerce clause itself establishes, between commerce "among the several States" and the internal concerns of a State. The same answer must be made to the contention that is based upon the serious economic situation which led to the passage of the Recovery Act,—the fall in prices, the decline in wages and employment, and the curtailment of the market for commodities. Stress is laid upon the great importance of maintaining wage distributions which would provide the necessary stimulus in starting "the cumulative forces making for expanding commercial activity." Without in any way disparaging this motive, it is enough to say that the recuperative efforts of the federal government must be made in a manner consistent with the authority granted by the Constitution.

We are of the opinion that the attempt through the provisions of the Code to fix the hours and wages of employees of defendants in their intrastate business was not a valid exercise of federal power.

On both the grounds we have discussed, the attempted delegation of legislative power, and the attempted regulation of intrastate transactions which affect interstate commerce only indirectly, we hold the code provisions here in question to be invalid and that the judgment of conviction must be reversed.

Justice CARDOZO delivered a concurring opinion with which Justice STONE concurred.

487. UNITED STATES v. ONE BOOK CALLED "ULYSSES"
5 Fed. Supp. 182
1933

This is the most notable opinion interpreting that section of the Tariff Act of 1890 which authorized Customs Bureau officials to confiscate imported books which were of an "obscene" character. Senator Cutting had already riddled this provision in his speech of Oct. 10, 1929. This form of censorship must be distinguished from that exercised by the Post Office authorities and by the States. See M. Ernst and W. Seagle, *To the Pure;* Alpert, "Judicial Censorship of Obscene Literature," 52 Harv. L. Rev. 40; M. Ernst and A. Lindey, *The Censor Marches On.*

WOOLSEY, J. The motion for a decree dismissing the libel herein is granted, and, consequently, of course, the Government's motion for a decree of forfeiture and destruction is denied. . . .

II. I have read "Ulysses" once in its entirety and I have read those passages of which the Government particularly complains several times. In fact, for many weeks, my spare time has been devoted to the consideration of the decision which my duty would require me to make in this matter.

III. The reputation of "Ulysses" in the literary world, however, warranted me taking such time as was necessary to enable me to satisfy myself as to the intent with which the book was written, for, of course, in any case where a book is claimed to be obscene it must first be determined, whether the intent with which it was written was what is called, according to the usual phrase, pornographic, —that is, written for the purpose of exploiting obscenity.

If the conclusion is that the book is pornographic that is the end of the inquiry and forfeiture must follow.

But in "Ulysses," in spite of its unusual frankness, I do not detect anywhere the leer of the sensualist. I hold, therefore, that it is not pornographic.

IV. In writing "Ulysses," Joyce sought to make a serious experiment in a new, if not wholly novel, literary genre. He takes persons of the lower middle class living in Dublin in 1904 and seeks not only to describe what they did on a certain day early in June of that year as they went about the City bent on their usual occupation, but also to tell what many of them thought about the while.

Joyce has attempted—it seems to me, with astonishing success—to show how the screen of consciousness with its ever-shifting kaleidoscopic impressions carries, as it were on a plastic palimpsest, not only what is in the focus of each man's observation of the actual things about him, but also in a penumbral zone residua of past impressions, some recent and some drawn up by association from the domain of the subconscious. He shows how each of these impressions affects the life and behavior of the character which he is describing.

What he seeks to get is not unlike the result of a double or, if that is possible, a multiple exposure on a cinema film which would give a clear foreground with a background visible but somewhat blurred and out of focus in varying degrees.

To convey by words an effect which obviously lends itself more appropriately to a graphic technique, accounts, it seems to me, for much of the obscurity which meets a reader of "Ulysses." And it also explains another aspect of the book, which I have further to consider, namely, Joyce's sincerity and his honest effort to show exactly how the minds of his characters operate.

If Joyce did not attempt to be honest in developing the technique which he has adopted in "Ulysses" the result would be psychologically misleading and thus unfaithful to his chosen technique. Such an attitude would be artistically inexcusable.

It is because Joyce has been loyal to his technique and has not funked its necessary implications, but has honestly attempted to tell fully what his characters think about, that he has been the subject of so many attacks and that his purpose has been so often misunderstood and misrepresented. For his attempt sincerely and honestly to realize his objective has required him incidentally to use certain words which are generally considered dirty words and has led at times to what many think is a too poignant preoccupation with sex in the thoughts of his characters.

The words which are criticized as dirty are old Saxon words known to almost all men and, I venture, to many women, and are such words as would be naturally and habitually used, I believe, by the types of folk whose life, physical and mental, Joyce is seeking to describe. In respect of the recurrent emergence of the theme of sex in the minds of his characters, it must always be remembered that his locale was Celtic and his season Spring.

Whether or not one enjoys such a technique as Joyce uses is a matter of taste on which disagreement or argument is futile, but to subject that technique to the standards of some other technique seems to me to be little short of absurd.

Accordingly, I hold that "Ulysses" is a sincere and honest book and I think that the criticisms of it are entirely disposed of by its rationale.

V. Furthermore, "Ulysses" is an amazing *tour de force* when one considers the success which has been in the main achieved with such a difficult objective as Joyce set for himself. As I have stated, "Ulysses" is not an easy book to read. It is brilliant and dull, intelligible and obscure by turns. In many places it seems to me to be disgusting, but although it contains, as I have mentioned above, many words usually considered dirty, I have not found anything that I consider to be dirt for dirt's sake. Each word of the book contributes like a bit of mosaic to the detail of the picture which Joyce is seeking to construct for his readers.

If one does not wish to associate with such folk as Joyce describes, that is one's own choice. In order to avoid indirect contact with them one may not wish to read "Ulysses"; that is quite understandable. But when such a real artist in words, as Joyce undoubtedly is, seeks to draw a true picture of the lower middle class in a European city, ought it to be impossible for the American public legally to see that picture?

To answer this question it is not sufficient merely to find, as I have found above, that Joyce did not write "Ulysses" with what is a commonly called pornographic intent, I must endeavor to apply a more objective standard to his book in order to determine its effect in the result, irrespective of the intent with which it was written.

VI. The statute under which the libel is filed only denounces, in so far as we are here concerned, the importation into the United States from any foreign country of "any obscene book." Section 305 of the Tariff Act of 1930, Title 19 United States Code, Section 1305. It does not marshal against books the spectrum of condemnatory adjectives found, commonly, in laws dealing with matters of this kind. I am therefore, only required to determine whether "Ulysses"

is obscene within the legal definition of that word.

The meaning of the word "obscene" as legally defined by the Courts is: tending to stir the sex impulses or to lead to sexually impure and lustful thoughts. . . .

Whether a particular book would tend to excite such impulses and thoughts must be tested by the Court's opinion as to its effect on a person with average sex instincts—what the French would call *l'homme moyen sensuel* —who plays, in this branch of legal inquiry, the same role of hypothetical reagent as does the "reasonable man" in the law of torts and "the man learned in the art" on questions of invention in patent law.

The risk involved in the use of such a reagent arises from the inherent tendency of the trier of facts, however fair he may intend to be, to make his reagent too much subservient to his own idiosyncrasies. Here, I have attempted to avoid this, if possible, and to make my reagent herein more objective than he might otherwise be, by adopting the following course.

After I had made my decision in regard to the aspect of "Ulysses," now under consideration, I checked my impressions with two friends of mine who in my opinion answered to the above stated requirements for my reagent.

These literary assessors—as I might properly describe them—were called on separately, and neither knew that I was consulting the other. They are men whose opinion on literature and on life I value most highly. They had both read "Ulysses," and, of course, were wholly unconnected with this cause.

Without letting either of my assessors know what my decision was, I gave to each of them the legal definition of obscene and asked each whether in his opinion "Ulysses" was obscene within that definition.

I was interested to find that they both agreed with my opinion: that reading "Ulysses" in its entirety, as a book must be read on such a test as this, did not tend to excite sexual impulses or lustful thoughts but that its net effect on them was only that of somewhat tragic and very powerful commentary on the inner lives of men and women.

It is only with the normal person that the law is concerned. Such a test as I have described, therefore, is the only proper test of obscenity in the case of a book like "Ulysses" which is a sincere and serious attempt to devise a new literary method for the observation and description of mankind.

I am quite aware that owing to some of its scenes "Ulysses" is a rather strong draught to ask some sensitive, though normal, persons to take. But my considered opinion, after long reflection, is that whilst in many places the effect of "Ulysses" on the reader undoubtedly is somewhat emetic, nowhere does it tend to be an aphrodisiac.

"Ulysses" may, therefore, be admitted into the United States.

488. THE RECOGNITION OF SOVIET RUSSIA
November 16, 1933

(Public Papers and Addresses of Franklin D. Roosevelt, Vol. II, p. 471 ff.)

Since the Revolution of 1917 the United States had steadfastly refused to recognize the government of Soviet Russia. The chief objection to recognition was the Soviet policy of supporting subversive propaganda in other countries; behind this was the widespread hostility to communism. The depression brought a need for improved trade relations with Russia, and the advent of the New Deal a more liberal attitude toward the Russian experiment. In an exchange of notes the Soviet government promised to refrain from supporting subversive activities in the United States; after seven years it is clear that that promise was not kept. Further exchanges pledged Russia to secure religious liberty and fair trials for Americans residing in Russia, promised a consular convention, and waived any claims Russia might have against the United States for intervention in Siberia. See F. L. Schuman, *American Policy toward Russia Since 1917;* Graham, "Russian-American Relations, 1917–1933: an Interpretation," 28 Am. Pol. Sci. Rev. 387.

The White House, Washington
November 16, 1933

My dear Mr. Litvinov:

I am very happy to inform you that as a result of our conversations the Government of the United States has decided to establish normal diplomatic relations with the Government of the Union of Soviet Socialist Republics and to exchange ambassadors.

I trust that the relations now established between our peoples may forever remain normal and friendly, and that our Nations henceforth may cooperate for their mutual benefit and for the preservation of the peace of the world.

I am, my dear Mr. Litvinov,
Very sincerely yours,
FRANKLIN D. ROOSEVELT

The White House, Washington
November 16, 1933

My dear Mr. Litvinov:

I am glad to have received the assurance expressed in your note to me of this date that it will be the fixed policy of the Government of the Union of Soviet Socialist Republics:

1. To respect scrupulously the indisputable right of the United States to order its own life within its own jurisdiction in its own way and to refrain from interfering in any manner in the internal affairs of the United States, its territories or possessions.

2. To refrain, and to restrain all persons in Government service and all organizations of the Government or under its direct or indirect control, including organizations in receipt of any financial assistance from it, from any act overt or covert liable in any way whatsoever to injure the tranquillity, prosperity, order, or security of the whole or any part of the United States, its territories or possessions, and, in particular, from any act tending to incite or encourage armed intervention, or any agitation or propaganda having as an aim, the violation of the territorial integrity of the United States, its territories or possessions, or the bringing about by force of a change in the political or social order of the whole or any part of the United States, its territories or possessions.

3. Not to permit the formation or residence on its territory of any organization or group —and to prevent the activity on its territory of any organization or group, or of representatives or officials of any organization or group—which makes claim to be the Government of, or makes attempt upon the territorial integrity of, the United States, its territories or possessions; not to form, sub-

sidize, support or permit on its territory military organizations or groups having the aim of armed struggle against the United States, its territories or possessions, and to prevent any recruiting on behalf of such organizations and groups.

4. Not to permit the formation or residence on its territory of any organization or group —and to prevent the activity on its territory of any organization or group, or of representatives or officials of any organization or group—which has as an aim the overthrow or the preparation for the overthrow of,

or the bringing about by force of a change in, the political or social order of the whole or any part of the United States, its territories or possessions.

It will be the fixed policy of the Executive of the United States within the limits of the powers conferred by the Constitution and the laws of the United States to adhere reciprocally to the engagements above expressed.

I am, my dear Mr. Litvinov,

Very sincerely yours,

FRANKLIN D. ROOSEVELT

489. PHILIPPINE INDEPENDENCE ACT
March 24, 1934

(*U. S. Statutes at Large,* Vol. XLVIII, p. 456)

January 13, 1933, Congress passed, over the veto of President Hoover, the Hawes-Cutting Act providing for Philippine independence on certain conditions. These conditions were unacceptable to the Filipinos, and the Act lapsed. The McDuffie-Tydings Bill of 1934 eliminated some of the unsatisfactory provisions of the earlier act, and was accepted by the Philippine legislature. The impetus behind the acts of 1933 and 1934 was not primarily the idealistic one of the anti-imperialist crusade of 1898–1900. Considerations of economics entered very largely into the decision of 1933–1934. Unrest in the Far East and the growing threat of Japanese imperialism after 1937 made it not improbable that the actual consummation of independence might be delayed until a more propitious time. See H. B. Hawes, *Philippine Uncertainty;* G. L. Kirk, *Philippine Independence.*

An Act to provide for the complete independence to the Philippine Islands, to provide for the adoption of a constitution and a form of government for the Philippine Islands, and for other purposes.

CONVENTION TO FRAME CONSTITUTION FOR PHILIPPINE ISLANDS

SEC. 1. The Philippine Legislature is hereby authorized to provide for the election of delegates to a constitutional convention, which shall meet . . . at such time as the Philippine Legislature may fix, but not later than October 1, 1934, to formulate and draft a constitution for the government of the Commonwealth of the Philippine Islands, subject to the conditions and qualifications prescribed

in this Act, which shall exercise jurisdiction over all the territory ceded to the United States by the treaty of peace concluded between the United States and Spain on the 10th day of December 1898, ...

CHARACTER OF CONSTITUTION—MANDATORY PROVISIONS

SEC. 2. (a) The constitution formulated and drafted shall be republican in form, shall contain a bill of rights, and shall, either as a part thereof or in an ordinance appended thereto, contain provisions to the effect that, pending the final and complete withdrawal of the sovereignty of the United States over the Philippine Islands—

(1) All citizens of the Philippine Islands shall owe allegiance to the United States.

(2) Every officer of the government of the Commonwealth of the Philippine Islands shall, before entering upon the discharge of his duties, take and subscribe an oath of office, declaring, among other things, that he recognizes and accepts the supreme authority of and will maintain true faith and allegiance to the United States.

(3) Absolute toleration of religious sentiment shall be secured and no inhabitant or religious organization shall be molested in person or property on account of religious belief or mode of worship.

(4) Property owned by the United States, cemeteries, churches, and parsonages or convents appurtenant thereto, and all lands, buildings, and improvements used exclusively

for religious, charitable, or educational purposes shall be exempt from taxation.

(5) Trade relations between the Philippine Islands and the United States shall be upon the basis prescribed in section 6.

(6) The public debt of the Philippine Islands and its subordinate branches shall not exceed limits now or hereafter fixed by the Congress of the United States; and no loans shall be contracted in foreign countries without the approval of the President of the United States.

(7) The debts, liabilities, and obligations of the present Philippine government, its Provinces, municipalities, and instrumentalities, valid and subsisting at the time of the adoption of the constitution, shall be assumed and paid by the new government.

(8) Provision shall be made for the establishment and maintenance of an adequate system of public schools, primarily conducted in the English language.

(9) Acts affecting currency, coinage, imports, exports, and immigration shall not become law until approved by the President of the United States.

(10) Foreign affairs shall be under the direct supervision and control of the United States.

(11) All acts passed by the Legislature of the Commonwealth of the Philippine Islands shall be reported to the Congress of the United States.

(12) The Philippine Islands recognizes the right of the United States to expropriate property for public uses, to maintain military and other reservations and armed forces in the Philippines, and, upon order of the President, to call into the service of such armed forces all military forces organized by the Philippine government.

(13) The decisions of the courts of the Commonwealth of the Philippine Islands shall be subject to review by the Supreme Court of the United States as provided in paragraph (6) of section 7.

(14) The United States may, by Presidential proclamation, exercise the right to intervene for the preservation of the government of the Commonwealth of the Philippine Islands and for the maintenance of the government as provided in the constitution thereof, and for the protection of life, property, and individual liberty and for the discharge of government obligations under and in accordance with the provisions of the constitution.

(15) The authority of the United States High Commissioner to the government of the Commonwealth of the Philippine Islands, as provided in this Act, shall be recognized.

(16) Citizens and corporations of the United States shall enjoy in the commonwealth of the Philippine Islands all the civil rights of the citizens and corporations, respectively, thereof.

(b) The constitution shall also contain the following provisions, effective as of the date of the proclamation of the President recognizing the independence of the Philippine Islands, as hereinafter provided:

(1) That the property rights of the United States and the Philippine Islands shall be promptly adjusted and settled, and that all existing property rights of citizens or corporations of the United States shall be acknowledged, respected, and safeguarded to the same extent as property rights of citizens of the Philippine Islands.

(2) That the officials elected and serving under the constitution adopted pursuant to the provisions of this Act shall be constitutional officers of the free and independent government of the Philippine Islands and qualified to function in all respects as if elected directly under such government, and shall serve their full terms of office as prescribed in the constitution.

(3) That the debts and liabilities of the Philippine Islands, its Provinces, cities, municipalities, and instrumentalities, which shall be valid and subsisting at the time of the final and complete withdrawal of the sovereignty of the United States, shall be assumed by the free and independent government of the Philippine Islands; and that where bonds have been issued under authority of an Act of Congress of the United States by the Philippine Islands, or any Province, city, or municipality therein, the Philippine government will make adequate provision for the necessary funds for the payment of interest and principal, and such obligations shall be a first lien on the taxes collected in the Philippine Islands.

(4) That the government of the Philippine Islands, on becoming independent of the United States, will assume all continuing

obligations assumed by the United States under the treaty of peace with Spain ceding said Philippine Islands to the United States. . . .

SUBMISSION OF CONSTITUTION TO THE PRESIDENT OF THE UNITED STATES

SEC. 3. Upon the drafting and approval of the constitution by the constitutional convention in the Philippine Islands, the constitution shall be submitted within two years after the enactment of this Act to the President of the United States, who shall determine whether or not it conforms with the provisions of this Act. . . .

SUBMISSION OF CONSTITUTION TO FILIPINO PEOPLE

SEC. 4. After the President of the United States has certified that the constitution conforms with the provisions of this Act, it shall be submitted to the people of the Philippine Islands for their ratification or rejection at an election to be held within four months after the date of such certification, on a date to be fixed by the Philippine Legislature, at which election the qualified voters of the Philippine Islands shall have an opportunity to vote directly for or against the proposed constitution and ordinances appended thereto. . . . If a majority of the votes cast shall be for the constitution, such vote shall be deemed an expression of the will of the people of the Philippine Islands in favor of Philippine independence, . . .

If a majority of the votes cast are against the constitution, the existing government of the Philippine Islands shall continue without regard to the provisions of this Act. . . .

RELATIONS WITH THE UNITED STATES PENDING COMPLETE INDEPENDENCE

SEC. 6 After the date of the inauguration of the government of the Commonwealth of the Philippine Islands trade relations between the United States and the Philippine Islands shall be as now provided by law, subject to the following exceptions:

(a) There shall be levied, collected, and paid on all refined sugars in excess of fifty thousand long tons, and on unrefined sugars in excess of eight hundred thousand long tons, coming into the United States from the Philippine Islands in any calendar year, the same rates of duty which are required by the laws of the United States to be levied, collected, and paid upon like articles imported from foreign countries. . . .

(d) In the event that in any year the limit in the case of any article which may be exported to the United States free of duty shall be reached by the Philippine Islands, the amount or quantity of such articles produced or manufactured in the Philippine Islands thereafter that may be so exported to the United States free of duty shall be allocated, under export permits issued by the government of the Commonwealth of the Philippine Islands, to the producers or manufacturers of such articles proportionately on the basis of their exportation to the United States in the preceding year; except that in the case of unrefined sugar the amount thereof to be exported annually to the United States free of duty shall be allocated to the sugar-producing mills of the islands proportionately on the basis of their average annual production for the calendar years 1931, 1932, and 1933, and the amount of sugar from each mill which may be so exported shall be allocated in each year between the mill and the planters on the basis of the proportion of sugar to which the mill and the planters are respectively entitled. The government of the Philippine Islands is authorized to adopt the necessary laws and regulations for putting into effect the allocation hereinbefore provided.

(e) The government of the Commonwealth of the Philippine Islands shall impose and collect an export tax on all articles that may be exported to the United States from the Philippine Islands free of duty under the provisions of existing law as modified by the foregoing provisions of this section, including the articles enumerated in subdivisions (a), (b), and (c), within the limitations therein specified, as follows:

(1) During the sixth year after the inauguration of the new government the export tax shall be 5 per centum of the rates of duty which are required by the laws of the United States to be levied, collected, and paid on like articles imported from foreign countries;

(2) During the seventh year after the inauguration of the new government the export tax shall be 10 per centum. . . .

(3) During the eighth year after the inauguration of the new government the export tax shall be 15 per centum. . . .

(4) During the ninth year after the inauguration of the new government the export tax shall be 20 per centum. . . .

(5) After the expiration of the ninth year after the inauguration of the new government the export tax shall be 25 per centum. . . .

The government of the Commonwealth of the Philippine Islands shall place all funds received from such export taxes in a sinking fund, and such funds shall, in addition to other moneys available for that purpose, be applied solely to the payment of the principal and interest on the bonded indebtedness of the Philippine Islands, its Provinces, municipalities, and instrumentalities, until such indebtedness has been fully discharged. . . .

SEC. 7. Until the final and complete withdrawal of American sovereignty over the Philippine Islands—. . . .

(4) The President shall appoint, by and with the advice and consent of the Senate, a United States High Commissioner to the government of the Commonwealth of the Philippine Islands who shall hold office at the pleasure of the President and until his successor is appointed and qualified. . . .

If the government of the Commonwealth of the Philippine Islands fails to pay any of its bonded or other indebtedness or the interest thereon when due or to fulfill any of its contracts, the United States High Commissioner shall immediately report the facts to the President, who may thereupon direct the High Commissioner to take over the customs offices and administration of the same, administer the same, and apply such part of the revenue received therefrom as may be necessary for the payment of such overdue indebtedness or for the fulfillment of such contracts. . . .

(6) Review by the Supreme Court of the United States of cases from the Philippine Islands shall be as now provided by law; and such review shall also extend to all cases involving the constitution of the Commonwealth of the Philippine Islands.

SEC. 8. (a) Effective upon the acceptance of this Act by concurrent resolution of the Philippine Legislature or by a convention called for that purpose, as provided in section 17—

(1) For the purposes of the Immigration Act of 1917, the Immigration Act of 1924 (except section 13 (c)), this section, and all other laws of the United States relating to the immigration, exclusion, or expulsion of aliens, citizens of the Philippine Islands who are not citizens of the United States shall be considered as if they were aliens. For such purposes the Philippine Islands shall be considered as a separate country and shall have for each fiscal year a quota of fifty. . . .

RECOGNITION OF PHILIPPINE INDEPENDENCE AND WITHDRAWAL OF AMERICAN SOVEREIGNTY

SEC. 10. (a) On the 4th day of July immediately following the expiration of a period of ten years from the date of the inauguration of the new government under the constitution provided for in this Act the President of the United States shall by proclamation withdraw and surrender all right of possession, supervision, jurisdiction, control, or sovereignty then existing and exercised by the United States in and over the territory and people of the Philippine Islands, including all military and other reservations of the Government of the United States in the Philippines (except such naval reservations and fueling stations as are reserved under section 5), and, on behalf of the United States, shall recognize the independence of the Philippine Islands as a separate and self-governing nation and acknowledge the authority and control over the same of the government instituted by the people thereof, under the constitution then in force. . . .

NEUTRALIZATION OF PHILIPPINE ISLANDS

SEC. 11. The President is requested, at the earliest practicable date, to enter into negotiations with foreign powers with a view to the conclusion of a treaty for the perpetual neutralization of the Philippine Islands, if and when Philippine independence shall have been achieved. . . .

TARIFF DUTIES AFTER INDEPENDENCE

SEC. 13. After the Philippine Islands have become a free and independent nation there shall be levied, collected, and paid upon all articles coming into the United States from the Philippine Islands the rates of duty which are required to be levied, collected, and paid upon like articles imported from other foreign countries: *Provided,* That at least one year prior to the date fixed in this Act for the independence of the Philippine Islands, there shall be held a conference of representatives of the Government of the United States and the government of the Commonwealth of the Philippine Islands, . . . for the purpose of formulating recommendations as to future trade relations between the Government of the United States and the independent government of the Philippine Islands. . . .

IMMIGRATION AFTER INDEPENDENCE

SEC. 14. Upon the final and complete withdrawal of American sovereignty over the Philippine Islands the immigration laws of the United States . . . shall apply to persons who were born in the Philippine Islands to the same extent as in the case of other foreign countries. . . .

EFFECTIVE DATE

SEC. 17. The foregoing provisions of this Act shall not take effect until accepted by concurrent resolution of the Philippine Legislature or by a convention called for the purpose of passing upon that question as may be provided by the Philippine Legislature.

490. THE JOHNSON ACT
April 13, 1934

(*U. S. Statutes at Large,* Vol. XLVIII, p. 574)

This law was an expression of the widespread indignation of the American people at the failure of debtor nations to meet their obligations to the United States. On the war debts see, H. G. Moulton and L. Pasvolsky, *World War Debt Settlements,* and *War Debts and World Prosperity;* National Industrial Conference Board, *Inter-Ally Debts and the United States.*

An Act to prohibit financial transactions with any foreign government in default on its obligations to the United States.

Be it enacted, That hereafter it shall be unlawful within the United States or any place subject to the jurisdiction of the United States for any person to purchase or sell the bonds, securities, or other obligations of, any foreign government or political subdivision thereof or any organization or association acting for or on behalf of a foreign government or political subdivision thereof, issued after

a passage of this Act, or to make any loan to such foreign government, political subdivision, organization, or association, except a renewal or adjustment of existing indebtedness while such government, political subdivision, organization, or association, is in default in the payment of its obligations, or any part thereof, to the Government of the United States. Any person violating the provisions of this Act shall upon conviction thereof be fined not more than $10,000 or imprisoned for not more than five years, or both.

SEC. 2. As used in this Act the term "person" includes individual, partnership, corporation, or association other than a public corporation created by or pursuant to special authorization of Congress, or a corporation in which the Government of the United States has or exercises a controlling interest through stock ownership or otherwise.

491. THE ABROGATION OF THE PLATT AMENDMENT
May 29, 1934

(*U. S. Statutes at Large,* Vol. XLVIII, p. 1682)

The Roosevelt-Hull policy of "the good neighbor" was given dramatic substantiation by the negotiation of a treaty abrogating the Platt Amendment. The protracted and violent strife in Cuba during 1933 and 1934 accounted in part for the willingness of the United States to ab-

dicate responsibility for Cuban affairs. See H. F. Guggenheim, *The United States and Cuba;* C. Beals, *The Crime of Cuba;* R. H. Fitzgibbon, *Cuba and the United States, 1900–1935;* P. G. Wright; *The Cuban Situation and Our Treaty Relations.*

The United States of America and the Republic of Cuba, being animated by the desire to fortify the relations of friendship between the two countries, and to modify, with this purpose, the relations established between them by the Treaty of Relations signed at Havana, May 22, 1903, have appointed, with this intention, as their plenipotentiaries: . . .

Who, after having communicated to each other their full powers, which were found to be in good and due form, have agreed upon the following articles:

Art. I. The Treaty of Relations which was concluded between the two contracting parties on May 22, 1903, shall cease to be in force, and is abrogated, from the date on which the present treaty goes into effect.

Art. II. All the acts effected in Cuba by the United States of America during its military occupation of the island, up to May 20, 1902, the date on which the Republic of Cuba was established, have been ratified and held as valid; and all rights legally acquired by virtue of those acts shall be maintained and protected.

Art. III. Until the two contracting parties agree to the modification or abrogation of the stipulations of the agreement in regard to the lease to the United States of America of lands in Cuba for coaling and naval stations signed by the President of the Republic of Cuba on February 16, 1903, and by the President of the United States of America on the 23rd day of the same month and year, the stipulations of that agreement with regard to the naval station of Guantanamo shall continue in effect. The supplementary agreement in regard to naval or coaling stations signed between the two governments on July 2, 1903, shall continue in effect in the same form and on the same conditions with respect to the naval station at Guantanamo. So long as the United States of America shall not abandon the said naval station of Guantanamo or the two governments shall not agree to a modification of its present limits, the station shall continue to have the territorial area that it now has, with the limits that it has on the date of the signature of the present treaty.

Art. IV. If at any time in the future a situation should arise that appears to point to an outbreak of contagious disease in the territory of either of the contracting parties, either of the two governments shall, for its own protection, and without its act being considered unfriendly, exercise freely and at its discretion the right to suspend communications between those of its ports that it may designate and all or part of the territory of the other party, and for the period that it may consider to be advisable.

Art. V. The present Treaty shall be ratified by the contracting parties in accordance with their respective Constitutional methods; and shall go into effect on the date of the exchange of their ratifications, which shall take place in the city of Washington as soon as possible.

492. ANTI-WAR TREATY OF NON-AGGRESSION AND CONCILIATION
Signed October 10, 1933; Ratified June 15, 1934

(Congressional Record, 73d. Congress, 2d. Sess., Vol. LXXVIII, p. 11910 ff.)

This Treaty, concluded at Rio de Janeiro by Argentina, Brazil, Chile, Mexico, Paraguay, and Uruguay and the United States, extended the Kellogg-Briand Pact to the American States and provided additional machinery for conciliation and arbitration.

The states designated below, in the desire to contribute to the consolidation of peace, and to express their adherence to the efforts made by all civilized nations to promote the spirit of universal harmony;

To the end of condemning wars of aggression and territorial acquisitions that may be obtained by armed conquest, making them impossible and establishing their invalidity through the positive provisions of this treaty, and in order to replace them with pacific solutions based on lofty concepts of justice and equity;

Convinced that one of the most effective means of assuring the moral and material benefits which peace offers to the world, is the organization of a permanent system of conciliation for international disputes, to be applied immediately on the violation of the principles mentioned;

Have decided to put these aims of non-aggression and concord in conventional form, by concluding the present treaty, to which end they have appointed the undersigned plenipotentiaries, who, having exhibited their respective full powers, found to be in good and due form, have agreed upon the following:

ART. I. The High Contracting Parties solemnly declare that they condemn wars of aggression in their mutual relations or those with other states, and that the settlement of disputes or controversies of any kind that may arise among them shall be effected only by the pacific means which have the sanction of international law.

ART. II. They declare that as between the High Contracting Parties, territorial questions must not be settled by violence, and that they will not recognize any territorial arrangement which is not obtained by pacific means, nor the validity of the occupation or acquisition of territories that may be brought about by force of arms.

ART. III. In case of non-compliance by any state engaged in a dispute, with the obligations contained in the foregoing articles, the contracting states undertake to make every effort for the maintenance of peace. To that end they will adopt in their character as neutrals a common and solidary attitude; they will exercise the political, juridical or economic means authorized by international law; they will bring the influence of public opinion to bear but will in no case resort to intervention either diplomatic or armed; subject to the attitude that may be incumbent on them by virtue of other collective treaties to which such states are signatories.

ART. IV. The High Contracting Parties obligate themselves to submit to the conciliation procedure established by this treaty, the disputes specially mentioned and any others that may arise in their reciprocal relations, without further limitations than those enumerated in the following article, in all controversies which it has not been possible to settle by diplomatic means within a reasonable period of time.

ART. V. The High Contracting Parties and the states which may in the future adhere to this treaty, may not formulate at the time of signature, ratification or adherence, other limitations to the conciliation procedure than those which are indicated below:

(a) Differences for the solution of which treaties, conventions, pacts or pacific agreements of any kind whatever may have been concluded, which in no case shall be considered as annulled by this agreement, but supplemented thereby in so far as they tend to assure peace; as well as the questions or matters settled by previous treaties;

(b) Disputes which the parties prefer to solve by direct settlement or submit by common agreement to an arbitral or judicial solution;

(c) Questions which international law leaves to the exclusive competence of each state, under its constitutional system, for which reason the parties may object to their being submitted to the conciliation procedure before the national or local jurisdiction has decided definitely; except in the case of manifest denial or delay of justice, in which case the conciliation procedure shall be initiated within a year at the latest;

(d) Matters which affect constitutional precepts of the parties to the controversy. In case of doubt, each party shall obtain the reasoned opinion of its respective tribunal or supreme court of justice, if the latter should be invested with such powers.

The High Contracting Parties may communicate, at any time and in the manner provided for by Article XV, an instrument stating that they have abandoned wholly or in part the limitations established by them in the conciliation procedure.

The effect of the limitations formulated by one of the contracting parties shall be that the other parties shall not consider themselves obligated in regard to that party save in the measure of the exceptions established.

ART. VI. In the absence of a permanent Conciliation Commission or of some other international organization charged with this mission by virtue of previous treaties in effect, the High Contracting Parties undertake to submit their differences to the examination and investigation of a Conciliation Commission which shall be formed as follows, unless there is an agreement to the contrary of the parties in each case; . . .

ART. X. It is the duty of the Commission to secure the conciliatory settlement of the disputes submitted to its consideration.

After an impartial study of the questions

in dispute, it shall set forth in a report the outcome of its work and shall propose to the Parties bases of settlement by means of a just and equitable solution. . . .

493. THE TAYLOR ACT
June 28, 1934
(*U. S. Statutes at Large,* Vol. XLVIII, p. 1269)

The prolonged droughts of the early 1930's and the accompanying dust storms advertised the fact that over-grazing in the Plains area had contributed to the creation of a "dust bowl" and dramatized the necessity of a new policy with respect to the grazing lands of the West. "The grazing resources of these lands" said the Report of the Committee on Public Lands, "are now being used without supervision or regulation, and there is constant competition among the various users who desire to obtain exclusive benefit from the forage growth. The result of this competitive practice has been lack of proper care, with the attendant evils of soil erosion and removal of protection in drainage areas. . . . Without regulation further destruction is inevitable." This Act proposed the creation of new grazing districts up to 80,000,000 acres in order to conserve the public range. On the problem of soil erosion in the High Plains see S. Chase, *Rich Land, Poor Land;* W. P. Webb, *The Great Plains;* U. S. Dept. of Agriculture, "The Western Range"; U. S. Dept. of Interior, "The Future of The Great Plains."

An act to stop injury to the public grazing lands by preventing overgrazing and soil deterioration, to provide for their orderly use, improvement, and development, to stabilize the livestock industry dependent upon the public range, and for other purposes.

Be it enacted, That in order to promote the highest use of the public lands pending its final disposal, the Secretary of the Interior is authorized, in his discretion, by order to establish grazing districts or additions thereto and/or to modify the boundaries thereof, not exceeding in the aggregate an area of eighty million acres of vacant, unappropriated, and unreserved lands from any part of the public domain of the United States (exclusive of Alaska), which are not in national forests, national parks and monuments, Indian reservations, [etc.] and which in his opinion are chiefly valuable for grazing and raising forage crops: *Provided,* That no lands withdrawn or reserved for any other purpose shall be included in any such district except with the approval of the head of the department having jurisdiction thereof. . . .

SEC. 2. The Secretary of the Interior shall make provision for the protection, administration, regulation, and improvement of such grazing districts as may be created under the authority of the foregoing section, and he shall make such rules and regulations and establish such service, enter into such cooperative agreements, and do any and all things necessary to accomplish the purposes of this Act and to insure the objects of such grazing districts, namely, to regulate their occupancy and use, to preserve the land and its resources from destruction or unnecessary injury, to provide for the orderly use, improvement, and development of the range; and the Secretary of the Interior is authorized to continue the study of erosion and floor control and to perform such work as may be necessary amply to protect and rehabilitate the areas subject to the provisions of this Act, through such funds as may be made available for that purpose, and any willful violation of the provisions of this Act or of such rules and regulations thereunder after actual notice thereof shall be punishable by a fine of not more than $500.

SEC. 3. That the Secretary of the Interior is hereby authorized to issue or cause to be issued permits to graze livestock on such grazing districts to such bona fide settlers, residents, and other stock owners as under his rules and regulations are entitled to participate in the use of the range, upon the payment annually of reasonable fees in each case to be fixed or determined from time to time. . . . Such permits shall be for a period of not more than ten years, subject to the preference right of the permittees to renewal in the discretion of the Secretary of the Interior, who shall specify from time to time numbers of stock and seasons of use. During periods of range depletion due to severe drought or other natural causes, or in case of a general epidemic of disease, during the life of the permit, the Secretary of the Interior is hereby authorized, in his discretion to remit, reduce, refund in whole or in part, or authorize postponement of payment of grazing fees for such depletion period so long as the emergency exists: *Provided further,* That nothing in this Act shall be construed or administered in any way to diminish or impair any right to the possession and use of water for mining, agriculture, manufacturing, or other purposes which has heretofore vested or accrued under existing law validly affecting the public lands or which may be hereafter initiated or acquired and maintained in accordance with such law. So far as consistent with the purposes and provisions of this Act, grazing privileges recognized and acknowledged shall be adequately safeguarded, but the creation of a grazing district or the issuance of a permit pursuant to the provisions of this Act shall not create any right, title, interest, or estate in or to the lands. . . .

SEC. 5. That the Secretary of the Interior shall permit, under regulations to be prescribed by him, the free grazing within such districts of livestock kept for domestic purposes. . . .

SEC. 7. That the Secretary is hereby authorized, in his discretion, to examine and classify any lands within such grazing districts which are more valuable and suitable for the production of agricultural crops than native grasses and forage plants, and to open such lands to homestead entry in tracts not exceeding three hundred and twenty acres in area. Such lands shall not be subject to settlement or occupation as homesteads until after same have been classified and opened to entry after notice to the permittee by the Secretary of the Interior, and the lands shall remain a part of the grazing district until patents are issued therefor, the homesteader to be, after his entry is allowed, entitled to the possession and use thereof: *Provided,* That upon the application of any person qualified to make homestead entry under the public-land laws, filed in the land office of the proper district, the Secretary of the Interior shall cause any tract not exceeding three hundred and twenty acres in any grazing district to be classified, and such application shall entitle the applicant to a preference right to enter such lands when opened to entry as herein provided.

SEC. 8. That where such action will pro-

mote the purposes of the district or facilitate its administration, the Secretary is authorized and directed to accept on behalf of the United States any lands within the exterior boundaries of a district as a gift, or, when public interests will be benefited thereby, he is authorized and directed to accept on behalf of the United States title to any privately owned lands within the exterior boundaries of said grazing district, and in exchange therefor to issue patent for not to exceed an equal value of survey grazing district land or of unreserved surveyed public land in the same State or within a distance of not more than fifty miles within the adjoining State nearest the base lands. . . .

SEC. 11. That when appropriated by Congress, 25 per centum of all moneys received from each grazing district on Indian lands ceded to the United States for disposition under the public-land laws during any fiscal year is hereby made available for expenditure by the Secretary of the Interior for the construction, purchase, or maintenance of range improvements; and an additional 25 per centum of the money received from grazing during each fiscal year shall be paid at the end thereof by the Secretary of the Treasury to the State in which said lands are situated, to be expended as the State legislature may prescribe for the benefit of public schools and public roads of the county or counties in which such grazing lands are situated. And the remaining 50 per centum of all money received from such grazing lands shall be deposited to the credit of the Indians pending final disposition under applicable laws, treaties, or agreements.

SEC. 13. That the President of the United States is authorized to reserve by proclamation and place under national-forest administration in any State where national forests may be created or enlarged by Executive order any unappropriated public lands lying within watersheds forming a part of the national forests which, in his opinion, can best be administered in connection with existing national-forest administration units, and to place under the Interior Department administration any lands within national forests, principally valuable for grazing, which, in his opinion, can best be administered under the provisions of this Act.

SEC. 16. Nothing in this Act shall be construed as restricting the respective States from enforcing any and all statutes enacted for police regulation, nor shall the police power of the respective States be, by this Act, impaired or restricted, and all laws heretofore enacted by the respective States or any thereof, or that may hereafter be enacted as regards public health or public welfare, shall at all times be in full force and effect: *Provided, however,* That nothing in this section shall be construed as limiting or restricting the power and authority of the United States.

494. HOME BUILDING AND LOAN ASSOCIATION v. BLAISDELL
290 U. S. 251
1934

Appeal from the Supreme Court of Minnesota. The facts of the case are set forth in the opinion of the court. This was the first notable case involving the interpretation of emergency legislation incident to the depression of 1929—. For an earlier case of the interpretation of emergency legislation, see Doc. No. 415. See J. P. Clark, "Emergencies and the Law," 49 Pol. Sci. Qt., 268; Corwin, "Moratorium over Minnesota," 82 U. of Pa. L. Rev. 311.

HUGHES, C. J. Appellant contests the validity of Chapter 339 of the Laws of Minnesota of 1933, p. 514, approved April 18, 1933, called the Minnesota Mortgage Moratorium Law, as being repugnant to the contract clause of the Fourteenth Amendment, of the Federal Constitution. The statute was sustained by the Supreme Court of Minnesota (249 N. W. 334, 893) and the case comes here on appeal.

The Act provides that, during the emergency declared to exist, relief may be had through authorized judicial proceedings with respect to foreclosures of mortgages, and execution sales, of real estates; that sales may be postponed and periods of redemption may be extended. . . .

The state court upheld the statute as an emergency measure. Although conceding that the obligations of the mortgage contract were impaired the court decided that what it thus described as an impairment was, notwithstanding the contract clause of the Federal Constitution, within the police power of the State as that power was called into exercise by the public economy emergency which the legislature had found to exist. Attention is thus directed to the preamble and first section of the statute which described the existing emergency in terms that were deemed to justify the temporary relief which the statute affords. . . .

. . . Aside from the extension of time, the other conditions of redemption are unaltered. While the mortgagor remains in possession he must pay the rental value as that value has been determined, upon notice and hearing, by the court. The rental value so paid is devoted to the carrying of the property by the application of the required payments to taxes, insurance, and interest on the mortgage indebtedness. While the mortgagee-purchaser is debarred from actual possession, he has, so far as rental value is concerned, the equivalent of possession during the extended period.

In determining whether the provision for this temporary and conditional relief exceeds the power of the State by reason of the clause in the Federal Constitution prohibiting impairment of the obligations of contracts, we must consider the relation of emergency to constitutional power, the historical setting of the contract clause, the development of the jurisprudence of this court in the construction of that clause, and the principles of construction which we may consider to be established.

Emergency does not create power. Emergency does not increase granted power or remove or diminish the restrictions imposed upon power granted or reserved. The Constitution was adopted in a period of grave emergency. Its grants of power to the Federal government and its limitations of the power of the States were determined in the light of emergency and they are not altered by emergency. What power was thus granted and what limitations were thus imposed are questions which have always been, and always will be, the subject of close examination under our constitutional system.

While emergency does not create power, emergency may furnish the occasion for the exercise of power. . . .

But full recognition of the occasion and general purpose of the clause does not suffice to fix its precise scope. Nor does an examination of the details of prior legislation in the States yield criteria which can be considered controlling. To ascertain the scope of the constitutional prohibition we examine the course of judicial decisions in its application. These put it beyond question that the prohibition is not an absolute one and is not to be read with literal exactness like a mathematical formula. . . .

Not only is the constitutional provision qualified by the measure of control which the State retains over remedial processes, but the State also continues to possess authority to safeguard the vital interests of its people. It does not matter that legislation appropriate to that end "has the result of modifying or abrogating contracts already in effect." *Stephenson* v. *Binford,* 287 U. S. 251, 276. Not only are existing laws read into contracts in order to fix obligations as between the parties, but the reservation of essential attributes of sovereign power is also read into contracts as a postulate of the legal order. The policy of protecting contracts against impairment presupposes the maintenance of a government in virtue of which contractual relations are worth while,—a government which retains adequate authority to secure the peace and good order of society. This principle of harmonizing the constitutional prohibition with the necessary residuum of state power has had progressive recognition in the decisions of this Court.

Undoubtedly, whatever is reserved of state power must be consistent with the fair intent of the constitutional limitation of that power. The reserved power cannot be construed so as to destroy the limitation, nor is the limitation to be construed to destroy the reserved power in its essential aspects. They must be construed in harmony with each other. This principle precludes a construction which would permit the State to adopt as its policy the repudiation of debts or the destruction of contracts or the denial of means to enforce them. But it does not follow that conditions may not arise in which a temporary restraint of enforcement may not be consistent with the spirit and purpose of the constitutional provision and thus found to be within the range of the reserved power

of the State to protect the vital interests of the community. It cannot be maintained that the constitutional prohibition should be so construed as to prevent limited and temporary interpositions with respect to the enforcement of contracts if made necessary by a great public calamity such as fire, flood, or earthquake. See *American Land Co.* v. *Zeiss,* 219 U. S. 47. The reservation of state power appropriate to such extraordinary conditions may be deemed to be as much a part of all contracts as is the reservation of state power to protect the public interest in the other situations to which we have referred. And if state power exists to give temporary relief from the enforcement of contracts in the presence of disasters due to physical causes such as fire, flood, or earthquake, that power cannot be said to be non-existent when the urgent public need demanding such relief is produced by other and economic causes.

It is manifest from this review of our decisions that there has been a growing appreciation of public needs and of the necessity of finding ground for a rational compromise between individual rights and public welfare. The settlement and consequent contraction of the public domain, the pressure of a constantly increasing density of population, the interrelation of the activities of our people and the complexity of our economic interests, have inevitably led to an increased use of the organization of society in order to protect the very bases of individual opportunity. Where, in earlier days, it was thought that only the concerns of individuals or of classes were involved, and that those of the State itself were touched only remotely, it has later been found that the fundamental interests of the State are directly affected; and that the question is no longer merely that of one party to a contract as against another, but of the use of reasonable means to safeguard the economic structure upon which the good of all depends.

It is no answer to say that this public need was not apprehended a century ago, or to insist that what the provision of the Constitution meant to the vision of that day it must mean to the vision of our time. If by the statement that what the Constitution meant at the time of its adoption it means today, it is intended to say that the great clauses of the Constitution must be confined to the interpretation which the framers, with the conditions and outlook of their time would have placed upon them, the statement carries its own refutation. It was to guard against such a narrow conception that Chief Justice Marshall uttered the memorable warning— "We must never forget it is a constitution we are expounding" (*Mc Culloch* v. *Maryland,* 4 Wheat, 316, 407) "a constitution intended to endure for ages to come, and, consequently, to be adapted to the various crises of human affairs." . . .

Nor is it helpful to attempt to draw a fine distinction between the intended meaning of the words of the Constitution and their intended application. When we consider the contract clause and the decisions which have expounded it in harmony with the essential reserve power of the States to protect the security of their peoples, we find no warrant for the conclusion that the clause has been warped by these decisions from its proper significance or that the founders of our Government would have interpreted the clause differently had they had occasion to assume that responsibility in the conditions of the later day. The vast body of law which has been developed was unknown to the fathers but it is believed to have preserved the essential content and the spirit of the Constitution. With a growing recognition of public needs and the relation of individual right to public security, the court has sought to prevent the perversion of the clause through its use as an instrument to throttle the capacity of the States to protect their fundamental interests. This development is a growth from the seeds which the fathers planted. . . .

We are of the opinion that the Minnesota statute as here applied does not violate the contract clause of the Federal Constitution. Whether the legislation is wise or unwise as a matter of policy is a question with which we are not concerned.

SUTHERLAND, J., with whom concurred VAN DEVANTER, J., McREYNOLDS, J., and BUTLER, J., delivered a dissenting opinion.

495. NEBBIA v. NEW YORK
291 U. S. 502
1934

Appeal from the County Court of Monroe County, New York. The facts of this case are stated in the opinion. The importance of the case derives not only from the judicial validation of price fixing, but also from the new interpretation of the historic concept of "affectation with a public interest" and of the nature of the police power. For the background of this question, see especially R. L. Mott, *Due Process of Law;* L. P. McGehee, *Due Process of Law under the Federal Constitution;* E. Freund, *The Police Power, Public Policy, and Constitutional Rights;* and the illuminating article by W. Hamilton, "Affectation with a Public Interest," 39 Yale Law J. 1104. On the Nebbia case see, Hale, "The Constitution and the Price System," 34 Col. Law Rev. 401; Goldsmith and Winks, "Price Fixing: From Nebbia to Guffey," 31 Ills. Law Rev. 179; Fraenkel, "Constitutional Issues in the Supreme Court, 1934 Term," 84 U. of Pa. Law Rev. 345; Cohen and Horack, "After the Nebbia Case," 8 U. of Cin. L. Rev. 219.

ROBERTS, J. The Legislature of New York established, by Chapter 158 of the Laws of 1933, a Milk Control Board with power, among other things, to "fix minimum and maximum . . . retail prices to be charged by . . . stores to consumers for consumption off the premises where sold." The Board fixed nine cents as the price to be charged by a store for a quart of milk. Nebbia, the proprietor of a grocery store in Rochester, sold two quarts and a five cent loaf of bread for eighteen cents; and was convicted for violating the Board's order. At his trial he asserted the statute and order contravene the equal protection clause and the due process clause of the Fourteenth Amendment, and renewed the contention in successive appeals to the county court and the Court of Appeals. Both overruled his claim and affirmed the conviction.

The question for a decision is whether the Federal Constitution prohibits a state from so fixing the selling price of milk. We first inquire as to the occasion for the legislation and its history.

During 1932 the prices received by farmers

for milk were much below the cost of production. The decline in prices during 1931 and 1932 was much greater than that of prices generally. The situation of the families of dairy producers had become desperate and called for state aid similar to that afforded the unemployed, if conditions should not improve. . . .

Various remedies were suggested, amongst them united action by producers, the fixing of minimum prices for milk and cream by state authority, and the imposition of certain graded taxes on milk dealers proportioned so as to equalize the cost of milk and cream to all dealers and so remove the cause of price-cutting.

The legislature adopted Chapter 158 as a method of correcting the evils, which the report of the committee showed could not be expected to right themselves through the ordinary play of the forces of supply and demand, owing to the peculiar and uncontrollable factors affecting the industry. . . .

Section 312 (e) on which the prosecution in the present case is founded, provides: "After the board shall have fixed prices to be charged or paid for milk in any form . . . it shall be unlawful for a milk dealer to sell or buy or offer to sell or buy milk at any price less or more than such price . . . and no method or device shall be lawful whereby milk is bought or sold . . . at a price less or more than such price . . . whether by any discount, or rebate, or free service, or advertising allowance, or a combined price for such milk together with another commodity or commodities, or service or services, which is less or more than the aggregate of the prices for the milk and the price or prices for such other commodity or commodities, or service or services, when sold or offered for sale separately or otherwise. . . ."

First. The appellant urges that the order of the Milk Control Board denies him the equal protection of the laws. . . .

Second. The more serious question is whether, in the light of the conditions disclosed, the enforcement of § 312 (e) denied the appellant the due process secured to him by the Fourteenth Amendment.

Save the conduct of railroads, no business has been so thoroughly regimented and regulated by the State of New York as the milk industry. Legislation controlling it in the in-

terest of the public health was adopted in 1862 and subsequent statutes, have been carried into the general codification known as the Agriculture and Markets Law. A perusal of these statutes discloses that the milk industry has been progressively subjected to a larger measure of control. The producer or dairy farmer is in certain circumstances liable to have his herd quarantined against bovine tuberculosis; is limited in the importation of dairy cattle to those free from Bang's disease; is subject to rules governing the care and feeding of his cows and the care of the milk produced, the condition and surroundings of his barns and buildings used for production of milk, the utensils used, and the persons employed in milking. Proprietors of milk gathering stations or processing plants are subject to regulation, and persons in charge must operate under license and give bond to comply with the law and regulations; must keep records, pay promptly for milk purchased, abstain from false or misleading statements and from combinations to fix prices. In addition there is a large volume of legislation intended to promote cleanliness and fair trade practices, affecting all who are engaged in the industry. The challenged amendment of 1933 carried regulation much farther than the prior enactments. Appellant insists that it went beyond the limits fixed by the Constitution.

Under our form of government the use of property and the making of contracts are normally matters of private and not of public concern. The general rule is that both shall be free of governmental interference. But neither property rights nor contract rights are absolute; for government cannot exist if the citizen may at will use his property to the detriment of his fellows, or exercise his freedom of contract to work them harm. Equally fundamental with the private right is that of the public to regulate it in the common interest. . . .

The Fifth Amendment, in the field of federal activity, and the Fourteenth, as respects state action, do not prohibit governmental regulation for the public welfare. They merely condition the exertion of the admitted power, by securing that the end shall be accomplished by methods consistent with due process. And the guaranty of due process, as has often been held, demands only that the law shall not be unreasonable, arbitrary or capricious, and that the means selected shall have a real and substantial relation to the object sought to be attained. It results that a regulation valid for one sort of business, or in given circumstances, may be invalid for another sort, or for the same business under other circumstances, because the reasonableness of each regulation depends upon the relevant facts.

The reports of our decisions abound with cases in which the citizens, individual or corporate, has vainly invoked the Fourteenth Amendment in resistance to necessary and appropriate exertion of the police power. . . .

The Constitution does not guarantee the unrestricted privilege to engage in a business or to conduct it as one pleases. Certain kinds of business may be prohibited; and the right to conduct a business, or to pursue a calling, may be conditioned. Regulation of a business to prevent waste of the state's resources may be justified. And statutes prescribing the terms upon which those conducting certain businesses may contract, or imposing terms if they do enter into agreements, are within the state's competency.

Legislation concerning sales of goods, and incidentally affecting prices, has repeatedly been held valid. . . .

But we are told that because the law essays to control prices it denies due process. Notwithstanding the admitted power to correct existing economic ills by appropriate regulation of business, even though an indirect result may be a restriction of the freedom of contract or a modification of charges for services or the price of commodities, the appellant urges that direct fixation of prices is a type of regulation absolutely forbidden. His position is that the Fourteenth Amendment requires us to hold the challenged statute void for this reason alone. The argument runs that the public control of rates or prices is *per se* unreasonable and unconstitutional, save as applied to businesses affected with a public interest; that a business so affected is one in which property is devoted to an enterprise of a sort which the public itself might appropriately undertake, or one whose owner relies on a public grant or franchise for the right to conduct the business, or in which he is bound to serve all who apply; in short, such as is commonly called a public utility; or a business in its nature a monopoly. The milk industry, it is said, possesses none of these

characteristics, and, therefore, not being affected with a public interest, its charges may not be controlled by the state. Upon the soundness of this contention the appellant's case against the statute depends.

We may as well say at once that the dairy industry is not, in the accepted sense of the phrase, a public utility. We think the appellant is also right in asserting that there is in this case no suggestion of any monopoly or monopolistic practice. It goes without saying that those engaged in the business are in no way dependent upon public grants or franchises for the privilege of conducting their activities. But if, as must be conceded, the industry is subject to regulation in the public interest, what constitutional principle bars the state from correcting existing maladjustments by legislation touching prices? We think there is no such principle. The due process clause makes no mention of sales or of prices any more than it speaks of business or contracts or buildings or other incidents of property. The thought seems nevertheless to have persisted that there is something peculiarly sacrosanct about the price one may charge for what he makes or sells, and that, however able to regulate other elements of manufacture or trade, with incidental effect upon price, the state is incapable of directly controlling the price itself. The view was negatived many years ago. *Munn. v. Illinois.* . . .

In the further discussion of the principle it is said that when one devotes his property to a use, "in which the public has an interest," he in effect "grants to the public an interest in that use" and must submit to be controlled for the common good. The conclusion is that if Munn and Scott wished to avoid having their business regulated they should not have embarked their property in an industry which is subject to regulation in the public interest.

The true interpretation of the court's language is claimed to be that only property voluntarily devoted to a known public use is subject to regulation as to rates. But obviously Munn and Scott had not voluntarily dedicated their business to a public use. They intended only to conduct it as private citizens, and they insisted that they had done nothing which gave the public an interest in their transactions or conferred any right of regulation. The statement that one has dedicated his property to a public use is, therefore, merely another way of saying that if one embarks in a business which public interest demands shall be regulated, he must know regulation will ensue. . . .

Many other decisions show that the private character of a business does not necessarily remove it from the realm of regulation of charges or prices. . . .

It is clear that there is no closed class or category of businesses affected with a public interest, and the function of courts in the application of the Fifth and Fourteenth Amendments is to determine in each case whether circumstances vindicate the challenged regulation as a reasonable exertion of governmental authority or condemn it as arbitrary or discriminatory. The phrase "affected with a public interest" can, in the nature of things, mean no more than that an industry, for adequate reason, is subject to control for the public good. In several of the decisions of this court wherein the expressions "affected with a public interest," and "clothed with a public use," have been brought forward as the criteria of the validity of price control, it has been admitted that they are not susceptible of definition and form an unsatisfactory test of the constitutionality of legislation directed at business practices or prices. These decisions must rest, finally, upon the basis that the requirements of due process were not met because the laws were found arbitrary in their operation and effect. But there can be no doubt that upon proper occasion and by appropriate measures the state may regulate a business in any of its aspects, including the prices to be charged for the products or commodities it sells.

So far as the requirement of due process is concerned, and in the absence of other constitutional restriction, a state is free to adopt whatever economic policy may reasonably be deemed to promote public welfare, and to enforce that policy by legislation adapted to its purpose. The courts are without authority either to declare such policy, or, when it is declared by the legislature, to override it. If the laws passed are seen to have a reasonable relation to a proper legislative purpose, and are neither arbitrary nor discriminatory, the requirements of due process are satisfied, and judicial determination to that effect renders a court *functus officio*. . . . And it is equally clear that if the legislative policy be to curb unrestrained and harmful competition by measures which are not arbitrary or discriminatory it does not lie with the courts to determine that the rule is unwise. With the wisdom of the policy adopted, with the adequacy or practicability of the law enacted to forward it, the courts are both incompetent and unauthorized to deal. . . .

The law-making bodies have in the past endeavored to promote free competition by laws aimed at trusts and monopolies. The consequent interference with private property and freedom of contract has not availed with the courts to set these enactments aside as denying due process. Where the public interest was deemed to require the fixing of minimum prices, that expedient has been sustained. If the law-making body within its sphere of government concludes that the conditions or practices in an industry make unrestricted competition an inadequate safeguard of the consumer's interests, produce waste harmful to the public, threaten ultimately to cut off the supply of a commodity needed by the public, or portend the destruction of the industry itself, appropriate statutes passed in an honest effort to correct the threatened consequences may not be set aside because the regulation adopted fixes prices reasonably deemed by the legislature to be fair to those engaged in the industry and to the consuming public. And this is especially so where, as here, the economic maladjustment is one of price, which threatens harm to the producer at one end of the series and the consumer at the other. The Constitution does not secure to anyone liberty to conduct his business in such fashion as to inflict injury upon the public at large, or upon any substantial group of the people. Price control, like any other form of regulation, is unconstitutional only if arbitrary, discriminatory, or demonstrably irrelevant to the policy the legislature is free to adopt, and hence an unnecessary and unwarranted interference with individual liberty.

Tested by these considerations we find no basis in the due process clause of the Fourteenth Amendment for condemning the provisions of the Agriculture and Markets Law here drawn into question.

The judgment is affirmed.

Justices McReynolds, Van Devanter, Sutherland and Butler dissented.

496. ROOSEVELT'S VETO OF THE SOLDIERS' BONUS BILL
May 22, 1935

(Public Papers and Addresses of Franklin D. Roosevelt, Vol. IV, p. 182)

As early as the Minneapolis meeting of 1919 the American Legion had considered favorably the suggestion of "adjusted compensation" for veterans of the World War. In 1922 a bonus bill passed both houses of Congress, but was vetoed by President Harding. A second effort, in 1923, was met by a veto from President Coolidge. In 1924, however, Congress passed over the Presidential veto a bill calling for adjusted compensation certificates to mature in 1945. The depression brought a demand for full and immediate payment of these certificates, Congress responded first by permitting veterans to borrow up to fifty per cent of the fact value of the certificates, and finally by complete capitulation. Congress failed to override this veto, but in January 1936 a similar bill was passed over the Presidential veto. President Roosevelt's second veto message can be found in the *Public Papers and Addresses,* Vol. V, p. 67. On the bonus, see K. Durham, *Billions for Veterans;* R. Burlingame, *Peace Veterans;* M. Duffield, *King Legion;* M. James, *History of the American Legion.*

Mr. Speaker, Members of the House of Representatives:

. . . At the outbreak of the war, the President and the Congress sought and established an entirely new policy in order to guide the granting of financial aid to soldiers and sailors. Remembering the unfortunate results that came from the lack of a veterans' policy after the Civil War, they determined that a prudent and sound principle of insurance should supplant the uncertainties and unfairness of direct bounties. At the same time, their policy encompassed the most complete care for those who had suffered disabilities in service. With respect to the grants made within the lines of this general policy, the President and the Congress have fully recognized that those who served in uniform deserved certain benefits to which other citizens of the Republic were not entitled, and in which they could not participate.

In line with these sound and fair principles, many benefits have been provided for veterans. . . .

We may measure the benefits extended from the fact that there has been expended up to the end of the last fiscal year more than $7,800,000,000 for these items in behalf of the veterans of the World War, not including sums spent for home or work relief. With our current annual expenditures of some $450,-000,000 and the liquidation of outstanding obligations under term insurance and the payment of the service certificates, it seems safe to predict that by the year 1945 we will have expended $13,500,000,000. This is a sum equal to more than three-fourths of the entire cost of our participation in the World War, and ten years from now most of the veterans of that war will be barely past the half-century mark.

Payments have been made and are being made only to veterans of the World War and their dependents, and not to civilian workers who helped to win that war.

In the light of our established principles and policies let us consider the case of adjusted compensation. Soon after the close of the war a claim was made by several veterans' organizations that they should be paid some adjusted compensation for their time in uniform. After a complete and fair presentation of the whole subject, followed by full debate in the Congress of the United States, a settlement was reached in 1924.

This settlement provided for adjustment in compensation during service by an additional allowance per day for actual service rendered. Because cash payment was not to be made immediately, this basic allowance was increased by 25 per cent and to this was added compound interest for 20 years, the whole to be paid in 1945. The result of this computation was that an amount two and one-half times the original grant would be paid at maturity.

Taking the average case as an example, the Government acknowledged a claim of $400 to be due. This $400, under the provisions of the settlement, with the addition of the 25 per cent for deferred payment and the compound interest from that time until 1945, would amount to the sum of $1,000 in 1945. The veteran was thereupon given a certificate containing an agreement by the Government to pay him this $1,000 in 1945 or to pay it to his family if he died at any time before 1945.

In effect it was a paid-up endowment policy in the average case for $1,000 payable in 1945, or sooner in the event of his death. Under the provisions of this settlement the total obligation of $1,400,000,000 in 1924 produced a maturity or face value of $3,500,000,000 in 1945.

Since 1924 the only major change in the original settlement was the act of 1931, under which veterans were authorized to borrow up to 50 per cent of the face value of their certificates as of 1945. Three million veterans have already borrowed under this provision an amount which, with interest charges, totals $1,700,000,000.

The bill before me provides for the immediate payment of the 1945 value of the certificates. It means paying $1,600,000,000 more than the present value of the certificates. It requires an expenditure of more than $2,200,000,000 in cash for this purpose. It directs payment to the veterans of a much larger sum than was contemplated in the 1924 settlement. It is nothing less than a complete abandonment of that settlement. It is a new straight gratuity or bounty to the amount of $1,600,000,000. It destroys the insurance protection for the dependents of the veterans provided in the original plan. For the remaining period of 10 years they will have lost this insurance.

This proposal, I submit, violates the entire principle of veterans' benefits so carefully formulated at the time of the war and also the entire principle of the adjusted-certificate settlement of 1924.

What are the reasons presented in this bill for this fundamental change in policy? They are set forth with care in a number of "whereas" clauses at the beginning of the bill.

The first of these states as reasons for the cash payment of these certificates at this time: That it will increase the purchasing power of millions of the consuming public; that it will provide relief for many who are in need because of economic conditions; and that it will lighten the relief burden of cities, counties, and States. The second states that payment will not create any additional debt. The third states that payment now will be an effective method of spending money to hasten recovery.

These are the enacted reasons for the passage of this bill. Let me briefly analyze them.

First, the spending of this sum, it cannot be denied, would result in some expansion of retail trade. But it must be noted that retail trade has already expanded to a condition that compares favorably with conditions before the depression. However, to resort to the kind of financial practice provided in this bill would not improve the conditions necessary to expand those industries in which we have the greatest unemployment. The Treasury notes issued under the terms of this bill we know from past experience would return quickly to the banks. We know, too, that the banks have at this moment more than ample credit with which to expand the activities of business and industry generally. The ultimate effect of this bill will not, in the long run, justify the expectations that have been raised by those who argue for it.

The next reason in the first "whereas" clause is that present payment will provide relief for many who are in need because of economic conditions. The Congress has just passed an act to provide work relief for such citizens. Some veterans are on the relief rolls. . . . Assume, however, that such a veteran served in the United States or overseas during the war; that he came through in fine physical shape as most of them did; that he received an honorable discharge; that he is today 38 years old and in full possession of his faculties and health; that like several million other Americans he is receiving from his Government relief and assistance in one of many forms—I hold that that able-bodied citizen should be accorded no treatment different from that accorded to other citizens who did not wear a uniform during the World War.

The third reason given in the first "whereas" clause is that payment today would lighten the relief burden of municipalities. Why, I ask, should the Congress lift that burden in respect only to those who wore the uniform? Is it not better to treat every able-bodied American alike and to carry out the great relief program adopted by this Congress in a spirit of equality to all? This applies to every other unit of government throughout the Nation.

The second "whereas" clause, which states that the payment of certificates will not create an additional debt, raises a fundamental question of sound finance. To meet a claim of one group by this deceptively easy method of payment will raise similar demands for the payment of claims of other groups. It is easy to see the ultimate result of meeting recurring demands by the issuance of Treasury notes. It invites an ultimate reckoning in uncontrollable prices and in the destruction of the value of savings, that will strike most cruelly those like the veterans who seem to be temporarily benefited. The first person injured by sky-rocketing prices is the man on a fixed income. Every disabled veteran on pension or allowance is on fixed income. This bill favors the able-bodied veteran at the expense of the disabled veteran. . . .

The statement in this same second "whereas" clause that payment will discharge and retire an acknowledged contract obligation of the Government is, I regret to say, not in accordance with the fact. It wholly omits and disregards the fact that this contract obligation is due in 1945 and not today. . . .

The final "whereas" clause, stating that spending the money is the most effective means of hastening recovery, is so ill considered that little comment is necessary. Every authorization of expenditure by the 73d Congress in its session of 1933 and 1934, and every appropriation by the 74th Congress to date, for recovery purposes, has been predicated not on the mere spending of money to hasten recovery, but on the sounder principle of preventing the loss of homes and farms, of saving industry from bankruptcy, of safeguarding bank deposits, and most important of all—of giving relief and jobs through public work to individuals and families faced with starvation. These greater and broader concerns of the American people have a prior claim for our consideration at this time. They have the right of way. . . .

To argue for this bill as a relief measure is to indulge in the fallacy that the welfare of the country can be generally served by extending relief on some basis other than actual deserving need.

The core of the question is that man who is sick or under some other special disability because he was a soldier should certainly be assisted as such. But if a man is suffering from economic need because of the depression, even though he is a veteran, he must be placed on a par with all of the other victims of the depression. The veteran who is disabled owes his condition to the war. The healthy veteran who is unemployed owes his troubles to the depression. Each presents a separate and different problem. Any attempt to mingle the two problems is to confuse our efforts.

Even the veteran who is on relief will benefit only temporarily by this measure, because the payment of this sum to him will remove him from the group entitled to relief if the ordinary rules of relief agencies are followed. For him this measure would give but it would also take away. In the end he would be the loser.

The veteran who suffers from this depression can best be aided by the rehabilitation of the country as a whole. His country with honor and gratitude returned him at the end of the war to the citizenry from which he came. He became once more a member of the great civilian population. His interests became identified with its fortunes and also with its misfortunes. . . .

It is generally conceded that the settlement by adjusted-compensation certificates made in 1924 was fair and it was accepted as fair by the overwhelming majority of World War veterans themselves. . . .

It is important to make one more point. In accordance with the mandate of the Congress, our Budget has been set. The public has accepted it. On that basis this Congress has made and is making its appropriations. That Budget asked for appropriations in excess of receipts to the extent of four billion dollars. The whole of that deficit was to be applied for work relief for the unemployed. That was a single-minded, definite purpose. Every unemployed veteran on the relief rolls was included in that proposed deficit; he will be taken care of out of it.

I cannot in honesty assert to you that to increase that deficit this year by two billion two hundred million dollars will in itself bankrupt the United States. Today the credit of the United States is safe. But it cannot ultimately be safe if we engage in a policy of yielding to each and all of the groups that are able to enforce upon the Congress claims for special consideration. To do so is to abandon the principle of government by and for the American people and to put in its place government by and for political coercion by minorities. We can afford all that we need; but we cannot afford all that we want.

I do not need to be a prophet to assert that if these certificates, due in 1945, are paid in full today, every candidate for election to the Senate or to the House of Representatives will in the near future be called upon in the name of patriotism to support general pension legislation for all veterans, regardless of need or age.

Finally I invite your attention to the fact that, solely from the point of view of the good credit of the United States, the complete failure of the Congress to provide additional taxes for an additional expenditure of this magnitude would in itself any by itself alone warrant disapproval of this measure. . . .

I believe the welfare of the Nation, as well as the future welfare of the veterans, wholly justifies my disapproval of this measure.

Therefore, Mr. Speaker, I return, without my approval, House of Representatives bill No. 3896, providing for the immediate payment to veterans of the 1945 face value of their adjusted-service certificates.

497. RAILROAD RETIREMENT BOARD v. ALTON RAILROAD CO.
295 U. S. 330
1935

Certiorari to the U. S. Court of Appeals for the District of Columbia. Congress, in 1934 passed an act establishing compulsory retirement and pensions for all carriers subject to the Interstate Commerce Act. The authority for this law was, apparently, in the commerce clause of the Constitution. The Court, however, held that there was no reasonable relation between pensions and the promotion of efficiency in interstate commerce, and invalidated the act. For an analysis of the role of the Court in restricting the commerce clause see E. S. Corwin, *Commerce Power versus States Rights,* and *Twilight of the Supreme Court,* and E. R. Johnson, *Government Regulation of Transportation.* For an interpretation of the decision, see Powell, "Commerce, Pensions and Codes," 49 Harv. L. Rev. 1 and 193; Gellhorn, "Validity of Federal Compensation for Transportation Employees," 25 Am. Labor Legislation Rev. 71.

ROBERTS, J. The respondents, comprising 134 Class I railroads, two express companies, and the Pullman Company, brought this suit in the Supreme Court of the District of Columbia, asserting the unconstitutionality of the Railroad Retirement Act and praying an injunction against its enforcement. . . .

The Act establishes a compulsory retirement and pension system for all carriers subject to the Interstate Commerce Act. There is provision for the creation of a fund to be deposited in the United States treasury and administered by a Board denominated an independent agency in the executive branch of the Government. The retirement fund for payment of these pensions and for the expenses of administration of the system will arise from compulsory contributions from present and future employees and the carriers. The sums payable by the employees are to be percentages of their current compensation, and those by each carrier double the total payable by its employees. The Board is to determine from time to time what percentage is required to provide the necessary funds, but until that body otherwise determines the employee contribution is to be 2% of compensation. Out of this fund annuities are to be paid to beneficiaries. . . .

The Supreme Court of the District of Columbia declared the establishment of such a system within the competence of Congress; but thought several inseparable features of the Act transcended the legislative power to regulate interstate commerce, and required a holding that the law is unconstitutional in its entirety. Our duty, like that of the court below, is fairly to construe the powers of Congress, and to ascertain whether or not the enactment falls within them, uninfluenced by predilection for or against the policy disclosed in the legislation. The fact that the compulsory scheme is novel is, of course, no evidence of unconstitutionality. Even should we consider the Act unwise and prejudicial to both public and private interest, if it be fairly within delegated power our obligation is to sustain it. On the other hand though we should think the measure embodies a valuable social plan and be in entire sympathy with its purpose and intended results, if the provisions go beyond the boundaries of constitutional power we must so declare. . . .

The petitioners assert that the questioned Act, fairly considered, is a proper and necessary regulation of interstate commerce; its various provisions have reasonable relation to the main and controlling purposes of the enactment, the promotion of efficiency, economy and safety; consequently it falls within the power conferred by the commerce clause and does not offend the principle of due process. The respondents insist that numerous features of the Act contravene the due process guaranty and further that the requirement of pensions for employees of railroads is not a regulation of interstate commerce within the meaning of the Constitution. . . .

. . . Broadly, the record presents the question whether a statutory requirement that retired employees shall be paid pensions is regulation of commerce between the States within Article I, § 8. . . .

5. It results from what has now been said that the Act is invalid because several of its inseparable provisions contravene the due process of law clause of the Fifth Amendment. We are of opinion that it is also bad for another reason which goes to the heart of the law, even if it could survive the loss of the unconstitutional features which we have discussed. The Act is not in purpose or effect a regulation of interstate commerce within the meaning of the Constitution.

Several purposes are expressed in § 2 (a), amongst them: to provide "adequately for the satisfactory retirement of aged employees"; "to make possible greater employment opportunity and more rapid advancement"; to provide by the administration and construction of the Act "the greatest practicable amount of relief from unemployment and the greatest possible use of resources available for said purpose and for the payment of annuities for the relief of superannuated employees." The respondents assert and the petitioners admit that though these may in and of themselves be laudable objects, they have no reasonable relation to the business of interstate transportation. The clause, however, states a further purpose, the promotion of "efficiency and safety in interstate transportation," and the respondents concede that an act, the provisions of which show that it actually is directed to the attainment of such a purpose, falls within the regulatory power conferred upon the Congress; but they contend that here the provisions of the statute emphasize the necessary conclusion that the plan is conceived solely for the promotion of the stated purposes other than efficient and safe operation of the railroads. The petitioners' view is that this is the true and only purpose of the enactment, and the other objects stated are collateral to it and may be disregarded if the law is found apt for the promotion of this legitimate purpose.

From what has already been said with respect to sundry features of the statutory scheme, it must be evident that petitioners' view is that safety and efficiency are promoted by two claimed results of the plan: the abolition of excessive superannuation, and the improvement of morale. . . .

In final analysis, the petitioners' sole reliance is the thesis that efficiency depends upon morale, and morale in turn upon assurance of security for the worker's old age. Thus pensions are sought to be related to efficiency of transportation, and brought within the commerce power. In supporting the Act the petitioners constantly recur to such phrases as "old age security," "assurance of old age security," "improvement of employee morale and efficiency through providing definite assurance of old age security," "assurance of old age support," "mind at ease," and "fear of old age dependency." These expressions are frequently connected with assertions that the removal of the fear of old age dependency will tend to create a better morale throughout the ranks of employees. The theory is that one who has an assurance against future dependency will do his work more cheerfully, and therefore more efficiently. The question at once presents itself whether the fostering of a contented mind on the part of an employee by legislation of this type, is in any just sense a regulation of interstate transportation. If that question be answered in the affirmative, obviously there is no limit to the field of so-called regulation. The catalogue of means and actions which might be imposed upon an employer in any business, tending to the satisfaction and comfort of his employees, seems endless. Provision for free medical attendance and nursing, for clothing, for food, for housing, for the education of children, and a hundred other matters, might with equal propriety be proposed as tending to relieve the employee of mental strain and worry. Can it fairly be said that the power of Congress to regulate interstate commerce extends to the prescription of any or all of these things? Is it not apparent that they are really and essentially related solely to the social welfare of the worker, and therefore remote from any regulation of commerce as such? We think the answer is plain. These matters obviously lie outside the orbit of Congressional power. The answer of the petitioners is that not all such means of promoting contentment have such a close relation to interstate commerce as pensions. This is in truth no answer, for we must deal with the principle involved and not the means adopted. If contentment of the employee were an object for the attainment of which the regulatory power could be exerted, the courts could not question the wisdom of methods adopted for its advancement. . . .

Certainly the argument is inconsistent with any thought that a plan imposed by statute, requiring the payment of a pension, will promote the same loyalty and continuity of service which were the ends and objects of the voluntary plans. It is going far to say, as petitioners do, that Congress chose the more progressive method "already tried in the laboratory of industrial experience," which they claim has been approved and recommended by those qualified to speak. In support of the assertion, however, they cite general works dealing with voluntary pension plans, and not with any such compulsory system as that with which we are concerned. We think it cannot be denied, and, indeed, is in effect admitted, that the sole reliance of the petitioners is upon the theory that contentment and assurance of security are the major purposes of the Act. We cannot agree that these ends if dictated by statute, and not voluntarily extended by the employer, encourage loyalty and continuity of service. We feel bound to hold that a pension plan thus imposed is in no proper sense a regulation of the activity of interstate transportation. It is an attempt for social ends to impose by sheer fiat non-contractual incidents upon the relation of employer and employee, not as a rule or regulation of commerce and transportation between the States, but as a means of assuring a particular class of employees against old age dependency. This is neither a necessary nor an appropriate rule or regulation affecting the due fulfilment

of the railroads' duty to serve the public in interstate transportation.

The judgment of the Supreme Court of the District of Columbia is

Affirmed.

HUGHES, C. J., dissenting. I am unable to concur in the decision of this case. The gravest aspect of the decision is that it does not rest simply upon a condemnation of particular features of the Railroad Retirement Act, but denies to Congress the power to pass any compulsory pension act for railroad employees. If the opinion were limited to the particular provisions of the Act, which the majority find to be objectionable and not severable, the Congress would be free to overcome the objections by a new statute. Classes of persons held to be improperly brought within the range of the Act could be eliminated. Criticisms of the basis of payments, of the conditions prescribed for the receipt of benefits, and of the requirements of contributions could be met. Even in place of a unitary retirement system another sort of plan could be worked out. What was thus found to be inconsistent with the requirements of due process could be exercised and other provisions substituted. But after discussing these matters, the majority finally raise a barrier against all legislative action of this nature by declaring that the subject matter itself lies beyond the reach of the congressional authority to regulate interstate commerce. In that view, no matter how suitably limited a pension act for railroad employees might be with respect to the persons to be benefited, or how appropriate the measure of retirement allowances, or how sound actuarilly the plan, or how well adjusted the burden, still under this decision Congress would not be at liberty to enact such a measure. That is a conclusion of such serious and far-reaching importance that it overshadows all other questions raised by the Act. Indeed, it makes their discussion superfluous. The final objection goes, as the opinion states, "to the heart of the law, even if it could survive the loss of the unconstitutional features" which the opinion perceives. I think that the conclusion thus reached is a departure from sound principles and places an unwarranted limitation upon the commerce clause of the Constitution. . . .

. . . I think that it is clear that the morale

of railroad employees has an important bearing upon the efficiency of the transportation service, and that a reasonable pension plan by its assurance of security is an appropriate means to that end. Nor should such a plan be removed from the reach of constitutional power by classing it with a variety of conceivable benefits which have no such close and substantial relation to the terms and conditions of employment. The appropriate relation of the exercise of constitutional power to the legitimate objects of that power is always a subject of judicial scrutiny. With approximately 82 per cent of railroad employees, 90 per cent of those employed in cable, telephone and telegraph companies, and about one-half of those in the servic of electric railways, light, heat and power companies under formal pension plans, with the extensive recognition by national, state and local governments of the benefit of retirement and pension systems for public employees in the interest of both efficiency and economy, it is evident that there is a widespread conviction that the assurance of security through a pension plan for retired employees is closely and substantially related to the proper conduct of business enterprises.

But with respect to the carriers' plans, we are told that as they were framed in the desire to promote loyalty and continuity of service in the employment of particular carriers, the accruing advantages were due to the fact that the plans were of a voluntary character. In short, that the reaction of the employees would be simply one of gratitude for an act of grace. I find no adequate basis for a conclusion that the advantages of a pension plan can be only such as the carriers contemplated or that the benefit which may accrue to the service from a sense of security on the part of employees should be disregarded. In that aspect, it would be the fact that protection was assured, and not the mo-

tive in supplying it, which would produce the desired result. That benefit would not be lost because the sense of security was fostered by a pension plan enforced as an act of justice. Indeed, voluntary plans may have the defect of being voluntary, of being subject to curtailment or withdrawal at will. And the danger of such curtailment or abandonment, with the consequent frustration of the hopes of a vast number of railroad workers and its effect upon labor relation in this enterprise of outstanding national importance, might well be considered as an additional reason for the adoption of a compulsory plan. . . .

The fundamental consideration which supports this type of legislation is that industry should take care of its human wastage, whether that is due to accident or age. That view cannot be dismissed as arbitrary or capricious. It is a reasoned conviction based upon abundant experience. The expression of that conviction in law is regulation. When expressed in the government of interstate carriers, with respect to their employees likewise engaged in interstate commerce, it is a regulation of that commerce. As such, so far as the subject matter is concerned, the commerce clause should be held applicable. . . .

The power committed to Congress to govern interstate commerce does not require that its government should be wise, much less that it should be perfect. The power implies a broad discretion and thus permits a wide range even of mistakes. Expert discussion of pension plans reveals different views of the manner in which they should be set up and a close study of advisable methods is in progress. It is not our province to enter that field, and I am not persuaded that Congress in entering it for the purpose of regulating interstate carriers has transcended the limits of the authority which the Constitution confers.

I think the decree should be reversed.

498. HUMPHREY'S EXECUTOR v. UNITED STATES
295 U. S. 602
1935

Certificate from the Court of Claims. Myers v. U. S. (Doc. No. 459) appeared to give judicial sanction to a very broad power of removal by the President. Did this power extend to removal of members of the independent quasi-legislative and quasi-judicial commissions such as the Federal Trade Commission? The Court here held unanimously that it did not. See, E. S. Corwin, *The President's Power of Removal Under the Constitution;* E. P. Herring, *Public Administra-*

tion and the Public Interest; W. E. Binkley, *The Powers of the President;* H. Laski, *The American Presidency.*

Sutherland, J. . . . . William E. Humphrey, the decedent, on December 10, 1931, was nominated by President Hoover to succeed himself as a member of the Federal Trade Commission, and was confirmed by the United States Senate. He was duly commissioned for a term of seven years expiring September 25, 1938; and, after taking the required oath of office, entered upon his duties. On July 25, 1933, President Roosevelt addressed a letter to the commissioner asking for his resignation, on the ground "that the aims and purposes of the Administration with respect to the work of the Commission can be carried out most effectively with personnel of my own selection," but disclaiming any reflection upon the commissioner personally or upon his services. The commissioner replied, asking time to consult his friends. After some further correspondence upon the subject, the President on August 31, 1933, wrote the commissioner expressing the hope that the resignation would be forthcoming and saying:

"You will, I know, realize that I do not feel that your mind and my mind go along together on either the policies or the administering of the Federal Trade Commission, and, frankly, I think it is best for the people of this country that I should have a full confidence."

The commissioner declined to resign; and on October 7, 1933, the President wrote him:

"Effective as of this date you are hereby removed from the office of Commissioner of the Federal Trade Commission."

Humphreys never acquiesced in this action, but continued thereafter to insist that he was still a member of the Commission, entitled to perform its duties and receive the compensation provided by law at the rate of $10,000 per annum. Upon these and other facts set forth in the certificate, which we deem it unnecessary to recite, the following questions are certified:

"1. Do the provisions of section 1 of the Federal Trade Commission Act, stating that 'any commissioner may be removed by the President for inefficiency, neglect of duty, or malfeasance in office,' restrict or limit the power of the President to remove a commis-

sioner except upon one or more of the causes named?

"If the foregoing question is answered in the affirmative, then—

"2. If the power of the President to remove a commissioner is restricted or limited as shown by the foregoing interrogatory and the answer made thereto, is such a restriction or limitation valid under the Constitution of the United States?" . . .

The Federal Trade Commission Act creates a commission of five members to be appointed by the President by and with the advice and consent of the Senate, and § 1 provides:

"Not more than three of the commissioners shall be members of the same political party. The first commissioners appointed shall continue in office for terms of three, four, five, six, and seven years, respectively, from the date of the taking effect of this Act, the term of each to be designated by the President, but their successors shall be appointed for terms of seven years, except that any person chosen to fill a vacancy shall be appointed only for the unexpired term of the commissioner whom he shall succeed. The Commission shall engage in any other business, vocation, or employment. Any commissioner may be removed by the President for inefficiency, neglect of duty, or malfeasance in office. . . ."

First. The question first to be considered is whether, by the provisions of § 1 of the Federal Trade Commission Act already quoted, the President's power is limited to removal for the specific causes enumerated therein. . . .

The Commission is to be non-partisan; and it must, from the very nature of its duties, act with entire impartiality. It is charged with the enforcement of no policy except the policy of the law. Its duties are neither political nor executive, but predominantly quasi-judicial and quasi-legislative. Like the Interstate Commerce Commission, its members are called upon to exercise the trained judgment of a body of experts "appointed by law and informed by experience." . . .

The legislative reports in both houses of Congress clearly reflect the view that a fixed term was necessary to the effective and fair administration of the law. . . .

The debates in both houses demonstrate that the prevailing view was that the commission was not to be "subject to anybody in the government but . . . only to the people of the United States"; free from "political domination or control" or the "probability or possibility of such a thing"; to be "separate and apart from any existing department of the government—not subject to the orders of the President." . . .

Thus, the language of the act, the legislative reports, and the general purposes of the legislation as reflected by the debates, all combine to demonstrate the Congressional intent to create a body of experts who shall gain experience by length of service—a body which shall be independent of executive authority, *except in its selection,* and free to exercise its judgment without the leave or hindrance of any other official or any department of the government. To the accomplishment of these purposes, it is clear that Congress was of opinion that length and certainty of tenure would vitally contribute. And to hold that, nevertheless, the members of the commission continue in office at the mere will of the President, might be to thwart, in large measure, the very ends which Congress sought to realize by definitely fixing the term of office.

We conclude that the intent of the act is to limit the executive power of removal to the causes enumerated, the existence of none of which is claimed here; and we pass to the second question.

Second. To support its contention that the removal provision of § 1, as we have just construed it, is an unconstitutional interference with the executive power of the President, the government's chief reliance is *Myers* v. *United States, 272 U. S. 52.* . . . In the course of the opinion of the court, expressions occur which tend to sustain the government's contention, but these are beyond the point involved and, therefore, do not come within the rule of *stare decisis.* In so far as they are out of harmony with the views here set forth, these expressions are disapproved. . . .

The office of a postmaster is so essentially unlike the office now involved that the decision in the *Myers* case cannot be accepted as controlling our decision here. A postmaster is an executive officer restricted to the performance of executive functions. He is charged with no duty at all related to either the legislative or judicial power. The actual decision in the *Meyers* case finds support in the theory that such an officer is merely one of the units in the executive department and, hence, inherently subject to the exclusive and illimitable power of removal by the Chief Executive, whose subordinate and aid he is. Putting aside *dicta*, which may be followed if sufficiently persuasive but which are not controlling, the necessary reach of the decision goes far enough to include all purely executive officers. It goes no farther;—much less does it include an officer who occupies no place in the executive department and who exercises no part of the executive power vested by the Constitution in the President.

The Federal Trade Commission is an administrative body created by Congress to carry into effect legislative policies embodied in the statute in accordance with the legislative standard therein prescribed, and to perform other specified duties as a legislative or as a judicial aid. Such a body cannot in any proper sense be characterized as an arm or an eye of the executive. Its duties are performed without executive leave and, in the contemplation of the statute, must be free from executive control. . . .

We think it plain under the Constitution that illimitable power of removal is not possessed by the President in respect of officers of the character of those just named. The authority of Congress, in creating quasi-legislative or quasi-judicial agencies, to require them to act in discharge of their duties independently of executive control cannot well be doubted; and that authority includes, as an appropriate incident, power to fix the period during which they shall continue in office, and to forbid their removal except for cause in the meantime. For it is quite evident that one who holds his office only during the pleasure of another, cannot be depended upon to maintain an attitude of independence against the latter's will.

The fundamental necessity of maintaining each of the three general departments of government entirely free from the control or coercive influence, direct or indirect, of either of the others, has often been stressed and is hardly open to serious question. . . .

The power of removal here claimed for the President falls within this principle, since its coercive influence threatens the independence of a commission, which is not only wholly disconnected from the executive department, but which, as already fully appears, was created by Congress as a means of carrying into operation legislative and judicial powers, and as an agency of the legislative and judicial departments. . . .

The result of what we now have said is this: Whether the power of the President to remove an officer shall prevail over the authority of Congress to condition the power by fixing a definite term and precluding a removal except for cause, will depend upon the character of the office; the *Myers* decision, affirming the power of the President alone to make the removal, is confined to purely executive officers; and as to officers of the kind here under consideration, we hold that no removal can be made during the prescribed term for which the officer is appointed, except for one or more of the causes named in the applicable statute. . . .

499. GROSJEAN v. AMERICAN PRESS CO.
297 U. S. 233
1935

Appeal from the District Court of the United States for the Eastern District of Louisiana. Louisiana, in 1934 levied a special tax upon newspapers and periodicals carrying advertising matter and with a weekly circulation of twenty thousand copies or over. It was widely thought at the time that this tax represented an effort of the Huey Long regime to punish certain opposition newspapers. Did such a tax infringe upon that freedom of the press guaranteed in the First and Fourteenth Amendments? The Supreme Court, in an opinion notable for its review of the historical background of the First Amendment, held that it did. See G. L. Patterson, *Free Speech and a Free Press;* Z. Chafee, *Freedom of Speech;* Corwin, "Freedom of Speech and Press under the First Amendment," 30 Yale Law J. 48; Willis, "Freedom of Speech and of the Press," 4 Indiana Law J. 445.

SUTHERLAND, J. This suit was brought by appellees, nine publishers of newspapers in the State of Louisiana, to enjoin the enforcement against them of the Provisions of § 1 of the act of the legislature of Louisiana known as Act No. 23, passed and approved July 12, 1934, as follows:

"That every person, firm, association, or corporation, domestic or foreign, engaged in the business of selling, or making any charge for, advertising or for advertisements, whether printed or published, or to be printed or published, in any newspaper, magazine, periodical or publication whatever having a circulation of more than 20,000 copies per week, or displayed and exhibited, or to be displayed and exhibited by means of moving pictures, in the State of Louisiana, shall, in addition to all other taxes and licenses levied and assessed in this State, pay a license tax for the privilege of engaging in such business in this State of two per cent. of the gross receipts of such business."

The nine publishers who brought the suit publish thirteen newspapers; and these thirteen publications are the only ones within the State of Louisiana having each a circulation of more than 20,000 copies per week, although the lower court finds there are four other daily newspapers each having a circulation of "slightly less than 20,000 copies per week" which are in competition with those published by appellees both as to circulation and as to advertising. In addition, there are 120 weekly newspapers published in the state, also in competition, to a greater or less degree, with the newspapers of appellees. The revenue derived from appellees' newspapers comes almost entirely from regular subscribers or purchasers thereof and from payments received for the insertion of advertisements therein. . . .

Failure to file the report or pay the tax as thus provided constitutes a misdemeanor and subjects the offender to a fine not exceeding $500, or imprisonment not exceeding six months, or both, for each violation. Any corporation violating the act subjects itself to the payment of $500 to be recovered by suit. All of the appellees are corporations. The lower court entered a decree for appellees and granted a permanent injunction. . . .

Third. The validity of the act is assailed as violating the Federal Constitution in two particulars—(1) that it abridges the freedom of the press in contravention of the due process clause contained in § 1 of the Fourteenth Amendment; (2) that it denies appellees the equal protection of the laws in contravention of the same Amendment.

1. The first point presents a question of the utmost gravity and importance; for, if well made, it goes to the heart of the natural right of the members of an organized society, united for their common good, to impart and acquire information about their common interests. The First Amendment to the Federal Constitution provides that "Congress shall make no law . . . abridging the freedom of speech, or of the press . . ." While this provision is not a restraint upon the powers of the states, the states are precluded from abridging the freedom of speech or of the press by force of the due process clause of the Fourteenth Amendment. . . .

In Powell v. Alabama, (287 U. S. 45) . . . we concluded that certain fundamental rights, safeguarded by the first eight amendments against federal action, were also safeguarded against state action by the due process of law clause of the Fourteenth Amendment, and among them the fundamental right of the accused to the aid of counsel in a criminal prosecution.

That freedom of speech and of the press are rights of the same fundamental character, safeguarded by the due process of law clause of the Fourteenth Amendment against abridgement by state legislation, has likewise been settled by a series of decisions of this Court beginning with Gitlow v. New York (268 U. S. 652), and ending with Near v. Minnesota (283 U. S. 697). The word "liberty" contained in that amendment embraces not only the right of a person to be free from physical restraint, but the right to be free in the enjoyment of all his faculties as well.

Appellant contends that the Fourteenth Amendment does not apply to corporations; but this is only partly true. A corporation, we have held, is not a "citizen," within the meaning of the privileges and immunities clause. (Paul v. Virginia, 8 Wall. 168.) But a corporation is a "person" within the meaning of the equal protection and due process of law clauses, which are the clauses involved here. (Covington & Lexington Turnpike Co. v. Sandford, 164 U. S. 578; Smyth v. Ames, 169 U. S. 466).

The tax imposed is designated a "license tax for the privilege of engaging in such business"—that is to say, the business of selling, or making any charge for, advertising.

As applied to appellees, it is a tax of two per cent. on the gross receipts derived from advertisements carried in their newspapers when, and only when, the newspapers of each enjoy a circulation of more than 20,000 copies per week. It thus operates as a restraint in a double sense. First, its effect is to curtail the amount of revenue realized from advertising, and, second, its direct tendency is to restrict circulation. This is plain enough when we consider that, if it were increased to a high degree, as it could be if valid, it well might result in destroying both advertising and circulation.

A determination of the question whether the tax is valid in respect of the point now under review, requires an examination of the history and circumstances which antedated and attended the adoption of the abridgement clause of the First Amendment, since that clause expresses one of those "fundamental principles of liberty and justice which lie at the base of all our civil and political institutions," and, as such, is embodied in the concept "due process of law," and, therefore, protected against hostile state invasion by the due process clause of the Fourteenth Amendment. (Cf. Powell v. Alabama, supra, pp. 67–68.) The history is a long one; but for present purposes it may be greatly abbreviated. . . . [reviews history in England, and background of First Amendment.]

It is impossible to concede that by the words "freedom of the press" the framers of the amendment intended to adopt merely the narrow view then reflected by the law of England that such freedom consisted only in immunity from previous censorship; for this abuse had then permanently disappeared from English practice. It is equally impossible to believe that it was not intended to bring within the reach of these words such modes of restraint as were embodied in the two forms of taxation already described.

In the light of all that has now been said, it is evident that the restricted rules of the English law in respect of the freedom of the press in force when the Constitution was adopted were never accepted by the American colonists, and that by the First Amendment it was meant to preclude the national government, and by the Fourteenth Amendment to preclude the states, from adopting any form of previous restraint upon printed publications, or their circulation, including that which had theretofore been effected by these two well-known and odious methods.

This court had occasion in Near v. Minnesota, supra, at pp. 713 et seq., to discuss at some length the subject in its general aspect. The conclusion there stated is that the object of the constitutional provisions was to prevent previous restraints on publication; and the court was careful not to limit the protection of the right to any particular way of abridging it. Liberty of the press within the meaning of the constitutional provision, it was broadly said, meant "principally although not exclusively, immunity from previous restraints or (from) censorship."

Judge Cooley has laid down the test to be applied—"The evils to be prevented were not the censorship of the press merely, but any action of the government by means of which it might prevent such free and general discussion of public matters as seems absolutely essential to prepare the people for an intelligent exercise of their rights as citizens." 2 Cooley's Constitutional Limitations, 8th ed., p. 886.

It is not intended by anything we have said to suggest that the owners of newspapers are immune from any of the ordinary forms of taxation for support of the government. But this is not an ordinary form of tax, but one single in kind, with a long history of hostile misuse against the freedom of the press.

The predominant purpose of the grant of immunity here invoked was to preserve an untrammeled press as a vital source of public information. The newspapers, magazines and other journals of the country, it is safe to say, have shed and continue to shed, more light on the public and business affairs of the nation than any other instrumentality of publicity; and since informed public opinion is the most potent of all restraints upon misgovernment, the suppression or abridgement of the publicity afforded by a free press cannot be regarded otherwise than with grave concern. The tax here involved is bad not because it takes money from the pockets of the appellees. If that were all, a wholly different question would be presented. It is bad because, in the light of its history and of its present setting, it is seen to be a deliberate and calculated device in the guise of a tax to limit the circulation of information to which the public is entitled in virtue of the constitutional guaranties. A free press stands as one of the great interpreters between the government and the people. To allow it to be fettered is to fetter ourselves.

In view of the persistent search for new subjects of taxation, it is not without significance that, with the single exception of the Louisiana statute, so far as we can discover, no state during the one hundred fifty years of our national existence has undertaken to impose a tax like that now in question.

The form in which the tax is imposed is in itself suspicious. It is not measured or limited by the volume of advertisements. It is measured alone by the extent of the circulation of the publication in which advertisements are carried, with the plain purpose of penalizing the publishers and curtailing the circulation of a selected group of newspapers.

2. Having reached the conclusion that the act imposing the tax in question is unconstitutional under the due process of law clause because it abridges the freedom of the press, we deem it unnecessary to consider the further ground assigned that it also constitutes a denial of the equal protection of the laws.

Decree affirmed.

500. THE NATIONAL LABOR RELATIONS ACT
July 5, 1935

(U. S. Statutes at Large, Vol. XLIX, p. 449)

The invalidation of the NRA necessitated new legislation for the peaceful settlement of labor disputes, and Congress promptly passed this act, commonly known as the Wagner Act after its chief sponsor, Sen. Robert F. Wagner of New York. The act set up an independent Board authorized to investigate complaints, issue cease and desist orders against unfair practices in labor relations affecting interstate commerce, safeguard the right to bargain collectively, and arbitrate labor disputes. Notwithstanding its phenomenal success in the peaceful settlement of disputes, the National Labor Relations Board was under continuous fire both from employers and from the A. F. of L. which charged discrimination in favor of the rival C. I. O. The Government Printing Office publishes annual volumes of the Decisions and Orders of the Board. See J. Rosenfarb, *The National Labor Policy and How It Works;* H. Harris, *American Labor;* R. R. Brooks, *Unions of Their Own Choosing;* E. Levinson, *Labor on the March;* D. Yoder, *Labor Economics and Labor Problems;* H. G. Taylor, *Labor Problems and Labor Law;* N.L.R.B. Division of Economic Research, "Governmental Protection of Labor's Right to Organize"; Garrison, "The National Labor Relations Act," 24 Survey Graphic, 596.

An Act to diminish the causes of labor disputes burdening or obstructing interstate and foreign commerce, to create a National Labor Relations Board, and for other purposes.

Be it enacted,

FINDINGS AND POLICY

SECTION 1. The denial by employers of the right of employees to organize and the refusal by employers to accept the procedure of collective bargaining lead to strikes and other forms of industrial strife or unrest, which have the intent or the necessary effect of burdening or obstructing commerce by (a) impairing the efficiency, safety, or operation of the instrumentalities of commerce; (b) occurring in the current of commerce; (c) materially affecting, restraining, or controlling the flow of raw materials or manufactured or processed goods from or into the channels of commerce, or the prices of such materials or goods in commerce; or (d) causing diminution of employment and wages in such volume as substantially to impair or disrupt the market for goods flowing from or into the channels of commerce.

The inequality of bargaining power between employees who do not possess full freedom of association or actual liberty of contract, and employers who are organized in the corporate or other forms of ownership association substantially burdens and affects the flow of commerce, and tends to aggravate recurrent business depressions, by depressing wage rates and the purchasing power of wage earners in industry and by preventing the stabilization of competitive wage rates and working conditions within and between industries.

Experience has proved that protection by law of the right of employees to organize and bargain collectively safeguards commerce from injury, impairment, or interruption, and promotes the flow of commerce by removing certain recognized sources of industrial strife and unrest, by encouraging practices fundamental to the friendly adjustment of industrial disputes arising out of differences as to wages, hours, or other working conditions, and by restoring equality of bargaining power between employers and employees.

It is hereby declared to be the policy of the United States to eliminate the causes of certain substantial obstructions to the free flow of commerce and to mitigate and eliminate these obstructions when they have occurred by encouraging the practice and procedure of collective bargaining and by protecting the exercise by workers of full freedom of association, self-organization, and designation of representatives of their own choosing, for the purpose of negotiating the terms and conditions of their employment or other mutual aid or protection.

SEC. 2. When used in this Act—

(1) The term "person" includes one or more individuals, partnerships, associations, corporations, legal representatives, trustees, trustees in bankruptcy, or receivers.

(2) The term "employer" includes any person acting in the interest of an employer, directly or indirectly, but shall not include the United States, or any State or political subdivision thereof, or any person subject to the Railway Labor Act, as amended from time to time, or any labor organization (other than when acting as an employer), or anyone acting in the capacity of officer or agent of such labor organization.

(3) The term "employee" shall include any employee, and shall not be limited to the employees of a particular employer, unless the Act explicitly states otherwise, and shall include any individual whose work has ceased as a consequence of, or in connection with, any current labor dispute or because of any unfair labor practice, and who has not obtained any other regular and substantially equivalent employment, but shall not include any individual employed as an agricultural

laborer, or in the domestic service of any family or person at his home, or any individual employed by his parent or spouse. . . .

(5) The term "labor organization" means any organization of any kind, or any agency or employee representation committee or plan, in which employees participate and which exists for the purpose, in whole or in part, of dealing with employers concerning grievances, labor disputes, wages, rates of pay, hours of employment, or conditions of work.

(6) The term "commerce" means trade, traffic, commerce, transportation, or communication among the several States, . . .

(7) The term "affecting commerce" means in commerce, or burdening or obstructing commerce or the free flow of commerce, or having led or tending to lead to a labor dispute burdening or obstructing commerce or the free flow of commerce. . . .

(9) The term "labor dispute" includes any controversy concerning terms, tenure or conditions of employment, or concerning the association or representation of persons in negotiating, fixing, maintaining, changing, or seeking to arrange terms or conditions of employment, regardless of whether the disputants stand in the proximate relation of employer and employee. . . .

NATIONAL LABOR RELATIONS BOARD

SEC. 3. (a) There is hereby created a board, to be known as the "National Labor Relations Board," which shall be composed of three members, who shall be appointed by the President, by and with the advice and consent of the Senate. One of the original members shall be appointed for a term of one year, one for a term of three years, and one for a term of five years, but their successors shall be appointed for terms of five years each, except that any individual chosen to fill a vacancy shall be appointed only for the unexpired term of the member whom he shall succeed. The President shall designate one member to serve as chairman of the Board. Any member of the Board may be removed by the President, upon notice and hearing, for neglect of duty or malfeasance in office, but for no other cause. . . .

SEC. 4. (a) Each member of the Board shall receive a salary of $10,000 a year, shall be eligible for reappointment, and shall not

engage in any other business, vocation, or employment. . . . The Board may establish or utilize such regional, local, or other agencies, and utilize such voluntary and uncompensated services, as may from time to time be needed. . . .

SEC. 6. (a) The Board shall have authority from time to time to make, amend, and rescind such rules and regulations as may be necessary to carry out the provisions of this Act. Such rules and regulations shall be effective upon publication in the manner which the Board shall prescribe.

RIGHTS OF EMPLOYEES

SEC. 7. Employees shall have the right of self-organization, to form, join, or assist labor organizations, to bargain collectively through representatives of their own choosing, and to engage in concerted activities, for the purpose of collective bargaining or other mutual aid or protection.

SEC. 8. It shall be an unfair labor practice for an employer—

(1) To interfere with, restrain, or coerce employees in the exercise of the rights guaranteed in section 7.

(2) To dominate or interfere with the formation or administration of any labor organization or contribute financial or other support to it: *Provided,* That subject to rules and regulations made and published by the Board pursuant to section 6 (a), an employer shall not be prohibited from permitting employees to confer with him during working hours without loss of time or pay.

(3) By discrimination in regard to hire or tenure of employment or any term or condition of employment to encourage or discourage membership in any labor organization: *Provided,* That nothing in this Act, or in the National Industrial Recovery Act (U. S. C., Supp. VII, title 15, secs. 701–712), as amended from time to time, or in any code or agreement approved or prescribed thereunder, or in any other statute of the United States, shall preclude an employer from making an agreement with a labor organization (not established, maintained, or assisted by any action defined in this Act as an unfair labor practice) to require as a condition of employment membership therein, if such labor organization is the representative of the employees as pro-

vided in section 9 (a), in the appropriate collective bargaining unit covered by such agreement when made.

(4) To discharge or otherwise discriminate against an employee because he has filed charges or given testimony under this Act.

(5) To refuse to bargain collectively with the representatives of his employees, subject to the provisions of Section 9 (a).

REPRESENTATIVES AND ELECTIONS

SEC. 9. (a) Representatives designated or selected for the purposes of collective bargaining by the majority of the employees in a unit appropriate for such purposes, shall be the exclusive representatives of all the employees in such unit for the purposes of collective bargaining in respect to rates of pay, wages, hours of employment, or other conditions of employment: *Provided,* That any individual employee or a group of employees shall have the right at any time to present grievances to their employer.

(b) The Board shall decide in each case whether, in order to insure to employees the full benefit of their right to self-organization and to collective bargaining, and otherwise to effectuate the policies of this Act, the unit appropriate for the purposes of collective bargaining shall be the employer unit, craft unit, plant unit, or subdivision thereof.

(c) Whenever a question affecting commerce arises concerning the representation of employees, the Board may investigate such controversy and certify to the parties, in writing, the name or names of the representatives that have been designated or selected. In any such investigation, the Board shall provide for an appropriate hearing upon due notice, either in conjunction with a proceeding under section 10 or otherwise, and may take a secret ballot of employees, or utilize any other suitable method to ascertain such representatives.

(d) Whenever an order of the Board made pursuant to section 10 (c) is based in whole or in part upon facts certified following an investigation pursuant to subsection (c) of this section, and there is a petition for the enforcement or review of such order, such certification and the record of such investigation shall be included in the transcript of the entire record required to be filed under subsections 10 (e) or 10 (f), and thereupon

the decree of the court enforcing, modifying, or setting aside in whole or in part the order of the Board shall be made and entered upon the pleadings, testimony, and proceedings set forth in such transcript.

PREVENTION OF UNFAIR LABOR PRACTICES

SEC. 10. (a) The Board is empowered, as hereinafter provided, to prevent any person from engaging in any unfair labor practice (listed in section 8) affecting commerce. This power shall be exclusive, and shall not be affected by any other means of adjustment or prevention that has been or may be established by agreement, code, law, or otherwise.

(b) Whenever it is charged that any person has engaged in or is engaging in any such unfair labor practice, the Board, or any agent or agency designated by the Board for such purposes, shall have power to issue and cause to be served upon such person a complaint stating the charges in that respect, and containing a notice of hearing before the Board or a member thereof, or before a designated agent or agency, at a place therein fixed, not less than five days after the serving of said complaint. Any such complaint may be amended by the member, agent, or agency conducting the hearing or the Board in its discretion at any time prior to the issuance of an order based thereon. The person so complained of shall have the right to file an answer to the original or amended complaint and to appear in person or otherwise and give testimony at the place and time fixed in the complaint. In the discretion of the member, agent or agency conducting the hearing or the Board, any other person may be allowed to intervene in the said proceeding and to present testimony. In any such proceeding the rules of evidence prevailing in courts of law or equity shall not be controlling.

(c) The testimony taken by such member, agent or agency or the Board shall be reduced to writing and filed with the Board. Thereafter, in its discretion, the Board upon notice may take further testimony or hear argument. If upon all the testimony taken the Board shall be of the opinion that any person named in the complaint has engaged in or is engaging in any such unfair labor practice, then the Board shall state its findings of fact and shall issue and cause to be served on such person an order requiring such person to cease and desist from such unfair labor practice, and to take such affirmative action, including reinstatement of employees with or without back pay, as will effectuate the policies of this Act. Such order may further require such person to make reports from time to time showing the extent to which it has complied with the order. If upon all the testimony taken the Board shall be of the opinion that no person named in the complaint has engaged in or is engaging in any such unfair labor practice, then the Board shall state its findings of fact and shall issue an order dismissing the said complaint. . . .

(e) The Board shall have power to petition any circuit court of appeals of the United States, or if all the circuit courts of appeals to which application may be made are in vacation, any district court of the United States, within any circuit or district, respectively, wherein the unfair labor practice in question occurred or wherein such person resides or transacts business, for the enforcement of such order and for appropriate temporary relief or restraining order, and shall certify and file in the court a transcript of the entire record in the proceeding, including the pleadings and testimony upon which such order was entered and the findings and order of the Board. Upon such filing, the court shall cause notice thereof to be served upon such person, and thereupon shall have jurisdiction of the proceeding and of the question determined therein, and shall have power to grant such temporary relief or restraining order as it deems just and proper, and to make and enter upon the pleadings, testimony, and proceedings set forth in such transcript a decree enforcing, modifying, and enforcing as so modified, or setting aside in whole or in part the order of the Board. No objection that has not been urged before the Board, its member, agent or agency, shall be considered by the court, unless the failure or neglect to urge such objection shall be excused because of extraordinary circumstances. The findings of the Board as to the facts, if supported by evidence, shall be conclusive. . . . The Board may modify its findings as to the facts, or make new findings, by reason of additional evidence so taken and filed, and it shall file

such modified or new findings, which, if supported by evidence, shall be conclusive, and shall file its recommendations, if any, for the modification or setting aside of its original order. The jurisdiction of the court shall be exclusive and its judgment and decree shall be final, except that the same shall be subject to review by the appropriate circuit court of appeals if application was made to the district court as hereinabove provided, and by the Supreme Court of the United States upon writ of certiorari or certification. . . .

(f) Any person aggrieved by a final order of the Board granting or denying in whole or in part the relief sought may obtain a review of such order in any circuit court of appeals of the United States in the circuit wherein the unfair labor practice in question was alleged to have been engaged in or wherein such person resides or transacts business. . . .

(g) The commencement of proceedings under subsection (e) or (f) of this section shall not, unless specifically ordered by the court, operate as a stay of the Board's order. . . .

(i) Petitions filed under this Act shall be heard expeditiously, and if possible within ten days after they have been docketed.

INVESTIGATORY POWERS

SEC. 11. For the purpose of all hearings and investigations, . . .

(1) The Board, or its duly authorized agents or agencies, shall at all reasonable times have access to, for the purpose of examination, and the right to copy any evidence of any person being investigated or proceeded against that relates to any matter under investigation or in question. Any member of the Board shall have power to issue subpenas requiring the attendance and testimony of witnesses and the production of any evidence that relates to any matter under investigation or in question, before the Board, its member, agent, or agency conducting the hearing or investigation. . . .

SEC. 12. Any person who shall willfully resist, prevent, impede, or interfere with any member of the Board or any of its agents or agencies in the performance of duties pursuant to this Act shall be punished by a fine of not more than $5,000 or by imprisonment for not more than one year, or both.

LIMITATIONS

SEC. 13. Nothing in this Act shall be construed so as to interfere with or impede or diminish in any way the right to strike. . . .

SEC. 15. If any provision of this Act, or the application of such provision to any person or circumstance, shall be held invalid, the remainder of this Act, or the application of such provision to persons or circumstances other than those as to which it is held invalid, shall not be affected thereby. . . .

501. N. L. R. B. v. JONES & LAUGHLIN STEEL CORPORATION
301 U. S. 1
1937

On Writ of Certiorari to the U. S. Circuit Court of Appeals for the Fifth District. This is the leading case on the constitutionality of the National Labor Relations Act of 1935 (see Doc. No. 500 and references). In the first five years of its existence the National Labor Relations Board was subjected to an attack far more severe than any in the history of the independent commissions, but its record of successes in the Courts was spectacular. See, Nathanson and Lyons, "Judicial Review of the N. L. R. B.," 33 Ills. Law, Rev. 749; Ward, "Discrimination under the N. L. R. Act," 48 Yale Law J. 1152; Gellhorn and Lynfield, "Politics and Labor Relations," 39 Col. Law Rev. 339; Ziskind, "The Use of Economic Data in Labor Cases," 6 U. of Chicago Law Rev., 607; Geffs and Hepburn, "The Wagner Labor Act Cases," 22 Minn. L. Rev. 1; Koening, "The National Labor Relations Act—an Appraisal," 2 Cornell L. Qt. 392; Donoho, "Jurisdiction of the National Labor Relations Board," 6 Geo. Wash. L. Rev. 436.

HUGHES, C. J. In a proceeding under the National Labor Relations Act of 1935, the National Labor Relations Board found that the petitioner, Jones & Laughlin Steel Corporation, had violated the Act by engaging in unfair labor practices affecting commerce. The proceeding was instituted by the Beaver Valley Lodge No. 200, affiliated with the Amalgamated Association of Iron, Steel and Tin Workers of America, a labor organization. The unfair labor practices charged were that the corporation was discriminating against members of the union with regard to hire and tenure of employment, and was coercing and intimidating its employees in order to interfere with their self-organization. The discriminatory and coercive action alleged was the discharge of certain employees.

The National Labor Relations Board, sustaining the charge, ordered the corporation to cease and desist from such discrimination and coercion, to offer reinstatement to ten of the employees named, to make good their losses in pay, and to post for thirty days notices that the corporation would not discharge or discriminate against members, or those desiring to become members, of the labor union. As the corporation failed to comply, the Board petitioned the Circuit Court of Appeals to enforce the order. The court denied the petition, holding that the order lay beyond the range of federal power. 83 F. (2d) 998. We granted certiorari.

The scheme of the National Labor Relations Act may be briefly stated. [See Doc. No. 500.] Respondent, appearing specially for the purpose of objecting to the jurisdiction of the Board, filed its answer. Respondent admitted the discharges, but alleged that they were made because of inefficiency or violation of rules or for other good reasons and were not ascribable to union membership or activities. As an affirmative defense respondent challenged the constitutional validity of the statute and its applicability in the instant case.

Contesting the ruling of the Board, the respondent argues (1) that the Act is in reality a regulation of labor relations and not of interstate commerce; (2) that the Act can have no application to the respondent's relations with its production employees because they are not subject to regulation by the federal government; and (3) that the provisions of the Act violate Section 2 of Article III and the Fifth and Seventh Amendments of the Constitution of the United States.

The facts as to the nature and scope of the business of the Jones & Laughlin Steel Corporation have been found by the Labor Board and, so far as they are essential to the determination of this controversy, they are not in dispute. The Labor Board has found: The corporation is organized under the laws of Pennsylvania and has its principal office at Pittsburgh. It is engaged in the business of manufacturing iron and steel in plants situated in Pittsburgh and nearby Aliquippa, Pennsylvania. It manufactures and distributes a widely diversified line of steel and pig iron, being the fourth largest producer of steel in the United States. With its subsidiaries—nineteen in number—it is a completely integrated enterprise, owning and operating ore, coal and limestone properties, lake and river transportation facilities and terminal railroads located at its manufacturing plants. It owns or controls mines in Michigan and Minnesota. It operates four ore steamships on the Great Lakes, used in the transportation of ore to its factories. It owns coal mines in Pennsylvania. It operates towboats and steam barges used in carrying coal to its factories. It owns limestone properties in various places in Pennsylvania and West Virginia. It owns the Monongahela connecting railroad which connects the plants of the Pittsburgh works and forms an interconnection with the Pennsylvania, New York Central and Baltimore and Ohio Railroad systems. It owns the Aliquippa and Southern Railroad Company which connects the Aliquippa works with the Pittsburgh and Lake Erie, part of the New York Central system. Much of its product is shipped to its warehouses in Chicago, Detroit, Cincinnati and Memphis,—to the last two places by means of its own barges and transportation equipment. In Long Island City, New York, and in New Orleans it operates structural steel fabricating shops in connection with the warehousing of semi-finished materials sent from its works. Through one of its wholly-owned subsidiaries it owns, leases and operates stores, warehouses and yards for the distribution of equipment and supplies for drilling and operating oil and gas mills and for pipe lines, refineries and pumping stations. It has sales offices in twenty cities in the United States and a wholly-owned subsidiary which is devoted exclusively to distributing its product in Canada. Approximately 75 per cent. of its product is shipped out of Pennsylvania.

Summarizing these operations, the Labor Board concluded that the works in Pittsburgh and Aliquippa "might be likened to the heart of a self-contained, highly integrated body. They draw in the raw materials from Michigan, Minnesota, West Virginia, Pennsylvania in part through arteries and by means controlled by the respondent; they transform the materials and then pump them out to all parts of the nation through the vast mechanism which the respondent has elaborated."

To carry on the activities of the entire steel industry, 33,000 men mine ore, 44,000 men mine coal, 4,000 men quarry limestone, 16,000 men manufacture coke, 343,000 men manufacture steel, and 83,000 men transport its product. Respondent has about 10,000 employees in its Aliquippa plant, which is located in a community of about 30,000 persons.

Practically all the factual evidence in the case, except that which dealt with the nature of respondent's business, concerned its relations with the employees in the Aliquippa plant whose discharge was the subject of the complaint. These employees were active leaders in the labor union.

While respondent criticises the evidence and the attitude of the Board, which is described as being hostile toward employers and particularly toward those who insisted upon their constitutional rights, respondent did not take advantage of its opportunity to present evidence to refute that which was offered to show discrimination and coercion. In this situation, the record presents no ground for setting aside the order of the Board so far as the facts pertaining to the circumstances and purpose of the discharge of the employees are concerned. Upon that point it is sufficient to say that the evidence supports the findings of the Board that respondent discharged these men "because of their union activity and for the purpose of discouraging membership in the union." We turn to the questions of law which respondent urges in contesting the validity and application of the Act.

First. The scope of the Act.—The Act is challenged in its entirety as an attempt to regulate all industry, thus invading the reserved powers of the States over their local concerns. It is asserted that the references in the Act to interstate and foreign commerce are colorable at best; that the Act is not a true regulation of such commerce or of matters which directly affect it but on the contrary has the fundamental object of placing under the compulsory supervision of the federal government all industrial labor relations within the nation. The argument seeks support in the broad words of the preamble and in the sweep of the provisions of the Act, and it is further insisted that its legislative history shows an essential universal purpose in the light of which its scope cannot be limited by either construction or by the application of the separability clause.

If this conception of terms, intent and consequent inseparability were sound, the Act would necessarily fall by reason of the limitation upon the federal power which inheres in the constitutional grant, as well as because of the explicit reservation of the Tenth Amendment. *Schechter Corporation* v. *United States,* 295 U. S. 495, 549, 550, 554. The authority of the federal government may not be pushed to such an extreme as to destroy the distinction, which the commerce clause itself establishes, between commerce "among the several States" and the internal concerns of a State. That distinction between what is national and what is local in the activities of commerce is vital to the maintenance of our federal system.

But we are not at liberty to deny effect to specific provisions, which Congress has constitutional power to enact, by superimposing upon them inferences from general legislative declarations of an ambiguous character, even if found in the same statute. The cardinal principle of statutory construction is to save and not to destroy. We have repeatedly held that as between two possible interpretations of a statute, by one of which it would be unconstitutional and by the other valid, our plain duty is to adopt that which will save the act. Even to avoid a serious doubt the rule is the same.

We think it clear that the National Labor Relations Act may be construed so as to operate within the sphere of constitutional authority. The jurisdiction conferred upon the Board, and invoked in this instance, is found in Section 10 (a), which provides:

Sec. 10 (a). The Board is empowered, as hereinafter provided, to prevent any person from engaging in any unfair labor practice (listed in section 8) affecting commerce.

The critical words of this provision, prescribing the limits of the Board's authority in dealing with the labor practices, are "affecting commerce." The Act specifically defines the "commerce" to which it refers (sec. 2 (6)):

There can be no question that the commerce thus contemplated by the Act (aside from that within a Territory or the District of Columbia) is interstate and foreign commerce in the constitutional sense. The Act also defines the term "affecting commerce" (sec. 2 (7)):

This definition is one of exclusion as well as inclusion. The grant of authority to the Board does not purport to extend to the relationship between all industrial employees and employers. Its terms do not impose collective bargaining upon all industry regardless of effects upon interstate or foreign commerce. It purports to reach only what may be deemed to burden or obstruct that commerce and, thus qualified, it must be construed as contemplating the exercise of control within constitutional bounds. It is a familiar principle that acts which directly burden or obstruct interstate or foreign commerce, or its free flow, are within the reach of the congressional power. Acts having that effect are not rendered immune because they grow out of labor disputes. It is the effect upon commerce, not the source of the injury, which is the criterion. Whether or not particular action does affect commerce in such a close and intimate fashion as to be subject to federal control, and hence to lie within the authority conferred upon the Board, is left by the statute to be determined as individual cases arise. We are thus to inquire whether in the instant case the constitutional boundary has been passed.

Second. The unfair labor practices in question.—The unfair labor practices found by the Board are those defined in Section 8, subdivisions (1) and (3). These provide:

Sec. 8. It shall be an unfair labor practice for an employer—

(1) To interfere with, restrain, or coerce employees in the exercise of the rights guaranteed in section 7.

(3) By discrimination in regard to hire or ten-

ure of employment or any term or condition of employment to encourage or discourage membership in any labor organization. . . .

Section 8, subdivision (1), refers to Section 7, which is as follows:

SEC. 7. Employees shall have the right to self-organization, to form, join, or assist labor organizations, to bargain collectively through representatives of their own choosing, and to engage in concerted activities, for the purpose of collective bargaining or other mutual aid or protection.

Thus, in its present application, the statute goes no further than to safeguard the right of employees to self-organization and to select representatives of their own choosing for collective bargaining or other mutual protection without restraint or coercion by their employer.

That is a fundamental right. Employees have as clear a right to organize and select their representatives for lawful purposes as the respondent has to organize its business and select its own officers and agents. Discrimination and coercion to prevent the free exercise of the right of employees to self-organization and representation is a proper subject for condemnation by competent legislative authority. Long ago we stated the reason for labor organizations. We said that they were organized out of the necessities of the situation; that a single employee was helpless in dealing with an employer; that he was dependent ordinarily on his daily wage for the maintenance of himself and family; that if the employer refused to pay him the wages that he thought fair, he was nevertheless unable to leave the employ and resist arbitrary and unfair treatment; that union was essential to give laborers opportunity to deal on an equality with their employer. *American Steel Foundries* v. *Tri-City Central Trades Council*, 257 U. S. 184, 209. We reiterated these views when we had under consideration the Railway Labor Act of 1926. Fully recognizing the legality of collective action on the part of employees in order to safeguard their proper interests, we said that Congress was not required to ignore this right but could safeguard it. Congress could seek to make appropriate collective action of employees an instrument of peace rather than of strife. We said that such collective action would be a mockery if representation were made futile

by interference with freedom of choice. Hence the prohibition by Congress of interference with the selection of representatives for the purpose of negotiation and conference between employers and employees, "instead of being an invasion of the constitutional right of either, was based on the recognition of the rights of both." We have reasserted the same principle in sustaining the application of the Railway Labor Act as amended in 1934.

Third. The application of the Act to employees engaged in production.—The principle involved.—Respondent says that whatever may be said of employees engaged in interstate commerce, the industrial relations and activities in the manufacturing department of respondent's enterprise are not subject to federal regulation. The argument rests upon the proposition that manufacturing in itself is not commerce.

The Government distinguishes these cases. The various parts of respondent's enterprise are described as interdependent and as thus involving "a great movement of iron ore, coal and limestone along well-defined paths to the steel mills, thence through them, and thence in the form of steel products into the consuming centers of the country—a definite and well-understood course of business." It is urged that these activities constitute a "stream" or "flow" of commerce, of which the Aliquippa manufacturing plant is the focal point, and that industrial strife at that point would cripple the entire movement. Reference is made to our decision sustaining the Packers and Stockyards Act. The Court found that the stockyards were but a "throat" through which the current of commerce flowed and the transactions which there occurred could not be separated from that movement.

Respondent contends that the instant case presents material distinctions.

We do not find it necessary to determine whether these features of defendant's business dispose of the asserted analogy to the "stream of commerce" cases. The congressional authority to protect interstate commerce from burdens and obstructions is not limited to transactions which can be deemed to be an essential part of a "flow" of interstate or foreign commerce. Burdens and obstructions may be due to injurious action springing from other sources. The fundamental principle is that the power to regulate commerce is the power to enact "all appropriate legislation" for "its protection and advancement"; to adopt measures "to promote its growth and insure its safety"; "to foster, protect, control and restrain." That power is plenary and may be exerted to protect interstate commerce "no matter what the source of the dangers which threaten it." Although activities may be intrastate in character when separately considered, if they have such a close and substantial relation to interstate commerce that their control is essential or appropriate to protect that commerce from burdens and obstructions, Congress cannot be denied the power to exercise that control. Undoubtedly the scope of this power must be considered in the light of our dual system of government and may not be extended so as to embrace effects upon interstate commerce so indirect and remote that to embrace them, in view of our complex society, would effectually obliterate the distinction between what is national and what is local and create a completely centralized government. The question is necessarily one of degree.

That intrastate activities, by reason of close and intimate relation to interstate commerce, may fall within federal control is demonstrated in the case of carriers who are engaged in both interstate and intrastate transportation. There federal control has been found essential to secure the freedom of interstate traffic from interference or unjust discrimination and to promote the efficiency of the interstate service. It is manifest that intrastate rates deal *primarily* with a local activity. But in rate-making they bear such a close relation to interstate rates that effective control of the one must embrace some control over the other. Under the Transportation Act, 1920, Congress went so far as to authorize the Interstate Commerce Commission to establish a state-wide level of intrastate rates in order to prevent an unjust discrimination against interstate commerce. Other illustrations are found in the broad requirements of the Safety Appliance Act and the Hours of Service Act. It is said that this exercise of federal power has relation to the maintenance of adequate instrumentalities of interstate commerce. But the

agency is not superior to the commerce which uses it. The protective power extends to the former because it exists as to the latter.

The close and intimate effect which brings the subject within the reach of federal power may be due to activities in relation to productive industry although the industry when separately viewed is local. This has been abundantly illustrated in the application of the federal Anti-Trust Act.

Upon the same principle, the Anti-Trust Act has been applied to the conduct of employees engaged in production.

It is thus apparent that the fact that the employees here concerned were engaged in production is not determinative. The question remains as to the effect upon interstate commerce of the labor practice involved.

Fourth. Effects of the unfair labor practice in respondent's enterprise.—Giving full weight to respondent's contention with respect to a break in the complete continuity of the "stream of commerce" by reason of respondent's manufacturing operations, the fact remains that the stoppage of those operations by industrial strife would have a most serious effect upon interstate commerce. In view of respondent's far-flung activities, it is idle to say that the effect would be indirect or remote. It is obvious that it would be immediate and might be catastrophic. We are asked to shut our eyes to the plainest facts of our national life and to deal with the question of direct and indirect effects in an intellectual vacuum. Because there may be but indirect and remote effects upon interstate commerce in connection with a host of local enterprises throughout the country, it does not follow that other industrial activities do not have such a close and intimate relation to interstate commerce as to make the presence of industrial strife a matter of the most urgent national concern. When industries organize themselves on a national scale, making their relation to interstate commerce the dominant factor in their activities, how can it be maintained that their industrial labor relations constitute a forbidden field into which Congress may not enter when it is necessary to protect interstate commerce from the paralyzing consequences of industrial war? We have often said that interstate commerce itself is a practical conception. It is equally true that interferences with that commerce must be appraised by a judgment that does not ignore actual experience.

Experience has abundantly demonstrated that the recognition of the right of employees to self-organization and to have representatives of their own choosing for the purpose of collective bargaining is often an essential condition of industrial peace. Refusal to confer and negotiate has been one of the most prolific causes of strife. This is such an outstanding fact in the history of labor disturbances that it is a proper subject of judicial notice and requires no citation of instances. But with respect to the appropriateness of the recognition of self-organization and representation in the promotion of peace, the question is not essentially different in the case of employees in industries of such a character that interstate commerce is put in jeopardy from the case of employees of transportation companies. And of what avail is it to protect the facility of transportation, if interstate commerce is throttled with respect to the commodities to be transported!

These questions have frequently engaged the attention of Congress and have been the subject of many inquiries. The steel industry is one of the great basic industries of the United States, with ramifying activities affecting interstate commerce at every point. The Government aptly refers to the steel strike of 1919–1920 with its far-reaching consequences. The fact that there appears to have been no major disturbance in that industry in the more recent period did not dispose of the possibilities of future and like dangers to interstate commerce which Congress was entitled to foresee and to exercise its protective power to forestall. It is not necessary again to detail the facts as to respondent's enterprise. Instead of being beyond the pale, we think that it presents in a most striking way the close and intimate relation which a manufacturing industry may have to interstate commerce and we have no doubt that Congress had constitutional authority to safeguard the right of respondent's employees to self-organization and freedom in the choice of representatives for collective bargaining.

Fifth. The means which the Act employs. —Questions under the due process clause and other constitutional restrictions.—Respondent asserts its right to conduct its business in an orderly manner without being subjected to arbitrary restraints. What we have said points to the fallacy in the argument. Employees have their correlative right to organize for the purpose of securing the redress of grievances and to promote agreements with employers relating to rates of pay and conditions of work. Restraint for the purpose of preventing an unjust interference with that right cannot be considered arbitrary or capricious.

The Act does not compel agreements between employers and employees. It does not compel any agreement whatever. It does not prevent the employer "from refusing to make a collective contract and hiring individuals on whatever terms" the employer may by unilateral action determine." The Act expressly provides in Section 9 (a) that any individual employee or a group of employees shall have the right at any time to present grievances to their employer. The theory of the Act is that free opportunity for negotiation with accredited representatives of employees is likely to promote industrial peace and may bring about the adjustments and agreements which the Act in itself does not attempt to compel. As we said in *Texas & N. O. R. Co.* v. *Railway Clerks, supra,* and repeated in *Virginian Railway Co.* v. *System Federation, No. 40,* the cases of *Adair* v. *United States,* 208 U. S. 161, and *Coppage* v. *Kansas,* 236 U. S. 1, are inapplicable to legislation of this character. The Act does not interfere with the normal exercise of the right of the employer to select its employees or to discharge them. The employer may not, under cover of that right, intimidate or coerce its employees with respect to their self-organization and representation, and, on the other hand, the Board is not entitled to make its authority a pretext for interference with the right of discharge when that right is exercised for other reasons than such intimidation and coercion. The true purpose is the subject of investigation with full opportunity to show the facts. It would seem that when employers freely recognize the right of their employees to their own organizations and their unrestricted right of representation there will be much less occasion for controversy in respect to the free and appropriate exercise of the right of selection and discharge.

The Act has been criticised as one-sided in its application; that it fails to provide a more comprehensive plan. But we are dealing with the power of Congress, not with a particular policy or with the extent to which policy should go. We have frequently said that the legislative authority, exerted within its proper field, need not embrace all the evils within its reach. The Constitution does not forbid "cautious advance, step by step," in dealing with the evils which are exhibited in activities within the range of legislative power. The question in such cases is whether the legislature, in what it does prescribe, has gone beyond constitutional limits.

Our conclusion is that the order of the Board was within its competency and that the Act is valid as here applied. The judgment of the Circuit Court of Appeals is reversed and the cause is remanded for further proceedings in conformity with this opinion. McREYNOLDS, J., VAN DEVANTER, J., SUTHERLAND, J., and BUTLER, J. dissented.

502. ASSOCIATED PRESS v. NATIONAL LABOR RELATIONS BOARD
301 U. S. 103
1937

On Writ of Certiorari to the U. S. Circuit Court of Appeals for the Second Circuit. The Jones and Laughlin decision (see Doc. No. 501) had already sustained the constitutionality of the Wagner Act on broad grounds. This case involved more particularly the question whether the act, in so far as it affected newspapers, abridged the freedom of the press guaranteed by the First Amendment. For references see Doc. No. 501, and notes in 25 Col. L. Rev. 710, and 32 Ills. L. Rev. 196.

ROBERTS, J. In this case we are to decide whether the National Labor Relations Act, as applied to the petitioner by an order of the National Labor Relations Board, exceeds the power of Congress to regulate commerce pursuant to Article I, Section 8, abridges the freedom of the press guaranteed by the First Amendment, and denies trial by jury in violation of the Seventh Amendment of the Constitution.

In October 1935 the petitioner discharged Morris Watson, an employee in its New York office. The American Newspaper Guild, a labor organization, filed a charge with the Board alleging that Watson's discharge was in violation of Section 7 of the National Labor Relations Act which confers on employes the right to organize, to form, join, or assist labor organizations to bargain collectively through representatives of their own choosing and to engage in concerted activities for the purpose of collective bargaining or other mutual aid or protection; that the petitioner had engaged in unfair labor practices contrary to subsections (1) and (3) of Section 8 by interfering with, restraining or coercing Watson in the exercise of the rights guaranteed him by Section 7 and by discriminating against him in respect of his tenure of employment and discouraging his membership in a labor organization. The Board served a complaint upon the petitioner charging unfair labor practices affecting commerce within the meaning of the statute. The petitioner answered admitting Watson's discharge but denying that it was due to his joining or assisting the Guild or engaging in union activities, and denying, on constitutional grounds, the validity of the act and the jurisdiction of the Board.

Second. Does the statute, as applied to the petitioner, abridge the freedom of speech or of the press safeguarded by the First Amendment? We hold that it does not. It is insisted that the Associated Press is in substance the press itself, that the membership consists solely of persons who own and operate newspapers, that the news is gathered solely for publication in the newspapers of members. Stress is laid upon the facts that this membership consists of persons of every conceivable political, economic, and religious view, that the one thing upon which the members are united is that the Associated Press shall be wholly free from partisan activity or the expression of opinions, that it shall limit its function to reporting events without bias in order that the citizens of our country, if given the facts, may be able to form their own opinions respecting them. The conclusion which the petitioner draws is that whatever may be the case with respect to employes in its mechanical departments it must have absolute and unrestricted freedom to employ and to discharge those who, like Watson, edit the news, that there must not be the slightest opportunity for any bias or prejudice personally entertained by an editorial employe to color or to distort what he writes, and that the Associated Press cannot be free to furnish unbiased and impartial news reports unless it is equally free to determine for itself the partiality or bias of editorial employes. So it is said that any regulation protective of union activities, or the right collectively to bargain on the part of such employes, is necessarily an invalid invasion of the freedom of the press.

We think the contention not only has no relevance to the circumstances of the instant case but is an unsound generalization. The ostensible reason for Watson's discharge, as embodied in the records of the petitioner, is "solely on the grounds of his work not being on a basis for which he has shown capability." The petitioner did not assert and does not now claim that he had shown bias in the past. It does not claim that by reason of his connection with the union he will be likely, as the petitioner honestly believes, to show bias in the future. The actual reason for his discharge, as shown by the unattacked finding of the Board, was his Guild activity and his agitation for collective bargaining. The statute does not preclude a discharge on the ostensible grounds for the petitioner's action; it forbids discharge for what has been found to be the real motive of the petitioner. These considerations answer the suggestion that if the petitioner believed its policy of impartiality was likely to be subverted by Watson's continued service, Congress was without power to interdict his discharge. No such question is here for decision. Neither before the Board, nor in the court below nor here has the petitioner professed such belief. It seeks to bar all regulation by contending that regulation in a situation not presented would be invalid. Courts deal with cases upon the basis of the facts disclosed, never with nonexistent and assumed circumstances.

The act does not compel the petitioner to employ anyone; it does not require that the petitioner retain in its employ an incompetent editor or one who fails faithfully to edit the news to reflect the facts without bias or prejudice. The act permits a discharge for any reason other than union activity or agitation for collective bargaining with employes. The restoration of Watson to his former position in no sense guarantees his continuance in petitioner's employ. The petitioner is at liberty, whenever occasion may arise, to exercise its undoubted right to sever his relationship for any cause that seems to it proper save only as a punishment for, or discouragement of, such activities as the act declares permissible.

The business of the Associated Press is not immune from regulation because it is an agency of the press. The publisher of a newspaper has no special immunity from the application of general laws. He has no special privilege to invade the rights and liberties of others. He must answer for libel. He may be punished for contempt of court. He is subject to the anti-trust laws. Like others he must pay equitable and nondiscriminatory taxes on his business. The regulation here in question has no relation whatever to the impartial distribution of news. The order of the Board in nowise circumscribes the full freedom and liberty of the petitioner to publish the news as it desires it published or to enforce policies of its own choosing with respect to the editing and rewriting of news for publication, and the petitioner is free at any time to discharge Watson or any editorial employe who fails to comply with the policies it may adopt.

The judgment of the Circuit Court of Appeals is affirmed.

SUTHERLAND, J., VAN DEVANTER, J., McREYNOLDS, J., and BUTLER, J. dissented.

503. THE SOCIAL SECURITY ACT
August 14, 1935

(U. S. Statutes at Large, Vol. XLIX, p. 620)

Social security legislation began in the States as early as 1929, but it was not until the depression had run its course for six years that the Federal government took action in the matter.

The assumption of national responsibility for general social security constitutes a notable chapter in the history of federal centralization in the United States. For social security, see A. Epstein,

Insecurity; I. M. Rubinow, *The Quest for Security;* P. Douglas and A. Director, *The Problem of Unemployment;* P. Douglas, *Social Security in the United States;* M. Stevenson and R. Spear, *The Social Security Program;* J. R. Commons, *Unemployment Insurance;* J. B. Ewing, *Job Insurance;* The Social Security Board, *Social Security in America; Economic Security Act: Hearings before the Committee on Finance,* U. S. Sen., 74th Cong. 1st sess. on S 1130; H. Malisoff, "Emergence of Unemployment Compensation" 54 Pol. Sci. Qt.

An Act to provide for the general welfare by establishing a system of Federal old-age benefits, and by enabling the several States to make more adequate provision for aged persons, blind persons, dependent and crippled children, maternal and child welfare, public health, and the administration of their unemployment compensation laws; to establish a Social Security Board; to raise revenue; and for other purposes.

Be it enacted by the Senate and House of Representatives of the United States of America in Congress assembled,

TITLE I—GRANTS TO STATES FOR OLD AGE ASSISTANCE

APPROPRIATION

SECTION 1. For the purpose of enabling each State to furnish financial assistance, as far as practicable under the conditions in such State, to aged needy individuals, there is hereby authorized to be appropriated for the fiscal year ending June 30, 1936, the sum of $49,750,000, and there is hereby authorized to be appropriated for each fiscal year thereafter a sum sufficient to carry out the purposes of this title. The sums made available under this section shall be used for making payments to States which have submitted, and had approved by the Social Security Board established by Title VII, State plans for old-age assistance.

STATE OLD-AGE ASSISTANCE PLANS

SEC. 2. (a) A State plan for old-age assistance must (1) provide that it shall be in effect in all political subdivisions of the State, and, if administered by them, be mandatory upon them; (2) provide for financial participation by the State; (3) either provide for the establishment or designation of a single State agency to administer the plan, or provide for the establishment or designation of a single State agency to supervise the administration of the plan; (4) provide for granting to any individual, whose claim for old-age assistance is denied, an opportunity for a fair hearing before such State agency; (5) provide such methods of administration (other than those relating to selection, tenure of office, and compensation of personnel) as are found by the Board to be necessary for the efficient operation of the plan; (6) provide that the State agency will make such reports, in such form and containing such information, as the Board may from time to time require, and comply with such provisions as the Board may from time to time find necessary to assure the correctness and verification of such reports; and (7) provide that, if the State or any of its political subdivisions collects from the estate of any recipient of old-age assistance any amount with respect to old-age assistance furnished him under the plan, one-half of the net amount so collected shall be promptly paid to the United States. Any payment so made shall be deposited in the Treasury to the credit of the appropriation for the purposes of this title.

(b) The Board shall approve any plan which fulfills the conditions specified in subsection (a), except that it shall not approve any plan which imposes, as a condition of eligibility for old-age assistance under the plan—

(1) An age requirement of more than sixty-five years, except that the plan may impose, effective until January 1, 1940, an age requirement of as much as seventy years; or

(2) Any residence requirement which excludes any resident of the State who has resided therein five years during the nine years immediately preceding the application for old-age assistance and has resided therein continuously for one year immediately preceding the application; or

(3) Any citizenship requirement which excludes any citizen of the United States.

PAYMENT TO STATES

SEC. 3. (a) From the sums appropriated therefor, the Secretary of the Treasury shall pay to each State which has an approved plan for old-age assistance, for each quarter, beginning with the quarter commencing July 1, 1935, (1) an amount, which shall be used exclusively as old-age assistance, equal to one-half of the total of the sums expended during such quarter as old-age assistance under the State plan with respect to each individual who at the time of such expenditure is sixty-five years of age or older and is not an inmate of a public institution, not counting so much of such expenditure with respect to any individual for any month as exceeds $30, and (2) 5 per centum of such amount, which shall be used for paying the costs of administering the State plan or for old-age assistance, or both, and for no other purpose: *Provided,* That the State plan, in order to be approved by the Board, need not provide for financial participation before July 1, 1937 by the State, in the case of any State which the Board, upon application by the State and after reasonable notice and opportunity for hearing to the State, finds is prevented by its constitution from providing such financial participation.

(b) The method of computing and paying such amounts shall be as follows:

(1) The Board shall, prior to the beginning of each quarter, estimate the amount to be paid to the State for such quarter under the provisions of clause (1) of subsection (a), such estimate to be based on (A) a report filed by the State containing its estimate of the total sum to be expended in such quarter in accordance with the provisions of such clause, and stating the amount appropriated or made available by the State and its political subdivisions for such expenditures in such quarter, and if such amount is less than one-half of the total sum of such estimated expenditures, the source or sources from which the difference is expected to be derived, (B) records showing the number of aged individuals in the State, and (C) such other investigation as the Board may find necessary. . . .

TITLE II—FEDERAL OLD-AGE BENEFITS

OLD-AGE RESERVE ACCOUNT

SECTION 201. (a) There is hereby created an account in the Treasury of the United States to be known as the "Old-Age Reserve Account." . . .

OLD-AGE BENEFIT PAYMENTS

SEC. 202. (a) Every qualified individual shall be entitled to receive, with respect to the period beginning on the date he attains the age of sixty-five, or on January 1, 1942, whichever is the later, and ending on the date of his death, an old-age benefit (payable as nearly as practicable in equal monthly installments) as follows:

(1) If the total wages determined by the Board to have been paid to him, with respect to employment after December 31, 1936, and before he attained the age of sixty-five, were not more than $3,000, the old-age benefit shall be at a monthly rate of one-half of 1 per centum of such total wages;

(2) If such total wages were more than $3,000, the old-age benefit shall be at a monthly rate equal to the sum of the following:

(A) One-half of 1 per centum of $3,000; plus

(B) One-twelfth of 1 per centum of the amount by which such total wages exceeded $3,000 and did not exceed $45,-000; plus

(C) One-twenty-fourth of 1 per centum of the amount by which such total wages exceeded $45,000.

(b) In no case shall the monthly rate computed under subsection (a) exceed $85. . . .

PAYMENTS UPON DEATH

SEC. 203. (a) If any individual dies before attaining the age of sixty-five, there shall be paid to his estate an amount equal to 3½ per centum of the total wages determined by the Board to have been paid to him, with respect to employment after December 31, 1936. . . .

PAYMENTS TO AGED INDIVIDUALS NOT QUALIFIED FOR BENEFITS

SEC. 204. (a) There shall be paid in a lump sum to any individual who, upon attaining the age of sixty-five, is not a qualified individual, an amount equal to 3½ per centum of the total wages determined by the Board to have been paid to him, with respect to employ·

ment after December 31, 1936, and before he attained the age of sixty-five.

(b) After any individual becomes entitled to any payment under subsection (a), no other payment shall be made under this title in any manner measured by wages paid to him, except that any part of any payment under subsection (a) which is not paid to him before his death shall be paid to his estate. . . .

SEC. 210. . . .

(b) The term "employment" means any service, of whatever nature, performed within the United States by an employee for his employer, except—

(1) Agricultural labor;

(2) Domestic service in a private home;

(3) Casual labor not in the course of the employer's trade or business;

(4) Service performed as an officer or member of the crew of a vessel documented under the laws of the United States or of any foreign country;

(5) Service performed in the employ of the United States Government or of an instrumentality of the United States;

(6) Service performed in the employ of a State, a political subdivision thereof, or an instrumentality of one or more States or political subdivisions;

(7) Service performed in the employ of a corporation, community chest, fund, or foundation, organized and operated exclusively for religious, charitable, scientific, literary, or educational purposes, or for the prevention of cruelty to children or animals, no part of the net earnings of which inures to the benefit of any private shareholder or individual. . . .

TITLE III—GRANTS TO STATES FOR UNEMPLOYMENT COMPENSATION ADMINISTRATION

APPROPRIATION

SECTION 301. For the purpose of assisting the States in the administration of their unemployment compensation laws, there is hereby authorized to be appropriated, for the fiscal year ending June 30, 1936, the sum of $4,000,000, and for each fiscal year thereafter the sum of 49,000,000, to be used as hereinafter provided.

PAYMENTS TO STATES

SEC. 302. (a) The Board shall from time to time certify to the Secretary of the Treasury for payment to each State which has an unemployment compensation law approved by the Board under Title IX, such amounts as the Board determines to be necessary for the proper administration of such law during the fiscal year in which such payment is to be made. The Board's determination shall be based on (1) the population of the State; (2) an estimate of the number of persons covered by the State law and the cost of proper administration of such law; and (3) such other factors as the Board finds relevant. The Board shall not certify for payment under this section in any fiscal year a total amount in excess of the amount appropriated therefor for such fiscal year. . . .

PROVISIONS OF STATE LAWS

SEC. 303. (a) The Board shall make no certification for payment to any State unless it finds that the law of such State, approved by the Board under Title IX, includes provisions for—

(1) Such methods of administration (other than those relating to selection, tenure of office, and compensation of personnel) as are found by the Board to be reasonably calculated to insure full payment of unemployment compensation when due; and

(2) Payment of unemployment compensation solely through public employment offices in the State or such other agencies as the Board may approve; and

(3) Opportunity for a fair hearing, before an impartial tribunal, for all individuals whose claims for unemployment compensation are denied; and

(4) The payment of all money received in the unemployment fund of such State, immediately upon such receipt, to the Secretary of the Treasury to the credit of the Unemployment Trust Fund established by section 904; and

(5) Expenditure of all money requisitioned by the State agency from the Unemployment Trust Fund, in the payment of unemployment compensation, exclusive of expenses of administration; and

(6) The making of such reports, in such

form and containing such information, as the Board may from time to time require, and compliance with such provisions as the Board may from time to time find necessary to assure the correctness and verification of such reports; and

(7) Making available upon request to any agency of the United States charged with the administration of public works or assistance through public employment, the name, address, ordinary occupation and employment status of each recipient of unemployment compensation, and a statement of such recipient's rights to further compensation under such law.

(b) Whenever the Board, after reasonable notice and opportunity for hearing to the State agency charged with the administration of the State law, finds that in the administration of the law there is—

(1) a denial, in a substantial number of cases, of unemployment compensation to individuals entitled thereto under such law; or

(2) a failure to comply substantially with any provision specified in subsection (a);

the Board shall notify such State agency that further payments will not be made to the State until the Board is satisfied that there is no longer any such denial or failure to comply. Until it is so satisfied it shall make no further certification to the Secretary of the Treasury with respect to such State. . . .

TITLE IV—GRANTS TO STATES FOR AID TO DEPENDENT CHILDREN

APPROPRIATION

SECTION 401. For the purpose of enabling each State to furnish financial assistance, as far as practicable under the conditions in such State, to needy dependent children, there is hereby authorized to be appropriated for the fiscal year ending June 30, 1936, the sum of $24,750,000, and there is hereby authorized to be appropriated for each fiscal year thereafter a sum sufficient to carry out the purposes of this title. The sums made available under this section shall be used for making payments to States which have submitted, and had approved by the Board, State plans for aid to dependent children. . . .

PAYMENT TO STATES

SEC. 403. (a) From the sums appropriated therefor, the Secretary of the Treasury shall pay to each State which has an approved plan for aid to dependent children, for each quarter, beginning with the quarter commencing July 1, 1935, an amount, which shall be used exclusively for carrying out the State plan, equal to one-third of the total of the sums expended during such quarter under such plan, not counting so much of such expenditure with respect to any dependent child for any month as exceeds $18, or if there is more than one dependent child in the same home, as exceeds $18 for any month with respect to one such dependent child and $12 for such month with respect to each of the other dependent children. . . .

DEFINITIONS

SEC. 406. When used in this title—

(a) The term "dependent child" means a child under the age of sixteen who has been deprived of parental support or care by reason of the death, continued absence from the home, or physical or mental incapacity of a parent, and who is living with his father, mother, grandfather, grandmother, brother, sister, stepfather, stepmother, step brother, stepsister, uncle, or aunt, in a place of residence maintained by one or more of such relatives as his or their own home. . . .

TITLE V—GRANTS TO STATES FOR MATERNAL AND CHILD WELFARE

PART 1—MATERNAL AND CHILD HEALTH SERVICES

APPROPRIATION

SECTION 501. For the purpose of enabling each State to extend and improve, as far as practicable under the conditions in such State, services for promoting the health of mothers and children, especially in rural areas and in areas suffering from severe economic distress, there is hereby authorized to be appropriated for each fiscal year, beginning with the fiscal year ending June 30, 1936, the sum of $3,800,000. The sums made available under this section shall be used for making payments to States which have submitted, and had approved by the Chief of the Children's Bureau, State plans for such services.

ALLOTMENTS TO STATES

SEC. 502. (a) Out of the sums appropriated pursuant to section 501 for each fiscal year the Secretary of Labor shall allot to each State $20,000, and such part of $1,800,000 as he finds that the number of live births in such State bore to the total number of live births in the United States, in the latest calendar year for which the Bureau of the Census has available statistics.

(b) Out of the sums appropriated pursuant to section 501 for each fiscal year the Secretary of Labor shall allot to the States $980,000 (in addition to the allotments made under subsection (a)), according to the financial need for each State for assistance in carrying out its State plan, as determined by him after taking into consideration the number of live births in such State. . . .

APPROVAL OF STATE PLANS

SEC. 503. (a) A State plan for maternal and child-health services must (1) provide for financial participation by the State; (2) provide for the administration of the plan by the State health agency or the supervision of the administration of the plan by the State health agency; (3) provide such methods of administration (other than those relating to selection, tenure of office, and compensation of personnel) as are necessary for the efficient operation of the plan; (4) provide that the State health agency will make such reports, in such form and containing such information, as the Secretary of Labor may from time to time require, and comply with such provisions as he may from time to time find necessary to assure the correctness and verification of such reports; (5) provide for the extension and improvement of local maternal and child-health services administered by local child-health units; (6) provide for cooperation with medical, nursing, and welfare groups and organizations; and (7) provide for the development of demonstration services in needy areas and among groups in special need. . . .

PART 2—SERVICES FOR CRIPPLED CHILDREN
APPROPRIATION

SEC. 511. For the purpose of enabling each State to extend and improve (especially in rural areas and in areas suffering from severe economic distress), as far as practicable under the conditions in such State, services for lo-

cating crippled children, and for providing medical, surgical, corrective, and other services and care, and facilities for diagnosis, hospitalization, and aftercare, for children who are crippled or who are suffering from conditions which lead to crippling, there is hereby authorized to be appropriated for each fiscal year, beginning with the fiscal year ending June 30, 1936, the sum of $2,850,000. The sums made available under this section shall be used for making payments to States which have submitted, and had approved by the Chief of the Children's Bureau, State plans for such services.

ALLOTMENTS TO STATES

SEC. 512. (a) Out of the sums appropriated pursuant to section 511 for each fiscal year the Secretary of Labor shall allot to each State $20,000, and the remainder to the States according to the need of each State as determined by him after taking into consideration the number of crippled children in such State in need of the services referred to in section 511 and the cost of furnishing such services to them.

PART 3—CHILD-WELFARE SERVICES

SEC. 521. (a) For the purpose of enabling the United States, through the Children's Bureau, to cooperate with State public-welfare agencies in establishing, extending, and strengthening, especially in predominantly rural areas, public-welfare services (hereinafter in this section referred to as "child-welfare services") for the protection and care of homeless, dependent, and neglected children, and children in danger of becoming delinquent, there is hereby authorized to be appropriated for each fiscal year, beginning with the fiscal year ending June 30, 1936, the sum of $1,500,000. Such amount shall be allotted by the Secretary of Labor for use by cooperating State public-welfare agencies on the basis of plans developed jointly by the State agency and the Children's Bureau, to each State, $10,000, and the remainder to each State on the basis of such plans, not to exceed such part of the remainder as the rural population of such State bears to the total rural population of the United States. The amount so allotted shall be expended for payment of part of the cost of district, county or other local child-welfare services in areas predominantly rural, and for developing State services for the encouragement and assistance of adequate methods of community child-welfare organization in areas predominantly rural and other areas of special need. . . .

PART 4—VOCATIONAL REHABILITATION

SEC. 531. (a) In order to enable the United States to cooperate with the States and Hawaii in extending and strengthening their programs of vocational rehabilitation of the physically disabled, and to continue to carry out the provisions and purposes of the Act entitled "An Act to provide for the promotion of vocational rehabilitation of persons disabled in industry or otherwise and their return to civil employment," approved June 2, 1920, . . . there is hereby authorized to be appropriated for the fiscal years ending June 30, 1936, and June 30, 1937, the sum of $841,000 for each such fiscal year in addition to the amount of the existing authorization, and for each fiscal year thereafter the sum of $1,938,000.

TITLE VI—PUBLIC HEALTH WORK

APPROPRIATION

SECTION 601. For the purpose of assisting States, counties, health districts, and other political subdivisions of the States in establishing and maintaining adequate public-health services, including the training of personnel for State and local health work, there is hereby authorized to be appropriated for each fiscal year, beginning with the fiscal year ending June 30, 1936, the sum of $8,000,000 to be used as hereinafter provided.

STATE AND LOCAL PUBLIC HEALTH SERVICES

SEC. 602. (a) The Surgeon General of the Public Health Service, with the approval of the Secretary of the Treasury, shall, at the beginning of each fiscal year, allot to the States the total of (1) the amount appropriated for such year pursuant to section 601; and (2) the amounts of the allotments under this section for the preceding fiscal year remaining unpaid to the States at the end of such fiscal year. The amounts of such allotments shall be determined on the basis of (1) the population; (2) the special health problems; and (3) the financial needs; of the

respective States. Upon making such allotments the Surgeon General of the Public Health Service shall certify the amounts thereof to the Secretary of the Treasury.

(b) The amount of an allotment to any State under subsection (a) for any fiscal year, remaining unpaid at the end of such fiscal year, shall be available for allotment to States under subsection (a) for the succeeding fiscal year, in addition to the amount appropriated for such year.

(c) Prior to the beginning of each quarter of the fiscal year, the Surgeon General of the Public Health Service shall, with the approval of the Secretary of the Treasury, determine in accordance with rules and regulations previously prescribed by such Surgeon General after consultation with a conference of the State and Territorial health authorities, the amount to be paid to each State for such quarter from the allotment to such State, and shall certify the amount so determined to the Secretary of the Treasury. Upon receipt of such certification, the Secretary of the Treasury shall, through the Division of Disbursement of the Treasury Department and prior to audit or settlement by the General Accounting Office, pay in accordance with such certification.

(d) The moneys so paid to any State shall be expended solely in carrying out the purposes specified in section 601, and in accordance with plans presented by the health authority of such State and approved by the Surgeon General of the Public Health Service.

INVESTIGATIONS

SEC. 603. (a) There is hereby authorized to be appropriated for each fiscal year, beginning with the fiscal year ending June 30, 1936, the sum of $2,000,000 for expenditure by the Public Health Service for investigation of disease and problems of sanitation. . . .

TITLE VII—SOCIAL SECURITY BOARD

ESTABLISHMENT

SECTION 701. There is hereby established a Social Security Board to be composed of three members to be appointed by the President, by and with the advice and consent of the Senate. During his term of membership on the Board, no member shall engage in any other business, vocation, or employment. Not more than two of the members of the Board shall be members of the same political party. Each member shall receive a salary at the rate of $10,000 a year and shall hold office for a term of six years, . . .

DUTIES OF SOCIAL SECURITY BOARD

SEC. 702. The Board shall perform the duties imposed upon it by this Act and shall also have the duty of studying and making recommendations as to the most effective methods of providing economic security through social insurance, and as to legislation and matters of administrative policy concerning old-age pensions, unemployment compensation, accident compensation, and related subjects. . . .

TITLE VIII—TAXES WITH RESPECT TO EMPLOYMENT

INCOME TAX ON EMPLOYEES

SECTION 801. In addition to other taxes, there shall be levied, collected, and paid upon the income of every individual a tax equal to the following percentages of the wages (as defined in section 811) received by him after December 31, 1936, with respect to employment (as defined in section 811) after such date:

(1) With respect to employment during the calendar years 1937, 1938, and 1939, the rate shall be 1 per centum.

(2) With respect to employment during the calendar years 1940, 1941, and 1942, the rate shall be 1½ per centum.

(3) With respect to employment during the calendar years 1943, 1944, and 1945, the rate shall be 2 per centum.

(4) With respect to employment during the calendar years 1946, 1947, and 1948, the rate shall be 2½ per centum.

(5) With respect to employment after December 31, 1948, the rate shall be 3 per centum.

DEDUCTION OF TAX FROM WAGES

SEC. 802. (a) The tax imposed by section 801 shall be collected by the employer of the taxpayer, by deducting the amount of the tax from the wages as and when paid. . . .

EXCISE TAX ON EMPLOYERS

SEC. 804. In addition to other taxes, every employer shall pay an excise tax, with respect to having individuals in his employ, equal to the following percentages of the wages (as defined in section 811) paid by him after December 31, 1936, with respect to employment (as defined in section 811) after such date:

(1) With respect to employment during the calendar years 1937, 1938, and 1939, the rate shall be 1 per centum.

(2) With respect to employment during the calendar years 1940, 1941, and 1942, the rate shall be 1½ per centum.

(3) With respect to employment during the calendar years 1943, 1944, and 1945, the rate shall be 2 per centum.

(4) With respect to employment during the calendar years 1946, 1947, and 1948, the rate shall be 2½ per centum.

(5) With respect to employment after December 31, 1948, the rate shall be 3 per centum. . . .

DEFINITIONS

SEC. 811. When used in this title— . . .

(b) The term "employment" means any service, of whatever nature, performed within the United States by an employee for his employer, except—

(1) Agricultural labor;

(2) Domestic service in a private home;

(3) Casual labor not in the course of the employer's trade or business;

(4) Service performed by an individual who has attained the age of sixty-five;

(5) Service performed as an officer or member of the crew of a vessel documented under the laws of the United States or of any foreign country;

(6) Service performed in the employ of the United States Government or of an instrumentality of the United States;

(7) Service performed in the employ of a State, a political subdivision thereof, or an instrumentality of one or more States or political subdivisions;

(8) Service performed in the employ of a corporation, community chest, fund, or foundation, organized and operated exclusively for religious, charitable, scientific, literary, or educational purposes, or for the

prevention of cruelty to children or animals, no part of the net earnings of which inures to the benefit of any private shareholder or individual.

TITLE IX—TAX ON EMPLOYERS OF EIGHT OR MORE
IMPOSITION OF TAX

SECTION 901. On and after January 1, 1936, every employer shall pay for each calendar year an excise tax, with respect to having individuals in his employ, equal to the following percentages of the total wages payable by him with respect to employment during such calendar year:

(1) With respect to employment during the calendar year 1936 the rate shall be 1 per centum;

(2) With respect to employment during the calendar year 1937 the rate shall be 2 per centum;

(3) With respect to employment after December 31, 1937, the rate shall be 3 per centum. . . .

CERTIFICATION OF STATE LAWS

SEC. 903. (a) The Social Security Board shall approve any State law submitted to it, within thirty days of such submission, which it finds provides that—

(1) All compensation is to be paid through public employment offices in the State or such other agencies as the Board may approve;

(2) No compensation shall be payable with respect to any day of unemployment occurring within two years after the first day of the first period with respect to which contributions are required;

(3) All money received in the unemployment fund shall immediately upon such receipt be paid over to the Secretary of the Treasury to the credit of the Unemployment Trust Fund. . . .

(5) Compensation shall not be denied in such State to any otherwise eligible individual for refusing to accept new work under any of the following conditions: (A) If the position offered is vacant due directly to a strike, lockout, or other labor dispute; (B) if the wages, hours, or other conditions of the work offered are substantially less fa-

vorable to the individual than those prevailing for similar work in the locality; (C) if as a condition of being employed the individual would be required to join a company union or to resign from or refrain from joining any bona fide labor organization.

UNEMPLOYMENT TRUST FUND

SEC. 904. (a) There is hereby established in the Treasury of the United States a trust fund to be known as the "Unemployment Trust Fund, . . ."

(b) It shall be the duty of the Secretary of the Treasury to invest such portion of the Fund as is not, in his judgment, required to meet current withdrawals. Such investment may be made only in interest bearing obligations of the United States or in obligations guaranteed as to both principal and interest by the United States. . . .

INTERSTATE COMMERCE

SEC. 906. No person required under a State law to make payments to an unemployment fund shall be relieved from compliance therewith on the ground that he is engaged in interstate commerce, or that the State law does not distinguish between employees engaged in interstate commerce and those engaged in intrastate commerce.

DEFINITIONS

SEC. 907. When used in this title—

(a) The term "employer" does not include any person unless on each of some twenty days during the taxable year, each day being in a different calendar week, the total number of individuals who were in his employ for some portion of the day (whether or not at the same moment of time) was eight or more. . . .

TITLE X—GRANTS TO STATES FOR AID TO THE BLIND
APPROPRIATION

SECTION 1001. For the purpose of enabling each State to furnish financial assistance, as far as practicable under the conditions in such State, to needy individuals who are blind, there is hereby authorized to be appropriated for the fiscal year ending June 30, 1936, the sum of $3,000,000, and there is hereby authorized to be appropriated for each fiscal year thereafter a sum sufficient to carry out the purposes of this title. The sums made available under this section shall be used for making payments to States which have submitted, and had approved by the Social Security Board, State plans for aid to the blind. . . .

504. STEWARD MACHINE CO. v. DAVIS
301 U. S. 548
1937

Writ of Certiorari of U. S. Circuit Court of Appeals. This case involved the constitutionality of the tax imposed by the Social Security Act of 1935. For refs. see Doc. No. 503 and Nicholson, "Recent Decisions on the Power to Spend for the General Welfare," 12 Temple L. Qt. 435; Herbert, "General Welfare Clauses in the Constitution of the U. S.," 7 Fordham L. Rev. 390; Brebner-Smith, "Judicial limitations on Federal appropriations," 25 Virginia L. Rev. 613; Lowndes," "The Supreme Court on Taxation, 1936 Term," 86 U. of Pa. L. Rev. 1; Denby, "The Case against the Constitutionality of the Social Security Act," 3 Law and Contemporary Problems, 315.

CARDOZO, J. The validity of the tax imposed by the Social Security Act on employers of eight or more is here to be determined.

Petitioner, an Alabama corporation, paid a tax in accordance with the statute, filed a claim for refund with the Commissioner of Internal Revenue, and sued to recover the payment (46.14), asserting a conflict between the statute and the Constitution of the United States. Upon demurrer the District Court gave judgment for the defendant dismissing the complaint, and the Circuit Court of Appeals for the Fifth Circuit affirmed. . . . An important question of constitutional law being involved, we granted certiorari.

The Social Security Act is divided into eleven separate titles, of which only Titles IX and III are so related to this case as to stand in need of summary. [See Doc. No. 503]. . . .

The assault on the statute proceeds on an extended front. Its assailants take the ground that the tax is not an excise; that it is not uniform throughout the United States as excises are required to be; that its exceptions are so many and arbitrary as to violate the Fifth Amendment; that its purpose was not revenue, but an unlawful invasion of the reserved powers of the states; and that the states in submitting to it have yielded to coercion and have abandoned governmental functions which they are not permitted to surrender.

The objections will be considered seriatim with such further explanation as may be necessary to make their meaning clear.

First: The tax, which is described in the statute as an excise, is laid with uniformity throughout the United States as a duty, an impost or an excise upon the relation of employment.

1. We are told that the relation of employment is one so essential to the pursuit of happiness that it may not be burdened with a tax. Appeal is made to history. From the precedents of colonial days we are supplied with illustrations of excises common in the colonies. They are said to have been bound up with the enjoyment of particular commodities. Appeal is also made to principle or the analysis of concepts. An excise, we are told, imports a tax upon a privilege; employment, it is said, is a right, not a privilege, from which it follows that employment is not subject to an excise. Neither the one appeal nor the other leads to the desired goal. . . .

The historical prop failing, the prop or fancied prop of principle remains. We learn that employment for lawful gain is a "natural" or "inherent" or "inalienable" right, and not a "privilege" at all. But natural rights, so called, are as much subject to taxation as rights of less importance. An excise is not limited to vocations or activities that may be prohibited altogether. It is not limited to those that are the outcome of a franchise. It extends to vocations or activities pursued as of common right. What the individual does in the operation of a business is amenable to taxation just as much as what he owns, at all events if the classification is not tyrannical or arbitrary. "Business is as legitimate an object of the taxing powers as property." *City of Newton* v. *Atchison*, 31 Kan. 151, 154 (per Brewer, J.). Indeed, ownership itself, as we had occasion to point out the other day, is only a bundle of rights and privileges invested with a single name. *Henneford* v. *Silas Mason Co., Inc.*, March 29, 1937, 300 U. S. 577. . . . Employment is a business relation, if not itself a business. It is a relation without which business could seldom be carried on effectively. The power to tax the activities and relations that constitute a calling considered as a unit is the power to tax any of them. The whole includes the parts.

The subject matter of taxation open to the power of the Congress is as comprehensive as that open to the power of the states, though the method of apportionment may at times be different. "The Congress shall have power to lay and collect taxes, duties, imposts and excises." Art. 1, § 8. If the tax is a direct one, it shall be apportioned according to the census or enumeration. If it is a duty, impost, or excise, it shall be uniform throughout the United States. Together, these classes include every form of tax appropriate to sovereignty. Whether the tax is to be classified as an "excise" is in truth not of critical importance. If not that, it is an "impost" or a "duty." A capitation or other "direct" tax it certainly is not. "Although there have been from time to time intimations that there might be some tax which was not a direct tax nor included under the words 'duties, imposts and excises,' such a tax for more than one hundred years of national existence has as yet remained undiscovered, notwithstanding the stress of particular circumstances has invited thorough investigation into sources of powers." *Pollock* v. *Farmers' Loan and Trust Co.*, 157 U. S. 429, 557. There is no departure from that thought in later cases, but rather a new emphasis of it. Thus, in *Thomas* v. *United States*, 192 U. S. 363, 370, it was said of the words "duties, imposts and excises" that "they were used comprehensively to cover customs and excise duties imposed on importation, consumption, manufacture and sale of certain commodities, privileges, particular business transactions, vocations, occupations and the like." At times taxpayers have contended that the Congress is without power to lay an excise on the enjoyment of a privilege created by state law. The contention has been put aside as baseless. Congress may tax the transmission of property by inheritance or will, though the states and not Congress have created the privilege of succession. Congress may tax the enjoyment of a corporate franchise, though a state and not Congress has brought the franchise into being. The statute books of the states are strewn with illustrations of taxes laid on occupations pursued of common right. We find no basis for a holding that the power in that regard which belongs by accepted practice to the legislatures of the states, has been denied by the Constitution to the Congress of the nation.

2. The tax being an excise, its imposition must conform to the canon of uniformity. There has been no departure from this requirement. According to the settled doctrine the uniformity exacted is geographical, not intrinsic. . . .

Second: The excise is not invalid under the provisions of the Fifth Amendment by force of its exemptions.

The statute does not apply, as we have seen, to employers of less than eight. It does not apply to agricultural labor, or domestic service in a private home or to some other classes of less importance. Petitioner contends that the effect of these restrictions is an arbitrary discrimination vitiating the tax.

The Fifth Amendment unlike the Fourteenth has no equal protection clause. But even the states, though subject to such a clause, are not confined to a formula of rigid uniformity in framing measures of taxation. They may tax some kinds of property at one rate, and others at another, and exempt others altogether. They may lay an excise on the operations of a particular kind of business, and exempt some other kind of business closely akin thereto. If this latitude of judgment is lawful for the states, it is lawful, a fortiori, in legislation by the Congress, which is subject to restraints less narrow and confining.

The classifications and exemptions directed by the statute now in controversy have support in considerations of policy and practical convenience that cannot be condemned as arbitrary. The classifications and exemptions would therefore be upheld if they had been adopted by a state and the provisions of the Fourteenth Amendment were invoked to annul them. This is held in two cases passed upon today in which precisely the same provisions were the subject of attack, the provisions being contained in the Unemployment Compensation Law of the State of Alabama. *Carmichael* v. *Southern Coal & Coke Co.*, No. 724, 301 U. S. 495, and *Carmichael* v. *Gulf States Paper Corp.*, No. 797, 301 U. S. ——. The opinion rendered in those cases covers the ground fully. It would be useless to repeat the argument. The act of Congress is therefore valid, so far at least as its system of exemptions is concerned, and this though we assume that discrimination, if gross enough, is equivalent to confiscation and subject under the Fifth Amendment to challenge and annulment.

Third: The excise is not void as involving the coercion of the States in contravention of the Tenth Amendment or of restrictions implicit in our federal form of government.

The proceeds of the excise when collected are paid into the Treasury at Washington, and therefore are subject to appropriation like public moneys generally. No presumption can be indulged that they will be misapplied or wasted. Even if they were collected in the hope or expectation that some other and collateral good would be furthered as an incident, that without more would not make the act invalid. This indeed is hardly questioned. The case for the petitioner is built on the contention that here an ulterior aim is wrought into the very structure of the act, and what is even more important that the aim is not only ulterior, but essentially unlawful. In particular, the 90 per cent credit is relied upon as supporting that conclusion. But before the statute succumbs to an assault upon these lines, two propositions must be made out by the assailant. There must be a showing in the first place that separated from the credit the revenue provisions are incapable of standing by themselves. There must be a showing in the second place that the tax and the credit in combination are weapons of coercion, destroying or impairing the autonomy of the states. The truth of each proposition being essential to the success of the assault, we pass for convenience to a consideration of the second, without pausing to inquire whether there has been a demonstration of the first.

To draw the line intelligently between duress and inducement there is need to remind ourselves of facts as to the problem of unemployment that are now matters of common knowledge. . . . The fact developed quickly that the states were unable to give the requisite relief. The problem had become national in area and dimensions. There was need of help from the nation if the people were not to starve. It is too late today for the argument to be heard with tolerance that in a crisis so extreme the use of the moneys of the nation to relieve the unemployed and their dependents is a use for any purpose narrower than the promotion of the general welfare. The nation responded to the call of the distressed. Between January 1, 1933 and July 1, 1936, the states (according to statistics submitted by the Government) incurred obligations of $689,291,802 for emergency relief; local subdivisions an additional $775,675,366. In the same period the obligations for emergency relief incurred by the national government were $2,929,307,125, or twice the obligations of states and local agencies combined. According to the President's budget message for the fiscal year 1938, the national government expended for public works and unemployment relief for the three fiscal years 1934, 1935, and 1936, the stupendous total of $8,681,000,000. The *parens patriae* has many reasons—fiscal and economic as well as social and moral—for planning to mitigate disasters that bring these burdens in their train.

In the presence of this urgent need for some remedial expedient, the question is to be answered whether the expedient adopted has overlept the bounds of power. The assailants of the statute say that its dominant end and aim is to drive the state legislatures under the whip of economic pressure into the enactment of unemployment compensation laws at the bidding of the central government. Supporters of the statute say that its operation is not constraint, but the creation of a larger freedom, the states and the nation joining in a coöperative endeavor to avert a common evil. Before Congress acted, unemployment compensation insurance was still, for the most part, a project and no more. Wisconsin was the pioneer. Her statute was adopted in 1931. At times bills for such insurance were introduced elsewhere, but they did not reach the stage of law. In 1935 four states (California, Massachusetts, New Hampshire and New York) passed unemployment laws on the eve of the adoption of the Social Security Act, and two others did likewise after the federal act and later in the year. The statutes differed to some extent in type, but were directed to a common end. In 1936, twenty-eight other states fell in line, and eight more the present year. But if states had been holding back before the passage of the federal law, inaction was not owing, for the most part to the lack of sympathetic interest. Many held back through alarm lest in laying such a toll upon their industries, they would place themselves in a position of economic disadvantage as compared with neighbors or competitors. See House Report, No. 615, 74th Congress, 1st session, p. 8; Senate Report, No. 628, 74th Congress, 1st session, p. 11. Two consequences ensued. One was that the freedom of a state to contribute its fair share to the solution of a national problem was paralyzed by fear. The other was that in so far as there was failure by the states to contribute relief according to the measure of their capacity, a disproportionate burden, and a mountainous one, was laid upon the resources of the Government of the nation.

The Social Security Act is an attempt to find a method by which all these public agencies may work together to a common end. Every dollar of the new taxes will continue in all likelihood to be used and needed by the nation as long as states are unwilling, whether through timidity or for other motives, to do what can be done at home. At least the inference is permissible that Congress so believed, though retaining undiminished freedom to spend the money as it pleased. On the other hand fulfillment of the home duty will be lightened and encouraged by crediting the taxpayer upon his account with the Treasury of the nation to the extent that his contributions under the laws of the locality have simplified or diminished the problem of relief and the probable demand upon the resources of the fisc. Duplicated taxes, or burdens that approach them, are recognized hardships that government, state or national, may properly avoid. If Congress believed that the general welfare would better be promoted by relief through local units than by the system then in vogue, the coöperating localities ought not in all fairness to pay a second time.

Who then is coerced through the operation of this statute? Not the taxpayer. He pays in fulfilment of the mandate of the local legisla-ture. Not the state. Even now she does not offer a suggestion that in passing the unemployment law she was affected by duress. For all that appears she is satisfied with her choice, and would be sorely disappointed if it were now to be annulled. The difficulty with the petitioner's contention is that it confuses motive with coercion. "Every tax is in some measure regulatory. To some extent it interposes an economic impediment to the activity taxed as compared with others not taxed." *Sonzinsky* v. *United States, supra,* March 29, 1937. In like manner every rebate from a tax when conditioned upon conduct is in some measure a temptation. But to hold that motive or temptation is equivalent to coercion is to plunge the law in endless difficulties. The outcome of such a doctrine is the acceptance of a philosophical determinism by which choice becomes impossible. Till now the law has been guided by a robust common sense which assumes the freedom of the will as a working hypothesis in the solution of its problems. The wisdom of the hypothesis has illustration in this case. Nothing in the case suggests the exertion of a power akin to undue influence, if we assume that such a concept can ever be applied with fitness to the relations between state and nation. Even on that assumption the location of the point at which pressure turns into compulsion, and ceases to be inducement, would be a question of degree, —at times, perhaps, of fact. The point had not been reached when Alabama made her choice. We cannot say that she was acting, not of her unfettered will, but under the strain of a persuasion equivalent to undue influence, when she chose to have relief administered under laws of her own making, by agents of her own selection, instead of under federal laws, administered by federal officers, with all the ensuing evils, at least to many minds, of federal patronage and power. There would be a strange irony, indeed, if her choice were now to be annulled on the basis of an assumed duress in the enactment of a statute which her courts have accepted as a true expression of her will. We think the choice must stand. . . .

Fourth: The statute does not call for a surrender by the states of powers essential to their quasi-sovereign existence.

Argument to the contrary has its source in two sections of the act. One section (903) defines the minimum criteria to which a state compensation system is required to conform if it is to be accepted by the Board as the basis for a credit. The other section (904) rounds out the requirement with complementary rights and duties. Not all the criteria or their incidents are challenged as unlawful. We will speak of them first generally, and then more specifically in so far as they are questioned. . . .

Even if opinion may differ as to the fundamental quality of one or more of the conditions, the difference will not avail to vitiate the statute. In determining essentials Congress must have the benefit of a fair margin of discretion. One cannot say with reason that this margin has been exceeded, or that the basic standards have been determined in any arbitrary fashion. In the event that some particular condition shall be found to be too uncertain to be capable of enforcement, it may be severed from the others, and what is left will still be valid.

We are to keep in mind steadily that the conditions to be approved by the Board as the basis for a credit are not provisions of a contract, but terms of a statute, which may be altered or repealed. Section 903 (a) (6). The state does not bind itself to keep the law in force. It does not even bind itself that the moneys paid into the federal fund will be kept there indefinitely or for any stated time. On the contrary, the Secretary of the Treasury will honor a requisition for the whole or any part of the deposit in the fund whenever one is made by the appropriate officials. The only consequence of the repeal or excessive amendment of the statute, or the expenditure of the money, when requisitioned, for other than compensation uses or administrative expenses, is that approval of the law will end, and with it the allowance of a credit, upon notice to the state agency and an opportunity for hearing. Section 903 (b) (c).

These basic considerations are in truth a solvent of the problem. Subjected to their test, the several objections on the score of abdication are found to be unreal. . . .

Finally and chiefly, abdication is supposed to follow from section 904 of the statute and the parts of section 903 that are complementary thereto. Section 903 (a) (3). By these the Secretary of the Treasury is authorized and directed to receive and hold in the Unemployment Trust Fund all moneys deposited therein by a state agency for a state unemployment fund and to invest in obligations of the United States such portion of the Fund as is not in his judgment required to meet current withdrawals. We are told that Alabama in consenting to that deposit has renounced the plenitude of power inherent in her statehood.

The same pervasive misconception is in evidence again. All that the state has done is to say in effect through the enactment of a statute that her agents shall be authorized to deposit the unemployment tax receipts in the Treasury at Washington. Alabama Unemployment Act of September 14, 1935, section 10 (i). The statute may be repealed. Section 903 (a) (6). The consent may be revoked. The deposits may be withdrawn. The moment the state commission gives notice to the depositary that it would like the moneys back, the Treasurer will return them. To find state destruction there is to find it almost anywhere. With nearly as much reason one might say that a state abdicates its functions when it places the state moneys on deposit in a national bank.

There are very good reasons of fiscal and governmental policy why a State should be willing to make the Secretary of the Treasury the custodian of the fund. His possession of the moneys and his control of investments will be an assurance of stability and safety in times of stress and strain. A report of the Ways and Means Committee of the House of Representatives, quoted in the margin, develops the situation clearly. Nor is there risk of loss or waste. The credit of the Treasury is at all times back of the deposit, with the result that the right of withdrawal will be unaffected by the fate of any intermediate investments, just as if a checking account in the usual form had been opened in a bank.

The inference of abdication thus dissolves in thinnest air when the deposit is conceived of as dependent upon a statutory consent, and not upon a contract effective to create a duty. By this we do not intimate that the conclusion would be different if a contract were discovered. Even sovereigns may contract without derogating from their sovereignty. The states are at liberty, upon obtaining the consent of Congress, to make agreements with one another. Constitution,

Art. I, section 10, par. 3. We find no room for doubt that they may do the like with Congress if the essence of their statehood is maintained without impairment. Alabama is seeking and obtaining a credit of many millions in favor of her citizens out of the Treasury of the nation. Nowhere in our scheme of government—in the limitations express or implied of our federal constitution—do we find that she is prohibited from assenting to conditions that will assure a fair and just requital for benefits received. But we will not labor the point further. An unreal prohibition directed to an unreal agreement will not vitiate an act of Congress, and cause it to collapse in ruin. . . .

The judgment is affirmed.

Justices McReynolds, Sutherland, Butler and Van Devanter dissented.

505. HELVERING et. al. v. DAVIS
301 U. S. 619
1937

On Writ of Certiorari to the U. S. Circuit Court of Appeals for the First Circuit. In the Stewart Machine Co. case the Supreme Court sustained that part of the Social Security Act which imposed an excise upon employers. The present case involved the constitutionality of the tax upon employees and presented the broad question of the nature and limits of taxation for the general welfare. The opinion is notable for its recognition of the economic background and motivation of the legislation under consideration. Compare this opinion with the opinion of the majority in the AAA case, Doc. No. 478. For references see Docs. No. 503 and 504.

Cardozo, J. The Social Security Act is challenged once again. . . .

In this case Titles VIII and II are the subject of attack. Title VIII . . . lays a special income tax upon employees to be deducted from their wages and paid by the employers. Title II provides for the payment of Old Age Benefits, and supplies the motive and occasion, in the view of the assailants of the statute, for the levy of the taxes imposed by Title VIII. . . .

Second: The scheme of benefits created by the provisions of Title II is not in contravention of the limitations of the Tenth Amendment.

Congress may spend money in aid of the "general welfare." Constitution, Art. I, section 8; *United States* v. *Butler,* 297 U. S. 1, 65; *Steward Machine Co.* v. *Davis.* There have been great statesmen in our history who have stood for other views. We will not resurrect the contest. It is now settled by decision. *United States* v. *Butler.* The conception of the spending power advocated by Hamilton and strongly reinforced by Story has prevailed over that of Madison, which has not been lacking in adherents. Yet difficulties are left when the power is conceded. The line must still be drawn between one welfare and another, between particular and general. Where this shall be placed cannot be known through a formula in advance of the event. There is a middle ground or certainly a penumbra in which discretion is at large. The discretion, however, is not confided to the courts. The discretion belongs to Congress, unless the choice is clearly wrong, a display of arbitrary power, not an exercise of judgment. This is now familiar law. "When such a contention comes here we naturally require a showing that by no reasonable possibility can the challenged legislation fall within the wide range of discretion permitted to the Congress." *United States* v. *Butler, supra,* p. 67. Nor is the concept of the general welfare static. Needs that were narrow or parochial a century ago may be interwoven in our day with the well-being of the nation. What is critical or urgent changes with the times.

The purge of nation-wide calamity that began in 1929 has taught us many lessons. Not the least is the solidarity of interests that may once have seemed to be divided. Unemployment spreads from state to state, the hinterland now settled that in pioneer days gave an avenue of escape. Spreading from state to state, unemployment is an ill not particular but general, which may be checked, if Congress so determines, by the resources of the nation. If this can have been doubtful until now, our ruling today in the case of the *Steward Machine Co.* has set the doubt at rest. But the ill is all one or at least not greatly different whether men are thrown out of work because there is no longer work to do or because the disabilities of age make them incapable of doing it. Rescue becomes necessary irrespective of the cause. The hope behind this statute is to save men and women from the rigors of the poor house as well as from the haunting fear that such a lot awaits them when journey's end is near.

Congress did not improvise a judgment when it found that the award of old age benefits would be conducive to the general welfare. The President's Committee on Economic Security made an investigation and report, aided by a research staff of Government officers and employees, and by an Advisory Council and seven other advisory groups. Extensive hearings followed before the House Committee on Ways and Means, and the Senate Committee on Finance. A great mass of evidence was brought together supporting the policy which finds expression in the act. Among the relevant facts are these: The number of persons in the United States 65 years of age or over is increasing proportionately as well as absolutely. What is even more important the number of such persons unable to take care of themselves is growing at a threatening pace. More and more our population is becoming urban and industrial instead of rural and agricultural. The evidence is impressive that among industrial workers the younger men and women are preferred over the older. In time of retrenchment the older are commonly the first to go, and even if retained, their wages are likely to be lowered. The plight of men and women at so low an age as 40 is hard, almost hopeless, when they are driven to seek for reemployment. Statistics are in the brief. A few illustrations will be chosen from many there collected. In 1930, out of 224 American factories investigated, 71, or almost one third, had fixed maximum hiring age limits; in 4 plants the limit was under 40; in 41 it was under 46. In the other 153 plants there were no fixed limits, but in practice few were hired if they were over 50 years of age. With the loss of savings inevitable in periods of idleness, the fate of workers over 65, when thrown out of work, is little less than desperate. A recent study of the Social Security Board informs us that "one-fifth of the aged in the United States were receiving old-age assistance, emergency relief, institutional care, employment under the works program, or some other form of aid from public or private funds; two-fifths to one-half were dependent on friends and relatives, one-eighth had some income from earnings; and possibly one-sixth had some savings or property. Approximately three out of four persons 65 or over were probably dependent wholly or partially on others for support." We summarize in the margin the results of other studies by state and national commissions. They point the same way.

The problem is plainly national in area and dimensions. Moreover, laws of the separate states cannot deal with it effectively. Congress, at least, had a basis for that belief. States and local governments are often lacking in the resources that are necessary to finance an adequate program of security for the aged. This is brought out with a wealth of illustration in recent studies of the problem. Apart from the failure of resources, states and local governments are at times reluctant to increase so heavily the burden of taxation to be borne by their residents for fear of placing themselves in a position of economic disadvantage as compared with neighbors or competitors. We have seen this in our study of the problem of unemployment compensation. *Steward Machine Co.* v. *Davis.* A system of old age pensions has special dangers of its own, if put in force in one state and rejected in another. The existence of such a system is a bait to the needy and dependent elsewhere, encouraging them to migrate and seek a haven of repose. Only a power that is national can serve the interests of all.

Whether wisdom or unwisdom resides in the scheme of benefits set forth in Title II, it is not for us to say. The answer to such inquiries must come from Congress, not the courts. Our concern here as often is with power, not with wisdom. Counsel for respondent has recalled to us the virtues of self-reliance and frugality. There is a possibility, he says, that aid from a paternal government may sap those sturdy virtues and breed a race of weaklings. If Massachusetts so believes and shapes her laws in that conviction, must her breed of sons be changed, he asks, because some other philosophy of government finds favor in the halls of Congress? But the answer is not doubtful. One might ask with equal reason whether the system of protective tariffs is to be set aside at will in one state or another whenever local policy prefers the rule of *laissez faire*. The issue is a closed one. It was fought out long ago. When money is spent to promote the general welfare, the concept of welfare or the opposite is shaped by Congress, not the states. So the concept be not arbitrary, the locality must yield. Constitution, Art. VI, Par. 2.

Ordered accordingly.

Mr. Justice McReynolds and Mr. Justice Butler are of opinion that the provisions of the Act here challenged are repugnant to the Tenth Amendment, and that the decree of the Circuit Court of Appeals should be affirmed.

506. CANADIAN RECIPROCAL TRADE AGREEMENT

Signed November 15, 1935; Ratified May 14, 1936

(U. S. Dept. of State. Executive Agreements Series, No. 91)

When the Democrats came into office in March 1933 they found in effect the highest tariff in our history. Instead of a general reduction through new tariff legislation, Pres. Roosevelt and his Secretary of State Cordell Hull determined to use the power to lower tariffs for bargaining purposes. The purpose of this policy was not only economic but political as well. The Trade Agreements Act of 1934 authorized the President to make reciprocal agreements with foreign nations lowering tariffs on particular articles up to fifty per cent. Under this authority Sec. Hull, in the following six years, negotiated twenty-two reciprocal pacts. The new policy resulted in a gratifying expansion of American exports and was not without effect in improving American relations with Latin-American nations. The Canadian reciprocity agreement here given aroused widespread opposition especially from Mid-western farming interests. See, R. L. Buell, *The Hull Trade Program and the American System* (World Affairs Pamphlets, no. 2); H. S. Patton, *The Mid-West and the Trade Agreements Program* (Dept. of State Commercial Policy Ser. no. 27); F. B. Sayre, *The Way Forward;* H. J. Tasca, *The Reciprocal Trade Policy of the United States.* For an earlier effort at reciprocity with Canada see L. E. Ellis, *Reciprocity, 1911.*

By the President of the United States of America

A PROCLAMATION

Whereas it it provided in the Tariff Act of 1930 of the Congress of the United States of America, as amended by the Act of June 12, 1934, entitled "An Act To Amend the Tariff Act of 1930" (48 Stat. 943), as follows:

"Sec. 350. (a) For the purpose of expanding foreign markets for the products of the United States (as a means of assisting in the present emergency in restoring the American standard of living, in overcoming domestic unemployment and the present economic depression, in increasing the purchasing power of the American public, and in establishing and maintaining a better relationship among various branches of American agriculture, industry, mining, and commerce) by regulating the admission of foreign goods into the United States in accordance with the characteristics and needs of various branches of American production so that foreign markets will be made available to those branches of American production which require and are capable of developing such outlets by affording corresponding market opportunities for foreign products in the United States, the President, whenever he finds as a fact that any existing duties or other import restrictions of the United States or any foreign country are unduly burdening and restricting the foreign trade of the United States and that the purpose above declared will be promoted by the means hereinafter specified, is authorized from time to time—

"(1) To enter into foreign trade agreements with foreign governments or instrumentalities thereof; and

"(2) To proclaim such modifications of existing duties and other import restrictions, or such additional import restrictions, or such continuance, and for such minimum periods, of existing customs or excise treatment of any article covered by foreign trade agreements, as are required or appropriate to carry out any foreign trade agreement that the President has entered into hereunder. No proclamation shall be made increasing or decreasing by more than 50 per centum any existing rate of duty or transferring any article between the dutiable and free lists. The proclaimed duties and other import restrictions shall apply to articles the growth, produce, or manufacture of all foreign countries, whether imported directly, or indirectly: *Provided,* That the President may suspend the application to articles the growth, produce, or manufacture of any country because of its discriminatory treatment of American commerce or because of other acts or policies which in his opinion tend to defeat the purposes set forth in this section; . . .

WHEREAS I, Franklin D. Roosevelt, President of the United States of America, have found as a fact that certain existing duties and other import restrictions of the United States of America and the Dominion of Canada are unduly burdening and restricting the foreign trade of the United States of America and that the purpose declared in the said Tariff Act of 1930, as amended by the said Act of June 12, 1934, will be promoted by a foreign trade agreement between the United States of America and the Dominion of Canada;

WHEREAS reasonable public notice of the intention to negotiate such foreign trade agreement was given and the views presented by persons interested in the negotiation of such agreement were received and considered;

WHEREAS, after seeking and obtaining information and advice with respect thereto from the United States Tariff Commission, the Departments of State, Agriculture, and Commerce, and from other sources, I entered into a foreign Trade Agreement on November 15, 1935, through my duly empowered plenipotentiary, with His Majesty the King of Great Britain, Ireland and the British dominions beyond the Seas, Emperor of India, in respect of the Dominion of Canada, through his duly empowered Plenipotentiary, which Agreement, is as follows:

The President of the United States of America and His Majesty the King of Great Britain, Ireland and the British dominions beyond the Seas, Emperor of India, in respect of the Dominion of Canada, being desirous of facilitating and extending the commercial relations existing between the United States of America and Canada by granting mutual and reciprocal concessions and advantages for the promotion of trade, have resolved to conclude a Trade Agreement as a step toward the lowering of the barriers impeding trade between their two countries, and for this purpose have through their respective Plenipotentiaries agreed upon the following Articles:

ARTICLE I

The United States of America and Canada will grant each other unconditional and unrestricted most-favored-nation treatment in all matters concerning customs duties and subsidiary charges of every kind and in the method of levying duties, and, further, in all matters concerning the rules, formalities and charges imposed in connection with the clearing of goods through the customs, and with respect to all laws or regulations affecting the sale or use of imported goods within the country.

Accordingly, natural or manufactured products having their origin in either of the countries shall in no case be subject, in regard to the matters referred to above, to any duties, taxes or charges other or higher, or to any rules or formalities other or more burdensome, than those to which the like products having their origin in any third country are or may hereafter be subject.

Similarly, natural or manufactured products exported from the territory of the United States of America or Canada and consigned to the territory of the other country shall in no case be subject with respect to exportation and in regard to the above-mentioned matters, to any duties, taxes or charges other or higher, or to any rules or formalities other or more burdensome, than those to which the like products when consigned to the territory of any third country are or may hereafter be subject.

Any advantage, favor, privilege or immunity which has been or may hereafter be granted by the United States of America or Canada in regard to the above-mentioned matters, to a natural or manufactured product originating in any third country or consigned to the territory of any third country shall be accorded immediately and without compensation to the like product originating in or consigned to the territory of Canada or the United States of America, respectively, and irrespective of the nationality of the carrier.

ARTICLE II

Neither the United States of America nor Canada shall establish any prohibition or maintain any restriction on imports from the territory of the other country which is not applied to the importation of any like article originating in any third country. Any abolition of an import prohibition or restriction which may be granted even temporarily by either country in favor of an article of a third country shall be applied immediately and unconditionally to the like article originating in the territory of the other country. These provisions equally apply to exports. . . .

ARTICLE III

Articles the growth, produce or manufacture of the United States of America, enumerated and described in Schedule I annexed to this Agreement, shall, on their importation into Canada, be exempt from ordinary customs duties in excess of those set forth in the said Schedule. The said articles shall also be exempt from all other duties, taxes, fees, charges, or exactions, imposed on or in connection with importation, in excess of those imposed on the day of the signature of this Agreement or required to be imposed thereafter under laws of Canada in force on the day of the signature of this Agreement. . . .

ARTICLE IV

Articles the growth, produce or manufacture of Canada, enumerated and described in Schedule II annexed to this Agreement, shall, on their importation into the United States of America, be exempt from ordinary customs duties in excess of those set forth and provided for in the said Schedule. . . .

ARTICLE V

The provisions of Articles III and IV of this Agreement shall not prevent the Government of either country from imposing on the importation of any product a charge equivalent to an internal tax imposed on a like domestic product or on a commodity from which the imported product has been manufactured or produced in whole or in part.

ARTICLE VI

Articles the growth, produce or manufacture of the United States of America or Canada shall, after importation into the other country, be exempt from all internal taxes, fees, charges or exactions other or higher than those payable on like articles of national origin or any other foreign origin. . . .

ARTICLE VII

No prohibitions, import or customs quotas, import licenses, or any other form of quantitative regulation, whether or not operated in connection with any agency of centralized control, shall be imposed by the United States of America on the importation or sale of any article the growth, produce or manufacture of Canada enumerated and described in Schedule II, nor by Canada on the importation or sale of any article the growth, produce or manufacture of the United States of America enumerated and described in Schedule I, except as specifically provided for in the said Schedules.

The foregoing provision shall not apply to quantitative restrictions in whatever form imposed by either country on the importation or sale of any article the growth, produce or manufacture of the other country in conjunction with governmental measures operating to regulate or control the production, market supply, or prices of like domestic articles, or tending to increase the labor costs of production of such articles. Whenever the Government of either country proposes to establish or change any restriction authorized by this paragraph, it shall give notice thereof in writing to the other Government and shall afford such other Government an opportunity within thirty days after receipt of such notice to consult with it in respect of the proposed action; and if an agreement with respect thereto is not reached within thirty days following receipt of the aforesaid notice, the Government which proposes to take such action shall be free to do so at any time thereafter, and the other Government shall be free within fifteen days after such action is taken to terminate this Agreement in its entirety on thirty days' written notice. . . .

ARTICLE IX

The tariff advantages and other benefits provided for in this Agreement are granted by the United States of America and Canada to each other subject to the condition that if the Government of either country shall establish or maintain, directly or indirectly, any form of control of foreign exchange, it shall administer such control so as to insure that the nationals and commerce of the other country will be granted a fair and equitable share in the allotment of exchange. . . .

ARTICLE X

In the event that a wide variation occurs in the rate of exchange between the currencies of the United States of America and Canada, the Government of either country, if it considers the variation so substantial as to prejudice the industries or commerce of the country, shall be free to propose negotiations for the modification of this Agreement; and if an agreement with respect thereto is not reached within thirty days following receipt of such proposal, the Government making such proposal shall be free to terminate this Agreement in its entirety on thirty days' written notice.

ARTICLE XI

In the event that the Government of either country adopts any measure which, even though it does not conflict with the terms of this Agreement, is considered by the Government of the other country to have the effect of nullifying or impairing any object of the Agreement, the Government which has adopted any such measure shall consider such representations and proposals as the other Government may make with a view to effecting a mutually satisfactory adjustment of the matter. . . .

ARTICLE XII

Nothing in this Agreement shall be construed to prevent the adoption of measures prohibiting or restricting the exportation or importation of gold or silver, or to prevent the adoption of such measures as either Government may see fit with respect to the con-

trol of the export or sale for export of arms, ammunition, or implements of war, and, in exceptional circumstances, all other military supplies.

Subject to the requirement that there shall be no arbitrary discrimination by either country against the other country in favor of any third country where similar conditions prevail, the provisions of this Agreement shall not extend to prohibitions or restrictions (1) imposed on moral or humanitarian grounds; (2) designed to protect human, animal or plant life; (3) relating to prison-made goods; (4) relating to the enforcement of police or revenue laws; (5) directed against misbranding, adulteration, and other fraudulent practices, such as are provided for in the pure food and drug laws of either country; and (6) directed against unfair practices in import trade. . . .

ARTICLE XIV

The Government of each country reserves the right to withdraw or to modify the concession granted on any article under this Agreement, or to impose quantitative restrictions on any such article if, as a result of the extension of such concession to third countries, such countries obtain the major benefit of such concession and in consequence thereof an unduly large increase in importations of such article takes place. . . .

Done in duplicate, at the City of Washington, this fifteenth day of November, 1935.

For the President of the United States of America:

CORDELL HULL
*Secretary of State
of the United States of America.*

For His Majesty the King of Great Britain, Ireland and the British dominions beyond the Seas, Emperor of India, for the Dominion of Canada:

W. L. MACKENZIE KING
Prime Minister

---

507. CARTER v. CARTER COAL CO. et. al.
298 U. S. 238
1936

On Writs of Certiorari to the U. S. Court of Appeals for the District of Columbia. The coal in-

dustry had long been recognized as "sick" and an appropriate object of federal regulation. The

Guffey Coal Act of 30 Aug., 1935, whose provisions are here set forth in some detail, represented an effort to regulate both production and labor. The Court, in this opinion, not only reaffirmed the doctrine of the Schechter case (see Doc. No. 486) but appeared to return to the position of the E. C. Knight case (see Doc. No. 339). Mr. C. J. Hughes in a separate opinion insisted that the invalidity of the labor provisions of the Guffey Act did not necessarily invalidate the price-fixing provisions. A second Guffey Coal Act was passed, 26 April, 1937. For conditions in the coal industry, see E. E. Hunt, ed. *What the Coal Commission Found:* W. Hamilton and H. R. Wright, *The Case of Bituminous Coal.* For the Carter case see E. S. Corwin, *Twilight of the Supreme Court* and *Commerce Power versus States Rights;* W. Hamilton and O. Adair, *The Power to Govern;* Black, "The Commerce Clause and the New Deal," 20 Cornell L. Qt. 169; Eisenstein, "The Final Phase of the Schechter Episode," 5 Brooklyn L. Rev. 454; Hetsko, "Congressional Power under the Commerce Clause, etc." 34 Mich. L. Rev. 1167.

SUTHERLAND, J. The purpose of the "Bituminous Coal Conservation Act of 1935," involved in these suits, as declared by the title, are to stabilize the bituminous coal-mining industry and promote its interstate commerce; to provide for cooperative marketing of bituminous coal; to levy a tax on such coal and provide for a drawback under certain conditions; to declare the production, distribution, and use of such coal to be affected with a national public interest; to conserve the national resources of such coal; to provide for the general welfare, and for other purposes. C. 824, 49 Stat. 991. The constitutional validity of the act is challenged in each of the suits.

By the terms of the act, every producer of bituminous coal within the United States is brought within its provisions.

Section 1 is a detailed assertion of circumstances thought to justify the act. It declares that the mining and distribution of bituminous coal throughout the United States by the producer are affected with a national public interest; and that the service of such coal in relation to industrial activities, transportation facilities, health and comfort of the people, conservation by controlled production and economical mining and marketing, maintenance of just and rational relations between the public, owners, producers and employees, the right of the public to constant and adequate supplies of coal at reasonable prices,

and the general welfare of the nation, require that the bituminous coal industry should be regulated as the act provides.

Section 1, among other things, further declares that the production and distribution by producers of such coal bear upon and directly affect interstate commerce, and render regulation of production and distribution imperative for the protection of such commerce; that certain features connected with the production, distribution, and marketing have led to waste of the national coal resources, disorganization of interstate commerce in such coal, and burdening and obstructing interstate commerce therein; that practices prevailing in the production of such coal directly affect interstate commerce and require regulation for the protection of that commerce; and that the right of mine workers to organize and collectively bargain for wages, hours of labor, and conditions of employment should be guaranteed in order to prevent constant wage cutting and disparate labor costs detrimental to fair interstate competition, and in order to avoid obstructions to interstate commerce that recur in industrial disputes over labor relations at the mines. These declarations constitute not enactments of law, but legislative averments by way of inducement to the enactment which follows.

The substantive legislation begins with § 2, which establishes in the Department of the Interior a National Bituminous Coal Commission, to be appointed and constituted as the section then specifically provides. Upon this commission is conferred the power to hear evidence and find facts upon which its orders and actions may be predicated.

Section 3 provides:

"There is hereby imposed upon the sale or other disposal of all bituminous coal produced within the United States an excise tax of 15 per centum on the sale price at the mine, or in the case of captive coal the fair market value of such coal at the mine, such tax, subject to the later provisions of this section, to be payable to the United States by the producers of such coal, and to be payable monthly for each calendar month, on or before the first business day of the second succeeding month, and under such regulations, and in such manner, as shall be prescribed by the Commissioner of Internal Revenue: *Provided,* That in the case of captive coal produced as aforesaid, the Commissioner of Internal Revenue shall fix a price therefor at the current market price for the comparable kind, quality, and size of coals in the locality where the same is produced: *Provided further,* That any such coal producer who has filed with the National Bituminous Coal Commission his acceptance of the code provided for in section 4 of this Act, and who acts in compliance with the provisions of such code, shall be entitled to a drawback in the form of a credit upon the amount of such tax payable hereunder, equivalent to 90 per centum of the amount of such tax, to be allowed and deducted therefrom at the time settlement therefor is required, in such manner as shall be prescribed by the Commissioner of Internal Revenue. . . .

Section 4 provides that the commission shall formulate the elaborate provisions contained therein into a working agreement to be known as the Bituminous Coal Code. These provisions require the organization of twenty-three coal districts, each with a district board the membership of which is to be determined in a manner pointed out by the act. . . .

Without repeating the long and involved provisions with regard to the fixing of minimum prices, it is enough to say that the act confers the power to fix the minimum price of coal at each and every coal mine in the United States, with such price variations as the board may deem necessary and proper. There is also a provision authorizing the commission, when deemed necessary in the public interest, to establish maximum prices in order to protect the consumer against unreasonably high prices.

All sales and contracts for the sale of coal are subject to the code prices provided for and in effect when such sales and contracts are made. Various unfair methods of competition are defined and forbidden.

The labor provisions of the code, found in Part III of the same section, require that in order to effectuate the purposes of the act the district boards and code members shall accept specified conditions contained in the code, among which are the following:

Employees to be given the right to organize and bargain collectively, through representatives of their own choosing, free from interference, restraint, or coercion of employers or their agents in respect of their concerted activities.

Such employees to have the right of peaceable assemblage for the discussion of the principles of collective bargaining and to select their own check-weighman to inspect the weighing or measuring of coal.

A labor board is created, consisting of three members, to be appointed by the President and assigned to the Department of Labor. Upon this board is conferred authority to adjudicate disputes arising under the provisions just stated, and to determine whether or not an organization of employees had been promoted, or is controlled or dominated by an employer in its organization, management, policy, or election of representatives. The board "may order a code member to meet the representatives of its employees for the purpose of collective bargaining."

Subdivision (g) of Part III provides:

"Whenever the maximum daily and weekly hours of labor are agreed upon in any contract or contracts negotiated between the producers of more than two-thirds the annual national tonnage production for the preceding calendar year and the representatives of more than one-half of the mine workers employed, such maximum hours of labor shall be accepted by all the code members. The wage agreement or agreements negotiated by collective bargaining in any district or group of two or more districts, between representatives of producers of more than two-thirds of the annual tonnage production of such district or each of such districts in a contracting group during the preceding calendar year, and representatives of the majority of the mine workers therein, shall be filed with the Labor Board and shall be accepted as the minimum wages for the various classifications of labor by the code members operating in such district or group of districts." . . .

The questions involved will be considered under the following heads:

1. The right of stockholders to maintain suits of this character.

2. Whether the suits were prematurely brought.

3. Whether the exaction of 15 *per centum* on the sale price of coal at the mine is a tax or a penalty.

4. The purposes of the act as set forth in § 1, and the authority vested in Congress by the Constitution to effectuate them.

5. Whether the labor provisions of the act can be upheld as an exercise of the power to regulate interstate commerce.

6. Whether subdivision (g) of Part III of the Code, is an unlawful delegation of power.

7. The constitutionality of the price-fixing provisions, and the question of severability— that is to say, whether, if either the group of labor provisions or the group of price-fixing provisions be found constitutionally invalid, the other can stand as separable. . . .

Third. The co-called excise tax of 15 *per centum* on the sale price of coal at the mine, or, in the case of captive coal the fair market value, with its drawback allowance of 13½% is clearly not a tax but a penalty. . . .

It is very clear that the "excise tax" is not imposed for revenue but exacted as a penalty to compel compliance with the regulatory provisons of the act. The whole purpose of the exaction is to coerce what is called an agreement—which, of course, it is not, for it lacks the essential element of consent. One who does a thing in order to avoid a monetary penalty does not agree; he yields to compulsion precisely the same as though he did so to avoid a term in jail. . . .

But it is not necessary to pursue the matter further. That the "tax" is in fact a penalty is not seriously in dispute. The position of the government, as we understand it, is that the validity of the exaction does not rest upon the taxing power but upon the power of Congress to regulate interstate commerce; and that if the act in respect of the labor and price-fixing provisions be not upheld, the "tax" must fall with them. With that position we agree and confine our consideration accordingly.

Fourth. Certain recitals contained in the act plainly suggest that its makers were of opinion that its constitutionality could be sustained under some general federal power, thought to exist, apart from the specific grants of the Constitution. The fallacy of that view will be apparent when we recall fundamental principles which, although hitherto often expressed in varying forms of words, will bear repetition whenever their accuracy seems to be challenged. The recitals to which we refer are contained in § 1 (which is simply a preamble to the act), and, among others, are to the effect that the distribution of bituminous coal is of national interest, affecting the health and comfort of the people and the general welfare of the nation; that this circumstance, together with the necessity of maintaining just and rational relations between the public, owners, producers, and employees, and the right of the public to constant and adequate supplies at reasonable prices, require regulation of the industry as the act provides. These affirmations—and the further ones that the production and distribution of such coal "directly affect interstate commerce," because of which and of the waste of the national coal resources and other circumstances, the regulation is necessary for the protection of such commerce—do not constitute an exertion of the *will* of Congress which is legislation, but a recital of considerations which in the *opinion* of that body existed and justified the expression of its will in the present act. Nevertheless, this preamble may not be disregarded. On the contrary it is important, because it makes clear, except for the pure assumption that the conditions described "directly" affect interstate commerce, that the powers which Congress undertook to exercise are not specific but of the most general character—namely, to protect the general public interest and health and comfort of the people, to conserve privately-owned coal, maintain just relations between producers and employees and others, and promote the general welfare, by controling nation-wide production and distribution of coal. These, it may be conceded, are objects of great worth; but are they ends, the attainment of which has been committed by the Constitution to the federal government? This is a vital question; for nothing is more certain than that beneficent aims, however great or well directed, can never serve in lieu of constitutional power.

The ruling and firmly established principle is that the powers which the general government may exercise are only those specifically enumerated in the Constitution, and such implied powers as are necessary and proper to carry into effect the enumerated powers. Whether the end sought to be attained by an act of Congress is legitimate is wholly a matter of constitutional power and not at all of legislative discretion. Legislative congressional discretion begins with the choice of means and ends with the adoption of methods and details to carry the delegated powers into effect. The distinction between these two things—power and discretion—is not only very plain but very important. For while the

powers are rigidly limited to the enumerations of the Constitution, the means which
may be employed to carry the powers into
effect are not restricted, save that they must
be appropriate, plainly adapted to the end,
and not prohibited by, but consistent with, the
letter and spirit of the Constitution. Thus,
it may be said that to a constitutional end
many ways are open; but to an end not within
the terms of the Constitution, all ways are
closed.

The proposition, often advanced and as
often discredited, that the power of the federal government inherently extends to purposes affecting the nation as a whole with
which the states severally cannot deal or
cannot adequately deal, and the related notion that Congress, entirely apart from those
powers delegated by the Constitution, may
enact laws to promote the general welfare,
have never been accepted but always definitely rejected by this court. . . .

The general rule with regard to the respective powers of the national and the state
governments under the Constitution, is not
in doubt. The states were before the Constitution; and, consequently, their legislative
powers antedated the Constitution. Those who
framed and those who adopted that instrument meant to carve from the general mass
of legislative powers, then possessed by the
states, only such portions as it was thought
wise to confer upon the federal government;
and in order that there should be no uncertainty in respect of what was taken and what
was left, the national powers of legislation
were not aggregated but enumerated—with
the result that what was not embraced by the
enumeration remained vested in the states
without change or impairment. . . . While
the states are not sovereign in the true sense
of that term, but only *quasi*-sovereign, yet
in respect of all powers reserved to them
they are supreme—"as independent of the
general government as that government within
its sphere is independent of the States." *The
Collector* v. *Day,* 11 Wall. 113, 124. And
since every addition to the national legislative
power to some extent detracts from or invades the power of the states, it is of vital
moment that, in order to preserve the fixed
balance intended by the Constitution, the
powers of the general government be not so
extended as to embrace any not within the

express terms of the several grants or the implications necessarily to be drawn therefrom.
It is no longer open to question that the
general government, unlike the states, *Hammer* v. *Dagenhart,* 247 U. S. 251, 275, possesses no *inherent* power in respect of the
internal affairs of the states; and emphatically
not with regard to legislation. The question
in respect of the inherent power of that government as to the external affairs of the
nation and in the field of international law is a
wholly different matter which it is not necessary now to consider.

The determination of the Framers Convention and the ratifying conventions to preserve
complete and unimpaired state self-government in all matters not committed to the
general government is one of the plainest facts
which emerges from the history of their deliberations. . . . Every journey to a forbidden end begins with the first step; and the
danger of such a step by the federal government in the direction of taking over the powers
of the states is that the end of the journey
may find the states so despoiled of their
powers, or—what may amount to the same
thing—so relieved of the responsibilities
which possession of the powers necessarily enjoins, as to reduce them to little more than
geographical subdivisions of the national
domain. It is safe to say that if, when the
Constitution was under consideration, it had
been thought that any such danger lurked
behind its plain words, it would never have
been ratified. . . .

We have set forth, perhaps at unnecessary
length, the foregoing principles, because it
seemed necessary to do so in order to demonstrate that the general purposes which the
act recites, and which, therefore, unless the
recitals be disregarded, Congress undertook
to achieve, are beyond the power of Congress
except so far, and only so far, as they may
be realized by an exercise of some specific
power granted by the Constitution. Proceeding by a process of elimination, which it is
not necessary to follow in detail, we shall
find no grant of power which authorizes Congress to legislate in respect of these general
purposes unless it be found in the commerce
clause—and this we now consider.

Fifth. Since the validity of the act depends
upon whether it as a regulation of interstate
commerce, the nature and extent of the

power conferred upon Congress by the commerce clause becomes the determinative question in this branch of the case. . . . We first inquire, then— What is commerce? The term, as this court many times has said, is one of extensive import. No all-embracing definition has ever been formulated. The question is to be approached both affirmatively and negatively—that is to say, from the points of view as to what it includes and what it excludes.

In *Veazie et al.* v. *Moor*, 14 How. 568, this court, after saying that the phrase could never be applied to transactions wholly internal, significantly added: "Nor can it be properly concluded, that, because the products of domestic enterprise in agriculture or manufactures, or in the arts, may ultimately become the subjects of foreign commerce, that the control of the means or the encouragements by which enterprise is fostered and protected, is legitimately within the import of the phase *foreign commerce,* or fairly implied in any investiture of the power to regulate such commerce. A pretension as far reaching as this, would extend to contracts between citizen and citizen of the same State, would control the pursuits of the planter, the grazier, the manufacturer, the mechanic, the immense operations of the collieries and mines and furnaces of the country; for there is not one of these avocations, the results of which may not become the subjects of foreign commerce, and be borne either by turnpikes, canals, or railroads, from point to point within the several States, towards an ultimate destination, like the one above mentioned. . . ." . . .

That commodities produced or manufactured within a state are intended to be sold or transported outside the state does not render their production or manufacture subject to federal regulation under the commerce clause. . . .

We have seen that the word "commerce" is the equivalent of the phrase "intercourse for the purposes of trade." Plainly, the incidents leading up to and culminating in the mining of coal do not constitute such intercourse. The employment of men, the fixing of their wages, hours of labor and working conditions, the bargaining in respect to these things—whether carried on separately or collectively—each and all constitute intercourse for the purposes of production, not of trade. The latter is a thing apart from the relation of employer and employee, which in all producing occupations is purely local in character. Extraction of coal from the mine is the aim and the completed result of local activities. Commerce in the coal mined is not brought into being by force of these activities, but by negotiations, agreements, and circumstances entirely apart from production. Mining brings the subject matter of commerce into existence. Commerce disposes of it.

A consideration of the foregoing, and of many cases which might be added to those already cited, renders inescapable the conclusion that the effect of the labor provisions of the act, including those in respect of minimum wages wage agreements, collective bargaining, and the Labor Board and its powers, primarily falls upon production and not upon commerce; and confirms the further resulting conclusion that production is a purely local activity. It follows that none of these essential antecedents of production constitutes a transaction in or forms any part of interstate commerce. Everything which moves in interstate commerce has had a local origin. Without local production somewhere, interstate commerce, as now carried on, would practically disappear. Nevertheless, the local character of mining, of manufacturing and of crop growing is a fact, and remains a fact, whatever may be done with the products. . . .

But § 1 (the preamble) of the act now under review declares that all production and distribution of bituminous coal "bear upon and directly affect its interstate commerce"; and that regulation thereof is imperative for the protection of such commerce. The contention of the government is that the labor provisions of the act may be sustained in that view.

That the production of every commodity intended for interstate sale and transportation has some effect upon interstate commerce may be, if it has not already been, freely granted; and we are brought to the final and decisive inquiry, whether here that effect is direct, as the "preamble" recites, or indirect. The distinction is not formal, but substantial in the highest degree, as we pointed out in the *Schechter* case, *supra,* p. 546, *et seq.* . . .

Whether the effect of a given activity or condition is direct or indirect is not always easy to determine. The word "direct" implies that the activity or condition invoked or blamed shall operate proximately—not mediately, remotely, or collaterally—to produce the effect. It connotes the absence of an efficient intervening agency or condition. And the extent of the effect bears no logical relation to its character. The distinction between a direct and an indirect effect turns, not upon the magnitude of either the cause or the effect, but entirely upon the manner in which the effect has been brought about. If the production by one man of a single ton of coal intended for interstate sale and shipment, and actually so sold and shipped, affects interstate commerce indirectly, the effect does not become direct by multiplying the tonnage, or increasing the number of men employed, or adding to the expense or complexities of the business, or by all combined. It is quite true that rules of law are sometimes qualified by considerations of degree, as the government argues. But the matter of degree has no bearing upon the question here, since that question is not— What is the *extent* of the local activity or condition, or the *extent* of the effect produced upon interstate commerce? but— What is the *relation* between the activity or condition and the effect?

Much stress is put upon the evils which come from the struggle between employers and employees over the matter of wages, working conditions, the right of collective bargaining, etc., and the resulting strikes, curtailment and irregularity of production and effect on prices; and it is insisted that interstate commerce is *greatly* affected thereby. But, in addition to what has just been said, the conclusive answer is that the evils are all local evils over which the federal government has no legislative control. The relation of employer and employee is a local relation. At common law, it is one of the domestic relations. The wages are paid for the doing of local work. Working conditions are obviously local conditions. The employees are not engaged in or about commerce, but exclusively in producing a commodity. And the controversies and evils, which it is the object of the act to regulate and minimize, are local controversies and evils affecting local work undertaken to accomplish that local result. Such effect as they may have upon commerce, however extensive it may be, is secondary and indirect.

An increase in the greatness of the effect adds to its importance. It does not alter its character.

The government's contentions in defense of the labor provisions are really disposed of adversely by our decision in the *Schechter* case, *supra*. The only perceptible difference between that case and this is that in the *Schechter* case, the federal power was asserted with respect to commodities which had come to rest after their interstate transportation; while here, the case deals with commodities at rest before interstate commerce has begun. That difference is without significance. . . . A reading of the entire opinion makes clear, what we now declare, that the want of power on the part of the federal government is the same whether the wages, hours of service, and working conditions, and the bargaining about them, are related to production before interstate commerce has begun, or to sale and distribution after it has ended.

Sixth. That the act, whatever it may be in form, in fact is compulsory clearly appears. . . .

Seventh. Finally, we are brought to the price-fixing provisions of the code. The necessity of considering the question of their constitutionality will depend upon whether they are separable from the labor provisions so that they can stand independently. Section 15 of the act provides:

"If any provision of this Act, or the application thereof to any person or circumstances, is held invalid, the remainder of the Act and the application of such provisions to other persons or circumstances shall not be affected thereby."

In the absence of such a provision, the presumption is that the legislature intends an act to be effective as an entirety—that is to say, the rule is against the mutilation of a statute; and if any provision be unconstitutional, the presumption is that the remaining provisions fall with it. The effect of the statute is to reverse this presumption in favor of inseparability, and create the opposite one of separability. Under the non-statutory rule, the burden is upon the supporter of the legislation to show the separability of the provisions involved. Under the statutory rule, the burden is shifted to the assailant to show their inseparability. But under either rule, the determination, in the end, is reached by applying the same test—namely, What was the intent of the lawmakers? . . .

The primary contemplation of the act is stabilization of the industry through the regulation of labor *and* the regulation of prices; for, since both were adopted, we must conclude that both were thought essential. The regulations of labor on the one hand and prices on the other furnish mutual aid and support; and their associated force—not one or the other but both combined—was deemed by Congress to be necessary to achieve the end sought. The statutory mandate for a code upheld by two legs at once suggests the improbability that Congress would have assented to a code supported by only one.

This seems plain enough; for Congress must have been conscious of the fact that elimination of the labor provisions from the act would seriously impair, if not destroy, the force and usefulness of the price provisions. The interdependence of wages and prices is manifest. Approximately two-thirds of the cost of producing a ton of coal is represented by wages. Fair prices necessarily depend upon the cost of production; and since wages constitute so large a proportion of the cost, prices cannot be fixed with any proper relation to cost without taking into consideration this major element. If one of them becomes uncertain, uncertainty with respect to the other necessarily ensues. . . .

Thus wages, hours of labor, and working conditions are to be so adjusted as to effectuate the purposes of the act; and prices are to be so regulated as to *stabilize* wages, working conditions, and hours of labor which have been or are to be fixed under the labor provisions. The two are so woven together as to render the probability plain enough that uniform prices, in the opinion of Congress, could not be fairly fixed or effectively regulated, without also regulating these elements of labor which enter so largely into the cost of production.

The conclusion is unavoidable that the price-fixing provisions of the code are so related to and dependent upon the labor provisions as conditions, considerations or compensations, as to make it clearly probable that the latter being held bad, the former would not have been passed. The fall of the latter, therefore, carries down with it the former.

The price-fixing provisions of the code are thus disposed of without coming to the question of their constitutionality; but neither this disposition of the matter, nor anything we have said, is to be taken as indicating that the court is of opinion that these provisions, if separately enacted, could be sustained. . . .

The decrees must be reversed and the causes remanded for further consideration in conformity with this opinion.

It is so ordered.

Mr. Justice CARDOZO, dissenting.

My conclusions compendiously stated are these:

(a) Part II of the statute sets up a valid system of price-fixing as applied to transactions in interstate commerce and to those in intrastate commerce where interstate commerce is directly or intimately affected. The prevailing opinion holds nothing to the contrary.

(b) Part II, with is system of price-fixing, is separable from Part III, which contains the provisions as to labor considered and condemned in the opinion of the court.

(c) Part II being valid, the complainants are under a duty to come in under the code, and are subject to a penalty if they persist in a refusal. . . .

First: I am satisfied that the Act is within the power of the central government in so far as it provides for minimum and maximum prices upon sales of bituminous coal in the transactions of interstate commerce and in those of intrastate commerce where interstate commerce is directly or intimately affected. Whether it is valid also in other provisions that have been considered and condemned in the opinion of the court, I do not find it necessary to determine at this time. Silence must not be taken as importing acquiescence. Much would have to be written if the subject, even as thus restricted were to be explored through all its implications, historical and economic as well as strictly legal. The fact that the prevailing opinion leaves the price provisions open for consideration in the future makes it appropriate to forego a fullness of elaboration that might otherwise be necessary. As a system of price fixing the Act is challenged upon three grounds: (1) because the governance of prices is not within the commerce clause; (2) because it is a denial of due process forbidden by the Fifth Amendment; and (3) because the standards for administrative action are indefinite, with the result that there has been an unlawful delegation of legislative power.

(1) With reference to the first objection, the obvious and sufficient answer is, so far as the Act is directed to interstate transactions, that sales made in such conditions constitute interstate commerce, and do not merely "affect" it. To regulate the price for such transactions is to regulate commerce itself, and not alone its antecedent conditions or its ultimate consequences. The very act of sale is limited and governed. Prices in interstate transactions may not be regulated by the states. They must therefore be subject to the power of the nation unless they are to be withdrawn altogether from the governmental supervision. If such a vacuum were permitted, many a public evil incidental to interstate transactions would be left without a remedy. This does not mean, of course, that prices may be fixed for arbitrary reasons or in an arbitrary way. The commerce power of the nation is subject to the requirement of due process like the police power of the states. Heed must be given to similar considerations of social benefit or detriment in marking the division between reason and oppression. The evidence is overwhelmingly that Congress did not ignore those considerations in the adoption of this Act. What is to be said in that regard may conveniently be postponed to the part of the opinion dealing with the Fifth Amendment.

Regulation of prices being an exercise of the commerce power in respect of interstate transactions, the question remains whether it comes within that power as applied to intrastate sales where interstate prices are directly or intimately affected. Mining and agriculture and manufacture are not interstate commerce considered by themselves, yet their relation to that commerce may be such that for the protection of the one there is need to regulate the other. Sometimes it is said that the relation must be "direct" to bring that power into play. In many circumstances such a description will be sufficiently precise to

meet the needs of the occasion. But a great principle of constitutional law is not susceptible of comprehensive statement in an adjective. The underlying thought is merely this, that "the law is not indifferent to considerations of degree." It cannot be indifferent to them without an expansion of the commerce clause that would absorb or imperil the reserved powers of the states. At times, as in the case cited, the waves of causation will have radiated, so far that their undulatory motion, if discernible at all, will be too faint or obscure, too broken by cross-currents, to be heeded by the law. In such circumstances the holding is not directed at prices or wages considered in the abstract, but at prices or wages in particular conditions. The relation may be tenuous or the opposite according to the facts. Always the setting of the facts is to be viewed if one would know the closeness of the tie. Perhaps, if one group of adjectives is to be chosen in preference to another, "intimate" and "remote" will be found to be as good as any. At all events, "direct" and "indirect," even if accepted as sufficient, must not be read too narrowly. The power is as broad as the need that evokes it. . . .

Within rulings the most orthodox, the prices for intrastate sales of coal have so inescapable a relation to those for interstate sales that a system of regulation for transactions of the one class is necessary to give adequate protection to the system of regulation adopted for the other. . . .

What has been said in this regard is said with added certitude when complainants' business is considered in the light of the statistics exhibited in the several records. In No. 636, the Carter case, the complainant has admitted that "sustantially all" (over 97½%) of the sales of the Carter Company are made in interstate commerce. In No. 649 the percentages of intrastate sales are, for one of the complaining companies, twenty-five per cent, for another one per cent, and for most of the others two per cent or four. The Carter Company has its mines in West Virginia; the mines of the other companies are located in Kentucky. In each of those states, moreover, coal from other regions is purchased in large quantities, and is thus brought into competition with the coal locally produced. Plainly, it is impossible to say either from the statute itself or from any figures laid before us that interstate sales will not be prejudicially affected in West Virginia and Kentucky if intrastate prices are maintained on a lower level. . . .

(2) The commerce clause being accepted as a sufficient source of power, the next inquiry must be whether the power has been exercised consistently with the Fifth Amendment. In the pursuit of that inquiry, *Nebbia* v. *New York,* lays down the applicable principle. There a statute of New York prescribing a minimum price for milk was upheld against the objection that price fixing was forbidden by the Fourteenth Amendment. We found it a sufficient reason to uphold the challenged system that "the conditions or practices in an industry make unrestricted competition an inadequate safeguard of the consumer's interests, produce waste harmful to the public, threaten ultimately to cut off the supply of a commodity needed by the public, or portend the destruction of the industry itself."

All this may be said, and with equal, if not greater force, of the conditions and practices in the bituminous coal industry, not only at the enactment of this statute in August, 1935, but for many years before. Overproduction was at a point where free competition had been degraded into anarchy. Prices had been cut so low that profit had become impossible for all except a lucky handful. Wages came down along with prices and with profits. There were strikes, at times nation-wide in extent, at other times spreading over broad areas and many mines, with the accompaniment of violence and bloodshed and misery and bitter feeling. The sordid tale is unfolded in many a document and treatise. During the twenty-three years between 1913 and 1935, there were nineteen investigations or hearings by Congress or by specially created commissions with reference to conditions in the coal mines. The hope of betterment was faint unless the industry could be subjected to the compulsion of a code. In the weeks immediately preceding the passage of this Act the country was threatened once more with a strike of ominous proportions. The plight of the industry was not merely a menace to owners and to mine workers: it was and had long been a menace to the public, deeply concerned in a steady and uniform supply of a fuel so vital to the national economy.

Congress was not condemned to inaction in the face of price wars and wage wars so pregnant with disaster. Commerce had been choked and burdened; its normal flow had been diverted from one state to another; there had been bankruptcy and waste and ruin alike for capital and for labor. The liberty protected by the Fifth Amendment does not include the right to persist in this anarchic riot. . . . The free competition so often figured as a social goods imports order and moderation and a decent regard for the welfare of the group. There is testimony in these records, testimony even by the assailants of the statute, that only through a system of regulated prices can the industry be stabilized and set upon the road of orderly and peaceful progress. If further facts are looked for, they are narrated in the findings as well as in congressional reports and a mass of public records. After making every allowance for difference of opinion as to the most efficient cure, the student of the subject is confronted with the indisputable truth that there were ills to be corrected, and ills that had a direct relation to the maintenance of commerce among the states without friction or diversion. An evil existing, and also the power to correct it, the law-makers were at liberty to use their own discretion in the selection of the means.

(3) Finally, and in answer to the third objection to the statute in its price-fixing provisions, there has been no excessive delegation of legislative power. . . .

I am authorized to state that Mr. Justice BRANDEIS and Mr. Justice STONE join in this opinion.

508. THE REPUBLICAN PLATFORM OF 1936
June 11, 1936

(*Proceedings* of the 21st Republican National Convention, p. 136)

The Republican National Convention met in Cleveland, Ohio, June 9, 1936, nominated Gov. A. F. Landon of Kansas to the Presidency and Col. Frank Knox of Illinois to the Vice-Presidency, and adopted a platform whose theme was expressed in its opening words. The campaign that followed was bitter but scarcely exciting. In the November election the Republican candidates carried two states—Maine and Vermont, and polled a total of 16,681,913 votes. See, Alfred M. Landon, *America at the Crossroads;* D. Dumond, *Roosevelt to Roosevelt;* C. A. and M. R. Beard, *America in Midpassage.*

America is in peril. The welfare of American men and women and the future of our youth are at stake. We dedicate ourselves to the preservation of their political liberty, their individual opportunity and their character as free citizens, which today for the first time are threatened by Government itself.

For three long years the New Deal Administration has dishonored American traditions and flagrantly betrayed the pledges upon which the Democratic Party sought and received public support.

The powers of Congress have been usurped by the President.

The integrity and authority of the Supreme Court have been flouted.

The rights and liberties of American citizens have been violated.

Regulated monopoly has displaced free enterprise.

The New Deal Administration constantly seeks to usurp the rights reserved to the States and to the people.

It has insisted on the passage of laws contrary to the Constitution.

It has intimidated witnesses and interfered with the right of petition.

It has dishonored our country by repudiating its most sacred obligations.

It has been guilty of frightful waste and extravagance, using public funds for partisan political purposes.

It has promoted investigations to harass and intimidate American citizens, at the same time denying investigations into its own improper expenditures.

It has created a vast multitude of new offices, filled them with its favorites, set up a centralized bureaucracy, and sent out swarms of inspectors to harass our people.

It had bred fear and hesitation in commerce and industry, thus discouraging new enterprises, preventing employment and prolonging the depression.

It secretly has made tariff agreements with our foreign competitors, flooding our markets with foreign commodities.

It has coerced and intimidated voters by withholding relief from those opposing its tyrannical policies.

It has destroyed the morale of many of our people and made them dependent upon Government.

Appeals to passion and class prejudice have replaced reason and tolerance.

To a free people these actions are insufferable. This campaign cannot be waged on the traditional differences between the Republican and Democratic parties. The responsibility of this election transcends all previous political divisions. We invite all Americans, irrespective of party, to join us in defense of American institutions.

CONSTITUTIONAL GOVERNMENT AND FREE ENTERPRISE

WE PLEDGE OURSELVES:

1. To maintain the American system of constitutional and local self government, and to resist all attempts to impair the authority of the Supreme Court of the United States, the final protector of the rights of our citizens against the arbitrary encroachments of the legislative and executive branches of Government. There can be no individual liberty without an independent judiciary.

2. To preserve the American system of free enterprise, private competition, and equality of opportunity, and to seek its constant betterment in the interests of all.

REEMPLOYMENT

The only permanent solution of the unemployment problem is the absorption of the unemployed by industry and agriculture. To that end, we advocate:

Removal of restricitons on production.

Abandonment of all New Deal policies that raise production costs, increase the cost of living, and thereby restrict buying, reduce volume and prevent reemployment.

Encouragement instead of hindrance to legitimate business.

Withdrawal of Government from competition with private payrolls.

Elimination of unnecessary and hampering regulations.

Adoption of such policies as will furnish a chance for individual enterprise, industrial expansion, and the restoration of jobs.

RELIEF

The necessities of life must be provided for the needy, and hope must be restored pending recovery. The administration of relief is a major failure of the New Deal. It has been faithless to those who most deserve our sympathy. To end confusion, partisanship, waste and incompetence,

WE PLEDGE:

1. The return of responsibility for relief administration to non-political local agencies familiar with community problems.
2. Federal grants-in-aid to the States and Territories while the need exists, upon compliance with these conditions: (a) a fair proportion of the total relief burden to be provided from the revenues of States and local governments; (b) all engaged in relief administration to be selected on the basis of merit and fitness; (c) adequate provision to be made for the encouragement of those persons who are trying to become self-supporting.
3. Undertaking of Federal public works only on their merits and separate from the administration of relief.
4. A prompt determination of the facts concerning relief and unemployment.

SECURITY

Real security will be possible only when our productive capacity is sufficient to furnish a decent standard of living for all American families and to provide a surplus for future needs and contingencies. For the attainment of that ultimate objective, we look to the energy, self-reliance and character of our people, and to our system of free enterprise.

Society has an obligation to promote the security of the people, by affording some measure of protection against involuntary unemployment and dependency in old age. The New Deal policies, while purporting to provide social security, have, in fact, endangered it.

We propose a system of old age security, . . .

We propose to encourage adoption by the States and Territories of honest and practical measures for meeting the problems of unemployment insurance.

The unemployment insurance and old age annuity sections of the present Social Security Act are unworkable and deny benefits to about two-thirds of our adult population, including professional men and women and all those engaged in agriculture and domestic service, and the self employed, while imposing heavy tax burdens upon all. The so-called reserve fund estimated at forty-seven billion dollars for old age insurance is no reserve at all, because the fund will contain nothing but the Government's promise to pay, while the taxes collected in the guise of premiums will be wasted by the Government in reckless and extravagant political schemes.

LABOR

The welfare of labor rests upon increased production and the prevention of exploitation. We pledge ourselves to:

Protect the right of labor to organize and to bargain collectively through representatives of its own choosing without interference from any source.

Prevent governmental job holders from exercising autocratic powers over labor.

Support the adoption of State laws and interstate compacts to abolish sweatshops and child labor, and to protect women and children with respect to maximum hours, minimum wages and working conditions. We believe that this can be done within the Constitution as it now stands.

AGRICULTURE

The farm problem is an economic and social, not a partisan problem, and we propose to treat it accordingly. . . .

Our paramount object is to protect and foster the family type of farm, traditional in American life, and to promote policies which will bring about an adjustment of agriculture to meet the needs of domestic and foreign markets. As an emergency measure, during the agricultural depression, Federal benefit payments or grants-in-aid when administered within the means of the Federal Government are consistent with a balanced budget.

WE PROPOSE:

1. To facilitate economical production and

increased consumption on a basis of abundance instead of scarcity.

2. A national land-use program, including the acquisition of abandoned and non-productive farm lands by voluntary sale or lease, subject to approval of the legislative and executive branches of the States concerned, and the devotion of such land to appropriate public use, such as watershed protection and flood prevention, reforestation, recreation, and conservation of wild life.

3. That an agricultural policy be pursued for the protection and restoration of the land resources, designed to bring about such a balance between soil-building and soil-depleting crops as will permanently insure productivity, with reasonable benefits to cooperating farmers on family-type farms, but so regulated as to eliminate the New Deal's destructive policy towards the dairy and live-stock industries.

4. To extend experimental aid to farmers developing new crops suited to our soil and climate.

5. To promote the industrial use of farm products by applied science.

6. To protect the American farmer against the importation of all livestock, dairy, and agricultural products, substitutes therefor, and derivatives therefrom, which will depress American farm prices.

7. To provide effective quarantine against imported livestock, dairy and other farm products from countries which do not impose health and sanitary regulations fully equal to those required of our own producers.

8. To provide for ample farm credit at rates as low as those enjoyed by other industries, including commodity and livestock loans, and preference in land loans to the farmer acquiring or refinancing a farm as a home.

9. To provide for decentralized, non-partisan control of the Farm Credit Administration and the election by National Farm Loan Associations of at least one-half of each Board of Directors of the Federal Land Banks, and thereby remove these institutions from politics.

10. To provide, in the case of agricultural products of which there are exportable surpluses, the payment of reasonable benefits upon the domestically consumed portion of such crops in order to make the tariff effective. These payments are to be limited to the production level of the family-type farm.

11. To encourage and further develop cooperative marketing.

12. To furnish Government assistance in disposing of surpluses in foreign trade by bargaining for foreign markets selectively by countries both as to exports and imports. We strenuously oppose so-called reciprocal treaties which trade off the American farmer.

13. To give every reasonable assistance to producers in areas suffering from temporary disaster, so that they may regain and maintain a self-supporting status.

TARIFF

Nearly sixty per cent of all imports into the United States are now free of duty. The other forty per cent of imports compete directly with the product of our industry. We would keep on the free list all products not grown or produced in the United States in commercial quantites. As to all commodities that commercially compete with our farms, our forests, our mines, our fisheries, our oil wells, our labor and our industries, sufficient protection should be maintained at all times to defend the American farmer and the American wage earner from the destructive competition emanating from the subsidies of foreign Governments and the imports from low-wage and depreciated-currency countries.

We will repeal the present Reciprocal Trade Agreement law. . . .

We will restore the principle of the flexible tariff in order to meet changing economic conditions here and abroad and broaden by careful definition the powers of the Tariff Commission in order to extend this policy along non-partisan lines.

We will adjust tariffs with a view to promoting international trade, the stabilization of currencies, and the attainment of a proper balance between agriculture and industry.

We condemn the secret negotiation of reciprocal trade treaties without public hearing or legislative approval.

MONOPOLIES

A private monopoly is indefensible and intolerable. It menaces and, if continued, will utterly destroy constitutional government and the liberty of the citizen.

We favor the vigorous enforcement of the criminal laws, as well as the civil laws, against monopolies and trusts and their officials, and we demand the enactment of such additional legislation as is necessary to make it impossible for private monopoly to exist in the United States.

We will employ the full powers of the Government to the end that monopoly shall be eliminated and that free enterprise shall be fully restored and maintained.

REGULATION OF BUSINESS

We recognize the existence of a field within which governmental regulation is desirable and salutary. The authority to regulate should be vested in an independent tribunal acting under clear and specific laws establishing definite standards. Their determinations on law and facts should be subject to review by the Courts. We favor Federal regulation, within the Constitution, of the marketing of securities to protect investors. We favor also Federal regulation of the interstate activities of public utilities.

CIVIL SERVICE

Under the New Deal, official authority has been given to inexperienced and incompetent persons. The Civil Service has been sacrificed to create a national political machine. As a result the Federal Government has never presented such a picture of confusion and inefficiency.

We pledge ourselves to the merit system, virtually destroyed by New Deal spoilsmen. It should be restored, improved and extended. . . .

GOVERNMENT FINANCE

The New Deal Administration has been characterized by shameful waste and general financial irresponsibility. It has piled deficit upon deficit. It threatens national bankruptcy and the destruction through inflation of insurance policies and savings bank deposits.

WE PLEDGE OURSELVES TO:

Stop the folly of uncontrolled spending.

Balance the budget—not by increasing taxes but by cutting expenditures, drastically and immediately.

Revise the Federal tax system and coordinate it with State and local tax systems.

Use the taxing power for raising revenue and not for punitive or political purposes.

MONEY AND BANKING

We advocate a sound currency to be preserved at all hazards.

The first requisite to a sound and stable currency is a balanced budget.

We oppose further devaluation of the dollar.

We will restore to the Congress the authority lodged with it by the Constitution to coin money and regulate the value thereof by repealing all the laws delegating this authority to the Executive.

We will cooperate with other countries toward stabilization of currencies as soon as we can do so with due regard for our national interests and as soon as other nations have sufficient stability to justify such action.

FOREIGN AFFAIRS

We pledge ourselves to promote and maintain peace by all honorable means not leading to foreign alliances or political commitments.

Obedient to the traditional foreign policy of America and to the repeatedly expressed will of the American people, we pledge that America shall not become a member of the League of Nations nor of the World Court nor shall America take on any entangling alliances in foreign affairs.

We shall promote, as the best means of securing and maintaining peace by the pacific settlement of disputes, the great cause of international arbitration through the establishment of free, independent tribunals, which shall determine such disputes in accordance with law, equity and justice.

NATIONAL DEFENSE

We favor an army and navy, including air forces, adequate for our National Defense.

We will cooperate with other nations in the limitation of armaments and control of traffic in arms.

BILL OF RIGHTS

We pledge ourselves to preserve, protect and defend, against all intimidation and threat, freedom of religion, speech, press and radio; and the right of assembly and petition and immunity from unreasonable searches and seizures.

We offer the abiding security of a government of laws as against the autocratic perils of a government of men.

FURTHERMORE

1. We favor the construction by the Federal Government of head-water storage basins to prevent floods, subject to the approval of the legislative and executive branches of the government of the States whose lands are concerned. . . .

5. We shall use every effort to collect the war debt due us from foreign countries amounting to $12,000,000,000—one-third of our national debt. No effort has been made by the present administration even to reopen negotiations.

6. We are opposed to legislation which discriminates against women in Federal and State employment.

CONCLUSION

We assume the obligations and duties imposed upon Government by modern conditions. We affirm our unalterable conviction that, in the future as in the past, the fate of the nation will depend, not so much on the wisdom and power of Government, as on the character and virtue, self-reliance, industry and thrift of the people and on their willingness to meet the responsibilities essential to the preservation of a free society.

Finally, as our party affirmed in its first Platform in 1856: "Believing that the spirit of our institutions as well as the Constitution of our country guarantees liberty of conscience and equality of rights among our citizens, we oppose all legislation tending to impair them," and "we invite the affiliation and cooperation of the men of all parties, however differing from us in other respects, in support of the principles herein declared."

The acceptance of the nomination tendered by this Convention carries with it, as a matter of private honor and public faith, an undertaking by each candidate to be true to the principles and program herein set forth.

509. THE DEMOCRATIC PLATFORM OF 1936
June 25, 1936
(*Proceedings* of the Democratic National Convention, 1936, p. 192)

The Democratic National Convention met in Philadelphia June 23, 1936, renominated President Roosevelt and Vice-President Garner, and adopted a platform reaffirming the New Deal. In the ensuing election Mr. Roosevelt carried 46 states, polled 523 electoral and 27,751,612 popular votes. Roosevelt's campaign speeches can be found in his *Public Papers and Addresses,* Vol. V. See also, D. Dumond, *Roosevelt to Roosevelt;* C. A. and M. R. Beard, *America in Midpassage.*

THE DEMOCRATIC PLATFORM

Adopted by the Democratic Party, in Convention, at Philadelphia, June, 1936

We hold this truth to be self-evident—that the test of a representative government is its ability to promote the safety and happiness of the people.

We hold this truth to be self-evident—that twelve years of Republican leadership left our nation sorely stricken in body, mind and

spirit; and that three years of Democratic leadership have put it back on the road to restored health and prosperity.

We hold this truth to be self-evident—that twelve years of Republican surrender of the dictatorship of a privileged few have been supplanted by a Democratic leadership which has returned the people themselves to the place of authority, and has revived in them new faith and restored the hope which they had almost lost.

We hold this truth to be self-evident—that this three-year recovery in all the basic values of life and the reestablishment of the American way of living has been brought about by humanizing the policies of the Federal Government as they affect the personal, financial, industrial and agricultural well-being of the American people.

We hold this truth to be self-evident—that government in a modern civilization has certain inescapable obligations to its citizens, among which are:

(1) Protection of the family and the home.

(2) Establishment of a democracy of opportunity for all the people.

(3) Aid to those overtaken by disaster.

These obligations, neglected through twelve years of the old leadership, have once more been recognized by American Government. Under the new leadership they will never be neglected.

FOR THE PROTECTION OF THE FAMILY AND THE HOME

. . . .

SAVINGS AND INVESTMENT

(2) We have safeguarded the thrift of our citizens by restraining those who would gamble with other people's savings, by requiring truth in the sale of securities; by putting the brakes upon the use of credit for speculation; by outlawing the manipulation of prices in stock and commodity markets; by curbing the overweening power and unholy practices of utility holding companies; by insuring fifty million banks accounts.

OLD AGE AND SOCIAL SECURITY

(3) We have built foundations for the security of those who are faced with the hazards of unemployment and old age; for the orphaned, the crippled and the blind. On the foundation of the Social Security Act we are determined to erect a structure of economic security for all our people, making sure that this benefit shall keep step with the ever-increasing capacity of America to provide a high standard of living for all its citizens.

CONSUMER

(4) We will act to secure to the consumer fair value, honest sales and a decreased spread between the price he pays and the price the producer receives.

RURAL ELECTRIFICATION

(5) This administration has fostered power rate yardsticks in the Tennessee Valley and in several other parts of the nation. As a result electricity has been made available to the people at a lower rate. We will continue to promote plans for rural electrification and for cheap power by means of the yardstick method.

HOUSING

(6) We maintain that our people are entitled to decent, adequate housing at a price which they can afford. In the last three years the Federal Government, having saved more than two million homes from foreclosure, has taken the first steps in our history to provide decent housing for people of meagre incomes. We believe every encouragement should be given to the building of new homes by private enterprise; and that the Government should steadily extend its housing program toward the goal of adequate housing for those forced through economic necessities to live in unhealthy and slum conditions.

VETERANS

(7) We shall continue just treatment of our war veterans and their dependents.

FOR THE ESTABLISHMENT OF A DEMOCRACY OF OPPORTUNITY

AGRICULTURE

We have taken the farmers off the road to ruin.

We have kept our pledge to agriculture to use all available means to raise farm income towards its pre-war purchasing power. . . .

By Federal legislation we have reduced the farmer's indebtedness and doubled his net income. In cooperation with the States and through the farmers' own committees, we are restoring the fertility of his land and checking the erosion of his soil. We are bringing electricity and good roads to his home.

We shall continue to improve the soil conservation and domestic allotment program with payments to farmers. . . .

We recognize the gravity of the evils of farm tenancy, and we pledge the full cooperation of the Government in the refinancing of farm indebtedness at the lowest possible rates of interest and over a long term of years.

We favor the production of all the market will absorb, both at home and abroad, plus a reserve supply sufficient to insure fair prices to consumers; we favor judicious commodity loans on seasonal surpluses; and we favor assistance within Federal authority to enable farmers to adjust and balance production with demand, at a fair profit to the farmers.

We favor encouragement of sound, practical farm cooperatives.

By the purchase and retirement of ten million acres of sub-marginal land, and assistance to those attempting to eke out an existence upon it, we have made a good beginning toward proper land use and rural rehabilitation.

The farmer has been returned to the road to freedom and prosperity. We will keep him on that road.

LABOR

We have given the army of America's industrial workers something more substantial than the Republicans' dinner pail full of promises. We have increased the worker's pay and shortened his hours; we have undertaken to put an end to the sweated labor of his wife and children; we have written into the law of the land his right to collective bargaining and self-organization free from the interference of employers; we have provided Federal machinery for the peaceful settlement of labor disputes.

We will continue to protect the worker and we will guard his rights, both as wage-earner and consumer, in the production and consumption of all commodities, including coal and water power and other natural-resource products. . . .

BUSINESS

We have taken the American business man out of the red. We have saved his bank and given it a sounder foundation; we have extended credit; we have lowered interest rates; we have undertaken to free him from the ravages of cut-throat competition. . . .

YOUTH

We have aided youth to stay in school; given them constructive occupation; opened the door to opportunity which twelve years of Republican neglect had closed. . . .

MONOPOLY AND CONCENTRATION OF ECONOMIC POWER

Monopolies and the concentration of economic power, the creation of Republican rule and privilege, continue to be the master of the producer, the exploiter of the consumer, and the enemy of the independent operator. This is a problem challenging the unceasing effort of untrammeled public officials in every branch of the Government. We pledge vigorously and fearlessly to enforce the criminal and civil provisions of the existing anti-trust laws, and to the extent that their effectiveness has been weakened by new corporate devices or judicial construction, we propose by law to restore their efficacy in stamping out monopolistic practices and the concentration of economic power. . . .

UNEMPLOYMENT

We believe that unemployment is a national problem, and that it is an inescapable obligational way. . . . Where business fails to supply such employment, we believe that work at prevailing wages should be provided in co-operation with State and local governments on useful public projects, to the end that the national wealth may be increased, the skill and energy of the worker may be utilized, his morale maintained, and the unemployed assured the opportunity to earn the necessities of life.

THE CONSTITUTION

The Republican platform proposes to meet many pressing national problems solely by action of the separate States. We know that drought, dust storms, floods, minimum wages, maximum hours, child labor and working conditions in industry, monopolistic and unfair business practices cannot be adequately handled exclusively by 48 separate State legislatures, 48 separate State administrations and 48 separate State courts. Transactions and activities which inevitably overflow State boundaries call for both State and Federal treatment.

We have sought and will continue to seek to meet these problems through legislation within the Constitution.

If these problems cannot be effectively solved by legislation within the Constitution, we shall seek such clarifying amendment as will assure to the legislatures of the several States and to the Congress of the United States, each within its proper jurisdiction, the power to enact those laws which the State and Federal legislatures, within their respective spheres, shall find necessary in order adequately to regulate commerce, protect public health and safety and safeguard economic security. Thus we propose to maintain the letter and spirit of the Constitution.

THE MERIT SYSTEM IN GOVERNMENT

For the protection of government itself and promotion of its efficiency, we pledge the immediate extension of the merit system through the classified civil service—which was first established and fostered under Democratic auspices—to all non-policy-making positions in the Federal service.

We shall subject to the civil service law all continuing positions which, because of the emergency, have been exempt from its operation.

CIVIL LIBERTIES

We shall continue to guard the freedom of speech, press, radio, religion and assembly which our Constitution guarantees; with equal rights to all and special privileges to none.

GOVERNMENT FINANCE

The Administration has stopped deflation, restored values and enabled business to go ahead with confidence.

When national income shrinks, government income is imperilled. In reviving national income, we have fortified government finance. We have raised the public credit to a position of unsurpassed security. The interest rate on Government bonds has been reduced to the lowest point in twenty-eight years. The same Government bonds which in 1932 sold under eighty-three are now selling over 104.

We approve the objective of a permanently sound currency so stabilized as to prevent the former wide fluctuations in value which injured in turn producers, debtors, and property owners on the one hand, and wage-earners and creditors on the other, a currency which will permit full utilization of the country's resources. We assert that today we have the soundest currency in the world.

We are determined to reduce the expenses of government. . . . Our retrenchment, tax and recovery programs thus reflect our firm determination to achieve a balanced budget and the reduction of the national debt at the earliest possible moment.

FOREIGN POLICY

In our relationship with other nations, this Government will continue to extend the policy of the Good Neighbor. We reaffirm our opposition to war as an instrument of national policy, and declare that disputes between nations should be settled by peaceful means. We shall continue to observe a true neutrality in the disputes of others; to be prepared, resolutely to resist aggression against ourselves; to work for peace and to take the profits out of war; to guard against being drawn, by political commitments, international banking or private trading, into any war which may develop anywhere.

We shall continue to foster the increase in our foreign trade which has been achieved by this administration; to seek by mutual agreement the lowering of those tariff barriers, quotas and embargoes which have been raised against our exports of agricultural and industrial products; but continue as in the past to give adequate protection to our farmers and manufacturers against unfair competition or the dumping on our shores of commodities and goods produced abroad by cheap labor or subsidized by foreign governments.

THE ISSUE

The issue in this election is plain. The American people are called upon to choose between a Republican administration that has and would again regiment them in the service of privileged groups and a Democratic administration dedicated to the establishment of equal economic opportunity for all our people.

We have faith in the destiny of our nation. We are sufficiently endowed with natural resources and with productive capacity to provide for all a quality of life that meets the standards of real Americanism.

Dedicated to a government of liberal American principles, we are determined to oppose equally, the despotism of Communism and the menace of concealed Facism.

We hold this final truth to be self-evident— that the interests, the security and the happiness of the people of the United States of America can be perpetuated only under the democratic government as conceived by the founders of our nation.

510. UNITED STATES v. CURTISS-WRIGHT EXPORT CORP.
299 U. S. 304
1936

Appeal from the District Court of the U. S. for the Southern District of New York. This case involved the question of the delegation of powers in the realm of foreign affairs, and furnished the occasion for an illuminating dissertation on the nature of the American Union. The facts of the case are set forth in the decision. See W. E. Binkley, *The Powers of the President;* Q. Wright, *The Control of American Foreign Relations;* E. S. Corwin, *The President's Control of Foreign Relations.*

SUTHERLAND, J. On January 27, 1936, an indictment was returned in the court below, the first count of which charges that appellees, beginning with the 29th day of May, 1934, conspired to sell in the United States certain arms of war, namely fifteen machine guns, to Bolivia, a country then engaged in armed conflict in the Chaco, in violation of the Joint Resolution of Congress approved May 28, 1934, and the provisions of a proclamation issued on the same day by the President of the United States pursuant to authority conferred by Sec. 1 of the resolution. In pursuance of the conspiracy, the commission of certain overt acts was alleged, details of which need not be stated. The Joint Resolution follows:

"Resolved by the Senate and House of Representatives of the United States of America in Congress assembled, That if the President finds that the prohibition of the sale of arms and munitions of war in the United States to those countries now engaged in armed conflict in the Chaco may contribute to the reestablishment of peace between those countries, and if after consultation with the governments of other American Republics and with their cooperation, as well as that of such other governments as he may deem necessary, he makes proclamation to that effect, it shall be unlawful to sell, except under such limitations and exceptions as the President prescribes, any arms or munitions or war in any place in the United States to the countries now engaged in that armed conflict, or to any person, company, or association acting in the interest of either country, until otherwise ordered by the President or by Congress.

"Sec. 2. Whoever sells any arms or munitions of war in violation of section 1 shall, on conviction, be punished by a fine not exceeding $10,000 or by imprisonment not exceeding two years, or both."

The President's proclamation, after reciting the terms of the Joint Resolution, declares:

"Now, therefore, I Franklin D. Roosevelt, President of the United States of America, acting under and by virtue of the authority conferred in me by the said joint resolution of Congress, do hereby declare and proclaim that I have found that the prohibition of the sale of arms and munitions of war in the United States to those countries now engaged in armed conflict in the Chaco may contribute to the reestablishment of peace between those countries, and that I have consulted with the governments of other American Republics and have been assured of the cooperation of such governments as I have deemed necessary as contemplated by the said joint resolution; and I do hereby admonish all citizens of the United States and every person to abstain from every violation of the provisions of the joint resolution above set forth, hereby made applicable to Bolivia and Paraguay, and I do hereby warn them that all violations of such provisions will be rigorously prosecuted. . . .

On November 14, 1935, this proclamation was revoked in the following termns: . . .

Appellees severally demurred to the first count of the indictment on the grounds (1) that it did not charge facts sufficient to show the commission by appellees of any offense against any law of the United States; . . .

The court below sustained the demurrers upon the first point, . . . The government appealed to this court under the provisions of the Criminal Appeals Act of March 2, 1907. . . .

First. It is contended that by the Joint Resolution, the going into effect and continued operation of the resolution was conditioned (a) upon the President's judgment as to its beneficial effect 'ipon the reestablishment of peace between the countries engaged in armed conflict in the Chaco; (b) upon the making of a proclamation, which was left to his unfettered discretion, thus constituting an attempted substitution of the President's will for that of Congress; (c) upon the making of a proclamation putting an end to the operation of the resolution, which again was left to the President's unfettered discretion; and (d) further, that the extent of its operation in particular cases was subject to limitation and exception by the President, controlled by no standard. In each of these particulars, appellees urge that Congress abdicated its essential functions and delegated them to the Executive.

Whether, if the Joint Resolution had related solely to internal affairs it would be open to the challenge that it constituted an unlawful delegation of legislative power to the Executive, we find it unnecessary to determine. The whole aim of the resolution is to affect a situation entirely external to the United States, and falling within the category of foreign affairs. The determination which we are called to make, therefore, is whether the Joint Resolution, as applied to that situation, is vulnerable to attack under the rule that forbids a delegation of the law-making power. In other words, assuming (but not deciding) that the challenged delegation, if it were confined to internal affairs, would be invalid, may it nevertheless be sustained on the ground that its exclusive aim is to afford a remedy for a hurtful condition within foreign territory?

It will contribute to the elucidation of the question if we first consider the differences between the powers of the federal government in respect of foreign or external affairs and those in respect of domestic or internal affairs. That there are differences between them, and that these differences are fundamental, may not be doubted.

The two classes of powers are different, both in respect of their origin and their nature. The broad statement that the federal government can exercise no powers except those specifically enumerated in the Constitution, and such implied powers as are necessary and proper to carry into effect the enumerated powers, is categorically true only in respect of our internal affairs. In that field, the primary purpose of the Constitution was to carve from the general mass of legislative powers *then possessed by the states* such portions as it was thought desirable to vest in the federal government, leaving those not included in the enumeration still in the States. *Carter* v. *Carter Coal Co.,* 298 U. S. 238, 294. That this doctrine applies only to powers which the states had, is self evident. And since the states severally never possessed international powers, such powers could not have been carved from the mass of state powers but obviously were transmitted to the United States from some other source. During the colonial period, those powers were possessed exclusively by and were entirely under the control of the Crown. By the Declaration of Independence, "the Representatives of the United States of America" declared the United (not the several) Colonies to be free and independent states, and as such to have "full Power to levy War, conclude Peace, contract Alliances, establish Commerce and to do all other Acts and Things which Independent States may of right do."

As a result of the separation from Great Britain by the colonies acting as a unit, the powers of external sovereignty passed from the Crown not to the colonies severally, but to the colonies in their collective and corporate capacity as the United States of America. Even before the Declaration, the colonies were a unit in foreign affairs, acting through a common agency—namely the Continental Congress, composed of delegates from the thirteen colonies. That agency exercised the powers of war and peace, raised an army, created a navy, and finally adopted the Declaration of Independence. Rulers come and go; governments end and forms of government change; but sovereignty survives. A political society cannot endure without a supreme will somewhere. Sovereignty is never held in suspense. When, therefore, the external sovereignty of Great Britain in respect of the colonies ceased, it immediately passed to the Union. *See Penhallow* v. *Doane*, 3 Dall. 54, 80–81. That fact was given practical application almost at once. The treaty of peace, made on September 23, 1783, was concluded between his Britanic Majesty and the "United States of America." 8 Stat.—European Treaties—80.

The Union existed before the Constitution, which was ordained and established among other things to form "a more perfect Union."

Prior to that event, it is clear that the Union, declared by the Articles of Confederation to be "perpetual," was the sole possessor of external sovereignty and in the Union it remained without change save in so far as the Constitution in express terms qualified its exercise. The Framers' Convention was called and exerted its powers upon the irrefutable postulate that though the states were several their people in respect of foreign affairs were one. . . .

It results that the investment of the federal government with the powers of external sovereignty did not depend upon the affirmative grants of the Constitution. The powers to declare and wage war, to conclude peace, to make treaties, to maintain diplomatic relations with other sovereignties, if they had never been mentioned in the Constitution, would have vested in the federal government as necessary concomitants of nationality. Neither the Constitution nor the laws passed in pursuance of it have any force in foreign territory unless in respect of our own citizens; and operations of the nation in such territory must be governed by treaties, international understandings and compacts, and the principles of international law. As a member of the family of nations, the right and power of the United States in that field are equal to the right and power of the other members of the international family. Otherwise, the United States is not completely sovereign. The power to acquire territory by discovery and occupation, the power to expel undesirable aliens, the power to make such international agreements as do not constitute treaties in the constitutional sense; none of which is expressly affirmed by the Constitution, nevertheless exist as inherently inseparable from the conception of nationality. This the court recognized, and in each of the cases cited found the warrant for its conclusions not in the provisions of the Constitution, but in the law of nations. . . .

Not only, as we have shown, is the federal power over external affairs in origin and essential character different from that over internal affairs, but participation in the exercise of the power is significantly limited. In this vast external realm, with its important, complicated, delicate and manifold problems, the President alone has the power to speak or listen as a representative of the nation. He *makes* treaties with the advice and consent of the Senate; but he alone negotiates. Into the field of negotiation the Senate cannot intrude; and Congress itself is powerless to invade it. . . .

It is important to bear in mind that we are here dealing not along with an authority vested in the President by an exertion of legislative power, but with such an authority plus the very delicate, plenary and exclusive power of the President as the sole organ of the federal government in the field of international relations—a power which does not require as a basis for its exercise an act of Congress, but which, of course, like every other governmental power, must be exercised in subordination to the applicable provisions of the Constitution. It is quite apparent that if, in the maintenance of our international relations, embarrassment—perhaps serious embarrassment—is to be avoided and success for our aims achieved, congressional legislation which is to be made effective through negotiation and inquiry within the international field must often accord to the President a degree of discretion and freedom from statutory restriction which would not be admissible were domestic affairs alone involved. Moreover he, not Congress, has the better opportunity of knowing the conditions which prevail in foreign countries, and especially is this true in time of war. He has his confidential sources of information. He has his agents in the form of diplomatic, consular and other officials. Secrecy in respect of information gathered by them may be highly necessary, and the premature disclosure of it productive of harmful results. Indeed, so clearly is this true that the first President refused to accede to a request to lay before the House of Representatives the instructions, correspondence and documents relating to the negotiation of the Jay Treaty. . . .

In the light of the foregoing observations, it is evident that this court should not be in haste to apply a general rule which will have the effect of condemning legislation like that under review as constituting an unlawful delegation of legislative power. The principles which justify such legislation find overwhelming support in the unbroken legislative practice which has prevailed almost from the inception of the national government to the present day.

Let us examine, in chronological order, the acts of legislation which warrant this conclusion: . . . [cites numerous Congressional acts.]

It well may be assumed that these legislative precedents were in mind when Congress passed the joint resolutions of April 22, 1898, March 14, 1912, and January 31, 1922, to prohibit the export of coal or other war material. . . .

We had occasion to review these embargo and kindred acts in connection with an exhaustive discussion of the general subject of delegation of legislative power in a recent case, *Panama Refining Co.* v. *Ryan,* 293 U. S. 388, 421–422, and in justifying such acts, pointed out that they confided to the President "an authority which was cognate to the conduct by him of the foreign relations of the government."

The result of holding that the joint resolution here under attack is void and unenforceable as constituting an unlawful delegation of legislative power would be to stamp this multitude of comparable acts and resolutions as likewise invalid. And while this court may not, and should not, hesitate to declare acts of Congress, however many times repeated, to be unconstitutional if beyond all rational doubt it finds them to be so, an impressive array of legislation such as we have just set forth, enacted by nearly every Congress from the beginning of our national existence to the present day, must be given unusual weight in the process of reaching a correct determination of the problem. A legislative practice such as we have here, evidenced not by only occasional instances, but marked by the movement of a steady stream for a century and a half of time, goes a long way in the direction of proving the presence of unassailable ground for the constitutionality of the practice, to be found in the origin and history of the power involved, or in its nature or in both combined. . . .

The uniform, long-continued and undisputed legislative practice just disclosed rests upon an admissible view of the Constitution which, even if the practice found far less support in principle than we think it does, we should not feel at liberty at this late day to disturb. . . .

The judgment of the court below must be reversed and the cause remanded for further proceedings in accordance with the foregoing opinion.

Reversed.

McREYNOLDS, J. dissented.

511. DE JONGE v. OREGON
299 U. S. 353
1937

Appeal from the Supreme Court of Oregon. The extent to which the due process clause of the Fourteenth Amendment has come to embrace the guarantees of the first eight amendments is here illustrated. The facts of the case are set forth in the opinion of the Court. See, Z. Chafee, *Freedom of Speech;* C. Warren, "The new 'Liberty' under the Fourteenth Amendment," 39 Harv. L. Rev. 431; Spencer, "Criminal Syndicalism—De Jonge v. Oregon," 16 Ore. L. Rev. 278; "The Supreme Court as Protector of Political Minorities," 46 Yale L. J. 862; Jarrett and Mund, "The Right of Assembly," 9 N. Y. U. L. Qt. Rev. 1; and the note on the comparable Hague Injunction case in 48 Yale L. J., 257.

HUGHES, C. J. Appellant, Dirk De Jorge, was indicted in Multnomah County, Oregon, for violation of the Criminal Syndicalism Law of that State. The act defines "criminal syndicalism" as "the doctrine which advocates crime, physical violence, sabotage or any unlawful acts or methods as a means of accomplishing or effecting industrial or political change or revolution."

With this preliminary definition the act proceeds to describe a number of offenses, embracing the teaching of criminal syndicalism, the printing or distribution of books, pamphlets, &c., advocating that doctrine, the organization of a society or assemblage which advocates it, and presiding at or assisting in conducting a meeting of such an organization, society or group. The prohibited acts are made felonies, punishable by imprisonment for not less than one year nor more than ten years, or by a fine of not more than $1,000, or by both.

We are concerned with but one of the described offenses and with the validity of the statute in this particular application. The charge is that appellant assisted in the conduct of a meeting which was called under the auspices of the Communist party, an organization advocating criminal syndicalism. The defense was that the meeting was public and orderly and was held for a lawful purpose; that while it was held under the auspices of the Communist party, neither criminal syndicalism nor any unlawful conduct was taught or advocated at the meeting either by appellant or by others.

Appellant moved for a direction of acquittal, contending that the statute as applied to him, for merely assisting at a meeting called by the Communist party at which nothing unlawful was done or advocated, violated the due process clause of the Fourteenth Amendment of the Constitution of the United States. This contention was overruled. Appellant was found guilty as charged and was sentenced to imprisonment for seven years. The judgment was affirmed by the Supreme Court of the State, which considered the constitutional question and sustained the statute as thus applied. 152 Ore. 315. The case comes here on appeal. . . .

The stipulation, after setting forth the charging part of the indictment, recites in substance the following:

That on July 27, 1934, there was held in Portland a meeting which had been advertised by hand-bills issued by the Portland section of the Communist party; that the number of persons in attendance was variously estimated at from 150 to 300; that some of those present, who were members of the Communist party, estimated that not to exceed 10 to 15 per cent of those in attendance were such members; that the meeting was open to the public without charge and no questions were asked of those entering with respect to their relation to the Communist party; that the notice of the meeting advertised it as a protest against illegal raids on workers' halls and homes and against the shooting of striking longshoremen by Portland police; that the chairman stated that it was a meeting held by the Communist party; that the first speaker dwelt on the activities of the Young Communist League.

That the defendant De Jonge, the second speaker, was a member of the Communist party and went to the meeting to speak in its name; that in his talk he protested against conditions in the county jail, the action of city police in relation to the maritime strike then in progress in Portland and numerous other matters; that he discussed the reason for the raids on the Communist headquarters and workers' halls and offices; that he told the workers that these attacks were due to efforts on the part of the steamship companies and stevedoring companies to break the maritime longshoremen's and seamen's strike; that they hoped to break the strike by pitting the longshoremen and seamen against the Communist movement; that there was also testimony to the effect that defendant asked those present to do more work in obtaining members for the Communist party and requested all to be at the meeting of the party to be held in Portland on the following evening and to bring their friends to show their defiance to local police authority and o assist them in their revolutionary tactics.

That there was also testimony that defendant urged the purchase of certain Communist literature which was sold at the meeting; that while the meeting was still in progress it was raided by the police; that the meeting was conducted in an orderly manner; that defendant and several others who were actively conducting the meeting were arrested by the police and that on searching the hall the police found a quantity of Communist literature.

The stipulation then set forth various extracts from the literature of the Communist party to show its advocacy of criminal syndicalism. The stipulation does not disclose any activity by the defendant as a basis for his prosecution other than his participation in the meeting in question. Nor does the stipulation show that the Communist literature distributed at the meeting contained any advocacy of criminal syndiaclism or of any unlawful conduct.

It was admitted by the Attorney General of the State in his argument at the bar of this court that the literature distributed in the meeting was not of that sort and that the extracts contained in the stipulation were taken from Communist literature found elsewhere. Its introduction in evidence was for the purpose of showing that the Communist party as such did advocate the doctrine of criminal syndicalism, a fact which is not disputed on this appeal.

On the theory that this was a charge that criminal syndicalism and sabotage were advocated at the meeting in question, defendant moved for acquittal insisting that the evidence was insufficient to warrant his conviction. The trial court denied his motion and error in this respect was assigned on appeal.

The Supreme Court of the State put aside that contention by ruling that the indictment did not charge that criminal syndicalism or sabotage was advocated at the meeting described in the evidence, either by defendant or by any one else. . . .

"What the indictment does charge, in plain and concise language, is that the defendant presided at, conducted and assisted in conducting an assemblage of persons, organization, society and group, to wit, the Communist party, which said assemblage of persons, organization, society and group was unlawfully teaching and advocating in Multnomah County the doctrine of criminal syndicalism and sabotage."

In this view, lack of sufficient evidence as to illegal advocacy or action at the meeting became immaterial. Having limited the charge to defendant's participation in a meeting called by the Communist party, the State Court sustained the conviction upon that basis regardless of what was said or done at the meeting.

We must take the indictment as thus construed. Conviction upon a charge not made would be sheer denial of due process. It thus appears that, while defendant was a member of the Communist party, he was not indicted for participating in its organization, or for joining it, or for soliciting members or for distributing its literature. He was not charged with teaching or advocating criminal syndicalism or sabotage or any unlawful acts, either at the meeting or elsewhere.

He was accordingly deprived of the benefit of evidence as to the orderly and lawful conduct of the meeting and that it was not called or used for the advocacy of criminal syndicalism or sabotage or any unlawful action. His sole offense as charged, and for which he was convicted and sentenced to imprisonment for

seven years, was that he had assisted in the conduct of a public meeting, albeit otherwise lawful, which was held under the auspices of the Communist party.

The broad reach of the statute as thus applied is plain. While defendant was a member of the Communist party, that membership was not necessary to conviction on such a charge. A like fate might have attended any speaker, although not a member who "assisted in the conduct" of the meeting. However innocuous the object of the meeting, however lawful the subjects and tenor of the addresses, however reasonable and timely the discussion, all those assisting in the conduct of the meeting would be subject to imprisonment as felons if the meeting were held by the Communist party.

This manifest result was brought out sharply at this bar by the concessions which the Attorney General made, and could not avoid, in the light of the decision of the State court. Thus if the Communist party had called a public meeting in Portland to discuss the tariff, or the foreign policy of the government, or taxation, or relief, or candidacies for the offices of President, members of Congress, Governor or State legislators, every speaker who assisted in the conduct of the meeting would be equally guilty with the defendant in this case, upon the charge as here defined and sustained. . . .

While the States are entitled to protect themselves from the abuse of the privileges of our institutions through an attempted substitution of force and violence in the place of peaceful political action in order to effect revolutionary changes in government, none of our decisions go to the length of sustaining such a curtailment of the right of free speech and assembly as the Oregon statute demands in its present application.

Freedom of speech and of the press are fundamental rights which are safeguarded by the due process clause of the Fourteenth Amendment of the Federal Constitution. The right of peaceable assembly is a right cognate to those of free speech and free press and is equally fundamental.

As this court said in *United States* v. *Cruikshank,* "The very idea of a government, republican in form, implies a right on the part of its citizens to met peaceably for consultation in respect to public affairs and to petition for a redress of grievances."

The First Amendment of the Federal Constitution expressly guarantees that right against abridgment by Congress. But explicit mention there does not argue exclusion elsewhere. For the right is one that cannot be denied without violating those fundamental principles of liberty and justice which lie at the base of all civil and political institutions, principles which the Fourteenth Amendment embodies in the general terms of its due process clause.

These rights may be abused by using speech or press or assembly in order to incite to violence and crime. The people, through their Legislatures, may protect themselves against that abuse. But the legislative intervention can find constitutional justification only by dealing with the abuse. The rights themselves must not be curtailed.

The greater the importance of safeguarding the community from incitements to the overthrow of our institutions by force and violence, the more imperative is the need to preserve inviolate the constitutional rights of free speech, free press and free assembly in order to maintain the opportunity for free political discussion, to the end that government may be responsive to the will of the people and that changes, if desired, may be obtained by peaceful means. Therein lies the security of the republic, the very foundation of constitutional government.

It follows from these considerations that, consistently with the Federal Constitution, peaceable assembly for lawful discussion cannot be made a crime. The holding of meetings for peaceable political action cannot be proscribed. Those who assist in the conduct of such meetings cannot be branded as criminals

on that score. The question, if the rights of free speech and peaceable assembly are to be preserved, is not as to the auspices under which the meeting is held, but as to its purpose; not as to the relations of the speakers, but whether their utterances transcend the bounds of the freedom of speech which the Constitution protects.

If the persons assemblying have committed crimes elsewhere, if they have formed or are engaged in a conspiracy against the public peace and order, they may be prosecuted for their conspiracy or other violation of valid laws.

But it is a different matter when the State, instead of prosecuting them for such offenses, seizes upon mere participation in a peaceable assembly and a lawful public discussion as the basis for a criminal charge.

We are not called upon to review the findings of the State court as to the objectives of the Communist party. Notwithstanding those objectives, the defendant still enjoyed his personal right of free speech and to take part in a peaceable assembly having a lawful purpose, although called by that party. The defendant was none the less entitled to discuss the public issues of the day and thus in a lawful manner, without incitement to violence or crime, to seek redress of alleged grievances. That was of the essence of his guaranteed personal liberty.

We hold that the Oregon statute as applied to the particular charge as defined by the State court is repugnant to the due process clause of the Fourteenth Amendment. The judgment of conviction is reversed and the cause is remanded for further proceedings not inconsistent with this opinion. It is so ordered.

512. WEST COAST HOTEL CO. v. PARRISH
300 U. S. 379
1937

Appeal from the Supreme Court of the State of Washington. The decision in Adkins v. Children's Hospital (Doc. No. 451) holding the due process clause of the Fifth Amendment a barrier against federal minimum wage legislation, had effectively blocked such legislation for years. In 1933 New York State attempted to legislate minimum wages for women, but this legislation

was invalidated in a five to four decision which asserted that legislatures are "without power . . . to prohibit, change, or nullify contracts between employers and adult women workers as to amount of wages to be paid." The present case reversed this as well as the Adkins decision. The history of the Washington statute in dispute is given in the decision. See, Powell, "The Judiciality of Minimum Wage Legislation," 37 Harv. Law Rev. 545; Black, "Wages and Hours Laws in the Courts," 5 U. of Pitt. Law Rev. 223; Brown, "Minimum Wage Cases in the Supreme Court," 11 So. Cal. Law Rev. 256.

HUGHES, C. J., this case presents the question of the constitutional validity of the minimum wage law of the State of Washington.

The Act, entitled "Minimum Wages for Women," authorizes the fixing of minimum wages for women and minors. . . . It provides:

Sec. 1. The welfare of the State of Washington demands that women and minors be protected from conditions of labor which have a pernicious effect on their health and morals. The State of Washington, therefore, exercising herein its police and sovereign power declares that inadequate wages and unsanitary conditions of labor exert such pernicious effect.

Sec. 2. It shall be unlawful to employ women or minors in any industry or occupation within the State of Washington under conditions of labor detrimental to their health or morals; and it shall be unlawful to employ women workers in any industry within the State of Washington at wages which are not adequate for their maintenance.

Sec. 3. There is hereby created a commission to be known as the "Industrial Welfare Commission" for the State of Washington, to establish such standards of wages and conditions of labor for women and minors employed within the State of Washington, as shall be held hereunder to be reasonable and not detrimental to health and morals, and which shall be sufficient for the decent maintenance of women.

Further provisions required the Commission to ascertain the wages and conditions of labor of women and minors within the State. Public hearings were to be held. If after investigation the Commission found that in any occupation, trade or industry the wages paid to women were "inadequate to supply them necessary cost of living and to maintain the workers in health," the Commission was empowered to call a conference of representatives of employers and employees together with disinterested persons representing the public. The conference was to recommend to the Commission, on its request, an estimate of a minimum wage adequate for the purpose above stated, and on the approval of such a recommendation it became the duty

of the Commission to issue an obligatory order fixing minimum wages. Any such order might be reopened and the question reconsidered with the aid of the former conference or a new one. Special licenses were authorized for the employment of women who were "physically defective or crippled by age or otherwise," and also for apprentices, at less than the prescribed minimum wage.

By a later Act the Industrial Welfare Commission was abolished and its duties were assigned to the Industrial Welfare Committee consisting of the Director of Labor and Industries, the Supervisor of Industrial Insurance, the Supervisor of Industrial Relations, the Industrial Statistician and the Supervisor of Women in Industry. Laws of 1921 (Washington) chap. 7.

The appellant conducts a hotel. The appellee Elsie Parrish was employed as a chambermaid and (with her husband) brought this suit to recover the difference between the wages paid her and the minimum wage fixed pursuant to the state law. The minimum wage was $14.50 per week of 48 hours. The appellant challenged the act as repugnant to the due process clause of the Fourteenth Amendment of the Constitution of the United States. The Supreme Court of the State, reversing the trial court, sustained the statute and directed judgment for the plaintiffs. *Parrish* v. *West Coast Hotel Co.*, 185 Wash. 581. The case is here on appeal.

The appellant relies upon the decision of this Court in *Adkins* v. *Children's Hospital*, which held invalid the District of Columbia Minimum Wage Act which was attacked under the due process clause of the Fifth Amendment. . . .

The recent case of *Morehead* v. *New York ex rel. Tipaldo*, 298 U. S. 587, came here on certiorari to the New York court which had held the New York minimum wage act for women to be invalid. A minority of this Court thought that the New York statute was distinguishable in a material feature from that involved in the *Adkins* case and that for that and other reasons the New York statute should be sustained. But the Court of Appeals of New York had said that it found no material difference between the two statutes and this Court held that the "meaning of the statute" as fixed by the decision of the state court "must be accepted here as if the meaning had been specifically expressed in the enactment." Id., p. 609. That view led to the affirmance by this Court of the judgment in the *Morehead* case, as the Court considered that the only question before it was whether the *Adkins* case was distinguishable and that reconsideration of that decision had not been sought. . . .

We think that the question which was not deemed to be open in the *Morehead* case is open and is necessarily presented here. The Supreme Court of Washington has upheld the minimum wage statute of that State. It has decided that the statute is a reasonable exercise of the police power of the State. In reaching that conclusion the state court has invoked principles long established by this Court in the application of the Fourteenth Amendment. The state court has refused to regard the decision in the *Adkins* case as determinative and has pointed to our decisions 'both before and since that case as justifying its position. We are of the opinion that this ruling of the state court demands on our part a reexamination of the *Adkins* case. The importance of the question, in which many States having similar laws are concerned, the close division by which the decision in the *Adkins* case was reached, and the economic conditions which have supervened, and in the light of which the reasonableness of the exercise of the protective power of the State must be considered, make it not only appropriate, but we think imperative, that in deciding the present case the subject should receive fresh consideration.

The history of the litigation of this question may be briefly stated. The minimum wage statute of Washington was enacted over twenty-three years ago. Prior to the decision in the instant case it had twice been held valid by the Supreme Court of the State. *Larsen* v. *Rice*, 100 Wash. 642; *Spokane Hotel Co.* v. *Younger*, 113 Wash. 359. The Washington statute is essentially the same as that enacted in Oregon in the same year. Laws of 1913 (Oregon) chap. 62. The validity of the latter act was sustained by the Supreme Court of Oregon in *Stettler* v. *O'Hara*, 69 Ore. 519, and *Simpson* v. *O'Hara*, 70 Ore. 261. These cases, after reargument, were affirmed here by an equally divided court, in 1917. 243 U. S. 629. The law of Oregon thus continued in effect. The District of Columbia Minimum Wage Law (40 Stat. 960) was en-

acted in 1918. The statute was sustained by the Supreme Court of the District in the *Adkins* case. Upon appeal the Court of Appeals of the District first affirmed that ruling but on rehearing reversed it and the case came before this Court in 1923. The judgment of the Court of Appeals holding the Act invalid was affirmed, but with Chief Justice Taft, Mr. Justice Holmes and Mr. Justice Sanford dissenting, and Mr. Justice Brandeis taking no part. The dissenting opinions took the ground that the decision was at variance with the principles which this Court had frequently announced and applied. In 1925 and 1927, the similar minimum wage statutes of Arizona and Arkansas were held invalid upon the authority of the *Adkins* case. The Justices who had dissented in that case bowed to the ruling and Mr. Justice Brandeis dissented. *Murphy* v. *Sardell*, 269 U. S. 530; *Donham* v. *West-Nelson Co.*, 273 U. S. 657. The question did not come before us again until the last term in the *Morehead* case, as already noted. In that case, briefs supporting the New York statute were submitted by the States of Ohio, Connecticut, Illinois, Massachusetts, New Hampshire, New Jersey and Rhode Island. 298 U. S., p. 604, *note*. Throughout this entire period the Washington statute now under consideration has been in force.

The principle which must control our decision is not in doubt. The constitutional provision invoked is the due process clause of the Fourteenth Amendment governing the States, as the due process clause invoked in the *Adkins* case governed Congress. In each case the violation alleged by those attacking minimum wage regulation for women is deprivation of freedom of contract. What is this freedom? The Constitution does not speak of freedom of contract. It speaks of liberty and prohibits the deprivation of liberty without due process of law. In prohibiting that deprivation the Constitution does not recognize an absolute and uncontrollable liberty. Liberty in each of its phases has its history and connotation. But the liberty safeguarded is liberty in a social organization which requires the protection of law against the evils which menace the health, safety, morals and welfare of the people. Liberty under the Constitution is thus necessarily subject to the restraints of due process, and regulation which is reasonable in relation to its subject and is adopted in the interests of the community is due process.

This essential limitation of liberty in general governs freedom of contract in particular. More than twenty-five years ago we set forth the applicable principle in these words, after referring to the cases where the liberty guaranteed by the Fourteenth Amendment had been broadly described:

But it was recognized in the cases cited, as in many others, that freedom of contract is a qualified and not an absolute right. There is no absolute freedom to do as one wills or to contract as one chooses. The guaranty of liberty does not withdraw from legislative supervision that wide department of activity which consists of the making of contracts, or deny to government the power to provide restrictive safeguards. Liberty implies the absence of arbitrary restraint, not immunity from reasonable regulations and prohibitions imposed in the interests of the community. *Chicago, Burlington & Quincy R. R. Co.* v. *McGuire,* 219 U. S. 549, 565.

This power under the Constitution to restrict freedom of contract has had many illustrations. That it may be exercised in the public interest with respect to contracts between employer and employee is undeniable. Thus statutes have been sustained limiting employment in underground mines and smelters to eight hours a day (*Holden* v. *Hardy*); in requiring redemption in cash of store orders or other evidences of indebtedness issued in the payment of wages (*Knoxville Iron Co.* v. *Harbison,* 183 U. S. 13); in forbidding the payment of seamen's wages in advance (*Patterson* v. *Bark Eudora,* 190 U. S. 169); in making it unlawful to contract to pay miners employed at quantity rates upon the basis of screened coal instead of the weight of the coal as originally produced in the mine (*McLean* v. *Arkansas,* 211 U. S. 539); in prohibiting contracts limiting liability for injuries to employees (*Chicago, Burlington & Quincy R. R. Co.* v. *McGuire*); in limiting hours of work of employees in manufacturing establishments (*Bunting* v. *Oregon*); and in maintaining workmen's compensation laws (*New York Central R. Co.* v. *White,* 243 U. S. 188; *Mountain Timber Co.* v. *Washington,* 243 U. S. 219). In dealing with the relation of employer and employed, the legislature has necessarily a wide field of discretion in order that there may be suitable protection of health and safety, and that peace and good order may be promoted through regulations designed to insure wholesome conditions of work and freedom from oppression. *Chicago, Burlington & Quincy R. R. Co.* v. *McGuire, supra,* p. 570.

The point that has been strongly stressed that adult employees should be deemed competent to make their own contracts was decisively met nearly forty years ago in *Holden* v. *Hardy, supra,* where we pointed out the inequality in the footing of the parties. . . .

It is manifest that this established principle is peculiarly applicable in relation to the employment of women in whose protection the State has a special interest. That phase of the subject received elaborate consideration in *Muller* v. *Oregon,* where the constitutional authority of the State to limit the working hours of women was sustained. . . . Again, in *Quong Wing* v. *Kirkendall,* 223 U. S. 59, 63, in referring to a differentiation with respect to the employment of women, we said that the Fourteenth Amendment did not interfere with state power by creating a "fictitious equality." We referred to recognized classifications on the basis of sex with regard to hours of work and in other matters, and we observed that the particular points at which that difference shall be enforced by legislation were largely in the power of the State. In later rulings this Court sustained the regulation of hours of work of women employees in *Riley* v. *Massachusetts,* 232 U. S. 671 (factories), *Miller* v. *Wilson,* 236 U. S. 373 (hotels), and *Bosley* v. *McLaughlin,* 236 U. S. 385 (hospitals).

This array of precedents and the principles they applied were thought by the dissenting Justices in the *Adkins* case to demand that the minimum wage statute be sustained. The validity of the distinction made by the Court between a minimum wage and a maximum of hours in limiting liberty of contract was especially challenged. That challenge persists and is without any satisfactory answer. . . .

One of the points which was pressed by the Court in supporting its ruling in the *Adkins* case was that the standard set up by the District of Columbia Act did not take appropriate account of the value of the services rendered. . . .

The minimum wage to be paid under the Washington statute is fixed after full consideration by representatives of employers, employees and the public. It may be assumed that the minimum wage is fixed in consideration of the services that are performed in the particular occupations under normal conditions. Provision is made for special licenses at less wages in the case of women who are incapable of full service. The statement of Mr. Justice Holmes in the *Adkins* case is pertinent:

This statute does not compel anybody to pay anything. It simply forbids employment at rates below those fixed as the minimum requirement of health and right living. It is safe to assume that women will not be employed at even the lowest wages allowed unless they earn them, or unless the employer's business can sustain the burden. In short the law in its character and operation is like hundreds of so-called police laws that have been upheld. 261 U. S., p. 570.

And Chief Justice Taft forcibly pointed out the consideration which is basic in a statute of this character:

Legislatures which adopt a requirement of maximum hours or minimum wages may be presumed to believe that when sweating employers are prevented from paying unduly low wages by positive law they will continue their business, abating that part òf their profits, which were wrung from the necessities of their employees, and will concede the better terms required by the law; and that while in individual cases hardship may result, the restriction will enure to the benefit of the general class of employees in whose interest the law is passed and so to that of the community at large. *Id.,* p. 563.

We think that the views thus expressed are sound and that the decision in the *Adkins* case was a departure from the true application of the principles governing the regulation by the State of the relation of employer and employed. Those principles have been reenforced by our subsequent decisions. Thus in *Radice* v. *New York,* 264 U. S. 292, we sustained the New York statute which restricted the employment of women in restaurants at night. In *O'Gorman* v. *Hartford Fire Insurance Company,* 282 U. S. 251, which upheld an act regulating the commissions of insurance agents, we pointed to the presumption of the constitutionality of a statute dealing with a subject within the scope of the police power and to the absence of any factual foundation

of record for deciding that the limits of power had been transcended. In *Nebbia* v. *New York,* dealing with the New York statute providing for minimum prices for milk, the general subject of the regulation of the use of private property and of the making of private contracts received an exhaustive examination and we again declared that if such laws "have a reasonable relation to a proper legislative purpose, and are neither arbitrary nor discriminatory, the requirements of due process are satisfied"; that "with the wisdom of the policy adopted, with the adequacy or practicability of the law enacted to forward it, the courts are both incompetent and unauthorized to deal"; that "times without number we have said that the legislature is primarily the judge of the necessity of such an enactment, that every possible presumption is in favor of its validity, and that though the court may hold views inconsistent with the wisdom of the law, it may not be annulled unless palpably in excess of legislative power."

With full recognition of the earnestness and vigor which characterize the prevailing opinion in the *Adkins* case, we find it impossible to reconcile that ruling with these well-considered declarations. What can be closer to the public interest than the health of women and their protection from unscrupulous and overreaching employers? And if the protection of women is a legitimate end of the exercise of state power, how can it be said that the requirement of the payment of a minimum wage fairly fixed in order to meet the very necessities of existence is not an admissible means to that end? The legislature of the State was clearly entitled to consider the situation of women in employment, the fact that they are in the class receiving the least pay, that their bargaining power is relatively weak, and that they are the ready victims of those who would take advantage of their necessitous circumstances. The legislature was entitled to adopt measures to reduce the evils of the "sweating system," the exploiting of workers at wages so low as to be insufficient to meet the bare cost of living thus making their very helplessness the occasion of a most injurious competition. The legislature had the right to consider that its minimum wage requirements would be an important aid in carrying out its policy of protection. The adoption of similar requirements by many States evidences a deep-seated conviction both as to the presence of the evil and as to the means adapted to check it. Legislative response to that conviction cannot be regarded as arbitrary or capricious and that is all we have to decide. Even if the wisdom of the policy be regarded as debatable and its effects uncertain, still the legislature is entitled to its judgment.

There is an additional and compelling consideration which recent economic experience has brought into a strong light. The exploitation of a class of workers who are in an unequal position with respect to bargaining power and are thus relatively defenceless against the denial of a living wage is not only detrimental to their health and well being but casts a direct burden for their support upon the community. What these workers lose in wages the taxpayers are called upon to pay. The bare cost of living must be met. We may take judicial notice of the unparalleled demands for relief which arose during the recent period of depression and still continue to an alarming extent despite the degree of economic recovery which has been achieved. It is unnecessary to cite official statistics to establish what is of common knowledge through the length and breadth of the land. While in the instant case no factual brief has been presented, there is no reason to doubt that the State of Washington has encountered the same social problem that is present elsewhere. The community is not bound to provide what is in effect a subsidy for unconscionable employers. The community may direct its law-making power to correct the abuse which springs from their selfish disregard of the public interest. The argument that the legislation in question constitutes an arbitrary discrimination, because it does not extend to men, is unavailing. This Court has frequently held that the legislative authority, acting within its proper field, is not bound to extend its regulation to all cases which it might possibly reach. The legislature "is free to recognize degrees of harm and it may confine its restrictions to those classes of cases where the need is deemed to be clearest." If "the law presumably hits the evil where it is most felt, it is not to be overthrown because there are other instances to which it might have been applied." There is no, "doctrinaire requirement" that the legislation should be couched in all embracing terms. This familiar principle has repeatedly been applied to legislation which singles out women, and particular classes of women, in the exercise of the State's protective power. Their relative need in the presence of the evil, no less than the existence of the evil itself, is a matter for the legislative judgment.

Our conclusion is that the case of *Adkins* v. *Children's Hospital, supra,* should be, and it is, overruled. The judgment of the Supreme Court of the State of Washington is affirmed.

SUTHERLAND, J., VAN DEVANTER, J., McREYNOLDS, J., and BUTLER, J. dissented.

513. HERNDON v. LOWRY
301 U. S. 242
1937

Appeal from the Supreme Court of Georgia. One of the most difficult problems which faces the Court is that of drawing the dividing line between the power of the State to protect itself against riot or insurrection and the freedom of speech guaranteed to the individual by the Federal Constitution. This opinion, holding that the mere possession of radical literature does not constitute violation of a law prohibiting the incitement to insurrection, riot or conspiracy, is notable for a more liberal attitude than that revealed in the Gitlow case (Doc. No. 456). See the *Monthly Bulletin* of the International Juridical Association, vol. VI, no. 2, and notes in 50 Harv. L. Rev. 1313, and 35 Mich. L. Rev. 1373.

ROBERTS, J. The appellant claims his conviction in a state court deprived him of his liberty contrary to the guarantees of the Fourteenth Amendment. He assigns as error the action of the Supreme Court of Georgia in overruling his claim and refusing him a discharge upon habeas corpus. The petition for the writ, presented to the Superior Court of Fulton County, asserted the appellant was unlawfully detained by the appellee as sheriff under the supposed authority of a judgment pronouncing him guilty of attempting to incite insurrection, as defined in 56 of the Penal Code and sentencing him to imprisonment for not less than eighteen nor more than twenty years. . . .

At the July Term 1932 of the Superior Court of Fulton County an indictment was returned charging against the appellant an attempt to induce others to join in combined resistance to the lawful authority of the state with intent to deny, to defeat, and to overthrow such authority by open force, violent means, and unlawful acts; alleging that insurrection was intended to be manifested and accomplished by unlawful and violent acts. The indictment specified that the attempt was made by calling and attending public assemblies and by making speeches for the purpose of organizing and establishing groups and combinations of white and colored persons under the name of the Communist Party of Atlanta for the purpose of uniting, combining, and conspiring to incite riots and to embarrass and impede the orderly processes of the courts and offering combined resistance to, and, by force and violence, overthrowing and defeating the authority of the state; that by speech and persuasion, the appellant solicited and attempted to solicit persons to join, confederate with, and become members of the Communist Party and the Young Communist League and introduced into the state and circulated, aided and assisted in introducing and circulating, booklets, papers, and other writings with the same intent and purpose. The charge was founded on § 56 of the Penal Code, one of four related sections. Section 55 defines insurrection, § 56 defines an attempt to incite insurrection, § 57 prescribes the death penalty for conviction of the offenses described in the two preceding sections unless the jury shall recommend mercy, and § 58 penalizes, by imprisonment, the introduction and circulation of printed matter for the purpose of inciting insurrection, riot, conspiracy, etc. . . .

In the present proceeding the Superior Court and Supreme Court of Georgia have considered and disposed of the contentions based upon the Federal Constitution. The scope of a habeas corpus proceeding in the circumstances disclosed is a state and not a federal question and since the state courts treated the proceeding as properly raising issues of federal constitutional right, we have jurisdiction and all such issues are open here. We must, then, inquire whether the statute as applied in the trial denied appellant rights safeguarded by the Fourteenth Amendment.

The evidence on which the judgment rests consists of appellant's admissions and certain documents found in his possession. The appellant told the state's officers that some time prior to his arrest he joined the Communist Party in Kentucky and later came to Atlanta as a paid organizer for the party, his duties being to call meetings, to educate and disseminate information respecting the party, to distribute literature, to secure members, and to work up an organization of the party in Atlanta; and that he had held or attended three meetings called by him. He made no further admission as to what he did as an organizer, or what he said or did at the meetings. When arrested he carried a box containing documents. After he was arrested he conducted the officers to his room where additional documents and bundles of newspapers and periodicals were found, which he stated were sent him from the headquarters of the Communist Party in New York. He gave the names of persons who were members of the organization in Atlanta, and stated he had only five or six actual members at the time of his apprehension. The stubs of membership books found in the box indicated he had enrolled more members than he stated. There was no evidence that he had distributed any of the material carried on his person and found in his room, or had taken any of it to meetings, save two circulars or appeals respecting county relief which are confessedly innocuous.

The newspapers, pamphlets, periodicals, and other documents found in his room were, so he stated, intended for distribution at his meetings. These the appellee concedes were not introduced in evidence. Certain documents in his possession when he was arrested were placed in evidence. . . .

All of these may be dismissed as irrelevant except those falling within the first and second groups. No inference can be drawn from the possession of the books mentioned, either that they embodied the doctrines of the Communist Party or that they represented views advocated by the appellant. The minutes of meetings contain nothing indicating the purposes of the organization or any intent to overthrow organized government; on the contrary, they indicate merely discussion of relief for the unemployed. The two circulars, admittedly distributed by the appellant, had nothing to do with the Communist Party, its aims or purposes, and were not appeals to join the party but were concerned with unemployment relief in the county and included appeals to the white and negro unemployed to organize and represent the need for further county aid. They were characterized by the Supreme Court of Georgia as "more or less harmless."

The documents of the first class disclose the activity of the appellant as an organizer but, in this respect, add nothing to his admissions.

The matter appearing upon the membership blanks is innocent upon its face however foolish and pernicious the aims it suggests. . . .

This vague declaration falls short of an attempt to bring about insurrection either immediately or within a reasonable time but amounts merely to a statement of ultimate ideals. The blanks, however, indicate more specific aims for which members of the Communist Party are to vote. They are to vote Communist for

"1. Unemployment and Social Insurance at the expense of the State and employers.

"2. Against Hoover's wage-cutting policy.

"3. Emergency relief for the poor farmers without restrictions by the government and banks; exemption of poor farmers from taxes and from forced collection of rents or debts.

"4. Equal rights for the Negroes and self-determination for the Black Belt.

"5. Against capitalistic terror: against all forms of suppression of the political rights of the workers.

"6. Against imperialist war; for the defense of the Chinese people and of the Soviet Union."

None of these aims is criminal upon its face. As to one, the 4th, the claim is that criminality may be found because of extrinsic facts. Those facts consist of possession by appellant of booklets and other literature of the second class illustrating the party doctrines. The State contends these show that the purposes of the Communist Party were forcible subversion of the lawful authority of Georgia. They contain, inter alia, statements to the effect that the party bases itself upon the revolutionary theory of Marxism, opposes "bosses' wars,"

approves of the Soviet Union, and desires the "smashing" of the National Guard, the C. M. T. C., and the R. O. T. C. But the State especially relies upon a booklet entitled "The Communist Position on the Negro Question," on the cover of which appears a map of the United States having a dark belt across certain Southern states and the phrase "Self-Determination for the Black Belt." The booklet affirms that the source of the Communist slogan "Right of Self-Determination of the Negroes in the Black Belt" is a resolution of the Communist International on the Negro question in the United States adopted in 1930, which states that the Communist Party in the United States has been actively attempting to win increasing sympathy among the negro population, that certain things have been advocated for the benefit of the Negroes in the Northern states, but that in the Southern portion of the United States the Communist slogan must be "The Right of Self-Determination of the Negroes in the Black Belt." . . .

There is no evidence the appellant distributed any writings or printed matter found in the box he carried when arrested, or any other advocating forcible subversion of governmental authority. There is no evidence the appellant advocated, by speech or written word, at meetings or elsewhere, any doctrine or action implying such forcible subversion. There is evidence tending to prove that the appellant held meetings for the purpose of recruiting members of the Communist Party and solicited contributions for the support of that party and there is proof of the doctrines which that party espouses. Appellant's intent to incite insurrection, if it is to be found, must rest upon his procuring members for the Communist Party and his possession of that party's literature when he was arrested.

Section 55 of the Georgia Penal Code defines insurrection as "combined resistance to the lawful authority of the State, with intent to the denial thereof, when the same is manifested or intended to be manifested by acts of violence." The appellant was not indicted under this section. Section 58 denounces the introduction, printing, or circulation, or assisting to print or circulate any document "for the purpose of inciting insurrection." The appellant was not indicted under this section.

Section 56, under which the indictment

is laid, makes no reference to force or violence except by the phrase "combined resistance to the lawful authority of the State." The Supreme Court evidently importing from the similar phraseology in § 55 the additional element contained in that section, namely, "manifested or intended to be manifested by acts of violence," has decided that intended resort to force is an essential element of the offense defined by § 56.

To ascertain how the Act is held to apply to the appellant's conduct we turn to the rulings of the state courts in his case. The trial court instructed the jury: "In order to convict the defendant, . . . it must appear clearly by the evidence that immediate serious violence against the State of Georgia was to be expected or advocated." The jury rendered a verdict of guilty. In the Supreme Court the appellant urged that the evidence was wholly insufficient to sustain the verdict under the law as thus construed. . . .

The affirmance of conviction upon the trial record necessarily gives § 56 the construction that one who seeks members for or attempts to organize a local unit of a party which has the purposes and objects disclosed by the documents in evidence may be found guilty of an attempt to incite insurrection.

The questions are whether this construction and application of the statute deprives the accused of the right of freedom of speech and of assembly guaranteed by the Fourteenth Amendment, and whether the statute so construed and applied furnishes a reasonably definite and ascertainable standard of guilt.

The appellant, while admitting that the people may protect themselves against abuses of the freedom of speech safeguarded by the Fourteenth Amendment by prohibiting incitement to violence and crime insists that legislative regulation may not go beyond measures forefending against "clear and present danger" of the use of force against the state. For this position he relies upon our decisions under the Federal Espionage Acts and cognate state legislation. . . .

The State, on the other hand, insists that our decisions uphold state statutes making criminal utterances which have a "dangerous tendency" towards the subversion of government. It relies particularly upon *Gitlow* v. *New York* (268 U. S. 652). There, however, we dealt with a statute which, quite unlike § 56 of the Georgia Criminal Code, denounced as criminal certain acts carefully and adequately described. . . .

It is evident that the decision sustaining the New York statute furnishes no warrant for the appellee's contention that under a law general in its description of the mischief to be remedied and equally general in respect of the intent of the actor, the standard of guilt may be made the "dangerous tendency" of his words.

The power of a state to abridge freedom of speech and of assembly is the exception rather than the rule and the penalizing even of utterances of a defined character must find its justification in a reasonable apprehension of danger to organized government. The judgment of the legislature is not unfettered. The limitation upon individual liberty must have appropriate relation to the safety of the state. Legislation which goes beyond this need violates the principle of the Constitution. If, therefore, a state statute penalize innocent participation in a meeting held with an innocent purpose merely because the meeting was held under the auspices of an organization membership in which, or the advocacy of whose principles, is also denounced as criminal, the law, so construed and applied, goes beyond the power to restrict abuses of freedom of speech and arbitrarily denies that freedom. And where a statute is so vague and uncertain as to make criminal an utterance or an act which may be innocently said or done with no intent to induce resort to violence or on the other hand may be said or done with a purpose violently to subvert government, a conviction under such a law cannot be sustained. . . .

1. The appellant had a constitutional right to address meetings and organize parties unless in so doing he violated some prohibition of a valid statute. The only prohibition he is said to have violated is that of § 56 forbidding incitement or attempted incitement to insurrection by violence. If the evidence fails to show that he did so incite, then, as applied to him, the statute unreasonably limits freedom of speech and freedom of assembly and violates the Fourteenth Amendment. We are of opinion that the requisite proof is lacking. From what has been said above with respect to the evidence offered at the trial it is apparent that the documents found upon the

appellant's person were certainly, as to some of the aims stated therein, innocent and consistent with peaceful action for a change in the laws or the constitution. The proof wholly fails to show that the appellant had read these documents; that he had distributed any of them; that he believed and advocated any or all of the principles and aims set forth in them, or that those he had procured to become members of the party knew or approved of any of these documents.

Thus, the crucial question is not the formal interpretation of the statute by the Supreme Court of Georgia but the application given it. In its application the offense made criminal is that of soliciting members for a political party and conducting meetings of a local unit of that party when one of the doctrines of the party, established by reference to a document not shown to have been exhibited to anyone by the accused, may be said to be ultimate resort to violence at some indefinite future time against organized government. It is to be borne in mind that the legislature of Georgia has not made membership in the Communist Party unlawful by reason of its supposed dangerous tendency even in the remote future. . . .

His membership in the Communist Party and his solicitation of a few members wholly fail to establish an attempt to incite others to insurrection. Indeed, so far as appears, he had but a single copy of the booklet the State claims to be objectionable; that copy he retained. The same may be said with respect to the other books and pamphlets, some of them of more innocent purport. In these circumstances, to make membership in the party and solicitation of members for that party a criminal offense, punishable by death, in the discretion of a jury, is an unwarranted invasion of the right of freedom of speech.

2. The statute, as construed and applied in the appellant's trial, does not furnish a sufficiently ascertainable standard of guilt. The Act does not prohibit incitement to violent interference with any given activity or operation of the state. By force of it, as construed, the judge and jury trying an alleged offender cannot appraise the circumstances and character of the defendant's utterances or activities as begetting a clear and present danger of forcible obstruction of a particular state function. Nor is any specified conduct or utterance of the accused made an offense.

The test of guilt is thus formulated by the Supreme Court of the state. Forcible action must have been contemplated but it would be sufficient to sustain a conviction if the accused intended that an insurrection "should happen at any time within which he might reasonably expect his influence to continue to be directly operative in causing such action by those whom he sought to induce." If the jury conclude that the defendant should have contemplated that any act or utterance of his in opposition to the established order or advocating a change in that order, might, in the distant future, eventuate in a combination to offer forcible resistance to the State, or as the State says, if the jury believe he should have known that his words would have "a dangerous tendency" then he may be convicted. To be guilty under the law, as construed, a defendant need not advocate resort to force. He need not teach any particular doctrine to come within its purview. In deed, he need not be active in the formation of a combination or group if he agitate for a change in the frame of government, however peaceful his own intent. If, by the exercise of prophesy, he can forecast that, as a result of a chain of causation, following his proposed action a group may arise at some future date which will resort to force, he is bound to make the prophecy and abstain, under pain of punishment, possibly of execution. Every person who attacks existing conditions, who agitates for a change in the form of government, must take the risk that if a jury should be of opinion he ought to have foreseen that his utterances might contribute in any measure to some future forcible resistance to the existing government he may be convicted of the offense of inciting insurrection. Proof that the accused in fact believed that his effort would cause a violent assault upon the state would not be necessary to conviction. It would be sufficient if the jury thought he reasonably might foretell that those he persuaded to join the party might, at some time in the indefinite future, resort to forcible resistance of government. The question thus proposed to a jury involves pure speculation as to future trends of thought and action. Within what time might one reasonably expect that an attempted organization of the Communist Party in the

United States would result in violent action by that party? If a jury returned a special verdict saying twenty years or even fifty years the verdict could not be shown to be wrong. The law, as thus construed, licenses the jury to create its own standard in each case. . . .

The statute, as construed and applied, amounts merely to a dragnet which may enmesh anyone who agitates for a change of government if a jury can be persuaded that he ought to have foreseen his words would have some effect in the future conduct of others. No reasonably ascertainable standard of guilt is prescribed. So vague and indeterminate are the boundaries thus set to the freedom of speech and assembly that the law necessarily violates the guarantees of liberty embodied in the Fourteenth Amendment.

The judgment is reversed. . . .

Mr. Justice VAN DEVANTER, with whom joined Mr. Justice McREYNOLDS, SUTHERLAND, and BUTLER, dissented.

514. THE NEUTRALITY ACT OF 1937
May 1, 1937

(*U. S. Statutes at Large*, Vol. L, p. 121)

Disillusionment with the results of American participation in the first World War, growing throughout the twenties, was aggravated by the depression as well as by the continuation of the "old diplomacy" in Europe, and deepened by the findings of the Nye Committee on Munitions Manufactures and by a host of books and articles arguing the desirability of isolation. The outbreak of the Italo-Ethiopian conflict in May, 1935 led to the hasty passage of the Joint Resolution of Aug. 31, 1935 designed to prevent American involvement in any international conflict. The following year Congress strengthened this act by prohibiting loans to belligerents, and in January, 1937 it took cognizance of the problem presented by civil wars by forbidding the export of munitions for the use of either of the opposing forces in the Spanish Civil War. Finally on May 1, 1937 a Joint Resolution recapitulated these earlier resolutions, strengthening them in some particulars and giving larger discretionary powers to the President. A notable characteristic of this neutrality act was its failure to distinguish between aggressor and victim nations. In a curious fashion the neutrality legislation of 1935–37 vindicated the position taken by Sec. of State Bryan in 1914–15. The outbreak of the second World War in September, 1939 forced a reconsideration of this act and the Neutrality Law of 1939 relaxed in important particulars the provisions of the present act. On the problem of neutrality see C. A. and M. R. Beard, *America in Midpassage;* E. Borchard and W. Lage, *Neutrality for the United States;* P. C. Jessup, *Neutrality, Today and Tomorrow;* H. W. Dulles and H. F. Armstrong, *Can America Stay Neutral;* F. P. Davidson and G. Viereck, *Before America Decides;* J. Raushenbush, *The Final Choice;* Dulles, "Cash and Carry Neutrality," 18 Foreign Affairs, 179;

"The Neutrality Act of 1937," For. Pol. Rep. Vol. XIII no. 14.

JOINT RESOLUTION

To amend the joint resolution, approved August 31, 1935, as amended.

Resolved . . .

EXPORT OF ARMS, AMMUNITION, AND IMPLEMENTS OF WAR

SECTION 1. (a) Whenever the President shall find that there exists a state of war between, or among, two or more foreign states, the President shall proclaim such fact, and it shall thereafter be unlawful to export, or attempt to export, or cause to be exported, arms, ammunition, or implements of war from any place in the United States to any belligerent state named in such proclamation, or to any neutral state for transshipment to, or for the use of, any such belligerent state.

(b) The President shall, from time to time, by proclamation, extend such embargo upon the export of arms, ammunition, or implements of war to other states as and when they may become involved in such war.

(c) Whenever the President shall find that a state of civil strife exists in a foreign state and that such civil strife is of a magnitude or is being conducted under such conditions that the export of arms, ammunition, or implements of war from the United States to such foreign state would threaten or endanger the peace of the United States, the President shall proclaim such fact, and it shall thereafter be unlawful to export, or attempt to export, or cause to be exported, arms, ammunition, or implements of war from any place in the United States to such foreign state, or to any neutral state for transshipment to, or for the use of, such foreign state.

(d) The President shall, from time to time by proclamation, definitely enumerate the arms, ammunition, and implements of war, the export of which is prohibited by this section. The arms, ammunition, and implements of war so enumerated shall include those enumerated in the President's proclamation Numbered 2163, of April 10, 1936, but shall not include raw materials or any other articles or materials not of the same general character as those enumerated in the said proclamation, and in the Convention for the Supervision of the International Trade in Arms and Ammunition and in Implements of War, signed at Geneva June 17, 1925.

(e) Whoever, in violation of any of the provisions of this Act, shall export, or attempt to export, or cause to be exported, arms, ammunition, or implements of war from the United States shall be fined not more than $10,000, or imprisoned not more than five years, or both. . . .

(f) In the case of the forfeiture of any arms, ammunition, or implements of war by reason of a violation of this Act, . . . such arms, ammunition, or implements of war shall be delivered to the Secretary of War for such use or disposal thereof as shall be approved by the President of the Unted States.

(g) Whenever, in the judgment of the President, the conditions which have caused him to issue any proclamation under the authority of this section have ceased to exist, he shall revoke the same, and the provisions of this section shall thereupon cease to apply with respect to the state or states named in such proclamation, except with respect to offenses committed, or forfeitures incurred, prior to such revocation.

EXPORT OF OTHER ARTICLES AND MATERIALS

SEC. 2. (a) Whenever the President shall have issued a proclamation under the authority of section 1 of this Act and he shall thereafter find that the placing of restrictions on the shipment of certain articles or materials in addition to arms, ammunition, and implements of war from the United States to belligerent states, or to a state wherein civil strife exists, is necessary to promote the security or preserve the peace of the United States or to protect the lives of citizens of the United States, he shall so proclaim, and it shall thereafter be unlawful, for any American vessel to carry such articles or materials to any belligerent state, or to any state wherein civil strife exists, named in such proclamation issued under the authority of section 1 of this Act, or to any neutral state for transshipment to, or for the use of, any such belligerent state or any such state wherein civil strife exists. The President shall by proclamation from time to time definitely enumerate the articles and materials which it shall be unlawful for American vessels to so transport. . . .

(c) The President shall from time to time by proclamation extend such restrictions as are imposed under the authority of this section to other states as and when they may be declared to become belligerent states under proclamations issued under the authority of section 1 of this Act.

(d) The President may from time to time change, modify, or revoke in whole or in part any proclamations issued by him under the authority of this section.

(e) Except with respect to offenses committed, or forfeitures incurred, prior to May 1, 1939, this section and all proclamations issued thereunder shall not be effective after May 1, 1939.

FINANCIAL TRANSACTIONS

SEC. 3. (a) Whenever the President shall have issued a proclamation under the authority of section 1 of this Act, it shall thereafter be unlawful for any person within the United States to purchase, sell, or exchange bonds, securities, or other obligations of the government of any belligerent state or of any state wherein civil strife exists, named in such proclamation, or of any political subdivision of any such state, or of any person acting for or on behalf of the government of any such state, or of any faction or asserted government within any such state wherein civil strife exists, or of any person acting for or on behalf of any faction or asserted government within any such state wherein civil strife exists, issued after the date of such proclamation, or to make any loan or extend any credit to any such government, political subdivision, faction, asserted government, or person, or to solicit or receive any contribution for any such government, political subdivision, faction, asserted government, or person: *Provided,* That if the President shall find that such action will serve to protect the commercial or cther interests of the United States or its citizens, he may, in his discretion, and to such extent and under such regulations as he may prescribe, except from the operation of this section ordinary commercial credits and short-time obligations in aid of legal transactions and of a character customarily used in normal peacetime commercial transactions. Nothing in this subsection shall be construed to prohibit the solicitation or collection of funds to be used for medical aid and assistance, or for food and clothing to relieve human suffering, when such solicitation or collection of funds is made on behalf of and for use by any person or organization which is not acting for or on behalf of any such government, political subdivision, faction, or asserted government, but all such solicitations and collections of funds shall be subject to the approval of the President and shall be made under such rules and regulations as he shall prescribe. . . .

(c) Whoever shall violate the provisions of this section or of any regulations issued hereunder shall, upon conviction thereof, be fined not more than $50,000 or imprisoned for not more than five years, or both. Should the violation be by a corporation, organization, or association, each officer or agent thereof participating in the violation may be liable to the penalty herein prescribed. . . .

EXCEPTIONS—AMERICAN REPUBLICS

SEC. 4. This Act shall not apply to an American republic or republics engaged in war against a non-American state or states, provided the American republic is not co-operating with a non-American state or states in such war.

NATIONAL MUNITIONS CONTROL BOARD

SEC. 5. (a) There is hereby established a National Munitions Control Board (hereinafter referred to as the 'Board') to carry out the provisions of this Act. The Board shall consist of the Secretary of State, who shall be chairman and executive officer of the Board, the Secretary of the Treasury, the Secretary of War, the Secretary of the Navy, and the Secretary of Commerce. Except as otherwise provided in this Act, or by other law, the administration of this Act is vested in the Department of State. The Secretary of State shall promulgate such rules and regulations with regard to the enforcement of this section as he may deem necessary to carry out its provisions. The Board shall be convened by the chairman and shall hold at least one meeting a year.

(b) Every person who engages in the business of manufacturing, exporting, or importing any of the arms, ammunition, or implements of war referred to in this Act, whether as an exporter, importer, manufacturer, or dealer, shall register with the Secretary of State his name, or business name, principal place of business, and places of business in the United States, and a list of the arms, ammunition, and implements of war which he manufactures, imports, or exports.

(c) Every person required to register under this section shall notify the Secretary of State of any change in the arms, ammunition, or implements of war which he exports, imports, or manufactures; . . .

(d) It shall be unlawful for any person to export, or attempt to export, from the United States to any other state, any of the arms, ammunition, or implements of war referred to in this Act, or to import, or attempt to import, to the United States from any other state, any of the arms, ammunition, or implements of war referred to in this Act, without first having obtained a license therefor. . . .

(k) The President is hereby authorized to proclaim upon recommendation of the Board from time to time a list of articles which shall be considered arms, ammunition, and implements of war for the purposes of this section.

AMERICAN VESSELS PROHIBITED FROM CARRYING ARMS TO BELLIGERENT STATES

Sec. 6. (a) Whenever the President shall have issued a proclamation under the authority of section 1 of this Act, it shall thereafter be unlawful, until such proclamation is revoked, for any American vessel to carry any arms, ammunition, or implements of war to any belligerent state, or to any state wherein civil strife exists, named in such proclamation, or to any neutral state for transshipment to, or for the use of, any such belligerent state or any such state wherein civil strife exists.

(b) Whoever, in violation of the provisions of this section, shall take, or attempt to take, or shall authorize, hire, or solicit another to take, any American vessel carrying such cargo out of port or from the jurisdiction of the United States shall be fined not more than $10,000, or imprisoned not more than five years, or both; and, in addition, such vessel, and her tackle, apparel, furniture, and equipment, and the arms, ammunition, and implements of war on board, shall be forfeited to the United States.

USE OF AMERICAN PORTS AS BASE OF SUPPLY

SEC. 7. (a) Whenever, during any war in which the United States is neutral, the President, or any person thereunto authorized by him, shall have cause to believe that any vessel, domestic or foreign, whether requiring clearance or not, is about to carry out of a port of the United States, fuel, men, arms, ammunition, implements of war, or other supplies to any warship, tender, or supply ship of a belligerent state, but the evidence is not deemed sufficient to justify forbidding the departure of the vessel as provided for by section 1, title V, chapter 30, of the Act approved June 15, 1917, and if, in the President's judgment, such action will serve to maintain peace between the United States and foreign states, or to protect the commercial interests of the United States and its citizens, or to promote the security or neutrality of the United States, he shall have the power and it shall be his duty to require the owner, master, or person in command thereof, before departing from a port of the United States, to give a bond to the United States, with sufficient sureties, in such amount as he shall deem proper, conditioned that the vessel will not deliver the men, or any part of the cargo, to any warship, tender, or supply ship of a belligerent state.

(b) If the President, or any person thereunto authorized by him, shall find that a vessel, domestic or foreign, in a port of the United States, has previously cleared from a port of the United States during such war and delivered its cargo or any part thereof to a warship, tender, or supply ship of a belligerent state, he may prohibit the departure of such vessel during the duration of the war.

SUBMARINES AND ARMED MERCHANT VESSELS

SEC. 8. Whenever, during any war in which the United States is neutral, the President shall find that special restrictions placed on the use of the ports and territorial waters of the United States by the submarines or armed merchant vessels of a foreign state, will serve to maintain peace between the United States and foreign states, or to protect the commercial interests of the United States and its citizens, or to promote the security of the United States, and shall make proclamation therefore, it shall thereafter be unlawful for any such submarine or armed merchant vessel to enter a port or the territorial waters of the United States or to depart therefrom, except under such conditions and subject to such limitations as the President may prescribe. Whenever, in his judgment, the conditions which have caused him to issue his proclamation have ceased to exist, he shall revoke his proclamation and the provisions of this section shall thereupon cease to apply.

TRAVEL ON VESSELS OF BELLIGERENT STATES

SEC. 9. Whenever the President shall have issued a proclamation under the authority of section 1 of this Act it shall thereafter be unlawful for any citizen of the United States to travel on any vessel of the state or states named in such proclamation, except in accordance with such rules and regulations as the President shall prescribe: . . .

ARMING OF AMERICAN MERCHANT VESSELS PROHIBITED

SEC. 10. Whenever the President shall have issued a proclamation under the authority of section 1, it shall thereafter be unlawful, until such proclamation is revoked, for any American vessel engaged in commerce with any belligerent state, or any state wherein civil strife exists, named in such proclamation, to be armed or to carry any armament, arms, ammunition, or implements of war, except small arms and ammunition therefor which the President may deem necessary and shall publicly designate for the preservation of discipline aboard such vessels.

REGULATIONS

SEC. 11. The President may, from time to time, promulgate such rules and regulations.

not inconsistent with law, as may be necessary and proper to carry out any of the provisions of this Act; and he may exercise any power or authority conferred on him by this Act through such officer or officers, or agency or agencies, as he shall direct. . . .

515. REFORM OF THE FEDERAL JUDICIARY
1937
(U. S. 75th Cong. 1st Sess. *Sen. Report* 711)

The judicial invalidation of a large part of the New Deal program revived the oft-expressed demand for judicial reform. President F. D. Roosevelt argued, as had Theodore Roosevelt, that the courts were out of harmony with democracy and that some way should be found to force them in line with the will of the people as expressed through the other branches of the government. President Roosevelt's specific program called for a reorganization of the inferior federal courts to attain greater efficiency, and the appointment of one new justice, up to six in number, for every justice of the Supreme Court who, having passed the age of seventy and served for ten years, failed to retire. The proposal shocked many who felt that it violated the spirit of the American constitutional system of checks and balances and threatened the independence of the judiciary. The ultimate rejection of the proposal by the Senate Judiciary Committee and by Congress was probably the most serious setback which the President suffered during his eight years of office, yet it is clear now that although he lost the battle he won the campaign. We have included here the proposed bill for the reorganization of the judiciary, the President's address on the bill, the adverse report of the Senate Judiciary Committee, and the emasculated reform act which finally emerged. See M. Ernst, *The Ultimate Power;* I. Brant, *Storm over the Constitution;* R. K. Carr, *Democracy and the Supreme Court;* D. Alfange, *The Supreme Court and the National Will;* W. Lippman, *The Supreme Court, Independent or Controlled;* J. Alsop and T. Catledge, *The 168 Days;* C. A. and M. R. Beard, *America in Midpassage;* C. A. Ewing, *Judges of the Supreme Court, 1789–1937;* C. Fairman, "Retirement of Federal Judges," 51 Harv. L. Rev. 397. The Hearings are published, in six parts, in U. S. 75th Cong. 1st Sess. Sen. Comm. on Judiciary, *Hearings* on 1392.

1. PROPOSED BILL.

Be it enacted, That—

(a) When any judge of a court of the United States, appointed to hold his office

during good behavior, has heretofore or hereafter attained the age of seventy years and has held a commission or commissions as judge of any such court or courts at least ten years, continuously or otherwise, and within six months thereafter has neither resigned nor retired, the President, for each such judge who has not so resigned or retired, shall nominate, and by and with the advice and consent of the Senate, shall appoint one additional judge to the court to which the former is commissioned: *Provided,* That no additional judge shall be appointed hereunder if the judge who is of retirement age dies, resigns, or retires prior to the nomination of such additional judge.

(b) The number of judges of any court shall be permanently increased by the number appointed thereto under the provisions of subsection (a) of this section. No more than fifty judges shall be appointed thereunder, nor shall any judge be so appointed if such appointment would result in (1) more than fifteen members of the Supreme Court of the United States, (2) more than two additional members so appointed to a circuit court of appeals, the Court of Claims, the United States Court of Customs and Patent Appeals, or the Customs Court, or (3) more than twice the number of judges now authorized to be appointed for any district or, in the case of judges appointed for more than one district, for any such group of districts. . . .

(d) An additional judge shall not be appointed under the provisions of this section when the judge who is of retirement age is commissioned to an office as to which Congress has provided that a vacancy shall not be filled.

SEC. 2. (a) Any circuit judge hereafter appointed may be designated and assigned from time to time by the Chief Justice of the

United States for service in the circuit court of appeals for any circuit. Any district judge hereafter appointed may be designated and assigned from time to time by the Chief Justice of the United States for service in any district court, or, subject to the authority of the Chief Justice, by the senior circuit judge of his circuit for service in any district court within the circuit. A district judge designated and assigned to another district hereunder may hold court separately and at the same time as the district judge in such district. . . . The designation and assignment of any judge may be terminated at any time by order of the Chief Justice or the senior circuit judge, as the case may be. . . .

SEC. 3 (a) The Supreme Court shall have power to appoint a proctor. It shall be his duty (1) to obtain and, if deemed by the Court to be desirable, to publish information as to the volume, character, and status of litigation in the district courts and circuit courts of appeals, and such other information as the Supreme Court may from time to time require by order, and it shall be the duty of any judge, clerk, or marshal of any court of the United States promptly to furnish such information as may be required by the proctor; (2) to investigate the need of assigning district and circuit judges to other courts and to make recommendations thereon to the Chief Justice; (3) to recommend, with the approval of the Chief Justice, to any court of the United States methods for expediting cases pending on its dockets; and (4) to perform such other duties consistent with his office as the Court shall direct. . . .

SEC. 5. When used in this Act—

(a) The term "judge of retirement age" means a judge of a court of the United States, appointed to hold his office during good behavior, who has attained the age of seventy years and has held a commission or commissions as judge of any such court or courts at least ten years, continuously or otherwise, and within six months thereafter, whether or not he is eligible for retirement, has neither resigned nor retired. . . .

2. ADDRESS BY THE PRESIDENT OF THE UNITED STATES, MARCH 9, 1937

. . . Tonight, sitting at my desk in the White House, I make my first radio report to the people in my second term of office. . . .

The American people have learned from the depression. For in the last three national elections an overwhelming majority of them voted a mandate that the Congress and the President begin the task of providing that protection—not after long years of debate, but now.

The courts, however, have cast doubts on the ability of the elected Congress to protect us against catastrophe by meeting squarely our modern social and economic conditions.

We are at a crisis in our ability to proceed with that protection. It is a quiet crisis. There are no lines of depositors outside closed banks. But to the far-sighted it is far-reaching in its possibilities of injury to America.

I want to talk with you very simply about the need for present action in this crisis—the need to meet the unanswered challenge of one-third of a nation ill-nourished, ill-clad, ill-housed.

Last Thursday I described the American form of government as a three-horse team provided by the Constitution to the American people so that their field might be plowed. The three horses are, of course, the three branches of government—the Congress, the executive, and the courts. Two of the horses are pulling in unison today; the third is not. Those who have intimated that the President of the United States is trying to drive that team overlook the simple fact that the President, as Chief Executive, is himself one of the three horses.

It is the American people themselves who are in the driver's seat.

It is the American people themselves who want the furrow plowed.

It is the American people themselves who expect the third horse to pull in unison with the other two.

I hope that you have reread the Constitution of the United States. Like the Bible, it ought to be read again and again.

It is an easy document to understand when you remember that it was called into being because the Articles of Confederation under which the Original Thirteen States tried to operate after the Revolution showed the need of a National Government with power enough to handle national problems. In its preamble the Constitution states that it was intended to form a more perfect Union and promote the general welfare; and the powers given to the Congress to carry out those purposes can be best described by saying that they were all the powers needed to meet each and every problem which then had a national character and which could not be met by merely local action.

But the framers went further. Having in mind that in succeeding generations many other problems then undreamed of would become national problems, they gave to the Congress the ample broad powers "to levy taxes * * * and provide for the common defense and general welfare of the United States."

That, my friends, is what I honestly believe to have been the clear and underlying purpose of the patriots who wrote a Federal Constitution to create a National Government with national power, intended as they said, "to form a more perfect union * * * for ourselves and our posterity."

For nearly 20 years there was no conflict between the Congress and the Court. Then, in 1803, . . . The Court claimed the power to declare it [a statute] unconstitutional and did so declare it. But a little later the Court itself admitted that it was an extraordinary power to exercise and through Mr. Justice Washington laid down this limitation upon it: "It is but a decent respect due to the wisdom. the integrity, and the patriotism of the legislative body, by which any law is passed, to presume in favor of its validity until its violation of the Constitution is proved beyond all reasonable doubt."

But since the rise of the modern movement for social and economic progress through legislation, the Court has more and more often and more and more boldly asserted a power to veto laws passed by the Congress and State legislatures in complete disregard of this original limitation.

In the last 4 years the sound rule of giving statutes the benefit of all reasonable doubt has been cast aside. The Court has been acting not as a judicial body, but as a policy-making body.

When the Congress has sought to stabilize national agriculture, to improve the conditions of labor, to safeguard business against unfair competition, to protect our national resources, and in many other ways to serve our clearly national needs, the majority of the Court has been assuming the power to pass on the wisdom of these acts of the Congress—and to approve or disapprove the public policy written into these laws.

That is not only my accusation. It is the accusation of most distinguished Justices of the present Supreme Court. I have not the time to quote to you all the language used by dissenting Justices in many of these cases. But in the case holding the Railroad Retirement Act unconstitutional, for instance, Chief Justice Hughes said in a dissenting opinion that the majority opinion was "a departure from sound principles," and placed "an unwarranted limitation upon the commerce clause." And three other Justices agreed with him.

In the case holding the A. A. A. unconstitutional, Justice Stone said of the majority opinion that it was a "tortured construction of the Constitution." And two other Justices agreed with him.

In the case holding the New York Minimum Wage Law unconstitutional, Justice Stone said that the majority were actually reading into the Constitution their own "personal economic predilections," and that if the legislative power is not left free to choose the methods of solving the problems of poverty, subsistence, and health of large numbers in the community, then "government is to be rendered impotent." And two other Justices agreed with him.

In the face of these dissenting opinions, there is no basis for the claim made by some members of the Court that something in the Constitution has compelled them regretfully to thwart the will of the people.

In the face of such dissenting opinions, it is perfectly clear that as Chief Justice Hughes has said, "We are under a Constitution, but the Constitution is what the judges say it is."

The Court in addition to the proper use of its judicial functions has improperly set itself up as a third House of the Congress—a superlegislature, as one of the Justices has called it —reading into the Constitution words and implications which are not there, and which were never intended to be there.

We have, therefore, reached the point as a Nation where we must take action to save the Constitution from the Court and the Court from itself. We must find a way to take an appeal from the Supreme Court to the Constitution itself. We want a Supreme Court which will do justice under the Constitution—not over it. In our courts we want a government of laws and not of men.

I want—as all Americans want—an independent judiciary as proposed by the framers of the Constitution. That means a Supreme Court that will enforce the Constitution as written—that will refuse to amend the Constitution by the arbitrary exercise of judicial power—amendment by judicial say-so. It does not mean a judiciary so independent that it can deny the existence of facts universally recognized.

How, then, could we proceed to perform the mandate given us? It was said in last year's Democratic platform, "If these problems cannot be effectively solved within the Constitution, we shall seek such clarifying amendment as will assure the power to enact those laws, adequately to regulate commerce, protect public health and safety, and safeguard economic security." In other words, we said we would seek an amendment only if every other possible means by legislation were to fail.

When I commenced to review the situation with the problem squarely before me, I came by a process of elimination to the conclusion that short of amendments the only method which was clearly constitutional, and would at the same time carry out other much-needed reforms, was to infuse new blood into all our courts. We must have men worthy and equipped to carry out impartial justice. But at the same time we must have judges who will bring to the courts a present-day sense of the Constitution—judges who will retain in the courts the judicial functions of a court and reject the legislative powers which the courts have today assumed.

In 45 out of 48 States of the Union, judges are chosen not for life but for a period of years. In many States judges must retire at the age of 70. Congress has provided financial security by offering life pensions at full pay for Federal judges on all courts who are willing to retire at 70. In the case of Supreme Court Justices, that pension is $20,-000 a year. But all Federal judges, once appointed, can, if they choose, hold office for life no matter how old they may get to be.

What is my proposal? It is simply this:

Whenever a judge or justice of any Federal court has reached the age of 70 and does not avail himself of the opportunity to retire on a pension, a new member shall be appointed by the President then in office, with the approval, as required by the Constitution, of the Senate of the United States.

That plan has two chief purposes: By bringing into the judicial system a steady and continuing stream of new and younger blood, I hope, first, to make the administration of all Federal justice speedier and therefore less costly; secondly, to bring to the decision of social and economic problems younger men who have had personal experience and contact with modern facts and circumstances under which average men have to live and work. This plan will save our National Constitution from hardening of the judicial arteries.

The number of judges to be appointed would depend wholly on the decision of present judges now over 70 or those who would subsequently reach the age of 70.

If, for instance, any one of the six Justices of the Supreme Court now over the age of 70 should retire as provided under the plan, no additional place would be created. Consequently, although there never can be more than 15, there may be only 14, or 13, or 12, and there may be only 9.

There is nothing novel or radical about this idea. It seeks to maintain the Federal bench in full vigor. It has been discussed and approved by many persons of high authority even since a similar proposal passed the House of Representatives in 1869.

Why was the age fixed at 70? Because the laws of many States, the practice of the civil service, the regulations of the Army and Navy, and the rules of many of our universities and of almost every great private business enterprise commonly fix the retirement age at 70 years or less.

The statute would apply to all the courts in the Federal system. There is general approval so far as the lower Federal courts are concerned. The plan has met opposition only so far as the Supreme Court of the United States itself is concerned. If such a plan is good for the lower courts, it certainly ought to be equally good for the highest court, from which there is no appeal.

Those opposing this plan have sought to

arouse prejudice and fear by crying that I am seeking to "pack" the Supreme Court and that a baneful precedent will be established.

What do they mean by the words "packing the Court"?

Let me answer this question with a bluntness that will end all honest misunderstanding of my purposes.

If by that phrase "packing the Court" it is charged that I wish to place on the bench spineless puppets who would disregard the law and would decide specific cases as I wished them to be decided, I make this answer: That no President fit for his office would appoint, and no Senate of honorable men fit for their office would confirm, that kind of appointees to the Supreme Court.

But if by that phrase the charge is made that I would appoint and the Senate would confirm Justices worthy to sit beside present members of the Court who understand those modern conditions; that I will appoint Justices who will not undertake to override the judgment of the Congress on legislative policy; that I will appoint Justices who will act as Justices and not as legislators—if the appointment of such Justices can be called "packing the Courts"—then I say that I, and with me the vast majority of the American people, favor doing just that thing—now.

Is it a dangerous precedent for the Congress to change the number of the Justices? The Congress has always had, and will have, that power. The number of Justices has been changed several times before—in the administrations of John Adams and Thomas Jefferson, both signers of the Declaration of Independence, Andrew Jackson, Abraham Lincoln, and Ulysses S. Grant.

I suggest only the addition of Justices to the bench in accordance with a clearly defined principle relating to a clearly defined age limit. Fundamentally, if in the future America cannot trust the Congress it elects to refrain from abuse of our constitutional usages, democracy will have failed far beyond the importance to it of any kind of precedent concerning the judiciary.

We think it so much in the public interest to maintain a vigorous judiciary that we encourage the retirement of elderly judges by offering them a life pension at full salary. Why then should we leave the fulfillment of this public policy to chance or make it de-

pendent upon the desire or prejudice of any individual Justice?

It is the clear intention of our public policy to provide for a constant flow of new and younger blood into the judiciary. Normally, every President appoints a large number of district and circuit judges and a few members of the Supreme Court. Until my first term practically every President of the United States had appointed at least one member of the Supreme Court. President Taft appointed five members and named a Chief Justice; President Wilson three; President Harding four, including a Chief Justice; President Coolidge one; President Hoover three, including a Chief Justice.

Such a succession of appointments should have provided a court well balanced as to age. But chance and the disinclination of individuals to leave the Supreme Bench have now given us a Court in which five Justices will be over 75 years of age before next June and one over 70. Thus a sound public policy has been defeated.

I now propose that we establish by law an assurance against any such ill-balanced Court in the future. I propose that hereafter, when a judge reaches the age of 70, a new and younger judge shall be added to the Court automatically. In this way I propose to enforce a sound public policy by law instead of leaving the composition of our Federal courts, including the highest, to be determined by chance or the personal decision of individuals.

If such a law as I propose is regarded as establishing a new precedent, is it not a most desirable precedent?

Like all lawyers, like all Americans, I regret the necessity of this controversy. But the welfare of the United States, and indeed of the Constitution itself, is what we all must think about first. Our difficulty with the Court today rises not from the Court as an institution but from human beings within it. But we cannot yield our constitutional destiny to the personal judgment of a few men who, being fearful of the future, would deny us the necessary means of dealing with the present.

This plan of mine is no attack on the Court; it seeks to restore the Court to its rightful and historic place in our system of constitutional government and to have it resume its high task of building anew on the Constitution "a system of living law."

I have thus explained to you the reasons that lie behind our efforts to secure results by legislation within the Constitution. I hope that thereby the difficult process of constitutional amendment may be rendered unnecessary. . . .

I am in favor of action through legislation—

First, because I believe that it can be passed at this session of the Congress.

Second, because it will provide a reinvigorated, liberal-minded judiciary necessary to furnish quicker and cheaper justice from bottom to top.

Third, because it will provide a series of Federal courts willing to enforce the Constitution as written, and unwilling to assert legislative powers by writing into it their own political and economic policies.

During the past half century the balance of power between the three great branches of the Federal Government has been tipped out of balance by the courts in direct contradiction of the high purposes of the framers of the Constitution. It is my purpose to restore that balance. You who know me will accept my solemn assurance that in a world in which democracy is under attack I seek to make American democracy succeed.

3. ADVERSE REPORT FROM THE COMMITTEE ON THE JUDICIARY.

The Committee on the Judiciary, to whom was referred the bill to reorganize the judicial branch of the Government, after full consideration, having unanimously amended the measure, hereby report the bill adversely with the recommendation that it do not pass. . . .

THE ARGUMENT

The committee recommends that the measure be rejected for the following primary reasons:

I. The bill does not accomplish any one of the objectives for which it was originally offered.

II. It applies force to the judiciary and in its initial and ultimate effect would undermine the independence of the courts.

III. It violates all precedents in the history of our Government and would in itself be a dangerous precedent for the future.

IV. The theory of the bill is in direct violation of the spirit of the American Constitution and its employment would permit alteration of the Constitution without the people's consent or approval; it undermines the protection our constitutional system gives to minorities and is subversive of the rights of individuals.

V. It tends to centralize the Federal district judiciary by the power of assigning judges from one district to another at will.

VI. It tends to expand political control over the judicial department by adding to the powers of the legislative and executive departments respecting the judiciary. . . .

OBJECTIVES AS ORIGINALLY STATED

As offered to the Congress, this bill was designed to effectuate only three objectives, described as follows in the President's message:

1. To increase the personnel of the Federal courts "so that cases may be promptly decided in the first instance, and may be given adequate and prompt hearing on all appeals";

2. To "invigorate all the courts by the permanent infusion of new blood";

3. To "grant to the Supreme Court further power and responsibility in maintaining the efficiency of the entire Federal judiciary."

The third of these purposes was to be accomplished by the provisions creating the office of the Proctor and dealing with the assignment of judges to courts other than those to which commissioned.

The first two objectives were to be attained by the provisions authorizing the appointment of not to exceed 50 additional judges when sitting judges of retirement age, as defined in the bill, failed to retire or resign. How totally inadequate the measure is to achieve either of the named objectives, the most cursory examination of the facts reveals. . . .

QUESTION OF AGE NOT SOLVED

The next question is to determine to what extent "the persistent infusion of new blood" may be expected from this bill.

It will be observed that the bill before us does not and cannot compel the retirement of any judge, whether on the Supreme Court or any other court, when he becomes 70 years of age. It will be remembered that the mere attainment of three score and ten by a particular judge does not, under this bill, require the appointment of another. The man on the bench may be 80 years of age, but this bill will not authorize the President to appoint a new judge to sit beside him unless he has served as a judge for 10 years. In other words, age itself is not penalized; the penalty falls only when age is attended with experience.

No one should overlook the fact that under this bill the President, whoever he may be and whether or not he believes in the constant infusion of young blood in the courts, may nominate a man 69 years and 11 months of age to the Supreme Court, or to any court, and if confirmed, such nominee, if he never had served as a judge, would continue to sit upon the bench unmolested by this law until he had attained the ripe age of 79 years and 11 months.

We are told that "modern complexities call also for a constant infusion of new blood in the courts, just as it is needed in executive functions of the Government and in private business." Does this bill provide for such? The answer is obviously no. As has been just demonstrated, the introduction of old and inexperienced blood into the courts is not prevented by this bill.

More than that, the measure, by its own terms, makes impossible the "constant" or "persistent" infusion of new blood. It is to be observed that the word is "new," not "young."

The Supreme Court may not be expanded to more than 15 members. No more than two additional members may be appointed to any circuit court of appeals, to the Court of Claims, to the Court of Customs and Patent Appeals, or to the Customs Court, and the number of judges now serving in any district or group of districts may not be more than doubled. There is, therefore, a specific limitation of appointment regardless of age. That is to say, this bill, ostensibly designed to provide for the infusion of new blood, sets up insuperable obstacles to the "constant" or "persistent" operation of that principle. . . .

It thus appears that the bill before us does not with certainty provide for increasing the personnel of the Federal judiciary, does not remedy the law's delay, does not serve the interest of the "poorer litigant" and does not provide for the "constant" or "persistent

infusion of new blood" into the judiciary. What, then, does it do?

THE BILL APPLIES FORCE TO THE JUDICIARY

The answer is clear. It applies force to the judiciary. It is an attempt to impose upon the courts a course of action, a line of decision which, without that force, without that imposition, the judiciary might not adopt. . . .

Those of us who hold office in this Government, however humble or exalted it may be, are creatures of the Constitution. To it we owe all the power and authority we possess. Outside of it we have none. We are bound by it in every official act.

We know that this instrument, without which we would not be able to call ourselves presidents, judges, or legislators, was carefully planned and deliberately framed to establish three coordinate branches of government, every one of them to be independent of the others. For the protection of the people, for the preservation of the rights of the individual, for the maintenance of the liberties of minorities, for maintaining the checks and balances of our dual system, the three branches of the Government were so constituted that the independent expression of honest difference of opinion could never be restrained in the people's servants and no one branch could overawe or subjugate the others. That is the American system. It is immeasurably more important, immeasurably more sacred to the people of America, indeed, to the people of all the world than the immediate adoption of any legislation however beneficial.

That judges should hold office during good behavior is the prescription. It is founded upon historic experience of the utmost significance. Compensation at stated times, which compensation was not to be diminished during their tenure, was also ordained. Those comprehensible terms were the outgrowths of experience which was deep-seated. . . . This judicial system is the priceless heritage of every American.

By this bill another and wholly different cause is proposed for the intervention of executive influence, namely, age. Age and behavior have no connection; they are unrelated subjects. By this bill, judges who have reached 70 years of age may remain on the bench and have their judgment augmented if they agree with the new appointee, or vetoed if they disagree. This is far from the independence intended for the courts by the framers of the Constitution. This is an unwarranted influence accorded the appointing agency, contrary to the spirit of the Constitution. The bill sets up a plan which has as its stability the changing will or inclination of an agency not a part of the judicial system. Constitutionally, the bill can have no sanction. The effect of the bill, as stated by the Attorney General to the committee, and indeed by the President in both his message and speech, is in violation of the organic law.

OBJECT OF PLAN ACKNOWLEDGED

No amount of sophistry can cover up this fact. The effect of this bill is not to provide for an increase in the number of Justices composing the Supreme Court. The effect is to provide a forced retirement or, failing in this, to take from the Justices affected a free exercise of their independent judgment. . . .

Let us, for the purpose of the argument, grant that the Court has been wrong, wrong not only in that it has rendered mistaken opinions but wrong in the far more serious sense that it has substituted its will for the congressional will in the matter of legislation. May we nevertheless safely punish the Court?

Today it may be the Court which is charged with forgetting its constitutional duties. Tomorrow it may be the Congress. The next day it may be the Executive. If we yield to temptation now to lay the lash upon the Court, we are only teaching others how to apply it to ourselves and to the people when the occasion seems to warrant. Manifestly, if we may force the hand of the Court to secure our interpretation of the Constitution, then some succeeding Congress may repeat the process to secure another and a different interpretation and one which may not sound so pleasant in our ears as that for which we now contend.

There is a remedy for usurpation or other judicial wrongdoing. If this bill be supported by the toilers of this country upon the ground that they want a Court which will sustain legislation limiting hours and providing minimum wages, they must remember

that the procedure employed in the bill could be used in another administration to lengthen hours and to decrease wages. If farmers want agricultural relief and favor this bill upon the ground that it gives them a Court which will sustain legislation in their favor, they must remember that the procedure employed might some day be used to deprive them of every vestige of a farm relief.

When members of the Court usurp legislative powers or attempt to exercise political power, they lay themselves open to the charge of having lapsed from that "good behavior" which determines the period of their official life. But, if you say, the process of impeachment is difficult and uncertain, the answer is, the people made it so when they framed the Constitution. It is not for us, the servants of the people, the instruments of the Constitution, to find a more easy way to do that which our masters made difficult.

But, if the fault of the judges is not so grievous as to warrant impeachment, if their offense is merely that they have grown old, and we feel, therefore, that there should be a "constant infusion of new blood," then obviously the way to achieve that result is by constitutional amendment fixing definite terms for the members of the judiciary or making mandatory their retirement at a given age. Such a provision would indeed provide for the constant infusion of new blood, not only now but at all times in the future. The plan before us is but a temporary expedient which operates once and then never again, leaving the Court as permanently expanded to become once more a court of old men, gradually year by year falling behind the times. . . .

A MEASURE WITHOUT PRECEDENT

This bill is an invasion of judicial power such as has never before been attempted in this country. It is true that in the closing days of the administration of John Adams, a bill was passed creating 16 new circuit judges while reducing by one the number of places on the Supreme Court. It was charged that this was a bill to use the judiciary for a political purpose by providing official positions for members of a defeated party. The repeal of that law was the first task of the Jefferson administration.

Neither the original act nor the repealer

was an attempt to change the course of judicial decision. And never in the history of the country has there been such an act. The present bill comes to us, therefore, wholly without precedent.

It is true that the size of the Supreme Court has been changed from time to time, but in every instance after the Adams administration, save one, the changes were made for purely administrative purposes in aid of the Court, not to control it. . . .

A PRECEDENT OF LOYALTY TO THE CONSTITUTION

Shall we now, after 150 years of loyalty to the constitutional ideal of an untrammeled judiciary, duty bound to protect the constitutional rights of the humblest citizen even against the Government itself, create the vicious precedent which must necessarily undermine our system? The only argument for the increase which survives analysis is that Congress should enlarge the Court so as to make the policies of this administration effective.

We are told that a reactionary oligarchy defies the will of the majority, that this is a bill to "unpack" the Court and give effect to the desires of the majority; that is to say, a bill to increase the number of Justices for the express purpose of neutralizing the views of some of the present members. In justification we are told, but without authority, by those who would rationalize this program, that Congress was given the power to determine the size of the Court so that the legislative branch would be able to impose its will upon the judiciary. This amounts to nothing more than the declaration that when the Court stands in the way of a legislative enactment, the Congress may reverse the ruling by enlarging the Court. When such a principle is adopted, our constitutional system is overthrown!

This, then, is the dangerous precedent we are asked to establish. When proponents of the bill assert, as they have done, that Congress in the past has altered the number of Justices upon the Supreme Court and that this is reason enough for our doing it now, they show how important precedents are and prove that we should now refrain from any action that would seem to establish one which could be followed hereafter whenever a Congress and an executive should become dissatisfied with the decisions of the Supreme Court.

This is the first time in the history of our country that a proposal to alter the decisions of the court by enlarging its personnel has been so boldly made. Let us meet it. Let us now set a salutary precedent that will never be violated. Let us, of the Seventy-fifth Congress, in words that will never be disregarded by any succeeding Congress, declare that we would rather have an independent Court, a fearless Court, a Court that will dare to announce its honest opinions in what it believes to be the defense of the liberties of the people, than a Court that, out of fear or sense of obligation to the appointing power, or factional passion, approves any measure we may enact. We are not the judges of the judges. We are not above the Constitution.

Even if every charge brought against the so-called "reactionary" members of this Court be true, it is far better that we await orderly but inevitable change of personnel than that we impatiently overwhelm them with new members. Exhibiting this restraint, thus demonstrating our faith in the American system, we shall set an example that will protect the independent American judiciary from attack as long as this Government stands. . . .

True it is, that courts like Congresses, should take account of the advancing strides of civilization. True it is that the law, being a progressive science, must be pronounced progressively and liberally; but the milestones of liberal progress are made to be noted and counted with caution rather than merely to be encountered and passed. Progress is not a mad mob march; rather, it is a steady, invincible stride. . . .

If, under the "hydraulic pressure" of our present need for economic justice, we destroy the system under which our people have progressed to a higher degree of justice and prosperity than that ever enjoyed by any other people in all the history of the human race, then we shall destroy not only all opportunity for further advance but everything we have thus far achieved. . . .

Even if the case were far worse than it is alleged to be, it would still be no argument in favor of this bill to say that the courts and some judges have abused their power. The courts are not perfect, nor are the judges. The Congress is not perfect, nor are Senators and Representatives. The Executive is not perfect. These branches of government and the office under them are filled by human beings who for the most part strive to live up to the dignity and idealism of a system that was designed to achieve the greatest possible measure of justice and freedom for all the people. We shall destroy the system when we reduce it to the imperfect standards of the men who operate it. We shall strengthen it and ourselves, we shall make justice and liberty for all men more certain when, by patience and self-restraint, we maintain it on the high plane on which it was conceived.

Inconvenience and even delay in the enactment of legislation is not a heavy price to pay for our system. Constitutional democracy moves forward with certainty rather than with speed. The safety and the permanence of the progressive march of our civilization are far more important to us and to those who are to come after us than the enactment now of any particular law. The Constitution of the United States provides ample opportunity for the expression of popular will to bring about such reforms and changes as the people may deem essential to their present and future welfare. It is the people's charter of the powers granted those who govern them. . . .

SUMMARY

We recommend the rejection of this bill as a needless, futile, and utterly dangerous abandonment of constitutional principle.

It was presented to the Congress in a most intricate form and for reasons that obscured its real purpose.

It would not banish age from the bench nor abolish divided decisions.

It would not affect the power of any court to hold laws unconstitutional nor withdraw from any judge the authority to issue injunctions.

It would not reduce the expense of litigation nor speed the decision of cases.

It is a proposal without precedent and without justification.

It would subjugate the courts to the will of Congress and the President and thereby destroy the independence of the judiciary, the only certain shield of individual rights.

It contains the germ of a system of centralized administration of law that would enable an executive so minded to send his judges into every judicial distr'ct in the land to sit

in judgment on controversies between the Government and the citizen.

It points the way to the evasion of the Constitution and establishes the method whereby the people may be deprived of their right to pass upon all amendments of the fundamental law.

It stands now before the country, acknowledged by its proponents as a plan to force judicial interpretation of the Constitution, a proposal that violates every sacred tradition of American democracy.

Under the form of the Constitution it seeks to do that which is unconstitutional.

Its ultimate operation would be to make this Government one of men rather than one of law, and its practical operation would be to make the Constitution what the executive or legislative branches of the Government choose to say it is—an interpretation to be changed with each change of administration.

It is a measure which should be so emphatically rejected that its parallel will never again be presented to the free representatives of the free people of America.

WILLIAM H. KING.
FREDERICK VAN NUYS.
PATRICK MCCARRAN.
CARL A. HATCH.
EDWARD R. BURKE.
TOM CONNALLY.
JOSEPH C. O'MAHONEY.
WILLIAM E. BORAH.
WARREN R. AUSTIN.
FREDERICK STEIWER.

4. Judiciary Reform Act of 1937, August 24, 1937.

An Act to provide for intervention by the United States, direct appeals to the Supreme Court of the United States, and regulation of the issuance of injunctions, in certain cases involving the constitutionality of Acts of Congress, and for other purposes.

Be it enacted, That whenever the constitutionality of any Act of Congress affecting the public interest is drawn in question in any court of the United States in any suit or proceeding to which the United States, or any agency thereof, or any officer or employee thereof, as such officer or employee, is not a party, the court having jurisdiction of the suit or proceeding shall certify such fact to the Attorney General. In any such case the court shall permit the United States to intervene and become a party for presentation of evidence (if evidence is otherwise receivable in such suit or proceeding) and argument upon the question of the constitutionality of such Act. In any such suit or proceeding the United States shall, subject to the applicable provisions of law, have all the rights of a party and the liabilities of a party as to court costs to the extent necessary for a proper presentation of the facts and law relating to the constitutionality of such Act.

SEC. 2. In any suit or proceeding in any court of the United States to which the United States, or any agency thereof, or any officer or employee thereof, as such officer or employee, is a party, or in which the United States has intervened and become a party, and in which the decision is against the constitutionality of any Act of Congress, an appeal may be taken directly to the Supreme Court of the United States by the United States or any other party to such suit or proceeding upon application therefor or notice thereof within thirty days after the entry of a final or interlocutory judgment, decree, or order; and in the event that any such appeal is taken, any appeal or cross-appeal by any party to the suit or proceeding taken previously, or taken within sixty days after notice of an appeal under this section, shall also be or be treated as taken directly to the Supreme Court of the United States. In the event that an appeal is taken under this section, the record shall be made up and the case docketed in the Supreme Court of the United States within sixty days from the time such appeal is allowed, under such rules as may be prescribed by the proper courts. Appeals under this section shall be heard by the Supreme Court of the United States at the earliest possible time and shall take precedence over all other matters not of a like character. This section shall not be construed to be in derogation of any right of direct appeal to the Supreme Court of the United States under existing provisions of law.

SEC. 3. No interlocutory or permanent injunction suspending or restraining the enforcement, operation, or execution of, or setting aside, in whole or in part, any Act of Congress upon the ground that such Act or any part thereof is repugnant to the Constitution of the United States shall be issued or granted by any district court of the United States, or by any judge thereof, or by any circuit judge acting as district judge, unless the application for the same shall be presented to a circuit or district judge, and shall be heard and determined by three judges, of whom at least one shall be a circuit judge. When any such application is presented to a judge, he shall immediately request the senior circuit judge (or in his absence, the presiding circuit judge) of the circuit in which such district court is located to designate two other judges to participate in hearing and determining such application. It shall be the duty of the senior circuit judge or the presiding circuit judge, as the case may be, to designate immediately two other judges from such circuit for such purpose, and it shall be the duty of the judges so designated to participate in such hearing and determination. Such application shall not be heard or determined before at least five days' notice of the hearing has been given to the Attorney General and to such other persons as may be defendants in the suit: *Provided,* That if of opinion that irreparable loss or damage would result to the petitioner unless a temporary restraining order is granted, the judge to whom the application is made may grant such temporary restraining order at any time before the hearing and determination of the application, but such temporary restraining order shall remain in force only until such hearing and determination upon notice as aforesaid, and such temporary restraining order shall contain a specific finding, based upon evidence submitted to the court making the order and identified by reference thereto, that such irreparable loss or damage would result to the petitioner and specifying the nature of the loss or damage. The said court may, at the time of hearing such application, upon a like finding, continue the temporary stay or suspension, in whole or in part, until decision upon the application. The hearing upon any such application for an interlocutory or permanent injunction shall be given precedence and shall be in every way expedited and be assigned for a hearing at the earliest practicable day. An appeal may be taken directly to the Supreme Court of the United States upon application therefor or notice thereof within thirty days after the entry of the order, decree, or judgment granting or denying, after notice and hearing, and interlocutory or permanent injunction in such case. In the event that an appeal is taken under this section, the record shall be made up and the case docketed in the Supreme Court of the United States within sixty days from the time such appeal is allowed, under such rules as may be prescribed by the proper courts. Appeals under this section shall be heard by the Supreme Court of the United States at the earliest possible time and shall take precedence over all other matters not of a like character. This section shall not be construed to be in derogation of any right of direct appeal to the Supreme Court of the United States under existing provisions of law.

SEC. 4. Section 13 of the Judicial Code, as amended, is hereby amended to read as follows:

"SEC. 13. Whenever any district judge by reason of any disability or absence from his district or the accumulation or urgency of business is unable to perform speedily the work of his district, the senior circuit judge of that circuit, or, in his absence, the circuit justice thereof, shall designate and assign any district judge of any district court within the same judicial circuit to act as district judge in such district and to discharge all the judicial duties of a judge thereof for such time as the business of the said district court may require. Whenever it is found impracticable to designate and assign another district judge within the same judicial circuit as above provided and a certificate of the needs of any such district is presented by said senior circuit judge or said circuit justice to the Chief Justice of the United States, he, or in his absence the senior associate justice, shall designate and assign a district judge of an adjoining judicial circuit if practicable, or if not practicable, then of any judicial circuit, to perform the duties of district judge and hold a district court in any such district as above provided.

516. THE WAGNER HOUSING ACT
September 1, 1937

(U. S. Statutes at Large, Vol. L, p.. 888)

Agitation for slum clearance and the construction of good low-cost housing dates back to the nineteenth century, but notwithstanding the efforts of philanthropists and reformers, little was accomplished, and it was notorious that in this field the United States lagged badly behind such countries as Austria, Germany, England, and Sweden. The NRA provided funds for slum clearance and the construction of low cost housing, but these were insufficient to make any real improvement in the situation. The Wagner Housing Act attempted to solve the problem by placing the enormous resources of the federal government behind the slum clearance program. For the background of the slum problem, see R. W. DeForest and L. Veiller, *The Tenement House Problem;* J. Riis, *How the Other Half Lives;* E. E. Wood, *Recent Trends in American Housing;* L. H. Pink, *The New Day in Housing;* L. Post, *The Challenge of Housing;* M. W. Straus and T. Wegg, *Housing Comes of Age.*

An Act to provide financial assistance to the States and political subdivisions thereof for the elimination of unsafe and insanitary housing conditions, for the eradication of slums, for the provision of decent, safe, and sanitary dwellings for families of low income, and for the reduction of unemployment and the stimulation of business activity, to create a United States Housing Authority, and for other purposes.

DECLARATION OF POLICY

SECTION 1. It is hereby declared to be the policy of the United States to promote the general welfare of the Nation by employing its funds and credit, as provided in this Act, to assist the several States and their political subdivisions to alleviate present and recurring unemployment and to remedy the unsafe and insanitary housing conditions and the acute shortage of decent, safe, and sanitary dwellings for families of low income, in rural or urban communities, that are injurious to the health, safety, and morals of the citizens of the Nation.

DEFINITIONS

SEC. 2. When used in this Act—

(1) The term "low-rent housing" means decent, safe, and sanitary dwellings within

the financial reach of families of low income, and developed and administered to promote serviceability, efficiency, economy, and stability, and embraces all necessary appurtenances thereto. The dwellings in low-rent housing as defined in this Act shall be available solely for families whose net income at the time of admission does not exceed five times the rental (including the value or cost to them of heat, light, water, and cooking fuel) of the dwellings to be furnished such families, except that in the case of families with three or more minor dependents, such ratio shall not exceed six to one.

(2) The term "families of low income" means families who are in the lowest income group and who cannot afford to pay enough to cause private enterprise in their locality or metropolitan area to build an adequate supply of decent, safe, and sanitary dwellings for their use.

(3) The term "slum" means any area where dwellings predominate which, by reason of dilapidation, overcrowding, faulty arrangement or design, lack of ventilation, light or sanitation facilities, or any combination of these factors, are detrimental to safety, health, or morals. . . .

UNITED STATES HOUSING AUTHORITY

SEC. 3. (a) There is hereby created in the Department of the Interior and under the general supervision of the Secretary thereof a body corporate of perpetual duration to be known as the United States Housing Authority, which shall be an agency and instrumentality of the United States.

(b) The powers of the Authority shall be vested in and exercised by an Administrator, who shall be appointed by the President, by and with the advice and consent of the Senate. The Administrator shall serve for a term of five years and shall be removable by the President upon notice and hearing for neglect of duty or malfeasance but for no other cause. . . .

SEC. 4. . . .

(e) The Authority, including but not limited to its franchise, capital, reserves, surplus, loans, income, assets, and property of any kind, shall be exempt from all taxation now or hereafter imposed by the United States or by any State, county, municipality, or local taxing authority. Obligations, including interest thereon, issued by public housing agencies in connection with low-rent-housing or slum-clearance projects, and the income derived by such agencies from such projects, shall be exempt from all taxation now or hereafter imposed by the United States. . . .

LOANS FOR LOW-RENT-HOUSING AND SLUM-CLEARANCE PROJECTS

SEC. 9. The Authority may make loans to public-housing agencies to assist the development, acquisition, or administration of low-rent-housing or slum-clearance projects by such agencies. Where capital grants are made pursuant to section 11 the total amount of such loans outstanding on any one project and in which the Authority participates shall not exceed the development or acquisition cost of such project less all such capital grants, but in no event shall said loans exceed 90 per centum of such cost. In the case of annual contributions in assistance of low rentals as provided in section 10 the total of such loans outstanding on any one project and in which the Authority participates shall not exceed 90 per centum of the development or acquisition cost of such project. Such loans shall bear interest at such rate not less than the going Federal rate at the time the loan is made, plus one-half of one per centum, shall be secured in such manner, and shall be repaid within such period not exceeding sixty years, as may be deemed advisable by the Authority.

ANNUAL CONTRIBUTIONS IN ASSISTANCE OF LOW RENTALS

SEC. 10. (a) The Authority may make annual contributions to public housing agencies to assist in achieving and maintaining the low-rent character of their housing projects. The annual contributions for any such project shall be fixed in uniform amounts, and shall be paid in such amounts over a fixed period of years. No part of such annual contributions by the Authority shall be made available for any project unless and until the State, city, county, or other political subdivision in which such project is situated shall contribute, in the form of cash or tax remissions, general or special, or tax exemptions, at least 20 per centum of the annual contributions herein provided. The Authority shall embody the provisions for such annual contributions in a contract guaranteeing their payment over such fixed period: *Provided,* That no annual contributions shall be made, and the Authority shall enter into no contract guaranteeing any annual contribution in connection with the development of any low-rent-housing or slum-clearance project involving the construction of new dwellings, unless the project includes the elimination by demolition, condemnation, and effective closing, or the compulsory repair or improvement of unsafe or insanitary dwellings situated in the locality or metropolitan area, substantially equal in number to the number of newly constructed dwellings provided by the project; except that such elimination may, in the discretion of the Authority, be deferred in any locality or metropolitan area where the shortage of decent, safe, or sanitary housing available to families of low income is so acute as to force dangerous overcrowding of such families.

(b) Annual contributions shall be strictly limited to the amounts and periods necessary, in the determination of the Authority, to assure the low-rent character of the housing projects involved. Toward this end the Authority may prescribe regulations fixing the maximum contributions available under different circumstances, giving consideration to cost, location, size, rent-paying ability of prospective tenants, or other factors bearing upon the amounts and periods of assistance needed to achieve and maintain low rentals. Such regulations may provide for rates of contribution based upon development, acquisition or administration cost, number of dwelling units, number of persons housed, or other appropriate factors. . . .

(e) The Authority is authorized, on and after the date of the enactment of this Act, to enter into contracts which provide for annual contributions aggregating not more than $5,000,000 per annum, on or after July 1, 1938, to enter into additional such contracts which provide for annual contributions aggregating not more than $7,500,000 per annum, and on or after July 1, 1939, to enter into additional such contracts which provide for annual contributions aggregating not more than $7,500,000 per annum. Without further authorization from Congress, no new contracts for annual contributions beyond those herein authorized shall be entered into by the Authority. The faith of the United States is solemnly pledged to the payment of all annual contributions contracted for pursuant to this section, and there is hereby authorized to be appropriated in each fiscal year, out of any money in the Treasury not otherwise appropriated, the amounts necessary to provide for such payments.

CAPITAL GRANTS IN ASSISTANCE OF LOW RENTALS

SEC. 11. (a) As an alternative method of assistance to that provided in section 10, when any public housing agency so requests and demonstrates to the satisfaction of the Authority that such alternative method is better suited to the purpose of achieving and maintaining low rentals and to the other purposes of this Act, capital grants may be made to such agency for such purposes. . . .

(b) Pursuant to subsection (a) of this section, the Authority may make a capital grant for any low-rent-housing or slum-clearance project, which shall in no case exceed 25 per centum of its development or acquisition cost. . . .

(d) The Authority is authorized, on or after the date of the enactment of this Act to make capital grants (pursuant to subsection (b) of this section) aggregating not more than $10,000,000, on or after July 1, 1938, to make additional capital grants aggregating not more than $10,000,000, and on or after July 1, 1939, to make additional capital grants aggregating not more than $10,000,000. Without further authorization from Congress, no capital grants beyond those herein authorized shall be made by the Authority.

(e) To supplement any capital grant made by the Authority in connection with the development of any low-rent-housing or slum-clearance project, the President may allocate to the Authority, from any funds available for the relief of unemployment, an additional capital grant to be expended for payment of labor used in such development: *Provided,* That such additional capital grant shall not exceed 15 per centum of the development cost of the low-rent-housing or slum-clearance project involved.

(f) No capital grant pursuant to this section shall be made for any low-rent-housing or slum-clearance project unless the public housing agency receiving such capital grant shall also receive, from the State, political subdivision thereof, or otherwise, a contribution for such project (in the form of cash, land, or the value, capitalized at the going Federal rate of interest, of community facilities or services for which a charge is usually made, or tax remissions or tax exemptions) in an amount not less than 20 per centum of its development or acquisition cost.

DISPOSAL OF FEDERAL PROJECTS

SEC. 12. . . .

(b) As soon as practicable the Authority shall sell its Federal projects or divest itself of their management through leases.

GENERAL POWERS OF THE AUTHORITY

SEC. 13. . . .

(5) No contract for any loan, annual contribution, or capital grant made pursuant to this Act shall be entered into by the Authority with respect to any project hereafter initiated costing more than $4,000 per family-dwelling-unit or more than $1,000 per room (excluding land, demolition, and non-dwelling facilities); except that in any city the population of which exceeds 500,000 any such contract may be entered into with respect to a project hereafter initiated costing not to exceed $5,000 per family-dwelling-unit or not to exceed $1,250 per room (excluding land, demolition, and non-dwelling facilities), if in the opinion of the Authority such higher family-dwelling-unit cost or cost per room is justified by reason of higher costs of labor and materials and other construction costs. With respect to housing projects on which construction is hereafter initiated, the Authority shall make loans, grants, and annual contributions only for such low-rent-housing projects as it finds are to be undertaken in such a manner (a) that such projects will not be of elaborate or expensive design or materials, and economy will be promoted both in construction and administration, and (b) that the average construction cost of the dwelling units (excluding land, demolition, and non-dwelling facilities) in any such project is not greater than the average construction cost of dwelling units

currently produced by private enterprise, in the locality or metropolitan area concerned, under the legal building requirements applicable to the proposed site, and under labor standards not lower than those prescribed in this Act.

FINANCIAL PROVISIONS

SEC. 17. The Authority shall have a capital stock of $1,000,000, which shall be subscribed by the United States and paid by the Secretary of the Treasury out of any available funds. . . .

SEC. 20. (a) The Authority is authorized to issue obligations, in the form of notes, bonds, or otherwise, which it may sell to obtain funds for the purposes of this Act. The Authority may issue such obligations in an amount not to exceed $100,000,000 on or after the date of enactment of this Act, an additional amount not to exceed $200,000,000 on or after July 1, 1938, and an additional amount not to exceed $200,000,000 on or after July 1, 1939. Such obligations shall . . . bear such rates of interest not exceeding 4 per centum per annum.

(b) Such obligations shall be exempt, both as to principal and interest, from all taxation (except surtaxes, estate, inheritance, and gift taxes) now or hereafter imposed by the United States or by any State, county, municipality, or local taxing authority.

(c) Such obligations shall be fully and unconditionally guaranteed upon their face by the United States as to the payment of both interest and principal, and, in the event that the Authority shall be unable to make any such payment upon demand when due, payments shall be made to the holder by the Secretary of the Treasury with money hereby authorized to be appropriated for such purpose out of any money in the Treasury not otherwise appropriated.

SEC. 21. . . .

(d) Not more than 10 per centum of the funds provided for in this Act, either in the form of a loan, grant, or annual contribution, shall be expended within any one State.

517. THE ECONOMIC CONDITIONS OF THE SOUTH
July 25, 1938

(Report to the President on the Economic Conditions of the South by the National Emergency Council)

"It is my conviction," wrote President Roosevelt, "that the South represents right now the Nation's No. 1 economic problem." This statement and the Report of the National Emergency Council which appeared to substantiate it, aroused widespread criticism. It has been thought best to incorporate in complete form two of the fifteen sections of the Report rather than attempt to give brief excerpts from each section. See, R. Vance, *Human Geography of the South*; H. Odum, *Southern Regions of the United States*; *Report* of the Land Planning Commission of the National Resources Board, Pt. II; E. A. Woods and C. B. Metzger, *America's Human Wealth*.

SECTION 2
SOIL

Nature gave the South good soil. With less than a third of the Nation's area, the South contains more than a third of the Nation's good farming acreage. It has two-thirds of all the land in America receiving a 40-inch annual rainfall or better. It has nearly half of the land on which crops can grow for 6 months without danger of frost.

This heritage has been sadly exploited. Sixty-one per cent of all the Nation's land badly damaged by erosion is in the Southern States. An expanse of southern farm land as large as South Carolina has been gullied and washed away; at least 22 million acres of once fertile soil has been ruined beyond repair. Another area the size of Oklahoma and Alabama combined has been seriously damaged by erosion. In addition, the sterile sand and gravel washed off this land has covered over a fertile valley acreage equal in size to Maryland.

There are a number of reasons for this wastage:

Much of the South's land originally was so fertile that it produced crops for many years no matter how carelessly it was farmed. For generations thousands of southern farmers plowed their furrows up and down the slopes, so that each furrow served as a ditch to hasten the run-off of silt-laden water after every rain. While many farmers have now learned the importance of terracing their land or plowing it on the contours, thousands still follow the destructive practices of the past.

Half of the South's farmers are tenants, many of whom have little interest in preserving soil they do not own.

The South's chief crops are cotton, tobacco, and corn; all of these are inter-tilled crops— the soil is plowed between the rows, so that it is left loose and bare of vegetation.

The top-soil washes away much more swiftly than from land planted to cover crops, such as clover, soybeans, and small grains. Moreover, cotton, tobacco, and corn leave few stalks and leaves to be plowed under in the fall; and as a result the soil constantly loses its humus and its capacity to absorb rainfall.

Even after harvest, southern land is seldom planted to cover crops which would protect it from the winter rains. This increases erosion tenfold.

Southeastern farms are the smallest in the Nation. The operating units average only 71 acres, and nearly one-fourth of them are smaller than 20 acres. A farmer with so little land is forced to plant every foot of it in cash crops; he cannot spare an acre for soil restoring crops or pasture. Under the customary tenancy system, moreover, he has every incentive to plant all his land to crops which will bring in the largest possible immediate cash return. The landlord often encourages him in this destructive practice of cash-cropping.

Training in better agricultural methods, such as planting soil-restoring crops, terracing, contour-plowing, and rotation, has been spreading, but such training is still unavailable to most southern farmers. Annually the South spends considerably more money for fertilizer than for agricultural training through its land-grant colleges, experiment stations, and extension workers.

Forests are one of the best protections against erosion. Their foliage breaks the force of the rain; their roots bind the soil so that it cannot wash away; their fallen leaves form a blanket of vegetable cover which soaks up the water and checks run-off. Yet the South has cut away a large part of its forest, leaving acres of gullied, useless soil. There has been comparatively little effort at systematic reforestation. Overgrazing, too, has resulted in serious erosion throughout the Southwest.

There is a close relationship between this erosion and floods, which recently have been causing a loss to the Nation estimated at about $35,000,000 annually. Rainfall runs off uncovered land much more rapidly than it does from land planted to cover crops or forest. Recent studies indicate that a single acre of typical corn land lost approximately 127,000 more gallons of rainfall in a single year than a similar field planted to grass. Another experiment showed that land sodded in grass lost less than 1 per cent of a heavy rain through immediate run-off, while nearby land planted to cotton lost 31 per cent. In short, unprotected land not only is in danger of destruction; it also adds materially to the destructive power of the swollen streams into which it drains.

These factors—each one reenforcing all the others—are causing an unparalleled wastage of the South's most valuable asset, its soil. They are steadily cutting down its agricultural income, and steadily adding to its cost of production as compared with other areas of the world which raise the same crops.

For example, it takes quantities of fertilizer to make worn-out, eroded land produce. The South, with only one-fifth of the Nation's income, pays three-fifths of the Nation's fertilizer bill. In 1929 it bought 5½ million tons of commercial fertilizer at a cost of $161,-000,000. And although fertilizer performs a valuable and necessary service, it does not restore the soil. For a year or two it may nourish a crop, but the land still produces meagerly and at high cost.

Moreover, southern farmers cannot pile on fertilizer fast enough to put back the essential minerals which are washing out of their land. Each year, about 27,500,000 tons of nitrogen and phosphorous compounds are leached out of southern soil and sent down the rivers to the sea.

The South is losing more than $300,000,000 worth of fertile topsoil through erosion every year. This is not merely a loss of income—it is a loss of irreplaceable capital.

SECTION 7

HEALTH

For years evidence has been piling up that food, clothing, and housing influence not only the sickness rate and death rate but even the height and weight of school children. In the South, where family incomes are exceptionally low, the sickness and death rates are unusually high. Wage differentials become in fact differentials in health and life; poor health, in turn, affects wages.

The low-income belt of the South is a belt of sickness, misery, and unnecessary death. Its large proportion of low-income citizens are more subject to disease than the people of any similar area. The climate cannot be blamed—the South is as healthful as any section for those who have the necessary care, diet, and freedom from occupational disease.

Several years ago the United States Public Health Service conducted syphilis-control demonstrations in selected rural areas in the South. These studies revealed a much higher ratio of syphilis among Negroes than among whites, but showed further than this higher ratio was not due to physical differences between races. It was found to be due to the greater poverty and lower living conditions of the Negroes. Similar studies of such diseases have shown that individual health cannot be separated from the health of the community as a whole.

The presence of malaria, which infects annually more than 2,000,000 people, is estimated to have reduced the industrial output of the South one-third. One of the most striking examples of the effect of malaria on industry was revealed by the Public Health Service in studies among employees of a cotton mill in eastern North Carolina. Previous to the attempts to control malaria, the records of the mill one month showed 66 looms were idle as a result of ill-health. After completion of control work, no looms were idle for that reason. Before control work, 238,046 pounds of cloth were manufactured in one month. After completion of the work production rose to 316,804 pounds in one month—an increase of 33⅓ per cent.

In reports obtained in 1935 from 9 lumber companies, owning 14 sawmill villages in 5 southern States, there was agreement that malaria was an important and increasing problem among the employees. During the year 7.6 per cent of hospital admissions, 16.4 per cent of physician calls, and 19.7 per cent of dispensary drugs were for malaria. The average number of days off duty per case of malaria was 9, while days in the hospital for the same cause were 5. Ten railroads in the South listed malaria as an economic problem and a costly liability. Four utility companies had full-time mosquito-fighting crews at work during the year. The average case admitted to a company hospital lasted 3 days and the average number of days off duty because of malaria was 11. Each case of malaria was said to cost the companies $40.

If we attempt to place a monetary value on malaria by accepting the figure of $10,000 as the value of an average life and using the death rate of 3.943 for malaria reported by the census for 1936, the annual cost of deaths from this disease is $39,500,000. To this figure could be added the cost of illness, including days of work lost.

The health-protection facilities of the South are limited. For example, there are only one-third as many doctors per capita in South Carolina as there are in California. The South is deficient in hospitals and clinics, as well as in health workers. Many counties have no facilities at all.

The South has only begun to look into its pressing industrial hygiene problems, although it has 26 per cent of the male mine workers in the United States and 14 per cent of the male factory workers. These are the workers with which modern industrial health protection is most concerned.

The experience as to pneumonia and tuberculosis among employees of the Tennessee Coal, Iron & Railroad Co. and their dependents during the 11-year period from 1925 to 1935 gives an indication of health conditions among miners in the South. The situation generally is probably worse than shown by the figures for this company, whose workers have relatively better protection against disease. For this period the number under observation averaged slightly more than 77,000 persons. There were 3,780 cases of pneumonia, of which 739 terminated fatally. This resulted

in an average frequency per 1,000 of approximately 4.9 pneumonia cases per year among surface workers, 4.7 among coal miners, and 10.6 among ore miners. The rate of 4.2 for dependents included also the pneumonia of childhood and infancy. A fatality rate of 30.7 deaths per 1,000 cases of pneumonia was found among surface workers, a rate of 26.8 among coal miners, and 24.8 among ore miners. Deaths from tuberculosis occurred at an annual rate of 1.467 per thousand workers among coal miners, 1.232 among ore miners, and 0.566 among surface workers.

Prior to 1936 only one State in the South gave consideration to industrial hygiene. Today, with the aid of Social Security funds, seven additional States have industrial-hygiene units, and approximately 7,000,000 of the 10,000,000 gainful workers are receiving some type of industrial-hygiene service. However, these industrial-hygiene units have started their programs only recently, and it will be some time before adequate health services will be available. The funds now being spent for this activity in the eight States which have industrial-hygiene services do not meet the problem of protecting and improving the health of these workers. Approximately $100,-000 is now being budgeted for this work, although it is known that the economic loss due to industrial injuries and illnesses among these workers is hundreds of millions of dollars.

Reports of one of the largest life-insurance companies show that more people in the southern area than elsewhere die without medical aid. The same company reported in a recent year a rise of 7.3 per cent in the death rate in the nine South Atlantic States, though in no other region had the death rate risen above 4.8 per cent, and in some sections it had declined.

The scourge of pellagra, that affects the South almost exclusively, is a disease chiefly due to inadequate diet; it responds to rather simple preventive measures, including suitable nourishing food. Even in southern cities from 60 to 88 per cent of the families of low incomes are spending for food less than enough to purchase an adequate diet.

518. CONNECTICUT GENERAL LIFE INS. CO. v. JOHNSON
303 U. S. 77
1938

Appeal from the Supreme Court of California. This case involved the constitutionality of a California law taxing the gross premiums of insurance companies doing business in the state. The Connecticut company challenged the constitutionality of the act in so far as it applied to reinsurance premiums on contracts made in and payable in other states. The Court held that the act in question violated the due process clause of the Fourteenth Amendment. Only the dissenting opinion is here given; its importance flows from the fact that it is the first clear-cut protest against the traditional interpretation of the Fourteenth Amendment which has come officially from any member of the Supreme Court for half a century For the recent interpretation of the meaning of that amendment, see Graham, "The Conspiracy Theory of the Fourteenth Amendment," 47 Yale L. J., 371; Boudin, "Truth and Fiction about the Fourteenth Amendment," 16 N. Y. U. Law Qt. Rev. 19.

BLACK, J., dissenting. I do not believe that this California corporate franchise tax has been proved beyond all reasonable doubt to be in violation of the Federal Constitution and I believe that the judgment of the Supreme Court of California should be affirmed. Traditionally, states have been empowered to grant or deny foreign corporations the right to do business within their borders, and "may exclude them arbitrarily or impose such conditions as [they] will upon their engaging in business within [their] jurisdiction."

California laid an annual tax upon gross insurance premiums which the Supreme Court of California has construed to be "a franchise tax exacted for the privilege of doing business." In measuring this franchise tax imposed upon corporations the state includes reinsurance premiums paid to the corporation on contracts made without the state, *where such reinsurance protects citizens of the State of California*. There is no attempt by this tax to regulate the business of the insurance company in any state except California.

The record does not indicate that California made any contract with this Connecticut corporation guaranteeing it a permanent franchise to do business in California on the same terms and conditions upon which it entered the state. . . .

But it is contended that the due process clause of the Fourteenth Amendment prohibits California from determining what terms and conditions should be imposed upon this Connecticut corporation to promote the welfare of the people of California.

I do not believe the word "person" in the Fourteenth Amendment includes corporations. "The doctrine of stare decisis, however appropriate and even necessary at times, has only a limited application in the field of constitutional law." This Court has many times changed its interpretations of the Constitution when the conclusion was reached that an improper construction had been adopted. . . . A constitutional interpretation that is wrong should not stand. I believe this Court should now overrule previous decisions which interpreted the Fourteenth Amendment to include corporations.

Neither the history nor the language of the Fourteenth Amendment justifies the belief that corporations are included within its protection. The historical purpose of the Fourteenth Amendment was clearly set forth when first considered by this Court in the Slaughter House Cases, . . .

Certainly, when the Fourteenth Amendment was submitted for approval, the people were not told that the states of the South were to be denied their normal relationship with the Federal Government unless they ratified an amendment granting new and revolutionary rights to corporations. This Court, when the Slaughter House Cases were decided in 1873, had apparently discovered no such purpose. The records of the time can be searched in vain for evidence that this amendment was adopted for the benefit of corporations. It is true that in 1882, twelve years after its adoption, and ten years after the Slaughter House Cases, an argument was made in this Court that a journal of the joint Congressional Committee which framed the amendment, secret and undisclosed up to that date, indicated the committee's desire to protect corporations by the use of the word "person." (*San Mateo County* v. *Southern Pacific Railroad*, 116 U. S. 138.) Four years later, in 1886, this Court in the case of *Santa Clara County*

v. *Southern Pacific Railroad*, 118 U. S. 394, decided for the first time that the word "person" in the amendment did in some instances include corporations. A secret purpose on the part of the members of the committee, even if such be the fact, however, would not be sufficient to justify any such construction. The history of the amendment proves that the people were told that its purpose was to protect weak and helpless human beings and were not told that it was intended to remove corporations in any fashion from the control of state governments. The Fourteenth Amendment followed the freedom of a race from slavery. Justice Swayne said in the Slaughter House Cases, that: "By 'any person' was meant *all* persons within the jurisdiction of the State. No distinction is intimated on account of race or color." Corporations have neither race nor color. He knew the amendment was intended to protect the life, liberty, and property of *human* beings.

The langauge of the amendment itself does not support the theory that it was passed for the benefit of corporations.

The first clause of section 1 of the amendment reads: "All *persons* born or naturalized in the United States, and subject to the jurisdiction thereof, are citizens of the United States and of the State wherein they reside." Certainly a corporation cannot be naturalized and "persons" here is not broad enough to include "corporations."

The first clause of the second sentence of section 1 reads: "No State shall make or enforce any law which shall abridge the privileges or immunities of citizens of the United States." While efforts have been made to persuade this Court to allow corporations to claim the protection of *this* clause, these efforts have not been successful.

The next clause of the second sentence reads: "Nor shall any State deprive any *person* of life, liberty, or property, without due process of law." It has not been decided that this clause prohibits a state from depriving a corporation of "life." This Court has expressly held that "the liberty guaranteed by the 14th Amendment against deprivation without due process of law is the liberty of *natural, not artificial persons*." Thus, the words "life" and "liberty" do not apply to corporations, and of course they could not have been so intended to apply. However, the

decisions of this Court which the majority follow hold that corporations are included in this clause in so far as the word "property" is concerned. In other words, this clause is construed to mean as follows:

"Nor shall any State deprive any *human being* of life, liberty or property without due process of law; nor shall any State deprive any corporation of property without due process of law."

The last clause of this second sentence of section 1 reads: "Nor deny to any person within its jurisdiction the equal protection of the laws." As used here, "person" has been construed to include corporations.

Both Congress and the people were familiar with the meaning of the word "corporation" at the time the Fourteenth Amendment was submitted and adopted. The judicial inclusion of the word "corporation" in the Fourteenth Amendment has had a revolutionary effect on our form of government. The states did not adopt the amendment with knowledge of its sweeping meaning under its present construction. No section of the amendment gave notice to the people that, if adopted, it would subject every state law and municipal ordinance, affecting corporations (and all administrative actions under them), to censorship of the United States courts. No word in all this amendment gave any hint that its adoption would deprive the states of their long-recognized power to regulate corporations.

The second section of the amendment informed the people that representatives would be apportioned among the several states "according to their respective numbers, counting the whole number of *persons* in each State, excluding Indians not taxed." No citizen could gather the impression *here* that while the word "persons" in the second section applied to human beings, the word "persons" in the first section *in some instances* applied to corporations. Section 3 of the amendment said that "no *person* shall be a Senator or Representative in Congress," (who "engaged in insurrection"). There was no intimation *here* that the word "person" in the first section *in some instances* included corporations.

This amendment sought to prevent discrimination by the states against classes or races. We are aware of this from words spoken in this Court within five years after its adoption, when the people and the courts were personally familiar with the historical background of the amendment. "We doubt very much whether any action of a State not directed by way of discrimination against the negroes as a class, or on account of their race, will ever be held to come within the purview of this provision." Yet, of the cases in this Court in which the Fourteenth Amendment was applied during the first fifty years after its adoption, less than one-half of 1 per cent invoked it in protection of the negro race, and more than 50 per cent asked that its benefits be extended to corporations.

If the people of this nation wish to deprive the states of their sovereign rights to deter-mine what is a fair and just tax upon corporations doing a purely local business within their own state boundaries, there is a way provided by the Constitution to accomplish this purpose. That way does not lie along the course of judicial amendment to that fundamental charter. An amendment having that purpose could be submitted by Congress as provided by the Constitution. I do not believe that the Fourteenth Amendment had that purpose, nor that the people believed it had that purpose, nor that it should be con-strued as having that purpose.

I believe the judgment of the Supreme Court of California should be sustained.

519. HELVERING v. GERHARDT
304 U. S. 405
1938

On Writs of Certiorari to the U. S. Circuit Court of Appeals for the Second Circuit. The question of reciprocal immunity of state and federal governments from taxation is an old and troublesome one. Marshall, in McCulloch v. Maryland, laid down the principle that the instrumentalities of the national government must be immune from taxation by the states, because the power to tax involved the power to destroy. The same principle was applied to the instrumentalities of the states, notably in Collector v. Day (Doc. No. 282). The immense enlargement of governmental personnel, the growth of government activities—many of them of a quasi-private character, and the acute financial problems presented by the depression all combined to force a reconsideration of these principles. What are governmental instrumentalities, and how far does immunity extend to those employed by state or federal governments? The Court in this and the Graves case attempted to distinguish between instrumentalities essential to the preservation of government and those non-essential—obviously a very difficult and somewhat arbitrary distinction. Justice Black, in his concurring opinion, called sensibly for a reconsideration of the whole question of intergovernmental tax immunity. See on this and the Graves case, U. S. Dept. of Justice, "Taxation of Government Bondholders and Employees—the Immunity Rule and the Sixteenth Amendment"; Graham, "Two Centuries of Tax Immunity," 18 N. Car. L. Rev. 16; Magill, "Problem of Intergovernmental Tax Exemption," 15 Tax Mag. 699; Shaw, "Recent Cases on the Doctrine of Intergovernmental Tax Immunity," 8 Brooklyn L. Rev. 38; Watkins, "The Power of State and Federal Governments to Tax one another," 24 Va. L. Rev. 475; Lewinson, "Tax-Exempt Salaries and Securities," 23 A. B. A. J. 685; Freedman "Government owned Corporations and Intergovernmental Tax Immunity," 24 Wash. U. L. Qt. 46; Lowndes, "Taxation in the Supreme Court 1937 Term," 87 U. of Pa. L. Rev. 1.

STONE, J. The question for decision is whether the imposition of a federal income tax for the calendar years 1932 and 1933 on salaries received by respondents, as employees of the Port of New York Authority, places an unconstitutional burden on the States of New York and New Jersey.

The Port Authority is a bi-state corporation, created by compact between New York and New Jersey. . . .

In conformity to the plan, and pursuant to further legislation of the two states, the Authority has constructed the Outerbridge Crossing Bridge, the Goethals Bridge, the Bayonne Bridge, and the George Washington Bridge [etc.]. . . .

The respondents during the taxable years in question, were respectively a construction engineer and two assistant general managers, employed by the Authority at annual salaries ranging between $8,000 and $15,000. All took oaths of office, although neither the compact nor the related statutes appears to have created any office to which any of the respondents were appointed, or defined their duties or prescribed that they should take an oath. The several respondents having failed to return their respective salaries as income for the taxable years in question, the commissioner determined deficiencies against them. The Board of Tax Appeals found that the Port Authority was engaged in the performance of a public function for the States of New York and New Jersey, and ruled that the compensation received by the Authority's employees was exempt from federal income tax. The Circuit Court of Appeals for the Second Circuit, affirmed without opinion on the authority of *Brush* v. *Commissioner*. We granted certiorari because of the public importance of the question presented.

The Constitution contains no express limitation on the power of either a state or the national government to tax the other, or its instrumentalities. The doctrine that there is an implied limitation stems from *McCulloch* v. *Maryland*, in which it was held that a state tax laid specifically upon the privilege of issuing bank notes, and in fact applicable alone to the notes of national banks, was invalid since it impeded the national government in the exercise of its power to establish and maintain a bank, implied as an incident to the borrowing, taxing, war and other powers specifically granted to the national government by article 1, § 8 of the Constitution. . . .

That the taxing power of the federal government is nevertheless subject to an implied restriction when applied to state instrumentalities was first decided in *Collector* v. *Day*, 11 Wall. 113, where the salary of a state officer, a probate judge, was held to be immune from federal income tax. The question there presented to the Court was not one of interference with a granted power in a field in which the federal government is supreme, but a limitation by implication upon the granted federal power to tax. In recognizing that implication for the first time, the Court was concerned with the continued existence of the states as governmental entities, and their preservation from destruction by the national taxing power. The immunity which it implied was sustained only because it was one deemed necessary to protect the states from destruction by the federal taxation of those governmental functions which they were exercising when the Constitution was adopted and which were essential to their continued existence. . . .

It is enough for present purposes that the state immunity from the national taxing power, when recognized in *Collector* v. *Day,* was narrowly limited to a state judicial officer engaged in the performance of a function which pertained to state governments at the time the Constitution was adopted, without which no state "could long preserve its existence."

There are cogent reasons why any constitutional restriction upon the taxing power granted to Congress, so far as it can be properly raised by implication, should be narrowly limited. One, as was pointed out by Chief Justice Marshall in *McCulloch* v. *Maryland,* and *Weston* v. *Charleston,* is that the people of all the states have created the national government and are represented in Congress. Through that representation they exercise the national taxing power. The very fact that when they are exercising it they are taxing themselves serves to guard against its abuse through the possibility of resort to the usual processes of political action which provides a readier and more adaptable means than any which courts can afford, for securing accommodation of the competing demands for national revenue, on the one hand, and for reasonable scope for the independence of state action, on the other.

Another reason rests upon the fact that any allowance of a tax immunity for the protection of state sovereignty is at the expense of the sovereign power of the nation to tax. Enlargement of the one involves diminution of the other. When enlargement proceeds beyond the necessity of protecting the state, the burden of the immunity is thrown upon the national government with benefit only to a privileged class of taxpayers. With the steady expansion of the activity of state governments into new fields they have undertaken the performance of functions not known to the states when the Constitution was adopted, and have taken over the management of business enterprises once conducted exclusively by private individuals subject to the national taxing power. In a complex economic society tax burdens laid upon those who directly or indirectly have dealings with the states, tend, to some extent not capable of precise measurement, to be passed on economically and thus to burden the state government itself. But if every federal tax which is laid on some new form of state activity, or whose economic burden reaches in some measure the state or those who serve it, were to be set aside as an infringement of state sovereignty, it is evident that a restriction upon national power, devised only as a shield to protect the states from curtailment of the essential operations of government which they have exercised from the beginning, would become a ready means for striking down the taxing power of the nation. Once impaired by the recognition of a state immunity found to be excessive, restoration of that power is not likely to be secured through the action of state legislatures; for they are without the inducements to act which have often persuaded Congress to waive immunities thought to be excessive.

In tacit recognition of the limitation which the very nature of our federal system imposes on state immunity from taxation in order to avoid an everexpanding encroachment upon the federal taxing power, this Court has refused to enlarge the immunity substantially beyond those limits marked out in *Collector* v. *Day*. It has been sustained where, as in *Collector* v. *Day,* the function involved was one thought to be essential to the maintenance of a state government. . . .

But the Court has refused to extend the immunity to a state conducted liquor business, or to a street railway business taken over and operated by state officers as a means of effecting a local public policy. It has sustained the imposition of a federal excise tax laid on the privilege of exercising corporate franchises granted by a state to public service companies. In each of these cases it was pointed out that the state function affected was one which could be carried on by private enterprise, and that therefore it was not one without which a state could not continue to exist as a governmental entity. The immunity has been still more narrowly restricted in those cases where some part of the burden of a tax, collected not from a state treasury but from individual taxpayers, is said to be passed on to the state. In these cases the function has been either held or assumed to be of such a character that its performance by the state is immune from direct federal interference; yet the individuals who personally derived profit or compensation from their employment in carrying out the function were deemed to be subject to federal income tax.

In a period marked by a constant expansion of government activities and the steady multiplication of the complexities of taxing systems, it is perhaps too much to expect that the judicial pronouncements marking the boundaries of state immunity should present a completely logical pattern. But they disclose no purposeful departure from, and indeed definitely establish, two guiding principles of limitation for holding the tax immunity of state instrumentalities to its proper function. The one, dependent upon the nature of the function being performed by the state or in its behalf, excludes from the immunity activities thought not to be essential to the preservation of state governments even though the tax be collected from the state treasury. . . . The other principle, exemplified by those cases where the tax laid upon individuals affects the state only as the burden is passed on to it by the taxpayer, forbids recognition of the immunity when the burden on the state is so speculative and uncertain that if allowed it would restrict the federal taxing power without affording any corresponding tangible protection to the state government; even though the function be thought important enough to demand immunity from a tax upon the state itself, it is not necessarily protected from a tax which well may be substantially or entirely absorbed by private persons.

With these controlling principles in mind we turn to their application in the circumstances of the present case. The challenged taxes are upon the net income of respondents, derived from their employment in common occupations not shown to be different in their methods or duties from those of similar employees in private industry. The taxpayers enjoy the benefits and protection of the laws of the United States. They are under a duty to support its government and are not beyond the reach of its taxing power. A nondiscriminatory tax laid on their net income, in common with that of all other members of the community, could by no reasonable probability be considered to preclude the performance of the function which New York and New Jersey have undertaken, or to obstruct it more than like private enterprises are obstructed by our taxing system. Even though, to some unascertainable extent, the tax deprives the states of the advantage of paying less than the standard rate for the services which they engage, it does not curtail any of those functions which have been thought hitherto to be essential to their continued existence as states. At most it may be said to increase somewhat the cost of the state governments because, in an interdependent economic society, the taxation of income tends to raise (to some extent which economists are not able to measure), the price of labor and materials. The effect of the immunity if allowed would be to relieve respondents of their duty of financial support to the national government, in order to secure to the state a theoretical advantage so speculative in its character and measurement as to be unsubstantial. A tax immunity devised for protection of the states as governmental entities cannot be pressed so far. . . .

The basis upon which constitutional tax immunity of a state has been supported is the protection which it affords to the continued existence of the state. To attain that end it is not ordinarily necessary to confer on the state a competitive advantage over private persons in carrying on the operations of its government. There is no such necessity here, and the resulting impairment of the federal power to tax argues against the advantage. The state and national governments must coexist. Each must be supported by taxation of those who are citizens of both. The mere fact that the economic burden of such taxes may be passed on to a state government and thus increase to some extent, here wholly conjectural, the expense of its operation, infringes no constitutional immunity. Such burdens are but normal incidents of the organization within the same territory of

two governments, each possessed of the taxing power. . . .

As was pointed out in *Metcalf & Eddy* v. *Mitchell,* there may be state agencies of such a character and so intimately associated with the performance of an indispensable function of state government that any taxation of it would threaten such interference with the functions of government itself as to be considered beyond the reach of the federal taxing power. If the tax considered in *Collector* v. *Day,* upon the salary of an officer engaged in the performance of an indispensable function of the state which cannot be delegated to private individuals, may be regarded as such an instance, that is not the case presented here.

Expressing no opinion whether a federal tax may be imposed upon the Port Authority itself with respect to its receipt of income or its other activities, we decide only that the present tax neither precludes nor threatens unreasonably to obstruct any function essential to the continued existence of the state government. So much of the burden of the tax laid upon respondents' income as may reach the state is but a necessary incident to the coexistence within the same organized government of the two taxing sovereigns, and hence is a burden the existence of which the Constitution presupposes. The immunity, if allowed, would impose to an inadmissible extent a restriction upon the taxing power which the Constitution has granted to the federal government.

Reversed.

BLACK, J. delivered a concurring opinion.
BUTLER, J. delivered a dissenting opinion in which McREYNOLDS, J. concurred.

520. GRAVES et. al. v. NEW YORK ex. rel. O'KEEFE
306 U. S. 466
1939

Writ of Certiorari to the Supreme Court of the State of New York. This case involved the validity of a New York State income tax on the salary of an employee of the federal Home Owners' Loan Corporation. For the problem of intergovernmental tax immunity and references, see Doc. No. 519.

STONE, J. We are asked to decide whether the imposition by the State of New York

of an income tax on the salary of an employee of the Home Owners' Loan Corporation places an unconstitutional burden upon the federal government.

Respondent, a resident of New York, was employed during 1934 as an examining attorney for the Home Owners' Loan Corporation at an annual salary of $2,400. In his income tax return for that year he included his salary as subject to the New York state income tax imposed by Art. 16 of the Tax Law of New York. Subdivision 2f of § 359, since repealed, exempted from the tax "Salaries, wages and other compensation received from the United States of officials or employees thereof, including persons in the military or naval forces of the United States. * * *" Petitioners, New York State Tax Commissioners, rejected respondent's claim for a refund of the tax based on the ground that his salary was constitutionally exempt from state taxation because the Home Owners' Loan Corporation is an instrumentality of the United States Government and that he, during the taxable year, was an employee of the federal government engaged in the performance of a governmental function. . . .

The Home Owners' Loan Corporation was created pursuant to § 4(a) of the Home Owners' Loan Act of 1933, which was enacted to provide emergency relief to home owners, particularly to assist them with respect to home mortgage indebtedness. The corporation, which is authorized to lend money to home owners on mortgages and to refinance home mortgage loans within the purview of the Act, is declared to be an instrumentality of the United States. Its shares of stock are wholly government-owned. Its funds are deposited in the Treasury of the United States, and the compensation of its employees is paid by drafts upon the Treasury.

For the purposes of this case we may assume that the creation of the Home Owners' Loan Corporation was a constitutional exercise of the powers of the federal government. As that government derives its authority wholly from powers delegated to it by the Constitution, its every action within its constitutional power is governmental action, and since Congress is made the sole judge of what powers within the constitutional grant are to be exercised, all activities of government constitutionally authorized by Congress must stand on a parity with respect to their constitutional immunity from taxation. And when the national government lawfully acts through a corporation which it owns and controls, those activities are governmental functions entitled to whatever tax immunity attaches to those

functions when carried on by the government itself through its departments.

The single question with which we are now concerned is whether the tax laid by the state upon the salary of respondent, employed by a corporate instrumentality of the federal government, imposes an unconstitutional burden upon that government. The theory of the tax immunity of either government, state or national, and its instrumentalities, from taxation by the other, has been rested upon an implied limitation on the taxing power of each, such as to forestall undue interference, through the exercise of that power, with the governmental activities of the other. That the two types of immunity may not, in all respects, stand on a parity has been recognized from the beginning, and possible differences in application, deriving from differences in the source, nature and extent of the immunity of the governments and their agencies, were pointed out and discussed by this Court in detail during the last term. *Helvering* v. *Gerhardt*.

So far as now relevant, those differences have been thought to be traceable to the fact that the federal government is one of delegated powers in the exercise of which Congress is supreme; so that every agency which Congress can constitutionally create is a governmental agency. And since the power to create the agency includes the implied power to do whatever is needful or appropriate, if not expressly prohibited, to protect the agency, there has been attributed to Congress some scope, the limits of which it is not now necessary to define, for granting or withholding immunity of federal agencies from state taxation. Whether its power to grant tax exemptions as an incident to the exercise of powers specifically granted by the Constitution can ever, in any circumstances, extend beyond the constitutional immunity of federal agencies which courts have implied, is a question which need not now be determined.

Congress has declared in § 4 of the Act that the Home Owners' Loan Corporation is an instrumentality of the United States and that its bonds are exempt, as to principal and interest, from federal and state taxation, except surtaxes, estate, inheritance and gift taxes. The corporation itself, "including its franchise, its capital, reserves and surplus, and its loans and income," is likewise exempted from taxation; its real property is subject to tax to the same extent as other real property. But Congress has given no intimation of any purpose either to grant or withhold immunity from state taxation of the salary of the corporation's employees, and the Congressional intention is not to be gathered from the statute by implication.

It is true that the silence of Congress, when it has authority to speak, may sometimes give rise to an implication as to the Congressional purpose. The nature and extent of that implication depend upon the nature of the Congressional power and the effect of its exercise. But there is little scope for the application of that doctrine to the tax immunity of governmental instrumentalities. The constitutional immunity of either government from taxation by the other, where Congress is silent, has its source in an implied restriction upon the powers of the taxing government. So far as the implication rests upon the purpose to avoid interference with the functions of the taxed government or the imposition upon it of the economic burden of the tax, it is plain that there is no basis for implying a purpose of Congress to exempt the federal government or its agencies from tax burdens which are unsubstantial or which courts are unable to discern. Silence of Congress implies immunity no more than does the silence of the Constitution. It follows that when exemption from state taxation is claimed on the ground that the federal government is burdened by the tax, and Congress has disclosed no intention with respect to the claimed immunity, it is in order to consider the nature and effect of the alleged burden, and if it appears that there is no ground for implying a constitutional immunity, there is equally a want of any ground for assuming any purpose on the part of Congress to create an immunity.

The present tax is a non-discriminatory tax on income applied to salaries at a specified rate. It is not in form or substance a tax upon the Home Owners' Loan Corporation or its property or income, nor is it paid by the corporation or the government from their funds. It is laid upon income which becomes the property of the taxpayer when

received as compensation for his services; and the tax laid upon the privilege of receiving it is paid from his private funds and not from the funds of the government, either directly or indirectly. The theory, which once won a qualified approval, that a tax on income is legally or economically a tax on its source, is no longer tenable, and the only possible basis for implying a constitutional immunity from state income tax of the salary of an employee of the national government or of a governmental agency is that the economic burden of the tax is in some way passed on so as to impose a burden on the national government tantamount to an interference by one government with the other in the performance of its functions.

In the four cases in which this Court has held that the salary of an officer or employee of one government or its instrumentality was immune from taxation by the other, it was assumed, without discussion, that the immunity of a government or its instrumentality extends to the salaries of its officers and employees. This assumption, made with respect to the salary of a governmental officer in *Dobbins* v. *Commissioners of Erie County,* 16 Pet. 435, and in Collector v. Day, 11 Wall. 113, was later extended to confer immunity on income derived by a lessee from lands leased to him by a government in the performance of a government function, *Gillespie* v. *Oklahoma,* 257 U. S. 501; *Burnet* v. *Coronado Oil & aGs Co.,* 285 U. S. 393, and cases cited, although the claim of a like exemption from tax on the income of a contractor engaged in carrying out a government project was rejected both in the case of a contractor with a state, *Metcalf & Eddy* v. *Mitchell,* and of a contractor with the national government, *James* v. *Dravo Contracting Co.*

The ultimate repudiation in *Helvering* v. *Mountain Producers Corp.,* supra, of the doctrine that a tax on the income of a lessee derived from a lease of government owned or controlled lands is a forbidden interference with the activities of the government concerned led to the reexamination by this Court, in the Gerhardt case, of the theory underlying the asserted immunity from taxation by one government of salaries of employees of the other. It was there pointed out that the implied immunity of one government and its agencies from taxation by the other should, as a principle of constitutional construction, be narrowly restricted. For the expansion of the immunity of the one government correspondingly curtails the sovereign power of the other to tax, and where that immunity is invoked by the private citizen it tends to operate for his benefit at the expense of the taxing government and without corresponding benefit to the government in whose name the immunity is claimed. It was further pointed out that, as applied to the taxation of salaries of the employees of one government, the purpose of the immunity was not to confer benefits on the employees by relieving them from contributing their share of the financial support of the other government, whose benefits they enjoy, or to give an advantage to that government by enabling it to engage employees at salaries lower than those paid for like services by other employers, public or private, but to prevent undue interference with the one government by imposing on it the tax burdens of the other.

In applying these controlling principles in the Gerhardt case the Court held that the salaries of employees of the New York Port Authority, a state instrumentality created by New York and New Jersey, were not immune from federal income tax, even though the Authority be regarded as not subject to federal taxation. It was said that the taxpayers enjoyed the benefit and protection of the laws of the United States and were under a duty, common to all citizens, to contribute financial support to the government; that the tax laid on their salaries and paid by them could be said to affect or burden their employer, the Port Authority, or the states creating it, only so far as the burden of the tax was economically passed on to the employer; that a non-discriminatory tax laid on the income of all members of the community could not be assumed to obstruct the function which New York and New Jersey had undertaken to perform, or to cast an economic burden upon them, more than does the general taxation of property and income which, to some extent, incapable of measurement by economists, may tend to raise the price level of labor and materials. The Court concluded that the claimed immunity would do no

more than relieve the taxpayers from the duty of financial support to the national government in order to secure to the state a theoretical advantage, speculative in character and measurement and too unsubstantial to form the basis of an implied constitutional immunity from taxation.

The conclusion reached in the Gerhardt case that in terms of constitutional tax immunity a federal income tax on the salary of an employee is not a prohibited burden on the employer makes it imperative that we should consider anew the immunity here claimed for the salary of an employee of a federal instrumentality. As already indicated, such differences as there may be between the implied tax immunity of a state and the corresponding immunity of the national government and its instrumentalities may be traced to the fact that the national government is one of delegated powers, in the exercise of which it is supreme. Whatever scope this may give to the national government to claim immunity from state taxation of all instrumentalities which it may constitutionally create, and whatever authority Congress may possess as incidental to the exercise of its delegated powers to grant or withhold immunity from state taxation, Congress has not sought in this case to exercise such power. Hence these distinctions between the two types of immunity cannot affect the question with which we are now concerned. The burden on government of a non-discriminatory income tax applied to the salary of the employee of a government or its instrumentality is the same, whether a state or national government is concerned. The determination in the Gerhardt case that the federal income tax imposed on the employees of the Port Authority was not a burden on the Port Authority made it unnecessary to consider whether the Authority itself was immune from federal taxation; the claimed immunity failed because even if the Port Authority were itself immune from federal income tax, the tax upon the income of its employees cast upon it no unconstitutional burden.

Assuming, as we do, that the Home Owners' Loan Corporation is clothed with the same immunity from state taxation as the government itself, we cannot say that the present tax on the income of its employees lays any unconstitutional burden upon it. All the reasons for refusing to imply a constitutional prohibition of federal income taxation of salaries of state employees, stated at length in the Gerhardt case, are of equal force when immunity is claimed from state income tax on salaries paid by the national government or its agencies. In this respect we perceive no basis for a difference in result whether the taxed income be salary or some other form of compensation, or whether the taxpayer be an employee or an officer of either a state or the national government, or of its instrumentalities. In no case is there basis for the assumption that any such tangible or certain economic burden is imposed on the government concerned as would justify a court's declaring that the taxpayer is clothed with the implied constitutional tax immunity of the government by which he is employed. That assumption, made in *Collector* v. *Day,* and in New York ex. rel. *Rogers* v. *Graves,* is contrary to the reasoning and to the conclusions reached in the Gerhardt case and in *Metcalf & Eddy* v. *Mitchell,* [etc.]. In their light the assumption can no longer be made. *Collector* v. *Day,* and New York ex rel. *Rogers* v. *Graves,* are overruled so far as they recognize an implied constitutional immunity from income taxation of the salaries of officers or employees of the national or a state government or their instrumentalities.

So much of the burden of a non-discriminatory general tax upon the incomes of employees of a government, state or national, as may be passed on economically to that government, through the effect of the tax on the price level of labor or materials, is but the normal incident of the organization within the same territory of two governments, each possessing the taxing power. The burden, so far as it can be said to exist or to affect the government in any indirect or incidental way, is one which the Constitution presupposes, and hence it cannot rightly be deemed to be within an implied restriction upon the taxing power of the national and state governments which the Constitution has expressly granted to one and has confirmed to the other. The immunity is not one to be implied from the Constitution, because if allowed it would impose to an inadmissible extent a restriction

on the taxing power which the Constitution has reserved to the state governments.

Reversed.

Mr. Chief Justice HUGHES concurs in the result.

Mr. Justice FRANKFURTER, concurring. I join in the Court's opinion but deem it appropriate to add a few remarks. . . .

The arguments upon which *McCulloch* v. *Maryland,* rested had their roots in actuality. But they had been distorted by sterile refinements unrelated to affairs. These refinements derived authority from an unfortunate remark in the opinion in *McCulloch* v. *Maryland.* Partly as a flourish of rhetoric and partly because the intellectual fashion of the times indulged a free use of absolutes, Chief Justice Marshall gave currency to the phrase that "the power to tax involves the power to destroy." This dictum was treated as though it were a constitutional mandate. But not without protest. One of the most trenchant minds on the Marshall court, Justice William Johnson, early analyzed the dangerous inroads upon the political freedom of the States and the Union within their respective orbits resulting from a doctrinaire application of the generalities uttered in the course of the opinion in *McCulloch* v. *Maryland.* The seductive cliché that the power to tax involves the power to destroy was fused with another assumption, likewise not to be found in the Constitution itself, namely the doctrine that the immunities are correlative—because the existence of the national government implies immunities from state taxation, the existence of state governments implies equivalent immunities from federal taxation. When this doctrine was first applied Mr. Justice Bradley registered a powerful dissent, the force of which gathered rather than lost strength with time. *Collector* v. *Day.*

All these doctrines of intergovernmental immunity have until recently been moving in the realm of what Lincoln called "pernicious abstractions." The web of unreality spun from Marshall's famous dictum was brushed away by one stroke of Mr. Justice Holmes's pen: "The power to tax is not the power to destroy while this Court sits." *Panhandle Oil Co.* v. *Mississippi,* 277 U. S. 218, 223 (dissent). Failure to exempt public functionaries from the universal duties of citizenship to pay for the cost of government was hypothetically transmuted into hostile action of one government against the other. A succession of decisions thereby withdrew from the taxing power of the States and Nation a very considerable range of wealth without regard to the actual workings of our federalism, and this, too, when the financial needs of all governments began steadily to mount. These decisions have encountered increasing dissent. . . . In this Court dissents have gradually become majority opinions, and even before the present decision the rationale of the doctrine had been undermined.

The judicial history of this doctrine of immunity is a striking illustration of an occasional tendency to encrust unwarranted interpretations upon the Constitution and thereafter to consider merely what has been judicially said about the Constitution, rather than to be primarily controlled by a fair conception of the Constitution. Judicial exegesis is unavoidable with reference to an organic art like our Constitution, drawn in many particulars with purposed vagueness so as to leave room for the unfolding future. But the ultimate touchstone of constitutionality is the Constitution itself and not what we have said about it. Neither *Dobbins* v. *Commissioners of Erie County,* and its offspring, nor *Collector* v. *Day,* and its, can stand appeal to the Constitution and its historic purposes. Since both are the starting points of an interdependent doctrine, both should be, as I assume them to be, overruled this day. Whether Congress may, by express legislation, relieve its functionaries from their civic obligations to pay for the benefits of the State governments under which they live is matter for another day.

521. THE CAROLENE PRODUCTS DOCTRINE
1938
(304 *U. S. Supreme Court Reports,* 144, footnote 4)

This famous footnote to an otherwise inconspicuous case announced what has come to be known as the "preferred freedoms" doctrine of the First Amendment; much of the judicial debate of the fifties centered on the validity and relevance of this doctrine as against the "balance of interest" doctrine espoused by Judge Frankfurter. On Carolene Products see A. T. Mason, *Harlan Fiske Stone;* S. J. Konefsky, *Chief Justice Stone and the Supreme Court;* Commager, *Majority Rule and Minority Rights;* Mason, "The Core of Free Government: Mr. Justice Stone and Preferred Freedoms," 65 *Yale Law J.* 597; Luksy, "Minority Rights and Public Interest," 52 *Yale Law. J.* 1; L. Hand, "Chief Justice Stone's Conception of the Judicial Function," 46 *Columbia Law Rev.* 696; H. Wechsler, "Stone and the Constitution," 46 *Columbia L. Rev.* 764; Bernard, "Liberties of the First Amendment," 50 *Mich. Law Rev.* 261.

STONE, C. J. . . . Regulatory legislation affecting ordinary commercial transactions is not to be pronounced unconstitutional unless in the light of the facts made known or generally assumed it is of such a character as to preclude the assumption that it rests upon some rational basis within the knowledge and experience of legislators.[4]

4. There may be narrower scope for operation of the presumption of constitutionality when legislation appears on its face to be within a specific prohibition of the Constitution, such as those of the first ten Amendments which are deemed equally specific when held to be embraced within the Fourteenth.

It is unnecessary to consider now whether legislation which restricts those political processes which can ordinarily be expected to bring about repeal of undesirable legislation, is to be subjected to a more exacting judicial scrutiny under the general prohibitions of the Fourteenth Amendment, than are most other types of legislation. . . .

Nor need we enquire whether similar considerations enter into the review of statutes directed at particular religions . . . or national . . . or racial minorities . . . whether prejudice against discrete and insular minorities may be a special condition, which tends seriously to curtail the operation of those political processes ordinarily to be relied upon to protect minorities, and which may call for a correspondingly more searching judicial inquiry.

522. THE NEW ORDER IN THE FAR EAST

United States Note to Japan Regarding Violations of American Rights in China
December 31, 1938

(U. S. Dept. of State, *Press Release*, Vol. XIX, No. 483)

The invasion of China by Japan in July, 1937, threatened American interests in the Far East and challenged the Open Door doctrine. On October 6, 1938 the United States sent a strong protest to Japan against the violation of American treaty rights and of the Open Door. To this note Japan replied, November 18, to the effect that a "new situation" had developed in the Far East and the Open Door policy was no longer applicable. The note of Dec. 31 is the American reply to this note. In June, 1939 the United States reaffirmed its position and the following month gave evidence of its seriousness by taking the initial step in abrogating the Commercial Treaty of 1911 with Japan. On Recent Far Eastern policy see H. L. Stimson, *The Far Eastern Crisis;* A. W. Griswold, *The Far Eastern Policy of the United States;* S. C. Y. Pan, *American Diplomacy concerning Manchuria;* N. Peffer, *Must We Fight in Asia;* and Foreign Policy Reports, Vol. 13, no. 23, "America's Role in the Far Eastern Conflict."

Text of a note which the American Ambassador to Japan, Mr. Joseph C. Grew, communicated, under instruction, to the Japanese Minister for Foreign Affairs, His Excellency Mr. Hachiro Arita, on December 31, 1938:

The Government of the United States has received and has given full consideration to the reply of the Japanese Government of November 18 to this Government's note of October 6 on the subject of American rights and interests in China.

In the light of facts and experience the Government of the United States is impelled to reaffirm its previously expressed opinion that imposition of restrictions upon the movements and activities of American nationals who are engaged in philanthropic, educational and commercial endeavors in China has placed and will, if continued, increasingly place Japanese interests in a preferred position and is, therefore, unquestionably discriminatory, in its effect, against legitimate American interests. Further, with reference to such matters as exchange control, compulsory currency circulation, tariff revision, and monopolistic promotion in certain areas of China,

the plans and practices of the Japanese authorities imply an assumption on the part of those authorities that the Japanese Government or the regimes established and maintained in China by Japanese armed forces are entitled to act in China in a capacity such as flows from rights of sovereignty and, further, in so acting to disregard and even to declare nonexistent or abrogated the established rights and interests of other countries, including the United States.

The Government of the United States expresses its conviction that the restrictions and measures under reference not only are unjust and unwarranted but are counter to the provisions of several binding international agreements, voluntarily entered into, to which both Japan and the United States, and in some cases other countries, are parties.

In the concluding portion of its note under reference, the Japanese Government states that it is firmly convinced that "in the face of the new situation, fast developing in East Asia, any attempt to apply to the conditions of today and tomorrow inapplicable ideas and principles of the past neither would contribute toward the establishment of a real peace in East Asia nor solve the immediate issues," and that "as long as these points are understood, Japan has not the slightest inclination to oppose the participation of the United States and other powers in the great work of reconstructing East Asia along all lines of industry and trade."

The Government of the United States in its note of October 6 requested, in view of the oft-reiterated assurances proffered by the Government of Japan of its intention to observe the principle of equality of opportunity in its relations with China, and in view of Japan's treaty obligations so to do, that the Government of Japan abide by these obligations and carry out these assurances in practice. The Japanese Government in its reply appears to affirm that it is its intention to make its observance of that principle conditional upon an understanding by the American Government and by other governments of a "new situation" and a "new order" in the Far East as envisaged and fostered by Japanese authorities.

Treaties which bear upon the situation in the Far East have within them provisions relating to a number of subjects. . . . The various provisions agreed upon may be said to have constituted collectively an arrangement for safeguarding, for the benefit of all, the correlated principles on the one hand of national integrity and on the other hand of equality of economic opportunity. Experience has shown that impairment of the former of these principles is followed almost invariably by disregard of the latter. Whenever any government begins to exercise political authority in areas beyond the limits of its lawful jurisdiction there develops inevitably a situation in which the nationals of that government demand and are accorded, at the hands of their government, preferred treatment, whereupon equality of opportunity ceases to exist and discriminatory practices, productive of friction, prevail.

The admonition that enjoyment by the nationals of the United States of nondiscriminatory treatment in China—a general and well-established right—is henceforth to be contingent upon an admission by the Government of the United States of the validity of the conception of Japanese authorities of a "new situation" and a "new order" in East Asia, is, in the opinion of this Government, highly paradoxical.

This country's adherence to and its advocacy of the principle of equality of opportunity do not flow solely from a desire to obtain the commercial benefits which naturally result from the carrying out of that principle. They flow from a firm conviction that observance of that principle leads to economic and political stability, which are conducive both to the internal well-being of nations and to mutually beneficial and peaceful relationships between and among nations; from a firm conviction that failure to observe that principle breeds international friction and ill-will, with consequences injurious to all countries, including in particular those countries which fail to observe it; and from an equally firm conviction that observance of that principle promotes the opening of trade channels thereby making available the markets, the raw materials and the manu-factured products of the community of nations on a mutually and reciprocally beneficial basis.

The principle of equality of economic opportunity is, moreover, one to which over a long period and on many occasions the Japanese Government has given definite approval. It is one to the observance of which the Japanese Government has committed itself in various international agreements and understandings. It is one upon observance of which by other nations the Japanese Government has of its own accord and upon its own initiative frequently insisted. It is one to which the Japanese Government has repeatedly during recent months declared itself committed.

The people and the Government of the United States could not assent to the establishment, at the instance of and for the special purposes of any third country, of a regime which would arbitrarily deprive them of the long-established rights of equal opportunity and fair treatment which are legally and justly theirs along with those of other nations.

Fundamental principles, such as the principle of equality of opportunity, which have long been regarded as inherently wise and just, which have been widely adopted and adhered to, and which are general in their application, are not subject to nullification by a unilateral affirmation.

With regard to the implication in the Japanese Government's note that the "conditions of today and tomorrow" in the Far East call for a revision of the ideas and principles of the past, this Government desires to recall to the Japanese Government its position on the subject of revision of agreements.

This Government had occasion in the course of a communication delivered to the Japanese Government on April 29, 1934, to express its opinion that "treaties can lawfully be modified or be terminated, but only by processes prescribed or recognized or agreed upon by the parties to them."

In the same communication this Government also said, "In the opinion of the American people and the American Government no nation can, without the assent of the other nations concerned, rightfully endeavor to make conclusive its will in situations where there are involved the rights, the obligations and the legitimate interests of other sovereign states." . . .

At various times during recent decades various powers, among which have been Japan and the United States, have had occasion to communicate and to confer with regard to situations and problems in the Far East. In the conducting of correspondence and of conferences relating to these matters, the parties involved have invariably taken into consideration past and present facts and they have not failed to perceive the possibility and the desirability of changes in the situation. In the making of treaties they have drawn up and have agreed upon provisions intended to facilitate advantageous developments and at the same time to obviate and avert the arising of friction between and among the various powers which, having interests in the region or regions under reference, were and would be concerned.

In the light of these facts, and with reference especially to the purpose and the character of the treaty provisions from time to time solemnly agreed upon for the very definite purposes indicated, the Government of the United States deprecates the fact that one of the parties to these agreements has chosen to embark—as indicated both by action of its agents and by official statements of its authorities—upon a course directed toward the arbitrary creation by that power by methods of its own selection, regardless of treaty pledges and the established rights of other powers concerned, of a "new order" in the Far East. Whatever may be the changes which have taken place in the situation in the Far East and whatever may be the situation now, these matters are of no less interest and concern to the American Government than have been the situations which have prevailed there in the past, and such changes as may henceforth take place there, changes which may enter into the producing of a "new situation" and a "new order," are and will be of like concern to this Government. This Government is well aware that the situation has changed. This Government is also well aware that many of the changes have been brought about by action

of Japan. This Government does not admit, however, that there is need or warrant for any one power to take upon itself to prescribe what shall be the terms and conditions of a "new order" in areas not under its sovereignty and to constitute itself the repository of authority and the agent of destiny in regard thereto. . . .

The United States has in its international relations rights and obligations which derive from international law and rights and obligations which rest upon treaty provisions. Of those which rest on treaty provisions, its rights and obligations in and with regard to China rest in part upon provisions in treaties between the United States and China, and in part upon provisions in treaties between the United States and several other powers, including both China and Japan. These treaties were concluded in good faith for the purpose of safeguarding and promoting the interests not of one only but of all their signatories. The people and the Government of the United States cannot assent to the abrogation of any of this country's rights or obligations by the arbitrary action of agents or authorities of any other country.

The Government of the United States has, however, always been prepared, and is now, to give due and ample consideration to any proposals based on justice and reason which envisage the resolving of problems in a manner duly considerate of the rights and obligations of all parties directly concerned by processes of free negotiation and new commitment by and among all of the parties so concerned. There has been and there continues to be opportunity for the Japanese Government to put forward such proposals. This Government has been and it continues to be willing to discuss such proposals, if and when put forward, with representatives of the other powers, including Japan and China, whose rights and interests are involved, at whatever time and in whatever place may be commonly agreed upon.

Meanwhile, this Government reserves all rights of the United States as they exist and does not give assent to any impairment of any of those rights.

523. "HANDS OFF THE WESTERN HEMISPHERE"
F. D. Roosevelt's Pan-American Day Address, April 14, 1939
(*New York Times,* April 15, 1939)

The American family of nations pays honor today to the oldest and most successful association of sovereign governments which exists in the world. . . .

For upwards of half a century the republics of the Western world have been working together to promote their common civilization under a system of peace. That venture, launched so hopefully fifty years ago, has succeeded; the American family is today a great co-operation group facing a troubled world in serenity and calm. . . .

What was it that has protected us from the tragic involvements which are today making the Old World a new cockpit of old struggles? The answer is easily found. A new and powerful ideal—that of the community of nations—sprang up at the same time that the Americans became free and independent. It was nurtured by statesmen, thinkers and plain people for decades. Gradually it brought together the Pan-American group of governments; today it has fused the thinking of the peoples, and the desires of their responsible representatives toward a common objective.

The result of this thinking has been to shape a typically American institution. This is the Pan-American group, which works in open conference, by open agreement. We hold our conferences not as a result of wars, but as the result of our will to peace.

Elsewhere in the world, to hold conferences such as ours, which meet every five years, it is necessary to fight a major war, until exhaustion or defeat at length brings governments together to reconstruct their shattered fabrics.

Greeting a conference at Buenos Aires in 1936, I took occasion to say:

"The madness of a great war in another part of the world would affect us and threaten our good in a hundred ways, and the economic collapse of any nation or nations must of necessity harm our own prosperity. Can we, the republics of the world, help the Old World to avert the catastrophe which impends? Yes, I am confident that we can."

I still have that confidence. There is no fatality which forces the Old World toward new catastrophe. Men are not prisoners of fate, but only prisoners of their own minds. They have within themselves the power to become free at any moment. . . .

No nation on this hemisphere has any will to aggression, or any desire to establish dominance or mastery. Equally, because we are interdependent, and because we know it, no American nation seeks to deny any neighbor access to the economic and other resources which it must have to live in prosperity.

In these circumstances dreams of conquest appear to us as ridiculous as they are criminal. Pledges designed to prevent aggression, accompanied by the open doors of trade and intercourse, and bound together by common will to co-operate peacefully, make warfare between us as outworn and useless as the weapons of the Stone Age. We may proudly boast that we have begun to realize in Pan-American relations what civilization in intercourse between countries really means.

If that process can be successful here, is it too much to hope that a similar intellectual and spiritual process may succeed elsewhere? Do we really have to assume that nations can find no better methods of realizing their destinies than those which were used by the Huns and Vandals fifteen hundred years ago?

The American peace which we celebrate today has no quality of weakness in it. We are prepared to maintain it, and to defend it to the fullest extent of our strength, matching force to force if any attempt is made to subvert our institutions, or to impair the independence of any one of our group.

Should the method of attack be that of economic pressure, I pledge that my own country will also give economic support, so that no American nation need surrender any fraction of its sovereign freedom to maintain its economic welfare. This is the spirit and intent of the declaration of Lima: The solidarity of the continent.

The American family of nations may also rightfully claim, now, to speak to the rest of the world. We have an interest, wider than that of the mere defense of our sea-ringed continent. We know now that the development of the next generation will so narrow the oceans separating us from the Old World, that our customs and our actions are necessarily involved with hers.

Beyond question, within a scant few years air fleets will cross the ocean as easily as today they cross the closed European seas. Economic functioning of the world becomes increasingly a unit; no interruption of it anywhere can fail, in the future, to disrupt economic life everywhere.

The past generation in Pan-American matters was concerned with constructing the principles and the mechanisms through which this hemisphere would work together. But the next generation will be concerned with the methods by which the New World can live together with the Old.

The issue is really whether our civilization is to be dragged into the tragic vortex of unending militarism punctuated by periodic wars, or whether we shall be able to maintain the ideal of peace, individuality and civilization as the fabric of our lives. We have the right to say that there shall not be an organization of world affairs which permits us no choice but to turn our countries into barracks unless we are to be vassals of some conquering empire.

The truest defense of the peace of our hemisphere must always lie in the hope that our sister nations beyond the seas will break the bonds of the ideas which constrain them toward perpetual warfare. By example we can at least show them the possibility. We, too, have a stake in world affairs.

Our will to peace can be as powerful as our will to mutual defense; it can command greater loyalty, devotion and discipline than that enlisted elsewhere for temporary conquest or equally futile glory. It will have its voice in determining the order of world affairs.

This is the living message which the New World can send to the Old. It can be light opening on dark waters. It shows the path of peace.

524. F. D. ROOSEVELT'S APPEALS FOR PEACE IN EUROPE
April 14, 1939 and August 23, 1939
(U. S. Dept. of State, *Press Releases*)

During the period from the Munich Conference of September, 1938 to the outbreak of war, September, 1939, Roosevelt's efforts to persuade the European powers, and especially Germany and Italy, to peace were unceasing.

"THE WHITE HOUSE
April 14, 1939

HIS EXCELLENCY ADOLF HITLER, CHANCELLOR OF THE GERMAN REICH,

You realize I am sure that throughout the world hundreds of millions of human beings are living today in constant fear of a new war or even a series of wars.

The existence of this fear—and the possibility of such a conflict—is of definite concern to the people of the United States for whom I speak, as it must also be to the peoples of the other nations of the entire Western Hemisphere. All of them know that any major war, even if it were to be confined to other continents, must bear heavily on them during its continuance and also for generations to come.

Because of the fact that after the acute tension in which the world has been living during the past few weeks there would seem to be at least a momentary relaxation—because no troops are at this moment on the march—this may be an opportune moment for me to send you this message.

On a previous occasion I have addressed you in behalf of the settlement of political, economic, and social problems by peaceful methods and without resort to arms.

But the tide of events seems to have reverted to the threat of arms. If such threats continue, it seems inevitable that much of the world must become involved in common ruin. All the world, victor nations, vanquished nations, and neutral nations will suffer. I refuse to believe that the world is, of necessity, such a prisoner of destiny. On the contrary, it is clear that the leaders of great nations have it in their power to liberate their peoples from the disaster that impends. It is equally clear that in their own minds and in their hearts the peoples themselves desire that their fears be ended.

It is, however, unfortunately necessary to take cognizance of recent facts.

Three nations in Europe and one in Africa have seen their independent existence terminated. A vast territory in another independent nation of the Far East has been occupied by a neighboring state. Reports, which we trust are not true, insist that further acts of aggression are contemplated against still other independent nations. Plainly the world is moving toward the moment when this situation must end in catastrophe unless a more rational way of guiding events is found.

You have repeatedly asserted that you and the German people have no desire for war. If this is true there need be no war.

Nothing can persuade the peoples of the earth that any governing power has any right or need to inflict the consequences of war on its own or any other people save in the cause of self-evident home defense.

In making this statement we as Americans speak not through selfishness or fear or weakness. If we speak now it is with the voice of strength and with friendship for mankind. It is still clear to me that international problems can be solved at the council table.

It is therefore no answer to the plea for peaceful discussion for one side to plead that unless they receive assurances beforehand that the verdict will be theirs, they will not lay aside their arms. In conference rooms, as in courts, it is necessary that both sides enter upon the discussion in good faith, assuming that substantial justice will accrue to both; and it is customary that they leave their arms outside the room where they confer.

I am convinced that the cause of world peace would be greatly advanced if the nations of the world were to obtain a frank statement relating to the present and future policy of governments.

Because the United States, as one of the nations of the Western Hemisphere, is not involved in the immediate controversies which have arisen in Europe, I trust that you may be willing to make such a statement of policy to me as the head of a nation far removed from Europe in order that I, acting only with the responsibility and obligation of a friendly intermediary, may communicate such declaration to other nations now apprehensive as to the course which the policy of your Government may take.

Are you willing to give assurance that your armed forces will not attack or invade the territory or possessions of the following independent nations: Finland, Estonia, Latvia, Lithuania, Sweden, Norway, Denmark, The Netherlands, Belgium, Great Britain and Ireland, France, Portugal, Spain, Switzerland, Liechtenstein, Luxemburg, Poland, Hungary, Rumania, Yugoslavia, Russia, Bulgaria, Greece, Turkey, Iraq, the Arabias, Syria, Palestine, Egypt and Iran.

Such an assurance clearly must apply not only to the present day but also to a future sufficiently long to give every opportunity to work by peaceful methods for a more permanent peace. I therefore suggest that you construe the word "future" to apply to a minimum period of assured non-aggression—ten years at the least—a quarter of a century, if we dare look that far ahead.

If such assurance is given by your Government, I will immediately transmit it to the governments of the nations I have named and I will simultaneously inquire whether, as I am reasonably sure, each of the nations enumerated above will in turn give like assurance for transmission to you.

Reciprocal assurances such as I have outlined will bring to the world an immediate measure of relief.

I propose that if it is given, two essential problems shall promptly be discussed in the resulting peaceful surroundings, and in those discussions the Government of the United States will gladly take part.

The discussions which I have in mind relate to the most effective and immediate manner through which the peoples of the world can obtain progressive relief from the crushing burden of armament which is each day bringing them more closely to the brink of economic disaster. Simultaneously the Government of the United States would be prepared to take part in discussions looking towards the most practical manner of opening up avenues of international trade to the end that every nation of the earth may be enabled to buy and sell on equal terms in the world market as well as to possess assurance of obtaining the materials and products of peaceful economic life.

At the same time, those governments other than the United States which are directly interested could undertake such political discussions as they may consider necessary or desirable.

We recognize complex world problems which affect all humanity but we know that study and discussion of them must be held in an atmosphere of peace. Such an atmosphere of peace cannot exist if negotiations are overshadowed by the threat of force or by the fear of war.

I think you will not misunderstand the spirit of frankness in which I send you this message. Heads of great governments in this hour are literally responsible for the fate of humanity in the coming years. They cannot fail to hear the prayers of their peoples to be protected from the foreseeable chaos of war. History will hold them accountable for the lives and the happiness of all—even unto the least.

I hope that your answer will make it possible for humanity to lose fear and regain security for many years to come.

A similar message is being addressed to the Chief of the Italian Government.

FRANKLIN D. ROOSEVELT

August 24, 1939

The following is the text of a communication, dispatched yesterday by the President and delivered today to the King of Italy by Ambassador Phillips:

Again a crisis in world affairs makes clear the responsibility of heads of nations for the fate of their own people and indeed of humanity itself. It is because of traditional accord between Italy and the United States and the ties of consanguinity between millions of our citizens that I feel that I can address Your Majesty in behalf of the maintenance of world peace.

It is my belief and that of the American people that Your Majesty and Your Majesty's Government can greatly influence the averting of an outbreak of war. Any general war would cause to suffer all nations whether belligerent or neutral, whether victors or van-quished, and would clearly bring devastation to the peoples and perhaps to the governments of some nations most directly concerned.

The friends of the Italian people and among them the American people could only regard with grief the destruction of great achievements which European nations and the Italian nation in particular have attained during the past generation.

We in America having welded a homogeneous nation out of many nationalities, often find it difficult to visualize the animosities which so often have created crises among nations of Europe which are smaller than ours in population and in territory, but we accept the fact that these nations have an absolute right to maintain their national independence if they so desire. If that be sound doctrine then it must apply to the weaker nations as well as to the stronger.

Acceptance of this means peace, because fear of aggression ends. The alternative, which means of necessity efforts by the strong to dominate the weak, will lead not only to war, but to long future years of oppression on the part of victors and to rebellion on the part of the vanquished. So history teaches us.

On April fourteenth last I suggested in essence an understanding that no armed forces should attack or invade the territory of any other independent nation, and that this being assured, discussions be undertaken to seek progressive relief from the burden of armaments and to open avenues of international trade including sources of raw materials necessary to the peaceful economic life of each nation.

I said that in these discussions the United States would gladly take part. And such peaceful conversations would make it wholly possible for governments other than the United States to enter into peaceful discussions of political or territorial problems in which they were directly concerned.

Were it possible for Your Majesty's Government to formulate proposals for a pacific solution of the present crisis along these lines you are assured of the earnest sympathy of the United States.

The Government of Italy and the United States can today advance those ideals of

Christianity which of late seem so often to have been obscured.

The unheard voices of countless millions of human beings ask that they shall not be vainly sacrificed again.

525. THE HATCH ACT
August 2, 1939
(*U. S. Statutes at Large,* Vol. LIII, p. 1147)

This act, forbidding "pernicious" political activities by federal officeholders, was part of the long-drawn-out struggle for civil service reform, but its immediate background was the widespread resentment against alleged exploitation of relief workers by political organizations. Perhaps its more lasting significance will derive from the extent to which it defederalizes party politics and transfers to local and state leaders power heretofore exercised by national party leaders.

An Act to prevent pernicious political activities.

Be it enacted, That it shall be unlawful for any person to intimidate, threaten, or coerce, or to attempt to intimidate, threaten, or coerce, any other person for the purpose of interfering with the right of such other person to vote or to vote as he may choose, or of causing such other person to vote for, or not to vote for, any candidate for the office of President, Vice President, Presidential elector, Member of the Senate, or Member of the House of Representatives at any election. . . .

SEC. 2. It shall be unlawful for any person employed in any administrative position by the United States, or by any department, independent agency, or other agency of the United States (including any corporation controlled by the United States or any agency thereof, and any corporation all of the capital stock of which is owned by the United States or any agency thereof), to use his official authority for the purpose of interfering with, or affecting the election or the nomination of any candidate for the office of President, Vice President, Presidential elector, Member of the Senate, or Member of the House of Representatives, Delegates or Commissioners from the Territories and insular possessions.

SEC. 3. It shall be unlawful for any person, directly or indirectly, to promise any employment, position, work, compensation, or other benefit, provided for or made possible in whole or in part by any Act of Congress, to any person as consideration, favor, or reward for any political activity or for the support of or opposition to any candidate or any political party in any election.

SEC. 4. Except as may be required by the provisions of subsection (b), section 9 of this Act, it shall be unlawful for any person to deprive, attempt to deprive, or threaten to deprive, by any means, any person of any employment, position, work, compensation, or other benefit provided for or made possible by any Act of Congress appropriating funds for work relief or relief purposes, on account of race, creed, color, or any political activity, support of, or opposition to any candidate or any political party in any election.

SEC. 5. It shall be unlawful for any person to solicit or receive or be in any manner concerned in soliciting or receiving any assessment, subscription, or contribution for any political purpose whatever from any person known by him to be entitled to or receiving compensation, employment, or other benefit provided for or made possible by any Act of Congress appropriating funds for work relief or relief purposes.

SEC. 6. It shall be unlawful for any person for political purposes to furnish or to disclose, or to aid or assist in furnishing or disclosing, any list or names of persons receiving compensation, employment, or benefits provided for or made possible by any Act of Congress appropriating, or authorizing the appropriation of, funds for work relief or relief puposes, to a political candidate, committee, campaign manager, or to any person for delivery to a political candidate, committee, or campaign manager, and it shall be unlawful for any person to receive any such list or names for political purposes.

SEC. 7. No part of any appropriation made by any Act, heretofore or hereafter enacted, making appropriations for work relief, relief, or otherwise to increase employment by providing loans and grants for public-works projects, shall be used for the purpose of, and no authority conferred by any such Act upon any person shall be exercised or administered for the purpose of, interfering with, restraining, or coercing any individual in the exercise of his right to vote at any election.

SEC. 8. Any person who violates any of the foregoing provisions of this Act upon conviction thereof shall be fined not more than $1,000 or imprisoned for not more than one year, or both.

SEC. 9. (a) It shall be unlawful for any person employed in the executive branch of the Federal Government, or any agency or department thereof, to use his official authority or influence for the purpose of interfering with an election or affecting the result thereof. No officer or employee in the executive branch of the Federal Government, or any agency or department thereof, shall take any active part in political management or in political campaigns. All such persons shall retain the right to vote as they may choose and to express their opinions on all political subjects. For the purposes of this section the term "officer" or "employee" shall not be construed to include (1) the President and Vice President of the United States; (2) persons whose compensation is paid from the appropriation for the office of the President; (3) heads and assistant heads of executive departments; (4) officers who are appointed by the President, by and with the advice and consent of the Senate, and who determine

policies to be pursued by the United States in its relations with foreign powers or in the Nation-wide administration of Federal laws.

(b) Any person violating the provisions of this section shall be immediately removed from the position or office held by him, and thereafter no part of the funds appropriated by any Act of Congress for such position or office shall be used to pay the compensation of such person.

SEC. 9A. (1) It shall be unlawful for any person employed in any capacity by any agency of the Federal Government, whose compensation, or any part thereof, is paid from funds authorized or appropriated by any Act of Congress, to have membership in any political party or organization which advocates the overthrow of our constitutional form of government in the United States.

(2) Any person violating the provisions of this section shall be immediately removed from the position or office held by him, and thereafter no part of the funds appropriated by any Act of Congress for such position or office shall be used to pay the compensation of such person.

SEC. 10. All provisions of this Act shall be in addition to, not in substitution for, of existing law.

SEC. 11. If any provision of this Act, or the application of such provision to any person or circumstance, is held invalid, the remainder of the Act, and the application of such provision to other persons or circumstances, shall not be affected thereby.

526. THE DECLARATION OF PANAMA
October 2, 1939

(U. S. Dept. of State *Bull.* I, Oct. 7, 1939)

This attempt of the American nations to establish a new principle of international law by creating a "safety belt" of three hundred miles around the American Continents was shortly flouted by both belligerents in the naval battle off Montevideo, Dec. 13, 1939.

The republics of America, meeting in Panama, have solemnly ratified their position as neutrals in the conflict which disturbs the peace of Europe. But as the present war may reach unexpected derivations, which by their gravitation may affect the fundamental interests of America, it is hereby declared

that nothing can justify that the interests of belligerents prevail over the rights of neutrals, causing upsets and sufferings of peoples who, by their neutrality in the conflict and their distance from the scene of the happenings, should not suffer its fatal dolorous consequences.

During the World War of 1914–1918, the Governments of Argentina, Brazil, Chile, Colombia and Ecuador presented or supported individual proposals seeking in principle a declaration of American republics which entreated the belligerent nations to abstain from engaging in bellicose activities within a prudent distance from the American coasts.

Therefore, it is imperative as a formula of immediate necessity to adopt urgent dispositions based on such precedents, and in guarantee of these interests to avoid a repetition of the damages and sufferings experienced by the American nations and their citizens in the 1914–1918 war.

There is no doubt that the governments of the American republics ought to foresee these dangers as a means of self-protection and to insist upon the determination that in their waters and up to a reasonable distance from their coasts no hostile acts may be engaged in or bellicose activities carried out by participants in a war in which the said [American] governments do not participate.

For these considerations the governments of the American republics resolve and herewith declare:

1. As a measure of continental protection, the American republics, as long as they maintain their neutrality, have the undisputed right to conserve free from all hostile acts by any belligerent non-American nation those waters adjacent to the American continents which they consider of primordial interest and direct utility for their relations, whether such hostile act is attempted or carried out by land, sea or air.

These waters described will be determined in the following manner:

All waters within the limits herewith specified, except the territorial waters of Canada, and of colonies and undisputed possessions of European countries within these limits.

Beginning at a point on the frontier between the United States and Canada at Passamaquoddy Bay, where the 44th degree 46 minutes and 36 seconds of North Latitude crosses the 66th degree 44 minutes and 11 seconds of West Longitude; from there, directly along parallel 44 degrees 46 minutes and 36 seconds to a point crossing 60 degrees West Longitude; from there directly south-ward to a point at 20 degrees North Latitude; from there by loxodromical line to a point at 5 degrees North Latitude and 24 degrees West Longitude; from there directly south to a point at 20 degrees South Latitude; from there by loxodromical line to a point at 58 degrees South Latitude and 57 degrees West Longitude; thence westward to a point at 80 degrees West Longitude; thence by loxodromical line to a point where the Equator crosses 97 degrees West Longitude; thence by loxodromical line to a point 15 degrees North Latitude and 120 degrees West Longitude thence by loxodromical line to a point at 48 degrees 29 minutes and 38 seconds North Latitude and 136 degrees West Longitude; thence directly east to the termination in the Pacific Ocean, at Jean de Fuqua Strait, on the frontier between the United States and Canada.

2. The governments of the American republics agree to make an effort to seek observance by the belligerents of the dispositions contained in this declaration through joint representations to the governments actually participating in hostilities or those that may participate in the future.

This procedure will in no wise affect the exercise of the individual rights of each State inherent in its sovereignty.

3. The governments of the American republics further declare that, whenever they consider it necessary, they will consult among themselves to determine what measures they can take individually or collectively for the purpose of obtaining fulfillment of the dispositions of this declaration.

4. The American republic, as long as there exists a state of war in which they themselves are not participating and whenever they consider it necessary, may carry out individual or collective patrols, whichever they may decide through mutual agreement or as far as the elements and resources of each one permit, in waters adjacent to their coasts within the zone already defined.

527. THE NEUTRALITY ACT OF 1939
November 4, 1939

(76th Congress, 2nd Session, *Public Resolution* No. 54)

The outbreak of the second World War, September 1939, and the widespread sympathy for England and France forced a reconsideration of the Neutrality Act of 1937. On Sept. 23, 1939 President Roosevelt appealed to Congress so to amend the existing neutrality laws as to permit belligerents to purchase and remove, at their own risk, war munitions and materials. After a long and bitter debate in which the forces of the isolationists were led by Senator Borah, Congress agreed to the "cash and carry" system, retaining, meanwhile, most of the safeguards of the earlier legislation. Of the sections here omitted, those dealing with Restrictions on Use of American Ports, Submarines and Armed Merchant Vessels, National Munitions Control Board, and Regulations, are substantially similar to the comparable provisions in the Act of 1937, Doc. No. 514.

JOINT RESOLUTION

To preserve the neutrality and the peace of the United States and to secure the safety of its citizens and their interests.

Whereas the United States, desiring to preserve its neutrality in wars between foreign states and desiring also to avoid involvement therein, voluntarily imposes upon its nationals by domestic legislation the restrictions set out in this joint resolution; and

Whereas by so doing the United States waives none of its own rights or privileges, or those of any of its nationals, under international law, and expressly reserves all the rights and privileges to which it and its nationals are entitled under the law of nations; and

Whereas the United States hereby expressly reserves the right to repeal, change or modify this joint resolution or any other domestic legislation in the interests of the peace, security or welfare of the United States and its people: Therefore be it *Resolved,*

PROCLAMATION OF A STATE OF WAR BETWEEN FOREIGN STATES

SECTION 1. (a) That whenever the President, or the Congress by concurrent resolution, shall find that there exists a state of war between foreign states, and that it is necessary to promote the security or preserve the peace of the United States or to protect the lives of citizens of the United States, the President shall issue a proclamation naming the states involved; and he shall, from time to time, by proclamation, name other states

as and when they may become involved in the war.

(b) Whenever the state of war which shall have caused the President to issue any proclamation under the authority of this section shall have ceased to exist with respect to any state named in such proclamation, he shall revoke such proclamation with respect to such state.

COMMERCE WITH STATES ENGAGED IN ARMED CONFLICT

SEC. 2. (a) Whenever the President shall have issued a proclamation under the authority of section 1 (a) it shall thereafter be unlawful for any American vessel to carry any passengers or any articles or materials to any state named in such proclamation.

(b) Whoever shall violate any of the provisions of subsection (a) of this section or of any regulations issued thereunder shall, upon conviction thereof, be fined not more than $50,000 or imprisoned for not more than five years, or both. Should the violation be by a corporation, organization, or association, each officer or director thereof participating in the violation shall be liable to the penalty herein prescribed.

(c) Whenever the President shall have issued a proclamation under the authority of section 1 (a) it shall thereafter be unlawful to export or transport, or attempt to export or transport, or cause to be exported or transported, from the United States to any state named in such proclamation, any articles or materials (except copyrighted articles or materials) until all right, title, and interest therein shall have been transferred to some foreign government, agency, institution, association, partnership, corporation, or national. . . .

(g) The provisions of subsections (a) and (c) of this section shall not apply to transportation by American vessels (other than aircraft) of mail, passengers, or any articles or materials (except articles or materials listed in a proclamation referred to in or issued under the authority of section 12 (i)) (1) to any port in the Western Hemisphere south of thirty-five degrees north latitude, (2) to any port in the Western Hemisphere north of thirty-five degrees north latitude and west of sixty-six degrees west longitude,

(3) to any port on the Pacific or Indian Oceans, including the China Sea, the Tasman Sea, the Bay of Bengal, and the Arabian Sea, and any other dependent waters of either of such oceans, seas, or bays, or (4) to any port on the Atlantic Ocean or its dependent waters south of thirty degrees north latitude. The exceptions contained in this subsection shall not apply to any such port which is included within a combat area as defined in section 3 which applies to such vessels. . . .

(i) Every American vessel to which the provisions of subsections (g) and (h) apply, and every neutral vessel to which the provisions of subsection (l) apply, shall, before departing from a port or from the jurisdiction of the United States, file with the collector of customs of the port of departure, or if there is no such collector at such port then with the nearest collector of customs, a sworn statement (1) containing a complete list of all the articles and materials carried as cargo by such vessel, and the names and addresses of the consignees of all such articles and materials, and (2) stating the ports at which such articles and materials are to be unloaded and the ports of call of such vessel. All transportation referred to in subsections (f), (g), (h), and (l) of this section shall be subject to such restrictions, rules, and regulations as the President shall prescribe; but no loss incurred in connection with any transportation excepted under the provisions of subsections (g), (h), and (l) of this section shall be made the basis of any claim put forward by the Government of the United States. . . .

(l) The provisions of subsection (c) of this section shall not apply to the transportation by a neutral vessel to any port referred to in subsection (g) of this section of any articles or materials (except articles or materials listed in a proclamation referred to in or issued under the authority of section 12 (i)) so long as such port is not included within a combat area as defined in section 3 which applies to American vessels.

COMBAT AREAS

SEC. 3. (a) Whenever the President shall have issued a proclamation under the authority of section 1 (a), and he shall thereafter find that the protection of citizens of the United States so requires, he shall, by proclamation, define combat areas, and thereafter it shall be unlawful, except under such rules and regulations as may be prescribed, for any citizen of the United States or any American vessel to proceed into or through any such combat area. The combat areas so defined may be made to apply to surface vessels or aircraft, or both.

(b) In case of the violation of any of the provisions of this section by any American vessel, or any owner or officer thereof, such vessel, owner, or officer shall be fined not more than $50,000 or imprisoned for not more than five years, or both. Should the owner of such vessel be a corporation, organization, or association, each officer or director participating in the violation shall be liable to the penalty hereinabove prescribed. In case of the violation of this section by any citizen traveling as a passenger, such passenger may be fined not more than $10,000 or imprisoned for not more than two years, or both.

(c) The President may from time to time modify or extend any proclamation issued under the authority of this section, and when the conditions which shall have caused him to issue any such proclamation shall have ceased to exist he shall revoke such proclamation and the provisions of this section shall thereupon cease to apply, except as to offenses committed prior to such revocation. . . .

TRAVEL ON VESSELS OF BELLIGERENT STATES

SEC. 5. (a) Whenever the President shall have issued a proclamation under the authority of section 1 (a) it shall thereafter be unlawful for any citizen of the United States to travel on any vessel of any state named in such proclamation, except in accordance with such rules and regulations as may be prescribed.

(b) Whenever any proclamation issued under the authority of section 1 (a) shall have been revoked with respect to any state the provisions of this section shall thereupon cease to apply with respect to such state, except as to offenses committed prior to such revocation.

ARMING OF AMERICAN MERCHANT VESSELS PROHIBITED

SEC. 6. Whenever the President shall have issued a proclamation under the authority of section 1 (a), it shall thereafter be unlawful, until such proclamation is revoked, for any American vessel, engaged in commerce with any foreign state to be armed, except with small arms and ammunition therefor, which the President may deem necessary and shall publicly designate for the preservation of discipline aboard any such vessel.

FINANCIAL TRANSACTIONS

SEC. 7. (a) Whenever the President shall have issued a proclamation under the authority of section 1 (a), it shall thereafter be unlawful for any person within the United States to purchase, sell, or exchange bonds, securities, or other obligations of the government of any state named in such proclamation, or of any political subdivision of any such state, or of any person acting for or on behalf of the government of any such state, or political subdivision thereof, issued after the date of such proclamation, or to make any loan or extend any credit (other than necessary credits accruing in connection with the transmission of telegraph, cable, wireless and telephone service) to any such government, political subdivision, or person. The provisions of this subsection shall also apply to the sale by any person within the United States to any person in state named in any such proclamation of articles or materials listed in a proclamation referred to in or issued under the authority of section 12 (i). . . .

SOLICITATION AND COLLECTION OF FUNDS AND CONTRIBUTIONS

SEC. 8. (a) Whenever the President shall have issued a proclamation under the authority of section 1 (a), it shall thereafter be unlawful for any person within the United States to solicit or receive a contribution for or on behalf of the government of any state named in such proclamation or for or on behalf of any agent or instrumentality of any such state. . . .

AMERICAN REPUBLICS

SEC. 9. This joint resolution (except section 12) shall not apply to any American republic engaged in war against a non-American state or states, provided the American republic is not cooperating with a non-American state or states in such war. . . .

NATIONAL MUNITIONS CONTROL BOARD

SEC. 12. (c) Every person required to register under this section shall notify the Secretary of State of any change in the arms, ammunition, or implements of war which he exports, imports, or manufactures; and upon such notification the Secretary of State shall issue to such person an amended certificate of registration, free of charge, which shall remain valid until the date of expiration of the original certificate. Every person required to register under the provisions of this section shall pay a registration fee of $100. Upon receipt of the required registration fee, the Secretary of State shall issue a registration certificate valid for five years, which shall be renewable for further periods of five years upon the payment for each renewal of a fee of $100; but valid certificates of registration (including amended certificates) issued under the authority of section 2 of the joint resolution of August 31, 1935, or section 5 of the joint resolution of August 31, 1935, as amended, shall, without payment of any additional registration fee, be considered to be valid certificates of registration issued under this subsection, and shall remain valid for the same period as if this joint resolution had not been enacted.

(d) It shall be unlawful for any person to export, or attempt to export, from the United States to any other state, any arms, ammunition, or implements of war listed in a proclamation referred to in or issued under the authority of subsection (i) of this section, or to import, or attempt to import, to the United States from any other state, any of the arms, ammunition, or implements of war listed in any such proclamation, without first having submitted to the Secretary of State the name of the purchaser and the terms of sale and having obtained a license therefor. . . .

(g) No purchase of arms, ammunition, or implements of war shall be made on behalf of the United States by any officer, executive department, or independent establishment of the Government from any person who shall have failed to register under the provisions of this joint resolution.

(h) The Board shall make a report to Congress on January 3 and July 3 of each year, copies of which shall be distributed as are other reports transmitted to Congress. Such reports shall contain such information and data collected by the Board as may be considered of value in the determination of questions connected with the control of trade in arms, ammunition, and implements of war, including the name of the purchaser and the terms of sale made under any such license. The Board shall include in such reports a list of all persons required to register under the provisions of this joint resolution, and full information concerning the licenses issued hereunder, including the name of the purchaser and the terms of sale made under any such license.

(i) The President is hereby authorized to proclaim upon recommendation of the Board from time to time a list of articles which shall be considered arms, ammunition, and implements of war for the purposes of this section; but the proclamation Numbered 2237, of May 1, 1937 (50 Stat. 1834) defin-

ing the term "arms, ammunition, and implements of war" shall, until it is revoked, have full force and effect as if issued under the authority of this subsection. . . .

GENERAL PENALTY PROVISION

SEC. 15. In every case of the violation of any of the provisions of this joint resolution or of any rule or regulation issued pursuant thereto where a specific penalt· is not herein provided, such violator or violators, upon conviction, shall be fined not more than $10,-000, or imprisoned not more han two years, or both. . . .

REPEALS

SEC. 19. The joint resolution of August 31, 1935, as amended, and the joint resolution of January 8, 1937, ar hereby repealed; but offenses committed ad penalties, forfeitures, or liabilities inc red under either of such joint resolutions ior to the date of enactment of this joint esolution may be prosecuted and punished and suits and proceedings for violations o either of such joint resolutions or of any ·e or regulation issued pursuant thereto ay be commenced and prosecuted, in tl same manner and with the same effect· if such joint resolutions had not been ·pealed.

528. CHAMBERS v. FLORIDA
309 U. S. 227
1940

On Writ of Certiorari to the Supreme Court of the State of Florida. The essential facts of the case are fully set forth in the opinion. On the use of the "third degree" see E. M. Borchard, *Convicting the Innocent; Report* of the Committee on Lawless Enforcement of the Law, 1 American Journal of Political Science, 575; *Report* of the National Commission on Law Observance and Enforcement, vol. IV. For the interpretation of due process as embracing the protections of the Federal bill of rights, see *Twining* v. *New Jersey,* 211 U. S. 78; *Palko* v. *Connecticut,* 302 U. S. 319; *Hague* v. *C. I. O.* 307 U. S. 496.

BLACK, J. The grave question presented by the petition for certiorari, granted in forma

pauperis, is whe·r proceedings in which confessions wer tilized, and which culminated in senten of death upon four young negro men in t State of Florida, failed to afford the saf rd of that due process of law guarantee·y the Fourteenth Amendment.

Second. T record shows—

About nir clock on the night of Saturday, May 1 933, Robert Darcy, an elderly white mar as robbed and murdered in Pompano, rida, a small town in Broward County a twelve miles from Fort Lauderdale, ounty seat. The opinion of the Supreme urt of Florida affirming petitioners' cor ion for this crime stated that "It wa of those crimes that induced an enraged community . . . ." And, as the dissenting judge pointed out, "The murder and robbery of the elderly Mr. Darcy . . . was a dastardly and atrocious crime. It naturally aroused great and well deserved indignation."

Between 9:30 and 10 o'clock after the murder, petitioner Charlie Davis was arrested, and within the next twenty-four hours from twenty-five to forty negroes living in the community, including petitioners Williamson, Chambers and Woodward, were arrested without warrants and confined in the Broward County jail, at Fort Lauderdale. Evidence of petitioners was that on the way to Miami a motorcycle patrolman drew up to the car in which the men were riding and the sheriff "told the cop that he had some negroes that he . . . taking down to Miami to escape a mob." This statement was not denied by the sheriff in his testimony and Williams did not testify at all.

It is clear from the evidence of both the State and petitioners that from Sunday, May 14, to Saturday, May 20, the thirty to forty negro suspects were subjected to questioning and cross questioning. From the afternoon of Saturday, May 20, until sunrise of the 21st, petitioners and possibly one or two others underwent persistent and repeated questioning.

So far as appears, the prisoners at no time during the week were permitted to see or confer with counsel or a single friend or relative. When carried singly from his cell and subjected to questioning, each found himself, a single prisoner, surrounded in a fourth floor jail room by four to ten men, the county sheriff, his deputies, a convict guard, and other white officers and citizens of the community.

The testimony is in conflict as to whether all four petitioners were continually threatened and physically mistreated until they finally, in hopeless desperation and fear of their lives, agreed to confess on Sunday morning just after daylight. Be that as it may, it is certain that by Saturday, May 20th, five days of continued questioning had elicited no confession. Admittedly, a concentration of effort—directed against a small number of prisoners including petitioners— on the part of the questioners, principally the sheriff and Williams, the convict guard,

began about 3:30 that Saturday afternoon. From that hour on, with only short intervals for food and rest for the questioners—"They all stayed up all night." "They bring one of them at a time backwards and forwards . . . until they confessed."

After one week's constant denial of all guilt, petitioners "broke."

Just before sunrise, the State officials got something "worthwhile" from petitioners which the State's attorney would "want"; again he was called; he came; in the presence of those who had carried on and witnessed the all night questioning, he caused his questions and petitioners' answers to be stenographically reported. These are the confessions utilized by the State to obtain the judgments upon which petitioners were sentenced to death. No formal charges had been brought before the confession. Two days thereafter, petitioners were indicted, were arraigned and Williamson and Woodward pleaded guilty; Chambers and Davis pleaded not guilty. Later the sheriff, accompanied by Williams, informed an attorney who presumably had been appointed to defend Davis that Davis wanted his plea of not guilty withdrawn. This was done, and Davis then pleaded guilty. When Chambers was tried, his conviction rested upon his confession and testimony of the other three confessors. The convict guard and the sheriff "were in the Court room sitting down in a seat." And from arrest until sentenced to death, petitioners were never—either in jail or in court —wholly removed from the constant observation, influence, custody and control of those whose persistent pressure brought about the sunrise confessions.

Third. The scope and operation of the Fourteenth Amendment have been fruitful sources of controversy in our constitutional history. However, in view of its historical setting and the wrongs which called it into being, the due process provision of the Fourteenth Amendment—just as that in the Fifth—had led few to doubt that it was intended to guarantee procedural standards adequate and appropriate, then and thereafter, to protect, at all times, people charged with or suspected of crime by those holding positions of power and authority. Tyrannical governments had immemorially utilized dictatorial criminal procedure and punishment to make scape goats of the weak, or of helpless political, religious, or racial minorities and those who differed, who would not conform and who resisted tyranny. The instruments of such governments were in the main, two. Conduct, innocent when engaged in, was subsequently made by fiat criminally punishable without legislation. And a liberty loving people won the principle that criminal punishments could not be inflicted save for that which proper legislative action had already by "the law of the land" forbidden when done. But even more was needed. From the popular hatred and abhorrence of illegal confinement, torture and extortion of confessions of violations of the "law of the land" evolved the fundamental idea that no man's life, liberty or property be forfeited as criminal punishment for violation of that law until there had been a charge fairly made and fairly tried in a public tribunal free of prejudice, passion, excitement and tyrannical power. Thus, as assurance against ancient evils, our country, in order to preserve "the blessings of liberty," wrote into its basic law the requirement, among others, that the forfeiture of the lives, liberties or property of people accused of crime can only follow if procedural safeguards of due process have been obeyed.

The determination to preserve an accused's right to procedural due process sprang in large part from knowledge of the historical truth that the rights and liberties of people accused of crime could not be safely entrusted to secret inquisitorial processes. The testimony of centuries, in governments of varying kinds over populations of different races and beliefs, stood as proof that physical and mental torture and coercion had brought about the tragically unjust sacrifices of some who were the noblest and most useful of their generations. The rack, the thumbscrew, the wheel, solitary confinement, protracted questioning and cross questioning, and other ingenious forms of entrapment of the helpless or unpopular had left their wake of mutilated bodies and shattered minds along the way to the cross, the guillotine, the stake and the hangman's noose. And they who have suffered most from secret and dictatorial proceedings have almost always been the poor, the ignorant, the numerically weak, the friendless, and the powerless.

This requirement—of conforming to fundamental standards of procedure in criminal trials—was made operative against the States by the Fourteenth Amendment. When one of several accused had limped into the trial court as a result of admitted physical mistreatment inflicted to obtain confessions upon which a jury had returned a verdict of guilty of murder, this Court recently declared, *Brown* v. *Mississippi*, that "It would be difficult to conceive of methods more revolting to the sense of justice than those taken to procure the confessions of these petitioners, and the use of the confessions thus obtained as the basis for conviction and sentence was a clear denial of due process."

Here, the record develops a sharp conflict upon the issue of physical violence and mistreatment, but shows, without conflict, the drag net methods of arrest on suspicion without warrant, and the protracted questioning and cross questioning of these ignorant young colored tenant farmers by State officers and other white citizens, in a fourth floor jail room, where as prisoners they were without friends, advisers or counselors, and under circumstances calculated to break the strongest nerves and the stoutest resistance. Just as our decision in *Brown* v. *Mississippi* was based upon the fact that the confessions were the result of compulsion, so in the present case, the admitted practices were such as to justify the statement that "The undisputed facts showed that compulsion was applied."

For five days petitioners were subjected to interrogations culminating in Saturday's (May 20th) all night examinations. Over a period of five days they steadily refused to confess and disclaimed any guilt. The very circumstances surrounding their confinement and their questioning without any formal charges having been brought, were such as to fill petitioners with terror and frightful misgivings. Some were practical strangers in the community; three were arrested in a one-room farm tenant house which was their home; the haunting fear of mob violence was around them in an atmosphere charged with excitement and public indignation. From virtually the moment of their arrest until their eventual confessions, they never knew just when any one would be called back to the fourth floor room, and there, surrounded by his accusers and others, interrogated by men who held their very lives—so far as these ignorant petitioners could know—in the balance. The rejection of petitioner Woodward's first "confession," given in the early hours of Sunday morning, because it was found wanting, demonstrates the relentless tenacity which "broke" petitioners' will and rendered them helpless to resist their accusers further. To permit human lives to be forfeited upon confessions thus obtained would make of the constitutional requirement of due process of law a meaningless symbol.

We are not impressed by the argument that law enforcement methods such as those under review are necessary to uphold our laws. The Constitution proscribes such lawless means irrespective of the end. And this argument flouts the basic principle that all people must stand on an equality before the bar of justice in every American court.

Today, as in ages past, we are not without tragic proof that the exalted power of some governments to punish manufactured crime dictatorially is the handmaid of tyranny. Under our constitutional system, courts stand against any winds that blow as havens of refuge for those who might otherwise suffer because they are helpless, weak, outnumbered, or because they are non-conforming victims of prejudice and public excitement. Due process of law, preserved for all by our Constitution, commands that no such practice as that disclosed by this record shall send any accused to his death. No higher duty, no more solemn responsibility, rests upon this Court, than that of translating into living law and maintaining this constitutional shield deliberately planned and inscribed for the benefit of every human being subject to our Constitution—of whatever race, creed or persuasion.

The Supreme Court of Florida was in error and its judgment is

Reversed.

529. UNITED STATES v. SOCONY-VACUUM OIL CO.
310 U. S. 150
1940

On Writs of Certiorari to the U. S. Circuit Court of Appeals for the Seventh Circuit. Only that portion of the case is presented which concerns the application to the Sherman Anti-Trust Act of the Rule of Reason. For the earlier vicissitudes of the Rule of Reason see Doc. No. 375. Justice Douglas' statement that price fixing agreements had always been unlawful under the Sherman Act appeared to indicate that this decision did not constitute a departure from the Rule of Reason, but many students held that the repudiation of the Rule of Reason was implicit in the opinion.

DOUGLAS, J. . . .

V. *Application of the Sherman Act*
A. Charge to the Jury

The court charged the jury that it was a violation of the Sherman Act for a group of individuals or corporations to act together to raise the prices to be charged for the commodity which they manufactured where they controlled a substantial part of the interstate trade and commerce in that commodity. The court stated that where the members of a combination had the power to raise prices and acted together for that purpose, the combination was illegal; and that it was immaterial how reasonable or unreasonable those prices were or to what extent they had been affected by the combination. It further charged that if such illegal combination existed, it did not matter that there may also have been other factors which contributed to the raising of the prices. In that connection, it referred specifically to the economic factors which we have previously discussed and which respondents contended were primarily responsible for the price rise and the spot markets' stability in 1935 and 1936, viz. control of production, the Connally Act, the price of crude oil, an increase in consumptive demand, control of inventories and manufacturing quotas, and improved business conditions. The court then charged that, unless the jury found beyond a reasonable doubt that the price rise and its continuance were "caused" by the combination and not caused by those other factors, verdicts of "not guilty" should be returned. It also charged that there was no evidence of governmental approval which would exempt the buying programs from the prohibitions of the Sherman Act; and that knowledge or acquiescence of officers of the government or the good intentions of the members of the combination would not give immunity from prosecution under that Act.

The Circuit Court of Appeals held this charge to be reversible error, since it was based upon the theory that such a combination was illegal per se. In its view respondents' activities were not unlawful unless they constituted an unreasonable restraint of trade. Hence, since that issue had not been submitted to the jury and since evidence bearing on it had been excluded, that court reversed and remanded for a new trial so that the character of those activities and their effect on competition could be determined. In answer to the government's petition respondents here contend that the judgment of the Circuit Court of Appeals was correct, since there was evidence that they had affected prices only in the sense that the removal of the competitive evil of distress gasoline by the buying programs had permitted prices to rise to a normal competitive level; that their activities promoted rather than impaired fair competitive opportunities; and therefore that their activities had not unduly or unreasonably restrained trade. And they also contend that certain evidence which was offered should have been admitted as bearing on the purpose and end sought to be attained, the evil believed to exist, and the nature of the restraint and its effect. By their cross-petition respondents contend that the record contains no substantial competent evidence that the combination, either in purpose or effect, unreasonably restrained trade within the meaning of the Sherman Act, and therefore that the Circuit Court of Appeals erred in holding that they were not entitled to directed verdicts of acquittal.

In *United States* v. *Trenton Potteries Co.,* 273 U. S. 392, this Court sustained a conviction under the Sherman Act where the jury was charged that an agreement on the part of the members of a combination, controlling a substantial part of an industry, upon the prices which the members are to charge for their commodity is in itself an unreasonable restraint of trade without regard to the reasonableness of the prices or the good intentions of the combining units. There the combination was composed of those who controlled some 82 per cent of the business of manufacturing and distributing in the United States vitreous pottery. Their object was to fix the prices for the sale of that commodity. In that case the trial court refused various requests to charge that the agreement to fix prices did not itself constitute a violation of law unless the jury also found that it unreasonably restrained interstate commerce. This Court reviewed the various price-fixing cases under the Sherman Act beginning with *United States* v. *Trans-Missouri Freight Association,* 166 U. S. 290, and *United States* v. *Joint Traffic Association,* 171 U. S. 505, and said ". . . it has since often been decided and always assumed that uniform price-fixing by those controlling in any substantial manner a trade or business in interstate commerce is prohibited by the Sherman Law, despite the reasonableness of the particular prices agreed upon." 273 U. S. page 398. This Court pointed out that the so-called "rule of reason" announced in *Standard Oil Co.* v. *United States,* 221 U. S. 1, and in *United States* v. *American Tobacco Co.,* 221 U. S. 106, had not affected this view of the illegality of price-fixing agreements. And in holding that agreements "to fix or maintain prices" are not reasonable restraints of trade under the statute merely because the prices themselves are reasonable, it said:

"The aim and result of every price-fixing agreement, if effective, is the elimination of one form of competition. The power to fix prices, whether reasonably exercised or not involves power to control the market and to fix arbitrary and unreasonable prices. The reasonable price fixed today may through economic and business changes become the unreasonable price of tomorrow. Once established, it may be maintained unchanged because of the absence of competition secured by the agreement for a price reasonable when fixed. Agreements which create such potential power may well be held to be in themselves unreasonable or unlawful restraints without the necessity of minute inquiry whether a particular price is reasonable or unreasonable as fixed and without placing on the government in enforcing the Sherman Law the burden of ascertaining from day to day whether it has become unreasonable through the mere variation of economic conditions. Moreover, in the absence of express legislation requiring it, we should hesitate to adopt a construction making the difference between legal and illegal conduct in the field of business relations depend upon so uncertain a test as whether prices are reasonable ——a determination which can be satisfactorily made only after a complete survey of our economic organization and a choice between rival philosophies."

In conclusion this Court emphasized that the Sherman Act is not only a prohibition against the infliction of a particular type of public injury, but also, as stated in *Standard Sanitary Mfg. Co. v. United States*, 226 U. S. 20, a "limitation of rights" which may be "pushed to evil consequences, and therefore restrained.

But respondents claim that other decisions of this Court afford them adequate defenses to the indictment. (Considers alleged precedents and dismisses them as irrelevant.) . . .

Thus for over forty years this Court has consistently and without deviation adhered to the principle that price-fixing agreements are unlawful per se under the Sherman Act and that no showing of so-called competitive abuses or evils which those agreements were designed to eliminate or alleviate may be interposed as a defense. . . .

The reasonableness of prices has no constancy due to the dynamic quality of the business facts underlying price structures. Those who fixed reasonable prices today would perpetuate unreasonable prices tomorrow, since those prices would not be subject to continuous administrative supervision and readjustment in light of changed conditions. Those who controlled the prices would control or effectively dominate the market. And those who were in that strategic position would have it in their power to destroy or drastically impair the competitive system. But the thrust of the rule is deeper and reaches more than monopoly power. Any combination which tampers with price structures is engaged in an unlawful activity. Even though the members of the price-fixing group were in no position to control the market, to the extent that they raised, lowered, or stabilized prices they would be directly interfering with the free play of market forces. The Act places all such schemes beyond the pale and protects that vital part of our economy against any degree of interference. Congress has not left with us the determination of whether or not particular price-fixing schemes are wise or unwise, healthy or destructive. It has not permitted the age-old cry of ruinous competition and competitive evils to be a defense to price-fixing conspiracies. It has no more allowed genuine or fancied competitive abuses as a legal justification for such schemes than it has the good intentions of the members of the combination. If such a shift is to be made, it must be done by the Congress. Certainly Congress has not left us with any such choice. Nor has the Act created or authorized the creation of any special exception in favor of the oil industry. Whatever may be its peculiar problems and characteristics, the Sherman Act, so far as price-fixing agreements are concerned, establishes one uniform rule applicable to all industries alike. There was accordingly no error in the refusal to charge that in order to convict the jury must find that the resultant prices were raised and maintained at "high, arbitrary and non-competitive levels." The charge in the indictment to that effect was surplusage. . . .

Under the Sherman Act a combination formed for the purpose and with the effect of raising, depressing, fixing, pegging, or stabilizing the price of a commodity in interstate or foreign commerce is illegal per se. Where the machinery for price-fixing is an agreement on the prices to be charged or paid for the commodity in the interstate or foreign channels of trade, the power to fix prices exists if the combination has control of a substantial part of the commerce in that commodity. Where the means for price-fixing are purchases or sales of the commodity in a market operation or, as here, purchases of a part of the supply of the commodity for the purpose of keeping it from having a depressive effect on the markets, such power may be found to exist though the combination does not control a substantial part of the commodity. In such a case that power may be established if as a result of market conditions, the resources available to the combinations, the timing and the strategic placement of orders and the like, effective means are at hand to accomplish the desired objective. But there may be effective influence over the market though the group in question does not control it. Price-fixing agreements may have utility to members of the group though the power possessed or exerted falls far short of domination and control. Monopoly power is not the only power which the Act strikes down, as we have said. Proof that a combination was formed for the purpose of fixing prices and that it caused them to be fixed or contributed to that result is proof of the completion of a price-fixing conspiracy under § 1 of the Act. The indictment in this case charged that this combination had that purpose and effect. And there was abundant evidence to support it. . . .

ROBERTS, J., and McREYNOLDS, J. dissented.

530. F. D. ROOSEVELT'S ADDRESS AT CHARLOTTESVILLE, VIRGINIA
June 10, 1940
(*The Public Papers of F. D. Roosevelt*, Vol. 9. p. 259)

This address, delivered the day after Italy entered the World War on the side of Germany, indicated that in so far as the President could control American foreign policy the United States had abandoned neutrality for "non-belligerency." The speech met with almost universal approval.

President Newcomb, my friends of the University of Virginia. . . .

Every generation of young men and women in America has questions to ask the world. Most of the time they are the simple but nevertheless difficult questions—questions of work to do, opportunities to find, ambitions to satisfy.

But every now and again in the history of the republic a different kind of question presents itself—a question that asks, not about the future of an individual or even of a generation, but about the future of the country, the future of the American people. . . .

There is such a time again today. Again today the young men and the young women of America ask themselves with earnestness and with deep concern this same question: "What is to become of the country we know?"

Now they ask it with even greater anxiety than before. They ask, not only what the future holds for this republic, but what the future holds for all peoples and all nations that have been living under democratic forms of government—under the free institutions of a free people.

It is understandable to all of us, I think, that they should ask this question. They read the words of those who are telling them that the ideal of individual liberty, the ideal of free franchise, the ideal of peace through justice is a decadent idea!

They read the word and hear the boast of those who say that a belief in force—force directed by self-chosen leaders—is the new and vigorous system which will overrun the earth. They have seen the ascendancy of this philosophy of force in nation after nation where free institutions and individual liberties were once maintained.

It is natural and understandable that the younger generation should first ask itself what the extension of the philosophy of force to all the world would lead to ultimately. We see today, for example, in stark reality some of the consequences of what we call the machine age.

Where control of machines has been retained in the hands of mankind as a whole, untotaled benefits have accrued to mankind. For mankind was then the master: The machine was the servant.

But in this new system of force the mastery of the machine is not in the hands of mankind. It is in the control of infinitely small groups of individuals who rule without a single one of the democratic sanctions that we have known.

The machine in the hands of irresponsible conquerors becomes the master; mankind is not only the servant, it is the victim too. Such mastery abandons with deliberate contempt all of the moral values to which even this young country for more than 300 years has been accustomed and dedicated.

Surely the new philosophy proves from month to month that it could have no possible conception of the way of life or the way of thought of a nation whose origins go back to Jamestown and Plymouth Rock.

And conversely, neither those who sprang from that ancient stock nor those who have come hither in later years can be indifferent to the destruction of freedom in their ancestral lands across the sea.

Perception to danger to our institutions may come slowly or it may come with a rush and shock as it has to the people of the United States in the past few months. This perception of danger—danger in a worldwide arena—has come to us clearly and overwhelmingly. We perceive the peril in this world-wide arena—an arena that may become so narrow that only the Americans will retain the ancient faiths.

Some indeed still hold to the now somewhat obvious delusion that we of the United States can safely permit the United States to become a lone island, a lone island in a world dominated by the philosophy of force.

Such an island may be the dream of those who still talk and vote as isolationists. Such an island represents to me and to the overwhelming majority of Americans today a helpless nightmare, the helpless nightmare of a people without freedom. Yes, the night-

mare of a people lodged in prison, handcuffed, hungry and fed through the bars from day to day by the contemptuous, unpitying masters of other continents.

It is natural also that we should ask ourselves how now we can prevent the building of that prison and the placing of ourselves in the midst of it.

Let us not hesitate—all of us—to proclaim certain truths. Overwhelmingly we, as a nation, and this applies to all the other American nations, we are convinced that military and naval victory for the gods of force and hate would endanger the institutions of democracy in the Western World—and that equally, therefore, the whole of our sympathies lie with those nations that are giving their life blood in combat against those forces.

The people and Government of the United States have seen with the utmost regret and with grave disquiet the decision of the Italian Government to engage in the hostilities now raging in Europe.

More than three months ago the chief of the Italian Government sent me word that because of the determination of Italy to limit, so far as might be possible, the spread of the European conflict, more than two hundred millions of people in the region of the Mediterranean had been enabled to escape the suffering and the devastation of war.

I informed the chief of the Italian Government that this desire on the part of Italy to prevent the war from spreading met with full sympathy and response on the part of the government and the people of the United States, and I expressed the earnest hope of this government and of this people that this policy on the part of Italy might be continued. I made it clear that in the opinion of the Government of the United States any extension of hostilities in the region of the Mediterranean might result in the still greater enlargement of the scene of the conflict, the conflict in the Near East and in Africa, and that if this came to pass no one could foretell how much greater the theatre of the war eventually might become.

Again, upon a subsequent occasion, not so far ago, recognizing that certain aspirations of Italy might form the basis of discussions between the powers most specifically concerned, I offered, in a message addressed to the chief of the Italian Government, to send to the Governments of France and Great Britain such specific indications of the desires of Italy to obtain readjustments with regard to her position as the chief of the Italian Government might desire to transmit through me.

While making it clear that the government of the United States in such an event could not and would not assume responsibility for the nature of the proposals submitted nor for agreements which might thereafter be reached, I proposed that if Italy would refrain from entering the war I would be willing to ask assurances from the other powers concerned that they would faithfully execute any agreement so reached, and that Italy's voice in any future peace conference would have the same authority as if Italy had actually taken part in the war as a belligerent.

Unfortunately, unfortunately to the regret of all of us, and to the regret of humanity, the chief of the Italian Government was unwilling to accept the procedure suggested, and he has made no counter-proposal. This government directed its efforts to doing what it could to work for the preservation of peace in the Mediterranean area, and it likewise expressed its willingness to endeavor to cooperate with the government of Italy when the appropriate occasion arose for the creation of a more stable world order, through the reduction of armaments and through the construction of a more liberal international economic system which would assure to all powers equality of opportunity in the world markets and in the securing of raw materials on equal terms.

I have likewise, of course, felt it necessary in my communications to Signor Mussolini to express the concern of the government of the United States because of the fact that any extension of the war in the region of the Mediterranean would inevitably result in great prejudice to the ways of life and government and to the trade and commerce of all the American republics.

The government of Italy has now chosen to preserve what it terms its "freedom of action" and to fulfill what it states are its promises to Germany. In so doing it has manifested disregard for the rights and security of other nations, disregard for the lives of the peoples of those nations which are directly threatened by the spread of this war; and has evidenced its unwillingness to find the means through pacific negotiations for the satisfaction of what it believes are its legitimate aspirations.

On this 10th day of June, 1940, the hand that held the dagger has struck it into the back of its neighbor.

On this 10th day of June, 1940, in this university founded by the first great American teacher of democracy we send forth our prayers and our hopes to those beyond the seas who are maintaining with magnificent valor their battle for freedom.

In our unity, in our American unity, we will pursue two obvious and simultaneous courses; we will extend to the opponents of force the material resources of this nation and, at the same time, we will harness and speed up the use of those resources in order that we ourselves in the Americas may have equipment and training equal to the task of any emergency and every defense.

All roads leading to the accomplishment of these objectives must be kept clear of obstructions. We will not slow down or detour. Signs and signals call for speed—full speed ahead.

Yes, it is right that each new generation should ask questions. But in recent months the principal question has been somewhat simplified. Once more the future of the nation and the future of the American people is at stake.

We need not and we will not, in any way, abandon our continuing efforts to make democracy work within our borders. Yes, we still insist on the need for vast improvements in our own social and economic life.

But that, that is a component part of national defense itself.

The program unfolds swiftly and into that program will fit the responsibility and the opportunity of every man and woman in the land to preserve our heritage in days of peril.

I call for effort, courage, sacrifice, devotion. Granting the love of freedom, all of these are possible.

And the love of freedom is still fierce, still steady in the nation today.

531. ALIEN REGISTRATION ACT, 1940
June 28, 1940

(Public Law No. 670, 76th Congress)

This law is notable as the first in which Congress followed the doctrine of guilt by association. It was directed not primarily to the problem of aliens but to subversive activities which were causing grave concern on the eve of war. See Z. Chafee, Jr., *Free Speech in the United States;* M. R. Konvitz, *Aliens and Asiatics in American Law;* W. M. Gilson, *Aliens and the Law.* See Docs. No. 101, 425.

An Act to prohibit certain subversive activities; to amend certain provisions of law with respect to the admission and deportation of aliens; to require the fingerprinting and registration of aliens; and for other purposes.

TITLE I

SECTION 1. (a) It shall be unlawful for any person, with intent to interfere with, impair, or influence the loyalty, morale, or discipline of the military or naval forces of the United States—

(1) to advise, counsel, urge, or in any manner cause insubordination, disloyalty, mutiny, or refusal of duty by any member of the military or naval forces of the United States; or

(2) to distribute any written or printed matter which advises, counsels, or urges insubordination, disloyalty, mutiny, or refusal of duty by any member of the military or naval forces of the United States.

SEC. 2. (a) It shall be unlawful for any person—

(1) to knowingly or willfully advocate, abet, advise, or teach the duty, necessity, desirability, or propriety of overthrowing or destroying any government in the United States by force or violence, or by the assassination of any officer of any such government;

(2) with the intent to cause the overthrow or destruction of any government in the United States, to print, publish, edit, issue, circulate, sell, distribute, or publicly display any written or printed matter advocating, advising, or teaching the duty, necessity, desirability, or propriety of overthrowing or destroying any government in the United States by force or violence;

(3) to organize or help to organize any society, group, or assembly of persons who teach, advocate, or encourage the overthrow or destruction of any government in the United States by force or violence; or to be or become a member of, or affiliate with, any such society, group, or assembly of persons, knowing the purposes thereof.

532. THE GOBITIS CASE
310 U. S. 586
1940

The Gobitis children were expelled from the public schools of Minersville, Pennsylvania, for refusing to salute the American flag as required by the local Board of Education. Their refusal was based on the belief that such an action would be contrary to scripture, an interpretation held by the Watch Tower Bible and Tract Society, the "Jehovah's Witnesses," of which they were members. Their father, Walter Gobitis, brought suit to enjoin the Board from requiring participation in the flag-salute ceremony as a requisite for attending school. The District Court and the Circuit Court both decided in his favor, and the school board appealed to the Supreme Court. See H. W. Barber, "Religious Liberty vs. the Police Power," *Am. Pol. Sci. Rev.,* Vol. XLI; V. Rotnem and F. G. Folsom, Jr., "Recent Restrictions upon Religious Liberty," *ibid.,* Vol. XXXVI, pp. 1053-1068; H. H. Stroup, *The Jehovah's Witnesses;* H. S. Commager, *Majority Rule and Minority Rights* is an analysis of issues presented by this case; W. G. Fennell, "The 'Reconstructed Court' and Religious Freedom: the Gobitis Case in Retrospect," *19 N.Y.U. Law Quart. Rev.,* 31 ff.; H. S. Commager, "Who is Loyal to America?" *Harpers,* Sept., 1947; T. R.

Powell, "Conscience and Constitution" in *Democracy and National Unity*. A. Mason, *Harlan F. Stone*, ch. 31.

On Writ of Certiorari to the United States Circuit Court of Appeals for the Third Circuit.

FRANKFURTER, J. A grave responsibility confronts this Court whenever in course of litigation it must reconcile the conflicting claims of liberty and authority. But when the liberty invoked is liberty of conscience, and the authority is authority to safeguard the nation's fellowship, judicial conscience is put to its severest test. Of such a nature is the present controversy.

Lillian Gobitis, aged twelve, and her brother William, aged ten, were expelled from the public schools of Minersville, Pennsylvania, for refusing to salute the national flag as part of a daily school exercise. The local Board of Education required both teachers and pupils to participate in this ceremony. The ceremony is a familiar one. The right hand is placed on the breast and the following pledge recited in unison: "I pledge allegiance to my flag, and to the Republic for which it stands; one nation indivisible, with liberty and justice for all." While the words are spoken, teachers and pupils extend their right hands in salute to the flag. The Gobitis family are affiliated with "Jehovah's Witnesses," for whom the Bible as the Word of God is the supreme authority. The children had been brought up conscientiously to believe that such a gesture of respect for the flag was forbidden by command of scripture.

The Gobitis children were of an age for which Pennsylvania makes school attendance compulsory. Thus they were denied a free education and their parents had to put them into private schools. To be relieved of the financial burden thereby entailed, their father, on behalf of the children and in his own behalf, brought this suit. He sought to enjoin the authorities from continuing to exact participation in the flag-salute ceremony as a condition of his children's attendance at the Minersville school. After trial of the issues, Judge Maris gave relief in the District Court on the basis of a thoughtful opin-

ion; his decree was affirmed by the Circuit Court of Appeals. Since this decision ran counter to several per curiam dispositions of this Court, we granted certiorari to give the matter full reconsideration. By their able submissions, the Committee on the Bill of Rights of the American Bar Association and the American Civil Liberties Union, as friends of the Court, have helped us to our conclusion.

We must decide whether the requirement of participation in such a ceremony, exacted from a child who refuses upon sincere religious grounds, infringes without due process of law the liberty guaranteed by the Fourteenth Amendment.

Centuries of strife over the erection of particular dogmas as exclusive or all-comprehending faiths led to the inclusion of a guarantee for religious freedom in the Bill of Rights. The First Amendment, and the Fourteenth through its absorption of the First, sought to guard against repetition of those bitter religious struggles by prohibiting the establishment of a state religion and by securing to every sect the free exercise of its faith. So pervasive is the acceptance of this precious right that its scope is brought into question, as here, only when the conscience of individuals collides with the felt necessities of society.

Certainly the affirmative pursuit of one's convictions about the ultimate mystery of the universe and man's relation to it is placed beyond the reach of law. Government may not interfere with organized or individual expression of belief or disbelief. Propagation of belief—or even of disbelief in the supernatural— is protected, whether in church or chapel, mosque or synagogue, tabernacle or meetinghouse. Likewise the Constitution assures generous immunity to the individual from imposition of penalties for offending, in the course of his own religious activities, the religious views of others, be they a minority or those who are dominant in government.

But the manifold character of man's relations may bring his conception of religious duty into conflict with the secular interests of his fellow-men. When does the constitutional guarantee compel exemption from doing what society thinks necessary for the promotion of some great common end, or from a penalty for conduct which appears dangerous to the general good? To state the problem is to recall the truth that no single principle can answer all of life's complexities. The right to freedom of religious belief, however dissident and however obnoxious to the cherished beliefs of others—even of a majority—is itself the denial of an absolute. But to affirm that the freedom to follow conscience has itself no limits in the life of a society would deny that very plurality of principles which, as a matter of history, underlies protection of religious toleration. Compare Mr. Justice Holmes in Hudson County Water Co. v. McCarter, 209 U.S. 349, 355. Our present task then, as so often the case with courts, is to reconcile two rights in order to prevent either from destroying the other. But, because in safeguarding conscience we are dealing with interests so subtle and so dear, every possible leeway should be given to the claims of religious faith.

In the judicial enforcement of religious freedom we are concerned with a historic concept. See Mr. Justice Cardozo in Hamilton v. Regents, 293 U.S. 245, at page 265. The religious liberty which the Constitution protects has never excluded legislation of general scope not directed against doctrinal loyalties of particular sects. Judicial nullification of legislation cannot be justified by attributing to the framers of the Bill of Rights views for which there is no historic warrant. Conscientious scruples have not, in the course of the long struggle for religious toleration, relieved the individual from obedience to a general law not aimed at the promotion or restriction of religious beliefs. The mere possession of religious convictions which contradict the relevant concerns of a political society does not relieve the citizen from the discharge of political responsibilities. The necessity for this adjustment has again and again been recognized. In a number of situations the exertion of political authority has been sustained, while basic considerations of religious freedom have been left inviolate. Reynolds v. United States, 98 U.S. 145; Davis v. Beason, 133 U.S. 333; Selective Draft Law Cases, 245 U.S. 366; Hamilton v. Regents, 293 U.S. 245. In all these cases the general laws in question, up-

held in their application to those who refused obedience from religious conviction, were manifestations of specific powers of government deemed by the legislature essential to secure and maintain that orderly, tranquil, and free society without which religious toleration itself is unattainable. Nor does the freedom of speech assured by Due Process move in a more absolute circle of immunity than that enjoyed by religious freedom. Even if it were assumed that freedom of speech goes beyond the historic concept of full opportunity to utter and to disseminate views, however heretical or offensive to dominant opinion, and includes freedom from conveying what may be deemed an implied but rejected affirmation, the question remains whether school children, like the Gobitis children, must be excused from conduct required of all the other children in the promotion of national cohesion. We are dealing with an interest inferior to none in the hierarchy of legal values. National unity is the basis of national security. To deny the legislature the right to select appropriate means for its attainment presents a totally different order of problem from that of the propriety of subordinating the possible ugliness of littered streets to the free expression of opinion through distribution of handbills. Compare Schneider v. State of New Jersey, 308 U.S. 147.

Situations like the present are phases of the profoundest problem confronting a democracy—the problem which Lincoln cast in memorable dilemma: "Must a government of necessity be too strong for the liberties of its people, or too weak to maintain its own existence?" No mere textual reading or logical talisman can solve the dilemma. And when the issue demands judicial determination, it is not the personal notion of judges of what wise adjustment requires which must prevail.

Unlike the instances we have cited, the case before us is not concerned with an exertion of legislative power for the promotion of some specific need or interest of secular society—the protection of the family, the promotion of health, the common defense, the raising of public revenues to defray the cost of government. But all these specific activities of government presuppose the existence of an organized political society. The ultimate foundation of a free society is the binding tie of cohesive sentiment. Such a sentiment is fostered by all those agencies of the mind and spirit which may serve to gather up the traditions of a people, transmit them from generation to generation, and thereby create that continuity of a treasured common life which constitutes a civilization. "We live by symbols." The flag is the symbol of our national unity, transcending all internal differences, however large, within the framework of the Constitution. This Court has had occasion to say that ". . . the flag is the symbol of the nation's power,—the emblem of freedom in its truest, best sense. . . . it signifies government resting on the consent of the governed; liberty regulated by law; the protection of the weak against the strong; security against the exercise of arbitrary power; and absolute safety for free institutions against foreign aggression." Halter v. Nebraska, 205 U.S. 34.

The case before us must be viewed as though the legislature of Pennsylvania had itself formally directed the flag-salute for the children of Minersville; had made no exemption for children whose parents were possessed of conscientious scruples like those of the Gobitis family; and had indicated its belief in the desirable ends to be secured by having its public school children share a common experience at those periods of development when their minds are supposedly receptive to its assimilation, by an exercise appropriate in time and place and setting, and one designed to evoke in them appreciation of the nation's hopes and dreams, its sufferings and sacrifices. The precise issue, then, for us to decide is whether the legislatures of the various states and the authorities in a thousand counties and school districts of this country are barred from determining the appropriateness of various means to evoke that unifying sentiment without which there can ultimately be no liberties, civil or religious. To stigmatize legislative judgment in providing for this universal gesture of respect for the symbol of our national life in the setting of the common school as a lawless inroad on that freedom of conscience which the Constitution protects, would amount to no less than the pronouncement of pedagogical and psycho-

logical dogma in a field where courts possess no marked and certainly no controlling competence. The influences which help toward a common feeling for the common country are manifold. Some may seem harsh and others no doubt are foolish. Surely, however, the end is legitimate. And the effective means for its attainment are still so uncertain and so unauthenticated by science as to preclude us from putting the widely prevalent belief in flag-saluting beyond the pale of legislative power. It mocks reason and denies our whole history to find in the allowance of a requirement to salute our flag on fitting occasions the seeds of sanction for obeisance to a leader.

The wisdom of training children in patriotic impulses by those compulsions which necessarily pervade so much of the educational process is not for our independent judgment. Even were we convinced of the folly of such a measure, such belief would be no proof of its unconstitutionality. For ourselves, we might be tempted to say that the deepest patriotism is best engendered by giving unfettered scope to the most crotchety beliefs. Perhaps it is best, even from the standpoint of those interests which ordinances like the one under review seek to promote, to give to the least popular sect leave from conformities like those here in issue. But the court-room is not the arena for debating issues of educational policy. It is not our province to choose among competing considerations in the subtle process of securing effective loyalty to the traditional ideals of democracy, while respecting at the same time individual idiosyncracies among a people so diversified in racial origins and religious allegiances. So to hold would in effect make us the school board for the country. That authority has not been given to this Court, nor should we assume it.

We are dealing here with the formative period in the development of citizenship. Great diversity of psychological and ethical opinion exists among us concerning the best way to train children for their place in society. Because of these differences and because of reluctance to permit a single, iron-cast system of education to be imposed upon a nation compounded of so many strains, we have held that, even though public education is one of our most cherished democratic institutions, the Bill of Rights bars a state from compelling all children to attend the public schools. Pierce v. Society of the Sisters of the Holy Names of Jesus and Mary, 268 U.S. 510. But it is a very different thing for this Court to exercise censorship over the conviction of legislatures that a particular program or exercise will best promote in the minds of children who attend the common schools an attachment to the institutions of their country.

What the school authorities are really asserting is the right to awaken in the child's mind considerations as to the significance of the flag contrary to those implanted by the parent. In such an attempt the state is normally at a disadvantage in competing with the parent's authority, so long—and this is the vital aspect of religious toleration—as parents are unmolested in their right to counteract by their own persuasiveness the wisdom and rightness of those loyalties which the state's educational system is seeking to promote. Except where the transgression of constitutional liberty is too plain for argument, personal freedom is best maintained—so long as the remedial channels of the democratic process remain open and unobstructed—when it is ingrained in a people's habits and not enforced against popular policy by the coercion of adjudicated law. That the flag-salute is an allowable portion of a school program for those who do not invoke conscientious scruples is surely not debatable. But for us to insist that, though the ceremony may be required, exceptional immunity must be given to dissidents, is to maintain that there is no basis for a legislative judgment that such an exemption might introduce elements of difficulty into the school discipline, might cast doubts in the minds of the other children which would themselves weaken the effect of the exercise.

The preciousness of the family relation, the authority and independence which give dignity to parenthood, indeed the enjoyment of all freedom, presuppose the kind of ordered society which is summarized by our flag. A society which is dedicated to the preservation of these ultimate values of civilization may in self-protection utilize the educational process for inculcating those almost unconscious feelings which bind men together in a comprehending loyalty, whatever may be their lesser differences and difficulties. That is to say, the process may be utilized so long as men's right to believe as they please, to win others to their way of belief, and their right to assemble in their chosen places of worship for the devotional ceremonies of their faith, are all fully respected.

Judicial review, itself a limitation on popular government, is a fundamental part of our constitutional scheme. But to the legislature no less than to courts is committed the guardianship of deeply-cherished liberties. Where all the effective means of inducing political changes are left free from interference, education in the abandonment of foolish legislation is itself a training in liberty. To fight out the wise use of legislative authority in the forum of public opinion and before legislative assemblies rather than to transfer such a contest to the judicial arena, serves to vindicate the self-confidence of a free people.

Reversed.

533. WEST VA. STATE BD. v. BARNETTE
319 U. S. 624
1943

Inspired by the decision in the Gobitis case, the West Virginia State Board of Education ordered the flag salute ceremony to be made compulsory in all public schools. Children who disobeyed were to be dismissed from school, and action could be taken against their parents on the grounds that the children were "unlawfully absent." Members of the Jehovah's Witnesses brought suit in the United States District Court to restrain enforcement against their sect; the lower court decided in their favor, and the West Virginia State Board of Education appealed the case directly to the U. S. Supreme Court. Justices Black, Douglas, and Murphy filed concurring decisions, Justices Roberts and Reed dissenting decisions. See previous Document.

JACKSON, J. This case calls upon us to reconsider a precedent decision, as the Court throughout its history often has been required to do. Before turning to the Gobitis case, however, it is desirable to notice certain characteristics by which this controversy is distinguished.

The freedom asserted by these respondents does not bring them into collision with rights asserted by any other individual. It is such conflicts which most frequently require intervention of the State to determine where the rights of one end and those of another begin. But the refusal of these persons to participate in the ceremony does not interfere with or deny rights of others to do so. Nor is there any question in this case that their behavior is peaceable and orderly. The sole conflict is between authority and rights of the individual. The State asserts power to condition access to public education on making a prescribed sign and profession and at the same time to coerce attendance by punishing both parent and child. The latter stand on a right of self-determination in matters that touch individual opinion and personal attitude.

As the present Chief Justice said in dissent in the Gobitis case, the State may "require teaching by instruction and study of all in our history and in the structure and organization of our government, including the guaranties of civil liberty which tend to inspire patriotism and love of country." 310 U.S. at page 604. Here, however, we are dealing with a compulsion of students to declare a belief. They are not merely made acquainted with the flag salute so that they may be informed as to what it is or even what it means. The issue here is whether this slow and easily neglected route to aroused loyalties constitutionally may be short-cut by substituting a compulsory salute and slogan. This issue is not prejudiced by the Court's previous holding that where a State, without compelling attendance, extends college facilities to pupils who voluntarily enroll, it may prescribe military training as part of the course without offense to the Constitution. It was held that those who take advantage of its opportunities may not on ground of conscience refuse compliance with such conditions. In the present case attendance is not optional. That case is also to be distinguished from the present one because, independently of college privileges or requirements, the State has power to raise militia and impose the duties of service therein upon its citizens.

There is no doubt that, in connection with the pledges, the flag salute is a form of utterance. Symbolism is a primitive but effective way of communicating ideas. The use of an emblem or flag to symbolize some system, idea, institution, or personality, is a short cut from mind to mind. Causes and nations, political parties, lodges and ecclesiastical groups seek to knit the loyalty of their followings to a flag or banner, a color or design. The State announces rank, function, and authority through crowns and maces, uniforms and black robes; the church speaks through the Cross, the Crucifix, the altar and shrine, and clerical raiment. Symbols of State often convey political ideas just as religious symbols come to convey theological ones. Associated with many of these symbols are appropriate gestures of acceptance or respect: a salute, a bowed or bared head, a bended knee. A person gets from a symbol the meaning he puts into it, and what is one man's comfort and inspiration is another's jest and scorn. . . .

It is also to be noted that the compulsory flag salute and pledge requires affirmation of a belief and an attitude of mind. It is not clear whether the regulation contemplates that pupils forego any contrary convictions of their own and become unwilling converts to the prescribed ceremony or whether it will be acceptable if they simulate assent by words without belief and by a gesture barren of meaning. It is now a commonplace that censorship or suppression of expression of opinion is tolerated by our Constitution only when the expression presents a clear and present danger of action of a kind the State is empowered to prevent and punish. It would seem that involuntary affirmation could be commanded only on even more immediate and urgent grounds than silence. But here the power of compulsion is invoked without any allegation that remaining passive during a flag salute ritual creates a clear and present danger that would justify an effort even to muffle expression. To sustain the compulsory flag salute we are required to say that a Bill of Rights which guards the individual's right to speak his own mind, left it open to public authorities to compel him to utter what is not in his mind.

Whether the First Amendment to the Constitution will permit officials to order observance of ritual of this nature does not depend upon whether as a voluntary exercise we would think it to be good, bad or merely innocuous. Any credo of nationalism is likely to include what some disapprove or to omit what others think essential, and to give off different overtones as it takes on different accents or interpretations. If official power exists to coerce acceptance of any patriotic creed, what it shall contain cannot be decided by courts, but must be largely discretionary with the ordaining authority, whose power to prescribe would no doubt include power to amend. Hence validity of the asserted power to force an American citizen publicly to profess any statement of belief or to engage in any ceremony of assent to one presents questions of power that must be considered independently of any idea we may have as to the utility of the ceremony in question.

Nor does the issue as we see it turn on one's possession of particular religious views or the sincerity with which they are held. While religion supplies respondents' motive for enduring the discomforts of making the issue in this case, many citizens who do not share these religious views hold such a compulsory rite to infringe constitutional liberty of the individual. It is not necessary to inquire whether non-conformist beliefs will exempt from the duty to salute unless we first find power to make the salute a legal duty.

The Gobitis decision, however, *assumed,* as did the argument in that case and in this, that power exists in the State to impose the flag salute discipline upon school children in general. The Court only examined and rejected a claim based on religious beliefs of immunity from an unquestioned general rule. The question which underlies the flag salute controversy is whether such a ceremony so touching matters of opinion and political attitude may be imposed upon the individual by official authority under powers committed to any political organization under our Constitution. We examine rather than assume

existence of this power and, against this broader definition of issues in this case, re-examine specific grounds assigned for the Gobitis decision.

1. It was said that the flag-salute controversy confronted the Court with "the problem which Lincoln cast in memorable dilemma: 'Must a government of necessity be too *strong* for the liberties of its people, or too *weak* to maintain its own existence?' " and that the answer must be in favor of strength. . . . Such oversimplification, so handy in political debate, often lacks the precision necessary to postulates of judicial reasoning. If validly applied to this problem, the utterance cited would resolve every issue of power in favor of those in authority and would require us to override every liberty thought to weaken or delay execution of their policies.

Government of limited power need not be anemic government. Assurance that rights are secure tends to diminish fear and jealousy of strong government, and by making us feel safe to live under it makes for its better support. Without promise of a limiting Bill of Rights it is doubtful if our Constitution could have mustered enough strength to enable its ratification. To enforce those rights today is not to choose weak government over strong government. It is only to adhere as a means of strength to individual freedom of mind in preference to officially disciplined uniformity for which history indicates a disappointing and disastrous end.

The subject now before us exemplifies this principle. Free public education, if faithful to the ideal of secular instruction and political neutrality, will not be partisan or enemy of any class, creed, party, or faction. If it is to impose any ideological discipline, however, each party or denomination must seek to control, or failing that, to weaken the influence of the educational system. Observance of the limitations of the Constitution will not weaken government in the field appropriate for its exercise.

2. It was also considered in the Gobitis case that functions of educational officers in states, counties and school districts were such that to interfere with their authority "would

in effect make us the school board for the country."

The Fourteenth Amendment, as now applied to the States, protects the citizen against the State itself and all of its creatures—Boards of Education not excepted. These have, of course, important, delicate, and highly discretionary functions, but none that they may not perform within the limits of the Bill of Rights. That they are educating the young for citizenship is reason for scrupulous protection of Constitutional freedoms of the individual, if we are not to strangle the free mind at its source and teach youth to discount important principles of our government as mere platitudes.

Such Boards are numerous and their territorial jurisdiction often small. But small and local authority may feel less sense of responsibility to the Constitution, and agencies of publicity may be less vigilant in calling it to account. The action of Congress in making flag observance voluntary and respecting the conscience of the objector in a matter so vital as raising the Army contrasts sharply with these local regulations in matters relatively trivial to the welfare of the nation. There are village tyrants as well as village Hampdens, but none who acts under color of law is beyond reach of the Constitution.

3. The Gobitis opinion reasoned that this is a field "where courts possess no marked and certainly no controlling competence," that it is committed to the legislatures as well as the courts to guard cherished liberties and that it is constitutionally appropriate to "fight out the wise use of legislative authority in the forum of public opinion and before legislative assemblies rather than to transfer such a contest to the judicial arena," since all the "effective means of inducing political changes are left free."

The very purpose of a Bill of Rights was to withdraw certain subjects from the vicissitudes of political controversy, to place them beyond the reach of majorities and officials and to establish them as legal principles to be applied by the courts. One's right to life, liberty, and property, to free speech, a free press, freedom of worship and assembly, and other fundamental rights may not be submitted to vote; they depend on the outcome of no elections.

In weighing arguments of the parties it is important to distinguish between the due process clause of the Fourteenth Amendment as an instrument for transmitting the principles of the First Amendment and those cases in which it is applied for its own sake. The test of legislation which collides with the Fourteenth Amendment, because it also collides with the principles of the First, is much more definite than the test when only the Fourteenth is involved. Much of the vagueness of the due process clause disappears when the specific prohibitions of the First become its standard. The right of a State to regulate, for example, a public utility may well include, so far as the due process test is concerned, power to impose all of the restrictions which a legislature may have a "rational basis" for adopting. But freedoms of speech and of press, of assembly, and of worship may not be infringed on such slender grounds. They are susceptible of restriction only to prevent grave and immediate danger to interests which the state may lawfully protect. It is important to note that while it is the Fourteenth Amendment which bears directly upon the State it is the more specific limiting principles of the First Amendment that finally govern this case.

Nor does our duty to apply the Bill of Rights to assertions of official authority depend upon our possession of marked competence in the field where the invasion of rights occurs. True, the task of translating the majestic generalities of the Bill of Rights, conceived as part of the pattern of liberal government in the eighteenth century, into concrete restraints on officials dealing with the problems of the twentieth century, is one to disturb self-confidence. These principles grew in soil which also produced a philosophy that the individual was the center of society, that his liberty was attainable through mere absence of governmental restraints, and that government should be entrusted with few controls and only the mildest supervision over men's affairs. We must transplant these rights to a soil in which the *laissez-faire* concept or principle of non-interference has withered at least as to economic affairs, and social advancements are increasingly sought through closer integration of society and through expanded and strengthened governmental controls. These changed conditions often deprive precedents of reliability and cast us more than we would choose upon our own judgment. But we act in these matters not by authority of our competence but by force of our commissions. We cannot, because of modest estimates of our competence in such specialties as public education, withhold the judgment that history authenticates as the function of this Court when liberty is infringed.

4. Lastly, and this is the very heart of the Gobitis opinion, it reasons that "National unity is the basis of national security," that the authorities have "the right to select appropriate means for its attainment," and hence reaches the conclusion that such compulsory measures toward "national unity" are constitutional. Upon the verity of this assumption depends our answer in this case.

National unity as an end which officials may foster by persuasion and example is not in question. The problem is whether under our Constitution compulsion as here employed is a permissible means for its achievement.

Struggles to coerce uniformity of sentiment in support of some end thought essential to their time and country have been waged by many good as well as by evil men. Nationalism is a relatively recent phenomenon but at other times and places the ends have been racial or territorial security, support of a dynasty or regime, and particular plans for saving souls. As first and moderate methods to attain unity have failed, those bent on its accomplishment must resort to an ever-increasing severity. As governmental pressure toward unity becomes greater, so strife becomes more bitter as to whose unity it shall be. Probably no deeper division of our people could proceed from any provocation than from finding it necessary to choose what doctrine and whose program public educational officials shall compel youth to unite in embracing. Ultimate futility of such attempts to compel coherence is the lesson of every such effort from the Roman drive to stamp out Christianity as a disturber of its pagan unity, the Inquisition,

as a means to religious and dynastic unity, the Siberian exiles as a means to Russian unity, down to the fast failing efforts of our present totalitarian enemies. Those who begin coercive elimination of dissent soon find themselves exterminating dissenters. Compulsory unification of opinion achieves only the unanimity of the graveyard.

It seems trite but necessary to say that the First Amendment to our Constitution was designed to avoid these ends by avoiding these beginnings. There is no mysticism in the American concept of the State or of the nature or origin of its authority. We set up government by consent of the governed, and the Bill of Rights denies those in power any legal opportunity to coerce that consent. Authority here is to be controlled by public opinion, not public opinion by authority.

The case is made difficult not because the principles of its decision are obscure but because the flag involved is our own. Nevertheless, we apply the limitations of the Constitution with no fear that freedom to be intellectually and spiritually diverse or even contrary will disintegrate the social organization. To believe that patriotism will not flourish if patriotic ceremonies are voluntary and spontaneous instead of a compulsory routine is to make an unflattering estimate of the appeal of our institutions to free minds. We can have intellectual individualism and the rich cultural diversities that we owe to exceptional minds only at the price of occasional eccentricity and abnormal attitudes. When they are so harmless to others or to the State as those we deal with here, the price is not too great. But freedom to differ is not limited to things that do not matter much. That would be a mere shadow of freedom. The test of its substance is the right to differ as to things that touch the heart of the existing order.

If here is any fixed star in our constitutional constellation, it is that no official, high or petty, can prescribe what shall be orthodox in politics, nationalism, religion, or other matters of opinion or force citizens to confess by word or act their faith therein. If there are any circumstances which permit an exception, they do not now occur to us.

We think the action of the local authorities in compelling the flag salute and pledge transcends constitutional limitations on their power and invades the sphere of intellect and spirit which it is the purpose of the First Amendment to our Constitution to reserve from all official control.

The decision of this Court in Minersville School District v. Gobitis and the holdings of those few per curiam decisions which preceded and foreshadowed it are overruled, and the judgment enjoining enforcement of the West Virginia Regulation is affirmed.

JJ. Frankfurter. Roberts. Reed. dissenting.

534. THE ACT OF HAVANA
Agreements Reached at the Havana Pan-American Conference
July 29, 1940
(*New York Times,* July 30, 1940)

The imminent threat of German or Italian occupation or control of French, English or Dutch possessions in the New World and the even more menacing threat of Nazi control of Latin American trade through barter agreements and political and military pressure, led to a notable conference of the American states in July, 1940. Secretary Hull quickly assumed leadership of this conference, and despite the opposition of the delegation from the Argentine succeeded in achieving substantially his objectives.

The text of the convention covering the legal phase of the plan to be acted upon regarding foreign possessions in the New World follows:

The governments represented in the second consultative meeting of American Foreign Ministers considering:

That, as a consequence of the acts which are developing on the European Continent, there might be produced in territories of possessions which some belligerent nations hold in America situations wherein that sovereignty may be extinguished or essentially affected, or the government suffers acephalism (becomes headless), generating peril for the peace of the Continent and creating a situation wherein the dominion of law and order and respect of life, liberty and property of the inhabitants disappears;

That the American republics would consider any transfer or attempt to transfer sovereignty, jurisdiction, possession or any interest or control in any of these regions to another non-American State as contrary to American sentiments, principles and rights of American States to maintain their security and political independence;

That the American republics would not recognize nor accept such transfer or intent to transfer or acquire interests or rights, direct or indirect, in any of these regions, whatever might be the form employed to realize it;

That the American republics reserve the right to judge through their respective organs of government if some transfer or intent to transfer sovereignty, jurisdiction, cession or incorporation of geographical regions in America owned by European countries until Sept. 1, 1939, may impair their political independence even though there has been no formal transfer or change in the status of the regions;

That for this reason it is necessary to establish for unforeseen cases as for any other which may produce acephalism of the government in the said regions a regime of provisional administration, while arriving at the objective for free determination of the peoples;

That the American republics, as an international community which acts integrally and forcefully, supporting itself on political and juridical principles which have been applied for more than a century, have the incontestable right, in order to preserve their unity and security, to take under their administration said regions and to deliberate over their destinies in accordance with their respective degrees of political and economic development;

That the provisional and transitory character of the measures agreed upon does not mean forgetfulness or abrogation of the principle of non-intervention, the regulator of inter-American life, a principle proclaimed by the American Institute, recognized by the celebrated committee of experts on international law which met at Rio de Janeiro and consecrated in all its amplitude in the seventh Pan-American conference held at Montevideo;

That this community, therefore, has the international juridical capacity to act in such matters;

That in such a case the most adequate regime is that of provisional administration.

Desiring to protect their peace and security and to promote the interests of any of the regions to which this (document) refers and which are understood to be within the foregoing consideration;

Have resolved to conclude the following convention:

First—If a non-American State attempts directly or indirectly to substitute for another non-American State in the sovereignty or control which that (other State) exerted over any territory situated in America, thereby threatening the peace of the continent, said territory automatically will be considered to be within the stipulations of this convention, and will be submitted to a regime of provisional administration.

Second—That administration shall be executed—as it is considered advisable in each case—by one or more American States by virtue of previous consent.

Third—When administration is established over a region it shall be executed in the interest of the security of America and to the benefit of the administered region looking toward its well-being and development, until the region is found to be in condition to administer itself or to return to its former status, so long as this is compatible with the security of the American republics.

Fourth—Administration of the territory shall operate under conditions which guarantee freedom of conscience and faith with the restrictions demanded by the maintenance of public order and good habits.

Fifth—The administration shall apply local laws, coordinating them with the objectives of this convention, but it may adopt in addition those decisions necessary to solve situations concerning which no such local laws exist.

Sixth—In all that concerns commerce and industry the American nations shall enjoy equal conditions and the same benefits, and the administrator never shall create a situation of privilege for himself or his compatriots or for any particular nations. Liberty of economic relations with all countries on a basis of reciprocity shall be maintained.

Seventh—The natives of the region shall participate as citizens in the public administration and tribunals of justice, with no other consideration than that of competence.

Eighth—In so far as possible rights of any kind shall be governed by local laws and customs, acquired to be protected in conformity with such laws.

Ninth—Forced labor shall be abolished in regions where it exists.

Tenth—The administration will provide means to diffuse public education in all grades, with the double aim of promoting the wealth of the region and better living conditions of the people, especially in regard to public and individual hygiene, and preparation of the exercise of political autonomy in the shortest time.

Eleventh—The natives of the region under administration shall have their own organic charter, which the administration shall establish, consulting the people in whatever way possible.

Twelfth—The administration shall submit an annual report to the inter-American organization charged with control of the administered regions, on the manner in which it carried out its mission, attaching accounts and measures adopted during the year in said region.

Thirteenth—The organization to which the preceding article refers shall be authorized to take cognizance of petitions which inhabitants of the region transmit through the intermediary of the administration with reference to the operation of the provisional administration. The administration shall remit, along with these petitions, such observations as it considers convenient.

Fourteenth—First the administration shall be authorized for a period of three years, at the termination of which, and in case of necessity, it shall be renewed for successive periods of not longer than a decade.

Fifteenth—Expenses incurred in the exercise of the administration shall be covered by revenues from the administered region, but in case these are insufficient the deficit shall be covered by the administering nation or nations.

Sixteenth—There shall be established a commission which shall be called the "Inter-American Commission of Territorial Administration" and shall be composed of one representative for each of the States which ratify this convention, and it shall be the international organization to which the convention refers.

Any country which ratifies it (the convention) may call the first meeting, indicating the most convenient city. The commission shall elect a president, complete its organization and fix a definite headquarters. Two-thirds of its members shall constitute a quorum and two-thirds of the members present may adopt agreements.

Seventeenth—The commission is authorized to establish a provisional administration over regions to which the present convention applies; it also is authorized to install the said administration so that it will be operated by the number of States which will be determined according to the case, and to legalize its execution in terms of the preceding articles.

Eighteenth—The present convention will be opened for signatures of the American republics in Havana and shall be ratified by the high contracting parties in accordance with their constitutional procedures. The Secretary of State of the Republic of Cuba shall transmit, as soon as possible, authentic copies certified to the various governments to obtain ratifications. Instruments of ratification shall be deposited in the archives of the Pan-American Union in Washington, which shall notify the signatory governments of said deposit; such notification shall be considered as exchange of ratifications.

Nineteenth—The present convention shall be effective when two-thirds of the American States shall have deposited their respective instruments of ratification.

535. HEMISPHERIC DEFENSE
August 18, 1940

(*Department of State Bulletin,* Aug. 24, 1940)

August 17 President Roosevelt and Prime Minister Mackenzie King of Canada met at Ogdensburg, New York, to discuss mutual Canadian-American problems of defense. The next day they issued the following joint statement:

The Prime Minister and the President have discussed the mutual problems of defense in relation to the safety of Canada and the United States.

It has been agreed that a Permanent Joint Board on Defense shall be set up at once by the two countries.

This Permanent Joint Board on Defense shall commence immediate studies relating to sea, land and air problems including personnel and matériel.

It will consider in the broad sense the defense of the north half of the Western Hemisphere.

The Permanent Joint Board on Defense will consist of four or five members from each country, most of them from the services. It will meet shortly.

536. EXCHANGE OF DESTROYERS FOR AIR AND NAVAL BASES
September 2, 1940

(*Department of State Bulletin,* Sept. 7, 1940, pp. 199–200)

In his Charlottesville speech the President had promised to "extend to the opponents of force the material resources of this nation." The urgent need of Britain for additional destroyers to protect her far-flung sea-lanes, and the equally urgent need of the United States for additional air and naval bases, suggested the desirability of an exchange. That exchange, consummated by the interchange of notes between the Marquess of Lothian and Secretary of State Hull, was characterized by the President as "the most important action in the reinforcement of our national defense that has been taken since the Louisiana Purchase."

Washington, September 2, 1940

SIR:

I have the honor under instructions from His Majesty's Principal Secretary of State for Foreign Affairs to inform you that in view of the friendly and sympathetic interests of His Majesty's Government in the United Kingdom in the national security of the United States and their desire to strengthen the ability of the United States to cooperate effectively with the other nations of the Americas in the defense of the Western Hemisphere, His Majesty's Government will secure the grant to the Government of the United States, freely and without consideration, of the lease for immediate establishment and use of naval and air bases and facilities for entrance thereto and the operation and protection thereof, on the Avalon Peninsula and on the southern coast of Newfoundland, and on the east coast and on the Great Bay of Bermuda.

Furthermore, in view of the above and in view of the desire of the United States to acquire additional air and naval bases in the Caribbean and in British Guiana, and with endeavoring to place a monetary or commercial value upon the many tangible and intangible rights and properties involved, His Majesty's Government will make available to the United States for immediate establishment and use naval and air bases and facilities for entrance thereto and the operation and protection thereof, on the eastern side of the Bahamas, the southern coast of Jamaica, the western coast of St. Lucia, the west coast of Trinidad in the Gulf of Paria, in the island of Antigua and in British Guiana within fifty miles of Georgetown, in exchange for naval and military equipment and material which the United States Government will transfer to His Majesty's Government.

All the bases and facilities referred to in the preceding paragraphs will be leased to the United States for a period of ninety-nine years, free from all rent and charges other than such compensation to be mutually agreed on to be paid by the United States in order to compensate the owners of private property for loss by expropriation or damage arising out of the establishment of the bases and facilities in question.

His Majesty's Government, in the leases to be agreed upon, will grant to the United States for the period of the leases all the rights, power and authority within the bases leased, and within the limits of the territorial waters and air spaces adjacent to or in the vicinity of such bases, necessary to provide access to and defense of such bases, and appropriate provisions for their control.

Without prejudice to the above-mentioned rights of the United States authorities and their jurisdiction within the leased areas, the adjustment and reconciliation between the jurisdiction of the authorities of the United States within these areas and the jurisdiction of the authorities of the territories in which these areas are situated, shall be determined by common agreement.

The exact location and bounds of the aforesaid bases, the necessary seaward, coast and anti-aircraft defenses, the location of sufficient military garrisons, stores and other necessary auxiliary facilities shall be determined by common agreement.

His Majesty's Government are prepared to designate immediately experts to meet with experts of the United States for these purposes. Should these experts be unable to agree in any particular situation, except in the case of Newfoundland and Bermuda, the matter shall be settled by the Secretary of State of the United States and His Majesty's Secretary of State for Foreign Affairs.

I have the honor to be, with the highest consideration, sir,

Your most obedient, humble servant.

LOTHIAN.

DEPARTMENT OF STATE
Washington, September 2, 1940

EXCELLENCY:

I have received your note of September 2, 1940 . . .

I am directed by the President to reply to your note as follows:

The Government of the United States appreciates the declarations and the generous action of His Majesty's Government as contained in your communication which are destined to enhance the national security of the United States and greatly to strengthen its ability to cooperate effectively with the other nations of the Americas in the defense of the Western Hemisphere. It therefore gladly accepts the proposals.

The Government of the United States will immediately designate experts to meet with experts designated by His Majesty's Government to determine upon the exact location of the naval and air bases mentioned in your communication under acknowledgment.

In consideration of the declarations above quoted, the Government of the United States will immediately transfer to His Majesty's Government fifty United States Navy destroyers generally referred to as the twelve hundred-ton type. . . .

CORDELL HULL.

537. F. D. ROOSEVELT'S "FOUR FREEDOMS" SPEECH
January 6, 1941

(The Public Papers of F. D. Roosevelt, Vol. 9, p. 663)

The "Four Freedoms," formulated in the President's annual message to the Congress, came to be accepted as the most succinct statement of the things for which the American people were prepared to fight.

TO THE CONGRESS OF THE UNITED STATES:

I address you, the Members of the Seventy-Seventh Congress, at a moment unprecedented in the history of the Union. I use the word "unprecedented," because at no previous time has American security been as seriously threatened from without as it is today. . . .

It is true that prior to 1914 the United States often had been disturbed by events in other Continents. We had even engaged in two wars with European nations and in a number of undeclared wars in the West Indies, in the Mediterranean and in the Pacific for the maintenance of American rights and for the principles of peaceful commerce. In no case, however, had a serious threat been raised against our national safety or our independence.

What I seek to convey is the historic truth that the United States as a nation has at all times maintained opposition to any attempt to lock us in behind an ancient Chinese wall while the procession of civilization went past. Today, thinking of our children and their children, we oppose enforced isolation for ourselves or for any part of the Americas.

Even when the World War broke out in 1914, it seemed to contain only small threat of danger to our own American future. But, as time went on, the American people began to visualize what the downfall of democratic nations might mean to our own democracy.

We need not over-emphasize imperfections in the Peace of Versailles. We need not harp on failure of the democracies to deal with problems of world deconstruction. We should remember that the Peace of 1919 was far less unjust than the kind of "pacification" which began even before Munich, and which is being carried on under the new order of tyranny that seeks to spread over every continent today. The American people have unalterably set their faces against that tyranny.

Every realist knows that the democratic way of life is at this moment being directly assailed in every part of the world—assailed either by arms, or by secret spreading of poisonous propaganda by those who seek to destroy unity and promote discord in nations still at peace. During sixteen months this assault has blotted out the whole pattern of democratic life in an appalling number of independent nations, great and small. The assailants are still on the march, threatening other nations, great and small.

Therefore, as your President, performing my constitutional duty to "give to the Congress information of the state of the Union,"

I find it necessary to report that the future and the safety of our country and of our democracy are overwhelmingly involved in events far beyond our borders.

Armed defense of democratic existence is now being gallantly waged in four continents. If that defense fails, all the population and all the resources of Europe, Asia, Africa and Australasia will be dominated by the conquerors. The total of those populations and their resources greatly exceeds the sum total of the population and resources of the whole of the Western Hemisphere—many times over.

In times like these it is immature—and incidentally untrue—for anybody to brag that an unprepared America, single-handed, and with one hand tied behind its back, can hold off the whole world.

No realistic American can expect from a dictator's peace international generosity, or return of true independence, or world disarmament, or freedom of expression, or freedom of religion—or even good business. Such a peace would bring no security for us or for our neighbors. "Those, who would give up essential liberty to purchase a little temporary safety, deserve neither liberty nor safety." As a nation we may take pride in the fact that we are soft-hearted; but we cannot afford to be soft-hearted. We must always be wary of those who with sounding brass and a tinkling cymbal preach the "ism" of appeasement. We must especially beware of that small group of selfish men who would clip the wings of the American eagle in order to feather their own nests.

I have recently pointed out how quickly the tempo of modern warfare could bring into our very midst the physical attack which we must expect if the dictator nations win this war.

There is much loose talk of our immunity from immediate and direct invasion from across the seas. Obviously, as long as the British Navy retains its power, no such danger exists. Even if there were no British Navy, it is not probable that any enemy would be stupid enough to attack us by landing troops in the United States from across thousands of miles of ocean, until it had acquired strategic bases from which to operate. But we learn much from the lessons of the past years in Europe—particularly the lesson of Norway, whose essential seaports were captured by treachery and surprise built up over a series of years. The first phase of the invasion of this Hemisphere would not be the landing of regular troops. The necessary strategic points would be occupied by secret agents and their dupes—and great numbers of them are already here, and in Latin America.

As long as the aggressor nations maintain the offensive, they—not we—will choose the time and the place and the method of their attack. That is why the future of all American Republics is today in serious danger. That is why this Annual Message to the Congress is unique in our history. That is why every member of the Executive branch of the government and every member of the Congress face great responsibility—and great accountability.

The need of the moment is that our actions and our policy should be devoted primarily—almost exclusively—to meeting this foreign peril. For all our domestic problems are now a part of the great emergency. Just as our national policy in internal affairs has been based upon a decent respect for the rights and dignity of all our fellowmen within our gates, so our national policy in foreign affairs has been based on a decent respect for the rights and dignity of all nations, large and small. And the justice of morality must and will win in the end.

Our national policy is this.

First, by an impressive expression of the public will and without regard to partisanship, we are committed to all-inclusive national defense.

Second, by an impressive expression of the public will and without regard to partisanship, we are committed to full support of all those resolute peoples, everywhere, who are resisting aggression and are thereby keeping war away from our Hemisphere. By this support, we express our determination that the democratic cause shall prevail; and we strengthen the defense and security of our own nation.

Third, by an impressive expression of the public will and without regard to partisanship we are committed to the proposition that principles of morality and considerations for our own security will never permit us to acquiesce in a peace dictated by aggressors and sponsored by appeasers. We know that enduring peace cannot be bought at the cost of other people's freedom.

In the recent national election there was no substantial difference between the two great parties in respect to that national policy. No issue was fought out on this line before the American electorate. Today, it is abundantly evident that American citizens everywhere are demanding and supporting speedy and complete action in recognition of obvious danger. Therefore, the immediate need is a swift and driving increase in our armament production. . . .

Our most useful and immediate role is to act as an arsenal for them as well as for ourselves. They do not need man power. They do need billions of dollars worth of the weapons of defense. . . .

Let us say to the democracies: "We Americans are vitally concerned in your defense of freedom. We are putting forth our energies, our resources and our organizing powers to give you the strength to regain and maintain a free world. We shall send you, in ever-increasing numbers, ships, planes, tanks, guns. This is our purpose and our pledge." In fulfillment of this purpose we will not be intimidated by the threats of dictators that they will regard as a breach of international law and as an act of war our aid to the democracies which dare to resist their aggression. Such aid is not an act of war, even if a dictator should unilaterally proclaim it so to be. When the dictators are ready to make war upon us, they will not wait for an act of war on our part. They did not wait for Norway or Belgium or the Netherlands to commit an act of war. Their only interest is in a new one-way international law, which lacks mutuality in its observance, and, therefore, becomes an instrument of oppression.

The happiness of future generations of Americans may well depend upon how effective and how immediate we can make our aid felt. No one can tell the exact character of the emergency situations that we may be called upon to meet. The Nation's hands must not be tied when the Nation's life is in danger. We must all prepare to make the sacrifices that the emergency—as serious as war itself—demands. Whatever stands in the way of speed and efficiency in defense preparations must give way to the national need.

A free nation has the right to expect full cooperation from all groups. A free nation has the right to look to the leaders of business, of labor, and of agriculture to take the lead in stimulating effort, not among other groups but within their own groups. The best way of dealing with the few slackers or trouble makers in our midst is, first, to shame them by patriotic example, and, if that fails, to use the sovereignty of government to save government.

As men do not live by bread alone, they do not fight by armaments alone. Those who man our defenses, and those behind them who build our defenses, must have the stamina and courage which come from an unshakable belief in the manner of life which they are defending. The mighty action which we are calling for cannot be based on a disregard of all things worth fighting for.

The Nation takes great satisfaction and much strength from the things which have been done to make its people conscious of their individual stake in the preservation of democratic life in America. Those things have toughened the fibre of our people, have renewed their faith and strengthened their devotion to the institutions we make ready to protect. Certainly this is no time to stop thinking about the social and economic problems which are the root cause of the social revolution which is today a supreme factor in the world.

There is nothing mysterious about the foundations of a healthy and strong democracy. The basic things expected by our people of their political and economic systems are simple. They are: equality of opportunity for youth and for others; jobs for those who can work; security for those who need it; the ending of special privilege for the few; the preservation of civil liberties for all; the enjoyment of the fruits of scientific progress in a wider and constantly rising standard of living.

These are the simple and basic things that must never he lost sight of in the turmoil and unbelievable complexity of our modern world. The inner and abiding strength of our economic and political systems is dependent upon the degree to which they fulfill these expectations.

Many subjects connected with our social economy call for immediate improvement. As examples: We should bring more citizens under the coverage of old age pensions and unemployment insurance. We should widen the opportunities for adequate medical care. We should plan a better system by which persons deserving or needing gainful employment may obtain it.

I have called for personal sacrifice. I am assured of the willingness of almost all Americans to respond to that call. . . .

In the future days, which we seek to make secure, we look forward to a world founded upon four essential human freedoms.

The first is freedom of speech and expression—everywhere in the world.

The second is freedom of every person to worship God in his own way—everywhere in the world.

The third is freedom from want—which, translated into world terms, means economic understandings which will secure to every nation a healthy peace time life for its inhabitants—everywhere in the world.

The fourth is freedom from fear—which, translated into world terms, means a worldwide reduction of armaments to such a point and in such a thorough fashion that no nation will be in a position to commit an act of physical aggression against any neighbor—anywhere in the world.

That is no vision of a distant millenium. It is a definite basis for a kind of world attainable in our own time and generation. That kind of world is the very antithesis of the so-called new order of tyranny which the dictators seek to create with the crash of a bomb.

To that new order we oppose the greater conception—the moral order. A good society is able to face schemes of world domination and foreign revolutions alike without fear.

Since the beginning of our American history we have been engaged in change—in a perpetual peaceful revolution—a revolution which goes on steadily, quietly adjusting itself to changing conditions—without the concentration camp or the quick-lime in the ditch. The world order which we seek is the cooperation of free countries, working together in a friendly, civilized society.

This nation has placed its destiny in the hands and heads and hearts of its millions of free men and women; and its faith in freedom under the guidance of God. Freedom means the supremacy of human rights everywhere. Our support goes to those who struggle to gain those rights or keep them. Our strength is in our unity of purpose.

To that high concept there can be no end save victory.

538. THE LEND LEASE ACT
March 11, 1941
(*U. S. Statutes at Large,* Vol. LV, p. 31)

Early in January the President submitted to Congress a program designed to enable the United States to aid the Allies notwithstanding the limitations of the Neutrality legislation. The proposal precipitated long and bitter debate but was eventually accepted by both Houses by substantial majorities.

Be it enacted That this Act may be cited as "An Act to Promote the Defense of the United States."

Section 3.

(a) Notwithstanding the provisions of any other law, the President may, from time to time, when he deems it in the interest of national defense, authorize the Secretary of War, the Secretary of the Navy, or the head of any other department or agency of the Government—

(1) To manufacture in arsenals, factories, and shipyards under their jurisdiction, or otherwise procure, to the extent to which funds are made available therefor, or contracts are authorized from time to time by

the Congress, or both, any defense article for the government of any country whose defense the President deems vital to the defense of the United States.

(2) To sell, transfer title to, exchange, lease, lend, or otherwise dispose of, to any such government any defense article, but no defense article not manufactured or procured under paragraph (1) shall in any way be disposed of under this paragraph, except after consultation with the Chief of Staff of the Army or the Chief of Naval Operations of the Navy, or both. The value of defense articles disposed of in any way under authority of this paragraph, and procured from funds heretofore appropriated, shall not exceed $1,300,000,000. The value of such defense articles shall be determined by the head of the department or agency concerned or such other department, agency or officer as shall be designated in the manner provided in the rules and regulations issued hereunder. Defense articles procured from funds hereafter appropriated to any department or agency of the Government, other than from funds authorized to be appropriated under this Act, shall not be disposed of in any way under authority of this paragraph except to the extent hereafter authorized by the Congress in the Acts appropriating such funds or otherwise.

(3) To test, inspect, prove, repair, outfit, recondition, or otherwise to place in good working order, to the extent to which funds are made available therefor, or contracts are authorized from time to time by the Congress, or both, any defense article for any such government, or to procure any or all such services by private contract.

(4) To communicate to any such government any defense information, pertaining to any defense article furnished to such government under paragraph (2) of this subsection.

(5) To release for export any defense article disposed of in any way under this subsection to any such government,

(b) The terms and conditions upon which any such foreign government receives any aid authorized under subsection (a) shall be those which the President deems satisfactory,

and the benefit to the United States may be payment or repayment in kind or property, or any other direct or indirect benefit which the President deems satisfactory.

(c) After June 30, 1943, or after the passage of a concurrent resolution by the two Houses before June 30, 1943, which declares that the powers conferred by or pursuant to subsection (a) are no longer necessary to promote the defense of the United States, neither the President nor the head of any department or agency shall exercise any of the powers conferred by or pursuant to subsection (a); except that until July 1, 1946, any of such powers may be exercised to the extent necessary to carry out a contract or agreement with such a foreign government made before July 1, 1943, or before the passage of such concurrent resolution, whichever is the earlier.

(d) Nothing in this Act shall be construed to authorize or to permit the authorization of convoying vessels by naval vessels of the United States.

(e) Nothing in this Act shall be construed to authorize or to permit the authorization of the entry of any American vessel into a combat area in violation of section 3 of the Neutrality Act of 1939.

Section 8

The Secretaries of War and of the Navy are hereby authorized to purchase or otherwise acquire arms, ammunition, and implements of war produced within the jurisdiction of any country to which section 3 is applicable, whenever the President deems such purchase or acquisition to be necessary in the interests of the defense of the United States.

Section 9

The President may, from time to time, promulgate such rules and regulations as may be necessary and proper to carry out any of the provisions of this Act; and he may exercise any power or authority conferred on him by this Act through such department, agency, or officer as he shall direct,

539. THE ATLANTIC CHARTER
August 14, 1941
(The Public Papers of F. D. Roosevelt, Vol. 10, p. 314)

In a dramatic meeting off Newfoundland, President Roosevelt and Winston Churchill formulated this statement of common war aims.

The President of the United States of America and the Prime Minister, Mr. Churchill, representing His Majesty's Government in the United Kingdom, being met together, deem it right to make known certain common principles in the national policies of their respective countries on which they base their hopes for a better future for the world.

First, their countries seek no aggrandizement, territorial or other;

Second, they desire to see no territorial changes that do not accord with the freely expressed wishes of the peoples concerned;

Third, they respect the right of all peoples to choose the form of government under which they will live; and they wish to see sovereign rights and self government restored to those who have been forcibly deprived of them;

Fourth, they will endeavor, with due respect for their existing obligations, to further the enjoyment by all States, great or small, victor or vanquished, of access, on equal terms, to the trade and to the raw materials of the world which are needed for their economic prosperity;

Fifth, they desire to bring about the fullest collaboration between all nations in the economic field with the object of securing, for all, improved labor standards, economic advancement and social security;

Sixth, after the final destruction of the Nazi tyranny, they hope to see established a peace which will afford to all nations the means of dwelling in safety within their own boundaries, and which will afford assurance that all the men in all the lands may live out their lives in freedom from fear and want;

Seventh, such a peace should enable all men to traverse the high seas and oceans without hindrance;

Eighth, they believe that all of the nations of the world, for realistic as well as spiritual reasons must come to the abandonment of the use of force. Since no future peace can be maintained if land, sea or air armaments continue to be employed by nations which threaten, or may threaten, aggression outside of their frontiers, they believe, pending the establishment of a wider and permanent system of general security, that the disarmament of such nations is essential. They will likewise aid and encourage all other practicable measures which will lighten for peace-loving peoples the crushing burden of armaments.

FRANKLIN D. ROOSEVELT
WINSTON S. CHURCHILL

540. PRESIDENT ROOSEVELT'S MESSAGE ASKING FOR WAR AGAINST JAPAN
December 8, 1941
(The Public Papers of F. D. Roosevelt, Vol. 10, p. 514)

The day after the attack on Pearl Harbor, President Roosevelt appeared before Congress and asked for a declaration of war against Japan. Congress responded that same afternoon, without a dissenting vote. H. Feis, *The Road to Pearl Harbor.*

Yesterday, December 7, 1941—a date which will live in infamy—the United States of America was suddenly and deliberately attacked by naval and air forces of the Empire of Japan.

The United States was at peace with that nation and, at the solicitation of Japan, was still in conversation with its Government and its Emperor looking toward the maintenance of peace in the Pacific. Indeed, one hour after Japanese air squadrons had commenced bombing in Oahu, the Japanese Ambassador to the United States and his colleague delivered to the Secretary of State a formal reply to a recent American message. While this reply stated that it seemed useless to continue the existing diplomatic negotiations, it contained no threat or hint of war or armed attack.

It will be recorded that the distance of Hawaii from Japan makes it obvious that the attack was deliberately planned many days or even weeks ago. During the intervening time the Japanese Government has deliberately sought to deceive the United States by false statements and expressions of hope for continued peace.

The attack yesterday on the Hawaiian Islands has caused severe damage to American naval and military forces. Very many American lives have been lost. In addition American ships have been reported torpedoed on the high seas between San Francisco and Honolulu.

Yesterday the Japanese Government also launched an attack against Malaya. Last night Japanese forces attacked Hong Kong. Last night Japanese forces attacked Guam. Last night Japanese forces attacked the Philippine Islands. Last night the Japanese attacked Wake Island. This morning the Japanese attacked Midway Island.

Japan has, therefore, undertaken a surprise offensive extending throughout the Pacific area. The facts of yesterday speak for themselves. The people of the United States have already formed their opinions and well understand the implications to the very life and safety of our nation.

As Commander-in-Chief of the Army and Navy, I have directed that all measures be taken for our defense.

Always will we remember the character of the onslaught against us.

No matter how long it may take us to overcome this premeditated invasion, the American people in their righteous might will win through to absolute victory.

I believe I interpret the will of the Congress and of the people when I assert that we will not only defend ourselves to the uttermost but will make very certain that this form of treachery shall never endanger us again.

Hostilities exist. There is no blinking at the fact that our people, our territory and our interests are in grave danger.

With confidence in our armed forces— with the unbonded determination of our people—we will gain the inevitable triumph —so help us God.

I ask that the Congress declare that since the unprovoked and dastardly attack by Japan on Sunday, December seventh, a state of war has existed between the United States and the Japanese Empire.

541. DECLARATION OF WAR ON GERMANY
December 11, 1941

(The Public Papers of F. D. Roosevelt, Vol. 10, p. 532)

See H. S. Quigley, *Far Eastern War;* Davis and Lindley, *How War Came;* T. A. Bisson et al, "The United States at War," *For Policy Repts.,* Vol. XVII, 246 ff.; W. P. Maddox, ed., "America and Japan," *An. Am. Ac. Pol. Soc. Sci.* Vol. 238; W. Langer and S. Gleason, *The Undeclared War;* W. Lord, *Day of Infamy.*

THE PRESIDENT'S MESSAGE

To the Congress of the United States:

On the morning of Dec. 11 the Government of Germany, pursuing its course of world conquest. declared war against the United States.

The long-known and the long-expected has thus taken place. The forces endeavoring to enslave the entire world now are moving toward this hemisphere.

Never before has there been a greater challenge to life, liberty and civilization.

Delay invites great danger. Rapid and united effort by all of the peoples of the world who are determined to remain free will insure a world victory of the forces of justice and of righteousness over the forces of savagery and of barbarism.

Italy also has declared war against the United States.

I therefore request the Congress to recognize a state of war between the United States and Germany, and between the United States and Italy.

FRANKLIN D. ROOSEVELT.

THE WAR RESOLUTION

Declaring that a state of war exists between the Government of Germany and the government and the people of the United States and making provision to prosecute the same.

Whereas the Government of Germany has formally declared war against the government and the people of the United States of America:

Therefore, be it

Resolved by the Senate and House of Representatives of the United States of America in Congress assembled, that the state of war between the United States and the Government of Germany which has thus been thrust upon the United States is hereby formally declared; and the President is hereby authorized and directed to employ the entire naval and military forces of the United States and the resources of the government to carry on war against the Government of Germany; and, to bring the conflict to a successful termination, all of the resources of the country are hereby pledged by the Congress of the United States.

542. UNITED STATES v. DARBY LUMBER CO.
312 U. S. 100
1941

The F. W. Darby Lumber Company and Fred W. Darby were indicted for violating Section 15 of the Fair Labor Standards Act. The principal questions in the case were whether Congress has the power to prohibit shipment in interstate Commerce of products made by employees whose wages were lower or whose hours were longer than Congress prescribed, and, secondly, whether Congress may prohibit employment of workers producing goods for interstate commerce, if their working conditions do not meet a standard determined by Congress. The case is particularly important in that the Court in a unanimous decision specifically overruled *Hammer v. Dagenhart,* which had declared government regulation of transportation of products of child labor unconstitutional. See Doc. No. 413.

Appeal from the District Court of the United States for the Southern District of Georgia.

STONE, J. The two principal questions raised by the record in this case are, first, whether Congress has constitutional power to prohibit the shipment in interstate commerce of lumber manufactured by employees whose wages are less than a prescribed minimum or whose weekly hours of labor at that wage are

greater than a prescribed maximum, and, second, whether it has power to prohibit the employment of workmen in the production of goods "for interstate commerce" at other than prescribed wages and hours. . . .

The Fair Labor Standards Act set up a comprehensive legislative scheme for preventing the shipment in interstate commerce of certain products and commodities produced in the United States under labor conditions as respects wages and hours which fail to conform to standards set up by the Act. Its purpose is to exclude from interstate commerce goods produced for the commerce and to prevent their production for interstate commerce, under conditions detrimental to the maintenance of the minimum standards of living necessary for health and general well-being; and to prevent the use of interstate commerce as the means of competition in the distribution of goods so produced, and as the means of spreading and perpetuating such substandard labor conditions among the workers of the several states. . . .

The prohibition of shipment of the proscribed goods in interstate commerce. Section 15 (a) (1) prohibits, and the indictment charges, the shipment in interstate commerce, of goods produced for interstate commerce by employees whose wages and hours of employment do not conform to the requirements of the Act. Since this section is not violated unless the commodity shipped has been produced under labor conditions prohibited by § 6 and § 7, the only question arising under the commerce clause with respect to such shipments is whether Congress has the constitutional power to prohibit them.

While manufacture is not of itself interstate commerce the shipment of manufactured goods interstate is such commerce and the prohibition of such shipment by Congress is undubitably a regulation of the commerce. The power to regulate commerce is the power "to prescribe the rule by which commerce is to be governed." Gibbons v. Ogden, 9 Wheat. 1, 196. It extends not only to those regulations which aid, foster and protect the commerce, but embraces those which prohibit it. It is conceded that the power of Congress to prohibit transportation in interstate commerce includes noxious articles, and articles such as intoxicating liquor or convict made goods, traffic in which is forbidden or restricted by the laws of the state of destination.

But it is said that the present prohibition falls within the scope of none of these categories; that while the prohibition is nominally a regulation of the commerce its motive or purpose is regulation of wages and hours of persons engaged in manufacture, the control of which has been reserved to the states and upon which Georgia and some of the states of destination have placed no restrictions; that the effect of the present statute is not to exclude the prescribed articles from interstate commerce in aid of state regulation as in Kentucky Whip & Collar Co. v. Illinois Central R. Co., but instead, under the guise of a regulation of interstate commerce, it undertakes to regulate wages and hours within the state contrary to the policy of the state which has elected to leave them unregulated.

The power of Congress over interstate commerce "is complete in itself, may be exercised to its utmost extent, and acknowledges no limitations, other than are prescribed by the constitution." That power can neither be enlarged nor diminished by the exercise or non-exercise of state power. Congress, following its own conception of public policy concerning the restrictions which may appropriately be imposed on interstate commerce, is free to exclude from the commerce articles whose use in the states for which they are destined it may conceive to be injurious to the public health, morals or welfare, even though the state has not sought to regulate their use.

Such regulation is not a forbidden invasion of state power merely because either its motive or its consequence is to restrict the use of articles of commerce within the states of destination and is not prohibited unless by other Constitutional provisions. It is no objection to the assertion of the power to regulate interstate commerce that its exercise is attended by the same incidents which attend the exercise of the police power of the states.

The motive and purpose of the present regulation is plainly to make effective the Congressional conception of public policy that interstate commerce should not be made the instrument of competition in the distribution of goods produced under substandard labor conditions, which competition is injurious to the commerce and to the states from and to which the commerce flows. The motive and purpose of a regulation of interstate commerce are matters for the legislative judgment upon the exercise of which the Constitution places no restriction and over which the courts are given no control. "The judicial cannot prescribe to the legislative departments of the government limitations upon the exercise of its acknowledged power." Veazie Bank v. Fenno, 8 Wall, 533, 548. Whatever their motive and purpose, regulations of commerce which do not infringe some constitutional prohibition are within the plenary power conferred on Congress by the Commerce Clause. Subject only to that limitation, presently to be considered, we conclude that the prohibition of the shipment interstate of goods produced under the forbidden substandard labor conditions is within the constitutional authority of Congress.

In the more than a century which has elapsed since the decision of Gibbons v. Ogden, these principles of constitutional in-

terpretation have been so long and repeatedly recognized by this Court as applicable
to the Commerce Clause, that there would
be little occasion for repeating them now
were it not for the decision of this Court
twenty-two years ago in Hammer v. Dagenhart, 247 U. S. 251. In that case it was held
by a bare majority of the Court over the
powerful and now classic dissent of Mr.
Justice Holmes setting forth the fundamental
issues involved, that Congress was without
power to exclude the products of child labor
from interstate commerce. The reasoning and
conclusion of the Court's opinion there cannot be reconciled with the conclusion which
we have reached, that the power of Congress
under the Commerce Clause is plenary to
exclude any article from interstate commerce
subject only to the specific prohibitions of
the Constitution.

Hammer v. Dagenhart has not been followed. The distinction on which the decision
was rested that Congressional power to prohibit interstate commerce is limited to articles which in themselves have some harmful or deleterious property—a distinction
which was novel when made and unsupported
by any provision of the Constitution—has
long since been abandoned. The thesis of the
opinion that the motive of the prohibition or
its effect to control in some measure the use
or production within the states of the article
thus excluded from the commerce can operate to deprive the regulation of its constitutional authority has long since ceased to have
force. And finally we have declared "The
authority of the Federal Government over
interstate commerce does not differ in extent
or character from that retained by the states
over interstate commerce." United States v.
Rock Royal Co-Operative, Inc., 307 U.S.
533, 569.

The conclusion is inescapable that Hammer v. Dagenhart, was a departure from the
principles which have prevailed in the interpretation of the commerce clause both before
and since the decision and that such vitality,
as a precedent, as it then had has long since
been exhausted. It should be and now is
overruled.

*Validity of the wage and hour require-
ments.* Section 15(a)(2) and §§ 6 and 7 require employers to conform to the wage and
hour provisions with respect to all employees
engaged in the production of goods for interstate commerce. . . . The validity of the
prohibition turns on the question whether
the employment, under other than the prescribed labor standards, of employees engaged in the production of goods for
interstate commerce is so related to the
commerce and so affects it as to be within
the reach of the power of Congress to regulate it. . . .

Without attempting to define the precise
limits of the phrase, we think the acts alleged
in the indictment are within the sweep of the
statute. The obvious purpose of the Act was
not only to prevent the interstate transportation of the proscribed product, but to stop
the initial step toward transportation, production with the purpose of so transporting
it. Congress was not unaware that most
manufacturing businesses shipping their
product in interstate commerce make it in
their shops without reference to its ultimate
destination and then after manufacture select
some of it for shipment interstate and some
intrastate according to the daily demands of
their business, and that it would be practically impossible, without disrupting manufacturing businesses, to restrict the prohibited
kind of production to the particular pieces
of lumber, cloth, furniture or the like which
later move in interstate rather than intrastate commerce. . . .

There remains the question whether such
restriction on the production of goods for
commerce is a permissable exercise of the
commerce power. The power of Congress
over interstate commerce is not confined to
the regulation of commerce among the states.
It extends to those activities intrastate which
so affect interstate commerce or the exercise
of the power of Congress over it as to make
regulation of them appropriate means to the
attainment of a legitimate end, the exercise
of the granted power of Congress to regulate
interstate commerce.

While this Court has many times found
state regulation of interstate commerce,
when uniformity of its regulation is of national concern, to be incompatible with the
Commerce clause even though Congress has
not legislated on the subject, the Court has
never implied such restraint on state control

over matters intrastate not deemed to be regulations of interstate commerce or its instrumentalities even though they affect the commerce. In the absence of Congressional legislation on the subject state laws which are not regulations of the commerce itself or its instrumentalities are not forbidden even though they affect interstate commerce.

But it does not follow that Congress may not by appropriate legislation regulate intrastate activities where they have a substantial effect on interstate commerce. A recent example is the National Labor Relations Act, for the regulation of employer and employee relations in industries in which strikes, induced by unfair labor practices named in the Act, tend to disturb or obstruct interstate commerce. But long before the adoption of the National Labor Relations Act, this Court had many times held that the power of Congress to regulate interstate commerce extends to the regulation through legislative action of activities intrastate which have a substantial effect on the commerce or the exercise of the Congressional power over it. . . .

Sometimes Congress itself has said that a particular activity affects the commerce as it did in the present act, the Safety Appliance Act, and the Railway Labor Act. In passing on the validity of legislation of the class last mentioned the only function of courts is to determine whether the particular activity regulated or prohibited is within the reach of the federal power.

Congress, having by the present Act adopted the policy of excluding from interstate commerce all goods produced for the commerce which do not conform to the specified labor standards, it may choose the means reasonably adapted to the attainment of the permitted end, even though they involve control of intrastate activities. Such legislation has often been sustained with respect to powers, other than the commerce power granted to the national government,

when the means chosen, although not themselves within the granted power, were nevertheless deemed appropriate aids to the accomplishment of some purpose within an admitted power of the national government. . . .

We think also that § 15(a) (2), now under consideration, is sustainable independently of § 15(a) (1), which prohibits shipment or transportation of the proscribed goods. As we have said the evils aimed at by the Act are the spread of substandard labor conditions through the use of the facilities of interstate commerce for competition by the goods so produced with those produced under the prescribed or better labor conditions; and the consequent dislocation of the commerce itself caused by the impairment or destruction of local businesses by competition made effective through interstate commerce. The Act is thus directed at the suppression of a method or kind of competition in interstate commerce which it has in effect condemned as "unfair," as the Clayton Act, 38 Stat. 730, has condemned other "unfair methods of competition" made effective through interstate commerce.

The means adopted by § 15(a) (2) for the protection of interstate commerce by the suppression of the production of the condemned goods for interstate commerce is so related to the commerce and so affects it as to be within the reach of the commerce power. Congress, to attain its objective in the suppression of nationwide competition in interstate commerce by goods produced under substandard labor conditions, has made no distinction as to the volume or amount of shipments in the commerce or of production for commerce by any particular shipper or producer. It recognized that in present day industry, competition by a small part may affect the whole and that the total effect of the competition of many small producers may be great. The legislation aimed at a whole embraces all its parts.

543. MITCHELL v. UNITED STATES et. al.
313 U. S. 80
1941

Appeal from the District Court of the U. S. for the Northern District of Illinois. Essential facts of the case are given in the opinion. See M. R. Konvitz, *Constitution and Civil Rights;* C. S. Johnson, *Patterns of Negro Segregation.*

HUGHES, J. Appellant, a Negro resident of Chicago, and a member of the House of Representatives of the United States, left Chicago for Hot Springs on the evening of April 20, 1937, over the lines of the Illinois Central Railroad Company to Memphis, Tennessee, and the Rock Island beyond, traveling on a round-trip ticket he had purchased at three cents per mile. He had requested a bedroom on the Chicago-Hot Springs Pullman sleeping car but none being available he was provided with a compartment as far as Memphis in the sleeper destined to New Orleans. Just before the train reached Memphis, on the morning after leaving Chicago, he had a Pullman porter transfer him to the Chicago-Hot Springs sleeper on the same train. Space was there available and the porter assigned him a particular seat in that car for which he was to pay the established fare of ninety cents. Shortly after leaving Memphis and crossing the Mississippi River into Arkansas, the train conductor took up the Memphis-Hot Springs portion of his ticket but refused to accept payment for the Pullman seat from Memphis and, in accordance with custom, compelled him over his protest and finally under threat of arrest to move into the car provided for colored passengers. This was in purported compliance with an Arkansas statute, requiring segregation of colored from white persons by the use of cars or partitioned sections providing "equal but separate and sufficient accommodations" for both races. Later the conductor returned the portion of the ticket he had taken up and advised appellant that he could get a refund on the basis of the coach fare of two cents

per mile from Memphis. That refund was not claimed from defendants and was not sought before the Commission, but it was found that the carriers stood ready to make it upon application. . . .

The Commission further found that the Pullman car contained ten sections of berths and two compartment drawing rooms; that the use of one of the drawing rooms would have amounted to segregation under the state law and ordinarily such combinations are available to colored passengers upon demand, the ninety cent fare being applicable. Occasionally they are used by colored passengers but in this instance both drawing rooms were already occupied by white passengers. The Pullman car was of modern design and had all the usual facilities and conveniences found in standard sleeping cars. It was air-conditioned, had hot and cold running water and separate flushable toilets for men and women. It was in excellent condition throughout. First-class white passengers had, in addition to the Pullman sleeper, the exclusive use of the train's only dining-car and only observation-parlor car, the latter having somewhat the same accommodations for day use as the Pullman car.

The coach for colored passengers, though of standard size and steel construction, was "an old combination affair," not air-conditioned, divided by partitions into three main parts, one for colored smokers, one for white smokers and one in the center for colored men and women, known as the women's section, in which appellant sat. There was a toilet in each section but only the one in the women's section was equipped for flushing and it was for the exclusive use of colored women. The car was without wash basins, soap, towels or running water, except in the women's section. The Commission stated that, according to appellant, the car was "filthy and foul smelling," but that the testimony of defendants' witnesses was to the contrary. . . .

The Commission, though treating the enforcement of the state law as a matter for state authorities, thought that in deciding the case on the facts presented it must recognize that the state law required the defendants to segregate colored passengers; that in these circumstances the present colored-passenger coach and the Pullman drawing rooms met the requirements of the Act; and that as there was comparatively little colored traffic and no indication that there was likely to be such demand for dining-car and observation-parlor car accommodations by colored passengers as to warrant the running of any extra cars or the construction of partitions, the discrimination and prejudice was "plainly not unjust or undue." The Commission observed that it was only differences in treatment of the latter character that were "unlawful and within the power of this Commission to condemn, remove, and prevent."

From the dismissal of the complaint, five Commissioners dissented.

The United States is a party to this suit to set aside the Commissioner's order. . . . The Government concludes that the Commission erroneously supposed that the Arkansas Separate Coach Law applied to an interstate passenger and erroneously determined that the small number of colored passengers asking for first-class accommodations justified an occasional discrimination against them because of their race. . . .

The undisputed facts showed conclusively that, having paid a first-class fare for the entire journey from Chicago to Hot Springs, and having offered to pay the proper charge for a seat which was available in the Pullman car for the trip from Memphis to Hot Springs, he was compelled, in accordance with custom, to leave that car and to ride in a second-class car and was thus denied the standard conveniences and privileges afforded to first-class passengers. This was manifestly a discrimination against him in the course of his interstate journey and admittedly that discrimination was based solely upon the fact that he was a Negro. The question whether this was a discrimination forbidden by the Interstate Commerce Act is not a question of segregation but one of equality of treatment. The denial to appellant of equality of accommodations because of his race would be an invasion of a fundamental individual right which is guaranteed against state action by the Fourteenth Amendment and in view of the nature of the right and of our constitutional policy it cannot be maintained that the discrimination as it was alleged was not essentially unjust. In that aspect it could not be deemed to lie outside the purview of the sweeping prohibitions of the Interstate Commerce Act.

We have repeatedly said that it is apparent from the legislative history of the Act that not only was the evil of discrimination the principal thing aimed at, but that there is no basis for the contention that Congress intended to exempt any discriminatory action or practice of interstate carriers affecting interstate commerce which it had authority to reach. . . .

We find no sound reason for the failure to apply this principle by holding the discrimination from which the appellant suffered to be unlawful and by forbidding it in the future. . . .

We take it that the chief reason for the Commission's action was the "comparatively little colored traffic." But the comparative volume of traffic cannot justify the denial of a fundamental right of equality of treatment, a right specifically safeguarded by the provisions of the Interstate Commerce Act. We thought a similar argument with respect to volume of traffic to be untenable in the application of the Fourteenth Amendment. We said that it made the constitutional right depend upon the number of persons who may be discriminated against, whereas the essence of that right is that it is a personal one. While the supply of particular facilities may be conditioned upon there being a reasonable demand therefor, if facilities are provided, substantial equality of treatment of persons traveling under like conditions cannot be refused. It is the individual we said, who is entitled to the equal protection of the laws, —not merely a group of individuals, or a body of persons according to their numbers. And the Interstate Commerce Act expressly extends its prohibitions to the subjecting of "any particular person" to unreasonable discriminations. . . .

The decree of the District Court is reversed and the cause is remanded with directions to set aside the order of the Commission and to remand the case to the Commission for further proceedings in conformity with this opinion.

544. UNITED STATES v. CLASSIC
313 U. S. 299
1941

One of the features of the American political system is that primary elections, while actually an important part of the constitutional structure, are formally under the control of private organizations. In this case the previous position of the Court that party primaries were private affairs was reversed. See Merriam and Overacker, *Primary Elections;* Stoney, "Suffrage in the South," *Survey Graphic,* Vol. 29, p. 163; see also Doc. No. 464.

Appeal from the District Court of the United States for the Eastern District of Louisiana.

STONE, J. Two counts of an indictment found in a federal district court charged that appellees, Commissioners of Elections, conducting a primary election under Louisiana law, to nominate a candidate of the Democratic Party for representative in Congress, willfully altered and falsely counted and certified the ballots of voters cast in the primary election. The questions for decision are whether the right of qualified voters to vote in the Louisiana primary and to have their ballots counted is a right "secured . . . by the Constitution" within the meaning of §§ 19 and 20 of the Criminal Code, and whether the acts of appellees charged in the indictment violate those sections.

The charge based on these allegations, was that the appellees conspired with each other and with others unknown, to injure and oppress citizens in the free exercise and enjoyment of rights and privileges secured to them by the Constitution and Laws of the United States, namely, (1) the right of qualified voters who cast their ballots in the primary election to have their ballots counted as cast for the candidate of their choice, and (2) the right of the candidates to run for the office of Congressman and to

have the votes in favor of their nomination counted as cast. The overt acts alleged were that the appellees altered eighty-three ballots cast for one candidate and fourteen cast for another, marking and counting them as votes for a third candidate, and that they falsely certified the number of votes cast for the respective candidates to the chairman of the Second Congressional District Committee. . . .

Section 19 of the Criminal Code condemns as a criminal offense any conspiracy to injure a citizen in the exercise "of any right or privilege secured to him by the Constitution or laws of the United States." Section 20 makes it a penal offense for anyone who, "acting under color of any law" "willfully subjects, or causes to be subjected, any inhabitant of any State . . . to the deprivation of any rights, privileges, or immunities secured or protected by the Constitution and laws of the United States." The Government argues that the right of a qualified voter in a Louisiana congressional primary election to have his vote counted as cast is a right secured by Article I, §§ 2 and 4 of the Constitution, and that a conspiracy to deprive the citizen of that right is a violation of § 19, and also that the willful action of appellees as state officials, in falsely counting the ballots at the primary election and in falsely certifying the count, deprived qualified voters of that right and of the equal protection of the laws guaranteed by the Fourteenth Amendment, all in violation of § 20 of the Criminal Code.

Article I, § 2 of the Constitution, commands that "The House of Representatives shall be composed of Members chosen every second Year by the People of the several States, and the Electors in each State shall have the qualifications requisite for Electors of the most numerous Branch of the State Legislature." By § 4 of the same article "The

Times, Places and Manner of holding Elections for Senators and Representatives, shall be prescribed in each State by the Legislature thereof; but the Congress may at any time by Law make or alter such Regulations, except as to the Places of chusing Senators." Such right as is secured by the Constitution to qualified voters to choose members of the House of Representatives is thus to be exercised in conformity to the requirements of state law subject to the restrictions prescribed by § 2 and to the authority conferred on Congress by § 4, to regulate the times, places and manner of holding elections for representatives.

We look then to the statutes of Louisiana here involved to ascertain the nature of the right which under the constitutional mandate they define and confer on the voter and the effect upon its exercise of the acts with which appellees are charged, all with the view to determining, first, whether the right or privilege is one secured by the Constitution of the United States, second, whether the effect under the state statute of appellee's alleged acts is such that they operate to injure or oppress citizens in the exercise of that right within the meaning of § 19 and to deprive inhabitants of the state of that right within the meaning of § 20, and finally, whether §§ 19 and 20 respectively are in other respects applicable to the alleged acts of appellees.

. . . The states are given, and in fact exercise a wide discretion in the formulation of a system for the choice by the people of representatives in Congress. In common with many other states Louisiana has exercised that discretion by setting up machinery for the effective choice of party candidates for representative in Congress by primary elections and by its laws it eliminates or seriously restricts the candidacy at the general election of all those who are defeated at the primary. All political parties, which are defined as those that have cast at least 5 per cent of the total vote at specified preceding elections, are required to nominate their candidates for representative by direct primary elections. . . . .

The right to vote for a representative in Congress at the general election is, as a matter of law, thus restricted to the successful party candidate at the primary, to those not candidates at the primary who file nomination papers, and those whose names may be lawfully written into the ballot by the electors. Even if, as appellees argue, contrary to the decision in Serpas v. Trebucq, supra, voters may lawfully write into their ballots, cast at the general election, the name of a candidate rejected at the primary and have their ballots counted, the practical operation of the primary law in otherwise excluding from the ballot on the general election the names of candidates rejected at the primary is such as to impose serious restrictions upon the choice of candidates by the voters save by voting at the primary election. In fact, as alleged in the indictment, the practical operation of the primary in Louisiana, is and has been since the primary election was established in 1900 to secure the election of the Democratic primary nominee for the Second Congressional District of Louisiana.

Interference with the right to vote in the Congressional primary in the Second Congressional District for the choice of Democratic candidate for Congress is thus as a matter of law and in fact an interference with the effective choice of the voters at the only stage of the election procedure when their choice is of significance, since it is at the only stage when such interference could have any practical effect on the ultimate result, the choice of the Congressman to represent the district. The primary in Louisiana is an integral part of the procedure for the popular choice of Congressman. The right of qualified voters to vote at the Congressional primary in Louisiana and to have their ballots counted is thus the right to participate in that choice.

We come then to the question whether that right is one secured by the Constitution. Section 2 of Article I commands that Congressmen shall be chosen by the people of the several states by electors, the qualifications of which it prescribes. . . .

Obviously included within the right to choose, secured by the Constitution, is the right of qualified voters within a state to cast their ballots and have them counted at Congressional elections. This Court has consistently held that this is a right secured by the Constitution. And since the constitutional command is without restriction or limitation, the right unlike those guaranteed by the Fourteenth and Fifteenth Amendments, is secured against the action of individuals as well as of states. Ex parte, Yarbrough, supra; Logan v. United States, supra.

But we are now concerned with the question whether the right to choose at a primary election, a candidate for election as representative, is embraced in the right to choose representatives secured by Article I, § 2. We may assume that the framers of the Constitution in adopting that section, did not have specifically in mind the selection and elimination of candidates for Congress by the direct primary any more than they contemplated the application of the commerce clause to interstate telephone, telegraph and wireless communication which are concededly within it. But in determining whether a provision of the Constitution applies to a new subject matter, it is of little significance that it is one with which the framers were not familiar. For in setting up an enduring framework of government they undertook to carry out for the indefinite future and in all the vicissitudes of the changing affairs of men, those fundamental purposes which the instrument itself discloses. Hence we read its words, not as we read legislative codes which are subject to continuous revision with the changing course of events, but as the revelation of the great purposes which were intended to be achieved by the Constitution as a continuing instrument of government. If we remember that "it is a Constitution we are expounding," we cannot rightly prefer, of the possible meanings of its words, that which will defeat rather than effectuate the Constitutional purpose.

That the free choice of the people of representatives in Congress, subject only to the restrictions to be found in §§ 2 and 4 of Article I and elsewhere in the Constitution, was one of the great purposes of our Constitutional scheme of government cannot be doubted. We cannot regard it as any the less the constitutional purpose or its words as any the less guarantying the integrity of that choice when a state, exercising its privilege

in the absence of Congressional action, changes the mode of choice from a single step, a general election, to two, of which the first is the choice at a primary of those candidates from whom, as a second step, the representative in Congress is to be chosen at the election.

Nor can we say that that choice which the Constitution protects is restricted to the second step because § 4 of Article I, as a means of securing a free choice of representatives by the people, has authorized Congress to regulate the manner of elections, without making any mention of primary elections. For we think that the authority of Congress, given by § 4, includes the authority to regulate primary elections when, as in this case, they are a step in the exercise by the people of their choice of representatives in Congress. . . . In Newberry v. United States, supra, four Justices of this Court were of opinion that the term "elections" in § 4 of Article I did not embrace a primary election since that procedure was unknown to the framers. A fifth Justice who with them pronounced the judgment of the Court, was of opinion that a primary, held under a law enacted before the adoption of the Seventeenth Amendment, for the nomination of candidates for Senator, was not an election within the meaning of § 4 of Article I of the Constitution, presumably because the choice of the primary imposed no legal restrictions on the election of Senators by the state legislatures to which their election had been committed by Article I, § 3. The remaining four Justices were of the opinion that a primary election for the choice of candidates for Senator or Representative were elections subject to regulation by Congress within the meaning of § 4 of Article I. The question then has not been prejudged by and decision of this Court.

. . . From time immemorial an election to public office has been in point of substance no more and no less than the expression by qualified electors of their choice of candidates.

Long before the adoption of the Constitution the form and mode of that expression had changed from time to time. There is no historical warrant for supposing that the framers were under the illusion that the method of effecting the choice of the electors would never change or that if it did, the change was for that reason to be permitted to defeat the right of the people to choose representatives for Congress which the Constitution had guaranteed. The right to participate in the choice of representatives for Congress includes, as we have said, the right to cast a ballot and to have it counted at the general election whether for the successful candidate or not. Where the state law has made the primary an integral part of the procedure of choice, or where in fact the primary effectively controls the choice, the right of the elector to have his ballot counted at the primary, is likewise included in the right protected by Article I, § 2. And this right of participation is protected just as is the right to vote at the election, where the primary is by law made an integral part of the election machinery, whether the voter exercises his right in a party primary which invariably, sometimes or never determines the ultimate choice of the representatives. Here, even apart from the circumstance that the Louisiana primary is made by law an integral part of the procedure of choice, the right to choose a representative is in fact controlled by the primary because, as is alleged in the indictment, the choice of candidates at the Democratic primary determines the choice of the elected representative. Moreover, we cannot close our eyes to the fact already mentioned that the practical influence of the choice of candidates at the primary may be so great as to affect profoundly the choice at the general election even though there is no effective legal prohibition upon the rejection at the election of the choice made at the primary and may thus operate to deprive the voter of his constitutional right of choice. This was noted and extensively commented upon by the concurring Justices in Newberry v. United States.

Unless the constitutional protection of the integrity of "elections" extends to primary elections, Congress is left powerless to effect the constitutional purpose, and the popular choice of representatives is stripped of its constitutional protection save only as Congress, by taking over the control of state elections, may exclude from them the influence of the state primaries. Such an expedient would end that state autonomy with respect to elections which the Constitution contemplated that Congress should be free to leave undisturbed, subject only to such minimum regulation as it should find necessary to insure the freedom and integrity of the choice. Words, especially those of a constitution, are not to be read with such stultifying narrowness. The words of §§ 2 and 4 of Article I, read in the sense which is plainly permissible and in the light of the constitutional purpose, require us to hold that a primary election which involves a necessary step in the choice of candidates for election as representatives in Congress, and which in the circumstances of this case controls that choice, is an election within the meaning of the constitutional provision and is subject to congressional regulation as to the manner of holding it. . . .

There remains the question whether §§ 19 and 20 are an exercise of the congressional authority applicable to the acts with which appellees are charged in the indictment. Section 19 makes it a crime to conspire to "injure" or "oppress" any citizen "in the free exercise . . . of any right or privilege secured to him by the Constitution." In Ex parte Yarbrough, supra, and in United States v. Mosley, supra, as we have seen, it was held that the right to vote in a congressional election is a right secured by the Constitution, and that a conspiracy to prevent the citizen from voting or to prevent the official count of this ballot when cast, is a conspiracy to injure and oppress the citizen in the free exercise of a right secured by the Constitution within the meaning of § 19. Conspiracy to prevent the official count of a citizen's ballot, held in United States v. Mosley, supra, to be a violation of § 19 in the case of a congressional election, is equally a conspiracy to injure and oppress the citizen when the ballots are cast in a primary election pre-requisite to the choice of party candidates for a congressional election. In both cases the right infringed is one secured by the Constitution. The injury suffered by the citizen in the exercise of the right is an injury which the statute describes and to which it applies in the one case as in the other.

The right of the voters at the primary to have their votes counted is, as we have stated, a right or privilege secured by the Constitution, and to this § 20 also gives protection. The alleged acts of appellees were committed in the course of their performance of duties under the Louisiana statute requiring them to count the ballots, to record the result of the count, and to certify the result of the election. Misuse of power, possessed by virtue of state law and made possible only because the wrongdoer is clothed with the authority of state law, is action taken "under color of" state law. Here the acts of appellees infringed the constitutional right and deprived the voters of the benefit of it within the meaning of § 20.

Justices DOUGLAS, BLACK, and MURPHY dissenting.

545. EDWARDS v. CALIFORNIA
314 U. S. 160
1941

During the depression of the 1930's thousands of farmers and casual farm laborers were driven from their marginal farm lands in the Southwest prairie states by the economic crisis and the terrible dust storms. Many migrated to California, lured by the climate, the relatively greater prosperity, and the hope for seasonal work picking fruits and vegetables, a trek graphically described in John Steinbeck's *Grapes of Wrath*. As the influx of poverty-stricken "Okies" began to exceed the demand, resentment arose in California against the entrance of more public charges, and a law was passed making it a misdemeanor to bring or aid in bringing into the state any nonresident person known to be indigent. In January, 1940, Fred F. Edwards, a resident of the state of California, went to Texas, picked up his wife's brother, a Texan resident, whom Edwards knew to be indigent, and drove him to his home in Marysville, California. The Justice Court sentenced him to six months' imprisonment for violating the statute, and the Superior Court of Yuba County sustained the verdict. No appeal to a higher court in California was open, so Edwards appealed to the U.S. Supreme Court, contending that the California statute was unconstitutional. It is interesting that the Court nullified the California Act as interference in interstate commerce rather than a violation of the privileges and rights of American citizens. See E. W. Adams, "State Control of Interstate Migration of Indigents," 40 *Mich. L. Rev.* 711 ff.; S. P. Meyers, "Federal Privileges and Immunities: Application to Ingress and Egress," 29 *Cornell L. Q.*, 489 ff.; J. Steinbeck, *Grapes of Wrath*; C. McWilliams, *Factories in the Field.*

Appeal from the Superior Court of the State of California in and for the County of Yuba.

BYRNES, J. The facts of this case are simple and are not disputed. Appellant is a citizen of the United States and a resident of California. In December, 1939, he left his home in Marysville, California, for Spur, Texas, with the intention of bringing back to Marysville, his wife's brother, Frank Duncan, a citizen of the United States and a resident of Texas. When he arrived in Texas, appellant learned that Duncan had last been employed by the Works Progress Administration. Appellant thus became aware of the fact that Duncan was an indigent person and he continued to be aware of it throughout the period involved in this case. The two men agreed that appellant should transport Duncan from Texas to Marysville in appellant's automobile. Accordingly, they left Spur on January 1, 1940, entered California by way of Arizona on January 3, and reached Marysville on January 5. When he left Texas, Duncan had about $20. It had all been spent by the time he reached Marysville. He lived with appellant for about ten days until he obtained financial assistance from the Farm Security Administration. During the ten day interval, he had no employment.

In Justice Court a complaint was filed against appellant under Section 2615 of the Welfare and Institutions Code of California, which provides: "Every person, firm, or corporation, or officer or agent thereof that brings or assists in bringing into the State any indigent person who is not a resident of the State, knowing him to be an indigent person, is guilty of a misdemeanor." . . . Appelant was convicted and sentenced to six months' imprisonment in the county jail, and sentence was suspended. . . .

Article I, Section 8 of the Constitution delegates to the Congress the authority to regulate interstate commerce. And it is settled beyond question that the transportation of persons is "commerce," within the meaning of that provision. It is nevertheless true that the States are not wholly precluded from exercising their police power in matters of local concern even though they may thereby affect interstate commerce. The issue presented in this case, therefore, is whether the prohibition embodied in Section 2615 against the "bringing" or transportation of indigent persons into California is within the police power of that State. We think that it is not, and hold that it is an unconstitutional barrier to interstate commerce.

The gravity and perplexity of the social and economic dislocation which this statute reflects is a matter of common knowledge and concern. We are not unmindful of it. We appreciate that the spectacle of large segments of our population constantly on the move has given rise to urgent demands upon the ingenuity of government. Both the brief of the Attorney General of California and that of the Chairman of the Select Committee of the House of Representatives of the United States as *amicus curiae* have sharpened this appreciation. . . .

In the words of Mr. Justice Cardozo: "The Constitution was framed under the dominion of a political philosophy less parochial in range. It was framed upon the theory that the peoples of the several states must sink or swim together, and that in the long run prosperity and salvation are in union and not division." Baldwin v. Seelig, 294 U.S. 511.

It is difficult to conceive of a statute more squarely in conflict with this theory than the Section challenged here. Its express purpose and inevitable effect is to prohibit the transportation of indigent persons across the California border. The burden upon interstate commerce is intended and immediate; it is the plain and sole function of the statute. Moreover, the indigent non-residents who are the real victims of the statute are deprived of the opportunity to exert political pressure upon the California legislature in order to obtain a change in policy. We think this statute must fail under any known test of the validity of State interference with interstate commerce. . . .

546. JAPANESE RELOCATION ORDER
February 19, 1942
(*Federal Register,* Vol. VII, No. 38)

Alarmed by the supposed danger of Japanese invasion of the Pacific coast after Pearl Harbor and under the apprehension that all persons of Japanese ancestry were a potential threat to the United States, the War Department persuaded the President to authorize the evacuation of some 112,000 West Coast Japanese, two-thirds of them American citizens to "relocation" centers. A Congressional Resolution of March 2i, 1942, made it a misdemeanor "to knowingly enter, remain in, or leave prescribed military areas" contrary to the orders of the commanding officer of the area. This Act which, in perspective seems to have been wholly unnecessary, has been called by E. S. Corwin "the most drastic invasion of the rights of citizens of the U.S. by their own government that has thus far occurred in the history of our nation." See Doc. No. 547 and M. Grodzins, *Americans Betrayed.*

EXECUTIVE ORDER
AUTHORIZING THE SECRETARY OF WAR TO PRESCRIBE MILITARY AREAS

Whereas the successful prosecution of the war requires every possible protection against espionage and against sabotage to national-defense materials, national-defense premises, and national-defense utilities. . . .

Now, therefore, by virtue of the authority

vested in me as President of the United States, and Commander in Chief of the Army and Navy, I hereby authorize and direct the Secretary of War, and the Military Commanders whom he may from time to time designate, whenever he or any designated Commander deems such action necessary or desirable, to prescribe military areas in such places and of such extent as he or the appropriate Military Commander may determine, from which any or all persons may be excluded, and with respect to which, the right of any person to enter, remain in, or leave shall be subject to whatever restrictions the Secretary of War or the appropriate Military Commander may impose in his discretion. The Secretary of War is hereby authorized to provide for residents of any such area who are excluded therefrom, such transportation, food, shelter, and other accommodations as may be necessary, in the judgment of the Secretary of War or the said Military Commander, and until other arrangements are made, to accomplish the purpose of this order. The designation of military areas in any region or locality shall supersede designations of prohibited and restricted areas by the Attorney General under the Proclamations of December 7 and 8, 1941,[1] and shall supersede the responsibility and authority of the Attorney General under the said Proclamations in respect of such prohibited and restricted areas.

I hereby further authorize and direct the Secretary of War and the said Military Commanders to take such other steps as he or the appropriate Military Commander may deem advisable to enforce compliance with the restrictions applicable to each Military area hereinabove authorized to be designated, including the use of Federal troops and other Federal Agencies, with authority to accept assistance of state and local agencies.

I hereby further authorize and direct all Executive Departments, independent establishments and other Federal Agencies, to assist the Secretary of War or the said Military Commanders in carrying out this Executive Order, including the furnishing of medical aid, hospitalization, food, clothing, transportation, use of land, shelter, and other supplies, equipment, utilities, facilities, and services. . . .

FRANKLIN D. ROOSEVELT

547. HIRABAYASHI v. UNITED STATES
320 U. S. 81
1943

This was the first of the cases testing the constitutionality of the Presidential evacuation order and the Act of Congress designed to effectuate that order. The facts of the case are set forth in the opinion. The second case, Koremarsu v. U.S., 323 U.S. 214, in general followed this precedent; there were two dissenting opinions, from Justices Murphy and Jackson. A third case, Ex parte Endo, 323 U.A. 283, granted a writ of habeas corpus to a loyal Japanese American, discharging her from custody. See M. Grodzins, *Americans Betrayed;* E. S. Corwin, *Total War and the Constitution;* N. Dembitz, "Racial Discrimination and the Military Judgment," *Col. L. Rev.,* March, 1945; C. Fairman, "Law of Martial Rule and the National Emergency," *Harv. L. Rev.,* June, 1942; E. V. Rostow, "The Japanese-American Cases—a Disaster," *Yale L. J.,* June, 1945.

On Certificate from the United States Circuit Court of Appeals for the Ninth Circuit.

STONE, J. Appellant, an American citizen of Japanese ancestry, was convicted in the district court of violating the Act of Congress of March 21, 1942, . . . which makes it a misdemeanor knowingly to disregard restrictions made applicable by a military commander to persons in a military area prescribed by him as such, all as authorized by an Executive Order of the President.

The questions for our decision are whether

[1] 6 F.R. 6420.

the particular restriction violated, namely that all persons of Japanese ancestry residing in such an area be within their place of residence daily between the hours of 8:00 P.M. and 6:00 A.M., was adopted by the military commander in the exercise of an unconstitutional delegation by Congress of its legislative power, and whether the restriction unconstitutionally discriminated between citizens of Japanese ancestry and those of other ancestries in violation of the Fifth Amendment. . . .

. . . Appellant asserted that the indictment should be dismissed because he was an American citizen who had never been a subject of and had never borne allegiance to the Empire of Japan, and also because the Act of March 21, 1942, was an unconstitutional delegation of Congressional power. . . .

The evidence showed that appellant had failed to report to the Civil Control Station on May 11 or May 12, 1942, as directed, to register for evacuation from the military area. He admitted failure to do so, and stated it had at all times been his belief that he would be waiving his rights as an American citizen by so doing. The evidence also showed that for like reason he was away from his place of residence after 8:00 P.M. on May 9, 1942. The jury returned a verdict of guilty on both counts and appellant was sentenced to imprisonment for a term of three months on each, the sentences to run concurrently. . . .

The curfew order which appellant violated, and to which the sanction prescribed by the Act of Congress has been deemed to attach, purported to be issued pursuant to an Executive Order of the President. In passing upon the authority of the military commander to make and execute the order, it becomes necessary to consider in some detail the official action which preceded or accompanied the order and from which it derives its purported authority. . . .

. . . On February 19, 1942, the President promulgated Executive Order No. 9066. The Order recited that "the successful prosecution of the war requires every possible protection against espionage and against sabotage to national-defense material, national-defense premises, and national-defense utilities. . . ."

. . . On March 2, 1942, General DeWitt promulgated Public Proclamation No. 1. The proclamation recited that the entire Pacific Coast "by its geographical location is particularly subject to attack, to attempted invasion by the armed forces of nations with which the United States is now at war, and in connection therewith, is subject to espionage and acts of sabotage, thereby requiring the adoption of military measures necessary to establish safeguards against such enemy operations" . . . .

On March 24, 1942, General DeWitt issued Public Proclamation No. 3. After referring to the previous designation of military areas by Public Proclamations No. 1 and 2, it recited that ". . . the present situation within these Military Areas and Zones requires as a matter of military necessity the establishment of certain regulations pertaining to all enemy aliens and all persons of Japanese ancestry within said Military Areas and Zones . . ." It accordingly declared and established that from and after March 27, 1942, "all alien Japanese, all alien Germans, all alien Italians, and all persons of Japanese ancestry residing or being within the geographical limits of Military Area No. 1 . . . shall be within their place of residence between the hours of 8:00 P.M. and 6:00 A.M., which period is hereinafter referred to as the hours of curfew." It also imposed certain other restrictions on persons of Japanese ancestry, and provided that any person violating the regulations would be subject to the criminal penalties provided by the Act of Congress of March 21, 1942. . . .

Appellant does not deny that he knowingly failed to obey the curfew order as charged in the second count of the indictment, or that the order was authorized by the terms of Executive Order No. 9066, or that the challenged Act of Congress purports to punish with criminal penalties disobedience of such an order. His contentions are only that Congress unconstitutionally delegated its legislative power to the military commander by authorizing him to impose the challenged regulation, and that, even if the regulation were in other respects lawfully authorized, the Fifth Amendment prohibits the discrimination made between citizens of Japanese descent and those of other ancestry.

It will be evident from the legislative history that the Act of March 21, 1942, contemplated and authorized the curfew order which we have before us. . . .

The conclusion is inescapable that Congress, by the Act of March 21, 1942, ratified and confirmed Executive Order No. 9066. . . .

. . . And so far as it lawfully could, Congress authorized and implemented such curfew orders as the commanding officer should promulgate pursuant to the Executive Order of the President. The question then is not one of Congressional power to delegate to the President the promulgation of the Executive Order, but whether, acting in cooperation, Congress and the Executive have constitutional authority to impose the curfew restriction here complained of. . . .

The war power of the national government is "the power to wage war successfully." See Charles Evans Hughes, War Powers Under the Constitution, 42 A. B.A.Rep. 232, 238. It extends to every matter and activity so related to war as substantially to affect its conduct and progress. The power is not restricted to the winning of victories in the field and the repulse of enemy forces. It embraces every phase of the national defense, including the protection of war materials and the members of the armed forces from injury and from the dangers which attend the rise, prosecution and progress of war. . . . Since the Constitution commits to the Executive and to Congress the exercise of the war power in all the vicissitudes and conditions of warfare, it has necessarily given them wide scope for the exercise of judgment and discretion in determining the nature and extent of the threatened injury or danger and in the selection of the means for resisting it. . . . Where, as they did here, the conditions call for the exercise of judgment and discretion and for the choice of means by those branches of the Government on which the Constitution has placed the responsibility of war-making, it is not for any court to sit in review of the wisdom of their action or substitute its judgment for theirs.

The actions taken must be appraised in the light of the conditions with which the President and Congress were confronted in the early months of 1942, many of which, since disclosed, were then peculiarly within the knowledge of the military authorities. . . .

. . . That reasonably prudent men charged with the responsibility of our national defense had ample ground for concluding that they must face the danger of invasion, take measures against it, and in making the choice of measures consider our internal situation, cannot be doubted.

The challenged orders were defense measures for the avowed purpose of safe-guarding the military area in question, at a time of threatened air raids and invasion by the Japanese forces, from the danger of sabotage and espionage. As the curfew was made applicable to citizens residing in the area only if they were of Japanese ancestry, our inquiry must be whether in the light of all the facts and circumstances there was any substantial basis for the conclusion, in which Congress and the military commander united, that the curfew as applied was a protective measure necessary to meet the threat of sabotage and espionage which would substantially affect the war effort and which might reasonably be expected to aid a threatened enemy invasion. The alternative which appellant insists must be accepted is for the military authorities to impose the curfew on all citizens within the military area, or on none. In a case of threatened danger requiring prompt action, it is a choice between inflicting obviously needless hardship on the many, or sitting passive and unresisting in the presence of the threat. We think that constitutional government, in time of war, is not so powerless and does not compel so hard a choice if those charged with the responsibility of our national defense have reasonable ground for believing that the threat is real. . . .

In the critical days of March, 1942, the danger to our war production by sabotage and espionage in this area seems obvious. . . . At a time of threatened Japanese attack upon this country, the nature of our inhabitants' attachments to the Japanese enemy was consequently a matter of grave concern. Of the 126,000 persons of Japanese descent in the United States, citizens and non-citizens, approximately 112,000 resided in California, Oregon and Washington at the time of the adoption of the military regulations. Of these approximately two-thirds are citizens because born in the United States. Not only did the great majority ·of such persons reside within the Pacific Coast states but they were concentrated in or near three of the large cities, Seattle, Portland and Los Angeles, all in Military Area No. 1.

There is support for the view that social, economic and political conditions which have prevailed since the close of the last century, when the Japanese began to come to this country in substantial numbers, have intensified their solidarity and have in large measure prevented their assimilation as an integral part of the white population. In addition, large numbers of children of Japanese parentage are sent to Japanese language schools outside the regular hours of public schools in the locality. Some of these schools are generally believed to be sources of Japanese nationalistic propaganda, cultivating allegiance to Japan. Considerable numbers, estimated to be approximately 10,000, of American-born children of Japanese parentage have been sent to Japan for all or a part of their education.

Congress and the Executive, including the military commander, could have attributed special significance, in its bearing on the loyalties of persons of Japanese descent, to the maintenance by Japan of its system of dual citizenship. Children born in the United States of Japanese alien parents, and especially those children born before December 1, 1924, are under many circumstances deemed, by Japanese law, to be citizens of Japan. No official census of those whom Japan regards as having thus retained Japanese citizenship is available, but there is ground for the belief that the number is large. . . .

As a result of all these conditions affecting the life of the Japanese, both aliens and citizens, in the Pacific Coast area, there has been relatively little social intercourse between them and the white population. The restrictions, both practical and legal, affecting the privileges and opportunities afforded to persons of Japanese extraction residing in the United States, have been sources of irritation and may well have tended to increase their isolation, and in many instances their attachments to Japan and its institutions.

Viewing these data in all their aspects, Congress and the Executive could reasonably have concluded that these conditions have encouraged the continued attachment of members of this group to Japan and Japanese institutions. These are only some of the many considerations which those charged with the responsibility for the national defense could take into account in determining the nature and extent of the danger of espionage and sabotage, in the event of invasion or air raid attack. The extent of that danger could be definitely known only after the event and after it was too late to meet it. Whatever views we may entertain regarding the loyalty to this country of the citizens of Japanese ancestry, we cannot reject as unfounded the judgment of the military authorities and of Congress that there were disloyal members of that population, whose number and strength could not be precisely and quickly ascertained. We cannot say that the war-making branches of the Government did not have ground for believing that in a critical hour such persons could not readily be isolated and separately dealt with, and constituted a menace to the national defense and safety, which demanded that prompt and adequate measures be taken to guard against it.

Appellant does not deny that, given the danger, a curfew was an appropriate measure against sabotage. It is an obvious protection against the perpetration of sabotage most readily committed during the hours of darkness. If it was an appropriate exercise of the war power its validity is not impaired because it has restricted the citizen's liberty. Like every military control of the population of a dangerous zone in war time, it necessarily involves some infringment of individual liberty, just as does the police establishment of fire lines during a fire, or the confinement of people to their houses during an air raid alarm—neither of which could be thought to be an infringement of constitutional right. Like them, the validity of the restraints of the curfew order depends on all the conditions which obtain at the time the curfew is imposed and which support the order imposing it.

But appellant insists that the exercise of the power is inappropriate and unconstitutional because it discriminates against citizens of Japanese ancestry, in violation of the Fifth Amendment. The Fifth Amendment contains no equal protection clause and it restrains only such discriminatory legislation by Congress as amounts to a denial of due process. Congress may hit at a particular danger where it is seen, without providing for others which are not so evident or so urgent.

Distinctions between citizens solely because of their ancestry are by their very nature odious to a free people whose institutions are founded upon the doctrine of equality. For that reason, legislative classification or discrimination based on race alone has often been held to be a denial of equal protection. We may assume that these considerations would be controlling here were it not for the fact that the danger of espionage and sabotage, in time of war and of threatened invasion, calls upon the military authorities to scrutinize every relevant fact bearing on the loyalty of populations in the danger areas. Because racial discriminations are in most circumstances irrelevant and therefore prohibited, it by no means follows that, in dealing with the perils of war, Congress and the Executive are wholly precluded from taking into account those facts and circumstances which are relevant to measures for our national defense and for the successful prosecution of the war, and which may in fact place citizens of one ancestry in a different category from others. "We must never forget, that it is a constitution we are expounding," "a constitution intended to endure for ages to come, and, consequently, to be adapted to the various crises of human affairs." The adoption by Government, in the crisis of war and of threatened invasion, of measures for the public safety, based upon the recognition of facts and circumstances which indicate that a group of one national extraction may menace that safety more than others, is not wholly beyond the limits of the Constitution and is not to be condemned merely because in other and in most circumstances racial distinctions are irrelevant.

Here the aim of Congress and the Executive was the protection against sabotage of war materials and utilities in areas thought to be in danger of Japanese invasion and air attack. We have stated in detail facts and circumstances with respect to the American citizens of Japanese ancestry residing on the Pacific Coast which support the judgment of the war-waging branches of the Government that some restrictive measure was urgent. We cannot say that these facts and circumstances, considered in the particular war setting, could afford no ground for differentiating citizens of Japanese ancestry from other groups in the United States. The fact alone that attack on our shores was threatened by Japan rather than another enemy power set these citizens apart from others who have no particular associations with Japan. . . .

The Constitution as a continuously operating charter of government does not demand the impossible or the impractical. The essentials of the legislative function are preserved when Congress authorizes a statutory command to become operative, upon ascertainment of a basic conclusion of fact by a designated representative of the Government. The present statute, which authorized curfew orders to be made pursuant to Executive Order No. 9066 for the protection of war resources from espionage and sabotage, satisfies those requirements. Under the Executive Order the basic facts, determined by the military commander in the light of knowledge then available, were whether that danger existed and whether a curfew order was an appropriate means of minimizing the danger. Since his findings to that effect were, as we have said, not without adequate support, the legislative function was performed and the sanction of the statute attached to violations of the curfew order. It is unnecessary to consider whether or to what extent such findings would support orders differing from the curfew order.

The conviction under the second count is without constitutional infirmity. Hence we have no occasion to review the conviction on the first count since, as already stated, the sentences on the two counts are to run concurrently and conviction on the second is sufficient to sustain the sentence. For this reason also it is unnecessary to consider the Government's argument that compliance with the order to report at the Civilian Control Station did not necessarily entail confinement in a relocation center.

Affirmed.

548. F. D. ROOSEVELT'S STATEMENT ON NORTH AFRICAN POLICY
November 17, 1942

(Department of State Bulletin, Vol. VII, p. 935)

When the armistice between France and Germany was concluded in June, 1940, France was divided into two parts: occupied France under German control, and unoccupied France, ruled by a government in Vichy headed by Marshal Petain, in which outright Nazi sympathizers like Pierre Laval played major roles. In order to maintain a listening post on the continent and to lessen German influence over the Vichy government, the United States continued diplomatic relations with France, a policy widely condemned by liberal groups in this country. When the Allies invaded North Africa in November, 1942, a conservative French army officer, General Henri Giraud, was chosen to attempt to halt French resistance to the landings, and, when his orders were not obeyed, General Eisenhower accepted the assistance of Admiral Darlan, vice-premier of Vichy France and a notorious collaborationist. Although Darlan was assassinated the next month, the Giraud government continued many of the practices and personnel of the Vichy regime. The State Department maintained that support of De Gaulle would be tantamount to choosing the leader of the new French government, a prerogative which belonged to the French people, while the deal with Darlan was defended on the grounds of military expediency. See W. Langer, *Our Vichy Gamble;* K. Pendar, *Adventure in Diplomacy;* Renee Bierre-Gosset, *Conspiracy in Algiers;* S. E. Morison, *Operations in North African Waters;* Ellen Hammer, "Hindsight on Vichy," *Pol. Sci. Q.,* Vol. LXI, pp. 175 ff.; J. MacVane, *Journey Into War.*

President Franklin D. Roosevelt's Statement on Political Arrangements in North Africa made by Lieut. General Dwight D. Eisenhower, Allied Commander in Chief in North Africa. Washington, November 17, 1942:

I have accepted General Eisenhower's political arrangements made for the time being in Northern and Western Africa.

I thoroughly understand and approve the feeling in the United States and Great Britain and among all the other United Nations that in view of the history of the past two years no permanent arrangement should be made with Admiral Darlan. People in the United Nations likewise would never understand the recognition of a reconstituting of the Vichy Government in France or in any French territory.

We are opposed to Frenchmen who support Hitler and the Axis. No one in our Army has any authority to discuss the future Government of France and the French Empire.

The future French Government will be established—not by any individual in metropolitan France or overseas—but by the French people themselves after they have been set free by the victory of the United Nations.

The present temporary arrangement in North and West Africa is only a temporary expedient, justified solely by the stress of battle.

The present temporary arrangement has accomplished two military objectives. The first was to save American and British lives on the one hand, and French lives on the other hand.

The second was the vital factor of time. The temporary arrangement has made it possible to avoid a "mopping up" period in Algiers and Morocco which might have taken a month or two to consummate. Such a period would have delayed the concentration for the attack from the West on Tunis, and we hope on Tripoli.

Every day of delay in the current operation would have enabled the Germans and Italians to build up a strong resistance, to dig in and make a huge operation on our part essential before we could win. Here again, many more lives will be saved under the present speedy offensive, than if we had had to delay it for a month or more.

It will also be noted that French troops, under the command of General Giraud, have already been in action against the enemy in Tunisia, fighting by the side of American and British soldiers for the liberation of their country.

Admiral Darlan's proclamation assisted in making a "mopping up" period unnecessary. Temporary arrangements made with Admiral Darlan apply, without exception, to the current local situation only.

I have requested the liberation of all persons in Northern Africa who had been imprisoned because they opposed the efforts of the Nazis to dominate the world, and I have asked for the abrogation of all laws and decrees inspired by Nazi Governments or Nazi idealogies. Reports indicate that the French of North Africa are subordinating all political questions to the formation of a common front against the common enemy.

549. FEDERAL POWER COMMISSION v. NATURAL GAS PIPELINE CO.
315 U. S. 575
1942

When the Natural Gas Pipeline Co. challenged a regulation of the Federal Power Commission, this crucial decision sustained the findings of administrative boards and established the Court's refusal to go behind the facts. Chief Justice Stone read an opinion sustaining the ruling of the Federal Power Commission. His reasoning, however, seemed timid to three members of the Court and they wrote a concurring opinion carrying the logic of the decision to its conclusion. Because this concurring opinion has commanded increasing support and because it affords a historical review of the whole rate evaluation question, it is given here instead of the opinion of Chief Justice Stone. Justice Frankfurter filed a separate opinion concurring with the findings of Stone. Compare with the Minnesota Rate Cases of 1890, Doc. No. 319. See also the opinion of Justice Brandeis in the Southwestern Bell Telephone Co. case, 262 U.S. 276; the O'Fallon case, 279 U.S. 461; the St. Joseph Stock Yard case, 298 U.S. 38; McCart v. Indianapolis Water Co., 302 U.S. 419. On the problem of valuation and judicial review see Bonbright, Valuation of Property; Hale, "The Fair Value Theory," 33 Ill. L. Rev., 517; Hale, "Conflicting Judicial Criteria of Utility Rates," 38 Col. L. Rev. 959; Henderson, "Railway Valuation and the Courts," 33 Harv. L. Rev. 1031.

BLACK, DOUGLAS, and MURPHY, JJ., concurring.

I.

We concur with the Court's judgment that the rate order of the Federal Power Commission, issued after a fair hearing upon findings of fact supported by substantial evidence, should have been sustained by the court below. But insofar as the Court assumes that, regardless of the terms of the statute, the due process clause of the Fifth Amendment grants it power to invalidate an order as unconstitutional because it finds the charges to be unreasonable, we are unable to join in the opinion just announced.

Rate making is a species of price fixing. In a recent series of cases, this Court has held that legislative price fixing is not prohibited by the due process clause. We believe that in so holding, it has returned in part at least to the constitutional principles which prevailed for the first hundred years of our history. The Munn and Peik cases, decided in 1877, Justices Field and Strong dissenting, emphatically declared price fixing to be a constitutional prerogative of the legislative branch, not subject to judicial review or revision.

In 1886, four of the Justices who had voted with him in the Munn and Peik cases no longer being on the Court, Chief Justice Waite expressed views in an opinion of the Court which indicated a yielding in part to the doctrines previously set forth in Mr. Justice Field's dissenting opinions, although the decision, upholding a state regulatory statute, did not require him to reach this issue. See Railroad Commission Cases, 116 U.S. 307. . . . By 1890, six Justices of the 1877 Court, including Chief Justice Waite, had been replaced by others. The new Court then clearly repudiated the opinion expressed for the Court by Chief Justice Waite in the Munn and Peik cases, in a holding which accorded with the views of Mr. Justice Field. Chicago, etc., Railway Co. v. Minnesota. Under those views, first embodied in a holding of this Court in 1890, "due process" means no less than "reasonableness judicially determined." In accordance with this elastic meaning which, in the words of Mr. Justice Holmes, makes the sky the limit of judicial power to declare legislative acts unconstitutional, the conclusions of judges, substituted for those of legislatures, become a broad and varying standard of constitutionality. We shall not attempt now to set out at length the reasons for our belief that acceptance of such a meaning is historically unjustified and that it transfers to courts powers which, under the Constitution, belong to the legislative branch of government. But we feel that we must record our disagreement from an opinion which, although upholding the action of the Commission on these particular facts, nevertheless gives renewed vitality to a "constitutional" doctrine which we are convinced has no support in the Constitution.

The doctrine which makes of "due process" an unlimited grant to courts to approve or reject policies selected by legislatures in accordance with the judges' notion of reasonableness had its origin in connection with legislative attempts to fix the prices charged by public utilities. And in no field has it had more paralyzing effects.

II.

We have here, to be sure, a statute which expressly provides for judicial review. Congress has provided in § 5 of the Natural Gas Act that the rates fixed by the Commission shall be "just and reasonable." The provision for judicial review states that the "finding of the Commission as to the facts, if supported by substantial evidence, shall be conclusive." But we are not satisfied that the opinion of the Court properly delimits the scope of that review under this Act. Furthermore, since this case starts a new chapter in the regulation of utility rates, we think it important to indicate more explicitly than

has been done the freedom which the Commission has both under the Constitution and under this new statute. While the opinion of the Court erases much which has been written into rate cases during the last half century, we think this is an appropriate occasion to lay the ghost of Smyth v. Ames, which has haunted utility regulation since 1898. That is especially desirable lest the reference by the majority to "constitutional requirements" and to "the limits of due process" be deemed to perpetuate the fallacious "fair-value" theory of rate making in the limited judicial review provided by the Act.

Smyth v. Ames held [See Doc. No. 319],

(1) This theory derives from principles of eminent domain. In condemnation cases the "value of property, generally speaking, is determined by its productiveness,—the profits which its use brings to the owner." But those principles have no place in rate regulation. In the first place, the value of a going concern in fact depends on earnings under whatever rates may be anticipated. The present fair value rule creates but offers no solution to the dilemma that value depends upon the rates fixed and the rates upon value. See Mr. Justice Brandeis, State of Missouri ex rel. Southwestern Bell Telephone Co. v. Public Service Commission, 262 U.S. 276. In the second place, when property is taken under the power of eminent domain the owner is "entitled to the full money equivalent of the property taken, and thereby to be put in as good position pecuniarily as it would have occupied, if its property had not been taken." United States v. New River Collieries Co., 262 U.S. 341. But in rate-making the owner does not have any such protection. We know without attempting any valuation that if earnings are reduced the value will be less. But that does not stay the hand of the legislature or its administrative agency in making rate reductions. As we have said, rate-making is one species of price-fixing. Price-fixing, like other forms of social legislation, may well diminish the value of the property which is regulated. But that is no obstacle to its validity. As stated by Mr. Justice Holmes "The fact that tangible property is also visible tends to give rigidity to our conception of our rights in it that we do not attach to others less con-

cretely clothed. But the notion that the former are exempt from the legislative modification required from time to time in civilized life is contradicted not only by the doctrine of eminent domain, under which what is taken is paid for, but by that of the police power in its proper sense, under which property rights may be cut down, and to that extent taken, without pay." Somewhat the same view was expressed in Nebbia v. People of New York, where this Court said: "The due process clause makes no mention of sales or of prices any more than it speaks of business or contracts or buildings or other incidents of property. The thought seems nevertheless to have persisted that there is something peculiarly sacrosanct about the price one may charge for what he makes or sells, and that, however able to regulate other elements of manufacture or trade, with incidental effect upon price, the state is incapable of ·directly controlling the price itself. This view was negatived many years ago. Munn v. Illinois. Explicit recognition of these principles will place the problems of rate-making in their proper setting under this statute."

(2) The rule of Smyth v. Ames, as construed and applied, directs the rate-making body in forming its judgment as to "fair-value" to take into consideration various elements—capitalization, book cost, actual cost, prudent investment, reproduction cost. But as stated by Mr. Justice Brandeis: "Obviously 'value' cannot be a composite of all these elements. Nor can it be arrived at on all these bases. They are very different, and must, when applied in a particular case, lead to widely different results. The rule of Smyth v. Ames, as interpreted and applied, means merely that all must be considered. What, if any, weight shall be given to any one, must practically rest in the judicial discretion of the tribunal which makes the determination. Whether a desired result is reached may depend upon how any one of many elements is treated." The risks of not giving weight to reproduction cost have been great. The havoc raised by insistence on reproduction cost is now a matter of historical record. Mr. Justice Brandeis in the Southwestern Bell Telephone case demonstrated how the rule of Smyth v. Ames has seriously im-

paired the power of rate-regulation and how the "fair value" rule has proved to be unworkable by reason of the time required to make the valuations, the heavy expense involved, and the unreliability of the results obtained. The result of this Court's rulings in rate cases since Smyth v. Ames has recently been summarized as follows: "Under the influence of these precedents, commission regulation has become so cumbersome and so ineffective that it may be said, with only slight exaggeration, to have broken down. Even the investor, on whose behalf the constitutional safeguards have been developed, has received no protection against the rebounds from the inflated stock-market prices that are stimulated by the 'fair-value' doctrine." Bonbright, Valuation of Property, p. 1154.

As we read the opinion of the Court, the Commission is now freed from the compulsion of admitting evidence on reproduction cost or of giving any weight to that element of "fair value." The Commission may now adopt, if it chooses, prudent investment as a rate base—the base long advocated by Mr. Justice Brandeis. And for the reasons stated by Mr. Justice Brandeis in the Southwestern Bell Telephone case there could be no constitutional objection if the Commission adhered to that formula and rejected all others.

Yet it is important to note, as we have indicated, that Congress has merely provided in § 5 of the Natural Gas Act that the rates fixed by the Commission shall be "just and reasonable." It has provided no standard beyond that. Congress, to be sure, has provided for judicial review. But § 19(b) states that the "finding of the Commission as to the facts, if supported by substantial evidence, shall be conclusive." In view of these provisions we do not think it is permissible for the courts to concern themselves with any issues as to the economic merits of a rate base. The Commission has a broad area of discretion for selection of an appropriate rate base. The requirements of "just and reasonable" embrace among other factors two phases of the public interest: (1) the investor interest; (2) the consumer interest. The investor interest is adequately served if the utility is allowed the opportunity to earn the cost of the service. That cost has been defined by Mr. Justice Brandeis as follows: "Cost includes, not only operating expenses, but also capital charges. Capital charges cover the allowance, by way of interest, for the use of the capital, whatever the nature of the security issued therefor, the allowance for risk incurred, and enough more to attract capital." State of Missouri ex rel. Southwestern Bell Telephone Co. v. Public Service Commission, 262 U.S. 291. Irrespective of what the return may be on "fair value," if the rate permits the company to operate successfully and to attract capital all questions as to "just and reasonable" are at an end so far as the investor interest is concerned. Various routes to that end may be worked out by the expert administrators charged with the duty of regulation. It is not the function of the courts to prescribe what formula should be used. The fact that one may be fair to investors does not mean that another would be unfair. The decision in each case must turn on considerations of justness and fairness which cannot be cast into a legalistic formula. The rate of return to be allowed in any given case calls for a highly expert judgment. That judgment has been entrusted to the Commission. There it should rest.

One *caveat* however should be entered. The consumer interest cannot be disregarded in determining what is a "just and reasonable" rate. Conceivably a return to the company of the cost of the service might not be "just and reasonable" to the public. The correct principle was announced by this Court in Covington & Lexington Turnpike Co. v. Sandford, 164 U.S. 578.

"It cannot be said that a corporation . . . is entitled as of right, and without reference to the interests of the public, to realize a given per cent, upon its capital stock. When the question arises whether the legislature has exceeded its constitutional power in prescribing rates to be charged by a corporation controlling a public highway, stockholders are not the only persons whose rights or interests are to be considered. The rights of the public are not to be ignored. It is alleged here that the rates prescribed are unreasonable and unjust to the company and its stockholders. But that involves an inquiry as to what is reasonable and just for the public. If the establishing of new lines of transportation should cause a diminution in the number of those who need to use a turnpike road, and, consequently, a diminution in the tolls collected, that is not, in itself, a sufficient reason why the corporation operating the road should be allowed to maintain rates that would be unjust to those who must or do use its property. The public cannot properly be subjected to unreasonable rates in order simply that stockholders may earn dividends."

This problem carries into a field not necessary to develop here. It reemphasizes however, that the investor interest is not the sole interest for protection. The investor and consumer interests may so collide as to warrant the rate-making body in concluding that a return on historical cost or prudent investment though fair to investors would be grossly unfair to the consumers. The possibility of that collision reinforces the view that the problem of rate-making is for the administrative experts not the courts and that the *ex post facto* function previously performed by the courts should be reduced to the barest minimum which is consistent with the statutory mandate for judicial review. That review should be as confined and restricted as the review, under similar statutes, of orders of other administrative agencies.

550. CASABLANCA CONFERENCE
Feb. 12, 1943

(The Public Papers of F. D. Roosevelt, Vol. 12, p. 71)

By the beginning of 1943 the military initiative had passed to the United Nations. The Casablanca Conference was necessary to step up the Tunisian campaign and plan a new offensive in Southern Europe. President Roosevelt outlined the purposes of the Casablanca Conference as

(1) to maintain the initiative, (2) to dispatch all aid to the Russians, and (3) to send assistance to the Chinese. Finally, the conference was called to help resolve the conflict between Giraud and de Gaulle. Roosevelt was the first President to leave the United States in wartime. Only Roosevelt and Churchill met at Casablanca; Stalin was invited but pleaded the necessity of remaining in Russia to give personal direction to the Russian campaign. The conference met from January 14 to 24, 1943. At Roosevelt's request, it was called the "Unconditional Surrender Conference," a phrase taken from Grant's letter to the Confederate commander of Forts Henry and Donelson. The official report of Jan. 24, 1943 did not contain the term "Unconditional Surrender." Because, in perspective, that was the real significance of the conference, we give here President Roosevelt's radio report of Feb. 12, 1943. See Elliott Roosevelt, *As He Saw It;* F. C. Balling, "Unconditional Surrender and a Unilated Declaration of Peace," *Am. Pol. Sci. Rev.* Vol. XXXIX, pp. 474 ff. Carol Thompson, "Casablanca and After," *Current History,* March, 1943.

The decisions reached and the actual plans made at Casablanca were not confined to any one theater of war or to any one continent or ocean or sea. Before this year is out, it will be made known to the world—in actions rather than in words—that the Casablanca Conference produced plenty of news; and it will be bad news for the Germans and Italians—and the Japanese.

We have lately concluded a long, hard battle in the Southwest Pacific and we have made notable gains. That battle started in the Solomons and New Guinea last summer. It has demonstrated our superior power in planes and, most importantly, in the fighting qualities of our individual soldiers and sailors.

American armed forces in the Southwest Pacific are receiving powerful aid from Australia and New Zealand and also directly from the British themselves.

We do not expect to spend the time it would take to bring Japan to final defeat merely by inching our way forward from island to island across the vast expanse of the Pacific.

Great and decisive actions against the Japanese will be taken to drive the invader from the soil of China. Important actions will be taken in the skies over China—and over Japan itself.

The discussions at Casablanca have been continued in Chungking with the Generalissimo by General Arnold and have resulted in definite plans for offensive operations.

There are many roads which lead right to Tokyo. We shall neglect none of them.

In an attempt to ward off the inevitable disaster, the Axis propagandists are trying all of their old tricks in order to divide the United Nations. They seek to create the idea that if we win this war, Russia, England, China, and the United States are going to get into a cat-and-dog fight.

This is their final effort to turn one nation against another, in the vain hope that they may settle with one or two at a time—that any of us may be so gullible and so forgetful as to be duped into making "deals" at the expense of our Allies.

To these panicky attempts to escape the consequences of their crimes we say—all the United Nations say—that the only terms on which we shall deal with an Axis government or any Axis factions are the terms proclaimed at Casablanca: "Unconditional Surrender." In our, uncompromising policy we mean no harm to the common people of the Axis nations. But we do mean to impose punishment and retribution in full upon their guilty, barbaric leaders. . . .

In the years of the American and French revolutions the fundamental principle guiding our democracies was established. The cornerstone of our whole democratic edifice was the principle that from the people and the people alone flows the authority of government.

It is one of our war aims, as expressed in the Atlantic Charter, that the conquered populations of today be again the masters of their destiny. There must be no doubt anywhere that it is the unalterable purpose of the United Nations to restore to conquered peoples their sacred rights.

551. MOSCOW CONFERENCE
October, 1943

(*Dept. of State Bulletin*, Vol. IX, pp. 307 ff.)

By the fall of 1943, almost two years after the entrance of America into the war, no "second front" had been opened on the European continent, and the Soviet Union complained bitterly, while many people, here and abroad, alleged that the failure to establish a "second front" was a political move directed against future Soviet power. The 15,000-mile air trip of Secretary of State Cordell Hull to Moscow and the success of the Moscow Conference in dispelling that atmosphere of distrust was one of the great diplomatic triumphs of the war. The Moscow Conference planned the new military phase of the war which would begin with the establishment of a "second front" in the West. Secretary Hull, Anthony Eden, British Foreign Secretary, and Soviet Foreign Commissar Molotov, together with the Chinese ambassador to the Soviet Union, signed a four power pact pledging their determination to establish a new world organization. The Tripartite Conference of Foreign Ministers met in Spiridonovka House in Moscow from October 19 to November 1 in twelve historic sessions. The conference dealt with political as well as military problems, notably in the appeal to the Austrians to break with Germany, and the decision to create an independent Austria; the plan to establish in London a European commission of foreign ministers; and the decision to revise the Mediterranean Commission to include representatives of Greece and Yugoslavia. See Jan Ciechanowski, *Defeat in Victory;* P. B. Potter, "Moscow; Cairo; Teheran," *Am. J. Int. Law* Vol. 38; S. B. Fay, "The meaning of the Moscow Conference," *Current History,* n.s. Vol. 5, pp. 289-94; Walter Lippmann, "The Four Policemen," *Vital Speeches* Vol. 10, pp. 138 ff.

The Moscow Conference
October, 1943

The conference of foreign secretaries of the United States of America, Mr. Cordell Hull; of the United Kingdom, Mr. Anthony Eden; and of the Soviet Union, Mr. V. M. Molotov; took place at Moscow from 19 to 30 October, 1943. There were twelve meetings. In addition to the foreign secretaries,

the following took part in the conference:

For the United States of America: Mr. W. Averell Harriman, Ambassador of the United States; Major General John R. Deane, United States Army; Mr. H. Hackworth, Mr. James C. Dunn and experts.

For the United Kingdom: Sir Archibald Clark Kerr, Ambassador; Mr. William Strang, Lieutenant General Sir Hastings Ismay and experts.

For the Soviet Union: Marshal K. E. Voroshilov, Marshal of the Soviet Union; Mr. A. Y. Vishinsky, Mr. M. M. Litvinov, Deputy People's Commissars for Foreign Affairs; Mr. V. Sergeyev, Deputy People's Commissar for Foreign Trade; Major General A. A. Gryzlov, of the general staff; Mr. G. F. Saksin, senior official for People's Commissariat for Foreign Affairs, and experts.

The agenda included all questions submitted for discussion by the three governments. Some of the questions called for final decisions, and these were taken. On other questions, after discussion, decisions of principle were taken: These questions were referred for detailed consideration to commissions specially set up for the purpose, or reserved for treatment through diplomatic channels. Other questions again were disposed of by an exchange of views. The governments of the United States, the United Kingdom, and the Soviet Union have been in close cooperation in all matters concerning the common war effort, but this is the first time that the foreign secretaries of the three governments have been able to meet together in conference.

In the first place there were frank and exhaustive discussions of the measures to be taken to shorten the war aaginst Germany and her satellites in Europe. Advantage was taken of the presence of military advisers representing the respective chiefs of staff in order to discuss definite military operations with regard to which decisions had been taken and which are already being prepared in order to create a basis for the closest military cooperation in the future between the three countries.

Second only to the importance of hastening the end of the war was the recognition by the three governments that it was essential in their own national interests and in the interest of all peace-loving nations to continue to present close collaboration and cooperation in the conduct of the war into the period following the end of hostilities, and that only in this way could peace be maintained and the political, economic, and social welfare of their people fully promoted.

This conviction is expressed in a declaration in which the Chinese Government joined during the conference and which was signed by the three Foreign Secretaries and the Chinese Ambassador at Moscow on behalf of their governments. This declaration provided for even closer collaboration in the prosecution of the war and in all matters pertaining to the surrender and disarmament of the enemies with which the four countries were respectively at war. It set forth the principles upon which the four governments agreed that a broad system of international cooperation and security should be based. Provision is made for the inclusion of all other peace-loving nations, great and small, in this system.

The conference agreed to set up machinery for insuring the closest cooperation between the three governments in the examination of European questions arising as the war developed. For this purpose the conference decided to establish in London a European advisory commission to study these questions and to make joint recommendations to the three . governments.

Provision was made for continuing when necessary the tri-partite consultations of representatives of the three governments in the respective capitals through the existing diplomatic channels.

The conference also agreed to establish an advisory council for matters relating to Italy, to be composed, in the first instance, of representatives of their three governments and of the French Committee of National Liberation. Provision is made for addition to this council of representatives of Greece and Yugoslavia in view of their special interests arising out of aggressions of Facist Italy upon their territory during the present war.

This council will deal with day to day questions other than military preparations and will make recommendations designed to coordinate allied policy with regard to Italy.

The three foreign secretaries considered it appropriate to reaffirm, by a declaration published today, the attitude of the allied governments in favor of the restoration of democracy in Italy.

The three foreign secretaries declared it to be the purpose of their governments to restore the independence of Austria. At the same time they reminded Austria that in the final settlement account will be taken of efforts that Austria may make toward its own liberation.

The foreign secretaries issued at the conference a declaration by President Roosevelt, Prime Minister Churchill and Premier Stalin containing a solemn warning that at the time of granting any armistice to any German government, those German officers and men and members of the Nazi party who have had any connection with atrocities and executions in countries overrun by German forces, will be taken back to the countries in which their abominable crimes were committed to be charged and punished according to the laws of those countries.

In an atmosphere of mutual confidence and understanding which characterized all the work of the conference, consideration was also given to other important questions. These included not only questions of a current nature, but also questions concerning treatment of Hitlerite Germany and its satellites, economic cooperation and assurance of general peace.

JOINT FOUR-NATION DECLARATION

The governments of the United States of America, United Kingdom, the Soviet Union and China;

United in their determination, in accordance with the declaration by the United Nations of January 1942, and subsequent declarations, to continue hostilities against those Axis powers with which they respectively are at war until such powers have laid down their arms on the basis of unconditional surrender;

Conscious of their responsibility to secure the liberation of themselves and the peoples allied with them from the menace of aggression;

Recognizing the necessity of insuring a rapid and orderly transition from war to peace and of establishing and maintaining international peace and security with the least diversion of the world's human and economic resources for armaments;

Jointly declare:

1. That their united action, pledged for the prosecution of the war against their respective enemies, will be continued for the organization and maintenance of peace and security.

2. That those of them at war with a common enemy will act together in all matters relating to the surrender and disarmament of that enemy.

3. That they will take all measures deemed by them to be necessary to provide against any violation of the terms imposed upon the enemy.

4. That they recognize the necessity of establishing at the earliest practicable date a general international organization, based on the principle of the sovereign equality of all peace-loving states, and open to membership by all such states, large and small, for the maintenance of international peace and security.

5. That for the purpose of maintaining international peace and security pending the re-establishment of law and order and the inauguration of a system of general security they will consult with one another and as occasion requires with other members of the United Nations, with a view to joint action on behalf of the community of nations.

6. That after the termination of hostilities they will not employ their military forces within the territories of other states except for the purposes envisaged in this declaration and after joint consultation.

7. That they will confer and cooperate with one another and with other members of the United Nations to bring about a practicable general agreement with respect to the regulation of armaments in the post-war period.

DECLARATION REGARDING ITALY

The Foreign Secretaries of the United States, the United Kingdom and the Soviet Union have established that their three governments are in complete agreement that

Allied policy toward Italy must be based upon the fundamental principle that Fascism and all its evil influence and configuration shall be completely destroyed and that the Italian people shall be given every opportunity to establish governmental and other institutions based upon democratic principles.

The Foreign Secretaries of the United States and United Kingdom declare that the action of their governments from the inception of the invasion of Italian territory, in so far as paramount military requirements have permitted, has been based upon this policy.

In furtherance of this policy in the future the Foreign Secretaries of the three governments are agreed that the following measures are important and should be put into effect:

1. It is essential that the Italian Government should be made more democratic by inclusion of representatives of those sections of the Italian people who have always opposed Fascism.

2. Freedom of speech, of religious worship, of political belief, of press and of public meeting shall be restored in full measure to the Italian people, who shall be entitled to form anti-Fascist political groups.

3. All institutions and organizations created by the Fascist regime shall be suppressed.

4. All Fascist or pro-Fascist elements shall be removed from the administration and from institutions and organizations of a public character.

5. All political prisoners of the Fascist regime shall be released and accorded full amnesty.

6. Democratic organs of local government shall be created.

7. Fascist chiefs and army generals known or suspected to be war criminals shall be arrested and handed over to justice.

In making this declaration the three Foreign Secretaries recognize that so long as active military operations continue in Italy the time at which it is possible to give full effect to the principles stated above will be determined by the Commander-in-Chief on the basis of instructions received through the combined chiefs of staff.

The three governments, parties to this

declaration, will, at the request of any one of them, consult on this matter. It is further understood that nothing in this resolution is to operate against the right of the Italian people ultimately to choose their own form of government.

DECLARATION ON AUSTRIA

The governments of the United Kingdom, the Soviet Union and the United States of America are agreed that Austria, the first free country to fall a victim to Hitlerite aggression, shall be liberated from German domination.

They regard the annexation imposed on Austria by Germany on March 15, 1938, as null and void. They consider themselves as in no way bound by any changes effected in Austria since that date. They declare that they wish to see re-established a free and independent Austria and thereby to open the way for the Austrian people themselves, as well as those neighboring States which will be faced with similar problems, to find that political and economic security which is the only basis for lasting peace.

Austria is reminded, however, that she has a responsibility, which she cannot evade, for participation in the war at the side of Hitlerite Germany, and that in the final settlement account will inevitably be taken of her own contribution to her liberation.

STATEMENT ON ATROCITIES

Signed by President Roosevelt, Prime Minister Churchill and Premier Stalin

The United Kingdom, the United States and the Soviet Union have received from many quarters evidence of atrocities, massacres and cold-blooded mass executions which are being perpetrated by Hitlerite forces in many of the countries they have overrun and from which they are now being steadily expelled. The brutalities of Nazi domination are no new thing, and all peoples or territories in their grip have suffered from the worst form of government by terror. What is new is that many of the territories are now being redeemed by the advancing armies of the liberating powers, and that in their desperation the recoiling Hitlerites and Huns are redoubling their ruthless cruelties.

This is now evidenced with particular clearness by monstrous crimes on the territory of the Soviet Union which is being liberated from Hitlerites, and on French and Italian territory.

Accordingly, the aforesaid three Allied powers, speaking in the interest of the thirty-two United Nations, hereby solemnly declare and give full warning of their declaration as follows:

At the time of granting of any armistice to any government which may be set up in Germany, those German officers and men and members of the Nazi party who have been responsible for or have taken a consenting part in the above atrocities, massacres and executions will be sent back to the countries in which their abominable deeds were done in order that they may be judged and punished according to the laws of these liberated countries and of free governments which will be erected therein. Lists will be compiled in all possible detail from all these countries having regard especially to invaded parts of the Soviet Union, to Poland and Czechoslovakia, to Yugoslavia and Greece including Crete and other islands, to Norway, Denmark, Netherlands, Belgium, Luxemburg, France and Italy.

Thus, Germans who take part in wholesale shooting of Polish officers or in the execution of French, Dutch, Belgian or Norwegian hostages or Cretan peasants, or who have shared in slaughters inflicted on the people of Poland or in territories of the Soviet Union which are now being swept clear of the enemy, will know they will be brought back to the scene of their crimes and judged on the spot by the peoples whom they have outraged.

Let those who have hitherto not imbued their hands with innocent blood beware lest they join the ranks of the guilty, for most assuredly the three Allied powers will pursue them to the uttermost ends of the earth and will deliver them to their accusors in order that justice may be done.

The above declaration is without prejudice to the case of German criminals, whose offenses have no particular geographical localization and who will be punished by joint decision of the governments of the Allies.

552. CAIRO CONFERENCE
November, 1943

(Dept. of State Bulletin, Vol. IX, p. 393)

By late November, 1943, the European war was going so well that the Allies could afford to fight in the Pacific on almost as great a scale as in Europe. From November 22 to 26, 1943, Roosevelt and Churchill met for the first time with Chiang Kai-Shek at Cairo. The conference was entirely concerned with Asia; hence, Russia was not represented. Military discussions were concerned with fleet allocations and the opening of supply lines to China from India and Burma. The conference gave China UN status as one of the Big Four. See H. G. Butcher, *My Three Years With Eisenhower;* S. B. Fay, "Moscow, Cairo, and Teheran," *Current History,* n.s., Vol. 6, pp. 97 ff.; Chiang Kai-Shek, *Resistance and Reconstruction.*

Released December 1, 1943

The several military missions have agreed upon future military operations against Japan. The Three Great Allies expressed their resolve to bring unrelenting pressure against their brutal enemies by sea, land, and air.

This pressure is already rising.

The Three Great Allies are fighting this war to restrain and punish the aggression of Japan. They covet no gain for themselves and have no thought of territorial expansion. It is their purpose that Japan shall be stripped of all the islands in the Pacific which she has seized or occupied since the beginning of the first World War in 1914, and that all the territories Japan has stolen from the Chinese, such as Manchuria, Formosa, and the Pescadores, shall be restored to the Republic of China. Japan will also be expelled from all other territories which she has taken by violence and greed. The aforesaid three great powers, mindful of the enslavement of the people of Korea, are determined that in due course Korea shall become free and independent.

With these objects in view the three Allies, in harmony with those of the United Nations at war with Japan, will continue to persevere in the serious and prolonged operations necessary to procure the unconditional surrender of Japan.

553. CONNALLY-FULBRIGHT RESOLUTIONS
November 5, 1943

(Congressional Record, Vol. 89, p. 7729, 9222)

One of the great fears of advocates of a world organization was that the United States Senate, which must ratify all treaties by a two-thirds vote, would fail to approve American entrance into such an organization, just as the plans of Woodrow Wilson for American participation in an effective League of Nations had been thwarted after the First World War. On March 16, 1943, Senators Joseph Ball (R., Minn.), Harold Burton (R., Ohio), Carl Hatch (D., N. Mex.), and Lister Hill (D., Ala.) began a bipartisan movement to commit the U.S. Senate to participation in an international organization. After much discussion on October 14, Senate Foreign Relations Committee reported out the Connally resolution. The debate took place while the Moscow Conference was going

on; when the Conference announced its declaration in favor of "a general international organization," the Senate incorporated a new paragraph into the Connally Resolution almost identical with Article 4 of the Moscow Declaration. In order to insure a greater vote for the Resolution, another paragraph was added specifically stating that all treaties enacted to carry out the purposes of the Resolution must be passed on by a vote of two-thirds of the Senate. On November 5, the Senate adopted the Resolution, as amended, by a vote of 85-5, well above the necessary two-thirds vote which would later be required to approve the new international organization. See bibliography for United Nations Participation Act. Also see bibliography for Docs. 435, 436.

The Fulbright Resolution

Passed by the House of Representatives 21 September 1943

RESOLVED by the House of Representatives (the Senate concurring), that the Congress hereby expresses itself as favoring the creation of appropriate international machinery with power adequate to establish and to maintain a just and lasting peace, among the nations of the world, and as favoring participation by the United States therein through its constitutional process.

The Connally Resolution

Passed by the Senate 6 November 1943

RESOLVED, That the war against all our enemies be waged until complete victory is achieved.

That the United States cooperate with its comrades-in-arms in securing a just and honorable peace.

That the United States, acting through its constitutional processes, join free and sovereign nations in the establishment and maintenance of international authority with power to prevent aggression and to preserve the peace of the world.

That the Senate recognize the necessity of there being established at the earliest practicable date a general international organization, based on the principle of the sovereign equality of all peace-loving states, and open to membership by all such states, large and small, for the maintenance of international peace and security.

That, pursuant to the Constitution of the United States, any treaty made to effect the purpose of this resolution, on behalf of the Government of the United States with any other nation or any association of nations, shall be made only by and with the advice and consent of the Senate of the United States, provided two-thirds of the Senators present concur.

554. TEHERAN CONFERENCE
December 1, 1943

(Dept. of State Bulletin, Vol. IX, p. 409)

From their conference at Cairo, President Roosevelt and Prime Minister Churchill flew to the Iranian capital of Teheran for their first meeting with Premier Stalin. For four days, from November 28 to December 1, 1943, the three men met and dined together constantly, discussing the military aspects of coordinating the Russian offensive with the forthcoming second front. It was at the Teheran conference that the details of the Allied invasions of France were worked out; the meetings had been long awaited, and the end of the second front issue resulted in increased good feeling among the Big Three. Only a vague, general communique was issued at the time of the conference, and the secrecy of the conference was widely criticized by the press. One of the political problems decided at the conference was the Iranian question. Iran had been jointly occupied by the Big Three; they issued a statement at the conference, pledging recall of their troops when the war ended. Not until March 24, 1947 did the State Department make public other decisions of the conference in respect to arming Yugoslav guerrillas and attempting to get Turkey to declare war against the Axis. See F. R. Dulles,

The Road to Teheran; D. Dallin, *The Big Three;* H. C. Nixon, "Big Four," *Va. Quart. Rev.,* Vol. 19 pp. 513 ff; Elliott Roosevelt, *As He Saw It.*

We—The President of the United States, the Prime Minister of Great Britain, and the Premier of the Soviet Union, have met these four days past, in this, the Capital of our Ally, Iran, and have shaped and confirmed our common policy.

We express our determination that our nations shall work together in war and in the peace that will follow.

As to war—our military staffs have joined in our round table discussions, and we have concerted our plans for the destruction of the German forces. We have reached complete agreement as to the scope and timing of the operations to be undertaken from the east, west and south.

The common understanding which we have here reached guarantees that victory will be ours.

And as to peace—we are sure that our concord will win an enduring Peace. We recognize fully the supreme responsibility resting upon us and all the United Nations to make a peace which will command the goodwill of the overwhelming mass of the peoples of the world and banish the scourge and terror of war for many generations.

With our Diplomatic advisers we have surveyed the problems of the future. We shall seek the cooperation and active participation of all nations, large and small, whose peoples in heart and mind are dedicated, as are our own peoples, to the elimination of tyranny and slavery, oppression and intolerance. We will welcome them, as they may choose to come, into a world family of Democratic Nations.

No power on earth can prevent our destroying the German armies by land, their U Boats by sea, and their war plants from the air.

Our attack will be relentless and increasing.

Emerging from these cordial conferences we look with confidence to the day when all peoples of the world may live free lives, untouched by tyranny, and according to their varying desires and their own consciences.

We came here with hope and determination. We leave here, friends in fact, in spirit and in purpose.

ROOSEVELT, CHURCHILL and STALIN

Declaration of the Three Powers Regarding Iran

(This declaration was published Dec. 7, 1943.)

The President of the United States, the Premier of the U.S.S.R. and the Prime Minister of the United Kingdom, having consulted with each other and with the Prime Minister of Iran, desire to declare the mutual agreement of their three Governments regarding their relations with Iran.

The Governments of the United States, the U.S.S.R. and the United Kingdom recognize the assistance which Iran has given in the prosecution of the war against the common enemy, particularly by facilitating the transportation of supplies from overseas to the Soviet Union.

The three Governments realize that the war has caused special economic difficulties for Iran, and they are agreed that they will continue to make available to the Government of Iran such economic assistance as may be possible, having regard to the heavy demands made upon them by their worldwide military operations and to the worldwide shortage of transport, raw materials and supplies for civilian consumption.

With respect to the post-war period, the Governments of the United States, the U.S.S.R. and the United Kingdom are in accord with the Government of Iran that any economic problems confronting Iran at the close of hostilities should receive full consideration, along with those of other members of the United Nations, by conferences or international agencies held or created to deal with international economic matters.

The Governments of the United States, the U.S.S.R and the United Kingdom are at one with the Government of Iran in their desire for the maintenance of the independence, sovereignty and territorial integrity of Iran. They count upon the participation of Iran, together with all other peace-loving nations, in the establishment of international peace, security and prosperity after the war, in accordance with the principles of the Atlantic Charter, to which all four Governments have subscribed.

WINSTON S. CHURCHILL
JOSEPH V. STALIN
FRANKLIN D. ROOSEVELT

Washington, March 24, 1947—The text of the military and other conclusions reached at the Teheran conference, as announced today by the State Department:

The conference:

(1) Agreed that the partisans in Yugoslavia should be supported by supplies and equipment to the greatest possible extent, and also by Commando operations;

(2) Agreed that, from the military point of view, it was most desirable that Turkey should come into the war on the side of the Allies before the end of the year;

(3) Took note of Marshal Stalin's statement that if Turkey found herself at war with Germany, and as a result Bulgaria declared war on Turkey or attacked her, the Soviet would immediately be at war with Bulgaria. The conference further took note that this fact could be explicitly stated in the forthcoming negotiations to bring Turkey into the war;

(4) Took note that Operation Overlord [the landings in Normandy] would be launched during May, 1944, in conjunction with an operation against southern France. The latter operation would be undertaken in as great a strength as availability of landing craft permitted. The conference further took note of Marshal Stalin's statement that the Soviet forces would launch an offensive at about the same time with the object of preventing the German forces from transferring from the eastern to the western front;

(5) Agreed that the military staffs of the three powers should henceforward keep in close touch with each other in regard to the impending operations in Europe. In particular it was agreed that a cover plan to mystify and mislead the enemy as regards these operations should be concerted between the staffs concerned.

FRANKLIN D. ROOSEVELT
JOSEPH V. STALIN
WINSTON S. CHURCHILL
Teheran, December 1, 1943.

555. AN ECONOMIC BILL OF RIGHTS
January 11, 1944

(The Public Papers of F. D. Roosevelt, Vol. 13, p. 32)

President Roosevelt's annual message to Congress in 1944 was especially notable for his espousal of the new bill of rights.

If ever there was a time to subordinate individual or group selfishness to the national good, that time is now. Disunity at home—bickerings, self-seeking partisanship, stoppages of work, inflation, business as usual, politics as usual, luxury as usual—these are the influences which can undermine the morale of the brave men ready to die at the front for us here.

Those who are doing most of the complaining are not deliberately striving to sabotage the national war effort. They are laboring under the delusion that the time is past when we must make prodigious sacrifices—that the war is already won and we can begin to slacken off. But the dangerous folly of that point of view can be measured by the distance that separates our troops from their ultimate objectives in Berlin and Tokyo—and by the sum of all the perils that lie along the way.

Let us remember the lessons of 1918. In the summer of that year the tide turned in favor of the Allies. But this Government did not relax. In fact, our national effort was stepped up. In August, 1918, the draft age limits were broadened from 21-31 to 18-45. The President called for "force to the utmost," and his call was heeded. And in November, only three months later, Germany surrendered.

That is the way to fight and win a war—all out—and not with half-an-eye on the battlefronts abroad and the other eye-and-a-half on personal, selfish, or political interests here at home.

Therefore, in order to concentrate all our energies and resources on winning the war, and to maintain a fair and stable economy at home, I recommend that the Congress adopt:

1. A realistic tax law—which will tax all unreasonable profits, both individual and corporate, and reduce the ultimate cost of the war to our sons and daughters. The tax bill now under consideration by the Congress does not begin to meet this test.

2. A continuation of the law for the renegotiation of war contracts—which will pre-

vent exorbitant profits and assure fair prices to the Government. For two long years I have pleaded with the Congress to take undue profits out of the war.

3. A cost of food law—which will enable the Government (a) to place a reasonable floor under the prices the farmer may expect for his production, and (b) to place a ceiling on the prices a consumer will have to pay for the food he buys. This should apply to necessities only; and will require public funds to carry out. It will cost in appropriations about 1 per cent of the present annual cost of the war.

4. Early enactment of the stabilization statute of October, 1942. This expires June 30, 1944, and if it is not extended well in advance the country might just as well expect price chaos by summer. We cannot have stabilization by wishful thinking. We must take positive action to maintain the integrity of the American dollar.

5. A national service law—which, for the duration of the war, will prevent strikes, and with certain appropriate exceptions, will make available for war production or for any other essential services every able-bodied adult in the nation.

These five measures together form a just and equitable whole. I would not recommend a national service law unless the other laws were passed to keep down the cost of living, to share equitably the burdens of taxation, to hold the stabilization line, and to prevent undue profits.

The Federal Government already has the basic power to draft capital and property of all kinds for war purposes on a basis of just compensation.

As you know, I have for three years hesitated to recommend a national service act. Today, however, I am convinced of its necessity. Although I believe that we and our Allies can win the war without such a measure, I am certain that nothing less than total mobilization of all our resources of manpower and capital will guarantee an earlier victory, and reduce the toll of suffering and sorrow and blood.

I have received a joint recommendation for this law from the heads of the War Department, the Navy Department, and the Maritime Commission. These are the men who bear responsibility for the procurement of the necessary arms and equipment, and for the successful prosecution of the war in the field. They say:

When the very life of the nation is in peril the responsibility for service is common to all men and women. In such a time there can be no discrimination between the men and women who are assigned by the Government to its defense at the battle front and the men and women assigned to produce the vital materials essential to successful military operations. A prompt enactment of a national service law would be merely an expression of the universality of this responsibility.

It is our duty now to begin to lay plans and determine the strategy for the winning of a lasting peace and the establishment of an American standard of living higher than ever before known. We cannot be content, no matter how high the general standard of living may be, if some fraction of our people—whether it be one-third or one-fifth or one-tenth—is ill-fed, ill-clothed, ill-housed, and insecure.

This Republic had its beginning, and grew to its present strength, under the protection of certain inalienable political rights—among them the right of free speech, free press, free worship, trial by jury, freedom from unreasonable searches and seizures. They were our rights to life and liberty.

As our nation has grown in size and stature, however—as our industrial economy expanded—these political rights proved inadequate to assure us equality in the pursuit of happiness.

We have come to a clear realization of the fact that true individual freedom cannot exist without economic security and independence. "Necessitous men are not free men." People who are hungry and out of a job are the stuff of which dictatorships are made.

In our day these economic truths have become accepted as self-evident. We have accepted, so to speak, a second Bill of Rights under which a new basis of security and prosperity can be established for all, regardless of station, race or creed.

Among these are:

The right to a useful and remunerative

job in the industries or shops or farms or mines of the nation;

The right to earn enough to provide adequate food and clothing and recreation;

The right of every farmer to raise and sell his products at a return which will give him and his family a decent living;

The right of every business man, large and small, to trade in an atmosphere of freedom from unfair competition and domination by monopolies at home or abroad;

The right of every family to a decent home;

The right to adequate medical care and the opportunity to achieve and enjoy good health;

The right to adequate protection from the economic fears of old age, sickness, accident and unemployment;

The right to a good education.

All of these rights spell security. And after this war is won we must be prepared to move forward, in the implementation of these rights, to new goals of human happiness and well-being.

America's own rightful place in the world depends in large part upon how fully these and similar rights have been carried into practice for our citizens. For unless there is security here at home there cannot be lasting peace in the world.

FRANKLIN D. ROOSEVELT

THE WHITE HOUSE,
January 11, 1944.

556. SMITH v. ALLWRIGHT
321 U. S. 649
1944

Lonnie E. Smith, a Negro citizen, brought action against S. E. Allwright, Election Judge of the Forty-eighth Precinct of Harris County, Texas, and his assistant, in the United States District Court for the Southern District of Texas, contending that he was denied a ballot in the Democratic primaries in Texas solely on the grounds of his race. His petition was denied and the Circuit Court, basing its action on Grovey v. Townsend, upheld the District Court. This decision overruled Grovey v. Townsend (295 U.S. 45), and the Court in this case took occasion to rehearse the history of judicial reversals and to reject the doctrine of *stare decisis* in the realm of Constitutional law. See Doc. and bibliography in U.S. v. Classic; R. E. Cushman, "The Texas 'White Primary' Case—Smith v. Allwright," 30 *Cornell L. Quart.*, pp. 66 ff.; F. E. Folsom, "Federal Elections and the 'White Primary,'" 33 *Col. L. Rev.*, pp. 1086 ff.; Stevenson, *Race Distinctions in American Law*.

On writ of Certiorari to the United States Circuit Court of Appeals for the Fifth Circuit.

REED, J. . . . The State of Texas by its Constitution and statutes provides that every person, if certain other requirements are met which are not here in issue, qualified by residence in the district or county "shall be deemed a qualified elector." Primary elections for United States Senators, Congressmen and state officers are provided for by Chapters Twelve and Thirteen of the statutes. Under these chapters, the Democratic Party was required to hold the primary which was the occasion of the alleged wrong to petitioned. . . . These nominations are to be made by the qualified voters of the party.

The Democratic Party of Texas is held by the Supreme Court of that state to be a "voluntary association," protected by Section 27 of the Bill of Rights, Art. 1, Constitution of Texas, from interference by the state except that:

"In the interest of fair methods and a fair expression by their members of their preferences in the selection of their nominees, the State may regulate such elections by proper laws."

The Democratic party on May 24, 1932 in a State Convention adopted the following resolution, which has not since been "amended, abrogated, annulled or avoided":

"Be it resolved that all white citizens of the State of Texas who are qualified to vote under the Constitution and laws of the State shall be eligible to membership in the Democratic party and, as such, entitled to participate in its deliberations."

It was by virtue of this resolution that the respondents refused to permit the petitioner to vote.

Texas is free to conduct her elections and limit her electorate as she may deem wise, save only as her action may be affected by the prohibitions of the United States Constitution or in conflict with powers delegated to and exercised by the National Government. The Fourteenth Amendment forbids a state from making or enforcing any law which abridges the privileges or immunities of citizens of the United States and the Fifteenth Amendment specifically interdicts any denial or abridgement by a state of the right of citizens to vote on account of color. Respondents appeared in the District Court and the Circuit Court of Appeals and defended on the ground that the Democratic party of Texas is a voluntary organization with members banded together for the purpose of selecting individuals of the group representing the common political beliefs as candidates in the general election. As such a voluntary organization, it was claimed, the Democratic party is free to select its own membership and limit to whites participation in the party primary. Such action, the answer asserted, does not violate the Fourteenth, Fifteenth or Seventeenth Amendments as officers of government cannot be chosen at primaries and the Amendments are applicable only to general elections where governmental officers are actually elected. Primaries, it is said, are political party affairs, handled by party not governmental officers.

The right of a Negro to vote in the Texas primary has been considered heretofore by this Court. Since Grovey v. Townsend and prior to the present suit, no case from Texas involving primary elections has been before this Court. We did decide, however, United States v. Classic. We there held that Section 4 of Article I of the Constitution authorized Congress to regulate primary as well as general elections, "where the primary is by law made an integral part of the election machinery." Consequently, in the Classic case, we upheld the applicability to frauds in a Louisiana primary of §§ 19 and 20 of the Criminal Code. Thereby corrupt acts of election officers were subjected to Congressional sanctions because that body had power to protect rights of Federal suffrage secured by the Constitution in primary as in general elections. This decision depended, too, on the determination that under the Louisiana statutes the primary was a part of the procedure for choice of Federal officials. By this decision the doubt as to whether or not such primaries were a part of "elections" subject to Federal control, which had remained unanswered since Newberry v. United States, was erased. The Nixon cases were decided under the equal protection clause of the Fourteenth Amendment without a determination of the status of the primary as a part of the electoral process. The exclusion of Negroes from the primaries by action of the State was held invalid under that Amendment. The fusing by the Classic case of the primary and general elections into a single instrumentality for choice of officers has a definite bearing on the permissibility under the Constitution of excluding Negroes from primaries. This is not to say that the Classic case cuts directly into the rationale of Grovey v. Townsend. This latter case was not mentioned in the opinion. Classic bears upon Grovey v. Townsend not because exclusion of Negroes from primaries is any more or less state action by reason of the unitary character of the electoral process but because the recognition of the place of the primary in the electoral scheme makes clear that state delegation to a party of the power to fix the qualifications of primary elections is delegation of a state function that may make the party's action the action of the state. When Grovey v. Townsend was written, the Court looked upon the denial of a vote in a primary as a mere refusal by a party of party membership. As the Louisiana statutes for holding primaries are similar to those of Texas, our ruling in Classic as to the unitary character of the electoral process calls for a reëxamination as to whether or not the exclusion of Negroes from a Texas party primary was state action.

It may now be taken as a postulate that the right to vote in such a primary for the nomination of candidates without discrimination by the State, like the right to vote in a general election, is a right secured by the Constitution.

We are thus brought to an examination

of the qualifications for Democratic primary electors in Texas, to determine whether state action or private action has excluded Negroes from participation.

We think that this statutory system for the selection of party nominees for inclusion on the general election ballot makes the party which is required to follow these legislative directions an agency of the state in so far as it determines the participants in a primary election. The party takes its character as a state agency from the duties imposed upon it by state statutes; the duties do not become matters of private law because they are performed by a political party. The plan of the Texas primary follows substantially that of Louisiana, with the exception that in Louisiana the state pays the cost of the primary while Texas assesses the cost against candidates. In numerous instances, the Texas statutes fix or limit the fees to be charged. Whether paid directly by the state or through state requirements, it is state action which compels. When primaries become a part of the machinery for choosing officials, state and national, as they have here, the same tests to determine the character of discrimination or abridgment should be applied to the primary as are applied to the general election. If the state requires a certain electoral procedure, prescribes a general election ballot made up of party nominees so chosen and limits the choice of the electorate in general elections for state offices, practically speaking, to those whose names appear on such a ballot, it endorses, adopts and enforces the discrimination against Negroes, practiced by a party entrusted by Texas law with the determination of the qualifications of participants in the primary. This is state action within the meaning of the Fifteenth Amendment.

The United States is a constitutional democracy. Its organic law grants to all citizens a right to participate in the choice of elected officials without restriction by any state because of race. This grant to the people of the opportunity for choice is not to be nullified by a state through casting its electoral process in a form which permits a private organization to practice racial discrimination in the election. Constitutional rights would be of little value if they could be thus indirectly denied.

The privilege of membership in a party may be, as this Court said in Grovey v. Townsend, no concern of a state. But when, as here, that privilege is also the essential qualification for voting in a primary to select nominees for a general election, the state makes the action of the party the action of the state. In reaching this conclusion we are not unmindful of the desirability of continuity of decision in constitutional questions. However, when convinced of former error, this Court has never felt constrained to follow precedent. In constitutional questions, where correction depends upon amendment and not upon legislative action this Court throughout its history has freely exercised its power to reëxamine the basis of its constitutional decisions. This has long been accepted practice, and this practice has continued to this day. This is particularly true when the decision believed erroneous is the application of a constitutional principle rather than an interpretation of the Constitution to extract the principle itself. Here we are applying, contrary to the recent decision in Grovey v. Townsend, the well established principle of the Fifteenth Amendment, forbidding the abridgement by a state of a citizen's right to vote. Grovey v. Townsend is overruled.

Judgment reversed.

557. YALTA (CRIMEA) CONFERENCE
February, 1945

(*New York Times,* March 15, 1945)

By February, 1945, the Allies had assumed the offensive once more in Europe. It was important for the Big Three to meet again to determine a program for the occupation of Germany, to discuss further plans for the new world organization, and to resolve political conflicts. The division of Europe into military spheres had resulted in political friction among the great powers, particularly in respect to unilateral action by Russia in Poland and by Britain in Greece. From February 4 to 11, 1945, the Big Three leaders, Roosevelt, Churchill, and Stalin, met for the second and last time in the summer palace of Czar Nicholas II near Yalta on the southern shore of the Crimean peninsula. Among important matters discussed were the Polish question, voting procedure in the Security Council of the new international organization, and the formation of democratic governments in Axis satellite nations. Probably the most important single result of the Yalta discussions was the calling of the San Francisco Conference to set up the new international organization. Important sections of the agreements were not made public until March 1947. See J. F. Byrnes, *Speaking Frankly;* W. S. Churchill, *Triumph and Tragedy;* J. R. Deane,. *The Strange Alliance;* E. R. Stettinius, *Roosevelt and the Russians: The Yalta Conference;* F. O. Wilcox, "The Yalta Voting Formula," *Am. Pol. Sci. Rev.,* Vol. 39, pp. 943 ff.; L. H. Woolsey, "Poland at Yalta and Dumbarton Oaks," 39 *Am. J. Int. L.,* pp. 295 ff.

Washington, March 24—The text of the agreements reached at the Crimea (Yalta) Conference between President Roosevelt, Prime Minister Churchill and Generalissimo Stalin, as released by the State Department today, follows:

PROTOCOL OF PROCEEDINGS OF CRIMEA
CONFERENCE

The Crimea Conference of the heads of the Governments of the United States of America, the United Kingdom, and the Union of Soviet Socialist Republics, which took place from Feb. 4 to 11, came to the following conclusions:

I. WORLD ORGANIZATION

It was decided:

1. That a United Nations conference on the proposed world organization should be summoned for Wednesday, 25 April, 1945, and should be held in the United States of America.

2. The nations to be invited to this conference should be:

(a) the United Nations as they existed on 8 Feb., 1945; and

(b) Such of the Associated Nations as have declared war on the common enemy by 1 March, 1945. (For this purpose, by the term "Associated Nations" was meant the eight Associated Nations and Turkey.) When the conference on world organization is held, the delegates of the United Kingdom and United States of America will support a proposal to admit to original membership two Soviet Socialist Republics, i.e., the Ukraine and White Russia.

3. That the United States Government, on behalf of the three powers, should consult the Government of China and the French Provisional Government in regard to decisions taken at the present conference concerning the proposed world organization.

4. That the text of the invitation to be issued to all the nations which would take part in the United Nations conference should be as follows:

"The Government of the United States of America, on behalf of itself and of the Governments of the United Kingdom, the Union of Soviet Socialistic Republics and the Republic of China and of the Provisional Government of the French Republic, invite the Government of ———— to send representatives to a conference to be held on 25 April, 1945, or soon thereafter, at San Francisco, in the United States of America, to prepare a charter for a general international organization for the maintenance of international peace and security.

"The above-named Governments suggest that the conference consider as affording a basis for such a Charter the proposals for the establishment of a general international organization which were made public last October as a result of the Dumbarton Oaks conference and which have now been supplemented by the following provisions for Section C of Chapter VI:

C. Voting

"1. Each member of the Security Council should have one vote.

" '2. Decisions of the Security Council on procedural matters should be made by an affirmative vote of seven members.

" '3. Decisions of the Security Council on all matters should be made by an affirmative vote of seven members, including the concurring votes of the permanent members; provided that, in decisions under Chapter VIII, Section A and under the second sentence of Paragraph 1 of Chapter VIII, Section C, a party to a dispute should abstain from voting.'

"Further information as to arrangements will be transmitted subsequently.

"In the event that the Government of ——————— desires in advance of the conference to present views or comments concerning the proposals, the Government of the United States of America will be pleased to transmit such views and comments to the other participating Governments."

Territorial trusteeship:

It was agreed that the five nations which will have permanent seats on the Security Council should consult each other prior to the United Nations conference on the question of territorial trusteeship.

The acceptance of this recommendation is subject to its being made clear that territorial trusteeship will only apply to (a) existing mandates of the League of Nations; (b) territories detached from the enemy as a result of the present war; (c) any other territory which might voluntarily be placed under trusteeship; and (d) no discussion of actual territories is contemplated at the forthcoming United Nations conference or in the preliminary consulations, and it will be a matter for subsequent agreement which territories within the above categories will be placed under trusteeship.

[*The section from this point to the next italicized note was published Feb. 13, 1945.*]

II. DECLARATION ON LIBERATED EUROPE

The following declaration has been approved:

The Premier of the Union of Soviet Socialist Republics, the Prime Minister of the United Kingdom and the President of the United States of America have consulted with each other in the common interests of the peoples of their countries and those of liberated Europe. They jointly declare their mutual agreement to concert during the temporary period of instability in liberated Europe the policies of their three Governments in assisting the peoples liberated from the domination of Nazi Germany and the peoples of the former Axis satellite states of Europe to solve by democratic means their pressing political and economic problems.

The establishment of order in Europe and the rebuilding of national economic life must be achieved by processes which will enable the liberated peoples to destroy the last vestiges of nazism and fascism and to create democratic institutions of their own choice. This is a principle of the Atlantic Charter— the right of all peoples to choose the form of government under which they will live— the restoration of sovereign rights and self-government to those peoples who have been forcibly deprived of them by the aggressor nations.

To foster the conditions in which the liberated peoples may exercise these rights, the three Governments will jointly assist the people in any European liberated state or former Axis satellite state in Europe where, in their judgment conditions require, (a) to establish conditions of internal peace; (b) to carry out emergency measures for the relief of distressed peoples; (c) to form interim governmental authorities broadly representative of all democratic elements in the population and pledged to the earliest possible establishment through free elections of Governments responsive to the will of the people; and (d) to facilitate where necessary the holding of such elections.

The three Governments will consult the other United Nations and provisional authorities or other Governments in Europe when matters of direct interest to them are under consideration.

When, in the opinion of the three Governments, conditions in any European liberated state or any former Axis satellite state in Europe make such action necessary, they will immediately consult together on the measures necessary to discharge the joint responsibilities set forth in this declaration.

By this declaration we reaffirm our faith in the principles of the Atlantic Charter, our pledge in the Declaration by the United Nations and our determination to build in cooperation with other peace-loving nations world order, under law, dedicated to peace, security, freedom and general well-being of all mankind.

In issuing this declaration, the three powers express the hope that the Provisional Government of the French Republic may be associated with them in the procedure suggested.

[*Here ends the previously published part of this section of the agreements.*]

III. DISMEMBERMENT OF GERMANY

It was agreed that Article 12 (a) of the Surrender Terms for Germany should be amended to read as follows:

"The United Kingdom, the United States of America and the Union of Soviet Socialist Republics shall possess supreme authority with respect to Germany. In the exercise of such authority they will take such steps, including the complete disarmament, demilitarization and dismemberment of Germany as they deem requisite for future peace and security."

The study of the procedure of the dismemberment of Germany was referred to a committee consisting of Mr. [Anthony] Eden [their Foreign Secretary] (chairman), Mr. [John] Winant [of the United States] and Mr. [Fedor T.] Gusev. This body would consider the desirability of associating with it a French representative.

IV. ZONE OF OCCUPATION FOR THE FRENCH AND CONTROL COUNCIL FOR GERMANY

It was agreed that a zone in Germany, to be occupied by the French forces, should be allocated to France. This zone would be formed out of the British and American zones and its extent would be settled by the British and Americans in consultation with the French Provisional Government.

It was also agreed that the French Provisional Government should be invited to become a member of the Allied Control Council for Germany.

V. REPARATION

The following protocol has been approved:

Protocol

On the Talks Between the Heads of Three Governments at the Crimean Conference on the Question of the German Reparations in Kind

1. Germany must pay in kind for the losses caused by her to the Allied nations in the course of the war. Reparations are to be received in the first instance by those countries which have borne the main burden of the war, have suffered the heaviest losses and have organized victory over the enemy.

2. Reparations in kind is to be exacted from Germany in three following forms:

(a) Removals within two years from the surrender of Germany or the cessation of organized resistance from the national wealth of Germany located on the territory of Germany herself as well as outside her territory (equipment, machine tools, ships, rolling stock, German investments abroad, shares of industrial, transport and other enterprises in Germany, etc.), these removals to be carried out chiefly for the purpose of destroying the war potential of Germany.

(b) Annual deliveries of goods from current production for a period to be fixed.

(c) Use of German labor.

3. For the working out on the above principles of a detailed plan for exaction of reparation from Germany an Allied reparations commission will be set up in Moscow. It will consist of three representatives—one from the Union of Soviet Socialist Republics, one from the United Kingdom and one from the United States of America.

4. With regard to the fixing of the total sum of the reparation as well as the distribution of it among the countries which suffered from the German aggression, the Soviet and American delegations agreed as follows:

"The Moscow reparation commission should take in its initial studies as a basis for discussion the suggestion of the Soviet Government that the total sum of the reparation in accordance with the points (a) and (b) of the Paragraph 2 should be 20 billion dollars and that 50 per cent of it should go to the Union of Soviet Socialist Republics."

The British delegation was of the opinion that, pending consideration of the reparation question by the Moscow reparation commission, no figures of reparation should be mentioned.

The above Soviet-American proposal has been passed to the Moscow reparation commission as one of the proposals to be considered by the commission.

VI. MAJOR WAR CRIMINALS

The conference agreed that the question of the major war criminals should be the subject of inquiry by the three Foreign Secretaries for report in due course after the close of the conference.

[The section from this point to the next italicized note was published Feb. 13, 1945.]

VII. POLAND

The following declaration on Poland was agreed by the conference:

"A new situation has been created in Poland as a result of her complete liberation by the Red Army. This calls for the establishment of a Polish Provisional Government which can be more broadly based than was possible before the recent liberation of the western part of Poland. The Provisional Government which is now functioning in Poland should therefore be reorganized on a broader democratic basis with the inclusion of democratic leaders from Poland itself and from Poles abroad. This new Government should then be called the Polish Provisional Government of National Unity.

"M. Molotov, Mr. Harriman and Sir A. Clark Kerr are authorized as a commission to consult in the first instance in Moscow with members of the present Provisional Government and with other Polish democratic leaders from within Poland and from abroad, with a view to the reorganization of the present Government along the above lines. This Polish Provisional Government of National Unity shall be pledged to the holding of free and unfettered elections as soon as possible on the basis of universal suffrage and secret ballot. In these elections all democratic and anti-Nazi parties shall have the right to take part and to put forward candidates.

"When a Polish Provisional Government of National Unity has been properly formed in conformity with the above, the Government of the U.S.S.R., which now maintains diplomatic relations with the present Provisional Government of Poland, and the Government of the United Kingdom and the Government of the United States of America will establish diplomatic relations with the new Polish Provisional Government of National Unity, and will exchange Ambassadors by whose reports the respective Governments will be kept informed about the situation in Poland.

"The three heads of Government consider that the eastern frontier of Poland should follow the Curzon Line with digressions from it in some regions of five to eight kilometers in favor of Poland. They recognize that Poland must receive substantial accessions of territory in the north and west. They feel that the opinion of the new Polish Provisional Government of National Unity should be sought in due course of the extent of these accessions and that the final delimitation of the western frontier of Poland should thereafter await the peace conference."

VIII. YUGOSLAVIA

It was agreed to recommend to Marshal Tito and to Dr. [Ivan] Subasitch:

(a) That the Tito-Subasitch agreement should immediately be put into effect and a new Government formed on the basis of the agreement.

(b) That as soon as the new Government has been formed it should declare:

(I) That the Anti-Fascist Assembly of the National Liberation (AVNOJ) will be extended to include members of the last Yugoslav Skupstina who have not compromised themselves by collaboration with the enemy, thus forming a body to be known as a temporary Parliament and

(II) That legislative acts passed by the Anti-Fascist Assembly of National Liberation (AVNOJ) will be subject to subsequent ratification by a Constituent Assembly; and that this statement should be published in the communiqué of the conference.

[Here ends the previously published section of the agreements.]

IX. ITALO-YUGOSLAV FRONTIER— ITALO-AUSTRIAN FRONTIER

Notes on these subjects were put in by

the British delegation, and the American and Soviet delegations agreed to consider them and give their views later.

X. YUGOSLAV-BULGARIAN RELATIONS

There was an exchange of views between the Foreign Secretaries on the question of the desirability of a Yugoslav-Bulgarian pact of alliance. The question at issue was whether a state still under an armistice regime could be allowed to enter into a treaty with another state. Mr. Eden suggested that the Bulgarian and Yugoslav Governments should be informed that this could not be approved. Mr. Stettinius suggested that the British and American Ambassadors should discuss the matter further with Mr. Molotov in Moscow. Mr. Molotov agreed with the proposal of Mr. Stettinius.

XI. SOUTHEASTERN EUROPE

The British delegation put in notes for the consideration of their colleagues on the following subjects:

(a) The Control Commission in Bulgaria.

(b) Greek claims upon Bulgaria, more particularly with reference to reparations.

(c) Oil equipment in Rumania.

XII. IRAN

Mr. Eden, Mr. Stettinius and Mr. Molotov exchanged views on the situation in Iran. It was agreed that this matter should be pursued through the diplomatic channel.

[*The section from this point to the next italicized note was published Feb. 13, 1945.*]

XIII. MEETINGS OF THE THREE FOREIGN SECRETARIES

The conference agreed that permanent machinery should be set up for consultation between the three Foreign Secretaries; they should meet as often as necessary, probably about every three or four months.

These meetings will be held in rotation in the three capitals, the first meeting being held in London.

[*Here ends the previously published section of the agreements.*]

XIV. THE MONTREUX CONVENTION AND THE STRAITS

It was agreed that at the next meeting of the three Foreign Secretaries to be held in London, they should consider proposals which it was understood the Soviet Government would put forward in relation to the Montreaux Convention, and report to their Governments. The Turkish Government should be informed at the appropriate moment.

The foregoing protocol was approved and signed by the three Foreign Secretaries at the Crimean Conference Feb. 11, 1945.

E. R. STETTINIUS JR.
M. MOLOTOV
ANTHONY EDEN

AGREEMENT REGARDING JAPAN

The leaders of the three great powers—the Soviet Union, the United States of America and Great Britain—have agreed that in two or three months after Germany has surrendered and the war in Europe has terminated, the Soviet Union shall enter into the war against Japan on the side of the Allies on condition that:

1. The status quo in Outer Mongolia (the Mongolian People's Republic) shall be preserved;

2. The former rights of Russia violated by the treacherous attack of Japan in 1904 shall be restored, viz.:

(a) The southern part of Sakhalin as well as the islands adjacent to it shall be returned to the Soviet Union;

(b) The commercial port of Dairen shall be internationalized, the pre-eminent interests of the Soviet Union in this port being safeguarded, and the lease of Port Arthur as a naval base of the U.S.S.R. restored;

(c) The Chinese-Eastern Railroad and the South Manchurian Railroad, which provide an outlet to Dairen, shall be jointly operated by the establishment of a joint Soviet-Chinese company, it being understood that the pre-eminent interests of the Soviet Union shall be safeguarded and that China shall retain full sovereignty in Manchuria;

3. The Kurile Islands shall be handed over to the Soviet Union.

It is understood that the agreement concerning Outer Mongolia and the ports and railroads referred to above will require concurrence of Generalissimo Chiang Kai-shek. The President will take measures in order to obtain this concurrence on advice from Marshal Stalin.

The heads of the three great powers have agreed that these claims of the Soviet Union shall be unquestionably fulfilled after Japan has been defeated.

For its part, the Soviet Union expresses its readiness to conclude with the National Government of China a pact of friendship and alliance between the U.S.S.R. and China in order to render assistance to China with its armed forces for the purpose of liberating China from the Japanese yoke.

JOSEPH V. STALIN
FRANKLIN D. ROOSEVELT
WINSTON S. CHURCHILL

February 11, 1945.

558. THE ACT OF CHAPULTEPEC
March 6, 1945

(*Congressional Record,* March 12, 1945, p. 2058)

Senator Connally, as American delegate to the Inter-American Conference on the Problems of the War, observed that the Act of Chapultepec was an adoption by the Latin American States of a multilateral policy of the Monroe Doctrine. The essence of it was the agreement that any attack against the territorial integrity or sovereignty of an American state should be considered an act of aggression against the other states signing the Pact. For background, see Docs. 521, 526, 534, and A. Whitaker, *The Western Hemisphere Idea.*

Part I. The Governments Represented at the Inter-American Conference on Problems of War and Peace Declare:

1. That all sovereign States are juridically equal among themselves.

2. That every State has the right to the respect of its individuality and independence, on the part of the other members of the international community.

3. That every attack of a State against the integrity or the inviolability of the territory, or against the sovereignty or political independence of an American State, shall, conformably to Part III hereof, be considered as an act of aggression against the other States which sign this Act. In any case invasion by armed forces of one State into the territory of another trespassing boundaries established by treaty and demarcated in accordance therewith shall constitute an act of aggression.

4. That in case acts of aggression occur or there are reasons to believe that an aggression is being prepared by any other State against the integrity or inviolability of the territory, or against the sovereignty or political independence of an American State, the States signatory to this Act will consult among themselves in order to agree upon the measures it may be advisable to take.

5. That during the war, and until the treaty recommended in Part II hereof is concluded, the signatories of this Act recognize that such threats and acts of aggression, as indicated in paragraphs 3 and 4 above, constitute an interference with the war effort of the United Nations, calling for such procedures, within the scope of their constitutional powers of a general nature and for war, as may be found necessary, including: recall of chiefs of diplomatic missions; breaking of diplomatic relations; breaking of consular relations; breaking of postal, telegraphic, telephonic, radio-telephonic relations; interruption of economic, commercial and financial relations; use of armed force to prevent or repel aggression.

6. That the principles and procedure contained in this Declaration shall become effective immediately, inasmuch as any act of aggression or threat of aggression during the present state of war interferes with the war effort of the United Nations to obtain victory. Henceforth, and to the end that the principles and procedures herein stipulated shall conform with the constitutional processes of each Republic, the respective Governments shall take the necessary steps to perfect this instrument in order that it shall be in force at all times.

Part II. The Inter-American Conference on Problems of War and Peace *Recom-*

mends:

That for the purpose of meeting threats or acts of aggression against any American Republic following the establishment of peace, the Governments of the American Republics consider the conclusion, in accordance with their constitutional processes, of a treaty establishing procedures whereby such threats or acts may be met by the use, by all or some of the signatories of said treaty, of any one or more of the following measures: recall of chiefs of diplomatic missions; breaking of diplomatic relations; breaking of consular relations; breaking of postal, telegraphic, telephonic, radio-tele-phonic relations; interruption of economic, commercial and financial relations; use of armed force to prevent or repel aggression.

Part III. The above Declaration and Recommendation constitute a regional arrangement for dealing with such matters relating to the maintenance of international peace and security as are appropriate for regional action in this Hemisphere. The said arrangement, and the pertinent activities and procedures, shall be consistent with the purposes and principles of the general international organization, when established.

This agreement shall be known as the *"Act of Chapultepec."*

559. NEW YORK STATE ANTI-DISCRIMINATION ACT
March 12, 1945
(Laws of New York, Chapter 118)

Although a long struggle was waged in Congress for a federal anti-discrimination act, the principle was succesful only in the states. See A. Wilson "The Proposed Legislative Knell of Private Discriminatory Practices," 31 *Va. L. Rev.,* pp. 798 ff.; R. C. Weaver, *Negro Labor;* H. R. Bernhardt, "The Right to a Job," 29 *Corn. L. Quart.,* pp. 489 ff.; H. R. Cayton and G. S. Mitchell, *Black Workers and the New Unions.*

An act to amend the executive law, in relation to prevention and elimination of practices of discrimination in employment and otherwise against persons because of race, creed, color or national origin, . . .

§ 125. *Purposes of article.* This article shall be known as the "Law Against Discrimination." It shall be deemed an exercise of the police power of the state for the protection of the public welfare, health and peace of the people of this state, and in fulfillment of the provisions of the constitution of this state concerning civil rights; and the legislature hereby finds and declares that practices of discrimination against any of its inhabitants because of race, creed, color or national origin are a matter of state concern, that such discrimination threatens not only the rights and proper privileges of its inhabitants but menaces the institutions and foundation of a free democratic state. A state agency is hereby created with power to eliminate and prevent discrimination in employment because of race, creed, color or national origin, either by employers, labor organizations, employment agencies or other persons, and to take other actions against discrimination because of race, creed, color or national origin, as herein provided; and the commission established hereunder is hereby given general jurisdicition and power for such purposes.

§ 126. *Opportunity for employment without discrimination a civil right.* The opportunity to obtain employment without discrimination because of race, creed, color or national origin is hereby recognized as and declared to be a civil right.

§ 128. *State commission against discrimination.* There is hereby created in the executive department a state commission against discrimination. Such commission shall consist of five members, to be known as commissioners, who shall be appointed by the governor, by and with the advice and consent of the senate, and one of whom shall be designated as chairman by the governor. The term of office of each member of the commission shall be for five years, provided, however, that of the commissioners first appointed, one shall be appointed for a term of one year, one for a term of two years, one for a term of three years, one for a term of four years, and one for a term of five years.

Each member of the commission shall receive a salary of ten thousand dollars a year. . . .

§ 129. *General policies of commission.* The commission shall formulate policies to effectuate the purposes of this article and may make recommendations to agencies and officers of the state or local subdivisions of government in aid of such policies and purposes.

§ 130. *General powers and duties of commission.* The commission shall have the following functions, powers and duties: 1. To establish and maintain its principal office in the city of Albany, and such other offices within the state as it may deem necessary.

5. To adopt, promulgate, amend, and rescind suitable rules and regulations to carry out the provisions of this article, and the policies and practice of the commission in connection therewith.

6. To receive, investigate and pass upon complaints alleging discrimination in employment because of race, creed, color or national origin.

7. To hold hearings, subpoena witnesses, compel their attendance, administer oaths, take the testimony of any person under oath, and in connection therewith, to require the production for examination of any books or papers relating to any matter under investigation or in question before the commission. The commission may make rules as to the issuance of subpoenas by individual commissioners.

8. To create such advisory agencies and conciliation councils, local, regional or statewide, as in its judgment will aid in effectuating the purposes of this article and of section eleven of article one of the constitution of this state, and the commission may empower them to study the problems of discrimination in all or specific fields of human relationships or in specific instances of discrimination because of race, creed, color or national origin, and to foster through community effort or otherwise good-will, cooperation and conciliation among the groups and elements of the population of the state, and make recommendations to the commission for the development of policies and procedures in general and in specific instances, and for programs of formal and informal education which the commission may recommend to the appropriate state agency. Such advisory agencies and conciliation councils shall be composed of representative citizens, serving without pay, but with reimbursement for actual and necessary traveling expenses; and the commission may make provision for technical and clerical assistance to such agencies and councils and for the expenses of such assistance.

9. To issue such publications and such results of investigations and research as in its judgment will tend to promote good-will and minimize or eliminate discrimination because of race, creed, color or national origin.

10. To render each year to the governor and to the legislature a full written report of all its activities and of its recommendations.

§ 131. *Unlawful employment practices.* It shall be an unlawful employment practice: 1. For an employer, because of the race, creed, color or national origin of any individual, to refuse to hire or employ or to bar or to discharge from employment such individual or to discriminate against such individual in compensation or in terms, conditions or privileges of employment.

2. For a labor organization, because of the race, creed, color or national origin of any individual, to exclude or to expel from its membership such individual or to discriminate in any way against any of its members or against any employer or any individual employed by an employer.

3. For any employer or employment agency to print or circulate or cause to be printed or circulated any statement, advertisement or publication, or to use any form of application for employment or to make any inquiry in connection with prospective employment, which expresses, directly or indirectly, any limitation, specification or discrimination as to race, creed, color or national origin, or any intent to make any such limitation, specification or discrimination, unless based upon a bona fide occupational

qualification.

4. For any employer, labor organization or employment agency to discharge, expel or otherwise discriminate against any person because he has opposed any practices forbidden under this article or because he has filed a complaint, testified or assisted in any proceeding under this article.

5. For any person, whether an employer or an employee or not, to aid, abet, incite, compel or coerce the doing of any of the acts forbidden under this article, or to attempt to do so.

§ 132. *Procedure*. Any person claiming to be aggrieved by an alleged unlawful employment practice may, by himself or his attorney-at-law, make, sign and file with the commission a verified complaint in writing which shall state the name and address of the person, employer, labor organization or employment agency alleged to have committed the unlawful employment practice complained of and which shall set forth the particulars thereof and contain such other information as may be required by the commission. The industrial commissioner or attorney-general may, in like manner, make, sign and file such complaint. Any employer whose employees, or some of them, refuse or threaten to refuse to cooperate with the provisions of this article, may file with the commission a verified complaint asking for assistance by conciliation or other remedial action. . . .

§ 135. *Construction*. The provisions of this article shall be construed liberally for the accomplishment of the purposes thereof.

560. BRIDGES v. WIXON
326 U. S. 135
1945

The historical background of the Bridges case is fully set forth in the concurring opinion by Justice Murphy. The opinions in this case, important in themselves, are particularly significant for the light they throw on the whole question of guilt by association. We have given here only those portions of the opinion of the Court that deal with the meaning of the baffling term "affiliation." In the summer of 1949 the government once more instituted deportation proceedings against Bridges, but was again frustrated.

Habeas corpus proceeding by Harry Bridges against I. F. Wixon, as District Director, Immigration and Naturalization Service, Department of Justice.

DOUGLAS, J. . . . The two grounds on which the deportation order rests—that Harry Bridges at one time had been both "affiliated" with the Communist party and a member of it—present different questions with which we deal separately.

Affiliation. The statute defines affiliation as follows:

"For the purpose of this section: (1) the giving, loaning, or promising of money or any thing of value to be used for the advising, advocacy, or teaching of any doctrine above enumerated shall constitute the advising, advocacy, or teaching of such doctrine; and (2) the giving, loaning or promising of money or any thing of value to any organization, association, society, or group of the character above described shall constitute affiliation therewith; but nothing in this paragraph shall be taken as an exclusive definition of advising, advocacy, teaching, or affiliation." 41 Stat. 1009. The doctrine referred to is the overthrow of the government by force or violence. The organizations or groups referred to are those which advise and teach that doctrine or which write, circulate, display and the like or have in their possession for such purpose any written or printed matter of that character.

In ruling on the question whether an alien had been "affiliated" with the Communist party and therefore could be deported, the court in United States ex rel. Kettunen v. Reimer, 2 Cir., 79 F.2d 315, 317, said that such an affiliation was not proved "unless the alien is shown to have so conducted himself that he has brought about a status of mutual recognition that he may be relied on to cooperate with the Communist Party on a fairly permanent basis. He must be more than merely in sympathy with its aims or even willing to aid it in a casual intermittent way. Affiliation includes an element of dependability upon which the organization can rely which, though not equivalent to membership duty, does rest upon a course of conduct that could not be abruptly ended without giving at least reasonable cause for the charge of a breach of good faith." The same idea was expressed by Dean Landis in the first Bridges' report. After stating that "affiliation" implies a "stronger bond" than "association," he went on to say: "In the corporate field its use embraces not the casual affinity of an occasional similarity of objective, but ties and connections that, though less than that complete control which parent possesses over subsidiary, are nevertheless sufficient to create a continuing relationship that embraces both units within the concept of a system. In the field of eleemosynary and political organization the same basic idea prevails." And he concluded: "Persons engaged in bitter industrial struggles tend to seek help and assistance from every available source. But the intermittent solicitation and acceptance of such help must be shown to have ripened into those bonds of mutual cooperation and alliance that entail continuing reciprocal duties and responsibilities before they can be deemed to come within the statutory requirement of affiliation. . . . To expand that statutory definition to embrace within its terms ad hoc cooperation on objectives whose pursuit is clearly allowable under our constitutional system, or friendly associations that have not been shown to have resulted in the employment of illegal means, is warranted neither by reason nor by law."

The legislative history throws little light on the meaning of "affiliation" as used in the statute. It imports, however, less than membership but more than sympathy. By the terms of the statute it includes those who contribute money or anything of value to an organization which believes in, advises, advocates, or teaches the overthrow of our government by force or violence. That example throws light on the meaning of the term "affiliation." He who renders financial assistance to any organization may generally be said to approve of its objectives or aims. So Congress declared in the case of an alien who contributed to the treasury of an organization whose aim was to overthrow the government by force and violence. But he who cooperates with such an organization only in its *wholly lawful activities* cannot by that fact be said as a matter of law to be "affiliated" with it. Nor is it conclusive that the cooperation was more than intermittent and showed a rather consistent course of conduct. Common sense indicates that the term "affiliation" in this setting should be construed more narrowly. Individuals, like nations, may cooperate in a common cause over a period of months or years though their ultimate aims do not coincide. Alliances for limited objectives are well known. Certainly those who joined forces with Russia to defeat the Nazis may not be said to have made an alliance to spread the cause of Communism. An individual who makes contributions to feed hungry men does not become "affiliated" with the Communist cause because those men are Communists. A different result is not necessarily indicated if aid is given to or received from a proscribed organization in order to win a legitimate objective in a domestic controversy. Whether intermittent or repeated the act or acts tending to prove "affiliation" must be of that quality which indicates an adherence to or a furtherance of the purposes or objectives of the proscribed organization as distinguished from mere cooperation with it in lawful activities. The act or acts must evidence a working alliance to bring the program to fruition.

We are satisfied that the term "affiliation" was not so construed either by Judge Sears or by the Attorney General. The reports made in this case contain no precise formulation of the standard which was employed. But the way in which the term "affiliation" was used and applied convinces us that it was given a looser and more expansive meaning than the statute permits. . . .

. . . When we turn to the facts of this case we have little more than a course of conduct which reveals cooperation with Communist groups for the attainment of wholly lawful objectives.

The associations which Harry Bridges had with various Communist groups seem to indicate no more than cooperative measures to attain objectives which were wholly legitimate. The link by which it is sought to tie him to subversive activities is an exceedingly tenuous one, if it may be said to exist at all. . . . Nor is there any finding that Bridges took over this project with the view of doing more than advancing the lawful cause of unionism. The advice to support for office certain candidates said to be Communists was based entirely on the platform on which they ran—cash relief; abolition of vagrancy laws; no evictions; gas, water and electricity for the unemployed; and unemployment relief. The advice to read Communist literature was not general; it was specifically addressed to the comparative merits of those publications and other papers on the truthfulness of labor news. The use of addresses of Communist organizations, especially stressed by the Attorney General, was said by Judge Sears to demonstrate "a close cooperation with the Communists and Communist Organizations." But close cooperation is not sufficient to establish an "affiliation" within the meaning of the statute. It must evidence a working alliance to bring the proscribed program to fruition.

It must be remembered that the Marine Workers Industrial Union was not a sham or pretense. It was a genuine union. It was found to have, and we assume it did have, the illegitimate objective of overthrowing the government by force. But it also had the objective of improving the lot of its members in the normal trade union sense. One who cooperated with it in promoting its legitimate objectives certainly could not by that fact alone be said to sponsor or approve of its general or unlawful objectives. But unless he also joined in that overall program,

he would not be "affiliated" with the Communist cause in the sense in which the statute uses the term.

Whether one could be a member of that union without becoming "affiliated" with the Communist party within the meaning of the statute, we need not decide. For Harry Bridges was never a member of it. To say that his cooperation with it made him in turn "affiliated" with the Communist party is to impute to him belief in and adherence to its general or unlawful objectives. In that connection, it must be remembered that although deportation technically is not criminal punishment . . . it may nevertheless visit as great a hardship as the deprivation of the right to pursue a vocation or a calling.

We cannot assume that Congress meant to employ the term "affiliation" in a broad, fluid sense which would visit such hardship on an alien for slight or insubstantial reasons. . . .

Inference must be piled on inference to impute belief in Harry Bridges of the revolutionary aims of the groups whose aid and assistance he employed in his endeavor to improve the lot of the workingmen on the water-front. That he enlisted such aid is not denied. He justified that course on the grounds of expediency—to get such help as he could to aid the cause of his union. But there is evidence that he opposed the Communist tactics of formenting strikes; that he believed in the policy of arbitration and direct negotiation to settle labor disputes, with the strike reserved only as a last resort. . . .

. . . We cannot construe "affiliation" as used in the statute to bring such conduct and attitudes within its reach. . . .

Chief Justice STONE, Justice ROBERTS, Justice FRANKFURTER dissenting.

561. ROOSEVELT'S DRAFT OF JEFFERSON DAY ADDRESS
April 13, 1945

(*Congressional Record,* April 16, 1945)

This address, never delivered, was the last written by Franklin D. Roosevelt. See D. P. Geddes, *Franklin D. Roosevelt: A Memorial;* Frances Perkins, *The Roosevelt I knew;* G. W. Johnson, *Dictator or Democrat;* Alden Hatch, *Franklin D. Roosevelt;* John Gunther, *Roosevelt in Retrospect;* R. Sherwood, *Roosevelt and Hopkins.*

Americans are gathered together this evening in communities all over the country to pay tribute to the living memory of Thomas Jefferson—one of the greatest of all democrats; and I want to make it clear that I am spelling that word "democrats" with a small "d."

I wish I had the power, just for this evening, to be present at all these gatherings.

In this historic year, more than ever before, we do well to consider the character of Thomas Jefferson as an American citizen of the world.

As minister to France, then as our first Secretary of State and as our third President, Jefferson was instrumental in the establishment of the United States as a vital factor in international affairs.

It was he who first sent our Navy into far distant waters to defend our rights. And the promulgation of the Monroe Doctrine was the logical development of Jefferson's far-seeing foreign policy.

Today this Nation which Jefferson helped so greatly to build is playing a tremendous part in the battle for the rights of man all over the world.

Today we are part of the vast Allied force—a force composed of flesh and blood and steel and spirit—which is today destroying the makers of war, the breeders of hate, in Europe and in Asia.

In Jefferson's time our Navy consisted of only a handful of frigates—but that tiny Navy taught nations across the Atlantic that piracy in the Mediterranean—acts of aggression against peaceful commerce and the enslavement of their crews was one of those things which, among neighbors, simply was not done.

Today we have learned in the agony of war that great power involves great responsibility. Today we can no more escape the consequence of German and Japanese aggression than could we avoid the consequences of attacks by the Barbary corsairs a century and a half before.

We, as Americans, do not choose to deny our responsibility.

Nor do we intend to abandon our determination that, within the lives of our children and our children's children, there will not be a third World War.

We seek peace—enduring peace. More than an end to war, we want an end to the beginnings of all wars—yes, an end to this brutal, inhuman and thoroughly impractical method of settling the differences between governments.

The once powerful, malignant Nazi state is crumbling, the Japanese war lords are receiving, in their home land, the retribution for which they asked when they attacked Pearl Harbor.

But the mere conquest of our enemies is not enough.

We must go on to do all in our power to conquer the doubts and the fears, the ignorance and the greed, which made this horror possible.

Thomas Jefferson, himself a distinguished scientist, once spoke of the 'brotherly spirit of science, which unites into one family all its votaries of whatever grade, and however widely dispersed throughout the different quarters of the globe.'

Today, science has brought all the different quarters of the globe so close together that it is impossible to isolate them one from another.

Today we are faced with the pre-eminent fact that, if civilization is to survive, we must cultivate the science of human relationships—the ability of all peoples, of all kinds, to live together and work together in the same world, at peace.

Let me assure you that my hand is the steadier for the work that is to be done, that

I move more firmly into the task, knowing that you—millions and millions of you—are joined with me in the resolve to make this work endure.

The work, my friends, is peace more than an end of this war—an end to the beginning of all wars, yes, an end, forever, to this impractical, unrealistic settlement of the differences between governments by the mass killing of peoples.

Today as we move against the terrible scourge of war—as we go forward toward the greatest contribution that any generation of human beings can make in this world— the contribution of lasting peace, I ask you to keep up your faith. I measure the sound, solid achievement that can be made at this time by the straight edge of your confidence and your resolve. And to you, and to all Americans who dedicate themselves with us to the making of an abiding peace, I say:

The only limit to our realization of tomorrow will be our doubts of today. Let us move forward with strong and active faith.

562. THE SURRENDER OF GERMANY
May 7, 1945
(*Department of State Bulletin*, July 22, 1945)

On March 7, for the first time since the Napoleonic invasion, the Rhine was crossed by foreign armies. As Russian and American armies poured into Germany, east and west, a new phase of the war began: the isolation and conquest of German pockets in central Europe. On May 6 the German commanders, Jodl and Friedeburg, appeared at Allied headquarters to capitulate. At 2:41 a.m., May 7, 1945, at General Eisenhower's headquarters in Rheims, Col. Gen. Gustav Jodl, Chief of Staff of the German Army, completed the signature of four surrender documents, one each for Great Britain, the United States, Russia, and France. After over five and a half years the war in Europe was at an end. See H. C. Butcher, *My Three Years with Eisenhower;* Walter Millis, *The Last Phase;* J. D. Dawson, *European Victory;* H. R. Trevor-Roper, *The Last Days of Hitler;* L. Clay, *Decision in Germany;* W. Churchill, *Triumph and Tragedy.*

Instrument of surrender of all German forces to General Dwight D. Eisenhower, Supreme Commander of the Allied Expeditionary Forces, and to the Soviet High Command

Rheims. *May 7, 1945.*

1. We the undersigned, acting by authority of the German High Command, hereby surrender unconditionally to the Supreme Commander, Allied Expeditionary Force and simultaneously to the Soviet High Command all forces on land, sea, and in the air who are at this date under German control.

2. The German High Command will at once issue orders to all German military, naval and air authorities and to all forces under German control to cease active operations at 2301 hours Central European time on 8 May and to remain in the positions occupied at that time. No ship, vessel, or aircraft is to be scuttled, or any damage done to their hull, machinery or equipment.

3. The German High Command will at once issue to the appropriate commanders, and ensure the carrying out of any further orders issued by the Supreme Commander, Allied Expeditionary Force and by the Soviet High Command.

4. This act of military surrender is without prejudice to, and will be superseded by any general instrument of surrender imposed by, or on behalf of the United Nations and applicable to Germany and the German armed forces as a whole.

5. In the event of the German High Command or any of the forces under their control failing to act in accordance with this Act of Surrender, the Supreme Commander, Allied Expeditionary Force and the Soviet High Command will take such punitive or other action as they deem appropriate.

Signed at Rheims at 0241 on the 7th day of May, 1945.

Statement by the Governments of the United States of America, Union of Soviet Socialist

Republics, the United Kingdom and the provisional Government of the French Republic on zones of occupation in Germany.

1. Germany, within her frontiers as they were on Dec. 31, 1937, will, for the purposes of occupation, be divided into four zones, one to be allotted to each power as follows:

An eastern zone to the Union of Soviet Socialist Republics;

A northwestern zone to the United Kingdom;

A southwestern zone to the United States of America;

A western zone to France.

The occupying forces in each zone will be under a commander in chief designated by the responsible power. Each of the four powers may, at its discretion, include among the forces assigned to occupation duties under the command of its commander in chief, auxiliary contingents from the forces of any other Allied power which has actively participated in military operations against Germany.

2. The area of "Greater Berlin" will be occupied by forces of each of the four powers. An inter-Allied governing authority (in Russian, Komendatura) consisting of four commandants, appointed by their respective commanders-in-chief, will be established to direct jointly its administration.

Statement by the Governments of the United States of America, Union of Soviet Socialist

Republics, United Kingdom, and the Provisional Government of the French Republic on control of machinery in Germany.

1. In the period when Germany is carrying out the basic requirements of unconditional surrender, supreme authority in Germany will be exercised, on instructions from their Governments, by the Soviet, British, United States and French commanders-in-chief, each in his own zone of occupation, and also jointly, in matters affecting Germany as a whole. The four commanders-in-chief will together constitute the Control Council. Each commander-in-chief will be assisted by a political adviser.

2. The Control Council, whose decisions shall be unanimous, will ensure appropriate uniformity of action by the commanders-in-chief in their respective zones of occupation and will reach agreed decisions on the chief questions affecting Germany as a whole.

3. Under the Control Council, there will be a permanent coordinating committee composed of one representative of each of the four commanders-in-chief and a control staff organized in the following divisions (which are subject to adjustment in the light of experience): Military; naval; air; transport; political; economic; finance; reparation, deliveries and restitution; internal affairs and communications; legal; prisoners of war and displaced persons; manpower. There will be four heads of each division, one designated by each power. . . .

563. MILITARY OCCUPATION OF JAPAN
October 4, 1945
(U. S. State Department, *The Axis in Defeat*)

General MacArthur, as supreme commander in the Pacific, was designated to direct the military occupation of Japan. Our occupation policy for Japan was prepared by the State, War and Navy departments and approved by President Truman on September 6, providing for the demilitarization of Japan, the trial of war criminals, the encouragement of democratic institutions, freedom of religious worship, the dissolution of great industrial and banking combines, and the subordination of the Emperor to General MacArthur. On September 10, the Imperial General Staff was ordered dissolved, and within the next week MacArthur ordered the dissolution of the Black Dragon Society and the arrest of its leaders; the establishment of American censorship over the Domei news agency; publication of the names of 40 Japanese leaders wanted as war criminals; and the creation of a program of re-education along democratic lines. On September 27, the Emperor, breaking all precedent, made a personal call on General MacArthur at his headquarters. MacArthur's most important order was announced on October 4, restoring civil liberties, freeing political prisoners, and abolishing the secret police. W. C. Johnstone, *Future of Japan; Occupation of Japan: Policy and Progress,* Dept. of State Publication 2671, Far Eastern Series 17; W. Fleisher, *What to Do With Japan; Report of the U. S. Education Mission to Japan,* Dept. of State Publication 2579, Far Eastern Series 11; Ruth Benedict, *The Chrysanthemum and the Sword.*

1. In order to remove restrictions on political, civil and religious liberties and discrimination on grounds of race, nationality, creed or political opinion, the Imperial Japanese Government will:

a. Abrogate and immediately suspend the operation of all provisions of all laws, decrees, orders, ordinances and regulations which:

(1) Establish or maintain restrictions on freedom of thought, of religion, of assembly and of speech, including the unrestricted discussion of the Emperor, the Imperial Institution and the Imperial Japanese Government.

(2) Establish or maintain restrictions on the collection and dissemination of information.

(3) By their terms or their applications, operate unequally in favor of or against any person by reason of race, nationality, creed or political opinion. . . .

c. Release immediately all persons now detained, imprisoned, under "protection or surveillance," or whose freedom is restricted in any other manner who have been placed in that state of detention, imprisonment, "protection and surveillance," or restriction of freedom:

(1) Under the enactments referred to in Para 1 a and b above.

(2) Without charge.

(3) By charging them technically with a minor offense, when, in reality, the reason for detention, imprisonment, "Protection and Surveillance," or restriction of freedom, was because of their thought, speech, religion, political beliefs, or assembly. The release of all such persons will be accomplished by 10 October 1945.

d. Abolish all organizations or agencies created to carry out the provisions of the enactments referred to in Para 1 a and b above and that part of, or functions of, other offices or sub divisions of other civil departments or organs which supplement or assist them in the execution of such provisions. These include, but are not limited to:

(1) All secret police organs.

(2) Those departments in the Ministry of Home Affairs, such as the Bureau of Police, charged with supervision of publications, supervision of public meetings and organizations, censorship of motion pictures, and such other departments concerned with the control of thought, speech, religion or assembly.

(3) Those departments, such as the special higher police (Tokubetsu, Koto, Keisatsu Bu), in the Tokyo Metropolitan Police, the Osaka Metropolitan Police, and other Metropolitan Police, the Police of the Territorial Administration of Hokkaido and the various prefectural police charged with supervision of publications, supervision of public meetings and organizations, censorship of motion pictures, and such other departments concerned with the control of thought, speech, religion or assembly.

(4) Those departments, such as the Protection and Surveillance Commission, and all Protection and Surveillance Stations responsible thereto, under the Ministry of Justice charged with protection and surveillance and control of thought, speech, religion, or assembly.

e. Remove from office and employment the Minister of Home Affairs, the Chief of the Bureau of Police of the Ministry of Home Affairs, the Chief of the Tokyo Metropolitan Police Board, the Chief of Osaka Metropolitan Police Board, the Chief of any other Metropolitan Police, the Chief of Police of the Territorial Administration of Hokkaido, the Chiefs of each prefectural police department, the entire personnel of the special higher police of all metropolitan, territorial and prefectural police departments, the guiding and protecting officials and all other personnel of the Protection and Surveillance Commission and of the Protection and Surveillance Stations. None of the above persons will be reappointed to any position under the Ministry of Home Affairs, the Ministry of Justice or any police organ in Japan. Any of the above persons whose assistance is required to accomplish the provisions of this directive will be retained until the directive is accomplished and then dismissed.

f. Prohibit any further activity of police officials, members of police forces, and other government, national or local, officials or employees which is related to the enactments referred to in Para 1 a and b above and to the organs and functions abolished by Para 1 d above.

g. Prohibit the physical punishment and mistreatment of all persons detained, imprisoned, or under protection and surveilliance under any and all Japanese enactments, laws, decrees, orders, ordinances and regulations. All such persons will receive at all times ample sustenance.

h. Ensure the security and preservation of all records and any and all other materials

of the organs abolished in Para 1 d. These records may be used to accomplish the provisions of this directive, but will not be destroyed, removed, or tampered with in any way.

i. Submit a comprehensive report to this Headquarters not later than 15 October 1945 describing in detail all action taken to comply with all provisions of this directive. This report will contain the following specific information prepared in the form of separate supplementary reports: . . .

2. All officials and subordinates of the Japanese Government affected by the terms of this directive will be held personally responsible and strictly accountable for compliance with and adherence to the spirit and letter of this directive.

564. TRUMAN'S STATEMENT ON FUNDAMENTALS OF AMERICAN FOREIGN POLICY
October 27, 1945

(Department of State Bulletin, XIII, pp. 653 ff.)

This was the first important statement of foreign policy after President Truman's return from the Potsdam Conference. Point 10 anticipated the subsequent fourth point of the Fair Deal program of 1949. H. S. Truman, *Memoirs*, Vol. I.

. . . 1. We seek no territorial expansion or selfish advantage. We have no plans for aggression against any other state, large or small. We have no objective which need clash with the peaceful aims of any other nation.

2. We believe in the eventual return of sovereign rights and self-government to all peoples who have been deprived of them by force.

3. We shall approve no territorial changes in any friendly part of the world unless they accord with the freely expressed wishes of the people concerned.

4. We believe that all peoples who are prepared for self-government should be permitted to choose their own form of government by their own freely expressed choice, without interference from any foreign

source. That is true in Europe, in Asia, in Africa, as well as in the Western Hemisphere.

5. By the combined and cooperative action of our war Allies, we shall help the defeated enemy states establish peaceful, democratic governments of their own free choice. And we shall try to attain a world in which Nazism, Fascism, and military aggression cannot exist.

6. We shall refuse to recognize any government imposed upon any nation by the force of any foreign power. In some cases it may be impossible to prevent forceful imposition of such a government. But the United States will not recognize any such government.

7. We believe that all nations should have the freedom of the seas and equal rights to the navigation of boundary rivers and waterways and of rivers and waterways which pass through more than one country.

8. We believe that all states which are accepted in the society of nations should have access on equal terms to the trade and the raw materials of the world.

9. We believe that the sovereign states of

the Western Hemisphere, without interference from outside the Western Hemisphere, must work together as good neighbors in the solution of their common problems.

10. We believe that full economic collaboration between all nations, great and small, is essential to the improvement of living conditions all over the world, and to the establishment of freedom from fear and freedom from want.

11. We shall continue to strive to promote freedom of expression and freedom of religion throughout the peace-loving areas of the world.

12. We are convinced that the preservation of peace between nations requires a United Nations Organization composed of all the peace-loving nations of the world who are willing jointly to use force if necessary to insure peace.

That is the foreign policy which guides the United States now. That is the foreign policy with which it confidently faces the future.

It may not be put into effect tomorrow or the next day. But none the less, it is our policy; and we shall seek to achieve it. It may take a long time, but it is worth waiting for, and it is worth striving to attain. . . .

565. UNITED NATIONS PARTICIPATION ACT
December 20, 1945
(Public Law 264, 79th Congress)

This measure, which passed the Senate by a vote of 65 to 7, the House by 344 to 15, made the United States a member of the United Nations. Readers should consult the text of the United Nations charter, which has been published in many places and is available upon application to the United Nations Secretariat. See P. Bidwell, *The United States and the United Nations;* K. Colegrove, *The American Senate and World Peace;* E. S. Corwin, The *Constitution and World Organization;* L. M. Goodrich and E. Hambro, *Charter of the United Nations;* Emery Reves, *Anatomy of Peace;* J. Robinson, *Human Rights and Fundamental Freedoms in the Charter of the United Nations;* C. Eagleton and F. O. Wilcox, "The United Nations: Peace and Security," *Am. Pol. Sci. Rev.,* Vol. 39, pp. 934 ff; Robert Summers, ed., *Dumbarton Oaks;* Wendell Willkie, *One World;* J. B. Whitton, ed., *The Second Chance: America and the Peace.*

An act—To provide for the appointment of representatives of the United States in the organs and agencies of the United Nations, and to make other provision with respect to the participation of the United States in such organiaztion.

SEC. 2. (a) The President, by and with the advice and consent of the Senate, shall appoint a representative of the United States at the seat of the United Nations who shall have the rank and status of envoy extraordinary and ambassador plenipotentiary, shall receive annual compensation of $20,000, and shall hold office at the pleasure of the President. Such representative shall represent the United States in the Security Council of the United Nations and shall perform such other functions in connection with the participation of the United States in the United Nations as the President may from time to time direct.

(b) The President, by and with the advice and consent of the Senate, shall appoint a deputy representative of the United States to the Security Council who shall have the rank and status of envoy extraordinary and minister plenipotentiary, shall receive annual compensation of $12,000, and shall hold office at the pleasure of the President. Such deputy representative shall represent the United States in the Security Council of the United Nations in the event of the absence or disability of the representative.

(c) The President, by and with the advice and consent of the Senate, shall designate from time to time to attend a specified session or specified sessions of the General Assembly of the United Nations not to exceed five representatives of the United States and such number of alternates as he may determine consistent with the rules of procedure of the General Assembly. One of the representatives shall be designated as the senior representative. Such representatives and alternates shall each be entitled to receive compensation at the rate of $12,000 per annum for such period as the President may specify, except that no member of the Senate or House of Representatives or officer of the United States who is designated under this subsection as a representative of the United States or as an alternate to attend any specified session or specified sessions of the General Assembly shall be entitled to receive such compensation.

(d) The President may also appoint from time to time such other persons as he may deem necessary to represent the United States in the organs and agencies of the United Nations, but the representative of the United States in the Economic and Social Council and in the Trusteeship Council of the United Nations shall be appointed only by and with the advice and consent of the Senate.

(e) Nothing contained in this section shall preclude the President or the Secretary of State, at the direction of the President, from representing the United States at any meeting or session of any organ or agency of the United Nations.

SEC. 3. The representatives provided for in section 2 hereof, when representing the United States in the respective organs and agencies of the United Nations, shall, at all times, act in accordance with the instructions of the President transmitted by the Secretary of State.

SEC. 4. The President shall, from time to time as occasion may require, but not less than once a year, make reports to the Congress of the activities of the United Nations and of the participation of the United States therein.

SEC. 5. (a) Notwithstanding the provisions of any other law, whenever the United States is called upon by the Security Council to apply measures which said Council has decided, pursuant to article 41 of said Charter, are to be employed to give effect to its decisions under said Charter, the President may, to the extent necessary to apply such measures, through any agency which he may designate, and under such orders, rules, and regulations as may be prescribed by him, investigate, regulate, or prohibit, in whole or in part, economic relations or rail, sea, air, postal, telegraphic, radio, and other means of comunication between any foreign country or any national thereof or any person therein and the United States or any person subject to the jurisdiction thereof, or involving any property subject to the jurisdiction of the United States.

SEC. 6. The President is authorized to negotiate a special agreement or agreements with the Security Council which shall be subject to the approval of the Congress by appropriate Act or joint resolution, providing for the numbers and types of armed forces, their degree of readiness and general location, and the nature of facilities and assistance, including rights of passage, to be made available to the Security Council on its call for the purpose of maintaining international peace and security in accordance with article 43 of said Charter. The President shall not be deemed to require the authorization of the Congress to make available to the Security Council on its call in order to take action under article 42 of said Charter and pursuant to such special agreement or agreements the armed forces, facilities, or assistance provided for therein: *Provided,* That nothing herein contained shall be construed as an authorization to the President by the Congress to make available to the Security Council for such purpose armed forces, facilities or assistance in addition to the forces, facilities, and assistance provided for in such special agreement or agreements.

Approved December 20, 1945.

566. CONSTITUTION OF UNESCO
1945
(Department of State Publication 3082, pp. 1-3)

In 1945 UNESCO was set up as one of the specialized agencies of the U. N. Economic and Social Council, and in 1946 the United States joined it, committing herself to its objectives of promoting collaboration through education, science, and culture. The Librarian of Congress, Luther Evans, became Director of UNESCO in 1953. See B. M. Tripp, *UNESCO in Perspective;* H. E. Wilson, *The Development of UNESCO;* J. Huxley, *UNESCO, Its Purpose and Its Philosophy;* T. Besterman, *UNESCO.*

The governments of the States parties to this Constitution on behalf of their peoples declare:

that since wars begin in the minds of men, it is in the minds of men that the defences of peace must be constructed;

that ignorance of each other's ways and lives has been a common cause, throughout the history of mankind, of that suspicion and mistrust between the peoples of the world through which their differences have all too often broken into war;

that the great and terrible war which has now ended was a war made possible by the denial of the democratic principles of the dignity, equality and mutual respect of men, and by the propagation, in their place, through ignorance and prejudice, of the doctrine of the inequality of men and races;

that the wide diffusion of culture, and the education of humanity for justice and liberty and peace are indispensable to the dignity of man and constitute a sacred duty which all the nations must fulfill in a spirit of mutual assistance and concern:

that a peace based exclusively upon the political and economic arrangements of governments would not be a peace which could secure the unanimous, lasting and sincere support of the peoples of the world, and that the peace must therefore be founded, if it is not to fail, upon the intellectual and moral solidarity of mankind.

For These Reasons, the States parties to this Constitution, believing in full and equal opportunities for education for all, in the unrestricted pursuit of objective truth, and in the free exchange of ideas and knowledge, are agreed and determined to develop and to increase the means of communication between their peoples and to employ these means for the purposes of mutual understanding and a truer and more perfect knowledge of each other's lives;

In Consequence Whereof they do hereby create the United Nations Educational, Scientific and Cultural Organization for the purpose of advancing, through the educational and scientific and cultural relations of the peoples of the world, the objectives of international peace and of the common welfare of mankind for which the United Nations Organisation was established and which its Charter proclaims.

ARTICLE I. PURPOSES AND FUNCTIONS

1. The purpose of the Organisation is to contribute to peace and security by promoting collaboration among the nations through education, science and culture in order to further universal respect for justice, for the rule of law and for the human rights and fundamental freedoms which are affirmed for the peoples of the world, without distinction of race, sex, language or religion, by the Charter of the United Nations.

2. To realise this purpose the Organisation will:

(a) collaborate in the work of advancing the mutual knowledge and understanding of peoples, through all means of mass communication and to that end recommend such international agreements as may be necessary to promote the free flow of ideas by word and image;

(b) give fresh impulse to popular education and to the spread of culture;

by collaborating with Members, at their request, in the development of educational activities;

by instituting collaboration among the nations to advance the ideal of equality of educational opportunity without regard to race, sex or any distinctions economic or social;

by suggesting educational methods best

suited to prepare the children of the world for the responsibilities of freedom;

(c) maintain, increase and diffuse knowledge;

by assuring the conservation and protection of the world's inheritance of books, works of art and monuments of history and science, and recommending to the nations concerned the necessary international conventions;

by encouraging cooperation among the nations in all branches of intellectual activity, including the international exchange of persons active in the fields of education, science and culture and

the exchange of publications, objects of artistic and scientific interest and other materials of information;

by initiating methods of international cooperation calculated to give the people of all countries access to the printed and published materials produced by any of them.

3. With a view to preserving the independence, integrity and fruitful diversity of the cultures and educational systems of the States Members of this Organisation, the Organisation is prohibited from intervening in matters which are essentially within their domestic jurisdiction. . . .

567. ASSOCIATED PRESS v. UNITED STATES
1946
326 U. S. 1

The Attorney-General filed a bill in a Federal District Court for an injunction against AP, charging that it had violated the Sherman Act as a combination and conspiracy in restraint of trade in news. The Government charged that the bylaws of the AP, which prohibited members from selling news to non-members, and which granted to each member the power to bar non-member competitors from membership, were violations of the Sherman Act, as was a contract between the AP and the Canadian Press, under which both groups agreed to furnish news exclusively to the other. The three-judge District Court enjoined the bylaws restricting admission of a competitor and the distribution of news to non-members and enjoined observance of the Canadian contract until the by-laws were amended. The Associated Press appealed the case to the Supreme Court, and the United States Government also appealed, for it wanted the decree broadened. See Oliver Gramling, *A.P., the Story of News,* Morris Ernst, *The First Freedom;* J. R. Wiggins, *Freedom or Security.*

BLACK, J. The publishers of more than 1200 newspapers are members of the Associated Press (AP), a cooperative association incorporated under the Membership Corporations Law of the State of New York, Consol. Laws c. 35. Its business is the collection, assembly and distribution of news. The news

it distributes is originally obtained by direct employees of the Association, employees of the member newspapers, and the employees of foreign independent news agencies with which AP has contractual relations, such as the Canadian Press. Distribution of the news is made through interstate channels of communication to the various newspaper members of the Association, who pay for it under an assessment plan which contemplates no profit to AP.

The United States filed a bill in a Federal District Court for an injunction against AP and other defendants charging that they had violated the Sherman Anti-Trust Act, in that their acts and conduct constituted (1) a combination and conspiracy in restraint of trade and commerce in news among the states, and (2) an attempt to monopolize a part of that trade.

The heart of the government's charge was that appellants had by concerted action set up a system of By-Laws which prohibited all AP members from selling news to non-members, and which granted each member powers to block its non-member competitors from membership. These By-Laws, to which all AP members had assented, were, in the context of the admitted facts, charged to be in violation of the Sherman Act. . . .

To put the issue into proper focus, it becomes necessary at this juncture to examine the By-Laws.

All members must consent to be bound by them. They impose upon members certain duties and restrictions in the conduct of their separate businesses. For a violation of the By-Laws severe disciplinary action may be taken by the Association. The Board of Directors may impose a fine of $1000.00 or suspend a member and such "action . . . shall be final and conclusive. No member shall have any right to question the same." The offending member may also be expelled by the members of the corporation for any reason "which in its absolute discretion it shall deem of such a character as to be prejudicial to the welfare of the corporation and its members, or to justify such expulsion. The action of the regular members of the corporation in such regard shall be final and there shall be no right of appeal against or review of such action."

These By-Laws, for a violation of which members may be thus fined, suspended, or expelled, require that each newspaper member publish the AP news regularly in whole or in part, and that each shall "promptly furnish to the corporation, through its agents or employees, all the news of such member's district, the area of which shall be determined by the Board of Directors." All members are prohibited from selling or furnishing their spontaneous news to any agency or publisher except to AP. Other By-Laws require each newspaper member to "conduct his or its business in such manner that the news furnished by the corporations" shall not be made available to any non-member in advance of publication. The joint effect of these By-Laws is to block all newspaper non-members from any opportunity to buy news from AP or any of its publisher members. Admission to membership in AP thereby becomes a prerequisite to obtaining AP news or buying news from any one of its more than twelve hundred publishers. The erection of obstacles to the acquisition of membership consequently can make it difficult, if not impossible for non-members to get any of the news furnished by AP or any of the individual members of this combination of American newspaper publishers.

The By-Laws provide a very simple and non-burdensome road for admission of a non-competing applicant. The Board of Directors in such case can elect the applicant without payment of money or the imposition of any other onerous terms. In striking contrast are the By-Laws which govern admission of new members who do compete. Historically, as well as presently, applicants who would offer competition to old members have a hard road to travel. . . .

The District Court found that the By-Laws in and of themselves were contracts in restraint of commerce in that the contained provisions designed to stifle competition in the newspaper publishing field. The court also found that AP's restrictive By-Laws had hindered and impeded the growth of competing newspapers. This latter finding, as to the *past* effect of the restrictions, is challenged. We are inclined to think that it is supported by undisputed evidence, but we do not stop to labor the point. For the court below found, and we think correctly, that the By-Laws on their face, and without regard to their past effect, constitute restraints of trade. Combinations are no less unlawful because they have not as yet resulted in restraint. An agreement or combination to follow a course of conduct which will necessarily restrain or monopolize a part of trade or commerce may violate the Sherman Act, whether it be "wholly nascent or abortive on the one hand, or successful on the other." For these reasons the argument, repeated here in various forms, that AP had not yet achieved a complete monopoly is wholly irrelevant. Undisputed evidence did show, however, that its By-Laws had tied the hands of all of its numerous publishers, to the extent that they could not and did not reach any of their non-member competitors. In this respect the Court did find, and that finding cannot possibly be challenged, that AP's By-Laws had hindered and restrained the sale of interstate news to non-members who competed with members.

Inability to buy news from the largest news agency, or any one of its multitude of members, can have most serious effects on the publication of competitive newspapers, both those presently published and those which but for these restrictions, might be published in the future. This is illustrated by the District Court's finding that in 26 cities of the United States, existing news-papers already have contracts for AP news and the same newspapers have contracts with United Press and International News Service under which new newspapers would be required to pay the contract holders large sums to enter the field. The net ef-fect is seriously to limit the opportunity of any new paper to enter these cities. Trade restraints of this character, aimed at the destruction of competition, tend to block the initiative which brings newcomers into a field of business and to frustrate the free enterprise system which it was the purpose of the Sherman Act to protect.

We need not again pass upon the conten-tion that trade in news carried on among the states is not interstate commerce, As-sociated Press v. National Labor Relations Board, 301 U.S. 103, or that because AP's activities are cooperative, they fall outside the sphere of business, American Medical Ass'n v. United States, 317 U.S. 519. It is significant that when Congress has desired to permit cooperatives to interfere with the competitive system of business, it has done so expressly by legislation.

Nor can we treat this case as though it merely involved a reporter's contract to de-liver his news reports exclusively to a single newspaper, or an exclusive agreement as to news between two newspapers in different cities. For such trade restraints might well be "reasonable," and therefore not in vio-lation of the Sherman Act. But however innocent such agreements might be, standing alone, they would assume quite a different aspect if utilized as essential features of a program to hamper or destroy competition. It is in this light that we must view this case.

It has been argued that the restrictive By-Laws should be treated as beyond the prohibitions of the Sherman Act, since the owner of the property can choose his asso-ciates and can, as to that which he has pro-duced by his own enterprise and sagacity, efforts or ingenuity, decide for himself whether and to whom to sell or not to sell. While it is true in a very general sense that one can dispose of his property as he pleases, he cannot "go beyond the exercise of this right, and by contracts or combinations, express or implied, unduly hinder or ob-struct the free and natural flow of commerce

in the channels of interstate trade." The Sherman Act was specifically intended to prohibit independent businesses from becom-ing "associates" in a common plan which is bound to reduce their competitor's oppor-tunity to buy or sell the things in which the groups compete. Victory of a member of such a combination over its business rivals achieved by such collective means cannot consistently with the Sherman Act or with practical, everyday knowledge be attributed to *individual* "enterprise and sagacity"; such hampering of business rivals can only be attributed to that which really makes it pos-sible—the collective power of an unlawful combination. That the object of sale is the creation or product of a man's ingenuity does not alter this principle. It is obviously fallacious to view the By-Laws here in issue as instituting a program to encourage and permit full freedom of sale and disposal of property by its owners. Rather, these pub-lishers have, by concerted arrangements, pooled their power to acquire, to purchase, and to dispose of news reports through the channels of commerce. They have also pooled their economic and news control power and, in exerting that power, have en-tered into agreements which the District Court found to be "plainly designed in the interest of preventing competition." . . .

Finally, the argument is made that to apply the Sherman Act to this association of publishers constitutes an abridgment of the freedom of the press guaranteed by the First Amendment. Perhaps it would be a sufficient answer to this contention to refer to the decisions of this Court in Associated Press v. N. L. R. B., and Indiana Farmer's Guide Publishing Co. v. Prairie Farmer Pub-lishing Co., 293 U.S. 268. It would be strange indeed however if the grave concern for freedom of the press which prompted adoption of the First Amendment should be read as a command that the government was without power to protect that freedom. The First Amendment, far from providing an argument against application of the Sher-man Act, here provides powerful reasons to the contrary. That Amendment rests on the assumption that the widest possible dissemi-nation of information from diverse and an-tagonistic sources is essential to the welfare of the public, that a free press is a condition of a free society. Surely a command that the government itself shall not impede the free flow of ideas does not afford non-governmental combinations a refuge if they impose restraints upon that constitutionally guaranteed freedom. Freedom to publish means freedom for all and not for some. Freedom to publish is guaranteed by the Constitution, but freedom to combine to keep others from publishing is not. Freedom of the press from governmental interference under the First Amendment does not sanction repression of that freedom by private interests. The First Amendment affords not the slightest support for the contention that a combination to restrain trade in news and views has any constitutional immunity. . . .

Affirmed.

568. UNITED STATES v. LOVETT, WATSON, AND DODD
328 U. S. 303
1946

Section 304 of the Emergency Deficiency Appropriation Act of 1943 provided that, after November 15, 1943, no salary was to be paid to Robert Morss Lovett, Secretary of the Virgin Islands, Goodwin B. Watson, and William E. Dodd, Jr., both on the staff of the Federal Communications Commission, for any government work. This action arose from a speech on February 1, 1943, by Rep. Martin Dies, chairman of the House Committee on Un-American Activities, stating that thirty-nine government employees were members of subversive, communist organizations, and that Congress should refuse to appropriate funds for their salaries. A special sub-committee of the House Committee on Appropriation investigated the charges and decided that three of the thirty-nine, Watson, Dodd, and Lovett were guilty, after which the House passed the act in question. The Senate voted down this section, 69-0, but the House was adamant, and the Senate was forced to concur in order to get the appropriations act passed. Lovett, Watson, and Dodd continued to work for the government after November 15, 1943, without salary, and filed suit in the Court of Claims for back salary, contending that the section was unconstitutional, violating the Fifth Amendment, being a bill of attainder, and a Congressional usurpation of executive power of removal. The Court of Claims found in favor of the plaintiffs, and the Government appealed the case to the Supreme Court. See Doc. No. 528; F. L. Schuman, " 'Bill of Attainder' in the Seventy-Eighth Congress," *Am. Pol. Sci. Rev.*, Vol. 37; A. R. Ogden, *The Dies Committee;* W. Gellerman, *Martin Dies;* M. Dies, *The Trojan Horse in America;* H. S. Commager, "Who is Loyal to America?" *Harper's,* September, 1947.

On Writs of Certiorari to the Court of Claims.

BLACK, J. In 1943 the respondents, Lovett, Watson, and Dodd, were and had been for several years working for the Government. The Government agencies which had lawfully employed them were fully satisfied with the quality of their work and wished to keep them employed on their jobs. Over the protest of those employing agencies, Congress provided in Section 304 of the Urgent Deficiency Appropriation Act of 1943, by way of an amendment attached to the House bill, that after November 15, 1943, no salary or compensation should be paid respondents out of any monies then or thereafter appropriated except for services as jurors or members of the armed forces, unless they were prior to November 15, 1943 again appointed to jobs by the President with the advice and consent of the Senate. Notwithstanding the Congressional enactment, and the failure of the President to reappoint respondents, the agencies kept all the respondents at work on their jobs for varying periods after November 15, 1943; but their compensation was discontinued after that date. To secure compensation for this post-November 15th work, respondents brought these actions in the Court of Claims. They urged that Section 304 is unconstitutional and void on the grounds that: (1) The Section, properly interpreted, shows a Congressional purpose to exercise the power to remove executive employees, a power not entrusted to Congress but to the Executive Branch of Government under Article II, Sections 1, 2, 3, and 4 of the Constitution; (2) the Section violates Article I, Section 9, Clause 3, of the Constitution which provides that "no bill of attainder or ex post facto law shall be passed";

(3) the Section violates the Fifth Amendment, in that it singles out these three respondents and deprives them of their liberty and property without due process of law. . . .

Our inquiry is thus confined to whether the actions in the light of a proper construction of the Act present justiciable controversies and if so whether Section 304 is a bill of attainder against these respondents involving a use of power which the Constitution unequivocally declares Congress can never exercise. . . .

We hold that the purpose of Section 304 was not merely to cut off respondents' compensation through regular disbursing channels but permanently to bar them from government service, and that the issue of whether it is constitutional is justiciable. The Section's language as well as the circumstances of its passage which we have just described show that no mere question of compensation procedure or of appropriations was involved, but that it was designed to force the employing agencies to discharge respondents and to bar their being hired by any other governmental agency. Any other interpretation of the Section would completely frustrate the purpose of all who sponsored Section 304, which clearly was to "purge" the then existing and all future lists of Government employees of those whom Congress deemed guilty of "subversive activities" and therefore "unfit" to hold a federal job. What was challenged therefore is a statute which, because of what Congress thought to be their political beliefs, prohibited respondents from ever engaging in any government work, except as jurors or soldiers. Respondents claimed that their discharge was unconstitutional; that they consequently rightfully continued to work for the Government and that the Government owes them compensation for services performed under contracts of employment. Congress has established the Court of Claims to try just such controversies. What is involved here is a Congressional proscription of Lovett, Watson, and Dodd, prohibiting their ever holding a Government job. Were this case to be not justiciable, Congressional action, aimed at three named individuals, which stigmatized their reputation and seriously impaired their chance to earn a living,

could never be challenged in any court. Our Constitution did not contemplate such a result. To quote Alexander Hamilton, ". . . a limited constitution . . . [is] one which contains certain specified exceptions to the legislative authority; such, for instance, as that it shall pass no bills of attainder, no ex post facto laws, and the like. Limitations of this kind can be preserved in practice no other way than through the medium of the courts of justice; whose duty it must be to declare all acts contrary to the manifest tenor of the Constitution void. Without this, all the reservations of particular rights or privileges would amount to nothing."

We hold that Section 304 falls precisely within the category of Congressional actions which the Constitution barred by providing that "No Bill of Attainder or ex post facto Law shall be passed." In Cummings v. State of Missouri, this Court said, "A bill of attainder is a legislative act which inflicts punishment without a judicial trial. If the punishment be less than death, the act is termed a bill of pains and penalties. Within the meaning of the Constitution, bills of attainder include bills of pains and penalties."

Section 304 was designed to apply to particular individuals. Just as the statute in the two cases mentioned it "operates as a legislative decree of perpetual exclusion" from a chosen vocation. This permanent proscription from any opportunity to serve the Government is punishment, and of a most severe type. It is a type of punishment which Congress has only invoked for special types of odious and dangerous crimes, such as treason; acceptance of bribes by members of Congress; or by other government officials; and interference with elections by Army and Navy officers.

Section 304, thus, clearly accomplishes the punishment of named individuals without a judicial trial. The fact that the punishment is inflicted through the instrumentality of an Act specifically cutting off the pay of certain named individuals found guilty of disloyalty, makes it no less galling or effective than if it had been done by an Act which designated the conduct as criminal. No one would think that Congress could have passed a valid law, stating that after investigation it had found Lovett, Dodd, and Watson "guilty" of the crime of engaging in "subversive activities," defined that term for the first time, and sentenced them to perpetual exclusion from any government employment. Section 304, while it does not use that language, accomplishes that result. The effect was to inflict punishment without the safeguards of a judicial trial and "determined by no previous law or fixed rule." The Constitution declares that that cannot be done either by a state or by the United States.

Those who wrote our Constitution well knew the danger inherent in special legislative acts which take away the life, liberty, or property of particular named persons, because the legislature thinks them guilty of conduct which deserves punishment. They intended to safeguard the people of this country from punishment without trial by duly constituted courts. . . . When our Constitution and Bill of Rights were written, our ancestors had ample reason to know that legislative trials and punishments were too dangerous to liberty to exist in the nation of free men they envisioned. And so they proscribed bills of attainder. Section 304 is one. Much as we regret to declare that an Act of Congress violates the Constitution, we have no alternative here.

569. CONSTITUTION OF THE CONGRESS OF INDUSTRIAL ORGANIZATIONS
1946

The failure of the American Federation of Labor to organize the unorganized and its adherence to the craft form of organization led to a breach within the ranks of organized labor. The Committee for Industrial Organization, formed in 1935, acquired members with great rapidity, and in 1937 took on the name, Congress of Industrial Organizations. This independent Constitution, adopted in 1946, was a consequence of the general conviction in the C.I.O. that unity between the two great labor organizations was unlikely in the calculable future. By 1947 the C.I.O. unions claimed a total paid membership of 6,000,000. Compare the Constitution of the A. F. of L., Doc. No. 473; see R. R. Brooks, *When Labor Organizes;* B. Stolberg, *The Story of the C.I.O.;* H. Harris, *American Labor;* E. Levinson, *Labor on the March.* See Doc. No. 626.

action into labor unions for their mutual aid and protection.

Second. To extend the benefits of collective bargaining and to secure for the workers means to establish peaceful relations with their employers, by forming labor unions capable of dealing with modern aggregates of industry and finance.

Third. To maintain determined adherence to obligations and responsibilities under collective bargaining and wage agreements.

Fourth. To secure legislation safeguarding the economic security and social welfare of the workers of America, to protect and extend our democratic institutions and civil rights and liberties, and thus to perpetuate the cherished traditions of our democracy.

ARTICLE I

NAME

This organization shall be known as the "Congress of Industrial Organizations" (CIO).

ARTICLE II

OBJECTS

The objects of the organization are:

First. To bring about the effective organization of the working men and women of America regardless of race, creed, color, or nationality, and to unite them for common

ARTICLE III

AFFILIATES

SECTION 1. The Organization shall be composed of affiliated national and international unions, organizing committees, local industrial unions and industrial union councils.

SEC. 2. Certificates of affiliation shall be issued to national and international unions and organizing committees by the Executive Board.

SEC. 3. Certificates of affiliation shall be issued to local industrial unions by the Executive Board. The Executive Board shall issue rules governing the conduct, activities, affairs, and the suspension and expulsion of local industrial unions. It shall be the duty of the Executive Board to combine local industrial unions into national or international unions or organizing committees. Any local industrial union or group of local industrial unions may request the Executive Board to authorize such combination. The decision of the Executive Board may be appealed to the convention, provided, however, that pending the appeal the decision shall remain in full force and effect.

SEC. 4. Certificates of affiliation shall be issued to industrial union councils by the Executive Board. Industrial Union Councils shall be organized upon a city, state or other regional basis as may be deemed advisable by the Executive Board and shall be composed of the locals of national unions, international unions and organizing committees, and local industrial unions and local industrial union councils within the territorial limits of such council. It shall be the duty of national and international unions and organizing committees to direct their locals to affiliate with the proper industrial union councils. It shall be the duty of all local industrial unions and local industrial union councils to affiliate with the proper industrial union councils. The Executive Board shall issue rules governing the conduct, activities, affairs, and the suspension and expulsion of industrial union councils. The decision of the Executive Board may be appealed to the convention, provided, however, that pending the appeal the decision shall remain in full force and effect.

SEC. 6. National or international unions and organizing committees may not be suspended or expelled except upon a two-thirds vote at the convention. This provision may not be amended except by a two-thirds vote at the convention.

ARTICLE IV

OFFICERS AND EXECUTIVE BOARD

SECTION 1. The officers shall consist of a president, secretary-treasurer, and nine vice presidents. Each officer shall be a member of an affiliate, shall be elected by a majority of the votes cast at each regular convention, shall serve for the term of one year and shall assume office immediately upon election. In the event that more than two candidates are nominated for any one of the foregoing offices, and no one candidate receives a majority of the votes cast, all except the two candidates receiving the highest votes shall be eliminated from the list of candidates, and a second vote taken. . . .

SEC. 3. The convention shall elect the Executive Board which shall be composed of one member from each affiliated national and international union and organizing committee. Each such affiliate shall nominate one of its duly qualified officers for such membership to the Executive Board. The President, Secretary-Treasurer and Vice Presidents shall be members of the Executive Board by virtue of their office. . . .

SEC. 5. National headquarters shall be maintained at Washington, D. C.

ARTICLE V

THE DUTIES OF THE OFFICERS

PRESIDENT

SECTION 1. The President shall preside over the convention and meetings of the Executive Board, exercise supervision of the affairs of the Organization, and function as the chief executive officer.

SEC. 2. The President shall interpret the meaning of the Constitution and his interpretation shall be subject to review by the Executive Board. Between sessions of the Executive Board he shall have full power to direct the affairs of the Organization, and his acts shall be reported to the Executive Board for its approval.

SEC. 3. The President shall have authority, subject to the approval of the Executive Board, to appoint, direct, suspend or remove, such organizers, representatives, agents and employees as he may deem necessary.

SEC. 4. The President shall make full reports of the administration of his office and of the affairs of the Organization to the convention. . . .

ARTICLE VI

DUTIES OF THE EXECUTIVE BOARD

SECTION 1. The Executive Board shall enforce the constitution and carry out the instructions of the conventions, and between conventions shall have power to direct the affairs of the Organization.

SEC. 7. The Executive Board shall have the power to file charges and conduct hearings on such charges against any officer of the Organization or other member of the Executive Board, on the ground that such person is guilty of malfeasance or maladministration, and to make a report to the convention recommending appropriate action. The Executive Board must serve such officer with a copy of the written charges a reasonable time before the hearing.

ARTICLE VII

CONVENTION

SECTION 1. The convention shall be the supreme authority of the Organization and except as otherwise provided in the Constitution, its decisions shall be by a majority vote.

SEC. 2. A convention shall be held each year during the months of October or November at a time and place designated by the Executive Board. The Executive Board shall give at least 30 days' notice of the time and place which it so designates. Special conventions may be called upon 30 days' notice by the Executive Board.

SEC. 3. The Call for a special convention must include a statement of the particular subject or subjects to be considered at the convention and no other business shall be transacted at such convention. A special convention shall be governed by the provisions for regular conventions.

SEC. 4. A majority of the delegates seated shall constitute a quorum.

SEC. 5. Each national and international union and organizing committee and each local industrial union shall be entitled to one vote for each member. Each industrial union council shall be entitled to one vote.

SEC. 6. Each national or international union and organizing committee shall be entitled to the number of delegates indicated in the following scale:

Up to	5,000	membership, 2 delegates
Over	5,000	membership, 3 delegates
Over	10,000	membership, 4 delegates
Over	25,000	membership, 5 delegates
Over	50,000	membership, 6 delegates
Over	75,000	membership, 7 delegates
100,000	membership, 8 delegates for the first 100.000 members and one additional delegate for each additional 50,000 or majority fraction thereof.	

Each local industrial union and industrial union council shall be entitled to one delegate. Local industrial unions may combine with other local industrial unions in a reasonable distance of one another and elect delegates to represent them.

570. EMPLOYMENT ACT OF 1946
February 20, 1946
(*Public Law 304, 79th Congress*)

The Employment Act of 1946 marked a new approach to the formulation of national economic policy by making explicit the government's responsibility for full employment. The act set up a Council of Economic Advisers authorized to study economic trends and to recommend to the President policies to alleviate the negative effects of the business cycle. Under the leadership of economists like Leon Keyserling and Arthur Burns, the Council came to exercise profound influence on the formulation of economic policies. See E. G. Nourse, *The 1950's Come First;* E. G. Nourse, *Economics in the Public Service;* S. E. Harris, *Economic Planning;* S. K. Bailey, *Congress Makes A Law.*

AN ACT

To declare a national policy on employment, production, and purchasing power, and for other purposes. . . .

SEC. 2. The Congress hereby declares that it is the continuing policy and responsibility of the Federal Government to use all practicable means consistent with its needs and obligations and other essential considerations of national policy, with the assistance and cooperation of industry, agriculture, labor, and State and local governments, to coordinate and utilize all its plans, functions, and resources for the purpose of creating and maintaining, in a manner calculated to foster and promote free competitive enterprise and the general welfare, conditions under which there will be afforded useful employment opportunities, including self-employment, for those able, willing, and seeking to work, and to promote maximum employment, production, and purchasing power.

SEC. 3. (a) The President shall transmit to the Congress within sixty days after the beginning of each regular session (commencing with the year 1947) an economic report setting forth (1) the levels of employment, production, and purchasing power obtaining in the United States and such levels needed to carry out the policy declared in section 2; (2) current and foreseeable trends in the levels of employment, production, and purchasing power; (3) a review of the economic program of the Federal Government and a review of economic conditions affecting employment in the United States or any considerable portion thereof during the preceding year and of their effect upon employment, production, and purchasing power; and (4) a program for carrying out the policy declared in section 2, together with such recommendations for legislation as he may deem necessary or desirable. . . .

SEC. 4. (a) There is hereby created in the Executive Office of the President a Council of Economic Advisers. The Council shall be composed of three members who shall be appointed by the President, by and with the advice and consent of the Senate, and each of whom shall be a person who, as a result of his training, experience, and attainments, is exceptionally qualified to analyze and interpret economic developments, to appraise programs and activities of the Government in the light of the policy declared in section 2, and to formulate and recommend national economic policy to promote employment, production, and purchasing power under free competitive enterprise. Each member of the Council shall receive compensation at the rate of $15,000 per annum. The President shall designate one of the members of the Council as chairman and one as vice chairman, who shall act as chairman in the absence of the chairman. . . .

(c) It shall be the duty and function of the Council—

(1) to assist and advise the President in the preparation of the Economic Report;

(2) to gather timely and authoritative information concerning economic developments and economic trends, both current and prospective, to analyze and interpret such information in the light of the policy declared in section 2 for the purpose of determining whether such developments and trends are interfering, or are likely to interfere, with the achievement of such policy, and to compile and submit to the President studies relating to such developments and trends;

(3) to appraise the various programs and activities of the Federal Government in the light of the policy declared in section 2 for the purpose of determining the extent to which such programs and activities are contributing, and the extent to which they are not contributing, to the achievement of such policy, and to make recommendations to the President with respect thereto;

(4) to develop and recommend to the President national economic policies to foster and promote free competitive enterprise, to avoid economic fluctuations or to diminish the effects thereof, and to maintain employment, production, and purchasing power;

(5) to make and furnish such studies, reports thereon, and recommendations with respect to matters of Federal economic policy and legislation as the President may request.

(d) The Council shall make an annual report to the President in December of each year. . . .

SEC. 5. (a) There is hereby established a Joint Committee on the Economic Report, to be composed of seven Members of the Senate, to be appointed by the President of the Senate, and seven Members of the House of Representatives, to be appointed by the

Speaker of the House of Representatives. The party representation on the joint committee shall as nearly as may be feasible reflect the relative membership of the majority and minority parties in the Senate and House of Representatives.

(b) It shall be the function of the joint committee—

(1) to make a continuing study of matters relating to the Economic Report;

(2) to study means of coordinating programs in order to further the policy of this Act; and

(3) as a guide to the several committees of the Congress dealing with legislation relating to the Economic Report, not later than May 1 of each year (beginning with the year 1947) to file a report with the Senate and the House of Representatives containing its findings and recommendations with respect to each of the main recommendations made by the President in the Economic Report, and from time to time to make such other reports and recommendations to the Senate and House of Representatives as it deems advisable. . . .

571. THE CONTROL OF ATOMIC ENERGY
November 15, 1946
(79th Congress, 2nd Session. Senate Comm. Monograph No. 1)

The atomic bomb had been created by the scientists of the United States, Great Britain, and Canada. The end of the war and the creation of the United Nations at once raised, in critical form, the question of the control of the new weapon. The American public, alarmed by the potentialities of Russian control of the atom bomb, insisted upon keeping the "secret" of the bomb, though physicists were generally agreed that this was a secret that could not be kept. American policy on the atomic bomb was formulated in a declaration made jointly by President Truman, the Prime Minister of the United Kingdom, and the Prime Minister of Canada. On January 24, 1946, the United Nations established an Atomic Energy Commission. The American position, as presented by Bernard Baruch, was that the atomic weapon should not be made available to other nations until adequate provisions for security and inspection had been agreed upon; the Russian position, as presented by Andrei Gromyko, was that manufacture of the bomb should be outlawed and stock piles destroyed at once, and that the American plan for control and inspection would involve an unwarranted interference with the domestic affairs of sovereign states. The American plan was, in effect, adopted. On the problem of atomic control, see Bernard Brodie, *Absolute Weapon;* P. S. M. Blackett, *Fear, War, and the Bomb;* Dexter Masters, ed. *One World or None;* E. L. Woodward, *Some Political Consequences of the Atomic Bomb;* U.S. Govt. Printing Office, *Essential Information on Atomic Energy;* J. P. Baxter, *Scientists Against Time.*

Text of the agreed declaration on atomic energy by the President of the United States, the Prime Minister of the United Kingdom, and the Prime Minister of Canada

The President of the United States, the Prime Minister of the United Kingdom, and the Prime Minister of Canada have issued the following statement:

1. We recognize that the application of recent scientific discoveries to the methods and practice of war has placed at the disposal of mankind means of destruction hitherto unknown, against which there can be no adequate military defense, and in the employment of which no single nation can in fact have a monopoly.

2. We desire to emphasize that the responsibility for devising means to insure that the new discoveries shall be used for the benefit of mankind, instead of as a means of destruction, rests not on our nations alone, but upon the whole civilized world. Nevertheless, the progress that we have

made in the development and use of atomic energy demands that we take an initiative in the matter, and we have accordingly met together to consider the possibility of international action—

(a) to prevent the use of atomic energy for destructive purposes;

(b) to promote the use of recent and future advances in scientific knowledge, particularly in the utilization of atomic energy, for peaceful and humanitarian ends.

3. We are aware that the only complete protection for the civilized world from the destructive use of scientific knowledge lies in the prevention of war. No system of safeguards that can be devised will of itself provide an effective guaranty against production of atomic weapons by a nation bent on aggression. Nor can we ignore the possibility of the development of other weapons or of new methods of warfare which may constitute as great a threat to civilization as the military use of atomic energy.

4. Representing, as we do, the three countries which possess the knowledge essential to the use of atomic energy, we declare at the outset our willingness, as a first contribution, to proceed with the exchange of fundamental scientific information and the interchange of scientists and scientific literature for peaceful ends with any nation that will fully reciprocate.

5. We believe that the fruits of scientific research should be made available to all nations, and that freedom of investigation and free interchange of ideas are essential to the progress of knowledge. In pursuance of this policy, the basic scientific information essential to the development of atomic energy for peaceful purposes has already been made available to the world. It is our intention that all further information of this character that may become available from time to time should be similarly treated. We trust that other nations will adopt the same policy, thereby creating an atmosphere of reciprocal confidence in which political agreement and cooperation will flourish.

6. We have considered the question of the disclosure of detailed information concerning the practical industrial application of atomic energy. The military exploitation of atomic energy depends, in large part, upon the same methods and processes as would be required for industrial uses.

We are not convinced that the spreading of the specialized information regarding the practical application of atomic energy, before it is possible to devise effective, reciprocal, and enforceable safeguards acceptable to all nations, would contribute to a constructive solution of the problem of the atomic bomb. On the contrary, we think it might have the opposite effect. We are, however, prepared to share, on a reciprocal basis with others of the United Nations, detailed information concerning the practical industrial application of atomic energy just as soon as effective enforceable safeguards against its use for destructive purposes can be devised.

7. In order to attain the most effective means of entirely eliminating the use of atomic energy for destructive purposes and promoting its widest use for industrial and humanitarian purposes, we are of the opinion that at the earliest practicable date a commission should be set up under the United Nations Organization to prepare recommendations for submission to the Organization.

The Commission should be instructed to proceed with the utmost dispatch and should be authorized to submit recommendations from time to time dealing with separate phases of its work.

In particular the Commission should make specific proposals—

(a) for extending between all nations the exchange of basic scientific information for peaceful ends;

(b) for control of atomic energy to the extent necessary to insure its use only for peaceful purposes;

(c) for the elimination from national armaments of atomic weapons and of all other major weapons adaptable to mass destruction;

(d) for effective safeguards by way of inspection and other means to protect complying States against the hazards of violations and evasions.

8. The work of the Commission should proceed by separate stages, the successful completion of each one of which will develop the necessary confidence of the world before the next stage is undertaken. Specifically it

is considered that Commission might well devote its attention first to the wide exchange of scientists and scientific information, and as a second stage to the development of full knowledge concerning natural resources of raw materials.

9. Faced with the terrible realities of the application of science to destruction, every nation will realize more urgently than before the overwhelming need to maintain the rule of law among nations and to banish the scourge of war from the earth. This can only be brought about by giving whole-hearted support to the United Nations Organization, and by consolidating and extending its authority, thus creating conditions of mutual trust in which all peoples will be free to devote themselves to the arts of peace. It is our firm resolve to work without reservation to achieve these ends.

HARRY S. TRUMAN,
President of the United States.
C. R. ATTLEE,
Prime Minister of the United Kingdom.
W. L. MACKENZIE KING,
Prime Minister of Canada.

572. THE ATOMIC ENERGY COMMISSION
August 1, 1946
(*Public Law 585, 79th Congress, 2nd Session*)

The general background of this measure is stated in Section 1. The act was amended in 1954 to provide for greater cooperation among the free nations and increased use of atomic power by private industry. See, H. D. Smyth, *Atomic Energy for Military Purposes*, B. Brodie, ed., *The Absolute Weapon: Atomic Power and the World Order;* Julia E. Johnsen, *The Atomic Bomb.*

AN ACT

For the development and control of atomic energy.

DECLARATION OF POLICY

SECTION 1. (a) FINDINGS AND DECLARATION.—Research and experimentation in the field of nuclear chain reaction have attained the stage at which the release of atomic energy on a large scale is practical. The significance of the atomic bomb for military purposes is evident. The effect of the use of atomic energy for civilian purposes upon the social, economic, and political structures of today cannot now be determined. It is a field in which unknown factors are involved. Therefore, any legislation will necessarily be subject to revision from time to time. It is reasonable to anticipate, however, that tapping this new source of energy will cause profound changes in our present way of life. Accordingly, it is hereby declared to be the policy of the people of the United States that, subject at all times to the paramount objective of assuring the common defense and security, the development and utilization of atomic energy shall, so far as practicable, be directed toward improving the public welfare, increasing the standard of living, strengthening free competition in private enterprise, and promoting world peace.

(b) PURPOSE OF ACT.—It is the purpose of this Act to effectuate the policies set out in section 1 (a) by providing, among others, for the following major programs relating to atomic energy:

(1) A program of assisting and fostering private research and development to encourage maximum scientific progress;

(2) A program for the control of scientific and technical information which will permit the dissemination of such information to encourage scientific progress, and for the sharing on a reciprocal basis of information concerning the practical industrial application of atomic energy as soon as effective and enforceable safeguards against its use for destructive purposes can be devised;

(3) A program of federally conducted research and development to assure the Government of adequate scientific and technical accomplishment;

(4) A program for Government control of the production, ownership, and use of fissionable material to assure the common defense and security and to insure the broadest possible exploitation of the fields; and

(5) A program of administration which

will be consistent with the foregoing policies and with international arrangements made by the United States, and which will enable the Congress to be currently informed so as to take further legislative action as may hereafter be appropriate.

ORGANIZATION

SEC. 2. (a) ATOMIC ENERGY COMMISSION.—

(1) There is hereby established an Atomic Energy Commission (herein called the Commission), which shall be composed of five members. Three members shall constitute a quorum of the Commission. The President shall designate one member as Chairman of the Commission.

(2) Members of the Commission shall be appointed by the President, by and with the advice and consent of the Senate.

(4) There are hereby established within the Commission—

(A) a General Manager, who shall discharge such of the administrative and executive functions of the Commission as the Commission may direct.

(B) a Division of Research, a Division of Production, a Division of Engineering, and a Division of Military Application. . . .

(b) GENERAL ADVISORY COMMITTEE.— There shall be a General Advisory Committee to advise the Commission on scientific and technical matters relating to materials, production, and research and development, to be composed of nine members, who shall be appointed from civilian life by the President. Each member shall hold office for a term of six years.

(c) MILITARY LIAISON COMMITTEE.— There shall be a Military Liaison Committee consisting of representatives of the Departments of War and Navy, detailed or assigned thereto, without additional compensation, by the Secretaries of War and Navy in such number as they may determine. The Commission shall advise and consult with the Committee on all atomic energy matters which the Committee deems to relate to military applications, including the development, manufacture, use, and storage of bombs, the allocation of fissionable material for military research, and the control of information relating to the manufacture or

utilization of atomic weapons. The Commission shall keep the Committee fully informed of all such matters before it and the Committee shall keep the Commission fully informed of all atomic energy activities of the War and Navy Departments. The Committee shall have authority to make written recommendations to the Commission on matters relating to military applications from time to time as it may deem appropriate. If the Committee at any time concludes that any action, proposed action, or failure to act of the Commission on such matters is adverse to the responsibilities of the Departments of War or Navy, derived from the Constitution, laws, and treaties, the Committee may refer such action, proposed action, or failure to act to the Secretaries of War and Navy. If either Secretary concurs, he may refer the matter to the President, whose decision shall be final.

RESEARCH

SEC. 3. (a) RESEARCH ASSISTANCE.—The Commission is directed to exercise its powers in such manner as to insure the continued conduct of research and development activities in the fields specified below by private or public institutions or persons and to assist in the acqustion of an ever-expanding fund of theoretical and practical knowledge in such fields. To this end the Commission is authorized and directed to make arrangements (including contracts, agreements, and loans) for the conduct of research and development activities relating to—

(1) nuclear processes;

(2) the theory and production of atomic energy, including processes, materials, and devices related to such production;

(3) utilization of fissionable and radioactive materials for medical, biological, health, or military purposes;

(4) utilization of fissionable and radioactive materials and processes entailed in the production of such materials for all other purposes, including industrial uses; and

(5) the protection of health during research and production activities.

PRODUCTION OF FISSIONABLE MATERIAL
SEC. 4.

. . . (b) PROHIBITION.—It shall be unlawful for any person to own any facilities for the production of fissionable material or for any person to produce fissionable material, except to the extent authorized by subsection (c).

(c) OWNERSHIP AND OPERATION OF PRODUCTION FACILITIES.—

(1) OWNERSHIP OF PRODUCTION FACILITIES.—The Commission, as agent of and on behalf of the United States, shall be the exclusive owner of all facilities for the production of fissionable material other than facilities which (A) are useful in the conduct of research and development activities in the fields specified in section 3, and (B) do not, in the opinion of the Commission, have a potential production rate adequate to enable the operator of such facilities to produce within a reasonable period of time a sufficient quantity of fissionable material to produce an atomic bomb or any other atomic weapon.

(2) OPERATION OF THE COMMISSION'S PRODUCTION FACILITIES.—The Commission is authorized and directed to produce or to provide for the production of fissionable material in its own facilities.

(e) MANUFACTURE OF PRODUCTION FACILITIES.—Unless authorized by a license issued by the Commission, no person may manufacture, produce, transfer, or acquire any facilities for the production of fissionable material.

CONTROL OF MATERIALS

SEC. 5. (a) FISSIONABLE MATERIALS.—

(2) GOVERNMENT OWNERSHIP OF ALL FISSIONABLE MATERIAL.—All right, title, and interest within or under the jurisdiction of the United States, in or to any fissionable material, now or hereafter produced, shall be the property of the Commission, and shall be deemed to be vested in the Commission by virtue of this Act.

(4) DISTRIBUTION OF FISSIONABLE MATERIAL.—Without prejudice to its continued ownership thereof, the Commission is authorized to distribute fissionable material owned by it, with or without charge, to applicants requesting such material (A) for the conduct of research or development activities either independently or under contract or other arrangement with the Commission, (B)

for use in medical therapy, or (C) for use pursuant to a license issued under the authority of section 7.

(7) PUBLIC LANDS.—All uranium, thorium, and all other materials determined pursuant to paragraph (1) of this subsection to be peculiarly essential to the production of fissionable material, contained, in whatever concentration, in deposits in the public lands are hereby reserved for the use of the United States subject to valid claims, rights, or privileges existing on the date of the enactment of this Act: The Secretary of the Interior shall cause to be inserted in every patent, conveyance, lease, permit, or other authorization hereafter granted to use the public lands or their mineral resources, under any of which there might result the extraction of any materials so reserved, a reservation to the United States of all such materials, whether or not of commercial value, together with the right of the United States through its authorized agents or representatives at any time to enter upon the land and prospect for, mine, and remove the same, making just compensation for any damage or injury occasioned thereby.

MILITARY APPPLICATIONS OF ATOMIC ENERGY

SEC. 6 (a) AUTHORITY.—The Commission is authorized to—

(1) conduct experiments and do research and development work in the military application of atomic energy; and

(2) engage in the production of atomic bombs, atomic bomb parts, or other military weapons utilizing fissionable materials; except that such activities shall be carried on only to the extent that the express consent and direction of the President of the United States has been obtained, which consent and direction shall be obtained at least once each year.

The President from time to time may direct the Commission (1) to deliver such quantities of fissionable materials or weapons to the armed forces for such use as he deems necessary in the interest of national defense or (2) to authorize the armed forces to manufacture, produce, or acquire any equipment or device utilizing fissionable material or atomic energy as a military weapon.

INTERNATIONAL ARRANGEMENTS

SEC. 8.

. . . (b) EFFECT OF INTERNATIONAL ARRANGEMENTS.—Any provision of this Act or any action of the Commission to the extent that it conflicts with the provisions of any international arrangement made after the date of enactment of this Act shall be deemed to be of no further force or effect.

PROPERTY OF THE COMMISSION

SEC. 9. (a) The President shall direct the transfer to the Commission of all interests owned by the United States or any Government agency in the following property:

(1) All fissionable material; all atomic weapons and parts thereof; all facilities, equipment, and materials for the processing, production, or utilization of fissionable material or atomic energy; all processes and technical information of any kind, and the source thereof (including data, drawings, specifications, patents, patent applications, and other sources) relating to the processing, production, or utilization of fissionable material or atomic energy; and all contracts, agreements, leases, patents, applications for patents, inventions and discoveries (whether patented or unpatented), and other rights of any kind concerning any such items;

(2) All facilities, equipment, and materials, devoted primarily to atomic energy research and development; and

(3) Such other property owned by or in the custody or control of the Manhattan Engineer District or other Government agencies as the President may determine.

CONTROL OF INFORMATION

SEC. 10. (a) POLICY.—It shall be the policy of the Commission to control the dissemination of restricted data in such a manner as to assure the common defense and security. Consistent with such policy, the Commission shall be guided by the following principles:

(1) That until Congress declares by joint resolution that effective and enforceable international safeguards against the use of atomic energy for destructive purposes have been established, there shall be no exchange of information with other nations with respect to the use of atomic energy for industrial purposes; and

(2) That the dissemination of scientific and technical information relating to atomic energy should be permitted and encouraged so as to provide that free interchange of ideas and criticisms which is essential to scientific progress.

(3) Whoever, with intent to injure the United States or with intent to secure an advantage to any foreign nation, acquires or attempts or conspires to acquire any document, writing, sketch, photograph, plan, model, instrument, appliance, note or information involving or incorporating restricted data shall, upon conviction thereof, be punished by death or imprisonment for life (but the penalty of death or imprisonment for life may be imposed only upon recommendation of the jury and only in cases where the offense was committed with intent to injure the United States); or by a fine of not more than $20,000 or imprisonment for not more than twenty years, or both.

PATENTS AND INVENTIONS

SEC. 11. (a) PRODUCTION AND MILITARY UTILIZATION.

(1) No patent shall hereafter be granted for any invention or discovery which is useful solely in the production of fissionable material or in the utilization of fissionable material or atomic energy for a military weapon. Any patent granted for any such invention or discovery is hereby revoked, and just compensation shall be made therefor.

(b) USE OF INVENTIONS FOR RESEARCH.—No patent hereafter granted shall confer any rights with respect to any invention or discovery to the extent that such invention or discovery is used in the conduct of research or development activities in the fields specified in section 3. Any rights conferred by any patent heretofore granted for any invention or discovery are hereby revoked to the extent that such invention or discovery is so used, and just compensation shall be made therefor.

(c) NONMILITARY UTILIZATION.—

(1) It shall be the duty of the Commission to declare any patent to be affected

with the public interest if (A) the invention or discovery covered by the patent utilizes or is essential in the utilization of fissionable material or atomic energy; and (B) the licensing of such invention or discovery under this subsection is necessary to effectuate the policies and purposes of this Act.

(2) Whenever any patent has been declared, pursuant to paragraph (1), to be affected with the public interest—

(A) The Commission is hereby licensed to use the invention or discovery covered by such patent in performing any of its powers under this Act.

GENERAL AUTHORITY

SEC. 12. (a) In the performance of its functions the Commission is authorized to—

(1) establish advisory boards to advise with and make recommendations to the Commission on legislation, policies, administration, research, and other matters;

(2) establish by regulation or order such standards and instructions to govern the possession and use of fissionable and byproduct materials as the Commission may deem necessary or desirable to protect health or to minimize danger from explosions and other hazards to life or property;

(3) make such studies and investigations, obtain such information, and hold such hearings as the Commission may deem necessary or proper to assist it in exercising any authority provided in this Act, or in the administration or enforcement of this Act, or any regulations or orders issued thereunder.

(5) acquire such materials, property, equipment, and facilities, establish or construct such buildings and facilities, and modify such buildings and facilities from time to time as it may deem necessary, and construct, acquire, provide, or arrange for such facilities and services (at project sites where such facilities and services are not available) for the housing, health, safety, welfare, and recreation of personnel employed by the Commission as it may deem necessary;

JOINT COMMITTEE ON ATOMIC ENERGY

SEC. 15. (a) There is hereby established a Joint Committee on Atomic Energy to be composed of nine Members of the Senate to be appointed by the President of the Senate, and nine Members of the House of Representatives to be appointed by the Speaker of the House of Representatives. In each instance not more than five members shall be members of the same political party.

(b) The joint committee shall make continuing studies of the activities of the Atomic Energy Commission and of problems relating to the development, use, and control of atomic energy. The Commission shall keep the joint committee fully and currently informed with respect to the Commission's activities. All bills, resolutions, and other matters in the Senate or the House of Representatives relating primarily to the Commission or to the development, use, or control of atomic energy shall be referred to the joint committee. The members of the joint committee who are Members of the Senate shall from time to time report to the Senate, and the members of the joint committee who are Members of the House of Representatives shall from time to time report to the House, by bill or otherwise, their recommendations with respect to matters within the jurisdiction of their respective Houses which are (1) referred to the joint committee or (2) otherwise within the jurisdiction of the joint committee.

573. THE FULBRIGHT ACT
August 1, 1946
(Public Law 584, 79th Congress, 2nd Session)

At the close of the war millions of dollars worth of surplus war materials were left in Allied countries. Senator Fulbright of Arkansas proposed that the money received from the sale of such war surplus to Allied governments should be used to finance cultural and educational interchange. A precedent for this plan could be found in the arrangements whereby the United States appropriated half of the indemnity received from China after the Boxer uprising to bring Chinese students to the United States.

AN ACT

To Amend the Surplus Property Act of 1944.

SEC. 2. Section 32 (b) (2) In carrying out the provisions of this section, the Secretary of State is hereby authorized to enter into an executive agreement or agreements with any foreign government for the use of currencies, or credits for currencies, of such government acquired as a result of such surplus property disposals, for the purpose of providing, by the formation of foundations or otherwise, for (A) financing studies, research, instruction, and other educational activities of or for American citizens in schools and institutions of higher learning located in such foreign country, or of the citizens of such foreign country in American schools and institutions of higher learning located outside the continental United States, Hawaii, Alaska (including the Aleutian Islands), Puerto Rico, and the Virgin Islands, including payment for transportation, tuition, maintenance, and other expenses incident to scholastic activities; or (B) furnishing transportation for citizens of such foreign country who desire to attend American schools and institutions of higher learning in the continental United States, Hawaii, Alaska (including the Aleutian Islands), Puerto Rico, and the Virgin Islands, and whose attendance will not deprive citizens of the United States of an opportunity to attend such schools and institutions: *Provided, however,* That no such agreement or agreements shall provide for the use of an aggregate amount of the currencies, or credits for currencies, of any one country in excess of $20,000,000 or for the expenditure of the currencies, or credits for currencies, of any one foreign country in excess of $1,000,000 annually at the official rate of exchange for such currencies, unless otherwise authorized by Congress, nor shall any such agreement relate to any subject other than the use and expenditure of such currencies or credits for currencies for the purposes herein set forth: *Provided further,* That for the purpose of selecting students and educational institutions qualified to participate in this program, and to supervise the exchange program authorized herein, the President of the United States is hereby authorized to appoint a Board of Foreign Scholarships, consisting of ten members, who shall serve without compensation, composed of representatives of cultural, educational, student and war veterans groups, and including representatives of the United States Office of Education, the United States Veterans' Administration, State educational institutions, and privately endowed educational institutions: *And Provided further,* That in the selection of American citizens for study in foreign countries under this paragraph preference shall be given to applicants who shall have served in the military or naval forces of the United States during World War I or World War II, and due consideration shall be given to applicants from all geographical areas of the United States.

574. THE TRUMAN DOCTRINE
March 12, 1947

(Congressional Record, March 12, 1947)

The immediate background of this message to Congress is stated in the text. The idea that the United States was to underwrite the defense of free states against "totalitarian regimes" was widely hailed as a sharp new turn in American foreign policy, a world-wide equivalent of the Monroe Doctrine. In the Soviet Union it was held to be an open threat on the part of the United States aaginst Russian-dominated areas and Russian expansion. See F. L. Schuman, *Soviet Politics;* E. H. Carr, *The Soviet Impact on the Western World;* E. A. Speiser, *The United States and the Near East;* D. E. Webster, *The Turkey of Ataturk;* H. Truman *Memoirs,* Vol. II.

The gravity of the situation which confronts the world today necessitates my appearance before a joint session of the Congress. The foreign policy and the national security of this country are involved.

One aspect of the present situation, which I wish to present to you at this time for your consideration and decision, concerns Greece and Turkey.

The United States has received from the Greek Government an urgent appeal for financial and economic assistance. Preliminary reports from the American Economic Mission now in Greece and reports from the American Ambassador in Greece corroborate the statement of the Greek Government that assistance is imperative if Greece is to survive as a free nation.

I do not believe that the American people and the Congress wish to turn a deaf ear to the appeal of the Greek Government.

The very existence of the Greek state is today threatened by the terrorist activities of several thousand armed men, led by Communists, who defy the Government's authority at a number of points, particularly along the northern boundaries. A commission appointed by the United Nations Security Council is at present investigating disturbed conditions in Northern Greece and alleged border violations along the frontiers between Greece on the one hand and Albania, Bulgaria and Yugoslavia on the other.

Meanwhile, the Greek Government is un-able to cope with the situation. The Greek Army is small and poorly equipped. It needs supplies and equipment if it is to restore the authority to the Government throughout Greek territory.

Greece must have assistance if it is to become a self-supporting and self-respecting democracy. The United States must supply this assistance. We have already extended to Greece certain types of relief and economic aid but these are inadequate. There is no other country to which democratic Greece can turn. No other nation is willing and able to provide the necessary support for a democratic Greek Government.

The British Government, which has been helping Greece, can give no further financial or economic aid after March 31. Great Britain finds itself under the necessity of reducing or liquidating its committments in several parts of the world, including Greece.

We have considered how the United Nations might assist in this crisis. But the situation is an urgent one requiring immediate action, and the United Nations and its related organizations are not in a position to extend help of the kind that is required.

. . .

Greece's neighbor, Turkey, also deserves our attention. The future of Turkey as an independent and economically sound state is clearly no less important to the freedom-loving peoples of the world than the future of Greece. The circumstances in which Turkey finds itself today are considerably different from those of Greece. Turkey has been spared the disasters that have beset Greece. And during the war, the United States and Great Britain furnished Turkey with material aid. Nevertheless, Turkey now needs our support.

Since the war Turkey has sought additional financial assistance from Great Britain and the United States for the purpose of effecting the modernization necessary for the maintenance of its national integrity.

That integrity is essential to the preservation of order in the Middle East.

The British Government has informed us

that, owing to its own difficulties, it can no longer extend financial or economic aid to Turkey. As in the case of Greece, if Turkey is to have the assistance it needs, the United States must supply it. We are the only country able to provide that help.

I am fully aware of the broad implications involved if the United States extends assistance to Greece and Turkey, and I shall discuss these implications with you at this time.

One of the primary objectives of the foreign policy of the United States is the creation of conditions in which we and other nations will be able to work out a way of life free from coercion. This was a fundamental issue in the war with Germany and Japan. Our victory was won over countries which sought to impose their will, and their way of life, upon other nations.

To ensure the peaceful development of nations, free from coercion, the United States has taken a leading part in establishing the United Nations. The United Nations is designed to make possible lasting freedom and independence for all its members. We shall not realize our objectives, however, unless we are willing to help free peoples to maintain their free institutions and their national integrity against aggressive movements that seek to impose on them totalitarian regimes. This is no more than a frank recognition that totalitarian regimes imposed on free peoples, by direct or indirect aggression, undermine the foundations of international peace and hence the security of the United States.

The peoples of a number of countries of the world have recently had totalitarian regimes forced upon them against their will. The Government of the United States has made frequent protests against coercion and intimidation, in violation of the Yalta Agreement, in Poland, Rumania and Bulgaria. I must also state that in a number of other countries there have been similar developments.

At the present moment in world history nearly every nation must choose between alternative ways of life. The choice is too often not a free one.

One way of life is based upon the will of the majority, and is distinguished by free institutions, representative government, free elections, guarantees of individual liberty, freedom of speech and religion, and freedom from political oppression.

The second way of life is based upon the will of the minority forcibly imposed upon the majority. It relies upon terror and oppression, a controlled press and radio, fixed elections, and the suppression of personal freedoms.

I believe that it must be the policy of the United States to support free peoples who are resisting attempted subjugation by armed minorities or by outside pressures.

I believe that we must assist free peoples to work out their own destinies in their own way.

I believe that our help should be primarily through economic and financial aid which is essential to economic stability and orderly political processes.

The world is not static, and the status quo is not sacred. But we cannot allow changes in the status quo in violation of the charter of the United Nations by such methods as coercion, or by such subterfuges as political infiltration. In helping free and independent nations to maintain their freedom, the United States will be giving effect to the principles of the charter of the United Nations.

It is necessary only to glance at a map to realize that the survival and integrity of the Greek nation are of grave importance in a much wider situation. If Greece should fall under the control of an armed minority, the effect upon its neighbor, Turkey, would be immediate and serious. Confusion and disorder might well spread throughout the entire Middle East.

Moreover, the disappearance of Greece as an independent state would have a profound effect upon those countries in Europe whose peoples are struggling against great difficulties to maintain their freedoms and their independence while they repair the damages of war.

It would be an unspeakable tragedy if these countries, which have struggled so long against overwhelming odds, should lose that victory for which they sacrificed so much. Collapse of free institutions and loss of independence would be disastrous not only for them but for the world. Discouragement and possibly failure would quickly be the lot of neighboring peoples striving to maintain their freedom and independence.

Should we fail to aid Greece and Turkey in this fateful hour, the effect will be far reaching to the west as well as to the east. We must take immediate and resolute action.

I therefore ask the Congress to provide authority for assistance to Greece and Turkey in the amount of $400,000,000 for the period ending June 30, 1948.

In addition to funds, I ask the Congress to authorize the detail of American civilian and military personnel to Greece and Turkey, at the request of those countries, to assist in the tasks of reconstruction, and for the purpose of supervising the use of such financial and material assistance as may be furnished. I recommend that authority also be provided for the instruction and training of selected Greek and Turkish personnel.

Finally, I ask that the Congress provide authority which will permit the speediest and most effective use, in terms of needed commodities, supplies, and equipment, of such funds as may be authorized. . . .

The seeds of totalitarian regimes are nurtured by misery and want. They spread and grow in the, evil soil of poverty `and strife. They reach their full growth when the hope of a` people for a better life has died. We must keep that hope alive. The free peoples of the world look to us for support in maintaining their freedoms.

If we falter in our leadership, we may endanger the peace of the world—and we shall surely endanger the welfare of this nation.

Great responsibilities have been placed upon us by the swift movement of events. I am confident that the Congress will face these responsibilities squarely.

575. AMERICAN AID TO GREECE AND TURKEY
May 22, 1947
(80th Congress, 1st Session. Senate Doc. 111)

Truman called, originally, for four hundred millions to implement the Truman Doctrine, see Doc. No. 574. As of Jan. 1, 1949, Congress had appropriated 625 millions for Greece and Turkey, and as the Greek Civil War continued unabated it was clear that further appropriations would be required.

AN ACT

To provide for assistance to Greece and Turkey.

Whereas the Governments of Greece and Turkey have sought from the Government of the United States immediate financial and other assistance which is necessary for the maintenance of their national integrity and their survival as free nations; and

Whereas the national integrity and survival of these nations are of importance to the security of the United States and of all freedom-loving peoples and depend upon the receipt at this time of assistance; and . . .

Whereas the furnishing of such assistance to Greece and Turkey by the United States will contribute to the freedom and independence of all members of the United Nations in conformity with the principles and purposes of the Charter: Now, therefore,

Be it enacted that, notwithstanding the provisions of any other law, the President may from time to time when he deems it in the interest of the United States furnish assistance to Greece and Turkey, upon request of their governments, and upon terms and conditions determined by him—

(1) by rendering financial aid in the form of loans, credits, grants, or otherwise, to those countries;

(2) by detailing to assist those countries any persons in the employ of the Government of the United States; . . .

(3) by detailing a limited number of members of the military services of the United States to assist those countries, in an advisory capacity only; . . .

(4) by providing for (A) the transfer to, and the procurement for by manufacture or otherwise and the transfer to, those coun-

tries of any articles, services, and information, and (B) the instruction and training of personnel of those countries; . . .

SEC. 3. As a condition precedent to the receipt of any assistance pursuant to this Act, the government requesting such assistance shall agree (a) to permit free access of United States Government officials for the purpose of observing whether such assistance is utilized effectively and in accordance with the undertakings of the recipient government; (b) to permit representatives of the press and radio of the United States to observe freely and to report fully regarding the utilization of such assistance; . . . and (f) to give full and continuous publicity within such country as to the purpose, source, character, scope, amounts, and progress of United States economic assistance carried on therein pursuant to this Act.

SEC. 4. . . . (b) There is hereby authorized to be appropriated to the President not to exceed $400,000,000 to carry out the provisions of this Act. . . .

SEC. 5. . . . The President is directed to withdraw any or all aid authorized herein under any of the following circumstances:

(1) If requested by the Government of Greece or Turkey, respectively, representing a majority of the people of either such nation;

(2) If the Security Council finds (with respect to which finding the United States waives the exercise of any veto) or the General Assembly finds that action taken or assistance furnished by the United Nations makes the continuance of such assistance unnecessary or undesirable;

(3) If the President finds that any purposes of the Act have been substantially accomplished by the action of any other intergovernmental organizations or finds that the purposes of the Act are incapable of satisfactory accomplishment; and

(4) If the President finds that any of the assurances given pursuant to section 3 are not being carried out.

SEC. 6. Assistance to any country under this Act may, unless sooner terminated by the President, be terminated by concurrent resolution by the two Houses of the Congress. . . .

SEC. 8. The chief of any mission to any country receiving assistance under this Act shall be appointed by the President, by and with the advice and consent of the Senate, and shall perform such functions relating to the administration of this Act as the President shall prescribe.

Approved May 22, 1947.

576. TRUMAN LOYALTY ORDER
March 22, 1947
(*Federal Register*, Vol. 12, p. 1935)

See H. S. Commager, "Washington Witch-Hunt," 164 *Nation*, 385; G. Seldes, *Witch Hunt;* Alan Barth, *Loyalty of Free Men;* H. D. Lasswell, *National Security and Individual Freedom;* J. L. O'Brian, *National Security and Individual Freedom.*

PART I

INVESTIGATION OF APPLICANTS

1. There shall be a loyalty investigation of every person entering the civilian employment of any department or agency of the Executive Branch of the Federal Government.

A. Investigations of persons entering the competitive service shall be conducted by the Civil Service Commission, except in such cases as are covered by a special agreement between the commission and any given department or agency.

B. Investigations of persons other than those entering the competitive service shall be conducted by the employing department or agency. Departments and agencies without investigative organizations shall utilize the investigative facilities of the Civil Service Commission.

2. The investigations of persons entering the employ of the Executive Branch may be conducted after any such person enters upon

actual employment therein, but in any such case the appointment of such person shall be conditioned upon a favorable determination with respect to his loyalty. . . .

3. An investigation shall be made of all applicants at all available pertinent sources of information and shall include reference to:

A. Federal Bureau of Investigation files.

B. Civil Service Commission files.

C. Military and Naval Intelligence files.

D. The files of any other appropriate government investigative or intelligence agency.

E. House Committee on un-American Activities files.

F. Local law-enforcement files at the place of residence and employment of the applicant, including municipal, county and state law-enforcement files.

G. Schools and colleges attended by applicant.

H. Former employers of applicant.

I. References given by applicant.

J. Any other appropriate source.

4. Whenever derogatory information with respect to loyalty of an applicant is revealed, a full field investigation shall be conducted. A full field investigation shall also be conducted of those applicants, or of applicants for particular positions, as may be designated by the head of the employing department or agency, such designations to be based on the determination by any such head of the best interests of national security.

PART II

INVESTIGATION OF EMPLOYES

1. The head of each department and agency in the Executive Branch of the Government shall be personally responsible for an effective program to assure that disloyal civilian officers or employes are not retained in employment in his department or agency.

A. He shall be responsible for prescribing and supervising the loyalty determination procedures of his department or agency, in accordance with the provisions of this order, which shall be considered as providing minimum requirements.

B. The head of a department or agency which does not have an investigative organization shall utilize the investigative facilities of the Civil Service Commission.

2. The head of each department and agency shall appoint one or more loyalty boards, each composed of not less than three representatives of the department or agency concerned, for the purpose of hearing loyalty cases arising within such department or agency and making recommendations with respect to the removal of any officer or employe of such department or agency on grounds relating to loyalty, and he shall prescribe regulations for the conduct of the proceedings before such boards.

A. An officer or employe who is charged with being disloyal shall have a right to an administrative hearing before a loyalty board in the employing department or agency. He may appear before such board personally, accompanied by counsel or representative of his own choosing, and present evidence on his own behalf, through witnesses or by affidavit.

B. The officer or employe shall be served with a written notice of such hearing in sufficient time, and shall be informed therein of the nature of the charges against him in sufficient detail, so that he will be enabled to prepare his defense. The charges shall be stated as specifically and completely as, in the discretion of the employing department or agency, security considerations permit, and the officer or employe shall be informed in the notice (1) of his right to reply to such charges in writing within a specified reasonable period of time, (2) of his right to an administrative hearing on such charges before a loyalty board, and (3) of his right to appear before such board personally, to be accompanied by counsel or representative of his own choosing, and to present evidence on his behalf, through witness or by affidavit.

3. A recommendation of removal by a loyalty board shall be subject to appeal by the officer or employe affected, prior to his removal, to the head of the employing department or agency or to such person or persons as may be designated by such head, under such regulations as may be prescribed by him, and the decision of the department or agency concerned shall be subject to appeal to the Civil Service Commission's Loyalty Review Board, hereinafter provided for, for an advisory recommendation.

4. The rights of hearing, notice thereof, and appeal therefrom shall be accorded to every officer or employe prior to his removal on grounds of disloyalty, irrespective of tenure, or of manner, method, or nature of appointment, but the head of the employing department or agency may suspend any officer or employe at any time pending a determination with respect to loyalty.

5. The loyalty boards of the various departments and agencies shall furnish to the Loyalty Review Board, hereinafter provided for, such reports as may be requested concerning the operation of the loyalty program in any such department or agency.

PART III

RESPONSIBILITIES OF CIVIL SERVICE COMMISSION

1. There shall be established in the Civil Service Commission a Loyalty Review Board of not less than three impartial persons, the members of which shall be officers or employes of the commission.

A. The board shall have authority to review cases involving persons recommended for dismissal on grounds relating to loyalty by the loyalty board of any department or agency and to make advisory recommendations thereon to the head of the employing department or agency. Such cases may be referred to the board either by the employing department or agency, or by the officer or employe concerned.

B. The board shall make rules and regulations, not inconsistent with the provisions of this order, deemed necessary to implement statutes and executive orders relating to employe loyalty.

C. The Loyalty Review Board shall also:

(1) Advise all departments and agencies on all problems relating to employe loyalty.

(2) Disseminate information pertinent to employe loyalty programs.

(3) Coordinate the employe loyalty policies and procedures of the several departments and agencies.

(4) Make reports and submit recommendations to the Civil Service Commission for transmission to the President from time to time as may be necessary to the maintenance of the employe loyalty program.

2. There shall also be established and maintained in the Civil Service Commission a central master index covering all persons on whom loyalty investigations have been made by any department or agency since Sept. 1, 1939. Such master index shall contain the name of each person investigated, adequate identifying information concerning each such person, and a reference to each department and agency which has conducted a loyalty investigation concerning the person involved. . . .

B. The reports and other investigative material and information developed by the investigating department or agency shall be retained by such department or agency in each case.

3. The Loyalty Review Board shall currently be furnished by the Department of Justice the name of each foreign or domestic organization, association, movement, group or combination of persons which the Attorney General, after appropriate investigation and determination, designates as totalitarian, Fascist, Communist or subversive, or as having adopted a policy of advocating or approving the commission of acts of force or violence to deny others their rights under the Constitution of the United States, or as seeking to alter the form of government of the United States by unconstitutional means.

A. The Loyalty Review Board shall disseminate such information to all departments and agencies.

PART IV

SECURITY MEASURES IN INVESTIGATIONS

1. At the request of the head of any department or agency of the Executive Branch an investigative agency shall make available to such head, personally, all investigative material and information collected by the investigative agency concerning any employe or prospective employe of the requesting department or agency, or shall make such material and information available to any officer or officers designated by such head and approved by the investigative agency.

2. Notwithstanding the foregoing requirement, however, the investigative agency may refuse to disclose the names of confidential informants, provided it furnishes sufficient

information about such informants on the basis of which the requesting department or agency can make an adequate evaluation of the information furnished by them, and provided it advises the requesting department or agency in writing that it is essential to the protection of the informants or to the investigation of other cases that the identity of the informants not be revealed. Investigative agencies shall not use this discretion to decline to reveal sources of information where such action is not essential.

3. Each department and agency of the Executive Branch should develop and maintain, for the collection and analysis of information relating to the loyalty of its employes and prospective employes, a staff specially trained in security techniques, and an effective security control system for protecting such information generally and for protecting confidential sources of such information particularly.

PART V

STANDARDS

1. The standard for the refusal of employment or the removal from employment in an executive department or agency on grounds relating to loyalty shall be that, on all the evidence, reasonable grounds exist for belief that the person involved is disloyal to the Government of the United States.

2. Activities and associations of an appli-

cant or employe which may be considered in connection with the determination of disloyalty may include one or more of the following:

A. Sabotage, espionage, or attempts or preparations therefor, knowingly associating with spies or saboteurs;

B. Treason or sedition or advocacy thereof;

C. Advocacy of revolution of force or violence to alter the constitutional form of Government of the United States;

D. Intentional, unauthorized disclosure to any person, under circumstances which may indicate disloyalty to the United States, of documents or information of a confidential or non-public character obtained by the person making the disclosure as a result of his employment by the Government of the United States;

E. Performing or attempting to perform his duties, or *otherwise acting, so as to serve the interests of another government in preference to the interests of the United States.*

F. Membership in, affiliation with or *sympathetic association* with any foreign or *domestic* organization, association, movement, *group or combination* of persons, designated by the Attorney General as totalitarian, Fascist, Communist, or *subversive,* or as having adopted a policy of advocating or approving the commision of acts of force or violence to deny other persons their rights under the Constitution of the United States, or as seeking to alter the form of Government of the United States by unconstitutional means.

577. THE MARSHALL PLAN
June 5, 1947

(*Congressional Record,* June 30, 1947)

On June 5, 1947, at a Harvard commencement, Secretary of State George C. Marshall delivered a notable address setting forth the basic principles of American policy toward the postwar rehabilitation of Europe. Secretary Marshall viewed the European economy as a unit, and suggested that European countries in need of American aid should join together in drawing up a program stating their needs. Great Britain and France, after consulting with Prime Minister Molotov of the Soviet Union, issued an invitation on July 3, 1947 to twenty-two European countries to participate in a conference, the purpose of which was to draw up a blueprint of European reconstruction to present to the United States. The Soviet Union took an increasingly hostile view of the undertaking, saw the Marshall Plan as the beginning of an anti-Russian bloc, and refused to participate. The conference of European countries opened at Paris on July 12, and submitted a general report on European needs, September 23, 1947. See Sidney B. Fay, "The Marshall Plan," *Current History,* September, 1947; *The New York Times,* September 24, 1947, for the conference report.

Remarks by the Honorable George C. Marshall, Secretary of State, at Harvard University on June 5, 1947

I need not tell you gentlemen that the world situation is very serious. That must be apparent to all intelligent people. I think one difficulty is that the problem is one of such enormous complexity that the very mass of facts presented to the public by press and radio make it exceedingly difficult for the man in the street to reach a clear appraisement of the situation. Furthermore, the people of this country are distant from the troubled areas of the earth and it is hard for them to comprehend the plight and consequent reactions of the long-suffering peoples, and the effect of those reactions on their governments in connection with our efforts to promote peace in the world.

In considering the requirements for the rehabilitation of Europe the physical loss of life, the visible destruction of cities, factories, mines, and railroads was correctly estimated, but it has become obvious during recent months that this visible destruction was probably less serious than the dislocation of the entire fabric of European economy. For the past 10 years conditions have been highly abnormal. The feverish preparation for war and the more feverish maintenance of the war effort engulfed all aspects of national economies. Machinery has fallen into disrepair or is entirely obsolete. Under the arbitrary and destructive Nazi rule, virtually every possible enterprise was geared into the German war machine. Long-standing commercial ties, private institutions, banks, insurance companies and shipping companies disappeared, through loss of capital, absorption through nationalization or by simple destruction. In many countries, confidence in the local currency has been severely shaken. The breakdown of the business structure of Europe during the war was complete. Recovery has been seriously retarded by the fact that 2 years after the close of hostilities a peace settlement with Germany and Austria has not been agreed upon. But even given a more prompt solution of these difficult problems, the rehabilitation of the economic structure of Europe quite evidently will require a much longer time and greater effort than had been foreseen.

There is a phase of this matter which is both interesting and serious. The farmer has always produced the foodstuffs to exchange with the city dweller for the other necessities of life. This division of labor is the basis of modern civilization. At the present time it is threatened with breakdown. The town and city industries are not producing adequate goods to exchange with the food-producing farmer. Raw materials and fuel are in short supply. Machinery is lacking or worn out. The farmer or the peasant cannot find the goods for sale which he desires to purchase. So the sale of his farm produce for money which he cannot use seems to him an unprofitable transaction. He, therefore, has withdrawn many fields from crop cultivation and is using them for grazing. He feeds more grain to stock and finds for himself and his family an ample supply of food, however short he may be on clothing and the other ordinary gadgets of civilization. Meanwhile people in the cities are short of food and fuel. So the governments are forced to use their foreign money and credits to procure these necessities abroad. This process exhausts funds which are urgently needed for reconstruction. Thus a very serious situation is rapidly developing which bodes no good for the world. The modern system of the division of labor upon which the exchange of products is based is in danger of breaking down.

The truth of the matter is that Europe's requirements for the next 3 or 4 years of foreign food and other essential products—principally from America—are so much greater than her present ability to pay that she must have substantial additional help, or face economic, social, and political deterioration of a very grave character.

The remedy lies in breaking the vicious circle and restoring the confidence of the European people in the economic future of their own countries and of Europe as a whole. The manufacturer and the farmer throughout wide areas must be able and willing to exchange their products for currencies the continuing value of which is not open to question.

Aside from the demoralizing effect on the world at large and the possibilities of disturbances arising as a result of the desperation of the people concerned, the consequences to the economy of the United States should be apparent to all. It is logical that the United States should do whatever it is able to do to assist in the return of normal economic health in the world, without which there can be no political stability and no assured peace. Our policy is directed not against any county or doctrine but against hunger, poverty, desperation, and chaos. Its purpose should be the revival of a working economy in the world so as to permit the emergence of political and social conditions in which free institutions can exist. Such assistance, I am convinced, must not be on a piecemeal basis as various crises develop. Any assistance that this Government may render in the future should provide a cure rather than a mere palliative. Any government that is willing to assist in the task of recovery will find full cooperation, I am sure, on the part of the United States Government. Any government which maneuvers to block the recovery of other countries cannot expect help from us. Furthermore, governments, political parties, or groups which seek to perpetuate human misery in order to profit therefrom politically or otherwise will encounter the opposition of the United States.

It is already evident that, before the United States Government can proceed much further in its efforts to alleviate the situation and help start the European world on its way to recovery, there must be some agreement among the countries of Europe as to the requirements of the situation and the part those countries themselves will take in order to give proper effect to whatever action might be undertaken by this Government. It would be neither fitting nor efficacious for this Government to undertake to draw up unilaterally a program designed to place Europe on its feet economically. This is the business of the Europeans. The initiative, I think, must come from Europe. The role of this country should consist of friendly aid in the drafting of a European program and of later support of such a program so far as it may be practical for us to do so. The program should be a joint one, agreed to by a number, if not all European nations.

An essential part of any successful action on the part of the United States is an understanding on the part of the people of America of the character of the problem and the remedies to be applied. Political passion and prejudice should have no part. With foresight, and a willingness on the part of our people to face up to the vast responsibility which history has clearly placed upon our country, the difficulties I have outlined can and will be overcome.

578. EVERSON v. BOARD OF EDUCATION
330 U. S. 1
1947

The rising costs of education, during the war and post-war years, led to demands from parochial and independent schools for some form of governmental aid. The Board of Education of Ewing, New Jersey, provided for free transportation for all pupils to public and parochial schools alike. The challenge to this act reintroduced the old controversy over the separation of church and state. The concurring and dissenting opinions in this case give abundant historical analysis and bibliographical references; see, also, J. M. O'Neill, *Religion and Education Under the Constitution;* A. W. Johnson, *Legal Status of Church-State Relationships in the United States;* Leo Pfeffer, *Church, State, and Freedom;* Leo Pfeffer, "Church and State, Something Less than Separation," 19 *U. of C. L. Rev.*, 1; E. S. Corwin, "Supreme Court as National School Board," 14 *Law and Cont. Problems, 3.*

Appeal from the Court of Errors and Appeals of the State of New Jersey.
Affirmed.

BLACK, J. . . . A New Jersey statute authorizes its local school districts to make rules and contracts for the transportation of children to and from schools. The appellee, a township board of education, acting pursuant to this statute authorized reimbursement to parents of money expended by them for the bus transportation of their children on regular busses operated by the public transportation system. Part of this money was for the payment of transportation of some children in the community to Catholic parochial schools. . . .

The appellant, in his capacity as a district taxpayer, filed suit in a State court challenging the right of the Board to reimburse parents of parochial school students. He contended that the statute and the resolution passed pursuant to it violated both the State and the Federal Constitutions. . . .

The only contention here is that the State statute and the resolution, in so far as they authorized reimbursement to parents of children attending parochial schools, violate the Federal Constitution in these two respects, which to some extent, overlap. First. They authorize the State to take by taxation the private property of some and bestow it upon others, to be used for their own private purposes. This, it is alleged violates the due process clause of the Fourteenth Amendment. Second. The statute and the resolution forced inhabitants to pay taxes to help support and maintain schools which are dedicated to, and which regularly teach, the Catholic Faith. This is alleged to be a use of State power to support church schools contrary to the prohibition of the First Amendment which the Fourteenth Amendment made applicable to the states. . . .

Insofar as the second phase of the due process argument may differ from the first, it is by suggesting that taxation for transportation of children to church schools constitutes support of a religion by the State. But if the law is invalid for this reason, it is because it violates the First Amendment's prohibition against the establishment of religion by law. This is the exact question raised by appellant's second contention, to consideration of which we now turn.

Second. The New Jersey statute is challenged as a "law respecting an establishment of religion." The First Amendment, as made applicable to the states by the Fourteenth, commands that a state "shall make no law respecting an establishment of religion, or prohibiting the free exercise thereof." These words of the First Amendment reflected in the minds of early Americans a vivid mental picture of conditions and practices which they fervently wished to stamp out in order to preserve liberty for themselves and for their posterity. Doubtless their goal has not been entirely reached; but so far has the Nation moved toward it that the expression "law respecting an establishment of religion," probably does not so vividly remind present-day Americans of the evils, fears, and political problems that caused that expression to be written into our Bill of Rights. Whether this New Jersey law is one respecting the "establishment of religion" requires an understanding of the meaning of that language, particularly with respect to the imposition of taxes. Once again, therefore, it is not inappropriate briefly to review the background and environment of the period in which that constitutional language was fashioned and adopted. . . .

This Court has previously recognized that the provisions of the First Amendment, in the drafting and adoption of which Madison and Jefferson played such leading roles, had the same objective and were intended to provide the same protection against governmental intrusion on religious liberty as the Virginia statute. Reynolds v. United States, supra, 98 U.S. at page 164, [etc.]. Prior to the adoption of the Fourteenth Amendment, the First Amendment did not apply as a restraint against the states. Most of them did soon provide similar constitutional protections for religious liberty. But some states persisted for about half a century in imposing restraints upon the free exercise of religion and in discriminating against particular religious groups. In recent years, so far as the provision against the establishment of a religion is concerned, the question has most frequently arisen in connection with proposed state aid to church schools and efforts to carry on religious teachings in the public schools in accordance with the tenets of a particular sect. Some churches have either sought or accepted state financial support for their schools. Here again the efforts to obtain state aid or acceptance of it have not been limited to any one particular faith. The state courts, in the main, have remained faithful to the language of their own constitutional provisions designed to protect religious freedom and to separate religions and governments. Their decisions, however, show the difficulty in drawing the line between tax legislation which provides funds for the welfare of the general public and that which is designed to support institutions which teach religion.

The meaning and scope of the First Amendment, preventing establishment of religion or prohibiting the free exercise thereof, in the light of its history and the evils it was designed forever to suppress, have been several times elaborated by the decisions of this Court prior to the application of the First Amendment to the states by the

Fourteenth. The broad meaning given the Amendment by these earlier cases has been accepted by this Court in its decisions concerning an individual's religious freedom rendered since the Fourteenth Amendment was interpreted to make the prohibitions of the First applicable to state action abridging religious freedom. There is every reason to give the same application and broad interpretation to the "establishment of religion" clause. The interrelation of these complementary clauses was well summarized in a statement of the Court of Appeals of South Carolina, quoted with approval by this Court, in Watson v. Jones, 13 Wall. 679: "The structure of our government has, for the preservation of civil liberty, rescued the temporal institutions from religious interference. On the other hand, it has secured religious liberty from the invasions of the civil authority."

The "establishment of religion" clause of the First Amendment means at least this: Neither a state nor the Federal Government can set up a church. Neither can pass laws which aid one religion, aid all religions, or prefer one religion over another. Neither can force nor influence a person to go to or to remain away from church against his will or force him to profess a belief or disbelief in any religion. No person can be punished for entertaining or professing religious beliefs or disbeliefs, for church attendance or non-attendance. No tax in any amount, large or small, can be levied to support any religious activities or institutions, whatever they may be called, or whatever form they may adopt to teach or practice religion. Neither a state nor the Federal Government can, openly or secretly, participate in the affairs of any religious organizations or groups and vice versa. In the words of Jefferson, the clause against establishment of religion by law was intended to erect "a wall of separation between Church and State." Reynolds v. United States, supra, 98 U.S. at page 164.

We must consider the New Jersey statute in accordance with the foregoing limitations imposed by the First Amendment. But we must not strike that state statute down if it is within the state's constitutional power even though it approaches the verge of that power. New Jersey cannot consistently with the "establishment of religion" clause of the First Amendment contribute tax-raised funds to the support of an institution which teaches the tenets and faith of any church. On the other hand, other language of the amendment commands that New Jersey cannot hamper its citizens in the free exercise of their own religion. Consequently, it cannot exclude individual Catholics, Lutherans, Mohammedans, Baptists, Jews, Methodists, Non-believers, Presbyterians, or the members of any other faith, *because of their faith, or lack of it,* from receiving the benefits of public welfare legislation. While we do not mean to intimate that a state could not provide transportation only to children attending public schools, we must be careful, in protecting the citizens of New Jersey against state-established churches, to be sure that we do not inadvertently prohibit New Jersey from extending its general State law benefits to all its citizens without regard to their religious belief.

Measured by these standards, we cannot say that the First Amendment prohibits New Jersey from spending tax-raised funds to pay the bus fares of parochial school pupils as a part of a general program under which it pays the fares of pupils attending public and other schools. It is undoubtedly true that children are helped to get to church schools. There is even a possibility that some of the children might not be sent to the church schools if the parents were compelled to pay their children's bus fares out of their own pockets when transportation to a public school would have been paid for by the State. The same possibility exists where the state requires a local transit company to provide reduced fares to school children including those attending parochial schools, or where a municipally owned transportation system undertakes to carry all school children free of charge. Moreover, state-paid policemen, detailed to protect children going to and from church schools from the very real hazards of traffic, would serve much the same purpose and accomplish

much the same result as state provisions intended to guarantee free transportation of a kind which the state deems to be best for the school children's welfare. And parents might refuse to risk their children to the serious danger of traffic accidents going to and from parochial schools, the approaches to which were not protected by policemen. Similarly, parents might be reluctant to permit their children to attend schools which the state had cut off from such general government services as ordinary police and fire protection, connections for sewage disposal, public highways and sidewalks. Of course, cutting off church schools from these services, so separate and so indisputably marked off from the religious function, would make it far more difficult for the schools to operate. But such is obviously not the purpose of the First Amendment. That Amendment requires the state to be a neutral in its relations with groups of religious believers and non-believers; it does not require the state to be their adversary. State power is no more to be used so as to handicap religions, than it is to favor them.

This Court has said that parents may, in the discharge of their duty under state compulsory education laws, send their children to a religious rather than a public school if the school meets the secular educational requirements which the state has power to impose. See Pierce v. Society of Sisters, 268 U.S. 510. It appears that these parochial schools meet New Jersey's requirements. The State contributes no money to the schools. It does not support them. Its legislation, as applied, does no more than provide a general program to help parents get their children, regardless of their religion, safely and expeditiously to and from accredited schools.

The First Amendment has erected a wall between church and state. That wall must be kept high and impregnable. We could not approve the slightest breach. New Jersey has not breached it here.

Affirmed.

579. TAFT-HARTLEY ACT
June 23, 1947
(*Public Law 101, 80th Congress*)

The National Labor Relations Act of 1935 placed limitations on the conduct of employers in labor-management disputes. See Doc. No. 500. The Taft-Hartley Act placed limitations on the conduct of trade unions in labor-management disputes. Some of the important provisions of the act banned the closed shop, permitted employers to sue unions for breaking contracts, forbade union contributions to political campaigns, and required unions to give 60 days' notice before inaugurating strikes. President Truman vetoed the act, but it was passed over his veto by a vote of 331 to 83 in the House and 68 to 25 in the Senate. After 1947, the trade union movement conducted a continuous campaign to repeal or amend this law. See H. A. Millis and E. C. Brown, *From the Wagner Act to Taft-Hartley;* J. Seidman, *American Labor from Defense to Reconversion;* F. A. Hartley, *Our New National Labor Policy.*

AN ACT

To amend the National Labor Relations Act, to provide additional facilities for the mediation of labor disputes affecting commerce, to equalize legal responsibilities of labor organizations and employers, and for other purposes. . . .

SEC. 101. The National Labor Relations Act is hereby amended to read as follows: . . . .

"SEC. 3. (a) The National Labor Relations Board (hereinafter called the 'Board') created by this Act prior to its amendment by the Labor Management Relations Act, 1947, is hereby continued as an agency of the United States, except that the Board shall consist of five instead of three members, appointed by the President by and with the advice and consent of the Senate. . . .

"SEC. 7. Employees shall have the right to self-organization, to form, join, or assist labor organizations, to bargain collectively through representatives of their own choosing, and to engage in other concerted activities for the purpose of collective bargaining or other mutual aid or protection, and shall also have the right to refrain from any or all of such activities except to the extent that such right may be affected by an agreement requiring membership in a labor organization as a condition of employment as authorized in section 8 (a) (3).

"SEC. 8. (a) It shall be an unfair labor practice for an employer—

"(1) to interfere with, restrain, or coerce employees in the exercise of the rights guaranteed in section 7;

"(2) to dominate or interfere with the formation or administration of any labor organization or contribute financial or other support to it: *Provided,* That subject to rules and regulations made and published by the Board pursuant to section 6, an employer shall not be prohibited from permitting employees to confer with him during working hours without loss of time or pay;

"(3) by discrimination in regard to hire or tenure of employment or any term or condition of employment to encourage or discourage membership in any labor organization: *Provided,* That nothing in this Act, or in any other statute of the United States, shall preclude an employer from making an agreement with a labor organization . . . to require as a condition of employment membership therein, (i) if such labor organization is the representative of the employees as provided in section 9 (a), in the appropriate collective-bargaining unit covered by such agreement when made; and (ii) if, following the most recent election held as provided in section 9 (e) the Board shall have certified that at least a majority of the employees eligible to vote in such election have voted to authorize such labor organization to make such an agreement: *Provided further,* That no employer shall justify any discrimination against an employee for nonmembership in a labor organization (A) if he has reasonable grounds for believing that such membership was not available to the employee on the same terms and conditions generally applicable to other members, or (B) if he has reasonable grounds for believing that membership was denied or terminated for reasons other than the failure of the employee to tender the periodic dues and the initiation fees uniformly required as a condition of acquiring or retaining membership;

"(4) to discharge or otherwise discriminate against an employee because he has filed charges or given testimony under this Act;

"(5) to refuse to bargain collectively with the representatives of his employees, subject to the provisions of section 9 (a).

"(b) It shall be an unfair labor practice for a labor organization or its agents—

"(1) to restrain or coerce (A) employees in the exercise of the rights guaranteed in section 7: *Provided,* That this paragraph shall not impair the right of a labor organization to prescribe its own rules with respect to the acquisition or retention of membership therein; or (B) an employer in the selection of his representatives for the purposes of collective bargaining or the adjustment of grievances;

"(2) to cause or attempt to cause an employer to discriminate against an employee in violation of subsection (a) (3) or to discriminate against an employee with respect to whom membership in such organization has been denied or terminated on some ground other than his failure to tender the periodic dues and the initiation fees uniformly required as a condition of acquiring or retaining membership;

"(3) to refuse to bargain collectively with an employer, provided it is the representative of his employees subject to the provision of section 9 (a);

"(4) to engage in, or to induce or encourage the employees of any employer to engage in, a strike or a concerted refusal in the course of their employment to use, manufacture, process, transport, or otherwise handle or work on any goods, articles, materials, or commodities or to perform any services, where an object thereof is: (A) forcing or requiring any employer or self-employed person to join any labor or employer organization or any employer or other person to cease using, selling, handling, transporting, or otherwise dealing in the products of any other producer, processor, or manufacturer, or to cease doing business with any other person; (B) forcing or requiring any other employer to recognize or bargain with a labor organization as the representative of his employees unless such labor organization has been certified as the representative of such employees under the provisions of section 9; (C) forcing or requiring any employer to recognize or bargain with a particular labor organization as the representative of his employees if another labor organization has been certified as the representative of such employees under the provisions of section 9; (D) forcing or requiring any employer to assign particular work to employees in a particular labor organization or in a particular trade, craft, or class rather than to employees in another labor organization or in another trade, craft, or class, unless such employer is failing to conform to an order or certification of the Board determining the bargaining representative for employees performing such work: *Provided,* That nothing contained in this subsection (b) shall be construed to make unlawful a refusal by any person to enter upon the premises of any employer (other than his own employer), if the employees of such employer are engaged in a strike ratified or approved by a representative of such employees whom such employer is required to recognize under this Act;

"(5) to require of employees covered by an agreement authorized under subsection (a) (3) the payment, as a condition precedent to becoming a member of such organization, of a fee in an amount which the Board finds excessive or discriminatory under all the circumstances. In making such a finding, the Board shall consider, among other relevant factors, the practices and customs of labor organizations in the particular industry, and the wages currently paid to the employees affected; and

"(6) to cause or attempt to cause an employer to pay or deliver or agree to pay or deliver any money or other thing of value, in the nature of an exaction, for services which are not performed or not to be performed.

"(c) The expressing of any views, argument, or opinion, or the dissemination thereof, whether in written, printed, graphic, or visual form, shall not constitute or be evidence of an unfair labor practice under any of the provisions of this Act, if such expression contains no threat of reprisal or force or promise of benefit.

"(d) . . . That where there is in effect a collective-bargaining contract covering employees in an industry affecting commerce, the duty to bargain collectively shall also mean that no party to such contract shall terminate or modify such contract, unless the party desiring such termination or modification—

"(1) serves a written notice upon the other party to the contract of the proposed termination or modification sixty days prior to the expiration date thereof, or in the event such contract contains no expiration date, sixty days prior to the time it is proposed to make such termination or modification;

"(2) offers to meet and confer with the other party for the purpose of negotiating a new contract or a contract containing the proposed modifications;

"(3) notifies the Federal Mediation and Conciliation Service within thirty days after such notice of the existence of a dispute, and simultaneously therewith notifies any State or Territorial agency established to mediate and conciliate disputes within the State or Territory where the dispute occurred, provided no agreement has been reached by that time; and

"(4) continues in full force and effect without resorting to strike or lock-out, all the terms and conditions of the existing contract for a period of sixty days after such notice is given or until the expiration date of such contract, whichever occurs later: . . .

"(h) No investigation shall be made by the Board of any question affecting commerce concerning the representation of employees, raised by a labor organization under subsection (c) of this section, no petition under section 9 (e) (1) shall be entertained, and no complaint shall be issued pursuant to a charge made by a labor organization under subsection (b) of section 10, unless there is on file with the Board an affidavit executed contemporaneously or within the preceding twelve-month period by each officer of such labor organization and the officers of any national or international labor organization of which it is an affiliate or constituent unit that he is not a member of the Communist Party or affiliated with such party, and that he does not believe in, and is not a member of or supports any organization that believes in or teaches, the overthrow of the United States Government by force or by any illegal or unconstitutional methods. The provisions of section 35 A of the Criminal Code shall be applicable in respect to such affidavits. . . .

SEC. 301. . . . (b) Any labor organization which represents employees in an industry affecting commerce as defined in this Act and any employer whose activities affect commerce as defined in this Act shall be bound by the acts of its agents. Any such labor organization may sue or be sued as an entity and in behalf of the employees whom it represents in the courts of the United States. Any money judgment against a labor organization in a district court of the United States shall be enforceable only against the organization as an entity and against its assets, and shall not be enforceable against any individual member or his assets. . . .

SEC. 303. (a) It shall be unlawful, for the purposes of this section only, in an industry or activity affecting commerce, for any labor organization to engage in, or to induce or encourage the employees of any employer to engage in, a strike or a concerted refusal in the course of their employment to use, manufacture, process, transport, or otherwise handle or work on any goods, articles, materials, or commodities or to perform any services, where an object thereof is—

(1) forcing or requiring any employer or self-employed person to join any labor or employer organization or any employer or other person to cease using, selling, handling, transporting, or otherwise dealing in the products of any other producer, processor or manufacturer, or to cease doing business with any other person;

(2) forcing or requiring any other employer to recognize or bargain with a labor organization as the representative of his employees unless such labor organization has been certified as the representative of such employees under the provisions of section 9 of the National Labor Relations Act;

(3) forcing or requiring any employer to recognize or bargain with a particular labor organization as the representative of his employees if another labor organization has been certified as the representative of such employees under the provisions of section 9 of the National Labor Relations Act;

(4) forcing or requiring any employer to assign particular work to employees in a particular labor organization or in a particular trade, craft, or class rather than to employees in another labor organization or in another trade, craft, or class unless such employer is failing to conform to an order of certification of the National Labor Relations Board determining the bargaining representative for employees performing such work. Nothing contained in this subsection shall be construed to make unlawful a refusal by any person to enter upon the premises of any employer (other than his own employer), if the employees

of such employer are engaged in a strike ratified or approved by a representative of such employees whom such employer is required to recognize under the National Labor Relations Act.

(b) Whoever shall be injured in his business or property by reason of any violation of subsection (a) may sue therefor in any district court of the United States subject to the limitations and provisions of section 301 hereof without respect to the amount in controversy, or in any other court having jurisdiction of the parties, and shall recover the damages by him sustained and the cost of the suit. . . .

SEC. 304. Section 313 of the Federal Corrupt Practices Act, 1925 (U. S. C., 1940 edition, title 2, sec. 251; Supp. V, title 50, App., sec. 1509), as amended, is amended to read as follows:

"SEC. 313. It is unlawful for any national bank, or any corporation organized by authority of any law of Congress, to make a contribution or expenditure in connection with any election to any political office, or in connection with any primary election or political convention or caucus held to select candidates for any political office, or for any corporation whatever, or any labor organization to make a contribution or expenditure in connection with any election at which Presidential and Vice Presidential electors or a Senator or Representative in or a Delegate or Resident Commissioner to Congress are to be voted for, or in connection with any primary election or political convention or caucus held to select candidates for any of the foregoing offices, or for any candidate, political committee, or other person to accept or receive any contribution prohibited by this section. . . .

SEC. 305. It shall be unlawful for any individual employed by the United States or any agency thereof including wholly owned Government corporations to participate in any strike. Any individual employed by the United States or by any such agency who strikes shall be discharged immediately from his employment, and shall forfeit his civil service status, if any, and shall not be eligible for reemployment for three years by the United States or any such agency. . . .

580. NATIONAL SECURITY ACT OF 1947
July 26, 1947
(Public Law 253, 80th Congress)

This act provided for the unification of the armed forces under the supervision of a new cabinet officer, the Secretary of Defense. It also provided for the creation of a National Security Council to co-ordinate the domestic, foreign, and military policies of the government relating to national security. The Security Council speedily became a kind of super-cabinet operating in the broad field of national security. See R. Cutler, "The Development of the National Security Council," 34 *Foreign Affairs,* 441; D. Anderson, "The President and National Security," *The Atlantic Monthly,* January, 1956.

AN ACT

To promote the national security by providing for a Secretary of Defense; for a National Military Establishment; for a Department of the Army, a Department of the Navy, and a Department of the Air Force; and for the coordination of the activities of the National Military Establishment with other departments and agencies of the Government concerned with the national security.

SEC. 101. (a) There is hereby established a council to be known as the National Security Council (hereinafter in this section referred to as the "Council").

The President of the United States shall preside over meetings of the Council: *Provided,* That in his absence he may designate a member of the Council to preside in his place.

The function of the Council shall be to advise the President with respect to the integration of domestic, foreign, and military policies relating to the national security so as to enable the military services and the other departments and agencies of the Government to cooperate more effectively in matters involving the national security.

The Council shall be composed of the President; the Secretary of State; the Secretary of Defense; the Secretary of the Army; the Secretary of the Navy; the Secretary of the Air Force; the Chairman of the National Security Resources Board; and such of the following named officers as the President may designate from time to time: The Secretaries of the executive departments, the Chairman of the Munitions Board, and the Chairman of the Research and Development Board; but no such additional member shall be designated until the advice and consent of the Senate has been given to his appointment to the office the holding of which authorizes his designation as a member of the Council.

(b) In addition to performing such other functions as the President may direct, for the purpose of more effectively coordinating the policies and functions of the departments and agencies of the Government relating to the national security, it shall, subject to the direction of the President, be the duty of the Council—

(1) to assess and appraise the objectives, commitments, and risks of the United States in relation to our actual and potential military power in the interest of national security, for the purpose of making recommendations to the President in connection therewith; and

(2) to consider policies on matters of common interest to the departments and agencies of the Government concerned with the national security, and to make recommendations to the President in connection therewith. . . .

(d) The Council shall, from time to time, make such recommendations, and such other reports to the President as it deems appropriate or as the President may require.

SEC. 102. (a) There is hereby established under the National Security Council a Central Intelligence Agency with a Director of Central Intelligence, who shall be the head thereof. . . .

(d) For the purpose of coordinating the intelligence activities of the several Government departments and agencies in the interest of national security, it shall be the duty of the Agency, under the direction of the National Security Council—. . . .

(3) to correlate and evaluate intelligence relating to the national security, and provide for the appropriate dissemination of such intelligence within the Government using where

appropriate existing agencies and facilities: . . . .

SEC. 103. (a) There is hereby established a National Security Resources Board (hereinafter in this section referred to as the "Board") to be composed of the Chairman of the Board and such heads or representatives of the various executive departments and independent agencies as may from time to time be designated by the President to be members of the Board. . . .

(c) It shall be the function of the Board to advise the President concerning the coordination of military, industrial, and civilian mobilization, including—

(1) policies concerning industrial and civilian mobilization in order to assure the most effective mobilization and maximum utilization of the Nation's manpower in the event of war;

(2) programs for the effective use in time of war of the Nation's natural and industrial resources for military and civilian needs, for the maintenance and stabilization of the civilian economy in time of war, and for the adjustment of such economy to war needs and conditions; . . . .

SEC. 201. (a) There is hereby established the National Military Establishment, and the Secretary of Defense shall be the head thereof.

(b) The National Military Establishment shall consist of the Department of the Army, the Department of the Navy, and the Department of the Air Force, together with all other agencies created under title II of this Act.

SEC. 202. (a) There shall be a Secretary of Defense, who shall be appointed from civilian life by the President, by and with the advice and consent of the Senate: *Provided,* That a person who has within ten years been on active duty as a commissioned officer in a Regular component of the armed services shall not be eligible for appointment as Secretary of Defense. The Secretary of Defense shall be the principal assistant to the President in all matters relating to the national security. Under the direction of the President and subject to the provisions of this Act he shall perform the following duties:

(1) Establish general policies and programs for the National Military Establishment and for all of the departments and agencies therein;

(2) Exercise general direction, authority, and control over such departments and agencies;

(3) Take appropriate steps to eliminate unnecessary duplication or overlapping in the fields of procurement, supply, transportation, storage, health, and research;

(4) Supervise and coordinate the preparation of the budget estimates of the departments and agencies comprising the National Military Establishment; formulate and determine the budget estimates for submittal to the Bureau of the Budget; and supervise the budget programs of such departments and agencies under the applicable appropriation Act: . . . .

SEC. 210. There shall be within the National Military Establishment a War Council composed of the Secretary of Defense, as Chairman, who shall have power of decision; the Secretary of the Army; the Secretary of the Navy; the Secretary of the Air Force; the Chief of Staff, United States Army; the Chief of Naval Operations; and the Chief of Staff, United States Air Force. The War Council shall advise the Secretary of Defense on matters of broad policy relating to the armed forces, and shall consider and report on such other matters as the Secretary of Defense may direct.

SEC. 211. (a) There is hereby established within the National Military Establishment the Joint Chiefs of Staff, which shall consist of the Chief of Staff, United States Army; the Chief of Naval Operations; the Chief of Staff, United States Air Force; and the Chief of Staff to the Commander in Chief, if there be one.

(b) Subject to the authority and direction of the President and the Secretary of Defense, it shall be the duty of the Joint Chiefs of Staff—

(1) to prepare strategic plans and to provide for the strategic direction of the military forces;

(2) to prepare joint logistic plans and to assign to the military services logistic responsibilities in accordance with such plans;

(3) to establish unified commands in strategic areas when such unified commands are in the interest of national security;

(4) to formulate policies for joint training of the military forces; . . . .

(c) The Joint Chiefs of Staff shall act as the principal military advisers to the President and the Secretary of Defense and shall perform such other duties as the President and the Secretary of Defense may direct or as may be prescribed by law. . . .

581. TRUMAN'S CIVIL RIGHTS MESSAGE
February 2, 1948

(80th Congress, 2d Session, *House Doc.* No. 516)

On December 5, 1946, President Truman appointed a Committee on Civil Rights, composed of leaders in church and education, and directed it to recommend "more adequate and effective means and procedures for the protection of the civil rights of the people of the United States." The following year the Committee issued a report, *To Secure These Rights,* calling for a comprehensive federal-state program to eliminate racial discrimination. President Truman then called on Congress to implement this program. Although this message produced little in the form of new legislation, it dramatized existing inequities. The proposals of the Truman administration were given some practical effect by the Supreme Court in 1954 in *Brown* v. *Board of Education,* Doc. No. 612. See B. H. Nelson, *The Fourteenth Amendment and The Negro Since 1920;* R. K. Carr, *Federal Protection of Civil Rights,* "Civil Rights in America," *Annals of the American Academy,* 1951. A bill incorporating some of Truman's proposals was finally enacted in 1957. See Doc. 626.

To the Congress of the United States:

In the state of the Union message on January 7, 1948, I spoke of five great goals toward which we should strive in our constant effort to strengthen our democracy and improve the welfare of our people. The first of these is to secure fully our essential human rights. I am now presenting to the Congress my recommendations for legislation to carry us forward toward that goal.

This Nation was founded by men and women who sought these shores that they might enjoy greater freedom and greater opportunity than they had known before. The founders of the United States proclaimed to the world the American belief that all men are created equal, and that governments are

instituted to secure the inalienable rights with which all men are endowed. In the Declaration of Independence and the Constitution of the United States they eloquently expressed the aspirations of all mankind for equality and freedom.

These ideals inspired the peoples of other lands, and their practical fulfillment made the United States the hope of the oppressed everywhere. Throughout our history men and women of all colors and creeds, of all races and religions, have come to this country to escape tyranny and discrimination. Millions strong, they have helped build this democratic Nation and have constantly reinforced our devotion to the great ideals of liberty and equality. With those who preceded them they have helped to fashion and strengthen our American faith—a faith that can be simply stated:

We believe that all men are created equal and that they have the right to equal justice under law.

We believe that all men have the right to freedom of thought and of expression and the right to worship as they please.

We believe that all men are entitled to equal opportunities for jobs, for homes, for good health, and for education.

We believe that all men should have a voice in their government, and that government should protect, not usurp, the rights of the people.

These are the basic civil rights which are the source and the support of our democracy.

Today the American people enjoy more freedom and opportunity than ever before. Never in our history has there been better reason to hope for the complete realization of the ideals of liberty and equality.

We shall not, however, finally achieve the ideals for which this Nation was founded so long as any American suffers discrimination as a result of his race, or religion, or color, or the land of origin of his forefathers.

Unfortunately there still are examples—flagrant examples—of discrimination which are utterly contrary to our ideals. Not all groups of our population are free from the fear of violence. Not all groups are free to live and work where they please or to improve their conditions of life by their own efforts. Not all groups enjoy the full privileges of citizenship and participation in the Government under which they live.

We cannot be satisfied until all our people have equal opportunities for jobs, for homes, for education, for health, and for political expression, and until all our people have equal protection under the law. . . .

The protection of civil rights is the duty of every government which derives its powers from the consent of the people. This is equally true of local, State, and National Governments. There is much that the States can and should do at this time to extend their protection of civil rights. Wherever the law-enforcement measures of State and local governments are inadequate to discharge this primary function of government, these measures should be strengthened and improved.

The Federal Government has a clear duty to see that constitutional guaranties of individual liberties and of equal protection under the laws are not denied or abridged anywhere in our Union. That duty is shared by all three branches of the Government, but it can be fulfilled only if the Congress enacts modern, comprehensive civil-rights laws, adequate to the needs of the day, and demonstrating our continuing faith in the free way of life.

I recommend, therefore, that the Congress enact legislation at this session directed toward the following specific objectives:

(1) Establishing a permanent Commission on Civil Rights, a Joint Congressional Committee on Civil Rights, and a Civil Rights Division in the Department of Justice.

(2) Strengthening existing civil-rights statutes.

(3) Providing Federal protection against lynching.

(4) Protecting more adequately the right to vote.

(5) Establishing a Fair Employment Practice Commission to prevent unfair discrimination in employment.

(6) Prohibiting discrimination in interstate transportation facilities.

(7) Providing home rule and suffrage in Presidential elections for the residents of the District of Columbia.

(8) Providing statehood for Hawaii and Alaska and a greater measure of self-government for our island possessions.

(9) Equalizing the opportunities for residents of the United States to become naturalized citizens.

(10) Settling the evacuation claims of Japanese-Americans. . . .

The legislation I have recommended for enactment by the Congress at the present session is a minimum program if the Federal Government is to fulfill its obligation of insuring the Constitutional guaranties of individual liberties and of equal protection under the law.

Under the authority of existing law the executive branch is taking every possible action to improve the enforcement of the civil-rights statutes and to eliminate discrimination in Federal employment, in providing Federal services and facilities, and in the armed forces.

I have already referred to the establishment of the Civil Rights Division of the Department of Justice. The Federal Bureau of Investigation will work closely with this new Division in the investigation of Federal civil-rights cases. Specialized training is being given to the Bureau's agents so that they may render more effective service in this difficult field of law enforcement.

It is the settled policy of the United States Government that there shall be no discrimination in Federal employment or in providing Federal services and facilities. Steady progress has been made toward this objective in recent years. I shall shortly issue an Executive order containing a comprehensive restatement of the Federal nondiscrimination policy, together with appropriate measures to ensure compliance.

During the recent war and in the years since its close we have made such progress toward equality of opportunity in our armed services without regard to race, color, religion, or national origin. I have instructed the Secretary of Defense to take steps to have the remaining instances of discrimination in the armed services eliminated as rapidly as possible. The personnel policies and practices of all the services in this regard will be made consistent.

I have instructed the Secretary of the Army to investigate the status of civil rights in the Panama Canal Zone with a view to eliminating such discrimination as may exist there. If legislation is necessary, I shall make appropriate recommendations to the Congress. . . .

The position of the United States in the world today makes it especially urgent that we adopt these measures to secure for all our people their essential rights.

The peoples of the world are faced with the choice of freedom or enslavement, a choice between a form of government which harnesses the state in the service of the individual and a form of government which chains the individual to the needs of the state.

We in the United States are working in company with other nations who share our desire for enduring world peace and who believe with us that, above all else, men must be free. We are striving to build a world family of nations—a world where men may live under governments of their own choosing and under laws of their own making.

As part of that endeavor, the Commission on Human Rights of the United Nations is now engaged in preparing an international bill of human rights by which the nations of the world may bind themselves by international covenant to give effect to basic human rights and fundamental freedoms. We have played a leading role in this undertaking designed to create a world order of law and justice fully protective of the rights and the dignity of the individual.

To be effective in these efforts, we must protect our civil rights so that by providing all our people with the maximum enjoyment of personal freedom and personal opportunity we shall be a stronger nation—stronger in our leadership, stronger in our moral position, stronger in the deeper satisfactions of a united citizenry.

We know that our democracy is not perfect. But we do know that it offers a fuller, freer, happier life to our people than any totalitarian nation has ever offered.

If we wish to inspire the peoples of the world whose freedom is in jeopardy, if we wish to restore hope to those who have already lost their civil liberties, if we wish to fulfill the promise that is ours, we must correct the remaining imperfections in our practice of democracy.

We know the way. We need only the will.

HARRY S TRUMAN.

582. THE VANDENBERG RESOLUTION
May 19, 1948
(*80th Congress, 2nd Session.* S. Res. 239)

During and after World War II Senator Vandenberg of Michigan emerged as one of the leaders of internationalism and one of the architects of the bipartisan foreign policy. This Resolution was commonly regarded as the forerunner of the Atlantic Pact.

Whereas peace with justice and the defense of human rights and fundamental freedoms require international cooperation through more effective use of the United Nations: Therefore be it

Resolved, That the Senate reaffirm the policy of the United States to achieve international peace and security through the United Nations so that armed force shall not be used except in the common interest, and that the President be advised of the sense of the Senate that this Government, by constitutional process, should particularly pursue the following objectives within the United Nations Charter:

(1) Voluntary agreement to remove the veto from all questions involving pacific settlements of international disputes and situations, and from the admission of new members.

(2) Progressive development of regional and other collective arrangements for individual and collective self-defense in accordance with the purposes, principles, and provisions of the Charter.

(3) Association of the United States, by Constitutional process, with such regional and other collective arrangements as are based on continuous and effective self-help and mutual aid, and as affect its national security.

(4) Contributing to the maintenance of peace by making clear its determination to exercise the right of individual or collective self-defense under article 51 should any armed attack occur affecting its national security.

(5) Maximum efforts to obtain agreements to provide the United Nations with armed forces as provided by the Charter, and to obtain agreement among member nations upon universal regulation and reduction of armaments under adequate and dependable guaranty against violation.

(6) If necessary, after adequate effort toward strengthening the United Nations, review of the Charter at an appropriate time by a General Conference called under article 109 or by the General Assembly.

583. McCOLLUM v. BOARD OF EDUCATION
333 U. S. 203
1948

Another aspect of the rising church-state controversy of the 'forties emerged from the widespread practice of devoting "released time" to religious instruction in the public schools. As of 1947 over two million pupils in some 2200 communities participated in released time programs. The Program of the Board of Education of Champaign County, Illinois, was challenged by Vashti McCollum on the ground that it violated the prohibitions of the First Amendment as embraced in the Fourteenth. The concurring opinion, by Justice Frankfurter, presents a full analysis of the historical background and many bibliographical references. See also J. M. O'Neill, *Religion and Education under the Constitution;* and, for a sharply critical review of the decision, E. S. Corwin, *"The Supreme Court as National School Board,"* 23 *Thought,* 665; A. W. Johnson and F. H. Yost, *Separation of Church and State;* R. F. Cushman, "Holy Bible and Public Schools," 40 *Cornell L. Q.,* 475.

Appeal from the Supreme Court of the State of Illinois.

Action for mandamus by the People of the State of Illinois, on the relation of Vashti McCollum, against the Board of Education of School District No. 71, Champaign County, Ill., and others to require the Board of Education to adopt and enforce rules and regulations prohibiting all instruction in and teaching of all religious education in all public schools in the district and in all public school houses and buildings in the district when occupied by public schools.

BLACK, J. This case relates to the power of a state to utilize its tax-supported public school system in aid of religious instruction insofar as that power may be restricted by the First and Fourteenth Amendments to the Federal Constitution.

The appellant, Vashti McCollum, began this action for mandamus against the Champaign Board of Education in the Circuit Court of Champaign County, Illinois. Her asserted interest was that of a resident and taxpayer of Champaign and of a parent whose child was then enrolled in the Champaign public schools. Illinois has a compulsory education law which, with exceptions, requires parents to send their children, aged seven to sixteen, to its tax-supported public schools where the children are to remain in attendance during the hours when the schools are regularly in session. Parents who violate this law commit a misdemeanor punishable by fine unless the children attend private or parochial schools which meet educational standards fixed by the State. District boards of education are given general supervisory powers over the use of the public school buildings within the school districts.

Appellant's petition for mandamus alleged that religious teachers, employed by private religious groups, were permitted to come weekly into the school buildings during the regular hours set apart for secular teaching, and then and there for a period of thirty minutes substitute their religious teaching for the secular education provided under the compulsory education law. The petitioner charged that this joint public-school religious-group program violated the First and Fourteenth Amendments to the United States Constitution. . . .

Although there are disputes between the parties as to various inferences that may or may not properly be drawn from the evidence concerning the religious program, the following facts are shown by the record without dispute. In 1940 interested members of the Jewish, Roman Catholic, and a few of the Protestant faiths formed a voluntary association called the Champaign Council on Religious Education. They obtained permission from the Board of Education to offer classes in religious instruction to public school pupils in grades four to nine inclusive. Classes were made up of pupils whose parents signed printed cards requesting that their children be permitted to attend; they were held weekly, thirty minutes for the lower grades, forty-five minutes for the higher. The council employed the religious teachers at no expense to the school authorities, but the instructors were subject to the approval and supervision of the superintendent of schools. The classes were taught in three separate religious groups by Protestant teachers, Catholic priests, and a Jewish rabbi, although for the past several years there have apparently been no classes instructed in the Jewish religion. Classes were conducted in the regular classrooms of the school building. Students who did not choose to take the religious instruction were not released from public school duties; they were required to leave their classrooms and go to some other place in the school building for pursuit of their secular studies. On the other hand, students who were released from secular study for the religious instructions were required to be present at the religious classes. Re-

ports of their presence or absence were to be made to their secular teachers.

The foregoing facts, without reference to others that appear in the record, show the use of tax-supported property for religious instruction and the close cooperation between the school authorities and the religious council in promoting religious education. The operation of the state's compulsory education system thus assists and is integrated with the program of religious instruction carried on by separate religious sects. Pupils compelled by law to go to school for secular education are released in part from their legal duty upon the condition that they attend the religious classes. This is beyond all question a utilization of the tax-established and tax-supported public school system to aid religious groups to spread their faith. And it falls squarely under the ban of the First Amendment (made applicable to the States by the Fourteenth) as we interpreted it in Everson v. Board of Education, 330 U.S. 1, 67 S.Ct. 504. There we said: "Neither a state nor the Federal Government can set up a church. Neither can pass laws which aid one religion, aid all religions, or prefer one religion over another. Neither can force nor influence a person to go to or to remain away from church against his will or force him to profess a belief or disbelief in any religion. No person can be punished for entertaining or professing religious beliefs or disbeliefs, for church attendance or nonattendance. No tax in any amount, large or small, can be levied to support any religious activities or institutions, whatever they may be called, or whatever form they may adopt to teach or practice religion. Neither a state nor the Federal Government can, openly or secretly, participate in the affairs of any religious organizations or groups, and vice versa. In the words of Jefferson, the clause against establishment of religion by law was intended to erect 'a wall of separation between Church and State.' " The majority in the Everson case, and the minority as shown by quotations from the dissenting views agreed that the First Amendment's language, properly interpreted, had erected a wall of separation between Church and State. They disagreed as to the facts shown by the record and as to the proper application of the

First Amendment's language to those facts.

Recognizing that the Illinois program is barred by the First and Fourteenth Amendments if we adhere to the views expressed both by the majority and the minority in the Everson case, counsel for the respondents challenge those views as dicta and urge that we reconsider and repudiate them. They argue that historically the First Amendment was intended to forbid only government preference of one religion over another, not an impartial governmental assistance of all religions. In addition they ask that we distinguish or overrule our holding in the Everson case that the Fourteenth Amendment made the "establishment of religion" clause of the First Amendment applicable as a prohibition against the States. After giving full consideration to the arguments presented we are unable to accept either of these contentions.

To hold that a state cannot consistently with the First and Fourteenth Amendments utilize its public school system to aid any or all religious faiths or sects in the dissemination of their doctrines and ideals does not, as counsel urge, manifest a governmental hostility to religious or religious teachings. A manifestation of such hostility would be at war with our national tradition as embodied in the First Amendment's guaranty of the free exercise of religion. For the First Amendment rests upon the premise that both religion and government can best work to achieve their lofty aims if each is left free from the other within its respective sphere. Or, as we said in the Everson case, the First Amendment has erected a wall between Church and State which must be kept high and impregnable.

Here not only are the state's tax-supported public school buildings used for the dissemination of religious doctrines. The State also affords sectarian groups an invaluable aid in that it helps to provide pupils for their religious classes through use of the state's compulsory public school machinery. This is not separation of Church and State.

The cause is reversed and remanded to the State Supreme Court for proceedings not inconsistent with this opinion.

584. SELECTIVE SERVICE ACT OF 1948
June 24, 1948
(Public Law 759, 80th Congress)

In 1916 and again in 1940, Congress made provision for drafting men during peacetime. Both of these acts were directed to a crisis in which war seemed imminent. In 1948, Congress acted to deal with a long-run situation of tension in the world. In this sense, the act of 1948 set a precedent. See President's Advisory Commission on Universal Training, *A Program for National Security;* W. Millis, *Arms and Men;* S. P. Huntington, *The Soldier and the State;* A. A. Ekirch, Jr., *The Civilian and the Military;* G. B. Turner, ed., *History of Military Affairs in Western Society,* chs. 14, 15.

AN ACT

To provide for the common defense by increasing the strength of the armed forces of the United States, including the reserve components thereof, and for other purposes.

SECTION 1.   (a) This Act may be cited as the "Selective Service Act of 1948."

(b) The Congress hereby declares that an adequate armed strength must be achieved and maintained to insure the security of this Nation.

(c) The Congress further declares that in a free society the obligations and privileges of serving in the armed forces and the reserve components thereof should be shared generally, in accordance with a system of selection which is fair and just, and which is consistent with the maintenance of an effective national economy. . . .

SEC. 2.   Notwithstanding any other provision of law, the authorized active duty personnel strength of the armed forces . . . is hereby established as follows: (1) Of the Army of the United States, 837,000 plus 110,000 one-year enlistees; (2) of the Navy, including the Marine Corps, the present authorized statutory strength of 666,882, plus 36,000 one-year enlistees; and (3) of the

Air Force of the United States, 502,000 plus 15,000 one-year enlistees. The strength herein established for each of the armed forces shall mean the daily average number of persons on active duty therein during the fiscal year.

SEC. 3. Except as otherwise provided in this title, it shall be the duty of every male citizen of the United States, and every other male person residing in the United States, who, on the day or days fixed for the first or any subsequent registration, is between the ages of eighteen and twenty-six, to present himself for and submit to registration at such time or times and place or places, and in such manner, as shall be determined by proclamation of the President and by rules and regulations prescribed hereunder.

SEC. 4. (a) Except as otherwise provided in this title, every male citizen of the United States, and every other male person residing in the United States, who is between the ages of nineteen and twenty-six, at the time fixed for his registration, or who attains the age of nineteen after having been required to register pursuant to section 3 of this title, shall be liable for training and service in the armed forces of the United States. . . . The President is authorized from time to time, whether or not a state of war exists, to select and induct into the armed forces of the United States for training and service in the manner provided in this title such number of persons as may be required to provide and maintain the personnel strengths (other than one-year enlistee personnel strengths) of the respective armed forces authorized by section 2 of this title. . . .

SEC. 5. (a) The selection of persons for training and service under section 4 shall be made in an impartial manner, under such rules and regulations as the President may prescribe, from the persons who are liable for such training and service and who at the time of selection are registered and classified, but not deferred or exempted. . . .

585. UNITED STATES NOTE ON BERLIN BLOCKADE AND AIRLIFT
July 6, 1948
(*Department of State Bulletin*, Vol. XIX, p. 86)

At the Potsdam Conference a four-power command was set up to govern Berlin. Although Berlin was surrounded by Soviet occupied territory, the city itself was divided into four zones occupied by American, British, French, and Russian troops. On June 20 and June 22, 1948, the Soviet occupation officials declared that they considered Berlin an integral part of the Soviet zone of Germany and would henceforth govern the city on a unilateral basis. On June 24, they halted all land and water traffic between the Western zones of Germany and Berlin. The United States and Britain responded with an air-lift of food, coal, etc., to the beleagured citizens of the Western zones. At its height, a plane was landing on the Berlin airstrips every minute, and the Allies were delivering some 4500 tons of supplies daily. On May 12, 1949, the Soviets abandoned their blockade and normal traffic was restored between the Western zones of Germany and Berlin. See H. Truman, *Memoirs, Vol. II*; L. Clay, *Decision in Germany*.

The United States Government wishes to call to the attention of the Soviet Government the extremely serious international situation which has been brought about by the actions of the Soviet Government in imposing restrictive measures on transport which amount now to a blockade against the sectors in Berlin occupied by the United States, United Kingdom and France. The United States Government regards these measures of blockade as a clear violation of existing agreements concerning the administration of Berlin by the four occupying powers.

The rights of the United States as a joint occupying power in Berlin derive from the total defeat and unconditional surrender of Germany. The international agreements undertaken in connection therewith by the Governments of the United States, United Kingdom, France and the Soviet Union defined the zones in Germany and the sectors in Berlin which are occupied by these powers. They established the quadripartite control of Berlin on a basis of friendly cooperation which the Government of the United States earnestly desires to continue to pursue.

These agreements implied the right of free access to Berlin. This right has long been confirmed by usage. It was directly specified in a message sent by President Truman to Premier Stalin on June 14, 1945, which agreed to the withdrawal of United States forces to the zonal boundaries provided satisfactory arrangements could be entered into between the military commanders, which would give access by rail, road and air to United States forces in Berlin. Premier Stalin replied on June 16 suggesting a change in date but no other alteration in the plan proposed by the President. Premier Stalin then gave assurances that all necessary measures would be taken in accordance with the plan. Correspondence in a similar sense took place between Premier Stalin and Mr. Churchill. In accordance with this understanding, the United States, whose armies had penetrated deep into Saxony and Thuringia, parts of the Soviet zone, withdrew its forces to its own area of occupation in Germany and took up its position in its own sector in Berlin. Thereupon the agreements in regard to the occupation of Germany and Berlin went into effect. The United States would not have so withdrawn its troops from a large area now occupied by the Soviet Union had there been any doubt whatsoever about the observance of its agreed right of free access to its sector of Berlin. The right of the United States to its position in Berlin thus stems from precisely the same source as the right of the Soviet Union. It is impossible to assert the latter and deny the former.

It clearly results from these undertakings that Berlin is not a part of the Soviet zone, but is an international zone of occupation. Commitments entered into in good faith by the zone commanders and subsequently confirmed by the Allied Control Authority, as well as practices sanctioned by usage, guarantee the United States together with other powers, free access to Berlin for the purpose of fulfilling its responsibilities as an occupying power. The facts are plain. Their meaning is clear. Any other interpretation would offend all the rules of comity and reason.

In order that there should be no misunderstanding whatsoever on this point, the United States Government categorically asserts that it is in occupation of its sector in Berlin with free access thereto as a matter of established right deriving from the defeat and surrender of Germany and confirmed by formal agreements among the principal Allies. It further declares that it will not be induced by threats, pressures or other actions to abandon these rights. It is hoped that the Soviet Government entertains no doubts whatsoever on this point. . . .

The responsibility which this Government bears for the physical well-being and the safety of the German population in its sector of Berlin is outstandingly humanitarian in character. This population includes hundreds of thousands of women and children, whose health and safety are dependent on the continued use of adequate facilities for moving food, medical supplies and other items indispensable to the maintenance of human life in the western sectors of Berlin. The most elemental of these human rights which both our Governments are solemnly pledged to protect are thus placed in jeopardy by these restrictions. It is intolerable that any one of the occupying authorities should attempt to impose a blockade upon the people of Berlin.

The United States Government is therefore obliged to insist that in accordance with existing agreements the arrangements for the movement of freight and passenger traffic between the western zones and Berlin be fully restored. There can be no question of delay in the restoration of these essential services, since the needs of the civilian population in the Berlin area are imperative. . . .

586. THE NORTH ATLANTIC TREATY
Signed, 4 April 1949

(*81st Congress, 1st Session.* Executive Document L)

The North Atlantic Pact, as it was popularly known, was designed to provide collective security to the democratic nations of the Atlantic Community against possible overt action by Russia or her satellite states. It was patterned closely on the Treaty of Rio de Janeiro of 1947. Although it marked a sharp departure from traditional American foreign policy, it was clearly consistent with the Truman Doctrine, the Marshall Plan, and the Vandenberg Resolution of 19 May 1948. Other signatory countries were Belgium, Canada, Denmark, France, Iceland, Italy, Luxembourg, Netherlands, Norway, Portugal, and the United Kingdom.

The Parties to this Treaty reaffirm their faith in the purposes and principles of the Charter of the United Nations and their desire to live in peace with all peoples and all governments.

They are determined to safeguard the freedom, common heritage and civilization of their peoples, founded on the principles of democracy, individual liberty and the rule of law.

They seek to promote stability and well-being in the North Atlantic area.

They are resolved to unite their efforts for collective defense and for the preservation of peace and security.

They therefore agree to this North Atlantic Treaty:

ART. 1. The Parties undertake, as set forth in the Charter of the United Nations, to settle any international disputes in which they may be involved by peaceful means in such a manner that international peace and security, and justice, are not endangered, and to refrain in their international relations from the threat or use of force in any manner inconsistent with the purposes of the United Nations.

ART. 2. The Parties will contribute toward the further development of peaceful and friendly international relations by strengthening their free institutions, by bringing about a better understanding of the principles upon which these institutions are founded, and by promoting conditions of stability and well-being. They will seek to eliminate conflict in their international economic policies and will encourage economic collaboration between any or all of them.

ART. 3. In order more effectively to achieve the objectives of this Treaty, the Parties, separately and jointly, by means of continuous and effective self-help and mutual aid, will maintain and develop their individual and collective capacity to resist armed attack.

ART. 4. The Parties will consult together whenever, in the opinion of any of them, the territorial integrity, political independence or security of any of the Parties is threatened.

ART. 5. The Parties agree that an armed attack against one or more of them in Europe or North America shall be considered an attack against them all; and consequently they agree that, if such an armed attack occurs, each of them, in exercise of the right of individual or collective self-defense recognized by Article 51 of the Charter of the United Nations, will assist the Party or Parties so attacked by taking forthwith, individually and in concert with the other Parties, such action as it deems necessary, including the use of armed force, to restore and maintain the security of the North Atlantic area.

Any such armed attack and all measures taken as a result thereof shall immediately be reported to the Security Council. Such measures shall be terminated when the Security Council has taken the measures necessary to restore and maintain international peace and security.

ART. 6. For the purpose of Article 5 an armed attack on one or more of the Parties is deemed to include an armed attack on the territory of any of the Parties in Europe or North America, on the Algerian departments of France, on the occupation forces of any Party in Europe, on the islands under the jurisdiction of any Party in the North Atlantic area north of the Tropic of Cancer or on the vessels or aircraft in this area of any of the Parties.

ART. 7. This Treaty does not affect, and shall not be interpreted as affecting, in any way the rights and obligations under the Charter of the Parties which are members of the United Nations, or the primary responsibility of the Security Council for the maintenance of international peace and security.

ART. 8. Each Party declares that none of the international engagements now in force between it and any other of the Parties or any third state is in conflict with the provisions of this Treaty, and undertakes not to enter into any international engagement in conflict with this Treaty.

ART. 9. The Parties hereby establish a council, on which each of them shall be represented, to consider matters concerning the implementation of this Treaty. The council shall be so organized as to be able to meet promptly at any time. The council shall set up such subsidiary bodies as may be necessary; in particular it shall establish immediately a defense committee which shall recommend measures for the implementation of Articles 3 and 5.

ART. 10. The Parties may, by unanimous agreement, invite any other European state in a position to further the principles of this Treaty and to contribute to the security of the North Atlantic area to accede to this Treaty. Any state so invited may become a party to the Treaty by depositing its instrument of accession with the Government of the United States of America. The Government of the United States of America will inform each of the Parties of the deposit of each such instrument of accession.

ART. 11. . . . The Treaty shall enter into force between the states which have ratified it as soon as the ratifications of the majority of the signatories, including the ratifications of Belgium, Canada, France, Luxembourg, the Netherlands, the United Kingdom and the United States, have been deposited and shall come into effect with respect to other states on the date of the deposit of their ratifications.

ART. 12. After the Treaty has been in force for ten years, or at any time thereafter, the Parties shall, if any of them so requests, consult together for the purpose of reviewing the Treaty, having regard for the factors then affecting peace and security in the North Atlantic area, including the development of universal as well as regional arrangements under the Charter of the United Nations for the maintenance of international peace and security.

ART. 13. After the Treaty has been in force for twenty years, any Party may cease to be a party one year after its notice of denunciation has been given to the Government of the United States of America, which will inform the Governments of the other Parties of the deposit of each notice of denunciation.

587. RECOGNITION OF ISRAEL
1948–49

(White House Press Releases, May 14, 1948, and January 31, 1949)

In 1947, the General Assembly of the United Nations adopted a plan for the partition of Palestine into independent Jewish and Arab states. On May 14, 1948, the Jewish community of Palestine proclaimed the creation of the independent state of Israel. On the same day, President Truman announced that the United States accorded *de facto* recognition to the government of Israel. *De jure* recognition was granted on January 31, 1949. The quick response of the United States to the Israeli plea for recognition established close relations between the two governments. These relations were further cemented when the United States supported Israel's successful application for admission to the United Nations in 1949. See J. C. Hurewitz, *The Struggle for Palestine;* J. C. Hurewitz, *Diplomacy in the Near and Middle East;* Abba Eban, *The Voice of Israel;* E. Rackman, *Israel's Emerging Constitution, 1948–1951.*

1. STATEMENT BY PRESIDENT TRUMAN, May 14, 1949

This Government has been informed that a Jewish state has been proclaimed in Palestine, and recognition has been requested by the provisional government thereof.

The United States recognizes the provisional government as the *de facto* authority of the new State of Israel.

2. STATEMENT BY PRESIDENT TRUMAN, January 31, 1949

On October 24, 1948, the President stated that when a permanent government was elected in Israel, it would promptly be given *de jure* recognition. Elections for such a government were held on January 25th. The votes have now been counted, and this Government has been officially informed of the results. The United States Government is therefore pleased to extend *de jure* recognition to the Government of Israel as of this date.

588. TRUMAN'S POINT FOUR PROGRAM
June 24, 1949

(81st Congress, 1st Session, *House Doc.* No. 240)

Following a proposal made in his inaugural address, President Truman sent a special message to Congress urging a program of technical assistance to underdeveloped areas. The President recommended a modest initial appropriation of $45 million to be expanded as future needs required. Congress enacted the President's proposal on June 5, 1950, and thus took another important step in the assumption of international responsibilities. See W. A. Brown, *American Foreign Assistance;* R. T. Mack, *Raising the World's Standard of Living;* M. Curti and K. Beir, *Prelude to Point Four;* J. B. Bingham, *Shirt-Sleeve Diplomacy.*

To the Congress of the United States:

In order to enable the United States, in cooperation with other countries, to assist the peoples of economically underdeveloped areas to raise their standards of living, I recommend the enactment of legislation to authorize an expanded program of technical assistance for such areas, and an experimental program for encouraging the outflow of private investment beneficial to their economic development. These measures are the essential first steps in an undertaking which will call upon private enterprise and voluntary organizations in the United States, as well as the government, to take part in a constantly growing effort to improve economic conditions in the less developed regions of the world.

The grinding poverty and the lack of economic opportunity for many millions of people in the economically underdeveloped parts of Africa, the Near and Far East, and certain regions of Central and South America, constitute one of the greatest challenges of the world today. In spite of their age-old economic and social handicaps, the peoples in these areas have, in recent decades, been stirred and awakened. The spread of industrial civilization, the growing understanding of modern concepts of government, and the impact of two World Wars have changed their lives and their outlook. They are eager to play a greater part in the community of nations.

All these areas have a common problem. They must create a firm economic base for the democratic aspirations of their citizens. Without such an economic base, they will be unable to meet the expectations which the modern world has aroused in their peoples. If they are frustrated and disappointed, they may turn to false doctrines which hold that the way of progress lies through tyranny. . . .

For these various reasons, assistance in the development of the economically underdeveloped areas has become one of the major elements of our foreign policy. In my inaugural address, I outlined a program to help the peoples of these areas to attain greater production as a way to prosperity and peace.

The major effort in such a program must be local in character; it must be made by the people of the underdeveloped areas themselves. It is essential, however, to the success of their effort that there be help from abroad. In such cases, the peoples of these areas will be unable to begin their part of this great enterprise without initial aid from other countries.

The aid that is needed falls roughly into two categories. The first is the technical, scientific, and managerial knowledge necessary to economic development. This category includes not only medical and educational knowledge, and assistance and advice in such basic fields as sanitation, communications, road building, and governmental services, but also, and perhaps most important, assistance in the survey of resources and in planning for long-range economic development.

The second category is production goods —machinery and equipment—and financial assistance in the creation of productive enterprises. The underdeveloped areas need capital for port and harbor development, roads and communications, irrigation and drainage projects, as well as for public utilities and the whole range of extractive, processing, and manufacturing industries. Much of the capital required can be provided by these areas themselves, in spite of their low standards of living. But much must come from abroad.

The two categories of aid are closely related. Technical assistance is necessary to lay the ground-work for productive investment. Investment, in turn, brings with it technical assistance. In general, however, technical surveys of resources and of the possibilities of economic development must precede substantial capital investment. Furthermore, in many of the areas concerned, technical assistance in improving sanitation, communications, or education is required to

create conditions in which capital investment can be fruitful. . . .

It has already been shown that experts in these fields can bring about tremendous improvements. For example, the health of the people of many foreign communities has been greatly improved by the work of United States sanitary engineers in setting up modern water supply systems. The food supply of many areas has been increased as the result of the advice of United States agricultural experts in the control of animal diseases and the improvement of crops. These are only examples of the wide range of benefits resulting from the careful application of modern techniques to local problems. The benefits which a comprehensive program of expert assistance will make possible can only be revealed by studies and surveys undertaken as a part of the program itself.

To inaugurate the program, I recommend a first year appropriation of not to exceed 45 million dollars. This includes 10 million dollars already requested in the 1950 Budget for activities of this character. The sum recommended will cover both our participation in the programs of the international agencies and the assistance to be provided directly by the United States.

In every case, whether the operation is conducted through the United Nations, the other international agencies, or directly by the United States, the country receiving the benefit of the aid will be required to bear a substantial portion of the expense.

589. TRUMAN ANNOUNCES HYDROGEN BOMB PROGRAM
January 31, 1950
(*Department of State Bulletin*, Vol. XXII, p. 229)

The first Russian atomic explosion of 1949 intensified the race to develop new and more efficient weapons of destruction. On January 31, 1950, President Truman announced the inauguration of an all-out effort to develop a hydrogen bomb substantially more powerful than existing atomic weapons. This program achieved its initial objective in November, 1952, when the first hydrogen bomb was detonated. See W. L. Laurence, *The Hell Bomb;* H. D. Smyth, *Atomic Energy for Military Purposes;* A. H. Compton, *Atomic Quest;* J. W. Camp-

bell, *The Atomic Story;* G. Dean, *Report on the Atom.*

It is part of my responsibility as Commander-in-Chief of the armed forces to see to it that our country is able to defend itself against any possible aggressor. Accordingly, I have directed the Atomic Energy Commission to continue its work on all forms of atomic weapons, including the so-called hydrogen or super-bomb. Like all other work in the field of atomic weapons, it is being and will be carried forward on a basis consistent with the over-all objectives of our program for peace and security.

This we shall continue to do until a satisfactory plan for international control of atomic energy is achieved. We shall also continue to examine all those factors that affect our program for peace and this country's security.

The activities necessary to carry out our program of technical aid will be diverse in character and will have to be performed by a number of different government agencies and private instrumentalities. It will be necessary to utilize not only the resources of international agencies and the United States Government, but also the facilities and the experience of the private business and non-profit organizations that have long been active in this work. . . .

In the economically underdeveloped areas of the world today there are new creative energies. We look forward to the time when these countries will be stronger and more independent than they are now, and yet more closely bound to us and to other nations by ties of friendship and commerce, and by kindred ideals. On the other hand, unless we aid the newly awakened spirit in these peoples to find the course of fruitful development, they may fall under the control of those whose philosophy is hostile to human freedom, thereby prolonging the unsettled state of the world and postponing the achievement of permanent peace.

Before the peoples of these areas we hold out the promise of a better future through the democratic way of life. It is vital that we move quickly to bring the meaning of that promise home to them in their daily lives.

HARRY S TRUMAN.

590. TRUMAN'S STATEMENT ON THE KOREAN WAR
June 27, 1950
(*Department of State Press Release*)

At the Cairo and Potsdam conferences, the Allied Powers promised the Korean people independence and self-government. After the defeat of Japan, the United States established a military government in Korea south of the 38th parallel and the U.S.S.R. established a similar government north of the parallel. A joint American-Soviet commission to work out the details of Korean unification failed to agree. Intervention by the United Nations was of no avail. Finally in 1948, the U.S. and the U.N. sponsored elections in South Korea, and shortly thereafter a government of the Republic of Korea was established to rule South Korea. In 1949, the United States granted *de jure* recognition and withdrew its troops. The Soviets responded by creating a North Korean government. On June 25, 1950, the North Koreans launched a full-scale attack on the South. Two days later the U. N. Security Council called on all members of the U. N. to assist South Korea to repel the attack and restore peace. President Truman then issued the following statement. See H. Truman, *Memoirs, Vol. II;* M. Clark, *From the Danube to the Yalu;* L. M. Goodrich, *Korea: A Study of U.S. Policy in the United Nations;* R. T. Oliver, *Why War Came in Ko-*

rea; Council on Foreign Relations, *The U. S. in World Affairs, 1950.*

In Korea the Government forces, which were armed to prevent border raids and to preserve internal security, were attacked by invading forces from North Korea. The Security Council of the United Nations called upon the invading troops to cease hostilities and to withdraw to the 38th parallel. This they have not done, but on the contrary have pressed the attack. The Security Council called upon all members of the United Nations to render every assistance to the United Nations in the execution of this resolution. In these circumstances I have ordered United States air and sea forces to give the Korean Government troops cover and support.

The attack upon Korea makes it plain beyond all doubt that Communism has passed beyond the use of subversion to conquer independent nations and will now use armed invasion and war. It has defied the orders of the Security Council of the United Nations issued to preserve international peace and security. In these circumstances the occupation of Formosa by Communist forces would be a direct threat to the security of the Pacific area and to the United States forces performing their lawful and necessary functions in that area. Accordingly I have ordered the Seventh Fleet to prevent any attack on Formosa. As a corollary of this action I am calling upon the Chinese Government on Formosa to cease all air and sea operations against the mainland. The Seventh Fleet will see that this is done. The determination of the future status of Formosa must await the restoration of security in the Pacific, a peace settlement with Japan, or consideration by the United Nations.

I have also directed that United States Forces in the Philippines be strengthened and that military assistance to the Philippine Government be accelerated.

I have similarly directed acceleration in the furnishing of military assistance to the forces of France and the Associated States in Indo-China and the dispatch of a military mission to provide close working relations with those forces.

I know that all members of the United Nations will consider carefully the consequences of this latest aggression in Korea in defiance of the Charter of the United Nations. A return to the rule of force in international affairs would have far reaching effects. The United States will continue to uphold the rule of law.

I have instructed Ambassador Austin, as the representative of the United States to the Security Council, to report these steps to the Council.

591. McCARRAN INTERNAL SECURITY ACT
September 23, 1950

(Public Law 831, 81st Congress)

The growth of Communist power in the postwar world aroused deep fears among many Americans who believed that Communism menaced America not only from without but from within. In 1947, President Truman inaugurated a loyalty program designed to keep the federal government free from subversive influence. See Doc. No. 574. In 1950, Congress went beyond the Truman program and acted to limit the operation of "subversive" groups in all areas of American life. Ignoring President Truman's warning that the act was unconstitutional, Congress overrode his veto by a voice-vote. See W. Gellhorn, *Individual Freedom and Governmental Restraints;* M. Ernst and D. L. Loth, *Report on the American Communist;* F. Biddle, *The Fear of Freedom;* C. Wilcox, ed., *Civil Liberties Under Attack;* H. D. Lasswell, *National Security and Individual Freedom;* C. McWilliams, *Witch Hunt;* S. A. Stouffer, *Communism, Conformity, and Civil Liberties;* H. Truman, *Memoirs, Vol. II.*

AN ACT

To protect the United States against certain un-American and subversive activities by requiring registration of Communist organizations, and for other purposes.

SEC. 2. As a result of evidence adduced before various committees of the Senate and House of Representatives, the Congress hereby finds that—

(1) There exists a world Communist movement which, in its origins, its development, and its present practice, is a world-wide revolutionary movement whose purpose it is, by treachery, deceit, infiltration into other groups (governmental and otherwise), espionage, sabotage, terrorism, and any other means deemed necessary, to establish a Communist totalitarian dictatorship in the countries throughout the world through the medium of a world-wide Communist organization. . . .

(4) The direction and control of the world Communist movement is vested in and exercised by the Communist dictatorship of a foreign country.

(5) The Communist movement in the United States is an organization numbering thousands of adherents,

rigidly and ruthlessly disciplined. Awaiting and seeking to advance a moment when the United States may be so far extended by foreign engagements, so far divided in counsel, or so far in industrial or financial straits, that overthrow of the Government of the United States by force and violence may seem possible of achievement, it seeks converts far and wide by an extensive system of schooling and indoctrination. Such preparations by Communist organizations in other countries have aided in supplanting existing governments. The Communist organization in the United States, pursuing its stated objectives, the recent successes of Communist methods in other countries, and the nature and control of the world Communist movement itself, present a clear and present danger to the security of the United States and to the existence of free American institutions, and make it necessary that Congress, in order to provide for the common defense, to preserve the sovereignty of the United States as an independent nation, and to guarantee to each State a republican form of government, enact appropriate legislation recognizing the existence of such world-wide conspiracy and designed to prevent it from accomplishing its purpose in the United States. . . .

SEC. 4. (a) It shall be unlawful for any person knowingly to combine, conspire, or agree with any other person to perform any act which would substantially contribute to the establishment within the United States of a totalitarian dictatorship, as defined in paragraph (15) of section 3 of this title, the direction and control of which is to be vested in, or exercised by or under the domination or control of, any foreign government, foreign organization, or foreign individual: *Provided, however,* That this subsection shall not apply to the proposal of a constitutional amendment. . . .

(f) Neither the holding of office nor membership in any Communist organization by any person shall constitute per se a violation of subsection (a) or subsection (c) of this section or of any other criminal statute. The fact of the registration of any person under section 7 or section 8 of this title as an officer or member of any Communist organization shall not be received in evidence against such person in any prosecution for any alleged violation of subsection (a) or subsection (c) of this section or for any alleged violation of any other criminal statute. . . .

SEC. 7. (a) Each Communist-action organization (including any organization required, by a final order of the Board, to register as a Communist-action organization) shall, within the time specified in subsection (c) of this section, register with the Attorney General, or on a form prescribed by him by regulations, as a Communist-action organization.

(b) Each Communist-front organization . . . shall . . . register with the Attorney General, on a form prescribed by him by regulations, as a Communist-front organization. . . .

(d) Upon the registration of each Communist organization under the provisions of this title, the Attorney General shall publish in the Federal Register the fact that such organization has registered as a Communist-action organization, or as a Communist-front organization, as the case may be, and the publication thereof shall constitute notice to all members of such organization that such organization has so registered. . . .

SEC. 12. (a) There is hereby established a board, to be known as the Subversive Activities Control Board, which shall be composed of five members, who shall be appointed by the President, by and with the advice and consent of the Senate. Not more than three members of the Board shall be members of the same political party. Two of the original members shall be appointed for a term of one year, two for a term of two years, and one for a term of three years, but their successors shall be appointed for terms of three years each, except that any individual chosen to fill a vacancy shall be appointed only for the unexpired term of the member whom he shall succeed. The President shall designate one member to serve as Chairman of the Board. Any member of the Board may be removed by the President, upon notice and hearing, for neglect of duty or malfeasance in office, but for no other cause. . . .

(e) It shall be the duty of the Board—

(1) upon application made by the Attorney General under section 13 (a) of this title, or by any organization under section 13 (b) of this title, to determine whether any organization is a "Communist-action organization" within the meaning of paragraph (3) of section 3 of this title, or a "Communist-front organization" within the meaning of paragraph (4) of section 3 of this title; and

(2) upon application made by the Attorney General under section 13 (a) of this title, or by any individual under section 13 (b) of this title, to determine whether any individual is a member of any Communist-action organization registered, or by final order of the Board required to be registered, under section 7 (a) of this title. . . .

SEC. 22. The Act of October 16, 1918 . . . is hereby amended to read as follows: "That any alien who is a member of any one of the following classes shall be excluded from admission into the United States:

"(1) Aliens who seek to enter the United States whether solely, principally, or incidentally, to engage in activities which would be prejudicial to the public interest, or would endanger the welfare or safety of the United States;

"(2) Aliens who, at any time, shall be or shall have been members of any of the following classes:

"(A) Aliens who are anarchists;

"(B) Aliens who advocate or teach, or who are members of or affiliated with any organization that advocates or teaches, opposition to all organized government;

"(C) Aliens who are members of or affiliated with (i) the Communist Party of the United States; (ii) any other totalitarian party of the United States; (iii) the Communist Political Association; (iv) the Communist or other totalitarian party of any State of the United States, of any foreign state, or of any political or geographical subdivision of any foreign state; (v) any section, subsidiary, branch, affiliate, or subdivision of any such association or party; or (vi) the direct predecessors or successors of any such association or party, regardless of what name such group or organization may have used, may now bear, or may hereafter adopt;

"(D) Aliens not within any of the other provisions of this paragraph (2) who advocate the economic, international, and governmental doctrines of world communism or the economic and governmental doctrines of any other form of totalitarianism, or who are members of or affiliated with any organization that advocates the economic, international, and governmental doctrines of world communism, or the economic and governmental doctrines of any other form of totalitarianism, either through its own utterances or through any written or printed publications issued or published by or with the permission or consent of or under the authority of such organization or paid for by the funds of such organization. . . .

"(F) Aliens who advocate or teach or who are members of or affiliated with any organization that advocates or teaches (i) the overthrow by force or violence or other unconstitutional means of the Government of the United States or of all forms of law; or (ii) the duty, necessity, or propriety of the unlawful assaulting or killing of any officer or officers (either of specific individuals or of officers generally) of the Government of the United States or of any other organized government, because of his or their official character; or (iii) the unlawful damage, injury, or destruction of property; or (iv) sabotage;

"(G) Aliens who write or publish, or cause to be written or published, or who knowingly circulate, distribute, print, or display, or knowingly cause to be circulated, distributed, printed, published, or displayed, or who knowingly have in their possession for the purpose of circulation, publication, or display, any written or printed matter, advocating or teaching opposition to all organized government, or advocating (i) the overthrow by force or violence or other unconstitutional means of the Government of the United States or of all forms of law; or (ii) the duty, necessity, or propriety of the unlawful assaulting or killing of any officer or officers (either of specific individuals or of officers generally) of the Government of the United States or of any other organized government; or (iii) the unlawful damage, injury, or destruction of property; or (iv) sabotage; or (v) the economic, international, and governmental doctrines of world communism or the economic and governmental doctrines of any other form of totalitarianism. . . .

SEC. 102. (a) In the event of any one of the following:

(1) Invasion of the territory of the United States or its possessions,

(2) Declaration of war by Congress, or

(3) Insurrection within the United States in aid of a foreign enemy,

and if, upon the occurrence of one or more of the above, the President shall find that the proclamation of an emergency pursuant to this section is essential to the preservation, protection and defense of the Constitution, and to the common defense and safety of the territory and people of the United States, the President is authorized to make public proclamation of the existence of an "Internal Security Emergency."

(b) A state of "Internal Security Emergency" (hereinafter referred to as the "emergency") so declared shall continue in existence until terminated by proclamation of the President or by concurrent resolution of the Congress. . . .

SEC. 103. (a) Whenever there shall be in existence such an emergency, the President, acting through the Attorney General, is hereby authorized to apprehend and by order detain, pursuant to the provisions of this title, each person as to whom there is reasonable ground to believe that such person probably will engage in, or probably will conspire with others to engage in, acts of espionage or of sabotage. . . .

592. TRUMAN'S VETO OF THE McCARRAN ACT
September 22, 1950

(81st Congress, 2nd Session, *House Doc.* No. 708)

To the House of Representatives:

I return herewith, without my approval, H. R. 9490, the proposed Internal Security Act of 1950.

I am taking this action only after the most serious study and reflection and after consultation with the security and intelligence agencies of the Government. The Department of Justice, the Department of Defense, the Central Intelligence Agency, and the Department of State have all advised me that the bill would seriously damage the security and the intelligence operations for which they are responsible. They have strongly expressed the hope that the bill would not become law.

This is an omnibus bill containing many different legislative proposals with only one

thing in common: they are all represented to be "anti-Communist." But when the many complicated pieces of the bill are analyzed in detail, a startling result appears.

H. R. 9490 would not hurt the Communists. Instead, it would help them.

It has been claimed over and over again that this is an "anti-Communist" bill—a "Communist control" bill. But in actual operation the bill would have results exactly the opposite of those intended.

It would actually weaken our existing internal security measures and would seriously hamper the Federal Bureau of Investigation and our other security agencies. . . .

I therefore most earnestly request the Congress to reconsider its action. I am confident that on more careful analysis most

Members of Congress will recognize that this bill is contrary to the best interests of our country at this critical time.

H. R. 9490 is made up of a number of different parts. In summary, their purposes and probable effects may be described as follows: . . . (Analysis of secs. 1-21, and 23)

Sections 22 and 25 of this bill would make sweeping changes in our laws governing the admission of aliens to the United States and their naturalization as citizens.

The ostensible purpose of these provisions is to prevent persons who would be dangerous to our national security from entering the country or becoming citizens. In fact, present law already achieves that objective.

What these provisions would actually do is to prevent us from admitting to our country, or to citizenship, many people who could make real contributions to our national strength. The bill would deprive our Government and our intelligence agencies of the valuable services of aliens in security operations. It would require us to exclude and to deport the citizens of some friendly non-Communist countries. Furthermore, it would actually make it easier for subversive aliens to become United States citizens. Only the Communist movement would gain from such actions.

Section 24 and sections 26 through 30 of this bill make a number of minor changes in the naturalization laws. None of them is of great significance—nor are they particularly relevant to the problem of internal security. These provisions, for the most part, have received little or no attention in the legislative process. I believe that several of them would not be approved by the Congress if they were considered on their merits, rather than as parts of an omnibus bill.

Section 31 of this bill makes it a crime to attempt to influence a judge or jury by public demonstration, such as picketing. While the courts already have considerable power to punish such actions under existing law, I have no objection to this section.

Sections 100 through 117 of this bill (title II) are intended to give the Government power, in the event of invasion, war, or insurrection in the United States in aid of a foreign enemy, to seize and hold persons who could be expected to attempt acts of espionage or sabotage, even though they had as yet committed no crime. It may be that legislation of this type should be on the statute books. But the provisions in H. R. 9490 would very probably prove ineffective to achieve the objective sought, since they would not suspend the writ of habeas corpus, and under our legal system to detain a man not charged with a crime would raise serious constitutional questions unless the writ of habeas corpus were suspended. Furthermore, it may well be that other persons than those covered by these provisions would be more important to detain in the event of emergency. This whole problem, therefore, should clearly be studied more thoroughly before further legislative action along these lines is considered.

In brief, when all the provisions of H. R. 9490 are considered together, it is evident that the great bulk of them are not directed toward the real and present dangers that exist from communism. Instead of striking blows at communism, they would strike blows at our own liberties and at our position in the forefront of those working for freedom in the world. At a time when our young men are fighting for freedom in Korea, it would be tragic to advance the objectives of communism in this country, as this bill would do.

Because I feel so strongly that this legislation would be a terrible mistake, I want to discuss more fully its worst features: sections 1 through 17 and sections 22 and 25. . . .

Unfortunately, these provisions are not merely ineffective and unworkable. They represent a clear and present danger to our institutions.

Insofar as the bill would require registration by the Communist Party itself, it does not endanger our traditional liberties. However, the application of the registration requirements to so-called Communist-front organizations can be the greatest danger to freedom of speech, press and assembly, since the alien and sedition laws of 1798. This danger arises out of the criteria or standards to be applied in determining whether an organization is a Communist-front organization.

There would be no serious problem if the bill required proof that an organization was controlled and financed by the Communist Party before it could be classified as a Communist-front organization. However, recognizing the difficulty of proving those matters, the bill would permit such a determination to be based solely upon "the extent to which the positions taken or advanced by it from time to time on matters of policy do not deviate from those" of the Communist movement.

This provision could easily be used to classify as a Communist-front organization any organization which is advocating a single policy or objective which is also being urged by the Communist Party or by a Communist foreign government. In fact, this may be the intended result, since the bill defines "organization" to include "a group of persons . . . permanently or temporarily associated together for joint action on any subject or subjects." Thus, an organization which advocates low-cost housing for sincere humanitarian reasons might be classified as a Communist-front organization because the Communists regularly exploit slum conditions as one of their fifth-column techniques.

It is not enough to say that this probably would not be done. The mere fact that it could be done shows clearly how the bill would open a Pandora's box of opportunities for official condemnation of organizations and individuals for perfectly honest opinions which happen to be stated also by Communists.

The basic error of these sections is that they move in the direction of suppressing opinion and belief. This would be a very dangerous course to take, not because we have any sympathy for Communist opinions, but because any governmental stifling of the free expression of opinion is a long step toward totalitarianism.

There is no more fundamental axiom of American freedom than the familiar statement: In a free country we punish men for the crimes they commit but never for the opinions they have. And the reason this is so fundamental to freedom is not, as many suppose, that it protects the few unorthodox from suppression by the majority. To permit freedom of expression is primarily for the benefit of the majority, because it protects criticism, and criticism leads to progress.

We can and we will prevent espionage, sabotage, or other actions endangering our national security. But we would betray our finest traditions if we attempted, as this bill would attempt, to curb the simple expression of opinion. This we should never do, no matter how distasteful the opinion may be to the vast majority of our people. The course proposed by this bill would delight the Communists, for it would make a mockery of the Bill of Rights and of our claims to stand for freedom in the world.

And what kind of effect would these provisions have on the normal expression of political views? Obviously, if this law were on the statute books, the part of prudence would be to avoid saying anything that might be construed by someone as not deviating sufficiently from the current Communist-propaganda line. And since no one could be sure in advance what views were safe to express, the inevitable tendency would be to express no views on controversial subjects.

The result could only be to reduce the vigor and strength of our political life—an outcome that the Communists would happily welcome, but that freemen should abhor.

We need not fear the expression of ideas —we do need to fear their suppression.

Our position in the vanguard of freedom rests largely on our demonstration that the free expression of opinion, coupled with government by popular consent, leads to national strength and human advancement. Let us not, in cowering and foolish fear, throw away the ideals which are the fundamental basis of our free society.

Not only are the registration provisions of this bill unworkable and dangerous, they are also grossly misleading in that all but one of the objectives which are claimed for them are already being accomplished by other and superior methods—and the one objective which is not now being accomplished would not in fact be accomplished under this bill either.

It is claimed that the bill would provide information about the Communist Party and its members. The fact is, the FBI already possesses very complete sources of information concerning the Communist movement in this country. If the FBI must disclose its sources of information in public hearings to require registration under this bill, its present sources of information, and its ability to acquire new information, will be largely destroyed.

It is claimed that this bill would deny income-tax exemptions to Communist organizations. The fact is that the Bureau of Internal Revenue already denies income-tax exemptions to such organizations.

It is claimed that this bill would deny passports to Communists. The fact is that the Government can and does deny passports to Communists under existing law.

It is claimed that this bill would prohibit the employment of Communists by the Federal Government. The fact is that the employment of Communists by the Federal Government is already prohibited and, at least in the executive branch, there is an effective program to see that they are not employed.

It is claimed that this bill would prohibit the employment of Communists in defense plants. The fact is that it would be years before this bill would have any effect of this nature—if it ever would. Fortunately, this objective is already being substantially achieved under the present procedures of the Department of Defense, and if the Congress would enact one of the provisions I have recommended—which it did not include in this bill—the situation would be entirely taken care of, promptly and effectively. . . .

Sections 22 and 25 of this bill are directed toward the specific questions of who should be admitted to our country, and who should be permitted to become a United States citizen. I believe there is general agreement that the answers to those questions should be: We should admit to our country, within the available quotas, anyone with a legitimate purpose who would not endanger our security, and we should admit to citizenship any immigrant who will be a loyal and constructive member of the community. Those are essentially the standards set by existing law. Under present law we do not admit to our country known Communists because we believe they work to overthrow our Government, and we do not admit Communists to citizenship because we believe they are not loyal to the United States.

The changes which would be made in the present law by sections 22 and 25 would not reinforce those sensible standards. Instead, they would add a number of new standards, which, for no good and sufficient reason, would interfere with our relations with other countries and seriously damage our national security.

Section 22 would, for example, exclude from our country anyone who advocates any form of totalitarian or one-party government. We, of course, believe in the democratic system of competing political parties, offering a choice of candidates and policies. But a number of countries with which we maintain friendly relations have a different form of government.

Until now no one has suggested that we should abandon cultural and commercial relations with a country merely because it has a form of government different from ours. Yet section 22 would require that. As one instance, it is clear that under the definitions of the bill the present Government of Spain, among others, would be classified as "totalitarian." As a result, the Attorney General would be required to exclude from the United States all Spanish businessmen, students, and other nonofficial travelers who support the present Government of their country. I cannot understand how the sponsors of this bill can think that such an action would contribute to our national security. . . .

Section 22 is so contrary to our national interests that it would actually put the Government into the business of thought control by requiring the deportation of any alien who distributes or publishes, or who is affiliated with an organization which distributes or publishes, any written or printed matter advocating (or merely expressing belief in) the economic and governmental doctrines of any form of totalitarianism. This provision does not require an evil intent or purpose on the part of the alien, as does a similar provision in the Smith Act. Thus, the Attorney General would be required to deport any alien operating or connected with a well-stocked bookshop containing books on economics or politics written by supporters of the present Governments of Spain, of Yugoslavia, or any one of a number of other countries. Section 25 would make the same aliens ineligible for citizenship. There should be no room in our laws for such hysterical provisions. The next logical step would be to "burn the books."

This illustrates the fundamental error of these immigration and naturalization provisions. It is easy to see that they are hasty and ill-considered. But far more significant—and far more dangerous—is their apparent underlying purpose. Instead of trying to encourage the free movement of people, subject only to the real requirements of national security, these provisions attempt to bar movement to anyone who is, or once was, associated with ideas we dislike and, in the process, they would succeed in barring many people whom it would be to our advantage to admit.

Such an action would be a serious blow to our work for world peace. We uphold—or have upheld till now, at any rate—the concept of freedom on an international scale. That is the root concept of our efforts to bring unity among the free nations and peace in the world.

The Communists, on the other hand, attempt to break down in every possible way the free interchange of persons and ideas. It will be to their advantage, and not ours, if we establish for ourselves an "iron curtain" against those who can help us in the fight for freedom. . . .

I do not undertake lightly the responsibility of differing with the majority in both Houses of Congress who have voted for this bill. We are all Americans; we all wish to safeguard and preserve our constitutional liberties against internal and external enemies. But I cannot approve this legislation, which instead of accomplishing its avowed purpose would actually interfere with our liberties and help the Communists against whom the bill was aimed.

This is a time when we must marshal all our resources and all the moral strength of our free system in self-defense against the threat of Communist aggression. We will fail in this, and we will destroy all that we seek to preserve, if we sacrifice the liberties of our citizens in a misguided attempt to achieve national security.

There is no reason why we should fail. Our country has been through dangerous times before, without losing our liberties to external attack or internal hysteria. Each of us, in Government and out, has a share in guarding our liberties. Each of us must search his own conscience to find whether he is doing all that can be done to preserve and strengthen them.

No considerations of expediency can justify the enactment of such a bill as this, a bill which would so greatly weaken our liberties and give aid and comfort to those who would destroy us. I have, therefore, no alternative but to return this bill without my approval, and I earnestly request the Congress to reconsider its action.

HARRY S TRUMAN.

593. DENNIS v. U. S.
341 U. S. 494
1951

The Truman administration opened its drive against internal Communism in 1948 by obtaining the indictment of eleven high-ranking Communist leaders for conspiring to teach and advocate the violent overthrow of the government in violation of the Smith Act of 1940. See Doc. No. 531. Convicted in the lower Courts, the Communists carried their case to the Supreme Court, which voted six to two to sustain the Smith Act and the conviction of the Communist leaders. This decision modified the "clear and present danger" doctrine of Justice Holmes by holding that offenders could be punished for conspiring to teach and advocate revolution. See M. L. Ernst and D. L. Loth, *Report on the American Communist;* C. H.

Pritchett, *Civil Liberties and the Vinson Court;* W. Mendelson, "Clear and Present Danger—From Schenck to Dennis," 52 Columbia Law Review, 313; N. L. Nathanson, "Communist Trial and the Clear and Present Danger Test" 63 *Harv. L. Rev.,* 1167 H. S. Commager, *Freedom, Loyalty and Dissent;* T. Draper, *Roots of American Communism.*

Appeal from the United States Court of Appeals for the second Circuit.

VINSON, C. J. Petitioners were indicted in July, 1948, for violation of the conspiracy provisions of the Smith Act, § 11, during the

period of April, 1945, to July, 1948. . . .
A verdict of guilty as to all the petitioners
was returned by the jury on October 14,
1949. The Court of Appeals affirmed the
convictions. 183 F. 2d 201. We granted certiorari limited to the following two questions: (1) Whether either § 2 or § 3 of the
Smith Act, inherently or as construed and
applied in the instant case, violates the First
Amendment and other provisions of the Bill
of Rights; (2) whether either § 2 or § 3 of
the Act, inherently or as construed and applied in the instant case, violates the First
and Fifth Amendments because of indefiniteness. . . .

The indictment charged the petitioners
with willfully and knowingly conspiring (1)
to organize as the Communist Party of the
United States of America a society, group
and assembly of persons who teach and advocate the overthrow and destruction of the
Government of the United States by force
and violence, and (2) knowingly and wilfully to advocate and teach the duty and
necessity of overthrowing and destroying the
Government of the United States by force
and violence. The indictment further alleged
that § 2 of the Smith Act proscribes these
acts and that any conspiracy to take such
action is a violation of § 3 of the Act. . . .

The obvious purpose of the statute is to
protect existing Government, not from
change by peaceable, lawful and constitutional means, but from change by violence,
revolution and terrorism. That it is within
the *power* of the Congress to protect the
Government of the United States from
armed rebellion is a proposition which requires little discussion. Whatever theoretical
merit there may be to the argument that
there is a "right" to rebellion against dictatorial governments is without force where
the existing structure of the government
provides for peaceful and orderly change.
We reject any principle of governmental
helplessness in the face of preparation for
revolution, which principle, carried to its
logical conclusion, must lead to anarchy. No
one could conceive that it is not within the
power of Congress to prohibit acts intended
to overthrow the Government by force and
violence. The question with which we are
concerned here is not whether Congress has
such *power*, but whether the *means* which

it has employed conflict with the First and
Fifth Amendments to the Constitution.

One of the bases for the contention that
the means which Congress has employed
are invalid takes the form of an attack on
the face of the statute on the grounds that
by its terms it prohibits academic discussion
of the merits of Marxism-Leninism, that it
stifles ideas and is contrary to all concepts
of a free speech and a free press. . . .

The very language of the Smith Act ne-
gates the interpretation which petitioners
would have us impose on that Act. It is
directed at advocacy, not discussion. Thus,
the trial judge properly charged the jury that
they could not convict if they found that
petitioners did "no more than pursue peaceful studies and discussions or teaching and
advocacy in the realm of ideas." He further
charged that it was not unlawful "to conduct in an American college and university
a course explaining the philosophical theories set forth in the books which have been
placed in evidence." Such a charge is in
strict accord with the statutory language,
and illustrates the meaning to be placed on
those words. Congress did not intend to eradicate the free discussion of political theories,
to destroy the traditional rights of Americans
to discuss and evaluate ideas without fear of
governmental sanction. Rather Congress was
concerned with the very kind of activity in
which the evidence showed these petitioners
engaged.

But although the statute is not directed
at the hypothetical cases which petitioners
have conjured, its application in this case
has resulted in convictions for the teaching
and advocacy of the overthrow of the Government by force and violence, which, even
though coupled with the intent to accomplish that overthrow, contains an element
of speech. For this reason, we must pay
special heed to the demands of the First
Amendment marking out the boundaries of
speech.

We pointed out in *Douds, supra,* that the
basis of the First Amendment is the hypothesis that speech can rebut speech, propaganda will answer propaganda, free debate
of ideas will result in the wisest governmental policies. It is for this reason that
this Court has recognized the inherent value
of free discourse. An analysis of the leading

cases in this Court which have involved direct limitations on speech, however, will demonstrate that both the majority of the Court and the dissenters in particular cases have recognized that this is not an unlimited, unqualified right, but that the societal value of speech must, on occasion, be subordinated to other values and considerations. . . .

The rule we deduce from these cases is that where an offense is specified by a statute in nonspeech or nonpress terms, a conviction relying upon speech or press as evidence of violation may be sustained only when the speech or publication created a "clear and present danger" of attempting or accomplishing the prohibited crime. . . .

In this case we are squarely presented with the application of the "clear and present danger" test, and must decide what that phrase imports. . . .

Obviously, the words cannot mean that before the Government may act, it must wait until the *putsch* is about to be executed, the plans have been laid and the signal is awaited. If Government is aware that a group aiming at its overthrow is attempting to indoctrinate its members and to commit them to a course whereby they will strike when the leaders feel the circumstances permit, action by the Government is required. The argument that there is no need for Government to concern itself, for Government is strong, it possesses ample powers to put down a rebellion, it may defeat the revolution with ease needs no answer. For that is not the question. Certainly an attempt to overthrow the Government by force, even though doomed from the outset because of inadequate numbers or power of the revolutionists, is a sufficient evil for Congress to prevent. The damage which such attempts create both physically and politically to a nation makes it impossible to measure the validity in terms of the probability of success, or the immediacy of a successful attempt. In the instant case the trial judge charged the jury that they could not convict unless they found that petitioners intended to overthrow the Government "as speedily as circumstances would permit." This does not mean, and could not properly mean, that they would not strike until there was certainty of success. What

was meant was that the revolutionists would strike when they thought the time was ripe. We must therefore reject the contention that success or probability of success is the criterion. . . .

The mere fact that from the period 1945 to 1948 petitioners' activities did not result in an attempt to overthrow the Government by force and violence is of course no answer to the fact that there was a group that was ready to make the attempt. The formation by petitioners of such a highly organized conspiracy, with rigidly disciplined members subject to call when the leaders, these petitioners, felt that the time had come for action, coupled with the inflammable nature of world conditions, similar uprisings in other countries, and the touch-and-go nature of our relations with countries with whom petitioners were in the very least ideologically attuned, convince us that their convictions were justified on this score. And this analysis disposes of the contention that a conspiracy to advocate, as distinguished from the advocacy itself, cannot be constitutionally restrained, because it comprises only the preparation. It is the existence of the conspiracy which creates the danger. Cf. *Pinkerton* v. *United States,* 328 U.S. 640 (1946); *Goldman* v. *United States,* 245 U.S. 474 (1918); *United States* v. *Rabinowich,* 238 U.S. 78 (1915). If the ingredients of the reaction are present, we cannot bind the Government to wait until the catalyst is added. . . .

We hold that § § 2 (a) (1), 2 (a) (3) and 3 of the Smith Act, do not inherently, or as construed or applied in the instant case, violate the First Amendment and other provisions of the Bill of Rights, or the First and Fifth Amendments because of indefiniteness. Petitioners intended to overthrow the Government of the United States as speedily as the circumstances would permit. Their conspiracy to organize the Communist Party and to teach and advocate the overthrow of the Government of the United States by force and violence created a "clear and present danger" of an attempt to overthrow the Government by force and violence. They were properly and constitutionally convicted for violation of the Smith Act. The judgments of conviction are

Affirmed.

JACKSON, V., concurring. This prosecution is the latest of never-ending, because never successful, quests for some legal formula that will secure an existing order against revolutionary radicalism. It requires us to reappraise, in the light of our own times and conditions, constitutional doctrines devised under other circumstances to strike a balance between authority and liberty.

Activity here charged to be criminal is conspiracy—that defendants conspired to teach and advocate, and to organize the Communist Party to teach and advocate, overthrow and destruction of the Government by force and violence. There is no charge of actual violence or attempt at overthrow.

The principal reliance of the defense in this Court is that the conviction cannot stand under the Constitution because the conspiracy of these defendants presents no "clear and present danger" of imminent or foreseeable overthrow. . . .

If we must decide that this Act and its application are constitutional only if we are convinced that petitioner's conduct creates a "clear and present danger" of violent overthrow, we must appraise imponderables, including international and national phenomena which baffle the best informed foreign offices and our most experienced politicians. We would have to foresee and predict the effectiveness of Communist propaganda, opportunities for infiltration; whether, and when, a time will come that they consider propitious for action, and whether and how fast our existing government will deteriorate. And we would have to speculate as to whether an approaching Communist *coup* would not be anticipated by a nationalistic fascist movement. No doctrine can be sound whose application requires us to make a prophecy of that sort in the guise of a legal decision. The judicial process simply is not adequate to a trial of such far-flung issues. The answers given would reflect our own political predilections and nothing more.

The authors of the clear and present danger test never applied it to a case like this, nor would I. If applied as it is proposed here, it means that the Communist plotting is protected during its period of incubation; its preliminary stages of organization and preparation are immune from the law; the

Government can move only after imminent action is manifest, when it would, of course, be too late.

The highest degree of constitutional protection is due to the individual acting without conspiracy. But even an individual cannot claim that the Constitution protects him in advocating or teaching overthrow of government by force or violence. I should suppose no one would doubt that Congress has power to make such attempted overthrow a crime. But the contention is that one has the constitutional right to work up a public desire and will to do what is a crime to attempt. I think direct incitement by speech or writing can be made a crime, and I think there can be a conviction without also proving that the odds favored its success by 99 to 1, or some other extremely high ratio.

The names of Mr. Justice Holmes and Mr. Justice Brandeis cannot be associated with such a doctrine of governmental disability. After the *Schenck* case, in which they set forth the clear and present danger test, they joined in these words of Mr. Justice Holmes, spoken for a unanimous Court:

". . . [T]he First Amendment while prohibiting legislation against free speech as such cannot have been, and obviously was not, intended to give immunity for every possible use of language. *Robertson* v. *Baldwin*, 165 U.S. 275, 281. We venture to believe that neither Hamilton nor Madison, nor any other competent person then or later, ever supposed that to make criminal the counselling of a murder within the jurisdiction of Congress would be an unconstitutional interference with free speech." *Frohwerk* v. *United States*, 249 U.S. 204.

The same doctrine was earlier stated in *Fox* v. *Washington*, 236 U.S. 273, 277, and that case was recently and with approval cited in *Giboney* v. *Empire Storage & Ice Co.*, 336 U.S. 490, 502.

As aptly stated by Judge Learned Hand in *Masses Publishing Co.* v. *Patten*, 244 F. 535, 540: "One may not counsel or advise others to violate the law as it stands. Words are not only the keys of persuasion, but the triggers of action, and those which have no purport but to counsel the violation of law cannot by any latitude of interpretation be a part of that public opinion which is the final source of government in a democratic state." . . .

BLACK, J., dissenting. . . .

At the outset I want to emphasize what the crime involved in this case is, and what it is not. These petitioners were not charged with an attempt to overthrow the Government. They were not charged with nonverbal acts of any kind designed to overthrow the Government. They were not even charged with saying anything or writing anything designed to overthrow the Government. The charge was that they agreed to assemble and to talk and publish certain ideas at a later date: The indictment is that they conspired to organize the Communist Party and to use speech or newspapers and other publications in the future to teach and advocate the forcible overthrow of the Government. No matter how it is worded, this is a virulent form of prior censorship of speech and press, which I believe the First Amendment forbids. I would hold § 3 of the Smith Act authorizing this prior restraint unconstitutional on its face and as applied.

But let us assume, contrary to all constitutional ideas of fair criminal procedure, that petitioners although not indicted for the crime of actual advocacy, may be punished for it. Even on this radical assumption, the only way to affirm these convictions, as the dissent of MR. JUSTICE DOUGLAS shows, is to qualify drastically or wholly repudiate the established "clear and present danger" rule. This the Court does in a way which greatly restricts the protections afforded by the First Amendment. The opinions for affirmance show that the chief reason for jettisoning the rule is the expressed fear that advocacy of Communist doctrine endangers the safety of the Republic. Undoubtedly, a governmental policy of unfettered communication of ideas does entail dangers. To the Founders of this Nation, however, the benefits derived from free expression were worth the risk. They embodied this philosophy in the First Amendment's command that Congress "shall make no law abridging . . . the freedom of speech, or of the press . . . ." I have always believed that the First Amendment is the keystone of our Government, that the freedoms it guarantees provide the best insur-

ance against destruction of all freedom. At least as to speech in the realm of public matters, I believe that the "clear and present danger" test does not "mark the furthermost constitutional boundaries of protected expression" but does "no more than recognize a minimum compulsion of the Bill of Rights." *Bridges* v. *California,* 314 U.S. 252, 263.

So long as this Court exercises the power of judicial review of legislation, I cannot agree that the First Amendment permits us to sustain laws suppressing freedom of speech and press on the basis of Congress' or our own notions of mere "reasonableness." Such a doctrine waters down the first Amendment so that it amounts to little more than an admonition to Congress. The Amendment as so construed is not likely to protect any but those "safe" or orthodox views which rarely need its protection. . . .

Public opinion being what it now is, few will protest the conviction of these Communist petitioners. There is hope, however, that in calmer times, when present pressures, passions and fears subside, this or some later Court will restore the First Amendment liberties to the high preferred place where they belong in a free society.

DOUGLAS, J., dissenting. If this were a case where those who claimed protection under the First Amendment were teaching the techniques of sabotage, the assassination of the President, the filching of documents from public files, the planting of bombs, the art of street warfare, and the like, I would have no doubts. The freedom to speak is not absolute; the teaching of methods of terror and other seditious conduct should be beyond the pale along with obscenity and immorality. . . .

So far as the present record is concerned, what petitioners did was to organize people to teach and themselves teach the Marxist-Leninest doctrine contained chiefly in four books: Foundations of Leninism by Stalin (1924), The Communist Manifesto by Marx and Engels (1848), State and Revolution by Lenin (1917), History of the Communist Party of the Soviet Union (B) (1939). . . .

I repeat that we deal here with speech alone, not with speech *plus* acts of sabotage or unlawful conduct. Not a single seditious act is charged in the indictment.

Free speech has occupied an exalted position because of the high service it has given our society. Its protection is essential to the very existence of a democracy. The airing of ideas releases pressures which otherwise might become destructive. When ideas compete in the market for acceptance, full and free discussion exposes the false and they gain few adherents. Full and free discussion even of ideas we hate encourages the testing of our own prejudices and preconceptions. Full and free discussion keeps a society from becoming stagnant and unprepared for the stresses and strains that work to tear all civilizations apart.

Full and free discussion has indeed been the first article of our faith. We have founded our political system on it. It has been the safeguard of every religious, political, philosophical, economic, and racial group amongst us. We have counted on it to keep us from embracing what is cheap and false; we have trusted the common sense of our people to choose the doctrine true to our genius and to reject the rest. This has been the one single outstanding tenet that has made our institutions the symbol of freedom and equality. We have deemed it more costly to liberty to suppress a despised minority than to let them vent their spleen. We have above all else feared the political censor. We have wanted a land where our people can be exposed to all the diverse creeds and cultures of the world.

There comes a time when even speech loses its constitutional immunity. Speech innocuous one year may at another time fan such destructive flames that it must be halted in the interests of the safety of the Republic. That is the meaning of the clear and present danger test. When conditions are so critical that there will be no time to avoid the evil that the speech threatens, it is time to call a halt. Otherwise, free speech which is the strength of the Nation will be the cause of its destruction.

Yet free speech is the rule, not the exception. The restraint to be constitutional must be based on more than fear, on more than passionate opposition against the speech, on more than a revolted dislike for its contents. There must be some immediate injury to society that is likely if speech is allowed. . . .

The nature of Communism as a force on the world scene would, of course, be relevant to the issue of clear and present danger of petitioners' advocacy within the United States. But the primary consideration is the strength and tactical position of petitioners and their converts in this country. On that there is no evidence in the record. If we are to take judicial notice of the threat of Communists within the nation, it should not be difficult to conclude that *as a political party* they are of little consequence. Communists in this country have never made a respectable or serious showing in any election. I would doubt that there is a village, let alone a city or county or state which the Communists could carry. Communism in the world scene is no bogey-man; but Communism as a political faction or party in this country plainly is. Communism has been so thoroughly exposed in this country that it has been crippled as a political force. Free speech has destroyed it as an effective political party. It is inconceivable that those who went up and down this country preaching the doctrine of revolution which petitioners espouse would have any success. In days of trouble and confusion when bread lines were long, when the unemployed walked the streets, when people were starving, the advocates of a short-cut by revolution might have a chance to gain adherents. But today there are no such conditions. The country is not in despair; the people know Soviet Communism; the doctrine of Soviet revolution is exposed in all of its ugliness and the American people want none of it.

How it can be said that there is a clear and present danger that this advocacy will succeed is, therefore, a mystery. Some nations less resilient than the United States, where illiteracy is high and where democratic traditions are only budding, might have to take drastic steps and jail these men for merely speaking their creed. But in America they are miserable merchants of unwanted ideas; their wares remain unsold. The fact that their ideas are abhorrent does not make them powerful. . . .

The First Amendment provides that "Congress shall make no law . . . abridging the freedom of speech." The Constitution provides no exception. This does not mean, however, that the Nation need hold its hand until it is in such weakened condition that there is no time to protect itself from incitement to revolution. Seditious conduct can always be punished. But the command of the First Amendment is so clear that we should not allow Congress to call a halt to free speech except in the extreme case of peril from the speech itself. The First Amendment makes confidence in the common sense of our people and in their maturity of judgment the great postulate of our democracy. Its philosophy is that violence is rarely, if ever, stopped by denying civil liberties to those advocating resort to force. The First Amendment reflects the philosophy of Jefferson "that it is time enough for the rightful purposes of civil government for its officers to interfere when principles break

out into overt acts against peace and good order." The political censor has no place in our public debates. Unless and until extreme and necessitous circumstances are shown our aim should be to keep speech unfettered and to allow the processes of law to be invoked only when the provocateurs among us move from speech to action.

Vishinsky wrote in 1948 in The Law of the Soviet State, "In our state, naturally there can be no place for freedom of speech, press, and so on for the foes of socialism."

Our concern should be that we accept no such standard for the United States. Our faith should be that our people will never give support to these advocates of revolution, so long as we remain loyal to the purposes for which our Nation was founded. . . .

594. THE RECALL OF GENERAL DOUGLAS MacARTHUR
April 11, 1951

(Department of State Bulletin, April 16, 1951)

The question of military strategy in the Korean war involved the over-all foreign policy of the United States. In October, 1950, the Chinese Communist government sent troops to aid the faltering North Koreans. To meet this situation, the commander of United States and United Nations troops in Korea, General Douglas MacArthur, proposed the use of air and naval forces to extend the war to Chinese territory. President Truman rejected this proposal and ordered MacArthur to conduct a limited war on the Korean peninsula. When MacArthur continued to press for more extensive military operations against the Chinese, President Truman relieved him of his command. Truman explained the reasons for his action in this address to the nation. See H. Truman, *Memoirs, Vol. II;* Council on Foreign Relations, *The United States in World Affairs,* 1950–1953; R. H. Rovere and A. M. Schlesinger, Jr., *The General and the President;* C. Whitney, *MacArthur: His Rendezvous with History;* C. A. Willoughby and J. Chamberlain, *McArthur, 1944–1951.*

I want to talk plainly to you tonight about what we are doing in Korea and about our policy in the Far East.

In the simplest terms, what we are doing

in Korea is this: We are trying to prevent a third world war.

I think most people in this country recognized that fact last June. And they warmly supported the decision of the Government to help the Republic of Korea against the Communist aggressors. Now, many persons, even some who applauded our decision to defend Korea, have forgotten the basic reason for our action.

It is right for us to be in Korea. It was right last June. It is right today.

I want to remind you why this is true.

The Communists in the Kremlin are engaged in a monstrous conspiracy to stamp out freedom all over the world. If they were to succeed, the United States would be numbered among their principal victims. It must be clear to everyone that the United States cannot—and will not—sit idly by and await foreign conquest. The only question is: When is the best time to meet the threat and how?

The best time to meet the threat is in the beginning. It is easier to put out a fire in the beginning when it is small than after it has become a roaring blaze.

And the best way to meet the threat of

aggression is for the peace-loving nations to act together. If they don't act together, they are likely to be picked off, one by one. . . .

This is the basic reason why we joined in creating the United Nations. And since the end of World War II we have been putting that lesson into practice—we have been working with other free nations to check the aggressive designs of the Soviet Union before they can result in a third world war.

That is what we did in Greece, when that nation was threatened by the aggression of international communism.

The attack against Greece could have led to general war. But this country came to the aid of Greece. The United Nations supported Greek resistance. With our help, the determination and efforts of the Greek people defeated the attack on the spot.

Another big Communist threat to peace was the Berlin blockade. That too could have led to war. But again it was settled because free men would not back down in an emergency. . . .

The question we have had to face is whether the Communist plan of conquest can be stopped without general war. Our Government and other countries associated with us in the United Nations believe that the best chance of stopping it without general war is to meet the attack in Korea and defeat it there.

That is what we have been doing. It is a difficult and bitter task.

But so far it has been successful.

So far, we have prevented World War III.

So far, by fighting a limited war in Korea, we have prevented aggression from succeeding and bringing on a general war. And the ability of the whole free world to resist Communist aggression has been greatly improved.

We have taught the enemy a lesson. He has found out that aggression is not cheap or easy. Moreover, men all over the world who want to remain free have been given new courage and new hope. They know now that the champions of freedom can stand up and fight and that they will stand up and fight.

Our resolute stand in Korea is helping the forces of freedom now fighting in Indo-

china and other countries in that part of the world. It has already slowed down the timetable of conquest. . . .

We do not want to see the conflict in Korea extended. We are trying to prevent a world war—not to start one. The best way to do this is to make plain that we and the other free countries will continue to resist the attack.

But you may ask: Why can't we take other steps to punish the aggressor? Why don't we bomb Manchuria and China itself? Why don't we assist Chinese Nationalist troops to land on the mainland of China?

If we were to do these things we would be running a very grave risk of starting a general war. If that were to happen, we would have brought about the exact situation we are trying to prevent.

If we were to do these things, we would become entangled in a vast conflict on the continent of Asia and our task would become immeasurably more difficult all over the world.

What would suit the ambitions of the Kremlin better than for our military forces to be committed to a full-scale war with Red China? . . .

The course we have been following is the one best calculated to avoid an all-out war. It is the course consistent with our obligation to do all we can to maintain international peace and security. Our experience in Greece and Berlin shows that it is the most effective course of action we can follow. . . .

If the Communist authorities realize that they cannot defeat us in Korea, if they realize it would be foolhardy to widen the hostilities beyond Korea, then they may recognize the folly of continuing their aggression. A peaceful settlement may then be possible. The door is always open.

Then we may achieve a settlement in Korea which will not compromise the principles and purposes of the United Nations.

I have thought long and hard about this question of extending the war in Asia. I have discussed it many times with the ablest military advisers in the country. I believe with all my heart that the course we are following is the best course.

I believe that we must try to limit war to Korea for these vital reasons: to make sure that the precious lives of our fighting men are not wasted; to see that the security of our country and the free world is not needlessly jeopardized; and to prevent a third world war.

A number of events have made it evident that General MacArthur did not agree with that policy. I have therefore considered it essential to relieve General MacArthur so that there would be no doubt or confusion as to the real purpose and aim of our policy.

It was with the deepest personal regret that I found myself compelled to take this action. General MacArthur is one of our greatest military commanders. But the cause of world peace is more important than any individual.

The change in commands in the Far East means no change whatever in the policy of the United States. We will carry on the fight in Korea with vigor and determination in an effort to bring the war to a speedy and successful conclusion.

The new commander, Lt. Gen. Matthew Ridgway, has already demonstrated that he has the great qualities of military leadership needed for this task.

We are ready, at any time, to negotiate for a restoration of peace in the area. But we will not engage in appeasement. We are only interested in real peace.

Real peace can be achieved through a settlement based on the following factors:

One: the fighting must stop.

Two: concrete steps must be taken to insure that the fighting will not break out again.

Three: there must be an end to the aggression.

A settlement founded upon these elements would open the way for the unification of Korea and the withdrawal of all foreign forces.

In the meantime, I want to be clear about our military objective. We are fighting to resist an outrageous aggression in Korea. We are trying to keep the Korean conflict from spreading to other areas. But at the same time we must conduct our military activities so as to insure the security of our forces. This is essential if they are to continue the fight until the enemy abandons its ruthless attempt to destroy the Republic of Korea.

That is our military objective—to repel attack and to restore peace.

In the hard fighting in Korea, we are proving that collective action among nations is not only a high principle but a workable means of resisting aggression. Defeat of aggression in Korea may be the turning point in the world's search for a practical way of achieving peace and security.

The struggle of the United Nations in Korea is a struggle for peace.

The free nations have united their strength in an effort to prevent a third world war.

That war can come if the Communist rulers want it to come. But this Nation and its allies will not be responsible for its coming.

We do not want to widen the conflict. We will use every effort to prevent that disaster. And in so doing we know that we are following the great principles of peace, freedom, and justice.

595. MacARTHUR'S SPEECH TO CONGRESS
April 19, 1951

(82nd Congress, 1st Session, *House Doc.* No. 36)

The dismissal of General MacArthur precipitated a major debate over American policy in the Far East. Two issues were raised in the debate: first, was President Truman right in removing General MacArthur from his command; second, was the strategy of limited war a valid one in the Korean conflict. General MacArthur presented his view of the situation in this address to a joint session of Congress. Thereafter, the Senate committees on Armed Services and Foreign Relations investigated the recall of MacArthur and the military situation in the Far East and unanimously concluded that the President was within his constitutional rights in asserting the dominance of civil over military power. They failed to reach any agreement on the wisdom of the policy of limited war. This issue remained a controversial one and was heatedly debated in the presidential campaign of 1952. But the Truman policy of self-restraint was eventually adopted by the Eisenhower administration. See R. H. Rovere and A. M. Schlesinger, Jr., *The General and the President;* C. Whitney, *MacArthur: His Rendezvous with History;* U.S. Senate Committee on Armed Services and Committee on Foreign Relations, 82nd Congress, *Joint Statement . . . on Relief of General MacArthur and on American Policy in Far East.*

. . . The Communist threat is a global one. Its successful advance in one sector threatens the destruction of every other sector. You cannot appease or otherwise surrender to communism in Asia without simultaneously undermining our efforts to halt its advance in Europe. . . .

. . . While I was not consulted prior to the President's decision to intervene in support of the Republic of Korea, that decision, from a military standpoint, proved a sound one, as we hurled back the invader and decimated his forces. Our victory was complete and our objectives within reach when Red China intervened with numerically superior ground forces. This created a new war and an entirely new situation—a situation not contemplated when our forces were committed against the North Korean invaders—a situation which called for new decisions in the diplomatic sphere to permit the realistic adjustment of military strategy. Such decisions have not been forthcoming.

While no man in his right mind would advocate sending our ground forces into continental China and such was never given a thought, the new situation did urgently demand a drastic revision of strategic planning if our political aim was to defeat this new enemy as we had defeated the old.

Apart from the military need as I saw it to neutralize the sanctuary protection given the enemy north of the Yalu, I felt that military necessity in the conduct of the war made mandatory:

1. The intensification of our economic blockade against China;

2. The imposition of a naval blockade against the China coast;

3. Removal of restrictions on air reconnaissance of China's coastal areas of Manchuria;

4. Removal of restrictions on the forces of the Republic of China on Formosa with logistical support to contribute to their effective operations against the common enemy.

For entertaining these views, all professionally designed to support our forces committed to Korea and bring hostilities to an end with the least possible delay and at a saving of countless American and Allied lives, I have been severely criticized in lay circles, principally abroad, despite my understanding that from a military standpoint the above views have been fully shared in past by practically every military leader concerned with the Korean campaign, including our own Joint Chiefs of Staff.

I called for reinforcements, but was informed that reinforcements were not available. I made clear that if not permitted to destroy the enemy buildup bases north of the Yalu; if not permitted to utilize the friendly Chinese force of some 600,000 men on Formosa; if not permitted to blockade the China coast to prevent the Chinese Reds from getting succor from without; and if there were to be no hope of major reinforcements, the position of the command from the military standpoint forbade victory. We could hold in Korea by constant maneuver and at an approximate area where our supply line advantages were in balance with the supply line disadvantages of the enemy, but we could hope at best for only an indecisive campaign, with its terrible and constant attrition upon our forces if the enemy utilized his full military potential. I have constantly called for new political decisions essential to a solution. Efforts have been made to distort my position. It has been said that I was in effect a warmonger. Nothing could be further from the truth. I know war as few other men now living know it, and nothing to me is more revolting. I have long advocated its complete abolition as its very destructiveness on both friend and foe has rendered it useless as a means of settling international disputes.

596. EUROPEAN RECOVERY PROGRAM
December 30, 1951

(Department of State Bulletin, Vol. XXVI, p. 43)

The Marshall Plan for aid to Europe was given practical effect by the Economic Cooperation Act of 1948. This act appropriated money for the rehabilitation of Europe and created an Economic Cooperation Administration to spend it. Additional legislation provided for aid to other parts of the world. Under the authority thus granted, the ECA gave assistance to countries throughout the world including Communist Yugoslavia after the Tito-Stalin break of 1948. The heart of the American program of economic aid remained the effort to secure the recovery of Western Europe. The terminal report of December 30, 1951, summarized the achievements of the ECA in Western Europe. See S. E. Harris, *The European Recovery Program;* J. A. Krout, ed., "American Foreign Aid Program," *Proc. of Amer. Academy of Pol. Sci., Vol. 23,* p. 345; J. K. Galbraith, "European Recovery: The Longer View," 12 *Rev. of Politics,* 165; J. H. Williams, "End of the Marshall Plan," 30 *Foreign Affairs,* 593.

The recovery of Europe from the chaos of 1947, when it was hungry, cold, disorderly, and frightened, can be measured in cold statistics: Industrial production, 64 percent above 1947 and 41 percent above prewar; steel production, nearly doubled in less than 4 years; coal production, slightly below prewar but still 27 percent higher than in 1947; aluminum, copper, and cement production, up respectively 69, 31, and 90 percent from 1947; food production, 24 percent above 1947 and 9 percent above prewar levels.

The Economic Cooperation Administration has expended nearly 12 billion dollars in grants and loans in carrying out the European Recovery Program—equal to nearly 80 dollars for every man, woman, and child in the United States. To this, the countries of Europe have added the equivalent of another 9 billion dollars in its own currencies to match the American grant-aid dollars. Of the U.S. funds, about 5.5 billion dollars have been used to purchase industrial commodities, mostly from the United States, and another 5.2 billion dollars for the purchase of food and other agricultural commodities such as cotton. Over 800 million dollars has alone gone into the cost of ocean freight for goods sent to Europe. The U.S. contribution to the setting up of the EPU was 350 million dollars and another 100 million dollars has been used since then to help the payments union over rough spots.

In their turn, the Marshall Plan countries in the past 3 years completed or are pushing to completion a total of 27 major projects for the increase of power and 32 major projects for modernizing and expanding the production of iron and steel. Major petroleum refining works number 11 and the volume of refining has quadrupled over prewar. Other industrial projects costing the equivalent of a million dollars or more bring the total of such projects to 132, costing the equivalent of over two billion dollars. About half a billion dollars of the U.S. commodity and technical aid has gone into these projects.

Into other major recovery projects have gone also the equivalent of billions of dollars of the counterpart currencies generated in the Marshall Plan countries to match American dollar aid. Such counterpart funds are used by the respective countries for recovery projects approved by the ECA. Biggest single use—equivalent to more than a billion dollars—has been for the improvement of electric, gas, and power facilities, an improvement that is helping to make possible Europe's rearmament program today.

Similarly vital to Europe's defense has been the rehabilitation of the continent's run-down and war-smashed railway network, with approved projects for use of counterpart funds totaling more than the equivalent of half a billion dollars. Similarly, counterpart projects for the reconstruction of merchant fleets, port and shipping facilities, and inland waterways have been completed or are in the process of completion in the Marshall Plan countries. Airports, too, have been built or improved with ECA-generated local currencies.

Through such double-barreled use of dollar aid and local funds, Marshall Plan nations, in less than 4 years, have rebuilt their economies to a point that could well persuade the Kremlin that the Europe which looked like such easy pickings in 1946 and 1947 is indeed a formidable bastion today.

Steel production, for example, so necessary to a strong peace or war economy, has risen from less than 31 million tons in 1947 to nearly 60 million tons in 1951. Soviet Russia and her satellites combined have a steel production rate of about 35 million tons.

The average volume of crude oil refined in Europe in prewar years was 12 million tons annually. In 1950–51 the volume of refined products reached 46.8 million tons, or nearly four times prewar.

In 1947, Europe's average monthly electrical production was 13½ million kilowatt hours. In mid-1951 the wheels of Europe's industry were being turned with 20½ million kilowatt hours per month. From a monthly cement production average of less than 2 million metric tons in 1947, Europe's production rose to 4 million tons monthly during the first half of 1951.

Cotton-yarn production in free Europe has risen from a monthly average of 82,000 metric tons in 1947 to 125,000 tons in 1951; wool yarn production is up from 33,000 tons monthly in 1947 to 44,000 tons in 1951.

One of the most dramatic improvements,

and one closely tied to Europe's defense capabilities, is in the production of motor vehicles. Monthly production, running at the rate of 54,000 vehicles in 1947, is up to 145,000 vehicles in 1951.

Agricultural production is up 9 percent over prewar and 24 percent over 1947–48, but at the same time there are many more mouths to feed (population is up from 250 million in 1938 to over 275 million in 1951) and Europe is not yet self-sufficient in food production.

Overall, Europe's gross national product —the total sum of its production of goods and services—rose by nearly 25 percent in the less than 4 years of Marshall Plan aid to over 125 billion dollars in 1950. This is a 15 percent increase over prewar levels.

But Europe by no means considers its job finished. Member countries of the OEEC recently issued a manifesto declaring their intention to work for an expansion of total production in Western Europe by 25 percent over the next 5 years.

With her industrial plant rebuilt to better than prewar years, Europe's hope for meeting or surpassing this goal must rest on improved production methods and greater productivity—increased output of goods with the same amount of manpower, machines, and management.

597. MUTUAL SECURITY ACT OF 1951
October 10, 1951
(*Public Law 165, 82nd Congress*)

The Truman Doctrine and the Marshall Plan committed the United States to large-scale programs of military and economic aid to friendly nations. The Military Defense Assistance Act of 1949 authorized military aid and the Economic Cooperation Acts of 1948 and 1949 and the Point Four Program of 1950 authorized economic and technical assistance to free nations throughout the world. See Docs. No. 572, 575, 588. At the end of 1951, Congress assigned the function of administering both the economic and the military aid programs to a new agency, the Mutual Security Administration. The significance of the Mutual Security Act of 1951 was twofold: first, it provided for the co-ordination of the military and economic aid programs; second, it marked a new emphasis of American policy on military, rather than eco-

nomic aid. See D. Middleton, *Defense of Western Europe;* H. L. Marx, ed., *Defense and National Security;* U.S. President, *Report to Congress on the Mutual Security Program,* 1951–.

AN ACT

To maintain the security and promote the foreign policy and provide for the general welfare of the United States by furnishing assistance to friendly nations in the interest of international peace and security.

SEC. 2. The Congress declares it to be the purpose of this Act to maintain the security and to promote the foreign policy of the United States by authorizing military, economic, and technical assistance to friendly countries to strengthen the mutual security and individual and collective defenses of the free world, to develop their resources in the interest of their security and independence and the national interest of the United States and to facilitate the effective participation of those countries in the United Nations system for collective security. The purposes of the Mutual Defense Assistance Act of 1949, as amended (22 U.S.C. 1571–1604), the Economic Cooperation Act of 1948, as amended, and the Act for International Development (22 U.S.C. 1557) shall hereafter be deemed to include this purpose.

TITLE I—EUROPE

SEC. 101. (a) In order to support the freedom of Europe through assistance which will further the carrying out of the plans for defense of the North Atlantic area, while at the same time maintaining the economic stability of the countries of the area so that they may meet their responsibilities for defense, and to further encourage the economic unification and the political federation of Europe, there are hereby authorized to be appropriated to the President for the fiscal year 1952 for carrying out the provisions and accomplishing the policies and purpose of this Act—

(1) not to exceed $5,028,000,000 for assistance pursuant to the provisions of the Mutual Defense Assistance Act of 1949, as amended, for countries which are parties to the North Atlantic Treaty and for any country of Europe (other than a country covered by another title of this Act), which the President determines to be of direct importance to the defense of the North Atlantic area and whose increased ability to defend itself the President determines is important to the preservation of the peace and security of the North Atlantic area and to the security of the United States. . . .

(2) not to exceed $1,022,000,000 for assistance pursuant to the provisions of the Economic Cooperation Act of 1948, as amended (including

assistance to further European military production), for any country of Europe covered by paragraph (1) of this subsection and for any other country covered by section 103 (a) of the said Economic Cooperation Act of 1948, as amended. . . .

TITLE II—NEAR EAST AND AFRICA

SEC. 201. In order to further the purpose of this Act by continuing to provide military assistance to Greece, Turkey, and Iran, there are hereby authorized to be appropriated to the President for the fiscal year 1952, not to exceed $396,250,000 for furnishing assistance to Greece and Turkey pursuant to the provisions of the Act of May 22, 1947, as amended, and for furnishing assistance to Iran pursuant to the provisions of the Mutual Defense Assistance Act of 1949, as amended (22 U.S.C. 1571–1604). In addition, unexpected balances of appropriations heretofore made for assistance to Greece and Turkey, available for the fiscal year 1951, pursuant to the Act of May 22, 1947, as amended, and for assistance to Iran pursuant to the Mutual Defense Assistance Act of 1949, as amended, are hereby authorized to be continued available through June 30, 1952, and to be consolidated with the appropriation authorized by this section.

SEC. 202. Whenever the President determines that such action is essential for the purpose of this Act, he may provide assistance, pursuant to the provisions of the Mutual Defense Assistance Act of 1949, as amended, to any country of the Near East area (other than those covered by section 201) and may utilize not to exceed 10 per centum of the amount made available (excluding balances of prior appropriations continued available) pursuant to section 201 of this Act: *Provided,* That any such assistance may be furnished only upon determination by the President that (1) the strategic location of the recipient country makes it of direct importance to the defense of the Near East area, (2) such assistance is of critical importance to the defense of the free nations, and (3) the immediately increased ability of the recipient country to defend itself is important to the preservation of the peace and security of the area and to the security of the United States.

SEC. 203. In order to further the purpose of this Act in Africa and the Near East, there are hereby authorized to be appropriated to the President, for the fiscal year 1952, not to exceed $160,000,000 for economic and technical assistance in Africa and the Near East in areas other than those covered by section 103 (a) of the Economic Cooperation Act of 1948, as amended. . . .

TITLE III—ASIA AND PACIFIC

SEC. 301. In order to carry out in the general area of China (including the Republic of the Philippines and the Republic of Korea) the provisions of subsection (a) of section 303 of the Mutual Defense Assistance Act of 1949, as amended, there are hereby authorized to be appropriated to the President for the fiscal year 1952, not to exceed $535,250,000. . . .

SEC. 302. (a) In order to further the purpose of this Act through the strengthening of the area covered in section 301 of this Act (but not including the Republic of Korea), there are hereby authorized to be appropriated to the President, for the fiscal year 1952, not to exceed $237,500,000 for economic and technical assistance in those portions of such area which the President deems to be not under Communist control. Funds appropriated pursuant to authority of this section shall be available under the applicable provisions of the Economic Cooperation Act of 1948, as amended, and of the Act for International Development. . . .

TITLE IV—AMERICAN REPUBLICS

SEC. 401. In order to further the purpose of this Act through the furnishing of military assistance to the other American Republics, there are hereby authorized to be appropriated to the President, for the fiscal year 1952, not to exceed $38,150,000 for carrying out the purposes of this section under the provisions of the Mutual Defense Assistance Act of 1949, as amended. . . .

TITLE V—ORGANIZATION AND GENERAL PROVISIONS

SEC. 501. (a) In order that the programs of military, economic, and technical assistance authorized by this Act may be administered as parts of a unified program in accordance with the intent of Congress and to fix responsibility for the coordination and supervision of these programs in a single person, the President is authorized to appoint in the Executive Office of the President a Director for Mutual Security. The Director on behalf of the President and subject to his direction, shall have primary responsibility for—

(1) continuous supervision and general direction of the assistance programs under this Act to the end that such programs shall be (A) effectively integrated both at home and abroad, and (B) administered so as to assure that the defensive strength of the free nations of the world shall be built as quickly as possible on the basis of continuous and effective self-help and mutual aid;

(2) preparation and presentation to the Congress of such programs of foreign military, economic, and technical assistance as may be required in the interest of the security of the United States;

(3) preparation for the President of the report to the Congress required by section 518 of this Act. . . .

SEC. 502. (a) The Economic Cooperation Administration and the offices of Administrator for Economic Cooperation. Deputy Administrator, United States Special Representative in Europe, and Deputy Special Representative are hereby abolished.

(b) To assist in carrying out the purpose of this Act—

(1) there is hereby established, its principal office at the seat of the government, a Mutual Security Agency, hereinafter referred to as the Agency, which shall be headed by the Director for Mutual Security; and

(2) there shall be transferred to the Director the powers, functions, and responsibilities conferred upon the Administration for Economic Cooperation by the Economic Cooperation Act of 1948, as amended, and by any other law, but no such powers, functions, and responsibilities, shall be exercised after June 30, 1952, except as provided in subsection (c) of this section.

(c) Not later than April 1, 1952, the President shall inform the Committee on Foreign Relations of the Senate and the

Committee on Foreign Affairs of the House of Representatives which of the powers, functions, and responsibilities transferred to the Director by subsection (b) (2) are found by the President to be necessary to enable the Director after June 30, 1952, to carry out the duties conferred upon him by section 503. The termination provisions of section 122 of the Economic Cooperation Act of 1948, as amended, shall come into effect on June 30, 1952, and none of the powers, functions, and responsibilities conferred by that Act shall be exercised after that date, except those powers, functions, and responsibilities found necessary to enable the Director to carry out the duties conferred on him by section 503 of this Act, which powers, functions, and responsibilities unless otherwise provided by law shall continue in effect until June 30, 1954. . . .

SEC. 503.   After June 30, 1952, the Director, on behalf of the President and subject to his direction, shall, in consultation with the Secretaries of State and Defense, continue to have primary responsibility for—

(a) the development and administration of programs of assistance designed to sustain and increase military effort, including production, construction, equipment and matériel in each country or in groups of countries which receive United States military assistance;

(b) the provision of such equipment, materials, commodities, services, financial, or other assistance as he finds to be necessary for carrying out mutual defense programs; and

(c) the provision of limited economic assistance to foreign nations for which the United States has responsibility as a result of participation in joint control arrangements when the President finds that the provision of such economic assistance is in the interest of the security of the United States. . . .

SEC. 513.   Whenever the President determines it to be necessary for the purpose of this Act, not to exceed 10 per centum of the funds made available under any title of this Act may be transferred to and consolidated with funds made available under any other title of this Act in order to furnish, to a different area, assistance of the kind for which such funds were available before transfer. Whenever the President makes any such determination, he shall forthwith notify the Committee on Foreign Relations of the Senate and the Committee on Foreign Affairs of the House of Representatives. In the case of the transfer of funds available for military purposes, he shall also forthwith notify the Committees on Armed Services of the Senate and House of Representatives.

SEC. 516.   It is hereby declared to be the policy of the Congress that this Act shall be administered in such a way as (1) to eliminate the barriers to, and provide the incentives for, a steadily increased participation of free private enterprise in developing the resources of foreign countries consistent with the policies of this Act, (2) to the extent that it is feasible and does not interfere with the achievement of the purposes set forth in this Act, to discourage the cartel and monopolistic business practices prevailing in certain countries receiving aid under this Act which result in restricting production and increasing prices, and to encourage where suitable competition and productivity, and (3) to encourage where suitable the development and strengthening of the free labor union movements as the collective bargaining agencies of labor within such countries. . . .

SEC. 529.   If the President determines that the furnishing of assistance to any nation—

(a) is no longer consistent with the national interest or security of the United States or the policies and purpose of this Act; or

(b) would contravene a decision of the Security Council of the United Nations; or

(c) would be inconsistent with the principle that members of the United Nations should refrain from giving assistance to any nation against which the Security Council or the General Assembly has recommended measures in case of a threat to, or breach of, the peace, or act of aggression,

he shall terminate all or part of any assistance furnished pursuant to this Act. The function conferred herein shall be in addition to all other functions heretofore conferred with respect to the termination of military, economic, or technical assistance. . . .

598. YOUNGSTOWN SHEET & TUBE CO. v. SAWYER
343 U. S. 579
1952

This decision is one of the few instances in our history where the court has restrained the executive power. In December, 1951, in the midst of the Korean War, steelworkers gave notice of intent to strike. Intervention by the Federal Mediation Service and the Wage Stabilization Board failed, and the steelworkers' union called a strike for April 4, 1952. On the ground that a strike would jeopardize national security, President Truman directed Secretary of Commerce Sawyer to take over and operate the affected steel mills. One of the mills challenged the constitutionality of this order and asked for an injunction against the Secretary of Commerce; the District Court granted the injunction; the Court of Appeals stayed the injunction, and the case came on appeal to the Supreme Court. See H. Truman, *Memoirs, Vol. II;* C. Rossiter, *Supreme Court and the Commander in Chief;* C. Rossiter, *Constitutional Dictatorship;* E.S. Corwin, *The President, Office and Powers;* B.M. Rich, *The Presidents and Civil Disorder;* Grover Cleveland, *The Government in the Chicago Strike of 1894;* E. Berman, *Labor Disputes and the President;* E.S. Corwin "Steel Seizure Case," 53 Columbia L. Rev., 53. Appendix I to this case provides a "synoptic analysis of Legislation authorizing seizure of Industrial Property."

BLACK, J. We are asked to decide whether the President was acting within his constitutional power when he issued an order directing the Secretary of Commerce to take possession of and operate most of the Nation's steel mills. The mill owners argue that the President's order amounts to lawmaking, a legislative function which the Constitution has expressly confided to the Congress and not to the President. The Government's position is that the order was made on findings of the President that his action was necessary to avert a national catastrophe which would inevitably result from a stoppage of steel production, and that in meeting this grave emergency the President was acting within the aggregate of his constitutional powers as the Nation's Chief Executive and the Commander in Chief of the Armed Forces of the United States. . . .

Two crucial issues have developed: *First.* Should final determination of the constitutional validity of the President's order be made in this case which has proceeded no further than the preliminary injunction stage? *Second.* If so, is the seizure order within the constitutional power of the President? . . .

The President's power, if any, to issue the order must stem either from an act of Congress or from the Constitution itself. There is no statute that expressly authorizes the President to take possession of property as he did here. Nor is there any act of Congress to which our attention has been directed from which such a power can fairly be implied. Indeed, we do not understand the Government to rely on statutory authorization for this seizure. There are two statutes which do authorize the President to take both personal and real property under certain conditions. However, the Government admits that these conditions were not met and that the President's order was not rooted in either of the statutes. The Government refers to the seizure provisions of one of these statutes (Sec. 201 (b) of the Defense Production Act) as "much too cumbersome, involved, and time-consuming for the crisis which was at hand."

Moreover, the use of the seizure technique to solve labor disputes in order to prevent work stoppages was not only unauthorized by any congressional enactment; prior to this controversy, Congress had refused to adopt that method of settling labor disputes. When the Taft-Hartley Act was under consideration in 1947, Congress rejected an amendment which would have authorized such governmental seizures in cases of emergency. Apparently it was thought that the technique of seizure, like that of compulsory arbitration, would interfere with the process of collective bargaining. Consequently, the plan adopted in that Act did not provide for seizure under any circumstances. Instead, the plan sought to bring about settlements by use of the customary devices of mediation, conciliation, investigation by boards of inquiry, and public reports. In some instances temporary injunctions were authorized to provide cooling-off periods. All this failing, unions were left free to strike after a secret vote by employees as to whether they wished to accept their employer's final settlement offer.

It is clear that if the President had authority to issue the order he did, it must be found in some provisions of the Constitution. And it is not claimed that express constitutional language grants this power to the President. The contention is that presidential power should be implied from the aggregate of his powers under the Constitution. Particular reliance is placed on provisions in Article II which say that "the executive Power shall be vested in a President . . ." ; that "he shall take Care that the Laws be faithfully executed"; and that he "shall be Commander in Chief of the Army and Navy of the United States."

The order cannot properly be sustained as an exercise of the President's military power as Commander in Chief of the Armed Forces. The Government attempts to do so by citing a number of cases upholding broad powers in military commanders engaged in day-to-day fighting in a theater of war. Such cases need not concern us here. Even though "theater of war" be an expanding concept, we cannot with faithfulness to our constitutional system hold that the Commander in Chief of the Armed Forces has the ultimate power as such to take possession of private property in order to keep labor disputes from stopping production. This is a job for the Nation's lawmakers, not for its military authorities.

Nor can the seizure order be sustained because of the several constitutional provisions that grant executive power to the President. In the framework of our Constitution, the President's power to see that the laws are faithfully executed refutes the idea that he is to be a lawmaker. The Constitution limits his functions in the lawmaking process to the recommending of laws he thinks wise and the vetoing of laws he thinks bad. And the Constitution is neither silent nor equivocal about who shall make laws which the President is to execute. The first section of the first article says that "All legislative Powers herein granted shall be vested in a Congress of the United States. . . ." After granting many powers to the Congress, Article I goes on to provide that Congress may "make all Laws which shall be necessary and proper for carrying into Execution the foregoing Powers and all other Powers vested by this Constitution in the Government of the United States, or in any Department or Officer thereof."

The President's order does not direct that a congressional policy be executed in a manner prescribed by Congress—it directs that a presidential policy be executed in a manner prescribed by the President. The preamble of the order itself, like that of many statutes, sets out reasons why the President believes certain policies should be adopted, proclaims that these policies as rules of conduct to be followed, and again, like a statute, authorizes a government official to promulgate additional rules and regulations consistent with the policy proclaimed and needed to carry that policy into execution. The power of Congress to adopt such public policies as those proclaimed by the order is beyond question. It can authorize the taking of private property for public use. It can make laws regulating the relationships between employers and employees, prescribing rules designed to settle labor disputes, and fixing wages and working conditions in certain fields of our economy. The Constitution did not subject this law-making power of Congress to presidential or military supervision or control.

It is said that other Presidents without congressional authority have taken possession of private business enterprises in order to settle labor disputes. But even if this be true, Congress has not thereby lost its exclusive constitutional authority to make laws necessary and proper to carry out the powers vested by the Constitution "in the Government of the United States, or in any Department or Officer thereof."

The Founders of this Nation entrusted the law making power to the Congress alone in both good and bad times. It would do no good to recall the historical events, the fears of power and the hopes for freedom that lay behind their choice. Such a review would but confirm our holding that this seizure order cannot stand.

The Judgment of the District Court is affirmed.

VINSON, C. J., dissenting: . . . In passing upon the question of Presidential powers in this case, we must first consider the context in which those powers were exercised.

Those who suggest that this is a case involving extraordinary powers should be mindful that these are extraordinary times. A world not yet recovered from the devastation of World War II has been forced to face the threat of another and more terrifying global conflict. . . . For almost two full years, our armed forces have been fighting in Korea, suffering casualties of over 108,000 men. Hostilities have not abated. The "determination of the United Nations to continue its action in Korea to meet the aggression" has been reaffirmed. Congressional support of the action in Korea has been manifested by provisions for increased military manpower and equipment and for economic stabilization, as hereinafter described. . . .

Even this brief review of our responsibilities in the world community discloses the enormity of our undertaking. Success of these measures may, as has often been observed, dramatically influence the lives of many generations of the world's peoples yet unborn. Alert to our responsibilities, which coincide with our own self preservation through mutual security, Congress has enacted a large body of implementing legislation. . . .

Congress recognized the impact of these defense programs upon the economy. Following the attack in Korea, the President asked for authority to requisition property and to allocate and fix priorities for scarce goods. In the Defense Production Act of 1950, Congress granted the powers requested and, *in addition,* granted power to stabilize prices and wages and to provide for settlement of labor disputes arising in the defense program. . . .

The President has the duty to execute the foregoing legislative programs. Their successful execution depends upon continued production of steel and stabilized prices for steel. Accordingly, when the collective bargaining agreements between the Nation's steel producers and their employees, represented by the United Steel Workers, were due to expire on December 31, 1951, and a strike shutting down the entire basic steel industry was threatened, the President acted to avert a complete shutdown of steel production. . . . We . . . assume without deciding that the courts may go behind a President's finding of fact that an emergency exists. But there is not the slightest basis for suggesting that the President's finding in this case can be undermined. Plaintiffs moved for a preliminary injunction before answer or hearing. Defendant opposed the motion, filing uncontroverted affidavits of Government officials describing the facts underlying the President's order.

Secretary of Defense Lovett swore that "a work stoppage in the steel industry will result immediately in serious curtailment of production of essential weapons and munitions of all kinds." He illustrated by showing that 84% of the national production of certain alloy steel is currently used for production of military-end items and that 35% of total production of another form of steel goes into ammunition, 80% of such ammunition now going to Korea. The Secretary of Defense stated that: "We are holding the line (in Korea) with ammunition and not with the lives of our troops."

Affidavits of the Chairman of the Atomic Energy Commission, the Secretary of the Interior, defendant as Secretary of Commerce, and the Administrators of the Defense Production Administration, the National Production Authority, the General Services Administration and the Defense Transport Administration were also filed in the District Court. These affidavits disclose an enormous demand for steel in such vital defense programs as the expansion of facilities in atomic energy, petroleum, power, transportation and industrial production, including steel production. Those charged with administering allocations and priorities swore to the vital part steel production plays in our economy. The affidavits emphasize the critical need for steel in our defense program, the absence of appreciable inventories of steel, and the drastic results of any interruption in steel production. . . .

Accordingly, if the President has any power under the Constitution to meet a critical situation in the absence of express statutory authorization, there is no basis whatever for criticizing the exercise of such power in this case.

The steel mills were seized for a public use. The power of eminent domain, invoked in this case, is an essential attribute of sovereignty and has long been recognized as a power of the Federal Government. . . .

Admitting that the Government could seize the mills, plaintiffs claim that the implied power of eminent domain can be exercised only under an Act of Congress; under no circumstances, they say, can that power be exercised by the President unless he can point to an express provision in enabling legislation. This was the view adopted by the District Judge when he granted the preliminary injunction. . . .

Under this view, the President is left powerless at the very moment when the need for action may be most pressing and when no one, other than he, is immediately capable of action. Under this view, he is left powerless because a power not expressly given to Congress is nevertheless found to rest exclusively with Congress.

Consideration of this view of executive impotence calls for further examination of the nature of the separation of powers under our tripartite system of Government. . . .

The whole of the "executive Power" is vested in the President. Before entering office, the President swears that he "will faithfully execute the Office of President of the United States, and will to the best of (his) ability, preserve, protect and defend the Constitution of the United States." Art. II, sec. 1.

This comprehensive grant of the executive power to a single person was bestowed soon after the country had thrown the yoke of monarchy. Only by instilling initiative and vigor in all of the three departments of Government, declared Madison, could tyranny in any form be avoided. . . . It is thus apparent that the Presidency was deliberately fashioned as an office of power and independence. Of course, the Framers created no autocrat capable of arrogating any power unto himself at any time. But neither did they create an automaton impotent to exercise the powers of Govern-

ment at a time when the survival of the Republic itself may be at stake.

In passing upon the grave constitutional question presented in this case, we must never forget, as Chief Justice Marshall admonished, that the Constitution is "intended to endure for ages to come, and consequently, to be adapted to the various *crises* of human affairs," and that "(i)ts means are adequate to its ends." Cases do arise presenting questions which could not have been foreseen by the Framers. In such cases, the Constitution has been treated as a living document adaptable to new situations. But we are not called upon today to expand the Constitution to meet a new situation. For, in this case, we need only look to history and time-honored principles of constitutional law—principles that have been applied consistently by all branches of the Government throughout our history. It is those who assert the invalidity of the Executive Order who seek to amend the Constitution in this case. . . .

The broad executive power granted by Article II to an officer on duty 365 days a year cannot, it is said, be invoked to avert disaster. Instead, the President must confine himself to sending a message to Congress recommending action. Under this messenger-boy concept of the Office, the President cannot even act to preserve legislative programs from destruction so that Congress will have something left to act upon. There is no judicial finding that the executive action was unwarranted because there was in fact no basis for the President's finding of the existence of an emergency for, under this view, the gravity of the emergency and the immediacy of the threatened disaster are considered irrelevant as a matter of law.

Seizure of the plaintiffs' property is not a pleasant undertaking. Similarly unpleasant to a free country are the draft which disrupts the home and military procurement which causes economic dislocation and compels adoption of price controls, wage stabilization and allocation of materials. The President informed Congress that even a temporary Government operation of plaintiffs' properties was "thoroughly distasteful" to him, but was necessary to prevent immediate paralysis of the mobilization program.

Presidents have been in the past, and any man worthy of the Office should be in the future, free to take at least interim action necessary to execute legislative programs essential to survival of the Nation. A sturdy judiciary should not be swayed by the un-pleasantness or unpopularity of necessary executive action, but must independently determine for itself whether the President was acting, as required by the Constitution, to "take Care that the laws be faithfully executed."

599. TRUMAN'S VETO OF THE McCARRAN-WALTER IMMIGRATION ACT
June 25, 1952

(82nd Congress, 2nd Session, *House Doc.* No. 520)

The McCarran-Walter Immigration Act continued the basic quota system of immigration adopted in 1924. It included new provisions to prevent the admission of possible subversives and to permit the expulsion of dangerous aliens. President Truman vetoed the bill on constitutional and other grounds, but Congress passed it over his veto by a vote of 278 to 133 in the House and 57 to 26 in the Senate. See P. Tyler, ed., *Immigration and the United States;* U.S. President's Commission on Immigration and Naturalization, *Whom We Shall Welcome;* B. M. Ziegler, ed., *Immigration.*

To the House of Representatives:

I return herewith, without my approval, H. R. 5678, the proposed Immigration and Nationality Act.

In outlining my objections to this bill, I want to make it clear that it contains certain provisions that meet with my approval. This is a long and complex piece of legislation. It has 164 separate sections, some with more than 40 subdivisions. It presents a difficult problem of weighing the good against the bad, and arriving at a judgment on the whole.

H. R. 5678 is an omnibus bill which would revise and codify all of our laws relating to immigration, naturalization, and nationality.

A general revision and modernization of these laws unquestionably is needed and long overdue, particularly with respect to immigration. But this bill would not provide us with an immigration policy adequate for the present world situation. Indeed, the bill, taking all its provisions together, would be a step backward and not a step forward. In view of the crying need for reform in the field of immigration, I deeply regret that I am unable to approve H. R. 5678.

In recent years our immigration policy has become a matter of major national concern. Long dormant questions about the effect of our immigration laws now assume first-rate importance. What we do in the field of immigration and naturalization is vital to the continued growth and internal development of the United States—to the economic and social strength of our country —which is the core of the defense of the free world. Our immigration policy is equally, if not more, important to the conduct of our foreign relations and to our responsibilities of moral leadership in the struggle for world peace.

In one respect, this bill recognizes the great international significance of our immigration and naturalization policy, and takes a step to improve existing laws. All racial bars to naturalization would be removed, and at least some minimum immigration quota would be afforded to each of the free nations of Asia.

I have long urged that racial or national barriers to naturalization be abolished. This was one of the recommendations in my civil-rights message to the Congress on February 2, 1948. On February 19, 1951, the House of Representatives unanimously passed a bill to carry it out.

But now this most desirable provision comes before me embedded in a mass of legislation which would perpetuate injustices of long standing against many other nations of the world, hamper the efforts we are making to rally the men of the east and west alike to the cause of freedom, and intensify the repressive and inhumane aspects of our immigration procedures. The price is too high and, in good conscience, I cannot agree to pay it. . . .

In addition to removing racial bars to naturalization, the bill would permit American women citizens to bring their alien husbands to this country as nonquota immigrants, and enable alien husbands of resident women aliens to come in under the quota in a preferred status. These provisions would be a step toward preserving the integrity of the family under our immigration laws, and are clearly desirable. . . .

But these few improvements are heavily outweighed by other provisions of the bill which retain existing defects in our laws, and add many undesirable new features.

The bill would continue, practically without change, the national origins quota system, which was enacted into law in 1924, and put into effect in 1929. This quota system—always based upon assumptions at variance with our American ideals—is long since out of date and more than ever unrealistic in the face of present world conditions.

This system hinders us in dealing with current immigration problems, and is a constant handicap in the conduct of our foreign relations. As I stated in my message to Congress on March 24, 1952, on the need for an emergency program of immigration from Europe:

> "Our present quota system is not only inadequate to meet present emergency needs, it is also an obstacle to the development of an enlightened and satisfactory immigration policy for the long-run future."

The inadequacy of the present quota system has been demonstrated since the end of the war, when we were compelled to resort to emergency legislation to admit displaced persons. If the quota system remains unchanged, we shall be compelled to resort to similar emergency legislation again, in order to admit any substantial portion of the refugees from communism or the victims of overcrowding in Europe.

With the idea of quotas in general there is no quarrel. Some numerical limitation must be set, so that immigration will be within our capacity to absorb. But the over-all limitation of numbers imposed by the national origins quota system is too small for our needs today, and the country by country limitations create a pattern that is insulting to large numbers of our finest citizens, irritating to our allies abroad, and foreign to our purposes and ideals.

The over-all quota limitation, under the law of 1924, restricted annual immigration to approximately 150,000. This was about one-seventh of 1 percent of our total population in 1920. Taking into account the growth in population since 1920, the law now allows us but one-tenth of 1 percent of our total population. And since the largest national quotas are only partly used, the number actually coming in has been in the neighborhood of one-fifteenth of 1 percent. This is far less than we must have in the years ahead to keep up with the growing needs of our Nation for manpower to maintain the strength and vigor of our economy.

The greatest vice of the present quota system, however, is that it discriminates, deliberately and intentionally, against many of the peoples of the world. The purpose behind it was to cut down and virtually eliminate immigration to this country from southern and eastern Europe. A theory was invented to rationalize this objective. The theory was that in order to be readily assimilable, European immigrants should be admitted in proportion to the numbers of persons of their respective national stocks already here as shown by the census of 1920. Since Americans of English, Irish, and German descent were most numerous, immigrants of those three nationalities got the lion's share—more than two-thirds—of the total quota. The remaining third was divided up among all the other nations given quotas.

The desired effect was obtained. Immigration from the newer sources of Southern and Eastern Europe was reduced to a trickle. The quotas allotted to England and Ireland remained largely unused, as was intended. Total quota immigration fell to a half or a third—and sometimes even less—of the annual limit of 154,000. People from such countries as Greece, or Spain, or Latvia were virtually deprived of any opportunity to come here at all, simply because Greeks or

Spaniards or Latvians had not come here before 1920 in any substantial numbers.

The idea behind this discriminatory policy was, to put it baldly, that Americans with English or Irish names were better people and better citizens than Americans with Italian or Greek or Polish names. It was thought that people of West European origin made better citizens than Rumanians or Yugoslavs or Ukrainians or Hungarians or Balts or Austrians. Such a concept is utterly unworthy of our traditions and our ideals. It violates the great political doctrine of the Declaration of Independence that "all men are created equal." It denies the humanitarian creed inscribed beneath the Statue of Liberty proclaiming to all nations, "Give me your tired, your poor, your huddled masses yearning to breathe free."

It repudiates our basic religious concepts, our belief in the brotherhood of man, and in the words of St. Paul that "there is neither Jew nor Greek, there is neither bond nor free, . . . for ye are all one in Christ Jesus."

The basis of this quota system was false and unworthy in 1924. It is even worse now. At the present time this quota system keeps out the very people we want to bring in. It is incredible to me that, in this year of 1952, we should again be enacting into law such a slur on the patriotism, the capacity, and the decency of a large part of our citizenry. . . .

The time to shake off this dead weight of past mistakes is now. The time to develop a decent policy of immigration—a fitting instrument for our foreign policy and a true reflection of the ideals we stand for, at home and abroad—is now. In my earlier message on immigration, I tried to explain to the Congress that the situation we face in immigration is an emergency—that it must be met promptly. I have pointed out that in the last few years, we have blazed a new trail in immigration, through our displaced persons program. Through the combined efforts of the Government and private agencies, working together not to keep people out, but to bring qualified people in, we summoned our resources of good will and human feeling to meet the task. In this program we have found better techniques to meet the immigration problems of the 1950's.

None of this fruitful experience of the last 3 years is reflected in this bill before me. None of the crying human needs of this time of trouble is recognized in this bill. But it is not too late. The Congress can remedy these defects, and it can adopt legislation to meet the most critical problems before adjournment. . . .

I now wish to turn to the other provisions of the bill, those dealing with the qualifications of aliens and immigrants for admission, with the administration of the laws, and with problems of naturalization and nationality. In these provisions, too, I find objections that preclude my signing this bill.

The bill would make it even more difficult to enter our country. Our resident aliens would be more easily separated from homes and families under grounds of deportation, both new and old, which would specifically be made retroactive. Admission to our citizenship would be made more difficult; expulsion from our citizenship would be made easier. Certain rights of native-born, first-generation Americans would be limited. All our citizens returning from abroad would be subjected to serious risk of unreasonable invasions of privacy. Seldom has a bill exhibited the distrust evidenced here for citizens and aliens alike—at a time when we need unity at home and the confidence of our friends abroad. . . .

I am asked to approve the reenactment of highly objectionable provisions now contained in the Internal Security Act of 1950 —a measure passed over my veto shortly after the invasion of South Korea. Some of these provisions would empower the Attorney General to deport any alien who has engaged or has had a purpose to engage in activities "prejudicial to the public interest" or "subversive to the national security." No standards or definitions are provided to guide discretion in the exercise of powers so sweeping. To punish undefined "activities" departs from traditional American insistence on established standards of guilt. To punish an undefined "purpose" is thought control.

These provisions are worse than the infamous Alien Act of 1798, passed in a time of national fear and distrust of foreigners, which gave the President power to deport any alien deemed "dangerous to the peace and safety of the United States." Alien residents were thoroughly frightened and citizens much disturbed by that threat to liberty.

Such powers are inconsistent with our democratic ideals. Conferring powers like that upon the Attorney General is unfair to him as well as to our alien residents. Once fully informed of such vast discretionary powers vested in the Attorney General, Americans now would and should be just as alarmed as Americans were in 1798 over less drastic powers vested in the President.

Heretofore, for the most part, deportation and exclusion have rested upon findings of fact made upon evidence. Under this bill, they would rest in many instances upon the "opinion" or "satisfaction" of immigration or consular employees. The change from objective findings to subjective feelings is not compatible with our system of justice. The result would be to restrict or eliminate judicial review of unlawful administrative action. . . .

Many of the aspects of the bill which have been most widely criticized in the public debate are reaffirmations or elabora-tions of existing statutes or administrative procedures. Time and again, examination discloses that the revisions of existing law that would be made by the bill are intended to solidify some restrictive practice of our immigration authorities, or to overrule or modify some ameliorative decision of the Supreme Court or other Federal courts. By and large, the changes that would be made by the bill do not depart from the basically restrictive spirit of our existing laws—but intensify and reinforce it.

These conclusions point to an underlying condition which deserves the most careful study. Should we not undertake a reassessment of our immigration policies and practices in the light of the conditions that face us in the second half of the twentieth century? The great popular interest which this bill has created, and the criticism which it has stirred up, demand an affirmative answer. I hope the Congress will agree to a careful reexamination of this entire matter. . . .

HARRY S TRUMAN.

600. UNITED STATES v. RUMELY
345 U. S. 41
1953

This is the leading case on the rights of witnesses before Congressional investigating committees. At a time when the investigative function of Congress was assuming increasing importance, it placed important limitations upon the powers of Congressional committees. The exact extent of these limitations was not clear, however, since the Court as a whole did not confront the constitutional questions discussed in the Douglas opinion. See T. Taylor, *Grand Inquest*; C. Fairman, *Mr. Justice Miller and the Supreme Court*; E. J. Eberling, *Congressional Investigations*; J. E. Johnson, *The Investigating Powers of Congress*; M. N. McGeary, *The Developments of Congressional Investigative Power*. For an analogous case in the lower courts, see Philip Wittenberg, ed., *The Lamont Case*.

DOUGLAS, J. . . . Of necessity I come to the constitutional questions. Respondent represents a segment of the American press. Some may like what his group publishes; others may disapprove. These tracts may be the essence of wisdom to some; to others their point of view and philosophy may be anathema. To some ears their words may be harsh and repulsive; to others they may carry the hope of the future. We have here a publisher who through books and pamphlets seeks to reach the minds and hearts of the American people. He is different in some respects from other publishers. But the differences are minor. Like the publishers of newspapers, magazines, or books, this publisher bids for the minds of men in the market place of ideas. The aim of the historic struggle for a free press was "to establish and preserve the right of the English people to full information in respect of the doings or misdoings of their government." Grosjean v. American Press Co., 297 U.S. 233, 247, . . . That is the tradition behind the First Amendment. Censorship or previous restraint is banned. . . . Discriminatory taxation is outlawed. . . . The privilege of pamphleteering, as well as the more orthodox types of publications, may neither be licensed, . . . Door to door distribution is privileged. . . . These are illustrative of the preferred position granted speech and the press by the First Amendment. . . .

If the present inquiry were sanctioned the press would be subjected to harassment that in practical effect might be as serious as censorship. A publisher, compelled to register with the federal government, would be subjected to vexatious inquiries. A requirement that a publisher disclose the identity of those who buy his books, pamphlets, or papers is indeed the beginning of surveillance of the press. True, no legal sanction is involved here. Congress has imposed no tax, established no board of censors, instituted no licensing system. But the potential restraint is equally severe. The finger of government leveled against the press is ominous. Once the government can demand of a publisher the names of the purchasers of his publications, the free press as we know it disappears. Then the spectre of a government agent will look over the shoulder of everyone who reads. The purchase of a book or pamphlet today may result in a subpoena tomorrow. Fear of criticism goes with every person into the bookstall. The subtle, imponderable pressures of the orthodox lay hold. Some will fear to read what is unpopular, what the powers-that-be dislike. When the light of publicity may reach any student, any teacher, inquiry will be discouraged. The books and pamphlets that are critical of the administration, that preach an unpopular policy in domestic or foreign affairs, that are in disrepute in the orthodox school of thought will be suspect and subject to investigation. The press and its readers will pay a heavy price in harrassment. But that will be minor in comparison with the menace of the shadow which government will cast over literature that does not follow the dominant party line. If the lady from Toledo can be required to disclose what she read yesterday and what she will read tomorrow, fear will take the place of freedom in the libraries, bookstores, and homes of the land. Through the harassment of hearings, investigations, reports, and subpoenas government will hold a club over speech and over the press. Congress could not do this by law. The power of investigation is also limited. Inquiry into personal and private affairs is precluded. . . . And so is any matter in respect to which no valid legislation could be had. . . . Since Congress could not by law require of respondent what the House demanded, it may not take the first step in an inquiry ending in fine or imprisonment.

601. EISENHOWER'S SECURITY PROGRAM— EXECUTIVE ORDER 10450
April 27, 1953
(*Federal Register*, Vol. 18, p. 2489)

President Eisenhower reorganized the government's security program in 1953. Executive Order 10450 extended the security system to all agencies of the government and replaced the Truman criterion of disloyalty as the basis for dismissing government employees with the new criterion of "security risk." See Doc. No. 576. This new criterion permitted the discharge of any person whose employment was for any reason not "clearly consistent with the interests of national security." In 1956 the Supreme Court held that this order applied only to workers in "sensitive" positions. See Doc. No. 619. See A. Yarmolinsky, *Case Studies in Personal Security;* W. Gellhorn, *Individual Freedom and Governmental Restraints;* J. R. Wiggins, *Freedom or Security; Current History,* October 1955.

WHEREAS the interests of the national security require that all persons privileged to be employed in the departments and agencies of the Government shall be reliable, trustworthy, of good conduct and character, and of complete and unswerving loyalty to the United States; and

WHEREAS the American tradition that all persons should receive fair, impartial, and equitable treatment at the hands of the Government requires that all persons seeking the privilege of employment or privileged to be employed in the departments and agencies of the Government be adjudged by mutually consistent and no less than minimum standards and procedures among the departments and agencies governing the employment and retention in employment of persons in the Federal service . . . it is hereby ordered as follows:

SECTION 1. In addition to the departments and agencies specified in the said act of August 26, 1950, and Executive Order No. 10237 of April 26, 1951, the provisions of that act shall apply to all other departments and agencies of the Government.

SEC. 2. The head of each department and agency of the Government shall be responsible for establishing and maintaining within his department or agency an effective program to insure that the employment and retention in employment of any civilian officer or employee within the department or agency is clearly consistent with the interests of the national security.

SEC. 3. (a) The appointment of each civilian officer or employee in any department or agency of the Government shall be made subject to investigation. The scope of the investigation shall be determined in the first instance according to the degree of adverse effect the occupant of the position sought to be filled could bring about, by virtue of the nature of the position, on the national security, but in no event shall the investigation include less than a national agency check (including a check of the fingerprint files of the Federal Bureau of Investigation), and written inquiries to appropriate local law-enforcement agencies, former employers and supervisors, references, and schools attended by the person under investigation: *Provided,* that upon request of the head of the department or agency concerned, the Civil Service Commission may, in its discretion, authorize such less investigation as may meet the requirements of the national security with respect to per-diem, intermittent, temporary, or seasonal employees, or aliens employed outside the United States. Should there develop at any stage of investigation information indicating that the employment of any such person may not be clearly consistent with the interests of the national security, there shall be conducted with respect to such person a full field investigation, or such less investigation as shall be sufficient to enable the head of the department or agency concerned to determine whether retention of such person is clearly consistent with the interests of the national security. . . .

SEC. 6. Should there develop at any stage of investigation information indicating that the employment of any officer or employee of the Government may not be clearly consistent with the interests of the national security, the head of the department or agency concerned or his representative shall immediately suspend the employment of the person involved if he deems such suspension necessary in the interests of the national security and, following such investigation and review as he deems necessary, the head of the department or agency concerned shall terminate the employment of such suspended officer or employee whenever he shall determine such termination necessary or advisable in the interests of the national security, in accordance with the said act of August 26, 1950.

SEC. 7. Any person whose employment is suspended or terminated under the authority granted to heads of departments and agencies by or in accordance with the said act of August 26, 1950, or pursuant to the said Executive Order No. 9835 or any other security or loyalty program relating to officers or employees of the Government, shall not be reinstated or restored to duty or reemployed in the same department or agency, and shall not be reemployed in any other department or agency, unless the head of the department or agency concerned finds that such reinstatement, restoration, or reemployment is clearly consistent with the interests of the national security, which finding shall be made a part of the records of such department or agency: *Provided,* that no person whose employment has been terminated under such authority thereafter may be employed by any other department or agency except after a determination by the Civil Service Commission that such person is eligible for such employment.

SEC. 8.(a) The investigations conducted pursuant to this order shall be designed to develop information as to whether the employment or retention in employment in the Federal service of the person being investigated is clearly consistent with the interests of the national security. Such information shall relate, but shall not be limited, to the following:

(1) Depending on the relation of the Government employment to the national security:

(i) Any behavior, activities, or associations which tend to show that the individual is not reliable or trustworthy.

(ii) Any deliberate misrepresentations, falsifications, or omission of material facts.

(iii) Any criminal, infamous, dishonest, immoral, or notoriously disgraceful conduct, habitual use of intoxicants to excess, drug addiction, or sexual perversion.

(iv) An adjudication of insanity, or treatment for serious mental or neurological disorder without satisfactory evidence of cure.

(v) Any facts which furnish reason to believe that the individual may be subjected to coercion, influence, or pressure which may cause him to act contrary to the best interests of the national security.

(2) Commission of any act of sabotage, espionage, treason, or sedition, or attempts thereat or preparation therefor, or conspiring with, or aiding or abetting, another to commit or attempt to commit any act of sabotage, espionage, treason, or sedition.

(3) Establishing or continuing a sympathetic association with a saboteur, spy, traitor, seditionist, anarchist, or revolutionist, or with an espionage or other secret agent or representative of a foreign nation, or any representative of a foreign nation whose interests may be inimical to the interests of the United States, or with any person who advocates the use of force or violence to overthrow the government of the United States or the alteration of the form of government of the United States by unconstitutional means.

(4) Advocacy of use of force or violence to overthrow the government of the United States, or of the alteration of the form of government of the United States by unconstitutional means.

(5) Membership in, or affiliation or sympathetic association with, any foreign or domestic organization, association, movement, group, or combination of persons which is totalitarian, Fascist, Communist, or subversive, or which has adopted, or shows, a policy of advocating or approving the commission of acts of force or violence to deny other persons their rights under the Constitution of the United States, or which seeks to alter the form of government of the United States by unconstitutional means.

(6) Intentional, unauthorized disclosure to any person of security information, or of other information disclosure of which is prohibited by law, or willful violation or disregard of security regulations.

(7) Performing or attempting to perform his duties, or otherwise acting, so as to serve the interests of another government in preference to the interests of the United States. . . .

DWIGHT D. EISENHOWER.

602. SUBMERGED LANDS ACT OF 1953
May 22, 1953
(Public Law 31, 83rd Congress)

This act settled a long-standing controversy over the development of natural resources, particularly oil, off the shores of the United States. The issue of state versus federal control over these resources involved two further questions: first, should these resources be exploited for the benefit of individual states or for the benefit of the nation as a whole; second, should these resources be developed by private corporations or by public agencies. In 1947 and again in 1950, the Supreme Court declared that the federal government had exclusive rights to these submerged lands, see U.S. v. California 332 U.S. 19, U.S. v. Louisiana 339 U.S. 699, and U.S. v. Texas 339 U.S. 707. In 1952, President Truman assigned the offshore oil resources to the Navy as a reserve for use in time of war. These actions were nullified by the Submerged Lands Act of 1953, which assigned federal rights to the offshore lands to the seaboard states. The question of the extent of state title to tidelands, however, remained to vex future administrations. See E. R. Bartley, *The Tidelands Oil Controversy;* Fulton, *Sovereignty of the Sea;* Masterson, *Jurisdiction in Marginal Seas;* Jessup, *Law of Territorial Waters and Maritime Jurisdiction.*

AN ACT

To confirm and establish the titles of the States to lands beneath navigable waters within State boundaries and to the natural resources within such lands and waters, to provide for the use and control of said lands and resources, and to confirm the jurisdiction and control of the United States over the natural resources of the seabed of the Continental Shelf seaward of State boundaries.

SEC. 3. *Rights of the States.—*
(a) It is hereby determined and declared to be in the public interest that (1) title to and ownership of the lands beneath navigable waters within the boundaries of the respective States, and the natural resources within such lands and waters and (2) the right and power to manage, administer, lease, develop, and use the said lands and natural resources all in accordance with applicable State law be, and they are hereby, subject to the provisions hereof, recognized, confirmed, established, and vested in and assigned to the respective States or the persons who were on June 5, 1950, entitled thereto under the law of the respective States in which the land is located, and the respective grantees, lessees, or successors in interest thereof;

(b) (1) The United States hereby releases and relinquishes unto said States and persons aforesaid, except as otherwise reserved herein, all right, title, and interest of the United States, if any it has, in and to all said lands, improvements, and natural resources; (2) the United States hereby releases and relinquishes all claims of the United States, if any it has, for money or damages arising out of any operations of said States or persons pursuant to State authority upon or within said lands and navigable waters; . . . .

(d) Nothing in this Act shall affect the use, development, improvement, or control by or under the constitutional authority of the United States of said lands and waters for the purposes of navigation or flood control or the production of power, or be construed as the release or relinquishment of any rights of the United States arising under the constitutional authority of Congress to regulate or improve navigation, or to provide for flood control, or the production of power; . . . .

SEC. 4. *Seaward Boundaries.—*The seaward boundary of each original coastal State is hereby approved and confirmed as a line three geographical miles distant from its coast line or, in the case of the Great Lakes, to the international boundary. Any State admitted subsequent to the formation of the Union which has not already done so may extend its seaward boundaries to a line three geographical miles distant from its coast line, or to the international boundaries of the United States in the Great Lakes or any other body of water traversed by such boundaries. Any claim heretofore or hereafter asserted either by constitutional provision, statute, or otherwise, indicating the intent of a State so to extend its boundaries is hereby approved and confirmed, without prejudice to its claim, if any it has, that its boundaries extend beyond that line. Nothing in this section is to be construed as questioning or in any manner prejudicing the existence of any State's seaward boundary beyond three geographical miles if it was so provided by its constitution or laws prior to or at the time such State became a member of the Union, or if it has been heretofore approved by Congress. . . .

SEC. 6. *Powers Retained by the United States.—*(a) The United States retains all its navigational servitude and rights in and powers of regulation and control of said lands and navigable waters for the constitutional purposes of commerce, navigation, national defense, and international affairs, all of which shall be paramount to, but shall not be deemed to include, proprietary rights of ownership, or the rights of management, administration, leasing, use, and development of the lands and natural resources which are specifically recognized, confirmed, established, and vested in and assigned to the respective States and others by section 3 of this Act.

(b) In time of war or when necessary for national defense, and the Congress or the President shall so prescribe, the United States shall have the right of first refusal to purchase at the prevailing market price, all or any portion of the said natural resources, or to acquire and use any portion of said lands by proceeding in accordance with due process of law and paying just compensation therefor. . . .

603. EISENHOWER'S ATOMS FOR PEACE PROGRAM
December 8, 1953
(*Department of State Publication 5314*)

Atomic power misused threatened to end human life; wisely used it held out the promise of a better life for all mankind. At the end of 1953, President Eisenhower directed the attention of the world community to the enormous potential for good inherent in the development of atomic energy. In a speech to the United Nations he proposed that the major scientific nations of the world jointly contribute to a pool of atomic power resources to be used for socially desirable purposes. The President thus aroused the hopes of the world that in the long run atomic energy would redound to the benefit of the world community. See International Conference on the Peaceful Uses of Atomic Energy, *Proceedings 1955;* A. H. Compton, *Atomic Quest;* G. Dean, *Report on the Atom;* R. E. Lapp, *Atoms and People;* U.S. Congress Joint Committee on Atomic Energy, *Peaceful Uses of Atomic Energy.*

MADAME PRESIDENT, MEMBERS OF THE GENERAL ASSEMBLY:

I feel impelled to speak today in a language that in a sense is new—one which I, who have spent so much of my life in the military profession, would have preferred never to use.

That new language is the language of atomic warfare.

The atomic age has moved forward at such a pace that every citizen of the world should have some comprehension, at least in comparative terms, of the extent of this development, of the utmost significance to every one of us. Clearly, if the peoples of the world are to conduct an intelligent search for peace, they must be armed with the significant facts of today's existence.

My recital of atomic danger and power is necessarily stated in United States terms, for these are the only incontrovertible facts that I know. I need hardly point out to this Assembly, however, that this subject is global, not merely national in character.

On July 16, 1945, the United States set off the world's first atomic explosion.

Since that date in 1945, the United States of America has conducted 42 test explosions.

Atomic bombs today are more than 25 times as powerful as the weapons with which the atomic age dawned, while hydrogen weapons are in the ranges of millions of tons of TNT equivalent.

Today, the United States' stockpile of atomic weapons, which, of course, increases daily, exceeds by many times the explosive equivalent of the total of all bombs and all shells that came from every plane and every gun in every theatre of war in all of the years of World War II.

A single air group, whether afloat or land-based, can now deliver to any reachable target a destructive cargo exceeding in power all the bombs that fell on Britain in all of World War II.

In size and variety, the development of atomic weapons has been no less remarkable. The development has been such that atomic weapons have virtually achieved conventional status within our armed services. In the United States, the Army, the Navy, the Air Force, and the Marine Corps are all capable of putting this weapon to military use.

But the dread secret, and the fearful engines of atomic might, are not ours alone.

In the first place, the secret is possessed by our friends and allies, Great Britain and Canada, whose scientific genius made a tremendous contribution to our original discoveries, and the designs of atomic bombs.

The secret is also known by the Soviet Union.

The Soviet Union has informed us that, over recent years, it has devoted extensive resources to atomic weapons. During this period, the Soviet Union has exploded a series of atomic devices, including at least one involving thermo-nuclear reactions.

If at one time the United States possessed what might have been called a monopoly of atomic power, that monopoly ceased to exist several years ago. Therefore, although our earlier start has permitted us to accumulate what is today a great quantitative advantage, the atomic realities of today comprehend two facts of even greater significance.

First, the knowledge now possessed by several nations will eventually be shared by others—possibly all others.

Second, even a vast superiority in numbers of weapons, and a constant capability of devastating retaliation, is no preventive, of itself, against the fearful material damage and toll of human lives that would be inflicted by surprise aggression.

The free world, at least dimly aware of these facts, has naturally embarked on a large program of warning and defense systems. That program will be accelerated and expanded.

But let no one think that the expenditure of vast sums for weapons and systems of defense can guarantee absolute safety for the cities and citizens of any nation. The awful arithmetic of the atomic bomb does not permit of any such easy solution. Even against the most powerful defense, an aggressor in possession of the effective minimum number of atomic bombs for a surprise attack could probably place a sufficient number of his bombs on the chosen targets to cause hideous damage.

Should such an atomic attack be launched against the United States, our reactions would be swift and resolute. But for me to say that the defense capabilities of the United States are such that they could inflict terrible losses upon an aggressor—for me to say that the retaliation capabilities of the United States are so great that such an aggressor's land would be laid waste—all this, while fact, is not the true expression of the purpose and the hope of the United States.

To pause there would be to confirm the hopeless finality of a belief that two atomic colossi are doomed malevolently to eye each other indefinitely across a trembling world. To stop there would be to accept helplessly the probability of civilization destroyed—the annihilation of the irreplaceable heritage of mankind handed down to us generation from generation—and the condemnation of mankind to begin all over again the age-old struggle upward from savagery toward decency, and right, and justice.

Surely no sane member of the human race could discover victory in such desolation. Could anyone wish his name to be coupled by history with such human degradation and destruction.

Occasional pages of history do record the faces of the "Great Destroyers" but the whole book of history reveals mankind's never-ending quest for peace, and mankind's God-given capacity to build.

It is with the book of history, and not with isolated pages, that the United States will ever wish to be identified. My country wants to be constructive, not destructive. It wants agreements, not wars, among nations. It wants itself to live in freedom, and in the confidence that the people of every other nation enjoy equally the right of choosing their own way of life.

So my country's purpose is to help us move out of the dark chamber of horrors into the light, to find a way by which the minds of men, the hopes of men, the souls of men everywhere, can move forward toward peace and happiness and well being.

In this quest, I know that we must not lack patience.

I know that in a world divided, such as ours today, salvation cannot be attained by one dramatic act.

I know that many steps will have to be taken over many months before the world can look at itself one day and truly realize that a new climate of mutually peaceful confidence is abroad in the world.

But I know, above all else, that we must start to take these steps—NOW. . . .

There is at least one new avenue of peace which has not yet been well explored—an avenue now laid out by the General Assembly of the United Nations.

In its resolution of November 18th, 1953, this General Assembly suggested—and I quote—"that the Disarmament Commission study the desirability of establishing a subcommittee consisting of representatives of the Powers principally involved, which should seek in private an acceptable solution . . . and report on such a solution to the General Assembly and to the Security Council not later than 1 September 1954."

The United States, heeding the suggestion of the General Assembly of the United Nations, is instantly prepared to meet privately with such other countries as may be "principally involved," to seek "an acceptable solution" to the atomic armaments race which overshadows not only the peace, but the very life, of the world.

We shall carry into these private or diplomatic talks a new conception.

The United States would seek more than the mere reduction or elimination of atomic materials for military purposes.

It is not enough to take this weapon out of the hands of the soldiers. It must be put into the hands of those who will know how to strip its military casing and adapt it to the arts of peace.

The United States knows that if the fearful trend of atomic military buildup can be reversed, this greatest of destructive forces can be developed into a great boon, for the benefit of all mankind.

The United States knows that peaceful power from atomic energy is no dream of the future. That capability, already proved, is here—now—today. Who can doubt, if the entire body of the world's scientists and engineers had adequate amounts of fissionable material with which to test and develop their ideas, that this capability would rapidly be transformed into universal, efficient, and economic usage.

To hasten the day when fear of the atom will begin to disappear from the minds of people, and the governments of the East and West, there are certain steps that can be taken now.

I therefore make the following proposals:

The Governments principally involved, to the extent permitted by elementary prudence, to begin now and continue to make joint contributions from their stockpiles of normal uranium and fissionable materials to an International Atomic Energy Agency. We would expect that such an agency would be set up under the aegis of the United Nations.

The ratios of contributions, the procedures and other details would properly be within the scope of the "private conversations" I have referred to earlier.

The United States is prepared to undertake these explorations in good faith. Any partner of the United States acting in the same good faith will find the United States a not unreasonable or ungenerous associate.

Undoubtedly initial and early contributions to this plan would be small in quantity. However, the proposal has the great virtue that it can be undertaken without the irritations and mutual suspicions incident to any attempt to set up a completely acceptable system of world-wide inspection and control.

The Atomic Energy Agency could be made responsible for the impounding, storage, and protection of the contributed fissionable and other materials. The ingenuity of our scientists will provide special safe conditions under which such a bank of fissionable material can be made essentially immune to surprise seizure.

The more important responsibility of this Atomic Energy Agency would be to devise methods whereby this fissionable material would be allocated to serve the peaceful pursuits of mankind. Experts would be mobilized to apply atomic energy to the needs of agriculture, medicine, and other peaceful activities. A special purpose would be to provide abundant electrical energy in the power-starved areas of the world. Thus the contributing powers would be dedicating some of their strength to serve the needs rather than the fears of mankind.

The United States would be more than willing—it would be proud to take up with others "principally involved" the development of plans whereby such peaceful use of atomic energy would be expedited.

Of those "principally involved" the Soviet Union must, of course, be one.

I would be prepared to submit to the Congress of the United States, and with every expectation of approval, any such plan that would:

First—encourage world-wide investigation into the most effective peacetime uses of fissionable material, and with the certainty that they had all the material needed for the conduct of all experiments that were appropriate;

Second—to begin to diminish the potential destructive power of the world's atomic stockpiles;

Third—allow all peoples of all nations to see that, in this enlightened age, the great powers of the earth, both of the East and of the West, are interested in human aspirations first, rather than in building up the armaments of war;

Fourth—open up a new channel for peaceful discussion, and initiate at least a new approach to the many difficult problems that must be solved in both private and public conversations, if the world is to shake off the inertia imposed by fear, and is to make positive progress toward peace.

Against the dark background of the atomic bomb, the United States does not wish merely to present strength, but also the desire and the hope for peace.

The coming months will be fraught with fateful decisions. In this Assembly; in the capitals and military headquarters of the world; in the hearts of men everywhere, be they governors or governed, may they be the decisions which will lead this world out of fear and into peace.

To the making of these fateful decisions, the United States pledges before you—and therefore before the world—its determination to help solve the fearful atomic dilemma—to devote its entire heart and mind to find the way by which the miraculous inventiveness of man shall not be dedicated to his death, but consecrated to his life. . . .

604. THE BRICKER AMENDMENT
January-February, 1954
(*Congressional Record*, January 28, February 4, 26, 1954)

The internationalist tendency of American foreign policy did not receive unanimous support from the American people. A powerful minority of neo-isolationists sought to check our increasing involvement in world affairs through the so-called Bricker amendment whose purpose was to restrict the power of the executive branch to make treaties and agreements that might limit American sovereignty. President Eisenhower expressed opposition to the Bricker amendment in a letter sent to the majority leader of the Senate on January 25, 1954. The Senate rejected the Bricker proposal on February 25 by a vote of 42 to 50. On February 26, Senator Walter F. George proposed a watered-down version of the Bricker amendment. This version received an affirmative two-thirds majority of 61 to 30 in its first test in the Senate. On the crucial motion to send the proposed amendment to the states the vote was 60 to 31, one less than the necessary two-thirds majority. This marked the high tide of support for the proposal to limit the treaty-making powers of the President. The whole incident is important not only as a manifestation of the struggle over interventionism in foreign policy but also as an example of the recurring struggle for power between the President and Congress. See G. A. Schubert, Jr., "Politics and the Constitution: the Bricker Amendment during 1953," 16 *Journal of Politics*, 257; Q. Wright, "Congress and the Treaty-Making Power," *Amer. Soc. of Int'l. Law Proceedings*, 1952, p. 43; H. S. Commager, "The Perilous Folly of Senator Bricker," *Reporter Magazine*, October 13, 1953.

1. PROPOSED AMENDMENT
"*Article*—

SEC. 1. Clause 2 of Article VI of the Constitution of the United States is hereby amended by adding at the end thereof; Notwithstanding the foregoing provisions of this clause, no treaty made after the establishment of this Constitution shall be the supreme law of the land unless made in pursuance of this Constitution.

SEC. 2. A provision of a treaty or other international agreement which conflicts with this Constitution shall not be of any force or effect.

SEC. 3. A treaty or other international

agreement shall become effective as internal law in the United States only through legislation by the Congress unless in advising and consenting to a treaty the Senate, by a vote of two-thirds of the Senators present and voting, shall provide that such treaty may become effective as internal law without legislation by the Congress.

SEC. 4. On the question of consenting to the ratification of a treaty the vote shall be determined by yeas and nays, and the names of the persons voting for and against shall be entered on the Journal of the Senate.

2. EISENHOWER LETTER ON THE BRICKER AMENDMENT

The White House
Washington, January 25, 1954.
DEAR SENATOR KNOWLAND:

In response to your inquiry, I give the following as my attitude toward the proposal for amending the treaty-making functions of the Federal Government.

I am unalterably opposed to the Bricker Amendment as reported by the Senate Judiciary Committee. It would so restrict the conduct of foreign affairs that our country could not negotiate the agreements necessary for the handling of our business with the rest of the world. Such an amendment would make it impossible for us to deal effectively with friendly nations for our mutual defense and common interests.

These matters are fundamental. We cannot hope to achieve and maintain peace if we shackle the Federal Government so that it is no longer sovereign in foreign affairs. The President must not be deprived of his historic position as the spokesman for the nation in its relations with other countries.

Adoption of the Bricker Amendment in its present form by the Senate would be notice to our friends as well as our enemies abroad that our country intends to withdraw from its leadership in world affairs. The inevitable reaction would be of major proportion. It would impair our hopes and plans for peace and for the successful achievement of the important international matters now under discussion. This would include the diversion of atomic energy from warlike to peaceful purposes.

I fully subscribe to the proposition that no treaty or international agreement can contravene the Constitution. I am aware of the feeling of many of our citizens that a treaty may override the Constitution. So that there can be no question on this point, I will gladly support an appropriate amendment that will make this clear for all time.
Sincerely,

DWIGHT D. EISENHOWER.

3. THE GEORGE RESOLUTION

"Article—

SEC. 1. A provision of a treaty or other international agreement which conflicts with this Constitution shall not be of any force or effect.

SEC. 2. An international agreement other than a treaty shall become effective as internal law in the United States only by an act of the Congress.

SEC. 3. On the question of advising and consenting to the ratification of a treaty the vote shall be determined by yeas and nays, and the names of the persons voting for and against shall be entered on the Journal of the Senate.

SEC. 4. This article shall be inoperative unless it shall have been ratified as an amendment to the Constitution by the legislatures of three-fourths of the several States within 7 years from the date of its submission.

605. SECRETARY DULLES' STRATEGY OF MASSIVE RETALIATION
January 12, 1954
(*Department of State Bulletin,* Vol. XXX, pp. 107–110)

The Eisenhower administration made two changes in the nation's military policy. First, the size of the military establishment was cut. Second, a new emphasis was placed upon atomic weapons in the nation's military planning. Secretary of State Dulles explained these changes as a new approach to military strategy, declaring that the United States planned in the future to rely on the threat of "massive retaliation" to "deter" Communist aggression. See J. R. Beal, *John Foster Dulles;* W. Reitzel, M. Kaplan and C. Coblenz, *United States Foreign Policy 1945-1955;* C. B. Marshall, *The Limits of Foreign Policy;* G. F. Kennan, *Realities of American Foreign Policy;* P. H. Nitze, "Atoms, Strategy and Policy," 34 *Foreign Affairs,* 187; T. K. Finletter, *Power and Policy;* H. A. Kissinger, "Military Policy and Defense of the 'Grey' Areas," 33 *Foreign Affairs,* 416.

We live in a world where emergencies are always possible, and our survival may depend upon our capacity to meet emergencies. Let us pray that we shall always have that capacity. But, having said that, it is necessary also to say that emergency measures—however good for the emergency—do not necessarily make good permanent policies. Emergency measures are costly; they are superficial; and they imply that the enemy has the initiative. They cannot be depended on to serve our long-time interests.

This "long time" factor is of critical importance. The Soviet Communists are planning for what they call "an entire historical era," and we should do the same. They seek, through many types of maneuvers, gradually to divide and weaken the free nations by overextending them in efforts which, as Lenin put it, are "beyond their strength, so that they come to practical bankruptcy." Then, said Lenin, "our victory is assured." Then, said Stalin, will be "the moment for the decisive blow."

In the face of this strategy, measures cannot be judged adequate merely because they ward off an immediate danger. It is essential to do this, but it is also essential to do so without exhausting ourselves.

When the Eisenhower administration applied this test, we felt that some transformations were needed. It is not sound military strategy permanently to commit U. S. land forces to Asia to a degree that leaves us no strategic reserves. It is not sound economics, or good foreign policy, to support permanently other countries; for in the long run, that creates as much ill will as good will. Also, it is not sound to become permanently committed to military expenditures so vast they lead to "practical bankruptcy."

Change was imperative to assure the stamina needed for permanent security. But it was equally imperative that change should be accompanied by understanding of our true purposes. Sudden and spectacular change had to be avoided. Otherwise, there might have been a panic among our friends and miscalculated aggression by our enemies. We can, I believe, make a good report in these respects.

We need allies and collective security. Our purpose is to make these relations more effective, less costly. This can be done by placing more reliance on deterrent power and less dependence on local defensive power.

This is accepted practice so far as local communities are concerned. We keep locks on our doors, but we do not have an armed guard in every home. We rely principally on a community security system so well equipped to punish any who break in and steal that, in fact, would-be aggressors are generally deterred. That is the modern way of getting maximum protection at a bearable cost. What the Eisenhower administration seeks is a similar international security system. We want, for ourselves and the other free nations, a maximum deterrent at a bearable cost.

Local defense will always be important. But there is no local defense which alone will contain the mighty land power of the Communist world. Local defenses must be reinforced by the further deterrent of massive retaliatory power. A potential aggressor must know that he cannot always prescribe battle conditions that suit him. Otherwise, for example, a potential aggressor, who is glutted with manpower, might be tempted to attack in confidence that resistance would be confined to manpower. He might be tempted to attack in places where his superiority was decisive.

The way to deter aggression is for the free community to be willing and able to respond vigorously at places and with means of its own choosing.

So long as our basic policy concepts were unclear, our military leaders could not be selective in building our military power. If an enemy could pick his time and place and method of warfare—and if our policy was to remain the traditional one of meeting aggression by direct and local opposition—then we needed to be ready to fight in the Arctic and in the Tropics; in Asia, the Near East, and in Europe; by sea, by land, and by air; with old weapons and with new weapons. . . .

Before military planning could be changed, the President and his advisers, as represented by the National Security Council, had to take some basic policy decisions. This has been done. The basic decision was to depend primarily upon a great capacity to retaliate, instantly, by means and at places of our choosing. Now the Department of Defense and the Joint Chiefs of Staff can shape our military establishment to fit what is *our* policy, instead of having to try to be ready to meet the enemy's many choices. That permits of a selection of military means instead of a multiplication of means. As a result, it is now possible to get, and share, more basic security at less cost.

Let us now see how this concept has been applied to foreign policy, taking first the Far East.

In Korea this administration effected a major transformation. The fighting has been stopped on honorable terms. That was possible because the aggressor, already thrown back to and behind his place of beginning, was faced with the possibility that the fighting might, to his own great peril, soon spread beyond the limits and methods which he had selected.

The cruel toll of American youth and the nonproductive expenditure of many billions have been stopped. Also our armed forces are no longer largely committed to the Asian mainland. We can begin to create a strategic reserve which greatly improves our defensive posture.

This change gives added authority to the warning of the members of the United Nations which fought in Korea that, if the Communists renewed the aggression, the United Nations response would not necessarily be confined to Korea.

I have said in relation to Indochina that, if there were open Red Chinese army aggression there, that would have "grave consequences which might not be confined to Indochina." . . .

In the ways I outlined we gather strength for the long-term defense of freedom. We do not, of course, claim to have found some magic formula that insures against all forms of Communist successes. It is normal that at some times and at some places there may be setbacks to the cause of freedom. What we do expect to insure is that any setbacks will have only temporary and local significance, because they will leave unimpaired those free world assets which in the long run will prevail.

If we can deter such aggression as would mean general war, and that is our confident resolve, then we can let time and fundamentals work for us. . . .

606. ATOMIC ENERGY COMMISSION DECISION IN OPPENHEIMER CASE
June 29, 1954
(U. S. Atomic Energy Commission Press Release)

Dr. J. Robert Oppenheimer played a major role in the development of the atomic bomb by American scientists during the Second World War. After the war, Dr. Oppenheimer served as consultant to the Atomic Energy Commission. In the spring of 1954, a special Personnel Security Board headed by Gordon Gray voted 2 to 1 to class Dr. Oppenheimer as a security risk, deny him access to restricted government data, and suspend him from his position as consultant to the Atomic Energy Program. The decision was accompanied by an unusual opinion which pronounced Oppenheimer devotedly loyal, unusually discreet, and a public servant whose contribution could never be repaid. On June 29, 1954, the Atomic Energy Commission upheld the decision of the Gray Board by a vote of 4 to 1. The majority and minority opinions of the AEC not only reflected basic differences in judgment of Dr. Oppenheimer but also basic differences in judgment concerning the proper approach to the problem of security in a democratic state. Informed opinion throughout the country was sharply critical of the conclusions of the majority of the Commission. See J. and S. Alsop, *We accuse;* W. Gellhorn, *Security, Loyalty, and Science;* U.S. Atomic Energy Commission, *In the Matter of J. Robert Oppenheimer;* E. Rabinowitch, "What Is a Security Risk?" *Bulletin of Atomic Scientists,* June 1954; C. P. Curtis, *The Oppenheimer Case;* Eleanor Bontecou, *The Federal Loyalty-Security Program;* Morton Grodzins, *The Loyal and the Disloyal;* Alan Westin, *The Constitution and Loyalty Programs;* Alan Barth, *Government by Investigation.*

UNITED STATES ATOMIC ENERGY COMMISSION

Washington 25, D. C., June 29, 1954.

The issue before the Commission is whether the security of the United States warrants Dr. J. Robert Oppenheimer's continued access to restricted data of the Atomic Energy Commission. The data to which Dr. Oppenheimer has had until recently full access include some of the most vital secrets in the possession of the United States.

Having carefully studied the pertinent documents—the transcript of the hearings before the Personnel Security Board (Gray Board), the findings and recommendation of the Board, the briefs of Dr. Oppenheimer's counsel, and the findings and recommendation of the General Manager—we have concluded that Dr. Oppenheimer's clearance for access to restricted data should not be reinstated.

The Atomic Energy Act of 1946 lays upon the Commissioners the duty to reach a determination as to "the character, associations, and loyalty" of the individuals engaged in the work of the Commission. Thus, disloyalty would be one basis for disqualification, but it is only one. Substantial defects of character and imprudent and dangerous associations, particularly with known subversives who place the interests of foreign powers above those of the United States, are also reasons for disqualification.

On the basis of the record before the Commission, comprising the transcript of the hearing before the Gray Board as well as reports of Military Intelligence and the Federal Bureau of Investigation, we find Dr. Oppenheimer is not entitled to the continued confidence of the Government and of this Commission because of the proof of fundamental defects in his "character."

In respect to the criterion of "associations," we find that his associations with persons known to him to be Communists have extended far beyond the tolerable limits of prudence and self-restraint which are to be expected of one holding the high positions that the Government has continuously entrusted to him since 1942. These associations have lasted too long to be justified as merely the intermittent and accidental revival of earlier friendships. . . .

In weighing the matter at issue, we have taken into account Dr. Oppenheimer's past contributions to the atomic energy program. At the same time, we have been mindful of the fact that the positions of high trust and responsibility which Dr. Oppenheimer has occupied carried with them a commensurately high obligation of unequivocal character and conduct on his part. A Government official having access to the most sensitive areas of restricted data and to the innermost details of national war plans and weapons must measure up to exemplary standards of reliability, self-discipline, and trustworthiness. Dr. Oppenheimer has fallen far short of acceptable standards.

The record shows that Dr. Oppenheimer has consistently placed himself outside the rules which govern others. He has falsified in matters wherein he was charged with grave responsibilities in the national interest. In his associations he has repeatedly exhibited a willful disregard of the normal and proper obligations of security. . . .

Dr. Oppenheimer's persistent and willful disregard for the obligations of security is evidenced by his obstruction of inquiries by security officials. The record shows . . . instances where Dr. Oppenheimer has refused to answer inquiries of Federal officials on security matters or has been deliberately misleading.

"Associations" is a factor which, under the law, must be considered by the Commission. Dr. Oppenheimer's close association with Communists is another part of the pattern of his disregard of the obligations of security.

Dr. Oppenheimer, under oath, admitted to the Gray Board that from 1937 to at least 1942 he made regular and substantial contributions in cash to the Communist Party. He has admitted that he was a "fellow traveler" at least until 1942. He admits that he attended small evening meetings at private homes at which most, if not all, of the others present were Communist Party members. He was in contact with officials of the Communist Party, some of whom had been engaged in espionage. His activities were of such a nature that these Communists looked upon him as one of their number.

However, Dr. Oppenheimer's early Communist associations are not in themselves a controlling reason for our decision.

They take on importance in the context of his persistent and continuing association with Communists, including his admitted meetings with Haakon Chevalier in Paris as recently as last December—the same individual who had been intermediary for the Soviet Consulate in 1943.

On February 25, 1950, Dr. Oppenheimer wrote a letter to Chevalier attempting "to clear the record with regard to your alleged involvement in the atom business." Chevalier used this letter in connection with his application to the State Department for a United States passport. Later that year Chevalier came and stayed with Dr. Oppenheimer for several days at the latter's home. In December 1953, Dr. Oppenheimer visited with Chevalier privately on two occasions in Paris, and lent his name to Chevalier's dealings with the United States Embassy in Paris on a problem which, according to Dr. Oppenheimer, involved Chevalier's clearance. Dr. Oppenheimer admitted that today he has only a "strong guess" that Chevalier is not active in Communist Party affairs.

These episodes separately and together present a serious picture. It is clear that for one who has had access for so long to the most vital defense secrets of the Government and who would retain such access if his clearance were continued, Dr. Oppenheimer has defaulted not once but many times upon the obligations that should and must be willingly borne by citizens in the national service.

Concern for the defense and security of the United States requires that Dr. Oppenheimer's clearance should not be reinstated.

Dr. J. Robert Oppenheimer is hereby denied access to restricted data.

LEWIS L. STRAUSS, *Chairman.*
EUGENE M. ZUCKERT, *Commissioner.*
JOSEPH CAMPBELL, *Commissioner.*

DISSENTING OPINION
OF HENRY DE WOLF SMYTH

I dissent from the action of the Atomic Energy Commission in the matter of Dr. J. Robert Oppenheimer. I agree with the "clear conclusion" of the Gray Board that he is completely loyal and I do not believe he is a security risk. It is my opinion that his clearance for access to restricted data should be restored.

In a case such as this, the Commission

is required to look into the future. It must
determine whether Dr. Oppenheimer's continued employment by the Government of
the United States is in the interests of the
people of the United States. This prediction
must balance his potential contribution to
the positive strength of the country against
the possible danger that he may weaken the
country by allowing important secrets to
reach our enemies.

Since Dr. Oppenheimer is one of the most
knowledgable and lucid physicists we have,
his services could be of great value to the
country in the future. Therefore, the only
question being determined by the Atomic
Energy Commission is whether there is a
possibility that Dr. Oppenheimer will intentionally or unintentionally reveal secret information to persons who should not have
it. To me, this is what is meant within our
security system by the term security risk.
Character and associations are important
only insofar as they bear on the possibility
that secret information will be improperly
revealed.

In my opinion the most important evidence in this regard is the fact that there
is no indication in the entire record that
Dr. Oppenheimer has ever divulged any secret information. The past 15 years of his
life have been investigated and reinvesti-
gated. For much of the last 11 years he has
been under actual surveillance, his movements watched, his conversations noted, his
mail and telephone calls checked. This professional review of his actions has been
supplemented by enthusiastic amateur help
from powerful personal enemies.

After reviewing the massive dossier and
after hearing some forty witnesses, the Gray
Board reported on May 27, 1954, that Dr.
Oppenheimer "seems to have had a high
degree of discretion reflecting an unusual
ability to keep to himself vital secrets." My
own careful reading of the complete dossier
and of the testimony leads me to agree with
the Gray Board on this point. I am confident
that Dr. Oppenheimer will continue to keep
to himself all the secrets with which he is
entrusted. . . .

The history of Dr. Oppenheimer's contributions to the development of nuclear weapons stands untarnished.

It is clear that Dr. Oppenheimer's past

associations and activities are not newly discovered in any substantial sense. They have
been known for years to responsible authorities who have never been persuaded that
they rendered Dr. Oppenheimer unfit for
public service. Many of the country's outstanding men have expressed their faith in
his integrity.

In spite of all this, the majority of the
Commission now concludes that Dr. Oppenheimer is a security risk. I cannot accept
this conclusion or the fear behind it. In my
opinion the conclusion cannot be supported
by a fair evaluation of the evidence.

To be effective a security system must be
realistic. In the words of the Atomic Energy
Commission security criteria:

"The facts of each case must be carefully
weighed and determination made in the
light of all the information presented, whether favorable or unfavorable. The judgment
of responsible persons as to the integrity
of the individuals should be considered. The
decision as to security clearance is an over-
all, commonsense judgment, made after
consideration of all the relevant information
as to whether or not there is risk that the
granting of security clearance would endanger the common defense or security."

Application of this standard of overall
commonsense judgment to the whole record
destroys any pattern of suspicious conduct
or catalog of falsehoods and evasions, and
leaves a picture of Dr. Oppenheimer as an
able, imaginative human being with normal
human weaknesses and failings. In my opinion the conclusion drawn by the majority
from the evidence is so extreme as to endanger the security system. . . .

With respect to the alleged disregard of
the security system, I would suggest that the
system itself is nothing to worship. It is a
necessary means to an end. Its sole purpose,
apart from the prevention of sabotage, is
to protect secrets. If a man protects the
secrets he has in his hands and his head, he
has shown essential regard for the security
system.

In addition, cooperation with security officials in their legitimate activities is to be
expected of private citizens and Government
employees. The security system has, however, neither the responsibility nor the right
to dictate every detail of a man's life. I

frankly do not understand the charge made by the majority that Dr. Oppenheimer has shown a persistent and willful disregard for the obligations of security, and that therefore he should be declared a security risk. No gymnastics of rationalization allow me to accept this argument. If in any recent instances, Dr. Oppenheimer has misunderstood his obligation to security, the error is occasion for reproof but not for a finding that he should be debarred from serving his country. Such a finding extends the concept of "security risk" beyond its legitimate justification and constitutes a dangerous precedent.

In these times, failure to employ a man of great talents may impair the strength and power of this country. Yet I would accept this loss if I doubted the loyalty of Dr. Oppenheimer or his ability to hold his tongue. I have no such doubts.

I conclude that Dr. Oppenheimer's employment "will not endanger the common defense and security" and will be "clearly consistent with the interests of the national security." I prefer the positive statement that Dr. Oppenheimer's further employment will continue to strengthen the United States.

I therefore have voted to reinstate Dr. Oppenheimer's clearance.

HENRY D. SMYTH, *Commissioner.*

607. AMERICAN INTERVENTION IN GUATEMALA
June 30, 1954
(State Department Press Release, June 30, 1954)

American diplomats devoted little time to the problems of Latin America in the years following the Second World War. Their activities centered upon Europe and Asia. During this period, Communism gained its first foothold in Latin America. The tiny state of Guatemala came under the control of a government willing and able to do business with the Communist bloc. When Guatemala received a shipment of arms from Communist Czechoslovakia, Secretary of State Dulles reacted vigorously. He secured the support of all North and South American states except Guatamala for a declaration condemning the spread of Communist influence to the Western Hemisphere, then encouraged anti-Communist groups in Guatemala to stage a successful revolt against the pro-Communist government. To allay widespread criticism of American policy, Secretary Dulles analyzed the whole Guatemalan situation in a radio address of June 30, 1954. See C. Urrutia-Aparitio, "Guatemala's Withdrawal from the Organization of Central American States," 48 *American Journal of International Law,* 145; A. P. Whitaker, *The Hemispheric Idea;* J. Gillin and K. H. Silvert, "Ambiguities in Guatemala," 34 *Foreign Affairs,* 469.

. . . In Guatemala, international Communism had an initial success. It began ten years ago when a revolution occurred in Guatemala. The revolution was not without justification. But the Communist seized on it, not as an opportunity for real reforms, but as a chance to gain political power.

Communist agitators devoted themselves to infiltrating the public and private organizations of Guatemala. They sent recruits to Russia and other Communist countries for revolutionary training and indoctrination in such institutions as the Lenin School in Moscow. Operating in the guise of "reformers" they organized the workers and peasants under Communist leadership. Having gained control of what they call "mass organizations" they moved on to take over the official press and radio of the Guatemalan Government. They dominated the Social Security organization and ran the agrarian reform program. Through the technique of the "popular front" they dictated to the Congress and the President.

The judiciary made one valiant attempt to protect its integrity and independence. But the Communists, using their control of the legislative body, caused the Supreme Court to be dissolved when it refused to give approval to a Communist-contrived law. Arbenz, who until this week was President of Guatemala, was openly manipulated by the leaders of Communism.

Guatemala is a small country. But its

power, standing alone, is not a measure of the threat. The master plan of international Communism is to gain a solid political base in this hemisphere, a base that can be used to extend Communist penetration to the other peoples of the other American Governments. It was not the power of the Arbenz Government that concerned us but the power behind it.

If world Communism captures any American State, however small, a new and perilous front is established which will increase the danger to the entire free world and require even greater sacrifices from the American people.

This situation in Guatemala had become so dangerous that the American States could not ignore it. At Caracas last March the American States held their Tenth Inter-American Conference. They then adopted a momentous statement. They declared that "the domination or control of the political institutions of any American State by the international communist movement . . . would constitute a threat to the sovereignty and political independence of the American States, endangering the peace of America."

There was only one American State that voted against this Declaration. That State was Guatemala.

This Caracas Declaration precipitated a dramatic chain of events. From their European base the Communist leaders moved rapidly to build up the military power of their agents in Guatemala. In May a large shipment of arms moved from behind the Iron Curtain into Guatemala. The shipment was sought to be secreted by false manifests and false clearances. Its ostensible destination was changed three times while en route.

At the same time, the agents of international Communism in Guatemala, intensified efforts to penetrate and subvert the neighboring Central American States. They attempted political assassinations and political strikes. They used consular agents for political warfare.

Many Guatemalan people protested against their being used by Communist dictatorship to serve the Communist's lust for power. The response was mass arrests, the suppression of constitutional guarantees, the killing of opposition leaders and other brutal tactics normally employed by Communism to secure the consolidation of its power.

In the face of these events and in accordance with the spirit of the Caracas Declaration, the nations of this hemisphere laid further plans to grapple with the danger. The Arbenz Government responded with an effort to disrupt the inter-American system. Because it enjoyed the full support of Soviet Russia, which is on the Security Council, it tried to bring the matter before the Security Council. It did so without first referring the matter to the American regional organization as is called for both by the United Nations Charter itself and by the treaty creating the American Organization.

The Foreign Minister of Guatemala openly connived in this matter with the Foreign Minister of the Soviet Union. The two were in open correspondence and ill-concealed privity. The Security Council at first voted overwhelmingly to refer the Guatemala matter to the Organization of American States. The vote was ten to one. But that one negative vote was a Soviet veto.

Then the Guatemalan Government, with a Soviet backing, redoubled its efforts to supplant the American States system by Security Council jurisdiction.

However, last Friday, the United Nations Security Council decided not to take up the Guatemalan matter, but to leave it in the first instance to the American States themselves. That was a triumph for the system of balance between regional organization and world organization, which the American States had fought for when the Charter was drawn up at San Francisco.

The American States then moved promptly to deal with the situation. Their "peace commission" left yesterday for Guatemala. Earlier the Organization of American States had voted overwhelmingly to call a meeting of their Foreign Ministers to consider the penetration of international Communism in Guatemala and the measures required to eliminate it. Never before has there been so clear a call uttered with such a sense of urgency and strong resolve.

Throughout the period I have outlined, the Guatemalan Government and Communist agents throughout the world have persistently attempted to obscure the real issue—that of Communist imperialism—by claiming that the United States is only interested in protecting American business. We regret that there have been disputes between the Guatemalan Government and the United Fruit Company. We have urged repeatedly that these disputes be submitted for settlement to an international tribunal or to international arbitration. That is the way to dispose of problems of this sort. But this issue is relatively unimportant. All who know the temper of the U.S. people and Government must realize that our overriding concern is that which, with others, we recorded at Caracas, namely the endangering by international Communism of the peace and security of this hemisphere.

The people of Guatemala have now been heard from. Despite the armaments piled up by the Arbenz Government, it was unable to enlist the spiritual cooperation of the people.

Led by Colonel Castillo Armas, patriots arose in Guatemala to challenge the Communist leadership—and to change it. Thus, the situation is being cured by the Guatemalans themselves.

Last Sunday, President Arbenz of Guatemala resigned and seeks asylum. Others are following his example.

Tonight, just as I speak, Colonel Castillo Armas is in conference in El Salvador with Colonel Monzon, the head of the Council which has taken over the power in Guatemala City. It was this power that the just wrath of the Guatemalan people wrested from President Arbenz who then took flight.

Now the future of Guatemala lies at the disposal of the Guatemalan people themselves. It lies also at the disposal of leaders loyal to Guatemala who have not treasonably become the agents of an alien despotism which sought to use Guatemala for its own evil ends.

608. COMMUNIST CONTROL ACT OF 1954
August 24, 1954
(*Public Law 637, 83rd Congress*)

The government's program to prevent subversion from within culminated in the Communist Control Act of 1954 outlawing the Communist Party. See Docs. No. 531, 574, 591, 601; S. H. Hofstadter, *The Fifth Amendment and the Immunity Act of 1954;* C. A. Auerbach, "Communist Control Act of 1954, 23 *U. of Chicago Law Review,* 173; M. L. Ernst and D. L. Loth, *Report on the American Communist;* R. K. Carr, *The House Committee on Un-American Activities, 1945–1950.*

AN ACT

To outlaw the Communist Party, to prohibit members of Communist organizations from serving in certain representative capacities, and for other purposes.

SEC. 2. The Congress hereby finds and declares that the Communist Party of the United States, although purportedly a political party, is in fact an instrumentality of a conspiracy to overthrow the Government of the United States. It constitutes an authoritarian dictatorship within a republic,

demanding for itself the rights and privileges accorded to political parties, but denying to all others the liberties guaranteed by the Constitution. Unlike political parties, which evolve their policies and programs through public means, by the reconciliation of a wide variety of individual views, and submit those policies and programs to the electorate at large for approval or disapproval, the policies and programs of the Communist Party are secretly prescribed for it by the foreign leaders of the world Communist movement. Its members have no part in determining its goals, and are not permitted to voice dissent to party objectives. Unlike members of political parties, members of the Communist Party are recruited for indoctrination with respect to its objectives and methods, and are organized, instructed, and disciplined to carry into action slavishly the assignments given them by their hierarchical chieftains. Unlike political parties, the Communist Party acknowledges no constitutional or statutory limitations upon its conduct or upon that of its members. The Communist

Party is relatively small numerically, and gives scant indication of capacity ever to attain its ends by lawful political means. The peril inherent in its operation arises not from its numbers, but from its failure to acknowledge any limitation as to the nature of its activities, and its dedication to the proposition that the present constitutional Government of the United States ultimately must be brought to ruin by any available means, including resort to force and violence. Holding that doctrine, its role as the agency of a hostile foreign power renders its existence a clear present and continuing danger to the security of the United States. It is the means whereby individuals are seduced into the service of the world Communist movement, trained to do its bidding, and directed and controlled in the conspiratorial performance of their revolutionary services. Therefore, the Communist Party should be outlawed.

SEC. 3. The Communist Party of the United States, or any successors of such party regardless of the assumed name, whose object or purpose is to overthrow the Government of the United States, or the government of any State, Territory, District, or possession thereof, or the government of any

political subdivision therein by force and violence, are not entitled to any of the rights, privileges, and immunities attendant upon legal bodies created under the jurisdiction of the laws of the United States or any political subdivision thereof; and whatever rights, privileges, and immunities which have heretofore been granted to said party or any subsidiary organzation by reason of the laws of the United States or any political subdivision thereof, are hereby terminated: *Provided, however,* That nothing in this section shall be construed as amending the Internal Security Act of 1950, as amended.

SEC. 4. Whoever knowingly and willfully becomes or remains a member of (1) the Communist Party, or (2) any other organization having for one of its purposes or objectives the establishment, control, conduct, seizure, or overthrow of the Government of the United States, or the government of any State or political subdivision thereof, by the use of force or violence, with knowledge of the purpose or objective of such organization, shall be subject to all the provisions and penalties of the Internal Security Act of 1950, as amended, as a member of a "Communist-action" organization. . . .

609. SOUTHEAST ASIA TREATY ORGANIZATION
September 8, 1954
(*Department of State Bulletin,* September 20, 1954)

The French withdrawal from Vietnam, together with the growing alarm at the spread of Communism in the undeveloped world (or the fear of such expansion), prompted Secretary of State John Foster Dulles to negotiate a defensive alliance, patterned after the NATO treaty, with certain governments of Southeast Asia and other interested parties—excluding, however, China, Vietnam, and Formosa. The treaty was signed in Manila by representatives of the United States, Australia, France, New Zealand, Pakistan, the Republic of the Philippines, Thailand, and the United Kingdom.

The Parties to this Treaty,

Recognizing the sovereign equality of all the Parties,

Reiterating their faith in the purposes and

principles set forth in the Charter of the United Nations and their desire to live in peace with all peoples and all governments,

Reaffirming that, in accordance with the Charter of the United Nations, they uphold the principle of equal rights and self-determination of peoples, and declaring that they will earnestly strive by every peaceful means to promote self-government and to secure the independence of all countries whose peoples desire it and are able to undertake its responsibilities,

Desiring to strengthen the fabric of peace and freedom and to uphold the principles of democracy, individual liberty and the rule of law, and to promote the economic well-being and development of all peoples in the treaty area,

Intending to declare publicly and formally their sense of unity, so that any potential aggressor will appreciate that the Parties stand together in the area, and

Desiring further to coordinate their efforts for collective defense for the preservation of peace and security,

Therefore agree as follows:

ARTICLE I

The Parties undertake, as set forth in the Charter of the United Nations, to settle any international disputes in which they may be involved by peaceful means in such a manner that international peace and security and justice are not endangered, and to refrain in their international relations from the threat or use of force in any manner inconsistent with the purposes of the United Nations.

ARTICLE II

In order more effectively to achieve the objectives of this Treaty, the Parties, separately and jointly, by means of continuous and effective self-help and mutual aid will maintain and develop their individual and collective capacity to resist armed attack and to prevent and counter subversive activities directed from without against their territorial integrity and political stability.

ARTICLE III

The Parties undertake to strengthen their free institutions and to cooperate with one another in the further development of eco-nomic measures, including technical assistance, designed both to promote economic progress and social well-being and to further the individual and collective efforts of governments toward these ends.

ARTICLE IV

1. Each Party recognizes that aggression by means of armed attack in the treaty area against any of the Parties or against any State or territory which the Parties by unanimous agreement may hereafter designate, would endanger its own peace and safety, and agrees that it will in the event act to meet the common danger in accordance with its constitutional processes. Measures taken under this paragraph shall be immediately reported to the Security Council of the United Nations.

2. If, in the opinion of any of the Parties, the inviolability or the integrity of the territory or the sovereignty or political independence of any Party in the treaty area or of any other State or territory to which the provisions of paragraph 1 of this Article from time to time apply is threatened in any way other than by armed attack or is affected or threatened by any fact or situation which might endanger the peace of the area, the Parties shall consult immediately in order to agree on the measures which should be taken for the common defense.

3. It is understood that no action on the territory of any State designated by unanimous agreement under paragraph 1 of this Article or on any territory so designated shall be taken except on the invitation or with the consent of the government concerned. . . .

610. EISENHOWER'S LETTER TO NGO DINH DIEM
October 23, 1954
(*Department of State Bulletin,* November 15, 1954)

In the spring of 1954, after years of civil war, Vietnamese nationalists under the communist leader Ho Chi Minh defeated the French army at Dienbienphu. The Geneva Agreements of July 1954 formalized the end of French control in Vietnam, prohibited military intervention in the area by any other foreign power, and provided for democratic elections and the eventual reunification of both halves of the country. Ngo Dinh Diem, a Vietnamese Catholic and aristocrat, who had opposed both the Communists and the French, became premier of South Vietnam with the strong moral backing of groups of influential Americans, whom he had impressed both with his anti-Communism and with his apparent enthusiasm for social reform. Eisenhower, however, was skeptical of any large-scale American commitment to Diem, and assured him only of economic assistance, and that in the most general terms. See Bernard Fall, *The Two Vietnams;* Jean Lacouture, *Vietnam: Between Two Truces;* Robert Scheer, *How the United States Got Involved in Vietnam.*

DEAR MR. PRESIDENT:

I have been following with great interest the course of developments in Vietnam, particularly since the conclusion of the conference at Geneva. The implications of the agreement concerning Vietnam have caused grave concern regarding the future of a country temporarily divided by an artificial military grouping, weakened by a long and exhausting war, and faced with enemies without and by their subversive collaborators within.

Your recent requests for aid to assist in the formidable project of the movement of several hundred thousand loyal Vietnamese citizens away from areas which are passing under a *de facto* rule and political ideology which they abhor, are being fulfilled. I am glad that the United States is able to assist in this humanitarian effort.

We have been exploring ways and means to permit our aid to Vietnam to be more effective and to make a greater contribution to the welfare and stability of the Government of Vietnam. I am, accordingly, instructing the American Ambassador to Vietnam [Donald R. Heath] to examine with you in your capacity as Chief of Government, how an intelligent program of American aid given directly to your Government can serve to assist Vietnam in its present hour of trial, provided that your Government is prepared to give assurances as to the standards of performance it would be able to maintain in the event such aid were supplied.

The purpose of this offer is to assist the Government of Vietnam in developing and maintaining a strong, viable state, capable of resisting attempted subversion or aggression through military means. The Government of the United States expects that this aid will be met by performance on the part of the Government of Vietnam in undertaking needed reforms. It hopes that such aid, combined with your own continuing efforts, will contribute effectively toward an independent Vietnam endowed with a strong Government. Such a Government would, I hope, be so responsive to the nationalist aspirations of its people, so enlightened in purpose and effective in performance, that it will be respected both at home and abroad and discourage any who might wish to impose a foreign ideology on your free people.

611. SENATE CENSURE OF SENATOR McCARTHY
December 2, 1954
(Senate Resolution 301, 83rd Congress, 2d Session)

Early in 1950, Senator Joseph R. McCarthy of Wisconsin inaugurated a campaign to prove that the government was infested with Communists and Communist sympathizers. At various times thereafter, he charged that Communist sympathizers had dictated American policy decisions and that such noted Americans as General George C. Marshall were Communist dupes. McCarthy's activities reached a climax in a full scale investigation of "Communist infiltration in the army." These hearings resulted in charges on the part of Army Secretary Stevens that McCarthy attempted to secure special privileges for his former aide Private G. David Schine and counter charges by Senator McCarthy that Stevens attempted to hide evidence of Communist infiltration from his committee and the public. On July 30, 1954, Senator Ralph Flan- ders of Vermont introduced a resolution in the Senate censuring McCarthy for improper conduct especially during the army investigation. A Senate Committee headed by Senator Watkins of Utah recommended censure; and the Senate accepted this recommendation by a vote of 67 to 22. Following this action by the Senate, McCarthy's influence waned. See J. Anderson and R. W. May, *McCarthy;* J. R. McCarthy, *McCarthyism, the Fight for America;* W. F. Buckley and L. B. Bozell, *McCarthy and His Enemies;* "McCarthy; A Documented Record," *The Progressive,* April, 1954; U.S. Senate Government Operations Committee, 83rd Congress, *Special Senate Investigation on charges and countercharges Involving Secretary of Army Robert T. Stevens . . . and Senator Joe McCarthy . . . pursuant to S. Res. 189;* U.S.

Senate Select Committee to Study Censure Charges, 83rd Congress, *Hearings . . . pursuant to S. Res. 301.*

Resolved, That the Senator from Wisconsin, Mr. McCarthy, failed to cooperate with the Subcommittee on Privileges and Elections of the Senate Committee on Rules and Administration in clearing up matters referred to that subcommittee which concerned his conduct as a Senator and affected the honor of the Senate and, instead, repeatedly abused the subcommittee and its members who were trying to carry out assigned duties, thereby obstructing the constitutional processes of the Senate, and that this conduct of the Senator from Wisconsin, Mr. McCarthy, is contrary to senatorial traditions and is hereby condemned.

SEC. 2. The Senator from Wisconsin, Mr. McCarthy, in writing to the chairman of the Select Committee to Study Censure Charges (Mr. Watkins) after the Select Committee had issued its report and before the report was presented to the Senate charging three members of the Select Committee with "deliberate deception" and "fraud" for failure to disqualify themselves; in stating to the press on November 4, 1954, that the special Senate session that was to begin November 8, 1954, was a "lynch party"; in repeatedly describing this special Senate session as a "lynch bee" in a nationwide television and radio show on November 7, 1954; in stating to the public press on November 13, 1954, that the chairman of the Select Committee (Mr. Watkins) was guilty of "the most unusual, most cowardly thing I've heard of" and stating further: "I expected he would be afraid to answer the questions, but didn't think he'd be stupid enough to make a public statement"; and in characterizing the said committee as the "unwitting handmaiden," "involuntary agent" and "attorneys-in-fact" of the Communist Party and in charging that the said committee in writing its report "imitated Communist methods—that it distorted, misrepresented, and omitted in its effort to manufacture a plausible rationalization" in support of its recommendations to the Senate, which characterizations and charges were contained in a statement released to the press and inserted in the *Congressional Record* of November 10, 1954, acted contrary to senatorial ethics and tended to bring the Senate into dishonor and disrepute, to obstruct the constitutional processes of the Senate, and to impair its dignity; and such conduct is hereby condemned.

612. BROWN v. BOARD OF EDUCATION OF TOPEKA
347 U. S. 483
1954

This case tested the validity of state laws providing for racial segregation in the public schools. The Court reversed the doctrine of *Plessy* v. *Ferguson* 163 U.S. 537 that the Fourteenth Amendment does not outlaw segregation so long as equal facilities are provided for each race. The Court here ruled that "Separate educational facilities are inherently unequal." The Court followed this ruling with another on May 31, 1955, which established the principle that desegregation must proceed with "all deliberate speed" and assigned to the lower courts the responsibility for applying this principle: 349 U.S. 294. These rulings inaugurated a substantial revolution in the legal status of Negroes not only in the field of education but in other areas as well. On November 7, 1955, the Interstate Commerce Commission followed the Court's reasoning in a ruling that segregation was illegal on interstate trains and buses. *NAACP* v. *St. Louis-San Francisco Railway Company.* Following these decisions, the struggle over segregation shifted from the realm of law to the realm of politics. See B. H. Nelson, *The Fourteenth Amendment and the Negro Since 1920;* H. S. Ashmore, *The Negro and the Schools;* P. A. Freund, "Understanding the School Decision," *Congressional Record,* March 28, 1956; J. D. Hyman, "Segregation and the Fourteenth Amendment," 4 *Vanderbilt L. Rev.,* 555; Thurgood Marshall et. al., *Brief for Appelants in the case of Brown v. Board of Education,* filed in the U.S. Supreme Court, November 16, 1953; Thurgood Marshall,

"Supreme Court as Protector of Civil Rights," *Annals Am. Academy of Pol. and Social Science*, May 1951.

Appeal from the U.S. Dist. Court, District of Kansas.

WARREN, C. J. These cases come to us from the States of Kansas, South Carolina, Virginia, and Delaware. They are premised on different facts and different local conditions, but a common legal question justifies their consideration together in this consolidated opinion.

In each of the cases, minors of the Negro race, through their legal representatives, seek the aid of the courts in obtaining admission to the public schools of their community on a nonsegregated basis. In each instance, they have been denied admission to schools attended by white children under laws requiring or permitting segregation according to race. This segregation was alleged to deprive the plaintiffs of the equal protection of the laws under the Fourteenth Amendment. In each of the cases other than the Delaware case, a three-judge federal district court denied relief to the plaintiffs on the so-called "separate but equal" doctrine announced by this Court in Plessy v. Ferguson, 163 U. S. 537. Under that doctrine, equality of treatment is accorded when the races are provided substantially equal facilities, even though these facilities be separate. In the Delaware case, the Supreme Court of Delaware adhered to that doctrine, but ordered that the plaintiffs be admitted to the white schools because of their superiority to the Negro schools.

The plaintiffs contend that segregated public schools are not "equal" and cannot be made "equal," and that hence they are deprived of the equal protection of the laws. Because of the obvious importance of the question presented, the Court took jurisdiction. Argument was heard in the 1952 Term, and reargument was heard this Term on certain questions propounded by the Court.

Reargument was largely devoted to the circumstances surrounding the adoption of the Fourteenth Amendment in 1868. It covered exhaustively consideration of the Amendment in Congress, ratification by the states, then existing practices in racial segregation, and the views of proponents and opponents of the Amendment. This discussion and our own investigation convince us that, although these sources cast some light, it is not enough to resolve the problem with which we are faced. At best, they are inconclusive. The most avid proponents of the post-War Amendments undoubtedly intended them to remove all legal distinctions among "all persons born or naturalized in the United States." Their opponents, just as certainly, were antagonistic to both the letter and the spirit of the Amendments and wished them to have the most limited effect. What others in Congress and the state legislatures had in mind cannot be determined with any degree of certainty.

An additional reason for the inconclusive nature of the Amendment's history, with respect to segregated schools, is the status of public education at that time. In the South, the movement toward free common schools, supported by general taxation, had not yet taken hold. Education of white children was largely in the hands of private groups. Education of Negroes was almost nonexistent, and practically all of the race were illiterate. In fact, any education of Negroes was forbidden by law in some states. Today, in contrast, many Negroes have achieved outstanding success in the arts and sciences as well as in the business and professional world. It is true that public education had already advanced further in the North, but the effect of the Amendment on Northern States was generally ignored in the congressional debates. Even in the North, the conditions of public education did not approximate those existing today. The curriculum was usually rudimentary; ungraded schools were common in rural areas; the school term was but three months a year in many states; and compulsory school attendance was virtually unknown. As a consequence, it is not surprising that there should be so little in the history of the Fourteenth Amendment relating to its intended effect on public education.

In the first cases in this Court construing the Fourteenth Amendment, decided shortly after its adoption, the Court interpreted it as proscribing all state-imposed discriminations against the Negro race. The doctrine of "separate but equal" did not make its appearance in this Court until 1896 in the case of Plessy v. Ferguson, supra, involving not education but transportation. American courts have since labored with the doctrine for over half a century. In this Court, there have been six cases involving the "separate but equal" doctrine in the field of public education. In Cumming v. Board of Education of Richmond County, 175 U. S. 528, and Gong Lum v. Rice, 275 U. S. 78, the validity of the doctrine itself was not challenged. In more recent cases, all on the graduate school level, inequality was found in that specific benefits enjoyed by white students were denied to Negro students of the same educational qualifications. State of Missouri ex rel. Gaines v. Canada, 305 U. S. 337; Sipuel v. Board of Regents of University of Oklahoma, 332 U. S. 631; Sweatt v. Painter, 339 U. S. 629; McLaurin v. Oklahoma State Regents, 339 U. S. 637. In none of these cases was it necessary to reexamine the doctrine to grant relief to the Negro plaintiff. And in Sweatt v. Painter, supra, the Court expressly reserved decision on the question whether Plessy v. Ferguson should be held inapplicable to public education.

In the instant cases, that question is directly presented. Here, unlike Sweatt v. Painter, there are findings below that the Negro and white schools involved have been equalized, or are being equalized, with respect to buildings, curricula, qualifications and salaries of teachers, and other "tangible" factors. Our decision, therefore, cannot turn on merely a comparison of these tangible factors in the Negro and white schools involved in each of the cases. We must look instead to the effect of segregation itself on public education.

In approaching this problem, we cannot turn the clock back to 1868 when the Amendment was adopted, or even to 1896 when Plessy v. Ferguson was written. We must consider public education in the light of its full development and its present place in American life throughout the Nation. Only in this way can it be determined if segregation in public schools deprives these plaintiffs of the equal protection of the laws.

Today, education is perhaps the most important function of state and local governments. Compulsory school attendance laws and the great expenditures for education both demonstrate our recognition of the importance of education to our democratic society. It is required in the performance of our most basic public responsibilities, even service in the armed forces. It is the very foundation of good citizenship. Today it is a principal instrument in awakening the child to cultural values, in preparing him for later professional training, and in helping him to adjust normally to his environment. In these days, it is doubtful that any child may reasonably be expected to succeed in life if he is denied the opportunity of an education. Such an opportunity, where the state has undertaken to provide it, is a right which must be made available to all on equal terms.

We come then to the question presented: Does segregation of children in public schools solely on the basis of race, even though the physical facilities and other "tangible" factors may be equal, deprive the children of the minority group of equal educational opportunities? We believe that it does.

In Sweatt v. Painter, supra [339 U. S. 629, 70 S.Ct. 850], in finding that a segregated law school for Negroes could not provide them equal educational opportunities, this Court relied in large part on "those qualities which are incapable of objective measurement but which make for greatness in a law school." In McLaurin v. Oklahoma State Regents, supra [339 U. S. 637, 70 S.Ct. 853], the Court, in requiring that a Negro admitted to a white graduate school be treated like all other students, again resorted to intangible considerations: ". . . his ability to study, to engage in discussions and exchange views with other students, and, in general, to learn his profession." Such considerations apply with added force to children in grade and high schools. To separate them from others of similar age and qualifications solely because of their race generates a feeling of inferiority as to their status in the community that may affect their hearts and minds in a way unlikely ever to be undone. The effect of this separation on their educational opportunities was well stated by a finding in the Kansas case by a court which nevertheless felt compelled to rule against the Negro plaintiffs:

"Segregation of white and colored children in public schools has a detrimental effect upon the colored children. The impact is greater when it has the sanction of the law; for the policy of separating the races is usually interpreted as denoting the inferiority of the Negro group. A sense of inferiority affects the motivation of a child to learn. Segregation with the sanction of law, therefore, has a tendency to retard the educational and mental development of Negro children and to deprive them of some of the benefits they would receive in a racially integrated school system."

Whatever may have been the extent of psychological knowledge at the time of Plessy v. Ferguson, this finding is amply supported by modern authority. Any language in Plessy v. Ferguson contrary to this finding is rejected.

We conclude that in the field of public education the doctrine of "separate but equal" has no place. Separate educational facilities are inherently unequal. Therefore, we hold that the plaintiffs and others similarly situated for whom the actions have been brought are, by reason of the segregation complained of, deprived of the equal protection of the laws guaranteed by the Fourteenth Amendment. This deposition makes unnecessary any discussion whether such segregation also violates the Due Process Clause of the Fourteenth Amendment.

Because these are class actions, because of the wide applicability of this decision, and because of the great variety of local conditions, the formulation of decrees in these cases presents problems of considerable complexity. On reargument, the consideration of appropriate relief was necessarily subordinated to the primary question—the constitutionality of segregation in public education. We have now announced that such segregation is a denial of the equal protection of the laws. In order that we may have the full assistance of the parties in formulating decrees, the cases will be restored to the docket, and the parties are requested to present further argument. . . . The Attorney General of the United States is again invited to participate. The Attorneys General of the states requiring or permitting segregation in public education will also be permitted to appear as *amici curiae* upon request to do so by September 15, 1954, and submission of briefs by October 1, 1954.

It is so ordered.

613. CONGRESSIONAL RESOLUTION ON THE DEFENSE OF FORMOSA
January 29, 1955
(*Public Law 4, 84th Congress*)

Communist China threatened in 1955 to attack and overcome the last strongholds of the Chinese nationalist government on Formosa and the neighboring Pescadores islands. At the urging of President Eisenhower, Congress passed a resolution declaring that Formosa and the neighboring islands were essential to American military security and authorizing the President to use American troops to defend the islands from Communist attack. This is a rare instance of Congressional action giving the President authority to involve the nation in war at his own discretion. See Doc. No. 660; A. Dean, "United States Foreign Policy and Formosa," 33 *Foreign Affairs*, 360; J. W. Ballantine, *Formosa, A Problem for United States Foreign Policy*; R. A. Smith, *The Rebirth of Formosa*; H. Feis, *The China Tangle*.

Whereas the primary purpose of the United States, in its relations with all other nations, is to develop and sustain a just and enduring peace for all; and

Whereas certain territories in the West Pacific under the jurisdiction of the Republic of China are now under armed attack, and threats and declarations have been and are being made by the Chinese Communists that such armed attack is in aid of and in preparation for armed attack on Formosa and the Pescadores.

Whereas such armed attack if continued would gravely endanger the peace and security of the West Pacific Area and particularly of Formosa and the Pescadores; and

Whereas the secure possession by friendly governments of the Western Pacific Island chain, of which Formosa is a part, is essential to the vital interests of the United States and all friendly nations in or bordering upon the Pacific Ocean; and

Whereas the President of the United States on January 6, 1955, submitted to the Senate for its advice and consent to ratification a Mutual Defense Treaty between the United States of America and the Republic of China, which recognizes that an armed attack in the West Pacific area directed against territories, therein described, in the region of Formosa and the Pescadores, would be dangerous to the peace and safety of the parties to the treaty: Therefore be it

Resolved by the Senate and House of Representatives of the United States of America in Congress assembled, That the President of the United States be and he hereby is authorized to employ the Armed Forces of the United States as he deems necessary for the specific purpose of securing and protecting Formosa and the Pescadores against armed attack, this authority to include the security and protection of such related positions and territories of that area now in friendly hands and the taking of such other measures as he judges to be required or appropriate in assuring the defense of Formosa and the Pescadores.

This resolution shall expire when the President shall determine that the peace and security of the area is reasonably assured by international conditions created by action of the United Nations or otherwise, and shall so report to the Congress.

614. THE NATIONAL HIGHWAY PROGRAM
February 22, 1955
(84th Congress, 1st Session, *House Doc.* No. 93)

By the mid-fifties, the vast increase in the number of automobiles and trucks, the increase in long-distance driving, and the deterioration of the road system, had created a problem of staggering proportions. As early as the Federal Highway Act of 1921, 42 Stat. 212, Congress had committed itself to the principle of aid in the construction of highways, and it was clear in any event that the states were unable to assume the burden of road-building on an adequate scale. President Eisenhower's message called for the expenditure of $101 billion by federal, state, and local governmental units for roads during the ten-year period following 1955. On June 30, 1956, Congress authorized the expenditure of $33 billion. Compare this message with that of Madison, Doc. 116; Monroe, Doc. 125; and Jackson, Doc. 138.

To the Congress of the United States:

Our unity as a nation is sustained by free communication of thought and by easy transportation of people and goods. The ceaseless flow of information throughout the Republic is matched by individual and commercial movement over a vast system of interconnected highways crisscrossing the country and joining at our national borders with friendly neighbors to the north and south.

Together, the uniting forces of our communication and transportation systems are dynamic elements in the very name we bear —United States. Without them, we would be a mere alliance of many separate parts.

The Nation's highway system is a gigantic enterprise, one of our largest items of capital investment. Generations have gone into its building. Three million three hundred and sixty-six thousand miles of road, traveled by 58 million motor vehicles, comprise it. The replacement cost of its drainage and bridge and tunnel works is incalculable. One in every seven Americans gains his livelihood and supports his family out of it. But, in large part, the network is inadequate for the Nation's growing needs.

In recognition of this, the governors in July of last year at my request began a study of both the problem and methods by which the Federal Government might assist the States in its solution. I appointed in September the President's Advisory Committee on a National Highway Program, headed by Lucius D. Clay, to work with the governors and to propose a plan of action for submission to the Congress. At the same time, a committee representing departments and agencies of the National Government was organized to conduct studies coordinated with the other two groups.

All three were confronted with inescapable evidence that action, comprehensive and quick and forward-looking, is needed.

First. Each year, more than 36,000 people are killed and more than a million injured on the highways. To the home where the tragic aftermath of an accident on an unsafe road is a gap in the family circle, the monetary worth of preventing that death cannot be reckoned. But reliable estimates place the measurable economic cost of the highway accident toll to the Nation at more than $4.3 billion a year.

Second. The physical condition of the present road net increases the cost of vehicle operation, according to many estimates, by as much as 1 cent per mile of vehicle travel. At the present rate of travel, this totals more than $5 billion a year. The cost is not borne by the individual vehicle operator alone. It pyramids into higher expense of doing the Nation's business. Increased highway transportation costs, passed on through each step in the distribution of goods, are paid ultimately by the individual consumer.

Third. In case of an atomic attack on our key cities, the road net must permit quick evacuation of target areas, mobilization of defense forces, and maintenance of every essential economic function. But the present system in critical areas would be the breeder of a deadly congestion within hours of an attack.

Fourth. Our gross national product, about $357 billion in 1954, is estimated to reach over $500 billion in 1965 when our population will exceed 180 million and, according to other estimates, will travel in 81 million vehicles 814 billion vehicle-miles that year. Unless the present rate of highway improvement and development is increased existing traffic jams only faintly foreshadow those of 10 years hence.

To correct these deficiencies is an obligation of government at every level. The highway system is a public enterprise. As the owner and operator, the various levels of government have a responsibility for management that promotes the economy of the Nation and properly serves the individual

user. In the case of the Federal Government, moreover, expenditures on a highway program are a return to the highway user of the taxes which he pays in connection with his use of the highways.

Congress has recognized the national interest in the principal roads by authorizing two Federal-aid systems, selected cooperatively by the States, local units, and the Bureau of Public Roads.

The Federal-aid primary system as of July 1, 1954, consisted of 234,407 miles, connecting all the principal cities, county seats, ports, manufacturing areas, and other traffic generating centers.

In 1944 the Congress approved the Federal-aid secondary system, which on July 1, 1954, totaled 482,972 miles, referred to as farm-to-market roads—important feeders linking farms, factories, distribution outlets, and smaller communities with the primary system.

Because some sections of the primary system, from the viewpoint of national interest, are more important than others, the Congress in 1944 authorized the selection of a special network, not to exceed 40,000 miles in length, which would connect by routes, as direct as practicable, the principal metropolitan areas, cities, and industrial centers, serve the national defense, and connect with routes of continental importance in the Dominion of Canada and the Republic of Mexico.

This national system of interstate highways, although it embraces only 1.2 percent of total road mileage, joins 42 State capital cities and 90 percent of all cities over 50,000 population. It carries more than a seventh of all traffic, a fifth of the rural traffic, serves 65 percent of the urban and 45 percent of the rural population. Approximately 37,600 miles have been designated to date. This system and its mileage are presently included within the Federal-aid primary system.

In addition to these systems, the Federal Government has the principal, and in many cases the sole, responsibility for roads that cross or provide access to federally owned land—more than one-fifth of the Nation's area.

Of all these, the interstate system must be given top priority in construction planning. But at the current rate of development, the interstate network would not reach even a reasonable level of extent and efficiency in half a century. State highway departments cannot effectively meet the need. Adequate right-of-way to assure control of access, grade separation structures, relocation and realinement of present highways—all these, done on the necessary scale within an integrated system, exceed their collective capacity.

If we have a congested and unsafe and inadequate system, how then can we improve it so that 10 years from now it will be fitted to the Nation's requirements?

A realistic answer must be based on a study of all phases of highway financing, including a study of the costs of completing the several systems of highways, made by the Bureau of Public Roads in cooperation with the State highway departments and local units of government. This study, made at the direction of the 83d Congress in the 1954 Federal-aid Highway Act, is the most comprehensive of its kind ever undertaken.

Its estimates of need show that a 10-year construction program to modernize all our roads and streets will require expenditure of $101 billion by all levels of Government.

The preliminary 10-year totals of needs by road systems are:

	Billions
Interstate (urban $11, rural $12 billion)	$23
Federal-aid primary (urban $10, rural $20 billion)	30
Federal-aid secondary (entirely rural)	15
Subtotal of Federal-aid systems (urban $21, rural $47 billion)	68
Other roads and streets (urban $16, rural $17 billion)	33
Total of needs (urban $37, rural $64 billion)	101

The Governors' Conference and the President's Advisory Committee are agreed that the Federal share of the needed construction program should be about 30 percent of the total, leaving to State and local units responsibility to finance the remainder.

The obvious responsibility to be accepted by the Federal Government, in addition to the existing Federal interest in our 3,366,000-mile network of highways, is the development of the interstate system with its most essential urban arterial connections.

In its report, the Advisory Committee recommends:

1. That the Federal Government assume principal responsibility for the cost of a modern interstate network to be completed by 1964 to include the most essential urban arterial connections; at an annual average cost of $2.5 billion for the 10-year period.

2. That Federal contributions to primary and secondary road systems, now at the rate authorized by the 1954 act of approximately $525 million annually, be continued.

3. That Federal funds for that portion of the Federal-aid systems in urban areas not on the interstate system, now approximately $75 million annually, be continued.

4. That Federal funds for forest highways be continued at the present $22.5 million per year rate.

Under these proposals, the total Federal expenditures through the 10-year period would be:

	Billions
Interstate system	$25.000
Federal-aid primary and secondary	5.250
Federal-aid urban	.750
Forest highways	.225
Total	31.225

The extension of necessary highways in the Territories and highway maintenance and improvement in National Parks, on Indian lands and on other public lands of the United States will continue to be treated in the budget for these particular subjects.

A sound Federal highway program, I believe, can and should stand on its own feet, with highway users providing the total dollars necessary for improvement and new construction. Financing of interstate and Federal-aid systems should be based on the planned use of increasing revenues from present gas and diesel oil taxes, augmented in limited instances with tolls.

I am inclined to the view that it is sounder to finance this program by special bond issues, to be paid off by the above-mentioned revenues which will be collected during the useful life of the roads and pledged to this purpose, rather than by an increase in general revenue obligations. . . .

DWIGHT D. EISENHOWER.

615. EISENHOWER'S OPEN SKIES PROPOSAL
Statement on Disarmament Presented at the Geneva Conference
July 21, 1955

(The Public Papers of the Presidents: Dwight D. Eisenhower, 1955, no. 166)

All through the fifties the competition for nuclear weapons and the search for a formula for disarmament commanded the most anxious attention of statesmen. During the "thaw" in Soviet-United States relations brought on by the truce in Korea, the cease-fire in the Formosa Strait, and the compromise peace in Vietnam, Eisenhower attended a summit conference in Geneva, announced that "the American people want to be friends with the Soviet peoples" and proposed disarmament and "open skies" inspection. The Russians would not hear of this proposal, however, and countered with a proposal for the prohibition of the manufacture of atomic weapons and a drastic limitation on ground forces of the great powers. For the problem of disarmament in a nuclear age see Pierre Gallois, *The Balance of Terror;* Bernard Brodie, *The Absolute Weapon;* Herman Kahn, *On Thermonuclear War;* George Kennan, *Russia, the Atom and the West;* Henry Kissinger, *Nuclear Weapons and Foreign Policy;* Ralph Lapp, *Atoms and Peace;* James Warburg, *Disarmament, The Challenge of the 1960s;* F. O. Miksche, *The Failure of Atomic Strategy;* Lester Pearson, *Diplomacy in the Nuclear Age;* Anthony Nutting, *Disarmament;* Philip Quigg, "Open Skies and Open Space," *Foreign Affairs,* October 1958.

Disarmament is one of the most important subjects on our agenda. It is also extremely difficult. In recent years the scientists have discovered methods of making weapons many, many times more destructive of opposing armed forces—but also of homes, and industries and lives—than ever known or even imagined before. These same scientific discoveries have made much more complex the problems of limitation and control and reduction of armament. . . .

The United States government is prepared to enter into a sound and reliable agreement making possible the reduction of armament. I have directed that an intensive and thorough study of this subject be made within our own government. From these studies, which are continuing, a very important principle is emerging to which I referred in my opening statement on Monday.

No sound and reliable agreement can be made unless it is completely covered by an inspection and reporting system adequate to support every portion of the agreement.

The lessons of history teach us that disarmament agreements without adequate reciprocal inspection increase the dangers of war and do not brighten the prospects of peace.

Thus it is my view that the priority attention of our combined study of disarmament should be upon the subject of inspection and reporting. . . .

Gentlemen, since I have been working on this memorandum to present to this Conference, I have been searching my heart and mind for something that I could say here that could convince everyone of the great sincerity of the United States in approaching this problem of disarmament.

I should address myself for a moment principally to the delegates from the Soviet Union, because our two great countries admittedly possess new and terrible weapons in quantities which do give rise in other parts of the world, or reciprocally, to the fears and dangers of surprise attack.

I propose, therefore, that we take a practical step, that we begin an arrangement, very quickly, as between ourselves—immediately. These steps would include:

To give to each other a complete blueprint of our military establishments, from beginning to end, from one end of our countries to the other; lay out the establishments and provide the blueprints to each other.

Next, to provide within our countries facilities for aerial photography to the other country—we to provide you the facilities within our country, ample facilities for aerial reconnaissance, where you can make all the pictures you choose and take them to your own country to study, you to provide exactly the same facilities for us and we to make these examinations, and by this step to convince the world that we are providing as between ourselves against the possibility of great surprise attack, thus lessening danger and relaxing tension. Likewise we will make more easily attainable a comprehensive and effective system of inspection and disarmament, because what I propose, I assure you, would be but a beginning. . . .

The quest for peace is the statesman's most exacting duty. Security of the nation entrusted to his care is his greatest responsibility. Practical progress to lasting peace is his fondest hope. Yet in pursuit of his hope he must not betray the trust placed in him as guardian of the people's security. A sound peace—with security, justice, wellbeing, and freedom for the people of the world—*can* be achieved, but only by patiently and thoughtfully following a hard and sure and tested road.

616. FORD FOUNDATION GRANT TO EDUCATION
December 13, 1955

(*New York Times,* December 13, 1955)

Private philanthropic foundations played an increasingly important role in American life after the Second World War. The largest of these organizations was the Ford Foundation. In 1955, the Ford Foundation allocated $500 million to improve the quality of higher education and medicine in the United States. Money granted the colleges and universities was to be used largely for increases in salaries of teachers. See D. McDonald, *The Ford Foundation;* A. Flexner, *Funds and Foundations.*

STATEMENT BY THE TRUSTEES OF THE FORD FOUNDATION

To supplement and encourage the efforts of the American people in meeting problems affecting the progress of the whole nation, the trustees of the Ford Foundation have approved special appropriations of $500,000,-000 for privately supported institutions in communities all over the land.

This sum is in addition to new appropriations for projects under the foundation's established program, the total of which was approximately $30,000,000.

The $500,000,000 appropriated for the special programs, which will be paid out over the next eighteen months, includes:

$210,000,000 for grants to 615 regionally accredited privately supported liberal arts and science colleges and universities in the United States to help them raise teachers' salaries. This supplements the $50,000,000 appropriated last spring for teachers' salaries.

$200,000,000 for approximately 3,500 privately supported hospitals to help them improve and extend their services to the public.

$90,000,000 for privately supported medical schools to help them strengthen their instruction.

In March, 1955, the trustees announced an appropriation of $50,000,000 to be spent in helping America's privately supported colleges and universities raise the level of their faculty salaries. In a statement at that time Henry Ford 2d, Chairman of the board of trustees said:

"All the objectives of higher education ultimately depend upon the quality of teaching. In the opinion of the foundation's trustees, private and corporate philanthropy can make no better investment of its resources than in helping to strengthen American education at its base—the quality of its teaching. . . .

"Nowhere are the needs of the private colleges more apparent than in the matter of faculty salaries. Merely to restore professors' salaries to their 1939 purchasing power would require an average increase of at least 20 per cent. Even this would not bring teachers in our private colleges to their economic position before World War II in relation to that of other professions and occupations. They have not begun to share the benefits of the expanded productive power of this nation, and the whole educational system suffers from this fact.

"Industry, commerce, government, the arts, the sciences and the professions—indeed our whole way of life—depends heavily upon the quality of our education. Recognizing this fact, the trustees of the Ford Foundation want to do everything they can to emphasize the cardinal importance of the college teacher to our society."

Shortly after this announcement an advisory committee was formed to study the problem, recommend a list of colleges which should receive the grants, and suggest a method by which the funds could be most effectively allocated. . . .

The program recommended by the advisory committee was approved by the Trustees and consists of two parts:

A sum approximating its 1954–55 payroll for instruction in the liberal arts and sciences would be given to each of the 615 private, regionally accredited, four-year colleges and universities in the United States. The income from the endowment grant would be used for increasing faculty salaries. The total amount appropriated for these grants is $210,000,000.

An additional sum approximating one-half of last year's faculty salaries in the liberal arts and sciences would be given to 126 institutions which have led the way in their regions in improving the status and compensation of American college teachers. Income from this additional grant could be spent by these institutions either for raising faculty salaries or for other pressing academic needs. The total sum appropriated for these grants is $50,000,000.

The schools to receive the additional grant were selected by the advisory committee on the basis of replies to questionnaires sent to every regionally accredited privately supported college and university in the country. The Committee emphasized that "it did not attempt to compare the caliber of these many different colleges, their general excellence or reputation. Indeed, our study confirms the belief so widely held that variety of excellence is a healthy aspect of our entire system of higher education, whether publicly or privately supported. This variety cannot be readily reduced to mathematical comparisons or scores. . . .

617. UNITED STATES v. LATTIMORE
127 Fed. Supp. 405
1955

Senator McCarthy's drive against alleged "Communist symphthizers" focused in 1952 upon one man, Professor Owen J. Lattimore, distinguished Far Eastern expert at the Johns Hopkins University. Testifying before a Senate subcommittee in 1952, Lattimore denied under oath that he was a "follower of the Communist line" or a "promotor of Communist causes." These statements were used as grounds for a perjury indictment against him. Federal Judge Luther Youngdahl dismissed the charges as too vague to be adjudicated in a court of law. See O. Lattimore, *Ordeal by Slander;* U.S. Senate Internal Security Subcommittee of Judiciary Committee, *Hearings on Subversive Influence in Educational Process . . . Feb. 10–March 10, 1953.*

YOUNGDAHL, District Judge.

Owen Lattimore was indicted October 7, 1954, on two counts of perjury allegedly

committed before the Senate Internal Security Subcommittee on or about February 27, 1952.

The first count charges that Lattimore perjured himself when he denied that he was a "follower of the Communist line." It avers that in his positions and policies as to political, diplomatic, military, economic and social matters, there can be found expressed in his statements and writings from 1935 to 1950, several hundred instances in which he followed the Communist line, meaning that he:

"... followed in time, conformed to, complied with and paralleled the positions taken, the policies expressed and propaganda issued on the same matters by the Government of the Soviet Union, the Communist Party of the Soviet Union, the Comintern and its successors, the various Communist governments, parties and persons adhering to Communism and accepting the leadership of the Soviet Communist Party." (Count I, paragraph 5).

The second count charges that Lattimore perjured himself when he testified he had never been a "promoter of Communist interests." Such a person is defined as one who: ". . . knowingly and intentionally contributed to the growth, enlargement and prosperity of Communism by acting to further, encourage and advance those objectives of political, diplomatic, military, economic and social interest to the Government of the Soviet Union, the Communist party of the Soviet Union, the Comintern and its successors, the various Communist governments, parties and persons adhering to Communism and accepting the leadership of the Soviet Communist party." (Count II, paragraph 5).

Defendant moved to dismiss the indictment, alleging that each of the two counts violate both the First and Sixth Amendments to the United States Constitution. The Court's holding that both counts should be dismissed on the ground of vagueness renders unnecessary a determination of their constitutionality under the First Amendment. . . .

When passing upon the Motion to Dismiss, ". . . the allegations of the indictment must be accepted as they are written." This we do, and are of the opinion that it does not, as a matter of law, inform the accused of the nature and cause of the accusation against him. Neither does it charge an offense with reasonable clarity so that the accused can make his defense, nor furnish the accused with such a description of the charge that he would be able to avail himself of his conviction or acquittal for protection against a further prosecution for the same cause.

In upholding the dismissal of the first count in the prior indictment Judge Prettyman, speaking for the Court of Appeals, aptly stated,

"Not only is it a basic rule that 'Criminal statutes must have an ascertainable standard of guilt or they

fall for vagueness', but it is equally well established that an indictment must charge an offense with such reasonable certainty that the accused can make his defense. The cases on the point are myriad, as reference to any authority quickly reveals."

Testing the two counts against this principle, the Court is satisfied that they fail to meet the prescribed standard of definiteness and so must fall for vagueness.

Under Count I, perjury is charged to the statement by Lattimore that he was not a follower of the Communist line. The Government supplies a definition of this phrase in the indictment. The Government is prompt to concede that no such definition was presented to the defendant at the Committee hearing in 1952; that it was formulated after Lattimore testified; that it was prepared after independent research conducted by the United States Attorney's Office. The sources of such research, however, do not appear. The Government contends that it is a matter of common knowledge as to what is meant by "follower of the Communist line" and that people differ but little in their understanding of the term; that it is not a minimal requirement of following the Communist line to zig and zag with it, since it does not always zigzag; and that the Communist line means the Soviet Communist line and all other organizations that followed the Soviet line. The Government claims a right to prove, by men who are familiar with the common usage of the phrase and by documents of defendant's, that the definition found in the indictment was the same definition which Lattimore had in mind when he testified; that the jury should be left to determine what is the Communist line, what it means to follow such a line, what Lattimore understood as the Communist line, what Lattimore meant by the word "follow," and lastly, having decided the above, that Lattimore, when he said he was not a follower of the Communist line, did not at that time believe in the truth of such testimony according to the meaning he ascribed to these words.

While the proper test of perjury is subjective, insofar as it is based upon the understanding of the witness himself regarding the words that he used, a criminal prosecution must have certain objective standards. Most often in perjury cases the objective standard is not hard to come by; what the accused considered his statements to mean is not in issue since the words or phrases involved have one clear, accepted and recognized meaning. Here, the phrase "follower of the Communist line" is subject to varying interpretations. It has no universally accepted definition. The Government has defined it in one way and seeks to impute its definition to the defendant. Defendant has declined to adopt it, offering a definition of his own. It would not necessitate great ingenuity to think up definitions differing from those offered either by the Government or defendant. By groundless surmise only could the jury determine which definition defendant had in mind.

The Court cannot escape the conclusion that "follower of the Communist line" is not a phrase with a meaning about which men of ordinary intellect could agree, nor one which could be used with mutual understanding by a questioner and answerer unless it were defined at the time it were sought and offered as testimony. This count, even with its apparent definition, is an open invitation to the jury to substitute, by conjecture, their understanding of the phrase for that of the defendant. The meaning of such a phrase varies according to a particular individual's political philosophy. To ask twelve jurors to agree and then decide that the definition of the Communist line found in the indictment is the definition that defendant had in mind and denied believing in, is to ask the jury to aspire to levels of insight to which the ordinary person is incapable, and upon which speculation no criminal indictment should hinge. We cannot debase the principle that:

> "The accused is entitled under the Constitution to be advised as to every element in respect to which it is necessary for him to prepare a defense."

When elements in an indictment are so easily subject to divergent interpretation, the accused is not adequately apprised of the charges as to enable him to prepare a defense. It therefore fails to conform to the requirements of the Sixth Amendment and Federal Rules. It cannot be cured by a bill of particulars.

The second count charges that Lattimore perjured himself when he testified he had never been a "promoter of Communist interest."

This entire perjury indictment arises out of, and is essentially founded upon, the statements, correspondence, and editorial comments of defendant. It does not rest upon alleged acts of espionage or such an act as membership in the Communist party. The Government pointed to the activities of an espionage agent as an example of how one might knowingly promote Communist interests without also being a knowing follower of the Communist line—whatever that may be. But the Government was quick to state that it was not charging defendant with being an espionage agent. It should be kept in mind that under this count only written comments and opinions are involved and are said to have produced a certain effect, namely, to have promoted Communist interests. Such writings and comments are not alleged to have produced the designated result over a short period of time, and in isolated instances, but over a fifteen-year period. By no stretch of the imagination can we comprehend how this consistent result (promoting Communist interests) could have been so attained had not the commentator been both aware of what the Communists were asserting during this extended period, and then knowingly adhered to these assertions (followed the Communist line). If defendant had contradicted the Communists' assertions, he could hardly be said to have promoted their interests.

Count II, thus dependent upon Count I, cannot stand, being anchored to, partaking of, and plagued by, all its vagueness and indefiniteness. While some paragraphs of Count II specifically refer to Count I, either for the definition of the Communist line or for topical references wherein defendant promoted Communist interests, all of the paragraphs, realistically appraised, are rooted in, and presume a prior finding of, the meaning of the phrase "follower of the Communist line."

The charges here serve only to inform the defendant that his sworn statements are to be tested against all his writings for chance parallelism with, or indirect support of, Communism regardless of any deliberate intent on his part. They demonstrate that the Government seeks to establish that at some time, in some way, in some places, in all his vast writings, over a fifteen-year period, Lattimore agreed with something it calls and personally defines as following the Communist line and promoting Communist interests.

Jury inquiries would be limitless. No charge by the Court could embody objective standards to circumscribe and guide the jury in its determination of what the witness might have meant regarding words he used. With so sweeping an indictment with its many vague charges, and with the existing atmosphere of assumed and expected loathing for Communism, it would be neither surprising nor unreasonable were the jury subconsciously impelled to substitute its own understanding for that of defendant.

To require defendant to go to trial for perjury under charges so formless and obscure as those before the Court would be unprecedented and would make a sham of the Sixth Amendment and the Federal Rule requiring specificity of charges.

The indictment will therefore be dismissed.

618. CONSTITUTION OF THE AFL-CIO
1955

(Report of the First Constitutional Convention of the AFL-CIO, 1955)

Labor's civil war ended in 1955 when the American Federation of Labor and the Congress of Industrial Organizations merged into a single federation of unions, the AFL-CIO. See Doc. No. 569. This brought into a single labor organization some 15 million workers. The constitution of the new organization granted to the new Federation more power over national union affairs than the constitution of the old American Federation of Labor. See Doc. No. 473. This reflected an increase in the importance of the functions performed by the central agencies of the labor movement. See A. J. Goldberg, *AFL-CIO Labor United;* E. Levinson, *Labor on the March;* J. Siedman, *American Labor from Defense to Reconversion.*

PREAMBLE

The establishment of this Federation through the merger of the American Federation of Labor and the Congress of Industrial Organizations is an expression of the hopes and aspirations of the working people of America.

We seek the fulfillment of these hopes and aspirations through democratic processes within the framework of our constitutional government and consistent with our institutions and traditions.

At the collective bargaining table, in the community, in the exercise of the rights and responsibilities of citizenship, we shall responsibly serve the interests of the American people.

We pledge ourselves to the more effective organization of working men and women; to the securing to them of full recognition and enjoyment of the rights to which they are justly entitled; to the achievement of ever higher standards of living and working conditions; to the attainment of security for all the people; to the enjoyment of the leisure which their skills make possible; and to the strengthening and extension of our way of life and the fundamental freedoms which are the basis of our democratic society.

We shall combat resolutely the forces which seek to undermine the democratic institutions of our nation and to enslave the human soul. We shall strive always to win full respect for the dignity of the human individual whom our unions serve.

With Divine guidance, grateful for the fine traditions of our past, confident of meeting the challenge of the future, we proclaim this constitution. . . .

ARTICLE II. *Objects and Principles*

The objects and principles of this Federation are:

1. To aid workers in securing improved wages, hours and working conditions with due regard for the autonomy, integrity and jurisdiction of affiliated unions.

2. To aid and assist affiliated unions in

extending the benefits of mutual assistance and collective bargaining to workers and to promote the organization of the unorganized into unions of their own choosing for their mutual aid, protection and advancement, giving recognition to the principle that both craft and industrial unions are appropriate, equal and necessary as methods of union organization.

3. To affiliate national and international unions with this Federation and to establish such unions; to form organizing committees and directly affiliated local unions and to secure their affiliation to appropriate national and international unions affiliated with or chartered by the Federation; to establish, assist and promote state and local central bodies composed of local unions of all affiliated organizations and directly affiliated local unions; to establish and assist trade departments composed of affiliated national and international unions and organizing committees.

4. To encourage all workers without regard to race, creed, color, national origin or ancestry to share equally in the full benefits of union organization.

5. To secure legislation which will safeguard and promote the principle of free collective bargaining, the rights of workers, farmers and consumers, and the security and welfare of all the people and to oppose legislation inimical to these objectives.

6. To protect and strengthen our democratic institutions, to secure full recognition and enjoyment of the rights and liberties to which we are justly entitled, and to preserve and perpetuate the cherished traditions of our democracy.

7. To give constructive aid in promoting the cause of peace and freedom in the world and to aid, assist and cooperate with free and democratic labor movements throughout the world.

8. To preserve and maintain the integrity of each affiliated union in the organization to the end that each affiliate shall respect the established bargaining relationships of every other affiliate and that each affiliate shall refrain from raiding the established bargaining relationship of any other affiliate and, at the same time, to encourage the elimination of conflicting and duplicating organizations and jurisdictions through the

process of voluntary agreement or voluntary merger in consultation with the appropriate officials of the Federation, to preserve, subject to the foregoing, the organizing jurisdiction of each affiliate.

9. To aid and encourage the sale and use of union made goods and union services through the use of the union label and other symbols; to promote the labor press and other means of furthering the education of the labor movement.

10. To protect the labor movement from any and all corrupt influences and from the undermining efforts of communist agencies and all others who are opposed to the basic principles of our democracy and free and democratic unionism.

11. To safeguard the democratic character of the labor movement and to protect the autonomy of each affiliated national and international union.

12. While preserving the independence of the labor movement from political control, to encourage workers to register and vote, to exercise their full rights and responsibilities of citizenship, and to perform their rightful part in the political life of the local, state and national communities.

ARTICLE VIII. *Executive Council*

SECTION 1. The Executive Council shall consist of the President, the Vice Presidents and the Secretary-Treasurer.

SEC. 2. The Executive Council shall be the governing body of this Federation between conventions. It is authorized and empowered to take such action and render such decisions as may be necessary to carry out fully and adequately the decisions and instructions of the conventions and to enforce the provisions contained in this constitution. Between conventions it shall have the power to direct the affairs of the Federation and to take such actions and render such decisions as are necessary and appropriate to safeguard and promote the best interests of the Federation and its affiliated unions, including the organization of unorganized industries by means most appropriate for that purpose.

SEC. 3. The Executive Council shall meet upon the call of the President at least three times within each year at a time and place designated by the President.

SEC. 4. It shall be the duty of the Executive Council to watch legislative measures directly affecting the interests of working people, and to initiate, wherever necessary, such legislative action as the convention may direct.

SEC. 5. The Executive Council shall prepare and present to the convention in printed form a statement of all matters of interest to the convention and of the activities of the Federation between conventions.

SEC. 6. The Executive Council shall have power to make rules to govern matters consistent with this constitution and shall report accordingly to the Federation.

SEC. 7. It is a basic principle of this Federation that it must be and remain free from any and all corrupt influences and from the undermining efforts of communist, fascist or other totalitarian agencies who are opposed to the basic principles of our democracy and of free and democratic trade unionism. The Executive Council, when requested to do so by the President or by any other member of the Executive Council, shall have the power to conduct an investigation, directly or through an appropriate standing or special committee appointed by the President, of any situation in which there is reason to believe that any affiliate is dominated, controlled or substantially influenced in the conduct of its affairs by any corrupt influence, or that the policies or activities of any affiliate are consistently directed toward the advocacy, support, advancement or achievement of the program or of the purposes of the Communist Party, any fascist organization or other totalitarian movement. Upon the completion of such an investigation, including a hearing if requested, the Executive Council shall have the authority to make recommendations or give directions to the affiliate involved and shall have the further authority, upon a two-thirds vote, to suspend any affiliate found guilty of a violation of this section. Any action of the Executive Council under this section may be appealed to the convention, provided, however, that such action shall be effective when taken and shall remain in full force and effect pending any appeal.

SEC. 8. Subject to the provisions of Article III, Section 7, the Executive Council shall use every possible means to assist affiliated unions in the organization of the unorganized and to organize new national and international unions, organizing committees, and directly affiliated local unions. . . .

SEC. 9. In carrying out the provisions of this Article the Executive Council shall recognize that both craft and industrial unions are appropriate, equal and necessary as methods of trade union organization and that all workers whatever their race, color, creed or national origin are entitled to share in the full benefits of trade union organization.

SEC. 10. A majority of the members of the Executive Council shall constitute a quorum for the transaction of the business of the Council.

SEC. 11. The Executive Council shall have the power to file charges and conduct hearings on such charges against any Executive Officer of the Federation or other member of the Executive Council on the ground that such person is guilty of malfeasance, or maladministration. and to make a report to the convention recommending appropriate action. The Executive Council must serve such officer with a copy of the written charges a reasonable time before the hearing. . . .

ARTICLE XI. *Department of Organization*

SECTION 1. The organizing work of this Federation as set forth in Article VIII, Section 8, shall be conducted by the Department of Organization under the general supervision of the President. The Department of Organization shall be provided the staff and resources necessary to conduct such activities.

SEC. 2. The Department of Organization shall be headed by a Director of Organization who shall be appointed by the President after consultation with the Executive Committee, subject to the approval of the Executive Council. . . .

ARTICLE XIII. *Committees and Staff Departments*

SECTION 1. The President of the Federation shall appoint the following standing committees and such other committees as may from time to time be necessary. The.

President with the approval of the Executive Council may combine standing committees. The committees, under the direction of the President, and subject to the authority of the Executive Council and the convention, shall carry out their functions as described herein:

(a) The Committee on Legislation shall undertake to carry out the policies and programs of the Federation in the Congress and in the legislatures of state and local governments;

(b) The Committee on Civil Rights shall be vested with the duty and responsibility to assist the Executive Council to bring about at the earliest possible date the effective implementation of the principle stated in this constitution of non-discrimination in accordance with the provisions of this constitution;

(c) The Committee on Political Education shall be vested with the duty and responsibility to assist the Executive Council in meeting the need for sound political education and in bringing about the effective implementation of the objectives stated in this constitution of encouraging workers to register and vote, to exercise their full rights and responsibilities of citizenship and to perform their rightful part in the political life of the city, state, and national communities;

(d) The Committee on Ethical Practices shall be vested with the duty and responsibility to assist the Executive Council in carrying out the constitutional determination of the Federation to keep the Federation free from any taint of corruption or communism, in accordance with the provisions of this constitution.

(e) The Committee on International Affairs shall be concerned with international developments facing our nation and the Federation's relationships with the international trade union movement;

(f) The Committee on Education shall promote the widest possible understanding among union members of the aims of the Federation, shall assist affiliated unions in developing their own educational programs and shall implement the Federation's interest in providing the nation with the highest standard of education at all levels;

(g) The Committee on Social Security shall have the responsibility of providing guidance and information in the fields of social insurance and welfare;

(h) The Committee on Economic Policy shall undertake to recommend programs and policies toward the end of promoting prosperity, full employment and full utilization of our resources. . . .

ARTICLE XVII. *Amendments*

This constitution can be amended or altered only by the convention, by a two-thirds vote of those present and voting, either by a show of hands, or, if a roll-call is properly demanded as provided in this constitution, by such roll-call. . . .

619. COLE v. YOUNG
351 U. S. 536
1956

This case dealt with the application of the Internal Security Act of 1950, Doc. No. 591, to government employees who have no contact with restricted information. The Court voided that part of Executive Order 10450 which extended the security program to all government employees. Following this decision, President Eisenhower ordered the Attorney General to modify the government's security program to apply only to sensitive positions in which employees have direct contact with restricted government documents. See 70 *Harvard Law Review* 165; 42 *American Bar Ass'n. Journal* 764.

Appeal from the United States Court of Appeals for the District of Columbia.

HARLAN, J. This case presents the question of the meaning of the term "national security" as used in the Act of August 26, 1950, giving to the heads of certain departments and agencies of the Government summary suspension and unreviewable dismissal powers over their civilian employees, when deemed necessary "in the interest of the national security of the United States."

Petitioner, a preference-eligible veteran under § 2 of the Veterans' Preference Act of 1944, 58 Stat. 387, held a position in the classified civil service as a food and drug inspector for the New York District of the Food and Drug Adminstration, Department of Health, Education, and Welfare. In November 1953 he was suspended without pay from his position pending investigation to determine whether his employment should be terminated. . . .

Thereafter the Secretary of the Department of Health, Education, and Welfare, after "a study of all the documents in [petitioner's] case," determined that petitioner's continued employment was not "clearly consistent with the interests of national security" and ordered the termination of his employment. . . .

The Act authorizes dismissals only upon a determination by the Secretary that the dismissal is "necessary or advisable in the interest of the national security." That determination requires an evaluation of the risk of injury to the "national security" that the employee's retention would create, which in turn would seem necessarily to be a function not only of the character of the employee and the likelihood of his misconducting himself, but also of the nature of the position he occupies and its relationship to the "national security." That is, it must be determined whether the position is one in which the employee's misconduct would affect the "national security." That of course would not be necessary if "national security" were used in the Act in a sense so broad as to be involved in *all* activities of the Government, for then the relationship to the "national security" would follow from the very fact of employment. For the reasons set forth below, however, we conclude (1) that the term "national security" is used in the Act in a definite and limited sense and relates only to those activities which are directly concerned with the Nation's safety, as distinguished from the general welfare; and (2) that no determination has been made that petitioner's position was affected with the "national security" as that term is used in the Act. It follows that his dismissal was not authorized by the 1950 Act.

As noted above, the issue turns on the meaning of "national security" as used in the

Act. While that term is not defined in the Act, we think it clear from the statute as a whole that that term was intended to comprehend only those activities of the Government that are directly concerned with the protection of the Nation from internal subversion or foreign aggression, and not those which contribute to the strength of the Nation only through their impact on the general welfare.

Virtually conclusive of this narrow meaning of "national security" is the fact that had Congress intended the term in a sense broad enough to include all activities of the Government, it would have granted the power to terminate employment "in the interest of the national security" to all agencies of Government. Instead, Congress specified 11 named agencies, to which the Act should apply, the character of which reveals, without doubt, a purpose to single out those agencies which are directly concerned with the national defense and which have custody over information the compromise of which might endanger the country's security, the so-called "sensitive" agencies. Thus, of the 11 named agencies, 8 are concerned with military operations or weapons development, and the other 3, with international relations, internal security, and the stock-piling of strategic materials. . . .

It is clear, therefore, both from the face of the Act and the legislative history, that "national security" was not used in the Act in an all-inclusive sense but was intended to refer only to the protection of "sensitive" activities. It follows that an employee can be dismissed "in the interest of the national security" under the Act only if he occupies a "sensitive" position, and thus that a condition precedent to the exercise of the dismissal authority is a determination by the agency head that the position occupied is one affected with the "national security." . . .

From our holdings (1) that not all positions in the Government are affected with the "national security" as that term is used in the 1950 Act and (2) that no determination has been made that petitioner's position was one in which he could adversely affect the "national security," it necessarily follows that petitioner's discharge was not authorized by the 1950 Act. . . . Since petitioner's discharge was not authorized by the 1950 Act and hence violated the Veterans' Preference Act, the judgment of the Court of Appeals is reversed and the case is remanded to the District Court for further proceedings not inconsistent with this opinion.

Reversed and remanded.

CLARK, J., dissenting . . . The President believed that the national security required the extension of the coverage of the Act to all employees. That was his judgment, not ours. He was given that power, not us. By this action the Court so interprets the Act as to intrude itself into presidential policy making. The Court should not do this especially here where Congress has ratified the President's action. As required by the Act the Executive Order was reported to the Congress and soon thereafter it came up for discussion and action in both the House and the Senate. It was the sense of the Congress at that time that the Order properly carried out the standards of the Act and was in all respects an expression of the congressional will. 99 Cong.Rec. 4511–4543, 5818–5990. In addition, Congress has made appropriations each subsequent year for investigations, etc., under its provisions. This in itself "stands as confirmation and ratification of the action of the Chief Executive." Fleming v. Mohawk Wrecking & Lumber Co., 331 U.S. 111, 116.

The President having extended the coverage of the Act to the Department of Health, Education, and Welfare, it became the duty of the Secretary to dismiss any employee whenever she deemed it "necessary or advisable in the interests of national security." She made such a finding. It is implicit in her order of dismissal. Her "evaluation as to the effect which continuance of [petitioner's] employment might have upon the 'national security' " has been made. She decided that he should be dismissed. Under the Act this determination is "conclusive and final." . . .

We believe the Court's order has stricken down the most effective weapon against subversive activity available to the Government. It is not realistic to say that the Government can be protected merely by applying the Act to sensitive jobs. One never knows just which job is sensitive. The janitor might prove to be in as important a spot security-wise as the top employee in the building. The Congress decided that the most effective way to protect the Government was through the procedures laid down in the Act. The President implemented its purposes by requiring that Government employment be "clearly consistent" with the national security. The President's standard is "complete and unswerving loyalty" not only in sensitive places but thoughout the Government. The President requires and every employee should give no less. This is all that the Act and the Order require. They should not be subverted by the technical interpretation the majority places on them today. We would affirm.

Justices Reed and Minton joined in the dissent.

620. PENNSYLVANIA v. NELSON
350 U. S. 497
1956

This case tested the validity of the sedition acts of Pennsylvania and several other states. The Court declared that the defense of the federal government from sedition was properly a function of the federal government rather than the states, and concluded that since Congress had preempted the field with a whole series of laws, the sedition acts of the various states were void. For an earlier example of this reasoning, see *Prigg* v. *Pennsylvania*, Doc. 158. See Hunt, "Federal Supremacy and State Legislation," 53 *Michigan Law Rev.*, 407.

Appeal from the decision of the Pennsylvania State Supreme Court.

WARREN, C. J. The respondent Steve Nelson, an acknowledged member of the Communist Party, was convicted in the Court of Quarter Sessions of Allegheny County, Pennsylvania, of a violation of the Pennsylvania Sedition Act and sentenced to imprisonment for twenty years and to a fine of $10,000 and to costs of prosecution in the sum of

$13,000. The Superior Court affirmed the conviction. 172 Pa.Super. 125. The Supreme Court of Pennsylvania, recognizing but not reaching many alleged serious trial errors and conduct of the trial court infringing upon respondent's right to due process of law, decided the case on the narrow issue of supersession of the state law by the Federal Smith Act. In its opinion, the court stated:

> "And, while the Pennsylvania statute proscribes sedition against either the Government of the United States or the Government of Pennsylvania, it is only alleged sedition against the United States with which the instant case is concerned. Out of all the voluminous testimony, we have not found, nor has anyone pointed to, a single word indicating a seditious act or even utterance directed against the Government of Pennsylvania."

The precise holding of the court, and all that is before us for review, is that the Smith Act of 1940, as amended in 1948, which prohibits the knowing advocacy of the overthrow of the Government of the United States by force and violence, supersedes the enforceability of the Pennsylvania Sedition Act which proscribes the same conduct. . . .

Where, as in the instant case, Congress has not stated specifically whether a federal statute has occupied a field in which the States are otherwise free to legislate, different criteria have furnished touchstones for decision. Thus,

> "[t]his Court, in considering the validity of state laws in the light of . . . federal laws touching the same subject, has made use of the following expressions: conflicting; contrary to; occupying the field; repugnance; difference; irreconcilability; inconsistency; violation; curtailment; and interference. But none of these expressions provides an infallible constitutional test or an exclusive constitutional yardstick. In the final analysis, there can be no one crystal clear distinctly marked formula." Hines v. Davidowitz. 312 U.S. 52, 67, 61.

And see Rice v. Santa Fe Elevator Corp., 331 U.S. 218, 230–321. In this case, we think that each of several tests of supersession is met.

First, "[t]he scheme of federal regulation [is] so pervasive as to make reasonable the inference that Congress left no room for the States to supplement it." Rice v. Santa Fe Elevator Corp., 331 U.S. at page 230. The Congress determined in 1940 that it was necessary for it to reenter the field of antisubversive legislation, which had been abandoned by it in 1921. In that year, it enacted the Smith Act which proscribes advocacy of the overthrow of any government—federal, state or local—by force and violence and organization of and knowing membership in a group which so advocates. Conspiracy to commit any of these acts is punishable under the general criminal conspiracy provisions in 18 U.S.C. § 371, 18 U.S.C.A. § 371. The Internal Security Act of 1950 is aimed more directly at Communist organizations. It distinguishes between "Communist-action organizations" and "Communist-front organizations," requiring such organizations to register and to file annual reports with the Attorney General giving complete details as to their officers and funds. Members of Communist-action organizations who have not been registered by their organization must register as individuals. Failure to register in accordance with the requirements of Sections 786–787 is punishable by a fine of not more than $10,000 for an offending organization and by a fine of not more than $10,000 or imprisonment for not more than five years or both for an individual offender—each day of failure to register constituting a separate offense. And the Act imposes certain sanctions upon both "action" and "front" organizations and their members. The Communist Control Act of 1954 declares "that the Communist Party of the United States, although purportedly a political party, is in fact an instrumentality of a conspiracy to overthrow the Government of the United States" and that "its role as the agency of a hostile foreign power renders its existence a clear present and continuing danger to the security of the United States." It also contains a legislative finding that the Communist Party is a " 'Communist-action' organization" within the meaning of the Internal Security Act of 1950 and provides that "knowing" members of the Communist Party are "subject to all the provisions and penalties" of that Act. It furthermore sets up a new classification of "Communist-infiltrated organizations" and provides for the imposition of sanctions against them.

We examine these Acts only to determine the congressional plan. Looking to all of them in the aggregate, the conclusion is inescapable that Congress has intended to occupy the field of sedition. Taken as a whole, they evince a congressional plan which makes it reasonable to determine that no room has been left for the States to supplement it. Therefore, a state sedition statute is superseded regardless of whether it purports to supplement the federal law. As was said by Mr. Justice Holmes in Charlestown & Western Carolina R. Co. v. Varnville Furniture Co., 237 U.S. 597, 604.

> "When Congress has taken the particular subject-matter in hand, coincidence is as ineffective as opposition, and a state law is not to be declared a help because it attempts to go farther than Congress has seen fit to go."

Second, the federal statutes "touch a field in which the federal interest is so dominant that the federal system [must] be assumed to preclude enforcement of state laws on the same subject." Rice v. Santa Fe Elevator Corp., 331 U.S. at page 230, citing Hines v. Davidowitz, supra. Congress has devised an all embracing program for resistance to the various forms of totalitarian aggression. Our external defenses have been strengthened, and a plan to protect against internal subversion has been made by it. It has appropriated vast sums, not only for our own protection, but also to strengthen freedom throughout the world. It has charged the Federal Bureau of Investigation and the Central Intelligence Agency with responsibility for intelligence concerning Communist seditious activities against our Government, and has denominated such activities as part of a world conspiracy. It accordingly proscribed sedition against all government in the nation—national, state and local. Congress declared that these steps were taken "to provide for the common defense, to preserve the sovereignty of the United States as an independent nation, and to guarantee to each State a republican form

of government. . . . Congress having thus treated seditious conduct as a matter of vital national concern, it is in no sense a local enforcement problem. As was said in the court below:

> "Sedition against the United States is not a *local* offense. It is a crime against the *Nation.* As such, it should be prosecuted and punished in the Federal courts where this defendant has in fact been prosecuted and convicted and is now under sentence. It is not only important but vital that such prosecutions should be exclusively within the control of the Federal Government. . . ."

Third, enforcement of state sedition acts presents a serious danger of conflict with the administration of the federal program. . . .

In his brief, the Solictor General states that forty-two States plus Alaska and Hawaii have statutes which in some form prohibit advocacy of the violent overthrow of established government. These statutes are entitled anti-sedition statutes, criminal anarchy laws, criminal syndicalist laws, etc. Although all of them are primarily directed against the overthrow of the United States Government, they are in no sense uniform. And our attention has not been called to any case where the prosecution has been successfully directed against an attempt to destroy state or local government. Some of these Acts are studiously drawn and purport to protect fundamental rights by appropriate definitions, standards of proof and orderly procedures in keeping with the avowed congressional purpose "to protect freedom from those who would destroy it, without infringing upon the freedom of all our people." Others are vague and are almost wholly without such safeguards. Some even purport to punish mere membership in subversive organizations which the federal statutes do not punish where federal registration requirements have been fulfilled.

When we were confronted with a like situation in the field of labor-management relations, Mr. Justice Jackson wrote:

> "A multiplicity of tribunals and a diversity of procedures are quite as apt to produce incompatible or conflicting adjudications as are different rules of substantive law."

Should the States be permitted to exercise a concurrent jurisdiction in this area, federal enforcement would encounter not only the difficulties mentioned by Mr. Justice Jackson, but the added conflict engendered by different criteria of substantive offenses.

Since we find that Congress has occupied the field to the exclusion of parallel state legislation, that the dominant interest of the Federal Government precludes state intervention, and that administration of state Acts would conflict with the operation of the federal plan, we are convinced that the decision of the Supreme Court of Pennsylvania is unassailable.

We are not unmindful of the risk of compounding punishments which would be created by finding concurrent state power. In our view of the case, we do not reach the question whether double or multiple punishment for the same overt acts directed against the United States has constitutional sanction. Without compelling indication to the contrary, we will not assume that Congress intended to permit the possibility of double punishment. Cf. Houston v. Moore, 5 Wheat. 1, 31, 75; Jerome v. United States, 318 U.S. 101, 105.

The judgment of the Supreme Court of Pennsylvania is affirmed.

Affirmed.

Justices Reed, Burton, and Minton dissenting.

621. EISENHOWER'S VETO OF NATURAL GAS BILL
February 17, 1956
(84th Congress, 2d Session, *House Doc.* No. 342)

On June 7, 1954, the Supreme Court affirmed the right of the Federal Power Commission to regulate the price of natural gas sold in interstate commerce. *Phillips Petroleum Co.* v. *Wisconsin* 347 U.S. 672. The producers of natural gas clamored for exemption from such regulation. Their appeals were met by the Natural Gas Bill which limited the extent of government regulation of the production and distribution of natural gas. President Eisenhower supported the bill while it was before Congress. But when the bill came to his desk for signature, the President was confronted with substantial evidence of unlawful lobbying by natural gas producers and thereupon vetoed the bill, basing his decision not on the content of the bill but on the manner of its passage.

To the House of Representatives:

I am unable to approve H. R. 6645, to amend the Natural Gas Act, as amended. This I regret because I am in accord with its basic objectives.

Since the passage of this bill a body of evidence has accumulated indicating that private persons, apparently representing only a very small segment of a great and vital industry, have been seeking to further their own interests by highly questionable activities. These include efforts that I deem to be so arrogant and so much in defiance of acceptable standards of propriety as to risk creating doubt among the American people concerning the integrity of governmental processes.

Legally constituted agencies of Government are now engaged in investigating this situation. These investigations cannot be concluded before the expiration of the 10-day period within which the President must act upon the legislation under the Constitution.

I believe I would not be discharging my own duty were I to approve this legislation before the activities in question have been fully investigated by the Congress and the Department of Justice. To do so under such conditions could well create long-term apprehension in the minds of the American people. It would be a disservice both to the people and to their Congress. Accordingly, I return H. R. 6645 without my approval.

At the same time, I must make quite clear that legislation conforming to the basic objectives of H. R. 6645 is needed. It is needed because the type of regulation of producers of natural gas which is required under present law will discourage individual initiative and incentive to explore for and develop new sources of supply.

In the long run this will limit supplies of

gas, which is contrary not only to the national interest but especially to the interest of consumers.

I feel that any new legislation, in addition to furthering the long-term interest of con-sumers in plentiful supplies of gas, should include specific language protecting consumers in their right to fair prices.

DWIGHT D. EISENHOWER

622. SOUTHERN DECLARATION ON INTEGRATION
March 12, 1956
(*New York Times*, March 12, 1956)

In the second Brown v. Board of Education decision (349 U.S. 294) the Court directed that integration proceed "with all deliberate speed." In the event, the deliberateness was far more conspicuous than the speed. Though there was at first some disposition to acquiesce in the judicial mandate, opposition grew and hardened. Hastily organized White Citizens Councils conspired to frustrate the operation of the Brown decision. On March 12 ninety-six Southern Congressmen—it was practically unanimous—issued a Declaration denouncing the Supreme Court decision as a violation of the Constitution and calling on their states to refuse obedience to it, and pledging themselves to resist it "by all lawful means."

See A. P. Blaustein and C. C. Ferguson, *Desegregation and the Law;* Sutherland, "The American Judiciary and Racial Segregation" 20 *Modern Law Rev.* 201; B. M. Ziegler, ed., *Segregation and the Supreme Court;* H. H. Hyman and P. B. Sheatsley, "Attitudes toward Desegregation," 195 *Scientific American*, 35; James F. Byrnes, "The Supreme Court Must Be Curbed," *U.S. News and World Report*, May 18, 1956; Robert B. McKay, "With All Deliberate Speed," 31 *N.Y.U. Law Rev.* 991; and Robert McKay, "With All Deliberate Speed: Legislative Reaction and Judicial Development, 1956–57," 43 *Virginia Law Rev.* 1205; Alexander Bickel "The Original Understanding and the Segregation Decision," 69 *Harvard Law Rev.* 1; C. V. Woodward, *Strange Career of Jim Crow.*

We regard the decision of the Supreme Court in the school cases as clear abuse of judicial power. It climaxes a trend in the Federal judiciary undertaking to legislate, in derogation of the authority of Congress, and to encroach upon the reserved rights of the states and the people.

The original Constitution does not men-tion education. Neither does the Fourteenth Amendment nor any other amendment. The debates preceding the submission of the Fourteenth Amendment clearly show that there was no intent that it should affect the systems of education maintained by the states.

The very Congress which proposed the amendment subsequently provided for segregated schools in the District of Columbia.

When the amendment was adopted in 1868, there were thirty-seven states of the Union. Every one of the twenty-six states that had any substantial racial differences among its people either approved the operation of segregated schools already in existence or subsequently established such schools by action of the same law-making body which considered the Fourteenth Amendment.

As admitted by the Supreme Court in the public school case (Brown v. Board of Education), the doctrine of separate but equal schools "apparently originated in Roberts v. City of Boston (1849), upholding school segregation against attack as being violative of a state constitutional guarantee of equality." This constitutional doctrine began in the North—not in the South—and it was followed not only in Massachusetts but in Connecticut, New York, Illinois, Indiana, Michigan, Minnesota, New Jersey, Ohio, Pennsylvania and other northern states until they, exercising their rights as states through the constitutional processes of local self-government, changed their school systems.

In the case of Plessy v. Ferguson in 1896 the Supreme Court expressly declared that under the Fourteenth Amendment no person was denied any of his rights if the states provided separate but equal public facilities. This decision has been followed in many other cases. It is notable that the Supreme Court, speaking through Chief Justice Taft, a former President of the United States, unanimously declared in 1927 in Lum v. Rice that the "separate but equal" principle is ". . . within the discretion of the state in regulating its public schools and does not conflict with the Fourteenth Amendment."

This interpretation, restated time and again, became a part of the life of the people of many of the states and confirmed their habits, customs, traditions and way of life. It is founded on elemental humanity and common sense, for parents should not be deprived by Government of the right to direct the lives and education of their own children.

Though there has been no constitutional amendment or act of Congress changing this established legal principle almost a century old, the Supreme Court of the United States, with no legal basis for such action, undertook to exercise their naked judicial power and substituted their personal political and social ideas for the established law of the land.

This unwarranted exercise of power by the court, contrary to the Constitution, is creating chaos and confusion in the states principally affected. It is destroying the amicable relations between the white and Negro races that have been created through ninety years of patient effort by the good people of both races. It has planted hatred and suspicion where there has been heretofore friendship and understanding.

Without regard to the consent of the governed, outside agitators are threatening immediate and revolutionary changes in our public school systems. If done, this is certain to destroy the system of public education in some of the states.

With the gravest concern for the explosive and dangerous condition created by this decision and inflamed by outside meddlers:

We reaffirm our reliance on the Constitution as the fundamental law of the land.

We decry the Supreme Court's encroachments on rights reserved to the states and to the people, contrary to established law and to the Constitution.

We commend the motives of those states which have declared the intention to resist forced integration by any lawful means.

We appeal to the states and people who are not directly affected by these decisions to consider the constitutional principles involved against the time when they too, on issues vital to them, may be the victims of judicial encroachment.

Even though we constitute a minority in the present Congress, we have full faith that a majority of the American people believe in the dual system of government which has enabled us to achieve our greatness and will in time demand that the reserved rights of the states and of the people be made secure against judicial usurpation.

We pledge ourselves to use all lawful means to bring about a reversal of this decision which is contrary to the Constitution and to prevent the use of force in its implementation.

In this trying period, as we all seek to right this wrong, we appeal to our people not to be provoked by the agitators and troublemakers invading our states and to scrupulously refrain from disorder and lawless acts.

623. BUTLER v. MICHIGAN
77 S. Ct.Rep. 524
1957

This is the first major censorship case to reach the Supreme Court; while technically it addressed itself only to the issue of applying standards of what was fit for children to the whole realm of literature, its implications are wide. See Z. Chafee, *The Blessings of Liberty;* A. Meiklejohn, *Free Speech: and its Relation to Self Government;* W. Gellhorn, *Individual Freedom and Governmental Restraints,* ch. 2; M. L. Ernst and W. Seagle, *To the Pure;* Marie Jahoda, *The Impact of Literature;* Paul Blanshard, *The Right to Read;* Frank Thayer, *Legal Control of the Press;* Lockhart and McClure, "Literature, the Law of Obscenity, and the Constitution," 38 *Minn. L. Rev.* 295; Alpert, "Judicial Censorship of Obscene Literature" 52 *Harv. L. Rev.* 40; Z. Chafee, "Censorship of Books and Plays," 1 *Bill of Rights Rev.* 16.

FRANKFURTER, J. This appeal from a judgment of conviction entered by the Recorder's Court of the City of Detroit, Michigan, challenges the constitutionality of the following provision, § 343, of the Michigan Penal Code, Comp.Laws Supp.1954, § 750.343:

"Any person who shall import, print, publish, sell, possess with the intent to sell, design, prepare, loan, give away, distribute or offer for sale, any book, magazine, newspaper, writing, pamphlet, ballad, printed paper, print, picture, drawing, photograph, publication or other thing, including any recordings, containing obscene, immoral, lewd or lascivious language, or obscene, immoral, lewd or lascivious prints, pictures, figures or descriptions, tending to incite minors to violent or depraved or immoral acts, manifestly tending to the corruption of the morals of youth, or shall introduce into any family, school or place of education or shall buy, procure, receive or have in his possession, any such book, pamphlet, magazine, newspaper, writing, ballad, printed paper, print, picture, drawing, photograph, publication or other thing, either for the purpose of sale, exhibition, loan or circulation, or with intent to introduce the same into any family, school or place of education, shall be guilty of a misdemeanor."

Appellant was charged with its violation for selling to a police officer what the trial judge characterized as "a book containing obscene, immoral, lewd, lascivious language, or descriptions, tending to incite minors to violent or depraved or immoral acts, manifestly tending to the corruption of the morals of youth." Appellant moved to dismiss the proceeding on the claim that application of § 343 unduly restricted freedom of speech as protected by the Due Process Clause of the Fourteenth Amendment in that the statute (1) prohibited distribution of a book to the general public on the basis of the undesirable influence it may have upon youth; (2) damned a book and proscribed its sale merely because of some isolated passages that appeared objectionable when divorced from the book as a whole; and (3) failed to provide a sufficiently definite standard of guilt. After hearing the evidence, the trial judge denied the motion, and, in an oral opinion, held that "the defendant is guilty because he sold a book in the City of Detroit containing this language [the passages deemed offensive], and also because the Court feels that even viewing the book as a whole, it [the objectionable language] was not necessary to the proper development of the theme of the book nor of the conflict expressed therein." Appellant was fined $100. . . .

It is clear on the record that appellant was convicted because Michigan, by § 343, made it an offense for him to make available for the general reading public (and he in fact sold to a police officer) a book that the trial judge found to have a potentially deleterious influence upon youth. The State insists that, by thus quarantining the general reading public against books not too rugged for grown men and women in order to shield juvenile innocence, it is exercising its power to promote the general welfare. Surely, this is to burn the house to roast the pig. Indeed, the Solicitor General of Michigan has, with characteristic candor, advised the Court that Michigan has a statute specifically designed to protect its children against obscene matter "tending to the corruption of the morals of youth." But the appellant was not convicted for violating this statute.

We have before us legislation not reasonably restricted to the evil with which it is said to deal. The incidence of this enactment is to reduce the adult population of Michigan to reading only what is fit for children. It thereby arbitrarily curtails one of those liberties of the individual, now enshrined in the Due Process Clause of the Fourteenth Amendment, that history has attested as the indispensable conditions for the maintenance and progress of a free society. We are constrained to reverse this conviction.

Reversed.

624. EISENHOWER ADDRESS ON AMERICAN POLICY IN THE MIDDLE EAST
February 20, 1957
(*New York Times*, February 21, 1957)

Bowing to American pressure and world opinion, Great Britain and France evacuated their troops from Egyptian territory at the end of 1956. See Doc. No. 625. Israeli troops were withdrawn from all occupied territory except the Gulf of Aqaba and the Gaza strip which had been used by Egypt for hostile acts against Israel. President Eisenhower assured the Israelis that the United States would support efforts to prevent the resumption of hostile acts by Egypt if Israel would withdraw her troops from these two areas. This commitment became binding when Israel complied with the President's request. The exact character of the commitment however was clouded in semantic ambiguity. See "United States Policy in the Middle East Sept. 1956–June 1957: Documents." Dept. of State Publication 6505.

I come to you again to talk about the situation in the Middle East. The future of the United Nations and peace in the Middle East may be at stake.

In the four months since I talked to you about the crisis in that area, the United Nations has made considerable progress in resolving some of the difficult problems. We are now, however, faced with a fateful moment as the result of the failure of Israel to withdraw its forces behind the Armistice lines, as contemplated by the United Nations Resolutions on this subject. . . .

When I talked to you last October, I pointed out that the United States fully realized that military action against Egypt resulted from grave and repeated provocations. But also I said that the use of military force to solve international disputes could not be reconciled with the principles and purposes of the United Nations, to which we had all subscribed. I added that our country could not believe that resort to force and war would for long serve the permanent interests of the attacking nations, which were Britain, France and Israel.

So I pledged that the United States would seek through the United Nations to end the conflict and to bring about a recall of the forces of invasion, and then make a renewed and earnest effort through that organization to secure justice, under international law, for all of the parties concerned.

Since that time much has been achieved and many of the dangers implicit in the situation have been avoided. The governments of Britain and France have withdrawn their forces from Egypt. Thereby they showed respect for the opinions of mankind as expressed almost unanimously by the eighty-nation members of the United Nations General Assembly. . . .

The Prime Minister of Israel, in answer to a personal communication, assured me early in November that Israel would willingly withdraw its forces if and when there should be created a United Nations force to move into the Suez Canal area. This force was, in fact, created and has moved into the canal area.

Subsequently, Israeli forces were withdrawn from much of the territory of Egypt which they had occupied. However, Israeli forces still remain outside the armistice lines, notably at the mouth of the Gulf of Aqaba which is about 100 miles from the nearest Israeli territory and in the Gaza Strip which, by the armistice agreement, was to be occupied by Egypt. This fact creates the present crisis. . . .

In view of the valued friendly relations which the United States has always had with the state of Israel, I wrote to Prime Minister Ben-Gurion on Feb. 3. I recalled his statement to me of Nov. 8 to the effect that the Israeli forces would be withdrawn under certain conditions, and I urged that, in view of the General Assembly resolutions of Feb. 2, Israel should complete that withdrawal.

However, the Prime Minister, in his reply, took the position that Israel would not evacuate its military forces from the Gaza Strip unless Israel retained the civil administration and police. This would be in contradiction to the armistice agreement. Also, the reply said that Israel would not withdraw from the Straits of Aqaba unless freedom of passage through the straits was assured.

It was a matter of keen disappointment to us that the Government of Israel, despite the United Nations action, still felt unwilling to withdraw.

However, in a further effort to meet the views of Israel in these respects, Secretary of State Dulles, at my direction, gave to the Government of Israel on Feb. 11 a statement of United States policy. This has now been made public. It pointed out that neither the United States nor the United Nations had authority to impose upon the parties a substantial modification of the Armistice agreement which was freely signed by Israel and Egypt. Nevertheless, the statement said, the United States as a member of the United Nations would seek such disposition of the United Nations Emergency Force as would assure that the Gaza Strip could no longer be a source of armed infiltration and reprisals.

The Secretary of State orally informed the Israeli Ambassador that the United States would be glad to urge and support, also, some participation by the United Nations, with the approval of Egypt, in the administration of the Gaza Strip. The principal population of the strip consists of about 300,000 Arab refugees, who exist largely as a charge upon the benevolence of the United Nations and its members.

With reference to the passage into and through the Gulf of Aqaba, we expressed the conviction that the gulf constitutes international waters and that no nation has the right to prevent free and innocent passage in the gulf. We announced that the United States was prepared to exercise this right itself and to join with others to secure general recognition of this right. . . .

We should not assume that if Israel withdraws, Egypt will prevent Israeli shipping from using the Suez Canal or the Gulf of Aqaba. If, unhappily, Egypt does hereafter violate the Armistice agreement or other international obligation, then this should be dealt with firmly by the society of nations.

The present moment is a grave one, but we are hopeful that reason and right will prevail. Since the events of last October and November, solid progress has been made, in conformity with the Charter of the United Nations. There is the cease-fire, the forces of Britain and France have been withdrawn, the forces of Israel have been partially withdrawn, and the clearing of the Canal nears completion. When Israel completes its withdrawal, it will have removed a definite block to further progress.

Once this block is removed, there will be serious and creative tasks for the United Nations to perform. There needs to be respect for the right of Israel to national existence and to internal development. Complicated provisions insuring the effective international use of the Suez Canal will need to be worked out in detail. The Arab refugee problem must be solved. As I said in my special message to Congress on Jan. 5, it must be made certain that all the Middle East is kept free from aggression and infiltration.

Finally, all who cherish freedom, including ourselves, should help the nations of the Middle East achieve their just aspirations for improving the well-being of their peoples.

What I have spoken about tonight is only one step in a long process calling for patience and diligence, but at this moment it is the critical issue on which future progress depends.

It is an issue which can be solved if only we will apply the principles of the United Nations.

That is why, my fellow Americans, I know you want the United States to continue to use its maximum influence to sustain those principles as the world's best hope for peace.

625. THE EISENHOWER DOCTRINE
March 9, 1957
(Public Law 7, 85th Congress)

The Suez crisis of 1956–57 created a situation which appeared to be highly favorable to Communist infiltration or overt attack. After persuading Britain, France, and Israel to withdraw their forces from Egyptian territory, President Eisenhower turned his attention to the larger problem of protecting the Middle East from Communist attack. The President asked for authority to send financial and military aid, at his discretion, to any Middle Eastern country threatened by Communist aggression. Congress endorsed the proposal for economic aid and modified the proposal dealing with military aid. Compare this doctrine with the Truman Doctrine, Doc. No. 574. See J. C. Hurewitz, *Middle East Dilemmas;* J. C. Campbell, "From 'Doctrine' to Policy in the Middle East," 35 *Foreign Affairs,* 441.

Resolved, That the President be and hereby is authorized to cooperate with and assist any nation or group of nations in the general area of the Middle East desiring such assistance in the development of economic strength dedicated to the maintenance of national independence.

SEC. 2. The President is authorized to undertake, in the general area of the Middle East, military assistance programs with any nation or group of nations of that area desiring such assistance. Furthermore, the United States regards as vital to the national interest and world peace the preservation of the independence and integrity of the nations of the Middle East. To this end, if the President determines the necessity thereof, the United States is prepared to use armed force to assist any such nation or group of nations requesting assistance against armed aggression from any country controlled by international communism: *Provided,* That such employment shall be consonant with the treaty obligations of the United States and with the Constitution of the United States.

SEC. 3. The President is hereby authorized to use during the balance of the fiscal year 1957 for economic and military assistance under this joint resolution not to exceed $200,000,000 from any appropriation now available for carrying out the provisions of the Mutual Security Act of 1954. . . .

SEC. 4. The President should continue to furnish facilities and military assistance, within the provisions of applicable law and established policies, to the United Nations Emergency Force in the Middle East, with a view to maintaining the truce in that region.

SEC. 5. The President shall within the months of January and July of each year report to the Congress his action hereunder.

SEC. 6. This joint resolution shall expire when the President shall determine that the peace and security of the nations in the general area of the Middle East are reasonably assured by international conditions created by action of the United Nations or otherwise except that it may be terminated earlier by a concurrent resolution of the two Houses of Congress.

626. CIVIL RIGHTS ACT OF 1957
September 9, 1957
(71 U. S. Statutes at Large, 634.)

Both Truman (see Doc. No. 581) and Eisenhower had requested legislation to provide federal enforcement of those guarantees of civil rights written into the Constitution and expounded by the Supreme Court. This hotly-contested act—the first of its kind since Reconstruction—went part way toward meeting these Presidential requests. It created a Federal Civil Rights Commission, established a Civil Rights division in the office of the Attorney-General, empowered federal prosecutors to obtain injunctions against those who denied any citizen his rights under the Constitution, and permitted trial of offenders in contempt of these injunctions without jury in civil cases, but with jury in criminal cases.

AN ACT

To provide means of further securing and protecting the civil rights of persons within the jurisdiction of the United States.

PART I—ESTABLISHMENT OF THE COMMISSION ON CIVIL RIGHTS

SEC. 101. (a) There is created in the executive branch of the Government a Commission on Civil Rights (hereinafter called the "commission").

(b) The commission shall be composed of six members who shall be appointed by the President by and with the advice and consent of the Senate. Not more than three of the members shall at any one time be of the same political party.

(c) The President shall designate one of the members of the commission as chairman and one as vice chairman. The vice chairman shall act as chairman in the absence or disability of the chairman, or in the event of a vacancy in that office.

(d) Any vacancy in the commission shall not affect its powers and shall be filled in the same manner, and subject to the same limitation with respect to party affiliations as the original appointment was made.

(e) Four members of the commission shall constitute a quorum.

RULES OF PROCEDURE OF THE COMMISSION

SEC. 102. (e) If the commission determines that evidence or testimony at any hearing may tend to defame, degrade or incriminate any person, it shall (1) receive such evidence or testimony in executive session; (2) afford such person an opportunity voluntarily to appear as a witness; and (3) receive and dispose of requests from such person to subpoena additional witnesses.

(g) No evidence or testimony taken in executive session may be released or used in public sessions without the consent of the commission. Whoever releases or uses in public without the consent of the commission evidence or testimony taken in executive

session shall be fined not more than $1,000, or imprisoned for not more than one year.

(h) In the discretion of the commission, witnesses may submit brief and pertinent sworn statements in writing for inclusion in the record. The commission is the sole judge of the pertinency of testimony and evidence adduced at its hearings.

(i) Upon payment of the cost thereof, a witness may obtain a transcript copy of his testimony given at a public session or, if given at an executive session, when authorized by the commission.

DUTIES OF THE COMMISSION

SEC. 104. (a). The commission shall—

(1) Investigate allegations in writing under oath or affirmation that certain citizens of the United States are being deprived of their right to vote and have that vote counted by reason of their color, race, religion or national origin; which writing, under oath or affirmation, shall set forth the facts upon which such belief or beliefs are based.

(2) Study and collect information concerning legal developments constituting a denial of equal protection of the laws under the Constitution; and

(3) Appraise the laws and policies of the Federal Government with respect to equal protection of the laws under the Constitution.

(b) The commission shall submit interim reports to the President (3) and to the Congress at such times as either the commission or the President shall deem desirable and shall submit to the President (4) and to the Congress a final and comprehensive report of its activities, findings, and recommendations not later than two years from the date of the enactment of this act.

(c) Sixty days after the submission of its final report and recommendations the commission shall cease to exist.

POWERS OF THE COMMISSION

SEC. 105 (a) (5). There shall be a full-time staff director for the commission who shall be appointed by the President by and with the advice and consent of the Senate and who shall receive compensation at a rate to be fixed by the President, not in excess of $22,500 a year. The President shall consult with the commission before submitting the nomination of any person for appointment to the position of staff director. Within the limitations of its appropriations, the commission may appoint (6) such other personnel as it deems advisable, in accordance with the civil service and classification laws, . . .

(b) The commission shall not accept or utilize services of voluntary or uncompensated personnel . . .

(c) The commission may constitute such advisory committees (i) within states composed of citizens of that state and may consult with governors, attorneys general and other representatives of state and local governments, and private organizations, as it deems advisable.

(e) All Federal agencies shall cooperate fully with the commission to the end that it may effectively carry out its functions and duties.

(f) The commission, or on the authorization of the commission any subcommittee of two or more members, at least one of whom shall be of each major political party, may, for the purpose of carrying out the provisions of this act, hold such hearings and act at such times and places as the commission or such authorized subcommittee may deem advisable. Subponeas for the attendance and testimony of witnesses or the production of written or other matter may be issued in accordance with the rules of the commission as contained in Section 102 (j) and (k) of this act, over the signature of the chairman of the commission or of such subcommittee, and may be served by any person designated by such chairman.

(g) In case of contumacy or refusal to obey a subpoena, any District Court of the United States or the United States Court of any territory or possession, or the District Court of the United States for the District of Columbia, within the jurisdiction of which the inquiry is carried on or within the jurisdiction of which said person guilty of contumacy or refusal to obey is found or resides or transacts business, upon application by the Attorney General of the United States shall have jurisdiction to issue to such person an order requiring such persons to appear before the commission or a subcommittee thereof, there to produce evidence if so ordered, or there to give testimony touching the matter under investigation; and any

failure to obey such order of the court may be punished by said court as a contempt thereof.

PART II—TO PROVIDE FOR AN ADDITIONAL ASSISTANT ATTORNEY GENERAL

SEC. III There shall be in the Department of Justice one additional assistant attorney general, who shall be appointed by the President, by and with the advice and consent of the Senate, who shall assist the Attorney General in the performance of his duties, and who shall receive compensation at the rate prescribed by law for other assistant attorneys generals.

PART IV—TO PROVIDE MEANS OF FURTHER SECURING AND PROTECTING THE RIGHT TO VOTE

SEC. 131. (c) Add, immediately following the present text, (13) four new subsections to read as follows:

(b) No person, whether acting under color of law or otherwise, shall intimidate, threaten, coerce or attempt to intimidate, threaten or coerce any other person for the purpose of interfering with the right of such other person to vote or to vote as he may choose, or of causing such other person to vote for, or not to vote for, any candidate for the office of President, Vice President, Presidential elector, member of the Senate or member of the House of Representatives, delegates or commissioners from the territories or possessions, at any general, special, or primary election held solely or in part for the purpose of selecting or electing any such candidate.

(c) Whenever any person has engaged or there are reasonable grounds to believe that any person is about to engage in any act or practice which would deprive any other person of any right or privilege secured by subsection (a) or (b), the Attorney General may institute for the United States, or in the name of the United States, a civil action or other proper proceeding for preventive relief, including an application for a permanent or temporary injunction, restraining order, or other order. In any proceeding hereunder the United States shall be liable for costs the same as a private person.

(d) The district courts of the United

States shall have jurisdiction of proceedings instituted pursuant to this section and shall exercise the same without regard to whether the party aggrieved shall have exhausted any administrative or other remedies that may be provided by law.

(e) (14) Any person cited for an alleged contempt under this act shall be allowed to make his full defense by counsel learned in the law; and the court before which he is cited or tried, or some judge thereof, shall immediately, upon his request, assign to him such counsel, not exceeding two, as he may desire, who shall have free access to him at all reasonable hours. He shall be allowed, in his defense to make any proof that he can produce by lawful witnesses, and shall have the like process of the court to compel his witnesses to appear at his trial or hearing, as is usually granted to compel witnesses to appear on behalf of the prosecution. If such person shall be found by the court to be financially unable to provide for such counsel, it shall be the duty of the court to provide such counsel.

PART V—TO PROVIDE TRIAL BY JURY FOR PROCEEDINGS TO PUNISH CRIMINAL CONTEMPTS OF COURT GROWING OUT OF CIVIL RIGHTS CASES AND TO AMEND THE JUDICIAL CODE RELATING TO FEDERAL JURY QUALIFICATIONS

SEC. 151. In all cases of criminal contempt arising under the provisions of this act, the accused, upon conviction, shall be punished by fine or imprisonment or both; Provided however, that in case the accused is a natural person the fine to be paid shall not exceed the sum of $1,000, nor shall imprisonment exceed the term of six months; Provided further, That in any such proceeding for criminal contempt, at the discretion of the judge, the accused may be tried with or without a jury; Provided further, however, That in the event such proceeding for criminal contempt be tried before a judge without a jury and the sentence of the court on conviction is a fine in excess of the sum of $300 or imprisonment in excess of forty-five days, the accused in said proceeding, upon demand therefor, shall be entitled to a trial de novo before a jury, which shall conform as near as may be to the practice in other criminal cases.

This section shall not apply to contempts committed in the presence of the court or so near thereto as to interfere directly with the administration of justice nor to the misbehavior, misconduct or disobedience, of any officer of the court in respect to the writs, orders, or process of the court.

Nor shall anything herein or in any other provision of law be construed to deprive courts of their power, by civil contempt proceedings, without a jury, to secure compliance with or to prevent obstruction of, as distinguished from punishment for violations of, any lawful writ, process, order, rule, decree, or command of the court in accordance with the prevailing usages of law and equity, including the power of detention. . . .

627. EISENHOWER'S ADDRESS ON THE SITUATION IN LITTLE ROCK
September 24, 1957

(Public Papers of the Presidents: Dwight D. Eisenhower, 1957, no. 198)

With the passing of time, Southern resistance to desegregation grew and became "massive." Within a few months, in 1956, five southern states adopted forty-two segregation measures. Georgia made it a felony for any school official to spend tax money for public schools in which the races were mixed; Mississippi made it a crime for any organization to institute desegregation proceedings in the state courts; Virginia went to the extreme of closing some of her public schools altogether. State resistance came to a head in Arkansas. In the late summer of 1957 Governor Orville Faubus called out the state National Guard under orders not to protect Negro children in their right to attend school, but to prevent them from exercising that right. These troops were withdrawn on order of the federal district judge. Mobs, aided and abetted by the local authorities, then prevented Negroes from entering the local high school. On September 24, President Eisenhower dispatched federal troops to Little Rock to preserve order and at the same time he addressed the nation on this subject. The people of Arkansas responded by reelecting Faubus to the governorship, and Faubus persisted in his tactics of obstruction until the following year. Eventually order was restored, the troops withdrawn, and token desegregation took place. See A. T. Mason and W. M. Beaney, *The Supreme Court in a Free Society;* C. V. Woodward, *The Strange Career of Jim Crow;* C. S. Mangum, *The Legal Status of the Negro;* Harry Ashmore, *The Negro and the Schools;* William Peters, *The Southern Temper;* Don Shoemaker, ed., *With All Deliberate Speed;* Albert Blaustein, and Clarence Ferguson, *Desegregation and the Law;* Benjamin Ziegler, *Desegregation and the Supreme Court.*

My Fellow Citizens. . . . I must speak to you about the serious situation that has arisen in Little Rock. . . . In that city, under the leadership of demagogic extremists, disorderly mobs have deliberately prevented the carrying out of proper orders from a federal court. Local authorities have not eliminated that violent opposition and, under the law, I yesterday issued a proclamation calling upon the mob to disperse.

This morning the mob again gathered in front of the Central High School of Little Rock, obviously for the purpose of again preventing the carrying out of the court's order relating to the admission of Negro children to that school.

Whenever normal agencies prove inadequate to the task and it becomes necessary for the executive branch of the federal government to use its powers and authority to uphold federal courts, the President's responsibility is inescapable.

In accordance with that responsibility, I have today issued an Executive Order directing the use of troops under federal authority to aid in the execution of federal law at Little Rock, Arkansas. This became necessary when my Proclamation of yesterday was not observed, and the obstruction of justice still continues.

It is important that the reasons for my action be understood by all our citizens.

As you know, the Supreme Court of the United States has decided that separate public educational facilities for the races are inherently unequal and therefore compulsory school segregation laws are unconstitutional. . . .

During the past several years, many communities in our southern states have instituted public school plans for gradual progress in the enrollment and attendance of school children of all races in order to bring themselves into compliance with the law of the land.

They thus demonstrated to the world that we are a nation in which laws, not men, are supreme.

I regret to say that this truth—the cornerstone of our liberties—was not observed in this instance. . . .

Here is the sequence of events in the development of the Little Rock school case.

In May of 1955, the Little Rock School Board approved a moderate plan for the gradual desegregation of the public schools in that city. It provided that a start toward integration would be made at the present term in the high school, and that the plan would be in full operation by 1963. . . . Now this Little Rock plan was challenged in the courts by some who believed that the period of time as proposed in the plan was too long.

The United States Court at Little Rock, which has supervisory responsibility under the law for the plan of desegregation in the public schools, dismissed the challenge, thus approving a gradual rather than an abrupt change from the existing system. The court found that the school board had acted in good faith in planning for a public school system free from racial discrimination.

Since that time, the court has on three separate occasions issued orders directing that the plan be carried out. All persons were instructed to refrain from interfering with the efforts of the school board to comply with the law.

Proper and sensible observance of the law then demanded the respectful obedience which the nation has a right to expect from all its people. This, unfortunately, has not been the case at Little Rock. Certain misguided persons, many of them imported into Little Rock by agitators, have insisted upon defying the law and have sought to bring it into disrepute. The orders of the court have thus been frustrated.

The very basis of our individual rights and freedoms rests upon the certainty that the President and the Executive Branch of Government will support and insure the carrying out of the decisions of the federal courts, even, when necessary with all the means at the President's command. . . .

Mob rule cannot be allowed to override the decisions of our courts.

Now, let me make it very clear that federal troops are not being used to relieve local and state authorities of their primary duty to preserve the peace and order of the community. . . .

The proper use of the powers of the Executive Branch to enforce the orders of a federal court is limited to extraordinary and compelling circumstances. Manifestly, such an extreme situation has been created in Little Rock. This challenge must be met and with such measures as will preserve to the people as a whole their lawfully protected rights in a climate permitting their free and fair exercise.

The overwhelming majority of our people in every section of the country are united in their respect for observance of the law— even in those cases where they may disagree with that law. . . .

A foundation of our American way of life is our national respect for law.

In the South, as elsewhere, citizens are keenly aware of the tremendous disservice that has been done to the people of Arkansas in the eyes of the nation, and that has been done to the nation in the eyes of the world.

At a time when we face grave situations abroad because of the hatred that communism bears toward a system of government based on human rights, it would be difficult to exaggerate the harm that is being done to the prestige and influence, and indeed to the safety, of our nation and the world.

Our enemies are gloating over this incident and using it everywhere to misrepresent our whole nation. We are portrayed as a violator of those standards of conduct which the peoples of the world united to proclaim in the Charter of the United Nations. There they affirmed "faith in fundamental human rights" and "in the dignity and worth of the human person" and they did so "without distinction as to race, sex, language or religion."

And so, with deep confidence, I call upon the citizens of the State of Arkansas to assist in bringing to an immediate end all interference with the law and its processes. If resistance to the federal court orders ceases at once, the further presence of federal troops will be unnecessary and the City of Little Rock will return to its normal habits of peace and order and a blot upon the fair name and high honor of our nation in the world will be removed.

Thus will be restored the image of America and of all its parts as one nation, indivisible, with liberty and justice for all.

628. YATES v. UNITED STATES
354 U. S. 298, at 339
1957

Appeal from U.S. District Court for Southern District of California. This case involving the alleged violation of the terms of the Smith Act by fourteen members of the Communist Party, qualified the Dennis decision in important particulars. We give here not the opinion of the Court, through Justice Harlan, but the concurring opinion by Justices Black and Douglas which covers somewhat broader ground more briefly. See references for Doc. 593, and Alexander Meiklejohn, *Free Speech and Its Relation to Self-Government;* Richardson, "Freedom of Expression and the Functions of the Courts," 65 *Harvard Law Rev.* 1.

Mr. Justice BLACK, with whom Mr. Justice DOUGLAS joins, concurring in part and dissenting in part:

I

I would reverse every one of these convictions and direct that all the defendants be acquitted. In my judgment the statutory provisions on which these prosecutions are based abridge freedom of speech, press, and assembly in violation of the First Amendment to the United States Constitution. See my dissent and that of Mr. Justice Douglas in Dennis v. United States, 341 U. S. 494, 579. Also see my opinion in American Communications Ass'n, C. I. O. v. Douds, 339 U. S. 382, 445.

The kind of trials conducted here are wholly dissimilar to normal criminal trials. Ordinarily these "Smith Act" trials are prolonged affairs lasting for months. In part this is attributable to the routine introduction in evidence of massive collections of books, tracts, pamphlets, newspapers, and manifestoes discussing communism, socialism, capitalism, feudalism and governmental institutions in general, which, it is not too much to say, are turgid, diffuse, abstruse, and just plain dull. Of course, no juror can or is expected to plow his way through this jungle of verbiage. The testimony of witnesses is comparatively insignificant. Guilt or innocence may turn on what Marx or Engels or someone else wrote or advocated as much as a hundred or more years ago. Elaborate, refined distinctions are drawn between "communism," "Marxism," "Leninism," "Trotskyism," and "Stalinism." When the propriety of obnoxious or unorthodox views about government is in reality made the crucial issue, as it must be in cases of this kind, prejudice makes conviction inevitable except in the rarest circumstances.

Since the Court proceeds on the assumption that the statutory provisions involved are valid, however, I feel free to express my views about the issues it considers. . . .

I agree with the Court insofar as it holds that the trial judge erred in instructing that persons could be punished under the Smith Act for teaching and advocating forceful overthrow as an abstract principle. But on the other hand, I cannot agree that the instruction which the Court indicates it might approve is constitutionally permissible. The Court says that persons can be punished for advocating action to overthrow the Government by force and violence, where those to whom the advocacy is addressed are urged "to *do* something, now or in the future, rather than merely to *believe* in something." Under the Court's approach, defendants could still be convicted simply for agreeing to talk as distinguished from agreeing to act. I believe that the First Amendment forbids Congress to punish people for talking about pub-

lic affairs, whether or not such discussion incites to action, legal or illegal. As the Virginia Assembly said in 1785, in its "Statute for Religious Liberty," written by Thomas Jefferson, "it is time enough for the rightful purposes of civil government, for its officers to interfere when principles break out into overt acts against peace and good order." . . .

The section under which this conspiracy indictment was brought, requires proof of an overt act done "to effect the object of the conspiracy." Originally, 11 such overt acts were charged here. These 11 have now dwindled to 2, and as the Court says:

> "Each was a public meeting held under Party auspices at which speeches were made by one or more of the petitioners extolling leaders of the Soviet Union and criticizing various aspects of the foreign policy of the United States. At one of the meetings an appeal for funds was made. Petitioners contend that these meetings do not satisfy the requirement of the statute that there be shown an act done by one of the conspirators 'to effect the object of the conspiracy.' The Government concedes that nothing unlawful was shown to have been said or done at these meetings, but contends that these occurrences nonetheless sufficed as overt acts under the jury's findings."

The Court holds that attendance at these lawful and orderly meetings constitutes an "overt act" sufficient to meet the statutory requirements. I disagree.

The requirement of proof of an overt act in conspiracy cases is no mere formality, particularly in prosecutions like these which in many respects are akin to trials for treason. Article III, Sect. 3, of the Constitution provides that "No Person shall be convicted of Treason unless on the Testimony of two Witnesses to the same overt Act, or on Confession in open Court." One of the objects of this provision was to keep people from being convicted of disloyalty to government during periods of excitement when passions and prejudices ran high, merely because they expressed "unacceptable" views. See Cramer v. United States, 325 U. S. 1, 48. The same reasons that make proof of overt acts so important in treason cases apply here. The only overt act which is now charged against these defendants is that they went to a constitutionally protected public assembly where they took part in lawful discussion of public questions, and where neither they nor anyone else advocated or suggested overthrow of the United States Government. Many years ago this Court said that "The very idea of a government, republican in form, implies a right on the part of its citizens to meet peaceably for consultation in respect to public affairs and to petition for a redress of grievances." United States v. Cruikshank, 92 U. S. 542. In my judgment defendants' attendance at these public meetings cannot be viewed as an overt act to effectuate the object of the conspiracy charged.

In essence, petitioners were tried upon the charge that they believe in and want to foist upon this country a different and to us a despicable form of authoritarian government in which voices criticizing the existing order are summarily silenced. I fear that the present type of prosecutions are more in line with the philosophy of authoritarian government than with that expressed by our First Amendment.

Doubtlessly, dictators have to stamp out causes and beliefs which they deem subversive to their evil regimes.

But governmental suppression of causes and beliefs seems to me to be the very antithesis of what our Constitution stands for. The choice expressed in the First Amendment in favor of free expression was made against a turbulent background by men such as Jefferson, Madison, and Mason—men who believed that loyalty to the provisions of this Amendment was the best way to assure a long life for this new nation and its Government. Unless there is complete freedom for expression of all ideas, whether we like them or not, concerning the way government should be run and who shall run it, I doubt if any views in the long run can be secured against the censor. The First Amendment provides the only kind of security system that can preserve a free government— one that leaves the way wide open for people to favor, discuss, advocate, or incite causes and doctrines however obnoxious and antagonistic such views may be to the rest of us.

Mr. Justice CLARK dissented.

629. PEREZ v. BROWNELL
1958
356 U. S. 44

Action by national of the United States by birth against Attorney General of United States for judgment declaring plaintiff to be a national. Section 401 of the Nationality Act of 1940 provided that a national of the United States shall lose his citizenship by voting in an election in a foreign state. This decision on the power of the Congress to deprive a native-born American of his citizenship represents perhaps the furthest reach of Congressional authority during peace time in the whole of our history. See Preuss, "International Law and Deprivation of Nationality," 23 George Washington Law J. 250; John B. Moore, Digest of International Law, v. 3 sec. 410; John Roche, "The Loss of American Nationality," 99 U. of Pa. Law Rev. 25; Louis Boudin, "Involuntary Loss of Citizenship," 73 Harvard Law Rev. 1510; Weiss, Nationality and Statelessness in International Law. This decision was reversed in Afroyim v. Rusk, 387 U.S. 253 (1967).

Mr. Justice FRANKFURTER: The first step in our inquiry must be to answer the question: what is the source of power on which Congress must be assumed to have drawn? Although there is in the Constitution no specific grant to Congress of power to enact legislation for the effective regulation of foreign affairs, there can be no doubt of the existence of this power in the law-making organ of the nation. See United States v. Curtiss-Wright Export Corp., 299 U. S. 304. The states that joined together to form a single nation and to create, through the Constitution, a Federal Government to conduct the affairs of that nation must be held to have granted that Government the powers indispensable to its functioning effectively in the company of sovereign nations. The Government must be able not only to deal affirmatively with foreign nations, as it does through the maintenance of diplomatic relations with them and the protection of American citizens sojourning within their territories. It must also be able to reduce to a minimum the frictions that are unavoidable in a world of sovereigns sensitive in matters touching their dignity and interests.

The inference is fairly to be drawn from the Congressional history of the Nationality Act of 1940, read in light of the historical background of expatriation in this country, that, in making voting in foreign elections (among other behavior) an act of expatriation, Congress was seeking to effectuate its power to regulate foreign affairs. The legislators, counseled by those on whom they rightly relied for advice, were concerned about actions by citizens in foreign countries that create problems of protection and are inconsistent with American allegiance. Moreover, we cannot ignore the fact that embarrassments in the conduct of foreign relations were of primary concern in the consideration of the Act of 1907, of which the loss of nationality provisions of the 1940 Act are a codification and expansion.

Broad as the power in the National Government to regulate foreign affairs must necessarily be, it is not without limitation. The restrictions confining Congress in the exercise of any of the powers expressly delegated to it in the Constitution apply with equal vigor when that body seeks to regulate our relations with other nations. Since Congress may not act arbitrarily, a rational nexus must exist between the content of a specific power in Congress and the action of Congress in carrying that power into execution. More simply stated, the means—in this case, withdrawal of citizenship—must be reasonably related to the end—here, regulation of foreign affairs. The inquiry—and, in the case before us, the sole inquiry—into which this Court must enter is whether or not Congress may have concluded not unreasonably that there is a relevant connection between this fundamental source of power and the ultimate legislative action.

Our starting point is to ascertain whether the power of Congress to deal with foreign relations may reasonably be deemed to include a power to deal generally with the active participation, by way of voting, of American citizens in foreign political elections.

Experience amply attests that in this day of extensive international travel, rapid communication and widespread use of propaganda, the activities of the citizens of one nation when in another country can easily cause serious embarrassments to the government of their own country as well as to their fellow citizens. We cannot deny to Congress the reasonable belief that these difficulties might well become acute, to the point of jeopardizing the successful conduct of international relations, when the citizen of one country chooses to participate in the political or governmental affairs of another country. The citizen may by his action unwittingly promote or encourage a course of conduct contrary to the interests of his own government; moreover, the people or government of the foreign country may regard his action to be the action of his government, or at least as a reflection if not an expression of its policy.

It follows that such activity is regulable by Congress under its power to deal with foreign affairs. And it must be regulable on more than an *ad hoc* basis. The subtle influences and repercussion with which the government must deal make it reasonable for the generalized, although clearly limited, category of "political election" to be used in defining the area of regulation. That description carries with it the scope and meaning of its context and purpose; classes of elections—nonpolitical in the colloquial sense —as to which participation by Americans could not possibly have any effect on the relations of the United States with another country are excluded by any rational construction of the phrase. The classification that Congress has adopted cannot be said to be inappropriate to the difficulties to be dealt with. Specific applications are of course open to judicial challenge, as are other general categories in the law, by a "gradual process of judicial inclusion and exclusion." Davidson v. New Orleans, 96 U. S. 97.

The question must finally be faced whether, given the power to attach some sort of consequence to voting in a foreign political election, Congress, acting under the Necessary and Proper Clause, could attach loss of nationality to it. Is the means, withdrawal of citizenship, reasonably calculated to effect the end that is within the power of Congress to achieve, the avoidance of embarrassment in the conduct of our foreign relations attributable to voting by American citizens in foreign political elections? The importance and extreme delicacy of the matters here sought to be regulated demand that Congress be permitted ample scope in selecting appropriate modes for accomplishing its purpose. The critical connection between this conduct and loss of citizenship is the fact that it is the possession of American citizenship by a person committing the act that makes the act potentially embarrassing to the American Government and pregnant with the possibility of embroiling this country in disputes with other nations. The termination of citizenship terminates the problem. Moreover, the fact is not without significance that Congress has interpreted this conduct, not irrationally, as importing not only something less than complete and unswerving allegiance to the United States but also elements of an allegiance to another country in some measure, at least, inconsistent with American citizenship.

It cannot be said, then, that Congress acted without warrant when, pursuant to its power to regulate the relations of the United States with foreign countries, it provided that anyone who votes in a foreign election of significance politically in the life of another country shall lose his American citizenship. To deny the power of Congress to enact the legislation challenged here would be to disregard the constitutional allocation of governmental functions that it is this Court's solemn duty to guard.

Judgment affirmed.

Mr. Chief Justice WARREN, with whom Mr. Justice BLACK and Mr. Justice DOUGLAS join, dissenting: Citizenship *is* man's basic right for it is nothing less than the right to have rights. Remove this priceless possession and there remains a stateless person, disgraced and degraded in the eyes of his countrymen. He has no lawful claim to protection from any nation, and no nation may assert rights on his behalf. His very existence is at the sufferance of the state within whose borders he happens to be. In this country the expatriate would presumably enjoy, at most, only the limited rights and privileges of aliens, and like the alien he might even be subject to deportation and thereby deprived of the right to assert any rights. This government was not established with power to decree this fate.

The people who created this government endowed it with broad powers. They created a sovereign state with power to function as a sovereignty. But the citizens themselves are sovereign, and their citizenship is not subject to the general powers of their government. Whatever may be the scope of its powers to regulate the conduct and affairs of all persons within its jurisdiction, a government *of* the people cannot take away their citizenship simply because one branch of that government can be said to have a conceivably rational basis for wanting to do so.

The fatal defect in the statute before us is that its application is not limited to those situations that may rationally be said to constitute an abandonment of citizenship. In specifying that any act of voting in a foreign political election results in loss of citizenship, Congress has employed a classification so broad that it encompasses conduct that fails to show a voluntary abandonment of American citizenship. "The connection between the fact proved and that presumed is not sufficient." Manley v. State of Georgia, 279 U.S. 1. The reach of this statute is best indicated by a decision of a former attorney general, holding that an American citizen lost her citizenship under Section 401 (e) by voting in an election in a Canadian town on the issue of whether beer and wine should be sold. Voting in a foreign election may be a most equivocal act, giving rise to no implication that allegiance has been compromised. Nothing could demonstrate this better than the political history of this country. It was not until 1928 that a presidential election was held in this country in which no alien was eligible to vote. Earlier in our history at least 22 states had extended the franchise to aliens. It cannot be seriously contended that this nation understood the vote of each alien who previously took advantage of this privilege to be an act of allegiance to this country, jeopardizing the alien's native citizenship. How then can we attach such significance to any vote of a United States citizen in a foreign election? It is also significant that of 84 nations whose nationality laws have been compiled by the United Nations, only this country specifically designates foreign voting as an expatriating act.

My conclusions are as follows. The Government is without power to take citizenship away from a native-born or lawfully naturalized American. The Fourteenth Amendment recognizes that this priceless right is immune from the exercise of governmental powers. If the Government determines that certain conduct by United States citizens should be prohibited because of anticipated injurious consequences to the conduct of foreign affairs or to some other legitimate governmental interest, it may within the limits of the Constitution proscribe such activity and assess appropriate punishment. But every exercise of governmental power must find its source in the Constitution. The power to denationalize is not within the letter or the spirit of the powers with which our Government was endowed. The citizen may elect to renounce his citizenship, and under some circumstances he may be found to have abandoned his status by voluntarily performing acts that compromise his undivided allegiance to his country. The mere act of voting in a foreign election, however, without regard to the circumstances attending the participation, is not sufficient to show a voluntary abandonment of citizenship. The record in this case does not disclose any of the circumstances under which this petitioner voted. We know only the bare fact that he cast a ballot. The basic right of American citizenship has been too dearly won to be so lightly lost.

630. EISENHOWER ANNOUNCES DISPATCH OF U. S. TROOPS TO LEBANON
July 15, 1958
(Public Papers of the Presidents: Dwight D. Eisenhower, 1958, no. 171

When in the spring of 1958 Syria and Egypt undertook to subvert the pro-Western government of Lebanon, President Chamoun appealed to the United Nations for help. The UN machinery worked slowly—or not at all—and when Iraq broke out in revolt, Chamoun turned directly to the United States for help. Eisenhower responded by ordering the Sixth Fleet to steam into the eastern Mediterranean and by dispatching eventually 14,000 Marines to Lebanon. An American proposal to turn the whole thing over to the United Nations was vetoed by the Soviet. When nearby Arab states agreed to refrain from intervention in Lebanon, and Chamoun agreed to retire, peace returned to the little country. In October, Eisenhower withdrew the Marines. See Doc. no. 625; Carleton Coon, *The Story of the Middle East;* Caractacus, *Revolution in Iraq;* John C. Campbell, *Defense of the Middle East;* Nicola Ziadeh, *Syria and Lebanon;* Walter Z. Laqueur, *The Soviet Union and the Middle East.*

Yesterday morning, I received from President Chamoun of Lebanon an urgent plea that some United States forces be stationed in Lebanon to help maintain security and to evidence the concern of the United States for the integrity and independence of Lebanon. President Chamoun's appeal was made with the concurrence of all the members of the Lebanese Cabinet.

President Chamoun made clear that he considered an immediate United States response imperative if Lebanon's independence, already menaced from without, were to be preserved in the face of the grave developments which occurred yesterday in Baghdad whereby the lawful government was violently overthrown and many of its members martyred.

In response to this appeal from the government of Lebanon, the United States has dispatched a contingent of United States forces to Lebanon to protect American lives and by their presence there to encourage the Lebanese government in defense of Lebanese sovereignty and integrity. These forces have not been sent as any act of war. They will demonstrate the concern of the United States for the independence and integrity of Lebanon, which we deem vital to the national interest and world peace. Our concern will also be shown by economic assistance. We shall act in accordance with these legitimate concerns.

The United States, this morning, will report its action to an emergency meeting of the United Nations Security Council. As the United Nations charter recognizes, there is an inherent right of collective self-defense. In conformity with the spirit of the charter, the United States is reporting the measures taken by it to the Security Council of the United Nations, making clear that these measures will be terminated as soon as the Security Council has itself taken the measures necessary to maintain international peace and security.

The United States believes that the United Nations can and should take measures which are adequate to preserve the independence and integrity of Lebanon. It is apparent, however, that in the face of the tragic and shocking events that are occurring nearby, more will be required than the team of United Nations observers now in Lebanon. Therefore, the United States will support in the United Nations measures which seem to be adequate to meet the new situation and which will enable the United States forces promptly to be withdrawn.

Lebanon is a small peace-loving state with which the United States has traditionally had the most friendly relations. There are in Lebanon about 2500 Americans and we cannot, consistently with our historic relations and with the principles of the United Nations, stand idly by when Lebanon appeals itself for evidence of our concern and when Lebanon may not be able to preserve internal order and to defend itself against indirect aggression.

631. NATIONAL DEFENSE EDUCATION ACT
September 2, 1958
(72 *U. S. Statutes at Large,* 1580 ff. Public Law 85–864)

The "baby-bulge" of the forties, which brought additional millions of children to schools and colleges, the rising costs of education, and the rapid obsolescence of existing facilities created an acute crisis in the decade of the fifties. As local school authorities found it difficult to raise enough money to do the job adequately, demand for federal aid became insistent. In 1947–48 the President's Commission on Higher Education proposed increased federal spending for higher education and in 1956 the President's Committee for the White House Conference on Education advocated an expanded program of federal support for primary and secondary education. President Eisenhower proposed a $2 billion school aid program in 1956, and President Kennedy asked for $3 billion in 1961, but such proposals invariably encountered strong opposition both from religious interests demanding aid for parochial schools and from states-rights conservatives who feared increasing federal control over education. At the college level, agreement was somewhat easier to achieve, and Congress in 1958 passed the National Defense Education Act, which was extended and broadened by subsequent acts of 1961, 1963 and 1964. The emphasis on science, readily apparent from the portions given below, reflected current alarm over Soviet successes in missile development—the "missile gap"—while the Communist disclaimer was a reminder that cold-war considerations gave an important impetus to the passage of this legislation. Later the scope of the program was broadened to include non-scientific subjects, and the Communist disclaimer was dropped.

TITLE I—GENERAL PROVISIONS

SEC. 101. The Congress hereby finds and declares that the security of the Nation requires the fullest development of the mental resources and technical skills of its young men and women. The present emergency demands that additional and more adequate educational opportunities be made available. The defense of this Nation depends upon the mastery of modern techniques developed from complex scientific principles. It depends as well upon the discovery and development of new principles, new techniques, and new knowledge.

We must increase our efforts to identify and educate more of the talent of our Nation. This requires programs that will give assurance that no student of ability will be denied an opportunity for higher education because of financial need; will correct as rapidly as possible the existing imbalances in our educational programs which have led to an insufficient proportion of our population educated in science, mathematics, and modern foreign languages and trained in technology.

The Congress reaffirms the principle and declares that the States and local communities have and must retain control over and primary responsibility for public education. The national interest requires, however, that the Federal Government give assistance to education for programs which are important to our defense.

To meet the present educational emergency requires additional effort at all levels of government. It is therefore the purpose of this Act to provide substantial assistance in various forms to individuals, and to States and their subdivisions, in order to insure trained manpower of sufficient quality and quantity to meet the national defense needs of the United States.

SEC. 102. Nothing contained in this Act shall be construed to authorize any department, agency, officer, or employee of the United States to exercise any direction, supervision, or control over the curriculum, program of instruction, administration, or personnel of any educational institution or school system.

TITLE II—LOANS TO STUDENTS IN INSTITUTIONS OF HIGHER EDUCATION

SEC. 201. For the purpose of enabling the Commissioner to stimulate and assist in the establishment at institutions of higher education of funds for the making of low-interest loans to students in need thereof to pursue their courses of study in such institutions, there are hereby authorized to be appropriated $47,500,000 for the fiscal year ending June 30, 1959, $75,000,000 for the fiscal year ending June 30, 1960, $82,500,000 for the- fiscal year ending June 30, 1961, $90,000,000 for the fiscal year ending June 30, 1962, and such sums for the fiscal year ending June 30, 1963, and each of the three succeeding fiscal years as may be necessary to enable students who have received a loan for any school year ending prior to July 1, 1962, to continue or complete their education. . . .

(b) In no case may the total of such Federal capital contributions to any institution of higher education for any fiscal year exceed $250,000.

SEC. 204. An agreement with any institution of higher education for Federal capital contributions by the Commissioner under this title shall—

(1) provide for establishment of a student loan fund by such institution; . . .

(4) provide that in the selection of students to receive loans from such student loan fund special consideration shall be given to (A) students with a superior academic background who express a desire to teach in elementary or secondary schools, and (B) students whose academic background indicates a superior capacity or preparation in science, mathematics, engineering, or a modern foreign language. . . .

SEC. 207. (a) Upon application by any institution of higher education with which he has made an agreement under this title, the Commissioner may make a loan to such institution for the purpose of helping to finance the institution's capital contributions to a student loan fund established pursuant to such agreement. . . .

TITLE III—FINANCIAL ASSISTANCE FOR STRENGTHENING SCIENCE, MATHEMATICS, AND MODERN FOREIGN LANGUAGE INSTRUCTION

SEC. 301. There are hereby authorized to be appropriated $70,000,000 for the fiscal year ending June 30, 1959, and for each of the three succeeding fiscal years, for (1) making payments to State educational agencies under this title for the acquisition of equipment (suitable for use in providing education in science, mathematics, or modern foreign language) and . . . (2) making loans authorized in section 305. . . .

SEC. 305. (a) The Commissioner shall allot, out of funds reserved for each fiscal year for the purposes of this section under the provisions of section 302 (a), to each State for loans under the provisions of this section an amount which bears the same ratio to such funds as the number of persons in such State enrolled in private nonprofit elementary and secondary schools bears to the total of such numbers for all States.

(b) From the sums allotted to each State under the provisions of this section the Commissioner is authorized to make loans to private nonprofit elementary and secondary schools in such State for the purposes for which payments to State educational agencies are authorized under the first sentence of section 301. . . .

TITLE IV—NATIONAL DEFENSE FELLOWSHIPS

SEC. 401. There are hereby authorized to be appropriated such sums as may be necessary to carry out the provisions of this title.

SEC. 402. During the fiscal year ending June 30, 1959, the Commissioner is authorized to award one thousand fellowships under the provisions of this title, and during each of the three succeeding fiscal years he is authorized to award one thousand five hundred such fellowships. Such fellowships shall be for periods of study not in excess of three academic years.

SEC. 403. (a) The Commissioner shall award fellowships under this title to individuals accepted for study in graduate programs approved by him under this section. The Commissioner shall approve a graduate program of an institution of higher education only upon application by the institution and only upon his finding:

(1) that such program is a new program or an existing program which has been expanded,

(2) that such new program or expansion of an existing program will substantially further the objective of increasing the facilities available in the Nation for the graduate training of college or university level teachers and of promoting a wider geographical distribution of such facilities throughout the Nation, and

(3) that in the acceptance of persons for study in such programs preference will be given to persons interested in teaching in institutions of higher education.

SEC. 404. (a) Each person awarded a fellowship under the provisions of this title shall receive a stipend of $2,000 for the first academic year of study after the baccalaureate degree, $2,200 for the second such year, and $2,400 for the third such year, plus an additional amount of $400 for each such year on account of each of his dependents.

(b) In addition to the amounts paid to persons pursuant to subsection (a) there shall be paid to the institution of higher education at which each such person is pursuing his course of study such amount, not more than $2,500 per academic year, as is determined by the Commissioner to constitute that portion of the cost of the new graduate program or of the expansion in an existing graduate program in which such person is pursuing his course of study, which is reasonably attributable to him.

TITLE V—GUIDANCE, COUNSELING, AND TESTING; IDENTIFICATION AND ENCOURAGEMENT OF ABLE STUDENTS

SEC. 501. There are hereby authorized to be appropriated $15,000,000 for the fiscal year ending June 30, 1959, and for each of the three succeeding fiscal years, for making grants to State educational agencies under this part to assist them to establish and maintain programs of testing and guidance and counseling. . . .

SEC. 503. (a) Any State which desires to receive payments under this part shall submit to the Commissioner, through its State educational agency, a State plan which meets the requirements of section 1004 (a) and sets forth—

(1) a program for testing students in the public secondary schools, and if authorized by law in other secondary schools, of such State to identify students with outstanding aptitudes and ability, and the means of testing which will be utilized in carrying out such program; and

(2) a program of guidance and counseling in the public secondary schools of such State (A) to advise students of courses of study best

suited to their ability, aptitudes, and skills, and (B) to encourage students with outstanding aptitudes and ability to complete their secondary school education, take the necessary courses for admission to institutions of higher education, and enter such institutions. . . .

TITLE X—MISCELLANEOUS PROVISIONS

. . . (f) No part of any funds appropriated or otherwise made available for expenditure under authority of this Act shall be used to make payments or loans to any individual unless such individual (1) has executed and filed with the Commissioner an affidavit that he does not believe in, and is not a member of and does not support any organization that believes in or teaches, the overthrow of the United States Government by force or violence or by any illegal or unconstitutional methods, and (2) has taken and subscribed to an oath or affirmation in the following form: "I do solemnly swear (or affirm) that I will bear true faith and allegiance to the United States of America and will support and defend the Constitution and laws of the United States against all its enemies, foreign and domestic." The provisions of section 1001 of title 18, United States Code, shall be applicable with respect to such affidavits. . . .

632. NAACP v. ALABAMA
357 U. S. 449
1958

Appeal from the Supreme Court of Alabama. The NAACP had spearheaded the struggle for Negro rights in the South. One method whereby Southern whites fought back against the Brown decision and the new program for civil rights was a rash of laws harassing the NAACP. On the surface these laws merely required of the NAACP—and of other organizations—full disclosure: membership lists, records, finances, and so forth. Clearly membership lists gave state and local authorities an opportunity to bring social or economic pressure on members of unpopular organizations. The task of weighing the right of the state to information about organizations against the right of privacy, the interest of society in full disclosure and the interest of society in voluntary association, was a difficult one. See Robison, "Protection of Associations from Compulsory Disclosure," 58 *Columbia Law Rev.* 614; Rankwich, "The Right of Privacy," 27 *Notre Dame Law Rev.* 499; Fly, "Full Disclosure: Public Safeguard," 168 *The Nation,* 299; and the elaborate discussion of some of these questions in American Communications Association v. Douds, 339 U.S. 382.

Mr. Justice HARLAN: We review from the standpoint of its validity under the Federal Constitution a judgment of civil contempt entered against the National Association for the Advancement of Colored People, in the courts of Alabama. The question presented is whether Alabama, consistently with the Due Process Clause of the Fourteenth Amendment, can compel petitioner to reveal to the State's Attorney General the names and addresses of all its Alabama members and agents, without regard to their positions or functions in the Association. The judgment of contempt was based upon petitioner's refusal to comply fully with a court order requiring in part the production of membership lists. Petitioner's claim is that the order, in the circumstances shown by this record, violated rights assured to petitioner and its members under the Constitution. . . .

Petitioner produced substantially all the data called for . . . except its membership lists, as to which it contended that Alabama could not constitutionally compel disclosure. . . .

The Association both urges that it is constitutionally entitled to resist official inquiry into its membership lists, and that it may assert, on behalf of its members, a right personal to them to be protected from compelled disclosure by the State of their affiliation with the Association as revealed by the membership lists. We think that petitioner argues more appropriately the rights of its members, and that its nexus with them is sufficient to permit that it act as their representative before this Court. In so concluding, we reject respondent's argument that the Association lacks standing to assert here constitutional rights pertaining to the members, who are not of course parties to the litigation. . . .

If petitioner's rank-and-file members are constitutionally entitled to withhold their connection with the Association despite the production order, it is manifest that this right is properly assertable by the Association. To require that it be claimed by the members themselves would result in nullification of the right at the very moment of its assertion. . . .

We thus reach petitioner's claim that the production order in the state litigation trespasses upon fundamental freedoms protected by the Due Process Clause of the Fourteenth Amendment. Petitioner argues that in view of the facts and circumstances shown in the record, the effect of compelled disclosure of the membership lists will be to abridge the rights of its rank-and-file members to engage in lawful association in support of their common beliefs. It contends that governmental action which, although not directly suppressing association, nevertheless carries this consequence, can be justified only upon some overriding valid interest of the State.

Effective advocacy of both public and private points of view, particularly controversial ones, is undeniably enhanced by group association, as this Court has more than once recognized by remarking upon the close nexus between the freedoms of speech and assembly.

It is beyond debate that freedom to engage in association for the advancement of beliefs and ideas is an inseparable aspect of the "liberty" assured by the Due Process Clause of the Fourteenth Amendment, which embraces freedom of speech. [Cites cases] Of course, it is immaterial whether the beliefs sought to be advanced by association pertain to political, economic, religious or cultural matters, and state action which may have the effect of curtailing the freedom to associate is subject to the closest scrutiny.

The fact that Alabama, so far as is relevant to the validity of the contempt judgment presently under review, has taken no direct action to restrict the right of petitioner's members to associate freely, does not end inquiry into the effect of the production order. In the domain of these indispensable liberties, whether of speech, press, or association, the decisions of this Court recognize that abridgement of such rights, even though unintended, may inevitably follow from varied forms of governmental action. . . .

It is hardly a novel perception that compelled disclosure of affiliation with groups engaged in advocacy may constitute as effective a restraint on freedom of association as the forms of governmental action in the cases above were thought likely to produce upon the particular constitutional rights there involved. This Court has recognized the vital relationship between freedom to associate and privacy in one's associations. When referring to the varied forms of governmental action which might interfere with freedom of assembly, it said in American Communications Ass'n v. Douds, 339 U. S. 402, "A requirement that adherents of particular religious faiths or political parties wear identifying arm-bands, for example, is obviously of this nature." Compelled disclosure of membership in an organization engaged in advocacy of particular beliefs is of the same order. Inviolability of privacy in group association may in many circumstances be indispensable to preservation of freedom of association, particularly where a group espouses dissident beliefs.

We think that the production order, in the respects here drawn in question, must be regarded as entailing the likelihood of a substantial restraint upon the exercise by petitioner's members of their right to freedom of association. Petitioner has made an uncontroverted showing that on past occasions revelation of the identity of its rank-and-file members has exposed these members to economic reprisal, loss of employment, threat of physical coercion, and other manifestations of public hostility. . . .

It is not sufficient to answer, as the State does here, that whatever repressive effect compulsory disclosure of names of petitioner's members may have upon participation by Alabama citizens in petitioner's activities follows not from *state* action but from *private* community pressures. The crucial factor is the interplay of governmental and private action, for it is only after the initial exertion of state power represented by the production order that private action takes hold. . . .

633. FIRST UNITARIAN CHURCH v. LOS ANGELES COUNTY
357 U. S. 513 at 529
1958

Appeal from Supreme Court of California. A California statute denied tax exemption to any "person or organization which advocates the overthrow of the government of the United States or of the State by force or violence . . ." and required that all who claimed tax exemption sign an elaborate loyalty oath. The law affected veterans who were entitled to tax exemption under the provisions of the California Constitution; in Speiser v. Randall, 357 U.S. 513 the Court struck down this application of the act as a violation of freedom of speech. We give here the concurring opinion in a case involving the right of a church to tax exemption; because it covers both the free speech and the freedom of religion issues, we give the concurring opinion of Justice Black. See Leo Pfeffer, *Church, State and Freedom;* Harold Hyman, *To Try Men's Souls;* and notes in 44 *Am. Bar Assoc. Law J.* 1196; 72 *Harvard Law Rev.* 185; 12 *Vanderbilt Law Rev.* 275.

Mr. Justice BLACK, whom Mr. Justice DOUGLAS joins, concurring: California, in effect, has imposed a tax on belief and expression. In my view, a levy of this nature is wholly out of place in this country; so far as I know such a thing has never even been attempted before. I believe that it constitutes a palpable violation of the First Amendment, which of course is applicable in all its particulars to the states. . . . The mere fact that California attempts to exact this ill-concealed penalty from individuals and churches and that its validity has to be considered in this Court only emphasizes how dangerously far we have departed from the fundamental principles of freedom declared in the First Amendment. We should never forget that the freedoms secured by that Amendment—Speech, Press, Religion, Petition and Assembly—are absolutely indispensable for the preservation of a free society in which government is based upon the consent of an informed citizenry and is dedicated to the protection of the rights of all, even the most despised minorities . . .

This case offers just another example of a wide-scale effort by government in this country to impose penalties and disabilities on everyone who is or is suspected of being a "Communist" or who is not ready at all times and all places to swear his loyalty to state and nation. Government employees, lawyers, doctors, teachers, pharmacists, veterinarians, subway conductors, industrial workers and a multitude of others have been denied an opportunity to work at their trade or profession for these reasons. Here a tax is levied unless the taxpayer makes an oath that he does not and will not in the future advocate certain things; in Ohio those without jobs have been denied unemployment insurance unless they are willing to swear that they do not hold specific views; and Congress has even attempted to deny public housing to needy families unless they first demonstrate their loyalty. These are merely random samples; I will not take time here to refer to innumerable others, such as oaths for hunters and fishermen, wrestlers and boxers and junk dealers.

I am convinced that this whole business of penalizing people because of their views and expressions concerning government is hopelessly repugnant to the principles of freedom upon which this nation was founded and which have helped to make it the greatest in the world. As stated in prior cases, I believe "that the First Amendment grants an absolute right to believe in any governmental system, [to] discuss all governmental affairs and [to] argue for desired changes in the existing order. This freedom is too dangerous for bad, tyrannical governments to permit. But those who wrote and adopted our First Amendment weighed those dangers against the dangers of censorship and deliberately chose the First Amendment's unequivocal command that freedom of assembly, petition, speech and press shall not be abridged. I happen to believe this was a wise choice and that our free way of life enlists such respect and love that our nation cannot be imperiled by mere talk."

Loyalty oaths, as well as other contemporary "security measures," tend to stifle all forms of unorthodox or unpopular thinking or expression—the kind of thought and expression which has played such a vital and beneficial role in the history of this nation. The result is a stultifying conformity which in the end may well turn out to be more destructive to our free society than foreign agents could ever hope to be. The course which we have been following the last decade is not the course of a strong, free, secure people, but that of the frightened, the insecure, the intolerant. I am certain that loyalty to the United States can never be secured by the endless proliferation of "loyalty" oaths; loyalty must arise spontaneously from the hearts of people who love their country and respect their government. I also adhere to the proposition that the "First Amendment provides the only kind of security system that can preserve a free government—one that leaves the way wide open for people to favor, discuss, advocate, or incite causes and doctrines however obnoxious and antagonistic such views may be to the rest of us." Yates v. United States, 345 U. S. 298, 344.

634. COOPER v. AARON
1958
358 U. S. 1

Certiorari to the Court of Appeals for the Eighth District. The background of this case is set forth in Doc. 627, and the legal situation fully analyzed in the body of the opinion. The case is notable because it was not only a unanimous judgment, but one in which each judge concurred by name and of which each judge was presumably joint author. See, in addition to references in Doc. 627, Leflar and Davis, "Segregation in Public Schools," 67 *Harvard Law Rev.* 377; McKay, "With All Deliberate Speed," 31 *N.Y.U. Law Rev.* 991; Charles Black, "The Lawfulness of the Segregation Decision," 69 *Yale Law J.* 421; Pollak, "Racial Discrimination and Judicial Integrity," 108 *U. of Pa. Law Rev.* 1; Charles Fairman, "Attack on Segregation Cases," 70 *Harvard Law Rev.* 83.

Opinion of the Court by the CHIEF JUSTICE, Mr. Justice BLACK, Mr. Justice FRANKFURTER, Mr. Justice DOUGLAS, Mr. Justice BURTON, Mr. Justice CLARK, Mr. Justice HARLAN, Mr. Justice BRENNAN, and Mr. Justice WHITTAKER:

As this case reaches us it raises questions of the highest importance to the maintenance of our federal system of government. It necessarily involves a claim by the governor and legislature of a state that there is no duty on state officials to obey federal court orders resting on this Court's considered interpretation of the United States Constitution. Specifically it involves actions by the governor and legislature of Arkansas upon the premise that they are not bound by our holding in Brown v. Board of Education, 347 U. S. 483. . . .

On May 17, 1954, this Court decided that enforced racial segregation in the public schools of a state is a denial of the equal protection of the laws enjoined by the Fourteenth Amendment. Brown v. Board of Education.

The Court postponed, pending further argument, formulations of a decree to effectuate this decision. That decree was rendered May 31, 1955. Brown v. Board of Education, 349 U. S. 294. In the formulation of that decree the Court recognized that good faith compliance with the principles declared in Brown might in some situations "call for elimination of a variety of obstacles in making the transition to school systems operated in accordance with the constitutional principles set forth in our May 17, 1954, decision." . . .

Under such circumstances, the district courts were directed to require "a prompt and reasonable start toward full compliance," and to take such action as was necessary to bring about the end of racial segregation in the schools "with all deliberate speed." . . .

On May 20, 1954, three days after the first Brown opinion, the Little Rock District School Board adopted, and on May 23, 1954, made public, a statement of policy entitled "Supreme Court Decision—Segregation in the Public Schools." In this statement the Board recognized that "It is our responsibility to comply with Federal Constitutional Requirements and we intend to do so when the Supreme Court of the United States outlines the method to be followed."

Thereafter the Board undertook studies of the administrative problems confronting the transition to a desegregated public school system in Little Rock. It instructed the Superintendent of Schools to prepare a plan . . . The plan provided for desegregation at the senior high school level (grades 10 through 12) as the first stage. Desegregation at the junior high and elementary levels was to follow. It was contemplated that desegregation at the high school level would commence in the fall of 1957, and the expectation was that complete desegregation of the school system would be accomplished by 1963. . . .

While the School Board was thus going forward with its preparation for desegregating the Little Rock school system, other state authorities, in contrast, were actively pursuing a program designed to perpetuate in Arkansas the system of racial segregation which this Court had held violated the Fourteenth Amendment. First came, in November 1956, an amendment to the State Constitution flatly commanding the Arkansas General Assembly to oppose "in every Constitutional manner the Unconstitutional desegregation decisions of May 17, 1954 and May 31, 1955 of the United States Supreme Court," Ark. Const. Amend. 44, and, through the initiative, a pupil assignment law. Pursuant to this state constitutional command, a law relieving school children from compulsory attendance at racially mixed schools, was enacted by the General Assembly in February, 1957. . . .

On September 2, 1957, the day before these Negro students were to enter Central High, the school authorities were met with drastic opposing action on the part of the Governor of Arkansas who dispatched units of the Arkansas National Guard to the Central High School grounds, and placed the school "off limits" to colored students. As found by the District Court in subsequent proceedings, the Governor's action had not been requested by the school authorities, and was entirely unheralded . . .

The next school day was Monday, September 23, 1957. The Negro children entered the high school . . . under the protection of the Little Rock Police Department and members of the Arkansas State Police. But the officers caused the children to be removed from the school during the morning because they had difficulty controlling a large and demonstrating crowd which had gathered at the high school. On September 25, however, the President of the United States dispatched federal troops to Central High School and admission of the Negro students to the school was thereby effected. Regular army troops continued at the high school until November 27, 1957. They were then replaced by federalized National Guardsmen who remained throughout the balance of the school year. Eight of the Negro students remained in attendance at the school throughout the school year.

We come now to the aspect of the proceedings presently before us. On February 20, 1958, the School Board and the Superintendent of Schools filed a petition in the District Court seeking a postponement of their program of desegregation. Their position in essence was that because of extreme hostility, which they stated had been engendered largely by the official attitudes and actions of the Governor and the Legislature, the maintenance of a sound educational program at Central High School, with the Negro students in attendance, would be impossible. The Board therefore proposed that the Negro students already admitted to the school be withdrawn and sent to segregated schools, and that all further steps to carry out the Board's desegregation program be postponed for a period later suggested by the Board to be two and one-half years. . . .

One may well sympathize with the position of the Board in the face of the frustrating conditions which have confronted it, but, regardless of the Board's good faith, the actions of the other state agencies responsible for those conditions compel us to reject the Board's legal position. . . .

The constitutional rights of respondents are not to be sacrificed or yielded to the violence and disorder which have followed upon the actions of the Governor and Legislature. . . .

. . . the constitutional rights of children not to be discriminated against in school admission on grounds of race or color declared by this Court in the Brown case can neither be nullified openly and directly by state legislators or state executive or judicial officers, nor nullified indirectly by them through evasive schemes for segregation whether attempted "ingeniously or ingenuously." Smith v. Texas, 311 U.S. 128.

What has been said, in the light of the facts developed, is enough to dispose of the case. However, we should answer the premise of the actions of the Governor and Legislature that they are not bound by our holding in the Brown case. It is necessary only to recall some basic constitutional propositions which are settled doctrine.

Article VI of the Constitution makes the Constitution the "supreme Law of the Land." In 1803, Chief Justice Marshall, speaking for a unanimous Court, referring to the Constitution as "the fundamental and paramount law of the nation," declared in the notable case of Marbury v. Madison that "It is emphatically the province and duty of the judicial department to say what the law is." This decision declared the basic principle that the federal judiciary is supreme in the exposition of the law of the Constitution, and that principle has ever since been respected by this Court and the country as a permanent and indispensable feature of our constitutional system. It follows that the interpretation of the Fourteenth Amendment enunciated by this Court in the Brown case is the supreme law of the land . . .

No state legislator or executive or judicial officer can war against the Constitution without violating his undertaking to support it . . .

It is, of course, quite true that the responsibility for public education is primarily the concern of the states, but it is equally true that such responsibilities, like all other state activity, must be exercised consistently with federal constitutional requirements as they apply to state action. The Constitution created a government dedicated to equal justice under law. The Fourteenth Amendment embodied and emphasized that ideal. State support of segregated schools through any arrangement, management, funds, or property cannot be squared with the Amendment's command that no state shall deny to any person within its jurisdiction the equal protection of the laws. The right of a student not to be segregated on racial grounds in schools so maintained is indeed so fundamental and pervasive that it is embraced in the concept of due process of law. Bolling v. Sharpe, 347 U.S. 497. The basic decision in Brown was unanimously reached by this Court only after the case had been briefed and twice argued and the issue had been given the most serious consideration. Since the first Brown opinion three new Justices have come to the Court. They are at one with the Justices still on the Court who participated in that basic decision as to its correctness, and that decision is now unanimously reaffirmed. The principles announced in that decision and the obedience of the states to them, according to the command of the Constitution, are indispensable for the protection of the freedoms guaranteed by our fundamental charter for all of us. Our constitutional ideal of equal justice under law is thus made a living truth.

635. EISENHOWER'S VETO OF WATER POLLUTION CONTROL ACT
February 23, 1959
(Public Papers of the Presidents: Dwight D. Eisenhower, 1960, no. 43)

With the industrialization of almost the entire country, and the rapid growth of big cities, the problem of the pollution of streams and lakes, and even of seashores became of urgent importance. Gradually the conviction grew that only the national government could deal adequately with the problem. Congress responded with an act voting substantial federal funds to fight water pollution. See "Water Pollution

Control," Hearings of the sub-committee of the Committee on Public Works, 87 Cong. 1st sess. on Sen. Re. 805; R. J. Hammond, *Benefit Cost Analysis and Water Pollution Control;* Otto Eckstein, *Water Resource Development;* C. B. Haver, *History and Status of Federal Resource Development Activities;* Louis Klein, *Aspects of River Pollution;* Ben Morrell, *Our Nation's Water Resources.*

To the House of Representatives:

I am returning herewith, without my approval, H. R. 3610, an enrolled bill "To amend the Federal Water Pollution Control Act to increase grants for construction of sewage treatment works, and for other purposes."

The bill would authorize an increase in federal grants to municipalities for assistance in the construction of sewage treatment works from $50 million to $90 million annually, and from $500 million to $900 million in the aggregate.

Because water pollution is a uniquely local blight, primary responsibility for solving the problem lies not with the federal government but rather must be assumed and exercised, as it has been, by state and local governments. This being so, the defects of H. R. 3610 are apparent. By holding forth the promise of a large-scale program of long-term federal support, it would tempt municipalities to delay essential water pollution abatement efforts while they waited for federal funds. . . .

Polluted water is a threat to the health and well-being of all our citizens. Yet, pollution and its correction are so closely involved with local industry processes and with public water supply and sewage treatment, that the problem can be successfully met only by state and local action rather than providing excuses for inaction—which an expanded program under H. R. 3610 would do . . .

I am requesting the Secretary of Health, Education and Welfare to arrange for a national conference on water pollution to be held next December.

636. UPHAUS v. WYMAN
360 U. S. 72
1959

No case, since the Dennis, attracted such widespread attention as did the case of the Rev. Willard Uphaus and his World Fellowship v. the State of New Hampshire. Constitutionally the case is interesting because it involved complex problems of freedom of association, freedom of religion, the right of privacy, as well as the more familiar problem of the authority of the state to investigate and its right to know. The facts of the case are set forth fully in the dissenting opinion. See notes in 45 *Am. Bar Assoc. Law Rev.* 1069; 47 *California Law Rev.* 930; 61 *Columbia Law Rev.* 725; 73 *Harvard Law Rev.* 161; 38 *Texas Law Rev.* 330.

Mr. Justice CLARK: This case is here again on appeal from a judgment of civil contempt entered against appellant by the Merrimack County Court and affirmed by the Supreme Court of New Hampshire. It arises out of appellant's refusal to produce certain documents before a New Hampshire legislative investigating committee which was authorized and directed to determine, *inter alia,* whether there were subversive persons or organizations present in the State of New Hampshire. Upon the first appeal from the New Hampshire court, we vacated the judgment, and remanded the case to it for consideration in the light of Sweezy v. State of New Hampshire, 1957, 354 U.S. 234. That court reaffirmed its former decision, 101 N.H. 139, deeming Sweezy not to control the issues in the instant case. For reasons which will appear, we agree with the Supreme Court of New Hampshire.

As in Sweezy, the Attorney General of New Hampshire, who had been constituted a one-man legislative investigating committee by Joint Resolution of the Legislature, was conducting a probe of subversive activities in the state. In the course of his investigation the Attorney General called appellant, Executive Director of World Fellowship, Inc., a voluntary corporation organized under the laws of New Hampshire and maintaining a summer camp in the state. Appellant testified concerning his own activities, but refused to comply with two subpoenas *duces tecum* which called for the production of certain corporate records for the years 1954 and 1955. The information sought consisted of: (1) a list of the names of all the camp's nonprofessional employees for those two summer seasons; (2) the correspondence which appellant had carried on with and concerning those persons who came to the camp as speakers; and (3) the names of all persons who attended the camp during the same periods of time. Met with appellant's refusal, the Attorney General, in accordance with state procedure, petitioned the Merrimack County Court to call appellant before it and require compliance with the subpoenas.

In court, appellant again refused to produce the information. He claimed that by the Smith Act, as construed by this Court in Commonwealth of Pennsylvania v. Nelson, 1956, 350 U.S. 497, Congress had so completely occupied the field of subversive activities that the states were without power to investigate in that area. Additionally, he contended that the Due Process Clause precluded enforcement of the subpoenas, first, because the resolution under which the Attorney General was authorized to operate was vague and, second, because the documents sought were not relevant to the inquiry. Finally, appellant argued that enforcement would violate his rights of free speech and association.

The Merrimack County Court sustained appellant's objection to the production of the names of the nonprofessional employees. The Attorney General took no appeal from that ruling, and it is not before us. Appellant's objections to the production of the names of the camp's guests were overruled, and he was ordered to produce them. Upon his refusal, he was adjudged in contempt of court and ordered committed to jail until he should have complied with the court order. On the demand for the correspondence and the objection thereto, the trial court made no ruling but transferred the question to the Supreme Court of New Hampshire. That court affirmed the trial court's action in regard to the guest list. Concerning the requested production of the correspondence, the Supreme Court entered no order, but directed that on remand the trial court "may exercise its discretion with respect to the entry of an order to enforce the command of the subpoena for the production of correspondence." 100 N. H. at page 448. No remand having yet been effected, the trial court has not acted upon this phase of the case, and there is no final judgment requiring the appellant to produce the letters. We therefore do not treat with that question. We now pass to a consideration of the sole question before us, namely, the validity of the order of contempt for refusal to produce the list of guests at World Fellowship, Inc., during the summer seasons of 1954 and 1955. In addition to the arguments appellant made to the trial court, he urges here that the "indefinite sentence" imposed upon him constitutes such cruel and unusual punishment as to be a denial of due process.

Appellant vigorously contends that the New Hampshire Subversive Activities Act of 1951 and the resolution creating the committee have been superseded by the Smith Act, as amended. In support of this position appellant cites Com. of Pennsylvania v. Nelson, *supra*. The argument is that Nelson, which involved a prosecution under a state sedition law, held that "Congress has intended to occupy the field of sedition." [350 U.S. 505, 76 S. Ct. 481.] This rule of decision, it is contended, should embrace legislative investigations made pursuant to an effort by the Legislature to inform itself of the presence of subversives within the state and possibly to enact laws in the subversive field. The appellant's argument sweeps too broad. In Nelson itself we said that the "precise holding of the court . . . is that the Smith Act . . . which prohibits the knowing advocacy of the overthrow of the Government of the United States by force and violence, supersedes the enforceability of the Pennsylvania Sedition Act which proscribes the *same conduct*." 350 U.S. at page 499. The basis of Nelson thus rejects the notion that it stripped the states of the right to protect themselves. All the opinion proscribed was a race between federal and state prosecutors to the courthouse door. The opinion made clear that a state could proceed with prosecutions for sedition against the state itself; that it can legitimately investigate in this area follows *a fortiori*. In Sweezy v. State of New Hampshire, *supra,* where the same contention was made as to the identical state Act, it was denied *sub silentio*. Nor did our opinion in Nelson hold that the Smith Act had proscribed state activity in protection of itself either from actual or threatened "sabotage or attempted violence of all kinds." In footnote 8 of the opinion it is pointed out that the state had full power to deal with internal civil disturbances.

Thus registration statutes, *quo warranto* proceedings as to subversive corporations, the subversive instigation of riots and a host of other subjects directly affecting state security furnish grist for the state's legislative mill. Moreover, the right of the state to require the production of corporate papers of a state-chartered corporation in an inquiry to determine whether corporate activity is violative of state policy is, of course, not touched upon in Nelson and today stands unimpaired, either by the Smith Act or the Nelson opinion.

Appellant's other objections can be capsuled into the single question of whether New Hampshire, under the facts here, is precluded from compelling the production of the documents by the Due Process Clause of the Fourteenth Amendment. Let us first clear away some of the underbrush necessarily surrounding the case because of its setting. First, the academic and political freedoms discussed in Sweezy v. State of New Hampshire, *supra*, are not present here in the same degree, since World Fellowship is neither a university nor a political party. Next, since questions concerning the authority of the committee to act as it did are questions of state law, Dreyer v. People of State of Illinois, 1902, 187 U.S. 71, 84, we accept as controlling the New Hampshire Supreme Court's conclusion that "[t]he legislative history makes it clear beyond a reasonable doubt that it [the Legislature] did and does desire an answer to these questions." Finally, we assume, without deciding, that Uphaus had sufficient standing to assert any rights of the guests whose identity the committee seeks to determine. See National Association for Advancement of Colored People v. State of Alabama, 1958, 357 U.S. 449. The interest of the guests at World Fellowship in their associational privacy having been asserted, we have for decision the federal question of whether the public interests overbalance these conflicting private ones. Whether there was "justification" for the production order turns on the "substantiality" of New Hampshire's interests in obtaining the identity of the guests when weighted against the individual interests which the appellant asserts. National Association for Advancement of Colored People v. State of Alabama, *supra*. What was the interest of the state? The

Attorney General was commissioned to determine if there were any subversive persons within New Hampshire. The obvious starting point of such an inquiry was to learn what persons were within the state. It is, therefore, clear that the requests relate directly to the Legislature's area of interest, i.e., the presence of subversives in the state, as announced in its resolution. Nor was the demand of the subpoena burdensome; as to time, only a few months of each of the two years were involved; as to place, only the camp conducted by the corporation; nor as to the lists of names, which included about 300 each year.

Moreover, the Attorney General had valid reason to believe that the speakers and guests at World Fellowship might be subversive persons within the meaning of the New Hampshire Act. The Supreme Court of New Hampshire found Uphaus' contrary position "unrelated to reality." Although the evidence as to the nexus between World Fellowship and subversive activities may not be conclusive, we believe it sufficiently relevant to support the Attorney General's action. The New Hampshire definition of subversive persons was born of the legislative determination that the Communist movement posed a serious threat to the security of the state. The record reveals that appellant had participated in "Communist front" activities and that "[n]ot less than nineteen speakers invited by Uphaus to talk at World Fellowship had either been members of the Communist Party or had connections or affiliations with it or with one or more of the organizations cited as subversive or Communist controlled in the United States Attorney General's list." While the Attorney General's list is designed for the limited purpose of determining fitness for federal employment, Wieman v. Updegraff, 1952, 344 U.S. 183, and guilt by association remains a thoroughly discredited doctrine, it is with a legislative investigation—not a criminal prosecution—that we deal here. Certainly the investigatory power of the state need not be constricted until sufficient evidence of subversion is gathered to justify the institution of criminal proceedings.

The nexus between World Fellowship and subversive activities disclosed by the record furnished adequate justification for the investigation we here review. The Attorney General sought to learn if subversive persons were in the state because of the legislative determination that such persons, statutorily defined with a view toward the Communist Party, posed a serious threat to the security of the state. The investigation was, therefore, undertaken in the interest of self-preservation, "the ultimate value of any society," Dennis v. United States, 1951, 341 U.S. 494, 509. This governmental interest outweighs individual rights in an associational privacy which, however real in other circumstances, cf. National Association for Advancement of Colored People v. State of Alabama, *supra*, were here tenuous at best. The camp was operating as a public one, furnishing both board and lodging to persons applying therefor. As to them, New Hampshire law requires that World Fellowship, Inc., maintain a register, open to inspection of sheriffs and police officers. It is contended that the list might be "circulated throughout the states and the Attorney Generals throughout the states have cross-indexed files, so that any guest whose name is mentioned in that kind of proceeding immediately becomes suspect, even in his own place of residence." Record, p. 7. The record before us, however, only reveals a report to the Legislature of New Hampshire made by the Attorney General in accordance with the requirements of the resolution. We recognize, of course, that compliance with the subpoena will result in exposing the fact that the persons therein named were guests at World Fellowship. But so long as a committee must report to its legislative parent, exposure—in the sense of disclosure—is an inescapable incident of an investigation into the presence of subversive persons within a state. And the governmental interest in self-preservation is sufficiently compelling to subordinate the interest in associational privacy of persons who, at least to the extent of the guest registration statute, made public at the inception the association they now wish to keep private. In the light of such a record we conclude that the state's interest has not been "pressed, in this instance, to a point where it has come into fatal collision with the overriding" constitutionally protected rights of appellant and those he may represent. Cantwell v. State of Connecticut, 1940, 310 U.S. 296, 307.

We now reach the question of the validity of the sentence. The judgment of contempt orders the appellant confined until he produces the documents called for in the subpoenas. He himself admitted to the court that although they were at hand, not only had he failed to bring them with him to court, but that, further, he had no intention of producing them. In view of appellant's unjustified refusal we think the order a proper one. As was said in Green v. United States, 1958, 356 U.S. 165, 197, (dissenting opinion): "Before going any further, perhaps it should be emphasized that we are not at all concerned with the power of courts to impose conditional imprisonment for the purpose of compelling a person to obey a valid order. Such coercion, where the defendant carries the keys to freedom in his willingness to comply with the court's directive, is essentially a civil remedy designed for the benefit of other parties and has quite properly been exercised for centuries to secure compliance with judicial decrees."

We have concluded that the committee's demand for the documents was a legitimate one; it follows that the judgment of contempt for refusal to produce them is valid. We do not impugn appellant's good faith in the assertion of what he believed to be his rights. But three courts have disagreed with him in interpreting those rights. If appellant chooses to abide by the result of the adjudication and obey the order of New Hampshire's courts, he need not face jail. If, however, he continues to disobey, we find on this record no constitutional objection to the exercise of the traditional remedy of contempt to secure compliance.

Affirmed.

Mr. Justice BRENNAN, with whom the CHIEF JUSTICE, Mr. Justice BLACK, and Mr. Justice DOUGLAS join, dissenting: The Court holds today that the constitutionally protected rights of speech and assembly of appellant and those whom he may represent are to be subordinated to New Hampshire's legislative investigation because, as applied in the demands made on him, the investigation is rationally connected with a discernible legislative purpose. With due respect for my Brothers' views, I do not agree that a showing of any requisite legislative purpose or other state interest that constitutionally can subordinate appellant's rights is to be found in this record. Exposure purely for the sake of exposure is not such a valid subordinating purpose. Watkins v. United States, 354 U.S. 178, 187; Sweezy v. State of New Hampshire, 354 U.S. 234; NAACP v. State of Alabama, 357 U.S. 449. This record, I think, not only fails to reveal any interest of the state sufficient to subordinate appellant's constitutionally protected rights, but affirmatively shows that the investigatory objective was the impermissible one of exposure for exposure's sake. I therefore dissent from the judgment of the Court. . . .

Only recently has the Court been required to begin a full exploration of the impact of the governmental investigatory function on these freedoms. Here is introduced the weighty consideration that the power of investigation, whether exercised in aid of the governmental legislative power, or in aid of the governmental power to adjudicate disputes, is vital to the functioning of free governments and is therefore necessarily broad. But where the exercise of the investigatory power collides with constitutionally guaranteed freedoms, that power too has inevitable limitations, and the delicate and always difficult accommodation of the two with minimum sacrifice of either is the hard task of the judiciary and ultimately of this Court. . . .

Of course . . . Government must have freedom to make an appropriate investigation where there appears a rational connection with the lawmaking process, the processes of adjudication, or other essential governmental functions. . . . But guide lines must be marked out by the courts. . . . On the facts of this case I think that New Hampshire's investigation, as applied to the appellant, was demonstrably and clearly outside the wide limits of the power which must be conceded to the state even though it be attended by some exposure. In demonstration of this I turn to the detailed examination of the facts which this case requires. . . .

The appellant, Uphaus, is executive director of a group called World Fellowship which runs a discussion program at a summer camp in New Hampshire, at which the public is invited to stay. Various speakers come to the camp primarily for discussion of political, economic, and social matters. The appellee reports that Uphaus and some of the speakers have been said by third persons to have a history of association with "Communist front" movements, to have followed the "Communist line," signed amnesty petitions and *amicus curiae* briefs, and carried on similar activities of a sort which have recently been viewed hostilely and suspiciously by many Americans. A strain of pacifism runs through the appellant's thinking, and the appellee apparently would seek to determine whether there should be drawn therefrom an inference of harm for our institutions; he conjectures, officially, whether "the advocacy of this so-called peace crusade is for the purpose of achieving a quicker and a cheaper occupation by the Soviet Union and Communism." There is no evidence that any activity of a sort that violates the law of New Hampshire or could in fact be constitutionally punished went on at the camp. What is clear was that there was some sort of assemblage at the camp that was oriented toward the discussion of political and other public matters. The activities going on were those of private citizens. The views expounded obviously were minority views. But the assemblage was, on its face, for purposes to which the First and Fourteenth Amendments give constitutional protection against incursion by the powers of government. . . .

The Legislature, upon receiving the report, extended the investigation for a further two years. It was during this period that the refusals of the appellant to furnish information with which we are now concerned took place. The Attorney General had already published the names of speakers at the World Fellowship camp. Now he wanted the correspondence between Uphaus and the speakers. The Attorney General admitted that it was unlikely that the correspondence between Uphaus and the speakers was going to contain a damning admission of a purpose to advocate the overthrow of the government (presumably of New Hampshire) by force and violence. He said that it might indicate a sinister purpose behind the advocacy of pacifism—"the purpose of achieving a quicker and a cheaper occupation by the Soviet Union and Communism." The guest list, the nonavailability of which to the Attorney General was commented on in the passage from the 1955 report was also desired. Appellant's counsel, at the hearing in court giving rise to the contempt finding under review, protested that appellant did not want to allow the Attorney General to have the names to expose them. The Attorney General also wished the names of the nonprofessional help at the camp—the cooks and dishwashers and the like. It was objected that the cooks and dishwashers were hired from the local labor pool and that if such employment were attended by a trip to the Attorney General's office and the possibility of public exposure, help might become hard to find at the camp. This last objection was sustained in the trial court, but the other two inquiries were allowed and appellant's failure to respond to the one relating to the guest list was found contemptuous. . . .

In examining the right of the State to obtain this information from the appellant by compulsory process, we must recollect what we so recently said in NAACP v. State of Alabama:

"Effective advocacy of both public and private points of view, particularly controversial ones, is undeniably enhanced by group association, as this Court has more than once recognized by remarking upon the close nexus between the freedoms of speech and assembly. It is beyond debate that freedom to engage in association for the advancement of beliefs and ideals is an inseparable aspect of the "liberty" assured by the Due Process Clause of the Fourteenth Amendment which embraces freedom of speech. Of course, it is immaterial whether the beliefs sought to be advanced by association pertain to political, economic, religious or cultural matters, and state action which may have the effect of curtailing the freedom to associate is subject to the closest scrutiny."

And in examining the state's interest in carrying out a legislative investigation, as was said in a similar context in United States v. Rumely, *supra*, we must strive not to be "that 'blind' Court, against which Mr. Chief Justice Taft admonished in a famous passage . . . that does not see what '[a]ll others can see and understand.' " The problem of protecting the citizen's constitutional rights from legislative investigation and exposure is a practical one, and we must take a practical, realistic approach to it. . . .

One may accept the Court's truism that preservation of the state's existence is undoubtedly a proper purpose for legislation. But, in descending from this peak of abstraction to the facts of this case, one must ask the question: What relation did this investigation of individual conduct have to legislative ends here? If bills of attainder were still a legitimate legislative end, it is clear that the investigations and reports might naturally have furnished the starting point (though only that) for a legislative adjudication of guilt under the 1951 Act. But what other legislative purpose was actually being fulfilled by the course taken by this investigation, with its overwhelming emphasis on individual associations and conduct?

The investigation, as revealed by the report, was overwhelmingly and predominantly a roving, self-contained investigation of individual and group behavior, and behavior in compulsory disclosure itself tends to have a repressive effect. We deal only with the power of the state to *compel* such a disclosure. We are asked, in this narrow context, only to give meaning to our statement in Watkins v. United States, "that the mere semblance of a legislative purpose would not justify an inquiry in the face of the Bill of Rights." Here we must demand some initial showing by the state sufficient to counterbalance the interest in privacy as it relates to freedom of speech and assembly. On any basis that has practical meaning, New Hampshire has not made such a showing here. I would reverse the judgment of the New Hampshire Supreme Court.

637. BARENBLATT v. U. S.
360 U. S. 109
1959

This was probably the most exhaustively argued of the many cases involving the reach of the investigatory power of Congressional committees. In the Watkins case (354 U.S. 178) the

Court had reversed a contempt citation of a witness before a Congressional committee because the committee had failed to make clear the pertinence of its questions to a legitimate legislative purpose, and the Sweezy case (Sweezy v. New Hampshire, 354 U.S. 234) had radiated the same doctrine. Barenblatt did not so much reverse as circumscribe the reach of these two decisions. See references to Doc. 600 and Wittke, *The History of English Parliamentary Privilege;* Finer, "Congressional Investigations: The British System," 18 *U. of Chicago Law Rev.* 521; Landis, "Constitutional Limitations on the Congressional Power of Investigation," 40 *Harvard Law Rev.* 153; Potts, "Power of Legislative Bodies to Punish for Contempt," 74 *U. of Pa. Law Rev.* 691; C. H. Pritchett, *The Political Offender and the Warren Court;* and notes in 47 *California Law Rev.* 930; 45 *Cornell Law Rev.* 354; 73 *Harvard Law Rev.* 159; 58 *Michigan Law Rev.* 406; and 27 *U. of Chicago Law Rev.* 315.

Mr. Justice HARLAN: Once more the Court is required to resolve the conflicting constitutional claims of Congressional power and of an individual's right to resist its exercise. The Congressional power in question concerns the internal process of Congress in moving within its legislative domain; it involves the utilization of its committees to secure "testimony needed to enable it efficiently to exercise a legislative function belonging to it under the Constitution." . . . The scope of the power of inquiry, in short, is as penetrating and far-reaching as the potential power to enact and appropriate under the Constitution.

Broad as it is, the power is not, however, without limitations. Since Congress may only investigate into those areas in which it may potentially legislate or appropriate, it cannot inquire into matters which are within the exclusive province of one or the other branch of the government. Lacking the judicial power given to the Judiciary, it cannot inquire into matters that are exclusively the concern of the Judiciary. Neither can it supplant the Executive in what exclusively belongs to the Executive. And the Congress, in common with all branches of the government, must exercise its powers subject to the limitations placed by the Constitution on governmental action, more particularly in the context of this case the relevant limitations of the Bill of Rights. . . .

In the present case Congressional efforts to learn the extent of a nationwide, indeed worldwide, problem have brought one of its investigating committees into the field of education. Of course, broadly viewed, inquiries cannot be made into the teaching that is pursued in any of our educational institutions. When academic teaching-freedom and its corollary learning-freedom, so essential to the well-being of the Nation, are claimed, this Court will always be on the alert against intrusion by Congress into this constitutionally protected domain. But this does not mean that the Congress is precluded from interrogating a witness merely because he is a teacher. An educational institution is not a constitutional sanctuary from inquiry into matters that may otherwise be within the constitutional legislative domain merely for the reason that inquiry is made of someone within its walls. . . .

We here review petitioner's conviction for contempt of Congress, arising from his refusal to answer certain questions put to him by a Subcommittee of the House Committee on Un-American Activities during the course of an inquiry concerning alleged Communist infiltration into the field of education. . . .

Pursuant to a subpoena, petitioner on June 28, 1954, appeared as a witness before this Congressional Subcommittee. After answering a few preliminary questions and testifying that he had been a graduate student and teaching fellow at the University of Michigan from 1947 to 1950 and an instructor in psychology at Vassar College from 1950 to shortly before his appearance before the Subcommittee, petitioner objected generally to the right of the Subcommittee to inquire into his "political" and "religious" beliefs or any "other personal and private affairs" or "associational activities," upon grounds set forth in a previously prepared memorandum which he was allowed to file with the Subcommittee. Thereafter petitioner specifically declined to answer each of the following five questions:

"Are you now a member of the Communist Party?
"Have you ever been a member of the Communist Party?

"Now, you have stated that you knew Francis Crowley. Did you know Francis Crowley as a member of the Communist Party?

"Were you ever a member of the Haldane Club of the Communist Party while at the University of Michigan?

"Were you a member while a student of the University of Michigan Council of Arts, Sciences, and Professions?"

In each instance the grounds of refusal were those set forth in the prepared statement. Petitioner expressly disclaimed reliance upon "the Fifth Amendment." . . .

We conceive the ultimate issue in this case to be whether petitioner could properly be convicted of contempt for refusing to answer questions relating to his participation in or knowledge of alleged Communist Party activities at educational institutions in this country. . . .

Petitioner's various contentions resolve themselves into three propositions: First, the compelling of testimony by the Subcommittee was neither legislatively authorized nor constitutionally permissible because of the vagueness of Rule XI of the House of Representatives, Eighty-third Congress, the charter of authority of the parent Committee. Second, petitioner was not adequately apprised of the pertinency of the Subcommittee's questions to the subject matter of the inquiry. Third, the questions petitioner refused to answer infringed rights protected by the First Amendment. . . .

The precise constitutional issue confronting us is whether the Subcommittee's inquiry into petitioner's past or present membership in the Communist Party transgressed the provisions of the First Amendment, which of course reach and limit Congressional investigations.

The Court's past cases establish sure guides to decision. Undeniably, the First Amendment in some circumstances protects an individual from being compelled to disclose his associational relationships. However, the protections of the First Amendment unlike a proper claim of the privilege against self-incrimination under the Fifth Amendment, do not afford a witness the right to resist inquiry in all circumstances. Where First Amendment rights are asserted to bar governmental interrogation, resolution of the issue always involves a balancing by the

courts of the competing private and public interests at stake in the particular circumstances shown. These principles were recognized in the Watkins case, where, in speaking of the First Amendment in relation to Congressional inquiries, we said: "It is manifest that despite the adverse effects which follow upon compelled disclosure of private matters, not all such inquiries are barred. . . . The critical element is the existence of, and the weight to be ascribed to, the interest of the Congress in demanding disclosures from an unwilling witness." . . .

The first question is whether this investigation was related to a valid legislative purpose, for Congress may not constitutionally require an individual to disclose his political relationships or other private affairs except in relation to such a purpose.

That Congress has wide power to legislate in the field of Communist activity in this Country, and to conduct appropriate investigations in aid thereof, is hardly debatable. The existence of such power has never been questioned by this Court, and it is sufficient to say, without particularization, that Congress has enacted or considered in this field a wide range of legislative measures, not a few of which have stemmed from recommendations of the very Committee whose actions have been drawn in question here. In the last analysis this power rests on the right of self-preservation, "the ultimate value of any society," Dennis v. United States, 341 U.S. 494, 509. Justification for its exercise in turn rests on the long and widely accepted view that the tenets of the Communist Party include the ultimate overthrow of the Government of the United States by force and violence, a view which has been given formal expression by the Congress. . . .

We think that investigatory power in this domain is not to be denied Congress solely because the field of education is involved. . . . Indeed we do not understand petitioner here to suggest that Congress in no circumstances may inquire into Communist activity in the field of education. Rather his position is in effect that this particular investigation was aimed not at the revolutionary aspects but at the theoretical classroom discussion of communism.

In our opinion this position rests on a too constricted view of the nature of the investigatory process. . . . Nor can it fairly be concluded that this investigation was directed at controlling what is being taught at our universities rather than at overthrow. . . .

Nor can we accept the further contention that this investigation should not be deemed to have been in furtherance of a legislative purpose because the true objective of the Committee and of the Congress was purely "exposure." So long as Congress acts in pursuance of its constitutional power, the judiciary lacks the authority to intervene on the basis of the motives which spurred the exercise of that power. . . .

Finally, the record is barren of other factors which in themselves might sometimes lead to the conclusion that the individual interests at stake were not subordinate to those of the state. There is no indication in this record that the Subcommittee was attempting to pillory witnesses. Nor did petitioner's appearance as a witness follow from indiscriminate dragnet procedures, lacking in probable cause for belief that he possessed information which might be helpful to the Subcommittee. And the relevancy of the questions put to him by the Subcommittee is not open to doubt.

We conclude that the balance between the individual and the governmental interests here at stake must be struck in favor of the latter, and that therefore the provisions of the First Amendment have not been offended.

We hold that the judgment of the Court of Appeals must be affirmed.

Mr. Justice BLACK, with whom the CHIEF JUSTICE, Justice DOUGLAS concur, dissenting. . . . The First Amendment says in no equivocal language that Congress shall pass no law abridging freedom of speech, press, assembly or petition. The activities of this Committee, authorized by Congress, do precisely that, through exposure, obloquy, and public scorn. The Court does not really deny this fact but relies on a combination of three reasons for permitting the infringement: (A) The notion that despite the First Amendment's command Congress can abridge speech and association if this Court decides that the governmental interest in abridging speech is greater than an individual's interest in exercising that freedom, (B) the Government's right to "preserve itself," (C) the fact that the Committee is only after Communists or suspected Communists in this investigation.

(A) I do not agree that laws directly abridging First Amendment freedoms can be justified by a Congressional or judicial balancing process. There are, of course, cases suggesting that a law which primarily regulates conduct but which might also indirectly affect speech can be upheld if the effect on speech is minor in relation to the need for control of the conduct. . . . But even such laws governing conduct, we emphasized, must be tested, though only by a balancing process, if they indirectly affect ideas. On one side of the balance, we pointed out, is the interest of the United States in seeing that its fundamental law protecting freedom of communication is not abridged; on the other the obvious interest of the state to regulate conduct within its boundaries. . . .

To apply the Court's balancing test under such circumstances is to read the First Amendment to say "Congress shall pass no law abridging freedom of speech, press, assembly and petition, unless Congress and the Supreme Court reach the joint conclusion that on balance the interests of the government in stifling these freedoms is greater than the interest of the people in having them exercised." This is closely akin to the notion that neither the First Amendment nor any other provision of the Bill of Rights should be enforced unless the Court believes it is *reasonable* to do so. Not only does this violate the genius of our *written* Constitution, but it runs expressly counter to the injunction to Court and Congress made by Madison when he introduced the Bill of Rights. "If they [the first ten amendments] are incorporated into the Constitution, independent tribunals of justice will consider themselves in a peculiar manner the guardians of those rights; they will be an impenetrable bulwark against *every* assumption of power in the Legislative or Executive; they will be naturally led to resist *every* encroachment upon rights expressly stipulated for in the Constitution by the declaration of rights." Unless we return to this view of our judicial function, unless we once again accept the notion that the Bill of Rights means what it says and that this Court must enforce that meaning, I am of the opinion that our great charter of liberty will be more honored in the breach than in the observance.

But even assuming what I cannot assume, that some balancing is proper in this case, I feel that the Court after stating the test ignores it completely. At most it balances the right of the government to preserve itself, against Barenblatt's right to refrain from revealing Communist affiliations. Such a balance, however, mistakes the factors to be weighed. In the first place, it completely leaves out the real interest in Barenblatt's silence, the interest of the people as a whole in being able to join organizations, advocate causes, and make political "mistakes" without later being subjected to governmental penalties for having dared to think for themselves. It is this right, the right to err politically, which keeps us strong as a nation. For no number of laws against communism can have as much effect as the personal conviction which comes from having heard its arguments and rejected them, or from having once accepted its tenets and later recognized their worthlessness. Instead, the obloquy which results from investigations such as this not only stifles "mistakes" but prevents all but the most courageous from hazarding any views which might at some later time become disfavored. This result, whose importance cannot be overestimated, is doubly crucial when it affects the universities, on which we must largely rely for the experimentation and development of new ideas essential to our country's welfare. It is these interests of society, rather than Barenblatt's own right to silence, which I think the Court should put on the balance against the demands of the government, if any balancing process is to be tolerated. Instead they are not mentioned, while on the other side the demands of the government are vastly overstated and called "self-preservation." It is admitted that this Committee can only seek information for the purpose of suggesting laws, and that Congress' power to make laws in the realm of speech and association is quite limited, even on the Court's test. Its interest in making such laws in the field of education, primarily a state function, is

clearly narrower still. Yet the Court styles this attenuated interest self-preservation and allows it to overcome the need our country has to let us all think, speak, and associate politically as we like and without fear of reprisal. Such a result reduces "balancing" to a mere play on words and is completely inconsistent with the rules this Court has previously given for applying a "balancing test" where it is proper. . . .

(B) Moreover, I cannot agree with the Court's notion that First Amendment freedoms must be abridged in order to "preserve" our country. That notion rests on the unarticulated premise that this nation's security hangs upon its power to punish people because of what they think, speak or write about, or because of those with whom they associate for political purposes. The government, in its brief, virtually admits this position when it speaks of the "communication of unlawful ideas." I challenge this premise, and deny that ideas can be proscribed under our Constitution. I agree that despotic governments cannot exist without stifling the voice of opposition to their oppressive practices. The First Amendment means to me, however, that the only constitutional way our government can preserve itself is to leave its people the fullest possible freedom to praise, criticize or discuss, as they see fit, all governmental policies and to suggest, if they desire, that even its most fundamental postulates are bad and should be changed; "Therein lies the security of the Republic, the very foundation of constitutional government." On that premise this land was created, and on that premise it has grown to greatness. Our Constitution assumes that the common sense of the people and their attachment to our country will enable them, after free discussion, to withstand ideas that are wrong. To say that our patriotism must be protected against false ideas by means other than these is, I think, to make a baseless charge. Unless we can rely on these qualities—if, in short, we begin to punish speech—we cannot honestly proclaim ourselves to be a free nation and we have lost what the Founders of this land risked their lives and their sacred honors to defend.

(C) The Court implies, however, that the ordinary rules and requirements of the

Constitution do not apply because the Committee is merely after Communists and they do not constitute a political party but only a criminal gang. . . . By accepting this charge and allowing it to support treatment of the Communist Party and its members which would violate the Constitution if applied to other groups, the Court, in effect, declares that Party outlawed. It has been only a few years since there was a practically unanimous feeling throughout the country and in our courts that this could not be done in our free land. . . . But the Party as a whole and innocent members of it could not be attained merely because it had some illegal aims and because some of its members were lawbreakers. . . .

The fact is that once we allow any group which has some political aims or ideas to be driven from the ballot and from the battle for men's minds because some of its members are bad and some of its tenets are illegal, no group is safe. Today we deal with Communists or suspected Communists. In 1920, instead, the New York Assembly duly elected legislators on the ground that, being Socialist, they were disloyal to the country's principles. In the 1830's the Masons were hunted as outlaws and subversives, and abolitionists were considered revolutionaries of the most dangerous kind in both North and South. Earlier still, at the time of the universally unlamented alien and sedition laws, Thomas Jefferson's party was attacked and its members derisively called "Jacobins." . . . History should teach us then, that in times of high emotional excitement minority parties and groups which advocate extremely unpopular social or governmental innovations will always be typed as criminal gangs and attempts will always be made to drive them out. It was knowledge of this fact, and of its great dangers, that caused the Founders of our land to enact the First Amendment as a guarantee that neither Congress nor the people would do anything to hinder or destroy the capacity of individuals and groups to seek converts and votes for any cause, however radical or unpalatable their principles might seem under the accepted notions of the time. Whatever the states were left free to do, the First Amendment sought to leave Congress devoid of any kind or quality of power to direct any type of national laws against the freedom of individuals to think what they please, advocate whatever policy they choose, and join with others to bring about the social, religious, political and governmental changes which seem best to them. Today's holding, in my judgment, marks another major step in the progressively increasing retreat from the safeguards of the First Amendment.

Ultimately all the questions in this case, really boil down to one—whether we as a people will try fearfully and futilely to preserve democracy by adopting totalitarian methods, or whether in accordance with our traditions and our Constitution we will have the confidence and courage to be free.

I would reverse this conviction.

Mr. Justice BRENNAN, dissenting: I would reverse this conviction. It is sufficient that I state my complete agreement with my Brother Black that no purpose for the investigation of Barenblatt is revealed by the record except exposure purely for the sake of exposure. This is not a purpose to which Barenblatt's rights under the First Amendment can validly be subordinated. An investigation in which the processes of lawmaking and law-evaluating are submerged entirely in exposure of individual behavior —in adjudication of a sort, through the exposure process—is outside the constitutional pale of Congressional inquiry. Watkins v. United States, 354 U. S. 178; see also Sweezy v. State of New Hampshire, 354 U. S. 234; NAACP v. State of Alabama, 357 U. S. 449; Uphaus v. Wyman, 360 U. S. 72.

638. THE U-2 AFFAIR
1960

Nineteen fifty-nine saw a brief thaw in the relations between the Soviet Union and the United States. In the fall of 1959, Premier Khrushchev toured the United States, visited President Eisenhower at Camp David, and invited the President to make a return visit to

Russia. Meantime the two leaders planned for yet another summit conference, to meet in Paris in May. But on May 5 Khrushchev announced that the Russians had brought down an American reconnaissance plane deep in the heart of Russia and captured its pilot, Francis Powers. We give here the Soviet Note on the U-2 affair, the brief official statement of the State Department, and the more elaborate explanation by President Eisenhower. Meantime Powers was tried in Russia for espionage and condemned to ten years imprisonment; in less than two years he was released and returned to the United States. Eisenhower called off further reconnaissance flights over Russia; when Khrushchev demanded apology, disavowal, and punishment, the President refused, and the Soviet Premier broke up the summit conference. See Jules Davids, *America and the World of Our Time;* Robert Osgood, *Limited War;* Richard Stebbins, *The United States in World Affairs, 1960;* W. W. Rostow, *The United States in the World Arena;* Chester Bowles, *The Coming Political Breakthrough;* John Lukacs, *A History of the Cold War;* George Kennan, "Peaceful Coexistence: A Western View," *Foreign Affairs,* Jan. 1960.

1. SOVIET NOTE ON THE U-2 INCIDENT
May 10, 1960

(Department of State Bulletin,
May 30, 1960)

On May 1 of this year at 5 hours 36 minutes, Moscow time, a military aircraft violated the boundary of the Union of Soviet Socialist Republics and intruded across the borders of the Soviet Union for a distance of more than 2,000 kilometers. The government of the Union of Soviet Socialist Republics naturally could not leave unpunished such a flagrant violation of Soviet state boundaries. When the intentions of the violating aircraft became apparent, it was shot down by Soviet rocket troops in the area of Sverdlovsk.

Upon examination by experts of all data at the disposal of the Soviet side, it was incontrovertibly established that the intruder aircraft belonged to the United States of America, was permanently based in Turkey and was sent through Pakistan into the Soviet Union with hostile purposes. . . .

Exact data from the investigation leave no doubts with respect to the purpose of the flight of the American aircraft which violated the U. S. S. R. border on May 1. This aircraft was specially equipped for reconnaissance and diversionary flight over the territory of the Soviet Union. It had on board apparatus for aerial photography for detecting the Soviet radar network and other special radio-technical equipment which form part of U. S. S. R. anti-aircraft defenses. At the disposal of the Soviet expert commission which carried out the investigation, there is indisputable proof of the espionage-reconnaissance mission of the American aircraft: films of Soviet defense and industrial establishments, a tape recording of signals of Soviet radar stations and other data.

Pilot Powers, . . . has indicated that he did everything in full accordance with the assignment given him. On the flight map taken from him there was clearly and accurately marked the entire route he was assigned after takeoff from the city of Adana (Turkey): Peshawar (Pakistan)–the Ural Sea–Sverdlovsk–Archangel–Murmansk, followed by a landing at the Norwegian airfield at Bude. The pilot has also stated that he served in subunit number 10–10 which under cover of the National Aeronautics and Space Administration is engaged in high altitude military reconnaissance. . . .

After it had been incontrovertibly proven that the American aircraft intruded across the borders of the Soviet Union for aggressive reconnaissance purposes, a new announcement was made by the U. S. State Department on May 7 which contained the forced admission that the aircraft was sent into the Soviet Union for military reconnaissance purposes and, by that very fact, it was admitted that the flight was pursuing aggressive purposes.

2. STATE DEPARTMENT STATEMENT ON U-2 INCIDENT
May 7, 1960

(Department of State Bulletin,
May 23, 1960)

The Department has received the text of Mr. Khrushchev's further remarks about the unarmed plane which is reported to have been shot down in the Soviet Union. As previously announced, it was known that a U-2 plane was missing. As a result of the inquiry ordered by the President it has been established that insofar as the authorities in Washington are concerned there was no authorization for any such flight as described by Mr. Khrushchev.

Nevertheless it appears that in endeavoring to obtain information now concealed behind the Iron Curtain a flight over Soviet territory was probably undertaken by an unarmed civilian U-2 plane.

It is certainly no secret that, given the state of the world today, intelligence collection activities are practiced by all countries, and postwar history certainly reveals that the Soviet Union has not been lagging behind in this field.

The necessity for such activities as measures for legitimate national defense is enhanced by the excessive secrecy practiced by the Soviet Union in contrast to the free world.

One of the things creating tension in the world today is apprehension over surprise attack with weapons of mass destruction.

To reduce mutual suspicion and to give a measure of protection against surprise attack the United States in 1955 offered its open-skies proposal—a proposal which was rejected out of hand by the Soviet Union. It is in relation to the danger of surprise attack that planes of the type of unarmed civilian U-2 aircraft have made flights along the frontiers of the free world for the past 4 years.

3. EISENHOWER'S STATEMENT ON THE U-2 INCIDENT
May 25, 1960
(White House Press Release)

(Public Papers of the Presidents: Dwight D. Eisenhower, 1960, no. 163)

You recall, of course, why I went to Paris ten days ago.

Last summer and fall I had many conversations with world leaders; some of these were with Chairman Khrushchev, here in America. Over those months a small improvement in relations between the Soviet Union and the West seemed discernible. A possibility developed that the Soviet leaders might at last be ready for serious talks about our most persistent problems—those of disarmament, mutual inspection, atomic control, and Germany, including Berlin.

To explore that possibility, our own and the British and French leaders met together, and later we agreed, with the Soviet leaders, to gather in Paris on May 16. . . .

Our safety, and that of the free world, demand, of course, effective systems for gathering information about the military capabilities of other powerful nations, especially those that make a fetish of secrecy. This involves many techniques and methods. In these times of vast military machines and nuclear-tipped missiles, the ferreting out of this information is indispensable to free-world security.

This has long been one of my most serious preoccupations. It is part of my grave responsibility, within the over-all problem of protecting the American people, to guard ourselves and our allies against surprise attack.

During the period leading up to World War II we learned from bitter experience the imperative necessity of a continuous gathering of intelligence information, the maintenance of military communications and contact, and alertness of command.

An additional word seems appropriate about this matter of communications and command. While the Secretary of Defense and I were in Paris, we were, of course, away from our normal command posts. He recommended that under the circumstances we test the continuing readiness of our military communications. I personally approved. Such tests are valuable and will be frequently repeated in the future.

Moreover, as President, charged by the Constitution with the conduct of America's foreign relations, and as Commander-in-Chief, charged with the direction of the operations and activities of our Armed Forces and their supporting services, I take full responsibility for approving all the various programs undertaken by our government to secure and evaluate military intelligence.

It was in the prosecution of one of these intelligence programs that the widely publicized U-2 incident occurred.

Aerial photography has been one of many methods we have used to keep ourselves and the free world abreast of major Soviet military developments. The usefulness of this work has been well established through four years of effort. The Soviets were well aware of it. Chairman Khrushchev has stated that he became aware of these flights several years ago. Only last week, in his Paris press conference, Chairman Khrushchev confirmed that he knew of these flights when he visited the United States last September.

Incidentally, this raises the natural question—why all the furor concerning one particular flight? He did not, when in America last September charge that these flights were any threat to Soviet safety. He did not then see any reason to refuse to confer with American representatives.

This he did only about the flight that unfortunately failed, on May 1, far inside Russia.

Now, two questions have been raised about this particular flight; first, as to its timing, considering the imminence of the summit meeting; second, our initial statements when we learned the flight had failed.

As to the timing, the question was really whether to halt the program and thus forgo the gathering of important information that was essential and that was likely to be unavailable at a later date. The decision was that the program should not be halted.

The plain truth is this: when a nation needs intelligence activity, there is no time when vigilance can be relaxed. Incidentally, from Pearl Harbor we learned that even negotiation itself can be used to conceal preparations for a surprise attack.

Next, as to our government's initial statement about the flight, this was issued to protect the pilot, his mission, and our intelligence processes, at a time when the true facts were still undetermined.

Our first information about the failure of this mission did not disclose whether the pilot was still alive, was trying to escape, was avoiding interrogation, or whether both plane and pilot had been destroyed. Protection of our intelligence system and the pilot, and concealment of the plane's mission, seemed imperative. It must be remembered that over a long period these flights had given us information of the greatest importance to the nation's security. In fact, their success has been nothing short of remarkable. . . .

I then made two facts clear to the public: first, our program of aerial reconnaissance had been undertaken with my approval; second, this government is compelled to keep abreast, by one means or another, of military activities of the Soviets, just as their government has for years engaged in espionage activities in our country and throughout the world. . . .

In fact, before leaving Washington I had directed that these U-2 flights be stopped. Clearly their usefulness was impaired. Moreover, continuing this particular activity in these new circumstances could not but complicate the relations of certain of our allies with the Soviets.

At the four-power meeting on Monday morning, he demanded of the United States four things: First, condemnation of U-2 flights as a method of espionage; second, assurance that they would not be continued; third, a public apology on behalf of the United States; and, fourth, punishment of all those who had any responsibility respecting this particular mission.

I replied by advising the Soviet leader that I had, during the previous week, stopped these flights and that they would not be resumed. I offered also to discuss the matter with him in personal meetings, while the regular business of the summit might proceed. Obviously, I would not respond to his extreme demands. He knew, of course, by holding to those demands the Soviet Union was scuttling the summit conference. . . .

A major American goal is a world of open societies.

Here in our country anyone can buy maps and aerial photographs showing our cities, our dams, our plants, our highways—indeed, our whole industrial and economic complex. We know that Soviet attachés regularly collect this information. Last fall Chairman Khrushchev's train passed no more than a few hundred feet from an operational ICBM, in plain view from his window. Our thousands of books and scientific journals, our magazines, newspapers and official publications, our radio and television, all openly describe to all the world every aspect of our society.

This is as it should be. We are proud of our freedom.

Soviet distrust, however, does still remain.

To allay these misgivings I offered five years ago to open our skies to Soviet reconnaissance aircraft on a reciprocal basis. The Soviets refused. That offer is still open. At an appropriate time America will submit such a program to the United Nations, together with the recommendation that the United Nations itself conduct this reconnaissance. Should the United Nations accept this proposal, I am prepared to propose that America supply part of the aircraft and equipment required.

639. SHELTON v. TUCKER
364 U. S. 479
1960

Appeal from U.S. District Court for Eastern District of Arkansas. The question presented here was similar to that presented in NAACP v. Alabama, Doc. no. 357 U.S. 449 and raised some of the questions raised by Adler v. Board of Education, 342 U.S. 485 and Belian v. Board of Higher Education 357 U.S. 399: how far may the state (or the school authorities) go in requiring full disclosure of membership and activities as a prerequisite for teaching in its schools? While on the surface the Arkansas statute proclaimed an interest of the state in all associations and affiliations, there was reason to suppose that it was primarily concerned with membership in the NAACP and similar organizations. See Freund, "Competing Freedoms in American Constitutional Law," 13 *U. of Chicago Conference Series* 26; Richardson, "Freedom of Expression and the Function of the Courts," 65 *Harvard Law Rev.* 1.

Mr. Justice STEWART: An Arkansas statute compels every teacher, as a condition of employment in a state-supported school or college, to file annually an affidavit listing without limitation every organization to which he has belonged or regularly contributed within the preceding five years. At issue in these two cases is the validity of that statute under the Fourteenth Amendment to the Constitution . . .

The statute in question is Act 10 of the Second Extraordinary Session of the Arkansas General Assembly of 1958. The provisions of the Act are summarized in the opinion of the District Court as follows:

"Act 10 provides in substance that no person shall be employed or elected to employment as a superintendent, principal or teacher in any public school in Arkansas, or as an instructor, professor or teacher in any public institution of higher learning in that state until such person shall have submitted to the appropriate hiring authority an affidavit listing all organizations to which he at the time belongs and to which he has belonged during the past five years, and also listing all organizations to which he at the time is paying regular dues or is making regular contributions, or to which within the past five years he has paid such dues or made such contributions. . . ."

The plaintiffs in the Federal District Court (appellants here) were B. T. Shelton, a teacher employed in the Little Rock Public School System, suing for himself and others similarly situated, together with the Arkansas Teachers Association. Shelton . . . declined to file the affidavit, and his contract for the ensuing school year was not renewed. At the trial the evidence showed that he was not a member of the Communist Party or of any organization advocating the overthrow of the government by force, and that he was a member of the National Association for the Advancement of Colored People. The court upheld Act 10, finding the information it required was "relevant," and relying on several decisions of this Court. . . .

I

It is urged here, as it was unsuccessfully urged throughout the proceedings in both the federal and state courts, that Act 10 deprives teachers in Arkansas of their rights to personal, associational, and academic liberty, protected by the Due Process Clause of the Fourteenth Amendment from invasion by state action. In considering this contention, we deal with two basic postulates.

First. There can be no doubt of the right of a state to investigate the competence and fitness of those whom it hires to teach in its schools, as this Court before now has had occasion to recognize. . . .

Second. It is not disputed that to compel a teacher to disclose his every associational tie is to impair that teacher's right of free association, a right closely allied to freedom of speech and a right which, like free speech, lies at the foundation of a free society. Such interference with personal freedom is conspicuously accented when the teacher serves at the absolute will of those to whom the disclosure must be made—those who any year can terminate the teacher's employment without bringing charges, without notice, without a hearing, without affording an opportunity to explain.

The statute does not provide that the information it requires be kept confidential. Each school board is left free to deal with the information as it wishes. The record contains evidence to indicate that fear of public disclosure is neither theoretical nor groundless. Even if there were no disclosure to the general public, the pressure upon a teacher to avoid any ties which might displease those who control his professional destiny would be constant and heavy. Public exposure, bringing with it the possibility of public pressures upon school boards to discharge teachers who belong to unpopular or minority organizations, would simply operate to widen and aggravate the impairment of constitutional liberty. . . .

II

The question to be decided here is not whether the State of Arkansas can ask certain of its teachers about all their organizational relationships. It is not whether the state can ask all of its teachers about certain of their associational ties. It is not whether teachers can be asked how many organizations they belong to, or how much time they spend in organizational activity. The question is whether the state can ask every one of its teachers to disclose every single organization with which he has been associated over a five-year period. The scope of the inquiry required by Act 10 is completely unlimited. The statute requires a teacher to reveal the church to which he belongs, or to which he has given financial support. It requires him to disclose his political party, and every political organization to which he may have contributed over a five-year period. It requires him to list, without number, every conceivable kind of associational tie—social, professional, political, avocational, or religious. Many such relationships could have no possible bearing upon the teacher's occupational competence or fitness.

In a series of decisions this Court has held that, even though the governmental purpose be legitimate and substantial, that purpose cannot be pursued by means that broadly stifle fundamental personal liberties when the end can be more narrowly achieved. The breadth of legislative abridgment must be viewed in the light of less drastic means for achieving the same basic purpose. . . .

The unlimited and undiscriminate sweep of the statute now before us brings it within the ban of our prior cases. The statute's comprehensive interference with associational freedom goes far beyond what might be justified in the exercise of the state's legitimate inquiry into the fitness and competency of its teachers. The judgments in both cases must be reversed.

It is so ordered.

Judgments reversed.

Justices FRANKFURTER, CLARK, HARLAN and WHITTAKER, dissenting.

640. EISENHOWER'S FAREWELL ADDRESS
January 17, 1961

(Public Papers of the Presidents: Dwight D. Eisenhower, 1960–61, no. 421)

On Eisenhower see Sherman Adams, *First-Hand Report: Story of the Eisenhower Administration;* Marquis Childs, *Eisenhower: Captive Hero;* Robert J. Donavan, *Eisenhower, the Inside Story;* Louis Koenig, *The Invisible Presidency;* Merlo J. Pusey, *Eisenhower The President;* Richard Rovere, *The Eisenhower Years: Affairs of State.*

My fellow Americans:

Three days from now, after half a century in the service of our country, I shall lay down the responsibilities of office as, in traditional and solemn ceremony, the authority of the Presidency is vested in my successor. . . .

We now stand ten years past the midpoint of a century that has witnessed four major wars among great nations. Three of them involved our own country. Despite these holocausts America is today the strongest, the most influential and most productive nation in the world. Understandably proud of this pre-eminence we yet realize that America's leadership and prestige depend, not merely upon our unmatched material progress, riches and military strength, but on how we use our power in the interests of world peace and human betterment.

Throughout America's adventure in free government, our basic purposes have been to keep the peace; to foster progress in human achievement, and to enhance liberty, dignity and integrity among people and among nations. To strive for less would be unworthy of a free and religious people. Any failure traceable to arrogance, or our lack of comprehension or readiness to sacrifice would inflict upon us grievous hurt both at home and abroad.

Progress toward these noble goals is persistently threatened by the conflict now engulfing the world. It commands our whole attention, absorbs our very beings. We face a hostile ideology—global in scope, atheistic in character, ruthless in purpose, and insidious in method. Unhappily the danger it poses promises to be of indefinite duration. To meet it successfully, there is called for, not so much the emotional and transitory sacrifices of crisis, but rather those which enable us to carry forward steadily, surely, and without complaint the burdens of a prolonged and complex struggle—with liberty the stake. Only thus shall we remain, despite every provocation, on our charted course toward permanent peace and human betterment. . . .

A vital element in keeping the peace is our military establishment. Our arms must be mighty, ready for instant action, so that no potential aggressor may be tempted to risk his own destruction.

Our military organization today bears little relation to that known by any of my predecessors in peacetime, or indeed by the fighting men of World War II or Korea.

Until the latest of our world conflicts, the United States had no armaments industry. American makers of plowshares could, with time and as required, make swords as well. But now we can no longer risk emergency improvisation of national defense; we have been compelled to create a permanent armaments industry of vast proportions. Added to this, three and a half million men and women are directly engaged in the defense establishment. We annually spend on military security more than the net income of all United States corporations.

This conjunction of an immense military establishment and a large arms industry is new in the American experience. The total influence—economic, political, even spiritual—is felt in every city, every statehouse, every office of the federal government. We recognize the imperative need for this development. Yet we must not fail to comprehend its grave implications. Our toil, resources, and livelihood are all involved; so is the very structure of our society.

In the councils of government, we must guard against the acquisition of unwarranted influence, whether sought or unsought, by the military-industrial complex. The potential for the disastrous rise of misplaced power exists and will persist.

We must never let the weight of this combination endanger our liberties or democratic processes. We should take nothing for granted. Only an alert and knowledgeable citizenry can compel the proper meshing of the huge industrial and military machinery of defense with our peaceful methods and goals, so that security and liberty may prosper together.

Akin to, and largely responsible for the sweeping changes in our industrial-military posture, has been the technological revolution during recent decades.

In this revolution, research has become central; it also becomes more formalized, complex, and costly. A steadily increasing share is conducted for, by, or at the direction of, the federal government. . . .

The prospect of domination of the nation's scholars by federal employment, project allocations, and the power of money is ever present—and is gravely to be regarded.

Yet, in holding scientific research and discovery in respect, as we should, we must also be alert to the equal and opposite danger that public policy could itself become the captive of a scientific-technological elite.

It is the task of statesmanship to mold, to balance, and to integrate these and other forces, new and old, within the principles of our democratic system—ever aiming toward the supreme goals of our free society.

Another factor in maintaining balance involves the element of time. As we peer into society's future, we—you and I, and our government—must avoid the impulse to live only for today, plundering, for our own ease and convenience, the precious resources of tomorrow. We cannot mortgage the material assets of our grandchildren without risking the loss also of their political and spiritual heritage. We want democracy to survive for all generations to come, not to become the insolvent phantom of tomorrow.

Down the long lane of the history yet to be written America knows that this world of ours, ever growing smaller, must avoid becoming a community of dreadful fear and hate, and be, instead, a proud confederation of mutual trust and respect.

Such a confederation must be one of equals. The weakest must come to the conference table with the same confidence as do we, protected as we are by our moral, economic, and military strength. That table, though scarred by many past frustrations, cannot be abandoned for the certain agony of the battlefield.

Disarmament, with mutual honor and confidence, is a continuing imperative. Together we must learn how to compose differences, not with arms, but with intellect and decent purpose. Because this need is so sharp and apparent I confess that I lay down my official responsibilities in this field with a definite sense of disappointment. As one who has witnessed the horror and the lingering sadness of war—as one who knows that another war could utterly destroy this civilization which has been so slowly and painfully built over thousands of years—I wish I could say tonight that a lasting peace is in sight.

Happily, I can say that war has been avoided. Steady progress toward our ultimate goal has been made. But, so much remains to be done. As a private citizen, I shall never cease to do what little I can to help the world advance along that road. . . .

641. JOHN F. KENNEDY'S INAUGURAL ADDRESS
January 20, 1961
(*Department of State Bulletin,* February 6, 1961)

Nominated on the first ballot at the Democratic convention in Los Angeles, Senator Kennedy won the 1960 election by a slim popular margin of 118,000 votes and a substantial majority of 303 to 219 votes in the Electoral College. On Kennedy see Theodore White, *The Making of the President,* 1960; Dean Acheson, *A Democrat Looks at his Party;* James Mc.G. Burns, *John F. Kennedy;* and Kennedy's own *The Strategy of Peace, Let Us Begin,* and *To Turn the Tide.*

VICE-PRESIDENT JOHNSON, MR. SPEAKER, MR. CHIEF JUSTICE, PRESIDENT EISENHOWER, VICE-PRESIDENT NIXON, PRESIDENT TRUMAN, REVEREND CLERGY, FELLOW CITIZENS:

We observe today not a victory of party but a celebration of freedom—symbolizing an end as well as a beginning—signifying renewal as well as change. For I have sworn before you and Almighty God the same solemn oath our forebearers prescribed nearly a century and three-quarters ago.

The world is very different now. For man holds in his mortal hands the power to abolish all forms of human poverty and all forms of human life. And yet the same revolutionary beliefs for which our forebearers fought are still at issue around the globe—the belief that the rights of man come not from the generosity of the state but from the hand of God.

We dare not forget today that we are the heirs of that first revolution. Let the word go forth from this time and place, to friend and foe alike, that the torch has been passed to a new generation of Americans—born in this century, tempered by war, disciplined by a hard and bitter peace, proud of our ancient heritage—and unwilling to witness or permit the slow undoing of those human rights to which this nation has always been committed, and to which we are committed today at home and around the world.

Let every nation know, whether it wishes us well or ill, that we shall pay any price, bear any burden, meet any hardship, support any friend, oppose any foe to assure the survival and the success of liberty.

This much we pledge—and more.

To those old allies whose cultural and spiritual origins we share, we pledge the loyalty of faithful friends. United, there is little we cannot do in a host of co-operative ventures. Divided, there is little we can do—for we dare not meet a powerful challenge at odds and split asunder.

To those new states whom we welcome to the ranks of the free, we pledge our word that one form of colonial control shall not have passed away merely to be replaced by a far more iron tyranny. We shall not always expect to find them supporting our view. But we shall always hope to find them strongly supporting their own freedom—and to remember that, in the past, those who foolishly sought power by riding the back of the tiger ended up inside.

To those people in the huts and villages of half the globe struggling to break the bonds of mass misery, we pledge our best efforts to help them help themselves, for whatever period is required—not because the Communists may be doing it, not because we seek their votes, but because it is right. If a free society cannot help the many who are poor, it cannot save the few who are rich.

To our sister republics south of our border, we offer a special pledge—to convert our good words into good deeds—in a new alliance for progress—to assist free men and free governments in casting off the chains of poverty. But this peaceful revolution of hope cannot become the prey of hostile powers. Let all our neighbors know that we shall join with them to oppose aggression or subversion anywhere in the Americas. And let every other power know that this hemisphere intends to remain the master of its own house.

To that world assembly of sovereign states, the United Nations, our last best hope in an age where the instruments of war have far outpaced the instruments of peace, we renew our pledge of support—to prevent it from becoming merely a forum for invective—to strengthen its shield of the new and the weak—and to enlarge the area in which its writ may run.

Finally, to those nations who would make themselves our adversary, we offer not a pledge but a request: that both sides begin anew the quest for peace, before the dark powers of destruction unleashed by science engulf all humanity in planned or accidental self-destruction.

We dare not tempt them with weakness. For only when our arms are sufficient beyond doubt can we be certain beyond doubt that they will never be employed.

But neither can two great and powerful groups of nations take comfort from our present course—both sides overburdened by the cost of modern weapons, both rightly alarmed by the steady spread of the deadly atom, yet both racing to alter that uncertain balance of terror that stays the hand of mankind's final war.

So let us begin anew—remembering on both sides that civility is not a sign of weakness, and sincerity is always subject to proof. Let us never negotiate out of fear. But let us never fear to negotiate.

Let both sides explore what problems unite us instead of belaboring those problems which divide us.

Let both sides, for the first time, formulate serious and precise proposals for the inspection and control of arms—and bring the absolute power to destroy other nations under the absolute control of all nations.

Let both sides seek to invoke the wonders of science instead of its terrors. Together let us explore the stars, conquer the deserts, eradicate disease, tap the ocean depths, and encourage the arts and commerce.

Let both sides unite to heed in all corners of the earth the command of Isaiah—to "undo the heavy burdens . . . [and] let the oppressed go free."

And if a beachhead of co-operation may push back the jungle of suspicion, let both sides join in creating a new endeavor, not a new balance of power, but a new world of law, where the strong are just and the weak secure and the peace preserved.

All this will not be finished in the first one hundred days. Nor will it be finished in the first one thousand days, nor in the life of this administration, nor even perhaps in our lifetime on this planet. But let us begin.

In your hands, my fellow citizens, more than mine, will rest the final success or failure of our course. Since this country was founded, each generation of Americans has been summoned to give testimony to its national loyalty. The graves of young Americans who answered the call to service surround the globe.

Now the trumpet summons us again—not as a call to bear arms, though arms we need —not as a call to battle, though embattled we are—but a call to bear the burden of a long twilight struggle, year in and year out, "rejoicing in hope, patient in tribulation"— a struggle against the common enemies of man: tyranny, poverty, disease, and war itself.

Can we forge against these enemies a grand and global alliance, North and South, East and West, that can assure a more fruit- ful life for all mankind? Will you join in that historic effort?

In the long history of the world, only a few generations have been granted the role of defending freedom in its hour of maximum danger. I do not shrink from this responsibility—I welcome it. I do not believe that any of us would exchange places with any other people or any other generation. The energy, the faith, the devotion which we bring to this endeavor will light our country and all who serve it—and the glow from that fire can truly light the world.

And so, my fellow Americans: ask not what your country can do for you—ask what you can do for your country.

My fellow citizens of the world: ask not what America will do for you, but what together we can do for the freedom of man.

Finally, whether you are citizens of America or citizens of the world, ask of us here the same high standards of strength and sacrifice which we ask of you. With a good conscience our only sure reward, with history the final judge of our deeds, let us go forth to lead the land we love, asking His blessing and His help, but knowing that here on earth God's work must truly be our own.

642. KENNEDY'S MESSAGE ON FEDERAL AID TO EDUCATION
February 20, 1961

(Public Papers of the Presidents: John F. Kennedy, 1961, no. 46)

Between 1920 and 1960 the population increased by about 75 per cent and the high school population by 500 per cent, while college and university enrollment increased six-fold. Inability of the poorer states to support public schools and universities adequately led to a widespread demand for federal aid to education at every level. In the late forties Senator Taft introduced a bill appropriating up to $250 million a year to aid public schools in the poorer states and guaranteeing appropriations of $40 a year for every school child in the country. This bill failed of passage as did similar bills during the Eisenhower administration. Meantime, however, federal appropriations for research in colleges and universities, and for scholarships to students of science had mounted to substantial sums. President Kennedy came to office committed to a program of federal aid to education at all levels, but his proposals ran into intransigent opposition from states rightists and from those who feared a crack in the "wall of separation between church and state." See James Conant, *The American High School Today;* Conant, *Slums and Suburbs;* Freeman Butts, *The American Tradition in Religion and Education;* Leo Pfeffer, *Church, State and Freedom;* James O'Neill, *Religion and Education Under the Constitution.*

1. ASSISTANCE TO PUBLIC ELEMENTARY AND SECONDARY SCHOOLS

. . . I recommend to the Congress a three-year program of general federal assistance for public elementary and secondary classroom construction and teachers' salaries.

Based essentially on the bill which passed the Senate last year (S. 8), although beginning at a more modest level of expenditures, this program would assure every state of no less than $15 for every public school student in average daily attendance, with the total amount appropriated ($666 million being authorized in the first year, rising to $866 million over a three-year period) distributed according to the equalization formula contained in the last year's Senate bill, and already familiar to the Congress by virtue of its similarity to the formulas contained in the Hill-Burton Hospital Construction and other acts. Ten per cent of the funds allocated to each state in the first year, and an equal amount thereafter, is to be used to help meet the unique problems of each state's "areas of special educational need"—depressed areas, slum neighborhoods, and others.

This is a modest program with ambitious goals. The sums involved are relatively small when we think in terms of more than 36 million public school children, and the billions of dollars necessary to educate them properly. Nevertheless, a limited beginning now—consistent with our obligations in other areas of responsibility—will encourage all states to expand their facilities to meet the increasing demand and enrich the quality of education offered, and gradually assist our relatively low-income states in the elevation of their educational standards to a national level.

The bill which will follow this message has been carefully drawn to eliminate disproportionately large or small inequities, and to make the maximum use of a limited number of dollars. In accordance with the clear prohibition of the Constitution, no elementary or secondary school funds are allocated for constructing church schools or paying church-school teachers' salaries; and thus nonpublic school children are rightfully not counted in determining the funds each state will receive for its public schools. Each state will be expected to maintain its own effort or contribution; and every state whose effort is below the national average will be expected to increase that proportion of its income which is devoted to public elementary and secondary education.

This investment will pay rich dividends in the years ahead—in increased economic growth, in enlightened citizens, in national excellence. For some 40 years, the Congress has wrestled with this problem and searched for a workable solution. I believe that we now have such a solution; and that this Congress in this year will make a land-mark contribution to American education. . . .

2. CONSTRUCTION OF COLLEGES AND UNIVERSITY FACILITIES

The burden of increased enrollments—imposed upon our elementary and secondary schools already in the fifties—will fall heavily upon our colleges and universities during the sixties. By the autumn of 1966, an estimated one million more students will be in attendance at institutions of higher learning than enrolled last fall—for a total more than twice as high as the total college enrollment of 1950. Our colleges, already hard-pressed to meet rising enrollments since 1950 during a period of rising costs, will be in critical straits merely to provide the necessary facilities, much less the cost of quality education.

The country as a whole is already spending nearly $1 billion a year on academic and residential facilities for higher education—some 20 per cent of the total spent for higher education. Even with increased contributions from state, local, and private sources, a gap of $2.9 billion between aggregate needs and expenditures is anticipated by 1965, and a gap of $5.2 billion by 1970.

The national interest requires an educational system on the college level sufficiently financed and equipped to provide every student with adequate physical facilities to meet his instructional, research, and residential needs.

I therefore recommend legislation which will:

(1) Extend the current College Housing Loan Program with a five year $250 million a year program designed to meet the federal government's appropriate share of residential housing for students and faculty. As a start, additional lending authority is necessary to speed action during fiscal 1961 on approvable loan applications already at hand.

(2) Establish a new, though similar, long-term, low-interest rate loan program for academic facilities, authorizing $300 million in loans each year for five years to assist in the construction of classrooms, laboratories, li-

braries, and related structures—sufficient to enable public and private higher institutions to accommodate the expanding enrollments they anticipate over the next five years; and also to assist in the renovation, rehabilitation, and modernization of such facilities.

. . . I recommend the establishment of a five-year program with an initial authorization of $26,250,000 of state-administered scholarships for talented and needy young people which will supplement but not supplant those programs of financial assistance to students which are now in operation.

Funds would be allocated to the states during the first year for a total of twenty-five thousand scholarships averaging $700 each, 37,500 scholarships the second year, and 50,000 for each succeeding year thereafter.

These scholarships, which would range according to need up to a maximum stipend of $1000, would be open to all young persons, without regard to sex, race, creed, or color, solely on the basis of their ability—as determined on a competitive basis—and their financial need. They would be permitted to attend the college of their choice, and free to select their own program of study. Inasmuch as tuition and fees do not normally cover the institution's actual expenses in educating the student, additional allowances to the college or university attended should accompany each scholarship to enable these institutions to accept the additional students without charging an undue increase in fees or suffering an undue financial loss.

643. KENNEDY'S MESSAGE ON THE PEACE CORPS
March 1, 1961
(*Department of State Bulletin,* March 20, 1961)

The Peace Corps was to the 1960's what Lend-Lease had been to the 1940's; like Lend-Lease it caught the popular imagination not only at home but abroad. The idea apparently originated with the President's brother-in-law, Sargent Shriver who was appointed its first director. In his message to Congress the President noted that the idea of a Peace Corps had received strong support from members of Congress, and from universities, student groups, labor unions, and others. First established on a pilot basis by Executive Order of March 1, the Peace Corps was put on a permanent statutory basis on September 22, when Congress appropriated $40 million for its operation during the fiscal year of 1962. The Peace Corps provided an effective outlet for the idealism of American youth. As the President said in his statement on signing the Executive Order, "Life in the Peace Corps will not be easy. There will be no salary, and allowances will be at a level sufficient only to maintain health and meet basic needs. . . . But every American who participates in the Peace Corps . . . will know that he or she is sharing in the great common task of bringing to man that decent way of life which is the foundation of freedom and a condition of peace."

To the Congress of the United States:

I recommend to the Congress the establishment of a permanent Peace Corps—a pool of trained American men and women sent overseas by the U.S. Government or through private organizations and institutions to help foreign countries meet their urgent needs for skilled manpower. . . .

Throughout the world the people of the newly developing nations are struggling for economic and social progress which reflects their deepest desires. Our own freedom, and the future of freedom around the world, depend, in a very real sense, on their ability to build growing and independent nations where men can live in dignity, liberated from the bonds of hunger, ignorance, and poverty.

One of the greatest obstacles to the achievement of this goal is the lack of trained men and women with the skill to teach the young and assist in the operation of development projects—men and women with the capacity to cope with the demands of swiftly evolving economies, and with the dedication to put that capacity to work in the villages, the mountains, the towns, and the factories of dozens of struggling nations.

The vast task of economic development urgently requires skilled people to do the work of the society—to help teach in the schools, construct development projects, demonstrate modern methods of sanitation in the villages, and perform a hundred other tasks calling for training and advanced knowledge.

To meet this urgent need for skilled manpower we are proposing the establishment of a Peace Corps—an organization which will recruit and train American volunteers, sending them abroad to work with the people of other nations.

This organization will differ from existing assistance programs in that its members will supplement technical advisers by offering the specific skills needed by developing nations if they are to put technical advice to work. They will help provide the skilled manpower necessary to carry out the development projects planned by the host governments, acting at a working level and serving at great personal sacrifice. There is little doubt that the number of those who wish to serve will be far greater than our capacity to absorb them. . . .

Last session, the Congress authorized a study of these possibilities. Preliminary reports of this study show that the Peace Corps is feasible, needed, and wanted by many foreign countries.

Most heartening of all, the initial reaction to this proposal has been an enthusiastic response by student groups, professional organizations, and private citizens everywhere —a convincing demonstration that we have in this country an immense reservoir of dedicated men and women willing to devote their energies and time and toil to the cause of world peace and human progress.

Among the specific programs to which Peace Corps members can contribute are teaching in primary and secondary schools, especially as part of national English language teaching programs; participation in the worldwide program of malaria eradication; instruction and operation of public health and sanitation projects; aiding in village development through school construction and other programs; increasing rural agricultural productivity by assisting local farmers to use modern implements and techniques. The initial emphasis of these programs will be on teaching. Thus the Peace Corps members will be an effective means of implementing the development programs of the host countries—programs which our technical assistance operations have helped to formulate.

The Peace Corps will not be limited to the young, or to college graduates. All Americans who are qualified will be welcome to join this effort. But undoubtedly the corps will be made up primarily of young people as they complete their formal education.

Because one of the greatest resources of a free society is the strength and diversity of its private organizations and institutions much of the Peace Corps program will be carried out by these groups, financially assisted by the federal government.

Peace Corps personnel will be made available to developing nations in the following ways:

1. Through private voluntary agencies carrying on international assistance programs.

2. Through overseas programs of colleges and universities.

3. Through assistance programs of international agencies.

4. Through assistance programs of the U.S. Government.

5. Through new programs which the Peace Corps itself directly administers.

In the majority of cases the Peace Corps will assume the entire responsibility for recruitment, training, and the development of oversea projects. In other cases it will make available a pool of trained applicants to private groups who are carrying out projects approved by the Peace Corps.

In the case of Peace Corps programs conducted through voluntary agencies and universities, these private institutions will have the option of using the national recruitment system—the central pool of trained manpower—or developing recruitment systems of their own.

In all cases men and women recruited as a result of federal assistance will be members of the Peace Corps and enrolled in the central organization. All private recruitment and training programs will adhere to Peace Corps standards as a condition of federal assistance.

In all instances the men and women of the Peace Corps will go only to those countries where their services and skills are genuinely needed and desired. U.S. operations missions, supplemented where necessary by special Peace Corps teams, will consult with leaders in foreign countries in order to determine where Peace Corpsmen are needed, the types of job they can best fill, and the number of people who can be usefully employed. The Peace Corps will not supply personnel for marginal undertakings without a sound economic or social justification. In furnishing assistance through the Peace Corps careful regard will be given to the particular country's developmental priorities.

Membership in the Peace Corps will be open to all Americans, and applications will be available shortly. Where application is made directly to the Peace Corps—the vast majority of cases—they will be carefully screened to make sure that those who are selected can contribute to Peace Corps programs, and have the personal qualities which will enable them to represent the United States abroad with honor and dignity. In those cases where application is made directly to a private group, the same basic standards will be maintained. Each new recruit will receive a training and orientation period varying from 6 weeks to 6 months. This training will include courses in the culture and language of the country to which they are being sent and specialized training designed to increase the work skills of re-

cruits. In some cases training will be conducted by participant agencies and universities in approved training programs. Other training programs will be conducted by the Peace Corps staff.

Length of service in the Corps will vary depending on the kind of project and the country, generally ranging from 2 to 3 years. Peace Corps members will often serve under conditions of physical hardship, living under primitive conditions among the people of developing nations. For every Peace Corps member service will mean a great financial sacrifice. They will receive no salary. Instead they will be given an allowance which will only be sufficient to meet their basic needs and maintain health. It is essential that Peace Corps men and women live simply and unostentatiously among the people they have come to assist. At the conclusion of their tours, members of the Peace Corps will receive a small sum in the form of severance pay based on length of service abroad to assist them during their first weeks back in the United States. Service with the Peace Corps will not exempt volunteers from selective service.

644. THE ALLIANCE FOR PROGRESS, 1961

Kennedy inherited a difficult and highly sensitive Latin-American situation, and tackled it with immense energy. For the background of the Latin-American problem see the analysis in Kennedy's address of March 13. We give here that address, and the formal charter (with a few minor omissions) of Punta Del Este, Uruguay, which was designed to implement the proposals set forth by the President. See Adlai Stevenson, "The Alliance for Progress: a Road Map to New Achievements," *Department of State Bulletin,* August 21, 1961; William Benton, *The Voice of Latin America;* Chester Bowles, *An American Purpose.*

1. PRESIDENT KENNEDY'S PROPOSAL

March 13, 1961

(*Department of State Bulletin,* April 3, 1961)

. . . One hundred and thirty-nine years ago the United States, stirred by the heroic

struggles of its fellow Americans, urged the independence and recognition of the new Latin-American republics. It was then, at the dawn of freedom throughout this hemisphere, that Bolívar spoke of his desire to see the Americas fashioned into the greatest region in the world, "greatest," he said, "not so much by virtue of her area and her wealth, as by her freedom and her glory."

Never, in the long history of our hemisphere, has this dream been nearer to fulfillment, and never has it been in greater danger. . . .

Throughout Latin America—a continent rich in resources and in the spiritual and cultural achievements of its people—millions of men and women suffer the daily degradations of hunger and poverty. They lack decent shelter or protection from disease. Their children are deprived of the education or the jobs which are the gateway to a better life. And each day the problems grow more urgent. Population growth is outpacing economic growth, low living standards are even further endangered, and discontent—the discontent of a people who know that abundance and the tools of progress are at last within their reach—that discontent is growing. In the words of José Figueres, "once dormant peoples are struggling upward toward the sun, toward a better life."

If we are to meet a problem so staggering in its dimensions, our approach must itself be equally bold, an approach consistent with the majestic concept of Operation Pan America. Therefore I have called on all people of the hemisphere to join in a new Alliance for Progress—*Alianza para Progreso*—a vast co-operative effort, unparalleled in magnitude and nobility of purpose, to satisfy the basic needs of the American people for homes, work and land, health and schools— *techo, trabajo y tierra, salud y escuela.*

Ten-Year Plan for the Americas

First, I propose that the American republics begin on a vast new ten-year plan for the Americas, a plan to transform the 1960's into an historic decade of democratic progress. These ten years will be the years of maximum progress, maximum effort—the years when the greatest obstacles must be overcome, the years when the need for assistance will be the greatest.

And if we are successful, if our effort is bold enough and determined enough, then the close of this decade will mark the beginning of a new era in the American experience. The living standards of every American family will be on the rise, basic education will be available to all, hunger will be a forgotten experience, the need for massive outside help will have passed, most nations will have entered a period of self-sustaining growth, and, although there will be still much to do, every American republic will be the master of its own revolution and its own hope and progress. . . .

If the countries of Latin America are ready to do their part—and I am sure they are—then I believe the United States, for its part, should help provide resources of a scope and magnitude sufficient to make this bold development plan a success, just as we helped to provide, against nearly equal odds, the resources adequate to help rebuild the economies of Western Europe. For only an effort of towering dimensions can insure fulfillment of our plan for a decade of progress.

Second, I will shortly request a ministerial meeting of the Inter-American Economic and Social Council, a meeting at which we can begin the massive planning effort which will be at the heart of the Alliance for Progress.

For if our alliance is to succeed, each Latin nation must formulate long-range plans for its own development—plans which establish targets and priorities, insure monetary stability, establish the machinery for vital social change, stimulate private activity and initiative, and provide for a maximum national effort. These plans will be the foundation of our development effort and the basis for the allocation of outside resources. . . .

Third, I have this evening signed a request to the Congress for $500 million as a first step in fulfilling the Act of Bogotá. This is the first large-scale inter-American effort —instituted by my predecessor President Eisenhower—to attack the social barriers which block economic progress. The money will be used to combat illiteracy, improve the productivity and use of their land, wipe out disease, attack archaic tax and land-tenure structures, provide educational opportunities, and offer a broad range of projects designed to make the benefits of increasing abundance available to all. We will begin to commit these funds as soon as they are appropriated.

Fourth, we must support all economic integration which is a genuine step toward larger markets and greater competitive opportunity. The fragmentation of Latin-American economies is a serious barrier to industrial growth. Projects such as the Central American common market and free-trade areas in South America can help to remove these obstacles.

Fifth, the United States is ready to co-operate in serious, case-by-case examinations of commodity market problems. Frequent violent changes in commodity prices seriously injure the economies of many Latin-American countries, draining their resources and stultifying their growth. Together we must find practical methods of bringing an end to this pattern.

Sixth, we will immediately step up our food-for-peace emergency program, help to establish food reserves in areas of recurrent drought, and help provide school lunches for children and offer feed grains for use in rural development. For hungry men and women cannot wait for economic discussions or diplomatic meetings; their need is urgent, and their hunger rests heavily on the conscience of their fellow men.

Seventh, all the people of the hemisphere must be allowed to share in the expanding wonders of science—wonders which have captured man's imagination, challenged the powers of his mind, and given him the tools for rapid progress. I invite Latin-American scientists to work with us in new projects in fields such as medicine and agriculture, physics and astronomy, and desalinization, and to help plan for regional research laboratories in these and other fields, and to strengthen co-operation between American universities and laboratories.

We also intend to expand our science-teacher training programs to include Latin-American instructors, to assist in establishing such programs in other American countries, and translate and make available revolutionary new teaching materials in physics, chemistry, biology, and mathematics so that the young of all nations may contribute their skills to the advance of science.

Eighth, we must rapidly expand the training of those needed to man the economies of rapidly developing countries. This means expanded technical training programs, for which the Peace Corps, for example, will be available when needed. It also means assistance to Latin-American universities, graduate schools, and research institutes.

We welcome proposals in Central America for intimate co-operation in higher education, co-operation which can achieve a regional effort of increased effectiveness and excellence. We are ready to help fill the gap in trained manpower, realizing that our ultimate goal must be a basic education for all who wish to learn.

Ninth, we reaffirm our pledge to come to the defense of any American nation whose independence is endangered. As confidence in the collective security system of the Organization of American States spreads, it will be possible to devote to constructive use a major share of those resources now spent on the instruments of war. Even now, as the government of Chile has said, the time has come to take the first steps toward sensible limitations of arms. And the new generation of military leaders has shown an increasing awareness that armies can not only defend their countries—they can, as we have learned through our own Corps of Engineers, help to build them.

Tenth, we invite our friends in Latin America to contribute to the enrichment of life and culture in the United States. We need teachers of your literature and history and tradition, opportunities for our young people to study in your universities, access to your music, your art, and the thought of your great philosophers. For we know we have much to learn.

In this way you can help bring a fuller spiritual and intellectual life to the people of the United States and contribute to understanding and mutual respect among the nations of the hemisphere.

With steps such as these we propose to complete the revolution of the Americas, to build a hemisphere where all men can hope for a suitable standard of living and all can live out their lives in dignity and in freedom.

POLITICAL FREEDOM AND SOCIAL PROGRESS

To achieve this goal political freedom must accompany material progress. Our Alliance for progress is an alliance of free governments—and it must work to eliminate tyranny from a hemisphere in which it has no rightful place. Therefore let us express our special friendship to the people of Cuba and the Dominican Republic—and the hope they will soon rejoin the society of free men, uniting with us in our common effort.

This political freedom must be accompanied by social change. For unless necessary social reforms, including land and tax reform, are freely made, unless we broaden the opportunity of all of our people, unless the great mass of Americans share in increasing prosperity, then our alliance, our revolution, our dream, and our freedom will fail. But we call for social change by free men—change in the spirit of Washington and Jefferson, of Bolívar and San Martín and Martí—not change which seeks to impose on men tyrannies which we cast out a century and a half ago. Our motto is what it has always been—progress yes, tyranny no—*progreso sí, tiranía no!*

But our greatest challenge comes from within—the task of creating an American civilization where spiritual and cultural values are strengthened by an ever-broadening base of material advance, where, within the rich diversity of its own traditions, each nation is free to follow its own path toward progress.

The completion of our task will, of course, require the efforts of all the governments of our hemisphere. But the efforts of governments alone will never be enough. In the end the people must choose and the people must help themselves.

And so I say to the men and women of the Americas—to the *campesino* in the fields, to the *obrero* in the cities, to the *estudiante* in the schools—prepare your mind and heart for the task ahead, call forth your strength, and let each devote his energies to the betterment of all so that your children and our children in this hemisphere can find an ever richer and a freer life.

Let us once again transform the American Continent into a vast crucible of revolutionary ideas and efforts, a tribute to the power of the creative energies of free men and women, an example to all the world that liberty and progress walk hand in hand. Let us once again awaken our American revolution until it guides the struggles of people everywhere—not with an imperialism of force or fear but the rule of courage and freedom and hope for the future of man.

2. THE CHARTER OF PUNTA DEL ESTE
August 17, 1961

(Department of State Bulletin, September 11, 1961)

PREAMBLE

We, the American republics, hereby proclaim our decision to unite in a common effort to bring our people accelerated economic progress and broader social justice within the framework of personal dignity and political liberty.

Almost two hundred years ago we began in this Hemisphere the long struggle for freedom which now inspires people in all parts of the world. Today, in ancient lands, men moved to hope by the revolutions of our young nations search for liberty. Now we must give a new meaning to that revolutionary heritage. For America stands at a turning point in history. The men and women of our Hemisphere are reaching for the better life which today's skills have placed within their grasp. They are determined for themselves and their children to have decent and ever-more-abundant lives, to gain access to knowledge and equal opportunity for all, to end those conditions which benefit the few at the expense of the needs and dignity of the many. It is our inescapable task to fulfill these just desires—to demonstrate to the poor and forsaken of our countries, and of all lands, that the creative powers of free men hold the key to their progress and to the progress of future generations. And our certainty of ultimate success rests not alone on our faith in ourselves and in our nations but on the indomitable spirit of free man which has been the heritage of American civilization.

Inspired by these principles, and by the principles of Operation Pan America and the Act of Bogotá, the American republics hereby resolve to adopt the following program of action to establish and carry forward an Alliance for Progress.

TITLE I

OBJECTIVES OF THE ALLIANCE FOR PROGRESS

It is the purpose of the Alliance for Progress to enlist the full energies of the peoples and governments of the American republics in a great co-operative effort to accelerate the economic and social development of the participating countries of Latin America, so that they may achieve maximum levels of well-being, with equal opportunities for all, in democratic societies adapted to their own needs and desires.

The American republics agree to work toward the achievement of the following fundamental goals in the present decade:

1. To achieve in the participating Latin-American countries a substantial and sustained growth of per capita incomes at a

rate designed to attain, at the earliest possible date, levels of income capable of assuring self-sustaining development, and sufficient to make Latin American income levels constantly larger in relation to the levels of the more industrialized nations. . . .

It is recognized that, in order to reach these objectives within a reasonable time, the rate of economic growth in any country of Latin America should be not less than 2.5 per cent per capita per year, and that each participating country should determine its own growth target in the light of its stage of social and economic evolution, resource endowment, and ability to mobilize national efforts for development.

2. To make the benefits of economic progress available to all citizens of all economic and social groups through a more equitable distribution of national income, raising more rapidly the income and standard of living of the needier sectors of the population, at the same time that a higher proportion of the national product is devoted to investment.

3. To achieve balanced diversification in national economic structures, . . .

4. To accelerate the process of rational industrialization so as to increase the productivity of the economy as a whole, taking full advantage of the talents and energies of both the private and public sectors, utilizing the natural resources of the country and providing productive and remunerative employment for unemployed or part-time workers. . . .

5. To raise greatly the level of agricultural productivity and output and to improve related storage, transportation, and marketing services.

6. To encourage, in accordance with the characteristics of each country, programs of comprehensive agrarian reform leading to the effective transformation, where required, of unjust structures and systems of land tenure and use, with a view to replacing latifundia and dwarf-holdings by an equitable system of land tenure. . . .

7. To eliminate adult illiteracy and by 1970 to assure, as a minimum, access to six years of primary education for each school-age child in Latin America; to modernize and expand vocational, secondary, and higher educational and training facilities, to strengthen the capacity for basic and applied

research, and to provide the competent personnel required in rapidly growing societies.

8. To increase life expectancy at birth by a minimum of five years, and to increase the ability to learn and produce, by improving individual and public health. . . .

9. To increase the construction of low-cost house for low-income families in order to replace inadequate and deficient housing and to reduce housing shortages; and to provide necessary public services to both urban and rural centers of population.

10. To maintain stable price levels, avoiding inflation or deflation and the consequent social hardships and maldistribution of resources, bearing always in mind the necessity of maintaining an adequate rate of economic growth.

11. To strengthen existing agreements on economic integration, with a view to the ultimate fulfillment of aspirations for a Latin-American common market that will expand and diversify trade among the Latin-American countries and thus contribute to the economic growth of the region.

12. To develop co-operative programs designed to prevent the harmful effects of excessive fluctuations in the foreign exchange earnings derived from exports of primary products, which are of vital importance to economic and social development; and to adopt the measures necessary to facilitate the access of Latin-American exports to international markets.

. . . . .

Chapter II.
National Development Programs

1. Participating Latin-American countries agree to introduce or strengthen systems for the preparation, execution and periodic revision of national programs for economic and social development consistent with the principles, objectives and requirements contained in this document. Participating Latin American countries should formulate, if possible within the next eighteen months, long-term development programs. Such programs should embrace, according to the characteristics of each country, the elements outlined in the Appendix.

2. National development programs should incorporate self-help efforts directed to:

a. The improvement of human resources

and widening of opportunities through raising general standards of education and health; improving and extending technical education and the training of professionals, with emphasis on science and technology; providing adequate remuneration for work performed; encouraging managerial, entrepreneurial, and salaried talent; providing more productive employment for underemployed manpower; establishing effective systems of labor relations, and procedures for consultation and collaboration among public authorities, employer associations, and labor organizations; promoting local institutions for basic and applied research; and improving the standards of public administration.

b. The wider development and more efficient use of natural resources, especially those which are now idle or underutilized, including measures for the processing of raw materials.

c. The strengthening of the agricultural base, progressively extending the benefits of the land to those who work it, and ensuring in countries with Indian populations the integration of these populations into the economic, social, and cultural processes of modern life. . . .

d. The more effective, rational, and equitable mobilization and use of financial resources through the reform of tax structures, including fair and adequate taxation of large incomes and real estate, and the strict application of measures to improve fiscal administration. . . .

e. The promotion through appropriate measures, including the signing of agreements for the purpose of reducing or eliminating double taxation, of conditions that will encourage the flow of foreign investments and help to increase the capital resources of participating countries in need of capital.

f. The improvement of systems of distribution and sales in order to make markets more competitive and prevent monopolistic practices.

Chapter III.
Immediate and Short-Term Action Measures

1. Recognizing that a number of Latin-American countries, despite their best efforts, may require emergency financial assistance, the United States will provide assistance from the funds which are or may be established for such purposes. . . .

2. Participating Latin-American countries should immediately increase their efforts to accelerate their development, giving special emphasis (in addition to the creation or strengthening of machinery for long-term development programming) to the following objectives:

a. The completion of projects already under way and the initiation of projects for which the basic studies have been made in order to accelerate their financing and execution.

b. The implementation of new projects which are designed:

   i. To meet the most pressing social needs and benefit directly the greatest number of people;

   ii. To concentrate efforts within each country in the less developed or more depressed areas in which particularly serious social problems exist;

   iii. To utilize idle capacity or resources, particularly underemployed manpower;

   iv. To survey and assess natural resources.

c. The facilitation of the preparation and execution of long-term programs through measures designed:

   i. To train teachers, technicians, and specialists;

   ii. To provide accelerated training to workers and farmers;

   iii. To improve basic statistics;

   iv. To establish needed credit and marketing facilities;

   v. To improve services and administration.

3. The United States will assist in the realization of these short-term measures with a view to achieving concrete results from the Alliance for Progress at the earliest possible moment. In connection with the measures set forth above, and in accordance with the statement of President Kennedy, the United States will provide assistance under the Alliance, including assistance for the financing of short-term measures, total-

ling more than one billion dollars in the year ending March 1962.

TITLE III

ECONOMIC INTEGRATION OF LATIN AMERICA

The American republics consider that the broadening of present national markets in Latin America is essential to accelerate the process of economic development in the Hemisphere. It is also an appropriate means for obtaining greater productivity through specialized and complementary industrial production which will, in turn, facilitate the attainment of greater social benefits for the inhabitants of the various regions of Latin America. The broadening of markets will also make possible the better use of resources under the alliance for Progress. Consequently, the American republics recognize that: . . .

11. The promotion and co-ordination of transportation and communications systems is an effective way to accelerate the integration process. In order to counteract abusive practices in relation to freight rates and tariffs, it is advisable to encourage the establishment of multinational transport and communication enterprises in the Latin-American countries, or to find other appropriate solutions.

12. In working toward economic integration and complementary economies, efforts should be made to achieve an appropriate co-ordination of national plans, or to engage in joint planning for various economies through the existing regional integration organizations. Efforts should also be made to promote an investment policy directed to the progressive elimination of unequal growth rates in the different geographic areas, particularly in the case of countries which are relatively less developed. . . .

14. The active participation of the private sector is essential to economic integration and development, and except in those countries in which free enterprise does not exist, development planning by the pertinent national public agencies, far from hindering such participation, can facilitate and guide it, thus opening new perspectives for the benefit of the community.

15. As the countries of the Hemisphere still under colonial domination achieve their independence, they should be invited to participate in Latin-American economic integration programs.

. . . . .

645. THE BAY OF PIGS: AMBASSADOR STEVENSON'S STATEMENT
1961

(*Department of State Bulletin,* May 8, 1961)

American opinion had, at first, welcomed the overthrow of the Cuban dictator, Batista, and the accession to power of the revolutionary leader Fidel Castro. Castro, however, speedily embarked upon three policies which alienated not only American but Latin-American sympathy as well: reckless confiscation of American and other foreign property without compensation; infiltration and subversion of other Latin-American states; and a close rapproachment to Soviet Russia. On January 3, 1961 Castro, in what amounted to an open declaration of hostility, ordered that the American Embassy be reduced to 11 persons; President Eisenhower countered by severing relations with Cuba. Meantime thousands of refugees from the Castro dictatorship had fled to nearby states in Latin America, and particularly to Florida, where they planned and drilled for a return to their home island and the overthrow of the dictator. There is no doubt that in this they were supported, financed, and armed by the U.S. Central Intelligence Agency. Castro charged that the United States was planning to invade his island, but at a press conference April 12 President Kennedy stated that "there will not under any conditions be . . . an intervention in Cuba by United States armed forces. This Government will do everything it possibly can—and I think it can meet its responsibilities—to make sure that there are no Americans involved in any actions inside Cuba." On the morning of April 15, airplanes stationed in Florida bombed the Cuban mainland, and on the morning of the 17th, the Cuban refugees took off from Florida and Guatemala in an attempted invasion of their home country. The invasion was a failure; almost all of the invaders were killed or captured. Cuba—supported by the Soviet— promptly charged that the United States had invaded her, and called upon the UN to brand her action that of an aggressor. We give here portions of Ambassador Adlai Stevenson's replies to these charges. See, C. Wright Mills, *Listen, Yankee;* Nathaniel Weyl, *Red Star Over Cuba;* Herbert Matthews, *The Cuban Story;* Robert F. Smith, *The United States and Cuba, 1917–1960.*

STATEMENT OF APRIL 17

Let me make it clear that we do not regard the Cuban problem as a problem between Cuba and the United States. The challenge is not to the United States but to the hemisphere and its duly constituted body, the Organization of American States. The Castro regime has betrayed the Cuban revolution. It is now collaborating in organized attempts by means of propaganda, agitation, and subversion to bring about the overthrow of existing governments by force and replace them with regimes subservient to an extracontinental power. These events help to explain why the Cuban government continues to bypass the Organization of American States, even if they do not explain why Cuba, which is thus in open violation of its obligations under inter-American treaties and agreements, continues to charge the United States with violations of these same obligations.

Soon after the Castro government assumed power, it launched a program looking to the export of its system to other countries of the hemisphere, particularly in the Caribbean area. The intervention of Cuban diplomatic personnel in the internal affairs of other nations of the hemisphere has become flagrant. Cuban diplomatic and consular establishments are used as distribution points for propaganda material calling on the peoples of Latin America to follow Cuba's example. Even Cuban diplomatic pouches destined for various Latin-American countries have been found to contain inflammatory and subversive propaganda directed against friendly governments.

In public support of these activities Prime Minister Castro, President Dorticós, Dr. Roa himself, and many other high-ranking members of the revolutionary government have openly stated that "the peoples of Latin America should follow Cuba's example." They have frankly declared that the Cuban system is for export. . . .

Statements of Soviet Russian and Chinese Communist leaders indicate that, by Dr. Castro's own actions, the Cuban revolution has become an instrument of the foreign policies of these extracontinental powers. The increasingly intimate relationship between Cuba and the Soviet Union, the People's Republic of China, and other countries associated with them, in conjunction with the huge shipments of arms, munitions, and other equipment from the Sino-Soviet bloc, must therefore be matters of deep concern to independent governments everywhere.

The Castro regime has mercilessly destroyed the hope of freedom the Cuban people had briefly glimpsed at the beginning of 1959. Cuba has never witnessed such political persecution as exists today. The arrests, the prisons bulging with political prisoners, and the firing squads testify to this. Since the Castro regime came to power, more than 600 persons have been executed, with a shocking disregard of the standards of due process of law and fair trial generally accepted and practiced in the civilized community of nations. The government has even threatened to replace its slogan for this year—"the year of education"—with a new slogan—"the year of the execution wall."

There is no democratic participation of the Cuban people in the determination of their destiny. Staged rallies, at which small percentages of the population are harangued and asked to express approval of policies by shouts or show of hands, represent the procedure of a totalitarian demagog and not free and democratic expression of opinion through the secret ballot.

The Cuban farm worker who was promised his own plot of land finds that he is an employee of the state working on collective or state-run farms. The independent labor movement, once one of the strongest in the hemisphere, is today in chains. Freely elected Cuban labor leaders, who as late as the end of 1960 protested the destruction of workers' rights, were imprisoned for their pains, or took asylum in foreign embassies, or fled the country to escape imprisonment.

When in addition the people are confronted, despite aid from the Sino-Soviet bloc, with a drastic reduction in their standard of living, it is not surprising opposition to their present master grows. . . .

The problem created in the Western Hemisphere by the Cuban revolution is not one of revolution. . . . The problem is that every effort is being made to use Cuba as a base to force totalitarian ideology into other parts of the Americas.

The Cuban government has disparaged the plans of the American states to pool their resources to accelerate social and economic development in the Americas. At the Bogotá meeting of the Committee of 21 in September, 1960, the Cuban delegation missed few opportunities to insult the representatives of other American states and to play an obstructionist role. They refused to sign the Act of Bogotá and thereby to take part in the hemisphere-wide co-operative effort of social reform to accompany programs of economic development. The Cuban official reaction to President Kennedy's Alliance for Progress program for the Americas was in a similar vein. In a speech on March 12, 1961, Dr. Castro denounced the program, portraying it as a program of "alms" using "usurious dollars" to buy the economic independence and national dignity of the countries which participate in the program. . . .

Dr. Castro has carefully and purposefully destroyed the great hope the hemisphere invested in him when he came to power two years ago. No one in his senses could have expected to embark on such a course as this with impunity. No sane man would suppose that he could speak Dr. Castro's words, proclaim his aggressive intentions, carry out his policies of intervention and subversion—and at the same time retain the friendship, the respect, and the confidence of Cuba's sister republics in the Americas. He sowed the wind and reaps the whirlwind.

It is not the United States which is the cause of Dr. Castro's trouble: It is Dr. Castro himself. It is not Washington which has turned so many thousands of his fellow countrymen against his regime—men who fought beside him in the Cuban hills, men who risked their lives for him in the underground movements in Cuban cities, men who lined Cuban streets to hail him as the liberator from tyrannny, men who occupied the most prominent places in the first government of the Cuban revolution. It is these men who constitute the threat—if threat there is—to Dr. Castro's hope of consolidating his power and intensifying his tyranny. . . .

The problem which the United States confronts today is our attitude toward such men as these. Three years ago many American citizens looked with sympathy on the cause espoused by Castro and offered hospitality to his followers in their battle against the tyranny of Batista. We cannot expect Americans today to look with less sympathy on those Cubans who, out of love for their country and for liberty, now struggle against the tyranny of Castro.

If the Castro regime has hostility to fear, it is the hostility of Cubans, not of Americans. If today Castro's militia are hunting down guerrillas in the hills where Castro himself once fought, they are hunting down Cubans, not Americans. If the Castro regime is overthrown, it will be overthrown by Cubans, not by Americans.

I do not see that it is the obligation of the United States to protect Dr. Castro from the consequences of his treason to the promises of the Cuban revolution, to the hopes of the Cuban people, and to the Democratic aspirations of the Western Hemisphere. . . .

Our only hope is that the Cuban tragedy may awaken the people and governments of the Americas to a profound resolve—a resolve to concert every resource and energy to advance the cause of economic growth and social progress throughout the hemisphere, but to do so under conditions of human freedom and political democracy. This cause represents the real revolution of the Americas. To this struggle to expand freedom and abundance and education and culture for all the citizens of the New World the free states of the hemisphere summon all the peoples in nations where freedom and independence are in temporary eclipse. We confidently expect that Cuba will be restored to the American community and will take a leading role to win social reform and economic opportunity, human dignity and democratic government, not just for the people of Cuba but for all the people of the hemisphere.

STATEMENT OF APRIL 18

The current uprising in Cuba is the product of the progressively more violent opposition of the Cuban people to the policies and practices of this regime. Let us not forget that there have been hundreds of freedom fighters in the mountains of central Cuba for almost a year; that during the last six months skirmishes with the Castro police, attacks upon individual members of his armed forces, nightly acts of sabotage by the revolutionaries, have been increasing in number and intensity. Protest demonstrations have taken place by workers whose trade-union rights have been betrayed, by Catholics whose freedom of expression and worship has been circumscribed, by professional men whose right to free association has been violated. The response of the Castro regime has been repression, arrests without warrant, trial without constitutional guarantees, imprisonment without term and without mercy, and, finally, the execution wall.

Let me be absolutely clear: that the present events are the uprising of the Cuban people against an oppressive regime which has never given them the opportunity in peace and by democratic process to approve or to reject the domestic and foreign policies which it has followed.

For our part, our attitude is clear. Many Americans looked with sympathy, as I have said, on the cause espoused by Dr. Castro when he came to power. They look with the same sympathy on the men who today seek to bring freedom and justice to Cuba—not for foreign monopolies, not for the economic or political interests of the United States or any foreign power, but for Cuba and for the Cuban people.

It is hostility of Cubans, not Americans, that Dr. Castro has to fear. It is not our obligation to protect him from the consequences of his treason to the revolution, to the hopes of the Cuban people, and to the democratic aspirations of the hemisphere.

The United States sincerely hopes that any difficulties which we or other American countries may have with Cuba will be settled peacefully. We have committed no aggression against Cuba. We have no aggressive purposes against Cuba. We intend no military intervention in Cuba. We seek to see a restoration of the friendly relations which once prevailed between Cuba and the United States. We hope that the Cuban people will settle their own problems in their own interests and in a manner which will assure social justice, true independence, and political liberty to the Cuban people. . . .

STATEMENT OF APRIL 20

I have some final words that I should like to say in this debate. I am grateful to those of my colleagues who have expressed respect for my country and for the honesty of its spokesmen here and in Washington.

First let me say that we don't deny that the exiles from Cuba have received the sympathy of many people inside and outside the United States—even as Dr. Castro had the sympathy of many in the United States, Mexico, and elsewhere. But the extent to which so many speakers have deliberately confused this with intervention and aggression by the United States Government has exceeded all bounds of fact or fancy.

Obviously the incessant repetition of such charges as though they had been proved reveals a greater anxiety to mislead and to corrupt world opinion than to keep the discussion on the tracks. . . .

I have heard a torrent—a deluge—of ugly words from Communist speakers here accusing the United States of aggression and invasion against Cuba. I will resist the temptation to invite attention to the record of aggression of the countries represented by some of those speakers—or to inquire as to which country has *really* intervened in Cuba, which country has perverted the Cuban revolution, and why these same speakers are so emotional about the revolt of the Cuban refugees against the new tyranny in Cuba and the new imperialism in the world.

Let me just ask—if this was a United States military operation, do you think it would succeed or fail? How long do you think Cuba could resist the military power of the United States? Perhaps the best evidence of the falsity of the shrill charges of American aggression in Cuba is the melancholy fact that this blow for freedom has not yet succeeded. And if the United States had been in charge I submit that fighting would hardly have broken out on the day debate was to start in this committee. . . .

The Cuban people have not spoken.

Their yearning to be free of Castro's executions, of his betrayal of the revolution, of his controlled press, and of his yoke and rule by mailed fist has not been extinguished. The more than 100,000 refugees from his tyranny are undeniable proof of the historic aspirations of the Cuban people for freedom. The Cubans will continue to look forward to the day when they can determine their own future by democratic processes and through free institutions.

And what are the lessons to be learned? For those Cuban patriots who gave their lives, the lesson is one of tragic finality. But what of those who live on and will shape the future? The events of the last few days are indelible reminders to all of us in the Western Hemisphere. The penetration of force from outside our hemisphere, dominating a puppet government and providing it with arms, tanks, and fighter aircraft, is already dangerously strong and deep. It is now demonstrably stronger, deeper, and more dangerous to all of us who value freedom than most Americans—and most of our neighbors in the Western Hemisphere—have been willing to think.

If there is hope in the events of the last few days it is that it will awaken all of us in the Americas to a renewed determination to mobilize every resource and energy to advance the cause of economic growth and social progress throughout the hemisphere—to foster conditions of freedom and political democracy. They summon all of us to expand freedom and abundance with education of all peoples. If we dedicate ourselves with renewed resolve to bringing greater social reform, greater economic opportunity, greater human dignity, the sacrifices of the last few days will not have been in vain. . . .

646. THE BERLIN CRISIS
1961

(*Department of State Bulletin,* August 14, 1961)

The long-simmering Berlin crisis reached another of its many climaxes in mid-summer of 1961. In the alternating seasons of thaw and freeze in Russian policy towards the West, this was a season of deep freeze. On June 4, Premier Khrushchev proposed the effective ending of the three-power control of West Berlin and the creation of a "demilitarized city" for Berlin. "The occupation regime now being maintained," he wrote, "has already outlived itself and has lost all connection with the purposes for which it was established, as well as with the Allied agreements concerning Germany that established the basis for its existence. The occupation rights will naturally be terminated upon the conclusion of a German peace treaty, whether it is signed with both German States or only with the German Democratic Republic (e.g. East Germany) within whose territory West Berlin is located." The West reacted sharply to this proposal; President Kennedy's address of July 25 breathed determination and defiance. The Soviet response was just as decided. On August 13, East German authorities—supported of course by the Soviet—closed the boundaries between the Eastern and the Western sectors of the hapless city. Not withstanding vigorous protests from the Western powers, East Germany then proceeded to erect a vast concrete wall between the two sectors, in part to prevent the continuous flow of refugees and escapees to the Western sector, in part to dramatize the separation of the two Berlins and to isolate the West Berliners. We give here President Kennedy's address of July 25 and the formal protest of the Western Commandants of August 15. The story can be followed in the successive issues of the *Department of State Bulletins* during the summer and fall of 1961.

An important by-product of the Berlin crisis was a lively public controversy over fall-out shelters, touched off by Kennedy's plea for a greatly enlarged program of civil defense. A wide variety of critics opposed large-scale construction of shelters on the grounds that it increased the risk of nuclear war and that in any case there was no adequate defense against all-out nuclear attack. The combination of this criticism and public apathy defeated efforts to commit the country to what was, in effect, a new nuclear strategy (as distinguished from the old strategy of deterrence by threat of retaliation)—the proposition that the country could survive a nuclear war and might therefore, under certain circumstances, be able to undertake a "pre-emptive first strike."

1. KENNEDY'S REPORT
July 25, 1961

Seven weeks ago tonight I returned from Europe to report on my meeting with Premier Khrushchev and the others. His grim warnings about the future of the world, his aide memoire on Berlin, his subsequent speeches and threats which he and his agents have launched, and the increase in the Soviet military budget that he has announced have all prompted a series of decisions by the administration and a series of consultations with the members of the NATO organization. In Berlin, as you recall, he intends to bring to an end, through a stroke of the pen, first, our legal rights to be in West Berlin and, secondly, our ability to make good on our commitment to the 2 million free people of that city. That we cannot permit.

We are clear about what must be done—and we intend to do it. I want to talk frankly with you tonight about the first steps that we shall take. These actions will require sacrifice on the part of many of our citizens. More will be required in the future. They will require, from all of us, courage and perseverance in the years to come. But if we and our allies act out of strength and unity of purpose—with calm determination and steady nerves, using restraint in our words as well as our weapons—I am hopeful that both peace and freedom will be sustained.

The immediate threat to free men is in West Berlin. But that isolated outpost is not an isolated problem. The threat is worldwide. Our effort must be equally wide and strong and not be obsessed by any single manufactured crisis. We face a challenge in Berlin, but there is also a challenge in southeast Asia, where the borders are less guarded, the enemy harder to find, and the danger of communism less apparent to those who have so little. We face a challenge in our own hemisphere and indeed wherever else the freedom of human beings is at stake.

Let me remind you that the fortunes of war and diplomacy left the free people of West Berlin in 1945 110 miles behind the Iron Curtain. . . .

We are there as a result of our victory over Nazi Germany, and our basic rights to be there deriving from that victory include both our presence in West Berlin and the enjoyment of access across East Germany. These rights have been repeatedly confirmed and recognized in special agreements with the Soviet Union. Berlin is not a part of East Germany, but a separate territory under the control of the allied powers. Thus our rights there are clear and deep-rooted. But in addition to those rights is our commitment to sustain—and defend, if need be—the opportunity for more than 2 million people to determine their own future and choose their own way of life.

Thus our presence in West Berlin, and our access thereto, cannot be ended by any act of the Soviet Government. The NATO shield was long ago extended to cover West Berlin, and we have given our word that an attack in that city will be regarded as an attack upon us all.

For West Berlin, lying exposed 110 miles inside East Germany, surrounded by Soviet troops and close to Soviet supply lines, has many roles. It is more than a showcase of liberty, a symbol, an island of freedom in a Communist sea. It is even more than a link with the free world, a beacon of hope behind the Iron Curtain, an escape hatch for refugees.

West Berlin is all of that. But above all it has now become, as never before, the great testing place of Western courage and will, a focal point where our solemn commitments, stretching back over the years since 1945, and Soviet ambitions now meet in basic confrontation.

It would be a mistake for others to look upon Berlin, because of its location, as a tempting target. The United States is there, the United Kingdom and France are there, the pledge of NATO is there, and the people of Berlin are there. It is as secure, in that sense, as the rest of us, for we cannot separate its safety from our own.

I hear it said that West Berlin is militarily untenable. And so was Bastogne. And so, in fact, was Stalingrad. Any dangerous spot is tenable if men—brave men—will make it so.

We do not want to fight, but we have fought before. And others in earlier times have made the same dangerous mistake of assuming that the West was too selfish and too soft and too divided to resist invasions of freedom in other lands. Those who threaten to unleash the forces of war on a dispute.

over West Berlin should recall the words of the ancient philosopher: "A man who causes fear cannot be free from fear."

We cannot and will not permit the Communists to drive us out of Berlin, either gradually or by force. . . .

In the days and months ahead, I shall not hesitate to ask the Congress for additional measures or exercise any of the Executive powers that I possess to meet this threat to peace. Everything essential to the security of freedom must be done; and if that should require more men, or more taxes, or more controls, or other new powers, I shall not hesitate to ask them. The measures proposed today will be constantly studied, and altered as necessary. But while we will not let panic shape our policy, neither will we permit timidity to direct our program.

Accordingly I am now taking the following steps:

(1) I am tomorrow requesting of the Congress for the current fiscal year an additional $3,247,000,000 of appropriations for the Armed Forces.

(2) To fill out our present Army divisions and to make more men available for prompt deployment, I am requesting an increase in the Army's total authorized strength from 875,000 to approximately 1 million men.

(3) I am requesting an increase of 29,000 and 63,000 men, respectively, in the active-duty strength of the Navy and the Air Force.

(4) To fulfill these manpower needs, I am ordering that our draft calls be doubled and tripled in the coming months. . . .

And let me add that I am well aware of the fact that many American families will bear the burden of these requests. Studies or careers will be interrupted; husbands and sons will be called away; incomes in some cases will be reduced. But these are burdens which must be borne if freedom is to be defended. Americans have willingly borne them before, and they will not flinch from the task now.

We have another sober responsibility. To recognize the possibilities of nuclear war in the missile age without our citizens' knowing what they should do and where they should go if bombs begin to fall would be a failure of responsibility. In May I pledged a new start on civil defense. Last week I assigned, on the recommendation of the Civil Defense Director, basic responsibility for this program to the Secretary of Defense, to make certain it is administered and coordinated with our continental defense efforts at the highest civilian level. Tomorrow I am requesting of the Congress new funds for the following immediate objectives: to identify and mark space in existing structures—public and private—that could be used for fallout shelters in case of attack; to stock those shelters with food, water, first-aid kits, and other minimum essentials for survival; to increase their capacity; to improve our air-raid warning and fallout detection systems, including a new household warning system which is now under development; and to take other measures that will be effective at an early date to save millions of lives if needed.

In the event of an attack, the lives of those families which are not hit in a nuclear blast and fire can still be saved—*if* they can be warned to take shelter and *if* that shelter is available. We owe that kind of insurance to our families—and to our country. In contrast to our friends in Europe, the need for this kind of protection is new to our shores. But the time to start is now. In the coming months I hope to let every citizen know what steps he can take without delay to protect his family in case of attack. I know that you will want to do no less. . . .

2. NOTE OF WESTERN COMMANDANTS TO SOVIET COMMANDANTS

August 15, 1961

(*Department of State Bulletin,* September 4, 1961)

During the night of August 12–13 the East German authorities put into effect illegal measures designed to turn the boundaries between the West sectors of Berlin and the Soviet sector into an arbitrary barrier to movement of German citizens resident in East Berlin and East Germany.

Not since the imposition of the Berlin blockade had there been such a flagrant violation of the four-power agreements concerning Berlin. The agreement of June 20, 1949, in which the U.S.S.R. pledged itself to facilitate freedom of movement within Berlin and between Berlin and the rest of Germany, had also been violated.

In disregard of these arrangements and of the wishes of the population of this city, for the welfare of which the four powers are jointly responsible, freedom of circulation throughout Berlin has been severely curtailed. Traffic between the East sector and the Western sectors of Berlin has been disrupted by the cutting of S-Bahn and U-Bahn service, the tearing up of streets, the erection of road blocks, and the stringing of barbed wire. In carrying out these illegal actions, military, and paramilitary units, which were formed in violation of four-power agreements and whose very presence in East Berlin is illegal, turned the Soviet sector of Berlin into an armed camp.

Moreover, the East German authorities have now prohibited the many inhabitants of East Berlin and East Germany who were employed in West Berlin from continuing to pursue their occupations in West Berlin. They have thus denied to the working population under their control the elementary right of free choice of place of employment.

It is obvious that the East German authorities have taken these repressive measures because the people under their control, deeply perturbed by the threats on Berlin recently launched by Communist leaders, were fleeing in large numbers to the West.

We must protest against the illegal measures introduced on August 13 and hold you responsible for the carrying out of the relevant agreements.

647. KENNEDY'S LETTER TO NGO DINH DIEM
December 14, 1961

(*Department of State Bulletin,* January 1, 1962)

For the background of the Vietnamese situation see Doc. No. 610. In spite of the reluctance of the Eisenhower administration to commit itself to full-scale support of Diem, the latter found many influential friends in this country, both in the government and without. The American Friends of Vietnam, organized by liberals in 1955, promoted Diem as a democratic alternative to Communism, and a group of political scientists at Michigan State University, supported by the Central Intelligence Agency (CIA), helped to organize the police force which in the absence of long-awaited land reforms became the mainstay of Diem's regime. Senator John F. Kennedy, introduced to Diem in 1952 by Supreme Court Justice William O. Douglas, became an early supporter of Diem, although it was under Kennedy's administration that the United States in 1963 finally abandoned the Diem regime to its fate—largely, it would appear, because Diem seemed finally to be more interested, in Kennedy's estimation, in quelling local opposition than in fighting the Communists. In the meantime, however—still hoping that Diem would become the nucleus of a workable democratic nationalism—Kennedy, accepting Diem's thesis that North Vietnam was seeking "to take over your country," stepped up American support by sending military "advisers" to South Vietnam, thereby drawing the United States further into a situation from which there seemed to be no turning back, yet the advantages of which became increasingly difficult to perceive. See also Docs. No. 660, 664, 665.

DEAR MR. PRESIDENT: I have received your recent letter in which you described so cogently the dangerous condition caused by North Vietnam's efforts to take over your country. The situation in your embattled country is well known to me and to the American people. We have been deeply disturbed by the assault on your country. Our indignation has mounted as the deliberate savagery of the Communist program of assassination, kidnapping, and wanton violence became clear.

Your letter underlines what our own information has convincingly shown—that the campaign of force and terror now being waged against your people and your Government is supported and directed from the outside by the authorities at Hanoi. They have thus violated the provisions of the Geneva Accords designed to ensure peace in Vietnam and to which they bound themselves in 1954.

At that time, the United States, although not a party to the Accords, declared that it "would view any renewal of the aggression in violation of the Agreements with grave concern and as seriously threatening international peace and security." We continue to maintain that view.

In accordance with that declaration, and in response to your request, we are prepared to help the Republic of Vietnam to protect its people and to preserve its independence. We shall promptly increase our assistance to your defense effort as well as help relieve the destruction of the floods which you describe. I have already given the orders to get these programs underway.

The United States, like the Republic of Vietnam, remains devoted to the cause of peace and our primary purpose is to help your people maintain their independence. If the Communist authorities in North Vietnam will stop their campaign to destroy the Republic of Vietnam, the measures we are taking to assist your defense efforts will no longer be necessary. We shall seek to persuade the Communists to give up their attempts of force and subversion. In any case, we are confident that the Vietnamese people will preserve their independence and gain the peace and prosperity for which they have sought so hard and so long.

648. BLACK POWER
1962

Following the Supreme Court's decision in Brown v. Board of Education (Doc. No. 612), the civil-rights movement entered a more militant phase, beginning with the Montgomery bus boycott of 1955–1956, in which civil-rights demonstrators led by Martin Luther King succeeded by non-violent methods in forcing desegregation of the city's buses. In 1960, demonstrators inspired by King's success discovered a new technique of agitation against segregation, the "sit-in" at segregated lunch counters. The sit-in movement, spreading rapidly through the South, led to widespread arrests and, in some cases, to the integration of lunch counters and other facilities. (It also raised constitutional questions explored by the Supreme Court in Bell v. Maryland, Doc. No. 657.) In 1961, the Congress of Racial Equality (CORE), one of a number of organizations which had sprung up out of discontent with the more conservative leadership of the National Association for the Advancement of Colored People (NAACP), sent "freedom riders" to several Southern cities in another attack on discrimination on buses and trains. The campaign for integration of schools also continued, spreading to the college level in 1962 when James Meredith succeeded in entering the all-white University of Mississippi. In 1963 and 1964 attention turned to the vote, with the Student Nonviolent Coordinating Committee now emerging as the vanguard of the civil-rights movement. SNCC, while still committed to integration, and to integration brought about by non-violent means, advocated energetic attempts to organize the Negro masses into an effective political force. These efforts came to a head in 1964 when delegates of the Freedom Democratic Party of Mississippi tried unsuccessfully to achieve recognition by the National Democratic Convention.

All these activities aimed at integration—the achievement of full and equal American citizenship for the Negro minority. Side by side with the civil-rights movement, however, there developed new and radically disaffected varieties of black nationalism, aiming not at integration but at complete separation from the white community. The Black Muslims, founded in the thirties but attaining their greatest influence in the early 1960's, professed an elaborate historical mythology of the "so-called" Negro people, tracing the American Negroes to the lost tribes of "Islam" and claiming kinship with the peoples of Islam. Underlying this theology, grotesque as it may have been, were several insights which, purged of their Muslim imagery, were later to reappear in the movement for "black power": an awareness of the uprising of colored peoples throughout the rest of the world (which black nationalists hoped would force changes in America as well); an appreciation of the psychological and moral damage which Negroes had brought on themselves by identifying with white culture; a strong class-consciousness, which enabled black nationalists to see how little had been accomplished by the Negro masses, whatever had been accomplished by the minority of athletes and entertainers; and above all, a sense of the powerful resistance to integration which white America could be expected to offer. Malcolm X was the most articulate spokesman for the Black Muslims (later he became an early architect of the "black power" doctrine, broke with Elijah Muhammad, and in 1965 was assassinated—presumably by the latter's agents). In March, 1962, he debated James Farmer of the Congress of Racial Equality at Cornell University. Their exchange poses quite clearly the issue between the integrationist and the separatist point of view, civil rights and black power. It should be added that Farmer himself later emerged as a strong advocate of independent political action, and that eventually both CORE and SNCC not only adopted the black power doctrine but took steps which seemed likely to lead to the expulsion of white members from those organizations.

1. MALCOLM X ON BLACK SEPARATISM
March 7, 1962
(Dialogue Magazine, May 1962)

. . . It so happens that you and I were born at a time of great change, when changes are taking place. And if we can't react intelligently to these changes, then we are going to be destroyed. When you look into the United Nations set-up, the way it is, we see that there is a change of power taking place, a change of position, a change of influence, a change of control. Wherein, in the past, white people used to exercise unlimited control and authority over dark mankind, today they are losing their ability to dictate unilateral terms to dark mankind. Whereas, yesterday dark nations had no voice in their own affairs, today the voice that they exercise in their own affairs is increasing, which means in essence that the voice of the white man or the white world is becoming more quiet every day, and the voice of the nonwhite world is becoming more loud every day. These are the facts of life and these are the changes that you and I, this generation, have to face up to on an international level, a national level, or a local level before we can get a solution to the problems that confront not only the white man, but problems that confront also the black man, or the non-white man. . . .

The same hand that has been writing on the wall in Africa and Asia is also writing on the wall right here in America. The same rebellion, the same impatience, the same anger that exists in the hearts of the dark people in Africa and Asia is existing in the hearts and minds of 20 million black people in this country who have been just as thoroughly colonized as the people in Africa and Asia. Only the black man in America has been colonized mentally, his mind has been destroyed. And today, even though he goes to college, he comes out and still doesn't even know he is a black man; he is ashamed of what he is, because his culture has been destroyed, his identity has been destroyed;

he has been made to hate his black skin, he has been made to hate the texture of his hair, he has been made to hate the features that God gave him. Because the honorable Elijah Muhammad is coming along today and teaching us the truth about black people to make us love ourselves. Instead of realizing that it is you who taught us to hate ourselves and our own kind, you accuse the honorable Elijah Muhammad of being a hate teacher and accuse him of being a racist. He is only trying to undo the white supremacy that you have indoctrinated the entire world with.

I might point out that it makes America look ridiculous to stand up in world conferences and refer to herself as the leader of the free world. Here is a country, Uncle Sam, standing up and pointing a finger at the Portuguese, and at the French, and at other colonizers, and there are 20 million black people in this country who are still confined to second-class citizenship, 20 million black people in this country who are still segregated and Jim-Crowed, as my friend, Dr. Farmer has already pointed out. And despite the fact that 20 million black people here yet don't have freedom, justice and equality, Adlai Stevenson has the nerve enough to stand up in the United Nations and point the finger at South Africa, and at Portugal and at some of these other countries. All we say is that South Africa preaches what it practices and practices what it preaches; America preaches one thing and practices another. And we don't want to integrate with hypocrites who preach one thing and practice another.

The good point in all of this is that there is an awakening going on among whites in America today, and this awakening is manifested in this way: two years ago you didn't know that there were black people in this country who didn't want to integrate with you; two years ago the white public had been brainwashed into thinking that every black man in this country wanted to force his way into your community, force his way into your schools, or force his way into your factories; two years ago you thought that all you would have to do is give us a little token integration and the race problem would be solved. Why? Because the people in the black community who didn't want integration were never given a voice, were never given a platform, were never given an opportunity to shout out the fact that integration would never solve the problem. And it has only been during the past year that the white public has begun to realize that the problem will never be solved unless a solution is devised acceptable to the black masses, as well as the black bourgeoisie—the upper class or middle class Negro. And when the whites began to realize that these integration-minded Negroes were in the minority, rather than in the majority, then they began to offer an open forum and give those who want separation an opportunity to speak their mind too.

We who are black in the black belt, or black community, or black neighborhood can easily see that our people who settle for integration are usually the middle-class so-called Negroes, who are in the minority. Why? Because they have confidence in the white man; they have absolute confidence that you will change. They believe that they can change you, they believe that there is still hope in the American dream. But what to them is an American dream to us is an American nightmare, and we don't think that it is possible for the American white man in sincerity to take the action necessary to correct the unjust conditions that 20 million black people here are made to suffer morning, noon, and night. And because we don't have any hope or confidence or faith in the American white man's ability to bring about a change in the injustices that exist, instead of asking or seeking to integrate into the American society we want to face the facts of the problem the way they are, and separate ourselves. And in separating ourselves this doesn't mean that we are anti-white or anti-American, or anti-anything. We feel, that if integration all these years hasn't solved the problem yet, then we want to try something new, something different and something that is in accord with the conditions as they actually exist. . . .

The only way you can solve the race problem as it exists, is to take into consideration the feelings of the masses, not the minority; the majority not the minority. And it is proof that the masses of white people don't want Negroes forcing their way into their neighborhood and the masses of black people

don't think it's any solution for us to force ourselves into the white neighborhood, so the only ones who want integration are the Negro minority, as I say, the bourgeoisie and the white minority, the so-called white liberals. And that same white liberal who professes to want integration whenever the Negro moves to his neighborhood, he is the first one to move out. And I was talking with one today who said he was a liberal and I asked him where did he live, and he lived in an all-white neighborhood and probably might for the rest of his life. This is conjecture, but I think it stands true.

So we think this, that when whites talk integration they are being hypocrites, and we think that the Negroes who accept token integration are also being hypocrites, because they are the only ones who benefit from it, the handful of hand-picked high-class, middle-class Uncle Tom Negroes. They are hand-picked by whites and turned loose in a white community and they're satisfied. But if all of the black people went into the white community, over night you would have a race war. If four or five little black students going to school in New Orleans bring about the riots that we saw down there, what do you think would happen if all of the black people tried to go to any school that they want, you would have a race war. So our approach to it, those of us who follow the honorable Elijah Muhammad, we feel that it is more sensible than running around here waiting for the whites to allow us inside their attic or inside their basement. . . .

2. JAMES FARMER ON INTEGRATION
March 7, 1962
(*Dialogue Magazine,* May 1962)

. . . The masses of Negroes are through putting up with segregation; they are tired of it. They are tired of being pushed around in a democracy which fails to practice what it preaches. The Negro students of the South who have read the Constitution, and studied it, have read the amendments to the Constitution, and know the rights that are supposed to be theirs—they are coming to the point where they themselves want to do something about achieving these rights, not depend on somebody else. The time has passed when we can look for pie in the sky, when we can depend upon someone else on high to solve the problem for us. The Negro students want to solve the problem themselves. Masses of older Negroes want to join them in that. We can't wait for the law. The Supreme Court decision in 1954 banning segregated schools has had almost eight years of existence, yet, less than eight percent of the Negro kids are in integrated schools. That is far too slow. Now the people themselves want to get involved, and they are. I was talking with one of the student leaders of the South only last week; he said, "I myself desegregated a lunch counter, not somebody else, not some big man, some powerful man, but me, little me. I walked the picket line and I sat in and the walls of segregation toppled. Now all people can eat there." One young prize fighter was a cell-mate of mine in the prisons of Mississippi as a freedom rider; he had won his last fight and had a promising career. I saw him three weeks ago, and asked him, "How are you coming along?" He said, "not very well, I lost the last fight and I am through with the prize ring, I have no more interest in it. The only fight I want now," said he, "is the freedom fight. Because I, a little man, can become involved in it, and can help to win freedom." So that's what's happening; you see, we are going to do something about freedom now, we are not waiting for other people to do it. The student sit-ins have shown it; we are winning. As a result of one year of the student sit-ins, the lunch counters were desegregated in more than 150 cities. The walls are tumbling down.

Who will say that lunch counters, which are scattered all over the country are not important? Are we not to travel? Picket lines and boycotts brought Woolworth's to its knees. In its annual report of last year, Woolworth's indicated that profits had dropped and one reason for the drop was the nationwide boycott in which many Northern students, including Cornellians participated. The picketing and the nationwide demonstrations are the reason that the walls came down in the south, because people were in motion with their own bodies marching with picket signs, sitting in, boycotting, withholding their patronage. In Savannah, Georgia, there was a boycott, in which ninety-nine percent of the Negroes participated. They stayed out of the stores. They registered to vote. The store owners then got together and said, "We want to sit down and talk; gentlemen, you have proved your point. You have proved that you can control Negroes' purchasing power and that you can control their votes. We need no more proof, we are ready to hire the people that you send." Negroes are hired in those stores now as a result of this community-wide campaign. In Lexington, Kentucky, the theatres were opened up by CORE as a result of picketing and boycotting. Some of the theatres refused to admit Negroes, others would let Negroes sit up in the balcony. They boycotted that one, picketed the others. In a short period of time, the theatre owners sat down to negotiate. All of the theatres there are open now. Using the same technique, they provided scores of jobs in department stores, grocery stores, and more recently as city bus drivers.

Then came the freedom rides. 325 people were jailed in Jackson, Mississippi, others beaten, fighting for freedom non-violently. They brought down many many barriers. They helped to create desegregation in cities throughout the South. . . . And then on Route 40. How many Negroes and interracial groups have driven Route 40 to Washington or to New York and carried their sandwiches, knowing that they could not eat between Wilmington and Baltimore. The freedom rides there, and some Cornell students participated in those freedom rides, brought down the barriers in more than half of those restaurants and each weekend, rides are taking place aimed at the others. By Easter we will have our Easter dinner in any place we choose on Route 40. At least 53 out of the 80 are now desegregated. In voter registration projects, we have registered 17,000 Negroes in South Carolina, previously unregistered. The politicians, segregationists, it's true, now call up our leaders and say, "I would like to talk to you because I don't believe in segregation as much as my opponent," or, "We would like to sit down and talk," or, "Can you come by my house and let's talk about this thing." Because they are realizing that now they have to be responsible to the votes of Negroes as well as the handful of whites, these are the things that are being done by people themselves in motion. Not waiting for someone else to do it, not looking forward to pie in the sky at some later date, not expecting a power on high to solve the problem for them; but working to solve it themselves and winning.

What are our objectives; segregation, separation? Absolutely not! The disease and the evils that we have pointed to in our American culture have grown out of segregation and its partner, prejudice. We are for integration, which is the repudiation of the evil of segregation. It is a rejection of the racist theories of DeGobineau, Lothrop Stoddard and all the others. It matters not whether they say that whites are superior to Negroes and Negroes are inferior, or if they reverse the coin and say that Negroes are superior and whites are inferior. The theory is just as wrong, just as much a defiance of history. We reject those theories. We are working for the right of Negroes to enter all fields of activity in American life. To enter business if they choose, to enter the professions, to enter the sciences, to enter the arts, to enter the academic world. To be workers, to be laborers if they choose. Our objective is to have each individual accepted on the basis of his individual merit and not on the basis of his color. On the basis of what he is worth himself. . . .

649. BAKER v. CARR
82 Supreme Court Reporter, 691
1962

Appeal from District Court for the Middle District of Tennessee. Not since Brown v. Topeka had any decision been awaited as eagerly as was this decision on the power of the courts to rule on questions of legislative apportionment in the states. The situation was familiar and widespread: rural control of state legislatures through the power over apportionment, and the refusal—often in the face of clear constitutional mandate—to carry through periodic reapportionments. A case involving issues similar to those in this case, Colegrove v. Green (328 U.S. 549, 1946) had been dismissed because the issue was held to be of a peculiarly political nature; but that case had been decided by a close vote of four to three. Only one of the four was still on the Court in 1962—Frankfurter—while two of the dissenters—Black and Douglas—participated in the Baker v. Carr case. See on the whole question of legislative apportionment and judicial review, Griffith, *Rise and Development of the Gerrymander;* Bone, "States Attempting to Comply with Reapportionment Requirements," 17 *Law and Contemporary Problems,* 387; Harvey, "Reapportionments of State Legislatures," 17 *Law and Contemporary Problems,* 364; Walter, "Reapportionment and Urban Representation," 105 *Annals of Am. Aca. of Pol. and Soc. Sci.* 11; Lewis, "Legislative Apportionment and the Federal Courts," 71 *Harvard Law Rev.* 1057; Durfee "Apportionment or Representation in the Legislature," 43 *Mich. Law Rev.* 1091; Senator Clark in 106 *Congressional Record,* 13827–13842 (June 29, 1960).

Mr. Justice BRENNAN:

This civil action was brought to redress the alleged deprivation of federal constitutional rights. The complaint, alleging that by means of a 1901 statute of Tennessee apportioning the members of the General Assembly among the state's 95 counties, "these plaintiffs and others similarly situated, are denied the equal protection of the laws accorded them by the Fourteenth Amendment to the Constitution of the United States by virtue of the debasement of their votes," was dismissed by a three-judge court in the Middle District of Tennessee. The court held that it lacked jurisdiction of the subject matter and also that no claim was stated upon which relief could be granted. We hold that the dismissal was error, and remand the cause to the District Court for trial and further proceedings consistent with this opinion. . . .

The Tennessee Constitution provides in Article II as follows:

"SEC. 4.   *Census.*—An enumeration of the qualified voters, and an apportionment of the Representatives in the General Assembly, shall be made in the year one thousand eight hundred and seventy-one, and within every subsequent term of ten years.

"SEC. 5.   *Apportionment of repre-*

sentatives.—The number of Representatives shall, at the several periods of making the enumeration, be apportioned among the several counties or districts, according to the number of qualified voters in each. . . .

"SEC. 6. *Apportionment of senators.*—The number of Senators shall, at the several periods of making the enumeration, be apportioned among the several counties or districts according to the number of qualified electors in each, and shall not exceed one-third in the number of representatives. . . ."

Thus, Tennessee's standard for allocating legislative representation among her counties is the total number of qualified voters resident in the respective counties, subject only to minor qualifications. Decennial reapportionment in compliance with the constitutional scheme was effected by the General Assembly each decade from 1871 to 1901. . . .

In the more than 60 years since that action, all proposals in both Houses of the General Assembly for reapportionment have failed to pass.

Between 1901 and 1961, Tennessee has experienced substantial growth and redistribution of her population. In 1901, the population was 2,020,616, of whom 487,380 were eligible to vote. The 1960 federal census reports the State's population at 3,567,089, of whom 2,092,891 are eligible to vote. The relative standings of the counties in terms of qualified voters have changed significantly. It is primarily the continued application of the 1901 Apportionment Act to this shifted and enlarged voting population which gives rise to the present controversy.

Indeed, the complaint alleges that the 1901 statute, even as of the time of its passage, "made no apportionment of Representatives and Senators in accordance with the constitutional formula . . . , but instead arbitrarily and capriciously apportioned representatives in the Senate and House without reference . . . to any logical or reasonable formula whatever." It is further alleged that "because of the population changes since 1900, and the failure of the legislature to reapportion itself since 1901," the 1901 statute became "unconstitutional and obsolete." Appellants also argue that, because of the composition of the legislature effected by the 1901 apportionment act, redress in the form of a state constitutional amendment to change the entire mechanism for reapportioning, or any other change short of that, is difficult or impossible. The complaint concludes that "these plaintiffs and others similarly situated, are denied the equal protection of the laws accorded them by the Fourteenth Amendment to the Constitution of the United States by virtue of the debasement of their votes." They seek a declaration that the 1901 statute is unconstitutional and an injunction restraining the appellees from acting to conduct any further elections under it. They also pray that unless and until the General Assembly enacts a valid reapportionment, the District Court should either decree a reapportionment by mathematical application of the Tennessee constitutional formulae to the most recent federal census figures, or direct the appellees to conduct legislative elections, primary and general, at large. They also pray for such other and further relief as may be appropriate. . . .

In light of the District Court's treatment of the case, we hold today only (a) that the court possessed jurisdiction of the subject matter; (b) that a justiciable cause of action is stated upon which appellants would be entitled to appropriate relief; and (c) because appellees raise the issue before this Court, that the appellants have standing to challenge the Tennessee apportionment statutes. Beyond noting that we have no cause at this stage to doubt the District Court will be able to fashion relief if violations of constitutional rights are found, it is improper now to consider what remedy would be most appropriate if appellants prevail at the trial. . . .

Article III, Sect. 2 of the federal Constitution provides that "the judicial Power shall extend to all Cases, in Law and Equity, arising under this Constitution, the Laws of the United States, and Treaties made, or which shall be made, under their Authority; . . ." It is clear that the cause of action is one which "arises under" the federal Constitution. The complaint alleges that the 1901 statute effects an apportionment that deprives the appellants of the.

equal protection of the laws in violation of the Fourteenth Amendment. Dismissal of the complaint upon the ground of lack of jurisdiction of the subject matter would, therefore, be justified only if that claim were "so attenuated and unsubstantial as to be absolutely devoid of merit." . . .

Since the complaint plainly sets forth a case arising under the Constitution, the subject matter is within the federal judicial power defined in Art. III, Sect. 2, and so within the power of Congress to assign to the jurisdiction of the District Courts. Congress has exercised that power. . . .

An unbroken line of our precedents sustains the federal courts' jurisdiction of the subject matter of federal constitutional claims of this nature.

A federal court cannot "pronounce any statute, either of a state or of the United States, void, because irreconcilable with the Constitution, except as it is called upon to adjudge the legal rights of litigants in actual controversies."

Have the appellants alleged such a personal stake in the outcome of the controversy as to assure that concrete adverseness which sharpens the presentation of issues upon which the court so largely depends for illumination of difficult constitutional questions? This is the gist of the question of standing. It is, of course, a question of federal law. . . .

We hold that the appellants do have standing to maintain this suit. Our decisions plainly support this conclusion. Many of the cases have assumed rather than articulated the premise in deciding the merits of similar claims. And Colegrove v. Green, squarely held that voters who allege facts showing disadvantage to themselves as individuals have standing to sue. A number of cases decided after Colegrove recognized the standing of the voters there involved to bring those actions.

These appellants seek relief in order to protect or vindicate an interest of their own, and of those similarly situated. Their constitutional claim is, in substance, that the 1901 statute constitutes arbitrary and capricious state action, offensive to the Fourteenth Amendment in its irrational disregard of the standard of apportionment prescribed by the state's constitution or of any standard, effecting a gross disproportion of representa-

tion to voting population. . . . A citizen's right to a vote free of arbitrary impairment by state action has been judicially recognized as a right secured by the Constitution, when such impairment resulted from dilution by a false tally, cf. United States v. Classic, 313 U.S. 299, or by a refusal to count votes from arbitrarily selected precincts, cf. United States v. Mosley, 238 U.S. 383, or by a stuffing of the ballot box, cf. Ex parte Siebold, 100 U.S. 371.

It would not be necessary to decide whether appellants' allegations of impairment of their votes by the 1901 apportionment will, ultimately, entitle them to any relief, in order to hold that they have standing to seek it. If such impairment does produce a legally cognizable injury, they are among those who have sustained it. They are asserting "a plain, direct and adequate interest in maintaining the effectiveness of their votes," Coleman v. Miller, 307 U.S. at 438. They are entitled to a hearing and to the District Court's decision on their claims. "The very essence of civil liberty certainly consists in the right of every individual to claim the protection of the laws, whenever he receives an injury." Marbury v. Madison, 5 U.S. 137, 163.

In . . . Colegrove v. Green, the court stated: "From a review of these decisions there can be no doubt that the federal rule . . . is that the federal courts . . . will not intervene in cases of this type to compel legislative reapportionment." 179 F. Supp. at 826. We understand the District Court to have read the cited cases as compelling the conclusion that since the appellants sought to have a legislative apportionment held unconstitutional, their suit presented a "political question" and was therefore nonjusticiable. We hold that this challenge to an apportionment presents no nonjusticiable "political question." The cited cases do not hold the contrary.

Of course the mere fact that the suit seeks protection of a political right does not mean it presents a political question. . . .

But it is argued that this case shares the characteristics of decisions that constitute a category not yet considered, cases concerning the Constitution's guaranty, in Art. IV, Sect. 4, of a republican form of government. A conclusion as to whether the case at bar does present a political question cannot be confidently reached until we have considered those cases with special care. We shall discover that Guaranty Clause claims involve those elements which define a "political question," and for that reason and no other, they are nonjusticiable. In particular, we shall discover that the nonjusticiability of such claims has nothing to do with their touching upon matters of state governmental organization. . . .

We come, finally, to the ultimate inquiry whether our precedents as to what constitutes a nonjusticiable "political question" bring the case before us under the umbrella of that doctrine. A natural beginning is to note whether any of the common characteristics which we have been able to identify and label descriptively are present. We find none: The question here is the consistency of state action with the federal Constitution. We have no question decided, or to be decided, by a political branch of government coequal with this Court. Nor do we risk embarrassment of our government abroad, or grave disturbance at home if we take issue with Tennessee as to the constitutionality of her action here challenged. Nor need the appellants, in order to succeed in this action, ask the Court to enter upon policy determinations for which judicially manageable standards are lacking. Judicial standards under the Equal Protection Clause are well developed and familiar, and it has been open to courts since the enactment of the Four-

teenth Amendment to determine, if on the particular facts they must, that a discrimination reflects *no* policy, but simply arbitrary and capricious action.

This case does, in one sense, involve the allocation of political power within a state, and the appellants might conceivably have added a claim under the Guaranty Clause. Of course, as we have seen, any reliance on that clause would be futile. But, because any reliance on the Guaranty Clause could not have succeeded it does not follow that appellants may not be heard on the Equal Protection claim which in fact they tender. True, it must be clear that the Fourteenth Amendment claim is not so enmeshed with those political question elements which render Guaranty Clause claims nonjusticiable as actually to present a political question itself. But we have found that not to be the case here. . . .

We conclude that the complaint's allegations of a denial of equal protection present a justiciable constitutional cause of action upon which appellants are entitled to a trial and a decision. The right asserted is within the reach of judicial protection under the Fourteenth Amendment.

The judgment of the District Court is reversed. . . .

Justices DOUGLAS, CLARK, and STEWART, filed concurring opinions. FRANKFURTER and HARLAN dissented.

650. THE CUBAN MISSILE CRISIS
October 27, 1962

(*Department of State Bulletin,* November 12, 1962)

For reasons that are not altogether clear, the Soviet Union, at Fidel Castro's request, decided to place intermediate-range ballistic missiles on Cuba—a reckless act which may have contributed to Khrushchev's downfall in October, 1964. Kennedy's decision to force removal of the missiles brought the world to the gravest crisis it had experienced since the Second World War, perhaps the gravest military crisis in history, since it carried with it the possibility of all-out nuclear war. For a week, the world trembled on the edge of catastrophe. Publicly the Russians proposed a deal: Russian missiles to be with-

drawn from Cuba in return for the removal of American missiles from Turkey, combined with pledges of non-aggression on the part of both major powers. Privately, in a letter the substance of which is repeated in Kennedy's reply (given here in its entirety), Khrushchev made no mention of a bargain and asked merely for an American assurance not to invade Cuba—a reminder, incidentally, that the Bay of Pigs incident (Doc. No. 645) had played some part in bringing about the present crisis. In effect, Khrushchev backed down, and Kennedy's prompt and gracious acceptance of his capitulation brought the crisis to an end. See Doc. No. 645; Arthur Schlesinger, Jr., *The Thousand Days;* Theodore Sorenson, *Kennedy.*

DEAR MR. CHAIRMAN: I have read your letter of October 26th with great care and welcomed the statement of your desire to seek a prompt solution to the problem. The first thing that needs to be done, however, is for work to cease on offensive missile bases in Cuba and for all weapons systems in Cuba capable of offensive use to be rendered inoperable, under effective United Nations arrangements.

Assuming this is done promptly, I have given my representatives in New York instructions that will permit them to work out this weekend—in cooperation with the Acting Secretary General and your representative—an arrangement for a permanent solution to the Cuban problem along the lines suggested in your letter of October 26th. As I read your letter, the key elements of your proposals—which seem generally acceptable as I understand them—are as follows:

1) You would agree to remove these weapons systems from Cuba under appropriate United Nations observation and supervision; and undertake, with suitable safeguards, to halt the further introduction of such weapons systems into Cuba.

2) We, on our part, would agree—upon the establishment of adequate arrangements through the United Nations to ensure the carrying out and continuation of these commitments—(a) to remove promptly the quarantine measures now in effect and (b) to give assurances against an invasion of Cuba. I am confident that other nations of the Western Hemisphere would be prepared to do likewise.

If you will give your representative similar instructions, there is no reason why we should not be able to complete these arrangements and announce them to the world within a couple of days. The effect of such a settlement on easing world tensions would enable us to work toward a more general arrangement regarding "other armaments", as proposed in your second letter which you made public. I would like to say again that the United States is very much interested in reducing tensions and halting the arms race; and if your letter signifies that you are prepared to discuss a detente affecting NATO and the Warsaw Pact, we are quite prepared to consider with our allies any useful proposals.

But the first ingredient, let me emphasize, is the cessation of work on missile sites in Cuba and measures to render such weapons inoperable, under effective international guarantees. The continuation of this threat, or a prolonging of this discussion concerning Cuba by linking these problems to the broader questions of European and world security, would surely lead to an intensification of the Cuban crisis and a grave risk to the peace of the world. For this reason I hope we can quickly agree along the lines outlined in this letter and in your letter of October 26th.

651. KENNEDY'S SPEECH AT AMERICAN UNIVERSITY
June 10, 1963
(Public Papers of the Presidents: John F. Kennedy,
1963, no. 232)

Both the USSR and the United States emerged somewhat sobered and chastened from the near-disaster of the Cuban missile crisis. In the spring of 1963, they initiated a series of quiet diplomatic conversations about disarmament and the general reduction of tensions; and whereas in the past disarmament negotiations had always degenerated into propaganda contests, this time both sides showed a serious interest in reducing the risk of nuclear confronta-tions like the one through which they had so recently passed. Kennedy's commencement speech at American University gave public notice that he had been reconsidering the whole question of Soviet–American relations and had come to the conclusion that it was time, in effect, to liquidate the cold war in Europe. At the time, this speech seemed to herald a new departure in American foreign policy—an abandonment of the anti-Communist crusade abroad and a renewed attack on mounting problems at home. In retrospect, one can see that the détente with the Soviet Union in Europe merely freed the United States for a more active role in Asia. The rapprochement with the USSR and Kennedy's enlarged commitments to Diem (see Doc. No. 647) were pieces of the same large pattern. Nevertheless, Kennedy's American University speech had an important affect on public discussion. For the first time, it became politically respectable to discuss foreign affairs without resorting automatically to the rhetoric of the cold war.

. . . Some say that it is useless to speak of world peace or world law or world disarmament—and that it will be useless until the leaders of the Soviet Union adopt a more enlightened attitude. I hope they do. I believe we can help them do it. But I also believe that we must reexamine our own attitude—as individuals and as a Nation—for our attitude is as essential as theirs. And every graduate of this school, every thoughtful citizen who despairs of war and wishes to bring peace, should begin by looking inward—by examining his own attitude toward the possibilities of peace, toward the Soviet Union, toward the course of the cold war and toward freedom and peace here at home.

First: Let us examine our attitude toward peace itself. Too many of us think it is impossible. Too many think it unreal. But that is a dangerous, defeatist belief. It leads to the conclusion that war is inevitable—that mankind is doomed—that we are gripped by forces we cannot control. . . .

Second: Let us reexamine our attitude toward the Soviet Union. . . .

No government or social system is so evil that its people must be considered as lacking in virtue. As Americans, we find communism profoundly repugnant as a negation of personal freedom and dignity. But we can still hail the Russian people for their many achievements—in science and space, in economic and industrial growth, in culture and in acts of courage.

Among the many traits the peoples of our two countries have in common, none is stronger than our mutual abhorrence of war. Almost unique, among the major world powers, we have never been at war with each other. And no nation in the history of battle ever suffered more than the Soviet Union suffered in the course of the Second World War. At least 20 million lost their lives. Countless millions of homes and farms were burned or sacked. A third of the nation's territory, including nearly two thirds of its industrial base, was turned into a wasteland—a loss equivalent to the devastation of this country east of Chicago.

Today, should total war ever break out again—no matter how—our two countries would become the primary targets. It is an ironic but accurate fact that the two strongest powers are the two in the most danger of devastation. All we have built, all we have worked for, would be destroyed in the first 24 hours. And even in the cold war, which brings burdens and dangers to so many countries, including this Nation's closest allies—our two countries bear the heaviest burdens. For we are both devoting massive sums of money to weapons that could be better devoted to combating ignorance, poverty, and disease. We are both caught up in a vicious and dangerous cycle in which suspicion on one side breeds suspicion on the other, and new weapons beget counterweapons.

In short, both the United States and its allies, and the Soviet Union and its allies, have a mutually deep interest in a just and genuine peace and in halting the arms race. Agreements to this end are in the interests of the Soviet Union as well as ours—and even the most hostile nations can be relied upon to accept and keep those treaty obligations, and only those treaty obligations, which are in their own interest.

So, let us not be blind to our differences—but let us also direct attention to our common interests and to the means by which those differences can be resolved. And if we cannot end now our differences, at least we can help make the world safe for diversity. For, in the final analysis, our most basic common link is that we all inhabit this small planet. We all breathe the same air. We all cherish our children's future. And we are all mortal.

Third: Let us reexamine our attitude toward the cold war, remembering that we are not engaged in a debate, seeking to pile up debating points. We are not here distributing blame or pointing the finger of judgment. We must deal with the world as it is, and not as it might have been had the history of the last 18 years been different. . . .

. . . The United States will make no deal with the Soviet Union at the expense of other nations and other peoples, not merely because they are our partners, but also because their interests and ours converge.

Our interests converge, however, not only in defending the frontiers of freedom, but in pursuing the paths of peace. It is our hope —and the purpose of allied policies—to convince the Soviet Union that she, too, should let each nation choose its own future, so long as that choice does not interfere with the choices of others. The Communist drive to impose their political and economic system on others is the primary cause of world tension today. For there can be no doubt that, if all nations could refrain from interfering in the self-determination of others, the peace would be much more assured.

This will require a new effort to achieve world law—a new context for world discussions. It will require increased understanding between the Soviets and ourselves. And increased understanding will require increased contact and communication. One step in this direction is the proposed arrangement for a direct line between Moscow and Washington, to avoid on each side the dangerous delays, misunderstandings, and misreadings of the other's actions which might occur at a time of crisis.

We have also been talking in Geneva about other first-step measures of arms control, designed to limit the intensity of the arms race and to reduce the risks of accidental war. Our primary long-range interest in Geneva, however, is general and complete disarmament—designed to take place by stages, permitting parallel political developments to build the new institutions of peace which would take the place of arms. The pursuit of disarmament has been an effort of this Government since the 1920's. It has been urgently sought by the past three administrations. And however dim the prospects may be today, we intend to continue this effort—to continue it in order that all countries, including our own, can better grasp what the problems and possibilities of disarmament are.

The one major area of these negotiations where the end is in sight, yet where a fresh start is badly needed, is in a treaty to outlaw nuclear tests. The conclusion of such a treaty, so near and yet so far, would check the spiraling arms race in one of its most dangerous areas. It would place the nuclear powers in a position to deal more effectively with one of the greatest hazards which man faces in 1963, the further spread of nuclear arms. It would increase our security—it would decrease the prospects of war. Surely this goal is sufficiently important to require our steady pursuit, yielding neither to the temptation to give up the whole effort nor the temptation to give up our insistence on vital and responsible safeguards.

I am taking this opportunity, therefore, to announce two important decisions in this regard.

First: Chairman Khrushchev, Prime Minister Macmillan, and I have agreed that high-level discussions will shortly begin in Moscow looking toward early agreement on a comprehensive test ban treaty. Our hopes must be tempered with the caution of history—but with our hopes go the hopes of all mankind.

Second: To make clear our good faith and solemn convictions on the matter, I now declare that the United States does not propose to conduct nuclear tests in the atmosphere so long as other states do not do so. We will not be the first to resume. Such a declaration is no substitute for a formal binding treaty, but I hope it will help us achieve one. Nor would such a treaty be a substitute for disarmament, but I hope it will help us achieve it. . . .

. . . The United States, as the world knows, will never start a war. We do not want a war. We do not now expect a war. This generation of Americans has already had enough—more than enough—of war and hate and oppression. We shall be prepared if others wish it. We shall be alert to try to stop it. But we shall also do our part to build a world of peace where the weak are safe and the strong are just. We are not helpless before that task or hopeless of its success. Confident and unafraid, we labor on—not toward a strategy of annihilation but toward a strategy of peace.

652. SCHOOL DISTRICT OF ABINGTON TOWNSHIP, PENNSYLVANIA v. SCHEMPP
83 Supreme Court Reporter 1560
1963

This decision involved a Pennsylvania law requiring Bible reading in public schools and a similar rule of the Baltimore school board which had given rise to the case of Murray v. Curlett, covered in the same opinion. In the first case, referred to in the Court's opinion as No. 142, a lower court had ruled that religious exercises in public schools amounted to an establishment of religion by the State and therefore violated the Constitution; in the Maryland case (No. 119), the lower court sided with the school board. The Supreme Court, in a controversial decision, upheld the former interpretation, Justice Stewart filing a lone dissent.

Applying the Establishment Clause principles to the cases at bar we find that the States are requiring the selection and reading at the opening of the school day of verses from the Holy Bible and the recitation of the Lord's Prayer by the students in unison. These exercises are prescribed as part of the curricular activities of students who are required by law to attend school. They are held in the school buildings under the supervision and with the participation of teachers employed in those schools. The trial court in No. 142 has found that such an opening exercise is a religious ceremony and was intended by the State to be so. We agree with the trial court's finding as to the religious character of the exercises. Given that finding, the exercises and the law requiring them are in violation of the Establishment Clause.

There is no such specific finding as to the religious character of the exercises in No. 119, and the State contends (as does the State in No. 142) that the program is an effort to extend its benefits to all public school children without regard to their religious belief. Included within its secular purposes, it says, are the promotion of moral values, the contradiction to the materialistic trends of our times, the perpetuation of our institutions and the teaching of literature. The case came up on demurrer, of course,

to a petition which alleged that the uniform practice under the rule had been to read from the King James version of the Bible and that the exercise was sectarian. The short answer, therefore, is that the religious character of the exercise was admitted by the State. But even if its purpose is not strictly religious, it is sought to be accomplished through readings, without comment, from the Bible. Surely the place of the Bible as an instrument of religion cannot be gainsaid, and the State's recognition of the pervading religious character of the ceremony is evident from the rule's specific permission of the alternative use of the Catholic Douay version as well as the recent amendment permitting nonattendance at the exercises. None of these factors is consistent with the contention that the Bible is here used either as an instrument for nonreligious moral inspiration or as a reference for the teaching of secular subjects.

The conclusion follows that in both cases the laws require religious exercises and such exercises are being conducted in direct violation of the rights of the appellees and petitioners. Nor are these required exercises mitigated by the fact that individual students may absent themselves upon parental request, for that fact furnishes no defense to a claim of unconstitutionality under the Establishment Clause. Further, it is no defense to urge that the religious practices here may be relatively minor encroachments on the First Amendment. The breach of neutrality that is today a trickling stream may all too soon become a raging torrent and, in the words of Madison, "it is proper to take alarm at the first experiment on our liberties."

It is insisted that unless these religious exercises are permitted a "religion of secularism" is established in the schools. We agree of course that the State may not establish a "religion of secularism" in the sense of affirmatively opposing or showing hostility to religion, thus "preferring those who

believe in no religion over those who do believe." We do not agree, however, that this
decision in any sense has that effect. In addition, it might well be said that one's education is not complete without a study of
comparative religion or the history of religion and its relationship to the advancement of civilization. It certainly may be said
that the Bible is worthy of study for its literary and historic qualities. Nothing we have
said here indicates that such study of the
Bible or of religion, when presented objec-
tively as part of a secular program of education, may not be effected consistently with
the First Amendment. But the exercises here
do not fall into those categories. They are
religious exercises, required by the States in
violation of the command of the First
Amendment that the Government maintain
strict neutrality, neither aiding nor opposing religion.

Finally, we cannot accept that the concept
of neutrality, which does not permit a State
to require a religious exercise even with the
consent of the majority of those affected,
collides with the majority's right to free exercise of religion.[10] While the Free Exercise
Clause clearly prohibits the use of state action to deny the rights of free exercise to
anyone, it has never meant that a majority
could use the machinery of the State to
practice its beliefs. Such a contention was
effectively answered by Mr. Justice Jackson

for the Court in West Virginia Board of
Education v. Barnette, 319 U. S. 624:

"The very purpose of a Bill of Rights was
to withdraw certain subjects from the vicissitudes of political controversy, to place
them beyond the reach of majorities and officials and to establish them as legal principles to be applied by the courts. One's right
to . . . freedom of worship . . . and other
fundamental rights may not be submitted
to vote; they depend on the outcome of no
elections."

The place of religion in our society is an
exalted one, achieved through a long tradition of reliance on the home, the church
and the inviolable citadel of the individual
heart and mind. We have come to recognize through bitter experience that it is not
within the power of government to invade
that citadel, whether its purpose or effect be
to aid or oppose, to advance or retard. In
the relationship between man and religion,
the State is firmly committed to a position
of neutrality. Though the application of that
rule requires interpretation of a delicate sort,
the rule itself is clearly and concisely stated
in the words of the First Amendment. Applying that rule to the facts of these cases, we
affirm the judgment in No. 142. In No. 119,
the judgment is reversed and the cause remanded to the Maryland Court of Appeals
for further proceedings consistent with this
opinion. . . .

653. THE NUCLEAR TEST BAN TREATY
September 24, 1963
(Department of State Bulletin, August 12, 1963)

This was the first fruit of the new Soviet–
American détente—the unexpected outcome of
the Cuban missile crisis (Doc. No. 650). The
treaty was signed on July 25, 1963 and ratified
by the Senate on September 24 by a vote of 80
to 19, by the Soviet Union the next day, and
by Great Britain—a third party to the negotiations—the following month. Eventually 99 other
nations ratified the treaty, with the conspicuous
exception of France, at that time the fourth nuclear power. De Gaulle's refusal to sign reflected,
among other things, his growing belief that
France could no longer rely on the military protection of NATO and, in general, his wish to
pursue a course independent of the United
States in all things.

The Governments of the United States of
America, the United Kingdom of Great
Britain and Northern Ireland, and the Union
of Soviet Socialist Republics, hereinafter
referred to as the "Original Parties",

Proclaiming as their principal aim the
speediest possible achievement of an agreement on general and complete disarmament
under strict international control in accordance with the objectives of the United Nations which would put an end to the armaments race and eliminate the incentive to
the production and testing of all kinds of
weapons, including nuclear weapons,

Seeking to achieve the discontinuance of all test explosions of nuclear weapons for all time, determined to continue negotiations to this end, and desiring to put an end to the contamination of man's environment by radioactive substances,

Have agreed as follows:

Article I

1. Each of the Parties to this Treaty undertakes to prohibit, to prevent, and not to carry out any nuclear weapon test explosion, or any other nuclear explosion, at any place under its jurisdiction or control:

(a) in the atmosphere; beyond its limits, including outer space; or underwater, including territorial waters or high seas; or

(b) in any other environment if such explosion causes radioactive debris to be present outside the territorial limits of the State under whose jurisdiction or control such explosion is conducted. It is understood in this connection that the provisions of this subparagraph are without prejudice to the conclusion of a treaty resulting in the permanent banning of all nuclear test explosions, including all such explosions underground, the conclusion of which, as the Parties have stated in the Preamble to this Treaty, they seek to achieve.

2. Each of the Parties to this Treaty undertakes furthermore to refrain from causing, encouraging, or in any way participating in, the carrying out of any nuclear weapon test explosion, or any other nuclear explosion, anywhere which would take place in any of the environments described, or have the effect referred to, in paragraph 1 of this Article. . . .

Article III

1. This Treaty shall be open to all States for signature. Any State which does not sign this Treaty before its entry into force in accordance with paragraph 3 of this Article may accede to it at any time. . . .

3. This Treaty shall enter into force after its ratification by all the Original Parties and the deposit of their instruments of ratification. . . .

Article IV

This Treaty shall be of unlimited duration. Each Party shall in exercising its national sovereignty have the right to withdraw from the Treaty if it decides that extraordinary events, related to the subject matter of this Treaty, have jeopardized the supreme interests of its country. It shall give notice of such withdrawal to all other Parties to the Treaty three months in advance. . . .

654. WESBERRY v. SANDERS
84 Supreme Court Reporter, 526
1964

Faced again with the politically explosive issue of reapportionment, the Court now clarified some of the issues it had avoided in Baker v. Carr (Doc. No. 649), in which it had held only that reapportionment was subject to judicial review. The present case concerned apportionment in the House of Representatives—specifically a Georgia statute of 1931 under which urban districts (as in most states) were heavily underrepresented in the House. Eight of the nine justices agreed in this case that questions of apportionment were justiciable, Justice Frankfurter's death having removed one of the two dissenters in Baker v. Carr. Both Justices Clark and Stewart, however, joined with Justice Harlan in dissenting from the Court's opinion as to the substance of this case. A six-man majority held that Georgia's malapportioned congressional districts contravened Article I, Section 2 of the Constitution, which in effect, they argued, laid down the principle of "one man, one vote." Justice Harlan based his dissent largely on historical grounds. See also Doc. No. 656.

BLACK, J. . . . The 1931 Georgia apportionment grossly discriminates against voters in the Fifth Congressional District. A single Congressman represents from two to three times as many Fifth District voters as are represented by each of the Congressmen from the other Georgia congressional districts. The apportionment statute thus contracts the value of some votes and expands that of others. If the Federal Constitution intends that when qualified voters elect members of Congress each vote be given as much weight as any other vote, then this statute cannot stand.

We hold that, construed in its historical context, the command of Art. I, § 2, that Representatives be chosen "by the People of the several States" means that as nearly as is practicable one man's vote in a congressional election is to be worth as much as another's. . . . To say that a vote is worth more in one district than in another would not only run counter to our fundamental ideas of democratic government, it would cast aside the principle of a House of Representatives elected "by the People," a principle tenaciously fought for and established at the Constitutional Convention. The history of the Constitution, particularly that part of it relating to the adoption of Art. I, § 2, reveals that those who framed the Constitution meant that, no matter what the mechanics of an election, whether statewide or by districts, it was population which was to be the basis of the House of Representatives. . . .

The question of how the legislature should be constituted precipitated the most bitter controversy of the Convention. One principle was uppermost in the minds of many delegates: that, no matter where he lived, each voter should have a voice equal with that of every other in electing members of Congress. . . .

Some delegates opposed election by the people. The sharpest objection arose out of the fear on the part of small States like Delaware that if population were to be the only basis of representation the populous States like Virginia would elect a large enough number of representatives to wield overwhelming power in the National Government. . . .

The dispute came near ending the Convention without a Constitution. . . . The deadlock was finally broken when a majority of the States agreed to what has been called the Great Compromise, based on a proposal which had been repeatedly advanced by Roger Sherman and other dele-

gates from Connecticut. It provided on the one hand that each State, including little Delaware and Rhode Island, was to have two Senators. . . . The other side of the compromise was that, as provided in Art. I, § 2, members of the House of Representatives should be chosen "by the People of the several States" and should be "apportioned among the several States . . . according to their respective Numbers." . . .

It would defeat the principle solemnly embodied in the Great Compromise—equal representation in the House of equal numbers of people—for us to hold that, within the States, legislatures may draw the lines of congressional districts in such a way as to give some voters a greater voice in choosing a Congressman than others. The House of Representatives, the Convention agreed, was to represent the people as individuals, and on a basis of complete equality for each voter. . . .

In urging the people to adopt the Constitution, Madison said in No. 57 of The Federalist:

"Who are to be the electors of the Federal Representatives? Not the rich more than the poor; not the learned more than the ignorant; not the haughty heirs of distinguished names, more than the humble sons of obscure and unpropitious fortune. The electors are to be the great body of the people of the United States. . . ."

Readers surely could have fairly taken this to mean, "one person, one vote."

While it may not be possible to draw congressional districts with mathematical precision, that is no excuse for ignoring our Constitution's plain objective of making equal representation for equal numbers of people the fundamental goal for the House of Representatives. That is the high standard of justice and common sense which the Founders set for us.

HARLAN, J., dissenting. . . . Disclaiming all reliance on other provisions of the Constitution, in particular those of the Fourteenth Amendment on which the appellants relied below and in this Court, the Court holds that the provision in Art. I, § 2, for election of Representatives "by the People" *means* that congressional districts are to be "as nearly as is practicable" equal in population. Stripped of rhetoric and a "historical context," which bears little resemblance to the evidence found in the pages of history, the Court's opinion supports its holding only with the bland assertion that "the principle of a House of Representatives elected 'by the People'" would be "cast aside" if "a vote is worth more in one district than in another," *i. e.*, if congressional districts within a State, each electing a single Representative, are not equal in population. The fact is, however, that Georgia's 10 Representatives *are* elected "by the People" of Georgia, just as Representatives from other States are elected "by the People of the several States." This is all that the Constitution requires.

Although the Court finds necessity for its artificial construction of Article I in the undoubted importance of the right to vote, that right is not involved in this case. All of the appellants do vote. The Court's talk about "debasement" and "dilution" of the vote is a model of circular reasoning, in which the premises of the argument feed on the conclusion. Moreover, by focusing exclusively on numbers in disregard of the area and shape of a congressional district as well as party affiliations within the district, the Court deals in abstractions which will be recognized even by the politically unsophisticated to have little relevance to the realities of political life. . . .

. . . Nothing that the Court does today will disturb the fact that although in 1960 the population of an average congressional district was 410,481, the States of Alaska, Nevada, and Wyoming each have a Representative in Congress, although their respective populations are 226,167, 285,278, and 330,066. In entire disregard of population, Art. I, § 2, guarantees each of these States and every other State "at Least one Repre-

sentative." It is whimsical to assert in the face of this guarantee that an absolute principle of "equal representation in the House of equal numbers of people" is "solemnly embodied" in Article I. All that there is is a provision which bases representation in the House, generally but not entirely, on the population of the States. The provision for representation of *each State* in the House of Representatives is not a mere exception to the principle framed by the majority; it shows that no such principle is to be found. . . .

. . . The Great Compromise concerned representation *of the States* in the Congress. In all of the discussion surrounding the basis of representation of the House and all of the discussion whether Representatives should be elected by the legislatures or the people of the States, there is nothing which suggests even remotely that the delegates had in mind the problem of districting within a State. . . .

. . . None of the Court's references to the ratification debates supports the view that the provision for election of Representatives "by the People" was intended to have any application to the apportionment of Representatives within the States; in each instance, the cited passage merely repeats what the Constitution itself provides: that Representatives were to be elected by the people of the States.

In sharp contrast to this unanimous silence on the issue of this case when Art. I, § 2, was being discussed, there are repeated references to apportionment and related problems affecting the States' selection of Representatives in connection with Art. I, § 4. The debates in the ratifying conventions . . . indicate that under § 4, the state legislatures, subject only to the ultimate control of Congress, could district as they chose. . . .

655. REYNOLDS v. SIMS
84 Supreme Court Reporter, 1363
1964

Whereas Wesberry v. Sanders (Doc. No. 654) dealt with apportionment in the House of Representatives, the present case raised the issue of apportionment in state legislatures. In language

even more sweeping than that of the Baker or Wesberry decisions, the Court now invoked the Equal Protection Clause of the Fourteenth Amendment to support its decision that both houses of a state legislature must be apportioned on the basis of population. The Court argued further that analogies with the system of representation in Congress, in which one house is based on population and the other on geography, were irrelevant to the case of state legislatures. In the subsequent cases of WMCA, Inc. v. Lomenzo and Lucas v. Forty-fourth General Assembly of Colorado (1964), the Court applied the same reasoning to apportionment schemes proposed by New York and Colorado, both of which it invalidated. Justice Harlan, dissenting in the present case as in the other apportionment cases, accused the Court of unwarranted judicial interference in political affairs—a charge that was soon taken up by the Court's critics in the country as a whole.

WARREN, C. J. . . . Undoubtedly, the right of suffrage is a fundamental matter in a free and democratic society. Especially since the right to exercise the franchise in a free and unimpaired manner is preservative of other basic civil and political rights, any alleged infringement of the right of citizens to vote must be carefully and meticulously scrutinized.

Legislators represent people, not trees or acres. Legislators are elected by voters, not farms or cities or economic interests. As long as ours is a representative form of government, and our legislatures are those instruments of government elected directly by and directly representative of the people, the right to elect legislators in a free and unimpaired fashion is a bedrock of our political system. It could hardly be gainsaid that a constitutional claim had been asserted by an allegation that certain otherwise qualified voters had been entirely prohibited from voting for members of their state legislature. And, if a State should provide that the votes of citizens in one part of the State should be given two times, or five times, or 10 times the weight of votes of citizens in another part of the State, it could hardly be contended that the right to vote of those residing in the disfavored areas had not been effectively diluted. It would appear extraordinary to suggest that a state could be constitutionally permitted to enact a law providing that certain of the state's voters could vote two, five, or 10 times for their legislative representatives, while voters living else-

where could vote only once. And it is inconceivable that a state law to the effect that, in counting votes for legislators, the votes of citizens in one part of the State would be multiplied by two, five, or 10, while the votes of persons in another area would be counted only at face value, could be constitutionally sustainable. Of course, the effect of state legislative districting schemes which give the same number of representatives to unequal numbers of constituents is identical. Overweighting and overvaluation of the votes of those living here has the certain effect of dilution and undervaluation of the votes of those living there. The resulting discrimination against those individual voters living in disfavored areas is easily demonstrable mathematically. Their right to vote is simply not the same right to vote as that of those living in a favored part of the State. Two, five, or 10 of them must vote before the effect of their voting is equivalent to that of their favored neighbor. Weighting the votes of citizens differently, by any method or means, merely because of where they happen to reside, hardly seems justifiable. One must be ever aware that the Constitution forbids "sophisticated as well as simple-minded modes of discrimination." . . .

. . . Since the achieving of fair and effective representation for all citizens is concededly the basic aim of legislative apportionment, we conclude that the Equal Protection Clause guarantees the opportunity for equal participation by all voters in the election of state legislators. Diluting the weight of votes because of place of residence impairs basic constitutional rights under the Fourteenth Amendment just as much as invidious discriminations based upon factors such as race, *Brown* v. *Board of Education*, 347 U. S. 483, [or economic status, *Griffin* v. *Illinois*, 351 U. S. 12, *Douglas* v. *California*, 372 U. S. 353]. Our constitutional system amply provides for the protection of minorities by means other than giving them majority control of state legislatures. And the democratic ideals of equality and majority rule, which have served this Nation so well in the past, are hardly of any less significance for the present and the future.

We are told that the matter of apportioning representation in a state legislature is a complex and many-faceted one. We are advised that States can rationally consider factors other than population in apportioning legislative representation. We are admonished not to restrict the power of the States to impose differing views as to political philosophy on their citizens. We are cautioned about the dangers of entering into political thickets and mathematical quagmires. Our answer is this: a denial of constitutionally protected rights demands judicial protection; our oath and our office require no less of us. . . .

IV.

We hold that, as a basic constitutional standard, the Equal Protection Clause requires that the seats in both houses of a bicameral state legislature must be apportioned on a population basis. Simply stated, an individual's right to vote for state legislators is unconstitutionally impaired when its weight is in a substantial fashion diluted when compared with votes of citizens living in other parts of the State. Since, under neither the existing apportionment provisions nor under either of the proposed plans was either of the houses of the Alabama Legislature apportioned on a population basis, the District Court correctly held that all three of these schemes were constitutionally invalid. Furthermore, the existing apportionment, and also to a lesser extent the apportionment under the Crawford-Webb Act, presented little more than crazy quilts, completely lacking in rationality, and could be found invalid on that basis alone. . . .

V.

Since neither of the houses of the Alabama Legislature under any of the three plans considered by the District Court was apportioned on a population basis, we would be justified in proceeding no further. However, one of the proposed plans, that contained in the so-called 67-Senator Amendment, at least superficially resembles the scheme of legislative representation followed in the Federal Congress. Under this plan, each of Alabama's 67 counties is allotted one senator, and no counties are given more than one Senate seat. Arguably, this is analogous to the allocation of two Senate seats, in the Federal Congress, to each of the 50 States, regardless of population. Seats in the Alabama House, under the proposed constitutional amendment, are distributed by giving each of the 67 counties at least one, with the remaining 49 seats being allotted among the more populous counties on a population basis. This scheme, at least at first glance, appears to resemble that prescribed for the Federal House of Representatives, where the 435 seats are distributed among the States on a population basis, although each State, regardless of its population, is given at least one Congressman. Thus, although there are substantial differences in underlying rationale and result, the 67-Senator Amendment, as proposed by the Alabama Legislature, at least arguably presents for consideration a scheme analogous to that used for apportioning seats in Congress.

Much has been written since our decision in *Baker* v. *Carr* about the applicability of the so-called federal analogy to state legislative apportionment arrangements. After considering the matter, the court below concluded that no conceivable analogy could be drawn between the federal scheme and the apportionment of seats in the Alabama Legislature under the proposed constitutional amendment. We agree with the District Court, and find the federal analogy inapposite and irrelevant to state legislative districting schemes. Attempted reliance on the federal analogy appears often to be little more than an after-the-fact rationalization offered in defense of malajusted state apportionment arrangements. The original constitutions of 36 of our States provided that representation in both houses of the state legislatures would be based completely, or predominantly, on population. And the Founding Fathers clearly had no intention of establishing a pattern or model for the apportionment of seats in state legislatures when the system of representation in the Federal Congress was adopted. Demonstrative of this is the fact that the Northwest Ordinance, adopted in the same year, 1787, as the Federal Constitution, provided for the apportionment of seats in territorial legislatures solely on the basis of population.

Thus, we conclude that the plan contained in the 67-Senator Amendment for apportioning seats in the Alabama Legislature cannot be sustained by recourse to the so-called federal analogy. Nor can any other inequitable state legislative apportionment scheme be justified on such an asserted basis. This does not necessarily mean that such a plan is irrational or involves something other than a "republican form of government." We conclude simply that such a plan is impermissible for the States under the Equal Protection Clause, since perforce resulting, in virtually every case, in submergence of the equal-population principle in at least one house of a state legislature.

Since we find the so-called federal analogy inapposite to a consideration of the constitutional validity of state legislative apportionment schemes, we necessarily hold that the Equal Protection Clause requires both houses of a state legislature to be apportioned on a population basis. . . .

HARLAN, J., dissenting. . . . The Court's elaboration of its new "constitutional" doctrine indicates how far—and how unwisely —it has strayed from the appropriate bounds of its authority. The consequence of today's decision is that in all but the handful of States which may already satisfy the new requirements the local District Court or, it may be, the state courts, are given blanket authority and the constitutional duty to supervise apportionment of the state legisla-tures. It is difficult to imagine a more intolerable and inappropriate interference by the judiciary with the independent legislatures of the States.

. . . These decisions give support to a current mistaken view of the Constitution and the constitutional function of this Court. This view, in a nutshell, is that every major social ill in this country can find its cure in some constitutional "principle," and that this Court should "take the lead" in promoting reform when other branches of government fail to act. The Constitution is not a panacea for every blot upon the public welfare, nor should this Court, ordained as a judicial body, be thought of as a general haven for reform movements. The Constitution is an instrument of government, fundamental to which is the premise that in a diffusion of governmental authority lies the greatest promise that this Nation will realize liberty for all its citizens. This Court, limited in function in accordance with that premise, does not serve its high purpose when it exceeds its authority, even to satisfy justified impatience with the slow workings of the political process. For when, in the name of constitutional interpretation, the Court *adds* something to the Constitution that was deliberately excluded from it, the Court in reality substitutes its view of what should be so for the amending process. . . .

656. ESCOBEDO v. ILLINOIS
378 U. S. 478
1964

The most important decisions of the Warren Court concerned themselves, broadly speaking, with four major areas: civil rights, reapportionment, religious freedom, and procedures of criminal investigation under the Bill of Rights. In the last of these, the general drift of the Court's opinions—opinions that were no less controversial than those concerning civil rights and reapportionment—was to set strict limits to the powers of the state in apprehending, interrogating, and prosecuting suspected criminals. In Mapp v. Ohio (1961) the Court held that evidence obtained by search and seizure in violation of the Fourth Amendment was inadmissible in state as well as federal courts; in Gideon v. Wainwright (1963), it affirmed the right to counsel in state criminal cases; in Jackson v. Denno (1964), it tightened its rule against forced confessions; and in the Miranda case (1966), it imposed additional restrictions on self-incrimination. In all of these cases, the chief constitutional issue was whether the guarantees contained in the Bill of Rights applied to the states as well as to agencies of the federal government, but even when that question was settled, additional issues, of enormous practical importance, remained. In the present case, Danny Escobedo, a 22-year old of Mexican extraction, had been convicted of murder on the basis of a confession secured before his formal indictment, during an interrogation in which he was denied access to his lawyer. The Supreme Court of Illinois first reversed the conviction and then, in a rehearing, ruled that the right to counsel applied only to persons formally indicted for a crime.

GOLDBERG, J. The critical question in this case is whether, under the circumstances, the refusal by the police to honor petitioner's request to consult with his lawyer during the course of an interrogation constitutes a denial of "the Assistance of Counsel" in violation of the Sixth Amendment to the Constitution as "made obligatory upon the States by the Fourteenth Amendment," *Gideon v. Wainwright*, 372 U. S. 335, 342, and thereby renders inadmissible in a state criminal trial any incriminating statement elicited by the police during the interrogation. . . .

The interrogation here was conducted before petitioner was formally indicted. But in the context of this case, that fact should make no difference. When petitioner requested, and was denied, an opportunity to consult with his lawyer, the investigation had ceased to be a general investigation of "an unsolved crime." Petitioner had become the accused, and the purpose of the interrogation was to "get him" to confess his guilt despite his constitutional right not to do so. At the time of his arrest and throughout the course of the interrogation, the police told petitioner that they had convincing evidence that he had fired the fatal shots. Without informing him of his absolute right to remain silent in the face of this accusation, the police urged him to make a statement. . . . Petitioner, a layman, was undoubtedly unaware that under Illinois law an admission of "mere" complicity in the murder plot was legally as damaging as an admission of firing of the fatal shots. . . . The "guiding hand of counsel" was essential to advise petitioner of his rights in this delicate situation. . . . This was the "stage when legal aid and advice" were most critical to petitioner. . . . It would exalt form over substance to make the right to counsel, under these circumstances, depend on whether at the time of the interrogation, the authorities had secured a formal indictment. Petitioner had, for all practical purposes, already been charged with murder. . . .

In *Gideon v. Wainwright*, 372 U.S. 335, we held that every person accused of a crime, whether state or federal, is entitled to a lawyer at trial. The rule sought by the State here, however, would make the trial no more than an appeal from the interrogation; and the "right to use counsel at the formal trial [would be] a very hollow thing

[if], for all practical purposes, the conviction is already assured by pretrial examination." *In re Groban*, 352 U.S. 330, 344 (BLACK, J., dissenting). "One can imagine a cynical prosecutor saying: 'Let them have the most illustrious counsel, now. They can't escape the noose. There is nothing that counsel can do for them at the trial.' " *Ex parte Sullivan*, 107 F. Supp. 514, 517–18.

We have learned the lesson of history, ancient and modern, that a system of criminal law enforcement which comes to depend on the "confession" will, in the long run, be less reliable and more subject to abuses than a system which depends on extrinsic evidence independently secured through skillful investigation. . . .

We have also learned the companion lesson of history that no system of criminal justice can, or should, survive if it comes to depend for its continued effectiveness on the citizens' abdication through unawareness of their constitutional rights. No system worth preserving should have to *fear* that if an accused is permitted to consult with a lawyer, he will become aware of, and exercise, these rights. If the exercise of constitutional rights will thwart the effectiveness of a system of law enforcement, then there is something very wrong with that system.

We hold, therefore, that where, as here, the investigation is no longer a general inquiry into an unsolved crime but has begun to focus on a particular suspect, the suspect has been taken into police custody, the police carry out a process of interrogations that lends itself to eliciting incriminating statements, the suspect has requested and been denied an opportunity to consult with his lawyer, and the police have not effectively warned him of his absolute constitutional right to remain silent, the accused has been denied "the Assistance of Counsel" in violation of the Sixth Amendment to the Constitution as "made obligatory upon the States by the Fourteenth Amendment," and that no statement elicited by the police during the interrogation may be used against him at a criminal trial. . . .

Nothing we have said today affects the powers of the police to investigate "an unsolved crime," by gathering information from witnesses and by other "proper investigative efforts." We hold only that when the process shifts from investigatory to accusatory—when its focus is on the accused and its purpose is to elicit a confession— our adversary system begins to operate, and,

under the circumstances here, the accused must be permitted to consult with his lawyer.

657. BELL v. MARYLAND
84 Supreme Court Reporter, 1814

1964

The issue here was whether the Fourteenth Amendment outlaws private discrimination as well as discrimination by state governments. The plaintiff in the case had been arrested in a sit-in at a segregated lunch counter. As in earlier cases involving the same question, the Court found grounds to evade the central issue. In a separate opinion, given below, Justices Douglas and Goldberg confronted this issue and argued for outright reversal of the conviction of civil-rights demonstrators in the Maryland courts. Justices Black, Harlan, and White dissented on the grounds that an attack on private discrimination was an attack on property.

The problem in this case, and in the other sit-in cases before us, is presented as though it involved the situation of "a private operator conducting his own business on his own premises and exercising his own judgment" as to whom he will admit to the premises.

The property involved is not, however, a man's home or his yard or even his fields. Private property is involved, but it is property that is serving the public. As my Brother GOLDBERG says, it is a "civil" right, not a "social" right, with which we deal. Here it is a restaurant refusing service to a Negro. But so far as principle and law are concerned it might just as well be a hospital refusing admission to a sick or injured Negro (cf. Simkins v. Moses H. Cone Memorial Hospital, 4 Cir., 323 F.2d 959), or a drug store refusing antibiotics to a Negro, or a bus denying transportation to a Negro, or a telephone company refusing to install a telephone in a Negro's home.

The problem with which we deal has no relation to opening or closing the door of one's home. The home of course is the essence of privacy, in no way dedicated to public use, in no way extending an invitation to the public. Some businesses, like the classical country store where the owner lives overhead or in the rear, make the store an extension, so to speak, of the home. But such is not this case. The facts of these sit-in cases have little resemblance to any institution of property which we customarily associate with privacy. . . .

The revolutionary change effected by an affirmance in these sit-in cases would be much more damaging to an open and free society than what the Court did when it gave the corporation the sword and the shield of the Due Process and Equal Protection Clauses of the Fourteenth Amendment. Affirmance finds in the Constitution a corporate right to refuse service to anyone "it" chooses and to get the State to put people in jail who defy "its" will. . . .

Affirmance would make corporate management the arbiter of one of the deepest conflicts in our society: corporate management could then enlist the aid of state police, state prosecutors, and state courts to force *apartheid* on the community they served, if *apartheid* best suited the corporate need; or, if its profits would be better served by lowering the barriers of segregation, it could do so. . . .

The point is that corporate motives in the retail field relate to corporate profits, corporate prestige, and corporate public relations. Corporate motives have no tinge of an individual's choice to associate only with one class of customers, to keep members of one race from his "property," to erect a wall of privacy around a business in the manner that one is erected around the home. . . .

BLACK, J., with whom Justice HARLAN and Justice WHITE, join, dissenting.

We are admonished that in deciding this case we should remember that "it is *a consti-*

tution we are expounding." We conclude as we do because we remember that it *is* a Constitution and that it is our duty "to bow with respectful submission to its provisions." And in recalling that it is a Constitution "intended to endure for ages to come," we also remember that the Founders wisely provided the means for that endurance: changes in the Constitution, when thought necessary, are to be proposed by Congress or conventions and ratified by the States. The Founders gave no such amending power to this Court. Our duty is simply to interpret the Constitution, and in doing so the test of constitutionality is not whether a law is offensive to our conscience or to the "good old common law," but whether it is offensive to the Constitution. Confining ourselves to our constitutional duty to construe, not to rewrite or amend, the Constitution, we believe that section 1 of the Fourteenth Amendment does not bar Maryland from enforcing its trespass laws so long as it does so with impartiality.

This Court has done much in carrying out its solemn duty to protect people from unlawful discrimination. And it will, of course, continue to carry out this duty in the future as it has in the past. But the Fourteenth Amendment of itself does not compel either a black man or a white man running his own private business to trade with anyone else against his will. We do not believe that section 1 of the Fourteenth Amendment was written or designed to interfere with a storekeeper's right to choose his customers or with a property owner's right to choose his social or business associates, so long as he does not run counter to valid state or federal regulation. The case before us does not involve the power of the Congress to pass a law compelling privately owned businesses to refrain from discrimination on the basis of race and to trade with all if they trade with any. We express no views as to the power of Congress, acting under one or another provision of the Constitution, to prevent racial discrimination in the operation of privately owned businesses, nor upon any particular form of legislation to that end. Our sole conclusion is that section 1 of the Fourteenth Amendment, standing alone, does not prohibit privately owned restaurants from choosing their own customers. It does not destroy what has until very recently been universally recognized in this country as the unchallenged right of a man who owns a business to run the business in his own way so long as some valid regulatory statute does not tell him to do otherwise. . . .

658. CIVIL RIGHTS ACT OF 1964
July 2, 1964
(78 *U. S. Statutes at Large,* 241 ff. Public Law 88–352)

Dissatisfaction with the ineffectiveness of the Civil Rights Act of 1957 (Doc. No. 626) had led to the passage of another civil-rights law in 1960, addressed primarily to the problem of voting but, like its predecessor, ineffective. Mounting pressure from the civil-rights movement (see introduction to Doc. No. 648) forced President Kennedy in 1963 to demand federal legislation against segregation in all businesses involved in interstate commerce and against job discrimination. President Johnson continued Kennedy's efforts. After a long struggle, capped by a three-month filibuster, Congress finally passed a bill, stronger than Kennedy's original proposal but weaker than some of the alternatives proposed by the House. It prohibited discrimination in places of public accommodation, forbade discrimination in employment, forbade discrimination in voting, and set up machinery of enforcement. This was the strongest civil-rights measure since Reconstruction, but in practice it was a qualified success at best.

TITLE I—VOTING RIGHTS

SEC. 101 (2). No person acting under color of law shall—

(A) in determining whether any individual is qualified under State law or laws to vote in any Federal election, apply any standard, practice, or procedure different from the standards, practices, or procedures applied under such law or laws to other individuals within the same county, parish, or similar political subdivision who have been found by State officials to be qualified to vote; . . .

(C) employ any literacy test as a qualification for voting in any Federal election unless (i) such test is administered to each individual wholly in writing; and (ii) a certified copy of the test and of the answers given by the individual is furnished to him within twenty-five days of the submission of his request made within the period of time during which records and papers are required to be retained and preserved pursuant to title III of the Civil Rights Act of 1960. . . .

TITLE II—INJUNCTIVE RELIEF AGAINST DISCRIMINATION IN PLACES OF PUBLIC ACCOMMODATION

SEC. 201. (a) All persons shall be entitled to the full and equal enjoyment of the goods, services, facilities, privileges, advantages, and accommodations of any place of public accommodation, as defined in this section, without discrimination or segregation on the ground of race, color, religion, or national origin.

(b) Each of the following establishments which serves the public is a place of public accommodation within the meaning of this title if its operations affect commerce, or if discrimination or segregation by it is supported by State action:

(1) any inn, motel, or other establishment which provides lodging to transient guests, other than an establishment located within a building which contains not more than five rooms for rent or hire and which is actually occupied by the proprietor of such establishment as his residence;

(2) any restaurant, cafeteria, lunch room, lunch counter, soda fountain, or other facility principally engaged in selling food for consumption on the premises . . .

(3) any motion picture house, the-ater, concert hall, sports arena, stadium or other place of exhibition or entertainment. . . .

(d) Discrimination or segregation by an establishment is supported by State action within the meaning of this title if such discrimination or segregation (1) is carried on under color of any law, statute, ordinance, or regulation; or (2) is carried on under color of any custom or usage required or enforced by officials of the State or political subdivision thereof. . . .

SEC. 202. All persons shall be entitled to be free, at any establishment or place, from discrimination or segregation of any kind on the ground of race, color, religion, or national origin, if such discrimination or segregation is or purports to be required by any law, statute, ordinance, regulation, rule, or order of a State or any agency or political subdivision thereof. . . .

SEC. 206. (a) Whenever the Attorney General has reasonable cause to believe that any person or group of persons is engaged in a pattern or practice of resistance to the full enjoyment of any of the rights secured by this title, the Attorney General may bring a civil action in the appropriate district court of the United States by filing with it a complaint . . . requesting such preventive relief, including an application for a permanent or temporary injunction, restraining order or other order against the person or persons responsible for such pattern or practice, as he deems necessary to insure the full enjoyment of the rights herein described.

TITLE VI—NONDISCRIMINATION IN FEDERALLY ASSISTED PROGRAMS

SEC. 601. No person in the United States shall, on the ground of race, color, or national origin, be excluded from participation in, be denied the benefits of, or be subjected to discrimination under any program or activity receiving Federal financial assistance.

659. GOLDWATER'S ACCEPTANCE SPEECH
July 16, 1964
(*New York Times,* July 17, 1964)

Meeting in Los Angeles, the Republican convention bypassed the moderate wing of the party and nominated Senator Barry Goldwater of Arizona, a man of the Right who had repeatedly deplored the compromises made by Republican liberals. Not since 1896 had a major party so decisively repudiated its traditional leadership. Goldwater's triumph, made possible by years of patient organization at the grassroots, represented a groundswell of discontent within the party, which—as in the Bryan campaign—had as its principal target a putative eastern and Europeanized elite which was accused of having betrayed the real interests of the people. In the campaign that followed, Goldwater scorned the usual fence-mending practices of successful candidates, made few overtures to his defeated adversaries, and based his appeal to the voters not on his willingness to compromise with political conventions but on his ideological purity. These tactics doubtless contributed to his overwhelming defeat. All of them were clearly foreshadowed in his acceptance speech to the nominating convention, remarkable for the absence of conciliatory gestures and for the round assertion—addressed to those who had accused Goldwater of extremism —that "extremism in the defense of liberty is no vice."

. . . Now my fellow Americans, the tide has been running against freedom. Our people have followed false prophets. We must, and we shall, return to proven ways— not because they are old, but because they are true.

We must, and we shall, set the tide running again in the cause of freedom. And this party, with its every action, every word, every breath and every heart beat, has but a single resolve, and that is freedom. . . .

During four futile years the Administration which we shall replace has distorted and lost that faith. It has talked and talked and talked and talked the words of freedom but it has failed and failed and failed in the works of freedom.

Now failure cements the wall of shame in Berlin; failures blot the sands of shame at the Bay of Pigs; failures marked the slow death of freedom in Laos; failures infest the jungles of Vietnam, and failures haunt the houses of our once great alliances and undermine the greatest bulwark ever erected by free nations, the NATO community.

Failures proclaim lost leadership, obscure purpose, weakening wills and the risk of inciting our sworn enemies to new aggressions and to new excesses.

And because of this Administration we are tonight a world divided. We are a nation becalmed. We have lost the brisk pace of diversity and the genius of individual creativity. We are plodding along at a pace set by centralized planning, red tape, rules without responsibility and regimentation without recourse.

Rather than useful jobs in our country, people have been offered bureaucratic makework; rather than moral leadership, they have been given bread and circuses; they have been given spectacles, and, yes, they've even been given scandals.

Tonight there is violence in our streets, corruption in our highest offices, aimlessness among our youth, anxiety among our elderly, and there's a virtual despair among the many who look beyond material success toward the inner meaning of their lives. And where examples of morality should be set, the opposite is seen. Small men seeking great wealth or power have too often and too long turned even the highest levels of public service into mere personal opportunity. . . .

Fellow Republicans, it is the cause of Republicanism to resist concentrations of power, private or public, which enforce such conformity and inflict such despotism. . . .

It is further the cause of Republicanism to restore a clear understanding of the tyranny of man over man in the world at large. It is our cause to dispel the foggy thinking which avoids hard decisions in the delusion that a world of conflict will somehow resolve itself into a world of harmony, if we just don't rock the boat or irritate the forces of aggression—and this is hogwash.

It is, further, the cause of Republicanism to remind ourselves, and the world, that only the strong can remain free; that only the strong can keep the peace.

Now I needn't remind you, or my fellow Americans regardless of party, that Republicans have shouldered this hard responsibility and marched in this cause before. It was Republican leadership under Dwight Eisenhower that kept the peace, and passed along to this Administration the mightiest arsenal for defense the world has ever known.

And I needn't remind you that it was the strength and the believable will of the Eisenhower years that kept the peace by using our strength, by using it in the Formosa Strait, and in Lebanon, and by showing it courageously at all times.

It was during those Republican years that the thrust of Communist imperialism was blunted. It was during those years of Republican leadership that this world moved closer not to war but closer to peace than at any other time in the last three decades.

And I needn't remind you, but I will, that it's been during the Democratic years that our strength to deter war has been stilled and even gone into a planned decline. It has been during Democratic years that we have weakly stumbled into conflicts, timidly refusing to draw our own lines against aggression, deceitfully refusing to tell even our own people of our full participation and tragically letting our finest men die on battlefields unmarked by purpose, unmarked by pride or the prospect of victory.

Yesterday it was Korea; tonight it is Vietnam. Make no bones of this. Don't try to sweep this under the rug. We are at war in Vietnam. And yet the President, who is the Commander in Chief of our forces, refuses to say, refuses to say mind you, whether or not the objective over there is victory, and his Secretary of Defense continues to mislead and misinform the Amer-ican people, and enough of it has gone by.

And I needn't remind you, but I will, it has been during Democratic years that a billion persons were cast into Communist captivity and their fate cynically sealed.

Today—today in our beloved country we have an Administration which seems eager to deal with Communism in every coin known—from gold to wheat; from consulates to confidence, and even human freedom itself.

Now the Republican cause demands that we brand Communism as the principal disturber of peace in the world today. Indeed, we should brand it as the only significant disturber of the peace. And we must make clear that until its goals of conquest are absolutely renounced, and its relations with all nations tempered, Communism and the governments it now controls are enemies of every man on earth who is or wants to be free. . . .

Anyone who joins us in all sincerity we welcome. Those, those who do not care for our cause, we don't expect to enter our ranks in any case. And let our Republicanism so focused and so dedicated not be made fuzzy and futile by unthinking and stupid labels.

I would remind you that extremism in the defense of liberty is no vice!

And let me remind you also that moderation in the pursuit of justice is no virtue! . . .

Our Republican cause is not to level out the world or make its people conform in computer-regimented sameness. Our Republican cause is to free our people and light the way for liberty throughout the world. Ours is a very human cause for very humane goals. This party, its good people, and its unquestionable devotion to freedom will not fulfill the purposes of this campaign which we launch here now until our cause has won the day, inspired the world, and shown the way to a tomorrow worthy of all our yesteryears.

660. THE TONKIN GULF INCIDENT
1964

After the fall of Diem (see introduction to Docs. No. 610 and 647), the South Vietnamese civil war entered a new phase. Communist-led guerillas (the National Liberation Front or Vietcong) gained control of larger and larger areas of the country, and a succession of military dictators proved ineffective in dealing with them. The Johnson administration, like the

Kennedy administration, interpreted the guerilla warfare in the south as evidence of North Vietnamese aggression, and increased its military and naval support of the South Vietnamese government. In August 1964, during the Presidential campaign in which Goldwater was accusing Johnson of laxity in combatting Communism, the administration claimed that North Vietnamese gunboats had fired on American destroyers in the Tonkin Gulf off the coast of North Vietnam. Johnson ordered aerial retaliation and then asked Congress to give him broad discretionary power to combat Communism in Southeast Asia. The House unanimously and the Senate with only two dissenting votes (Morse of Oregon and Gruening of Alaska) passed a joint resolution to this effect on August 7. It was this resolution that furnished the legal basis for the subsequent escalation of the war (see Doc. No. 664).

1. PRESIDENT JOHNSON'S MESSAGE TO CONGRESS
August 5, 1964
(*Department of State Bulletin,* August 24, 1964)

Last night I announced to the American people that the North Vietnamese regime had conducted further deliberate attacks against U.S. naval vessels operating in international waters, and that I had therefore directed air action against gunboats and supporting facilities used in these hostile operations. This air action has now been carried out with substantial damage to the boats and facilities. Two U.S. aircraft were lost in the action.

After consultation with the leaders of both parties in the Congress, I further announced a decision to ask the Congress for a resolution expressing the unity and determination of the United States in supporting freedom and in protecting peace in southeast Asia.

These latest actions of the North Vietnamese regime have given a new and grave turn to the already serious situation in southeast Asia. Our commitments in that area are well known to the Congress. They were first made in 1954 by President Eisenhower. They were further defined in the Southeast Asia Collective Defense Treaty approved by the Senate in February 1955.

This treaty with its accompanying proto-

col obligates the United States and other members to act in accordance with their constitutional processes to meet Communist aggression against any of the parties or protocol states.

Our policy in southeast Asia has been consistent and unchanged since 1954. I summarized it on June 2 in four simple propositions:

1. *America keeps her word.* Here as elsewhere, we must and shall honor our commitments.

2. *The issue is the future of southeast Asia as a whole.* A threat to any nation in that region is a threat to all, and a threat to us.

3. *Our purpose is peace.* We have no military, political, or territorial ambitions in the area.

4. *This is not just a jungle war, but a struggle for freedom on every front of human activity.* Our military and economic assistance to South Vietnam and Laos in particular has the purpose of helping these countries to repel aggression and strengthen their independence.

The threat to the free nations of southeast Asia has long been clear. The North Vietnamese regime has constantly sought to take over South Vietnam and Laos. This Communist regime has violated the Geneva accords for Vietnam. It has systematically conducted a campaign of subversion, which includes the direction, training, and supply of personnel and arms for the conduct of guerrilla warfare in South Vietnamese territory. In Laos, the North Vietnamese regime has maintained military forces, used Laotian territory for infiltration into South Vietnam, and most recently carried out combat operations—all in direct violation of the Geneva agreements of 1962.

In recent months, the actions of the North Vietnamese regime have become steadily more threatening. . . .

As President of the United States I have concluded that I should now ask the Congress, on its part, to join in affirming the national determination that all such attacks will be met, and that the United States will continue in its basic policy of assisting the free nations of the area to defend their freedom.

As I have repeatedly made clear, the

United States intends no rashness, and seeks no wider war. We must make it clear to all that the United States is united in its determination to bring about the end of Communist subversion and aggression in the area. We seek the full and effective restoration of the international agreements signed in Geneva in 1954, with respect to South Vietnam, and again in Geneva in 1962, with respect to Laos. . . .

2. JOINT RESOLUTION OF CONGRESS
H. J. Res. 1145
August 7, 1964

(Department of State Bulletin, August 24, 1964)

Resolved by the Senate and House of Representatives of the United States of America in Congress assembled, That the Congress approves and supports the determination of the President, as Commander in Chief, to take all necessary measures to repel any armed attack against the forces of the United States and to prevent further aggression.

SEC. 2. The United States regards as vital to its national interest and to world peace the maintenance of international peace and security in southeast Asia. Consonant with the Constitution of the United States and the Charter of the United Nations and in accordance with its obligations under the Southeast Asia Collective Defense Treaty, the United States is, therefore, prepared, as the President determines, to take all necessary steps, including the use of armed force, to assist any member or protocol state of the Southeast Asia Collective Defense Treaty requesting assistance in defense of its freedom.

SEC. 3. This resolution shall expire when the President shall determine that the peace and security of the area is reasonably assured by international conditions created by action of the United Nations or otherwise, except that it may be terminated earlier by concurrent resolution of the Congress.

661. ECONOMIC OPPORTUNITY ACT OF 1964
August 20, 1964

(78 U. S. Statutes at Large, 580 ff. Public Law 88–452)

Next to the Civil Rights Act of 1964 (Doc. No. 658), the present legislation, which initiated the "war on poverty," was the most important item in President Johnson's program, one of the principal components of his "Great Society." Whereas the Civil Rights Act had been inherited from the Kennedy administration, the "anti-poverty" bill originated with Johnson, having been proposed in his State of the Union message of January 1964. Overcoming the considerable opposition in Congress was an impressive feat of executive leadership; and the measure was passed much as the President had asked. It created an Office of Economic Opportunity (as director of which the President appointed Sargent Shriver) and provided a great variety of measures against poverty, the most important of which are indicated in the excerpts that follow. The whole program, however, was chronically short of funds.

SEC. 2. Although the economic well-being and prosperity of the United States have progressed to a level surpassing any achieved in world history, and although these benefits are widely shared throughout the Nation, poverty continues to be the lot of a substantial number of our people. The United States can achieve its full economic and social potential as a nation only if every individual has the opportunity to contribute to the full extent of his capabilities and to participate in the workings of our society. It is, therefore, the policy of the United States to eliminate the paradox of poverty in the midst of plenty in this Nation by opening to everyone the opportunity for education and training, the opportunity to work, and the opportunity to live in decency and dignity. It is the purpose of this Act to strengthen, supplement, and coordinate efforts in furtherance of that policy.

TITLE I—YOUTH PROGRAMS
PART A—JOB CORPS

SEC. 101. The purpose of this part is to prepare for the responsibilities of citizenship and to increase the employability of young men and young women aged sixteen through twenty-one by providing them in rural and urban residential centers with education, vocational training, useful work experience, including work directed toward the conservation of natural resources, and other appropriate activities.

SEC. 102. In order to carry out the purposes of this part, there is hereby established within the Office of Economic Opportunity (hereinafter referred to as the "Office"), established by title VI, a Job Corps (hereinafter referred to as the "Corps").

SEC. 103. The Director of the Office (hereinafter referred to as the "Director") is authorized to—

(a) enter into agreements with any Federal, State, or local agency or private organization for the establishment and operation, in rural and urban areas, of conservation camps and training centers; . . .

(b) arrange for the provision of education and vocational training of enrollees in the Corps . . .

(c) provide or arrange for the provision of programs of useful work experience and other appropriate activities for enrollees . . .

SEC. 105. (a) Enrollees may be provided with such living, travel, and leave allowances, and such quarters, subsistence, transportation, equipment, clothing, recreational services, medical, dental, hospital, and other health services, and other expenses as the Director may deem necessary or appropriate for their needs. Transportation and travel allowances may also be provided, in such circumstances as the Director may determine, for applicants for enrollment to or from places of enrollment, and for former enrollees from places of termination to their homes. . . .

PART B—WORK-TRAINING PROGRAMS

SEC. 111. The purpose of this part is to provide useful work experience opportunities for unemployed young men and young women, through participation in State and community work-training programs, so that their employability may be increased or their education resumed or continued and so that public agencies and private nonprofit organizations (other than political parties) will be enabled to carry out programs which will permit or contribute to an undertaking or service in the public interest that would not otherwise be provided, or will contribute to the conservation and development of natural resources and recreational areas. . . .

PART C—WORK-STUDY PROGRAMS

SEC. 121. The purpose of this part is to stimulate and promote the part-time employment of students in institutions of higher education who are from low-income families and are in need of the earnings from such employment to pursue courses of study at such institutions. . . .

SEC. 123. The Director is authorized to enter into agreements with institutions of higher education (as defined by section 401 (f) of the Higher Education Facilities Act of 1963 (P.L. 88–204)) under which the Director will make grants to such institutions to assist in the operation of work-study programs as hereinafter provided.

SEC. 124. An agreement entered into pursuant to section 123 shall—

(a) provide for the operation by the institution of a program for the part-time employment of its students in work—

(1) for the institution itself, or

(2) for a public or private nonprofit organization when the position is obtained through an arrangement between the institution and such an organization and—

(A) the work is related to the student's educational objective, or

(B) such work (i) will be in the public interest and is work which would not otherwise be provided, (ii) will not result in the displacement of employed workers or impair existing contracts for services, and (iii) will be governed by such conditions of employment as will be appropriate and reasonable in light of such factors as the type of work performed, geographical region, and proficiency of the employee:

Provided, however, That no such work shall involve the construction, operation, or maintenance of so much of any facility used or to be used for sectarian instruction or as a place for religious worship . . .

TITLE II—URBAN AND RURAL COMMUNITY ACTION PROGRAMS

PART A—GENERAL COMMUNITY ACTION PROGRAMS

SEC. 201. The purpose of this part is to provide stimulation and incentive for urban and rural communities to mobilize their resources to combat poverty through community action programs.

SEC. 202. (a) The term "community action program" means a program—

(1) which mobilizes and utilizes resources, public or private, of any urban or rural, or combined urban and rural, geographical area (referred to in this part as a "community"), including but not limited to a State, metropolitan area, county, city, town, multicity unit, or multicounty unit in an attack on poverty;

(2) which provides services, assistance, and other activities of sufficient scope and size to give promise of progress toward elimination of poverty or a cause or causes of poverty through developing employment opportunities, improving human performance, motivation, and productivity, or bettering the conditions under which people live, learn, and work;

(3) which is developed, conducted, and administered with the maximum feasible participation of residents of the areas and members of the groups served; and

(4) which is conducted, administered, or coordinated by a public or private nonprofit agency (other than a political party), or a combination thereof.

(b) The Director is authorized to prescribe such additional criteria for programs carried on under this part as he shall deem appropriate. . . .

PART B—ADULT BASIC EDUCATION PROGRAMS

SEC. 212. It is the purpose of this part to initiate programs of instruction for individuals who have attained age eighteen and whose inability to read and write the English language constitutes a substantial impairment of their ability to get or retain employment commensurate with their real ability, so as to help eliminate such inability and raise the level of education of such individuals with a view of making them less likely to become dependent on others, improving their ability to benefit from occupational training and otherwise increasing their opportunities for more productive and profitable employment, and making them better able to meet their adult responsibilities.

SEC. 213. (a) From the sums appropriated to carry out this title, the Director shall make grants to States which have State plans approved by him under this section. . . .

PART C—VOLUNTARY ASSISTANCE PROGRAM FOR NEEDY CHILDREN

SEC. 219. The purpose of this part is to allow individual Americans to participate in a personal way in the war on poverty, by voluntarily assisting in the support of one or more needy children, in a program coordinated with city or county social welfare agencies.

SEC. 220. (a) In order to carry out the purposes of this part, the Director is authorized to establish a section within the Office of Economic Opportunity to act as an information and coordination center to encourage voluntary assistance for deserving and needy children. Such section shall collect the names of persons who voluntarily desire to assist financially such children and shall secure from city or county social welfare agencies such information concerning deserving and needy children as the Director shall deem appropriate. . . .

TITLE III—SPECIAL PROGRAMS TO COMBAT POVERTY IN RURAL AREAS

SEC. 301. It is the purpose of this title to meet some of the special problems of rural poverty and thereby to raise and maintain the income and living standards of low-income rural families and migrant agricultural employees and their families.

PART A—AUTHORITY TO MAKE GRANTS AND LOANS

SEC. 302. (a) The Director is authorized to make—
>   (1) loans having a maximum maturity of 15 years and in amounts not exceeding $2,500 in the aggregate to any low income rural family where, in the judgment of the Director, such loans have a reasonable possibility of effecting a permanent increase in the income of such families by assisting or permitting them to—
>   (A) acquire or improve real estate or reduce encumbrances or erect improvements thereon,
>   (B) operate or improve the operation of farms not larger than family sized, including but not limited to the purchase of feed, seed, fertilizer, livestock, poultry, and equipment, or
>   (C) participate in cooperative associations; and/or to finance non-agricultural enterprises which will enable such families to supplement their income. . . .

PART B—ASSISTANCE FOR MIGRANT, AND OTHER SEASONALLY EMPLOYED, AGRICULTURAL EMPLOYEES AND THEIR FAMILIES

SEC. 311. The Director shall develop and implement as soon as practicable a program to assist the States, political subdivisions of States, public and nonprofit agencies, institutions, organizations, farm associations, or individuals in establishing and operating programs of assistance for migrant, and other seasonally employed, agricultural employees and their families which programs shall be limited to housing, sanitation, education, and day care of children. Institutions, organizations, farm associations, or individuals shall be limited to direct loans. . . .

TITLE IV—EMPLOYMENT AND INVESTMENT INCENTIVES

SEC. 401. It is the purpose of this title to assist in the etablishment, preservation, and strengthening of small business concerns and improve the managerial skills employed in such enterprises; and to mobilize for these objectives private as well as public managerial skills and resources.

SEC. 402. The Director is authorized to make, participate (on an immediate basis) in, or guarantee loans, repayable in not more than fifteen years, to any small business concern (as defined in section 3 of the Small Business Act (15 U.S.C. 632) and regulations issued thereunder), or to any qualified person seeking to establish such a concern, when he determines that such loans will assist in carrying out the purposes of this title, with particular emphasis on employment of the long-term unemployed . . .

TITLE VI—ADMINISTRATION AND COORDINATION

SEC. 601. (a) There is hereby established in the Executive Office of the President the Office of Economic Opportunity. The Office shall be headed by a Director who shall be appointed by the President, by and with the advice and consent of the Senate. There shall also be in the Office one Deputy Director and three Assistant Directors who shall be appointed by the President, by and with the advice and consent of the Senate. The Deputy Director and the Assistant Directors shall perform such functions as the Director may from time to time prescribe. . . .

SEC. 616. No part of any funds appropriated or otherwise made available for expenditure under authority of this Act shall be used to make payments to any individual unless such individual has executed and filed with the Director an affidavit that he does not believe in, and is not a member of and does not support any organization that believes in or teaches the overthrow of the United States Government by force or violence or by any illegal or unconstitutional methods.

662. THE WARREN REPORT
September 24, 1964

On November 22, 1963, President Kennedy was assassinated while riding in a motorcade in Dallas. The Dallas police arrested Lee Harvey Oswald, a former Marine, and charged him with the crime. Before Oswald could be brought to trial, he himself was assassinated (November 24) by Jack Ruby, a nightclub operator, while being transferred, before millions of television viewers, from the police headquarters to the Dallas county jail. One of Lyndon Johnson's first acts as President was to appoint an official commission, headed by Chief Justice Earl Warren, to conduct a full investigation into the assassination of President Kennedy and the murder of Oswald. The commission, which included Senators Russell and Cooper, Representatives Hale Boggs and Gerald Ford, Allen Dulles (former director of CIA), and John J. McCloy (former U.S. High Commissioner for Germany), concluded that Oswald had acted alone, that there was no relationship between Oswald and Ruby, and that there was no conspiracy to assassinate the President. The issues surrounding the case, however, were extremely complicated, and the Warren Report did not silence speculation about a possible conspiracy. For a judicious but critical examination of the Commission and its findings, see Edward Jay Epstein, *Inquest*.

. . . These conclusions represent the reasoned judgment of all members of the Commission and are presented after an investigation which has satisfied the Commission that it has ascertained the truth concerning the assassination of President Kennedy to the extent that a prolonged and thorough search makes this possible.

1. The shots which killed President Kennedy and wounded Governor Connally were fired from the sixth floor window at the southeast corner of the Texas School Book Depository. This determination is based upon the following:

(a) Witnesses at the scene of the assassination saw a rifle being fired from the sixth floor window of the Depository Building, and some witnesses saw a rifle in the window immediately after the shots were fired.

(b) The nearly whole bullet found on Governor Connally's stretcher at Parkland Memorial Hospital and the two bullet fragments found in the front seat of the Presidential limousine were fired from the 6.5-millimeter Mannlicher-Carcano rifle found on the sixth floor of Depository Building to the exclusion of all other weapons.

(c) The three used cartridge cases found near the window on the sixth floor at the southeast corner of the building were fired from the same rifle which fired the above-described bullet and fragments, to the exclusion of all other weapons.

(d) The windshield in the Presidential limousine was struck by a bullet fragment on the inside surface of the glass, but was not penetrated.

(e) The nature of the bullet wounds suffered by President Kennedy and Governor Connally and the location of the car at the time of the shots establish that the bullets were fired from above and behind the Presidential limousine, striking the President and the Governor as follows:

(1) President Kennedy was first struck by a bullet which entered at the back of his neck and exited through the lower front portion of his neck, causing a wound which would not necessarily have been lethal. The President was struck a second time by a bullet which entered the right-rear portion of his head, causing a massive and fatal wound.

(2) Governor Connally was struck by a bullet which entered on the right side of his back and traveled downward through the right side of his chest, exiting below his right nipple. This bullet then passed through his right wrist and entered his left thigh where it caused a superficial wound.

(*f*) There is no credible evidence that the shots were fired from the Triple Underpass, ahead of the motorcade, or from any other location.

2. The weight of the evidence indicates that there were three shots fired.

3. Although it is not necessary to any essential findings of the Commission to determine just which shot hit Governor Connally, there is very persuasive evidence from the experts to indicate that the same bullet which pierced the President's throat also caused Governor Connally's wounds. However, Governor Connally's testimony and certain other factors have given rise to some difference of opinion as to this probability but there is no question in the mind of any member of the Commission that all the shots which caused the President's and Governor Connally's wounds were fired from the sixth floor window of the Texas School Book Depository.

4. The shots which killed President Kennedy and wounded Governor Connally were fired by Lee Harvey Oswald. This conclusion is based upon the following:

(*a*) The Mannlicher-Carcano 6.5-millimeter Italian rifle from which the shots were fired was owned by and in the possession of Oswald.

(*b*) Oswald carried this rifle into the Depository Building on the morning of November 22, 1963.

(*c*) Oswald, at the time of the assassination, was present at the window from which the shots were fired.

(*d*) Shortly after the assassination, the Mannlicher-Carcano rifle belonging to Oswald was found partially hidden between some cartons on the sixth floor and the improvised paper bag in which Oswald brought the rifle to the Depository was found close by the window from which the shots were fired.

(*e*) Based on testimony of the experts and their analysis of films of the assassination, the Commission has concluded that a rifleman of Lee Harvey Oswald's capabilities could have fired the shots from the rifle used in the assassination within the elapsed time of the shooting. The Commission has concluded further that Oswald possessed the capability with a rifle which enabled him to commit the assassination.

(*f*) Oswald lied to the police after his arrest concerning important substantive matters.

(*g*) Oswald had attempted to kill Maj. Gen. Edwin A. Walker (Resigned, U.S. Army) on April 10, 1963, thereby demonstrating his disposition to take human life.

5. Oswald killed Dallas Police Patrolman J. D. Tippit approximately 45 minutes after the assassination. . . .

9. The Commission has found no evidence that either Lee Harvey Oswald or Jack Ruby was part of any conspiracy, domestic or foreign, to assassinate President Kennedy. . . .

(*f*) No direct or indirect relationship between Lee Harvey Oswald and Jack Ruby has been discovered by the Commission, nor has it been able to find any credible evidence that either knew the other, although a thorough investigation was made of the many rumors and speculations of such a relationship.

(*g*) The Commission has found no evidence that Jack Ruby acted with any other person in the killing of Lee Harvey Oswald.

11. On the basis of the evidence before the Commission it concludes that Oswald acted alone. Therefore, to determine the motives for the assassination of President Kennedy, one must look to the assassin himself. Clues to Oswald's motives can be found in his family history, his education or lack of it, his acts, his writings, and the recollections of those who had close contacts with him throughout his life. The Commission has presented with this report all of the background information bearing on motivation which it could discover. Thus, others may study Lee Oswald's life and arrive at their own conclusions as to his possible motives.

The Commission could not make any definitive determination of Oswald's motives. It has endeavored to isolate factors which contributed to his character and which might have influenced his decision to assassinate President Kennedy. These factors were:

(*a*) His deep-rooted resentment of all authority which was expressed in a hostility toward every society in which he lived;

(b) His inability to enter into meaningful relationships with people, and a continuous pattern of rejecting his environment in favor of new surroundings;

(c) His urge to try to find a place in history and despair at times over failures in his various undertakings;

(d) His capacity for violence as evidenced by his attempt to kill General Walker;

(e) His avowed commitment to Marxism and communism, as he understood the terms and developed his own interpretation of them; this was expressed by his antagonism toward the United States, by his defection to the Soviet Union, by his failure to be reconciled with life in the United States even after his disenchantment with the Soviet Union, and by his efforts, though frustrated, to go to Cuba.

Each of these contributed to his capacity to risk all in cruel and irresponsible actions. . . .

663. THE BERKELEY STUDENT REVOLT
1964

Student protest became a prominent feature of academic life, for the first time, in the 1960's. The first major student "revolt," and possibly the prototype, was the Free Speech Movement at the University of California at Berkeley, led by students who had worked in the civil-rights movement but involving, at its peak in December 1964, large numbers of undergraduates. The immediate precipitant of the rebellion was an order of the university administration prohibiting various forms of political agitation on the campus, but the scope of the protest widened until it became an attack on the impersonality, excessive specialization, and prostitution of knowledge which the students associated with the "multiversity"—a concept of the university of which Clark Kerr, president of the University of California, happened to be the leading spokesman. The following speech by Mario Savio, an undergraduate philosophy major who emerged as the leader of the FSM, was delivered during a sit-in of eight hundred students in Sproul Hall during the night of December 2, and it shows that much more was involved, for the students, than a narrow issue of university procedure. Eventually the faculty voted its support of the program of the FSM, but the deeper issues remained, as the statement by acting chancellor Meyerson, in the wake of the crisis, makes clear. And beyond the pedagogical and academic issues he analyzes, there lay the still deeper issue of the generational rift and the rejection of American society by increasing numbers of young people—feelings which would soon be further stirred by the war in Vietnam, which subsequently became the principal focus of student demonstrations.

1. MARIO SAVIO: "AN END TO HISTORY"
December 2, 1964

(*Humanity,* December, 1964)

. . . In our free speech fight at the University of California, we have come up against what may emerge as the greatest problem of our nation—depersonalized, unresponsive bureaucracy. We have encountered the organized status quo in Mississippi, but it is the same in Berkeley. Here we find it impossible usually to meet with anyone but secretaries. Beyond that, we find functionaries who cannot make policy but can only hide behind the rules. We have discovered total lack of response on the part of the policy makers. To grasp a situation which is truly Kafkesque, it is necessary to understand the bureaucratic mentality. And we have learned quite a bit about it this fall, more outside the classroom than in.

As bureaucrat, an administrator believes that nothing new happens. He occupies an a-historical point of view. In September, to get the attention of this bureaucracy which had issued arbitrary edicts suppressing student political expression and refused to discuss its action, we held a sit-in on the campus. We sat around a police car and kept it immobilized for over thirty-two hours. At last, the administrative bureaucracy agreed to negotiate. But instead, on the following Monday, we discovered that a committee had been appointed, in accordance with usual regulations, to resolve the dispute. Our attempt to convince any of the administrators that an event had occurred, that something new had happened, failed. They saw this simply as something to be handled by normal University procedures.

The same is true of all bureaucracies. They begin as tools, means to certain legitimate goals, and they end up feeding their own existence. The conception that bureaucrats have is that history has in fact come to an end. No events can occur now that the Second World War is over which can change American society substantially. We proceed by standard procedures as we are. . . .

This free speech fight points up a fascinating aspect of contemporary campus life. Students are permitted to talk all they want so long as their speech has no consequences.

One conception of the university, suggested by a classical Christian formulation, is that it be in the world but not of the world. The conception of Clark Kerr, by contrast, is that the university is part and parcel of this particular stage in the history of American society; it stands to serve the need of American industry; it is a factory that turns out a certain product needed by industry or government. Because speech does often have consequences which might alter this perversion of higher education, the university must put itself in a position of censorship. It can permit two kinds of speech, speech which encourages continuation of the status quo, and speech which advocates changes in it so radical as to be irrelevant in the foreseeable future.

. . . The University is well structured, well tooled, to turn out people with all the sharp edges worn off, the well-rounded person. The University is well equipped to produce that sort of person, and this means that the best among the people who enter must for four years wander aimlessly much of the time questioning why they are on campus at all, doubting whether there is any point in what they are doing, and looking toward a very bleak existence afterward in a game in which all of the rules have been made up, which one cannot really amend.

It is a bleak scene, but it is all a lot of us have to look forward to. Society provides no challenge. American society in the standard conception it has of itself is simply no longer exciting. The most exciting things going on in America today are movements to change America. America is becoming ever more the Utopia of sterilized, automated contentment. The "futures" and "careers" for which American students now prepare are for the most part intellectual and moral wastelands. This chrome-plated consumers paradise would have us grow up to be well-behaved children. But an important minority of men and women coming to the front today have shown that they will die rather than be standardized, replaceable and irrelevant.

2. STATEMENT BY ACTING CHANCELLOR MARTIN MEYERSON
January 13, 1965

. . . The world sees in the University of California perhaps the most impressive effort ever made to provide the best possible higher education to the largest possible numbers of students. Our successes in this area appear to the rest of the world as so impressive that a steady stream of observers and visitors come to learn from us. For example, in Britain today, many concerned with the plans to increase sharply the numbers attending university there point to the University of California as the proof that a democratic state may maintain excellent universities without limiting admission to a small potential elite as Britain has done up to now. It is, of course, not only those who seek to enlarge the size of their educational establishment who look to California for a model. But though others praise us, we are aware that we are only at the beginning of the effort to combine excellence and numbers. We know our defects better than do any of our observers.

However, we are not so sure of the directions we must take to improve education at Berkeley. I shall review some of the questions that we must ask ourselves. Berkeley is so pre-eminent as a center of research that again and again the question is asked—is not teaching, and in particular undergraduate education, slighted by the emphasis on research and the recruitment of great research scholars? I am convinced, as I believe all who have thought deeply about contemporary higher education are convinced, that the best teachers are very often the best researchers. Most disciplines are undergoing such rapid change and development that it is generally those who are contributing to the transformation of each field of study who are best able to teach it. This is true even for elementary courses; the teaching of the elements effectively requires knowing the frontiers and it is difficult in most subjects to remain in contact with new advances exclusively by reading the research literature. Our problem is how to develop a better relationship between research and teaching, and in particular between research and undergraduate teaching.

. . . One way of doing this may be to include early in the student's career in the university a number of small classes, laboratories, tutorials, or research seminars. When he is inducted in the style and content of higher learning, he can perhaps more easily take advantage of large lecture classes.

Our objective must be to ensure that every student has meaningful educational experiences which bring him into close personal contact with one or more members of the faculty and at the beginning of his career as a student. Our point of view must always be concerned with the education of the student—and not an abstract idea of the number or distribution of courses a student must take to graduate. We can never cover all knowledge. Our aim must be to graduate students who can continue learning.

We can expand the number of these educational experiences by relating our univerity in more ways to its setting. There is the Bay Area in this exciting and rapidly growing state. Our interest must not be to control or limit the experiences that come out of the community onto the campus, but to expand them. And at the same time we would hope to contribute to the cultural and civic life of the Bay Area and California.

Then there is the wider Pacific area. Our university is in an unrivaled position to develop interesting new courses that could be a model to the rest of the country, bringing together the work of different disciplines to illuminate the problems of Asia, the Pacific Basin, and Latin America. These interdisciplinary approaches and courses should be brought to the undergraduate, not left solely to graduate school. . . .

It is essential to develop centers on the campus with which students can identify. I have already indicated my conviction that size as such is not a problem. Size offers advantages. It means, for example, that students who have particular points of view and special interests, even if minority points of view and interests, can find other students and perhaps faculty who share them and thus paradoxically can overcome isolation and forced conformity in a large university where they could not do so in a smaller school. But just as these students can find a center of identification in an organization or activity, so we must make it possible for all of our students to escape from a feeling of anonymity, to find a point of location, of loyalty, of identification. We have to think seriously how this can be done. We have to consider what we can learn from other universities, and, indeed, other campuses of the University of California. Perhaps we can make better use of our various kinds of living quarters to develop stronger centers of identification for some of our students. We may be able to develop improved physical facilities for students, such as special rooms or centers for work and study, perhaps in conjunction with libraries, while students are on campus. We have to consider whether these should be organized around disciplines, or on some other basis. Certainly relations between departments and their students should be strengthened. . . .

These are the sorts of questions concerning our educational policies that I think the university community must explore. . . .

664. "AGGRESSION FROM THE NORTH":
STATE DEPARTMENT WHITE PAPER ON VIETNAM
February 27, 1965
(*Department of State Bulletin,* March 22, 1965)

Following his overwhelming defeat of Goldwater, and armed with the Congressional mandate he had received after the Tonkin Gulf incident (Doc. No. 660), President Johnson embarked on a new military strategy for defeating the Communists in Vietnam—strategic bombing of North Vietnam. Hitherto the fighting had been confined to South Vietnam, and Americans had participated in the role of military "advisers" to the Army of the Republic of Vietnam. The new policy required not only the saturation bombing of North Vietnam but the dispatch of large numbers of American troops to South Vietnam, until the total by 1967 had reached almost 500,000. Both measures presupposed an interpretation of the conflict as "aggression from the North"—not, as critics of the war insisted, a civil war between the National Liberation Front (Vietcong) and the successive military regimes in Saigon. This thesis—that South Vietnam was the victim of "aggression" analogous to the invasion of South Korea in 1950 or of Czechoslovakia in 1938—was spelled out at length in the State Department's "White Paper" of February 1965, which became the justification of subsequent escalations of the American effort in Southeast Asia.

South Vietnam is fighting for its life against a brutal campaign of terror and armed attack inspired, directed, supplied, and controlled by the Communist regime in Hanoi. This flagrant aggression has been going on for years, but recently the pace has quickened and the threat has now become acute.

The war in Vietnam is a new kind of war, a fact as yet poorly understood in most parts of the world. Much of the confusion that prevails in the thinking of many people, and even many governments, stems from this basic misunderstanding. For in Vietnam a totally new brand of aggression has been loosed against an independent people who want to make their own way in peace and freedom.

Vietnam is *not* another Greece, where in-digenous guerrilla forces used friendly neighboring territory as a sanctuary.

Vietnam is *not* another Malaya, where Communist guerrillas were, for the most part, physically distinguishable from the peaceful majority they sought to control.

Vietnam is *not* another Philippines, where Communist guerrillas were physically separated from the source of their moral and physical support.

Above all, the war in Vietnam is *not* a spontaneous and local rebellion against the established government.

There are elements in the Communist program of conquest directed against South Vietnam common to each of the previous areas of aggression and subversion. But there is one fundamental difference. In Vietnam a Communist government has set out deliberately to conquer a sovereign people in a neighboring state. And to achieve its end, it has used every resource of its own government to carry out its carefully planned program of concealed aggression. North Vietnam's commitment to seize control of the South is no less total than was the commitment of the regime in North Korea in 1950. But knowing the consequences of the latter's undisguised attack, the planners in Hanoi have tried desperately to conceal their hand. They have failed and their aggression is as real as that of an invading army.

This report is a summary of the massive evidence of North Vietnamese aggression obtained by the Government of South Vietnam. This evidence has been jointly analyzed by South Vietnamese and American experts.

The evidence shows that the hard core of the Communist forces attacking South Vietnam were trained in the North and ordered into the South by Hanoi. It shows that the key leadership of the Vietcong (VC), the officers and much of the cadre, many of the technicians, political organizers, and propagandists have come from the North and operate under Hanoi's direction. It shows that the training of essential military personnel and their infiltration into the South is directed by the Military High Command in Hanoi.

The evidence shows that many of the weapons and much of the ammunition and other supplies used by the Vietcong have been sent into South Vietnam from Hanoi. In recent months new types of weapons have been introduced in the VC army, for which all ammunition must come from outside sources. Communist China and other Communist states have been the prime suppliers of these weapons and ammunition, and they have been channeled primarily through North Vietnam.

The directing force behind the effort to conquer South Vietnam is the Communist Party in the North, the Lao Dong (Workers) Party. As in every Communist state, the party is an integral part of the regime itself. North Vietnamese officials have expressed their firm determination to absorb South Vietnam into the Communist world.

Through its Central Committee, which controls the Government of the North, the Lao Dong Party directs the total political and military effort of the Vietcong. The Military High Command in the North trains the military men and sends them into South Vietnam. The Central Research Agency, North Vietnam's central intelligence organization, directs the elaborate espionage and subversion effort. . . .

Under Hanoi's overall direction the Communists have established an extensive machine for carrying on the war within South Vietnam. The focal point is the Central Office for South Vietnam with its political and military subsections and other specialized agencies. A subordinate part of this Central Office is the Liberation Front for South Vietnam. The front was formed at Hanoi's order in 1960. Its principal function is to influence opinion abroad and to create the false impression that the aggression in South Vietnam is an indigenous rebellion against the established Government.

For more than 10 years the people and the Government of South Vietnam, exercising the inherent right of self-defense, have fought back against these efforts to extend Communist power south across the 17th parallel. The United States has responded to the appeals of the Government of the Republic of Vietnam for help in this defense of the freedom and independence of its land and its people.

In 1961 the Department of State issued a report called *A Threat to the Peace*. It described North Vietnam's program to seize South Vietnam. The evidence in that report had been presented by the Government of the Republic of Vietnam to the International Control Commission (ICC). A special report by the ICC in June 1962 upheld the validity of that evidence. The Commission held that there was "sufficient evidence to show beyond reasonable doubt" that North Vietnam had sent arms and men into South Vietnam to carry out subversion with the aim of overthrowing the legal Government there. The ICC found the authorities in Hanoi in specific violation of four provisions of the Geneva Accords of 1954.

Since then, new and even more impressive evidence of Hanoi's aggression has accumulated. The Government of the United States believes that evidence should be presented to its own citizens and to the world. It is important for free men to know what has been happening in Vietnam, and how, and why. That is the purpose of this report. . . .

The record is conclusive. It establishes beyond question that North Vietnam is carrying out a carefully conceived plan of aggression against the South. It shows that North Vietnam has intensified its efforts in the years since it was condemned by the International Control Commission. It proves that Hanoi continues to press its systematic program of armed aggression into South Vietnam. This aggression violates the United Nations Charter. It is directly contrary to the Geneva Accords of 1954 and of 1962 to which North Vietnam is a party. It shatters the peace of Southeast Asia. It is a fundamental threat to the freedom and security of South Vietnam.

The people of South Vietnam have chosen to resist this threat. At their request, the United States has taken its place beside them in their defensive struggle.

The United States seeks no territory, no military bases, no favored position. But we have learned the meaning of aggression elsewhere in the post-war world, and we have met it.

If peace can be restored in South Vietnam,

the United States will be ready at once to reduce its military involvement. But it will not abandon friends who want to remain free. It will do what must be done to help them. The choice now between peace and continued and increasingly destructive conflict is one for the authorities in Hanoi to make.

665. JOHNSON'S SPEECH ON VIETNAM, JOHNS HOPKINS UNIVERSITY
April 7, 1965
(Department of State Bulletin, April 26, 1965)

At the time of its delivery, this speech was widely taken as an indication of the Johnson administration's willingness to negotiate a conclusion to the Vietnamese war—a solution, it seemed, that was prevented only by the intransigence of North Vietnam. Later it became clear that the administration had consistently passed up opportunities for negotiation—a fact which suggested that the United States still hoped for decisive military victory. President Johnson's speech is notable not so much for his commitment to "unconditional negotiations" —a phrase that in practice proved to be open to a great variety of interpretations—as for his reiteration, once again, of the ideological justification for a greatly expanded American intervention. Once again Johnson insisted that the war in South Vietnam was the result of aggression from the North. The speech also resorts to the "domino theory" of Asian politics, according to which a Communist victory in South Vietnam would almost automatically lead to a Communist victory in Thailand, which would in turn lead to a Communist victory in Burma, and so on until all of Asia had fallen under the Communist yoke. This interpretation presupposed a conspiratorial view of revolution, according to which wars of national liberation were planned and directed, in the last resort, from Peking; and it also implied a military view of history which gave very little weight to the local, non-military sources of social revolution. Such at least was the argument of Johnson's critics.

. . . Over this war, and all Asia, is the deepening shadow of Communist China. The rulers in Hanoi are urged on by Peking. This is a regime which has destroyed freedom in Tibet, attacked India, and been condemned by the United Nations for aggression in Korea. It is a nation which is helping the forces of violence in almost every continent. The contest in Vietnam is part of a wider pattern of aggressive purpose.

Why are these realities our concern? Why are we in South Vietnam? We are there because we have a promise to keep. Since 1954 every American President has offered support to the people of South Vietnam. We have helped to build, and we have helped to defend. Thus, over many years, we have made a national pledge to help South Vietnam defend its independence. And I intend to keep our promise.

To dishonor that pledge, to abandon this small and brave nation to its enemy, and to the terror that must follow, would be an unforgivable wrong.

We are also there to strengthen world order. Around the globe, from Berlin to Thailand, are people whose well-being rests, in part, on the belief that they can count on us if they are attacked. To leave Vietnam to its fate would shake the confidence of all these people in the value of American commitment, the value of America's word. The result would be increased unrest and instability, and even wider war.

We are also there because there are great stakes in the balance. Let no one think for a moment that retreat from Vietnam would bring an end to conflict. The battle would be renewed in one country and then another. The central lesson of our time is that the appetite of aggression is never satisfied. To withdraw from one battlefield means only to prepare for the next. We must say in Southeast Asia, as we did in Europe, in the words of the Bible: "Hitherto shalt thou come, but no further."

There are those who say that all our effort there will be futile, that China's power is such it is bound to dominate all Southeast Asia. But there is no end to that argument until all the nations of Asia are swallowed up.

There are those who wonder why we have

a responsibility there. We have it for the same reason we have a responsibility for the defense of freedom in Europe. World War II was fought in both Europe and Asia, and when it ended we found ourselves with continued responsibility for the defense of freedom.

Our objective is the independence of South Vietnam, and its freedom from attack. We want nothing for ourselves, only that the people of South Vietnam be allowed to guide their own country in their own way.

We will do everything necessary to reach that objective. And we will do only what is absolutely necessary.

In recent months, attacks on South Vietnam were stepped up. Thus it became necessary to increase our response and to make attacks by air. This is not a change of purpose. It is a change in what we believe that purpose requires.

We do this in order to slow down aggression.

We do this to increase the confidence of the brave people of South Vietnam who have bravely borne this brutal battle for so many years and with so many casualties.

And we do this to convince the leaders of North Vietnam, and all who seek to share their conquest, of a very simple fact:

We will not be defeated.

We will not grow tired.

We will not withdraw, either openly or under the cloak of a meaningless agreement. . . .

Once this is clear, then it should also be clear that the only path for reasonable men is the path of peaceful settlement.

Such peace demands an independent South Vietnam securely guaranteed and able to shape its own relationships to all others, free from outside interference, tied to no alliance, a military base for no other country.

These are the essentials of any final settlement.

We will never be second in the search for such a peaceful settlement in Vietnam.

There may be many ways to this kind of peace: in discussion or negotiation with the governments concerned; in large groups or in small ones; in the reaffirmation of old agreements or their strengthening with new ones.

We have stated this position over and over again fifty times and more, to friend and foe alike. And we remain ready, with this purpose, for unconditional discussions.

And until that bright and necessary day of peace we will try to keep conflict from spreading. We have no desire to see thousands die in battle, Asians or Americans. We have no desire to devastate that which the people of North Vietnam have built with toil and sacrifice. We will use our power with restraint and with all the wisdom we can command. But we will use it. . . .

We will always oppose the effort of one nation to conquer another nation.

We will do this because our own security is at stake.

But there is more to it than that. For our generation has a dream. It is a very old dream. But we have the power and now we have the opportunity to make it come true.

For centuries, nations have struggled among each other. But we dream of a world where disputes are settled by law and reason. And we will try to make it so.

For most of history men have hated and killed one another in battle. But we dream of an end to war. And we will try to make it so.

For all existence most men have lived in poverty, threatened by hunger. But we dream of a world where all are fed and charged with hope. And we will help to make it so.

The ordinary men and women of North Vietnam and South Vietnam—of China and India—of Russia and America—are brave people. They are filled with the same proportions of hate and fear, of love and hope. Most of them want the same things for themselves and their families. Most of them do not want their sons ever to die in battle, or see the homes of others destroyed. . . .

Every night before I turn out the lights to sleep, I ask myself this question: Have I done everything that I can do to unite this country? Have I done everything I can to help unite the world, to try to bring peace and hope to all the peoples of the world? Have I done enough?

Ask yourselves that question in your homes and in this hall tonight. Have we done all we could? Have we done enough? . . .

666. JOHNSON'S STATEMENT ON AMERICAN INTERVENTION IN THE DOMINICAN REPUBLIC
May 2, 1965
(*State Department Bulletin,* May 17, 1965)

In April 1965, as recounted in the following press release, the administration received alarming reports from the Dominican Republic that a movement to restore former President Juan Bosch, a democrat earlier driven from office by a military coup, had been captured by Communists under the influence of Fidel Castro. With great dispatch, and without inquiring any further into the accuracy of these reports, President Johnson ordered American forces to the Dominican Republic. Despite his professions of neutrality, the effect of this maneuver was to assist the military junta in preventing the restoration of Bosch. As for the alleged threat of a Communist takeover, it seems to have existed only in the imagination of Ambassador W. Tapley Bennett, Jr., and the CIA. President Johnson was bitterly criticized for this action, one of the most controversial of his Presidency.

. . . Last week our observers warned of an approaching political storm in the Dominican Republic. I immediately asked our Ambassador to return to Washington at once so that we might discuss the situation and might plan a course of conduct. But events soon outran our hopes for peace.

Saturday, April 24—8 days ago—while Ambassador Bennett was conferring with the highest officials of your Government, revolution erupted in the Dominican Republic. Elements of the military forces of that country overthrew their government. However, the rebels themselves were divided. Some wanted to restore former President Juan Bosch. Others opposed his restoration. President Bosch, elected after the fall of Trujillo and his assassination, had been driven from office by an earlier revolution in the Dominican Republic.

Those who opposed Mr. Bosch's return formed a military committee in an effort to control that country. The others took to the street, and they began to lead a revolt on behalf of President Bosch. Control and effective government dissolved in conflict and confusion. . . .

On Wednesday afternoon there was no longer any choice for the man who is your President. I was sitting in my little office reviewing the world situation with Secretary Rusk, Secretary McNamara, and Mr. McGeorge Bundy. Shortly after 3 o'clock I received a cable from our Ambassador, and he said that things were in danger; he had been informed the chief of police and governmental authorities could no longer protect us. We immediately started the necessary conference calls to be prepared.

At 5:14, almost 2 hours later, we received a cable that was labeled "critic," a word that is reserved for only the most urgent and immediate matters of national security.

The cable reported that Dominican law enforcement and military officials had informed our Embassy that the situation was completely out of control and that the police and the government could no longer give any guarantee concerning the safety of Americans or any foreign nationals.

Ambassador Bennett, who is one of our most experienced Foreign Service officers, went on in that cable to say that only an immediate landing of American forces could safeguard and protect the lives of thousands of Americans and thousands of other citizens of some 30 other countries. Ambassador Bennett urged your President to order an immediate landing.

In this situation hesitation and vacillation could mean death for many of our people, as well as many of the citizens of other lands.

I thought that we could not and we did not hesitate. Our forces, American forces, were ordered in immediately to protect American lives. They have done that. They have attacked no one, and although some of our servicemen gave their lives, not a single American civilian or the civilian of any other nation, as a result of this protection, lost their lives. . . .

The revolutionary movement took a tragic turn. Communist leaders, many of them trained in Cuba, seeing a chance to increase disorder, to gain a foothold, joined the revolution. They took increasing control. And what began as a popular democratic revolution, committed to democracy and social justice, very shortly moved and was taken over and really seized and placed into the hands of a band of Communist conspirators. . . .

The American nations cannot, must not, and will not permit the establishment of another Communist government in the Western Hemisphere. This was the unanimous view of all the American nations when, in January 1962, they declared, and I quote: 'The principles of communism are incompatible with the principles of the Inter-American system.' . . .

To those who fight only for liberty and justice and progress I want to join with the Organization of American States in saying— in appealing to you tonight to lay down your arms and to assure you there is nothing to fear. The road is open for you to share in building a Dominican democracy, and we in America are ready and anxious and willing to help you. Your courage and your dedication are qualities which your country and all the hemisphere need for the future. You are needed to help shape that future. And

neither we nor any other nation in this hemisphere can or should take it upon itself to ever interfere with the affairs of your country or any other country.

We believe that change comes, and we are glad it does, and it should come through peaceful process. But revolution in any country is a matter for that country to deal with. It becomes a matter calling for hemispheric action only—repeat, only—when the object is the establishment of a Communist dictatorship.

Let me also make clear tonight that we support no single man or any single group of men in the Dominican Republic. Our goal is a simple one. We are there to save the lives of our citizens and to save the lives of all people. Our goal, in keeping with the great principles of the inter-American system, is to help prevent another Communist state in this hemisphere. And we would like to do this without bloodshed or without large-scale fighting.

The form and the nature of the free Dominican government, I assure you, is solely a matter for the Dominican people. . .

667. GRISWOLD v. CONNECTICUT
85 Supreme Court Reporter, 1678
1965

Appellants in this case gave contraceptive information and advice to married persons, in violation of a Connecticut law forbidding the use of contraceptive devices and punishing anyone assisting in this offense. Their conviction was upheld in lower courts. By a 7 to 2 majority, the Supreme Court held that the Connecticut birth control law unconstitutionally violated the right of privacy. Justice Harlan concurred on narrower grounds. In this case as in Bell v. Maryland (Doc. No. 657), Justice Black, joined in dissent by Justice Stewart, emerged rather unexpectedly as an advocate of judicial self-restraint, arguing that the Court was now reading its own prejudices into the Constitution, in the area of civil liberties, just as earlier justices had done in the field of economic legislation.

Appeal from Connecticut Supreme Court of Errors.

DOUGLAS, J. . . . We have had many controversies over these penumbral rights of

"privacy and repose." . . . These cases bear witness that the right of privacy which presses for recognition here is a legitimate one.

The present case, then, concerns a relationship lying within the zone of privacy created by several fundamental constitutional guarantees. And it concerns a law which, in forbidding the *use* of contraceptives rather than regulating their manufacture or sale, seeks to achieve its goals by means having a maximum destructive impact upon that relationship. Such a law cannot stand in light of the familiar principle, so often applied by this Court, that a "governmental purpose to control or prevent activities constitutionally subject to state regulation may not be achieved by means which sweep unnecessarily broadly and thereby invade the area of protected freedoms." NAACP v. Alabama, 377 U.S. 288, 307. Would we allow the police to search the sacred precincts of marital bedrooms for telltale signs of the use of contraceptives? The very idea is repulsive to the notions of privacy surrounding the marriage relationship.

We deal with a right of privacy older than the Bill of Rights—older than our political parties, older than our school system. Marriage is a coming together for better or for worse, hopefully enduring, and intimate to the degree of being sacred. It is an association that promotes a way of life, not causes; a harmony in living, not political faiths; a bilateral loyalty, not commercial or social projects. Yet it is an association for as noble a purpose as any involved in our prior decisions.

Reversed.

BLACK, J., with whom Justice STEWART joined, dissenting. . . . The Court talks about a constitutional "right of privacy" as though there is some constitutional provision or provisions forbidding any law ever to be passed which might abridge the "privacy" of individuals. But there is not. There are, of course, guarantees in certain specific constitutional provisions which are designed in part to protect privacy at certain times and places with respect to certain activities. Such, for example, is the Fourth Amendment's guarantee against "unreasonable searches and seizures." But I think it belittles that Amendment to talk about it as though it protects nothing but "privacy." To treat it that way is to give it a niggardly interpretation, not the kind of liberal reading I think any Bill of Rights provision should be given. The average man would very likely not have his feelings soothed any more by having his property seized openly than by having it seized privately and by stealth. He simply wants his property left alone. And a person can be just as much, if not more, irritated, annoyed and injured by an unceremonious public arrest by a policeman as he is by a seizure in the privacy of his office or home.

One of the most effective ways of diluting or expanding a constitutionally guaranteed right is to substitute for the crucial word or words of a constitutional guarantee another word, more or less flexible and more or less restricted in its meaning. This fact is well illustrated by the use of the term "right of privacy" as a comprehensive substitute for the Fourth Amendment's guarantee against "unreasonable searches and seizures." "Privacy" is a broad, abstract and ambiguous concept which can easily be shrunken in meaning but which can also, on the other hand, easily be interpreted as a constitutional ban against many things other than searches and seizures. I have expressed the view many times that First Amendment freedoms, for example, have suffered from a failure of the courts to stick to the simple language of the First Amendment in construing it, instead of invoking multitudes of words substituted for those the Framers used. . . . For these reasons I get nowhere in this case by talk about a constitutional "right of privacy" as an emanation from one or more constitutional provisions. I like my privacy as well as the next one, but I am nevertheless compelled to admit that government has a right to invade it unless prohibited by some specific constitutional provision. For these reasons I cannot agree with the Court's judgment and the reasons it gives for holding this Connecticut law unconstitutional. . . .

668. SOCIAL SECURITY AMENDMENTS OF 1965 (MEDICARE)
July 30, 1965

(79 *U. S. Statutes at Large,* 286 ff. Public Law 89–97)

When the Social Security Acts (Doc. No. 503) were debated in 1935, some advocates of social security insisted that it ought to provide not only retirement benefits but a system of health insurance for people over 65. The strongest opposition to such a program came from the American Medical Association and its allies in Congress, who attacked it as "socialized medicine." In 1962 President Kennedy revived the issue, but Congress rejected his proposal. In 1964 Congress once again defeated a bill providing medical care for elderly people. Finally, after

Johnson's landslide victory in the Presidential elections of 1964, a health insurance program was adopted by Congress over the strong opposition of the AMA. An amendment to the Social Security Act, the bill provided a basic plan which automatically covered anyone over 65 (except aliens with less than five years' residence, aliens without status as permanent residents, and federal employees eligible for government health insurance under another law) and paid for hospitalization, nursing home care, home visits, and diagnostic services according to rather complicated rules laid down in Title XVIII, part A and elsewhere in the measure. In addition, a voluntary supplementary plan (part B), to which subscribers paid $3 a month, covered physicians' charges—not covered in the basic plan—together with additional home visits and diagnostic services. The basic plan contained a $40 deductible, the supplementary plan a deductible of $50. The whole program was to be financed in part from increases in the social security tax and in part from other revenues. In addition to the medical features of the bill, it also extended retirement benefits under the Social Security Act to include some categories of persons not previously covered and raised the amount one could earn and still qualify for retirement benefits from $1200 to $1500 a year. Only the medical provisions are given below.

TITLE XVIII—HEALTH INSURANCE FOR THE AGED

PART A—HOSPITAL INSURANCE BENEFITS FOR THE AGED

. . . SEC. 1812. (a) The benefits provided to an individual by the insurance program under this part shall consist of entitlement to have payment made on his behalf (subject to the provisions of this part) for—

(1) inpatient hospital services for up to 90 days during any spell of illness;

(2) post-hospital extended care services for up to 100 days during any spell of illness;

(3) post-hospital home health services for up to 100 visits . . . after the beginning of one spell of illness and before the beginning of the next; and

(4) outpatient hospital diagnostic services. . . .

PART B—SUPPLEMENTARY MEDICAL INSURANCE BENEFITS FOR THE AGED

SEC. 1831. There is hereby established a voluntary insurance program to provide medical insurance benefits in accordance with the provisions of this part for individuals 65 years of age or over who elect to enroll under such program, to be financed from premium payments by enrollees together with contributions from funds appropriated by the Federal Government.

SEC. 1832. (a) The benefits provided to an individual by the insurance program established by this part shall consist of—

(1) entitlement to have payment made to him or on his behalf (subject to the provisions of this part) for medical and other health services, except those described in paragraph (2) (B); and

(2) entitlement to have payment made on his behalf (subject to the provisions of this part) for—

(A) home health services for up to 100 visits during a calendar year; and

(B) medical and other health services (other than physicians' services unless furnished by a resident or intern of a hospital) furnished by a provider of services or by others under arrangements with them made by a provider of services.

(b) For definitions of 'spell of illness', 'medical and other health services', and other terms used in this part, see section 1861.

SEC. 1833. (a) Subject to the succeeding provisions of this section, there shall be paid from the Federal Supplementary Medical Insurance Trust Fund, in the case of each individual who is covered under the insurance program established by this part and incurs expenses for services with respect to which benefits are payable under this part, amounts equal to—

(1) in the case of services described in section 1832(a)(1)—80 percent of the reasonable charges for the services . . . and

(2) in the case of services described in section 1832(a)(2)—80 percent of the reasonable cost of the services. . . .

(b) Before applying subsection (a) with respect to expenses incurred by an individual during any calendar year, the total amount of the expenses incurred by such individual during such year (which would, except for this subsection, constitute incurred expenses from which benefits payable under subsection (a) are determinable) shall be reduced by a deductible of $50 . . .

SEC. 1839. (a) The monthly premium of each individual enrolled under this part for each month before 1968 shall be $3. . . .

PART C—MISCELLANEOUS PROVISIONS
DEFINITIONS OF SERVICES,
INSTITUTIONS, ETC.

SEC. 1861. For purposes of this title—
(a) The term 'spell of illness' with respect to any individual means a period of consecutive days—

(1) beginning with the first day (not included in a previous spell of illness) (A) on which such individual is furnished inpatient hospital services or extended care services, and (B) which occurs in a month for which he is entitled to benefits under part A, and

(2) ending with the close of the first period of 60 consecutive days thereafter on each of which he is neither an inpatient of a hospital nor an inpatient of an extended care facility.

(b) The term 'inpatient hospital services' means the following items and services furnished to an inpatient of a hospital and (except as provided in paragraph (3) by the hospital—

(1) bed and board;

(2) such nursing services and other related services, such use of hospital facilities, and such medical social services as are ordinarily furnished by the hospital for the care and treatment of inpatients, and such drugs, biologicals, supplies, appliances, and equipment, for use in the hospital, as are ordinarily furnished by such hospital for the care and treatment of inpatients; and

(3) such other diagnostic or therapeutic items or services, furnished by the hospital or by others under arrangements with them made by the hospital, as are ordinarily furnished to inpatients either by such hospital or by others under such arrangements;

excluding, however—

(4) medical or surgical services provided by a physician, resident, or intern; and

(5) the services of a private-duty nurse or other private-duty attendant. . . .

(s) The term 'medical and other health services' means any of the following items or services (unless they would otherwise constitute inpatient hospital services, extended care services, or home health services):

(1) physicians' services;

(2) services and supplies (including drugs and biologicals which cannot, as determined in accordance with regulations, be self-administered) furnished as an incident to a physician's professional service, of kinds which are commonly furnished in physicians' offices and are commonly either rendered without charge or included in the physicians' bills, and hospital services (including drugs and biologicals which cannot, as determined in accordance with regulations, be self-administered) incident to physicians' services rendered to outpatients;

(3) diagnostic X-ray tests, diagnostic laboratory tests, and other diagnostic tests;

(4) X-ray, radium, and radioactive isotope therapy, including materials and services of technicians;

(5) surgical dressings, and splints, casts, and other devices used for reduction of fractures and dislocations;

(6) rental of durable medical equipment, including iron lungs, oxygen tents, hospital beds, and wheelchairs used in the patient's home.

(including an institution used as his home);

(7) ambulance service where the use of other methods of transportation is contraindicated by the individual's condition, but only to the extent provided in regulations;

(8) prosthetic devices (other than dental) which replace all or part of an internal body organ, including replacement of such devices; and

(9) leg, arm, back, and neck braces, and artificial legs, arms, and eyes, including replacements if required because of a change in the patient's physical condition.

No diagnostic tests performed in any laboratory which is independent of a physician's office or a hospital shall be included within paragraph (3) unless such laboratory—

(10) if situated in any State in which State or applicable local law provides for licensing of establishments of this nature, (A) is licensed pursuant to such law, or (B) is approved, by the agency of such State or locality responsible for licensing establishments of this nature, as meeting the standards established for such licensing; and

(11) meets such other conditions relating to the health and safety of individuals with respect to whom such tests are performed as the Secretary may find necessary. . . .

SEC. 1862. (a) Notwithstanding any other provision of this title, no payment may be made under part A or part B for any expenses incurred for items or services—

(7) where such expenses are for routine physical checkups, eyeglasses or eye examinations for the purpose of prescribing, fitting, or changing eyeglasses, hearing aids or examinations therefor, or immunizations; . . .

(10) where such expenses are for cosmetic surgery or are incurred in connection therewith, except as required for the prompt repair of accidental injury or for improvement of the functioning of a malformed body member; . . .

(12) where such expenses are for services in connection with the care, treatment, filling, removal, or replacement of teeth or structures directly supporting teeth. . . .

SEC. 106. (a) Subsection (a) of section 213 of the Internal Revenue Code of 1954 (relating to allowance of deduction) is amended to read as follows:

(a) ALLOWANCE OF DEDUCTION.—There shall be allowed as a deduction the following amounts, not compensated for by insurance or otherwise—

(1) the amount by which the amount of the expenses paid during the taxable year (reduced by any amount deductible under paragraph (2) for medical care of the taxpayer, his spouse, and dependents (as defined in section 152) exceeds 3 percent of the adjusted gross income, and

(2) an amount (not in excess of $150) equal to one-half of the expenses paid during the taxable year for insurance which constitutes medical care for the taxpayer, his spouse, and dependents. . . .

669. JOHNSON'S STATEMENT ON THE RIOT IN WATTS
August 20, 1965

(Public Papers of the Presidents: Lyndon B. Johnson, 1965, no. 436)

On August 11, 1965, a Negro section of Los Angeles (Watts) erupted in a major riot, touched off by a minor incident involving a drunken driver and a white policeman. It required 13,000 National Guardsmen to suppress the riot with tear gas, rifles, and machine guns. Thirty-six people died, almost 900 were injured, 4,000 were arrested, 209 buildings were burned, 787 were damaged, and the property loss was estimated at $46 million. The riot in Watts was only one of a series of riots that became annual occurrences in the Negro ghettoes of Northern cities—New York, Rochester, Philadelphia, and Chicago in 1964; Cleveland in 1966; Newark and Detroit in 1967. All of these disturbances reflected, among other things, the disparity between general American affluence and the misery of the black ghettoes. Of the population of Watts, two-thirds of the adults had less than a high-school education, an eighth were illiterate; 30 per cent of the children came from broken homes. Watts had the lowest per capita income of any area in Los Angeles except its Skid Row. The area contained more than 500 parolees from California prisons, and it had an abnormally high rate of narcotics addiction, alcoholism, prostitution, and crime. The following remarks of President Johnson were delivered at a White House Conference on Equal Employment Opportunities.

If there is one thing I think we have learned from the civil rights struggle, it is that the problem of bringing the Negro American into an equal role in our society is more complex, and is more urgent, and is much more critical than any of us have ever known. Who of you could have predicted 10 years ago, that in this last, sweltering, August week thousands upon thousands of disenfranchised Negro men and women would suddenly take part in self-government, and that thousands more in that same week would strike out in an unparalleled act of violence in this Nation?

Our conscience cries out against the hatred that we heard last week. It bore no relation to the orderly struggle for civil rights that has ennobled the last decade. Every leader in that struggle has condemned this outrage against the laws of the land. And during the few days that preceded it, I had spent all week at the White House visiting individually with Dr. King, Mr. Farmer, Dr. Roy Wilkins, Mr. Philip Randolph—all talking about the great meeting that we had to have here later in the fall, because the cities of this Nation and the Negro family in this Nation are two of our most pressing, most important problems. Well, the bitter years that preceded the riots, the death of hope where hope existed, their sense of failure to change the conditions of life—these things no doubt led to these riots. But they did not justify them.

I hope that every American who believes in equal opportunity for his fellow men, understands this distinction that I have made. For we shall never achieve a free and prosperous and hopeful society until we have suppressed the fires of hate and we have turned aside from violence—whether that violence comes from the nightriders of the Klan, or the snipers and the looters in the Watts district. Neither old wrongs nor new fears can ever justify arson or murder. . . .

With . . . rights comes responsibility.

And with responsibility there goes obligation.

We cannot, and we must not, in one breath demand laws to protect the rights of all of our citizens, and then turn our back, or wink, or in the next breath allow laws to be broken that protect the safety of our citizens. There just must never come the hour in this Republic when any citizen, whoever he is, can ever ignore the law or break the law with impunity.

And so long as I am your President I intend to preserve the rights of all of our citizens, and I intend to enforce the laws that protect all of our citizens—without regard to race, religion, region, or without fear or favor.

A rioter with a Molotov cocktail in his hands is not fighting for civil rights any more than a Klansman with a sheet on his back and a mask on his face. They are both more or less what the law declares them: lawbreakers, destroyers of constitutional rights and liberties, and ultimately destroyers of a free America. They must be exposed and they must be dealt with.

It is our duty—and it is our desire—to open our hearts to humanity's cry for help. It is our obligation to seek to understand what could lie beneath the flames that scarred that great city. So let us equip the poor and the oppressed—let us equip them for the long march to dignity and to well-being. But let us never confuse the need for decent work and fair treatment with an excuse to destroy and to uproot.

Ours is an open society. The world is always witness to whatever we do—sometimes, I think (results of the cooperation of some of my friends) to some things we don't do. We would not have it otherwise. For the brave story of the Negro American is related to the struggle of men on every continent for their rights as sons of God. It is a compound of brilliant promises and stunning reverses. Sometimes, as in the past week when the two are mixed on the same pages of our newspapers and television screens, the result is baffling to all the world. And it is baffling to me, and to you, and to us. And always there is the danger that hours of disorder may erase the accumulated goodwill of many months and many years. And I warn and plead with all thinking Americans to contemplate this for a due period.

Yet beneath the discord we hear another theme. That theme speaks of a day when Americans of every color, and every creed, and every religion, and every region, and every sex can be trained for decent employment, can find it, can secure it, can have it preserved, and can support their families in an enriching and a rewarding environment. . . .

670. GINZBURG v. UNITED STATES
86 Supreme Court Reporter, 942
1966

Ralph Ginzburg, publisher of *Eros* magazine and other publications, was convicted in the U.S. District Court for the Eastern District of Pennsylvania of violating the federal obscenity statute, which prohibits the mailing of obscene materials. His conviction was upheld by a higher court. In Roth v. U.S. (1957), the Supreme Court had ruled that the test of obscenity lay in the content of the materials in question, but in the present case the Court, upholding Ginzberg's conviction, ruled that the manner in which the materials were advertised might constitute evidence of "pandering" to salacious interests.

BRENNAN, J. . . . In the cases in which this Court has decided obscenity questions since *Roth*, it has regarded the materials as sufficient in themselves for the determination of the question. In the present case, however, the prosecution charged the offense in the context of the circumstances of production, sale, and publicity and assumed that, standing alone, the publications themselves might not be obscene. We agree that the question of obscenity may include consideration of the setting in which the publications were presented as an aid to determining the question of obscenity, and assume without deciding that the prosecution could not have succeeded otherwise. . . . We view the publications against a background of commercial exploitation of erotica solely for the sake of their prurient appeal. The record in that regard amply supports the decision of the trial judge that the mailing of all three publications offended the statute.

The three publications were EROS, a hard-cover magazine of expensive format; Liaison, a bi-weekly newsletter; and *The Housewife's Handbook on Selective Promiscuity* (hereinafter the *Handbook*), a short book. . . .

Besides testimony as to the merit of the material, there was abundant evidence to show that each of the accused publications was originated or sold as stock in trade of the sordid business of pandering—"the business of purveying textual or graphic matter openly advertised to appeal to the erotic interest of their customers." EROS early sought mailing privileges from the postmasters of Intercourse and Blue Ball, Pennsylvania. The trial court found the obvious, that these hamlets were chosen only for the value their names would have in furthering petitioners' efforts to sell their publications on the basis of salacious appeal; the facilities of the post offices were inadequate to handle the anticipated volume of mail, and the privileges were denied. Mailing privileges were then obtained from the postmaster of Middlesex, New Jersey. EROS and Liaison thereafter mailed several million circulars soliciting subscriptions from that post office; over 5,500 copies of the *Handbook* were mailed.

The "leer of the sensualist" also permeates the advertising for the three publications. The circulars sent for EROS and Liaison stressed the sexual candor of the respective publications, and openly boasted that the publishers would take full advantage of what they regarded an unrestricted license allowed by law in the expression of sex and sexual matters. The advertising for the

Handbook, apparently mailed from New York, consisted almost entirely of a reproduction of the introduction of the book, written by one Dr. Albert Ellis. Although he alludes to the book's informational value and its putative therapeutic usefulness, his remarks are preoccupied with the book's sexual imagery. The solicitation was indiscriminate, not limited to those, such as physicians or psychiatrists, who might independently discern the book's therapeutic worth. Inserted in each advertisement was a slip labeled "GUARANTEE" and reading, "Documentary Books, Inc. unconditionally guarantees full refund on the price of THE HOUSEWIFE'S HANDBOOK ON SELECTIVE PROMISCUITY if the book fails to reach you because of U.S. Post Office censorship interference." Similar slips appeared in the advertising for EROS and Liaison; they highlighted the gloss petitioners put on the publications, eliminating any doubt what the purchaser was being asked to buy.

This evidence, in our view, was relevant in determining the ultimate question of obscenity and, in the context of this record, serves to resolve all ambiguity and doubt. The deliberate representation of petitioners' publications as erotically arousing, for example, stimulated the reader to accept them as prurient; he looks for titillation, not for saving intellectual content. Similarly, such representation would tend to force public confrontation with the potentially offensive aspects of the work; the brazenness of such an appeal heightens the offensiveness of the publications to those who are offended by such material. And the circumstances of presentation and discrimination of material are equally relevant to determining whether social importance claimed for material in the courtroom was, in the circumstances, pretense or reality—whether it was the basis upon which it was traded in the marketplace or a spurious claim for litigation purposes. Where the purveyor's sole emphasis is on the sexually provocative aspects of his publications, that fact may be decisive in the determination of obscenity. Certainly in a prosecution which, as here, does not necessarily imply suppression of the materials involved, the fact that they originate or are used as a subject of pandering is relevant to the application of the *Roth* test.

A proposition argued as to EROS, for example, is that the trial judge improperly found the magazine to be obscene as a whole, since he concluded that only four of the fifteen articles predominantly appealed to prurient interest and substantially exceeded community standards of candor, while the other articles were admittedly non-offensive. But the trial judge found that "[t]he deliberate and studied arrangement of EROS is editorialized for the purpose of appealing predominantly to prurient interest and to insulate through the inclusion of non-offensive material." However erroneous such a conclusion might be if unsupported by the evidence of pandering, the record here supports it. EROS was created, represented and sold solely as a claimed instrument of the sexual stimulation it would bring. Like the other publications, its pervasive treatment of sex and sexual matters rendered it available to exploitation by those who would make a business of pandering to "the widespread weakness for titillation by pornography." Petitioners' own expert agreed, correctly we think, that "[i]f the object [of a work] is material gain for the creator through an appeal to the sexual curiosity and appetite," the work is pornographic. In other words, by animating sensual detail to give the publication a salacious cast, petitioners reinforced what is conceded by the Government to be an otherwise debatable conclusion. . . .

BLACK, J., dissenting. Only one stark fact emerges with clarity out of the confusing welter of opinions and thousands of words written in this and two other cases today. That fact is that Ginzburg, petitioner here, is now finally and authoritatively condemned to serve five years in prison for distributing printed matter about sex which neither Ginzburg nor anyone else could possibly have known to be criminal. Since, as I have said many times, I believe the Federal Government is without any power whatever under the Constitution to put any type of burden on speech and expression of ideas of any kind (as distinguished from conduct), . . . I would reverse Ginzburg's conviction on this ground alone. Even assuming, however, that the Court is correct in holding today that Congress does have power to clamp official censorship on some subjects selected by the Court, in some ways approved by it, I believe that the federal obscenity statute as enacted by Congress and as enforced by the Court against Ginzburg in this case should be held invalid on two other grounds.

I

Criminal punishment by government, although universally recognized as a necessity in limited areas of conduct, is an exercise of one of government's most awesome and dangerous powers. Consequently, wise and good governments make all possible efforts to hedge this dangerous power by restricting it within easily identifiable boundaries. Experience, and wisdom flowing out of that experience, long ago led to the belief that agents of government should not be vested with power and discretion to define and punish as criminal past conduct which had not been clearly defined as a crime in advance. To this end, at least in part, written laws came into being, marking the boundaries of conduct for which public agents could thereafter impose punishment upon people. In contrast, bad governments either wrote no general rules of conduct at all, leaving that highly important task to the unbridled discretion of government agents at the moment of trial, or sometimes, history tells us, wrote their laws in an unknown tongue so that people could not understand them or else placed their written laws at such inaccessible spots that people could not read them. It seems to me that these harsh expedients used by bad governments to punish people for conduct not previously clearly marked as criminal are being used here to put Mr. Ginzburg in prison for five years. . . . The Court has in effect rewritten the federal obscenity statute and thereby imposed on Ginzburg standards and criteria that Congress never thought about; or if it did think about them, certainly it did not adopt them. Consequently, Ginzburg is, as I see it, having his conviction and sentence affirmed upon the basis of a statute amended by this Court for violation of which amended statute he was not charged in the courts below. Such an affirmance we have said vio-

lates due process. Quite apart from this vice in the affirmance, however, I think that the criteria declared by a majority of the Court today as guidelines for a court or jury to determine whether Ginzburg or anyone else can be punished as a common criminal for publishing or circulating obscene material are so vague and meaningless that they practically leave the fate of a person charged with violating censorship statutes to the unbridled discretion, whim and caprice of the judge or jury which tries him. . . .

II

It is obvious that the effect of the Court's decisions in the three obscenity cases handed down today is to make it exceedingly dangerous for people to discuss either orally or in writing anything about sex. Sex is a fact of life. Its pervasive influence is felt throughout the world and it cannot be ignored. Like all other facts of life it can lead to difficulty and trouble and sorrow and pain. But while it may lead to abuses, and has in many instances, no words need be spoken in order for people to know that the subject is one pleasantly interwoven in all human activities and involves the very substance of the creation of life itself. It is a subject which people are bound to consider and discuss whatever laws are passed by any government to try to suppress it. Though I do not suggest any way to solve the problems that may arise from sex or discussions about sex, of one thing I am confident, and that is that federal censorship is not the answer to these problems. I find it difficult to see how talk about sex can be placed under the kind of censorship the Court here approves without subjecting our society to more dangers than we can anticipate at the moment. It was to avoid exactly such dangers that the First Amendment was written and adopted. For myself I would follow the course which I believe is required by the First Amendment, that is, recognize that sex at least as much as any other aspect of life is so much a part of our society that its discussion should not be made a crime.